Contemporary Authors

Permanent Series

Contemporary Authors

Permanent Series

A BIO-BIBLIOGRAPHICAL GUIDE TO CURRENT AUTHORS AND THEIR WORKS

CHRISTINE NASSO

Editor

volume 2

GALE RESEARCH COMPANY • BOOK TOWER • DETROIT, MICHIGAN 48226

CONTEMPORARY AUTHORS

Published by
Gale Research Company, Book Tower, Detroit, Michigan 48226

Frederick G. Ruffner, *Publisher*   James M. Ethridge, *Editorial Director*

Christine Nasso, *Editor*
Ann Evory, *Associate Editor*
Michael L. Auty, Robin Farbman, Peter M. Gareffa,
Margaret Mazurkiewicz, Linda Metzger, Larry J. Moore,
Nancy M. Rusin, and Frank Michael Soley, *Assistant Editors*
Jane Bowden and Frances Carol Locher, *Contributing Editors*
Ellen Koral, Norma Sawaya, and Shirley Seip, *Editorial Assistants*
Michaeline Nowinski, *Production Manager*

Copyright © 1965, 1966, 1967, 1968, 1969, 1970, 1971, 1972, 1973, 1978
GALE RESEARCH COMPANY

Library of Congress Catalog Card Number 75-13539
ISBN 0-8103-0037-0

Preface

In 1975 Gale began publishing the *Contemporary Authors—Permanent Series*. The purpose of the *Permanent Series* was to remove from the revision cycle entries for deceased authors and authors past normal retirement age who were presumed to be no longer actively writing. Since revised volumes of *Contemporary Authors* were consistently larger than original volumes, and since Gale knew that future revised volumes would continue to grow, it seemed reasonable to list separately in the *Permanent Series* those entries which would not require future revision. This procedure was both logical in itself and comparable to the practices of other biographical reference-book publishers. For example, sketches removed from *Who's Who in America* are published periodically in *Who Was Who in America*.

Experience has proved, however, that a cumulative series devoted entirely to authors cannot effectively be treated in the same way as a repetitive series devoted to noteworthy persons in general. The *Permanent Series* is, therefore, being discontinued after the publication of Volume 2. Hereafter, all entries appearing in a given volume of *Contemporary Authors* will be retained in that volume when it is revised, whether the subjects of the sketches are active or inactive, living or dead.

Questions and Answers about
Contemporary Authors—Permanent Series

Which original volumes of *Contemporary Authors* were utilized for the *Permanent Series*? The *Permanent Series* is composed of sketches removed from volumes 9-36 of *Contemporary Authors* when these volumes were revised.

Sketches placed in the *Permanent Series* are not duplicated in revised volumes or in any other part of the *Contemporary Authors* series. Is that correct? Yes. The *Permanent Series* contains unduplicated sketches which are an integral part of *Contemporary Authors*. Although the *Permanent Series* is being discontinued, the two volumes will be kept in print to provide access to all authors covered in the *Contemporary Authors* series.

Are sketches in *Permanent Series* volumes simply reprinted from the original *Contemporary Authors* volumes, since the subjects of the sketches are deceased or inactive? No, they are not simply reprinted. Every part of every sketch was reviewed, and changed if research warranted it. About 85% of all sketches in *Permanent Series* volumes have been changed. The nature and extent of revision in the *Permanent Series* can be seen by comparing original listings for Euell Gibbons, Hermann Hesse, Martin Luther King, Jr., and Andre Malraux with the revised permanent sketches in this volume.

How were *Permanent Series* volumes prepared? *Permanent Series* volumes were compiled in conjunction with regular revised volumes. In the revision process, clippings of their previously published sketches were sent to the authors. After these clippings were returned, deceased authors and authors approaching or past retirement age who indicated that they had no recently published books and no *new* work in progress were designated for inclusion in the *Permanent Series*.

How do you revise previously published sketches if the authors do not return marked clippings? First, every attempt is made to reach authors through previous home addresses, business affiliations, publishers, organizations, or other practicable means either by mail or telephone. When necessary, searches are made to determine whether the authors may have died. A number of sources are checked for obituaries, including indexes of magazines and other news media.

If living authors fail to respond, or if authors are now deceased, work proceeds on verifying and updating the previously published information. Biographical dictionaries are checked (a task made easier through the use of Gale's *Biographical Dictionaries Master Index* and new *Author Biographies Master Index*), as are additional bibliographical sources, such as *Cumulative Book Index, The National Union Catalog,* etc. In other words, all steps are taken which can reasonably be expected to confirm or invalidate previous information, or to provide additional information. Sketches not personally verified by the authors are marked as follows:

† Research has yielded new information which has been added to the sketch
† † Research has yielded no new information

Why does the "Work in Progress" section appear in some of the sketches in *Permanent Series* volumes? Often, books and projects described in "Work in Progress" add a new dimension to the author's work. Even though this information no longer serves its original purpose, it is believed to be sufficiently useful to list in the final version of the author's entry.

Cumulative Index Should Always Be Consulted

The cumulative index published in alternate new volumes of *CA* will continue to be the user's guide to the location of an individual author's listing. Volume references for authors in the *Permanent Series* indicate both the volume in which the author's sketch originally appeared and the pertinent volume of the *Permanent Series.* A typical reference would read as follows:

King, Martin Luther, Jr.
1929-1968. . . . . CAP-2
Earlier sketch in CA 25-28

As always, suggestions from users concerning revision or any other aspect of *CA* will be welcomed.

CONTEMPORARY AUTHORS

Permanent Series

† Research has yielded new information which has been added to the sketch, but the author has not personally verified the entry in this edition.

† † Research has yielded no new information, but the author has not personally verified the entry in this edition.

ABBOTT, Freeland K(night) 1919-1971

PERSONAL: Born May 31, 1919, in Hartford, Conn.; son of Frank Knight (a clergyman) and Annabelle (Matthews) Abbott; married Isabel Bradshaw Bennett, July 3, 1943; children: Freeland Knight, Jr., Deborah Ann, Ernest Bennett, John Bradshaw. *Education:* Tufts University, A.B., 1942, A.M., 1947, Ph.D., 1952. *Home:* 14 Sawyer Ave., Medford, Mass. 02155. *Office:* Department of History, Tufts University, Medford, Mass. 02155.

CAREER: Miami University, Oxford, Ohio, assistant professor of history, 1947-49; Tufts University, Medford, Mass., instructor, 1949-51, assistant professor, 1951-56, associate professor, 1956-64, professor of history, beginning 1964. *Military service:* U.S. Army Air Forces, 1942-46; served in India and China. *Member:* American Historical Association, Association for Asian Studies, Middle East Society, New England Historical Society, Phi Beta Kappa. *Awards, honors:* Ford Foundation research fellow in Pakistan, 1953-55; Fulbright research scholar in Pakistan, 1959-60.

WRITINGS: (Contributor) Donald Smith, editor, *Religion and Politics in South Asia*, Princeton University Press, 1966; *Islam and Pakistan*, Cornell University Press, 1968. Contributor to *Asian Survey, Muslim World, Saturday Review*, and other journals.

WORK IN PROGRESS: Studies in comparative history; studies of Pakistan.†

(Died February 24, 1971)

*   *   *

ABRAHAMS, Robert David 1905-

PERSONAL: Born September 24, 1905, in Philadelphia, Pa.; son of William and Anne (David) Abrahams; married Florence Kohn, November 21, 1929; children: Richard Irving, Roger David, Marjorie. *Education:* Dickinson School of Law, LL.B., 1925. *Religion:* Jewish. *Home:* Morning Star, Fig Tree, Nevis, West Indies. *Office:* Land Title Building, Philadelphia, Pa. 19110.

CAREER: Admitted to Pennsylvania Bar, 1925; secretary to commissioner general to Europe for Sesquicentennial Exposition, Philadelphia, Pa., 1925; assistant city solicitor, Philadelphia, 1927-32; consul for Dominican Republic, Philadelphia, 1931-62; Legal Aid Society, Philadelphia, assistant chief counsel, 1933-50, chief counsel, 1950-73. Partner, Abrahams & Loewenstein (law firm), Philadelphia. Has taught courses at Temple University. Founder, Philadelphia Neighborhood Law Office Plan (first successful legal service plan for middle income group), 1939; president of Community Health Center, 1945-52, Jewish Family Service, 1951-54, and Pennsylvania Prison Society; executive director, Community Legal Service, 1966-67. Trustee, Dickinson School of Law.

MEMBER: National Legal Aid Association (vice-president, 1957), International Bar Association, American Bar Association, Pennsylvania Bar Association, Philadelphia Bar Association (chairman of committee on public service, 1961-62), Philadelphia Consular Club, Tau Epsilon Rho, Philmont Country Club, Locust Club. *Awards, honors:* Order of Duarte, 1945, and Order of Christopher Columbus, 1957 (both from Dominican Republic); Reginald Heber Smith Award of National Legal Aid Association, 1962.

WRITINGS—Adult: Come Forward (poems), Humphries, 1928; *New Tavern Tales* (fiction), Walter Neale, 1930; (with M. J. Meyer) *Handbook of Collection Practice for Attorneys, Collection Agencies, Credit Houses, Managers and Business Men*, Soney & Sage, 1931; *The Pot-Bellied Gods* (poems), Dorrance, 1932; *Death after Lunch* (novel), Phoenix Press, 1941; *Death in 1-2-3* (novel), Phoenix Press, 1942; *Three Dozen* (poems), Dorrance, 1945.

Juvenile: *Mr. Benjamin's Sword*, Jewish Publication Society, 1948; *The Commodore: Uriah P. Levy*, Jewish Publication Society, 1954; *The Uncommon Soldier: Major Alfred Mordecai*, Farrar, Straus, 1959; *Sir David Salomons: Sound of Bow Bells*, Farrar, Straus, 1962; *Humphrey's Ride*, Crowell, 1965; *The Bonus of Redonda*, Routledge & Kegan Paul, 1968, Macmillan, 1969. Also author of *Room for a Son*, 1954.

Contributor to legal journals; also contributor of articles and poems to *Esquire, Story, Saturday Evening Post*, and other magazines. Editor, *Independent* (weekly), 1932.†

*   *   *

ABRAMS, Charles 1901-1970

PERSONAL: Born September 20, 1901, in Vilna, Poland; brought to United States, 1904, naturalized, 1916; son of Abraham (a merchant) and Freda (Rabinowitz) Abrams;

married Ruth Davidson (a painter), December 22, 1928; children: Abby (Mrs. Thomas Baratta), Judith. *Education:* St. Lawrence University, LL.B., 1922. *Politics:* Democrat. *Home:* 18 West Tenth St., New York, N.Y. 10011. *Office:* 654 Madison Ave., New York, N.Y. 10021.

CAREER: Admitted to New York Bar, 1923; private practice of law, New York City, 1923-70, specializing in private and public housing law. Counsel for New York City Housing Authority, (drafter of Municipal Housing Authorities Law), 1934-37, American Federation of Housing Authorities, 1937-39, and Federal Public Housing Authority, 1939-40. New School for Social Research, New York City, member of the faculty, visiting professor and trustee, 1936-51; University of Pennsylvania, Philadelphia, member of planning faculty, 1951-55; Massachusetts Institute of Technology, Cambridge, visiting professor of urban land economics, 1955-64; Columbia University, New York City, professor of urban planning, 1965-70, also chairman of Division of Urban Planning of the School of Architecture, 1965-67, and chairman of the Executive Committee of the Institute of Urban Environment; Harvard University, Cambridge, Mass., visiting Williams Professor at the School of Design, 1968-69. Served on advisory council of the department of sociology at Princeton University; visiting lecturer, University College, London, England, 1968; frequent lecturer at many institutions, including Pratt Institute, Johns Hopkins University, University of Chicago, and University of Wisconsin; participated in design reviews at various schools of architecture.

Cabinet member during New York State Administration of Governor Averell Harriman, State Rent Administration and chairman of New York State Commission Against Discrimination, 1955-59; served as chairman of the Subcommittee of Housing and Redevelopment for Mayor Robert F. Wagner, New York City, and as chairman of the Task Force on Housing for Mayor John V. Lindsay, 1966; appointed member of Citizen's Advisory Committee of the Housing and Development Administration by Mayor Lindsay, 1968.

Head of United Nations housing missions to Ghana and Turkey, 1954, Pakistan, 1957, Philippines, 1958, Japan, 1960, and International Cooperation Administration missions to Jamaica and Bogota, Colombia, 1961; advisor to other United Nations missions to Bolivia, Ireland, Japan, Colombia, Nigeria, and Singapore, 1959-63; invited to represent the United States at an international conference on the role of the United Nations in urbanization, 1962, also invited by the United Nations to be an observer at Moscow Roundtable Conference on the Planning and Development of New Towns, 1964. Advisor to the Governments of Puerto Rico, Israel, Barbados, and Venezuela; consultant to Ford Foundation projects in Calcutta, India, and in Chile; founder of Middle East Technical University, Ankara, Turkey, 1955. Testified before hearings of various Congressional subcommittees in connection with urban problems. Member of several committees concerned with integrated housing and urban development, such as National Committee Against Discrimination in Housing (member of board), and Housing and Planning Subcommittee of the Citizen's Union (chairman). Trustee of Loula D. Lasker Fellowship Trust.

MEMBER: American Institute of Planners, New York County Lawyers Association, Association of the Bar of the City of New York, American Institute of Architects (honorary associate member). *Awards, honors:* Pultizer Prize nominee for articles in *New York Post,* c.1948; League for Industrial Democracy annual award, 1954; Catholic Interracial Council brotherhood award, 1959; S. L. Strauss award

of the New York Society of Architects, 1965; guest of honor at First Annual Award Banquet of the National Committee Against Discrimination in Housing, 1967; citation from the *Engineering News Record,* 1968.

WRITINGS: Revolution in Land, Harper, 1939; *The Future of Housing* (Book-of-the-Month Club dividend book), Harper, 1946; *A Housing Program for America,* 1947; *Race Bias in Housing,* American Civil Liberties Union, 1947; *Urban Land Problems and Policies,* United Nations, 1953 (issued in three languages); *Forbidden Neighbors: A Study of Prejudice in Housing,* Harper, 1955 reprinted, Kennikat, 1971; *Squatter Settlements: The Problem and the Opportunity,* Division of International Affairs of the Department of Housing and Urban Development, 1956; (with Otto Koenigsberger) *A Housing Program with Special Reference to Refugee Rehabilitation,* United Nations Technical Assistance Administration, 1957.

Man's Struggle for Shelter in an Urbanizing World, M.I.T. Press, 1964 (published in England as *Housing in the Modern World,* Faber, 1966); *The Negro American,* Cambridge University Press, 1965; (with L. N. Bloomberg) *United Nations Mission to Kenya on Housing,* United Nations Department of Economics and Social Affairs, 1965; (author of foreword) Robert L. Carter and others, *Equality,* Pantheon, 1965; *The City is the Frontier,* Harper, 1967; (with Robert Kolodny) *Home Ownership for the Poor: A Program for Philadelphia,* Praeger, 1970; (with Kolodny) *The Language of Cities: A Glossary of Terms,* Viking, 1971.

Urban and housing studies include: *Report on Housing in the Gold Coast,* 1956; *Boston's Waterfront: Some Ideas for Study,* for the Greater Boston Chamber of Commerce, 1961; *Housing in California* (report of the California Governor's Advisory Commission on Housing Problems), 1963; *The Negro Housing Problem: A Program for Philadelphia,* for the Community Renewal Program of Philadelphia, 1966; *Housing the Alaska Native,* for the Alaska State Housing Authority, 1967; *The Role and Responsibilities of the Federal Highway System in Baltimore,* 1968. Also author of reports on housing and development in other countries, for United Nations. Housing columnist, *New York Post,* 1947-49. Contributor to numerous periodicals, including *Nation, New Republic, Scientific American,* and Architectural Record.

BIOGRAPHICAL/CRITICAL SOURCES: New York Times, February 23, 1970.†

(Died February 22, 1970)

*   *   *

ACHESON, Dean (Gooderham)   1893-1971

PERSONAL: Born April 11, 1893, in Middletown, Conn.; son of Edward Campion (Episcopal Bishop of Connecticut) and Eleanor (Gooderham) Acheson; married Alice Stanley, May 5, 1917; children: Jane (Mrs. Dudley B. W. Brown), David Campion, Mary Eleanor (Mrs. William P. Bundy). *Education:* Yale University, B.A., 1915; Harvard University, LL.B., 1918. *Politics:* Democrat. *Religion:* Episcopalian. *Home:* 2805 P St., Washington, D.C. *Office:* Covington & Burling, Union Trust Building, Washington, D.C.

CAREER: Private secretary to Justice Louis D. Brandeis of the U.S. Supreme Court, Washington, D.C., 1919-21; Covington, Burling & Rublee (law firm), associate, 1921-33; appointed Undersecretary of the Treasury in May, 1933, resigned in November, 1933; Covington, Burling, Rublee, Acheson & Shorb, partner, 1934-41; Assistant Secretary of

State under President Roosevelt, 1941-45, and Undersecretary of State under President Truman, 1945-47; resumed practice of law as partner of Covington, Burling, Acheson, O'Brian & Shorb, 1947-49; Secretary of State under President Truman, 1949-53; private practice of law as member of Covington & Burling, beginning 1953. Vice-chairman of Commission on Organization of the Executive Branch of the Government (first Hoover Commission); chairman of American section of Canadian-U.S. Permanent Joint Defense Board, 1947-49, and of advisory committee on civil rules, U.S. Judicial Conference, beginning 1959. Fellow of Yale Corporation, 1936-61. Member of board of directors, Franklin D. Roosevelt Foundation and Harry S Truman Library Institute. Advisor to Presidents Kennedy, Johnson, and Nixon. *Military service:* U.S. Navy, ensign, 1917-18.

MEMBER: American Bar Association, American Society of International Law, American Academy of Arts and Sciences, Foreign Policy Association, Scroll and Key, District of Columbia Bar Association, Phi Beta Kappa, Delta Kappa Epsilon, Metropolitan Club (Washington, D.C.), Chevy Chase Club (Chevy Chase, Md.), Century Association (New York). *Awards, honors:* M.A., 1936, and LL.D., 1962, both from Yale University; LL.D. from Wesleyan University (Middletown, Conn.), 1947, Harvard University, 1950, Cambridge University, 1958, and Johns Hopkins University, 1963; D.C.L. from Oxford University, 1952, and University of Michigan, 1967; D.H.L. from Brandeis University, 1956; Pulitzer Prize, 1970, for *Present at the Creation.* Foreign decorations include Order of Vasa (Sweden), Grand Cross of the Order of Leopold (Belgium), Order of the Rising Sun (Japan), Order of the Aztec Eagle (Mexico), Great Cross of the Order of Boyaca (Colombia), National Order of the Southern Cross (Brazil), and Grand Cross of the Royal Order of Cambodia.

WRITINGS: Strengthening the Forces of Freedom (selected speeches and statements), U.S. Government Printing Office, 1950; *The Pattern of Responsibility,* edited by McGeorge Bundy, introduction by Douglas Southall Freeman, Houghton, 1952; *A Democrat Looks at His Party,* Harper, 1955; *An American Vista,* Hamish Hamilton, 1956; *A Citizen Looks at Congress,* Harper, 1957; *Power and Diplomacy* (William L. Clayton lectures), Harvard University Press, 1958; *Sketches from Lives of Men I Have Known,* Harper, 1961; *Morning and Noon* (autobiography of his youth and early career), Houghton, 1965; *Private Thoughts on Public Affairs* (contains *A Citizen Looks at Congress* and *A Democrat Looks at His Party*), Harcourt, 1967; *Present at the Creation: My Years in the State Department* (autobiography), Norton, 1969; *Fragments of my Fleece,* Norton, 1971; *Korean War,* Norton, 1971; *Grapes from Thorns,* Norton, 1972; *Struggle for a Free Europe* (based largely on material in *Present at the Creation*), Norton, 1973; *This Vast External Realm* (collection of addresses, essays, and lecturers), Norton, 1973.

Addresses, lectures, and statements published by U.S. Department of State or Government Printing Office, except as noted: *The Place of Bretton Woods in Economic Collective Security,* 1945; *The Credit to Britain, the Key to Expanded Trade,* 1946, published as *The Credit to Britain and World Trade,* 1946; *The Requirements of Reconstruction,* 1947; *The Meaning of the North Atlantic Pact,* 1949; *The United States Balance of Payments Problem,* 1949; *Waging Peace in the Americas,* 1949; *Economic Policy and the ITO Charter,* 1949; *The Current Situation in Germany,* 1949; *The Quality of American Patriotism,* 1950; *United Action for the Defense of a Free World,* 1950; *The Shield of Faith,*

1950; *Courage and Common Sense in Time of Crisis,* 1950; *United States Policy toward Asia,* 1950; *The ITO Charter: A Code of Fair Trade Practices,* 1950; *The Peace the World Wants,* 1950; *Plowing a Straight Furrow,* 1950; *The Strategy of Freedom,* 1950; *Crisis in Asia: An Examination of U.S. Policy,* 1950; *The Problem of International Organization among Countries of Europe and the North Atlantic Area,* 1950; *The Task of Today's Diplomacy,* 1950; *Tensions between the United States and the Soviet Union,* 1950; *Threats to Democracy and Its Way of Life,* 1950; *American Policy toward China,* 1951; *It Has Fallen to Us,* 1951; *The Measure of Today's Emergency,* 1951; *Our Far Eastern Policy,* 1951; *The Partnership for Freedom,* 1951; *What Is Point Four?,* 1952; *Achieving the Goals of the Charter,* 1952; *Strength and Unity,* 1952; *The Problem of Peace in Korea,* 1952; *Meetings at the Summit: A Study in Diplomatic Method,* University of New Hampshire Press, 1958; *Prelude to Independence,* [Williamsburg, Va.], 1959; *Fifty Years After,* Overbrook Press, 1961; *Real and Imagined Handicaps of Our Democracy in the Conduct of Its Foreign Relations,* Institute for National and International Affairs, 1962; *The Dilemmas of Our Times* (Brien McMahon lectures), University of Connecticut Press, 1963.

Contributor to *Harper's, Saturday Evening Post, Reporter, American Heritage, Yale Review, Esquire,* and other magazines and newspapers.

SIDELIGHTS: With his appointment as Undersecretary of the Treasury in 1933, Dean Acheson began his career in government service. He later became the fiftieth Secretary of State and one of the principal designers of much of the U.S. cold war strategy, including the post-World War II policy of containment of the Soviet Union through U.S. military strength and political alliances. Considered controversial yet knowledgeable, he was an experienced and valuable source for presidents and other high governmental officials to tap. Stephen S. Rosenfeld wrote: "Dean Acheson had great professional talents in the ways of cultural sensibility and friendship. He was a complete, a completed personality to an extent that few people are: someone who, at least to an outsider's view, had lived through a grand cycle and had done and experienced all those things that could conceivably have lain within the ambit of a man of his culture and class." Peter Steinfels, however, felt that "the full complexity of the man can be seen in a paradoxical comment of James Reston after [Acheson's] death: 'Dean Acheson was a very dogmatic man. He hated the narrow-minded duffers and voluble windbags of politics.' A dogmatism which is very sure about the dogmatism of others is complicated indeed. Reston then quotes an oft-quoted bit of Achesonia: 'On one thing only I feel a measure of assurance—on the rightness of contempt for sanctimonious self-righteousness which, joined with a sly worldliness, beclouds the dangers and opportunities of our time with an unctuous film.' Dean Acheson could never realize how sanctimonious, how self-righteous, how tainted with worldliness, more pompous than sly, and even how unctuous his own rolling expression of contempt could sound. That is his tragedy. His triumph is that his is one of the few leaders of our time who set forth standards by which he himself might be judged severely."

Discussing *Present at the Creation: My Years in the State Department,* Kenneth Younger wrote: "Dean Acheson's memoirs of his years in the State Department provide a panorama of the earth-shaking years of war and peace from 1941 until the end of 1952. After a period of apprenticeship in government during the war, he was almost continuously at the centre of events in the capital of the most powerful country in the world at a time when the shape of international politics for the remainder of the twentieth century was being determined." It was during these few years that the world witnessed the Korean War, the Berlin Blockade, the crisis in Iran, the birth of Israel, the implementation of the Marshall Plan and the forging of the North Atlantic Treaty. Younger went on to say that "during his years as Secretary of State (1949-52) Dean Acheson was subjected to vicious and wholly unjustified attacks in the United States for being 'soft on communism.' He met these with great courage but one feels that they ended by producing in him a certain defensive rigidity, which eventually began to colour his judgement in a rapidly changing world situation. This applies especially to Far Eastern affairs, on which the attack on him largely concentrated. One is left feeling that these years saw the forming of some American attitudes which were later to contribute to miscalculations over Vietnam. On such issues opinions may differ. What is beyond dispute is the moral stature of the man who guided U.S. foreign policy in these years and the high intelligence which he brought to tasks of overwhelming complexity and decisive significance for the world."

AVOCATIONAL INTERESTS: Cabinet making, gardening.

BIOGRAPHICAL/CRITICAL SOURCES: Dean Acheson, *Morning and Noon,* Houghton, 1965; *Newsweek,* October 13, 1969, December 22, 1969; *Vogue,* October 15, 1969; *Washington Post,* October 29, 1969, October 21, 1971; *Best Sellers,* November 1, 1969; Dean Acheson, *Present at the Creation: My Years in the State Department,* Norton, 1969; *Spectator,* May 2, 1970; *Commonweal,* October 29, 1971; David S. McLellan, *Dean Acheson: The State Department Years,* Dodd, 1976.†

(Died October 12, 1971)

*   *   *

ACKERMAN, Nathan W(ard)   1908-1971

PERSONAL: Born November 22, 1908, in Bessarabia, Russia; naturalized American citizen; son of David (a pharmacist) and Bertha (Frankel) Ackerman; married Gwendolyn Hills, October 10, 1937; children: Jean (Mrs. Barry Curhan), Deborah. *Education:* Columbia University, B.A., 1929, M.D., 1933. *Religion:* Jewish. *Home:* 124 East 84th St., New York, N.Y. 10028. *Office:* 149 East 78th St., New York, N.Y. 10021.

CAREER: Montefiore Hospital, New York City, intern, 1933-34, assistant resident, 1934-35; Menninger Clinic and Sanitarium, Topeka, Kan., resident in neuropsychiatry, 1935-36, psychiatrist, 1935-37; private practice of psychiatry, New York City, beginning 1937; Columbia University, New York City, lecturer at School of Social Work, 1946-65, clinical professor of psychiatry at College of Physicians and Surgeons, beginning 1947. Chief psychiatrist, Child Guild Institute, Jewish Board of Guardians, 1942-50; supervising psychiatrist, Family Mental Health Clinic, Jewish Family Services, 1956-65. Director, Child Development Center, 1946-51; director of professional program, Family Institute, New York City, beginning 1960; former assistant medical director, Southard School, Topeka, and Stony Lodge, New York. Visiting professor, Tulane University, beginning 1950; visiting lecturer, Albert Einstein Medical School. Diplomate, American Board of Psychiatry and Neurology. Consultant to science department, American Jewish Committee.

MEMBER: American Psychiatric Association, American Orthopsychiatric Association, American Psychoanalytic Association, American Group Therapy Association, American Psychopathological Association, Academy of Psychoanalysts, Association for Applied Psychoanalysis (honorary member), Association for Psychoanalytic Medicine (former president), Mexican Psychoanalytic Society, New York Academy of Medicine, New York Council of Child Psychiatry (former vice-president). *Awards, honors:* Adolph Meyer Award of Eastern Group Psychiatry Association, 1959.

WRITINGS: (With C.A.L. Binger, A. E. Cohn, H. A. Schroeder, and J. M. Steele) *Personality in Arterial Hypertension,* Brunner, 1945; (with Marie Jahoda) *Anti-Semitism and Emotional Disorders: A Psychoanalytic Interpretation,* Harper, 1950; *Psychodynamics of Family Life: Diagnosis and Treatment of Family Relationships,* Basic Books, 1958; *Treating the Troubled Family,* Basic Books, 1966; (editor with others) *Expanding Theory and Practice in Family Therapy,* Family Service Association of America, 1967; (editor and contributor) *Family Therapy in Transition,* Little, Brown, 1970; (editor) *Family Process Reader,* Basic Books, 1970. Contributor to professional journals. Chairman of board of editors, *Family Process.*†

(Died, 1971)

*   *   *

ADAMOV, Arthur   1908-1970

PERSONAL: Born August 23, 1908, in Kislovodsk, Russia; came to Paris at age of twelve; son of Sourene (an oil-well proprietor) and Helene (Bagatourov) Adamov; married Jacqueline Austrusseau. *Education:* Educated in Switzerland and in Mainz, Germany. *Home:* 52, rue de Seine, Paris 6, France.

CAREER: Was a member of Surrealist circles in Paris, and edited an avant-garde periodical, *Discontinuite.* Also edited *L'Heure Nouvelle* following World War II. Author and playwright.

WRITINGS—Plays: La Parodie [and] *L'Invasion* (*L'Invasion* produced, 1950; *La Parodie* produced, 1952), Charlot, 1950; *La Grande et la petite manoeuvre* (produced, 1950), [Paris], 1950; *Tous contre tous* (produced, 1953), L'Avant-scene (Paris), 1952; *Theatre I* (containing "La Parodie," "L'Invasion," "La Grande et la petite manoeuvre," "Tous contre tous," and "Le Professeur Tarranne" [produced, 1953]), Gallimard, 1953, new edition, 1970; "Comme nous avons ete," published in *Nouvelle Revue Francaise,* March, 1953, translation by Richard Howard published as "As We Were," in *Evergreen Review,* number 4, 1957; *Theatre II* (containing "Le Sens de la marche" [produced, 1953], "Les Retrouvailles," and "Le Ping-pong" [produced, 1955]), Gallimard, 1955; *Paolo Paoli* (produced, 1956), Gallimard, 1957; (with Guy Demoy and Maurice Regnaut) *Theatre de societe* (containing "Intimite," "Je ne suis pas Francais," and "La Complainte du ridicule"), Editeurs Francais Reunis, 1958; *Les Ames mortes* (after the poem by Nicolai Gogol; produced, 1963), Gallimard, 1960; *Le Printemps 71* (produced, 1963), Gallimard, 1961; *Theatre III* (containing "Paolo Paoli," "La Politique des restes," and "Sainte Europe"), Gallimard, 1966; *Theatre IV* (containing "M. le Modere" and "Le Printemps 71"), Gallimard, 1968; *Off Limits* (produced, 1969), Gallimard, 1969; *Si l'ete revenait,* Gallimard, 1970. Author of radio play, "En Fiacre," 1959.

Translation of his plays into English: *Ping-pong,* translated by Richard Howard, Grove, 1959 (produced in New York); *Paolo Paoli,* translated by Geoffrey Brereton, J. Calder,

1959; "Professor Taranne," in *Four Modern French Comedies*, Capricorn, 1960; *Two Plays* ("Professor Taranne," translated by Peter Meyer, and "Ping-pong," translated by Derek Prouse), J. Calder, 1962.

Other writings: (Editor) Claudine Chonez, *Il est temps*, Editions de l'Ilot, 1941; *L'Aveu* (autobiographical confession), Editions du Sagittaire, 1946 (one section translated by Richard Howard and published as "The Endless Humiliation," in *Evergreen Review*, spring, 1958); (author of preface) Strindberg, *Inferno*, Editions du Griffon, 1948; (with Maurice Gravier) *Auguste Strindberg, Dramaturge*, L'Arche, 1955; (author of introduction) Roger Gilbert-Lecomte, *Testament*, Gallimard, 1955; (editor) *La Commune de Paris*, Editions Sociales, 1959; (with others) *Connaissance de Don Ramon Maria del Valle-Inclan*, Julliard, 1963; *Ici et maintenant*, Gallimard, 1964; *L'Homme et l'enfant* (autobiographical), Gallimard, 1968; *Je ils*, Gallimard, 1969; (contributor with others) *Antonin Artaud et le theatre de notre temps*, new edition, Gallimard, 1969.

Translator: Carl Jung, *Le Moi et l'inconscient*, Nouvelle Revue Francaise, 1938; (with Marie Geringer) Rainer Maria Rilke, *Le Livre de la pauvrete et de la mort*, Bonnard (Lausanne), 1941; (with Marthe Robert) George Buechner, *Theatre Complet*, Editions de l'Arche, 1953; Kleist, "La Cruche cassee," in *Theatre Populaire*, March-April, 1954; Fyodor Dostoyevsky, *Crime et Chatiment*, Club Francaise du Livre, 1956; Nikolai Gogol, *Les Aventures de Tchitchikov, ou, Les Ames mortes*, La Guilde du Livre (Lausanne), 1956; Gogol, *Le Revisor*, Editions de l'Arche, 1958; Maxim Gorki, *Vassa Geleznova*, Editions de l'Arche, 1958; Anton Chekhov, *L'Esprit des bois*, Gallimard, 1958; Gorki, *La Mere*, Club Francais du Livre, 1958; Chekhov, *Theatre*, Club Francais du Livre, 1958; August Strindberg, *Le Pere*, Editions de l'Arche, 1958; Ivan Gontcharov, *Oblomov* (novel), Club Francais du Livre, 1959; Gogol, *Cinq Recits*, Club des Libraires de France, 1961; (with Claude Sebisch) Erwin Piscator, *Le Theatre politique*, Editions de l'Arche, 1962; Gorki, *Theatre Complet*, Volumes I and II (with Genia Cannac and Georges Daniel), Editions de l'Arche, 1963, Volume IV (with Cannac), 1964.

Adaptor: George Buechner, "La Mort de Danton," produced, 1948; Maxim Gorki, *Les Petits bourgeois* (produced, 1959), Editions de l'Arche, 1958.

Contributor of articles to *L'Heure Nouvelle*, *Theatre Populaire*, and *Cahiers de la Compagnie M. Renaud—Jean-Louis Barrault*.

SIDELIGHTS: Adamov's plays may be divided for convenience of analysis into the absurdist, surrealistic dramas he wrote prior to 1957 and the epic, realistic dramas he wrote after that point. The genesis of the earlier plays, of which *Ping-pong* is the acknowledged masterpiece, was an incident which occured when he was first reading Strindberg. Adamov began to see loneliness everywhere and to listen to snatches of conversation between people who passed him on the street. One day he saw a blind beggar ignored by two girls who were singing a popular song. He said, "I had closed my eyes, it was wonderful!" This led him to want to portray "on the stage, as crudely and as visibly as possible, the loneliness of man, the absence of communication." He once wrote that "a stage play ought to be the point of intersection between the visible and invisible worlds, or, in other words, the display, the manifestation of the hidden, latent contents that form the shell around the seeds of drama." In 1938 he believed that "the words in our aging vocabularies are like very sick people. Some may be able to

survive, others are incurable." He did his best to rectify this situation. Jean Vilar praised him for renouncing "the lace ornaments of dialogue and intrigue, for having given back to the drama its stark purity."

Adamov evolved a theory of the theatre which emphasized human isolation, the impossibility of any real communication or sympathy between people, and the absurdity of death. George Wellworth wrote that, in Adamov's plays, "nothing decisive ever happens, except the inevitable, meaningless and reasonless death at the end. . . . During the play the characters move aimlessly in mutually exclusive spheres running on courses unfathomable to their occupants." David I. Grossvogel noted that each person in his plays "is hardly more than a negative quantity, a victim whose capacity to exist is real only to the extent that the physical instruments of his torture are real and will be used on him: it is only by comparison with these instruments that he is found to have significance greater than that of the rudimentary and static object."

Adamov wrote in "The Endless Humiliation": "I want to make this truth contagious, virulent: every private fault, every individual guilt, whether the guilty person is conscious of it or not, transcends the individual to identify itself with the fault of all men everywhere and forever—the great original prevarication which is named Separation. . . . I do not know what name to give what I am separated from, but I am separated from it. Once it was called God. Now there is no longer any name. . . . When a terrifying vision assails me and I become a prey to fear, I perform a ritual of exorcism to conquer it, and my fear diminishes. But the legions of multiform terrors all derive from a single principle: the fear of death." In *La Parodie*, a character says that everyone is dead. Wallace Fowlie believed this "summarizes two major characteristics of Adamov's world as reflected in his [early] plays: everything moves toward death, and death has no reason. Adamov seems to be preparing the advent of tragedy and at the same time denying the authenticity or the competence of tragedy. In this sense, his world is a 'parody.' If fate is the same for everyone, then there is no fate." Wellworth noted that, for Adamov, "the climax of a human event must always involve the relentless destruction of the hero." Yet even this is futile, for, said Adamov, "in this life of which the basic circumstances themselves are terrifying, where the same situations fatally recur, all we can do is destroy, and too late at that, what we consider, mistakenly, to be the real obstacle, but what in fact is merely the last item in a maleficent series."

While the general outlook may remind one of Kafka, Adamov denied that his theatre derived from Kafka or that it strived for metaphysical allusions. Adamov had been accused of unallayed pessimism, but he wrote in the 'forties: "We are accused of pessimism, as though pessimism were but one among a number of possible attitudes, as if man were capable of choosing between two alternatives—optimism and pessimism." He believed, rather, that the crisis of the time was "essentially a religious crisis. It is a matter of life or death. . . . From whatever point he starts, whatever path he follows, modern man comes to the same conclusion: behind its visible appearances, life hides a meaning that is eternally inaccessible to penetration by the spirit that seeks for its discovery, caught in the dilemma of being aware that it is impossible to find it, and yet also impossible to renounce the hopeless quest." Esslin wrote that Adamov believed that this was not, "strictly speaking, a philosophy of the absurd, because it still presupposes the conviction that the world *has* a meaning, although it is of necessity outside the reach of human consciousness."

After the mid-'fifties, however, Adamov, in effect, rejected all the plays that could be classified as belonging to the "Theatre of the Absurd." He maintained that "the theatre must show, simultaneously but well-differentiated, both the curable and the incurable aspect of things. The incurable aspect, we all know, is that of the inevitability of death. The curable aspect is the social one." Wellworth noted that "with this step Adamov leaves the death-oriented hopelessness that is the avant-garde drama's chief philosophical standpoint and returns to a belief in the temporal hopes that exist in the illusion-laden world of social humanity.... Adamov has abandoned the deterministic play for a more flexible psychological drama. The characters are no longer helpless automatons but human beings endowed with free will." Esslin wrote that Adamov regarded Brecht as his mentor, and "puts him next to Shakespeare, Chekhov, and Buechner among the dramatists of world literature he admires most." Esslin continued: "Adamov has become the main spokesman of the committed political theatre in France. At the same time, he is regarded as one of the masters of a noncommitted, anti-political theatre of the soul. Like one of his own characters, he is the embodiment of two conflicting tendencies coexisting within the same person."

Esslin spoke of two Adamovs, "Adamov the dramatist of dream, neurosis, and futility, and Adamov the Brechtian epic realist, [who] may not be so far apart as they appear. It is only too easy to understand why Adamov should repudiate his earlier plays today. They are the expression of a past he has outgrown, the fossilized remains of a former self that he is only too happy to have put behind him." Also, "Adamov today regards his plays from *La Parodie* to *Les Retrouvailles* as too schematic, crude, and lacking in a proper appreciation of the needs and prospects of remedial revolutionary action in the face of social injustice. Yet these criticisms, even if they were entirely relevant, miss the point—these plays are true and have a powerful impact because they are the genuine expressions of a soul in torment [which was] real when it was felt—and it remains a very profound insight into the workings of the human mind and retains the power of all deeply felt poetic statements. It was, after all, Adamov himself, who pointed out that neurosis sharpens the perceptions and enables the sufferer to look into depths not usually open to the healthy eye. The works inspired by Adamov's neurosis may be more profound than those of an Adamov reconciled to the world, though still determined to change its institutions." Esslin also believed that the more recent Adamov plays combined the elements of the absurdist theatre and the more conventional theatre, and cited as an example the three short pieces he contributed to *Theatre de societe*, two being allegorical and one realistic, and the latter an acknowledged failure.

In the 'forties Adamov turned to Communism. But, wrote Esslin, "he finds in Communism no supernatural, sacred element. Its ideology confines itself to purely human terms, and for him it remains open to question 'whether anything that confines itself to the human sphere could ever attain anything but the subhuman.... If we turn to Communism nevertheless, it is merely because one day, when it will seem quite close to the realization of its highest aim—the victory over all the contradictions that impede the exchange of goods among men—it will meet, inevitably, the great "no" of the nature of things, which it thought it could ignore in its struggle.'" Esslin reported that after 1958 and the emergence of General de Gaulle, Adamov more actively supported the extreme Left. Yet in 1960 he said he still subscribed to what he had written earlier on this subject.

BIOGRAPHICAL/CRITICAL SOURCES: Yale French Studies, winter, 1954-55; Frederick Lumley, *Trends in Twentieth-Century Drama*, Barrie & Rockliff, 1956; David I. Grossvogel, *The Self-Conscious Stage*, Columbia University Press, 1958; Marc Beigbeder, *Le Theatre en France depuis la liberation*, Bordas, 1959; Wallace Fowlie, *Dionysus in Paris*, Meridian, 1960; Martin Esslin, *The Theatre of the Absurd*, Doubleday, 1961; L. C. Pronko, *Avant-Garde: The Experimental Theatre in France*, University of California Press, 1962; George Wellworth, *The Theatre of Protest and Paradox*, New York University Press, 1964; *Contemporary Literary Criticism*, Volume IV, Gale, 1975.†

(Died March 16, 1970)

*   *   *

ADAMS, Herbert Mayow   1893-

PERSONAL: Born February 9, 1893, in Sydenham, London, England; son of George Francis (a civil servant) and Rose Lilian (Barnby) Adams; married Geraldine Constance Mary Ley, October 4, 1926. *Education:* Educated at Christ Church, Oxford. *Religion:* Church of England. *Home:* 26 Newton Rd., Cambridge, England.

CAREER: Cambridge University, Trinity College, Cambridge, England, librarian, 1924-58. *Military service:* British Army, 1914-19; became lieutenant; received Military Cross.

WRITINGS: (Compiler) *Catalogue of Books Printed on the Continent of Europe, 1501-1600, in Cambridge Libraries*, Cambridge University Press, 1967.

*   *   *

ADAMS, Richard P(errill)   1917-1977

PERSONAL: Born August 17, 1917, in Mound City, Kan.; son of Jesse Bliss (a teacher) and Josephine (Perrill) Adams; married Jean Abel (a counselor), June 27, 1941; children: Lucy (Mrs. Louis Carrio), Ellen (Mrs. John Levy), Thomas. *Education:* University of Illinois, B.A., 1939, M.A., 1940; Columbia University, Ph.D., 1951. *Home:* 1020 Burdette St., New Orleans, La. 70118. *Office:* Department of English, Tulane University, New Orleans, La. 70118.

CAREER: Member of faculty, Long Island University, Rutgers University, and Lafayette College; Tulane University, New Orleans, La., professor of English, 1953-77, chairman of department, 1967-77. Fulbright lecturer in France, 1959-60, 1965-66. *Military service:* U.S. Army Air Forces, 1942-45; became second lieutenant. U.S. Air Force Reserves, beginning 1945; became major. *Member:* Modern Langauge Association of America, American Association of University Professors (secretary-treasurer), American Studies Association, South Central Modern Language Association (president, 1971-72).

WRITINGS: Faulkner: Myth and Motion, Princeton University Press, 1968. Contributor of articles and reviews to professional journals.

WORK IN PROGRESS: Altair Five and *The Eden Affair*, novels; a critical study of Wallace Stevens.

SIDELIGHTS: Richard P. Adams told *CA*, "I am a scholar of the Romantic tradition in American literature." Adams had lived in England and France.†

(Died March 25, 1977)

ADRIAN, Arthur A(llen) 1906-

PERSONAL: Born April 24, 1906, in Moundridge, Kan.; son of Peter Paul (a farmer) and Helena (Harms) Adrian; married Vonna Hicks, 1947. *Education:* Attended Tabor College, 1924-25; Kansas State Teachers College, B.S., 1929; University of Kansas, M.A., 1935; University of Chicago, graduate study, 1939-40; Western Reserve University (now Case-Western Reserve University), Ph.D., 1946. *Religion:* Presbyterian. *Home:* 1099 Mount Vernon Blvd., Cleveland Heights, Ohio 44112.

CAREER: Rural school teacher, Halstead, Kan., 1925-27; high school teacher of English in Alma, Kan., and Paola, Kan., 1929-36; instructor in English at University of Kansas, Lawrence, 1936-39, Oregon State College (now University), Corvallis, 1940-44; Case-Western Reserve University, Cleveland, Ohio, assistant professor, 1946-49, associate professor, 1950-62, professor of English, 1962-74, professor emeritus, 1974—. *Member:* International Association of University Professors of English, Modern Language Association of America, English-Speaking Union (member of board, 1963-66), Dickens Fellowship. *Awards, honors:* Grants from American Philosophical Society, 1954, 1962, and 1964, and American Council of Learned Societies, 1962; Huntington Library fellowship, 1955.

WRITINGS: Georgina Hogarth and the Dickens Circle, Oxford University Press, 1957; *Mark Lemon: First Editor of Punch*, Oxford University Press, 1966. Contributor to *PMLA, Modern Philology, Huntington Quarterly*, and other learned journals.

WORK IN PROGRESS: The Parent-Child Relationship in the Novels of Charles Dickens.

SIDELIGHTS: Adrian's research travels in Europe include a seven-month stay in Great Britain in 1962. He is proficient in German and French.

*   *   *

AFNAN, Ruhi Muhsen 1899-1971

PERSONAL: Born December, 1899, in Acre, Palestine; son of Seyed Muhsen and Tooba Khanum (Abbas) Afnan; married Zahra Jalal Shahid, 1938; children: Iraj, Parviz. *Education:* Syrian Protestant College (now American University of Beirut), B.A., 1921. *Politics:* "International in feeling." *Religion:* Baha'i. *Home:* Number 6, Lagvardi St., Ghaffari Ave., 25 Shahrivar Pl., Teheran, Iran.

CAREER: On completion of his studies was employed briefly as private secretary to his grandfather, Abdu'l-Baha, the son of the founder of the Baha'i faith; private secretary to Shoghi Effendi, the guardian of the Baha'i faith, 1922-37 (during this period Afnan made two trips to the United States and lectured extensively in this country and Canada); retired to a life of private study, mainly on the philosophic implications of Baha'ism, 1938.

WRITINGS: Mysticism and the Baha'i Revelation: A Contrast (collection of articles), Baha'i Publishing Committee (New York), 1934; *The Great Prophets: Moses, Zoroaster, Jesus*, Philosophical Library, 1960; *Zoroaster's Influence on Greek Thought*, Philosophical Library, 1965; *Zoroaster's Influence on Anaxagoras, the Greek Tragedians, and Socrates*, Philosophical Library, 1969; *The Revelation of Baha'u'llah and The Bab*, Volume I: *Descartes, Theory of Knowledge*, Philosophical Library, 1970; *Two Schools of Existentialism* (originally written in Persian), privately printed, Volume I: *The Trend of Atheist Thoughts—Jean Paul Sartre*, 1970, Volume II: *The Trend of Christian Thoughts—Gabriel Marcel*, 1970.

WORK IN PROGRESS: Further books on *The Revelation of Baha'u'llah and The Bab.*†

(Died May 8, 1971)

*   *   *

AGNEW, Peter L(awrence) 1901-1969

PERSONAL: Born May 17, 1901, in Lynn, Mass.; son of Peter L. and Susan A. (Lydon) Agnew. *Education:* Boston University, B.B.A., 1923; New York University, M.A., 1928, Ph.D., 1940; Harvard University, M.Ed., 1931. *Office:* Office of the Vice-President for Business Affairs, New York University, Washington Sq., New York, N.Y. 10003.

CAREER: Merrill Business School, Stamford, Conn., administrative assistant, 1924-26; Orange High School, Orange, N.J., head of commercial education department, 1926-31; New York University, New York, N.Y., instructor, 1931-41, assistant professor, 1941-45, associate professor, 1945-48, professor of education, 1948-69, professor emeritus of business administration, 1969, assistant dean of School of Education, 1948-54, chairman of department of business education, 1955-59, budget coordinator and executive vice-president of the University, 1959-62, assistant executive vice-president, 1963-64, vice-president for business affairs, 1964-69. Ford Foundation consultant to Ministry of Education, Ghana, West Africa, summers, 1963, 1964. President of board of directors, West Square Corp., 1964-69; member of board of directors, Gramercy-Greenwich Association, 1964-69, and Greenwich Village Chamber of Commerce, 1964-69.

MEMBER: International Society for Business Education, National Association for Business Teacher Education (president, 1948), National Business Teachers Association, American Business Education Association (board member, 1948-50), American Association of School Administrators, National Office Management Association (board member, 1950-53), Eastern Business Education Association (president, 1939-40), New York Academy for Public Education (board member, beginning 1957), Phi Delta Kappa, Delta Pi Epsilon (national vice-president, 1942-43), Pi Omega Pi. *Awards, honors:* Named distinguished business educator for 1964 by Business Education Association.

WRITINGS: (With Paul S. Lomax) *Problems of Teaching Bookkeeping*, Prentice-Hall, 1930; (editor) *Fundamentals of Mimeograph Duplication*, A. B. Dick Co., 1936; (contributor) M. E. Jansson, editor, *Handbook of Applied Mathematics*, 2nd edition, Van Nostrand, 1936; *Principles and Problems of Office Practice*, New York University Bookstore, 1938, revised edition, 1940; (with R. C. Goodfellow) *Ten-Key Adding Listing Machine Course*, Southwestern, 1939, 3rd edition (with William R. Pasewark), 1963; (with Goodfellow) *Full Keyboard Adding and Listing Machine Course*, Southwestern, 1939, 3rd edition (with Pasewark), 1963; (editor) *The Improvement of Classroom Teaching in Business Education*, Eastern Commercial Teachers' Association, 1939; (with Foster W. Loso and C. W. Hamilton) *Secretarial Office Practice*, Southwestern, 1939, 7th edition (with others), 1966.

Office Machines, Bellman, 1941; (with Goodfellow) *Crank Driven Calculator Course*, 2nd edition, Southwestern, 1942; (with Goodfellow) *Key-driven Calculator Course*, 2nd edition, Southwestern, 1942, 4th edition (with Pasewark), 1962; (with Ernest D. Bassett) *Business Filing and Records Control*, Southwestern 1943, 3rd edition, 1963; *Office Machines Course—Adding and Calculating Machines*, Southwestern, 1944, 3rd edition (with Nicholas J. Cornelia), 1962; (with

Goodfellow) *Key-driven Calculator Course for the Burroughs Calculator and Comptometer,* 3rd edition, Southwestern, 1949.

(With Loso) *Clerical Office Practice,* Southwestern, 1950, 4th edition (with Pasewark and James R. Meehan), 1967; (with Mary M. Brady) *Advanced Key-driven Calculator Course,* Southwestern, 1958; *Machine Office Practice,* Southwestern, 1959; *Typewriting Office Practice,* Southwestern, 3rd edition, 1960; (with Meehan and Loso) *Project for Secretarial and Office Practice,* 1960; (with Pasewark) *Rotary Calculator Course,* Southwestern, 4th edition, 1962; *Filing Office Practice,* Southwestern, 1963. Also author with others of *Vocational Efficiency Drills,* 1945.

Contributor to business education journals. *Yearbook* editor, Eastern Commerical Teachers Association, 1939-40.†

(Died September 5, 1969)

*   *   *

AGNON, S(hmuel) Y(osef Halevi) 1888-1970

PERSONAL: Name originally Shmuel Yosef Czaczkes; born July 17, 1888, in Buczacz, Galicia (then Austria-Hungary, now Poland); son of Shalom Mordecai (an ordained rabbi, merchant, and scholar) and Esther (Farb-Hacohen) Czaczkes; married Esther Marx, May 6, 1919; children: Emuna (daughter), Shalom Mordecai Hemdat. *Education:* Spent six years in various private hadarim and a short period at the Baron Hirsch School. Received no other formal education. *Religion:* Jewish. *Home:* Talpiot, Jerusalem, Israel.

CAREER: Lived in Galicia, 1888-1908; his first published verses appeared in Hebrew and Yiddish when he was fifteen; first went to Jaffa, Palestine in 1908 and became first secretary of the Jewish court in Jaffa and secretary of the National Jewish Council; went to Germany, 1913, and was a lecturer in Hebrew literature, 1920-24, and a tutor in Hebrew; returned to Palestine in 1924 to settle there permanently. *Member:* Hebrew Language Academy, Mekitzei Nirdanim (society for the publication of ancient manuscripts; president, 1950-70). *Awards, honors:* Fellow, Bar Ilan University; Bialik Prize for Literature, 1934, for *Bilevav Yamin (In the Heart of the Seas),* and again in the 1950's; D.H.L., Jewish Theological Seminary of America, 1936; Hakhnasat Kala, 1937; Ussishkin Prize, 1950, for *Tmol Shilshom;* Israel Prize, 1958; Ph.D., Hebrew University, Jerusalem, 1959; was made an honorary citizen of Jerusalem, 1962; Nobel Prize for Literature, 1966.

WRITINGS: Ve-Hayah he-'Akov le-Mishor, [Jaffa], 1911/12, Juedischer Verlag (Berlin), 1919; (editor with Ahron Eliasberg) *Das Buch von den Polnischen Juden* (folk tales), Juedischer Verlag, 1916; (editor) *Moaus Zur: Ein Chanukkahbuch,* Juedischer Verlag, 1918; *Giv 'at ha-Hol,* Juedischer Verlag, 1919.

Sipur ha-Shanim ha-Tovot (II Title: *Ma'aseh ha-Rav Veha-Orah*), [Tel-Aviv], c. 1920; *Be-Sod Yesharim,* Juedischer Verlag, 1921; *Me-Hamat ha-Metsik,* Juedischer Verlag, 1921; *'Al Kapot ha-Man'ul,* Juedischer Verlag, 1922; *Polin* (fiction), Hedim (Tel-Aviv), 1924/25; *Ma'aseh ha-meshulah me-erets ha-Kedosha,* [Tel-Aviv], 1924/25; *Ma'aseh rabi Gadiel ha-Tinok,* [Berlin], 1925; *Ha-Nidah,* 1926; *Agadat ha-sofer,* [Tel-Aviv], 1929.

Laylot, [Tel-Aviv], 1930/31; *Bi-levav Yamim,* Schocken (Berlin), 1935, translation by Israel Meir Lask published as *In the Heart of the Seas: A Story of a Journey to the Land of Israel,* Schocken (New York), 1948; *Kovets Sipurim,* [New York], 1937; *Yamim Nora'im,* Schocken (Jerusalem and Berlin), 1938, 4th edition, Schocken (New York), 1956, translation by Maurice T. Galpert, revised by Jacob Sloan, published as *Days of Awe: Being a Treasury of Traditions, Legends and Learned Commentaries Concerning Rosh ha-Shanah, Yom Kippur and the Days Between, Culled from Three Hundred Volumes, Ancient and New,* condensed and edited by Nahum N. Glatzer, Schocken, 1948; *Pi Shenaim o me-Husar Yom,* [Tel-Aviv], 1939.

Shevu'ath Emunim, [Jerusalem], 1943, translation by Walter Lever published as "Betrothed" in *Two Tales: Betrothed* [and] *Edo and Enam* (translation of *Edo ve-Enam*), Schocken, 1966; *Sipurim ve-Agadot,* edited by Jehiel Ben-Num, [Tel-Aviv], 1944; *'Al Berl Kazenelson,* [Tel-Aviv], 1944; *Sipurim,* [Jerusalem, Tel-Aviv], 1945.

Edo ve-Enam, Schocken (Jerusalem), 1950 (see above for translation); *Sifrehem shel Anshe Butshatsh* (reprinted from "Sefer Butsats"), [Tel-Aviv], 1956; (with others) *Tehilla, and Other Israeli Tales,* Abelard, 1956; (editor) *Atem re'item,* [Jerusalem], 1959.

Kelev Hutsot, [Jerusalem], 1960; (compiler) *Sifrehem shel Tsadikim,* [Jerusalem], 1961; *Ha-Esh ve-Ha'etsim,* Schocken, 1962; *Ve-Hayah he-Akov le-Mishor,* edited by Naftali Ginaton, [Israel], 1966; *Sipurim,* [Israel], 1966; *Sipurim,* edited by Ginaton, [Israel], 1967; *Sipure Yom ha-Kipurim,* edited by Ginaton, [Israel], 1967.

Selected Stories of S. Y. Agnon (Hebrew text), edited, with introduction, interpretations, and vocabulary, by Samuel Leiter, Tarbuth Foundation, 1970; *Twenty-One Stories,* edited by Nahum N. Glatzer, Schocken (New York), 1970; *Shirah,* [Israel], 1971; *Ir u-Melo'ah,* [Israel], 1973.

"Kol Sipurav" (collected works), eleven volumes, Schocken (Berlin, Tel-Aviv, and Jerusalem), Volume I and II: *Hakhnasath Kallah,* 1931, translation by I. M. Lask published as *The Bridal Canopy,* Doubleday, 1937, reprinted, Gollancz, 1968; Volume III: *Me-Az ume-Ata,* 1931; Volume IV: *Sippurei Ahayim,* 1931; Volume V: *Sippur Pashut,* 1935; Volume VI: *Be-Shuva u-ve-Natat,* 1935; Volume VII: *Ore'ah Nata Lalun,* 1937, translation by Misha Louvish and others published as *A Guest for the Night,* Schocken (New York), 1968; Volume VIII: *Elu va-Elu,* 1941 (later published in a revised edition as Volume II of collected works); Volume IX: *Tmol Shilshom,* 1945 (a section of this was published as *Kelev Hutsot,* [Merhavya], 1950); Volume X: *Samukh ve-Nireh,* 1950; Volume XI: *Ad Heinah,* 1953; volumes issued under title "Kol Sipurav Shel Agnon," [Jerusalem, Tel-Aviv], beginning, 1947, 4th edition, Schocken, 1957, standard edition, edited by Agnon, Schocken, 1953-62.

Contributor to numerous books, including: *Festschrift fuer A. Freimann,* [Berlin], 1935; *Minhah Ledavid,* [Jerusalem], 1935; *Sefer ha'Shanah shel Eretz Yisrael,* [Tel-Aviv], 1935; *Jewish Studies ... in Honour ... of J. L. Lendau,* [Tel-Aviv], 1936; *Sefer ha-Shabbat,* [Tel-Aviv], 1936; Leo W. Schwarz, editor, *A Golden Treasury of Jewish Literature,* Farrar & Rinehart, 1937; *Luah ha-Arets,* [Tel-Aviv], 1944; *Sefer Hashabat,* [New York], 1947; *Me-otuar ha-Sifrut ha-Hadashah,* [New York], 1948; Philip Goodman, editor, *The Purim Anthology,* Jewish Publication Society, 1949; Nathan Ausubel, editor, *A Treasury of Jewish Humor,* Doubleday, 1952; Azriel Eisenberg, editor, *The Bar Mitzvah Treasury,* Behrman, 1952; Abraham E. Millgram, editor, *Sabbath: The Day of Delight,* Jewish Publication Society, 1952; Joseph Leftwich, editor, *Yisroel,* Behrman, 1952; Azriel Eisenberg, editor, *The Confirmation Reader,* Behrman, 1953; M. Z. Frank, editor, *Sound the Great Trumpet,* Whittier Books,

1955; Sholom J. Kahn, editor, *A Whole Loaf: Stories from Israel*, Vanguard, 1962; Joel Blocker, editor, *Israeli Stories*, Schocken, 1962; Saul Bellow, editor, *Great Jewish Short Stories*, Dell, 1963; Samuel Sobel, editor, *A Treasury of Jewish Sea Stories*, Jonathan David, 1965; Leo W. Schwarz, editor, *The Jewish Caravan*, Farrar, Straus, 1965; S. Y. Penueli and A. Ukhmani, editors, *Hebrew Short Stories*, Volume I, Institute for the Translation of Hebrew Literature, and Megiddo Publishing Co. (Tel-Aviv), 1965. Contributor to *Haaretz* (daily newspaper), *Palestine Review*, *Commentary*, *Gazith*, *Congress Bi-Weekly*, and other publications.

SIDELIGHTS: "I am not a modern writer," Agnon once commented. "I am astounded that I have even one reader. I don't see the reader before me.... I never wanted to know the reader. I wanted to work in my own way." It is true that, though Agnon was the dominant figure among Hebrew fiction writers for many years, and though his works are considered classics, he was, until he won the Nobel Prize, virtually unknown outside the Jewish reading public. Yet his advent as a writer early in this century reversed the trend of Jewish literature from what Menachem Ribalow called "the general European spirit." Agnon "reversed the trend from Europe homeward again, from alien ways back to the native road.... He said not a single word *pro* or *contra*. He simply began to write in a different manner, different from all other Hebrew writers of that time. His novelty lay in his old-fashionedness. His uniqueness consisted in his return to the old sources, to the folk-character and its traits of simplicity and sincerity, purity and piety."

Agnon had sensed the alien aspects of European culture and initiated a return to Jewish folk material, to Medieval Hebrew, and to the traditions and laws that he found in ancient sources. His prose, which is lyrical, ironic, humorous, and deceptively simple, reads as though it had been written ages ago. "With Agnon," wrote Ribalow, "the Hebrew short story reaches artistic heights. He has the secret of the perfect blend of content and form, style and rhythm, inner beauty and outer grace. He has tapped new sources of Jewish ethical and esthetic values, revealing the spiritual grandeur in Jewish life. He has done what others have sought in vain to do: to convert simplicity and folk-naivete into a thing of consummate art and beauty. To the jangled nerves of this troubled generation, Agnon's stories bring balm and comfort." Edmund Wilson considered him "a man of unquestionable genius."

Agnon revived ancient forms of storytelling, forms unlike those of the modern Hebrew "realistic" story. Rueben Wallenrod said that "because of its [apparent] lack of frame, Agnon's story flows without effort, and events follow one another in loose sequence. The time of the events is very seldom indicated. In the continuous shift of his relationships, he lives mainly within his memories, and the boundary between the actual and the imaginary has become blurred to such an extent that the confines of time are gone...." According to David Patterson, "the first impressions of apparent simplicity soon give way to a realization of the overtones, references and allusions arising from the author's complete familiarity with the whole vast corpus of Hebrew literature. The ancient vocabulary of Hebrew is pregnant with associations of all kinds, and the skillful juxtaposition of words and phrases can be made to yield a variety of nuances. Linguistically, as well as thematically, Agnon's writings can be read at different levels."

Arnold J. Band wrote: "For some readers, Agnon is the epitome of traditional Jewish folk-literature; for others, he is

the most daring of modernists. For the older reader, Agnon conjures up memories of Jewish life in Eastern Europe; for the younger reader, he wrestles with the central universal problems of our agonized century." Band took issue with those who saw Agnon as merely a reviver of Jewish folk material and techniques. He pointed out that Agnon read widely in German and Scandinavian literatures, and also read Russian and French novelists in German translation. "To attribute Agnon's literary technique to Jewish folk-literature alone, as many tend to do, is sheer nonsense; Agnon was well-acquainted with the best in modern European literature at a relatively early age."

Agnon's characters are the pious and the humble men of faith whom he endowed "with divine qualities without making an effort to emphasize the mystical," wrote Ribalow. He, as well as his characters, believed that righteousness will ultimately triumph and that the cruel aspects of reality can be transcended by pity and love. He wrote about the dispossessed of the earth, he himself having twice lost his home in a fire. Robert Alter wrote that in 1924 Agnon's home in Hamburg burned down, "and everything he owned went up in the flames, including his library of four thousand books and the manuscript of an autobiographical novel (which he never attempted to begin again)." Other manuscripts, all unpublished, were also destroyed. In 1929, his home in Jerusalem was ravaged by Arab rioters, and a good part of his library was lost. In 1948, during the Israeli liberation, Agnon had to evacuate his home in Talpiot. He returned after the end of the hostilities.

Agnon took his pen name, which later became his legal name, from the title of his first published story, "Agunot," which appeared in Jaffa in 1909. Baruch Hochman explained that the Hebrew word *agunah* refers to a Jewish grass widow, i.e., a woman who is separated from her husband. "Owing to conditions of life in the Diaspora, war, plague and political accident carried men off, leaving the *agunah* as living testament to the vicissitudes of both life in the Diaspora and the rigors of the impersonal Law. It would seem no accident that Agnon took his name from the tale. The very word is redolent of loss, but also of the infinite yearning and ineffable tenderness elicited by loss. All of Agnon's work was to pivot on such feeling. First there was the sort of loss rendered in this tale: of loved ones torn away in the midst of life, by chance, by fate, by death or desire. Then there was historical loss: the submergence of the world of origins to which one's feelings are bound, in the abyss of history. Finally, there was metaphysical loss: of transcendent objects of desire in the bewilderment of modernity...."

His work has been compared to that of Cervantes and, even more frequently, to Kafka's, though his relation with the former is tenuous, and Agnon had reportedly denied any knowledge of Kafka. Alter noted that Agnon was not unlike Kafka in that he possessed "something of the same sense of a world where terrible things are waiting to spring out from the shadows of experience. Also ... his Hebrew has much the same unexcited, deliberately restrained tone of narration as Kafka's German, and achieves a very convincing Kafkaesque *frisson*, often through the imagery of sounds." But Kafka's world, unlike Agnon's, was amoral, and the distinction between good and evil was vague.

Agnon once stated his reasons for writing in Hebrew: "Out of affection for our language and love of the holy, I burn midnight oil over the teachings of the Torah and deny myself food for the words of our sages that I may store them up within me to be ready upon my lips. If the Temple were standing, I would take my place on the platform with my fellow choristers and would recite each day the song that the Levites used to say in the Holy Temple. [Agnon traced his ancestry to the tribe of Levi.] But since the Temple is destroyed and we have neither Priests in their service nor Levites in their chorus and song, I devote myself to the Torah, the Prophets, the latter Scriptures, the Mishnah, Halachah and Aggada, the Tosefta, rabbinical commentaries and textual glosses. When I look at their words and see that of all our precious possessions in ancient times only the memory is left us, I am filled with sorrow. And that sorrow makes my heart tremble. And from that trembling I write stories, like a man banished from his father's palace who builds himself a small shelter and sits there telling the glory of his ancestral home.'' Alter noted that ''like generations of Jews before him, Agnon regards Hebrew as the Jew's indispensable means of entrance into the sphere of sanctity.'' For Agnon, the Hebrew characters comprised ''the alphabet of holiness.''

Although Agnon's stories reflect the tragedy and death that lurk in the background, David Patterson wrote that ''one positive element alone remains constant—Jerusalem herself, which in Agnon's stories is endowed with a personality of her own, and becomes a symbol for all that is meaningful and permanent and harmonious in life. It is as though the holy city alone contains the seeds which might restore that wholeness of spirit and oneness [with the world] that are slipping through the nerveless fingers of our unhappy generation.''

After his immigration in 1924 until his death, Agnon wrote about life in Israel. The style remained the same, wrote Ribalow, ''epically quiet and midrashically wise. But more and more do present realities play a part, together with all of their difficulties and sufferings, their problems and contradictions.'' And Wallenrod observed that ''the new form of Agnon's stories has not changed the former content. The criterion for the human being is still his humaneness. . . .''

Agnon's entire life had been devoted to writing, and, with a permanent annual stipend from his publisher, Schocken Books, he was able to support himself on his writings alone. (In 1916 Salman Schocken promised to find a publisher for Agnon, and redeemed this promise by becoming a publisher in order to issue Agnon's writings.) He was known to be a perfectionist who sometimes set aside a story for as long as fifteen years before he felt ready to rework it and submit it for publication. Agnon had revised stories he published more than thirty years previously. He described his writing habits for the *New York Times*: ''When I was healthy I used to work standing. I felt myself fresh and good and sometimes worked that way all day and into the night. I recommend it to every writer. But now I must sit to work and keep this [nitroglycerine] for the heart condition I have had for fifteen years.'' The street in Talpiot on which he lived was closed to traffic, and a sign at the head of the street read: ''Quiet. Agnon is Writing.''

He read less in his later years, his vision failing, but when he did it was to the Talmud that he turned. He apologized to one American interviewer for not being able to speak English, and added: ''I made a contract with the Almighty, that for every language I did not learn he would give me a few words in Hebrew. . . . [Also], in order that I shouldn't have to go many places, I don't learn English.'' One place he wanted to, and did, visit, however, was Stockholm to receive the Nobel Prize from the king. It would be a rare pleasure, he said beforehand, ''because there is a special benediction one says before a king, and I have never met a king.''

His works have been translated into at least sixteen languages.

BIOGRAPHICAL/CRITICAL SOURCES—Books: Fritz Mordechai Kaufmann, *Vier Essais Ueber ostjuedische Dichtung und Kultur*, [Berlin], 1919; Eliezer Meir Lipschuetz, *Sh. Y. Agnon*, 1926; Eliezer Raphael Malachi, *Dr. Sh. Y. Agnon*, Hadoar (New York), 1935/36; Menachem Ribalow, *Dichter und Shafer fuer neu-Hebraish*, [New York], 1936; Elias Hurwicz, *Aus Agnons dichterischen Schaffen*, [Berlin], 1936; Yosef Seh-Lavan, *Shmuel Yosef Agnon*, [Tel-Aviv], 1947; Baruch Kurzweil, *Masekhet ha-Roman*, [Tel-Aviv], 1953; Dob Kimhi, *Soferim*, J. Sreberk (Tel-Aviv), 1953; Rueben Wallenrod, *The Literature of Modern Israel*, Abelard, 1956; Ephraim Zoref, *Sh. Y. Agnon*, [Tel-Aviv], 1957; Baruch Kurzweil, editor, *Yuval Shal* (a festschrift dedicated to Agnon on his seventieth birthday), 1958; Menachem Ribalow, *The Flowering of Modern Hebrew Literature*, Twayne, 1959; Dob Sadan, *Al Shai Agnon*, [Tel-Aviv], 1959; S. I. Penuell, *Yetsirato shel Sh. Y. Agnon*, [Tel-Aviv], 1960; Arnold J. Band, *Nostalgia and Nightmare: A Study in the Fiction of S. Y. Agnon*, University of California Press, 1968; B. Hojman, *The Fiction of S. Y. Agnon*, Cornell University Press, 1970.

Articles: *Commentary*, August, 1961, December, 1966; *Ariel* (Jerusalem), Number 11, 1965; *Daedalus*, fall, 1966; *New York Times Book Review*, September 18, 1966; *New York Times*, October 21, 1966; *Congress Bi-Weekly*, November 7, 1966; *New Statesman*, December 9, 1966; *Nation*, December 12, 1966; *Adam International Review*, Number 307-8-9, 1966; *Ariel* (entire issue devoted to Agnon), Number 17, 1966/67; *Contemporary Literary Criticism*, Volume IV, Gale, 1975.†

(Died Feburary 17, 1970)

* * *

AGUS, Irving A(braham) 1910-

PERSONAL: Name legally changed, 1937; born February 20, 1910, in Swislocz, Poland; came to United States in 1927, naturalized citizen; son of Leib (a rabbi) and Beila (Bereznicki) Agushewitz; married Tema Gerber, October 2, 1939; children: Rachel Ann (Mrs. Murry Varat), Ronald Ellis. *Education:* Hebrew University of Jerusalem, student, 1926-27; New York University, B.S., 1932; Dropsie College for Hebrew and Cognate Learning, Ph.D., 1937. *Home:* 208 West 179th St., Bronx, N.Y. 10453. *Office:* Department of History, Yeshiva University, New York, N.Y. 10032.

CAREER: Educational director of a Jewish congregation in Memphis, Tenn., 1939-45; principal of Jewish schools on Long Island, N.Y., 1945-47, and Philadelphia, Pa., 1949-51; Harry Fischel Institute for Research in Talmud, Jerusalem, Israel, dean, 1947-49; Yeshiva University, New York, N.Y., associate professor of history, 1950-55, professor of Jewish history and chairman of Jewish Division, beginning 1956, director of Graduate Summer School, beginning 1953. *Awards, honors:* La Med Prize, 1948, for *Rabbi Meir of Rothenburg*.

WRITINGS: Rabbi Meir of Rothenburg, two volumes, Dropsie College for Hebrew and Cognate Learning, 1947; *Teshuvot ba'ale ha-Tosafot: Responsa of the Tosaphists*, Yeshiva University Press, 1954; *Divrei yemei Yisroel: History of the Jewish People*, World Zionist Organization, Volume I, 1957, Volume II, 1967; *Urban Civilization in Pre-Crusade Europe*, two volumes, Yeshiva University Press, 1965; (contributor) Cecil Roth, editor, *The World History of the Jewish People*, second series, Volume II: *The Dark Ages*, Rutledge University Press, 1966; *The Heroic Age of Franco-German Jewry*, Yeshiva University Press, 1969.

Editor, Shainberg Library, five volumes, 1945. Member of editorial board, *Jewish Quarterly Review.*

* * *

AIKEN, Clarissa Lorenz   1899-

PERSONAL: Born January 28, 1899, in Milwaukee, Wis.; daughter of Louis Robert (a manufacturer) and Mary (Mich) Lorenz; married Conrad Aiken (the poet and critic), February 27, 1930 (divorced, 1937; died, 1973). *Education:* Attended New England Conservatory of Music. *Politics:* Democrat. *Home and office:* 290 Marlborough St., Boston, Mass. 02116. *Agent:* Bertha Case, 42 West 53rd St., New York, N.Y. 10019.

CAREER: Brookline Music School, Brookline, Mass., piano teacher, 1960-73.

WRITINGS: Junket to Japan (teen-age book) Little, Brown, 1960.

WORK IN PROGRESS: A memoir, tentatively entitled *Angel of Darkness.*

SIDELIGHTS: Clarissa Aiken lived for six years in Sussex, England. *Avocational interests:* Sewing, cooking, tennis, swimming.

* * *

ALEXANDER, Franklin Osborne   1897-

PERSONAL: Born November 3, 1897, in St. Louis, Mo.; son of Franklin Rittenhouse and Blanche (Osborne) Alexander; married Blanche Stanley, December 27, 1924; children: Mimi (Mrs. Everett D. Simson), Carolyn (Mrs. Harold Russek II). *Education:* Northwestern University, student, 1916-17, 1919-20. *Politics:* Nonpartisan. *Religion:* Episcopalian. *Home:* Beaver Hill Apartments, No. 328, Jenkintown, Pa. 19046. *Office address:* Box 262, Jenkintown, Pa. 19046.

CAREER: Free-lance commercial cartoonist in Chicago, Ill., 1919-24; cartoonist doing comic strips for Western Newspaper Union, 1924-31; creator of "Hairbreadth Harry," appearing in daily and Sunday papers, 1931-38; free-lance cartoonist in Philadelphia, Pa., 1938-42; editorial cartoonist for *Philadelphia Evening and Sunday Bulletin,* Philadelphia, 1942-67; cartoonist, syndicated by United Feature Service, New York, N.Y., 1955-67. *Military service:* U.S. Army, Ambulance Corps and Corps of Engineers, 1917-19. *Member:* Association of American Editorial Cartoonists, Sigma Chi. *Awards, honors:* National Headliners Award, 1945; Christopher Award, 1955; awards from National Safety Council, 1948 and 1958, Freedoms Foundation, 1949-67, National Conference of Christians and Jews, 1956, Boy Scouts of America, 1957 and 1958, Disabled American Veterans, 1961, United World Federalists, 1961, and Temple University, 1969.

WRITINGS—Self-illustrated: *Joe Doakes' Great Quest,* John Knox, 1968. Editorial cartoons have appeared in *Saturday Evening Post, Presbyterian Life, Christian Herald,* and other periodicals; regular cartoonist for several years for *Church News* (Episcopalian diocesan monthly).

SIDELIGHTS: Franklin Alexander told *CA:* "As an unabashed ivory-tower idealist, I use the allegorical form of story-telling, and as a cartoonist, I use the cartoon [as a device for taking] some of the curse out of what words often do to a 'message.'" Alexander's collection of editorial cartoons is maintained by the Carnegie Library at Syracuse University.

AVOCATIONAL INTERESTS: Freshwater fishing ("the vocation of expectancy").

* * *

ALIHAN, Milla

PERSONAL: Born in Vladikavkaz (now Dzaudzhikau), Russia; daughter of Alexander A. (a landowner) and Maria Sidamon (Tolpar) Alihan; married Bertram Cecil Eskell (a physician), July 16, 1938 (deceased). *Education:* Smith College, M.A.; Columbia University, Ph.D., 1938. *Religion:* Russian Orthodox. *Home:* 10 New St., Port Washington, Long Island, N.Y. 10050. *Agent:* Mrs. Maxwell Ruth Aley, 145 East 35th St., New York, N.Y. 10016. *Office:* Milla Alihan Associates, 25 East 83rd St., New York, N.Y. 10028.

CAREER: Wartime work for U.S. Government as an associate in research and preparation of civil defense program, 1941, as editor-in-chief of two magazines, *America* and *Illustrated America,* both sponsored by Departments of State and Defense for overseas distribution, 1944, and as a simultaneous interpreter at Nuremberg Trials, 1946; Standard-Kollsmann Corp., Elmhurst and Syosset, N.Y., director of public and human relations, 1945-59; Milla Alihan Associates, New York, N.Y., president, beginning 1945. Licensed psychologist, working in field of industrial and clinical psychology, in sociology and human relations; director, Institute for Research in Hypnosis; management consultant to Eastern Airlines, McKinsey & Co., Genesco, Inc., McGraw-Hill, Inc., Manpower, Inc., and others. Former director, American Federation of International Institutes; director, Russian Orthodox Theological Fund; trustee and member of supervisory psychological staff, Morton Prince Clinic for Hypnotherapy.

MEMBER: American Sociological Association (fellow), American Psychological Association, International Society for Clinical and Experimental Hypnosis, Aviation Writers Association, International Platform Association, Mensa. *Awards, honors:* Cited as one of the outstanding women of New Jersey by New Jersey Tercentenary Committee, 1964.

WRITINGS: Social Ecology: A Critical Analysis, Columbia University Press, 1938, reprinted, Cooper Square, 1964; *Corporate Etiquette,* Weybright, 1970. Wrote dubbed English script for Soviet motion picture, "Wait for Me," for MGM International, 1946; translated Nicolai Pogodin's four-act play, "The Aristocrats." Contributor to *Good Housekeeping* and other publications. Editorial adviser, *Canadian Forum;* editor-in-chief, *Newsletter* of Society for Clinical and Experimental Hypnosis, 1966-67.

WORK IN PROGRESS: A book on hypnotherapy; writing on what makes a successful consultant.

SIDELIGHTS: Milla Alihan grew up in China; she learned English in a French convent in Tsingtao, a German city on Chinese soil at that time under Japanese rule. She spent some years in British Columbia before coming to the United States. She writes: "If you had ever been in a vacuum without air, you would realize how essential air is, and this is the way I feel about liberty. We take liberty so completely for granted until we lose it—then and only then do we become aware of its life sustaining value. Because my life in other countries has made me acutely aware of how important liberty is, I am a staunch believer in the rights of an individual, in free enterprise and in the four freedoms."

Corporate Etiquette has been published in Portuguese and German editions.

ALLARD, Sven   1896-1975

PERSONAL: Born July 6, 1896, in Tjaellmo, Sweden; married Margaretha Silfverschioeld, April 10, 1933; children: Sven Otto, Nils Urban. *Education:* University of Uppsala, B.A., 1918, LL.B., 1920. *Religion:* Protestant. *Home:* Porlezza, Provincia di Como, Italy.

CAREER: Swedish diplomat; entered Foreign Office, 1921; third secretary at Swedish embassies in Warsaw, Poland, 1922, and Riga, Latvia, 1923-24; second secretary in Brussels, Belgium, 1925-26, The Hague, Netherlands, 1927, and Foreign Office, Stockholm, Sweden, 1927-30; consul in London, England, 1930-32; first secretary in Warsaw, 1932, Rome, Italy, 1933, and Paris, France, 1934; commercial counsellor in Paris, 1934-38; charge d'affaires in Athens, Greece, 1938, Ankara, Turkey, 1939-40, and Sofia, Bulgaria, 1941-43; minister to China, 1943-47; delegate for commercial negotiation, Foreign Office, Stockholm, 1947-49; minister to Rumania and Bulgaria, 1949-51, Hungary, 1949-54, Czechoslovakia, 1951-54, and Austria, 1954-56; ambassador to Austria, 1956-64; Swedish government representative to United Nations Food and Agriculture Organization, Rome, 1964-69. Swedish government representative diplomatic adviser, Swedish-International Red Cross relief action to Greece, 1942-43. *Awards, honors:* Grand Cross of the North Star of Sweden; Order of the Fenix of Greece; Austrian Order of Merit; Chinese Golden Harvest.

WRITINGS: Ryskt utspel i Wien, Norstedt, 1965, revised and enlarged edition published as *Russia and the Austrian State Treaty: A Case Study of Soviet Policy in Europe,* Pennsylvania State University Press, 1970; *Stalin och Hitler,* Norstedt, 1970. Contributor to Swedish magazines.†

(Died August 17, 1975)

*   *   *

ALLEN, A(rthur) B(ruce)   1903-1975
(Borough Trice)

PERSONAL: Born February 12, 1903, in Westgate-on-Sea, Kent, England; son of Sidney Bruce (a farmer) and Edith Nellie (Trice) Allen; married Frances Eleanor Peters. *Education:* Attended Saltley College, Birmingham, England, and University of London; Licentiate of College of Preceptors, 1930, Diploma in Theology, 1941. *Home:* "Glenfinlas," 5 Castle Villas, Castle St., Stroud, Gloucestershire GL5 2HP, England.

CAREER: Schoolmaster in Birmingham, and then Hendon, England, 1923-35; Winsor & Newton Ltd. (publishers), London, England, art lecturer, educational organizer, and editor of house magazine, *Colour Review,* 1935-41; Great Haseley Endowed School, Oxfordshire, England, headmaster, 1941-46; Peterborough Teachers Training College, Peterborough, England, senior lecturer in art and warden of student hostel, 1946-48; Stroud High School, Stroud, England, English and divinity master, 1948-50; ordained priest of Church of England, 1950; chaplain to Gloucester Prison, 1950-52, and Longfords Approved School, 1952-56; Rector of Enmore and Goathurst, Somerset, 1954-56; Vicar of Selsley, 1956-60; Vicar of Bisley, 1960-67; Vicar of Moreton Valence with Whitminister, 1967-75. Artist, with one-man shows in London, the English provinces, Paris, and Dublin, prior to World War II; honorary art tutor at College of the Sea, London, 1930-75, and Wandsworth Prison, London, 1930-40; lecturer on art on tours in Northern Ireland, Ireland, and Soviet Union, 1935-40. Actor, writer, producer, and designer with amateur theater groups; founder and

director of youth clubs wherever he has worked; broadcaster for radio and television, including the B.B.C. series "Our Village." *Wartime service:* Home Guard, section commander during World War II; also camouflage consultant to Army Officers Emergency Reserve, 1938-41. *Member:* Royal Society of Arts (fellow), Royal Society of St. George (fellow), Society of Authors, Council for the Preservation of Rural England, American Geographical Society, Authors' Club (London).

WRITINGS: (With wife, F. E. Allen) *Art and Artistic Handicrafts for the School,* three volumes, Harrap, 1932; *The Teaching of Colours in Schools,* Winsor & Newton, 1935; (self-illustrated) *Colour Town* (fairy tale), Winsor & Newton, 1935; *Lino Craft in School,* Winsor & Newton, 1935; (self-illustrated) *Colour Harmony for Beginners: The Ostwald Theory,* Warne, 1936; (with Evan H. Williams) *The Psychology of Punishment: The New School Discipline,* Allman & Son, 1936; *Drama Through the Centuries and Play Production To-day,* Allman & Son, 1936; *"Let's Go!": Being A Faithful Account of All That Happened to Billy and Binks When They Ran Away into the Greenwood,* Blackwood & Co., 1937; *Puppetry and Puppet Plays for Infants, Juniors, and Seniors,* Allman & Son, 1937; *The Teaching of Art to Infants and Junior Children,* Warne, 1937; *The Romance of the Alphabet,* Warne, 1937; *Colour Harmony: Its Theory and Practice,* Warne, 1937; *Puppet Plays for Infants and Juniors,* Allman & Son, 1937; *Puppet Plays for Seniors,* Allman & Son, 1937; *Poster Designing for Beginners,* Warne, 1938; *Selected Puppet Plays,* Allman & Son, 1938; *The Pyromaniac* (novel), Blackwood & Co., 1938; *The Teaching of Art in Senior Schools,* Warne, 1938; *Imagination and Reality in Colour: An Art Manual for Teachers,* Warne, 1939.

Graphic Art in Easy Stages, Wells Gardner, Darton & Co., 1940; *Design and the New Art,* Warne, 1940; *Puppetry for Beginners, in Three Stages,* Wells Gardner, Darton & Co., 1940; *At the Sign of the Griffin Inn* (fiction), Wells Gardner, Darton & Co., 1940; *Live English,* Collins, 1941; (under pseudonym Borough Trice) *'Orrible Murder* (fiction), Wells Gardner, Darton & Co., 1941; *Art in the Secondary School,* Warne, 1945; *Linocraft for Beginners,* Winsor & Newton, 1945; (with O.R.S. Hudson) *Citizenship,* Allman & Son, 1948; *The Bible and the Teacher,* Warne, 1948; *The Dawn of Art,* Warne, 1948; *Art in the Primary School,* Warne, 1948; *Art Through the Ages,* Warne, 1948.

The Model Theatre, Wells Gardner, Darton & Co., 1950; *Rural Education,* two volumes, Allman & Son, 1950; *Religious Drama for Amateur Players,* Faber, 1958.

Bible Handbook for Teachers of Religious Instruction, Barrie & Rockliff, 1960; *A Tale That Is Told: A Pageant of English Literature, 1900-1950,* Barrie & Rockliff, 1960, Dufour, 1966.

"The Rockliff New Project" series; published by Barrie & Rockliff, many with companion "Practical Books": *The Elizabethan House,* 1949; *The Spacious Days of Queen Elizabeth: The Background Book,* 1950; *The Middle Ages, 1154-1485: The Background Book,* 1951; *Norman England to 1154: The Complete Background Book,* 1953; *Stuart England: The Complete Background Book,* 1954; *Eighteenth-Century Buildings,* 1955; *Eighteenth-Century England: The Complete Background Book,* 1955; *The Nineteenth Century Up to 1850: The Complete Background Book,* 1956; *Victorian England, 1850-1900: The Complete Background Book,* 1956; *Twentieth-Century England: The Complete Background Book,* 1959.

Editor: (With O. J. Tonks) Friedrich W. Ostwald, *Individual Art Cards*, Series II (Allen not associated with previous series), Winsor & Newton, 1935; "Golden Galley Series of Junior Classics," Golden Galley Press, 1946-50; *Religious Drama Scenes*, Allman & Son, 1950; John Lees, *Brief Geography of the World*, revised edition (Allen not associated with previous edition), Allman & Son, 1959; *Concise English History*, Allman & Son, 1960. Contributor to *Times Educational Supplement, Country Fair, Countryman*, and other educational and regional publications. Editor, *Old Lutonian*, 1960-75, and *Gloucester Diocesan Gazette*, 1961-75.

WORK IN PROGRESS: Kalendar of Old English Customs.

SIDELIGHTS: Father Allen once told *CA:* "[I am] a dyed-in-the-wool countryman, of a long line of English farmers [and have] a passion for the countryside and the country way of life. Special hatred: All town-planners and 'improvers of the English countryside.' No one special hobby. Love reading and more reading. Gardening. Building stone walls. Painting. Drama in all its forms. Music. Love singing but can't sing—have the voice of a hoarse crow. Can't live without dogs and horses."

Allen's religious plays have been performed in Britain, South Africa, Northern Ireland, Ireland, and the United States.†

(Died January 17, 1975)

*   *   *

ALLEN, Cecil J(ohn)   1886-1973
(Mercury, Voyageur)

PERSONAL: Born January 25, 1886; son of John Freeman (a shipping agent) and Lucy (Nislop) Allen; married Lily Charlton, December 30, 1912 (died, 1963); children: Geoffrey Freeman. *Education:* City and Guilds of London (Technical), City and Guilds Certificate, 1903. *Politics:* Tory. *Religion:* Methodist.

CAREER: Great Eastern Railway, London, England, engineering assistant, 1903-08, inspector of materials, 1908-16, in general manager's office, 1916-18, chief inspector of materials, 1918-22; London & North Eastern Railway, London, with engineers department, Southern Area, 1922-46; Ian Allan Ltd. (publishers), Shepperton, Middlesex, England, a director, beginning 1947. Professional lecturer and broadcaster on railway subjects. *Member:* Royal Society of Arts (fellow), Institute of Transport, Institution of Locomotive Engineers (associate member), Fleet St. Railway Circle (president), Railway Club (past president).

WRITINGS—All published by Ian Allan, except as noted: *Modern British Permanent Way*, Railway News, 1915; *The Iron Road*, John F. Shaw, 1925; *The Steel Highway*, Longmans, Green, 1928; *Famous Trains*, Meccano, 1928; *Railways of To-day, Their Engineering, Equipment and Operation*, Warne, 1929; *"Coronation" and Other Famous Trains*, Nicholson & Watson, 1937, 2nd edition, 1957; *Titled Trains of Great Britain*, 1946, 5th edition, 1967; *Locomotive Practice and Performance in the Twentieth Century*, Heffer, 1949, 2nd edition, 1950; *The Locomotive Exchanges*, 1949, 2nd edition, 1950.

Switzerland's Amazing Railways, Thomas Nelson, 1953, 4th edition, 1965; *The Great Eastern Railway*, 1955, 5th edition, 1968; *Modern Railways: Their Engineering, Equipment and Operation*, Faber, 1959; *British Pacific Locomotives*, 1962, 3rd edition, 1967; *The North Eastern Railway*, 1964; *Two*

Million Miles of Train Travel (autobiography), 1965; *The London & North Eastern Railway*, 1966; *Hymns and the Christian Faith*, Pickering & Inglis, 1966; *Switzerland: Its Railways and Cableways, Mountain Roads and Lake Steamers*, 1967; *British Atlantic Locomotives*, 1968; (editor) *Locospotters Annual, 1969*, 1968.

Juveniles: *My Railway Book*, John F. Shaw, 1924; *Romantic Story of the Iron Road*, Hutchinson, 1940; *Eagle Book of Trains*, Hulton Press, 1953, 5th edition, Longacre Press, 1960; *British Railways*, Thomas Nelson, 1958, 3rd edition, 1961.

Author of a number of other booklets and brochures on railroads. Magazine contributions include "British Locomotive Practice and Performance" series, which ran for 535 consecutive installments in *Railway*, 1909-58, and a 200-installment series in *Modern Railways;* some magazine articles have appeared under pseudonyms Mercury and Voyageur. Editor, *Crusader*, 1931-58; also editor of *Trains Illustrated* and *Trains Annual* for many years; consulting editor, *Railway*.†

(Died, 1973)

*   *   *

ALLEN, John D(aniel)   1898-1972

PERSONAL: Born May 18, 1898, in Latta, S.C.; son of David Smith (a farmer) and Mary Jane (Coleman) Allen; married Elizabeth Joan Schaad, November 9, 1928; children: John Daniel, Jr., David Wakeman. *Education:* University of Georgia, B.A., 1926, M.A., 1929; Vanderbilt University, Ph.D., 1939. *Politics:* Democrat. *Religion:* Episcopalian. *Home:* 1113 Welbourne St., Johnson City, Tenn. 37601.

CAREER: Mercer University, Macon, Ga., 1928-46, became associate professor of English and chairman of department of journalism; Northwestern State College of Louisiana, Natchitoches, professor of English and publicity director, 1946-47; Sul Ross State College (now University), Alpine, Tex., director of Division of Languages, 1947-50; East Tennessee State University, Johnson City, professor of English, 1950-68. *Military service:* U.S. Army, 1917-19. *Member:* South Atlantic Modern Language Association, Tennessee Folklore Society, Tennessee Philological Society, Phi Beta Kappa.

WRITINGS: (Contributor) W. T. Couch, editor, *Culture in the South*, University of North Carolina Press, 1934; *Philip Pendleton Cooke* (critical biography), University of North Carolina Press, 1939; *Quantitative Studies in Prosody*, East Tennessee State University Press, 1968; (editor and author of introduction) *Philip Pendleton Cooke: Poet, Critic, Novelist*, Research Advisory Council, East Tennessee State University, 1969. Columnist, *Macon Telegraph*, 1944-46. Contributor of reviews to periodicals, including *New Republic*.

WORK IN PROGRESS: Verbal Music in English Verse: Four Major Means.

AVOCATIONAL INTERESTS: Gardening (flower and vegetable), rock hunting, geology.†

(Died October 25, 1972)

*   *   *

ALLEN, Shirley Walter   1883-

PERSONAL: Born October 14, 1883, in Sherman, N.Y.; son of Walter Ozias (a minister) and Harriet (Richardson) Allen; married Helen Brown, March 23, 1913; married second wife, Sara Elizabeth Fuldauer, September 10, 1961; children: (first marriage) Elizabeth Harriet (Mrs. James Barret Thompson), Robert Shirley. *Education:* Simpson College, student, 1903-04; Iowa State College of Agriculture and Mechanic Arts (now Iowa State University of Science and Technology), B.S., 1909, M.Forestry, 1929. *Politics:* Democrat. *Religion:* Congregationalist.

CAREER: U.S. Forest Service, 1909-14, began as forest assistant, became deputy forest supervisor in California; New York State College of Forestry (now State University of New York College of Environmental Science and Forestry), Syracuse, 1914-18, began as assistant professor, became associate professor in Forest Extension; U.S. Forest Service, industrial examiner, Madison, Wis., 1918-19, forest supervisor, Los Angeles, Calif., 1921-22; American Forestry Association, Washington, D.C., forester, 1924-28; University of Michigan, School of Natural Resources, Ann Arbor, professor of forestry, 1929-53, professor emeritus, 1953—. Forestry consultant, National Park Service, 1933-34; delegate from U.S. Department of Interior and state of Michigan to Second World Forestry Congress, Budapest, 1936; Michigan Conservation Commission, member, 1954-58, chairman, 1957; member of public lands committee, Interstate Oil Compact Commission, 1956-58; chairman, Michigan Nature Area Council, 1958. Member, Citizens Council of Ann Arbor, 1950-58.

MEMBER: Society of American Foresters (fellow; president, 1946-47), American Association for the Advancement of Science (fellow), American Forestry Association (forester, 1924-29), Wilderness Society (member of advisory committee, 1943-52), International Association of Fish, Game and Conservation Commissioners, Michigan Academy of Science, Arts, and Letters, Alpha Zeta, Delta Sigma Rho, Phi Kappa Phi. *Awards, honors:* Award of Merit, Michigan United Conservation Clubs, 1959.

WRITINGS: An Introduction to American Forestry, McGraw, 1938, 3rd edition (with Grant William Sharpe), 1960; *Conserving Natural Resources: Principles and Practice in a Democracy,* McGraw, 1955, 3rd edition (with Justin Wilkinson Leonard), 1966. Contributor to scientific journals and popular periodicals, 1918-67. Member of editorial board, *Journal of Forestry,* 1930.

WORK IN PROGRESS: Revision of *An Introduction to American Forestry* for a fourth edition; a history of the conservation movement in the United States.

SIDELIGHTS: Shirley Allen represented the American Forestry Association on sixteen trips of Trail-Riders of the Wilderness, 1936-53, traveling on horseback and by canoe.†

* * *

ALLENDOERFER, Carl (Barnett) 1911-1974

PERSONAL: Born April 4, 1911, in Kansas City, Mo.; son of Carl William (a banker) and Winfred (Barnett) Allendoerfer; married Dorothy Holbrook, June 26, 1937; children: Robert Duff, James Holbrook, William Barnett. *Education:* Haverford College, B.S., 1932; Oxford University, B.A., 1934, M.A., 1939; Princeton University, Ph.D., 1937. *Politics:* Republican. *Religion:* Protestant. *Home:* 4300 53rd Ave. N.E., Seattle, Wash. 98105. *Office:* University of Washington, Seattle, Wash. 98105.

CAREER: University of Wisconsin, Madison, instructor in mathematics, 1937-38; Haverford College, Haverford, Pa., instructor, 1938-39, assistant professor, 1939-42, associate professor, 1942-46, professor of mathematics, 1946-51; Uni-

versity of Washington, Seattle, professor of mathematics, 1951-74, executive officer of department, 1951-62. Fulbright lecturer at Cambridge University, 1957-58; visiting professor at New York University and Massachusetts Institute of Technology; member of Institute for Advanced Study, Princeton, N.J. Consultant in operations research, U.S. Army and Navy, World War II; member of Division on Mathematics, National Research Council, 1956-58, 1962-65. Member of Commission on Mathematics, College Entrance Examination Board, 1955-58. Producer of mathematical films.

MEMBER: Mathematical Association of America (president, 1959-60), American Association for the Advancement of Science (fellow), American Mathematical Society, National Council of Teachers of Mathematics, Society for Industrial and Applied Mathematics, Institute of Mathematical Statistics, Phi Beta Kappa, Sigma Xi. *Awards, honors:* Rhodes scholar at Oxford University, 1934.

WRITINGS: (With C. O. Oakley) *Principles of Mathematics,* McGraw, 1955, 2nd edition, 1963; (with C. O. Oakley) *Fundamentals of Freshman Mathematics,* McGraw, 1959, 3rd edition, 1972; *Mathematics for Parents,* Macmillan, 1965; (with C. O. Oakley) *Fundamentals of College Algebra,* McGraw, 1967. Contributor to professional journals. Editor, *American Mathematical Monthly,* 1952-56; consulting editor in mathematics, Macmillan Co.

AVOCATIONAL INTERESTS: Hiking and sailing.†

(Died September 29, 1974)

* * *

ALLGIRE, Mildred J. 1910-

PERSONAL: Born October 15, 1910, in Kalida, Ohio. *Education:* St. Joseph's Hospital School of Nursing, Fort Wayne, Ind., R.N., 1933; Indiana University, B.S. in nursing education, 1942; Stanford University, R.P.T. and M.A., 1950. *Politics:* Independent. *Religion:* Methodist. *Home:* 1812 North Emerson Ave., Indianapolis, Ind. 46218. *Office:* State Department of Welfare, 100 North Senate, Indianapolis, Ind. 46204.

CAREER: Visiting Nurse Association, Fort Wayne, Ind., staff nurse, 1936-41; Van Buren County Health Department, Paw Paw, Mich., and W. K. Kellogg Foundation, staff nurse, 1943-45; internship in rehabilitation in Detroit, Mich., 1946; Indiana State Department of Welfare, Indianapolis, field consultant, 1946-56, supervisor of consulting services for rehabilitation of crippled children, beginning 1956. Regular guest speaker at Indiana University, 1947-65. Has conducted many seminars on rehabilitation. *Member:* American Nurses Association, American Physical Therapy Association.

WRITINGS: (With Ruth R. Denney) *Nurses Can Give and Teach Rehabilitation,* Springer Publishing, 1960, 2nd edition (as sole author), 1968. Contributor to professional journals.

AVOCATIONAL INTERESTS: Oil painting, collecting art glass and china, rose cultivation.

* * *

ALSCHULER, Rose H. 1887-

PERSONAL: Born December 17, 1887, in Chicago, Ill.; daughter of Charles (a ranch owner and cattle commissioner) and Mary (Greenebaum) Haas; married Alfred S. Alschuler (an architect), December 17, 1907 (deceased); children: Marian (Mrs. Leon M. Despres), Frances (Mrs. Edward Gudeman), Alfred S., Jr., Richard H., John H. *Education:*

Attended University of Chicago, 1903-04, 1906-07, and Vassar College, 1905-06. *Politics:* Independent—usually Democratic. *Religion:* Jewish. *Home:* 777 Sheridan Rd., Highland Park, Ill. 60035.

CAREER: Organizer and staff director of first public school nursery in the United States, Franklin Public School Nursery, Chicago, Ill., 1925-31; also organizer and staff director of Garden Apartment Nursery Schools in the first Black housing project in Chicago, 1927-33, of Winnetka Public School Nursery and Junior Kindergarten, Winnetka, Ill., 1926-40, and of eighteen Works Progress Administration nursery schools in Chicago, 1933-40. Lecturer, San Francisco State College (now University), summer, 1949; lecturer at University of London, University of Oslo, University of Rome, University of Calcutta, and Hebrew University of Jerusalem. Chairman, National Commission for Young Children, 1941-43; consultant to Federal Public Housing Authority on building and equipping nursery schools for war housing, 1942-43. Member of board, Federated Jewish Charities of Chicago, 1938-41. *Member:* American Educational Research Association. *Awards, honors:* University of Chicago Alumni Citation for public service, 1944; honored by Technion, Haifa, Israel, and by Founders of Roosevelt University.

WRITINGS: (With associates on primary faculty of Winnetka public schools) *Two to Six,* Morrow, 1933; (with Christine Heinig) *Play: The Child's Response to Life,* Houghton, 1937; *Children's Centers,* Morrow, 1942; (with L. W. Hattwick) *Painting and Personality: A Study of Young Children,* University of Chicago Press, 1947, revised abridged edition, 1969. Contributor of numerous articles to educational journals.

* * *

AMERMAN, Lockhart 1911-1969

PERSONAL: Born September 11, 1911, in New York, N.Y.; son of William Libbey and Carrie (Lockhart) Amerman; married Louise S. Landreth, March 29, 1940; children: Peter, S. Phillips, Emily, Lucy. *Education:* Haverford College, B.A., 1931; Princeton University, M.A., 1935; Princeton Theological Seminary, B.D., 1935; attended University of Edinburgh, 1937, 1938. *Politics:* Republican. *Home:* 1 Pine Grove, Bristol, Pa. 19007.

CAREER: Fifth Avenue Presbyterian Church, New York, N.Y., assistant minister, 1935-37; Sewickley Presbyterian Church, Sewickley, Pa., minister, 1939-68. Visiting professor of homeletics, Pittsburgh Theological Seminary, Pittsburgh, Pa., 1943-45, and Princeton Theological Seminary, Princeton, N.J., 1945-46. President, Sewickley Public Library Board, 1946-56. *Member:* Church Service Society, Players Club (New York). *Awards, honors:* D.D., Grove City College, 1944, and Washington and Jefferson College, 1949.

WRITINGS: Where the Saints Have Trod, Gibson Press, 1943; *Wheat for a Penny,* Thistle House, 1945; *Guns in the Heather* (juvenile), Harcourt, 1963; *Cape Cod Casket* (juvenile), Harcourt, 1964; *The Sly One* (juvenile), Harcourt, 1966.

Contributor of articles and poetry to church journals, including *Living Church, Presbyterian Life,* and *Christianity Today.*

WORK IN PROGRESS: Another book for children.

AVOCATIONAL INTERESTS: Golf, cricket, tennis, soccer.††

(Died November 20, 1969)

AMES, Charles Edgar 1895-1972

PERSONAL: Born May 3, 1895, in Boston, Mass.; son of Oakes (a manufacturer) and Florence (Ingalls) Ames; married Eleanor Erving King, May, 1924; children: Charles Oakes, Cornelia King (Mrs. David M. Abbot), Eleanor Erving (Mrs. John W. Mattern). *Education:* Harvard University, A.B., 1917. *Home:* Laurel Hollow, Syosset, N.Y. 11791.

CAREER: Kean, Taylor & Co. (members of New York Stock Exchange), New York City, partner, 1925-59; Kidder, Peabody & Co. (investment bankers), New York City, limited partner and vice-president, 1960-65. Director and member of executive committee, Kansas City Southern Railroad. Former governor, Association of Stock Exchange Firms. *Military service:* U.S. Army, Infantry, 1917-19; became second lieutenant; received Silver Star and Purple Heart. U.S. Naval Reserve, active duty, 1942-45; became captain; received Navy Commendation.

WRITINGS: Pioneering the Union Pacific: A Reappraisal of the Builders of the Railroad, Appleton, 1969.†

(Died, 1972)

* * *

AMES, Winslow 1907-

PERSONAL: Born July 3, 1907, in Maullin, Chile; son of Edward Winslow and Katherine Millicent (Johnson) Ames; married Anna Rebecca Gerhard, June 27, 1931; children: Millicent Winslow (Mrs. Gary Adamson), Ann Willing (Mrs. Barry F. Deetz), Eliza Middleton (Mrs. Lee Littlefield), Alison Winthrop, Katrine Woolsey. *Education:* Columbia University, A.B., 1929; Harvard University, A.M., 1932 (as of 1930). *Politics:* "Vote-splitter." *Religion:* Episcopalian. *Home:* 80 Ferry Rd., Saunderstown, R.I. 02874.

CAREER: Lyman Allyn Museum, New London, Conn., director, 1930-42; Springfield Art Museum, Springfield, Mo., director, 1947-50; Gallery of Modern Art (including the Huntington Hartford Collection), New York, N.Y., director, 1957-61; Hollins College, Roanoke, Va., lecturer in art, 1964-65; University of Rhode Island, Kingston, lecturer in art, 1966-75. Columbia University, member of advisory council to department of art history and archaeology, beginning 1958, and co-chairman of exhibition committee. Episcopal Peace Fellowship, treasurer, 1948-68, chairman, 1968-69. Member of North Kingstown (R.I.) School Building and Planning Committee, 1966-67, and Historical Preservation Commission, State of Rhode Island, beginning 1968.

MEMBER: Society of Architectural Historians (member of board of directors, beginning 1976), Archives of American Art, Victorian Society (England), Victorian Society in America, Royal Society of Arts (London), Drawing Society, Society for the Preservation of New England Antiquities, Rhode Island Historical Society, Antiquarian & Landmarks Society of Connecticut, Order of Colonial Lords of Manors in America.

WRITINGS: Great Master Drawings of All Time, Volume I: *Italian Drawings,* Shorewood, 1962; *Italian Drawings from the 15th to the 19th Century,* Shorewood, 1963; *Prince Albert and Victorian Taste,* Viking, 1968. Contributor to *Gazette des Beaux-Arts, Museum News, Victorian Studies, Master Drawings,* and *Journal* of the Society of Architectural Historians.

WORK IN PROGRESS: Translating and updating Joseph Meder's *Die Handzeichnung. Ihre Entwicklung und Technik* (Schroll, 1919); with Anna Wells Rutledge, a book, for European readers, about American art.

ANDERSON, Alan Ross   1925-1973

PERSONAL: Born April 11, 1925, in Portland, Ore.; son of Ross E. and Selma (Wetteland) Anderson; married Carolyn Willson, June 11, 1949; children: Nicholas, Jeffrey, Elizabeth, Timothy. *Education:* Yale University, B.A., 1950; Ph.D., 1955; Cambridge University, M.Litt., 1952. *Home:* 4215 Bigelow Blvd., Pittsburgh, Pa. 15213. *Office:* Department of Philosophy, University of Pittsburgh, Pittsburgh, Pa. 15213.

CAREER: Dartmouth College, Hanover, N.H., instructor in philosophy, 1954-55; Yale University, New Haven, Conn., instructor, 1955-56, assistant professor, 1956-60, associate professor, 1961-63, professor of philosophy, 1963-65; University of Pittsburgh, Pittsburgh, Pa., professor of philosophy, 1966-73, chairman of department, 1967-70, senior research associate of Center for the Philosophy of Science, and Knowledge Availability Systems Center, 1965-73. Fulbright lecturer, University of Manchester, 1964-65. Research positions with National Security Agency, Office of Naval Research, and National Science Foundation. Member of board of directors, Basic Education, Inc., 1950-63, and Foote School, 1960-62. Member of selection committee, Woodrow Wilson Fellowship Foundation, 1961-64, and American Council of Learned Societies, 1970-73; member of screening committee for Fulbright-Hays grants, 1968-73. *Military service:* U.S. Army, Signal Corps, 1943-46.

MEMBER: International Union for the History and Philosophy of Science (secretary, 1967-69), American Philosophical Association (executive committee member, 1960-63; member of board of officers, 1970-73), Association for Symbolic Logic (member of council and executive committee, 1963-66), Mind Association (England; American treasurer, 1961-73), Connecticut Academy of Arts and Sciences (vice-president, 1963-64), Alexander Philosophical Society (England; honorary president, 1964-65), Phi Beta Kappa, Chi Delta Theta. *Awards, honors:* Fulbright fellow, 1950-52; Betts fellow, 1960-61; Morse fellow, 1960-61; Guggenheim fellow, 1964-65.

WRITINGS: (Editor with Maurice Mandelbaum and Francis W. Gramlich) *Philosophic Problems: An Introductory Book of Readings*, Macmillan, 1957, 2nd edition (with Mandelbaum, Gramlich, and Jerome B. Schneewind), 1967; (editor) *Minds and Machines*, Prentice-Hall, 1964; (with Moore) *The Responsive Environments Project*, Learning Research and Development Center, University of Pittsburgh, 1967; (editor with Nicholas Rescher, and others) *Essays in Honor of Carl G. Hempel*, D. Reidel, 1969; (with Nuel D. Belnap) *Entailment: The Logic of Relevance and Necessity*, Volume I, Princeton University Press, 1974.

Contributor: Joan H. Criswell, Herbert Solomon, and Patrick Suppes, editors, *Mathematical Methods in Small Group Processes*, Stanford University Press, 1962; *Philosophy of Science, 1961-62: University of Delaware Seminar in the Philosophy of Science*, Interscience, 1962; O. J. Harvey, editor, *Motivation and Social Interaction: Cognitive Determinants*, Ronald, 1963; *Boston Studies in the Philosophy of Science*, D. Reidel, 1963; Paul Benaceraff and Hilary Putnam, editors, *Philosophy of Mathematics: Selected Readings*, Prentice-Hall, 1964; David Braybrooke, editor, *Philosophical Problems of the Social Sciences*, Macmillan, 1965; Layman Allen and Mary Caldwell, editors, *Communication Sciences and Law: Reflections from the Jurimetrics Conference*, Bobbs-Merrill, 1965; Bruce J. Biddle and Edwin J. Thomas, editors, *Role Theory*, Wiley,

1966; Gordon J. Direnzo, editor, *Concepts, Theory, and Explanation in the Behavioral Sciences*, Random House, 1966; Nicholas Rescher, editor, *The Logic of Decision and Action*, University of Pittsburgh Press, 1966; Irving M. Copi and James A. Gould, editors, *Contemporary Readings in Logical Theory*, Macmillan, 1967; Gloria B. Levitas, editor, *Culture and Consciousness*, Braziller, 1967; Robert Hess and Roberta Meyer Bear, editors, *Early Education*, Aldine, 1968; David Goslin, editor, *Handbook of Socialization Theory and Research*, Rand McNally, 1968; J. W. Davis, D. J. Hockney, and W. K. Wilson, editors, *Philosophical Logic*, D. Reidel, 1969. Also author and co-author of technical reports for U.S. Office of Naval Research, 1956-61. Author, with Omar K. Moore, of three-part documentary film, "Easy Reading and Writing," for Basic Education, Inc., 1960.

Contributor to *Encyclopedia of Library and Information Science*. Contributor of numerous articles and book reviews to scientific and philosophical journals, including *Mathematical Reviews*, *Philosophical Review*, *Philosophical Studies*, and *Review of Metaphysics*. *Journal of Symbolic Logic*, consulting editor, 1958-73, editor, 1960, 1962; consulting editor, *Jurimetrics Journal*, 1959-69, *American Philosophical Quarterly*, 1962, *Metaphilosophy*, 1968-73; member of editorial board, *Journal of Philosophical Logic*, 1970-73. Member of reviewing staff, *Zentralblatt fur Mathematik*, 1961-73, *Mathematical Reviews*, 1963-73.†

(Died December 5, 1973)

*   *   *

ANDERSON, Alpha E.   1914-1970

PERSONAL: Born July 6, 1914, in Ashland, Wis.; daughter of Lars August (a minister) and Dagmar (Hall) Almquist; married Richard B. Anderson (a missionary), May 21, 1944; children: Philip, Elaine, Paul. *Education:* University of Nebraska, R.N., 1937, B.S., 1940; Stanislaus State College (now California State College, Stanislaus), graduate study, 1960-61. *Politics:* Republican. *Home:* 622 Park St., Turlock, Calif. 95380.

CAREER: St. Luke's Hospital, Denver, Colo., night supervisor of nurses, 1940-41; Evangelical Free Church of America, medical missionary and Bible school teacher in Republic of Congo, 1942-66; Elness Nursing Home, Turlock, Calif., charge nurse, 1967-68; medical missionary, 1968-70.

WRITINGS: *Pelendo, God's Prophet in the Congo*, Free Church Publications, 1964.†

(Died June, 1970)

*   *   *

ANDERSON, George Christian   1907-1976

PERSONAL: Born January 30, 1907, in Bootle, Lancashire, England; son of George and Marie (Reid) Anderson. *Education:* University of Pennsylvania, student, 1928-31; Divinity School of the Protestant Episcopal Church, Philadelphia, S.T.B., 1933; Oxford University, graduate study, 1937-39; additional study at Columbia University and Union Theological Seminary, New York, N.Y. *Home:* 518 Cedar Lane, Swarthmore, Pa. 19081.

CAREER: Ordained to the Episcopal ministry, 1933; Diocese of Philadelphia, Philadelphia, Pa., clergyman, beginning 1934; Trinity Episcopal Church, Swarthmore, Pa., rector, 1943-50. Associate chaplin, St. Luke's Hospital, 1951. Delivered Mary Hemingway Rees Memorial Lecture at World Federation for Mental Health, Amsterdam, 1963; lecturer at Columbia University. Consultant to Harvard Divinity School, Yeshiva University, and Loyola University. Consul for Paraguay, Philadelphia, 1945-72. *Member:* Academy of Religion and Mental Health (founder, 1954; president, 1970-73), American Association for the Advancement of Science, New York Academy of Medicine (associate fellow). *Awards, honors:* Medal of City of Istanbul (Turkey), 1958; D.D. from Divinity School of the Protestant Episcopal Church, Philadelphia, 1969.

WRITINGS: Man's Right to Be Human, Morrow, 1959; *Your Religion: Neurotic or Healthy,* Doubleday, 1970. Contributor of more than one hundred articles to theological, medical, psychiatric and other journals, and to newspapers.

WORK IN PROGRESS: A book on human emotions and values.†

(Died December 19, 1976)

* * *

ANDERSON, George K(umler) 1901-

PERSONAL: Born October 20, 1901, in Springfield, Ill.; son of George E. (a diplomat) and Mary (Kumler) Anderson; married Ethel Humphrey, October 30, 1933; children: Margaret (Mrs. H. Stephen Holske), John H. *Education:* Harvard University, A.B., 1920, A.M., 1921, Ph.D., 1925. *Politics:* Independent. *Religion:* Unitarian Universalist. *Home:* 169 Power St., Providence, R.I. 02906. *Office:* Department of English, Brown University, Providence, R.I. 02912.

CAREER: George Washington University, Washington, D.C., instructor in English, 1924-27; Brown University, Providence, R.I., assistant professor, 1927-30, associate professor, 1930-47, professor of English, 1947-72, professor emeritus, 1972—, chairman of department, 1950-60. Visiting professor, Middlebury College, Bread Loaf School of English, most summers, beginning 1931, State University of New York at Albany, 1938-39. *Member:* Modern Language Association of America, American Association of University Professors, Mediaeval Academy of America, Renaissance Society of America, College English Association, New England College English Association (president, 1967-68). *Awards, honors:* Guggenheim fellow, 1945; A.M., Brown University, 1957; Litt.D., Middlebury College, 1966, L.H.D., Rhode Island College, 1973.

WRITINGS: (With George B. Woods and Homer A. Watt) *The Literature of England: An Anthology and a History,* two volumes, Scott Foresman, 1936, abridged edition, with Karl J. Holzknecht, one volume, 1953, 5th edition, edited with William E. Buckler, two volumes, 1966, 2nd abridged edition, edited with Buckler, one volume, 1967; (editor with Eda Lou Walton, and contributor) *This Generation: A Selection of British and American Literature from 1914 to the Present, with Historical and Critical Essays,* Scott, Foresman, 1939, revised edition, 1949; *The Literature of the Anglo-Saxons,* Princeton University Press, 1949, revised edition, 1966; (editor with Robert Warnock) *The World in Literature,* two-volume edition and four-volume edition, Scott, Foresman, 1950-51, one-volume edition, 1959, revised edition, two volumes, 1967; *Old and Middle English Literature from the Beginnings to 1485,* enlarged edition (Anderson not associated with earlier edition), Collier Books, 1962; *The Legend of the Wandering Jew,* Brown University Press, 1965; *Bread Loaf School of English: The First Fifty Years,* Middlebury College Press, 1969. Contributor of about seventy-five articles to journals.

WORK IN PROGRESS: A study of Chaucer.

SIDELIGHTS: George Anderson commented: "I write out of an interest in a given subject and because I think what I have to say may be of interest to others.... I have no idea how much may prove to be publishable and I am not particularly concerned; for me from now on it is to be cakes and ale." Anderson is competent in all western European languages. *Avocational interests:* Music, travel, sports.

* * *

ANDERSON, Harold H(omer) 1897-

PERSONAL: Born October 23, 1897, in Dakota City, Neb.; son of Samuel Lilley and Mary (Inglis) Anderson; married Gladys Marie Lowe (a psychologist), June 30, 1927 (died June 17, 1965); married Thelma Chapman Jean, April 28, 1969; children: (first marriage) Janet Lowe (Mrs. John W. Twente, Jr.), Theodore Inglis. *Education:* Harvard University, S.B., 1922, law student, 1922-23; Rousseau Institute, Geneva, Switzerland, diploma, 1928; University of Geneva, Certificat de Pedagogie, 1928, Ph.D., 1929. *Religion:* Unitarian Universalist. *Home:* 282 Maplewood Dr., East Lansing, Mich. 48823. *Office:* Department of Psychology, 116 Olds Hall, Michigan State University, East Lansing, Mich. 48823.

CAREER: University of Iowa, Iowa Child Welfare Research Station, Iowa City, research assistant professor of psychology, 1929-36; University of Illinois, Urbana, assistant professor, 1936-41, associate professor of psychology, 1941-46; Michigan State University, East Lansing, professor of psychology and head of department, 1946-55, research professor of psychology, 1955-66, professor emeritus, 1966—. Visiting professor at University of California, Berkeley, 1942-43; Fulbright research professor at University of Frankfurt, 1953-54; research lecturer at the Universities of Stockholm, Oslo, and Helsinki, 1954; visiting summer professor at other universities in America. Director of cross-national research program with school children in Mexico, Brazil, Puerto Rico, and five countries of western Europe, 1952-63; has lectured widely in Europe, Mexico, and South America. Principal investigator, Research in Creativity, beginning 1956. Member of board of directors, Rehabilitation Medical Center, Inc., and Rehabilitation Industries, Inc., Lansing, Mich., 1954-60, and chairman, 1958-60.

MEMBER: American Psychological Association (fellow), American Orthopsychiatric Association (fellow; member of board of directors, 1948-50; vice-president, 1952-53), Interamerican Society of Psychology (treasurer, 1957-59; president-elect, 1959-63; president 1963-64), American Educational Research Association, Society for Research in Child Development, American Association for Humanistic Psychology, American Association for the Advancement of Science, American Association of University Professors, International Society for General Semantics, Society for General Systems Research, Midwest Psychological Association, Michigan Psychological Association (president, 1950-51), Sigma Xi. *Awards, honors:* Programming research grant from Michigan State University for Mexico and Brazil, 1961.

WRITINGS: Les cliniques psychologiques pour l'enfance aux Etats-Unis et l'oeuvre du Dr. Healy, Delachaux & Niestle, 1929; *Children in the Family,* Appleton, 1937; (editor with Gladys Lowe Anderson) *An Introduction to Projective Techniques,* Prentice-Hall, 1951; (editor, contributor, and author of introduction) *Creativity: And Its Cultivation,* Harper, 1959; (editor and contributor) *Creativity in Childhood and Adolescence: A Diversity of Approaches,* Science & Behavior Books, 1965.

Contributor: P. Witty and C. E. Skinner, editors, *Mental Hygiene in Modern Education,* Farrar & Rinehart, 1929; M. Jung, editor, *Modern Marriage,* Crofts, 1940; R. G. Barker, J. S. Kounin, and H. F. Wright, editors, *Child Behavior and Development,* McGraw, 1943; L. A. Pennington and I. A. Berg, editors, *An Introduction to Clinical Psychology,* Ronald, 1948; L. Carmichael, editor, *Manual of Child Psychology,* 2nd edition, Wiley, 1954; H. David and H. von Bracken, editors, *Perspectives in Personality Theory: An International Symposium,* Basic Books, 1956; Wilma Donahue and others, editors, *Freetime: Challenge to Later Maturity,* University of Michigan Press, 1958; Ira J. Gordon, editor, *Human Development: Readings in Research,* Scott, Foresman, 1965; E. J. Amidon and J. B. Hough, editors, *Interaction Analysis: Theory, Research, and Application,* Addison-Wesley, 1967. Author of monographs published in *Genetic Psychology Monographs, Review of Educational Research,* and *Applied Psychology Monographs.* Contributor to *McGraw-Hill Encyclopedia of Science and Technology, Encyclopedia Americana,* and *Childcraft;* contributor of about one hundred articles and reviews to periodicals, mainly professional journals.

WORK IN PROGRESS: Reporting results of a cross-national research project dealing with social values of teachers and children, the comparison of fourth- and seventh-grade children in regard to social values in eight countries, and teacher-child and parent-child conflict resolution.

SIDELIGHTS: Anderson speaks and reads French and German; he also reads Spanish and Portuguese. Several of his books and monographs have been translated into Spanish, French, German, and Portuguese.

BIOGRAPHICAL/CRITICAL SOURCES: MSU Reporter, Volume III, number 6, April, 1959.†

*   *   *

ANDREWS, Burton (Allen)   1906-

PERSONAL: Born July 31, 1906, in Tonkawa, Okla.; son of Edwin Alvia (a clergyman) and Bessie Pearl (Evinger) Andrews; married Mary Avard Meeker, November 24, 1961 (deceased). *Education:* Greenville College, A.B., 1927; University of Michigan, A.M., 1932, J.D., 1933. *Home:* 374 Morris St., Albany, N.Y. 12208. *Office:* Albany Law School, Union University, Albany, N.Y. 12208.

CAREER: Admitted to the Bar of New York State, 1936; Flint Junior College, Flint, Mich., professor of political science and sociology, 1931-34; National Gypsum Co., Buffalo, N.Y., associate of general counsel, 1934-44; Cravath, Swaine & Moore (law firm), New York, N.Y., associate, 1944-47; University of Florida, College of Law, Gainesville, professor of law, 1947-48; Union University, Albany Law School, Albany, N.Y., professor of law, 1948-76, professor emeritus, 1976—. *Member:* World Peace Through Law Center, United World Federalists.

WRITINGS: Cases: New York Public Corporations, Matthew Bender, 1951; *Cases: Introduction to Law,* privately printed, 1967. Contributor to *New York State Bar Journal, Albany Law Review,* and *Commercial and Financial Chronicle.*

WORK IN PROGRESS: Conflict of Laws; Legal Analysis and Synthesis; Elements of Religious Philosophy.

*   *   *

ANDREWS, Donald H(atch)   1898-197(?)

PERSONAL: Born June 11, 1898, in Southington, Conn.; son of Russell Gad (a manufacturer) and Mary (Hatch) Andrews; married Josephine Adair Veeder; married Elizabeth Howland, September 23, 1950; children: (first marriage) Donald Hatch, Jr. *Education:* Yale University, B.A., 1920, Ph.D., 1923. *Politics:* Republican. *Religion:* Episcopalian. *Home:* 750 Northeast 33rd St., Boca Raton, Fla. 33432.

CAREER: Research fellow at University of California, 1924-25, University of Leiden, 1925-26, Bartol Research Foundation of Franklin Institute, 1926-27; Johns Hopkins University, Baltimore, Md., associate, 1927-29, associate professor, 1929-30, professor, 1930-57, B.N. Baker Professor of Chemistry, 1957-63, professor emeritus, beginning 1963, chairman of department and director of chemistry laboratory, 1936-44, director of cryogeny laboratory, 1943-48; Florida Atlantic University, Boca Raton, professor of chemistry, 1963-64, distinguished professor of chemistry, 1964-67, distinguished professor emeritus, beginning 1967, distinguished professor of biophysics, 1968-70. Consultant to General Motors Corp., Proctor & Gamble, and Los Alamos Scientific Laboratory; member of first scientific commission, L'Institut Internationale de Froid. *Member:* American Chemical Society (vice-chairman, 1933; chairman, 1934), American Physical Society (fellow), American Mathematical Society, American Philosophical Society, Royal Chemical Society (fellow), Phi Beta Kappa, Sigma Xi.

WRITINGS: (With Richard J. Kokes) *Fundamental Chemistry* and *Laboratory Manual for Fundamental Chemistry,* Wiley, 1962, 2nd edition, 1965; *The Symphony of Life,* Unity, 1967; *Quimica Geral,* University of Sao Paulo Press, 1968; *Introductory Physical Chemistry,* McGraw, 1970; *Chemistry: A Humanistic View,* McGraw, 1974.†

(Deceased)

*   *   *

ANDRUS, Vera   1895-

PERSONAL: Born December 9, 1895, in Winoosky, Wis.; daughter of Hjalmer B. J. (a butter-maker) and Ethel (Caldwell) Andrus. *Education:* Studied literature and art at University of Minnesota, and art at St. Paul School of Art, Minneapolis Institute of Art, and Art Students League, New York. *Religion:* Christian Science. *Home:* 6 Pleasant St., Rockport, Mass. 01966.

CAREER: Professional flutist in Minneapolis, Minn., and with traveling concert companies, 1919-27; held civil service positions in offices of Minneapolis city clerk and city engineer during early career; Metropolitan Museum of Art, New York City, supervisor of photograph research and sales, 1929-57; artist and writer. City College (now City College of the City University of New York), New York City, art teacher in adult education, 1945-55. Has had one-woman shows at Smithsonian Institution, American Museum of Natural History, University of Maine, Essex Institute, Salem, Mass., and other galleries; work is owned by Metropolitan Museum of Art, Boston Museum of Fine Arts, Boston Public Library, Minneapolis Institute of Arts, University of Minnesota, and other institutions.

MEMBER: National Association of Women Artists, National League of American Pen Women (North Shore branch), Hudson Valley Art Association (past president), Rockport Art Association. *Awards, honors:* Minneapolis Institute of Art Prize, 1928; Medal of Honor, National Association of Women Artists, 1942; Metropolitan Museum grant to study abroad, 1950; Albert H. Wiggins Memorial Prize of the Boston Printmakers, 1954; other awards from

Westchester Federation of Women's Clubs, and Hudson Valley, Rockport, and Brockton Art Associations.

WRITINGS: Sea-Bird Island, Harcourt, 1939; *Sea Dust* (poetry, drawings, and lithographs), Wake-Brook, 1955; *Black River, a Wisconsin Story,* Little, Brown, 1967. Contributor of poems and articles to magazines and newspapers.

WORK IN PROGRESS: A book on El Greco and his times; a volume of poems; *Forty Years of Lithography;* a book on Cape Ann, with Pen Women; research centered on the sixteenth century in Europe, particularly the Mediterranean countries.

SIDELIGHTS: Vera Andrus' show, held at Essex Institute, Salem, Mass., in 1975, was a large exhibition of her art work and books.

*   *   *

ANGLE, Paul M(cClelland)   1900-1975

PERSONAL: Born December 25, 1900, in Mansfield, Ohio; son of John Elmer (a grocer) and Nellie Laverne (McClelland) Angle; married Vesta Verne Magee, June 17, 1926; children: Paula, John Edwin. *Education:* Oberlin College, student, 1918-19; Miami University, Oxford, Ohio, A.B. (magna cum laude), 1922; University of Illinois, M.A., 1924. *Home:* 1802 Lincoln Park West, Chicago, Ill. 60614.

CAREER: Textbook salesman for American Book Co., 1924-25; Abraham Lincoln Association (originally Lincoln Centennial Association), Springfield, Ill., executive secretary, 1925-32; Illinois State Historical Library, Springfield, librarian and state historian, 1932-45; Chicago Historical Society, Chicago, Ill., director and secretary, 1945-65, secretary, 1965-70. Illinois Sesquicentennial Commission, director of historical publications, 1966-75. *Member:* Phi Beta Kappa. *Awards, honors:* Litt.D., Augustana College, 1941; LL.D., Knox College, 1944; L.H.D., Illinois College, 1947; other honorary degrees from Lake Forest College and Miami University, Oxford, Ohio.

WRITINGS: Abraham Lincoln: An Authentic Story of His Life, Springfield Life Insurance Co., 1926; *Lincoln in the Year 1858,* Lincoln Centennial Association, 1926; *Lincoln in the Year 1859,* Lincoln Centennial Association, 1927; *Lincoln in the Year 1860,* Lincoln Centennial Association, 1927; *Lincoln in Springfield,* Lincoln Centennial Association, 1927; *"Atlantic Monthly" Lincoln Letters Spurious,* Lincoln Centennial Association, 1928; *One Hundred Years of Law: An Account of the Law Office which John T. Stuart Founded in Springfield, Illinois, a Century Ago,* Brown, Hay & Stephens, 1928; *Lincoln in the Year 1855,* Abraham Lincoln Association, 1929.

Lincoln in the Year 1856, Abraham Lincoln Association, 1930; *Lincoln in the Year 1857,* Abraham Lincoln Association, 1930; (with Carl Sandburg) *Mary Lincoln, Wife and Widow,* Harcourt, 1932; *Lincoln, 1854-1861: Being the Day-by-Day Activities of Abraham Lincoln from January 1, 1854 to March 4, 1861,* Abraham Lincoln Association, 1933; *Here I Have Lived: A History of Lincoln's Springfield, 1821-1865,* Abraham Lincoln Association, 1935, new edition, Abraham Lincoln Book Shop (Chicago), 1971; (compiler) *Suggested Readings in Illinois History,* Illinois State Historical Society, 1935; *Nathaniel Pope, 1784-1850: A Memoir,* privately printed, 1937.

(With Richard L. Beyer) *A Handbook of Illinois History: A Topical Survey with References for Teachers and Students,* Illinois State Historical Society, 1943; (editor and author of introduction and notes) *The Great Chicago Fire, Described*

in Seven Letters by Men and Women Who Experienced Its Horrors, and Now Published in Commemoration of the Seventy-Fifth Anniversary of This Catastrophe, Chicago Historical Society, 1946, enlarged edition published as *The Great Chicago Fire, October 8-10, 1871, Described by Eight Men and Women Who Experienced Its Horrors and Testified to the Courage of Its Inhabitants,* 1971; *A Shelf of Lincoln Books: A Critical, Selective Bibliography of Lincolniana,* Rutgers University Press, in association with Abraham Lincoln Association, 1946; (editor and author of introduction) *The Lincoln Reader* (Book-of-the-Month Club selection), Rutgers University Press, 1947; (compiler and author of introduction) *Abraham Lincoln: His Autobiographical Writings Now Brought Together for the First Time,* Rutgers University Press, 1948.

(Editor and author of foreword and notes) *Abraham Lincoln, By Some Men Who Knew Him,* American House, 1950; *Bloody Williamson: A Chapter in American Lawlessness,* Knopf, 1952, published as *Resort to Violence: A Chapter in American Lawlessness,* Lane, 1954; (editor) *By These Words: Great Documents of American Liberty, Selected and Placed in Their Contemporary Settings,* Rand McNally, 1954; (editor with Earl Schenck Miers) *The Living Lincoln: The Man, His Mind, His Times, and the War He Fought, Reconstructed from His Own Writings,* Rutgers University Press, 1955; *The Chicago Historical Society, 1856-1956: An Unconventional Chronicle,* Rand McNally, 1956; (with James R. Getz) *A Visitor to Chicago in Indian Days,* Caxton Club (Chicago), 1957; (with Miers) *Books: The Image of America and Doorways to American Culture,* Kingsport Press, 1958; (editor) *Created Equal?: The Complete Lincoln-Douglas Debates of 1858,* University of Chicago Press, 1958; (editor) *The American Reader: From Columbus to Today; Being a Compilation or Collection of the Personal Narratives, Relations and Journals Concerning the Society, Economy, Politics, Life and Times of Our Great and Many-Tongued Nation, By Those Who Were There,* Rand McNally, 1958, selections published in five volumes, Fawcett, Volume I: *A New Continent and a New Nation,* Volume II: *The New Nation Grows,* Volume III: *The Nation Divided,* Volume IV: *The Making of a World Power,* Volume V: *The Uneasy World,* all 1960; *The Library of Congress: An Account, Historical and Descriptive,* Kingsport Press, 1958; (editor) James Austin Connolly, *Three Years in the Army of the Cumberland: Letters and Diary,* Indiana University Press, 1959; (author of introduction and notes) *Herndon's Life of Lincoln: The History and Personal Recollections of Abraham Lincoln as Originally Written by William H. Herndon and Jesse W. Weik,* Fine Editions Press, 1959.

(With Miers) *Tragic Years, 1860-1865: A Documentary History of the American Civil War,* Simon & Schuster, 1960; (editor with Miers, and author of introduction) *American Culture: Some Beginnings,* privately printed, 1961; (with Fairfax Downey) *Texas and the War with Mexico* (juvenile), American Heritage Publishing, 1961; (compiler and editor with Miers) *The American Family: An Album of Self-Reliant People,* privately printed, 1963; *Crossroads: 1913,* Rand McNally, 1963; (with Miers) *Abraham Lincoln in Peace and War* (juvenile), American Heritage Publishing, 1964; (editor) John G. Nicolay and John Hay, *Abraham Lincoln: A History,* abridged edition (Angle not associated with earlier edition), University of Chicago Press, 1966; *A Pictorial History of the Civil War Years,* Doubleday, 1967; *We Asked* (series of interviews), Community Development Division, Illinois Bell Telephone Co. (Chicago), eight volumes in one, 1966-67, excerpt published as *We Asked Delyte Morris about Education in Illinois*, 1968; (editor) John Woods, *Two Years' Residence on the English Prairie of Illinois*, Lakeside Press, 1968; (editor with Richard G. Case) Robert Todd Lincoln, *A Portrait of Abraham Lincoln in Letters by His Oldest Son*, Chicago Historical Society, 1968; (compiler and editor with Mary Lynn McCree) *Prairie State: Impressions of Illinois, 1673-1967, by Travelers and Other Observers*, University of Chicago Press, 1968.

(Editor) *Pioneers: Narratives of Noah Harris Letts and Thomas Allen Banning, 1825-1865*, Lakeside Press, 1972; *On a Variety of Subjects*, Chicago Historical Society, 1974; *Phillip K. Wrigley: The Diary of a Modest Man*, Rand McNally, 1975.

SIDELIGHTS: The *New York Times* noted that "in 1928, when the *Atlantic Monthly* magazine began publishing 'Lincoln the Lover,' a series of letters and memorandums ascribed to Lincoln concerning his early romance with Ann Rutledge, Mr. Angle was one of the experts who swiftly challenged their authenticity. His arguments ranged from the handwriting and form of the letters to their portrayal of Lincoln—'an individual mawkish and bombastic, when Lincoln was neither.' Politically, he showed that in the period of the supposed letters Lincoln had given up hope of public office although they depicted him as still ambitious. The magazine dropped the series."

While Angle's books all received wide acclaim, the *New York Times* went on to state that it was nothing like the public response to *The Lincoln Reader*. Charles Poore said of Mr. Angle's introduction to each chapter, "The selections from the works of the different authors are introduced in turn so unobtrusively that the transitions from one point of view to another and from one style to another seldom jar."

BIOGRAPHICAL/CRITICAL SOURCES: New York Times, May 13, 1975; *Washington Post*, May 15, 1975.†

(Died May 11, 1975)

*　　　*　　　*

ANKENBRAND, Frank, Jr.　1905-

PERSONAL: Born October 2, 1905, in Philadelphia, Pa.; son of Frank (an interior decorator) and Catherine (Meeks) Ankenbrand; married Hazel Hall (a teacher), July 3, 1928; children: Frank III. *Education:* Charles Morris School of Journalism, diploma, 1930; Temple University, B.Sc. in Ed., 1941; University of Pennsylvania, graduate study, 1945-46. *Religion:* Society of Friends. *Home:* The Anchorage, Greenwich, N.J. 08328. *Office:* 436 Kings Hwy., Haddonfield, N.J. 08033.

CAREER: Vineland Historical and Antiquarian Society, Vineland, N.J., assistant secretary, 1937-38, historian, 1938-39, librarian, 1939-40, co-editor, 1937-41, then contributing editor of historical quarterly, 1941-60; Lindenweld, N.J., public schools, teacher, 1941-43; Valley Forge Military Academy and Junior College, Wayne, Pa., instructor, 1943-44, assistant professor, 1944-45, associate professor, 1945-53; Memorial High School, Haddonfield, N.J., teacher of English, beginning 1953. Artist, exhibiting woodcuts, collages, and gouaches. President of Philadelphia Graphic Arts Forum, 1960-61, and New Jersey Scholastic Press Association, 1962-63. *Military service:* U.S. Army, Transportation Corps, 1941-43; became second lieutenant.

MEMBER: National Education Association, National Federation of State Poetry Societies (national chancellor, 1962), American Poetry League, Walt Whitman Association, New Jersey Education Association, Society of New Jersey Artists (president, 1952-53), Philadelphia Art Alliance (president, Penn Laurel Poets, 1965-67), Haddonfield Fine Arts Association, Salmagundi Club (New York). *Awards, honors:* Author awards from New Jersey Association of English Teachers, 1961, for *Plum Blossom Scrolls*, 1964, for *Hemingway Mystique*, and 1965, for the foreword to *Gold of Goethe*.

WRITINGS: (With Isaac Benjamin) *The House of Vanity*, Leibman Press, 1928; (translator) Goethe, *The Erlking and Other Poems*, privately printed, 1932; *Fantasy for a Beggar's Opera*, Alpress, 1935; *Firebrands*, Alpress, 1935; *Chinese Legend*, Alpress, 1935; *Danse Macabre*, Alpress, 1936; *A Persian Rose Garden*, Bradford Press, 1936; (translator) *The Poems of Li Po*, William Lewis Washburn, 1941; *Kings in Omar's Rose Garden*, Offhand Press, 1959; *Walt Whitman Crosses*, Alpress, 1960; *Plum Blossom Scrolls* (haiku), Windward Press, 1961; *Hemingway Mystique*, Hors Commerce Press, 1964; *Fireflies* (haiku), Schori, 1965; *Selected Poems*, Roma, 1966; *Shower of Haiku*, Art Press, 1967; *Scroll of Birthday Haiku*, Central Connecticut State College, 1967.

Author of forewords and introductions to other books, including: James Russell Lowell, *The Courtin'*, Washburn Publications, 1936; *Omar Khayyam*, translation by Frederick York Powell, Sunnyside Press, 1937; *Gold of Goethe*, translation by J. S. Height, Schori, 1964; Vicki Silvers, *Echoes in the Wind*, Candor Press, 1967; Jaye Giammarino, *Wine in a Gold Cup*, Prairie Press, 1967; Anna Land Butters, *High Noon*, Prairie Press, 1967.

WORK IN PROGRESS: I Am the Earth, a third collection of haiku; *Collected Poems*, for Mitre Press; two anthologies; *Vignettes of Omar Khayyam of Naishapur*, for Schori Press; a translation.

BIOGRAPHICAL/CRITICAL SOURCES: Harold Henderson, *English Haiku*, Japan Society, 1966.††

*　　　*　　　*

APPLETON, Victor
[Collective pseudonym]

WRITINGS: "Don Sturdy" series; published by Grosset: *Don Sturdy in the Land of Volcanoes; or, The Trail of the Ten Thousand Smokes*, 1925; *. . . in the Tombs of Gold; or, The Old Egyptian's Great Secret*, 1925; *. . . on the Desert of Mystery; or, Autoing in the Land of Caravans*, 1925; *. . . with the Big Snake Hunters; or, Lost in the Jungles of the Amazon*, 1925; *. . . across the North Pole; or, Cast Away in the Land of Ice*, 1925; *. . . Captured by Head Hunters; or, Adrift in the Wilds of Borneo*, 1928; *. . . in Lion Land; or, The Strange Clearing in the Jungle*, 1929.

Don Sturdy in the Land of Giants; or, Captives of the Savage Patagonians, 1930; *. . . on the Ocean Bottom; or, The Strange Cruise of the Phantom*, 1931; *. . . in the Temples of Fear; or, Destined for a Strange Sacrifice*, 1932; *. . . Trapped in the Flaming Wilderness; or, Unearthing Secrets in Central Asia*, 1934; *. . . with the Harpoon Hunters; or, The Strange Cruise of the Whaling Ship*, 1935.

"Movie Boys" series; published by Garden City Publishing Co.: *The Movie Boys and the Flood; or, Perilous Days on the Mighty Mississippi*, 1926; *. . . and the Wreckers; or, Facing the Perils of the Deep*, 1926; *. . . at Seaside Park; or, The Rival Photo Houses of the Boardwalk*, 1926; *. . . at the Big Fair; or, The Greatest Film Ever Exhibited*, 1926; *The Movie Boys' First Show House; or, Fighting for a Foothold* *in Fairlands*, 1926; *The Movie Boys in Earthquake Land; or, Filming Pictures amid Strange Perils*, 1926; *. . . in Peril; or, Strenuous Days along the Panama Canal*, 1926; *. . . in the Jungle; or, Lively Times among the Wild Beasts*, 1926; *. . . in the Wild West; or, Stirring Days Among the Cowboys and Indians*, 1926; *The Movie Boys' New Idea; or, Getting the Best of Their Enemies*, 1926; *The Movie Boys on Broadway; or, The Mystery of the Missing Cash Box*, 1926; *. . . on Call; or, Filming the Perils of a Great City*, 1926; *The Movie Boys' Outdoor Exhibition; or, The Film That Solved a Mystery*, 1926; *The Movie Boys under Fire; or, The Search for the Stolen Film*, 1926; *. . . under the Sea; or, The Treasure of the Lost Ship*, 1926; *. . . under Uncle Sam; or, Taking Pictures for the Army*, 1926; *The Movie Boys' War Spectacle; or, the Film That Won the Prize*, 1927.

"Tom Swift" series; published by Grosset: *Tom Swift and His Airship*, 1910; *. . . and His Electric Runabout; or, The Speediest Car on the Road*, 1910; *. . . and His Motorcycle; or, Fun and Adventures on the Road*, 1910; *. . . and His Motor-Boat*, 1910; *. . . and His Submarine Boat; or, Under the Ocean for Sunken Treasure*, 1910; *. . . and His Sky Racer; or, The Quickest Flight on Record*, 1911; *. . . among the Diamond Makers; or, The Secret of Phantom Mountain*, 1911; *. . . and His Electric Rifle; or, Daring Adventure in Elephant Land*, 1911; *. . . in the Caves of Ice; or, The Wreck of the Airship*, 1911; *. . . in the City of Gold; or, Marvelous Adventures Underground*, 1912; *. . . and His Great Search-light; or, On the Border for Uncle Sam*, 1912; *. . . in Captivity; or, A Daring Escape by Airship*, 1912; *. . . and His Air Glider; or, Seeking the Platinum Treasure*, 1912; *. . . and His Wizard Camera; or, Thrilling Adventures While Taking Moving Pictures*, 1912; *. . . and His Photo Telephone; or, The Picture that Saved a Fortune*, 1914; *. . . and His Big Tunnel; or, The Hidden City of the Andes*, 1916.

Tom Swift and His Undersea Search; or, The Treasure on the Floor of the Atlantic, 1920; *. . . and His Chest of Secrets; or, Tracing the Stolen Inventions*, 1925; *. . . and His Talking Pictures; or, The Greatest Invention on Record*, 1928; *. . . and His House on Wheels; or, A Trip to the Mountain of Mystery*, 1929.

Tom Swift and His Dirigible; or, Adventure over the Forest of Fire, 1930; *. . . and His Sky Train; or, Overland through the Clouds*, 1931; *. . . and His Giant Magnet; or, Bringing Up the Lost Submarine*, 1932; *. . . and His Television Detector; or, Trailing the Secret Plotters*, 1933; *. . . and His Ocean Airport; or, Foiling the Haargolanders*, 1934; *. . . and His Planet Stone; or, Discovering the Secret of Another World*, 1935.

SIDELIGHTS: See **ADAMS, Harriet S.,** **STRATEMEYER, Edward L.,** and **SVENSON, Andrew E.**†

*　　*　　*

ARENT, Arthur 1904-1972

PERSONAL: Born September 29, 1904, in Jersey City, N.J.; son of Herman (a haberdasher and hotel owner) and Eva (Levy) Arent; married Blanche Englander, July 3, 1936. *Education:* Attended Lafayette College, 1923, and New York University, 1924-25. *Home:* 35 East Ninth St., New York, N.Y. 10003. *Agent:* Brandt & Brandt, 101 Park Ave., New York, N.Y. 10017.

CAREER: Author of plays, collectively called the "Living Newspaper," and writer for television, radio, and films. Writer of sketches for musical revues, 1935, and plays for Federal Theatre Project, 1935-39; writer for Warner Brothers, 1941-42, and for U.S. Office of War Information, 1942-

44; wrote or adapted plays for radio and television, 1944-56; staff writer, Columbia Broadcasting System, 1956-57, editor of "U.S. Steel Hour," 1957-58. Summer instructor, New York University, 1954. *Member:* Authors League, Television Writers Guild, Players Club. *Awards, honors:* Guggenheim fellow, 1938.

WRITINGS: (Contributor) Pierre de Rohan, editor, *Federal Theatre Plays* (includes: *Triple-A Plowed Under*, produced at Biltmore Theatre, March 14, 1936; *Power: A Living Newspaper*, produced at Ritz Theatre, February 23, 1937; and *One-Third of A Nation*, produced at Adelphi Theatre, January 17, 1938), Random House, 1938; (contributor) H. William Fitelson, editor, *The Theatre Guild on the Air*, Rinehart, 1947; *Gravedigger's Funeral* (espionage novel), Grossman, 1967; *The Laying-On of Hands*, Little, Brown, 1969.

Unpublished plays: "Ethiopia," produced at Biltmore Theatre, January 23, 1936; "1935," produced at Biltmore Theatre, May 12, 1936; "Injunction Granted," produced at Biltmore Theatre, July 24, 1936; (with Marc Blitzstein, Emanuel Eisenberg, Charles Friedman, and David Gregory) "Pins and Needles" (revue), presented by International Ladies' Garment Workers' Union Players, November 27, 1937; "It's Up to You," for U.S. Department of Agriculture, 1943.

Television play: "The Idyll of Red Gulch," U.S. Steel Hour, 1955.

Television adaptations; produced by U.S. Steel Hour: H.M. Harwood, "The Man in Possession," 1953; (with Raphael Hays) Lawrence Williams, "The Rise of Carthage," 1954; Sylvia Regan, "Morning Star," 1954; Elmer Rice, "The Grand Tour," 1954; W.E.C. Fairchild, "The Man with the Gun," 1954; Henry Bernstein, "The Thief," 1955; Muriel Box and Sidney Box, "The Seven Veils, 1955. Also wrote or adapted television plays for "Hallmark Hall of Fame," 1952-56, including "The Corn Is Green."

Radio plays: Wrote or adapted works for radio, including Dupont's "Calvadcade of America," 1944-49, and "The Theatre Guild on the Air," for which he adapted some one hundred Broadway plays, including "Strange Interlude," "Ah Wilderness," "Candida," "Craig's Wife," "Green Pastures," and "The Age of Innocence."

AVOCATIONAL INTERESTS: Gardening, music, billiards.

BIOGRAPHICAL/CRITICAL SOURCES: New York Times, May 20, 1972; *Variety*, May 24, 1972.†

(Died May 18, 1972)

*　　*　　*

ARMAND, Louis 1905-1971

PERSONAL: Born January 17, 1905, in Cruseilles, France; son of Jean-Marie (a teacher) and Marie-Clotilde (Masson) Armand; married Genevieve Gazel, September 24, 1928; children: Maurice, Joseph, Jeannine (Mme. du Pre de Saint-Maur), France-Marie (Mme. Lefevre de Ladonchamps). *Education:* Graduated from Ecole Polytechnique, 1924, and Ecole Nationale Superieure des Mines de Paris, 1926. *Home:* 30 Avenue de Villiers, Paris 17, France. *Office:* Union Internationale des Chemins de Fer, 14 rue Jean Rey, Paris 15, France.

CAREER: Began career as mining engineer in France; Societe National des Chemins de Fer Francais (S.N.C.F.), 1934-58, joined railway staff, 1934, became assistant general manager, 1946, general manager, 1949-55, chairman of board of directors, 1955-58; president, Euratom Commission, 1958-59; Union Internationale des Chemins de Fer, secretary-general, beginning 1961, and president; Westinghouse-Europe, president, beginning 1969. French Atomic Energy Commission, chairman of Industrial Equipment Committee, beginning 1956, and member of Scientific Council. Director, Compagnie International des Wagons-Lits, Union des Banques, Petrofina, Publicis, and other companies. Chairman of board, Ecole Polytechnique; chairman of board and honorary professor, Ecole National d'Administration. Worked in Resistance during Occupation of France in World War II, organizing a sabatoge group, Resistance-Fer, 1943. *Military service:* French artillery, 1926; became second lieutenant.

MEMBER: Academie Francaise, Academie des Sciences Morales et Politiques, Association Francaise de Normalisation (president), La Protectrice (president). *Awards, honors:* Compagnon de la Liberation; Grand Officier de la Legion d'Honneur; Croix de Guerre, 1939-45; Medal of Freedom; Knight Commander, Order of the British Empire.

WRITINGS: Some Aspects of the European Energy Problem: Suggestions for Collective Action, Organisation for European Economic Cooperation, 1955; (with Francis Perrin) *L'Euratom* (report given to l'Assemblee Nationale, July 5, 1956), [Paris], 1956; *Savoie* (geographical, historical, and archaeological notes by Pierre Moreau; photographs by Loic Jahan), Hachette, 1958; *Discours devant l'Assemblee parlementaire europeenne, 23 juin 1958,* Service des Publications des Communautes Europeennes, 1958; (with Michel Drancourt) *Plaidoyer pour l'avenir,* Calmann-Levy, 1961; *Notice sur la vie et les travaux de Paul-Gaultier, 1872-1960,* Firmin-Didot, 1962; *Histoire des chemins de fer en France* (S.N.F.C. anniversary presentation), Presses Modernes, 1963; *Discours de reception de M. Louis Armand a l'Academie francaise* [and] *Response de M. Jean Rostand,* Calmann-Levy, 1964; *Louis Armand: Trois fois vingt ans,* Journaux Regionaux Associes, 1965; *Simples propos,* Fayard, 1968; (with Drancourt) *Le Pari europeen,* Fayard, 1968, translation by Patrick Evans published as *The European Challenge,* Atheneum, 1970; (with others) *Ma mere,* Presses de la Cite, 1969; *Apres le diplome: ou, Les Statistiques de la reussite* (report presented to Rotary International), R. Laffont, 1969; *Propos ferroviaires,* Fayard, 1970.

Also author, with Franz Etzel and Francesco Giordani, of *Un Objectif pour Euratom,* an unpublished report submitted at the request of the governments of Belgium, France, German Federal Republic, Italy, Luxembourg, and the Netherlands, 1957. Author of a monthly column in *Realities.*

BIOGRAPHICAL/CRITICAL SOURCES: Louis Armand: Trois fois vingt ans, Journaux Regionaux Associes, 1965; *Best Sellers,* September 15, 1970.†

(Died August 30, 1971)

*   *   *

ARMSTRONG, Terence Ian Fytton   1912-1970
(John Gawsworth)

PERSONAL: Born June 29, 1912, in Kensington, London, England; son of F. P. and E. L. (Jackson) Armstrong; twice divorced; married third wife, Doreen Emily Ada (Rowley) Downie, 1955. *Education:* Attended Manor House School, Sussex, Linton House School, London, and Merchant Taylors' School, London. *Home:* 35 Sutherland Place, London W.2, England. *Agent:* Howard Moorepark, 444 East 82nd St., New York, N.Y. 10028.

CAREER: Freeman of the City of London, and of Merchant Taylors' Company, London, England, 1935; coordinator of Neo-Georgian lyric poetry movement, 1937; Delegue General de la Societe des Ecrivains de l'Afrique du Nord, Tunis, 1943; Royal Asiatic Society of Bengal, lecturer, 1945; succeeded as third King of Redonda (an island in the British West Indies), 1947-67, abdicating for reasons of health. Brandaris Insurance Co. Ltd., Amsterdam, Holland, London archivist, 1960. *Military service:* Royal Air Force, 1944-46; became flying officer, 1946. *Member:* Royal Society of Literature (fellow), Cairene Salamander Society of Poets (London president). *Awards, honors:* Benson Medal of the Royal Society of Literature, 1939.

WRITINGS—Poetry, under pseudonym John Gawsworth: *Confession,* Twyn Barlwm Press, 1931; *Epithalamium,* Press of the Blue Moon, 1931; *Fifteen Poems: Three Friends,* Twyn Barlwm Press, 1931; *Kingcup: Suite Sentimentale,* Twyn Barlwm Press, 1932; *Lyrics to Kingcup,* E. Larh, 1932; *Mishka and Madeleine: A Poem Sequence for Marcia,* Twyn Barlwm Press, 1932; *Song for Nancy,* privately printed, 1932; *Poems, 1930-1932,* Rich, 1933; *Flesh of Cypris,* E. H. Samuel, 1936; *Poems,* Richards, 1938; *New Poems,* Secker, 1939; *Mind of Man,* Richards, 1940; *Marlow Hill,* Richards, 1941; *Legacy to Love: Selected Poems, 1931-1941,* Collins, 1943; *Snow and Sand,* Susil Gupta (Calcutta), 1945; *Blow No Bugles,* Susil Gupta, 1945; (contributor) *Essays by Divers Hands,* Royal Society of Literature, 1946; *Collected Poems of John Gawsworth,* Sidgwick, 1948.

Other writings, under pseudonym John Gawsworth: *Above the River,* Ulysses Bookshop, 1931; *Apes, Japes and Hitlerism: A Study and Bibliography of P. Wyndham Lewis,* Unicorn, 1932; *Ten Contemporaries: Notes Toward Their Definitive Bibliography* (two series), Benn, 1932, Joiner & Steele, 1933; *The Twyn Barlwm Press, 1931-32,* privately printed, 1933; *Annotations on Some Minor Writings of T. E. Lawrence,* Scholartis Press, 1935; (with Matthew P. Shiel) *The Invisible Voices,* Richards, 1935; *The Dowson Legend,* Oxford University Press, 1939.

Editor, under pseudonym John Gawsworth: (And author of introduction) *Known Signatures: An Anthology of Modern Poetry,* Rich, 1932, revised edition with title *Fifty Years of Modern Verse,* Secker, 1938, abridged edition with title *Fifty Modern Poems by Forty Famous Poets,* Susil Gupta, 1945; *Backwaters: Excursions in the Shades,* Search Publications, 1932; *Strange Assembly: New Stories by H. Crackanthorpe* [and others], Unicorn, 1932; Richard Barham Middleton, *Pantomime Man,* Rich, 1933; *Full Score* (anthology of short stories), Rich, 1933; *Poets of Merchant Taylors' School,* Rich, 1934; *Poets of Harrow School,* Rich, 1934; *Poets of Eton College,* Rich, 1934; *Thirty New Tales of Horror,* Hutchinson, 1935; *Crimes, Creeps, and Thrills* (anthology of short stories), E. H. Samuel, 1936; Havelock Ellis, *Poems,* Richards Press, 1937; *The Muse of Monarchy: Poems by Kings and Queens of England,* E. Grant, 1937; *The Garland of Erica* (anthology), 1938; Matthew P. Shiel, *Best Short Stories,* Gollancz, 1948; Thomas Burke, *Best Stories,* Phoenix, 1950; Havelock Ellis, *From Marlowe to Shaw: Studies, 1876-1936,* Williams & Norgate, 1950; Alfred, Lord Tennyson, *Selected Poetical Works,* Coward, 1951; Havelock Ellis, *Sex and Marriage: Eros in Contemporary Life,* Williams & Norgate, 1951, Random House, 1952; John Milton, *Complete English Poems,* Macdonald, 1953. *English Digest,* founding editor, 1939-41, London editor, 1957-58; London editor, *Literary Digest,* 1946-49; editor,

Poetry Review, 1948-52; acting editor, *Enquiry*, 1949; British editor, *Ellery Queen's Mystery Magazine*, 1958.

WORK IN PROGRESS: Collected poems; collected literary essays.†

(Died September 23, 1970)

* * *

ARNDT, Ernst H(einrich) D(aniel) 1899-

PERSONAL: Born May 27, 1899, in Bloemfontein, Orange Free State, South Africa; son of Johannes (a missionary) and Luise (Gruetzner) Arndt; married Ruth Elisabeth Spence, August 6, 1926; children: David Ernst Spence, Wenonah Margarethe (Mrs. Joop Venter). *Education:* Grey University College (now University of the Orange Free State), B.A., 1920; Columbia University, M.A., 1922, Ph.D., 1924. *Home:* 292 Orient St., Pretoria, 0002, Transvaal, South Africa.

CAREER: University of Pretoria, Pretoria, South Africa, professor of economics, 1925-36, professor of banking, 1936-42; South African Treasury, Pretoria, registrar of banks and building societies, 1942-51; South African Reserve Bank, Pretoria, deputy governor, 1951-61; South African Land and Agricultural Bank, Pretoria, director, 1962-73. Chairman of South African Decimalisation Board, Pretoria, 1959-63. *Member:* Economic Society of South Africa (president, 1937-39), Suid-Afrikaanse Akademie vir Wetenskap en Kuns, Bankers' Institute of South Africa (president, 1956-57), Institute of Building Societies in South Africa. *Awards, honors:* D.Com., University of Pretoria, 1958; D.Sc. (Econ.), University of Witwatersrand, 1962; Diploma of Honour, University of the Orange Free State, 1963.

WRITINGS: Banking and Currency Development in South Africa, Juta, 1928; *An Analysis of the Investment Policies of Life Insurance Companies in South Africa,* University of Pretoria Press, 1937; *Safeguarding the Investor,* University of Pretoria Press, 1938; *The South African Mints,* University of Pretoria Press, 1939; *Ons Finansies: Geld en Bankwese,* Van Schaik, 1939; *Insuring Our Insurance,* Union Booksellers, 1941; *An Experiment in Agricultural Credit,* University of Pretoria Press, 1942; *The Union's Gold Reserve,* South African Reserve Bank, 1956; (contributor) W. F. Crick, editor, *Commonwealth Banking Systems,* Clarendon Press, 1965.

* * *

ARNOLD, Lloyd R. 1906-1970

PERSONAL: Born July 31, 1906, in Council Bluffs, Iowa; son of William R. (in glass business) and Iva (Van Atta) Arnold; married Erma M. Oviatt, March 31, 1928. *Education:* Attended high school for three years. *Religion:* Protestant. *Address:* Box 884, Sun Valley, Idaho 83353.

CAREER: Professional motion picture and still photographer. Mayor of Ketchum, Idaho, 1955-59. *Military service:* U.S. Army Air Forces, World War II; became warrant officer.

WRITINGS: High on the Wild with Hemingway, Caxton, 1968. Contributor of feature articles to periodicals.†

(Died March 21, 1970)

* * *

ARNOLD, Richard E(ugene) 1908-

PERSONAL: Born December 5, 1908, in Springfield, Mo.; son of James Aloysius and M. Rose (Sims) Arnold. *Educa-*

tion: St. Louis University, A.B., 1931, M.A., 1932, Ph.L., 1935, Ph.D., 1936, S.T.L., 1941. *Home and office:* Marquette University, 1404 West Wisconsin, Milwaukee, Wis. 53233.

CAREER: Entered Order of Society of Jesus (Jesuits), 1927, ordained Roman Catholic priest, 1940; St. Louis University High School, St. Louis, Mo., teacher of classical langauges, 1936-37; St. Louis University, St. Louis, university assistant, 1938-41, instructor, 1941-46, assistant professor of classical languages, 1946; Regis College, Denver, Colo., head of department of classical languages, 1946-48; Marquette University, Milwaukee, Wis., assistant professor, 1948-50, associate professor, 1950-53, professor of classics, beginning 1953, acting chairman of classics department, 1961-62. Consultant, National Association of Standard Medical Vocabulary. *Member:* American Philological Association, American Classical League, Classical Association of Middle West and South, Classical Club of St. Louis (president, 1945-46), Eta Sigma Phi.

WRITINGS: (With W. R. Hennes) *Iris,* St. Louis University Book Store, 1942; (editor) *Classical Essays Presented to James A. Kleist, S.J.,* Classical Bulletin, 1946; (with L. A. Kennedy and A. E. Millward) *The Universal Treatise of Nicholas of Autrecourt,* Marquette University Press, 1971. Contributor to new edition of *Du Cange Dictionary of Mediaeval Latin from Herman of Tournai;* contributor of book reviews to periodicals. Editor, *Classical Bulletin,* 1945-46; member of editorial board, "Mediaeval Philosophical Texts in Translation" series, beginning 1948.

WORK IN PROGRESS: Collaborating with others on an edition of Coemans' *Breves notitiae* and *Introductio in studium instituti et annotationes in formulam instituti II;* contributing to a forthcoming volume in "Mediaeval Philosophical Texts in Translation" series; translating and editing, *De Ente finito.*

SIDELIGHTS: Richard Arnold, whose hobbies include the teaching of Gregorian Chant and classical symphony classes, is competent in Latin and Greek, and has a reading knowledge of French and German.

* * *

ARUNDEL, Honor (Morfydd) 1919-1973

PERSONAL: Born August 15, 1919, in North Wales; daughter of Huber (an engineer) and Constance (Sawyer) Arundel; married Alex McCrindle (an actor), 1952; children: Suzanna, Catherine, Jessica; one stepdaughter. *Education:* Attended Somerville College, Oxford, 1938-39. *Religion:* None. *Home:* 3 Castle Wynd North, Edinburgh 1, Scotland. *Agent:* Scottish Casting Office, Television, Theatre, Screen Ltd. (S.C.O.T.T.S.), 2 Clifton St., Glasgow G3 7LA, Scotland.

CAREER: Writer. *Member:* Scottish P.E.N. *Awards, honors:* Scottish Arts Council Writing Award, 1972, for *A Family Failing.*

WRITINGS: (Editor with Maurice Carpenter and others) *New Lyrical Ballads,* Editions Poetry London, 1945; *Green Street,* Hamish Hamilton, 1965, Hawthorn, 1970; *The Freedom of Art,* Lawrence & Wishart, 1965; *The High House* (juvenile; illustrated by Eileen Armitage), Hamish Hamilton, 1966, Meridith, 1968; *The Amazing Mr. Prothero,* Hamish Hamilton, 1968, Thomas Nelson, 1972; *The Two Sisters* (Junior Literary Guild selection), Heinemann, 1968, Meridith, 1969; *Emma's Island* (Junior Literary Guild selection), Hamish Hamilton, 1968, Hawthorn, 1970; *The*

Longest Weekend, Hamish Hamilton, 1969, Thomas Nelson, 1970; *Emma in Love,* Hamish Hamilton, 1970, Thomas Nelson, 1972; *The Girl in the Opposite Bed,* Hamish Hamilton, 1970, Thomas Nelson, 1971; *The Terrible Temptation,* Thomas Nelson, 1971; (contributor) M. R. Hodgkin, editor, *Young Winter's Tales,* Macmillan, 1971; *A Family Failing,* Thomas Nelson, 1972; *The Blanket Word,* Thomas Nelson, 1973.

Plays: "The Home Game," produced by B.B.C. Sound, 1960. Contributor of poetry, critical articles, and reviews to British journals.

WORK IN PROGRESS: The Puritans, a novel; her autobiography; a collection of poems, for St. Columba Press.†

(Died June 8, 1973)

* * *

ASHMORE, Jerome 1901-

PERSONAL: Born January 26, 1901, in Niagara Falls, N.Y.; son of Deane Matheson (an electrical technician) and Blanche (Tucker) Ashmore; married Frances Seeley, May 1, 1935. *Education:* Attended University of Pennsylvania, 1918-19; University of Michigan, A.B., 1924, A.M., 1936; Columbia University, Ph.D., 1954. *Office:* Division of Special Interdisciplinary Studies, Crawford Hall, Case Western Reserve University, Cleveland, Ohio 44106.

CAREER: Case Western Reserve University, Cleveland, Ohio, lecturer, 1955-60, assistant professor, 1960-66, associate professor of philosophy, beginning 1966. *Member:* American Philosophical Association, American Society for Aesthetics, Society for Phenomenology and Existential Philosophy, Society for the Study of Process Philosophies, Ohio Philosophical Association. *Awards, honors: Journal of Aesthetics* essay prize, 1955, for "Some Differences between Abstract and Non-Objective Painting"; Matchette Foundation Prize for essay, "Santayana's Mistrust of Fine Art," also published in *Journal of Aesthetics,* 1956.

WRITINGS: Santayana, Art, and Aesthetics, Press of Western Reserve University, 1966; (contributor) O. B. Hardison, Jr., editor, *The Quest for Imagination,* Press of Case Western Reserve University, 1971. Contributor of more than twenty-five articles and occasional reviews to *Modern Drama, Physics Today, Monist,* and other journals.

WORK IN PROGRESS: Research on the foundation and character of meaning, expected to result in a book-length manuscript; other research centered on imagination and on essence.††

* * *

ASTURIAS, Miguel Angel 1899-1974

PERSONAL: Surname pronounced As-*too*-ree-ahs; born October 19, 1899, in Guatemala City, Guatemala; son of Ernesto (a Supreme Court magistrate, later an importer) and Maria (Rosales) Asturias; married Clemencia Amado; married second wife, Blanca Mora y Araujo; children: Rodrigo, Miguel Angel. *Education:* Universidad de San Carlos de Guatemala, Doctor of Laws, 1923; studied at the Sorbonne, University of Paris, 1923-28. *Residence:* Paris, France.

CAREER: Diplomat, writer; co-founder of Universidad Popular de Guatemala (a free evening college), 1921, and Associacion de Estudiantes Universitarios (Unionist party group). Left Guatemala for political reasons in 1923; went to Paris where he studied South American cultures and religions; European correspondent for Central American and Mexican newspapers, 1923-32; returned to Guatemala in 1932; worked as a journalist and founded a periodical, *El Diario del Aire;* elected deputy to Guatemalan national congress, 1942; joined diplomatic service, 1945; cultural attache to Mexico, 1946-47; minister-counselor in Buenos Aires, 1947-52; minister in Paris, 1952-53; ambassador to El Salvador, 1953-54; stripped of Guatemalan citizenship and forced into exile during the regime of Colonel Carlos Castillo Armas; lived in Argentina for eight years and worked as a correspondent for *El Nacional,* a Caracas newspaper, and as adviser to Editorial Losada (publishers), Buenos Aires; returned to Guatemala and the diplomatic service following the election of a new president, 1966; ambassador to France, 1966-70. *Member:* International P.E.N. *Awards, honors:* Prix Sylla Monsegur, Paris, 1931, for *Leyendas de Guatemala;* Prix du Meilleur Roman Etranger, 1952, for *El senor presidente;* Lenin Peace Prize, 1966; Nobel Prize for Literature, 1967.

WRITINGS: Rayito de Estrella (poetry), privately printed, 1925; (translator from the French with J. M. Gonzalez de Mendoza) *Anales de los xahil de los indios cakchiqueles,* published between 1925-27, 2nd edition, Tipografia nacional, 1967; (translator with Gonzalez de Mendoza and Georges Raynaud) *Popol Vuh: El libro del consejo,* published between 1925-27, 3rd edition, Universidad Nacional Autonoma de Mexico, 1964; *Leyendas de Guatemala,* Ediciones Oriente (Madrid), 1930, 4th edition, Editorial Losada (Buenos Aires), 1970; *Emulo Lipolidon,* Tipografia "America," 1935.

Anoche, 10 de marzo de 1543 (poetry), Ediciones del Aire (Guatemala), 1943; *El senor presidente* (novel), Editorial Costa-Amic (Mexico), 1946, translation by Frances Partridge published as *The President,* Gollancz, 1963, same translation published as *El Senor Presidente,* Atheneum, 1964; *Sien de alondra* (poetry), Argos (Buenos Aires), 1949; *Hombres de maiz,* Editorial Losada, 1949, translation by Gerald Martin published as *Men of Maize,* Delacorte, 1975.

Viento fuerte (novel), Editorial del Ministerio de Educacion Publica, 1950, translation by Darwin Flakoll and Claribel Alegria published as *The Cyclone,* Owen, 1967, translation by Gregory Rabassa published as *Strong Wind,* Delacorte, 1968; *Ejercicios poeticos en forma de soneto sobre temas de Horacio,* Botella al Mar (Buenos Aires), 1951; *El papa verde* (novel), Editorial Losada, 1954, translation by Rabassa published as *The Green Pope,* Delacorte, 1971; *Soluna: Comedia prodigiosa en dos jornadas y un final* (play; also see below), Ediciones Losange (Buenos Aires), 1955; *Bolivar* (poetry), El Salvador (San Salvador), 1955; *Week-end en Guatemala* (short stories), Editorial Goyanarte (Buenos Aires), 1956; *La audiencia de los confines: Cronica en tres andanzas* (play; also see below), Editorial Ariadna (Buenos Aires), 1957; *Messages indiens* (original in Spanish), translation by Claude Couffon, Seghers (Paris), 1958; *Nombre custodio, e Imagen pasajera* (poetry), La Habana, 1959.

(Editor) *Poesia precolombina,* Compania General Fabril Editora (Buenos Aires), 1960; (with Jean Mazon and F. Diez de Medina) *Bolivie, cet astre ignore* (original in Spanish), translation by Antoinette de Montmollin, La Baconniere, 1960, translation by Frances Hogarth-Gaute published as *Bolivia: An Undiscovered Land,* Harrap, 1961; *Leyendas,* Ministerio de Cultura (San Salvador), 1960; *Los ojos de los enterrados* (novel), Editorial Losada, 1960, translation by Gregory Rabassa published as *The Eyes of the Interred,* Delacorte, 1973; *El alhajadito,* Editorial Goyanarte, 1961, translation by Martin Shuttleworth published as *The Bejeweled Boy,* Doubleday, 1971; *Mulata de tal,* Editorial Losada,

1963, translation by Rabassa published as *Mulata*, Delacorte, 1967 (published in England as *The Mulatta and Mr. Fly*, Owen, 1967); (editor) *Paginas de Ruben Dario*, Editorial Universitaria de Buenos Aires, 1963; *Teatro: Chantaje, Dique seco, Soluna, La Audiencia de los Confines*, Editorial Losada, 1964; *Rumania, su nueva imagen*, Universidad Veracruzana, 1964; *Juan Girador*, Centre de recherches de l'Institut d'etudes hispaniques, 1964; *Clarivigilia primaveral* (poetry), Editorial Losada, 1965; *El espejo de Lida Sal*, Siglo Veintiuno Editores, 1967; (translator from the Rumanian) *Antologia de la prosa rumana*, Editorial Losada, 1967; *Latinoamerica y otros ensayos*, Guadiana de Publicaciones, 1968; (with Pablo Neruda) *Megkostoltuk Magyarorszagot* (original in Spanish), Corvina (Budapest), 1968, published as *Comiendo en Hungria*, Editorial Lumen (Barcelona), 1969; *Maladron*, Editorial Losada, 1969; *Hector Poleo*, Villand & Golanis (Paris), 1969.

El novelista en la universidad, Sociedad General Espanola de Libreria, 1971; *The Talking Machine* (juvenile; original in Spanish), translation by Beverly Koch, Doubleday, 1971; *Viernes de dolores*, Editorial Losada, 1971; *Trois de quatre soleils* (original in Spanish), translation by Claude Couffon, Albert Skira, 1971; *Mi mejor obra*, Organizacion Editorial Novaro, 1973, published as *Lo Mejor de mi obra*, 1974.

Omnibus volumes: *Obras escogidas*, Aguilar (Madrid), 1955, 2nd edition, 1964; *Torotumbo* (original in Spanish), translation by Rene L. F. Durand, Seghers, 1966, first Spanish edition published as *Torotumbo, La Audienica de los Confines, Mensajes indios*, Plaza & Janes (Barcelona), 1967; *Obras Completas*, three volumes, Aguilar, 1967; *Antologia de Miguel Angel Asturias*, edited by Pablo Palomino, Costa-Amic, 1968; *Miguel Angel Asturias: Semblanza para el estudio de su vida y obra, con una seleccion de poemas y prosas*, Cultural Centroamericana Libreria Proa (Guatemala), 1968; *El problema social del indio y otros textos*, edited by Claude Couffon, Centre de recherches de l'Institut d'etudes hispaniques, 1971; *Novelas y cuentos de juventud*, edited by Couffon, Centre de recherches de l'Institut de'etudes hispaniques, 1971; *America: Fabula de fabulas y otros ensayos*, compiled by Richard Callan, Monte Avila (Caracas), 1972.

Also author of *La arquitectura de la vida nueva* (lectures), 1920, *Sonetos*, 1936, *Alclasan* (poetry), 1939, *Fantomina* (poetry), 1940, and *Con el rehen en los dientes* (poetry), 1946. Co-founder of *Tiempos Nuevos*, a weekly newspaper, during the twenties.

SIDELIGHTS: When he received the Nobel Prize for Literature in 1967, Miguel Asturias was the second Latin American writer to be honored by the Swedish Academy. Upon reception of the award Asturias said, "My work will continue to reflect the voice of the peoples, gathering their myths and popular beliefs and at the same time seeking to give birth to a universal consciousness of Latin American problems."

Reviewing Asturias' first novel, *El senor presidente*, Thomas Lask of the *New York Times* wrote: "... it is an impressive piece of work. As a study of the way a Latin-American dictatorship corrupts all society, his novel has few superiors. The dictatorship brought out the worst of all men, making them gutless, bestial and callous. It operated like the great chain of being. Every part of society was allied through lies, cruelty, double-dealing and physical aggression. Mr. Asturias is powerfully vivid and eloquent in showing how the mythic force of the dictatorship kept the state together. We seldom see the President, but we feel his presence all the time."

In his review of *The Green Pope*, Geoffrey Wagner wrote that "Asturias is a great writer and has created in his central character George Maker Thompson a clever summa of mercantile culture. His universe, a Central American republic with 'the shape of a pistol holster,' is vividly real, and we share throughout in a common awareness of true sophistication. The descriptive material is superb, and probably unmatched by compositional ability, . . ."

David Gallagher called *Strong Wind* "a work of crude but not unpersuasive propaganda." He went on to state, however, that "the main reason for the ultimate failure of this often pleasantly exotic novel is that Asturias is an incompetent manipulator of plot. Characters make elaborate entrances then disappear, never to be heard of again."

Maladron, according to Thomas E. Lyon, ". . . bears the mark of what Fernando Alegria has termed 'automatic writing'—the author merely lets his interior thoughts and feelings flow forth, the better to capture, supposedly, the essence of life. The problem with this kind of writing, and with this particular novel, is that it often lacks stylistic polish and purposeful narrative organization."

Miguel Asturias once told a *Washington Post* reporter: "When the book is ripe and ready I get down to work. In the first version, I let out everything that crosses my mind. I type, because if I wrote by hand I wouldn't be able to read my writing afterwards. . . . The first version is completely automatic. I go straight through it, without ever turning back to see what I've left behind. . . . What I obtain from automatic writing is the mating or juxtaposition of words which, as the Indians say, have never met before."

El senor presidente was made into a film with the same title by Imago Producciones, Argentina.

BIOGRAPHICAL/CRITICAL SOURCES: Enrique Anderson-Imbert, *Spanish American Literature: A History*, translation by John V. Falconieri, Wayne State University Press, 1963; *Times Literary Supplement*, October 18, 1963, September 28, 1967; *New Stateman*, October 25, 1963, September 29, 1967; *Book Week*, February 2, 1964; *Punch*, October 11, 1967; *New York Times*, October 20, 1967, January 2, 1971, June 10, 1974; *Observer Review*, October 22, 1967; *National Observer*, October 23, 1967, February 17, 1969; *Christian Science Monitor*, October 26, 1967, May 10, 1969; *Books and Bookmen*, November, 1967; *Best Sellers*, November 1, 1967, February 1, 1969, March 15, 1971; *New York Times Book Review*, November 19, 1967, January 26, 1969; Hugo Cerezo Dardon, editor, *Coloquio con Miguel Angel Asturias*, Editorial Universitario, 1968; *Saturday Review*, January 25, 1968; *Books Abroad*, winter, 1968, spring, 1968, summer, 1969, autumn, 1970, winter, 1971; Aurora Sierra Franco, *Miguel Angel Asturias en la literatura*, Editorial Istmo (Guatemala), 1969; *Washington Post*, February 11, 1969, June 10, 1974; *Nation*, February 17, 1969; *New Republic*, February 22, 1969; *National Review*, April 6, 1971; *Commonweal*, April 30, 1971; *Detroit News*, December 19, 1971; *Contemporary Literary Criticism*, Volume III, Gale, 1975.†

(Died June 9, 1974)

*   *   *

AULETA, Michael S. 1909-

PERSONAL: Born August 21, 1909, in New York, N.Y.; son of Francis A. (a medical doctor) and Concettina (Acampora) Auleta; married Alice Joan Cambridge, December 28, 1940; children: Gregory F., Nancy Jo (Mrs. Stephen Smigocki). *Education:* Fordham University, B.A., 1932; New York University, M.A., 1939, Ed.D., 1947. *Religion:* Roman Catholic. *Residence:* Stuart, Fla.

CAREER: Elementary teacher in Mamaroneck, N.Y., 1937-39; State Teachers College (now State University of New York College at Oswego), principal of Laboratory School, 1939-43; State Teachers College (now State University of New York College at Fredonia), assistant professor of education, 1947-49; State University of New York College at Brockport, professor of education and chairman of department, 1949-67; University of South Florida, Tampa, professor of early childhood education, beginning 1967. Consultant in early childhood education to state of Florida. *Military service:* U.S. Coast Guard, 1943-45. *Member:* Association for Early Childhood Education, National Association for the Education of Young Children, Torch Club International, Kappa Delta Pi, Phi Delta Kappa.

WRITINGS: (Editor and contributor) *Foundations of Early Childhood Education: Readings,* Random House, 1969. Contributor of more than fifteen articles to education journals.

WORK IN PROGRESS: Research on a variety of childhood problems, especially a child's concept of parents as persons and children's secrets.

AVOCATIONAL INTERESTS: Horseback riding, golf, painting in water color, music.†

*   *   *

AUSTIN, Elizabeth S.   1907-

PERSONAL: Born January 23, 1907, in New York, N.Y.; married Oliver L. Austin, Jr., September 10, 1930; children: Anthony, Timothy. *Office:* Florida State Museum, University of Florida, Gainesville, Fla. 32601.

CAREER: University of Florida, Florida State Museum, Gainesville, research associate, beginning 1960. Author of children's books. *Member:* American Ornithologists Union, National League of American Pen Women.

WRITINGS: (Editor and compiler) *Frank M. Chapman in Florida: His Journals and Letters,* University of Florida Press, 1967; *Penguins: The Birds with Flippers,* Random House, 1968; *The Birds That Stopped Flying* (juvenile), Random House, 1969; (with husband, Oliver L. Austin, Jr.) *The Random House Book of Birds,* Random House, 1970. Contributor to *Golden Book Encyclopedia of Natural Science* and to periodicals. Writer of weekly column, "Wild Adventure," *Florida Times-Union Sunday Magazine,* 1961-66.

*   *   *

AVERBACH, Albert   1902-1975

PERSONAL: Born February 22, 1902, in Bender, Bessarabia; came to United States in 1906; son of Matus and Eva (Kirchen) Averbach. *Education:* Union University, Albany, N.Y., LL.B., 1923. *Politics:* Democrat. *Religion:* Jewish. *Home:* R.D. 6 (Sennett), Auburn, N.Y. 13021. *Office:* 30 State Falls, Seneca Falls, N.Y. 13148; 333 East Onondaga St., Syracuse, N.Y.; 350 Fifth Ave., New York, N.Y. 10001.

CAREER: Admitted to Bar of New York State, 1924, and began practice as member of firm of Freshman & Averbach, Syracuse, N.Y., 1924-30; practiced privately and in partnership, continously in Syracuse, N.Y., 1941-75, Seneca Falls, N.Y., 1941-75, and New York, N.Y., 1966-75. Vice-presi-

dent and general counsel of Rumsey Manufacturing Corp., 1941-47, and Rumsey Products, Inc., 1943-47. Lecturer on medico-legal subjects at medical and legal conventions in United States and foreign countries.

MEMBER: International Academy of Law and Science (fellow), International Academy of Trial Lawyers (past president; chairman of board of directors, 1954-56), International Bar Association, National Association of Claimants' Counsel of America (past vice-president; member of board of governors), American Trial Lawyers Association (past vice-president; member of board of governors), American Bar Association, American Judicature Society, Justinian Legal Society, Society of Medical Jurisprudence, Federal Bar associations of New York, New Jersey, and Connecticut, New York State Bar Association, New York State Association of Plaintiffs' Trial Lawyers, Scribes.

WRITINGS: Handling Accident Cases, seven volumes, Lawyers Cooperative Publishing, 1958-63, with supplements, 1961—, Volume IV and Volume V published as *Handling Automobile Cases,* with supplements, 1961—, Volume VI and Volume VII (with H. A. Gair and R. Tuby); (editor with M. M. Belli) *Tort and Medical Yearbook,* Bobbs-Merrill, Volume I, 1961, Volume II, 1962; (editor with Gair and Tuby) *Courtroom Projection on Trauma,* two volumes, Lawyers Cooperative Publishing, 1963, with supplements, 1963—; (editor with Charles Price) *The Verdicts Were Just: Eight Famous Lawyers Present Their Most Memorable Cases,* Lawyers Cooperative Publishing, 1966. Contributor of more than fifty articles to law and medical journals. Member of legal advisory board, *Traumatic Medicine and Surgery for the Attorney,* a ten-volume encyclopedia. Associate editor, NACCA Law Journal (National Association of Claimants Compensation Attorneys), 1954-75, *American Trial Lawyers* (journal), 1963-75, and *Journal of the International Academy of Law and Science,* 1966.

WORK IN PROGRESS: Two books, *Rx for Malpractice,* and *Pain,* both for publication by Lawyers Cooperative Publishing.†

(Died May 10, 1975)

*   *   *

AXFORD, Joseph Mack   1879-1970

PERSONAL: Born November 19, 1879; son of William (an attorney) and Harriett (Wood) Axford; married Mary Sophia Weeks, September 2, 1902 (deceased); children: Mary Rose (Mrs. John Woodford), Virginia (Mrs. Henry Horton), Wylie F. *Education:* Left school in the seventh grade ("the rest of my education was from personal reading and studying every book I could get hold of"). *Politics:* Republican. *Religion:* Episcopalian. *Address:* P.O. Box 697, Tombstone, Ariz. 85638.

CAREER: Cowboy, 1894-1910; general manager of Lisos Mine in Mexico, 1906; superintendent of Green Cattle Co., 1907-10; salesman for Union Oil Co., 1921-30; rancher in Maupin, Ore., 1930-50; salesman for Woodbury Hardware Co., Tombstone, Ariz., 1951-57. Deputy sheriff under three sheriffs, Cochise County, Arizona Territory, in his early years; member of Tombstone Vigilantes and Tombstone Restoration Commission. *Member:* Pioneer Cowboys Association, Kiwanis Club.

WRITINGS: Around Western Campfires, University of Arizona Press, 1969.†

(Died June 26, 1970)

AYEARST, Morley 1899-

PERSONAL: Surname is pronounced Ay-erst; born October 15, 1899, in Courtright, Ontario, Canada; son of John A. (a clergyman) and Maude (Crothers) Ayearst; married Marjorie Douglas Jones, June 15, 1929; children: Patricia Anne. *Education:* University of Toronto, B.A., 1921, M.A., 1924; Princeton University, Ph.D., 1932. *Home:* 245 Old Stone Hwy., East Hampton, N.Y. 11937.

CAREER: New York University, New York, N.Y., instructor, 1930-38, assistant professor, 1938-45, associate professor, 1945-62, professor of government, and chairman of department of government and international affairs, 1962-66, professor emeritus, 1966—, director of Westchester Center, White Plains, 1948-50, director of evening studies, Washington Square College, 1950-59. U.S. Government, chief of intelligence section, Board of Economic Welfare, Washington, D.C., 1943, senior intelligence officer, U.S. Embassy, England, and Supreme Headquarters of Expeditionary Allied Forces, in France, Belgium, and Germany, 1943-45; consultant to War Histories Division, Bureau of the Budget, 1946. *Member:* American Political Science Association, International Political Science Association, New York University Faculty Club at Washington Square, Preservation Society of East End (president), Springs Improvement Society (vice-president). *Awards, honors:* Ontario Government scholar in France, 1922-23; Fulbright scholar in British West Indies, 1953-54.

WRITINGS: (With William Bennett Munro) *Governments of Europe,* 4th edition (Ayearst was not associated with earlier editions), Macmillan, 1954; *The British West Indies: The Search for Self-Government,* New York University Press, 1960; (contributor) J. Dunner, editor, *Handbook of World History: Concepts and Issues,* Philosophical Library, 1968; *The Republic of Ireland: Its Government and Politics,* New York University Press, 1970. Special editor, *Collier's Young Peoples' Encyclopedia.* Contributor of articles and reviews to social science and economic journals in United States, Canada, Jamaica.

AVOCATIONAL INTERESTS: Foreign travel (especially wintering in Mexico), conservation (particularly as it concerns Long Island land, water, and wildlife), local politics.

* * *

AYUB KHAN, Mohammad 1907-1974

PERSONAL: Born May 14, 1907, in Rehana, Haripur, Pakistan; son of Risaldar Mirdad Khan (an army officer); married Zubeida Khatoon; children: Akhtar (son), Gohar (son), Naseem Aurangzeb (daughter), Shaukat (son), Jamila Amirzeb (daughter), Tahir (son), Shakeela Najibullah (daughter). *Education:* Educated at Aligarh Muslim University, 1922-26, and Royal Military Academy, Sandhurst, England, 1926-28. *Politics:* Pakistan Muslim League. *Religion:* Islam.

CAREER: Commissioned an officer in Royal Fusiliers, 1928, rising to command battalion in British Indian Army during World War II; first commander of East Pakistan Division (as major general), 1948-50; first Pakistani commander-in-chief of Pakistan Army (as general), 1951-58; also Pakistan Minister of Defence, 1954-55; in the space of three weeks, following the Pakistan cabinet crisis of October, 1958, became chief martial law administrator, then succeeded Iskander Mirza to the presidency; President of Pakistan, 1958-69, as first elected head of that country, 1960-69. Made field marshal, 1959. *Awards, honors—Military:* Hila-i-Jurat; Knight of St. Michael and St. George. Civil: Nishan-i-Pakistan.

WRITINGS: Friends Not Masters: A Political Autobiography, Oxford University Press, 1967; *Agricultural Revolution in Pakistan,* edited by Rana Khudadad Khan, Rana Tractors and Equipment (Lahore), 1968; *Ideology and Objectives,* edited by Syed Shabbir Hussain, Pakistan Muslim League, 1968; *President Ayub on Educational Revolution,* Sardar Mohammad Aslam Khan (Rawalpindi), 1968.

SIDELIGHTS: President Ayub Khan was known for his interest in building up Pakistan into a strong, modern, and industrially advanced country. His first book, *Friends Not Masters,* has been translated into Urdu, Bangla, Arabic, Japanese, and German. *Avocational interests:* Riding, shooting, reading, golf, horticulture.

BIOGRAPHICAL/CRITICAL SOURCES: Syed Shabbir Hussain, *Lengthening Shadows: The Story of Pakistan's Politics and Politicians from Advent of Pakistan to Fall of Ayub,* Mujahid Publications (Rawalpindi), 1970; *New York Times,* April 21, 1974.†

(Died April 19, 1974)

* * *

BABB, Lawrence 1902-

PERSONAL: Born December 1, 1902, in Columbia, Mo.; married Frances Creagan, March 27, 1932; children: Lawrence Alan. *Education:* University of Missouri, B.A., 1923, M.A., 1926; Yale University, Ph.D., 1933. *Home:* 632 Kedzie Dr., East Lansing, Mich. 48823.

CAREER: Michigan State University, East Lansing, instructor, 1939-43, assistant professor, 1943-47, associate professor, 1947-51, professor of English, 1951-72.

WRITINGS: The Elizabethan Malady, Michigan State University Press, 1951; *Sanity in Bedlam,* Michigan State University Press, 1959; (editor) Robert Burton, *The Anatomy of Melancholy: A Selection,* Michigan State University Press, 1965; *The Moral Cosmos of Paradise Lost,* Michigan State University Press, 1970. Contributor of articles and reviews to professional journals.

* * *

BACK, Joe W. 1899-

PERSONAL: Born April 12, 1899, in Montpelier, Ohio; son of Albert Edward (a physician) and Martha A. (Wyatt) Back; married Mary W. Cooper (an artist), February 19, 1933. *Education:* Formal education ended with grade school; studied at Art Institute of Chicago, 1925-27, 1929-31. *Politics:* Republican. *Religion:* Protestant. *Address:* Box 26, Dubois, Wyo. 82513.

CAREER: "In the past, as my type of work [in art] indicates, I have been mostly a stock hand, cowboy, ranch hand, freighter, camp cook, horse wrangler, guide, and packer. From 1916 up till 1960. And that's what kind of life I write about and model and paint." *Military service:* U.S. Navy, 1918-19. *Member:* Wyoming Art Association, Wind River Valley Artist Guild, American Legion.

WRITINGS—All self-illustrated: Horses, Hitches and Rocky Trails, Sage Books, 1959; *Mooching Moose and Mumbling Men,* Johnson Publishing (Boulder, Colo.), 1963; *The Sucker's Teeth,* Sage Books, 1965. Contributor to *Western Horseman.*

WORK IN PROGRESS: A novel, not yet titled.

AVOCATIONAL INTERESTS: Hunting, fishing, horse

raising and training; conservation of wilderness, game, fish, and all natural resources.

*   *   *

BACKUS, Oswald P(rentiss) III   1921-1972

PERSONAL: Born March 11, 1921, in Rochester, N.Y.; son of Oswald and Elma Adelaide (Muller) Backus; married Barbara Jean Swanton (a librarian), April 9, 1944; children: Mary Elizabeth (Mrs. Robert Whitaker), Frances Dudley, Robert Henry, Oswald Prentiss IV, Anthony Stoddard, Richard Swanton. *Education:* Yale University, B.A., 1942, Ph.D., 1949; Columbia University, M.A., 1943; Harvard University, LL.B., 1959. *Religion:* Lutheran. *Office:* Department of History, University of Kansas, Lawrence, Kan. 66044.

CAREER: Rutgers University, New Brunswick, N.J., lecturer in history, 1948-50; University of Kansas, Lawrence, assistant professor, 1950-55, associate professor, 1955-59, professor of history, 1959-72, chairman of department, 1960-62, director of Slavic and Soviet area studies, 1962-72. Visiting professor at University of Chicago, 1960, University of Marburg, 1965-66, and University of Bonn, summer, 1966. *Military service:* U.S. Army Air Forces, 1943-46.

MEMBER: American Historical Association, American Association for the Advancement of Slavic Studies (member of board of directors, 1965-67), Phi Beta Kappa. *Awards, honors:* Ford Foundation faculty fellow, 1954-55; Fulbright research fellow in Helsinki, Finland, 1957-58; Social Science Research Council fellow at Harvard Law School, 1958-59; grants from American Council of Learned Societies and University of Washington, Seattle, for work in Soviet Russia, Finland, and Poland, 1964-66, from Inter-University Committee on Travel Grants for work in Soviet Union and Finland, 1967, and from American Council of Learned Societies for research, 1971.

WRITINGS: (Translator and editor) Sigismund Freiherr von Heberstein, *Commentaries on Muscovite Affairs,* University of Kansas Press, 1956; *Motives of West Russian Nobles in Deserting Lithuania for Moscow, 1377-1514,* University of Kansas Press, 1957. Contributor to *Jahrbuecher fuer Geschichte Osteuropas.*

WORK IN PROGRESS: Comparison of Muscovite and Volynian land grants, 1490-1641; research on theft in the history of Russian law in the tenth through the early eighteenth centuries.

SIDELIGHTS: Oswald P. Backus spoke, read, and wrote Finnish, French, German, Italian, and Russian; he read Latin, Polish, Portuguese, and Ukrainian.†

(Died July 9, 1972)

*   *   *

BACON, Peggy   1895-

PERSONAL: Born May 2, 1895, in Ridgefield, Conn.; daughter of Charles Roswell (an artist) and Elizabeth (an artist; maiden name, Chase) Bacon; married Alexander Brook (an artist), May 4, 1920 (divorced, 1939); children: Belinda Brook Collins, Alexander Bacon Brook. *Education:* Kent Place School, Summit, N.J., graduate, 1913; further study at Art Students' League, New York, N.Y. *Politics:* Independent. *Religion:* None. *Home:* Langsford Rd., Cape Porpoise, Me. 04014. *Agent:* (Literary) Curtis Brown Ltd., 575 Madison Ave., New York, N.Y. 10022; (art) Kranshaar Gallery, 1055 Madison Ave., New York, N.Y.

CAREER: Artist, beginning 1920; author and illustrator of books. Paintings, drawings, and prints have been exhibited nationally, and at twenty-seven, one-woman shows in New York, N.Y.; teacher of painting, drawing, and composition for more than thirty years, instructing at Fieldston School, 1933-39, Art Students' League, Corcoran Art School, New School for Social Research, and at other schools, summer camps, art workshops, and private classes; work represented in permanent collections of Metropolitan Museum of Art, Brooklyn Museum, Museum of Modern Art, and other museums. *Member:* National Institute of Arts and Letters (former vice-president). *Awards, honors:* Guggenheim fellowship, 1933-34; National Academy of Art and Letters grant, 1941; honorary degrees from Mills College, and Nasson College.

WRITINGS—Author and illustrator: *The True Philosopher,* Four Seas Co., 1919; *Funerealities,* Aldergate, 1925; *The Lion-hearted Kitten,* Macmillan, 1927; *Mercy and the Mouse,* Macmillan, 1928; *The Ballad of Tangle Street,* Macmillan, 1929; *The Terrible Nuisance,* Harcourt, 1931; *Animosities,* Harcourt, 1931; *Mischief in Mayfield,* Harcourt, 1933; *Off With Their Heads,* McBride, 1934; *Catcalls,* McBride, 1934; *The Mystery of East Hatchett,* Viking, 1939; *Starting from Scratch,* Messner, 1945; *The Inward Eye,* Scribner, 1952; *The Good American Witch,* F. Watts, 1953; *The Oddity,* Pantheon, 1962; *The Ghost of Opalina; or, Nine Lives,* Little, Brown, 1967; *The Magic Touch,* Little, Brown, 1968.

Illustrator of more than forty other books. Writer and illustrator of series of children's stories appearing in *Delineator;* contributor to many other national magazines, including *Dial* (decorations), *Harper's Bazaar* (illustrations), *Vogue* (illustrations), *Vanity Fair* (decorations and poems), *Scribner's* (illustrations), *Stage* (series of caricatures), *New Yorker* (caricatures, poems, stories), *Fortune* (drawings), *Today* (series of political cartoons), *Mademoiselle, Promenade,* and *Yale Review* (short stories for adults); illustrator of brochures for American Medical Association, Abbott Laboratories, and other firms.

WORK IN PROGRESS: Tell Me True.

SIDELIGHTS: Miss Bacon told *CA:* "Conservation, birth control, and civil rights seem to me the most important issues today. Read French easily, but no longer speak it. Lived two years in France as a child, one year in London and Paris after I was grown."

Young Readers' Review called *The Ghost of Opalina* "a rich, varied collection of short stories, full of humor and excitement and replete with delicious thumbnail sketches of unusual people. . . . It is for good readers and is a fine read-aloud book. . . . It gives a good picture of social customs through the years."

AVOCATIONAL INTERESTS: Needlework, ceramics, gardening, reading.

BIOGRAPHICAL/CRITICAL SOURCES: Fields of Learning, Harper, 1961; *Literary Review,* spring, 1963; *Young Readers' Review,* October, 1967.

*   *   *

BACOTE, Clarence A(lbert)   1906-

PERSONAL: Born February 24, 1906, in Kansas City, Mo.; son of Samuel William (a minister) and Lucy (Bledsoe) Bacote; married Lucia Moore, August 3, 1931; children: Lucia Jean (Mrs. Charles James III), Samuel William. *Education:* University of Kansas, A.B., 1926; University of

Chicago, A.M., 1929, Ph.D., 1955. *Politics:* Democrat. *Religion:* Baptist. *Home:* 478 Thackeray Pl. S.W., Atlanta, Ga. 30311. *Office:* Department of History, Atlanta University, Atlanta, Ga. 30314.

CAREER: Western Baptist College, Kansas City, Mo., faculty member, 1926-27; Florida Agricultural and Mechanical College (now University), Tallahassee, professor of history, 1927-28, 1929-30; Atlanta University, Atlanta, Ga., assistant professor, 1930-39, professor of history, beginning 1939. Visiting professor, Wiley College, 1934; lecturer at colleges and universities, including University of Notre Dame, 1967, and Johns Hopkins University, 1969. Member of Georgia advisory committee, U.S. Civil Rights Commission, beginning 1962, and American Civil Liberties Union (to Georgia branch), 1962-67. Member, Georgia State Democratic Executive Committee, 1966; chairman, Atlanta All-Citizens Registration Committee, 1946-60. Fulton County Jury Commission, member, 1965-71, chairman, 1969-71; member, Atlanta Charter Commission, beginning 1971.

MEMBER: American Historical Association, Association for the Study of Negro Life and History (member of executive council), Organization of American Historians, Southern Historical Association (member of executive council, 1965-67), Alpha Phi Alpha, Sigma Pi Phi.

WRITINGS: (Contributor) Charles E. Wynes, editor, *The Negro in the South since 1865: Selected Essays in American Negro History,* University of Alabama Press, 1965; (contributor) Dwight W. Hoover, editor, *Understanding Negro History,* Quadrangle, 1968; *The Story of Atlanta University: A Century of Service, 1865-1965,* Princeton University Press, for Atlanta University, 1969. Contributor to historical journals. Member of editorial board, *Phylon.*†

* * *

BADGER, Ralph E(astman) 1890-

PERSONAL: Born February 3, 1890, in Lowell, Mass.; son of William Eastman (an engineer) and Jennie (Tinker) Badger; married Agnes G. Landry, 1922 (died, 1946); married Ann L. Lang, December 15, 1956; children: (first marriage) Shirley Badger Everett (died, 1961). *Education:* Dartmouth College A.B., 1913, M.C.S., 1914; Yale University, Ph.D., 1921. *Religion:* Episcopalian. *Office:* 333 North Ocean Blvd., #1622, Deerfield Beach, Fla. 33441.

CAREER: Brown University, Providence, R.I., professor of economics, 1921-29; Union Guardian Trust Co., Detroit, Mich., executive vice-president, 1929-43; Investment Counsel, Inc., Detroit, Mich., president, 1933-52; Ralph E. Badger Associates, Inc., president in Detroit, Mich., 1952-66, and Deerfield Beach, Fla., beginning 1967. Associate, Standard Research Consultants, Inc., New York, N.Y., 1950-71; consulting economist, Iranian Seven-Year Plan, 1950.

WRITINGS: Valuation of Industrial Securities, Prentice-Hall, 1925; *Investment Principles and Practices,* Prentice-Hall, 1928; *Problems in Investments,* Prentice-Hall, 1930; *A Complete Guide to Investment Analysis,* McGraw, 1967. Contributor to journals and technical publications.

* * *

BAHN, Margaret (Elizabeth) Linton 1907-1969

PERSONAL: Born April 23, 1907, in Maybole, Scotland; daughter of Archibald (a business man) and Agnes G. (Stewart) Linton; married Eugene Bahn (a professor of speech at Wayne State University), September 12, 1939.

Education: University of Glasgow, M.A., 1928; Sorbonne, University of Paris, graduate study, 1929. *Religion:* Presbyterian. *Home:* 1386 Grayton, Grosse Pointe Park, Mich. 48230.

CAREER: My Weekly Reader, American Education Press, Columbus, Ohio, editor, 1942-43; American School, Thessaloniki, Greece, teacher, 1959-60. Member of council, International Institute of Detroit. *Member:* American Association of University Women (vice-president of Grosse Pointe branch, 1959-60). *Awards, honors:* Honored posthumously by establishment of Margaret Elizabeth Bahn fellowship.

WRITINGS: (With husband, Eugene Bahn) *History of the Oral Interpretation of Literature,* Burgess, 1970. Short stories included in *The Communicative Act of Oral Interpretation,* Allyn & Bacon, 1967, and *Literature for Listening,* Allyn & Bacon, 1968.††

(Died April 6, 1969)

* * *

BAILY, Leslie 1906-1976

PERSONAL: Born December 14, 1906, in St. Albans, England; son of James T. (a Quaker schoolmaster who pioneered in teaching crafts in schools) and Lucy (Allott) Baily; married Margaret Jesper, June 16, 1928; children: June (Mrs. Patrick Bell), John. *Education:* Attended Quaker School, Sibford, England, and Cheltenham Grammar School. *Religion:* Quaker. *Home and office:* "The Granary," Shipley-by-Beningborough, York, England.

CAREER: Staff reporter on *Yorkshire Evening News,* 1924-28; free-lance journalist and broadcaster, 1928-36, with work including originating and writing (among other radio programs), the "Scrapbook" series, 1936-66; editor of radio supplement for *Sunday Referee,* London, England; joined British Broadcasting Corp., London, England, as first staff scriptwriter, 1936, and remained with BBC until 1946; free-lance writer, and research consultant for British Broadcasting Corp. radio and television, 1946-76.

WRITINGS: (With C. Brewer) *The BBC Scrapbooks,* Hutchinson, 1937; *Travellers' Tales,* Allen & Unwin, 1945; *The Gilbert & Sullivan Book* (dual biographies), Cassell, 1952, revised and enlarged edition, 1956; (editor; selections made by father, James T. Baily) *A Craftsman's Anthology,* Allen & Unwin, 1953; *Scrapbook, 1900-1914,* Muller, 1957; *Scrapbook for the Twenties,* Muller, 1959; *Craftsman and Quaker,* Allen & Unwin, 1959; *Leslie Baily's BBC Scrapbooks,* Volume I: *1896-1914,* British Broadcasting Corporation, 1966, Volume II: *1918-1939,* Fernhill, 1968; *Gilbert and Sullivan and Their World,* Thames & Hudson, 1973; *Gilbert and Sullivan: Their Life and Times,* Viking, 1974.

Author with S. Gilliat of filmscript for "The Story of Gilbert & Sullivan," produced by London Film Productions, and sole author of radio series also based on his *The Gilbert & Sullivan Book.* Other major radio programs include "Trial of William Penn," "South with Shackleton," "Travellers' Tales," and "The Schubert Discoveries."

Contributor of articles on modern history, radio, and television to *Times* (London), *Radio Times,* and other newspapers and magazines.

SIDELIGHTS: Baily's foremost identification was with the "Scrapbook," modern history documentaries, each one covering a year; they still are running as the longest established feature of BBC radio; he was a research consultant for that program (and others), expanding the research for the book compilations. *The Gilbert & Sullivan Book,* a best seller among biographies, was reprinted in England in 1967 for a total of six printings.

AVOCATIONAL INTERESTS: Painting, music.†

(Died February 21, 1976)

* * *

BAKER, Elsworth F. 1903-

PERSONAL: Born February 5, 1903, in Summit, S.D.; son of Niles Albert and Effie Anna (Cartwright) Baker; married Marguerite M. Mayberry, September 28, 1941; children: Courtney Fredrick, Allan Elsworth, Michael Bruce. *Education:* Student at Regina College, Regina, Saskatchewan, 1920-21, and Regina Normal School, 1921; University of Manitoba, M.D. (cum laude), 1928; University of Vienna, Certificate in Neurology and Psychiatry, 1929. *Politics:* Conservative Republican. *Religion:* None. *Home:* 51 Hance Rd., Fair Haven, N.J. 07701.

CAREER: General Hospital, Vancouver, British Columbia, intern, 1927-28; New Jersey State Hospital, Greystone Park, resident, 1928-31; New Jersey State Hospital, Marlboro, chief of women's service, 1931-48; Monmouth Medical Center, Long Branch, N.J., assistant psychiatrist, 1940-48; Orgone Energy Clinic, Forest Hills, N.Y., director, 1949-52; Orgonomic Publications, New York, N.Y., president, beginning 1967. Trustee, William Reich Foundation, 1949-56; member, Orgonomic Research Foundation, beginning 1967. Diplomate, American Board of Psychiatry and Neurology, 1936.

MEMBER: American Psychiatric Association (fellow), American Medical Association, American Association for the Advancement of Science (fellow), American Association for Medical Orgonomy, American College of Orgonomy (fellow; president, beginning 1968), New Jersey Neuro-Psychiatric Association (charter member), Monmouth County Medical Society (secretary-treasurer, 1946-48). *Awards, honors:* Award from New Jersey Association of Teachers of English, 1967, for *Man in the Trap;* Wilhelm Reich Award, American College of Orgonomy, 1972, for contributions to the science of Orgonomy; Knight Commander of Justice, Sovereign Order of St. John of Jerusalem, 1973; Knights of Malta, 1973.

WRITINGS: Main in the Trap, Macmillan, 1967. Contributor to medical journals. Editor, *Orgonomic Medicine,* 1955-56, and *Journal of Orgonomy,* beginning 1967.

* * *

BAKER, Howard 1905-

PERSONAL: Born April 5, 1905, in Philadelphia, Pa.; son of Howard W. (a California orange grower) and Bertha (Stavely) Baker; married Dorothy Dodds (a writer), September 2, 1930 (died June 17, 1968); married Virginia De Camp Beattie, 1969; children: (first marriage) Ellen, Jean Baker Fry. *Education:* Whittier College, B.A., 1927; Stanford University, M.A., 1929; attended the Sorbonne, University of Paris, 1929-31; University of California, Berkeley, Ph.D., 1937. *Politics:* Democrat. *Home:* Route 1, Box 11, Terra Bella, Calif. 93270.

CAREER: Lived among the expatriates in Paris during the late twenties; Harvard University, Cambridge, Mass., instructor in English, 1937-43; raises oranges and olives on his ranch in California. Visiting professor of English at University of California, Berkeley, 1958-59, Davis, 1963-66. Member of board of directors, Lindsay Ripe Olive Co., 1956-67, Tulare Co. (fruit exchange), Porterville, Calif., be-

ginning, 1963; president of board, Grand View Heights Citrus Association, Terra Bella, Calif., beginning, 1963. A founding member of, and occasional participant in, The Barn Theater, Porterville, Calif.

WRITINGS: Orange Valley (novel), Coward, 1931; *Induction to Tragedy: A Study in a Development of Form in Gorboduc, The Spanish Tragedy, and Titus Andronicus,* Louisiana State University Press, 1939, reprinted, Russell, 1965; *Letter From the Country* (poems), New Directions, 1941; *Ode to the Sea, and Other Poems,* A. Swallow, 1966; (with wife, Dorothy Baker) *The Ninth Day* (play), Proscenium Press (Dixon, Calif.), 1967. With Dorothy Baker, author of play, "Trio," first produced in New York, 1944. Work represented in many anthologies including, *Oxford Book of American Verse,* Oxford University Press, 1950; *Understanding Poetry,* Holt, 1960; *A Western Sampler,* Talisman, 1963. Contributor to *Southern Review* and other publications.

WORK IN PROGRESS: Research for a project in the interpretation of ancient Greek civilization in the Aegean.

SIDELIGHTS: William Van O'Connor noted that Baker "writes a quiet poem that is obviously the work of a considerable critical intelligence and careful craftsmanship. He is steeped in the culture of Greece, and many poems [in *Ode to the Sea*] have to do with Greek literature, legends, and culture. But some have to do with other subjects: the Mardi Gras, valleys in California, or Dr. Johnson. Mr. Baker belongs to a group that appears to be a rarer and rarer phenomenon: he is a true man of letters." Joseph Slater added "Dissident and conservative, [Baker] rejects the fashions of his time, counsels a 'program . . . of informed tenacity' . . . and 'frugal narrow-mindedness.' 'Be much hedged in,' he says; 'rehearse the ancient ways,' and await the return of the masters. In this hard light his archaism is delightful and significant, and the poems that are most his own, especially his disciplined, imaginative sonnets, seem stronger for being part of a program."

BIOGRAPHICAL/CRITICAL SOURCES: Poetry, December, 1966; *Saturday Review,* December 31, 1966.†

* * *

BAKWIN, Harry 1894-1973

PERSONAL: Born November 19, 1894, in Utica, N.Y.; son of Simon and Anna (Nadel) Bakwin; married Ruth Morris (a physician), February 2, 1925; children: Edward M., Patricia (Mrs. Frederick R. Selch), Barbara (Mrs. William S. Rosenthal), Michael. *Education:* Columbia University, B.S., 1915, M.D., 1917; Universities of Vienna and Berlin, postdoctoral study, 1924-25.

CAREER: Bellevue Hospital, New York, N.Y., intern, 1917-18; Columbia University, New York, N.Y., instructor in pediatrics, 1925-30; Bellevue Hospital, assistant visiting physician, 1925-30, associate attending physician, 1930-43, visiting physician, Children's Medical Service, 1943-73; New York University, New York, N.Y., assistant professor, 1939-40, associate professor, 1940-49, professor of clinical pediatrics, 1950-73. Consulting physician to New York Infirmary and Doctor's Hospital, both New York, N.Y., and other hospitals in Middletown, Mount Vernon, and Tarrytown, N.Y., Norwalk, Conn., and Newark, N.J. Member of advisory board, Association for Mentally Ill Children in Manhattan. Director of American Chess Foundation. *Military service:* U.S. Army, Medical Corps, 1918-19; became first lieutenant.

MEMBER: American Medical Association (fellow), American Academy of Pediatrics (president, 1955-56), American Pediatric Society, American Association for the Advancement of Science, American Association of Physical Anthropology, New York Academy of Medicine; and other medical societies, including honorary membership in a number abroad; Sigma Xi, Alpha Omega Alpha.

WRITINGS: (With wife, Ruth Morris Bakwin) *Psychologic Care During Infancy and Childhood,* Appleton, 1942; (with R. M. Bakwin) *Clinical Management of Behavior Disorders in Children,* Saunders, 1953, 4th edition, 1972. Author of more than 180 articles on physiology of the newborn, growth problems, and behavior problems of children.

AVOCATIONAL INTERESTS: Art collecting, chamber music, and chess.†

(Died December 25, 1973.)

* * *

BALL, Joseph H. 1905-

PERSONAL: Born November 3, 1905, in Crookston, Minn.; son of Joseph (a teacher, lawyer, and real estate agent) and Florence (Hurst) Ball; married Elizabeth Robbins (an artist), April 28, 1928; children: Jennifer Ann (Mrs. John Hulsizer), Peter J., Sara E. (Mrs. Charles E. Lister). *Education:* Studied at Antioch College, 1923-25, Eau Claire Normal School (now University of Wisconsin, Eau Clare), 1925-26, and University of Minnesota, 1926-27. *Politics:* Republican ("conservative or 19th-century liberal"). *Religion:* Agnostic. *Home:* Route 3, Front Royal, Va. 22630.

CAREER: Minneapolis Journal, Minneapolis, Minn., reporter, 1927-28; free-lance writer of fiction, 1928-29; *St. Paul Pioneer Press* and *St. Paul Dispatch,* St. Paul, Minn., reporter and political editor, 1930-40; U.S. Senator from Minnesota, 1940-48; Association of American Ship Owners, Washington, D.C., vice-president, 1949-53; States Marine Lines, New York, N.Y., vice-president, 1953-62; farmer and writer in Front Royal, Va., beginning 1962. *Awards, honors:* LL.D., Macalester College and Syracuse University.

WRITINGS: Collective Security: The Why and How, World Peace Foundation, 1943; *The Government Subsidized Union Monopoly: A Study of Labor Practices in the Shipping Industry,* Labor Policy Association (Washington), 1966; *The Implementation of Federal Manpower Policy, 1961-1971: A Study in Bureaucratic Competition and Intergovernmental Relations,* National Technical Information Service, 1972. Writer of numerous short stories for pulp magazines, 1928-29, and pamphlets and articles, 1940-50. Editor, *Washington Labor Letter,* 1949-53.

* * *

BALLINGER, Harry (Russell) 1892-

PERSONAL: Born September 4, 1892, in Port Townsend, Wash.; son of James Guy (a captain, U.S. Coast Guard) and Lourena (Russell) Ballinger; married Katharine Rice (an artist), October 12, 1951. *Education:* Studied at Art Students' League, New York, N.Y., at Academie Colorossi, Paris, France, and under Harvey Dunn. *Studio address:* RFD 2, New Hartford, Conn. 06057; and Rockport, Mass.

CAREER: Illustrator for national magazines, 1917-35; artist, specializing in landscape, portrait, and marine painting, beginning 1930. Teacher of illustration, 1928-33; instructor in painting, Grand Central Art School, 1930-36, Central Connecticut College, 1945-58; instructor in marine painting,

University of Hawaii, 1960. Represented by oils and watercolors in New England museums including: New Britain Museum of American Art, Wadsworth Atheneum, Springfield Art Museum, and Arts and Crafts Society. *Military service:* U.S. Coast Guard, 1918-19.

MEMBER: National Academy of Design (associate member), Allied Artists, Audubon Artists, American Watercolor Society, Salamagundi Club, Connecticut Academy, Kent Art Association, Rockport Art Association, North Shore Art Association. *Awards, honors:* Awards from Salamagundi Club for watercolor, 1944, 1952, 1954, 1958, 1970, for oils, 1958-61, 1963, 1965, 1966, 1969, 1970; award from Connecticut Academy, 1944; five awards from Rockport Art Association, 1953-63; and others.

WRITINGS—All published by Watson-Guptill: *Painting Surf and Sea,* 1957; *Painting Boats and Harbors,* 1959; *Painting Landscapes,* 1965, new enlarged edition, 1973; *Painting Sea and Shore,* 1966.†

* * *

BALLOU, Ellen B(artlett) 1905-

PERSONAL: Born September 24, 1905, in Pittsburgh, Pa.; daughter of Dwight Kellogg and Maud (Orr) Bartlett; married Norman Vaughn Ballou, June 29, 1932 (deceased). *Education:* Wellesley College, B.A., 1927; Northwestern University, M.A., 1929. *Address:* P.O. Box 271, Dublin, N.H. 03444.

CAREER: Albee Keith Stock Co., Providence, R.I., actress, summers, 1926, 1927; New Playwrights' Theatre, New York, N.Y., actress, 1927-28; Wheaton College, Wheaton, Mass., director of drama in English department, 1929-41; U.S. Office of Strategic Services, Washington, D.C., worked in Research and Analysis Section, 1944-46; Katharine Gibbs School, Providence, academic dean, 1947-55; Brown University, Providence, part-time instructor in English department, 1955-62. *Member:* Boston Authors Club, Garden Club of America, Garden Club of Dublin.

WRITINGS: The Building of the House: Houghton Mifflin's Formative Years, Houghton, 1970. Contributor to *New England Galaxy, Texas Historical Journal,* and other journals.

WORK IN PROGRESS: A biography of Frances Sargent Osgood (1811-1850); poetry.

SIDELIGHTS: Ellen Ballou wrote *CA:* "I enjoy research, especially when I am dealing with primary sources. I find writing difficult and do so only because I do not wish to become a Doctor Cassubon absorbed in 'mouldy futilities'." *Avocational interests:* Conservation, gardening, golf.

BIOGRAPHICAL/CRITICAL SOURCES: New York Times, January 31, 1970; *New York Times Book Review,* March 1, 1970; *Christian Science Monitor,* March 6, 1970.

* * *

BALOGH, Penelope 1916-1975

PERSONAL: Surname is pronounced Ball-og; born June 16, 1916; daughter of Henry Bernard (a priest, Church of England) and Stella (Hodgson) Tower; married Oliver Gatty (a physical chemist at Cambridge University), January 31, 1939 (deceased); married Thomas Balogh (a reader in economics at Oxford University), March 17, 1945 (divorced, 1970); children: (first marriage) Mrs. Tirril Harris; (second marriage) Stephen, Christopher, Tessa. *Education:* Oxford University, diploma in experimental psychology, 1947. *Poli-*

tics: Socialist ("belonged to left wing elements of Labour Party since age of 22"). *Home and office:* Association of Group and Individual Psychotherapy, 29 St. Mark's Crescent, London NW1, England.

CAREER: Psychotherapist, 1951-71; Well Walk Centre for Psychotherapy, London, England, member of staff, 1963-75; London Hospital, London, part-time psychotherapist, 1968-75. *Member:* Association of Psychotherapists (founder member), Medical Association for the Prevention of War, Society of Authors, Farmers Club, Imago.

WRITINGS: Up with the Joneses (juvenile), Gollancz, 1966; *I'm Glad I Was Analyzed,* Pergamon, 1968; *Life of Freud,* Studio Vista, 1971.

WORK IN PROGRESS: Dan Jones and the Onion Man (juvenile); *Meeting at Montignac* (novel); *'Always Is a Long Time' Said St. Mark;* a book about the life and work of Jesus.

SIDELIGHTS: Penelope Balogh traveled widely in Europe, Australia, North Africa, and United States.†

(Died, 1975)

*   *   *

BAMBERGER, Carl 1902-

PERSONAL: Born February 21, 1902, in Vienna, Austria; came to United States in 1937; son of Gustav and Melanie (Prossnitz) Bamberger; married Lotte Hammerschlag (a violist). *Education:* Studied theory and piano with Henrich Schenker in Vienna, and musicology and philosophy at University of Vienna. *Religion:* Jewish. *Home:* 171 West 79th St., New York, N.Y. 10024. *Office:* Mannes College of Music, 157 East 74th St., New York, N.Y. 10021.

CAREER: Opera conductor in Danzig, Germany (now part of Poland), 1924-27, and Darmstadt, 1927-31; guest conductor in many European cities; director of opera and orchestra department at Mannes College of Music, New York, N.Y., beginning 1938. Contributor for Spring Festival, Columbia, S.C., 1943-50, and City Center Opera, New York, since early 1950's; guest conductor elsewhere in United States and South America. Founder, New Choral Group of Manhattan and Brooklyn Oratorio Society. *Member:* American Symphony Orchestra League, Photographic Society of America, New York Colorslide Club. *Awards, honors:* Awards for photographs in international exhibits.

WRITINGS: (Editor and author of introduction) *The Conductor's Art,* McGraw, 1965; (contributor) D. J. Gillis, editor, *Furtwaengler Recalled,* DeGraff, 1966. Contributor to *Encyclopedia Americana,* 1967.

SIDELIGHTS: Bamberger has recorded for Columbia Records, RCA Victor, Nonesuch, and other labels.

*   *   *

BANCROFT, Caroline 1900-

PERSONAL: Born September 11, 1900, in Denver, Colo.; daughter of George Jarvis (a mining engineer) and Ethel (Norton) Bancroft. *Education:* Smith College, B.A., 1923; University of Denver, M.A., 1943. *Politics:* Republican. *Religion:* Episcopalian. *Home:* 1081 Downing St., Denver, Colo. 80218. *Agent:* McIntosh & Otis, Inc., 475 Fifth Ave., New York, N.Y. 10017.

CAREER: Denver Post, Denver, Colo., literary editor, 1928-33, and writer of "Literary Flashlights" column, 1928-33; University of Colorado Extension, Denver, instructor in creative writing, 1931-35; University of Denver Extension,

Denver, instructor in creative writing, 1936; Randell School, Denver, teacher of Colorado history, 1947-51; Matchless Mine Museum, Leadville, Colo., Denver chairman, beginning 1953; chronicler of Colorado history, including the original works on which the opera, "The Ballad of Baby Doe," and the musical comedy, "The Unsinkable Molly Brown," were based. Interviewed Tagore in India for *London Observer,* 1928; did special series in Europe on contemporary literary greats of London, Paris, and Netherlands for *New York Evening Post,* 1929. *Member:* Western Historical Association, Colorado Authors' League (vice-president, 1959-61), Colorado Folklore Society (various offices, including presidency, 1948-60), Westerners (Denver and New York posses), Rocky Mountain Railroad Club, Leadville Assembly (vice-president), Gilpin County Arts Association, Central City Opera House Association (Colorado history chairman). *Awards, honors:* Plaques for "contribution to the heritage of the state" from Central City Opera House Association, 1952, 1963, Century Club of the University of Denver, 1970, Denver Public Library, 1972, and others; Colorado Authors' League award for best non-fiction book published in 1969, for *Trail Ridge Country: Estes Park and Grand Lake.*

WRITINGS—All published by Golden Press, except as noted: *Silver Queen: The Fabulous Story of Baby Doe Tabor,* 1950, 6th edition, Johnson Publishers, 1959; *Famous Aspen: It's Fabulous Past—It's Lively Present,* 1954, revised edition, 1967; The *Brown Palace in Denver,* 1955; *The Unsinkable Mrs. Brown: S.S. Titantic Heroine,* 1956.

All published by Johnson Publishers, except as noted: *Gulch of Gold: A History of Central City,* Sage Books, 1958; *Colorful Colorado,* Sage Books, 1959; *Tabor's Matchless Mines and Lusty Leadville,* 1960; *Unique Ghost Towns and Mountain Spots,* 1961; *Colorado's Lost Gold Mines and Buried Treasure,* 1961; *Six Racy Madams of Colorado,* 1965; (with May B. Wills) *The Unsinkable Molly Brown Cookbook,* Sage Books, 1966; *Two Burros of Fairplay: Morsels of History for Young and Old,* 1968; *Trail Ridge Country: Estes Park and Grand Lake,* 1969. Also author of *A Guide to Central City,* 1946, and *The Melodrama of Walhurst,* 1952.

Contributor to *Colorado and Its People* and *Columbia Encyclopedia.* Author of a play for television biographical series of American Telephone & Telegraph Co., produced by American Broadcasting Co. network, 1956-57. Contributor to *New York Evening Post, New York Herald Tribune, New York Times, Town and Country, Woman's Home Companion, Western Folklore Quarterly, Colorado, Westerner's Brand Book* (both Denver and New York), and other magazines and newspapers, 1929-72.

WORK IN PROGRESS: The Storied San Juans: Creede, Lake City, Silverton, Ouray and Telluride.

SIDELIGHTS: Miss Bancroft's own screen treatment of *The Unsinkable Mrs. Brown* was nationally broadcast by American Broadcasting Companies in 1957 as "The Unsinkable Molly Brown." Miss Bancroft told *CA* that, although the Meridith Willson-Richard Morris Broadway musical (and the subsequent Metro-Goldwyn-Mayer film, scripted by Helen Deutsch) was based on her material, she was given no official credit for her work.

*   *   *

BANGHAM, Mary Dickerson 1896-

PERSONAL: Born December 31, 1896, in Bedford, Ohio; daughter of William Hudson (a clergyman) and Lizzie (Hollingshead) Dickerson; married Norman Clifford Bangham (a clergyman), July 14, 1921; children: Jeanne (Mrs. Truman R. Temple), Norman. *Education:* Ohio Wesleyan University, A.B., 1921; completed fiction course at Famous Writers School, 1968. *Religion:* Methodist. *Home:* 221 Gardner Ct., Washington Court House, Ohio 43160.

CAREER: Teacher in Ohio public schools, 1915-16, 1919-20; substitute teacher of English in Ohio high schools, beginning 1945. Also teacher of journalism in education therapy clinic of Veterans Administration Neuropsychiatric Hospital near Chillicothe, Ohio, 1950-52, of drama in summer youth fellowships, and Biblical poetry in community training course, Dayton, Ohio. *Member:* Theta Alpha Phi. *Awards, honors:* First Place in *Epworth Herald* national college short story contest, 1921; honorable mention in *Reader's Digest* contest, "Why I Go to Church," 1947.

WRITINGS: When Jesus Was Four—or Maybe Five, Augsburg, 1968. Contributor of some four hundred poems, articles, stories, and short plays to religious and secular periodicals; two plays, one short story, and several poems have been anthologized, and two poems were set to music and published by Willis Music Co., 1960.

WORK IN PROGRESS: Revising a half-hour dramatic program for television, and a religious play.

AVOCATIONAL INTERESTS: Camping, coaching dramatics.

* * *

BANTA, R(ichard) E(lwell) 1904-

PERSONAL: Born February 16, 1904, in Martinsville, Ind.; son of William Atley (a realtor) and Pearle (Elwell) Banta; married Caroline K. French, November 29, 1926; children: Kathleen Ann (Mrs. Charles E. Scott). *Education:* Attended Wabash College, 1925. *Politics:* Republican. *Home:* 715 Sycamore Dr., Crawfordsville, Ind. 47933.

CAREER: Bookseller and publisher in Crawfordsville, Ind., 1928-69. Assistant to the president, Wabash College, 1937-56. *Member:* Organization of American Historians, American Academy of Political and Social Science, Indiana Historical Society. *Awards, honors:* Litt.D., Wabash College, 1961.

WRITINGS: Rivers of America: The Ohio, Rinehart, 1949; *Indiana Authors and Their Books,* Wabash College, 1949; *The South,* Fideler, 1951; (editor) *Hoosier Caravan: A Treasury of Indiana Life & Lore,* Indiana University Press, 1951, new edition, 1975; *The Ohio Valley,* Teachers College Press, 1966.

* * *

BARBER, Willard F(oster) 1909-

PERSONAL: Born March 21, 1909, in Mitchell, S.D.; son of William A. (a teacher) and Martha A. (Foster) Barber; married Gladys R. Dorris (director of Overseas Education Fund of League of Women Voters), July, 1928; children: Martha (Mrs. D. H. Montgomery). *Education:* Stanford University, A.B., 1928, M.A., 1929; Columbia University, graduate studies in international affairs, 1931-33; National War College, diploma, 1948. *Politics:* Republican. *Religion:* Protestant. *Home:* 3718 University Ave. N.W., Washington, D.C. 20016.

CAREER: City College (now City College of the City University of New York), New York, N.Y., instructor in government, 1930-38; U.S. Department of State, officer, 1938-

62, with posts including deputy Assistant Secretary of State for Inter-American Affairs, 1949-50, counselor of embassy and charge d'affaires at U.S. embassies in Lima, Peru, 1950-53, Bogota, Columbia, 1953-56, and Warsaw, Poland, 1956-57, director of senior officer training, Foreign Service Institute, Washington, D.C., 1957-59, and chairman of Mutual Security evaluation teams to Turkey, Iran, and Pakistan, 1960-62; University of Maryland, College Park, lecturer in international affairs, beginning 1962. Visiting Mershon Professor, Ohio State University, 1964-65. Visitor to NATO Defense College, Paris, and Imperial Defence College, London, 1957; director of department of political affairs, National War College, 1957-58; consultant to Government of Burma on organization and curriculum of Defense College, 1959. Lecturer throughout United States, speaking at colleges and universities, for professional organizations, and women's and service clubs.

MEMBER: American Political Science Association, American Society for Public Administration, American Association of University Professors, Retired Foreign Service Officers Association, Pi Sigma Alpha, Phi Kappa Phi.

WRITINGS: (With W. B. Guthrie) *American Government,* Globe, 1935; (with C. N. Ronning) *Internal Security and Military Power: Counter Insurgency and Civic Action in Latin America,* Ohio State University Press, 1966. Contributor of articles and reviews to professional journals, magazines, and newspapers, among them *Saturday Review, New York Times, Dalhousie Review, American Journal of International Law, Military Review, Baltimore Evening Sun, Washington Post.*

* * *

BARBOUR, Russell B. 1906-

PERSONAL: Born May 23, 1906, in Philadelphia, Pa.; son of George and Mary (Brown) Barbour; married first wife, named Flora, 1933; married Ruth Barlow (a teacher), September 4, 1941; children: Jean (Mrs. Joel Peterson), Nancy (Mrs. Gene Miller), Sally Louise (Mrs. Thomas Gottshall), Robin (Mrs. Steven March). *Education:* Attended Pendle Hill Graduate Center, 1935-36; Ursinus College, A.B., 1939; Colgate Rochester Divinity School, B.D., 1942. *Politics:* Democrat. *Residence:* Perkiomenville, Pa. 18074.

CAREER: Protestant minister in Morristown, N.J., 1948-55; field representative, Pennsylvania State Human Relations Commission, 1962-67; Human Relations Commission, Allentown, Pa., executive director, 1967-72. Interim pastor of United Church of Christ. *Member:* National Association of Intergroup Relations Officials, National Conference of Christians and Jews (local chairman, 1951-55).

WRITINGS: Religious Ideas for Arts and Crafts, United Church, 1958; *Black and White Together,* United Church, 1968. Also author of *Breakthrough for Spirit in Groups,* and *Stories for Children.* Contributor to religious periodicals.

* * *

BARDSLEY, Cuthbert K(illick) N(orman) 1907-

PERSONAL: Born March 28, 1907, in Ulverston, Lancashire, England; son of J.U.N. (a canon of the Church of England) and Mabel (Killick) Bardsley. *Education:* New College, Oxford, M.A., 1931. *Home:* The Bishop's House, Coventry, Warwickshire, England.

CAREER: Clergyman of Church of England; All Hallows Church, Barking-by-the-Tower, London, England, curate, 1932-34; rector of Woolwich, London, 1940-44; provost of

Southwark, London, 1944-47; suffragan bishop of Croydon, Surrey, 1947-56; bishop of Coventry, Warwickshire, England, beginning 1956. Honorary canon in Canterbury Cathedral and Archbishop of Canterbury's representative with the three Armed Forces, 1948-56. *Member:* Army and Navy Club. *Awards, honors:* Commander of Order of the British Empire, 1952.

WRITINGS: Bishop's Move, Mowbray, 1952; *Sundry Times, Sundry Places,* Mowbray, 1962; (with William Purcell) *Him We Declare,* Mowbray, 1967, Word Books, 1968; *I Believe in Mission,* Mowbray, 1970.

*   *   *

BARGEBUHR, Frederick P(erez)   1904-

PERSONAL: Born May 24, 1904, in Hamburg, Germany; son of Arnold A. (a physician) and Ida (Friedman) Bargebuhr; divorced. *Education:* Attended Universities of Munich, 1922, Hamburg, 1926-29, Bonn, 1930, Frankfurt, 1930-32, and Paris (Sorbonne), 1932; University of Munich, Ph.D., 1933; Harvard University, additional study, 1949-50. *Religion:* Jewish. *Office:* Religious Studies Program, Southern Illinois University, Carbondale, Ill. 62901.

CAREER: Free-lance architect in Palestine, 1934-47; University of Iowa, Iowa City, instructor, 1951-52, assistant professor, 1952-56, associate professor, 1957-63, professor of religion, 1964-70. Visiting professor of Judaic studies, Free University of Berlin, Berlin, Germany, 1964-65; visiting professor, Religious Studies Program, Southern Illinois University, Carbondale, beginning 1970. Fulbright professor of Judaic studies at Free University of Berlin and in Heidelberg and Bonn, Germany, 1960-62. *Military service:* British Army, 1940-45; served as civilian interpreter. *Member:* American Oriental Society (former president, Midwest branch), Middle East Studies Association of North America, American Association of University Professors, British Museum Society, Royal Asiatic Society (England; fellow). *Awards, honors:* Four annual grants, American Philosophical Society, 1949-53; Bollingen fellowship in London and Rome, 1956-58; grant-in-aid, American Council of Learned Societies, 1964.

WRITINGS: (With Gerhard Liebes) *Haq-qol Medabber* (title means "The Voice Speaks"), Schocken (Tel Aviv), 1946; *El Palacio de la Alhambra en el siglo XI* (originally written in English but published in Spanish), University of Iowa (Iowa City and Mexico City), 1966, revised edition published as *The Alhambra: A Cycle of Studies on the Eleventh Century in Moorish Spain,* Walter de Gruyter (Berlin), 1968. Contributor to *Journal of the Warburg and Courtauld Institute* (University of London), *Review of Religion* (Columbia University), *Atlantis, Gazith, Castrum Peregrini,* and to *Encyclopaedia Britannica.*

WORK IN PROGRESS: A book on Solomon ibn Gabirol; a book on the Via Latina Catacomb in Rome, to be published in Holland.

SIDELIGHTS: A student of Hebrew, Arabic, Greek, and Latin, Frederick Bargebuhr is pursuing studies "aimed at the elucidation and acculturation and interculturation, e.g., between the Arabs and the Mediterranean world, the Roman world and Near Eastern (Judeo-Christian) influences." Bargebuhr told *CA* he is "totally at home in the Near East, in Europe and on the two American continents."††

*   *   *

BARGER, Harold   1907-

PERSONAL: Born April 27, 1907, in London, England; came to United States in 1939, naturalized in 1944; son of George (a professor of biochemistry) and Florence Emily (Thomas) Barger; married Anne Walls, July 8, 1937 (died, July 12, 1954); married Gwyneth Kahn, December 10, 1955. *Education:* Kings College, Cambridge, B.A., 1930; London School of Economics and Political Science, Ph.D., 1937. *Home:* 54 Morningside Dr., New York, N.Y. 10025. *Office:* Department of Economics, School of General Studies, Columbia University, New York, N.Y. 10027.

CAREER: University College, University of London, London, England, lecturer in political economy, 1931-39; Columbia University, New York, N.Y., instructor, 1939-43, assistant professor, 1943-47, associate professor, 1947-54, professor of economics, beginning, 1954, chairman of department, 1961-64. Staff member of National Bureau of Economic Research, 1940-54; assistant division chief, U.S. Department of State, 1945-46. *Military service:* U.S. Army, Office of Strategic Services, 1943-45; became first lieutenant. *Member:* American Economic Association, Royal Economic Society, Econometric Society, American Association of University Professors, American Civil Liberties Union.

WRITINGS: Foreign Trade, Gollancz, 1936, Kraus Reprint, 1972; *Outlay and Income in the United States, 1921-38,* National Bureau of Economic Research, 1942; (with H. H. Landsberg) *American Agriculture, 1899-1939: A Study of Output, Employment and Productivity,* National Bureau of Economic Research, 1942; (with S. H. Schurr) *The Mining Industries, 1899-1939: A Study of Output, Employment and Productivity,* National Bureau of Economic Research, 1944, reprinted, Arno Press, 1972; *The Transportation Industries, 1889-1946: A Study of Output, Employment and Productivity,* National Bureau of Economic Research, 1951; *Distribution's Place in the American Economy Since 1869,* National Bureau of Economic Research, 1955; *Money, Banking and Public Policy,* Rand McNally, 1962, 2nd edition, 1968; *The Management of Money: A Survey of American Experience,* Rand McNally, 1964. Contributor to *Journal of the American Statistical Association.*

WORK IN PROGRESS: Research in innovation, investment, productivity changes and growth rates, especially in Europe; research in national income and product estimation and analysis, and in monetary theory and policy.

SIDELIGHTS: Barger is fluent in French and has good command of German. He can read and make himself understood in Italian and Spanish and he reads Dutch, Swedish, and modern Greek.

*   *   *

BARKER, Elsa (McCormick)   1906-
    (E. M. Barker)

PERSONAL: Born March 29, 1906, in Sibley, Ill.; daughter of Ivor B. (a dentist) and Nelle (Jordan) McCormick; married S. Omar Barker (a professional writer), July 1, 1927. *Education:* New Mexico Highlands University, B.A., 1959. *Politics:* Conservative Republican. *Religion:* Protestant. *Home and office:* 1118 Ninth St., Las Vegas, N.M. 87701. *Agent:* Paul R. Reynolds, Inc., 12 East 41st St., New York, N.Y. 10017.

CAREER: Full-time writer, 1931-58; Las Vegas Junior High School, Las Vegas, N.M., chairman of English department, beginning 1960. *Member:* National Education Association, National Council of Teachers of English, Western Writers of America (president, 1972-73), New Mexico Education Association (building representative, 1964-66), P.E.O. Sisterhood.

WRITINGS—All Western novels, under name E. M. Barker: *Riders of the Ramhorn,* Stanley Paul, 1956; *Clouds Over the Chupaderos,* Stanley Paul, 1957; *Cowboys Can't Quit,* John Long, 1957; *Showdown at Pernasco Pass,* John Long, 1958; *War on the Big Hat,* John Long, 1959; *Secret of the Badlands,* John Long, 1960. Author of two serials distributed by King Features Syndicate, "Not by Guns Alone," 1957-60, and "Heiress to Murder," 1958-60. About 150 novelettes, short stories and serials were published in *True Romances, Ranch Romances* (now defunct), *Thrilling Western, Best Western, Mike Shayne's Mystery Magazine,* and other magazines, 1931-60.

SIDELIGHTS: Elsa Barker is the wife of writer S. Omar Barker, and sister of Wilfred McCormick, who is the author of some fifty sports novels for boys, among them the "Bronc Burnett" series. She has practiced a great deal of horseback riding, trout fishing, and some hunting in the Rockies (once shot a mountain lion). While she has concentrated on teaching during the past few years, her books have continued to come out in translations abroad, particularly in France and in the Netherlands, where six have been published in Dutch.

*   *   *

BARKER, S. Omar 1894-
(Jose Canusi, Phil Squires; Dan Scott, a house pseudonym)

PERSONAL: Born June 16, 1894, in Beulah, N.M.; son of Squire Lender (a rancher) and Priscilla Jane (McGuire) Barker; married Elsa McCormick (a writer under names, E. M. Barker and Elsa Barker, and a teacher of English), July 1, 1927. *Education:* New Mexico Highlands University, B.A., 1924. *Politics:* Conservative Republican. *Religion:* Protestant. *Home:* 1118 Ninth St., Las Vegas, N.M. 87701.

CAREER: High school teacher of English and Spanish, Tularosa, N.M., 1913-14; high school teacher and principal, Santa Rosa, N.M., 1914-16; instructor in English, New Mexico Highlands University, Las Vegas, 1921-22; member of New Mexico Legislature, 1925-26; writer, beginning 1926. Operated small ranch in New Mexico Rockies, 1929-56. Also worked as U.S. forest ranger; secretary of Las Vegas Cowboys' Reunion Rodeo and trombonist in Doc Patterson's Cowboy Band. Chairman of Las Vegas Heart Fund Drive, 1962; member of Las Vegas Hospital board, beginning 1962. *Military service:* U.S. Army, Engineers, 1917-19; served with American Expeditionary Forces in France; became sergeant. *Member:* Western Writers of America (president, 1958-59), American Poetry League, Wildlife Conservation Association, Western Historical Association, Westerners (Denver Posse), American Legion, Veterans of Foreign Wars, Disabled American Veterans. *Awards, honors:* Spur Award for best western short story of 1955, for "Bad Company," co-winner of Spur Award for best western nonfiction of 1958, for contribution to *This Is the West,* Justin Golden Boot Award, 1961, for distinguished writing in western field, 1954-61, Spur Award for best western poem of 1967, for "Empty Saddles at Christmas," Levi Strauss Golden Saddleman Award, 1967, for bringing dignity and honor to the western legend, all from Western Writers of America; honorary chief of Kiowa Tribe, Anadarko, Okla., 1959; Litt.D., New Mexico Highlands University, 1960; named lifetime honorary president of Western Writers of America, 1975.

WRITINGS: Winds of the Mountains (poetry), Santa Fe New Mexican Press, 1922; *Buckaroo Ballads* (poetry), Santa Fe New Mexican Press, 1928; *Born to Battle* (story collection), University of New Mexico Press, 1951; *Songs of the Saddlemen* (poetry), Sage Books, 1954; *Sunlight Through the Trees* (poetry), New Mexico Highlands University Press, 1954; (editor and contributor) *Legends and Tales of the Old West,* Doubleday, 1962; *Little World Apart* (novel), Doubleday, 1966; *Rawhide Rhymes,* Doubleday, 1968. Also edited two Western Writers of America anthologies, *Frontiers West* and *Spurs West.*

"Bret King of Rimrock Ranch" series for boys, under house pseudonym (property of Grosset & Dunlap) Dan Scott; all published by Grosset: *The Mystery of Ghost Canyon,* 1960; *The Secret of Hermit's Peak,* 1960; *The Range Rodeo Mystery,* 1960; *The Mystery of Rawhide Gap,* 1960; *The Secret of Fort Pioneer,* 1961; *The Mystery at Blizzard Mesa,* 1961; *The Mystery of the Comanche Caves,* 1963; *The Phantom of Wolf Creek,* 1963; *The Mystery of Bandit Gulch,* 1964.

Stories, poems, articles, and anecdotes have appeared in about seventy anthologies and in some twenty texts on American literature. Stories and poems anthologized in: John Gunther, *Inside U.S.A.,* Harper, 1947, revised edition, 1951; Harriet M. Lucas and Herman M. Ward, editors, *Prose and Poetry for Enjoyment,* 4th edition, Dent, 1950; Noel M. Loomis, editor, *Holsters and Heroes,* Macmillan, 1954; Harry E. Maule, editor, *The Fall Roundup,* Random, 1955; Don Ward, editor, *Branded West,* Houghton, 1956; Mark A. Neville, editor, *Interesting Friends,* Rand McNally, 1958; Jim Kjelgaard, editor, *Wild Horse Roundup,* Dodd, 1958; Fairfax D. Downey, compiler, *My Kingdom for a Horse,* Doubleday, 1960; E. N. Brandt, editor, *Saturday Evening Post Reader of Western Stories,* Doubleday, 1960; F. D. Downey, compiler, *Great Dog Stories of All Time,* Doubleday, 1962; E. D. Mygatt, editor, *Search for the Hidden Places,* McKay, 1963; Kenneth Fowler, editor, *Rawhide Men,* Doubleday, 1965; W. R. Cox, editor, *Rivers to Cross,* Dodd, 1966. Also contributor to *This Is the West,* edited by Robert West Howard, Rand McNally, 1957. Approximately 1,500 short stories, 1,000 pieces of nonfiction, and 2,500 poems have been published in more than 100 periodicals in America, England, and Canada; they have appeared in *Saturday Evening Post, Reader's Digest, Country Gentlemen, Farm Journal, Argosy, Adventure, Field and Stream, Ranch Romances* (now defunct), *Western Story* (now defunct), and *Maclean's Magazine,* among others. Author of a series of cowboy humor stories in *Wild West Weekly* (now defunct) under pseudonym Phil Squires.

WORK IN PROGRESS: Historical and humorous text to be "interlarded" between beefsteak recipes collected by Carol Truax for Grosset's *Cattleman's Steak Book;* selecting, from his magazine-published poetry, material for two collections, one western and one general.

SIDELIGHTS: Barker told *CA:* "The predominant wordage of my writing since 1925 has been in western short stories of the oldtime working cowboy, emphasis on humor, plus hundreds of cowboy poems. I have also written and published in magazines about 1,000 brief humorous verses of general interest, usually four to eight lines. My most successful individual piece of work is 'A Cowboy's Christmas Prayer' from *Songs of the Saddlemen.* Not only widely quoted and reprinted, but also used on Christmas TV programs of Ernie Ford and Jimmy Dean, and recorded as a reading by Jimmy Dean on his 'Christmas Record,' 1965." Barker's only book-length story, *Little World Apart,* is the partly autobiographical story of a pioneer New Mexico family—called a novel because the publishers couldn't find any other way to classify it. He has digressed from purely western lore (on which he does some speaking) to write stories and poems about animals, World War I, hunting and fishing, trees, and other nature and outdoor subjects. Between 1929-56, Barker and his wife, Elsa, did their writing on a ranch in a timbered cove named Rincon Montoso, about eight thousand feet up in the Rockies. While ranching there, their brand was Lazy S O B.

* * *

BARLOW, Claude W(illis)   1907-1976

PERSONAL: Born August 2, 1907, in Stafford, Conn.; son of George M. (a grocer) and Myrtie E. (Willis) Barlow. *Education:* Amherst College, B.A., 1928; Indiana University, M.A., 1930; Yale University, Ph.D., 1935; American Academy in Rome, additional study, 1935-38. *Home:* 22 Vincent Ave., Worcester, Mass. 01603.

CAREER: Indiana University, Bloomington, instructor in classics, 1930-31; Yale University, New Haven, Conn., instructor in classics,1934-35; Mount Holyoke College, South Hadley, Mass., instructor in classics, 1938-42; University of Tennessee, Knoxville, assistant professor of classics, 1947; Clark University, Worcester, Mass., assistant professor, 1947-52, associate professor, 1952-61, professor of classics, 1961-72. *Military service:* U.S. Army Air Forces, 1942-45; became staff sergeant. *Member:* American Philological Association, Archaeological Institute of America, Mediaeval Academy of America, Classical Association of New England (secretary-treasurer, 1953-63; president, 1968-69), Descendants of Old Plymouth Colony (president, 1966-69), Phi Betta Kappa. *Awards, honors:* American Academy in Rome fellow, 1935-38; Guggenheim fellow, 1945-46.

WRITINGS: (Editor) Lucius Annaeus Seneca, *Epistolae Senecae ad Paulum et Pauli ad Senecam,* American Academy in Rome, 1938; (editor) Saint Martin of Braga, *Opera omnia,* Yale University Press, 1950; (translator) *The Iberian Fathers,* two volumes, Catholic University of America Press, 1969.

WORK IN PROGRESS: Studies on the plays and editions of Terence, and on Spanish monasticism.

SIDELIGHTS: In addition to the classical languages taught, Claude Barlow read and worked in French, Italian, German, Spanish, and Portuguese.†

(Died January, 1976)

* * *

BARLOW, (Emma) Nora   1885-

PERSONAL: Born December 22, 1885, in Cambridge, England; daughter of Horace (a maker and designer of scientific instruments) and Ida (Farrer) Darwin; married Sir Alan Barlow (a civil servant), April, 1911 (deceased); children: Joan Helen (deceased), Thomas Erasmus, Erasmus Darwin, Andrew Dalmahoy, Hilda Horatia (Mrs. John Padel), Horace. *Education:* Educated at a private school in Wimbledon; attended lectures at Cambridge University. *Home:* Sellenger, Sylvester Rd., Cambridge, England.

WRITINGS—Editor: The Beagle Diary, 1831-1836, Cambridge University Press, 1933; *Charles Darwin and the Voyage of the Beagle,* Pilot Press, 1945, Philosophical Library, 1946; (and author of notes) *The Autobiography of Charles Darwin, 1809-1882,* Harcourt, 1958; *Darwin and Henslow: The Growth of an Idea; Letters, 1831-1860,* University of California Press, 1967. Contributor to *Cornhill Magazine, Science Progress, Notes and Records of the Royal Society,* and other publications in England.

SIDELIGHTS: Lady Barlow, a granddaughter of Charles Darwin, told *CA:* "A very early copy of my grandfather's complete diary of 'HMS Beagle' first aroused my interest. [It was] typed on an early typewriter by my father, Horace Darwin, whose interests were mechanical. From that time I felt a desire to go back to original manuscripts rather than accept the shortened versions of C.D.'s works." Accordingly, Lady Barlow's edition of Darwin's autobiogrpahy included those passages latterly deleted by him.

BIOGRAPHICAL/CRITICAL SOURCES: Times Literary Supplement, September 21, 1967; *Book World,* February 25, 1968.

* * *

BARNARD, Mary (Ethel)   1909-

PERSONAL: Born December 6, 1909, in Vancouver, Wash.; daughter of Samuel Melvin (a lumberman) and Bertha (Hoard) Barnard. *Education:* Reed College, B.A., 1932. *Politics:* Independent. *Religion:* Presbyterian. *Home:* 7100 Southeast Evergreen Highway, Vancouver, Wash. 98664. *Agent:* Russell & Volkening, Inc., 551 Fifth Ave., New York, N.Y. 10017.

CAREER: Did social work during the thirties; University of Buffalo, Lockwood Memorial Library, Buffalo, N.Y., curator of poetry collection, 1939-43; research assistant to Carl Van Doren in New York, N.Y., 1943-50; has done other free-lance literary work. *Member:* American Association of University Women, Fort Vancouver Historical Society. *Awards, honors:* Levinson Award of *Poetry* Magazine, 1935.

WRITINGS: (Contributor) *Five Young American Poets, 1940,* New Directions, 1940; *A Few Poems,* Reed College Press, 1952; (translator) *Sappho: A New Translation,* University of California Press, 1958; *The Mythmakers,* Ohio University Press, 1967.

AVOCATIONAL INTERESTS: Art, history, mythology.

BIOGRAPHICAL/CRITICAL SOURCES: Hudson Review, Volume XVIII, number 2, summer, 1965.

* * *

BARNES, Leonard (John)   1895-

PERSONAL: Born July 21, 1895, in London, England; son of John Albert (a civil servant) and Kate (Oakeshott) Barnes; married Beatrice Ingram Davies, 1900 (died, 1943); married Margaret Dinning Blackburn, July 1, 1943. *Education:* University College, Oxford, B.A., (first class honors), 1921, M.A., 1948. *Home:* Great Haseley, Oxfordshire, England.

CAREER: Colonial Office, London, England, civil servant, 1921-25; cotton farmer in South Africa and journalist on *Cape Times* and *Johannesburg Star,* 1925-32; free-lance writer and journalist in England, 1932-36; University of Liverpool, Liverpool, England, senior lecturer in education, 1936-45; Oxford University, Oxford, England, head of department of social and administrative studies, 1947-62. Member of commission advising the government of Malaya on formation of a new university, 1947; adviser on primary education to High Commissioner of Malaya, 1950; special consultant to United Nations Economic Commission for Africa, Addis Ababa, Ethiopia, 1964-69. *Military service:* British Army, 1914-18; served on Western Front; became captain; received Military Cross with bar.

WRITINGS: *Caliban in Africa: An Impression of Colour-Madness*, Gollancz, 1930; *The New Boer War*, Hogarth, 1932; *Youth at Arms*, (World War I poetry), P. Davies, 1933; *Zulu Paraclete: A Sentimental Record*, P. Davies, 1935; *The Duty of Empire*, Gollancz, 1935; *The Future of Colonies*, Hogarth, 1936; *Skeleton of the Empire* (monograph), Fact Ltd., 1937; *Empire or Democracy? A Study of the Colonial Question*, Gollancz, 1939; *Soviet Light on the Colonies*, Penguin, 1944; *Youth Service in an English County*, King George's Jubilee Trust, 1945; *The Outlook for Youth Work*, King George's Jubilee Trust, 1948; *The Homecoming* (poem), P. Davies, 1961; *African Renaissance*, Gollancz, 1969, Bobbs-Merrill, 1970; *Africa in Eclipse*, Gollancz, 1971, St. Martin's, 1972. Author of various pamphlets on colonial matters. Work included in *The War Poets, 1914-18* and *Up the Line to Death*, Methuen, 1964.

WORK IN PROGRESS: His memoirs.

SIDELIGHTS: Between 1964 and 1969 Leonard Barnes visited thirty-two countries in Africa. He has also traveled widely in Europe.

BIOGRAPHICAL/CRITICAL SOURCES: Sir Cosmo Parkinson, *Colonial Office from Within, 1909-1945*, Faber, 1947; Cyril Falls, *The First World War*, Longmans, Green, 1960; William Plomer, *Turbott Wolfe*, Morrow, 1965; *Punch*, January 29, 1969.

*   *   *

BARNES, Phoebe   1908-

PERSONAL: Born May 10, 1908, in Worcester, Mass.; daughter of Reginald (a manufacturer) and Dorcas (Bradford) Washburn; married Charles B. Barnes (a lawyer), June 15, 1929; children: Phoebe (Mrs. John E. Z. Caner), Josephine Lea (Mrs. John J. Iselin), Charles B., Jr., Cornelia Bradford. *Education:* Attended Radcliffe College, 1930-31. *Politics:* Liberal Republican. *Religion:* Protestant. *Home:* 13 Fairgreen Pl., Chestnut Hill, Mass. 02167.

WRITINGS: *Through Prisms*, Humphries, 1961; *Soundings and Bearings*, Branden, 1967. Contributor of articles on salmon fishing to *Atlantic Monthly*, *Salmon Magazine*, and *Boston Magazine*.

SIDELIGHTS: Mrs. Barnes has accompanied her husband on salmon fishing trips in Europe, Quebec, New Brunswick, and at Ungava Bay, north of Hudson Bay. They have a shooting camp on Cape Cod, and a summer place in Maine. *Avocational interests.* Sailing, needlepoint, and reading and arguing about politics and religion.

*   *   *

BARNES, Ralph M(osser)   1900-

PERSONAL: Born October 17, 1900, in Clifton Mills, W.Va.; son of John J. (a merchant) and Martha (Mosser) Barnes; wife deceased; children: Elizabeth (Mrs. Walter Parks), Carolyn (Mrs. Bruce Lemm). *Education:* West Virginia University, B.S.M.E., 1923, M.E., 1928; Cornell University, M.S., 1924, Ph.D., 1933. *Home:* 12304 Fifth Helena Dr., Los Angeles, Calif. *Office:* University of California, 405 Hilgard Ave., Los Angeles, Calif.

CAREER: Worked in industry at intervals, 1923-26; University of Illinois, College of Commerce, Urbana, instructor in industrial management, 1926-28; University of Iowa, College of Engineering, Iowa City, 1928-49, started as assistant professor of industrial engineering, professor, 1934-49, director of personnel, 1936-49; University of California, Los Angeles, professor of engineering and production manage-

ment, beginning, 1949. Consultant to Government of Spain in establishment of School of Industrial Administration in Madrid; consultant to industry in Norway, Sweden, Uruguay, Mexico, and other countries; conductor of management seminars and lecturer in European countries, Japan, and South America. *Member:* American Association for the Advancement of Science, American Institute of Industrial Engineers (fellow; former western region vice-president), American Society of Mechanical Engineers, Society for the Advancement of Management (former vice-president), American Society for Engineering Education, Industrial Management Society, Sigma Xi, Tau Beta Pi, Sigma Iota Epsilon, Pi Tau Sigma, Alpha Pi Mu, Beta Gamma Sigma. *Awards, honors:* Gilbreth Medal for outstanding achievement in the field of management, 1941, and Industrial Incentive Award for work in the field of work measurement and financial incentives, 1951, both from Society for the Advancement of Management.

WRITINGS: *Industrial Engineering and Management*, McGraw, 1931; *An Investigation of Some Hand Motions Used in Factory Work*, University of Iowa, 1936; *Motion and Time Study*, Wiley, 1937, 5th edition with title *Motion and Time Study: Design and Measurement of Work*, 1963, 6th edition, 1968; (with Marvin E. Mundel) *Studies of Hand Motions and Rhythm Appearing in Factory Work*, University of Iowa, 1938; (with Mundel) *A Study of Hand Motions Used in Small Assembly Work*, University of Iowa, 1939; (with Mundel) *A Study of Simultaneous Symmetrical Hand Motions*, University of Iowa, 1939; (with Mundel and John M. MacKenzie) *Studies of One- and Two-Handed Work*, University of Iowa, 1940; (with James S. Perkins and J. M. Juran) *A Study of the Effect of Practice on the Elements of a Factory Operation*, University of Iowa, 1940; *Motion and Time Study Applications*, Wiley, 1942, 4th edition, 1961; *Work Methods Manual*, Wiley, 1944; *Work Measurement Manual*, [Iowa City], 1944, 4th edition, W. C. Brown, 1951; *Work Methods Training Manual*, [Iowa City], 1945, 3rd edition, W. C. Brown, 1950; (with Norma A. Englert) *Bibliography of Industrial Engineering and Management Literature to January 1, 1946*, W. C. Brown, 1946; *Work Sampling*, W. C. Brown, 1956, 2nd edition, Wiley, 1957; *Motion and Time Study Problems and Projects*, Wiley, 1956, 2nd edition, 1961; (with J. L. McKinney) *Industrial Engineering Survey*, University of California, 1957. Member of editorial board, *International Journal of Production Research*, 1962.

WORK IN PROGRESS: A study of work measurement and motivation of workers; measuring work by physiological methods; development of management training programs.

SIDELIGHTS: Barnes's books have been translated into six languages, including Portuguese and Japanese.†

*   *   *

BARNITZ, Harry W.   1920-1973

PERSONAL: Born May 25, 1920, in Atlanta, Ga.; son of Henry L. and Elizabeth (Downing) Barnitz; married Mary van Zyverden, April 14, 1946; children: Robin, Wendy, Anne. *Education:* Attended College of the Academy of the New Church and the Theological School of the Lord's New Church, Nova Hierosolyma, both in Bryn Athyn, Pa. *Politics:* Non-partisan. *Home:* 22 Tudor Lane, Yonkers, N.Y. 10201. *Office:* Chapel of the New Church, 50 Granatan Dr., Yonkers, N.Y.

CAREER: Swedenborgian clergyman, ordained, 1944; pastor at Chapel of the New Church, Yonkers, N.Y., and lecturer in New York City area, 1960-73. Organist; composer of about two hundred songs, hymns, and choral and piano works. *Member:* Swedenborgian Foundation (life member).

WRITINGS: Existentialism and the New Christianity: Towards a New Universal Synthesis, Philosophical Library, 1969. Author of several pamphlets, privately printed.

WORK IN PROGRESS: Three books on religious, philosophical, and scientific subjects.†

(Died, 1973)

*   *   *

BARNUM, Richard
[Collective pseudonym]

WRITINGS—"Kneetime Animal" series; published by Barse & Hopkins: *Mappo, the Merry Monkey,* 1915; *Slicko, the Jumping Squirrel,* 1915; *Squinty, the Comical Pig,* 1915.

SIDELIGHTS: See ADAMS, Harriet S., STRATEMEYER, Edward L., and SVENSON, Andrew E.†

*   *   *

BARRETT, Anne Mainwaring (Gillett) 1911-

PERSONAL: Born May 7, 1911, in Southsea, Hampshire, England; daughter of Owen Francis (an admiral, Royal Navy) and Mabel (Cavenagh-Mainwaring) Gillett; married Hugh Myles Boxer, August 1, 1933 (divorced, 1940); married Wilfrid Kenyon Tufnell Barrett, June 10, 1941 (divorced, 1960); children: (second marriage) Alison Gay Tufnell (Mrs. A.V.N. Doggart). *Education:* Educated in Dorsetshire, England. *Agent:* Curtis Brown Ltd., 1 Craven Hill, London W2 3EW, England.

CAREER: Children's Film Foundation, London, England, associate and story editor, 1959-64; writer for young people.

WRITINGS: Caterpillar Hall, Collins, 1950; *Stolen Summer,* Collins, 1951, Dodd, 1953; *The Dark Island,* Collins, 1952; *The Journey of Johnny Rew,* Collins, 1954, Bobbs-Merrill, 1955; *Sheila Burton: Dental Assistant,* John Lane, 1956; *Songberd's Grove,* illustrations by N. H. Bodecker, Bobbs-Merrill, 1957, published with illustrations by David Knight, Collins, 1957; *Midway,* illustrations by Margery Gill, Collins, 1967, Coward, 1968. Author of screenplays; contributor of short stories and articles to periodicals.

BIOGRAPHICAL/CRITICAL SOURCES: Times Literary Supplement, May 25, 1967; *Young Readers' Review,* May, 1968.†

*   *   *

BARROWS, (Ruth) Marjorie
(R. M. Barrows, Ruth Barrows; pseudonyms: Jack Alden, Noel Ames, Ruth Dixon, Hugh Graham)

PERSONAL: Born in Chicago, Ill.; daughter of Ransom Moore (a physician) and Caroline A. P. (Dixon) Barrows. *Education:* Special student at Northwestern University, 1916-17, and University of Chicago, 1917-19. *Politics:* Republican. *Religion:* Presbyterian. *Home:* 1615 Hinman Ave., Evanston, Ill. 60201.

CAREER: Compton's Pictured Encyclopedia, contributing editor, 1920; secretary and plots assistant for a short story writer, 1920-21; *Child Life,* Chicago, Ill., associate editor, 1922-31, editor, 1931-38; Consolidated Books, co-editor, 1943-48; *Children's Hour,* editor-in-chief, 1952-62; *Treasure Trails,* editor, 1954-56; *Junior Treasure Chest of Family*

Weekly, editor, 1954-62. Advisory editor, *Highlights for Children,* 1956-66. Has served as a director of Midwest Writers' Conference. *Member:* International P.E.N. (New York center), Society of Midland Authors (director, beginning 1938; contest judge), Chicago Drama League (former director; little theater judge), English-Speaking Union, Evanston Drama Club, Arts Club (Chicago), Cordon Club (Chicago; honorary member). *Awards, honors:* Chicago Foundation of Literature award, 1956, for contribution to the literary heritage of Chicago.

WRITINGS—All children's literature: (Under name Ruth Barrows) *Bunny's Book,* Carrington, 1923; (under name Ruth Barrows) *Ella Phant,* Carrington, 1923; *The Magic Umbrella,* Rockwell, 1928, published as *The Magic Umbrella Abroad,* Follett, 1930; *My Rhyme and Picture Book,* Whitman Publishing, 1928; *Chip's Chums,* Whitman Publishing, 1929.

Who's Who in the Zoo, Reilly & Lee, 1932; *Ezra the Elephant,* Grosset, 1934; *Little Duck,* Grosset, 1935; *Johnny Giraffe,* Grosset, 1935; *Snuggles,* Rand McNally, 1935, published under pseudonym Ruth Dixon as *Snuggles: A Real Live Animal Book,* 1958; (author of text) *The Francis Tipton Hunter Picture Book,* Whitman Publishing, 1936; *The Pirate of Pooh* (plays), Rand McNally, 1936; (under pseudonym Ruth Dixon) *Yip and Yap,* Rand McNally, 1936, published as *Yip and Yap: A Real Live Animal Book,* 1958; *Whiskers,* Rand McNally, 1937.

Fraidy Cat, Rand McNally, 1942; *Let's Fly to Bermuda,* Albert Whitman, 1942; *The Funny Hat,* Rand McNally, 1943; *Timothy Tiger,* Rand McNally, 1943; (under pseudonym Jack Alden) *Cocky the Little Helicopter,* Rand McNally, 1943; (under pseudonym Hugh Graham) *The Runaway Airplane,* Rand McNally, 1943; *Jo Jo,* Rand McNally, 1944; *Sukey,* James and Jonathan Press, 1944, published as *Sukey, You Shall Be My Wife, and Other Stories,* Samuel Lowe, 1944; *Pet Show,* James and Jonathan Press, 1944; *Waggles,* Rand McNally, 1945; *Lancelot,* Rand McNally, 1946; *Hoppity,* Rand McNally, 1947; *Pudgy the Little Black Bear,* Rand McNally, 1948; *Scamper,* Rand McNally, 1949.

Nursery Tales, John Martin's House, 1950; *Tut! Tut! Tales,* Garden City Books, 1950; *That Parade,* Rand McNally, 1967; *The Little Red Boot,* Rand McNally, 1967.

"Muggins Mouse" series; published by Rand McNally, except as noted: *Muggins Mouse,* Reilly & Lee, 1932; *More About Muggins,* 1964; *Muggins Takes Off,* 1964; *The Rand McNally Book of Favorite Muggins Mouse Stories,* 1965; *Muggins' Big Balloon,* 1967; *Muggins Becomes a Hero,* 1968.

Wrote a series of twenty-five-cent books for Rand McNally, under pseudonym Ruth Dixon, except as noted, including: *Three Little Bunnies,* 1950; *Three Little Puppies,* 1951; *Little Friends: Kittens, Puppies, Bunnies,* 1951; *Scalawag the Monkey,* 1953; *Bartholomew the Beaver,* 1953; *Four Little Puppies,* 1957; (under name Marjorie Barrows) *Four Little Kittens,* 1957.

Compiler: *One Hundred Best Poems for Boys and Girls,* Whitman Publishing, 1930; *A Book of Famous Poems for Older Boys and Girls,* Whitman Publishing, 1931; *Favorite Pages from Child Life,* Rand McNally, 1931; *Child Life Story Book,* Rand McNally, 1932; *The Picture Book of Poetry,* Rand McNally, 1932; (with Frances Cavanah) *Child Life Mystery-Adventure Book,* Rand McNally, 1936; *The Organ Grinder's Garden,* Rand McNally, 1938; *Two Hundred Best Poems for Boys and Girls,* Whitman Publishing, 1938.

Pulitzer Prize Poems, Random House, 1941; (under name R. M. Barrows; with E. X. Pastor) *The Kit Book for Soldiers, Sailors, and Marines,* Consolidated Books, 1942; (with George Eaton) *Box Office,* Ziff-Davis Publishing, 1943; *Children's Treasury,* two volumes, Consolidated Books, 1944; *Let's Neck,* [Chicago], 1944; (under name R. M. Barrows) *Eleven of the World's Great War and Spy Stories,* Consolidated Books, 1944; (under name R. M. Barrows; with Eaton) *Twelve of the World's Great Humor Stories,* Consolidated Books, 1944; (under name R. M. Barrows; with Mathilda Schirmer) *Home Was Never Like This,* [Chicago], 1944; (under name R. M. Barrows; with Schirmer) *The Lady is Fresh, Delicious, Delectable, Delightful!,* [Chicago], 1944; *The Family Reader,* Consolidated Books, 1946; *One Thousand Beautiful Things,* Spencer Press, 1947; (under pseudonym Noel Ames) *These Wonderful People,* Consolidated Books, 1947; (under pseudonym Hugh Graham) *An American Treasury,* Consolidated Books, 1949, published as *One Thousand American Things,* Spencer Press, 1956; *The Peoples' Reader,* Spencer Press, 1949; *In Green Pastures,* Halcyon Press, 1949.

Indoor Play Book, Garden City Books, 1950; (with Schirmer) *The Children's Hour,* sixteen volumes, Spencer Press, 1953-54; *The Quintessence of Beauty and Romance,* Spencer Press, 1955; (with Bennett Cerf and Schirmer) *A Treasury of Humor,* Spencer Press, 1955; *Read Aloud Poems Every Young Child Should Know,* Rand McNally, 1957; *Treasure Trail Parade,* Spencer Press, 1958.

Contributor of about one hundred articles to *Compton's Pictured Encyclopedia;* light verse to *Ladies' Home Journal, Chicago Evening Post, Chicago Daily News,* and *Chicago Tribune,* mostly in the 1920's; also book reviewer for *Continent, Chicago Evening Post,* and *Chicago Daily News,* during the twenties.

WORK IN PROGRESS: A "light-hearted" autobiography; more children's books.

SIDELIGHTS: Favorites among Marjorie Barrows' own books are *Muggins Mouse* ("even Walt Disney sent him Christmas cards"), *The Pirate of Pooh, Fraidy Cat,* and *Tut! Tut! Tales.* Of the anthologies, she is proudest of *One Thousand Beautiful Things,* which has been reissued again and again, most recently by Hawthorn; another compilation, *One Hundred Best Poems* ranks among the fifty best-selling books of the past half century.

During her college days, Miss Barrows was an associate editor of an intercollegiate poetry magazine, *Youth, Poetry of Today;* on its student-professor board of editors at the time were John Erskine, Maxwell Anderson, and Stephen Vincent Benet. Members of the University of Chicago Poetry Club included Glenway Westcott, and Vincent Sheean—a "stimulating group," she says, that included future Pulitzer Prize poets and Harper Prize novelists.

Long a collector of autographed first editions, she has parted with three thousand books ("I *still* collect"). Many of the first editions have gone to the rare book collections of Northwestern University, University of Chicago, Roosevelt University, and Hiram College libraries. She also has collected much material to be taped for the blind.

*　*　*

BARTH, Charles P.　1895-
(Buffalo Chuck)

PERSONAL: Born October 1, 1895, in Buffalo, N.Y.; son of Charles Otto (a butcher) and Katherine (Wolfarth) Barth.

Education: Attended high school at night for three years. *Politics:* Independent. *Religion:* "Embrace them all."

CAREER: Roamed most of his life, working as a seaman on Great Lakes and Pacific Ocean vessels and then as an itinerant steeplejack for twenty-five years; when he became too old for high climbing, did painting and interior decorating for Van Schaack & Co. in Denver, Colo. Author of greeting card verse, 1938-42; former roving correspondent and staff member of *Bowery News,* New York, using the byline of Buffalo Chuck. Active in Skid Row rehabilitation work in Denver. *Military service:* U.S. Army, 1918-39; served in France. *Member:* Brotherhood of Painters, Decorators and Paperhangers of America, Veterans of Foreign Wars.

WRITINGS: Shep: A Reminiscence, Whitmore, 1969; *Hobo Trail to Nowhere,* Whitmore, 1969. Contributor of short stories and articles to *Hobo News* and *Bowery News,* and articles to *Denver Post, Western Family, American Baby,* and other periodicals.

SIDELIGHTS: Barth says he was steered away from skid row in the late 1930's by a part-Cherokee Indian lady, Little Tipping Toe, who encouraged him to write. His chief interest is the displaced American worker, including ranch hands and railroad workers.††

*　*　*

BARTLETT, Nancy W.　1913-1972

PERSONAL: Born September 14, 1913, in Cambridge, Mass.; daughter of Percival M. and Mary Esty (Cliff) White; married first husband, Edward B. Cole, 1935; married second husband, Calvin Page Bartlett (a partner in a law firm), 1947; children: (first marriage) Mary (Mrs. Peter Hugens), Matilda (Mrs. Malcolm Ticknor). *Education:* Radcliffe College, A.B., 1935. *Politics:* Democrat. *Religion:* Unitarian Universalist. *Home:* 32 Martin Rd., Concord, Mass. 01742.

CAREER: Headmistress of Ratcliff School, Brookline, Mass., and teacher of remedial reading for children.

WRITINGS: Then Pity, Then Embrace (novel), Macmillan, 1967.

WORK IN PROGRESS: A second novel.

SIDELIGHTS: Mrs. Bartlett began writing seriously when her daughters went off to college, doing a play first and then a short memoir of her childhood in Cambridge, Mass. She was encouraged by the writer and historian Barbara Tuchman, a college friend, and Cecil Scott, editor-in-chief of Macmillan, to expand her memoir into the novel, *Then Pity, Then Embrace.*†

(Died December 27, 1972)

*　*　*

BARTLETT, Paul　1909-

PERSONAL: Born July 13, 1909, in Moberly, Mo.; married Elizabeth Winters (a poet and editor), April 19, 1943; children: Steven. *Education:* Attended Oberlin College, University of Arizona, and National University of Mexico. *Home:* Calle Juarez 103, Comala, Colima, Mexico.

CAREER: University of California, Santa Barbara, editor of publications, 1964-70. Free-lance artist and writer. Instructor in creative writing, Georgia State College (now University), 1955. *Awards, honors:* Huntington Hartford Foundation writing fellowship, 1960 and 1961; Montalvo Foundation writing fellowship, 1961-62; Carnegie authors' fund grant, 1961 and 1971; Yaddo fellowship, 1970.

WRITINGS: When the Owl Cries (novel), Macmillan, 1960. Short stories anthologized in two New School for Social Research anthologies, 1961 and 1963, and in *Accent Anthology,* 1942. Contributor of short stories to *Coastlines, Chicago Review, Arizona Quarterly, Kenyon Review, Southwest Review, Literary Review, Forum, Mexican Life, Prairie Schooner,* and other literary journals.

WORK IN PROGRESS: The Journal of Leonardo da Vinci in a wholly new form; a film novel.

SIDELIGHTS: Bartlett told *CA:* "I have completed 300 pen and ink drawings of the haciendas, the first art record of them. These have been purchased by the University of Texas Latin American Library. This project has required many trips, 50,000 miles of travel through Mexico, since 1942."

* * *

BARTLETT, Philip A.
[Collective pseudonym]

WRITINGS—"Roy Stover Mystery" series; published by Grosset: *The Lakeport Bank Mystery,* 1929; *The Mystery of the Snowbound Express,* 1929; *The Cliff Island Mystery,* 1930; *Mystery of the Circle of Fire,* 1934.

SIDELIGHTS: See **ADAMS, Harriet S., STRATEMEYER, Edward L.,** and **SVENSON, Andrew E.**†

* * *

BARTON, Humphrey (Douglas Elliott)   1900-

PERSONAL: Born March 9, 1900, in England; son of P. F. (a physician) and Anne (Fox) Barton; married Jessie Gutch, 1930 (died, 1959); children: Peter, Patricia (Mrs. Michael Pocock). *Education:* Attended Haileybury and Imperial Service College, 1914-17. *Politics:* Conservative. *Religion:* Church of England. *Office:* Laurent Giles & Partners Ltd., 4 Quay Hill, Lymington, Hampshire, England.

CAREER: Engineer and marine surveyor; Laurent Giles & Partners Ltd. (naval architects), Lymington, Hampshire, England, director, beginning 1936. Harbor commissioner, Lymington, 1953-59. *Military service:* Royal Air Force, pilot, 1918-19; Royal Engineers, 1939-45; became major. *Member:* Royal Institute of Naval Architects (associate member), Ocean Cruising Club (founder and admiral); several English yacht clubs.

WRITINGS: Vertue XXXV, Adlard Coles, 1950; *Westward Crossing,* Norton, 1950; *The Sea and Me,* Adlard Coles, 1952, Macmillan, 1953; *Atlantic Adventurers: Voyages in Small Craft,* Adlard Coles, 1953, Van Nostrand, 1955, 2nd edition, Adlard Coles, 1962. Contributor of short stories to yachting magazines.

SIDELIGHTS: Barton lives aboard his thirty-four foot auxiliary sloop, "Rose Rambler," cruising the north Atlantic. He has made seven trans-Atlantic trips in that sloop, and a total of twelve crossings in craft less than fifty-five feet in overall length.††

* * *

BARTON, Mary Neill   1899-

PERSONAL: Born March 20, 1899, in Winchester, Va.; daughter of Samuel M. (a college professor) and Mary Millicent (Tidball) Barton. *Education:* Agnes Scott College, B.A., 1922; Columbia University, B.S., 1927, M.S., 1945. *Religion:* Episcopalian. *Home and office:* 500 West University Pkwy., Baltimore, Md. 21210.

CAREER: Enoch Pratt Free Library, Baltimore, Md., reference assistant, 1927-29, first assistant in reference department, 1929-38, head of general reference department, 1938-59; has done advisory work and other special assignments, and served as part-time librarian in department of embryology at Carnegie Institution of Washington in Baltimore, Md. Instructor at Drexel Institute, 1937, at Columbia University School of Library Service, summers of 1943, 1946. *Member:* American Library Association (council member, 1951-53, 1957-58; organizer and first president of references service division, 1957-58), Maryland Library Association, Baltimore Bibliophiles, Phi Beta Kappa. *Awards, honors:* Isadore Gilbert Mudge Award of American Library Association for distinguished contributions to reference librarianship, 1959.

WRITINGS: (With Virginia W. Kennedy) *Samuel Taylor Coleridge: A Selected Bibliography,* Enoch Pratt Free Library, 1935, reprinted, Kaus Reprint Co., 1969; (contributor) *Reference Function of the Library,* edited by Pierce Butler, University of Chicago Press, 1943; (compiler) *Reference Books: A Brief Guide for Students and Other Users of the Library,* Enoch Pratt Free Library, 1947, 7th edition (assisted by Marion V. Bell), 1970; (assisted by E. F. Watson) *General Reference Department Manual,* Enoch Pratt Free Library, 1950; (contributor) *The Library as a Community Information Center,* Illini Bookstore, 1959. Contributor to professional journals.

AVOCATIONAL INTERESTS: Art and travel.†

* * *

BARTON, May Hollis
[Collective pseudonym]

WRITINGS—"Barton Books for Girls" series; published by Cupples & Leon: *Hazel Hood's Strange Discovery,* 1928; *Little Miss Sunshine,* 1928; *Two Girls and a Mystery,* 1928; *Kate Martin's Problem,* 1929; *The Girls of Lighthouse Island,* 1929; *The Girl in the Top Flat,* 1930; *The Search for Peggy Ann,* 1930; *Charlotte Cross and Aunt Deb,* 1931; *Sallie's Test of Skill,* 1931; *Virginia's Venture,* 1932.

SIDELIGHTS: See **ADAMS, Harriet S., STRATEMEYER, Edward L.,** and **SVENSON, Andrew E.**†

* * *

BARTRAN, Margaret   1913-1976

PERSONAL: Born May 23, 1913, in Green Bay, Wis.; daughter of William Henry, Jr. (a physician and surgeon) and Clara (Barkhausen) Bartran. *Education:* University of Wisconsin, B.A., 1934; School of the Art Institute of Chicago, B.F.A., 1941. *Politics:* Republican. *Religion:* Congregational (NACCC). *Home:* 1043 South Quincy St., Green Bay, Wis. 54301.

CAREER: Bartran Galleries, Inc. (known as the Palmer House Galleries), Chicago, Ill., owner and operator, 1954-63. *Military service:* U.S. Naval Reserve (Women's Reserve), 1943-45; became lieutenant junior grade.

WRITINGS: A Guide to Color Reproductions, Scarecrow, 1966, revised edition, 1971.†

(Died November 12, 1976)

* * *

BASKIN, Wade   1924-1974

PERSONAL: Born July 24, 1924, in Harmony, Ark.; son of Dewey Buchanan (a teacher) and Essie (Jacobs) Baskin;

married Vlasta Kolenova (a teacher), January 1, 1949; children: Wade, Jr., Daniel Gregory, Michael Kenmar. *Education:* Sorbonne, University of Paris, certificat d'etudes, 1946; College of the Ozarks, B.A., 1947; Columbia University, M.A., 1949, Ed.D., 1956; also attended National University of Mexico, 1947, and Louisiana State University, 1948. *Politics:* Democrat. *Religion:* Presbyterian. *Home:* 1730 Oak Hills Dr., Durant, Okla. 74701. *Office:* Southeastern State College, Durant, Okla. 74701.

CAREER: College of the Ozarks, Clarksville, Ark., instructor in Romance languages, 1947-49; teacher in New Jersey public schools, 1949-52; Academy of Applied Linguistics, New York City, director of language teaching, 1951-56; Southern State College, Magnolia, Ark., assistant professor of foreign languages, 1956-59; Southeastern State College, Durant, Okla., associate professor, 1959-62, professor of foreign languages, 1962-74, head of department, 1959-62, adviser to foreign students, 1959-71. Teacher in New York City public schools, 1952-56. Originator and linguistics consultant, Choctaw Bilingual Education Program, 1968-71. Member, Oklahoma Commission for Improvement of Instruction, 1962-63. Elder of Presbyterian Church, 1962-74. *Military service:* U.S. Army, Eighth Armored Division, 1943-46.

MEMBER: American Association of Teachers of French (president of Oklahoma chapter, 1967), American Association of Teachers of Spanish and Portuguese (president of Oklahoma chapter, 1963), Modern Language Association of America, American Association of Teachers of German, South-Central Modern Language Association, Linguistic Circle of New York, Alpha Mu Gamma. *Awards, honors:* U.S. Department of State grant, 1947; Teacher of the Year, Southeastern State College faculty, 1963; Teacher of the Year, Blue Key (honorary student society), 1963; portrait hangs in International Portrait Gallery (New York).

WRITINGS—All published by Philosophical Library, except as noted: (Editor and author of foreword) *The Philosophy of Existentialism,* 1965, published as *Essays in Existentialism,* Citadel, 1967; (editor) *Of Human Freedom,* 1966; (editor) *Classics in Education,* 1966; (editor with G. Pat Powers) *New Outlooks in Psychology,* 1968; (with Powers) *Sex Education: Issues and Directives,* 1969; (with H. E. Wedeck) *Dictionary of Pagan Religions,* 1971; (with Wedeck) *Dictionary of Spiritualism,* 1971; *Dictionary of Satanism,* 1971; (compiler) *Classics in Chinese Philosophy,* 1972; (with Richard N. Runes) *Dictionary of Black Culture,* 1973; *The Sorcerer's Handbook,* 1974.

Editor and translator: Henri Bergson, *The Philosophy of Poetry,* 1959; Leonardo Da Vinci, *Philosophical Diary,* 1959; Voltaire, *Philosophical Dictionary,* 1961; Jean-Paul Sartre, *Essays in Aesthetics,* 1963; Andre Gide, *The White Notebook,* 1964; Gide, *Urien's Voyage,* 1964; Collin de Plancy, *Dictionary of Demonology,* 1965; de Plancy, *Dictionary of Witchcraft,* 1965; Marquis de Sade, *Crime of Passion,* Castle Books, 1965; Sartre, *The Wisdom of Jean-Paul Sartre: A Selection,* 1966; R. M. Alberes and Pierre de Boisdeffre, *Kafka: The Torment of Man,* 1968; Gide, *The Notebooks of Andre Walter,* P. Owen, 1968.

Translator: Paul Claudel, *The Essence of the Bible,* 1957; Andre Leroi-Gourhan, *Prehistoric Man,* 1957; Henri Bergson, *The World of Dreams,* 1958; Ferdinand de Saussure, *Course in General Linguistics,* 1959; Justus Streller, *To Freedom Condemned,* 1960; Alberes, *Philosopher without Faith,* 1961; Jean Rostand, *Human Heredity,* 1961; Emil Kraepelin, *One Hundred Years of Psychiatry,* 1962; Kurt

Kolle, *An Introduction to Psychiatry,* 1963; Emile Brehier, *History of Philosophy,* six volumes, University of Chicago Press, 1965-68.

Co-translator: (With Paul Selver) *Khrushchev of the Ukraine,* 1957; (with wife, Vlasta Baskin) Ernst Kretschmer, *Hysteria, Reflex and Instinct,* 1960.

Contributor: Robert E. Morrison, editor, *Primitive Existentialism,* 1968; Dagobert D. Runes, *Philosophy for Everyman,* 1969.

SIDELIGHTS: Baskin once told *CA:* "The Saussurean view of language has dominated my thinking for the past twenty years. I am still elaborating the consequences of Saussure's findings."†

(Died March 5, 1974)

* * *

BASS, Althea 1892-

PERSONAL: Born September 5, 1892, in Colfax, Ill.; daughter of Aaron and Tamazin (Roberts) Bierbower; married John Harvey Bass, August 25, 1917 (deceased); children: John Harvey, Jr. *Education:* University of Chicago, student, 1910-11; Fairmont College (now Wichita State University), Wichita, Kan., B.A., 1913; University of Oklahoma, M.A., 1921. *Politics:* Republican. *Religion:* Episcopalian. *Home:* 713 Cruce St., Norman, Okla. 73069.

CAREER Writer. *Member:* Association of American Indian Affairs, English-Speaking Union, Cherokee National Historical Society (life member), Oklahoma Historical Society (life member), Oklahoma Anthropoligical Society, Friends in Council of Chicago, Phi Beta Kappa, Delta Gamma. *Awards, honors:* Oklahoma Arts and Humanities Nonfiction Award, 1967.

WRITINGS: Now That the Hawthorn Blossoms, Humphries, 1931; *Cherokee Messenger,* University of Oklahoma Press, 1936, reprinted, 1968; *Young Inquirer,* Prairie, 1937; *A Cherokee Daughter of Mount Holyoke,* Prairie, 1937; *The Thankful People,* Caxton, 1950; *The Story of Tullahassee,* Semco Press, 1960; *The Arapaho Way,* C. N. Potter, 1966. Contributor of articles and fiction to *American Heritage, Saturday Review, Colophon, Sewanee Review, Woman's Day,* and other periodicals.

* * *

BASSETT, Richard 1900-

PERSONAL: Born February 21, 1900, in Durham, N.C.; son of John Spencer and Jessie (Lewellin) Bassett; married Henrietta Durant, September 10, 1937; married second wife, Claire Birge Albright, October 12, 1966; children: (first marriage) Edward. *Education:* Harvard University, A.B., 1919. *Politics:* Democrat. *Home:* 1017 Brook Rd., Milton, Mass. 02186.

CAREER: Milton Academy, Milton, Mass., head of art department, 1945-65. As a painter has had one-man shows in several cities including New York and Boston. *Military service:* U.S. Army, 1918, 1942-45; became captain. *Member:* National Association of Independent Schools (chairman of art committee, 1955-62; chairman of special committee on the teaching of art, 1960-65), Independent Schools Art Instructor Association (chairman, 1968-69), Harvard Club of Boston.

WRITINGS: (Editor) John Spencer Bassett, *A Short History of the United States,* Macmillan, 1939; (editor and contributor) *The Open Eye in Learning,* M.I.T. Press, 1969.

WORK IN PROGRESS: A history of the Independent Schools Art Instructor Association; studies in educational theory and the function of the humanities in education.

*   *   *

BATCHELDER, Howard T(imothy) 1909-

PERSONAL: Born November 24, 1909, in Greensboro Bend, Vt.; son of Carleton Harvey and Marcia Abigail (Fayer) Batchelder; married Mary Lockwood Sternenberg, August 27, 1931; children: William Howard, Robert Wesley. *Education:* West Texas State University, B.S., 1936; University of Michigan, A.M., 1938, Ph.D., 1942. *Home:* 1213 Pickwick Pl., Bloomington, Ind. 47401.

CAREER: School principal in Wildorado, Tex., 1931-34, Dimmitt, Tex., 1935-37; Mississippi State College for Women, Columbus, professor of social science and education, 1939-41, professor of education and head of department, 1942-43; Indiana University, School of Education, Bloomington, associate dean, beginning 1954, professor of education, beginning 1947. McGraw-Hill Book Co., editor of films in teacher education, 1945-57. *Military service:* U.S. Naval Reserve, 1942-46; became lieutenant commander. *Member:* National Education Association, American Association of University Professors, Phi Delta Kappa, Phi Kappa Phi, Pi Gamma Mu.

WRITINGS: (With Maurice McGlasson and Raleigh Schorling) *Student Teaching in Secondary Schools,* 4th edition (Batchelder not associated with earlier editions), McGraw, 1964. Contributor to educational journals.

AVOCATIONAL INTERESTS: Gardening, photography, and fishing.††

*   *   *

BAUDOUY, Michel-Aime 1909-

PERSONAL: Born April 1, 1909, in Le Vernet, Ariege, France; children: three. *Education:* Studied at Ecole Normale Superieure de l'Enseignement Technique in Paris, University of Toulouse, and Sorbonne, University of Paris. *Religion:* Roman Catholic.

CAREER: Novelist and writer for young people; professor of literature at Lycee Raspail, Paris, France. *Member:* Societe des Gens de Lettres, Societe des Auteurs et Compositeurs Dramatiques. *Awards, honors:* Prix de la Tribune de Paris, 1953, for children's literature; Prix Enfance du Monde, 1957; Prize, 1957, for play, "Pitie pour le Heros"; Prix de la Societe des Auteurs et Compositeurs Dramatiques, 1958; Honor Book award, Hans Christian Andersen International Children's Book Medal awards, 1960.

WRITINGS—Adult: *Nous n'etions que des hommes* (stories), Editions Stock, 1946; *Tandis que les peres* (novel), Calmann-Levy, 1948; *Le Ciel est bleu* (novel), Calmann-Levy, 1954; *La Quadrille Sarda* (novel), Plon, 1957; *J'ai vu naitre le France,* Editions du Temps, 1961; *Civilisation contemporaine: Aspects et problemes,* A. Hatier, 1965; *Europe, mon pays,* Editions de l'Amitie, 1967.

Youth books: *L'Enfant aux aigles,* translation by Audrey Clark published as *Noel and the Eagles,* Dent, 1955; *Bruno, roi de la montagne,* Editions de l'Amitie, 1953, translation by Marie Ponsot published as *Bruno, King of the Mountain,* Harcourt, 1960 (published in England as *Bruno, King of the Wild,* Bodley Head, 1962); *Les Vagabonds de la Marisma,* Editions de l'Amitie, 1955, translation by Gerard Hopkins published in England as *The Children of the Marshes,* Bodley Head, 1958, and in America under same title, Pan-

theon, 1959; *Les Princes du vent,* Rageot, 1956; *Le Seigneur des Hautes-Buttes,* Editions de l'Amitie, 1957, translation by Marie Ponsot published as *Old One-Toe,* Harcourt, 1959; *Mick et la P. 105,* Editions de l'Amitie, 1959, translation by Marie Ponsot published as *More than Courage,* Harcourt, 1961 (published in England as *Mick and the P. 105,* Bodley Head, 1961); *Le Chant de la voile.* Editions de l'Amitie, 1960; *Flashes sur le France,* Editions de l'Amitie, 1961, translation by Fanny Louise Neago published as *Deception at St.-Nazaire,* Harcourt, 1963 (published in England as *Tom and the S.S. France,* Bodley Head, 1964); *Mystere a Carnac,* Editions de l'Amitie, 1962, translation by Anne Carter published as *Secret of the Hidden Painting,* Harcourt, 1965; *Le "Onze" de mon village,* Editions de l'Amitie, 1963; *Zabo,* La Bacconniere, 1966; *Le Garcon du barrage,* translation by Thelma Niklaus published as *The Boy Who Belonged to No One,* Harcourt, 1967 (published in England as *The Boy on the Dam,* Brockhampton Press, 1970).

Plays: "Pitie pour le Heroes," first performed in Paris at Comedie de Paris, 1957. Also author of four plays produced on French radio and television.

SIDELIGHTS: Michel-Aime Baudouy wrote *L'Enfant aux aigles* while a prisoner of war in Germany in 1942. His books, translated into many languages, have brought him letters from young readers all over the world; he says that he has corresponded with a number of them.††

*   *   *

BAUER, Florence Marvyne

PERSONAL: Born in Elgin, Ill.; daughter of John Charles and Mary Rebecca (Williams) Chetwynd-Marvyne; married W. W. Bauer (a physician, writer, and lecturer), February 8, 1920; children: John R., Charles M., Ann (Mrs. Maurice Frederick Wetzel). *Education:* Studied at Church School of Art, Art Institute of Chicago, and Layton School of Art. *Politics:* Republican. *Religion:* Protestant. *Home and office:* Apartment 2230, 400 East Randolph St., Chicago, Ill. 60601.

CAREER: Writer. *Member:* National League of American Pen Women, Society of Midland Authors. *Awards, honors:* Friends of Literature Award in fiction, 1947, for *Behold Your King.*

WRITINGS: Behold Your King, Bobbs-Merrill, 1945 (chapter included in *The World Lives On,* Brentano, 1951); *Abram, Son of Terah,* Bobbs-Merrill, 1948 (chapter included in *The Old Testament and Fine Arts,* C. P. Maus, 1954); *Daughter of Nazareth,* Broadman, 1955; *Lady Besieged,* Bobbs-Merrill, 1960; (with husband, W. W. Bauer) *Way to Womanhood,* Doubleday, 1965; (with W. W. Bauer) *To Enjoy Marriage,* Doubleday, 1967. Writer of articles, plays for amateur productions, and radio scripts.

WORK IN PROGRESS: A novelette for Broadman, *Journey to Bethlehem.*†

*   *   *

BAUERNFEIND, Harry B. 1904-

PERSONAL: Born April 24, 1904, in St. Paul, Minn.; son of Samuel B. (a banker) and Ida (Wolf) Bauernfeind; married Georgianna Hoover (an organ and piano instructor), June 1, 1930; children: Lois (Mrs. Russell Peithman), John. *Education:* North Central College, B.S., 1926; graduate study at Ball State University, 1931, 1932, and Duquesne University, 1932, 1935; Northwestern University, M.A., 1943. *Religion:*

Presbyterian. *Home:* Crab Orchard Lake Rd., Carbondale, Ill. 62901.

CAREER: Northwestern University, Evanston, Ill., director of instruction, 1942-44; McGraw-Hill Book Co., Chicago, Ill., special representative, 1944-48; Gregg College, Chicago, Ill., dean of instruction, 1948-50; Detroit Business Institute, Detroit, Mich., director of education, 1950-51; Southern Illinois University, Carbondale, assistant dean of technical education, 1951-60, professor of business, beginning 1960. *Member:* American Vocational Association, National Business Teachers Association, Southern Illinois Business Teachers Association (past president), Illinois Vocational Association, Pi Omega Pi, Delta Pi Epsilon.

WRITINGS: Code Typing, Gregg Publishing Co., 1943; *How to Use Business Machines,* McGraw, 1961, 3rd edition, 1969. Contributor to professional journals.

WORK IN PROGRESS: Calculating Machines Laboratory, publication expected by Stipes.

*   *   *

BEACH, Charles Amory
[Collective pseudonym]

WRITINGS—"Air Service Boys" series; published by G. Sully: *Air Service Boys Flying for France,* 1918; *Air Service Boys over the Rhine,* 1918.

SIDELIGHTS: See **ADAMS, Harriet S., STRATEMEYER, Edward L.,** and **SVENSON, Andrew E.** †

*   *   *

BEAGLEHOLE, J(ohn) C(awte)   1901-1971

PERSONAL: Born June 13, 1901, in Wellington, New Zealand; son of David Ernest (a secretary and accountant) and Jane (Butler) Beaglehole; married Elsie Mary Holmes, February 17, 1930; children: John Robin, Timothy Holmes, Giles Cawte. *Education:* Victoria University of Wellington, B.A., 1923, M.A., 1924; University of London, Ph.D., 1929. *Politics:* Labour Party. *Home:* 6 Messines Rd., Wellington W.3, New Zealand.

CAREER: Tutor in and organizer of adult education programs in Otago and Waikato Districts, New Zealand, 1930-31; Auckland University College (now University of Auckland), Auckland, New Zealand, lecturer in history, 1932; Victoria University of Wellington, Wellington, New Zealand, lecturer, 1936-46, senior lecturer in history, 1947-48, senior research fellow and lecturer in colonial history, 1949-63, professor of British Commonwealth history, 1963-66, emeritus professor, 1967-71. Chairman of board of management, New Zealand University Press, 1947-61. President of New Zealand Council for Civil Liberties, beginning 1952; member of New Zealand Historic Places Trust, beginning 1955; member of New Zealand Arts Advisory Council, 1960-64. *Member:* Royal Society of New Zealand (fellow). *Awards, honors:* Condliffe Memorial Award of University of Canterbury, 1952; Gill Memorial Award of Royal Geographical Society, 1957; Companion of St. Michael and St. George, 1958; Ernest Scott Prize of University of Melbourne, 1962; D.Litt., Oxford University, 1966; Order of Merit, England, 1970.

WRITINGS: Captain Hobson and the New Zealand Company, Smith College Press, 1928; *The Exploration of the Pacific,* A. & C. Black, 1934, 3rd edition, Stanford University Press, 1966; *New Zealand: A Short History,* Allen & Unwin, 1936; *The University of New Zealand,* New Zealand Council for Educational Research, 1937; *The Discovery*

of New Zealand, New Zealand Department of Internal Affairs, 1939, 2nd edition, Oxford University Press, 1961; *Victoria University College: An Essay towards a History,* Victoria University College, 1949; (contributor) Peter Munz, editor, *The Feel of Truth: Essays in New Zealand and Pacific History,* A. H. & A. W. Reed for Victoria University, 1969; *The Life of Captain James Cook,* Stanford University Press, 1974.

Editor: *Abel Janszoon Tasman and the Discovery of New Zealand,* New Zealand Department of Internal Affairs, 1942; *New Zealand and the Statute of Westminster,* Victoria University College, 1944; *The Journals of Captain James Cook,* Cambridge University Press, Volume I: *The Voyage of the Endeavour,* 1955, Volume II: *The Voyage of the Resolution and Adventure,* 1961, Volume III: *The Voyage of the Resolution and Discovery,* 1967; *The Endeavour Journal of Joseph Banks,* two volumes, Public Library of New South Wales, 1962, 2nd edition, Angus & Robertson, 1963; Ruth M. Allen, *Nelson: A History of Early Settlement,* A. H. & A. W. Reed, 1965; G. Arnold Wood, *The Discovery of Australia,* Macmillan (Australia), 1969. Contributor to historical and geographical journals in New Zealand and abroad.

SIDELIGHTS: The Feel of Truth was presented to Beaglehole upon retirement from Victoria University of Wellington. At the time of his death, the *New York Times* said, "He was a musician, a poet, a mountain climber, a gardener, an art connoisseur, and a typographer."†

(Died October 10, 1971)

*   *   *

BECHTEL, Louise Seaman   1894-

PERSONAL: Surname is pronounced *Beck*-tel; born June 29, 1894, in Brooklyn, N.Y.; daughter of Charles Francis (a railroad accountant) and Anna (Van Brunt) Seaman; married Edwin De Turck Bechtel, February 28, 1929 (died, 1957). *Education:* Vassar College, A.B., 1915; Yale University, graduate study, 1915-18. *Home:* Bedford 4 Corners, Mount Kisco, N.Y.

CAREER: Macmillan Co., New York City, head of juvenile department, 1919-34; *New York Herald Tribune Book Review,* New York City, editor of reviews of children's books, 1949-56. *Member:* Metropolitan Museum of Art (fellow for life), Morgan Library (fellow), Bedford Garden Club (former president), Cosmopolitan Club, New York Botanical Garden.

WRITINGS: Books in Search of Children (R. R. Bowker Memorial Lecture), New York Public Library, 1946; *The Brave Bantam* (juvenile), Macmillan, 1946; *Mr. Peck's Pet's* (juvenile), Macmillan, 1947; *The Boy with the Star Lantern: Edwin De Turck Bechtel, 1880-1957* (memior), privately printed, 1960; *Books in Search of Children: Speeches and Essays,* compiled and with an introduction by Virginia Haviland, Macmillan, 1969. Writings include a pamphlet, ... *About Bedford Four Corners and Our Home on One Corner,* 1963. *Horn Book,* former associate editor, honorary director, beginning 1935.

SIDELIGHTS: The Brave Bantam has been translated into Norwegian.

*   *   *

BECKER, Albert B.   1903-1972

PERSONAL: Born November 12, 1903, in Pleasantville, Iowa; son of Elias and Elizabeth (Kommers) Becker; married Elizabeth Smith (a former teacher), July 16, 1942; children: John, David, Margaret, Paul. *Education:* Western Michigan University, B.A., 1927; University of Michigan, M.A., 1932; Northwestern University, Ph.D., 1949. *Religion:* United Methodist. *Home:* 404 East Bridge St., Plainwell, Mich. 49080.

CAREER: Rural teacher in Ottawa County, Mich., 1921-23; high school speech and English teacher in Hastings, Mich., 1927-37; Western Michigan University, Kalamazoo, began as instructor, became professor of speech. Member of Plainwell City Council. *Military service:* U.S. Army, 1942-43. *Member:* Michigan Speech Association (former president), Michigan Retired Teachers Association, Rotary.

WRITINGS: A School Assemblies Handbook, Western Michigan University, 1957; *Ideas for Your Next Assembly,* Western Michigan University, 1960; (with Karl F. Robinson) *Effective Speech for the Teacher,* McGraw, 1970.†

(Died, 1972)

*   *   *

BEER, Ethel S(ophia)   1897-1975

PERSONAL: Born May 14, 1897, in New York, N.Y.; daughter of Walter Eugene (a volunteer in charity organizations) and Bella (Nathan) Beer. *Education:* Educated at private schools in New York City, and then in France, 1912-14; also attended Columbia University, New York University, and New School for Social Research. *Home:* 41 Fifth Ave., New York, N.Y. 10003.

CAREER: Board member and volunteer social worker with various organizations in New York City, 1918-48; free-lance writer. *Member:* Society of Woman Geographers, National Council on Family Relations, National Committee for the Day Care of Children, National Conference of Social Work, International Conference of Social Work, National Book League (England), Women's Press Club (New York), Pen and Brush Club (New York).

WRITINGS: The Day Nursery, Dutton, 1938; *Working Mothers and the Day Nursery,* Morrow, 1957; *Marvelous Greece,* Walker & Co., 1967; *Greek Odyssey of an American Nurse: Adapted from the Unfinished Autobiography of Emilie Willms, R.N.,* Verry, 1973. Contributor of more than one hundred articles, primarily on the care of children of working mothers and on travel in Greece, to *Christian Science Monitor, Today's Health,* and to social work periodicals and metropolitan newspapers in United States and England.

WORK IN PROGRESS: Travel articles.†

(Died March 7, 1975)

*   *   *

BEHNKE, Charles A(lbert)   1891-

PERSONAL: Born September 21, 1891; son of Gustav (a packer) and Adeline (Palenske) Behnke; married Frieda Louise Neumann, August 14, 1918 (deceased); children: Anita Ruth (Mrs. Clifford Edward Sears), Lois Ruth (Mrs. David Amerman). *Education:* Attended Concordia College, Milwaukee, Wis. (graduate, summa cum honore), Concordia Seminary, St. Louis, Mo., and Colgate-Rochester Divinity School.

CAREER: Lutheran clergyman. Lutheran Church-Missouri Synod, Eastern district, vice-president, 1939-44, president, 1944-54, chairman of Board of Social Welfare, 1952-54, member of Board of European Affairs, 1955-61, member of

Chaplaincy Service Committee, beginning 1961. Served as interpreter and conducted services for German prisoners of war during World War II. *Member:* American Academy of Political and Social Science, Friends of the Rochester Public Library. *Awards, honors:* D.D., Concordia Seminary, St. Louis, Mo., 1946, for work in pastoral psychology.

WRITINGS: (With H. W. Bartels) *From Tragedy to Triumph,* Concordia, 1944; *New Frontiers for Spiritual Living,* Concordia, 1959; *Today and Tomorrow: Devotions for People Who are Growing with the Years,* Concordia, 1965. Editor, "Strength for the Day," devotional booklets for television program, "This Is the Life." Contributor to religious journals.

WORK IN PROGRESS: Through the Years, a devotional book for senior citizens.††

*   *   *

BELCASTRO, Joseph   1910-

PERSONAL: Born March 12, 1910, in St. John, Cosenza, Italy; son of Biagio (a shoe-cobbler) and Rose (Pisa) Belcastro; married Alberta Ida Cheeseman, August 20, 1939; children: David, Michael. *Education:* Attended Bethany College, Bethany, W.Va., 1930-31; Phillips University, A.B., 1934, M.A., 1935, B.D., 1936; Ohio State University, graduate study, 1937-40; Southern Baptist Theological Seminary, Ph.D., 1942. *Politics:* Democrat. *Home:* 129 South Napoleon Ave., Columbus, Ohio 42313.

CAREER: Clergyman of Disciples of Christ. East Columbus Christian Church, Columbus, Ohio, pastor, beginning 1942. *Member:* Disciples Ministerial Association, Masons, Lions Club, Sertoma Club. *Awards, honors:* D.Minn., Vanderbilt University, 1974.

WRITINGS: The Relationship of Baptism to Church Membership, Bethany Press, 1963.

WORK IN PROGRESS: A book, tentatively entitled *The Church Challenges the Charismatic-Tongues.*

*   *   *

BELLER, Jacob   1896-

PERSONAL: Born December 11, 1896, in Grodzisko, Austria; son of Nathan (a businessman) and Taube (Kalb) Beller; married Rachel Feingold, June 15, 1932. *Education:* Attended Hebrew Teachers Seminary, Lemberg, Austria, 1914-17, and Export Academy, Vienna, Austria, 1920-22; University of Buenos Aires, extention course in journalism, 1925-27. *Religion:* Hebrew.

CAREER: Free-lance journalist, editor, and author. Editor, *Journal of Hebrew Liturgy,* 1935; *Israeli Davar,* special correspondent in Latin America, 1948; *Hebrew Daily Journal,* Toronto, Ontario, managing editor, 1954-56; special correspondent in Latin America for *Toronto Globe and Mail,* Toronto, and *Jewish Daily Forward,* New York, N.Y., 1961. *Military service:* Austrian Army, World War I; became second lieutenant. *Awards, honors:* Surovich Award, Congress for Jewish Culture, New York, 1955, for *Across Twenty Latin American Countries.*

WRITINGS: From My Home Town (short stories), [London], 1927; *Over the Wide Oceans* (short stories), Hudson-LaPlata, 1942; *Eretz Israel, 1948,* Union Israelita de Galitzia en Buenos Aires, 1948; *Across Twenty Latin American Countries,* Editorial-Idisch, 1953; *Jews in Latin America,* Jonathan David, 1968. Contributor to *Heritage, Pioneer Women, World Over,* and to Jewish newspapers and periodicals in Canada, United States, and Latin America.

WORK IN PROGRESS: A history of the Inquisition and Crypto Jews in Spain, Portugal, and Latin America.

SIDELIGHTS: Beller has traveled as a journalist throughout North America, South and Central America, Portugal, Spain, Morocco, Israel, western Europe, England, and the Scandinavian countries.††

* * *

BENDIT, Laurence John 1898-1974

PERSONAL: Born May 14, 1898, in Marseille, France; son of Edmund (a merchant) and Emily (Westerman) Bendit; married P. D. Payne, September 15, 1939 (deceased); children: Michael, Deirdre Bendit Schweitzer. *Education:* Queen's College, Cambridge, M.A., 1920, M.D., B.Chir.; University College Hospital Medical School, London, M.R.C.S. and L.R.C.P., 1923; Maudsley Hospital, Diploma in Psychological Medicine, 1930. *Residence:* Ojai, Calif.

CAREER: Practiced medicine in England.

WRITINGS: (With wife, P. D. Payne) *The Psychic Sense,* Faber, 1943, Dutton, 1949, 2nd edition, Faber, 1958, Quest Books, 1967; *Paranormal Cognition,* Faber, 1944; (with P. D. Payne) *This World and That,* Faber, 1950, Theosophical Publishing, 1969; (with P. D. Payne) *Man Incarnate,* Theosophical Publishing, 1957, published as *The Etheric Body of Man,* 1977; *Man and His Universe,* Theosophical Publishing, 1957; *Key Words of the Wisdom of Tradition,* Theosophical Publishing, 1963; *The Mirror of Life and Death,* Theosophical Publishing, 1965; *The Changing Face of Theosophy and Other Articles,* Theosophical Publishing, 1965; *Self-Knowledge: A Yoga for the West,* Quest Books, 1967; (with P. D. Payne) *The Transforming Mind,* Theosophical Publishing, 1970; *The Mysteries Today, and Other Essays,* Theosophical Publishing, 1973. Author of a number of pamphlets, and contributor of articles to journals.

SIDELIGHTS: Bendit traveled in India and Europe.†

(Died September, 1974)

* * *

BENEDICT, Lois Trimble 1902-1967

PERSONAL: Born June 29, 1902, in North Tonawanda, N.Y.; daughter of William D. (a real estate man) and Bertha (Todd) Trimble; married Clinton S. Benedict (a civil engineer); children: Clinton S., Jr. *Education:* Buffalo State Teachers College, Diploma and Life Teaching Certificate, 1923; Simpson College, B.A., 1925. *Religion:* Methodist. *Home:* 23 High St., Katonah, N.Y. 10536.

CAREER: Elementary teacher in Katonah, N.Y., before marriage; operator of private kindergarden in her home, Katonah, N.Y., 1932-40; writer for young people. *Member:* National League of American Pen Women, Woman's Society of Christian Service (secretary of New York conference), Woman's Civic Club (Katonah), Lionets, King's Daughters.

WRITINGS: Canalboat Mystery, Atheneum, 1963. Writer of church school teacher's guides published by Friendship. Contributor of thirty stories and forty articles to *Scholastic Magazine, Boys' Life, Child Guidance, Juniors, Horticulture, Instructor, McCall's Needlework,* and other educational and denominational magazines (Catholic, Jewish, and Baptist, as well as Methodist).

WORK IN PROGRESS: A book on falconry and history of

the early settlement of Iceland; a book on scavenger animals, birds, and fish of the world.††

(Died April 8, 1967)

* * *

BENNETT, Frances Grant 1899-

PERSONAL: Born September 23, 1899, in Salt Lake City, Utah; daughter of Heber Jeddy (a minister) and Emily (Wells) Grant; married Wallace F. Bennett (a U.S. Senator), September 6, 1922; children: Wallace G., Rosemary (Mrs. Robert C. Fletcher), David W., Frances (Mrs. Lawrence S. Jeppson), Robert F. *Education:* Radcliffe College, special student, 1919, 1920-21; University of Utah, A.B., 1921. *Politics:* Republican. *Religion:* Mormon.

WRITINGS: Glimpses of a Mormon Family, Deseret, 1968.

* * *

BENNETT, Melba Berry 1901-1968

PERSONAL: Born August 2, 1901, in Los Angeles, Calif.; daughter of William Henry and Edna (Bush) Berry; married Frank H. Bennett, May 11, 1921; children: Peter, Ethel (Mrs. Ralph Busch, Jr.). *Education:* Attended Stanford University, 1918-21. *Politics:* Republican. *Religion:* Episcopalian. *Home:* 10 Lakeview Circle, Palm Springs, Calif.

CAREER: Writer. Lecturer in literature and politics to professional groups and students, 1935-68; trustee, Welwood Murray Memorial Library, Palm Springs, Calif., 1950-64; member of executive board, Occidental College Library, 1967-68. *Member:* Palm Springs Historical Society (president), Robinson Jeffers Society (president), Alpha Phi. *Awards, honors:* Literature Award, Commonwealth Club of California, 1966.

WRITINGS: Robinson Jeffers and the Sea, Grabhorn Press, 1936, reprinted, Folcroft Library Editions, 1971; *Often I Wonder* (poetry), Quercus Press, 1939; *In Review* (poetry), Grabhorn Press, 1946; *The Stone Mason of Tor House,* Ward Ritchie, 1966. Also author of "Palm Springs Garden Book," 1957, and "Historical Libraries of Europe" (series of monographs), Anthoensen Press, 1958-66.

WORK IN PROGRESS: A history of Palm Springs; further work on "Historical Libraries of Europe" series.†

(Died September 15, 1968)

* * *

BENNETT, Mildred R. 1909-

PERSONAL: Born September 8, 1909, in Elk Point, S.D.; daughter of Bert and Mary (Rowland) Rhoads; married Wilbur K. Bennett (a physician and surgeon), May 17, 1934; children: William G., Alicia Ann Engstrom. *Education:* Union College, Lincoln, Neb., B.A., 1931; University of Nebraska, M.A., 1938. *Religion:* Congregational. *Home:* 329 North Cedar, Red Cloud, Neb. 68970.

CAREER: Teacher of Spanish and English in Union College Preparatory School, Lincoln, Neb., 1931-32, and Inavale, Neb., 1932-34; Orthopedic Hospital, Lincoln, member of occupational therapy staff, 1935-38; Nebraska School for the Deaf, Omaha, teacher of reading and English, 1938-42. Co-organizer of drive to establish Willa Cather Pioneer Memorial in Red Cloud, Neb., 1955, and active since in supporting the memorial building. *Member:* National League of American Pen Women (Nebraska president, 1963), Nebraska Writers Guild (president, 1958-60), American Name Society, Nebraska Folklore Society. *Awards, honors:* National League of American Pen Women prize, 1960, for article on Willa Cather in *Prairie Schooner.*

WRITINGS: The World of Willa Cather, Dodd, 1951, paperback edition with additional notes, University of Nebraska Press, 1961; (editor and author of notes and commentary) *Early Stories of Willa Cather,* Apollo, 1957; (author of introduction) *Collected Short Fiction of Willa Cather,* University of Nebraska Press, 1965. Publications include Cliff's study guides for Willa Cather's *My Antonia* and *Death Comes to the Archbishop.* Contributor to *Collier's Encyclopedia.*

WORK IN PROGRESS: A book on Willa Cather for young people; a juvenile about a deaf boy's efforts to earn a Ph.D.

SIDELIGHTS: Bennett's research on Willa Cather began when she was teaching school in Inavale, Neb., and living among children of the people about whom Miss Cather wrote.

*   *   *

BENTEL, Pearl B(ucklen)   1901-

PERSONAL: Born October 23, 1901, in Rochester, Pa.; daughter of George Louis and Carrie (Veiock) Bucklen; married Charles Albert Bentel, March 10, 1925; children: Barbara (Mrs. Myles N. Murray), Susan (Mrs. Richard T. Bieniasz). *Education:* Attended University of Pittsburgh in 1920's, 1940's and 1950's and Microphone Playhouse, Pittsburgh, 1940. *Religion:* Protestant. *Agent:* Betty J. Russell, Russylvania, R.R. 1, Valparaiso, Ind. 46383.

CAREER: Clerk for industrial firm, Freedom, Pa., 1918-25; copywriter for advertising agency, Pittsburgh, Pa., 1941; continuity writer for Radio Station WWSW, Pittsburgh, 1942-44; writer of two hundred-episode radio serial, "Happiness Ahead," aired in Pittsburgh, with Gimbel Brothers as sponsor, 1946-47; writer for teens and young adults, beginning 1952. *Member:* Authors Guild.

WRITINGS: Program for Christine (Junior Literary Guild selection), Longmans, Green, 1953; *I'll Know My Love,* Longmans, Green, 1955; *Freshman at Large,* Longmans, Green, 1959; *Co-Ed Off Campus,* McKay, 1965.

WORK IN PROGRESS: Third book in college-girl series ("being a procrastinator, cannot guess when it will be finished").

SIDELIGHTS: Pearl Bentel told *CA:* "All my books have been inspired by teen-agers I have known. Digging out their stories is exciting." *Avocational interests:* Camping and tramping through national parks and forest camps in America, and camping in Europe.††

*   *   *

BERGEL, Egon Ernst   1894-1969

PERSONAL: Born November 6, 1894, in Vienna, Austria; came to United States in 1938, naturalized in 1944; married Emma Jahoda (a psychologist), April 7, 1923; children: Susanne (Mrs. John B. Mitchell), Ernest W. *Education:* University of Vienna, Dr.Jur., 1918, studies in philosophy, 1919-22; Harvard University, M.A., 1941, Ph.D., 1942. *Politics:* Independent. *Religion:* Protestant. *Home:* 730 Riverside Dr., New York, N.Y. 10031. *Office:* C. W. Post College, Long Island University, Brookville, N.Y.

CAREER: Attorney-at-law in Vienna, Austria, 1923-38; Friends University, Wichita, Kan., professor of sociology, 1942-44; U.S. Office of War Information, Washington, D.C., control editor, 1944-45; Montclair (N.Y.) Development Board, research consultant, 1946; Whitman College, Walla Walla, Wash., associate professor of sociology, 1946-

47; Springfield College, Springfield, Mass., professor of sociology and chairman of department of social sciences, 1947-63; Long Island University, C. W. Post College, Brookville, N.Y., professor of sociology, 1963-69. Visiting professor, University of Vienna, 1962. *Member:* American Sociological Association, American Association of University Professors, Eastern Sociological Association.

WRITINGS: System der Koerperschaftssteuer, Manz (Vienna), 1931; *Urban Sociology,* McGraw, 1955; *Social Stratification,* McGraw, 1962; (contributor) T.K.K.N. Unnithan and others, editors, *Towards a Sociology of Culture in India: Essays in Honour of Professor D. P. Mukerji,* Prentice-Hall, 1965. Contributor to *Slavonic Encyclopedia;* also contributor of articles to journals.

WORK IN PROGRESS: Principles of Sociology.

SIDELIGHTS: Urban Sociology has also been published in Spanish.

BIOGRAPHICAL/CRITICAL SOURCES: New York Times, October 26, 1969.†

(Died October 24, 1969)

*   *   *

BERGONZO, Jean Louis   1939-19(?)

PERSONAL: Born August 17, 1939, in Paris, France; son of Jean (a postal inspector) and Odette (Richard) Bergonzo; married Marie Christine Robin, May 6, 1961; children: Eleonore, Jerome. *Education:* Attended Ecole Communale; awarded bachelor's degrees from both Lycee Charlemagne and Lycee Henri IV; Faculte des Lettres, licence de philosophie. *Politics:* Left. *Religion:* Non-practicing Catholic. *Home:* 5 rue Chabanais, Paris 2e, France.

CAREER: Lycee Camille See, Paris, France, and Lycee Carnot Turgot, Paris, professor, 1961-64; *Siemens,* Paris, member of publicity staff, 1965-70; Mohawk Data Science, France, advertising manager, beginning 1970.

WRITINGS: L'Auberge espagnole, Editions de Minuit, 1966, translation by Helen R. Lane published as *The Spanish Inn,* Grove, 1968; *Les Murs du havre* (novel), Gallimard, 1969. Also author of a radio play, "Les Voyageurs," produced by station ORTF.

WORK IN PROGRESS: A novel, as yet untitled, and "perhaps a play."

SIDELIGHTS: Bergonzo told *CA* that he likes vacations, the movies, music, and cars, and that he is also very fond of sleeping. He added that he is interested in politics and that he would like to work in publishing. Bergonzo said he finds writing very difficult because he's lazy. He commented, however, that he would like to try writing for the cinema.

BIOGRAPHICAL/CRITICAL SOURCES: Combat, September 9, 1966; *La Quizaine Litteraire,* September 15, 1966; *La Tribune des Nations,* September 16, 1966; *L'Express,* September 26, 1966; *Arts-Loisirs,* September, 1966; *Le Monde,* October 8, 1966; *Le Figaro,* October 17, 1966; *Le Figaro Litteraire,* October 27, 1966; *Le Nouvel Observateur,* November 2, 1966; *Realites,* November, 1966.†

(Deceased)

*   *   *

BERKEMEYER, William C.   1908-

PERSONAL: Born April 18, 1908, in Allentown, Pa.; son of Charles F. (a newspaperman) and Emma P. (Clauss) Berkemeyer; married Mary Frances Hausman, October 14, 1936.

Education: Muhlenberg College, A.B., 1929; Lutheran Theological Seminary, Philadelphia, B.D., 1932, S.T.M., 1934. *Home and office:* 232 West Albemerle Ave., Lansdowne, Pa.

CAREER: Clergyman of Lutheran Church, beginning 1932. St. Matthew's Evangelical Lutheran Church, Bethlehem, Pa., pastor, 1936-61; Grace Evangelical Lutheran Church, Drexel Hill, Pa., pastor, 1961-73; consultant to Division for Mission in North America, Lutheran Church in America, beginning 1973. Part-time instructor in New Testament at Lutheran Theological Seminary, Philadelphia, Pa., 1932-34, Lutheran Theological Seminary, Gettysburg, Pa., 1947-48, and Moravian Theological Seminary, Bethlehem, 1948-50. Chairman of board, Philadelphia Lutheran Seminar, member of board, Board of College Education of Lutheran Church in America, Mary J. Drexel Home and Deaconess Motherhouse, and Muhlenberg College. *Member:* Society of Biblical Literature, Hymn Society of America, Lutheran Society for Worship, Music and the Arts, American Guild of Organists. *Awards, honors:* D.D., Muhlenberg College, 1953.

WRITINGS: (Contributor) Herbert Alleman, editor, *The Lutheran Commentary,* Fortress, 1936; *Diary of a Disciple,* Fortress, 1954; *Paul's Gospel* (adult education course), Fortress, 1967. Writer of study units; contributor to religious journals.

AVOCATIONAL INTERESTS: Music (former member of Bethlehem Bach Choir and Philadelphia Chamber Chorus).

* * *

BERKEY, Helen 1898-

PERSONAL: Born July 18, 1898, in St. Paul, Minn.; daughter of Charles Walter (a news bureau telegrapher) and Edna I. (Baldwin) Lamar; married Ira F. Berkey (a teacher), August 25, 1920 (deceased); children: Peter Andrew. *Education:* Studied at Reed College, two years; also studied summers at University of Hawaii, University of Oregon, and University of California, Berkeley. *Politics:* Republican. *Religion:* Congregational. *Home:* 1020 Green St., No. 413, Honolulu, Hawaii 96822. *Office:* Mutual of Omaha, 830 Ala Moana, Honolulu, Hawaii.

CAREER: Paradise of the Pacific, Honolulu, Hawaii, feature writer, 1945-51; Mutual of Omaha (insurance), saleswoman in Honolulu, beginning 1951. *Member:* Pan Pacific Women, Republican Club (Honolulu), Honolulu Community Theatre.

WRITINGS: Mele and the Firewoman, Tongg, 1940; *Ghost Dog,* Advertiser, 1942; *Aunty Penan's Banyan Tree,* Tuttle, 1967; *Hawaiian Tales,* C. E. Merrill, 1968; *Secret Cave of Kamanawa,* Tuttle, 1968. Also author of *Katsu the Fisherman: Tuna Fishing in Hawaii,* with Deborah Woodhull, 1940. Contributor to *Beacon* (Honolulu). Editor of *To Do Today* during World War II.

WORK IN PROGRESS: The Little Temple of Pu-u-ka-pu; a novel, *A House in a Thousand Palms.*††

* * *

BERLE, Adolf A(ugustus) 1895-1971

PERSONAL: Born January 29, 1895, in Boston, Mass.; son of Adolf A. (a minister) and Mary Augusta (Wright) Berle; married Beatrice Bend Bishop (a physician), December 17, 1927; children: Alice (Mrs. Clan Crawford), Beatrice (Mrs. Dean Meyerson), Peter A. A. *Education:* Harvard University, A.B., 1913, A.M., 1914, LL.B., 1916. *Politics:* Demo-

crat. *Religion:* Protestant. *Home:* 142 East 19th St., New York, N.Y. 10003. *Office:* Berle & Berle, 70 Pine St., New York, N.Y. 10005.

CAREER: Practice of law in Boston, Mass., 1916-17; senior partner in Berle, Berle & Brunner, and successor law firms of Berle, Berle, Agee & Land, and Berle & Berle, New York City, 1919-70. Columbia University School of Law, New York City, professor of corporation law, 1927-64, professor emeritus, 1964-71. Expert on staff, American Committee to Negotiate Peace with Germany, 1918-19; special counsel, Reconstruction Finance Corporation, 1933-38; assistant U.S. Secretary of State, 1938-44; U.S. Ambassador to Brazil, 1945-46; co-founder and chairman of liberal party, 1952-55; special assistant to Secretary of State, 1961, and chairman of President Kennedy's Task Force on Latin American Policy. Sucrest Corp., director, treasurer, and chairman of board, 1946-65, consultant, 1966-71; past director and counsel, Savings Bank Trust Co.; director of Nationwide Corp., and Michigan Life Insurance Co. Trustee and chairman of board, Twentieth Century Fund, 1935-71. *Military service:* U.S. Army, 1917-19; became first lieutenant.

MEMBER: American Philosophical Society, Council on Foreign Relations, Pan American Society of the United States, Phi Beta Kappa, Century Association, Army and Navy Club, Harvard Club of New York City. *Awards, honors:* Received Southern Cross from government of Brazil; Page One Award in Public Affairs, from New York Newspaper Guild, 1960, for "persistent fight for freedom in the world." LL.D. from Oberlin College, Yankton College, Wesleyan University, Columbia University, Queens University of Kingston, University of the Andes, and University of Aix-Marseilles; Doctor Honoris Causa, University of Brazil.

WRITINGS: Studies in the Law of Corporations Finance, Callaghan & Co., 1928; *Cases and Materials in the Law of Corporation Finance,* West Publishing, 1930, new edition, R. F. Magill, 1942; (with Gardiner C. Means) *The Modern Corporation and Private Property,* Macmillan, 1932, revised edition, Harcourt, 1968; (editor with C. Wilcox, H. F. Fraser, and P. M. Makin) *America's Recovery Program,* Oxford University Press, 1934; (with Victoria J. Pederson) *Liquid Claims and National Wealth: An Exploratory Study in the Theory of Liquidity,* Macmillan, 1934; *L'Homme et la propriete: Resolution du systeme de la propriete,* Hermann, 1939.

New Directions in the New World, Harper, 1940; *National Realism and Christian Faith,* American Unitarian Association, 1940; (editor with William C. Warren) *Cases and Materials on the Law of Business Organizations (Corporations),* Foundation Press, 1947.

Natural Selection of Political Forces, University of Kansas Press, 1950, revised edition, 1968; *The Emerging Common Law of Free Enterprise: Antidote to the Omnipotent State?,* Brandeis Lawyers' Society, 1951; *The Twentieth-Century Capitalist Revolution,* Harcourt, 1954; (contributor) A. W. Macmakon, editor, *Federalism Mature and Emergent,* Doubleday, 1955; *Economic Power and the Free Society,* Fund for the Republic, 1957; *Tides of Crisis: A Primer of Foreign Relations,* Reynal, 1957, published as *A Primer of Foreign Relations: Tides of Crisis,* Apollo Editions, 1962; (contributor) Walter Mills and John Courtney Murray, editors, *Foreign Policy and the Free Society,* Oceana, 1958; *The Bank the Banks Built: The Story of Savings Banks Trust Company, 1933-58,* Harper, 1959; *Power without Pro-*

perty: A New Development in American Political Economy, Harcourt, 1959.

The Motive Power of Political Economy, New York Society for Ethical Culture, 1960; *Background Readings on Planned Growth and a Free Market Economy,* [New York], 1960; *The Cold War in America,* Storrs, 1961; *Latin America: Diplomacy and Reality,* Harper, 1962; *The American Economic Republic,* Harcourt, 1965; *The Three Faces of Power* (essays), Harcourt, 1968; *Power* (includes the essays originally published as *The Three Faces of Power*), Harcourt, 1969; *Leaning against the Dawn: An Appreciation of the Twentieth Century Fund and Its Fifty Years of Adventure in Seeking to Influence American Development toward a More Effectively Just Civilization, 1919-1969,* Twentieth Century Fund, 1969. Also editor, with others, of *Hungary under Soviet Rule: A Survey of Developments,* 1957, *Hungary under Soviet Rule III: A Survey of Developments from the Revolution to August 1959, with Special Annex: Tibet—An Asian Hungary,* 1959, *Hungary under Soviet Rule IV: A Survey of Developments from August 1959 to August 1960,* c. 1960, and *The Unresolved Case of Soviet-Occupied Hungary, 1956-63: Hungary under Soviet Rule VII,* 1963. Contributor to *Enclopedie Francaise,* and to publications, including *Reporter* and *New York Times.*

SIDELIGHTS: The Modern Corporation and Private Property is considered by many to be a classic in its field. It was originally written in 1932, and the 1968 revision, although it left the basic text unchanged, offered new prefaces by both authors, and a new statistical appendix. Robert Lekachman noted, in his review of the 1968 edition, that Berle and Means "struck a blow, possibly decisive, at the school which has sought early and late to break up large corporations and restore a regime of atomistic competition. For even in describing desirable corporate reforms, [they] were affirming the legitimacy of the large corporation as very nearly a sovereign economic power."

"Throughout his book," wrote William S. Schlamm of *Power,* "Mr. Berle's intelligence, the nobility of his purpose, the accuracy of his recollections remain undisputable. Yet the book, though its literary form is the recapitulation of personal experience in public office (over the impressively long period 1917 to 1969), demands and merits attention as a definitive scholarly study of power—and it may well be the book on power to end all books on power. For here it is all displayed, all the knowledge and all the insight of contemporary 'political science.'" "Those who might object," Schlamm continued, "that a philosophical essay ought to be judged on the basis of its content, not its language, fail to see that language is the only observable dimension of truth; so that nothing that is badly expressed can be well thought out. I begin with a few observations on Berle's . . . style because this is the only book I know that succeeds . . . in presenting lean and recognizable truth. This is quite a problem, one must admit; and, in pondering it, I have arrived, I think, at a stunning conclusion: if a valid theory of power can be successfully stated in the style and language of camp, then the theory itself may be camp. Mr. Berle, in short, by convincing me of the adequacy of his comprehension of power, has also convinced me that our comprehension of power is inadequate. And I urgently recommend his book, not only because it is a surprising victory of thought over language, but also because, for this very reason, it questions the validity of our (his) thoughts on power."

Berle recorded "The Bill of Rights and the Economic Republic" for Center for the Study of Democratic Institutions.

BIOGRAPHICAL/CRITICAL SOURCES: New York Times Book Review, September 15, 1968; *Time,* October 31, 1969, March 1, 1971; *National Review,* December 17, 1969; *New York Times,* February 19, 1971; *Newsweek,* March 1, 1971.†

(Died February 17, 1971)

*   *   *

BERNSTEIN, Jerry Marx   1908-1969
(Jerry Marx)

PERSONAL: Born June 7, 1908, in Niagara Falls, N.Y.; son of Morris J. (a jeweler) and Sophia (Marx) Bernstein; married Carolyn Gugino (a dental assistant), March 19, 1944; children: Carol Louise (Mrs. Calvin Davis). *Education:* University of Wisconsin, student, 1927-30. *Religion:* Unitarian Universalist. *Office:* Oklahoma Department of Public Safety, Oklahoma City, Okla. 73111.

CAREER: Radio Station KTHS, Hot Springs, Ark., announcer, 1937-43; Radio Station KOMA, Oklahoma City, Okla., news director, 1943-49; Oklahoma Department of Public Safety, Oklahoma City, director of public information, 1949-69. *Member:* American Society of Safety Engineers, Association of State and Provincial Safety Coordinators, Oklahoma Council of Safety Supervisors, Sigma Delta Chi.

*WRITINGS—*Under name Jerry Marx: *Officer, Tell Your Story,* C. C Thomas, 1967. Associate editor, *Oklahoma Peace Officer.*

WORK IN PROGRESS: Short stories.††

(Died August 12, 1969)

*   *   *

BERRY, Katherine F(iske)   1877-19(?)

PERSONAL: Born August 31, 1877, in Bath, Me.; daughter of John Cutting (a missionary doctor) and Maria (Gove) Berry. *Education:* Attended Doshisha Girls' School in Japan, and schools in Germany and Massachusetts; Smith College, A.B., 1902. *Politics:* Republican. *Religion:* Congregational. *Home:* 36 Roxbury St., Worcester, Mass. 01609; (summer) Wynburg on the New Meadows, Star Route 4, Bath, Me.

CAREER: Lived in Okayama and Kyoto, Japan, until 1893; returned to Japan to teach at Doshisha Girls' School, Kyoto, 1919-20; back home in Worcester, Mass., wrote travelogues for radio, and free-lance feature articles for *Worcester-Telegram-Gazette* for many years. Organizer of Worcester Children's World Friendship Committee; member of Salisbury Associates of Worcester Art Museum, Worcester Science Museum, and Friends of the Worcester Public Library. *Member:* National League of American Pen Women (past president of Worcester branch; past director of New England region), Pen and Brush Club (New York), Victoria Society of Maine Women, Phippsburg Historical Society (Maine). *Awards, honors:* First prize in National League of American Pen Women Life Sketch Contest, 1958.

WRITINGS: A Pioneer Doctor in Old Japan, Revell, 1940; *Camping Characters on Casco Bay,* Falmouth Publishing, 1954; *Katie-san—From Maine Pastures to Japan Shores,* Dresser, 1963. Author of radio scripts and a children's pageant.†

(Deceased)

BERRY, William Turner 1888-

PERSONAL: Born August 19, 1888, in Wandsworth, London, England; son of John (a saddler) and Fanny Frances (Turner) Berry; married Amelia Johnson, 1920; children: Richard, Olive Berry Waters. *Education:* Studied at London School of Economics and Political Science, 1909-11, and took other classes in librarianship. *Religion:* Church of England. *Home:* Crossways, Newnham Sittingbourne, Kent, England.

CAREER: Lambeth Libraries, London, England, library assistant, 1908-12; St. Bride Printing Library, London, librarian, 1913, 1919-57. *Military service:* British Army, 1914-19; served in East African campaign. *Member:* Typographers Guild (honorary), Double Crown Club (honorary), Gallery Club (honorary).

WRITINGS: (With A. F. Johnson) *Catalogue of Specimens of Printing Types of English and Scottish Foundries 1665-1830,* Oxford University Press, 1935; (with Johnson) *Encyclopaedia of Type Faces,* Blandford, 1953, 4th edition, 1969; (with H. Edmund Poole) *Annals of Printing,* Blandford, 1966.

AVOCATIONAL INTERESTS: Gardening, water-color painting.

* * *

BEST, (Evangel) Allena Champlin 1892-1974 (Erick Berry, Anne Maxon)

PERSONAL: Born January 4, 1892, in New Bedford, Mass.; daughter of George Greenman (a librarian) and May (Allen) Champlin; married Carroll Thayer Berry, January 4, 1916; married second husband, Herbert Best (a writer), July 12, 1926; children: (first marriage) Allen Carroll Berry (deceased). *Education:* Attended Albany Academy for Girls, Albany, N.Y., Pennsylvania Academy of Fine Arts, and various art schools in New York and Paris. *Religion:* Protestant. *Residence:* Sharon, Conn. 06069.

CAREER: Author and illustrator, writing primarily for young people. *Member:* Society of Women Geographers.

WRITINGS—Under pseudonym Erick Berry, with one exception noted; almost all books self-illustrated: *Girls in Africa,* Macmillan, 1928; *Black Folk Tales: Retold from the Haussa of Northern Nigeria, West Africa,* Harper, 1928.

Penny-Whistle, Macmillan, 1930; *Illustrations of Cynthia: A Story of an Art School,* Harcourt, 1931; *Mom Du Jus: The Story of a Little Black Doll,* Doubleday, Doran, 1931; *Humbo the Hippo and the Little Boy-Bumbo,* Harper, 1932; *Careers of Cynthia,* Harcourt, 1932; *Juma of the Hills: A Story of West Africa,* Harcourt, 1932; *The Winged Girl of Knossos,* Appleton, 1933; (under pseudonym Anne Maxon; illustrations under pseudonym Erick Berry) *The House that Jill Built,* Dodd, 1934; *Sojo: The Story of Little Lazy-Bones,* Harper, 1934; *Strings to Adventure,* Lothrop, 1935; *Sunhelmet Sue,* Lothrop, 1936; *Cynthia Steps Out,* Goldsmith, 1937; *Homespun,* Lothrop, 1937; *Nancy Herself,* Goldsmith, 1937; *Honey of the Nile,* Oxford University Press, 1938, revised edition, Viking, 1963; *Your Cup and Saucer,* Thomas Nelson, 1938; *One-String Fiddle* (music by Lilian Webster), Winston, 1939; *The Potter's Wheel,* Thomas Nelson, 1939; *Go and Find the Wind,* Oxford University Press, 1939.

Lock Her Through, Oxford University Press, 1940; *The Tinmaker Man of New Amsterdam,* Winston, 1941; *Mad Dogs and Englishmen,* M. Joseph, 1941; *Hudson Frontier,* Oxford University Press, 1942; *There Is the Land,* Oxford University Press, 1943; (with husband, Herbert Best) *Concertina Farm,* M. Joseph, 1943; *Hearth-stone in the Wilderness,* Macmillan, 1944 (published in England as *Flight of the Wild Goose,* Hutchinson, 1946); *Harvest of the Hudson,* Macmillan, 1945; *A Pretty Little Doll,* Oxford University Press, 1946; *The Little Farm in the Big City,* Viking, 1947; (with H. Best) *Writing for Children,* Viking, 1947, 2nd edition, University of Miami Press, 1964; *Seven Beaver Skins, a Story of the Dutch in New Amsterdam,* Winston, 1948; *Forty-seven Keys,* Macmillan, 1949.

The Road Runs Both Ways, Macmillan, 1950; *Sybil Ludington's Ride,* Viking, 1952; *The Wavering Flame: Connecticut, 1776,* Scribner, 1953; *Hay-foot, Straw-foot,* Viking, 1954; *Green Door to the Sea,* Viking, 1955; *Horses for the General,* Macmillan, 1956; *The King's Jewel,* Viking, 1957; *The Land and People of Finland,* Lippincott, 1959, revised edition, 1972; *Beckoning Landfall,* Day, 1959; *Men, Moss, and Reindeer: The Challenge of Lapland,* Coward, 1959; *The Land and People of Iceland,* Lippincott, 1959, revised edition, 1972.

Stars in My Pocket (juvenile novel based on the life of Maria Mitchell), Day, 1960; *Leif the Lucky, Discoverer of America,* Garrard, 1961; *Valiant Captive: A Story of Margaret Eames, Captured in 1676 by the Indians,* Chilton, 1962; *Robert E. Peary, North Pole Conqueror,* Garrard, 1963; *Eating and Cooking Around the World,* Day, 1963; *The Four Londons of William Hogarth,* McKay, 1964; *You Have to Go Out!: The Story of the United States Coast Guard,* McKay, 1964; *Charles Proteus Steinmetz, Wizard of Electricity,* Macmillan, 1966; *Mr. Arctic: An Account of Vilhjalmur Stefansson,* McKay, 1966; *The Springing of the Rice: A Story of Thailand,* Macmillan, 1966; *When Wagon Trains Rolled to Santa Fe,* Garrard, 1966; *Underwater Warriors: Story of the American Frogmen,* McKay, 1967; (with H. Best) *Men Who Changed the Map,* Funk, Volume I, 1968; (with H. Best) *Polynesian Triangle,* Funk, 1968; *The Magic Banana and Other Polynesian Tales,* Day, 1968; *A World Explorer, Fridtjof Nansen,* Garrard, 1969; *The Valiant Little Potter,* Ginn, 1973.

Books by Herbert Best illustrated by Erick Berry include: *Garram the Hunter: A Boy of the Hill Tribes,* Doubleday, Doran, 1930; *Son of the White Man,* Doubleday, Doran, 1931; *Garram the Chief: The Story of the Hill Tribes,* Doubleday, Doran, 1932; *The Mystery of the Flaming Hut,* Harper, 1932; *Flag of the Desert,* Viking, 1936; *Tal of the Four Tribes,* Doubleday, Doran, 1938; *The Gunsmith's Boy,* Winston, 1942; *The Long Portage: A Story of Ticonderoga and Lord Howe,* Viking, 1948 (published in England as *The Road to Ticonderoga,* Penguin, 1954); *Watergate: A Story of the Irish on the Erie Canal,* Winston, 1951; *Not Without Danger: A Story of the Colony of Jamaica in Revolutionary Days,* Viking, 1951; *Ranger's Ransom: A Story of Ticonderoga,* Aladdin Books, 1953.

Other books illustrated: Gertrude Robinson, *White Heron Feather,* Harper, 1930; Felicite Lefevre (pseudonym of Margaret Smith-Masters), *Little Henry and the Tiger,* Harper, 1931; Veronica S. Hutchinson, *The Circus Comes to Town,* Minton, Balch, 1932; Louisa M. Alcott, *Little Men,* Harper, 1933; Achmed Abdullah, *The Cat Had Nine Lives,* Farrar, Straus, 1933; Eva K. Witte, *Araminta,* Minton, Balch, 1935; Eva K. Witte, *Jerome Anthony,* Putnam, 1936; Mildred Wasson, *Nancy Sails,* Harper, 1936; May Justus, *House in No-End Hollow,* Doubleday, Doran, 1938; Eleanor W. Nolen, *A Shipment for Susannah,* Thomas Nelson, 1938; Eva K. Evans, *Key Corner,* Putnam, 1938; Eva K. Evans, *Araminta's Goat,* Putnam, 1938; Halsa Alison

Kyser, *Little Cumsee in Dixie,* Longmans, Green, 1938; Paul L. Dunbar, *Little Brown Baby and Other Poems for Young People,* Dodd, 1940, reprinted, 1966; Eva K. Evans, *Mr. Jones and Mr. Finnigan,* Oxford University Press, 1941; May Justus, *Fiddle Away,* Grosset, 1942; Mary W. Thompson, *Blueberry Muffin,* Longmans, Green, 1942; Keith Robertson, *Pilgrim Goose,* Viking, 1956.

WORK IN PROGRESS: With Herbert Best, Volumes II-IV of *Men Who Changed the Map;* three books for Garrard, *Hopi Indians, King Philip,* and *Scott of the Antarctic; Hindu Folk Tales;* and *Tales from an Indian Jungle.*

SIDELIGHTS: Stories from *The Magic Banana and Other Polynesian Tales* were recorded as "South Sea Island Tales," read by Manu Tupou, Caedmon, 1974. See BEST, (Oswald) Herbert.†

(Died February, 1974)

*   *   *

BEST, (Oswald) Herbert 1894-

PERSONAL: Born March 25, 1894, in Chester, England; son of John Dugdale (a clergyman) and Julia (Deacon) Best; married (Evangel) Allena Champlin (an author and illustrator), July 12, 1926 (died February, 1974). *Education:* Attended King's School, Chester, England; Queens' College, Cambridge, LL.B., 1914. *Politics:* "Non-mobocratic." *Religion:* "Philosophical, perhaps animistic." *Residence:* Sharon, Conn. 06069.

CAREER: British Colonial Civil Service, district officer in Northern Nigeria, 1919-32, holding administrative and judicial posts, including commissioner of Supreme Court; author, beginning 1930, working usually in some degree of collaboration with his wife (best known under the pseudonym Erick Berry). *Military service:* British Army, Royal Engineers, 1914-19; became lieutenant. *Member:* Royal Geographical Society (London; fellow).

WRITINGS—Most books prior to 1960 illustrated by his wife (and signed with her pseudonym, Erick Berry): *Garram the Hunter: A Boy of the Hill Tribes,* Doubleday, Doran, 1930; *Son of the White Man,* Doubleday, Doran, 1931; *The Mystery of the Flaming Hut,* Harper, 1932; *Garram the Chief: The Story of the Hill Tribes,* Doubleday, Doran, 1932; *The Skull Beneath the Eaves,* Grayson & Grayson, 1933; *Flag of the Desert,* Viking, 1936; *Winds Whisper,* Hurst & Blackett, 1937; *Low River,* Hurst & Blackett, 1937; *Tal of the Four Tribes,* Doubleday, Doran, 1938.

The Twenty-fifth Hour, Random House, 1940; *The Gunsmith's Boy,* Winston, 1942; (with Erick Berry) *Concertina Farm,* M. Joseph, 1943; *Young'un,* Macmillan, 1944; *Border Iron,* Viking, 1945; *Whistle, Daughter, Whistle,* Macmillan, 1947; (with Berry) *Writing for Children,* Viking, 1947, 2nd edition, University of Miami Press, 1964; *The Long Portage: A Story of Ticonderoga and Lord Howe,* Viking, 1948 (published in England as *The Road to Ticonderoga,* Penguin, 1954).

Watergate: A Story of the Irish on the Erie Canal, Winston, 1951; *Not Without Danger: A Story of the Colony of Jamaica in Revolutionary Days,* Viking, 1951; *Ranger's Ransom: A Story of Ticonderoga,* Aladdin Books, 1953; *The Columbus Cannon,* Viking, 1954; *The Sea Warriors,* Macmillan, 1959.

Desmond's First Case, Viking, 1961; *Bright Hunter of the Skies,* Macmillan, 1961; *Carolina Gold,* Day, 1961; *The Webfoot Warriors: The Story of UDT, the U.S. Navy's Underwater Demolition Team,* Day, 1962; *A Rumor of Drums,* McKay, 1962; *Desmond the Dog Detective: The Case of the Lone Stranger,* Viking, 1962; *Parachute to Survival,* Day, 1964; *Desmond and the Peppermint Ghost,* Viking, 1965; (with Berry) *Men Who Changed the Map,* Volume I, Funk, 1968; *Desmond and Dog Friday,* Viking, 1968; (with Berry) *The Polynesian Triangle,* Funk, 1968; *Desmond the Dog Detective,* Viking, 1969.

WORK IN PROGRESS: Books on a wide range of historical and geographical subjects; research on the conflict between individual and group survival factors in modern civilizations.

SIDELIGHTS: "Many of our books are educational, to ourselves as well as to others," Best told *CA.* "Perhaps we were thwarted scholars when young, and have since compensated. Some travel in Asia, Africa, much of Europe, West Indies, Fiji, Polynesia (brief or extending for years) has appetised rather than sated an interest in ethnology and archaeology. Add an interest in farming, gardening, snorkeling, rifle- and pistol-shooting, woodworking and handicrafts in general. What a mixture!"†

*   *   *

BETHMANN, Erich Waldemar 1904-

PERSONAL: Surname is pronounced Bate-man; born September 4, 1904, in Berlin, Germany; son of Carl Louis and Anna-Elisa (Mueller) Bethmann; first wife's name: Zora; married Olivia Lattof, August 4, 1954; children: Erika (Mrs. Marcus Schaaf), Claus Waldemar, Hans George. *Education:* Theological Seminary, Friedensau, Germany, Lic.Theol. (B.D. equivalent), 1925; Seventh Day Adventist Theological Seminary, Takoma Park, Md., M.A., 1949; also studied at Livingstone College, London, England, and American University, Cairo, Egypt, 1926-27. *Religion:* Protestant. *Home:* 1830 R St. N.W., Washington, D.C. 20009.

CAREER: Member of Seventh Day Adventist educational mission in Egypt, 1928-32, director of missions in Transjordan, 1933-37, Iraq, 1937-39, and India, 1939-46; writer and lecturer in United States, 1946-50; American Friends of the Middle East, Washington, D.C., director of research and lecturer, 1951-69. *Member:* American Oriental Society, International Platform Association, Iran-American Society, Middle East Institute.

WRITINGS: Bridge to Islam, Nashville Publishers Association, 1950; *Decisive Years in Palestine,* American Friends of the Middle East, 1954; *The Fate of Muslims Under Soviet Rule,* American Friends of the Middle East, 1955; *Yemen on the Threshold,* American Friends of the Middle East, 1960; *Steps Toward Understanding Islam,* American Friends of the Middle East, 1966. Editor, "Basic Fact Series on Middle East"; editor, Continuing Committee of Muslim-Christian Cooperation.

WORK IN PROGRESS: Studying Islamic problems in the modern world; *Mid-East Vignettes.*

SIDELIGHTS: Bethmann speaks Arabic and French (in addition to his native German); reads Urdu and Persian. *Avocational interests:* History, including postal history.

*   *   *

BETHURUM, F(rances) Dorothy 1897-

PERSONAL: Surname is pronounced Beth-u-rum; born April 5, 1897, in Franklin, Tenn.; daughter of George Reid (a merchant) and Mary (Sinclair) Bethurum; married Roger Sherman Loomis (a writer), January 12, 1963 (deceased).

Education: Vanderbilt University, B.A., 1919, M.A., 1922; Yale University, Ph.D., 1930. *Politics:* Democrat. *Home:* 76 Great Neck Rd., Waterford, Conn.

CAREER: Randolph-Macon Woman's College, Lynchburg, Va., instructor, 1922-24, assistant professor of English, 1924-25; Lawrence College (now University), Appleton, Wis., associate professor, 1927-29, professor of English, 1929-40; Connecticut College, New London, professor of English and chairman of department, 1940-62, teaching scholar, 1962-65. Visiting summer professor at Bread Loaf School of English, 1951, University of Minnesota, 1956, Harvard University, 1961; Vanderbilt University, and Smith College. English Institute, member of supervising committee, 1942-47, chairman, 1947. Vanderbilt University Alumni Board, member, 1953-56.

MEMBER: Modern Language Association of America, National Humanities Faculty (chairman, 1969-70), Mediaeval Academy of America, American Association of University Professors (member of council, and first vice-president, 1962-64), Phi Beta Kappa, Kappa Alpha Theta. *Awards, honors:* Litt.D., Lawrence College, 1947; L.H.D., Colby College, 1959; Guggenheim fellow, 1937-38; Fulbright fellow at Oxford University, 1954-55; American Council of Learned Societies fellow, 1962-63.

WRITINGS: (With Randall Stewart) *Masterpieces of American Literature,* Scott, 1954; (with Stewart) *Masterpieces of English Literature,* Scott, 1955; (editor) *The Homilies of Wulfstan,* Clarendon Press, 1957, revised edition, 1971; (editor) *Critical Approaches to Mediaeval Literature,* Columbia University Press, 1960; (editor) Chaucer, *Squire's Tale,* Clarendon Press, 1965. Contributor of twenty-five articles to professional journals.

WORK IN PROGRESS: Neoplatonism in the Middle Ages with special reference to Chaucer.

SIDELIGHTS: Ms. Bethurum reads French, Italian, German, Latin, and Greek. *Avocational interests:* Music, travel, medieval art.

*   *   *

BEVIS, H(erbert) U(rlin)   1902-

PERSONAL: Surname is pronounced *Bee*-vis; born December 27, 1902, in Bascom, Fla.; son of Robert Calhoun (a grocer) and Mary Augusta (Etheridge) Bevis; married Jennie Anderson, November 7, 1928; children: Herbert A., Patricia Ann (Mrs. K. M. Beville), Virginia (Mrs. Jack F. Gamble). *Education:* Attended high school in Greenwood, Fla. *Politics:* Democrat (conservative). *Religion:* Christian (nondenominational). *Home and office:* 109 Northeast 11th St., Gainesville, Fla. 32601.

CAREER: Spent most of his teen years on a farm in west Florida; seaman with U.S. Coast Guard, 1922-23, and other marine occupations, 1923-27; house painter in Perry and Gainesville, Fla., 1928-30; sign painter in Florida, beginning 1930. Also has done abstract of title work intermittently since the 1920's.

WRITINGS—All science fiction; edited by Alice Sachs: *Space Stadium,* Lenox Hill, 1970; *The Star Rovers,* Lenox Hill, 1970; *The Time Winder,* Lenox Hill, 1970.

WORK IN PROGRESS: Another science fiction book, *The Alien Abductors;* expanding short stories (unsold) to book length.

BIOGRAPHICAL/CRITICAL SOURCES: Gainesville Sun (Gainesville, Fla.), March 14, 1970.

BEYER, Evelyn M.   1907-

PERSONAL: Born March 24, 1907, in Auburn, N.Y.; daughter of Lynn Ellison and Mabel (Coursen) Beyer. *Education:* University of Rochester, B.A., 1929; Bank Street College of Education, graduate study, 1931; New York University, M.A., 1945, and further graduate courses. *Home:* 23A Elm St., Fryeburg, Me. 04037.

CAREER: University of Rochester, Rochester, N.Y., librarian, 1930; Mount Kemble School, Morristown, N.J., teacher of preschool and primary children, 1932-35; Works Progress Administration (W.P.A.), supervisor of nursery schools in New York State, 1936; Harriet Johnson Nursery School, New York, N.Y., teacher and assistant director, 1937; Sarah Lawrence College, Bronxville, N.Y., teacher of child development, 1938-44, director of Nursery School, 1938-44, 1957-70; Rochester Child Health Institute, Rochester, Minn., director of preschool activities, 1945-52; Smith College, Northampton, Mass., associate professor of child study and director of Nursery School, 1952-57. *Member:* National Association for Nursery Education (governing board member), National Association for the Education of Young Children, New England Association for Nursery Education, Phi Beta Kappa.

WRITINGS: Just Like You (juvenile), Scott, 1949; *Who Likes Dinner?* (juvenile), Wonder Books, 1952; (with Lois Murphy) *Personality in Young Children,* Basic Books, 1956; (contributor) *Montessori in Perspective,* National Association for the Education of Young Children, 1966; (editor, and author of foreword) *Play and Playthings for the Preschool Child,* Penguin, 1967; *Teaching Young Children,* Western Publishing, 1968. Writer of pamphlets for National Association for Nursery Education, articles on child development and early childhood education for professional journals, and stories and verse for young children.

WORK IN PROGRESS: Children's stories.

*   *   *

BIDDLE, William W(ishart)   1900-19(?)

PERSONAL: Born June 19, 1900, in Chicago, Ill.; son of Henry Chalmers (a professor of chemistry) and Margaret M. (Wishart) Biddle; married Loureide Jeannette Cobb, July 9, 1925; children: Bruce Jesse, Katherine Joyce (Mrs. Robert L. Austin). *Education:* Pomona College, B.A. (magna cum laude), 1923; Union Theological Seminary, New York, N.Y., graduate study, 1924-27; Columbia University, M.A., 1928, Ph.D., 1932. *Religion:* Society of Friends (Quaker). *Home:* 1624 Merion Way, Apartment 39A, Seal Beach, Calif. 90740.

CAREER: Western Reserve University (now Case Western Reserve University), Cleveland, Ohio, instructor in group work, School of Applied Social Science, 1930-33; Colgate University, Hamilton, N.Y., instructor in education, 1934-35; Wisconsin State Teachers College (now University of Wisconsin), Milwaukee, professor of psychology and education and head of department of psychology, 1935-44; U.S. Department of Agriculture, Washington, D.C., senior health specialist and chief of community cooperative services, Farmers Home Administration, 1944-47; Earlham College, Richmond, Ind., director of community dynamics, 1947-60; United Presbyterian Church in the U.S.A., Board of National Missions, New York, N.Y., consultant in community development, 1960-65.

MEMBER: American Psychological Association (fellow), American Sociological Association (fellow), Adult Education Association of the U.S.A. (chairman of community development section, 1957-59), Society for International Development, International Society for Community Development, National Social Welfare Assembly, Phi Beta Kappa.

WRITINGS: Education and Propaganda, Bureau of Publications, Teachers College, Columbia University, 1932, reprinted, 1972. *The Cultivation of Community Leaders,* Harper, 1953; (with wife, Loureide J. Biddle) *Growth Toward Freedom,* Harper, 1957; *Community Dynamics Processes,* privately printed, 1961; (with Loureide J. Biddle) *The Community Development Process,* Holt, 1965; (with Loureide J. Biddle) *Encouraging Community Development,* Holt, 1968. Contributor to college and church bulletins, and to professional journals. Editor, *Community Development Bulletin* (quarterly publication of Institute of Strategic Studies, United Presbyterian Church in the U.S.A.).†

(Deceased)

*   *   *

BILLINGSLEY, Edward Baxter 1910-

PERSONAL: Born June 18, 1910, in Melbourne, Ark.; son of Edmund (a merchant) and Harriet (Baxter) Billingsley; married Patricia Mary Malloy, December 28, 1929. *Education:* University of Arkansas, student, 1926-28; U.S. Naval Academy, B.S., 1932; Northwestern University, M.A., 1947; University of North Carolina, Ph.D., 1964. *Politics:* Independent Democrat. *Religion:* Unitarian Universalist. *Office:* Department of History, University of South Florida, Tampa, Fla. 33620.

CAREER: U.S. Navy, 1928-59, commissioned ensign, 1932, captain, 1950-59, retired as rear admiral; Methodist College, Fayetteville, N.C., assistant professor of history, 1964-65; North Carolina State University at Raleigh, Fort Bragg Branch, Fayetteville, assistant professor of history, 1965-67; University of South Florida, Tampa, assistant professor, 1967-71, associate professor of history, beginning 1971. Served on gunboats at China Station, 1934-37; commanded two destroyers in World War II, mainly in North Atlantic and Mediterranean, and participated in invasions of Normandy, Southern France, and Okinawa; commanding officer of Naval Station at Subic Bay, Philippine Islands, 1955-57. *Member:* American Historical Association, Latin American Studies Association, Naval Historical Foundation, Southern Historical Society, Southeast Conference on Latin American Studies, Florida Historical Society. *Awards, honors*—Military: Bronze Star and Silver Star.

WRITINGS: In Defense of Neutral Rights: The United States Navy and the Wars of Independence in Chile and Peru, University of North Carolina Press, 1967.

WORK IN PROGRESS: Studying American naval discipline in the early nineteenth century; a study of Commodore Catesby ap Roger Jones' abortive seizure of Monterey in 1842.

*   *   *

BIRSE, A(rthur) H(erbert) 1889-

PERSONAL: Surname rhymes with "nurse"; born February 23, 1889, in St. Petersburg (now Leningrad), Russia; son of British subjects, John (a merchant) and Marion (Anderson) Birse; married Millicent Dare; children: Joscelyn, Peter Caird. *Education:* Educated in Russia. *Home:* Wick Lodge, Catsey Lane, Bushey, Hertfordshire, England. *Agent:* John Johnson, 12-13 Henrietta St., London WC2E 8LF, England.

CAREER: Lived in Russia until the Revolution of 1917 wiped out the family's business and farm; official in various banks in Poland and Italy, 1921-28; manager of Amstelbank, Amsterdam, Netherlands, 1932-36; assistant manager of Martins Bank Ltd., London, England, 1936-40; transferred from Army duty in Cairo to join the newly created British Military Mission in Moscow, 1941, and called, as a result of the illness of a Foreign Office interpreter, as an interpreter for Winston Churchill at his first meeting with Stalin, 1942; continued as Churchill's interpreter in conferences with the Russians at the Teheran, Yalta, and Potsdam meetings, 1943-45; foreign manager of Martins Bank Ltd., London, England, 1945-52. *Military service:* Fought with White Russian forces, 1919. British Army, 1940-42; became major. *Awards, honors:* Commander, Order of the British Empire; Order of the Red Banner of Labour (Soviet Union).

WRITINGS: Memoirs of an Interpreter (autobiographical), Coward, 1967.

SIDELIGHTS: Things Russian have punctuated Birse's quiet career in banking in ways other than his role as super-discreet interpreter for Winston Churchill; he was also involved in the breaking of the Soviet spy ring in Australia, an incident now known as the Petrov case. Birse speaks German, Polish, Italian, French, and Dutch.

BIOGRAPHICAL/CRITICAL SOURCES: Observer Review, June 11, 1967; *Book World,* November 19, 1967.†

*   *   *

BISCHOFF, Julia Bristol 1909-1970
(Julie Arnoldy)

PERSONAL: Born March 2, 1909, in Almont, Mich.; daughter of William Howard (a lawyer and farmer) and Charlotte (Kelsey) Bristol; married Francis N. Arnoldy (a major, U.S. Army; died, 1949); married William Henry Bischoff (a newspaper editor and free-lance writer), May 4, 1956; children: (first marriage) Irene Simone (Mrs. Jack North). *Education:* Attended Eastern Michigan University, 1926-27, and University of Grenoble, 1927-28, *Home:* Volcan de Buenos Aires, Costa Rica, Central America.

CAREER: During her early career taught in country schools in Almont Township, Mich.; *Detroit News,* Detroit, Mich., travel writer, 1937-39; *Miami News,* Miami, Fla., assistant editor of Sunday Magazine, "Florida Living," 1956-58; free-lance writer. In 1965 retired with her husband to a ranch in Costa Rica. *Member:* Audubon Society.

WRITINGS: Great-Great Uncle Henry's Cats, W. R. Scott, 1965; *A Dog for David,* W. R. Scott, 1966; *Paddy's Preposterous Promises,* W. R. Scott, 1968; *Mystery on the Rancho Grande,* W. R. Scott, 1969. Author of 150 broadcast radio plays, and a three-act play produced by Detroit Community Theatre; contributor of more than three hundred articles and a few short stories to magazines, many of them published under the name of Julie Arnoldy.

SIDELIGHTS: Julia Bristol Bischoff lived in Europe for three years. She told *CA* that her ambition is "to write a series of young people's books with Latin American settings (Latin American history has been my hobby for many years)."†

(Died, 1970)

*   *   *

BISHOP, Crawford M. 1885-

PERSONAL: Born August 29, 1885, in Baltimore, Md.;

married Luella Huelster, June 8, 1912; children: J. Bashford, Crawford M., Jr., Richard W., Leighton S. *Education:* Dartmouth College, B.A., 1906; University of Maryland, LL.B., 1909; Columbia University, M.A., 1917, Ph.D., 1931. *Politics:* Republican. *Religion:* Assembly of God.

CAREER: Admitted to Maryland Bar, 1909, Bar of the U.S. Court for China, Shanghai, 1912; Robert College, Constantinople (now Istanbul), Turkey, professor, 1906-07; U.S. Consular Service, vice consul in China, 1910-1915; attorney in New York, N.Y., for American International Corp., 1916-18, Asia Banking Corp., 1918-20; United States and Mexico Claims Commission, Washington, D.C., attorney, 1924-39; Headquarters, Supreme Commander of Allied Powers in Japan (SCAP), Tokyo, legal counsel, 1946-47; National Association of Evangelicals, representative in Tokyo, Japan, 1949-52; Northwest College, Kirkland, Wash., professor of foreign missions, 1954-60. Director of Latin American legal research, Library of Congress Law Library, 1940-44. *Member:* American Bar Association, Federal Bar Association, American Society of International Law, Phi Beta Kappa.

WRITINGS: International Arbitral Procedure, John Byrne, 1931; *Legal Codes of the Latin American Republics,* Library of Congress, 1942; *Law and Legal Literature of Cuba, Haiti, and Domincan Republic,* Library of Congress, 1943; *Missionary Legal Manual,* Moody, 1965. Contributor to law and literary journals.

SIDELIGHTS: Bishop is competent in French, German, Spanish, and Chinese.†

* * *

BISHOP, John L(yman) 1913-1974

PERSONAL: Born September 25, 1913, in Manila, Philippine Islands; son of Ancil Hiram (a businessman) and Amelia (Schmidt) Bishop. *Education:* Harvard University, A.B., 1937, M.A., 1938, Ph.D., 1953. *Home:* 6 Walnut St., Boston, Mass. 02108. *Office:* Department of Far Eastern Languages and Literature, Harvard University, 2 Divinity Ave., Cambridge, Mass. 02138.

CAREER: Eaglebrook School, Deerfield, Mass., English instructor, 1938-42; Phillips Academy, Andover, Mass., English instructor, 1942-43; Waynflete School, Portland, Me., head of English department, 1948-50; Beaver Country Day School, Chestnut Hill, Mass., English instructor, 1954-57; Harvard University, Cambridge, Mass., lecturer in Far Eastern languages, 1958-74. *Military service:* U.S. Naval Reserve, 1943-46; became lieutenant. *Member:* Association for Asian Studies.

WRITINGS: The Colloquial Short Story in China: A Study of the San-Yen Collections, Harvard University Press, 1956; (editor) *Studies in Chinese Literature,* Harvard University Press, 1965; (editor) *Studies of Governmental Institutions in Chinese History,* Harvard University Press, 1968. Editor, *Harvard Journal of Asiatic Studies,* 1957-74; contributing editor, *Books Abroad.*

WORK IN PROGRESS: Traditional Chinese fiction; Chinese poetry of the Sung dynasty.

BIOGRAPHICAL/CRITICAL SOURCES: New York Times, March 30, 1974.†

(Died March 24, 1974)

BISHOP, Tania Kroitor 1906-
(Tetiana Shevchuk; Virlyana Semkiw, a pseudonym)

PERSONAL: Given name, Tetiana; born February 5, 1906, in Canora, Saskatchewan, Canada; daughter of Andrew (a farmer) and Barbara (Semkiw) Shevchuk; married Peter P. Kroiter (a teacher; deceased); married Ralph J. Bishop (an architect), June 19, 1947; children: (first marriage) Roman B. *Education:* Attended Saskatoon Teachers' College and Queen's University at Kingston. *Home:* 1526 West Riverside Ave., Spokane, Wash. 99201.

CAREER: Public school teacher in Saskatchewan; social service worker in Winnipeg, Manitoba. Volunteer worker, Spokane Crisis Services. *Member:* National League of American Pen Women.

WRITINGS: A Record of the Spirit, Willing, 1959; (under name Tetiana Shevchuk) *Awakening of the Soul* (originally published in Ukrainian), Trident, 1960; (under name Tetiana Shevchuk) *Pilgrimage to Kiev* (originally published in Ukrainian), Trident, 1963; (under name Tetiana Shevchuk) *Na prestil malbutnikh dniv: An Overture to Future Days* (poetry in English and Ukrainian; preface in English), [Winnipeg], 1964, Trident, 1965; *Born of the Spirit,* Philosophical Library, 1968. Contributor to *Our Life, Woman's World,* and other magazines.

WORK IN PROGRESS: Translating Ukrainian poetry into English.

AVOCATIONAL INTERESTS: Man's relationship to God and nature, ecology, bird sanctuaries, organic gardening, dream significance as pioneered by Jung and Fromm.

* * *

BLACK, Duncan 1908-

PERSONAL: Born May 23, 1908, in Motherwell, England; son of Duncan (a boilermaker) and Margaret (Muir) Black; married Almut Uffenorde, November 16, 1946. *Education:* University of Glasgow, M.A. (mathematics and physics), 1929, M.A. (economics and politics), 1932, Ph.D., 1937. *Politics:* Liberal. *Religion:* Presbyterian. *Home:* 67 Penrhos Rd., Bangor, North Wales.

CAREER: University College of North Wales, Bangor, professor of economics, 1952-68, professor emeritus, 1968—.

WRITINGS: The Incidence of Income Taxes, Macmillan, 1939, reprinted, A. M. Kelley, 1965. *Committtee Decisions with Complementary Valuation,* Hodge & Co., 1951; *The Theory of Committees and Elections,* Cambridge University Press, 1958.

WORK IN PROGRESS: An edition of Lewis Carroll's *Principles of Parliamentary Representation;* a book, *Lewis Carroll and Logic.*

SIDELIGHTS: Black is competent in French, Italian, and German. *Avocational interests:* Cricket and philosophy.†

* * *

BLACK, Eugene R(obert) 1898-

PERSONAL: Born May 1, 1898, in Atlanta, Ga.; son of Eugene R. (a banker) and Gussie (Grady) Black; married Susette Heath, January 25, 1930; children: (previous marriage) Elizabeth Black Campbell, Eugene R., Jr.; (present marriage) William. *Education:* University of Georgia, A.B., 1917. *Home:* 178 Columbia Heights, Brooklyn, N.Y. 10001. *Office:* 1 Chase, Manhattan, N.Y. 10005.

CAREER: Harris Forbes and Co. and successor firm, Chase-Harris, Forbes Corp. (investment bankers), Atlanta, Ga., 1919-33, became vice-president; Chase National Bank, New York, N.Y., second vice-president, 1933-37, vice-president, 1937-47, senior vice-president, 1949; International Bank for Reconstruction and Development (World Bank), Washington, D.C., executive director representing the United States, 1947-49, president and chairman of executive directors, 1949-62; currently special consultant to Secretary-General of United Nations. Former president of World Bank affiliated organizations, International Finance Corp., and International Development Association. Trustee of Ford Foundation, Population Council, Inc., and Johns Hopkins University. *Member:* Phi Beta Kappa, River Club (New York), Chevy Chase Club (Washington), Athenaeum Club (London). *Awards, honors:* U.S. Chamber of Commerce Award as "great living American." Honorary degrees include LL.D. from Columbia University, 1954, Rutgers University, 1959, Yale University, 1960, and Harvard University, 1960; Doctor of Economics and Social Sciences, University of Hamburg, 1962.

WRITINGS: The Diplomacy of Economic Development, Harvard University Press, 1960; *Alternative in Southeast Asia,* foreword by Lyndon B. Johnson, Praeger, 1969.

* * *

BLACK, Matthew W(ilson) 1895-

PERSONAL: Born April 14, 1895, in Altoona, Pa.; son of William George (a railroad employee) and Della Gertrude (Yeager) Black; married Dorothy S. Dinsmore, June 20, 1929; children: Ann Bockee, Matthew Wilson, Jr. *Education:* Pennsylvania State University, A.B., 1915; University of Pennsylvania, M.A., 1916, Ph.D., 1927. *Politics:* Republican. *Religion:* Presbyterian. *Home:* 1143 Edgewood Rd., Berwyn, Pa. 19312.

CAREER: University of Pennsylvania, Philadelphia, instructor, 1916-23, assistant professor, 1923-33, associate professor, 1933-39, professor of English literature, 1939-65, professor emeritus, 1965—. Visiting professor at Southern Illinois University, 1965-67, and Ursinus College, 1967-68. Member, National Shakespeare Festival Committee, 1964. *Military service:* U.S. Army, 1917-18. *Member:* Modern Language Association of America.

WRITINGS: (With Matthias A. Shaaber) *Shakespeare's Seventeenth-Century Editors,* Modern Language Association of America, 1935; (editor) *Elizabethan and Seventeenth-Century Lyrics,* Lippincott, 1938; (editor with Felix E. Schelling) *Typical Elizabethan Plays,* Harper, 1949; (editor) Shakespeare, *Richard II* (new variorum edition), Modern Language Association of America, 1955; (editor and author of introduction) Thomas Middleton, *The Changeling,* University of Pennsylvania Press, 1966; (editor and author of introduction) Shakespeare, *Midsummer Night's Dream,* Barnes & Noble, 1967.

WORK IN PROGRESS: Supplementary bibliography for a reissue of *Richard II;* a new variorum edition of *Titus Andronicus.*

* * *

BLAIR, Everetta Love 1907-

PERSONAL: Born July 21, 1907, in Whitesboro, Grayson County, Tex.; daughter of Carl Everett (in real estate) and Cleta (Fitch) Love; married Arnold David Blair (a retired lieutenant colonel, U.S. Army), September 3, 1939. *Educa-*

tion: Southern Methodist University, student, 1925-26; University of Texas, A.B., 1929; University of South Carolina, M.A., 1954, Ph.D., 1964; studied at Institute of International Education, University of Edinburgh, summer, 1963, and Oxford University, summer, 1964. *Politics:* Democrat. *Religion:* Episcopalian. *Address:* c/o William F. Love, 4660 Sawtelle Blvd., Culver City, Calif. 90230. *Agent:* Annie Laurie Williams, Inc., 18 East 41st St., New York, N.Y. 10016.

CAREER: Houston Chronicle, Houston, Tex., feature writer and reporter, 1930; National Broadcasting Co., New York City, writer of feature articles and special promotion, 1934-36; U.S. First Army, Information Headquarters, New York City, feature writer, 1944-45; U.S. Far East Command Headquarters, Public Information Office, Tokyo, Japan, feature writer, 1951; Newberry College, Newberry, S.C., assistant professor of English, 1965-66. Secretary of operating board, United Service Organizations (U.S.O), Columbia, S.C., 1963-66. *Member:* Quill Club, English-Speaking Union, Daughters of the American Revolution, South Atlantic Modern Language Association, Theta Sigma Phi, South Caroliniana Society, Business and Professional Women's Club. *Awards, honors:* Certificate of Achievement, Far East Command Headquarters, 1951, for coverage of Special Services activities on the Korean War front.

WRITINGS: Jesse Stuart: His Life and Works, introduction by Jesse Stuart, University of South Carolina Press, 1967.

WORK IN PROGRESS: McClellanville—The Archibald Rutledge Country; Morale Front, a book on Blair's Korean War experiences; *Kabuki and I,* an account of personal experiences with the classical theater of Japan, 1969.

AVOCATIONAL INTERESTS: Music, historic restorations, photography.

* * *

BLAIR-FISH, Wallace Wilfrid 1889-1968
(Blair, Wilfrid Blair)

PERSONAL: Born September 25, 1889, in London, England; son of William David (a civil servant) and Louisa (Hawkins) Fish; married Hilary Margaret Burgis, June 3, 1914; married second wife, Hilary May Heaton, October 30, 1930; children (first marriage) Margaret Ann Blair-Fish MacLeod, John Michael Burgis. *Education:* Educated privately, and at Pembroke College, Oxford, 1908-10. *Politics:* Independent. *Religion:* Agnostic. *Home:* Fladbury Mill, near Pershore, Worcestershire, England.

CAREER: Journalist and playwright. Contributor to *Punch,* London, England, 1908-17, and member of the literary staff of two London newspapers, *Sunday Times* and *Sunday Chronicle* in that period; served in British Ministry of Food, 1917-19, and on Supreme Economic Council, 1919; Shakespeare Head Press, Oxford, England, publisher and joint managing director, 1921-22; Rural Industries Bureau, director, 1926-27; Rotary International, secretary for Great Britain and Ireland, 1928-37, and editor, 1928-42. *Member:* Oxford Union, Oxford Society. *Awards, honors: Evening Standard* award as radio playwright of the year (the award was made during the 1940's, but the exact year is not known).

WRITINGS—Under pseudonym Wilfrid Blair, except as noted: *Poets on the Isis, and Other Perversions,* Basil Blackwell, 1910; *Sa Muse S'Amuse* (poems reprinted from various periodicals), Basil Blackwell, 1914; *For Belgium* (war poems), Basil Blackwell, 1914; *Consarnin' Sairey 'Uggins* (one-act play), Samuel French, 1914; *"'Tis Simple Mirth"* (war poems and humor), Basil Blackwell, 1915; *1915, and Other Poems*, Basil Blackwell, 1915; *The Death of Shakespeare* (two-act play), Basil Blackwell, 1916; (with E.H.W.M.) *Black and White Magic* (poems), Basil Blackwell, 1917; *Herbs of Grace* (poems reprinted from *Punch*), Basil Blackwell, 1918; *The Life and Death of Mrs. Tidmuss*, Appleton, 1923; (under pseudonym Blair) *Oxford Ways: A Description of Undergraduate Life*, Basil Blackwell, 1925; *For Home—Or Country* (extravaganza), H.W.F. Deane, 1957; (under pseudonym Blair) *Tides and Fashions* (poems), Adlard, 1969.

Unpublished plays: "Whimsies," produced, 1915; "The Private Life of P. C. Pettifer," produced, 1916; "Old King Cole," produced, 1942; "The Beggar Maid," produced, 1943; "Gather Ye Rosebuds," produced, 1943; "Blimpton Won't Budge," produced, 1945; "Genius Ltd.," produced, 1945; "Born Again," produced, 1949; "Ivory Tower," produced, 1949; "Civvy Street," produced, 1949; "Pyrrhus Had Three Wives," produced, 1959; "Tragedy at Evesham," produced, 1965. Author of about forty radio plays, 1943-68.

AVOCATIONAL INTERESTS: Country life, reading, seeing plays written by others.††

(Died April, 1968)

* * *

BLIXEN, Karen (Christentze Dinesen) 1885-1962
(Isak Dinesen; other pseudonyms: Pierre Andrezel, Tania B., Osceola)

PERSONAL: Born April 17, 1885, in Rungsted, Denmark; daughter of Wilhelm (an army officer and writer under his own name and his Indian name Boganis) and Ingeborg (Westenholz) Dinesen; married Baron Bror Blixen-Finecke (a big-game hunter and writer, he was Miss Dinesen's second cousin), January 14, 1914 (divorced, 1921). *Education:* Studied English at Oxford University, 1904; studied painting at Royal Academy in Copenhagen, in Paris, 1910, and in Rome. *Home:* Rungstedlund, Rungsted Kyst, Denmark.

CAREER: Writer from 1907 to 1962, from 1934 writing in English and translating her own work into Danish. With her husband Baron Bror Blixen, she managed a coffee plantation in British East Africa (now Nairobi, Kenya), 1913-21, then took over the management herself until failing coffee prices forced her to give up the farm in 1931. Commissioned by three Scandinavian newspapers to write a series of twelve articles on wartime Berlin, Paris, and London, 1940. *Member:* American Academy of Arts and Letters (honorary member), National Institute of Arts and Letters (honorary member), Bayerische Akademie der Schoenen Kuenste (corresponding member), Danish Academy, Cosmopolitan Club (New York). *Awards, honors:* Ingenio et Arti Medal from King Frederick IX of Denmark, 1950; The Golden Laurels, 1952; Hans Christian Andersen Prize, 1955; Danish Critics' Prize, 1957; Henri Nathansen Memorial Fund award, 1957.

WRITINGS—Published in Danish under name Karen Blixen and in English under pseudonym Isak Dinesen: *Sandhedens Haevn* (play; title means "The Revenge of Truth"; first produced at Royal Theatre, Copenhagen, 1936), [Tilskueren], 1926, Gyldendal (Copenhagen), 1960; *Seven Gothic Tales* (Book-of-the-Month Club selection; contains "The Deluge at Norderney," "The Old Chevalier," "The

Monkey," "The Roads Round Pisa," "The Supper at Elsinore," "The Dreamers," and "The Poet"), Smith & Haas, 1934, reissued with new introduction, Modern Library, 1961, Danish translation published as *Syv Fantastiske Fortaellinger*, Reitzels, 1935, reprinted, Gyldendal, 1968; *Out of Africa* (Book-of-the-Month Club selection), Putnam (London), 1937, Random House, 1938, reprinted, 1970, Danish translation published as *Den Afrikanske Farm*, Gyldendal, 1937, reprinted, 1964; *Winter's Tales* (Book-of-the-Month Club selection), Random House, 1942, reprinted, Books for Libraries, 1971, Danish translation published as *Vinter-Eventyr*, Gyldendal, 1942; (under pseudonym Pierre Andrezel) *Gengaeldelsens Veje* (title means "The Ways of Retribution"), Danish translation by Clara Svendsen, Gyldendal, 1944, published as *The Angelic Avengers* (Book-of-the-Month Club selection), Putnam, 1946, Random House, 1947; *Om revtskrivning 23-24 marts 1938*, Gyldendal, 1949.

Farah, Wivel (Copenhagen), 1950; *Daguerreotypier* (two radio talks presented January, 1951), Gyldendal, 1951; *Babettes Gaestebud* (title means "Babette's Feast"), Fremad (Copenhagen), 1952; *Omkring den Nye Lov om Dyreforsoeg*, Politikens Forlag (Copenhagen), 1952; *Kardinalens tredie Historie* (title means "The Cardinal's Third Tale"), Gyldendal, 1952; *En Baaltale med 14 Aars Forsinkelse* (title means "Bonfire Speech 14 Years Delayed"), Berlingske Forlag (Copenhagen), 1953; *Spoegelseshestene*, Fremad, 1955; *Last Tales*, Random House, 1957, Danish translation published as *Sidste Fortaellinger*, Gyldendal, 1957; *Anecdotes of Destiny* (contains "The Diver," "Babette's Feast," "Tempests," "The Immortal Story," and "The Ring"), Random House, 1958, reprinted, 1974, Danish translation published as *Skaebne-Anekdoter*, Gyldendal, 1958.

Skygger paa Graesset, Gyldendal, 1960, published as *Shadows on the Grass* (Book-of-the-Month Club selection), Random House, 1961; (author of introduction) Truman Capote, *Holly* (an edition of *Breakfast at Tiffany's*), Gyldendal, 1960; (author of introduction) Olive Schreiner, *The Story of an African Farm*, Limited Editions Club, 1961; *On Mottoes of My Life* (originally published under name Isak Dinesen in *Proceedings of The American Academy of Arts and Letters and The National Institute of Arts and Letters*, Second Series, Number 10, 1960), Ministry of Foreign Affairs (Copenhagen), 1962; (author of introduction) Hans Christian Andersen, *Thumbelina, and Other Stories*, Macmillan, 1962; *Osceola* (posthumously published collection of early stories and poems), Gyldendal, 1962; (author of introduction) Basil Davidson, *Det Genfundne Africa*, Gyldendal, 1962; *Ehrengard* (posthumously published), Random House, 1963, Danish translation by Clara Svendsen, Gyldendal, 1963; *Karen Blixen* (memorial edition of principal works), Gyldendal, 1964; *Essays*, Gyldendal, 1965; *Efterladte Fortallinger*, Gyldendal, 1975.

Contributor of short stories, articles, and reviews to *Ladies' Home Journal, Saturday Evening Post, Atlantic, Harper's Bazaar, Vogue, Botteghe Oscure*, and *Heretica*. She has recorded excerpts from her books for Gyldendal, and has made two films, consisting of readings, for *Encyclopaedia Britannica*.

SIDELIGHTS: "A long time ago, in Africa, Isak Dinesen saw two lions attack an ox. Unarmed but for a stock whip, she flew at the kings of the jungle and lashed them into retreat. Unarmed but for a pen, Isak Dinesen . . . has spent the . . . years of her writing life routing the brute realities of the 20th century from her prose. Minute in output but masterful in style and content, [she] pursues gothic romance in preference to realism, the aristocratic spirit above democratic camaraderie, fate before fact," a *Time* reviewer wrote. "A major literary phenomenon of this century," a *Virginia Quarterly Review* reviewer stated, Isak Dinesen was "a Danish woman of genius who loved Shakespeare and preferred to write in English, . . . a lover of Africa and its people, and a superb literary stylist." When Ernest Hemingway accepted his Nobel Prize in 1958, he said that it should have been given to Isak Dinesen.

Miss Dinesen wrote in English, Hannah Arendt reported, "out of loyalty to her dead lover's language." Her lover, Denys Finch-Hatton, was an adventurous man who lived at her coffee plantation between safaris. His death in a plane crash desolated her, and in *Out of Africa* she hinted, "by the most tenuous, rarefied allusions, at the underlying story of a *grande passion,* which was then, and probably remained to the end, the source of her storytelling," Miss Arendt commented. While Finch-Hatton was away she made up stories which she told him when he returned.

She used her maiden name, Dinesen, and preceded it with a man's name, Isak, which in Hebrew means "one who laughs." She did not disclose her identity until after the success of her first book, *Seven Gothic Tales.* Miss Arendt stated that "Isak Dinesen 'never once wanted to be a writer.' . . . She 'had an intuitive fear of being trapped.'" She believed that a profession would be a trap, because it would necessitate taking a role, and might mean giving up other possibilities in life. Later, Miss Arendt said, Miss Dinesen realized that "the chief trap in life was one's own identity," the author being publicly identified with the private person. She began writing to fill time, when she lived in Africa, but did not consider herself a writer. "Only once—much later, during the Second World War," Miss Arendt stated, "had she 'created some fiction to make money,' and though this fiction, the novel *The Angelic Avengers,* did make money, it turned out to be 'terrible.'" Miss Dinesen began to write seriously because she felt that she could do only two things, cook, and possibly write.

English was the Baroness' second language, and her style in English, like Beckett's in French, was considered formal and classical, "a style which could pass, glissando, from the very florid to the succinct details," wrote Parmenia Migel. "She dips a branch of memory into the pool of the past," wrote a *Time* reviewer, "until it is crystallized with insights, landscapes, literature, and animals that seem as if painted by Henri Rousseau." Dorothy Canfield Fisher wrote about *Seven Gothic Tales:* "Where, you will ask yourself, puzzled, have I ever encountered such strange slanting beauty of phrase, clothing such arresting but controlled fantasy? As for me, I don't know where. . . . The light in it is strange, not at all the good straight downward noon-day stare of the every day sun. But it is a clear light, and in it we see a series of vigorously presented, outrageously unexpected, sometimes horrifying, but perfectly real human beings. They seem endowed with a sort of legendary intensity of living, almost beyond the possible, but that may be the result of the eerie light in which they are shown." Eudora Welty described Miss Dinesen's achievement: "Of a story she made an essence; of the essence she made an elixir; and of the elixir she began once more to compound the story."

Robert Langbaum spoke of Miss Dinesen's "coherence and relevance to modern life. . . . It is because she shows herself in her work such an excellent critic of the romantic tradition, because she sums it up and carries it a step forward, that she is in the mainstream of modern literature." She understood literature, especially the literary tradition in which she

wrote, and she was "faithful to the romantic ideal." Langbaum stated: "The combination of hardness and ineffable sweetness, of a humanity which gains outline and authenticity through the formality of its surface, is the quality of Isak Dinesen's art at its best." He contended that she is a modern writer because she was "deliberately anachronistic."

Miss Dinesen's themes did not vary greatly throughout her writings. She was concerned with the nobility and pride of the aristocracy, which earned her some criticism, especially from the Danes. "There was no greater aristocrat in spirit," Miss Migel stated. "What she did despise was that no man's land of humanity—those dull bourgeois who, with no pride in their separate destinies, live in slavish imitation of their millions of neighbors, the ones whom Saint-Exupery called 'the docile, passive, unprotesting cattle.'" Referring to these "cattle" in *Out of Africa,* Miss Dinesen commented: "The true aristocracy and the true proletariat of the world are both in understanding with tragedy. To them it is the fundamental principle of God, and the key—the minor key—to existence. They differ in this way from the bourgeoisie of all classes, who deny tragedy, who will not tolerate it, and to whom the word of tragedy means in itself unpleasantness." She spoke to Hudson Strode of the good and bad points of Danish democracy: "When I returned to Kenya it struck me how things come out so right on paper, but seldom in life. With democracy, we seem to give up all ideals that are higher than those that can be reached. It's a mediocre happiness, . . . purchased at the price of no great art, no great music. With complete democracy the quality is bound to come down. I don't think it's well for a nation to give up completely its elite. There should be a few versed in the classics."

Miss Dinesen's idea of aristocratic pride was usually enmeshed with the Scandinavian view of fate. In *Out of Africa* she noted: "Pride is faith in the idea that God had, when he made us. A proud man is conscious of the idea, and aspires to realize it. He does not strive toward a happiness, or comfort, which may be irrelevant to God's idea of him. His success is the idea of God, successfully carried through, and he is in love with its destiny. As the good citizen finds his happiness in the fulfilment of his duty to the community, so does the proud man find happiness in the fulfilment of his fate." Eric O. Johannesson expanded this view: "All of life becomes a great story in which we human beings have our own little story to enact to the best of our ability and knowledge. The characters who have faith in the story are rewarded with a sign or an image, discover their identity, and accept their destiny. Some of them are tragic figures, others are comic; but whether they are villains, victims, or fools does not seem to matter in the long run, for ultimately they are all marionettes and thus in the hands of God and the storyteller. In the final analysis, the marionettes in Dinesen's world are performing in stories which illustrate two central themes in Dinesen's view of life: The theme of aristocratic pride and the theme of acceptance."

Langbaum wrote that the two most frequent references in Miss Dinesen's writing are to marionettes and to the Book of Job. "They are both used to answer the same question—how to find the ideal in the real, the absolute in the relative. . . . She likes the extremely natural and the extremely artificial; she is a nature writer and a writer about styles of art and civilization. Her references to Job tell about . . . the intensification of the natural to yield the ideal. But her references to marionettes tell about . . . the imagination with which she bodies forth the ideal and the satire which invokes the ideal to criticize the real."

Miss Dinesen used in her writing the idea which, according to Langbaum, Thomas Mann explained: "'The apparently objective and accidental' is 'a matter of the soul's own contriving,' that 'the giver of all given conditions resides in ourselves.'" In early history the ego became aware of itself by assuming the identity of a god or hero. Various people such as Caesar and Cleopatra in a sense lived out the lives of earlier figures. Many of Miss Dinesen's characters are godlike, as Langbaum wrote, "like Mann's antique figures, artists of their own personalities in that they know what powers they draw upon." They knew that they are playing these lives again, and they do so blithely, with a kind of "gaiety." Miss Dinesen used elements of tragicomedy and Langbaum referred to her stories as "witty."

Isak Dinesen was born "in a Danish literary shrine, Rungstedlund, a rambling, redtiled house near Copenhagen, overlooking the sea." Johannes Ewald, the greatest lyric poet of Denmark, lived and worked there, and Miss Dinesen used Ewald's room as her study. She lived there again in her later years. She liked to have mottoes to live by, and began with "Navigare necesse est, vivere non necesse est." She later adopted the motto of Finch-Hatton's family crest, "Je responderay" ("I shall give account"). Miss Dinesen had been in ill health for many years, and eventually wasted away to 70 pounds. Her face was finely etched with the story of her life and her large luminous eyes were considered the most expressive part of her face. She was constantly painted and photographed by artists such as Carl Van Vechten, Richard Avedon, Brofferio, and Rene Bouche. Philip Callow, comparing her to Dame Edith Sitwell wrote: "In her 70's, emaciated and grotesquely wrinkled, just about able to balance on her brittle birdlike legs, she was more of a siren than ever." Carson McCullers was prompted to write: "She was very, very frail and old but as she talked her face was lit like a candle in an old church. My heart trembled when I saw her fragility." Philip Callow felt that "she seemed most proud of the title given her once by one of her Somali servants, who began a letter with 'Honourable Lioness.'" Langbaum wrote: "It is because Africa figures as a paradise lost—both in Isak Dinesen's life and in the life of Europe that *Out of Africa* is an authentic pastoral, perhaps the best pastoral of our time." Miss Dinesen settled on the coffee farm with her husband; later she met Denys Finch-Hatton and shared the experiences of living in Africa with him. She was extremely sensitive to her people, to the land and the animals, to the very air that she breathed there in the mountains. She said once that of the four elements, air was the most important, and the one which she tried to embody in her writing. Africa is used in her book, Langbaum believed, "to give us both an acute sense of history and a sense of the timeless life of nature at the unseen heart of things, where men and animals merge with each other and the landscape and the seen event merges all its unseen occurrences." She felt a great responsibility to and for the people who lived on her land, and she spent many hours taking care of their medical problems and arbitrating their disputes. The society of her farm was a feudal one, and she was in the position of the lord of the manor. "We see the relation of nature, the old order and the sense of tragedy in the story of her people's insistence on remaining together after she sold the farm," Langbaum stated. "They were to be resettled in the Kikuyu Reserve, where there was no stretch of unoccupied land big enough for all of them. She spent her last months in Africa haunting Government offices on their behalf. Her efforts were finally

successful. But when the authorities suggested that there was really no need for all her people to remain together, she thought of King Lear and his reply to the ungrateful daughters who wanted to strip him of the last few symbols of his royal identity. '"Oh reason not the need," I thought, "our basest beggars are in the poorest things superfluous."'"

This is the essence of the tragic view, that it is symbols not things that matter to human beings." Her vision of Africa was both quite true and quite special, because she brought to Africa with her the total of her cultural experience of the past.

Miss Dinesen used "tale," not in the sense of fairy tales, but in the sense of Shakespeare's *The Winter's Tale. Seven Gothic Tales,* Langbaum felt was "a great book about Europe," because of its "large historical and cultural range." "The Poet," in *Seven Gothic Tales,* Langbaum said, "comes from Kierkegaard, and suggests that Isak Dinesen is in substance an Existentialist writer—though she did not consider herself an Existentialist and disclaimed any extensive understanding of Existentialist philosophy. It is safe to say that Isak Dinesen is an Existentialist in the way that all romantic writers either are or are on their way to being Existentialists. For it is a basic tenet of romanticism that existence precedes essence, that experience is more fundamental than idea."

The Baroness was devoted to her father, who had lived among the Chippewa Indians for three years, and who killed himself when she was ten. Miss Arendt wrote that "the earlier part of her life had taught her that although you can tell stories or write poems about life, you cannot make life poetic, live it as if it were a work of art, . . . or use it for the realization of an 'idea.' . . . But life itself is neither essence nor elixir, and if you treat it as such it will only play its tricks on you. It was perhaps the bitter experience of life's tricks that prepared her . . . to be seized by the *grande passion* that is indeed no less rare than a *chef-d'oeuvre.* Storytelling, at any rate, is what in the end made her wise—and, incidentally, not a 'witch' . . . as her entourage admiringly called her." After Miss Dinesen returned to Denmark she was, Callow believed, "a sort of high priestess of the Heretica group of writers," and young writers made pilgrimages to see her. A *Time* reviewer commented that Miss Dinesen felt that she "had the gift of laughter, and something more, 'the pure joy of living, a sort of triumph simply because one exists.'"

Lawrence Durrell said of her style: "Her delicate, pointed prose style, always brushing against poetry, was quite unique and matched a witty and compassionate mind-fitted it like a glove. In an age flooded with shapeless and hasty writing her stories stand out with none of the aristocratic aloofness of which I once heard her unjustly accused. [Hers was a] patrician style, perfectly expressing the temper of a patrician mind." "She enriched the literature of her time," Louise Bogan stated, "with her power of imagination and her gift of fortitude." Hudson Strode commented: "In being *femme du monde,* she never lost contact with the soil; her roots went deep into Danish and African earth. Once while working in the Kenya maize fields, Karen Blixen amused herself by speaking in native rhymes to the young Swahili laborers. When she stopped, they begged, 'Speak again. Speak like the rain.' In her seven books she will doubtless go on speaking to the perceptive of the future in her own inimitable way." Clara Svendsen, Miss Dinesen's secretary and companion, and now the executor of her literary estate, has written: "She retained to the last her ever-longing heart, open and ready for unbounded joy. When she could no longer walk out in the woods to hear the nightingales in spring she located a spot where she could get by car, and sat lost and listening to the unstinted never-ending singing.''

"It is because Isak Dinesen had courage," Langbaum believed, "—both courage in the ordinary sense and the existential courage to be one's self and follow the logic of one's own nature—that her life and work are all of a piece: that she was able to write stories distinguished by the courage that in art we call style, and to create for herself a life and personality as audacious, extravagant, surprising and, yes, shocking, too, as her stories."

Miss Dinesen's estate is in the custody of the Rungstedlund Foundation in Denmark. She is buried under her favorite beech tree at Rungstedlund.

Orson Welles adapted "The Immortal Story," a short story, for the film with the same title which was released by Altura in 1968; another short story, "Echoes," has been adapted for filming by Mary Lee Settle.

BIOGRAPHICAL/CRITICAL SOURCES: Seven Gothic Tales, introduction by Dorothy Canfield Fisher, Modern Library, 1961; *Time,* January 6, 1961, September 27, 1968; Eric O. Johannesson, *The World of Isak Dinesen,* University of Washington, 1961; *Saturday Review,* March 16, 1963; Clara Svendsen, editor, *Isak Dinesen: A Memorial,* Random House, 1964; Robert Langbaum, *The Gayety of Vision: A Study of Isak Dinesen's Art,* Random House, 1965, published as *The Life and Destiny of Isak Dinesen,* University of Chicago Press, 1976; Parmenia Migel, *Titania: The Biography of Isak Dinesen,* Random House, 1967; *Books and Bookmen,* February, 1968; *New Yorker,* November 9, 1968; *Virginia Quarterly Review,* autumn, 1968; Clara Svendsen, editor, *The Life and Destiny of Isak Dinesen,* Random House, 1970.†

(Died September 7, 1962)
[Sketch approved by Clara Svendsen]

* * *

BLOCHMAN, Lawrence G(oldtree)   1900-1975

PERSONAL: Born February 17, 1900, in San Diego, Calif.; son of Lucien A. and Haidee (Goldtree) Blochman; married Marguerite Maillard, February 13, 1926. *Education:* University of California, Berkeley, A.B., 1921; Armed Forces Institute of Pathology, certificate in forensic pathology, 1952. *Home:* 370 Riverside Dr., New York, N.Y. 10025. *Agent:* Anita Diamant, 51 East 42 St., New York, N.Y. 10017.

CAREER: Worked for California newspapers in early years, as sports writer, police and courts reporter, city editor, and editor; *Japan Advertiser,* Tokyo, assistant night editor, 1921; *South China Morning Post,* Hong Kong, special writer, 1922; *Englishman,* Calcutta, India, feature writer and staff photographer, 1922-23; *Chicago Tribune,* European edition, assistant night editor, Paris, France, later editor of Riviera supplement, Nice, France, 1923-25; *Paris Times,* Paris, France, editorial and feature writer, 1925-27; full-time free-lance writer, 1928-75, with exception of stint in Hollywood as script writer for Universal Pictures, 1933-34, government service with Overseas Branch, U.S. Office of War Information, 1941-46, and six months as copy editor of *Business International,* 1960. Special correspondent, *New York Herald Tribune* in Guatemala, 1931, and for *American Weekly* in Paris, 1959. Consultant to Commission on Government Security, 1957, and U.S. Information Agency, 1962, 1964, 1967; public member, U.S. Department of State, Foreign Service Selection Boards, 1966.

MEMBER: Mystery Writers of America (president, 1948-49), Overseas Press Club of America (vice-president, 1956-57; member of board of governors). *Awards, honors:* Edgar Allan Poe Award (Edgar) of Mystery Writers of America, 1950, for *Diagnosis: Homicide.*

WRITINGS—Fiction: *Bombay Mail,* Little, Brown, 1934; *Bengal Fire,* Dell, 1937; *Red Snow at Darjeeling,* Saint Mystery Library, 1938; *Midnight Sailing,* Harcourt, 1938; *Blowdown,* Harcourt, 1939; *Wives to Burn,* Harcourt, 1940; *See You at the Morgue,* Duell, Sloan & Pearce, 1941; *Death Walks in Marble Halls,* Dell, 1942; *Diagnosis: Homicide* (story collection), Lippincott, 1950; *Pursuit,* Quinn Handibooks, 1951; *Rather Cool for Mayhem,* Lippincott, 1951; *Recipe for Homicide,* Lippincott, 1952; *Clues for Doctor Coffee* (story collection), Lippincott, 1964.

General: *Here's How: Round-the-World Bar Book of the Overseas Press Club,* New American Library, 1957; *Doctor Squibb: The Life and Times of a Rugged Idealist,* Simon & Schuster, 1958; (with Evangelia Callas) *My Daughter, Maria Callas,* Fleet, 1960; (with Stanley Stein) *Alone No Longer,* Funk, 1963; (with Harlan Logan) *Are You Misunderstood?,* Funk, 1965; (with Michael V. DiSalle) *The Power of Life or Death,* Random House, 1965; (with DiSalle) *Second Choice,* Hawthorn, 1966; *Wake Up Your Body,* McKay, 1969; (with Herbert Fensterheim) *Help Without Psychoanalysis,* Stein & Day, 1971; (with A. J. Cervantes) *Mister Mayor,* Nash Publishing, 1974.

Translator from the French: *The Unknown Warriors,* Simon & Schuster, 1949; *Caroline Cherie,* Prentice-Hall, 1952; *Caroline Coquette,* Prentice-Hall, 1953; *Love Camp,* Pyramid Books, 1953; *African Mistress,* Pyramid Books, 1954; *The Redhead from Chicago,* Pyramid Books, 1954; *Savage Triangle,* Pyramid Books, 1954; *The Damned One,* Pyramid Books, 1956; *The Man from Paris,* Pyramid Books, 1956; *In Search of Man,* Hawthorn, 1957; *The Heroes of God,* Hawthorn, 1959; *The Bride Was Much Too Beautiful,* Pyramid Books, 1959; (with Anthony Boucher) *The Shorter Cases of Inspector Maigret,* Doubleday, 1959; *Murder in Montmartre,* Dell, 1960; *A Month Among the Girls,* Pyramid Books, 1960; *The Deadly Species,* Dell, 1961; *A Month Among the Men,* Pyramid Books, 1962; *The Flesh,* Pyramid Books, 1962; *Three Beds in Manhattan,* Doubleday, 1964.

Ghost writer of three other books, one on laboratory medicine for a doctor. Author of several motion picture scripts, and numerous radio and television programs. His several hundred short stories include the "Daniel Webster Coffee, M.D." series, which appeared in *Collier's* at intervals for ten years, and stories in *Saturday Evening Post, Argosy, American Magazine, Adventure, Ellery Queen's Mystery Magazine,* and *This Week.* Contributor to *Encyclopaedia Britannica.*

WORK IN PROGRESS: A work of fiction, for Gold Medal.

SIDELIGHTS: Five of Blochman's works have been adapted for motion pictures—*Bombay Mail* for a film released by Universal, 1934, *Death Walks in Marble Halls,* Twentieth Century-Fox, *Pursuit,* Metro-Goldwyn-Mayer, 1935, *The Secret of the Chateau,* Universal, 1935, and *Chinatown Squad,* Universal, 1935.

He was bilingual in French, had a good working knowledge of Spanish, a colloquial knowledge of Japanese and German, and a smattering of Italian, Hindustani, and Malay.

(Died January 22, 1975)

BLUMBERG, Dorothy Rose 1904-

PERSONAL: Born March 3, 1904, in Baltimore, Md.; daughter of Isaac A. and Florence (Burgunder) Oppenheim; married Harold B. Cahn, June 9, 1923 (divorced, 1932); married Albert E. Blumberg (a professor of philosophy at Rutgers University), August 10, 1933; children: (first marriage) Patricia Cahn Gates, Frank B. Cahn II. Education: Goucher College, A.B., 1924; Columbia University, M.A., 1963. Home: 628 West 151st St., New York, N.Y. 10031.

MEMBER: American Historical Association, Labor Historians, Organization of American Historians, Phi Beta Kappa.

WRITINGS: Florence Kelley: The Making of a Social Pioneer, Augustus Kelley, 1966; Whose What? Aaron's Beard to Zorn's Lemma, Holt, 1969. Contributor to Encyclopedia of Social Work and Encyclopedia of American Biography; contributor of articles to Labor History.

WORK IN PROGRESS: A biography of Populist leader Mary Elizabeth Lease (1850-1933).

* * *

BLUMENFELD, Hans 1892-

PERSONAL: Born October 18, 1892, in Ornabrueck, Germany; son of Martin Jacob and Anna (Warburg) Blumenfeld. Education: Polytechnical Institute of Darmstadt, Master in Architecture, 1921. Politics: Independent Marxist. Religion: Atheist. Home: 66 Isabella St., Apt. 2602, Toronto, Ontario, Canada.

CAREER: Architect and city planner in Germany, Austria, Soviet Union, United States, and Canada; lecturer, University of Montreal, Montreal, Quebec; now lecturer at University of Toronto, Toronto, Ontario, and planning consultant. Member: American Institute of Planners, Town Planning Institute of Canada (fellow), Corporation des Urbanistes de Quebec (honorary), American Association of Planning Officials (honorary).

WRITINGS: Moderne Nahverkehrsplanug, Erich Schmidt Verlag, 1961; The Modern Metropolis: Its Origins, Growth, Characteristics, and Planning (essays), edited by Paul D. Spreiregen, M.I.T. Press, 1967. Contributor to professional journals in Canada, United States, Germany, Denmark, Sweden, Mexico, and Soviet Union.

SIDELIGHTS: Blumenfeld is competent in French, and knows some Russian and Italian.

* * *

BLUNDEN, Edmund (Charles) 1896-1974

PERSONAL: Born November 1, 1896, son of joint-headmasters of a London school; married Claire Margaret Poynting, 1945; children: four daughters. Education: Queen's College, Oxford, M.A. and C.Lit. Home: Long Melford, Suffolk, England.

CAREER: Joined the staff of The Athenaeum, 1920, as assistant to Middleton Murry and continued (until 1924) as a regular contributor when The Athenaeum was amalgamated with The Nation, returned, 1928; Tokyo University, Tokyo, Japan, professor of English, 1924-27; Oxford University, Oxford, England, fellow and tutor in English literature at Merton College, 1931-43, staff member of Senior Training Corps, 1940-44; worked with United Kingdom liaison mission in Tokyo, 1948-50; University of Hong Kong, professor of English, 1953-64; Oxford University Chair of Poetry, 1966-68. Military service: Royal Sussex Regiment, 1916-19;

served in France and Belgium; Military Cross, 1917. Member: Royal Society of Literature (fellow), Japan Academy (honorary). Awards, honors: Hawthornden Prize, 1922, for The Shepherd; Commander, Order of the British Empire, 1951; Queen's Gold Medal for Poetry, 1956; Benson Medal, Royal Society of Literature; Order of the Rising Sun, third class, Japan, 1963; Litt.D., University of Leeds.

WRITINGS—Poetry: Poems, [Horsham], 1914; Poems Translated from the French, [Horsham], 1914; Three Poems, J. Brooker, 1916; Pastorals: A Book of Verses, E. Macdonald, 1916.

The Barn with Certain Other Poems, Sidgwick & Jackson, 1920, Knopf, 1921; The Waggoner and Other Poems, Sidgwick & Jackson, 1920; The Shepherd, and Other Poems, Knopf, 1922; To Nature: New Poems, Beaumont Press, 1923; Edmund Blunden, Benn, 1925; English Poems, Cobden-Sanderson, 1925, Knopf, 1926; Masks of Time: A New Collection of Poems Principally Meditative, Beaumont Press, 1925; (contributor) Edward Thompson, editor, The Augustan Books of Modern Poetry, Benn, 1925, reissued as one part of Modern Poetry, L. B. Hill, 1925; Japanese Garland, Beaumont Press, 1928; Retreat, Doubleday, Doran, 1928; Winter Nights: A Reminiscence, Faber & Gwyer, 1928; Near and Far: New Poems, Cobden-Sanderson, 1929, Harper, 1930.

The Poems of Edmund Blunden, 1914-1930, Cobden-Sanderson, 1930, Harper, 1932; A Summer's Fancy, Beaumont Press, 1930; To Themis: Poems on Famous Trials, with Other Pieces, Beaumont Press, 1931; Halfway House: A Miscellany of New Poems, Cobden-Sanderson, 1932, Macmillan, 1933; Choice or Chance: New Poems, Cobden-Sanderson, 1934; Verses: To H. R. H. The Duke of Windsor, Alden Press, 1936; An Elegy and Other Poems, Cobden-Sanderson, 1937; On Several Occasions, by a Fellow of Merton College, Corvinus Press, 1938.

Poems, 1930-1940, Macmillan, 1940; Shells by a Stream: New Poems, Macmillan, 1944; After the Bombing, and Other Short Poems, Macmillan, 1949, reprinted, Books for Libraries Press, 1971.

Edmund Blunden (a selection of poetry and prose made by Kenneth Hopkins), Hart-Davis, 1950, Horizon, 1962, reprinted, Books for Libraries Press, 1970; Poems of Many Years, Collins, 1957; A Hong Kong House, Poetry Book Society, 1959 (published in England as A Hong Kong House: Poems 1951-1961, Collins, 1962).

Eleven Poems, Golden Head Press, 1965; The Midnight Skaters (chosen and introduced by C. Day Lewis), Bodley Head, 1968.

Prose: The Bonadventure: A Random Journal of an Atlantic Holiday, Cobden-Sanderson, 1922, Putnam, 1923; Christ's Hospital: A Retrospect, Christophers, 1923; On the Poems of Henry Vaughn: Characteristics and Intimations, with His Principal Latin Poems Carefully Translated into English Verse, Cobden-Sanderson, 1927, reprinted, Russell, 1969; Leigh Hunt's "Examiner" Examined, Cobden-Sanderson, 1928, Harper, 1931, reprinted, Archon Books, 1967; Undertones of War (narrative), Cobden-Sanderson, 1928, Doubleday, Doran, 1929, with new preface by the author, Oxford University Press, 1956, revised edition, Collins, 1965, Harcourt, 1966; Nature in English Literature, Harcourt, 1929, reprinted, Kennikat, 1970.

De Bello Germanico: A Fragment of Trench History, G. A. Blunden, 1930; Leigh Hunt and His Circle, Harper, 1930 (published in England as *Leigh Hunt: A Biography,* Cobden-Sanderson, 1930), reprinted as *Leigh Hunt: A Biography,* Archon Books, 1970; *The Somme Battle: Selected Chapters from Undertones of War,* Velhagen & Klasing, c. 1930; *In Summer,* privately printed for Fytton Armstrong, 1931; *Votive Tablets: Studies Chiefly Appreciative of English Authors and Books,* Cobden-Sanderson, 1931, Harper, 1932, reprinted, Books for Libraries Press, 1967; *The Face of England in a Series of Occasional Sketches,* Longmans, Green, 1932; *Fall in, Ghosts: An Essay on a Battalion Reunion,* White Owl Press, 1932; *Charles Lamb and His Contemporaries, Being the Clark Lectures Delivered at Trinity College, Cambridge, 1932,* Cambridge, The University Press, 1933, published as *Charles Lamb and His Contemporaries,* 1937, reprinted, Archon Books, 1967; (with Sylva Norman) *We'll Shift Our Ground: or, Two on a Tour,* Cobden-Sanderson, 1933; *The Mind's Eye: Essays,* J. Cape, 1934, reprinted, Books for Libraries Press, 1967; *Edward Gibbon and His Age,* J. W. Arrowsmith, 1935, reprinted, Folcroft, 1974; *Keat's Publisher: A Memoir of John Taylor (1781-1864),* J. Cape, 1936.

English Villages, Collins, 1941; *Thomas Hardy,* Macmillan, 1941, reprinted, St. Martin's, 1967; *Cricket Country,* Collins, 1944; *Shelley: A Life Story,* Collins, 1946, Viking, 1947, 2nd edition, Oxford University Press, 1965; *Shakespeare to Hardy,* Kenkyusha, 1948, reprinted with corrections, 1949, reprint of 1948 edition, Folcroft, 1969; *Shelley's Defence of Poetry and Blunden's Lectures on "Defence",* Hokuseido, 1948, reprinted, Folcroft, 1969; *Sons of Light: A Series of Lectures of English Writers,* Hosei University Press, 1949, Folcroft, 1969; *Addresses on General Subjects Connected with English Literature,* Kenkyusha, 1949, 2nd edition, 1958; *Poetry and Science and Other Lectures,* [Osaka], 1949.

Favorite Studies in English Literature, [Tokyo], 1950; *Influential Books,* [Tokyo], 1950; *Reprinted Papers: Partly Concerning Some English Romantic Poets,* [Tokyo], 1950, Folcroft Library Editions, 1971; *Chaucer to "B. V.",* [Tokyo], 1950, reprinted, Folcroft Library Editions, 1971; *A Wanderer in Japan,* [Tokyo], 1950; *John Keats,* Longmans, Green, 1950, 2nd revised edition, 1966; *Lectures in English Literature,* 2nd edition, Kodokwan, 1952; *The Dede of Pittie* (poems and prose), Christ's Hospital, 1953; *Charles Lamb,* Longmans, Green, 1954, revised edition, 1964; *War Poets, 1914-1918,* Longmans, Green, 1958; *Three Young Poets: Critical Sketches of Byron, Shelley and Keats,* Folcroft, 1959.

English Scientists as Men of Letters, Hong Kong University Press, 1961; *John Clare: Beginner's Luck,* Bridge Books, 1971.

Editor: (With Alan Porter) John Clare, *Poems,* Cobden-Sanderson, 1920; Christopher Smart, *A Song to David, with Other Poems,* Cobden-Sanderson, 1924; John Clare, *Madrigals and Chronicles,* Beaumont Press, 1924; *Shelley and Keats as They Struck Their Contemporaries,* C. W. Beaumont, 1925, Folcroft Library Editions, 1970, reprint of 1925 edition, Haskell, 1971; Benjamin Robert Hayden, *Autobiography,* Oxford University Press, 1927; (compiler) *A Hundred English Poems from the XIVth Century to the XIXth,* [Tokyo], 1927, 2nd revised edition, Kenkyusha, 1968; (author of introduction and compiler with Cyril Falls, H. M. Tomlinson, R. Wright) *The War, 1914-1918: A Booklist,* The Reader, 1929; *English Poems,* revised edition, Duckworth, 1929; William Collins, *The Poems,* Haslewood Books, 1929.

Great Short Stories of the War: England, France, Germany, America, Eyre & Spottiswoode, 1930; John Clare, *Sketches in the Life of John Clare,* Cobden-Sanderson, 1931; Wilfred Owen, *Poems,* Chatto & Windus, 1933, new edition, 1947, New Directions, 1949, author of introduction to amended edition entitled *Collected Poems,* New Directions, 1964; (compiler) *Charles Lamb: His Life Recorded by His Contemporaries,* Hogarth Press, 1934; (with Earl Leslie Griggs) *Coleridge: Studies by Several Hands on the Hundredth Anniversary of His Death,* Constable, 1934, reprinted, Russell, 1970.

Return to Husbandry, J. M. Dent, 1943; Christopher Smart, *Hymns for the Amusement of Children,* Luttrell Society, 1947; Francis Carey Slater, *Selected Poems,* Oxford University Press, 1947.

(With others) *The Christ's Hospital Book,* Hamish Hamilton, 1953; Ivor Gurney, *Poems,* Hutchinson, 1954; John Keats, *Selected Poems,* Norton, 1955; Percy Bysshe Shelley, *Poems,* Collins, 1955.

Alfred, Lord Tennyson, *Selected Poems,* Heinemann, 1960; Thomas Bewick, *A Memoir of Thomas Bewick, Written by Himself, 1822-1828,* Centaur Press, 1961, Southern Illinois University Press, 1962; (with Bernard Mellor) *Wayside Poems of the Early Eighteenth Century: An Anthology,* Oxford University Press, 1963; (author of introduction) William Wordsworth, *The Solitary Song: Poems for Young Readers,* Bodley Head, 1970.

Also author of numerous pamphlets and booklets on literary subjects. Translator of the poetry of Mezzetin and Loret, and of Henry Vaughan's Latin verse. Author of libretto for Gerald Finzi's "An Ode For St. Cecilia's Day," Boosey & Hawkes, 1947. Contributor to *Times Literary Supplement.*

SIDELIGHTS: Margaret Willy has said of Blunden: "[He is] in direct line of descent from Crabbe and Clare—his roots firmly planted in the sturdy pastoral tradition of English poetry." Another critic, Charles Morgan, noted: "Blunden has within his range both the poetry of observation penetrated and the poetry of the unperceived. In the first respect, he has an affinity with Wordsworth; in the second, with Coleridge...." This was not to say, however, that he merely continued a tradition. According to Hugh I'Anson Fausset, Blunden "seldom treads ground which his imagination has not intimately worked, circumscribed as that ground may be. Consequently the tradition which he maintains, he also renews." He "followed no school or fashion," wrote Alec M. Hardie. "The post-war disillusion hit hard at the literary world, old gods apparently had feet of clay, and newness, originality and revolt were the catchwords. To believe [as Blunden did] in the immediate past was [according to many of his contemporaries] to believe in sterility and decadence. Edmund Blunden was [erroneously] labelled a 'Georgian' by many of the rebels...." G. S. Fraser added: "... With Sassoon, Read and Graves, Blunden is a last important survivor of that generation of first world war poets who passed through and surmounted an ordeal of initiation.... [He] is the last surviving poet of the school of Hardy, the last writer of a natively English poetry...."

Fausset allowed that the dismissal of Blunden by certain contemporaries was possibly somewhat justified: "The charge brought against him that he has failed to come to grips with contemporary reality and is for that reason inevitably only a minor poet has some truth in it. His very virtues are here his defects. His rootedness in the past and the soil make him impervious to the distractions, the mechanized tensions, the life-and-death struggle of the modern world. He does not stand between two worlds, one dead, one struggling to be born, but in a world of his own, secure and at peace, though tempests rage without or its tranquil air quivers now and then at the thud of distant explosions.''

Yet within the limits he had set for himself, Blunden was a notable poet. His subjects include English rural life (for which he is probably best known, though he is no ''bucolic escapist,'' wrote Richard Church) and trench warfare during World War I. He also wrote occasional verse and 'personal' poems which Hardie saw as representing ''the pilgrimage of a poet often bewildered and in doubt, but rarely in despair, and it is hardly to be wondered at that his imagination and thought have explored more widely the metaphysical realms in ever-increasing persistence.... A similar atmosphere pervades his purely imaginative poems; he opens his wings in the clouds of mystery, the kingdom of 'The Ancient Mariner' and 'Christabel'. The riddle of man's power and mind are challenged.''

Hardie continued: ''''Blunden's country' cannot be confined. He has found a common link between England and France, England and Japan. Imaginative and poetic reasoning is his country. He seems the legitimate inheritor of the legacy of English literature, and has increased the value of his inheritance, not least by his modesty, tolerance and artistic sincerity.''

Blunden was a scholar as well. He was considered to be a leading authority on the English Romantic poets, and was responsible for rediscovering John Clare. Hardie wrote ''English literature owes much to him for his biographical discoveries, critical originality and perspicuity; literary periods are now the fuller for his researches.''

BIOGRAPHICAL/CRITICAL SOURCES: Robert Bridges, *The Dialectical Words in Blunden's Poems,* [Oxford], 1921; J. C. Squire, *Essays on Poetry,* Heinemann, 1923; Charles Williams, *Poetry at Present,* Clarendon, 1930; Frank Swinnerton, *The Georgian Scene,* Farrar & Rinehart, 1934; Richard Church, *Eight for Immortality,* Dent, 1941; *Poetry,* May, 1941; Hugh I'Anson Fausset, *Poets and Pundits,* Yale University Press, 1947; Charles Morgan, *Reflections in a Mirror,* second series, Macmillan, 1947; Oliver Edwards, *Talking of Books,* Heinemann, 1957; *English,* fall, 1957; Alec M. Hardie, *Edmund Blunden,* Longmans, Green, for the British Council, 1958; *London Magazine,* April, 1966; *Contemporary Literary Criticism,* Volume II, Gale, 1974.†

(Died January 20, 1974)

*   *   *

BOASE, Thomas Sherrer Ross   1898-1974

PERSONAL: Born August 31, 1898, in Dundee, Scotland; son of Charles Millet and Anne (Ross) Boase. *Education:* Oxford University, M.A., 1925. *Home:* 6, Atherton Dr., Wimbledon Common, London SW19 5LB, England.

CAREER: Hertford College, Oxford University, Oxford, England, fellow and tutor, 1922-37; University of London, London, England, professor of art history and director of Courtauld Institute of Art, 1937-47; Oxford University, president of Magdalen College, 1947-68, vice-chancellor of the university, 1958-60. Temporary civil servant, British Air Ministry, in Cairo, Egypt, and United Kingdom, 1939-43; chief representative in Middle East, British Council, 1943-45. Trustee of National Gallery, 1947-53, Shakespeare Birthplace Trust, beginning 1949, and British Museum, 1950-69; governor of Rugby School, 1951-63, Shakespeare

Memorial Theatre, beginning 1952; commissioner for ''Exhibition of 1851,'' beginning 1956. *Military service:* British Army, Oxford and Bucks Light Infantry, 1917-19; became lieutenant; received Military Cross.

MEMBER: British Archaeological Association (president, 1969-72), British Academy (fellow), American Philosophical Society (foreign member), Oxford and Cambridge Club (London). *Awards, honors:* D.C.L., Oxford University; LL.D., University of St. Andrews, University of Melbourne, and Rockefeller Institute; D.Litt., University of Durham and University of Reading.

WRITINGS: Boniface VIII, Constable, 1933; *St. Francis of Assisi,* Duckworth, 1936; (editor) *Oxford History of English Art,* Oxford University Press, 1949; *English Art 1100-1216,* Clarendon Press, 1953; *English Art 1800-1870,* Clarendon Press, 1959; *Castles and Churches of the Crusading Kingdom* (photographs by Richard Cleave), Oxford University Press, 1967; (contributor of critical essay) *The Sculpture of David Wynne, 1949-1967,* M. Joseph, 1968; *Kingdoms and Strongholds of the Crusades,* Thames & Hudson, 1971; *Death in the Middle Ages: Mortality, Judgement and Remembrance,* McGraw, 1972. Also co-author of *Nebuchadnezzar,* 1972. Editor, *Journal of the Warburg and Courtauld Institutes.*†

(Died April 14, 1974)

*   *   *

BOBBE, Dorothie de Bear   1905-1975

PERSONAL: Surname rhymes with ''hobby''; born March 1, 1905, in London, England; daughter of Bernard (a school principal) and Hannah (Bobbe) de Bear; married Sidney S. Bobbe (an attorney), June 28, 1928. *Education:* Education in England at Wordsworth College, London, 1915-23, and Oxford University, 1923-25. *Residence:* New York, N.Y.

CAREER: Daily Sketch (newspaper), London, England, an assistant editor, 1925-27; Gregg Publishing Co., New York, N.Y., an assistant editor, 1927-28; biographer. Active in various relief organizations during World War II.

WRITINGS: Abigail Adams, Minton, Balch, 1929, reprinted, Putnam, 1966; *Mr. and Mrs. John Quincy Adams,* Minton, Balch, 1930; *Fanny Kemble,* Minton, Balch, 1931; *De Witt Clinton,* Minton, Balch, 1933, new edition with a foreword by Henry Steele Commager, Friedman, 1962; *John Quincy Adams,* Putnam, 1971; *The New World Journey of Anne MacVicar,* Putnam, 1971. Contributor of section on Erie Canal, 1933-63, to Scribner's *Dictionary of American History;* also contributor to *American Heritage* and *New York Times Magazine.*

WORK IN PROGRESS: Three books in the juvenile field, for Putnam.

SIDELIGHTS: Mrs. Bobbe told *CA:* ''[I am] proud of my friendships with descendants of the subjects of the biographies, including Owen Wister, who was Fanny Kemble's grandson; also including the great-great-grandson of Alexander Hamilton, the subject of one of my articles in *American Heritage.*''

BIOGRAPHICAL/CRITICAL SOURCES: Edward H. O'Neill, *A History of American Biography,* University of Pennsylvania Press, 1935.†

(Died March 19, 1975)

*   *   *

BOCK, Carl H(einz)   1930-19(?)

PERSONAL: Born March 12, 1930, in New York, N.Y.;

son of Carl Heinrich (a landscape architect) and Meta (Meyer) Bock; married Trude Thelen, June 14, 1958; children: Patricia Barbara, Alexander Michael. *Education:* Attended Champlain College, 1947-49; University of Pennsylvania, B.A. (with honors), 1951, M.A., (with honors), 1952; University of Marburg, Dr. phil. (magna cum laude), 1961. *Home:* Im Wellengewann 36, 69 Heidelberg, Germany. *Office:* European Division, University of Maryland, Zengerstrasse 1, 69 Heidelberg, Germany.

CAREER: Milford School, Milford, Conn., history master, 1956-57; Buckley Country Day School, Roslyn, N.Y., history teacher, 1957; University of Maryland, European Division, Heidelberg, Germany, part-time lecturer in history, 1961-65, assistant director, beginning 1965. U.S. Army, Northern Area Command Headquarters, Frankfurt, Germany, civilian information specialist, 1962-63; Amerika Haus, Heidelberg, Germany, lecturer. *Military service:* U.S. Navy, 1952-55; became lieutenant junior grade. *Member:* American Historical Association, Organization of American Historians, Academy of Political Science, American Academy of Political and Social Science, Naval Institute (associate member), Phi Beta Kappa, Alpha Sigma Lambda, Phi Alpha Theta, American-German Friendship Club (Heidelberg).

WRITINGS: Prelude to Tragedy: The Negotiation and Breakdown of the Tripartite Convention of London, October 31, 1861, University of Pennsylvania Press, 1966. European Division editor, *Marab: A Review* (publication of University of Maryland Abroad).†

(Deceased)

*   *   *

BOLIN, Luis (A.)   1894-1969

PERSONAL: Surname is pronounced Bo-*lin*; born April 24, 1894, in Malaga, Spain; son of Manuel and Carmen (Bidwell) Bolin; married Mercedes Saavedra, October 3, 1929; married second wife, Cecilia McCallum Parker, March 9, 1963; children: (first marriage) Fernando, Marisol (daughter); (second marriage; stepchildren) Mrs. Philip Geyelin, Chauncey G. Parker III. *Education:* Secondary Institute, Malaga, B.A., 1910; University of Granada, Barrister, 1915; read for the Bar at Middle Temple, London, England; also studied at University of Madrid. *Religion:* Roman Catholic. *Home:* 1239 30th St. N.W., Washington, D.C.; and Doctor Fleming 1, Madrid, Spain. *Agent:* Collins-Knowlton-Wing, Inc., 575 Madison Ave., New York, N.Y. 10022.

CAREER: War correspondent with British Forces in France, 1916-18; Spanish Embassy, London, England, press attache, 1919-20; League of Nations Secretariat, Geneva, Switzerland, member, 1920-22; Spanish National Tourist Office, Seville, regional delegate, 1928-31; Spanish National Tourist Department, Madrid, director general, 1938-52; Spanish Embassy, Washington, D.C., counselor, 1952-63. London correspondent, *La Epoca,* Madrid, Spain, at various intervals, 1916-36. Chairman of European Travel Commission, New York, N.Y., 1957-60; consultant on tourism, World Bank and United Nations, 1964-65. *Military service:* Spanish Foreign Legion, honorary captain, 1936-69; attached to General Franco's Headquarters at Salamanca, 1936-38. *Awards, honors:* Grand Cross of the Order of Civil Merit and Grand Cross of Isabel la Catolica, both bestowed by Spanish Government; Commander of the Crown of Italy.

WRITINGS: (Published anonymously) *The Spanish Republic,* Eyre & Spottiswoode, 1933; *Parques Nacionales Northeamericanos,* Editora Nacional (Madrid), 1960, translation published as *The National Parks of the United States,* Knopf, 1961; *Spain: The Vital Years* (partly autobiographical), Lippincott, 1967. Contributor to Spanish-and English-language magazines and newspapers.

WORK IN PROGRESS: Research on sixteenth- to twentieth-century historical subjects.

SIDELIGHTS: The first chapter of *Spain: The Vital Years* recaps the opening days of the Spanish Civil War when Bolin was organizer of the flight that brought General Franco from the Canary Islands to Morocco in July, 1936, a flight that sparked the War. *Avocational interests:* Reading, art, travel, music, hunting, conservation.

BIOGRAPHICAL/CRITICAL SOURCES: Spain: The Vital Years, Lippincott, 1967.†

(Died September 3, 1969)

*   *   *

BOMANS, Godfried J(an) A(rnold)   1913-1971

PERSONAL: Born March 2, 1913, in The Hague, Netherlands; son of Jan Michiel (minister of the interior for the Netherlands Home Department) and Arnolda (von Beck) Bomans; married Gertrude Verscheure, August 17, 1945; children: Eva. *Education:* Studied law at University of Amsterdam and psychology at Catholic University of Nijmegen. *Religion:* Roman Catholic. *Home:* 10 Parkweg, Bloemendaal, Netherlands.

CAREER: Author. Appeared weekly on Dutch television. *Member:* Dickens Fellowship (London; vice-president).

WRITINGS: Sprookjes (fairy tales), Elsevier, 1946; *Kopstukken,* Elsevier, 1947; *Memoires of gedenkschriften van Minister Pieter Bas,* Het Spectrum, c. 1947; (with others) *Het Hildebrand monument van Prof. J. Bronner,* Elsevier, 1948; (with Antoon Coolen) *Liefde, dood en minne,* [Netherlands], 1948; *Buitelingen: Aforismen, buitelingen en capriolen,* [Netherlands], 1949; (with others) *Omnibus naar het geluk* (short stories), P. Brand, 1950; (with Josiah de Gruyter) *Meesters van de spotprent van Daumier tot Steinberg,* Boucher, 1952; *De Aventuren van tante Pollewop,* [Netherlands], 1953; *Capriolen,* Elsevier, 1953; *Erik, of het klein insectenboek,* [Netherlands], 1955; *Nieuwe buitelingen: Facetten en aspecten* (essays), Elsevier, 1955; *Wandelingen door Rome,* Elsevier, 1956; *Het doosje,* Nederlandsche Vereeniging voor Druk- en Boek-kunst, 1956; *Wonderlijke nachten,* [Netherlands], c. 1956; *Op het vinkentouw,* De Lanteern, 1957; *Noten kraken* (essays), Elsevier, 1962; *Op de keper beschouwd* (collection of articles), Elsevier, 1963; *Sprookjesboek,* Elsevier, 1965, translation by Patricia Crampton published as *The Wily Wizard and the Wicked Witch, and Other Weird Stories,* F. Watts, 1969; *Van de hak op de tak* (collection of essays), Elsevier, 1965; *Denkend aan Vlaanderen,* Lannoo, 1967; (with others) *Waarom ik geloof,* Semper Agendo, 1968; *Mijmeringen,* Elsevier, 1968; *Van hetzelfde,* Elsevier, 1969; *The Wily Witch, and All the Other Fairy Tales and Fables,* translation by Crampton, Stemmer House, 1977.

WORK IN PROGRESS: Research on the Victorian Age, especially on Dickens.

SIDELIGHTS: All of Bomans' books have been translated into several languages; many of them have run into numerous reprints in Dutch. He was competent in French, Italian, German, English, Spanish, Japanese, Greek (ancient), Latin, and Hebrew.†

(Died December 22, 1971)

BOND, Marshall, Jr. 1908-

PERSONAL: Born February 10, 1908, in Los Angeles, Calif.; son of Marshall (in mining) and Amy Louise (Burnett) Bond; married Louise Lincoln, May 31, 1945. *Education:* Yale University, Ph.B., 1931. *Politics:* Independent. *Religion:* Agnostic. *Home:* 990 Tornoe Rd., Santa Barbara, Calif. 93105. *Office:* 1900 State St., Santa Barbara, Calif. 93105.

CAREER: Independent real estate and insurance broker, associated with John E. Timmons & Co., Santa Barbara, Calif. *Military service:* U.S. Army, 1942-45; became master sergeant. *Member:* Sierra Club.

WRITINGS: Gold Hunter: The Adventures of Marshall Bond, University of New Mexico Press, 1969. Contributor to *Pacific Discovery.*

WORK IN PROGRESS: Adventures with Peons, Princes and Tycoons.

SIDELIGHTS: Marshall Bond is an ardent camper, photographer, and explorer. He has covered the Green and Colorado rivers by raft, explored three rivers in Mexico, and made one of his five trips to Europe aboard a sailing yacht. His interests include education, the theatre, and the arts.

* * *

BOND, Richmond Pugh 1899-

PERSONAL: Born September 16, 1899, in Magnolia, Miss.; son of Albert Richmond and Ruth (Pugh) Bond; married Marjorie Eliza Nix, September 3, 1924. *Education:* Vanderbilt University, A.B., 1920; Harvard University, A.M., 1923, Ph.D., 1929. *Home:* 101 Pine Lane, Chapel Hill, N.C. 27514.

CAREER: Instructor in English at Baylor University, Waco, Tex., 1921-22, Hollins College, Hollins, Va., 1923-24, and Indiana University, Bloomington, 1924-26; University of North Carolina, Chapel Hill, assistant professor, 1929-34, associate professor, 1934-39, professor of English, 1955-70. University of London, honorary lecturer, University College, 1949-51, special lecturer in the university, 1950-51; visiting summer professor at Duke University, New York University, and University of Texas. *Military service:* U.S. Naval Reserve, active duty, 1942-45; became lieutenant commander; received Navy Unit Commendation.

MEMBER: Modern Language Association of America, English Association (London), Augustan Reprint Society, South Atlantic Modern Language Association, Phi Beta Kappa. *Awards, honors:* Dexter traveling fellow, Harvard University, 1927, 1928-29; Sterling research fellow, Yale University, 1937-38; citation award, Society of Colonial Wars, 1952; resident fellow, Newberry Library, 1963.

WRITINGS: English Burlesque Poetry, 1700-1750, Harvard University Press, 1932, reprinted, Russell, 1964; (editor) *Chesterfield: Letters and Other Pieces,* Doubleday, Doran, 1935; (with Katherine K. Weed) *Studies of British Newspapers and Periodicals from Their Beginning to 1800: A Bibliography,* University of North Carolina Press, 1946; *Queen Anne's American Kings,* Clarendon Press, 1952; (editor) *Studies in the Early English Periodical,* University of North Carolina Press, 1957; (editor) *New Letters to the Tatler and Spectator,* University of Texas Press, 1959; *The Tatler: The Making of a Literary Journal,* Harvard University Press, 1971. Contributor of articles and reviews to journals.

WORK IN PROGRESS: Further research on the early English periodic press.

BONHAM CARTER, (Helen) Violet (Asquith) 1887-1969

PERSONAL: Born April 15, 1887, in London, England; daughter of Herbert Henry (first Earl of Oxford and Asquith, and Prime Minister of Great Britain, 1908-16) and Helen Kelsall (Melland) Asquith; married Sir Maurice Bonham Carter, November 30, 1915 (died, 1960); children: Helen Cressida (Mrs. Jasper Ridley), Laura Miranda (Mrs. Joseph Grimond), Mark Raymond, Raymond Henry. *Education:* Educated privately at home, and in Dresden and Paris. *Politics:* Liberal. *Religion:* Church of England. *Home:* 21 Hyde Park Sq., London W.2, England.

CAREER: Was active in Great Britain's political and cultural affairs as Lady Violet Bonham Carter until 1964 when she received peerage as Baroness Asquith of Yarnbury. President of Women's Liberal Federation, 1923-25, 1939-45; Liberal vice-president, Winston Churchill's Focus in Defence of Freedom and Peace, 1936-39; president of Liberal Party Organization, 1945-47, vice-president, 1947-65; contested Wells Division of Somersetshire as Liberal candidate, 1945, and Colne Valley, 1951; vice-chairman of United Europe Movement, 1947; delegate to Commonwealth Relations Conference in Canada, 1949. Governor of British Broadcasting Corp., 1941-46, of Old Vic, 1945-69; member of Royal Commission on the Press, 1947-49; trustee of Glyndebourne Arts Trust, 1955-69; president of Royal Institute of International Affairs, 1964-69. Falconer lecturer at University of Toronto, 1953; Romanes lecturer at Oxford University of Toronto, 1953; Romanes lecturer at Oxford University, 1963. *Awards, honors:* Dame of Order of the British Empire, 1953; LL.D., University of Sussex, 1963; life peerage, 1964.

WRITINGS: Winston Churchill: An Intimate Portrait, Harcourt, 1965 (published in England as *Winston Churchill as I Knew Him,* Eyre & Spottiswoode and Collins, 1965). Writer of radio and television scripts. Contributor of articles to newspapers and magazines.†

(Died February 19, 1969)

* * *

BONIME, Walter 1909-

PERSONAL: Born July 12, 1909, in Montville, Conn.; son of Ellis (a physician) and Reba (Strongin) Bonime; married second wife, Florence Levine (a writer), September 5, 1953; children: Karen, Stephen; step-children: Frank, Norma (Mrs. Alan Lovins). *Education:* University of Wisconsin, B.A., 1933; Columbia University, College of Physicians and Surgeons, M.D., 1938; New York Medical College, certificate in psychoanalysis, 1947. *Home:* 37 Washington Sq. W., New York, N.Y. 10011. *Office:* 10 Park Ave., New York, N.Y. 10016.

CAREER: Sinai Hospital of Baltimore, Baltimore, Md., interne, 1938-39; Central Islip State Hospital, Central Islip, N.Y., resident psychiatrist, 1939-42; New York Medical College, New York, beginning 1947, began as instructor, became associate professor of psychiatry, clinical professor, beginning 1973. Flower and Fifth Avenue Hospitals, New York, N.Y., associate attending psychiatrist, beginning 1947; Metropolitan Hospital, New York, N.Y., associate attending psychiatrist, 1961. *Wartime service:* U.S. Public Health Service, 1943-46; became assistant surgeon. *Member:* World Federation of Mental Health, American Medical Association, American Psychiatric Association (life fellow), Academy of Psychoanalysis (charter fellow),

Society of Medical Psychoanalysts (president, 1963-64), American Association for the Advancement of Science (fellow), Association for the Psychophysiological Study of Sleep, Association for Mental Health Aid to Israel, New York County Medical Society.

WRITINGS: (Contributor) Alfred Herman Rifkin, editor, *Schizophrenia in Psychoanalytic Office Practice,* Grune, 1957; *The Clinical Use of Dreams,* Basic Books, 1962; (contributor) Jules Hymen Masserman, editor, *Current Psychiatric Therapies,* Grune, 1962; (contributor) Silvano Arieti, editor, *American Handbook of Psychiatry,* Volume III, Basic Books, 1966.

SIDELIGHTS: Bonime told *CA:* "I thoroughly enjoy practice, teaching and writing in psychoanalysis and expect to continue all three aspects as long as I live. I love visiting the country but wouldn't want to live anywhere but [New York] City (except perhaps Paris). The theatre is one of my chief enjoyments outside my profession."

*   *   *

BONNEY, Merl E(dwin)   1902-

PERSONAL: Born October 26, 1902, in Pomeroy, Wash.; son of Harry H. (in real estate) and Margaret (Blakeman) Bonney; married Myrle Doane (a librarian), 1937; children: Lewis Alfred, Carol Ann. *Education:* Willamette University, A.B., 1925; Stanford University, M.A., 1927; Columbia University, Ph.D., 1935. *Politics:* Republican. *Religion:* Presbyterian. *Office:* Department of Psychology, North Texas State University, Denton, Tex. 76203.

CAREER: Oregon College of Education, Monmouth, assistant professor of educational psychology, 1927-31; Western State College of Colorado, Gunnison, assistant professor of educational psychology, 1934-35; North Texas State University, Denton, associate professor, 1936-48, professor of psychology, beginning 1948. Summer lecturer, University of Colorado, 1951, 1952, Portland State College (now University), 1954, 1955, and Chico State College (now California State University, Chico), 1953, 1957. *Member:* American Psychological Association, Southwestern Psychological Association, Texas Psychological Association (president, 1950). *Awards, honors:* Alumni award for best teacher, North Texas State University, 1971.

WRITINGS: Techniques of Appeal and Social Control, G. Banta, 1934; *Intelligence, Social Acceptance, and Social Mindedness,* Hogg Foundation, University of Texas, 1945; *Development of Social Attitudes,* Hogg Foundation, University of Texas, 1946; *Popular and Unpopular Children: A Sociometric Study* (monograph), Beacon House, 1947; *Bonney-Eessenden Sociograph with Manual,* California Text Bureau, 1955; *Mental Health in Education,* Allyn & Bacon, 1960; (contributor) J. L. Moreno and others, editors, *The Sociometry Reader,* Free Press, 1960; (with Richard S. Hampleman) *Personal-Social Evaluation Techniques,* Center for Applied Research in Education, 1962; *Interpersonal Relations and the Challenge of Leadership,* Hogg Foundation, University of Texas, 1964; (contributor) *Feelings and Learning,* Childhood Association of America, 1965; *The Normal Personality,* McCutchan, 1969. Contributor to *Journal of Social Psychology, Social Forces, Journal of Applied Psychology, Sociometry,* other publications. Editor, *Sociometry,* 1950.

WORK IN PROGRESS: Personality and Interpersonal Attraction.

BOOS, Frank Holgate   1893-1968

PERSONAL: Born August 27, 1893, in Battle Creek, Mich.; son of Frank (an agent for Anheuser Busch Co.) and Ella Ada (Bishop) Boos; first wife, Jane Petit; married second wife, Kathryn Besancon, September 14, 1934; children: Frank Holgate III. *Education:* Attended Detroit College of Law. *Politics:* Republican. *Religion:* "Left Catholic Church to become an Episcopalian." *Home:* 960 Trombley Rd., Grosse Pointe, Mich. 48230.

CAREER: Attorney in Detroit, Mich., for fifty years; former partner in firm of Baldwin & Boos; former consultant in law. *Military service:* U.S. Army, Infantry, World War I; became second lieutenant. *Member:* Michigan Bar Association (past president), Detroit Bar Association (past president), Detroit Club, Detroit Athletic Club, Grosse Pointe Club, Cooley Club.

WRITINGS: (Author of text in English and Spanish) *Las Urnas zapotecas en el Real Museo de Ontario* (portfolio of plates), National Institute of Anthropology and History (Mexico), 1964; *The Ceramic Sculptures of Ancient Oaxaca,* A. S. Barnes, 1966. Contributor to museum publications and to law journals.

BIOGRAPHICAL/CRITICAL SOURCES: Times Literary Supplement, February 2, 1967.††

(Died July 13, 1968)

*   *   *

BOREMAN, Jean   1909-

PERSONAL: Born November 24, 1909, in Pueblo, Colo.; daughter of Harry Clare (a manufacturer) and Grace (Lea) Pollok; married Edmund Boreman, January 23, 1937; married second husband, Carl E. Graeber (a fire department engineer), August 20, 1955; children: (first marriage) Barbara (Mrs. Frank Wallace), Arla (Mrs. Jay Crane). *Education:* University of California, Los Angeles, B.A., 1931. *Politics:* Republican. *Religion:* Episcopalian.

CAREER: Elementary teacher in Los Angeles, Calif., beginning 1931, teaching at every level from kindergarten through eighth grade. *Member:* Association for Childhood Education, American Association of University Women, Delta Zeta.

WRITINGS: Bullito, Griffin Patterson, 1945; *Quackie Goes to Town,* Griffin Patterson, 1946; *Moo Loo,* Melmont, 1955; *Bantie and Her Chicks,* Melmont, 1967.

"Rescue" series, with Molly C. Gorelick, published by Ritchie: *Fire on Sun Mountain,* 1967; *Flood at Dry Creek,* 1967; *Storm at Sand Point,* 1967; *Fog Over Sun City,* 1968; *Snow Storm at Green Valley,* 1968.††

*   *   *

BOSE, N(irmal) K(umar)   1901-1972
(Nirmala-Kumara Vasu)

PERSONAL: Born January 22, 1901, in Calcutta, India; son of Biman Bihari and Kiranashi Basu. *Education:* University of Calcutta, B.Sc. (honours), 1921, M.Sc., 1925, research fellow, 1929-30. *Home:* 37A Bosepara Lane, Calcutta 3, India.

CAREER: University of Calcutta, Calcutta, India, assistant lecturer in anthropology, 1938-42, lecturer, then reader in human geography, 1945-61. Visiting scholar, University of California, Berkeley, University of Chicago, University of Wisconsin, and University of Michigan, 1957-58; director of the Anthropological Survey of India, for the Government of

India, 1959-64. Visiting professor, Indian Institute of Advanced Study, 1965; Mahatma Gandhi Visiting Professor, Gauhati University, 1969; guest lecturer at Hiroshima University, Hiroshima, Japan, and at various American universities, 1965. Examiner in anthropology, political science, and folk literature at Indian universities. Member of the civil disobedience movement of Gandhi, doing "constructive work" in a village in Bengal, India, 1930-36, and participating in the Quit India Movement with Gandhi, 1942-45. Commissioner for Scheduled Castes and Scheduled Tribes, 1967-70. Assistant secretary, Ramakrishna Mission Institute of Culture, 1971.

MEMBER: Asiatic Society (anthropological secretary; fellow, 1971; president, 1972), Indian National Science Academy (fellow), Indian Science Congress Association (life member), Indian Anthropological Society (life member), Geographical Society of India (life member), Institute of Historical Study (life member), Bangiya Sahitya Parisad (secretary; vice-president; president, 1971-72), Nikhil Bharat Banga Bhasha Prasar Samiti (life member), Bangiya Vijnan Parisad (life member), Bangiya Jatiya Krida O Sakti Sangha (life member), St. John's Ambulance Association (life member), Bengal Library Association (life member). *Awards, honors:* Asiatic Society, Annandale Gold Medal, 1948, Saratchandra Roy Gold Medal, 1966, both for distinguished work in anthropology; Bronze Medal, University of Hiroshima, 1965; fellow, Sanskrit College, 1966; President's Award of *Padmashri*, 1966; Ramapran Gupta Award, Bangiya Sahitya Parisad.

WRITINGS: Cultural Anthropology, [Calcutta], 1929, revised edition, Associated Publishing Co. (Calcutta), 1953, Asia Publishing House, 1961; (editor and translator) *Canons of Orissan Architecture* (passages from native works in Sanskrit and Oriya), R. Chatterjee (Calcutta), 1932; (editor) *Selections from Gandhi*, Navajivan Publishing House (Ahmedabad), 1938, 2nd enlarged edition, 1957; (with Dharani Sen) *Excavations in Mayurbhanj*, University of Calcutta, 1948; *My Days with Gandhi*, Nishana (Calcutta), 1953; *Modern Bengal* (lectures delivered before the South Asia Colloquium, Berkeley, Calif., November-December, 1957), Center for South Asia Studies, Institute of International Studies, University of California, 1958; (with William Fielding Ogburn, with the assistance of Jyoti R. Moyee Sarma) *On the Trail of the Wolf Children*, Journal Press, 1959.

Readings for Indian Civilization, University of Chicago Press, 1961; *Gandhiji: The Man and His Mission* (pamphlet), Bharatiya Vidya Bhavan (Bombay), 1966; *Problems of National Integration* (lectures), Indian Institute of Advanced Study, 1967; (with P. H. Patwardhan) *Gandhi in Indian Politics*, Lalvani Publishing House, 1967; *Culture and Society in India*, Asia Publishing House, 1967; (editor) *Peasant Life in India: A Study in Indian Unity and Diversity*, 2nd edition, Manager of Publications (Delhi), 1967; *Calcutta, 1964: A Social Survey*, Lalvani Publishing House, 1968; *A Study of Satyagraha*, University of Poona, 1968.

Gandhism and Modern India, Department of Publication, University of Gauhati, 1970; *Tribal Life in India*, National Book Trust, 1971; *Lectures on Gandhism*, Navajivan Publishing House, 1971; *Problems of Indian Nationalism* (pamphlet), Indian Institute of Advance Study, 1971; *Anthropology and Some Indian Problems*, Institute of Social Research and Applied Anthropology (Calcutta), 1972. Also author of books in Bengali, 1926-72, and of booklets on anthropolopy and Gandhi. Editor with D. N. Majumdar, K. P.

Chattopadhyaya, R. C. Ray, and B. C. Ray, of *Man in India*, 1951-1958, sole editor, beginning 1958.

BIOGRAPHICAL/CRITICAL SOURCES: Aspects of Indian Culture and Society: Essays in Felicitation of Professor Nirmal Kumar Bose, Indian Anthropological Society, 1972.†

(Died October 15, 1972)

*   *   *

BOUGHNER, Daniel C(liness)   1909-1974

PERSONAL: Surname is pronounced *Buff*-ner; born April 19, 1909, in Cincinnati, Ohio; son of A. Brown (a newspaperman) and Caroline (Cliness) Boughner; married Rosalind Farr, July 11, 1937; children: Alan, Martin. *Education:* West Virginia University, A.B., 1930; Tufts University, A.M., 1932; Princeton University, Ph.D., 1938. *Politics:* Independent. *Religion:* Methodist. *Home:* 5321 Beverly Rd., Brooklyn, N.Y. 11203.

CAREER: Instructor in English at West Virginia University, Morgantown, 1934, and West Virginia Wesleyan College, Buckhannon, 1934-35; Northwestern University, Evanston, Ill., instructor, 1938-42, assistant professor of English, 1942-50; Evansville College (now University of Evansville), Evansville, Ind., professor of English, 1950-56; Brooklyn College of the City University of New York, Brooklyn, N.Y., assistant professor, 1958-60, associate professor, 1960-64, professor of English, beginning 1964. *Member:* Modern Language Association of America, Renaissance Society of America. *Awards, honors:* Newberry Library fellow, 1953, 1960; Folger Library fellow, 1954; Huntington Library fellow, 1956, 1963; Guggenheim fellow, 1956-57; Fulbright research fellow in Italy, 1957-58.

WRITINGS: The Braggart in Renaissance Comedy: A Study in Comparative Drama from Aristophanes to Shakespeare, University of Minnesota Press, 1954; *The Devil's Disciple*, Philosophical Library, 1968. Contributor to literature journals.

WORK IN PROGRESS: Shakespeare's Golden Comedy.†

(Died May 8, 1974)

*   *   *

BOURNE, Dorothy D(ulles)   1893-19(?)

PERSONAL: Born November 24, 1893, in New York, N.Y.; daughter of William, Jr. (a lawyer) and Sophea (Rhea) Dulles; married James R. Bourne (administrator with Puerto Rico Emergency Relief Administration; deceased) April 6, 1918; children: Nancy (Mrs. Terrell C. Myers), Robert Dulles. *Education:* Smith College, B.A., 1915; New York School of Social Work, certificate, 1917. *Politics:* Democrat. *Religion:* Protestant.

CAREER: Government of Puerto Rico, San Juan, director of rural social work, 1930-33; University of Puerto Rico, Rio Piedras, director of School of Social Work, 1933-36; Bard College, Annandale-on-Hudson, N.Y., professor of sociology and dean, 1949-62. President, Dutchess County Committee for Economic Opportunity; member of board of directors of Dutchess County Community Chest and Family Counseling Service. *Member:* American Sociological Society, American Association of University Women, League of Women Voters, Business and Professional Women's Club. *Awards, honors:* Eleanor Roosevelt Memorial Award, 1965; D.H.L., Bard College, 1967; Urban Service Award of the Office of Economic Opportunity, 1968; Smith College Medal, 1968.

WRITINGS: (With husband, James R. Bourne) *Thirty Years of Change in Puerto Rico,* Praeger, 1966. Contributor to professional journals.†

(Deceased)

*   *   *

BOURNE, James R.   1897-19(?)

PERSONAL: Born April 6, 1897, in New Haven, Conn.; son of Edward Gaylord (a college professor and author) and Annie (Nettleton) Bourne; married Dorothy W. Dulles (a sociologist; deceased), April 6, 1918; children: Nancy (Mrs. Terrell C. Myers), Robert Dulles. *Education:* Yale University, B.A., 1918. *Politics:* Democrat. *Religion:* Protestant.

CAREER: Owner of diary and fruit farm, 1919-29; manager of fruit cannery in Puerto Rico, 1929-32; administrator, Puerto Rico Emergency Relief Administration, 1933-36; owner of business and manufacturing firms in Rhinebeck, N.Y., 1937-56. During World War II held government posts in Washington, D.C., with U.S. Navy, Foreign Economic Administration, and other agencies. Chairman of Rhinebeck Zoning Board, 1953-66. *Military service:* U.S. Army, Field Artillery, 1918-19; became 2nd lieutenant. *Member:* Rotary Club (Rhinebeck).

WRITINGS: (With wife, Dorothy D. Bourne) *Thirty Years Of Change in Puerto Rico,* Praeger, 1966.

WORK IN PROGRESS: La Prera, the story of the Puerto Rico Emergency Relief Administration.†

(Deceased)

*   *   *

BOWEN, Elizabeth (Dorothea Cole)   1899-1973

PERSONAL: Born June 7, 1899, in Dublin, Ireland; daughter of Henry Cole and Florence Isabella Pomeroy (Colley) Bowen; married Alan Charles Cameron (a professor), August 4, 1923 (died, 1952). *Education:* Studied at Downe House, Downe, Kent, England. *Home:* Bowen's Court, Kildorrery, County Cork, Ireland.

CAREER: Worked in a shell-shock hospital near Dublin, Ireland; worked for Ministry of Information, London, England, during World War II, serving nights as an air-raid warden. *Member:* American Academy of Arts and Letters (honorary member), Irish Academy of Letters. *Awards, honors:* Commander, Order of the British Empire, 1948; D.Litt., Trinity College, Dublin, 1949, Oxford University, 1956; Companion of Literature, Royal Society of Literature, 1965; James Tait Black Memorial Prize, 1970, for *Eva Trout.*

WRITINGS: Encounters (stories; also see below), Sidgwick & Jackson, 1923, Boni & Liveright, 1926, new edition, Sidgwick & Jackson, 1949; *The Hotel* (novel), Constable, 1927, Dial, 1928; *Ann Lee's and Other Stories* (also see below), Boni & Liveright, 1928, reprinted, Books for Libraries, 1969; *Joining Charles and Other Stories,* Dial, 1929; *The Last September* (novel), Dial, 1929, new edition, with new author's preface, Knopf, 1952.

Friends and Relations (novel), Dial, 1931; *To the North* (novel), Gollancz, 1932, Knopf, 1933; *The Cat Jumps and Other Stories,* Gollancz, 1934; *The House in Paris* (novel), Gollancz, 1935, Knopf, 1936; (contributor) Charles Davy, editor, *Footnotes to the Film,* Oxford University Press, 1937, reprinted, Arno, 1970; *The Death of the Heart* (novel), Gollancz, 1938, Knopf, 1939.

Look at All Those Roses (stories), Knopf, 1941; *Bowen's Court* (non-fiction), Knopf, 1942, 2nd edition, 1964; *English Novelists,* Hastings House, 1942; *Seven Winters* (autobiography), Cuala Press (Dublin), 1942, published as *Seven Winters: Memories of a Dublin Childhood,* Longmans, Green, 1943; *The Demon Lover and Other Stories,* J. Cape, 1945, published as *Ivy Gripped the Steps and Other Stories,* Knopf, 1946; *Anthony Trollope: A New Judgement,* Oxford University Press, 1946; *Selected Stories,* M. Fridberg, 1946; (contributor) John Irwin, compiler, *How I Write My Novels,* Spearman, 1948; *Why Do I Write?: An Exchange of Views Between Elizabeth Bowen, Graham Greene, and V. S. Pritchett,* Marshall, 1948; *The Heat of the Day* (novel; Literary Guild selection), Knopf, 1948.

Collected Impressions (non-fiction), Knopf, 1950; *The Shelbourne: A Centre of Dublin Life for More than a Century,* Harrap, 1951, published as *The Shelbourne Hotel,* Knopf, 1951; *Early Stories* (includes *Encounters* and *Ann Lee's*), Knopf, 1951; *A World of Love* (novel), Knopf, 1955; (contributor) Dorothy Wilson, editor, *Family Christmas Book,* Prentice-Hall, 1957; *A Time in Rome* (non-fiction), Knopf, 1959; *Stories,* Knopf, 1959; (author of introduction) Anthony Trollope, *Doctor Thorne,* Houghton, 1959.

(Author of afterword) Virginia Woolf, *Orlando: A Biography,* New American Library, 1960; *After-Thought: Pieces About Writing* (essays and addresses), Longmans, Green, 1962, Knopf, 1964; *The Little Girls* (novel), Knopf, 1963; (contributor) *These Simple Things,* Simon & Schuster, 1965; *The Good Tiger* (juvenile), Knopf, 1965; *A Day in the Dark and Other Stories,* J. Cape, 1965; *Eva Trout; or, Changing Scenes* (novel), Knopf, 1968.

Pictures and Conversations, Knopf, 1975.

Editor: *The Faber Book of Modern Stories,* Faber, 1937; Katherine Mansfield, *Stories,* Vintage, 1956 (published in England as *34 Short Stories,* Collins, 1957).

Contributor of literary criticism and book reviews to *Tatler* and other journals; has done scripts for British Broadcasting Corp.

SIDELIGHTS: Orville Prescott called Miss Bowen a "sensitive, fastidious and astute Anglo-Irish woman." She was "a highly conscious artist," wrote Walter Allen, "who has evolved over the years a prose style that has the elaboration, the richness of texture, the allusiveness of poetry, a prose as carefully wrought, as subtle in its implications, as that of Henry James in his last phase. She has, too, an intense awareness of, and sensitivity to, place and weather, to the living character of houses, for example, and the indefinable yet readily palpable relation set up between them and the people who dwell in them." Critics generally consider *The Death of the Heart* her best novel; some call it one of the best English novels of the century.

"When I write, I am re-creating what was created for me," wrote Miss Bowen. "The gladness of vision, in writing, is my own gladness, but not at my own vision." Indeed, "vision" and "illumination" are key words to much of the criticism of her work. L. A. G. Strong said: "First of all, she is an Irish writer—as Irish as Yeats. That means, among other things, that she is very strongly conscious of light." He added: "Everything she sees is seen through an intensely personal prism: thus far she is introverted. The external details are seen with a vivid and accurate eye: in that she is extraverted. . . . She can suggest disquiet, whether moral, physical, or psychic, to a degree unequalled among her contemporaries. She can convey the very texture and perfume of happiness. All these things are the result of a merciless and unfaltering precision of awareness and of expression.

All belong to what, for me at least, is the essential quality of her work, illumination.''

Much of her art operates by implication and subtlety. Her characters are largely "cultivated, liberal upper middle-class." Walter Allen wrote: "Her first reputation was as a witty observer of manners, a delicate satirist of social absurdities; but from *To the North* (1932), social comedy, though always there, if sometimes uneasily, has been secondary to a conception of human relations verging upon the tragic. It is as though Henry James has been superimposed upon Jane Austen." Sean O'Faolain noted that she "has not assumed that the intellect must be abdicated by the modern novelist. She hovers patiently over her subjects. But the prime technical characteristic of her work, as of other modern women writers, such as Virginia Woolf, is that she fills the vacuum which the general disintegration of belief has created in life by the pursuit of sensibility."

Speaking of writing in *Collected Impressions*, Miss Bowen wrote: "Characters pre-exist. They are *found*. They reveal themselves slowly to the novelist's perception—as might fellow-travellers seated opposite one in a very dimly-lit railway carriage. . . . In each of the characters, while he or she is acting, the play and pull of alternatives must be felt. It is in being seen to be capable of alternatives that the character becomes, for the reader, valid. . . . A novel must contain at least one *magnetic* character. At least one character capable of keying the reader up, as though he (the reader) were in the presence of someone he is in love with. . . ." O'Faolain generalized thus about her characters: "There is an atmosphere of ancient fable behind all of Miss Bowen's fiction. Her persons are recognizable temperaments rather than composed characters. . . . Her characters are the modern, sophisticated, naturalistic novelist's versions of primitive urges. One feels that if she had lived three hundred and fifty years ago when passions rode freely and fiercely she would have described the dreams that drove Ophelia, Juliet and Desdemona to love and to death."

"Plot," wrote Miss Bowen, "might seem to be a matter of choice. It is not. The particular plot is something the novelist is driven to. It is what is left after the whittling-away of alternatives. . . . Plot is diction. Action of language, language of action. . . . Plot is story. It is also 'a story' in the nursery sense-lie. The novel lies, in saying that something happened that did not. It must, therefore, contain uncontradictable truth, to warrant the original lie. . . . Plot must further the novel towards its object. What object? The non-poetic statement of a poetic truth. . . . The essence of a poetic truth is that no statement of it can be final. . . . (Much to be learnt from storytelling to children. Much to be learnt from the detective story—especially non-irrelevance. . . . Plot must not cease to move forward. The *actual* speed of the movement must be even. *Apparent* variations in speed are good, necessary, but there must be no actual variations in speed. . . .''

Prescott noted that, in her short stories, Miss Bowen "has followed the examples of Chekhov and Katherine Mansfield, concentrating on creation of a mood, insight into character and emotional atmosphere. . . ." Miss Bowen, however, felt a certain ambivalence about the short story form which she has practiced since she was twenty. She told Harvey Breit: "I feel happiest, in the sense of poetic truth, in the short story. Yet if I wrote only short stories, I should feel I was shirking. The novel is more of an ethical thing. The short story has the dangers of perfection. Of course, there should be in the novel both the perfections: the sort of architectural proportions and the poetic truth—which are most possible in the short story."

AVOCATIONAL INTERESTS: Music, movies, and detective stories.

BIOGRAPHICAL/CRITICAL SOURCES: L.A.G. Strong in *Living Writers*, edited by Gilbert Phelps, Sylvan Press, 1947; Elizabeth Bowen, *Collected Impressions*, Knopf, 1950; Orville Prescott, *In My Opinion*, Bobbs-Merrill, 1952; Sean O'Faolain, *The Vanishing Hero*, Little, Brown, 1956; Harvey Breit, *The Writer Observed*, World Publishing, 1956; *New York Times Book Review*, January 26, 1964; *Critique*, spring, 1964; Walter Allen, *The Modern Novel*, Dutton, 1965; *New Statesman*, March 26, 1965, August 6, 1965; *Times Literary Supplement*, July 8, 1965; *Critique*, spring-summer, 1966; *Contemporary Literary Criticism*, Gale, Volume I, 1973, Volume III, 1975, Volume VI, 1976.†

(Died February 22, 1973)

* * *

BOWER, Louise 1900-

PERSONAL: Born September 15, 1900, in Vesta, Minn.; married Paul H. Bower; children: Dale Haack. *Education:* Ripley School of Nursing, graduate, 1921; additional study at University of Minnesota Extension. *Politics:* Republican. *Religion:* Methodist. *Home:* 1620 Concordia, St. Paul, Minn. 55104.

CAREER: Did private and institutional nursing in Minneapolis and St. Paul, Minn., 1921-39. Member of board of directors, Rolling Acres Home for Retarded Children, Excelsior, Minn., three years.

WRITINGS—With Ethel Tigue: *The Secret of Willow Coulee*, Abingdon, 1966; *Packy*, Abingdon, 1967. Contributor to *Child Life, Children's Friend, All Pets*, and *Minneapolis Star-Journal*. Edited newsletter for Rolling Acres Home, 1959-65.

WORK IN PROGRESS: Two books with Ethel Tigue, *The Stopping House* and *The Silver Dollar Saw-Mill*.

SIDELIGHTS: As the mother of a retarded son, Mrs. Bower's chief interest is working for improvement in the care and welfare of exceptional children.

AVOCATIONAL INTERESTS: Boating, knitting, raising African violets.††

* * *

BOWLES, Jane (Sydney) 1917-1973

PERSONAL: Born February 22, 1917, in New York, N.Y.; daughter of Sydney and Claire (Stajer) Auer; married Paul Bowles (a writer-composer), February 21, 1938. *Education:* Attended Stoneleigh; was tutored at Leysin, Switzerland, for two years. *Home:* Inmueble Itesa, Calle Campoamor, Tangier, Morocco.

WRITINGS: Two Serious Ladies (novel), Knopf, 1943; *In the Summer House* (two-act play, produced in New York, 1954, starring Judith Anderson, background music by Paul Bowles), Random House, 1954; *Plain Pleasures* (stories), P. Owen, 1966; *The Collected Works of Jane Bowles* (with introduction by Truman Capote; includes all of the above), Farrar, Straus, 1966. A puppet play, "Quarreling Pair," was published in *Mademoiselle*, December, 1966. Contributor to *Harper's Bazaar, Vogue*, and *Mademoiselle*.

SIDELIGHTS: Stephen Koch believed Mrs. Bowles was "one of the best writers around," one who wanted "to raise fiction to the condition of poetry. When her work first appeared, it was the closest thing around in the impoverished postwar period to fiction with the consciousness of language, fantasy, and form that makes real art," wrote Koch. Other writers, such as Truman Capote and James Purdy, have also praised her work, Purdy calling her "the eagle-woman of American letters." Her reputation was astonishing when compared to the quantity of work she published: one novel, two plays, and seven short stories. John Ashbery called her "a writer's writer," and added: "Few surface literary reputations are as glamorous as the underground one she has enjoyed since her novel *Two Serious Ladies* was published in 1943. The extreme rarity of the book, once it went out of print, has augmented its legend. When a London publisher wanted to reprint it [in 1964], even Mrs. Bowles was unable to supply him with a copy."

Mrs. Bowles called her *Collected Works* "a style book, very hard to describe." One critic, Patricia MacManus, described the writing as naturalistically surrealistic, wherein "reality and the absurd meet head-on and the most banal actions assume allusively dream-like connotations. Themes merge, then re-emerge to glide off in varying directions with scarcely a nod over the shoulder." Her prose is both colloquial and oblique; its charm is attested to by some of its severest critics. Ashbery, a highly favorable critic, wrote: "It is impossible to deduce the end of a sentence from its beginning, or a paragraph from the one that preceded it, or how one of the characters will reply to another. And yet the whole flows marvelously and inexorably to its cruel, lucid end; it becomes itself as we watch it. No other contemporary writer can consistently produce surprise of this quality, the surprise that is the one essential ingredient of great art. Jane Bowles deals almost exclusively in this rare commodity."

Her sensibility has been called original, personal, eccentric. She possessed a fine wit by which she evoked what Ashbery called "visions of a nutty America that we have to recognize as ours." Koch believed her humor was "decidedly arcane. . . . She is a dead-pan humorist whose self-consciously flat prose sets up in its less fantastic way situations like Purdy's Malcolm searching for his father. . . . The presiding genius of both writers . . . is doubtless Buster Keaton—that master of the motiveless character ambling through impossibility." Koch also suspected that *Two Serious Ladies*, with its "whimsical narrative technique," may have provided an inspiration for such writers as Purdy and Edward Albee.

Written in New York when Mrs. Bowles was in her early twenties, *Two Serious Ladies* was hailed as "one of the finest first novels of its kind." At one time, Geoffrey Wagner called it "incredibly bad." It is—for those who do not accept what Koch calls "an exercise in style *as* narrative," for those who search for motivations and reasons, or those who like their stories directed by logic. Koch thinks the novel is basically a good one, lacking only in energy and tempo. Miss MacManus called it "a very funny novel—a kind of daymare about two eminently respectable women who, each on her own, break loose from long-fixed patterns of living and plunge into bizarre experiences which they see as epitomizing the rich, full life."

Women are always primary in Mrs. Bowles's writings. The weak are pitted against the strong and neither gains victory. Miss MacManus wrote: "Her characters drift into one another's orbits, their lives fugitively overlapping but rarely joined in even an illusory permanence; singleness and separation from the mainstream of existence seem, ultimately, to be their natural condition." At her best, Mrs. Bowles had, as Koch noted, "a firm fast eye and ear for resonance of detail, flawless clips of speech, and certain half-visual, half-

auditory richness so subjective that it can only be found in prose of a very high order."

Most of Mrs. Bowles's published work was written in the United States. She did, however, wander across Europe, Central America, and Mexico, settling after the War in a boardinghouse which also housed her husband, Paul Bowles, as well as Richard and Ellen Wright, Oliver Smith, Gypsy Rose Lee, Carson McCullers, Benjamin Britten, a chimpanzee trainer with his animal, and W. H. Auden. Later, she went abroad again, traveled the Sahara Desert, and lived in Paris and Ceylon, and, after 1952, in Tangier. Along the way she taught herself to speak French, Spanish, and Moghrebi. In 1966, Truman Capote recalled the Mrs. Bowles he had known more than twenty years before: "Even then she had seemed the eternal urchin, appealing as the most appealing of nonadults, yet with some substance cooler than blood invading her veins, and with a wit, an eccentric wisdom no child, not the strangest *Wunderkind*, ever possessed." On a questionnaire she would list her occupation as housewife.

With the publication of *Collected Works* she could no longer be considered an underground writer. Ashbery hoped that "she will now be recognized for what she is: one of the finest modern writers of fiction, in any language. At the same time it should be pointed out that she is not quite the sort of writer that her imposing list of Establishment admirers seems to suggest. Her work is unrelated to theirs, and in fact it stands alone in contemporary literature, though if one can imagine George Ade and Kafka collaborating on a modern version of Bunyan's *Pilgrim's Progress* one will have a faint idea of the qualities of *Two Serious Ladies*." *In the Summer House* was acquired for filming in 1969.

AVOCATIONAL INTERESTS: Cooking and mimicry.

BIOGRAPHICAL/CRITICAL SOURCES: New York Times Book Review, May 9, 1943, January 29, 1967, February 12, 1967; *Book Week*, May 16, 1943, February 12, 1967; *Mademoiselle*, December, 1966; *New York Review of Books*, December 15, 1966; *Saturday Review*, January 14, 1967; *Commonweal*, February 3, 1967; *Contemporary Literary Criticism*, Volume III, Gale, 1975.†

(Died May 4, 1973)

* * *

BRAASCH, William Frederick 1878-

PERSONAL: Born July 6, 1878, in Lyons, Iowa; son of John Ernst (a merchant) and Albertina (Claasen) Braasch; married Nellie Stinchfield, November 11, 1908 (deceased); children: Marion (Mrs. James R. Watson), Elizabeth (Mrs. Frederick Graham), John W. *Education:* University of Minnesota, B.S., 1900, M.D., 1903. *Politics:* Republican. *Religion:* Protestant. *Office:* Graduate School of Medicine, University of Minnesota, Minneapolis, Minnesota.

CAREER: Minneapolis City Hospital, Minneapolis, Minn., intern in pathology, 1903-04, assistant city physician, 1905-07; Mayo Clinic, Rochester, Minn., staff member, beginning 1907, head of urology section, 1907-46; University of Minnesota, Graduate School of Medicine, Minneapolis, professor of urology, 1915-46; professor emeritus, 1946—. *Member:* American Medical Association (vice-president of board of trustees), Minnesota Medical Society (president). *Awards, honors:* Outstanding Service Award, University of Minnesota; Distinguished Service Award, Minnesota State Medical Association.

WRITINGS: Pyelography, Saunders, 1915; (with Benjamin

H. Hager) *Urography,* 2nd edition (Braasch not associated with earlier edition), Saunders, 1927; (with J. L. Emmett) *Clinical Urology,* Saunders, 1951; *Early Days of the Mayo Clinic,* C. C Thomas, 1969. Contributor of more than two hundred papers in the field of urology to medical journals.†

* * *

BRADFIELD, Richard 1896-

PERSONAL: Born April 29, 1896, in West Jefferson, Ohio; son of Bayard Taylor (a farmer) and Martha Anderson (Truitt) Bradfield; married Ethel May Hill, June 21, 1923; married Hannah Amelia Stillman, August 6, 1926; children: (first marriage) Richard II; (second marriage) Robert Browning, David Maurice, Patricia Bradfield Baasel, James Worthington. *Education:* Otterbein College, A.B., 1917; Ohio State University, Ph.D., 1922. *Politics:* Independent. *Religion:* Protestant. *Address:* 1715 Northwest 22nd Terrace, Gainesville, Fla.

CAREER: University of Missouri, Columbia, instructor, 1920-22, assistant professor, 1922-23, associate professor of soils, 1923-29; Ohio State University, Columbus, professor of soils, 1930-37; Cornell University, Ithaca, N.Y., professor of soil technology, 1937-62, head of department of agronomy, 1937-55, professor emeritus, 1962—. Rockefeller Foundation, part-time consultant, 1941-62, trustee, 1957-61, special consultant in agriculture, International Rice Research Institute, Manila, Philippines, 1962-71. Consultant soil scientist, U.S. Department of Agriculture, 1941-52; member of committee on plant and crop ecology, National Research Council, 1950-53.

MEMBER: American Chemical Society, American Society of Agronomy (fellow; president, 1942), Soil Science Society of America (president, 1937; honorary member), International Soil Science Society (president, 1956-60; honorary member), American Association for the Advancement of Science (fellow), Crop Science Society of the Philippines (honorary fellow), Sigma Xi, Alpha Zeta. *Awards, honors:* Guggenheim fellow in Germany, 1927-28; D.Sc., Otterbein College, 1941, Ohio State University, 1970; Otterbein College, distinguished alumni award, 1957, distinguished scientific achievement award, 1970; American Society of Agronomy Award for Services to International Agriculture, 1973.

WRITINGS: (With E. C. Stakman and P. C. Mangelsdorf) *Campaigns Against Hunger,* Belknap Press, 1968. Contributor of technical papers to a number of journals. Member of editorial board, *Agronomy Journal,* beginning 1940; consultant editor, *Soil Science,* beginning 1935.

WORK IN PROGRESS: Research on intensive multiple cropping systems for tropical regions, especially the rice belt of South Asia.

* * *

BRADLEY, Erwin S(tanley) 1906-

PERSONAL: Born March 30, 1906, in Saltillo, Pa.; son of William Harrison (a farmer) and Ida (Moreland) Bradley; married Vivian Wright (a librarian), 1941. *Education:* Juniata College, B.S., 1930; University of Michigan, M.A., 1934; Pennsylvania State University, Ph.D., 1952. *Politics:* Republican. *Religion:* Methodist.

CAREER: Teacher in public schools of Pennsylvania, 1924-39; Jefferson Military College, Washington, Miss., adjutant, 1941-43, 1945-47; Pennsylvania State University, University Park, graduate assistant in history, 1949-50; Union College,

Barbourville, Ky., professor of history and chairman of Division of Social Studies, 1953-73, curator, Library of Lincolniana, 1968-73. *Military service:* U.S. Army, 1943-45; served in Europe; received four battle stars. *Member:* National Historical Society, American Historical Association, Scottish Rite Consistory. *Awards, honors:* Iota Sigma Nu Award for distinguished scholarship, 1966; American Philosophical Society scholar, 1964.

WRITINGS: Union College: 1879-1954, Union College, 1954; *The Triumph of Militant Republicanism,* University of Pennsylvania Press, 1964; *Simon Cameron: Lincoln's Secretary of War,* University of Pennsylvania Press, 1966. Contributor to *Encyclopedia Americana.*

AVOCATIONAL INTERESTS: Music, numismatics.†

* * *

BRADWAY, John S(aeger) 1890-

PERSONAL: Born February 17, 1890, in Swarthmore, Pa.; son of William (a banker) and Jennie (Saeger) Bradway; married Mary Henderson, June 11, 1921 (deceased). *Education:* Haverford College, A.B., 1911, A.M., 1915; University of Pennsylvania, LL.B., 1914. *Politics:* Republican. *Home:* 536 Leavenworth St., San Francisco, Calif. 94109. *Office:* California Western School of Law, United States International University, San Diego, Calif. 92106.

CAREER: Admitted to Pennsylvania Bar, 1914, later to State Bar of California and North Carolina Bar; Philadelphia Legal Aid Society, Philadelphia, Pa., assistant attorney, 1914-20; Philadelphia Municipal Legal Aid Bureau, Philadelphia, chief counsel, 1920-22; private practice of law, Philadelphia, 1920-29; University of Southern California, Los Angeles, professor of law and director of legal aid clinic, 1929-31; Duke University, Durham, N.C., professor of law and director of legal aid clinic, 1931-59; University of California, Hastings College of the Law, San Francisco, professor of law, 1960-65; United States International University, California Western School of Law, San Diego, professor of law, 1965-74, professor emeritus, 1974—. Visiting professor at School of Social Work, University of North Carolina, 1950-59. National Association of Legal Aid Organizations, secretary, 1922-40, president, 1940-42. *Military service:* U.S. Naval Reserve, 1917-19; became lieutenant. *Member:* American Bar Association (chairman of legal aid committee, 1938-39; secretary of family law section, 1958-59), American Judicature Society, Association of American Law Schools, Phi Beta Kappa, Order of the Coif. *Awards, honors:* LL.D., Haverford College, 1959; D.H.L., California Western School of Law, 1976.

WRITINGS: (Compiler) *Laws of Pennsylvania Relating to Social Work,* Public Charities Association of Pennsylvania, 1929; *Law and Social Work: An Introduction to the Study of the Legal-Social Field for Social Workers,* University of Chicago Press, 1929; *The Bar and Public Relations,* Bobbs-Merrill, 1934; (compiler) *Legal Aid Bureaus: Their Organization and Administration,* Public Administration Service (Chicago), 1935, supplement published as *How to Organize a Legal Aid Clinic,* Edwards Brothers, 1938; *The Work of Legal Aid Committees of Bar Associations,* American Bar Association, 1938; *Legal Aid Clinic Instruction at Duke University,* Duke University Press, 1944; *Clinical Preparation for Law Practice,* Duke University Press, 1946, revised edition published as *The Duke University Legal Aid Clinic Handbook,* 1954; *Basic Legal Aid Clinic Materials and Exercises on Taking Hold of a Case at Law,* Duke University Press, 1950; *The History of a Lawsuit,* Duke University

Press, 1958; *How to Practice Law Effectively,* Oceana, 1958; *Selected Materials of Legal Aid Clinic Drills,* Duke University, 1959; (editor) *Selected Readings on the Legal Profession,* West Publishing, 1962. Contributor of numerous articles to professional journals. Special editor, *Progress in Family Law,* Volume 383 of *Annals of American Academy of Political and Social Science,* 1969. Special editor for several issues of *Law and Contemporary Problems,* and other legal journals.

*   *   *

BRAIDER, Donald   1923-1976

PERSONAL: Born April 30, 1923, in New York, N.Y.; son of Clifford Arthur (an organist) and Josephine (Giglio) Braider; married Elizabeth Ringo, October 3, 1943; married second wife, Carol Newton (a bookseller), June 22, 1946; children: (second marriage) Christopher, Susan, Jackson. *Education:* Attended Swarthmore College, Rutgers University, University of Grenoble, Merton College, Oxford, and Middlebury College, 1940-61. *Politics:* Radical. *Religion:* "Lapsed Anglican." *Residence:* Cooperstown, N.Y. *Agent:* Paul R. Reynolds, Inc., 12 East 41st St., New York, N.Y. 10017.

CAREER: United World Federalists, New York City, director of public relations, 1948-49; free-lance public relations representative, New York City, 1949-50; bookseller, East Hampton, N.Y., 1953-57; Wooster School, Danbury, Conn., head of French department, 1957-63, director of development, 1970-73; Kirkland College, Clinton, N.Y., director of development, 1973-75. Free-lance writer, 1951-76; copy editor, Farrar, Strauss & Giroux; textbook editor, Harcourt Brace Jovanovich. Member of Democratic Town Committee, Redding, Conn., beginning 1972; delegate to Connecticut Democratic Convention, 1972. *Military service:* U.S. Army, Military Intelligence, 1942-46; served in France.

WRITINGS: The Palace Guard, Viking, 1958; *Putnam's Guide to the Art Centers of Europe,* Putnam, 1965; *Color from a Light Within: A Novel Based on the Life of El Greco,* Putnam, 1967 (published in England as *The Master Painter: A Novel Based on the Life of El Greco,* Bodley Head, 1968); *Rage in Silence,* Putnam, 1969; *Five Early American Painters,* Meredith, 1969; *An Epic Joy,* Putnam, 1971; *George Bellows and the Ashcan School of Painting,* Doubleday, 1971; *The Niagara,* Holt, 1972; *The Life, History and Magic of the Horse,* Grosset, 1973; *Solitary Sam: A Biography of Sam Houston,* Putnam, 1974.

WORK IN PROGRESS: God Was a Redhaired Woman, for Doubleday; *Noble Substance,* fiction; *In Questionable Taste,* a book on the contemporary art market, for Morrow; *All Honor Bound: France in World War II,* for Doubleday.

AVOCATIONAL INTERESTS: Anything that appears in movable type, painting, sculpture, music, travel in Europe, dogs, and women.†

(Died June 22, 1976)

*   *   *

BRAND, C(larence) E(ugene)   1895-

PERSONAL: Born November 8, 1895, in Marion, Ala.; son of Romulus (a farmer) and Mary Elizabeth (Dew) Brand; married Frances Christian, August 11, 1921; married second wife, Katherine Hough, May 28, 1948; children: (first marriage) John S., Eugene D. *Education:* University of Texas, B.A. and M.A., 1917; University of Virginia, law student,

1930-31; Yale University, LL.B., 1933, D.C.L., 1936. *Politics:* Democrat. *Religion:* None. *Home:* 345 Morningside Dr., San Antonio, Tex. 78209.

CAREER: U.S. Army, 1917-49, commissioned second lieutenant, 1917, retired as colonel, 1949; Broadway National Bank, San Antonio, Tex., president, 1949-60; Pan American National Bank, San Antonio, Tex., chairman of board, beginning 1961. Director and secretary, Stull Chemical Co., San Antonio, Tex. Admitted to Connecticut Bar, 1933, and later to Bars of New York, Texas, and U.S. Supreme Court. Former president of Bexar County Legal Aid Association; member of board of directors and treasurer, San Antonio Chapter of American Cancer Society, 1958-64. *Member:* American Bar Association, American Judicature Society, Texas Bar Association, San Antonio Bar Association, Phi Beta Kappa, Order of the Coif. *Awards, honors*—Military: Legion of Merit, Bronze Star, Legion of Honor (France), and Croix de Guerre with two palms (France).

WRITINGS: Roman Military Law, University of Texas Press, 1968. Contributor to military and legal journals.

SIDELIGHTS: Brand is "reasonably" competent in Latin, French, German, Spanish, and knows some Italian.†

*   *   *

BRANDHORST, Carl T(heodore)   1898-

PERSONAL: Born August 24, 1898, in Lincoln, Neb.; son of Charles William (businessman) and Alwina (Backhaus) Brandhorst; married Louise Koeneke, June 28, 1922; children: Dorothy (Mrs. William Johnstone), Adeline (Mrs. E. P. Costello), Olivia (Mrs. Joseph Ishikawa), L. Carl, Ellen (Mrs. Edward Wiesehan), Charlotte (Mrs. D. W. Rohren), Curt W., Mark T. *Education:* Concordia Teachers College, Seward, Neb., diploma, 1917; Fort Hays Kansas State College, B.S. in Ed., 1939, M.S., 1941; University of Nebraska, Ph.D., 1961. *Politics:* Democrat. *Religion:* Lutheran. *Home:* 55 Pearl, Seward, Neb. 68434.

CAREER: Teacher in private schools, 1917-38; Concordia Teachers College, Seward, Neb., associate professor, 1938-57, professor of biology and chairman of department, 1957-65. Visiting associate professor and researcher, San Fernando Valley State College (now California State University, Northridge), 1962-63. Former member of television commission and former chairman of audiovisual board, Lutheran Church-Missouri Synod. *Member:* American Association for the Advancement of Science, National Association of Biology Teachers, Ecological Society of America, Nebraska Academy of Science (past president), Kansas Academy of Science, Sigma Xi, Phi Kappa Phi.

WRITINGS: (With Robert Sylweste) *Tale of Whitefoot* (juvenile), Simon & Schuster, 1968. Associate editor, *Issues in Christian Education* and *A Brief History of Concordia Teachers College,* Concordia Teachers College. Contributor to scientific publications.

WORK IN PROGRESS: Jewels in the Grass, a children's book on water; research on plant galls of southwestern desert areas.

*   *   *

BRATTON, Helen   1899-

PERSONAL: Born July 17, 1899, in Albany, N.Y.; daughter of Hiram and Josephine (Ashton) Stott; married George S. Bratton, September 27, 1923; children: Joyce (Mrs. W. R. Derlacki), Betty (Mrs. E. S. Smith), Carol (Mrs. J. H. Lienhard). *Education:* Studied at Washington

University, St. Louis, Mo., 1925-26, St. Louis Institute of Art, four years, and St. Louis Institute of Music, six years. *Address:* P.O. Box 2325, Carmel, Calif. *Agent:* Lenniger Literary Agency, Inc., 437 Fifth Ave., New York, N.Y. 10016.

CAREER: Civil Service employee in Washington, D.C., 1918-20; assistant court reporter and public stenographer in Aberdeen, Miss., 1920-23.

WRITINGS—Young adult fiction: *It's Morning Again,* McKay, 1964; *Amber Flask,* McKay, 1964; *Only in Time,* McKay, 1967.

AVOCATIONAL INTERESTS: Literature, art, music, gardening, and adult education.

* * *

BRAUNTHAL, Julius 1891-1972

PERSONAL: Born May 5, 1891, in Vienna, Austria; son of Meier and Clara (Gelles) Braunthal. *Education:* Attended secondary school in Vienna, Austria. *Home:* 20 The Grove, Teddington, Middlesex, England.

CAREER: Bookbinder in Austria, 1905-12; Austrian Ministry of the Armed Forces, Vienna, assistant to Secretary of State, 1918-20; *Arbeiter-Zeitung,* Vienna, political editor, 1920-34; *Der Kampf,* Vienna, editor, 1923-34; *Das Kleine Blatt,* Vienna, editor, 1926-34; *Tribune,* London, England, foreign editor, 1937-38; Labour and Socialist International, assistant secretary, 1938-39; *International Socialist Forum,* London, England, editor, 1941-48; Socialist International, general secretary, 1950-56; *Socialist International Information,* editor, 1951-56. *Military service:* Austria-Hungarian Army, 1914-18; became lieutenant; received Silver Medal for bravery. *Member:* International Institute of Social History (member of board of directors, beginning 1951), Society for the Study of Labour History. *Awards, honors:* Theodor-Korner-Stiftung Award for both *Otto Bauer: Ein Lebensbild* and *Victor und Friedrich Adler.*

WRITINGS: Die Sozialpolitik der Republik, Wiener Volksbuchhandlung, 1919; *Die Arbeiterraete in Deutschoesterreich,* Wiener Volksbuchhandlung, 1919; *Kommunisten und Sozialdemokraten,* Wiener Volksbuchhandlung, 1920; *Vom Kommunismus zum Imperialismus,* Wiener Volksbuchhandlung, 1922; *Need Germany Survive?,* Gollancz, 1943; *In Search of the Millennium,* Gollancz, 1945; *The Paradox of Nationalism: An Epilogue to the Nuremberg Trials,* introduction by Leonard Woolf, St. Botolph Publishing Co., 1946; *The Tragedy of Austria,* Gollancz, 1948; *L'Antitesi Ideologica fra Socialismo e Communismo,* Opere Nuove, 1956; *The Significance of Israeli Socialism,* Lincolns-Prager Publishers, 1958; *Il Socialismo in Asia,* Opere Nuove, 1959; *Otto Bauer: Ein Lebensbild,* Wiener Volksbuchhandlung, 1961; *Geschichte der Internationale,* Dietz, Volume I, 1961, Volume II, 1963, translation by Henry Collins and Kenneth Mitchell published as *History of the International,* Volume I, *1864-1914,* and Volume II, *1914-1943,* Praeger, 1967; *Victor und Friedrich Adler,* Wiener Volksbuchhandlung, 1966.

Editor: Siegmund Kunfi, *Gestalten und Ereignisse,* Wiener Volksbuchhandlung, 1930; Kunfi, *Die Neugestaltung der Welt,* Wiener Volksbuchhandlung, 1930; *Austerlitz Spricht,* Wiener Volksbuchhandlung, 1931; *Socialistische Weltstimmen,* Dietz, 1958; *Stimme aus dem Chaos,* Nest Verlag, 1960. Also editor of *Yearbook of the International Socialist Labour Movement,* 1956-1961 and 1957-1962, published by Lincolns-Prager. Contributor to *Encyclopaedia Britannica* and to journals in United States, Europe, and India.

SIDELIGHTS: George Lichtheim noted that Braunthal's *History of the International* "is the first integrated account of socialism and communism yet undertaken. It is going to be the inevitable point of departure for all subsequent efforts in this direction."

BIOGRAPHICAL/CRITICAL SOURCES: Joseph Fraenkel, editor, *The Jews of Austria,* Valentine, Mitchell, 1967; *Listener,* February 1, 1968.†

(Died April 28, 1972)

* * *

BRECHT, Edith 1895-1975

PERSONAL: Born April 7, 1895, in Lancaster City, Pa.; daughter of Milton J. (an educator and public service commissioner) and Mary M. (Wolfe) Brecht. *Education:* Studied at National School of Elocution, Philadelphia, and Millersville State College. *Politics:* Independent. *Religion:* Presbyterian. *Home address:* East Earl Route 1, Lancaster County, Pa. 17519. *Agent:* Curtis Brown Ltd., 575 Madison Ave., New York, N.Y. 10022.

CAREER: Writer.

WRITINGS—All children's books: *Ada and the Wild Duck,* Viking, 1964; *Timothy's Hawk,* Viking, 1965; *The Mystery at the Old Forge,* Viking, 1966; *Benjy's Luck,* Lippincott, 1967; *The Little Fox,* Lippincott, 1968. Contributor of poetry and stories to magazines, including *Poetry World, Chatelaine, Toronto Star Weekly, Woman's Day, Ladies' Home Journal, McCall's, Farm Journal, Seventeen,* and others.

WORK IN PROGRESS: An Amish story, *Slow Poke Sadie;* and a book of fairy tales.

SIDELIGHTS: Many of Edith Brecht's stories have been published in Danish and Swedish. *Avocational Interests:* The study of Amish and Mennonite people of Lancaster County; nature.†

(Died August 16, 1975)

* * *

BREEN, Quirinus 1896-1975

PERSONAL: Born March 3, 1896, in Orange City, Iowa; son of Everett (a minister) and Tona (De Fouw) Breen; married Helena De Valois, August 26, 1923; children: Elizabeth Edna (Mrs. A. B. Petersen), Quentin Lee. *Education:* Calvin College, A.B., 1920; University of Chicago, Ph.D., 1931. *Politics:* Democrat. *Home:* 100 Sunset Dr., Eugene, Ore. 97403.

CAREER: Hillsdale College, Hillsdale, Mich., assistant professor of history, 1931-33; Albany College, Albany, Ore., professor of history, 1933-38; University of Oregon, Eugene, instructor in history and social science, 1938-39, assistant professor, 1939-45, associate professor, 1945-50, professor of history, 1950-64, professor emeritus, 1964-75. Resident, Institute for Advanced Study, Princeton, N.J., 1964-65; professor of history, Grand Valley State College, Allendale, Mich., 1965-68. *Member:* American Historical Association, Society for Reformation Research, American Society of Church History (president, 1956). *Awards, honors:* Fulbright research scholar in Italy, 1956-57; D.Litt., Carthage College, 1968.

WRITINGS: John Calvin: A Study in French Humanism (revision of author's thesis at University of Chicago), Eerdmans, 1931, revised and augmented edition, Shoe String, 1968; (editor and author of critical notes) Marius Nizolius,

De Veris principiis philosophia, Fratelli Bocca, 1956; *Christianity and Humanism: Studies in the History of Ideas,* edited by Nelson Peter Ross, Eerdmans, 1968; (with others) Jerold C. Brauer, editor, *Essays in Divinity,* Volume II: *The Impact of the Church Upon Its Culture: Reappraisals of the History of Christianity,* University of Chicago Press, 1968. Contributor to *Oregon Law Review* and journals in his field.

WORK IN PROGRESS: A critical edition of Agricola's *De Inventione Dialectia.*†

(Died March 21, 1975)

* * *

BRETON, Andre   1896-1966

PERSONAL: Born February 19, 1896, in Tinchebray (Orne), France; son of Louis (an accountant) and Marguerite (Le Gongues) Breton; married Simone Kahn, September, 1921 (divorced); married Jacqueline Lamba, August, 1934 (divorced); married Elisa Bindhoff, August 20, 1945; children: (second marriage) Aube (Mrs. Yves Elesnet). *Education:* Attended College Chaptal, Paris, 1906-12, Faculte de Medicine, Paris, 1913-15. *Home:* 42 rue Fontaine, Paris 9e, France.

CAREER: Major participant in Dadaist literary movement, 1916-21; contributor to *Phalange, SIC,* and *Nord-Sud,* 1914-19; founder and editor, with Luis Aragon and Philippe Soupault, of the journal *Litterature,* 1919, sole editor, 1922-24; secured interview with Freud after having utilized his methods of psychoanalysis and recorded monologues of patients, 1921; founder of Bureau of Surrealist Research, 1924; editor of *La Revolution Surrealiste,* 1925-29; editor of *Le Surrealisme au Service de la Revolution,* 1930-33; principal director of a literary and art review, *Minotaure,* 1933-39; lecturer on surrealism in Brussels, Prague, and the Canary Islands, 1935; founder, with others, of the Commission of Inquiry into the Moscow Trials, 1936; in Mexico, with Leon Trotsky and Diego Rivera, he established the *Federation Internationale de l'Art Revolutionnaire Independant,* 1938; guest of the Committee of American Aid to Intellectuals in Marseilles, 1940-41; following censorship of some of his works and interrogation by the Vichy government, Breton went to Martinique where he was arrested and confined in a concentration camp; succeeded in coming to the United States, 1941; in New York City, he was founder and editor, with Marcel Duchamp, Max Ernst, and David Hare of the magazine *VVV,* 1942-44; speaker for the "Voice of America," 1942-45; delivered address at Yale University, 1942; studied occultism in the rites of Indian tribes in Arizona, New Mexico, and the West Indies; gave a series of lectures on surrealism in Haiti which precipitated an insurrection there, 1945; returned to France, 1946; adhered to the *Front Humain* movement which became the *Citoyens du Monde,* 1948-49; member of the Committee for the Defence of Garry Davis, 1949; director of the Galerie a l'Etoile Scellee, 1952-54; editor of *Le Surrealisme, Meme,* 1956-57; editor of the surrealist review, *La Breche,* 1961-66; organized several exhibitions of surrealism, in London, 1936, Paris, 1938 (fourteen countries represented), 1947, 1958, and 1965, Prague, 1948, New York, 1942 and 1960, Milan, 1961. *Wartime service:* Medical assistant in army psychiatric centers, 1915-19; medical director of the Ecole de Pilotage at Poitiers, 1939-40.

WRITINGS—Prose works: *Manifeste du surrealisme [et] Poisson-soluble,* Editions du Sagittaire, 1924, revised edition augmented with *Lettre aux voyantes,* Simon Kra, 1929; *Les Pas Perdus,* N.R.F., 1924, revised edition, Gallimard, 1969;

Legitime defense, Editions Surrealistes, 1926; *Introduction au discours sur le peu de realite,* N.R.F., 1927; *Nadja,* Gallimard, 1928, revised edition, 1963, translation by Richard Howard published in America as *Nadja,* Grove, 1960; *Le Surrealisme et la peinture,* Gallimard, 1928, revised edition, 1965, translation by Simon W. Taylor published as *Surrealism and Painting,* Macdonald & Co., 1972; *Second manifeste du surrealisme,* Simon & Kra, 1930; *Misere de la poesie: "L'Affaire Aragon" devant l'opinion publique,* Editions Surrealistes, 1932; *Les Vases communicants,* Editions des Cahiers Libres, 1932, reprinted, Gallimard, 1970; *Point du jour,* Gallimard, 1934, revised edition, 1970; *Qu'est-ce que le Surrealisme?* (text of lecture given in Brussels), R. Henriquez, 1934, translation by David Gascoyne published as *What is Surrealism?,* Faber, 1936; *Du temps que les surrealistes avaient raison,* Editions Surrealistes, 1935; *Position politique du surrealisme* (collection of Breton's lectures, speeches, and interviews), Editions du Sagittaire, 1935, reprinted, J. J. Pauvert, 1971; *Au lavoir noir,* Editions G.L.M., 1936; *L'Amour fou,* Gallimard, 1937, reprinted, 1966; *Limites non frontiers du surrealisme,* N.R.F., 1937; (editor and contributor) *Trajectoire du reve,* Editions G.L.M., 1938.

(Editor) *Anthologie de l'humour noire,* Editions du Sagittaire, 1940, definitive edition, 1966; *Arcane 17,* Brentano's, 1944; *Situation du surrealisme entre les deux guerres* (text of lecture given at Yale), Editions de la Revue Fontaine, 1945; *Yves Tanguy* (bilingual edition with translation by Bravig Imbs), Pierre Matisse Editions (New York), 1946; *Arcane 17, ente d'Ajours,* Editions du Sagittaire, 1947, revised edition augmented with *Andre Breton ou la transparence,* by Michael Beaujour, Plon, 1965; *Les Manifestes du Surrealisme,* [suivis de] *Prolegomenes a un troisieme manifeste du surrealisme ou non,* Editions du Sagittaire, 1947, revised edition augmented with *Du surrealisme en ses oeuvres vives et d'Ephemerides surrealistes,* 1955; *La Lampe dans l'horloge,* Robert Marin, 1948; *Flagrant delit: Rimbaud devant la conjuration de l'imposture et du truquage,* Thesee, 1949; (editor) *Judas, ou Le Vampire surrealiste,* by Ernest de Gengenbach, Les Editions Premieres, 1949; *Entretiens 1913-1952* (text of radio interviews with Breton), Gallimard, 1952, revised edition, 1969; *La Cle des champs,* Editions du Sagittaire, 1953; *Adieu ne plaise* (text of speech at the funeral of Francis Picabia, December 4, 1953), Editions P.A.B., 1954.

(Author of text) *Gardenas,* Feigen Gallery, 1961; (author of text) *Les Inpires et leurs demeurs* (photographs by Gilles Ehrmann), Editions du Temps, 1962; (author of text) *Un Art a l'etat brut: Peintures et sculptures des aborigenes d'Australie,* by Karc Kupka, La Guilde du Livre (Lausanne), 1962; *Manifestes du Surrealisme,* definitive edition, J. J. Pauvert, 1962, complete edition, 1972, translation by Richard Seaver and Helen R. Lane published as *Manifestoes of Surrealism,* University of Michigan Press, 1969; (author of text) *Pierre Moiliner* (film by Raymond Borde), Le Terrain Vague, 1964; (author of text) *L'ecart absolu,* L'Oeil galerie d'art, 1965; (editor) *Le Surrealisme au service de la revolution,* Arno Press, 1968; *Perspective cavaliere,* edited by Marguerite Bonnet, Gallimard, 1970; *L'Un dans l'autre,* E. Losfeld, 1970; *Communication de Andre-Yves Breton sur l'activite de la 6e Commission depuis 1965,* City of Paris, 1971. Author of *Le Roman francais au XVIIIe siecle* published by Boivin & Cie.

Poetry and prose poetry: *Mont de piete,* Au Sans Pareil, 1919; (with Philippe Soupault) *Les Champs magnetiques,* Au Sans Pareil, 1920, reprinted, Gallimard, 1971; *Claire de terre,* Collection Litterature, 1923, reprinted, Gallimard,

1966; (with Rene Char and Paul Eluard) *Ralentir travaux*, Editions Surrealistes, 1930, reprinted, J. Corti, 1968; *L'Union libre*, [Paris], 1931; *Le Revolver a cheveux blancs*, Editions des Cahiers Libres, 1932; (with others) *Violette Nozieres*, Nicolas Flamel (Brussels), 1933; *L'Air de l'eau*, Editions Cahiers d'Art, 1934; *Le Chateau Etoile*, Editions Albert Skira, 1937; *Fata Morgana*, Editions des Lettres Francaises (Buenos Aires), 1942, translation by Clark Mills published under same title, Black Swan Press, 1969; *Pleine marge*, Editions Karl Nierendorf (New York), 1943; *Young Cherry Trees Secured Against Hares: Jeunes cerisiers garantis contreles lievres*, bilingual edition with translation by Edouard Roditi, View (New York), 1946, reprinted, University of Michigan Press, 1969; *Ode a Charles Fourier*, Editions de la Revue Fontaine, 1947, revised edition with an introduction and notes by Jean Gaulmier, Librairie Klincksieck, 1961, bilingual edition, with translation by Kenneth White, published as *Ode to Charles Fourier*, Cape Goliard Press, 1969; (with Andre Masson) *Martinique, charmeuse de serpents*, Editions du Sagittaire, 1948, new edition, J. J. Pauvert, 1972; *Poemes*, Gallimard, 1948; *Au regard des divinites*, Editions Messages, 1949; *Constellations* (with 22 gouaches of Joan Miro), Pierre Matisse (New York), 1959; *Le la*, Editions P.A.B., 1961; *Signe ascendant, suivi de Fata Morgana, les Etats generaux, Des Epingles tremblantes, Xenophiles, Ode a Charles Fourier, Constellations, Le la*, Gallimard, 1968; *Selected Poems*, translated by Kenneth White, J. Cape, 1969.

Co-author: (With Luis Aragon) *Permettez*, [Paris], 1927; (with Paul Eluard) *L'Immaculee conception*, Editions Surrealistes, 1930, reprinted, Seghers, 1968; (with Paul Eluard) *Notes sur la poesie*, Editions G.L.M., 1936; (with Luis Aragon and Paul Eluard) *Lautremont envers et contre tout*, [Paris], 1937; (with Jindrich Heisler and Benjamin Peret) *Toyen*, Sokolova (Paris), 1953; (with Gerard Legrand) *L'Art magique*, Formes et Reflets, 1957; (with others) *Antonin Artaud, ou, La Sante des poetes*, La tour de feu, 1959; (with Antoine Adam and R. Etiemble) *L'Affaire Rimbaud*, J. J. Pauvert, 1962; (with Marcel Duchamp) *Surrealist Intrusion in the Enchanteurs Domain*, Libraire Fischbacker, 1965; (with others) *Le Groupe, la rupture*, Editions du Seuil, 1970.

Contributor: Herbert Read, editor, *Surrealism*, Faber, 1936, Praeger, 1971; *Ubu enchaine et l'objet aime*, Imprimerie de Rocroy, 1937; *La Terre n'est pas une vallee des larmes*, Editions "La Boetie," 1945; Maurice Nadeau, editor, *Documents Surrealistes*, Editions du Seuil, 1948; *Donati*, W. N. Dennis, 1949; *Farouche a quatre feuilles*, Grasset, 1954; Robert Lebel, *Sur Marcel Duchamp*, Editions Trianon, 1959, translation by George Heard published as *Marcel Duchamp*, Grove, 1959; *La poesie dans ses meubles*, Officina Undici (Rome), 1964; Michael Benedikt and George E. Wellwarth, editors and translators, *Modern French Theatre*, Dutton, 1964.

Author of introduction or preface: Jean Genbach (Ernst de Gengenbach), *Satan a Paris*, H. Meslin, 1927; Man Ray, *La Photographie n'est pas l'art*, Editions G.L.M., 1937; M. Guggenheim, editor, *Art of This Century*, Art Aid Corporation, 1942; Benjamin Peret, *La Parole est a Peret*, Editions Surrealistes, 1943; Francis Picabia, *Choix de poemes*, Editions G.L.M., 1947; Aime Cesaire, *Cahier d'un retour au pays natal*, Bordas, 1947; Jacques Vache, *Les Lettres de guerre de Jacques Vache, suivies d'une nouvelle*, K Editeur, 1949; Maurice Fourre, *A La Nuit du Rose-hotel*, Gallimard, 1950; Xavier Forneret, *Oeuvres*, Arcanes, 1952; Achim d'Arnim, *Contes bizarres*, Arcanes, 1953; Jean Ferry, *Une Etude sur Raymond Roussel*, Arcanes, 1953; J. Ferry, *Le*

Mecanicien, Gallimard, 1953; Georges Darien, *Le Voleur*, Union general d'editions, 1955; Oscar Panizza, *Concile d'amour*, J. J. Pauvert, 1960; Pierre Mabille, *Le Miroir de merveilleux*, Editions de Minuit, 1962; Jean-Pierre Duprey, *Derriere son double*, Le Soleil Noir, 1964; *Konrad Klapheck*, [Paris], 1965; Charles Maturin, *Melmouth, l'homme errant*, Editions G. P., 1965.

Contributor to many anthologies, including *Petite anthologie poetique du surrealisme*, edited by Georges Hugnet, Editions Jeanne Bucher, 1934; *New Directions in Prose and Poetry: 1940*, New Directions, 1940; *Anthologie du poeme en prose*, edited by Maurice Chapelan, Julliard, 1947; *The Dada Painters and Poets*, edited by Robert Motherwell, Wittenborn, Schultz, 1951; *Mid-Century Anthology of Modern French Poetry from Baudelaire to the Present Day*, edited by C. A. Hackett, Macmillan, 1956; *Le Poeme en prose*, edited by Suzanne Bernard, Libraire Nizet, 1959; *La Poesie surrealiste*, edited by Jean-Louis Bedouin, Editions Seghers, 1964; *Twentieth-Century French Literature to World War II*, edited by Harry T. Moore, Teffer & Simons, 1966.

Introductions to catalogues of art exhibitions: *La Peinture surrealiste*, Galerie Pierre, 1925; *Crise de l'objet*, Charles Ratton, 1936; (with Paul Eluard) *Dictionnaire abrege du surrealisme*, Galerie Beaux-Arts, 1938; *Mexique*, Renou et Colle, 1939; *First Papers of Surrealism*, Coordinating Council of French Relief Societies, 1942; *Exposition Baya: Derriere le miroir*, Galerie Maeght, 1947; *Exposition Toyen*, Galerie Denise Rene, 1947; *Jacques Herold*, Cahiers d'Art, 1947; *Preliminaires sur matta: Surrealisme et la Peinture*, Galerie Rene Drouin, 1947; *Seconde Arche*, Fontaine, 1947; *Le Surrealisme en 1947*, Galerie Maeght, 1947; *Le Cadavre exquis*, Galerie Nina Dousset, 1948; *Oceanie*, Andree Olive, 1948; (with Michel Tapie) *Les Statues magiques de Maria*, Galerie Rene Drouin, 1948; *491, Jumelles pour yeux bandes*, Galerie Rene Drouin, 1949; *Yves Laloy*, La Cour d'Ingres, 1958; (with Jose Pierre) *Enseignes sournoises*, Galerie Mona Lisa, 1964; *Magritte, Le Sens Propre*, Galerie Alexandre Iolas, 1964.

Contributor to numerous art, literary, political, historical, and other journals worldwide.

SIDELIGHTS: In a statement for *CA*, Breton summarized the scope and purpose of his literary career. "My principle objective," he stated, "has been to promote in art pure psychic automatism 'removed from all control exercised by the reason and disengaged from all esthetic or moral preoccupations' [*Manifeste du surrealisme*, 1924]. My entire life has been devoted to exalting the values of *poetry, love*, and *liberty*. I flatter myself in being one of the very first writers to have denounced the 'Moscow trials.' I have not deviated from that to which I committed myself at the beginning of my career. I have striven, with others, to pursue the struggle that leads to a *recasting of human understanding*. To that end, surrealism was proposed as a means to transform, first and foremost, man's sensibilities. In my opinion, it has not fallen far short of this goal."

The surrealist movement in literature was founded by Breton in the early twenties and dominated the period between the two wars. It was an outgrowth of the postwar defeatism as well as a reaction against the nihilism of Dada. Breton and his associates audaciously sought to bring about a revolution in man's consciousness, a state of "surreality," the objective of which was "the total liberation of the mind." What was envisaged was an emancipation from reason and logic, thought processes which he believed deaden man's sensitivity. The surrealists decried not so much the absurdity of the world of realities or the deficiencies of man's mind as they did the "limited utilization of the mind and of the objects of experience," writes Anna Balakian. Breton's concern was the intensification of the human experience, the realization of what he called "an ever clearer and at the same time an ever more passionate consciousness of the world perceived by the senses." Only when reason loses its control over the psyche and one approaches the "fantastic," he stated, does "the most profound emotion of the individual have the fullest opportunity to express itself." Once the fetters of rationality are removed, then it is by means of "pure psychic automatism" that "the true functioning of thought" is brought to light.

As an ardent student of the theories and methodology of Freud, Breton sought limitless human potentialities, heretofore untapped, within the realm of dreams and the subconscious. Therefore, at the outset of the surrealistic movement, a systematic investigation of these subliminal forces was conducted. Breton and his colleagues, who included, among others, Philippe Soupault, Paul Eluard, Robert Desnos, and Rene Crevel, experimented daily with writing "automatic texts" in a state of semi-trance, recounting dreams while in a hypnotically invoked sleep or when awake, inducing hallucination, and simulating in writing states of mental derangement. The prose poems of Breton and Soupault, *Les Champs magnetiques,* are perhaps the best example of the "automatic texts," writings poured out as rapidly as possible, free from forethought or reconsideration. In *Les Vases communicants* Breton describes the dream and the state of wakefulness as being perpetually interwoven and enriched by one another. Following this experimentation, Breton states that he found within the dream "the principle of the conciliation of opposites." Commenting in 1930 on the past development of surrealism, Breton further stated: "Everything leads to the belief that there exists a certain point in the mind at which life and death, the real and the imaginary, the past and the future, what is communicable and what is incommunicable, the heights and the depths, cease to be perceived as contradictory. It is in vain that one would seek any other motive for surrealist activity than the hope of determining this point." (*Second manifeste du surrealisme,* 1930)

There is, however, less emphasis in the *Second manifeste* on automatic writing and more on the "automatic life" as epitomized in Breton's work *Nadja* (1928). This work is an autobiographical account of his chance meeting with a woman named Nadja who looks fixedly at the surface of her bath water and says, "I am the thought on the bath in the room without mirrors." Life, in Nadja's possession, is magically permeated with sublime and startling coincidences, repeated chance encounters, prescience of objectively insignificant incidents, and spontaneous, poetic reactions to the quotidian as well as to the heart rending. She is the embodiment of Breton's preoccupations with intuitive imagination and "*le hasard objectif,*" objective chance or coincidence which together contribute to the "marvelous" in life.

Breton defined chance as being "the encounter of an external causality and an internal finality, a form of manifestation of the external necessity making its ways in the human unconscious." An individual who can submit himself to the laws of the subconscious is one who then partakes of the "marvelous" because his conscious mind is attuned to both the most fundamental subjective and objective realities. By freeing the imagination, one can conceive of the infinite possibilities of such a harmony. For Breton the imagination alone accounts for what can be. It is the imaginary, he wrote, that tends to become reality. And frequently in the use of the word "imagination" he denoted intuition. Clairvoyance also was a highly respected phenomena among the surrealists.

It is significant to note that in 1925 in his *Lettre aux voyantes,* published in 1929, Breton stated, "There are people who pretend that the war has taught them something; they are less well off than I who know what the year 1939 is reserving for me." In a sense, surrealism is a form of atheistic mysticism that not only identifies spirit and matter, but challenges man to be his own master, perhaps his own God, by exploiting the resources deep within his mind.

The releasing of these forces had immediate social and political implications, for, as Breton stated in *What is Surrealism?,* the liberation of the mind demands as a primary condition the liberation of man. Consequently, there existed in the period between the two wars an alliance between surrealism and the French Communist Party which sought the political and economic emancipation of man. Like the communists, the surrealists adhered to the philosophy of dialectic materialism. However, this alliance was never complete, for Breton adamantly refused to surrender the freedom and integrity of the writer and artist by subjugating creativity to an ideology. As a result, he expelled from the surrealist group those writers who thus compromised their liberty, broke officially with the Communist Party in 1935, and vociferously protested Stalinist communism. Breton also despised nationalism in any of its forms and strove for a new consciousness of life common to all artists and writers.

For the poet, this passionate dedication to liberty necessitated a liberation from the rules of art. All literary conventions and stylized forms had to be abandoned. Prose achieved a new status in Breton's writings, which was a natural form for automatic writing which demands an "uninterrupted flow of words." His prose, writes Marcel Raymond, "ambles along at a regular pace, fluid and smooth as a piece of pliable wood without knots." His writing is marked by a stream of images consisting of bizarre and illogical metaphors and the juxtaposition of opposites. "Breton called ideas vain and ineffective compared to the force of the sudden unexpected image" and believed that images should "not be directed by thoughts but be conducive to them," writes Anna Balakian. Translation of titles of poems such as "Soluble Fish," "The Whitehaired Revolver," and "Fertile Eyes" set forth the disparity and contradiction inherent in Breton's images. In his tract, *What is Surrealism?,* Breton commented: ". . . He who still refuses to see, for instance, a horse galloping on a tomato should be looked upon as a cretin. A tomato is also a child's balloon—surrealism . . . having suppressed the word 'like'."

What is most frequently revered in Breton's poetry and prose is his treatment of love. Maurice Nadeau remarks that Breton "brought back to poetry the long lost figure of woman as embodiment of magic powers [and as a] creature of grace and promise. . . ." Breton unequivocally proclaims the supremacy of love. "Today," he wrote, "it is up to man unhesitatingly to deny everything that can enslave him, and if necessary, to die on a barricade of flowers, if only to give body to a chimera, to woman, and perhaps to her alone, to rescue both that which she brings with her and that which lifts her up.—Silence!—There is no solution outside love." Professor Balakian told *CA* that Breton's writings as well as his personal interviews were marked by the quality of impersonality. She stated that he refrained from injecting his most subjective self into his poetry and quite deliberately kept his personal life from the eyes of the public. This detachment, as it was explained, contributes to the elements of permanence and universality that are characteristic of his writings which deal with themes such as love and war.

The impact of surrealism on the twentieth century is evident in the novel, poetry, philosophy, painting, photography, the cinema, the theater, and architecture. Surrealism has been described as "one of the most far-reaching attempts at changing not only literature and painting, but psychology, ethics, and man himself." (Peyre, *Yale French Studies*, no. 31.) Eugene Ionesco remarked, "I place Breton on the same level as Einstein, Freud, Jung, and Kafka." Breton himself took account of the effects of the movement when he stated that surrealism "has provoked new states of consciousness and overthrown walls beyond which it was immemorially supposed to be impossible to see; it has modified the sensibility . . . and taken a decisive step towards the unification of the personality, which it found threatened by an ever more profound dissociation." In an interview which took place in 1964, Breton said, "I may live ten more years, but my work is done." Two years later, at the age of seventy, he died from a heart attack.

BIOGRAPHICAL/CRITICAL SOURCES: Marcel Raymond, *De Baudelaire au Surrealisme*, R. A. Correa, 1933, translation by G.M. published as *From Baudelaire to Surrealism*, Wittenborn, Schultz, 1950; David Gascoyne, *A Short Survey of Surrealism*, Cogden-Sanderson, 1936; Georges Lemaitre, *From Cubism to Surrealism in French Literature*, Harvard University Press, 1941; Maurice Nadeau, *Histoire du Surrealisme*, Editions du Seuil, 1946, translation by Richard Howard published as *The History of Surrealism*, Macmillan, 1965; Anna Balakian, *The Literary Origins of Surrealism: A New Mysticism in French Poetry*, New York University Press, 1947; Claude Mauriac, *Andre Breton*, Editions de Flore, 1949; Victor Crastre, *Andre Breton*, Arcanes, 1952; Ferdinand Alquie, *Philosophie du Surrealisme*, Flammarion, 1955, translation by Bernard Waldrop published as *Philosophy of Surrealism*, University of Michigan Press, 1965; Anna Balakian, *Surrealism: The Road to the Absolute*, Noonday, 1959.

Wallace Fowlie, *Age of Surrealism*, Indiana University Press, 1960; Andre Breton, *Poesie et Autre*, edited by Gerard Legrand, Club du Meilleur Livre, 1960; Matthew Josephson, *Life Among the Surrealists: A Memoir*, Holt, 1962; *Yale French Studies*, Number 31, 1964; *Saturday Review*, March 12, 1966, October 29, 1966; *Le Monde*, September 29, 1966; *New York Times*, September 29, 1966, October 9, 1966; *Figaro Litteraire*, October 6, 1966; *Nouvelles Litteraires*, October 6, 1966; M. A. Caws, *Surrealism and the Literary Imagination*, Humanities, 1966; Clifford Browder, *Andre Breton: Arbiter of Surrealism*, Librairie Droz (Geneva), 1967; *Homage to Andre Breton*, Wittenborn, 1967; A. E. Balakian, *Andre Breton: Magus of Surrealism*, Oxford University Press, 1971; M. A. Caws, *Andre Breton*, Twayne, 1971; *Contemporary Literary Criticism*, Volume II, Gale, 1974.†

(Died September 28, 1966)

* * *

BREUER, Bessie   1893-1975

PERSONAL: Born October 19, 1893, in Cleveland, Ohio; married Henry Varnum Poor III (an artist; deceased); children: Anne Poor Kahler, Peter Varnum. *Education.* Attended University of Missouri. *Agent:* Brandt & Brandt, 101 Park Ave., New York, N.Y. 10017.

CAREER: Reporter for *St. Louis Times*, St. Louis, Mo.; editor, *New York Tribune*, New York, N.Y.; national director of publicity, American Red Cross; staff member, *Ladies' Home Journal;* editor, *Charm* (magazine). Worked in Office of War Information during World War II. Novelist, short story writer, and playwright. *Awards, honors:* O. Henry Memorial Award, 1944, for short story "Home Is a Place."

WRITINGS: Memory of Love, Simon & Schuster, 1935; *The Daughter*, Simon & Schuster, 1938; *The Bracelet of Wavia Lea* (short story collection), Sloane, 1947; *The Actress*, Harper, 1957; *Take Care of My Roses*, Atheneum, 1961. Author of play, "Sundown Beach," produced at Actors Studio. Short stories published in *New Yorker* and *Harper's Bazaar*, and anthologized in *Prize Stories: The O. Henry Awards*, 1944, and in other collections in United States and England. Contributor of articles to *Harper's* and *Pictorial Review*.

WORK IN PROGRESS: A novel for Atheneum.

SIDELIGHTS: Bessie Breuer's novels have been translated for European publication. One, *Memory of Love*, was filmed as "In Name Only," with Cary Grant and Carole Lombard.

BIOGRAPHICAL/CRITICAL SOURCES: New York Times, September 28, 1975.††

(Died September 26, 1975)

* * *

BREUER, Ernest Henry   1902-1972

PERSONAL: Surname rhymes with "lawyer"; born May 2, 1902, in Hungary; son of Henry Joseph and Esther (Greenfield) Breuer; married Minna Hirschfeld, August 26, 1932; children: Elizabeth Esta. *Education:* New York University, B.C.S., 1925; Harvard University, LL.B., 1929; Pratt Institute, B.L.S., 1948. *Home:* 143 Melrose Ave., Albany, N.Y. 12203. *Office:* New York State Law Library, Education Building, Albany, N.Y. 12203.

CAREER: National Association of Credit Men, New York, N.Y., special investigation, 1925-26; attorney in private practice, New York, N.Y., 1930-38, and Cincinnati, Ohio, 1938-43; American Red Cross, field director, Tinian, Mariana Islands, 1944-45; attorney in private practice, New York, N.Y., 1945-48; New York State Library, Albany, assistant law librarian, 1948-51, state law librarian, 1951-72. Consultant to other public law libraries in New York State. *Military service:* U.S. Army, 1942. *Member:* American Association of Law Libraries (executive board, 1959-61), American Society for Legal History (executive secretary, Northeast branch, 1962-72), Law Library Association of Greater New York (board of directors, 1961; president, 1965), Association of Law Libraries of Upstate New York (founder and president, 1954-57).

WRITINGS: Constitutional Developments in New York, 1777-1958, New York State Library, 1958, *Supplement, 1958-1967*, 1967, *A Second Supplement, April 4-September 26, 1967*, 1970; *The New York State Court of Claims*, New York State Library, 1959; *Moreland Act Investigations in New York: 1907-65*, New York State Library, 1965. Contributor to legal and law library journals.

AVOCATIONAL INTERESTS: Spectator football, travel, the theater, and opera.†

(Died, 1972)

BREWER, J(ohn) Mason 1896-1975

PERSONAL: Born March 24, 1896, in Goliad, Tex.; son of John Henry (a grocer and barber) and Minnie (a teacher; maiden name, Tate) Brewer; married Mae Thornton Hickman, October 18, 1928; married second wife, Ruth Helen Brush (a kindergarten teacher), August 22, 1959; children: (first marriage) John Mason, Jr. *Education:* Wiley College, A.B., 1917; Indiana University, M.A., 1950. *Home:* 2824 Laurel Lane, Commerce, Tex. 75428.

CAREER: Livingstone College, Salisbury, N.C., professor of English, 1959-69; East Texas State University, Commerce, Distinguished Visiting Professor of English, 1969-75. Visiting professor of anthropology, North Carolina Agricultural and Technical State University, 1967-69. Lecturer at Yale University, University of Toronto, University of Texas, Fisk University, Clark College, Tuskegee Institute, Duke University, University of Colorado, University of Arizona, and at International Folk Festival, 1955. *Member:* American Folklore Society (second vice-president, 1954; only member of his race to serve on research committee and council), National Folk Festival Association (member of board of directors), South Central Modern Language Association of America (chairman of folklore section), Texas Institute of Letters, North Carolina Folklore Society (first vice-president), Louisiana Folklore Society (life member, 1970). *Awards, honors:* Litt.D. from Paul Quinn College, 1951; Chicago Book Fair award, 1968, for *American Negro Folklore;* Twenty-first Annual Writers Roundup award for one of the outstanding books written by a Texas author, 1969, for *American Negro Folklore;* grants for research in Negro folklore from American Philosophical Society, Piedmont University Center for the Study of Negro Folklore, Library of Congress, National Library of Mexico, National University of Mexico.

WRITINGS: Echoes of Thought (poems), Progressive Printing Co. (Fort Worth, Texas), 1922; *Negrito: Negro Dialect Poems of the Southwest,* illustrations by Tom Smith, Naylor, 1933, reprinted, Books for Libraries, 1972; *Negro Legislators of Texas and Their Descendants: A History of the Negro in Texas Politics from Reconstruction to Disfranchisement,* introduction by Herbert P. Grambell, Mathis, Van Norton & Co., 1935, reprinted, R & E Research Associates, 1970, revised edition published as *Negro Legislators of Texas and Their Descendants,* introductions by Gambrell and Alwyn Barr, Jenkins Publishing, 1970; (editor) *Heralding Dawn: An Anthology of Negro Poets in Texas,* privately printed, 1936; *The Life of Dr. John Wesley Anderson* (verse), C. C. Cockrell & Son, 1938; *Little Dan from Dixieland: A Story in Verse,* Bookcraft, 1940; (editor) *Negro Folktales from Texas,* Webster Publishing, 1942; (editor) *Humorous Folktales of the South Carolina Negro,* South Carolina Negro Folklore Guild, 1945; *More Truth than Poetry,* privately printed, 1947; *The Word on the Brazos: Negro Preacher Tales from the Brazos Bottoms of Texas,* foreword by J. Frank Dobie, University of Texas Press, 1953; *Aunt Dicy Tales,* privately printed, 1956; *Dog Ghosts and Other Texas Negro Folk Tales,* University of Texas Press, 1958; *Worser Days and Better Times: The Folklore of the North Carolina Negro,* preface and notes by Warren E. Roberts, Quadrangle, 1965; *American Negro Folklore,* illustrated by Richard Lowe, Quadrangle, 1968.

Contributor to anthologies: *A Treasury of Southern Folklore,* edited by B. A. Botkin, Crown, 1949; *Texas Folk and Texas Folklore,* Texas Folklore Society, 1954; *A Treasury of American Anecdotes,* Random House, 1957; *The Illus-trated Book of American Folklore,* edited by Carl Whithers and Botkin, Grosset, 1958; *The Book of Negro Folklore,* edited by Arna Bontemps, Dodd, 1958; *Laughing on the Outside,* edited by Philip Sterling, Grosset, 1965; *The Book of Negro Humor,* edited by Langston Hughes, Dodd, 1966; *African Animal Tales,* North Carolina Folklore Society, 1968; *Black Expression,* edited by Addison Gayle, Weybright, 1969. General editor, "Negro Heritage" series, Pemberton Press. Contributor to *Journal of American Folklore, Phylon, Ebony, Crisis, Interracial Review,* and other journals.

WORK IN PROGRESS: The Negro in Mexican Folklore.

SIDELIGHTS: American Negro Folklore was the basis for a five film series by WTVI (North Carolina).

BIOGRAPHICAL/CRITICAL SOURCES: James W. Byrd, *J. Mason Brewer, Folklorist,* Steck, 1968; *Virginia Quarterly Review,* summer, 1969.†

(Died January 24, 1975)

* * *

BRIEFS, Goetz Antony 1889-1974

PERSONAL: Born January 1, 1889, in Eschweiler, Rhinelands, Germany; son of Francis (a merchant) and Ann (Vieten) Briefs; married Ann Stephany Weltmann, 1919 (died, 1946); married Elinor Castendyk Sturve, March 26, 1951; children: (first marriage) Godfrey, Henry, Angela Briefs Carpenter, Elisabeth Briefs Clancy; (second marriage) Regina. *Education:* Studied at University of Munich, 1908-09, University of Bonn, 1909-10, and University of Freiburg, 1911-12; received degree, Dr. rerum politicarum. *Religion:* Roman Catholic. *Home:* 1413 44th St. N.W., Washington, D.C.

CAREER: University of Freiburg, Freiburg, Germany, privatdocent (lecturer), 1913-19, assistant professor, 1919-20; University of Wuerzburg, Wuerzburg, Germany, assistant professor, 1921-22; University of Freiburg, professor of economics, 1922-26; Technical University, Berlin, Germany, professor of economics, 1926-34, professor emeritus, 1948-74; Catholic University of America, Washington, D.C., visiting professor, 1934-37; Georgetown University, Washington, D.C., professor of labor economics, 1937-62, professor emeritus, 1962-74. Summer lecturer, Columbia University, 1938-48; also lecturer at University of Vienna and University of Berne. Consultant to the German Government, 1915-19, and to the Pentagon, and Office of Strategic Services, 1944.

MEMBER: American Economic Association, German Sociological Society (formerly member of board), Mount Pelerin Society, German Social Political Association (formerly member of board), Pi Gamma Mu. *Awards, honors:* Grand Cross of Merit (Federal Republic of Germany), 1959; honorary degrees from University of Milan, University of Munich, Institute of Commerce and Business Administration (St. Gall, Switzerland), University of Freiburg, St. Mary's College of California, and Georgetown University.

WRITINGS: Das Spirituskartell, Braun, 1912; *Untersuchungen zur klassischen Nationaloekonomie,* G. Fischer, 1915; (with Martha Voss-Zietz and Maria Stegemann-Runk) *Die Hauswirtschaft im Kriege,* R. Hobbing, 1917; (editor) *Probleme der sozialen Betriebspolitik,* J. Springer, 1930; (editor) *Probleme der sozialen Werkspolitik,* Dunker & Humblot, 1930-35; *Betriebsfuehrung und Betriebsleben in der Industrie,* Ferdinand Enke Verlag, 1934; *The Proletariat: A Challenge to Western Civilization,* translated by Ruth A.

Eckhart, McGraw, 1937; *Can Labor Sit in the Office?*, National Industrial Conference Board, 1948; *Zwischen Kapitalismus und Syndikalismus*, A. Francke, 1952; *Die Verantwortung des christlichen Unternehmers Heute*, J. P. Bachem, c. 1955; *Unionism Reappraised*, American Enterprise Association, 1960; *Laissez-faire-Pluralism*, Duncker & Humblot, 1966; *Mitbestimmung?*, Seewald, 1967; *Trade Unionism Yesterday and Today*, Knapp, 1968. Contributor of about 170 articles to journals. Editor, *Economics and Labor* (Berlin); co-editor, *Archives of the Philosophy and Law of Economics* (Berlin).†

(Died May 18, 1974)

* * *

BRIGGS, Peter 1921-1975

PERSONAL: Born April 15, 1921, in St. Paul, Minn.; son of Allan and Winifred (Douglas) Briggs; divorced; children: Andy. *Education:* University of Chicago, B.A., 1942. *Home:* 240 East 35th St., New York, N.Y. *Agent:* McIntosh & Otis, Inc., 475 Fifth Ave., New York, N.Y. 10017.

CAREER: Worked in book advertising department at A. S. Barnes, and as promotion manager at Columbia University Press, Henry Holt, G. P. Putnam's Sons, John Day & Co., and Coward McCann, 1946-51; *Ladies' Home Journal*, New York, N.Y., articles editor, 1951-63; free-lance writer, 1963-75. *Military service:* U.S. Navy, World War II; became ensign.

WRITINGS—For young people: *Water, The Vital Essence*, Harper, 1967; *Men in the Sea*, Simon & Schuster, 1968; *The Great Global Rift*, Weybright, 1969; *Science Ship: A Voyage Aboard the Discoverer*, Simon & Schuster, 1969; *Rivers in the Sea*, Weybright, 1969; *Mysteries of the Sea*, McKay, 1969; *Mysteries of Our World: Unanswered Questions about the Continents, the Seas, the Atmosphere, the Origins of Life*, McKay, 1969; *Buccaneer Harbor: The Fabulous History of Port Royal, Jamaica*, Simon & Schuster, 1970; *Laboratory at the Bottom of the World*, McKay, 1970; *200,000,000 Years Beneath the Sea*, Holt, 1971; *What Is the Grand Design?: The Story of Evolving Life and the Changing Planet on Which It Is Lived*, McKay, 1973; *Will California Fall into the Sea*, McKay, 1973; *Rampage: The Story of Disastrous Floods, Broken Dams, and Human Fallibility*, McKay, 1973; *Population Policy: The Social Dilemma*, British Book Center, 1974.†

(Died July 18, 1975)

* * *

BRISSENDEN, Paul F(rederick) 1885-1974

PERSONAL: Surname is accented on first syllable; born September 21, 1885, in Benzonia, Mich.; son of James Thomas (a farmer) and Maretta (Lewis) Brissenden; married Margaret Geer, September 30, 1926 (deceased); children: Donald, Hoke and Arik (twins). *Education:* University of Denver, A.B., 1908; University of California, A.M., 1912; Columbia University, Ph.D., 1918. *Home:* Edgewater Hotel, Honolulu, Hawaii. *Office:* Hawaii Hall, University of Hawaii, Honolulu, Hawaii.

CAREER: U.S. Commission on Industrial Relations, special agent, 1914; U.S. Bureau of Labor Statistics, special agent, 1915-20; New York University, New York, N.Y., assistant professor of economics, 1920-21; Columbia University, New York, N.Y., 1921-55, started as lecturer, became professor of economics and chairman of the industry-labor relations department. University of Hawaii, Honolulu,

senior visiting scholar, Institute of Advanced Projects, East-West Center. Impartial chairman under various labor agreements, 1937-74. U.S. Office of Production Management and War Production Board, consultant and member of clothing advisory committee, 1941-43; U.S. Bureau of Labor Statistics, special consultant, 1941-43; National War Labor Board, mediator, arbitrator, and referee, 1942; Regional War Labor Board, vice-chairman and public member, 1943-45. National Consumers League, chairman of board of directors, 1939-40; International Rescue and Relief Committee, past member of board of directors.

MEMBER: National Academy of Arbitrators (charter member), American Arbitration Association (industrial tribunal member, 1939-74), American Economic Association, Sigma Alpha Epsilon, Beta Gamma Sigma.

WRITINGS: The Launching of the Industrial Workers of the World, University of California Publications in Economics, 1913, reprinted, Haskell House, 1971; *The I.W.W.: A Study of American Syndicalism*, Longmans, Green, 1918, 2nd edition, 1920; (with Emil Frankel) *Labor Turnover in Industry*, Macmillan, 1922; *Earnings of Factory Workers, 1899 to 1927: An Analysis of Pay-Roll Statistics*, U.S. Bureau of the Census, 1929, reprinted, Burt Franklin, 1971; *The Great Hawaiian Dock Strike*, 1953; *The Labor Injunction in Hawaii*, Public Affairs Press, 1956; *Arbitration in Australia and the United States*, 1960; (editor with H. S. Roberts) *Challenge of Industrial Relations*, East-West Center Press, 1965; *The Settlement of Labor Disputes on Rights in Australia*, University of California Institute of Industrial Relations, 1966. Author of reports and monographs. Contributor to *Industrial Relations* and other journals.†

(Died November 29, 1974)

* * *

BROCKWAY, Thomas P(armelee) 1898-

PERSONAL: Born November 21, 1898, in Clinton, N.Y.; son of Thomas Clinton (a clergyman) and Isabelle (Parmelee) Brockway; married Jean Lambert, June 14, 1927; children: Joan (Mrs. Robin E. Esch, a cellist). *Education:* Reed College, B.A., 1921; Oxford University, B.Litt., 1925; Yale University, Ph.D., 1937. *Home:* Matteson Rd., North Bennington, Vt.

CAREER: Instructor at St. John's College, Annapolis, Md., Dartmouth College, Hanover, N.H., and Yale University, New Haven, Conn., 1925-33; Bennington College, Bennington, Vt., professor of history and political science, 1933-66, acting president, 1950-51, 1963-64, dean, 1952-62. Foreign Economic Administration, Board of Economic Warfare, Washington, D.C., administrative officer, 1941-44. American Council of Learned Societies, executive associate, 1960-61, 1966. Vermont Forums, president, 1951-52. *Military service:* U.S. Army, 1918. *Member:* American Historical Association. *Awards, honors:* Rhodes scholar, 1922-25.

WRITINGS: Battles Without Bullets: The History of Economic Warfare, Foreign Policy Association, 1939; (editor) *Basic Documents of United States Foreign Policy*, Van Nostrand, 1957; (editor) *Language and Politics*, Heath, 1965.

WORK IN PROGRESS: A history of Bennington College.

AVOCATIONAL INTERESTS: Abstract photography, tennis, shaping wood on a bandsaw (especially fish for mobiles).

BRODERICK, John F. 1909-

PERSONAL: Born September 17, 1909, in Lynn, Mass.; son of Patrick W. and Margaret (Leonard) Broderick. *Education:* Boston University, A.B., 1931; Weston College, Weston, Mass., M.A., 1942, S.T.L., 1946; Gregorian University, Rome, H.E.D., 1951. *Home:* Campion Center, Weston, Mass. 02193.

CAREER: Roman Catholic priest of Society of Jesus (Jesuits); Boston College, Weston School of Theology, Cambridge, Mass., professor of ecclesiastical history, 1951-76, professor emeritus, 1976—. Staff editor, *New Catholic Encyclopedia,* 1967.

WRITINGS: The Holy See and the Irish Movement for Repeal of the Union with England: 1829-1847, Gregorian University Press, 1951; *Documents of Vatican Council I,* Liturgical Press, 1971. Contributor to *Encyclopaedia Britannica,* and *Encyclopedia Americana;* also contributor to *Theological Studies, America,* and other journals. *Catholic Historical Review,* advisory editor, 1962-65, and contributor.

*   *   *

BROEK, J(an) O(tto) M(arius) 1904-1974

PERSONAL: Surname pronounced Brook; born December 8, 1904, in Utrecht, Netherlands; became U.S. citizen in 1942; son of Jan (a physician) and Gertrude (Van Zwicht) Broek; married Orletta Ruth Heineck (an author), May 25, 1931; children: Orletta Marianne (Mrs. J. M. Leffingwall), Gertrude Juliana (Mrs. G. A. Williams), Jan Maarten. *Education:* University of Utrecht, student, 1924-29, Ph.D., 1932; graduate study at London School of Economics and Political Science, London, 1929, University of California, Berkeley, and other American universities, 1930-31. *Religion:* Protestant. *Home:* 235 Southampton Ave., Berkeley, Calif. 94707.

CAREER: Netherlands Railways, Utrecht, Netherlands, staff member, Division of Commerce, 1933-36; University of California, Berkeley, assistant professor, 1936-40, associate professor of geography, 1940-46; University of Utrecht, Utrecht, Netherlands, professor of social geography, 1946-48; University of Minnesota, Minneapolis, professor of geography, 1948-70, professor emeritus, 1970-74, chairman of department, 1948-56. Consultant to geography branch of Military Intelligence, U.S. Army, 1943-44; assistant to chief of Far Eastern Division, Office of Strategic Services, 1944. Visiting professor, University of Indonesia, 1947; honorary research associate, University College, London, 1961-62; University of California, Berkeley, visiting professor, 1970-72, research associate, 1972-74.

MEMBER: Association of American Geographers (vice-president, 1960; president, 1961), Association for Asian Studies, American Geographical Society, Royal Netherlands Geographical Society (corresponding member), Netherlands Society for Economic and Social Geography, El Instituto de la Produccion (University of Buenos Aires; corresponding member), Campus Club (University of Minnesota). *Awards, honors:* Rockefeller Foundation fellow, 1929-31; Fulbright professor, University of Malaya, 1954-55; American Council of Learned Societies-Social Science Research Council award, 1961-62.

WRITINGS: The Santa Clara Valley, California, Oosthoek (Utrecht), 1932; *The Economic Development of the Netherlands Indies,* Institute of Pacific Relations, 1942, reprinted, Russell, 1971; *Indonesia,* Doubleday, 1962; *Ma-*

laya, Doubleday, 1963; (with John W. Webb) *Selected Chapters of Human Geography,* Burgess, 1964; *Geography, Its Scope and Spirit,* C. E. Merrill, 1965, abridged edition published as *Compass of Geography,* 1966; (contributor) H. R. Friis, editor, *The Pacific Basin: A History of Its Geographical Exploration,* American Geographical Society, 1967; (with Webb) *A Geography of Mankind,* McGraw, 1968, 2nd edition, 1973. Contributor to *Encyclopaedia Britannica* and scholarly journals. Member of editorial board, Netherlands Society for Economic and Social Geography, 1946-67, and Royal Netherlands Geographical Society, 1946-48; member of editorial advisory board, Association for Asian Studies, 1950-53; advisory editor, *Terrae Incognitae: The Annals of the Society for the History of Discoveries,* 1967-74.†

(Died August 23, 1974)

*   *   *

BROOKS, A(lfred) Russell 1906-

PERSONAL: Born May 19, 1906, in Montgomery, Ala; son of John Randolph (a clergyman) and Eliza (Wallace) Brooks; married Sara Tucker Boome (an elementary school librarian), August 18, 1967; children: Dwight, George, Ann. *Education:* Morehouse College, B.A., 1931; University of Wisconsin, M.A., 1934, Ph.D., 1958; also studied at University of Edinburgh, 1938-39. *Home:* 415 College Park Dr., Frankfort, Ky. 40601.

CAREER: Atlanta University, Atlanta, Ga., instructor in English, university high school, 1932-33; Agricultural and Technical College of North Carolina (now North Carolina Agricultural and Technical State University), Greensboro, chairman of English department, 1934-44; Morehouse College, Atlanta, Ga., associate professor of English, 1946-60; Kentucky State College, Frankfort, professor of English and chairman of department, 1960-72. *Member:* Modern Language Association of America, National Council of Teachers of English, College English Association, College Language Association, American Association of University Professors, South Atlantic Modern Language Association.

WRITINGS: James Boswell, Twayne, 1971.

WORK IN PROGRESS: Preparing an anthology of works of self-directed satire by American Blacks.

*   *   *

BROWN, Beth
(Beth A. Retner)

PERSONAL: Born in New York, N.Y.; daughter of Alex and Sophia (Lane) Brown; formerly married to John Barry; children: Betty. *Education:* Studied at Columbia University, New York University, and University of Southern California. *Home:* Magic Mountain, Montrose, N.Y. *Office:* 325 West End Ave., New York, N.Y. 10023.

CAREER: Writer with headquarters in Manhattan. Film writer in Hollywood for Metro-Goldwyn-Mayer and Paramount Pictures Corp.; gathered material for specific books by working as nursemaid in an orphanage (*Little Girl Blue*), stripper with a burlesque troupe (*Applause*), check room girl in a night spot (*Mister Broadway*), and other jobs. *Member:* Society of Magazine Writers.

WRITINGS: Ballyhoo!, Dial, 1927; *Applause,* Liveright, 1928; *For Men Only,* C. Kendall, 1930; *Wedding Ring,* Doubleday, 1930; *Man and Wife,* C. Kendall, 1933, published as *Wives and Men,* Jarrolds, 1937; *Lady Hobo,* Coward, 1935; *Riverside Drive,* Dutton, 1936; *Universal Station,*

Regent, 1944; *Mr. Jolly's Hotel for Dogs*, Regent, 1947; *Everybody's Dog Book*, Winston, 1953, published as *All About Dogs: A Practical Handbook*, Collier, 1961; *Blinkie*, Prentice-Hall, 1956; (editor) *All Horses Go to Heaven* (anthology), Grosset, 1963; *Play Your Hunch—It May Be a Miracle*, Hawthorn, 1967; *Hurricane*, Prentice-Hall, 1968; *Hurricane's Colt*, Prentice-Hall, 1968; *Book of Cat Care*, Popular Library, 1968; *Dogs That Work for a Living*, Funk, 1968; *Beth Brown's Dog Parade*, Lion Press, 1968; *Dogs*, photography by Walter Chandoha, Lion Press, 1968; *Cats*, Hewitt House, 1970; *The House without a Home*, Lion Press, 1970. Also author of *Mr. Broadway*.

Compiler: *All Dogs Go to Heaven*, Arco, 1943; *All Cats Go to Heaven* (anthology), Grosset, 1960; *The Wonderful World of Cats*, Harper, 1961; *The Wonderful World of Dogs*, Harper, 1961; *Animal Street* (anthology), Collier, 1962; *The Wonderful World of Horses*, Harper, 1967.

Under pseudonym Beth A. Retner: *That's That!*, Doubleday, 1925; *The Tired Trolley Car*, Doubleday, 1926 (published in England as *The Weary Tram*); *Little Girl Blue*, Doubleday, 1926.

WORK IN PROGRESS: Inspirational books; a biography of Clara Barton; two juveniles, *The Night the Sun Shone* and *Come on a Merry-Go-Round*.†

(Deceased)

* * *

BROWN, Ida Mae 1908-

PERSONAL: Born September 24, 1908, in Baltimore, Md.; daughter of Albert and Rosa Brown; married Louis L. Snyder (a professor of history), June 26, 1936. *Education:* Columbia University, B.S. (magna cum laude), 1955. *Home and office:* 21 Dogwood Lane, Princeton, N.J. 08540.

CAREER: Formerly a social worker for City of New York, N.Y., and an editor for Van Nostrand Co., Princeton, N.J. *Member:* Phi Beta Kappa.

*WRITINGS—*With husband, Louis L. Snyder: *Bismarck and German Unification* (juvenile), F. Watts, 1966; *Frederick the Great: Prussian Warrior* (juvenile), F. Watts, 1968. Former assistant editor of Van Nostrand's "Anvil" series of paperbacks in history and the social sciences.

* * *

BROWN, Mark H(erbert) 1900-

PERSONAL: Born July 6, 1900, in Wellman, Iowa; son of William John (a farmer) and Harriett (Varney) Brown; married Alice Mildred Hansell (a teacher), June 9, 1934; children: John Herbert, Judith Harriett (deceased). *Education:* Iowa State College of Agriculture and Mechanic Arts (now Iowa State University of Science and Technology), B.S., 1924, M.S., 1930, Ph.D., 1932 *Religion:* Protestant. *Home:* Trails End Farm, Alta, Iowa 51002. *Agent:* Paul R. Reynolds, Inc., 12 East 41st St., New York, N.Y. 10017.

CAREER: U.S. Department of Agriculture, Soil Conservation Service, soil scientist in various parts of the country, 1934-54; Trails End Farm, Alta, Iowa, farmer, beginning 1954. Writer about the American West. *Military service:* U.S. Army, 1918. U.S. Army Air Forces and U.S. Air Force, active duty as Intelligence officer, 1942-53, Reserve service, 1953-62; became lieutenant colonel; received Bronze Star Medal, 1945. *Awards, honors:* Buffalo Award of New York Posse of the Westerners for best nonfiction western book of 1955, *The Frontier Years*.

WRITINGS: (With W. R. Felton) *The Frontier Years*, Holt, 1955; (with Felton) *Before Barbed Wire*, Holt, 1956; *The Plainsmen of the Yellowstone*, Putnam, 1961; *The Flight of the Nez Perce*, Putnam, 1967. Contributor to periodicals.

WORK IN PROGRESS: A book dealing with the western frontier.

* * *

BROWN, Muriel W(hitbeck) 1892-

PERSONAL: Born October 29, 1892, in Brighton, N.Y.; daughter of William Mortimer and Helen (Hood) Brown. *Education:* Wellesley College, B.A., 1915; Stanford University, M.A., 1924; Johns Hopkins University, Ph.D., 1926. *Home address:* Route 1, Box 268, Stephens City, Va. 22655.

CAREER: High school teacher of English in Philadelphia, Pa., 1916-18; White-Williams Foundation, Philadelphia, staff member, 1918-20; supervisor of special education, Pennsylvania State Department of Public Instruction, 1920-22; Society for the Prevention of Cruelty to Children, Rochester and Monroe County, N.Y., director of child study, 1927-33; National Council of Parent Education, New York, N.Y., research associate, 1933-35; regional supervisor of parent education, California State Department of Education, 1935-37; assistant professor of psychology at University of Tulsa, Tulsa, Okla., and specialist in family life and parent education for Tulsa public schools, 1937-40; U.S. Office of Education, Washington, D.C., consultant in family life education with the Home Economics Education Service, 1940-53, community development specialist and program officer with the International Division, 1953-56; U.S. Children's Bureau, Washington, D.C., parent education specialist, 1956-62; writer, lecturer, and consultant. Visiting professor, University of Hawaii, 1952. Consultant on mental health, child development, and community education with missions abroad, assisting with organization of West German mental health movement, 1952-53, and with establishment of home economics colleges in Pakistan, 1956-57. Trustee, American Toy Manufacturers' Research Institute.

MEMBER: World Federation for Mental Health, International Federation of Schools for Parents, American Academy of Political and Social Science, American Association for the Advancement of Science (fellow), American Home Economics Association, American Social Health Association (honorary life member), National Council on Family Relations, Society of Women Geographers, American Association of University Women, United Nations Association of the United States of America, Council of the Southern Mountains, Phi Beta Kappa, Sigma Xi, Omicron Nu (honorary member).

WRITINGS: (Contributor) Morris Fishbein and Ruby Jo Reeves, editors, *Modern Marriage and Family Living*, Oxford University Press, 1957; (contributor) *Handbook on Marriage and Family Living*, Rand McNally, 1964; (with Margaret Mead) *The Wagon and the Star: A Study in American Community Initiative*, Rand McNally, 1967. Author of government pamphlets, including "Prenatal Care," published by U.S. Children's Bureau. Contributor to professional journals and to magazines.

* * *

BROWN, William E(nglish) 1907-1975

PERSONAL: Born January 24, 1907, in Racine, Wis.; son of John Abner (a local steamship company agent) and Callista (English) Brown; married Mildred Conley (a teacher), October 1, 1932; children: Ann Fleur (Mrs. John Shepherd), Monica Ruth, Elizabeth Maria (Mrs. Francis Butler), Miriam Julie, Peter William. *Education:* Attended Marquette University, 1924; University of Notre Dame, A.B., 1929; University of Wisconsin, J.D., 1930. *Politics:* Independent, chiefly Democrat. *Religion:* Roman Catholic. *Home and office:* 920 East Mason St., Milwaukee, Wis. 53202.

CAREER: Admitted to Wisconsin bar; practiced law in Racine, Wis., 1930-32; Allis-Chalmers Manufacturing Company, Milwaukee, Wis., attorney, 1932-52, assistant general attorney in charge of law department, 1952-69. Former member of advisory board of St. Anthony Hospital, Milwaukee; member of board of trustees of Clarke College, Dubuque, Iowa; consultant to Sisters of Charity of the Blessed Virgin Mary, Dubuque. *Member:* National Conference of Christians and Jews (member, national board of directors and Wisconsin board of directors), American Civil Liberties Union, Center for the Study of Democratic Institutions, Common Cause, National Catholic Conference for Interracial Justice, Milwaukee Archdiocesan Council of Catholic Men (vice president), Milwaukee Catholic Interracial Council, Milwaukee Bar Association, Milwaukee Urban League, Milwaukee Archdiocesan Task Force on Education.

WRITINGS: (With Andrew M. Greeley) *Can Catholic Schools Survive?,* Sheed, 1970. Contributor of articles to *Notre Dame Lawyer, Wisconsin Bar Bulletin, Ave Maria, America, National Catholic Reporter, Overview,* and *U.S. Catholic-Jubilee.*

WORK IN PROGRESS: Research in Catholic school financing and Catholic parish, diocesan, and national councils; a monograph, *The Response Ability to Supply the Financial Requirements of a Roman Catholic Diocese and its Parishes.*

SIDELIGHTS: In 1969, William Brown told *CA* that he retired early "because of my concern about the increasing polarizations and deterioration of community relations in the civic community in general and in the Catholic Church in particular.... Hence my interest in (1) decision-making Church councils in which all elements of Church membership are represented, and (2) re-orientation of schools so that children and youths are educated and motivated to be competent, authentically human, community-minded citizens.

"*Can Catholic Schools Survive?* was written because of a slow burn mounting into a subdued rage over the anomie and malaise into which the Catholic educational venture has fallen ... during the last few years. There have been a number of excellent books and research reports describing the present situation, the history leading to it, and things that might be done about it. But all of them are cool, almost casual, instead of concerned and urgent. Catholic education is too important and its situation too desperate for a restrained academic approach, valuable as that is, to be sufficient. Someone had to get down to the nitty-gritty and provide specific, practical, integrated, hopeful answers. Someone had to get angry enough to pinpoint responsibility.... I hope [our book] will raise a minimum of defensiveness and an optimum of action. It does not pretend to be the last word, only the first; but hopefully the kind of first that will provide a sound foundation upon which all concerned may build authentic Christian approaches to Catholic education—in purpose, in programming, in structuring, and in financing—so that our young people and the adult society they will soon become

may be prepared to cope with change and avoid Future Shock."†

(Died May 26, 1975)

*   *   *

BROWNE, E(lliott) Martin   1900-

PERSONAL: Born January 29, 1900, in Zeals, Wiltshire, England; son of Percival John (a British Army officer) and Bernarda Gracia (Lees) Browne; married Henzie Raeburn (an actress), December 20, 1924 (died October 27, 1973); married Audrey Rideont, November 24, 1974; children: (first marriage) Denis, Christopher. *Education:* Attended Eton College, 1913-18; Christ Church, Oxford, B.A., 1921, M.A., 1923. *Home:* 20 Lancaster Grove, London N.W. 3, England. *Agent:* David Higham Associates Ltd., 5-8 Lower John St., Golden Sq., London W1R 4HA, England.

CAREER: Began with Doncaster Folkhouse, Doncaster, England, working in adult education, 1924-26; theatrical director-producer (and sometimes actor), beginning 1927, making first appearance on the London stage in "David," 1927, and New York debut in "Murder in the Cathedral," which he also directed, 1938; assistant professor of speech and drama at Carnegie Institute of Technology (now Carnegie-Mellon University), Pittsburgh, Pa., 1927-30; returned to England as director of religious drama for Diocese of Chichester, 1930-34; director of Pilgrim Players, in association with Arts Council of Great Britain, 1939-48; concurrently director of Mercury Theatre, producing verse plays, 1945-48; director of British Drama League, 1948-57; visiting professor of religious drama at Union Theological Seminary, New York, N.Y., for six months of each year, 1956-62. Honorary drama adviser to Coventry Cathedral, beginning 1962. Danforth visiting lecturer at American colleges, 1962-65; lecturer at Tufts University (in London), beginning 1967. Productions include all the plays of T. S. Eliot, many of Shakespeare and Christopher Fry, the first full-scale revival of the "York Cycle of Mystery Plays," 1951, and subsequent revivals of the cycle, and Edinburgh and Canterbury Festival plays. *Military service:* Grenadier Guards, 1918-19; became second lieutenant. *Member:* Royal Society of Literature (fellow). *Awards, honors:* Commander, Order of the British Empire, 1952; D.Litt., 1971.

WRITINGS: (Editor) *Religious Drama II,* Living Age Books, 1958; (contributor) Allen Tate, editor, *T. S. Eliot: The Man and His Work,* Chatto & Windus, 1967; (abridger) *The Mysteries,* Samuel French, 1967; *The Making of T. S. Eliot's Plays,* Cambridge University Press, 1969.

SIDELIGHTS: The Mysteries represents a condensation of the "Lincoln Cycles of Mystery Plays," which took sixteen hours to perform in the original cycle, into a two-hour performance. *Avocational interests:* Reading, walking.

*   *   *

BROWNE, George Stephenson   1890-1970

PERSONAL: Born August 5, 1890, in Melbourne, Victoria, Australia; son of George (a business manager) and Lydia Mary (Purcell) Browne; married Rosalind Haig Malcolm, March 3, 1923 (died, 1938); children: Shirley Malcolm (Mrs. Colin Baldwin). *Education:* University of Melbourne, M.A., 1912; Balliol College, Oxford, graduate study, 1918-20, M.A., 1928. *Politics:* Liberal. *Religion:* Church of England. *Home:* 50 The Avenue, Parkville N.2, Victoria, Australia.

CAREER: High school master in Victoria, Australia, 1912-

14; visited United States and Germany on Oxford travelling scholarship in education, 1922; Teachers College, Lancaster, England, vice-principal, 1922-33, University of Melbourne, Melbourne, Australia, professor of education and dean of Faculty of Education, 1934-56, professor emeritus, 1956-70. Visiting lecturer, University of California (now University of California, Berkeley), 1931; visiting professor, Portland State College (now University), 1953. Educational adviser and lecturer, Royal Australian Air Force, 1930-45. Station GTV-9, Melbourne, television commentator on current affairs, 1957-65, and lecturer for series, "Improve Your English," beginning 1965. Trustee in Australia, Northcote Farm School (for British children). *Military service:* Australian Imperial Force, 1916-18; served in France and was severely wounded in action; received Military Cross. *Member:* Melbourne Club, Naval and Military Club (Melbourne), Legacy Club.

WRITINGS: (Editor and contributor) *Education in Australia,* Macmillan (London), 1927; *Australia: A General Account,* Thomas Nelson, 1929; *The Case for Curriculum Revision,* Melbourne University Press, 1932; (with various collaborators on different editions) *Modern World Geographies,* five volumes, F. W. Cheshire, 1934, numerous revised editions, 1934-65; (with Norman Denholm Harper) *Our Pacific Neighbours,* F. W. Cheshire, 1953, revised edition, 1960; (with John Francis Cramer) *Contemporary Education: A Comparative Study of National Systems,* Harcourt, 1956, 2nd edition, 1965; (with Ian G. Coghill and Donald Dunstan Harris) *Southern World: A Physical and Regional Geography for Australian Schools,* F. W. Cheshire, 1962. Also author of *The Making of an Army Instructor,* 1943, *Report on Democratic Tendencies in Japanese Education,* 1947, and *Secondary Education To-Day and To-Morrow,* 1953.

WORK IN PROGRESS: Revision of earlier books, particularly *Modern World Geographies* and *Contemporary Education.*

SIDELIGHTS: George Stephenson Browne's interest in anthropology extended to American Indians, especially the Apache and Navajo. He visited, lived with, and studied the Polynesian Island groups and the Australian aborigine. *Avocational interests:* Tennis, golf.†

(Died May 23, 1970)

* * *

BRUNETTI, Cledo 1910-1971

PERSONAL: Born April 1, 1910, in Virginia, Minn.; son of Nazzareno (a merchant) and Serafina (Cavalieri) Brunetti; children: Marlene Marie (Mrs. Clyde Dias), Ronald David. *Education:* University of Minnesota, B.E.E., 1932, Ph.D., 1937. *Office address:* FMC Corp., Box 1201, San Jose, Calif. 95108.

CAREER: University of Minnesota, Minneapolis, instructor in electrical engineering, 1932-37; Lehigh University, Bethlehem, Pa., instructor, 1937-39, assistant professor of electrical engineering, 1939-41; National Bureau of Standards, Washington, D.C., research and development engineer, 1941-42, head of production engineering section, 1943-45, chief of ordnance engineering section, 1945-47, chief of engineering electronics 1947-48; Stanford University, Stanford, Calif., associate director, Stanford Research Institute and university lecturer, 1949-53; General Mills, Inc., Minneapolis, Minn., managing director of engineering research and development, 1953-57; FMC Corp., San Jose, Calif., executive assistant to executive vice-president for engineering and

ordnance, 1957-58; Grand Central Rocket Co. (FMC subsidiary), Redlands, Calif., vice-president and general manager, 1958-60, president and general manager, 1960-61; FMC Corp., assistant to president and director of missile and space programs, 1961-67, director of long range planning, 1967-71. Member of board of directors, Lewis & Kaufman Electronics Corp., Cascade Research Corp., Evergreen Western Corp., Snow Hills, Inc., II Communications Corp., and Sensors, Inc. Consultant to Office of Scientific Research and Development, 1942-46; chairman of advisory group on assemblies and assembly techniques, Office of the Secretary of Defense, 1955-60; special adviser to Vice-President of the United States, 1964-68. Member of national advisory group, National Radio Institute, 1948-62; member of space advisory committees, Stanford Research Institute and University of Texas, 1960-71. *Military service:* U.S. Army, Signal Reserve, 1932.

MEMBER: American Institute of Electrical and Electronics Engineers (fellow), American Institute of Aeronautics and Astronautics (formerly American Rocket Society; charter senior member), National Industrial Conference Board, American Studies Association, Washington Academy of Sciences, Association of the U.S. Army, Marine Technology Society, Sigma Xi, Tau Beta Pi, Eta Kappa Nu (national director), Pi Tau Pi, Scabbard and Blade.

AWARDS, HONORS: Cited by Eta Kappa Nu as America's outstanding young electrical engineer, 1941; U.S. Naval Ordnance Development Award, 1945; certificates for outstanding service from U.S. War Department, Army-Navy, and Office of Scientific Research and Development, 1945; National Materials and Methods Achievement Grand Award, 1947; Outstanding Achievement Award, University of Minnesota, 1958.

WRITINGS: (With Roger W. Curtis) *Printed Circuit Techniques,* U.S. Government Printing Office, 1947; *The Meaning of Automation* (pamphlet), General Mills, 1956; (with Geoffrey W. Drummer and others) *Electronic Equipment Design and Construction,* McGraw, 1961; (with C. H. Higgerson) *Your Future in a Changing World* (juvenile), Richards Rosen, 1970. Writer of five textbooks for National Radio Institute. Contributor of more than 150 articles to scientific and business journals.

AVOCATIONAL INTERESTS: Worldwide scuba diving.†

(Died May 22, 1971)

* * *

BRUYN, Kathleen 1903-

PERSONAL: Surname is pronounced Bruin; born January 23, 1903, in Niagara Falls, N.Y.; daughter of John A. (a civil engineer) and Hattie N. (Kean) Reynolds; married Marcel Bruyn, November 4, 1933 (deceased); children: Ruth Angeline Bruyn Pritchard. *Education:* Educated by private tutors. *Home:* 549 Pennsylvania St., Denver, Colo. 80203. *Agent:* Gerald Keenan, Boulder, Colo. 80302. *Office:* 1428 Pearl, Boulder, Colo. 80302.

CAREER: Niagara Falls Gazette, Niagara Falls, N.Y., reporter and columnist, 1927-33; free-lance writer. Worked on public relations for Central City Opera House Association, Denver, Colo., for many years until 1965.

WRITINGS: Uranium Country, University of Colorado Press, 1955; *"Aunt" Clara Brown: The Story of a Black Pioneer,* Pruett, 1971. Writer of biographical sketches for Colorado Historical Society; contributor to *Bulletin of Atomic Scientists* and other publications.

WORK IN PROGRESS: Several literary projects.††

BRYANT, Verda E. 1910-

PERSONAL: Born January 28, 1910, in Norfolk, Neb.; daughter of Ambrose (a laborer) and Frances Hannah (Simpson) Bilger; married Stele A. Bryant (a photographic technician), February 15, 1930; children: Blair Burt, Barbara Beth. *Education:* Attended public schools in Omaha, Neb. *Politics:* Independent. *Religion:* Reorganized Church of Jesus Christ of Latter-day Saints. *Home:* 415 North Eubank, Independence, Mo. 64050.

CAREER: Writer of religious materials for Reorganized Church of Jesus Christ of Latter-day Saints. Lecturer in seven states on the Holy Land and other world areas; also world-wide tour director.

WRITINGS—All published by Herald House: *Between the Covers of the Book of Mormon,* 1945; *Between the Covers of the Doctrine and Convenants,* 1958; *Organizing and Conducting Vacation Church Schools,* 1963; *Between the Covers of the Old Testament,* 1965. Writer of stories for church school papers, quarterlies for church school classes, courses of study for children, and lessons for adults.

WORK IN PROGRESS: Between the Covers of the New Testament.

*   *   *

BUCK, John N(elson) 1906-

PERSONAL: Born April 9, 1906, in Germantown, Pa.; son of Clifford Ross (an engineer) and Gertrude (Nelson) Buck; married Frances Sandidge, October 8, 1927; children: Barbara Sandidge (Mrs. John M. Robeson III), Gurdon Saltonstall. *Education:* Attended University of North Carolina, 1925, 1927, Washington School for Secretaries, 1927-28, Swarthmore College, 1943-44, and University of Virginia, 1944-45. *Politics:* Independent. *Religion:* Episcopalian. *Home:* 3180 Wellington Rd., Lumberton, N.C. 28358.

CAREER: Lynchburg Training School and Hospital, Lynchburg, Va., junior psychologist, 1929-38, senior psychologist, 1938-43, chief psychologist, 1945-51. Consulting psychologist to Hughes Memorial School, Danville, Va., 1945-51, and Richmond Professional Institute, Richmond, Va., 1951-53. Conducted seminars and workshops at University of Virginia, Emory University, Richmond Professional Institute, and various Veterans Administration hospitals. Lecturer at University of Pennsylvania and Duke University. *Member:* American Association on Mental Deficiency (former vice-president; honorary member), United States Chess Federation.

WRITINGS: (With George Koltanowski) *Your Chess Companion for 1940,* privately printed, 1939; *The House-Tree-Person Technique, a Qualitative and Quantitative Scoring Manual,* Journal of Clinical Psychology, 1948, revised and published as *The House-Tree-Person Technique–Revised Manual,* Western Psychological Services, 1966; *The House-Tree-Person Manual Supplement,* Western Psychological Services, 1964; (editor with Dr. Emanuel F. Hammer) *Advances in the House-Tree-Person Technique: Variations and Applications,* Western Psychological Services, 1969. Contributor to *Virginia Mental Hygiene Survey, American Journal of Mental Deficiency, Journal of Clinical Psychology, Journal of Applied Psychology, Journal of Projective Techniques, Journal of the National Education Association, De Paul Hospital Bulletin,* and *Revista de Psicologia General y Aplicad* (Madrid). Former contributing chess editor, *Lynchburg Daily Advance.*

SIDELIGHTS: Buck lists his major vocational interests as projective techniques, personality analysis, measurement of intelligence, and the licensing and certification of clinical psychologists. *Avocational interests:* Chess (Buck has won several chess tournaments) and cats.

*   *   *

BUCK, Stratton 1906-

PERSONAL: Born September 14, 1906, in Baltimore, Md.; son of Charles Elton (a salesman) and Helen (Sparks) Buck; married Emily Bailey, September 11, 1929; children: Helen (Mrs. Albert B. Reynolds), Sally Kelso (Mrs. Edward McCrady III). *Education:* University of Michigan, A.B., 1928; Columbia University, A.M., 1929; University of Chicago, Ph.D., 1941. *Politics:* Democrat. *Religion:* Episcopalian. *Home:* Running Knob Hollow Lake, Sewanee, Tenn. 37375. *Office:* University of the South, Sewanee, Tenn. 37375.

CAREER: University of Tennessee, Knoxville, instructor, 1929-37, assistant professor of Romance languages, 1937-42; University of the South, Sewanee, Tenn., associate professor, 1942-48, professor of French, 1948-71, emeritus professor, 1971—. *Member:* American Association of Teachers of French (president, Tennessee chapter, 1956-57), South Atlantic Modern Language Association, Tennessee Philological Association (president, 1957). *Awards, honors:* Chevalier de L'Ordre des Palmes academiques.

WRITINGS: Gustave Flaubert, Twayne, 1966. Contributor to *Sewanee Review, Revue d'Histoire litteraire de la France, Tennessee Studies in Literature,* and other journals.

WORK IN PROGRESS: Studies on the nineteenth-century French novel, especially works of Flaubert and Balzac.†

*   *   *

BUELL, Robert Kingery 1908-1971
(Brother Bob)

PERSONAL: Born November 10, 1908, in Humbolt, Neb.; son of Albert S. (a minister) and Lulu (Kingery) Buell; married Harriette Taylor (a security officer for California Department of Employment), August 26, 1950. *Education:* Took special courses at University of California, Berkeley, 1931-32, and Columbia University, 1933. *Politics:* Democrat. *Religion:* Methodist. *Home:* 921 Mercy St., Mountain View, Calif. 94040.

CAREER: Mountain View Standard Register Leader, Mountain View, Calif., reporter, beginning 1935. Writing coach, privately and by correspondence.

WRITINGS: Land of Dreams (poem), privately printed, 1932; *Verse Writing Simplified,* Stanford University Press, 1938; *Silent Speech,* Interstate Publishing (Mountain View, Calif.), 1939; *Wings of the Dawn* (poem), Interstate Publishing, 1941; *California Stepping Stones,* Stanford University Press, 1948; (with Madge Haines and Leslie Morrill) *Between Sea and Mountains,* Century Schoolbook, 1959; (with Haines and Morrill) *Gate Swings Open,* Century Schoolbook, 1959; (with Jane Jordan) *Everybody's Riches,* Century Schoolbook, 1959; (with Irene Tamany) *Two Nations, United States and Canada,* Century Schoolbook, 1965; (with Emily Watson Hallin) *Wild White Wings,* McKay, 1965; (with Hallin) *Follow the Honey Bird,* McKay, 1967; (with Charlotte Northcote Skladal) *Sea Otters and the China Trade,* McKay, 1968. As Brother Bob, wrote for monthly newsletter of International Society for Crippled Children for seventeen years.†

(Died May 1, 1971)

BUHLER, Charlotte B(ertha)   1893-197(?)

PERSONAL: Born December 20, 1893, in Berlin, Germany; came to United States in 1940, naturalized citizen. 1945; daughter of Hermann and Rose (Kristeller) Malachowski; married Karl L. Buhler (a psychologist), April 4, 1916; children: Ingeborg (Mrs. Alf-Jorgen Aas), Rolf D. *Education:* Attended Universities of Freiburg, Berlin, and Munich; University of Munich, Ph.D., 1918; postdoctoral study at University of Vienna and Columbia University.

CAREER: University of Vienna, Vienna, Austria, instructor, later associate professor of psychology, 1923-38; University of Oslo, Oslo, Norway, professor of psychology, 1938-40; director of child guidance clinics in Vienna, 1930-38, London, 1930-35, and Oslo, 1938-40; College of St. Catherine, St. Paul, Minn., professor of psychology, 1940-42; Minneapolis General Hospital, Minneapolis, Minn., chief clinical psychologist, 1942-45; Los Angeles County General Hospital, Los Angeles, Calif., chief clinical psychologist, 1945-53; University of Southern California, School of Medicine, Los Angeles, assistant clinical professor of psychiatry, 1953-58, professor emeritus, beginning, 1958. Psychologist in private practice, Los Angeles and Beverly Hills, Calif. Diplomate in clinical psychology, American Board of Examiners in Professional Psychology; certified psychologist, state of California.

MEMBER: American Association for Humanistic Psychology (director, beginning, 1961; president, 1965-66), American Psychological Association (fellow), American Orthopsychiatric Association (fellow), American Association for Gerontology, International Psychological Association (board member; director), Psychologists Interested in the Advancement of Psychotherapy (fellow; member of board of directors), American Group Psychotherapy Association (fellow), Society for Projective Techniques (fellow), California State Psychological Association (fellow), Southern California Group Psychotherapy Association (president, 1958-59), Los Angeles Society of Practicing Psychologists. *Awards, honors:* Rockefeller Foundation fellowships, 1924-25, 1935; medal of honor from the city of Vienna, 1964.

WRITINGS: Das Maerchen und die Phantasie des Kindes (title means "Fairy Tales and the Child's Fantasy"), J. A. Barth (Leipzig), 1918, 4th edition, with J. Bilz and Hildegard Hetzer, 1958.

Das Seelenleben des Jugendlichen (title means "The Psychology of Adolescence"), G. Fischer (Jena, Germany), 1922, 6th edition, 1967; (editor) *Tagebuch eines jungen Maedchens* (title means "Diary of a Young Girl"), G. Fischer, 1922, 2nd edition published as *Jugendtagebuch und Lebenslauf: Zwei Maedchentagebuecher* (title means "Adolescent Diary and Course of Life: Two Girls' Diaries"), 1932; (editor) *Zwei Knabentagebuecher* (title means "Two Boys' Diaries"), G. Fischer, 1925; (with Hetzer and Beatrix Tudor-Hart) *Soziologische und psychologische Studien ueber das erste Lebensjahr,* G. Fischer, 1927; *Die ersten sozialen Reaktionen des Kindes* (title means "The First Social Reactions of Infants"), 1927; (with Hetzer) *Inventar der Verhaltungsweisen des ersten Lebensjahres,* [Germany], 1927, translation by Pearl Greenberg and Rowena Ripin published as *The First Year of Life,* Day, 1930; *Kindheit und Jugend* (title means "Childhood and Adolescence"), Hirzel (Leipzig), 1928, 4th edition, Verlag fuer Psychologie Hogrefe, 1967.

(Contributor) C. A. Murchison, editor, *A Handbook of Child Psychology,* 2nd edition, Clark University Press,

1931; *Kleinkinder Tests,* J. A. Barth, 1932, translation by Henry Beaumont published as *Testing Children's Development from Birth to School Age,* Farrar & Rinehart, 1935; *Der menschliche Lebenslauf als psychologisches Problem* (title means "The Human Course of Life as a Psychological Problem"), Hirzel, 1933, 3rd edition, Verlag fuer Psychologie Hogrefe, 1960; *Drei Generationen im Jugendtagebuch,* (title means "Three Generations in Diaries"), G. Fischer, 1934; *From Birth to Maturity: An Outline of the Psychological Development of the Child,* translated by Esther Menaker and William Menaker, Paul, Trench, Trubner & Co., 1935, 8th edition, 1950; (with others) *Kind und Familie,* G. Fischer, 1937, translation by Henry Beaumount published as *The Child and His Family,* Harper, 1939, reprinted, Greenwood Press, 1972; *Praktische Kinderpsychologie* (title means "Practical Child Psychology"), O. Lorenz (Prague and Vienna), 1938.

(With E. Hoehn) *The World Test: Manual and Material,* New York Psychological Corp., 1941; (with D. Welty Lefever) *A Rorschach Study on the Psychological Characteristics of Alcoholics,* Hillhouse Press for Section of Studies on Alcohol, Yale University, 1948.

(With G. Kelly Lumry and H. Carroll) *World Test Standardization Studies,* Child Care Monograph, 1951; (with Faith Smitter and Sybil Richardson) *Childhood Problems and the Teacher,* Holt, 1952; (with M. P. Manson) *The Five-Task Test,* Western Psychological Services, 1955; (with Manson) *The Picture World Test* (with manual), Western Psychological Services, 1956; (contributor) G. Seward, editor, *Clinical Studies in Culture Conflict,* Ronald, 1958.

(Author of introduction) R. Wisser, editor, *Sinn und Sein* (title means "Meaning and Being"), Niemeyer (Tuebingen), 1960; (contributor) *Handbuch der Neurosenlehre und Psychotherapie,* Urban & Schwarzenberg (Munich), 1960; (contributor) R. W. Kleemeier, editor, *Aging and Leisure,* Oxford University Press, 1961; (with others) *Values in Psychotherapy,* Free Press of Glencoe, 1962; *Die Psychologie im Leben unserer Ziet,* Droemer Knar (Munich), 1962, 5th edition. 1964, translation by Hella F. Bernays published as *Psychology for Contemporary Living,* Hawthorn, 1969; (contributor) Lotte Schenk-Danzinger, editor, *Gegenwartsprobleme der Entwicklungspsychologie,* Verlag fuer Psychologie (Goettingen), 1963; (contributor) Frank T. Severin, editor, *Humanistic Viewpoints in Psychology,* McGraw, 1965; (contributor) Clark Moustakas, editor, *Existential Moments in Psychotherapy,* Basic Books, 1966; (contributor) Herbert A. Otto, editor, *Explorations in Human Potentialities,* C. C Thomas, 1966; *Psychologische Probleme unserer Zeit: Drei Vortraege,* G. Fischer (Stuttgart), 1968; (editor with Fred Massarik) *The Course of Human Life: A Study of Goals in the Humanistic Perspective,* Springer Publishing, 1968; *Wenn das Leben gelingen soll: Psychologische Studien ueber Lebenswartungen und Lebensergebnisse,* Droemer Knaur, 1969, translation by David J. Baker published as *The Way to Fulfillment: Psychological Techniques,* Hawthorn, 1971; (with Melanie Allen) *Introduction to Humanistic Psychology,* Brooks/Cole, 1972.

Deviser of other psychological tests. Contributor to *Encyclopedia for Child Guidance,* and about 150 articles to professional journals in United States and Europe; also writer of popular articles and studies on the psychology of art. Co-editor of *Journal of Humanistic Psychology,* and *The Nervous Child,* both published in America, and the British *Journal of Educational Psychology.*

SIDELIGHTS: The Buhlers lost their entire Viennese library to the Nazis, but not Mrs. Buhler's record of almost fifty years of writings in developmental, humanistic, and clinical psychology. There have been more than sixty translations of her works into some fifteen languages, including Hungarian, Icelandic, Russian, Hebrew, and most western European languages.†

(Died, 197[?])

* * *

BULEY, R(oscoe) Carlyle 1893-1968

PERSONAL: Born July 8, 1893, in Georgetown, Ind.; son of David Marion (a physician) and Nora (Keithley) Buley; married Esther Giles, 1919 (died, 1921); married Evelyn Barnett, August 5, 1926. *Education:* Indiana University, A.B., 1914, A.M., 1916; University of Wisconsin, Ph.D., 1925. *Politics:* Republican. *Home address:* Route 7, Box 90, Bloomington, Ind. *Office:* Lindlay Hall, Indiana University, Bloomington, Ind.

CAREER: High school teacher in Delphi and Muncie, Ind., 1914-18; head of history department and assistant principal at high school in Springfield, Ill., 1919-23; assistant instructor, University of Wisconsin, 1923-25; Indiana University, Bloomington, 1925-64, began as instructor, became professor of history, professor emeritus, 1964-68. *Military service:* U.S. Army, 1918-19; became sergeant. *Member:* American Historical Association, Organization of American Historians, Indiana Historical Society, Ohio Historical Society. *Awards, honors:* Pulitzer Prize in history, 1951, for *The Old Northwest: Pioneer Period, 1815-1840;* Elizur Wright Award, 1954, for *The American Life Convention, 1906-1952;* D.Litt., Coe College, 1958.

WRITINGS: (With Madge E. Pickard) *The Midwest Pioneer: His Ills, Cures and Doctors,* R. E. Banta, 1945, 2nd edition, Schuman, 1946; (editor) Logan Esarey, *The Indiana Home,* R. E. Banta, 1947; *The Old Northwest: Pioneer Period, 1815-1840,* two volumes, Indiana Historical Society, 1950, 3rd edition, Indiana University Press, 1963; *The American Life Convention, 1906-1952: A Study in the History of Life Insurance,* two volumes, Appleton, 1953; *The Equitable Life Assurance Society of the United States, 1859-1964,* two volumes, Appleton, 1967.

WORK IN PROGRESS: *The Red Lilly,* history of Eli Lilly and Co.

BIOGRAPHICAL/CRITICAL SOURCES: *Indiana Magazine of History,* March, 1952.†

(Died April 25, 1968)

* * *

BULLIS, Harry Amos 1890-1963

PERSONAL: Born October 7, 1890, in Hastings, Neb.; son of George Amos and Ella (Gould) Bullis; married Irma Elizabeth Alexander, 1919 (died, 1947); married Countess Maria Robert Smorczewska, December 29, 1948. *Education:* Simpson Academy, Indianola, Iowa, graduate, 1913; University of Wisconsin, B.A., 1917; London School of Economics and Political Science, graduate study, spring, 1919. *Religion:* Methodist. *Home:* Charleston Acres, 2401 Meeting St., Wayzata, Minn.

CAREER: Worked way through high school and college, and became assistant to a vice-president of Chase National Bank, New York, N.Y., 1917; Washburn Crosby Co. (predecessor of General Mills), Minneapolis, Minn., began as

ordinary mill hand, 1919, comptroller, 1925-28; General Mills, Inc., Minneapolis, Minn., started as secretary and comptroller, 1928, director, 1930-63, member of executive committee, 1931-63, president, 1943-48, chairman of board, 1948-59. Northwest Bancorporation, Minneapolis, Minn., director, 1947-63. Speaker on business topics, international relations, labor relations, and foreign trade. Chairman of International Development Advisory Board, 1958-59, and member of other government commissions and committees under Presidents Truman and Eisenhower. Member of national advisory council, American Association for the United Nations; president of American Freedom from Hunger Foundation, 1962-63; member of board of directors of U.S. Chamber of Commerce, 1946-59, Fund for Adult Education, 1953-61, and Council for Financial Aid to Education; chairman of numerous civic and charitable drives. Trustee of National Trust for Historical Preservation, 1954-59; currently trustee of National Planning Association, U.S. Council of International Chamber of Commerce, Simpson College, Hamline University, University of Wisconsin Foundation, University of Wisconsin Alumni Research Foundation, and other educational groups. *Military service:* U.S. Army, 1917-19; served overseas for eighteen months; became captain.

MEMBER: National Association of Manufacturers (former director), National Association of Cost Accountants (president, 1932-33), Wisconsin Alumni Association (national president, 1936-37), Phi Beta Kappa, Artus, Minneapolis Club, Minikadha Country Club, Wayzata Country Club. *Awards, honors:* Honorary degrees from eleven colleges and universities, 1943-60, among them University of Wisconsin and Simpson College, 1943, Hamline University, 1957, and Occidental College, 1960; Charles Coolidge Parlin Award of American Marketing Association, 1949; named Man of the Year, National Association of Manufacturers, 1953; other awards from Freedoms Foundation, 1952, U.S. National Student Association, 1956, and Free Enterprise Awards Association, 1957.

WRITINGS: *Manifesto for Americans,* McGraw, 1961. Contributor of articles to business and other journals.

AVOCATIONAL INTERESTS: Walking, football games, golf.

BIOGRAPHICAL/CRITICAL SOURCES: *Banco Times* (annual publication of Bancorporation), December 19, 1961; G. Zehnprennig, *Harry A. Bullis, Champion American,* Denison, 1964.†

(Died September 28, 1963)

* * *

BUNN, John W. 1898-

PERSONAL: Born September 26, 1898, in Wellston, Ohio; son of Peter H. (an engineer) and Lena M. (Janke) Bunn; married Bonnie Huff, April 24, 1921. *Education:* University of Kansas, B.S.Engr., 1921, M.S., 1936; attended courses at University of California, Los Angeles, 1926, Stanford University, 1930-36, and University of Iowa, 1947. *Politics:* Republican. *Religion:* Seventh-Day Adventist. *Address:* Ventura Estates, Newbury Park, Calif. 91320.

CAREER: University of Kansas, Lawrence, instructor in mechanical engineering, 1920-23, assistant professor of industrial engineering, 1923-27, then of physical education, 1927-30; Stanford University, Stanford, Calif., professor of physical education and head basketball coach, 1930-38, dean of men, 1938-46; Springfield College, Springfield, Mass., basketball coach, and director of athletics, 1946-56; Colorado State College (now University of Northern Colorado), Greeley, basketball coach, 1956-63.

WRITINGS: Scientific Principles of Coaching, Prentice-Hall, 1955; *The Art of Officiating Sports,* Prentice-Hall, 1957, 3rd edition, 1967; *The Basketball Coach: Guides to Success,* Prentice-Hall, 1961; *Basketball Techniques and Team Play,* Prentice-Hall, 1964.

SIDELIGHTS: Bunn won ten varsity letters in football, basketball, and baseball at University of Kansas—more than any student before or since. At Stanford he led the basketball team to the national title in 1937, and conference championships from 1936 to 1938. He has conducted programs pertaining to basketball and its rules in Europe, Australia, the Far East, and throughout the United States.

* * *

BURBANK, Natt B(ryant) 1903-

PERSONAL: Born December 4, 1903, in Danville, Vt.; son of Harvey (a superintendent of country schools) and Lillian (a teacher; maiden name, Bryant) Burbank; married Vivian E. Hubbard, December 22, 1934; children: Alice (Mrs. Fred M. Rhodes, Jr.), Joyce (Mrs. James Grow). *Education.* University of Vermont, A.B., 1925; Columbia University, A.M., 1931; further graduate study at Stanford University and Harvard University. *Home:* Plymouth 9A, Century Village, West Palm Beach, Fla. 33409.

CAREER: Teacher in Vermont schools, 1925-30; superintendent of schools in Morrisville, Vt., 1930-31, Danville, Vt., 1932-36, Bellows Falls, Vt., 1936-40, Concord, N.H., 1940-42, 1946-47, Melrose, Mass., 1947-49, and Boulder, Colo., 1949-64; Lehigh University, Bethlehem, Pa., professor of education, 1964-71, School of Education, director of Secondary Division, 1966-69, assistant dean of school, 1969-71. Instructor in school administration and supervision at University of Colorado, 1950-62, University of Maine, 1959, Montana State University, 1963, 1964, 1965, and Western State College, 1964. Chairman, Boulder Community Chest-United Fund, 1959-61; past vice-president, Boulder Chamber of Commerce. *Military service:* U.S. Army Reserve, active duty, 1942-46; commandant of European branch, U.S. Armed Forces Institute, 1944-45; retired as lieutenant colonel after twenty-eight years of reserve service.

MEMBER: American Association of School Administrators (member of executive committee, 1956-60; vice-president, 1961-62; president, 1963-64), Phi Delta Kappa, Rotary International (past president of clubs in Bellows Falls and Boulder). *Awards, honors:* LL.D., University of Vermont, 1963.

WRITINGS: (Contributor) David W. Beggs and R. B. McQuigg, editors, *America's Schools and Churches,* Indiana University Press, 1966; *The Superintendent of Schools–His Headaches and Rewards,* Interstate, 1968.

* * *

BURGER, Carl 1888-1967

PERSONAL: Born June 18, 1888, in Maryville, Tenn.; son of Joseph (a banker) and Elizabeth (Knox) Burger; married Margaret Rothery, September 18, 1920; children: Knox. *Education:* Attended Maryville College, Maryville, Tenn., and Stanford University; Cornell University, B.Arch., 1912; also studied for three years at School of Museum of Fine Arts, Boston. *Religion:* "No formal church." *Home and office:* 192 Bedford Rd., Pleasantville, N.Y.

CAREER: Onetime art director of the advertising firms of N. W. Ayer & Sons in Philadelphia, Pa., and Batten, Barton, Durstine and Osborn in New York, N.Y.; illustrator of books and magazines, and writer. Work as an artist includes large murals for the Bronx Zoo and New York Aquarium, and landscapes in watercolor. *Military service:* U.S. Army, Infantry, 1917-20; became captain. *Member:* American Museum of Natural History, New York Zoological Society, Cornell Club of New York.

WRITINGS—All self-illustrated: All About Fish, Random House, 1960; *All About Dogs,* Random House, 1962; *All About Elephants,* Random House, 1965; *All About Cats,* Random House, 1966; *Beaver Skins and Mountain Men,* Dutton, 1968.

Illustrator: Will Barker, *Familiar Animals of North America,* Harper, 1957; Will Barker, *Winter-Sleeping Wildlife,* Harper, 1958; Fred Gipson, *Recollection Creek,* Harper, 1959; Will Barker, *Familiar Insects of America,* Harper, 1960; Shiela Burnsford, *The Incredible Journey,* Little, Brown, 1960; Eugene Ackerman, *Tonk and Tonka,* Dutton, 1962; Fred Gipson, *Savage Sam,* Harper, 1962; Howard T. Walden, *Familiar Fresh Water Fishes,* Harper, 1964; Sterling North, *Little Rascal,* Dutton, 1965; Sterling North, *Hurry Spring!,* Dutton, 1966; Fred Gipson, *Old Yeller,* Harper, 1966. Also illustrator of other books. Contributor to magazines, mostly articles on natural history subjects.

SIDELIGHTS: Burger spoke French fairly well, and had good basic knowledge of German, and some knowledge of Spanish and Italian. *Avocational interests:* Fly fishing for trout and salmon.

BIOGRAPHICAL/CRITICAL SOURCES: Washington Post, January 2, 1968.†

(Died December, 1967)

* * *

BURGER, Nash K(err) 1908-

PERSONAL: Born September 8, 1908, in Jackson, Miss.; son of Nash Kerr (a salesman) and Clara (Eddy) Burger; married Marjorie Williams, December 26, 1938; children: Nash, Peter, Stephen. *Education:* Millsaps College, student, 1925-27; University of the South, B.A., 1930; University of Virginia, M.A., 1935. *Religion:* Episcopalian. *Home:* 1624 Mason Lane, Charlottesville, Va. 22901.

CAREER: Jackson (Miss.) city schools, head of department of English, 1932-37; St. Christopher's School, Richmond, Va., teacher of English and French, 1937-39; Historical Records Survey, editor in Jackson, Miss., 1939-42; Ingalls Shipbuilding Corp., Pascagoula, Miss., editor of house organ, 1942-44; *New York Times Book Review,* New York, N.Y., copy editor and writer, 1945-74. Historiographer, Episcopal Diocese of Mississippi, 1940-58.

WRITINGS: (With John K. Bettersworth) *South of Appomattox,* Harcourt, 1958; *Confederate Spy: Rose O'Neale Greenhow* (teen-age book), F. Watts, 1967. Contributor of articles and reviews to historical and other magazines and journals.

* * *

BURGESS, W(arren) Randolph 1889-

PERSONAL: Born May 7, 1889, in Newport, R.I.; son of Isaac Bronson and Ellen (Wilbur) Burgess; married May Ayres, May 17, 1917 (died July, 1953); married Helen Hamilton Woods, March 5, 1955; children: (first marriage)

Leonard Randolph, Julian Ayres. *Education:* Brown University, A.B., 1912; Columbia University, Ph.D., 1920. *Home:* Bowlingly, Queentown, Md. *Office:* Atlantic Council, 1616 H St. N.W., Washington, D.C. 20006.

CAREER: Federal Reserve Bank, New York City, member of staff, 1920-30, deputy governor, 1930-36, vice-president, 1936-38; First National City Bank of New York, New York City, vice-chairman, 1938-48, chairman of executive committee, 1948-52; U.S. Treasury Department, Washington, D.C., deputy to Secretary of Treasury, 1953-54, undersecretary, 1955-57; U.S. permanent representative to North Atlantic Treaty Organization, 1957-61; Atlantic Council, Washington, D.C., director, beginning 1961, chairman, beginning 1971. Chairman of New York State War Finance Committee, 1943-44; director, Discount Corp., International Banking Corp., Union Pacific Railroad, and Royal-Liverpool Group Insurance Companies in U.S. Fellow, Brown University, 1937-69. Trustee, Teachers College, Columbia University. Regent Professor, University of California, Berkeley, 1962.

MEMBER: Per Jacobssen Foundation (president), American Statistical Association (fellow; president, 1937), Academy of Political Science (president, 1939), American Bankers Association (president, 1944-45), American Economic Association, American Philosophical Society, Foreign Policy Association (director), Association of Reserve City Bankers (president, 1952), New York State Bankers Association (president, 1940-41), Phi Beta Kappa, Delta Upsilon; Metropolitan Club, Chevy Chase Club, Cosmos Club (all Washington); Century Association, University Club, River Club (all New York). *Awards, honors:* LL.D., Brown University, 1937, University of Rochester, 1948, Bowdoin College, 1959, and University of California, 1962; Commander, Friends Legion of Honor.

WRITINGS: Trends of School Costs, Russell Sage, 1920; *The Reserve Banks and the Money Market,* Harper, 1927, 3rd edition, 1946; (editor) *Interpretations of Federal Reserve Policy in the Speeches and Writings of Benjamin Strong,* Harper, 1930; (with George P. Roberts) *Our National Debt and the National Welfare,* Committee on Public Debt Policy, 1947; (with James R. Huntley) *Europe and America: The Next Ten Years,* Walker & Co., 1970. Contributor to professional journals.

*   *   *

BURLINGAME, Virginia (Struble)   1900-
(Virginia Struble)

PERSONAL: Born August 16, 1900, in West Liberty, Iowa; daughter of Linton Williams (a physician) and Maude (Wright) Struble; married Merrill G. Burlingame (a professor of history and author), September 12, 1936; children: Ray L. *Education:* Augustana College, A.B., 1928; Columbia University, B.S. in L.S., 1933. *Politics:* "Varies." *Religion:* Disciples of Christ. *Home:* 1419 South Wilson Ave., Bozeman, Mont. 59715.

CAREER: University of Iowa, Iowa City, member of library staff, 1926-27, 1931-36; Kansas State College of Pittsburg, teacher and member of library staff, 1927-30. *Member:* American Association of University Women, Wilderness Association, Audubon Society, National Wildlife Association, Montana Society of Natural and Earth Sciences, Montana Institute of Arts, Montana Library Association.

WRITINGS: (Under name Virginia Struble) *Cactus: The Story of a Porcupine,* Bethany Press, 1958; (under name Virginia Struble) *The Little Ducks Who Swam Away from*

Home, A. S. Barnes, 1961; *Larry Two-Feathers of the Nine Bar Ranch,* Bethany Press, 1967. Contributor of about fifty short stories and articles to magazines.

*   *   *

BURNET, George Bain   1894-

PERSONAL: Surname is pronounced *Bur*-net; born January 3, 1894, in Aberdeenshire, Scotland; son of James and Margaret (Thomson) Burnet; married Mildred Sinclair, December 22, 1953. *Education:* University of Edinburgh, M.A., 1915; New College, Edinburgh, Diploma in Theology (honours), 1921; University of Glasgow, Ph.D., 1936, D.Litt., 1961. *Home:* The Old Manse, Wamphray, Moffat DG10 9NG, England.

CAREER: Clergyman of Church of Scotland (Presbyterian). *Military service:* British Army, Royal Army Medical Corps and Royal Artillery, 1915-19; became lieutenant.

WRITINGS: Teaching the Old Testament in the Sunday School, Church of Scotland, 1948; *The History That Made Us,* Church of Scotland, 1949; *The Story of Quakerism in Scotland,* James Clarke, 1952; *The Book of the Abiding Christ,* Saint Catherine Press, 1955; *The Holy Communion in the Reformed Church of Scotland, 1560-1960,* Oliver & Boyd, 1960. Occasional contributor to *Scots Magazine.*

*   *   *

BURNETT, Whit(ney Ewing)   1899-1973

PERSONAL: Born August 14, 1899, in Salt Lake City, Utah; son of Benjamin James (a contractor) and Ann Marian (Christensen) Burnett; married Martha Foley, June, 1930 (divorced, 1942); married Hallie Southgate Abbett (an author and editor), November 2, 1942; children: (first marriage) David (deceased); (second marriage) John, Whitney Ann Beekman (Mrs. Robert Stevens). *Education:* Attended University of Southern California, 1918, University of Utah, 1920, University of California, Berkeley, 1922. *Religion:* Episcopalian. *Home:* 174 Huckleberry Hill Rd., Wilton, Conn. 06897. *Office:* Scholastic Magazines, Inc., 50 West 44th St., New York, N.Y. 10036. *Agent:* Theron Raines, 244 Madison Ave., New York, N.Y. 10016.

CAREER: Salt Lake City newspapers, reporter, 1916-18; *Evening Express,* Los Angeles, Calif., reporter, 1918; Associated Press, editor, Los Angeles, Calif., 1919-20, and San Francisco, Calif., 1921, assistant city editor, New York, N.Y., 1926-27; *New York Times,* New York, N.Y., copy desk editor, 1924-25; *New York Herald,* Paris edition, city editor, 1927-28; organizer of Balkan news service for *New York Sun* Foreign Service, and Consolidated Press, Vienna, Austria, 1929-31; with former wife Martha Foley, founded *Story* magazine, Vienna, Austria, 1931 (transferred to New York, N.Y., 1933), editor or co-editor, 1931-65, 1966-71 (publication acquired by Scholastic Magazines, Inc., 1966), director of *Story* College Creative Awards, 1966-71. Editor of The Story Press, and affiliated with J. B. Lippincott, E. P. Dutton, and Harper, 1935-52; editor, Hawthorn Books, 1958-61. Instructor in advanced creative writing, Columbia University, 1937-43; instructor at Queens College (now of the City University of New York), 1940, and Hunter College (now of the City University of New York), 1957-58. *Member:* P.E.N. (secretary, 1943), Overseas Press Club (member of board of governors, 1963-65, 1967-69, 1971-73), Anglo-American Press Association (Vienna; charter member), Poetry Society of America (member of executive board, 1971-73).

WRITINGS: *The Maker of Signs: A Variety*, Smith & Haas, 1934, reprinted, Books for Libraries, 1970; *The Literary Life and the Hell with It*, Harper, 1939.

Editor: (With Martha Foley) *Story Anthology, 1931-33*, Vanguard, 1933; (with Foley) *Story in America, 1933-34*, Vanguard, 1934; (with Foley) *The Flying Yorkshireman: A Book of Novellas*, Harper, 1937; *This Is My Best*, Dial, 1942, 5th edition, 1944; *Two Bottles of Relish*, Dial, 1943; *18 Great Stories of Today*, Avon, 1944; *The Seas of God*, Lippincott, 1944, reprinted as *Great Stories of the Human Spirit*, Garden City Books, 1954; *The Story Pocket Book*, Pocket Books, 1945; *Time to Be Young*, Lippincott, 1945; (with Charles Slatkin) *American Authors Today*, Ginn, 1947.

The World's Best, Dial, 1950; *This Is My Best Humor*, Dial, 1955, abridged edition published as *This Is My Funniest*, Perma Books, 1957; *The Spirit of Adventure*, Holt, 1956; *Animal Spirits*, Lippincott, 1957; *This Is My Philosophy*, Harper, 1957; *The Scarlet Treasury of Great Confessions by World-Famous Diarists, Letter-Writers and Lovers*, Pyramid Books, 1958; *The Spirit of Man*, Hawthorn, 1958 (published in England as *The Human Spirit*, Allen & Unwin, 1960).

Firsts of the Famous, Ballantine, 1962; *Thomas Hardy: The Return of the Native*, Barnes & Noble, 1966; *Discovery*, Four Winds, 1967, 3rd edition, 1968; *Henry Fielding: Joseph Andrews*, Barnes & Noble, 1968; *That's What Happened to Me*, Four Winds, 1969; *This Is My Best: In the Third Quarter of the Century*, Doubleday, 1970; *Black Hands on a White Face*, Dodd, 1971.

Editor with wife, Hallie Burnett: *Story: The Fiction of the Forties*, Dutton, 1949; *Sextet*, McKay, 1951; *Story*, Books 1 and 2, McKay, 1951-52, Books 3 and 4, Wynn, 1953; *The Tough Ones*, Popular Library, 1954; *19 Tales of Terror*, Bantam, 1957; *Fiction of a Generation*, MacGibbon & Kee, Volume I, 1960, Volume II, 1961; *Things with Claws*, Ballantine, 1961; *Best College Writing, 1961*, Random House, 1962; *Prize College Stories*, Random House, 1963; *The Modern Short Story in the Making*, Hawthorn, 1964; *The Stone Soldier*, Fleet, 1964; *Story Jubilee: Thirty-three Years of Story*, Doubleday, 1965. Also editors of *Story: The Yearbook of Discovery* (College Creative Awards selections), Four Winds, 1968-71.

Author, with John Pen, of novella, "Immortal Bachelor: The Love Story of Robert Burns," 1942.

WORK IN PROGRESS: Editing various anthologies.

SIDELIGHTS: Burnett once told *CA*: "[I] have devoted 40-odd years of publishing (with co-editors and associates) of more or less unknown young authors who later turn out to be William Saroyan, Carson McCullers, Truman Capote, Tennessee Williams, Ludwig Bemelmans, Joseph Heller, Mary O'Hara, Jerome Weidman, Norman Mailer, Gladys Schmitt, J. D. Salinger, Stephen Birmingham, Hallie Burnett, Elizabeth Janeway, etc.

"After four decades, I can see now that newspaperwork was writing on water, and teaching and editing is channeling most of your own small trickle of the creative stream to other folks' fields. However, I suppose I would do it all over again in about the same way, given enough helpers. Writing your own stuff must be the final satisfaction, but editors have theirs, in their own way, too."

The film rights to "Immortal Bachelor: The Love Story of Robert Burns" were sold to Daryl F. Zanuck.

BIOGRAPHICAL/CRITICAL SOURCES: *Connecticut Review*, spring, 1973.†

(Died April 22, 1973)

*   *   *

BURNS, Betty   1909-

PERSONAL: Given name, Elizabeth; born June 5, 1909, in Nashville, Tenn.; daughter of James Brantley and Ada (Newsom) Burns. *Education:* University of Tennessee, B.A., 1932. *Politics:* Pacifist. *Religion:* Methodist.

CAREER: Reporter for *Nashville Tennessean*, Nashville, Tennessee, 1932-37, and *Chicago Sun*, Chicago, Ill., 1941-46; writer with advertising agencies in Honolulu, Hawaii, and Nashville, Tenn., 1946-60; Methodist Publishing House, Nashville, Tenn., editorial assistant, 1960-65; Methodist Board of Evangelism, Nashville, Tenn., associate editor, 1965-66, Methodist Board of Education, Division of Higher Education, staff writer, beginning 1967.

WRITINGS: *With God As Thy Companion*, Broadman, 1965.

WORK IN PROGRESS: A religious book, and another for children.

AVOCATIONAL INTERESTS: Golf ("duffer").††

*   *   *

BURNS, John V.   1907-

PERSONAL: Born April 15, 1907, in Philadelphia, Pa. *Education:* St. Joseph's College, Princeton, N.J., B.A., 1929; Niagara University, M.A., 1935; Fordham University, Ph.D., 1950. *Home and office:* St. Vincent's Seminary, 500 East Chelten Ave., Philadelphia, Pa. 19144.

CAREER: Ordained Roman Catholic priest, 1934; priest in Philadelphia, Pa., Brooklyn, N.Y., and Buffalo, N.Y., 1934-72; Niagara University, Niagara University, N.Y., assistant professor of classical languages, 1934-35; St. John's University, New York, N.Y., assistant professor, 1935-39, professor of philosophy, 1939-60, chairman of department, 1956-59; Niagara University, professor of philosophy, 1960-72. *Wartime service:* U.S. Army specialized training program, instructor in basic engineering, 1943-44. *Member:* American Catholic Philosophical Association, American Catholic Philosophical Association, American Academy of Political and Social Science, Mediaeval Academy of America. *Awards, honors:* Freedoms Foundation Award, 1955, for *Concept of Freedom*.

WRITINGS: (Editor with Carl W. Grindel) *Concept of Freedom*, Regnery, 1955; *The Problem of Specific Natures*, New Scholasticism, 1956; *Dynamism in the Cosmology of Christian Wolff*, Exposition, 1966; *Hope Will Save Your Life*, Liguorian, 1969. Contributor to *New Catholic Encyclopedia*.

*   *   *

BURNS, Ralph J.   1901-
(Ralph Byrne)

PERSONAL: Born December 25, 1901, in Cambridge, Mass.; son of Edward F. P. (a businessman) and Katherine T. (Farrell) Burns; married November 18, 1924; wife's name, Mary (died, 1950); married Helene F. Lawlor, December 17, 1960; children: (first marriage) Paul, Mary (Mrs. Guy Giboine), Jere, Robert; (second marriage) Ralph, Jr., Helena Marie. *Education:* Attended Pace Institute (now Pace College), Boston University, and University of California, Los Angeles. *Politics:* Independent. *Home and office:* 39 Betts Rd., Belmont, Mass. 02178.

CAREER: During his early career worked on farms, was boardboy for a New York broker, and traveled as a model, packer, and salesman for a men's clothing manufacturer in Chicago, Ill.; entered the men's clothing business with his father in 1921, and in 1926 became president of E.F.P. Burns Co., Boston, Mass. City of Belmont, chairman of finance committee, 1952-68, member of board of assessors, beginning 1969. Chairman of board, Taunton State Hospital, 1952-62. *Member:* Cap and Gown Association of America (manufacturers; past president), Belmont Historical Society, Knights of Columbus, Mid-Ocean Club (Bermuda), Lexington (Mass.) Golf Club.

WRITINGS: Angel on Horseback, (novel), Colonial Publishing, 1945; *Golden Years in Belmont* (novelette), Belmont Herald Publishing, 1959; *Out of the Mist* (novel), Branden Press, 1969. Contributor to newspapers and magazines under various pseudonyms.

WORK IN PROGRESS: Legacy No. 1.

AVOCATIONAL INTERESTS: Golf (won four senior championships between 1956 and 1967), piano.††

* * *

BURTT, Harold E(rnest) 1890-

PERSONAL: Born April 26, 1890, in Haverhill, Mass.; son of Winslow J. and Annie B. (Boyer) Burtt; married Ruth M. Macintosh, June 7, 1916; children: Benjamin P. *Education:* Dartmouth College, A.B., 1911; Harvard University, A.M., 1913, Ph.D., 1915. *Home:* 1874 Riverside Dr. Apt. 2, Columbus, Ohio 43212. *Office:* Ohio State University, 1945 North High St., Columbus, Ohio 43210.

CAREER: Instructor in psychology at Simmons College, Boston, Mass., 1915-18, Harvard University, Cambridge, Mass., 1916-18; Ohio State University, Columbus, instructor, 1919-20, assistant professor, 1920-22, professor of psychology, 1922-60, professor emeritus, 1960—, chairman of department, 1939-60. Consultant to Adjutant General's Office, U.S. Army, World War II. *Military service:* U.S. Aviation Service, 1918; became captain. *Member:* American Association for the Advancement of Science (vice-president, Section I, 1936), American Psychological Association (fellow; member of council, 1943-46), American Statistical Association, Psychometric Society, Audubon Society, Torch Club, Wheaton Club, Kit Kat Club. *Awards, honors:* Service Medal, Ohio State University, 1963.

WRITINGS: Employment Psychology, Houghton, 1926, revised edition, 1942; *Legal Psychology,* Prentice-Hall, 1931; *Applied Psychology,* Prentice-Hall, 1948, 3rd edition, 1957; *Bird Psychology,* Macmillan, 1967. Contributor to psychology and ornithology journals.

AVOCATIONAL INTERESTS: Bryology, ornithology, general nature study, photography, amateur radio.

* * *

BUSH, John W(illiam) 1917-1976

PERSONAL: Born September 10, 1917, in Buffalo, N.Y.; son of John J. (in furniture business) and Mary (Schwanekamp) Bush. *Education:* Loyola University, Chicago, Ill., A.B., 1941; Woodstock College, Licentiate in Theology, 1950; Georgetown University, M.A., 1951; Fordham University, Ph.D., 1960; Sorbonne, University of Paris, postdoctoral study, 1968-69. *Politics:* Democrat. *Office:* Department of History, LeMoyne College, Syracuse, N.Y. 13214.

CAREER: Roman Catholic priest, member of Society of Jesus (Jesuits); Fordham University, New York, N.Y., instructor, 1951-56, assistant professor of European history, 1956-60; LeMoyne College, Syracuse, N.Y., assistant professor, 1960-64, associate professor of history, 1964-76 (on leave, 1975-76), chairman of department of history and political science, 1962-1967, chairman of department of history, 1967-71; St. Louis University, St. Louis, Mo., chairman of department of history, 1975-76. Visiting lecturer, Syracuse University, 1969. *Member:* American Historical Association, Society for French Historical Studies, Societe d'histoire modern, Jesuit Historical Association (past president), New York State Association of European Historians (past president). *Awards, honors:* Fulbright fellowship in France, 1958-59; summer fellowship at Cambridge Center for Social Studies, 1970.

WRITINGS: (Contributor) John C. Olin, editor, *Desiderius Erasmus: Christian Humanism and the Reformation,* Harper, 1964; *Venetia Redeemed: Franco-Italian Relations, 1864-1866,* Syracuse University Press, 1967; (contributor) Gaetano L. Vincitorio, editor, *Crisis in the Great Republic,* Fordham University Press, 1969. Contributor of articles to *New Catholic Encyclopedia, Heights,* and to historical journals; contributor of book reviews to *Cross Currents, Italica,* and *Catholic Historical Review.*

WORK IN PROGRESS: Jesuit Education and French Society, 1880-1901.†

(Died May 2, 1976)

* * *

BUTLER, Charles Henry 1894-19(?)

PERSONAL: Born November 26, 1894, in Sullivan, Ill.; son of Squire Thomas and Austine (Roane) Butler; married Agnes Peterson, August 11, 1922 (deceased). *Education:* Attended University of Illinois, 1913-15; University of Chicago, Ph.B., 1921, A.M., 1922; University of Missouri, Ph.D., 1931. *Politics:* Republican ("generally"). *Religion:* Presbyterian.

CAREER: University of Missouri, Columbia, principal of University High School, 1924-37; Western Michigan University, Kalamazoo, assistant professor, 1937-43, associate professor, 1943-49, professor of mathematics, 1949-64, head of department, 1951-60. *Military service:* U.S. Army, 1918-19. *Member:* Mathematical Association of America, National Council of Teachers of Mathematics, Michigan Council of Teachers of Mathematics.

WRITINGS: (With F. Lynwood Wren) *The Teaching of Secondary Mathematics,* McGraw, 1941, 5th edition (with Wren and J. Houston Banks), 1970; (with Wren) *Trigonometry for Secondary Schools,* Heath, 1948, 4th edition, 1965; *Arithmetic for High Schools,* Heath, 1953; (with Glade Wilcox) *Industrial Calculating Devices,* Holt, 1962.†

(Deceased)

* * *

BUTLER, Erica Bracher 1905-

PERSONAL: Born December 4, 1905, in Clifton, Tex.; daughter of Max Gotthard (a building contractor) and Olga (Ninow) Bracher; married G. Paul Butler (an author-editor), May 29, 1938; children: William Eric and Renate (twins), Jolyan Anthony. *Education:* Pasadena Junior College, student, 1925-27. *Politics:* Republican. *Religion:* Lutheran. *Home and office:* Casa Coral, 114 Southwest 57th Ter., Cape Coral, Fla. 33904.

CAREER: Writer, usually in collaboration with husband.

WRITINGS: (With husband, G. Paul Butler) *South America,* Van Nostrand, 1960; (with G. P. Butler) *Mexico,* Van Nostrand, 1960; (with G. P. Butler) *Caribbean and Central America and the Bahamas and Bermuda,* Van Nostrand, 1960; *Mexico,* Hastings, for United Nations Children's Fund (UNICEF), 1961. Translated several foreign sermons included in *Best Sermons,* edited by G. Paul Butler.

WORK IN PROGRESS: With husband, *Europe and the Mediterranean;* new editions of travel guides to Mexico, South America, and the Caribbean; two novels.

AVOCATIONAL INTERESTS: Music, art, biography.††

* * *

BUTLER, G(eorge) Paul 1900-

PERSONAL: Born October 23, 1900, in Chester, Pa.; son of William Austin (jeweler and jewelry designer) and Katherine Maud (Anthony) Butler; married Erica Bracher (a writer), May 29, 1938; children: G. Paul II, William Eric and Renate (twins), Jolyan Anthony. *Education:* Lawrence College (now Lawrence University), A.B., 1923; studied at Drew Theological Seminary (now Drew University), 1924-26, Columbia University, 1924-28, 1936-38; Milton University, Ph.D., 1929; University of Southern California, M.A., 1938. *Home and office:* Casa Coral, 114 Southwest 57th Ter., Cape Coral, Fla. 33904.

CAREER: Ordained Methodist minister, 1923. Pastor of Methodist churches in Wisconsin and New Jersey, 1920-24; *New York Times,* New York, N.Y., staff member, 1924-27; Silver Bay School, head of department of history, 1928-29; Southwestern University, Los Angeles, Calif., head of department of history, 1929-38; Los Angeles City College, Los Angeles, Calif., member of English faculty, 1930-38; Chapman College (formerly California Christian College), Los Angeles, Calif., head of departments of English literature and history, 1936-38; *New York Mirror,* New York, N.Y., editor of material concerning books, churches, and schools, 1938-63; lecturer, editor, free-lance writer. *Member:* Modern History Association, Modern Language Association of America, P.E.N., Monday Club (New York). *Awards, honors:* Citations from National Council of Christians and Jews, Freedoms Foundation, and U.S. Air Force, all 1956.

WRITINGS: (Editor with others) *Modern College Readings,* Prentice-Hall, 1936; *Best Sermons,* Volumes I-IX, Harper, 1943-50, Macmillan, 1951, McGraw-Hill, 1955, Crowell, 1959, Van Nostrand, 1961-64, Simon & Schuster, 1965-66; (co-author) *Guide to Practical Writing,* 1944; (with wife, Erica Bracher Butler) *South America,* Van Nostrand, 1960; (with E. B. Butler) *Mexico,* Van Nostrand, 1960; (with E. B. Butler) *Caribbean and Central America and the Bahamas and Bermuda,* Van Nostrand, 1960; (editor) *Great Catholic Sermons,* Sheed & Ward, 1963.

WORK IN PROGRESS: Volumes X-XII of *Best Sermons;* with wife, *Europe and the Mediterranean;* new editions of travel guides to Mexico, South America and the Caribbean.

* * *

BUTLER, Mildred Allen 1897-

PERSONAL: Born May 23, 1897, in Newton, Mass.; daughter of Charles Clifford (a hotel manager) and Sarah Louise (Boutwell) Butler; married Amandus J. Engdahl, April 2, 1932; children: Sylvia Louise. *Education:* Wellesley College, B.A., 1918; Columbia University, additional study, 1924-25; University of Oregon, M.A., 1952. *Religion:* Episcopalian. *Residence:* Portland, Ore.

CAREER: High school teacher of English in Wilton, N.H., 1918-19, in Newburyport, Mass., 1919-20, in Marblehead, Mass, 1920-24; Little Theatre League, Richmond, Va., director, 1925-27; Portland Civic Theatre, Portland, Ore., director, 1927-29; Cheviot Hills Community Players, Los Angeles, Calif., director, 1949-51; Theatre for Youth, Santa Barbara, Calif., director, 1953-54; Portland Civic Theatre, director, 1954-56; Theatre for Youth, director, 1959-60.

WRITINGS: *Literature Dramatized* (textbook for junior high school) Harcourt, 1926; *Actress in Spite of Herself: The Life of Anna Cora Mowatt* (juvenile), Funk, 1966; *Twice Queen of France: Anne of Brittany* (juvenile; Literary Guild selection), Funk, 1967; *Rapier for Revenge* (juvenile), Funk, 1969; *Ward of the Sun King* (juvenile), Funk, 1970.

Children's plays: (With Robert Pierik) *Beauty and the Beast,* Harlequin Press, 1958; *Mischievous Harlequin,* Harlequin Press, 1959; (with Pierik) *In the Forest of Fancy,* Harlequin Press, 1960. Contributor to speech and theater journals.

WORK IN PROGRESS: The Disobedient Queen: Katherine of Valois; a book for young people on the relationship between Elizabeth I of England and Mary Queen of Scots.

SIDELIGHTS: The ideas for Mildred Butler's more recent books came while she was vacationing in France, much of the research coming from French sources.†

* * *

BUXBAUM, Edith 1902-

PERSONAL: Born April 20, 1902, in Vienna, Austria; daughter of Samuel (a businessman) and Jeannette (Seidler) Buxbaum; married Fritz A. Schmidl (a social worker), August 16, 1944 (deceased). *Education:* University of Vienna, Ph.D., 1924; Institute for Psychoanalysis, Vienna, Austria, graduate, 1932. *Religion:* Jewish. *Home:* 6036 Upland Ter. S., Seattle, Wash. 98118. *Office:* Northwest Clinic for Psychiatry and Neurology, 4033 East Madison, Seattle, Wash. 98102.

CAREER: High school teacher in Vienna, Austria, prior to 1935; psychoanalyst training analyst in Seattle, Wash., beginning 1947, became associated with Northwest Clinic for Psychiatry and Neurology. University of Washington Medical School, Seattle, clinical professor in department of psychiatry, 1953-68. Consultant, Ryther Child Center. *Member:* International Psychoanalytic Association, American Psychoanalytic Association, Association for Child Analysis, American Orthopsychiatric Association, Seattle Psychoanalytic Society.

WRITINGS: (Contributor) *The Psychoanalytic Study of the Child,* International Universities Press, Volume I, 1945, Volume IX, 1954, Volume XV, 1960, Volume XIX, 1964; (with Florence Swanson) *Your Child Makes Sense: A Guidebook for Parents,* International Universities Press, 1949, published as *Understanding Your Child,* Grove, 1962; (contributor) *Case Studies in Childhood Emotional Disabilities,* Volume I, American Orthopsychiatric Association, 1953; (contributor) Morton Levitt, editor, *Readings in Psychoanalytic Psychology,* Appleton, 1959; *Troubled Children in a Troubled World,* International Universities Press, 1969. Contributor of articles, translations, and reviews to professional journals.

* * *

CAHALANE, Victor H(arrison) 1901-

PERSONAL: Born October 17, 1901, in Charlestown,

N.H.; son of David Victor and Elizabeth (Harrison) Cahalane; married Isabelle Porter, September 23, 1928; children: Margaret. *Education:* University of Massachusetts, B.S., 1924; Yale University, M.F., 1927; University of Michigan, graduate study, 1928-29. *Residence:* Clarksville, N.Y.

CAREER: Michigan Department of Conservation, Lansing, deer investigator, 1928-30; Cranbrook Institutions, Institute of Science, Bloomfield Hills, Mich., director, 1930-34; National Park Service, Washington, D.C., chief biologist, 1934-55; New York State Museum, Albany, assistant director, 1955-67. Consultant, National Parks Board of Trustees of South Africa, and U.S. National Park Service. *Member:* Wildlife Society (president, 1940-41), Defenders of Wildlife (president, 1964-71), American Committee for International Wildlife Protection (vice-president, 1963-70; historian, beginning 1970), American Ornithologists' Union, American Society of Mammalogists, Nature Conservancy, Fauna Preservation Society, Adirondack Mountain Club, Sierra Club, Boone & Crockett Club, Cosmos Club (Washington, D.C.). *Awards, honors:* Fellow of Cranbrook Institute of Science and Rochester Museum of Arts and Sciences.

WRITINGS: (Co-author) *Fading Trails: The Story of Vanishing American Wildlife,* Macmillan, 1942; *Meeting the Mammals,* Macmillan, 1943; *Mammals of North America,* Macmillan, 1947, reprinted, 1966; *A Biological Survey of Katmai National Monument,* Smithsonian Institution, 1959; (editor) *National Parks: A World Need,* American Committee for International Wildlife Protection, 1962; (editor) John J. Audubon and John Bachman, *The Imperial Collection of Audubon Animals* (Book-of-the-Month Club alternate selection), Hammond, Inc., 1967; (editor) Audubon and Bachman, *A Selected Treasury for Sportmen: Audubon Game Animals,* Hammond, Inc., 1968; (with C. C. Johnson) *Alive in the Wild,* Prentice-Hall, 1969. Contributor to scientific journals and popular magazines, including *Saturday Evening Post, National Geographic,* and *Natural History.*

WORK IN PROGRESS: Bears of the World, completion expected in 1980; a history of the American Committee for International Wildlife Protection.

SIDELIGHTS: Victor Cahalane has done research all over the United States, and in Europe and Africa. He is competent in French. *Avocational interests:* Nature photography.

BIOGRAPHICAL/CRITICAL SOURCES: Coronet, July, 1955.

* * *

CAHILL, Jane (Miller)   1901-

PERSONAL: Born January 12, 1901, in Philadelphia, Pa.; daughter of John Milton and Amelia (Welles) Miller; married Edward H. Cahill, July 19, 1924. *Education:* Attended private schools in Atlantic City, N.J. *Home:* Thomas Wynne Apartments, No. 412A, Wynnewood, Pa. 19096. *Office:* Office of Older Adults, Court House, Norristown, Pa. 19041.

CAREER: Fairchild Publications, Philadelphia, Pa., reporter and editor, 1941-66, writer of regular feature, "Experiences of Smaller Stores," for *Women's Wear Daily,* 1951-66; currently member of SCORE (counseling division, Small Business Administration), and writer of newsletter for senior citizens. *Member:* Washington Press Club, Fashion Group.

WRITINGS: Success on a Shoe String, Fairchild, 1953; *Experiences of Smaller Stores,* Fairchild, 1955; *Backbone of Retailing,* Fairchild, 1960; *Can a Smaller Store Succeed?,* Fairchild, 1966.

CAHN, Zvi   1896-
(Harry C. Laurie)

PERSONAL: Born July 8, 1896, in Warsaw, Poland; son of Isaac and Feiga (Zgersky) Cahn; married Haya Glauberman; children: Sulamith, Ruby. *Education:* Rabbinical Seminary, Warsaw, Poland, Rabbi 1918; graduate study at Universities of Berlin and Vienna, 1919-20; Dropsie College (now University), Ph.D., 1928.

CAREER: Hebrew Schools of Montreal, Montreal, Quebec, Canada, executive director, 1929-34; *Truth* (weekly), editor, 1935-36; *Jewish Daily Forward,* New York, N.Y., feature editor and columnist, beginning 1936. *Member:* American Sociological Association, Authors Guild, P.E.N., Jewish Writers Union.

WRITINGS: Fables (published in Hebrew), [Warsaw], 1914; *From the Deepness of My Heart* (poems in Hebrew), [Warsaw], 1915; *Blackbook* (in Hebrew), [Lodz], 1917; *Canadian Jewry,* [Toronto], 1932; *Halachah of the Karaites,* [New York], 1935; *The Rise of the Karaite Sect: A New Light on the Halakah and Origin of the Karaites,* M. Tausner, 1937; *Dos lid fun Oysleyzung,* [New York], 1938; *Idishkayt farn modernem Id,* [New York], 1941; *Der rebi fun Kotsk* (play; title means "The Rabbi of Kotzk"), [New York], 1950; *Der Rebi fun Barditshev* (play; title means "The Rabbi of Bardichev"), [New York], 1953; *Sheloshah Ketarim* [Tel Aviv], 1954; *Di filozofye fun identum,* [New York], 1958; *Shturmishe dayres* (novel; title means "Stormy Generations"), [Buenos Aires], 1959; *Di heldn in der veltgeshikhte* (title means "The Heroes of the World"), [Tel Aviv], 1961; *The Philosophy of Judaism,* Macmillan, 1962.

WORK IN PROGRESS: Everyday Psychology; a book of fiction, *One Hundred Romantic Nights;* and *Psychology of Religion.*††

* * *

CAINE, Sydney   1902-

PERSONAL: Born June 27, 1902, in Neasden, England; son of Harry Edward (a railway clerk) and Jane Harker (Buckley) Caine; married Muriel Anne Harris, August 15, 1925 (died, 1962); married Doris Winifred Folkard, March 23, 1965 (died, 1973); married Elizabeth Crane Bowyer, October 4, 1975; children: (first marriage) Michael. *Education:* London School of Economics and Political Science, B.Sc. (first class honors in economics), 1922. *Home:* 37 Belsize Pk., London NW3, England.

CAREER: Assistant inspector of taxes, British Civil Service, 1923-26; with Colonial Office, 1926-48, as financial secretary, Hong Kong, 1937-40, assistant secretary, London, England, 1940-42, financial adviser to secretary of state for the colonies, 1942-44, assistant undersecretary of state for the colonies, 1944-47, and deputy undersecretary of state, 1947-48; Treasury, London, third secretary, 1948-49, head of United Kingdom Treasury and Supply Delegation, Washington, D.C., 1949-51; University of Malaya, Singapore, vice-chancellor, 1952-56; University of London, London School of Economics and Political Science, London, director, 1957-67. Independent Television Authority, London, member, 1960-64, deputy chairman, 1964-67; governor, Reserve Bank of Rhodesia, London, 1965-67. Lecturer on tours in Australia and New Zealand, 1959, and Mexico, Colombia, Peru, and Venezuela, 1962. Member of executive of British Council, beginning 1957.

MEMBER: Royal Economic Society (president, 1966-68), Reform Club (London). *Awards, honors:* Companion of St.

Michael and St. George, 1945; grand officer, Order of Orange Nassau, 1946; Knight Commander of St. Michael and St. George, 1947; LL.D., University of Malaya, 1956; grand officer, Order of Dannebrog, 1966.

WRITINGS: History of the Foundation of the London School of Economics, London School of Economics and Political Science, 1963; *Prices for Primary Producers*, Institute of Economic Affairs (London), 1963; *Paying for TV?*, Institute of Economic Affairs, 1968, Transatlantic, 1969; *British Universities: Purpose and Prospects*, Bodley Head, 1969. Author or co-author of various government reports on the sugar industry, development of Ceylon, and finance. Contributor to *Lloyd's Bank Review, Political Quarterly, Foreign Affairs,* and other periodicals.

BIOGRAPHICAL/CRITICAL SOURCES: Washington Post, June 28, 1969; *Times Literary Supplement,* July 31, 1969.

* * *

CALDWELL, C(harles) Edson 1906-1974

PERSONAL: Born July 4, 1906, in Winters, Calif.; son of Charles Jarvis and Anna Lauer (Randall) Caldwell; married Ruth Wells, March 7, 1931; children: Constance Lucille (Mrs. George Fry), Catherine Elida. *Education:* Chico State College (now California State University, Chico), A.B., 1934; University of California, Berkeley, Ed.D., 1953. *Politics:* Nonpartisan. *Religion:* Presbyterian. *Home:* 5705 McAdoo Ave., Sacramento, Calif. 95819.

CAREER: Teacher in elementary schools in northern California, 1934-42; junior high school teacher in Vallejo, Calif., 1942-43, vice-principal, 1943-47; Vallejo Junior College (now Solano College), Vallejo, Calif., coordinator of student affairs, 1947-48; California State University, Sacramento, registrar, 1948-51, assistant professor, 1951-55, associate professor, 1955-60, professor of education, 1960-72. *Member:* American Personnel and Guidance Association, National Society for Programmed Instruction, Adult Education Association of the U.S.A., Phi Delta Kappa.

WRITINGS: Sociometric Techniques, Fearon, 1958; *Guidance Techniques for the Classroom Teacher,* Science Research Associates, 1960; (with Clarence Mahler) *Group Counseling for Secondary Schools,* Science Research Associates, 1961; (with Don Dinkmeyer) *Developmental Counseling and Guidance: A Comprehensive Approach,* McGraw, 1970.†

(Died March 23, 1974)

* * *

CALLAHAN, Charles C(lifford) 1910-

PERSONAL: Born March 23, 1910, in Jackson, Ohio; son of George Clifford (a shop superintendent) and Jennie Julia (Morrow) Callahan; married Violet S. Bander (a social worker), September 10, 1951; children: Judith A., Louesa T. (Mrs. John A. Barlow), John C. *Education:* Ohio State University, B.Sc., 1932, J.D., 1934; Yale University, J.S.D., 1937. *Religion:* Congregationalist. *Home:* 331 East Torrence Rd., Columbus, Ohio 43214. *Office:* Ohio State University, 1659 North High St., Columbus, Ohio 43210.

CAREER: Yale University, New Haven, Conn., lecturer, 1938-39, assistant professor of law, 1939-43; Ohio State University, Columbus, professor of property law, beginning 1943. *Member:* American Judicature Society, Ohio State Bar Association, Columbus Bar Association.

WRITINGS: (Contributor) *American Law of Property,* Little, Brown, 1952; *Principles of Ohio Water Rights Law,* Department of Natural Resources, State of Ohio, 1957; *Adverse Possession,* Ohio State University Press, 1961. Contributor to *Encyclopaedia Britannica,* and to legal encyclopedias and periodicals.

WORK IN PROGRESS: Compilation of teaching materials on the law of property.††

* * *

CALLIHAN, E(lmer) L(ee) 1903-

PERSONAL: Born December 6, 1903, in Lockhart, Tex.; son of Jefferson Davis and Elizabeth (Horner) Callihan; married Lillian Edwards, November 28, 1928. *Education:* University of Texas, B.J., 1929; Northwestern University, M.S.J., 1939, further graduate study, 1945. *Politics:* Republican. *Religion:* Baptist. *Home:* Rancho Poquito, Route 2, Nance Rd., Sunnyvale, Tex. 75149.

CAREER: Free-lance writer, and reporter and editor on Texas newspapers, 1923-30; *Sherman Daily Democrat,* Sherman, Tex., reporter and sports editor, 1930-32; Fort Worth (Tex.) public schools, publicity director and instructor in journalism, 1933-40; professor of journalism and chairman of department at Drake University, Des Moines, Iowa, 1940-45, and Baylor University, Waco, Tex., 1945-46; Southern Methodist University, Dallas, Tex., professor of journalism and chairman of department, 1946-69, professor emeritus, 1969—; part-time journalism textbook consultant, Chilton Book Co., 1969-74. Conducts a national writer's service. Former secretary, Sunnyvale (Tex.) Independent School District, fifteen years.

MEMBER: American Society of Journalism School Administrators (charter member), Association for Education in Journalism, Southwest Journalism Forum (associate chairman), Sigma Delta Chi, Kappa Tau Alpha (former national president and vice-president), Press Club of Dallas and Press Club Foundation. *Awards, honors:* Awards from Southwest Journalism Forum, 1961, 1968, American Society of Journalism School Administrators, 1962, Sigma Delta Chi, 1962, and Press Club of Dallas, 1969.

WRITINGS: (Contributor) *Careers in Journalism,* Quill & Scroll Foundation, 1946, 2nd revised edition, 1966; *Grammar for Journalists,* Ronald, 1957, revised edition, Chilton, 1969; (with Harold Nelson and Wayne Danielson) *Exercises and Tests for Journalists,* with teacher's manual, Chilton, 1970. Publications include a journalism course of study for Fort Worth public schools, 1938, and a guide to high school news publicity, Texas High School Press Association, 1940. Contributor to journalism and educational journals. Editor, Drake Creative Awards anthologies, 1940-45.

* * *

CAMPBELL, Camilla 1905-

PERSONAL: Born April 15, 1905, in Fort Worth, Tex.; daughter of Stanley (an attorney) and Clota (Terrell) Boykin; married Dan W. Campbell (a testing engineer), June 10, 1929. *Education:* Attended Texas Christian University, 1922-24, and University of Missouri, 1927-28. *Home:* 430 Corona St., San Antonio, Tex. 78209.

CAREER: Elementary teacher in Fort Worth, Tex., 1924-27, 1928-29; feature writer for *Fort Worth Star Telegram,* Fort Worth, 1943-44; writer for young people. Member of Girl Scout board, San Antonio, 1954-58, and Friends of the

Library, 1959-63; leader of as many as four senior Girl Scout troops at one time. *Member:* Texas Historical Association, Texas Institute of Letters (member of executive council, 1959-60), Theta Sigma Phi. *Awards, honors:* Horn Book honor selection, 1956, for *Star Mountain and Other Legends of Mexico;* Cokesbury Award, Texas Institute of Letters, 1958, for *Coronado and His Captains.*

WRITINGS: Galleons Sail Westward, Mathis, Van Nort, 1939; *Star Mountain and Other Legends of Mexico,* Whittlesey House, 1946, edition with new illustrations, McGraw, 1968; *The Bartletts of Box B Ranch* (Junior Literary Guild selection), Whittlesey House, 1949; *Coronado and His Captains,* Follett, 1958; *Viva la Patria,* Hill & Wang, 1970. Contributor of stories and plays to children's publications, and adult poetry and articles to magazines.

WORK IN PROGRESS: A biography of William Barrett Travis, commander of the Alamo; a novel on colonial Texas.

SIDELIGHTS: Campbell devotes much of her writing to historical subjects because she believes "it is a mistake for young people to be isolated in time (the present) as well as geographically." She has traveled extensively in Mexico; one summer she took ten high school girls to Mexico. A German edition of *Star Mountain* was published in Vienna in 1950, illustrated by a Viennese artist who "made the Mexicans look like American Indians."

BIOGRAPHICAL/CRITICAL SOURCES: San Antonio Light, March 15, 1959; *San Antonio News,* June 15, 1962.

* * *

CAMPBELL, John W(ood)   1910-1971
(Arthur McCann, Don A. Stuart, Karl Van Campen)

PERSONAL: Born June 8, 1910, in Newark, N.J.; son of John W. (a telephone engineer) and Dorothy (Strahorn) Campbell; married Margaret Winter (a consultant on crewel embroideries), June 15, 1950; children: Philinda (Mrs. James Hammond), Leslyn S. *Education:* Massachusetts Institute of Technology, student, 1928-31; Duke University, B.Sc., 1933. *Politics:* "May the best man win." *Religion:* Unitarian Universalist.

CAREER: Free-lance writer of science fiction, 1930-37; Conde-Nast Publishing Co., New York, N.Y., 1937-71, editor of *Astounding Science Fiction, Analog Science Fact,* and *Science Fiction.*

WRITINGS: The Atomic Story (science text), Holt, 1947; *The Mightiest Machine,* Hadley Publishing Co., 1947, reprinted, Ace Books, 1972; *Who Goes There?: Seven Tales of Science Fiction,* Shasta, 1948; *The Incredible Planet,* Fantasy Press, 1949; *The Moon Is Hell!,* Fantasy Press, 1951, reprinted, Ace Books, 1973; (editor) *Astounding Tales of Space and Time,* Berkley Publishing, 1951; *Cloak of Aesir,* Shasta, 1952; (editor) *The Astounding Science Fiction Anthology,* Simon & Schuster, 1952; *The Black Star Passes,* Fantasy Press, 1953, reprinted, Ace Books, 1972; (editor) *The First Astounding Science Fiction Anthology,* Grayson, 1954; (editor) *The Second Astounding Science Fiction Anthology,* Grayson, 1954; *Islands of Space,* Fantasy Press, 1956.

Invaders from the Infinite, Gnome Press, 1961; (editor) *Prologue to Analog,* Doubleday, 1962; (editor) *Analog I* (science fiction anthology), Doubleday, 1963, and annual volumes, 1964-70; *Collected Editorials from Analog,* edited by Harry Harrison, Doubleday, 1966; *The Planeteers,* Ace Books, 1966; *The Ultimate Weapon,* Ace Books, 1966; *The*

John W. Campbell Anthology, Doubleday, 1973; *The Best of J. W. Campbell,* Sidgwick & Jackson, 1974.

SIDELIGHTS: Who Goes There? was adapted for the motion picture, "The Thing." *Avocational Interests:* Photography, electronics, working in wood and metal, experiments in extrasensory perception.†

(Died July 11, 1971)

* * *

CANER, Mary Paul   1893-

PERSONAL: Born July, 1893, in Philadelphia, Pa.; daughter of Henry Neill (a lawyer) and Margaret (Butler) Paul; married G. Colket Caner (a physician), June 5, 1924; children: George C., Jr., Emily (Mrs. Henry Parkman), Lila (Mrs. Robert D. Mehlman). *Education:* Columbia-Presbyterian Hospital Training School for Nurses, R.N., 1920. *Religion:* Presbyterian. *Home:* 63 Marlboro St., Boston, Mass. 02116; (summer) Manchester-by-the-Sea, Mass. 01944.

CAREER: Presbyterian Hospital, New York, N.Y., head nurse, 1921; Massachusetts General Hospital, Boston, head nurse, beginning 1923. *Member:* National League of American Pen Women, Women's City Club of Boston, Chilton Club, Massachusetts Society of Colonial Dames, Shirley Eustis House Association (president).

WRITINGS: Time Against the Sky, Dresser, 1966. Writer of articles on the 1747 Shirley Eustis House. Editor, *Garden Club of America Bulletin,* 1950-60.

WORK IN PROGRESS: Research on old houses and restorations.

* * *

CANG, Joel   1899-1974

PERSONAL: Born March 8, 1899, in Lublin, Poland; son of Abraham and Alexandra (Lipsman) Cang; married Annabela Cynberg, 1927; children: Stephen. *Education:* University of London, D.Litt., 1926. *Religion:* Jewish. *Home:* 45 Aberdare Gardens, London N.W. 6, England.

CAREER: Correspondent in Warsaw, Poland, for *News Chronicle* and *Manchester Guardian,* 1930-39, and London *Times,* 1945-48; *Jewish Chronicle,* London, England, foreign editor, 1948-63; London *Times,* London, special correspondent for Russian and east European affairs, 1952-59. *Member:* National Union of Journalists.

WRITINGS: The Silent Millions: A History of the Jews in the Soviet Union, Rapp & Whiting, 1969, Taplinger, 1970.

WORK IN PROGRESS: A history of political trials in the Soviet Union.

AVOCATIONAL INTERESTS: Gardening, fishing, walking.†

(Died November, 1974)

* * *

CAPLAN, Harry   1896-

PERSONAL: Born January 7, 1896, in Hoag's Corners, Rensselaer County, N.Y.; son of Jacob and Sarah (Tolchin) Caplan. *Education:* Cornell University, A.B., 1916, A.M., 1917, Ph.D., 1921. *Religion:* Jewish. *Residence:* East Greenbush, N.Y. *Office:* 121 Goldwin Smith Hall, Cornell Univeristy, Ithaca, N.Y. 14850.

CAREER: Cornell University, Ithaca, N.Y., instructor in public speaking, 1919-23, instructor in classics, 1924-25, assistant professor, 1925-30, professor of classics, 1930-67, chairman of department of classics, 1929-46, Goldwin Smith Professor of Classical Languages and Literature, 1941-67, Goldwin Smith Professor Emeritus, 1967—. Visiting summer professor at University of Wisconsin, 1925, University of Michigan, 1932, Northwestern University, 1938, Stanford University, 1942, 1948, University of Chicago, 1945, Columbia University, 1946; visiting professor at University of Pittsburgh, 1967-68, University of Washington, 1968, Brandeis University, 1968, University of Minnesota, 1969, Stanford University, spring 1969, and University of Illinois, 1970-71. *Military service:* U.S. Army, 1918-19.

MEMBER: American Philological Association (president, 1955), Mediaeval Academy of America (fellow), Speech Association of America, Renaissance Society of America, Modern Language Association of America, Linguistic Society of America, Classical Association of England and Wales, American Association of University Professors, Phi Beta Kappa, Delta Sigma Rho, Phi Eta Sigma, Phi Delta Kappa, Phi Kappa Phi. *Awards, honors:* Guggenheim fellow, 1928-29, 1956; fellow of the Center for Advanced Studies, Wesleyan University, 1962-63, 1964.

WRITINGS: (Editor) Gianfrancesco Pico della Mirandola, *On the Imagination,* Yale University Press, 1930; (editor) *Mediaeval Artes Praedicandi,* Cornell University Press, 1934, and *A Supplementary Hand-List,* 1936; (editor and translator) Cicero, *Rhetorica ad Herennium,* Harvard University Press, 1954; *The Classical Tradition,* Cornell University Press, 1966; (editor with Anne King and Helen North) *Of Eloquence: Studies in Ancient and Mediaeval Rhetoric,* Cornell University Press, 1970. Also editor of *A Late Mediaeval Tractate on Preaching,* 1925, and with H. H. King of *Pulpit Eloquence—English,* 1955, and *Pulpit Eloquence—German,* 1956, both special issues of *Speech Monographs.* Contributor of articles and reviews on classical and medieval literature to journals. Assistant editor, *Quarterly Journal of Speech,* 1923; joint editor, "Cornell Studies in Classical Philology," 1929-67.

WORK IN PROGRESS: With Isaac Rabinowitz, an annotated translation of Judah Messer Leon's *The Book of the Honeycomb's Flow;* an edition of the medieval Latin commentary by Alanus on the *Rhetorica ad Herennium.*†

* * *

CARBONNIER, Jeanne 1894-1974

PERSONAL: Born November 25, 1894, in Paris, France; daughter of Charles (an organist and composer) and Nicolle (a concert pianist; maiden name, Jeanne) Carbonnier. *Education:* University of Paris, Doctor of Medicine, 1920. *Office:* 30 East 40th St., New York, N.Y. 10016.

CAREER: Physician. *Member:* Authors Guild, American College of Obstetrics and Gynecology (fellow). *Awards, honors:* Boys' Clubs of America Junior Book Award for *Congo Explorer.*

WRITINGS: Congo Explorer, Scribner, 1960; *Above All a Physician,* Scribner, 1961; *Barber-Surgeon: A Life of Ambroise Pare,* Pantheon, 1965.

WORK IN PROGRESS: Research on Inca civilization; a biography of J. B. Lully; *Histoire du Theatre du Palais-Royal* (in French).

SIDELIGHTS: Dr. Carbonnier traveled to Spain, Italy, France, Switzerland, Canada, Mexico, Guatemala, Peru, Chile, and Japan. *Avocational interests:* Music.†

(Died May 19, 1974)

CARLETON, William G(raves) 1903-

PERSONAL: Born November 19, 1903, in Evansville, Ind.; son of William Barnet (a journalist) and May (Ruston) Carleton. *Education:* Indiana University, A.B., 1926, M.A., 1935; University of Florida, J.D., 1931; University of North Carolina, graduate study, 1933. *Home:* 216 Southwest 12th St., Gainesville, Fla. 32601. *Office:* Peabody Hall, University of Florida, Gainesville, Fla. 32601.

CAREER: University of Florida, Gainesville, instructor in history and political science, 1926-31, associate professor of political science, 1936-40, head professor of social sciences, 1940-57, graduate professor of history and political science, 1957-62, professor emeritus, 1962—. Regular lecturer at Federal Executive Seminar at King's Point, N.Y., and at Berkeley, Calif.; member of national panel of speakers for Phi Beta Kappa. *Member:* American Political Science Association, American Historical Association, Southern Political Science Association, Florida Historical Association, Phi Beta Kappa, Phi Delta Phi, Phi Kappa Phi.

WRITINGS: The Revolution in American Foreign Policy, Doubleday, 1954, 4th edition, Random House, 1967; *Technology and Humanism: Some Exploratory Essays for Our Times,* Vanderbilt University Press, 1970. Articles (has written more than two hundred) have been reprinted in about fifty books. Regular contributor to *American Scholar, Antioch Review, Current History, Yale Review, Harper's,* and *Virginia Quarterly Review;* has also contributed to other professional journals and to reference works, including *World Book* and *Dictionary of American Biography.*

WORK IN PROGRESS: A People Blessed, a People Damned: A Historical Portraiture of the Americans and Their Society, a book on the historical origin and development of basic American cultural values; articles on revisionist views of American history and on political and social trends.

BIOGRAPHICAL/CRITICAL SOURCES: Aid DiPace Donald, *John F. Kennedy and the New Frontier,* Hill & Wang, 1966; James T. Crown, *The Kennedy Literature,* New York University Press, 1968.

* * *

CARLEY, V(an Ness) Royal 1906-1976

PERSONAL: Born August 14, 1906, in Bridgeport, Conn.; son of Albert H. and Maud (Orelup) Carley; married Beatrice Carpenter (a dietician), December 12, 1931; children: Neal, Bruce, Jay, Seth, Ross, Roy. *Education:* Pratt Institute, graduate, 1930. *Religion:* Protestant. *Home:* 166 Pearsall Pl., Bridgeport, Conn. 06605.

CAREER: Van Ness Service (advertising and promotional art), Bridgeport, Conn., owner, 1941-76. Wrote, produced, and appeared on television shows, 1955-68. Lecturer for many years to civic and religious groups.

WRITINGS—All published by C. R. Gibson: (Self-illustrated) *That Lazy Cat* (juvenile), 1969; *The 23rd Psalm for Today* (with photographs by the author), 1971; *The Dimensions of Gods Love,* 1972; (editor and illustrator) *The Lords Prayer for Today Together with Other Choice Portions of Holy Scripture,* 1974; *Beatitudes for Today,* 1975.

AVOCATIONAL INTERESTS: Aiding youth activities, photography.†

(Died August 15, 1976)

CARLS, (John) Norman 1907-

PERSONAL: Born December 22, 1907, in Virginia, Ill.; son of John H. (a farmer) and Katherine (Bins) Carls; married Catharine Driver, July 11, 1945; children: Catharine Trice. Education: Illinois State Normal University (now Illinois State University), B.Ed., 1932; Clark University, A.M., 1934, Ph.D., 1935. Residence: New Market, Va. 22844.

CAREER: Oregon College of Education, Monmouth, instructor, later assistant professor of geography, 1935-40; Eastern Illinois University, Charleston, associate professor of geography, 1940-46 (on military leave, 1942-46); U.S. Bureau of the Census, Washington, D.C., chief of operations, Geography Division, 1946-47; American University, Washington, D.C., associate professor, 1949-51, professor of geography, 1951-55; University of Pittsburgh, Pittsburgh, Pa., professor of geography, 1955-61, adjunct professor, 1961-64, chairman of department of geography, 1955-58; Columbia University, Teachers College, New York, N.Y., visiting professor of geography, 1963-64; Shippensburg State College, Shippensburg, Pa., professor of geography, 1964-73, professor emeritus, 1973—, chairman of department, 1966-73. Delegate, Mid-Century White House Conference on Youth, 1950; member, Pan American Consultation on Geography, 1952. Military service: U.S. Naval Reserve, active duty, 1942-46; became lieutenant commander.

MEMBER: Association of American Geographers, National Council for Geographic Education (president, 1956), National Council for the Social Studies, National Education Association, American Geographical Society, Association of Pacific Coast Geographers, Pennsylvania Council for Geographic Education (president, 1970-71), Gamma Theta Upsilon, Pi Gamma Mu, Theta Alpha Phi.

WRITINGS: (With Frank E. Sorenson) Neighbors Across the Seas, Holt, 1950; (with Sorenson and Margery D. Howart) Neighbors in Latin America, Holt, 1951; (with Sorenson and Howarth) Our United States in a World of Neighbors, Holt, 1958; (with Sorenson) Knowing Our Neighbors in Canada and Latin America, Holt, 1964; (with Sorenson and Phillip Bacon) Knowing Our Neighbors in the United States, Holt, 1966; (with Sorenson and Elaine M. Templin) Knowing Our Neighbors Around the Earth, Holt, 1966; (with Sorenson) Knowing Our Neighbors in the Eastern Hemisphere, Holt, 1968.†

*   *   *

CARLSON, William H(ugh) 1898-

PERSONAL: Born September 5, 1898, in Waverly, Neb.; son of Swan August (a farmer) and Christina (Johansdotter) Carlson; married Claire Agnes Dyer, June 17, 1924; children: Ruth Sherrill. Education: University of Nebraska, A.B., 1924; New York State Library School (now State University of New York at Albany), Certificate, 1926; University of California, Berkeley, M.A. in Librarianship, 1937. Politics: Independent. Religion: Congregationalist. Home: 1468 Northwest 20th Place, Corvallis, Ore. 97330.

CAREER: Farmer in Waverly, Neb., 1919-22; reporter in Aurora, Neb., 1923-24; Nebraska Legislative Reference Bureau Library, Lincoln, assistant, 1924-25; University of Iowa, Iowa City, supervisor of departmental libraries, 1926-29; librarian at University of North Dakota, Grand Forks, 1929-35, Vanderbilt University, Nashville, Tenn., 1935-36, University of Arizona, Tucson, 1937-42, and Oregon State University, Corvallis, 1945-65; Oregon State System of Higher Education, Corvallis, director of libraries, 1945-65, library planning and research associate, 1965-68; Willamette

University, Salem, Ore., acting librarian, 1968-69. Consultant, chiefly in buildings and surveys, to universities and state libraries. Trustee of Oregon State Library, 1955-63. Military service: U.S. Army, bugler, 1918-19.

MEMBER: American Library Association (president of library education division, 1952-53), Association of College and Research Libraries (president, 1947-48), Canadian Library Association, Pacific Northwest Library Association (president, 1952-53), Sigma Delta Chi, Phi Kappa Phi.

WRITINGS: (With Elizabeth Senning and E. D. Bullock) Nebraska Voters' Handbook, Nebraska Legislative Reference Bureau, 1924; Development and Financial Support of Seven Western and Northwestern State University Libraries, University of California Press, 1938; (with others) College and University Libraries and Librarianship, American Library Association, 1946; (contributor) R. B. Downs, editor, The Status of American College and University Librarians, American Library Association, 1958; (contributor) The Changing Environment for Library Services in the Metropolitan Area, Graduate School of Library Science, University of Illinois, 1966; In a Grand and Awful Time (illustrations by Nelson Sandgren), Oregon State University Press, 1967; The Carlson Family of Rockneby, Sweden, and Waverly, Nebraska, privately printed, 1967. Co-author of survey reports on Texas A&M College Library (with Robert W. Orr), 1950, and Portland High Schools (with Carl Hintz), 1959; author of centennial history of Oregon State University Library. Contributor of about 100 articles and reviews to journals.

WORK IN PROGRESS: Genealogical research, chiefly in the Scandinavian countries; articles for Encyclopedia of Library and Information Science, and Dictionary of American Library Biography.

SIDELIGHTS: William Carlson is competent in Swedish, Norwegian, and Danish; he has some ability in Spanish, French, and German.

BIOGRAPHICAL/CRITICAL SOURCES: PNLA Quarterly, April, 1966, July, 1966; William H. Carlson, In a Grand and Awful Time, Oregon State University Press, 1967.

*   *   *

CARMICHAEL, Peter A(rchibald) 1897-

PERSONAL: Born April 19, 1897, in Anniston, Ala.; son of Archibald Alexander (a cemetery superintendent) and Mary Frances (Conn) Carmichael; married Louise Harris (died, 1964). Education: Johns Hopkins University, B.S., 1927; Columbia University, M.A., 1928; University of North Carolina, Ph.D., 1930. Home: 4859 Tulane Dr., Baton Rouge, La. 70808. Office: Department of Philosophy, Louisiana State University, Baton Rouge, La. 70803.

CAREER: Newspaper writer in Anniston, Ala., 1919-21, Winston-Salem, N.C., 1921, and Roanoke, Va., 1922-24; Baltimore Evening Sun, Baltimore, Md., copyreader, 1924-27; College of William and Mary, Richmond Division, Richmond, Va., professor of philosophy and psychology, 1931-33; Converse College, Spartanburg, S.C., professor of philosophy and psychology, 1933-34; U.S. Department of Labor, Conciliation Service, commissioner, 1935-36; Louisiana State University, Baton Rouge, associate professor, 1936-37, professor of philosophy, 1937-67, professor emeritus, 1967—. Arbitrator of industrial disputes, National War Labor Board, 1942-46, Federal Mediation and Conciliation Service, beginning 1942. Visiting scholar, Clemson University, 1968-69. *Member:* American Philosophical Association, American Arbitration Association, American Society for Aesthetics, Association for Symbolic Logic, Southern Society for Philosophy and Psychology (president, 1946), Southwestern Philosophical Society (president, 1941-45).

WRITINGS: The South and Segregation, Public Affairs Press, 1965. Contributor to *Journal of Philosophy, Journal of Aesthetics and Art Criticism,* and other professional periodicals.

WORK IN PROGRESS: A biography; studies in logic and philosophical analysis.†

* * *

CARMICHAEL, Thomas N(ichols) 1919-1972

PERSONAL: Born December 30, 1919, in Pelham, N.Y.; son of Cyril (a broker) and Edith (Nichols) Carmichael; married Marcelle Tessendorf, October 20, 1945; children: Thomas Nichols, Jr. *Education:* Princeton University, B.A., 1942. *Politics:* "99% independent, 1% Democratic." *Home:* Nicolas Bravo 29, Ajijic, Jalisco, Mexico. *Agent:* Theron Raines, Raines & Raines, 475 Fifth Ave., New York, N.Y. 10017.

CAREER: Life (magazine), New York, N.Y., began as researcher, became reporter, writer, chief of domestic and foreign staffs, and assistant to the managing editor, 1945-66, military consultant in Mexico, 1966-72. *Military service:* U.S. Army, 1942-45; became captain; received Silver Star, Purple Heart, Presidential Citation.

WRITINGS: The Ninety Days, Geis, 1971.

WORK IN PROGRESS: A book on the Napoleonic conquest of Europe.

SIDELIGHTS: Thomas N. Carmichael told *CA* his main interest was the military, which he thought was "a rather neglected subject in the U.S. A better understanding of military history might just lead to a slightly less nonsensical U.S. military policy than is currently in vogue. My feelings on Westmoreland, Calley, Viet Nam, etc. would be unprintable—even today."

BIOGRAPHICAL/CRITICAL SOURCES: New York Times, October 26, 1972.†

(Died October 24, 1972)

* * *

CARRELL, Norman (Gerald) 1905-

PERSONAL: Surname is pronounced Ca-*rell;* born July 4, 1905, in London, England; son of Herbert Alfred (a businessman) and Edith (Sharp) Carrell; married; children: Elisabeth Marilyn Denise. *Education:* Attended College of Art and Technology, Bournemouth, England, 1923-24. *Politics:* Conservative. *Religion:* Protestant. *Home:* 14 Vineyard Hill Rd., Wimbledon, London SW19 7JH, England.

CAREER: Bournemouth Symphony Orchestra, Bournemouth, England, viola player, 1925-30; British Broadcasting Corp., London, England, viola player in BBC Symphony Orchestra, 1930-41, music booking manager, 1948-69. Specialist string examiner, Trinity College of Music. Arranger of Bach's "lost" concertos and adapter of various works of Bach for brass ensemble. *Military service:* British Army, Artillery, 1941-48; became major; received Africa Star. *Awards, honors:* Member of Order of the British Empire, 1963.

WRITINGS: Bach's "Brandenburg" Concertos, Allen & Unwin, 1963; *Bach the Borrower,* Allen & Unwin, 1967,

Hillary, 1968. Writer of program notes for Oxford Bach Festival and other concerts.

WORK IN PROGRESS: Expansion of *Bach's Concertos* for another book.

SIDELIGHTS: Carrell also plays piano and violin, and has a working knowledge of guitar, recorder, trumpet, horn, clarinet, and cello. *Avocational interests:* Painting, handicrafts, stamps, travel, violin making.

* * *

CARROLL, Donald K(ingery) 1909-

PERSONAL: Born April 16, 1909, in Hartington, Neb.; son of Charles Eden (a minister and university professor) and Blanche (Kingery) Carroll. *Education:* Harvard University, A.B., 1930; University of Miami, Miami, Fla., graduate student, 1932-33; University of Florida, J.D., 1935. *Politics:* Democrat. *Religion:* Methodist. *Home:* 100 Cadiz St., Apartment 111, Tallahassee, Fla. 32301.

CAREER: Nation, Boston, Mass., assistant to editor, 1930-31; admitted to bar of Florida, 1935; Milam, McIlvaine, Carroll & Wattles (law firm), Jacksonville, Fla., member of firm, 1938-57; assistant attorney general of Florida, 1941; District Court of Appeal, Tallahassee, Fla., judge, 1957-73, chief judge, 1961-63. Florida Citizenship Clearing House, president, 1958-61. *Military service:* U.S. Army, 1942-46; became captain; received Bronze Star. *Member:* American Bar Association (house of delegates, 1955-59), American Legion (commander, department of Florida, 1951-52), American Judicature Society (executive committee, 1956), National Conference of Bar Presidents (executive council, 1955-56), Florida Bar (president, 1955-56), Jacksonville Bar Association (president, 1949), Jacksonville Junior Chamber of Commerce (president, 1941).

WRITINGS: (Editor) *Handbook for Judges,* American Judicature Society, 1961. Author of pamphlets; contributor to legal journals.

WORK IN PROGRESS: Two books, *The Christian Way of Life* and *Participation by Citizens in Public Affairs.*

* * *

CARTER, Albert Howard 1913-1970

PERSONAL: Born November 10, 1913, in Chicago, Ill.; son of Albert Howard (a physician) and Elizabeth Malcolm (Stewart) Carter; married Marjorie Dargan (a college teacher), July 20, 1940; children: Albert Howard, Avise Elizabeth (Mrs. David Henry Stuart). *Education:* Attended Northwestern University, 1930-31; University of Chicago, Ph.B. and A.M., 1934, Ph.D., 1940. *Religion:* Presbyterian. *Home:* 401 Lake Maggiore Blvd., St. Petersburg, Fla. 33705.

CAREER: University of Chicago, Chicago, Ill., instructor in English, 1935-42; U.S. War Department, Washington, D.C., research analyst, 1942-47; University of Arkansas, Fayetteville, professor, 1947-60, chairman of department of English, 1947-54, chairman of humanities, 1948-60; Florida Presbyterian College (now Eckerd College), St. Petersburg, professor of literature and chairman of Division of Humanities, 1960-70. Fulbright professor, University of Munich, 1963-64. Vice-moderator, Presbyterian Synod of Florida, 1962.

MEMBER: American Council of Learned Societies (regional associate member, 1956-60), Modern Language Association of America, College English Association, Milton

Society of America, Renaissance Society of America, American Association of University Professors, American Civil Liberties Union (president of St. Petersburg branch, 1966-68), South-Central Modern Language Association (vice-president, 1948-49), Ozark Folklore Association (founder, 1949), South-Central Renaissance Conference (founder; president, 1955), Arkansas Folklore Society (president, 1956-57), Florida College English Association (founder; president, 1961), Phi Beta Kappa. *Awards, honors:* Meritorious Civilian Service Award, U.S. Army, 1946; Folger Shakespeare Library fellow, 1946-47; Fund for the Advancement of Education research fellow at University of California, 1954-55.

WRITINGS: Reading Recent American Literature (an English-language reader for German students), Moritz Diesterweg (Frankfurt am Main), 1967; *For Magi, Shepherds, and Us* (poetry), John Knox, 1970. Contributor of articles, stories, poems, and reviews to periodicals. Contributing editor, *Filibuster,* 1946-47, and *Books Abroad;* editorial associate, *Literature East & West,* 1964-67.

WORK IN PROGRESS: Studies of the signification of characters' names in Shakespeare.

SIDELIGHTS: Carter was competent in French, German, Italian, Latin, Sanskrit, Finnish, Old French, Anglo-Saxon, Spanish, and Dutch.†

(Died November 4, 1970)

* * *

CARTER, Paul J(efferson), Jr. 1912-1975

PERSONAL: Born December 9, 1912, in Los Angeles, Calif.; son of Paul Jefferson (a contractor) and Jean (Taylor) Carter; married Adelia Honeywood Pilkington, 1937; children: Adelia Honeywood (Mrs. William Conroy), Karen Webb, Paul J. III. *Education:* Centre College of Kentucky, A.B., 1934; University of Kentucky, M.A., 1935; University of Cincinnati, Ph.D., 1939. *Politics:* Democrat. *Religion:* Protestant. *Home:* 756 18th St., Boulder, Colo. 80302. *Office:* Hellems 105 West, University of Colorado, Boulder, Colo. 80302.

CAREER: DePauw University, Greencastle, Ind., instructor, 1939-41, assistant professor of English, 1941-42; Western Reserve University (now Case Western Reserve University), Cleveland College, Cleveland, Ohio, assistant professor of English, 1946-47; University of Colorado, Boulder, associate professor, 1947-56, professor of English, 1956-75. *Military service:* U.S. Naval Reserve, active duty, served as instructor at U.S. Naval Academy, 1942-46; became lieutenant commander; Inactive Reserve, 1949-67; became commander. *Member:* Modern Language Association of America (served as chairman of bibliography committee of Literature and Society group, and secretary-treasurer of American literature section), American Studies Association, College English Association, Rocky Mountain Modern Language Association. *Awards, honors:* Ford Foundation faculty fellow, 1955-56.

WRITINGS: Waldo Frank, Twayne, 1967; (editor with George K. Smart) *Literature and Society, 1961-1965: A Selective Bibliography,* University of Miami Press, 1967. Contributor to scholarly journals. Editor, *Colorado Quarterly,* 1953-75.

WORK IN PROGRESS: Social and political attitudes of Mark Twain; Waldo Frank and Marxism.

AVOCATIONAL INTERESTS: Tennis, golf.†

(Died March 14, 1975)

CASE, Josephine Young 1907-

PERSONAL: Born February 16, 1907, in Lexington, Mass.; daughter of Owen D. (an industrialist) and Josephine (Edmonds) Young; married Everett Case (president emeritus of Colgate University), June 27, 1931; children: Josephine, James H., Samuel, John P. *Education:* Bryn Mawr College, B.A., 1928; Radcliffe College, M.A., 1934. *Politics:* Democrat. *Religion:* Universalist. *Residence:* Van Hornesville, N.Y. 13475.

CAREER: Bryn Mawr College, Bryn Mawr, Pa., director, 1935-55; Skidmore College, Saratoga Springs, N.Y., chairman of board of trustees, 1960-71. Instructor in English at Colgate University, Hamilton, N.Y., 1961, and New York University, New York, N.Y., 1963-64. Member of board of directors and educational consultant, Radio Corporation of America, 1962-72. Member of board of directors, Fund for the Advancement of Education, 1965-67; member, President's Advisory Committee on Foreign Aid, 1965-69. Also on executive committee of National Book Committee, 1964-70, and trustee of American Assembly. *Awards, honors:* Litt.D. from Elmira College, 1946, Skidmore College, 1957, and St. Lawrence University, 1959; L.H.D. from Colgate University, 1962; Bryn Mawr Alumnae Award.

WRITINGS: At Midnight on the 31st of March (poem), Houghton, 1938; *Written in Sand,* Houghton, 1945; *Freedom's Farm* (poems), Houghton, 1946; *This Very Tree* (novel), Houghton, 1969. Writing anthologized in *America Remembers: Our Best-Loved Customs and Traditions.*

WORK IN PROGRESS: With her husband, Everett Case, a biography of her father, Owen D. Young.

AVOCATIONAL INTERESTS: Nature, travel (has visited forty countries and all fifty states).

BIOGRAPHICAL/CRITICAL SOURCES: Harper's, May, 1969.

* * *

CASE, Maurice 1910-1968

PERSONAL: Born July 4, 1910, in Reims, France; son of Jeral Silbere (a manufacturer) and Dina (Zilbone) Case; married Phyllis Eleanor Shapiro (a supervisor of recreation), January 18, 1936; children: Stephen Michael (died, 1964), Robert Ian. *Education:* City College (now City College of the City University of New York), B.S., 1932; New York School of Social Work, graduate student, 1933-35; New York University, M.A., 1955, Ed.D. (honors), 1963. *Politics:* Democrat. *Religion:* Jewish. *Residence:* New York, N.Y.

CAREER: New York (N.Y.) Department of Welfare, supervisor, 1932-42; New York State Department of Social Welfare, New York, researcher, 1942-45; New York Association for the Blind, New York, manager of recreation and camping services, 1945-65; State University of New York Agricultural and Technical College at Farmingdale, professor of sociology and chairman of department, 1965-68. Lecturer, Center for Instruction in Care of the Aged; assistant professor of health sciences, Kingsborough Community College; consultant, Adult Consultation Center of New York; member of board of directors, New York Association of Senior Centers. Lecturer at Hunter College of the City University of New York. *Member:* National Association of Social Workers, American Association of University Professors, American Sociological Association, Academy of Certified Social Workers, Phi Delta Kappa. *Awards, honors:* New York University Founder's Day Award, 1964; Special Service Award of Phi Delta Kappa, 1966.

WRITINGS: Recreation for Blind Adults, C. C Thomas, 1965. Contributor to journals.

WORK IN PROGRESS: Introductory Sociology, intended for community college students.

AVOCATIONAL INTERESTS: Sailing, scuba diving, skindiving; "to ponder, wonder, discuss, contemplate, advocate greater skepticism."†

(Died May 2, 1968)

* * *

CASTAGNA, Edwin 1909-

PERSONAL: Surname is pronounced Kas-*tah*-nya; born May 1, 1909, in Petaluma, Calif.; son of Frank (a farmer and butcher) and Eugenia (Burgle) Castagna; married Rachel Dent, May 3, 1943. *Education:* Santa Rosa Junior College, Junior Certificate, 1930; University of California, Berkeley, A.B., 1935, Certificate in Librarianship, 1936; graduate study at University of Nevada, 1948-49, Glendale College, 1950, and Long Beach City College, 1951. *Politics:* Democrat. *Home:* 3601 Greenway, Baltimore, Md. 21218. *Office:* Enoch Pratt Free Library, 400 Cathedral St., Baltimore, Md. 21201.

CAREER: Before entering the University of California worked as a merchant seaman, lumber camp worker, construction worker on the Coolidge Dam, and ranch hand; Ukiah (Calif.) Public Library, city librarian, 1937-40; Washoe County (Nev.) Library, director, 1940-49; Glendale (Calif.) Public Library, chief librarian, 1949-50; Long Beach (Calif.) Public Library, city librarian, 1950-60; Enoch Pratt Free Library, Baltimore, Md., director, beginning 1960. University of Southern California, teacher of library administration, 1958-60; University of California School of Librarianship, member of advisory council, 1954-60. *Military service:* U.S. Army, 1942-46; served in Europe with 771st Tank Battalion; became captain; received Bronze Star Medal and Purple Heart.

MEMBER: American Library Association (council, 1948-49, 1956-59; vice-president, 1963-64; president, 1964-65), Adult Education Association of the U.S.A., American Association for the United Nations (president, Long Beach, 1956-57; member of board of directors, Maryland, 1965), California Library Association (president, 1954), Nevada Library Association (president, 1946-47). Maryland Library Association, Maryland Historical Society, Maryland Academy of Sciences, Citizens Planning and Housing Association of Baltimore, Union de Bibliofilos Taurinos, Rotary Club, 14 West Hamilton Street Club, Baltimore Bibliofiles. *Awards, honors:* Edna H. Yelland Award, 1965, for article, "Why Is It Always So Bad in California?" in *California Librarian.*

WRITINGS: History of the 771st Tank Battalion, Lederer Street & Zeus, 1946; (editor with Kate Coplan and contributor) *The Library Reaches Out,* Oceana, 1965; *Three Who Met the Challenge: Joseph L. Wheeler, Lawrence Clark Powell, Frances Clarke Sayers,* Peacock, 1965; *Long, Warm Friendship: H. L. Mencken and the Enoch Pratt Free Library,* Peacock, 1966. Contributor to library journals.

SIDELIGHTS: Castagna told *CA:* "Among books that had a special influence on me are: Tolstoi's *War and Peace,* Richard Harding Davis' *Two Years Before the Mast,* Walt Whitman's *Leaves of Grass,* Mark Twain's books, John Steinbeck's *Grapes of Wrath,* Galbraith's *The Affluent Society,* and Walter Prescott Webb's *The Great Frontier,* in addition to many others. As a Californian transplanted to Baltimore, I find myself increasingly interested in the history and literature of this area, and especially in H. L. Mencken." He told Lawrence Clark Powell: "From my reading I have learned to admire courage, compassion, and charity. In books I have found myself as I am and as I would like to be. Everything I read adds something to my understanding. Life without books would be intolerable."

Castagna mentions special interest in "peace, good government, and investigating other parts of the world." He has traveled extensively throughout the United States and Canada, and has visited the South Seas, Mexico, Guatemala, Europe, Peru, Ecuador, Bolivia, Europe, and North and East Africa, and South Asia. He has "small competence in spoken German and ability to read French if it is not too technical." *Avocational interests:* Travel, bullfighting, collecting literature on bullfighting.

BIOGRAPHICAL/CRITICAL SOURCES: Baltimore Morning Sun, April 15, 1960; *Wilson Library Bulletin,* September, 1963.

* * *

CASTLE, Marian (Johnson)

PERSONAL: Born in Kendall County, Ill.; daughter of Oliver C. (a Presbyterian minister) and Anna (an author and lecturer; maiden name, French) Johnson; married Edward Carrick Castle, May 24, 1924. *Education:* Attended Carroll Academy and College and Millikin University; University of Chicago, Ph.B., 1920. *Religion:* Presbyterian. *Home:* 933 West Bonita Ave., Claremont, Calif. *Agent:* Paul R. Reynolds, Inc., 12 East 41st St., New York, N.Y. 10017.

CAREER: Handled publicity for summer concert and lecture tours, 1918-19; Young Women's Christian Association, Albuquerque, N.M., general secretary, 1921-22; free-lance writer for magazines, beginning 1930. *Member:* National League of American Pen Women (Claremont branch), Colorado Authors League, Denver Woman's Press Club, Zeta Tau Alpha. *Awards, honors:* Alumni Merit Award from Millikin University, 1962; honorary Litt.D. from Carroll College, 1950; numerous Tophand Awards from Colorado Authors League.

WRITINGS—Novels: *Deborah,* Morrow, 1946; *The Golden Fury,* Morrow, 1949; *Roxana,* Morrow, 1955; *Silver Answer,* Morrow, 1960. Contributor of stories and articles to magazines, including *Harper's, Atlantic Monthly, Forum, Woman's Home Companion, Liberty, Collier's, Good Housekeeping, Better Homes and Gardens, Reader's Digest.*

WORK IN PROGRESS: Short pieces for magazines.

SIDELIGHTS: Mrs. Castle's first novel, *Deborah,* was serialized in *Woman's Home Companion* and translated into seven foreign languages; *Silver Answer* was published in Dutch and made into a talking book for the blind. Her novel, *Golden Fury,* was the selection of five different book clubs.

* * *

CATTAUI, Georges 1896-1974
(Michel Francis)

PERSONAL: Surname is pronounced *Cata*-we; born September 14, 1896, in Paris, France; son of Adolphe (an Egyptologist) and Rachel (Francis) Cattaui. *Education:* Attended Lycee Carnot, Paris, 1910-13; Universite de Paris, faculte de Droit de Paris, Bachelier es-lettres, 1914, Licencie en droit, 1917; Ecole libre des sciences politiques, Diplome, 1925; University of Fribourg, theological studies, 1939-46.

Politics: Gaullist. *Religion:* Roman Catholic. *Home:* 7 rue Clement Marot, Paris 8e, France. *Agent:* A. J. Pilet, 66 avenue Victor Hugo, Paris, France.

CAREER: Secretary of Egyptian legation in Prague, Czechoslovakia, 1925, Bucharest, Romania, 1926-27, and London, England, 1927-35; author and poet. *Awards, honors:* Prix Femina-Vacaresco, 1953, for *Marcel Proust;* prizes of French Academy, 1958, for *T. S. Eliot,* and 1966, for *Orphisme et Prophetie;* Prix du Rayounement Francais, 1970.

WRITINGS: L'Amitie de Proust (with a letter from Paul Morand and a previously unpublished letter from Marcel Proust), Gallimard, 1935; (contributor with Paul Claudel and others) *Les Juifs* (symposium), [Paris], 1937; *Charles De Gaulle* (biography), Portes de France, 1944, revised and enlarged edition, 1946; *Symbole de la France: Le Mistere francais—Louis et l'ordre temporel chretien,* Neuchatel, 1944; *La Terre visitee,* Egloff (Paris), 1945; *Trois poetes* (Hopkins, Yeats, Eliot), Librairie Universelle de France, 1947; *Outre nuit* (poems), G.L.M., 1948; (with Rene Cattaui) *Mohammed Aly et l'Europe,* Geuthner (Paris), 1950; *Marcel Proust: Proust et son temps, Proust et le temps,* preface by Henri Daniel-Rops, Julliard, 1952; *Leon Bloy,* Editions Universitaires, 1954; (editor and author of preface and notes) Marcel Proust, *Documents iconographiques,* P. Cailler (Geneva), 1956; *T. S. Eliot,* Editions Universitaires, 1957, translation by Claire Pace and Jean Stewart published under same title, Funk, 1966; *Marcel Proust,* foreword by Pierre de Boisdeffre, Editions Universitaires, 1958, revised edition, 1971, translation by Ruth Hall published under same title, Merlin Press, 1966, Funk, 1968.

Charles DeGaulle: L'Homme et son destin, Fayard, 1960; *Saint Bernard de Clairvaux; ou, L'Esprit du Cantique des cantiques,* Gabalda (Paris), 1960, translation by Ena Dargan published as *Saint Bernard of Clairvaux,* Burns & Oates, 1966; (with Pierre Bourget) *Jules Hardouin Mansart,* Vincent, Freal (Paris), 1960; (with Maurice Hubert Raval) *Claude-Nicolas Ledoux, 1736-1806,* Electa Editrice (Milan), 1961; *L'Architettura Barocca,* Editrice Studium (Rome), 1962; *Proust perdu et retrouve,* Plon, 1963; *Peguy, temoin du temporel chretien,* Editions du Centurion (Paris), 1964; (author of introduction) Konstantinos Kabaphes, *Constantin Cavafy,* Seghers, 1964; *Orphisme et prophetie chez les poetes francais, 1850-1950* (Hugo, Nerval Baudelaire, Mallarme, Rimbaud, Valery, Claudel), Plon, 1965; (contributor) *Entretiens sur Marcel Proust,* Mouton (Paris), 1966; (editor with E. de LaRochefoucauld and A. Lanoux) *Claire Goll,* Seghers, 1967; *Claudel: Le Cycle des Coufontaine et le Mystere d'Israel,* Desclee de brouwer, 1968; *Proust et ses metamorphoses,* A. G. Nizet, 1972; *Baroque et rococo,* Arthaud, 1973.

Also author with Jean Mauriac of *Charles DeGaulle,* Plon; wrote script for film on architect Jules Hardouin Mansart, 1955. Contributor to periodicals under pseudonym Michel Francis.

WORK IN PROGRESS: Gerard Manley Hopkins; Recollections.

SIDELIGHTS: There have been German, Spanish, and Italian editions of several of Cattaui's books.†

(Died July, 1974)

*   *   *

CAUMAN, Samuel   1910-1971

PERSONAL: Surname is pronounced "common"; born June 29, 1910, in Boston, Mass.; son of Meyer (a manufacturer) and Anne (Waldstein) Cauman; married Leigh Davis Steinhardt (an editor), October 13, 1940; children: Thomas Edward, John Henry. *Education:* Harvard University, A.B., 1931, A.M., 1940; Massachusetts Institute of Technology, student, 1929-30. *Politics:* "Left of center." *Religion:* Jewish. *Home:* 420 Riverside Dr., New York, N.Y. 10025.

CAREER: Plays, Inc., Boston, Mass., assistant to publisher, 1940-42; Coolidge, Shepley, Bulfinch & Abbott, Boston, architectural draftsman, 1942; Submarine Signal Co., Boston, director of publications, 1943-46; Cauman & Pfeufer, Inc., Boston, creative director, 1946-50; New York University, New York, N.Y., research scientist in graphic arts, 1956-61; writer, free-lance editor, and typographer. An editor, Harry N. Abrams, Inc. (publisher), New York, N.Y., 1958-60. Lecturer in visual design, Boston University. Consultant, American-Scandinavian Foundation.

WRITINGS: The Living Museum, New York University Press, 1958; *Jonah Bondi Wise,* Crown, 1967; (with H. W. Janson and D. J. Janson) *Short History of Art,* Abrams, 1969; (with H. W. Janson) *History of Art for Young People,* Abrams, 1971; (with H. W. Janson) *A Basic History of Art,* Prentice-Hall, 1973. Assistant editor, *Harper's Encyclopedia of Art.*

WORK IN PROGRESS: Discovering Art, for Abrams; a study and biography of Gyorgy Kepes.

BIOGRAPHICAL/CRITICAL SOURCES: New York Times, March 7, 1971.†

(Died March 6, 1971)

*   *   *

CAVANAGH, John Richard   1904-

PERSONAL: Born July 21, 1904, in Brooklyn, N.Y.; son of Richard A. and Mary (Powers) Cavanagh; married Alberta Barth, October 17, 1933; children: Patricia Louise (Mrs. Harry Anger), Judith Ann, Maria Antonia (Mrs. William Johnson). *Education:* Georgetown University, B.S., 1928, M.D., 1930; postdoctoral study at University of Pennsylvania, 1944, and School of Tropical Medicine, 1945. *Religion:* Roman Catholic. *Office:* 3225 Garfield St. N.W., Washington, D.C. 20008.

CAREER: Diplomate, American Board of Neurology and Psychiatry, 1949. Providence Hospital, Washington, D.C., intern, 1930-31; Georgetown University, School of Medicine, Washington, D.C., assistant in clinical research, 1931-33, associate clinical professor of medicine, 1935-36; Georgetown University Hospital, Washington, D.C., Medical Service, 1933-46, chief of Medical Service, 1945-46; Washington Hospital Center, Washington, D.C., chief of department of psychiatry, 1962-64; physician in private practice of psychiatry, Washington, D.C., beginning, 1931. National Catholic School of Social Service, lecturer in medicine, 1933-42, in psychiatry, 1945-47; lecturer in medicine, Georgetown Dental College, 1934-38; special lecturer, Catholic University of America, School of Religious Studies, beginning, 1939; lecturer in mental hygiene, Trinity College, 1954-61. Member of Papal Commission on Birth Control, beginning, 1964. *Military service:* U.S. Naval Reserve, 1941-45; transferred to regular Navy, 1947, resigning, 1950; U.S. Naval Reserve, commander, 1950-60.

MEMBER: American Medical Association, American Psychiatric Association (fellow), American College of Physicians (fellow), Guild of Catholic Psychiatrists (executive committee, 1955-70; treasurer, 1959-70), World Federation for Mental Health, National Federation of Catholic Physicians' Guilds (president, beginning, 1974), Southern Medical Association, and local medical societies, International Club of Washington, Columbia Country Club (Chevy Chase). *Awards, honors:* Knight of St. Gregory the Great (Papal honor), 1941, and Knight Commander, 1961; Vicennial Medal, Georgetown University Medical School, 1953; Benemerenti Medal, 1964.

WRITINGS: (With James B. McGoldrick) *Fundamental Psychiatry,* Bruce, 1953, revised edition, 1966; *Fundamental Pastoral Counseling: Technic and Psychology,* Bruce, 1962; *Fundamental Marriage Counseling: A Catholic Viewpoint,* Bruce, 1963; *The Popes, the Pill, and the People,* Bruce, 1965; *Counseling the Invert,* Bruce, 1966. Contributor to medical journals. *Bulletin* of Guild of Catholic Psychiatrists, associate editor, 1952-58, editor, 1958-70; associate editor, *Linacre Quarterly* of National Federation of Catholic Physicians' Guilds.

*　*　*

CAWLEY, Robert Ralston 1893-1973

PERSONAL: Born July 18, 1893, in Canasaraga, N.Y.; son of Frank Edward (a miller) and Sarah Haseltine (Brown) Cawley; married Elizabeth Hoon (a visiting professor of English at Rider College), September 18, 1937; children: Margaret Elizabeth. *Education:* Harvard University, A.B., 1914, A.M. (with honors), 1915, Ph.D., 1921; postdoctoral study at University of London, University of Berlin, and University of Paris, 1921-22. *Politics:* Independent. *Religion:* Presbyterian (elder). *Home:* 228 Western Way, Princeton, N.J. 08540. *Office:* Rider College, Trenton, N.J. 08602.

CAREER: Thacher School, Ojai, Calif., master of French, German, and Spanish, 1915-18; Massachusetts Institute of Technology, Cambridge, instructor in French, German, and Spanish, 1919-20; Princeton University, Princeton, N.J., instructor, 1922-25, assistant professor, 1925-27, associate professor, 1927-44, professor of English, 1944-62, acting chairman of department, 1948-49, 1951-52; City University of New York (now City College of the City University of New York), New York, N.Y., distinguished professor, 1962-63; Rider College, Trenton, N.J., visiting professor of English, 1963-73. Researcher in British Museum, 1921-22, 1929-31, 1933-34, 1935, 1939, 1949, and at Bodleian, 1955. *Military service:* U.S. Army, Quartermaster Reserve Corps, 1918; became second lieutenant.

MEMBER: Modern Language Association of America (chairman of advisory board, 1947, 1951; chairman of Milton group, 1948), American Association of University Professors, London Scholars Group of American University Union (president), Alpha Phi Sigma, Princeton Club. *Awards, honors:* Harvard traveling fellowship, 1921-22.

WRITINGS: The Voyagers and Elizabethan Drama, Oxford University Press, 1938; *Unpathed Waters: Studies in the Influence of the Voyagers on Elizabethan Literature,* Princeton University Press, 1940; *Milton's Literary Craftsmanship,* Princeton University Press, 1941; (editor) Henry Peacham, *Truth of Our Times,* Columbia University Press, 1942; *Milton and the Literature of Travel,* Princeton University Press, 1951; (with George Yost) *Studies in Sir Thomas Browne,* University of Oregon Press, 1965; (with Arthur Link) *The First Presbyterian Church of Princeton: Two Centuries of History,* Princeton University Press, 1967; *Henry Peacham: His Contribution to English Poetry,* Pennsylvania State University Press, 1971. Contributor to *Encyclopaedia Britannica,* and to professional journals, including

Journal of Historical Studies, PMLA, and *Studies in Philology.*†

(Died May 11, 1973)

*　*　*

CERF, Bennett (Alfred) 1898-1971

PERSONAL: Born May 25, 1898, in New York, N.Y.; son of Gustave (a lithographer) and Fredericka (Wise) Cerf; married Sylvia Sidney, 1935 (divorced); married Phyllis Fraser (an editor), 1940; children: (second marriage) Christopher Bennett, Jonathan Fraser. *Education:* Columbia University, A.B., 1919; Columbia School of Journalism, Litt.B., 1920. *Home:* 132 East 62nd St., New York, N.Y.; Orchard Rd., Mt. Kisco, N.Y. *Office:* 457 Madison Ave., New York, N.Y. 10022.

CAREER: New York Herald Tribune, reporter, and New York Stock Exchange, clerk, 1921-23; Boni and Liveright (publishers), New York, N.Y., vice-president, 1923-25; Modern Library, Inc. (publishers), New York, N.Y., founder, and president, 1925-70; Random House, Inc. (publishers), New York, N.Y., founder with Donald S. Klopfer, and president, 1927-66, chairman of the board, 1966-70. Director, Bantam Books, New York, N.Y., 1945-67. Panelist on "What's My Line," Columbia Broadcasting System, 1952-67; Peabody Awards Committee, member, 1950-67, 69-70, chairman, 1955-67; member of board of directors, Metro-Goldwyn-Mayer, Inc., and Alfred A. Knopf, Inc. *Military service:* Served in Officers Training Corps, 1918. *Member:* Overseas Press Club, Pi Lambda Phi, Phi Beta Kappa, Pi Delta Epsilon, Dutch Treat, Century Country Club (both New York). *Awards, honors:* New York Philanthropic League, Distinguished Service Award, 1964.

WRITINGS: Good For a Laugh: A New Collection of Humorous Tidbits and Anecdotes From Aardvark to Zythum, Hanover House, 1952; *New Book of Jokes,* Maco Magazine Corp., 1958; *Bennett Cerf's Best Jokes,* edited by Haskel Frankel, Maco Magazine Corp., 1959; *Book of Laughs,* Beginner Books, 1959; *Book of Riddles,* Beginner Books, 1960; *More Riddles,* Beginner Books, 1961; *Bennett Cerf's Little Riddle Book,* Random House, 1964; *Book of Animal Riddles,* Beginner Books, 1964; *Silliest Pop-Up Riddles,* Random House, 1967; *Bennett Cerf's Treasury of Atrocious Puns,* Harper, 1968; *Bennett Cerf's The Sound of Laughter,* Doubleday, 1970; *Just For Fun: A Collection of Bennett Cerf's Best Stories,* Stanyan Books, 1971; *Stories to Make You Feel Better,* introduction by John Charles Daly, Random House, 1972.

Editor: *Great German Short Novels and Stories,* Modern Library, 1933; (with Henry C. Moriarty) *The Bedside Book of Famous British Stories,* Random House, 1940, reissued as *An Anthology of Famous British Stories,* Modern Library, 1952; (with Van H. Cartmell) *Sixteen Famous American Plays,* Garden City, 1941; *The Pocket Book of Modern American Plays,* Pocket Books, 1942; (with Cartmell) *Sixteen Famous British Plays,* Garden City, 1942; *Great Modern Short Stories,* Modern Library, 1942; *The Pocket Book of War Humor,* Pocket Books, 1943; *The Pocket Book of Cartoons,* Pocket Books, 1943; (with Cartmell) *Fifteen Famous European Plays,* Random House, 1943; (with Cartmell) *Thirty Famous One-Act Plays,* Modern Library, 1943; *Famous Ghost Stories,* Random House, 1944; *Try and Stop Me: A Collection of Anecdotes and Stories, Mostly Humorous,* Simon & Schuster, 1944; *S.R.O.: The Most Successful Plays in The History of the American Stage,* Doubleday, Doran, 1944; *Laughing Stock,* Grosset & Dunlap, 1945; *The*

Pocket Book of Jokes, Pocket Books, 1945; *Modern American Short Stories,* World Publishing Co., 1945; (with Cartmell) *Famous Plays of Crime and Detection, from Sherlock Holmes to Angel Street,* Blakiston, 1946; *Anything For a Laugh,* Grosset & Dunlap, 1946; *The Unexpected,* Bantam, 1948; *Shake Well Before Using: A New Collection of Impressions and Anecdotes Mostly Humorous,* Simon & Schuster, 1948.

Laughter, Incorporated: The Cream of the Recent Crop of Stories and Anecdotes, Harvested, Assorted and Prepared for Market, Garden City, 1950; (with John Angus Burrell) *An Anthology of Famous American Stories,* Modern Library, 1953; *An Encyclopedia of Modern American Humor,* Doubleday, 1954; *The Life of the Party,* Hanover House, 1956; *Vest Pocket Book for All Occasions,* Random House, 1956; *Reading for Pleasure,* Harper, 1957; *Jokes of the Year, 1957,* MACO Magazine Corp., 1957; (with Cartmell) *24 Favorite One-Act Plays,* Doubleday, 1958; *The Laugh's on Me,* Doubleday, 1959; *Bennett Cerf's Bumper Crop of Anecdotes and Stories, Mostly Humorous, About the Famous and Near Famous,* Garden City, 1959; *The Arabian Nights' Entertainments,* Modern Library, 1959; *Out on a Limerick: A Collection of over 300 of the World's Best Printable Limericks, Assembled, Revised, Dry-Cleaned, and Annotated by Mister Cerf,* Harper, 1960; *Four Contemporary American Plays,* Vintage, 1961; *Six American Plays for Today,* Modern Library, 1961; *Riddle-De-Dee: 458, Count Them, 458 Riddles Old and New for Children from 12 to 112,* Random House, 1962; *Houseful of Laughter,* Random House, 1963; (with Leonora Hornblow) *Bennett Cerf's Take Along Treasury,* Doubleday, 1963; *An Anthology of Famous American Stories,* Modern Library, 1963; *Great Modern Short Stories,* Vintage, 1966; *Plays of Our Time,* Random House, 1967; *Bennett Cerf's Pop-Up Limericks,* Random House, 1967. Wrote daily feature, "Try and Stop Me," for King Features Syndicate. Contributor to *This Week* Magazine and *Saturday Review.*

SIDELIGHTS: Random House began when Mr. Cerf and Mr. Klopfer purchased 109 Modern Library titles from the publishing firm of Boni & Liveright. This venture made literary classics easily available to the U.S. public. With the formation of the publishing firm, Cerf immediately sought the current literary giants. He signed Eugene O'Neill and Robinson Jeffers and then sailed to Europe to see James Joyce about the publication of *Ulysses* in the U.S. Upon his return, his copy of the book was promptly seized at customs and with an attorney, Morris Ernst, Cerf took the case to court. The historic decision by Judge John Woolsey was not only a victory for Cerf; it also proved to be a landmark in the struggle against censorship.

"Every publisher," said Cerf, "thinks of himself as an idealist, although the idealism is in the back of his head." Cerf tried to fulfill his idealistic responsibility "by publishing poetry, belles-lettres, the first novels you know won't sell a copy. We do two or three of those a year." Nevertheless he conceded that "it's awfully hard to turn down a book that's going to make money. If I thought nobody else was going to publish it, it wouldn't matter. But the thought that if I don't, somebody else will—I can't stand that. Besides, the real excitement is having somebody new come along, helping him get famous and watching him move to Hollywood and start calling me a son of a bitch." Jason Epstein, W. H. Auden's editor, explained: "Bennett runs Random House as a conservative branch of show business. The company is vulgar to a degree. But what makes the difference with Bennett is how important he feels it is to have Philip Roth and William

Styron on the list. Some other publisher would know a thousand ways to get rich without having one author like that. Bennett Cerf doesn't."

Cerf spent a good deal of his time coddling his authors. One of his temperamental clients was Sinclair Lewis. Once, when Lewis spent the night at Cerf's apartment, "Bill Faulkner called up and said he was in town," commented Cerf. "I told Lewis and asked him, could Bill come over? Lewis said, 'Certainly not. This is my night!' Then at 9:30, Lewis went to bed. At 10:30, he shouted downstairs, 'Bennett!' I answered him, and he said, ' I just wanted to see if you sneaked out to see Faulkner'."

A *New York Times* writer estimated that Bennett Cerf "differed from both his ivory-tower predecessors and his contemporaries. One of these was his avid engagement in non-publishing activities, chiefly "What's My Line?," on which he started in 1951. The show, in which panelists attempted to guess the occupation of various guests, made Mr. Cerf a national celebrity. "I have to remind people I'm a publisher," he once said as he was being sought out for his autograph.

BIOGRAPHICAL/CRITICAL SOURCES: New York Times, December 7, 1965; *Time,* December 16, 1966.†

(Died August 27, 1971)

*   *   *

CERF, Jay H(enry) 1923-1974

PERSONAL: Born May 17, 1923, in Chicago, Ill.; son of Norman Randolph (a businessman) and Blanche (Ruth) Cerf; married Carol Montgomery McGovern, June 13, 1951; children: Jay Randolph, Christopher David, William Montgomery. *Education:* University of Wisconsin, B.A., 1948, M.A., 1951; Yale University, M.A., 1952, Ph.D., 1957; studied abroad at University of Heidelberg, 1949, and Free University of Berlin, 1953-54. *Religion:* Episcopalian. *Home:* 3521 Ordway St. N.W., Washington, D.C. *Office:* Chamber of Commerce of the United States, 1615 H St. N.W., Washington, D.C. 20006.

CAREER: U.S. government, Washington, D.C., research analyst, 1949-51, legislative assistant to Congress, 1955-56; Foreign Policy Clearing House, Washington, D.C., director, 1957-61; U.S. Department of Commerce, Washington, D.C., special assistant to Secretary of Commerce, 1961, deputy assistant secretary of commerce for international affairs, 1961-62; Chamber of Commerce of the United States, Washington, D.C., secretary of U.S.-Mexico and foreign policy committees, 1962-74. Secretary of U.S. management advisory committee to Organization for Economic Co-operation and Development; trustee of U.S. Council of International Chamber of Commerce and U.S. Inter-American Council. *Military service:* U.S. Naval Reserve, active duty, 1943-46.

MEMBER: American Academy of Political and Social Science, American Political Science Association, Washington Institute of Foreign Affairs, National Press Club, Yale Club. *Awards, honors:* Fulbright fellowship to Germany, 1953-54.

WRITINGS: The Intellectual Basis of Nazism, 1951; *History of the Free University,* 1954; (editor with Walter Pozen) *Strategy for the 60's,* Praeger, 1961. Also editor of *A Strategic Doctrine of East-West Trade.*†

(Died August 15, 1974)

CERUTTY, Percy Wells 1895-1975

PERSONAL: Surname rhymes with "rarity"; born January 10, 1895, in Victoria, Australia; son of Harry and Emily (Nielsen) Cerutty; married Dorothy Barwell, November 11, 1921 (divorced); married Nancy Armstrong, March 10, 1955; children: Nielson Arnold. ("Never believed this world was worth bringing a child into. Took fine care never [to have] another. Have *adopted* several since.") *Education:* Self-educated, mostly at night schools. ("Realised: if one has a good brain: better never to have been to a University.") *Politics:* "Revolutionary Anarchist (natural radical). Do not have faith in the extremes, *viz:* capitalism, communism. Believe in profit sharing and incentives." *Religion:* "Christian Atheist. ALL religions have something: NO religion has the lot." *Home:* Hotham Road, Portsea Village, Victoria, Australia 3944.

CAREER: Educated and employed at managerial level in the telephone industry; became dissatisfied and tried many occupations, among them business managerial consultant, investor, owner of a women's apparel shop ("could have made a 'million' but tired of it"), laborer, free-lance journalist, and lecturer at universities. In early 1960's worked for a year doing a "strong man act" in stores all over Australia. Administrator of International Athletic Centre, Portsea Village, Victoria. "Spent most of my life studying and experimenting. To hear of a thing was for me to master it. Hence studies as to business, science, etc. Believe over a long lifetime a man with brains can master many things." Regarding *military service:* "Hate the military and all associated with it. Consider any and all who can accept or tolerate the military and similar as sub-normal in fundamental intelligence." *Memberships:* "None: I am a natural loner. On the whole I don't need people, saviours, heavenly fathers; heavens, rewards, nothing. Live above all such." *Awards, honors:* Received a gold medal at the Tokyo Games in recognition of his work in athletics.

WRITINGS: Running with Cerutty, [Los Angeles], 1959; *Athletics: How to Become a Champion,* Stanley Paul, 1960; *Schoolboy Athletics,* Stanley Paul, 1963; *Middle-Distance Running,* Pelham, 1964; *Sport Is My Life,* Stanley Paul, 1966; *Be Fit! Or Be Damned!,* Pelham, 1967; *Success: In Sport and Life,* Pelham, 1967. Contributor of articles about athletics, philosophy, musical criticism, and other topics, to numerous magazines.

WORK IN PROGRESS: Three books, *A New Approach to Athletics and Sport,* one book on disease and medicine, and another on Japan. "I have many hundreds of thousands of words written, but do not get time to get ready for publication: many subjects, including the Origin and Nature of the Universe, and on the Nature of women, love and marriage, etc."

SIDELIGHTS: Cerutty told *CA:* "I have done most things and been most places. I am a natural truth seeker and student, chronic migraine sufferer, and a ceaseless worker. I am very interested in political affairs, was a personal friend of the late Harold Holt (Prime Minister of Australia), and can be said to know, or have known, most of the top political big shots in Australia.

"I belong to no political party, no clubs or organizations. I am completely universal and cosmopolitan in my nature and ideas, and realise that all religious dogmas, political doctrines, nationalisms and racialisms, essential as they would appear to be for many, have no place in my ideas, nature, consciousness. All they do is *separate* people."

Cerutty also mentioned his home, "where I conduct the International Athletic Centre: visited by athletes, and others, from many countries (many from the U.S.A.), including the coach of the great middle-distance runner Jim Ryun. Every Australian in the athletic history of Australia to set a world record has visited the I.A.C. at Portsea. Believe that my teachings and techniques will revolutionise athletics and sport generally when fully understood."

At the age of 43, Cerutty had a severe physical breakdown. He wrote: "I was hardly able to walk a mile and unable to run 20 yards at any slow pace. I pulled myself out of this by studying medicine, naturalism and natural diet . . . and completely rebuilt my physical body. . . . I became so enthused that I started to run seriously and eight years after this breakdown (when it was thought by the doctors I would never work again and I felt I wouldn't live another two years), I found myself the Native Victorian Marathon Champion and record-holder at 51 years of age. I went on to set the best times then recorded in Australia for 30, 50, and 60 miles and am one of four Australians to cover 100 or better miles in 24 hours or less."

Cerutty concluded: "I look upon another 20 to 25 years of work and activity as normal for me. Retirement is similar to suicide: I banish the idea completely. REAL Men, that is, truly masculine men, die in harness—when they are sick to death of the idiocies of this so-called civilization."

BIOGRAPHICAL/CRITICAL SOURCES: Graeme Kelly, *Mr. Controversial: The Life of Percy Wells Cerutty,* Stanley Paul, 1964.†

(Died August 14, 1975)

* * *

CHADWICK, Lester
[Collective pseudonym]

WRITINGS—All published by Cupples & Leon: "Baseball Joe" series: *Baseball Joe on the School Nine,* 1912; . . . *of the Silver Stars,* 1912; . . . *at Yale,* 1913; . . . *in the World Series,* 1917; . . . *Home Run King,* 1922; . . . *Captain of the Team,* 1924; . . . *Champion of the League,* 1925; . . . *Pitching Wizard,* 1928.

"College Sports" series: *The Rival Pitchers: A Story of College Baseball,* 1910; *A Quarter-Back's Pluck,* 1910; *Winning Touchdown,* 1911; *Batting to Win,* 1911; *For the Honor of Randall,* 1912; *The Eight-Oared Victors,* 1913.

SIDELIGHTS: See ADAMS, Harriet S., STRATEMEYER, Edward L., and SVENSON, Andrew E.†

* * *

CHALMERS, Floyd S(herman) 1898-
(John Duke)

PERSONAL: Born September 14, 1898, in Chicago, Ill.; son of James Keeler (a salesman) and Anna (Dusing) Chalmers; married Jean A. Boxall, April 28, 1921; children: Wallace G., Margaret Joan. *Education:* Attended high school in Ontario, Canada, and college in Ripon, England. *Home:* Apartment 4611, 44 Charles St. W., Toronto, Ontario, Canada M4Y 1R8. *Office:* Room 805, 481 University Ave., Toronto, Ontario, Canada M5W 1A7.

CAREER: Toronto World and *Toronto News,* Toronto, Ontario, reporter, 1916-17; *Financial Post,* Toronto, reporter, 1919-25, editor, 1925-42; Maclean-Hunter Ltd. (magazine publishers), Toronto, executive vice-president, 1942-52, president, 1952-64, chairman of board, 1964-69. Director of Clarke, Irwin & Co., Toronto, 1969-74, Macmillan of

Canada, beginning 1974, Karsh of Ottawa Ltd., and Little Wings Ltd. Chancellor, York University, 1967-72. President, Canadian Opera Company, 1957-61; president, Stratford Shakespearean Festival Foundation, 1965-67; chairman, Floyd S. Chalmers Foundation (performing arts). *Military service:* Canadian Army, Tanks, 1917-19; served overseas.

MEMBER: Canadian Club (president, 1932-33), Empire Club, York Club, Toronto Golf Club, Ticker Club (founding president, 1929-30). *Awards, honors:* LL.D. from University of Western Ontario, 1962, Waterloo Lutheran University, 1963; Litt.D. from Trent University, 1968; Liveryman of Worshipful Company of Stationers and Newspapermakers (London); Freeman of City of London; B.F.A., York University, 1973; Diplome d'Honneur, Canadian Conference of the Arts, Canadian News Hall of Fame, 1975.

WRITINGS: A Gentleman of the Press (biography of John Bayne Maclean), Doubleday, 1969. Contributor of articles to newspapers, magazines, and business publications, many under pseudonym John Duke.

WORK IN PROGRESS: An autobiography.

*   *   *

CHAMBERLAIN, Samuel   1895-1975
(Phineas Beck)

PERSONAL: Born October 28, 1895, in Cresco, Iowa; son of George Ellsworth (a surgeon) and Cora Lee (Summers) Chamberlain; married Narcissa Gellatly (a writer), April 23, 1923; children: Narcisse, Stephanie. *Education:* Studied at University of Washington, Seattle, 1913-15, Massachusetts Institute of Technology, 1915-17, 1919-20, in Paris with Edouard Leon, 1925, and at Royal College of Art, London, 1926-27. *Politics:* Democrat. *Religion:* Episcopalian. *Home and studio:* 5 Tucker St., Marblehead, Mass. 01945.

CAREER: Traveled in Europe and contributed to architectural magazines, 1919-25; University of Michigan, Ann Arbor, assistant professor of architecture, 1925-26; full-time writer and illustrator, 1926-75. Lecturer in graphic arts at Massachusetts Institute of Technology, 1931-40. Work is represented in Bibliotheque Nationale (Paris), Art Institute of Chicago, Library of Congress, British Museum, Victoria and Albert Museum, and elsewhere. *Military service:* U.S. Army, ambulance driver attached to French Army Air Forces, 1917-18; received Croix de Guerre. U.S. Army Air Forces, 1943-45; became major; received Legion of Merit and Bronze Star.

MEMBER: National Academy of Design, Society of American Graphic Artists, American Academy of Arts and Sciences (fellow), Photographic Society of America (associate member), Societe de la Gravure Originale en Noir, Phi Delta Theta. *Awards, honors:* Honorable mention, Paris Salon, 1925; Guggenheim fellowship, 1926; Society of American Etchers, Kate W. Arms prize, 1933, and John Taylor Arms prize, 1936; M.A., Marlboro College, 1968; Chevalier de la Legion d'honneur (France); Stella della Solidarieta (Italy); special award, National Trust for Historic Preservation.

WRITINGS—Self-illustrated with photographs, except as noted; published by Hastings House, except as noted: *Tudor Homes of England* (illustrated with sketches and photographs), Architectural Book Publishing, 1929; *Through France with a Sketchbook* (illustrated with drawings), McBride, 1929.

An Architect Revisits France, Ludowici-Celadon, 1932; *A*

Small House in the Sun: The Visage of Rural New England, 1936, special anniversary edition, 1971; *Beyond New England Thresholds,* 1937; *Open House in New England,* S. Daye, 1937, 5th revised edition, Hastings House, 1948; *Cape Cod in the Sun,* 1937; *Historic Boston in Four Seasons,* 1938; *Gloucester and Cape Ann,* 1938; *Historic Salem in Four Seasons,* 1938; *Longfellow's Wayside Inn,* 1938; *New England Doorways,* 1939; *Nantucket,* 1939; *Lexington and Concord,* 1939.

Portsmouth, New Hampshire, 1940; *Old Marblehead,* 1940; *France Will Live Again: The Portrait of a Peaceful Interlude, 1919-1939* (illustrated with etchings, lithographs, sketches, and photographs), 1940; *The Coast of Maine,* 1941; *Martha's Vineyard,* 1941; (editor and designer) *This Realm, This England: The Citadel of a Valiant Race Portrayed by Its Greatest Etchers,* 1941; *Historic Cambridge in Four Seasons,* 1942; (editor and designer) *Fair Is Our Land,* 1942, 8th edition, 1967; (under pseudonym Phineas Beck) *Clementine in the Kitchen,* 1943, 9th revised and enlarged edition, 1963; *Ever New England,* 1944; *Behold Williamsburg: A Pictorial Tour of Virginia's Colonial Capital,* 1947; *Springtime in Virginia,* 1947; (editor) *Rockefeller Center: A Photographic Narrative,* 1948, 2nd revised edition, 1961; *Six New England Villages,* 1948.

Salem Interiors: Two Centuries of New England Taste and Decoration, 1950; *Princeton in Spring,* 1950; *Old Sturbridge Village,* 1951; (with wife, Narcissa Chamberlain as translator and adapter of French recipes) *Bouquet de France: An Epicurean Tour of the French Provinces,* Gourmet Books, 1952, 2nd revised edition, 1966; (with Henry N. Flynt) *Frontier of Freedom: The Soul and Substance of America Portrayed in One Extraordinary Village—Old Deerfield, Mass.,* 1952, 2nd revised and enlarged edition published as *Historic Deerfield: Houses and Interiors,* 1965; *Cape Ann through the Seasons,* 1953; *Cape Cod: A Photographic Sketchbook,* 1953; *Nantucket: A Photographic Sketchbook,* 1955; *A Tour of Old Sturbridge Village,* 1955, 2nd revised edition, 1965; (with Narcissa Chamberlain) *Southern Interiors of Charleston, South Carolina,* 1956; *The Berkshires,* 1956; (with Narcissa Chamberlain as translator and adapter of Italian recipes) *Italian Bouquet: An Epicurean Tour of Italy* (illustrated with prints, drawings, and photographs), 1958; *Mystic Seaport,* 1959, revised edition, 1961.

The New England Image, 1962; (with Narcissa Chamberlain as adapter of British recipes) *British Bouquet: An Epicurean Tour of Britain,* Gourmet Books, 1963; *The New England Scene,* 1965; *Etched in Sunlight: Fifty Years in the Graphic Arts,* Boston Public Library, 1968; *A Stroll through Historic Salem,* 1969; *New England in Color: A Collection of Color Photographs,* 1969; *Lexington and Concord in Color,* 1970; (with Narcissa Chamberlain) *The Chamberlain Selection of New England Rooms, 1639-1863,* 1972.

Illustrator: *The Education of Henry Adams,* Houghton, 1935; Mary Antony DeWolfe Howe, *Boston Landmarks,* 1946; George Francis Marlowe, *Churches of Old New England: Their Architecture and Their Architects, Their Pastors and Their People,* Macmillan, 1947; Donald Moffat, *Fair Harvard,* 1948; Walter Dumaux Edmonds, *The First Hundred Years, 1848-1948: Oneida Community,* Oneida Community, 1948; James Lincoln Huntington, *Forty Acres: The Story of the Bishop Huntington House,* 1949; Harry Hansen, *North of Manhattan,* 1950; Robert D. French, *The Yale Scene,* Yale University Press, 1950; Paul Hollister, *Beauport at Gloucester: The Most Fascinating House in America,* 1951; Mark Anthony DeWolfe Howe, *Who Lived Here: A Baker's Dozen of Historic New England Houses and Their Occupants,* Little, Brown, 1952; *Soft Skies of France,* 1953; *A Brief History of Old Deerfield, including a Description of Places Open to the Public, as well as Miscellaneous Information Pertaining Thereto,* Old Deerfield (Mass.), 1961; Marjorie Drake Ross, *The Book of Boston: The Victorian Period, 1837-1901,* 1964; *New England Legends and Folklore,* 1967; Jack Denton Scott, *The Complete Book of Pasta: An Italian Cookbook,* Morrow, 1968; Harry Hansen, *Longfellow's New England,* 1972.

Portfolio of architectural sketches drawn in northern Spain was issued by Architectural Book Publishing, 1926, and a similar portfolio, drawn in rural France, was issued in 1928. Regular contributor to *Gourmet.*

SIDELIGHTS: The publication of *Etched in Sunlight: Fifty Years in the Graphic Arts* was the occasion which prompted Edward Weeks to recall: "In the early twenties Sam acquired the economy and discipline which were to make his drawings so desirable; he went to France on a shoestring, sought out the old houses, the chateaus, the old towers, city gates, and bridges where the line of light and shade could be most beautifully depicted. He learned as he traveled, studying lithography in the studio of Gaston Dorfinant, and etching in the atelier of Edouard Leon on the Left Bank; and when he was joined by his attractive wife, Narcissa, who had just as fine a palate and a better memory for recipes, his mastery of black and white and his knowledge of good cooking and good wine began to approach perfection."

Weeks concluded at that time: "His artistry has covered half a century, at a time when the new medium of photography would have driven a lesser man out of business. With his zest for food and wine and his gift for friendship, Chamberlain has become, and I do not exaggerate, the most welcome and appreciative American in France and the adjoining gastronomic provinces of Italy and Britain."

BIOGRAPHICAL/CRITICAL SOURCES: Atlantic, September, 1968.†

(Died January 10, 1975)

* * *

CHANCELLOR, John 1900-1971

PERSONAL: Born March 1, 1900, in London, England. *Address:* c/o Lloyd's Bank Ltd., Clare, Suffolk, England. *Agent:* A. M. Heath & Co. Ltd., 40-42 William IV St., London WC2N 4DD England.

CAREER: At the age of fourteen, worked as office-boy with the *Daily Sketch,* London, England; became sub-editor for *Ideas,* a weekly owned by the *Daily Sketch* firm and edited by the Welsh novelist Caradoc Evans; became the editor and entire staff of *Ideas* during World War I at the age of sixteen; on his return from the war in 1919 he held various jobs with the same firm until he became London editor for the *Manchester Empire News;* began freelancing in 1922; between 1925 and 1930, he was an extra correspondent for the Allied Newspapers (now Thomson Newspapers) in Paris and Berlin. *Military service:* Royal Air Force, 1917-19. Royal Artillery, 1939-45; became warrant officer Class I; mentioned in dispatches for service in North Africa.

WRITINGS: Stolen Gold (novel), Hutchinson, 1925; *Mystery at Angel's End* (novel), Hutchinson, 1926; *How to be Happy in Paris,* Arrowsmith, 1926, Holt, 1927; *The Prim Windows* (novel), J. Cape, 1967; *The Farther Off from England* (novel), Cassell, 1969; *The Train with Misted Windows,* Macmillan, 1971. Author of play "King of the Damned," presented at Piccadilly and Lyceum Theatres, London, 1935.

SIDELIGHTS: "King of the Damned" was filmed by Gaumont-British. Chancellor spoke French and once served as interpreter for United States General Lyman Lemnitzer.†

(Died September, 1971)

* * *

CHAO, Yuen Ren 1892-

PERSONAL: Born November 3, 1892, in Tientsin, China; naturalized U.S. citizen; son of Heng Nien and Lai Sun (Feng) Chao; married Buwei Yang (a physician), June 1, 1921; children: Rulan (Mrs. Ted Pian), Xinna Nova (Mrs. P. Y. Huang), Lensey (Mrs. Isaac Namioka), Bella Chao Chiu. *Education:* Cornell University, A.B., 1914, graduate study, 1914-15; Harvard University, Ph.D., 1918. *Politics:* "Registered Democrat." *Religion:* Agnostic. *Home:* 1059 Cragmont Ave., Berkeley, Calif. 94708. *Office:* Department of Oriental Languages, University of California, Berkeley, Calif. 94720.

CAREER: Cornell University, Ithaca, N.Y., instructor in physics, 1919-20; National Peking University, Peking, China, interpreter for Bertrand Russell, 1920-21; Harvard University, Cambridge, Mass., instructor in philosophy and Chinese, 1921-24; National Tsing Hua University, Peking, China, research professor of Chinese, 1925-29; Academia Sinica, Peking, China, chief of linguistic section and director of linguistic survey, 1929-38; visiting professor of Chinese at University of Hawaii, Honolulu, 1938-39, and Yale University, New Haven, Conn., 1939-41; Harvard University, lecturer in Chinese, 1941-46, and civilian head of Chinese program, Army Specialized Training, 1943-44; University of California, Berkeley, professor of Oriental languages, 1947-48, Agassiz Professor of Oriental Languages and Literature, 1948-63, professor emeritus, 1963—. Held China Foundation chair in linguistics at National Taiwan University and was Fulbright research scholar at Kyoto University, 1959. Former member of committee on unification of the national language, Chinese Ministry of Education, and former director of Chinese Education Mission, Washington, D.C. Consultant to Bell Telephone Laboratories, 1943-46, and Ramo-Wooldridge Corp., 1962.

MEMBER: American Academy of Arts and Sciences (fellow), American Oriental Society (president, 1960), Linguistic Society of America (president, 1945), Modern Language Association of America, International Phonetic Association (member of council), Comite International Permanent des Linguistics, Association of Asian Studies, American Anthropological Association, History of Science Society, Academia Sinica, Philosophy of Science Association, American Association for the Advancement of Science (fellow), Science Society of China (co-founder, 1915), Phi Beta Kappa, Sigma Xi, Commonwealth Club (San Francisco). *Awards, honors:* Litt.D., Princeton University, 1946; Guggenheim fellow, 1954-55, 1968-69; LL.D., University of California, Berkeley, 1962; L.H.D., Ohio State University, 1971.

WRITINGS: A Phonograph Course in the Chinese National Language, Commercial Press (Shanghai), 1925; *Studies in Modern Wu Dialects,* Tsing Hua University Press (Peking, China), 1928; *Cantonese Primer,* Harvard University Press, 1947; (with Lien Sheng Yang) *Concise Dictionary of Spoken Chinese,* Harvard University Press, 1947; (translator from the Chinese) Buwei Yang Chao, *Autobiography of a Chinese Woman,* [New York], 1947; *Mandarin Primer: An Intensive Course in Spoken Chinese,* Harvard University Press, 1948; *A Grammar of Spoken*

Chinese, University of California Press, 1965; (editor) *Linguistics in East Asia and South East Asia,* Mouton & Co., 1967; *Language and Symbolic Systems,* Cambridge University Press, 1968; *Readings in Sayable Chinese,* three volumes, Asian Language Publications, 1968-69. Also author of books and pamphlets in Chinese on Chinese language and linguistics. Composer of *Songs of Contemporary Poems,* 1928, and *Children's Festival Songs,* 1934. Contributor to *Encyclopaedia Britannica, Collier's Encyclopedia,* and to journals in his field.

WORK IN PROGRESS: Research in "general Chinese".

*   *   *

CHAPELLE, Howard I(rving)   1901-1975

PERSONAL: Surname is pronounced Sha-*pell;* born February 1, 1901, in Tolland, Mass.; son of Irving George (a packer) and Sarah (Hardy) Chapelle; married Alice Zayma Galvin, July 16, 1935. *Education:* Educated in public schools of Waterbury and New Haven, Conn., and at Webb Institute, New York, N.Y. Tutored in Naval Architecture, Jacksonville, Fla.

CAREER: Naval architect in Cambridge, Md., 1932-57, as designer and treasurer of William A. Robinson Co. (shipyard), 1936-40, and president of Eastern Shore Industries, 1940-43; Smithsonian Institution, Washington, D.C., curator of transportation, 1957-67, senior historian, Museum of History and Technology, 1967-71. Visiting professor of American maritime studies, Munson Institute, Mystic, Conn., 1964-69. Chairman of technical committee on restoration of Admiral Perry's flagship, "Niagara"; consultant to Turkey, United Nations Food and Agriculture Organization, 1956-57. Member of board of trustees, Maritime Museum of Canada and Kirkland College, Easton, Md. *Military service:* U.S. Army, Transportation Corps, 1943-47; chief of Marine Branch, Research and Development Division, 1945-46; became lieutenant colonel; received Commendation Medal with oak-leaf cluster. *Member:* Society of Naval Architects and Marine Engineers, Society for Nautical Research (England), Marine Research Guild. *Awards, honors:* Guggenheim fellowship, 1950; Secretary's Exceptional Service Gold Medal, Smithsonian Institution, 1971.

WRITINGS: The Baltimore Clipper, Marine Research Society (Salem, Mass.), 1930; *History of the American Sailing Ship,* Norton, 1935; *American Sailing Craft,* Kenedy, 1936; *Yacht Design and Planning,* Norton, 1937; *Boatbuilding,* Norton, 1940; *A History of the American Sailing Navy,* Norton, 1949; *American Small Sailing Craft,* Norton, 1951; *National Watercraft Collection,* U.S. Government Printing Office, for Smithsonian Institution, 1957; (with Edwin Tappan Adney) *The Bark Canoes and Skin Boats of North America,* U.S. Government Printing Office, 1964; *The Search for Speed Under Sail,* Norton, 1967; *The Constellation Question,* U.S. Government Printing Office, 1970; *The American Fishing Schooners,* Norton, 1973. Writer of published report on fishing boats for Government of Turkey, 1957. Contributor of more than forty articles to encyclopedias and periodicals.

BIOGRAPHICAL/CRITICAL SOURCES: Washington Post, November 13, 1970.†

(Died June 30, 1975)

*   *   *

CHAPMAN, Allen
[Collective pseudonym]

WRITINGS: "Boys of Pluck" series: *The Young Land*

Agent; or, The Secret of the Borden Estate, Cupples & Leon, 1911.

"Boys of Business" series; published by Cupples & Leon: *The Young Express Agent; or, Bart Stirling's Road to Success,* 1906; *Two Boy Publishers; or, From Typecase to Editor's Chair,* 1906; *Mail Order Frank; or, A Smart Boy and His Chances,* 1907; *A Business Boy; or, Winning Success,* 1908.

"The Darewell Chums" series; published by Cupples & Leon: *The Darewell Chums; or, The Heroes of the School,* 1908; *. . . in the City; or, The Disappearance of Ned Wilding,* 1908; *. . . in the Woods; or, Frank Roscoe's Secret,* 1908; *. . . on a Cruise; or, Fenn Masterson's Odd Discovery,* 1909; *. . . in a Winter Camp,* 1911.

"The Radio Boys" series; published by Grosset: *The Radio Boys' First Wireless; or, Winning the Ferberton Prize,* 1922; *The Radio Boys with the Flood Fighters; or, Saving the City in the Valley,* 1925; *. . . Aiding the Snow Bound; or, Starvation Days at Lumber Run,* 1928; *. . . on the Pacific; or, Shipwrecked on an Unknown Island,* 1929; *. . . to the Rescue; or, The Search for the Barrmore Twins,* 1930.

"Railroad" series; published by Grosset, unless otherwise indicated: *Ralph of the Roundhouse; or, Bound to Become a Railroad Man,* Mershon, 1906; *. . . in the Switch Tower; or, Clearing the Track,* Chatterton-Peck, 1907; *. . . on the Engine; or, The Young Fireman of the Limited Mail,* 1909; *. . . on the Overland Express,* 1910; *. . . on the Midnight Flyer; or, The Wreck at Shadow Valley,* 1923; *. . . and the Train Wreckers; or, The Secret of the Blue Freight Cars,* 1928.

SIDELIGHTS: See **ADAMS, Harriet S., STRATEMEYER, Edward L.,** and **SVENSON, Andrew E.**†

*   *   *

CHARNOCK, Joan   1903-
(Joan Thomson)

PERSONAL: Born March 12, 1903, in Cambridge, England; daughter of Joseph John (a physicist and master of Trinity College, Cambridge University) and Rose Elisabeth (Paget) Thomson; married Harry Horsfield Charnock, September 10, 1946 (died January 3, 1963); children: Ann Rosemary, Joan (Mrs. John Edridge). *Education:* Educated in Cambridge, England. *Politics:* "Open-minded Tory." *Religion:* Church of England. *Home:* 6 Adams Rd., Cambridge CB3 9AD, England. *Agent:* Richmond Towers & Benson Ltd., 14 Essex St., Strand, London W.C.2, England.

CAREER: After leaving school acted as secretary to her physicist-father; during World War II worked for British Ministry of Labour, for censorship board, and with the Red Cross and Soldiers', Sailors' and Airmen's Families Association. *Member:* Cambridge Reading Circle.

WRITINGS—All juveniles, except as indicated: (Under name Joan Thomson) *The Making of Russia,* Oxford University Press, 1943; (under name Joan Thomson) *Russia: The Old and the New,* J. Murray, 1948; *Russia, the Land and the People* (adult), Bodley Head, 1960; *The Russian Twins,* J. Cape, 1963, Dufour, 1964; *David and Carol as Cooks,* J. Cape, 1964; *The Land and People of Poland,* Macmillan, 1967; *Red Revolutionary: The Life of Lenin,* Methuen, 1968, Hawthorn, 1970.

WORK IN PROGRESS: Research on Anton Chekhov.

AVOCATIONAL INTERESTS: Collecting early English watercolors, cooking, gardening.

BIOGRAPHICAL/CRITICAL SOURCES: Best Sellers, October 15, 1970.

CHAUNDLER, Christine   1887-1972
(Peter Martin)

PERSONAL: Surname is pronounced *Chawnd*-ler; born September 5, 1887; daughter of Henry (a solicitor) and Constance Julia (Thompson) Chaundler. *Education:* Attended Queen Anne's School, Caversham, and St. Winifred's School, Bangor, N. Wales. *Home:* Fleet Cottage, Fittleworth, Sussex, England.

CAREER: Cassell & Co., London, England, sub-editor of *Little Folks*, 1914-17; Nisbet & Co., London, children's editor, 1919-23; book reviewer, *Quiver Magazine*, 1923-48; Robert Hale Ltd., reader, beginning 1939. *Member:* Society of Authors, College of Psychic Science.

WRITINGS: (With Eric Wood) *My Book of Beautiful Legends*, Funk, 1916; *The Magic Kiss*, Cassell, 1916; *Little Squirrel Tickletail*, Cassell, 1917; *My Book of Stories from the Poets*, Cassell, 1919, Funk, 1920; *Ronald's Burglar*, Thomas Nelson, 1919; *The Reputation of the Upper Fourth*, Nisbet, 1919.

The Thirteenth Orphan, Nisbet, 1920; *Arthur and His Knights*, Nisbet, 1920; *Just Gerry*, Nisbet, 1920; *Snuffles for Short*, Nisbet, 1921; *The Right St. John's*, Oxford University Press, 1921; *The Binky Books*, Nisbet, 1921; *The Fourth Form Detectives*, Nisbet, 1921; *The Reformation of Dormitory Five*, Nisbet, 1922; *A Fourth Form Rebel*, Nisbet, 1922; *Captain Cara*, Nisbet, 1923; *Jan of the Fourth*, Nisbet, 1923; *Dickie's Day*, Thomas Nelson, 1924; *Winning Her Colours*, Nisbet, 1924; *Sally Sticks It Out*, S. W. Partridge, 1924; *Tomboy Toby*, S. W. Partridge, 1924; *Judy the Tramp*, Nisbet, 1924; *Princess Carroty-Top and Timothy*, Warne, 1924; *Jill the Outsider*, Cassell, 1924; *An Unofficial Schoolgirl*, Nisbet, 1925; *Bounty of the Blackbirds*, Nisbet, 1925, Collins, 1941; *The Adopting of Mickie*, Religious Tract Society, 1925; *A Credit to Her House*, Ward, Lock, 1926; *Twenty-six Christine Chaundler School Stories for Girls*, Girl's Own Paper, 1926; *The Exploits of Evangeline*, Nisbet, 1926; *Reforming the Fourth*, Ward, Lock, 1927; *The Chivalrous Fifth*, Thomas Nelson, 1927; *Philippa's Family*, Nisbet, 1927; *Meggy Makes Her Mark*, Nisbet, 1928; *The Games Captain*, Ward, Lock, 1928; *Friends in the Fourth*, Ward, Lock, 1929.

The Technical Fifth, Ward, Lock, 1930; *A Disgrace to the Fourth*, Thomas Nelson, 1930; *The New Girl in Four A*, Nisbet, 1930; *The Madcap of the School*, Thomas Nelson, 1930; *Two in Form Four*, Cassell, 1931; *The Junior Prefect*, Ward, Lock, 1931; *The Story-Book School*, Oxford University Press, 1931; *The Amateur Patrol*, Nisbet, 1932; *Jill of the Guides*, Nisbet, 1932; *Five B and Evangeline*, George Newnes, 1932; *Feud with the Sixth*, Nisbet, 1932; *Cinderella Ann*, Ward, Lock, 1932; *Pat's Third Term*, Oxford University Press, 1934; *The Children's Author: A Writer's Guide to the Juvenile Market*, Pitman, 1934; *The Lonely Garden*, Thomas Nelson, 1934; *Tales of Nicky-Nob*, W. & R. Chambers, 1937; *The Children's Story Hour*, Evans Brothers, 1938, new edition, Museum Press, 1946; *The Odd Ones*, Country Life, 1941, revised edition, 1950; *Curious Creatures: Verses*, The Naturist, 1944; *Winkie-Wee Tales*, Museum Press, 1945; *Prize for Gardening*, Thomas Nelson, 1948; *The Children's Christmas Book*, Mowbray, 1949; *More Stories for the Children's Hour*, R. Hale, 1949; *A Child Is Born*, Evans Brothers, 1949.

The Golden Years, R. Hale, 1950; *A Year-Book of Fairy Tales*, Mowbray, 1952; *The Blue Book of Saints' Stories*, Retold, Mowbray, 1952; *The Brown Book of Saints' Stories*, Retold, Mowbray, 1952; *The Red Book of Saints' Stories*, Retold, Mowbray, 1952; *A Year-Book of Legends, Collected and Retold*, Mowbray, 1954; *A Year-Book of the Stars: Legends Retold*, Mowbray, 1956; *A Year-Book of Customs*, Morehouse-Gorham, 1957; *A Year-Book of Saints*, Mowbray, 1958; *A Year-Book of Folklore*, Mowbray, 1959; *Through the Christian Year*, Mowbray, 1960; *Everyman's Book of Legends*, Mowbray, 1963; *A Year-Book of Nursery Tales*, Mowbray, 1963; *Everyman's Book of Ancient Customs*, Mowbray, 1968; *Every Man's Book of Superstitions*, Philosophical Library, 1970.

WORK IN PROGRESS: Legends of the Zodiac.

SIDELIGHTS: Christine Chaundler told *CA:* "As the eldest member of a large Victorian family—eldest to survive infancy that is—I have always had much to do with children. Most of my work has been for them. I am also greatly interested in folklore and in psychic things. Although not possessing E.S.P. powers myself, I have had much experience of them."†

(Died December, 1972)

*   *   *

CHAVCHAVADZE, Paul   1899-1971

PERSONAL: Surname is pronounced Chaf-cha-*vad*-zy; born June 27, 1899, in St. Petersburg (now Leningrad), Russia; came to United States in 1927, naturalized U.S. citizen; son of Prince Alexander (an army colonel) and Marie (Rodzianko) Chavchavadze; married Nina Romanoff (a princess of Russia), September 3, 1922; children: David. *Education:* Graduated from a Russian gymnasium, 1917. *Religion:* Russian Orthodox. *Residence:* Wellfleet, Mass. 02667. *Agent:* Maurice Crain, Inc., 18 East 41st St., New York, N.Y. 10017.

CAREER: Cunard Steamship Co., New York City, executive clerk, 1927-39; Tolstoy Foundation, New York City, member of staff, 1941-42; American National Red Cross, attached to 3rd U.S. Army, taking care of displaced persons in Europe, 1943-45, special representative in Korea and China, 1946-47; author.

WRITINGS: Family Album (family reminiscences), Houghton, 1949; *The Mountains of Allah* (novel), Doubleday, 1952; *Father Vikenty* (novel), Houghton, 1955; *Because the Night Was Dark* (novel), Macmillan (London), 1966; *Marie Avinov: Pilgrimage Through Hell* (her autobiography as told to Chavchavadze), Prentice-Hall, 1968; (translator) Svetlana Alliluyeva, *Only A Year*, Harper, 1969. Also author of novel, *The Judas Child*. Author of play, "Russian's Pond," produced in Orleans Arena Theater, Cape Cod, 1956.

BIOGRAPHICAL/CRITICAL SOURCES: New Yorker, September 27, 1969; *Variety*, August 4, 1971.†

(Died July 9, 1971)

*   *   *

CHENAULT, Lawrence R(oyce)   1897-

PERSONAL: Born July 3, 1897, in Hico, Tex.; son of Stephen A. (a merchant) and Bettie (Hand) Chenault; married Minetta Littleton, December 31, 1928; children: Laurel (Mrs. Charles R. Buhrman), Jeannie. *Education:* University of Texas, B.B.A., 1920; Wayne (now Wayne State) University, M.A., 1932; Columbia University, Ph.D., 1938. *Religion:* Unitarian Universalist.

CAREER: Auditor with private firm, 1920-21, for U.S. Treasury Department, 1922-26; Simpson & Chenault (public accountants), partner, 1926-28; certified public accountant, state of Texas, 1928; Socony Mobil Co., accountant, 1929-32; University of Puerto Rico, Rio Piedras, assistant professor of economics, 1935-36; Hunter College (now Hunter College of the City University of New York), New York, N.Y., associate professor, 1936-54, professor of economics and chairman of department, 1955-65. Visiting professor of economics at College of William and Mary, 1945, and New York University, 1949-50. *Member:* American Economic Association, American Institute of Certified Public Accountants, Metropolitan Economic Association.

WRITINGS: (Contributor) B. Singh, editor, *The Frontiers of Social Science,* Macmillan, 1955; (contributor) *The Future of the Champlain Basin,* New York-Vermont Interstate Commission, 1961; (with K. H. Smith) *Economics,* Doubleday, 1965. Contributor to technical journals.††

* * *

CHENEY, Brainard (Bartwell)   1900-

PERSONAL: Born June 3, 1900, in Fitzgerald, Ga.; son of Brainard Bartwell (a lawyer) and Mattie Lucy (Mood) Cheney; married Frances Neel (a college professor of library science), June 21, 1928. *Education:* Attended The Citadel, 1917-19, University of Georgia, 1924, and Vanderbilt University, 1924-25. *Politics:* Independent Democrat. *Religion:* Roman Catholic. *Home and office:* 112 Oak St., Smyrna, Tenn. 37167.

CAREER: Bank clerk in Lavonia, Ga., 1919-20; timber dealer in Lumber City, Ga., 1920-21; school principal in Jonesville, Ga., 1921-22, in Scotland, Ga., 1922-23, and in Bostwick, Ga., 1923-24; *Nashville Banner,* Nashville, Tenn., member of editorial staff and police reporter, 1925-42; executive secretary to U.S. Senator Tom Stewart of Tennessee, 1942-45; self-employed writer and editor, 1945-52; member of public relations staff of Tennessee Governor Frank Clement, 1952-58; novelist. Member of board, Samaritans Inc. *Awards, honors:* Guggenheim fellow, 1941; literary award of Georgia Writers Association, 1958, for *This Is Adam.*

WRITINGS—Novels: *Lightwood,* Houghton, 1939; *River Rogue,* Houghton, 1942; *This Is Adam,* Obolensky, 1958; *Devil's Elbow,* Crown, 1969. Two of his plays have been produced, "Strangers in This World" and "I Choose to Die." Contributor of short stories and articles to *Coronet, Georgia Review, Sewanee Review,* and other periodicals.

WORK IN PROGRESS: A novel.

AVOCATIONAL INTERESTS: Swimming, hunting woodchucks.

BIOGRAPHICAL/CRITICAL SOURCES: Washington Post, August 21, 1969.

* * *

CHESSMAN, Ruth (Green)   1910-

PERSONAL: Born December 3, 1910, in Cambridge, Mass.; daughter of Judah Harry (a realtor) and Nettie (Freed) Green; married Ben Chessman, August 8, 1937 (died December 19, 1969); children: Michael, Daniel, Jane. *Education:* Attended Massachusetts Institute of Technology for two and one-half years. *Home:* 19 Ellison Rd., Newton, Mass. 02159.

WRITINGS: Bound for Freedom, Abelard, 1965. Contributor of short stories and articles to magazines, including *Ellery Queen's Mystery Magazine, Four Quarters, Woman's Day,* and *Manhunt.*

CHILDS, Harwood Lawrence   1898-1972

PERSONAL: Born May 1, 1898, in Gray, Me.; son of Herman Andrew (a minister) and Eudora (Whittemore) Childs; married Willa Patricia Whitson, June 28, 1922 (died June 8, 1972); children: Elisabeth Ann (Mrs. Arthur E. Rowse), Margaret Frances (Mrs. Richard S. Armstrong), Martha Louise (Mrs. L. Edwin Sproul, Jr.). *Education:* Dartmouth College, A.B., 1919, M.A., 1921; Harvard University, law student, 1921-22; University of Chicago, Ph.D., 1928. *Home and office:* 51 Lake Lane, Princeton, N.J. 08540.

CAREER: Dartmouth College, Hanover, N.H., instructor in public speaking, 1919-20, instructor in economics, 1920-21; Syracuse University, Syracuse, N.Y., assistant professor of economics, 1922-24; College of William and Mary, Williamsburg, Va., associate professor of government, 1925-27; Bucknell University, Lewisburg, Pa., professor of government and head of department of political science, 1928-31; Princeton University, Princeton, N.J., associate professor, 1932-46, professor of politics, 1946-68. Specialist in Overseas Branch, U.S. Office of War Information, Washington, D.C., 1943-45; technical assistant for United Nations at School of Public Administration, Rio de Janeiro, Brazil, 1953-54; Haynes Foundation visiting lecturer, University of Southern California, Los Angeles, 1957. *Military service:* U.S. Navy, 1918.

MEMBER: American Political Science Association, American Association for Public Opinion Research. *Awards, honors:* Social Science Research Council fellowship in Germany, 1931-32; Guggenheim Foundation fellowship in Germany, 1937.

WRITINGS: Labor and Capital in National Politics, Ohio State University Press, 1928; *A Reference Guide to the Study of Public Opinion,* Princeton University Press, 1934; (editor) *Pressure Groups and Propaganda* (Volume 179 of the Association's *Annuals),* American Association of Political and Social Science, 1935; (editor with Fritz Morstein Marx and others) *Propaganda and Dictatorship,* Princeton University Press, 1936; (translator) *The Nazi Primer,* Harper, 1938; *An Introduction to Public Opinion,* Wiley, 1940; (contributor, and editor with J. B. Whitton) *Propaganda by Short Wave,* Princeton University Press, 1943; (contributor) American Political Science Association Research Committee, *Research in Political Science,* University of North Carolina Press, 1948; *Public Opinion: Nature, Formation, Role,* Van Nostrand, 1965; (editor) A. L. Lowell, *Public Opinion and Popular Government,* Johnson Reprint, 1969. Also contributor to *The American Political Scene,* 1956; contributor to journals. *Public Opinion Quarterly,* founder, 1937, managing editor, 1937-41, editor, 1964-68.†

(Died June 8, 1972)

* * *

CHISHOLM, R(obert) F(erguson)   1904-

PERSONAL: Born October 16, 1904, in Battleford, Saskatchewan, Canada; son of Robert Ferguson (a lawyer) and Eva (Kitson) Chisholm; married Dorothy Alice Pinchin, April 7, 1934 (died, 1960); married Rosemary Fennell, January 3, 1963; children: (first marriage) Judie (Mrs. Donald L. Wilson), Janet Forstner. *Education:* University of Toronto, B. Commerce, 1926. *Religion:* Protestant. *Office:* William Mara Co. Ltd., 234 Eglinton Ave. E., Toronto, Ontario, Canada.

CAREER: DeForest Crosley Radio Ltd., Toronto, Ontario, assistant to managing director, 1926-33; J. D. Woods & Co. Ltd., Toronto, industrial engineer, 1933-37; Gordon Mackay & Co. Ltd., Toronto, vice-president and general manager, 1937-56; Dominion Stores Ltd., Toronto, executive vice-president and director, 1956-69; chairman of the board, Thompson Paper Box Co. Ltd., and William Mara Co. Ltd., Toronto, beginning 1969. Director of wholesale and retail distribution during World War II, Canadian Wartime Prices and Trade Board. Director of R. L. Crain Ltd., Confederation Life Association, Capital Growth Fund Ltd., Formosa Brewery Ltd., Benson & Hedges Ltd., Quaker Oats of Canada Ltd., Merry Packaging Ltd., and Supermarket Institute. President of Toronto Symphony Orchestra, 1968-69, and Japan Fund of Canada, 1969-72. Member of board of governors, University of Toronto; member of board of regents, Victoria University. *Member:* Toronto Club, Rosedale Golf Club, and University Club (all Toronto); St. James's Club (Montreal), Canadian Club (president, 1950-51, 1960). *Awards, honors:* Order of the British Empire, 1947.

WRITINGS: Your Own Store and How to Run It, Crowell, 1945; *The Darlings: The Mystique of the Supermarket,* Chain Store Age Books, 1970.

*   *   *

CHOMMIE, John C(ampbell)   1914-1974

PERSONAL: Born September 5, 1914, in Thief River Falls, Minn.; son of Hans Olaf (an attorney) and Florence (Campbell) Chommie; married Genevieve Smyth, October 1, 1938 (deceased); married June Ray, July 5, 1947; children: (first marriage) Barbara (Mrs. Lloyd Tosse); (second marriage) Frances (Mrs. Philip Knox), Johanna, Karen, Catherine, John. *Education:* Attended University of Minnesota, 1932-33, 1935-36, and University of North Dakota, 1934-35; William Mitchell College of Law, LL.B., 1941, B.S.L., 1942; University of Southern California, LL.M., 1953; New York University, LL.M., 1956, J.S.D., 1960. *Home:* 9225 Southwest 63rd St., Miami, Fla. 33143. *Office:* School of Law, University of Miami, Coral Gables, Fla. 33124.

CAREER: Southwestern University, Los Angeles, Calif., professor of law, 1948-53; Dickinson College of Law, Carlisle, Pa., professor of law, 1953-56; University of Miami, Coral Gables, Fla., associate professor of law, 1956-57; Harvard University, School of Law, Cambridge, Mass., research assistant, 1957-58; University of Miami, associate professor, 1958-60, professor of law, beginning 1960. Visiting professor, Louisiana State University, 1965. Tax consultant to August, Nimkoff & Goldstone (attorneys), Miami, Fla. *Military service:* U.S. Merchant Marine, 1943-44. *Member:* Inter-American Bar Association, National Tax Association, American Association of University Professors. *Awards, honors:* Kenneson fellowship, New York University, summers, 1954-56.

WRITINGS: The World Tax Series and Taxation in the United Kingdom, Law School, New York University, 1958; *Handling Tax Avoidance Exchanges and Transfers Involving Foreign Corporations under Section 367,* Prentice-Hall, 1960; (contributor) *Law Governing International Transactions,* American Law Institute, 1960; (editor) *El Derecho de los Estados Unidos,* University of Miami Press, 1963; (with George Eder) *Taxation in Colombia,* Commerce Clearing House, 1964; *The Law of Federal Income Taxation,* West Publishing, 1968, 2nd edition, 1973; *The Internal Revenue Service,* Praeger, 1970. Contributor of articles on taxation to numerous law reviews and tax journals.

WORK IN PROGRESS: A study of the Ways and Means Committee and tax policy issues.

AVOCATIONAL INTERESTS: Travel, painting.†

(Died May, 1974)

*   *   *

CHOUKAS, Michael (Eugene)   1901-

PERSONAL: First syllable of surname rhymes with "two"; born November 16, 1901, on Samos Island, Greece; came to United States, 1916, became U.S. citizen, 1924; son of Nicholas (a merchant) and Calliope (Doukas) Choukas; married Gertrude Spitz, June 20, 1927; children: Michael, Jr. (headmaster at Vermont Academy). *Education:* Dartmouth College, A.B. (summa cum laude), 1927; Columbia University, A.M., 1928, Ph.D., 1934. *Politics:* Liberal Republican. *Religion:* Greek Orthodox. *Home:* Rye, N.H. 03870. *Office:* Pierce College, Athens, Greece.

CAREER: Worked on a Greek newspaper, New York, N.Y., before entering college; Dartmouth College, Hanover, N.H., instructor, 1929-35, assistant professor, 1935-40, professor of sociology, beginning 1940, head of department of sociology and anthropology, beginning 1949; Pierce College, Athens, Greece, provost, beginning 1971. Summer professor at Johns Hopkins University and Bates College. Director of study on alcoholism for state of New Hampshire, 1946. *Military service:* U.S. Office of Strategic Services, chief of plans and production for Morale Operations, 1944-45. *Member:* American Sociological Association, American Association of University Professors, Byzantine Fellowship, Phi Beta Kappa, Alpha Tau Omega. *Awards, honors:* Comparative Studies Center fellowship, 1964.

WRITINGS: Black Angels of Athos, S. Daye, 1934; *Propaganda Comes of Age,* Public Affairs Press, 1965. Contributor of articles and reviews to periodicals.

WORK IN PROGRESS: Translating from the Greek, *The Pre-History of the Theatre;* further research for a book, *Islanders of the Aegean.*

SIDELIGHTS: Choukas lived with the monks of Mount Athos during the summer of 1931, collecting material for his book on that monastic community of five thousand monks and twenty monasteries. "There was a whole library of books on that thousand-year-old womanless community," he reported, "but not one had treated it from the sociological view." He returned to the Aegean the summer of 1964 to gather material for a book on the islanders. He is fluent in Greek and French, taught himself English during his early years in America by reading the *New York Times* (with the aid of a dictionary), and then entered Columbia Grammar School at the age of twenty-one.

BIOGRAPHICAL/CRITICAL SOURCES: Columbia Grammar School, winter, 1965.

*   *   *

CHRISTENSEN, Francis   1902-19(?)

PERSONAL: Born May 9, 1902, in Salt Lake City, Utah; son of Lorenzo and Hilma (Carlson) Christensen; married Fern Jorgensen, September 5, 1925; married second wife, Bonniejean McGuire (a teacher), August 10, 1967; children: (first marriage) Ellen (Mrs. Charles A. Micaud), Margaret (Mrs. Charles Clark); (adopted children) Isabel Lyn, Jonathan Francis, Bonnie Aldine. *Education:* University of Utah, A.B., 1925; University of California, Berkeley, M.A., 1927; Harvard University, M.A., 1931, Ph.D., 1934.

CAREER: University of Wisconsin, Madison, instructor in English, 1934-37; DePauw University, Greencastle, Ind., instructor in English, 1938; University of Southern California, Los Angeles, assistant professor, 1939-45, associate professor, 1946-49, professor of English, beginning 1950, university editor, 1945-50. *Member:* Modern Language Association of America, National Council of Teachers of English, Conference on College Composition and Communication, Philological Association of the Pacific Coast, American Civil Liberties Union. *Awards, honors:* Carnegie Corporation grant, 1964; University Associates Award for creative scholarship and research, 1966.

WRITINGS: The Rhetoric of Short Units of the Composition, University of Nebraska Press, 1965; *Notes Toward a New Rhetoric: Six Essays for Teachers,* Harper, 1967; *The Christensen Rhetoric Program,* Harper, 1968. Contributor to journals in his field.

WORK IN PROGRESS: A Generative Rhetoric, a text.†

(Deceased)

* * *

CHRISTENSON, Cornelia V(os) 1903-

PERSONAL: Born September 5, 1903, in Grand Rapids, Mich.; daughter of Bert John (a language professor) and Rene (Moelker) Vos; married Carroll L. Christenson (a professor), June 11, 1929; children: John Martin, Ann Louise (Mrs. Lester Schonbrun). *Education:* Indiana University, A.B., 1924, M.A., 1927. *Politics:* Democrat. *Religion:* Unitarian. *Home:* 508 South Highland Ave., Bloomington, Ind. 47401. *Office:* Institute for Sex Research, Indiana University, Bloomington, Ind. 47401.

CAREER: Tucson High School, Tucson, Ariz., teacher, 1924-26; Indiana University, Bloomington, instructor in English, 1926-28; Oak Park High School, Oak Park, Ill., English teacher, 1928-30; Indiana University, Institute for Sex Research, member of staff, beginning 1950, research associate and trustee, beginning 1956, curator, beginning 1960. *Member:* Sex Information and Education Council of the United States (member of board of directors), Authors Guild, American Psychological Association, Phi Beta Kappa. *Awards, honors:* Indiana Author's Day award for best biography, 1971, for *Kinsey: A Biography.*

WRITINGS: (With P. H. Gebhard, W. B. Pomeroy, and C. E. Martin) *Pregnancy, Birth and Abortion,* Harper, 1958; (with Gebhard, Pomeroy, and J. H. Gagnon) *Sex Offenders: An Analysis of Types,* Harper, 1965; (editor with Theodore Bowie) *Studies in Erotic Art,* Basic Books, 1970; *Kinsey: A Biography,* Indiana University Press, 1971.

WORK IN PROGRESS: Research in erotic art, geriatrics, and sex.

* * *

CHRISTGAU, Alice Erickson 1902-

PERSONAL: Born November 15, 1902, in Scandia, Minn.; daughter of Alfred (a farmer) and Selma (Gustafson) Erickson; married Rufus John Christgau, June 22, 1927; children: Alice Kathleen (Mrs. Patrick Devaney), Roger Alfred, John Frederick. *Education:* Mankato State College, diploma, 1925; University of Minnesota, B.S., 1955. *Home:* 22 Home Pl., West Oakland, Calif. 94610.

CAREER: Teacher of English and history, and school principal in Minnesota, 1924-27; elementary and junior high school teacher in Minneapolis, Minn., 1942-50; teacher of

adult education classes in San Francisco and Berkeley, Calif., 1958-61; free-lance writer. *Member:* American Association of University Women (president, Oakland chapter, 1963-65), California Writers Club.

WRITINGS: Runaway to Glory, W. R. Scott, 1965; *Rosabel's Secret,* W. R. Scott, 1967; *The Laugh Peddler,* W. R. Scott, 1968. Contributor to magazines, including *Parents', American Mercury, Your Life, American Home,* and *Hygeia.*

WORK IN PROGRESS: My Friend Wowinapa, a juvenile novel dealing with the Minnesota Souix uprising, and a book of memoirs.

SIDELIGHTS: Alice Christgau has competence in Scandinavian languages. *Avocational interests:* History of Swedish immigration to United States, and early American history.

* * *

CHRISTIE, Trevor L. 1905-1969

PERSONAL: Born March 3, 1905, in San Francisco, Calif.; married Dorothy Fisher (a fabric specialist), 1930; children: Joyce Christie Stewart, Michael R. S. *Education:* Michigan State University, B.A., 1927. *Home:* 44 West 10th St., New York, N.Y. 10011.

CAREER: Writer for Associated Press and *Newsweek,* and formerly for *New York Herald Tribune. Member:* Overseas Press Club (New York).

WRITINGS: Legacy of a Pharaoh, Lippincott, 1966; *Antiquities in Peril,* Lippincott, 1967; *Recapturing America's Past,* Lippincott, 1967; *Etched in Arsenic,* Lippincott, 1968.†

(Died, 1969)

* * *

CLAASSEN, Harold 1905-
(Hub[bard] Pomeroy)

PERSONAL: Surname is pronounced Clawson; born September 21, 1905, in Sibley, Iowa; son of Eilt J. (a clothier) and Ollie (Harberts) Claassen; married Esther Boeke, June 11, 1931; children: Joan (Mrs. Charles E. Shinnick). *Education:* University of Iowa, B.A., 1928. *Politics:* Republican. *Religion:* Presbyterian. *Home:* 33 High Hollow Rd., Roslyn Heights, N.Y.

CAREER: Des Moines Register, Des Moines, Iowa, sports writer, 1928-37; Associated Press, general reporter, Kansas City, Mo., 1937-41, sports writer, New York, N.Y., 1941-56, executive sports editor, New York, N.Y., beginning 1956.

WRITINGS: (Compiler and editor with Steve Boda, Jr.) *Ronald Encyclopedia of Football,* Ronald, 1960, 3rd edition, 1963; *The History of Professional Football,* Prentice-Hall, 1963; *Football's Unforgettable Games,* Ronald, 1963. Contributor to sports magazines and other periodicals.

WORK IN PROGRESS: Writing on David Hand, famed whaling captain of the early 1800's, and on Fra Lippo Lippi and his son, fifteenth-century painters in Florence.††

* * *

CLARK, Andrew Hill 1911-1975

PERSONAL: Born April 29, 1911, in Fairford, Manitoba, Canada; came to United States in 1938, naturalized in 1945; son of Jeremiah Simpson (a physician) and Jessie Belle (Pratt) Clark; married Louise Emma Sassmann, December

28, 1940; children: Charles Dougald, John Roderick and Stephen Peter (twins), Mary Elizabeth. *Education:* Mc-Master University, B.A., 1930; University of Manitoba, graduate study, 1931-32; University of Toronto, M.A., 1938; University of California, Berkeley, Ph.D., 1944. *Politics:* Independent liberal. *Religion:* Humanist. *Home:* 5101 Coney Wiston Pl., Madison, Wis. 53705. *Office:* Department of Geography, University of Wisconsin, Madison, Wis. 53706.

CAREER: Manufacturers Life Insurance Co., Toronto, Ontario, member of actuarial department, 1932-35; University of New Zealand, Christchurch, lecturer in geography, 1941-42; Johns Hopkins University, Baltimore, Md., instructor in geography, 1943-44; U.S. Government, Washington, D.C., geographer in Office of Strategic Services and State Department, 1944-46; Rutgers University, New Brunswick, N.J., associate professor, 1946-49, professor of geography and chairman of department, 1949-51; University of Wisconsin—Madison, professor, 1951-64, research professor of geography, 1965-66, Vernor Clifford Finch Research Professor of Geography, 1966-75, chairman of department, 1958-61.

MEMBER: Association of American Geographers (honorary president, 1961-62), American Geographical Society, Agricultural History Society, Economic History Association, Canadian Association of Geographers, American Association of University Professors, Madison Literary Club (president, 1968-69). *Awards, honors:* Guggenheim fellow and Fulbright research scholar, 1961-62; Social Science Research Council fellow, 1962; Albert J. Beveridge Award Committee special commendation for the best book published in Canadian history, 1969, for *Acadia: The Geography of Early Nova Scotia to 1760;* Canadian Association of Geographers award for scholarly distinction, 1974.

WRITINGS: (With others) *New Zealand,* University of California Press (Berkeley), 1947; *The Invasion of New Zealand by People, Plants, and Animals,* Rutgers University Press, 1949 (published in Australia as *The Invasion of New Zealand by Exotic Plants and Animals* by Whitcombe & Tombs); (contributor) P. E. James and C. F. Jones, editors, *American Geography, Inventory and Prospect,* Syracuse University Press, 1954; (contributor) *Man's Role in Changing the Face of the Earth,* University of Chicago Press, 1956; *Three Centuries and the Island: The Historical Geography of Agriculture and Settlement in Prince Edward Island, Canada,* University of Toronto Press, 1959; (contributor) M. McCaskill, editor, *Land and Livelihood,* New Zealand Geographical Society (Christchurch), 1962; (editor with E. R. Officer) *Symposium on the Great Lakes Basin,* American Association for the Advancement of Science, 1962; (contributor) J. Andrews, editor, *Frontiers and Men,* F. W. Cheshire (Melbourne), 1966; (contributor) *Canada: A Geographical Interpretation,* Methuen, 1968; *Acadia: The Geography of Early Nova Scotia to 1760,* University of Wisconsin Press, 1968. Contributor to a number of journals. Editor, *A.A.G. Monographs* (publications of the Association of American Geographers), Volumes I-III, 1961, 1962, 1963, and *Journal of Historical Geography,* Volume I, 1975.

WORK IN PROGRESS: A volume on the historical geography of Nova Scotia, 1760-1867; various studies of Canadian habitat and overseas expansion of European culture and economy.

SIDELIGHTS: Clark was born on an Indian Reserve where his father was medical officer, and is registered (in error) as an Ojibwa Indian. He owned an island on Rough Rock Lake, north of Kenora, Ontario, and spent his summers there reading, writing, canoeing, and fishing.†

(Died May 21, 1975)

*   *   *

CLARK, C. H. Douglas 1890-

PERSONAL: Born July 10, 1890, in Bristol, England; son of Charles Henry (a clergyman) and Lily (Cornall) Clark; married Lyllian Wilson, September 6, 1937. *Education:* Attended Trent College, Derbyshire, England; University of London, B.Sc., 1912; Royal College of Science, graduate (first class honors in chemistry), 1915; University of Leeds, M.Sc., 1926, D.Sc. (London), 1935. *Home:* Peacehaven, 49 Green Lane, Cookridge Village, Leeds 16, England.

CAREER: Royal College of Science, London, England, demonstrator, 1920; University of Leeds, Leeds, England, faculty of chemistry department, 1920-55, lecturer, 1923-45, senior lecturer in department of structural and inorganic chemistry, 1945-55. Local preacher in Methodist church; composer of about fifty hymns; a principal in several public debates with exponents of scientific humanism. *Military service:* British Army, Royal Engineers, 1915-20; served four years in France; became lieutenant. *Member:* Royal College of Science (associate), Royal Institute of Chemistry (associate). *Awards, honors:* Dilpoma of Imperial College of Science and Technology, 1921.

WRITINGS: Basis of Modern Atomic Theory, Methuen, 1926; *Electronic Structure and Properties of Matter,* Chapman & Hall, 1934; *The Fine Structure of Matter,* three volumes, Chapman & Hall, 1938; *The Story of the Atomic Bomb,* Machinery Publishing Co., 1945; *Christianity and Bertrand Russell,* Lutterworth, 1958; *The Scientist and the Supernatural,* Epworth, 1966; *God within the Shadow,* Regency, 1970. Contributor of about fifty articles on spectoscopy and atomic and molecular physics to scientific journals; also has published 450 chess problems. First editor, *Royal College of Science Chemical Society Journal* (now *Scientific Journal of the Imperial College of Science*), 1915.

WORK IN PROGRESS: Further work in the relation of science and religion.

SIDELIGHTS: Christianity and Bertrand Russell, which also has been published in Japanese, is Clark's rebuttal of the famous philosopher's denials of religion; his target in *The Scientist and the Supernatural* is Julian Huxley. *Avocational interests:* Chess, music, amateur dramatics, swimming.†

*   *   *

CLARK, Harry Hayden 1901-1971

PERSONAL: Born July 8, 1901, in New Milford, Conn.; son of Robert Britton and Nellie (Keeler) Clark; married Kathleen Deady, June 27, 1925 (deceased); children: Jean Audrey (Mrs. Walter Marshall), Robert Carter, Roger Warner (deceased). *Education:* Trinity College, Hartford, Conn., B.A., 1923; Harvard University, M.A., 1924; Yale University, graduate study, 1924-25. *Politics:* No party. *Home:* 734 Seneca Pl., Madison, Wis. 53711. *Office:* Department of English, University of Wisconsin, Madison, Wis. 53706.

CAREER: Yale University, New Haven, Conn., instructor in English, 1924-25; Middlebury College, Middlebury, Vt., assistant professor of English, 1925-28; University of Wisconsin—Madison, assistant professor, 1928-32, associate professor, 1932-36, professor of English, beginning 1936.

Smith-Mundt Visiting Professor at University of Uppsala and University of Stockholm, 1953-54; visiting summer professor at Stanford University, Northwestern University, University of Iowa, University of Southern California, and Bread Loaf School of English, Middlebury College.

MEMBER: Modern Language Association of America (president of American literature section, 1952), International Association of University Professors, Wisconsin Academy of Sciences, Arts and Letters (president, 1965-66), Phi Beta Kappa, Sigma Nu. *Awards, honors:* Guggenheim fellowship, 1931-32; Library of Congress fellowship, 1945-46; LL.D. from Bowling Green State University, 1951; Michigan State University, Certificate of Merit, 1953, and Centennial Award, 1955; Litt.D. from Trinity College, Hartford, Conn., 1963.

WRITINGS: (Contributor with others) Floyd Stovall, editor, *The Development of American Literary Criticism,* University of North Carolina Press, 1955; *American Literature: Poe through Garland,* Appleton, 1970.

Editor: (And author of critical introduction) *Poems of Philip Freneau,* Hafner, 1929, reprinted 1960; *Major American Poets,* American Book Co., 1936; (and author of introduction and contributor) *Six New Letters of Thomas Paine,* University of Wisconsin Press, 1939; (with Gay Wilson Allen) *Literary Criticism: Pope to Croce,* American Book Co., 1941, reprinted, Wayne State University Press, 1962; (and author of introduction) Philip M. Freneau, *Letters on Various Interesting and Important Subjects,* Scholars Facsimilies & Reprints, 1943; (and author of introduction) *Thomas Paine: Representative Selections,* American Book Co., 1944, revised edition, Hill & Wang, 1961; (with Norman Foerster) *James Russell Lowell: Representative Selections,* American Book Co., 1947; *Transitions in American Literary History,* Duke University Press, for Modern Language Association of America, 1954.

General editor, "American Writers" series, 24 volumes, American Book Co., 1934-47, "American Literature" series, American Book Co., 1935-56, and "American Fiction" series, American Book Co., 1937-38. Contributor to *Dictionary of American Biography, Encyclopaedia Britannica, Collier's Encyclopedia,* and *World Book Encyclopedia.* Contributor of numerous studies to *Transactions* of Wisconsin Academy of Sciences, Arts and Letters, and to professional and scholarly journals. Member of editorial board, *American Literature,* 1943-55.

WORK IN PROGRESS: American Literary Criticism, 1865-1905.†

(Died June 6, 1971)

* * *

CLARK, Joseph D(eadrick) 1893-

PERSONAL: Born June 14, 1893, in Jonesboro, Tenn.; son of Joseph Lee (a physician) and Susannah Matilda (Crouch) Clark; married Elsie Estes, August 24, 1923; children: Joseph Lee. *Education:* Columbia College (now Columbia University), B.A., 1914; study at Oxford University, 1919; Harvard University, M.A., 1921; further study at University of Chicago, summers, 1925, 1927. *Politics:* Independent Democrat. *Religion:* United Church of Christ. *Home:* 15 Furches St., Raleigh, N.C. 27607.

CAREER: English teacher and head of department in high school in Johnson City, Tenn., 1914-16; principal of high school in Chase City, Va., 1919-22; Virginia Polytechnic Institute (now Virginia Polytechnic Institute and State Uni-

versity), Blacksburg, instructor in English, 1922-23; North Carolina State University at Raleigh, assistant professor, 1923-27, associate professor, 1927-29, professor of English, 1929-62, professor emeritus, 1962—. Member of Raleigh, N.C., school board, 1947-57. Chairman, Parks and Recreation Advisory Committee of Raleigh, 1950-57. *Military service:* U.S. Army, 1917-19; became sergeant. U.S. Army Reserve, 1919-25. *Member:* American Association of University Professors, Phi Kappa Phi. *Awards, honors:* Brown-Hudson Award, North Carolina Folklore Society, 1972.

WRITINGS: (Editor with A. P. Hudson and L. B. Hurley) *College Caravan,* Thomas Nelson, 1936, 3rd edition, Ronald, 1942; (with Philip Davis and A.B.R. Shelley) *Handbook of English,* Ginn, 1951; *Beastly Folklore,* Scarecrow, 1968. Contributor to folklore journals.

* * *

CLARK, Joseph James 1893-1971

PERSONAL: Born November 12, 1893, near Pryor, Okla.; son of William Andrew and Lillie Belle (Berry) Clark; married fourth wife, Olga Choubaroff, June 12, 1964; children: (prior marriage) Mary Louise, Catherine Carol. *Education:* Attended Oklahoma Agricultural and Mechanical College (now Oklahoma State University); U.S. Naval Academy, B.S., 1918. *Politics:* Democrat. *Religion:* Episcopalian. *Home:* 655 Park Ave., New York, N.Y. *Agent:* Allied Literary Co., 1104 South Robertson, Los Angeles, Calif. *Office:* Hegeman Harris Co., Inc., 1270 Avenue of the Americas, New York, N.Y. 10020.

CAREER: U.S. Navy, career officer, 1917-53, advancing to command of 7th Fleet and retiring as admiral; Hegeman Harris Co., Inc., New York, N.Y., executive, 1964-71, chairman of board, 1964-71. *Member:* Navy League of the United States, Military Order of the World Wars, Reserve Officers Association, Larchmont Yacht Club, Wings Club, New York Athletic Club, New York Yacht Club, Chevy Chase Club (Maryland). *Awards, honors—Military:* Navy Distinguished Service Medal (twice), Army Distinguished Service Medal, Navy Cross, Navy Commendation, Army Commendation, Silver Star, Legion of Merit.

WRITINGS: (With Dwight H. Barnes) *Sea Power and Its Meaning,* F. Watts, 1966; (with Clark G. Reynolds) *Carrier Admiral* (partial autobiography), McKay, 1967. Contributor to *Outdoor Life.*†

(Died July, 1971)

* * *

CLARK, Joseph L(ynn) 1881-

PERSONAL: Born July 27, 1881, in Hood County, Tex.; son of Randolph (co-founder of AddRan Male and Female College, which became Texas Christian University) and Ella Blanche (Lee) Clark; married Sallie Frances Chism, August 28, 1913 (deceased). *Education:* Texas Christian University, B.A., 1906; summer graduate study at University of Virginia, 1907, and University of California, 1915; Columbia University, M.A., 1917. *Politics:* Democrat ("inclined toward liberalism"). *Religion:* Disciples of Christ. *Home and office:* 1421 West 14th, Huntsville, Tex. 77340. *Agent:* R. L. Clark, 5031 Braes Valley Dr., Houston, Tex. 77025.

CAREER: During his college days was deputy county and district clerk of Deaf Smith County, Tex., and deputy county clerk and stenographer of Johnson County, Tex.; teacher of history and English at AddRan-Jarvis College, Thorp Spring, Tex., 1906-09, and Tarleton State College,

Stephenville, Tex., 1909-10; Sam Houston State College (now University), Huntsville, Tex., secretary to president, part-time librarian, and registrar, 1910-14, teacher of history and English, 1914-20, chairman of department of history, 1920-32, director of Division of Social Sciences, 1932-51; now retired. University of Texas, visiting summer teacher, 1940. Southern Conference on Education and Race Relations, past chairman; Texas Commission on Interracial Cooperation, co-founder, 1923, past president; Texas Commission on Human Relations, member of board of directors. Texas Christian University, member of development board.

MEMBER: Texas Association of College Teachers (co-founder, past president, and life member), Texas Academy of Science (life member), Texas State Teachers Association (life member), Southwestern Historical Association (fellow; past vice-president), East Texas Historical Association (co-organizer; past president), Pi Gamma Mu (past chancellor of Southwest division), Pi Sigma Alpha, Alpha Kappa Delta. *Awards, honors:* Citation of Texas Centennial Commission, 1936, of Texas Council on Human Relations, 1958; LL.D., Texas Christian University, 1941; knighthood of Sons of the Republic of Texas, 1964.

WRITINGS: A New History of Texas (elementary text), Heath, 1928; (with F. M. Stuart) *The Constitution and Government of Texas* (college text), Heath, 1930; *The History of Texas: Land of Promise* (high school text), Heath, 1940; (with Dorothy A. Linder) *The Story of Texas* (junior high school text), Heath, 1955, 2nd edition, 1963; (with E. M. Scott) *The Texas Gulf Coast: Its History and Industrial Development,* two volumes, Lewis Historical Publishing, 1955; *Thank God, We Made It! A Family Affair with Education,* University of Texas, 1969. Author of twelve Texas history classroom charts, published by Denoyer-Geppert. Author of research papers; contributor to journals. Member of board of editors, *Handbook of Texas,* two volumes, Texas State Historical Association, 1952.

WORK IN PROGRESS: Two Sons and a Seminary. The Biography of a Family; editing *Diaries and Memoirs of Joseph Addison Clark and His Sons, 1815-1935.*

SIDELIGHTS: Clark worked for many years on the development of the Sam Houston home and grounds, and the creation of the Sam Houston Memorial Museum.⁻

*   *   *

CLARK, William Smith II   1900-1969

PERSONAL: Born September 13, 1900, in Baltimore, Md.; son of Hubert Lyman and Frances Lee (Snell) Clark; married Gladys Hathaway, June 26, 1926; children: Stirrat Holman, Penelope Francis. *Education:* Amherst College, B.A. (magna cum laude), 1921; Harvard University, M.A., 1924, Ph.D., 1926. *Religion:* Protestant. *Home:* 2212 Bedford Ter., Cincinnati, Ohio 45208. *Office:* Department of English, University of Cincinnati, Cincinnati, Ohio 45221.

CAREER: American Board of Commissioners for Foreign Missions, student work and teaching at Hokkaido Imperial University, Sapporo, Japan, 1921-23; Amherst College, Amherst, Mass., instructor in English, 1926-31; University of Cincinnati, Cincinnati, Ohio, assistant professor, 1931-37, associate professor, 1937-40, professor of English, 1940-59, Nathaniel Ropes Professor of Comparative Literature, 1959-69, chairman of department of English, 1943-66. Visiting summer professor, Johns Hopkins University, 1940. In Japan on educational mission, sponsored by U.S. Department of State, Japanese Ministry of Education, and Hok-

kaido University, 1956, and as Department of State specialist, 1960.

MEMBER: Modern Language Association of America, American Society for Theatre Research, Society for Theatre Research (London), American Committee on Irish Studies, American Association of University Professors, Cincinnati Literary Club, MacDowell Society (Cincinnati; past president). *Awards, honors:* Guggenheim fellowship for research on Irish stage history in Great Britain, 1939; Sachs Prize of Cincinnati Institute of Fine Arts, 1948.

WRITINGS: (Editor) *Dramatic Works of Roger Boyle, Earl of Orrery,* two volumes, Harvard University Press, 1937; *Chief Patterns of World Drama,* Houghton, 1946; (editor) *James Russell Lowell: Essays, Poems, Letters,* Odyssey, 1948; *The Early Irish Stage: The Beginnings to 1720,* Clarendon Press, 1955; *The Irish Stage in the Country Towns: 1720-1800,* Clarendon Press, 1965. Contributor to professional journals.

WORK IN PROGRESS: The Stage in Dublin, Ireland: 1720-1760, in two volumes.

SIDELIGHTS: William Clark traveled in Asia (including Siberia), the Near East, some Mediterranean countries, and western Europe.††

(Died July 16, 1969)

*   *   *

CLARKE, Arthur G(ladstone)   1887-

PERSONAL: Born December 25, 1887, in Paulton, England; son of Alfred John (an accountant) and Albena (Durston) Clarke; married Nellie Pettifer, November 30, 1916 (died, 1961); children: Arnold John, Edna Katherine (Mrs. J. Parnham), David Howell. *Education:* Missionary School of Medicine, London, England, diploma, 1914. *Address:* c/o 222 Cheese Spring Rd., Wilton, Conn. 06897.

CAREER: Worked in marine insurance, London, England, 1904-12; missionary in Shantung, China, 1914-45; bible teacher in Bermuda, 1951-60; currently travels as a bible teacher and preacher.

WRITINGS: Decachords—Student's Guide to Homoeopathic Materia Medica, Missionary School of Medicine, 1923; *Analytical Studies in the Book of Psalms,* John Ritchie, 1949; *New Testament Church Principles,* John Ritchie, 3rd edition, Loizeaux, 1961; *The Song of Songs,* Walterick Publishers, 1967. Writer of various booklets in Chinese.†

*   *   *

CLARKE, Austin   1896-1974

PERSONAL: Born May 9, 1896, in Dublin, Ireland; son of Augustine and Ellen Patten (Browne) Clarke; married Nora Walker; children: Donald, Aidan, Dardis (all sons). *Education:* Attended Belvedere College, Dublin; University College, Dublin, M.A. *Home:* Bridge House, Templeogue, Dublin 14, Ireland.

CAREER: University College, Dublin, Ireland, followed Thomas McDonagh as English lecturer, 1918-22; National University of Ireland, Dublin, assistant examiner in matriculation, 1923-37; book reviewer in London, England, 1923-37; assistant editor of *Argosy* magazine, Edinburgh, Scotland, 1929; returned to Dublin, 1937, became broadcaster for Radio Eireann, beginning, 1937, also became free-lance writer. *Member:* Irish P.E.N. (president, 1939-42, 1946-49), Irish Academy of Letters (foundation member, 1932; president, 1952-54), Dublin Verse Speaking Society (chairman), Lyric Theatre Company (chairman). *Awards, honors:* National Award for poetry, Tailteann Games, 1932; D.Litt., Trinity College, Dublin; Denis Devlin Foundation memorial prize; Gregory Medal, Irish Academy of Letters, 1968.

WRITINGS—Poetry: *The Vengeance of Fionn* (based on the Irish saga, "Pursuit of Diarmuid and Ghrainne"), Maunsel (Dublin), 1917, 2nd edition, 1918; *The Fires of Baal,* Maunsel & Roberts (Dublin), 1921; *The Sword of the West,* Maunsel & Roberts, 1921; *The Cattledrive in Connaught, and Other Poems* (based on prologue to the "Tain bo Cualigne," with other free versions from Irish sagas), Allen & Unwin, 1925; *Pilgrimage, and Other Poems,* Allen & Unwin, 1929, Farrar & Rinehart, 1930; *The Collected Poems of Austin Clarke,* introduction by Padraic Colum, Allen & Unwin, 1936; *Night and Morning,* Orwell Press (Dublin), 1938; *Ancient Lights,* privately printed, 1955; *Too Great a Vine: Poems and Satires,* 2nd series, Bridge Press (Dublin), 1957; *The Horse-Eaters: Poems and Satires,* 3rd series, Bridge Press, 1960; *Collected Later Poems,* Dolmen Press (Dublin), 1961; *Forget-Me-Not,* Dolmen Press, 1962; *Flight to Africa, and Other Poems,* Dolmen Press, 1963; (with Tony Connor and Charles Tomlinson) *Poems: A Selection,* Oxford University Press, 1964; *Mnemosyne Lay in Dust,* drawings by Jack Coughlin, Dolmen Press, 1966; *Old-Fashioned Pilgrimage, and Other Poems,* Dufour, 1967; *A Sermon on Swift, and Other Poems,* Bridge Press, 1968; *The Echo at Coole, and Other Poems,* Dufour, 1968; *Orphide, and Other Poems,* privately printed, 1970; *Tiresias: A Poem,* Bridge Press, 1971; *The Wooing of Becfola,* Poem-of-the-Month Club (London), 1973; *Collected Poems,* edited by Liam Miller, Dolmen Press, 1974; Thomas Kinsella, editor, *The Selected Poetry of Austin Clarke,* Wake Forest Press, 1976.

Verse plays: *The Son of Learning* (three-act comedy; based on medieval Irish tale, "Aislinge Meic Conglinne"; produced in Cambridge, 1927), Allen & Unwin, 1927; *The Flame* (one-act; produced in Edinburgh, 1932), Allen & Unwin, 1930; *Sister Eucharia,* Orwell Press, 1939; *Black Fast* (one-act farce; produced in Dublin, 1941), Orwell Press, 1941; *As the Crow Flies* (lyric radio play), Orwell Press, 1943; *The Viscount of Blarney, and Other Plays* (produced in Dublin, 1944), Bridge Press, 1944; *The Second Kiss* (comedy; produced in Dublin, 1946), Bridge Press, 1946; *The Plot Succeeds* (pantomime; produced in Dublin, 1950), Bridge Press, 1950; *The Moment Next to Nothing* (three-act; produced in Dublin, 1958), Bridge Press, 1953; *Collected Plays,* Dolmen Press, 1963; *The Third Kiss* (comedy), Bridge Press, 1967; *The Frenzy of Sweeney,* Bridge Press, 1967; *Two Interludes Adapted from Cervantes: La Cueva de Salamanca* (The Student from Salamanca) [and] *El Viejo celoso* (The Silent Lover), Dolmen Press, 1968; *The Impuritans* (one-act play), Dolmen Press, 1973. Also author of *St. Patrick's Purgatory,* 1967.

Prose: *The Bright Temptation: A Romance* (romantic novel), Morrow, 1932, revised edition, 1965; *The Singing-Men at Cashel* (novel), Allen & Unwin, 1936; *First Visit to England, and Other Memories,* Bridge Press, 1945; *Poetry in Modern Ireland* (literary criticism), illustrations by Louis Le Brocquy, published for Cultural Relations Committee of Ireland by Colm O Lochlainn (Dublin), 1951, 2nd edition, 1961; *The Sun Dances at Easter* (novel), Andrew Melrose, 1952; *Twice Round the Black Church: Early Memories of Ireland and England,* Routledge & Kegan Paul, 1962; (editor and author of introduction) Joseph Campbell, *The Poems of Joseph Campbell,* Allen Figgis (Dublin), 1963; *A*

Tribute to Austin Clarke on His Seventieth Birthday, 9 May, 1966, compiled and edited by John Montague and Liam Miller, Dufour, 1966; *Beyond the Pale* (memoirs), 1967; (author of introduction) George Fitzmaurice, *The Plays of George Fitzmaurice,* Volume 1: *Dramatic Fantasies,* Dufour, 1967; *A Penny in the Clouds: More Memories of Ireland and England,* Routledge & Kegan Paul, 1968; *The Celtic Twilight and the Nineties* (criticism), Dolmen Press, 1969.

Poems included in numerous anthologies, including *Oxford Book of Irish Verse,* chosen by Donagh MacDonagh and Lennox Robinson, Oxford University Press (London), 1958, *New Poets of Ireland,* edited by Donald Carroll, Alan Swallow, 1963, and *New Modern Poetry,* edited by M. L. Rosenthal, Macmillan, 1967.

SIDELIGHTS: A reviewer for the *Times Literary Supplement* wrote: "Austin Clarke's answer to Robert Frost's question about what kind of verse he wrote has become justly famous: 'I load myself with chains and try to get out of them.' But looking at Mr. Clarke's new book [*Old-Fashioned Pilgrimage*] one wonders how accurate the *mot* is. The bag of technical tricks is indeed a fancy one: first-syllable rhymes, homonymic rhymes ... internal assonance, and rhymes that pun. Yet one's impression is not of a calculating master-craftsman but of a garrulous, rambling old Irishman, too impatient with getting on to the next story to be bothering very much about technique.... This slapdash, good-hearted naivety is not found in Mr. Clarke's poems on Irish topics, and luckily there are some of these in the new book. Here is the familiar Clarke country: priest-ridden, bigoted, suffering from Peck-sniffery, with birth-control banned and the natural pagan delights stifled. It is parish-pump stuff, but none the worse for that."

Samuel French Morse of *Poetry* magazine agreed that "Austin Clarke has his eccentricities, but they seldom if ever get in the way of the poem.... The real substance of the book is in the poems about Ireland: caustic, compassionate, curiously mannered in their play on words.... [Some poems] remind one a little of Yeats's more bitter poems on Ireland; but Clarke's invective is neither so lofty nor so ambiguous, nor, perhaps, so memorable, and yet its humaneness is very admirable indeed.... Neither visionary nor mere nationalist, Austin Clarke remains a distinguished Irish poet."

BIOGRAPHICAL/CRITICAL SOURCES: Times Literary Supplement, March 16, 1967; *Observer Review,* March 26, 1967, July 28, 1968; *Poetry,* May, 1968; *Contemporary Literary Criticism,* Gale, Volume VI, 1976.†

(Died March 20, 1974)

*   *   *

CLAUS, Marshall R. 1936-1970

PERSONAL: Born June 28, 1936, in St. Paul, Minn.; son of Robert and Ella (Faust) Claus; married Lois J. Duxbury (a secretary), August 13, 1966. *Education:* University of Iowa, B.S., 1960; Michigan State University, M.A., 1961. *Religion:* Methodist. *Home:* 125 Claremont Ave., Long Beach, Calif. 90803.

CAREER: Long Beach Unified School District, Long Beach, Calif., physical education teacher, 1962-70. Held commercial and instrument flight ratings and taught flying on a part-time basis. Member of three U.S. gymnastic teams; adviser on gymnastics programs to Young Men's Christian Associations (YMCA). *Military service:* U.S. Army Reserve.

WRITINGS: A Teacher's Guide to Gymnastics, National Press, 1969; Better Gymnastics for Boys, Dodd, 1970.††

(Died November 22, 1970)

* * *

CLAY, Roberta 1900-

PERSONAL: Born December 30, 1900, in Dublin, Tex.; daughter of William James (a teacher) and Lucy (Higginbotham) Clay. Education: Texas Woman's University (formerly College of Industrial Arts), B.A., 1921; attended University of Colorado, 1922, 1950; University of Missouri, 1924-25, B.J., 1931; Northwestern University, M.S.J., 1937; Columbia Univeristy, M.A., 1941. Politics: Liberal Democrat. Religion: Methodist. Agent: Max Siegel & Associates, 154 East Erie, Chicago, Ill. 60611.

CAREER: English teacher in Texas high schools, 1921-24; Wichita Falls Times, Wichita Falls, Tex., reporter, 1925-29; Stephenville Empire-Tribune, Stephenville, Tex., reporter, sub-editor, 1930-31; Tarleton State College (now University), Stephenville, associate professor and publicity director, 1931-36; College of the Ozarks, Clarksville, Ark., associate professor of English, 1937-45; State College of Arkansas, Teachers College, Conway, Ark., associate professor of English and journalism, 1945-65. Director, Arkansas High School Press Association. Member: American Civil Liberties Union, American Association of University Professors, American Association of University Women, Association for Education in Journalism, Foreign Policy Association Council, American for Democratic Action, League of Conservation Voters, Texas Conservation Council. Awards, honors: Award as distinguished college newspaper adviser, Columbia Scholastic Press Association, 1957.

WRITINGS: The College Newspaper, Pageant Press, 1965; Promotion in Print: A Guide for Publicity Chairman, A. S. Barnes, 1970.

Contributor of articles and verse to Journalism Quarterly, Christian Science Monitor, Texas Outlook, Arkansas Gazette, and Arkansas Democrat.

WORK IN PROGRESS: A study of sermon subjects in small churches; reminiscences and the philosophy of teaching; a nature study of the local area.

SIDELIGHTS: Roberta Clay once described herself, for CA, as an "activist for peace, justice . . . prison reform, conservation, better newspaper writing." Since her retirement, she has written "400-500 letters to editors or to legislators . . . in support of various causes."†

* * *

CLEMMONS, Robert S(tarr) 1910-

PERSONAL: Born October 21, 1910, in New London, Ohio; son of William Edward and Tella (Starr) Clemmons; married Beatrice Marian Winter, August 27, 1936; children: Lynne Marie (Mrs. Judson H. Morris, Jr.), David Robert. Education: Ohio Wesleyan University, A.B., 1933; Union Theological Seminary, M.Div., 1936; Oberlin College, D.Min., 1951; additional study at Vanderbilt University, George Peabody College for Teachers, University of Pittsburgh, and Columbia University. Home: 2019 Overhill Dr., Nashville, Tenn. 37215. Office: Methodist Board of Discipleship, 1001 19th Ave., S., Nashville, Tenn. 37203.

CAREER: Ordained minister of the Methodist Church, 1934. Church of All Nations, New York, N.Y., staff member, 1934-36; minister in Brecksville, Ohio, 1936; Kent State University, Kent, Ohio, director of Wesley Foundation, 1940-45; Methodist Board of Education, Nashville, Tenn., staff member, beginning 1945, member of young adult work committee, 1945-57, director of council on adult work, 1957-68, assistant to general secretary for program design and coordination, 1967. The Methodist Church, member of curriculum committee, 1945-68, member of general committee on family life, 1957-68, assistant to general secretary for educational design, director of ministries with ethnic constituencies, beginning 1972. Member: Academy of Religion, Adult Education Association, American Academy of Arts and Sciences, Methodist Conference on Christian Education (member of adult section), World Futurist Society.

WRITINGS: Dynamics of Christian Education, Abingdon, 1958; Young Adults and the Churches, Abingdon, 1959; Education for Churchmanship, Abingdon, 1966. Contributor to Widening Horizons of Christian Adult Education, University of Pittsburgh Press, and to Dictionary of Christian Education, Westminster.

WORK IN PROGRESS: Church Dynamics.

* * *

CLINE, Denzel C(ecil) 1903-

PERSONAL: Born March 11, 1903, near Woodsfield, Ohio; son of Martin Luther and Mary (Hogue) Cline; married Ida Riste, December 22, 1924; children: Denzel R., Marta (Mrs. Albert L. Shutt). Education: University of Washington, Seattle, B.A., 1925, M.A., 1926; Princeton University, Ph.D., 1933. Religion: Protestant. Home: 306 Leasia St., Williamston, Mich. 48895.

CAREER: University of Idaho, Moscow, instructor in economics, 1926-27; Princeton University, Princeton, N.J., instructor, 1927-33, assistant professor of economics, 1933-38; Michigan State University, East Lansing, associate professor, 1938-48, professor of economics, 1948-69, professor emeritus, 1969—. Fulbright lecturer in public finance, Ankara University, 1962-63. Tax research economist for various state surveys in New Jersey and Michigan, including Michigan Tax Study, 1957-58, and Michigan Highway Fiscal Study, 1961-62. Member of Governor's Advisory Committee on Michigan School Needs, 1954-55, and Michigan Committee on Financing School Building Construction, 1956-58. Member: American Economic Association (life member), Phi Beta Kappa.

WRITINGS: Pay the Piper: A Study of Michigan Taxes, Michigan State University Press, 1953; (with James Papke and Milton C. Taylor) Michigan Highway Fiscal Study, State of Michigan, 1961; (with M. C. Taylor) Michigan Tax Reform, Michigan State University Press, 1966. Contributor of fifty articles to professional journals.

* * *

CLITHERO, Myrtle E(ly) 1906-
(Sally Clithero)

PERSONAL: Born September 12, 1906, in Mazon, Ill.; daughter of John Maurice and Vallie (Fuller) Ely; married Loren L. Clithero (died, 1956); children: William Maurice. Education: Illinois State University, student, 1925-26, 1927-28; further study in extension courses. Residence: Mazon, Ill.

CAREER: Before marriage taught in a one-room school for two years, and in Oak Park, Ill., for three years; primary teacher in Sterling (Ill.) public schools, 1948-65. Member:

Daughters of the American Revolution, The Questers, National Federation of Republic Women, Retired Teachers Association.

WRITINGS: (Compiler under name Sally Clithero) *Beginning-To-Read Poetry,* illustrations by Erik Blegvad, Follett, 1967.

AVOCATIONAL INTERESTS: Collecting antique cow cream pitchers, playing bridge.

*   *   *

CLOUGH, William A.   1899-

PERSONAL: Surname rhymes with "rough"; born August 2, 1899, in Pompey, N.Y.; son of William M. (a farmer) and Nellie (Jennings) Clough; married Helen Gardner (deceased); children: Faith (Mrs. John Degenhart). *Education:* Syracuse University, B.S. in Journalism, 1925. *Politics:* Republican. *Religion:* Congregationalist.

CAREER: Morristown Jerseyman, Morristown, N.J., reporter, 1925-26; *New Bedford Standard-Times,* New Bedford, Mass., successively reporter, city editor, and Sunday editor, 1926-46; free-lance magazine writer, 1946-51; Will, Folsom and Smith, Inc. (fund raising counsel), New York, N.Y., director of Boston office, 1951-57.

WRITINGS: Father, We Thank Thee, Abingdon, 1949; *How to Claim Your Good,* Unity, 1960. Regular columnist, *Unity* (magazine), beginning 1959; contributor to more than forty other magazines.††

*   *   *

CLUNE, Francis Patrick   1893-1971
(Frank Clune)

PERSONAL: Born November 27, 1893, in Sydney, Australia; son of George (a laborer) and Teresa (Cullen) Clune; married Thelma Smith, March 9, 1923; children: Anthony, Terry. *Education:* Attended St. Benedict's School, Sydney, Australia, seven years. *Politics:* None. *Religion:* Roman Catholic. *Home:* 15 Princes Ave., Vaucluse, Sydney, New South Wales, Australia.

CAREER: Roamed in his early years in Australia, United States, Canada, and at sea; later accountant in Australia; author, 1934-71. *Military service:* With 15th U.S. Cavalry at Fort Leavenworth, Kan., 1912. Australian Army, World War I; wounded at Gallipoli, 1915; honorary major with Australian forces in Libya, Palestine, and New Guinea, 1942-43.

WRITINGS—All under name Frank Clune; all published by Angus & Robertson, except as noted: *Try Anything Once: The Autobiography of a Wanderer,* 1934, 9th edition, 1947; *Rolling around the Lachlan,* 1935; *Roaming around the Darling,* 1936; *Dig: A Drama of Central Australia,* 1937; *Free and Easy Land,* 1938; *Sky High to Shanghai,* 1939.

To the Isles of Spice with Frank Clune, 1940, published as *Isles of Spice,* Dutton, 1942; *All Aboard for Singapore,* 1941; *Chinese Morrison,* Bread and Cheese Club (Melbourne), 1941; *D'Air Devil: The Story of "Pard" Mustar,* 1941; *Last of the Australian Explorers,* 1942; *Prowling through Papua,* 1943; *Tobruk to Turkey,* 1943; *The Red Heart,* Hawthorn Press (Melbourne), 1944; *Captain Starlight,* Hawthorn Press, 1945; *The Forlorn Hope,* Hawthorn Press, 1945; *The Greatest Liar on Earth,* Hawthorn Press, 1945; *Pacific Parade* (autobiography), Hawthorn Press, 1945; *Dark Outlaw,* Invincible Press, c.1945, published as *Gunman Gardiner,* F. W. Cheshire, 1951, and as *King of*

the Road, Angus & Robertson, 1967; *Try Nothing Twice,* 1946; *Golden Goliath,* Hawthorn Press, 1946; *Song of India,* Invincible Press, 1946, revised edition, 1947; *Ben Hall, the Bushranger,* 1947; *Roaming around Australia,* Hawthorn Press, 1947; *High-Ho to London,* 1948; *Wild Colonial Boys,* 1948; *Land of Hope and Glory,* 1949; *Land of My Birth,* Invincible Press, 1949.

All Roads Lead to Rome, Invincible Press, 1950; *Ashes of Hiroshima,* 1950; *Hands across the Pacific,* 1951; *Somewhere in New Guinea,* 1951, Philosophical Library, 1952; *Castles in Spain,* 1952; *Flying Dutchman,* 1953; *Land of Australia,* Hawthorn Press, 1953; *Kelly Hunters,* 1954; (with P. R. Stephensen) *Viking of Van Diemen's Land,* 1954; *Roaming around Europe,* 1954; *Overland Telegraph,* 1955; *Captain Melville,* 1956; *Martin Cash,* 1956, revised edition, 1968; *Roaming around New Zealand,* 1956; *The Fortune Hunters,* 1957; *Scandals of Sydney Town,* 1957; *Flight to Formosa,* 1958; *A Tale of Tahiti,* 1958; *The Blue Mountains Murderer,* Horwitz, 1959; *Jimmy Governor,* Horwitz, 1959; *Murders on Maunga-Tapu,* 1959.

Journey to Canberra, 1960; *The Odyssey of Onehunga,* [Onehunga], c.1961; *Across the Snowy Mountains,* 1962; (with P. R. Stephensen) *The Pirates of the Brig Cyprus,* Hart-Davis, 1962, Morrow, 1963; *Saga of Sydney,* 1962, revised edition, 1963; *Bound for Botany Bay,* 1964; *Journey to Kosciusko* (condensed and combined version of *Journey to Canberra* and *Across the Snowy Mountains*), 1965; *Journey to Pitcairn,* 1966, Tri-Ocean, 1967; *Search for the Golden Fleece,* 1966; *The Norfolk Island Story,* 1967; *Serenade to Sydney,* 1967; *Scallywags of Sydney Cove,* 1968; *Scottish Martyrs,* 1969; *Captain Bully Hayes,* 1971.

AVOCATIONAL INTERESTS: Golf, travel.†

(Died March 11, 1971)

*   *   *

COAN, Otis W(elton)   1895-

PERSONAL: Surname is pronounced Ko-*ann;* born April 21, 1895, in Iberia, Mo.; son of Ernest Ellwood and Ellen (Schubert) Coan; married Dorothy Wilson, June, 1925; married second wife, Berenice Ellman, September 3, 1940; children: (first marriage) Donald Wilson, Richard Welton; (second marriage) Eugene Victor. *Education:* Hastings College, A.B., 1922; graduate study at University of Kansas and University of Arizona; University of California, Berkeley, M.A., 1928. *Home and office:* 455 Grant Ave., Apt. 14, Palo Alto, Calif. 94306.

CAREER: University of Tennessee, Knoxville, instructor in English, 1924-25; Central Junior College, El Centro, Calif., instructor in English, 1925-26; Los Angeles City College, Los Angeles, Calif., 1929—, began as instructor in English, currently professor emeritus. *Military service:* U.S. Army, 1918-19. *Member:* American Civil Liberties Union, American Friends Service Committee, Fellowship of Reconciliation, Friends Committee on Legislation.

WRITINGS: Rocktown, Arkansas (novel), Exposition, 1953; *America in Fiction: An Annotated List of Novels that Interpret Aspects of Life in the United States,* Stanford University Press, 1941, 5th edition (with Richard G. Lillard), Pacific Books, 1968; *Traveling* (poems), privately printed, 1970. Contributor to education, civil rights, and consumer publications.

*   *   *

COBRIN, Harry Aaron   1902-

PERSONAL: Born July 21, 1902, in New York, N.Y.; son

of Julius and Bessie Cobrin; married Ella Ruckmore, August 9, 1935; children: Elizabeth, Peter. *Education:* Cornell University, A.B., 1924. *Home:* 37 Riverside Dr., New York, N.Y.

CAREER: Clothing Manufacturers Association of the U.S.A., New York, N.Y., executive secretary, 1940-68; consulting economist to various groups and businesses. Member of business advisory council, Bureau of Labor Statistics, U.S. Department of Labor.

WRITINGS: The Men's Clothing Industry: Colonial through Modern Times, Fairchild, 1970.††

* * *

COCKCROFT, John (Douglas) 1897-1967

PERSONAL: Born May 27, 1897, in Todmorden, England; son of John A. (textile manufacturer) and A. M. (Fielden) Cockcroft; married E. Elizabeth Crabtree, August, 1925; children: Dorothea, Jocelyn, Elizabeth, Catherine, Christopher. *Education:* University of Manchester, B.Sc., 1919, M.Sc., 1922; St. John's College, Cambridge, B.A., 1924, Ph.D., 1928. *Politics:* Liberal. *Home and office:* Churchill College, Cambridge, England.

CAREER: Cambridge University, Cambridge, England, fellow of St. John's College, 1928-46, Jacksonian Professor of Natural Philosophy, 1939-46; British Ministry of Supply, chief superintendent of Air Defence, Research and Development Establishment, 1941-44; National Research Council of Canada, director of Atomic Energy Division in Montreal, Quebec, 1944-45, director of Chalk River Laboratory in Chalk River, Ontario, 1945-46; British Ministry of Supply, director of Atomic Energy Research Establishment, Harwell, 1946-58; United Kingdom Atomic Energy Authority, member for scientific research, 1954-59, part-time member, 1959-67; Cambridge University, master of Churchill College, 1959-67. Member of scientific advisory committee, British Broadcasting Corp., 1948-52, and governing board of National Institute for Research in Nuclear Science, 1957-65. Member of court, University of London, 1959-66; chancellor of Australian National University, Canberra, 1961-67; president of Manchester College of Science and Technology, 1961-67. *Military service:* British Army, 1915-18; became lieutenant.

MEMBER: Royal Society (London; fellow), British Association (president, 1962), Institute of Physics and Physical Society (fellow; president, 1961-62), Institution of Electrical Engineers, Royal Swedish Academy (foreign member), Royal Danish Academy (foreign member), Australian Academy of Sciences (foreign member), American Academy of Arts and Sciences (honorary foreign member); honorary member of various engineering institutes in England; Savile Club and Athenaeum Club (both London).

AWARDS, HONORS: Commander, Order of the British Empire, 1944; knighted, 1948; Chevalier de la Legion d'Honneur, 1950; Nobel Prize for physics (with Ernest Thomas Sinton Walton), 1951; Knight Commander of the Bath, 1953; Knight Commander, Military Order of Christ (Portugal), 1955; Order of Merit, 1957; Grand Cross, Order of Alfonso X (Spain), 1958; Atoms for Peace Award (United States), 1961. Medal of Freedom with golden palms (United States), 1947; J. A. Ewing Medal of Institution of Civil Engineering, 1948; Royal Medal of Royal Society, 1954; Feraday Medal of Institution of Electrical Engineers, 1955; Kelvin Medal (joint engineering institutions award), 1956; Churchill Gold Medal of Society of Engineers, 1958; Niels Bohr Medal (Denmark), 1958; Wilhelm Exner Medal

(Austria), 1961. More than twenty honorary degrees from universities and colleges in England, Ireland, Scotland, Australia, Canada, United States, and the Netherlands, including Oxford University, University of Dublin, Temple University, University of St. Andrews, Dalhousie University, Cambridge University, and University of Western Australia.

WRITINGS: (With others) *Atomic Challenge* (symposium), Winchester (London), 1947; *The Development and Future of Nuclear Energy,* Clarendon Press, 1950; *The Development of Radiation Chemistry and Radiochemistry,* Royal Institute of Chemistry, 1954; *Problems of Disarmament* (lecture), [London], 1962; (editor) *The Organization of Research Establishments,* Cambridge University Press, 1965. Also editor of *Science, Technology and Productivity,* Liberal Publications Department, and author of *Technology for Developing Countries,* Overseas Development Institute, both 1966. Papers on nuclear physics published in *Proceedings* of Royal Society, and technical papers in *Journal of Institute of Electrical Engineers.*

WORK IN PROGRESS: Autobiography.†

(Died September 18, 1967)

* * *

COCKRELL, Marian (Brown) 1909-

PERSONAL: Born March 15, 1909, in Birmingham, Ala.; daughter of George Summers (a surgeon) and Lucy May (Bradford) Brown; married Francis Marion Cockrell (a writer), November 3, 1931; children: Nancy Summers. *Education:* Attended Sophie Newcomb College, 1926-29, Metropolitan Art School, New York, N.Y., 1929-30. *Politics:* Democrat. *Religion:* Episcopalian. *Home and office:* 910 El Paseo, Ojai, Calif. 93023. *Agent:* Paul R. Reynolds, Inc., 12 East 41st St., New York, N.Y. 10017.

CAREER: Fiction writer since 1930's. *Member:* Ventura County Humane Society (president), Children's Home Society (Ventura), Kappa Kappa Gamma.

WRITINGS: Yesterday's Madness, Harper, 1943; *Lillian Harley,* Harper, 1944; *Shadow Castle* (juvenile), Whittlesey House, 1945; *Something Between,* Harper, 1946; *The Revolt of Sarah Perkins,* McKay, 1965. Author with husband, Francis Cockrell of *Saturday Evening Post* serial, "Dark Waters," 1944, and of screenplay of same name; has done other screen writing and television scripts ("mostly early Alfred Hitchcock"). Contributor of short stories to popular magazines during 1930's.

WORK IN PROGRESS: A novel about a small town family.

SIDELIGHTS: Marian Cockrell told *CA:* [I] "am very much concerned about lack of communication and compassion between individuals and nations, but don't know how to do anything about it ... I am not a scholar.... I enjoy writing fiction, inventing stories and people."††

* * *

COCTEAU, Jean (Maurice Eugene Clement) 1889-1963

PERSONAL: Born July 5, 1889, in Maisons-Laffitte (Seine-et-Oise), France; son of Georges (a lawyer) and Eugenie (Lecomte) Cocteau. *Education:* Studied at Lycee Condorcet, Paris; attended private classes.

CAREER: Poet, playwright, novelist, essayist, painter; became an early celebrity after a reading of his first poems at the Theatre Femina, Paris, 1906; founded the review, *Scheherazade,* with Maurice Rostand and others; met Diaghilev, 1912, and wrote his first scenario for ballet, "Le Dieu Bleu"; during World War I, went to Rheims as a civilian ambulance driver, and later to Belgium where he joined a group of marine-riflemen, until it was discovered that his presence was unauthorized; served for a while with an auxiliary corps in Paris; founded Editions de la Sirene with Blaise Cendrars, 1918; contributor on the arts to *Paris-Midi,* March to August, 1919; in 1936, made a trip around the world in eighty days, after a wager with *France-Soir;* wrote a regular series for *Ce Soir,* 1937-38; produced his first cartoon for a tapestry, commissioned by Gobelins, 1948; visited the United States in late 1948; presented the film "Le Testament d'Orphee" in Warsaw, Poland, 1960. *Member:* Academie Francaise, Academie Royale de Belgique, Academie Mallarme, American Academy, German Academy (Berlin), Academie de Jazz (president), Academie du Disque, Association France-Hongrie, National Institute of Arts and Letters (New York; honorary member). *Awards, honors:* Prix Louions-Delluc, 1946; Grand Prix de la Critique Internationale, 1950; Grand Prix du Film Avant-garde, 1950, for *Orphee;* D.Litt., Oxford University, 1956; Commandeur de la Legion d'Honneur, 1961.

WRITINGS—Poetry: *La Lampe d'Aladin,* Societe d'Editions, 1909; *Le Prince frivole,* Mercure de France, 1910; *La Danse de Sophocle,* Mercure de France, 1912; *Le Cap de Bonne-Esperance,* Editions de la Sirene, 1919; *L'Ode a Picasso,* Francois Bernouard, 1919; (with Andre Lhote) *Escales,* Editions de la Sirene, 1920; *Poesies: 1917-20,* Editions de la Sirene, 1920; *Vocabulaire,* Editions de la Sirene, 1922; *Plain-Chant,* Stock, 1923; *Poesie, 1916-23,* Gallimard, 1924; *La Rose de Francois,* F. Bernouard, 1924; *Cri ecrit,* Imprimerie de Montane (Montpellier), 1925; *Pierre Mutilee,* Editions des Cahiers Libres, 1925; *L'Ange heurtebise,* Stock, 1925; *Opera: Oeuvres poetiques 1925-27,* Stock, 1927, revised edition, 1959, published as *Oeuvres poetiques: 1925-27,* Dutilleul, 1959; *Morceaux choisis,* Gallimard, 1932, published as *Poemes,* H. Kaeser (Lausanne), 1945; *Mythologie* (poems written on lithographic stones; contains 10 original lithographs by Giorgio di Chirico), Editions de Quatre-Chemins, 1934; *Allegories,* Gallimard, 1941; *Leone,* Nouvelle Revue Francaise, 1945, translation by Alan Neame published as *Leoun,* [London], 1960; *La Crucifixion,* Morihien, 1946; *Poemes,* Gallimard, 1948; *Le Chiffre sept,* Seghers, 1952; *Appogiatures* (with a portrait of Cocteau by Modigliani), Editions du Rocher (Monaco), 1953; *Dentelle d'eternite,* Seghers, 1953; *Clair-Obscur,* Editions du Rocher, 1954; *Poemes: 1916-55,* Gallimard, 1956; (contributor) Paul Eluard, *Corps memorabiles,* Seghers, 1958; *De la Brouille,* Editions Dynamo (Liege), 1960; *Ceremonial espagnol du Phoenix* [suivi de] *La Partie d'echecs,* Gallimard, 1961; *Le Requiem,* Gallimard, 1962; *Faire-Part* (ninety-one previously unpublished poems), foreword by Jean Marais and Claude-Michel Cluny, Librairie Saint-Germain des Pres, 1968.

Novels: *Le Potomak,* Societe Litteraire de France, 1919, definitive edition, Stock, 1924; (self-illustrated) *Le Grand ecart,* Stock, 1923, reprinted, 1970, translation by Lewis Galantiere published as *The Grand Ecart,* Putnam, 1925, translation by Dorothy Williams published as *The Miscreant,* P. Owen, 1958; *Thomas l'imposteur,* Nouvelle Revue Francaise, 1923, revised edition, edited by Bernard Garniez, Macmillan, 1964, translation and introduction by Galantiere published as *Thomas the Impostor,* Appleton, 1925, translation by Williams published as *The Impostor,*

Noonday Press, 1957; *Les Enfants terribles,* Grasset, 1929, reprinted, 1963, revised edition, edited by Jacques Hardre, Blaisdell, 1969, translation by Samuel Putnam published as *Enfants Terribles,* Harcourt, 1930, translation by Rosamund Lehmann published in England as *The Children of the Game,* Harvill, 1955, same translation published as *The Holy Terrors* (not the same as translation of *Les Monstres sacres,* below), New Directions, 1957; *La Fin du Potomak,* Gallimard, 1940; *Deux travestis* (contains lithographs by Cocteau), Fournier, 1947.

Plays: *Les Maries de la tour Eiffel,* Nouvelle Revue Francaise, 1924, translation by Dudley Fitts published as "The Eiffel Tower Wedding Party," in *The Infernal Machine, and Other Plays,* New Directions, 1963, translation by Michael Benedikt published as "The Wedding on the Eiffel Tower," in *Modern French Plays,* Faber, 1964; *Orphee,* Stock, 1927, translation by Carl Wildman published as *Orphee: A Tragedy in One Act* (first produced in New York at Living Theatre as "Orpheus," September 30, 1954), Oxford University Press, 1933, translation by John Savacool published as *Orphee,* New Directions, 1963; *Antigone,* Nouvelle Revue Francaise, 1928, translation by Wildman published in *Four Plays,* MacGibbon & Kee, 1961; *La Voix humaine* (first produced in Paris at Comedie Francaise, February 17, 1930), Stock, 1930, translation by Wildman published as *The Human Voice,* Vision Press, 1951; *La Machine infernale,* Grasset, 1934, reprinted, Livre de Poche, 1974, published in England in French, under the original title, with an introduction and notes by W. M. Landers, Harrap, 1957, translation and introduction by Wildman published as *The Infernal Machine,* Oxford University Press, 1936, translation by Albert Bermel published as *The Infernal Machine,* New Directions, 1963; *Les Chevaliers de la table ronde,* Gallimard, 1937, reprinted, 1966, translation by W. H. Auden published as *The Knights of the Round Table,* New Directions, 1963; *Les Parents terribles,* Gallimard, 1938, reprinted, 1972, revised edition, edited by R. K. Totton, Methuen, 1972, translation by Charles Frank published as *Intimate Relations,* MacGibbon & Kee, 1962.

Les Monstres sacres, Gallimard, 1940, translation by Edward O. Marsh published as *The Holy Terrors,* MacGibbon & Kee, 1962; *La Machine a ecrire,* Gallimard, 1941, translation by Ronald Duncan published as *The Typewriter,* Dobson, 1957; *Renaud et Armide,* Gallimard, 1943; *L'Aigle a deux tetes,* Gallimard, 1946, reprinted, 1973, translation by Duncan published as *The Eagle Has Two Heads,* Funk, 1948, translation by Wildman published as *The Eagle with Two Heads,* MacGibbon & Kee, 1962; (adaptor) Tennessee Williams, *Un Tramway nomme desir* (first produced in Paris at Theatre Edouard VII, October, 1949), Bordas, 1949; *Bacchus,* Gallimard, 1952, translation by Mary C. Hoeck published as *Bacchus: A Play,* New Directions, 1963; (translator and adaptor) Jerome Kilty, *Cher menteur* (first produced in Paris at Theatre de l'Athenee, October 4, 1960), Paris-Theatre, 1960; *L'Impromptu du Palais-Royal,* Gallimard, 1962. Also author of "Parade," 1917, and "Le Boeuf sur le toit," 1920.

Opera: *Oedipus rex: Opera-oratorio en deux actes d'apres Sophocle,* Boosey & Hawkes, 1949.

Films; scenarist and adaptor: (And director) *Le Sang d'un poete* (produced, 1930), scenario, with photographs, published by Editions du Rocher, 1948, augmented edition, 1957, translation by Lily Pons published as *Blood of a Poet,* Bodley Press, 1949; "La Comedie du bonheur," produced, 1940; "Le Baron fantome" (appeared also as actor), produced, 1942; (and co-director with Jean Delannoy) *L'Eternel* retour (scenario and photographs; produced, 1943), Nouvelles Editions Francaises, 1948; "Les Dames du Bois du Boulogne," produced, 1944; (and director) La Belle et la bete (based on a fairy tale by Mme. Leprince de Beaumont; produced, 1945), Editions du Rocher, 1958, bilingual edition, New York University Press, 1970; Ruy Blas (adaptation of the play by Victor Hugo; produced, 1947), Editions du Rocher, 1947; "La Voix humaine" (adaptation of his one-act play), produced, 1947; (and director) "L'Aigle a deux tetes" (adaptation of his play), produced, 1947; "Noces de sable," produced 1948; (and director) Les Parents terribles (adaptation of his play; scenario and photographs; produced, 1948), Le Monde Illustre, 1949, translation and adaptation by Charles Frank produced under title "Intimate Relations" (also known as "Disobedient"), 1952; "Les Enfants terribles" (adaptation of his novel; he also speaks commentary; directed by J. P. Melville), produced, 1948; (and director) Orphee (scenario and photographs; speaks a few lines as "author"; produced, 1949; printed in limited edition, with Cocteau's drawings, by Larry Jordan, La Parade, 1951), Andre Bonne, 1951; (and director) "Santo Sospiro" (short film), produced, 1951; "Ce Siecle a cinquante ans" (short film), produced, 1952; "La Coronna nagra," produced, 1952; (and director) "Le Rouge est mis" (short film), produced, 1952; (and director) Le Testament d'Orphee (produced, 1959), Editions du Rocher, 1959.

Nonfiction: Le Coq et l'arlequin (notes on music, with a portrait of Cocteau by Picasso), Editions de la Sirene, 1918, translation by Rollo H. Myers published as Cock and Harlequin: Notes Concerning Music, Egoist Press (London), 1921; Dans le ciel de la patrie, Societe Spad, 1918; Le Secret professionnel, Stock, 1922; Dessins, Stock, 1923, translation published as Drawings, Dover, 1972; Picasso, Stock, 1923; Lettre a Jacques Maritain, Stock, 1926 (selected excerpts in English included in Journals, 1956, below), published as Lettre a Maritain: Reponse a Jean Cocteau (including response by Maritain), Stock, 1964; Le Rappel a l'ordre, Stock, 1926, translation by Myers published as A Call to Order, Faber & Gwyer, 1926, reprinted, Haskell House, 1974; Romeo et Juliette: Pretexte a mise en scene d'apres le drame de William Shakespeare, Se Vend au Sans Pareil, 1926; Le Mystere laic (an essay on indirect study), Editions de Quatre Chemins, 1928, published as Essai de critique indirecte: Le mystere laic—Des beaux arts consideres comme un assassinat, introduction by Bernard Grasset, Grasset, 1932; (self illustrated) Opium: Journal d'une desintoxication, Stock, 1930, reprinted, 1972, translation by Ernest Boyd published as Opium: The Diary of an Addict (contains twenty-seven illustrations by Cocteau), Longmans, Green, 1932, translation by Margaret Crosland and Sinclair Road published as Opium: The Diary of a Cure, P. Owen, 1957, revised edition, 1968, Grove, 1958; Le Livre blanc, Editions du Signe, 1930, reprinted, B. Laville, 1970, published as The White Paper, Olympia Press (Paris), 1957, Macaulay, 1958, translated with an introduction by Crosland, containing woodcuts by Cocteau, published as Le Livre blanc, P. Owen, 1969; (self-illustrated) Portraits-Souvenir, 1900-1914, Grasset, 1935, translation by Crosland published as Paris Album, 1900-1914, W. H. Allen, 1956; (contributor) Gea Augsbourg, La Vie de Darius Milhaud, Correa, 1935; 60 dessins pour "Les Enfants terribles", Grasset, 1935; Mon premier voyage: Tour du monde en 80 jours, Gallimard, 1936, translation by Stuart Gilbert published as Round the World Again in Eighty Days, G. Routledge, 1937, translation by W. J. Strachan published as My Journey Round the World, P. Owen, 1958.

Dessins en marge du texte des "Chevaliers de la table ronde," Gallimard, 1941; Le Greco, Le Divan, 1943; Portrait de Mounet-Sully (contains sixteen drawings by Cocteau), F. Bernouard (Paris), 1945; La Belle et la bete: Journal d'un film, Janin, 1946, translation by Ronald Duncan published as Diary of a Film, Roy, 1950, revised edition published as Beauty and the Beast: Diary of a Film, Dover, 1972; Poesie critique (poetry criticism), edited by Henri Parisot, Editions des Quatre Vents, 1946, published in two volumes, Gallimard, 1959; (with Paul Claudel, Paul Eluard, and Stephane Mallarme) De la musique encore et toujours!, preface by Paul Valery, Editions du Tambourinaire, 1946; La Difficulte d'etre, P. Morihien, 1947, translation by Elizabeth Sprigge published as The Difficulty of Being, introduction by Ned Rorem, P. Owen, 1966, Coward, 1967; Le Foyer des artistes, Plon, 1947; L'Eternel retour, Nouvelles Editions Francaises, 1947; Art and Faith: Letters between Jacques Maritain and Jean Cocteau, Philosophical Library, 1948; (self-illustrated) Drole de menage, P. Morihien, 1948; Lettre aux Americains, Grasset, 1949; (editor) Almanach du theatre et du cinema, Editions de Flore, 1949; Maalesh: Journal d'une tournee de theatre, Gallimard, 1949, translation by Mary C. Hoeck published as Maalesh: A Theatrical Tour in the Middle East, P. Owen, 1956; (editor) Choix de lettres de Max Jacob a Jean Cocteau: 1919-1944, P. Morihien, 1949.

Dufy, Flammarion, 1950; (with Andre Bazin) Orson Welles, Chavane, 1950; Modigliani, F. Hazin (Paris), 1950; (with others) Portrait de famille, Fini, 1950; Jean Marais, Calmann-Levy, 1951, reprinted, 1975; Entretiens autour de cinematographe, recueillis par Andre Fraigneau, A. Bonne, 1951, translation by Vera Traill published as Cocteau on Film: A Conversation Recorded by Andre Fraigneau, Roy, 1954, reprinted, Dover, 1972; Journal d'un inconnu, Grasset, 1952, translation by Alec Brown published as The Hand of a Stranger, Elek Books (London), 1956, Horizon, 1959; Reines de la France, Grasset, 1952; (with Julien Green) Gide vivant (includes commentary by Cocteau and excerpts from the diary of Green), Amiot-Dumont, 1952; Carte blanche (prose sketches with drawings, watercolors and photographs by Cocteau), Mermod (Lausanne), 1953; (with others) Prestige de la danse, Clamart, 1953; Discours de reception de M. Jean Cocteau a l'Academie francaise et reponse de M. Andre Maurois, Gallimard, 1955; Look to the Glory of Your Firm and the Excellence of Your Merchandise, for If You Deem These Good, Your Welfare Becomes the Welfare of All, translated by Lewis Galantiere, Draeger (Montrouge), c.1955; Aux confins de la Chine, Edition Caracteres, 1955; Colette: Discours de reception a l'Academie Royale de Belgique, Grasset, 1955 (extracts in English published in My Contemporaries, 1967, below); Lettre sur la poesie, Dutilleul, 1955; Le Dragon des mers, Georges Guillot, 1955; (contributor) Marbre et decoration, Federation Marbriere de France, c.1955.

Journals (contains sixteen drawings by Cocteau), edited and translated with an introduction by Wallace Fowlie, Criterion Books, 1956; Adieu a Mistinguett, Editions Dynamo, 1956; Art et sport, Savonnet (Limoges), 1956; Impression: Arts de la rue, Editions Dynamo, 1956; (author of introduction and notes) Jean Dauven, compiler, Jean Cocteau chez les sirens: Une experience de linguistic sur le discours de reception a l'Academie francaise de M. Jean Cocteau (illustrations by Picasso), Editions du Rocher, 1956; Temoignage (with portrait and engraving by Picasso), P. Bertrand, 1956; Le Discours de Strasbourg, Societe Messine d'Editions et d'Impressions (Metz), 1956; Le Discours d'Oxford, Gallimard, 1956, translation by Jean Stewart published as "Poetry and Invisibility," in *London Magazine*, January, 1957; (with Louis Aragon) *Entretiens sur le Musee de Dresde*, Cercle d'Art, 1957; *Erik Satie*, Editions Dynamo, 1957; *La Chapelle Saint Pierre, Villefranche sur Mer*, Editions du Rocher, 1957; *La Corrida du premier mai*, Grasset, 1957; *Comme un miel noir* (in French and English), L'Ecole Estienne, 1958; (with Roloff Beny and others) *Merveilles de la Mediterranee*, Arthaud, 1958; *Paraprosodies precedees de 7 dialogues*, Editions Du Rocher, 1958; (contributor) G. Coanet, *De bas en haut*, La Societe Messine d'Editions et d'Impressions (Metz), 1958; *La Salle des mariages, Hotel de ville de Menton*, Editions du Rocher, 1958; *La Canne blanche*, Editions Estienne, 1959; *Gondole des morts*, All'Insegne del Pesce d'Oro (Milan), 1959.

Guide a l'usage des visiteurs de la Chapelle Saint Blaise des Simples, Editions du Rocher, 1960, reprinted, 1975; *De la brouille*, Editions Dynamo, 1960; *Notes sur "Le Testament d'Orphee,"* Editions Dynamo, 1960; (editor) *Amedeo Modigilani: Quinze dessins*, Leda, 1960; *Decentralisation*, [Paris], 1961; *Du Serieux*, [Paris], 1961; (with others) *Insania pingens*, Ciba (Basle), 1961, published as *Petits maitres de la folies*, Clairfontaines (Lausanne), 1961; *Le Cordon ombilical*, Plon, 1962; *Picasso: 1916-1961* (with twenty-four original lithographs by Picasso), Editions du Rocher, 1962; *Discours a l'Academie royale de langue et de litterature francaises*, Editions Dynamo, 1962; *Hommage*, Editions Dynamo, 1962; *Interview par Jean Breton* (preceded by two poems by Cocteau, "Malediction au laurier," and "Hommage a Igor Stravinsky"), [Paris], 1963; *Adieu d'Antonio Ordonez*, Editions Forces Vives, 1963; (contributor) *La Comtesse de Noailles*, Librairie Academique Perrin, 1963; (contributor) *Exposition les peintres temoins de leur temps* (catalog), Musee Galliera (Paris), 1963; (contributor) *Toros muertos*, Editions Forces Vives, 1963; *La Mesangere*, De Tartas, 1963; *Jean Cocteau: Entretien avec Roger Stephane* (interview), J. Tallandier, 1964; (contributor) *Exposition Lucien Clergue* (catalog), Le Musee (Luneville), 1964; *Entretien avec Andre Fraigneau* (interview), preface by Pierre de Boisdeffre, Union Generale d'Editions, 1965; *Pegase*, Nouveau Cercle Parisien du Livre, 1965; *My Contemporaries*, translated, edited, and introduced by Crosland, P. Owen, 1967, Chilton, 1968; *Entre Radiguet et Picasso*, Editions Hermann, 1967; *Professional Secrets: The Autobiography of Jean Cocteau* (not related to 1922 book), translated by Richard Howard, edited by Robert Phelps, Farrar, Straus, 1970; *Lettres a Andre Gide avec quelques reponses d'Andre Gide*, La Table Ronde, 1970; (with Raymond Radiguet) *Paul et Virginie*, Edition Speciale, 1973; *Lettres a Milorad*, Editions Saint-Germain-des-Pres, 1975. Also author of an unpublished ballet scenario, "Le Dieu bleu," 1912.

Forewords, introductions, and prefaces: *Paris de jour*, Arts et Metiers Graphiques, 1937; Tran Van Tung, *Bach-yen; ou, La Fille au coeur fidele* (novel), Susse, 1946; Jacques Vienot, *L. Cappiello, sa vie et son oeuvre*, Editions de Clermont, 1946; Denise Bourdet, *Edouard Bourdet et ses amis*, La Jeune Parque, c.1946; Georgette Leblanc, *La Machine a courage*, Janin, 1947; Roger Lannes, *Hommage a la danse* (text in French, Spanish, and English), Editions de la Revue Masques, 1947; Jean-Pierre Aumont, *L'Empereur de Chine* (play), Nagel, 1948; Abbe Antoine Francois Prevost, *Manon Lescaut*, Stock, 1948; Charles Trenet, *La Bonne planete* (novel), Brunier, 1949; Marcel Vertes, *Le Cirque*, Livres Merveilleux (Monaco), 1949; Dore Ogrizek, *Paris tel qu'on l'aime*, Ode, 1949.

Odette Joyeux, *Le Chateau du Carrefour*, Gallimard, 1951; *Nicole's Guide to Paris*, Amiot-Dumont, 1951; Roland Toutain, *Mes 400 coups*, Amiot-Dumont, 1951; *Le Roman de Renart*, Editions des Arceaux (Montpellier), 1952; Nicholas Blake, *Poesie pour tous*, Seghers, 1953; Jean Harold, *Les Images qui ont fait rire Charlie Chaplin*, Presse de Livre Francais, 1953; *Feux vifs et flammes mortes pour un astre eteint*, Presses de Livre Francais, 1953; Claude Glayman, *Claire*, Seghers, 1954; Georges Detaille and Gerard Mulys, *Les Ballets de Monte Carlo: 1911, 1944*, Editions Arc-en-ciel, 1954; Ghislaine Costa de Beauregard, *Tete la premiere*, Seghers, 1954; Rene Bertrand, *Sagesse et chimeres*, Grasset, 1954; Jean Berthet, *Graffiti: 1930-1953*, L'Auteur, 1954; Charles Delauney, *Django Reinhardt*, Editions Jazz-hot, 1954; Dore Ogrizek, *L'Allemagne*, Ode, 1954; Jean Rene Legrand, *Meditations cabbalistiques sur des symboles traditionnels*, Editions des Champs-Elysees, 1955; Helene Jourdan-Morhange, *Mes amis musiciens*, Editeurs Francais Reunis, 1955; Keith Goesch, *Raymond Radiguet*, La Palatine (Geneva), 1955; Georges Coanet, *Vibrafaune* (poem), [Metz], 1955; Ambrose Bierce, *Le Dictionnaire du diable* ("Devil's Dictionary"), translated by Jacques Papy, Les Quatre Jeudi, 1955; Aga Khan III, *Memoires*, Michel, 1955; Pierre Borel, *Des mots*, Milas-Martin, 1955.

Ballet espagnol, Societe Francaise du Livre, 1956; Raymond Radiguet, *Le Diable au corps*, Georges Guillot, 1956; *Le Decor de theatre dans le monde depuis 1950*, Editions Elsevier, 1956; Edmond Petit, *Heures de vol*, Emile-Paul, 1956; Jimmy Guieu, *Black-out sur les soucoupes volantes*, Editions Fleuve Noir, 1956; Louis de Gonzague Frick, *Oddiaphanies*, Nouvelles Editions Debresse, 1956; *Epitaphes grecques*, Les Impenitents, 1956; Marcel Lobet, *Panorama du ballet d'aujourd'hui*, Dutilleul, 1956; Raymond Radiguet, *Le Bal du compte d'Orgel*, Livre Club du Libraire, 1956; Fereydoun Hoveyda, *Petite histoire du roman policier*, Editions du Pavillon, 1956; Jean-Marie Magnan, *La Nuit d'Arles*, Seghers, 1957; Andre Daguesseau, *Quelques fleurs de la vie: Poemes*, Editions de la Revue Moderne, 1957; Albert Simonin, *Le Petit Simonin illustre*, Pierre Amiot, 1957; Paul Eluard, *Corps memorables*, Seghers, 1957; Andre Fraigneau, *Venise que j'aime*, Editions Sun, 1957, translation by Ruth Whipple Fermaud published by Tudor, 1957; Jacques Veysset, *Le Palais Farnese*, Edizioni Cosmopolita (Rome), 1958; *Andre Lhote*, Presses Artistiques, 1958; Dante Alighieri, *Une Descente aux enfers*, Galerie de Ventadour, 1958; Michel Sima, *21 visages d'artistes*, Nathan, 1959; *Plus on est de fous*, edited by Gabriel Perreux, Hachette, 1959; *Les Meilleurs poemes anglais et americains d'aujourd'hui*, edited by Paul Ginestier, Societe d'Edition d'Enseignement Superieur, 1959; Roger Peyrefitte, *L'Exile du Capri*, Flammarion, 1959; *Exposition van Dongen* (catalog), Galerie des Ponchettes (Nice), 1959; Rollo Myers, *Erik Satie*, Gallimard, 1959; Annie Moberly and Eleanor Jourdain, *Les Fantomes de Trianon*, Editions du Rocher, 1959; Micheline Meunier, *Un Acteur-poete Jean Marais*, Nouvelles Editions Debresse, 1959; Dore Ogrizek, *La France: Un Portrait en couleurs*, Ode, 1959; Georges Peeters, *Monstres sacres du ring*, Editions de la Table Ronde, 1959.

Serge Lido, *Panorama de la danse*, Societe Francaise du Livre, 1960; *Retrospective Guy Pierre Fauconnet*, Musee Alfred-Bonno (Chelles), 1960; Nicole Houssa, *Comme un collier brise: Poemes*, Editions des Artistes (Brussels), 1960; Roger Pillaudin, *Jean Cocteau tourne son dernier film*, Editions de La Table Ronde, 1960; La Fontaine, *20 fables*, Jaspard, Solus et Cie (Monaco), 1961; Jacques Baroche, *Vedettes au microscope*, Contact-Editions, 1961; Henrik

Ibsen, *Theatre I,* Perrin, 1961; Alexander Liberman, *Les Maitres de l'art contemporain,* Arthaud, 1961; Odette Lutgen, *En depit de leur gloire,* Del Duca, 1961; George Bernard Shaw and Mrs. Patrick Campbell, *Correspondance* (translation of letters), Calmann-Levy, 1961; Henri Matarasso and Pierre Petitfils, *Vie d'Arthur Rimbaud,* Hachette, 1962; Joe Hamman, *Du Far-West a Montmartre,* Editeurs Francais Reunis, 1962; Pierre Borel, *Les Signes du ciel,* Editions du Cercle d'Etudes Litteraires Francaises, 1962; Pierre Perrin, *Avant le clair de lune:* (poems), Grassin, 1962; Guido Marinelli, *Biennales de Paris: 1959-1961,* M.A.O. (Turin), 1962; *Chefs-d'oeuvres de l'art,* Hachette, 1963; *Sequences* (anthology of contemporary French poetry), Grassin, 1963; *La Mesangere,* P. de Tartas, 1963; Henrik Ibsen, *Maison de poupee* [suivi de] *Les Revenants,* Perrin, 1964; Dore Ogrzek, *L'allemagne,* Ode, 1964; Robert Goffin, *Fil d'Ariane pour la poesie,* A. G. Nizet, 1964; Michel Oliver, *Cooking Is Child's Play,* Random House, 1965; Leon Moussinac, *Le Theatre des origines a non jours,* Flammarion, 1966; Alain Valery Alberto, *Nouveaux fotras,* Editions Dynamo, 1966.

Omnibus volumes: *Call to Order* (contains *Cock and Harlequin, Professional Secrets,* and other critical essays), translated by Rollo H. Myers, Holt, 1923, reprinted, Haskell House, 1974; *Oedipe Roi* [et] *Romeo et Julliette,* Plon, 1923; *Jean Cocteau* (contains a study of Roger Lannes, poems, and a bibliography), Seghers, 1945, revised edition, 1969; *Oeuvres completes,* Marguerat (Lausanne), Volume I contains *Le Grand ecart, Thomas l'imposteur, Les Enfants terribles,* "Le Fantome de Marseille," Volume II contains *Le Potomak, 1913-1914,* "Un Prospectus," *La Fin du Potomak,* Volume III contains *Le Cap de Bonne-Esperance, Poesies, Vocabulaire, Plain-Chant, Cri ecrit,* "Neige," Volume IV contains "Discours du grand sommeil," *Opera,* "Enigme," "Allegories," "Les Fils de l'air," Volume V contains "Orphee," "Oedipe Roi," "Antigone," "La Machine infernale," Volume VI contains *Romeo et Julliette,* "Les Chevaliers de la table ronde," "Renaud et Armide," Volume VII contains "Les Maries de la Tour Eiffel," "La Voix humaine," "Les Parents terribles," "Parade," "Le Boeuf sur le toit," Volume VIII contains "Le Machine a ecrire," "Les Monstres sacres," "L'Ecole des veuves," "Le Bel indifferent," "Anna la bonne," "La Dame de Monte Carlo," "Le Fantome de Marseille," Volume IX contains *Le Rappel a l'ordre,* "Le Numero Barbette," *Lettre a Jacques Maritain,* "La Jeunesse et le scandale," "Une Entrevue sur la critique avec Maurice Rouzaud," *Rousseau,* Volume X contains *Le Mystere laic, Opium, Des Beauxarts consideres comme un assassinat,* "Quelques articles," "Prefaces," "Le Mythe du Greco," "Coupures de press," 1947-50.

Theatre, Gallimard, Volume I contains "Antigone," "Les Maries da la Tour Eiffel," "Les Chevaliers de la table ronde," "Les parents terribles," Volume II contains "Les Monstres sacres," "La Machine a ecrire," "Renaud et Armide," "L'Aigle a deux tetes," both 1948, augmented edition, Grasset, Volume I contains same works as original first volume and "Orphee," "La Voix humaine," "La Machine infernale," "Oedipie Roi," Volume II contains same works as original second volume and "Bacchus," "Theatre de poche," "Arguments sceniques et choregraphiques," both 1957; *Poemes* (contains *Leone, Allegories, La Crucifixion,* and "Neiges"), Gallimard, 1948; *Theatre de Poche* (contains "Parade," "Le Boeuf sur le toit; ou, The Nothing Doing Bar," "Le Pauve Matelot," "L'Ecole des veuves," "Le Bel indifferent," "Le Fantome de Marseille," "Anna la bonne," "La Dame de Monte Carlo,"

"Le Fils de l'air," "Le Menteur," "Par la fenetre," "Je l'ai perdue," "Lis ton journal," "La Farce du chateau," and fourteen drawings by Cocteau), P. Morihien, 1949, published as *Nouveau theatre de poche* (contains above with the addition of "L'Epouse injustement soupconne"), Editions du Rocher, 1960; *Anthologie poetique de Jean Cocteau,* Le Club Francais du Livre, 1951; *Venise images par Ferruccio Leiss* [et] *L'Autre face de Venise par Jean Cocteau,* D. Guarnati (Milan), 1953; *Le Grand ecart* [et] *La Voix humaine,* Club des Editeurs, 1957; *Impression* [suivi de] *Arts de la rue* [et de] *Eloge de l'imprimerie,* Editions Dynamo, 1957.

Ceremonial espagnal du phenix [suivi de] *La Partie d'eches,* Gallimard, 1961; *Cocteau par Lui-meme,* edited by Andre Fraigneau, Editions du Seuil, 1957; *Five Plays* (contains "Orphee," "Antigone," "Intimate Relations," "The Holy Terrors," "The Eagle with Two Heads"), Hill & Wang, 1961; *Orpheus, Oedipus Rex,* [and] *The Infernal Machine,* translated with a foreword and introductory essay by Wildman, Oxford University Press, 1962; *Four Plays* (contains "Antigone," "Intimate Relations," "The Holy Terrors," "The Eagle with Two Heads"), translation, MacGibbon & Kee, 1962; *Les Enfants terribles* [et] *Les Parents terribles,* Club des Libraries de France, 1962; *Special Cocteau: Les Maries de la Tour Eiffel* [et] *Les Chevaliers de la table ronde,* [Paris], 1966; *Opera* [suivi de] *Le Discours du grand sommeil,* preface by Jacques Brosse, Gallimard, 1967; *The Infernal Machine, and Other Plays,* New Directions, 1967; *Opera* [suivi de] *Plain-Chant,* Livre de Poche, 1967; *Le Cap de Bonne Esperance* [suivi de] *Discours du grand sommeil,* Gallimard, 1967; *Pages choisies,* edited by Robert Prat, Hachette, 1967; *Opera* [suivi de] *Des mots, De mon style,* Tchou, 1967; *Two Screenplays: The Blood of a Poet* [and] *The Testament of Orpheus,* translated by Carol Martin-Sperry, Orion Press, 1968; *Screenplays and Other Writings on the Cinema* (contains "Blood of a Poet," "Beauty and the Beast," "Testament of Orpheus"), Orion Press, 1968; *White Paper* [with] *The Naked Beast at Heaven's Gate,* the latter by P. Angelique, Greenleaf Classics, 1968; *Three Screenplays: L'Eternal retour, Orphee, La Belle et la bete,* translated by Carol Martin-Sperry, Orion Press, 1968; *Cocteau's World* (anthology), translated and edited by Margaret Crosland, P. Owen, 1971, Dodd, 1973; *Du cinematographie* (collected works), edited by Andre Bernard and Claude Gauteur, P. Belfond, 1973; *Entretiens sur le cinematographie,* edited by Bernard and Gauteur, P. Belfond, 1973; *Mon Premier voyage, Des beaux-arts consideres comme un assassinat, Lettre a Maritan,* Vialetay, 1973; *Orphee: Extraits de la tragedie d'Orphee ainsi que des films Orphee et Le Testament d'Orphee,* Bordas, 1973; *Poesie de journalism, 1935-1938,* P. Belfond, 1973. Also published *Paraprosodies* [precedees de] *Sept dialogues avec le Seigneur qui est en nous,* Editions du Rocher.

SIDELIGHTS: Wallace Fowlie has said of Cocteau, "Variousness is the clue to his genius." Listing some of his many achievements, Fowlie reported: "When Cocteau played the drums in a jazz band, he helped launch the fashion of jazz. His first film, 'Le Sang d'un poete,' initiated a use of the *merveilleux* in cinema art that is still being copied. . . . With *Antigone* and *Orphee,* in which he played Angel Heurtebise in the Pitoeff production, he rejuvenated the theatre of antiquity. . . . He was also among the very first to call attention to the art of Picasso and the art of Louis Armstrong." The *National Observer* writer suggests that, "of the artistic generation whose daring gave birth to Twentieth Century Art, Cocteau came closest to being a Renaissance man."

His versatility, however, caused some damage to his reputation as a serious artist. Henri Peyre wrote, "It became customary to be entertained by Cocteau's chameleon-like metamorphoses and to treat him considerably as a 'juggler.'" But he went on to point out that: "The illusionist in Cocteau . . . was the outward mask which he liked to offer to the public in self-defence." According to Fowlie, the serious purposes behind his work emerged when he was awarded high academic honors: "It became apparent that the long career had not been motivated by the ambition to amuse, that . . . Cocteau was an indefatigable worker, a man believing that a supernatural force always directed the natural forces, . . . whose seeming facility was his method of work."

Cocteau was born into a social milieu whose members, according to Elizabeth Sprigge and Jean-Jacques Kihm, "led an enchanted existence, in which the arts were recognised as an essential part of good living." As a child he formed a lifelong passion for the theatre, which he described many times as, "the fever of crimson and gold." Fowlie reported: "The atmosphere of the theatre became a world for him. . . . Every detail of a theatre production fascinated him, from the luminously painted backdrop to the women selling caramels in the intermission." Writing of Cocteau's own work in the theater, Peyre contended that "*La Machine infernale* remains the best modernization of the Oedipus story in our generation."

Cocteau has also been especially highly praised for his films. Andre Fraigneau gave this assessment of the screen version of "Orphee": "Like a poem, a great novel, or a sequence in music, [it] can and calls out to be seen and heard again. There is no example of cinema in which the decline of the genre is contradicted with greater force." In this film, Cocteau's concern with unusual effects was given full play; Sprigge and Kihm noted that he "was able to indulge his obsession with mirrors to the full." They continued: "He greatly enjoyed both the real mirrors and the ingenious semblance of mirrors: frames framing a void, the construction of twin rooms and twin objects, which if you were quick enough you could see not to be perfectly inverted, Maria Casares playing back to back with her double, Jean Marais disappearing through a void, which in the next shot was filled with a mirror. . . ." When considering such effects, Fowlie pointed out that "it is well to remember Cocteau's statement that he is not a maker of films in the ordinary sense. He calls himself a poet using the camera as a vehicle for the projection of dreams."

Summing up the whole of Cocteau's achievement, Fowlie gave him a high place in the French critical tradition: "All of Cocteau's work can justifiably be called a 'poetry of criticism,' because in it he gives himself over without effort to the delight of judging, to the enjoyment of a game of ideas which forms the basis of criticism. Cocteau is one of those French writers—novelists, poets, dramatists—who are critics, and among the finest that France has produced, critics not only in their critical essays but also in their creative works."

There are several recordings of Cocteau's works in French, and also a conversation with William Fifield, *Jean Cocteau: A Self-Portrait* (with French-English text), issued by Caedmon.

Opium: Journal of a Cure has been dramatized by Roc Brynner and produced in Dublin and London, 1969, and in New York, 1970.

Cocteau is buried at Milly-la-Foret, in the garden of the chapel Saint-Blaise-des Simples, which he designed himself.

BIOGRAPHICAL/CRITICAL SOURCES—Books: Roger Lannes, *Jean Cocteau*, Seghers, 1945; Andre Fraigneau, *Jean Cocteau: Entretiens autour du cinematographe*, Andre Bonne, 1951, translation by Vera Traill published as *Cocteau on the Film: A Conversation Recorded by Andre Fraigneau*, Dobson, 1954; Margaret Crosiand, *Jean Cocteau*, Knopf, 1956; *The Journals of Jean Cocteau*, edited and translated, with an introduction, by Wallace Fowlie, Criterion, 1956; Fraigneau, *Cocteau par lui-meme*, Editions du Seuil, 1957, translation by Donald Lehmkuhl published as *Cocteau*, Grove, 1961; Rene Gilson, *Jean Cocteau* (on his film work), Seghers, 1964, Crown, 1969; Fraigneau, *Jean Cocteau: Entretiens a la radio*, preface by Pierre de Boisdeffre, Union Generale d'Editions, 1965; Wallace Fowlie, *Jean Cocteau: The History of a Poet's Age*, Indiana University Press, 1966; Elizabeth Sprigge and Jean-Jacques Kihm, *Jean Cocteau: The Man and the Mirror*, Gollancz, 1968; Frederick Brown, *An Impersonation of Angels: A Biography of Jean Cocteau*, Viking, 1968; Francis Steegmullen, *Cocteau*, Little, Brown, 1970; Bettina L. Knapp, *Jean Cocteau*, Twayne, 1970; Richard Howard, editor, *Professional Secrets: An Autobiography of Jean Cocteau*, translated by Richard Howard, Farrar, Straus, 1970; *Contemporary Literary Criticism*, Volume I, Gale, 1973.

Articles: *Empreintes* (Brussels), May, June, July, 1950; *La Table Ronde*, October, 1955; *Adam*, No. 300, 1965; *New York Times Book Review*, December 25, 1966; *London Magazine*, March, 1967; *National Observer*, June 12, 1967; *Commonweal*, November 17, 1967; *New Yorker*, September 27, 1969; *Commentary*, April, 1971; *Choice*, November, 1973; *American Imago*, summer, 1976.†

(Died October 11, 1963)

*   *   *

COFFIN, Patricia   1912-1974

PERSONAL: Born March 17, 1912, in New York, N.Y.; daughter of William (in foreign service) and Mabel (Rees) Coffin; married Theodore L. Gaillard, September 12, 1936 (divorced, 1949); married Merrill Kirk Lindsay (an editor and writer), December 12, 1949; children: (first marriage) Theodore L., Jr., Tristam Coffin; (second marriage) Dionis Coffin. *Education:* Attended Chapin School, New York, N.Y., Art Students League, and Grand Central School of Art. *Home:* 50 East 96th St., New York, N.Y. 10028. *Agent:* Ellen Levine, Curtis Brown Ltd., 575 Madison Ave., New York, N.Y. 10022.

CAREER: New York World-Telegram, New York City, columnist and feature writer, 1938-42; *Look* Magazine, New York City, editor, 1942-71, modern living editor, 1955-71; *Life* Magazine, New York City, consulting editor, beginning 1971. *Member:* Poetry Society of America (director), Wharf Rat's Club of Nantucket. *Awards, honors:* Theta Sigma Chi award for magazine writing, 1972.

WRITINGS: The Gruesome Green Witch, Walker & Co., 1969; *Nantucket*, Viking, 1971; *1,2,3,4,5,6: How to Understand and Enjoy the Years that Count*, Macmillan, 1972. Contributor to *Prairie Schooner, Poet Lore, Harper's, McCall's*, and *Ladies' Home Journal*. Contributing editor, *Panache Magazine*.

WORK IN PROGRESS: My Own Backyard, an ecological-biographical book; *Islands on My Mind*, a book of poetry; *Doors*, a collection of water color paintings.†

(Died May 30, 1974)

COFFMAN, Paul B(rown)   1900-

PERSONAL: Born December 20, 1900, in Columbus, Ohio; son of Elmer and Helen (Brown) Coffman; married Ruth Marcella Hudson, October 14, 1922; married second wife, Christine Mary Araman, August 12, 1960; children: (first marriage) Louise Joan, Earle Merritt Wesley. *Education:* Ohio State University, B.S., 1923; Harvard University, M.B.A., 1926. *Religion:* Methodist. *Home:* Twelve Acres, West Barnstable, Mass. 02668.

CAREER: Lecturer or instructor at Northeastern University and Boston University, Boston, Mass., 1923-27; College of William and Mary, Williamsburg, Va., assistant professor, 1926-27; Harvard University, School of Business Administration, Boston, Mass., 1927-35, began as instructor, became assistant professor and tutor; Poor's Publishing Co., New York City, and Wellesley, Mass., executive vice-president and general manager, 1930-32; Standard Statistics Co., New York City, vice-president and director, 1935-40; Standard & Poor's Corp., New York City, vice-president, 1941-44, director, 1941-66, member of executive committee, 1941-65; Standard Research Consultants, Inc., New York City, president and director, 1944-66, chairman of board, beginning 1966. Chairman of executive committee, Squire, Schilling & Skiff, 1944-61; president and director of Overseas Consultants, and Standard Research Consultants, International, 1957-61. Consultant to U.S. War Department, 1941-46, and Office of Secretary of Defense, 1947-49.

MEMBER: American Society of Appraisers (fellow; life member; president, 1959-61), Society of Professional Management Consultants, National Association of Accountants, American Academy of Political and Social Science (life member), Japan Society, Newcomen Society in North America, Beta Alpha Psi, Masons, Harvard Club (Boston and New York), University Club and India House (New York), Hyannis Yacht Club, Craigville Beach Club (Centerville, Mass.).

WRITINGS: (With Arnold Edward Hanson) *Problems in Auditing,* McGraw, 1930; (with Thomas Henry Sanders) *Problems in Industrial Accounting,* 2nd edition, McGraw, 1930; (with Ralph Eastman Badger) *The Complete Guide to Investment Analysis,* McGraw, 1967. Writer of column, "The Business Climate," for *Journal of Accountancy and Business Review and Forecast in Technical Valuation,* 1955-60. Chairman of editorial board, and editor, *Appraisal and Valuation Manual,* American Society of Appraisers, 1956-61; member of advisory council, *Executive* (publication of Harvard Business School), 1957-64.

*   *   *

COFFMAN, Ramon Peyton   1896-
(Uncle Ray)

PERSONAL: Born July 24, 1896, in Indianapolis, Ind.; son of Walter McDowell (a mechanical engineer and inventor) and Effie (Stringer) Coffman; married Nelle Ruth Gratton, December 14, 1929; children: Gratton Eugene, Peyton, Roger, Kathleen. *Education:* Attended Yale University, 1915-16, New School for Social Research, 1918-19; University of Wisconsin, A.B., 1926. *Religion:* Unitarian Universalist. *Residence:* Fort Lauderdale, Fla.

CAREER: Founder and editor of *Typical Boy* (magazine), 1912-14; reporter, later children's editor on newspapers in Milwaukee, Wis., 1920-22; began writing newspaper feature for children as Uncle Ray, 1922, and daily column, "Uncle Ray's Corner," has been syndicated in American newspapers, beginning 1925. Author of juvenile books, beginning 1924; founding editor and publisher of *Uncle Ray's Magazine,* 1946-57. *Member:* Sigma Delta Chi.

WRITINGS: The Child's Story of the Human Race, Dodd, 1924; *The Story of America,* six books, F. A. Owen, 1927-34; *Our America,* Dodd, 1930; (author of brief text) *Picture Story of Robinson Crusoe,* illustrated by Frank C. Pape, Reilly & Lee, 1932; *Uncle Ray's Story of the Stone-Age People,* Rand McNally, 1936; (under pseudonym Uncle Ray) *The Child's Story of Science,* Putnam, 1939.

(With Nathan G. Goodman) *Famous Explorers for Boys and Girls,* A. S. Barnes, 1942, reissued as *Famous Explorers for Young People,* Dodd, 1956; (with N. G. Goodman) *Famous Authors for Boys and Girls,* A. S. Barnes, 1943, also issued as *Famous Authors for Young People,* Dodd, 1943; (with N. G. Goodman) *Famous Generals and Admirals for Boys and Girls,* A. S. Barnes, 1944; (with N. G. Goodman) *Famous Pioneers for Young People,* A. S. Barnes, 1945; *Famous Kings and Queens for Young People,* A. S. Barnes, 1947.

WORK IN PROGRESS: A sixteen-volume set of writings.

SIDELIGHTS: Coffman has made seven trips to Europe and traveled around the world, writing about customs in other lands for young readers. Newspaper articles and books have been translated into a total of four languages.††

*   *   *

COLEAN, Miles Lanier   1898-

PERSONAL: Surname is pronounced Ko-leen; born August 4, 1898, in Peoria, Ill.; son of William Henry (a manufacturer) and Frances (Putman) Colean; married Marion Feltman, January 21, 1925; children: Mary Catherine (Mrs. E. E. Etherington). *Education:* Attended University of Wisconsin, 1916-17; Columbia University, B.Arch., 1922. *Religion:* Episcopalian. *Home:* 5001 Macomb St. N.W., Washington, D.C. 20016. *Office:* 1125 15th St. N.W., Washington, D.C. 20005.

CAREER: Began with architectural firm of R. H. Dana, New York City, 1922-24; Holabird & Root, Chicago, Ill., chief draftsman, 1925-28; Cowles & Colean (architects), Chicago, partner, 1928-34; Federal Housing Administration, Washington, D.C., technical director, 1934-37, assistant administrator, 1937-40; Twentieth Century Fund, New York City, director of housing survey, 1940-42; Starrett Brothers & Eken, Inc. (builders), New York City, vice-president, 1942-44; National Bureau of Economic Research, New York City, staff member, 1947-50; Investors Central Management Corp., New York City, chairman of board, beginning 1956. Private consultant in finance and construction, beginning 1940. Chairman of U.S. delegation, International Congress on Planning and Housing, Mexico City, 1938; member of Advisory Committee on National Defense, 1940; chairman of Business Research Advisory Committee, U.S. Bureau of Labor Statistics, 1953-54; member of President's Committee on Housing Policies and Programs, 1953, and Building Research Advisory Board of National Research Council, 1956-57. Consultant to National Resources Planning Board, 1942, Congressional committees on postwar policy and planning, 1944-46, Bureau of the Census, and other government agencies. Trustee of Urban Land Institute and Federal City Council.

MEMBER: Conference of Business Economists (chairman, 1960), American Institute of Architects (fellow), American Statistical Association (fellow), American Association for the Advancement of Science (fellow); Cosmos Club, Metropolitan Club, and Chevy Chase Club (all Washington, D.C.). *Awards, honors:* University Medal, Columbia University, 1943.

WRITINGS: Quest, Dutton, 1923; *American Housing: Problems and Prospects,* Twentieth Century Fund, 1944; *Impact of Government on Real Estate Finance in the United States,* National Bureau of Economic Research, 1950; (with Robinson Newcomb) *Stabilizing Construction: The Record and Potential,* McGraw, 1952; *Renewing Our Cities,* Twentieth Century Fund, 1953, reprinted, Kraus Reprint, 1975; *Mortgage Companies and Their Place in the Financial Structure,* Prentice-Hall, 1962. Also author of reports and pamphlets on housing, construction, and building codes, published by Twentieth Century Fund, National Planning Association, and U.S. Government Printing Office, 1942-46.

*   *   *

COLEMAN, Almand R(ouse)   1905-

PERSONAL: Born July 16, 1905, in Smithfield, Va.; son of Archer Almand (a life insurance salesman) and Ruby Booth (Rouse) Coleman; married Clare Merryman Whitfield, April 13, 1940 (died January, 1961); married Louise Hudson Foster, May 21, 1962; children: (first marriage) Lisa Crane (Mrs. Frederick Eppes Rose), William Stephen; (second marriage) Charles Almand; (stepchildren) Emily (Mrs. John Pickering), Edmund Palmer Foster, George William Foster. *Education:* Washington and Lee University, A.B., 1926, B.S. in Commerce, 1927; Harvard University, M.B.A., 1934. *Religion:* Episcopalian. *Home:* 1867 Field Rd., Charlottesville, Va. 22903. *Office:* Graduate School of Business Administration, University of Virginia, Box 3607, Charlottesville, Va. 22903.

CAREER: Certified public accountant in the state of Virginia, 1929; A. M. Pullen & Co., Richmond, Va., senior accountant, 1928-33; Farm Credit Administration, Washington, D.C., acting chief of Financial Analysis and Statistical Section, 1934-35; State Planters Bank & Trust Co., Richmond, assistant trust officer and assistant cashier, 1935-39; Washington and Lee University, Lexington, Va., associate professor, 1939-41, professor of accounting, 1941-54; University of Virginia, Graduate School of Business Administration, Charlottesville, professor, 1955-72, Charles C. Abbott Professor of Business Administration, beginning 1972. Visiting professor of accounting, Harvard University, 1954-1955. Member of board of directors of various corporations, including Lipscomb Lumber Co., W. H. Harris Grocery Co., and Rockbridge National Bank. *Military service:* U.S. Army, Office of the Chief of Army Ordnance, 1942-45; became major. U.S. Army Reserve, 1950-54; became lieutenant colonel.

MEMBER: National Association of Accountants, Financial Executives Institute, American Accounting Association (vice-president, 1956), American Institute of Certified Public Accountants, Raven Society, Phi Beta Kappa, Beta Gamma Sigma.

WRITINGS: (Editor) *Simplified Banking Forms and Procedure,* American Bankers Association, 1940; *Financial Accounting: A General Management Approach,* Wiley, 1970. Contributor to professional journals.

WORK IN PROGRESS: Research in the area of financial accounting, management accounting, and management control systems; research into computer fraud.

COLGRAVE, Bertram   1888-1968

PERSONAL: Born June 5, 1888, in England; son of Thomas and Esther (Abrahams) Colgrave; married Hilda K. Derry, September 4, 1936. *Education:* University of Birmingham, M.A., 1911; Cambridge University, M.A., 1921. *Home:* Evenwood, Church End, Coton, Cambridge, England.

CAREER: University of Durham, Durham, England, lecturer and reader, 1920-55. Visiting professor at University of North Carolina, University of Texas, University of Kansas, University of Colorado, and Mount Holyoke College. Sir Israel Gollancz Memorial Lecturer for British Academy, 1957. *Member:* Society of Antiquaries (fellow), Royal Historical Society (fellow), Mediaeval Academy of America (fellow). *Awards, honors:* University of Durham, M.A., 1930, and Litt.D., 1955.

WRITINGS: (Translator and author of notes) *Eddins' Life of Wilfrid,* Cambridge University Press, 1934; (translator and author of notes) *Two Lives of St. Cuthbert,* Cambridge University Press, 1940, reprinted, Greenwood Press, 1969; *Durham Castle: An Illustrated Survey of the Ancient Castle of the Bishops of Durham,* English Life Publications, 1953; (editor and translator) Felix, *Life of St. Guthlac,* Cambridge University Press, 1956; (editor, translator, and author of notes) *Earliest Life of Gregory the Great by an Anonymous Monk of Whitley,* University of Kansas Press, 1968; (editor with Roger Mynors) *Bede's Ecclesiastical History,* Oxford University Press, 1969. Sir Israel Gollancz Memorial Lecture, "The Earliest Saints' Lives Written in England," was published in *Proceedings* of British Academy, Volume XLIV, 1959. Editor-in-chief, "Early English Manuscripts in Facsimile," published by Johns Hopkins Press and Rosenkilde & Bagger (Denmark), 1951-63.†

(Died January 13, 1968)

*   *   *

COLLIGAN, Francis J(ames)   1908-19(?)

PERSONAL: Born December 27, 1908, in San Francisco, Calif.; son of Francis J. and Mary (Barrett) Colligan; married Margaret Clara Haxton, August 1, 1933; children: Francis Sherwin. *Education:* University of San Francisco, A.B. (honors), 1929; University of California, Berkeley, A.M., 1933, Ph.D., 1941.

CAREER: University of San Francisco (now San Francisco State University), Calif., instructor, later assistant professor of English, 1931-35; City College of San Francisco, San Francisco, Calif., organizer and director of library services and chairman of English department, 1935-42; U.S. Department of State, cultural relations attache, U.S. Embassy, Quito, Ecuador, 1942-44, posts in Washington, D.C., beginning, 1944, including chief, Division of Exchange of Persons, 1948-52, deputy director, International Educational Exchange Service, 1952-56, director of cultural planning and development staffs, 1958-64, director of Policy Review and Coordination Staff, Bureau of Educational and Cultural Affairs, and also executive secretary, Interagency Council on International Education and Cultural Affairs, beginning, 1964. U.S. representative or member of delegation at international conferences in Thailand, France, Switzerland, England, and other countries; participant in seminars on foreign policy and related subjects. Member of advisory council, Georgetown University's Institute of Languages and Linguistics, National Symphony Association, and Children's Hospital Association, Washington, D.C.

MEMBER: Society for International Development, International Studies Association, Modern Language Association of America, American Academy of Political and Social Science, Foreign Service Association, Cosmos Club and International Club (both Washington, D.C.), Commonweal Associates (New York), Commonwealth Club of California (San Francisco). *Awards, honors:* Honorary professor, School of Letters and Education, Central University of Ecuador, 1943; Rockefeller Public Service Award, 1955, utilized as visiting fellow at Princeton University, 1956, and independent researcher in western Europe, 1957; Superior Service Award, U.S. Department of State, 1966.

WRITINGS: (With Lloyd Luckmann) *Fundamentals of Public Speaking,* California Book Co., 1935; (co-author) *Report on the Foreign Student in the U.S.A.,* National Association of Foreign Student Advisors and Langmuir Foundation, 1962; (with Walter Johnson) *The Fulbright Program: A History,* University of Chicago Press, 1965. Contributor to *Dictionary of American History, New Catholic Encyclopedia,* and other publications.

WORK IN PROGRESS: International relations—educational, cultural, and developmental.

SIDELIGHTS: Colligan was fluent in Spanish and competent in French.†

(Deceased)

* * *

COLVIN, Ian G(oodhope) 1912-1975

PERSONAL: Born November 23, 1912, in London, England; son of Ian Duncan (an author) and Sophie (Robson) Colvin; married Moira Muntz, August 26, 1939; children: Diana, Clare, Andrew. *Education:* Attended Bradfield College, Berkshire, England; also studied in Paris at College of France and at Sorbonne, University of Paris. *Politics:* Conservative. *Religion:* Church of England. *Home:* 51 Cadogan Pl., London S.W. 1, England. *Agent:* A. M. Heath, 42 William IV St., London W.C. 2, England. *Office: Daily Telegraph,* London E.C. 4, England.

CAREER: Reuter, *News Chronicle,* and *Daily Telegraph,* London, England, journalist and leader writer, 1933-75. Author. *Military service:* Royal Marines, 1941-46; became temporary captain. *Member:* Royal Commonwealth Society, Press Club (London).

WRITINGS: Chief of Intelligence, Gollancz, 1950, published as *Master Spy,* McGraw, 1951; *The Unknown Courier,* Kimber, 1953; *Flight 777,* Evans Brothers, 1956; *None So Blind: A British Diplomatic View of the Origins of World War II,* Harcourt, 1965 (published in England as *Vansittart in Office: An Historical Survey of the Origins of the Second World War Based on the Papers of Sir Robert Vansittart,* Gollancz, 1965); *The Rise and Fall of Moise Tshombe: A Biography,* Leslie Frewin, 1968; *The Chamberlain Cabinet: How the Meetings in 10 Downing Street, 1937-39, Led to the Second World War,* Taplinger, 1971; (with Andre Brissaud) *Canaris,* Weidenfeld & Nicholson, 1973. Writer of articles and verse.

WORK IN PROGRESS: The History of British Foreign Policy in the Second World War.

SIDELIGHTS: Colvin was an authority on pre-war Germany and spoke French as well as German. He traveled widely in Africa and the Middle East.

(Died April 20, 1975)

COMSTOCK, Henry B. 1908-

PERSONAL: Born December 9, 1908, in New York, N.Y.; son of Enos B. (an illustrator and author of juvenile books) and Frances (a watercolorist; maiden name, Bassett) Comstock; married Mary Dalnodar, June 25, 1933; children: Carol D. (Mrs. Clinton J. Faille), Robert H. *Education:* Attended high school in Leonia, N.J.; studied art privately. *Politics:* Independent. *Religion:* Protestant. *Home and office:* 334 North Greenbush Rd., Blauvelt, N.Y. 10913. *Agent:* Evelyn Singer Agency, Box 163, Briarcliff Manor, N.Y. 10510.

CAREER: Arthur Kudner Advertising Agency, New York City, staff member in art department, 1937-38; *Railroad Magazine,* New York City, associate editor, 1939-42, editor, 1942-51; *Popular Science Monthly,* New York City, associate editor, 1952-61; free-lance writer and illustrator, beginning 1962. Member, Blauvelt (N.Y.) School Board, 1940-45.

WRITINGS: The Iron Horse, Crowell, 1971. Author and illustrator of brochures for industrial clients. Contributor to magazines.

WORK IN PROGRESS: Writing and illustrating a book on the construction of Gothic cathedrals.

AVOCATIONAL INTERESTS: Travel, beginning in 1927 with an eleven-hundred-mile ten-day bicycle ride from New York City to Milwaukee; for several years Henry Comstock test-drove new automobiles for *Popular Science Monthly,* giving them seven-thousand-mile workouts on roundabout transcontinental runs.††

* * *

CONNELL, K(enneth) H(ugh) 1917-1973

PERSONAL: Born September 6, 1917, in Southampton, England; son of James and Susanna (Cambridge) Connell; married Hanna Schumer (a university teacher), July 3, 1945; children: Myra Caroline, Monica Bridget. *Education:* London School of Economics and Political Science, B.Sc. (first class honors), 1940, Ph.D., 1948; Oxford University, M.A., 1950. *Home:* 15 Osborne Park, Belfast BT9 6JN, Northern Ireland. *Office:* Department of Economic and Social History, Queen's University, Belfast BT7 1NN, Northern Ireland.

CAREER: University of Wales, University College of Wales, Aberystwyth, assistant lecturer in economic history, 1941; University of Liverpool, Liverpool, England, lecturer in economic history, 1941-45; University of London, London School of Economics and Political Science, London, England, assistant lecturer in economic history, 1946-49; Oxford University, Oxford, England, official fellow of Nuffield College, 1949-52, lecturer in economics, 1950-52; Queen's University of Belfast, Belfast, Northern Ireland, senior lecturer, 1953-66, reader, 1966-67, professor and head of department of economic and social history, 1967-70, professor of social history, 1970-73. Visiting fellow, Research School of Social Sciences, Australian National University, 1965-66, and All Souls College, Oxford University, 1970-71. Member of economic and social history committee, Social Science Research Council, London, 1968-72.

MEMBER: Royal Irish Academy, Royal Historical Society (fellow), Economic History Society (member of council), Irish Economic History Society (founding member), International Union for the Scientific Study of Population. *Awards, honors:* Madden Prize of Trinity College, Dublin, 1951.

WRITINGS: *The Population of Ireland, 1750-1845,* Clarendon Press, 1950, reprinted, Greenwood Press, 1975; *Irish Peasant Society: Four Historical Essays,* Clarendon Press, 1968. Contributor to social science and history journals. Member of editorial committee, Royal Irish Academy's *A New History of Ireland;* general editor and contributor to multi-volume economic and social history of Ireland since the seventeenth century.

WORK IN PROGRESS: Further work on Ireland's history, especially on marriage and peasant society since the eighteenth century.†

(Died, 1973)

*   *   *

CONNELY, Willard   1888-1967

PERSONAL: Born July 1, 1888, in Atlantic City, N.J.; son of George Washington and Anne (Willard) Connely; married third wife, Agnes Lauchlan (an actress), September 18, 1948; children: (first marriage) Nancy (Mrs. A. D. Van Nostrand); (second marriage) Susan (Mrs. I. L. E. Rands), Sally. *Education:* Stevens Institute of Technology, student, 1906-08; Dartmouth College, B.Sc., 1911; Harvard University, M.A., 1921; New College, Oxford, B.A., 1927, M.A., 1931. *Politics:* Republican. *Religion:* Episcopalian. *Home and office:* Whitegates, Godalming, Surrey, England.

CAREER: Writer or editor in New York, N.Y., for *New York Sunday American,* 1911-13, *Harper's Weekly,* 1913-14, *McClure's,* 1913-15, International Film Service, 1916-17; Harvard University, Cambridge, Mass., instructor in English, 1920-25, assistant in Greek, 1925; *Sunday Express,* London, England, staff member, 1927-28; American University Union, London, England, director, 1930-46. Biographer, living and writing in England, 1927-67. In early 1930's instituted (under Carnegie Endowment of New York) weekend lectureships and one-term professorships at British universities for American professors; secretary to International Conference on Examinations, Carnegie Corp., 1931-38; consultant on European universities to U.S. Department of State, 1944. Byron Foundation lecturer at University of Nottingham, 1936; lecturer to H. M. Forces on America in the war, 1941-43. *Military service:* U.S. Naval Reserve, 1917-18; chief yeoman.

MEMBER: Royal Society of Literature (fellow), English-Speaking Union (committee for British-American schoolboy scholarship exchange member, 1930-67), Horatian Society (vice-chairman), Phi Beta Kappa. *Awards, honors:* Medalist, Carnegie Corp. of New York, 1936; grants from Carnegie Foundation, 1939, and American Council of Learned Societies, 1942.

WRITINGS: *Brawny Wycherley,* Scribner, 1930; *Sir Richard Steele,* Scribner, 1934, reprinted, Kennikat Press, 1967; *The True Chesterfield,* Cassell, 1939; *The Reign of Beau Brummell,* Greystone, 1940; *Young George Farquhar,* Cassell, 1949; *Count D'Orsay,* Cassell, 1952; *Beau Nash,* Laurie, 1955; *Adventures in Biography,* Laurie, 1956, Horizon, 1960; *Laurence Sterne as Yorick,* Bodley Head, 1958; *Louis Sullivan as He Lived: The Shaping of American Architecture,* Horizon, 1960. Contributor to *Chambers' Encyclopaedia,* 1946-47, *Encyclopaedia Britannica,* 1962; also contributor to *Puck, McClure's, Metropolitan, Classical Journal, Everybody's, Listener, Spectator.*

WORK IN PROGRESS: Autobiography.

SIDELIGHTS: Connely told *CA:* "Reading of Strachey and of Maurois led to my writing of biography. Vital: that young Americans can best learn to write English by reading and writing in French." Connely read the whole of Homer in the Greek (he considered this important to his career), and he spoke French and some Italian. He listed classical, French, and Italian literature as an avocational interest; collecting books, antique furniture, paintings, and china as hobbies.

BIOGRAPHICAL/CRITICAL SOURCES: *New York Times,* March 29, 1967.†

(Died March 26, 1967)

*   *   *

CONNOLLY, Cyril (Vernon)   1903-1974
(Palinurus)

PERSONAL: Born September 10, 1903, in Coventry, England; son of Matthew (an army major) and Muriel (Vernon) Connolly; married Deirdre Craig, 1959; children: one son, one daughter. *Education:* Attended Balliol College, Oxford. *Home:* Bushey Lodge, Firte, Lewes, Sussex, England.

CAREER: Writer for the *New Statesman* and other periodicals, 1927-74; weekly contributor to the *Sunday Times,* 1951-74; *Horizon,* London, England, founder, editor, and writer, 1939-50; *Observer,* London, literary editor, 1942-43. *Member:* Royal Society of Literature (fellow), White's, Pratt's, Beefsteak. *Awards, honors:* Chevalier de la Legion d'Honneur; Brackenbury Scholar; D.Litt., Trinity College, Dublin; Companion of Honour, L'Academie Francaise. Knighted; Commander of the Order of the British Empire, 1972.

WRITINGS: *The Rock Pool* (fiction), Scribner, 1936; *Enemies of Promise,* Routledge & Kegan Paul, 1938, Little, Brown, 1939, revised edition, Macmillan, 1948; (editor) *Horizon Stories,* Faber, 1943, Vanguard, 1946; (translator) Jean Bruller, under pseudonym Vercors, *Silence of the Sea,* Macmillan, 1944 (published in England as *Put Out the Light,* Macmillan, 1944); (under pseudonym Palinurus) *The Unquiet Grave: A Word Cycle,* Horizon (London), 1944, Harper, 1945, revised edition, Hamish Hamilton, 1945; *The Condemned Playground* (essays), Routledge & Kegan Paul, 1945, Macmillan, 1946; *The Missing Diplomats,* Queen Anne Press, 1952; *Ideas and Places,* Harper, 1953; *The Golden Horizon,* Weidenfeld & Nicolson, 1953, University Books, 1955; (editor and author of introduction) *Great English Short Novels,* Dial, 1953; (with Jerome Zerbe) *Les Pavillons: French Pavilions of the Eighteenth Century,* Macmillan, 1962; *Previous Convictions: Selected Writings of a Decade,* Harper, 1963; *The Modern Movement: 100 Key Books from England, France, and America,* Deutsch, 1965, Atheneum, 1966; (translator with Simon W. Taylor) Alfred Jarry, *The Ubu Plays* (contains *Ubu Rex, Ubu Cuckolded,* and *Ubu Enchained*), Grove, 1969; *The Evening Colonnade,* Harcourt, 1975. Contributor of article to *Art and Literature.*

SIDELIGHTS: Cyril Connolly related his "Georgian boyhood" in Eton College in the last part of his formidable work, *Enemies of Promise.* He believed that he was a spoiled child who suffered all the miseries of the English public school caste system, while managing to acquire an excellent education. With a sharp tongue he wasn't afraid to use, he was at times a critic of the literary world, at times a self-critic. Remembering a "very nasty review" he had written on Hemingway's *The Green Hills of Africa,* Connolly remarked that "the first time I met Hemingway I was introduced to him, just after I had reviewed this book, in Sylvia Beach's bookshop in Paris. When he realised who I was, he turned to Sylvia Beach and he said: 'This is a very bad moment for both of us.' That, I think, is a lovely remark: you see, he forgave me, because I was minding terribly the tactlessness of being introduced to him after writing this review, and he showed that he minded the review. We had dinner together and we became great friends, because after all I had liked his earlier books and said so.''

The *New Yorker* critic found *Enemies of Promise* to be ''a collection of searching and idea-packed literary essays, precisely noting the temper of current writing and pointing out the pitfalls that beset the beginning or the successful author.'' To Geoffrey Grigson, the complete book was most interesting, sociologically, ''as a specimen [and] as a piece from the war between the ninety per cent art-gentlemen and his gentility. It is good to see conscience at work in an art-gentleman.'' James Stern reflected that ''had I a son, whether destined for Eton, Dalton or the dogs, I would place a copy of *Enemies of Promise* in his hands at an early age. For this book is an education, a warning, an encouragement, a preparation for the literary life....''

In 1968, responding to questions about the whole of his own ''literary life'' and the things which influenced it, Connolly told interviewer Richard Kershaw that his own family ''would have liked me most of all, I think, to go into the Foreign Office; failing that, they'd have liked me to take some kind of nice job, like a clerk in the House of Commons, or perhaps the Lords, or anything but the thing that I did do—which was to waste a lot of time and be very extravagant and get so into debt that I spent years trying to get out of it.''

Kershaw queried Connolly if involvement in politics had prevented him from doing writing he ought to have done, to which Connolly replied: ''I would say only myself has prevented me doing the writing I ought to have done. A writer ought to have politics, but when it comes to the executive side of politics, standing for Parliament, speaking at a lot of meetings, being on committees, writing a lot of pamphlets, unless you're that kind of writer it must be bad for you. A writer has a vintage product which is him. He produces his little *vin ordinaire* called Chateau Connolly or whatever it is. Well, that wine results from his personality being kept in a certain condition, a certain temperature, a certain soil; and if you take him too far away from that, he becomes indistinguishable from other products of the new political soil. The Spanish war produced its best work from writers who were not involved in the running of the war but who made private sorties into it.'' Connolly attested, ''I could never do more than write for some political cause. But I was political. So were Auden and Spender and Isherwood, of the people I knew who were slightly younger than me, and many people of my own age. But for us, the Spanish war was the crux of everything, and it was such a disaster to our hopes: it was so awful to see the side we were convinced was right totally defeated, with the democracies looking on, either sadly or cheering. It made one feel nothing could be done by politics. You had to give up all that side. And then go back into the ivory tower...''

To the Virginia Woolf idea, that it is essential for a writer to have a room of his own and a private income, Connolly responded: ''Well, I think the room of one's own—don't forget, half of one's life one is married and hasn't got a room of one's own, unless you have a large study of your own—is a great help. There is no doubt that one's best thoughts come reading at night when you have gone to bed. If you can't read half the night your tank doesn't fill up for the next day. And a private income is very, very good too, if it isn't too big or too small. Eliot had a tiny income, which was no good to him. When he was offered to leave the bank where he worked, in return for a fixed income of 250 pounds a year subscribed by his admirers, he refused to leave: 'With that income I would still have to work for my living. I would do just as much journalism as if I didn't have an income at all. I'd rather stay in the bank.' Which he did for another few years ... A good writer rises above everything and it's an alibi to say: 'I can't write, I haven't got a room of my own ...' 'I can't write, I haven't got a private income ...' 'I can't write, I'm a journalist,' and so on. Those are all alibis. But I have seen in my contemporaries a great many who could have been much better if it hadn't been for two or three things: social climbing, drink and unhappy love affairs, due to flaws in themselves which made their love affairs go on for too long, or become too unhappy. All novelists,'' Connolly reflected, ''have got to be social animals, I think. You can't write a novel if you don't go to parties. And even poets have got to take a lot of their material from daily life or from things they do.''

Kershaw asked Connolly if he thought Freud, Marx, politicians, and great mass movements had destroyed the ability to be a writer in the sense that Connolly wished to be thirty or forty years ago, when he had started. Connolly answered: ''Each has made it harder. Freud has made it very much harder. For a critic Freud is invaluable as a tool to help you to understand other writers and the processes derived from their childhood. But in yourself Freud is a blocker: the moment you know enough Freud you know your own motives. Take, for instance, condemnation. Part of a critic's professional talent is his ability to abuse other people, especially if he can do it with moral indignation. Well, when you read Freud, who says, 'Whatever you blame you wish to do yourself,' you cannot blame in the same way.... I think nowadays [that the 'enemies of promise' are] the pressure of instant success, the enormous sums to be made by one book and the pathetically small ones to be made by the other ninety-nine. And, of course, the general visual impact of the television world—that is very bad for the writer, who has based himself for 2,000 years on the idea of the private person writing in his lavatory for someone who is going to read him in their lavatory. The totally private life of the writer,'' Connolly observed, ''has become economically impossible. The cottage in the country where the Georgian poet did his own cooking and wrote his imitation Elizabethan sonnets—all that has become rather ridiculous. You couldn't live like that now. You'd get nothing but a lot of brown envelopes from the Income Tax.'' Connolly felt strongly ''that all human beings are sentenced to death and that as the sentence will never be commuted, we are all entitled to the amenities of the condemned cell....''

BIOGRAPHICAL/CRITICAL SOURCES: Boston Transcript, October 10, 1936; *New York Times Book Review,* October 11, 1936, October 7, 1945; *Spectator,* November 12, 1938; *Manchester Guardian,* December 13, 1938; *New Yorker,* April 8, 1939, October 27, 1945; *New Republic,* July 15, 1946, January 31, 1948; *New York Herald Tribune Weekly Book Review,* February 27, 1949; *New Statesman and Nation,* May 30, 1953; Kingsley Martin, editor, *New Statesman Profiles,* Phoenix House, 1958; *Encounter,* February, 1964; D. J. Enright, *Conspirators and Poets,* Dufour, 1966; *Time,* March 25, 1966; *Listener,* April 11, 1968.†

(Died November 26, 1974)

CONRAD, Edna (G.)   1893-

PERSONAL: Born November 4, 1893, in Philadelphia, Pa.; daughter of John S. and Florence (Garrett) Conrad. *Education:* New York University, B.S., 1927. *Address:* P.O. Box 84, Belmont, Vt. 05730.

CAREER: Elementary school teacher in Friends' school in Brooklyn, N.Y., 1919-46; junior high school teacher in New York City, 1946-64; Mills College of Education, New York City, English tutor, 1965-71; College of St. Joseph the Provider, Rutland, Vt., English tutor, 1974-76. Dietitian and counselor, American Friends' Society summer work camps, Mexico and the United States, for nine years. *Member:* United Federation of Teachers, Community Historical Society (Belmont).

WRITINGS: (With Mary Van Dyke) *History on the Stage,* Van Nostrand, 1971.

WORK IN PROGRESS: Writing a design for education for Mt. Holly, Vt.

SIDELIGHTS: Edna Conrad told *CA* of the background of *History on the Stage:* "Mrs. Van Dyke, a drama teacher, and I, a classroom teacher, had worked with 7th grade children for over ten years dramatizing historical fiction for assembly programs. The results always amazed us. We felt that other people should know about our methods, and the wide range and vividness of the learnings that the children garnered through the process. We had our class help us write *History on the Stage.*"

AVOCATIONAL INTERESTS: Gardening, cooking, sewing, playing the recorder, reading.

*　　　*　　　*

CONVERSE, Paul D(ulaney)   1889-1968

PERSONAL: Born March 8, 1889, in Morristown, Tenn.; son of James B. (a minister and writer) and Eva Almeda (Dulaney) Converse; wife deceased; children: Paul L., Louise Converse Walker. *Education:* Washington and Lee University, B.A., 1913, M.A. and certificate of commerce, 1914; also studied summers at Columbia University, 1914, and University of Wisconsin, 1916. *Religion:* Presbyterian.

CAREER: Washington and Lee University, Lexington, Va., instructor in economics, 1912-15; University of Pittsburgh, Pittsburgh, Pa., 1915-24, began as instructor, became professor; University of Illinois, Urbana, 1924-57, began as associate professor, became professor of marketing, professor emeritus, 1957-68. Visiting professor at University of Texas, Austin, 1959, University of Oregon, 1962; visiting summer professor at other universities. Consultant and teacher with European Productivity Agency, France and Italy, 1959-60. *Member:* American Marketing Association (president, 1931), American Economic Association, Phi Beta Kappa, Delta Sigma Rho, Rotary Club. *Awards, honors:* LL.D., Washington and Lee University, 1944; American Marketing Association named its highest achievement award the Paul D. Converse Award, 1949.

WRITINGS: Marketing Methods and Policies, Prentice-Hall, 1921, revised edition, 1924, later revisions published as *The Elements of Marketing,* Prentice-Hall, 1930, 7th edition (with H. W. Huegy and Robert Mitchell), 1965, teacher's manual (with Huegy), Prentice-Hall, 1940; *Middlemen,* American Institute of Agriculture (Chicago), 1922; *Selling Policies,* Prentice-Hall, 1927; *Business Mortality of Illinois Retail Stores from 1925 to 1930,* University of Illinois, 1932; *Essentials of Distribution,* Prentice-Hall, 1936; *A Study of Retail Trade Areas in East Central Illinois,* University of

Illinois, 1943; *Should I Start My Own Business?,* University of Illinois, 1945; (with Huegy) *Establishing and Operating a Hardware Store,* Armed Forces Institute, 1945; (with Fred M. Jones) *Introduction to Marketing,* Prentice-Hall, 1948; (contributor) *Changing Perspectives in Marketing,* University of Illinois, 1951; *Fifty Years of Marketing in Retrospect,* Bureau of Business Research, University of Texas, 1959; *The Beginning of Marketing Thought in The United States,* Bureau of Business Research, University of Texas, 1959.

Writer of research monographs on marketing and consumer surveys, the majority published by Bureau of Business Research, University of Illinois. Contributor to *Dictionary of American History* and *Encyclopaedia Britannica;* more than one hundred articles have appeared in magazines and journals, including *Saturday Evening Post, Mercurio* (Rome), *Engineering Experiment, Bankers Magazine,* and marketing, economics, and education periodicals.

WORK IN PROGRESS: Two books, *The Story of Marketing* and *Business and the Bible.*

AVOCATIONAL INTERESTS: Gathering folk stories and stories of historical interest during travels in America, Europe, and Canada.

BIOGRAPHICAL/CRITICAL SOURCES: Journal of Marketing, July, 1951, October, 1958; *Champaign-Urbana Courier,* March 27, 1957.†

(Died October, 1968)

*　　　*　　　*

COON, Martha Sutherland   1884-

PERSONAL: Born June 6, 1884, in Beaver Dam, Wis.; daughter of John (an attorney) and Linnie (Aiken) Sutherland; married Julius McCowen Coon (an attorney), November 5, 1913 (died May 3, 1947); children: John Marshall, Evalin (Mrs. Edwin James Moore), Robert Runyon. *Education:* Student at Northwestern University, 1902-03, and Sioux Falls College, 1906-07; Grand Island College (later merged with Sioux Falls College), A.B., 1909; University of South Dakota, M.A., 1950. *Politics:* Republican. *Religion:* Presbyterian. *Home:* Oklahoma Methodist Manor, 4134 East 31st St., Tulsa, Okla. 74135.

CAREER: Sioux Falls College, Sioux Falls, S.D., full-time teacher of Latin and Greek, 1909-10, and Latin and English, 1943-55, part-time teacher, 1913-43; Tulsa (Okla.) public schools, substitute teacher in high schools, 1956-64. *Member:* American Association of University Women. *Awards, honors:* Litt.D., Sioux Falls College, 1961.

WRITINGS: Georgie's Capital (juvenile), Harvey House, 1967; *Oahe Dam: Master of the Missouri* (teen-age nonfiction), Harvey House, 1970. Poems published in anthologies and magazines, and stories in Sunday school papers.

WORK IN PROGRESS: Short stories for young readers.

SIDELIGHTS: Martha Coon began studying Latin at the age of eight when she was enrolled in Pierre University, a Presbyterian school in South Dakota which offered secondary and college-level courses. She studied Caesar and geology the next year, and Vergil and rhetoric the following year, and entered public school for the first time in the fifth grade. Mrs. Coon told *CA* that she wrote *Georgie's Capital* "to explain to my grandchildren how one might enjoy a type of life that seems to them primitive, but was lived by our family with pride and pleasure.... [I] intend to keep on writing as long as my mind and my eyes behave helpfully."

COOPER, Charles W(illiam) 1904-

PERSONAL: Born January 12, 1904, in Edgewood, Pa.; son of Clarence Lincoln (an accountant) and Virginia (Schmid) Cooper; married Edris M. Burgess, June 30, 1928; children: Charles William, Jr. *Education:* Attended Whittier College, 1921-22; University of California, Los Angeles, A.B. (with highest honors), 1925; University of California, Berkeley, M.A., 1926, Ph.D., 1931. *Politics:* Republican liberal. *Religion:* Quaker. *Home:* 900 Calle de los Amigos, D-303, Santa Barbara, Calif. 93105. *Office:* Whittier College, Whittier, Calif. 90601.

CAREER: San Bernardino Valley Junior College, San Bernardino, Calif., instructor in English, 1927-33, and chairman of department; Whittier College, Whittier, Calif., associate professor of English, 1933-36; Fresno State College (now California State University, Fresno), associate professor of English, 1936-38; Whittier College, professor of English, 1938-55, professor-at-large, 1955-68, professor emeritus, 1968—, director of Poet Theatre, 1938-46, assistant to the president of the college, 1960-68, director of Whittier College at Copenhagen Program, 1962-63. Visiting lecturer, Harvard University, 1948. Educational adviser, Pasadena Playhouse School of the Theatre, 1942-45. Co-director, Centre Quaker International, Paris, 1957-59. *Member:* Phi Beta Kappa (honorary member).

WRITINGS: (With E. J. Robins) *The Term Paper: A Manual and Model,* Stanford University Press, 1934, 4th edition, 1967; (with P. H. Houston) *Main Currents of English Literature,* revised edition, F. S. Crofts, 1934; (with Paul A. Camp) *Designing the Play,* F. S. Crofts, 1942; (with John Holmes) *Preface to Poetry,* Harcourt, 1946; *The Arts and Humanity,* Philosophical Library, 1952; (with wife, Edris B. Cooper) *The Letter Writer,* Stanford University Press, 1954; *Preface to Drama,* Ronald, 1955; (editor) Shakespeare, *Julius Caesar, A Midsummer Night's Dream, Romeo and Juliet* (modern revised version), Laidlaw Brothers, 1957; *The A. Wardman Story,* Whittier College Press, 1961; *Whittier: Independent College in California,* Ritchie, 1967.

Plays produced: "The Mystic Touch," Los Angeles Play Shop, 1929; "No More Yesterdays," Pasadena Playhouse Laboratory Theatre, 1935; "Venus in the House," University Street Playhouse, Fresno State College, 1938; "The Hoosier Parsonage," Poet Theatre, Whittier College, 1945. Composer of a symphony and several other musical works played locally. Also editor of *Break the New Ground: Seven Essays by Contemporary Quakers,* 1969. Contributor and consultant, *World Book Encyclopedia,* beginning 1959.

WORK IN PROGRESS: A novel based on characters and incidents developed for an unproduced musical comedy, "Beau Marche U.S.A."

SIDELIGHTS: The Term Paper has been in print for thirty-five years; a million copies of the third edition were sold, 1947-67, and well over half a million copies of the fourth edition were sold, 1967-75.

*   *   *

COOPER, Frank E(dward) 1910-1968

PERSONAL: Born July 3, 1910, in Detroit, Mich.; son of Frank Lee and Edith M. (Ruehle) Cooper; married Margaret Ellen Hayes, June 27, 1936; children: Frank, Edward, William. *Education:* University of Michigan, A.B., 1931, J.D., 1934. *Politics:* Republican. *Religion:* Episcopal. *Home:* 87 Merriweather Rd., Grosse Pointe Farms, Mich. 48236. *Office:* Beaumont, Smith & Harris, 1100 Ford Building, Detroit, Mich. 48226.

CAREER: Admitted to Michigan Bar, 1934. Beaumont, Smith & Harris (law firm), Detroit, Mich., member, 1943-68. Wayne State University, Detroit, professor of law during the 1940's; University of Michigan Law School, Ann Arbor, professor of administrative law and legal writing, 1950-68. General counsel, Michigan Manufacturers' Association, 1952-68. Member of Hoover Commission, and Model Act consultant. *Member:* American Bar Association (former chairman; member of board of directors of Administrative Law Section for many years), American Judicature Society, American Law Institute, Michigan Bar Association, Detroit Bar Association, Phi Beta Kappa, Sigma Delta Chi, Order of Coif, Cooley Club, Scribes. *Awards, honors:* Ross essay award of the American Bar Association, 1942; tributes from State of Michigan House of Representatives, Regents of the University of Michigan, Michigan Manufacturers' Association, and others.

WRITINGS: Administrative Agencies and the Courts, University of Michigan Press, 1951; *Effective Legal Writing,* Bobbs-Merrill, 1953; (with E. B. Stason) *The Law of Administrative Tribunals,* 3rd edition (Cooper was not associated with earlier editions), Callaghan, 1957; *The Lawyer and Administrative Agencies,* Prentice-Hall, 1957; *Living the Law,* Bobbs-Merrill, 1958; *Writing in Law Practice,* Bobbs-Merrill, 1963; *State Administrative Law,* Bobbs-Merrill, 1965. Contributor to law journals. Faculty editor, *Prospectus: A Journal of Law Reform.*†‡

(Died February 16, 1968)

*   *   *

COOPER, John R.
[Collective pseudonym]

WRITINGS—"Mel Martin Baseball Stories" series; published by Garden City Books, except as noted: *The Southpaw's Secret,* Cupples & Leon, 1947; *The Mystery at the Ball Park,* Cupples & Leon, 1947; *First Base Jinx,* 1952; *The Phantom Homer,* 1952; *The College League Mystery,* 1953; *The Fighting Shortstop,* 1953.

SIDELIGHTS: See **ADAMS, Harriet S., STRATEMEYER, Edward L.,** and **SVENSON, Andrew E.**†

*   *   *

COOPER, Sylvia 1903-
(Sylvia Paul Jerman)

PERSONAL: Born 1903, in New York, N.Y.; daughter of Lee Ashley and Virginia (Fitz Randolph) Grace; married second husband, John Arnold Cooper, September 6, 1941; children: Sylvia (Mrs. H. T. Fitch), Virginia (Mrs. R. M. McFarland), Anthony, Maud Danger. *Education:* Attended Radcliffe College.

CAREER: Formerly with Hearst Newspapers and *Cue* magazine. *Member:* Detroit Women Writers.

WRITINGS—Under name Sylvia Paul Jerman: *Prelude to Departure,* Harper, 1933; *Set Free,* H. Smith, 1934; *Attention: Miss Wells,* Harcourt, 1938.

Under name Sylvia Cooper: *Thunder Stone,* Simon & Schuster, 1955; *Self-Made Man,* Random House, 1960.††

*   *   *

COOPERMAN, Stanley 1929-1976

PERSONAL: Born October 22, 1929, in New York, N.Y.;

son of Samuel (a shoemaker) and Esta (Fisher) Cooperman; married Ruth Duernberg, 1952; married second wife, Charlotte Alexander, 1960; married third wife, Jenifer Svendsen, 1962; children: (third marriage) Galila-Yael, Amichai Kester. *Education:* New York University, B.A., 1951, graduate study, 1952-55; Indiana University, Ph.D., 1961. *Religion:* Jewish. *Home:* 4527 Marineview Crescent, North Vancouver, British Columbia, Canada.

CAREER: University of Oregon, Eugene, instructor, 1961-62, assistant professor of English, 1962-63; Hofstra University, Hempstead, New York, assistant professor of English, 1963-65; Simon Fraser University, Burnaby, British Columbia, beginning 1965, began as associate professor, became professor of English. Writer. Has given many poetry readings at U.S. and Canadian colleges and universities and on television. Has filmed lectures. *Member:* Modern Language Association of America, Association of Canadian University Teachers of English, National Council of Teachers of English, Canadian Association of University Teachers, League of Canadian Poets.

WRITINGS: Hemingway's "For Whom the Bell Tolls": A Critical Commentary, Barrister Publishing, 1966; *Hemingway's "The Old Man and the Sea": A Critical Commentary,* Barrister Publishing, 1966; *World War I and the American Novel,* Johns Hopkins Press, 1967; *The Day of the Parrot and Other Poems,* University of Nebraska Press, 1968; *The Owl Behind the Door* (poems), McClelland & Stewart (Toronto), 1968; (contributor) *How Do I Love Thee: Sixty Poets of Canada (and Quebec) Select and Introduce Their Favourite Poems* (anthology), edited by John Robert Colombo, Hurtig, 1970; *Cappelbaum's Dance* (poems), University of Nebraska Press, 1970; *Cannibals* (poems), Oberon Press, 1972; *Canadian Gothic and Other Poems,* Intermedia Press, 1976. Contributor of essays to *Yale Review, Modern Language Quarterly, Criticism, Shakespeare Studies, Literature and Psychology, College English,* and other publications; contributor of over 300 poems to eighty magazines.

WORK IN PROGRESS: Poetry; studies of Melville, Fitzgerald and Roth; a novel.

AVOCATIONAL INTERESTS: Fishing, gardening, and traveling.

BIOGRAPHICAL/CRITICAL SOURCES: Canadian Forum, April, 1968, December, 1968; *Nation,* June 24, 1968; *Minnesota Review,* Volume VIII, 1968; *New Leader,* April 14, 1969; *Carleton Miscellany,* summer, 1969; *South Atlantic Quarterly,* winter, 1969; *Virginia Quarterly Review,* winter, 1969; *Christian Century,* September 30, 1970.†

(Died April 25, 1976)

*   *   *

COOPERSMITH, Harry   1903-

PERSONAL: Born December 5, 1903, in Russia; son of Max and Pauline Coopersmith; married Ethel Kane (a school pyschologist), April 5, 1936; children: Penina. *Education:* Columbia University, B.S., 1924, M.A., 1933; studied at Juilliard School of Music, 1924-26, and in Vienna, Austria, 1930-32. *Home:* 3340 McCaw Ave., Santa Barbara, Calif. 93105.

CAREER: Music director for Board of Jewish Education, Chicago, Ill., 1926-30, Anshe Emet Synagogue, Chicago, Ill., 1933-40, Jewish Education Committee of New York, New York, N.Y., 1940-72.

WRITINGS: Songs of Zion, Behrman, 1942; *The Songs We*

Sing, United Synagogue of America, 1952; *Friday Eve Service,* Transcontinental Music Co., 1963; *The New Jewish Song Book,* Behrman, 1965; *High Holiday Service,* Transcontinental Music Co., 1965; *More of the Songs We Sing,* United Synagogue of America, 1971. Editor, "Holiday Records" series, Jewish Education Committee, 1965-66.

*   *   *

COPELAND, Melvin T.   1884-1975

PERSONAL: Born July 17, 1884, in Brewer, Me.; son of Salem Dwight (a mason) and Livonia (Pierce) Copeland; married Else Helbling, June 25, 1912 (died, 1954); children: Elsie Marie (Mrs. Chester Z. Brown), Martha (Mrs. David R. Bott). *Education:* Bowdoin College, A.B., 1906; Harvard University, A.M., 1907, Ph.D., 1910. *Politics:* Republican. *Religion:* Congregational. *Home:* Adams Hill Rd., Annisquam, Mass. 01930.

CAREER: Harvard University, Cambridge, Mass., instructor in economics, 1909-10; New York University, New York, N.Y., instructor in economics, 1911-12; Harvard University, instructor, 1912-15, assistant professor, 1915-19, professor of business administration, 1919-53, professor emeritus, 1953-75, director of research, 1916-26, 1942-53. Secretary of commercial economic board, Council of National Defense, 1917-18; executive secretary of conservation division, War Industries Board, 1918; member of purchase policy advisory committee, U.S. War Department, 1943. Member of Massachusetts Commission of Cost of Living, 1916-17; chairman, Massachusetts Commission on Post-War Readjustment, 1941-46; member of Gloucester (Mass.) Board of Appeals-Zoning Ordinance, 1952-75. Bowdoin College, member of board of overseers, 1934-47, trustee, 1947-61, trustee emeritus, 1961-75. *Member:* American Statistical Association (fellow), Phi Beta Kappa, Beta Theta Pi. *Awards, honors:* David A. Wells prize, Harvard University, 1912; medal from National Association of Cotton Manufacturers, 1921; Sc.D., Bowdoin College, 1931.

WRITINGS: Cotton Manufacturing Industry of the United States, Harvard University Press, 1912; (editor) *Business Statistics,* Harvard University Press, 1917; *Problems in Marketing,* A. W. Shaw, 1920, 4th edition, McGraw, 1931; *Principles of Merchandising,* A. W. Shaw, 1924; *Raw Material Prices and Business Conditions,* Harvard Business School, 1933; (with Edmund P. Learned) *Merchandising of Cotton Textiles,* Harvard Business School, 1933; (with W. Homer Turner) *Production and Distribution of Silk and Rayon Broad Goods,* Textile Foundation and National Federation of Textiles (New York), 1935; *A Raw Commodity Revolution,* Harvard Business School, 1938; (with Andrew R. Towl) *The Board of Directors and Business Management,* Harvard Business School, 1947; *The Executive at Work,* Harvard University Press, 1951; *And Mark an Era: The Story of the Harvard Business School,* Little, Brown, 1958; (with Elliott C. Rogers) *The Saga of Cape Ann,* Wheelwright, 1960. Contributor to economic and business journals, and to other publications.

BIOGRAPHICAL/CRITICAL SOURCES: New York Times, March 29, 1975.†

(Died March 27, 1975)

*   *   *

CORSON, Fred Pierce   1896-

PERSONAL: Born April 11, 1896, in Millville, N.J.; son of Jeremiah and Mary E. (Payne) Corson; married Frances

Beaman, March 22, 1922; children: Hampton Payne. *Education:* Dickinson College, A.B. (cum laude), 1917, A.M., 1920, D.D., 1931; Drew University, B.D., 1920. *Home and office:* Cornwall Manor, Cornwall, Pa. 12016.

CAREER: Ordained to ministry of Methodist Episcopal Church, 1920; pastor in Connecticut and New York, 1920-29; superintendent of Brooklyn South District of New York East Conference, 1930-34; Dickinson College, Carlisle, Pa., president, 1934-44; The Methodist Church, Philadelphia, Pa., bishop, beginning 1944. President of Methodist General Board of Education, 1948-60, of Council of Bishops, 1952-53, and of World Methodist Council, 1961-66. Distinguished lecturer at Southern Methodist University, Duke University, and a number of other universities and seminaries, 1944-61. Chairman of U.S. Secretary of War's Clergy Commission to Inspect Occupied Countries of Europe, and religious advisor to Armed Forces, 1948; chaplain at national Republican and Democratic conventions, 1948, 1952; delegate-observer at Second Vatican Council, 1962-65. Trustee of Drew University, Lycoming College, Pennington School, Wyoming Seminary, Wesley College, and a number of other seminaries; honorary chairman, Temple University.

MEMBER: Newcomen Society, Sons of the American Revolution, Phi Beta Kappa, Tau Kappa Alpha, Omicron Delta Kappa, Kappa Sigma, Tau Delta Kappa, Masons (past grand prelate of Pennsylvania Commandery of Knights Templer), Union League Club (New York and Philadelphia). *Awards, honors:* More than forty honorary degrees from colleges and universities, including Drew University, Syracuse University, Catholic University of America, Wilberforce University, and University of Pennsylvania. Yorktown Medal of the Society of Cincinnati, for distinguished service; St. George's Medal of World Methodist Church; World Outlook Award as Methodist of the year, 1963; St. Olav Medal (Norway), 1964; Gourgas Medal (highest Masonic decoration), 1964; Petrean Medal of St. Peter's College, 1965; Lycoming College Award, 1966; Peace Medal Award from Third Order Secular of St. Francis of Assisi, 1967; Rerum Novarum Medal from Pope Paul VI, 1967; Distinguished American Award of the National Football Foundation, 1968; John Wesley Ecumenical Medal, 1968; citations from Commonwealth of Pennsylvania legislature, and city of Philadelphia; distinguished Sun Yat Sen Medal.

WRITINGS: The Pattern of a Church, Methodist Church (Nashville), 1946; *Your Church and You,* John C. Winston Co., 1951; *Pattern for Successful Living,* John C. Winston Co., 1953; *The Christian Imprint,* Abingdon, 1955; (contributor) J. A. O'Brien, editor, *Steps to Christian Unity,* Doubleday, 1964; (contributor) Walter M. Abbott, editor, *Documents of the Vatican Two,* Association Press, 1966; (contributor) Stjepan Schmidt, editor, *Augustin Cardinal Bea: Spiritual Profile,* Geoffrey Chapman, 1971. Editor, Wesley translation of New Testament. Author of monographs on church-related subjects. Contributor to religious journals.

*　　*　　*

COTHRAN, J(oseph) Guy 1897-

PERSONAL: Born May 24, 1897, in Belton, S.C.; son of John C. (a farmer) and Esther (Cooley) Cothran; married Mary Louise Riley, June 23, 1925; children: Joseph Guy, Jr., Mary Virginia (Mrs. Ramsey), William Albert, John Clark, Riley, David Enoch. *Education:* Furman University, A.B., 1922; Southern Baptist Theological Seminary, Th.M., 1925; also attended University of Georgia. *Home:* 2241 August St., Greenville, S.C. 29605.

CAREER: Ordained to Baptist ministry; pastor in Panama City, Fla., Benton, Ark., Princeton, Ky., 1925-43; affiliated with Campaign for Baptist Schools, Kentucky, 1943-46; First Church, Arkadelphia, Ark., pastor, 1946-51. *Military service:* U.S. Naval Reserves, 1918. *Member:* Rotary International, Kiwanis International, American Legion.

WRITINGS: The Christian Family: A Complete Guidebook in the Principles of Christian Living, for Engaged Couples, for Parents and Homemakers, for Children, for the Elderly and Retired, Greenwich Book, 1960; *The Victorious Christian Life: Sermon Messages,* Exposition, 1963; *The Christian's Home in Glory,* Exposition, 1965; *Timely Messages for Times Like These,* Droke, 1970. Author of various tracts, 1943-46.

SIDELIGHTS: J. Guy Cothran has traveled in many foreign countries, and in all of the United States except Hawaii.

*　　*　　*

COTTLER, Joseph 1899-

PERSONAL: Born October 26, 1899, in Russia; son of David (a mechanic) and Gertrude (Meltzer) Cottler; married Elizabeth Steinbrook, December 27, 1927 (died November, 1975). *Education:* University of Pennsylvania, B.S., 1921. *Politics:* Nonpartisan. *Religion:* Jewish. *Home:* Mill Rd., Elkins Park, Pa. 19117.

CAREER: Teacher and counselor in Philadelphia, Pa., 1922-58. *Military service:* U.S. Navy, 1918.

WRITINGS—Juvenile books: (With Haym Jaffe) *Heroes of Civilization,* Little, Brown, 1931, revised edition, 1969; (with Jaffe) *Mapmakers,* Little, Brown, 1933; (with Harold Brecht) *Careers Ahead,* Little, Brown, 1934; *Champions of Democracy,* Little, Brown, 1935; *Man with Wings,* Little, Brown, 1942; *Alfred Wallace,* Little, Brown, 1966; (with Jaffe) *More Heroes of Civilization,* Little, Brown, 1969. Contributor of articles, and of reviews on recordings to journals.

SIDELIGHTS: Cottler has played the violin professionally and continues to play with chamber music groups. He has lived for extended periods in Europe and Mexico.

*　　*　　*

COUCH, Helen F(ox) 1907-
(V. Helen Fox)

PERSONAL: Born January 7, 1907, in Compton, Ill.; daughter of Jesse (a banker) and Emma (Tullis) Fox; married Harvey W. Couch, August 22, 1934; children: Emmaly Sue. *Education:* Studied at Cornell College, Mount Vernon, Iowa, at Northwestern University, and Northern Illinois University. *Politics:* Democrat. *Religion:* Methodist. *Home:* 2609 Woodlawn Dr., Nashville, Tenn. 37212. *Office:* Editorial Division, Methodist Board of Education, 201 Eighth Ave., S., Nashville, Tenn. 37203.

CAREER: Teacher in elementary schools in Illinois and Arkansas, 1929-34; War Manpower Commission, Hot Springs, Ark., employment counselor, 1942-46; director of Christian education at Methodist churches in Hot Springs, Ark., 1946-50, El Dorado, Ark., 1950-55; Methodist Board of Education, Editorial Division, Nashville, Tenn., editor of *Church School* and *Sunday Nighter,* 1955-61, of *Christian Home,* beginning 1961. Member of Committee on Family Life, The Methodist Church; member of Commission on Marriage and the Family, National Council of Churches. Member of board of directors of Outlook Nashville, Inc., 1960-64, Nashville Regional Eye Bank, Inc., beginning 1964.

Member: National Council on Family Relations, Child Study Association of America, American Association for the United Nations, Pilot Club (Nashville; member of board, 1959-62; president, 1961-62).

WRITINGS—With Sam S. Barefield: *Devotions for Junior Highs,* Abingdon, 1960; *Worship Sourcebook for Youth,* Abingdon, 1962; *Devotions for Young Teens,* Abingdon, 1965. Writer of worship and curriculum materials, and poems, articles, and reviews (some under pseudonym), for church publications.

AVOCATIONAL INTERESTS: Drama, music, and cooking.††

* * *

COURNOS, John   1881-1966
(Mark Gault)

PERSONAL: Born March 6, 1881, in Kiev, Russia; son of Gregory and Euphrosyne (Khatavner) Korshoon; Cournos is his stepfather's name; married Helen Kestner Satterthwaite (an author under pseudonyms John Hawk and Sybil Norton), January 1, 1924 (deceased); stepchildren: Alfred Satterthwaite, Mrs. Donald Sternbergh. *Education:* Educated privately in Russian village under tutor and governess. *Home and office:* 33 Washington Square W., New York, N.Y. 10011.

CAREER: Came to America with his family at the age of ten, knowing no English; worked as a newsboy in Philadelphia slums, and as a mill hand in a woolen mill; became an office boy for *Philadelphia Record,* and eventually assistant Sunday editor; left in 1912 for London, England, where he began his literary career in earnest; member of Gordon Craig's Committee for the School of the Theatre, 1916; decoded Russian government messages at Marconi House, London, England, 1917; appointed by British Foreign Office as a member of the Anglo-Russian Commission to Petrograd, where he remained for six months during the Bolshevik Revolution, 1918; member of British Ministry of Information, later transferred to political intelligence department of Foreign Office, resigned in 1920 to continue literary work; went to central Europe as investigator of famine areas for the Save the Children Fund of London, 1920. Was a regular reviewer for *New York Sun* until it closed in 1950. Lecturer at universities, including Bryn Mawr and New York University; appointed member of New York University faculty, as consultant on literature, 1965. *Awards, honors:* Announced as recipient of British Hawthornden Prize for his first novel, *The Mask,* but, as an American, was not entitled to it.

WRITINGS—Novels: *The Mask,* Doran, 1919; *The Wall,* Doran, 1921; *Babel,* Boni & Liveright, 1922; *The New Candide,* Boni & Liveright, 1924; *Miranda Masters,* Knopf, 1926; *O'Flaherty the Great,* Knopf, 1927; *Grandmother Martin Is Murdered,* Farrar & Rinehart, 1930; *Wandering Women,* Boni, 1930; *The Devil Is an English Gentleman,* two volumes, Farrar & Rinehart, 1932; (under pseudonym Mark Gault) *Face of Death,* Methuen, 1934.

Poems: *In Exile,* Boni & Liveright, 1923; *With Hey, Ho [and] The Man with the Spats,* Astra Books, 1963; *The Lost Leader: An Elegy for John Fitzgerald Kennedy,* Astra Books, 1964.

Plays: *Sport of Gods* (three-act; based on an episode from his novel, *Babel*), Benn, 1925.

Nonfiction: *London under the Bolsheviks: A Londoner's Dream on Returning from Petrograd,* Russian Liberation

Committee, 1919; *A Modern Plutarch* (biography), Bobbs-Merrill, 1928; *Autobiography,* Putnam, 1935; *An Open Letter to Jews and Christians,* Oxford University Press, 1938 (published in England as *Hear, O Israel,* Methuen, 1938); (with C. E. Silcox) *An Epistle to the Hebrews,* Ryerson, 1938.

Juveniles: *A Boy Named John,* Scribner, 1941; (with Sybil Norton, pseudonym of his wife) *Famous Modern American Novelists,* Dodd, 1952; (with Norton) *Famous British Novelists,* Dodd, 1952; (with Norton) *Famous British Poets,* Dodd, 1952; (with Norton) *Pilgrimage to Freedom: The Story of Roger Williams,* Holt, 1953; (with Norton) *Candidate for Truth: The Story of Daniel Webster,* Holt, 1953; (with Norton) *John Adams: Independence Forever,* Holt, 1954.

Translator from the Russian: Fedor K. Teternikov (under pseudonym Feodor Sologub) *The Old House and Other Tales,* M. Secker, 1915; (with Richard Aldington) Teternikov, *The Little Demon,* Knopf, 1916; Teternikov, *The Created Legend,* Frederick A. Stokes, 1916; Alexei Remizov, *Clock,* Knopf, 1924; (and editor) *Short Stories Out of Soviet Russia,* Dutton, 1929; Anton Chekhov, *That Worthless Fellow Platonov,* Dutton, 1930; D. S. Merezhkovskii, *Secret of the West,* Brewer and Warren, 1931; I. A. Bunin, *Grammar of Love,* H. Smith, 1934; A. L. Mikhelson, *I Came Out Alive,* Little, Brown, 1935 (published in England as *A Schoolboy Caught in the Russian Revolution: The Record of a Nightmare Adolescence,* Putnam, 1935); V. L. Durov, *My Circus Animals,* Houghton, 1936; V. I. Nemirov-Danchenko, *My Life in the Russian Theatre,* Putnam, 1935, Little, Brown, 1936, new edition (with an introduction by Joshua Logan), Theatre Arts Books, 1968; P. G. Tupikov, *Ocean,* Harper, 1936; E. V. Tarle, *Bonaparte,* Knight Publications, 1937; B. N. Bugaev (under pseudonym Andrey Biely) *St. Petersburg,* Grove, 1959.

Editor: (With E.J.H. O'Brien) *British Short Stories of 1922-1927,* six volumes, Dodd, 1922-27; *Fifteen Finest Short Stories,* Dodd, 1928; *Shylock's Choice* (anthology of Imagist poems), 1930; *American Short Stories of the Nineteenth Century,* Dutton, 1930, 2nd edition, 1960; (and author of introduction) *A Book of Prophecy from the Egyptians to Hitler,* Scribner, 1942; (and author of introduction) *A Treasury of Russian Life and Humor,* Coward, 1943, reprinted as *A Treasury of Classic Russian Literature,* Capricorn Books, 1962; (with Hiram Haydn) *A World of Great Stories,* Crown, 1947.

Editor with Sybil Norton of volumes of *Best World Short Stories* (annual), published by Appleton. Contributor to *Atlantic, Yale Review, Virginia Quarterly Review, The Studio, Criterion, Fortnightly Review, Times Literary Supplement,* and other periodicals.

WORK IN PROGRESS: A translation of a Lermontov poem; a book on poetry; two volumes of poems; a large work on human nature; a volume of epigrams; a work of fiction.

SIDELIGHTS: Cournos wrote to *CA:* "As translator I introduced to the Anglo-American public several writers, including Feodor Sologub, Aleksey Remizov, and Andrey Biely, the latter's *St. Petersburg* [originally published in 1916], a work which established the prose style of the period and probably influenced Boris Pasternak." According to Cournos, his early translations "represented an effort to learn English way back about 1910 or 11."

Cournos visited practically all of Europe, except Spain and Greece. "Music," he said, "is my chief recreation."

BIOGRAPHICAL/CRITICAL SOURCES: New York *Times,* August 29, 1966.†

(Died August 27, 1966)

* * *

COURTIER, S(idney) H(obson) 1904-197(?)
(Rui Chestor)

PERSONAL: Born January 28, 1904, in Kangaroo Flat, Victoria, Australia; son of Sidney Ernest and Maud McKenzie (Hobson) Courtier; married Audrey Jennie George, December 28, 1932; children: Colin, Brian, Lynne (Mrs. Graham Main). *Education:* University of Melbourne, Certificate in Education (first honors). *Politics:* Liberal ("in Australian politics, Conservative"). *Religion:* Methodist. *Home:* 2 Ian Rd., Safety Beach, Victoria 3936, Australia. *Agent:* Gerald Pollinger, Laurence Pollinger Ltd., 18 Maddox St., Mayfair, London W1R 0EU, England.

CAREER: Teacher in primary schools of Victoria, Australia, then principal for twelve years of Melbourne schools which were used for teacher training. Lecturer on literary subjects at teacher colleges; judge in short story competitions. *Military service:* Australian Imperial Forces, 1942-44. *Member:* International P.E.N. (president of Melbourne branch, 1954-57, 1958-61), British Crime Writers' Association, Masons.

WRITINGS—Novels; all published by Hammond, Hammond, except as noted: *The Glass Spear,* A. A. Wyn, 1950; *Gold for My Fair Lady,* A. A. Wyn, 1951; *One Cried Murder,* Rinehart, 1954; (with R. G. Campbell) *The Mudflat Million,* Angus & Robertson, 1955; *Come Back to Murder,* 1957; *Now Seek My Bones,* 1957; *A Shroud for Unlac,* 1958; *Death in Dream Time,* 1959; *Gently Dust the Corpse,* 1960; *Let the Man Die,* 1961; *Swing High Sweet Murder,* 1962; *Who Dies for Me?,* 1962; *A Corpse Won't Sing,* 1964; *Mimic a Murderer,* 1964; *The Ringnecker,* 1965; *A Corpse at Least,* 1966; *See Who's Dying,* 1967; *Murder's Burning,* Random House, 1967; *No Obelisk for Emily,* Jenkins, 1970; *Ligny's Lake,* Simon & Schuster, 1971; *Some Village Borgia,* R. Hale, 1971; *Dead If I Remember,* R. Hale, 1972; *Into the Silence,* R. Hale, 1973; *Listen to the Mocking Bird,* R. Hale, 1974; *A Window in Chungking,* R. Hale, 1975; *The Smiling Trip,* R. Hale, 1976.

Contributor of about two hundred short stories to magazines in Australia, United States, Great Britain, and other European countries; some of the short stories were published under the pseudonym Rui Chestor.

SIDELIGHTS: Many of S. H. Courtier's books have been issued in German translation by Wilhelm Goldmann Verlag.†

(Deceased)

* * *

COWARD, Noel (Peirce) 1899-1973
(Hernia Whittlebot)

PERSONAL: Born December 16, 1899, in Teddington-on-Thames, Middlesex, England; son of Arthur Sabin (a clerk in music publishing house and piano salesman) and Violet Agnes (Veitch) Coward. *Education:* Attended Chapel Royal School, Clapham; drama instruction at Miss Italia Conti's Academy, Liverpool; privately educated. *Home:* Les Avants, sur Montreux, Switzerland.

CAREER: Playwright, author, composer, songwriter, actor, singer, director, producer, and nightclub entertainer. First appearance on stage as Prince Mussel in a children's play, "The Goldfish," Little Theatre (London), 1911. Other roles include (all London productions except where otherwise indicated): Cannard in "The Great Name," Prince of Wales Theatre, 1911; William in "Where the Rainbow Ends," Savoy Theatre, 1911 (both with Charles Hawtrey's Company); dancer in ballet, "An Autumn Idyll," Savoy Theatre, 1911; one of the Angels of Light in "Hannele," Liverpool Repertory Theatre, 1913; Tommy in "War in the Air," Palladium Theatre, 1913; the Boy in "A Little Fowl Play," Coliseum, 1913 (with Charles Hawtrey's Company); Slightly in "Peter Pan," Duke of York's Theatre, 1913; toured as Charley Wykeham in "Charley's Aunt," 1916; Basil Pyecroft in "The Light Blues," Shaftesbury Theatre, 1916; Jack Morrison in "The Happy Family," Prince of Wales Theatre, 1916; Ripley Guildford in "The Saving Grace," Garrick Theatre, 1917; Courtney Borner in "Scandal," Strand Theatre, 1918; Ralph in "The Knight of the Burning Pestle," Birmingham Repertory Theatre, 1919; Clay Collins in "Polly With a Past," St. James Theatre, 1921; Lewis Dodd in "The Constant Nymph," New Theatre, 1926; Clark Storey in "The Second Man," Playhouse, 1928; Captain Stanhope in "Journey's End" (three performances), Victoria Theatre (Singapore, China), ca. 1930; King Magnus in "The Apple Cart," Haymarket Theatre, 1953; narrator of "Carnival of Animals," Carnegie Hall (New York), 1956 (see also, *WRITINGS*). Film roles include: "Hearts of the World," Comstock World, 1918; "The Scoundrel," Paramount Pictures, 1935; "Around the World in 80 Days," United Artists, 1956; "Our Man in Havana," Columbia, 1960; "Surprise Package," Columbia, 1960; "Paris When It Sizzles," Paramount Pictures, 1964; "Bunny Lake is Missing," Columbia, 1965; "Boom!," Universal, 1968; "The Italian Job," Paramount Pictures, 1968 (see also, *WRITINGS*). Producer of "Blithe Spirit," United Artists, 1945, and "This Happy Breed," Universal, 1946. President of Actors' Orphanage, 1934-56. *Military service:* British Army, Artists' Rifles, six months, 1918; entertained troops during World War II. *Member:* Royal Society of Literature (fellow). *Awards, honors:* New York Drama Critics Circle award for best foreign play, 1942, for *Blithe Spirit;* special Academy Award ("Oscar") for outstanding production achievement from Academy of Motion Picture Arts and Sciences, 1942, for "In Which We Serve;" special Antoinette Perry Award ("Tony"), 1970; D.Litt., University of Sussex, 1972.

WRITINGS—Plays: (Author and actor) *"I'll Leave It to You"* (first produced in London at New Theatre, 1920), French, 1920; (author and actor) *The Young Idea* (first produced in London at Savoy Theatre, 1923), French, 1924; *The Rat Trap,* Benn, 1924; (author and actor) *The Vortex* (first produced in London at Everyman Theatre, 1924; actor and director, with Basil Dean, of Broadway production, Henry Miller's Theater, 1925), Harper, 1925; *Fallen Angels* (first produced in London at Globe Theatre, 1925; produced in New York at Playhouse, 1956), Benn, 1925, French (New York), 1958; *Hay Fever* (first produced in London at Ambassador's Theatre, 1925; produced in New York at Maxine Elliot's Theatre, 1925), Harper, 1925, revised edition, French, 1927, with an introduction by author, Heinemann, 1965; *Easy Virtue* (first produced in London at St. Martin's Theatre, 1926), Benn, 1926; *This Was a Man* (first produced in London), Harper, 1926; *The Marquise* (first produced in London at Criterion Theatre, 1927; produced in New York at Biltmore Theatre, 1927), Benn, 1927; *Home Chat* (first produced in London at Duke of York's Theatre, 1927), M.

Secker, 1927; *Sirocco* (first produced in London at Daly's Theatre, 1927), M. Secker, 1927; (author, composer, and lyricist) *Charles B. Cochran's Revue* (first produced in London at London Pavilion, 1931), Chappell, 1928.

(Author and director) *Bitter Sweet* (operetta; first produced in London at His Majesty's Theatre, 1929; Broadway production directed by Coward at Times Square Theatre, 1931), Heinemann, 1930, Doubleday, 1931; *Post-Mortem,* Doubleday, 1931; (author and director) *Cavalcade* (first produced in London at Drury Lane Theatre, 1931), Heinemann, 1932, Doubleday, 1933; (author and actor; producer with Alfred Lunt and Lynn Fontanne) *Design for Living* (first produced in New York at Ethel Barrymore Theatre, 1933), Doubleday, 1933; (author and actor) *Conversation Piece* (first produced in London at His Majesty's Theatre, 1934; Broadway production directed by Coward at 44th Street Theatre, 1934), Doubleday, 1934; (author and director) *Point Valaine* (first produced in New York at Ethel Barrymore Theater, 1935), Doubleday, 1935; (author, composer, and lyricist) *Operette* (first produced in London at His Majesty's Theatre, 1938), Heinemann, 1938; *The Astonished Heart,* French, 1938, *Family Album,* French, 1938, *Fumed Oak,* French, 1938, *Hands Across the Sea,* French, 1938, *Red Peppers* (musical interlude), French, 1938, *Shadow Play* (musical), French, 1938, *Still Life,* French, 1938, *Ways and Means,* French, 1938, *We Were Dancing,* French, 1938 (preceding nine plays produced as *Tonight at 8:30,* below).

(Author and actor) *Blithe Spirit* (first produced in London at Piccadilly Theatre, 1941; produced in New York at Morosco Theater, 1941), Doubleday, 1941; (author and director) *Relative Values* (first produced in London at Savoy Theatre, 1951), Heinemann, 1942; (author, actor, and director) *Present Laughter* (first produced in England, 1942; produced in London at Haymarket Theatre, 1943; produced in Paris at Theatre Edouard VII, 1948, with title "Joyeux Chagrins"), Heinemann, 1943, Doubleday, 1947; (author, actor, and director) *This Happy Breed* (first produced in London at Haymarket Theater, 1943), Heinemann, 1943, Doubleday, 1947; *Peace in Our Time,* Heinemann, 1947, Doubleday, 1948.

(Author and director) *Quadrille* (first produced in London at Phoenix Theatre, 1952; produced in New York at Coronet Theater, 1954), Heinemann, 1952, Doubleday, 1955; (author, composer, and lyricist) *After the Ball* (operetta; based on Oscar Wilde's *Lady Windermere's Fan;* first produced in London at Globe Theatre, 1954), Chappell, 1954; *South Sea Bubble* (first produced in London at Lyric Theatre, 1956), Heinemann, 1956; (author and actor; director with John Gielgud) *Nude With Violin* (first produced in New York at Belasco Theater, 1957), Heinemann, 1957, Doubleday, 1958, revised acting edition, French, 1958; *Look After Lulu* (based on Georges Feydeau's *Occupe-toi d'Amelie;* first produced in London at Royal Court Theatre, 1959; produced in New York at Henry Miller's Theatre, 1959), Heinemann, 1959.

Waiting in the Wings (first produced in London at Duke of York's Theatre, 1960), Heinemann, 1960, Doubleday, 1961; (author, composer, lyricist, and director) *Sail Away* (libretto; first produced in New York at Broadhurst Theater, 1961), Bonard Productions, 1961; (author and actor) *Suite in Three Keys* (includes "A Song at Twilight," "Shadows of the Evening," and "Come Into the Garden, Maud"; first produced in London at Queen's Theatre, 1966), Heinemann, 1966, Doubleday, 1967; *Shadows of the Evening,* French, 1967; *Come Into the Garden Maud,* French, 1967; *A Song at Twilight,* French, 1967; *Private Lives* (first produced in London at Phoenix Theatre, 1930), Doubleday, 1968.

Omnibus volumes: *Three Plays: The Rat Trap, The Vortex [and] Fallen Angels* (with Coward's reply to his critics), Benn, 1925; *The Plays of Noel Coward,* first series (contains "Sirocco," "Home Chat," and "The Queen Was in the Parlour"), Doubleday, 1928; *Bitter Sweet, and Other Plays* (contains "Bitter Sweet," "Easy Virtue," and "Hay Fever"; with notes by W. Somerset Maugham), Doubleday, 1929; *Collected Sketches and Lyrics,* Hutchinson, 1931, Doubleday, 1932; *Play Parade* (contains "Design for Living," "Cavalcade," "Private Lives," "Bitter Sweet," "Post-Mortem," "The Vortex," and "Hay Fever"), Doubleday, 1933, revised edition, Heinemann, 1949; (author, actor, and director) *Tonight at 8:30* (three volumes; Volume I: "The Astonished Heart," "Red Peppers," and "We Were Dancing"; Volume II: "Fumed Oak," "Hands Across the Sea," and "Shadow Play"; Volume III: "Family Album," "Still Life," and "Ways and Means"; "The Astonished Heart," "Family Album," "Fumed Oak," "Hands Across the Sea," "Red Peppers," and "Shadow Play" originally produced in London at Phoenix Theatre, 1936, with title "Tonight at 7:30"; entire series produced in New York at National Theater, 1936, as "Tonight at 8:30"), Doubleday, 1936; *Second Play Parade* (contains "This Year of Grace," "Words and Music," "Operette," and "Conversation Piece"), Heinemann, 1939, 2nd edition published as *Play Parade, Volume II,* with addition of "Fallen Angels" and "Easy Virtue," 1950; *Curtain Calls* (contains "Tonight at 8:30," "We Were Dancing," "The Astonished Heart," "Red Peppers," "Hands Across the Sea," "Fumed Oak," "Shadow Play," "Ways and Means," "Still Life," "Family Album," "Conversation Piece," "Easy Virtue," "Point Valaine," and "This Was a Man"), Doubleday, 1940.

Play Parade, Volume III (contains "The Queen Was in the Parlour," "'I'll Leave It to You'," "The Young Idea," "Sirocco," "The Rat Trap," "This Was a Man," "Home Chat," and "The Marquise"), Heinemann, 1950; *Play Parade, Volume IV* (contains "Tonight at 8:30," "Present Laughter," and "This Happy Breed"), Heinemann, 1952; *Play Parade, Volume V,* Heinemann, 1958; *Play Parade, Volume VI,* Heinemann, 1962; *Three Plays by Noel Coward: Blithe Spirit, Hay Fever, [and] Private Lives,* with an introduction by Edward Albee, Dell, 1965.

Other plays: (Author, composer, and lyricist with Ronald Jeans; actor) "London Calling," first produced in London at Duke of York's Theatre, 1923; (with others) "Charlot's Revue," first produced in London at Prince of Wales Theatre, 1924; (author and composer with others) "On With the Dance" (revue), first produced in London, 1925; (author, composer, and actor) "This Year of Grace" (revue; published in *Second Play Parade,* above), first produced in New York at Selwyn Theater, 1928; (author, composer, and lyricist) "Words and Music" (revue; published in *Second Play Parade*), first production directed and conducted by Coward in London at Adelphi Theatre, 1932; "Biography," first produced in London at Globe Theatre, 1934; (composer and lyricist) "Set to Music" (revue), first production directed by Coward in New York at Music Box, 1939; (author and actor) "Sigh No More" (revue), first produced in London at Piccadilly Theatre, 1945; (author and director) "Pacific 1860" (musical), first produced in London at Drury Lane Theatre, 1946; (author and director) "Ace of Clubs" (musical), first produced in London at Cambridge Theatre, 1950; (author and director) "Island Fling," 1951; (author of scenario and score) "London Morning" (ballet), 1959; (author, composer, and lyricist) "The Girl Who Came to Supper" (based on *The Sleeping Prince*, by Terence M. Rattigan), first produced in New York at Broadway Theater, 1963; (author and director) "High Spirits" (musical adaptation, by Coward, of *Blithe Spirit*), first produced in New York at Alvin Theater, 1964; (contributor of material with others) "Carol Channing with 10 Stout-Hearted Men" (revue), first produced in London at Drury Lane Theatre, 1970.

Other writings: (Compiler) *Terribly Intimate Portraits*, Boni & Liveright, 1922; *A Withered Nosegay* (imaginary biographies), Christophers, 1922; (under pseudonym Hernia Whittlebot; real name cited as editor) *Chelsea Buns* (poems), Hutchinson, 1925; (editor) *Spangled Unicorn* (anthology), Hutchinson, 1932, Doubleday, 1933; *Present Indicative* (autobiography), Doubleday, 1937; *To Step Aside* (seven short stories), Doubleday, 1939; *Australia Visited, 1940* (broadcast series), Heinemann, 1941; *Middle East Diary*, Doubleday, 1944; *Star Quality* (six short stories), Doubleday, 1951; *Noel Coward Song Book*, Simon & Schuster, 1953; *Future Indefinite* (autobiography; sequel to *Present Indicative*), Doubleday, 1954; *Short Stories, Short Plays, and Songs*, Dell, 1955; (editor) Frederick Thomas Bason, *Last Bassoon*, Parrish, 1960; *Pomp and Circumstance* (novel), Doubleday, 1960; (translator) J. Dramese, *Les Folies du Musichall*, Blond, 1962; *Collected Short Stories*, Heinemann, 1962, new edition published as *The Collected Short Stories of Noel Coward*, 1969; *Seven Stories*, Doubleday, 1963; *Pretty Polly Barlow, and Other Stories*, Heinemann, 1964, published as *Pretty Polly, and Other Stories*, Doubleday, 1965; *The Lyrics of Noel Coward*, Heinemann, 1965, Doubleday, 1967; *Bon Voyage and Other Stories*, Heinemann, 1967, published as *Bon Voyage*, Doubleday, 1968; *Not Yet the Dodo and Other Verses*, Heinemann, 1967, Doubleday, 1968; Dick Richards, compiler, *The Wit of Noel Coward*, Frewin, 1968; (author of introduction) Michael Arlen, *The London Venture*, Cassell, 1968; (author of foreword) Raymond Mander and Joe Mitchenson, *Musical Comedy: A Story in Pictures*, P. Davies, 1969, Taplinger, 1970; (author of text) John Hadfield, editor, *A Last Encore* (pictures), Little, Brown, 1973.

Several revues based on excerpts from Coward's works, including: "And Now Noel Coward," retitled "Noel Coward's Sweet Potato," both produced in New York, 1968; "Cowardy Custard," produced in New York, 1972, published as *Cowardy Custard: The World of Noel Coward*, Heinemann, 1973; "Oh Coward!" produced in New York, 1972, published as *Oh Coward! A Musical Comedy Revue*, Doubleday, 1974.

Films: (Author of dialogue and lyrics) "Bitter Sweet," United Artists, 1933; (producer, actor, composer, co-director, and writer) "In Which We Serve," United Artists, 1942; (writer and producer) "Brief Encounter," (adaptation of *Still Life* and *Fumed Oak*), Universal, 1946 (screenplay published in *Three British Screen Plays*, edited by Roger Manvell, Methuen, 1950); (actor and contributor of material) "The Astonished Heart," Universal, 1950; (actor and contributor of material) "Meet Me Tonight" (adaptation of *Tonight at 8:30*), 1952. Also actor in and contributor of material to "Together With Music," a television play produced by Ford Star Jubilee, CBS-TV, 1955.

SIDELIGHTS: Coward's "music has been played by innumerable dance orchestras," writes Frank Swinnerton. "His plays have been booed (Coward facing the boos with every appearance of dignity) and extolled. He has been billed, in the cinemas of England, as the greatest living dramatist. He has been inaccurately reported as marooned upon a desert island; plays of his have been banned by the censor in England; he has written prefaces (and they have been printed) in italics. He knows all the smart people, and he neither drinks nor stays up late. He is liked wherever he goes; and might at any time, if it has not happened already, be mobbed by those outrageous harpies who molest actors and actresses at stage doors in London. His plays are denied wit by the dramatic critics, and yet in their way are wittier than most other smart plays except those by Frederick Lonsdale.

"It would appear that exception has been taken to some of Coward's work on the ground that it directly encourages immorality. That is very strange. His plays are among the most moral plays ever written. . . . He has been one of the most successful playwrights of modern times, and he has had much applause.

"Why should he be banned? The answer is, according to Coward, that the Middle Classes impose the weight of their 'massed illiteracy' upon the theatre. He says: 'I do resent very deeply, on my own behalf and on behalf of those young writers who are sincerely attempting to mirror contemporary life honestly and truthfully . . . that this weight of bourgeois ignorance and false sentimentality should not only be allowed to force those in authority to crush down rising talent for the sole reason that its outlook doesn't quite conform with the moral traditions of twenty-five years ago, but that it should be encouraged in every possible way by the press.'

"It is his object to mirror contemporary life. Not all contemporary life, but a section of it. And the part he mirrors is a part given to promiscuity, drunkenness, drugging, and fighting. . . . The only trouble is that these plays about neurotics do not quite satisfy us that neuroticism is a completely valuable theme; or that (assuming it to be a valuable theme) Coward has seen it more than superficially. The plays are written with much verve, and many lively sallies adorn them. The chit-chat they contain is insulting, irreverent, cheeky, and full of surprise. They are less good when Coward is serious; for then he gropes a little in the profundities, and his long theatrical experience does him an ill turn by making him specious. Therefore his lighter plays, or the lighter moments in his less frivolous plays, are best. . . . His wit, though it is not of the most subtle and distinguished kind, is fresh and amusing. . . ."

As an actor, Coward was both praised and panned. John Weightman, reviewing the 1966 production of "Suite in Three Keys," in which Coward played, wrote: "[Coward] had a way of getting up from his seat and moving jerkily about the stage or fiddling with the drinks tray that said quite clearly: 'I must vary things here with a bit of business.' More than once he appeared so bored with his lines he couldn't even remember them, and the clear, feminine voice of the prompter rang through the hush. And the pace! He lobbed the witticisms into the audience and waited for the crash of Philistine mirth. It usually occurred, but with the disjointed automatism of canned applause. . . . In short, Mr. Coward was a sad disappointment to me. . . ."

Others believe Coward's subtle style of "non-acting" was both polished and natural. Of his own work, Coward told Michael Macowan: ". . . Acting is not a state of being; it is giving an impression of feeling. . . . I believe that all acting is a question of control, the control of the actor of himself, and through himself of the audience." Coward said that he preferred playing someone else's work to his own; he added: "I always forget when I'm playing in my own plays that I am the author. Not at rehearsals, when I'm after the others, but when I'm actually doing it."

Coward had little admiration for the contemporary English and American theaters, which, for him, were characterized by sloppy acting, lack of flair, and bad plays. He saw this development as the result of modern disrespect for the "sanctity" of the theater (he always rehearsed in a freshly pressed suit, regardless of his role, and abhorred the blue jeans and old sweaters that he saw at the rehearsals of new plays). He told Macowan: "In the old days, before the war, in the 'twenties and the 'thirties, whenever I was about to do a new production in England I always used to go to New York for a fortnight and go to every single play, because the tempo and the wonderful speed and vitality of the American theatre was then far superior to the English. Since the war, the American theatre has deteriorated, I think, enormously; in England the standard is immensely high among young actors. But owing to the dearth of light-comedy playwrights it is rather fashionable now to say the day of the well-made play is over. That is nonsense. What they mean is that many of the playwrights don't know enough about it to construct a play properly. But in the last few years in the English theatre I think too much emphasis has been placed on the lower orders of life, so that it is now considered out of the question for a duchess to suffer labour pains—just wouldn't be possible because she has a big income. That has made a slight bias, so that all the young people have lost a certain style that we had in the old days." He did, however, respect Harold Pinter, whose contemporary plays have elicited much critical acclaim: "Oh, [Pinter is] an absolutely meticulous director," he told Macowan. "Every pause is professionally timed and the net result is, I think, remarkable. I think he is a very extraordinary writer and also a remarkable theatre man."

As he told Albin Krebs, Coward had the following advice for playwrights: "Consider the public. Treat it with tact and courtesy. It will accept much from you if you are clever enough to win it to your side. Never fear it nor despise it. Coax it, charm it, interest it, stimulate it, shock it now and then if you must, make it laugh, make it cry, but above all, dear pioneers . . . never, never, never bore the living hell out of it."

By reputation Coward was a sophisticated and urbane playboy, as trim and dapper at sixty-seven as he was in the 'twenties. "The legend of my playboyishness," he told Harvey Breit, "has lasted into my vintage. If the legend were true, how could I have managed to get anything done?" Breit asked Coward how he did manage. "I get up at 6," Coward replied. "I start work at 7 and work four and a half hours, and I *still* get to the beach before lunch. The thing is to have time, and peace." Coward worked fast and did little rewriting. "With a play I go straight on until I'm finished," he told Breit. "I do it straight on the typewriter. It was five days for *Blithe Spirit.* No, no changes. It was all complete. Maybe a few typographical errors. The quicker I write my plays, the better they are. I know this is a dangerous fact for would-be writers."

Although Coward had many critics, his success as a writer and performer and his devotion to the theater have long been firmly established. Jere Real feels that "inherent in Coward's work is a perceptive comic sense of the foibles of the human condition that transcends both the topical and the intellectual." And Brendan Gill once asserted, "Coward is the greatest of English theatrical figures in the multifariousness of his gifts." As T. E. Kalem notes, Coward "was never cool about the theater. . . . It was his cross, his sword, and his crown. He served it with undeviating grace, wit and loyalty."

Numerous film adaptations have been made of Coward's work, including: "Private Lives," Metro-Goldwyn-Mayer, 1931; "Design for Living," Paramount Pictures, 1933; "We Were Dancing" (based in part on *Tonight at 8:30*), Metro-Goldwyn-Mayer, 1942; "A Matter of Innocence" (based on short story "Pretty Polly"), Universal, 1967; also, "Heart of a Woman" (adaptation of *Cavalcade*).

The musical "Mr. and Mrs.," an adaptation of *Still Life* and *Fumed Oak,* was produced in London, 1968. Coward was the subject of a television special, "David Frost Presents Noel Coward," 1969. He also recorded a reading from *Private Lives* for Odeon, "Noel and Gertie."

BIOGRAPHICAL/CRITICAL SOURCES: Present Indicative (autobiography), Doubleday, 1937; Frank Swinnerton, *The Georgian Literary Scene,* Dent, 1938, revised edition, 1951; *Future Indefinite* (autobiography), Doubleday, 1954; Harvey Breit, *The Writer Observed,* World Publishing, 1956; interview by Michael Macowan, in *The Listener,* April 7, 1966; *Encounter,* July, 1966; Sheridan Morley, *A Talent to Amuse: A Biography of Noel Coward,* Doubleday, 1969; *Contemporary Literary Criticism,* Volume I, Gale, 1973.†

(Died March 26, 1973)

*   *   *

COWELL, Cyril   1888-

PERSONAL: Born July 21, 1888, in Canterbury, England; son of John (an architect) and Jessie Elizabeth (Ashenden) Cowell; married Edith Nellie Warner, March 21, 1929. *Education:* Attended school in Redhill, Surrey, England. *Religion:* Church of England.

CAREER: Writer and artist. *Military service:* British Army, Artillery, 1915-17.

WRITINGS: Adam the Gardener, Daily Express, 1946, latest revised edition, 1951; *Your Gardening Book,* Faber, 1954; (self illustrated) *Your Book of Animal Drawing,* Transatlantic, 1956, 2nd edition, Faber, 1962, Transatlantic, 1963; (self-illustrated) *Your Book of Figure Drawing,* Transatlantic, 1964.

Children's books: (Self-illustrated) *Larry Lop-ear,* Grout, 1945; *Larry Laughs Last,* Grout, 1946.††

*   *   *

COX, Hugh S(towell)   1874-1969

PERSONAL: Born July 23, 1874, in Bear River, Nova Scotia, Canada; son of George Davenport (a Baptist minister) and Ada (Davison) Cox; married Gertrude Izette, September 16, 1903; children: Myrl (Mrs. Frank Snow). *Education:* Attended St. John Business College, 1894-96.

CAREER: United Carr Fastener Co., Cambridge, Mass., head of receiving department, 1925-54.

WRITINGS: God Through Isaiah Speaks to Israel, Hebrew edition, Jerusalem Post Press, 1965, English edition, privately printed, 1966, revised and enlarged by E. T. Lenfest, 1976; *Revelation,* privately printed, 1965; *Ezekiel,* privately printed, 1965; *Jeremiah: A Helping Hand for Bible Students,* privately printed, 1967; *The Minor Prophets: Hosea to Malachi,* privately printed, 1967.

SIDELIGHTS: As pastor of a Bible Study group in Boston, wrote E. T. Lenfest, Cox was "impressed that it was time to bring Good Tidings of God's favor returning to the Jews," and he began the study of Hebrew in 1954. "After two seasons," Lenfest continued, "he found no response at the Milton Temple, and none were able to speak the language.

So he proceeded in an intensive study of Revelation . . . , writing the conclusions reached. That study and writing has continued through the books of Isaiah, Ezekiel, Jeremiah and the Minor Prophets."†

(Died December 21, 1969)

* * *

COX, Warren E(arle) 1895-1977

PERSONAL: Born August 27, 1895, in Oak Park, Ill.; son of William John and Ella Barret (Gile) Cox; married Ann Elizabeth Pierson, June 7, 1918. *Education:* Attended schools in New Jersey, Pennsylvania, and Missouri. *Politics:* None. *Religion:* None. *Home:* 201 East 37th St., New York, N.Y. 10016. *Office:* 6 East 39th St., New York, N.Y. 10016.

CAREER: Warren E. Cox Associates, Inc. (dealer in antiques and oriental art), New York, N.Y., president, beginning 1918. Designer of art objects, lamps, etc.; painter. *Military service:* U.S. Army, Infantry, World War I; became second lieutenant. *Member:* American Society of Appraisers.

WRITINGS: The Book of Pottery and Porcelain, Crown, 1944, revised edition, 1970; *Chinese Ivory Sculpture,* Crown, 1946, revised edition, 1966; (editor) *The Home-lovers Book,* Frost & Read (Bristol, England), c.1950; *Lighting and Lamp Design,* Crown, 1952; *Manual for Collectors of Oriental Art,* Shorewood Press, c.1967. Also author of "Hokusai Mangwa" and "The Autobiography of a Siamese Cat." Art director and art editor, *Encyclopaedia Britannica,* 14th edition, 1929-39. Contributor of articles to *Country Life, Connoisseur, Oriental Art,* and other publications.

WORK IN PROGRESS: An illustrated volume, *Drinking Vessels and Drinking Customs.*

SIDELIGHTS: Cox told *CA:* "My basic theory in art is that rich people have fine homes and often good taste. We consider ourselves top craftsmen and have endeavored to supply lamps that would go in such homes. (Mike Angelo was only a decorator when he did the Sistine Chapel.) We aim not for originality but for the best of craftsmanship. I have at present a jade lamp valued at $25,000 and am proud to say I worked for over three months making the repousse silver base for it. I consider that all artists of the best periods were basically craftsmen doing their best to fulfill a need. I am opposed to the high and mighty attitudes of 'modern' artists, who paint some subjective thing and then hope to sell it. In the article on 'Aesthetics' in the Britannica, I came to the conclusion that ART is nothing but human appeals as varied as the personalities of all mankind."†

(Died May 22, 1977)

* * *

CRABTREE, Arthur B(amford) 1910-

PERSONAL: Born May 5, 1910, in Stalybridge, England; son of George (a metal worker) and Harriet (Bamford) Crabtree; married Hanna Utzinger (a receptionist), September 10, 1938; children: Martin. *Education:* University of Manchester, B.A., 1933, B.D., 1935; University of Zurich, Dr. Theol., 1946; University of Tuebingen, postdoctoral student, 1964-65. *Home:* 6355 Lancaster Ave., Philadelphia, Pa. 19151. *Office:* Department of Religious Studies, Villanova University, Villanova, Pa. 19085.

CAREER: Baptist minister; pastor in Fleetwood, England,

1938-39, and Leeds, England, 1939-44; Baptist Union of Britain, London, England, administrator, 1944-49; Baptist Theological Seminary, Zurich, Switzerland, professor of theology, 1949-57; Eastern Baptist Theological Seminary, Philadelphia, Pa., professor of theology, 1957-68; Villanova University, Villanova, Pa., professor of theology, 1968—.

WRITINGS: Jonathan Edward's View of Man, Religious Education Press, 1947; (translator) Wilhelm Vischer, *The Witness of the Old Testament to Christ,* Lutterworth, 1947; *The Restored Relationship,* Judson, 1963.

WORK IN PROGRESS: History of Protestant Thought; Ecumenism in an Ecological Age.

* * *

CRAIG, John David 1903-

PERSONAL: Born April 28, 1903, in Cincinnati, Ohio; son of John (a business efficiency engineer) and Marie Johanna (Leuchsenring) Craig; married Mildred E. Day, August 12, 1939; children: Sharon Day, Kathleen Jane. *Education:* Attended University of Southern California and UTOCO Engineering College, 1920-24, and Calcutta University, 1926; four years world travel with tutor, 1924-28. *Religion:* Protestant. *Home:* 31532 Crystal Sands Dr., South Laguna, Calif. 92677. *Office:* 733 North Highland Ave., Hollywood, Calif. 90038.

CAREER: Petroleum engineer in California, 1922-24; director of world-wide research for Osborne-Craig Co., 1924-30; director and cameraman for motion picture productions in various parts of the world, 1931-39; director and producer of adventure, travel, documentary, and oceanography films in California, beginning 1948. President of Crayne Television Productions, Inc., and Underwater Technologists Associates, Inc., both Hollywood, Calif. Developer of helium-oxygen self-contained diving apparatus, and underwater camera and lighting equipment. Certified advanced scuba diving instructor; holder of U.S. Navy deep diving certificate. Lecturer. *Military service:* U.S. Army Air Forces, 1942-47; became lieutenant colonel; received Legion of Merit, Purple Heart, Distinguished Flying Cross, Air Medal with ten oak leaf clusters, Distinguished Unit Citation with three clusters, Africa Star, ten battle stars.

MEMBER: American Polar Society, Air Force Association, Retired Officers Association, Kiwanis International (honorary life member), Adventurers Club (Chicago), Savage Club (London).

WRITINGS: Danger Is My Business (Literary Guild selection), Simon & Schuster, 1938; *Invitation to Skin and Scuba Diving,* Simon & Schuster, 1965. Contributor to magazines, including *Esquire, Cosmopolitan, American, Popular Mechanics, Rotarian, Coronet.*

* * *

CRAIGIE, E(dward) Horne 1894-

PERSONAL: Born June 24, 1894, in Edinburgh, Scotland; son of Alfred Horne (a merchant) and Margaret Wilson (Deuchars) Craigie; married Marguerite Cecile Homuth, July 5, 1919; children: Margaret Florilla, Louise Cecile (Mrs. Allen Livingston Browne). *Education:* University of Toronto, B.A., 1916, Ph.D., 1920; other graduate study at University of Chicago, summers, 1915, 1917, Wistar Institute, 1918, Instituto Cajal, 1927, and Central Institute for Brain Research, Amsterdam, 1927. *Home:* 52 Strathgowan Ave., Toronto, Canada M4N 1B9.

CAREER: University of Toronto, Toronto, Ontario, lecturer, 1920-25, assistant professor, 1925-33, associate professor, 1933-45, professor of comparative anatomy and neurology, 1945-62, professor emeritus, 1962—. Member: American Association for the Advancement of Science, Royal Society of Canada, Royal Canadian Institute, American Association of Anatomists (member of executive council, 1941-48), Toronto Guild for Colour Photography (president, 1953-54).

WRITINGS: Anatomy of the Central Nervous System of the Rat, University of Toronto Press, 1925, revised edition (with W. Zeman and J.R.M. Innes) published as Craigie's Neuroanatomy of the Rat, Academic Press, 1963; (translator from the Spanish) Santiago Ramon y Cajal, Recollections of My Life, American Philosophical Society, 1937; (author of revision) Bensley's Practical Anatomy of the Rabbit, 6th edition, University of Toronto Press, 1938, 8th edition, 1948; A Laboratory Guide to the Anatomy of the Rabbit, University of Toronto Press, 1951, 2nd edition, 1966; A Laboratory Outline for the Dissection of the Lamprey, of the Dogfish, and of the Skate, University of Toronto Press, 1957; (contributor) George Austin, editor, The Spinal Cord, C. C Thomas, 1961; (with W. C. Gibson) The World of Ramon y Cajal, C. C Thomas, 1968. Contributor of about seventy articles to learned journals. Editor for Section V, Transactions of Royal Society of Canada, 1941-61; editor, Transactions of the Royal Canadian Institute, 1945-48, and Canadian Journal of Zoology, 1947-55.

AVOCATIONAL INTERESTS: Amateur archaeology, color photography; travel, especially in Middle America.

*   *   *

CRANFORD, Robert J(oshua)   1908-

PERSONAL: Born August 28, 1908, in Troy, N.C.; son of Eli Wade (a teacher and editor) and Vernia (Zachary) Cranford; married Sara Kathryn Croxton, January 1, 1932; children: Bobbie Jean (Mrs. Walter H. Simmons). Education: Duke University, A.B., 1928; University of South Carolina, A.M., 1950; University of Iowa, Ph.D., 1953. Politics: Republican-Independent. Home: 2908 South 25th St., Lincoln, Neb. 68502. Office: 319 Nebraska Hall, University of Nebraska, Lincoln, Neb. 68508.

CAREER: Charlotte News, Charlotte, N.C., reporter and editor, 1929-34, 1944-48; Associated Press, staffer in Charlotte, N.C., 1934-44; University of South Carolina, Columbia, public relations director, 1948-51, acting dean of School of Journalism, 1950-51; University of Iowa, Iowa City, instructor in journalism, 1951-53; Northwestern University, Evanston, Ill., associate professor of journalism, 1953-57; University of Nebraska, Lincoln, professor of journalism and mass communications, beginning 1957. Consultant, Nebraska Press Association, 1962, Omaha Sun Newspapers, 1965. Director of education division, Lincoln Community Chest, 1964. Military service: U.S. Naval Reserve, lieutenant, 1942.

MEMBER: Association for Education in Journalism (secretary-treasurer of newspaper division), National Council of College Publications Advisers (past chairman of committee on high school relations), Sigma Delta Chi, Kappa Tau Alpha (executive council). Awards, honors: Named adviser of the year, National Council of College Publications Advisers, 1962.

WRITINGS: Copy Editing Workbook, Holt, 1958, 2nd edition, 1967; The State Editor and His Problems, University of Nebraska Press, 1961; A Correspondent's Manual, University of Nebraska Press, 1962; The Nebraska Press Coverage of the 1960 Presidential Campaign, University of Nebraska Press, 1964. Contributor of poetry and articles to journals.

WORK IN PROGRESS: A Tear for Inverness, a novel; a collection of poems; readership surveys for a major magazine and a newspaper chain.†

*   *   *

CRAWFORD, John E(dmund)   1904-1971

PERSONAL: Born January 21, 1904, in Pittsburgh, Pa.; son of Edmund Miley (an engineer) and Charlotte Wesley (Perrett) Crawford; married Dorathea Marie Bohm, 1936. Education: University of Pittsburgh, B.S., 1932, M.S., 1934, Ed.D., 1940; Columbia University, postdoctoral study, 1942. Home: 520 Washington Rd., Apartment 601, Pittsburgh, Pa. 15228.

CAREER: Certified psychologist, states of Pennsylvania, New Jersey, and Ohio. Pittsburgh (Pa.) public schools, classroom teacher, 1930-43; John A. Roebling's Sons Co., Trenton, N.J., training specialist, 1943-46; Wagner College, Staten Island, N.Y., professor of psychology, and director of guidance, 1947-51; Lawrence County (Pa.) public schools, clinical psychologist and supervisor of special services, 1954-62; Millersville State College, Millersville, Pa., professor of psychology and director of research; Eastern State School and Hospital, Trevose, Pa., clinical psychologist; Allegheny County (Pa.) public schools, clinical psychologist, 1967-71. Private practice as consulting psychologist for children, 1945-71. Consultant to Art Institute of Pittsburgh, 1971. Member: American Psychological Association (fellow), Pennsylvania Psychological Association (fellow).

WRITINGS: Practical Electricity (text for slow learners in vocational schools), Bruce, 1939; Case Studies in Human Relations, Supervision Publishing Co., 1941; (with Luther E. Woodward) Better Ways of Growing Up, Lutheran Press (Philadelphia), 1949, revised edition (sole author), Fortress, 1964; Teens . . . How to Meet Your Problems, Morrow, 1953; Milestones for Modern Teens, Morrow, 1954; More Power to You, Muhlenberg Press, 1957; P.S. to Puzzled Parents, Christian Education Press, 1959; Go With Courage, Christian Education Press, 1961; Children With Subtle Perceptual-Motor Difficulties, Stanwix, 1966; Being the Real Father Now That Your Teenager Will Need, Fortress, 1968.

Evaluation and aptitude tests: Crawford Spatial Relations Test (designed for use in guidance centers for young adults), Psychological Corp. (New York), 1942; Point-Motion Test (for engineering aptitude), Psychological Corp., 1942; Block-Projection Test (for engineering aptitude), C. A. Gregory, 1944; Small Parts Dexterity Test (for industrial use), Psychological Corp., 1950.

Contributor of more than thirty professional articles to Vocational Education and other journals, 1930-40; writer of weekly page under heading "This Business of Living" for Methodist periodical, Classmate, 1953-59.

WORK IN PROGRESS: A series of 16 mm color and sound films, "Teaching Exceptional Children"; further research on children with subtle brain damage; a text for physicians and pediatricians.†

(Died October 12, 1971)

CRAWFORD, Matsu W(offord) 1902-

PERSONAL: Born February 28, 1902, in Laurens, S.C.; daughter of John Albert (a farmer) and Cleo (Cunningham) Wofford; married Vernon A. Crawford (a Presbyterian minister), September 2, 1925; children: John Richard, Vernon A., Jr. (deceased). *Education:* Winthrop College, A.B., 1923; Mercer University, M.Ed., 1952. *Religion:* Presbyterian. *Home:* 308 West Arlington Ave., Greer, S.C. 29651.

CAREER: Taught high school English in South Carolina before her marriage; lived in Japan where her husband was a Presbyterian missionary, 1929-40; member of staff of Federal Housing Administration office, Warner Robins, Ga., 1942-45; high school English teacher in St. Petersburg, Fla., 1957-61.

WRITINGS: For Every Red Sea (novel), Zondervan, 1964; *Love is Like an Acorn,* Zondervan, 1968. Contributor to religious publications.

WORK IN PROGRESS: Another novel, *A Striving With Wind;* and short stories and articles.

* * *

CRAWFORD, Robert Platt 1893-

PERSONAL: Born December 7, 1893, in Council Bluffs, Iowa; son of Nelson Antrim (a lawyer) and Fanny (Vandercook) Crawford. *Education:* University of Nebraska, A.B., 1917; Columbia University, A.M., 1926.

CAREER: Nebraska State Journal, Lincoln, reporter, 1914-16; U.S. Department of Agriculture, Washington, D C., assistant editor, 1918; *Nebraska Farmer,* Lincoln, associate editor, 1919-21; University of Nebraska, Lincoln, historical research, 1922, assistant professor, 1923, associate professor, 1924-26, professor of journalism, 1926-59, professor emeritus, 1959—, assistant to chancellor, 1928-38. Wartime posts with U.S. government included field representative, later specialist in business and finance, Office of War Information, 1944-45, member of journalism faculty, Department of Defense University, Florence, Italy, 1945, and senior publications analyst, Headquarters, Supreme Commander of the Allied Powers in Japan, Tokyo, 1946-47. *Member:* American Economic Association, Royal Economic Society (fellow), Society of Midland Authors (vice-president for Nebraska), Authors Club (London), Nebraska Writers Guild (honorary).

WRITINGS: These Fifty Years, University of Nebraska Press, 1925; *The Magazine Article,* McGraw, 1931; *Think for Yourself,* Whittlesey House, 1937, new edition, Fraser, 1964; *The Techniques of Creative Thinking,* Hawthorn, 1954, new edition, Fraser, 1964; *Direct Creativity with Attribute Listing,* Fraser, 1964. Writer of syndicated newspaper column, "Dollars and Sense," in the 1920's, and of series on real estate for *Financial World,* 1952-60; contributor to *Barron's, Country Gentleman,* and other periodicals.

WORK IN PROGRESS: Two books.††

* * *

CREELMAN, Marjorie B(roer) 1908-

PERSONAL: Born December 5, 1908, in Toledo, Ohio; daughter of William F. and Ethel (Griffin) Broer; married George Douglas Creelman, June 29, 1932 (divorced December 2, 1958); children: Carleton Douglas, Stewart Elliott, Katherine Creelman Skrobela. *Education:* Attended Pine Manor Junior College, 1926-27, and University of Wisconsin, 1927-28; Vassar College, A.B. (with honors), 1931;

Columbia University, M.A., 1932; Western Reserve (now Case Western Reserve) University, Ph.D., 1954; also studied at Cleveland College, 1946-47, 1959-60. *Politics:* Independent. *Home and office:* 2433 Lamberton Rd., Cleveland, Ohio 44118.

CAREER: New York Psychiatric Institute, New York, N.Y., assistant psychologist, 1932-33; Sunny Acres Sanitorium, Cleveland, Ohio, assistant psychologist, 1947-48; Western Reserve (now Case Western Reserve) University, Cleveland, clinical assistant, 1947-49, supervisor of field work and director of practicum training program, 1949-53; Creelman Associates, Cleveland, senior associate and partner, 1954-58; also private practice as psychotherapist, Cleveland, 1954-61; St. Elizabeth's Hospital, Washington, D.C., research psychologist, 1963-65, director of program in psychophysiology, 1965-67; private practice in Washington, D.C., 1964-69; Alexandria Community Mental Health Center, Alexandria, Va., director of psychological services, 1967-69; Cleveland State University, Cleveland, professor of psychology, 1969-75; private practice of psychotherapy, Cleveland, beginning 1969. Lecturer in psychology, Fenn College (now Cleveland State University), 1960-61. Member of training faculty for Gestalt Institute of Cleveland, 1969.

MEMBER: American Society for Group Psychotherapy and Psychodrama (fellow; member of council, beginning 1973), International Council of Psychologists (fellow; secretary, 1964-65), American Academy of Psychotherapists, American Psychological Association, International Society for General Semantics (associate member), World Federation for Mental Health (associate member), Ohio Psychological Association (fellow), Cleveland Institute for Gestalt Therapy (fellow; member of executive board, 1956-60), Cleveland Academy of Clinical Psychologists (former chairman and secretary), Psi Chi, Sigma Delta Epsilon.

WRITINGS: The Experimental Investigation of Meaning, Springer Publishing, 1966. Contributor to professional journals. Editor, *Persona,* 1947-50; *Ohio Psychologist,* 1955-59; directory editor, American Academy of Psychotherapists, 1963-66.

WORK IN PROGRESS: Research in psychotherapy.

AVOCATIONAL INTERESTS: Creative writing, music, sculpture and painting.

* * *

CRENA de IONGH, Daniel 1888-1970

PERSONAL: Born April 21, 1888, in Dordrecht, Netherlands; son of Adrianus Cornelis (a lawyer) and Cornelie Madeleine (van Eck) Crena de Iongh; married A. E. Gransberg, May 8, 1916; married second wife, Mary Dows Herter (an author and translator), July 3, 1947; children: (first marriage) Cornelis Adriaan, Elisabeth Crommelin, Cornelie Madeleine van Ravesteyn, Pauline McHarg. *Education:* University of Leiden, D.L. 1914. *Religion:* Protestant. *Home:* 30 Shadow Lane, Wilton, Conn. 06897.

CAREER: Nederlandsche Handel-Maatschappij, first at Rotterdam, then at Amsterdam, Netherlands, various positions up to president, 1914-39; Netherlands Indies Exchange Control, Batavia, head, 1940-42; Netherlands Indies Government in Exile, London, England, financial adviser, 1942-43; Board for Netherlands Indies, Surinam, and Curacao, New York, N.Y., chairman, 1943-46; International Bank for Reconstruction and Development, Washington, D.C., treasurer, 1946-52, executive director, 1953-55; International Monetary Fund, Washington, D.C., executive director,

1953-55. *Member:* Metropolitan Club (New York, N.Y., and Washington, D.C.), Reform Club (London, England). *Awards, honors:* Knight of Order of the Netherlands Lion; Commander, French Legion of Honor; Great Officer of Order of the Falcon of Iceland.

WRITINGS: Byzantine Aspects of Italy, Norton, 1967. Member of editorial board, *de Gids,* 1930-39.

SIDELIGHTS: Daniel Crena de Iongh had a lifelong interest in art, religion, and history; on retirement, Crena de Iongh selected Byzantium as his special field of interest, and studied and traveled in the areas that once belonged to the Byzantine Empire, including Turkey, Greece, Sinai, Lebanon, Egypt, Yugoslavia, Cyprus, and Italy.†

(Died November 26, 1970)

* * *

CREW, Francis Albert Eley   1888-1973

PERSONAL: Born March 2, 1888, in Tipton, Staffordshire, England; son of Thomas (a company director) and Annie (Eley) Crew; married Helen Campbell Dykes, 1913 (died, 1971); married Margaret Ogilvie Withof-Keus, 1972; children: Graeme Campbell Eley, Cicely Francis Ely (Mrs. Ruthven Todd). *Education:* Attended University of Birmingham; University of Edinburgh, M.B. and Ch.B., 1912, M.D., 1921, D.Sc., 1923. *Politics:* Radical. *Religion:* Atheist. *Home:* Upton's Mill, Framfield, Sussex, England.

CAREER: University of Edinburgh, Edinburgh, Scotland, director of Institute of Animal Genetics, 1921-44, Buchanan Professor of Animal Genetics, 1928-44, professor of public health and social medicine, 1944-55. Professor of preventive and social medicine, Ain Shams University, Cairo, Egypt, 1956; United Nations World Health Organization Visiting Professor at Rangoon University, 1957-58, and Topiwala National Medical College, Bombay University, 1959-60. Special lecturer at University of Birmingham, 1927, University of Edinburgh, 1962, and to medical societies. Chairman of board of management, Edinburgh Central Group of Hospitals, and member of British Army Health Advisory Committee, 1946-56; advisor in population genetics to Central Family Planning Institute of Delhi for Ministry of Overseas Development, 1966-67. Commander of Edinburgh Special Constabulary, 1938-39. *Military service:* British Army, 1914-18; served in India and France. Royal Army Medical Corps, 1939-45; director of medical research, War Office, 1942-46; became brigadier. First Edinburgh Home Guard, lieutenant colonel, 1954-56.

MEMBER: Royal Society of London (fellow), Royal Society of Edinburgh (fellow), Royal College of Physicians of Edinburgh (fellow), Genetical Society (president, 1938-39), Society for Social Medicine, National Veterinary Medical Association (honorary member), Physiological Society of India (honorary member), Czecho-Slovakian Academy of Agriculture (foreign member), Athenaeum Club (London). *Awards, honors:* Keith Prize of Royal Society of Edinburgh, 1937-39; Order of St. John of Jerusalem; Order of Polonia Restituta; D.Sc., Banaras Hindu University; LL.D., University of Edinburgh.

WRITINGS: Animal Genetics, Oliver & Boyd, 1925; *Organic Inheritance in Man,* Oliver & Boyd, 1927; (with Rowena Lamy) *The Genetics of the Budgerigar,* Watmough, 1931; (with J. N. Pickard) *Scientific Aspects of Rabbit Breeding,* Watmough, 1931; *Sex-Determination,* Methuen, 1933, 4th edition, Dover, 1965; *Genetics in Relation to Clinical Medicine,* Oliver & Boyd, 1947; *Measure-*

ments of the Public Health: Essays in Social Medicine, Oliver & Boyd, 1948; *Man Must Wage War,* Watts, 1952; *Official Medical History (British Army) of the Second World War,* seven volumes, H.M.S.O., 1953-66; *Health: Its Nature and Conservation,* Pergamon, 1965; *The Foundations of Genetics,* Pergamon, 1965. Author of essays and papers on social medicine and hygiene. Co-founder and first editor of *Journal of Preventive Medicine* and *Journal of Experimental Biology.*

WORK IN PROGRESS: Research in genetics of the Indian game bantam plumage color, of the Australian zebra finch, and of the Indian munas.†

(Died May, 1973)

* * *

CRISSEY, Elwell   1899-

PERSONAL: Born February 1, 1899, in Windsor, Mo.; son of William Ernest and Dora (Greene) Crissey; married Julia John, August 26, 1930 (divorced); married Densie Virene Lawsha (a secretary at Illinois State University), June 9, 1945; children: (first marriage) William Elwell; (second marriage) Faith Lenore, Brian Laird. *Education:* Studied at Central Methodist College, 1918-21, Columbia University, 1927-28, and took summer courses at Northwestern University. *Politics:* "Free-lance Democrat. Keenly interested in politics but no party man." *Religion:* Methodist. *Home:* 409 East Beecher St., Bloomington, Ill. 61701. *Office:* Words at Work, 215 East Front St., Bloomington, Ill. 61701.

CAREER: Kansas City Star, Kansas City, Mo., reporter, 1922-25; Associated Press, bureau editor in Philadelphia, Pa., 1925-26; magazine writer and editor, New York, N.Y., 1927-30; promotion director for professional fund-raising agencies, New York, N.Y., and Chicago, Ill., 1931-55; Words at Work (business communications), Bloomington, Ill., founder-owner, beginning 1953. Educational director, U.S. War Production Board, Washington, D.C., 1942-45. Lecturer on the religious beliefs of George Washington and Abraham Lincoln. *Awards, honors:* George Washington Medal of Honor of Freedoms Foundation (twice) for essays-lectures; winner of seven literary awards.

WRITINGS: Lincoln's Lost Speech: Pivot of His Career, Hawthorn, 1967; *Centennial History of Peoples Bank of Bloomington Illinois,* Pantagraph Press, 1969. Contributor of feature articles to magazines. Associate editor, *Popular Science Monthly,* 1927-28.

WORK IN PROGRESS: Abraham Lincoln the Orator; Did Abe Lincoln Love Ann Rutledge? An Affirmation; a new history of the Supreme Council of Freemasons.

* * *

CROCKER, Lionel (George)   1897-

PERSONAL: Born January 17, 1897, in Ann Arbor, Mich.; son of George (an engineer) and Jennie (Musson) Crocker; married Geraldine M. Hamilton (a physician and county health commissioner), August 15, 1925; children: Joan Elizabeth, Laurence G., Thomas Hamilton (deceased). *Education:* University of Michigan, A.M., 1918, M.A., 1921, Ph.D., 1933. *Politics:* Republican. *Religion:* American Baptist Convention. *Home:* 423 East College St., Granville, Ohio 43023. *Office:* Department of Speech, Denison University, Granville, Ohio. 43023.

CAREER: Instructor in speech at University of Minnesota, Minneapolis, 1919, and University of Michigan, Ann Arbor, 1920-21, 1922-26, and 1927-28; Waseda University, Tokyo,

Japan, professor of speech, 1921-22; American Floating University, professor of speech on world cruise, 1926-27; Denison University, Granville, Ohio, head of department of speech, 1928-67, senior professor of speech, 1954-67, professor emeritus, 1967—. Has done summer teaching at University of Colorado, University of Maine, Indiana State University, Stanford University, and other universities. Research fellow, Ministers Research Foundations, Inc. Speechwriter for Republican candidates Thomas Dewey and John Bricker, 1944. *Military service:* U.S. Army, Medical Corps, 1918-19. *Member:* Speech Association of America (vice president, 1951; president, 1952), American Association of University Professors, Rotary International, Phi Beta Kappa, Tau Kappa Alpha (secretary), Theta Chi, Omicron Delta Kappa. *Awards, honors:* D.Ph. from Otterbein College, 1967; D.H. from Drury College, 1967.

WRITINGS: Henry Ward Beecher's Art of Preaching, University of Chicago Press, 1934, published as *Henry Ward Beecher's Speaking Art,* Revell, 1937; *Public Speaking for College Students,* American Book Co., 1941, 3rd edition and *Workbook,* 1956, 4th edition (with Herbert W. Hildebrandt), 1965; *Argumentation and Debate,* American Book Co., 1944, revised edition, American Bankers Association, 1959; (with L. M. Eich) *Oral Reading,* Prentice-Hall, 1947, 2nd revised edition, 1962; *Effective Speaking,* American Bankers Association, 1948, revised edition, 1959; *Business and Professional Speech,* Ronald, 1951; *Interpretive Speech,* Prentice-Hall, 1952; *Rhetorical Analysis of Speeches,* Allyn & Bacon, 1966. Also author of *Effective Debating,* 1961.

Editor: *Essays for Freshmen by Freshmen,* Wahr, 1921; *Essays on American College Life,* Waseda University Press, 1922; (with P. A. Carmack) *Readings in Rhetoric,* C. C Thomas, 1965; *Analysis of Lincoln and Douglas as Public Speakers and Debaters,* C. C Thomas, 1968; *Harry Emerson Fosdick's Art of Preaching: An Anthology,* C. C Thomas, 1971. Editor, *Speaker* (publication of Tau Kappa Alpha), 1938-40, and *Central States Speech Journal,* 1948-50; associate editor, *Quarterly Journal of Speech,* 1937-44, and *Journal of Communication,* 1962-63.

WORK IN PROGRESS: A one-act play, "Lincoln Goes to Cooper Union"; *A Survey of American Public Address.*

* * *

CROFTS, John E(rnest) V(ictor) 1887-1972

PERSONAL: Born May 6, 1887, in Dalton, Lancashire, England; son of John (a clergyman) and Maud (Gronshaw) Crofts; married Sibyl Ann Hony, September, 1915; children: James, Martin. *Education:* Queen's College, Oxford, first class honors in English language and literature, 1909, B.Litt., 1914. *Home:* Stonethwaite, Borrowdale, Keswick, England.

CAREER: University College (now University of Reading), Reading, England, assistant lecturer in English, 1912-19; University of Bristol, Bristol, England, Winterstoke Professor of English, 1919-41, public orator, 1929-36; John Lewis Partnership Ltd., London, England, partners' counsellor, 1941-52. Co-opted member, Bristol Education Committee, 1938-41. *Military service:* British Army, 101st Field Ambulance, 1915-18.

WRITINGS: Field Ambulance Sketches, John Lane, 1920; (author of introduction and notes) *Gray: Poetry and Prose,* Oxford University Press, 1926; *Shakespeare and the Posthorses,* Arrowsmith, 1927; (editor) William Shakespeare, *Romeo and Juliet,* Blackie & Co., 1938; *Wordsworth and*

the Seventeenth Century, (Warton lecture), Routledge & Kegan Paul, 1940; (contributor) Helen Gardner, editor, *John Donne: A Collection of Critical Essays,* Prentice-Hall, 1962; *Packhorse, Waggon and Post: Land Carriage and Communications under the Tudors and Stuarts,* University of Toronto Press, 1967.

WORK IN PROGRESS: A Stuart Miscellany, prose; *Illumined, Obstinate and Unbeatable,* an impression of the pre-gospel Jesus.†

(Died, 1972)

* * *

CROW, Martin M(ichael) 1901-

PERSONAL: Born October 30, 1901, in Crow's Mills, Pa.; son of Wylie Lee (a farmer and livestock breeder) and Minnie Vilora (Scott) Crow. *Education:* Washington and Jefferson College, A.B., 1924; Harvard University, A.M., 1925; University of Chicago, Ph.D., 1934. *Politics:* Democrat. *Religion:* Presbyterian. *Home:* 1303 Bradwood Rd., Austin, Tex. 78722. *Office:* 230 Parlin Hall, University of Texas, Austin, Tex. 78712.

CAREER: University of Arkansas, Fayetteville, instructor in English, 1925-28; Washington and Jefferson College, Washington, Pa., instructor, 1928-30, assistant professor of English, 1930-31; University of Texas, Austin, assistant professor, 1934-45, associate professor, 1945-50, professor of English, 1950-72, professor emeritus, 1972—, chairman of department, 1946-49. Visiting professor, University of Chicago, summers of 1941 and 1942, and in 1955-56, University of Minnesota, summer, 1953. *Military service:* U.S. Army Air Forces, 1942-44. U.S. Air Force Reserve, 1944-53; became captain.

MEMBER: Modern Language Association of America (Chaucer Library committee member, beginning 1967), Mediaeval Academy of America (councillor, 1965-68), Modern Humanities Research Association (consultative board member, 1967-70), Conference of College Teachers of English, American Association of University Professors, International Arthurian Society, English-Speaking Union, South Central Modern Language Association, Texas Folklore Society, Phi Beta Kappa. *Awards, honors:* Research grants, University of Texas Research Institute, 1952-53, 1954-55, 1958, 1966-67; grant-in-aid, American Council of Learned Societies, 1958-59, 1967-68.

WRITINGS: (Editor with C. C. Olson) *Chaucer's World,* Columbia University Press, 1948; (editor with C. C. Olson) *Chaucer Life-Records,* University of Texas Press, 1966. Contributor to *Speculum, Modern Philology, Texas Studies in English,* and *Texas Library Chronicle.* Editor, *Texas Studies in English,* 1949-51.

WORK IN PROGRESS: A biography of Chaucer for the general scholarly reader; articles on Chaucer.

SIDELIGHTS: Crow is competent in French, German, and Latin. *Avocational interests:* Genealogy.

* * *

CROXTON, Frederick E(mory) 1899-

PERSONAL: Born May 23, 1899, in Washington, D.C.; son of Fred C. and Mattie M. (Stocks) Croxton; married Rosetta R. Harpster, September 14, 1921; children: Frederick Emory, Jr., Rosetta Harpster (Mrs. William A. Clark). *Education:* Ohio State University, A.B., 1920, A.M., 1921; Columbia University, Ph.D., 1926. *Residence:* Leonia, N.J.

CAREER: Ohio Wesleyan University, Delaware, Md., lecturer in statistics, 1920-21; Ohio State University, Columbus, instructor, 1921-26 (on leave, 1924-26); Columbia University, New York, N.Y., university fellow, 1924-26, lecturer in statistics, 1926-27, assistant professor, 1927-37, associate professor, 1937-44, professor of statistics, 1944-64, professor emeritus, 1964—. Lecturer in statistics at University of Chicago, summer, 1926, New York School of Social Work, 1930-32, 1944, and University of Colorado, summer, 1948. Military service: U.S. Army, Infantry, 1918-19; became second lieutenant. Member: American Association for the Advancement of Science (fellow), American Statistical Association (fellow), Phi Beta Kappa, Phi Delta Kappa, Beta Gamma Sigma.

WRITINGS: (With Pierce Williams) Corporation Contributions to Organized Community Welfare Service, National Bureau of Economic Research, 1930; (with D. J. Cowden) Practical Business Statistics, Prentice-Hall, 1934, 4th edition, 1969; Workbook in Applied General Statistics, Prentice-Hall, 1937, 5th edition (with Sidney Klein), 1967; (with Cowden) Applied General Statistics, Prentice-Hall, 1939, 3rd edition (with Cowden and Klein), 1967; Elementary Statistics with Applications in Medicine and the Biological Sciences, Dover, 1953. Also author of pamphlets and articles.

*   *   *

CULVER, Elsie Thomas   1898-

PERSONAL: Born January 3, 1898, in Danielson, Conn.; daughter of Dudley Nicholas and Orie (Streeter) Thomas; children: Helen Celestia (Mrs. Ralph E. Peterson). Education: University of California, Berkeley, A.B. (with honors in political science), 1918; Pacific School of Religion, M.A., 1941, B.D., 1942. Politics: Liberal. Religion: "Ecumenical." Home: 1056 Stannage Ave., Albany, Calif. 94706.

CAREER: Prior to 1938, held editorial and advertising positions on California dailies, and did free-lance writing for national magazines and trade journals in Chicago, Ill.; Church World Service, New York, N.Y., director of national promotion, 1942-48; ordained to Congregational ministry (specifically for a writing and ecumenical ministry), 1944; director of public relations for World Council of Churches, traveling in Europe, Asia, and Africa, 1949-57; Senior Peacebuilders, Inc., Berkeley, Calif., founder-director, beginning 1958. Lecturer in religious communications, New York University, 1956. Worked on press coverage for Fourth National Workshop for Christian Unity (inter-faith), Berkeley, Calif. 1967; worked as delegate on materials for First White House Conference on Aging. Member: Religious Public Relations Council (chairman of professional standards committee, 1956-58), California Writers Club.

WRITINGS: Tell the Folks Back Home, Foreign Missions Conference, 1949; New Church Programs with the Aging, Association Press, 1961; Women in the World of Religion, Doubleday, 1967. Contributor of articles and short stories to Collier's, Toronto Star, New York Times Magazine, other secular publications, and most Protestant periodicals. American editor, Ecumenical Press Service, 1950-57; editor, Cornerstone (quarterly).

WORK IN PROGRESS: The role of women, secular as well as religious; interfaith ecumenicity; ecology as a sociological concept; American history prior to the Mayflower.

CUNNINGHAM, James F.   1901-

PERSONAL: Born September 26, 1901, in Danbury, Conn.; son of James Edward (a hatter) and Mary (Lynch) Cunningham. Education: Catholic University, B.A., 1928, M.A., 1930. Politics: Democrat.

CAREER: Ordained Roman Catholic priest in Congregation of St. Paul (Paulists), 1930; served as assistant pastor in Los Angeles, Calif., 1930-34, and New York, N.Y., 1934-36; Mission Trailer Band, Winchester, Tenn., pastor, 1936-40; Paulist Fathers, New York, N.Y., superior general, 1946-52; Santa Susanna's American Church, Rome, Italy, pastor, 1952-64; Old Saint Mary's Church, Chicago, Ill., pastor, beginning 1964. Military service: U.S. Navy, 1940-46; served as chaplain in Panama, Puerto Rico, and on U.S.S. South Dakota; became commander; received Purple Heart, Bronze Star Medal, and nine battle stars. Member: New York Athletic Club, Illinois Athletic Club, Circolo del Golf (Rome).

WRITINGS: The Life of Jesus, Sunday Visitor, 1938; American Pastor in Rome, Doubleday, 1966.††

*   *   *

CUNZ, Dieter   1910-1969

PERSONAL: Born August 4, 1910, in Hoechstenbach, Germany; came to United States in 1938, naturalized in 1944; son of Paul and Hedwig (Silbersiepe) Cunz. Education: University of Frankfurt, Ph.D., 1934. Religion: Lutheran. Residence: Worthington, Ohio.

CAREER: Newspaperman in Switzerland, 1935-38; University of Maryland, College Park, instructor, 1939-43, assistant professor, 1943-47, associate professor, 1947-49, professor of German, 1949-57, resident dean of university's Foreign Study Center, Zurich, Switzerland, 1947-48; Ohio State University, Columbus, professor of German literature and chairman of department of German, 1957-69. Member: American Association of Teachers of German, Modern Language Association of America, Society for the History of the Germans in Maryland (secretary, 1944-56; honorary member), Ohio Historical Society, Phi Beta Kappa (honorary member). Awards, honors: Carl Schurz Memorial Foundation fellow, 1939-42; Officers Cross of Merit (Federal Republic of Germany), 1962; Alfred J. Wright Award, Ohio State University, 1964.

WRITINGS: Ulrich Zwingli (biography), Sauerlander (Switzerland), 1937; The Maryland Germans: A History, Princeton University Press, 1948, reprinted, Kennikat, 1972; (co-author) German for Beginners, Ronald, 1958, revised edition, 1965; (editor) Ricarda Huch, Der letzte Sommer, Norton, 1963; They Came from Germany, Dodd, 1966; (editor) Johann Heinrich Jung-Stilling, Henrich Stillings Jugend, Juenglingsjahre, Reclam (Stuttgart), 1968. Contributor of articles on the history of German immigration to journals. Editor, Reports of the Society for the History of the Germans in Maryland, 1942-56; editor, annual Americana-Germanica bibliography in American-German Review, 1945-60.

WORK IN PROGRESS: Research in German literature of the eighteenth century. Avocational interests: Classical music.†

(Died, 1969)

*   *   *

CURRY, Estell H.   1907-

PERSONAL: Born July 3, 1907, in Pine River, Minn.; son

of William C. (a farmer) and Alice (McLaughlin) Curry; married Nelda Damrow, April 21, 1930 (deceased); children: Betty (Mrs. William Rohde), Virginia Lee (Mrs. Richard Whiteherst). *Education:* Stout State University, B.S., 1931; Wayne State University, M.A., 1936; University of Missouri, graduate study, 1954. *Religion:* Lutheran. *Office:* Vocational Education, Detroit Board of Education, 5057 Woodward Ave., Detroit, Mich. 48202.

CAREER: Detroit (Mich.) public schools, teacher, 1930-40; Wayne State University, Detroit, Mich., critic teacher, 1940-50; Detroit (Mich.) Board of Education, vocational department head, 1950-56, supervisor of industrial arts, 1956-61, assistant director, beginning 1961. *Member:* American Industrial Arts Association, American Vocational Association, National Education Association, Michigan Industrial Education Society, Michigan Education Association, Engineering Society of Detroit, Mu Sigma Pi (president), Phi Delta Kappa, Iota Lambda Sigma, American Speakers Club (president). *Awards, honors:* Named Michigan industrial education teacher of the year, 1950; award of Industrial Arts Division of American Vocational Association, 1967.

WRITINGS: (With G. Harold Silvius) *Teaching Successfully the Industrial Education Subjects,* McKnight & McKnight, 1953, 2nd edition, 1967; (with Silvius) *Teaching Multiple Activities in Industrial Education,* McKnight & McKnight, 1956, 2nd edition, 1971; (with Rolland Pardonnet and Russell Symes) *General Industrial Arts,* Van Nostrand, 1967. Contributor to professional journals.

AVOCATIONAL INTERESTS: Travel, golf, pitching horseshoes, bowling, fishing, photography, playing bridge, reading, shuffling, playing organ, modernizing cottage, and playing the stock market.†

*   *   *

CURTIS, Lewis Perry   1900-1976

PERSONAL: Born November 30, 1900, in Southport, Conn.; son of Roderick Perry (a businessman) and Louisa (Wells) Curtis; married Jeanet Ellinwood Sullivan, December 26, 1929; children: Lewis Perry, Jr., Nancy Ellinwood (Mrs. Michael D. Padnos). *Education:* Yale University, B.A., 1923, Ph.D., 1926. *Politics:* Independent. *Home:* 479 Whalley Ave., New Haven, Conn. 06511.

CAREER: Yale University, New Haven, Conn., instructor in English literature, 1927-31, instructor in history and literature, 1933-37, assistant professor of history, 1937-44, associate professor, 1944-67, Colgate Professor of History, 1967-1969. *Member:* American Historical Association, Phi Beta Kappa. *Awards, honors:* American Council of Learned Societies fellowship, 1931-32; Guggenheim fellowship, 1941-42.

WRITINGS: The Politicks of Laurence Sterne, Oxford University Press, 1929; (editor) *Letters of Laurence Sterne,* Clarendon Press, 1935, 2nd edition, 1965; (with H. W. Liebert) *Esto Perpetua: The Club of Dr. Johnson and His Friends,* Archon Books, 1963; *Coercion and Conciliation in Ireland, 1880-1892,* Princeton University Press, 1963; *Anglican Moods of the Eighteenth Century,* Archon Books, 1966; *Chichester Towers,* Yale University Press, 1966. Editor, "Yale Historical Publications," 1950-57.

SIDELIGHTS: Curtis told *CA:* "My interest in open aristocracy stands as the basic principle of all my work, once I finished my studies of Laurence Sterne. I coursed over a wide field: English civilization, from the early seventeenth

century to the present; French civilization from Louis XIV (and Descartes) to 1794. For me, teaching always came first."†

(Died April 8, 1976)

*   *   *

CURTIS BROWN, Beatrice   1901-1974

PERSONAL: Born August 24, 1901, in London, England; daughter of Albert (a journalist and literary agent) and Caroline (Lord) Curtis Brown; married A.V.J. Horton, July, 1938 (divorced, 1945). *Education:* Attended St. Felix School, Southwold, Suffolk, England, 1916-19. *Religion:* Church of England. *Agent:* Curtis Brown Ltd., 575 Madison Ave., New York, N.Y. 10022.

CAREER: Free-lance journalist and writer, 1923-36; in British civil service, 1940-46; British Broadcasting Corp., talks producer, 1947-56; teacher and lecturer in English literature and oral communication, 1958-63.

WRITINGS: Elizabeth Chudleigh, Duchess of Kingston, Viking, 1927; *Alas Queen Anne,* Bobbs-Merrill, 1929 (published in England as *Anne Stuart, Queen of England,* Bles, 1929); *For the Delight of Antonio,* Houghton, 1932; *Jonathan Bing and Other Verses* (poetry for children), Oxford University Press, 1934, new edition with additional poems, Lothrop, 1968; *The Sancroft Sisters* (novel), Putnam, 1935; (editor) *Letters of Queen Anne,* McClelland & Stewart, 1935; *Southwards from Swiss Cottage* (reminiscences), Home & Van Thal, 1948; *Anthony Trollope,* A. Swallow, 1949; *Isabel Fry,* Barker, 1960. Also author of *Polly Polloo.* Contributor to *Spectator, Times* (London), *Guardian,* and other publications.

WORK IN PROGRESS: Studies in Oral Communication; and *Essays on the Technique of Living.*†

(Died April 18, 1974)

*   *   *

CURTISS, John S(helton)   1899-

PERSONAL: Born July 15, 1899, in Buffalo, N.Y.; son of Harlow C. (an attorney) and Ethel (Mann) Curtiss; married Edna Sutter, September 25, 1925; children: John Sutter, Anne (Mrs. Merwin Fong). *Education:* Princeton University, A.B., 1921; Columbia University, M.A., 1929, Ph.D., 1940. *Politics:* Democrat. *Home:* 4418 Guess Rd., Durham, N.C. 27705. *Office:* Department of History, Duke University, Durham, N.C. 27706.

CAREER: In business, Buffalo, N.Y., 1921-25, and farming in Arizona, 1925-28; high school teacher of history in Buffalo, N.Y., 1930-33; Columbia University, New York, N.Y., part-time teacher of history, 1934-36; City College (now City College of the City University of New York), New York, N.Y., tutor in history, 1935-36; Brooklyn College (now Brooklyn College of the City University of New York), Brooklyn, N.Y., teacher of history in evening session, 1936-41; Franklin D. Roosevelt Library, Hyde Park, N.Y., junior archivist, 1941-42; research analyst, U.S. Office of Strategic Services, 1942-45; Duke University, Durham, N.C., associate professor, 1945-51, professor of history, 1952-66, James B. Duke Professor of History, 1966-69, James B. Duke Professor Emeritus, 1969—. Exchange professor to Institute of History, Academy of Sciences, Union of Soviet Socialist Republics, 1963-64.

MEMBER: American Historical Association, American Association for the Advancement of Slavic Studies,

Southern Historical Association, Southern Conference on Slavic Studies (president, 1962-63). *Awards, honors:* Herbert Baxter Adams Prize of American Historical Association, 1940, for *Church and State in Russia: 1900-1917;* Guggenheim fellow, 1954-55; American Council of Learned Societies senior fellow, 1963-64.

WRITINGS: Church and State in Russia: 1900-1917, Columbia University Press, 1940; *An Appraisal of the Protocols of Zion,* Columbia University Press, 1941; *The Russian Church and the Soviet State,* Little, Brown, 1953; *Russian Revolutions of 1917,* Van Nostrand, 1957; (editor) *Essays in Russian and Soviet History,* Columbia University Press, 1963; *The Russian Army under Nicholas I: 1825-1855,* Duke University Press, 1965; *The Peasant in Nineteenth-Century Russia,* Stanford University Press, 1968. Contributor to *American Historical Review, Slavic Review, South Atlantic Quarterly.*

SIDELIGHTS: Curtiss has traveled and done research in the Soviet Union, Austria, Finland, Czechoslovakia, Switzerland, and England. He is competent in Russian and French, and reads German and Spanish.†

* * *

D'ABREU, Gerald Joseph 1916-19(?)

PERSONAL: Surname is pronounced Dah-*brer;* born January 19, 1916, in India; son of Gerald Basil (an engineer) and Clare (Dee) D'Abreu; married Marjorie Dealtry, August 12, 1944. *Education:* Royal Academy of Music, London, England, L.R.S.M., 1936, L.R.A.M., 1941, L.L.C.M. (T.D.), 1959.

CAREER: Ballet Guild, London, England, musical director, 1945-46; London Ballet, London, England, musical director, 1946; London College of Music, London, England, professor of piano, harmony, and composition, and music examiner, 1947-61; high school music teacher in London, England, 1961-63, in Bancroft, Ontario, 1965-66; public school music teacher, Ottawa, Ontario, 1966-67; private instructor in piano and harmony, beginning, 1967. Concert pianist; composer of works for orchestra and string quartet, and of instrumental music.

WRITINGS: Playing the Piano with Confidence, Faber, 1964, St. Martin's, 1965.

WORK IN PROGRESS: A book on teaching the piano; a play; a novel.

AVOCATIONAL INTERESTS: Painting in oils, especially portraits.†

(Deceased)

* * *

DAHLBERG, Edwin T(heodore) 1892-

PERSONAL: Born December 27, 1892, in Fergus Falls, Minn.; son of Elof (a farmer) and Christine (Ring) Dahlberg; married Emilie Louise Loeffler, August 27, 1918; children: Margaret Emilie (Mrs. Gordon M. Torgersen), Bruce Theodore, Keith Ramel. *Education:* University of Minnesota, B.A., 1914; Rochester Theological Seminary, B.D., 1918. *Politics:* Independent.

CAREER: Ordained Baptist minister, 1918; pastor in Potsdam, N.Y., 1918-21, Buffalo, N.Y., 1921-31, St. Paul, Minn., 1931-39, Syracuse, N.Y., 1939-50; Delmar Baptist Church, St. Louis, Mo., pastor, 1950-62, pastor emeritus, 1962—; Crozer Theological Seminary, Chester, Pa., minister in residence, beginning, 1962. Interfaith Peace Mission

to Vietnam, member, 1965. American Baptist Convention, president, 1946-48; World Council of Churches, member of Central Committee, 1948-54; National Council of Churches of Christ in the U.S.A., president, 1957-60. *Member:* American Foundation on Non-Violence (vice-president), National Committee on Migratory Farm Labor, National Committee for a Sane Nuclear Policy, Iron Wedge (University of Minnesota). *Awards, honors:* Ghandi Peace Prize of Promoting Enduring Peace, Inc.; Distinguished Alumni award, University of Minnesota; D.D., Keuka College, 1940, Kalamazoo College, 1947, Denison University, 1960; LL.D., Franklin College, 1959.

WRITINGS: Youth and the Homes of Tomorrow, Judson, 1934; *This Is the Rim of East Asia,* Friendship, 1962; (editor) *Herald of the Evangel: Sixty Years of American Christianity,* Bethany, 1965. Contributor to religion journals.

WORK IN PROGRESS: Prisoners are Persons; two other books, tentatively titled *Nights Alone With God* and *Track of the Bull Wheel.*

SIDELIGHTS: Dahlberg traveled on Christmas missions to American Armed Forces in the Alaskan Command, 1957, Spain and Morocco, 1958, Taiwan and the Pacific Islands, 1959. He made seven other trips to Europe, 1947-62, and four to Southeast Asia, 1952-65. Several lectureships and memorials have been established in recognition of his work for peace, including the Dahlberg Peace Award of the American Baptist Convention.††

* * *

DAKIN, (David) Julian 1939-1971

PERSONAL: Born July 17, 1939, in England; son of Samuel Arthur and Lili (Furness) Dakin; married Carmen Guijarro (a teacher), November 24, 1966. *Education:* Attended Sorbonne, University of Paris, 1956-57; Trinity College, Cambridge, B.A., 1960; University of Leeds, Diploma in English as a Second Language, 1963. *Home:* Mulberry House, Chestnut Ave., Guildford, Surrey, England.

CAREER: British Council, London, England, administrative assistant, 1960-63; assistant teacher in a primary school, Huddersfield, England, 1963-64; University of Edinburgh, Edinburgh, Scotland, lecturer in applied linguistics, 1964-71. Specialist assistant professor, Institute of English, Calcutta, India, 1968-69; research officer, Centre for Information on Language Teaching, London, 1969.

WRITINGS: Songs and Rhymes for the Teaching of English, Longmans, Green, 1968; (with H. G. Widdowson and B. Tiffen) *Language in Education: The Problem in Commonwealth Africa and the Indo-Pakistan Subcontinent,* Oxford University Press, 1968; *The Language Laboratory and Language Learning,* Longman, 1973; (contributor with Anthony Howatt) J.P.B. Allen and S. Pit Corder, editors, *Techniques in Applied Linguistics,* Oxford University Press, 1974.

WORK IN PROGRESS: A study of the language laboratory and language learning.†

(Died October 22, 1971)

* * *

DALE, James 1886-

PERSONAL: Born February 27, 1886; son of Bernard (a lawyer) and Katherine (Jacomb-Hood) Dale; married Marguerite Adamson, February, 1911; children: Celia Margery (Mrs. Cecil Ramsey). *Education:* Attended Haileybury College, 1900-02. *Politics:* "Continued Tory, verging on extreme." *Religion:* Pagan. *Home:* Branch Hill, Hampstead, London, Middlesex, England.

CAREER: Actor in England, beginning 1908. Instructor, Royal Academy of Dramatic Art. *Military service:* British Army, Infantry, served in World War I. *Member:* Savage Club (London).

WRITINGS: "A Conversation at the Styx" (play), first produced in London at Little Theatre, 1912; "Honorable Women" (play), first produced on West End at Ambassadors Theatre, 1913; "Wild Justice" (play), first produced on West End at Savoy Theatre, 1930; *Pulling Faces for a Living,* Gollancz, 1970. Also author of two radio plays, "September Rose" and "Come All Ye Faithful." Contributor of articles to periodicals and newspapers.

WORK IN PROGRESS: Fiction; Shakespearean criticism.

SIDELIGHTS: James Dale told *CA:* "I am interested in politics up to a certain extent. But painting is my favorite study and hobby. I dislike the tag of writing and the worse tag of acting. I enjoy walking, the society of my contemporaries and the very young, especially boys. I enjoy discussions on art and theatre. I am bored by well meaning people and feel at home with soldiers and service people."

BIOGRAPHICAL/CRITICAL SOURCES: Punch, May 20, 1970.

*   *   *

DALEY, Arthur (John)   1904-1974

PERSONAL: Born July 31, 1904, in New York, N.Y.; son of Daniel Michael (a sales executive) and Mary (Greene) Daley; married Betty Blake, November 28, 1928; children: Robert, Kevin, Patricia (Mrs. John F. Trout), Katharine. *Education:* Fordham University, B.A., 1926. *Religion:* Roman Catholic. *Home:* 120 Stonehedge Dr. N., Greenwich, Conn. 06830. *Office:* New York Times, Times Square, New York, N.Y. 10036.

CAREER: New York Times, New York, N.Y., sports writer, 1926-74, columnist, "Sports of the Times," 1942-74. *Awards, honors:* Pulitzer Prize for reporting, 1956; Grantland Rice Award, 1961; Sportswriter of the Year Award, 1963.

WRITINGS: (With John Kieran) *The Story of the Olympic Games,* Stokes Publishing, 1936, revised edition published as *The Story of the Olympic Games, 776 B.C. to 1968,* Lippincott, 1969, 2nd revised edition published as *The Story of The Olympic Games, 776 B.C. to 1972,* 1973; (contributor) E. V. McLoughlin, editor, *The Story of Our Time–Encyclopedia Yearbook,* Grolier Society, 1947; *Times at Bat: A Half Century of Baseball,* Random House, 1950, published as *Inside Baseball: Times at Bat, A Half Century of Baseball,* Grosset, 1961; *Sports of the Times,* Dutton, 1959; *Knute Rockne: Football Wizard of Notre Dame,* Kenedy, 1960; *Kings of the Home Run,* Putnam, 1962, published as *All the Home Run Kings,* 1972; *Pro Football's Hall of Fame: The Official Book,* Quadrangle, 1963; (with John Arlott) *Pageantry of Sport: From the Age of Chivalry to the Age of Victoria,* Hawthorne, 1968. Contributor of articles to periodicals, including *Reader's Digest, Collier's,* and *Literary Digest.*†

(Died January 3, 1974)

*   *   *

DALY, Anne   1896-

PERSONAL: Born May 22, 1896, in County Cork, Ireland; daughter of Daniel (a farmer) and Margaret Daly. *Education:* Educated in Lancashire, England. *Religion:* Roman Catholic. *Home:* Sherwood Cross, Douglas Rd., Cork, Ireland.

CAREER: Lecturer in teacher training college, 1929-32.

WRITINGS: Green Eyes (juvenile), Hollis & Carter, 1943; *Leave It to the Doctor* (play; produced in Dublin at Abbey Theatre, 1959), Progress House, 1961; *The Window on the Square* (play; produced in Dublin at Abbey Theatre, 1951), Progress House, 1968.

WORK IN PROGRESS: Editing the journal of her late sister, who published five novels under the pen name of Margaret Hassett.

BIOGRAPHICAL/CRITICAL SOURCES: Drama, summer, 1968.††

*   *   *

DALY, Elizabeth   1878-1967

PERSONAL: Born October 15, 1878, in New York, N.Y.; daughter of Joseph F. (a judge) and Emma (Barker) Daly. *Education:* Bryn Mawr College, B.A., 1901; Columbia University, M.A., 1902. *Politics:* Democrat. *Home:* 99 Huntington Rd., Port Washington, N.Y.

CAREER: Bryn Mawr College, Bryn Mawr, Pa., reader in English, 1904-06; tutor in French and English, and producer of amateur plays and pageants in schools and clubs; mystery novelist. *Member:* Mystery Writers of America (honorary member). *Awards, honors:* Edgar Allan Poe award, 1960.

*WRITINGS—*All published by Farrar & Rinehart: *Unexpected Night,* 1940; *Deadly Nightshade,* 1940; *The Street Has Changed,* 1941; *Murders in Volume 2 (also see below),* 1941; *The House Without the Door,* 1942; *Evidence of Things Seen (also see below),* 1943; *Nothing Can Rescue Me,* 1943; *Arrow Pointing Nowhere,* 1944; *The Book of the Dead (also see below),* 1944; *Any Shape or Form,* 1945.

All published by Rinehart: *Somewhere in the House,* 1946; *The Wrong Way Down,* 1946; *Night Walk,* 1947; *Book of the Lion,* 1948; *And Dangerous to Know,* 1949; *Death and Letters,* 1950; *The Book of Crime,* 1951; *An Elizabeth Daly Mystery Omnibus: Three Henry Gamadge Novels* (includes *Murders in Volume 2, Evidence of Things Seen,* and *The Book of the Dead),* 1960.†

(Died September 2, 1967)

*   *   *

DANIELOU, Jean   1905-1974

PERSONAL: Born May 14, 1905, in Paris, France; son of Charles (a journalist) and Madeleine (Clamorgan) Danielou. *Education:* College Sainte Croix de Neuilly, Agrege de l'Universite; Sorbonne, University of Paris, Docteur en lettres, 1927; Faculte de theologie de Lyon, Docteur en theologie, 1944. *Home:* Rue Monsieur 15, Paris, France.

CAREER: Entered Society of Jesus (Jesuits), 1929, ordained priest, 1938, consecrated archbishop of Taormina, 1969, created cardinal, 1969; Institut Catholique de Paris, Paris, France, professor of primitive Christianity, 1943-74, dean, 1962-74. Visiting professor, University of Notre Dame, summer, 1950. Lecturer on the ecumenical movement. Founder of Circle St. Jean Baptiste (a Catholic center). Editor, Editions du Cerf. *Military service:* French Army, 1939. *Awards, honors:* Chevalier de la Legion d'Honneur.

WRITINGS: Le Signe du temple; ou, de la presence de

Dieu, Gallimard, 1942, translation by Walter Roberts, published as *Presence of God,* Helicon, 1960; *Platonisme et theologie mystique: Essai sur la doctrine spirituelle de Saint Gregoire de Nysse,* Editions Montaigne, 1944; *Le Mystere du salut des nations,* Editions du Seuil, 1945, translation by Angeline Bouchard published as *The Salvation of the Nations,* Sheed (London), 1949, Sheed (New York), 1950; *Dialogues avec les marxistes, les existentialistes, les protestants, les juifs, l'hindouisme,* Le Portulan, 1948; *Le Mystere de l'avent,* Editions du Seuil, 1948, translation by Rosemary Sheed published as *Advent,* Sheed (London), 1950, Sheed (New York), 1951, published as *The Advent of Salvation: A Comparative Study of Non-Christian Religions and Christianity,* Paulist Press, 1962; *Origene,* La Table Ronde, 1948, translation by Walter Mitchell published as *Origen,* Sheed, 1955.

Sacramentum futuri: Etudes sur les origines de la typologie biblique, Beauchesne, 1950, translation by Wulstan Hibbard published as *From Shadow to Reality: Studies in the Biblical Typology of the Father,* Burns & Oates, 1960; *Bible et liturgie: La Theologie biblique des sacraments et des fetes d'apres les Peres de l'Eglise,* Editions du Cerf, 1950, translation published as *The Bible and the Liturgy,* University of Notre Dame Press, 1956; *Sur l'incomprehensibilite de Dieu: Cinq homelies,* Editions du Cerf, 1951; *Essai sur le mystere de l'histoire,* Editions du Seuil, 1952, translation by Nigel Abercrombie published as *The Lord of History: Reflections on the Inner Meaning of History,* Regnery, 1958; *Dieu et nous,* Grasset, 1956, revised edition, 1963, translation by Walter Roberts published as *God and the Ways of Knowing,* Meridian Books, 1957 (published in England as *God and Us,* Mowbray, 1957); *Les Saints "paiens" de l'Ancien Testament,* Editions de Seuil, 1956, translation by Felix Faber published as *Holy Pagans of the Old Testament,* Helicon, 1957; *The Angels and Their Mission, According to the Fathers of the Church* (originally published in French as *Les Anges et leur mission d'apres les peres de l'Eglise*), translation by David Heimann, Newman Press, 1957; *Les Manuscrits de la Mer Morte et les origines du Christianisme,* Editions de l'Orante, 1957, translation by Salvator Attanasio published as *The Dead Sea Scrolls and Primitive Christianity,* Helicon, 1958.

Christian Today (originally published in French), translation by Kathryn Sullivan, Desclee, 1960; *Approaches du Christ,* Grasset, 1960, translation by Walter Roberts published as *Christ and Us,* Sheed, 1961; *Les Symboles chretiens primitifs,* Editions du Seuil, 1961, translation by Donald Attwater published as *Primitive Christian Symbols,* Helicon, 1964; (editor and author of introduction) *St. Gregory of Nyssa: From Glory to Glory—Texts from His Mystical Writings* (originally published in French), translated and edited by Herbert Musurillo, Scribner, 1961; (editor with Herbert Vorgrimier and contributor) *Sentire Ecclesiam: Das Bewustsein von der Kirche als gestaltende Kraft der Froemmigkeit,* Herder, 1961; *Scandeleuse verite,* Fayard, 1961, translation by W. J. Kerrigan published as *The Scandal of Truth,* Helicon, 1962; *Message evangelique et culture hellenistique aux IIe et IIIe siecles,* Desclee, 1961, translation by John A. Baker published as *Gospel Message and Hellenistic Culture,* Westminster, 1973; (editor) *Les Laics et la mission de l'Eglise: Etudes et documents du Cercle St. Jean Baptiste,* Editions du Centurion, 1962; (with M. Hayek and others, and editor) *Unite des Chretiens et conversion du monde: Themes de reflexion et de priere,* Editions du Centurion, 1962.

Dialogue avec Israel, Palatine, 1963, translation by Jean Marie Roth published as *Dialogue with Israel,* response by Jacob B. Agus, Helicon, 1968; *Au Commencement, Genese I-II,* Editions du Seuil, 1963, translation by Julien L. Randolf published as *In the Beginning . . . Genesis I-II,* Helicon, 1965; (with Henri Marrou) *Des Origines a Saint Gregoire le Grand,* Editions du Seuil, 1963; (with others) *Si les Astres sont habites,* edited by Henri Duquaire, Palatine, 1963; (with others) *Reponses aux questions de Simone Weil,* Aubier, 1964; *Jean-Baptiste, temoin de l'Agneau,* Editions du Seuil, 1964, translation by Joseph A. Horn published as *The Work of John the Baptist,* Helicon, 1966; *Evangile et monde moderne: Petit Traite de morale a l'usage de laics,* Desclee, 1964; (with others) *Introduction to the Great Religions* (originally published in French), translation by Albert J. La Mothe, Jr., Fides, 1964; (with Henri Marrou) *The Christian Centuries: A New History of the Catholic Church,* Volume I: *The First Six Hundred Years* (originally published in French), translation by Vincent Cronin, McGraw, 1964; *The Development of Christian Doctrine before the Council of Nicaea,* Volume I: *The Theology of Jewish Christianity* (originally published in French), translated and edited by John A. Baker, Darton, Longman & Todd, 1964; *L'Oraison, probleme politique,* Fayard, 1965, translation by J. R. Kirwan published as *Prayer as a Political Problem,* Sheed, 1967.

Mythes paiens, mystere chretien, Fayard, 1966, translation by P. J. Hepburne-Scott published as *Twentieth-Century Encyclopedia of Catholicism,* Volume VIII: *Myth and Mystery,* Hawthorn, 1968; *Etudes d'exegese judeo-chretienne (les Testimonia),* Beauchesne, 1966; (with Jean Bose) *L'Eglise face au monde,* Palatine, 1966; *Le Message chretien et la pensee grecque au IIe siecle,* Faculte de Theologie, Institut Catholique de Paris, 1966; (with Andre Chouraqui) *Les Juifs: Dialogue entre Jean Danielou et Andre Chouraqui,* Beauchesne, 1966, translation published as *The Jews, Views and Counterviews: A Dialogue between Jean Danielou and Andre Chouraqui,* Newman Press, 1967; *L'Entree dans l'histoirie du salut: Bapteme et confirmation,* Editions du Cerf, 1967; *Les Evangiles de l'enfance,* Editions du Seuil, 1967, translation by Rosemary Sheed published as *The Infancy Narratives,* Herder & Herder, 1968; (editor and author of introduction and notes) *La Colombe et la tenebre,* Editions de L'Orante, 1967; *L'Avenir de la religion,* Fayard, 1968; *La Catechese aux premiers siecles,* edited by Regine du Charlat, Fayard-Mame, 1968; *Tests,* Beauchesne, 1968; (with J. P. Jossua) *Christianisme de masse ou d'elite: Dialogue entre Jean Danielou et J. P. Jossua,* Beauchesne, 1968; *La Trinite et le mystere de l'existence,* Desclee, 1968, translation by Jeremy Leggat published as *God's Life in Us,* Dimension Books, 1969; *La Crise actuelle de l'intelligence,* Apostolat des Editions, 1969, translation published as "The Crisis of Intelligence" in *Media of Communication: Art and Morals,* edited by Sister Mary Dominic, Society of St. Paul, 1970; *La Foi de toujours et l'homme d'aujourd'hui,* Beauchesne, 1969, translation by Paul Joseph published as *The Faith Eternal and the Man of Today,* Franciscan Herald, 1970; (contributor) Arnold Toynbee, editor, *The Crucible of Christianity: Judaism, Hellenism, and the Historical Background to the Christian Faith,* World Publishing, 1969; *La Resurrection,* Editions du Seuil, 1969; (with A. H. Couratin and John Kent) *The Pelican Guide to Modern Theology,* Volume II: *Historical Theology,* edited by R.P.C. Hanson, Penguin, 1969.

L'Etre et le temps chez Gregoire de Nysee, R. J. Brill, 1970; *L'Eglise des apotres,* Editions du Seuil, 1970; *Nouveaux tests,* Beauchesne, 1970; (with others) *Jesus ou le Christ?,*

Desclee de Brouwer, 1970; (with Candido Pozo) *Iglesia y secularizacion*, La Editorial Catolica, 1971; *Pourquoi l'Eglise?*, Fayard, 1972; *La Culture trahie par les sirens*, Epi, 1972; *La Speranza*, ERI (Torino), 1973; (with Wladimir d'Ormesson) *Discours de reception de S. E. le Cardinal Jean Danielou a l'Academie francaise et reponse de M. Wladimir d'Ormesson*, Fayard, 1973.

Also author of *Le IIIeme Siecle: Origene, Le IVeme Siecle: Gregoire de Nysee et son milieu*, and *Le Judaisme au temps du Christ*, all published by Faculte de Theologie, Institut Catholique de Paris; author of numerous pamphlets and monographs on religion. Founder in 1942 of "Sources chretiennes," a series of French translations of the Greek and Roman Fathers; translator of some works for the collection, and author of introductions to many.

SIDELIGHTS: Jean Cardinal Danielou was described as "a man of known wit and heart" by critic Michael Novak, and his book on philosophical and theological themes, *The Scandal of Truth*, was called "a seminal, fertile book. . . . It yields a deep sense of Catholicism." Although Cardinal Danielou was criticized by a *Christian Century* reviewer who found that "behind his elegant thought forms [he] relies on a flat-out dogmatism," L.F.X. Mayhew, praised *Christ and Us*. He called it "fresh in treatment, original in its insights and thoroughly in contact with contemporary religious needs." Cardinal Danielou analyzed various approaches to Christ and Christianity because he felt that "the fact of Christianity, its simple and continuing existence, is something every thinking person must ultimately examine," said J. J. Keating. Mayhew called *Christ and Us* "a kind of Summa of Christology. . . . [Cardinal Danielou] is able to define so lucidly the essence of each question and to indicate so clearly both his own ideas and those which disagree with his."

Cardinal Danielou proposed that the Church work within society, based in civilization's realities. As P. J. Weber noted in *Prayer as a Political Problem:* "Danielou asks an old question of a renewing Church. Should the People of God be limited to the angelic purists living heroic lives in an alien culture? Or should they be the Church of the poor—the Church of the masses? Pere Danielou is not on the side of the angels." Further, Weber commented that "Pere Danielou does not limit his vision to Christian prayer. But he does see Christianity as the revealed religion ultimately adaptable to all civilizations." At the same time that he stressed engagement in the world, he also propounded "with prophetic vigor the essentially theocentric rather than anthrocentric character of true religion," according to Mayhew.

Cardinal Danielou was not only "one of the leading Catholic theologians in Europe," according to R. F. Harvanek, but also an historian making valuable contributions to our knowledge of the early Church. In particular, he was author of the history of the first three hundred years in Volume I of *The Christian Centuries*, which R. M. Grant observed "will inevitably become a standard authority."

Cardinal Danielou's books have appeared in multiple translations, including German, Spanish, and Italian.

BIOGRAPHICAL/CRITICAL SOURCES: Commonweal, September 16, 1960, October 13, 1961, March 15, 1963; *Catholic World*, November, 1960, September, 1961; *America*, March 30, 1963, June 2, 1965, October 7, 1967; *Christian Century*, May 1, 1963; *Times Literary Supplement*, December 31, 1964, July 29, 1965; *Critic*, February, 1965; *Journal of Religion*, July, 1965; *Saturday Review*, No-

vember 11, 1967; *New York Times*, March 29, 1969, July 6, 1969, January 31, 1970; *Judeo-christianisme recherches historiques et theologiques offertes en homage au cardinal Jean Danielou*, Recherches de science religieuse, 1972; Jacques Fontaine and Charles Kannengiesser, editors, *Epektasis: Melanges patristiques offerts au cardinal Jean Danielou*, Beauchesne, 1972; *Newsweek*, July 1, 1974; *Time*, July 1, 1974; *National Review*, October 11, 1974.†

(Died May 20, 1974)

* * *

DARINGER, Helen Fern 1892-

PERSONAL: Born June 24, 1892, in Matoon, Ill.; daughter of William (a manufacturer of window sash and doors) and Cora (Ballah) Daringer. *Education:* University of Chicago, Ph.B., 1918; Columbia University, M.A., 1921, Ph.D., 1932. *Politics:* Democrat. *Religion:* Protestant. *Home:* Meadow Lakes 21-08, Hightstown, N.J. 08520.

CAREER: Eastern Illinois State College (now University), Charleston, teacher of English, 1918-20, 1921-25; Columbia University, Teachers College, Lincoln School, New York, N.Y., teacher of English, 1925-49; writer, mostly for juveniles. *Member:* English-Speaking Union, Authors Guild, Asia Society.

WRITINGS—All published by Harcourt: (Editor) *Poet's Craft* (anthology), 1935; *Grammar for Everyday Use*, 1940; *Adopted Jane*, 1947; *Mary Montgomery: Rebel*, 1948; *Pilgrim Kate*, 1949; *Debbie of Green Gate*, 1950; *Country Cousin*, 1951; *Stepsister Sally*, 1952; *Keepsake Ring*, 1953; *Bigity Anne*, 1954; *Like a Lady*, 1955; *Golden Thorn*, 1956; *Flower of Araby*, 1958; *Turnabout Twins*, 1960; *Yesterday's Daughter*, 1964.

AVOCATIONAL INTERESTS: Travel.

* * *

DARLINGTON, Alice B(enning) 1906-1973

PERSONAL: Born 1906, in Two Harbors, Minn.; married Charles F. Darlington (a businessman and author), 1931; children: three. *Education:* Studied at Washburn College (now University) and under Karl Menninger, M.D., of the Menninger Clinic; University of Chicago, Ph.B., 1929. *Home:* 30 East 72nd St., New York, N.Y. 10021.

CAREER: Scott, Foresman & Co. (publishers), Chicago, Ill., editorial assistant, 1927-28; Council on Foreign Relations, Chicago, executive secretary, 1929-31; member, American Committee to the League of Nations, 1930; U.S. Office of Economic Opportunity, Washington, D.C., coordinator of consultants for Project Head Start, 1965-66. Board member at various times of Hillcrest Home (Washington, D.C.), United Hospital Fund of New York, Spence-Chapin Adoption Service (New York), Memorial Sloan-Kettering Cancer Center (New York), and Hillcrest Center for Children (Bedford Hills, N.Y.); long active in, and formerly managing director of, Metropolitan Opera Guild, Inc. (New York); active in other community and public service organizations. *Awards, honors:* Citation from University of Chicago, 1960, for distinguished public service.

WRITINGS: (With husband, Charles F. Darlington) *African Betrayal*, McKay, 1968.†

(Died March 24, 1973)

* * *

DARLINGTON, Charles F. 1904-

PERSONAL: Born September 13, 1904, in New York,

N.Y.; married Alice Nelson Benning (a businesswoman and author), 1931 (died March 24, 1973); children: three. *Education:* Harvard University, A.B., 1926; graduate study at New College, Oxford, 1927, and University of Geneva, 1928. *Home:* 30 East 72nd St., New York, N.Y. 10021.

CAREER: Secretariat of League of Nations, Geneva, Switzerland, member of Economic and Financial Section, 1929-31; Bank for International Settlements, Basle, Switzerland, member of Central Banking Department, 1931-34; U.S. Department of State, Washington, D.C., assistant chief of Division of Trade Agreements, 1935-39, chief of Petroleum Division, 1945; General Motors Overseas Operations, foreign exchange manager, 1940-41; Socony Mobil Oil Co., Inc., executive, 1946-61, with positions including London representative, vice-president and director of Socony Vacuum Overseas Supply Co., Middle East adviser, president of Near East Development Corp., and director of Iraq Petroleum Co. and Iranian Consortium; U.S. Ambassador to Republic of Gabon, appointed by President Kennedy, 1961-65. Secretary of Steering Committee and Executive Committee, United Nations Conference on International Organization, San Francisco, 1945. Member and secretary, Taconic State Park Commission, 1958-62. *Military service:* U.S. Navy, 1943-44; served in Mediterranean theater; became lieutenant commander. *Member:* Council on Foreign Relations (New York).

WRITINGS: (With wife, Alice B. Darlington) *African Betrayal,* McKay, 1968.

*   *   *

DARROCH, Maurice A. 1903-19(?)

PERSONAL: Surname is pronounced Darrow; born April 1, 1903, in Paisley, Ontario, Canada; son of Archie Buie and Ann (Buchanan) Darroch; married Ruth B. McCaffrey, December 10, 1924; children: Robert E., Maureen (Mrs. Robert McCarron). *Education:* University of Michigan, B.A., 1925; Moody Bible Institute, student, 1932; Northern Baptist Theological Seminary, Th.B. and B.D., 1935; Los Angeles Baptist Theological Seminary, Th.D., 1942.

CAREER: Baptist clergyman; pastor in Utica, Ill., 1933-37; Moody Bible Institute, Chicago, Ill., director of extension department and Christian Workers Bureau, 1937-42; pastor in Newark, N.J., 1942-47; North American home director, Sudan Interior Mission, 1946-58. *Member:* Interdenominational Foreign Mission Association of North America.

WRITINGS: True Revival, Moody, 1935; *Missions' Race Against Time,* Moody, 1955, revised and enlarged edition, Sudan Interior Mission Publications, 1956; *How Shall They Hear?,* Zondervan, 1958. Author of pamphlets.

WORK IN PROGRESS: Revision of *Missions' Race Against Time;* writing *World Religions: Missions Today and Tomorrow.*†

(Deceased)

*   *   *

DAS, Durga 1900-1974

PERSONAL: Born November 23, 1900, in Punjab, India; son of Ishwar and Uttam (Devi) Das; married Rattan Devi; children: Savitri Das Uggarsain, Inder Jit, Vikarma Jit, Satya Jit, Brahma Jit, Rani Das Tarneja. *Education:* D.A.V. College, Lahore, student, 1916-18. *Politics:* Progressive. *Religion:* Hindu. *Home:* 2 Tolstoy Lane, New Delhi-1, India. *Office:* Durga Das Pvt. Ltd., 10 Parliament St., New Delhi-1, India.

CAREER: Parliamentary correspondent and editor, Associated Press of India, 1918-37; *Statesman,* Calcutta, India, special representative, 1938-44; *Hindustan Times,* New Delhi, India, joint editor, 1944-57, chief editor, 1957-60; Durga Das Pvt. Ltd., New Delhi, managing director, and editor-in-chief of India News and Feature Alliance and *States* (English-language bimonthly), beginning 1960. Chairman, Press Gallery Committee of Indian Parliament, 1951-60, 1962-63; member, Press Council of India, beginning 1967. *Member:* All-India Newspaper Editors' Conference (president, 1959-61), Indian and Eastern Newspapers Society, Press Club of India (president, 1959-62).

WRITINGS: India and the World (collection of articles), Hindustan Times, 1958; *India: From Curzon to Nehru and After,* Collins, 1969, John Day, 1970; *Gandhi in Cartoons,* Navajivan Publishing House, 1969; (editor) *Sardar Patel's Correspondence, 1945-1950,* Navajivan Publishing House, 1971.†

(Died May 17, 1974)

*   *   *

DAVIES, Ada Hilton 1893-

PERSONAL: Born June 10, 1893, in Orwell, N.Y.; daughter of Hobart Harwell (a teacher) and Rose Catherine (Shepard) Hilton; married Thomas Morgan Davies, August 30, 1910 (deceased). *Education:* University of Montana, B.P.D., 1914. *Politics:* Democrat. *Home:* 311 Maynard St., San Francisco, Calif. 94112.

CAREER: High school and junior college teacher in Billings and Park City, Mont., 1915-19; *Berkeley Daily Gazette,* Berkeley, Calif., and *Oakland Post-Enquirer,* Oakland, Calif., columnist, news and advertising writer, 1921-28; later advertising manager of department store, and account executive with advertising agencies in San Francisco, Calif. *Member:* California Writers Club, Armed Forces Writer's League. *Awards, honors:* First prize for poem, Western Writers Conference, 1942.

WRITINGS: Signature (verse), Golden Quill, 1964. Contributor of poems to *Poetry, Voices, Number, Variegation,* and other journals.

WORK IN PROGRESS: A science-fiction novel; science-fiction stories; *Two Views from One Window,* nonfiction.

*   *   *

DAVIES, Oliver 1905-

PERSONAL: Born May 7, 1905, in London, England; son of Ernest and Eleanor (Taylor) Davies. *Education:* Exeter College, Oxford, B.A., 1927, M.A., 1930; University of Dublin, D.Litt., 1946. *Home:* 63 St. Patrick's Rd., Pietermaritzburg, South Africa. *Office:* Natal Museum, Loop St., Pietermaritzburg, South Africa.

CAREER: Queen's University of Belfast, Belfast, Northern Ireland, began as lecturer, became reader in ancient history and archaeology; University of Natal, Durban, South Africa, professor of classics, 1948-51; University of Ghana, Legon, Accra, began as reader, became professor of archaeology; affiliated with Natal Museum, Pietermaritzburg, South Africa. *Member:* Royal Anthropological Institute.

WRITINGS: Roman Mines in Europe, Clarendon Press, 1935; *Natal Archaeological Studies,* University of Natal Press, 1952; *Archaeology in Ghana,* Thomas Nelson, 1961; *The Quaternary in the Coastlands of Guinea,* Jackson, Son & Co., 1964; *West Africa before the Europeans,* Barnes & Noble, 1967.

WORK IN PROGRESS: Study of quaternary shorelines in southern Africa, on behalf of the International Quaternary Association; Tertiary-Quaternary formations in South Africa, for the Geological Survey.

* * *

DAVIS, Arthur Kyle, Jr. 1897-19(?)

PERSONAL: Born September 20, 1897, in Petersburg, Va.; son of Arthur Kyle (a college president) and Lucy Pryor (McIlwaine) Davis. *Education:* University of Virginia, B.A., 1917, M.A., 1919, Ph.D., 1924; Balliol College, Oxford, Diploma in Economics and Political Science, 1921, B.Litt., 1923. *Politics:* Democrat or independent. *Religion:* Episcopalian.

CAREER: University of Virginia, Charlottesville, instructor in English, 1923-24, assistant professor, 1924-27, associate professor, 1927-40, professor, beginning, 1940. Visiting professor, Harvard University, 1926, Sweet Briar College, 1926-27. *Military service:* U.S. Army, 1918-19; became second lieutenant. U.S. Naval Reserve, 1943-45; became lieutenant commander. *Member:* Modern Language Association of America (chairman of popular literature group, 1936-38), College English Association (vice-president, 1948-50), American Folklore Society (advisory board member, beginning, 1962), Southeastern Folklore Society (president, 1940-41), Phi Beta Kappa. *Awards, honors:* Rhodes scholar, 1920-23; Sterling Research Fellow, Yale University, 1928-29; American Council of Learned Societies grant to study Virginia folk songs, 1932; Chicago Folklore Prize, University of Chicago, 1961.

WRITINGS: Traditional Ballads of Virginia, Harvard University Press, 1929; *Folk-Songs of Virginia,* Duke University Press, 1949; *More Traditional Ballads of Virginia,* University of North Carolina Press, 1960; (editor) *Matthew Arnold's Letters: A Descriptive Checklist,* University Press of Virginia for Bibliographical Society of Virginia, 1968. Contributor to *Saturday Review, Sewanee Review,* and other journals. Editor-in-chief, *College Verse,* 1936-37; advisory editor, *Southern Folklore Quarterly.*

WORK IN PROGRESS: Other Folk-Songs of Virginia.†

(Deceased)

* * *

DAVIS, Edwin Adams 1904-
(E. Adams Davis)

PERSONAL: Born May 10, 1904, in Alba, Mo.; son of Frank Byrd (a farmer and judge) and Willie (Greever) Davis; married La Verna Mae Rowe (an editor of research manuscripts), May 8, 1925; children: Edwin Adams, Jr. *Education:* Kansas State College of Pittsburg (now Pittsburg State University), B.S. in Ed., 1925; University of Iowa, M.A., 1931; Louisiana State University, Ph.D., 1936. *Politics:* "Democrat (usually vote Republican)." *Religion:* Episcopalian. *Home:* 506 Stanford Ave., Baton Rouge, La. 70808.

CAREER: High school teacher and then principal in Kansas and Missouri, 1925-30; Drury College, Springfield, Mo., associate professor of history and acting head of department, 1931-32; Louisiana State University, Baton Rouge, instructor, 1934-36, assistant professor, 1936-42, associate professor, 1942-50, professor of history, 1950-73, head of department, 1952-63, founder and head of department of archives, 1935-46, special assistant to president of the university, 1962-68. State sponsor, Louisiana Historical Records Survey, 1937-43; chairman, Louisiana Committee for the Con-

servation of Cultural Resources, 1941-45; director, Louisiana Tidelands Historical Survey, 1955-57; senior consultant, Louisiana State Archives and Records Service, beginning 1956. Television lecturer, presenting Louisiana history series, 1960-61, 1964.

MEMBER: Southern Historical Association (founding member; member of executive council, 1947-50), Louisiana Historical Association (president, 1958; member of executive committee and board of directors, 1958-62). *Awards, honors:* Rosenwald research fellowships, 1939-41; Social Science Research Council grants, 1946, 1954-55; Louisiana State University grants, 1946, 1948, 1950, 1952, 1954.

WRITINGS: (Editor) Bennet H. Barrow, *Plantation Life in the Florida Parishes of Louisiana,* Columbia University Press, 1943; (under name E. Adams Davis) *Of the Night Wind's Telling: Legends from the Valley of Mexico,* University of Oklahoma Press, 1946, reprinted, 1976; (with William Ransom Hogan) *William Johnson's Natchez: The Ante-Bellum Diary of a Free Negro,* Louisiana State University Press, 1951; (with Hogan) *The Barber of Natchez,* Louisiana State University Press, 1954; *Louisiana, the Pelican State,* Louisiana State University Press, 1959, 4th edition, 1975; (author of Volume I, editorial consultant on Volumes II-IV) *The Story of Louisiana,* four volumes, Hyer Publishing, 1960-63, revised edition of Volume I published as *Louisiana: A Narrative History,* Claitor's, 1961, 3rd revised edition, 1970; (with Martin Hardwick Hall) *A Campaign from Santa Fe to the Mississippi: Being a History of the Old Sibley Brigade,* Stagecoach, 1961; (with Hall) *Fallen Guidon: The Forgotten Saga of General Jo Shelby's Confederate Command,* Stagecoach, 1962; *Heroic Years: Louisiana in the War for Southern Independence* (television lecture series), Bureau of Educational Materials and Research, Louisiana State University, 1964; *Heritage of Valor: The Picture Story of Louisiana in the Confederacy,* Louisiana State Archives and Records Service, 1965; *Louisiana: Its Horn of Plenty,* Panoramic Teaching Aids, 1968; (editor) *The Rivers and Bayous of Louisiana,* Bureau of Educational Materials and Research, Louisiana State University, 1968.

Writer and narrator of record album, "Dramatic Moments in Louisiana History," Stanley Projection Co., 1967. Contributor to *Dictionary of American History, World Book Encyclopedia,* and about twenty articles and one hundred reviews to professional journals and newspapers. Editorial associate, *Journal of Southern History,* 1935-36; founding managing editor, *Louisiana History,* 1960-62.

WORK IN PROGRESS: Two books, *The Fabulous Old City of Mexico, The Governors of Louisiana,* and two long-term editorial projects, *Dictionary of Louisiana Biography* and *Encyclopedia of Louisiana History.*

SIDELIGHTS: Davis did his most recent research in Europe in 1968-75; he previously has researched Southern and Louisiana history and the history of Mexico City in libraries and archives throughout United States, and in Mexico, Seville, Madrid, London, and Paris. *Avocational interests:* Tennis, music, Mexico, the acquisition of paintings.

* * *

DAVIS, H(enry) Grady 1890-

PERSONAL: Born June 5, 1890, in Monroe County, Tenn.; son of William Henry (a farmer) and Margaret (Shaffer) Davis; married Madge Mitchell, June 7, 1917; children: Henry Grady, Jr., Margaret (Mrs. John A. Laughner). *Education:* Roanoke College, A.B., 1910; Lutheran Theological Seminary, Philadelphia, Pa., B.D., 1916; also studied at

University of Tennessee and University of Chicago. *Home:* 1612 South 13th Ave., Maywood, Ill. 60153.

CAREER: Ordained Lutheran minister, 1910; pastor in Greene County, Tenn., 1910-13, in Trenton, N.J., 1916-18, in Kingsport, Tenn., 1918-21; Weidner Institute, Mulberry, Ind., president, 1921-24; pastor in Whitestown, Ind., 1924-37; Chicago Lutheran Theological Seminary (now Lutheran School of Theology), Maywood, Ill., professor of functional theology, beginning 1937. *Awards, honors:* D.D., Wittenberg College, 1938.

WRITINGS: Design for Preaching, Muhlenberg Press, 1958; *Why We Worship,* Fortress, 1961; (contributor) Philip Hefner, editor, *The Scope of Grace,* Fortress, 1964; (with Arthur Voobus) *The Gospels in Study and Preaching: Trinity Sunday to the Ninth Sunday after Trinity,* Volume I, Fortress, 1966.

WORK IN PROGRESS: Volume II of *The Gospels in Study and Preaching;* studies on the nature of biblical preaching, and on human existence as seen in the work of modern poets.††

* * *

DAVIS, Mary Octavia   1901-
   (Dutz)

PERSONAL: Born May 11, 1901, in Castroville, Tex.; daughter of Fletcher (a newspaper publisher and writer) and Roberta Octavia (Hopp) Davis. *Education:* Our Lady of the Lake College, B.A., 1930; additional study at University of Texas; graduate of Famous Writers School, 1966. *Religion:* Roman Catholic. *Home and office:* 125 Adams, San Antonio, Tex. 78210.

CAREER: Primary teacher in San Antonio (Tex.) public schools, 1931-69. Has also been camp counselor, playground director, active in children's theatre, and exhibitor in art shows. *Member:* National League of American Pen Women, Poetry Society of Texas, River Art Group, King William Conservation Society.

WRITINGS—Self-illustrated, with illustrations under pseudonym Dutz: *Pinkie,* Steck, 1952; *Rickie,* Steck, 1955; *Mouse Trail,* Steck, 1965; *Going to the Fair,* Steck, 1968. Conductor of poetry page and children's columnist in *Fletcher's Farming;* contributor of poetry to other periodicals.

WORK IN PROGRESS: Six children's books, *Dinkie Doodle Bug, Boss, Sunday Haus, Yanaquana Boy, Bird Boy,* and *Old House;* composing songs and dances for children, and adult songs.††

* * *

DAVIS, W(arren) Jefferson   1885-1973

PERSONAL: Born March 17, 1885, in Front Royal, Va.; son of George C. and Sarah Maude Davis; married Beatrice Merrill, 1923; married second wife, Ione Dismukes, 1927. *Education:* George Washington University, B.Sc., 1911; Georgetown University, LL.B., 1911; University of Virginia, graduate study; University of Koenigsberg, LL.D., 1928. *Home:* 7442 Caminito Rialto, La Jolla, Calif. 92037.

CAREER: Admitted to California Bar, 1913; attorney practicing in California, beginning 1913. Counsel for U.S. Government at International Aviation Congress at Prague; former special assistant to military attaché, American Embassy in Berlin; also former chairman of California Commission on Uniform State Laws and member of other govern-

mental bodies concerned with uniform laws and aeronautical law; founder of first exchange fellowship in air law between American and European universities. *Military service:* U.S. Army, liaison officer in Office of Director of Military Aeronautics, 1918-19; later organized and commanded a reserve pursuit squadron and pursuit group. California Air National Guard; became colonel.

MEMBER: American Bar Association, American Law Institute (life member), American Academy of Public Affairs (Los Angeles; former president), Phi Sigma Kappa, Phi Delta Phi, Pi Gamma Mu, Masons. *Awards, honors:* Officer, Order of the Crown (Italy), 1922; Officer, Legion of Honor (France), 1927; Aero Educational Research Organization award, 1930, for *Air Conquest.*

WRITINGS: Kent's Notes on Rhetoric, University of Virginia, c. 1925; *Putting Laws Over Wings,* Newsprint (Whittier, Calif.), 1926; *Highways and Airways: Their Relation to Commerce and National Defense,* Newsprint, 1926; *The World's Wings,* Simmons-Bordman, 1927; *Japan, the Air Menace of the Pacific,* Christopher, 1928, reprinted, 1970; *Radio Law,* Parker, Stone & Baird, 1929, 2nd edition, 1930; *Aeronautical Law,* Parker, Stone & Baird, 1930, supplement, 1933; *Air Conquest,* Parker, Stone & Baird, 1930; *The Law of Air Carriers,* Parker, Stone & Baird, 1934; *Law of the Land,* Carlton, 1962; (contributor) Bryton Barron, *Dream Becomes a Nightmare: The U.S. Today,* Crestwood, 1964. Also author of "The Supremacy of the Constitution" series, 1972.†

(Died November 21, 1973)

* * *

DAWSON, Elmer A.
   [Collective pseudonym]

WRITINGS—All published by Grosset: "The Buck and Larry Stories" series: *Buck's Winning Hit,* 1930; *Larry's Fadeaway,* 1930; *The Pick-up Nine,* 1930; *Buck's Home Run Drive,* 1931; *Larry's Speed Ball,* 1932.

"Garry Grayson Football Stories" series: *Garry Grayson's Winning Kick,* 1928; *Garry Grayson Hitting the Line,* 1929; *Garry Grayson's Winning Touchdown,* 1930; *. . . Double Signals,* 1931; *. . . Forward Pass,* 1932.

SIDELIGHTS: See **ADAMS, Harriet S., STRATEMEYER, Edward L.,** and **SVENSON, Andrew E.**†

* * *

DAWSON, Giles E(dwin)   1903-

PERSONAL: Born March 4, 1903, in Columbus, Ohio; son of William Leon (an ornithologist) and Frances Etta (Ackerman) Dawson; married Margaret Williams, 1926 (died 1957); married Margaret White, January 24, 1959; children: (first marriage) Pamela (Mrs. J. Pierrepont Moffat), G. Nicholas; (second marriage) Victoria, Geoffrey Odo, Seth Quintus Adams. *Education:* Oberlin College, A.B., 1925; Cornell University, A.M., 1926, Ph.D., 1931; Western Reserve University (now Case Western Reserve University), graduate study, 1929-30. *Politics:* Democrat. *Religion:* Episcopalian. *Home:* 1217 34th St. N.W., Washington, D.C. 20007.

CAREER: Instructor in English at University of North Dakota, Grand Forks, 1926-27, and Western Reserve University (now Case Western Reserve University), Cleveland, Ohio, 1927-32; Folger Shakespeare Library, Washington, D.C., reference librarian, 1932-46, curator of books and manuscripts, 1946-68; Catholic University of America,

Washington, D.C., adjunct professor, 1946-67, professor of English literature, 1967-71, professor emeritus, 1971—; Howard University, Washington, D.C., assistant professor, 1971—. Visiting professor, Johns Hopkins University, 1950-52. *Military service:* U.S. Naval Reserve, active duty, 1942-45; became lieutenant commander. *Member:* Malone Society (England). *Awards, honors:* Senior fellow at Southeast Institute of Medieval and Renaissance Studies, Duke University, 1975.

WRITINGS: (Editor) *The Seven Champions of Christendom,* Western Reserve University Press, 1929; (editor) *July and Julian,* Malone Society, 1955; *Life of William Shakespeare,* Folger Shakespeare Library, 1957; (with Laetitia Kennedy-Skipton) *Elizabethan Handwriting: A Manual,* Norton, 1966. Contributor to learned journals. Associate editor, *Shakespeare Quarterly,* 1950-72; member of advisory board, *Shakespeare Studies.*

WORK IN PROGRESS: Research on Elizabethan letters on marriage, and on letters by students at Oxford University, 1576-1621, both projects utilizing letters from the Bogot Collection at the Folger Shakespeare Library.

SIDELIGHTS: Dawson was sued for libel in 1948 in the District Court, Washington, D.C., as the result of a letter using contemptuous language about a believer in the theory that the Earl of Oxford wrote the plays of Shakespeare. After two years the plaintiff dropped the suit, which stirred up further newspaper activity on the issue. Dawson also notes that he was the subject ("or object") of two disapproving articles in *Baconiana* following his Third Programme broadcasts for BBC in London in 1950.

*   *   *

DAY, Albert Edward   1884-1973

PERSONAL: Born November 18, 1884, in Euphemia, Ohio; son of Elam Mansfield (an editor) and Mary Ellen (Bright) Day; married Emma Reader, September 28, 1904 (deceased); children: Ruth Lucile (Mrs. Pierre LeMunycn), Helen M., Dorothy (Mrs. George Johnson), Ben Wilson, Mary Ellen (Mrs. Ronald O'Neill). *Education:* Taylor University, A.B., 1904; University of Cincinnati, M.A., 1916. *Politics:* Independent. *Home and office:* 3402 Siesta Dr., Falls Church, Va. 22042.

CAREER: Ordained to ministry of Methodist Church, 1904; held pastorates in Ohio and Pennsylvania, 1904-32; Mount Vernon Place Church, Baltimore, Md., pastor, 1932-37; First Methodist Church, Pasadena, Calif., pastor, 1937-45; director of New Life Movement and editor of *New Life,* 1945-47; Mount Vernon Place Church, Baltimore, pastor, 1948-57. Special mediator for National War Labor Board, 1942-43. Lyman Beecher lecturer at Yale University, 1934; Fondren lecturer at Southern Methodist University, 1940; distinguished lecturer at other universities, colleges, and seminaries. Member of Methodist Board of Foreign Missions, 1924-36; vice-president of Federal Council of Churches in Christ, 1942-44; founder of Disciplined Order of Christ, 1945. *Military service:* U.S. Army, chaplain, 1918-19.

MEMBER: Masons, Sigma Alpha Epsilon. *Awards, honors:* D.D., Taylor University, 1918, Ohio Wesleyan University, 1926, and Alleghany College, 1936; Litt.D., University of Southern California, 1939; chosen one of six leading preachers of America by *Christian Century* poll, 1940, and one of ten most influential living Methodists by *Christian Advocate* poll, 1947.

WRITINGS: Present Perils in Religion, Abingdon, 1928; (with others) *Whither Religion,* Harper, 1929; *Revitalizing Religion,* Abingdon, 1930; *Jesus and Human Personality,* Abingdon, 1934; *God in Us: We in God,* Abingdon, 1938; *The Evangel of a New World,* Cokesbury Press, 1939; *The Faith We Live: The Fondren Lectures for 1940,* Cokesbury Press, 1940; *Discipline and Discovery,* Upper Room, 1947; *An Autobiography of Prayer,* Harper, 1952; *Existence under God,* Abingdon, 1958; *Dialogue and Destiny,* Harper, 1961; *The Cup and the Sword,* Pantheon, 1962; *Letters on the Healing Ministry,* Methodist Evangelistic Materials, 1964.

WORK IN PROGRESS: Writing on spiritual healing, on group dynamics, and on prayer therapy.

BIOGRAPHICAL/CRITICAL SOURCES: E. Oursler, *The Healing Power of Faith,* Hawthorn, 1957.†

(Died October 12, 1973)

*   *   *

DAZEY, Agnes J(ohnston)
(Agnes Christine Johnston)

PERSONAL: Born in Swissville, Pa.; daughter of John Parry and Isabel (MacElheney) Johnston; married Frank M. Dazey (a writer); children: Ruth (Mrs. Jack D. Phelan), Mitchell H., Frank Cadwallader. *Education:* Attended Radcliffe College. *Agent:* Reece Halsey Agency, 8733 Sunset Blvd., Los Angeles, Calif. 90069.

CAREER: Joined Vitagraph Co. in Hollywood in 1915, and, while still in her teens, wrote the filmscript for Mary Pickford's biggest moneymaker, "Daddy Long Legs"; collaborated with husband on scripts for Pathe, Paramount, Metro-Goldwyn-Mayer, Allied Artists, and other studios over a span of years, doing among other filmplays, most of the "Hardy Family" series featuring Mickey Rooney and Lewis Stone; in 1954 the Dazeys were sent to Munich, Germany, to write propaganda films for U.S. Department of State; went to Mexico in 1960, intending to write, but became involved in a free medical clinic for the poor, Dr. Banda Dispensario in Colonia Seattle, and worked as assistant manager of the clinic, until 1966; resumed writing after this lapse, with fiction on the good neighbor theme.

WRITINGS: (With husband, Frank M. Dazey) *Pepe, the Bad One* (juvenile), Westminster, 1966.

Screenplays; under name Agnes Christine Johnston: (With F. M. Dazey) "Nobody's Fool," Universal, 1936; "Out West with the Hardys," Metro-Goldwyn-Mayer, 1939; "All Women Have Secrets," Paramount, 1939; (with F. M. Dazey) "The Hardy's Ride High," Metro-Goldwyn-Mayer, 1939; "Seventeen," Paramount, 1940; "Life Begins for Andy Hardy," Metro-Goldwyn-Mayer, 1941; "Double Date," Universal, 1941; "The Courtship of Andy Hardy," Metro-Goldwyn-Mayer, 1942; (with F. M. Dazey) "Andy Hardy's Double Life," Metro-Goldwyn-Mayer, 1943; "Andy Hardy's Blonde Trouble," Metro-Goldwyn-Mayer, 1944; "The Time, Place and Girl," Warner Bros., 1946; "Janie Gets Married," Warner Bros., 1946; "Black Beauty," New Trends, 1946; "Black Gold," Allied Artists, 1947; "Mickey," Eagle Lion, 1948; "Stage Struck," Monogram, 1949; "Alarm Clock Andy"; "Show People"; (with F. M. Dazey) "The Shine Girl"; (with F. M. Dazey) "Hour's Leave"; "Henry Aldrich"; (with F. M. Dazey) "Movie Crazy" (for Harold Lloyd); (with F. M. Dazey) "Janice"; and about thirty more original screenplays or adaptations. She also collaborated with her husband on television plays for "Lux Theatre" and "Fireside Theatre." Contributor of fiction to *This Week, Cosmopolitan, Good Housekeeping, American,* and other magazines.

WORK IN PROGRESS: Left-Over House, another juvenile; research for further stories on Mexico.

SIDELIGHTS: Mrs. Dazey once told *CA:* "When it comes to screenplay credits, we go way, way back. We wrote so many pictures, we can't remember the names and dates of them all. . . . At the time we started [their work in the Mexican clinic] the death rate in our village was very high—a coffin being carried out almost every day. But after a year or so the death rate was lower than that of Guadalajara, a city with fine doctors and rich people. Thus, for six years we did almost no writing—it is hard to concentrate on fiction when one is dealing with matters of life and death. However, the experience was most rewarding and gave us knowledge of the Mexican people—hence our first book, *Pepe, the Bad One.*" The book was purchased by Walt Disney Productions for filming.†

*   *   *

DAZEY, Frank M.

PERSONAL: Son of Charles T. (an author) and Lucy (Harding) Dazey; married Agnes Christine Johnston (a writer); children: Ruth (Mrs. Jack D. Phelan), Mitchell H., Frank Cadwallader. *Education:* Harvard University, B.A. *Agent:* Reece Halsey Agency, 8733 Sunset Blvd., Los Angeles, Calif. 90069.

CAREER: When just out of Harvard, wrote "Manhattan Madness" for Paramount Pictures, Douglas Fairbanks Sr.'s first great hit; subsequently collaborated with his wife on filmscripts for Pathe, Warner Brothers, Metro-Goldwyn-Mayer, Allied Artists, and other studios over a span of years; also was scenario editor in Hollywood for Selznick Pictures and Warner Brothers; writer, with wife, of propaganda films for U.S. Department of State, Munich, Germany, 1954; manager of Dr. Banda Dispensario, a free clinic for the poor, in Colonia Seattle, Mexico, 1960-66. *Military service:* U.S. Army, Field Artillery, World War I; became captain. *Member:* Harvard Club of New York.

WRITINGS: (With wife, Agnes J. Dazey) *Pepe, the Bad One* (juvenile), Westminister, 1966.

Screenplays; with wife, under her maiden name, Agnes Christine Johnston, except as indicated: "Nobody's Fool," Universal, 1936; (sole author) "13 Hours by Air," Paramount, 1936; "The Hardy's Ride High," Metro-Goldwyn-Mayer, 1939; "Andy Hardy's Double Life," Metro-Goldwyn-Mayer, 1943; (sole author) "Helldorado," Republic, 1946; "The Shine Girl"; "Hour's Leave"; "Movie Crazy" (for Harold Lloyd); "Janice," and over twenty-five more original screenplays. He also collaborated with his wife on television plays for "Lux Theatre" and "Fireside Theatre," and other series. Contributor of fiction to a number of national magazines.

WORK IN PROGRESS: Left-Over House, a juvenile; research for further stories on Mexico.

SIDELIGHTS: See listing for Agnes J. Dazey.†

*   *   *

DEALEY, E(dward) M(usgrove)   1892-1969
(Ted Dealey)

PERSONAL: Born October 5, 1892, in Dallas, Tex.; son of George Bannerman (a newspaperman) and Olivia (Allen) Dealey; married Clara MacDonald, March 1, 1916 (de-

ceased); married Trudie Lewellen, June 29, 1951; children: (first marriage) Edward M. (deceased), Joseph M., Clara Patricia (Mrs. Robert J. Brooks). *Education:* University of Texas, B.A., 1913; Harvard University, M.A., 1914, graduate study, 1914-15. *Politics:* Independent Democrat. *Religion:* Presbyterian. *Home:* 3525 Turtle Creek Blvd., Dallas, Tex. 75219. *Office: Dallas News,* Dallas, Tex. 75222.

CAREER: Dallas News, Dallas, Tex., reporter, 1915-20, staff correspondent, 1920-24, Sunday editor and editorial writer, 1924-28; A. H. Belo Corp. (publishers of *Dallas Morning News* and *Texas Almanac*), Dallas, Tex., assistant to publisher, 1928-32, vice-president, 1932-40, president, 1940-69, chairman, 1960-69, publisher, 1964-69. First vice-president, Associated Press, 1948; director, Southland Paper Mills, Inc. Trustee, Texas Research Foundation. *Military service:* U.S. Army, 1942-43; became major.

MEMBER: American Newspaper Publishers Association (director, 1940-45), Advertising Federation of America (director, 1936-41), English-Speaking Union, Southern Newspaper Publishers Association (president, 1937-38; chairman of board, 1938-39), Texas Newspaper Publishers Association (president, 1935-37), Dallas Historical Society, Dallas Citizens Council, Advertising Club, Order of the T (University of Texas football), Phi Delta Theta, Sigma Delta Chi, Masons, Dallas Country Club, Skeet and Gun Club, Koon Kreek Hunting and Fishing Club, Carmen Mountain Hunting Club (Coahuila, Mexico), Pine Island Hunting and Fishing Club.

WRITINGS—Under name Ted Dealey: *"Colonel Bill," One of the Last of the Old-Time Personal Journalists,* privately printed, 1939; *Sunset in the East,* privately printed, 1945; *Three Men of Texas and a Texas Institution, "The Dallas Morning News,"* Newcomen Society in North America, 1957; *The Dallas Spirit: The Last Fool Flight,* privately printed, 1959; *Report from Russia,* privately printed, 1959; *The Low-Down on Down Under,* privately printed, 1963; *Travels in a Troubled World,* privately printed, 1964; *Diaper Days of Dallas,* Abingdon, 1966. Member of editorial board, *This Week.* Contributor of fiction to periodicals.†

(Died November, 1969)

*   *   *

DEARMER, Geoffrey   1893-

PERSONAL: Born March 21, 1893, in London, England; son of Percy (Canon of Westminster) and Mabel (White) Dearmer; married Margaret Helen Procter, March, 1936; children: Juliet. *Education:* Attended Westminster School, 1907-10, and Christ Church, Oxford, 1911-13. *Home:* 68 Walsingham, St. John's Wood Park, London N.W. 8, England.

CAREER: Writer. Examiner of plays to Lord Chamberlain, 1936-58; staff of "Children's Hour," British Broadcasting Corp., 1936-60. *Military service:* British Army, 1914-20; became captain. *Member:* Garrick Club (London). *Awards, honors:* Member of Royal Victorian Order (M.V.O.).

WRITINGS: Poems, McBride, 1918; *The Day's Delight* (poems), J. Murray, 1923; *Man with a Cane: A School Comedy,* Baker Plays, 1929; *St. Paul* (three-act historical play), Heinemann, 1929; (with Clifford Bax) *Chronicles of Cupid: Being a Masque of Love Throughout the Ages,* Samuel French, 1931; (with W. H. Andrews) *Referee* (one-act farce), H.W.F. Deane, 1931; *Saint on Holiday* (novel), Heinemann, 1933; *They Chose to be Birds* (novel), Heinemann,

1935; (compiler) *Told on the Air: Broadcast Stories of Children,* Latimer House, 1948; *Aught for Your Comfort?* (poems), privately printed, 1967. Wrote script for the Selsey pageant, "Tides of Invasion," 1965.

* * *

DeCHANT, John A(loysius) 1917-1974

PERSONAL: Surname is pronounced DeShahnt; born June 21, 1917, in Milwaukee, Wis.; son of John Henry and Frances Irene (McGee) DeChant; married Mary Elizabeth Knoernschild, May 30, 1944; children: John David, Robert Thomas, Michael Patrick, Richard Dennis, James Francis. *Education:* Marquette University, Ph.B., 1939. *Home:* 4710 Bethesda Ave., Bethesda, Md.

CAREER: Public relations work for Catholic agencies in Milwaukee, Wis., 1939-41, and Washington, D.C., 1941-42; news editor of *New World,* 1940-41; War Assets Administration, Washington, D.C., field information chief, 1946; director of community relations for Aircraft Industries Association, Washington, D.C., 1946-47, and for steel industries, Hill & Knowlton, Inc., New York City, 1947-49; U.S. Government, Washington, D.C., field counseling officer with Economic Cooperation Administration, 1949, senior public relations consultant, Office of Civil Defense, 1950-51, and director of national public affairs and administrator of public education program, Federal Civil Defense Administration, 1951-54; American Heritage Foundation, New York City, executive director, 1954-55; Crusade for Freedom, New York City, and Washington, D.C., vice-president, 1955-56; associated with private public relations firms in Washington, D.C., 1957-65, DeChant and Key, partner, 1960-64, John A. DeChant & Associates, head, 1964-65; U.S. Department of Labor, Washington, D.C., director of information, Bureau of Employment, 1965-68, special assistant to director of information, Manpower Administration, 1968-74. Member of National Defense Executive Reserve, Office of Emergency Planning, 1962. Vice-president of Marine Corps Memorial Foundation. *Military service:* U.S. Marine Corps, 1942-46; served as chief press officer for Air Wing; became captain; received Navy Ribbon with four battle stars. U.S. Marine Corps Reserve; became colonel.

MEMBER: Public Relations Society of America, American Legion, Marine Corps Reserve Officers Association (executive council member, 1950-54), Sigma Delta Chi, National Press Club. *Awards, honors:* National Air Council fellowship, 1947; Distinguished Service Award, Federal Civil Defense Administration; gold medal of Swedish Civil Defense League.

WRITINGS: (With Richard Hubler) *Flying Leathernecks,* Doubleday, 1944; *Devilbirds: Marine Aviation in World War II,* Harper, 1947; *The Modern United States Marine Corps,* Van Nostrand, 1966.†

(Died October 9, 1974)

* * *

deCOSTE, Fredrik 1910-

PERSONAL: Born November 24, 1910, in Boston, Mass.; son of George and Mary (Duffy) deCoste. *Education:* Attended Transylvania University, 1932-33, and University of San Marcos, Peru, 1936-37. *Politics:* None. *Religion:* Roman Catholic.

CAREER: Writer for *West Coast Leader,* Lima, Peru, during late 1930's, then assistant director of Experiment in International Living, Putney, Vt.; with U.S. Government in Central America, 1941-44; U.S. International Book Association, New York City, and Mexico City, Mexico, director for Mexico, 1946-48; Council for Inter-American Cooperation, New York City, assistant director, 1948-51; National Foreign Trade Council, New York City, worked on international education affairs, 1951-62; writer. *Military service:* U.S. Naval Reserve, World War II.

WRITINGS: True Tales of Old St. Augustine, Great Outdoors Publishing, 1966. Author of booklet, "First Child of Spanish Florida," St. Augustine Historical Society, 1965. Contributor to newspapers and magazines. Editor, *Noticias* (weekly news digest), 1950-60.

WORK IN PROGRESS: A Short History of Colonial Florida; a volume of short stories on Spanish and British Florida.††

* * *

DeFOREST, Charlotte B. 1879-1971

PERSONAL: Born February 23, 1879, in Osaka, Japan; daughter of John Hyde (a clergyman and missionary) and Elizabeth (Starr) DeForest. *Education:* Smith College, B.A., 1901, M.A., 1907; also studied at Chicago Theological Seminary, Hartford School of Missions, and Oxford University. *Religion:* United Church of Christ. *Residence:* Claremont, Calif.

CAREER: American Board of Commissioners for Foreign Missions, Boston, Mass., missionary assigned to educational work in Japan, 1903-50; Kobe College for Women, Kobe, Japan, teacher of English and Bible, 1905-15, president, 1915-40; social worker for Japanese detained in Boston, 1942-43; teacher of Japanese to an Army student training unit at Pomona College, Claremont, Calif., 1943-44; did welfare work (under U.S. Government) at Japanese Relocation Center, Manzanar, Calif., 1944-45; returned to Kobe College on her own to teach and rally alumnae scattered by the war, 1947-50. Former member of directorate, Japan Christian Education Association; member of women's planning committee, Japan International Christian University. *Member:* American Association for the United Nations, American Association of Retired Persons, American Civil Liberties Union. *Awards, honors:* L.H.D., Smith College, 1916; Order of the Sacred Treasure, fifth grade, 1940, and fourth grade, 1950, both decorations from Imperial Household Bureau, Japan, for educational service.

WRITINGS: The Evolution of a Missionary: John Hyde DeForest, Revell, 1914; *The Woman and the Leaven in Japan,* Central Committee on United Study of Foreign Missions, 1923; *Handbook of Memorials in New Campus,* [Japan], 1934; *History of Kobe College* (for 75th anniversary), Kobe College Corp. (Chicago), 1950; *Poems down the Years,* Kobe College Alumnae Association, 1960; (translator) *The Prancing Pony: Nursery Rhymes from Japan,* Walker & Co., 1968. Occasional contributor of articles on Japan and education to periodicals; author of twelve short autobiographical sketches published serially in Japanese in *Kobe Shimbun* (newspaper), 1967.

WORK IN PROGRESS: Translation of Japanese nurse-maids' songs.

SIDELIGHTS: Charlotte DeForest had audiences with both the Emperor and Empress of Japan. *Avocational interests:* Poetry.†

(Died, 1971)

De JAEGHER, Raymond-Joseph 1905-
(Lei Chen Yuan)

PERSONAL: Born September 13, 1905, in Courtrai, Belgium; son of August and Josephine (Voos) De Jaegher. *Education:* Catholic University of Louvain, M.A., 1925, Institut Superieur de Philosophie, M.A., 1927, graduate of the School of Theology, 1930. *Office:* East Asian Research Institute, 86 Riverside Dr., New York, N.Y.

CAREER: Roman Catholic priest. Teacher and missionary in China (De Jaegher's name in Chinese is Lei Chen Yuan), 1931-41; elected Mayor of An-Kwo District, 1937; rector of the Chinese Seminary of An-Kwo, 1941-43; prisoner in Japanese concentration camp, Weihsien, Shantung, China, 1943-45; relief worker in Chinese provinces of Hopei, Shantung, Shansi, Chagar and Suiyuan, 1945-49; regent of Institute of Far Eastern Studies, Seton Hall University, South Orange, N.J., 1951-54; accompanied Ngo Dinh-Diem (then a revolutionary leader in Vietnam) on American and European tours in the early 1950's, and served as his unofficial adviser during his premiership and presidency, 1955-63; founder of Free Pacific Association of Vietnam, 1955, and head of the association, 1955-63; also founder of Free Pacific News Agency and *Free Pacific* (monthly), Saigon, Vietnam, and two high schools, Free Pacific Institute and Ming Yuen High School; staff member of East Asian Research Institute, New York, N.Y. Former director of Saigon Chinese-language newspaper, *New Viet-Nam*. Lecturer in United States and Canada for the Asian Speakers Bureau of the Free Pacific Association. Trustee of Hwakang Yang Ming Shan (the China Academy), Taipei. *Member:* International Press Association (Saigon branch), Confucian Society (Saigon), Rotary Club (Saigon West). *Awards, honors:* Prize Syvio Pellico, 1954, for *Tempete sur la Chine.*

WRITINGS: Que Penser du Communisme Chinois?, [Louvain], 1947; *Father Lebbe, Apostle of China,* St. Paul's Press (New York), 1950; (with Irene C. Kuhn) *The Enemy Within,* Doubleday, 1952; *Tempete sur la Chine,* Plon, 1953; *Life of Archbishop Paul Yu Pin,* Free Pacific Association (Saigon), 1958; (with Stephen Pan) *Peking's Red Guards,* Twin Circle, 1968. Contributor of more than one hundred articles in Chinese to *Free Pacific* (magazine), and articles in French, English, and Latin to other publications. Editor of magazine published in English as *Free Front,* and in French as *Front de la Liberte,* Saigon, 1957-63.

WORK IN PROGRESS: Research on Communism.

SIDELIGHTS: The Kuhn-De Jaegher collaboration, *The Enemy Within,* was translated for Chinese, Spanish, French, Dutch, Italian, Vietnamese, and Indian editions. Father De Jaegher began his travels in Asia in 1930, visited Inner Mongolia, 1930-31, and ranged over much of China, visiting all the Chinese bishops from January to June, 1937, during his years as an educator and missionary there. He lived under the Chinese Communists from 1937 to 1943. He made a number of visits to Communist territory, 1945-49, annual visits to the Republic of China, 1950-67, many trips to Europe, to Japan (fifteen times), Korea, and other Southeast Asian countries. Each year De Jaegher visits Vietnam. In his review of *Peking's Red Guards,* an account of Mao's "cultural revolution" and the "Red Guard" upheaval, M. S. Evans writes: "The Pan-De Jaegher narrative may be read for systematic instruction about the ills of Chinese society and flashes of insight into our own."

BIOGRAPHICAL/CRITICAL SOURCES: National Review, August 13, 1968.

DE JOVINE, F(elix) Anthony 1927-1976

PERSONAL: Born June 29, 1927, in Cleveland, Ohio; son of Anthony and Lena (Chimera) De Jovine. *Education:* Case Western Reserve University, B.A., 1959, M.A., 1963; Ohio State University, Ph.D., 1967. *Address:* P.O. Box 1002, Athens, Ohio 45701. *Office:* Department of English, Ohio University, Athens, Ohio 45701.

CAREER: Teacher in Cleveland, Ohio high school, 1959-63; Ohio State University, Columbus, instructor in English and education, 1963-65; Miami University, Oxford, Ohio, assistant professor of English, 1965-68; Youngstown State University, Youngstown, Ohio, assistant professor of English, 1969-70; Ohio University, Athens, associate professor of English, 1970-76. Visiting professor of education, Ohio State University, 1968-69; visiting professor of English, Kansai University of Foreign Studies, 1969. Curriculum consultant, Ohio schools. Chairman, Committee on Teacher Preparation in Ohio. *Military service:* U.S. Navy, 1945-59. *Member:* National Council of Teachers of English, English Association of America, Conference of English Education.

WRITINGS: The Young Hero in Fiction: A Motif for Teaching Literature, Appleton, 1971.

AVOCATIONAL INTERESTS: Italian language and linguistics.†

(Died March 22, 1976)

*   *   *

DENDY, Marshall C(oleman) 1902-

PERSONAL: Born June 4, 1902, in Lavonia, Ga.; son of Samuel Knox (a merchant) and Josey (Wilkes) Dendy; married Nan Copeland, June 30, 1926; children: Nancy Elizabeth (Mrs. Dallas M. Ryle, Jr.), Marshall Coleman, Jr. *Education:* Presbyterian College, Clinton, S.C., A.B., 1923; Columbia Seminary, Decatur, Ga., B.D., 1926; University of Tennessee, M.A., 1943. *Politics:* Independent. *Home:* 1717 Gay Dr., Orlando, Fla. 32803.

CAREER: Ordained minister of Presbyterian Church, 1926; pastor in Crawfordville, Ga., 1926-28, Newberry, S.C., 1928-31, Gainesville, Ga., 1931-38, Knoxville, Tenn., 1938-42, Orlando, Fla., 1945-52; Presbyterian Church of the United States, Board of Christian Education, Richmond, Va., executive secretary, 1953-68; interim pastor of First Presbyterian Church, Thomasville, Ga., 1970, Bristol, Tenn., 1971-72. Moderator, Presbyterian Synod of Florida, 1948, General Assembly of Presbyterian Church of the United States, 1967. Chairman of Department of Christian Education, National Council of Churches of Christ; lecturer at World Council of Christian Education, Tokyo, 1958. President of Orlando (Fla.) Community Chest, 1950; trustee of Agnes Scott College. *Member:* Kiwanis Club (president, Gainesville, Ga., 1937, and Orlando, Fla., 1950).

WRITINGS: Changing Patterns in Christian Education, John Knox, 1964; *A Study of the Catechism: The Westminster Shorter Catechism for Families,* CLC Press, 1966.

AVOCATIONAL INTERESTS: Music, hunting, golf.

*   *   *

den HOLLANDER, A(rie) Nicolaas Jan 1906-1976

PERSONAL: Born April 23, 1906, in Rotterdam, Netherlands; son of Paul (director of a municipal department) and Maria C. E. (Mighorst) den Hollander. *Education:* University of Amsterdam, Ph.D., 1933. *Religion:* Protestant. *Home:* 46 Watteaustraat, Amsterdam, Netherlands. *Office:*

American Institute, Jodenbreestrasse 9, Amsterdam, Netherlands.

CAREER: University of Amsterdam, Amsterdam, Netherlands, professor of sociology and American studies, beginning 1946, and director of America Institute. Visiting professor at University of Chicago, Northwestern University, University of California, and ten other American universities, and at universities in France, Switzerland, Germany, Norway, Sweden, Austria, Rumania, Italy, and Belgium. Head of UNESCO Social Science Team in Pakistan, 1952-53; president of UNESCO Centre of the Netherlands; member of bureau, UNESCO Committee of the Netherlands. Trustee, Academy for Physical Education. *Member:* International Sociological Association (vice-president, 1956-59), Sociological Association of the Netherlands (president, 1957-63), European Association for American Studies (chairman, beginning 1968). *Awards, honors:* Knight, Order of Pro Deo et Patria.

WRITINGS—Indexed in some sources under surname Hollander: *De Landelijke Arme Blanken in het Zuiden der Verenigde Staten* (title means "The Rural 'Poor Whites' in the Southern United States"), Wolters, 1933; *Het Andere Volk* (booklet; title means "As Others See Us"), Sijthoff, 1946; *Nederzettingsvormen en -problemen in de Grote Hongaarse Laagvlakte* (title means "Patterns of Settlement in the Great Hungarian Plain"), Meulenhoff, 1947; *Mens en Wereldhuishouding* (title means "Resource Patterns and Man"), Ensie, 1948; (co-editor) *Drift en Koers,* Van Gorcum, 1962; (with M. A. Klompe and S. Groenman) *25 Jaar Nederlandse Sociologische Vereniging,* Van Gorcum, 1964; (with O. D. van den Muijzenberg, J. D. Spechmann, and W. F. Wertheim) *De Plurale Samenleving: Begripzonder Toekomst?,* J. A. Boom, 1966; *Visie en Verwoording* (title means "Perception and Verbalization"), Van Gorcum, 1968; (editor with Sigmund Skard) *American Civilisation: An Introduction,* Longmans, Green, 1968; *Americana,* J. S. Boom, 1970; (editor) *Diverging Parallels: A Comparison of American and European Thought and Action,* E. J. Brill, 1971; (editor) *Contagious Conflict: The Impact of American Dissent on European Life,* E. J. Brill, 1973; *De verbeeldingswereld van Edgar Allan Poe en enkele tijdgenoten,* Athenaeum-Polak & Van Gennep, 1974.

Contributor: W. T. Couch, editor, *Culture in the South,* University of North Carolina Press, 1933; K. F. Proost and J. Romein, editors, *Geestelijk Nederland, 1920-1940,* Kosmos, 1949; *De Wereld der Mensen,* Wolters, 1953; *Het Leven,* University of Ghent, 1960; A. Silbermann, editor, *Militanter Humanismus,* Fischer (Frankfurt), 1966; *La Sociologia Contemporanea nell' Europa Occidentale a nelle Americhe,* [Rome], 1967; D. G. Jongmans and P.C.W. Gutkind, *Anthropologists in the Field,* Van Gorcum, 1967. Contributor of about forty articles to Dutch, French, German, Italian, American, and Spanish journals and magazines; occasional contributor of articles and reviews to newspapers. Co-editor, *Mens en Maatschappij* and *Sociologia Neerlandica.*

WORK IN PROGRESS: Research on the image of the United States in various European countries since 1783.

SIDELIGHTS: Arie Nicolaas Jan den Hollander's travels covered all of Europe, and parts of the United States, Canada, Asia, and North Africa. *Avocational interests:* Collecting art and antiques.†

(Died June 16, 1976)

de ROBECK, Nesta   1886-

PERSONAL: Born July 28, 1886, in Eastbourne, England; daughter of Charles and Elinor Parry (Oreden) de Robeck. *Education:* Educated privately. *Religion:* Roman Catholic. *Home:* Borgo Aretino 7, Assisi, Italy.

WRITINGS: Music of the Italian Renaissance, Medici Society (London), 1928; *Among the Franciscan Tertiaries,* Dent, 1929, Dutton, 1930; *The Christmas Crib,* Burns & Oates, 1938, Bruce Publishing, 1956; *St. Clare of Assisi,* Bruce Publishing, 1951; *Saint Elizabeth of Hungary: A Story of Twenty-Four Years,* Bruce Publishing, 1954; *Padre Pio,* Bruce Publishing, 1958; *Vico Necchi,* Franciscan Herald, 1960; *St. Francis of Assisi, His Holy Life and Love of Poverty,* Franciscan Herald, 1964; (compiler) *Praise the Lord* (anthology), Franciscan Herald, 1967.

* * *

DETHERAGE, May   1908-

PERSONAL: Born July 5, 1908, in Lebanon, Mo.; daughter of Marion Walker (in construction) and Nellie Belle (Jones) Detherage. *Education:* Southwestern Baptist Theological Seminary, Diploma in Christian Training, 1929; Mississippi Women's College (now William Carey College), B.A., 1932. *Religion:* Southern Baptist. *Home:* 3438 Masonic Dr., Apt. 111, Alexandria, La. 71301.

CAREER: Manager of Baptist book stores in Phoenix, Ariz., 1943-44, Alexandria, La., 1948-52, and New Orleans, La., 1952-73. *Member:* New Orleans Librarians Association, Profetts (New Orleans Seminary; past president). *Awards, honors:* Alumnus of the Year, William Carey College, 1966.

WRITINGS: (Compiler) *Sunrise to Starlight,* Abingdon, 1966. Writer of booklet, "Planning Your Wedding," published by C. R. Gibson, 1950.

* * *

DETJEN, Ervin W(infred)   1909-

PERSONAL: Born January 24, 1909, in Green Bay, Wis.; son of August Charles and Jennie (Lages) Detjen; married Mary Elizabeth Ford, June 14, 1938; children: Ervin W., Jr. *Education:* University of Illinois, B.S., 1931; University of Louisville, M.A., 1946. *Politics:* Independent. *Religion:* Methodist. *Home:* 1956 Deer Park Ave., Louisville, Ky.

CAREER: Louisville (Ky.) public schools, junior high school teacher of industrial arts, 1931-46, elementary school principal, 1946-71, principal of Hazelwood Elementary School, 1958-71. University of Louisville, lecturer in elementary education and guidance, 1947-60. Member of board of directors, Children's Theatre of Louisville. *Member:* National Education Association, Association for Supervision and Curriculum Development, Kentucky Education Association, Kappa Phi Kappa, Kappa Delta Pi, Tau Kappa Epsilon, Masons, Shrine.

WRITINGS: Home Room Guidance Programs for the Junior High School Years, Houghton, 1940; *Your Plans for the Future,* McGraw, 1947; *Your High School Days,* McGraw, 1947, revised edition, 1958; *Elementary School Guidance,* McGraw, 1952, revised edition, 1963; *So You're in High School,* Whittlesey House, 1958; *Orientacion Educacional en la Escuela Primaria,* Editorial Kapelusz (Buenos Aires), 1959. Contributor to *Child-Family Digest, Better Homes and Gardens.*

AVOCATIONAL INTERESTS: Fishing, swimming, hunting, archery, music, woodcraft, building construction, and furniture-making.

BIOGRAPHICAL/CRITICAL SOURCES: Better Homes and Gardens, April, 1950; *Louisville Courier-Journal,* May 17, 1952, May 1, 1958, May 17, 1963.

* * *

DETZ, Phyllis 1911-

PERSONAL: Born January 9, 1911, in Marysville, Pa.; daughter of Gerald A. and Rena (Heany) Dissinger; married J. Ernest Detz (a banker), June 4, 1938; children: Deborah (Mrs. Phillip Friday). *Education:* Millersville State College, B.S., 1954; Pennsylvania State University, M.Ed., 1961. *Politics:* Republican. *Religion:* Protestant. *Home:* 317 Maple Ave., Marysville, Pa. 17053.

CAREER: Social studies teacher in Marietta, Pa., 1930-34, in Marysville, Pa., 1934-54; junior and senior high school librarian in Duncannon, Pa., 1954-61; West Shore School District, Lemoyne, Pa., library coordinator, 1961-70. *Member:* National Education Association (life member).

WRITINGS: (Editor and compiler with Kermit M. Stover) *On This Day* (poetry and prose anthology), J. G. Ferguson, 1970.

* * *

DEVADUTT, Vinjamuri E(verett) 1908-

PERSONAL: Born December 16, 1908, in Pithapuram, India; came to United States in 1953, naturalized in 1963; son of Ramaniya V. and Krishna Veni (Swyampakala) Vinjamuri; married Sushila Silas (a public school teacher), June 19, 1934; children: Sudhir (son), Sumati (Mrs. Alec Hazlett), Premanjali (Mrs. Joseph Stulberg). *Education:* Serampore College, B.D., 1931; Andhra University, M.A., 1936; Victoria University, Th.D., 1949. *Politics:* Registered Democrat. *Home:* 77 Highland Pkwy., Rochester, N.Y. 14620.

CAREER: Clergyman of American Baptist Convention. University of Nagpur, Hislop College, Nagpur, India, lecturer, later assistant professor of philosophy, 1937-39; Serampore College, Serampore India, professor of philosophy and history of religions, 1940-53, chairman of department of philosophy and dean of theology, 1950-53; Princeton University, Princeton, N.J., visiting professor of religion, 1953-54; Ohio Wesleyan University, Delaware, professor of religion, 1954-56; Colgate Rochester Divinity School, Rochester, N.Y., professor of ecumenical theology, 1956-74. Part-time professor of religion, University of Rochester, beginning 1956; visiting fellow, Manchester College, Oxford, spring, 1969. Member of board of managers, commission on missionary education of National Council of Churches, beginning 1963, and American Baptist Foreign Mission Society, 1963-68. Co-chairman, Committee of Protestants and Catholics of Rochester on Ecumenism. *Member:* Association for Asian Studies, American Oriental Society, Asia Society, American Association for the United Nations. *Awards, honors:* D.D., Acadia University, 1954.

WRITINGS: (Contributor) Allan Richardson, editor, *Biblical Authority for Today,* S.C.M. Press, 1950, Westminster, 1952; (contributor) Donald Bailey, editor, *Inter-Communion,* S.C.M. Press, 1952; (contributor) Philip Maurey, editor, *History's Lessons for Tomorrow's Mission,* World's Student Christian Federation, 1959; *The Bible and Faith of Men,* Friendship, 1967. Contributor to professional journals and religious publications. Editor, *Indian Journal of Theology,* 1950-54.

WORK IN PROGRESS: A history of Hinduism.

DEVER, Joseph 1919-1970

PERSONAL: Surname rhymes with "never"; born September 1, 1919, in Somerville, Mass.; son of Bernard James (a salesman) and Rosealeen (Feeney) Dever; married Margaret Kermode (a college professor), June 10, 1945; children: Gregory Joseph, Miriam Therese, Monica Margaret, Catherine, Elizabeth. *Education:* Boston College, B.A., 1942. *Politics:* Registered Democrat. *Religion:* Roman Catholic.

CAREER: Bruce Publishing Co., Milwaukee, Wis., assistant fiction editor, 1946-48; Archdiocese of Chicago, administrative assistant and speech writer for Bishop Bernard J. Sheil, 1949-51; Building Service International Union, president of Local 397, 1953-55; *Horsemen's Journal,* assistant editor, 1955-58; Massachusetts Registrar of Motor Vehicles, public relations assistant, 1958-62; *Boston Sunday Herald,* Boston, Mass., feature writer, beginning, 1963; *Philadelphia Bulletin,* Philadelphia, Pa., society editor. Author, 1947-70. Editorial consultant to Cardinal Cushing, 1963-64; public relations consultant to Commonwealth of Massachusetts and City of Boston Park Department. *Military service:* U.S. Army Air Forces, 1942-46; editor of camp newspaper and *Yank* correspondent. *Member:* Newspaper guild. *Awards, honors:* First prize in world-wide *Yank* Short Story Contest, 1944, for "Fifty Missions"; Funk & Wagnalls literary fellowship to Bread Loaf Writers' Conference, 1957.

WRITINGS: No Lasting Home (novel), Bruce, 1947; *A Certain Widow* (novel), Bruce, 1951; *Three Priests* (novel), Doubleday, 1958; *Cushing of Boston: A Candid Portrait* (biography), Humphries, 1965; (with Stewart L. Udall) *National Parks of America,* Putnam, 1966; (with others) *This Treasured Land,* Putnam, 1966. Short story, "Fifty Missions," was anthologized in *The Best from Yank,* Dutton, and *Our Father's House,* Sheed; it was also adapted by the author for television, and produced on the "Catholic Hour," National Broadcasting System, 1954. Contributor of critical articles to anthologies of current fiction, and verse to *New York Times* and *America.*

WORK IN PROGRESS: A nonfiction book, *Old Boston Churches.*†

(Died December 13, 1970)

* * *

DEWEY, Godfrey 1887-

PERSONAL: Born September 3, 1887, in New York, N.Y.; son of Melvil (a librarian, creator of Dewey Decimal Classification System, and executive) and Annie (Godfrey) Dewey; married Marjorie Kinne, May 28, 1914 (deceased); children: Kinne (deceased), Katharin (Mrs. H. Winthrop Martin), Arthur Kinne (deceased), Margaret, Stuart Kinne (deceased). *Education:* Harvard University, A.B., 1909, Ed.M., 1921, Ed.D., 1926. *Politics:* Republican (conservative). *Religion:* Episcopalian. *Home:* White Pines, Lake Placid Club, N.Y. 12946. *Office:* Lake Placid Education Foundation, Lake Placid Club, N.Y. 12946.

CAREER: Lake Placid Co., Lake Placid Club, N.Y., various executive positions, 1909-62; Dewey Shorthand Corp., Lake Placid Club, president and treasurer, 1937-71; Forest Press, Inc., Lake Placid Club, president, 1951-61. Lake Placid Education Foundation (founded by his father), trustee, beginning 1924, vice-president, 1924-32, and beginning 1957; Emerson College, trustee, 1940-51, president, 1949-51; chairman of board, Northwood School, 1954-59. Secretary, Simplified Spelling Board, 1921-46. III Olympic Winter Games, Lake Placid, 1932, president of organizing committee, 1929-32. *Military service:* U.S. Army, Engineers, 1918; became captain.

MEMBER: National Education Association, International Reading Association, Simpler Spelling Association, Phonemic Spelling Council, National Shorthand Reporters Association (honorary member), New York State Shorthand Reporters Association (honorary member), Phi Delta Kappa, American Legion, Masons, Grange. *Awards, honors:* Freedoms Foundation Award, 1950; named to National Ski Hall of Fame, 1970.

WRITINGS: Personal Shorthand (basic text), World Book Co., 1922; *Personal Shorthand Reader,* World Book Co., 1922; *Personal Shorthand Exercises,* World Book Co., 1922; *Demotic Shorthand Compend,* Forest Press, 1923; *Demotic Shorthand Reader,* Forest Press, 1923; *Demotic Shorthand Examination,* Forest Press, 1923; *Irving's "Rip Van Winkle" Written in Personal Shorthand,* World Book Co., 1923; *English Heterografy, or How We Spel!,* Simplified Spelling Board, 1923, published as *How We Spell!,* Lake Placid Club Education Foundation, 1968; *Relativ Frequency of English Speech Sounds,* (Volume IV, "Harvard Studies in Education"), Harvard University Press, 1923, revised, enlarged edition, 1950.

General Shorthand (basic text), Personal Shorthand Corp., 1936; *The GS Teacher,* Personal Shorthand Corp., 1936; *The GS Reader,* Personal Shorthand Corp., 1936; *Script Shorthand* (basic text), General Shorthand Corp., 1938; *Script Shorthand Exercises,* General Shorthand Corp., 1938; *Script Shorthand Teacher,* General Shorthand Corp., 1938; *Script Shorthand Dictation Course,* General Shorthand Corp., 1939; *Script Shorthand Dictation Course: Teacher's Handbook,* General Shorthand Corp., 1939.

Supplementary Dictation Exercises, General Shorthand Corp., 1940; *Supplementary Dictation Exercises: Teacher's Handbook,* General Shorthand Corp., 1940; *Script Shorthand Dictionary,* General Shorthand Corp., 1941; *Script Shorthand Penmanship,* General Shorthand Corp., 1942; *Dewey Shorthand at a Glance,* Dewey Shorthand Corp., 1947; *Dewey Shorthand Basic Text,* Dewey Shorthand Corp., 1947; *Dewey Shorthand Workbooks,* Dewey Shorthand Corp., 1947; *Dewey Shorthand Teacher,* Dewey Shorthand Corp., 1947; *Dewey Shorthand Dictation Course,* Dewey Shorthand Corp., 1948; *Dewey Shorthand Dictation Course: Teacher's Handbook,* Dewey Shorthand Corp., 1948; *Dewey Shorthand for Personal Use,* Dewey Shorthand Corp., 1949.

World English Spelling Dictionary, Simpler Spelling Association, 1969; *Relative Frequency of English Spellings,* Teachers College Press, 1970; *English Spelling: Roadblock to Reading,* Teachers College Press, 1971.

Editor, *Dewey Decimal Classification and Relative Index,* 15th edition, revised, Forest Press, 1951, and 7th abridged edition, 1952. Contributor of articles, chiefly on spelling reform, shorthand, and winter sports to magazines and professional journals. Editor, *Script Shorthand News, Dewey Shorthand News,* and *The Scribe,* 1938-46.

WORK IN PROGRESS: Phonemic notations as initial teaching media.

SIDELIGHTS: Godfrey Dewey's lifelong interest in spelling reform and related aspects of education goes back to his father, who in 1876 was chiefly responsible for formation of the American Library Association as well as the Spelling Reform Association. He also has been influenced, he noted, by a thirty-five year association with Sir James Pitman, au-

thor of the initial teaching alphabet and grandson of Sir Isaac Pitman, "the outstanding spelling reformer as well as shorthand inventor of the 19th century in Great Britain."

* * *

DEWEY, Irene Sargent 1896-

PERSONAL: Born July 3, 1896, in Broken Bow, Neb.; daughter of Randall Benedict (a farmer) and Elizabeth (Chrisman) Sargent; married Alan Scott Dewey, June 12, 1922; children: Alan, Douglas, Tom, Dorothy Dewey Tyrrell, Dennis (deceased). *Education:* University of Nebraska, B.S. in Ed., 1964. *Politics:* Republican. *Religion:* Methodist. *Home:* 745 North F St., Broken Bow, Neb. 68822.

CAREER: Elementary teacher for 37 years in rural and town schools in Nebraska, including Custer County, Scottsbluff County, Thomas County, Franklin County, and Adams County; elementary teacher, Kenesaw, Neb., beginning 1966. *Member:* Chaparral Poets, Nebraska Ars Poetica.

WRITINGS: Mulberry Musings (poems), A. Swallow, 1964.

AVOCATIONAL INTERESTS: Music.††

* * *

DEWHURST, J(ames) Frederic 1895-1967

PERSONAL: Born March 23, 1895, in Seattle, Wash.; son of Clarence Eli (a businessman) and Sara Seeley (Robertson) Dewhurst; married Julie Gill, July 1, 1949 (died, 1962); children: (previous marriage) John Richard. *Education:* University of Washington, Seattle, B.S., 1918; University of Pennsylvania, M.A., 1922, Ph.D., 1928.

CAREER: University of Pennsylvania, Philadelphia, 1920-30, began as instructor, professor of industry, 1929-30; director of economic research for Federal Reserve Bank of Philadelphia, Philadelphia, Pa., 1921-28, for U.S. Department of Commerce, Washington, D.C., 1930-32; economist with American Iron and Steel Institute, New York, N.Y., 1933, and Twentieth Century Fund, New York, N.Y., 1933-35; Social Science Research Council, New York, N.Y., director of Commission on Social Security, 1935-37, staff consultant, 1937-45; Twentieth Century Fund, economist, 1937-53, executive director, 1953-56, economic adviser and director of survey of Europe's needs and resources, 1957-60, and later trustee. Lecturer in marketing at University of Pennsylvania, 1941-42. Technical adviser to American delegation at International Conference on Government Statistics, League of Nations, 1928, and at World Economic Conference, 1932. *Military service:* U.S. Army, Cavalry, World War I; served with American Expeditionary Forces; became captain.

MEMBER: American Economic Association, American Statistical Association (fellow), American Academy of Arts and Sciences (fellow), Cosmos Club (Washington, D.C.), Army and Navy Club (New York). *Awards, honors:* Elected to Distribution Hall of Fame; Paul D. Converse Award, 1957; D.Sc., University of Pennsylvania, 1962.

WRITINGS: (With J. H. S. Bossard) *University Education for Business,* Press of the University of Pennsylvania, 1931; (with P. W. Stewart) *Does Distribution Cost Too Much?,* Twentieth Century Fund, 1939; (with others) *America's Needs and Resources,* Twentieth Century Fund, 1947, updated edition, 1955; (with others) *Europe's Needs and Resources,* Twentieth Century Fund, 1961; *The New Europe and Its Economic Future,* Macmillan, 1964. Also writer of articles and reports on economic subjects.†

(Died May 27, 1967)

DIACK, Hunter 1908-1974

PERSONAL: Born October 5, 1908, in Kemnay, Aberdeenshire, Scotland; son of James Adam (a tailor) and Margaret (Hunter) Diack; married Elsie Jones, December 14, 1947; children: Anne Denise, James Hunter. *Education:* University of Aberdeen, M.A. (first class honors), 1930. *Home:* 12 Derby Rd., Bramcote, Nottinghamshire, England. *Office:* Institute of Education, University of Nottingham, University Park, Nottingham, England.

CAREER: University of Nottingham, Institute of Education, Nottingham, England, senior tutor, 1950-74. Member of national advisory council, Reading Reform Foundation (United States; only member outside North America), 1967-1974. Director, Ray Palmer Ltd. (publishers), Nottingham. *Military service:* Royal Air Force, 1940-46. *Member:* Association of University Teachers.

WRITINGS: (With R. F. Mackenzie) *Road Fortune: A Cycle Journey through Europe*, Macmillan, 1935.

(With J. C. Daniels) "Royal Road Readers" series, twelve books, teacher's book, eighteen supplementaries, Chatto & Windus, 1954-58; *Royal Road Reader Card Apparatus*, Philip & Tracy, 1955; *Learning and Teaching English Grammar*, Chatto & Windus, 1956; *How Words Work*, Chatto & Windus, 1956; (with Daniels) *Progress in Reading*, Institute of Education, University of Nottingham, 1956; (with Daniels) *Standard Reading Tests*, Chatto & Windus, 1958, revised edition, 1960.

Reading and the Psychology of Perception, Peter Skinner, 1960; (with Daniels) *Progress in Reading in the Infants School*, Institute of Education, University of Nottingham, 1960; *The Flying Wonder* (juvenile), Peter Skinner, 1961; *Thinking in Numbers*, Peter Skinner, 1961; *The Alphabet Word Book*, Chatto & Windus, 1963; *Arithmetic in the Decimal Age*, Ray Palmer, 1963; *Boy in a Village* (autobiographical), Ray Palmer, 1963; *Improve Your English*, three books, New English Library, 1965; *That Village on the Don* (autobiographical), Ray Palmer, 1965; *The Teaching of Reading*, Philosophical Library, 1965 (published in England as *In Spite of the Alphabet: A Study in the Teaching of Reading*, Chatto & Windus, 1965); *Learning to Talk and to Read*, British Medical Association, 1966; *Language for Teaching*, Chatto & Windus, 1966; (contributor) Carl Friedrich Schmitt, editor, *Die Lese Synthese*, Moritz Diesterweg, 1966; *Writing: The Easy Way*, Transworld, 1967; *Spelling: The Easy Way*, Transworld, 1967; *Study: The Easy Way*, Transworld, 1967; *101 Aids to Exam Success*, Dickens Press, 1967.

Beneath the Visited Moon, privately printed, 1973; *Short of the Margin*, privately printed, 1973; *The First R*, privately printed, 1974; *Improving Your Spelling*, privately printed, 1974; *Standard Literacy Tests: A Measure of Vocabulary*, Hart-Davis, 1975, published as *Test Your Own Wordpower: Your Vocabulary and Its Measurement*, Paladin Books, 1975; *Literacy Tests for Schools*, Hart-Davis, 1975; *Speaking and Reading* (booklet), British Medical Association, 1975.

Contributor to newspapers and journals. London correspondent, *Scottish Educational Journal;* radio critic, *Times Educational Supplement;* dramatic critic, *Spectator.* Former editor, *Further Education;* joint editor, *North-East Review.*

SIDELIGHTS: Hunter Diack told *CA*: "The obscure village I was brought up in Aberdeenshire had a very close contacts with America. Granite workers used to commute between the village and America. As a young student, travelled a great deal in Europe and America, financed chiefly by travel articles.... Cycled 2,000 miles in New York State, Quebec, Ontario, and subsequently through France, Italy, and Germany.

"Although I greatly enjoyed writing the light-hearted biographies, *Boy in a Village* and *That Village on the Don,* my greatest satisfaction has come from writing *Language for Teaching,* which I hope will have some influence in reducing the amount of word-mongering that goes on in the name of education."†

(Died December 12, 1974)

*   *   *

DICKASON, David Howard 1907-1974

PERSONAL: Born August 21, 1907, in Wooster, Ohio; son of John Howard (a professor of Latin) and Blanche (Garrett) Dickason; married Marjorie Hicks (an art teacher), December 27, 1937; children: Christie (Mrs. Gary Waldhorn), Theresa (Mrs. John Cederholm), Cynthia. *Education:* College of Wooster, B.A., 1929; University of California, Berkeley, M.A., 1931; Ohio State University, Ph.D., 1940. *Politics:* Democrat. *Home:* 2301 Moore's Pike, Bloomington, Ind. 47401. *Office:* Department of English, Indiana University, Bloomington, Ind. 47401.

CAREER: Collegio Americano, Barranquilla, Colombia, instructor in English, 1929-30; Prince Royal's College, Chiangmai, Thailand, instructor in English, 1931-35; Rangoon University, Rangoon, Burma, instructor in English, 1935-36; Indiana University, Bloomington, instructor, 1939-44, assistant professor, 1944-48, associate professor, 1948-53, professor of English, 1953-74. Director of orientation programs for foreign students, Institute of International Education,1950-54. Visiting professor of American literature, San Marcos University, Lima, Peru, 1961. Technical adviser, Ministry of Education, Bangkok, 1956-58. *Military service:* U.S. Office of Strategic Services, Liaison Officer for Research and Secret Intelligence branches of Far East Division, 1944-46; received Certificate of Merit.

MEMBER: Modern Language Association of America, American Studies Association, Phi Beta Kappa, Delta Sigma Rho. *Awards, honors:* Huntington Library research grant, 1943; Guggenheim fellowship, 1954-55; American Philosophical Society grant, 1959-60; Smith-Mundt State Department grant for teaching in Peru, 1961; Fulbright senior research fellowship to England, 1963-64.

WRITINGS: The Daring Young Men: The Story of the American Pre-Raphaelites, Indiana University Press, 1953; *Introduction to Literature in English*, Thai Ministry of Education, 1958; (editor) William Williams, *Mr. Penrose: The Journal of Penrose Seaman*, Indiana University Press, 1969; *William Williams: Novelist and Painter of Colonial America, 1727-1792*, Indiana University Press, 1970.

Photographer: W. A. R. Wood, *Land of Smiles*, [Bangkok], 1935; H. G. Deignan, *Birds of Northern Thailand*, Smithsonian Institution Press, 1945.

Assistant editor, "Research Monographs" series, Indiana University Press. Also contributor of articles to art, literature, and history journals, and contributor of photographs to national periodicals, including *Asia, National Geographic,* and *Travel.*

WORK IN PROGRESS: Collecting writings of artist and author Rembrandt Peale, for a biography; a critical anthology of the literature of the Caribbean.

AVOCATIONAL INTERESTS: Gardening, travel, theater.†

(Died April, 1974)

* * *

DICKERSON, William E(ugene)   1897-1971

PERSONAL: Born February 3, 1897, in Chicago, Ill.; son of William J. and Helen (Driscoll) Dickerson; married Lola Mayfield, June 28, 1923; children: William Eugene, Dale Mayfield. *Education:* University of Washington, Seattle, B.B.A., 1921, M.B.A., 1923; University of Chicago, Ph.D., 1926. *Home:* 265 East Schreyer Pl., Columbus, Ohio 43214. *Office:* Ohio State University, Columbus, Ohio 43210.

CAREER: University of Chicago, Chicago, Ill., instructor in accounting, 1926-27; University of Kentucky, Lexington, assistant professor, 1927-28; University of Pittsburgh, Uniontown, Pa., assistant professor, 1928-29; Ohio State University, Columbus, associate professor, 1929-46, professor of accounting, 1946-66, professor emeritus, 1966-71. Visiting professor at University of Hawaii, 1963, University of Colorado, 1964, Florida Atlantic University, 1966, and Western Washington State College, 1967. Certified public accountant in Ohio, 1933-71. *Member:* American Accounting Association (vice-president, 1961-62), National Accounting Association, American Institute of Certified Public Accountants, Financial Executives Institute of America, Ohio Society of Certified Public Accountants (past director), Beta Alpha Psi (national president, 1951).

WRITINGS: (With J. Weldon Jones) *Ohio C.P.A. Problems and Solutions,* Ohio State University Bookstore, 1931, revised edition (with William B. Jencks and Richard C. Rea), Tri-State Offset, 1946; (with J. Brooks Heckert) *Drug Store Accounting,* McGraw, 1943; (with Horace W. Domigan) *Tax Accounting: State and Local Taxes,* W. C. Brown, 1951; (with Leo D. Stone) *Federal Income Tax Fundamentals,* Wadsworth, 1961, 3rd edition, 1968. Contributor to professional journals. Past editor, *Ohio Certified Public Accountant.*†

(Died July 13, 1971)

* * *

DICKINSON, (William) Stirling   1909-

PERSONAL: Born December 22, 1909, in Chicago, Ill.; son of Francis Reynolds (a lawyer) and Alice May (Stirling) Dickinson. *Education:* Princeton University, B.A. (cum laude), 1931; studied art at Art Institute of Chicago, three years, and at Fontainebleau School of Fine Arts in France. *Politics:* Democrat. *Religion:* Episcopalian. *Home:* Santo Domingo 38, San Miguel de Allende, Guanajuato, Mexico. *Office:* Allende Institute, San Miguel de Allende, Guanajuato, Mexico.

CAREER: University School of Fine Arts, San Miguel de Allende, Guanajuato, Mexico, associate director, 1938-51; Allende Institute (college-level school of arts, crafts, writing, and Spanish), San Miguel de Allende, president and director, beginning 1951. Has exhibited work at Art Institute of Chicago and in Mexico. Public lecturer on Mexico and his travels elsewhere; speaker at world orchid conferences in Medellin, Colombia, Long Beach, Calif., and Frankfort, Germany. San Miguel de Allende baseball team, manager, beginning 1937, and former player; member of board of

directors, San Miguel de Allende Hospital. *Wartime service:* Civilian posts overseas with U.S. Naval Intelligence and U.S. Office of Strategic Services during World War II. *Member:* San Miguel Garden Club (president), Audubon Society (member of board), San Miguel Social Club (manager), 24 Hour Association (president), Malanquin Golf Club (secretary). *Awards, honors:* Adopted son of San Miguel, 1942; Lane Bryant Award, 1970, for outstanding contributions by an American living abroad in field of social welfare, international relations.

WRITINGS: (Author with Heath Bowman, and illustrator with woodcuts) *Mexican Odyssey,* Willett Clark, 1935; (author with Bowman, and illustrator with woodcuts) *Westward from Rio,* Willett Clark, 1936; (with Bowman) *Death Is Incidental: A Story of Revolution,* Willett Clark, 1937; (with Tom Scott) *San Miguel de Allende,* Brandenburgh Press, 1971. Translator of *Imperial Cuzco* by Cossio del Pomar, 1940. Contributor to *AOS Bulletin* (publication of American Orchid Society) and other orchid periodicals.

SIDELIGHTS: Dickinson has made four hiking trips in Nepal and traveled extensively in Africa, South America, Thailand, Australia, New Guinea, and other countries. He has the largest orchid collection in Mexico, gathered personally on travels as well as through exchange with orchid fanciers all over the world.

* * *

DIEKHOFF, John S(iemon)   1905-1976

PERSONAL: Born October 23, 1905, in Ann Arbor, Mich.; son of Tobias J. C. (a professor) and Julia (Schacht) Diekhoff; married Vera Johnston (an editor), December 18, 1929. *Education:* University of Michigan, A.B., 1926, M.A., 1927; Oxford University, graduate study, 1927-28; Western Reserve University (now Case Western Reserve University), Ph.D., 1937. *Home:* 3102 Van Aken Blvd., Shaker Heights, Ohio 44120.

CAREER: University of Michigan, Ann Arbor, instructor in rhetoric, 1928-29; Oberlin College, Oberlin, Ohio, instructor in English, 1929-40; Queens College (now Queens College of the City University of New York), Flushing, N.Y., assistant professor, 1940-48, associate professor of English, 1948-53; Hunter College (now Hunter College of the City University of New York), New York, N.Y., professor of education and director of Office of Institutional Research, 1953-56; Western Reserve University (now Case Western Reserve University), Cleveland, Ohio, professor and dean of Cleveland College, 1956-63; University of Michigan, Center for the Study of Higher Education, professor of higher education, 1963-65; Case Western Reserve University, professor of English, 1965-70, professor emeritus, 1970-76, chairman of department, 1968-70, associate dean of the Faculty of Arts and Sciences, 1965-67, acting dean of the Graduate School, 1967, vice-provost, 1967-70, member of board of overseers, 1976. Lecturer and director of Center for the Study of Liberal Education for Adults, University of Chicago, 1951-53. Research consultant, City of New York Board of Higher Education, 1947-48, 1950-51. Member of Commission on Colleges and Secondary Schools, North Central Association of Colleges and Secondary Schools, 1958-67; member of board of advisers, American Foundation for Continuing Education, 1967-71. Member, Cuyahoga County Welfare Commission Task Force on Dental Health, 1969. *Military service:* U.S. Army, 1943-46; became captain.

MEMBER: Modern Language Association of America (chairman of commission on trends in education, 1965-68),

Milton Society of America (president, 1957-58), National Council of Teachers of English (vice-chairman of committee on education of college teachers, 1960-63). *Awards, honors:* Rockefeller Foundation postwar fellowship in humanities, 1947-48; L.H.D., Rutgers University, 1959; Honored Scholar, Milton Society of America, 1970.

WRITINGS: (Editor) *Milton on Himself,* Oxford University Press, 1939, reprinted, Humanities, 1965; *Milton's "Paradise Lost": A Commentary on the Argument,* Columbia University Press, 1946; *Democracy's College,* Harper, 1950; *The Domain of the Faculty,* Harper, 1956; (with Marjorie B. Smiley) *Prologue to Teaching,* Oxford University Press, 1959; *Tomorrow's Professors,* Fund for the Advancement of Education, 1959; (contributor) *On Teaching Adults* (anthology), Center for the Study of Liberal Education for Adults, 1960; (contributor) Van Cleve Morris, editor, *Becoming an Educator,* Houghton, 1963; *NDEA and Modern Foreign Languages,* Modern Language Association of America, 1965; (author of foreword) James Holly Hanford, *John Milton: Poet and Humanist,* Press of Western Reserve University, 1966; (editor) *A Maske at Ludlow,* Press of Case Western Reserve University, 1968; (with Ida Long Rogers) *Private Higher Education in Tennessee,* Tennessee Council of Private Colleges, 1970.

Member of editorial board, *Complete Prose Works of John Milton,* Yale University Press, 1948-60, 1965-76. Contributor of more than fifty articles on English literature and education to professional journals; contributor of poem to *Milton Quarterly;* also contributor to *Saturday Review.* Editorial consultant, *Journal of Higher Education,* 1950-61; member of editorial board, *Journal of General Education,* 1963-71.

BIOGRAPHICAL/CRITICAL SOURCES: Milton Quarterly, Volume IV, number 2, 1970; Joseph Anthony Wittreich, Jr., editor, *Calm of Mind: Tercentenary Essays on "Paradise Regained" and "Samson Agonistes" in Honor of John S. Diekhoff,* Press of Case Western Reserve University, 1971.†

(Died August 20, 1976)

* * *

DIGGES, Sister Mary Laurentia 1910-

PERSONAL: Born August 16, 1910, in Roswell, N.M.; daughter of John (a printer) and Mary Adele (Bryan) Digges. *Education:* Mount St. Mary's College, Los Angeles, Calif., B.A., 1945; Catholic University of America, M.A., 1949, Ph.D., 1952. *Politics:* Democrat. *Home and office:* Mount St. Mary's College, 12001 Chalon Rd., Los Angeles, Calif. 90049.

CAREER: Roman Catholic nun, member of Congregation St. Joseph. Teacher in parochial grammar and high schools; Mount St. Mary's College, Los Angeles, Calif., professor of English, beginning 1952, chairman of department, beginning 1964. *Member:* Modern Language Association of America, College English Association. *Awards, honors:* First prize ($1,000) in literary contest sponsored jointly by Thomas More Association and Farrar, Straus & Cudahy, 1957, for manuscript of *Transfigured World.*

WRITINGS: Transfigured World, Farrar, Straus, 1957; *Adam's Haunted Sons,* Volume I, Macmillan, 1966. Contributor of about twenty-five articles to professional and popular journals.

WORK IN PROGRESS: Volume II of *Adam's Haunted Sons;* a book of explications of modern poetry.

SIDELIGHTS: Three of her creative writing students won top prizes three consecutive years in the annual *Atlantic Monthly* contests for college students—with a first for poetry, 1962, for essay, 1963, and for short story, 1964.

BIOGRAPHICAL/CRITICAL SOURCES: Los Angeles Times, June 17, 1964, January 15, 1967.†

* * *

DILLENBECK, Marsden V.

PERSONAL: Born in Ghent, N.Y.; son of Andrew L. (a minister) and Stella (Whitbeck) Dillenbeck; married Winifred Purdy (an office manager), July 9, 1938. *Education:* Hamilton College, A.B., 1930; further study at New York College for Teachers (now State University of New York at Albany), summers, 1932-35, and Syracuse University Extension, 1937. *Politics:* Republican. *Religion:* Lutheran. *Office:* Language Arts Department, Rye High School, Rye, N.Y. 10580.

CAREER: Teacher of English at Hartwick Seminary (now Hartwick College), Oneonta, N.Y., 1930-34, in Potsdam, N.Y., 1935-37, and Hamilton, N.Y., 1937-42; principal in Ephratah, N.Y., 1934-35; Colgate University, Hamilton, head of Flight Division at U.S. Naval Flight School, 1942-44, university instructor in physics and English, 1944-46; Rye High School, Rye, N.Y., chairman of language arts department, beginning 1946. President, Rye Town Singers, 1949. *Member:* National Council of Teachers of English, New York State Education Association, Westchester County Teachers Association.

WRITINGS—Editor of textbook editions: (With Ellen Brooks) Kenneth Grahame, *The Wind in the Willows,* Scribner, 1964; (with Marion Warren) John Galsworthy, *A Man of Property,* Scribner, 1965; (with John C. Schweitzer) *Seven Novellas,* Scribner, 1966.

SIDELIGHTS: Dillenbeck has traveled in all parts of the United States, Canada, and Mexico, and in Europe, Turkey, and Africa. *Avocational interests:* Reading, playing poker, barbecuing.†

* * *

DIMMETTE, Celia (Puhr) 1896-

PERSONAL: Surname is pronounced Dim-*mette;* born September 21, 1896, in Brookings County, S.D.; daughter of Frank (a farmer) and Susanna (Miller) Puhr; married Charles L. Dimmette, January 21, 1918 (deceased). *Education:* Attended University of Akron and Actual Business College. *Home:* 131 Fairweather Lane, Fort Myers Beach, Fla. 33931.

CAREER: Poet. *Member:* Poetry Society of America, Ohio Poetry Society. *Awards, honors:* Lyric Award, Ohio Poetry Society, 1942, 1951, 1967; Midwestern Writers' Conference book award, 1948, for *Toward the Metal Sun;* Max Corman Award, Poetry Society of America, 1967.

WRITINGS—Poems: *Toward the Metal Sun,* Bruce H. Humphries, 1950; *Horizon Far as Ocean,* Amerian Weave Press, 1965; *The Winds Blow Promise,* Golden Quill, 1969; (editor) *Lake of Memory,* privately printed, 1969; (with Emily Dare Werner) *Time of Brave Men,* privately printed, 1969; (with Werner) *Hill Country Home,* privately printed, 1970.

WORK IN PROGRESS: A nonfiction book on the Midwest in the early twentieth century.

SIDELIGHTS: Celia Dimmette advises aspiring writers to

"keep working. Write and rewrite. Perfect your style. Reach into yourself and your own life for material."

* * *

DIXON, Marjorie (Mack) 1887-
(Marjorie Mack)

PERSONAL: Born April 17, 1887, in Norfolk, England; daughter of John (in British Army) and Henrietta (Packard) Mack; married Harold Dixon (a farmer), April 21, 1918; children: Jeremy, Nicholas. *Education:* Educated at Allenswood, Wimbledon Park, England, 1900-03; later took secretarial training in London. *Politics:* Conservative. *Religion:* Church of England ("nominally"). *Home:* Mere Hill Cottage, Merle Common, Oxted, Surrey, England.

CAREER: Worked as private secretary, four years for the foreign editor of the *Times,* London, England, and during his absences abroad, for Lovat Fraser, Lord Lloyd, and Lady Astor; reader of the foreign press (for publishers), 1916-19; after her marriage in 1918 went to live at Gincox Farm, Oxted, Surrey, England. Member of Unicorn Theatre Club, which specializes in plays for children. *Awards, honors:* First prize, British Drama League, 1932.

WRITINGS: The King of the Fiddles, Faber, 1941, Transatlantic, 1943; *Runaway Boy,* Faber, 1942, Transatlantic, 1943; (with Richard Kennedy) *The Green-Coated Boy,* Faber, 1957, A. S. Barnes, 1959; *The Forbidden Island,* Criterion, 1960; *Breton Fairy Tales,* Gollancz, 1971.

Under name Marjorie Mack: *The Red Centaur,* Faber, 1939; *Velveteen Jacket,* Faber, 1941; *Hannaboy's Farm,* Faber, 1942; *The Educated Pin,* Faber, 1944.

WORK IN PROGRESS: An autobiography, *Edwardian Typist;* a novel about Ireland, *To the Mountain.*

AVOCATIONAL INTERESTS: Weaving.

* * *

DOBIE, Edith 1894-1975

PERSONAL: Born February 10, 1894, in Bradford, Pa.; daughter of William (a businessman) and Phebe Ann (Derry) Dobie. *Education:* Syracuse University, A.B., 1914; University of Chicago, M.A., 1922; Stanford University, Ph.D., 1926. *Religion:* Presbyterian. *Home:* 4337 15th Ave. N.E., Seattle, Wash. 98105.

CAREER: Stanford University, Stanford, Calif., instructor in problems of citizenship, 1926; University of Washington, Seattle, assistant professor, 1926-31, associate professor, 1937-52, professor of history, 1952-57, professor emeritus and research consultant, 1957-75. Visiting professor at University of Alberta, 1961, and Elmira College, 1961-62. *Member:* American Historical Association, American Association of University Professors, Phi Beta Kappa, Delta Delta Delta. *Awards, honors:* Social Science Research Council grant-in-aid, 1936-37; Fulbright scholarship, 1953-54.

WRITINGS: Political Career of Stephen Mallory White: A Study of Party Activities Under the Convention System, Stanford University Press, 1927, reprinted, AMS Press, 1972; (editor with Charles E. Martin) *Problems in International Understanding,* Publications of Social Science Faculty, University of Washington, 1928; (contributor) J. B. Harrison, editor, *If Men Want Peace,* Macmillan, 1946; (contributor) Robin W. Winks, editor, *The Historiography of British Empire Commonwealth,* Duke University Press, 1966; *Malta's Road to Independence,* University of Oklahoma Press, 1967.†

(Died April 24, 1975)

DOBROVOLSKY, Sergei P(avlovich) 1908-

PERSONAL: Born October 8, 1908, in Vladivostok, Russia; came to United States in 1941, naturalized in 1946; son of Paul E. and Claudia (Politova) Dobrovolsky; married Tamara Remelman (a librarian), June 12, 1967. *Education:* Faculty of Law, Harbin, Manchuria, diploma, 1931; Columbia University, M.A., 1942, Ph.D., 1949. *Religion:* Greek Orthodox. *Home:* 249 Elm St., San Mateo, Calif. 94401. *Office:* Department of Economics, Rensselaer Polytechnic Institute, Troy, N.Y. 12181.

CAREER: China United Lamp Co., Shanghai, China, accountant and branch manager, 1932-41; National Bureau of Economic Research, New York, N.Y., researcher, 1942-45; U.S. Office of Strategic Services, Washington, D.C., researcher, 1945-46; Wayne University (now Wayne State University), Detroit, Mich., assistant professor, 1948-53, associate professor of economics, 1953-57; Rensselaer Polytechnic Institute, Troy, N.Y., professor of economics, 1957-74, professor emeritus, 1974—, chairman of department, 1957-67. Visiting professor, Rice University, 1963-64, McGill University, 1974-76; lecturer, University of California, Berkeley, summer, 1977. *Member:* American Economic Association, American Finance Association. *Awards, honors:* Social Science Research Council award, 1946-47.

WRITINGS: Corporate Income Retention, National Bureau of Economic Research, 1951; (with others) *Capital in Manufacturing and Mining,* Princeton University Press, 1960; (contributor) *Historical Statistics of the United States,* U.S. Bureau of Census, 1960; *The Economics of Corporation Finance,* McGraw, 1971. Contributor to economics journals.

* * *

DODDS, Robert H(ungerford) 1914-1976

PERSONAL: Born October 25, 1914, in Carroll, Iowa; son of John Simpson (a civil engineer) and Josephine (Hungerford) Dodds; married Malene Fletcher, October 3, 1942; children: Susanna Hawley (Mrs. Jonathan Baker Cobb), Matthew Sanford. *Education:* Iowa State University, B.S., 1936, licensed as civil engineer, 1946; Northwestern University, M.S., 1948. *Politics:* Republican. *Religion:* Protestant. *Home:* 72 Davis Rd., Port Washington, N.Y. 11050.

CAREER: Engineering News-Record, New York City, editorial assistant, 1937-40, associate editor, 1948-57; Colorado State University, Fort Collins, associate professor of civil engineering, 1946-47; Lockwood, Kessler & Bartlett (consulting engineers), Syosset, N.Y., development engineer, 1955-57; Gibbs & Hill, Inc. (consulting engineers), New York City, project engineer, 1957-64, personnel and public relations manager, 1964-73; *Engineering News-Record,* New York City, manager of business data department, 1973-76. *Military service:* U.S. Naval Reserve, Civil Engineer Corps, 1942-46; became lieutenant commander. *Member:* American Society of Civil Engineers, American Congress on Surveying and Mapping, National Society of Professional Engineers.

WRITINGS: Writing for Technical and Business Magazines, Wiley, 1969. Also co-author of *History of World War II, 1945-6.* Contributor to technical, business, and professional publications.

SIDELIGHTS: Robert H. Dodds told *CA:* "Writing for

Technical and Business Magazines is aimed at professional people who would write about their own work. In turn, I wrote about a substantial part of my career's work.''†

(Died November 25, 1976)

* * *

DOGGETT, Frank 1906-

PERSONAL: Born May 4, 1906, in Jacksonville, Fla.; son of John L. (an attorney) and Carrie (Van Deman) Doggett; married Dorothy Emerson, March 16, 1934; children: Dorothy Jean (Mrs. Herschel E. Shepard), John L. *Education:* Rollins College, A.B., 1931; Emory University, M.A., 1933. *Religion:* Episcopalian. *Home:* 310 Sixth St., Atlantic Beach, Fla. 32003.

CAREER: D. U. Fletcher Senior High School, Neptune Beach, Fla., principal, 1937-69. *Military service:* U.S. Naval Reserve, 1943-65; retired as lieutenant commander. *Member:* Modern Language Association of America. *Awards, honors:* D. Let., University of Florida.

WRITINGS: Stevens' Poetry of Thought, Johns Hopkins Press, 1966. Contributor to *PMLA, English Literary History, Studies in English Literature,* and other journals.

* * *

DOUGLAS, Leonard M(arvin) 1910-?

PERSONAL: Born April 8, 1910, in Cheyenne, Okla.; son of John W. (a farmer) and Laura (Dykes) Douglas; married Bonnie Rose King (a teacher), January 16, 1929; children: Betty Rose Douglas Rios, Lynne Marlene Douglas Hartsell. *Education:* Central State College (now University), Edmond, Okla., B.S., 1938; Northeast Missouri State Teachers College (now Northeast Missouri State University), M.A., 1949; Colorado State College of Education (now University of Northern Colorado), Ed.D., 1956. *Politics:* Democrat. *Religion:* Methodist. *Office:* New Mexico State University, University Park, N.M. 88001.

CAREER: Teacher and principal in elementary and high schools, 1936-44; Sinclair-Prairie Oil Co., Tulsa, Okla., clerk and warehouseman, 1944-45; superintendent of public schools, Callao, Mo., 1946-51; New Mexico Western College (now Western New Mexico University), Silver City, associate professor of education, 1951-58; New Mexico State University, University Park, associate professor of education, 1958-61, and beginning 1963, director of teacher corps, 1968-70. Business education adviser in Georgetown, Guyana for U.S. Agency for International Development, 1961-63. Certified lay speaker of Methodist Church. *Member:* National Education Association, American Vocational Association, Association for Student Teaching (New Mexico state membership chairman, beginning 1967), Association for Higher Education, Association for Supervision and Curriculum Development, New Mexico Education Association, New Mexico Classroom Teachers Association, Phi Delta Kappa, Masons.

WRITINGS: The Secondary Teacher at Work, Heath, 1967. Writer of three survey reports on business education in Guyana (then British Guiana), 1961-63. Contributor to education journals.

AVOCATIONAL INTERESTS: Fishing, photography, do-it-yourself projects.†

(Deceased)

DOUGLAS-HOME, Robin 1932-1968

PERSONAL: Born May 8, 1932, in London, England; nephew of Sir Alec Douglas-Home, the former Prime Minister; married Sandra Paul (a fashion model), 1959 (divorced, 1965); children: Sholto (son). *Education:* Attended Eton College, 1945-50. *Residence:* Sussex, England. *Agent:* David Higham Associates Ltd., 5-8 Lower John St., London W1R 4HA, England.

CAREER: Writer, songwriter, photographer, pianist. Once worked for an advertising agency; columnist for *Daily Express,* London, England, 1959-66; often worked as a pianist in better clubs. *Military service:* British Army, 1950-56; became captain. *Awards, honors:* Award for best first novel of 1965, for *Hot for Uncertainties.*

WRITINGS: Sinatra (biography), M. Joseph, 1962; *Hot for Uncertainties* (novel), Longmans, Green, 1965; *When the Sweet Talking's Done* (novel), Frewin, 1968; *The Faint Aroma of Performing Seals* (novel), Frewin, 1969. Feature writer for *Daily Mirror, News of the World,* and *Harper's Bazaar.* Contributing editor, *Queen.*

WORK IN PROGRESS: Why Did I Buy Those Blue Pyjamas?, a novel.

SIDELIGHTS: Douglas-Home was to have worked with Leslie Frewin on the production of the film version of *The Faint Aroma of Performing Seals.* Douglas-Home traveled around Europe and the Middle East, and in America, India, and Africa. *Avocational interests:* Ornithology.

BIOGRAPHICAL/CRITICAL SOURCES: New York Times, October 16, 1968.†

(Died October 15, 1968).

* * *

DOW, Sterling 1903-

PERSONAL: Born November 19, 1903, in Portland, Me.; son of Sterling Tucker (a railroad executive) and Alice Gertrude (Verrill) Dow; married Elizabeth Sanderson Flagg, June 5, 1931; children: Elizabeth (Mrs. Robert George Lown), Sterling III. *Education:* Harvard University, A.B., 1925, A.M., 1928, Ph.D., 1936; graduate study at Trinity College, Cambridge, 1925-26, and American School of Classical Studies, Athens, Greece, 1931-32, 1935-36. *Politics:* Republican. *Home:* 159 Brattle, Cambridge, Mass. 02138. *Office:* Widener Library 690, Harvard University, Cambridge, Mass. 02138; and Boston College, Chestnut Hill, Mass. 02167.

CAREER: Harvard University, Cambridge, Mass., instructor and tutor in history, 1936-41, associate professor, 1941-46, professor of history and Greek, 1946-49, and John E. Hudson Professor of Archaeology, 1949-70, professor emeritus, 1970—, war archivist, 1944-45; Boston College, Chestnut Hill, Mass., visiting professor of Greek civilization and history, beginning 1970. Served with U.S. Office of Strategic Services in Washington, D.C., and Cairo, Egypt, 1942-44. Sather Professor at University of California, Berkeley, 1964; annual professor at American School of Classical Studies, Athens, 1966-67. Founder, and trustee of American Research Centre in Egypt, 1950-53, 1955-59; trustee of Byzantine Institute, Radcliffe College, 1953-55; member of advisory board, Guggenheim Foundation, 1955-67; director, El Centro Arqueologico Hispano-Americano, beginning 1955.

MEMBER: Archaeological Institute of America (president, 1946-48; honorary president, 1949-60), American Philological Association, American Classical League (vice-president, 1949-54), Council for Basic Education, Deutsches Archaeologisches Institut (honorary member), Society for Promotion of Hellenic Studies (England; honorary life member; honorary American secretary, beginning 1957), Society for Promotion of Roman Studies (England; honorary American secretary, beginning 1957), Classical Association of New England (president, 1955-56), Teachers of Classics in New England (founder member; president, 1947-60), Massachusetts Historical Society, Phi Beta Kappa (honorary member), Tavern Club (Boston). *Awards, honors:* Guggenheim fellowships, 1934-35, 1959-60, 1966-67; William and Frances White Emerson scholarship, Cambridge Historical Society, 1957; LL.D., University of California, Berkeley; Litt.D., St. Francis College; L.H.D., Boston College.

WRITINGS: Fifty Years of Sathers: The Sather Professorship of Classical Literature in the University of California, Berkeley, 1913/4-1963/4, University of California Press, 1965; (with Robert F. Healey) *A Sacred Calendar of Eleusis,* Harvard University Press, 1965. Author of booklets, *The Law Codes of Athens,* Bobbs-Merrill, 1959, *The Greeks in the Bronze Age,* Bobbs-Merrill, 1960, and *Conventions in Editing: A Suggested Reformation of the Leiden System,* Duke University, 1969; also author of *Scholarly Aids in Classical Studies.* Contributor of about 125 articles and reviews to scholarly journals in America and abroad. Founder of *Archaeology* (quarterly publication of Archaeological Institute of America).†

*   *   *

DREW-BEAR, Robert 1901-

PERSONAL: Born January 2, 1901, in London, England; son of Emile (an engineer) and Jessie (Henderson) Drew-Bear; married Lotte Blumenthal (director of R. Feigen Gallery), August 22, 1942; children: Thomas, Annette. *Education:* Harvard University, B.S., 1927, M.B.A., 1931. *Politics:* Democrat. *Religion:* Unitarian Universalist. *Home:* 260 Centre Ave., New Rochelle, N.Y. 10805.

CAREER: Wadsworh Atheneum, Hartford, Conn., assistant director, 1932-42; University of Massachusetts, Amherst, professor of marketing, 1957-69; Center for Integrative Education, New Rochelle, N.Y., executive secretary, 1969-77. Also taught at Trinity College, Hartford, Conn., and American University, Washington, D.C. *Military service:* U.S. Army, 1942. *Member:* Friends of the Earth.

WRITINGS: Mass Merchandising: Revolution and Evolution, Fairchild, 1970.

WORK IN PROGRESS: A pilot study of interdisciplinary courses given in American colleges and universities.

*   *   *

DRIVER, Godfrey Rolles 1892-1975

PERSONAL: Born August 20, 1892, in Oxford England; son of Samuel Rolles (canon of Christ Church and Regius Professor, Oxford University) and Mabel (Burr) Driver; married Madeleine Mary Goulding, December 18, 1924; children: Mary Madeleine, Susanna (Mrs. H. Charman), Joanna (Susanna and Joanna are twins). *Education:* New College, Oxford, B.A., 1915, M.A., 1919. *Religion:* Church of England. *Home:* 41 Park Town, Oxford, England.

CAREER: Magdalen College, Oxford University, Oxford, England, fellow, 1919-62, classical tutor, 1919-28, librarian, 1923-40, vice-president, 1931-32; Oxford University, lecturer, 1927-28, reader, 1928-38, professor of Semitic philology, 1938-62. Also lecturer in Hebrew at St. John's College, Oxford University, 1928-38, and deputy professor of Hebrew, 1953-54, 1959-60; visiting professor at University of Chicago, 1925, University of Louvain, 1950, University of Birmingham, 1958, and Queen's University of Belfast, 1960. Schweich Lecturer at British Academy, 1944, distinguished lecturer at British universities. *Military service:* British Army (Intelligence Corps), 1915-19, 1940-42; became major; received Military Cross, 1917.

MEMBER: British Academy (fellow), International Organization for the Study of the Old Testament (president, 1953-59). *Awards, honors:* Leverhulme research fellow, 1939 (resigned because of war); Burkitt Medal of British Academy for Biblical Studies, 1953; Commander, Order of the British Empire, 1958; Knight Bachelor, 1968. D.D., University of Aberdeen, 1946; D.Litt., University of Durham, 1948, University of Manchester, 1956, and Cambridge University, 1965; honorary fellow of Magdalen College, Oxford University, 1962, School of Oriental and African Studies, University of London, 1963, and New College, Oxford University, 1975.

WRITINGS: Letters of the First Babylonian Dynasty, Oxford University Press, 1924; *A Grammar of Colloquial Arabic of Syria and Palestine,* Probsthain, 1925; (with L. Hodgson) *Nestorius: The Bazaar of Heracleides,* Oxford University Press, 1925; (editor, translator, and author of commentary with John C. Miles) *The Assyrian Laws,* Clarendon Press, 1935; *Problems of the Hebrew Verbal System,* T. & T. Clark, 1936; *Reginald Campbell Thompson, 1876-1941,* Cambridge University Press, 1946; *Semitic Writing from Pictograph to Alphabet,* Oxford University Press, 1948, 3rd edition, 1973; *The Hebrew Scrolls from the Neighborhood of Jericho and the Dead Sea,* Oxford University Press, 1951; (editor, translator, and author of commentary with Miles) Hammurabi, *Babylonian Laws,* Oxford University Press, Volume I, 1952, Volume II, 1955; (editor, translator, and author of commentary with E. Mittwock and others) *Aramaic Documents of the Fifth Century B.C.,* Clarendon Press, 1954, abridged edition, 1957; *Canaanite Myths and Tales from Ugarit (now Ras-as Shamrah),* T. & T. Clark, 1956; *The Judean Scrolls: The Problem and a Solution,* Basil Blackwell, 1965, Schocken, 1966.

Director, *New English Bible,* 1962-75. Contributor of articles on the language and the Old Testament to journals in England and abroad. Editor, *Journal of Theological Studies,* 1933-40.

WORK IN PROGRESS: Old Testament, for *New English Bible;* a revised edition of *Oxford Hebrew Lexicon;* various studies in Hebrew grammar.†

(Died April 22, 1975)

*   *   *

DUDLEY, Guilford, Jr. 1907-

PERSONAL: Born June 23, 1907, in Nashville, Tenn.; son of Guilford and Anne (Dallas) Dudley; married Jane Anderson, June 24, 1950; children: Guilford III, Robert Lusk, Trevania Dallas. *Education:* Vanderbilt University, B.A., 1929. *Politics:* Republican. *Religion:* Protestant Episcopal. *Home:* 2201 Harding Pl., Nashville, Tenn. 37215. *Office:* Life & Casualty Insurance Co., Nashville, Tenn. 37219; and 1820 South Ocean, Palm Beach, Fla. 33480.

CAREER: Life & Casualty Insurance Co., Nashville, Tenn., beginning 1930, began as agent, assistant vice-president, 1936-37, vice-president, 1937-51, executive vice-president, 1951-52, president, 1952-69, member of board, 1946-69, beginning 1972. U.S. Ambassador to Denmark, 1969-72. Member of board of directors of Third National Bank. Horse breeder, with horses racing under his colors in United States, England, Ireland, and France. Member of board of Vanderbilt University, Cumberland College, American General Insurance Co., American Century Marketing Investors, STP Corp., WLAC-Radio, Channing Funds, and other civic and philanthropic organizations. *Military service:* U.S. Naval Air Force, 1942-46.

WRITINGS: The Skyline is a Promise, Holt, 1965.

AVOCATIONAL INTERESTS: Fox hunting, skiing, golfing, tennis, and painting.

*   *   *

DUFFY, Elizabeth   1904-19 (?)

PERSONAL: Born May 6, 1904, in New Bern, N.C.; daughter of Francis (a physician) and Lida (Patterson) Duffy; married John T. Baker, 1928; married John E. Bridgers, Jr. (a professor of English), August 27, 1938 (died February 16, 1966); children: (second marriage) Elizabeth Duffy Bridgers. *Education:* North Carolina College for Women (now University of North Carolina at Greensboro), A.B., 1925; Columbia University, M.A., 1926, Johns Hopkins University, Ph.D., 1928. *Politics:* Democrat (liberal wing). *Office:* Department of Psychology, University of North Carolina at Greensboro, Greensboro, N.C.

CAREER: Columbia University, New York, N.Y., postdoctoral research fellow, 1928-29; Sarah Lawrence College, Bronxville, N.Y., member of social sciences faculty, 1929-37; University of North Carolina at Greensboro, professor of psychology, beginning, 1937. National Science Foundation, lecturer, Virginia Visiting Scientists Program, 1959-60, member of panel for awarding graduate fellowships, 1963, consultant on research proposals. Greensboro Redevelopment Commission (urban renewal), member, 1951-64, vice-chairman, 1951-60; Greensboro Community Council, member, 1958-62.

MEMBER: American Psychological Association (fellow; Division I, member of executive committee, 1952-55, president, 1961-62), Society for Psychophysiological Research, Psychonomic Society, American Association for the Advancement of Science (fellow), American Association of University Professors, Southern Society for Philosophy and Psychology (member of council, 1942-47, 1950-51; president, 1949-50), Southeastern Psychological Association, North Carolina Psychological Association (member of executive committee, 1952-56; president, 1954-55), American Civil Liberties Union, Americans for Democratic Action, Phi Beta Kappa, Sigma Xi, Greensboro Country Club, Dunes Club (Morehead City, N.C.). *Awards, honors:* Southern Fellowships Fund grantee, 1959; City of Greensboro, certificate of meritorious service, 1964.

WRITINGS: Activation and Behavior, Wiley, 1962.

Contributor: *Walter Clinton Jackson Essays in the Social Sciences,* University of North Carolina Press, 1942; Douglas Candland, editor, *Emotion: Bodily Change,* Van Nostrand, 1962; Chalmers L. Stacey and Manfred L. Demartino, editors, *Understanding Human Motivation,* Howard Allen, 1963; R. N. Haber, editor, *Current Research in Motivation,* Holt, 1966; N. S. Greenfield and Richard Sternbach, editors, *Handbook of Psychophysiology,* Holt, 1967. Also contributor to *Encyclopedia of*

Vocational Guidance, Philosophical Library, 1948, and about twenty-five articles to psychology journals.

SIDELIGHTS: Elizabeth Duffy wrote: "Think the field of psychology is in somewhat of a muddle due to lack of sufficient attention to the nature and exactitude of the concepts which it employs. . . . My chief interest has been in the criticism and attempted improvement of concepts, with an eye on the explanation, in strict scientific terms, of the responses of the whole human being."†

(Deceased)

*   *   *

DUKE, Vernon   1903-1969
(Vladimir Dukelsky)

PERSONAL: Original name Vladimir Dukelsky; legally changed in 1936; born October 10, 1903, in Pskoff, Russia; came to United States in 1922, naturalized in 1936; son of Alexander (a civil engineer) and Anna (Kopylov) Dukelsky; married Kay McCracken (a singer; professional name, Katherine Duke), October 30, 1957. *Education:* Educated at a private school in Kiev, Russia, and then at Kiev Conservatory, 1917-20 (studies interrupted by war). *Politics:* "Democrat, more or less." *Religion:* Greek Orthodox. *Home:* 507 Almoloya Dr., Pacific Palisades, Calif. 90272. *Agent:* Bertha Klausner International Literary Agency, Inc., 71 Park Ave., New York, N.Y. 10016.

CAREER: Left Russia in 1920, and spent two years in Constantinople before migrating to United States; retained name Vladimir Dukelsky for concert music and, at the suggestion of George Gershwin, adopted name Vernon Duke for majority of his other compositions; began career as composer in America, composing orchestral and instrumental works, and music for ballets, Broadway shows, and films; also did lyrics for a number of popular songs. Ballets include: "Zephyr and Flora," produced by Sergei Diaghilev, 1925; "Jardin Public," 1936; "Entr'acte," 1938; "La Bal des Balnchisseuses," produced in Paris, 1946. Musical shows include: "Yvonne," 1926; "Yellow Mask," 1928; "Open Your Eyes," 1930; "Garrick Gaieties," 1930; "Walk a Little Faster," 1932; "Ziegfeld Follies," 1934, 1935; "The Show Is On," 1936; "Cabin in the Sky," 1940; "Banjo Eyes," 1941; "Dancing in the Streets," 1943; "Tars and Spars," 1944; "Sadie Thompson," 1944; and a number of others. Songs include: "April in Paris," "This Is Romance," "Taking a Chance on Love," "Time Remembered," "Autumn in New York," and "What Is There to Say." His first two symphonies were performed by the Warsaw Philharmonic, London Philharmonic, and Boston Symphony Orchestra, 1927-28, and his "Third Symphony" was initially performed in 1946. In addition to complete scores and incidental music for motion pictures, he composed for opera, chorus, piano, violin, and other instruments. *Military service:* U.S. Coast Guard, 1942-45; enlisted as coxswain, became lieutenant commander in Reserve. *Member:* Russian Nobility Association in America. *Awards, honors:* Chevalier of Order of St. Brigitte.

WRITINGS: Passport to Paris (autobiography), Little, Brown, 1955; *Poslaniia* (Russian poetry; title means "Epistles"), Baschkirzew (Munich), 1962; *Stradaniia nemolodogo Vetera* (Russian poetry; title means "The Sufferings of the Not-so-Young Werther"), Baschkirzew, 1962; *Listen Here! A Critical Essay on Music Depreciation,* Obolensky, 1963. Also author of two volumes of Russian poetry published by Baschkirzew, 1965, 1968.

Published music, under name Vladimir Dukelsky: *Surrealist*

Suite, Sprague-Coleman, 1940; *Five Victorian Songs,* Sprague-Coleman, 1942; *Homage to Boston,* Sprague-Coleman, 1943; *Album of Song Hits from the United States Coast Guard Production, "Tars and Spars"* (book and lyrics by Howard Dietz), C. Fischer, 1944; *Music for Moderns,* Robbins Music Corp., 1944; *Concerto for Violin and Orchestra; Violin and Piano,* C. Fischer, 1944; *Sweet Bye and Bye* (lyrics by Ogden Nash), Harms, 1946; *Ogden Nash's Musical Zoo,* Little, 1947; *Paris aller et retour,* Amphion (Paris), 1948; *Milord L'Arsouille* (book by Paul Gibson and Nino Frank), P. Seghers (Paris), 1952; *Le Boheme et mon couer* (poems by Francis Carco), Amphion, 1949; *Symphony Number 3 in E,* C. Fischer, 1950.

Recorded two albums of his own music, 1959, 1961. Contributor of more than one hundred articles to *Variety, Stage, New York Times, Music Publishing Journal,* and other periodicals and newspapers.

WORK IN PROGRESS: An anthology of Russian emigre poetry, in collaboration with Merrill Sparks.

SIDELIGHTS: Vernon Duke was the first composer to write a ballet specifically for film; he composed the famous water ballet in the film *Goldwyn Follies,* 1937.†

(Died January 16, 1969)

* * *

DULLES, Allen W(elsh)   1893-1969

PERSONAL: Born April 7, 1893, in Watertown, N.Y.; son of Allen Macy (a Presbyterian minister) and Edith (Foster) Dulles; married Clover Todd, October 16, 1920; children: Clover Todd (Mrs. Jens H. Jebsen), Joan Dulles Buresch, Allen Macy. *Education:* Princeton University, B.A., 1914, M.A., 1916; George Washington University, LL.B., 1926. *Politics:* Republican. *Religion:* Presbyterian. *Home:* 2723 Que St. N.W., Washington, D.C. 20007.

CAREER: Teacher of English in Allahabad, India, for one year before entering U.S. Diplomatic Service, 1916; served at legations in Vienna, Berne, Paris, Berlin, and Constantinople, 1916-22, and then as chief of Division of Near East Affairs, Department of State, Washington, D.C., 1922-26; Sullivan & Cromwell (attorneys), New York, N.Y., lawyer, 1926-42, 1945-51; Central Intelligence Agency, Washington, D.C., deputy director, 1951-53, director, 1953-61; Sullivan & Cromwell, "of counsel," 1962-69. Member of U.S. delegations or legal adviser in Geneva to Inter-National Conference on Arms Traffic, 1925, Preparatory Disarmament Commission, 1926, Three Power Naval Conference, 1927, and General Disarmament Conference, 1932-33; member of President's Commission on the Assassination of President Kennedy, 1963-64. Trustee of Princeton University, 1961-63. *Wartime service:* U.S. Office of Strategic Services, 1942-45.

MEMBER: Council on Foreign Relations (member of board of directors), Phi Beta Kappa; Century Association and Piping Rock Club (New York); Alibi Club and Metropolitan Club (Washington, D.C.). *Awards, honors:* Medal for Merit, 1946; Medal of Freedom, 1946; Order of S.S. Maurizio e Lazzaro (Italy), 1946; Officer, Legion of Honor (France), 1947; Officer of Order of Leopold (Belgium), 1948; National Security Medal, 1961. LL.D. from Brown University, 1947, Temple University, 1952, Columbia University, 1955, Princeton University, 1957, George Washington University, 1959, Boston University, 1961, University of South Carolina, 1962, and Williams College, 1965. Awards from U.S. organizations include: Bernard Baruch Gold Medal

from Veterans of Foreign Wars, annual citation of Salvation Army, and Golden Rule Award of St. George Association.

WRITINGS: (With Hamilton Fish Armstrong) *Can We Be Neutral?,* privately printed, 1935; (with Armstrong) *Can America Stay Neutral?,* privately printed, 1939; *Germany's Underground,* Macmillan, 1947; *The Craft of Intelligence,* Harper, 1963; *The Secret Surrender,* Harper, 1967; (editor) *Great True Spy Stories,* Harper, 1968; (editor) *Great Spy Stories from Fiction,* Harper, 1969. Also author of *The Boer War,* written at the age of eight.

BIOGRAPHICAL/CRITICAL SOURCES: London *Times,* January 31, 1969.†

(Died January 29, 1969)

* * *

DUNCAN, Hugh Dalziel   1909-1970

PERSONAL: Born October 6, 1909, in Bo'ness, Scotland; naturalized U.S. citizen; son of Alexander Kerr (a grocery chain executive) and Ellen Murray (Dalziel) Duncan; married Minna Green (a social worker), March 29, 1940. *Education:* Drake University, B.A. (cum laude), 1931; University of Chicago, M.A., 1933, Ph.D., 1948. *Politics:* Liberal Democrat. *Home address:* R.F.D. 2, Box 20, Cobden, Ill. 62920.

CAREER: Before going to college worked as stock boy in department store, and in chain groceries and book stores during his college years; copywriter for advertising agency in Chicago, Ill., 1931-32; lived and worked at Hull House, Chicago, Ill., 1933-34, and then taught school in Des Moines, Iowa, for two years; began writing in 1946 and supported this with part-time teaching at University of Chicago, Chicago, Ill., and Northwestern University, Evanston, Ill., 1948-52; to further finance writing, organized a real estate syndicate to buy golf course in Olympia Fields, Ill., 1953, and managed the development of a subdivision; visiting professor of sociology at Carleton College, Northfield, Minn., 1961, and Rice University, Houston, Tex., 1962-63; Illinois Institute of Technology, Chicago, professorial lecturer in sociology, 1963-64; Southern Illinois University, Carbondale, visiting professor of sociology, 1964-65, professor of sociology and English, 1965-70. *Military service:* U.S. Army, 1942-46; became captain.

MEMBER: American Sociological Association (fellow), American Studies Association, National Society for the Study of Communication, Midwest Sociological Society, Phi Beta Kappa. *Awards, honors:* Grant-in-aid from Social Science Research Council, 1949; Graham Foundation for Advanced Studies in the Fine Arts fellowship, 1962; National Institute of Mental Health research grant, 1964.

WRITINGS: Language and Literature in Society: A Sociological Essay on Theory and Method in the Interpretation of Linguistic Symbols, with a Bibliographical Guide to the Sociology of Literature, University of Chicago Press, 1953; *Communication and Social Order,* Bedminister, 1962; *The Rise of Chicago as a Literary Center: A Sociological Essay in American Culture,* Bedminster, 1964; *Culture and Democracy: The Struggle for Form in Society and Architecture in Chicago and the Middle West During the Life and Times of Louis H. Sullivan,* Bedminster, 1965; *Symbols in Society: Axiomatic, Theoretical, and Methodological Propositions on the Social Function of Symbols,* Oxford University Press, 1968; *Symbols and Social Theory,* Oxford University Press, 1969.

Contributor: Howard Becker and Alvin Boskoff, editors,

Modern Sociological Theory, Dryden, 1957; Kurt H. Wolff, editor, *George Simmel, 1858-1918*, Ohio State University Press, 1959; Wolff, editor, *Emile Durkheim, 1858-1917*, Ohio State University Press, 1960; (author of introduction) A. S. Siegel, editor, *Chicago's Famous Buildings: A Photographic Guide to the City's Architectural Landmarks and Other Notable Buildings*, University of Chicago Press, 1965; (author of introduction) Kenneth Burke, *Permanence and Change: An Anatomy of Purpose*, Bobbs-Merrill, 1965; Lee Thayer, editor and compiler, *Communication Theory and Research: Proceedings of the First International Symposium*, C. C Thomas, 1967; Frank E. Dance, editor, *Human Communication Theory: Original Essays*, Holt, 1967; Floyd W. Matson and Ashley Montagu, editors, *The Human Dialogue: Perspectives on Communication*, Free Press, 1967. Contributor of articles and reviews to professional journals.

WORK IN PROGRESS: Courtship: The Drama of Hierarchy; and *Rules: A Sociological Inquiry.*

BIOGRAPHICAL/CRITICAL SOURCES: Scientific American, January, 1963; *Bedminster Letter*, Number 2, 1963.†

(Died August 8, 1970)
*   *   *

DUNCAN, Julia K.
[Collective pseudonym]

WRITINGS—"Doris Force" series; published by Henry Altemus Co.: *Doris Force at Cloudy Cove*, 1931; *... at Locked Gates*, 1931; *... at Barry Manor*, 1932; *... at Raven Rock*, 1932.

SIDELIGHTS: See **ADAMS, Harriet S., STRATEMEYER, Edward L.,** and **SVENSON, Andrew E.**†
*   *   *

DUNKIN, Paul S(haner) 1905-1975

PERSONAL: Born September 28, 1905, in Flora, Ind.; son of Edgar Ward and Daisy (Shaner) Dunkin; married Gladys Hammond, March 17, 1935; children: Anne (Mrs. Brad Willis). *Education:* DePauw University, A.B., 1929; University of Illinois, A.M., 1931, B.S. in L.S., 1935, Ph.D., 1937. *Politics:* Democrat. *Religion:* Methodist. *Home:* 817 South Mitchell St., Bloomington, Ind. 47401.

CAREER: Folger Shakespeare Library, Washington, D.C., senior cataloger, 1937-50, chief of technical services, 1950-59; Rutgers University, Graduate School of Library Service, New Brunswick, N.J., professor, 1959-71, professor emeritus, 1971-75. *Member:* American Library Association (chairman of cataloging section, 1961-62; president, Resources and Technical Services Division, 1964-65), Bibliographical Society (London), Bibliographical Society of the University of Virginia, Bibliographical Society of America. *Awards, honors:* Margaret Mann Citation for cataloging, American Library Association, 1968.

WRITINGS: Post-Aristophanic Comedy, University of Illinois Press, 1946; *How to Catalog a Rare Book*, American Library Association, 1951, revised edition, 1973; (author of commentary) Seymour Lubetzky, *Code of Cataloging Rules*, American Library Association, 1960; *Cataloging U.S.A.*, American Library Association, 1969; *Tales of Melvil's Mouser; or Much Ado about Libraries*, Bowker, 1970; *Bibliography: Tiger or Fat Cat?*, Shoe String, 1975. Contributor to library and bibliographical journals. Editor, *Library Resources and Technical Services*, 1967-71.†

(Died, 1975)

DUNKMAN, William E(dward) 1903-

PERSONAL: Born February 3, 1903, in Cincinnati, Ohio; son of William F. and Clara (Lorenz) Dunkman; married Cornelia Engle, August 9, 1933; children: Elizabeth Dunkman Riesz, W. Bruce. *Education:* University of Cincinnati, Com.E., 1926; Columbia University, M.S., 1928, Ph.D., 1933. *Religion:* Presbyterian. *Home:* 475 Newton Dr., Rochester, N.Y. 14618.

CAREER: Washington and Lee University, Lexington, Va., instructor in accounting, 1926-27; National Bureau of Economic Research, New York City, assistant, 1928; Columbia University, New York City, lecturer in money and banking, 1929-33; University of Rochester, Rochester, N.Y., assistant professor, 1933-39, associate professor, 1939-47, professor of economics, 1947-68, professor emeritus, 1968—, chairman of department of economics and business administration, 1948-56; Rochester Institute of Technology, Rochester, visiting professor of economics, beginning 1968. Fulbright lecturer, Tohoku University, 1956-57. Chief of Division of Research and Statistics, New York State Banking Department, 1944-46; economic consultant to public and private agencies. *Member:* American Economic Association, American Finance Association, Appalachian Finance Association (president, 1967-68), Eastern Finance Association (founding director), New York State Economic Association (president, 1948-49), Beta Gamma Sigma.

WRITINGS: Qualitative Credit Control, Columbia University Press, 1933; *Questions on Money and Banking*, Columbia University Press, 1941; *Savings and Savings Facilities in New York State*, New York Bankers Association, 1953; *A Survey of Courses in Banking and Finance*, American Bankers Association, 1966; *Money, Credit, and Banking*, Random House, 1970. Contributor to finance journals.

WORK IN PROGRESS: Writing on Federal Reserve policy.

*   *   *

DUNN, Alan (Cantwell) 1900-1974

PERSONAL: Born August 11, 1900, in Belmar, N.J.; son of George Warren (a lawyer) and Sarah Benton (Brown) Dunn; married Mary Petty (an artist), December 8, 1927. *Education:* Attended Columbia University, 1918-19, National Academy of Design Art Schools, 1919-23, Louis Comfort Tiffany Foundation, Oyster Bay, Long Island, 1921-28, and Fontainebleau Ecole des Arts, France, 1923. *Home:* 12 East 88th St., New York, N.Y. *Office:* c/o *New Yorker* Magazine, 25 West 43rd St., New York, N.Y. 10036.

CAREER: Cartoonist, portrait and landscape painter, and writer. *New Yorker*, New York City, staff contributor, 1926-74; *Architectural Record*, New York City, editorial cartoonist, 1936-74; paintings and cartoons have been exhibited throughout the world; work is represented in the permanent collections of various museums, including the Metropolitan Museum, New York City. *Military service:* U.S. Army, Student Training Corps, Columbia University, 1918. *Member:* Authors Guild, Century Association, Phi Gamma Delta. *Awards, honors:* Fellow, American Academy in Rome, 1923-24.

WRITINGS—Collections of cartoons: *Rejections*, Knopf, 1931; *Who's Paying for This Cab?*, Simon & Schuster, 1945;

The Last Lath, Architectural Record, 1947; *Should It Gurgle?,* Simon & Schuster, 1956; *A Portfolio of Social Cartoons,* Simon & Schuster, 1968; *Architecture Observed,* Architectural Record, 1971.

Prose-picture novels: *East of Fifth,* Simon & Schuster, 1948; (with Eric Hodgins) *Enough Time?,* Time, Inc., 1959; *Is There Intelligent Life on Earth?,* Simon & Schuster, 1960.

SIDELIGHTS: Alan Dunn told *CA* that in 1926 his interest "shifted entirely to the field of social comment art, one of the oldest and most historical art forms since it portrays the life of the times. Both the ideas and the drawings are this artist's own, thus combining writing and picture into a single art."

There is a comprehensive collection of Dunn's work at the Library of Congress, and an Alan Dunn Manuscript Collection at Syracuse University.†

(Died May 20, 1974)

*   *   *

DUNN, Waldo H(ilary) 1882-1969

PERSONAL: Born October 4, 1882, in Rutland, Ohio; son of Arthur Marion (a teacher) and Isabel (Fowler) Dunn; married Fern D. Greenwald, June 11, 1907; children: Dorothy (Mrs. Herman D. Beatty), Lorna (Mrs. Charles W. Mann), Arthur Yale, Mary (Mrs. H. Cuyler Anderson). *Education:* Attended University of Cincinnati, 1902, and College of Wooster, 1903-05; Yale University, B.A., 1906, M.A., 1909; University of Glasgow, Litt.D., 1916. *Politics:* Republican. *Religion:* Presbyterian. *Home:* 1212 North Bever St., Wooster, Ohio 44691.

CAREER: Teacher in Ohio public schools, 1900-02; Davis and Elkins College, Elkins, W.Va., professor of English, 1906-07; College of Wooster, Wooster, Ohio, adjunct professor of English, 1907-13, professor of rhetoric and English composition, 1913-16, professor of English and head of department, 1916-34, acting dean, 1924-25; Scripps College, Claremont, Calif., visiting professor, 1931-32, professor of English and head of department, 1934-52, professor emeritus, 1952-69, acting president, 1939-40. Visiting professor, Western Reserve (now Case Western Reserve) University, Graduate School, 1930-31. *Member:* Modern Language Association of America (life member), English Association (Great Britain), Virgil Society (Great Britain), Facsimile Text Society, Richard Doddridge Blackmore Society (London; life president), Rowfant Club (Cleveland; honorary life member). *Awards, honors:* LL.D., College of Wooster, 1950.

WRITINGS: Vanished Empire, Robert Clark Co., 1904; (with Lucy Lilian Notestein) *The Modern Short-Story,* A. S. Barnes, 1914; *English Biography,* Dutton, 1916, reprinted, AMS Press, 1973; *Life of Donald G. Mitchell (Ik Marvel),* Scribner, 1922; *Froude and Carlyle: A Study of the Froude-Carlyle Controversy,* Longmans, Green, 1930, reprinted, Kennikat, 1969; *Three Eminent Victorians,* Scripps College Press, 1932; (with Nathaniel Wright Stephenson) *George Washington,* Oxford University Press, 1940; *R. D. Blackmore: The Author of Lorna Doone, A Biography,* Longmans, Green, 1956, reprinted, Greenwood Press, 1975; *James Anthony Froude,* Oxford University Press, Volume I, 1961, Volume II, 1963; (with Ivor L. M. Richardson) *Sir Robert Stout,* A. M. & A. W. Reed, 1961.

Editor: (With James Holly Hanford) Milton, *De Doctrina Christiana,* Columbia University Press, 1933-34; (with Howard Lowry and Karl Young) Matthew Arnold, *Note-*

Books, Oxford University Press, 1952. Contributor to *Encyclopedia Americana, Twentieth Century,* and other periodicals. Editor, *Wooster Quarterly* (now *Wooster Alumni Magazine*), 1907-21.

SIDELIGHTS: Most of Dunn's books have had British editions. He was competent in French, German, Italian, Spanish, Latin, modern and ancient Greek, and had some knowledge of Russian.

BIOGRAPHICAL/CRITICAL SOURCES: College Courant (journal of Graduates Association of University of Glasgow), Volume IV, number 7, 1951; *London Times,* May 17, 1969.†

(Died May 5, 1969)

*   *   *

DURAND, Loyal, Jr. 1902-1970

PERSONAL: Born July 12, 1902, in Milwaukee, Wis.; son of Loyal and Lucia Relf (Kemper) Durand; married Dorothy Lee, December 25, 1929; children: Loyal III, Philip Poyntel, Lee McVickar, Kemper Bartlett. *Education:* University of Wisconsin, B.A., 1924, M.A., 1925, Ph.D., 1930. *Religion:* Episcopalian. *Home:* 3940 Wilani Rd., Knoxville, Tenn. 37919. *Office:* Department of Geography, University of Tennessee, Knoxville, Tenn. 37916.

CAREER: University of Wisconsin, Madison, instructor, 1928-30, assistant professor of geography, 1930-44; University of Tennessee, Knoxville, associate professor, 1944-46, professor of geography, 1946-70. Summer visiting professor at Pennsylvania State University, 1938, 1940, 1953, University of Utah, 1943, University of California, Los Angeles, 1947, University of Michigan, 1966, and elsewhere; visiting professor at University of Hawaii, 1957-58. National Resources Board, land planning consultant, 1934-35, special land planning consultant, 1941; member of National Academy of Sciences-National Research Council advisory committee to U.S. Office of Naval Research, 1951-54. *Member:* National Council of Geography Teachers (president, 1950), Association of American Geographers (vice-president, 1951), American Association of University Professors, Wisconsin Academy of Sciences, Arts and Letters (secretary-treasurer, 1935-44), Phi Beta Kappa, Sigma Xi.

WRITINGS: Home Regions of Wisconsin, Macmillan, 1933; (with R. H. Whitbeck and J. R. Whitaker) *The Working World: An Economic Geography,* American Book, 1938, 2nd revised edition, 1947; (with George T. Renner, C. Langdon White, and Weldon B. Gibson) *World Economic Geography,* Crowell, 1951; *World Geography,* Holt, 1954, revised edition, 1958; (with Prudence Cutright) *Living Together as American Neighbors,* Macmillan, 1958, 3rd edition, 1966; (with Cutright, J. Hubert Anderson, and John J. Brooks) *Living Together as World Neighbors,* Macmillan, 1959, 3rd edition, 1966; (with Saul Israel and Norma Roemer) *World Geography Today,* Holt, 1962, 2nd edition, 1966. Geographical editor, Macmillan's "Social Studies" series. Contributor to *Encyclopaedia Britannica, Grolier's Encyclopedia,* and *World Book Encyclopedia;* also contributor of more than fifty research articles to professional journals and the proceedings of learned societies. Contributing editor, *Economic Geography,* beginning 1947.

WORK IN PROGRESS: A book; research articles.†

(Died October 14, 1970)

*   *   *

DUTHIE, Charles S. 1911-

PERSONAL: Born January 6, 1911, in Rosehearty, Scotland; son of Andrew May (a grocer) and Christian (Wood) Duthie; married Annie Cowie Fulerton, May 31, 1941; children: Andrew Stewart, Eileen Mary (Mrs. Gordon Miller). *Education:* University of Aberdeen, M.A. (first class honors), 1932; Scottish Congregational College, B.D. (with distinction), 1935; additional study at University of Edinburgh, 1934-35, and University of Tubingen, 1935-36. *Home:* Principal's Lodge, New College, 527 Finchley Rd., London N.W.3, England. *Office:* New College, University of London, 527 Finchley Rd., London N.W.3, England.

CAREER: Clergyman of Congregational Church; Paton College, Nottingham, England, tutor in theology, 1936-38; Congregational minister in Bathgate, England, 1938-40; Scottish Congregational College, Edinburgh, principal, 1944-64; University of London, New College, London, England, principal, beginning 1964. Lecturer, Post-Graduate School of Theology, University of Edinburgh, 1946-64. President, Congregational Church in England and Wales, 1971-72. *Military service:* British Army, chaplain, 1940-44; served in France, Egypt, Libya, and Palestine. *Awards, honors:* D.D., University of Aberdeen, 1952.

WRITINGS: God in His World, Independent Press, 1955, Abingdon, 1956; *Outline of Christian Belief,* Abingdon, 1968. Contributor to theology and religion journals.

WORK IN PROGRESS: A book on the Christian life.

* * *

DYKEMA, Karl W(ashburn) 1906-1970

PERSONAL: Born January 31, 1906, in Yonkers, N.Y.; son of Peter William (a college professor) and Jessie Margaret (Dunning) Dykema; married Christine Lillian Rhoades (an associate professor of French), June 16, 1931; children: Nicholas Edmund, Patricia Caroline Dykema Geisler, Christopher Rhoades. *Education:* Antioch College, student, 1923-25; Columbia University, B.A., 1928, M.A., 1932, further graduate study, 1934-37; also studied at Alliance Francaise, Paris, 1930, and University of Berlin, 1931. *Politics:* Independent. *Address:* Box 182, Route 3, Western Reserve Rd., Canfield, Ohio 44406. *Office:* Department of English, Youngstown State University, Youngstown, Ohio 44503.

CAREER: Teacher of music in Towson, Md., 1928-29, and Chateau de Bures School for Boys, near Orgeval, Seine-et-Oise, France, 1929-30; Gogebic Community College (now Ironwood Junior College), Ironwood, Mich., instructor in German and English, 1932-36; Youngstown State University, Youngstown, Ohio, beginning 1937, began as instructor, became professor of English and dean of the College of Arts and Sciences. *Member:* National Council of Teachers of English, Conference on College Composition and Communication, American Dialect Society (member of board of directors, 1953-57), American Name Society, American Association of University Professors, Ohio College English Association, English Association of Ohio (president, 1962-63).

WRITINGS: (Reviser) Porter G. Perrin, *Writer's Guide and Index to English,* 3rd edition, Scott, Foresman, 1959, 4th edition (reviser with Wilma R. Ebbitt), 1965, published as *Writer's Guide* and *Index to English,* two volumes, 1966.

Contributor: Harold B. Allen, editor, *Readings in Applied English Linguistics,* Appleton, 1958, 2nd edition, 1964; John A. Rycenga and Joseph Schwartz, editors, *Perspectives in Language,* Ronald, 1963; Graham Wilson, editor, *A Linguistic Reader,* Harper, 1967. Contributor to *Encyclopedia Americana, Encyclopaedia Britannica,* and to professional

journals. Editorial adviser, *College English* and *American Speech.*†

(Died July 16, 1970)

* * *

EAGLE, Robert H(arold) 1921-1969

PERSONAL: Born October 17, 1921, in Jacksonville, Fla.; son of Harold S. and Annie P. Eagle; married Elizabeth McBride, September 20, 1954. *Education:* University of North Carolina, B.S., 1948, graduate study. *Home:* Wood View, Pine Bluff Trail, Chapel Hill, N.C.

CAREER: U.S. Government, management engineer with Rural Electrification Administration, 1950-53, staff member of Second Hoover Commission, 1953-55, Federal Supply Service, 1955-59, and Federal Aviation Agency, 1960-61. *Military service:* U.S. Navy, 1942-46.

WRITINGS: (With James W. Prichard) *Modern Inventory Management,* Wiley, 1965.†

(Died, 1969)

* * *

EARLEY, Tom 1911-

PERSONAL: Surname is pronounced "early"; born September 13, 1911, in Mountain Ash, Glamorganshire, Wales; son of Tom (a colliery blacksmith) and Annie (Powell) Earley; married Elizabeth Robinson (a lecturer and course tutor at Brixton College), April 13, 1939; children: Jean, Kathleen. *Education:* Attended Trinity College, Carmarthen, Wales, 1929-31. *Politics:* "Libertarian socialist and Welsh nationalist." *Religion:* None. *Home:* 21 Bloomsbury Sq., London W.C.1, England.

CAREER: English and physical education teacher in secondary schools in Maidenhead, Berkshire, England, 1931-38, and in London's East End schools, 1938-45; St. Dunstan's College, London, England, teacher of spoken English, 1945-71; full-time writer, beginning 1971. *Member:* Poetry Society, Peace Pledge Union, Plaid Cymru, Yr Academi Gymreig, City Literary Institute, London Welsh Association.

WRITINGS—Poems: *Welshman in Bloomsbury,* Outposts Publications, 1966; *The Sad Mountain,* Wesleyan University Press, 1970. Formerly regular contributor of articles on education and on pacificism to *Freedom* (anarchist paper).

WORK IN PROGRESS: A third book of verse.

SIDELIGHTS: Tom Earley has been a lifelong socialist and pacifist, active for many years in the anarchist movement. He took part in the first Aldermaston march and in the first civil disobedience protest with Bertrand Russell; at different times between 1939 and 1945 both Earley and his wife spent periods in prison for opposing the war.

BIOGRAPHICAL/CRITICAL SOURCES: New Statesman, June, 1970; *Western Mail,* Cardiff, Wales, June 8, 1970.

* * *

ECKELBERRY, Grace Kathryn 1902-

PERSONAL: Born December 16, 1902, in Braymer, Mo.; daughter of John H. (a teacher) and Zella O. (McVicker) Eckelberry. *Education:* Stephens College, Columbia, Mo., A.A., 1922; Damrosch School of Music, teacher's certificate, 1928; Columbia University, B.S., 1935, M.S., 1953; Yale University, M.S. (nursing), 1938. *Politics:* Republican.

Religion: Protestant. *Home:* 61 Rennell St., Bridgeport, Conn. 06604. *Agent:* Charles Bollinger, Park Ave. S., New York, N.Y. *Office:* College of Nursing, University of Bridgeport, 75 Linden Ave., Bridgeport, Conn. 06602.

CAREER: Stephens College, Columbia, Mo., instructor in piano, 1923-24; Settlement Music School, Philadelphia, Pa., teacher of musicianship, 1928-35; Visiting Nurse Association, New Haven, Conn., staff nurse and assistant to educational director, 1938-39, 1944-45; Yale University, School of Nursing, New Haven, instructor in nursing, 1939-44; Syracuse University, School of Nursing, Syracuse, N.Y., associate professor of nursing, 1945-54; Visiting Nurse Association, Bridgeport, Conn., team nurse leader, 1954; University of Bridgeport, College of Nursing, Bridgeport, Conn., associate professor of public health nursing, beginning 1954. Chairman, State Committee of Public Health Nurse Coordinators, 1948-54. *Member:* American Nurses Association, National League on Nursing, American Public Health Association, Connecticut Public Health Association, P.E.O. Sisterhood.

WRITINGS: Administration of Comprehensive Nursing Care: The Nature of Professional Nursing Practice, Appleton, 1971.

WORK IN PROGRESS: A book on teaching-learning situations in nursing.

SIDELIGHTS: Grace Eckelberry told *CA:* "I write to clarify my thinking and to express ideas to which I am deeply committed. I was under the impression that a writer must select a reader audience and address that audience at all times. In time, I found I must write for myself and for no-one else. The excitement and very real satisfaction I received from getting to know my own thoughts were my greatest rewards. Publication became un-important. Were a young writer to seek my advice, I would urge him to develop the art of thinking and to cherish those images which have become a part of his self. Then try to clothe them in words."

*   *   *

ECKER, H(erman) Paul   1922-1976

PERSONAL: Born May 15, 1922, in Appleton, Wis.; son of Herman Fred (a traffic manager) and Lillie Clara (Tank) Ecker; married Louise Gayle Wassner, June 13, 1945; children: Caryn Brooke. *Education:* Pomona College, Claremont, Calif., B.A., 1948; Claremont Graduate School, M.A., 1949, Ph.D., 1967. *Home:* 8 Meadow Pl., Carmel Valley, Calif. 93924. *Office:* Defense Resources Management Education Center, Naval Postgraduate School, Monterey, Calif. 93940.

CAREER: Kimberly Clark Paper Corp., laboratory technician in physics, 1940-42, 1945-46; San Jose State College (now University), San Jose, Calif., instructor 1949-52; assistant professor and associate director of Institute of Industrial Relations, 1952-55, associate professor of economics, 1955-57; U.S. Naval Postgraduate School, Monterey, Calif., associate professor, 1957-59, professor of economics, beginning 1959, chairman of business administration and economics, 1962-65, executive director of Defense Resources Management Education Center, beginning 1965. Director, Northern California Council on Economic Education, 1956-57. Consultant to North Atlantic Treaty Organization (NATO) and to Italian, German, and Canadian Ministries of Defense. *Military service:* U.S. Navy, aviator, 1942-45; became lieutenant junior grade. *Member:* American Economic Association, Academy of Management.

WRITINGS: (With Vernon Ouellette, John Macrae, and Charles Telford) *Handbook for Supervisors,* Prentice-Hall, 1959, second edition (with Ouellete and Macrae), 1969. Contributor to management journals.†

(Died, 1976)

*   *   *

EDGREN, Harry D(aniel)   1899-

PERSONAL: Born December 20, 1899, in Chicago, Ill.; son of Charles and Lena (Lindal) Edgren; married Helen Hammerstrom, November 6, 1926; children: Jack, Donald. *Education:* Young Men's Christian Association College (now George Williams College), B.P.E., M.P.E., 1926; University of Chicago, B.P.H., M.Ed., 1935; New York University, Ed.D., 1943. *Politics:* Independent. *Religion:* Protestant. *Home:* 1734 Summit Dr., West Lafayette, Ind. 47906.

CAREER: George Williams College, Downers Grove, Ill., professor of recreation education, 1924-51; Fulbright professor in India, 1954-55; Purdue University, Lafayette, Ind., professor of recreation education, 1956-66. *Military service:* U.S. Army, 1918. *Member:* Kappa Delta Pi.

WRITINGS: 1000 Games and Stunts, Abingdon, 1945, reprinted, 1961; (with Earl H. Regnier) *Fun with the Family,* Stipes, c.1958; (with Gunnar A. Peterson) *The Book of Outdoor Winter Activities,* Association Press, 1962; (with Joseph J. Gruber) *Teacher's Handbook of Indoor and Outdoor Games,* Prentice-Hall, 1963; *Fun for the Family,* Abingdon, 1967; (with Peterson) *The Fun in Winter Camping,* Association Press, 1967. Contributor to education and other journals.††

*   *   *

EDWARDS, Margaret (Alexander)   1902-

PERSONAL: Born October 23, 1902, in Childress, Tex.; daughter of Claud Elvon and Hadena (Crews) Alexander; married Philip H. Edwards, March 29, 1945 (deceased). *Education:* Trinity University, Waxahachie, Tex., A.B., 1922; Columbia University, A.M., 1928, B.S. in L.S., 1937. *Politics:* Democrat. *Home:* 3613 Clayton Rd., R.D. 3, Joppa, Md. 21085.

CAREER: Teacher of English and Latin in public schools in Forney, Tex., Vernon, Tex., and Towson, Md., 1923-32; Enoch Pratt Free Library, Baltimore, Md., coordinator of young adult services, 1932-62. Visiting teacher in library schools at McGill University, Rutgers University, Catholic University, Texas University, and University of Montana. Conducted workshops and lectured throughout United States. *Member:* American Civil Liberties Union, American Library Association (honorary member), League of Women Voters (president of Harford County Chapter, 1968-70), Maryland Library Association (honorary member). *Awards, honors:* Grolier Award, American Library Association, 1957.

WRITINGS: The Fair Garden and the Swarm of Beasts: The Library and the Young Adult, Hawthorn, 1969. Contributor to library journals and other periodicals.

SIDELIGHTS: Margaret Edwards told *CA:* "My West Texas pioneer and frontier background is probably responsible for many of my good and reprehensible characteristics. The fact that I bawled out a supervisor and was fired from teaching is responsible for my finding my true vocation with teenagers and books." She added, "I am concerned: 1. That public and school librarians give increased stress to the promotion of the individual's reading for pleasure and enrichment; 2. That the nation's individual citizens be more concerned for the nation's problems, particularly its minorities; 3. That the great potential in modern youth become a force for constructive change in America."

AVOCATIONAL INTERESTS: Owns a small farm in Maryland where she maintains a herd of registered Herefords.

*　　*　　*

EDWARDS, T(homas) Bentley 1906-

PERSONAL: Born December 18, 1906, in Birmingham, England; son of Thomas William (manager of an institution) and Annie Elizabeth (Polson) Edwards; married Beryl Bamford, April 30, 1930; children: Diane Elizabeth (Mrs. Robert Connor Gass), Thomas David. *Education:* University of British Columbia, B.A., 1930; University of Washington, Seattle, M.S., 1938; University of California, Berkeley, Ph.D., 1949. *Home:* 8624 Edgehill Ct., El Cerrito, Calif. 94530. *Office:* School of Education, University of California, Berkeley, Calif. 94720.

CAREER: High school science teacher in Vancouver, British Columbia, 1930-46; St. Mary's College of California, Moraga, instructor in chemistry, 1947-49; Chico State College (now California State University, Chico), assistant professor of physical science, 1949-52; director of northern California regional project in secondary education, 1952-53; University of California, Berkeley, assistant professor, 1953-55, associate professor, 1955-61, professor of education, 1961-73, professor emeritus, 1973—. Visiting professor at University of Baghdad, 1966-67. *Member:* National Society for the Study of Education, Association for Supervision and Curriculum Development, American Association for the Advancement of Science, Phi Delta Kappa.

WRITINGS: (With H. O. English and D. M. Flather) *Science and Life,* Dent, 1941; (with English and others) *Science and Progress,* Dent, 1946; *The Regional Project in Secondary Education,* University of California Press, 1956; (with J. Cecil Parker and William B. Stegeman) *Curriculum in America,* Crowell, 1962; (editor with Frederick M. Wirt) *School Desegregation in the North,* Chandler Publishing, 1967.

WORK IN PROGRESS: Science and Education; articles on education of the culturally different.

SIDELIGHTS: In 1946 Edwards sailed with his family from Vancouver, Canada, to Berkeley, Calif., aboard a thirty-two foot ketch. They lived aboard the boat for two years while he completed his doctorate.†

*　　*　　*

EFRON, Alexander 1897-

PERSONAL: Surname rhymes with "Teflon"; born December 26, 1897, in Grodno, Russia; became U.S. citizen; son of Benjamin (an artist) and Anna (Yudkofsky) Efron; married Rose Kunitz, January 31, 1919; children: Edith, Robert. *Education:* Columbia University, A.B., 1918, E.E., 1921, M.A., 1931, Ph.D., 1938. *Politics:* Democrat ("moderate orientation"). *Home:* 1500 Bay Rd., Apt. 1412, Miami Beach, Fla. 33139.

CAREER: New York (N.Y.) public schools, teacher of physics, 1923-67, chairman of physical science department at John Adams High School, 1930-40, chairman of physics department at Stuyvesant High School, 1940-67, principal of Stuyvesant Evening High and Trade School, 1937-39, roving science supervisor in summer and evening high schools,

1952-66. Member of examination committee, New York State Board of Regents, 1940-45 and College Entrance Examination Board, 1948-54. *Military service:* U.S. Army, 1918. *Member:* American Association of Physics Teachers, American Institute of Physics, Physics Club of New York (president, 1926-27). *Awards, honors:* Award of honor by Physics Club of New York, 1964; award as "outstanding secondary school teacher of science in New York" from New York section of Institute of Electrical and Electronics Engineers, 1965.

WRITINGS: Basic Physics, J. F. Rider, 1957, *Laboratory Workbook,* 1961, published as *Exploring Modern Physics,* with *Laboratory Manual and Teacher Manual,* Hayden, 1968; *Heat,* J. F. Rider, 1957, published as *Exploring Heat,* Hayden, 1969; *Sound,* J. F. Rider, 1957, published as *Exploring Sound,* Hayden, 1969; *Light,* J. F. Rider, 1958, published as *Exploring Light,* Hayden, 1969; *Liquids and Gases,* J. F. Rider, 1958; *Mechanics,* J. F. Rider, 1958, published as *Exploring Mechanics,* Hayden, 1969; *Nuclear Energy,* J. F. Rider, 1958, published as *Exploring Matter and Nuclear Energy,* Hayden, 1969; *Magnetic and Electrical Fundamentals,* J. F. Rider, 1959; *Direct Current Electricity,* J. F. Rider, 1960; *Alternating Current Electricity,* J. F. Rider, 1961; *Experimental Physics for Young People,* J. F. Rider, 1962. Contributor to *Collier's Science Encyclopedia, Harper's Science Encyclopedia,* and to education journals.

WORK IN PROGRESS: Energy: Past, Present, and Future.

SIDELIGHTS: Alexander Efron has traveled extensively; he has studied art and paints floral subjects. Dr. Efron speaks five languages.†

*　　*　　*

EGBERT, Donald Drew 1902-1973

PERSONAL: Born May 12, 1902, in Norwalk, Conn.; son of George Drew (a Congregational minister) and Kate Estelle (Powers) Egbert; married Virginia Wylie (a researcher in medieval art), August 9, 1946. *Education:* Princeton University, B.A., 1924, M.F.A., 1927, further graduate study in art and archaeology, 1927-29. *Home:* 164 Moore St., Princeton, N.J. 08540.

CAREER: Princeton University, Princeton, N.J., instructor, 1929-35, assistant professor, 1935-44, associate professor, 1944-46, professor of art, archaeology, and architecture, 1946-70, Butler Professor of the History of Architecture, 1968-70, professor emeritus, 1970-73, American Civilization Program, 1942-70. Lecturer in ancient architecture at Bryn Mawr College, 1930. Color photographer with one-man shows at Princeton University Library, 1957, and George Eastman House, Rochester, N.Y., 1958. *Member:* Society of Architectural Historians, College Art Association, Mediaeval Academy of America, American Historical Association, American Studies Association, Renaissance Society of America, Academy of Political Science, American Academy of Political and Social Science, American Society for Aesthetics, Metropolitan Museum of Art (life fellow), Phi Beta Kappa. *Awards, honors:* Haskins Medal from Mediaeval Academy of America for distinguished scholarship in the field of the Middle Ages, 1943.

WRITINGS: The Tickhill Psalter and Related Manuscripts, New York Public Library, 1940; *Princeton Portraits,* Princeton University Press, 1947; (editor with Stow Persons, and contributor) *Socialism and American Life,* two volumes, Princeton University Press, 1952; *Socialism and*

American Art in the Light of European Utopianism, Marxism, and Anarchism, Princeton University Press, 1967; *Social Radicalism and the Arts, Western Europe: A Cultural History from the French Revolution to 1968,* Knopf, 1970; *On Arts in Society: Selections from the Periodical Writings of Donald Drew Egbert,* American Life Foundation, 1970. Contributor to art, history, and architecture journals.

WORK IN PROGRESS: Volumes II and III of *Social Radicalism and the Arts,* covering the Soviet Union and the United States.

SIDELIGHTS: Egbert traveled widely in Europe, including Soviet Russia and most other Iron Curtain countries, and in Egypt and the Near East.†

(Died January 3, 1973)

*   *   *

EHRENZWEIG, Albert A(rmin)   1906-1974

PERSONAL: Born April 1, 1906, in Herzogenburg, Austria; came to United States in 1939, naturalized in 1945; son of Albert (a professor of law) and Emma (Bachrachova) Ehrenzweig; married Erica Witrofsky (a braillist), April 9, 1933; children: Elizabeth (Mrs. David T. Steffen), Joan (Mrs. Egon van Kaschnitz). *Education:* University of Vienna, Dr.utr.jur., 1928; University of Bristol, Intermediate LL.B., 1939; University of Chicago, Dr.Jur., 1942; Columbia University, LL.M., 1942, S.J.D., 1952. *Office:* School of Law, University of California, Berkeley, Calif. 94720.

CAREER: Austrian Courts, secretary to judges, 1929-33, judge, 1933-38; University of Vienna, Vienna, Austria, privatdocent, 1937-38; State of New York Law Revision Commission, Ithaca, research assistant, 1942-44; Cravath, Swaine & Moore (law firm), New York, N.Y., associate, 1944-48; University of California, Berkeley, professor of law, 1948-74. Fulbright professor at University of Tokyo, 1956, and University of Pavia, 1960; University of Vienna, honorary professor, 1961-74, honorary senator, 1965-74; NATO (North Atlantic Treaty Organization) professor of private international law at Leyden, Netherlands, spring, 1964.

MEMBER: American Bar Association, American Foreign Law Association, American Society for Political and Legal Philosophy, International Association of Insurance Law (honorary president), Society for Private International Law (Japan; honorary member), International Academy of Comparative Law, Bar Association of City of New York. *Awards, honors:* Guggenheim fellowship, 1952; Dr. Hon. Causa, University of Stockholm, 1969.

WRITINGS: Irrtum und Rechtswidrigkeit, M. Perles, 1931; *Die Schuldhaftung im Schadenersatzrecht,* Manz, 1936; *Zur Erneuerung des Schadenersatzrechts,* Manz, 1937; (with F. E. Koch and others) *Income Tax Treaties: The Income Tax Conventions of the United States with Great Britain, Canada and Other Countries,* Commerce Clearing House (Chicago), 1950; *Negligence without Fault,* University of California Press, 1951; *"Full Aid" Insurance for the Traffic Victim,* University of California Press, 1954; *American-Greek Private International Law,* Oceana, 1957; *Conflict of Laws, Part I: Jurisdiction and Judgments,* West Publishing, 1959; *A Treatise on the Conflict of Laws* (includes revision of *Jurisdiction and Judgments),* West Publishing, 1962; *American-Japanese Private International Law,* Oceana, 1964; (with David W. Louisell) *Jurisdiction in a Nutshell: State and Federal,* West Publishing, 1964, 3rd edition, 1973;

Conflicts in a Nutshell, West Publishing, 1965, 3rd edition, 1974; (co-author) *Selected Problems of Conflict of Laws,* School of Law, University of California, 1965; *Private International Law: A Comparative Treatise on American International Conflicts Law,* Oceana, Volume I, 1967, Volume II (with Erik Jayme), 1973; (contributor) *Specific Principles of Private Transnational Law,* Academy of International Law (Hague), 1968; *Psychoanalytic Jurisprudence,* Oceana, 1971. Contributor of about two hundred and fifty articles and reviews to American and foreign legal periodicals.

BIOGRAPHICAL/CRITICAL SOURCES: California Law Review, October, 1974.†

(Died June 4, 1974)

*   *   *

EHRMANN, Herbert B(rutus)   1891-1970

PERSONAL: Born December 15, 1891, in Louisville, Ky.; son of Hilmar and Ernestine (Heissman) Ehrmann; married Sara Emilie Rosenfeld, May 12, 1917; children: H. Bruce, Robert Lincoln. *Education:* Harvard University, A.B., 1912, LL.B., 1914. *Religion:* Jewish. *Home:* 14 Irving St., Brookline, Mass.

CAREER: Admitted to Massachusetts Bar, 1915, and began practice of law in Boston that same year; member of Goulston & Storrs (law firm), Boston, Mass., beginning 1921. Counsel with William G. Thompson for Sacco and Vanzetti, 1926-27. Member of Massachusetts Minimum Wage Commission, U.S. Shipping Board, 1917-18, War Labor Policies Board, 1918-19, Massachusetts Judicial Council, 1934-37, and Massachusetts Civil Service Commission, 1939-45. Member of board of directors, U.S. Trust Co., Boston. American Jewish Committee, president, 1959-61, honorary president, beginning 1961. Trustee of Massachusetts Training Schools, 1933-37, and Social Law Library, Boston; former president of Hale House Association and Greater Boston Federation of Neighborhood Houses. *Member:* American Bar Association, American Arbitration Association (arbitrator), Massachusetts Bar Association, Boston Bar Association (council member), Old South Association, Delta Sigma Rho, Boston Author's Club, Harvard Club (Boston). *Awards, honors:* Mystery Story Writers of America Edgar Allan Poe Award, 1969, for *The Case That Will Not Die.*

WRITINGS: Criminal Courts of Cleveland, Ohio, Cleveland Foundation, 1921; *The Untried Case,* Vanguard, 1933, reissued, 1960; *The Case That Will Not Die: Commonwealth vs. Sacco and Vanzetti,* Little, Brown, 1969. Author of a play, "Under This Roof," produced in Westboro, Mass., at Red Barn Theatre, 1940, and on Broadway, 1942. Contributor to legal and other periodicals.†

(Died June 17, 1970)

*   *   *

ELDREDGE, Laurence H(oward)   1902-

PERSONAL: Born March 18, 1902, in Cold Spring, N.J.; son of Irvin H. (a merchant) and Marie Louise (Benton) Eldredge; married Helen Biddle Gans, September 30, 1926; children: Mary Harriet, Deborah (Mrs. D. Eldredge duPont), Helen Louise (Mrs. James W. Bradley). *Education:* Lafayette College, B.S., 1924; University of Pennsylvania, LL.B., 1927. *Home:* 3741 Broderick St., San Francisco, Calif. 94123. *Office:* Hastings College of the Law, University of California, San Francisco, Calif. 94102.

CAREER: Public Ledger, Philadelphia, Pa., reporter, 1924-

25; syndicated news writer, 1925-27; admitted to Pennsylvania Bar, 1927; attorney in Philadelphia, 1927-71, as associate of Montgomery & McCracken, 1927-38, and member of firm of Norris, Lex, Hart & Eldredge, 1944-56; admitted to California State Bar, 1972; University of California, San Francisco, Hastings College of the Law, professor of law, beginning 1972. Temple University, professor of law, 1928-33, adjunct professor, 1947-52; University of Pennsylvania, associate in law, 1933-34, 1937-38, professor of law, 1938-44, lecturer on medical jurisprudence in Medical School, 1940-68; visiting professor of law, Columbia University, 1941, 1946. Special deputy attorney general of Pennsylvania, 1948-49. President of Episcopal Hospital, 1946-53, Philadelphia Art Alliance, 1949-66, and Museum Council of Philadelphia, 1958-59; Magee Memorial Hospital, trustee, 1946-59, secretary-treasurer, 1953-59; member of board of directors, Hospital Council, 1952-60; past president, Better Business Bureau of Philadelphia. *Military service:* U.S. Coast Guard Reserve, superintendent of Voluntary Training School, Philadelphia, during World War II; became commander.

MEMBER: American Law Institute, American Bar Association, Pennsylvania Bar Association, California Bar Association, San Francisco Bar Association, Philadelphia Bar Association (chairman of board of governors, 1960-61), Lafayette College Alumni Association (president, 1961-62), Phi Beta Kappa, Delta Upsilon, Order of the Coif, Franklin Inn Club, Penn Club, Union League, Racquet Club, Lawyers Club of Philadelphia, Bohemian Club and University Club (both San Francisco). *Awards, honors:* Citation from Lafayette College, 1960; Meritorious Service award, Delta Upsilon, 1961; Medal of Achievement, Philadelphia Art Alliance, 1966.

WRITINGS: Pennsylvania Annotations to Restatement, Torts, American Law Institute, Volume I, 1938, Volume II, 1939; *Modern Tort Problems,* Bisel, 1941; *Trials of a Philadelphia Lawyer* (autobiographical), Lippincott, 1968. Contributor of articles and reviews to legal journals and newspapers. Editor, *Pennsylvania Bar Association Quarterly,* 1938-42; state reporter, Supreme Court of Pennsylvania, 1942-68.

*   *   *

ELLENBERGER, Henri F(rederic) 1905-

PERSONAL: Born November 6, 1905, in Northern Rhodesia; son of Victor and Evangeline (Christol) Ellenberger; married Emilie Von Bachst (an artist), 1930; children: Michel, Helene (Mrs. Pierre Koppel), Andre, Irene (Mrs. Gilles Boisvert). *Education:* University of Paris, Faculte de Medecine, diploma, 1934; also studied in Strasbourg; psychiatric studies in Paris and in Switzerland. *Religion:* Protestant. *Home:* 4846 Madison Ave., Montreal, Quebec, Canada H3X-3T. *Office:* University of Montreal, Montreal, Quebec, Canada.

CAREER: Taught psychiatry at Menninger School of Psychiatry, 1953-59; McGill University, Montreal, Quebec, associate professor of psychiatry, 1960-63; University of Montreal, Montreal, professor of criminology, beginning 1963. Psychiatric consultant, Institut Philippe Pinel de Montreal, 1965-72; psychiatrist, Hotels Dieu de Montreal Hospital, beginning 1972. *Awards, honors:* Golden Medal of the Beccaria Prize, German Criminological Society, 1970.

WRITINGS: (Editor with Rollo May and others) *Existence: A New Dimension in Psychiatry and Psychology,* Basic Books, 1958; *The Discovery of the Unconscious: The History and Evolution of Dynamic Psychiatry,* Basic Books, 1970. Contributor to encyclopedias. Contributor of about one hundred fifty articles to professional journals.

SIDELIGHTS: The Discovery of the Unconscious: The History and Evolution of Dynamic Psychiatry has been translated into French, Italian, Spanish, and Japanese.

*   *   *

ELLIN, E(lizabeth) M(uriel) 1905-

PERSONAL: Born March 22, 1905, in Waiuku, New Zealand; daughter of Ernest Morely (a farmer) and Edith (Sorby) Ellin. *Education:* Educated in Auckland, New Zealand. *Home:* 42 Beach Rd., Castor Bay, Auckland 9, New Zealand.

CAREER: "Jack of all trades ... here, there and anywhere."

WRITINGS: The Children of Clearwater Bay (juvenile), Macmillan, 1969.

WORK IN PROGRESS: Bound for New Zealand and *The Greenstone Axe,* both children's stories of early New Zealand.

BIOGRAPHICAL/CRITICAL SOURCES: Times Literary Supplement, October 16, 1969.††

*   *   *

ELLIS, Amanda M. 1898-1969

PERSONAL: Born April 30, 1898, in Jefferson City Mo.; daughter of Barna Harris and Lillie (Grieshammer) Ellis. *Education:* Colorado College, A.B. (with honors), 1920; University of Iowa, M.A., 1922; University of Illinois, graduate study, 1926-27. *Politics:* Democrat. *Home:* 1130 Wood Ave., Colorado Springs, Colo. 80903.

CAREER: University of Iowa, Iowa City, instructor in English, 1920-22; Des Moines University, Des Moines, Iowa, instructor, 1922-23, assistant professor of English, 1924-26; University of Illinois, Urbana, visiting professor, 1926-27; Colorado College, Colorado Springs, assistant professor, 1927-31, associate professor, 1931-60, professor of English, 1960-67, professor emeritus, 1967-69, writer in residence, 1958-67. *Member:* National Council of Teachers of English (national vice-president, 1942), College English Association, American Association of University Women (state president, 1946), Modern Language Association of America, Authors League of America, Colorado Authors League, Colorado Springs Symphony Guild, Phi Beta Kappa, Theta Sigma Phi (honorary). *Awards, honors:* Order of the Rose Award from Delta Gamma.

WRITINGS: (Editor) *Representative Short Stories,* Thomas Nelson, 1928, revised edition, 1938; *The Literature of England,* Little, Brown, 1938; *Elizabeth the Woman* (novel), Dutton, 1951; *The Strange, Uncertain Years: An Informal Account of Life in Six Colorado Communities,* Shoe String, 1966; *Rebels and Conservatives: Dorothy and William Wadsworth and Their Circle,* Indiana University Press, 1967. Author of *Recent Continental Literature* and *Continental Literature Today,* for the American Association of University Women; also author of *The Colorado Springs Story,* 1954, *Bonanza Towns: Leadville and Cripple Creek,* 1954, *Legends and Tales of the Rockies,* 1954, *Pioneers,* 1955, and *The Romance of Uranium,* 1955. Writer of two television scripts for "Alcoa Presents," American Broadcasting Co. network. Contributor of about seventy articles to magazines and journals, and reviews to *New York Times, St. Louis Post-Dispatch,* and other newspapers.

WORK IN PROGRESS: A book on three medieval women.†

(Died May 11, 1969)

ELLIS, Clyde T(aylor) 1908-

PERSONAL: Born December 21, 1908, near Garfield, Ark.; son of Cecil Oscar (a farmer) and Minerva Jane (Taylor) Ellis; married Izella Baker, December 20, 1931; married Camille Waldron Fitzhugh, September 23, 1966; children: (first marriage) Patricia Suzanne, Mary Lynn. *Education:* University of Arkansas, B.S., 1958; George Washington University, graduate study. *Politics:* Democrat. *Religion:* Episcopalian. *Home:* 5317 Kenwood Ave., Chevy Chase, Md.

CAREER: Superintendent of schools in Garfield, Ark., 1920-34; admitted to Arkansas Bar, 1933; attorney in private practice, Garfield and Bentonville, Ark., 1934-43; National Rural Electric Cooperative Association, Washington, D.C., general manager, 1943-67; appointed to National Water Commission by President Johnson, 1968-70; assistant to Senator John A. McClellan, Washington, D.C., beginning 1971. Member of Arkansas General Assembly, 1933-34, Arkansas Senate, 1935-36, and of U.S. House of Representatives, 1941-43. Consultant in government relations. *Military service:* U.S. Naval Reserve, World War II. *Member:* Arkansas Bar Association, Washington (D.C.) Bar Association, Tau Kappa Alpha, Blue Key, Masons, Cosmos Club, Congressional Country Club.

WRITINGS: A Giant Step, Random House, 1967.†

* * *

ELLIS, J(ames) H(ervey) S(tewart) 1893-

PERSONAL: Born May 23, 1893, in Rensselaer, Ind.; son of James Hervey Stewart (a merchant) and Jessie (Dayhuff) Ellis; married Gwen Parsons, August 19, 1918; married second wife, Maxine Courtney Ford, April 17, 1945; married third wife, Catherine Jones Wheeler, November 6, 1958; children: (first marriage) James Parsons, Daniel Clyde. *Education:* University of Virginia, student, 1912-13; University of Chicago, Ph.B., 1917. *Politics:* Republican. *Religion:* Protestant. *Address:* P.O. Box 2448, Reno, Nev. 89505.

CAREER: Arthur W. Shaw Co., Chicago, Ill., staff of promotion department, 1917-18; William H. Rankin Co., Chicago, vice-president, 1919-28; Erwin Wasey & Co., Chicago, and New York City, copy chief, 1928-35; Kudner Agency, Inc., New York City, executive vice-president, 1935-45, president, 1945-58. Former chairman of board, National Outdoor Advertising Bureau; former director, American Association of Advertising Agencies; member, U.S. Post Office Advisory Committee, 1953-61. *Military service:* American Expeditionary Forces, Tank Corps, 1918-19 (his corporal's warrant was signed "D. D. Eisenhower Capt. Inf."). *Member:* Farmington Country Club (Charlottesville, Va.).

WRITINGS: Billboards to Buicks: Advertising as I Lived It, Abelard, 1968, published as *The Jumping Frog From Jasper County; or, The Hoosier Boy Lands on Madison Avenue,* Intext, 1970.

AVOCATIONAL INTERESTS: Shopwork, photography.

* * *

ELLIS, Ray C. 1898-

PERSONAL: Born March 31, 1898, in Warren, Mass.; son of George and Fannie (Stebbins) Ellis; married Wilhelmina Powers, September 1, 1921 (died September 30, 1971); married Aline L. Henderson, April 5, 1972; children: (first marriage) Ruth, Ray, Jr., Herbert. *Education:* Tri-State College, Angola, Ind., B.Sc. (engineering), 1922; additional study at Massachusetts Institute of Technology. *Member:* Republican. *Religion:* Protestant. *Home:* Dark Harbor, Me.

CAREER: General Motors, various posts, 1921-36, general manager of Delco Radio Division, Kokomo, Ind., 1936-41; U.S. War Production Board, Washington, D.C., deputy director of Radio and Radar Division, 1941-44; Raytheon Co., Lexington, Mass., vice-president, 1945-62. During World War II also served with Office of Scientific Research and Development and other war committees. Chairman of Maine Educational Television Advisory Council.

WRITINGS: (With Charles Olson) *Export or Die,* Dartnell, 1966.

* * *

EMERSON, Alice B.
[Collective pseudonym]

WRITINGS—All published by Cupples & Leon: "Betty Gordon Stories" series: *Betty Gordon at Ocean Park,* 1923; *. . . and Her School Chums,* 1924; *. . . on the Campus,* 1928; *. . . and the Hale Twins,* 1929; *. . . at Mystery Farm,* 1930; *. . . on No-trail Island,* 1931; *. . . and the Mystery Girl,* 1932.

"Ruth Fielding Stories" series: *Ruth Fielding and the Gypsies,* 1915; *. . . on the St. Lawrence,* 1922; *. . . in the Far North,* 1924; *. . . at Cameron Hall,* 1928; *. . . Clearing Her Name,* 1929; *. . . in Talking Pictures,* 1930; *. . . and Baby June,* 1931; *. . . and Her Double,* 1932; *. . . and Her Greatest Triumph,* 1933; *. . . and Her Crowning Victory,* 1934; *. . . in the Saddle,* c. 1938.

SIDELIGHTS: See **ADAMS, Harriet S., STRATEMEYER, Edward L.,** and **SVENSON, Andrew E.**†

* * *

EMERSON, H(enry) O(liver) 1893-
(Oliver Gordon)

PERSONAL: Born August 21, 1893, in Thornaby, England; son of Thomas (a stock-taker) and Mary Elizabeth (Oliver) Emerson; married Adrienne Cohen van Dunnegem, April 20, 1925; children: Hubert, Denise (Mrs. Geoffrey Shaw), Monica Emerson Hamilton. *Education:* University College, Nottingham (now University of Nottingham), B.A., 1914. *Home and office:* 16 Old Sneed Rd., Bristol 9, England.

CAREER: Harvey Grammar School, Folkestone, England, former head of modern languages department, and headmaster at various times. Served as private secretary to Gordon Selfridge. Lecturer at Oxford University, University of Bristol, University of Lancaster, for British Broadcasting Corp. (in both French and English), and at colleges in United States and Mexico; chief examiner in French for General Certificate of Education, Associated Examining Board. *Military service:* British Army, 1914-19; became major. *Member:* Institute of Journalists, (honorary secretary/treasurer of British District Branch), Press Club (London). *Awards, honors:* Chevalier des Palmes Academiques (France).

WRITINGS: (With H. R. Morris, translator and author of notes) *Toto, Policier de France,* Hachette, 1929; *Easy French for the Forces,* Continental (London), 1940; "Modern French," four-part course, Continental, 1940, revised edition, 1955; *A Practical French Course for Evening, Technical, and Commercial Schools,* three parts, Continental, 1940; *A Picture Book of Free Composition in French,* Continental, 1940; *Petits Contes Amusants,* Continental, 1943; *Nouveaux Contes d'aujourd'hui,* Continental, 1943;

Comedies d'aujourd'hui, Continental, 1943; (with F. Evans) *From Lands of Tale and Legend*, Hachette, 1947; *Guidance and Practice in French*, Hulton Educational Publications, 1965; *Pierre qui Roule*, Macmillan, 1966; *Images Francaises*, Macmillan, 1970. Also author of *Le Cirque Carlini, Free Composition in French for First Examinations, Contes d'aujourd'hui, Premier Contes*, and *Victoria: Gare du Nord*, all published by Hachette.

General editor, Brodie's "Modern French" series: *Hints for Ordinary Level Candidates in French; Contes de nos Jours; Contes et Comedies; Jean Lemaire: Contrebandier; Un peu de Tout*. Also editor of *Five One-Act Plays*, published by Hachette. Contributor to newspapers in Great Britain and the United States; regular reviewer for *The Teacher* (London).

WORK IN PROGRESS: Continuing work on "Modern French" series; revising *Modern French*.

* * *

EMMRICH, Curt   1897-1975
(Kurt Emmrich; Peter Bamm, a pseudonym)

PERSONAL: Born October 20, 1897, in Hochneukirch, Germany; son of Johannes and Beatrice (Schomburg) Emmrich; married Ruth von Stangen, March 15, 1942; children: Sylvia (Mrs. Dieter Biedenkopf). *Education:* Medical student at Universities of Goettingen, Freiburg, and Frankfurt, 1919-22; University of Berlin, dr.med., 1923; specialized work in sinology at Universities of Berlin, Paris, and Goettingen, 1923-28, and in surgery in Berlin and Hamburg, 1934. *Home:* 25 Seestrasse, Zollikon, Switzerland. *Agent:* Felix Guggenheim, 725 North Roxbury Dr., Beverly Hills, Calif.; and Mrs. Ruth Liepman, Marienburgweg 23, Zurich, Switzerland.

CAREER: General surgeon in German hospitals, 1934-40; collaborator on British broadcasts in Hamburg, Germany, 1945-47; full-time writer, 1947-75. *Military service:* German Army, 1914-18, 1940-45; served in France in World War I; commanding officer of surgical theater at the front in Russia in World War II. *Member:* Deutsche Akademie fuer Sprache und Dichtung, Comite Medico-Juridique de Monaco, Comite de Medicine et de Pharmacie Militaries (Belgium), Historisch Genootschap (Netherlands), P.E.N. *Awards, honors:* Military Order of St. Heinrich; Paracelcus Medal of German Medical Association.

WRITINGS—All under pseudonym Peter Bamm, except as indicated: (Under name Kurt Emmrich) *Die unregelmaessigen Verteidigungen der Damenbauerereoffnung*, [Berlin], 1924; (under name Kurt Emmrich) *Die unregelmaessigen Spielanfaenge*, [Berlin], 1925; *C₁₈fi₂₂fi₂fl fiie Geschichte einer Entdeckung* (booklet on estrone), Schering, 1939; (translator) James Johnston Abraham, *Am puls des lebens, blaetter aus dem tagebuch eines arztes*, Deutsche Verlagsanstalt, 1939; *Ex Ovo: Essays ueber die Medizin*, Deutsche Verlagsanstalt, 1948; *Feuilletons* (selections from *Die kleine Weltlaterne, I-Punkt*, and *Der Hahnenschwanz*), 1949, published as *Die kleine Weltlaterne*, Deutsche Verlagsanstalt, 1951, subsequent editions published as *Anarchie mit Liebe; Die unsichtbare Flagge* (personal narratives of World War II), Koesel-Verlag, 1952, translation by Frank Herrmann published as *The Invisible Flag*, John Day, 1956; *Fruehe Staetten der Christenheit*, Koesel-Verlag, 1955, translation by Stanley Godman published as *Early Sites of Christianity*, Pantheon, 1957; (editor) Roloff Beny, *Wiege unserer Welt: Staetten alter Kulturen am Mittelmeer*, Droemersche Verlagsanstalt Theodore Knaur Nachf, 1958; *Welten des Glau-*

bens Aus den Fruehzeiten des Christentums, Droemersche Verlagsanstalt Theodore Knaur Nachf, 1959, translation and adaptation by Christopher Holme published as *The Kingdoms of Christ from the Days of the Apostles to the Middle Ages*, McGraw, 1959.

An den Kuesten des Lichts: Variationen ueber das Thema Aegaeis, Koesel-Verlag, 1961; *Anarchie mit Liebe*, Deutsche Verlagsanstalt, 1962; *Alexander: Oder, Die Verwandlung der Welt*, Droemer, 1965, translation by J. Maxwell Brownjohn published in an illustrated edition as *Alexander the Great: Power as Destiny*, McGraw, 1968; *Werke*, two volumes (Volume I includes *Fruehe Staetten der Christenheit, An den Kuesten des Lichts*, and *Alexander*; Volume II includes *Die unsichtbare Flagge, Ex Ovo, Die kleine Weltlaterne*, and *Anarchie mit Liebe*), Droemer, 1967; *Adam und der Affe* (essays), Deutsche Verlagsanstalt, 1969; *Eines Menschen Zeit*, Droemer, 1972; *Kleines Kaleidoskop: Betrachtungen eines Chronisten*, Voss Verlag, 1973; *Am Rande der Schoepfung*, Deutsche Verlagsanstalt, 1974; *Ein Leben lang*, Deutsche Verlagsanstalt, 1976. Also author of *Die Kleine Weltlaterne*, 1935, *I-Punkt*, 1937, and *Der Hahnenschwantz*, 1939. Contributor of about one thousand essays and reviews to magazines and daily newspapers.

SIDELIGHTS: Die unsichtbare Flagge has appeared in eleven languages, and five other books by Emmrich have been published in seven or more languages. He has done scientific research on travels in China, South America, Mexico, the Near East, all western European countries, and in East, West, and North Africa.

BIOGRAPHICAL/CRITICAL SOURCES: Book World, December 15, 1968; Rudolf Riedler, *Drei Gespraeche: Luise Rinser, Peter Bamm, Johannes Mario Simmel*, Auer, 1974.†

(Died March 30, 1975)

* * *

ENGEL, Salo   1908-1972

PERSONAL: Born July 31, 1908, in Austria; naturalized U.S. citizen, 1952; son of Wolfgang (a businessman) and Fanny (Tuchmann) Engel; married Rosel Brauner, June 29, 1933; children: Michael. *Education:* University of Frankfurt, Referendar (cum laude), 1931; studied at University of Geneva and Graduate Institute of International Studies, Geneva, 1933-36; Graduate Institute of International Studies, Doctorate es sciences politiques (summa cum laude), 1936; Academy of International Law, The Hague, postdoctoral fellow, 1937. *Religion:* Jewish. *Office:* Department of Political Science, University of Tennessee, Knoxville, Tenn. 37916.

CAREER: Law practice in attorney's office, Frankfurt am Main, Germany, 1931-33; Geneva Research Center, Geneva, Switzerland, research associate, 1937-40; Permanent Court of International Justice, Geneva, special assistant to registrar, J. Lopez Olivan, 1941-46; University of Tennessee, Knoxville, professor of political science and international law, beginning 1947. Visiting consultant on comparative law, Harvard University, 1958-59; visiting professor of government, Louisiana State University, 1967; Cordell Hull lecturer, Middle Tennessee State University, 1971. Legal codification adviser to Panama, 1955-57.

MEMBER: American Society of International Law, American Political Science Association, International Studies Association, American Association of University Professors, Southern Political Science Association. *Awards, honors:* Knight of Panamanian Order Nacional de Vasco Nunez de Balboa, 1957; Ford Foundation law faculty fellow, 1963-64; Rockefeller Foundation research grant, 1964-65; University of Tennessee faculty grants, 1970, 1971-72; nominated as senior Fulbright scholar in Israel, 1971.

WRITINGS: Art. 5 und Art. 14, Satz 3 der Voelkerbundsatzung, Rosnoblet, 1936; (contributor) Karl Strupp, editor, *Bibliographie du droit des gens et des relations internationales,* [Leyden], 1939; *League Reform: An Analysis of Official Proposals and Discussions 1936-1939,* Geneva Research Centre, 1940; *Recueil des lois usuelles suisses,* Fiches Juridiques Suisses, 1946; (contributor) *Yearbook of World Affairs,* Praeger, 1953; *The Changing Charter of the United Nations* (booklet), London Institute of World Affairs, 1958; *Legislacion Panamena,* Universidad de Panama, Volume I, 1958; (editor with R. A. Metall) *Law, State and International Legal Order: Essays in Honor of Hans Kelsen,* University of Tennessee Press, 1964.

Contributing editor, *Schweizer Lexikon in sieben Baenden,* [Zurich], 1945, and *Dictionary of Political Science,* 1964. Contributor to *Anuario de Derecho* (Panama), *American Journal of International Law, Revue de droit international et de legislation comparee,* and other journals.

WORK IN PROGRESS: Handbook of International Treaties and Documents, 1815-1970; Volume II of *Legislacion Panamena;* a revision of Hans Kelsen's *The Law of the United Nations;* editing *The U.N.—One Generation After,* a symposium; editing *Cordell Hull: A Centennial Evaluation.*

SIDELIGHTS: Salo Engel spoke and wrote in French and Spanish, spoke Hebrew and Yiddish, and read Latin.†

(Died, 1972)

* * *

ENGELS, Norbert (Anthony) 1903-

PERSONAL: Born September 4, 1903, in Green Bay, Wis.; son of William P. (a tailor) and Euphrasia (Dave) Engels; married Eleanore Perry, June 19, 1929 (died, 1966); married Laone Gagnon, 1968; children: (first marriage) John, David, Julie. *Education:* University of Notre Dame, B.Mus., 1926, M.A., 1927. *Religion:* Roman Catholic. *Home and office:* Half Moon Lake, Pound, Wis. 54161.

CAREER: Professional musician (trombonist and arranger) in United States and Europe, 1922-30; University of Notre Dame, Notre Dame, Ind., instructor, 1927-45, professor of English literature, 1945-69, professor emeritus, 1969—. *Military service:* U.S. Naval Reserve, 1919-22. *Member:* American Association of University Professors.

WRITINGS: Man Around the House, Prentice-Hall, 1948; *Thou Art My Strength* (poems), Benedictine Press, 1949; (with son, John Engels) *Writing Techniques,* McKay, 1962; (with John Engels) *Experience and Imagination,* McKay, 1965. Contributor to *Popular Mechanics, Saturday Evening Post, Popular Science, Commonweal, America, American Home,* and other periodicals; also contributor of Sunday features on travel to newspapers. Contributing editor, *Science and Mechanics,* 1950-60.

WORK IN PROGRESS: A study of imagery in Shakespeare's plays as a key to his environment and experience.

SIDELIGHTS: Engels told *CA:* "I do not publish much academic material in so-called learned journals because I believe the publish-or-perish principle to be absurd as a measure of a good teacher, and also because it is responsible for loading these journals with ostentatious trash." *Avocational interests:* Cabinet-making, outdoors activities.

* * *

ENGLISH, O(liver) Spurgeon 1901-

PERSONAL: Born September 27, 1901, in Presque Isle, Me.; son of George Wesley (a farmer) and Annie Louise (Hemphill) English; married Ellen Mary Brown, February 28, 1933; children: Wesley J., Carroll A., Cheryl A. (Mrs. Kenneth Hall). *Education:* University of Maine, student, 1918-20; Jefferson Medical College, M.D., 1924; Harvard University, postgraduate study, 1929-32. *Politics:* Democrat. *Religion:* Unitarian Universalist. *Home:* 449 Righters Mill Rd., Penn Valley, Narberth, Pa. 19072. *Agent:* Marie Wilkerson, Park Avenue Literary Agency, 230 Park Ave., New York, N.Y. 10017.

CAREER: Jefferson Medical College Hospital, Philadelphia, Pa., intern, 1924-27; Boston Psychopathic Hospital, Boston, Mass., resident physician, 1927-28; Montefiore Hospital, New York, N.Y., resident, 1928-29; Charity Hospital, Berlin, Germany, volunteer in psychology, 1929-30; Harvard University, Cambridge, Mass., instructor in psychiatry, 1929-32; Philadelphia General Hospital, Philadelphia, physician in psychopathic department, 1933-47; Temple University, Philadelphia, clinical professor, 1933-38, professor of psychiatry, beginning 1938, head of department of psychiatry, 1938-64; private practice of psychiatry, beginning 1964.

MEMBER: American Medical Association, American Psychoanalytic Association (fellow), American Psychiatric Association (fellow), American College of Physicians (fellow), Philadelphia County Medical Society, Philadelphia College of Physicians. *Awards, honors:* Sc.D., University of Maine, 1960; American Academy of Psychotherapists Award for outstanding contribution to the art and science of psychotherapy, 1968.

WRITINGS: (With Edward Weiss) *Psychosomatic Medicine: A Clinical Study of Psychophysiologic Reactions,* Saunders, 1943, 3rd edition, 1957; (with Gerald H. J. Pearson) *Emotional Problems of Living: Avoiding the Neurotic Pattern,* Norton, 1945, 3rd edition, 1963; (with Stuart M. Finch) *Emotional Problems of Growing Up,* Science Research Associates, 1951; (with Constance J. Foster) *Fathers Are Parents, Too,* Putnam, 1951, 2nd edition, Belmont Books, 1962; (with Foster) *Your Behavior Problems,* Science Research Associates, 1952; *Personality Manifestations in Psychosomatic Illness: Visual Aid Charts to Psychotherapy,* Stern, 1953; (with Finch) *Introduction to Psychiatry,* Norton, 1954, 3rd edition, 1964; (with Foster) *A Guide to Successful Fatherhood,* Science Research Associates, 1954; (with others) *Direct Analysis and Schizophrenia,* Grune, 1961; (with Pearson) *Common Neuroses of Children and Adults,* Norton, 1964.

AVOCATIONAL INTERESTS: Golf, tennis, photography, folk music.

* * *

ERICKSON, Arvel Benjamin 1905-1974

PERSONAL: Born September 15, 1905, in Eveleth, Minn.; son of Gustav and Anna (Mallom) Erickson; married Alva C. Roslund, June 9, 1932; children: Lynn Garrett (Mrs. Thomas Burnett). *Education:* University of Minnesota, B.A., 1929; University of Washington, Seattle, M.A., 1933; Western Reserve University (now Case Western Reserve

University), Ph.D., 1939. *Home:* 3432 Clarendon Rd., Cleveland Heights, Ohio 44118. *Office:* Case Western Reserve University, Euclid Ave., Cleveland, Ohio 44106.

CAREER: Case Institute of Technology (now Case Western Reserve University), Cleveland, Ohio, instructor in history, 1938-40; Western Reserve University (now Case Western Reserve University), instructor in history, 1940-42; regional economist, U.S. Office of Price Administration, 1942-45; Case Western Reserve University, assistant professor, 1945-47; associate professor, 1947-51; professor of history, 1951-74. Visiting summer professor at University of Manitoba, 1962, and University of Victoria, 1963. *Member:* American Historical Association, Conference on British Studies, American Association of University Professors, Ohio Academy of History, Omicron Delta Kappa. *Awards, honors:* Research grants from Social Science Research Council, 1953, and American Philosophical Society, 1953, 1961; Carl F. Wittke Distinguished Teacher Award, Western Reserve University, 1964; *Journal of Military Affairs* essay prize.

WRITINGS: The Public Career of Sir James Graham, Press of the Western Reserve University, 1952, reprinted, Greenwood Press, 1974; *Edward T. Cardwell: Peelite,* American Philosophical Society, 1959; (editor with Martin J. Havran) *Readings in English History,* Scribner, 1967; (with Harvan) *England: Prehistory to the Present,* Doubleday, 1968; (with Wilbur D. Jones) *The Peelites, 1846-1857,* Ohio State University Press, 1972. Contributor to professional journals. Associate editor, *Journal of Social History.*

SIDELIGHTS: Erickson traveled extensively in Europe and had a general knowledge of French and German.†

(Died November 24, 1974)

*   *   *

ERNEST, Victor (Hugo)   1911-

PERSONAL: Born April 17, 1911; son of Hugo James (a telegrapher) and Blanch Lavern (Walters) Ernest; married Alice Schmoldt (a secretary and typist), June 1, 1935; children: John Paul, Marianne Jewell. *Education:* Attended Bemidji State College, Northwestern Bible College (now Northwest College of the Assemblies of God), and Bethel College and Seminary, St. Paul, Minn. *Politics:* Republican. *Office:* Park Baptist Church, 1145 Dayton Ave., St. Paul Park, Minn. 55071.

CAREER: Entered Christian ministry, 1932, ordained, 1935; Park Baptist Church, St. Paul Park, Minn., pastor.

WRITINGS: I Talked with Spirits, Tyndale, 1970.

WORK IN PROGRESS: Demonism; a book dealing with personal experiences and Biblical commentary of spiritualism and witchcraft.††

*   *   *

ESKELUND, Karl   1918-1972

PERSONAL: Born January 7, 1918, in Holte, Denmark; son of Niels (a dentist) and Bergliot Eskelund; married Chi-yun Fei (a writer), September 9, 1939; children: Mei-mei (daughter). *Education:* Attended high school in Denmark; studied later at Yenching University, Peking, China, and at University of Missouri. *Residence:* Hareskovby, Denmark.

CAREER: World traveler and writer.

WRITINGS: Min Kone spiser med Pinde, Gyldendal, 1945, published as *Pa kryss og tvers med kinesisk kone,* 1959, translation published as *My Chinese Wife,* Doubleday, 1945;

My Danish Father, Doubleday, 1945; *Med hovedit i lommen,* Gyldendal, 1949, translation published as *Headhunting in Ecuador,* Burke Publishing, 1953, published as *Vagabond Fever: A Gay Journal in the Land of the Andes,* Rand McNally, 1954.

Dollargrin og Alvor, Gyldendal, 1950; *Hendes kinesiske familie,* Gyldendal, 1951; *Heads in Pocket,* Clerke, 1952; *Ka Korte vi til Indien,* Gyldendal, 1952; *Kejserens nye klaeder: En beretning fra Japan,* Gyldendal, 1953, translation published as *The Emperor's New Clothes,* Burke Publishing, 1955; *Brune tommermaend: Rejse gennem Indonesien,* Gyldendal, 1953, translation published as *Indonesian Adventure,* Burke Publishing, 1954; *Kaerlighendens kaktus: En skildring fra Mexico,* Gyldendal, 1955, translation published as *The Cactus of Love: Travels in Mexico,* Redman, 1957, Taplinger, 1961; *I den sorte gryde: Rejseoplevelser fra Guldkysten,* Gyldendal, 1956, translation published as *Black Man's Country: A Journey Through Ghana,* Redman, 1956; *De rode mandariner,* Gyldendal, 1957, translation published as *The Red Mandarins: Travels in Red China,* Redman, 1959, Taplinger, 1961; (with wife, Chi-yun Eskelund) *Banduru, Boy of Ghana, in West Africa,* Methuen, 1958; *Den glemte dal,* Gyldendal, 1958, translation published as *The Forgotten Valley: A Journey into Nepal,* Redman, 1959, Taplinger, 1960; *Sort, hvid og kaffebrun: Rejseskildring fra Brasilien,* Gyldendal, 1959, translation published as *Drums in Bahia: Travels in Brazil,* Redman, 1960.

Men Gud sov: En rejse i Afrika, Gyldendal, 1960, translation published as *While God Slept: Travels in Africa,* Redman, 1961; *Sort kaviar og rod optimisme: En rejse i Rushland,* Gyldendal, 1961, translation published as *Black Caviar and Red Optimism: Travels in Russia,* Redman, 1962; *Sla Rommen i glasset: En rejse fra Cuba til Guyana,* Gyldendal, 1962, translation published as *Revolt in the Tropics: Travels in the Caribbean,* Redman, 1963; *Jeg gik mig over a og vand: En rejse blandt primitive stammer i Filipinerne,* Gyldendal, 1963, translation published as *Sun, Slaves, and Sinners: Travels in the Philippines,* Redman, 1964; *Sig det til Shah: En rejse i Persien,* Gyldendal, 1964, translation published as *Behind the Peacock Throne,* Redman, 1965; *Den gale krig: En rejse i Vietnam,* Gyldendal, 1966; *Stille flyder Ganges,* Gyldendal, 1967.

SIDELIGHTS: Some of Eskelund's books have also been published in Norway, Sweden, Germany, and Yugoslavia.†

(Died, 1972)

*   *   *

ESPINOSA, Jose E(dmundo)   1900-1967

PERSONAL: Born September 5, 1900, in New Mexico; son of Celso de Jesus (a rancher) and Rafaela Martinez (Valdez) Espinosa y Montoya; married first wife, Margaret Gallivan; married second wife, Julia Hanna (a university professor), December 27, 1956; children: (first marriage) Mary Catherine (Mrs. Ceferino Martin). *Education:* Washington Conservatory of Music, graduate, 1922; George Washington University, A.B., 1929, M.A., 1931; Cornell University, Ph.D., 1934. *Religion:* Roman Catholic. *Residence:* Detroit, Mich.

CAREER: Cornell University, Ithaca, N.Y., member of faculty, 1931-37; University of Detroit, Detroit, Mich., associate professor of Spanish, 1937-42; George Washington University, Washington, D.C., associate professor of Spanish, 1942-45; University of Detroit, professor of Spanish and Spanish-American histories and literatures, 1945-67, professor emeritus, 1967. Visiting summer professor at George

Washington University of New Mexico, and University of Albuquerque. *Member:* American Association of Teachers of Spanish and Portuguese (past president of Michigan chapter), Catholic Association of Foreign Language Teachers (founding member; president, 1955-56), National Board of Catholic Authors, New Mexico Historical Society, New Mexico Institute of Archaeology, Delta Phi Epsilon.

WRITINGS: Compendium of Spanish Grammar, Thrift Press, 1936; *The Spanish Subjunctive* (pamphlet), Thrift Press, 1936; (editor) *Anthology of Spanish Literature,* Thrift Press, 1937; *Spanish Proverbs,* Thrift Press, 1939; (editor with E. A. Mercado) Alvar Nunez Cabeza de Vaca, *Los Naufragios y relacion,* Heath, 1941; *A Practical Spanish Vocabulary,* Thrift Press, 1941; *Saints in the Valleys: The Saints in the History and Religious Folk Art of Spanish New Mexico, 1540-1957,* University of New Mexico Press, 1960, 2nd edition, 1967; *An Introduction to Spanish Phonetics* (experimental edition), University of Detroit Press, 1962. Original Spanish poetry published in *Santa Fe New Mexican,* 1938-47; contributor of articles to *Hispania, El Palacio, La Revista Catolica,* and reviews to *Books Abroad.*††

(Died December 22, 1967)

* * *

ETTLESON, Abraham 1897-

PERSONAL: Born October 2, 1897, in Medzhbish, Podolia, Russia; son of Enoch (a cap-maker) and Faigie Ettleson; married Dora Moldofsky, January 17, 1925. *Education:* Attended Crane Junior College, Chicago, Ill., 1918-20; University of Illinois, M.D., 1924. *Religion:* Jewish.

CAREER: Neurologist and neurosurgeon in private practice in Phoenix, Ariz. *Military service:* U.S. Navy, Medical Corps, 1941-46; became captain. *Member:* American Medical Association, American Association of Neurological Surgeons, Arizona Medical Association, Maricopa County Medical Society.

WRITINGS: Lewis Carroll's Through the Looking-Glass Decoded, Philosophical Library, 1966.††

* * *

EVANS, G(eraint) N(antglyn) D(avies) 1935-1971

PERSONAL: Born August 21, 1935, in Cardiff, Wales; son of Daniel John Huxley (a professor and clergyman) and Anne (Davies) Evans; married Ursula Ruth Burmeister, December 21, 1963. *Education:* Trinity College, London, associate, 1954; Cambridge University, B.A., 1957, M.A., 1960; Salzburg Seminar in American Studies, United Kingdom scholar, 1958; Lehigh University, M.A., 1961; Yale University, M.A., 1962, Ph.D., 1964. *Home:* 406 West 46th St., New York, N.Y. 10036. *Office:* Department of History, Richmond College of the City University of New York, Staten Island, N.Y. 10301.

CAREER: Malvern College, Malvern, England, instructor in history, 1958; Lafayette College, Easton, Pa., instructor in history, 1959; McGill University, Montreal, Quebec, assistant professor of history, 1963-66; Southern Illinois University, Carbondale, assistant professor of history, 1966-67; Richmond College of the City University of New York, Staten Island, N.Y., associate professor of history and American studies, beginning 1967. Visiting fellow, Dalhousie University, 1969; visiting professor, Chapman College, 1970-71.

MEMBER: American Historical Association, Canadian Historical Association, American Studies Association (pres-ident of Metropolitan New York branch, 1969-70), Institute of Early American History, Canadian Association for American Studies, British Association for American Studies, Organization of American Historians, American Association of University Professors. *Awards, honors:* Fulbright scholar, 1958-63; Canada Council postdoctoral fellow, 1965; senior research fellow at Centre d'-Etudes Canadiennes-Francaises, McGill University, 1966; Danforth associate, 1969-72.

WRITINGS: The Loyalists in Canada (booklet), Copp, 1968; *Allegiance in America: The Case of the Loyalists,* Addison-Wesley, 1968; *Uncommon Obdurate: The Public Careers of J. F. W. DesBarres,* Peabody Museum (Salem, Mass.), 1969. Contributor to history journals.

WORK IN PROGRESS: Migrants to the Maritimes: the Loyalist Movement to Atlantic Canada; A History of Canada, a book for American readers; an edition of a hitherto unknown Loyalist diary, dealing with New York, 1776-1779.††

(Died December 28, 1971)

* * *

EVANS, Melbourne G(riffith) 1912-

PERSONAL: Born January 23, 1912, in Portland, Ore.; son of Griffith Edward and Agnes (Brown) Evans; married Pauline Davidson (an associate professor of physics), September 6, 1950; children: Lynn Janet (Mrs. Jerry Van Drew), Brian Griffith. *Education:* Reed College, B.A., 1937; University of California, Berkeley, M.A., 1940, Ph.D., 1948. *Home:* 5801 Coors Blvd. S.W., Albuquerque, N.M. 87105. *Office:* Department of Philosophy, University of New Mexico, Albuquerque, N.M. 87106.

CAREER: Syracuse University, Syracuse, N.Y., instructor in philosophy, 1948-51; American Council of Learned Societies, New York, N.Y., scholar, 1951-53; University of Alabama, Tuscaloosa, visiting associate professor of philosophy, 1955; University of New Mexico, Albuquerque, lecturer in philosophy and mathematics, 1955-60, associate professor, 1960-67, professor of philosophy, beginning 1967, professor emeritus, 1977—, acting chairman of department, 1968-69. *Military service:* U.S. Army, 1942-45; became technical sergeant. *Member:* American Philosophical Association.

WRITINGS: The Physical Philosophy of Aristotle, University of New Mexico Press, 1964. Contributor to philosophy journals.

WORK IN PROGRESS: Historical and critical investigations in the Special Theory of Relativity; investigations leading to the extension of the truth-functional concept to the entire domain of formal logic.

SIDELIGHTS: Melbourne Evans told *CA:* "One whose profession has been the teaching of philosophy is hardly an author in the usual sense. Yet the use of language as a tool to create and express abstract ideas is an art, at once as difficult and demanding as it is rewarding. In the past, philosophy—and even science—was often graced by men of great literary power. The virtual absence of such men from the contemporary scene, and our general failure today to insist that the form of expression has value, are trends that bode no good for the future."

* * *

EVANS, Robert F(ranklin) 1930-1974

PERSONAL: Born January 9, 1930, in Akron, Ohio; son of

Charles Robert (a businessman) and Lola (Boyd) Evans; married Lilian Alder, September 26, 1956; children: Danielle Louise, Nicole Estelle. *Education:* Yale University, B.A., 1951, Ph.D., 1959; Cambridge University, B.A., 1954, M.A., 1961. *Home:* 504 South 46th St., Philadelphia, Pa. 19143.

CAREER: Assistant minister at St. Thomas Episcopal Church in Washington, D.C., 1958-60; Western Michigan University, Kalamazoo, instructor in religion, 1960-61; University of Pennsylvania, Philadelphia, lecturer, 1961-62, assistant professor, 1962-67, associate professor, 1968-73, professor of religion, 1973-74. Church organist and choir director. *Member:* Society for Religion in Higher Education, American Academy of Religion, American Society of Church History. *Awards, honors:* Lilly fellowship for postdoctoral study in religion, 1965-66; Society for Religion in Higher Education Fellowship, 1970-71.

WRITINGS: Making Sense of the Creeds, Association Press, 1964; *Pelagius: Inquiries and Reappraisals* (six essays), Seabury, 1968; *Four Letters of Pelagius,* Seabury, 1968; *One and Holy: The Church in Latin Patristic Thought,* Allenson, 1972. Contributor to *Journal of Theological Studies* (Oxford, England), and *Studies in Medieval Culture.*

BIOGRAPHICAL/CRITICAL SOURCES: Encounter, Volume XXX, number 1, 1968; *Commonweal,* April 11, 1969.†

(Died May 30, 1974)

*   *   *

EYLES, Wilfred Charles 1891-

PERSONAL: Born August 1, 1891, in Camden, New South Wales, Australia; son of Charles and Alma Beatrice Eyles. *Education:* Attended high school in Stroud, New South Wales, Australia. *Politics:* None. *Religion:* None. *Home:* 40 Ewart St., West Marrickville, New South Wales, Australia. *Agent:* Paul Flesch & Co., 259 Collins St., Melbourne, Australia.

CAREER: Geologist and mineralogist. *Member:* Western Suburbs Lapidary Society (honorary member).

WRITINGS: The Book of Opals, Tuttle, 1964.

WORK IN PROGRESS: The Autobiography of an Australian Yank.††

*   *   *

FABRI, Ralph 1894-1975

PERSONAL: First syllable of surname rhymes with "mob"; born April 23, 1894, in Budapest, Hungary; came to United States in 1921, naturalized in 1927; son of Henrik Lipot (an industrialist) and Helen (Fischer) Fabri. *Education:* Royal State Gymnasium, Budapest, Hungary, B.A., 1912; Royal Institute of Technology, Budapest, architecture study, 1912-14; Royal Academy of Fine Arts, Budapest, M.A., 1918. *Home:* 54 West 74th St., New York, N.Y. 10023. *Office: Today's Art,* 25 West 45th St., New York, N.Y. 10036.

CAREER: Painter, exhibiting in major shows in America, and in Europe, Far and Middle East, and Africa; teacher of art and art historian. Parsons School of Design, New York, N.Y., instructor in drawing and painting, 1947-49; Newark School of Fine and Industrial Art, Newark, N.J., art historian, 1949-50; City College (now City College of the City University of New York), New York, N.Y., associate pro-

fessor of art history, 1951-65; National Academy School of Fine Arts, New York, N.Y., instructor in art, 1960-75; Syndicate Magazines, Inc., New York, N.Y., editor of *Today's Art,* 1961-75. Paintings (in oil, casein, and polymer) exhibited in one-man shows at Smithsonian Institution, 1942, Honolulu Academy of Fine Arts, 1943, in Budapest, 1946, and elsewhere, 1938-74; represented in permanent collections of National Academy, Metropolitan Museum of Art, Library of Congress, Rosenwald Collection, and many others; staff critic, Pictures on Exhibit, 1950-61.

MEMBER: National Academy of Design (treasurer, 1962-69), Royal Society of Arts (London; fellow), Audubon Artists (honorary life president), National Society of Painters in Casein (president, 1955-57, 1959-61; honorary life president), Allied Artists of America (president, 1973-75), Society of American Graphic Artists, American Watercolor Society, Painters and Sculptors Society of New Jersey, Boston Printmakers, Washington Printmakers, American Association of University Professors. *Awards, honors:* Most recent awards include Walter E. Meyer Prize, 1959, J. J. Newman Medal, 1963, Medal of Honor (New Jersey), 1964, Grumbacher Award, 1965, 1972, 1973, Bainbridge Award, 1967, Motilla Award, 1972.

WRITINGS: Learn to Draw, Authentic Publications, 1945; *Oil Painting: How-To-Do-It,* Jay Press, 1953; *Sculpture in Paper,* Watson-Guptill, 1966; *Guide to Polymer Painting,* Reinhold, 1966; *Color: A Complete Guide for Artists,* Watson-Guptill, 1967; *Complete Guide to Flower Painting,* Watson-Guptill, 1968; *Painting Outdoors,* Watson-Guptill, 1969; *History of the American Watercolor Society,* American Watercolor Society, 1969; *Painting Cityscapes,* Watson-Guptill, 1970; *Artist's Guide to Composition,* Watson Guptill, 1971. Art editor, *Funk & Wagnalls Universal Standard Encyclopedia,* 1958-60, *Funk & Wagnalls New Encyclopedia,* 1969-70; book reviewer, *American Artist.*

SIDELIGHTS: Fabri traveled abroad every summer since 1954, covering all the American countries, all of Europe, most of Africa, the South Sea Islands, Australasia, Caribbean, and Near, Far, and Middle East.†

(Died February 12, 1975)

*   *   *

FAIRFAX-LUCY, Brian (Fulke Cameron-Ramsay) 1898-1974

PERSONAL: Title after succeeding brother as fifth baronet in 1965 was Major Sir Brian Fulke Cameron-Ramsay-Fairfax-Lucy; born December 18, 1898, in Scotland; son of Henry William Cameron Ramsay-Fairfax (a colonel, British Army) and Ada Christina Lucy; married Alice Caroline Helen Buchan (an author), July 29, 1933; children: Edmund John William Hugh, Mary (Mrs. James Scott). *Education:* Attended Eton College, 1912-16, and Royal Military College, Sandhurst, 1916. *Politics:* Conservative. *Religion:* Church of England. *Home:* Charlecote Park, Warwickshire, England; and The Mill, Fossebridge, Cheltenham, England. *Agent:* A. P. Watt & Son, 26/28 Bedford Row, London WC1R 4HL, England.

CAREER: Regular officer in the British Army, 1916-33, 1939-45; began service with the Queen's Own Cameron Highlanders during World War I (was wounded); stationed on the Northwest Frontier, India, 1919-25, and in Germany, 1926; adjutant of Second Cameron Highlanders, 1927-30; aide-de-camp to Lord High Commissioner to General Assembly of Church of Scotland, 1931-33. National Greyhound Racing Club, steward, 1928-33, stipendiary steward, 1933-36; during World War II served principally as a major with the Cameron Highlanders.

WRITINGS—Children's books: *Horses in the Valley,* Oxford University Press, 1941; *The Horse from India,* Muller, 1944; *Albert: The Adventures of a Farmyard Duck,* Partridge Publications, 1944; *The Cat Did It,* Oxford University Press, 1951; (with Philippa Pearce) *The Children of the House,* Lippincott, 1968.

WORK IN PROGRESS: His autobiography.

SIDELIGHTS: The Children of the House, a partially autobiographical novel, was written originally by Brian Fairfax-Lucy for adult readers and was adapted by Philippa Pearce for children. Barbara Wersta described the book as "the story of Sir Robert and Lady Hatton, two impoverished aristocrats struggling to maintain a way of life. The victims of this struggle were the Hatton children. . . ." Polly Goodwin wrote, "Theirs was a small, contained, lonely world, however infinitely strange to today's youth, in which they were far closer to kindly servants than to parents who ruled with an iron hand." Relief finally came for them in the form of World War I, and three of the children joined the war effort to escape their unhappy home. Wersta summarized: "These are the memories of Brian Fairfax-Lucy's childhood. . . . The simplicity, truth, and lack of emphasis in this story are virtually Chekhovian, and it is a stouthearted reader who will not weep."

AVOCATIONAL INTERESTS: All games from cricket to football, and fishing, shooting, and riding; also a love of music and live theatre.

BIOGRAPHICAL/CRITICAL SOURCES: Children's Book World, November 3, 1968; *New York Times Book Review,* November 3, 1968.†

(Died, 1974)

* * *

FALK, Charles J(ohn)   1899-1971

PERSONAL: Born December 29, 1899, in Evansville, Ind.; son of Rudolph (a millwright) and Frances (Langhans) Falk; married Helen Maler, May 2, 1931; children: Margaret Ann (Mrs. James F. Goss), Linda Louise (Mrs. Frank Alessio, Jr.). *Education:* St. Patrick's Seminary, Menlo Park, Calif., graduate, 1923; Urban University, Rome, Italy, S.T.B., 1924, S.T.L., 1925, S.T.D., 1926; University of California, Los Angeles, graduate study in education, 1935, 1948-49; Claremont Graduate School, graduate study in education and administration, 1937-39. *Religion:* Episcopalian. *Home:* 4293 Summit Dr., La Mesa, Calif. 92041. *Office* San Diego State University, San Diego, Calif. 92115.

CAREER: St. Charles College, Catonsville, Md., teacher of history and languages, 1926-28; St. Patrick's Seminary, Menlo Park, Calif., professor of Scripture and languages, 1928-30; San Diego (Calif.) public schools, teacher and supervisor of adult social-civic education, 1934-36, adult high school principal and dean of junior college, 1936-39, coordinator of instruction, 1939-43, assistant to superintendent and secretary of board of education, 1943-46; U.S. Office of Military Government, Bavaria, successively chief of secondary education, elementary education, and educational adviser to military governor, 1946-48; San Diego public schools, assistant to superintendent, secretary of board of education, and director of publications and public relations, 1948-52; Occidental College, Los Angeles, Calif., associate professor of education and school administration, 1952-55; U.S. Depart-

ment of State, International Cooperation Administration, chief of Education Division, Saigon, Vietnam, then evaluator of U.S.-Indian university contacts, Delhi, India, 1955-57; San Diego State College (now University), San Diego, assistant professor, 1957-61, associate professor, 1961-65, professor of education, beginning 1965. Visiting professor of education at Claremont Graduate School, 1940-45, and at Pomona College and California Western University.

MEMBER: American Association of University Professors, Far Western Philosophy of Education Association, California Teachers Association, San Diego Historical Society, Phi Delta Kappa.

WRITINGS: (With Lacey Easthorn and Victor Kelley) *Planning Your Life for School and Society,* Scribner, 1939; *Educational Survey of Central Vietnam,* International Cooperation Administration, 1955; *Education in the Pays Montagnard du Sud,* International Cooperation Administration, 1955; *Higher Education in Vietnam,* International Cooperation Administration, 1956; *The Development and Organization of Education in California,* Harcourt, 1968. Contributor to educational periodicals. Editor, California Educational Press (California Teachers Association), 1953-54.

WORK IN PROGRESS: Further research in history and philosophy of education.

SIDELIGHTS: Charles Falk spoke German, French, Italian; read Latin, Greek, Spanish, Swedish.†

(Died April, 1971)

* * *

FALKNER, Murry (Charles)   1899-

PERSONAL: Born June 26, 1899, in Ripley, Miss.; son of Murry Cuthbert (business manager, University of Mississippi) and Maud (Butler) Falkner; married Suzanne Coqterre, August 24, 1944. *Education:* University of Mississippi, LL.B., 1922. *Politics:* Conservative. *Home:* 3700 San Juan Dr., Mobile, Ala. 36609. *Agent:* Daniel S. Mead, 915 Broadway, New York, N.Y. 10010.

CAREER: Attorney practicing in Oxford, Miss., 1922-24; special agent with Federal Bureau of Investigation, stationed in cities throughout the country, 1925-28, 1934-42, 1946-65. *Military service:* U.S. Marine Corps, American Expeditionary Forces in France, 1918-19; received French Brigade Citation and Purple Heart. U.S. Army, Counter-Intelligence Corps, 1942-46; served in Europe, Africa, and Middle East; became major. *Member:* Sigma Alpha Epsilon.

WRITINGS: The Falkners of Mississippi: A Memoir, Louisiana State University Press, 1967. Contributor of articles to *American Heritage, Southern Review,* and *Private Pilot.*

WORK IN PROGRESS: Who Live by the Gun.

SIDELIGHTS: The only surviving brother of William Faulkner (who added a "u" to the name). Murry is the third of four Falkner brothers to produce a book. The late John Falkner wrote *My Brother Bill;* the difference between that book and *The Falkners of Mississippi,* Lewis P. Simpson points out in his introduction to the latter, is "that we seem to be seeing the Falkners and their world in, so to speak, pre-Yoknapatawpha times." Murry Falkner's list of writers "who have influenced me most and whom I have enjoyed most": Voltaire, Dryden, Hugo, Kipling, Conrad, Cabell, Churchill. He was formerly a licensed pilot (his three brothers also held licenses), used to own a plane, and was the only FBI agent authorized to fly his own craft on official business. Falkner also noted that he is a fair amateur astronomer, and that he speaks French adequately.

BIOGRAPHICAL/CRITICAL SOURCES: New York Times Book Review, December 17, 1967; *Virginia Quarterly Review,* spring, 1968; *Georgia Review,* fall, 1968.

*   *   *

FARNSWORTH, Paul Randolph 1899-

PERSONAL: Born August 15, 1899, in Waterbury, Conn.; son of Hiland Randolph (a mechanical engineer) and Elisabeth (March) Farnsworth; married Helen Cherington (a professor of economics), August 31, 1926 (deceased); children: Elliott Cherington, Susan March (Mrs. Aimery P. Caron). *Education:* Ohio State University, B.A., 1921, M.A., 1923, Ph.D., 1925. *Home:* 37 Pearce Mitchell Pl., Stanford, Calif. 94305. *Office:* Psychology Department, Stanford University, Stanford, Calif. 94305.

CAREER: Ohio State University, Columbus, instructor in psychology, 1922-24; Stanford University, Stanford, Calif., instructor, 1925-26, assistant professor, 1926-31, associate professor, 1931-42, professor of psychology, 1942-64, professor emeritus, 1964—. Visiting summer professor, Ohio State University, 1931; University of Wisconsin (now University of Wisconsin—Madison), summer lecturer, 1938, acting professor, 1939-40; summer lecturer, University of Chicago, 1942.

MEMBER: American Psychological Association (president of Arts Division, 1945-51; member of board of directors, 1953-56), American Association for the Advancement of Science (vice-president of Section I, 1950), American Society for Aesthetics (trustee, 1949-52, 1958-61, 1964-67), American Musicological Society (member of executive board, 1943-46, 1949-52), Western Psychological Association (president, 1938), California Psychological Association (secretary-treasurer, 1949-52), Phi Beta Kappa, Sigma Xi, Phi Delta Kappa, Pi Mu Epsilon.

WRITINGS: (With Richard T. LaPiere) *Social Psychology,* McGraw, 1936, 3rd edition, 1949; (contributor) Robert Holmes Seashore, editor, *Fields of Psychology: An Experimental Approach,* Holt, 1942; (contributor) Philip Lawrence Harriman, editor, *The Encyclopedia of Psychology,* Philosophical Library, 1946; *Musical Taste: Its Measurement and Cultural Nature,* Stanford University Press, 1950; *The Social Psychology of Music,* Dryden, 1958, 2nd edition, Iowa State University Press, 1969. Contributor to professional journals. Editor, *Annual Review of Psychology,* 1955-68.

SIDELIGHTS: The Social Psychology of Music has been translated into Japanese and German.

*   *   *

FAY, Frederic L(eighton) 1890-

PERSONAL: Born June 9, 1890, in Spencer, Mass.; son of Amasa C. (a minister) and Jennie (Leighton) Fay. *Education:* Attended Gordon College, 1916; Hartford School of Religious Education (now Hartford Seminary Foundation), B.R.E., 1934. *Religion:* Baptist. *Home:* 66 Commonwealth Ave., Chestnut Hill, Mass. 02167.

CAREER: Director of Christian education for Union Congregational Church, Boston, Mass., 1914-20, South Congregational Church, New Britain, Conn., 1920-27, Reformed Church, Bronxville, N.Y., 1928-33, Trinity Episcopal Church, Buffalo, N.Y., 1935-37, Asylum Hill Congregational Church, Hartford, Conn., 1938-40, and First Congregational Church, Binghamton, N.Y., 1941-43; Whittemore Associates, Inc., Boston, salesman of religious goods, 1945-

66. President of New England Guild of English Handbell Ringers, 1959-64.

WRITINGS: Student's Bible Dictionary, Whittemore, 1956; *A Map Book for Bible Students,* Whittemore, 1966.

WORK IN PROGRESS: Research on Christian church year festivals.

AVOCATIONAL INTERESTS: Music and handbell ringing.††

*   *   *

FEAVER, J(ohn) Clayton 1911-

PERSONAL: Born June 24, 1911, in Fowler, Calif.; son of Ernest Albion and Agnes Katherine (Hansen) Feaver; married Margaret Storsand, June 21, 1936; children: John Hansen, Katherine Elaine, Margaret Ellen. *Education:* Fresno State College (now California State University, Fresno), A.B., 1933; San Francisco Theological Seminary, further study, 1933-34; Pacific School of Religion, B.D., 1936; Yale University, Ph.D., 1949. *Home:* 900 East Boyd, Norman, Okla. 73069. *Office:* Department of Philosophy, University of Oklahoma, Norman, Okla. 73069.

CAREER: Berea College, Berea, Ky., 1941-51, began as assistant professor, became associate professor of philosophy; University of Oklahoma, Kingfisher College, Norman, professor of the philosophy of religion and ethics, beginning 1951, David Ross Boyd Professor of Philosophy, beginning 1959. Chairman of executive committee, Oklahoma College of Continuing Education, 1960-71; vice-chairman of executive committee, Southwest Center for Human Relations Studies, 1961-69, chairman, beginning 1969. Member, Oklahoma Governor's Committee on Children and Youth, beginning 1967. *Member:* American Philosophical Association, American Association of University Professors, Southern Society for Philosophy of Religion, Southwestern Philosophical Society (president, 1960), Phi Beta Kappa, Omicron Delta Kappa.

WRITINGS: (Editor with William Horosz) *Religion in Philosophical and Cultural Perspective,* Van Nostrand, 1967; (contributor) George L. Cross, editor, *The World of Ideas: Essays on the Past and Future,* University of Oklahoma Press, 1968.

*   *   *

FEILDING, Charles (Rudolph) 1902-

PERSONAL: Surname pronounced "fielding"; born January 16, 1902, in Whitford, Wales; son of John Basil and Emily Margaret (Tod) Feilding; married Ann Truslow, August 20, 1935; children: Geoffrey Truslow, Goodith (Mrs. Brian Heeney). *Education:* King's College, Halifax, Nova Scotia, B.A., 1926; General Theological Seminary, New York, N.Y., S.T.B., 1929, S.T.D., 1949. *Home:* 10 Avoca Ave., Apt. 803, Toronto, Ontario, Canada M4T 2B7. *Office:* Trinity College, University of Toronto, Toronto, Ontario, Canada M5S 1H8.

CAREER: Anglican clergyman; General Theological Seminary, New York City, fellow and tutor, 1929-35; St. Mary's Church, New York City, rector, 1935-40; University of Toronto, Trinity College, Toronto, Ontario, professor of moral theology, 1940-70, professor emeritus, 1970—, dean of divinity, 1946-61. Chairman, Toronto Graduate School of Theological Studies, 1946-52; visiting fellow, Yale University, 1961-62. Director of research in practical training for the ministry, American Association of Theological Schools, 1962-64; founder member of Canadian Council for Supervised Pastoral Education and of Toronto Institute for Pastoral Training. Consultant in theological education in the Caribbean, Great Britain, United States, and other countries. *Member:* Canadian Institute of Religion and Gerontology (vice-president, 1975). *Awards, honors:* D.D. from Presbyterian College of Montreal, 1968, and Acadia University, 1969.

WRITINGS: (With H.R.S. Ryan) *Marriage in Church and State,* Anglican Church of Canada, 1965; (with others) *Education for Ministry,* American Association of Theological Schools, 1966.

BIOGRAPHICAL/CRITICAL SOURCES: Christian Century, April 26, 1967.

* * *

FEINGOLD, Jessica 1910-

PERSONAL: Born December 28, 1910, in New Orleans, La.; daughter of M. W. (a merchant) and Jessie (Schwabacker) Feingold. *Education:* Vassar College, B.A., 1931; Columbia University, M.A., 1933. *Residence:* New York, N.Y. *Office:* Jewish Theological Seminary of America, 3030 Broadway, New York, N.Y. 10027.

CAREER: Jewish Theological Seminary of America, New York, N.Y., administrative secretary, 1943-56, director of Institute for Religious and Social Studies, beginning 1951, executive vice-president of Conference on Science, Philosophy and Religion, beginning 1956, director of intergroup activities, beginning 1959. *Awards, honors:* First Conference on Science, Philosophy and Religion Medal, 1956.

WRITINGS: (Editor with Clarence H. Faust) *Aspects of Education for Character: Strategies for Change in Higher Education,* Columbia University Press, 1969. Has done editorial work on numerous books of others.

* * *

FEIS, Ruth (Stanley-Brown) 1892-

PERSONAL: Surname rhymes with "mice"; born August 3, 1892, in Mentor, Ohio; daughter of Joseph and Mary (Garfield) Stanley-Brown; married Herbert Feis (a historian); children: Mary Felicia (Mrs. Jerome A. Gomes). *Education:* Vassar College, B.A., 1915. *Politics:* Democrat. *Religion:* Protestant. *Home:* 1161 Willa Vista Tr., Maitland, Fla. 32751. *Agent:* Curtis Brown Ltd., 60 East 56th St., New York, N.Y. 10022.

CAREER: Publishers' Weekly, New York, N.Y., editorial staff, 1916-18; Macmillan Co., New York, N.Y., writer of trade leaflets, 1918-20; *Dial* (magazine), New York, N.Y., advertising manager, 1920-22; *League of Nations News,* New York, N.Y., editor, 1925-29.

WRITINGS: (Editor) *Magic in Herbs,* M. Barrows, 1941; *Mollie Garfield in the White House,* Rand McNally, 1962.

WORK IN PROGRESS: Rachael Field: Her Life and Her Books.

AVOCATIONAL INTERESTS: Gardening, travel.

* * *

FEISE, Ernst 1884-1966

PERSONAL: Born June 8, 1884, in Braunschweig, Germany; came to United States, 1908, naturalized, 1931; son of Johannes and Auguste (Witzell) Feise; married Dorothy Findlay, September 6, 1910; children: Richard, Dorelen Feise Bunting, Frederik. *Education:* Attended University of Berlin, 1902-03, University of Munich, 1903-05; University

of Leipzig, Ph.D., 1908. *Home:* 1103 Rolandvue Ave., Ruxton, Md.

CAREER: University of Wisconsin, Madison, instructor, 1908-12, assistant professor, 1912-15, associate professor of German, 1915-17; Colegio Aleman, Mexico City, Mexico, professor of modern languages, 1920-23; Ohio State University, Columbus, assistant professor of German, 1924-27; Johns Hopkins University, Baltimore, Md., associate professor, 1927-28, professor of German, 1928-51, professor emeritus, 1951-66. Middlebury College, Middlebury, Vt., director of School of German, summers, 1931-48; Whittier College, Whittier, Calif., Whitney Professor, 1953-54; Goucher College, Baltimore, Md., visiting lecturer, 1954-58. *Member:* Modern Language Association of America (member of council, 1945-48), American Association of Teachers of German (president, 1939-41), American Association of University Professors, American Goethe Society (past president), Phi Beta Kappa. *Awards, honors:* Order of Merit First Class of Republic of Germany; Goethe Medal of Goethe Institute (Munich); Litt.D., Middlebury College, 1949.

WRITINGS: (Translator) Goethe, *Die Leiden des Jungen Werther,* Oxford University Press, 1914, Scribner, 1916; (translator) Goethe, *Hermann und Dorothea,* Oxford University Press, 1914, Scribner, 1916; (translator) Hauptmann, *Einsame Menschen,* Holt, 1930; *Xenion* (essays), Johns Hopkins Press, 1951; (translator) *Heine's Lyric Poems and Ballads,* University of Pittsburgh Press, 1961. Contributor to learned journals.††

(Died June 17, 1966)

* * *

FENNER, H(arry) Wolcott 1911-1972

PERSONAL: Born March 24, 1911, in Norfolk, Va.; son of Harry Mosely (in industrial banking) and Ruby (Davis) Fenner; married Mildred Sandison (editor of *Today's Education*), February 1, 1940. *Education:* University of Virginia, B.S., 1934; George Washington University, law student, 1935. *Politics:* Democrat. *Religion:* Episcopalian. *Home:* 530 N St. S.W., Washington, D.C. 20024. *Office:* Ringling Brothers, Barnum & Bailey Circus, 1015 18th St. N.W., Washington, D.C. 20036.

CAREER: Mark Winkler Management (real estate), Washington, D.C., property manager, 1937-52; Feld Brothers (producers of concerts), Washington, D.C., controller, 1952-57; Ringling Brothers, Barnum & Bailey Circus, Washington, D.C., vice-president of advertising and promotion, 1957-71, senior vice-president, 1971-72.

WRITINGS: (Editor with wife, Mildred Sandison Fenner) *The Circus: Lure and Legend,* Prentice-Hall, 1970.

WORK IN PROGRESS: A collection of circus fiction.

AVOCATIONAL INTERESTS: Singing ("a good legitimate baritone").†

(Died October 14, 1972)

* * *

FERNALD, John (Bailey) 1905-

PERSONAL: Surname is pronounced *Fer*-nald; born November 21, 1905, in Mill Valley, Calif.; son of Chester Bailey (a playwright) and Josephine (Harker) Fernald; married Mary Cecil Kidd (divorced); married Jenny Laird (an actress), May 27, 1942; children: Martin Chester, Karin. *Education:* Attended Marlborough College, Wiltshire, England, 1920-23, and Trinity College, Oxford, 1924-28. *Politics:* "Supporter of British Labour Government." *Home:* 2 Daleham Mews, Hampstead, London N.W.3, England. *Agent:* Curtis Brown Ltd., 1 Craven Hill, London W2 3EW, England.

CAREER: Produced plays for amateurs in England, 1926-28; stage manager for "Journey's End," London, England, 1928-29; *Pall Mall* (magazine), London, drama editor, 1929; director of innumerable plays in London, 1929-36, most notably "The Duchess of Malfi," 1929, "Mr. Eno," 1930, "She Passed through Lorraine," 1931, "Below the Surface," 1932, "The Mocking Bird," 1933, "The Dominant Sex," 1934, "Crime and Punishment," 1935, and "Storm Song," 1936; Associated British Pictures, London, associate producer, 1937; returned to the theatre and directing, 1938-39, producing "Oscar Wilde," 1938, "The Doctor's Dilemma," and "Major Barbara," 1939; Reunion Theatre, director of productions, 1946; Liverpool Playhouse, Liverpool, England, director of more than forty productions, 1946-49, including the first performances of "Young Wives' Tale" (as "Wings to Fly With"), "The Human Touch," and "The Silver Curlew"; Arts Theatre, London, director, 1949-65, with productions including "John Gabriel Borkman," "Ivanov," "Heartbreak House," "Nightmare Abbey," "Dial 'M' for Murder," "Uncle Vanya," "The Seagull," "No Escape," "Saint Joan," "Peter Pan," "The Remarkable Mr. Pennypacker," "Tea and Sympathy," "Ghosts," and "The Affair"; John Fernald Company of Meadow Brook Theatre, Rochester, Mich., artistic director, beginning 1966, producing, among other plays, "Caucasian Chalk Circle," "Three Sisters," "King Lear," and "The Cherry Orchard"; New York University, New York, N.Y., professor of theatre, 1970-71. Royal Academy of Dramatic Art, London, member of teaching staff, 1934-40, principal, 1955-65; Shute lecturer in the art of theatre, University of Liverpool, 1948; professor of dramatic art, Meadow Brook Theatre, Rochester, Mich., 1966-70. *Military service:* Royal Naval Volunteer Reserve, 1940-45; became lieutenant commander; awarded Atlantic Star. *Member:* Royal Society of Arts (fellow), Garrick Club (London), The Players (New York). *Awards, honors:* Silver medal, Royal Society of Arts, 1966.

WRITINGS: The Play Produced: An Introduction to the Technique of Producing Plays, Year Book Press, 1933; *Destroyer from America,* Macmillan, 1942; (with wife, Jenny Laird) *And No Birds Sing* (play), Samuel French, 1947; *Sense of Direction,* Seeker & Warburg, 1968, Stein & Day, 1969. Contributor to various theatrical journals, including *Journal of the Royal Society of Arts.*

WORK IN PROGRESS: An autobiography.

AVOCATIONAL INTERESTS: Travel, contemplating cats, sailing and navigation, reading, and listening to music.

BIOGRAPHICAL/CRITICAL SOURCES: Best Sellers, August 1, 1968; *Times Literary Supplement,* September 19, 1968.†

*   *   *

FERRE, Nels F(redrik) S(olomon)   1908-1971

PERSONAL: Surname is pronounced *Fer*-ray; born June 8, 1908, in Luleaa, Sweden; came to United States in 1921, naturalized in 1931; son of Frans August (a clergyman) and Maria (Wickman) Ferre; married Katharine Louise Pond, June 8, 1932; children: Frederick Pond, Mariel Esther (Mrs. David J. Dumin), Katharine Kerstin (Mrs. Stephen S. Large), Faith (Mrs. Robert B. Harriman, Jr.). *Education:*

Boston University, A.B., 1931; Andover Newton Theological School, B.D., 1934; Harvard University, A.M., 1936, Ph.D., 1938; additional study at University of Uppsala and University of Lund, 1936-37. *Politics:* Independent. *Office:* Department of Philosophy, College of Wooster, Wooster, Ohio 44691.

CAREER: Ordained Congregational minister, 1934; Andover Newton Theological School, Newton Center, Mass., instructor, 1937-38, assistant professor, 1938-40, Abbot Professor of Christian Theology, 1940-50, 1957-65; Vanderbilt University, Divinity School, Nashville, Tenn., professor of philosophical theology, 1950-57; Parsons College, Fairfield, Iowa, scholar-in-residence, 1965-68; College of Wooster, Wooster, Ohio, Ferris Professor of Philosophy, 1968-71. Fulbright lecturer, Oxford University, 1951-52; visiting lecturer at Harvard University, 1947-48, Hartley-Victoria College, Manchester, England, 1956, Boston University, 1959-60, Doshisha University, Kyoto, 1961, and Near East School of Theology, Beirut, 1962. Distinguished lecturer at Pacific School of Religion, Southern Methodist University, Vanderbilt University, and at various seminaries.

MEMBER: American Philosophical Association, American Theological Society (president, 1957-58), Society for Religion in Higher Education, Phi Beta Kappa. *Awards, honors:* Sheldon traveling fellow of Harvard University in Europe, 1936-37; Carnegie grant-in-aid, 1950; D.D. from Boston University, 1956.

WRITINGS: Swedish Contributions to Modern Theology, Harper, 1939, revised edition, 1967; *The Christian Fellowship,* Harper, 1940; *The Christian Faith,* Harper, 1942; *Return to Christianity,* Harper, 1943; *Faith and Reason,* Harper, 1946, reprinted, Books for Libraries Press, 1971; *Evil and the Christian Faith,* Harper, 1947, reprinted, Books for Libraries Press, 1971; *Pillars of Faith,* Harper, 1948; *Christianity and Society,* Harper, 1950; *Strengthening the Spiritual Life,* Harper, 1951; *The Christian Understanding of God,* Harper, 1951; *The Sun and the Umbrella,* Harper, 1953; *Christian Faith and Higher Education,* Harper, 1954; *Making Religion Real,* Harper, 1955; *Christ and the Christian,* Harper, 1958; *Know Your Faith,* Harper, 1959; *The Atonement and Mission* (booklet), London Missionary Society, 1960; *Searchlights on Contemporary Theology,* Harper, 1961; *God's New Age,* Harper, 1962; *The Finality of Faith,* Harper, 1963; *Reason in Religion,* Thomas Nelson, 1963; *A Theology for Christian Prayer,* Tidings, 1963; *The Living God of Nowhere and Nothing,* Epworth, 1966, Westminster, 1967; *A Theology of Christian Education,* Westminster, 1967; *The Universal Word,* Westminster, 1969; *Swedish Contributions to Modern Theology: With Special Reference to Lundension Thought,* Gannon, 1970.

Contributor: W. K. Anderson, editor, *Methodism,* Methodist Publishing House, 1947; J. Richard Spann, editor, *Fruits of Faith,* Abingdon-Cokesbury, 1950; A. William Loos, editor, *Religious Faith and World Culture,* Prentice-Hall, 1951; D. W. Soper, editor, *Room for Improvement,* Wilcox & Follett, 1951; D. W. Soper, editor, *These Found the Way,* Westminster, 1951; Charles Kegley and Robert Bretall, editors, *The Theology of Paul Tillich,* Macmillan, 1952; John Ferguson, editor, *Studies in Christian Social Commitment,* Independent Press (London), 1954; *Meeting God in Scripture,* Upper Room, 1964; A. W. Hastings and E. Hastings, editors, *Theologians of Our Time,* T. & T. Clark, 1966; LeRoy S. Rouner, editor, *Philosophy, Religion and World Civilization: Essays in Honor of William Ernest Hocking,* Nijhoff, 1966; George and Wolfgang Roth, editors, *The Church in the Modern World,* Ryerson Press, 1967.

Articles included in other books, and a sermon in *Best Sermons, 1955,* McGraw, 1955; also contributor of sections to symposium volumes of Conference on Science, Philosophy, and Religion published by Harper, 1942, 1943, 1947, 1948, 1949, 1953, and about 250 articles and more than 260 reviews to journals and newspapers.

WORK IN PROGRESS: A book on ethics.

SIDELIGHTS: Ferre's theological method and thought were the subject of nine doctoral dissertations at American universities and seminaries, 1952-67; a tenth was written by a Jesuit at St. Thomas University in Rome. *Strengthening the Spiritual Life* is the most widely translated of his books, with Hindi, Urdu, Spanish, and Chinese editions. Three other books have been published in Japanese.

BIOGRAPHICAL/CRITICAL SOURCES: Robert E. Bruce, *A Chronicle of Achievement,* Boston University Press, 1948; Davis Wesley Soper, *Major Voices in American Theology,* Westminster, 1952; *Preacher's Magazine,* September, 1956, October, 1956, November, 1956; *Hibbert Journal,* April, 1958; Robert Clyde Johnson, *Authority in Protestant Theology,* Westminster, 1959; *Canadian Journal of Theology,* October, 1960, October, 1962; A. F. Nelson and G. S. Ferre, *Basic Philosophical Issues,* Educational Publishers, 1962; Frank N. Magill, editor, *Masterpieces of Christian Literature,* Harper, 1963; *Theology and Life,* summer, 1963; *British Weekly,* November 25, 1965, December 2, 1965, December 9, 1965; *Japanese Religions,* March, 1966; Kenneth Hamilton, *Revolt against Heaven,* Eerdmans, 1965; John Hick, editor, *Prospect for Theology,* Nisbet, 1966.†

(Died February 6, 1971)

* * *

FERRIS, James Cody
[Collective pseudonym]

WRITINGS: Thunder Canyon, Collins, 1930.

"The X Bar X Boys" series; published by Grosset, except as noted: *The X Bar X Boys at Nugget Camp,* 1928; *... at Grizzly Pass,* 1929; *... at Rustlers' Gap,* 1929; *X Bar X Ranch,* Collins, 1930; *The X Bar X Boys Lost in the Rockies,* 1930; *... Riding for Life,* 1931; *... in Smoky Valley,* 1932; *... at Copperhead Gulch,* 1933; *... Branding the Wild Herd,* 1934; *... at the Strange Rodeo,* 1935; *... with the Secret Rangers,* 1936; *... Hunting the Prize Mustangs,* 1937; *... at Triangle Mine,* 1938; *... and the Sagebrush Mystery,* 1939; *... in the Haunted Gully,* 1940; *... Seeking the Lost Troopers,* 1941; *... Following the Stampede,* 1942.

SIDELIGHTS: See ADAMS, Harriet S., STRATEMEYER, Edward L., and SVENSON, Andrew E.†

* * *

FEUERLICHT, Ignace

PERSONAL: Born in Austria; naturalized U.S. citizen; son of Herman and Rachel Feuerlicht. *Education:* Studied at University of Lyon, 1930-31; University of Vienna, Ph.D., 1932; further study at Columbia University, New York University, and National University of Mexico. *Home:* 110 West 96th St., New York, N.Y. 10025.

CAREER: Realgymnasium, Vienna, Austria, teacher of French and German, 1932-38; Ecole Normale, Seine, France, teacher of German, 1938-39; high school teacher in

New York and New Jersey, 1943-46; Sampson College, assistant professor of German, 1946-47; State University of New York College at New Paltz, associate professor, 1947-57, professor of German and French, beginning 1957. *Member:* American Association of Teachers of German, Modern Language Association of America. *Awards, honors:* Travel grant from Austrian Government; grants from the State University of New York.

WRITINGS: Thomas Mann und die Grenzen des Ich, Winter (Heidelberg), 1966; *Thomas Mann,* Twayne, 1968. Contributor to language journals.

* * *

FIGH, Margaret Gillis   1896-

PERSONAL: Born July 12, 1896, in Brewton, Ala.; daughter of Daniel (a teacher and banker) and Martha (Hobdy) Gillis; married John Poston Figh III, August 18, 1925 (deceased); children: John Poston IV. *Education:* Judson College, A.B., 1916; University of Alabama, M.A., 1917; Columbia University, M.A., 1925. *Politics:* Independent. *Religion:* United Methodist. *Home:* 2442 Agnew St., Montgomery, Ala. 36106. *Office:* Department of English, Huntingdon College, Montgomery, Ala. 36106.

CAREER: High school teacher of English in Alabama, 1917-24; Huntingdon College, Montgomery, Ala., assistant professor, 1925-27, associate professor of English, 1927-73, professor emeritus, 1973—. Instructor, Montgomery Center, University of Alabama, 1937-42. *Member:* South Atlantic Modern Language Association, Alabama College English Teachers Association. *Awards, honors:* Carnegie Foundation grants for research in Southern folklore, 1947, 1948, 1949.

WRITINGS: (Contributor) *Historic Homes of Alabama and Their Traditions,* Birmingham Publishing Co., 1935; (contributor) Benjamin A. Botkin and Carl Withers, *The Illustrated Book of American Folklore,* Grosset, 1958; (with Kathryn Tucker Wyndham) *Thirteen Alabama Ghosts and Jeffry,* Strode, 1970. Contributor to folklore journals and other periodicals.

WORK IN PROGRESS: Further research on the folktale in Alabama.

SIDELIGHTS: Margaret Figh told *CA* that the purpose behind much of her writing is the "preserving of folk settings, tales and language in entertaining form." She reported that she was influenced by "Stephen Benet's humorous tales growing out of folklore."

* * *

FINCK, Furman J(oseph)   1900-

PERSONAL: Born October 10, 1900, in Chester, Pa.; son of Henri Auguste (a master designer) and Caroline (Smith) Finck; married Mildred Price (a composer), June 18, 1938; children: Nicolas. *Education:* Pennsylvania Academy of the Fine Arts, student, 1921-24; Ecole des Beaux Arts and Academie Julian, Paris, student, 1924. *Home:* 285 Central Park W., New York, N.Y. 10024.

CAREER: Artist. Temple University, Philadelphia, Pa., Oak Lane Country Day School, head of art department, 1926-34; Tyler School of Art, professor of painting, 1934-64, professor of drawing and anatomy, 1964-67, professor emeritus, 1967—. Instructor of drawing and painting, Cheltenham Art Center, Cheltenham, Pa., beginning 1966; professor of portrait painting, Philadelphia Museum of Art, beginning 1969; dean, duCret School of the Arts, Plainfield, N.J., beginning 1969; tutorial counselor, Fordham University, 1969. Works have appeared in national and international group exhibitions; also in public collections of National Portrait Gallery, Toledo Museum, and Temple University Health Science Center.

MEMBER: American Artist's Fellowship (vice-president), English-Speaking Union of the U.S., Players (co-chairman of fine arts), Salmagundi Club (chairman of public relations), St. Georges Society of New York, Twenty-Five Year Club of Temple University, Dutch Treat. *Awards, honors:* National Academy of Design, Andrew Carnegie Prize, 1943, first Altman Prize, 1955; Popular award, Worcester Museum, 1945; D.F.A., Muhlenberg College, 1954; Krindler Prize, Slamagundi Annual, 1964.

WRITINGS: The Meaning of Art in Education, Teachers College, Columbia University Press, 1938; (with Victor D'Amico) *The Artist as Teacher,* Appleton, 1946; *Complete Guide to Portrait Painting,* Watson-Guptill, 1970. Contributor to journals.

WORK IN PROGRESS: With Dudley duCret, working on a revision of Arthur Guptill's *Sketching as a Hobby.*†

*   *   *

FINKEL, George (Irvine)   1909-1975
(E. M. Pennage)

PERSONAL: Born May 13, 1909, in Durham, England; son of George Edward (a farmer) and Grace Amy (Stephenson) Finkel; married Lena Almond, January, 1930; children: Ian Derek, Anne Deirdre (Mrs. Leslie Beckhouse), Christopher Thomas George, David Michael. *Education:* Educated at Bede Collegiate School, 1919-26, and in Royal Navy. *Politics:* "Floating voter." *Religion:* Anglican. *Home:* 18 Coolabah Rd., Valley Heights, New South Wales, Australia.

CAREER: Began in chemical engineering; became aviator, flying pioneer routes in Africa, 1935-39; career officer in Royal Navy, 1939-58, leaving service with rank of lieutenant commander; University of New South Wales, Kensington, New South Wales, Australia, planning engineer, 1958-69. Author. *Member:* Australian Society of Authors, Children's Book Council of New South Wales.

WRITINGS—All published by Angus & Robertson, except as indicated: *The Mystery of Secret Beach,* 1962; *Ship in Hiding,* 1963; *Cloudmaker,* Roy, 1965; *The Singing Sands,* 1966; *Watch Fires to the North,* Viking, 1967 (published in England as *Twilight Province,* 1967); *The Long Pilgrimage,* 1967, Viking, 1969; *The Loyal Virginian,* Viking, 1968 (published in Australia as *The 'Loyall Virginian,'* 1968); *Navigator and Explorer: James Cook* (booklet), Wentworth Books, 1969; *Journey to Jorsala,* 1969; *The Peace Seekers,* 1970; *James Cook: Royal Navy,* 1970; *William Light,* 1972; *The Stranded Duck,* 1973; *Matthew Flinders: Explorer and Scientist,* Collins, 1973; *New South Wales, 1788-1900,* Thomas Nelson, 1974; *Victoria, 1834-1900,* Thomas Nelson, 1974; *The Dutchman Gold: The Story of Angus Tasman,* 1975. Also author of twelve topic books for the South Australian Education Department, published by Thomas Nelson. Author of monthly motoring column in *Avalon News,* New South Wales.

SIDELIGHTS: According to information George Finkel gave *CA, The Stranded Duck* and a book entitled *The Crew of the "Ingrid"* were to have been published under the pseudonym E. M. Pennage; however, *The Stranded Duck* has now appeared under his own name. *Avocational interests:* Desert travel, Anglo-Saxon and Byzantine history, ancient voyages.†

(Died, 1975)

FINNEY, Charles G(randison)   1905-

PERSONAL: Born December 1, 1905, in Sedalia, Mo.; son of Norton Jameson (a railroad superintendent) and Florence (Bell) Finney; married Marie Doyle, September 10, 1939; children: Sheila (Mrs. Peter C. Boulay), Felice (Mrs. Gary Jarrold). *Education:* Attended University of Missouri, one and one-half years. *Politics:* Democrat. *Religion:* Roman Catholic. *Home:* 2702 East 18th St., Tucson, Ariz. 85716. *Agent:* Barthold Fles Literary Agency, 507 Fifth Ave., New York, N.Y. 10017.

CAREER: Arizona Daily Star, Tucson, Ariz., proofreader, 1930-45, night wire editor, 1945-53, copy reader, 1953-65, financial editor, 1965-70. *Military service:* U.S. Army, 1927-30. *Awards, honors:* National Booksellers Award for most original novel of 1935, *The Circus of Dr. Lao.*

WRITINGS: The Circus of Dr. Lao, Viking, 1935, reprinted, Avon, 1976; *The Unholy City,* Vanguard, 1937; *Past the End of the Pavement,* Holt, 1939; *The Old China Hands,* Doubleday, 1962; *The Ghosts of Manacle* (contains short stories and a novella, "The End of the Rainbow"), Pyramid Publications, 1964; *The Magician Out of Manchuria* [and] *The Unholy City,* Pyramid Publications, 1968. His story, "The Iowan's Curse," was included in *Best American Short Stories,* 1959. Contributor of short stories to *New Yorker, Paris Review, Point West,* and *Fantasy and Science Fiction.*

SIDELIGHTS: Finney's panoply of legendary creatures created a sensation when *The Circus of Dr. Lao* was published in 1935. A *New York Times* critic felt that Finney's fantasy "entered a field of humor pretty well pre-empted" by Thorne Smith's satyrs. And William Rose Benet wrote in the *Saturday Review:* "I don't wonder the publishers accepted this book by acclamation. It may not mean anything, but it is a remarkable excursion into the fantastic. . . . Don't run away with the idea that Mr. Finney's extraordinary brainstorm won't occasionally horrify or disgust you. It will. It isn't a book for babies. But it certainly is funny." *The Circus of Dr. Lao,* which F. H. Britten called "licentious, irreverent, insolent and quite amusing," was adapted by Charles Beaumont for the film, "The Seven Faces of Dr. Lao."

Finney's next two books disappointed the critics, and more than two decades passed before publication of *The Old China Hands,* semidocumentary stories of the American army in China. Finney did not abandon fiction in the interval, but continued to publish short stories. One of them, "Life and Death of a Western Gladiator," the biography of a rattlesnake, first appeared in *Harper's* in 1958, and has been reprinted in a total of nine textbooks. It was adapted for a television documentary for ABC-TV in 1976.

BIOGRAPHICAL/CRITICAL SOURCES: Saturday Review of Literature, July 20, 1935; *New York Times,* July 28, 1935; *Books,* August 4, 1935; *Forum,* October, 1935.

*   *   *

FISCHEL, Walter J(oseph)   1902-1973

PERSONAL: Born November 12, 1902, in Frankfurt am Main, Germany; son of Hugo and Zerline (Kahn) Fischel; married Irene Markrich (a scientific illustrator and artist), June 13, 1954; children: Corinne Zipporah. *Education:* University of Heidelberg, student, 1921-22; University of

Frankfurt, Dr.Rer.Pol., 1924; University of Giessen-Heidelberg, Ph.D., 1926. *Religion:* Jewish. *Home:* 2954 Russell St., Berkeley, Calif. 94705. *Office:* Department of Near Eastern Languages, University of California, Berkeley, Calif. 94720.

CAREER: Rabbinical College, Frankfurt, Germany, teacher and lecturer, 1922-24; Hebrew University of Jerusalem, School of Oriental Studies, Jerusalem, Israel, faculty member, 1926-45; University of California, Berkeley, visiting professor, 1945-46, professor of Semitic languages and literature beginning 1946, chairman of department of Near Eastern languages, 1948-58. Member of scientific expeditions to Syria, Turkey, Iran, Kurdistan, and India, 1930, 1936; lecturer in South America, 1938, South Africa, 1940, United States and Canada, 1943-44, and in the Near and Middle East, Iran, and India. *Member:* American Oriental Society (member of executive committee, 1951-53), Society of Biblical Literature (president of Pacific Coast branch, 1948-51), American Academy for Jewish Research (fellow), American Association for Jewish Education (member of board of governors), Royal Asiatic Society (fellow). *Awards, honors:* Guggenheim fellowship, 1959-60; Fulbright senior research award for work in India, 1963-64; Humanities Institute Award of University of California, 1967.

WRITINGS: Jews in the Economic and Political Life of Mediaeval Islam (monograph), Royal Asiatic Society, 1937, with new introduction, Ktav, 1969; (editor) *Semitic and Oriental Studies in Honor of William Popper,* University of California Press, 1951; (editor and translator) *Ibn Khaldun and Tamerlane: Their Historic Meeting in Damascus, 1401 A.D.,* University of California Press, 1952; *ha-Yehudim be-Hodu* (title means "The Jews of India"), Ben-Zvi Institute, Hebrew University of Jerusalem, 1960; (contributor) Louis Finkelstein, editor, *The Jews: Their History, Culture and Religion* Harper, 1960; (editor) Ibn Taghri Birdi, *History of Egypt* (extract from *Chronicle*), English translation by William Popper, American Oriental Society, 1967; *Ibn Khaldun in Egypt: His Public Functions and Historical Research, a Study in Islamic Historiography,* University of California Press, 1967; (editor and author of introduction) *Unknown Jews in Unknown Lands: The Travels of Rabbi David d'Beth Hillel,* Ktav, 1973. Also author of *The Jews of Persia and Central Asia and Their Literature.*

Contributor of numerous monographs, articles, and studies to *Harvard Theological Review, Journal of the Economic and Social History of the Orient, Historia Judaica, Revue des Etudes Juives,* and other learned journals. Chairman of editorial board, University of California publications in Semitic philology, beginning 1949; member of editorial staff, "Near Eastern Series," University of California, beginning 1960.

SIDELIGHTS: In addition to his native German, Walter Fischel was competent in French, Dutch, Spanish, Hebrew, Arabic, Farsi, and other Near Eastern languages.†

(Died July 14, 1973)

* * *

FISCHER, Ann 1919-1971

PERSONAL: Born May 22, 1919, in Kansas City, Kan.; daughter of Thomas W. and Gertrude A. (Miller) Kindrick; married John Lyle Fischer (a professor of anthropology), July 9, 1949; children: Madeleine Nikko, Mary Anne. *Education:* University of Kansas, A.B., 1941; Harvard University, Ph.D., 1957. *Politics:* Democrat. *Religion:* None. *Home:* 1133 Lowerline, New Orleans, La. 70118. *Office:*

Department of Anthropology, Tulane University of Louisiana, New Orleans, La. 70118.

CAREER: Pacific Science Board fellow in Truk, Caroline Islands, 1949-50; teacher of English and field worker in Ponape, Caroline Islands, 1950-53; member of field team working on Six Cultures project in a New England village, 1954-55; Harvard University, Cambridge, Mass., research assistant, 1955-57; Children's Hospital, Boston, Mass., research associate on Russell Sage Foundation project, 1957-58; Tulane University of Louisiana, New Orleans, part-time teacher in University College, 1958-59, began as lecturer in School of Public Health and Tropical Medicine, professor, beginning 1960, faculty member of School of Social Work, 1960-65, associate professor, 1963-65, faculty member of department of anthropology, beginning 1964, professor of anthropology, beginning 1965. Visiting summer professor, University of Hawaii, 1966. Consultant to Peace Corps on Micronesia, 1966.

MEMBER: American Anthropological Association (fellow). *Awards, honors:* National Institute of Mental Health grants for work with Houma Indians, 1960, and for Negro family study, 1964-66; U.S. Children's Bureau and Tulane Research Council grants for research at Center for Advanced Study in the Behavioral Sciences, 1965-66.

WRITINGS: (With husband, John L. Fischer) "The New Englanders of Orchard Town U.S.A.," in *Six Cultures: Studies of Child Rearing,* edited by Beatrice Whiting, Wiley, 1963, published separately, 1966; (contributor) Leigh Minturn Triandis and William Lambert, editors, *Mothers in Six Societies,* Wiley, 1964; (contributor) Peggy Golde, editor, *Women in the Field,* Aldine, 1970. Also contributor to *Japan and the Ryukyus,* for Natural History Press. Book review editor, *American Anthropologist,* beginning 1970. Contributor to medical, anthropology, and sociology journals.

WORK IN PROGRESS: Co-director of family survey of metropolitan New Orleans, supported by U.S. Children's Bureau.†

(Died, 1971)

* * *

FISCHTROM, Harvey 1933-1974
(Harve Zemach)

PERSONAL: Born December 5, 1933, in Newark, N.J.; son of Mac and Ida Fischtrom; married Margot Zemach (an illustrator of children's books), January 29, 1957; children: Kaethe, Heidi, Rachel, Rebecca. *Education:* Wesleyan University, Middletown, Conn., B.A., 1955; University of Vienna, graduate study, 1955-56; Brandeis University, M.A., 1959. *Residence:* London, England.

CAREER: Instructor in history and social science at Boston University, College of Basic Studies, Boston, Mass., 1960-65, and University of Massachusetts, Amherst, beginning 1965. Author of juvenile books. *Member:* Phi Beta Kappa. *Awards, honors:* Fulbright scholar in Austria, 1955-56; first prize at World Children's Book Festival, 1965, for *Salt: A Russian Tale;* Caldecott Honor Book award, 1970, for *The Judge: An Untrue Tale.*

WRITINGS—Under pseudonym Harve Zemach; all juveniles; illustrated by his wife, Margot Zemach: *A Small Boy Is Listening,* Houghton, 1959; *A Hat with a Rose,* Dutton, 1961; *Nail Soup: A Swedish Folk Tale Retold,* Follett, 1964; (adaptor) Alexei Afansev, *Salt: A Russian Tale,* translated by Benjamin Zemach, Follett, 1965; *The Tricks of Master*

Dabble, Holt, 1965; (adaptor) *The Speckled Hen: A Russian Nursery Rhyme,* Holt, 1966; (adaptor) *Mommy, Buy Me a China Doll,* Follett, 1966; (adaptor) *Too Much Nose: An Italian Tale,* Holt, 1967; *The Judge: An Untrue Tale,* Farrar, Straus, 1969; *Awake and Dreaming,* Farrar, Straus, 1970; *Penny a Look: An Old Story,* Farrar, Straus, 1971; *Duffy and the Devil,* Farrar, Straus, 1973; (with daughter, Kaethe Zemach) *The Princess and Froggie,* Farrar, Straus, 1975.

BIOGRAPHICAL/CRITICAL SOURCES: New York Times Book Review, January 25, 1970.†

(Died November 2, 1974)

*   *   *

FISHER, Alden L(owell)   1928-1970

PERSONAL: Born April 22, 1928, in Potter, Neb.; son of Arlo Emmet and Alice (Nelson) Fisher; married Rosemary Fitzpatrick (a teacher), August 25, 1955; children: Marc, Anne. *Education:* St. Louis University, B.S., 1951, M.A., 1953; University of Louvain, Ph.D., 1956. *Religion:* Roman Catholic. *Home:* 7241 Colgate, St. Louis, Mo. 63130. *Office:* St. Louis University, 221 North Grand, St. Louis, Mo. 63103.

CAREER: St. Louis University, St. Louis, Mo., instructor, 1956-59, assistant professor, 1959-62, associate professor, 1962-66, professor of philosophy, beginning 1966, assistant psychologist, beginning 1960, director of university honors program, 1961-64. Visiting research specialist, Veterans Administration Hospital, Lexington, Ky., summer, 1961. *Military service:* U.S. Army, 1946-49; became first lieutenant. *Member:* American Philosophical Association, American Psychological Association (fellow), Metaphysical Society of America, New York Academy of Sciences. *Awards, honors:* Fulbright scholar in Belgium, 1953-55.

WRITINGS: (Translator from the French) Maurice Merleau-Ponty, *The Structure of Behavior,* Beacon Press, 1963; (editor) *The Essential Writings of Merleau-Ponty,* Harcourt, 1969; (editor with George B. Murray) *Philosophy and Science as Modes of Knowing,* Appleton, 1969. Contributor to professional journals. Associate editor, *Modern Schoolman* and *New Scholasticism.*

WORK IN PROGRESS: Translating Alphonse de Waelhens' *Existence et signification.*†

(Died November, 1970)

*   *   *

FISK, McKee   1900-

PERSONAL: Born February 4, 1900, in Alton, Ill.; son of Elmer McReynolds and Maud Ella (McKee) Fisk; married Laura R. Best (a nurse), November 26, 1931; children: Donald, Karolus A., Patricia. *Education:* Oklahoma City University, A.B., 1923; University of Southern California, A.M., 1926; Yale University, Ph.D., 1936. *Home:* 880 West Cliff Dr., Santa Cruz, Calif. 95060. *Office:* Graduate School of Business, University of Santa Clara, Santa Clara, Calif. 95053.

CAREER: High school teacher in Denison, Tex., 1923-25; Santa Ana Junior College, Santa Ana, Calif., instructor in business, 1925-26, dean, 1926-35; Yale University, New Haven, Conn., instructor, 1935-36; professor of business education and head of department at Oklahoma State University of Agriculture and Applied Sciences, Stillwater, 1936-40, and at University of North Carolina at Greensboro,

1940-43; U.S. Veterans Administration, Division of Vocational Rehabilitation and Education, Washington, D.C., chief of business and sales training, 1943-45; McGraw-Hill Book Co., New York, N.Y., business education editor, 1945-48; Fresno State College (now California State University, Fresno), professor of business administration and dean of School of Business, 1948-69, professor emeritus and dean emeritus, beginning 1969; University of Santa Clara, Santa Clara, Calif., professor of business administration, beginning 1969. Summer professor at other colleges and universities, including University of Michigan, University of Pittsburgh, University of Southern California, Indiana University, and Stanford University; Distinguished Lecturer, Sacramento State College (now California State University, Sacramento), 1968. Consultant to dean of Faculty of Business Administration, University of Karachi, 1962, 1964. Chairman, Committee on Taxonomy of Business Education, U.S. Office of Education. Member of Accrediting Commission for Business Schools, 1956-68.

MEMBER: American Association of Collegiate Schools of Business, National Business Education Association (honorary member), California Business Education Association (president, 1953), Phi Kappa Phi, Beta Gamma Sigma, Beta Alpha Psi, Delta Pi Epsilon (national president, 1939-41), Sigma Alpha Epsilon, Alpha Kappa Psi, Pi Omega Pi, Phi Chi Theta (honorary member), Omicron Delta Epsilon, Kiwanis Club. *Awards, honors:* Distinguished service awards of United Business Schools Association, 1955, Accrediting Commission for Business Schools, 1959, and California Business Education Association, 1969; John Robert Gregg Award in Business Education, 1968.

WRITINGS: (With W. E. Grimes) *Farm Accounting,* University Publishing, 1937; (with David A. Pomeroy) *Applied Business Law,* South-Western, 5th revised edition (Fisk was not associated with earlier editions) 1944, 7th revised edition (with James C. Snapp), 1955, 10th revised edition (with Norbert J. Mietus), 1972; *Introduction to Business Law,* South-Western, 1958, revised edition, 1968. Contributor to *Collier's Encyclopedia, National Business Education Yearbook,* 1966, and to periodicals. Editor, yearbooks of National Business Teachers Federation, 1940-43; business education editor, *American Vocational Journal.*

SIDELIGHTS: Sales of *Applied Business Law* had exceeded one million copies by January, 1967, when the publishers presented a gold-bound copy of the book to Fisk.

*   *   *

FISKIN, A(bram) M. I.   1916-1975

PERSONAL: Born April 3, 1916, in Winnipeg, Manitoba, Canada; son of Isor (a merchant) and Esther (De Leon) Fiskin; married Ingfried Jackson (a college teacher), February 2, 1949. *Education:* University of Manitoba, B.A., 1936; University of Minnesota, M.A., 1941, Ph.D., 1964. *Home:* 2465 South Dahlia Lane, Denver, Colo. 80222.

CAREER: Teacher at University of Minnesota, Minneapolis, 1942-43, Northwestern University, Evanston, Ill., 1943-47, and University of Denver, Denver, Colo., 1948-51; self-employed in Denver, 1951-64; Drake University, Des Moines, Iowa, associate professor of English, 1964-66; Pennsylvania State University, University Park, associate professor of English, beginning 1967. Member of faculty, Chapman College, floating campus, 1966-67. Member of advisory board, Colorado Polytechnic College. *Member:* Modern Language Association of America, American Business Writing Association, Society of Technical Writers and Publishers (senior member).

WRITINGS: (Editor and contributor) *Writers of Our Years*, University of Denver Press, 1951.

Study guides: William Congreve, *Way of the World*, Cliff's Notes, 1966; Richard Sheridan, *The Rivals and The School for Scandal*, Cliff's Notes, 1967; Ben Jonson, *The Alchemist*, Cliff's Notes, 1967. Contributor to *Britannica Junior Encyclopaedia;* contributor of articles and reviews to *Chicago Sun, Humanist, Western Folklore, Denver Post, Denver Quarterly, Italica,* and other publications. Poetry editor, *Humanist,* 1947-49; associate editor, *Faulkner Quarterly,* 1952-53.

WORK IN PROGRESS: A book on writing the company annual report; a study of Eugene O'Neill's plays; a study of how Shakespeare used his sources to create dramatic plots and effects.†

(Died June 8, 1975)

* * *

FITCH, Edwin M(edbery) 1902-

PERSONAL: Born June 10, 1902, in Wakonda, S.D.; son of George William (a life insurance salesman) and Edith (Medbery) Fitch; married Gertrude Rossman, 1929; married second wife, Charlotte Warner, August 30, 1935; children: (first marriage) Jean Fitch Costa; (second marriage) Mary Fitch Harahan, Kathryn Medbery Fitch. *Education:* Yankton College, B.A., 1923; Oxford University, B.A. (second class honors), 1926; University of Wisconsin, Ph.D., 1933. *Politics:* Democrat. *Religion:* Unitarian Universalist. *Home:* 1601 Longfellow St., McLean, Va. 22101.

CAREER: New York University, New York City, instructor in economics, 1926-27; University of South Dakota, Vermillion, associate professor of economics, 1927-29; American Association for Labor Legislation, New York City, research assistant, 1930-31; W. T. Raleigh Co., Freeport, Ill., economist, 1931-32; National Recovery Administration, Bituminous Coal Section, Washington, D.C., statistician, 1934; Federal Co-ordinator of Transportation, Washington, D.C., assistant director of labor relations, 1934-36; Railroad Retirement Board, Washington, D.C., chief statistician, 1936-42; U.S. Office of Defense Transportation, Washington, D.C., 1942-44, began as assistant director, became associate director of Division of Transport Personnel; Air Transport Association, Washington, D.C., director of personnel relations, 1944-47; Alaska Railroad (operated under U.S. Department of Interior prior to 1967; now under U.S. Department of Transportation), Washington, D.C., 1947-68, began as industrial relations adviser, became assistant to general manager. Lecturer on labor relations, Graduate School, George Washington University, 1950-54.

MEMBER: National Defense Transportation Association (life member), Association of American Rhodes Scholars, Society for the Preservation and Encouragement of Barber Shop Quartet Singing in America (president of Alexandria [Va.] chapter, 1962-63). *Awards, honors:* Rhodes scholar, 1923-26.

WRITINGS: The Alaska Railroad, Praeger, 1967; (with John F. Shanklin) *The Bureau of Outdoor Recreation,* Praeger, 1970. Author of a number of government monographs in the fields of labor and transportation and contributor to journals in those two fields.

AVOCATIONAL INTERESTS: Developing a 110-acre wilderness area in the Bull Run Mountains of Virginia for family use.

FITZHUGH, Louise 1928-1974

PERSONAL: Born October 5, 1928, in Memphis, Tenn.; daughter of Millsaps (an attorney) and Louise (Perkins) Fitzhugh. *Education:* Attended Bard College, Art Students League, and Cooper Union. *Residence:* Bridgewater, Conn. *Agent:* McIntosh & Otis, 475 Fifth Ave., New York, N.Y. 10017.

CAREER: Author, illustrator, and artist. *Awards, honors:* Sequoyah Award, 1967, for *Harriet the Spy;* Brooklyn Art Books for Children citation, for *Bang, Bang, You're Dead.*

WRITINGS: (With Sandra Scoppettone) *Suzuki Beane,* Doubleday, 1961; *Harriet the Spy,* Harper, 1964; *The Long Secret,* Harper, 1965; (with Scoppettone) *Bang, Bang, You're Dead,* Harper, 1969; *Nobody's Family Is Going to Change,* Farrar, Straus, 1974.

SIDELIGHTS: Louise Fitzhugh lived a year in Italy and a year in France. *Avocational interests:* Played the flute.

BIOGRAPHICAL/CRITICAL SOURCES: New York Times Book Review, November 5, 1967, February 25, 1968; *New York Times,* November 21, 1974; *Children's Literature Review,* Volume I, Gale, 1976.†

(Died November 19, 1974)

* * *

FLAYDERMAN, Phillip C(harles) 1930-1969

PERSONAL: Born December 12, 1930, in Boston, Mass.; son of Benjamin and Shirley (Bellar) Flayderman; married Marilyn Krugman (a teacher); children: Bruce David, Stephen Mark Jon. *Education:* Amherst College, A.B. (magna cum laude), 1952; Columbia University, M.A., 1962. *Politics:* None. *Religion:* None. *Agent:* John Schaffner Literary Agency, 425 East 51st St., New York, N.Y. 10022.

CAREER: Columbia University, New York City, lecturer in German, 1952-53, teacher in university grammar school, 1959-62; Washington Square Press, Inc., New York City, editor-in-chief, 1962-65; New American Library, Inc., New York City, education editor, 1966-67; Dell Publishing Co., Inc., New York City, senior editor, 1967-69. Lecturer, New York University, beginning 1966. *Military service:* U.S. Army, 1954-56.

WRITINGS: Sarpedon, William-Frederick, 1952; (translator) Boris Pasternak, *Sister My Life* (poems), Washington Square, 1967; (editorial assistant) Hugh Auchincloss Brown, *Cataclysms of the Earth,* Twayne, 1967; (editor) *Great Narrative Poems,* Pyramid Publications, 1968; (editor) *One Hundred Great Poems,* Pyramid Publications, 1968.

WORK IN PROGRESS: The Art of Collecting Antiques, in collaboration with father, Benjamin Flayderman; *A Short History of Man's Major Ideas.*

SIDELIGHTS: Flayderman spoke, read, and wrote German, Russian, Latin, and Greek (ancient).†

(Died, 1969)

* * *

FLEISCHMANN, Harriet 1904-

PERSONAL: Born March 11, 1904, in Philadelphia, Pa.; daughter of Enos Hesser (a builder) and Edith (Livezey) Drakeley; married Rudolf Fleischmann, August 25, 1934 (deceased); children: Edith. *Education:* University of Pennsylvania, B.S. in Ed., 1926. *Politics:* Republican. *Religion:* Protestant. *Home:* 127 West Queen Lane, Philadelphia, Pa. 19144.

CAREER: Teacher of French, 1926-34, and librarian, 1952-58, both in Philadelphia, Pa. *Member:* Violet Oakley Foundation, Alpha Zi Delta, University Women's Club.

WRITINGS: The Great Enchantment, Chilton, 1967. Contributor to *Philadelphia Inquirer.*

WORK IN PROGRESS: Research on seventeenth-century France for a novel.

AVOCATIONAL INTERESTS: Music (pianist, occasionally presenting recitals).

BIOGRAPHICAL/CRITICAL SOURCES: Germantown Courier, April 27, 1967.††

* * *

FLEMING, Harold M(anchester)   1900-19(?)

PERSONAL: Born May 26, 1900, in Salem, Mass.; son of Charles H. (a life insurance agent) and Abbie (Kimball) Fleming; wife died, 1963. *Education:* Harvard University, A.B., 1920. *Politics:* Republican. *Home and office:* Antrim, N.H. 03440.

CAREER: Spent 1920-24 abroad, working in England, France, and for American Relief Administration in Prague, Moscow, and Samara, 1920-23, and for Chinese Bureau of Economic Information and Shanghai newspapers, 1923-24; continued roaming on return to America, doing stints with San Francisco Bureau of Governmental Research, New Orleans Joint Traffic Bureau, and Bureau of Railway Economics, Washington, D.C., 1924-27; Eastman, Dillon & Co., security analyst, Chicago, Ill., 1928-30; market-letter writer in New York City, 1931-34, for Smith, Graham and Rockwell, 1932-34; *Christian Science Monitor,* Wall Street correspondent, New York City, 1933-52; free-lance writer, beginning 1952. Correspondent (weekly story) for *Sunday Times,* London, 1937-39, *Goteborg Handels-Tidningen* (Swedish newspaper), 1945-52, and *Financial Times,* London, 1947-49; did research and writing for Young & Rubicam, 1942-45, and wrote a syndicated column for General Electric Co., 1946-49. Weekly radio commentator for Mutual Network, 1940, and National Broadcasting Co., 1943-44. *Member:* New York Financial Writers Association (charter member), Harvard Club of New York.

WRITINGS: Ten Thousand Commandments: A Story of the Antitrust Laws, Prentice-Hall, 1951, reprinted, Arno, 1972; *Oil Prices and Competition,* American Petroleum Institute, 1953; *States, Contracts and Progress: The Dynamics of International Wealth,* Oceana, 1960; *American Achievement,* American Can Co., 1962; *Gasoline Prices and Competition,* Appleton, 1966. Contributor to magazines, including *Nation's Business, Saturday Evening Post, Atlantic, Woman's Day, Harper's.* Editor, *A.R.A. Review* (published every year or two for veterans of Herbert Hoover's overseas and U.S. operations), 1936-65.

WORK IN PROGRESS: A second book on antitrust Laws.

SIDELIGHTS: Fleming sometimes wrote sixty hours a week in the winter when snowed in at his woods home. He handled the winter supply problem by stocking about 600 pounds of canned goods and "instant everything"; other items were hoisted to the house via a pulley from the garage, adjacent to a sometimes passable road. Fleming considered economists' writing "duller than dishwater." *Avocational interests:* Sculpture, photography.

BIOGRAPHICAL/CRITICAL SOURCES: Peterborough Transcript, October 13, 1966.†

(Deceased)

FLORY, Julia McCune   1882-1971

PERSONAL: Born February 2, 1882, in Newark, Ohio; daughter of John Holbrook (a merchant) and Elnora Phoebe (Brown) McCune; married Walter L. Flory, October 2, 1908; children: John, Elizabeth (Mrs. John W. Kelly), Phoebe. *Education:* Attended Denison University, 1901-03. *Politics:* Republican. *Religion:* Unitarian Universalist. *Residence:* Shaker Heights, Ohio.

CAREER: Co-founder and associate of the Cleveland Playhouse, beginning 1915.

WRITINGS: The Cleveland Playhouse: How It Began, Western Reserve University Press, 1965; (self-illustrated) *India: In Glittering Chariot,* Edwards Brothers, 1971.†

(Died April 23, 1971)

* * *

FOFF, Arthur R(aymond)   1925-1973
(A. R. Lawrence, Karl Lawrence)

PERSONAL: Born November 12, 1925, in San Francisco, Calif.; son of Frank Arthur (a banker) and Eunice (Lawrence) Foff; married Antonette Fereva (a painter and writer), November 23, 1944; children: Erika Leon, Frieda Lawrence, Hedda, Greta. *Education:* University of California, Berkeley, A.A. (with honors), 1942, A.B. (magna cum laude), 1944; Stanford University, Ed.D., 1955. *Agent:* Russell & Volkening, 551 Fifth Ave., New York, N.Y. 10017. *Office:* Department of English, San Francisco State University, San Francisco, Calif. 94132.

CAREER: San Francisco State University, San Francisco, Calif., 1948-73, chairman of department of creative writing, 1948-58, became professor of English literature and creative writing. Professor of American literature, Hiroshima University, Hiroshima, Japan, 1958-60; professor of American literature and cultural advisor, Damascus University, Damascus, Syria, 1961-64; professor of American literature, American University of Beirut, Beirut, Lebanon, 1965-67. *Wartime service:* Office of Strategic Services, 1943-46. *Member:* American Association of University Professors, Association of Literature (Netherlands), Phi Beta Kappa, Phi Delta Kappa, Big C, Mill Valley Country Club (member of board of directors, 1968-70). *Awards, honors:* Joseph Henry Jackson Literary Awards, 1944, 1945.

WRITINGS: Beautiful Golden-Haired Mamie (stories), Harcourt, 1945; *Sawdust,* Little, Brown, 1946; *Glorious in Another Day* (novel), Lippincott, 1947; (editor with J. D. Grambs) *Readings in Education,* Harper, 1956; *North of Market* (novel), Harcourt, 1957; (editor with Daniel Knapp) *Story: An Introduction to Prose Fiction,* Wadsworth, 1964. Contributor to *New York Times Book Review* and *San Francisco Chronicle.*

WORK IN PROGRESS: Analyses of Modern Short Stories; Cries and Comedy of Samuel Beckett; Stone, or the Last Days of the K. O. Koral.

SIDELIGHTS: Arthur Foff traveled in the Far East, Middle East, Canada, Balkan countries, Scandinavia, Mexico, U.S., Guam, Wake Islands, Western and Eastern Europe, Ireland, Scotland, and England. *Avocational interests:* Literature, painting, and sunny days.†

(Died, 1973)

* * *

FOLKMAN, Jerome (Daniel)   1907-

PERSONAL: Born September 25, 1907, in Cleveland, Ohio;

son of Ben (a manufacturer) and Rose (Tronstein) Folkman; married Bessie Schomer, December 14, 1930; children: Moses Judah, David Hillel, Joy (Mrs. Arthur J. Moss). *Education:* University of Cincinnati, A.B., 1928; Hebrew Union College (now Hebrew Union College—Jewish Institute of Religion), B.H.L., 1928; University of Michigan, graduate study, 1934-36; Ohio State University, Ph.D., 1953. *Politics:* Democrat. *Religion:* Reform Judaism. *Home:* 2531 Maryland Ave., Columbus, Ohio 43209. *Office:* 1810 College Rd., Columbus, Ohio 43210.

CAREER: Ordained rabbi, 1928; rabbi in congregations in Jackson, Mich., and Grand Rapids, Mich., 1931-47; Temple Israel, Columbus, Ohio, rabbi, 1947-73, rabbi emeritus, 1973—. Adjunct professor of sociology, Ohio State University, beginning 1963. Englander Memorial Lecturer, Hebrew Union College (now Hebrew Union College—Jewish Institute of Religion), 1957; McKinley Visiting Scholar, Walsh College, Malone College, and Mount Union College, 1976; Benjamin Tintner Memorial Lecturer, New York Association of Reformed Rabbis, 1976. Member of board of governors, Hebrew Union College, 1952-56; president, Ohio Conference on Family Relations. 1955-57; member of board of directors, Better Business Bureau of Central Ohio, beginning 1977. Member of board of directors and board of trustees for various state and local organizations. Participated in "House Divided" programs, WBNS-TV, 1962-66.

MEMBER: International Council of Christians and Jews, Central Conference of American Rabbis (member of executive board, 1957-59; financial secretary, 1969-71), American Sociological Association (fellow), Union of American Hebrew Congregations (member of board of trustees, 1960-64), American Association of University Professors, National Council on Family Relations (member-at-large of executive committee, 1961-63), Society for the Study of Social Problems, Family Service Association of America (director, 1965-68), B'nai B'rith (president of district No. 6, 1943-44), Alpha Kappa Delta, Faculty Club (Ohio State University), Torch Club (president, 1976-77). *Awards, honors:* D.D., Hebrew Union College, 1957; Sanford Lakin Award, B'nai B'rith, 1961; Citizen of the Year Award, Frontiers International, 1967; Governor's Award, State of Ohio, 1968.

WRITINGS: The Cup of Life: A Jewish Marriage Manual, Jonathan David, 1955; *Design for Jewish Living,* Union of American Hebrew Congregations, 1955; (with Nancy M. K. Clatworthy) *Marriage Has Many Faces,* C. E. Merrill, 1970. Contributor to scholarly journals and popular magazines. Member of editorial advisory board, *Highlights for Children,* beginning 1953.

*   *   *

FOLMSBEE, Stanley J(ohn)   1899-1974

PERSONAL: Born November 29, 1899, in South Valley, N.Y.; son of Arthur and Clara (Somers) Folmsbee; married Ocie L. Buckner, April 6, 1927. *Education:* Dickinson College, A.B., 1922; University of Pennsylvania, A.M., 1926, Ph.D., 1932. *Politics:* Independent. *Religion:* United Methodist. *Home:* 1715 Birdsong St., Knoxville, Tenn. 37915. *Office:* Department of History, University of Tennessee, Knoxville, Tenn. 37916.

CAREER: University of Tennessee, Knoxville, instructor, 1928-34, assistant professor, 1934-43, associate professor, 1943-46, professor of history, 1946-69, professor emeritus, 1969-74. Managing editor of publications, East Tennessee Historical Society, 1936-74. Trustee, Fort Loudoun Association; director, Blount Mansion Association; consultant,

James White Fort Association. *Member:* American Historical Association, Organization of American Historians, Southern Historical Association (executive council member, 1963-67), Sons of the Revolution (president of Tennessee branch), Tennessee Historical Society, Phi Beta Kappa, Exchange Club (Knoxville).

WRITINGS: Sectionalism and Internal Improvements in Tennessee, 1796-1845, East Tennessee Historical Society, 1939; (editor with H. C. Amick) *Tennessee Social Science Maps,* Denoyer-Geppert, 1940; *Blount College and East Tennessee College, 1794-1840: The First Predecessors of the University of Tennessee,* University of Tennessee, 1946; (with Joseph H. Parks) *The Story of Tennessee,* Harlow Publishing, 1954, 4th edition, 1968; *East Tennessee University, 1840-1879: Predecessor of the University of Tennessee,* University of Tennessee, 1959; (with Robert E. Corlew and Enoch L. Mitchell) *History of Tennessee,* four volumes, Lewis Historical Publishing Co., 1960, abridged and revised edition of Volumes I-II published as *Tennessee: A Short History,* University of Tennessee Press, 1969; *Tennessee Establishes a State University: First Years of the University of Tennessee, 1879-1887,* University of Tennessee, 1961. Contributor to *Encyclopedia Americana, Collier's Encyclopedia,* to other encyclopedias, and to historical journals. Member of board of editors, Tennessee Historical Society, 1943-59, and Southern Historical Association, 1953-55.

WORK IN PROGRESS: An annotated edition of the autobiography of David Crockett, with the late J. A. Shackford; a history of the University of Tennessee, 1794-1970, with James R. Montgomery.

BIOGRAPHICAL/CRITICAL SOURCES: East Tennessee Historical Society Publications, Number 34, 1962; J.G.M. Ramsey, *The Annals of Tennessee to the End of the Eighteenth Century,* reprinted, East Tennessee Historical Society, 1967.†

(Died September 6, 1974)

*   *   *

FOLSOM, Marion Bayard   1893-

PERSONAL: Born November 23, 1893, in McRae, Ga.; son of William B. and Margaret Jane (McRae) Folsom; married Mary Davenport, November 16, 1918; children: Marion Bayard, Jr., Frances (Mrs. Charles T. Bundy II). *Education:* University of Georgia, A.B. (with honors), 1912; Harvard University, M.B.A. (with distinction), 1914. *Politics:* Republican. *Religion:* Presbyterian. *Home:* 106 Oak Lane, Rochester, N.Y. *Office:* Eastman Kodak Co., 343 State St., Rochester, N.Y.

CAREER: Eastman Kodak Co., Rochester, N.Y., began 1914, treasurer, 1935-53, director, 1947-52; Eastman Savings and Loan Association, Rochester, N.Y., president, 1947-52; U.S. Government, undersecretary of the Treasury, 1953-55, Secretary of Health, Education, and Welfare, 1955-58; Eastman Kodak Co., director, beginning 1958. Director of Lincoln Rochester Trust Co., 1929-49, Buffalo Branch of Federal Reserve Bank of New York, 1938-47, Federal Reserve Bank of New York, 1949-53; trustee of Rochester Savings Bank, 1931-49, beginning 1958. Member of President's Advisory Council on Economic Security, 1934-35, Business Council, beginning 1936, Federal Advisory Council on Social Security, 1937-38 and 1963-65, Federal Hospital Council, 1965-68, Advisory Council for Economic Security, 1966-70, National Health Advisory Council, beginning 1970; Committee for Economic Development, trustee, beginning 1942, chairman of trustees, 1950-52, vice-chairman, 1960-68;

director, National Bureau for Economic Research, beginning 1961. Member of state and local government councils and of boards of universities and economic institutions. *Military service:* U.S. Army, 1917-19.

MEMBER: National Education Association (honorary life member), American College of Hospital Administrators (honorary fellow), Academy of Medicine (honorary fellow), American Hospital Association, Academy of Arts and Sciences, Phi Beta Kappa, Sigma Nu, University Club, Rochester Country Club, Genesee Valley Club, Pundit Club (Rochester), Metropolitan Club (Washington, D.C.), Harvard Club of New York City. *Awards, honors:* Albert Einstein Medal for Citizenship, Yeshiva University, 1958; Warren B. Stockberger Award of Society for Personnel Administration, 1959; Edward Moore Award of Monroe County Medical Society, 1970. Honorary degrees from University of Rochester, Hobart and William Smith Colleges, Syracuse University, Tufts University, Brown University, Swarthmore College, Rollins College, New York University, Hamilton College, Springfield College.

WRITINGS: Executive Decisions in Business and Government, McGraw, 1962. Author of management and economic reports. Contributor of articles to proceedings and annuals of learned societies.

BIOGRAPHICAL/CRITICAL SOURCES: Saturday Evening Post, December 3, 1955.†

*   *   *

FOLTIN, Lore Barbara   1913-19(?)

PERSONAL: Born July 22, 1913, in Vienna, Austria; daughter of I. J. (a farmer) and Adelheid (von Zwicker) Dentsch; married Edgar M. Foltin (a professor of psychology), August 16, 1941. *Education:* Masaryk University, student, 1933-35; German University of Prague, J.U.Dr., 1938.

CAREER: College of William and Mary, Williamsburg, Va., instructor in German, 1945-49; University of Pittsburgh, Pittsburgh, Pa., instructor, 1949-56, assistant professor, 1956-61, associate professor, 1961-71, professor of Germanic languages and literature, beginning 1971. *Member:* Modern Language Association of America, American Association of Teachers of German, International Arthur Schnitzler Research Association, Pennsylvania Modern Language Association. *Awards, honors:* Cultural and education exchange grant, 1952; Ford Foundation grant, 1962; faculty fellowship, 1968.

WRITINGS: Aus Nah und Fern, Houghton, 1950, 2nd edition, 1963; *Deutsche Welt,* Houghton, 1958; (editor) *Franz Werfel, 1890-1945,* University of Pittsburgh Press, 1961; (compiler with Hubert Heinen) *Paths to German Poetry: An Introductory Anthology,* Dodd, 1969; *Franz Werfel* (biography), Metzler, 1972. Contributor of articles and reviews to language journals; member of editorial board, *Modern Austrian Literature.*†

(Deceased)

*   *   *

FOOTE, Dorothy Norris (McBride)   1908-

PERSONAL: Born June 7, 1908, in Webster City, Iowa; daughter of Harry Eugene (a salesman) and Daisy Belle (Smith) McBride; married Henry L. Foote, April 20, 1956. *Education:* University of Iowa, B.A., M.A., Ph.D., the last in 1932; graduate study at University of Washington, Seattle, 1940, and Columbia University, 1948. *Politics:* Democrat. *Religion:* Presbyterian. *Agent:* Ruth Cantor, 156 Fifth Ave., New York, N.Y. 10010.

CAREER: University of Redlands, Redlands, Calif., associate professor, 1945-49; California State College at Los Angeles (now California State University, Los Angeles), associate professor, 1952-54; San Jose State College (now University), associate professor of literature, 1954-65. *Member:* National Council of Teachers of English, College English Association, Modern Language Association of America, Shakespeare Association of America, Authors Guild.

WRITINGS: (With Martha Heasley Cox) *A Reading Approach to College Writing,* Chandler Publishing, 1959, 4th edition, 1965; *The Constant Star,* Scribner, 1959. Contributor to *Shakespeare Notes, Explicator,* and other professional journals.

WORK IN PROGRESS: Four textbooks in composition and literature.

AVOCATIONAL INTERESTS: Music, travel.††

*   *   *

FORBES, Graham B.
[Collective pseudonym]

WRITINGS—"Frank Allen" series; all published by Garden City Publishing, 1926: *Frank Allen and His Motor Boat; . . . and His Rivals; . . . at Gold Fork; . . . at Rockspur Ranch; . . . at Zero Camp; . . . Captain of the Team; . . . Head of the Crew; . . . in Camp; . . . in Winter Sports; . . . Pitcher; . . . Playing to Win; Frank Allen's Schooldays.*

SIDELIGHTS: See **ADAMS, Harriet S., STRATEMEYER, Edward L.,** and **SVENSON, Andrew E.**†

*   *   *

FORD, Agnes Gibbs   1902-

PERSONAL: Born December 27, 1902, in Carthage, Tenn.; daughter of Frederick Calvin (a building contractor) and Lucy (Warren) Gibbs; married Arthur Thomas Ford, October 14, 1938 (deceased). *Education:* George Peabody College for Teachers, B.A., 1955, M.A., 1964. *Politics:* Democrat. *Religion:* Baptist.

CAREER: Baptist Sunday School Board, Nashville, Tenn., advertising copywriter, public relations, and publicity projects, 1928-49, 1950-67. Interim public relations director, Belmont College, beginning 1969. *Member:* Baptist Public Relations Association (charter member), Religious Public Relations Council (charter member; president, Nashville chapter), National League of American Pen Women (former president, Nashville chapter), Women's National Book Association, Middle Tennessee Business Press Club (former president).

WRITINGS: (Compiler) *Prayers for Everyone,* Baker Book, 1967. Author of three religious booklets, published by Augsburg and C. R. Gibson. Contributor to Baptist and secular periodicals.

WORK IN PROGRESS: A children's book, *Pink Music;* a religious book, *The Face in the Pew;* a collection of unusual materials on Christmas.

AVOCATIONAL INTERESTS: Interior decorating.†

*   *   *

FORD, Robert E.   1913-1975

PERSONAL: Born November 9, 1913, in Decatur, Tex. *Education:* Attended Baylor University, Decatur Baptist College; University of Texas, B.A. *Home:* 4236 Greenbrier,

Dallas, Tex. *Agent:* McIntosh & Otis, 475 Fifth Ave., New York, N.Y. 10017.

CAREER: Associated Press, Dallas, Tex., Texas State editor, 1945-75. *Military service:* U.S. Marine Corps; became lieutenant colonel; received Purple Heart. *Member:* Authors Guild.

WRITINGS: Sergeant Sutton, Hawthorn, 1970.

WORK IN PROGRESS: A novel.†

(Died July 1, 1975)

* * *

FOREMAN, Kenneth Joseph 1891-

PERSONAL: Born September 4, 1891, in Fort Edward, N.Y.; son of Charles Waldo (a Presbyterian pastor) and Mary Elisabeth (Benedict) Foreman; married Susan Allison Lewis, December 23, 1920 (died, 1959); children: Kenneth Joseph, Jr. *Education:* Davidson College, B.A., 1911; Union Theological Seminary, Richmond, Va., graduate study, 1918-19; Princeton Theological Seminary, S.T.B., 1921, S.T.M., 1922; Princeton University, M.A., 1922; Yale University, Ph.D., 1935. *Politics:* Independent. *Address:* Box 488, Montreat, N.C. 28757.

CAREER: Clergyman of Presbyterian Church in the United States; Davidson College, Davidson, N.C., associate professor of German, 1922-24, Sprunt Professor of Bible and Philosophy, 1924-47; Louisville Presbyterian Theological Seminary, Louisville, Ky., professor of systematic theology, 1947-62, professor emeritus, 1962—. Visitor in residence, Union Theological Seminary, 1962-64; editor, Board of Christian Education, Presbyterian Church in the United States, 1962-64. *Military service:* U.S. Navy, 1917-18. *Member:* Phi Beta Kappa. *Awards, honors:* D.D., Washington and Lee University, 1933.

WRITINGS: From This Day Forward, Outlook Publishers, 1950; *God's Will and Ours,* Outlook Publishers, 1954; *Candles on the Glacier,* Association Press, 1956; (contributor with others) Balmer H. Kelly, general editor, *Layman's Bible Commentary,* John Knox, Volume I: *Introduction to the Bible,* 1959, Volume XXI: *Romans,* 1961; *Identification: Human and Divine,* John Knox, 1963; *Methuselah,* John Knox, 1968. Weekly columnist for *Presbyterian Outlook* for more than twenty-five years; also writer of "The Bible Speaks," weekly column syndicated to more than five hundred U.S. and Canadian newspapers, for ten years.†

* * *

FOREST, Ilse 1896-

PERSONAL: Born January 4, 1896, in New York, N.Y.; daughter of Hermann and Helene (Greanelle) Bosch; married June 26, 1917 (husband deceased); children: Robert. *Education:* Attended Hunter College (now Hunter College of the City University of New York), 1918-20; Columbia University, B.S., 1922, M.A., 1923, Ph.D. (education), 1927; Yale University, Ph.D. (philosophy), 1939. *Religion:* Roman Catholic.

CAREER: Bryn Mawr College, Bryn Mawr, Pa., associate professor, 1927-42; Brooklyn College (now Brooklyn College of the City University of New York), Brooklyn, N.Y., associate professor, 1946-57; Western Reserve University (now Case Western Reserve University), Cleveland, Ohio, associate professor, 1957-66; St. John College, Cleveland, Ohio, professor of education, beginning 1966. Lecturer at Lake Erie College, 1965-66, in adult education program at

Case Western Reserve University, beginning 1966. Consultant on humanities curriculum, Educational Research Council of Greater Cleveland. *Member:* American Association of University Professors, Kappa Delta Pi.

WRITINGS: Preschool Education, Macmillan, 1927; *Child Life and Religion,* R. R. Smith, 1932; *School for the Child from Two to Eight,* Ginn, 1934; *Early Years At School,* McGraw, 1949; *Child Development,* McGraw, 1954; (with R. Mulhauser and M. Eriksson) *Foreign Languages in the Elementary School,* Prentice-Hall, 1964. Contributor to *Thomist, American Journal of Orthopsychiatry,* and educational journals.

WORK IN PROGRESS: New Insights in Early Education and a book on adult learning.

* * *

FORMAN, Jonathan 1887-1974

PERSONAL: Born September 30, 1887, in Austinburg, Ohio; son of Cassius Clay (a farmer) and Alice Florence (Coup) Forman; married Doris Marie Andrews, November 1, 1923; children: Alice, Cynthia, Jonathan II. *Education:* Ohio State University, A.B., 1910; Starling-Ohio Medical College, M.D., 1913; Harvard University, graduate study, summers, 1912-16. *Politics:* Republican. *Home:* 4425 Olentangy Blvd., Columbus, Ohio 43214.

CAREER: Ohio State University, College of Medicine, Columbus, assistant in pathology, 1913-14, instructor, 1914-16, assistant professor, 1916-19; Harvard University, Cambridge, Mass., Austin teaching fellow, 1919-20; in private practice of medicine, Columbus, Ohio, beginning 1920; Ohio State University, special lecturer in allergy, 1933-34, lecturer in medicine, 1933-45, professor of history of medicine, 1945-57, professor emeritus, 1957-74. Diplomate, American Board of Internal Medicine; former pathologist and gastroenterologist for hospitals and clinics. Trustee, Louis Bromfield Malabar Farm; chairman, Friends of the Land, 1952-60. *Military service:* U.S. Navy, 1917-19; became lieutenant.

MEMBER: American Medical Association (fellow), American College of Allergists (fellow; president, 1949-50), American Academy of Allergy, International College of Applied Nutrition (founding member), International Correspondence Society of Allergists (director-general), Society of Comprehensive Medicine, American Gerontology Society, American Geriatric Society, Argentine Society for Study of Allergy (honorary member), Alpha Omega Alpha, Delta Sigma Chi, Phi Rho Sigma, Sigma Tau Delta. *Awards, honors:* Louis Bromfield Gold Medal for contributions to soil conservation, 1961; Clemens von Pirquet Gold Medal, 1964; Ainsley Griffin Gold Medal of Phi Rho Sigma.

WRITINGS: (With J. W. Mercer) *Surgical Pathology,* 2nd edition (Forman was not associated with earlier edition), Stoneman Press, 1914; *History of the University of Michigan School of Medicine,* Phi Rho Sigma Fraternity, 1931; *History of the Ohio State University College of Medicine,* Ohio State University, 1934; (editor with O. E. Fink) *Soil, Food, and Health,* Friends of the Land, 1948; (editor with Fink) *Water and Man: A Study in Ecology,* Friends of the Land, 1950. Also editor of *Directory of Physicians Interested in Clinical Allergy,* 1948. Contributor to medical journals. Editor, *Ohio State Medical Journal,* 1935-57; editor-in-chief, *Clinical Physiology,* 1959-65; editor, *Archives of Clinical Ecology.*†

(Died, 1974)

FOSKETT, Reginald   1909-1973

PERSONAL: Born March 30, 1909, in Derby, England; son of Albert Ernest (a civil engineer) and Ellen Elizabeth (Dicken) Foskett; married Daphne Kirk, 1937; children: Patricia Ann (Mrs. Michael Middleton), Helen Margaret (Mrs. Neil Godfrey). *Education:* Oxford University, B.A. (second class honors), 1931, M.A., 1935; University of Nottingham, Ph.D., 1957. *Home and office:* Field Broughton Place, Field Broughton, Grange-over-Sands, Lancashire, England.

CAREER: Ordained deacon, Church of England, 1932, and priest, 1933; curate, 1932-37; curate in charge, Rainworth Conventional District, 1937-43; rector of Ordsall, Nottinghamshire, 1943-47, surrogate, 1943-47, 1948-57; vicar of Ilkeston, Derbyshire, 1948-57, and rural dean, 1950-57; canon of Derby Cathedral, 1954-57; provost of St. Mary's Cathedral, Edinburgh, Scotland, 1957-67; Bishop Suffragan of Penrith, England, 1967-70; assistant bishop of Carlisle, beginning 1971. Examining chaplain to bishop of Derby, 1952-57, bishop of Edinburgh, 1959-67. Divinity lecturer at Nottinghamshire County Training College for Teachers, 1946-50.

WRITINGS: Some Scottish Links with the American Episcopal Church, 1685-1785, J. A. Birkbeck, 1962; (editor) *The Zambesi Doctors,* Edinburgh University Press, 1964; (editor) *The Zambesi Journal and Letters of Dr. John Kirk,* two volumes, Oliver & Boyd, 1965. Contributor to religion and history journals.

WORK IN PROGRESS: A Reforming Bishop: A Study of the Episcopate of John Kaye of Bristol and Lincoln, 1820-1853; Kirk of Zanzibar, the biography of Sir John Kirk.

SIDELIGHTS: Foskett told *CA,* "My interest in East Africa stems from the fact that my wife's grandfather was a pioneer in East Africa and a companion of David Livingston."†

(Died November, 1973)

* * *

FOSTER, Marguerite H.   1909-

PERSONAL: Born January 2, 1909, in Engle, Tex.; daughter of Frank (a rancher) and Valasta (Gallia) Herzik; divorced; children: Karen, Allen, William. *Education:* Rice University, B.A., 1930; University of California, Berkeley, M.A., 1934, Ph.D., 1941. *Home:* 634 Wildwood lane, Palo Alto, Calif. 94303. *Office:* Department of Philosophy, DeAnza College, 21250 Stevens Creek Blvd., Cupertino, Calif. 95014.

CAREER: University of California, Berkeley, lecturer in speech, 1946-49, lecturer in philosophy, 1951-53; San Jose State College (now University), San Jose, Calif., visiting assistant professor of philosophy, 1953-54; Mills College, Oakland, Calif., visiting assistant professor of humanities, 1954-55; Lawrence Radiation Laboratory, Berkeley, Calif., technical editor, 1955-60; University of Colorado, Boulder, visiting assistant professor of philosophy, 1960-63; Moorhead State College, Moorhead, Minn., associate professor of philosophy, 1964-65; Chico State College (now University), Chico, Calif., assistant professor of philosophy, 1965-66; Metropolitan State College, Denver, Colo., associate professor of philosophy, 1966-67; DeAnza College, Cupertino, Calif., head of philosophy department, beginning 1967. *Member:* American Philosophical Association, Minnesota Academy of Sciences, Phi Beta Kappa.

WRITINGS: (Editor with Michael Martin) *Probability*

Confirmation, and Simplicity, Odyssey, 1966. Contributor to *Journal of Philosophy* and *Convivo.*

WORK IN PROGRESS: Newton, Darwin and Freud: Scientific Methodology; Aging in the United States.

* * *

FOWLER, Mary Elizabeth   1911-

PERSONAL: Born December 16, 1911, in Lewiston, Idaho; daughter of Herbert Eugene (a professor) and Mary Josephine (Keatinge) Fowler. *Education:* Attended Western Washington College of Education (now Western Washington State College), 1928-30; University of Washington, Seattle, B.A., 1933, M.A., 1939; New York University, Ph.D., 1954. *Home:* 46 Selden Hill Dr., West Hartford, Conn. 06107.

CAREER: Teacher and dean of girls at a Connecticut high school, 1940-43; high school teacher in Massachusetts, 1943-44; Central Connecticut State College, New Britain, assistant professor, 1946-54, associate professor, 1954-60, professor of English, 1960-73. *Member:* National Council of Teachers of English, Conference on College Composition and Communication, Conference on English Education, New England Association of Teachers of English (president, 1960-62), Connecticut Council of Teachers of English.

WRITINGS: Teaching Language, Composition, and Literature, McGraw, 1965. Contributor to education journals.

WORK IN PROGRESS: A textbook on literature for young adults; writing on the reading interests of young adults and on teaching composition at the secondary level.†

* * *

FOX, Samuel   1905-

PERSONAL: Born March 18, 1905, in Chicago, Ill.; son of M. Bert (an insurance executive) and Sara (Nestor) Fox; married Genevieve Kubreener (an attorney), January 29, 1928; children: Stanley K., Lawrence Nestor, Stephen Richard. *Education:* Medill Junior College, A.A., 1922; University of Chicago, Ph.B., 1924, M.B.A., 1947; Loyola University, Chicago, Ill., J.D., 1927, LL.M., 1928; University of Notre Dame, Ph.D., 1950; registered Certified Public Accountant, 1962. *Home:* Suite 7311, John Hancock Center, Chicago, Ill. 60611. *Office:* Roosevelt University, 430 South Michigan, Chicago, Ill. 60605.

CAREER: Member of Illinois Bar. Luster & Luster, Chicago, Ill., attorney, 1928-31; Fox & Fox, Attorneys, Chicago, partner, 1931-40; U.S. Rubber Co., Mishawaka, Ind., budget accountant, 1940-41; Bell & Thorn, Inc., Chicago, controller, 1941-42; Bendix Aviation Corp., South Bend, Ind., inventory control, 1942; U.S. Office of Price Administration, Chicago, regional enforcement attorney, 1943-46; University of Illinois at Chicago Circle, professor of accountancy, 1946-73; Roosevelt University, Chicago, professor of accountancy, beginning 1973. Loyola University, Chicago, lecturer in law, 1928-31; Illinois Institute of Technology, lecturer in accounting control, 1949-53; North Park College, lecturer in labor management, 1953-58; American University of Beirut, visiting professorial lecturer, 1963; Al-Hikma University, Baghdad, Fulbright lecturer, 1966; Peruvian University of Science and Technology, lecturer, 1967; Agency for International Development, Lima, Peru, cost accounting specialist, 1967.

MEMBER: American Taxation Association, Academy of International Business, American Accounting Association American Association for the Advancement of Science, In ternational Academy of Law and Science (fellow), Academy of Management, American Economic Association, National Association of Accountants, American Institute of Certified Public Accountants, American Association of Attorney-Certified Public Accountants, American Society for Engineering Education, American Business Law Association (executive vice-president, 1963-64), American Judicature Society, Illinois State Bar Association, Illinois Society of Certified Public Accountants, Wisconsin Institute of Certified Public Accountants, Chicago Regional Business Law Association (founder and first president).

WRITINGS: Law of Decedents Estates, Loyola Press, 1928; *Fundamental Cost Accounting*, Stipes, 1958; *Management and the Law*, Appleton, 1966. Also author of *Managerial Law Workbook*. Contributor to business and law journals; contributor of reviews to *Choice*. Sports columnist, *Park Ridge Herald*, and drama critic, *Des Plaines Suburban Times*, 1946-66.

WORK IN PROGRESS: Business Law; Introduction to Business; International Accounting.

SIDELIGHTS: Samuel Fox told *CA* that he speaks German, Arabic, and Spanish "meagerly."

* * *

FRAENKEL, Osmond K. 1888-

PERSONAL: Born October 17, 1888, in New York, N.Y.; son of Joseph E. (a mining engineer) and Emily (Kessler) Fraenkel; married Helene Esberg, December 11, 1913; children: Carol (Mrs. Mack Lipkin), Nancy (Mrs. James A. Wechsler), George. *Education:* Harvard University, A.B., 1907 (as of class of '08), A.M., 1908; Columbia University, LL.B., 1911. *Politics:* Independent. *Religion:* "None." *Home:* 25 West 11th St., New York, N.Y. 10011. *Office:* 120 Broadway, New York, N.Y. 10005.

CAREER: Lawyer, practicing in New York, N.Y., beginning 1911. Yale University, New Haven, Conn., instructor in labor law in mid-1940's. New York (N.Y.) Department of Welfare, chairman of review board, 1935-51; War Labor Board, member of panel of arbitrators, 1943-45; American Civil Liberties Union, general counsel, beginning 1955. *Member:* National Lawyers Guild (past vice-president and board member), New York County Lawyers Association, Association of the Bar of the City of New York.

WRITINGS: The Sacco-Vanzetti Case, Knopf, 1931; (editor) *The Curse of Bigness*, Viking, 1935; *Our Civil Liberties*, Viking, 1943; *The Supreme Court and Civil Liberties*, Oceana, 1960, revised edition, 1963; *The Rights We Have*, Crowell, 1971. Contributor to legal journals.

SIDELIGHTS: Fraenkel speaks and reads French and German. *Avocational interests:* Collecting first editions of modern English and American writers, and reading them; hiking, playing bridge, music (has large collection of records).

* * *

FRAMPTON, Merle E(lbert) 1903-

PERSONAL: Born September 15, 1903, in Smithfield, W.Va.; son of Clark Sylvester (an engineer) and Ethel Pearl (von Betzer) Frampton; married Iris C. Coldwell, December 30, 1923; children: Scott Athearn, Iris Merle, Diane Joyce. *Education:* Boston University, B.R.E., 1925, A.M., 1926, M.Sc., 1927; Harvard University, A.M., 1930, Ph.D., 1934. *Politics:* Republican. *Religion:* Presbyterian. *Home:* 14000 North Como Dr., Route 1, Box 627R, Tucson, Ariz. 85704.

CAREER: Chicago Commons Settlement House, Chicago, Ill., boys' worker, 1921-23; College of the Ozarks, Clarksville, Ark., professor of economics and vice-president, 1930-33; Westminster Foundation, Boston, Mass., director, 1933-35; Columbia University, Teachers College, New York City, professor of education and founder and head of department of the handicapped, 1935-44; New York Institute for the Education of the Blind, New York City, principal, beginning 1935; Hunter College of the City University of New York, New York City, professor of education, beginning 1952. Director of study on special education and rehabilitation, U.S. House of Representatives Committee on Education and Labor; first vice-chairman, President's Committee on Employment of the Handicapped, 1947; president, Eyes Right Foundation for Handicapped Children; aided with programs for the physically handicapped and the exceptional in Argentina, Mexico, Cuba, Costa Rica, Chile, Italy, Uruguay, and Paraguay. Member of board of directors, American Printing House for the Blind and Society for the Prevention of Cruelty to Children; member of executive committee, Bronx Council of Social Agencies. *Military service:* U.S. Naval Reserve, active duty, World War II; became commander.

MEMBER: American Sociological Association, National Education Association, American Association of Instructors and Workers for the Blind, American Federation of Physically Handicapped (chairman of Conference on the Severely Disabled), National Conference of Christians and Jews, John Milton Society, Bronx Rotary Club (president, 1951-52), National Republican Club, University Club of New York, National Arts Club (Harvard), New York Athletic Club. *Awards, honors:* LL.D., College of the Ozarks, 1932; Litt.D., Missouri Valley College, 1940; Order of Merit awarded by President of Paraguay, 1963.

WRITINGS: Family and Society, Van Nostrand, 1935; (editor with Hugh Grant Rowell) *Education of the Handicapped,* World Book Co., Volume I, 1938, Volume II, 1940; (editor) *Education of the Blind,* World Book Co., 1940; *Our Present Revolution,* Edwin Gould Printery, 1943; (editor with Clarence R. Athearn) *The School Assembly as an Educational Force,* New York Institute for the Education of the Blind, 1941; *Rehabilitation in Theory and Practice,* New York Institute for the Education of the Blind, 1947; (with Paul C. Mitchell) *Camping for Blind Youth,* New York Institute for the Education of the Blind, 1949; (with Ellen Kerney) *The Residential School for the Blind,* Edwin Gould Printery, 1952; (editor with Elena D. Gall) *Special Education for the Exceptional,* three volumes, Sargent, 1955-56, an adaptation published as *Resources for Special Education,* Sargent, 1956, and an excerpt as *The Intellectually Gifted,* Sargent, 1956; *Tragedy,* New York Institute for the Education of the Blind, 1965; (with others) *Forgotten Children: A Program for the Multihandicapped,* Sargent, 1969. Also author of survey reports on the physically handicapped for schools, agencies, and industry; contributor of articles on special education in the twentieth century to journals.

* * *

FRANCIS, R. Mabel 1880-19(?)

PERSONAL: Born July 26, 1880, in Cornish, N.H.; daughter of Edward and Martha (Williams) Francis. *Education:* Attended Gordon College, Nyack Missionary College (now Nyack College), and Defiance College.

CAREER: Evangelist, and Christian and Missionary Alliance missionary in Japan, 1909-1965. *Awards, honors:* Made honorary citizen of Matsuyama City; received Fifth Order of the Sacred Treasure from Emperor of Japan.

WRITINGS: (With G. Smith) *One Shall Chase a Thousand* (autobiography), Christian Publications, 1968.†

(Deceased)

* * *

FRANCO, Jean 1914-1971

PERSONAL: Born July 17, 1914, in Nice, France; son of Jean and Anne (Garro) Franco; married Jeanne Gaudo, 1941; children: Simone Franco Joubert, Michel. *Education:* Ecole Normale, Nice, Diplome, Brevet Superieur, 1933. *Home:* Chalet le Lyrure, 74400 Les Praz, Chamonix, France.

CAREER: Nice, France, schoolmaster, 1934-41, school inspector, 1941-45; College National des Praz de Chamonix, Chamonix, France, director, 1946-50; U.N.C.M., secretary general, 1950-57; Ecole Nationale de Ski et d'Alpinisme, Chamonix, director, 1957-71, inspector general, 1971. Federation Francais de la Montagne, secretary general, 1952-58. Head of three French expeditions to the Himalayas, Makalu, 1954-55, and Jannu, 1959. Honorary professor at the mountain school of Spain. *Military service:* French Army, artillery officer. *Member:* Groupe de Haut Montagne (president, 1956-61), Comite de l'Himalaya, Haut Comite des Sports, Association Internationale pour l'Enseignement du Ski (president, beginning 1968). *Awards, honors:* Chevalier de la Legion d'Honneur; Commandeur du merite sportif; gold medal of the Academie des Sports.

WRITINGS: Makalu, Arthaud, 1955; (with M. Mora) *Ski de France,* Arthaud, 1961; (with L. Terray) *Bataille pour Jannu,* Gallimard, 1964; *Le Ski,* Presses Universitaires de France, 1966.

WORK IN PROGRESS: A book on the "Technique of Alpinism."†

(Died December 2, 1971)

* * *

FRANK, Irving 1910-

PERSONAL: Born June 5, 1910, in New York, N.Y.; son of David and Yetta (Green) Frank; married Rosanne Krcek (an instructor at Northern Illinois University), 1939; children: Marilyn L. (Mrs. Paul Stromborg), Rebecca J. (Mrs. Sanford Cohen). *Education:* New York University, B.S., 1933; Chicago Medical School, M.D., 1938; Northern Illinois University, M.S.Ed., 1962, Ed.D., 1966. *Religion:* Jewish. *Home and office:* 135 South Sacramento, Sycamore, Ill. 60178.

CAREER: St. Joseph's Hospital, Bellingham, Wash., intern, 1938-39; Civilian Conservation Corps, physician, 1939-40; in private practice, Chicago, Ill., 1940-42; U.S. Office of Indian Affairs, physician at Kiowa, Navajo, and Washington Reservations, 1946-49; in private practice as both general family physician and psychiatrist, beginning 1949. Sycamore Municipal Hospital, Sycamore, Ill., chief of staff, 1959-60, chief of medical psychology department, beginning 1964; Chicago Medical School, Chicago, Ill., clinical associate, department of psychiatry, beginning 1966. DeKalb County Courts, alienist, beginning 1955. Registered psychologist, State of Illinois. *Military service:* U.S. Army, Medical Corps, 1942-46; became captain.

MEMBER: American Medical Association, American Psychiatric Association, American Psychological Association, American Academy of Psychotherapists, Society for Research in Child Development, American Academy of Psychosomatic Medicine, Royal Society of Health, Illinois Medical Society (member of mental health committee), DeKalb Medical Society (past president), Phi Delta Kappa.

WRITINGS: (With Marvin Powell) *Psychosomatic Ailments in Childhood and Adolescents,* C. C Thomas, 1967. Contributor to medical journals.

WORK IN PROGRESS: The Art of Guidance and Counseling for the General Practitioner, in collaboration with wife, Rosanne Krcek Frank, for C. C Thomas.†

* * *

FRASER, Blair 1909-1968

PERSONAL: Born April 17, 1909, in Sydney, Nova Scotia, Canada; son of John Hugh and Margaret (Blair) Fraser; married Jean MacLeod, September 28, 1931; children: John, Graham. *Education:* Acadia University, B.A., 1928. *Home:* 150 Acacia Ave., Ottawa, Ontario, Canada. *Office:* Press Gallery, House of Commons, Ottawa, Ontario, Canada.

CAREER: Newspaperman in Montreal, Quebec, 1929-43, working on the three English dailies, with last post as associate editor and book review editor of *Montreal Gazette,* 1940-43; *Maclean's Magazine,* Toronto, Ontario, Ottawa editor, 1944-60, 1962-68, editor-in-chief, Toronto, 1960-62, overseas editor, London, 1962. Canadian Broadcasting Corp., radio commentator, beginning 1944, television commentator, beginning 1953. *Member:* Canadian Institute of International Affairs, Rideau Club (Ottawa), University Club (Montreal), Royal Canadian Yacht Club (Toronto). *Awards, honors:* President's Medal, Governor-General's award board, for best articles written by a Canadian, 1951, and 1961; D.C.L., Acadia University, 1953.

WRITINGS: The Search for Identity: Canada, 1945-67, Doubleday, 1967; *Blair Fraser Reports: Selection, 1944-1968* (collection of articles and columns written for *Maclean's Magazine*), edited by sons, John Fraser and Graham Fraser, Macmillan, 1969. Contributor of essays to various collections.

WORK IN PROGRESS: Two books on aspects of Canadian politics, with special reference to separatist movements in Quebec.

SIDELIGHTS: The final volume in Doubleday's Canadian history series was aptly titled *The Search for Identity,* according to Walter O'Hearn, because this identity crisis "ceased to be the Canadian parlor game and [became] the Canadian preoccupation." O'Hearn approved Fraser's qualifications for writing the history because he was "a member of Ottawa's 'in group'" and he wrote "with firm authority about incidents where he was so close an onlooker as to be almost a participant." O'Hearn recommended that "the reader who honestly wants to know something about Canada could not do better than read this frankly journalistic account. It is never dull."

On assignments for *Maclean's Magazine,* Fraser made two visits to mainland China, three to Taiwan, five to India, and several to the Middle East.

BIOGRAPHICAL/CRITICAL SOURCES: New York Times Book Review, February 4, 1968; *New York Times,* May 14, 1968.†

(Died May 12, 1968)

FRASER, W(aller) B(rown) 1905-
(Brown Waller)

PERSONAL: Born April 29, 1905; son of William Caswell and Molly (Keller) Fraser. *Education:* University of Tennessee, A.B., 1929, A.M., 1930; University of Michigan, graduate study, 1936-37. *Politics:* Independent. *Religion:* Baptist.

CAREER: High school teacher of history and English in Maynardville, Tenn., 1931; Missionary Baptist College, Sheridan, Ark., teacher of history and English, 1932-33; Plymouth Motor Co., Detroit, Mich., employed in shipping and receiving departments, 1937-59.

WRITINGS—Under name Brown Waller: *Last of the Great Western Train Robbers,* A. S. Barnes, 1968.

AVOCATIONAL INTERESTS: Study of politics and economics.††

* * *

FRAZIER, George 1911-1974

PERSONAL: Born June 10, 1911, in Boston, Mass.; son of George II and Catherine (Minihan) Frazier; married Mimsi Madden, 1941 (divorced); children: George IV, J. Pepper. *Education:* Harvard University, A.B., 1933. *Politics:* Democrat. *Religion:* Roman Catholic. *Home:* 52 East 81st St., New York, N.Y. 10028.

CAREER: Free-lance writer. *Life,* New York, N.Y., entertainment editor, 1941-46; *Boston Herald,* Boston, Mass., daily columnist, 1961-65; columnist for *Esquire,* 1967-74, and *Boston Globe,* 1970-74. Media critic for "CBS Morning News"; commentator for WNAC-TV in Boston. *Awards, honors: Down Beat* Silver Medal for contributions to the growth of jazz.

WRITINGS: The One with the Mustache Is Costello, Random House, 1947. Also author of other books on movies and men's fashions. Contributor of articles on jazz, literature, sports, stage, and cinema to magazines.†

(Died June 13, 1974)

* * *

FREDGE, Frederique 1906-

PERSONAL: Born January 9, 1906, in Bale, Switzerland; daughter of Jacques-Joseph and Anne (Le Blanc) Glass; married Paul Leon Fredge, October 19, 1930 (divorced); children: Gladys-Ruth (Mrs. James Bruce Harvey), Lionel-Ralph. *Education:* Studied at Ecole des Arts et Metiers, Geneva, 1921-25, and University of Geneva, 1927-29; took journalism courses at University of Wisconsin Extension, Milwaukee, and University of Nevada. *Politics:* Non-partisan. *Religion:* Protestant. *Agent:* Larry Sternig, 742 Robertson St., Milwaukee, Wis. 53213.

CAREER: Tour director for study seminars in Europe for ten years; instructor in French and creative writing in continuing education classes at Marquette University, Milwaukee, Wis., beginning 1957. Lecturer on Americana at service and women's clubs across the country.

WRITINGS: Chattemite (novel), Editions Atar (Geneva), 1927; *Cooking 'Round the World with a Wooden Spoon,* Doubleday, 1965; *There We Were Again* (autobiographical novel), Norton, 1966. Contributor of short stories and feature articles to magazines and newspapers, including *Mademoiselle, Esquire, Daily Express* (London), *Toronto Star Weekly, New Yorker, Milwaukee Journal* and *Everywoman.*

WORK IN PROGRESS: Reminiscences as a tour director in Europe; studying the story of Saint Sarah.

SIDELIGHTS: Mrs. Fredge told *CA:* "I have eaten chicken a la king twice a day, three weeks in a row, lecturing to women's clubs, half-cooked hamburgers and lima beans in Rotary, Kiwanis, and Lions clubs twice a day, three weeks in a row, and I can't look them in the face. That is why I wrote a cookbook." That book, *Cooking 'Round the World with a Wooden Spoon,* was run serially in the *Philadelphia Inquirer,* 1966, and is used as a text by the author in the gourmet courses she occasionally gives.††

* * *

FREEDMAN, Maurice 1920-1975

PERSONAL: Born December 11, 1920, in London, England; son of Harry (a tailor) and Minnie (Glazer) Freedman; married Judith Djamour (an editor), August 15, 1946. *Education:* King's College, London, B.A. (honors), 1941; London School of Economics and Political Science, M.A., 1948, Ph.D., 1956. *Religion:* Jewish. *Home:* 187 Gloucester Pl., London NW1 6BU, England. *Office:* Institute of Social Anthropology, 51 Banbury Rd., Oxford OX2 6PF, England.

CAREER: University of London, London School of Economics and Political Science, London, England, lecturer, 1951-57, reader, 1957-65, professor of anthropology, 1965-70; Oxford University, Institute of Social Anthropology, Oxford, England, professor of social anthropology, 1970-75. Visiting professor at Yale University, 1960-61, University of Malaysia, 1962, and Cornell University, 1965. Malinowski Memorial Lecturer, 1962. Has done field research in Singapore, Indonesia, and Hong Kong. *Military service:* British Army, Royal Artillery, 1941-45; became captain. *Member:* Royal Anthropological Institute (president, 1967-69), Association of Social Anthropologists, Institute of Race Relations, Association for Asian Studies, Association of British Orientalists. *Awards, honors:* Colonial Social Science Research Council research fellow in Singapore, 1949-50.

WRITINGS: (Editor) *A Minority in Britain,* Vallentine, Mitchell, 1955; *Chinese Family and Marriage in Singapore,* H.M.S.O., 1957; *Lineage Organization in Southeastern China,* Athlone Press, 1958; *Chinese Lineage and Society: Fukien and Kwangtung,* Athlone Press, 1966, Humanities, 1971; *Rights and Duties, or Chinese Marriage,* London School of Economics and Political Science, 1967; (editor) *Social Organization: Essays presented to Raymond Firth,* Cass, 1967; (editor) *Family and Kinship in Chinese Society,* Stanford University Press, 1970. Contributor to anthropology journals. *Jewish Journal of Sociology,* managing editor, 1959-71, editor, 1971-75.

WORK IN PROGRESS: Research on Chinese religion.

BIOGRAPHICAL/CRITICAL SOURCES: Listener, December 28, 1967.†

(Died July 14, 1975)

* * *

FREER, Harold Wiley 1906-

PERSONAL: Born November 15, 1906, in Cleveland, Ohio; son of Willis Miles and Addie (Barnhill) Freer; married Dorothy Clark, August 15, 1932; children: Arthur Douglas, Deirdre Mae. *Education:* University of Southern California, B.A., 1931; Union Theological Seminary, New York, N.Y., B.D., 1934. *Home:* 2430 East Elm St., Phoenix, Ariz. 85016.

CAREER: Ordained minister of United Church of Christ, 1934; Spiritual Life Clinic, director in Westlake, Ohio, and Phoenix, Ariz., beginning 1955.

WRITINGS: (With F. B. Hall) *Two or Three Together,* Harper, 1954; *Christian Disciplines,* Pageant, 1960; *Growing in the Life of Prayer,* Abingdon, 1962; *God Meets Us Where We Are,* Abingdon, 1967.

* * *

FRENCH, Edward L(ivingstone) 1916-1969

PERSONAL: Born December 15, 1916, in Scunthorpe, England; naturalized U.S. citizen; son of William M. and Elizabeth (Picken) French; married Jean Parker Wingate, June 27, 1942; children: Elizabeth Jean, Jean, Edward L., Jr. *Education:* Ursinus College, A.B., 1938; University of Pennsylvania, M.A., 1947, Ph.D., 1950. *Home:* 267 Walker Rd., Wayne, Pa. 19087. *Office:* Devereux Foundation, 19 South Waterloo Rd., Devon, Pa. 19333.

CAREER: Chestnut Hill Academy, Chestnut Hill, Pa., teacher, 1938-43; Vineland Training School, Vineland, N.J., chief psychologist, 1949-50; Devereux Schools (nonprofit residential treatment center for retarded and emotionally disturbed children and adolescents), Devon, Pa., director of psychology and education, 1950-57; Devereux Foundation, Devon, Pa., director, 1957-69, president, 1960-69. President of Clinical Biochemistry and Behavioral Research Institute, 1964-69; trustee of National Association of Private Psychiatric Hospitals. *Military service:* U.S. Army, 1943-46; became sergeant; received Bronze Star Medal.

MEMBER: American Psychological Association (fellow; president, 1967-68), American Association on Mental Deficiency (fellow), Society for Research in Child Development (fellow), American Academy on Mental Retardation, American Association for the Advancement of Science (fellow), American Management Association, Pennsylvania Psychological Association (fellow), New York Academy of Sciences.

WRITINGS: (With J. Clifford Scott) *Child in the Shadows,* Lippincott, 1960, revised edition published as *How to Help Your Retarded Child,* 1967; (contributor) *Therapeutic Education,* Special Child, 1966; (contributor) *The Exceptional Child,* Holt, 1967. Author of six booklets dealing with mental deficiency and retardation. Contributor to professional journals.

WORK IN PROGRESS: "Residential Therapy," a chapter for *Special Education Programs Throughout the United States,* for C.C Thomas; editing a book of readings, *Impeded Children,* for Harper.†

(Died November 23, 1969)

* * *

FRENCH, R(obert) B(utler) D(igby) 1904-

PERSONAL: Born May 26, 1904, in Londonderry, Ireland; son of Arthur Cowan Digby (a clergyman) and Synolda (Butler) French. *Education:* Trinity College, Dublin, B.A. (first class honors), 1928, M.A., 1931. *Religion:* Anglican. *Home:* Newtown Verney, Kilternan, County Dublin, Ireland.

CAREER: Leader-writer for *Irish Times* before World War II; British Broadcasting Corp., member of Overseas Division, 1942-45; University of Dublin, Trinity College, Dublin, Ireland, lecturer in English literature, 1937, editor of *Trinity,* 1949-68, in charge of college relations with the press,

1957-61, college tutor, 1962, and senior lecturer in English literature, 1968-74, former secretary of university council. *Awards, honors:* Page scholar of English-Speaking Union in United States, 1940.

WRITINGS: P. G. Wodehouse, Oliver & Boyd, 1966, Barnes & Noble, 1967. Writer of commentary for films, "Building for Books" (documentary) and "Ireland," and revue sketches, songs, and lyrics, mainly for amateur production. Correspondent for *Times* (London); contributor to a number of other newspapers. Contributor to *Hermathena.*

* * *

FRERICHS, A(lbert) C(hristian) 1910-

PERSONAL: Born June 8, 1910, in Talmage, Neb.; son of Fred (a farmer) and Anna (Fahrenholz) Frerichs; married Sylvia Regine Fritz, June 16, 1943; children: David Michael (deceased), Catherine Elizabeth, Angela Margaret, Jonathan Charles, Paul Albert, Peter George, Ruth, Sylvia Ann. *Education:* Wartburg Seminary, graduate, 1934; St. Olaf College, B.A., 1935; University of Nebraska, graduate study, one year. *Politics:* Republican. *Religion:* Lutheran.

CAREER: Clergyman; missionary in New Guinea, 1937-75; currently pastor in Fargo, N.D. Founder of the first teacher's college in the highlands of New Guinea. *Awards, honors:* D.D., Wartburg Theological Seminary.

WRITINGS: Anutu Conquers in New Guinea, Wartburg Press, 1957, revised edition, Augsburg, 1969. Contributor to religious journals and newspapers.

SIDELIGHTS: A. C. Frerichs is fluent in Kote and can speak two other New Guinea languages, Graged and Komano. He is also fluent in German.

* * *

FREUDENHEIM, Yehoshua (Oskar) 1894-1975

PERSONAL: Born March 11, 1894, in Przemysl, Poland; son of Kalman (an industrialist) and Paula (Hermelin) Freudenheim; married Isabella Herzenstein, December 22, 1918; married second wife, Hermina Langer, November 27, 1930; children: (first marriage) Uriel. *Education:* University of Vienna, Doctor of Law, 1919. *Religion:* Jewish. *Home:* R'chov Harav, Chaim Berlin 30, Bert Karrmah, Jerusalem, Israel.

CAREER: During his earlier career was an advocate in Vienna, Austria; lawyer in Jerusalem, Israel, and legal adviser to Jewish Agency on Pensions for Israel, 1946-65. *Military service:* Austro-Hungarian Army. *Member:* Chamber of Advocates (Jerusalem). *Awards, honors:* Ruppin Prize of City of Haifa for *Hashilton bi-Medinat Jisrael,* 1953.

WRITINGS: Hashilton bi-Medinat Jisrael, Reuwen Mass (Jerusalem), 1953, 3rd edition, 1959, English translation by Meir Silverstone and Chaim Ivor Goldsmith published as *Government in Israel,* Oceana, 1967. Contributor to Israeli newspapers.

SIDELIGHTS: Freudenheim spoke German, English, French.†

(Died February 14, 1975)

* * *

FRIEDER, Emma 1891-

PERSONAL: Born January 1, 1891, in Debrecen, Hungary; daughter of Marcus (a silk manufacturer) and Bertha (Kertes) Frieder. *Education:* Barnard College, A.B., 1913; Columbia University, M.A., 1918. *Religion:* "Ethical culture." *Home:* 317 West 89th St., New York, N.Y. 10024.

WRITINGS: Altar Fires: Essays in Sacred Literature, Hurst Publishing, 1957, 3rd edition, 1971; *Essays in Religion,* Exposition Press, 1968, 2nd edition, Hurst Publishing, 1971.†

*   *   *

FRIEDLAND, Ronald Lloyd   1937-1975
  (Ronald Lloyd)

PERSONAL: Born July 6, 1937, in East Orange, N.J.; son of Walter Albert (a painter and sculptor) and Anne (Sherman) Friedland; married Patricia Ann Burnham, July 14, 1962. *Education:* Middlebury College, B.A., 1959; Columbia University, M.A., 1960, Ph.D., 1967. *Politics:* "Socialist by way of Edmund Burke." *Religion:* Skeptic. *Home:* 46 West 65th St., New York, N.Y. 10023.

CAREER: Columbia University, New York, N.Y., member of English faculty, 1962; University of Hawaii, Honolulu, member of English faculty, 1962-65; Hampton Institute, Hampton, Va., member of English faculty, 1965-66; Borough of Manhattan Community College, New York, N.Y., member of English faculty, 1966-67; Fordham University, Bronx, N.Y., professor of English, 1967-71.

WRITINGS: (Editor and author of introduction) D. H. Lawrence, *Lady Chatterly's Lover,* Bantam, 1970; *Bringing It All Back Home* (novel), Lippincott, 1971; (under pseudonym Ronald Lloyd) *France* (juvenile), F. Watts, 1975; *American Film Directors: The World as They See It* (juvenile), F. Watts, 1976. Contributor of articles and stories to *Dissent, New York Times,* and other periodicals and newspapers.

WORK IN PROGRESS: A novel.

SIDELIGHTS: Ronald Lloyd Friedland lived in Paris for several years, spent considerable time in Asia, visited Europe frequently, and in his younger days did construction work in Sondrestrom, Greenland.†

(Died July 27, 1975)

*   *   *

FRIEND, Joseph H(arold)   1909-1972

PERSONAL: Born April 14, 1909, in Toledo, Ohio; son of Louis (a tailor) and Rose (Gould) Friend; married Vita Lauter, 1932; married second wife, Irja G. Koski, 1939; married third wife, Jewell Anne Ryan (dean of College of Liberal Arts at Southern Illinois University, Carbondale), August 16, 1967; children: (second marriage) George M., Daniel K. *Education:* University of Wisconsin, B.A., 1932; Columbia University, M.A., 1941; Indiana University, Ph.D., 1962. *Politics:* Independent. *Religion:* No affiliation. *Home address:* R.F.D. 1, Makanda, Ill. 62958. *Office:* Center for English as a Second Language, Southern Illinois University, Carbondale, Ill. 62901.

CAREER: Indiana University, instructor in English at Bloomington and Indianapolis campuses, 1933-43; World Publishing Co., Cleveland, Ohio, editor in charge of lexicography, 1944-48; Western Reserve University (now Case Western Reserve University), Cleveland, lecturer, 1946-47, assistant professor, 1948-62, associate professor, 1962-65, professor of English, 1965-66; Southern Illinois University, Carbondale, professor of English and director of Center for English as a Second Language, beginning 1966. Consultant in linguistics, Project English Demonstration Center, Cleveland, 1963-64.

MEMBER: Linguistic Society of America, National

Council of Teachers of English, Conference on College Composition and Communication (member of executive committee, 1966-68), Teachers of English to Speakers of Other Languages. *Awards, honors:* Martha Kinney Cooper Ohioana Library Association Award for lexicographical work, given for general editorship of *Webster's New World Dictionary of the American Language.*

WRITINGS: (General editor) *Webster's New World Dictionary of the American Language,* World Publishing, 1951, college edition, 1953; *The Development of American Lexicography 1798-1864,* Mouton & Co., 1967; *An Introduction to English Linguistics,* World Publishing, 1967, revised edition with Japanese annotations, Kinseido (Tokyo), 1968. Contributor to *Encyclopaedia Britannica* and professional journals. General editor, "New World Language and Linguistics Series," 1967.

AVOCATIONAL INTERESTS: Music, the theatre.†

(Died November, 1972)

*   *   *

FRILLMANN, Paul W.   1911-1972

PERSONAL: Born June 12, 1911, in Melrose Park, Ill.; married Louise Kluender, June 5, 1946; children: Juliana Mary, Kristin Louise. *Education:* Studied at Concordia College, Milwaukee, Wis., Concordia Seminary, and Harvard University. *Home:* 186 Riverside Dr., New York, N.Y. 10024. *Office:* Harold L. Oram, Inc., 677 Fifth Ave., New York, N.Y. 10002.

CAREER: Went to China as a Lutheran missionary in 1936, and remained after the Japanese invasion to guard the Lutheran compound in Hankow; U.S. Foreign Service, consul in Mukden and then Shanghai, China, and Hong Kong, 1946-53; Harvard University, Cambridge, Mass., assistant to dean of the Divinity School; Harold L. Oram, Inc. (public relations and fund-raising firm), New York, N.Y., executive vice-president, 1953-72. *Military service:* American Volunteer Group (Flying Tigers), chaplain, 1941-42. U.S. Army Air Forces, 1942-46; became major; received Bronze Star, Legion of Merit, White Cloud Banner (China).

WRITINGS: (With Graham Peck) *China: The Remembered Life,* Houghton, 1968.

BIOGRAPHICAL/CRITICAL SOURCES: Christian Science Monitor, June 11, 1968; *New York Times Book Review,* February 9, 1969.†

(Died August 19, 1972)

*   *   *

FRINK, Maurice   1895-1972

PERSONAL: Born May 21, 1895, in Elkhart, Ind.; son of Charles Walter (a physician) and Maude (Robinson) Frink; married Edith Raut, June 1, 1918; children: Elizabeth Frink McCain, Maurice, Jr., William R., Susanna Frink Habenicht. *Education:* Columbia University, student, 1915-16. *Politics:* Independent. *Religion:* Protestant.

CAREER: Daily Truth (newspaper), Elkhart, Ind., member of editorial staff, 1913-47, managing editor, 1947-51; University of Colorado, Boulder, instructor and lecturer in School of Journalism, 1951-54; State Historical Society of Colorado, Boulder, executive director, 1954-62. Volunteer worker with wife, Edith Frink, on Navajo reservation for Volunteers in Service to America (VISTA), 1965-66. *Military service:* U.S. Army, 1918. *Member:* Colorado Authors League, Denver Westerners (president, 1954-56). *Awards, honors:* Tophand Award of Colorado Authors League, 1956, for *When Grass Was King.*

WRITINGS: Cow Country Cavalcade: 80 Years of Wyoming Stock Growers Association, Old West, 1954; (with W. Turrentine Jackson and Agnes Wright Spring) *When Grass Was King,* University of Colorado Press, 1956; *The Boulder Story,* Pruett, 1965; (with Casey E. Barthelmess) *Photographer on an Army Mule,* University of Oklahoma Press, 1965; *Fort Defiance and the Navajos,* Pruett, 1968. Editor, *Denver Westerners Brand Book: IX,* 1954. Contributor to magazines and journals, including *Out West, Outing, Sports Afield, Outdoor America, Nature, Saturday Review, Outdoor Life, Colorado Quarterly, Nebraska History.*

WORK IN PROGRESS: Pine Ridge Medicine Man, a biography of James Riley Walker, an Indian Service doctor with the Oglala Sioux, 1878-1914.†

(Died March 25, 1972)

*   *   *

FROBOESS, Harry (August)   1899-

PERSONAL: Born October 23, 1899, in Dresden, Germany; son of Hans August (a civil engineer) and Gertrud (Lessing) Froboess; married Hertha Muller, June 25, 1927. *Education:* University of Vienna, Master Degree in Phy. Ed., 1924. *Religion:* Lutheran.

CAREER: Teacher of physical education, Davos, Switzerland, 1925-29; professional athlete, giving exhibitions throughout the world, 1930-45; aerial gymnast, also on world tours, 1946-56; artist and writer of nonfiction. Producer of amateur aquatic shows; consultant and instructor, Red Cross Water Safety Program, beginning 1943; consultant, Swiss and German Olympic Committees. *Member:* Santa Fe Art Association (president, 1960-62). *Awards, honors:* Gold Medal in high diving, Paris Olympics, 1924; Gold Medal in gymnastics, Amsterdam Olympics, 1928; blue ribbons for drawing at art shows in America and abroad.

WRITINGS—All self-illustrated: *Die Kunst des Wasser-Springens,* Rex (Vienna), 1948; *The Reminiscing Champ* (autobiography), Pageant, 1953; *Official Guide to Diving,* Fell, 1965; *Gluecklich Ueberlebt,* Schweizer Verlaghaus, 1969. Column, ''The Reminiscing Champ,'' appeared in eight European magazines, 1950-52.

SIDELIGHTS: Froboess has competence in German, French, Dutch, and Norwegian.

BIOGRAPHICAL/CRITICAL SOURCES: The Reminiscing Champ, Pageant, 1953.†

*   *   *

FROHMAN, Charles E(ugene)   1901-1976

PERSONAL: Born August 9, 1901, in Sandusky, Ohio; son of Daniel and Helen (Wagner) Frohman; married Ruth Elisabeth Dunsmore, June 10, 1933; children: David James, Daniel Charles. *Education:* University of Pennsylvania, B.S., 1923; Yale University, LL.B., 1926. *Home and office:* 1313 Cedar Point Rd., Sandusky, Ohio 44870.

CAREER: Engaged in practice of law in Sandusky, Ohio, with King, Ramsey & Flynn, 1926-32, King, Flynn & Frohman, 1932-36, and Flynn, Frohman, Buckingham, Py & Kruse, 1936-46; Hinde & Dauch Paper Co., Sandusky, general counsel, 1932-48, director, 1939-58, vice-president, 1941-49, president, 1949-58; Hinde & Dauch Paper Co. of Canada Ltd., director, 1940-59, vice-chairman, 1951-59. Vice-president and director, O-P Craft Co., Inc., 1935-70;

Third National Bank of Sandusky, director, beginning 1938, vice-president, beginning 1952. Other directorships include Sandusky Chamber of Commerce, 1930-39, 1951-57, American Crayon Co., 1938-57, Cedar Point, Inc., 1948-51, Lake Erie Broadcasting Co., 1950-53, National Industrial Conference Board, 1951-57, Sky Tours, Inc., 1953-56, West Virginia Pulp & Paper Co., 1953-66, Corrugated Paper Box Co., 1954-58, Hilton Bros. Ltd., 1954-58, and Who's Who in America, 1960-69. Member of paperboard products advisory committee, U.S. Office of Price Administration, 1941-45; chairman, Erie County War Savings Committee, 1942-43; member of Sandusky appeals panel, War Manpower Commission, 1943-45. Good Samaritan Hospital, trustee, 1936-51, president, 1937-48, fund trustee, 1943-65; trustee, Dawes Arboretum, 1961-63.

MEMBER: American Institute of Management (fellow; director, 1959-70), American Bar Association, American Academy of Political and Social Science (life member), Academy of Political Science (life member), Western Reserve Historical Society, Great Lakes Historical Society (life member; trustee, 1946-54), Maumee Valley Historical Society, Ohio Historical Society (trustee, beginning 1956; vice-president, 1959-61; president, 1961-63), Ohioana Library Association (trustee, 1951-55), Rutherford B. Hayes Foundation (trustee, beginning 1970), Erie County Historical Society, Firelands Historical Society (life member), Delta Theta Phi, Theta Alpha Phi, Beta Gamma Sigma, Masons, Elks, Yale Club (New York), Rockwell Trout Club, Sandusky Yacht Club. *Awards, honors:* D.B.A. from Bowling Green State University, 1958.

WRITINGS—All published by Ohio Historical Society: *A History of Sandusky and Erie County,* 1965; *Rebels on Lake Erie,* 1966; *Sandusky's Yesterdays,* 1968; *Cedar Point Yesterdays,* 1969, 3rd edition, 1972; *Put-in-Bay,* 1971; *Sandusky's Third Dimension,* 1971; *Sandusky's Editor,* 1972. Also author of *Sandusky Area Miscellany,* 1973, and *Sandusky Potpourri,* 1974. Contributor of articles on local history to journals. Member of board of editors, *Yale Law Journal,* 1925-26.†

(Died September 10, 1976)

*   *   *

FROST, S. E., Jr.   1899-

PERSONAL: Born September 20, 1899, in Fort Worth, Tex.; son of Severe E. (a teacher) and Mary Elizabeth (Hamner) Frost; married Maude Disbrow, July 23, 1927; children: John S. E. *Education:* Southern Methodist University, B.A., 1922; Yale Divinity School, B.D., 1924; Columbia University, M.A., 1925, Ph.D., 1939; additional study at Texas Christian University, Vanderbilt University, and University of Texas. *Politics:* Republican. *Home:* 2140-B Ronda Granada, Laguna Hills, Calif. 92653.

CAREER: Ordained minister of Congregational Church, 1925; pastor in Cocoanut Grove, Fla., 1925; *Miami Daily News,* Miami, Fla., church and literary editor, 1925-28; Miami Chamber of Commerce, Miami, Fla., director of public relations, 1928-29; pastor in Austin, Tex., 1929-35; Adelphi College, Garden City, N.Y., chairman of department of education, 1937-40; high school teacher of English, Floral Park, N.Y., 1940-41, 1943-46; Brooklyn College (now Brooklyn College of the City University of New York), Brooklyn, N.Y., instructor, 1941-43, assistant professor, 1946-64, associate professor of education, 1964-68. Hofstra College (now University), part-time faculty member, 1952-63. *Member:* National Education Association, National Society for the Study of Education, National Society of College Teachers of Education, American Academy of Political and Social Science, Phi Delta Kappa, Kappa Delta Pi. *Awards, honors:* Carnegie grant for research in radio and education, 1935-37.

WRITINGS: Theses and Dissertations Written at the Institutions of Higher Education of Texas, University of Texas Press, 1934; *Is American Radio Democratic?,* University of Chicago Press, 1937; *Education's Own Stations,* University of Chicago Press, 1937; *Basic Teachings of the Great Philosophers,* Garden City Books, 1942, revised edition. Doubleday, 1962; (editor) *The Sacred Writings of the World's Great Religions,* Balkiston Co., 1943; (editor) *The World's Great Sermons,* Garden City Books, 1943; (editor) *Great Religious Stories,* Garden City Books, 1945; (editor) *Masterworks in Philosophy,* Doubleday, 1946; *Essentials of History of Education,* Barron's, 1947; *Favorite Stories from the Bible,* Permabooks, 1950; *Introduction to American Education,* Doubleday, 1962; *Historical and Philosophical Foundations of Western Education,* C. E. Merrill, 1966, 2nd edition (with Kenneth P. Bailey), 1973. Contributor of articles and book reviews to educational journals.

WORK IN PROGRESS: A book, *Philosophical Roots of American Education;* studies of the life of John Amos Comenius.

*   *   *

FULDA, Carl H. 1909-1975

PERSONAL: Born August 22, 1909, in Berlin, Germany; came to United States in 1936, naturalized in 1941; married Gaby Gros (a piano teacher and voice coach), 1935; children: Thomas R., John A. *Education:* University of Freiburg, J.U.D., 1931; Yale University, LL.B., 1938. *Politics:* Democrat. *Home:* 3410 Shinoak Dr., Austin, Tex. 78731. *Office:* School of Law, University of Texas, 2500 Red River, Austin, Tex. 78705.

CAREER: Attorney and law secretary in Berlin, Germany, 1931-33; Victoria Insurance Co., Paris, France, executive assistant, 1933-35; State Law Revision Commission, Ithaca, N.Y., research assistant, 1938-41; attorney for U.S. Department of the Treasury, 1942, and Office of Price Administration, 1942-46, both Washington, D.C.; Rutgers University, Newark, N.J., assistant professor, 1946-49, associate professor, 1949-52, professor of law, 1952-54; Ohio State University, Columbus, professor of law, 1954-64; University of Texas at Austin, professor of law, 1964-65, Hugh Lamar Stone Professor of Law, beginning 1965. Consultant to U.S. Department of Commerce, 1950, and Agency for International Development, New Delhi, India, 1967; member of White House Task Force on Antitrust Policy, 1968; member of American Bar Association Commission to study Federal Trade Commission, 1969. Visiting professor at Columbia University, 1952, Seminar of American Studies, Salzburg, Austria, 1960, Louisiana State University, 1962, University of Frankfurt, Germany, 1962, University of Tuebingen, Germany, 1964, 1970, and Hastings College of Law, University of California, 1972. Member of State Bars of New York, and Texas, and Travis County (Tex.) Bar. *Member:* American Bar Association, American Society of International Law, American Foreign Law Association, American Association of University Professors. *Awards, honors:* Ford Foundation law faculty fellow, 1959-60.

WRITINGS: Competition in Regulated Industries: Transportation, Little, Brown, 1961; *Einfuehring in das Recht der U.S.A.* (title means "Introduction to the Law of the United States"), Nomos, 1966; (with Warren Schwartz) *Cases and Materials on the Regulation of International Trade and Investment,* Foundation Press, 1970. Contributor of numerous articles to legal periodicals. Member of board of editors, *American Journal of Comparative Law* and *Transportation Law Journal.*

WORK IN PROGRESS: Writing on the regulation of business for Volume XVII of the *International Encyclopedia of Comparative Law.†*

(Died January 5, 1975)

*   *   *

FULLER, Lon L(uvois) 1902-

PERSONAL: Born June 15, 1902, in Hereford, Tex.; son of Francis Bartow (a banker) and Mary Salome (Moore) Fuller; married Gail Thompson, July, 1926 (died, 1960); married Marjorie Chapple, November 5, 1960; children: (first marriage) Francis Brock, Cornelia Hopfield. *Education:* University of California, student, 1919-20; Stanford University, A.B., 1924, J.D., 1926. *Politics:* Democrat. *Home:* 16 Traill St., Cambridge, Mass. 02138. *Office:* Law School, Harvard University, Cambridge, Mass. 02138.

CAREER: University of Oregon, Eugene, assistant professor, 1926-27, associate professor of law, 1927-28; University of Illinois (now University of Illinois at Urbana-Champaign), Urbana, associate professor, 1928-30, professor of law, 1930-31; Duke University, Durham, N.C., professor of law, 1931-39; Harvard University, Cambridge, Mass., professor of law, 1940-48, Carter Professor of General Jurisprudence, beginning 1948. Practice of law, Ropes, Gray, Best, Coolidge & Rugg, Boston, Mass., 1942-45. Summer lecturer at University of Chicago, 1930-33, University of Washington, 1931, University of North Carolina, 1934, University of Southern California, 1937, and University of California, Berkeley, 1971.

MEMBER: American Academy of Arts and Sciences, Massachusetts Bar Association, Phi Beta Kappa, Order of the Coif. *Awards, honors:* Phillips Award of American Philosophical Association, 1935, for essay on American legal realism.

WRITINGS: The Law in Quest of Itself (Julius Rosenthal Foundation lectures at Northwestern University, 1940), Foundation Press (Chicago), 1940, reprinted, Beacon Press, 1966; *Reason and Fiat in Case Law* (Benjamin N. Cardozo lecture), American Book-Stratford Press, 1943; (editor) *Basic Contract Law,* West Publishing, 1947, 2nd edition (with Robert Braucher), 1964; (editor) *The Problems of Jurisprudence: A Selection of Readings,* Foundation Press (Brooklyn), 1949; *Human Purpose and Natural Law* (originally published in *Journal of Philosophy,* 1956), Notre Dame Law School, 1958; *The Morality of Law* (Storrs lectures, 1963), Yale University Press, 1964, revised edition, 1969; *Legal Fictions,* Stanford University Press, 1967; *Anatomy of the Law,* Praeger, 1968. Also author of journal articles on law, some of which have been translated and published as pamphlets in Spanish. Writer of course materials for Association of American Law Schools and American Bar Association conferences.

WORK IN PROGRESS: Two articles.

BIOGRAPHICAL/CRITICAL SOURCES: New Statesman, February 14, 1969.

*   *   *

FURFEY, Paul Hanly 1896-

PERSONAL: Born June 30, 1896, in Cambridge, Mass.; son

of James Arthur (a prison official) and Margaret (Connell) Furfey. *Education:* Boston College, A.B., 1917; Catholic University of America, Ph.D., 1926; studied at St. Mary's Seminary, Baltimore, Md., 1918-19, and Sulpician Seminary, Washington, D.C., 1919-22; postdoctoral study at University of Berlin and University of Frankfurt, 1931-32. *Politics:* Independent ("active in liberal causes"). *Home:* 3619 12th St. N.E., Washington, D.C. 20017. *Office:* Catholic University of America, Washington, D.C. 20017.

CAREER: Roman Catholic priest with title of right reverend monsignor. Catholic University of America, Washington, D.C., instructor, 1925-31, associate professor, 1931-40, professor of sociology, 1940-66, professor emeritus, 1966—, co-director of Bureau of Social Research, beginning 1959. Honorary professor, Universidad de America, 1956. *Awards, honors:* Named domestic prelate, 1958; LL.D., Duquesne University, 1944; L.H.D., St. John's University, Jamaica, N.Y., 1964.

WRITINGS: Gang Age, Macmillan, 1926; *Parish and Play,* Dolphin Press, 1928; *Social Problems of Childhood,* Macmillan, 1929; *You and Your Children,* Benziger, 1929; *The Growing Boy,* Macmillan, 1930; *New Lights on Pastoral Problems,* Bruce, 1931; *Fire on the Earth,* Macmillan, 1936; *Three Theories of Society,* Macmillan, 1937; *This Way to Heaven,* Preservation Press, 1939; *History of Social Thought,* Macmillan, 1942; *The Mystery of Iniquity,* Bruce, 1944; *Scope and Method of Sociology,* Harper, 1953; *The Respectable Murderers,* Herder & Herder, 1966; *The Morality Gap,* Macmillan, 1968; *Interaction of Deaf and Hearing in Baltimore City, Maryland,* Catholic University of America Press, 1968. Also author of *The Subculture of the Washington Ghetto.*

SIDELIGHTS: Monsignor Furfey told *CA:* "I am quite active in three sorts of social movements, namely, anti-war, relief of poverty, equal rights for Negroes and women. I can get around in the principal European languages; but I am better at reading than speaking foreign languages."

BIOGRAPHICAL/CRITICAL SOURCES: Commonweal, April 18, 1969.

*   *   *

FYSON, J(enny) G(race)   1904-

PERSONAL: Born October 3, 1904, in Bromley, Kent, England; daughter of Cholmondeley (a local government administrator of education) and Jenny Maud (Mann) Harrison; married Christopher Fyson, March, 1939 (deceased); children: Charles. *Education:* Educated by a governess at home, in a private village school, and at St. Swithun's, Winchester, England, 1918-21. *Politics:* "No party." *Religion:* Ecumenical. *Home:* Near Maidstone, Kent, England.

CAREER: Painter, 1921-37; playwright, 1934-38; author of children's books.

WRITINGS—Juvenile: The Three Brothers of Ur, Oxford University Press, 1964, Coward, 1966; *The Journey of the Eldest Son,* Oxford University Press, 1965, Coward, 1967; (contributor) Edward Blishen, editor, *Miscellany V,* Oxford University Press, 1968. Writer of two educational scripts on Saul and David for radio.

WORK IN PROGRESS: Let the Waters Bring, a picture book about God and evolution for under-sevens; *Andrew and His Friend Fire; The Fox Has a White Face,* a novel on life in a village during World War II as seen through a young boy's eyes.

SIDELIGHTS: Kept out of school by poor health in her late teens, Mrs. Fyson fell back on painting, reading, and literature. "It was then," she recalls, "that Darwin's *Origin of Species* and Bernard Shaw came like earthquakes, upsetting accepted and unquestioned philosophy. Gibbon interested me in the past and Frazer's *Golden Bough* provided a solution for the sacrifice of Isaac. Abraham was a brave man throwing off the shackles of an old custom." Current interests in addition to evolution: Jung, archaeology, the causes of war, gardening.

*   *   *

GABO, Naum   1890-

PERSONAL: Name originally Naum Neemia Pevsner; born August 5, 1890, in Briask, Russia; son of Boris (a manufacturer) and Fanya (Asersky) Pevsner; married Miriam Israels (an artist), October 13, 1936; children: Nina S. *Education:* Studied at University of Munich.

CAREER: Sculptor. Teacher in School of Design, Harvard University, one semester. *Member:* Institute of Arts and Letters, Academy of Arts and Sciences, Swedish Academy. *Awards, honors:* Honorary doctorate, Royal College of Art, London, England; Brandeis Award; Logan medal for sculpture; Knight Commander of Order of the British Empire.

WRITINGS: (Editor with James Lee Martin and Ben Nicholson) *Circle: International Survey of Constructive Art,* Faber, 1937; (with J. J. Sweeney and Katherine Drier) *Three Lectures on Modern Art,* Philosophical Library, 1949, new edition, 1971; *Gabo: Constructions, Sculpture, Paintings, Drawings, and Engravings,* Harvard University Press, 1957; *Of Divers Arts* (A. W. Mellon lectures in the fine arts), Pantheon, 1962.

*   *   *

GAGE, William   1915-1973

PERSONAL: Born August 8, 1915, in Detroit, Mich.; son of William Henry (an insurance man) and Jessie (Campbell) Gage. *Education:* Yale University, B.A., 1938. *Politics:* Republican. *Religion:* Christian. *Home:* 266 Rivard, Grosse Pointe, Mich. 48230. *Agent:* Russel & Volkening, Inc., 551 Fifth Ave., New York, N.Y. 10017.

CAREER: Campbell-Ewald Co. (advertising agency), Detroit, Mich., 1939-73, account executive, 1947-50, account supervisor, 1950-52, vice-president, 1952-73. President, Friends of Detroit Public Library, 1969-71. *Military service:* U.S. Navy, 1940-45; became lieutenant commander. *Member:* University Club and Recess Club (both Detroit).

WRITINGS: Appointment with Dishonor, Little, Brown, 1958; *The Cruel Coast,* New American Library, 1966.

SIDELIGHTS: "I aspire to be a good yarn-spinner, and nothing more," William Gage told *CA.* "Once a plot has occurred to me (in rough form), I find that the research, travel, correspondence and interviews with authorities are tremendously rewarding in a personal way—above and beyond the actual written words."†

(Died December 29, 1973)

*   *   *

GALBRAITH, Madelyn   1897-1976

PERSONAL: Born August 31, 1897, in San Antonio, Tex.; daughter of George William (an engineer) and Julia Ann (Long) Galbraith. *Education:* Attended public schools in San Antonio, Tex. *Religion:* Reorganized Church of Jesus Christ of Latter-day Saints. *Home:* 1203 Breeden, Apt. 6, San Antonio, Tex. 78212.

CAREER: Bridal consultant, 1930-59.

WRITINGS: *Feather in the Wind,* Herald House, 1954; *There Is a Book,* Herald House, 1971; *Village in the Sun,* Herald House, 1975.

WORK IN PROGRESS: Two works, *No Continuing City* and *The Book,* a book of Mormon prophesies now being fulfilled.

SIDELIGHTS: Miss Galbraith made ten trips through Mexico and Yucatan.†

(Died August 2, 1976)

* * *

GALLOWAY, John C. 1915-1970

PERSONAL: Born June 15, 1915, in Cabot, Ark.; son of John C. (a merchant) and Blanche (Bradford) Galloway; married Jean Davidson (a teacher), January 29, 1949; children: Spence C., Pamela G. *Education:* American University, A.B., 1941, M.A., 1950; Columbia University, Ph.D., 1956. *Office:* Department of Art, Oakland University, Rochester, Mich. 48063.

CAREER: American University, Washington, D.C., instructor in art, 1947-50; University of Alabama, University, began as assistant professor, became associate professor of art; Southern Illinois University, Carbondale, professor of art history, 1958-60; Oakland University, Rochester, Mich., professor of art and chairman of department, 1960-70. Visiting professor, Indiana University, summer 1957. Television and public lecturer on African and contemporary art. *Military service:* U.S. Army, 1942-46; became captain. *Member:* Royal Anthropological Institute (fellow), College Art Association, American Association of University Professors, Friends of Modern Art (past secretary), Midwestern Art Conference, Founders' Society of Detroit Institute of Arts. *Awards, honors:* Fulbright research scholar in Europe, 1957-58.

WRITINGS: (With Harry Elmer Barnes and others) *An Intellectual and Cultural History of the Western World,* three volumes, Dover, 1965; *Origins of Modern Art, 1905-1914,* McGraw, 1965; (with Andreas Lommel and Luis Pericot-Garcia) *Le Grande epoche dell'arte: La preistoria e i primitivi attuali,* Sansoni Editore (Florence), 1967, published as *Prehistoric and Primitive Art,* Abrams, 1968; *Modern Art: The Nineteenth and Twentieth Centuries,* W. C. Brown, 1967; *Picasso,* McGraw, 1969. Contributor to professional journals. Consultant, *Choice,* 1965-70.†

(Died April 17, 1970)

* * *

GANSHOF, Francois-Louis 1895-

PERSONAL: Born March 14, 1895, in Bruges, Belgium; son of Arthur (a lawyer) and Louise (van der Meersch) Ganshof; married Nelly Kirkpatrick, September 14, 1920; children: Louis, Christiane, Francoise (Mrs. Philippe Godding), Denyse (Mrs. Henri Mairesse). *Education:* University of Ghent, D.Lit., 1921; University of Paris, LL.D., 1922. *Religion:* Protestant. *Home:* 12 rue Jacques Jordaens, Brussels, Belgium.

CAREER: Served at the Bar in Brussels, 1922-23; University of Ghent, lecturer, 1923-29; professor of medieval and legal history, 1929-1961, professor emeritus, 1961—. *Military service:* Belgian Army, World Wars I and II; became major. *Member:* American Historical Association, Royal Historical Society (London; both honorary). *Fellow:* Royal Flemish Academy of Sciences (Belgium), Institut de France (Academie des Inscriptions et Belles Lettres), British Academy, Medieval Academy of America, Royal Academy of Sciences of Netherland (Amsterdam), Academy of Sciences of Vienna, Academy of Sciences of Berlin. *Awards, honors:* Honorary degrees from the Universities of Montpellier, Grenoble, Bordeaux, Lille, Glasgow, Paris, Strasbourg, London, Poitiers, Rennes, Dijon, Alger, and Cambridge.

WRITINGS: *Etudes sur les ministeriales en Flandre et en Lotharingie,* Academie Royale de Belgique, 1926; *Recherches sur les tribunaux de chatellenie en Flandre avant le milieu du XIIIe siecle,* Sainte Catherine Press, 1932; (with F. Lot and C. Pfister) *Les destinees de l'Empire en Occident de 395 a 888,* Presses Universitaires de France, 1934, 2nd edition, 1940; *De Zuidelijke Nederlanden in de XViie en XVIIIe eeuw,* Nijhoff, 1935; *Pages d'histoire,* Editions Universitaires, 1941, 2nd edition, 1944; *Over Stadsontwikkeling tusschen Loire en Rijn gedurende de Middeleeuwen,* De Standaard Boekhandel, 1941, 2nd edition, 1944; *La Flandre sous les premiers comtes,* La Renaissance du Livre, 1943, 3rd edition, 1949; *Qu'est-ce que la Feodalite?,* Office de Publicite, 1944, 4th edition, 1969, translation by Philip Grierson published as *Feudalism,* Longmans, Green, 1952, Harper, 1961, 3rd edition, 1964; *The Imperial Coronation of Charlemagne: Theories and Facts,* Jackson, Son & Co., 1949, 2nd edition, 1971.

(Editor with Coenraad Dirk Jan) *De Geschiedenis van onze tijd, 1914-1915,* W. de Haan, 1951; *Le Moyen Age,* Hachette, 1953, 4th edition, 1968, translation by Remy Inglis Hall published as *The Middle Ages: A History of International Relations,* 1971; *Wat waren de Capitularia?,* Koninklijke Vlaamse Academie voor Wetenschappen van Belgie, 1955; *Histoire des institutions francaises au Moyen Age,* Presses Universitaires de France, 1957; *Recherches sur les Capitulaires,* Sirey, 1958; *La Belgique Carolingienne,* La Renaissance du Livre, 1958; *Das Hochmittelalter* (in *Propylaen Weltgeschichte,* Volume V, general editor, Golo Mann), Propylaen Verlag Ullstein, 1963; *En historicus uit de vie eeuw: Gregorius van Tours,* Paleis der Academien, 1966; *Frankish Institutions under Charlemagne,* translation by Bryce Lyon and Mary Lyon, Brown University Press, 1968; *Droit Romain dans les Capitulaires,* Guiffre, 1969; *Le Droit de la faillite dans les etats de la Communaute economique europeenne,* Centre Interuniversitaire de Droit Compare, 1969; *The Carolingians and the Frankish Monarchy,* translation by Janet Sondheimer, Cornell University Press, 1971.

Contributor to *Karl der Grosse,* Volume I: *Persoenlichkeit und Geschichte,* edited by Helmut Beumann. Also author of numerous history pamphlets.

* * *

GARCEAU, Oliver 1911-

PERSONAL: Born November 22, 1911, in Boston, Mass.; son of Edgar (a physician) and Sally Holmes (Morse) Garceau; married Iris V. Thistle, August 18, 1934; children: Laurence. *Education:* Harvard University, A.B., 1933, M.B.A., 1935, M.A., 1939, Ph.D., 1940; Oxford University, graduate study, 1933; University of Chicago, post-doctoral study, 1943-44. *Address:* P.O. Box 8, Sedgwick, Me. 04676.

CAREER: Harvard University, Cambridge, Mass., taught in government department, 1940-41, 1945-46; University of Maine, Orono, associate professor of government, 1946-47; Social Science Research Council, New York City, staff associate, 1947-48; Bennington College, Bennington, Vt., professor of government, 1948-58; Ford Foundation, New York City, executive associate and consultant, 1955-57; Harvard University, Cambridge, research professor of government, 1959-60. Visiting professor, Williams College, 1952. Member of executive board, Inter-University Case Program in Public Administration, 1952-58; member of board of trustees, St. Andrews Hospital, 1959-69; member, Governor of Maine's Task Force on Government Reorganization, 1967-69. *Military service:* U.S. Naval Reserve, active duty, 1941-45; became lieutenant commander. *Member:* American Political Science Association (member of executive council, 1951-53), Social Science Research Council (member of committee on political behavior, 1950-64), Lincoln County Cultural and Historical Association (president, 1963-64; director, 1966-69), Castine Scientific Society (member of council, beginning 1970), Sedgwick Historical Society (director, beginning 1970; president, 1972-73), Phi Beta Kappa.

WRITINGS: The Political Life of the American Medical Association, Harvard University Press, 1941; *The Public Library in the Political Process,* Columbia University Press, 1949, reprinted, Gregg, 1972; (editor and contributor) *Political Research and Political Theory,* Harvard University Press, 1968. Contributor to professional journals. Associate editor, publications of Society for Applied Anthropology, 1956-66.

BIOGRAPHICAL/CRITICAL SOURCES: Virginia Quarterly Review, spring, 1969.

*   *   *

GARDNER, Dorothy E. M.   1900-1972

PERSONAL: Born July 27, 1900, in India; daughter of Henry Montfort (an army officer) and Marion (Edge) Gardner. *Education:* University of London, Certificate in Child Development, 1935; University of Leeds, M.A., 1940. *Home:* Lindfield, 10 Shalford Rd., Guildford, Surrey, England.

CAREER: Elementary teacher in Edinburgh, Scotland, and London, England, 1920-30; Bishop Otter College, Chichester, Sussex, England, lecturer in education, 1930-36; City of Leeds Training College, Leeds, Yorkshire, England, head of department of infant and junior education, 1936-42; Bolton Education Authority, Bolton, Lancashire, England, supervisor of schools, 1942-43; University of London, London, England, head of department of child development, Institute of Education, 1943-68, university reader, 1951-68. Lecturer in United States, Canada, and New Zealand. Served terms of six years each as member of Central Advisory Council for Education, British Ministry of Education, and of Central Training Council for Child Care, British Home Office. *Member:* Nursery School Association of Great Britain and Northern Ireland (vice chairman), British Psychological Society. *Awards, honors:* Officer of Order of the British Empire, 1967.

WRITINGS: The Children's Play Centre, Methuen, 1937; *Testing Results in the Infant School,* Methuen, 1942; *Education under Eight,* Longmans, Green, 1949; *Long Term Results of Infant School Methods,* Methuen, 1950; *The Education of Young Children,* Methuen, 1956; (with J. Cass) *The Role of the Teacher in Infant and Nursery Schools,* Pergamon, 1965; *Experiment and Tradition in Primary Schools,* Methuen, 1966; *Susan Isaacs,* Methuen, 1969. Author of television scripts. Contributed to journals.

WORK IN PROGRESS: Research in personality develop-

ment as affected by different forms of primary school education.†

(Died April, 1972)

*   *   *

GARDNER-SMITH, Percival   1888-

PERSONAL: Born Feburary 3, 1888, in Wadingham, Lincolnshire, England; son of Robert (a clergyman) and Mary (Alexander) Gardner-Smith; married Sophia Dorothy Leeke, September 30, 1913; married second wife, Catharine Elizabeth Leeke, November 30, 1961. *Education:* Jesus College, Cambridge, B.A., 1909, M.A., 1912, B.D., 1926. *Home:* 11 Cranmer Rd., Cambridge, England.

CAREER: Clerk in Holy Orders; vicar of Comberton, 1916-22; Jesus College, Cambridge University, Cambridge, England, dean, 1922-56, fellow, beginning 1923, president, 1948-58. Cambridge University, lecturer in theology, 1922-53, senior proctor, 1926-27, member of financial board, 1949-55. Member of City Council of Cambridge, 1950-56. *Member:* Modern Churchmen's Union (former vice-president).

WRITINGS: The Narratives of the Resurrection, Methuen, 1928; (contributor) J. F. Bethune Baker, editor, *The Christian Religion,* Volume III, Cambridge University Press, 1930; *The Christ of the Gospels,* Heffer, 1937; *St. John and the Synoptic Gospels,* Cambridge University Press, 1938; (editor) *The Roads Converge,* Edward Arnold, 1963, St. Martin's, 1964. Contributor to dictionaries, encyclopedias, and journals.††

*   *   *

GARRETT, Eileen J(eanette)   1893-1970
(Jean Lyttle)

PERSONAL: Born March 17, 1893, in Beau Park, County Meath, Ireland; daughter of Anthony and Ann (Brownell) Vancho; adopted daughter (after death of parents) of William and Martha Lyttle; married Clive Barry, 1909; married second husband, J. W. Garrett, 1918; children: one daughter, two sons. *Education:* Educated at national and private schools in Ireland and England. *Office:* Parapsychology Foundation, Inc., 29 West 57th St., New York, N.Y. 10019.

CAREER: Trained as a trance medium under the direction of James Hewat McKenzie of the British College of Psychic Science. Founder and publisher, Creative Age Press, 1941-51; founder and editor, *Tomorrow* (a literary monthly magazine), 1941-51; Parapsychology Foundation, Inc., New York City, founder and president, 1951-70; Garrett Publications, New York City, founder, owner, and president, 1951-70; founder and editor, *Tomorrow* (a quarterly review of psychical research), 1952-62; editor, *International Journal of Parapsychology,* 1959-68.

WRITINGS: My Life as a Search for the Meaning of Mediumship, Opuaga Press, 1939, reprinted, Arno, 1975; *Telepathy: In Search of a Lost Faculty,* Creative Age Press, 1941, reprinted, with a new introduction, Garrett Publications, 1968; (under pseudonym Jean Lyttle) *Today the Sun Rises,* Creative Age Press, 1942; (under pseudonym Jean Lyttle) *You Are France, Lisette,* Creative Age Press, 1943; *Awareness,* Creative Age Press, 1943, 2nd edition, Helix Press Books, 1960; (under pseudonym Jean Lyttle) *Sheila Lacey,* Creative Age Press, 1944; (with Abril Lamarque) *Man, The Maker: A Pictorial Record of Man's Inventiveness,* Creative Age Press, 1946; *Adventures in the Supernormal: A Personal Memoir,* Creative Age Press, 1949, reprinted, Paperback Library, 1968.

(Editor) *Does Man Survive Death?: A Symposium,* Holborn

Publishing, 1950, Helix Press Books, 1957; *The Sense and Nonsense of Prophecy,* Creative Age Press, 1950; *Life Is the Healer,* Dorrance, 1957; (editor) *Beyond the Five Senses* (collection of articles from *Tomorrow*), Lippincott, 1957; (under pseudonym Jean Lyttle) *Threads of Destiny,* Dorrance, 1961; (under pseudonym Jean Lyttle) *Many Voices: The Autobiography of a Medium,* Putnam, 1968.

BIOGRAPHICAL/CRITICAL SOURCES: Washington Post, September 18, 1970; A. Angoff, *Eileen Garrett and the World Beyond the Senses,* Morrow, 1974.†

(Died in Nice, France, September 15, 1970)

* * *

GARTON, Nina R. 1905-

PERSONAL: Born February 27, 1905, in Missoula, Mont.; daughter of William (a surveyor) and Bessie (Watson) Engle; husband deceased. *Education:* Seattle University, B.S.S., 1951; University of Montana, Diploma in Social Work, 1952; University of Utah, M.S.W., 1961. *Religion:* Roman Catholic. *Office:* Coos County Public Welfare, Child Welfare Division, Coos Bay, Ore. 97420.

CAREER: Social worker in Japan, 1953-55, and Canada, 1958-60; social worker for State Hospital, Salem, Ore., 1961-64, Mental Health Clinic, Coquille, Ore., 1964-66, and Child Welfare Division of Coos County Public Welfare, Coos Bay, Ore., beginning 1966. *Member:* National Association of Social Workers, American Group Psychotherapy Association, International Federation of Business and Professional Women's Clubs, Oregon Mental Health Association, Oregon Social Welfare Association, Oregon Association of Child Care Workers, Northwest Institute for Family Therapy (fellow), Soroptomists.

WRITINGS: (With Herbert A. Otto) *Development of Theory and Practice in Social Casework,* C. C Thomas, 1964, 2nd edition, 1968.

AVOCATIONAL INTERESTS: Traveling.††

* * *

GATES, Lillian Francis 1901-

PERSONAL: Born October 7, 1901, in Liverpool, England; daughter of Edward and Rachel B. (Higginson) Cowdell; married Paul Wallace Gates (a professor of American history at Cornell University), August 7, 1929; children: Edward W., Lillian F. (Mrs. Richard E. Goodman), Annette R. (Mrs. Preston W. Shimer), Rosemary W. (Mrs. Joseph Campos). *Education:* University of British Columbia, B.A., 1924; Clark University, Worcester, Mass., M.A., 1926; Radcliffe College, Ph.D., 1956. *Religion:* Episcopalian. *Home:* 1202 Ellis Hollow Rd., Ithaca, N.Y. 14850.

CAREER: Instructor in history at Wheaton College, Norton, Mass., 1926-28, and Cornell University, Ithaca, N.Y., 1942-44; Ithaca College, Ithaca, assistant professor, 1946-51.

WRITINGS: Land Policies of Upper Canada, University of Toronto Press, 1968. Contributor to *Canadian Historical Review* and *Ontario History.*

WORK IN PROGRESS: A biography of William L. Mackenzie.

* * *

GAZAWAY, Rena 1910-

PERSONAL: Born May 26, 1910, in Hume, Mo.; daughter of John Marcellus and Lula Tennessee (McMillan) Ga-

zaway. *Education:* Columbia University, B.S., 1948; University of Cincinnati, M.A., 1952; St. John's University, Jamaica, N.Y., Ph.D., 1961. *Politics:* Republican. *Religion:* Episcopalian. *Home:* 294 West Kemper Rd., Cincinnati, Ohio 45246. *Office:* College of Nursing and Health, University of Cincinnati, Proctor Hall, 3100 Vine, Cincinnati, Ohio 45219.

CAREER: Babies' Milk Fund Association, Cincinnati, Ohio, assistant educational director and field instructor, 1946-50; University of Cincinnati, College of Nursing and Health, Cincinnati, assistant professor, 1950-72, associate professor of research and studies, beginning 1972. University of Kentucky Medical Center, College of Medicine, Lexington, research associate in department of community health, 1962-63, assistant professor, 1963-64, visiting professor of community medicine, beginning 1964. Member of health commission, Council of the Southern Mountains, Berea, Ky; member of board of trustees, Daniel Drake Memorial Hospital, Cincinnati, beginning 1962. *Member:* American Public Health Association, National League for Nursing, American Sociological Association, Adult Education Association of the U.S.A., Association of Reserve Officers of U.S. Public Health Service, Professional Association of the Commissioned U.S. Public Health Service. *Awards, honors:* Selected as one of ten Women of the Year by *Cincinnati Enquirer,* 1972; Distinguished Alumnus Award, University of Kansas Nurses Alumni Association, 1974.

WRITINGS: (With W. J. Hayes) *Human Relations in Nursing,* Saunders, 1955, 3rd revised edition, 1964, and *Teacher's Guide,* 1959; *Source Book for Teachers to Accompany Human Relations in Nursing,* Saunders, 1964; *Culture Change, Mental Health, and Poverty,* University of Kentucky Press, 1969; *The Longest Mile,* Doubleday, 1969. Abstracter for *Nursing Research,* beginning 1961.

BIOGRAPHICAL/CRITICAL SOURCES: New York Times Book Review, November 2, 1969.

* * *

GECYS, Casimir C. 1904-

PERSONAL: Surname is pronounced Ge-cheese; born February 9, 1904, in Utena, Lithuania; naturalized U.S. citizen; son of Thomas and Stase (Vitas) Gecys. *Education:* State University at Vilnius, Th.D., 1935; Fordham University, Ph.D., 1952. *Religion:* Roman Catholic. *Home:* 731 Morris Park Ave., Bronx, N.Y. 10462. *Office:* Fordham University, Box 690, Bronx, N.Y. 10458.

CAREER: Teacher of languages in Lithuanian state high schools, 1928-30, principal, 1938-40; Fordham University, Bronx, N.Y., assistant professor of Russian history, beginning, 1958. *Member:* American Political Science Association, American Association for the Advancement of Slavic Studies, Lithuanian Academy of Sciences.

WRITINGS: (Editor) *Die Massigkeitsbruderschaften der Diozese Samogitien in den Jahren 1858-1864,* Zorza (Vilnius), 1935; (contributor) *Lithuania in a Teutonic Clutch,* 1945; (editor) *Katalikiskoji Lietuva,* Draugas, 1946; (contributor) *Religion in the USSR,* Institute for the Study of the USSR, 1960; (editor) *Two Worlds,* Institute for Contemporary Russian Studies, 1964; (with William F. Walsh) *Shadow and Substance: The Words and Deeds of Communism,* Institute for Contemporary Russian Studies, 1964. Contributor to *Ukrainian Quarterly, Russian Review, Lituanus.*

SIDELIGHTS: Gecys is competent in Lithuanian, Russian,

Polish, German, and English. He travels in western Europe every second summer.††

* * *

GELLHORN, Ernst 1893-1973

PERSONAL: Born January 7, 1893, in Breslau, Germany; came to United States in 1929, naturalized in 1935; son of Moritz (a merchant) and Hulda (Stein) Gelhorn; married Hilde Obermeier, 1925; children: Irene (deceased), Helen Hartmann, Ernest, Joyce Greene. *Education:* University of Heidelberg, M.D., 1919; University of Muenster, Ph.D., 1919. *Religion:* Unitarian Universalist. *Home:* 2 Fellowship Circle, Santa Barbara, Calif.

CAREER: University of Halle, Halle, Germany, assistant professor, 1921-25, associate professor of physiology, 1925-29; University of Oregon, Eugene, associate professor, 1929-31, professor of physiology, 1931-32; University of Illinois Medical School, Chicago, professor, 1932-43; University of Minnesota, Minneapolis, professor of neurophysiology, 1943-60, professor emeritus, 1960-73. *Member:* American Physiological Society, Society for Experimental Biology and Medicine, American Electroencephalographic Society, American Association for the Advancement of Science, New York Academy of Science, Pavlovian Society (honorary member), International League Against Epilepsy (honorary member), Sigma Xi. *Awards, honors:* Morrison Prize of New York Academy, 1930; Alvarenga Prize of College of Physicians, Philadelphia, 1934; prize of the Carbon Dioxide Research Association, 1957.

WRITINGS: Autonomic Regulations, Interscience, 1934; (with E. Lambert) *Vasomotor System in Anoxia,* University of Illinois Press, 1939; *Physiological Foundations of Neurology and Psychiatry,* University of Minnesota Press, 1953; *Autonomic Imbalance and the Hypothalamus,* University of Minnesota Press, 1957; (with G. Loofbourrow) *Emotions and Emotional Disorders,* Hoeber Medical Division, 1963; *Autonomic-somatic Integrations,* University of Minnesota Press, 1966; (compiler) *Biological Foundations of Emotions: Research and Commentary,* Scott, Foresman, 1968. Author of more than 350 published scientific papers.†

(Died, April 13, 1973)

* * *

GELZER, Matthias 1886-1974

PERSONAL: Born December 19, 1886, in Liestal, Switzerland; son of Karl (a minister) and Elisabeth (Vischer) Gelzer; married Marianne Wackernagel, April 1, 1913 (died January 18, 1928); married Katharina Brauer, September 30, 1929; children: (first marriage) Heinrich, Verena (Mrs. Paul Handschin), Alexander, Ursus. *Education:* Humanistisches Gymnasium, Basel, Switzerland, Dr. Phil., 1909. *Religion:* Reformed Church.

CAREER: Professor of ancient history at University of Freiburg, Freiburg im Breisgau, Germany, 1912-15, University of Greifswald, Greifswald, Germany, 1915-18, and University of Strasbourg, Strasbourg, France, 1918; University of Frankfurt, Frankfurt am Main, Germany, professor of ancient history, 1919-55, professor emeritus, 1955-74. *Member:* German Academy, Norwegian Academy, Swedish Academy, Heidelberg Academy (corresponding fellow), Bavarian Academy (corresponding fellow), British Academy (corresponding fellow), Society for the Promotion of Roman Studies (honorary member). *Awards, honors:* Dr. jur., University of Frankfurt, 1956; Dr. phil., University of Basel, 1959.

WRITINGS: Studien yur byzantinischen Verwaltung Aegyptens, Quelle & Meyer Verlag, 1909; *Die Nobilitaet der roemischen Republik,* Teubner Verlagsgesellschaft, 1912, translation by Robin Seager published as *The Roman Nobility,* A. S. Barnes, 1969; *Caesar: Der Politiker und Staatsmann,* Deutsche Verlags-anstalt, 1921, 6th edition, with others, 1960, translation by Peter Needham published as *Caesar: Politician and Statesman,* Harvard University Press, 1968; *Die Archaica im Geschichtswerk des Polybios,* Akademie der Wissenschaften (Berlin), 1940; *Cn. Pompeius Strabo und der Aufstieg seines Sohnes Magnus,* Akademie der Wissenschaften, 1942; *Das erste Konsulat des Pompeius und die Uebertragung der Grossen Imperien,* Akademie der Wissenschaften, 1943; ... *Vom Roemischen Staat: Zur Politik und Gesellschaftsgeschichte der Romishen Republik* (collection of papers and essays), Koehler & Amelang, 1944; *Pompeius,* Verlag F. Bruckmann, 1949, 2nd edition, 1959; *Uber die Arbeitsweise des Polybios,* [Heidelberg], 1956; *Kleine Schriften,* Franz Steiner Verlag, Volume I, 1962, Volume II, 1963, Volume III, 1964; *Cicero und Caesar,* Franz Steiner Verlag, 1968; *Cicero: Ein biographischer Versuch,* Franz Steiner Verlag, 1969.

BIOGRAPHICAL/CRITICAL SOURCES: Times Literary Supplement, April 16, 1970.†

(Died, 1974)

* * *

GEORGE, N(orvil) L(ester) 1902-

PERSONAL: Born December 2, 1902, in Manchester, Okla.; son of Evart R. (a farmer) and Lucinda (Smith) George; married Ida Mae Jensen, August 6, 1929; children: Gwendolyn Elaine (Mrs. John W. Ehlers). *Education:* University of Oklahoma, B.S., 1926, Ed.M., 1931; Columbia University, Ed.D., 1947. *Religion:* Methodist. *Home:* 2619 Northwest 67th, Oklahoma City, Okla. 73116.

CAREER: Teacher in rural schools of Grant County, Okla., 1921-22; University of Oklahoma, Norman, assistant in administration, university high school, 1924-26; superintendent of schools in Geary, Okla., 1926-35, and Duncan, Okla., 1936-41; Oklahoma City (Okla.) public schools, administrative posts, including assistant superintendent, 1941-68. Summer instructor at University of Denver, University of Colorado, University of Oklahoma, and other universities. School plant consultant, Oklahoma City University, 1970-71; consultant to more than thirty other school systems. *Member:* National Education Association, Oklahoma Education Association, Phi Beta Sigma, Phi Delta Kappa, Masons, Rotary.

WRITINGS: School Custodian Training Manual, with study guide, Bureau of Education Research and Services, University of Houston, 1954, 2nd edition, 1961; (with Ruth D. Heckler) *School Food Centers,* Ronald, 1960; *Effective School Maintenance,* Parker Publishing, 1969. Contributor of more than sixty articles to periodicals.

* * *

GERSHMAN, Herbert S. 1926-1971

PERSONAL: Born June 3, 1926, in Brooklyn, N.Y.; married Sally Tiesdell, 1956; children: Michael B., Diane L. *Education:* City College (now City College of the City University of New York), B.A., 1949; Free University of Brussels, Licence es Lettres, 1951; Washington University, St. Louis, Mo., Ph.D., 1953.

CAREER: Oberlin College, Oberlin, Ohio, instructor in

French, 1953-56; University of Missouri—Columbia, assistant professor, 1956-60, associate professor, 1960-65, professor of French, 1965-69, chairman of department of Romance languages, 1962-65; Washington University, St. Louis, Mo., professor of French, 1970-71. *Military service:* U.S. Army, 1944-46. *Member:* Modern Language Association of America, Linguistic Society of America, American Association of Teachers of French, Midwest Modern Language Association, Linguistic Circle of New York, Phi Beta Kappa. *Awards, honors:* Fulbright award to Belgium, 1949-50; American Council of Learned Societies grant to Linguistics Institute at University of Michigan, 1956; American Philosophical Society travel grant, 1960.

WRITINGS: (Compiler with K. B. Whitworth) *Anthology of Critical Prefaces to the Nineteenth-Century French Novel,* University of Missouri Press, 1962; *The Surrealist Revolution in France,* University of Michigan Press, 1969; *A Bibliography of the Surrealist Revolution in France,* University of Michigan Press, 1969. Contributor to *Yale French Studies, Italica, Books Abroad,* and other journals.

WORK IN PROGRESS: Nineteenth- and twentieth-century French literature.

AVOCATIONAL INTERESTS: Travel, swimming, tennis.

BIOGRAPHICAL/CRITICAL SOURCES: Saturday Review, May 31, 1969; *New York Times Book Review,* July 31, 1969.†

(Died March 31, 1971)

*   *   *

GERWIG, Anna Mary (Gerwig)   1907-

PERSONAL: Born August 22, 1907, in Wilkinsburg, Pa.; daughter of Frederick Henry Nicholas (executive of a blast furnace firm) and Agnes (Ferguson) Gerwig; married Frank Gerwig (an accountant for Pabst Brewing Co.), July 22, 1944 (deceased October, 1971). *Education:* Wellesley College, B.A., 1928; Columbia University, M.A., 1929; University of Pittsburgh, Ph.D., 1945. *Politics:* Republican. *Religion:* Presbyterian.

CAREER: Teacher of Latin and Spanish at Winchester-Thurston School, Pittsburgh, Pa., 1931-45, Latin School of Chicago, Chicago, Ill., 1947-59; Evanston Township High School, Evanston, Ill., teacher of Latin and chairman of department of classics, 1959-1971. *Member:* Classical Association of the Middle West and South, National Education Association, Illinois Classical Conference, Chicago Classical Association.

WRITINGS: How to Prepare for College Board Achievement Tests: Latin, Barron's, 1965. Has done translations of English dialogue into Latin for educational films produced by Encyclopaedia Britannica Films.

AVOCATIONAL INTERESTS: Golf, bridge, theater, art, and people.

BIOGRAPHICAL/CRITICAL SOURCES: Pittsburgh Post-Gazette, January 15, 1943.

*   *   *

GIBBONS, Euell (Theophilus)   1911-1975

PERSONAL: Given name rhymes with "jewel"; born September 8, 1911, in Clarksville, Tex.; son of Ely Joseph (a roamer who worked variously as a carpenter, blacksmith, grocer, rancher, and contractor) and Laura Agusta (Bowers) Gibbons; married Anna Swanson, September 12, 1935 (divorced); married Freda Fryer (a teacher), December 17, 1949; children: (first marriage) Ronald Euell, Michael Darian. *Education:* Studied at University of Hawaii, 1947-50, Temple University, part-time, 1953-54, and Pendle Hill (Quaker study center), part-time, 1955-60. *Politics:* Left-wing Democrat. *Religion:* Quaker. *Residence:* Beavertown, Pa. 17813.

CAREER: Left home at fifteen, working for the next five or six years as harvest hand, cowboy, carpenter, and trapper in Texas and New Mexico; hopped a freight for California in 1933, lived at times in hobo camps, and was a laborer in a San Jose can company before enlisting in the Army, 1934-36; when Army hitch ended, had various jobs in Washington State, then joined the Communist Party and became a district organizer (resigned from party after Soviets attacked Finland in 1939); civilian boat builder with U.S. Navy at Pearl Harbor during World War II; failing as a private boat-building contractor in the latter days of the war, he turned beachcomber, living in a thatched hut in Hawaii and subsisting on foraged wild food, 1945-47; entered University of Hawaii as a freshman at age thirty-six, working at the same time for the *Honolulu Advertiser,* 1947-50; teacher of carpentry and boat building at Maui Vocational School, Wailuku, Hawaii, 1951-53, and teacher at a Quaker school in Moorestown, N.J., 1953-54; farmer in Greenfield, Ind., 1954-55, as co-founder of an agricultural cooperative community that subsequently failed; member of buildings and grounds staff at Pendle Hill, Wallingford, Pa., 1955-60, also taking courses at the study center those years; full-time writer, 1960-75. Professional lecturer. *Member:* Academy of Natural Sciences, Wildlife Federation, Nature Study Association. *Awards, honors:* Banks Memorial Award, University of Hawaii, 1948; D.Sc., Susquehanna University, 1972.

WRITINGS: Stalking the Wild Asparagus (see also below), McKay, 1962; *Stalking the Blue-Eyed Scallop* (see also below), McKay, 1964; *Stalking the Healthful Herbs* (see also below), McKay, 1966; *Euell Gibbons' Beachcomber's Handbook,* McKay, 1967; (with brother, Joe Gibbons) *Feast on a Diabetic Diet,* McKay, 1969, 2nd revised edition, Fawcett, 1974; *Stalking the Good Life: My Love Affair with Nature* (illustrated by wife, Freda Gibbons), McKay, 1971; *Stalking the Faraway Places,* McKay, 1973; *The Ewell Gibbons Stalking Library* (includes *Stalking the Wild Asparagus, Stalking the Blue-Eyed Scallop,* and *Stalking the Healthful Herbs*), McKay, 1975. Nature editor and monthly columnist, *Organic Gardening and Farming;* contributor of poetry to *Friends Journal,* and what he terms "biological verse" (prose) to *Frontiers.*

SIDELIGHTS: "My career is a bit hairy," Gibbons told *CA,* "as I have been a job-hopper and wanderer. . . . Although I received less than 6 years formal schooling, and had never been in high school at all, I easily passed the requirements for a high school diploma from McKinley Adult High School in Honolulu, receiving the diploma after three weeks of testing. All my life I studied and wrote, no matter what else I was doing at the time . . . [and] sought out material on ethnobotany from nearby universities and libraries, besides reading all the journals and reports of early explorers that I could lay my hands on, searching for material on the culture of the aborigines, especially their cuisine and even more especially, the wild plants they made use of for food or crafts."

The unpublished writing that Gibbons did through the years—sonnets, short stories, and novel outlines—now is in the Euell Gibbons Collection at Boston University Library. While his wife supported him by teaching school, he spent a year producing a novel about a schoolteacher in the world of wild food, then worked another year transforming the non-selling novel into nonfiction and his first success, *Stalking the Wild Asparagus.*

Gibbons' mother and maternal grandmother both were self-taught naturalists with great interest in wild foods; as a boy he concocted wild food recipes, and once kept the family alive on foraged food for several weeks when the father was away looking for work. According to John McPhee, who made a six-day living-off-the-land trip with Gibbons and wrote about it for the *New Yorker,* Gibbons gathers, cooks, and eats everything he writes about. Gibbons received national exposure through a television cereal commercial and appearances on talk shows. The Gibbons named their home near Beavertown, Pa., "It Wonders Me."

BIOGRAPHICAL/CRITICAL SOURCES: Harper's Bazaar, February, 1964; *Saturday Evening Post,* July 25, 1964; *Life,* September 23, 1966; John McPhee, "A Forager" (Profiles), *New Yorker,* April 6, 1968.

(Died December 29, 1975)

*   *   *

GIBBS, Anthony   1902-1975

PERSONAL: Born March 9, 1902, in Bolton, England; son of Sir Philip (a journalist and novelist) and Agnes (Rowland) Gibbs; married Ysobel Maisie Martin, September 15, 1928; children: Philip Martin, Frances Jocelyn (Mrs. Ian McElwaine). *Education:* Attended Stonyhurst College, Blackburn, England, 1918, Royal Academy of Music, 1919, and Oxford University, 1920. *Politics:* Ex-Liberal. *Religion:* Ex-Roman Catholic. *Home:* Spurfold House, Peaslake, Surrey GU5 952, England. *Agent:* Curtis Brown Ltd., 1 Craven Hill, London W2 3EW, England.

CAREER: Gibbs was exposed at an early age to the literary celebrities of the day, due to his famous father, whom he sometimes accompanied on journalistic trips; his own career as a novelist was punctuated with such side excursions as London correspondent for the *New Yorker,* 1929, script writer in California for Twentieth Century-Fox, war correspondent, 1939 ("actual combat neatly avoided"), and parliamentary candidate, 1945; following the war he "became immersed" in publishing, serving as director of Allan Wingate Ltd., London, 1948-57, and of Anthony Gibbs & Phillips Ltd., Anthony Gibbs (Publishers) Ltd., and Library Reprints Ltd.; he also founded Tandem Books (paperbacks), 1965, and later sold out to Universal Publishing & Distributing Co., New York.

WRITINGS—Novels, except as noted: *Peter Vacuum,* Dial, 1925 (published in England as *Little Peter Vacuum,* Hutchinson, 1925); *The Elder Brother,* Dial, 1926; *High Endeavour,* Hutchinson, 1927; *Enter the Greek,* Harper, 1928 (published in England as *Enter—a Greek,* Hutchinson, 1928); *Young Apollo,* Harper, 1929; *Heydey,* Doubleday, 1931; *The New Crusade,* Hutchinson, 1931, Doubleday, 1932; *London Symphony,* Hutchinson, 1934; *The Dramatist,* Doubleday, 1935; (with uncle, Cosmo Hamilton) *The Aunt of England* (three-act play; first produced on the West End at Savoy Theatre, 1938), Samuel French, 1935; *Uncle Lazarus and Other Stories* (short stories), Hutchinson, 1936; *Royal Exchange: The Gay Adventures of Prince Heinrich in the Land of the Upper Lower Middle Classes,* Hutchinson, 1938; *Restoration Comedy,* Hutchinson, 1939; *Here Lies To-Morrow,* Laurie, 1949; *Daybreak,* Laurie, 1950; *Gibbs and the Phoney War* (autobiographical), Dawnay, 1967; *In My Own Good Time* (autobiographical), P. Davies, 1969,

Gambit, 1970; *Oh My God, Is That You?,* Wingate, 1972; *A Passion for Cars,* David & Charles, 1974.

Film scripts for Alexander Korda: "Private Life of Henry VIII," United Artists, 1933; "Men of Tomorrow," Munda, 1935; "Return of the Scarlet Pimpernel," United Artists, 1938. Also author of "Cash." Regular contributor of stories to *Nash's Magazine.*

SIDELIGHTS: In My Own Good Time, which Anthony Gibbs called "cynical autobiography," includes an account of his triumphs and disasters in America, when he was trying to sway U.S. sentiment towards Britain's war cause. According to the American publisher, the autobiography was written in three installments: the first on the Kordas was sold as a magazine serial, but withdrawn when it was threatened with sixteen libel actions; the war section was censored by Anthony Eden; the third section was written after the termination of Gibbs's association with the Wingate publishing house.

British critics found *In My Own Good Time* "brilliantly amusing" and "a most lively, witty relaxed piece of writing." But Gibbs said: "Like all superficially lighthearted people, I am a glutton for punishment within. My view of the world at the moment is that science has now made FAITH impossible, and that when organized religion goes out the window, civilizations historically founded on, say, the Christian ethic, are bound to collapse from the inside.... The cure could be to found an ethic, not on faith but on observable fact. I think we know enough, now, to do this. But who am I?"

Gibbs lived in Massachusetts for two years, and for one in Westwood, Calif. He took out first papers for American citizenship, but "was persuaded back [to England] by parents and wife's parents. Both glad and sorry." He traveled extensively in all European countries except Russia, and in Canada and the United States.

BIOGRAPHICAL/CRITICAL SOURCES—Autobiographies: *Gibbs and the Phoney War,* Dawnay, 1967; *In My Own Good Time,* P. Davies, 1969, Gambit, 1970.†

(Died March 11, 1975)

*   *   *

GIBBS, William E.   1936-19(?)

PERSONAL: Born March 6, 1936, in Asheville, N.C.; son of Preston E. (an accountant) and Lyda (Magee) Gibbs; married Patricia R. Phillips (a teacher), August 13, 1960; children: Jeffrey Stephen, Lezlie Suzanne, Lauren Michele. *Education:* Long Beach State College (now California State University, Long Beach), B.S., 1959.

CAREER: Excelsior High School, Norwalk, Calif., teacher of business education, 1961-66; California State College, Los Angeles (now California State University, Los Angeles), assistant supervisor of directed teaching, 1967; University of California, Los Angeles, associate in education, 1967-68. *Military service:* U.S. Naval Reserve, 1953-61. *Member:* California Business Education Association.

WRITINGS: Basic Rules of Alphabetic Filing (programmed instruction), South-Western, 1965. Contributor of articles on programmed instruction to professional journals.

WORK IN PROGRESS: The Basic Bookkeeping Cycle, for South-Western.†

(Deceased)

GIERGIELEWICZ, Mieczyslaw
(Feliks Bielski, M. G.)

PERSONAL: Born in Poland; son of Julian and Zenobia (Bielska) Giergielewicz; married Ewa Telichowska, April 14, 1950 (deceased, 1974); children: Christine. *Education:* University of Warsaw, B.A., M.A., Ph.D., the last in 1930. *Office:* Department of Slavic Languages and Literature, University of Pennsylvania, Philadelphia, Pa. 19104.

CAREER: Gebethner & Wolff (publishers), Warsaw, Poland, editorial director, 1938-39; Polish University in Exile, London, England, professor of Slavic and poetics, beginning 1952; Alliance College, Cambridge Springs, Pa., professor of Slavic, 1957-58; University of California, Berkeley, lecturer in Polish and Slavic literature, 1958-59; University of Pennsylvania, Philadelphia, professor of Polish and Slavic literature, beginning 1959. *Member:* Polish Society of Arts and Sciences Abroad (London), Shevchenko Ukrainian Scientific Society (New York), American Association for the Advancement of Slavic Studies, Polish Institute of Arts and Sciences in America, American Association of Slavic and East European Languages, Polish Heritage Society of Philadelphia.

WRITINGS: O nowej ortografii (title means "On the New Polish Spelling"), [Warsaw], 1936; *Technika popularyzacji,* [London], 1944; *Drogi Mickiewicza* (title means "Ways of Mickiewicz"), [London], 1945; (editor) Cyprian Kamil Norwid, *Laur dojrzaly* (poems and tales), [London], 1946; (editor) Juliusz Slowacki, *Poematy* (narrative poems), Volume I, [London], 1947; (editor) Slowacki, *Wiersze wybrane* (lyrical poems), [London], 1947; (editor) Slowacki, *Balladyna,* [London], 1947; (editor) Antoni Malczewski, *Maria,* [London], 1947; *Element prawa w tworczosci Slowackiego* (title means "Element of Law in Slowacki's Poetry"), [London], 1951; *Zarys kultury polskiej 1918-1953* (title means "Outline of Polish Culture 1918-1953"), [London], 1953; *Obraz tworczosci Adama Mickiewicza* (title means "Outline of Mickiewicz's Poetic Heritage"), [London], 1955; *Rym i wiersz* (title means "Rhyme and Verse"), [London], 1957; *Gastronomia Mickiewicza i jej rodowod literacki,* [London], 1958; *Prus-Goncharov,* [The Hague], 1964; *Henryk Sienkiewicz's American Resonance,* [Rome], 1966; *Henryk Sienkiewicz,* Twayne, 1968; *Introduction to Polish Versification,* University of Pennsylvania Press, 1970.

Contributor: Herminia Naglerowa, editor, *Wyspianski zywy,* [London], 1957; Wladyslaw Gunther, editor, *Krasinski zywy,* [London], 1959; Gunther, editor, *Norwid zywy,* [London], 1962; *U Stolittya Smerti Tarasa Shevchenka,* [Philadelphia], 1962; Waclaw Lednicki and others, editors, *Zygmunt Krasinski, Romantic Universalist,* Mouton & Co., 1964; *Literatura polska na obczyznie,* [London], 1964; Gunther, editor, *Sienkiewicz zyy,* [London], 1967; Kazimierz Sowinski and Tymon Terlecki, editors, *O Tadeuszu Sulkowskim,* [London], 1967. Also contributor to *Studies in Russian and Polish Literature,* edited by Z. Folejewski, 1962. Contributor of articles, sketches, epigrams, reviews, and translations to many publications.

WORK IN PROGRESS: Preparation of collective volume, *Major Problems of Polish Social Life and Culture;* research on structural problems in the novels of H. Sienkiewicz; study of the opera "Ostrolenka" by the German composer J. H. Bonawitz.

SIDELIGHTS: An historian of Polish literature, Giergielewicz is most interested in comparative research. Languages used in his writings include Polish, Russian, French, German, Ukrainian, Spanish, Italian, and Byelorussian. He has traveled widely in Europe and Canada in connection with his studies and attended international meetings of scholars, including the Congress of Slavists in Sofia, Bulgaria, in 1963.

AVOCATIONAL INTERESTS: Chess.

* * *

GIFFORD, Edward S(tewart), Jr. 1907-

PERSONAL: Born October 10, 1907, in Philadelphia, Pa.; son of Edward Stewart (a physician) and Emma (Ruff) Gifford; married Virginia Mason (an artist), June 8, 1931; children: George Mason. *Education:* University of Pennsylvania, A.B., 1930, M.D., 1933. *Politics:* Independent. *Religion:* "No affiliation." *Home and office:* 1913 Spruce St., Philadelphia, Pa. 19103.

CAREER: Certified ophthalmologist, 1940; Frankford Hospital, Philadelphia, Pa., intern, 1933-34; Woman's Hospital, Philadelphia, Pa., consulting ophthalmologist, 1948-63; University of Pennsylvania, Philadelphia, assistant professor of ophthalmology, beginning 1952; Pennsylvania Hospital, Philadelphia, chief ophthalmologist, 1954-1973, consulting ophthalmologist, beginning 1973. *Member:* American Medical Association, Academy of Ophthalmology and Otolaryngology, Philadelphia College of Physicians, Franklin Inn Club, Philadelphia Art Alliance. *Awards, honors:* Philadelphia Athenaeum Literary Award, 1967, for *Father Against the Devil.*

WRITINGS: The Evil Eye: Studies in the Folklore of Vision, Macmillan, 1958; *The Charms of Love,* Doubleday, 1962; *Father Against the Devil,* Doubleday, 1966.

WORK IN PROGRESS: Philadelphia Takes the British, 1777-1778.

* * *

GILLETT, Mary (Bledsoe)

PERSONAL: Born in Jefferson, N.C.; daughter of John Tyrrell (a farmer) and Sara Jane (Tulbert) Bledsoe; married Rupert Gillett (an editorial writer), October 5, 1926; children: John Bledsoe, Jane (Mrs. Louis Estes). *Education:* University of Texas, B.A., 1920. *Politics:* Republican. *Religion:* Episcopalian. *Agent:* Lenninger Literary Agency, 437 Fifth Ave., New York, N.Y. 10016.

CAREER: San Antonio Express, San Antonio, Tex., reporter, 1920-21; Library of Congress, Washington, D.C., cataloguer, 1921-22; *Richmond News Leader,* Richmond, Va., feature writer, 1922-24; publicity staff member, Chesapeake & Ohio Railroad, 1924-26; Ayer & Gillett (advertising), Charlotte, N.C., vice-president and head copywriter, 1953-63. Member of board, Charlotte Symphony Orchestra, 1953, and Charlotte Nature Museum, 1959-62. *Awards, honors:* American Association of University Women (North Carolina Division), Juvenile Award, 1969, for *Bugles at the Border.*

WRITINGS: Shadows Slant North (adult novel), Lothrop, 1937; *Bugles at the Border* (juvenile novel), Blair, 1968. Also editor of two juvenile anthologies, *Child Life Reader,* for Rand McNally, and *Read Aloud Stories.*

WORK IN PROGRESS: A historical book for girls, *Goodbye, Blue Mountains;* a historical novel for boys, *Musketeers of Alamogardo.*†

GILLIES, Mary Davis   1900-

PERSONAL: Born May 1, 1900, in Partridge, Kan.; daughter of Robert A. L. (a businessman) and Harriet (Rehm) Davis; married Robert C. Gillies, May 5, 1929 (divorced, 1938); married Joseph E. Johnston, July 14, 1940. *Education:* University of Washington, Seattle, B.S., 1924, M.A., 1925. *Religion:* Protestant. *Home:* 444 South State St., Apt. 209, Bellingham, Wash. 98225. *Agent:* Lucy Goldthwaite, 67 Martinique, Tampa, Fla. 33606.

CAREER: University of Oregon, Eugene, instructor in applied design, 1925-26; U.S. Department of Agriculture, Bureau of Home Economics, Washington, D.C., writer in Textile Division, 1927-28; Gardner Advertising Agency, New York City, account executive, 1928-29; *McCall's,* New York City, decorating and building editor, 1929-67; decorating consultant and lecturer, beginning 1967. Consultant to Alderman Studios and Allied Chemical Co. *Member:* National Society of Interior Designers, Fashion Group, National Home Fashions League (president, 1956), Authors League of America. *Awards, honors:* Dorothy Daw Award of National Association of Furniture Manufacturers, 1948, 1954, 1961; Gold Medal of Freedoms Foundation for instigating Yardsville U.S.A. and community clean-up campaign, 1949.

WRITINGS: Popular Home Decoration, William H. Wise, 1940, revised edition, 1948; *All About Modern Decorating,* Harper, 1948; *How to Keep House,* Harper, 1948, revised edition, 1968; *McCall's Book of Modern Houses,* Simon & Schuster, 1951, revised edition, 1958; *McCall's Decorating Book,* Random House, 1964.

WORK IN PROGRESS: Interior Design for the 70's.

SIDELIGHTS: As the decorating editor of *McCall's,* Mary Davis Gillies originated the magazine's Congress on Better Living and its conference technique of gathering information on what women really want in their homes; almost a million women entered the various building and home decorating contests she developed.

AVOCATIONAL INTERESTS: Travel, painting, a wildflower garden.

*   *   *

GILLMOR, Frances   1903-

PERSONAL: Born May 21, 1903, in Buffalo, N.Y.; daughter of Abner Churchill (a businessman) and Annie (McVicar) Gillmor. *Education:* Attended University of Chicago, 1921-23; University of Arizona, B.A., 1928, M.A., 1931; graduate study at Indiana University, 1946, National School of Anthropology and History, Mexico, 1952; National University of Mexico, Doctora en Letras, 1957. *Politics:* Democrat. *Religion:* Episcopalian. *Address:* Box 4605, Tucson, Ariz. 81717.

CAREER: University of New Mexico, Albuquerque, instructor in English, 1932-34; University of Arizona, Tucson, assistant professor, 1934-44, associate professor, 1944-52, professor of English, 1952-73, became professor emeritus, 1973, chairman of university folklore committee and director of Folklore Archive, 1943-73. *Member:* American Folklore Society (fellow; vice-president, 1958, 1964), American Anthropological Association (fellow), Modern Language Association of America, Authors League of America, Sociedad Folklorica de Mexico, Folklore Society (England), Arizona Pioneer and Historical Society, Phi Beta Kappa, Phi Kappa Phi. *Awards, honors:* Guggenheim fellowship for research in Spanish folk plays, 1959-60.

WRITINGS: Thumbcap Weir (novel; Book-of-the-Month Club alternate selection), Minton, Balch, 1929; *Windsinger* (novel), Minton, Balch, 1930; (with Louisa Wade Wetherill) *Traders to the Navajos,* Houghton, 1934; *Fruit Out of the Rock* (novel), Duell, Sloan & Pearce, 1940; *Flute of the Smoking Mirror* (biography of Nezahualcoyotl), University of New Mexico Press, 1949; *The King Danced in the Market Place* (biography of Moteczuma Ilhuicamina), University of Arizona Press, 1964.

Also author of book-length publications of Spanish texts of dance dramas of Mexican villages, University of Arizona, 1942, and English summary, 1943. Contributor of short stories to *Mademoiselle* and *Southwest Review,* articles to *Tomorrow, Forth, Journal of American Folklore,* Mexican and Brazilian journals, and Southwest quarterlies, and more than sixty reviews to *Journal of American Folklore, Arizona Quarterly, Folk-Lore* (London), *Western Folklore,* and other journals.

WORK IN PROGRESS: A book on folk plays in Mexican and Spanish villages.

SIDELIGHTS: Ms. Gillmor travels in Spain and Mexico, gathering material and photographs on folk plays at village fiestas; also has done research in folklore archives of other European countries; competent in Spanish.

*   *   *

GINGERICH, Melvin   1902-1975

PERSONAL: Born January 29, 1902, in Kalona, Iowa; son of John (a farmer) and Lydia (Reber) Gingerich; married Verna Mae Roth, August 30, 1925; children: Owen Jay. *Education:* Goshen College, B.A., 1926; University of Iowa, M.A., 1930, Ph.D., 1938. *Religion:* Mennonite. *Home:* 405 Marilyn Ave., Goshen, Ind. 46526.

CAREER: High school teacher in Washington, Iowa, 1927-41; Bethel College, North Newton, Kan., assistant professor of history, 1941-47; Mennonite Research Foundation, Goshen, Ind., director of research, 1947-59; Mennonite Historical and Research Committee, Goshen, executive secretary, 1959-1970. Teacher of history, Washington Junior College, 1930-41; part-time professor of history, Goshen College, 1949-61. Worked for Mennonite Central Committee in Tokyo, Japan, 1955-57. Lecturer on Japan and other topics. *Member:* Society of American Archivists, State Historical Society of Iowa (life member).

WRITINGS: The Mennonites in Iowa, State Historical Society of Iowa, 1939; (assistant editor) *Who's Who among the Mennonites,* Bethel College Press, 1943; *Service for Peace,* Mennonite Central Committee, 1949; *Youth and Christian Citizenship,* Herald Press, 1949; *What of Noncombatant Service?,* Mennonite Central Committee, 1949; *The Christian and Revolution,* Herald Press, 1968; *Four Centuries of Mennonite Costume,* Pennsylvania German Society, 1970. Managing editor, *Mennonite Encyclopedia,* beginning 1948; editor, *Mennonite Historical Bulletin;* managing editor, *Mennonite Quarterly Review,* 1958-71; columnist, *Mennonite Weekly Review,* beginning 1942.†

(Died June 24, 1975)

*   *   *

GINGRICH, F(elix) Wilbur   1901-

PERSONAL: Born September 27, 1901, in Annville, Pa.; son of Felix Moyer (a minister) and Minnie (Shiffer) Gingrich; married Lola Engel, March 28, 1929; children: John W., Barbara Gingrich Stokes, Carol Sue (Mrs. Charles J.

Kaucher). *Education:* Lafayette College, A.B., 1923; University of Chicago, A.M., 1927, Ph.D., 1932. *Politics:* Republican. *Religion:* United Methodist. *Home:* 1502 North 12th St., Reading, Pa. 19604.

CAREER: Albright College, Reading, Pa., assistant professor of Latin and German, 1923-26, professor of Greek and Bible, 1927-55, professor of Greek, 1955-72, became professor emeritus, 1972. *Member:* Society of Biblical Literature, Pennsylvania German Society. *Awards, honors:* Lindback Award for distinguished teaching, 1965; G. W. Kidd Alumni Award, Lafayette College, 1971.

WRITINGS: (With E. H. Barth) *A History of Albright College, 1856-1956*, Albright College, 1956; (editor and translator with W. F. Arndt) *A Greek-English Lexicon of the New Testament*, University of Chicago Press, 1957; (editor) *A Shorter Lexicon of the Greek New Testament*, University of Chicago Press, 1965. Contributor to *Interpreter's Dictionary of the Bible;* also contributor to scholarly journals and other periodicals.

WORK IN PROGRESS: A revision of *A Greek-English Lexicon of the New Testament*.

*   *   *

GISOLFI, Anthony M. 1909-

PERSONAL: Born November 13, 1909, in San Felice, Italy; son of Ernest Edward and Vincenza (Prisco) Gisolfi; married Eleanor Hayes (a teacher), June 29, 1935. *Education:* City College (now City College of the City University of New York), A.B., 1930; Columbia University, A.M., 1931, Ph.D., 1959. *Home:* 25 Merriam Ave., Bronxville, N.Y. 10708. *Office:* State University of New York at Albany, Albany, N.Y. 12203.

CAREER: High School of Music and Art, New York, N.Y., teacher of Italian and Spanish, 1937-63; State University of New York at Albany, associate professor of Romance languages, beginning 1964. City College (now City College of the City University of New York), lecturer in Italian, Division of Adult Education, 1947-63; summer lecturer at Wellesley College, 1948, Columbia University, 1958-63. U.S. Office of War Information, Overseas Branch, regional specialist, in London, Rome, and Washington, D.C., 1943-45. *Member:* American Association of Teachers of Italian (vice-president, 1959-60), Modern Language Association of America, Dante Society of America.

WRITINGS: (With S. Colman) *Classical Italian Songs*, S. F. Vanni, 1955; *On Classic Ground: A Family Holiday in Italy*, Bookman Associates, 1962; *The Essential Matilde Serao*, Las Americas, 1968. Contributor to *Italica* and other journals.

*   *   *

GIUSEPPI, John (Anthony) 1900-

PERSONAL: Born July 23, 1900, in London, England; son of Montague Spencer (assistant keeper at Public Land Record Office) and Emilie Louise (Hardinge) Giuseppi; married Annie Matilda Willis, September 26, 1926; children: Gerald St. Aubyn, Joanna Mary (Mrs. C. J. Watkins). *Education:* Attended St. Paul's School, London, England, 1913-19 ("obtained scholarship in history at Lincoln College, Oxford, but was unable to take it up"). *Politics:* Conservative. *Religion:* Roman Catholic. *Home:* 19 Ember Lane, Esher, Surrey, England.

CAREER: Bank of England, London, 1921-60, archivist in charge of historical records, bank museum, and art collec-

tions, 1936-60. Co-opted member of Records and Antiquities Committee of Surrey County Council, 1962-74. *Military service:* Home Guard, 1940-44; became lieutenant. Army Cadet Corps, 1944-50; became captain. *Member:* Society of Antiquaries of London (fellow), Surrey Archaeological Society, Surrey Record Society.

WRITINGS: The Bank of England: A History From Its Foundation in 1694, Regnery, 1966. Contributor of monographs and articles to magazines and journals. Honorary editor, *Business Archives*, 1960-68.

*   *   *

GLICK, Virginia Kirkus 1893-
(Virginia Kirkus)

PERSONAL: Born December 7, 1893, in Meadville, Pa.; daughter of Frederick Maurice (a clergyman) and Isabella (Clark) Kirkus; married Frank Glick, June 4, 1936. *Education:* Vassar College, A.B., 1916; Columbia University, graduate study, 1917. *Politics:* Democrat. *Religion:* Episcopalian. *Residence:* Redding Ridge, Conn.

CAREER: Teacher of English and history, Wilmington, Del., 1917; *Pictorial Review*, New York City, editorial work in fashion; *McCall's*, New York City, back-of-the-book editor; Harper & Brothers, New York City, head of children's book department, 1926-32; Virginia Kirkus Service, Inc., New York City, president, 1933-62. During World War II served on Booksellers Authority, Washington, D.C., and on selection board for Armed Services Editions. President of Mark Twain Library, 1953-54; member of Connecticut Governor's Commission on Rural Libraries, 1961-64. *Member:* American Library Association, P.E.N. (New York board member, 1962-65), League of Women Voters, Vassar Club (Fairfield County, Conn.).

WRITINGS: A House for the Weekends, Little, Brown, 1945; (under name Virginia Kirkus) *The First Book of Gardening*, F. Watts, 1956, revised edition, 1976. Frequent contributor of feature articles to *Saturday Review*.

WORK IN PROGRESS: Round the World at 70.

*   *   *

GLIDDEN, Frederick D(illey) 1908-1975
(Luke Short)

PERSONAL: Born 1908, in Kewanee, Ill.; son of Wallace Dilley and Fannie Mae (Hurff) Glidden; married Florence Elder, 1934; children: James (deceased), Kate Hirson, Daniel. *Education:* University of Missouri, degree in journalism, 1930. *Agent:* H. N. Swanson, 8523 Sunset Blvd., Los Angeles, Calif. 90069. *Office address:* Box 356, Aspen, Colo.

CAREER: Began career as a newspaperman ("I've read or heard that all newspapermen are disappointed writers, but in me you behold a writer who is a disappointed newspaperman. I've been fired from more newspapers than I like to remember, even if I could"); spent two years in Northern Canada as a trapper; helped form a thorium corporation in Colorado, 1955. *Awards, honors:* Western Writers of America Levi Strauss Golden Saddleman Award, 1969; National Cowboy Hall of Fame and Western Heritage Center, Western Heritage Award, 1974.

*WRITINGS—*Under pseudonym Luke Short: *The Feud at Single Shot*, Farrar & Rinehart, 1936; *Man on the Blue*, Dell, 1937, reprinted, 1975; *King Colt*, Bantam, 1937, reprinted, Dell, 1975; *Guns of the Double Diamond*, Collins, 1937; *Marauder's Moon*, Dell, 1937; *Bull-Foot Ambush*,

Collins, 1938; *Misery Lode,* Collins, 1938; *The Branded Man,* Dell, 1938 (published in serial form in *Adventure* magazine, under title "Rustler's Range"); *Weary Range,* Collins, 1939; *Six Guns of San Jon,* Collins, 1939; *Gold Rustlers,* Collins, 1939; *Raiders of the Rimrock,* Doubleday, 1939; *Flood Water,* Collins, 1939, published as *Hard Money,* Doubleday, 1940.

Bounty Guns, Collins, 1940; *Brand of Empire,* Collins, 1940; *War on Cimarron,* Doubleday, 1940 (published in England as *Hurricane Range,* Collins, 1940), reprinted, Bantam, 1975; *Bought with a Gun,* Dell, 1940; *Dead Freight for Piute,* Doubleday, 1940 (published in England as *Western Freight,* Collins, 1941); *Gunman's Chance,* Doubleday, 1941 (first serialized in *Saturday Evening Post,* under title "Blood on the Moon," March 15-April 26, 1941; published in England as *Blood on the Moon,* Collins, 1943); *Ride the Man Down,* Doubleday, 1942 (serialized in *Saturday Evening Post,* April 4-May 16, 1942), reprinted, Bantam, 1975; *Hardcase,* Doubleday, 1942; *Sunset Graze,* Doubleday, 1942; *Ramrod,* Macmillan, 1943 (serialized in *Saturday Evening Post,* March 27-May 8, 1943), reprinted, Popular Library, 1969; *Gauntlet of Fire,* Collins, 1944; *And the Wind Blows Free,* Macmillan, 1945; *Coroner Creek,* Macmillan, 1946 (serialized in *Saturday Evening Post,* May 19-July 7, 1945), reprinted, Bantam, 1975; *Fiddlefoot,* Houghton, 1946 (serialized in *Saturday Evening Post,* March 2-April 13, 1946); *Station West,* Houghton, 1946 (serialized in *Saturday Evening Post,* October 19-November 30, 1946); *High Vermillion,* Houghton, 1948 (serialized in *Saturday Evening Post,* May 31-July 5, 1947), reprinted, Bantam, 1972; *Ambush,* Houghton, 1949 (serialized in *Saturday Evening Post,* December 25, 1948-February 12, 1949).

Play a Lone Hand, Houghton, 1950 (serialized in *Collier's,* November 4-December 9, 1950); *Vengeance Valley,* Houghton, 1950 (serialized in *Saturday Evening Post,* December 3, 1949-January 14, 1950); *Barren Land Murders,* Fawcett, 1951 (serialized in *Adventure* magazine under title "Spy of the North"); *The Whip,* Bantam, 1951 (serialized in *Collier's* and *Saturday Evening Post,* under title "Doom Cliff"); *Saddle by Starlight,* Houghton, 1952, reprinted, Bantam, 1975; *Silver Rock,* Houghton, 1953 (serialized in *Collier's,* August 21-October 2, 1953); *Rimrock,* Random House, 1955 (serialized in *Saturday Evening Post,* under title "Fool's Treasure," April 16-May 28, 1955), reprinted, Bantam, 1974; (contributor) *Riders West,* Dell, 1956; (editor) *Colt's Law,* Bantam, 1968; (editor) *Rawhide and Bobwire,* Bantam, 1958.

First Claim, Hammond, Hammond, 1961; *Last Hunt,* Hammond, Hammond, 1963; *Desert Crossing,* Hammond, Hammond, 1963; *The Some-Day Country,* Bantam, 1964; *First Campaign,* Bantam, 1964; *Trigger Country,* Hammond, Hammond, 1965; *Paper Sheriff,* Bantam, 1966; *Savage Range,* Bantam, 1966; *Primrose Try,* Bantam, 1967; *Guns of Hanging Lake,* Bantam, 1968; *Donovan's Gun,* Bantam, 1968.

The Outrider, Bantam, 1972; *The Stalkers,* Bantam, 1973; *The Man From Two Rivers,* Bantam, 1974; *Savage Range,* Bantam, 1974; *Barren Land Showdown,* Fawcett World, 1974; *The Man with a Summer Name,* Bantam, 1974; *The Deserters,* Bantam, 1975; *Bold Rider,* Dell, 1975; *Trouble Country,* Bantam, 1976.

WORK IN PROGRESS: Sunset Gaze, for Bantam.

SIDELIGHTS: Glidden was considered a leader in western fiction. His brother, Jonathan Glidden, who wrote under the pseudonym Peter Dawson, had also achieved success in this

field before his death in 1957. G. W. Harris, who praised Short's versatility in a review of *Dead Freight for Piute,* said of *Ride the Man Down:* "A complicated but lively story, filled with swift action, suspense, violence and bloodshed. And it is cleverly plotted and well written, with the sure skill that Luke Short has shown in half a dozen earlier excellent westerns." His scenes, setting, and plot varied from the early cowboy to modern western detective. Early travels and an extended stay in New Mexico before settling in Colorado supplied some of the scenery. Glidden successfully avoided publicity for years and with seeming modesty wrote this preface to a serial in *Saturday Evening Post,* "When I remember that the *Post* audience has been brought up on the western stories of Eugene Manlove Rhodes, I have an impulse to duck."

Many of Glidden's books have been adapted for movies, including *Ramrod,* released by United Artists Corp. under the same title in 1947. Paramount Pictures adapted *Dead Freight for Piute* for the movie "Albuquerque," in 1948, and *High Vermillion* for the movie "Silver City," in 1951. RKO released two movies, "Blood on the Moon" and "Station West," in 1948 based on Glidden's books of the same name; Columbia Pictures Corp. produced "Coroner Creek" the same year. The titles *Ambush,* and *Vengeance Valley* were retained for two movies released by Metro-Goldwyn Mayer in 1950 and 1951, respectively. Republic released "Ride the Man Down," in 1952, and "Hell's Outpost," based on *Silver Rock,* in 1955.

BIOGRAPHICAL/CRITICAL SOURCES: New York Times Book Review, February 9, 1941, January 24, 1943; *Saturday Evening Post,* March 15, 1941; *Chicago Sunday Tribune,* January 11, 1953.†

(Died August 18, 1975)

* * *

GLUECK, Eleanor T(ouroff) 1898-1972

PERSONAL: Surname is pronounced to rhyme with "book"; born April 12, 1898, in New York, N.Y.; daughter of Bernard L. (an industrialist) and Anna (Wodzislawski) Touroff; married Sheldon Glueck (Roscoe Pound Professor Emeritus of Law, Harvard University), April 16, 1922; children: Joyce Glueck Rosberg (deceased). *Education:* Barnard College, A.B., 1920; New York School of Social Work, diploma, 1921; Harvard University, Ed.M., 1923, Ed.D., 1925. *Politics:* Independent. *Religion:* Jewish. *Office:* Westengard House, 3 Garden St., Cambridge, Mass. 02138.

CAREER: Dorchester (Mass.) Welfare Center, head social worker, 1921-22; Harvard University, Cambridge, Mass., researcher in criminology in department of social ethics, 1925-28, research assistant in criminology, Law School, 1929-53, research associate, Law School, 1953-64, and co-director of Research Project into the Causes, Treatment and Prevention of Juvenile Delinquency, 1929-64. Technical consultant, White House Conference on Children and Youth, 1960; member of delinquency committee, American Medical Association Conference on Mental Health, 1961; member, Massachusetts State Committee on Action for Mental Health, 1962; trustee and member of executive committee, Judge Baker Guidance Center, Boston, Mass.

MEMBER: American Academy of Arts and Sciences (fellow), American Society of Criminology, National Association of Social Workers, National Conference of Social Welfare, American Association of University Women, International Society of Criminology, International Conference of Social Work, International Society of Social Defense, World Federation for Mental Health, Medical Correctional Association, United Prison Association (member of corporation), German Society of Criminology, League of Women Voters.

AWARDS, HONORS—All except honorary degree are joint awards shared with husband, Sheldon Glueck: Herbert C. Parsons Memorial Award of United Prison Association of Massachusetts, 1946; Distinguished Service Award, Boston Juvenile Court, 1952; S.D. from Harvard University, 1958; August Vollmer Award of American Society of Criminology, 1961; Special Gold Medal, Institute of Criminal Anthropology, University of Rome, 1964; First Beccaria Gold Medal of German Society of Criminology, 1964.

WRITINGS: The Community Use of Schools, Williams & Wilkins, 1927; *Extended Use of School Buildings,* U.S. Government Printing Office, 1927; *Evaluative Research in Social Work,* Columbia University Press, 1936; *The Gluecks' Adventure in Japan,* Obun (Japan), 1962.

With husband, Sheldon Glueck: *Five Hundred Criminal Careers,* Knopf, 1930; *One Thousand Juvenile Delinquents,* Harvard University Press, 1934; *Five Hundred Delinquent Women,* Knopf, 1934; (editor) *Preventing Crime: A Symposium,* McGraw, 1936; *Later Criminal Careers,* Commonwealth Fund-Oxford University Press, 1937; *Juvenile Delinquents Grown Up,* Commonwealth Fund-Oxford University Press, 1940; *Criminal Careers in Retrospect,* Commonwealth Fund-Oxford University Press, 1943; *After-Conduct of Discharged Offenders,* Macmillan, 1944; *Unraveling Juvenile Delinquency,* Commonwealth Fund-Harvard University Press, 1950; *Delinquents in the Making,* Harper, 1952; *Physique and Delinquency,* Harper, 1956; *Predicting Delinquency and Crime,* Harvard University Press, 1959; *Family Environment and Delinquency,* Houghton, 1962; *Ventures in Criminology,* Tavistock Publications, 1964; *Delinquents and Non-Delinquents in Perspective,* Harvard University Press, 1968. Also author of *Toward a Topology of Juvenile Offenders,* 1970.

Contributor of monographs and articles to professional journals. Former member of advisory editorial board, *International Journal of Social Psychiatry* and *Psychiatric Opinion.*

BIOGRAPHICAL/CRITICAL SOURCES: Saturday Review, April 6, 1963; *U.S. News & World Report,* April 25, 1965; *Pictorial Living* (Sunday supplement to *Boston Advertiser*), June 13, 1965.†

(Died September 25, 1972)

*   *   *

GLUECK, Nelson   1900-1971

PERSONAL: Surname is pronounced Glick; born June 4, 1900, in Cincinnati, Ohio; son of Morris and Anna (Rubin) Glueck; married Helen Iglauer (a physician), March 26, 1931; children: Charles Jonathan. *Education:* Hebrew Union College (now Hebrew Union College-Jewish Institute of Religion), Cincinnati, Ohio, B.H.L., 1918, Rabbi, 1923; University of Cincinnati, A.B., 1920; University of Jena, Ph.D., 1926. *Politics:* Democrat. *Home:* 162 Glenmary Ave., Cincinnati, Ohio 45220. *Office:* Hebrew Union College-Jewish Institute of Religion, 3101 Clifton Ave., Cincinnati, Ohio 45220.

CAREER: American School of Oriental Research, Jerusalem, Palestine, Morgenthau fellow, 1928-29; Hebrew Union College (now Hebrew Union College-Jewish Institute of Religion), Cincinnati, Ohio, instructor, 1929-31, assistant professor, 1932-33, associate professor, 1934-35, professor

of Bible and biblical archaeology, 1936-71, president, 1947-50 (also president of Jewish Institute of Religion, New York, 1949-50); Hebrew Union College-Jewish Institute of Religion, Cincinnati, Los Angeles, New York, and Jerusalem, president, 1950-1971. University of Cincinnati, lecturer on biblical literature, 1932-36; American Schools of Oriental Research, director in Jerusalem, 1932-33, 1936-40, 1942-47, annual professor in Baghdad, 1933-34, and field director in Baghdad, 1942-47. Director of archaeological excavations at Khirbet Tannur and Tell-el-Kheleifeh, and member of exploration and survey teams elsewhere in Palestine and Transjordan. Trustee of American Schools of Oriental Research, John F. Kennedy Memorial Library, and Cincinnati Art Museum. *Military service:* Office of Strategic Services, 1942-47.

MEMBER: American Philosophical Society, American Schools of Oriental Research, American Oriental Society, Archaeological Institute of America, Israel Exploration Society, Central Conference of American Rabbis, Phi Beta Kappa; Explorers Club and P.E.N. (both New York), Literary Club and University Club (both Cincinnati), Cosmos Club (Washington, D.C.), Harvard Club (Boston).

AWARDS, HONORS: Cincinnati Fine Arts Award, 1940; Ohioana Career Medal, 1956; Ohioana Book Award in nonfiction for *Rivers in the Desert,* 1960; selected to give benediction at inauguration of President John F. Kennedy, 1961, Ohio Governor's Award, 1965. Honorary degrees from University of Cincinnati, University of Pennsylvania, Miami University (Oxford, Ohio), Jewish Theological Seminary of America, Jewish Institute of Religion (now Hebrew Union College-Jewish Institute of Religion), Dropsie College, Lincoln College (Lincoln, Ill.), Delaware Valley College of Science and Agriculture, College of the Holy Cross, Kenyon College, Drake University, Brandeis University, Wayne State University, and New York University, 1936-65.

WRITINGS: Das Wort Hesed im alttestamentlichen Sprachgebrauche, A. Topelmann, 1927, translation by Alfred Gottschalk, published as *Hesed in the Bible,* Hebrew Union College Press, 1967; *The Other Side of the Jordan,* American Schools of Oriental Research, 1940; *The River Jordan,* Westminster, 1946; *Rivers in the Desert: A History of the Negev,* Farrar, Straus, 1959; *Deities and Dolphins: The Story of the Nabataeans,* Farrar, Straus, 1965; *Dateline: Jerusalem; A Diary,* Hebrew Union College Press, 1968; *Near Eastern Archaeology in the Twentieth Century,* Doubleday, 1970; (contributor) Hans Goedicke, editor, *Near Eastern Studies in Honor of William Foxwell Albright,* Johns Hopkins University Press, 1971. Author of *Explorations in Eastern Palestine* (annuals of American School of Oriental Research), Volume XIV, 1934, Volume XV, 1935, Volume XVIII-XIX, 1939, Volume XXV-XXVIII, 1951. Contributor of articles on archaeology and Bible to books, encyclopedias, and magazines.†

(Died February 12, 1971)

*   *   *

GO, Puan Seng   1904-

PERSONAL: Born July 28, 1904, in Amoy, China; son of Keng (a newspaper editor) and Kien Ti Go; married Felisa Velasco (general manager of *Fookien Times*), October 20, 1932; children: Betty (Mrs. Feliciano Belmonte, Jr.), Cecily (Mrs. David Chua Eoan), Dorcy (Mrs. Thomas Lam), Elsie (Mrs. Maoyeh Lu), Andrew Velasco, Grace (Mrs. Lu Beng Tek). *Education:* Attended a private school in Amoy,

China, 1909-18, and took English courses at National University, Manila, and Far Eastern University, Manila. *Religion:* Christian. *Home:* 385 Eulogio Rodriguez St., Quezon City, Philippines. *Agent:* Shirley Hector Agency, 29 West 46th St., New York, N.Y. 10036. *Office: Fookien Times,* 1117 Soler St., Manila, Philippines.

CAREER: Newspaperman, beginning 1925; Fookien Times Co., Inc. (newspaper publishers), Manila, Philippines, publisher and editor, beginning 1948. Member of executive board, International Press Institute, Zurich, Switzerland, beginning 1970. *Member:* National Press Club of the Philippines (charter member), Manila Overseas Press Club (past governor), Manila Rotary Club (member of board of directors, 1970-71), Manila Polo Club, Army & Navy Club, El Club Filipino, Baguio Country Club. *Awards, honors:* Seniority in Journalism Award, National Press Club of the Philippines, 1958; Presidential Award of Merit, Junior Chamber of Commerce of the Philippines, 1965; honorary doctorate, Indian Christian University, 1973.

WRITINGS: Refuge and Strength, Prentice-Hall, 1970 (published in England as *Exile,* M. Joseph, 1970), published as *Jimmy Go,* Logos International, 1976.

SIDELIGHTS: Puan Seng Go, an elder in Chinese journalism, has visited the United States eight times since 1957, and has traveled from this country to Europe, the Middle East, and other parts of Asia. During the Japanese occupation of the Philippines there was a high price set on his head.

Go told *CA:* "My fight against aggression and for freedom before and during World War II were important motivating factors in my career as a newspaperman. I served twice on the Executive Committee of the International Press Institute (IPI) upholding the freedom of the Press."†

*   *   *

GODFREY, Henry F.   1906-1975

PERSONAL: Born October 22, 1906, in Hempstead, N.Y.; son of Henry Fletcher and Marie (Havemeyer) Godfrey; married Marie Louise Gray, June 15, 1929; children: Marie-Louise (Mrs. Lowell P. Weicker, Jr.), William Gray, Richard D. *Education:* Harvard University, A.B., 1929. *Politics:* Independent Democrat. *Religion:* Episcopalian. *Home:* 700 Arlington, DeLand, Fla. 32720 (winter); Water St., Marion, Mass. 02738 (summer). *Agent:* Anita Diamant, 51 East 42nd St., New York, N.Y. 10017.

CAREER: Clark-Hooper, Inc., New York City, executive vice-president, 1934-41; Schenley Distillers, New York City, advertising research manager, 1946-48; J. Walter Thompson Co., New York City, copy and media research director, 1948-56; Stetson University, DeLand, Fla., professor of business administration, 1956-63. *Military service:* U.S. Naval Reserve, active duty, 1941-46; became lieutenant commander. *Member:* Beverly Yacht Club (Marion, Mass.), Harvard Club of New York, Apawamis Club (Rye, N.Y.).

WRITINGS: Your Yucatan Guide, Funk, 1967; *Your El Salvador Guide,* Funk, 1968; *Your Central America Guide,* Funk, 1970.

WORK IN PROGRESS: Your Guatemala Guide, left uncompleted at time of death.

SIDELIGHTS: Henry Godfrey told *CA:* "Winters my wife and I travel extensively in Central America, whose lands we know and love. Summers are spent in research for forthcoming trips—and in sailing my small boat on Buzzards Bay. Original book (on Yucatan) sprang from research which

demonstrated that no decent guide to the area had been written since John Lloyd Stephens, . . . in 1841."†

(Died October 4, 1975)

*   *   *

GOEDERTIER, Joseph M.   1907-

PERSONAL: Born February 10, 1907, in Gijzegem, Belgium; son of Aloysius and Mary (Michielsen) Goedertier. *Education:* Attended Institute of Philosophy, Nijmegen, Netherlands, 1925-27, Institute of Theology, Louvain, Belgium, 1927-31, and Yale University, 1947; Columbia University, M.A., 1949. *Home:* 2-28-5 Matsubara Setagaya-Ku, 156 Tokyo, Japan.

CAREER: Roman Catholic priest. Did missionary work in Central Mongolia, 1931-46; missionary in Japan, beginning 1950. Professor of philosophy, Seishin University, Okayama, Japan, 1953-64.

WRITINGS: A Dictionary of Japanese History, Weatherhill, 1968. Also author of *Kulturele Geschiedenis van Japan,* Volume I: *Die Klassieke Letteren,* Volume II: *De Godsdiensten,* Volume III: *De Kunsten,* in Dutch, and *Wroeging* (short stories translated from the Chinese).

WORK IN PROGRESS: A Dictionary of Japanese Biographies.

*   *   *

GOERLING, Lars   1931-1966

PERSONAL: Born August 23, 1931, in Stockholm, Sweden; son of Roland and Elizabeth (Norstrom) Goerling; divorced; children: Ingrid Cecilia, Lars Anders. *Home and office:* Lyckebo, Jarna, Sweden.

CAREER: Author and movie producer.

WRITINGS: Triptyk (novel), Bonniers, 1961; *491* (novel), Bonniers, 1962, English translation by Anselm Hollo published as *491,* Grove, 1966; *Hela Apparaten* (novella), Bonniers, 1964. Author of two plays in Swedish, "Intrusion" and "All Ready for the Night," and of three filmscripts, including "491," Janus, 1966. Also author of several radio plays and one television drama.

WORK IN PROGRESS: A novel; two filmscripts.

SIDELIGHTS: R. E. Lindgren noted that Goerling "sprang into notoriety with *491,* an immediate best seller and popular film in Sweden. Its theme of alienation, a non-hero and an anti-novel, plus immediate consciousness of rutty juvenile gangs on Stockholm's streets attracted fascinated attention." Its title is derived from Matthew 18:21-25, wherein is related Jesus' dictum concerning the maximum number of times that a man may be forgiven: "Until seventy times seven." Therefore, the 491st sin becomes unforgivable. However, Gertrude Samuels commented that Goerling, "a dutiful detractor of mankind, throws into his nightmare of a novel more than one unforgivable sin." Miss Samuels said that the "brainless sadism" portrayed in the novel is unconvincing, and compares the book unfavorably to Golding's *Lord of the Flies.* "[Golding's children] could feel compassion and weep for the end of innocence. [Goerling's] one-dimensional delinquents are given no such saving grace. Man is evil; forgiveness is stupid." The *Times Literary Supplement* was equally unreceptive, explaining that Goerling "appears to have based his book upon a literary acquaintanceship ranging from the Marquis de Sade to Frank Harris, and written it in the prose of Mickey Spillane; amusing that the translator has been faithful to the original."

According to the *New York Times,* Goerling's first novel was extremely well-received in Sweden, and the author became known as "one of Sweden's angriest young men [who] often attacked authority in his works." He told *CA,* "I am 'one of a kind' in Sweden, and making my living off it." He added that he was "very interested in politics and 'social security.'"

The film version of *491* was extremely controversial—banned in several countries and heavily censored in others.

AVOCATIONAL INTERESTS: Traveling in Europe.

BIOGRAPHICAL/CRITICAL SOURCES: Saturday Review, July 23, 1966; *New York Times Book Review,* July 31, 1966; *New York Times,* August 3, 1966; *Times Literary Supplement,* November 24, 1966.††

(Died August 1, 1966)

* * *

GOLDBERG, M(ilton) A(llan) 1919-1970

PERSONAL: Born April 26, 1919, in Chicago, Ill.; son of Isadore and Marion (Rose) Goldberg; married Hannah Friedman (a professor of history), June 18, 1956; children: Lisa Rachel. *Education:* University of New Mexico, A.B. (with honors and distinction), 1948; University of Chicago, A.M., 1949; Johns Hopkins University, Ph.D., 1955. *Home:* 222 West Whiteman St., Yellow Springs, Ohio 45387. *Office:* Literature Department, Antioch College, Yellow Springs, Ohio 45387.

CAREER: Instructor in English at LeMoyne College (now LeMoyne-Owen College), Memphis, Tenn., 1949-52, Johns Hopkins University, Baltimore, Md., 1954-55, and University of New Mexico, Albuquerque, 1955-57; Antioch College, Yellow Springs, Ohio, assistant professor, 1957-59, associate professor, 1959-66, professor of literature, 1966-70, chairman of department, 1964, 1966-67, chairman of humanities area, 1968-70. Visiting associate professor, University of Washington, Seattle, 1963. *Military service:* U.S. Army, 1941-45.

WRITINGS: Smollett and the Scottish School: Studies in Eighteenth Century Thought, University of New Mexico Press, 1959; (contributor) S. K. Kumar and K. S. McKean, editors, *Critical Approaches to Fiction,* McGraw, 1968; *The Poetics of Romanticism: Toward a Reading of John Keats,* Kent State University Press, 1969. Writer of "Metamorphosis," a three-act play in verse, based on a novel by Franz Kafka, with music by Michael White, produced at Theater of the Living Arts, Philadelphia, 1968. Editor of special edition of *Antioch Review,* "Shakespeare and the Renaissance: A Mid-Twentieth Century Prospective," 1964. Contributor of articles and reviews to professional journals.

WORK IN PROGRESS: The World Within: Studies in Fictional Form, a study of the novel since the eighteenth century; an untitled novel.†

(Died May 26, 1970)

* * *

GOLDEN, Ruth I(sbell) 1910-

PERSONAL: Born December 21, 1910, in Mount Pleasant, Mich.; daughter of Elbert Archie (a salesman) and Roseanna (Chard) Isbell; married David Leslie Golden, June 20, 1936; children: Patricia Gayle Steinhoff. *Education:* Central Michigan University, A.B., 1931; Wayne State University, M.A., 1942, Ed.D., 1963. *Home:* 234 Elm Grove Drive,

Tecumseh, Ontario, Canada (summer), and 487 Naish Ave., Cocoa Beach, Fla. 32931 (winter).

CAREER: Teacher of English in New Haven, Mich., later in Van Dyke, Mich., 1931-43; Detroit (Mich.) Board of Education, high school teacher of English, 1945-53, head of department of English at various Detroit high schools successively, 1953-65, 1967-72. Researcher on speech problems of inner-city children under Ford Foundation grant, 1955-56; principal investigator and director of Changing Dialects Research Project in Detroit public schools under National Defense Education Act grants, 1960-62, 1965-67; consultant at conferences and institutes on teaching English to the culturally disadvantaged. President of Community Council, Highland Park, Mich., 1946-48.

MEMBER: American Dialect Society, National Council of Teachers of English, National Education Association, Michigan Education Association, Alpha Delta Kappa (international president, 1965-67), Order of the Eastern Star, Detroit Women Administrators Club, Metropolitan Linguistics Club. *Awards, honors:* Named to Michigan governor's list of outstanding business and professional women, 1964.

WRITINGS: The 3 Book: Communications Skills, privately printed, 1954; *Improving Patterns of Language Usage,* Wayne State University Press, 1960, 2nd edition, 1966; (contributor) *Improving English Skills of Culturally Different Youth,* U.S. Office of Education, 1964. Writer of taped "The Golden Series of American English Language Lessons," privately produced, 1963; (contributor) R. W. Shuy, editor, *Social Dialects and Language Learning,* National Council of Teachers of English, 1964. Also writer of two three-act plays, "Sweet Adversity" and "Rummage," and a dramatization of *Silas Marner,* produced on stage.

Has made tapes and recordings for changing dialect patterns of urban primary children, and has authored reports on the teaching of standard English for the U.S. Office of Education.

WORK IN PROGRESS: Mr. Peepers, My Poodle, audiolingual and visual series for kindergarten and primary children introducing some metric system vocabulary.

SIDELIGHTS: More than forty school systems are using the curriculum that she helped develop to teach English as a "second language" to speakers of non-standard English (*Time,* February 18, 1966). The technique involves the use of tapes or records, giving users of folk language untiring models of standard informal language to imitate and practice. "The child must feel that both he and his language are accepted," Mrs. Golden stresses, "but that the latter just has its limitations. We offer him standard English as a second language for which he may have wider use." The Changing Dialects Project has involved research throughout the United States, and in Canada, Mexico, and five European countries.

BIOGRAPHICAL/CRITICAL SOURCES: Detroit News, January 30, 1963, May 15, 1965; *Alpha Delta Kappan,* fall, 1965; *Time,* February 18, 1966.

* * *

GOLDMANN, Lucien 1913-1970

PERSONAL: Born June 20, 1913, in Bucharest, Rumania; became French citizen; son of Joseph (a lawyer) and Serafina (Birnbaum) Goldmann; married Annie Taieb, June 26, 1956; children: Michel, Philippe. *Education:* Received early education in Rumania, at Faculty of Law of Bucharest; University of Zurich, Ph.D., 1944; Paris, Faculty of Law; Sorbonne, University of Paris, Docteur es Lettres, 1956. *Home:* 98 Rue de Rennes, Paris 6e, France. *Office:* Ecole Pratique des Hautes Etudes, VIe section, 54 Rue de Varenne, Paris 7e, France.

CAREER: University of Brussels, Institute of Sociology, Brussels, Belgium, director of research, 1946-58; Ecole Pratique des Hautes Etude, VIe section, Paris, France, director of studies, 1958-70. Visiting professor at University of Montreal, Free University of Berlin, Johns Hopkins University, and then at Northwestern University, 1967, and Columbia University, 1969; lecturer in Europe, United States, Canada, Mexico, and Venezuela.

WRITINGS: Mensch, gemeinschatz und welt in der philosophie Immanuel Kant (thesis), Europa Verlag, 1945, translation by author published as *La Communaute humaine et l'univers chez Kant,* Presses Universitaires de France, 1948, published as *Introduction a la philosophie chez Kant,* Gallimard, 1967, translation by Robert Black published as *Immanuel Kant,* NLB, 1971, Humanities, 1972; *Sciences humaines et philosophie,* Presses Universitaires de France, 1952, revised and augmented edition, Gonthier, 1966, translation by Hayden V. White and Robert Anchor published as *The Human Sciences and Philosophy,* Grossman, 1969; *Jean Racine, dramaturge,* L'Arche, 1956, revised edition published as *Racine, essai,* 1970, translation by Alastair Hamilton published as *Racine,* Rivers Press, 1972; *La Dieu cache: Etude sur la vision tragique dans les pensees de Pascal et dans le theatre de Racine,* Gallimard, 1956, translation by Philip Thody published as *The Hidden God: A Study of Tragic Vision in the Pensees of Pascal and the Tragedies of Racine,* Humanities, 1964; (editor) Martin de Barcos, *Correspondence,* Presses Universitaires de France, 1956; *Recherches dialecti,* Gallimard, 1959.

(Contributor) *Problems d'une sociologie du roman,* Institut de Sociologie, Universite Libre, 1963; *Pour une sociologie du roman,* Gallimard, 1964, revised and augmented edition, 1965, translation by Alan Sheridan published as *Towards a Sociology of the Novel,* Tavistock, 1975; (with Maurice Patronnier de Gandillac and Jean Piaget) *Entretians sur les notions de genese de structure,* Mouton & Co., 1965; (contributor) *Jean Piaget et les sciences sociales,* Droz, 1966; *Et teatro de Jean Genet,* Monte Avila Editores, 1968; *Der christliche Buerger und die Aufkalaerung,* Luchterhand, 1968, translation by Henry Maas published as *The Philosophy of the Enlightenment: The Christian Burgess and the Enlightenment,* M.I.T. Press, 1973.

Marxisme et sciences humaines, Gallimard, 1970; *Structures mentales et creation culturelle,* Editions Anthropos, 1970; *La Creation culturelle dans la societe moderne,* Gonthier, 1971, translation published as *Cultural Creation in Modern Society,* Telos Press, 1976; *Power and Humanism* (pamphlet), Bertrand Russell Peace Foundation, 1971; *Situation de la critique racinienne,* L'Arche, 1971; *Lukacs et Heidegger,* edited by Yonssef Ishaghpour, Gonthier, 1973.

SIDELIGHTS: Edward W. Said wrote: "The reason Goldmann will seem novel to English-speaking readers is that we have no one who does what he does. Although he writes about literature he is not really a literary critic. . . . He is, I suppose, a sociologist of mind, which is to say that he is concerned with studying the historical appearances or incarnations of certain structures of mind: he says in *The Hidden God* that he aims to construct a typology of 'world visions.'" Goldmann, in *Towards a Sociology of the Novel,* according to the *New York Times,* "attempted to develop a semi-Marxist-semistructuralist method of analysis of the

novel that the author was notably to apply to novels of Alain Robbe-Grillet and the theater of Jean Genet."

BIOGRAPHICAL/CRITICAL SOURCES: Times Literary Supplement, November 5, 1964; *Partisan Review,* summer, 1966; *New York Times,* October 10, 1970; *Christianity Today,* September 14, 1973; *Economist,* November 3, 1973; *Choice,* September, 1974.†

(Died October 3, 1970)

* * *

GOLDNER, Jack 1900-

PERSONAL: Born April 27, 1900, in Austria; son of Selig (a government official) and Ann (Krisnapoller) Goldner; married Martha R. Isgor, September 7, 1935; children: George S., Marlene B. (Mrs. Edwin Jay Sheldon). *Education:* Attended Pace College, 1929-30, New York University, 1931-35, and Columbia University, 1950-52. *Home:* 61-37 81st St., Middle Village, N.Y. 11379. *Office:* 101 Park Ave., New York, N.Y. 10017.

CAREER: Certified public accountant with own practice, New York City, 1938-65; senior partner, Goldner & Goldner (certified public accountants), New York City, beginning 1965. *Member:* American Institute of Certified Public Accountants, American Accounting Association, New York State Society of Certified Public Accountants, New York State Association of Professions.

WRITINGS: Accounting Manual for Export-Import Companies, Matthew Bender, 1960; *Foreign Trade Accounting and Management Handbook,* Commerce Clearing House, 1968. Contributor of numerous articles to professional journals.

* * *

GOMBROWICZ, Witold 1904-1969

PERSONAL: Born August 4, 1904, in Warsaw, Poland; son of Jan and Antonina (Kotkowska) Gombrowicz; married Marie Labrosse, January, 1969. *Education:* University of Warsaw, B.A. and licence en droit.

CAREER: Emigrated from Poland to Buenos Aires, Argentina, 1939, worked as a bank employee, gave courses in philosophy in cafes, and lived there until 1962; returned to Europe and, along with other writers such as Michel Butor and artists such as Masson, was invited by the Ford Foundation to live in West Berlin, 1963-64; then lived in Paris, Abbaye de Royaumont, and in the Alpes-Maritimes, 1964-69. Full-time writer. *Awards, honors:* Prix International de Litterature (formerly the Prix Formentor; $20,000), 1967, for *Le Cosmos.*

WRITINGS: Pamietnik z okresu dojrzewania (stories), Roj (Warsaw), 1933; *Ferdydurke* (novel), Roj, 1937, translation by Eric Mosbacher published under same title, Harcourt, 1961, 2nd edition, 1967; *Iwona: Ksiezniczka Burgunda* (comedy; produced in Warsaw, 1957), Roj, 1937, translation by Krystyna Griffith-Jones and Catherine Robins published as *Ivona: Princess of Burgundia,* Grove, 1969 (translation published in England as *Princess Ivona,* Calder & Boyars, 1969); *Slub* (play; produced in Paris at Theatre Recamier, 1963), Julliard, 1947, translation by Louis Iribarne published as *The Marriage,* Grove, 1969; *Trans-Atlantyk [and] Slub* (the former is a novel), with commentary by author, Instytut Literacki (Paris), 1953; *Bakakaj* (short stories), Wydawnictwo Literacki (Krakow), 1957; *Dziennik, 1953-1956* (journal), Instytut Literacki, 1957.

Pornografia (novel), Instytut Literacki, 1960, translation by Alastair Hamilton published under same title, Calder & Boyars, 1966, Grove, 1967; *Dziennik, 1957-1961,* Instytut Literacki, 1962; *Kosmos* (novel), Instytut Literacki, 1965, translation by Eric Mosbacher published as *Cosmos,* Grove, 1967; *Operetka,* Instytut Literacki, 1966, translation by Louis Iribarne published as *Operetta,* Calder & Boyars, 1971; *Dziennik, 1961-1966,* Instytut Literacki, 1966; *Entretiens avec Gombrowicz,* edited by Dominique de Roux, P. Belfond (Paris), 1968, translation by Alastair Hamilton published as *A Kind of Testament,* Temple University Press, 1973; *Kziela zebrane,* Instytut Literacki, Volume I: *Ferdydurke,* 1969, Volume II: *Trans-Atlantyk,* 1970, Volume III: *Pornografia,* 1970, Volume IV: *Kosmos,* 1970, Volume V: *Teatr,* 1971; Volume VI: *Dziennik, 1953-1956,* 1971, Volume VII: *Dziennik, 1957-1961,* 1971, Volume VIII: *Dziennik, 1961-1966,* 1971, Volume IX: *Opowiadania,* 1972; *Gombrowicz,* edited by Constantin Jelenski and Dominique de Roux, Editions de l'Herne (Paris), 1971.

Work represented in many anthologies, including *Ten Contemporary Polish Stories,* edited by Edmund Ormond, Wayne State University Press, 1958; *Sechzehn polnische Erzaehler,* edited by Marcel Reich-Ranicki, Rororo-Taschenbach Ausgabe, 1962; *Explorations in Freedom: Prose, Narrative, and Poetry from Kultura,* edited by Leopold Tyrmand, Free Press, 1970.

SIDELIGHTS: "They have assured me over 300 times that I was a genius. But what have I sold in France? Perhaps 300 books." This was 1965, and even then, when *L'Express* called him "the greatest unknown writer of our time," Gombrowicz was exaggerating. Since then his popularity as a satirist and storyteller has grown in the non-communist world and his books have been translated into over thirty languages.

Since Gombrowicz was what Eliot Fremont-Smith called "a satirist of an extreme sort, a seditionist of the soul whose pose is one of bitter, jeering delight," he had trouble in his native Poland. *Ferdydurke* caused a literary sensation, then a scandal, when it first appeared in Warsaw in 1937. During the war it was forgotten. Between 1946 and 1956, the first ten years of the communist regime in Poland, publication of Gombrowicz's work was forbidden, although remaining copies of *Ferdydurke* circulated from person to person. When Gomulka came to power he allowed *Ferdydurke* to be reprinted in an edition of 10,000 copies which immediately sold out. Gombrowicz was hailed by Artur Sandauer, a leading Polish critic, as "the pride of the nation." *Iwona* was produced and compared favorably with the work of Beckett and Ionesco. *Slub* was about to be produced when the government decided that literary liberty again had to be suppressed, and that Gombrowicz's influence on younger Polish authors was detrimental to the good of the country. The *Times Literary Supplement* noted that Gombrowicz provoked the Polish government with his contempt for patriotism in such statements as "the Nation and its romanticism constituted for me an undrinkable potion concocted to spite and anger me." Gombrowicz said that the officials attacked him "for such base reasons, on such a low level."

Then the West discovered Gombrowicz. In France, Francois Bondy called him brilliant, Mario Maurin compared *Ferdydurke* to Sartre's *La Nausee,* and K. A. Jelenski called it a "strange masterpiece." When *Ferdydurke* was finally published in English, Richard Winston wrote: "If laughter is seditious, *Ferdydurke* would be condemned by any kind of sober-minded society. . . . The humor is irresistible, the nonsense ineffable, and the sense inescapable. If a combination

of Ionesco, S. J. Perelman, and Ilf and Petrov is conceivable, this is it." "The diversity of the book," wrote T. P. McConnell, "its dimensional complexity, its Rabelais-on-the-couch outrageous humor, must astonish the casual as well as the sophisticated reader. . . . Gombrowicz cannot be considered an even cleverly derivative writer but a highly original innovator. . . . *Ferdydurke* at last possesses that quality of poetry which withholds more than it tells." Pawel Mayewski called it "a brilliant tour de force, . . . inventive to the point of being irritating. . . . Gombrowicz's strange talent for mingling poetry and psychology so that at times they become one is unique among contemporary writers." Geoffrey Grigson, on the other hand, thought it tiresome.

Critics have sought to explain *Ferdydurke* by calling it variously a satire on almost everything, a game of ideas, a psychic exploration of heart and mind, an existentialist novel, a surrealistic novel, political allegory, and what the *Times Literary Supplement* called "calculated lunacy." Madeleine Chapsal said that, according to Gombrowicz, the novel is "a picture of the battle that a man in love with immaturity fights in favor of his true maturity." Gombrowicz himself good-naturedly offered these comments: "What a bore is the everlasting question: What did you mean by *Ferdydurke*? Come, come, be more sensuous, less cerebral, start dancing with the book instead of asking for meanings. Why take so much interest in the skeleton if it's got a body? See rather whether it is capable of pleasing and is not devoid of grace and passion. . . . For the time being—if you wish to let me know that the book pleased you—when you see me simply touch your right ear. If you touch your left ear, I shall know that you didn't like it, and if you touch your nose it will mean that you are not sure. . . . Thus we shall avoid uncomfortable and even ridiculous situations and understand each other in silence."

Gombrowicz's effort always was, as he said, to direct our attention to "the real speech, the speech without words, beyond words and full of meaning that words could not convey." He defined himself thus: "I am neither a communist nor a fascist, not a Polish nobleman nor a conservative, not an Argentine nor a Pole nor a member of the Polish avant-garde. I am nothing at all. I am an artist. And even that is saying too much. I am Gombrowicz. And even that is too much. I am who I am."

Insofar as it can be said that he had a "philosophy," it was contained in a system of ideas very close to existentialism. He very much admired Sartre. Yet Gombrowicz's existentialism was something which he claimed to have discovered himself, intuitively, before he had ever read Sartre. Gombrowicz's philosophy consisted basically in the opposition of youth and age. Albert Goldman called this ". . . his obsessive theme: the treacherous, hostile, mutually corruptive relations of youth and maturity." For Gombrowicz, youth was inferior in every respect except in the possession of beauty. He said that "culture is the work of the adult, or the moribund. An old man finds himself gripped between these two tendencies: on the one hand is his attraction toward youth, toward inferiority; on the other hand is his desire to attain culture, power, and superiority. I believe that here is the one key to the comprehension of man and culture. We are not sufficiently conscious of this, we deny too much our tendency toward inferiority. Yet beauty inclines toward the lowly." Gombrowicz admired youth, not maturity: "After the age of thirty, men lapse into monstrosity." In *Pornografia* he graphically depicted the conflict between youth and age. Fremont-Smith noted also that *Pornografia,* which missed winning the Prix International in 1965 by one vote, "extends the earlier novel's formal proposition that 'men create each other by imposing forms on each other' and its abrasive corollary that man, at odds with his own form, 'is also a constant producer of form; he secretes form tirelessly, just as the bee secretes honey'."

Gombrowicz, who had little to say about his writings, once did say that *Trans-Atlantyk* was difficult to translate from the rich Polish in which it was written into what he called the "rigid" French language. *Kosmos,* which one critic called "a poetic, savagely satirical, highly personal description of a world where the surreal intrudes upon the banal," was, according to Gombrowicz, simply "an arbitrary organization of reality."

Gombrowicz strived to pursue the essence of man, and to do so with wit and vitality. He called the literature of his day, "so tiresome. It lacks poetry, freshness, interest; it is even repugnant. And such boredom! I try to do just the opposite; I do my best to be fresh, attractive and easy. If I do not attain these goals, it is not because I haven't wished to." Miss Chapsal considered his work to be the product of "a voice who remains himself, with his contradictions, his anguish, his suffering, his narcissism, and, when necessary, his *demoniaque.* His objective is to propose that man become himself."

Gombrowicz spoke French, Spanish, German, and Russian.

BIOGRAPHICAL/CRITICAL SOURCES: Times Literary Supplement, February 3, 1961, November 3, 1966; *New Statesman,* February 17, 1961; *Spectator,* March 3, 1961; *New York Herald Tribune Lively Arts,* June 4, 1961; *Commonweal,* June 23, 1961; *New York Times Book Review,* July 30, 1961; *Saturday Review,* September 9, 1961, December 10, 1966; *L'Express,* July 25, 1965, May 8-14, 1967; *New York Times,* May 3, 1967, May 12, 1967; *TriQuarterly,* spring, 1967; *The Drama Review,* Volume XIV, number 1, 1969, and number 3, 1970; Dominique de Roux, *Gombrowicz,* Union generale d'editions, 1971; Carolyn Riley, editor, *Contemporary Literary Criticism,* Gale, Volume IV, 1975, Volume VII, 1977.†

(Died July 25, 1969)

*   *   *

GOODMAN, Paul   1911-1972

PERSONAL: Born September 9, 1911, in New York, N.Y.; son of Barnett (a businessman) and Augusta Goodman; married (common-law) to second wife, Sally; children: (first marriage) Susan; (second marriage) Mathew R. (deceased), Daisy J. *Education:* City College of New York (now City College of the City University of New York), B.A., 1931; attended lectures at Columbia and Harvard, though he was never officially registered at either institution; University of Chicago, Ph.D., 1940 (received, 1954). *Residence:* New York, N.Y.; and North Stratford, N.H.

CAREER: Worked as an outside reader for Metro-Goldwyn-Mayer, 1931; University of Chicago, instructor, 1939-40; Manumit School of Progressive Education, Pawling, N.Y., instructor in Latin, physics, history, and mathematics; later an instructor at Black Mountain College, Black Mountain, N.C.; has taught at New York University and Sarah Lawrence College; was Knapp Professor, University of Wisconsin, 1964; taught at Experimental College of San Francisco State College, 1966; and University of Hawaii, 1971-72. Lecturer on college campuses. Has conducted seminars on "Education and the Great Society" at Institute for Policy Studies, Washington, D.C. Practiced as lay psychotherapist with the New York Institute for Gestalt Therapy. *Awards, honors:* American Council of Learned Societies fellowship, 1940; award from the National Institute of Arts and Letters, 1953.

WRITINGS—Poetry: *Stop-light,* Vinco Publishing, 1941; (contributor) *Five Young American Poets,* New Directions, 1945; *The Well of Bethlehem,* privately printed, c.1950; *Red Jacket,* privately printed, c.1956; *The Lordly Hudson: Collected Poems,* Macmillan, 1962; *Day, and Other Poems,* privately printed, c.1960; *Hawkweed,* Random House, 1967; *North Percy,* Black Sparrow, 1968; *Homespun of Oatmeal Gray,* Random House, 1970; *Collected Poems,* Random House, 1974.

Fiction: *The Grand Piano, or, The Almanac of Alienation* (novel), Colt, 1942; *The Facts of Life* (stories), Vanguard, 1945; *State of Nature* (novel), Vanguard, 1946; *The Break-Up of Our Camp and Other Stories,* New Directions, 1949; *The Dead of Spring* (novel), privately printed, 1950; *Parents' Day* (novel), 5x8 Press, 1951; *The Empire City* (collected novels), Bobbs-Merrill, 1959; *Our Visit to Niagara* (stories), Horizon Press, 1960; *Making Do* (novel), Macmillan, 1963; *Adam and His Works* (stories), Random House, 1968.

Non-fiction: (With Meyer Leben and Edward Roditi) *Pieces of Three,* 5x8 Press, 1942; *Art and Social Nature* (essays), Arts and Science Press, 1946; *Kafka's Prayer* (criticism), Vanguard, 1947; (with brother, Percival Goodman) *Communitas: Means of Livelihood and Ways of Life,* University of Chicago Press, 1947, 2nd edition, Vintage, 1960; (with Frederick S. Perls and Ralph Hefferline) *Gestalt Therapy,* Messner, 1951; *The Structure of Literature* (criticism), University of Chicago Press, 1954; *Censorship and Pornography on the Stage and Are Writers Shirking Their Political Duty?* [New York], c.1959; *Growing Up Absurd: Problems of Youth in the Organized System,* Random House, 1960; *The Community of Scholars,* Random House, 1962; *Utopian Essays and Practical Proposals,* Random House, 1962; *Drawing the Line,* Random House, 1962; *The Society I Live In is Mine,* Horizon Press, 1963; *Compulsory Mis-Education,* Horizon Press, 1964; *People or Personnel: Decentralizing and the Mixed System,* Random House, 1965; *Five Years: Thoughts During a Useless Time* (partial autobiography), Brussell & Brussell, 1967; *Like a Conquered Province: The Moral Ambiguity of America* (Massey Lectures, Canadian Broadcasting Corp.), Random House, 1967; *The Open Look,* Funk, 1969; *The Individual and Culture,* Dorsey, 1969; *New Reformation: Notes of a Neolithic Conservative,* Random House, 1970; *Speaking and Language: Defense of Poetry* (criticism), Random House, 1971; *Little Prayers and Finite Experience,* Harper, 1972.

Plays: *Childish Jokes: Crying Backstage* (first produced in New York by Living Theatre, August, 1951), 5x8 Press, 1958; "The Cave at Machpelah", first produced in New York at Living Theatre Playhouse, June 1959; *Three Plays: The Young Disciple* (first produced in New York by Living Theatre, October, 1955), *Faustina* (first produced in New York at Cherry Lane Theatre, May, 1952), *Jonah* (first produced in New York at American Place Theater, February, 1966), Random House, 1965; *Tragedy and Comedy: Four Cubist Plays,* Black Sparrow, 1970.

Other: (Contributor) M. R. Stein, A. J. Vidick, and D. M. White, editors, *Identity and Anxiety,* Free Press, 1960; (contributor) Herbert Gold, editor, *First Person Singular: Essays for the Sixties,* Dial, 1963; (editor) *Seeds of Liberation,* Braziller, 1965; (compiler) *Essays in American Colonial His-*

tory, Holt, 1967. Contributor to *Dissent, Commentary, Harper's, Commonweal, Poetry, Playboy, Salamagundi, Esquire, Symposium, Mademoiselle, Nation, New York Review of Books,* and other publications. Edited *Complex* magazine; former film editor, *Partisan Review;* served as television critic, *New Republic.* An editor of *Liberation,* 1960-72.

SIDELIGHTS: During the wave of radicalism which swept college campuses in the sixties, students who believed they could trust no one over thirty made an exception for Paul Goodman. Journalists have noted that Goodman was the only writer consistently quoted by the Free Speech Movement in Berkeley. According to George Steiner, "Goodman's is about the only American voice that young English pacifists and nuclear disarmers find convincing." Students see him "as the prophet and exemplar of a free life in a bureaucratic society," wrote Richard Kostelanetz. He in turn saw the students as "the major exploited class," whose education is for the most part a waste of time. "To Goodman, drop-outs, delinquents, and college beatniks are all victims of the same process," said Peter Schrag, "and have all refused to accept the terms of organized society and the empty rat race (his phrase) which it imposes."

Society's terms are precisely what Goodman always refused to accept. He was what Michael Harrington calls "a devotee of that genuinely American cult of experience in which the natural man refuses to obey, or rather, seeks to destroy conventional society." He admired the individual and despised organizational personnel and any "enterprises extrinsically motivated and interlocked with other centralized systems." (Goodman said that his liberalism often took him close to the position held by the radical Right.) All of the instances of dissatisfaction that Goodman enumerated were directly concerned with his belief that, as Steiner explains, "the health of society [is] indivisible from the mental state and psychopathology of the individual," an individual who is always a social animal. To arrive at his philosophical position, Goodman "linked doctrines of anarchism, non-violence, and decentralization derived from Kropotkin, Gandhi, and Jefferson, to the heritage of Freud and, more specifically, of Wilhelm Reich." Kostelanetz noted that "essentially, Goodman believes that man is creative, loving, and communal; but often the institutions and roles of behavior that he creates serve to alienate him from his natural self. Moreover, once society's organizations become more important than the individuals who comprise them, then man must suppress his humanity to suit the inhuman system." Kostelanetz added that, throughout Goodman's lectures, books, and public statements, "what particularly impresses the young (and perhaps disturbs the old) is Goodman's personal integrity. He has always lived by his ideals, defying whatever bureaucratic systems he touched, practicing conspicuously the non-conformist sexual behavior he preached (resulting in his being fired from his first three teaching positions), forbidding editors to bowdlerize what he had written, attaining such a mastery over poverty that he could never succumb to money, and having a sense of purpose that made him resistant to flattery or vanity."

Steiner felt that he continued to "sustain dialogue amid the chaotic loudness of mass society.... Between the closing walls of technological determinism and political cliche, he is trying to hack out elbow room for the imagination. The novels, the poems, the polemics, the tough-minded reveries of the utopian, spring from an axiom of hope: from the assertion that the imperatives of our social and political condition are only apparent, that they do not enshrine the only possi-

bility." Goodman once said "It is false that I write about many subjects. I have only one, the human beings I know in their man-made scene." He was a self-described "community anarchist" whose concern was the improvement of society through the efforts of individuals and voluntary groups. He said optimistically: "If ten thousand people in all walks of life will stand up on their two feet and talk out and insist, we shall get back our country."

Writing was Goodman's principal vocation, though it was not a profitable one until the publication of *Growing Up Absurd.* Steiner believes that "roughly, Goodman's career falls into three periods: a stage of intellectually brilliant but not unconventional radicalism in the 1930's, culminating in his novel, *The Empire City* (1942); a fairly long eclipse, during which his work was known to a small circle of passionate admirers; ... and the breakthrough, after *Growing Up Absurd* in 1960, and the re-issue of *Communitas....*" *Growing Up Absurd,* an argument in defense of America's youth, "defines the chaos of society that they sense but cannot clarify," writes Kostelanetz. Goodman continued to write about the young, especially in relation to education. "Fundamentally," he said, "there is no right education except growing up into a worthwhile world. Indeed, our excessive concern with problems of education at present simply means that the grown-ups do not have such a world." He favors small colleges where students would be guided by "intrinsic motivation," and has proposed voluntary attendance on all levels of education. The components of our present system, he believed, "are a uniform world-view, the absence of any viable alternative, confusion about the relevance of one's own experience and feelings, and a chronic anxiety, so that one clings to the one world-view as the only security. This *is* brainwashing." Dropping-out, as he saw it, is a sound alternative. In *Compulsory Mis-Education,* Goodman, a Ph.D., states that long schooling is not only inept, it is psychologically, politically and professionally damaging." He further believes that we should be experimenting with different kinds of schools, no school at all, the real city as school, farm schools, practical apprenticeships, guided travel, work camps, little theaters and local newspapers, community service."

On the basis of his proposals for an improved educational system, Goodman's critics labelled him a romantic, a dreamer, an anti-intellectual. Schrag notes that "his chief villains—men like James B. Conant—are people who see education as training ground for the demands that this culture makes." While reviewing *The Community of Scholars,* wherein Goodman advocated a return to the ideal of the medieval university, D. M. Grunschlag was disconcerted because Goodman apparently showed a greater concern for student happiness, administrative fluency, and 'growing up' than [for] education." On the other hand, Goodman has become "a sort of roving prophet," says Schrag, "for the independent students who are establishing free universities and similar para-academic organizations."

Yet even those who admire his ideas find some of his solutions unworkable. Nat Hentoff writes: "Goodman's solutions to the various problems he confronts are often debatable and are sometimes impossible of achievement without a prior social revolution that he does not know how to instigate. His highest and most stimulating function, therefore, is as a nay-sayer. What makes him so readable is that all his years in exacerbated opposition have not made him chronically self-righteous or humorless. ... However one may disagree with Goodman's theories, it is invigorating to attend his indignant, sardonic, and often devastatingly accurate assaults on specific examples of obtuseness in the culture." Some of his discourses have also been attacked as either poorly written or lacking in sound judgment. In response to one attack on his alleged imprecision and wooliness, he wrote: "I suppose I ought to say something about the [charge] that I don't do my homework, since other profound scholars . . . have accused me of the same. (Indeed, I seem to some people to be a village idiot.) Now Aristotle points out that it is the sign of an ignorant man to be more precise than the subject warrants. In books like *Growing Up, Gestalt Therapy,* and *Communitas* I am trying to say something about the whole man in an indefinitely complicated organism/environment field. My experience in reading in this interesting subject is that those authors say the best things who keep their visions central and concrete, . . . who draw on what they know intimately, and are not afraid to risk being passionately involved. Their strong errors, as St. Thomas says, are better than weak truths."

Goodman's books teem with suggestions for man's improvement. He proposed, instead of a reliance on drugs, a return to revitalizing leisure activity; the non-interference of the state in one's sexual life ("to license sex is absurd"); withdrawal from Vietnam; banning private automobiles in Manhattan; building dormitories in housing projects to allow children to safely get away from home; and removing national boundaries by encouraging economic regionalism and international functions. Certain critics, such as Edmund Fuller, believe that Goodman is "a sage in some areas and a screwball in others." Goodman simply held to his position that "to make positive decisions for one's community, rather than being regimented by others' decisions, is one of the noble acts of man."

"First, I'm a humanist," said Goodman. "Anything I write on society is pragmatic—it aims to accomplish something. . . . Apart from that I'm also an artist. That's a different internal spring. You don't create an artwork from the same motivation. I write songs, for instance, but that's the same as writing a poem. Also, it's impossible to be a dramatist without being a musician or a choreographer. I'm a man of letters."

His fiction, poetry, and literary criticism are as provocative and inventive as his social essays. Robert Phelps called *Empire City,* which includes Goodman's favorite book, *The Dead of Spring,* "a book originating in good will, mature candor, and an urgently fermenting, more than secular morality. . . . The spirit inside, and the text itself, which seems not so much written as whistled, laughed, teased, prayed, come as close to imparting a man's gratuitous love for his own kind as mere language ever can." Denise Levertov wrote of his poems: "Rhythmically, most of the story poems tend to go flat, and inventive though Paul Goodman is he cannot put life, for me, into the long-since-dead ballade. But the sonnets are among the few readable sonnets of the century. . . . [Some of the other poems are] marvels of true, peculiar, irreducible poetry." Laurence Lieberman wrote of Goodman's poetry: "It is his lover's quarrel with the country that I'm grateful to find he's keeping alive in the poems, and that is what gives his poetry a kind of superabundant life that is rare today." Goodman once said: "I must write, freely, the kind of poems and stories that belong to a person who dutifully takes on these other responsibilities of citizenship. Yet the task is too much for me." Steiner sees "both the moral choice and the statement of defeat [as] Jewish. But as one looks at the prodigious amount of work done, there is no sense of failure; only the exhilarating sight of a man fighting windmills which have, in fact, turned out to

be Philistine giants. Mr. Goodman is a *mensch.* The species is getting rare."

BIOGRAPHICAL/CRITICAL SOURCES: Times Literary Supplement, October 22, 1954; *New York Herald Tribune Book Review,* June 28, 1959, November 18, 1962; *Commentary,* June, 1960, August, 1963; *New York Herald Tribune Lively Arts,* January 15, 1961; *Saturday Review,* February 17, 1962, February 18, 1967; *Nation,* April 13, 1963; *Reporter,* July 18, 1963, January 26, 1967; *New York Times Book Review,* September 27, 1964; *Atlantic,* August, 1965; *New York Times Magazine,* April 3, 1966; Carolyn Riley, editor, *Contemporary Literary Criticism,* Gale, Volume I, 1973, Volume II, 1974, Volume IV, 1975, Volume VII, 1977.†

(Died August 2, 1972)

*   *   *

GORDON, Frederick [Collective pseudonym]

WRITINGS—All published by Graham & Matlack: *Sammy Brown's Treasure Hunt,* 1912; *The Young Crusoes of Pine Island,* 1912; *Bob Bouncer's Schooldays,* 1912.

SIDELIGHTS: See **ADAMS, Harriet S., STRATEMEYER, Edward L.,** and **SVENSON, Andrew E.**†

*   *   *

GORDON, Ida L. 1907-

PERSONAL: Born November 14, 1907, in Wakefield, England; daughter of Alfred and Ada (Wilson) Pickles; married E. V. Gordon (a university professor), July, 1930 (deceased); children: Bridget Mary (Mrs. Alex MacKenzie), Christine Ann, Janet Margaret, Robert Andrew (deceased). *Education:* University of Leeds, B.A. (honors), 1928, Ph.D., 1930. *Home:* 14 Middlepenny Rd., Langbank, Renfrewshire, Scotland.

CAREER: University of Manchester, Manchester, England, lecturer, 1938-60, senior lecturer in English language and literature, 1960-68. Visiting professor, University of Victoria, Victoria, British Columbia, summer, 1970. *Member:* Viking Society for Northern Research.

WRITINGS: (Editor) *The Seafarer* (Old English poem), Methuen, 1960; *The Double Sorrow of Troilus: A Study of Ambiguities in "Troilus and Criseyde,"* Oxford University Press, 1970.

WORK IN PROGRESS: Chaucerian studies.

SIDELIGHTS: Ida Gordon has visited Iceland twice, spending six months there at one period to study the saga literature. Several years ago she traveled in Ethiopia.

*   *   *

GORELIK, Mordecai 1899-

PERSONAL: Surname is pronounced Go-*re*-lik; born August 25, 1899, in Shchedrin, Minsk, Russia; son of Morris and Bertha (Dirskin) Gorelik; married Frances Strauss, 193? (deceased); married Loraine Kabler, 1972; children: one son, one daughter. *Education:* Pratt Institute, graduate 1920; studied for theater under Robert Edmond Jones, Norman Bel Geddes, and others. *Home:* 19532 Sandcastle Lane, Huntington Beach, Calif. 92648.

CAREER: Began career in the theater as scene painter and technician with Neighborhood Playhouse and Provincetown Players, New York City, 1920-21; instructor-designer for

School of the Theatre, New York City, 1921-22; designer of more than fifty professional productions for Broadway; director and designer for civic and university theaters; production designer for Hollywood films, beginning 1944; Southern Illinois University, Carbondale, beginning 1960, began as research professor of theater, became professor emeritus. Broadway productions designed include Theatre Guild's "Processional," 1925, "Success Story," 1932, "Men in White," 1933, "Golden Boy," 1937, "Tortilla Flat," 1938, "All My Sons," 1947, "The Flowering Peach," 1954, and "A Distant Bell," 1960; production designer for the films, "Days of Glory," 1944, "Our Street," 1944, "None but the Lonely Heart," 1944, "Salt to the Devil," 1949, and the French film, "L'Ennemi publique numero 1," 1954; American scenic supervisor for visiting productions of Comedie Francaise of Paris and the Old Vic Co. of London, 1956. Instructor in theater at American Academy of Dramatic Arts, 1926-32, New School for Social Research, 1940-41, Biarritz American University, 1945-46, University of Toledo and New York University, 1956, University of Hawaii and Bard College, 1959, Brigham Young University, 1961, California State College, 1964, San Jose State College (now University), 1965, Long Island University, 1972, and University of Southern California, 1975. Consultant for theater, U.S. Military Government in Germany, 1949.

AWARDS, HONORS: Guggenheim fellowship for study of European theater, 1936-37; Rockefeller Foundation grant for study of European theater, 1949-51; Fulbright grant for study of Australian theater under auspices of Australian-American Educational Foundation, 1967; Theta Alpha Phi medal of honor, 1971.

WRITINGS: New Theatres for Old, Samuel French, 1940, reprinted, Octagon, 1975; (translator) Max Frisch, *Firebug,* Hill & Wang, 1963. Play adaptations include "The Annotated Hamlet," presented under his direction at Southern Illinois University, 1961, and "The Firebugs," presented at Maidman Playhouse, 1963; author of "Paul Thompson Forever," premiered in 1947, and "Rainbow Terrace," premiered in 1966. Contributor to *Theatre Arts, Drama Survey, New York Times, Quarterly Journal of Speech,* and other publications. Contributor also to *Encyclopaedia Britannica, Encyclopedia Americana, Collier's Encyclopedia.*

WORK IN PROGRESS: The Scenic Imagination; three plays, "The Big Day," "Andrus, or the Vision," and "Yes and No."

AVOCATIONAL INTERESTS: Fishing.

*   *   *

GORMAN, Katherine   ?-1972

PERSONAL: Born in Philadelphia, Pa.; daughter of Vernon Harris and Margaret (Gilboyne) Bonsey; married William F. Gorman. *Education:* Studied at Columbia University, Ringling School of Art, and Eliot O'Hara Watercolor School. *Home:* Lake Palms Apartments, 750 Burlington Ave. N., St. Petersburg, Fla. 33701.

MEMBER: National League of American Pen Women (national contests chairman, 1952-54; national features editor, 1954-56; novels chairman, 1956-58; Florida poetry chairman, 1964-66, 1968-70; national markets chairman, 1968-69), National Federation of State Poetry Societies, Poetry Society of America, Academy of American Poets, League of Women Voters (vice-president, 1950), Florida Federation of the Arts (secretary, 1953-54), Toastmistress Club, Stuart Society, St. Petersburg Arts Centre (charter and life member), St. Petersburg Museum of Fine Arts (charter member).

Awards, honors: First prize of National Federation of State Poetry Societies, 1968, for *Flesh the Only Coin.*

*WRITINGS—*Poetry: *Flesh the Only Coin,* South & West, 1968; *Album,* Olivant, 1968. Contributor of short stories and articles to *Good Housekeeping, Cosmopolitan,* and other periodicals; contributor of poetry to *Atlantic, Human Voice, Epos, Commonweal, Mademoiselle, New York Herald-Tribune,* and other periodicals. Editor, *Florida Speaks,* 1950-54; Southeast regional editor, *Pen Woman,* 1970-72.

WORK IN PROGRESS: A collection of poems, *Company I Have Kept.*

AVOCATIONAL INTERESTS: Travel, ceramic sculpture.†

(Died, 1972)

*   *   *

GOULD, Beatrice Blackmar   1898-

PERSONAL: Born October 27, 1898, in Emmetsburg, Iowa; daughter of Harry E. (a teacher) and Mary Kathleen (Fluke) Blackmar; married Charles Bruce Gould (a writer and editor), October 4, 1923; children: Sesaly (Mrs. Frederic Burton Krafft). *Education:* University of Iowa, B.A., 1922; Columbia University, M.S., 1925. *Religion:* Protestant. *Residence:* Hopewell, N.J. 08525. *Agent:* Curtis Brown Ltd., 575 Madison Ave., New York, N.Y. 10022.

CAREER: Newspaper reporter in New York City, and later women's editor of *New York Sunday World,* 1926-29; writer for magazines, 1929-35; editor with husband of *Ladies' Home Journal,* Philadelphia, Pa., 1935-62, an editorship that boosted the once languishing magazine to the highest paid circulation of the day; General Foods, New York City, director, 1959-62. Member of women's advisory committee, War Manpower Commission, 1942-45. *Member:* Cosmopolitan Club, Oxford Club, Cambridge Club, Theta Sigma Phi, Kappa Kappa Gamma. *Awards, honors:* Shared with her husband the Distinguished Service Award of University of Missouri School of Journalism, 1946, and William Freeman Snow Award, 1951; Freedom Foundations Award, 1952; Columbia University Alumni Association, award for outstanding achievement in journalism, 1955.

WRITINGS: (With husband, Bruce Gould) *American Story* (autobiographical), Harper, 1968.

Plays, with Bruce Gould: "Man's Estate," produced in New York by the Theatre Guild, spring, 1929; "The Terrible Turk," produced in California at Pasadena Playhouse, 1934; "First Gentlemen of Her Time." Contributor to *Saturday Evening Post* and other national magazines.

BIOGRAPHICAL/CRITICAL SOURCES: New York Times Book Review, July 14, 1968.

*   *   *

GOULETT, Harlan M(ador)   1927-1969

PERSONAL: Born November 14, 1927, in Minneapolis, Minn.; son of John Burnell (a printer) and Lillian (Leifur) Goulett; married Diane Mayhew (a speech therapist), June 23, 1951; children: Harlan, Jr., Elizabeth, Dale. *Education:* University of Minnesota, B.S.L., 1951, LL.B., 1953. *Home:* 2609 Robins St., Minneapolis, Minn. 55410.

CAREER: State of Minnesota, special assistant attorney general, 1955-56; Office of Prosecuting Attorney, Minneapolis, Minn., assistant county attorney, beginning 1956. Trustee, Minnesota State County Attorneys Association. *Military service:* U.S. Navy, 1946-47. *Member:* Minnesota

State Bar Association (secretary of criminal law committee; chairman of insanity subcommittee), National District Attorneys Association (associate director).

WRITINGS: The Insanity Defense in Criminal Trials, West Publishing, 1965. Contributor to *Eroto.*

AVOCATIONAL INTERESTS: Gardening, bird watching, and horseshoes.†

(Died, 1969)

*   *   *

GOW, Ronald   1897-

PERSONAL: Born November 1, 1897, in Heaton Moor, near Manchester, England; son of Anthony (a banker) and Clara (Ashworth) Gow; married Wendy Hiller (an actress), January 25, 1937; children: Ann, Anthony. *Education:* Manchester University, B.Sc. *Home:* 9 Stratton Rd., Beaconsfield, Buckinghamshire, England. *Agent:* Laurence Fitch Ltd., 113-117 Wardour St., London, W.1, England.

CAREER: Playwright; formerly employed as research chemist and schoolmaster. *Military service:* British Army, 1918.

WRITINGS—Plays: *Breakfast at Eight,* Samuel French, 1922; *Under the Skull and Bones: A Piratical Play with Songs,* Baker International Play Bureau, 1929; *Higgins, the Highwayman of Cranford,* Walter H. Baker, 1930; *Henry; or, the House on the Moor,* Walter H. Baker, 1931; *The Golden West: A Farce on the Instalment Plan,* Walter H. Baker, 1932; *Gallows Glorious* (produced at Shaftsbury Theatre, London, 1933, retitled "John Brown" and produced in New York, 1934), Goilancz, 1933; *The Vengeance of the Gang,* Walter H. Baker, 1933; *Plays for the Classroom,* J. Murray, 1933; *O.H.M.S.,* H.W.F. Deane, 1933; *My Lady Wears a White Cockade* (first produced at Embassy Theatre, London, 1934), Garamond, 1935; *Compromise,* H.W.F. Deane, 1935; *Lawyer of Springfield,* H.W.F. Deane, 1935; *Ma's Bit o'Brass* (originally designed in scenario form for the film "Lancashire Luck," 1937), Walter H. Baker, 1938; *Scuttleboom's Treasure,* Samuel French, 1938; *Grannie's a Hundred,* Walter H. Baker, 1939.

Adaptor: Walter Greenwood, *Love on the Dole* (first produced at Garrick Theatre, London, 1935, produced at Shubert Theatre, New York, 1936), J. Cape, 1935, Samuel French, 1936; "Jenny Jones" (musical based on stories by Rhys Davis), first produced at Hippodrome, London, 1944; Thomas Hardy, "Tess of the D'Urbervilles," first produced, 1946; Norah Lofts, "Jassy," first produced, 1947; H. G. Wells, "Ann Veronica," first produced at Picadilly Theatre, London, 1949, new musical adaptation with Frank Wells first produced at Cambridge Theatre, London, April, 1969; Vita Sackville-West, "The Edwardians," first produced at Saville Theatre, London, 1959; Henry James, "A Boston Story," produced at Duchess Theatre, London, 1968. Also writer of film and radio scripts, including a daily propaganda serial, "Front Line Family," during World War II.

BIOGRAPHICAL/CRITICAL SOURCES: National Observer, September 22, 1968; *Statesman,* September 27, 1968; *Punch,* October 2, 1968; *Variety,* January 29, 1969, April 30, 1969; *Stage,* July 30, 1970.

*   *   *

GRAHAM, Donald W(ilkinson)   1903-

PERSONAL: Born June 17, 1903, in Fort William, Ontario,

Canada; son of Donald Campbell and Robina (Wilkinson) Graham; married Phyllis Hopson (a writer and illustrator), June 14, 1946; children: Donald Hopson and Kenneth Douglas (twins), Jeanne Elizabeth. *Education:* Attended Stanford University, 1921-23, and Chouinard Art Institute, 1923-27. *Home:* 21058 West Hillside Dr., Topanga, Calif. 90290.

CAREER: Chouinard Art Institute, Los Angeles, Calif., instructor in perspective, 1924-27; New Orleans Art School, New Orleans, La., instructor in drawing, 1928-30; Chouinard Art Institute, instructor in drawing, 1930-36; Walt Disney Training School, Los Angeles, instructor in drawing, 1932-41; Chouinard Art Institute, instructor in drawing, 1942-47; Tacoma Art Center, Tacoma, Wash., instructor in drawing, 1947-49; Chouinard Art Institute, instructor in drawing and composition, 1949-71, chairman of faculty.

WRITINGS: Composing Pictures, Van Nostrand, 1970.

WORK IN PROGRESS: A book on drawing.††

*   *   *

GRAHAM, Howard Jay   1905-

PERSONAL: Born August 16, 1905, in Dows, Iowa; son of Roderick Morrison (a merchant) and Anna (Johnson) Graham; married Mary Wilson (a teacher), December 21, 1929; children: Donald Wilson, Anna Ruth. *Education:* Whitman College, B.S. (with honors), 1927; University of California, Berkeley, M.A., 1930, Certificate of Librarianship, 1939. *Politics:* Democratic. *Religion:* Protestant. *Home:* 630 Pearson St., Walla Walla, Wash. 99362.

CAREER: Los Angeles County Law Library, Los Angeles, Calif., order librarian, 1939-50, bibliographer, 1950-59; writer and researcher, beginning 1959. Prepared historical memorandum on the antislavery backgrounds and origins of the Fourteenth Amendment for National Association for the Advancement of Colored People counsel briefing in the 1953 school desegregation cases before the U.S. Supreme Court. *Member:* American Historical Association, Organization of American Historians, Bibliographical Society, Selden Society (London), State Historical Society of Wisconsin, Phi Beta Kappa. *Awards, honors:* First prize in *New Republic* Essay Contest, 1929; fellow, University of California, Berkeley, 1936-39; Guggenheim fellowships, 1953-54, 1957-58; first prize for essay in Golden Jubilee Contest sponsored by American Association of Law Libraries, 1956; LL.D., Whitman College, 1969.

WRITINGS: (Contributor) *Selected Essays in Constitutional Law,* Volume I, Association of American Law Schools, 1938; *Everyman's Constitution: Historical Essays on the Fourteenth Amendment, the "Conspiracy Theory," and American Constitutionalism,* State Historical Society of Wisconsin, 1968. Also author of "When the Bay Bridge Was a Joke," serialized in *San Francisco News,* 1934; contributor of more than forty articles and reviews to legal and historical journals and to popular periodicals, including *New Republic, Westways,* and *California Monthly.*

WORK IN PROGRESS: Monographs and articles: "The Early Tudor Origins of Royal Privilege and Copyright"; a survey, dating, and redating of the *English Year Books,* 1490-1540; "New Light on English Law Printing, 1510-1540"; and "Format and the Rise of Constitutionalism."

BIOGRAPHICAL/CRITICAL SOURCES: Nation, June 23, 1969.†

GRANBERRY, Edwin 1897-

PERSONAL: Born April 18, 1897, in Meridian, Miss.; son of James Asaph (an educator) and Elizabeth Jane (Phillips) Granberry; married Mable Leflar, March 22, 1924; children: Edwin Jr., Julian Maddux, Hal Maurice. Education: University of Florida, student, 1916-18; Columbia University, A.B., 1920; Harvard University, drama studies at 47 Workshop, 1922-24. Religion: Protestant. Home: 201 Phelps Ave., Winter Park, Fla. 32789. Agent: Harold Matson Co., Inc., 22 East 40th St., New York, N.Y. 10016. Office: Rollins College, Winter Park, Fla. 32791.

CAREER: Miami University, Oxford, Ohio, assistant professor of Romance languages, 1920-22; Stevens School, Hoboken, N.J., Latin and French master, 1925-30; Rollins College, Winter Park, Fla., associate professor, 1933-40, Irving Bacheller Professor of Creative Writing, beginning 1940. Military service: U.S. Marine Corps, World War I. Member: Authors League, Authors Guild. Awards, honors: O. Henry Memorial Award, 1932, for best short-short story published in an American magazine, "A Trip to Czardis."

WRITINGS—Fiction: The Ancient Hunger, Macaulay, 1927; Strangers and Lovers, Macaulay, 1928; The Erl King, Macaulay, 1930; A Trip to Czardis, Trident, 1967.

Translations from the French: Dominique Dunois, A Lover Returns, Macaulay, 1930; Jacques de Lacretalle, A Man's Life, Holt, 1932; Andre Chamson, The Mountain Tavern, Holt, 1934.

Plays: "Hitch Your Wagon to a Star," produced by 47 Workshop, Harvard University, 1924; "The Falcon," produced at Annie Russel Theatre, Rollins College, 1951. Contributor of short stories and articles to numerous magazines.

SIDELIGHTS: Granberry introduced the Florida "cracker" in fiction with his novel, Strangers and Lovers. His book A Trip for Czardis, was adapted for television by Robert Herridge. Avocational interests: Florida's folklore, fauna, and flora.

BIOGRAPHICAL/CRITICAL SOURCES: John Bradbury, Renaissance in the South, University of North Carolina Press, 1963.

* * *

GRANT, Dorothy Fremont 1900-

PERSONAL: Born October 8, 1900, in New York, N.Y.; daughter of Francis Murray and Henrietta (Addison) Fremont; married Douglas Malcolm Grant (an artist), May 3, 1922; children: one foster child. Education: Attended Starkey Seminary, Lakemont, N.Y., 1914-18. Politics: Independent. Religion: Roman Catholic.

CAREER: Founder, owner, and editor, Patter, Manhasset, N.Y., 1932-38; owner of Honey Rock Kennels, 1953-58; copywriter for radio and television, 1957-60; founder, owner, and manager of Grandma's Attic, Asheville, N.C., beginning 1967; author. Asheville Community Theatre, member of board of directors, 1962-63, president, 1964-65. Military service: U.S. Naval Reserve Forces, 1918-20. Member: North Carolina Society for Prevention of Cruelty to Animals.

WRITINGS: What Other Answer, Bruce Publishing, 1943; (compiler) War Is My Parish, Bruce Publishing, 1944; Margaret Brent, Adventurer, Longmans, Green, 1944; Night of Decision (novel), Longmans, Green, 1946; So! You Want to Get Married, Bruce Publishing, 1947; Devil's Food (novel), Longmans, Green, 1949; John England, American Christo-pher, Bruce Publishing, 1949; Born Again, Bruce Publishing, 1950; ". . . For I Have Sinned," Bruce Publishing, 1952; The Fun We've Had: Highlights of a Happy Marriage, Bruce Publishing, 1954; Adventurous Lady: Margaret Brent of Maryland, Kenedy, 1957; Rose Greenhow, Confederate Secret Agent, Kenedy, 1961.

WORK IN PROGRESS: A book about a European among southern Indians, 1736-44; research for contemporary nonfiction (humorous).††

* * *

GRANT, Jane (Cole) 1895-1972

PERSONAL: Born May 29, 1895, in Joplin, Mo.; daughter of Robert T. (a merchant) and Sophrona (Cole) Grant; married Harold W. Ross (founder and editor of New Yorker), March 27, 1920 (divorced, 1929); married William B. Harris (a banker), June 3, 1939. Education: Educated in public and private schools in Missouri, Kansas, and New York. Home: 480 Park Ave., New York, N.Y. 10022; and Litchfield, Conn. Office: New Yorker, 25 West 43rd St., New York, N.Y. 10036.

CAREER: Collier's Weekly (magazine), New York City, staff member, 1912-14; New York Times, New York City, reporter, 1914-30; New Yorker, New York City, co-founder and administrator, 1925-31, consultant, beginning 1942; free-lance writer, 1925-72; co-owner with husband, William Harris, White Flower Farm (retail plant and seed operation), Litchfield, Conn. Member of board of directors, Pack Medical Group; vice-chairman, Connecticut Committee for Equal Rights, beginning 1951. Member: Overseas Press Club, National Council of Women, National Trust for Historic Preservation, Lucy Stone League (president, beginning 1950), New York Newspaper Women's Club (co-founder).

WRITINGS: Ross, "The New Yorker" and Me, Reynal, 1968. Contributor to Saturday Evening Post, American Mercury, and other periodicals.

WORK IN PROGRESS: I Saw What I Could, a book about Russia; Dennis O'Connor, a novel.

SIDELIGHTS: Jane Grant was the city room's first woman reporter at the New York Times. She organized the Lucy Stone League in 1921 which "was a crusade on behalf of women who wanted to work, vote, travel and campaign under their maiden names," making it, according to the New York Times, "a forerunner of the Women's Liberation movement."

BIOGRAPHICAL/CRITICAL SOURCES: Time, March 15, 1968; Harper's, March, 1968; Best Sellers, April 1, 1968; Atlantic, April, 1968; Book World, May 5, 1968; New York Times, March 17, 1972.†

(Died March 16, 1972)

* * *

GRANT, Mary A(melia) 1890-

PERSONAL: Born November 10, 1890, in Topeka, Kan.; daughter of Emerson Warren (a civil engineer) and Jennie (Bradbury) Grant. Education: University of Kansas, A.B., 1913, A.M., 1914; Bryn Mawr College, graduate student, 1914-15; University of Wisconsin, Ph.D., 1919; postdoctoral study at American Academy in Rome, 1919-20, and American School in Athens, summer, 1936. Politics: Republican. Religion: Congregational. Home: 1444 Engel Rd., Lawrence, Kan. 66044.

CAREER: Western College for Woman (now Western College), Oxford, Ohio, instructor in Latin, 1916-17; University of Kansas, Lawrence, instructor in Latin, 1921-22, assistant professor of Latin and Greek, 1922-27, associate professor, 1927-60, curator of Wilcox Museum of Classical Antiquities, 1944-60. *Member:* American Philological Association, Classical League, Classical Association of the Middle West and South, American Association of University Professors, National League of American Pen Women, Phi Beta Kappa, Pi Lambda Theta. *Awards, honors:* University of Wisconsin postdoctoral traveling fellowship, 1919-20.

WRITINGS: The Ancient Rhetorical Theories of the Laughable, University of Wisconsin Studies in Language and Literature, 1921; (editor) G. C. Fiske, *Cicero's De Oratore and Horace's Ars Poetica,* University of Wisconsin Studies in Language and Literature, 1929; (translator and editor) *The Myths of Hyginus,* University of Kansas Press, 1960; *Folktale and Hero Tale Motifs in the Odes of Pindar,* University of Kansas Press, 1967. Poetry was published in six issues of *Atlantic Monthly,* 1943-47, and in *Spirit.*

* * *

GRANT, Ozro F. 1908-

PERSONAL: Born September 6, 1908, in Durham, Okla.; son of James Lafayette (a farmer) and Mary Etta (Mills) Grant; married Ollie Jameson; children: Mrs. Tom Baxter, Mrs. Herman Brown, Ruth Beebe, Laurel Spawn, Margaret. *Politics:* Independent. *Religion:* Protestant. *Address:* Route 3 Box 258 M, Charleston, Ark. 72933.

CAREER: College of the Sequoias, Visalia, Calif., teacher of creative writing, 1956-63; currently a part-time rancher in Arkansas. Board member, Arts and Crafts Festival, Greenwood, Ark. *Member:* Authors League of America.

WRITINGS: Bad 'Un, Ace Books, 1954; *From Diapers to Diplomas,* Vantage, 1956; *Kick the Dog Gently,* Bobbs-Merrill, 1965. Contributor to periodicals, including *Rosicrucian Digest* and *Koppers News.*

WORK IN PROGRESS: Farewell Dear Charley; research on Pancho Villa and the Mexican campaign, and on postal service, 1928-63.

AVOCATIONAL INTERESTS: Metaphysics, occultism, politics, psychology.

* * *

GRANTHAM, Alexander (William George Herder) 1899-

PERSONAL: Born March 15, 1899, in London, England; son of F. W. and A. (Von Herder) Grantham; married Maurine Samson, October 28, 1925. *Education:* Pembroke College, Cambridge, B.A., 1922, M.A., 1925. *Home:* 90 Piccadily, London, England.

CAREER: Called to Bar of Inner Temple, 1934; British Colonial Service, colonial secretary in Bermuda, 1935-38, and Jamaica, 1938-41, chief colonial secretary in Nigeria, 1942-44, governor of Fiji and high commissioner for Western Pacific, 1945-47, governor of Hong Kong, 1947-57. Political adviser to Shell Co. in Far East, 1959-62. Governor of Wellington College. *Military service:* British Army, 18th Hussars, 1917-19. *Member:* Naval and Military Club. *Awards, honors:* Knighted (Knight Commander of St. Michael and St. George), 1945; LL.D., University of Hong Kong; honorary fellow, Pembroke College, Cambridge University.

WRITINGS: Via Ports, Hong Kong University Press, 1965.

GRAY, Dwight E(lder) 1903-

PERSONAL: Born July 6, 1903, in Knoxville, Ohio; son of Lorenzo L. (a minister) and Mary Emma (Elder) Gray; married Helen Baldwin, September 5, 1931. *Education:* Muskingum College, A.B., 1925; Ohio State University, M.S., 1929, Ph.D., 1932. *Home:* 1001 Spring St., Apt. 1105, Silver Spring, Md. 20910.

CAREER: High school teacher in Ohio, 1925-29; University of Akron, Akron, Ohio, 1932-43, started as instructor, became associate professor of physics; Harvard University, Underwater Sound Laboratory, Cambridge, Mass., editor, 1943-45; Johns Hopkins University, Applied Physics Laboratory, Silver Spring, Md., supervisor of technical reports, 1945-50; U.S. Library of Congress, Washington, D.C., chief of Technical Information Division, 1950-55; National Science Foundation, Washington, D.C., program director, 1955-63; Library of Congress, chief of Science and Technology Division, 1963-65; American Institute of Physics, Washington, D.C., Washington representative, 1966-72. Adviser to technical information branch, U.S. Atomic Energy Commission, 1950. *Member:* American Physical Society, American Association for the Advancement of Science, National Association of Science Writers, Society for Technical Communication, Sigma Xi, Sigma Pi Sigma.

WRITINGS: (With John H. Martens) *Radiation Monitoring in Atomic Defense,* Van Nostrand, 1951; (coordinating editor) *American Institute of Physics Handbook,* McGraw, 1957, 3rd edition, 1972; (with J. W. Coutts) *Man and His Physical World,* Van Nostrand, 1942, 4th edition, 1966; *So You have to Write a Technical Report,* Information Resources Press, 1970.

* * *

GRAY, J(ohn) Stanley 1894-

PERSONAL: Born November 8, 1894, in Freeport, Ohio; son of Thomas Andrew and Elizabeth (Johnston) Gray; married Gunborg Berglund, June 18, 1923; children: Mary Catherine (Mrs. W. R. Myles, Jr.), J. Stanley II, Olga Ruth. *Education:* Muskingum College, A.B., 1920; University of Michigan, A.M., 1924; Ohio State University, Ph.D., 1929.

CAREER: Gustavus Adolphus College, St. Peter, Minn., professor of speech, 1921-24; University of Minnesota, Minneapolis, assistant professor of speech, 1924-25; University of Oregon, Eugene, assistant professor of speech, 1924-27; University of Pittsburgh, Pittsburgh, Pa., associate professor of psychology, 1931-46; University of Denver, Denver, Colo., professor of psychology, 1946-47; University of Georgia, Athens, professor of psychology, 1947-62. Visiting professor at University of Texas, 1956-57, and Southern Illinois University. *Military service:* U.S. Army, Medical Corps, 1917-18; became sergeant. *Member:* American Psychological Association.

WRITINGS: Psychological Foundations of Education, American Book Co., 1935; *Psychology in Use,* American Book Co., 1941, 2nd edition, 1951; *Psychology Applied in Human Affairs,* McGraw, 1946, 2nd edition, 1954; *Psychology in Industry,* McGraw, 1952; (with Karl Garrison) *Educational Psychology,* Appleton, 1955, 2nd edition, 1964. Contributor to professional journals.††

* * *

GREEN, Mary McBurney 1896-

PERSONAL: Born October 1, 1896, in Englewood, N.J.; daughter of George Thomas (a stockbroker) and Mary Burd

(Peale) Green. *Education:* Columbia University, B.S., 1929, M.A., 1934. *Religion:* Christian.

CAREER: Teacher at Harriet Johnson Nursery School, Bank St., New York, N.Y., 1934-38, and Green Acres School, Bethesda, Md., 1942-49; Wheaton College, Norton, Mass., associate professor of education and director of nursery school, 1949-56. Has exhibited her art work, which includes painting, etching, dry point, engraving, and lithography. Secretary, Brookfield Craft Center, Brookfield, Conn., 1957-60. *Member:* National Association for the Education of Young Children, League of Women Voters, Flanders Nature Center (Woodbury, Conn.).

WRITINGS—Children's books: *Everybody Has a House,* W. R. Scott, 1944; *Is It Hard? Is It Easy?,* W. R. Scott, 1949; *Everybody Eats,* W. R. Scott, 1950; *Whose Little Red Jacket?,* F. Watts, 1965; *When Will I Whistle?,* F. Watts, 1967; *Everybody Grows Up,* F. Watts, 1969.†

* * *

GREENBLATT, M(anuel) H(arry) 1922-1972

PERSONAL: Born November 26, 1922, in Philadelphia, Pa.; son of Louis (a jeweler) and Anna (Sutan) Greenblatt; married Nora Hymes (a music teacher), 1945; children: Harriet Karen, Barbara Sue. *Education:* University of Pennsylvania, A.B., 1943, Ph.D., 1948. *Religion:* Jewish. *Home:* 60 Wittmer Ct., Princeton, N.J. 08540.

CAREER: Radio Corporation of America, Princeton, N.J., research engineer, 1948-68. *Member:* American Physical Society, Institute of Electrical and Electronics Engineers, Sigma Xi.

WRITINGS: Mathematical Entertainments, Crowell, 1965; *Multiple Sclerosis and Me,* C. C Thomas, 1972. Contributor to *American Scientist, Review of Scientific Instruments, American Journal of Physics,* and other journals.

WORK IN PROGRESS: Research leading to a collection of examples for a reasonable and proper understanding of current and extant theories in physics and mathematics.†

(Died December 25, 1972)

* * *

GREENE, Harry A. 1889-

PERSONAL: Born October 1, 1889, in Cedar Rapids, Iowa; son of William W. and Fannie B. (Paterson) Greene; married Iva I. Kratzer, August 20, 1913; children: William Franklin. *Education:* Coe College, B.S., 1911; University of Iowa, M.A., 1916, Ph.D., 1919. *Politics:* Republican. *Religion:* Protestant. *Home:* 100 Randall Road, Princeton, N.J.

CAREER: University of Iowa, Iowa City, 1919-1955, became professor of education and director of Bureau of Educational Research and Service, professor emeritus, beginning 1955. Visiting summer professor at University of West Virginia and University of California, Los Angeles. *Member:* American Educational Research Association (past president and past secretary-treasurer), National Society for the Study of Education, National Education Association, Phi Delta Kappa. *Awards, honors:* Ed.D., Coe College, 1965.

WRITINGS: Measurement and Evaluation in Elementary School, Longmans, Green, 1943; (with A. N. Jorgensen and J. R. Gerberich) *Measurement and Evaluation in Secondary School,* Longmans, Green, 1943; (with McBroom, Ashley, and others) *Building Better English,* Harper, 1944, 4th edition, 1965; (with Walter T. Petty) *Developing Language*

Skills in the Elementary School, Allyn & Bacon, 1959, 4th edition, 1971; (with A. N. Jorgensen and J. R. Gerberich) *Measurement and Evaluation in the Modern School,* McKay, 1962. Former editor, *Review of Educational Research.*

* * *

GREENER, Leslie 1900-1974

PERSONAL: Born February 13, 1900, in Cape Town, South Africa; son of Herbert (a military officer) and Helen (Bennett) Greener; married Rhona Haszard, December 20, 1925 (deceased); married Margaret Edmunds, April 20, 1934 (deceased); married Dorothy Henry, July 30, 1968; children: (second marriage) Guy. *Education:* Graduate of Royal Military College at Sandhurst, 1919; studied art at Academie Julien, Paris, France, 1927-28, and did external work at University of London, 1930. *Politics:* Independent ("for international understanding"). *Religion:* Pagan. *Home:* 3 Lambert Ave., Hobart, Tasmania, 7005, Australia.

CAREER: British Indian Army, career officer, 1919-24; Victoria College, Alexandria, Egypt, teacher of art and French, 1928-31; University of Chicago, Oriental Institute Expedition, Luxor, Egypt, archaeological artist, 1931-36; Associated Newspapers, Sydney, Australia, journalist, 1937-41, 1945-49; Australian Army, 1941-45, taken prisoner in Malaya and held by Japanese for three and one-half years (received promotion to captain from the ranks); director of adult education, Tasmania, Australia, 1949-54; University of Chicago, Oriental Institute Expedition, archaeological artist, 1958-67. Author. *Member:* Society of Australian Writers. *Awards, honors:* Commonwealth of Australia literary fellowship, 1957.

WRITINGS: He Lived in My Shoes, Harrap, 1948; *No Time to Look Back,* Viking, 1950; *Moon Ahead,* Viking, 1951; *Wizard Boatman of the Nile,* Harrap, 1957; *High Dam over Nubia,* Viking, 1962; *The Discovery of Egypt,* Cassell, 1966, Viking, 1967. Also author with Norman Laird of *Ross Bridge and the Sculpture of Daniel Herbert.* Writer of numerous radio and television scripts for Australian Broadcasting Commission; also writer of script for "Aborigines of Van Dieman's Hand," a documentary film for Tasmanian Government Film Unit.

WORK IN PROGRESS: Further Discovery in Egypt, a continuation of *The Discovery of Egypt,* using material gathered during the 1966-67 expedition.

SIDELIGHTS: Leslie Greener told *CA:* "Interests are living men and the history that made them as they are. Also interested in all ancient history, including remains of vanished stone-age people of Tasmania, who were living when white men first came. Believe modern man still in untamed savage state; yet am not pessimistic. . . . Individual life is, to me, pointless in terms of human comprehension; yet it is sufficiently enthralling an experience to be worth living. Intend to live until I am at least 140 years old. My country home in Tasmania burnt to the ground in a forest fire last February. Lost all notes and files. Also birth certificate; hence old age postponed."†

(Died December 8, 1974)

* * *

GREENSPUN, H(erman) M(ilton) 1909-
(Hank Greenspun)

PERSONAL: Born August 27, 1909, in Brooklyn, N.Y.; son of Samuel J. and Anna (Fleischman) Greenspun; married Barbara Joan Ritchie (treasurer of *Las Vegas Sun*), May 21, 1944; children: Susan Gail, Brian Lee, Jane Toni, Daniel Alan. *Education:* St. John's College, Brooklyn, N.Y., LL.B., 1934. *Politics:* Republican. *Home:* Regency Towers, Las Vegas, Nev. *Office: Las Vegas Sun,* 121 South Highland, Las Vegas, Nev. 89106.

CAREER: Admitted to New York Bar, 1936; private law practice, New York, N.Y., 1936-46; *Las Vegas Life* (magazine), Las Vegas, Nev., publisher, 1946-47; *Las Vegas Sun* (newspaper), Las Vegas, owner, publisher, editorial writer, and columnist, beginning 1950. Owner, KLAS-TV, Las Vegas, 1954-68. *Military service:* U.S. Army, 1941-46; became major; received Croix de Guerre with silver star. *Member:* National Press Club, Overseas Press Club, Nevada State Press Association (president, 1957), American Legion, Veterans of Foreign Wars, Disabled American Veterans. *Awards, honors:* Outstanding Journalist Award, Jewish War Veterans, 1957; Nevada State Press Association award for best column, 1959.

WRITINGS: (Under name Hank Greenspun, with Alex Pelle) *Where I Stand,* McKay, 1966. Contributor to *Collier's* and other magazines.

*   *   *

GRIERSON, John 1909-1977

PERSONAL: Born January 2, 1909, in Liverpool, England; son of John (a cotton broker) and Edith Jessie (Cairns) Grierson; married Frances Hellyer, April 16, 1936; children: Nicola Rosamund (Mrs. David Mackrill), Bruce John, Peter Angus Hellyer. *Education:* Attended Royal Air Force College, Cranwell, 1928-29. *Home:* Beauregard, Beauregard Lane, St. Peter Port, Guernsey, Channel Islands. *Agent:* A. M. Heath & Co. Ltd., 40-42 William IV St., London, WC2 England.

CAREER: Royal Air Force, regular service, 1928-31, reserve service, 1932-45; Hawker Siddeley Aviation, Brooklands, Coventry and Gloucester, England, test pilot, 1938-45; United Whalers, flight commodore, 1946-47; deputy director of civil aviation in Germany, 1948-49; de Havilland Engine Co., sales executive in Leaverden, England, 1950-55, superintendent of flight development in Hatfield, England, 1955-62, sales manager for de Havilland Aircraft & Hawker Siddeley, 1962-64, California representative for Hawker Siddeley Dynamics, 1964-65. Main speaker at National Air and Space Museum Symposium on fiftieth anniversary of Lindbergh's solo flight, 1977. *Member:* Royal Geographical Society (fellow; council, 1963-65), Army and Navy Club, Royal Channel Isles Yacht Club.

WRITINGS: Through Russia By Air, Foulis & Co., 1934; *High Failure,* Hodge & Co., 1935; *Jet Flight,* Sampson Low, Marston & Co., 1945; *Air Whaler,* Sampson Low, Marston & Co., 1948; *Sir Hubert Wilkins: Enigma of Exploration,* R. Hale, 1961; *Challenge to the Poles,* foreword by Charles A. Lindbergh, Archon Books, 1964; *Heroes of the Polar Skies,* Heinemann, 1967. Contributor to *Flight* and *Times* (London).

AVOCATIONAL INTERESTS: Flying.

(Died May, 1977)

*   *   *

GRIFFITHS, G(ordon) D(ouglas) 1910-1973

PERSONAL: Born July 19, 1910, in Wallasey, Cheshire, England; son of Harold Ernest (a jeweler) and May (James) Griffiths; married Edith Grace Chalmers Lane (a librarian),

October 14, 1948. *Education:* Attended St. Luke's College, Exeter, 1957-58. *Politics:* Liberal. *Religion:* Church of England. *Home:* Shute Hill House, Teignmouth, Devonshire, England.

CAREER: Engaged in farming prior to World War II; teacher of French, Latin, and Greek in various Devonshire preparatory schools, the last being Exeter Cathedral School, 1959-60. Publisher's reader and free-lance writer. *Military service:* British Army, Intelligence Corps, 1943-46; became acting sergeant.

WRITINGS: (With wife, Edith Grace Griffiths) *History of Teignmouth,* Brunwsick Press, 1965; *Mattie: The Story of a Hedgehog* (children's book; illustrated by Elsie Wrigley), World's Work, 1967; *Silver Blue,* World's Work, 1970; *Abandoned,* World's Work, 1973. Contributor of articles on fishing to *Angler, Caravan Life, Angling Times,* and other periodicals.

WORK IN PROGRESS: More books for children.

SIDELIGHTS: Griffiths told *CA:* "Am not primarily a naturalist; such knowledge as I have of wild life has been acquired incidentally while following outdoor pursuits. Interested in farming, gardening, shooting, fishing, reading, and solving crossword puzzles. Detest mawkish sentimentality about animals and hypocrisy of any kind."†

(Died July, 1973)

*   *   *

GRISEWOOD, Harman (Joseph Gerard) 1906-

PERSONAL: Born February 8, 1906, in Broxbourne, England; son of Harman (a lieutenant colonel in the British Army) and Lucille (Cardozo) Grisewood; married Margaret Bailey, September 14, 1940; children: Sabina. *Education:* Attended Worcester College, Oxford, 1924-27. *Religion:* Roman Catholic. *Address:* c/o Coutts & Co., 10 Mount St., London W1Y 6DP, England.

CAREER: British Broadcasting Corp., London, England, member of repertory company, 1929-33, announcer, 1933-36, assistant to program organizer, 1936-39, assistant director of program planning, 1939-41, assistant controller of European Division, 1941-45, acting controller of European Division, 1945-46, director of talks, 1946-47, planner of Third Programme, 1947-48, controller of Third Programme, 1948-52, director of the Spoken Word, 1952-55, chief assistant to the director-general, 1955-64. Vice-president, European Broadcasting Union, 1953-54. Welsh national lecturer, 1966. *Member:* Royal Society of Arts (fellow). *Awards, honors:* King Christian X Freedom Medal, 1946; Commander of the Order of the British Empire, 1960; Knight of Order of Malta, 1960.

WRITINGS: (Editor) *Ideas and Beliefs of the Victorians,* Dutton, 1949; *Broadcasting and Society,* S.C.M. Press, 1949; (editor) *Epoch and Artist: Selected Writings of David Jones,* Faber, 1959; *The Recess* (novel), Macdonald & Co., 1963; *The Last Cab on the Rank* (novel), Macdonald & Co., 1964; *David Jones: Artist and Writer* (booklet), British Broadcasting Corp., 1966; *One Thing at a Time* (autobiography), Hutchinson, 1968; *The Painted Kipper: A Study of the Spurious in the Contemporary Scene* (essay), C. A. Watts, 1970. Editor, *Dublin Review* (religious quarterly), 1949-52.

BIOGRAPHICAL/CRITICAL SOURCES: London Magazine, May, 1968; *Books and Bookmen,* May, 1968; *One Thing at a Time* (autobiography), Hutchinson, 1968.

GROOM, Bernard 1892-

PERSONAL: Born September 20, 1892, in London, England; son of Frank Sutherland (a corn merchant) and Alice Emma (Bailhache) Groom. Education: University College, London, B.A., 1914, M.A. (with distinction), 1915; Magdalen College, Oxford, B.A., 1917, M.A., 1921. Politics: Conservative. Religion: Anglican.

CAREER: Clifton College, Bristol, England, master of senior English, 1919-40; University of Montevideo, Montevideo, Uruguay, professor of English, 1941-48; McMaster University, Hamilton, Ontario, associate professor, 1949-57, professor of English, 1957-60. Member of Libraries and Museum Committee, Weston super Mare, 1967. Awards, honors: Essay prize, Society for Pure English, 1937.

WRITINGS: Poems, Elkin Mathews, 1924; (editor) John Keats, Selections, Macmillan, 1927; (editor) Alexander Pope, The Rape of the Lock, Macmillan, 1929; A Literary History of England, Longmans, Green, 1929, 4th edition published as A History of English Literature, 1947; A Short History of English Words, Macmillan, 1934, 7th edition, 1966; (editor) Wordsworth, a Selection, Edward Arnold, 1936; (editor) William Shakespeare, Macbeth, Clarendon Press, 1939, reprinted with corrections, 1959; The Diction of Poetry from Spenser to Bridges, University of Toronto Press, 1955, 2nd edition, 1960; (editor) Edward Gibbon, The Autobiography of Edward Gibbon, St. Martin's, 1956; The Unity of Wordsworth's Poetry, Macmillan, 1966. Contributor to Encyclopedia of Poetry and Poetics, Princeton University Press, 1965, Essays and Studies of the English Association, and Society for Pure English tracts.

WORK IN PROGRESS: "W. P. Ker and the Teaching of Literature," an article to be included in a collection of Groom's essays.

SIDELIGHTS: A History of English Literature was translated into Spanish and published in Montevideo, 1947. Groom is competent in French and Spanish, and a student of Greek, Latin, German, and Italian. Avocational interests: Theology.†

*   *   *

GROSECLOSE, Elgin 1899-

PERSONAL: Born November 25, 1899, in Waukomis, Okla.; son of Clarence and Della (Wishard) Groseclose; married Louise Williams, June 25, 1927; children: Jane (Mrs. Peter Theodoropoulos), Nancy (Mrs. Herold Witherspoon), Hildegarde (Mrs. Earl Bender), Suzy (Mrs. Kenneth Labaugh). Education: University of Oklahoma, A.B., 1920; American University, M.A., 1924, Ph.D., 1928. Home: 4813 Woodway Lane N.W., Washington, D.C. 20016. Office: Groseclose, Williams & Associates, 1010 Vermont Ave. N.W., Washington, D.C. 20005.

CAREER: Teacher at Presbyterian Mission School in Tabriz, Persia (now Iran), and secretary of Persia Relief Commission, 1920-23; U.S. Department of Commerce, Washington, D.C., special agent, 1923-26, assistant U.S. Trade Commissioner, 1926; Guaranty Trust Co., New York City, staff member, 1927-30; Fortune (magazine), New York City, associate editor, 1930-32; University of Oklahoma, Norman, assistant professor of economics, 1932-38; U.S. Government, Washington, D.C., economist with Federal Communications Commission, 1935-38, and Treasury Department, 1938-43; Treasurer-General of Iran by appointment of Iranian Parliament, 1943; Elgin Groseclose (economic consultant), Washington, D.C., head of firm, 1944-59; Groseclose,

Williams & Associates (financial and investment consultants), Washington, D.C., head of firm, beginning 1959; Institute for Monetary Research, Washington, D.C., founder, executive director, beginning 1960. Lecturer in banking and finance, City College (now City College of the City University of New York), 1930-32; founder, president, Welfare of the Blind, Inc., Washington, D.C., 1956-68. Washington City Bible Society, trustee, beginning 1945, president, 1968-73.

MEMBER: National Association of Business Economists, Phi Beta Kappa, National Economists Club (founding member), Cosmos Club (Washington, D.C.). Awards, honors: American Booksellers Award, 1939, and Foundation for Literature Award, 1940, both for Ararat.

WRITINGS: Money: The Human Conflict, University of Oklahoma Press, 1934; The Persian Journey of the Rev. Ashley Wishard and His Servant Fathi, Bobbs-Merrill, 1939; Ararat, Carrick & Evans, 1939; The Firedrake, Lippincott, 1942; Introduction to Iran, Oxford University Press, 1947; (contributor) Frances Brentano, editor, The Word Lives On, Doubleday, 1951; The Carmelite, Macmillan, 1955; The Scimitar of Saladin, Macmillan, 1956; Money and Man, Ungar, 1961; Fifty Years of Managed Money: The Story of the Federal Reserve, Books, Inc., 1966.

Monographs: The Decay of Money, Institute for Monetary Research, 1962; The Monetary Uses of Silver, Institute for Monetary Research, 1965; The Siken Metal: Silver, Past, Present Prospective, Institute for Monetary Research, 1975.

BIOGRAPHICAL/CRITICAL SOURCES: Harry R. Warfel, American Novelists of Today, American Book Co., 1951.

*   *   *

GROSS, John J. 1912-1970

PERSONAL: Born March 20, 1912, in Walla Walla, Wash.; son of John Jefferson (a farmer) and Millie (Hale) Gross; married Beth J. Brockman, 1933 (divorced); married Cleo Sibley, August 7, 1945 (divorced); married Stefania Engelhardt (director of a language laboratory), August 18, 1960; children: (first marriage) John Derek Lewis, Jeffrey Gil Lewis; (third marriage) Katherine, Margaret. Education: Attended Oregon State University, 1929-31; University of Oregon, B.A., 1934, M.A., 1942; University of Iowa, Ph.D., 1955. Religion: Episcopalian. Home: 868 Carol Rd., Bowling Green, Ohio 43402. Office: Department of English, Bowling Green State University, Bowling Green, Ohio 43402.

CAREER: Instructor in English at Washington State University, Pullman, 1944-46, and at Oregon State University, Corvallis, 1946; Lewis and Clark College, Portland, Ore., assistant professor, 1946-47, associate professor of English, 1947-53; University of Iowa, Iowa City, instructor in English, 1953-55; San Jose State College (now University), San Jose, Calif., assistant professor of English, 1955-56; Indiana University, Kokomo Campus, assistant professor, 1956-57, associate professor of English, 1957-62; Bowling Green State University, Bowling Green, Ohio, professor of English, 1962-70. Fulbright professor, University of Helsinki, 1957-59. Visiting summer professor at University of Warsaw, 1958, and University of Turku and Abo Academy, 1968. Member: Modern Language Association of America, Modern Language Society of Finland (honorary member), American Association of University Professors.

WRITINGS: John P. Marquand, Twayne, 1963; (with

Richard C. Carpenter) *The Examined Life,* World Publishing, 1967; *James Joyce,* Viking, 1970 (published in England as *Joyce,* Fontana Books, 1971). Contributor of essays, criticism, and reviews to literary journals.

WORK IN PROGRESS: Sir Thomas Browne, for Twayne; and *The Community Theme in American Literature.*†

(Died September 13, 1970)

*   *   *

GROSS, John Owen   1894-1971

PERSONAL: Born July 9, 1894, in Folsom, Ky.; son of William (a carpenter) and Anna Marie (Chrisman) Gross; married Harriet Blatzer, June 30, 1920 (died May 9, 1966); children: George Albert, John Birney, Harriet Lucille (Mrs. Edwin E. Smith). *Education:* Asbury College, A.B., 1918; Boston University, S.T.B., 1921; graduate study at University of Cincinnati and University of Kentucky. *Home:* 3415 West End Ave., Apt. 903, Nashville, Tenn. 37203.

CAREER: Ordained elder of Methodist Episcopal Church, 1921; pastor, then district superintendent, Barbourville, Ky., 1921-29; Union College, Barbourville, Ky., president, 1929-38; Simpson College, Indianola, Iowa, president, 1938-41; The Methodist Church, Board of Education, Nashville, Tenn., executive secretary of Department (later Division) of Educational Institutions, 1941-65; educational consultant, beginning 1965. Trustee of American University and a number of Methodist colleges. *Member:* National Education Association, Phi Beta Kappa, Kiwanis Club, Old Oak Club, Cumberland Club, Cosmos Club. *Awards, honors:* Degrees from twenty-six colleges and universities, including De Pauw University, University of Chattanooga, Iowa Wesleyan University, and Boston University; Order of Achievement, Lambda Chi Alpha.

WRITINGS: Education for Life, Abingdon, 1949; *Martin Ruter: Christian Educator,* Board of Education, Methodist Church, 1956; *Methodist Beginnings in Higher Education,* Abingdon, 1958; *Beginnings of American Methodism,* Abingdon, 1961. Contributor to *Christian Century* and Methodist church school publications.

WORK IN PROGRESS: History of Higher Education in the Methodist Church; a book on John Wesley and education; section on higher education for *Dictionary of World Methodism,* for Abingdon.

SIDELIGHTS: In a page devoted to the expansion of Methodist college campuses, *Time* credited Gross with sparking the growth of the education empire, citing the three hundred new college buildings and five new campuses opened between 1957-61. Gross also raised a $300,000 annual scholarship fund for students at Methodist institutions, administered under a loan plan.

BIOGRAPHICAL/CRITICAL SOURCES: Time, February 3, 1961.†

(Died February, 1971)

*   *   *

GROSSMAN, William L(eonard)   1906-

PERSONAL: Born April 4, 1906, in New York, N.Y.; son of William (an attorney) and Carrie (Basch) Grossman; married Mignon Soire, May 22, 1929; children: Ruth C. (Mrs. Richard B. Hadlock), Elizabeth A. (Mrs. Earl Hammond). *Education:* Harvard University, B.A., 1927, M.A., 1928, LL.B., 1932; New York University, J.S.D., 1936. *Home:* 50 Marshall St., Brookline, Mass. 02146.

CAREER: Attorney in New York City, and Washington, D.C., 1933-35; New York University, New York City, faculty member, 1937-48; Instituto Tecnologico de Aeronautica, Sao Jose dos Campos, S.P., Brazil, chairman of department of transport economics, 1948-52; New York University, faculty member, 1952-73, professor of business administration and law of commerce, 1965-73. Consultant to government agencies and transportation companies. *Member:* Brazilian Academy of Letters, Portuguese Language Society. *Awards, honors:* Machado de Assis Medal of Brazilian Academy of Letters, 1960; Commander of the Order of Rio Branco from Brazilian government, 1969, for translations of Brazilian authors into English.

WRITINGS: Air Passenger Traffic, Remsen Press, 1947; (with Jack W. Farrell) *The Heart of Jazz,* New York University Press, 1956; *Ocean Freight Rates,* Cornell Maritime, 1956; *Fundamentals of Transportation,* Simmons-Boardman, 1959.

Translator from the Portuguese: Machado de Assis, *Epitaph of a Small Winner,* Noonday, 1952; (with James L. Taylor) Jorge Amado, *Gabriela, Clove and Cinnamon,* Knopf, 1962; (with Helen Caldwell) Machado de Assis, *The Psychiatrist and Other Stories,* University of California Press, 1962; (and author of introduction, biographical notes, and commentary) *Modern Brazilian Short Stories,* University of California Press, 1967. Also contributor of translations to *New World Writing* and *Odyssey Review.*

Contributor of articles on literature (mainly Brazilian) and reviews to *Americas, Commonweal, Hispania, Saturday Review, Crisis, New York Times Book Review,* and other journals; contributor of articles on music to *Jazz Today, Metronome, Village Voice,* and other periodicals; contributor of articles on transportation to *Air Transport, Collier's Yearbook, Journal of Air Law and Commerce, New York University Law Review,* and *Railway Age,* as well as other publications; also contributor of articles on a variety of subjects to *American Labor Legislation Review, Yale Law Journal, Nation, Commercial and Financial Chronicle,* and *American Mercury.*

SIDELIGHTS: Early in his professional life Grossman became a New Deal lawyer, "one of the so-called bright young men." When his specialization in transportation led to work for the Brazilian government, he learned Portuguese, in the field, and discovered the literature of Brazil. He has since pursued, according to Alexander Coleman, "his persistent and quite justified avocation and translation of Brazilian novels." Most importantly, he discovered Machado de Assis and introduced him, in translation, to American readers. He frequently lectures on Machado de Assis, and has been a consultant to several publishers in selecting Brazilian works for publication in English.

BIOGRAPHICAL/CRITICAL SOURCES: New York Times Book Review, July 9, 1967.

*   *   *

GROUT, Ruth E(llen)   1901-

PERSONAL: Born October 4, 1901, in Princeton, Mass.; daughter of Edgar Homer and Laura (Miller) Grout. *Education:* Mount Holyoke College, A.B., 1923; Yale University, M.P.H., 1930, Ph.D., 1939. *Politics:* Independent. *Religion:* Congregational. *Home:* 6 Brandon Road, Chapel Hill, N.C. 27514.

CAREER: Teacher of biology in secondary schools in Connecticut, 1923-31; director of school health education study in Cattaraugus County, N.Y., 1931-38; consultant on health education to Tennessee Valley Authority, Chattanooga, Tenn., 1939-42, U.S. Office of Education, Washington, D.C., 1942-43; University of Minnesota, Minneapolis, associate professor, 1943-52, professor of health education, School of Public Health and College of Education, 1952-67, professor emeritus, 1967—. World Health Organization, consultant in Europe, 1952-53, 1956-57, Thailand, 1959, Nigeria, Togo, Ghana, 1962, and eastern Mediterranean region, 1966. Trustee of Northwestern Hospital, Minneapolis.

MEMBER: American Public Health Association (fellow; chairman of health education section, 1952-53), American School Health Association (fellow), American Association of Retired Persons, American Association of University Women, American Association for Health, Physical Education and Recreation, Society of Public Health Educators, Quota Club (Minneapolis). *Awards, honors:* Elizabeth Severance Prentiss National Award, 1958.

WRITINGS: A Project in Rural School Health Education, Milbank Memorial Fund, 1935; (editor) *Handbook of Health Education,* Doubleday, Doran, 1936; *Evaluation of a Rural School Health Education Project,* Milbank Memorial Fund, 1938; *Health Teaching in Schools,* Saunders, 1948, 5th edition, 1968. Editor of World Health Organization seminar reports; contributor to professional journals.

AVOCATIONAL INTERESTS: Travel, cooking, and birds.†

*   *   *

GROVES, Ruth Clouse   1902-

PERSONAL: Born March 23, 1902, in Cunningham, Kan.; daughter of Johnathan (a building contractor) and Lillie Mae (Dotson) Clouse; married Everett C. Groves (a newspaperman), June 22, 1929; children: Everett, Jr., Yvonne (Mrs. Thomas A. Dailey), Homer. *Education:* Attended University of Kansas, 1919-20, 1921-22; University of Nebraska, A.B., 1924, graduate study, 1927; also graduate study at University of Chicago, 1930, and Northwestern University, 1938, 1941. *Religion:* Baptist. *Home:* 834 Sixteenth St., Wilmette, Ill. 60091.

CAREER: Teacher of English in junior and senior high schools in Kansas, 1922-27, and Dallas, Tex., 1927-29; operator of private kindergarten in Elmwood Park, Ill., 1932-33; part-time teacher of English at New Trier Township High School and New Trier Adult Evening School, Winnetka, Ill. Volunteer publicity writer for Wilmette Family Service, 1942, Hospitalized Veterans Writing Project, 1950, and various civic groups in Wilmette, Ill. *Member:* National League of American Pen Women, American Association of University Women, Theta Sigma Phi. *Awards, honors:* Eunice Tiejens Award, Midwest Writers' Conference, 1942; first place award in free verse, Poets and Patrons Poetry Contest, Chicago.

WRITINGS: Harp on the Willow, Schori, 1964. Editor of "Growth in Good English" series, teachers' manuals for grades seven and eight. Contributor to education journals.

BIOGRAPHICAL/CRITICAL SOURCES: Sigma Kappa Triangle, spring, 1965; *Pen Women,* summer, 1966.††

*   *   *

GRUSD, Edward Elihu   1904-

PERSONAL: Surname rhymes with "buzzed"; born June 15, 1904, in Cincinnati, Ohio; son of Moses and Rose (Morris) Grusd; married Elizabeth Franklin, July 8, 1932;

children: David F., Dulcy (Mrs. Michael J. Brightman). *Education:* Ohio State University, B.Sc., 1926. *Politics:* Democrat. *Religion:* Jewish. *Home:* 3707 Morrison St. N.W., Washington, D.C. 20015.

CAREER: Reporter in Columbus, Ohio, 1925, and Cincinnati, Ohio, 1926-27; *Ohio State Journal,* Columbus, Ohio, feature writer in Europe, 1927; reporter in Omaha, Neb., 1928; *National Jewish Monthly,* Washington, D.C., editor, 1928-70. *L'Univers Israelite,* U.S. correspondent, 1929-39. *Member:* Sigma Delta Chi.

WRITINGS: B'nai B'rith: The Story of a Covenant, Appleton, 1966.

*   *   *

GUDSCHINSKY, Sarah C(aroline)   1919-1975

PERSONAL: Born May 8, 1919, in Bay City, Mich.; daughter of Eduard E. (a letter carrier) and Ursula E. (MacFarlane) Gudschinsky. *Education:* Central State Teachers College (now Central Michigan University), B.Sc., 1940; University of Pennsylvania, M.A., 1956, Ph.D., 1958. *Office:* Summer Institute of Linguistics, Huntington Beach, Calif. 92648.

CAREER: Teacher in rural elementary schools in Michigan, 1937-38, 1940-46; Summer Institute of Linguistics, linguistic and literacy field worker in Mixtec and Mazatec, Mexico, 1948-55, chairman, Technical Studies Department of Brazil branch, Rio de Janeiro, Brazil, 1958-66, literacy coordinator, directing workshops and seminars in Latin America, Australia, and New Guinea, beginning 1965. Instructor in linguistics and literacy, University of Oklahoma, summers, 1950-69; collaborating professor, University of Brasilia, Brazil, 1962-63, 1964-65; visiting professor, University College, University of London, 1964, Annamalai University, India, 1967; linguistic specialist, U.S. Agency for International Development, 1966-67; adjunct professor of linguistics, University of Texas at Arlington, 1970-71, 1971-72. Visiting lecturer, Museu Nacional, Rio de Janeiro, Brazil, Museu Goeldi, Belem, University of Bahia, and other universities and museums, 1958-63. Linguistic specialist, U.S. Agency for International Development, 1966-67; literacy specialist, Literacy House, Lucknow, India, 1967-68. Member, Inter-American Progressive Linguistics and Language Teaching, beginning 1963. Consultant, Crow Bilingual Education Program, 1971, Cherokee, 1972, Seminole, 1972-73.

WRITINGS: Handbook of Literacy, Summer Institute of Linguistics, 1951, 3rd edition, 1957; *Proto-Popotecan: A Comparative Study of Popolocan and Mixtecan,* Williams & Wilkins, 1959; *How to Learn an Unwritten Language,* Holt, 1967; *A Manual of Literacy for Preliterate Peoples,* Summer Institute of Linguistics, 1973.

Contributor: J. Mattoso Camera, Jr., *Introducao as linguas indigenas brasilerias,* Museo Nacional (Rio de Janeiro), 1965; *El Simposio de Bloomington., agosta de 1964: Actas, Informes, y Comunicaciones,* Instituto Caro y Cuervo (Bogota), 1967; *Idiomas, Cosmovisiones y Cultura,* Universidad Nacional del Litoral (Rosario, Argentina), 1968; Robert Wauchope, editor, *Handbook of Middle American Indians,* Volume V, University of Texas Press, 1968; *Conference on Navajo Orthography, Albuquerque, N.M., May 2-3, 1969,* Center for Applied Linguistics, 1969; William K. Durr, editor, *Reading Difficulties: Diagnosis, Correction and Remediation,* International Reading Association, 1970; Richard E. Hodges and E. Hugh Rudorf, editors, *The Nature of the Writing System: Pedagogical Implications, in Language and Learning to Read,* Houghton, 1972. Contributor of articles to *Language Learning, International Journal of American Linguistics, Word, Language, Fundamental and Adult Education, Current Anthropology, Notes on Translation, Kivung* (journal of the Linguistic Society of University of Papua and New Guinea), *Read, Bible Translator,* and other professional journals.†

(Died July 9, 1975)

*   *   *

GUILD, Lurelle Van Arsdale 1898-

PERSONAL: Born August 19, 1898, in New York, N.Y.; son of Thomas Lurelle (a cotton broker) and Alice (Gumble) Guild; married Louise Eden, November 26, 1929; children: Cynthia Eden (Mrs. Hugh Hitchens). *Education:* Syracuse University, Bachelor of Painting, 1920; further study at University of Berlin. *Religion:* Presbyterian. *Home:* 188 Long Neck Point Rd., Darien, Conn. 06820.

CAREER: Industrial designer, New York City, beginning 1927; president of Lurelle Guild Associates, New York City, and Dale Decorators, Darien, Conn., beginning 1929, and Milestone Village Museum (restoration of a colonial town), Noroton, Conn., beginning 1927. Adviser, National Housing Authority, 1942-44; director, Regional Planning Commission, New York City, 1952-55. Industrial designs include interiors of Alcoa steamships and small appliances for Westinghouse; work has been exhibited in Museum of Modern Art, Metropolitan Museum, and other galleries. *Member:* American Institute of Decorators, American Society of Industrial Designers (fellow); Art Directors Club, Coffee House, Dutch Treat Club, and Yale Club (all New York). *Awards, honors:* Art Directors Club Medal, 1924, for paintings and drawings done for J. Walter Thompson Advertising Agency; Fashion Academy Award, 1951, for household products; and other awards.

WRITINGS: (Self-illustrated) *The Geography of American Antiques,* Doubleday, 1927, revised edition (with Carl William Drepperd) published as *New Geography of American Antiques,* Doubleday, 1948; *The American Home Course in Period Furniture* (taken from material first published in *American Home,* 1930-32), Art Education Press, 1933; *Designed for Living,* Scranton Lace Co., 1936. Contributor to *Ladies' Home Journal, House and Garden, House Beautiful, Better Homes and Gardens,* and other magazines. Former associate editor, *Pictorial Review, American Home,* and *Delineator.*

WORK IN PROGRESS: Three books, *Suddenly It Happened, How to be an Expert on Antiques in Three Hours,* and *1812.*†

*   *   *

GUNNING, Robert 1908-

PERSONAL: Born May 21, 1908, in Glen Jean, W. Va.; son of John Robert (a public official) and Grace Gunning; married Mary Hadley Lewis; children: Nora, Thomas, Grace, Seth. *Education:* Ohio State University, B.A., 1930. *Politics:* Democrat. *Religion:* Unaffiliated. *Home and office:* 7495 East Broad St., Blacklick, Ohio 43004.

CAREER: Columbus Citizen, Columbus, Ohio, reporter, 1930-33; *Akron Beacon Journal,* Akron, Ohio, reporter, 1933-35; American Education Press, Columbus, editor, 1935-44; Robert Gunning Associates (writing consultants to business), Blacklick, Ohio, president, beginning 1944. *Member:* American Business Writers Association, Phi Beta Kappa, University Club of Columbus.

WRITINGS: Clear News Writing, Scripps-Howard Newspapers, 1950; *Clear Technical Writing,* Standard Oil of New Jersey, 1951; *The Technique of Clear Writing,* McGraw, 1952, revised and enlarged edition, 1968; *More Effective Writing,* Cahners Books (Boston), 1963; *How to Take the Fog Out of Writing,* Dartnell, 1964. Writer of sound-slide film, "How to Write Clear, Concise, and Effective Business Letters."

AVOCATIONAL INTERESTS: Travel, tennis, sculpture.

*   *   *

GUTMANN, James 1897-

PERSONAL: Born April 11, 1897, in New York, N.Y.; son of Carl (a merchant) and Lilly (Liebmann) Gutmann; married Jeanette Mack, February 3, 1920 (died, 1960); children: Barbara (Mrs. Paul Rosenkrantz), Carl Mack, Alice (Mrs. Martin Brandfonbrener). *Education:* Columbia University, A.B., 1918, M.A., 1919, Ph.D., 1936. *Home:* 39 Claremont Ave., New York, N.Y. 10027. *Office:* Columbia University, New York, N.Y. 10027.

CAREER: Columbia University, New York, N.Y., lecturer, 1920-30, instructor, 1930-36, assistant professor, 1936-42, associate professor, 1942-48, professor of philosophy, 1948-62, emeritus professor, 1962—, chairman of department, 1952-60, director of university seminars, 1970-76. Member of executive committee, New York Committee Against Capital Punishment; chairman of board of directors Encampment for Citizenship. *Member:* American Philosophical Association, American Association of University Professors, Conference on Method in Philosophy and Science (chairman), American Civil Liberties Union, Phi Beta Kappa, New York Philosophy Club, Columbia Faculty Club. *Awards, honors:* Great Teacher Award and Nicholas Murray Butler Medal for Philosophy, Columbia University.

WRITINGS: (With J. J. Cross and others) *Introduction to Reflective Thinking,* Houghton, 1923; (with Jacques Barzun) *Syllabus of an Introduction to Contemporary Civilization,* Columbia University Press, 1931; (editor, translator, and author of critical introduction and notes) F.W.J. von Schelling, *Of Human Freedom,* Open Court, 1938; (with others) *A College Program in Action,* Columbia University Press, 1945; (translator with others) Ernst Cassirer, *Rousseau, Kant, Goethe: Two Essays,* Princeton University Press, 1945; (editor and author of introduction) Baruch Spinoza, *Ethics,* Hafner, 1949; (with E. J. Sternglass and others) *Horizons of a Philosopher,* E. J. Brill, 1963; (editor) Salvatore Attanasio, translator, *Philosophy A to Z: Based on the Work of Alwin Diemer and Others,* Grosset, 1963; (editor) *Meditations of Marcus Aurelius,* Washington Square, 1963.

Contributor: H. J. Bridges, editor, *Aspects of Ethical Religion,* American Ethical Union, 1926; Alan W. Brown, editor, *Bibliography of Important Books,* American Library Association, 1940; P. A. Schilpp, editor, *The Philosophy of Ernst Cassirer,* Northwestern University Press, 1949; Corliss Lamont and Mary Redmer, editors, *Dialogue on George Santayana,* Horizon, 1959; Lamont, editor, *Dialogue on John Dewey,* Horizon, 1959; John P. Anton, editor, *Naturalism and Historical Understanding,* State University of New York Press, 1967; Howard E. Kiefer and Milton K. Munitz, editors, *Ethics and Social Justice,* State University of New York Press, 1968. Managing editor, *Standard;* member of editorial board, *Studies in Romanticism.*

WORK IN PROGRESS: Brand Blanshard's Philosophy of Education, for Library of Living Philosophers.

HABER, Tom Burns 1900-

PERSONAL: Born May 5, 1900, in Rossburg, Ohio; son of Charles Andrew and Lottie Sarah (Burns) Haber; married Grace Hamilton Stevenson (an instructor in English), August 3, 1929. Education: Ohio Northern University, A.B., 1921, B.Sc. in Ed., 1922; Ohio State University, A.M., 1925, Ph.D., 1929. Home: 220 Canyon Dr., Columbus, Ohio 43214.

CAREER: High school teacher of English in Ohio, 1921-24; Ohio State University, Columbus, instructor in English language and literature, 1927-49, assistant professor, 1949-66, associate professor, 1966-67, professor of humanities, beginning 1968. Director of Writers' Workshop, Columbus branch of American Association of University Women, 1941-44. Secretary of board of trustees, Ohioana Library, 1944-49; member of board of directors, Ohio Poetry Day. Member: Bibliographical Society of America, American Association of University Professors, English Association of Ohio (treasurer, 1962-65), Columbus Rose Club, Alpha Phi Gamma (founder).

WRITINGS: Comparative Study of the Beowulf and the Aeneid, Princeton University Press, 1931, reprinted, Phaeton Press, 1968; Two Centuries of Anecdotes, Christopher, 1932; Writer's Handbook of American Usage, Longmans, Green, 1942; Handbook of Basic English, Appleton, 1945; (editor) A. E. Housman, The Manuscript Poems, University of Minnesota Press, 1955; Thirty Housman Letters to Witter Bynner, Knopf, 1957; (editor) A. E. Housman, Complete Poems (Centennial edition), Holt, 1959; The Making of a Shropshire Lad, University of Washington Press, 1966; A. E. Housman, Twayne, 1967. Contributor of articles and reviews to professional journals in United States and abroad.

SIDELIGHTS: Haber is proficient in Latin, French, and German.†

* * *

HABER, William 1899-

PERSONAL: Born March 6, 1899, in Rumania; brought to United States in 1900; son of Leon and Anna (Stern) Haber; married Fannie Gallas, August 31, 1924; children: Ralph, Alan. Education: University of Wisconsin, B.A., 1923, M.A., 1926, Ph.D., 1927; Harvard University, graduate study, 1924-25. Home: 530 Hillspur Rd., Barton Hills, Ann Arbor, Mich. Office: University of Michigan, Ann Arbor, Mich. 48104.

CAREER: Hart, Schaffner & Marx, labor manager, 1923; University of Wisconsin—Madison, instructor in economics, 1926-27; Michigan State College (now University), Lansing, associate professor of economics, 1927-36; University of Michigan, Ann Arbor, professor of economics, beginning 1936, chairman of department, 1962-63, dean of College of Literature, Science, and the Arts, 1963-68, advisor to executive officers of the university, beginning 1968. Government posts include chairman of Committee on Long-Range Work and Relief Policy, beginning 1941, special assistant to director of Bureau of the Budget, 1942, director of Bureau of Program Requirement, War Manpower Commission, 1943, and assistant executive director, 1944, chairman of Federal Advisory Council on Employment Security, 1948-58, member of President's Task Force on Depressed Areas, 1961, and member of Public Advisory Committee, Area Redevelopment Administration, 1962. Consultant to secretaries of labor during six administrations. Member of executive committee, American-Jewish Committee, beginning

1945; member of board of directors, United Service for New Americans, beginning 1947; chairman of National Hillel Commission, B'nai B'rith, beginning 1949; president of central board, World ORT Union (Organization for Rehabilitation Through Training), beginning 1955. Oakland Housing Corp., member of board of directors, beginning 1934, chairman of the board, beginning 1972; director, Huron Valley National Bank, beginning 1964; president, Washtenaw County United Way, 1974.

MEMBER: American Economic Association, American Society for Public Administration, Industrial Relations Research Association (president, 1960), American Public Welfare Association, National Academy of Arbitrators, American Arbitration Association. Awards, honors: John Dewey Award of League for Industrial Democracy, 1960; L.H.D. from Michigan State University, 1970, and Hebrew University of Jerusalem, 1971; Doctor of Law, Brandeis University, 1975.

WRITINGS: Industrial Relations in the Building Industry, Harvard University Press, 1930, reprinted, Arno, 1971; Unemployment Relief and Economic Security, State of Michigan, 1936; (co-author) Post War Economic Reconstruction, Public Affairs Institute, 1945; (editor) Readings in Social Security, Irwin, 1948; The Cost of Financing Unemployment Insurance in Michigan, Michigan Employment Security Commission, 1952; (co-editor) Manpower in the United States, Industrial Relations Research Association, 1954; (with H. L. Levinson) Labor Relations and Productivity in the Building Trades, Bureau of Industrial Relations, University of Michigan, 1955; (with others) Maintenance of Way Employment on United States Railroads, [Detroit], 1957; The Michigan Economy: Its Potentials and Its Problems, Upjohn, 1960; (editor with Wilbur J. Cohen) Social Security Programs: Problems and Policies, Irwin, 1961; (with others) The Impact of Technological Change, Upjohn, 1963; (with D. H. Kruger) The Role of the United States Employment Service in a Changing Economy, Upjohn, 1964; (with others) Programs in Aid of the Unemployed in the 1960's, Upjohn, 1965; (co-author) Michigan in the 1970's: An Economic Forecast, Bureau of Business Research, University of Michigan, 1965; (editor) Labor in a Changing America, Basic Books, 1966; (with M. G. Murray) Unemployment Insurance in the American Economy, Irwin, 1966. Contributor to public administration and sociology journals.

* * *

HACKER, Mary Louise 1908-

PERSONAL: Born December 30, 1908, in London, England; daughter of William and Louise (Adams) Hacker; married B. Lloyd Page (an industrialist), November 7, 1933; children: Gillian Mary, Charles Martin, Richard William. Education: University of London, B.A., 1930. Home: Manor House, Mackerve End, Harpenden, Hertfordshire, England. Agent: A. P. Watt & Son, 26/28 Bedford Row, London, WC1R 4HL England.

CAREER: Hearst Newspapers, London Bureau, journalist, 1930-33; now part-time writer. Member: P.E.N. (England).

WRITINGS: The Charming Boy, J. Cape, 1955; The Kind Young Man, J. Cape, 1957. Poetry anthologized in P.E.N. Poems, 1963. Contributor of poems to Punch, Spectator, Times Literary Supplement, and of short stories to various periodicals.

WORK IN PROGRESS: A novel and short stories.

SIDELIGHTS: Mary Hacker has made several trips to Spain, Morocco, Yugoslavia, and France. She is competent in French.††

*   *   *

HADDEN, Maude Miner   1880-1967

PERSONAL: Born June 29, 1880, in Leyden, Mass.; daughter of James Rathbone and Mary Elizabeth (Newcomb) Miner; married Alexander Mactier Hadden, May 6, 1924 (deceased). *Education:* Smith College, B.A., 1901; Columbia University, M.A., 1906, Ph.D., 1917. *Politics:* Republican. *Religion:* Episcopalian. *Home:* Primavera, Twin Lakes, Salisbury, Conn.; and 167 Seaview Ave., Palm Beach, Fla. (winter). *Office:* Institute of World Affairs, 527 Madison Ave., New York, N.Y. 10022.

CAREER: Hood College, Frederick, Md., professor of mathematics, 1901-04, professor of history, 1904-05; Magistrates Courts, New York, N.Y., probation officer, 1907-09; Waverly House, New York, N.Y., founder, 1908; Girls' Service League, New York, N.Y., founder, 1908, president, 1929-41; Institute of World Affairs, New York, N.Y., founder, 1924, president, beginning, 1945. Conducted institutes, New York School of Social Work, 1917, 1918, 1924; taught courses on social problems, Columbia University, Teachers College, 1919-21. Founder and president, Youth Foundation, Inc.; Palm Beach Round Table, founder, 1933, later president. Member of New York State Probation Committee, 1918-19. Trustee, Henry Morrison Flagler Museum.

MEMBER: American Academy of Political and Social Science, National Institute of Social Sciences, American Academy of Poets, American Association of University Women, National Committee for Mental Hygiene, English-Speaking Union, Foreign Policy Association, Poetry Society of America, League of Nations Association, League of Women Voters, Quills, Women's National Republican Club, Women's University Club, Society of Four Arts (Palm Beach), Phi Beta Kappa, Phi Beta Kappa Associates (vice-president, beginning 1964), Colony Club (New York), Everglades Club and Bath and Tennis Club (both Palm Beach). *Awards, honors:* L.H.D., Russell Sage College, 1949; Stetson University award for leadership in international relations.

WRITINGS: Slavery of Prostitution—A Plea for Emancipation, Macmillan, 1917; *Garnet Rock* (verse), Comet Press, 1944; *High Horizons* (verse), Whittier Books, 1957. Also author of *Reformatory Girls,* 1906, and *The Institute of World Affairs: Its Beginning,* 1947. Author of pamphlets; contributor to journals.

WORK IN PROGRESS: Her autobiography.†

(Died April, 1967)

*   *   *

HAIGHT, Anne Lyon   1895-

PERSONAL: Born May 11, 1895, in St. Paul, Minn.; daughter of Tracy (an engineer) and Frances (Gilbert) Lyon; married Sherman Post Haight, July 2, 1914; children: Frederick Everest II, Frances Tracy (Mrs. George Griswold), Sherman Post, Jr. *Education:* Privately educated. *Politics:* Republican. *Religion:* Episcopalian. *Home:* 820 Fifth Ave., New York, N.Y. 10021.

CAREER: Writer and lecturer. Chairman of Winston Churchill Memorial Library, Fulton, Mo., and Colony Club Library, New York, N.Y.; former chairman of Garden Club of American Library; member of women's advisory commit-tee, New York Public Library and American Museum of Natural History; chairman of social service at New York City Hospital for forty years and founder of hospital library. *Member:* Colonial Dames of America (chairman of book award committee), Hroswitha Club (book collectors' organization; president).

WRITINGS: Banned Books: Notes on Some Books Banned for Various Reasons at Various Times and in Various Places, Bowker, 1935, 3rd edition, revised and enlarged, 1970; *Morals, Manners, Etiquette and the Three R's,* Overbrook Press, 1950; *Portrait of Latin America as Seen by Her Print Makers* (bilingual edition in English and Spanish), Hastings House, 1946; (editor) *Hroswitha of Gandersheim: Her Life, Times, and Works,* Hroswitha Club (New York), 1965. Contributor to *Bookmaking on the Distaff Side,* American Institute of Graphic Arts. Contributor of essays and articles to *Colophon, Saturday Review, Publishers' Weekly,* and other periodicals.

WORK IN PROGRESS: A biography of Belle da Costa Greene.

SIDELIGHTS: Mrs. Haight collected Eskimo artifacts on six expeditions to the Arctic (Alaska, Northwest Territory, and Greenland), later giving the works to the Stefansson Collection at Dartmouth College. She also collected artifacts for the American Museum of Natural History on four trips to Africa, accompanied William Beebe on expeditions to Central and South America, and has visited the king of Saudi Arabia several times. The Ford Foundation has reprinted her *Banned Books* for distribution to schools and universities; the book has also been translated into Arabic and German and published in England.††

*   *   *

HAIGHT, Gordon S(herman)   1901-

PERSONAL: Born February 6, 1901, in Muskegon, Mich.; son of Louis Pease and Grace (Carpenter) Haight; married Mary Nettleton, June 24, 1937. *Education:* Yale University, B.A., 1923, Ph.D., 1933. *Home:* 145 Peck Hill Rd., Woodbridge, Conn. 06525.

CAREER: Master in English, Kent School, Kent, Conn., 1924-25, Hotchkiss School, Lakeville, Conn., 1925-30; Yale University, New Haven, Conn., faculty member, 1933-68, fellow of Calhoun College, 1933-49, master of Pierson College, 1949-53, professor of English, 1950-68, Emily Sanford Professor of English Literature, 1966-68, professor emeritus, 1968—. Visiting professor of English, Graduate School, Columbia University, 1946-47, and University of Oregon, 1949. *Member:* Modern Language Association of America, Modern Humanities Research Association, Royal Society of Literature (fellow), British Academy (corresponding fellow), Connecticut Academy of Arts and Sciences, Yale Club, Century Club (New York City), Elizabethan Club (New Haven), Berzelius, Zeta Psi, Torch Club. *Awards, honors:* Guggenheim fellowships, 1947, 1953, 1960; James Tait Black Memorial Prize, 1969, Heinemann Award for Literature, 1969, Van Wyck Brooks Award, 1969, and National Institute of Arts and Letters Award, 1970, all for *George Eliot: A Biography.*

WRITINGS: Mrs. Sigourney, the Sweet Singer of Hartford, Yale University Press, 1930; *The Publication of Quarles' Emblems,* Bibliographical Society (London), 1934; *The Sources of Quarles' Emblems,* Bibliographical Society, 1935; (editor) J. W. De Forest, *Miss Ravenal's Conversion,* Harper, 1939, 2nd edition, Rinehart, 1955; *George Eliot and John Chapman, with Chapman's Diaries,* Yale University

Press, 1940, 2nd edition, Archon Books, 1969; *George Eliot: A Biography,* Oxford University Press, 1968.

Editor and author of introduction: Benjamin Franklin, *Autobiography,* Walter J. Black, 1941; *The Best of Ralph Waldo Emerson,* Walter J. Black, 1941; Francis Bacon, *Essays,* Walter J. Black, 1942; Omar Khayyam, *Rubaiyat,* translation by Edward Fitzgerald, Walter J. Black, 1942; Henry David Thoreau, *Walden,* Walter J. Black, 1942; Walt Whitman, *Selected Poems,* Walter J. Black, 1942; George Eliot, *Adam Bede,* Rinehart, 1948; *The George Eliot Letters,* seven volumes, Yale University Press, 1954-55; Eliot, *Middlemarch,* Houghton, 1955; Eliot, *The Mill on the Floss,* Houghton, 1961; *A Century of George Eliot Criticism,* Houghton, 1965; *The Viking Portable Victorian Reader,* Viking, 1972.

Contributor to *The Literary History of the United States,* Macmillan, 1948; also contributor to *Dictionary of American Biography, Encyclopaedia Britannica, Notable American Women.*

Editorial advisor: *Nineteenth Century Fiction, Victorian Studies, PMLA, Studies in English Literature, Wellesley Index to Victorian Periodicals.*

SIDELIGHTS: Haight's study of George Eliot, begun in 1933, culminated in *George Eliot: A Biography,* which has won four important awards since its publication in 1968. During those thirty-five years, Haight produced several preliminary books. *George Eliot and John Chapman,* in which the details of her life with the London publisher, first discussed in detail, offered, according to the *Times Literary Supplement* reviewer, "unexpected, even startling information" about her. With the publication of the seven volumes of *The George Eliot Letters* it became obvious that "no one knew more than Haight about the life of George Eliot." This edition proved a powerful force in restoring George Eliot to the critical esteem she enjoyed a century ago. Lionel Trilling finds that the "tact, the intelligence, and the large learning" of Haight have produced "a great edition." In the succeeding years Mr. Haight's editions of several of her novels demonstrated to the *Times Literary Supplement* that he "was also a perceptive critic." *George Eliot: A Biography* has been equally well reviewed. Thomas Lask praises the "majestic ease with which Haight moves through the material." Saul Maloff calls the book "scrupulous," "affectionate," and "indisputably definitive." Jean Stafford finds the edition "an illuminating portrait of the luminous woman."

AVOCATIONAL INTERESTS: Photography; gardening, especially the growing of varieties of fuchsias; water colors.

BIOGRAPHICAL/CRITICAL SOURCES: *Times Literary Supplement,* November 19, 1954, August 10, 1956, October 3, 1968; *New York Times Book Review,* December 18, 1955, October 1, 1968; *Sunday Times,* June 17, 1956; *Books and Bookmen,* January, 1968; *Newsweek,* September 30, 1968; *Book Week,* October 6, 1968; *Statesman,* October 11, 1968; *Canadian Forum,* April, 1969; *Punch,* April 12, 1970.

* * *

HALL, H(essel) Duncan 1891-1976

PERSONAL: Born March 8, 1891, in Glen Innes, New South Wales, Australia; son of William Hessel (a minister) and Jeannie (Duncan) Hall; married second wife, Jenny Waelder (a physician), September 10, 1943; children: (previous marriage) one son, three daughters. *Education:* University of Sydney, B.A. (first class honors), 1913, M.A.

(first class honors), 1915; Balliol College, Oxford, B.Litt., 1920. *Office:* 7501 Fairfax Rd., Bethesda, Md. 20014.

CAREER: Oxford University, Oxford, England, tutorial class lecturer, 1917-20; University of Sydney, Sydney, Australia, examiner in history department and tutorial class lecturer, 1921-25; Syracuse University, Maxwell Graduate School, Syracuse, N.Y., professor of international affairs, 1926-27; League of Nations Secretariat, Geneva, Switzerland, senior official, 1927-39; Harvard University, Cambridge, Mass., visiting professor of international affairs, summer, 1940, and researcher, 1940-42; British Raw Materials Mission, Washington, D.C., member, 1942-45; British Embassy, Washington, D.C., historical adviser and director of British official war histories (civil), 1945-55. Australian correspondent, *Manchester Guardian,* 1922-26. Australian delegate to Institute of Pacific Relations conferences, 1925, 1927, 1939; official observer at eight British Commonwealth Parliamentary conferences between 1935-59. *Member:* Royal Institute of International Affairs, American Historical Association, Cosmos Club (Washington, D.C.). *Awards, honors:* Guggenheim fellowship, 1955, for book on history of the British Commonwealth of Nations.

WRITINGS: *The British Commonwealth of Nations,* Methuen, 1920; *Historical and Technical Study of Dangerous Drugs Limitation Convention of 1931,* League of Nations, 1937; (contributor) *Conference on Canadian-American Affairs,* Ginn, 1941; (editor with W. Y. Elliott, and contributor) *The British Commonwealth at War,* Knopf, 1943, reprinted, Books for Libraries, 1971; *Mandates, Dependencies, and Trusteeship,* Carnegie Endowment for International Peace, 1948; *North American Supply,* H.M.S.O., 1955; (with C. C. Wrigley) *Studies of Overseas Supply,* H.M.S.O., 1956; (contributor) *Studies in International History,* Longmans, Green, 1967; *Commonwealth: A History of the British Commonwealth of Nations, 1900-1957,* introduction by Sir Robert Menzies, Van Nostrand, 1971. Contributor of more than one hundred articles to *Manchester Guardian, Spectator, Nation, Atlantic, New York Times, Times* (London), and scholarly journals; writer of several series of syndicated articles in England, Australia, New Zealand, South Africa, and Canada.

BIOGRAPHICAL/CRITICAL SOURCES: *American Political Science Review,* December, 1953; *Journal of Commonwealth Political Studies,* November, 1962.†

(Died July 12, 1976)

* * *

HALL, Livingston 1903-

PERSONAL: Born May 5, 1903, in Chicago, Ill.; son of James Parker (a law teacher) and Evelyn (Movius) Hall; married Elizabeth Blodgett, September 13, 1930; children: Thomas L., Margaret Hall Whitfield, Elizabeth Hall Richardson, John K. *Education:* University of Chicago, Ph.B., 1923; Harvard University, LL.B. (magna cum laude), 1927. *Politics:* Republican. *Religion:* Episcopalian. *Home:* c/o Simon's Rock, Great Barrington, Mass. 01230. *Office:* Harvard Law School, Cambridge, Mass. 02138.

CAREER: Admitted to New York Bar, 1929, Massachusetts Bar, 1934; with Root, Clark, Buckner, Howland & Ballantine, New York, N.Y., 1927-31; assistant U.S. Attorney, Southern District of New York, 1931-32; Harvard University Law School, Cambridge, Mass., assistant professor, 1932-37, professor of law, beginning 1937, Roscoe Pound Professor of Law, 1964-71, professor emeritus, 1971—, vice-dean, 1938-58, acting dean, 1959. Regional price and enforcement attorney, U.S. Office of Price Administration, Boston, Mass., 1942-43. Moderator, Town of Weston, 1947-49, Town of Concord, 1957-67. *Military service:* U.S. Army Air Forces, 1943-45; became lieutenant colonel; received Medal of Freedom. *Member:* American Bar Association (house of delegates member, 1964-74), Massachusetts Bar Association (president, 1963-64), Massachusetts Judicial Council, Phi Beta Kappa.

WRITINGS: (With Warren A. Seavy) *Cases on Agency,* West Publishing, 1956; (with Sheldon Glueck) *Cases on Criminal Law and Enforcement,* West Publishing, 1958; (with Y. Kamisar, Wayne LaFave, and Jerold Israel) *Modern Criminal Procedure,* West Publishing, 1969.

* * *

HALL, Rubylea (Ray) 1910-

PERSONAL: Born March 3, 1910, in Greenwood, Fla.; daughter of David Everett and Amanda Cohran (Pittman) Ray; divorced; children: Bettyre Powell, Richard Lynn Hall. *Education:* Florida State University, teacher's license, 1936, special courses, 1942-43; University of Florida, special courses, 1937-38. *Home:* Columbia Residence, 628 West 114th St., New York, N.Y. 10025.

CAREER: Teacher in Florida public schools, 1927-32, 1936-43; government work with Federal Emergency Relief Administration, 1932-33, and as civilian clerk at Camp Blanding, Fla., 1943-44; University of Florida, Gainesville, librarian in Chem-Pharm Library, 1944-49; Q-Tips, Inc., Long Island City, N.Y., director of customer services, beginning, 1959. *Member:* National League of American Pen Women, Sigma Tau Delta. *Awards, honors:* Bohnenberger Award of Southeastern Conference of Libraries for best novel of the South, 1947-48, for *The Great Tide.*

WRITINGS—Novels: *The Great Tide,* Duell, Sloan & Pearce, 1947; *Davey,* Duell, Sloan & Pearce, 1952; *Flamingo Prince,* Duell, Sloan & Pearce, 1954; *God Has A Sense of Humor,* Duell, Sloan & Pearce, 1960.

WORK IN PROGRESS: A novel on fifteenth-century Paris; two contemporary works.

SIDELIGHTS: The Great Tide has been in print continuously since publication, and has been translated into French as *La Fureure du Temps.*††

* * *

HALL, Ted Byron 1902-

PERSONAL: Born December 10, 1902, in Whitefield, Indian Territory (now Okla.); son of William Solomon (a merchant) and Daisy Caroline (Hendrix) Hall; married Louthena Jane McCoy (a genealogist), May 30, 1926; children: Theodore Byron, Marjorie Lou (Mrs. Frank M. Young). *Education:* Attended Oklahoma Agricultural and Mechanical College (now Oklahoma State University), 1922-23, 1926, 1927, and Northeastern State College, 1960-61. *Politics:* Democrat. *Religion:* Presbyterian. *Home address:* Box 67, 1320 Jamestown Dr., Tahlequah, Okla. 74464.

CAREER: Teacher and principal in schools in Oklahoma, 1922-28; peanut farmer in Whitefield, Okla., 1924; Veteran's Administration Hospital, Muskogee, Okla., assistant librarian, 1925; U.S. Department of the Interior, Bureau of Indian Affairs, Osage Agency, Pawhuska, Okla., field clerk, 1928-29; Atkinson, Warren & Henley Co., Oklahoma City, Okla., farm loan inspector, 1929; Pierce Petroleum Co., Elk City, Okla., commission agent, 1929-30; U.S. Department

of the Interior, Bureau of Indian Affairs, appraiser at Quapaw Indian Agency, Miami, Okla., 1930, field clerk (allotting agent) at Pima Indian Agency, Sacaton, Ariz., 1930-33, superintendent of Leupp (Navajo) Agency, Ariz., 1933-34, Papago Agency, Sells, Ariz., 1934-40, and Osage Agency, Pawhuska, 1940-54, assistant area director at Gallup Area Office, Gallup, N.M., 1954-59. President, First National Building (Pawhuska), 1940; member of board of directors, Osage Federal Savings and Loan Association, 1940-48. *Military service:* U.S. Army, Coast Artillery Corps, 1918.

MEMBER: National Association of Retired Federal Employees, Indian Territory Historical and Genealogical Society, Alpha Gamma Rho. *Awards, honors:* Distinguished service award from U.S. Department of the Interior, 1959.

WRITINGS: (Editor with others) *The Osage People and Their Trust Property,* Osage Agency, 1953; *Oklahoma Indian Territory,* American Reference Publishers, 1971.

WORK IN PROGRESS: A series, "Diary of an Indian Agent," Volume I: *The Oklahoma Years* (with the Osages and the Quapaws), Volume II: *The Arizona Years* (with the Pimas, the Navajos, and the Papagos), Volume III: *The New Mexico Years* (with the Apaches, Navajos, Pueblos, and Utes).

SIDELIGHTS: Ted Byron Hall told *CA:* "I've embarked on writing a series of three books on my day to day activities and observations (I've kept a daily journal since November, 1933) as an employee and officer of the Bureau of Indian Affairs, in the hope my records will shed one more ray of light on the impact that Amer-European culture has had and is having on the socio-economic affairs of such Indian tribes as the New Mexico, and Utah, the Osages in Oklahoma and elsewhere, the Pimas and Papagos of Arizona, the Pueblos and Zunis in New Mexico, the Quapaws of Oklahoma, and the Colorado Utes."

* * *

HALSEY, Elizabeth 1890-

PERSONAL: Born August 27, 1890, in Oshkosh, Wis.; daughter of Rufus Henry (an educational administrator) and Emma Lavinia (Cole) Halsey. *Education:* University of Chicago, B.Ph., 1911; Wellesley College, M.A., 1922; University of Michigan, Ph.D., 1940. *Politics:* Democrat. *Religion:* Congregational. *Home address:* Carmel Valley Manor, P.O. Box 6087, Carmel, Calif. 93921.

CAREER: High school teacher of physical education in Fort Atkinson, Wis., 1911-14; Wellesley College, Wellesley, Mass., instructor in physical education, 1916-22; Near East Relief, recreation director in Constantinople and Athens, Greece, 1922-24; University of Iowa, Iowa City, 1924-55, became professor of physical education and head of department. Visiting summer professor at University of Oregon, University of California, Berkeley, and other universities; visiting lecturer at University of Michigan, 1929-31. *Member:* American Academy of Physical Education (fellow), American Association for Health, Physical Education and Recreation (member of council), National Association for Physical Education of College Women (past president), American Association of University Professors, League of Women Voters, Colorado Authors' League. *Awards, honors:* Citation for community service, University of Chicago; Honor Award, American Association for Health, Physical Education and Recreation.

WRITINGS: Public Recreation in Metropolitan Chicago,

Chicago Recreation Commission, 1941; *Physical Education for Children,* Holt, 1958, 2nd edition, 1963; *Women in Physical Education,* Putnam, 1961; *Inquiry and Invention in Physical Education,* Lea & Febiger, 1964. Contributor to professional journals.

WORK IN PROGRESS: A biography of a well-known woman physician.

AVOCATIONAL INTERESTS: Swimming, croquet, reading, music, discussion groups.††

* * *

HAMBURGER, Max 1897-1970

PERSONAL: Born May 31, 1897, in Kitzingen am Main, Bavaria, Germany; son of Louis (a merchant) and Nathalie (Kahn) Hamburger; married Charlotte Weinstein. *Education:* Koenigliches Neues Gymnasium, Wurzberg, Germany, graduate (with distinction), 1916; studied at University of Wurzburg and University of Heidelberg, 1918-21, Dr. jur. et rer. pol. (Wurzburg), 1921. *Home:* 626 West End Ave., New York, N.Y. 10024. *Office:* New School for Social Research, 12th St., New York, N.Y. 10011.

CAREER: Attorney and legal publicist, Wurzburg, Germany, 1924-39; researcher and lecturer in field of ancient and legal philosophy, London, England, 1939-48; New School for Social Research, New York, N.Y., member of department of philosophy and political science, specializing in ancient, comparative and legal philosophy, 1949-70. Lecturer at Columbia University, 1952. *Member:* Royal Institute of Philosophy (London), American Academy of Political and Social Science, Renaissance Society of America.

WRITINGS: Treu und Glauben im Verkehr, Bensheimer (Germany), 1930; *Deflation und Rechtsordnung,* Bensheimer, 1933; *The Awakening of Western Legal Thought,* Allen & Unwin, 1942, reprinted with a new introduction by the author, Biblo & Tannen, 1969; *Morals and Law: The Growth of Aristotle's Legal Theory,* Yale University Press, 1951, new edition, Biblo & Tannen, 1965. Writer of articles on law, philosophy, political science, and rhetoric; also writes poetry in English and German.

WORK IN PROGRESS: Equitable Law from Hammurabi to Justinian; Man, Community and State: From Homer to Plato; Aristotle and Confucius: A Comparison; Aristotle's Logic: A Reappraisal; A Golden Book of Pre-Confucian, Confucian, and Confucianist Philosophy; Philo of Alexandria: A Study; W.A. Mozart: Music's Universal Genius.†

(Died February 7, 1970)

* * *

HAMILL, Robert H(offman) 1912-1975

PERSONAL: Born September 2, 1912, in Indianapolis, Ind.; son of Charles Barker (an insurance salesman) and Leola (Hoffman) Hamill; married Hannah Jewett, August 29, 1935 (died May, 1968); married Geneva S. Shue, March 15, 1969; children: (first marriage) Dennis W., Timothy J., Gwendolyn J., Gregory P. *Education:* Northwestern University, B.S., 1933; Yale University, B.D., 1936. *Politics:* Democrat. *Office:* Office of University Chaplain, Boston University, Boston, Mass.

CAREER: Ordained in the Methodist Church, 1937; pastor of several Methodist churches in the Midwest, 1936-57; University Methodist Church, Madison, Wis., pastor, 1957-62; Boston University, Boston, Mass., university chaplain, 1962-75. Member of general conference, United Methodist

Church, 1960; creator of Teen Overseas Project, an annual travel-camp program for sixteen-year-old American youth in western Europe; campus preacher and lecturer.

WRITINGS: Gods of the Campus, Abingdon, 1949; *How Free Are You?,* Abingdon, 1956; *Plenty and Trouble: The Impact of Technology on People,* Abingdon, 1971. Author of "Skeptics Corner," a monthly column in *Motive,* 1940-54. Contributor to religious periodicals.

AVOCATIONAL INTERESTS: Woodcarving, photography, golf.†

(Died February 8, 1975)

* * *

HAMILTON, Raphael N(oteware) 1892-

PERSONAL: Born November 5, 1892, in Omaha, Neb.; son of Charles William (a banker) and Maud (Noteware) Hamilton. *Education:* Educated privately in France, 1907-08; Creighton University, A.B., 1913; St. Louis University, M.A., 1919, Ph.D., 1932. *Home:* 1404 West Wisconsin Ave., Milwaukee, Wis. 53233.

CAREER: Entered Society of Jesus (Jesuits), 1913, ordained priest, 1926; Campion College, Prairie du Chien, Wis., assistant professor, 1920-21, professor of history and head of department, 1921-23; St. Louis University, St. Louis, Mo., instructor in history, 1928-29; Marquette University, Milwaukee, Wis., assistant professor, 1930-32, professor of history, 1932-61, professor emeritus, 1961—, head of history department, 1932-56, dean of Graduate School, 1939-43, university archivist, 1961-73. Member, Wisconsin Governor's Commission for Celebration of Tercentenary of Father Marquette, 1968-73; member, Milwaukee Mayor's Landmarks Commission. *Member:* American Historical Association, American Catholic Historical Association, Society of American Archivists, State Historical Society of Wisconsin, Phi Alpha Theta, Alpha Sigma Nu. *Awards, honors:* Citation and medal, Society of Colonial Wars (New York), 1971, for *Marquette's Explorations: The Narratives Re-examined.*

WRITINGS: The Story of Marquette University, Marquette University Press, 1953; *Father Marquette,* Eerdmans, 1970; *Marquette's Explorations: The Narratives Re-examined,* University of Wisconsin Press, 1970. Contributor to historical journals.

WORK IN PROGRESS: Writing on Pere Marquette and on Robert de La Salle.

* * *

HAMMEN, Oscar J(ohn) 1907-

PERSONAL: Born February 28, 1907, in Adell, Wis.; son of Christian (a farmer) and Emma (Fehse) Hammen; married Barbara Sharland Schloesser, August 26, 1933; children: Philip D., Richard F., John R. *Education:* Northwestern College, Watertown, Wis., B.A., 1929; University of Wisconsin, B.A., 1930, Ph.D., 1941. *Home:* 637 Blaine St., Missoula, Mont. 59801. *Office:* Department of History, University of Montana, Missoula, Mont. 59801.

CAREER: Idaho State College (now Idaho State University), Pocatello, assistant professor of history, 1941-44; University of Nebraska, Lincoln, visiting professor of history, 1944-45; University of Utah, Salt Lake City, visiting professor of history and political science, 1945-46; Westminster College, Salt Lake City, Utah, professor of history, 1946-47; University of Montana, Missoula, professor of history, beginning 1947, chairman of department, 1956-58. Visiting professor at University of Wisconsin, 1959, and University of Colorado, summer, 1961. *Member:* American Historical Association, Phi Alpha Theta (national councillor, 1956-59; member of advisory board, 1959-63). *Awards, honors:* Social Science Research Council grant-in-aid, 1949, 1963; American Philosophical Society grant, 1963.

WRITINGS: The Red '48ers, Karl Marx and Friedrich Engels, Scribner, 1969. Contributor to *South Atlantic Quarterly, Contract Social,* and other journals.

WORK IN PROGRESS: Principles of Communism, the Manifesto and Democracy.

SIDELIGHTS: Oscar Hammen traveled to Germany and the Netherlands for research on Marx and Engels. He is competent in German, and has a reading knowledge of French, Dutch, and Italian.

*   *   *

HANDLIN, Mary (Flug) 1913-1976

PERSONAL: Born September 14, 1913, in New York, N.Y.; daughter of Harry (a merchant) and Fanny (Schuh) Flug; married Oscar Handlin (a professor of history and an author), September 18, 1937; children: Joanna F., David P., Ruth B. *Education:* Brooklyn College (now Brooklyn College of the City University of New York), B.A., 1933; Columbia University, M.A., 1934; London School of Economics and Political Science, further study, 1937-38. *Home:* 18 Agassiz St., Cambridge, Mass. 02140. *Office:* Harvard University, Widener 783, Cambridge, Mass. 02138.

CAREER: Department of Welfare, New York City, investigator, 1934-35; U.S. Railroad Retirement Board, Washington, D.C., analyst, 1935-37; New York State Department of Labor, New York City, analyst, 1938-39; U.S. Wage and Hour Division, Boston, Mass., analyst, 1939-42; Social Science Research Council, Cambridge, Mass., research historian, 1942-46; Harvard University, Cambridge, research editor, 1958-76. *Member:* American Association of University Women. *Awards, honors:* Robert H. Lord Award from Emmanuel College, 1972.

WRITINGS—All with husband, Oscar Handlin: *Commonwealth: Government in American Economy,* Harvard University Press, 1947; (editors with others) *Harvard Guide to American History,* Harvard University Press, 1954; *Dimensions of Liberty,* Harvard University Press, 1961; *Popular Sources of Political Authority,* Harvard University Press, 1966; *The American College and American Culture,* McGraw, 1970; *Facing Life: Youth and the Family in American History,* Little, Brown, 1971; *The Wealth of the American People: A History of American Influence,* McGraw, 1975. Contributor to professional journals.†

(Died May 24, 1976)

*   *   *

HARD, Frederick 1897-

PERSONAL: Born August 24, 1897, in Bessemer, Ala.; son of James Henry (a businessman) and Augusta (Giles) Hard; married Beverly Stephens, May 28, 1931; children: Beverly (Mrs. James R. Davies), Frederick Parham. *Education:* University of the South, B.A., 1922; University of North Carolina, M.A., 1924; Johns Hopkins University, Ph.D., 1928. *Politics:* Democrat. *Religion:* Episcopalian. *Home:* 325 14th Ave., Santa Cruz, Calif. 95062.

CAREER: University of the South, Sewanee, Tenn., in-

structor in English, 1922-23; University of North Carolina, Chapel Hill, instructor in music, 1923-24; Johns Hopkins University, Baltimore, Md., instructor in English, 1925-27; Tulane University, New Orleans, La., assistant professor, 1927-31, associate professor, 1931-38, professor of English and dean of Newcomb College, 1938-44; Scripps College, Claremont, Calif., president, 1944-64, provost of the five Claremont Colleges, 1947-48, 1953-55, 1958-59, 1963-64; University of California, Santa Cruz, professor of English literature, 1965-74, professor emeritus, 1974—. Visiting summer professor at University of Alabama, 1930-34, 1936, Columbia University, 1939-42, 1950, and University of Hawaii, 1954; visiting professor at University of Pittsburgh, winter, 1965. Tulane University, member of board of visitors, beginning 1954, president of board, 1954-57; Council on Library Resources, member of board of directors, beginning 1956, member of executive committee, 1961-64. Councilman, City of Claremont, 1947-48. Trustee of Scripps College, Southwest Museum, and Hospital of the Good Samaritan (Los Angeles).

MEMBER: Modern Language Association of America (member of executive council, 1941-46), American Council on Education, Association of American Colleges (member of board), American Council of Learned Societies (member of advisory council), American School of Classical Studies in Athens, Western College Association (president, 1949), Independent Colleges of Southern California (founding member), Southern California Archaeological Society, Phi Beta Kappa (member of senate of united chapters, beginning 1951; member of executive committee of senate, beginning 1958), Alpha Tau Omega, Omicron Delta Kappa, University Club (Claremont and Los Angeles), California Club. *Awards, honors:* Fellow of Huntington Library, 1936-37; D.C.L., University of the South, 1944; Litt.D., Occidental College, 1949; LL.D., Tulane University, 1955; fellow of Folger Shakespeare Library, 1964.

WRITINGS: (With R. R. Kirk and H. L. Marcoux) *Writing and Reading English Prose,* Farrar & Rinehart, 1941; *The Sculptured Scenes from Shakespeare* (monograph), Folger Shakespeare Library, 1959; (contributor) *Shakespeare Celebrated,* Cornell University Press, 1966; (editor and author of introduction and notes) Sir Henry Wotton, *The Elements of Architecture: A Facism,* University Press of Virginia, 1968; *Louis B. Wright: A Bibliography and an Appreciation,* University Press of Virginia, 1968. Contributor to *Collier's Encyclopedia,* 1948-50; also contributor of articles, chiefly on the literature and art of the English Renaissance, and reviews to learned journals.

WORK IN PROGRESS: An article on mythology for Scribner's *Dictionary of the History of Ideas;* continuing studies on relations between literature and the arts in the English Renaissance.

*   *   *

HARDINGE, Helen (Mary Cecil) 1901-

PERSONAL: Born May 11, 1901, in London, England; daughter of Edward (a soldier) and Violet (Maxse) Cecil; married Alexander Hardinge (Baron Hardinge of Penshurst), February 8, 1920 (died May, 1960); children: George Edward Charles, Winifred, Elizabeth. *Education:* Educated privately. *Politics:* "Just deeply interested." *Religion:* Church of England. *Home:* South Park, Penshurst, Kent, England. *Agent:* Curtis Brown Group Ltd., 1 Craven Hill, London W2 3EW, England.

CAREER: As Lady Hardinge of Penshurst and now the

Dowager Lady Hardinge, her interests have centered on charitable, historical, and literary matters. *Member:* Society of Authors, Writers Circle (Tunbridge Wells).

WRITINGS: The Path of Kings, Blandford, 1952; (translator from the French) Gabriel Marcel, editor, *Fresh Hope for the World,* Longmans, Green, 1960; *Loyal to Three Kings: A Memoir of Alec Hardinge, Private Secretary to the Sovereign, 1920-1943,* Kimber & Co., 1967. Has written scripts for "Woman's Hour," a BBC television program, radio programs, and articles for periodicals.

WORK IN PROGRESS: Historical research with Robert Lacey.

AVOCATIONAL INTERESTS: Archeology, botany, ornithology, and wildlife conservancy.

BIOGRAPHICAL/CRITICAL SOURCES: Times Literary Supplement, October 19, 1967.

* * *

HARDY, Alice Dale
[Collective pseudonym]

WRITINGS—"Riddle Club" series; published by Grosset: *The Riddle Club at Sunrise Beach,* 1925; . . . *at Rocky Falls,* 1929. "Flyaway" series also written under this pseudonym.

SIDELIGHTS: See **ADAMS, Harriet S., STRATEMEYER, Edward L.,** and **SVENSON, Andrew E.**†

* * *

HARKNESS, Marjory Gane   1880-19(?)

PERSONAL: Born March 8, 1880, in Yonkers, N.Y.; daughter of Thomas Frederick (a businessman) and Sarah (Jones) Gane; married Frank E. Harkness, January 5, 1918. *Education:* Smith College, B.L., 1901. *Religion:* Protestant. *Residence:* Tamworth, N.H. 03886. *Agent:* Russell & Volkening, Inc., 551 Fifth Ave., New York, N.Y. 10017.

CAREER: Former secretary and director, New Hampshire Board of Realtors.

WRITINGS: "A Brook of Our Own": A Few Notes From the Films of a Mountain Real Estate Office, Knopf, 1945, 2nd edition, Richard D. Smith, 1965; (editor) *Percy Lubbock Reader,* Wheelwright, 1957; *The Tamworth Narrative,* Wheelwright, for Tamworth Foundation and Tamworth Historical Society, 1958; (editor) *James Welch, High Sheriff, Being the Reminiscences of James Welch, Former Sheriff of Carroll County, New Hampshire,* Tamworth Historical Society, 1960; (editor) *The Fishbasket Papers: The Diaries, 1768-1823, of Bradbury Jewell, esq. of Tamworth,* Noone House, 1963.†

(Deceased)

* * *

HARRINGTON, Mark Raymond   1882-1971
(Ramon de las Cuevas, Jiskogo, Tonashi)

PERSONAL: Born July 6, 1882, in Ann Arbor, Mich.; son of Mark Walrod (an astronomer) and Rose Martha (Smith) Harrington; former three wives deceased; married Marie Walsh, April 23, 1949; children: (second marriage) Johns Heye. *Education:* University of Michigan, student, 1903-05; Columbia University, B.S., 1907, A.M., 1908. *Politics:* Democrat. *Religion:* Roman Catholic. *Home:* 11039 Memory Park Ave., Mission Hills, Calif. 91345.

CAREER: Did earliest work in ethnology and archaeology with American Museum of Natural History, Peabody Mu-

seum of Harvard University, and Museum of the American Indian; University of Pennsylvania Museum, Philadelphia, assistant curator of American section, 1911-14; Heye Foundation, Museum of the American Indian, New York, N.Y., archaeologist and ethnologist, 1915-17, 1919-28; Southwest Museum, Los Angeles, Calif., director of research, 1928-29, curator, 1928-64. Carnegie Institution of Washington, research associate, 1930-71; National Park Service, collaborator, 1943-71; University of California, Los Angeles, research associate, 1949-71. Discoverer of Ozark Bluff Dweller culture in Arkansas and Missouri; consultant on restoration of several early California missions. *Member:* American Association for the Advancement of Science (fellow), Society for American Archaeology, Western Writers of America, Archeological Survey Association of Southern California (honorary life member), San Fernando Valley Historical Society (honorary life member). *Awards, honors:* Honorary doctorate, Occidental College, 1956.

WRITINGS: Sacred Bundles of the Sac and Fox Indians, University of Pennsylvania Museum, 1914; *Certain Caddo Sites in Arkansas,* Museum of the American Indian, 1920; *Religion and Ceremonies of the Lenape,* Museum of the American Indian, 1921; *Cuba Before Columbus,* two volumes, Museum of the American Indian, 1921; *Cherokee and Earlier Remains on Upper Tennessee River,* Museum of the American Indian, 1922; (with L. L. Loud) *Lovelock Cave,* University of California Press, 1929; *Gypsum Cave, Nevada,* Southwest Museum, 1933; *Dickon Among the Lenape Indians,* Winston, 1938 (abbreviated edition published in England as *Dickon Among the Indians,* Harmondsworth, 1949, U.S. edition reissued as *The Indians of New Jersey,* Rutgers University Press, 1963); *How to Build a California Adobe,* Ward Ritchie and Southwest Museum, 1948; *An Ancient Site at Borax Lake, California,* Southwest Museum, 1948; *The Ozark Bluff Dwellers,* Museum of the American Indian, 1960; *The Iroquois Trail,* Rutgers University Press, 1964.

Author of brochure on San Fernando Mission, and leaflets on Indian life for Southwest Museum and New York State Museum. Contributor of articles to *Masterkey* (Southwest Museum quarterly); writer of other scientific articles and some fiction.

WORK IN PROGRESS: Occasional articles.†

(Died June 30, 1971)

* * *

HARRISON, George Russell   1898-

PERSONAL: Born July 14, 1898, in San Diego, Calif.; son of Ernest (a dry goods merchant) and Magda (Lincke-Tiesel) Harrison; married Florence Kent, 1922 (died, 1955); married Betty Cavanna (a writer), March 9, 1957; children: (first marriage) Mary Lou, Nancy (Mrs. Kurt H. Grab), David Kent. *Education:* Stanford University, B.S., 1919, M.A., 1920, Ph.D., 1922. *Home:* Barnes Hill Rd., Concord, Mass. 01742. *Office:* Massachusetts Institute of Technology, 77 Massachusetts Ave., Cambridge, Mass. 02139.

CAREER: Stanford University, Stanford, Calif., instructor in physics, 1919-23; Harvard University, Cambridge, Mass., research fellow, 1923-25; Stanford University, assistant professor, 1925-27, associate professor of physics, 1927-30; Massachusetts Institute of Technology, Cambridge, professor of physics, 1930-64, dean of science, 1942-64, became dean emeritus, 1964. Harvard University, research associate, 1930-31; National Defense Research Committee, chief of optics division, 1942-46, chief of physics division, 1945-

46; General MacArthur's Headquarters, chief of research section, 1944. Director of Bausch & Lomb, Inc., and Colt Industries. Trustee of Boston Museum of Science, Corning Glass Museum, and Babson Institute.

MEMBER: Optical Society of America (president, 1946-48), American Philosophical Society, American Academy of Arts and Sciences (vice-president, 1944-46), American Association for the Advancement of Science (vice-president, 1953). *Awards, honors:* Rumford Medal of American Academy of Arts and Sciences, 1939; Medal of Freedom, 1946; Presidential Medal of Merit, 1948; Ives Medal, 1949; Cresson Medal of Franklin Institute, 1953; Pittsburgh Spectrographic Award, 1957; and Mees Medal. D.Sc., Northeastern University, 1943, and St. Lawrence University, 1952; LL.D., Middlebury College, 1955; D.Eng., Drexel Institute of Technology, 1956.

WRITINGS: Atoms in Action, Morrow, 1938, 3rd edition, 1955; *M.I.T. Wavelength Tables,* Wiley, 1938; *How Things Work,* Morrow, 1941; (with Lord and Loofbourow) *Practical Spectroscopy,* Prentice-Hall, 1948; *What Man May Be,* Morrow, 1956; *First Book of Light,* F. Watts, 1962; *First Book of Energy,* F. Watts, 1965; *The Conquest of Energy,* Morrow, 1968; *Lasers,* F. Watts, 1971. Illustrator (photographs) of "Around the World Today," series of twelve books, written by wife, Betty Cavanna, and published by F. Watts, 1960-67. Editor, *Journal* of Optical Society of America, 1940-50.

* * *

HART, Albert Gailord 1909-

PERSONAL: Born March 9, 1909, in Oak Park, Ill.; son of Hastings Hornell and Josephine (Newton) Hart; married Ann Webster (a social worker), July 28, 1936; children: Josephine (Mrs. Melvin Bristol), Molly (Mrs. Robert Lewis), Stephen. *Education:* Harvard University, B.A. (summa cum laude), 1930; graduate study in Vienna and Germany, 1930-31, London, 1934-35; University of Chicago, Ph.D., 1936. *Politics:* Republican. *Home:* 54 Morningside Dr., New York, N.Y. 10025. *Office:* 1005 International Affairs, Columbia University, New York, N.Y. 10027.

CAREER: Iowa State College (now Iowa State University of Science and Technology), Ames, associate professor, 1939-42, professor of economics, 1942-45; Committee for Economic Development, Chicago, Ill., research economist, 1945-46; Columbia University, New York, N.Y., visiting professor, 1946-47, professor of economics, beginning 1947, chairman of department, 1958-64. Research director of economic stabilization project, Twentieth Century Fund, 1949-52; research associate, Institut de Science Economique Appliq:ue, Paris, France, 1952-53; visiting professor, University of Chile, 1962; Fulbright professor, University of Frankfurt, 1967. Consultant, U.S. Treasury Department, 1943-53, and beginning 1961; United Nations consultant and technical assistance economist in Chile, 1961-62, Mexico, 1963, and Argentina, 1964.

MEMBER: American Economic Association (vice-president, 1962), Royal Economic Society (fellow), Econometric Society, Phi Beta Kappa. *Awards, honors:* Ford faculty research fellowship, 1956-57.

WRITINGS: How the National Income Is Divided, University of Chicago Press, 1937; *Debts and Recovery: A Study of Changes in the Internal Debt Structure From 1929 to 1937,* Twentieth Century Fund, 1938; *Economic Policy for Rearmament,* University of Chicago Press, 1940; *Anticipations, Uncertainty, and Dynamic Planning,* University of

Chicago Press, 1940; (with Edward D. Allen) *Paying for Defense,* Blakiston, 1941; (with Mary Jean Bowman) *Food Management and Inflation,* Iowa State College Press, 1943; (with John Richard Hicks) *Social Framework of the American Economy: An Introduction to Economics,* Oxford University Press, 1945, 2nd edition, 1953; (with P. B. Kenen) *Money, Debt, and Economic Activity,* Prentice-Hall, 1948, 4th edition, 1969.

Defense Without Inflation, with Recommendations of the Committee on Economic Stabilization, Twentieth Century Fund, 1951; (with C. Cary Brown) *Financing Defense: Federal Tax and Expenditure Policies,* Twentieth Century Fund, 1951; *Defense and the Dollar: Federal Credit and Monetary Policies with Recommendations of the Committee on Economic Stabilization,* Twentieth Century Fund, 1953; (with Paul Thomas Homan and others) *Economic Order,* Harcourt, 1958; (with Nicholas Kaldor and Jan Tinbergen) *The Case for an International Commodity Reserve Currency,* United Nations, 1964; (author of introduction) John R. Hicks, *Estructura de la economia,* [Mexico], 1965. Also co-author of *Jobs and Markets in the Transition,* 1946, and *International Compensation for Fluctuations in Commodity Trade,* 1961; writer of technical reports for United Nations. Contributor of articles and reviews to periodicals.

WORK IN PROGRESS: Research in expectational economics—the image of the future held by businessmen and households, where they get this image, and how far it is a real element in decisions; a comparative study of short-term economic indicators available for Latin America and other underdeveloped economies.

SIDELIGHTS: Albert Hart can teach and write in Spanish and German. *Avocational interests:* Directing small groups in Renaissance-baroque music.

* * *

HARTICH, Alice 1888-

PERSONAL: Surname is pronounced *Har*-tick; born April 26, 1888, in Brooklyn, N.Y.; daughter of Joseph Buxton (a hat dealer) and Alice (Doughty) Hartich. *Education:* Attended Brooklyn Training School for Teachers; Adelphi College, B.S., 1927; New York University, M.A., 1940. *Politics:* Republican. *Religion:* Protestant.

CAREER: Brooklyn (N.Y.) public schools, elementary teacher and principal, 1910-55. *Member:* Poetry Society of America, Delta Kappa Gamma.

WRITINGS: (Co-author) *Play Days* (workbook), American Book Co., 1937; *Gift of Light* (poetry), Fine Editions, 1949; *Pure White Flame* (poetry), Golden Quill, 1964. Author of short stories for children.

WORK IN PROGRESS: Society Rebel—The Story of Grace H. Dodge; four juveniles, including two picture books.††

* * *

HARTMAN, Louis F(rancis) 1901-1970

PERSONAL: Born January 17, 1901, in New York, N.Y.; son of Louis Francis and Josephine (Grennan) Hartman. *Education:* Attended Mount St. Alphonsus Seminary, Esopus, N.Y., 1922-28, and Catholic University of America, 1929; Pontifical Biblical Institute, Rome, Italy, Licentiate in Sacred Scripture, 1932, Licentiate in Oriental Languages, 1934. *Politics:* Independent. *Home:* Holy Redeemer College, 3112 Seventh St. N.E., Washington, D.C. 20017.

CAREER: Entered Congregation of the Most Holy Redeemer (Redemptorists), 1922, and was ordained priest, 1927; Mount St. Alphonsus Seminary, Esopus, N.Y., professor of Sacred Scripture, 1932-34, 1936-48; Catholic Biblical Association of America, Washington, D.C., executive secretary, 1948-70; Catholic University of America, Washington, D.C., assistant professor, 1950-53, associate professor, 1953-62, professor of Semitics, 1962-70, head of department, 1965-67. Annual professor at American School of Oriental Research in Jerusalem, 1959-60. *Member:* Society of Biblical Literature, American Oriental Society. *Awards, honors:* Citation from St. Bonaventure University, 1958, for outstanding contributions to Catholic biblical scholarship.

WRITINGS: (Co-editor and contributor) *Commentary on the New Testament,* Sadlier, 1942; (contributor) F. X. Murphy, editor, *A Monument to Saint Jerome: Essays on Some Aspects of His Life, Works and Influence,* Sheed, 1952; (co-editor) *Confraternity Version of the Bible,* St. Anthony Guild Press, Volume I: *Genesis to Ruth,* 1952, Volume II: *Job to Sirach,* 1955, Volume IV: *Isaiah to Malachi,* 1961; (editor) *Lives of the Saints,* John J. Crawley, Volume II, 1962; (translator and adapter) *Encyclopedic Dictionary of the Bible* (based on A. van den Borne's *Bijbels Woordenboek*), McGraw, 1963; (translator) *The Imitation of Christ,* John J. Crawley, 1964; (contributor) J. P. Lerhinan, editor, *Background to Morality,* Desclee, 1964; (with Betty Morrow) *Jewish Holidays: A Holiday Book,* Garrard, 1967. Staff editor, *The New Catholic Encyclopedia.* Author with A. Leo Oppenheim of a book-length supplement to *Journal of the American Oriental Society,* "On Beer and Brewing Techniques in Ancient Mesopotamia," 1950; contributor of occasional articles and about forty reviews to *Catholic Biblical Quarterly* and other journals.

WORK IN PROGRESS: The Book of Daniel, for "Anchor Bible."

SIDELIGHTS: Hartman was competent in Latin, Greek, German, French, Dutch, Spanish, Italian, Akkadian, Ugaritic, Sumerian, Syriac, Hebrew, and Aramaic. *Avocational interests:* Bird watching.

BIOGRAPHICAL/CRITICAL SOURCES: Catholic Biblical Quarterly, Volume XXIX, 1967.†

(Died August 22, 1970)

* * *

HARTMAN, Robert S. 1910-1973

PERSONAL: Born January 27, 1910, in Berlin, Germany; came to United States, 1941; naturalized citizen; married Rita S. Emanuel, August 30, 1936; children: Jan. *Education:* Attended German College of Political Science, 1926-27, University of Paris, 1927-28, University of London, 1928-29; University of Berlin, LL.B., 1932; National University of Mexico, graduate student, 1941; Northwestern University, Ph.D., 1946. *Home:* Apartado 422, Cuernavaca, Morelos, Mexico.

CAREER: University of Berlin, Berlin, Germany, instructor in philosophy of law, 1932-33; District Court Berlin-Charlottenburg, assistant judge, 1932-33; Walt Disney Enterprises, representative in Scandinavia and Baltic States, 1934-37, in Mexico and Central America, 1937-41; Lake Forest Academy, Lake Forest, Ill., teacher of language, history, and philosophy, 1942-45; College of Wooster, Wooster, Ohio, instructor, later assistant professor of philosophy, 1945-48; Ohio State University, Columbus, associate professor of philosophy, 1948-55; National University of Mex-

ico, Mexico City, U.S. State Department exchange professor, 1956-57, research professor of philosophy, 1957-73. Visiting professor at Massachusetts Institute of Technology, 1955-56, Yale University, 1966. Council of Profit Sharing Industries, Chicago, Ill., organizing chairman, 1947, executive secretary, 1947-49; co-founder, Institute fuer Sozialwirtschaftliche Betriebsgestaltung, Duesseldorf, Germany, 1952. Consultant to American corporations, including General Electric, General Foods, and International Business Machines, 1949-73, and to National Profit Sharing Commission of Mexico, 1963.

MEMBER: American Philosophical Association, Allegemeine Gesellschaft fuer Philosophie in Deutschland, National Education Association, American Association of University Professors, Delta Phi Alpha (honorary member).

WRITINGS: Profit Sharing Manual, Council of Profit Sharing Industries, 1948; *Axiologia Formal: La Ciencia de la Valoracion,* National University of Mexico, 1957; *Die Partnerschaft von Kapital und Arbeit: Theorie und Praxis eines neuen Wirtschaftssystems* (title means "The Partnership of Capital and Labor: Theory and Practice of a New Economic System"), Westdeutscher Verlag, 1958; *La Estructura del Valor,* Fondo de Cultura Economica, 1959, revised edition published as *La Ciencia del Valor,* National University of Mexico, 1965, later revision published as *El Conocimiento del Bien: Critica de la Razon Axiologica,* Fondo de Cultura Economica, 1965 (English translation published as *The Structure of Value: Foundations of Scientific Axiology,* Southern Illinois University Press, 1966); *The Hartman Value Inventory,* Miller Associates, 1966; *The Hartman Value Profile,* Research Concepts, 1973.

Co-author: *The Philosophy of Ernst Cassirer,* Northwestern University Press, 1949; *Perspectives in Philosophy,* Ohio State University Press, 1953; *The Language of Value,* Columbia University Press, 1957; *New Knowledge in Human Values,* Harper, 1958; *Chronique de Philosophie, 1949-1955,* International Institute of Philosophy, 1959.

Translator, editor: (Swedish into German) A. Strindberg, *Der Sohn der Magd,* Buechergilde Gutenberg, 1936; (German into English) G. W. F. Hegel, *Reason in History: A General Introduction to the Philosophy of History,* Liberal Arts Press, 1953; (German into Spanish) Helmut Coing, *El Sentido del Derecho,* National University of Mexico, 1959; (German into Spanish) Ernst von Aster, *La Filosofia del Presente,* National University of Mexico, 1964; (English into Spanish) L. Susan Stebbing, *Introduccion Moderna a la Logica,* National University of Mexico, 1965; (German into English; with Wolfgang Schwartz) Immanuel Kant, *Logic,* Bobbs-Merrill, 1974.

Contributor: (Introduction) Max Picard, *Hitler in Our Selves,* Regnery, 1947; *The Philosophy of Ernst Cassirer,* Library of Living Philosophers, 1949; (introduction) Kenneth M. Thompson, *Profit Sharing: Democratic Capitalism in American Industry,* Harper, 1949; *Philosophie: Chronique des annees 1949-1955,* Volume II, Nuova Italia, 1958; *Primer Coloquio Mexicano de Historia de la Ciencia,* Sociedad Mexicana de Historia de la Ciencia y de la Tecnologia, 1964. Contributor to *Dianoia, Anuario de Filosofia,* National University of Mexico, and to other yearbooks and proceedings; more than one hundred articles and reviews have appeared in philosophy and social science journals in North and Latin America, Europe, Asia, and Australia. Member of editorial board, *Kant-Studien,* beginning 1952, *Darshana* (India), beginning 1961, *Journal of Humanistic Psychology,* beginning 1961.

WORK IN PROGRESS: Grundriss der Geschichte der Philosophie.

SIDELIGHTS: Hartman spoke German, French, Spanish, and Swedish.†

(Died September 21, 1973)

*   *   *

HATCH, Preble D(elloss) K(ellogg)   1898-

PERSONAL: Born December 8, 1898, in Troy, Me.; son of Charles Albert (a farmer) and Nellie V. (Gould) Hatch; married Marion E. Johnson (a teacher; writes under the name of Mary Ann Hatch), August 18, 1920; children: Philip Norman, Everett Stanley. *Education:* Attended Shaw Business College, 1918, and National School of Accountancy, 1919; American Institute of Grapho-Analysis, C.G.A.P., 1948. *Residence:* Bangor, Me.

CAREER: Assistant high school principal, Mapleton, Me., 1920; Aroostook School of Accountancy, Presque Isle, Me., principal, 1921-27; furniture store credit manager, 1928-29; Bangor Credit Bureau, Inc., Bangor, Me., president, 1929-67; writer of humorous books. *Military service:* U.S. Navy, 1918.

WRITINGS—Novels: *Don't Shoot the Bill Collector,* Crowell, 1951; *Homer the Handy Man,* Crowell, 1952; *Eat Now–Burp Later,* Coach House, 1968. Also author of *Anything for Money.* Writer of some course materials for correspondence schools and articles on handwriting analysis.

AVOCATIONAL INTERESTS: Landscape painting in oil (also does forestcraft pictures and pictures in clay).††

*   *   *

HATCHER, Harlan (Henthorne)   1898-

PERSONAL: Born September 9, 1898, in Ironton, Ohio; son of Robert Elison and Linda (Leslie) Hatcher; married Frank W. Colfax, 1922 (deceased); married Anne Gregory Vance, April 3, 1942; children: (second marriage) Robert Leslie, Anne Linda. *Education:* Ohio State University, A.B., 1922, A.M., 1923, Ph.D., 1927; University of Chicago, graduate study, 1925. *Home:* 841 Greenhills Dr., Ann Arbor, Mich. 48105.

CAREER: Ohio State University, Columbus, assistant professor, 1928-32, professor of English, 1932-51, dean of College of Arts and Sciences, 1944-48, vice-president of university, 1948-51; University of Michigan, Ann Arbor, president, 1951-67, president emeritus, 1967—. Lecturer at other universities. Director of Federal Writers' Project, Ohio, 1937-38. Head of Ford Foundation study missions to Soviet Union, 1959, and South America, 1962; head of American delegation to Tokyo conference of International Association of Universities, 1965. Chairman, Developing Great Lakes Megalopolis Research Project, Inc., 1969; chairman, University Residential Theatre Association, beginning 1970. Member, Ford Foundation Fellowship Advisory Board, 1961-65. Trustee of Institute for Defense Analyses; director of Detroit Edison Co., Ann Arbor Bank, and Tecumseh Products Co. *Military service:* U.S. Army, 1918. U.S. Naval Reserve, 1942-44; became lieutenant.

MEMBER: Association of American Universities (past president), National Council of Teachers of English, Modern Language Association of America, American Association of University Professors, American Historical Society, Great Lakes Historical Society, Phi Beta Kappa, Economic Club (Detroit; member of board of directors),

Detroit Athletic Club, Century Club (New York), Rotary. *Awards, honors:* Ohio Governor's Award, 1949; Ohioana Grand Medal, 1950; Commander, Order of Orange Nassau (Netherlands), 1952; Star of Italian Solidarity, 1962; Second Order of Merit with the Middle Cordon of the Rising Sun (Japan), 1962; Companion, Order of the White Elephant (Thailand), 1965; Wolverine Frontiersman Award. Twenty-eight honorary degrees from universities and colleges in United States, Mexico, and Japan, including Ohio State University, New York University, University of California, Berkeley, and National University of Mexico.

WRITINGS: The Versification of Robert Browning, Ohio State University Press, 1928, reprinted, Phaeton, 1968; *Tunnell Hill,* Bobbs-Merrill, 1931; *Patterns of Wolfpen,* Bobbs-Merrill, 1934; *Creating the Modern American Novel,* Farrar & Rinehart, 1935, reprinted, Russell, 1965; *Central Standard Time,* Farrar & Rinehart, 1937; *The Buckeye Country: A Pageant of Ohio,* Putnam, 1940; (editor) *The Ohio Guide,* Oxford University Press, 1940; (editor) *Modern Continental, British and American Dramas,* three volumes, Harcourt, 1941 (reissued in a shorter edition as *Modern Dramas,* Harcourt, 1944); *The Great Lakes,* Oxford University Press, 1944; *Lake Erie,* Bobbs-Merrill, 1945, reprinted, Greenwood Press, 1971; *The Western Reserve: The Story of New Connecticut in Ohio,* Bobbs-Merrill, 1949, revised edition, World Publishing, 1966; *A Century of Iron and Men,* Bobbs-Merrill, 1950; (editor) *A Modern Repertory,* Harcourt, 1953; *Giant from the Wilderness,* World Publishing, 1955; (with Erich A. Walter) *A Pictorial History of the Great Lakes,* Crown, 1963; *The Persistent Quest for Values: What Are We Seeking?,* University of Missouri Press, 1966. Contributor of articles and fiction to journals. Book critic, *Columbus Citizen,* 1938-44; editorial adviser, *College English,* 1938-44.†

*   *   *

HAUN, Paul   1906-1969

PERSONAL: Born April 23, 1906, in Arkansas City, Kan.; son of John Evans (a railroad station agent) and Mary Alice (Finch) Haun; married Ruth Walton (an associate professor of social work). *Education:* Attended Colorado College, 1923-26; Columbia University, A.B., 1928, M.D., 1931, Med.Sc.D., 1936. *Religion:* Methodist. *Home:* 22 South Eastfield Ave., Trenton, N.J. 08618. *Office:* 135 West Hanover St., Trenton, N.J. 08625.

CAREER: Resident in neurology and psychiatry at hospitals in New York, N.Y., Boston, Mass., and Worcester, Mass., 1932-37; Colorado State Hospital, Pueblo, member of staff, 1937-38; neurologist and psychiatrist in private practice, medical director of Mount Airy Sanitarium, assistant neurologist at Denver General Hospital, and on staffs of various hospitals, Denver, Colo., 1938-42; certified in psychiatry by American Board of Psychiatry and Neurology, 1946; U.S. Veterans Administration, Washington, D.C., chief of hospital construction unit, Psychiatry and Neurology Division, 1946-52; Wake Forest College (now University), Bowman Gray School of Medicine, Winston-Salem, N.C., clinical director, 1952-55, assistant professor, 1952-54, associate professor of psychiatry, 1955; Eastern Pennsylvania Psychiatric Institute, Philadelphia, director of professional education, 1955-57; New Jersey Department of Institutions and Agencies, Trenton, director of psychiatric education, 1957-69. Instructor in psychiatry, Harvard University, 1936-37; assistant professor of psychiatry, Georgetown University, 1947-49; clinical associate professor of psychiatry, New Jersey College of Medicine and Dentistry, 1960-69. *Military service:* U.S. Army, 1942-46; served in South Pacific; became captain. *Member:* American Psychiatric Association, Group for the Advancement of Psychiatry, American College of Psychiatrists, New Jersey Neuropsychiatric Association, Philadelphia Psychiatric Society.

WRITINGS: Psychiatric Sections in General Hospitals, F. W. Dodge Corp., 1950; (contributor) Louis Linn, editor, *Frontiers in General Hospital Psychiatry,* International Universities, 1961; (contributor) J. K. Owen, editor, *Modern Concepts of Hospital Administration,* Saunders, 1962; *Recreation: A Medical Viewpoint,* compiled and edited by Elliott M. Avedon and Frances B. Arje, Teachers College Press, 1965. Contributor to proceedings of recreation congresses, and to psychiatric, nursing, hospital, and recreation journals.†

(Died October, 1969)

* * *

HAUSMANN, Bernard A(ndrew) 1899-

PERSONAL: Born January 24, 1899, in Cleveland, Ohio; son of August (a day laborer) and Mary (Wagner) Hausmann. *Education:* Gonzaga University, M.A., 1925; St. Louis University, graduate study, 1928-32; Yale University, Ph.D., 1937. *Home and office:* Carmelite Monastery, 3501 Silver Lake Rd., Traverse City, Mich. 49684.

CAREER: Roman Catholic priest, member of Society of Jesus (Jesuits); University of Detroit, Detroit, Mich., instructor in mathematics, 1925-26; St. Ignatius High School, Cleveland, Ohio, teacher of Latin, 1926-28; professor of mathematics at University of Detroit, 1937-44, West Baden College, West Baden Springs, Ind., 1944-64, Bellarmine School of Theology, North Aurora, Ill., 1964-66, and University of Detroit, 1966-68; Carmelite Monastery, Traverse City, Mich. chaplain, beginning 1968.

WRITINGS: Learning the Breviary, Benziger, 1932; (translator) *Our Best Friend,* Bruce, 1934; *From an Ivory Tower,* Bruce, 1960; *Learning the New Breviary,* Benziger, 1961. Editor of *Breviarium Romanum,* published by Benziger, beginning 1940.

AVOCATIONAL INTERESTS: Pyrogravure (woodburning) of portraits, pencil drawing.

* * *

HAWLEY, Mabel C.
[Collective pseudonym]

WRITINGS—"Four Little Blossoms" series; published by Cupples & Leon: *Four Little Blossoms at Sunrise Beach,* 1929; . . . *Indoors and Out,* 1930.

SIDELIGHTS: See ADAMS, Harriet S., STRATEMEYER, Edward L., and SVENSON, Andrew E.†

* * *

HAYES, Francis Clement 1904-

PERSONAL: Born December 14, 1904, in Buncombe County, N.C.; son of Julius Franklin (a merchant) and Laura (Starnes) Hayes; married Helen Oldham, June 5, 1931. *Education:* University of North Carolina, A.B., 1928, Ph.D., 1936; University of Madrid, graduate study, 1929; Columbia University, A.M., 1930. *Religion:* Quaker. *Home:* 2035 Northwest Seventh Lane, Gainesville, Fla. 32601. *Office:* University of Florida, Gainesville, Fla. 32601.

CAREER: Instructor in Spanish at New York University,

New York, N.Y., 1928-30, and University of North Carolina, Chapel Hill, 1930-31; Charleston College, Charleston, S.C., associate professor of Spanish and French, 1931-32; University of North Carolina, instructor in Spanish, 1932-40; Guilford College, Greensboro, N.C., associate professor of Spanish and French and chairman of foreign language department, 1940-46; University of Florida, Gainesville, professor of Spanish literature, 1946-73, professor emeritus, 1973—, chairman for Spanish, Division of Language and Literature, 1946-50. Visiting professor (U.S. Department of State), University of Sucre, Sucre, Bolivia, 1944-45; visiting summer professor, University of California, Los Angeles, 1947.

MEMBER: Modern Language Association of America, American Association of Teachers of Spanish and Portuguese (chairman of literary section, 1948-49), American Association of University Professors, Council for Basic Education, South Atlantic Modern Language Association (chairman of Spanish selection, 1953), Phi Beta Kappa.

WRITINGS: (Editor with Guillermo Francovich) Stephen Vincent Benet, *America* (text in English, with notes and vocabulary in Spanish), U.S. Department of State (Sucre), 1945; (with P. V. Fernandez) *Beginning Spanish,* Houghton, 1949; *Gestures: A Working Bibliography,* University of Florida Library, 1957; *Lope de Vega,* Twayne, 1967. Contributor to *Encyclopedia Americana;* contributor of more than twenty-five articles to professional journals and magazines, including *Modern Language Journal* and *Collier's.* Member of editorial board, *Southern Folklore Quarterly,* beginning 1946; associate editor, *South Atlantic Bulletin,* 1948-72.

WORK IN PROGRESS: Dicionario historico de refranes espanoles, a compilation of some 75,000 Spanish proverbs on file in the University of Florida Library.

AVOCATIONAL INTERESTS: Folk gestures around the world; chess.

* * *

HAYS, Paul R. 1903-

PERSONAL: Born April 2, 1903, in Des Moines, Iowa; son of Everett Hollingsworth and Fae Susan (Hatch) Hays; married, 1924 (divorced, 1943); married second wife, Elinor Rice, November 19, 1949; children: (first marriage) Rhys Williams. *Education:* Columbia University, A.B., 1925, A.M., 1927, LL.B., 1933. *Religion:* Protestant. *Home:* 276 Riverside Dr., New York, N.Y.

CAREER: Instructor in Greek and Latin at New York University, 1926, and Columbia University, 1926-32, both New York, N.Y.; Cravath, de Gersdorff, Swaine & Wood (law firm), New York, N.Y., associate, 1933-34; National Recovery Administration, Washington, D.C., counsel, 1934-35; Cravath, de Gersdorff, Swaine & Wood, associate, 1935-36; Columbia University, New York, N.Y., assistant professor, 1936-38, associate professor, 1938-43, professor of law, 1943-57, Nash Professor of Law, 1957-61, professor of law, beginning 1961; judge (appointed) of U.S. Court of Appeals, Second Circuit, beginning 1961. Legal consultant to New York State Banking Department, 1936-37, New York State Law Revision Commission, 1937-45, U.S. Department of Justice, 1944-45. Labor arbitrator and impartial chairman for many industries, 1940-61. Chairman of New York Governor's Committee on Welfare Funds, 1957-60, and Liberal Party, 1960-61. Presidential elector, 1960.

MEMBER: American Bar Association (secretary of section

on labor relations law, 1959-60), New York State Bar Association, Association of the Bar of City of New York, New York County Lawyers Association, Phi Beta Kappa.

WRITINGS: (With Joseph P. Chamberlain and Noel T. Dowling) *The Judicial Function in Federal Administrative Agencies,* New York Commonwealth Fund, 1942; *Cases and Materials on Civil Procedure,* Foundation Press, 1947; (with Milton Handler) *Cases on Labor Law,* West Publishing, 1950, 4th revised edition, 1963; *Labor Arbitration: A Dissenting View,* Yale University Press, 1966. Contributor to periodicals.

*   *   *

HAYWOOD, Richard Mansfield   1905-1977

PERSONAL: Born June 12, 1905, in Lynn, Mass.; son of Charles Edward (a lawyer) and Anne (Moulton) Haywood; married Margaret Rider Mowbray, September 6, 1930; children: Richard Mowbray, Anne Mowbray, Mary Coale (Mrs. Donald L. Metz). *Education:* Dartmouth College, A.B., 1926; Johns Hopkins University, Ph.D., 1932. *Religion:* Episcopalian. *Home address:* Route 6, Box 245, Charlottesville, Va. 22901.

CAREER: Johns Hopkins University, Baltimore, Md., associate in Latin, 1932-44; Hotchkiss School, Lakeville, Conn., associate in Latin, 1944-50; New York University, New York, N.Y., associate, 1950-52, assistant professor, 1952-58, associate professor, 1958-60, professor of classics, 1960-73, professor emeritus, 1973-77. *Member:* American Philological Association, Phi Beta Kappa. *Awards, honors:* Guggenheim fellowship, 1939-40; Fulbright fellowship for research in Italy, 1960-61.

WRITINGS: Studies on Scipio Africanus, Johns Hopkins Press, 1933, reprinted, Greenwood Press, 1973; (contributor) Irwin Isenberg, editor, *An Economic Survey of Ancient Rome,* Johns Hopkins Press, 1938; *Ancient Rome,* Johns Hopkins Press, 1938, text edition, McKay, 1967; *The Myth of Rome's Fall,* Crowell, 1958; *Ancient Greece and the Near East,* McKay, 1964; *The Ancient World,* McKay, 1971. Also author of *Roman Africa.* Contributor of articles and reviews to classical journals.

WORK IN PROGRESS: Imperial City: Ancient Rome at Its Height.†

(Died March 31, 1977)

*   *   *

HEALEY, F(rancis) G(eorge)   1903-

PERSONAL: Born April 20, 1903, in Lifton, Devonshire, England; son of Garnet John (a local government official) and Ellen Louisa (Down) Healey; married Mary Isabel Dixon, November 7, 1931; children: John, Margaret Dixon (Mrs. Gordon Stewart), Elizabeth Henderson (Mrs. Isaac Ormyron), Norman. *Education:* University of Birmingham, B.A., 1926; Westminster College, Cambridge, England, theological studies, 1926-30; Cambridge University, B.A., 1938, M.A., 1931. *Home:* 14 Brownlow Rd., Cambridge, England.

CAREER: Clergyman of Presbyterian Church of England. Missionary in Formosa and China, 1930-39, and professor of theology in Taiwan, Formosa, 1935-39; British Foreign Office, member of staff in Tokyo, 1939-41; Swarthmore College, Swarthmore, Pa., associate professor of philosophy and religion, 1941-42; British Foreign Office, staff member in Washington, D.C., 1942-45, and London, England, 1945; Presbyterian Church of England, minister at Southend,

1945-48, overseas secretary, London, 1948-51, and general secretary, London, 1951-60, moderator of General Assembly, 1965-66; Westminster College, Cambridge, England, professor of systematic theology and apologetics, 1960-73. *Member:* Society for Study of Theology (England).

WRITINGS: Rooted in Faith: Three Centuries of Nonconformity 1662-1962, Independent Press, 1961; *Religion and Reality: The Theology of John Oman,* Oliver & Boyd, 1965; (editor) *Prospect for Theology: Essays in Honour of H. H. Farmer,* Nisbet, 1966; *Fifty Key Words in Theology,* John Knox, 1967; (editor) *What Theologians Do,* Eerdmans, 1971.

SIDELIGHTS: Healey formerly lectured in Chinese (Fukienese) and Japanese; reads German and French. *Avocational interests:* Gardening, chess.

*   *   *

HEARD, (Henry Fitz) Gerald   1889-1971
(H. F. Heard)

PERSONAL: Born October 6, 1889, in London, England; came to the United States in 1937; son of Henry James (a prebendary of the Church of England) and Maude (Bannatyne) Heard. *Education:* Gonville and Caius College, Cambridge, honors in history, 1911, graduate work, 1911-12. *Home:* 322 East Rustic Rd., Santa Monica, Calif. 90402. *Agent:* Russell & Volkening, Inc., 551 Fifth Ave., New York, N.Y. 10017.

CAREER: Worked with Agricultural Co-op Movement in Ireland, 1919-23, in England, 1923-27. Author, lecturer, researcher. Radio lecturer, 1929-71; science commentator, British Broadcasting Corp., 1930-34; lecturer, Oxford University, 1929-31; visiting lecturer, Washington University, St. Louis, Mo., 1951, 1952, 1955-56; Haskell Foundation Lecturer at Oberlin College and Macliesh Lecturer at Rockford College, both 1958. *Awards, honors:* Bollingen Foundation grant, 1955-56; Henrietta Hertz Award of the British Academy, for *The Ascent of Humanity.*

WRITINGS: Narcissus: An Anatomy of Clothes, Dutton, 1924; *The Ascent of Humanity,* Harcourt, 1929; *The Social Substance of Religion,* Harcourt, 1931; *The Emergence of Man,* J. Cape, 1931, Harcourt, 1932; *This Surprising World: A Journalist Looks at Science,* Cobden-Sanderson, 1932; *These Hurrying Years: An Historical Outline, 1900-1933,* Oxford University Press, 1934; *The Source of Civilization,* J. Cape, 1935; *Science in the Making,* Faber, 1935; *Exploring the Stratosphere,* Thomas Nelson, 1936; *Science Front,* Cassell, 1936; (contributor) *The New Pacificism* (essays), Allenson, 1936, reprint edited by Gerald K. Hibbert, Garland Publishing, 1972; *The Third Morality,* Morrow, 1937; *Pain, Sex, and Time,* Harper, 1939; *A Quaker Mutation,* Pendle Hill, 1940; *Man the Master,* Harper, 1941; *The Creed of Christ,* Harper, 1941; *The Code of Christ,* Harper, 1941; *Training for the Life of the Spirit,* Cassell, 1942; *A Dialogue in the Desert,* Harper, 1942; *A Preface to Prayer,* Harper, 1944; *The Recollection,* James Delkin, 1944; *The Gospel According to Gamaliel,* Harper, 1945; *The Eternal Gospel,* Harper, 1946; *Is God Evident?: An Essay toward Natural Theology,* Harper, 1948; *Prayers and Meditations,* Harper, 1949.

The Riddle of the Flying Saucers: Is Another World Watching?, Carroll & Nicholson, 1950, published as *Is Another World Watching?: The Riddle of the Flying Saucers,* Harper, 1951; *Is God in History?: An Inquiry into Human and Prehuman History in Terms of the Doctrine of Creation, Fall and Redemption,* Harper, 1950; *Morals since*

1900, Harper, 1950; *Ten Questions on Prayer* (pamphlet), Pendle Hill, 1951; *The Black Fox: A Novel of the Seventies*, Harper, 1951; *Gabriel and the Creatures*, Harper, 1952 (published in England as *Wishing Well: An Outline of the Evolution of the Mammals Told as a Series of Stories about How the Animals Got Their Wishes*, Faber, 1953); *The Human Venture*, Harper, 1955; (with others) *Kingdom without God: Road's End for the Social Gospel*, Foundation for Social Research, 1956; *Training for a Life of Growth*, Wayfarer Press, 1959; *The Five Ages of Man*, Julian Press, 1963.

Under name H. F. Heard: *A Taste for Honey*, Vanguard, 1941, reprinted, Lancer Books, 1964; *Reply Paid: A Mystery*, Vanguard, 1942; *Murder by Reflection*, Vanguard, 1942; *The Great Fog, and Other Weird Tales*, Vanguard, 1944, published as *The Great Fog: Weird Tales of Terror and Detection*, Sun Dial Press, 1946; *Dopplegangers: An Episode of the Fourth, the Psychological Revolution, 1997*, Vanguard, 1947; *The Lost Cavern, and Other Tales of the Fantastic*, Vanguard, 1948; *The Notched Hairpin*, Vanguard, 1949.

SIDELIGHTS: Graham Hunter called Heard "one of the small and scattered number of men who, knowing the extensive field of modern knowledge in its essentials, are able to think in cosmic terms." He had already established his reputation as a writer before he left England for America in 1937. After delving into the past and studying old religions, Heard's theories concerning a new form of religion took shape. His ideas were considered by many to be quite controversial, but he had, as Reinhold Niebuhr said, "gifts of art and imagination which are quite independent of his religious dogmas."

BIOGRAPHICAL/CRITICAL SOURCES: Saturday Review, August 17, 1929, January 30, 1932, September 8, 1934, March 15, 1947, April 28, 1951, February 29, 1964; *New Republic*, August 21, 1929, February 24, 1932; *New York Times*, October 13, 1929, January 17, 1932, September 9, 1934, May 9, 1937, September 19, 1937, January 6, 1946, September 15, 1946, April 29, 1951; *Nation*, October 16, 1929, September 26, 1934; *New Statesman*, December 7, 1929, April 14, 1934, February 22, 1936; *Spectator*, November 21, 1931, April 27, 1934, January 15, 1937; *Times Literary Supplement*, December 21, 1935, October 20, 1950; *Commonweal*, March 5, 1937; *Christian Century*, December 25, 1940, December 19, 1945, November 6, 1946; *San Francisco Chronicle*, October 20, 1946, March 9, 1947, April 29, 1951; *New Yorker*, January 20, 1951; *New York Times Book Review*, January 5, 1964.†

(Died August 14, 1971)

*   *   *

HEDDEN, Worth Tuttle 1896-
(Winifred Woodley)

PERSONAL: Born January 10, 1896, in Raleigh, N.C.; daughter of Daniel Herndon (a clergyman) and Amelia (Wescott) Tuttle; married Walter Page Hedden (a transportation consultant), July 23, 1919; children: Daniel, Page (Mrs. Ian Wilson), Mark. *Education:* Trinity College (now Duke University), A.B., 1916; Columbia University, graduate student, 1917-18. *Politics:* Democrat. *Religion:* Agnostic. *Home and office:* 191 Greens Farms Rd., Westport, Conn. 06880. *Agent:* Elizabeth McKee, McIntosh, McKee & Dodds, Inc., 22 East 40th St., New York, N.Y. 10016.

CAREER: Women's Vocational Bureau, Richmond, Va., secretary, 1916-17; assistant to Socialist leader Norman

Thomas, New York City, 1917-18, and to author-educator Walter B. Pitken, New York City, 1918-19; American Red Cross, New York City, veterans' aide, 1919-20; Straight College (now Dillard University), New Orleans, La., teacher of English, 1920-21; *Encyclopaedia Britannica*, New York City, staff writer, 1927-28; novelist. *Member:* P.E.N., Phi Beta Kappa (honorary member). *Awards, honors:* Prize ($600) for short story published in *New Pierson*; Anisfield-Wolf Award (for best book concerned with racial problems), and Southern Authors' National Democratic Organization Award, 1948, both for *The Other Room*.

WRITINGS: Wives of High Pasture (novel), Doubleday, 1944; *The Other Room* (novel), Crown, 1947; *Love Is a Wound* (novel), Crown, 1952; (under pseudonym Winifred Woodley) *Two and Three Make One* (memoir), Crown, 1956. Contributor to anthologies; short stories and articles published in *Smart Set, Atlantic, Harper's, New Republic, World Tomorrow, American Scholar, New York Times, New York Herald Tribune*, and *Saturday Review*.

WORK IN PROGRESS: An autobiograhical novel, objectively treated, focused on "consuming interest and to-date conclusions about women, marriage, minorities."

SIDELIGHTS: In 1966 Mrs. Hedden told *CA:* "The subject I, at seventy, consider vital is personal vitality—living to the best of one's ability without (consciously) preventing others doing the same, politically, socially, religiously. At seventeen, in a small southern town, 'others' for me became the local minorities: mill hands, share croppers, colored people—even well-to-do women who, to keep *In*, had to suppress brains or talent. Most of my writing has been about Negroes and about women-in-the-minority; my theme—look for the individual in all races, creeds, and previous conditions of servitude.

"My motivation has always been mental, never manual; hence my detestation of housekeeping which, except for very odd times, has prevented my reading-and-writing (other wives-and-mothers, more generally skilled than I, have done both)." As a child, Mrs. Hedden loved the moves that took her family to a succession of North Carolina towns. Since 1948 she has traveled over most of the globe with her husband, missing only the Arctic regions, Australasia, South Africa, and northwestern United States. She still considers her writing an avocation, along with reading philosophy, anthropology, and archaeology, and gardening.

BIOGRAPHICAL/CRITICAL SOURCES: New York Herald Tribune, July 6, 1947; *San Francisco Chronicle*, July 10, 1947; *Survey Graphic*, August, 1947; Harry R. Warfel, *American Novelists of Today*, American Book Co., 1951; *Wilson Library Bulletin*, February, 1957.

*   *   *

HEDGES, Trimble R(aymond) 1906-

PERSONAL: Born September 24, 1906, in Banner, Okla.; son of Arthur L. (a farmer) and Cleo B. (Williams) Hedges; married Charlsie Hynds Jordon, 1927; children: Charles A., David M. *Education:* Oklahoma State University, B.S., 1928; University of Illinois, M.S., 1933, Ph.D., 1938. *Politics:* Democrat. *Religion:* Unitarian Universalist. *Home:* 20 Parkside Dr., Davis, Calif. 95616. *Office:* Department of Agricultural Economics, University of California, Davis, Calif. 95616.

CAREER: County agricultural agent, Custer County, Okla., 1928-31; Oklahoma State University, Stillwater, assistant professor, 1935-37, associate professor, 1937-38; field officer of southern division, Agricultural Adjustment Administration, 1938; University of Arkansas, Fayetteville, associate professor, 1938-41, professor and agricultural economist, 1941-45, head of department, 1945-47; University of California, Davis, associate professor, 1947-54, professor of agricultural economics, beginning 1954. Agricultural economist, Giannini Foundation, beginning 1947; agricultural economist and chief of Plans and Programs Section, for U.S. Mutual Security Agency, Paris, France, 1952-53; Fulbright lecturer, University of Naples, 1963-64. *Military service:* U.S. Naval Reserve, 1931-35; became lieutenant commander. *Member:* American Farm Economic Association, American Society of Farm Managers and Rural Appraisers, Society for International Development, Western Economic Association, Western Farm Economics Association, California Society of Farm Managers and Rural Appraisers.

WRITINGS: (With Gordon R. Sitton) *Farm Management Manual,* National Press, 1956, revised edition, 1965; *Farm Management Decisions,* Prentice-Hall, 1963. Contributor of about 150 bulletins, research reports, and articles to journals.

WORK IN PROGRESS: Writing on economics of mechanical cotton harvesting and irrigation water availability in the San Joaquin Valley; land tenure in relation to laws and institutions, and its effect on farm organization and management and on family earnings; vegetable crops in California; farm production and income in Brazil; farm fragmentation and consolidation in Europe; irrigation water supplies and costs in the Sacramento Valley.

SIDELIGHTS: Hedges speaks French, German, Italian, and Portuguese.†

* * *

HEDLEY, George (Percy) 1899-

PERSONAL: Born September 24, 1899, in Tientsin, China; son of John (a clergyman) and Annie Smith (Whitehead) Hedley; married Helen Louise Campbell, May 14, 1922; children: Sheila C. (Mrs. Charles W. Bodemer). *Education:* University of Southern California, B.A., 1920, M.A., 1921; Maclay School of Religion, B.D., 1924; Pacific School of Religion, D.Theol., 1928. *Politics:* Democrat. *Home:* 1306 Euclid Ave., Berkeley, Calif. 94708.

CAREER: Ordained to the Methodist ministry, 1924; ordained to priest's orders of the Protestant Episcopal Church (retaining Methodist status), 1959. College of Puget Sound (now University of Puget Sound), Tacoma, Wash., professor of religious education and Biblical literature, 1923-26; Pacific School of Religion, Berkeley, Calif., assistant professor of Biblical literature, 1928-33; Hartford Theological Seminary, Hartford, Conn., acting assistant professor of Biblical literature, 1933-34; Pacific Coast Labor School, Berkeley, Calif., director, 1935-41; Mills College, Oakland, Calif., associate professor, 1940-48, professor of sociology and economics and chaplain, 1948-65, professor and chaplain emeritus, 1965—. James A. Gray Lecturer, Duke University, 1955; Clark Lecturer, Pomona College, 1957. Recorder and photographer, Tellen-Nasbeh Expedition of the Palestine Institute, 1927 and 1929. *Military service:* U.S. Army, World War I. *Member:* Phi Beta Kappa, City Commons Club (Berkeley). *Awards, honors:* Silver Medal of Commonwealth Club of California, 1946, for *The Christian Heritage in America;* D.D., Pacific School of Religion, 1958.

WRITINGS: A Christian Year, Macmillan, 1934; *The San Francisco Strike As I Have Seen It,* Church Council for Social Education, 1934; *Books: Backgrounds and Foregrounds,* Eucalyptus Press, 1940; *Reconsiderations,* Mills College, 1942; *Again From the Dead* (verse), Eucalyptus Press, 1943; *Credo ut Videam* (verse), Eucalyptus Press, 1943; *In Brief* (verse), Eucalyptus Press, 1945; *The Christian Heritage in America* (Religious Book Club selection), Macmillan, 1946; *The Symbol of the Faith,* Macmillan, 1948.

The Superstitions of the Irreligious, Macmillan, 1951; *Christian Worship: Some Meanings and Means* (Religious Book Club selection), Macmillan, 1953; *Religion on the Campus,* Macmillan, 1955; *Jericho to Jerusalem* (verse), Mansfield Advertiser Press, 1956; *The Minister Behind the Scenes,* Macmillan, 1956; *Aurelia Henry Reinhardt: Portrait of a Whole Woman,* Mills College, 1961; *When Protestants Worship,* Abingdon, 1961; *Religion and the Natural World,* University of Washington Press, 1962; *The Magical Madness of Mills* (verse), Mills College, 1964; *Nativity* (verse), Edmonds Press, 1965; *The Holy Trinity,* Fortress, 1967.

Author of pamphlets. Contributor to *Harper's, Religion in Life, Vital Speeches,* and other periodicals; contributor of book reviews and daily verse to *San Francisco Chronicle,* 1936-40; weekly columnist, *Oakland Tribune,* beginning 1965.

BIOGRAPHICAL/CRITICAL SOURCES: Time, December 21, 1959.††

* * *

HEDRICK, Addie M. 1903-

PERSONAL: Born August 22, 1903, in Black Rock, Ark.; daughter of William Henry (a farmer) and Mary Elizabeth (Lunsford) Underwood; married Joseph A. Hedrick, November 21, 1920; children: Louise (Mrs. L. J. Caranna), Joseph A., Jr. *Education:* Attended public schools in Arkansas.

MEMBER: National League of American Pen Women, World Poetry Society, Poetry Society of Tennessee, Arkansas Authors, Composers, & Artists.

WRITINGS: Sentient Dust, Stovall Press, 1952; *Mumbaloo, and Other Poems,* Stovall Press, 1967; *A Cup of Stars,* Golden Quill, 1969. Poetry included in several anthologies; contributor to poetry magazines and to *Christian Science Monitor, Portland Oregonian, Arkansas Gazette, Denver Post, Colorado Quarterly, Louisville Times-Courier,* and other publications.

AVOCATIONAL INTERESTS: Gardening, nature, and oil painting.

* * *

HEILIG, Matthias R. 1881-?

PERSONAL: Born January 15, 1881, in Stroudsburg, Pa.; son of Theophilus (a clergyman) and Mary Alice (Davis) Heilig; married Mary Beetern, February 10, 1909; married second wife, Alsiee Raymond, July 4, 1965; children: (first marriage) Alice (Mrs. Walter Douglas Halsted), David. *Education:* Muhlenberg College, M.A., 1903; Mount Airy Theological Seminary, further study, 1905-08.

CAREER: Lutheran clergyman, with pastorates in Dansville, N.Y., 1909-14, and Downington, Pa., 1914-37; Unitarian (now Unitarian Universalist) clergyman, beginning 1943, with pastorates in Waterloo, Iowa, 1943-46, Philadelphia, Pa., 1947-48, and Southold, Long Island, N.Y., 1949-

57. Also part-time teacher in public schools of Downigtown, Pa., for one year. *Member:* Curtis Institute (Southold), Wranglers Club (Philadelphia).

WRITINGS: With Sullivan in 1779, Stroudsburg Times, 1907; *A Pioneer Through Time,* American Press, 1963; *Conversations on the Styx,* Philosophical Library, 1967; *Discussions on the Styx,* Philosophical Library, 1969.†

(Deceased)

*　*　*

HELLMAN, Hugo E.　1908-

PERSONAL: Born August 18, 1908, in Muenster, Tex.; son of August (a rancher) and Anda (Fette) Hellman; married Margaret Schuengel, July 18, 1937; children: John, Robert. *Education:* Marquette University, Ph.B., 1931, M.A., 1934, Ph.D., 1940. *Politics:* Independent. *Religion:* Catholic. *Home:* 1530 Church St., Milwaukee, Wis. *Office:* Marquette University, 625 North 15th St., Milwaukee, Wis.

CAREER: High school teacher in Milwaukee, Wis., 1931-36; Marquette University, Milwaukee, Wis., instructor, 1936-38, professor of speech, 1938-40, director of School of Speech, 1940-68, dean, 1968-73, dean emeritus, 1973—, Law School, lecturer in parliamentary law, beginning 1970. Parliamentarian, American Bowling Congress; parliamentary consultant to American Dental Hygiene Association, and other organizations. *Member:* American Institute of Parliamentarians (member of board of directors), Speech Association of America, American Forensic Association (president, 1954-58), American Academy of Political and Social Science.

WRITINGS: Building Model Scenery, privately printed, 1948; (with Joseph M. Staudacher) *Speech in Groups,* Edwards, 1965; (with Staudacher and William Lamers) *Speech Arts,* Macmillan, 1966; *Parliamentary Procedure,* Macmillan, 1966; (with Staudacher) *Fundamentals of Speech: A Group Speaking Approach,* Random House, 1969. Also author of *How to Debate the Annual High School Propositions,* published annually by Edwards. Regular contributor to *American Parliamentary Journal.*

WORK IN PROGRESS: An edition of *Robert's Rules for Parliamentary Practice.*

AVOCATIONAL INTERESTS: Freshwater sailing; boat designing.†

*　*　*

HELPS, Racey　1913-1971

PERSONAL: Born February 2, 1913, in Bristol, England; son of Clifford Racey (an advertising man) and Dorothy Lucy (Davis) Helps; married Renee Orr; children: Anne Rosemary (Mrs. Michael Plumley), Julian Racey. *Education:* Studied at West of England College of Art. *Religion:* Pantheist. *Home:* Lake, Barnstaple, North Devonshire, England. *Agent:* Mark Paterson, 42 Canonbury Sq., London, England.

CAREER: Former antiquarian bookseller; writer and illustrator of books for children, beginning 1946.

WRITINGS—All self-illustrated; all published by Collins, except where noted: *Footprints in the Snow,* 1946; *Upside Down Medicine,* 1946; *My Friend Wilberforce,* 1947; *Barnaby Camps Out,* 1947; *Tippetty's Treasure,* 1949; *Little Dill's Party, a Counting Story,* John Martin's House, 1951; *Prickly Pie,* 1975, Chilton, 1968.

All published by Chilton, except where noted: *Kingsup Cot-*

tage, Medici Society, 1962; *Pinny Takes a Bath,* 1966; *Two From a Teapot,* 1966; *Mr. Roley to the Rescue,* 1966; *The Blow-Away Balloon,* 1967; *Selina, the Circus Seal,* 1967; *The Clean Sweep,* 1967; *Two's Company,* 1968. Stories and poems included in children's annuals. Has done newspaper strips for *Bristol Evening World, Gleaner* (Jamaica), and *Woman's Friend,* and also created card games and jigsaw puzzles.

SIDELIGHTS: Helps' books also have been published in Scandinavia, Germany, and Yugoslavia. He wrote his first children's stories for his daughter; he did his writing and illustrating in his cottage-home in a small village near the sea and Exmoor. Helps told *CA* that his disappointments were: "Not to have had classical education; not to have carried out early ambition to write good historical novels."†

(Died, 1971)

*　*　*

HEMLEBEN, Sylvester John　1902-

PERSONAL: Born February 25, 1902, in La Crosse, Wis.; son of Albert Lawrence and Jeanette (Elligen) Hemleben; married Mary Ruth Bingham, April 16, 1938; children: Sylvester John, Jr., Scott Parker. *Education:* University of Iowa, B.A., 1927, M.A., 1928; graduate study at Columbia University, 1928-29, and Cambridge University, 1929; Fordham University, Ph.D., 1931; postdoctoral study at Harvard University, 1935, and University of Munich, 1936; University of Mississippi, L.L.B. (with distinction), 1963, J.D., 1968. *Politics:* Democrat. *Religion:* Episcopalian.

CAREER: College of New Rochelle, New Rochelle, N.Y., staff member, 1927-35, department head, 1931-35; Fordham University, School of Education, Bronx, N.Y., lecturer, 1931-35, associate professor of history and social studies and head of department of social studies, 1935-45; U.S. War Department, Chemical Corps, Washington, D.C., editor in historical branch, 1945-47; University of Southwestern Louisiana, Lafayette, professor of history, 1947-61; University of Mississippi, University, associate professor of law, 1963-65; private practice of law, 1965-66; Brevard Community College, Cocoa, Fla., professor of political science, 1966-72.

MEMBER: American Bar Association, American Political Science Association, Royal Historical Society (fellow), Association of Political Science Instructors, Mississippi State Bar, Brevard County Historical Society, Phi Delta Phi, Pi Gamma Mu, Phi Alph Theta, Phi Delta Kappa. *Awards, honors:* Award for best comment published in *Mississippi Law Journal* in 1962.

WRITINGS: Outlines of Modern European History, 1500-1830, Southern New England Typographic Service, 1934; *Plans for World Peace through Six Centuries,* University of Chicago Press, 1943, reprinted with new introduction, Garland Publishing, 1972; *Mississippi Workmen's Compensation: Selected Cases,* University of Mississippi Press, 1964. Contributor of articles and reviews to legal and education journals. Former articles editor, *Mississippi Law Journal.*

WORK IN PROGRESS: A history of the University of Mississippi School of Law.

*　*　*

HENDERLEY, Brooks
[Collective pseudonym]

WRITINGS—"The Y.M.C.A. Boys" series; published by Cupples & Leon: *The Y.M.C.A. Boys of Cliffwood,* 1916; *. . . on Bass Island,* 1916.

SIDELIGHTS: See **ADAMS, Harriet S., STRATEMEYER, Edward L.,** and **SVENSON, Andrew E.†**

*   *   *

HENDERSON, Ian   1910-1969

PERSONAL: Born April 13, 1910, in Edinburgh, Scotland; son of Alexander (a publisher's manager) and Elizabeth (Gaudie) Henderson; married Kathrine Margaret Macartney (a teacher), September 8, 1947; children: Alexander William, Elizabeth Camilla. *Education:* University of Edinburgh, M.A. (first class honors in philosophy), 1933, B.D. (distinction in systematic theology), 1936; also studied at University of Zurich, 1935, and University of Basel, 1936, 1937. *Home:* Kirkland, Campsie Glen, near Glasgow, Scotland. *Office:* University of Glasgow, Glasgow W. 2, Scotland.

CAREER: Ordained minister, Church of Scotland (Presbyterian), 1938; parish minister in Fraserburgh, Scotland, 1938-42, and Kilmany, Scotland, 1942-48; University of Glasgow, Glasgow, Scotland, professor of systematic theology, 1948-69. External examiner in theology at University of St. Andrews, 1945-48, The Queen's University of Belfast, 1950, University of Aberdeen, 1951, and University of Manchester, 1954. *Member:* Association of University Teachers of the United Kingdom. *Awards, honors:* D.D., University of Edinburgh, 1954.

WRITINGS: (Translator with J.L.M. Haire) Karl Barth, *Knowledge and Service of God,* Hodder & Stoughton, 1938; (translator with Haire) Walter Luethi, *In Time of Earthquake,* Hodder & Stoughton, 1939; *Can Two Walk Together?,* Nisbet, 1948; *Myth in the New Testament,* S. C. M. Press, 1953; *Rudolf Bultmann,* John Knox, 1966. Theological articles included in *Grolier's Encyclopedia,* 1965; *Power Without Glory,* Hutchinson, 1967, John Knox, 1969; *Scotland, Kirk and People,* Butterworth, 1969.

WORK IN PROGRESS: Ecumenicity and Power, a study of Anglo-Scottish ecclesiastical relations and of the influences of the power factor on church and theology; a study of hermeneutics, still in the early stages.

SIDELIGHTS: Henderson visited Germany a number of times. He was critical of the ecumenical movement, while "welcoming better Catholic-Protestant relations." He lived in the country (and gardened as a hobby), and commuted to classes in Glasgow.†

(Died April 8, 1969)

*   *   *

HENRY, Joseph B.   1901-

PERSONAL: Born February 2, 1901, in Germantown, Ohio; son of Burton R. (a tobacco buyer) and Pearl (Bennett) Henry; married Ruth C. Fornshell, September 7, 1933 (deceased); married Harriette Howe, April 12, 1958; children: Joseph R.; stepchildren: Marilyn (Mrs. J. D. Smith), Gary Garnett. *Education:* Otterbein College, A.B., 1926; United Theological Seminary, M.Th., 1935; summer study at University of California, Los Angeles, 1946, and University of Cincinnati, 1948. *Home and office:* 423 Santa Rosa Rd., Arcadia, Calif. 91006.

CAREER: Clergyman of Evangelical United Brethren Church, now clergyman of United Methodist Church. Minister of churches in Miamisburg, Ohio, 1929-36, Greenville, Ohio, 1936-43, and Dayton, Ohio, 1943-48; American Institute of Family Relations, Los Angeles, Calif., director of public education, 1949-53; private counseling practice (marriage and family life), Arcadia, Calif., beginning 1953. Part-

time minister of visitation, Santa Anita Church, Arcadia, California, beginning 1972. Past director of Community Services and Civil Defense, Darke County, Ohio; president of board of directors, Santa Fe Trail Council, Camp Fire Girls, 1945-46. *Member:* National Council on Family Relations, California State Marriage Counselors Association, National Alliance for Family Life (founding member). *Awards, honors:* Award for study in radio and television, National Council of Churches, 1946; L.H.D., Otterbein College, 1966.

WRITINGS: Fulfillment in Marriage, Revell, 1966. Writer of radio and television scripts.

WORK IN PROGRESS: Research for writings on life's meanings.

AVOCATIONAL INTERESTS: Growing roses, and collecting humorous incidents from sacred places.

*   *   *

HENRY, Vera

PERSONAL: Born in Forest, Ontario, Canada; daughter of Hugh Thomas (a contractor) and Myrtle (Gammon) Johnson; married James A. Henry; children: James H., Kevin M. *Residence:* Royal Oak, Mich. *Agent:* Lenniger Literary Agency, 437 Fifth Ave., New York, N.Y. 10016.

CAREER: Free-lance writer, 1942-75. Teacher in adult education program, Ferndale, Mich., beginning 1964; editorial associate, *Writer's Digest,* 1966-75. Staff member of Detroit Women Writers-Oakland University Writers Conference, 1962-74; staff member at conferences in Sarnia and London, Ontario. *Member:* Detroit Women Writers (membership chairman, 1961-75), Quota International (honorary member). *Awards, honors:* Writer of the year award, Detroit Women Writers, 1954, 1957, and book author of the year award, 1966; headliner award of Theta Sigma Phi, 1958.

WRITINGS: A Lucky Number, Lippincott, 1957; *Mystery of Cedar Valley,* Avalon, 1964; *Ong, the Wild Gander,* Lippincott, 1966; *Portrait in Fear,* Caravelle, 1967. Also author of two fiction correspondence courses for *Writer's Digest.* Writer of television and radio scripts. Contributor of more than three hundred short stories and articles to magazines, including *Red Book, Good Housekeeping, Seventeen.*

WORK IN PROGRESS: One adult and two juvenile novels.

SIDELIGHTS: Mrs. Henry told *CA:* "I think that being a writer is the most challenging, exasperating, wonderful job in the world and it surprises me anyone ever wants to do anything else." Her radio and television scripts have been translated into Spanish, Italian, French, Danish, Norwegian, and Swedish. Mrs. Henry's manuscripts have been deposited at the University of Oregon.

*   *   *

HERNANDEZ, Al   1909-

PERSONAL: Original name Alfredo Eufronio Guillermo Antonio Ornez de Hernandez; born June 25, 1909, in Iloilo City, Philippine Islands; son of Don Julio (a publisher, lawyer, architect, and inventor) and Aurelia (Ornez) de Hernandez; married Nene Witte (a commercial artist); married second wife, Maria Penelope Lachonas (formerly Miss Greece, and a model, dancer, and choreographer), January 5, 1943; children: (first marriage) Angela, Alfred, Rita; (second marriage) Alana. *Education:* Studied radio, theater, television, and films at various institutes, 1929-52; studied espionage and sea, jungle, and combat intelligence at Fraser Commando School, Australia, 1943-60. *Politics:* Republican. *Religion:* Roman Catholic. *Home:* 2305 Driftwood Dr., Las Vegas, Nev. 89107. *Agent:* W. Gerdes-Testa, 8923 Sunset Blvd., Hollywood, Calif.

CAREER: During early career in show business, worked as a dance director in Hollywood, Calif., producer of Far Eastern Exposition in Manila, Philippine Islands, 1937, and show producer in Chicago, Ill. *Movie News,* Hollywood, Calif., publisher and writer, beginning 1946. Other jobs include instructor at Glickman College of Fine Arts, 1941, film production in Hollywood, Calif., 1948, advertising creator for Ed Humphries Advertising, Chicago, Ill., 1952, producer of television advertisements in Hollywood, Calif., 1956, director of International Film Festival, Las Vegas, Nev., 1966. *Military service:* U.S. Army, Intelligence, during World War II; served in the Pacific; became second lieutenant; received Legion of Merit, Bronze Star. U.S. Army Reserve, about 9 years. *Member:* American Guild of Variety Artists, American Legion, Veterans of Foreign Wars, Reserve Officers Association.

WRITINGS: (With Earle Dixon) *Bahala Na,* foreword by Douglas MacArthur, Howell-North, 1961. Also author of *Found on Dress Rehearsal, On a Dollar Boat on My Way to Dollar Land,* and *How Party Second.* Contributor of articles to magazines and newspapers.

BIOGRAPHICAL/CRITICAL SOURCES: Los Angeles Examiner, June 11, 1961; *Las Vegas Scene Sunday Magazine,* March 31, 1963; *Las Vegas Review-Journal,* January 6, 1965; *Graphic Magazine,* November 1, 1967.

* * *

HERRING, Ralph A(lderman) 1901-19(?)

PERSONAL: Born August 18, 1901, in Pender County, N.C.; son of David Wells (a missionary to China) and Alice (Rea) Herring; married Willeen Tull, August 5, 1925; children: Ralph, Jr., David, Jackson, Margaret Herring Mc-Surely. *Education:* Wake Forest College (now Wake Forest University), B.A., 1921; Southern Baptist Theological Seminary, Th.M., 1925, Ph.D., 1929. *Home:* 711 Continental Apartments, West End Ave., Nashville, Tenn.

CAREER: Baptist minister, beginning 1924, with pastorates in Crestwood, Ky., 1924-29, Ashland, Ky., 1929-36, and Winston-Salem, N.C., 1936-61; Southern Baptist Seminaries (six seminaries), Nashville, Tenn., director of seminary Extension Department, beginning 1961. Visited missions or participated in Baptist conferences in South America, 1949, Hong Kong, 1956, Mexico and South America, 1959, Japan and Taiwan, 1963, Mexico, 1964. President of North Carolina Baptist State Convention, 1943-45. Trustee of Wake Forest College (now University), 1942-46, Campbell College, 1950-54, and Southeastern Baptist Seminary, 1951-61. *Member:* Rotary International. *Awards, honors:* D.D., Wake Forest College, 1940.

WRITINGS: Studies in Philippians, Broadman, 1952, revised edition published as *To Live Is Christ,* 1954; *God Being My Helper,* Broadman, 1955; *The Cycle of Prayer,* Broadman, 1966. Contributor to books and denominational journals.†

(Deceased)

* * *

HERRON, Ima Honaker 1899-

PERSONAL: Born March 9, 1899, in Farmersville, Tex.; daughter of William Patrick (a teacher and merchant) and Beulah Alice (Honaker) Herron. *Education:* Kidd Key Junior College, A.A., 1919; Southern Methodist University, B.A., 1921, M.A., 1926; University of Chicago, summer graduate student, 1924; Duke University, Ph.D., 1935. *Politics:* Democrat. *Religion:* Methodist. *Home:* 3001 University Blvd., Dallas, Tex. 75205.

CAREER: High school teacher of English and French in Farmersville, Tex., 1921-23; Kidd Key Junior College, Sherman, Tex., instructor in English, 1923-24, chairman of department, 1926-27; Southern Methodist University, Dallas, Tex., instructor, 1927-31, assistant professor, 1934-42, associate professor, 1942-46, professor of English and American literature, 1946-62, chairman of department, 1951-53, E. A. Lilly Professor of American Literature, 1962-64, professor emeritus, 1964—, part-time teacher of graduate seminars, 1964-66. Contributing member, Colophon, Southern Methodist University.

MEMBER: Modern Language Association of America (member of American literature group bibliography committee, 1932-53), South Central Modern Language Association (vice-president, 1952), South Central College English Association (secretary, 1957), Southwestern American Literature Association (charter member, 1969), American Studies Association of Texas, Texas Conference of College Teachers of English (past councillor), Phi Beta Kappa, Mortar Board, Chi Omega. *Awards, honors:* Carnegie Foundation grant, 1951; Faculty Achievement Award, Southern Methodist University, 1962; Danforth Foundation research grants, 1963, 1964; Woman of Achievement Award, Southern Methodist University, 1965; Outstanding Chi Omega Award, 1973.

WRITINGS: The Small Town in American Literature, Duke University Press, 1939, reprinted, Haskell House, 1970; (with J. W. Bowyer, G. D. Bond, and J. L. Brooks) *Better College English,* Appleton, 1950; *The Small Town in American Drama,* Southern Methodist University Press, 1969. Contributor to *Collier's Encyclopedia* and to literary and education journals.

WORK IN PROGRESS: A semi-historical novel, tentatively entitled, *The Glory Road;* a monograph on the fiction of Conrad Richter.

BIOGRAPHICAL/CRITICAL SOURCES: Variety, July 30, 1969; *Dallas Morning News,* December 28, 1969.

* * *

HERSHEY, Burnet 1896-1971

PERSONAL: Born December 13, 1896, in Bucharest, Rumania; brought to United States in 1899; son of Joseph (a sculptor) and Bertha (Bughici) Hershey; married Thyrza Putnam Sturgeis, June, 1935 (divorced). *Education:* Attended Columbia University, 1916-18, Sorbonne, University of Paris, 1921-22, London School of Economics and Political Science, 1945. *Home:* 91 Central Park W., New York, N.Y. 10023.

CAREER: Foreign correspondent and author. Covered the Ford Peace Expedition to Europe (the youngest reporter aboard) for *New York Evening Post,* 1915; accredited war correspondent in France, Belgium, and Germany, 1917-18, and Paris correspondent for *New York Sun,* 1917-20; subsequently foreign correspondent for *Philadelphia Ledger* in London, Berlin, Geneva, and for *Philadelphia Ledger and Times* in the Far East and Asia Minor, 1920-21; accredited war correspondent during World War II, and special correspondent for *New York Post* in England and North Africa, 1942-43, and for *Liberty* at Allied Headquarters, 1944-45; New York and Washington correspondent for *Tribune de Geneva;* also affiliated at various times with *New York Tribune, New York World, Brooklyn Eagle,* and International News Service. Major stories covered include the Versailles Peace Conference (he was accredited to the American Commission to Negotiate Peace, and to thirty-two international conferences). *Member:* Overseas Press Club of America (founder, president), American War Correspondents Association (president, 1949). *Awards, honors:* Legion of Honor (France); Palmes Academiques (France); Officier del'Instruction Publique (France); African and ETO (European Theatre of Operations) ribbons of U.S. War Department.

WRITINGS: (With Walter Bodin) *It's a Small World,* Coward, 1934 (published in England as *World of Midgets,* Jarrolds, 1935); *The Air Future,* Duell, Sloan & Pearce, 1934; *Skyways of Tomorrow,* Foreign Policy Association (New York), 1944; *Bloody Record of Nazi Atrocities,* World Publishing, 1944; *Dag Hammarskjold, Soldier of Peace,* Encyclopaedia Britannica, 1961; *From a Reporter's Little Black Book* (short stories), Pilot Books, 1966; *The Odyssey of Henry Ford and the Great Peace Ship,* Taplinger, 1967, published as *Get the Boys Out of the Trenches,* Pyramid Books, 1968; *You Can't Go to Heaven on a Roller Skate* (novel), Living Books, 1969; *Nymph and the Brass* (novel), Living Books, 1970.

Plays: "Scattered Seed," 1936; "Dealers in Death," produced in New York at Criterion Theater, 1938; "The Brown Danube," produced in New York at Lyceum Theatre, 1939; "Murder by Appointment," produced in New Haven and other cities, 1938; "Love Costs Money," produced in Whitestone Landing, N.Y., 1940. Author of scripts for more than 120 documentaries produced by Warner Brothers, Fox, RKO, and others.

Compiler and editor, *A Documentary History of the Versailles Conference,* fifteen volumes, Repository of Yeshiva University, 1945. Contributor to *Saturday Evening Post, Look, Reader's Digest, This Week, Liberty National Observer,* and other national magazines. Contributor to six Overseas Press Club anthologies. Associate editor of *Encyclopaedia of American Crime.*

WORK IN PROGRESS: A novel; his autobiography.

BIOGRAPHICAL/CRITICAL SOURCES: New York Times Book Review, August 27, 1967.†

(Died December 13, 1971)

*   *   *

HESKY, Olga   ?-1974

PERSONAL: Born in London, England; daughter of Lewis and Rachel (Franks) Cowen; married Mark Lynford; married second husband, George Hesky, 1954; children: (first marraige) Adam, Gabrielle (Mrs. Russel Logan). *Education:* Attended University of London, 1930-31. *Religion:* Jewish. *Home:* Hope House, Hedgerley, Buckinghamshire, England. *Agent:* Curtis Brown Ltd., 1 Craven Hill, London W2 3EW, England.

CAREER: Prior to 1949 was reporter, sub-editor, and film and theater critic on newspapers in England and South Africa; editor of *Wizo in Israel,* Tel Aviv, 1949-59; full-time writer, beginning 1959.

WRITINGS: The Painted Queen (historical novel), Anthony Blond, 1961, Obolensky, 1962; *The Purple Armchair,*

Anthony Blond, 1961; *Number the Dust* (historical novel), Constable, 1963; *Say Not Goodnight,* Constable, 1964; *The Serpent's Smile,* John Long, 1966, Dodd, 1967; *Time for Treason,* John Long, 1967, Dodd, 1968; *The Sequin Syndicate,* Dodd, 1969; *The Different Night,* John Long, 1970. Author of plays for South African Broadcasting Corp. and documentary films shown in Israel.

WORK IN PROGRESS: A novel.

SIDELIGHTS: Mrs. Hesky felt that her two historical novels were by far her best work ("according also to responsible critics"), but she had been writing thrillers "because though the others were freely borrowed from libraries, these were bought." She had traveled most of the world except the Far East. In addition to English and Hebrew, she was fluent in French and German.

AVOCATIONAL INTERESTS: Painting, reading, gardening, bridge, driving, and her dog.†

(Died, 1974)

*   *   *

HESSE, Hermann   1877-1962
(Hermann Lauscher, Emil Sinclair)

PERSONAL: Born July 2, 1877, in Calw, Wuerttemberg, Germany; Swiss citizen, 1924-62; son of Johannes (a religious journalist, publisher, and missionary) and Marie (Gundert) Hesse; married Maria Bernoulli, 1904 (divorced, 1923); married Ruth Wenger, January, 1924 (divorced, 1927); married Ninon Auslaender Dolbin, November, 1931 (died September 22, 1966); children: (first marriage) Bruno, Heiner, Martin. *Education:* Attended preparatory Latin school of Rector Otto Bauer, Goeppingen, Germany, 1890-91; studied theology at Seminar Maulbronn, 1891-92, ran away in 1892; attended Gymnasium at Cannstadt, expelled in 1893. *Home:* Montagnola, near Lugano, Switzerland.

CAREER: After his expulsion from the Gymnasium at Cannstadt, Hesse was apprenticed to a bookseller in Esslingen, Germany, but he ran away after three days and returned to Calw where he worked for six months as assistant to his father at Calwer Verlagsverein, a publishing association. In 1894 he became an apprentice in the clock factory of Heinrich Perrot, in Calw, where he assembled steeple clocks. From 1895 to 1898, he was an apprentice in the Heckenhauer bookshop in Tuebingen, Germany, and an assistant there from 1898 to 1899. In 1899 he began work with a bookdealer in Basel, Switzerland, returning to Calw late in 1901. From 1903 until his death in 1962, Hesse devoted most of his time to writing articles, essays, poetry, and fiction.

As eye trouble prevented him from entering the regular military, he served as a volunteer worker through the German consulate in Bern, Switzerland, on behalf of the German prisoners of war (1914-18). During the period 1916-18, Hesse underwent psychoanalysis. From 1907 to 1912, he edited the periodical *Maerz;* during World War I he edited the periodical for prisoners of war, *Sonntagsbote fuer deutsche Kriegsgefangene;* he served as co-editor of *Deutsche Internierten-Zeitung* from 1916 to 1917, and of *Vivos Voco* from 1919 to 1920. *Member:* Prussian Academy of Poets (resigned in 1926 when he lost faith in German politics), Schweizerischer Schriftstellerverein (Zuerich). *Awards, honors:* Wiener Bauernfeldpreis, 1904; Fontanepreis, 1920, for *Demian* (Hesse declined this award as it was intended for new writers); Gottfried-Keller Prize for literature (Zuerich), 1936; Nobel Prize for Literature, 1946; Goethe-Preis (Frankfurt), 1946; honorary doctorate, University of Bern,

1947; Wilhelm Raabe-Preis, 1950; Peace Prize of the German Book Trade, 1955; Knight of the order Pour le Merite (Friedensklasse), 1955.

WRITINGS—Poetry: *Romantische Lieder,* E. Pierson, 1899; (under pseudonym Hermann Lauscher) *Hinterlassene Schriften und Gedichte,* Reich, 1901, published under name Hermann Hesse as *Hermann Lauscher,* S. Fischer, 1933; *Gedichte,* G. Grote, 1902; *Unterwegs,* Mueller, 1911, supplement with title *Zeitgedichte,* 1915; *Aus Indien: Aufzeichnungen von einer indischen Reise,* S. Fischer, 1913; *Musik des Einsamen,* E. Salzer, 1915; *Gedichte des Malers,* Verlag Seldwyla, 1920; *Ausgewaehlte Gedichte,* S. Fischer, 1921; *Italien,* Euphorion-Verlag, 1923; *Verse im Krankenbett,* Staempfli, 1927; *Vom "grossen" und vom "kleinen" Dichtertum,* O. Harrassowitz, 1928; *Trost der Nacht: Neue Gedichte,* S. Fischer, 1929.

Jahreszeiten, Gebruder Fretz, 1931; *Blumengiessen,* 1933; *Besinnung,* Erasmusdruck, 1934; *Leben einer Blume,* Erasmusdruck, 1934; *Vom Baum des Lebens,* Insel Verlag, 1934; *Schmerzen,* Erasmusdruck, 1935; *Jahreslauf,* Orell Fuessli, 1936; *Ein Traum Josef Knechts,* privately printed by Erasmusdruck, 1936; *Das Haus der Traeume* (an incomplete poem), Vereinigung Oltner Buecherfreunde, 1936; *Stunden im Garten: Eine Idylle,* Bermann-Fischer, 1936; *Chinesisch,* S. Fischer, 1937; *Orgelspiel,* Erasmusdruck, 1937; *Der lahme Knabe: Eine Erinnerung aus der Kindheit,* Gebruder Fretz, 1937; *Neue Gedichte,* S. Fischer, 1937; *Foehnige Nacht,* S. Fischer, 1938; *Der letzte Glasperlenspieler,* S. Fischer, 1938; *Zehn Gedichte,* privately printed by Staempfli, 1939.

Die Gedichte (collected poems), Fretz & Wasmuth, 1942, 5th enlarged edition, 1956; *Fuenf Gedichte,* privately printed by Franz Schmitt, 1942; *Krankennacht,* 1942; *Stufen: Noch ein Gedicht Josef Knechts,* Bezirksschule fuer das graphische Gewerbe in Thueringen, 1943; *Der Bluetenzweig,* Fretz & Wasmuth, 1945; *Friede 1914 [und] Dem Frieden entgegen 1945: Zwei Friedensgedichte,* K. H. Silomon, 1945; *Spaete Gedichte,* privately printed by Tschudy, 1946; *In Sand geschreiben,* Neue Zuercher Zeitung, 1947; *Drei Gedichte,* Conzett & Huber, 1948.

Jugendgedichte, G. Grote, 1950; *Zwei Gedichte,* privately printed by Tschudy, 1951; *Rueckblick* (fragment), Conzett & Huber, 1951; *Zwei Idyllen: Stunden im Garten [und] Der lahme Knabe,* Suhrkamp, 1952; *Gedichte,* Suhrkamp, 1953; *Alter Maler in der Werkstatt* (for Hans M. Purrmann), 1954; *Klage und Trost,* 1954; *Zum Frieden,* Tschudy, 1956; *Wanderer im Spaetherbst,* [Montagnola], 1956, Staempfli, 1958; *Wenkenhof: Eine romantische Jugenddichtung,* National-Zeitung, 1957; *Das Lied von Abels Tod,* [Montagnola], 1957; *24 ausgewaehlte Gedichte,* edited by Hans R. Hilty, Tschudy, 1958; *Treue Begleiter,* Tschudy, 1958; *Gedichte,* Tschudy, 1958; *Besinnung [und] Stufen,* Tschudy, 1959; *Vier spaete Gedichte,* privately printed by Tschudy, 1959; *Freund Peter: Bericht an die Freunde,* privately printed by Gebrueder Fretz, 1959, published as *Bericht an die Freunde: Letzte Gedichte,* Vereinigung Oltner Buecherfreunde, 1960.

Stufen: Alte und neue Gedichte in Auswahl, Suhrkamp, 1961, 2nd edition, 1966; *Die spaeten Gedichte,* Insel Verlag, 1963; *Buchstaben,* Kumm, 1965; *Poems,* selected and translated by James Wright, Farrar, Straus, 1970; *Stufen: Ausgewaehlte Gedichte,* Suhrkamp, 1972; *Poems,* Bantam, 1974.

Novels: *Peter Camenzind,* S. Fischer, 1904, translation by Walter J. Strachan, P. Owen, 1961, translation by Michael Roloff, Farrar, Straus, 1969; *Unterm Rad,* S. Fischer, 1906,

translation by Strachan published as *The Prodigy,* Vision Press, 1957, translation by Michael Roloff published as *Beneath the Wheel,* Farrar, Straus, 1969; *Gertrud,* A. Langen, 1910, translation by Hilda Rosner published as *Gertrude,* Vision Press, 1955, revised translation, Farrar, Straus, 1969; *Rosshalde,* S. Fischer, 1914, translation by Ralph Manheim, Farrar, Straus, 1970; (under pseudonym Emil Sinclair) *Demian: Die Geschichte von Emil Sinclairs Jugend,* S. Fischer, 1919, translation by N. H. Friday published as *Demian,* Boni & Liveright, 1923, new edition with foreword by Thomas Mann published as *Demian: The Story of a Youth,* Holt, 1948, new translation by Michael Roloff and Michael Lebeck, with introduction by Thomas Mann, published as *Demian: The Story of Emil Sinclair's Youth,* Harper, 1965.

Siddhartha: Eine indische Dichtung, S. Fischer, 1922, translation by Hilda Rosner published as *Siddhartha,* New Directions, 1951; *Aufzeichnungen eines Herrn im Sanatorium* (fragment), Phaidon-Verlag, 1925, published as *Haus zum Frieden: Aufzeichnungen eines Herrn im Sanatorium,* Johannespresse, 1947; *Der Steppenwolf,* S. Fischer, 1927, translation by Basil Creighton published as *Steppenwolf,* Holt, 1929, revised edition, 1963; *Narziss und Goldmund,* S. Fischer, 1930, translation by Geoffrey Dunlop published as *Death and the Lover,* Dodd, 1932 (later published in England by P. Owen as *Goldmund,* 1959, and as *Narziss and Goldmund,* 1965), new translation by Ursule Molinaro published as *Narcissus and Goldmund,* Farrar, Straus, 1968; *Die Morgenlandfahrt: Eine Erzaehlung,* S. Fischer, 1932, translation by Hilda Rosner published as *The Journey to the East,* Vision Press, 1956, Noonday, 1957; *Das Glasperlenspiel: Versuch einer Lebensbeschreibung des Magister Ludi Josef Knecht samt Knechts hintelassenen Schriften,* two volumes, Fretz & Wasmuth, 1943, translation by Mervyn Savill published as *Magister Ludi,* Holt, 1949, 2nd edition, Aldus, 1957, new translation by Richard Winston and Clara Winston published as *The Glass Bead Game (Magister Ludi),* Holt, 1969, and as *Magister Ludi (The Glass Bead Game),* Bantam, 1970; *Berthold* (fragment), Fretz & Wasmuth, 1945.

Short fiction: *Eine Stunde hinter Mitternacht,* E. Diederichs, 1899; *Diesseits* (five tales), S. Fischer, 1907, new edition, 1930; *Nachbarn* (five tales), S. Fischer, 1908; *Umwege* (five tales), S. Fischer, 1912; *Der Hausierer,* Stuttgart, 1914; *Anton Schievelbeyns ohn-freiwillige Reisse nachher ost-Indien,* H. F. S. Bachmair, 1914; *Knulp: Drei Geschichten aus dem Leben Knulps* (published in part in 1908), S. Fischer, 1915, new edition with introduction, notes, and vocabulary by William Diamond and Christel B. Schomaker, Oxford University Press, 1932, translation by Ralph Manheim published as *Knulp: Three Tales from the Life of Knulp,* Farrar, Straus, 1971; *Am Weg* (eight tales), Reuss & Itta, 1915, published as *Am Weg: Erzaehlungen,* W. Classen, 1946, enlarged edition published as *Am Weg: Fruehe Erzaehlungen,* 1970; *Schoen ist die Jugend* (two tales), S. Fischer, 1916, new edition with introduction, notes, German questions, and vocabulary by Theodore Geissendoerfer, Prentice-Hall, 1932, original edition published as *Schoen ist die Jugend und der Zyklon: Zwei Erzaehlungen,* Suhrkamp, 1961; *Hans Dierlamms Lehrzeit* (a tale), Kuenstlerdank-Gesellschaft, 1916; *Alte Geschichten* (two tales), Buecherzentrale fuer deutsch Kriegsgefangene, 1918; *Zwei Maerchen* (two tales), Buecherei fuer deutsche Kriegsgefangene, 1918; *Maerchen,* S. Fischer, 1919, translation by Denver Lindley published as *Strange News from Another Star and Other Tales,* Farrar, Straus, 1972.

Im Presselschen Gartenhaus: Eine Erzaehlung dem alten Tuebingen (a tale), Lehmann, 1920; *Klingsors letzter Sommer* (three tales), S. Fischer, 1920, translation by Richard Winston and Clara Winston published as *Klingsor's Last Summer*, Farrar, Straus, 1970; *Die Offizina Bodoni* (miscellany), J. Hegner, 1923; *Psychologia balnearia oder Glossen eines Badener Kurgastes,* privately printed in Montagnola, 1924, published as *Kurgast: Aufzeichnungen von einer Badener Kur,* S. Fischer, 1925; *Die Verlobung* (tales), Verein fuer Verbreitung guter Schriften, 1924; *Piktors Verwandlungen* (a tale), Gesellschaft deutsche Buecherfreunde, 1925; *Die Nuernberger Reise* (a tale), S. Fischer, 1927; *Der Zyklon und andere Erzaehlungen* (tales), S. Fischer, 1929.

Weg nach Innen: Vier Erzaehlungen (four tales), S. Fischer, 1932; *Hermann Hesse* (selections), edited by Alfred Simon, E. Reinhardt, 1932; *Kleine Welt* (seven revised tales and poems from *Nachbarn, Umwege,* and *Aus Indien*), S. Fischer, 1933; *Fabulierbuch* (tales), S. Fischer, 1935; *Tragisch* (a tale), H. Reichner, 1936.

In der alten Sonne (a tale), P. Reclam, 1943; *Der Pfirsichbaum und andere Erzaehlungen* (tales), Buechergilde Gutenberg, 1945; *Traumfaehrte: Neue Erzaehlungen und Maerchen* (early tales, 1910-32), Fritz & Wasmuth, 1945; *Kurgast [und] Die Nuernberger Reise: Zwei Erzaehlungen* (two tales), Fretz & Wasmuth, 1946; *Heumond [und] Aus Kinderzeiten: Erzaehlungen,* Gute Schriften, 1947; *Weg nach Innen: Vier Erzaehlungen* (four tales; different selection than *Weg nach Innen* above), Suhrkamp, 1947; *Geheimnisse* (tales), Conzett & Huber, 1947, published as *Geheimnisse: Letzte Erzaehlungen,* Suhrkamp, 1955; *Kinderseele* (three tales), Duckworth, 1948; *Fruehe Prosa,* Fretz & Wasmuth, 1948; *Kinderseele und Ladidel* (two tales), edited, with introduction, notes, and vocabulary, by W. M. Dutton, Harrap, 1948, Heath, 1952; *Zwei Erzaehlungen: Der Novalis [und] Der Zwerg,* edited, with introduction, notes, and vocabulary, by Anna Jacobson and Anita Asher, Appleton, 1948, 2nd edition, 1950; *Der Bettler* (a tale), privately printed by Tschudy, 1949; *Glueck* (a tale), privately printed by Tschudy, 1949; *Hermann Hesse* (collection of early tales), two volumes, edited by Ernst Rheinwald and Otto Hartmann [Turbingen and Stuttgart], 1949.

Drei Erzaehlungen (three tales), edited by Waldo C. Peebles, American Book Co., 1950; *Weihnacht mit zwei Kindergeschichten,* Neue Zuercher Zeitung, 1951; *Bericht aus Normalien* (fragment) [Montagnola], 1951; *Die Verlobung und andere Erzaehlungen* (tales), Deutsche Buch-Gemeinschaft, 1951; *Spaete Prosa* (collected tales, 1944-50), Suhrkamp, 2nd edition, 1967, American text edition edited by Theodore Ziolkowski, Harcourt, 1966; *Glueck* (eleven tales), [Vienna], 1952; *Diesseits. Kleine Welt. Fabulierbuch,* Suhrkamp, 1954; *Diesseits: Erzaehlungen,* with a foreword by the author, Diogenes Verlag, 1954; *Der Wolf und andere Erzaehlungen* (tales), edited by Martha Ringier, Schweizer, 1955; *Floetentraum,* Arethusa Pers, 1955, 8th edition, 1969; *Zwei jugendliche Erzaehlungen* (two tales), Vereinigung Oltner Buecherfreunde, 1956; *Der Zwerg* [Bamberg], 1956; *Augustus, Der Dichter, [und] Ein Mensch mit Namen Ziegler,* edited by Thomas E. Colby, Norton, 1957, published as *Drei Erzaehlungen: Augustus, Der Dichter, [und] Ein Mensch mit Namen Ziegler,* Methuen, 1960; *Klein und Wagner* (a tale), Suhrkamp, 1958, 2nd edition published as *Klein und Wagner: Novelle,* 1973; *Der Lateinschueler,* Gute Schriften, 1958.

Tractat vom Steppenwolf, Suhrkamp, 1961; *Drei Erzaehlungen* (three tales), Suhrkamp, 1961; *Tessiner Erzaehlungen* (tales), with watercolors by the author, Fretz, 1962; *Weg nach Innen: Fuenf Erzaehlungen* (five tales), Deutscher Buecherbund, 1965; *Prosa aus dem Nachlass,* edited by Ninon Hesse, Suhrkamp, 1965; *Der vierte Lebenslauf Josef Knechts,* edited by Ninon Hesse, Suhrkamp, 1966; *Aus Kinderzeiten und andere Erzaehlungen,* Verlag der Arche, 1968; *Der Dichter,* Arethusa Pers, 1969; *Stories of Five Decades,* edited, with introduction, by Theodore Ziolkowski, translated by Ralph Manheim and Denver Linley, Farrar, Straus, 1972; *Weg nach Innen: Hermann Hesse* (five tales; different selection than *Weg nach Innen* with five tales above), Suhrkamp, 1973; *Iris: Ausgewaehlt Maerchen* (selected tales), Suhrkamp, 1973; *Tales of Student Life,* edited, with introduction, by Theodore Ziolkowski, translated by Ralph Manheim, Farrar, Straus, 1975.

Nonfiction: *Boccaccio* (monograph), Schuster & Loeffler, 1904; *Franz von Assisi* (monograph), Schuster & Loeffler, 1904; *Faust und Zarathustra,* Bremer Verlag, 1909.

Zum Sieg, [Stuttgart], 1915; *Kriegslektuere,* Thomas, 1915; *Lektuere fuer Kriegsgefangene,* Staempfli, 1916; (with sister, Adele Hesse) *Zum Gedaechtnis unseres Vatres* (biography of their father, Johannes Hesse), Polygraphisches Institut, 1916, Wunderlich, 1930; (under pseudonym Emil Sinclair) *Eigensinn,* 1918; (published anonymously) *Zarathustras Wiederkehr: Ein Wort an die deutsche Jugend,* Staempfli, 1919.

(With Richard Woltereck) *Kindergenesungsheim Milwaukee: Ein Aufruf an die gebuertigen Deutschen im Auslande,* Seemann, 1920; *Wanderung, Aufzeichnungen: Mit farbigen Bildern vom Verfasser,* S. Fischer, 1920, translation by James Wright published as *Wandering: Notes and Sketches,* Farrar, Straus, 1972; *Blick ins Chaos* (three essays), Verlag Seldwyla, 1920, translation by Stephen Hudson published as *In Sight of Chaos,* Verlag Seldwyla, 1923; *Erinnerung an Lektuere,* Braumueller, 1925; *Betrachtungen,* S. Fischer, 1928; *Eine Bibliothek der Weltliteratur,* Reclam-Verlag, 1929, Ungar, 1945, supplemented edition includes *Magie des Buches,* W. Classen, 1946.

Magie des Buches, Poeschel & Trepte, 1930; *Beim Einzug ins neue Haus,* privately printed in Montagnola, 1931; *Gedenkblaetter,* S. Fischer, 1937, 3rd edition, Suhrkamp, 1950.

Der Novalis: Aus dem Papieren eines Altmodischen, Vereinigung Oltner Buecherfreunde, 1940; *Kleine Betrachtungen* (six essays), Staempfli, 1941; *Das seltene Buch,* K. H. Silomon, 1942; *Gedenkblatt fuer Franz Schall,* Fretz & Wasmuth, 1943; *Nachruf auf Christoph Schrempf,* Fretz & Wasmuth, 1944; *Zwischen Sommer und Herbst,* privately printed in Zurich, 1944; *Erinnerung an Klingsors Sommer,* Fretz & Wasmuth, 1944; *Zwei Aufsaetze* (two essays), privately printed by Gebrueder Fretz, 1945; *Maler und Schriftsteller,* Museum Solothurn, 1945; *Danksagung und moralisierende Betrachtung,* [Montagnola], 1946; *Statt eines Briefes,* [Montagnola], 1946; *Dank an Goethe* (four essays), W. Classen, 1946; *Der Europaeer* (five essays), Suhrkamp, 1946; *Feuerwerk* (essay), privately printed by Vereinigung Oltner Buecherfreunde, 1946; *Krieg und Frieden: Betrachtungen zu Krieg und Politik seit dem Jahre 1914* (twenty-nine essays), Fretz & Wasmuth, 1946, supplemented edition, [Berlin], 1949, translation by Ralph Manheim published as *If the War Goes On: Reflections on War and Politics,* Farrar, Straus, 1971; *Mein Glaube,* Conzett & Huber, 1946; *Ansprache in der ersten Stunde des Jahres 1946,* Neue Zuercher Zeitung, 1946; *Eine Konzertpause,* Neue Zuercher Zeitung, 1947; *Stufen der Menschwerdung* (first published in *Neue Rundschau,* number 43, 1932), Vereinigung Oltner Buecherfreunde, 1947; *Antwort auf Bitt-*

briefe, privately printed in Montagnola, 1947; *Die kulturellen Werte des Theaters*, 1947; *Berg und See*, Buechergilde Gutenberg, 1948; *Ueber Romain Rolland*, 1948; *Traumtheater*, National-Zeitung, 1948; *Begegnungen mit Vergagenem*, [Montagnola], 1949; *Gedenkblatt fuer Martin*, Neue Zuercher Zeitung, 1949; *Gedenkblatt fuer Adele*, privately printed by Gebrueder Fretz, 1949; *Stunden am Schreibtisch*, National-Zeitung, 1949; *Wege zu Hermann Hesse* (essay; excerpt from *Gedichten und Prosa*), edited by Walter Haussmann, Metzler, 1949.

Erinnerung an Andre Gide, Tschudy, 1951; *Ueber "Peter Camenzind*," Neue Zuercher Zeitung, 1951; *Gedanken ueber Gottfried Keller*, National-Zeitung, 1951; *Die Dohle*, Neue Zuercher Zeitung, 1951; *Grossvaeterliches*, privately printed by Tschudy, 1952; *Herbstliche Erlebnisse: Gedenkblatt fuer Otto Hartmann*, Tschudy, 1952; *Lektuere fuer Minuten: Ein paar Gedanken aus meinen Buechern und Briefen*, privately printed by Staempfli, 1952; *Nachruf fuer Marulla*, Gebrueder Fretz, 1953; *Kaminfegerchen*, privately printed by Tschudy, 1953; *Ueber das Alter*, Vereinigung Oltner Buecherfreunde, 1954; *Notizblaetter um Ostern*, Neue Zuercher Zeitung, 1954; *Abendwolken* [und] *Bei den Massageten* (two essays), Tschudy, 1956; *Hilfsmaterial fuer den Literaturunterricht*, Volk und Wissen Volksigener, 1956; *Der Trauermarsch: Gedenkblatt fuer einen Jugendfreund*, Tschudy, 1957; *Tessin*, Verlag der Arche, 1957; (with Gunter Boehmer) *Festliches Tessin*, [Frankfurt-am-Main], 1957; *In Italien vor fuenfzig Jahren*, National-Zeitung, 1958.

Eine Bodensee-Erinnirung, [Basel], 1961; *Aerzte: Ein paar Erinnerungen*, Vereinigung Oltner Buecherfreunde, 1963; *Ein Blatt von meinem Baum*, Hyperion-Verlag, 1964; *Neue deutsche Buecher: Literaturberichte fuer Bonniers Letteraera Magasin, 1935-36*, edited by Bernard Zeller, Schiller-Nationalmuseum, 1965.

Politische Betrachtungen, compiled by Siegfried Unseld, Suhrkamp, 1970; *Mein Glaube: Eine Dokumentation*, compiled, with afterword, by Siegfried Unseld, Suhrkamp, 1971; *Autobiographical Writings*, edited, with introduction, by Theodore Ziolkowski, translated by Denver Lindley, Farrar, Straus, 1972; *Eigensinn: Autobiographische Schriften*, compiled, with afterword, by Siegfried Unseld, Suhrkamp, 1972; *Schriften zur Literatur*, two volumes, Suhrkamp, 1972; *Die Kunst des Mussiggangs: Kurze Prosa aus dem Nachlass*, edited, with afterword, by Volker Michels, Suhrkamp, 1973; *My Belief: Essays on Life and Art*, edited, with introduction, by Ziolkowski, translated by Lindley and Manheim, Farrar, Straus, 1974.

Letters: *Der Junge Dichter: Ein Brief an Viele*, A. Langen, 1910, reprinted as *An einen jungen Dichter*, Callwey, 1932.

Zwei Briefe (correspondence with Thomas Mann), Tschudy, 1945; *Ein Brief nach Deutschland*, National-Zeitung, 1946; *Brief an Adele*, Neue Zuercher Zeitung, 1946; *Der Autor an einen Korrektor*, Kantonales Amt fuer berufliche Ausbildung, 1947; *Zwei Briefe ueber das Glasperlenspiel*, National-Zeitung, 1947; *An einen jungen Kollegen in Japan*, privately printed by Gebrueder Fretz, 1947; *Versuch einer Rechtfertigung* (correspondence with Max Brod), Conzett & Huber, 1948; *Blaetter vom Tage*, privately printed by Gebrueder Fretz, 1948; *Preziositaet* (letter to Eduard Korrodi), Neue Zuercher Zeitung, 1948; *Auszuege aus zwei Briefen*, Conzett & Huber, 1949; *An einen jungen Kuenstler*, privately printed at Montagnola, 1949.

Zwei Briefe: An einen jungen Kuenstler [und] *Das junge Genie*, Tschudy, 1950, published as *Das junge Genie: Brief an einen Achtzehnjaehrigen*, 1950, also published as *Das junge Genie: Antwort an einen Achtzehnjaehrigen*, Neue Zuercher Zeitung, 1950; *An einen "einfachen Mann aus dem arbeitenden Volk*," National-Zeitung, 1950; *Ein Brief zu Thomas Manns 75. Geburtstag*, S. Fischer, 1950; *Kriegsangst: Antwort auf Briefe aus Deutschland*, National-Zeitung, 1950; *An die Herausgeber der "Dichterbuehne*," E. Blaschker Verlag, 1950; *Brief an einen schwaebischen Dichter* (letter to Otto Heuschele), Vereinigung Oltner Buecherfreunde, 1951; *Glueckwunsch fuer Peter Suhrkamp*, 1951; *Briefe* (collection), Suhrkamp, 1951, 2nd enlarged edition, 1964; *Eine Handvoll Briefe* (collection), Buechergilde Gutenberg, 1951; *Ahornschatten*, Neue Zuercher Zeitung, 1952; *Letzter Gruss an Otto Hartmann*, 1952; *Allerlei Post: Rundbrief an Freunde*, Neue Zuercher Zeitung, 1952; *Geburtstag Ein Rundbrief*, 1952; *Engadiner Erlebnisse: Ein Rundbrief*, Conzett & Huber, 1953; [*Correspondence with Romain Rolland*], Fretz & Wasmuth, 1954; *Beschwoerungen; Rundbrief im Februar 1954*, Tschudy, 1954; *Rundbrief aus Sils-Maria*, Neue Zuercher Zeitung, 1954; *Ueber Gewaltpolitik, Krieg und das Boese in der Welt*, National-Zeitung, 1955; *Ein paar Leserbrief an Hermann Hesse*, privately printed in Montagnola, 1955; *Antworten*, privately printed by Tschudy, 1958; *Ein paar indische Miniaturen*, National-Zeitung, 1959.

An einen Musiker, Vereinigung Oltner Buecherfreunde, 1960; *Kindheit und Jugend vor Neunzehnhundert: Hermann Hesse in Briefen und Lebenszeugnissen, 1877-95*, compiled and edited by Ninon Hesse, Suhrkamp, 1966; *Briefwechsel: Hermann Hesse-Thomas Mann*, edited by Anni Carlsson, Suhrkamp, 1968; *Briefwechsel, 1945-59: [Von] Hermann Hesse* [und] *Peter Suhrkamp*, edited by Siegfried Unseld, Suhrkamp, 1969.

Hermann Hesse, Helene Voigt-Diederichs: Zwei Autorenportraets in Briefen, 1897 bis 1900, Diederichs, 1971, also published as *Zwei Autorenportraets in Briefen, 1897 bis 1900: Hermann Hesse* [und] *Helen Voigt-Diederichs*, 1971; *Briefwechsel aus der Naehe* [bei] *Hermann Hesse* [und] *Karl Kerenyi*, edited, with commentary, by Magda Kerenyi, Langen-Mueller, 1972; *D'une rive a l'autre: Hermann Hesse et Romain Rolland*, Albin Michel, 1972.

Other published work: *Selma Lagerlof* (excerpt from *Hinterlassene Schriften und Gedichte*), A. Langen, 1908; *Kleiner Garten: Erlebnisse und Dichtungen* (miscellany), E. P. Tal, 1919; *Heimkehr* (first act of a play), 1920; *Elf Aquarelle aus dem Tessin*, O. C. Recht, 1921; (under pseudonym Emil Sinclair) *Sinclairs Notizbuch: Mit einer mehr farbigen Tafel nach einem Aquarelle des Verfassers*, Rasher, 1923; *Bilderbuch*, S. Fischer, 1926; *Krisis: Ein Stueck Tagebuch*, S. Fischer, 1928; *Kurzgefasster Lebenslauf*, edited by Erwin Ackerknecht, Herrcke & Lebeling, 1929.

Kastanienbaeume, Kunstgewerbeschule, 1932; *Mahnung: Erzaehlungen und Gedichte*, privately printed by Werkstatt der Gothaer gewerbliche Berufsschule (Gotha), 1933; *Hieroglyphen*, Erasmusdruck, 1936; *Drei Bilder aus einem alten Tessiner Park*, Oprecht, 1938; *Prosa: Auf einen Dichter*, Fretz & Wasmuth, 1942; *Bildschmuck im Eisenbahnwafen*, Weltwoche-Verlag, 1944; *Rigi-Tagebuch, 1945*, Staempfli, 1945; *Indischer Lebenslauf* (excerpts from *Das Glasperlenspiel*), Gute Schriften, 1946; *Spaziergang in Wuerzburg*, privately printed by Tschudy, 1947; *Fuer Max Wassmer, zum 60. Geburtstag*, Der Bund, 1947; *Beschreibung einer Landschaft: Ein Stueck Tagebuch*, privately printed by Staempfli, 1947; *Legende vom indischen Koenig*, Berner Handpresse E. Jenzer, 1948; *Der Stimmen und der Heilige* (first published as "Ein Stueck Tagebuch" in *Betrachtung-*

en), privately printed by Johannespresse, 1948; *Fragment aus der Jugendzeit*, Neue Zuercher Zeitung, 1948; *Notizen aus diesen Sommertagen*, National-Zeitung, 1948; *Musikalische Notizen*, Conzett & Huber, 1948; *Gerbersau* (collected early writings), two volumes, R. Wunderlich, 1949; *Alle Buecher dieser Welt: Ein Almanach fuer Buecherfreunde*, edited by K. H. Silomon, Verlag die Wage, 1949; *Aus vielen Jahren* (poetry, stories, pictures, and other items), Staempfli, 1949.

Das Lied des Lebens, Neue Zuercher Zeitung, 1950; *Eine Arbeitsnacht*, Neue Zuercher Zeitung, 1950; *Aus dem "Tagebuch eines Entgleisten,"* National-Zeitung, 1950; *Aus einem Notizbuch*, Tschudy, 1951; *Noergeleien*, National-Zeitung, 1951; *Eine Sonate*, National-Zeitung, 1951; *Das Werk von Hermann Hesse: Ein Brevier* (selections of fiction with excerpts from letters), edited by Siegfried Unseld, Suhrkamp, 1952; *Aprilbrief*, Neue Zuercher Zeitung, 1952; *Dank fuer die Briefe und Glueckwuensche zum 2 Juli 1952*, privately printed in Montagnola, 1952; *Kauf einer Schreibmaschine*, National-Zeitung, 1952; *Regen im Herbst (Gruss und Glueckwunsch)*, privately printed in Montagnola, 1953; *Der Schlossergeselle*, National-Zeitung, 1953; *Doktor Knoelges Ende*, National-Zeitung, 1954; *Die Nikobaren*, National-Zeitung, 1954; *Knopf-Annaehen*, National-Zeitung, 1955; *Tagebuchblatt: Ein Maulbronner Seminarist*, Tschudy, 1955; *Aquarelle aus dem Tessin*, W. Klein, 1955; *Beschwoerungen: Spaete Prosa, neue Folge*, Suhrkamp, 1955; *Magie des Buches: Betrachtungen und Gedichte*, Hoehere Fachschule fuer das Graphische Gewerbe, 1956; *Gedichte und Prosa*, Schroedel, 1956; *Cesco und der Berg*, National-Zeitung, 1956; *Weihnachtsgaben und anderes*, privately printed in Montagnola, 1956; *Wiederbegegnung mit zwei Jugendgedichten*, Westermann, 1956; *Welkes Blatt*, Schiller-National-Museum, 1957; *Gute Stunde*, Laetare-Verlag, 1957; *Malfreunde, Malsorgen*, Neue Zuercher Zeitung, 1957; *Betrachten und Briefe*, Suhrkamp, 1957; *Hermann Hesse: Ein Auswahl*, edited by Reinhard Buchward, Velhagen & Klasing, 1957; *Knulp, Peter Camenzind, [und] Briefe*, edited, with notes by A. Rossen, Kastalia, 1958; *Chinesische Legende*, privately printed by Tschudy, 1959; *Sommerbrief aus dem Engadin*, privately printed by Tschudy, 1959.

Rueckgriff, privately printed by Tschudy, 1960; *Ein Paar Aufzeichnungen und Briefe*, privately printed by Tschudy, 1960; *Aus einem Tagebuch des Jahres 1920*, Verlag der Arche, 1960; *Das Wort*, Conzett & Huber, 1960; *Schreiben und Schriften*, privately printed by Tschudy, 1961; *Zen*, privately printed by Tschudy, 1961; *Dichter und Weltburger* (selections), edited by Gisela Stein, Holt, 1961; *Der Beichvater* (selection from *Das Glasperlenspiel*), Furche-Verlag, 1962; *Prosa und Gedichte*, compiled, with interpretation, by Franz Baumer, Koesel-Verlag, 1963; *Erwin*, William Matheson, 1965; *Hermann Hesse: Eine Auswahl fuer Auslaender* (selections in German for foreigners), compiled, with supplement, by Gerhard Kirchhoff, Hueber, 1966.

Lectuere fuer Minuten: Gedanken aus seinen Buechern und Briefen, compiled by Volker Michels, Suhrkamp, 1971; *Beschreibung einer Landschaft*, Neske, 1971; *Glueck, Spaete Prosa, und Betrachtungen: Hermann Hesse*, Suhrkamp, 1973; *Hermann Hesse und der ferner Osten*, Buechergilde Gutenberg, 1973; *Reflections: Selections from his Books and Letters*, compiled by Volker Michels, translated by Ralph Manheim, Farrar, Straus, 1974.

Collected works: *Gesammelte Dictungen*, six volumes, Suhrkamp, 1952; *Gesammelte Schriften*, seven volumes, Suhrkamp, 1957; *Gesammelte Werke*, twelve volumes, Suhrkamp, 1970, 3rd edition, 1973; *Die Erzaehlungen: Hermann Hesse*, compiled by Volker Michels, Suhrkamp, 1973; *Gesammelte Briefe*, edited by Volker Michels and Ursula Michels, with Heiner Hesse, Suhrkamp, 1973.

Editor: (With Martin Lang and Emil Strauss) *Der Lindenbaum* (German folksongs), S. Fischer, 1910; August J. Liebeskind, *Morgenlaendische Erzaehlungen*, Insel Verlag, 1913, 2nd edition, 1957; Josef von Eichendorff, *Gedichte und Novellen*, Deutsche Bibliothek, 1913, new edition, 1945; Jean Paul, *Titan*, Insel Verlag, 1913; Ludwig Achim von Arnim and Clemens Brentano, compilers, *Des Knaben Wunderhorn* (old German songs), Deutsche Bibliothek, 1913; *Das Meisterbuch*, Deutsche Bibliothek, 1913, new edition, 1918; Christian Wagner, *Gedichte*, Georg Mueller, 1913; *Der Zauberbrunnen* (German romantic songs), Kiepenheuer, 1913; *Lieder deutscher Dichter*, A. Langen, 1914; Matthias Claudius, *Der Wandsbecker Bote*, Insel Verlag, 1915; *Gesta Romanorum*, Insel Verlag, 1915; *Alemannenbuch*, Verlag Seldwyla, 1919, new edition, 1920; (with Walter Stich) *Ein Schwabenbuch fuer die deutschen Kriegsgefangenen*, Verlag der Buecherzentrale fuer deutsche Kriegsgefangene, 1919.

Xaver Schnyder von Wartensee, *Ein Luzerner Junker vor hundert Jahren* (excerpt from memoirs), Verlag Seldwyla, 1920; Salomon Gessner, *Dichtungen*, Haessel, 1922; *Geschichten aus dem Mittelalter*, K. Hoenn, 1925; *Maerchen und Legenden aus der Gesta Romanorum*, Insel Verlag, 1926; Goethe, *30 Gedichte*, Lesezirkel Hottingen, 1932.

Series editor: (with Richard Woltereck) "Buecherei fuer deutsche Kriegsgefangene," twenty titles, Verlag der Buecherzentrale fuer deutsche Kriegsgefangene, 1918-19; "Merkwuerdige Geschichten," six titles, Verlag Seldwyla, 1922-24; "Merkwuerdige Geschichten und Menschen," seven titles, S. Fischer, 1925-27.

Work represented in many anthologies, including *Versuchung*, Kamp, 1963; *Bodenseebuch*, edited by Guntram Brummer, Buecherfabrik Bodan, 1965; Kurt Ziegler, *Calw*, privately printed, 1965.

Selected sections of Hesse's fiction have been recorded, including "Hermann Hesse: Sprechplatte," Suhrkamp, 1971; "Hermann Hesse: Traktat vom Steppenwolf und andere Texte," Deutschen Grammophon Gesellschaft, 1973.

Hesse's work also has been scored or adapted for musical compositions for the following recordings: Franz Dietsch, "Wege und Ziel," Wildt, 1956; Anton Huller, "Stufen," Doblinger, 1962; Karl Heinz Taubert, "Von Baum des Lebens," Semrock, 1962; Paul Mueller-Zuerich, "Bergnacht," Hug, 1963; Mueller-Zuerich, "Reiselied," Hug, 1963; Hans Kracke, "Sonne leuchte nur ins Herz hinein," Boehm, 1963; Rudolf Mauersberger, "Drei weltliche Choere a cappella," Breitkopf & Huertel, 1963; Wolfgang Steffen, "Zyklus: Opus 19," Bate & Bock, 1963; Anton Wuerz, "Sprache des Fruehlings," Leuckart, 1963.

SIDELIGHTS: When Hesse was twelve years old, he read Hoelderlin's poem "Die Nacht" and decided that he must become a poet. Eva J. Engel wrote: "Quite clearly such an experience is something like a miracle which can be encountered only once in a lifetime. The individual thus summoned, alone and wondering, doubting his own fitness, is suddenly aware that he is completely set apart from all those around him by a heightened capacity, the capacity of 'individuation.' As part of this painful and yet wonderful process of 'coming into being' he will experience shocks which reveal things that were hidden to him and stood in the way of his inner progress."

As a young poet, Hesse attempted to escape from modern civilization. He was "overcome by an intensity of suffering," noted Miss Engel, and he refused to face the antitheses engendered by civilization. He felt himself incapable of either choosing or rejecting the "essential loneliness of the artist" (Engel). Thus, Hesse sought the serenity of nature, and his earliest work fell within the tradition of German Romanticism. He began by observing, feeling, and recording. The observation of nature brought insight into the beauty and mystery of nature and Hesse progressed to a recognition of self as external to the natural world of his observations. Hesse's early poetry, documenting his first interpretations of this duality of self and world, became the Goethean poetry of confession. He had begun to impose the discipline of ratiocination upon the spontaneity of observation. Miss Engel wrote: "... the content of Hesse's work began to show more and more clearly that it was groping towards 'Erkenntnis' [In a footnote Engel added: "For Hesse this word would seem to stand for 'gaining insight into existence and its meaning'"]. This search begins with innumerable attempts to seek and describe the individual self, the real self, the essential self."

Hesse's search for self-definition eventually led to a more cogent definition of his opponent—the external world. Ralph Freedman stated: "This alien reality or 'world' is variously identified with anything seemingly external to the self, including objects of perception, non-intuitive reasoning, social pressures, or mercantilism; in short, it is a very wide concept and includes the very world of perception as well as contemporary reality." Once conscious of the adversary, Hesse began his lifelong pursuit of the ultimate acceptance or resolution of the conflict. (His quest, however, was not wholly selfish. Miss Engel commented that Hesse wrote: "I am a poet, I seek and profess. It is my task to serve sincerity and truth.... I have a mission: those who also search I must help to understand and to endure life.") But he was yet unable to comprehend the nature of his goal. He became critical of his Romantic sentiments, of Christianity, and of Western thought, and he began the study of Eastern religions and philosophies in an effort to learn the technique of impersonal analysis through which the wisdom and depth of Chinese poetry is manifested. Ernst Rose said: "The Romantic quatrains were replaced by free verse and a more involved syntax. But Hesse still could not overcome his self.... There emerged a new clarity and simplicity, no longer naive, and almost brittle in its observation of distance. These mature poems still let the poetic self shine through, but the objective image now claimed the center of attention. Their quality is that of a wise serenity.... In such poems the real world has become ephemeral, a shell and a dress for the infinite. Hesse now seeks to be nothing more than a mirror, in which passing visions and images momentarily appear." Rose commented that Hesse himself said: "I had advanced far enough on the Eastern path of Lao-tse and of the *I Ching,* so I knew exactly how accidental and changeable was this so-called reality."

The influence of his study of Oriental philosophy was reflected in *Siddhartha.* "For Western readers," explained Rose, "*Siddhartha* climaxed centuries of effort to penetrate Eastern thought and religion and to understand that God had revealed himself to mankind in different ways." But as Hesse had become discontented with the formal religions of the West, so he concluded that Oriental dogma did not define the ultimate relationship between self and world in a fully acceptable manner. The "East" which he sought became a metaphor for the transcendental self. He was, never-

theless, assured of the existence of an omnipresent *divinity* (not a *deity* in the sense of a certain being) which, according to Rose, "could never be expressed in concrete anthropomorphic images, but was always accessible to mystic intuition." Hesse's study of the various formalized systems thus became part of a process of individuation; he realized that the goal of his personal quest could only be derived from his own interpretations of self and externality. Miss Engel noted: "Though he would never join Nietzsche in his clamouring for a 'revaluing of all values,' Hesse does accept, with distress, that 'God is dead'; he accepts the consequences that the individual must rethink metaphysical concepts by himself, that is without the support of recognized religions." Ralph Freedman stated: "As it confronts the world, the self seeks to absorb its opponent." And it was the necessity for selectivity in this absorption that forced Hesse to assume various stances in his confrontation with the world. His technique, then, must be the postulation, by an act of will, of creative illusion in which self and world are imposed upon one another. Freedman believes that, if Hesse's goal is to be the projection of the conflict between self and world into an ego that can unify them, he must employ either "mystical revelation" or "the illusion induced by art." Freedman remarked: "For Hesse, these two realms are interdependent—the mystic's vision encompassing more fully any unity achieved by art, the poet's apprehension sustaining in time the harmonies briefly envisioned in the mystic's trance.... The moment of reconciliation must be frozen in time. To elicit 'magic' from the materials of crude experience, Hesse must represent unity within the flow of time. The artist must capture the mystic's vision through his medium of words." (Rose told us that "in his most inspired moments, Hesse did not want to be called a poet or an artist, but a magician.") "Throughout Hesse's novels, stories, and fairy tales," Freedman continued, "idyllic moments and scenes occur as essential structural elements through which the hero's quest is accentuated and ultimately defined.... Hesse's protagonists, and occasionally the author himself, depict their experiences so as to unify past, present, and future in a single moment of apprehension."

It was through the medium of his fiction, then, that Hesse presented himself in opposition to the world. But his work is not autobiographical in the usual sense. Rather, he used "aesthetic self-portraits achieved through representative heroes" (Freedman). Freedman explained Hesse's employment of this device thus: "The perennial split between the individual and the world beyond him is portrayed, not in dramatic action, but in symbolic or allegorical self-representation. Echoing Novalis' idea of the artist as a supreme mimic dissolving alien existence in himself, Hesse renders his conflicts as symbolic 'self-portraits'.... These psychological self-portraits include particularly Hesse's versions of the 'eternal self' regulating the 'I' of poet and hero. Besides functioning as a Freudian superego, or, more pertinently, as a Jungian collective unconscious, this higher aspect of self acts as a *daemon* who guards its activities and comments upon them ironically.... Hermann Hesse's lyrical novels reconcile an inner vision with a universe of consecutive events. His success in creating an adequate form in the spirit of Novalis is his most important distinction as a modern writer and transcends many of his difficulties and imperfections. Combining allegorical narrative with psychological and philosophical self-portraits, he achieved a vision of man and ideas with an immediacy usually unobtainable in conventional narrative."

Thus Hesse's fiction uses the terms and processes of the real world to approach an ego operative in the realm of illusion. *Steppenwolf* was an important product of Hesse's thinking at this time. Rose commented: "It was the first German novel to include a descent into the cellars of the subconscious in its search for spiritual integration. With Freud it recognized the *libido,* and with Jung it discovered in the subconscious a reservoir of spiritual archetypes and formative ideas." But Hesse realized that his achievement in *Steppenwolf* was merely another step toward his goal. Miss Engel observed that twenty years later he wrote in *Das Glasperlenspiel:* ". . . To transcend, rather like to awake, too, was a truly magic term for me. It was demanding, encouraging; it consoled and promised. My life, so I decided, was to consist of transcendence. It was to move with measured tread from step to step. I was to pass through and leave behind one zone after another in the way in which a piece of music deals with theme after theme and different tempi by playing them, completing them, dismissing them, never wearying or falling asleep, on the contrary, fully awake and alert." Rose concluded: "With *Steppenwolf,* Hesse reached the end of his 'confessional' period. The poet realized that an exclusive concern with his own soul would never lead to the desired integration of man and society. Unity could be reached only by his immersion in the full stream of life, and in his last novels he chose to depict life as a whole."

At one time Hesse considered, although not seriously, becoming a musician and abandoning his writing. Music, for Hesse, functioned as the integration of the conflicting elements in self and world, producing either dissonance, which the artist must hopelessly attempt to resolve, or harmony in the achievement of art. Freedman believed that Hesse expressed his desire to be a musician in *Der Kurgast:* "If I were a musician I could write without difficulty a melody in two voices, a melody which consists of two notes and sequences which correspond to each other, which in any event stand to one another in the closest and liveliest reciprocity and mutual relationship. And anyone who could read music, could read my double melody, could see and hear in each tone its counterpoint, the brother, the enemy, the antipode. Well, and just this double-voiced melody and externally moving antithesis, this double line I want to express with my own material, with words, and I work myself sore at it, and it doesn't work." Freedman further explained that "as a writer, Hesse longs to be a musician, not because he might feel more at home in a non-literary metier, but because music embodies the very concept of harmony within dissonance which is his prevailing theme. The clash of opposites and their reconciliation is not only heard and made visually apparent to the reader of musical notations; it is also dramatized. . . . In its function of presenting simultaneously the harmony and dissonance of opposing motifs, music seems to solve the conflicts in self and world."

In 1931, Hesse began *Das Glasperlenspiel* ("The Bead Game"), a novel on which he worked for eleven years. "As early as 1935," related Rose, "Hesse called [this work] the final goal of his life and poetic activity." The novel postulates the achievement of a transcendental harmony of self and divinity wherein human existence finds its ultimate meaning. Miss Engel said of the novel: "By the Utopian nature of this ideal alliance Hesse refers us to accomplishment, to endeavor in a foreseeable future. He would not have turned to the future if he had considered the present congenial to such ideas. He could not reject the present without looking at it closely. Hence, his search is no longer concerned with the 'self in the past' but with the self in the present-day world. We are first of all concerned with the ego

and the intellectual stimulus it received." Rose explained the premise and function of the novel for Hesse: ". . . Since man is forever removed from [divinity], he can attain the ultimate only in symbolic form. This form is embodied in the bead game, a game played with glass beads strung on wires, with each bead representing a special theme or idea. . . . Things are set in proper perspective and are recognized in their transcendental relationship. They become translucent glass beads which anticipate the cosmic unity meant by the deity. The dreams of the subconscious are correlated to the abstractions of the intellect; the revelations of art to the systems of philosophy; romantic and Platonic visions to Chinese and Indian speculations; Nicholas of Cusa to Leibnitz and Hegel. The idea is to pursue the disparate elements of modern culture, and of every culture, to a common divine fountainhead. The bead game is no mere sport for jaded intellectuals. . . . For in Hesse's view, the elements of culture are by no means unimportant. They are not the inconsequential veil of Maya, but retain their weight and individuality. . . . This time Hesse wants to live life in earnest and find an applicable and practical solution for the problem of human existence." Miss Engel summarized: ". . . It is Hesse's extraordinary achievement, and good fortune, to have been able to jettison belief in dualism and to attempt to see life in terms of integration of phenomenon and idea. From a belief in opposites . . ., he advanced to the acceptance of polarity. . . ." "Hesse's view of man," wrote Rose, "can best be described as a poetic image of the total personality adumbrated by anthropological psychology. Here the individual stands in the spheres of nature and society just as much as he is indissolubly linked with history and with the forces of transcendency."

Music also functions as a symbol integral to the progress of the novel. Freedman stated: "It resolves dissonance by organizing experience and directing it toward a total vision rather than toward its consecutive or analytic explication. In this way, music can be seen . . . as the quintessence of imagination. It is 'the infinite within the finite, the element of genius present in all forms of art.' Its language, composed of magic formulae, is apt to frighten away philistines as new, indefinable worlds are opened up. An example of this use of music is Hesse's famous distinction in *Der Steppenwolf* between *rauschende* and *heitere Musik.* The former is chaotic music, likened to that of Wagner. A deceptive vision of unity is achieved by massive sound which blurs boundaries between contradictory elements and themes. Its chaos, apparently triumphant, merely reflects diversity in an indistinguishable mass. The latter is clear, detached music likened to that of Mozart. Its ordered harmonies show the interplay of contrasting motifs with precision; its detachment prevents the blurring of boundaries between self and world and so reflects an independent unity. . . . Music deepens the melody of life and catches it in art. . . ."

In whatever manner Hesse presented his philosophical convictions, however, "he never wrote in the abstract terms of rational philosophy. His was the more suggestive language of art. . . ." (Rose). Miss Engel wrote: "[His was] a predilection for specific, generally onomatopoeic words, and above all, for the rhythmic pattern of his prose. The prose is as flexible as the theme, and yet has a recognizable musicality of its own (only the *Glasperlenspiel* must be excepted). The sentence structure is beautifully clear, characterized by a throng of adjectives and a complex differentiation of content and emphasis by paraphrase. Antithetical structure has as much symbolic significance as the tripartite, graduated statement." The result of such writing observed Rose, is the "achievement of transparency. The clarity of the vision gains depth and becomes mysterious." Rose believed, however, that Hesse's simplicity is often misunderstood. "The clarity of Hesse's language," he asserted, "was meant as a defense against chaos. . . . A transparent world is no accidental array of realistic details to which one has to adapt by compromise. It demands commitment."

Robin White, in the early 1960's, wrote: "Although Hermann Hesse received the Nobel Prize for literature in 1946, his work, with the possible exception of *Steppenwolf*, has remained relatively unknown in the United States." Freedman explored this lack of interest among non-German-speaking readers: "The reasons are not too far to seek; they lie in his choice of the lyrical genre. In the English-speaking world, for example, this form appears alien to the novel, vaguely experimental, without the substance of character and plot required even of poetic novelists like Hardy or D. H. Lawrence. Nor does Hesse seem to be a 'symbolic' writer like Faulkner or Joyce."

In the following decade, however, Hesse's work sold well over six million copies in English translation. The *London Times Literary Supplement* explained his rise from unknown lyrical experimentalist to literary cult hero: "The Hesse we read today is in fact no longer the bittersweet elegist of Wilhelmine Germany, the anguished intellectual entre deux guerres, the serene hermit of Montagnola apres Nobel. The cult has adjusted the kaleidoscope of Hesse's works in such a way as to bring into focus a Hesse for the 1970's: environmentalist, war opponent, enemy of a computerized technocracy, who seeks heightened awareness . . . , and who is prepared to sacrifice anything but his integrity for the sake of his freedom."

Although it is doubtful that he was aware of his illness, Hesse had leukemia. At the age of eighty-five, he died in his sleep from a brain hemorrhage.

Siddhartha was filmed in 1972 by Lotus Films and *Steppenwolf* in 1974 by D/R Films Inc.

AVOCATIONAL INTERESTS: Watercolor painting, music.

BIOGRAPHICAL/CRITICAL SOURCES: Gustav Emil Mueller, *Philosophy of Literature,* Philosophical Library, 1948; Henry Stuart Hughes, *Consciousness and Society: The Reorientation of European Social Thought, 1890-1930,* Knopf, 1958; Joseph Mileck, *Hermann Hesse and His Critics,* University of North Carolina Press, 1958; Bernhard Zeller, *Eine Chronik in Bildern,* Suhrkamp, 1960; Oskar Seidlin, *Essays in German and Comparative Literature,* University of North Carolina Press, 1961; Helmut Waibler, *Hermann Hesse: Eine Biblographie,* Francke-Verlag, 1962; Alex Natan, editor, *German Men of Letters, Volume II,* Oswald Wolff, 1963; Ralph Freedman, *The Lyrical Novel: Studies in Hermann Hesse, Andre Gide, and Virginia Woolf,* Princeton University Press, 1963; Ernst Rose, *Faith From the Abyss,* New York University Press, 1965; Mark Boulby, *Herman Hesse: His Mind and Art,* Cornell University Press, 1967; Theodore Ziolkowski, *The Novels of Hermann Hesse: A Study in Theme and Structure,* Princeton University Press, 1967; F. Baumer, *Hermann Hesse,* Ungar, 1969; G. W. Field, *Hermann Hesse,* Twayne, 1970; B. Zeller, *Portrait of Hesse: An Illustrated Biography,* translation by Mark Hollebone, McGraw, 1971; M. Serrano, *C. G. Jung and Hermann Hesse,* Routledge & Kegan Paul, 1971; Volker Michels, compiler, *Materialien zu Hermann Hesses "Der Steppenwolf,"* Suhrkamp, 1972; Volker Michels,

compiler, *Materialien zu Hermann Hesses "Das Glasperlenspiel,"* Suhrkamp, 1973; Siegfried Unseld, *Hermann Hesse: Eine Werkgeschichte,* Suhrkamp, 1973; Volker Michels, *Hermann Hesse: Leben und Werk im Bild,* Insel-Verlag, 1973; Theodore Ziolkowski, editor, *Hesse,* Prentice-Hall, 1973; R. H. Farquharson, *An Outline of the Works of Hermann Hesse,* Forum House, 1973; Martin Pfeifer, *Hermann Hesse-Bibliographie: Primarschrifttum und Sekundaerschrifttum in Auswahl,* Erich Schmidt, 1973; Carolyn Riley, editor, *Contemporary Literary Criticism,* Gale, Volume I, 1973, Volume II, 1974, Volume III, 1975, Volume VI, 1976.†

(Died August 9, 1962)

*   *   *

HESTER, Kathleen B.   1905-

PERSONAL: Born February 13, 1905, in Allentown, Pa.; daughter of Robert James (a land developer) and Regina F. (Sier) Hester. *Education:* Carnegie Institute of Technology (now Carnegie-Mellon University), B.S., 1926; University of Pittsburgh, M.A., 1931, Ph.D., 1938. *Religion:* Roman Catholic.

CAREER: Teacher at public schools in Mount Lebanon, Pa., 1935-43; University of Pittsburgh, Pittsburgh, Pa., director of reading laboratory, 1940-43; Merrick Demonstration School, Miami, Fla., supervising teacher, 1943-45; University of Miami, Coral Gables, Fla., director of reading laboratory, 1943-45; Eastern Michigan University, Ypsilanti, professor of education, beginning 1945. Visiting professor, University of Miami, Coral Gables, Fla., 1950-53; reading consultant, Puerto Rico Department of Public Instruction, 1959-61. *Member:* National Council of Teachers in English, International Reading Association, Michigan Reading Association (member of council).

WRITINGS: Teaching Every Child to Read, Harper, 1955, 2nd edition, 1964; (with G. A. Yoakam and Louise Abney) "Laidlaw Supplementary Readers," primary series and intermediate series, Laidlaw, 1955; *Teachers' Manual for Use with New Horizons Through Reading and Literature,* Book I, Laidlaw, 1958, Book II (with William A. Mills), 1958; (with Harold G. Shane) "Gateways to Reading Treasures," seven readers, Laidlaw, 1960, revised editions, 1965; (contributor) Albert J. Harris, editor, *Readings on Reading Instruction,* McKay, 1963; (with Angeles Pastor, Vda Guzman, Rosa de Capo, and Carmen G. Tejera) "Por el mundo del cuento y la aventura," ten basic readers for Spanish America, Laidlaw, 1963; (co-author) "The Laidlaw English Program," eight books, Laidlaw, 1967; (co-author) "The Urban Reading Series," four readers, Laidlaw, 1967. Contributor of articles and reviews to journals. Member of editorial advisory board, International Reading Association.

WORK IN PROGRESS: A series of intermediate level readers for urban areas.

SIDELIGHTS: Kathleen Hester is fluent in Spanish.††

*   *   *

HIEBERT, Paul Gerhardt   1892-

PERSONAL: Born July 17, 1892, in Pilot Mound, Manitoba, Canada; son of John and Maria (Penner) Hiebert; married Dorothea Cunningham, 1926. *Education:* University of Manitoba, B.A., 1916; University of Toronto, M.A., 1917, M.Sc., 1921; McGill University, Ph.D., 1924. *Home:* 118 Wilde Ave., Carman, Manitoba, Canada.

CAREER: University of Manitoba, Winnipeg, member of

chemistry faculty, 1924-53, professor of chemistry, 1943-54. *Awards, honors:* Stephen Leacock Medal for best humorous book published by a Canadian author, 1948, for *Sarah Binks;* L.L.D., University of Manitoba, 1924; D.Litt., Brandon University, 1925.

WRITINGS: Sarah Binks (novel), Oxford University Press, 1947; *Tower in Siloam* (nonfiction), McClelland & Stewart, 1966; *Willows Revisited,* McClelland & Stewart, 1967.

AVOCATIONAL INTERESTS: Philosophy, gardening.

* * *

HILBORN, Harry (Warren) 1900-

PERSONAL: Born April 16, 1900, in Blair, Ontario, Canada; son of Joseph (a miller) and Sophia (Hagey) Hilborn; married Marguerite Mary Carr, June 7, 1932 (died March 20, 1973); children: Kenneth Harry. *Education:* University of Chicago, student, 1925; University of Toronto, B.A., 1923, M.A., 1925, Ph.D., 1935. *Home:* 244 Frontenac St., Kingston, Ontario, Canada.

CAREER: University of Toronto, Toronto, Ontario, lecturer in Italian and Spanish, 1923-27; Acadia University, Wolfville, Nova Scotia, associate professor, 1927-41, professor of Romance languages, 1941-50, head of department, 1949-50; Queen's University, Kingston, Ontario, professor of Spanish and Italian, 1950-70, professor emeritus, 1970—, head of department, 1950-66. *Member:* Modern Language Association of America (chairman of group, 1951-52), Canadian Association of Hispanists (secretary-treasurer, 1968-70, 1974-76; president, 1970-72), North-East Modern Language Association (chairman of group, 1969-70), Ontario Modern Language Teachers' Association (vice-president, 1962; president, 1963-64). *Awards, honors:* Quebec Bonne Entente Prize, 1923; J. J. MacLaren Gold Medal in Modern Languages, 1923; D.Litt., Acadia University, 1961.

WRITINGS: A Chronology of the Plays of D. Pedro Calderon de la Barca, University of Toronto Press, 1938; (translator and annotator) Jose Luis Martinez, editor, *The Modern Mexican Essay,* University of Toronto Press, 1965. Contributor of articles to *Dalhousie Review, Queen's Quarterly, Ontario Modern Language Review, Modern Language Notes, Hispanic Review, Publications of the Modern Language Association,* and other professional journals.

SIDELIGHTS: Harry Hilborn told *CA:* "My principle interests have centered on certain alien cultures, with a view to broadening my outlook on life. My professional obligations caused me to concentrate on Hispanic culture, but this was the result of circumstances rather than an initial preference. I have devoted myself extensively to French and Italian cultures as well." *Avocational interests:* Music, theatre.

* * *

HILL, Grace Brooks
[Collective pseudonym]

WRITINGS—"Corner House Girls" series: *The Corner House Girls Solve a Mystery,* Barse & Hopkins, 1923.

SIDELIGHTS: See **ADAMS, Harriet S., STRATEMEYER, Edward L.,** and **SVENSON, Andrew E.**†

* * *

HINDLE, W(ilfred) H(ope) 1903-1967

PERSONAL: Born December 12, 1903, in Barrow in Furness, England; son of Isaiah (a businessman) and Janet (Hope) Hindle; married Annette Zeiss, 1929 (divorced, 1946); married Eilana Bent, January 30, 1948; children: (first marriage) Mrs. Robert Bamberg, Mrs. Claudio Cintoli. *Education:* Oxford University, Diploma in Education, 1925; also studied at Sorbonne, University of Paris. *Address:* c/o Athenaeum Club, Pall Mall, London S.W.1, England.

CAREER: Yorkshire Post, Leeds, England, leader writer, 1926; *Times,* London, England, editorial staff, 1927-33; *Evening Standard,* London, England, literary editor, 1934-36; *Morning Post,* London, England, leader writer, 1936-37; British Foreign Service, 1938-43, with posts in Prague, 1938-39, Budapest, 1939-41, and Teheran, 1941-43; British Information Services, Washington, D.C., and New York, N.Y., editor of *British* (magazine), 1943-45; special assistant to U.S. representative of Anglo-Iranian Oil Co., 1945-46; Henry Holt & Co., New York, N.Y., foreign editor, 1946; United Nations, New York, N.Y., precis-writer and senior translator in English Section, 1947-55, editorial control officer, 1956-60, chief of editorial control, 1961-64, and was editorial consultant at intervals to United Nations, 1964-66. Writer. *Member:* Athenaeum Club (London), Lotos Club (New York).

WRITINGS: The Morning Post, 1772-1937: Portrait of a Newspaper, Routledge & Kegan Paul, 1937; (editor) *We Were There, by Twelve Foreign Correspondents,* Putnam, 1939 (published in England as *Foreign Correspondent: Personal Adventures Abroad in Search of the News by Twelve British Correspondents,* Harrap, 1939); *A Guide to Writing for the United Nations,* United Nations, 1965. Also author of *Cartoon History of the (between Wars) Disarmament Conference* and *Songs for New Soldiers,* both published in 1936. Contributor to British and American periodicals. Editor, *Review of Reviews,* 1933-36.

SIDELIGHTS: Hindle spoke French, Russian, German, and Spanish.††

(Died June 1, 1967)

* * *

HINTZE, Guenther 1906-

PERSONAL: Born July 8, 1906, in Breslau, Germany; came to United States in 1945, naturalized in 1954; son of Erwin (a museum director) and Elisabeth (Tottman) Hintze; married Else Martinec, June 30, 1939; children: Klaus, Dagmar (Mrs. Frank Hayo), Peter. *Education:* Technical University of Breslau, B.S.E.E., 1927, M.S., 1929. *Religion:* Methodist.

CAREER: General Electric Co., Breslau, Germany, electronic engineer, 1929-35; Osram Philips, Berlin, Germany, operating manager, 1935-40; German Rocket Research Center, Peenemunde, research engineer, guidance and control, 1942, chief of design section for system evaluation, and adviser on production and test firings, 1943-45; U.S. Army Ordnance, 1945-68, head of missile evaluation, Ordnance Research and Development Division, Fort Bliss, Tex., 1946-49, chief of System Analysis Branch, Redstone Arsenal, Ala., 1949-52, scientist at White Sands Missile Range, N.M., 1953-68, serving as chief of Dynamic Systems Branch, 1953-57, chief of Flight Simulation Laboratory, 1957-64, director of Computer Directorate, 1965-66, and director of Analysis and Computation Directorate, 1966-68; George Washington University, Washington, D.C., research professor, beginning 1968. Lecturer in engineering, University of Texas at El Paso, 1958-68. *Military service:* German Army, 1940-41. *Member:* American Academy of

Arts and Sciences, American Society for Cybernetics, Society for General Systems Research. *Awards, honors:* Ph.D., New Mexico State University, 1962; Scientific achievement award, U.S. Department of the Army, 1962.

WRITINGS: Fundamentals of Digital Machine Computing, Springer-Verlag, 1966. Contributor of articles on missile flight simulation and real-time flight analysis and control to journals.†

* * *

HIPSKIND, Verne K(enneth)   1925-1975

PERSONAL: Born June 28, 1925, in Seattle, Wash.; son of Carl Frederick (a welder) and Effie May (Odle) Hipskind; married Maggie Jo Ramey (a claims clerk), June 7, 1947; children: Verlene, Chris, Mark. *Education:* University of Louisville, certificate of completion, Southern Police Institute, 1962; further study at Texas A & M University and Baylor University. *Religion:* Baptist. *Home:* 3638 Gaspar Dr., Dallas, Tex. 75220.

CAREER: General Paint Corp., Seattle, Wash., salesman, 1942, 1945-48; Dallas Police Department, Dallas, Tex., 1948-75, began as police officer, safety director, 1962-75. Instructor, American Red Cross. *Military service:* U.S. Army, 1942-45; served in Pacific Theater; became sergeant; received two battle stars. *Member:* American Society of Safety Engineers (Southwest chapter), National Safety Council (member of executive committee; instructor), Boy Scouts of America, Texas Police Association, Texas Safety Association, Dallas Council of Safety Supervisors, Dallas Citizens' Traffic Commission. *Awards, honors:* Dallas (Tex.) *Times-Herald* Community Service Award, 1956; other community awards.

WRITINGS: Personnel Safety for Public Employees, C. C Thomas, 1965. Writer of training pamphlets; contributor to police journals.

WORK IN PROGRESS: Further research on police personnel safety.†

(Died April 7, 1975)

* * *

HIRSCHBERG, Cornelius   1901-

PERSONAL: Born March 28, 1901, in Mount Vernon. N.Y.; son of Alexander (a lawyer) and Lillian (Coon) Hirschberg; married Anna Kopple, July 2, 1925; children: Betty (Mrs. Irwin Rosenblum). *Education:* Attended elementary school in New York, N.Y. *Politics:* "None—rarely vote." *Religion:* Jewish. *Home:* 64 Hawthorne Pl., Montclair, N.J. 07042. *Agent:* John Schaffner, 896 Third Ave.. New York, N.Y. 10022.

CAREER: Held numerous jobs in retailing and store management, 1915-60; Yormark Watch Co., New York, N.Y., salesman, beginning 1960. *Member:* Mystery Writers of America, Crime Writers of England. *Awards, honors:* Edgar Allan Poe Award of Mystery Writers of America, 1963, for *Florentine Finish.*

WRITINGS: The Priceless Gift, Simon & Schuster, 1960; *Florentine Finish,* Harper, 1963. Contributor to periodicals.

WORK IN PROGRESS: A novel with a Swiss background

BIOGRAPHICAL/CRITICAL SOURCES: Reporter, October 27, 1960.

* * *

HISLOP, Codman   1906-

PERSONAL: Born January 5, 1906, in Brooklyn, N.Y.; son of John Clifford (an architect) and Florence Elizabeth (Frost) Hislop; married Gertrude Horstmeyer, September 26, 1946; children: Marjorie (Mrs. George F. Hanson; stepdaughter). *Education:* Union College, Schenectady, N.Y., B.A., 1931; Columbia University, M.A., 1935; Harvard University, Ph.D., 1953. *Politics:* Independent. *Residence:* Dorset, Vt. 05251.

CAREER: Union College, Schenectady, N.Y., assistant to the president, 1932-33, instructor, 1935-40, assistant professor, 1940-47, associate professor, 1947-53, professor, 1953-64, research professor of American civilization, beginning 1964. *Military service:* U.S. Army Air Forces, Combat Intelligence, 1942-45; became major. *Member:* American Association of University Professors, Paleontological Society, Sigma Phi. *Awards, honors:* Union College, Bailey Prize, 1931, and Litt.D., 1972.

WRITINGS: Albany: Dutch, English, and American, Argus, 1936; (with W. H. Richardson) *The Lost Plays of John Howard Payne,* Princeton University Press, 1940; *The Mohawk,* Rinehart, 1947; *Eliphalet Nott,* Wesleyan University Press, 1971. Contributor to *Colophon, Saturday Evening Post, New York History, New England Quarterly,* and *Vermont History.* Consultant, *Life.*

WORK IN PROGRESS: Treason at West Point.

SIDELIGHTS: Codman Hislop has traveled to England, France, Italy, Greece, and Pacific Islands.

* * *

HITREC, Joseph George   1912-1972

PERSONAL: Born February 28, 1912, in Zagreb, Yugoslavia; came to United States, 1946, naturalized citizen, 1951; son of Thomas and Gisele (Molnar) Hitrec; married Leyla Jeanette Saygin, September 19, 1946; children: Vesna Gilda. *Education:* Royal University of Zagreb, M.A., 1934; Columbia University, graduate study. *Home:* 155 Riverside Dr., New York, N.Y. 10024. *Agent:* Shirley Hector Agency, 29 West 46th St., New York, N.Y. 10036. *Office:* Kingsborough College, 2001 Oriental Blvd., Manhattan Beach, New York, N.Y.

CAREER: Started working for British advertising agency in London, England, 1935, later transferring to Indian branches in Calcutta and Bombay, and heading Indian branch operation, 1938-46; copywriter and executive with several advertising agencies, New York, N.Y., 1947-65; instructor in American and world literature, Kingsborough College, New York, N.Y., 1965-72. Author and translator; lecturer in eastern United States. During World War II, worked in Central Planning Unit, Ministry of Broadcasting and Information, New Delhi, India. *Member:* International Advertising Association, Authors Guild. *Awards, honors:* Harper Prize ($10,000), 1948, for *Son of the Moon.*

WRITINGS: Poems, Gaj (Zagreb), 1932; *Rulers' Morning* (stories of India), Harper, 1946; *Son of the Moon* (novel of modern India), Harper, 1948; *Angel of Gaiety* (novel of India), Harper, 1953; (translator from the Yugoslavian) Ivo Andric, *Bosnian Chronicle,* Knopf, 1961; (translator) Ivo Andric, *The Woman from Sarajevo,* Knopf, 1961; *Terrorists* (story collection), Znanje (Zagreb), 1963; (translator) Ivo Andric, *The Pasha's Concubine and Other Tales,* Allen & Unwin, 1970. Contributor of short fiction, articles, and reviews to periodicals in America, England, India, Yugoslavia, and Austria, including *Harper's, Harper's Bazaar, Reporter, Saturday Review, New York Times, New York Herald Tribune, Tomorrow, Horizon,* and *New English Review.*†

(Died August 22, 1972)

HOCKING, Brian   1914-1974

PERSONAL: Born September 22, 1914, in London, England; son of Sidney Blake and Alice Elizabeth (Fisher) Hocking; married Jocelyn May Hicks, January 17, 1938; children: Martin Blake, Drake, Linnet Elizabeth (Mrs. Duncan MacGregor Murray). *Education:* Imperial College of Science and Technology, London, B.Sc. (honors), 1937; University of Alberta, M.Sc., 1948; University of London, Ph.D., 1953. *Home:* 1151 75th Ave., Edmonton, Alberta, Canada. *Office:* Department of Entomology, University of Alberta, Edmonton, Alberta, Canada.

CAREER: Scientific work in India, 1938-42; University of Alberta, Edmonton, Alberta, assistant professor, 1946-51, associate professor, 1951-54, professor of entomology and chairman of department, beginning 1954. Consultant on filariasis to World Health Organization, Rangoon, Burma, 1964. *Military service:* Indian Army, 1942-45; became major. *Member:* Entomological Society of Canada (president, 1960), Entomological Society of America, Royal Entomological Society of London, Institute of Biology, American Mosquito Control Association, Bee Research Association, Entomological Society of Alberta, Entomological Society of Ontario.

WRITINGS: (With E. H. Strickland and G. E. Ball) *A Laboratory Manual for Insect Morphology,* Scholar's Library, 1958; *Smell in Insects: A Bibliography with Abstracts,* Defence Research Board (Canada), 1960; *The Ultimate Science: A Layman's Account of Biology,* Canadian Broadcasting Corp., 1963; (with I. M. Besler and L. R. Tolman) *Laboratory Exercises for Elements of Biology,* McGraw, 1963; (with others) *Laboratory Exercises for Introductory Biology,* Department of Education, Province of Alberta, 1964; (with others) *Senior High School Curriculum Guide for Biology 20, Biology 32 and Biology 30,* Department of Education, Province of Alberta, 1965; *Biology—or Oblivion: Lessons from the Ultimate Science,* Schenkman, 1965; *Six-Legged Science,* Schenkman, 1968. Editor, *Quaestiones Entomologicae.*

WORK IN PROGRESS: Two books, *Essays in Entomology* and *Outline Text in Biology;* research in general entomology, sense organs and behavior, and insect flight; *Skeleton for Life,* a book, is being finished by his son, Drake, for Schenkman.

SIDELIGHTS: Hocking was competent in German and French and he knew some Bengali and Urdu. He had traveled in the Canadian Arctic, Europe, Africa, and Burma on entomological matters.†

(Died May 23, 1974)

*   *   *

HODGE, Marshall Bryant   1925-19(?)

PERSONAL: Born September 3, 1925, in Albany, Ore.; son of Arthur R. (a Presbyterian minister) and Mary (Bryant) Hodge; married Barbara Aultman (an elementary teacher), March 24, 1948; children: Kathleen, Douglas. *Education:* Whitworth College, B.A. (magna cum laude), 1949; San Francisco Theological Seminary, B.D. (magna cum laude), 1952; University of Southern California, Ph.D., 1960. *Politics:* Democrat.

CAREER: Presbyterian clergyman. Minister in Petaluma, Calif., 1952-55, and Los Angeles, Calif., 1955-56; Los An-

geles County (Calif.) Mental Health Department, supervising counselor, 1956-59; Fullerton Junior College, Fullerton, Calif., instructor in psychology, 1959-61; private practice as marriage and family counselor, Claremont, Calif., beginning 1959; Ingelside Psychiatric Hospital, Rosemead, Calif., marriage and family counselor, beginning 1967. *Military service:* U.S. Army, Infantry, 1943-46; received Bronze Star. *Member:* American Psychological Association, Southern California Group Psychotherapy Association (member of board of directors).

WRITINGS: Your Fear of Love, Doubleday, 1967.

WORK IN PROGRESS: A book with working title, *So You're Thinking of Getting Help: A Guide for Those Considering Psychotherapy or Marriage Counseling.*†

(Deceased)

*   *   *

HODGSON, Marshall G. S.   1922-1968

PERSONAL: Surname is pronounced Hod-son; born April 11, 1922, in Richmond, Ind.; son of James Goodwin (a librarian) and Gertrude Elizabeth (Simms) Hodgson; married Phyllis E. Walker, May 25, 1958; children: Sara Elizabeth and Beverly Ruth (twins; both deceased), Cynthia Susan. *Education:* University of Colorado, B.A., 1943; Earlham College, B.A., 1943; University of Chicago, Ph.D., 1951. *Religion:* Society of Friends (Quaker). *Home:* Route 1, Avoca, Wis. 53506.

CAREER: University of Chicago, Chicago, Ill., 1953-68, started as research associate, professor of history and chairman of committee on social thought (an interdisciplinary department). *Member:* American Historical Association, American Oriental Society, American Society for the Study of Religion, American Association of University Professors, Phi Beta Kappa.

WRITINGS: The Order of Assassins: The Struggle of the Early Nizari Ismailis Against the Islamic World, Mouton & Co., 1955; *The Venture of Islam: Conscience and History in a World Civilization,* three volumes, University of Chicago Press, 1975. Also author of *Introduction to Islamic Civilization: Course Syllabus and Selected Readings,* published by University of Chicago Press, 1958, for limited distribution. Contributor to *UNESCOPE, Courier, Diogenes,* and other scholarly journals.

WORK IN PROGRESS: A general history of Islamicate civilization; studies on the unity of world history and on the mythos of the microcosmic return.

SIDELIGHTS: Marshall Hodgson read French, German, Italian, Spanish, Danish, Latin, Arabic, Persian, and some Greek, Urdu, and Turkish; he had studied several other languages more limitedly.†

(Died June 10, 1968)

*   *   *

HOFF, Carol   1900-

PERSONAL: Born February 24, 1900, in Tucson, Ariz.; daughter of Charles Frederick (a real estate dealer) and Helen (Eckhardt) Hoff. *Education:* University of Texas, LL.B., 1922; University of Colorado, summer graduate study; Texas Woman's University, M.L.S., 1954. *Politics:* Independent. *Religion:* Presbyterian. *Home:* 318 Delany Dr., Seguin, Tex. 78155.

CAREER: Yorktown (Tex.) public schools, high school teacher of English, 1924-50, school librarian, 1950-66; substitute teacher and volunteer worker in public library. Library Board, member, 1945-60, chairman, 1950-58. *Member:* Texas State Teachers Association, Texas Library Association, Texas Institute of Letters, Delta Kappa Gamma, Kappa Beta Pi, Beta Phi Mu, Key Allegro Landscape Club (secretary, beginning 1967). *Awards, honors:* Charles W. Follett Award and Cokesbury Award of Texas Institute of Letters, 1950, both for *Johnny Texas;* Boys' Clubs of America Junior Book Award, 1956, for *Wilderness Pioneer.*

WRITINGS—Juvenile; all published by Follett, except where noted: *Johnny Texas,* 1950; *Johnny Texas on the San Antonio Road,* 1953; *Wilderness Pioneer,* 1955; *Head to the West,* 1957; *The Four Friends,* 1958; *Chris,* 1960.

Adult basic education books: *They Served America,* Steck, 1966; *Holidays and History,* Steck, 1967.

WORK IN PROGRESS: Jesse, story of a Mexican-American boy in south Texas; two other juveniles set in early Texas; a book dealing with propaganda, and a reader, both for basic adult education.

SIDELIGHTS: Most of Carol Hoff's juveniles are set in early Texas and are based on experiences of her great-grandparents, who were Texas pioneers. *Avocational interests:* Reading, gardening, listening to symphonic music, playing bridge, collecting stamps, and designing clothes.

* * *

HOFFMANN, Felix 1911-1975

PERSONAL: Born April 11, 1911, in Aarau, Switzerland; son of Emil Adolf (a music director) and Mina (Froehlich) Hoffmann; married Gretel Kienscherf, January 18, 1936; children: Sabine Hoffmann Muischneek, Cristiane Hoffmann Affolter, Susanne Hoffmann-Grendelweier, Dieter Hoffmann Gottstein. *Education:* Attended Kunstakademie Karlsruhe, Germany, 1931-33, and Kunstakademie Berlin, 1934-35. *Religion:* Protestant. *Home:* Ruetliweg 2, CH-5000-Aarau, Switzerland.

CAREER: Illustrator of books for young people and children, 1932-75; free-lance artist and painter in Aarau, Switzerland, 1935-75, executed stained glass windows for churches, school buildings, and municipal buildings, wall murals and mosaics for various other structures in Switzerland; illustrator of bibliophile books for German and American publishers, 1951-75. *Military service:* Swiss Army. *Member:* Gesellschaft schweizer Maler, Bildhauer und Architekten, Bund deutscher Buchkunstler, Xylon, Vereinigung der Holzschneider. *Awards, honors:* Schweizer Jugendbuchpreis, 1957; International Board on Books for Children, Hans Christian Andersen Award honor list, 1960 and 1962, Hans Christian Andersen Award, 1972; Children's Spring Book Festival award, *New York Herald Tribune,* 1963; Premio Fondatione Carmine (Florence), 1969.

WRITINGS—Illustrator: Werner Bergengruen, *Die drei Falken,* Trajanus-Presse (Frankfurt am Main), 1956; Giovanni Boccaccio, *Die Nymphe von Fiesole,* Trajanus-Presse, 1958; Hans Christian Andersen, *Der standhafte Zinnsoldat: Ein Maerchen,* Aargauer Tagblatt (Aarau), 1960; *Bilderbibel* (includes 100 lithographs by Hoffmann, text by Paul Erismann), Zwingli Verlag (Zurich), 1961; Thomas Mann, *The Magic Mountain,* Limited Editions Club, 1962; Apuleius Madaurensis, *Amor und Psyche,* Verlag Ars (Frankfurt am Main), 1963; *Das hohe Lied (The Song of Solomon* from the Old Testament), Flamberg-Verlag (Zurich), 1964; *Die Shoepfung der Welt (Genesis,* I-II, from the Old Testament), Verlag Ars, 1965; Bram Sto-

ker, *Dracula,* Limited Editions Club, 1965; *A Boy Went Out to Gather Pears* (old nursery rhyme), Harcourt, 1966; Aesopus, *Drei Dutzend Fabeln von Aesop,* Angelus-Drucke (Bern), 1967; Anton Pavlovich Chekhov, *Der wartende Kutscher,* Paulus Verlag (Recklinghausen), 1968; Max Voegeli, *The Wonderful Lamp,* Houghton, 1969; *Die sieben Todsuenden* (includes seven etchings by Hoffmann, and verses from *Das Narrenschiff* by Sebastian Brant), Sauerlaender (Aarau), 1969; *Es taget von dem Walde* (thirty-six Swiss folk songs), [Aarau], 1974; (and adaptor) *The Story of Christmas: A Picture Book,* Atheneum, 1975; Jean Froissart, *Les Bourgeois de Calais,* Langewiesche-Brandt, 1976.

Illustrator of children's picture books of fairy tales by the Grimm Brothers: *Der Wolf and die sieben Geisslein,* Sauerlaender, 1957, translation by Katya Sheppard published as *The Wolf and the Seven Kids,* Oxford University Press, 1958, Harcourt, 1959; *Dornroeschen,* Sauerlaender, 1959, translation by Peter Collier published as *Sleeping Beauty,* Harcourt, 1959; *Rapunzel,* Sauerlaender, 1960, translation published under same title, Harcourt, 1961; *Die sieben Raben,* Sauerlaender, 1962, translation published as *The Seven Ravens,* Harcourt, 1963; *Die vier kunstreichen Brueder,* Sauerlaender, 1966, translation published as *The Four Clever Brothers,* Harcourt, 1967; *King Thrushbeard,* Harcourt, 1970; (and editor) *Hans im Glueck,* Sauerlaender, 1975, translation published as *Hans in Luck,* Atheneum, 1975.

Illustrations also included in *The Favorite Fairy Tales Told in Poland,* edited by Virginia Haviland, Little, Brown, 1963.

WORK IN PROGRESS: Passion, twenty-one etchings with the bible as text.

SIDELIGHTS: Felix Hoffmann told *CA* that his Grimm fairy tale books were created for the use of his own children when they were young, between 1945 and 1951. The most recent books were inspired by his two grandchildren. All the picture books are composed of original chromolithographs, color separations which he printed himself, using either lithograph stones or acetate, both less expensive methods than photographic reproduction.

BIOGRAPHICAL/CRITICAL SOURCES: Philobiblon, 1960; *Texas University Quarterly,* spring, 1962; *Der Polygraph,* June, 1969; *Felix Hoffmann,* Sauerlaender, 1971.†

(Died June 16, 1975)

* * *

HOGAN, Willard N(ewton) 1909-

PERSONAL: Born March 26, 1909, in Dry Ridge, Ky.; son of Ellie B. (a businessman) and Mary Vernon (Jones) Hogan; married Hildur Canter, April 3, 1937; children: Carolyn Hogan Rounds, Jeannette Hogan Tighe, Edward. *Education:* Transylvania College (now University), A.B., 1930; University of Kentucky, M.A., 1934; Brookings Institution, graduate study, 1935-36; University of Chicago, Ph.D., 1939. *Politics:* Democrat. *Religion:* Protestant. *Home:* 1115 Idylwild Dr., Lincoln, Neb. 68503.

CAREER: U.S. Government, Washington, D.C., research and administrative positions, 1937-45; Berea College, Berea, Ky., associate professor of history and political science, 1945-49; State University of New York College at New Paltz, professor of political science, 1949-63; University of Nebraska, Lincoln, professor of political science, 1963-74, chairman of department, 1967-70. Consultant on United Nations Project, Brookings Institution, 1951-53. Chairman, New Paltz (N.Y.) Zoning Commission, 1958-63.

WRITINGS: (With Amry Vandenbosch) *The United Nations,* McGraw, 1952; *International Conflict and Collective Security,* University of Kentucky Press, 1955; (with Vandenbosch) *Toward World Order,* McGraw, 1963; *Representative Government and European Integration,* University of Nebraska Press, 1967. Contributor to professional journals.

AVOCATIONAL INTERESTS: Travel, chess, and gardening.

*   *   *

HOLBORN, Hajo   1902-1969

PERSONAL: Born May 18, 1902, in Berlin, Germany; came to United States in 1934, naturalized in 1940; son of Ludwig (a physicist) and Helene (Bussmann) Holborn; married Annemarie Bettmann, October 2, 1926; children: Frederick, Hanna (Mrs. Charles M. Gray). *Education:* University of Berlin, Ph.D., 1924. *Home:* 233 Santa Fe Ave., Hamden, Conn. 06517. *Office:* Department of History, Yale University, New Haven, Conn. 06520.

CAREER: University of Heidelberg, Heidelberg, Germany, assistant professor of history, 1926-31; Carnegie Professor of History and International Relations at School of Politics, Berlin, Germany, and lecturer at University of Berlin, 1931-33; Yale University, New Haven, Conn., visiting professor of history, 1934-38, associate professor, 1938-40, professor of history, 1940-46, Randolph W. Townsend Professor of History, 1946-59, Sterling Professor of History, 1959-69. On leave from Yale University to serve with U.S. Office of Strategic Services, Washington, D.C., 1943-45. Professor of diplomatic history, Fletcher School of Law and Diplomacy, Tufts University, 1936-42; visiting lecturer or professor at Harvard University, 1941-42, Stanford University, 1948, Columbia University, 1950-51, and University of Vienna, 1955. Consultant to U.S. Department of State, 1947-49.

MEMBER: American Historical Association (president, 1967), American Academy of Arts and Sciences, American Society of Church History, Council on Foreign Relations. *Awards, honors:* Commander's Cross of Merit (Federal Republic of Germany); M.A., Yale University, 1940; Ph.D. from University of Chicago and Free University of Berlin, both 1967; first Inter Nations award, 1969.

WRITINGS: Ulrich von Hutter and the German Reformation, translated by Roland H. Bainton, Yale University Press, 1937, reprinted, Harper, 1966; *American Military Government: Its Organization and Policies,* Infantry Journal Press, 1947; *The Political Collapse of Europe,* Knopf, 1951; *A History of Modern Germany,* Knopf, Volume I: *The Reformation,* 1959, Volume II: *1648-1840,* 1963, Volume III: *1840-1945,* 1969; *Hajo Holborn* (essays and speeches), Inter Nationes (Bonn), 1969; *Germany and Europe: Historical Essays,* Doubleday, 1970; *History and the Humanities,* Doubleday, 1972; *Republic to Reich: The Making of the Nazi Revolution* (essays), translated by Ralph Manheim, Pantheon, 1972.

Editor: (With wife, Annemarie Holborn) Desiderius Erasmus, *Ausgewaehlte werke,* Beck, 1964; Joseph Maria von Radowitz, *Aufzeichnungen und Erinnerungen,* Biblio Verlag, 1967. Also author of numerous monographs in German. Former co-editor of *The Journal of Modern History* and *The Journal of the History of Ideas.*

SIDELIGHTS: Gordon A. Craig wrote of Holborn: "A historian of remarkable scope and penetration, he wrote with equal authority about politics and ideas, about the classical world and the age of the Reformation, about the development of modern strategical theory and the diplomacy of great powers, and his books . . . were models of meticulous scholarly analysis and exposition."

BIOGRAPHICAL/CRITICAL SOURCES: L. Krieger and F. Stern, editors, *The Responsibility of Power: Historical Essays in Honor of Hajo Holborn,* Doubleday, 1968; *New York Times,* June 21, 1969; *New York Times Book Review,* August 24, 1969.†

(Died June 20, 1969)

*   *   *

HOLBORN, Louise W.   1898-19(?)

PERSONAL: Born August 8, 1898, in Berlin, Germany. *Education:* Social Work School, Berlin, State Diploma, 1923; study in political science at University of Berlin and University of Heidelberg, 1929-33; School of Politics, Berlin, Diploma, 1933; Harvard University, M.A., 1936, Ph.D., 1938. *Religion:* Protestant.

CAREER: Smith College, Northampton, Mass., visiting lecturer in international relations, 1946-47; Connecticut College, New London, professor of government, 1947-63; Harvard University Extension, Radcliffe Seminars, Cambridge, Mass., professor of international relations and comparative government, 1963-64, beginning 1965; Radcliffe Institute, Cambridge, research scholar, 1963-64, 1965-69. Consultant to Cooperative for American Relief Everywhere (CARE), 1957-59, to Intergovernmental Committee of European Migration, Geneva, 1961-63, and to U.S. Department of Health, Education, and Welfare Cuban Refugee Program, 1964-65.

MEMBER: American Political Science Association, International Political Science Association, American Society of International Law, American Association of University Women, American Civil Liberties Union, League of Women Voters, International Institute (Boston), World Affairs Council (Boston), Phi Beta Kappa. *Awards, honors:* Senior scholarship in international relations from Rockefeller Foundation, 1961-62.

WRITINGS: (Compiler and editor) *War and Peace Aims of the U.N., 1939-45,* two volumes, World Peace Foundation, 1948; *The International Refugee Organization, 1946-52,* Oxford University Press, 1956; (editor with G. M. Carter and J. W. Herz) *Documents of Major Foreign Powers,* Harcourt, 1968; (editor with Carter and Herz) *German Constitutional Documents since 1871,* Praeger, 1970. Contributor to political science journals.

WORK IN PROGRESS: History of the U.N. High Commissioner for Refugees.†

(Deceased)

*   *   *

HOLCOMBE, Arthur N(orman)   1884-

PERSONAL: Born November 3, 1884, in Winchester, Mass.; son of Franklin Gibbons (a lawyer) and Inez Norman (Maynard) Holcombe; married Carolyn Hawley Crossett, August 30, 1910 (died, 1956); married Hadassah Moore Leeds Parrot, October 8, 1964; children: (first marriage) Waldo Hawley, Mary (Mrs. Richard T. Fisher, Jr.), Robert Crossett, Jane (Mrs. Bradley Dewey, Jr.), Richard M. *Education:* Harvard University, A.B., 1906, Ph.D., 1909; also studied at University of Berlin, University of Paris, University of Munich, and London School of Economics and Political Science. *Politics:* Republican. *Religion:* Unitarian Universalist. *Home:* 180 Canton Ave., Milton, Mass. 02187.

CAREER: Taught at Harvard University, Cambridge, Mass., 1909-55, professor emeritus, 1955—. Lecturer at Johns Hopkins University, 1959-60; lecturer at national universities in China, 1928, 1935, at College of Europe, 1952, and at University of California, Stanford University, University of Michigan, Massachusetts Institute of Technology, and other universities. U.S. Government posts include member of U.S. Bureau of Efficiency, 1917-19, and of President's Committee on Administrative Management, 1936; chairman of appeals board, War Production Board, 1942-45. Chairman of Commission to Study the Organization of Peace (affiliate of United Nations Association), 1955-64; chairman of International Commission to Study the Organization of Peace (affiliate of World Federation of United Nations Associations), 1965.

MEMBER: American Political Science Association (president, 1936), American Association of University Professors (councillor), American Academy of Arts and Sciences (councillor), Cosmos Club (Washington, D.C.). *Awards, honors:* Davis A. Wells Prize, 1909-10 for manuscript of *Public Ownership of Telephones on the Continent of Europe;* Bancroft Prize of Columbia University and Franklin D. Roosevelt Prize of American Political Science Association, 1951, for *Our More Perfect Union;* L.H.D., Columbia University, 1954.

WRITINGS: Public Ownership of Telephones on the Continent of Europe, Houghton, 1911; *State Government in the United States,* Macmillan, 1916, 3rd edition, revised and enlarged, 1931; *The Foundations of the Modern Commonwealth,* Harper, 1923; *The Political Parties of To-day,* Harper, 1924, reprinted, Arno, 1974; *The Chinese Revolution: A Phase in the Regeneration of a World Power,* Harvard University Press, 1930, reprinted, Fertig, 1974; *The Spirit of the Chinese Revolution* (Lowell Institute lectures), Knopf, 1930, reprinted, Hyperion Press (Westport, Conn.), 1973; *The New Party Politics,* Norton, 1933; *Government in a Planned Democracy,* Norton, 1935.

The Middle Classes in American Politics, Harvard University Press, 1940, reprinted, Russell, 1965; *Dependent Areas in the Post-War World,* World Peace Foundation, 1941; *Politics in Action: The Problems of Representative Government,* National Education Association, 1943; *Human Rights in the Modern World* (James Stokes lectures), New York University Press, 1948; *Our More Perfect Union: From Eighteenth-Century Principles to Twentieth-Century Practice,* Harvard University Press, 1950, 2nd edition, 1958; *The United Nations and American Foreign Policy* (booklet; James lecture), Institute of Government and Public Affairs, University of Illinois, 1957; *Securing the Blessings of Liberty: The Constitutional System,* introduction by Hubert H. Humphrey, Scott, Foresman, 1964, revised edition, 1969; *A Strategy of Peace in a Changing World,* Harvard University Press, 1967.

As chairman of Commission to Study the Organization of Peace, various reports of the commission, including *Strengthening the United Nations, A Universal United Nations,* and *Peaceful Coexistence* have been published under his name. Contributor to many journals.†

*   *   *

HOLISHER, Desider 1901-1972

PERSONAL: Born February 2, 1901, in Budapest, Hungary; son of Leopold (a goldsmith-jeweler) and Anna (Weiner) Holisher; married Myra Zlatogorsky, December 25, 1928; children: Leo. *Education:* University of Berlin, M.Econ., 1926; attended Berlin Photography Academy, 1927-28. *Religion:* Jewish. *Home:* 611 West 111th St., New York, N.Y. 10025.

CAREER: Reporter Feature Syndicate, Berlin, Germany, feature writer and photo editor, 1929-33; Rome correspondent for European newspapers and magazines, 1933-38; writer, photographic illustrator, and teacher in United States, beginning, 1938. Sometime instructor in pictorial arts and photography at Rutgers University, and City College of the City University of New York.

WRITINGS: Roma Centro Mondiale, Andrea Scattini (Rome), 1937; *The Eternal City: Rome of the Popes,* Ungar, 1943; *The House of God,* Crown, 1946; *Pilgrims Path: The Story of Plymouth,* Stephen-Paul Publishers, 1947; (with Clarence W. Hall) *Protestant Panorama,* Farrar, Strauss, 1951; *Capitol Hill: The Story of Congress,* Schuman, 1952; *The Synagogue and Its People,* Abelard, 1955; *Growing Up in Israel,* Viking, 1963.

Contributor of photographs: William Bridges, *Big Zoo,* Viking, 1941; Theodore McClintock, *Animal Close-Ups,* Abelard, 1958.

Author of over three hundred illustrated articles and photo-stories in periodicals in the United States and Europe; American magazines include *National Geographic;* also contributor to publications of the U.S. Army Civil Affairs Division for Europe.

SIDELIGHTS: As an accredited correspondent in Rome, 1933-38, Holisher was the first newspaperman permitted to photograph the daily life and activities within the Vatican State. His illustrated articles went to magazines and newspapers in Switzerland, France, England, Netherlands, Austria, and Hungary, and were republished throughout Europe. He spoke German, Italian, and French.†

(Died August 11, 1972)

*   *   *

HOLLIDAY, Joseph 1910-
(Joe Holliday; pseudonyms: Jack Bosco, Jack Dale)

PERSONAL: Born December 14, 1910, in Gibraltar; son of Joseph (a laborer) and Julia Francis (Bosco) Holliday; married Gladys Muriel Squier, November 30, 1935; children: Anne June (Mrs. Stanley Hotchkiss), Marilyn Jane (Mrs. Tony Cucci). *Education:* Attended public schools in Toronto, Ontario, and took night classes in art, advertising, and other subjects. *Politics:* Liberal ("generally—not firm"). *Religion:* Anglican ("generally—not firm"). *Home:* 26 Porter Crescent, Scarborough, Ontario, Canada. *Office:* Wadham Publications Ltd., 109 Vanderhoof Ave., Suite 101, Toronto, Ontario, Canada M4G 2J2.

CAREER: Prior to 1940 was associate editor of *Sporting News,* did publicity for a radio station, and was manager of a theater, all in Toronto, Ontario; de Havilland Aircraft, Toronto, member of publicity staff and chief photographer, 1940-45; Imperial Oil Ltd., Toronto, publicity and editorial work, 1945-56; Weston Publishing Co., Toronto, editor, 1956-70; Wadham Publications Ltd., Toronto, editor, beginning 1970. *Member:* Canadian Authors Association (chairman of headquarters committee, 1959-71), Canadian Business Press Association (member of board of directors, 1960), Canadian Aviation Historical Society. *Awards, honors:* Centennial Medal from Canadian Government, 1967; Allan Sangstor Memorial Award, 1973.

WRITINGS: Oil Trails in Headless Valley (juvenile), Longmans, Green, 1954; *Mosquito: The Wooden Wonder Aircraft of World War II,* Doubleday, 1970. Also author of an autobiography, *Frantic Til Fifty.*

"Dale of the Mounted" juvenile series: *Dale of the Mounted on the West Coast,* Thomas Allen, 1954; . . . *in Newfoundland,* Thomas Allen, 1955; . . .: *Dew Line Duty,* Thomas Allen, 1957; . . . *Submarine Hunt,* Thomas Allen, 1958, Pennington Press, 1959; *Dale of the Mounted,* Pennington Press, 1959; . . . *Atomic Plot,* Thomas Allen, 1959; . . .: *Atlantic Assignment,* Pennington Press, 1959; . . . *in Hong Kong,* Thomas Allen, 1962. Also author of *Dale of the Mounted in the Northwest, Dale of the Mounted in the Artic, Dale of the Mounted on the St. Lawrence,* and *Dale of the Mounted at the U.N.*

Contributor of articles on a variety of subjects to *Toronto Star, Financial Post, Chatelaine, Industrial Canada, Air Classics Quarterly, Airtrails, RCMP Quarterly,* and other magazines, trade journals, and newspapers in Canada and the United States; some of the articles were published under name Joe Holliday and the pseudonyms Jack Bosco and Jack Dale. Editor, *Canadian Author & Bookman Quarterly,* 1955-60, 1976, and *Automative, Petroleum & TBA Marketer.*

AVOCATIONAL INTERESTS: Photography (has a collection of 3,500 color slides taken on travels in Europe, Japan, Hong Kong, and elsewhere), wood carving, metal sculpture, making tape recordings.†

*   *   *

HOLLISTER, George E(rwin)   1905-

PERSONAL: Born July 9, 1905, in Erwin, S.D.; son of Arthur R. (a druggist) and Mary (Lattin) Hollister; married Helen M. Schoepp, June 19, 1928; children: Carolyn Hope (Mrs. Donald C. Thompson). *Education:* General Beadle State College (now Dakota State College), B.S., 1930; George Peabody College for Teachers, M.A., 1932; University of Minnesota, Ph.D., 1947. *Religion:* Unitarian Universalist. *Home:* 1213 Harney, Laramie, Wyo. 82070. *Office:* College of Education, University of Wyoming, Laramie, Wyo. 82070.

CAREER: Teacher in South Dakota, 1926-29; Macalester College, St. Paul, Minn., instructor in education, 1940; University of Wyoming, Laramie, 1940-43, and beginning 1947, became professor of elementary education, director of Division of Undergraduate Teacher Education, 1955-60. *Military service:* U.S. Army Air Forces, 1943-46; became captain. *Member:* National Council of Teachers of Mathematics, Association for Supervision and Curriculum Development, Association for Student Teaching (member of national executive committee), National Education Association (life member), National Council for Social Studies, Wyoming Education Association (president, 1963), Kappa Delta Pi, Phi Delta Kappa, Pi Kappa Delta.

WRITINGS: (With Agnes Gunderson) *Teaching Arithmetic in Grades I and II,* Heath, 1954, revised edition published as *Teaching Arithmetic in the Primary Grades,* 1964; (with others) "Learning to Use Arithmetic," series, Heath, 1962. Contributor to education journals.††

*   *   *

HOLMES, Paul Allen   1901-

PERSONAL: Born June 20, 1901, in Milton, Wis.; son of David Alfred (a leaf-tobacco dealer) and Jeannette

(Spaulding) Holmes; married Miriam O'May, August 5, 1954; children: Janet, Paul Allen III. *Education:* Attended Milton College, 1917-18; University of Wisconsin, A.B., 1921; Marquette University, law study, 1924-27. *Politics:* Republican. *Religion:* Protestant. *Home and office:* 380 Southeast Fifth Court, Pompano Beach, Fla. 33060. *Agent:* Scott Meredith, 580 Fifth Ave., New York, N.Y. 10036.

CAREER: Member of editorial staff of newspapers in Chicago, Ill., 1917-19, Madison, Wis., 1920-21, Milwaukee, Wis., 1922-24; *Milwaukee Sentinel,* Milwaukee, Wis., reporter, 1921-22, 1924-29, city editor, 1930-34, executive editor, 1934-38; *Milwaukee Post,* Milwaukee, Wis., editor, 1939-40; *Chicago Tribune,* Chicago, Ill., staff writer, 1941-66. Admitted to Wisconsin bar, 1927. Member of Oak Park (Ill.) Board of Education, 1963-66. *Member:* Chicago Press Club. *Awards, honors:* Special award, Mystery Writers of America, 1961, for *The Sheppard Murder Case.*

WRITINGS: Murder Buttoned Up, Dutton, 1948; *The Sheppard Murder Case,* McKay, 1961; (with Stephen Sheppard) *My Brother's Keeper,* McKay, 1964; *The Candy Murder Case,* Bantam, 1966; *Re-Trial: Murder and Dr. Sam Sheppard,* Bantam, 1966. Contributor of articles to *Chicago Tribune Magazine. Family Weekly, Marquette Law Review,* and of reviews to *Chicago Tribune Books Today.*

*   *   *

HOLMES, Urban T(igner)   1900-1972

PERSONAL: Born July 13, 1900, in Washington, D.C.; son of Urban Tigner (a commander, U.S. Navy) and Florence Fielding (Lawson) Holmes; married Margaret Allen Gemmell, June 22, 1922; children: Mary Cleland (Mrs. Louis Leon Bernard), Florence Anne (Mrs. Hampton Hubbard), Urban T. Holmes III. *Education:* U.S. Naval Academy, midshipman, 1916-17; University of Pennsylvania, A.B., 1920; Harvard University, A.M., 1921, Ph.D., 1923; University of Paris, graduate study, 1922-23. *Politics:* Democrat. *Religion:* Episcopalian.

CAREER: University of Missouri, Columbia, assistant professor of French, 1923-25; University of North Carolina, Chapel Hill, associate professor, 1925-27, professor, 1927-45, Kenan Professor of Romance Philology, beginning 1945. Visiting professor at University of Chicago, 1929, University of Southern California, 1939, Louisiana State University, 1949; distinguished visiting professor at Michigan State University, 1959, consulting professor, 1960-62. Lecturer at Mediaeval Institute, University of Notre Dame, 1948, 1956; Fulbright lecturer at University of Melbourne, 1960. Member of advisory committee, Southern Fellowship Fund, 1960-63; member of screening committee, Fulbright-Hayes Committee, 1961-67. *Military service:* U.S. Naval Reserve, seaman, 1918. Office of Strategic Services, liaison officer, 1943-44.

MEMBER: Modern Language Association of America (member of executive council, 1940-43), Mediaeval Academy of America (fellow), Linguistic Society of America, American Association of Teachers of French, Societe de Linguistique de Paris, American Numismatic Society, Society of Antiquaries (London), Royal Numismatic Society, Royal Archaeological Institute, Anglo-Norman Text Society (American secretary), Society of Federal Linguists, South Atlantic Modern Language Association (president, 1941), Phi Beta Kappa, Delta Phi. *Awards, honors:* Litt.D., Washington and Lee University, 1948, Western Michigan University, 1965; Chevalier, Legion of Honor (France), 1950; John Keble Award of American Church Union (Episcopal Church), 1968.

WRITINGS: *A French Composition: Consisting of Original French Text with English Paraphrase,* Lucas Brothers, 1925; *Books of Travel,* University of North Carolina Press, 1927, 2nd edition, 1929.

The French Novel in English Translation, University of North Carolina Press, 1930; (with Hugo Giduz) *Sept contes de la vieille France,* Heath, 1930; (editor) *The Works of Guillaume de Salluste, sieur du Bartas,* University of North Carolina Press, 1935; (with Alexander H. Schutz) *A History of the French Language,* Hedrick, 1935; (with Schutz) *A Source Book for the History of the French Language,* Hedrick, 1940; (compiler with C. M. Woodward and G. C. S. Adams) *Census of French and Provencal Dialect Dictionaries in American Libraries,* Linguistic Society of America, 1937; *A History of Old French Literature: From the Origins to 1300,* Crofts, 1937, revised edition, Russell, 1962.

(Editor) Adenet le Roi, *Berte aus grans Pies,* University of North Carolina Press, 1946; (editor) *Critical Bibliography of French Literature,* Volume I, 1947; (editor with A. J. Denomy) *Mediaeval Studies in Honor of Jeremiah Denis Mathias Ford,* Harvard University Press, 1948; *A New Interpretation of Chretien's conte del Graal,* University of North Carolina Press, 1948.

(Editor with A. G. Engstrom and S. E. Leavitt) *Romance Studies Presented to William Morton Dey,* University of North Carolina Press, 1950; (editor with R. W. Linker) Willi Apel, *French Secular Music of the Late Fourteenth Century,* Mediaeval Academy of America, 1950; *Daily Living in the Twelfth Century, Based on the Observations of Alexander Neckam in London and Paris,* University of Wisconsin Press, 1952; *Samuel Pepys in Paris, and Other Essays,* University of North Carolina Press, 1954; (with Sister Mary Amelia Klenke) *Chretien de Troyes and the Grail,* University of North Carolina Press, 1956.

(Editor with K. R. Scholberg) *French and Provencal Lexicography: Essays Presented to Honor Alexander H. Schutz,* Ohio State University Press, 1964; (editor) *Romance Studies in Memory of Edward Billings Ham,* California State College, 1967.

Contributor to encyclopedias and language journals. Editor, "North Carolina Studies in Romance Languages and Literature," beginning 1940, and *Romance Notes,* beginning 1960; member of editorial board, *Speculum* and *Studies in Philology.*

WORK IN PROGRESS: Books on Chretien de Troyes, Marie de France, medieval houses, and medieval man's concept of human nature; with Rupert Pickens, an edition of *Philippe de Thaun.*

SIDELIGHTS: Urban Holmes spoke French, Portuguese, Spanish, Italian; he could read all the Romance languages, German, Latin, ancient Greek, Gaelic, Welsh, "and some others less well." *Avocational interests:* Singing (bass).

BIOGRAPHICAL/CRITICAL SOURCES: J. Mahoney and J. E. Keller, editors, *Mediaeval Studies in Honor of Urban Tigner Holmes, Jr.,* University of North Carolina Press, 1966.†

(Died May 12, 1972)

*   *   *

HOOD, Dora (Ridout)   1885-

PERSONAL: Born January 23, 1885, in Toronto, Ontario, Canada; daughter of George (a businessman) and Elizabeth (Fisken) Ridout; married Frederick Hood (a physician), December 2, 1918 (died, 1927); children: Wharton, Mary Glen Hood Bell. *Education:* Eudcated privately in Canada, and at Perse School, Cambridge, England; Havergal College, Toronto, graduate, 1905. *Religion:* Anglican.

CAREER: Founder and operator of Dora Hood's Book Room (dealing in rare and out-of-print Canadian books), Toronto, Ontario, 1928-54. *Member:* Ontario Historical Society, Architectural Conservancy of Ontario, Royal Ontario Museum.

WRITINGS: *The Side Door: 26 Years in My Book Room* (autobiographical), Ryerson, 1958; *Davidson Black* (biography of the Canadian anatomist and anthropologist), University of Toronto Press, 1964. Writer of essays on rare books.

WORK IN PROGRESS: Historical research on places and persons in Canada.††

*   *   *

HOPKINS, Prynce (C.)   1885-1970
(Pryns Hopkins)

PERSONAL: Born March 5, 1885, in Oakland, Calif.; son of Charles Harris (a stockbroker) and Mary Isabel (Booth) Hopkins; married Eileen Thomas, January 12, 1920 (deceased); married Fay Cartledge, December 20, 1933 (divorced, 1946); children: Eileen (Mrs. Thomas Ames), Jennifer (Mrs. Jurgen Hansen), David. *Education:* Yale University, Ph.B., 1906; Columbia University, M.A., 1910; University College, London, Ph.D., 1927. *Politics:* Democrat. *Religion:* Ethical Culture Movement. *Home and office:* 1920 Garden St., Santa Barbara, Calif. *Agent:* Alex Jackinson, 55 West 42nd St., New York, N.Y. 10036.

CAREER: Owner and supervisor of Boy Land Experimental School in California, 1912-18, and Chateau de Bures School for Boys, Morainvilliers, France, 1925-38; University of London, University College, London, England, honorary lecturer in psychology, 1928-40; Claremont Graduate School, Claremont, Calif., lecturer in psychology, 1941-46; writer on social problems from psychological angle, and lecturer, 1947-70. Board member or committee chairman of Santa Barbara branches of United World Federalists, American Association for the United Nations, National Committee on Alcoholism, and Mental Health Association; vice president of American Ethical Union. *Member:* American Psychological Association (fellow), American Sociological Society, British Psychological Association (fellow), Royal Geographic Society (fellow), British Psycho-Analytic Association (associate member), California State Psychological Society, California Sociological Society, Los Angeles Psychoanalytic Society (affiliate).

WRITINGS—All under the name Pryns Hopkins, except as indicated: (Under name Prynce Hopkins) *Father or Sons?,* K. Paul, Trench, & Trubner, 1927; *Psychology of Social Movements,* Norton, 1938; *Aids to Successful Study,* Allen & Unwin, 1941; *From Gods to Dictators,* Haldeman-Julius, 1944; *World Culture,* Freedom Publications, 1945; *A Westerner Looks East,* Warren F. Lewis, 1951; (under name Prynce Hopkins) *Both Hands before the Fire,* Traversity Press, 1962; *The Social Psychology of Religious Experience,* Paine-Whitman, 1962; *Orientation, Socialization and Individuations,* Asia Publishing House, 1963; *World Invisible: A Study of Sages, Saints, and Saviours,* Traversity Press, 1963. Also author of *Gone up in Smoke: A Study of Tobacconism,* 1948. Editor and publisher of *Freedom* magazine, 1941-46.

WORK IN PROGRESS: Violence: Its Norms, Pathology, and Control.

SIDELIGHTS: Hopkins was competent in French and German and spoke Italian and Spanish. He often visited the principal countries of Europe, North Africa, and Asia, and, occasionally, Southeast Asia and Latin America.†

(Died, 1970)

* * *

HOPKINS, Vivian C. 1909-

PERSONAL: Born September 2, 1909, in Troy, N.Y.; daughter of Richard and Josephine (Brown) Hopkins. *Education:* Wellesley College, B.A., 1930; University of Michigan, M.A., 1931, Ph.D., 1943; Radcliffe College, M.A., 1939. *Religion:* Methodist. *Home:* 824 Second Ave., Troy, N.Y. 12182.

CAREER: English teacher in high schools in Connecticut and New York, 1931-36; Russell Sage College, Troy, N.Y., instructor in English, 1935-36; Medina Collegiate Center, Medina, N.Y., instructor in English, 1936-37; Pine Manor Junior College, Wellesley, Mass., instructor in English, 1937-38; University of Michigan, Avery Hopwood Awards, Ann Arbor, secretary to director, 1939-41; State University of New York at Albany, instructor in English and speech, 1941-48, associate professor, 1948-53, professor of English and American literature, 1953-71, professor emeritus, 1971—. *Member:* Modern Language Association of America, American Studies Association, American Association of University Women, New York State Historical Association, Albany Wellesley Club, Albany Institute of History and Art, Rensselaer County Historical Society. *Awards, honors:* Avery Hopwood Award for a play, from University of Michigan, 1931; American Association of University Women fellowship, 1948-49; Guggenheim fellowship, 1956-57; summer fellowships, Research Foundation, State University of New York, 1958, 1960, and 1964.

WRITINGS: Spires of Form: A Study of Emerson's Aesthetic Theory, Harvard University Press, 1951; *Prodigal Puritan: A Life of Delia Bacon,* Harvard University Press, 1959. Contributor of articles to literature journals.

WORK IN PROGRESS: Francis Bacon in America: 1800-1865; De Witt Clinton and the Empire State.

AVOCATIONAL INTERESTS: Playing piano, photography.

* * *

HORI, Ichiro 1910-1974

PERSONAL: Born March 19, 1910, in Osaka, Japan; son of Motoo (a banker) and Fusa Hori; married Michi Yanagita. *Education:* Tokyo Imperial University, B.A., 1932, graduate study, 1932-35; University of Tokyo, Ph.D., 1953. *Home:* 631 Seijo-machi, Setagaya-ku, Tokyo, Japan.

CAREER: Former professor of history of religion at University of Tokyo and Kokugakuin University, both in Tokyo, Japan. *Member:* Japanese Association for Religious Studies (president, 1968-70), Folklore Society of Japan (director, beginning 1952), Japanese Association of Indian and Buddhist Studies (member of council). *Awards, honors:* Japan Academy Prize, 1956.

WRITINGS: Folk Religion in Japan: Continuity and Change, edited by Joseph M. Kitagawa and Alan L. Miller, University of Chicago Press, 1968. Contributor of articles to journals in Japanese and English.

WORK IN PROGRESS: Social Anxiety and the Folk Religion; research in religion and social change.†

(Died August 10, 1974)

* * *

HORNER, George F(rederick) 1899-1974

PERSONAL: Born July 16, 1899, in York, Pa.; son of William Rudolph and Henrietta (Wortz) Horner; married Elizabeth Ward, 1949. *Education:* Pennsylvania State University, B.A., 1921, M.A., 1924; Harvard University, graduate study, 1924-26; University of North Carolina, Ph.D., 1938. *Politics:* Democrat. *Religion:* Lutheran. *Home:* 408 46th Ave. N., Myrtle Beach, S.C. 29577. *Office:* Department of English, University of North Carolina at Chapel Hill, Chapel Hill, N.C. 27514.

CAREER: Pennsylvania State University, State College, instructor in English, 1921-24; University of North Carolina at Chapel Hill, 1926-74, began as instructor, became professor of English, professor emeritus, 1966-74. *Military service:* U.S. Army, 1917. U.S. Naval Reserves, 1943-45. *Member:* Modern Language Association of America, College English Association, Conference on College, Composition and Communication, South Atlantic Modern Language Association.

WRITINGS: Cooper's Pocket Handkerchief, privately printed, 1946; (with Robert N. Bain) *Colonial and Federal American Writing,* Odyssey, 1966.†

(Died, 1974)

* * *

HORNOS, Axel 1907-

PERSONAL: "H" in surname is silent; born July 3, 1907, in Buenos Aires, Argentina; became American citizen, 1958; son of Claudio B. (a diplomat) and Rosa (Valle) Hornos; married Mary A. Wassington, May 10, 1930; children: Maribel Hornos Gotzmer, Serge. *Home:* 177 Long Meadow Circle, Pittsford, N.Y. 14534.

CAREER: Eastman Kodak Co., International Markets Division, Rochester, N.Y., worked in creative advertising in several photographic areas, 1944-68. President, Association for Teen-Age Diplomats (affiliate of American Field Service), 1954, 1955, 1957.

WRITINGS: Argentina, Paraguay, and Uruguay (youth book), Thomas Nelson, 1969.

Translator into Spanish: John Hodgson Bradley, *Autobiography of the Earth,* Editorial Sudamericana (Buenos Aires), 1939; G. Russell Harrison, *Atoms in Action,* Editorial Sudamericana, 1942; David Dietz, *The History of Science,* [Buenos Aires], 1943; Jerry Mangione, *Mount Allegro,* Editorial Futuro (Buenos Aires), 1944. Contributor to *Atlantic, Saturday Review, American Mercury, Dance,* and *Rochester Democrat and Chronicle.*

WORK IN PROGRESS: Two juveniles, *Storm over the Pampas* and *Shadows in the Forest;* an adult book on Argentina, tentatively entitled *The Silver Land;* research for a book on Guidobaldo and Elisabetta di Montefeltro, Duke and Duchess of Urbino.

SIDELIGHTS: Axel Hornos was a resident of Europe for ten years, living in France, Italy, Spain, and Switzerland. He still travels a great deal in South America and Europe, mostly for research purposes. *Avocational interests:* Biography, the visual arts, classical music, sociology, world politics.

BIOGRAPHICAL/CRITICAL SOURCES: Best Sellers, August 1, 1969.††

* * *

HORROCKS, Edna M. 1908-

PERSONAL: Born June 29, 1908, in Cleveland, Ohio; daughter of Walter E. (an engineer) and Agnes (Vale) Horrocks. Education: Western Reserve University (now Case Western Reserve University), B.A., 1939, M.A., 1942; graduate study at Columbia University and University of Wisconsin. Religion: Methodist. Home: 573 Edinborough Dr., Bay Village, Ohio 44140. Office: Cleveland Board of Education, 1380 East Sixth St., Cleveland, Ohio 44114.

CAREER: Cleveland (Ohio) public schools, elementary teacher, 1928-40, assistant principal and principal, 1941-49, directing supervisor of language arts, 1949-64, director of elementary schools, beginning 1964. Instructor in reading and dramatics, Western Reserve University (now Case Western Reserve University), 1946-50. Member: National Council of Teachers of English (national elementary director), Association for Supervision and Curriculum Development, International Reading Association, Women's National Book Association, Delta Kappa Gamma.

WRITINGS: (With Matilda Bailey) Our English Language (Grades 1-6), American Book Co., 1956, 1960; (with Esther Torreson) Language Learnings (Kindergarten and Grades 1-2), American Book Co., 1956, 1960; (with Theresa Norwick) Word Study Charts and Manual, Ginn, 1958; (with Ralph Staiger, Grace Sackett, Edith Evans, and Florence Linsenmeier) Spelling (Grades 1-8), Ginn, 1965-66. Editor, "Books Too Good to Miss," Western Reserve University Press, 1953-59.

WORK IN PROGRESS: Spelling books.

AVOCATIONAL INTERESTS: Sports, travel.††

* * *

HOSKINS, Katherine (de Montalant) 1909-

PERSONAL: Born May 25, 1909, in Indian Head, Md.; daughter of Henry Ellis and Katherine (Peck) Lackey; married Albert Learnard Hoskins, November 10, 1935; children: Camilla. Education: Smith College, A.B. (honors), 1931.

CAREER: Poet. Awards, honors: Brandeis University creative arts award (citation), 1957-58; Guggenheim fellowship, 1958; Longview Award, 1958.

WRITINGS—All poetry: A Penitential Primer, Cummington Press, 1945; Villa Narcisse, Noonday Press, 1956; Out in the Open, Macmillan, 1959; Excursions, Atheneum, 1967. Has contributed both prose and poetry to Hudson Review, Sewanee Review, Yale Review, Poetry, Nation, and New Republic.

SIDELIGHTS: Katherine Hoskins' poetry has been described as "austerely excellent," and "written with precision and exactness." According to Louis Simpson, "Katherine Hoskins could write anything if she had a mind to." "The main mission Mrs. Hoskins has given herself," notes James Dickey, "is to . . . compress until the poem chokes and quivers with its own held-down violence. One can feel the strain: one reads these poems with tight jaws and the beginnings of sweat on the forehead. . . . But . . . she depends entirely too much on what might be called the wordiness of words, or on giving the initiative to words. . . . Her assumption seems to be that words themselves will do everything that needs to be done. . . . The result of her practice is a curiously bookish, heavy, pontificating diction." Laurence Lieberman agrees: "Her work offers some of the same obstacles to an impatient reader as do the poems of Thomas Hardy: lumbering, choppy meters; eccentric, hand-picked oddities of diction; unnatural syntax." He adds, however, that "these qualities are not so much overcome as made to work, in many of her good poems."

Regarding a poem included in Excursions, Lieberman writes: "It is that beautifully rare specimen of poetry, in any age, that seems to spring from a bedrock of daily experience that is but scantily explored in literature—the purely uncritical love that exists between the very old and the very young. And this is one subject Miss Hoskins has made perfectly her own." In reviewing the same volume Joel Connarroe says: "The dominant theme . . . is transience, expressed most often in terms of nostalgia for the joys of childhood. Many of the poems are about children, and these are pervaded by a kind of fairy tale imagery that soon cloys." Stafford, however, sees this concentration on the young an "engaging trend." "Mainly," he continues, "the new poems bring a certain point of view, a realization of maturity. . . ." Lieberman finds another new trend in her work. "She has learned to reveal her very rich poetic gifts," he writes, "and show them to advantage as never before, by developing a new line movement, and a new variant of form that is much closer to free verse than her previous work. . . . It would seem that formally patterned stanzas usually have a constricting effect on Miss Hoskins's line. . . . But a relatively open form frees her line, and gives her busy verbal antics a wider, more elastic field to move in. The result is that we find a new authority—even a kind of necessity—inhering in her very special vocabulary, which, in these new poems, seems to be perfectly rooted in the experience she transmits to the reader."

BIOGRAPHICAL/CRITICAL SOURCES: Yale Review, autumn, 1956, autumn, 1968; Shenandoah, summer, 1967; New York Times Book Review, June 18, 1967; Harper's, August, 1967; Poetry, December, 1967.

* * *

HOUGHTON, Neal D(oyle) 1895-

PERSONAL: Born May 8, 1895, in Putnam County, Mo.; son of William Dudley (a farmer) and Engeline (Lawson) Houghton; married Esther Mae Steele, June 26, 1915 (died May 1, 1965); married Katherine C. Sowanick, May 19, 1967; children: (first marriage) Neal D., Jr., Charles William, Virginia (Mrs. Frank R. Culhabe). Education: Northeast Missouri State Teachers College (now Northeast Missouri State University), B.S., 1921; University of Missouri, M.A., 1923; University of Illinois, Ph.D., 1927. Politics: Democrat. Home: 2134 East Sixth St., Tucson, Ariz. 85719. Office: Department of Political Science, University of Arizona, Tucson, Ariz. 85721.

CAREER: University of Illinois, Urbana, instructor in political science, 1923-25; Northeast Missouri State Teachers College (now Northeast Missouri State University), Kirksville, 1925-28, professor of political science and head of Division of Social Sciences; University of Arizona, Tucson, assistant professor, 1928-31, associate professor, 1932-36, professor of political science, beginning 1937. Visiting professor at University of Illinois, 1929, University of Missouri, 1934, University of Washington, Seattle, 1957-58, and University of Saskatchewan, 1965-66. Vice-chairman, Arizona Power Authority, 1946-55. Member: American Political Science Association (member of executive council, 1937-40), American Society of International Law, International Studies Association, American Association of University Professors, Western Political Science Association (president, 1952), Phi Beta Kappa, Phi Kappa Phi.

WRITINGS: Realities of American Government, Macmillan, 1937; (editor) *Struggle against History: U.S. Foreign Policy in an Age of Revolution,* Washington Square Press, 1968. Contributor of monographs and research articles to journals, including *International Conciliation, Background,* and *California Law Review, American Law Review, United States Law Review, American Political Science Review, Western Political Quarterly, Social Science.*

WORK IN PROGRESS: Challenges to Political Scientists in Contemporary International Politics and American Foreign Policy; other writings on foreign policy; research on aspects of the United States diplomatic recognition of governmental changes in Mexico and Central America.

*   *   *

HOWARD, Harold P.   1905-

PERSONAL: Born August 7, 1905, in Vermillion, S.D.; son of Joseph Henry (a college professor) and Mary Ellen (Lowe) Howard; married Katherine Thomas, December 26, 1926; children: Jacqueline (Mrs. R. M. Miller), Harold P., Jr. *Education:* University of South Dakota, B.A., 1925. *Politics:* Republican. *Religion:* Protestant. *Home:* 404 Main, Stickney, S.D. 57375. *Office:* Argus Printers, 21 Main, Stickney, S.D. 57375.

CAREER: News-American, Aberdeen, S.D., reporter, 1925; *Daily Republican,* Mitchell, S.D., city reporter, 1925; Associated Press, reporter in Pierre, S.D., 1926, and in Chicago, Ill., 1926-27; *Sioux City Journal,* Sioux City, Iowa, night city desk editor, 1927; partner, *Armour Chronicle,* Armour, S.D., 1928-31, *Canby News-Press,* Canby, Minn., 1931-33, and *Spencer Advocate,* Spencer, Neb., 1933-34; Argus Printers, Stickney, S.D., owner, beginning 1934.

WRITINGS: "Sacajawea," Indian Girl with Lewis and Clark, University of Oklahoma Press, 1971. Also author of numerous historical brochures.

AVOCATIONAL INTERESTS: History and travel.

*   *   *

HOWARD, Munroe   1913-1974
(Philip St. Clair)

PERSONAL: Born November 20, 1913, in New York, N.Y.; son of Philip (a physician) and Jennie (Goldberg) Horowitz; married Barbara Kraut, December 28, 1956. *Education:* Lehigh University, B.A., 1934. *Home:* 305 San Vicente Blvd., Santa Monica, Calif. 90402.

CAREER: Larrimore Ltd. (men's wear), New York, N.Y., advertising manager, 1935-36; Columbia Photograph Co., New York, N.Y., public relations director, 1936-37; Howard Emery Co. (mining), Peekskill, N.Y., president, 1939-43; Margaret Ettinger Public Relations, Los Angeles, Calif., staff member, 1943-45; Philsen Ceramics, Los Angeles, Calif., advertising and sales manager, 1945-48; Lisle Sheldon Advertising Agency, Los Angeles, Calif., account executive, 1953-54. *Awards, honors:* Freedom Foundation Award for articles on the American way of life, 1951, 1952, 1961, 1962, and annually, 1964-67.

WRITINGS: Understanding the Stock Market, Motivation Associates, 1961; *Call Me Brick,* Grove, 1967; *Run Sheep Run,* Dell, 1970; *Molly,* Dell, 1971; *Call Him Rod,* Dell, 1972. Contributor of articles and stories to periodicals, some under pseudonym Philip St. Clair.

WORK IN PROGRESS: Two novels, *Bedeviled,* and *Love in All Seasons;* two historical novels, *This Dream Will Last,* an American Revolution story, and *To the Torch,* the latter on the Napoleonic era; also writing the book for a musical play, "The Recurring Itch."

BIOGRAPHICAL/CRITICAL SOURCES: New York Times Book Review, September 17, 1967.†

(Died September 20, 1974)

*   *   *

HOWE, Helen   1905-1975

PERSONAL: Born January 11, 1905, in Boston, Mass.; daughter of Mark Antony De Wolfe (a writer) and Fanny Huntington (Quincy) Howe; married Alfred Reginald Allen (a library collection curator), May 31, 1946. *Education:* Radcliffe College, student, 1923-24. *Politics:* Democrat. *Religion:* Episcopalian. *Home:* 1158 Fifth Ave., New York, N.Y. 10029.

CAREER: Monologuist, beginning 1936, appearing throughout the United States in the character sketches she wrote; has presented one-woman shows in New York and London theaters and in supper clubs.

WRITINGS—All published by Simon & Schuster, except where noted: *The Whole Heart* (novel), 1943; *We Happy Few* (novel), 1946; *The Circle of the Day* (novel), 1950; *The Success* (novel), 1956; *Fires of Autumn* (novel), Harper, 1959; *The Gentle Americans, 1864-1900* (biography), Harper, 1965.

SIDELIGHTS: During her career as a monologuist, Helen Howe was invited twice to appear at the White House.†

(Died February 1, 1975)

*   *   *

HOWES, Royce (Bucknam)   1901-1973

PERSONAL: Born January 3, 1901, in Minneapolis, Minn.; son of George Royce (an insurance agent) and Alice (Bucknam) Howes; married Dorothy Jane Chandler, May 7, 1924 (died, 1971); children: Geoffrey, Jane (Mrs. Jerry Flint). *Education:* Studied at University of Minnesota, one year. *Home:* 141 Colorado Ave., Highland Park, Mich. 48203.

CAREER: Detroit News, Detroit, Mich., staff of business office, 1924-26; Detroit Steel Products Co., Detroit, Mich., editor of house publications, 1926-27; *Detroit Free Press,* editorial staff, 1927-66, editorial writer and columnist, 1942-55, associate editor, 1955-61, editorial director, 1961-66. Wayne State University, part-time instructor in journalism, 1931-41, 1966. *Military service:* U.S. Army, 1943-46; became lieutenant colonel; received Bronze Star, Meritorious Unit Citation, battle star. *Member:* American Society of Newspaper Editors, Detroit Historical Society, Friends of the Detroit Public Library (director, 1961-65), Detroit Fire Fighters Association (honorary member), Detroit Press Club. *Awards, honors:* Pulitzer prize for editorial writing, 1955; National Headliners Award for editorial writing, 1955.

WRITINGS—All published by Doubleday Crime Club, except as indicated: *Death on the Bridge,* 1935; *The Callao Clue,* 1936; *Night of the Garter Murder,* 1937; *Death Dupes a Lady,* 1937; *Murder at Maneuvers,* 1938; *Death Rides a Hobby,* 1939; *The Nasty Name Murders,* 1939; *The Case of* the Copy Hook Killing, Dutton, 1945; (contributor) Detroit Murders, Duell, Sloan & Pearce, 1948; Edward G. Guest (biography), Reilly & Lee, 1953. Contributor of short stories to Saturday Evening Post and other magazines.

WORK IN PROGRESS: A history of the Detroit Free Press.

AVOCATIONAL INTERESTS: Fire fighters and fire fighting.†

(Died March 18, 1973)

* * *

HSIA, Tsi-an   1916-1965

PERSONAL: Surname is pronounced Shia; born August 12, 1916, in Soochow, China; son of Ta-tung (in banking) and Yun-chih (Ho) Hsia. Education: Kuang-hua University, B.A., 1940.

CAREER: National Taiwan University, Taipei, 1950-59, began as lecturer, became professor in department of foreign languages; University of Washington, Seattle, visiting associate professor, 1959-60; University of California, Berkeley, Center for Chinese Studies, research associate linguist, 1960-65.

WRITINGS: The Gate of Darkness: Studies on the Leftist Literary Movement in China, posthumously published, University of Washington Press, 1968.

Monographs; all published by Center for Chinese Studies, University of California: Metaphor, Myth, Ritual, and the People's Commune, 1961; Enigma of the Five Martyrs, 1962; A Terminological Study of the Hsia-fang Movement, 1963; The Commune in Retreat as Evidenced in Terminology and Semantics, 1964. Editor, Wen-hsueh Tsa-chih (literary review), Taipei, 1956-60.

BIOGRAPHICAL/CRITICAL SOURCES: Hsien-tci Wen-hsueh, Number 25, July, 1965 (entire issue of this modern literature quarterly published in Taipei was devoted to Hsia's accomplishments); Yung-chiu ti huai-nien (memorial volume), published by T. A. Hsia Commemorative Volume Committee, Taipei, 1967; Nation, February 24, 1969; New York Review of Books, October 23, 1969.††

(Died February 23, 1965)

* * *

HUDSON, (Arthur) Palmer   1892-

PERSONAL: Born May 14, 1892, in Attala County, Miss.; son of William Arthur (a farmer) and Lou Garnett (Palmer) Hudson; married Grace McNulty Noah, September 12, 1916; children: William Palmer (deceased), Margaret Louise (Mrs. Almand R. Coleman), Ellen Noah (Mrs. Charles Graham). Education: University of Mississippi, B.S., 1913, M.A., 1920; University of Chicago, M.A., 1925; University of North Carolina, Ph.D., 1930. Politics: Democrat. Religion: Episcopalian. Home: Chapel Hill Nursing Home, Chapel Hill, N.C. 27514.

CAREER: High school principal in Gulfport, Miss., 1913-18, and teacher at Gulf Coast Military Academy, Gulfport, 1918-19; Oxford (Miss.) city schools, superintendent, 1919-20; University of Mississippi, Oxford, assistant professor, 1920-24, associate professor, 1924-27, professor of English, 1927-30; University of North Carolina, Chapel Hill, associate professor, 1930-35, professor of English, 1935-51, Kenan Distinguished Professor, 1951-62, professor emeritus, 1963—. Visiting summer professor, University of Florida, 1938-39.

MEMBER: Modern Language Association of America, Society of American Historians (fellow), College English Association (past director), American Folklore Society (fellow), South Atlantic Modern Language Association, North Carolina Folklore Society (past vice-president; secretary-treasurer, 1942-64; life member), Phi Beta Kappa. Awards, honors: Smith Research Prize of University of North Carolina, 1930; Rockefeller Foundation grant, 1934-35.

WRITINGS: (Editor) Specimens of Mississippi Folklore, Edwards Brothers, 1928; (editor) Humor of the Old Deep South, Macmillan, 1936, reprinted, Kennikat, 1970; Folksongs of Mississippi and Their Background, University of North Carolina Press, 1936; (with G. Herzog) Folk Tunes from Mississippi, National Service Bureau, 1937; (co-editor) The College Survey of English Literature, Harcourt, 1942; (editor with H. M. Belden) The Frank C. Brown Collection of North Carolina Folklore, Volume II: Ballads from North Carolina, Volume III: Folksongs from North Carolina, Duke University Press, 1952; (with J. T. Flanagan) Folklore in American Literature, Row, Peterson & Co., 1958; Folklore Keeps the Past Alive, University of Georgia Press, 1962; Songs of the Carolina Charter Colonists, 1663-1963, Carolina Tercentenary Commission, 1962.

Contributor to Dictionary of American History, 1940, Literary History of United States, 1948, Chambers's Encyclopaedia, Encyclopedia Americana, and Collier's Encyclopedia. Contributor to professional journals. Editor, Journal of North Carolina Folklore, 1954-64; advisory editor, Mississippi Quarterly, and Southern Folklore.

WORK IN PROGRESS: An autobiography, The Days and Works of Arthur Palmer Hudson.

SIDELIGHTS: Hudson told CA that his life has been influenced by his association with several people: two of his teachers at the University of Mississippi, his golfing friend, William Faulkner, and sociologist, Howard W. Odum, who encouraged him to collect folklore.

* * *

HUGHES, Dorothy (Berry)   1910-

PERSONAL: Born April 17, 1910, in St. Louis, Mo.; daughter of Samuel Wheeler (a realtor) and Eugenia (Berry) Hughes. Education: Barnard College, B.A., 1936; Columbia University, B.S.L.S., 1940.

CAREER: Horace Mann School, New York City, assistant librarian, 1932-40; Columbia University, New York City, assistant librarian, 1940-42; New York Public Library, New York City, assistant in cataloging office, 1942-65; writer. Member: Poetry Society of America. Awards, honors: DeWitt Award, Poetry Society of America, 1969; recipient award in literature from American Academy of Arts and Letters, and National Institute of Arts and Letters, 1973; Borestone Mountain poetry awards.

WRITINGS—Poems: The Green Loving, Scribner, 1953; The Great Victory Mosaic, University of Missouri Press, 1971.

* * *

HUGHES, (Charles James) Pennethorne   1907-1967
(C. J. Pennethorne Hughes, James Pennethorne Hughes)

PERSONAL: Born October 29, 1907, on Isle of Wight, England; son of Charles Ernest (a clergyman) and Margaret (Pennethorne) Hughes; married Bea Landauer, June 21, 1948 (died, 1962). Education: Hertford College, Oxford,

B.A. (honors in history), 1929. *Religion:* Church of England. *Home:* Blakemore Cottage, Keevil, near Trowbridge, Wiltshire, England.

CAREER: Oundle School, Peterborough, Northhamptonshire, England, history master, 1930-35; British Broadcasting Corp., London, England, staff, 1935-63, successively as talks producer, head of programming for West of England, director in Middle East, 1942-45, director in New Delhi, 1945-47, head of Eastern Service, and head of staff training; retired in 1964 to devote time to literature, occasional broadcasting for BBC, and lecturing. *Member:* American Name Society.

WRITINGS: (Under name C. J. Pennethorne Hughes) *The Nineteenth Century and the World War,* Gollancz, 1935; *While Shepheard's [sic] Watched,* Chatto & Windus, 1949; *Witchcraft,* Longmans, Green, 1952; (under name James Pennethorne Hughes) *How You Got Your Name,* Phoenix House, 1959, revised edition, 1961, Aldine, 1963; (under name James Pennethorne Hughes) *Is Thy Name Want?,* Phoenix House, 1965; *The Shell Guide to the Isle of Wight,* Faber, 1967; *Your Book of Surnames,* Faber, 1967, Transatlantic, 1968. Writer of radio and television scripts, plays, talks, and features. Contributor of short stories, poems, articles, and reviews to periodicals.

WORK IN PROGRESS: The Shell Guide to Kent.

SIDELIGHTS: Hughes was an "Oxford poet" in the twenties, contributing poetry, short stories, and reviews to magazines of the day. His writing lapsed during years with British Broadcasting Corp., but he kept up on history by constant reviewing in the field. He was regarded by the popular press ("in its undiscriminating way," says Hughes) as an expert on witchcraft and the origin of surnames. Hughes lived in a fifteenth-century cottage in the country, but visited London frequently.††

(Died November 3, 1967)

*   *   *

HUGHES, Philip   1895-1967

PERSONAL: Born May 11, 1895, Manchester, England; son of Joseph (an engineer) and Elizabeth (Gough) Hughes. *Education:* Attended St. Bede's College, Manchester, England, and Ushaw College (seminary); University of Louvain, Licencie es Sciences historiques (with the greatest distinction), 1921. *Home and office:* University of Notre Dame, Notre Dame, Ind.

CAREER: Ordained Roman Catholic priest in Diocese of Salford, England, August 8, 1920; named domestic prelate to the pope, 1957. Research work in Vatican Archives, 1921-23; College of St. Thomas, St. Paul, Minn., faculty, 1923-24; parish work in Manchester, England, 1924-31; Archdiocese of Westminster, London, England, archivist, 1931-43; duties interrupted by illness, 1943-54; University of Notre Dame, Notre Dame, Ind., professor of history, 1955-63, scholar in residence, 1963-67. *Member:* American Catholic Historical Association (president, 1966). *Awards, honors:* Docteur en Philosophie et Lettres, University of Louvain, 1956; D.Litt., National University of Ireland, 1956, Villanova University, 1957; LL.D., University of Portland, 1961, and University of Notre Dame, 1963; D.H.L., College of St. Thomas, St. Paul, Minn., and Seton Hall University, 1962.

WRITINGS: The Catholic Question, 1688-1829, Sheed (London), 1929; *A History of the Church,* three volumes, Sheed (London), 1933, 1934, 1947; *St. John Fisher,* Burns & Oates, 1935; *Meditations for Lent from St. Thomas Aqui-*

nas, Burns & Oates, 1937; *Life of Pius XI,* Burns and Oates, 1937; *The Faith in Practice,* Longmans, Green, 1937, revised edition published as *The Catholic Faith in Practice,* Dimension, 1965; *A Popular History of the Catholic Church,* Burns & Oates, 1938, new edition (with final chapter by E. E. Y. Hales) published as *A Short History of the Catholic Church,* 1967; *Rome and the Counter-Reformation in England,* Burns & Oates, 1942; *The Popes' New Order,* Burns & Oates, 1943; *The English Catholics,* Burns & Oates, 1950; *The Reformation in England,* three volumes, Hollis & Carter, 1951, 1952, 1954; *A Popular History of the Reformation,* Doubleday, 1957; *The Church in Crisis: A History of the General Councils, 325-1870,* Doubleday, 1961. Frequent contributor to *Tablet* (London), *Times Literary Supplement* (London), *Clergy Review,* and *Dublin Review.*

WORK IN PROGRESS: Europe in the Age of the Catholic Reformation (1559-1610); also, the correspondence of John Lingard (1771-1851).†

(Died October 6, 1967)

*   *   *

HUGILL, Stan(ley) James   1906-

PERSONAL: Surname rhymes with "bugle"; born November 19, 1906, in Hoylake, Cheshire, England; son of Henry James (in Royal Navy) and Florence Mary (Southwood) Hugill; married Bronwen Irene Benbow, April 2, 1963; children: Philip James, Martin John. *Education:* School of Oriental and African Studies, University of London, Diploma in Japanese, 1949. *Religion:* Church of England. *Home:* 34 Copperhill St., Aberdovey, Merionethshire, Wales.

CAREER: Seaman in sail and steam, including service with Blue Funnel Line of Liverpool, England, 1922-40; Outward Bound Sea School, Aberdovey, Merionethshire, Wales, instructor and bosun, 1950-75. Singer of sea chanties at folk concerts and for folksong groups; also recorded songs for an album, "Shanties of the Seven Seas." Anchorman on British Broadcasting Corp. television program, "Dance and Skylark," 1965-66. *Member:* Merseyside Folk Song Federation (president), Argonauts Club (Liverpool; vice-president, 1951-53). *Awards, honors:* First prize in *Seafarer* literary competition, 1937.

WRITINGS: Shanties of the Seven Seas, Dutton, 1961, 2nd edition, 1967; (self-illustrated) *Sailortown* (nonfiction), Dutton, 1967, 2nd edition, 1968; *Shanties and Sailor's Songs,* Praeger, 1969. Contributor to *Groves Dictionary of Music and Musicians.* Translator of technical materials from the Japanese, 1951-59. Monthly columnist, "Bosun's Locker," in *Spin* (Liverpool folksong magazine).

WORK IN PROGRESS: Research in folklore of the sea, origins of nauticalisms, sea superstitions, and sea songs (both naval and merchant); *Sailing Ships, Sailormen and Sealore,* for Dutton.

SIDELIGHTS: Hugill is competent in Spanish as well as in Japanese; he has studied Polynesian dialects, Maori, Malay, Chinese. During his years at sea he spent much time ashore in New Zealand, Australia, and South America. *Avocational interests:* Painting in oils.

BIOGRAPHICAL/CRITICAL SOURCES: New York Times Book Review, November 5, 1967.

HUNT, Francis
  [Collective pseudonym]

WRITINGS—"Mary and Jerry Mystery Stories" series; published by Grosset: *The Messenger Dog's Secret,* 1935; *The Mystery of the Toy Bank,* 1935; *The Story the Parrot Told,* 1935; *The Secret of the Missing Clown,* 1936; *The Mystery of the Crooked Tree,* 1937.

SIDELIGHTS: See **ADAMS, Harriet S., STRATEMEYER, Edward L.,** and **SVENSON, Andrew E.**†

* * *

HUNT, (Leslie) Gordon   1906-1970

PERSONAL: Born August 14, 1906, in East Grinstead, Sussex, England; son of Edward (an organist and musician) and Mary (Gallagher) Hunt; married Joan Brooke Thorman, 1937; married second wife, Valerie Smith Hochfelden, October 22, 1959; children: (first marriage) Simon Christopher Brooke, Jeremy John Thorman. *Education:* Educated in Tunbridge Wells, Kent, England. *Politics:* Conservative. *Religion:* Church of England. *Home:* Hunters Lodge, Seaview Rd., Port Elizabeth, South Africa. *Agent:* Epoque Ltd., 12-15 Bouverie St., London E.C.4, England. *Office address:* P.O. Box 5080, Port Elizabeth, South Africa.

CAREER: Steele Brothers, Burma, timber manager, 1927-42; Colonial Development Corp., London, England, timber manager, traveling throughout the British colonies, including Nyasaland and Swaziland, 1947-53 (largely instrumental in starting the Usutu Forest in Swaziland, claimed to be the largest contiguous man-made forest in the world); Rhodesia Congo Border Power Corp., Kitwe, Zambia, managing director, 1952-61; free-lance writer, living in Port Elizabeth, South Africa. *Military service:* British Intelligence Corps-Far East, served in India, 1942-45, and Burma, 1945-47; became lieutenant colonel. *Member:* Speical Forces Club and Junior Carlton Club (both London).

WRITINGS: *One More River,* illustrations by Victor Ambrus, Collins, 1965; *The Forgotten Land,* Bles, 1967; (contributor) *Three Great Adventure Stories,* Collins, 1969.

WORK IN PROGRESS: *Shuttered Windows,* about his army intelligence work; a novel, largely autobiographical.

SIDELIGHTS: *The Forgotten Land* describes Gordon Hunt's life in the prewar teak forests of Burma, and *One More River* is the story of his escape with nine others from the Japanese by means of an arduous trek across the mountainous divide between Burma and Yunan. Working in the Congo during the chaotic years of 1960-61, Hunt witnessed battles in the streets of Elisabethville and acted as messenger from Moise Tshombe to the world when Tshombe went into hiding in September, 1961.

BIOGRAPHICAL/CRITICAL SOURCES: *Times Literary Supplement,* December 28, 1967.††

(Died July 13, 1970)

* * *

HURLEY, Wilfred G(eoffrey)   1895-1973

PERSONAL: Born November 15, 1895, in Old Town, Me.; son of James Francis and Mary Ella (Jordan) Hurley. *Education:* Colby College, B.A., 1916; Harvard University, graduate study, 1916-18; Catholic University of America, M.A., 1924. *Home:* 611 West Boston Blvd., Detroit, Mich.

CAREER: Entered Congregatio Sancti Pauli (Paulist order), 1919, ordained priest, 1924; missionary in Portland, Ore., 1924-28; head of mission group, San Francisco, Calif., 1923-

38; rector of Old St. Mary's Church, San Francisco, Calif., 1940-45, and Santa Suzanna Church, Rome, Italy, 1945-53. *Military service:* U.S. Navy, line officer, 1917-19. *Awards, honors:* Knight commander, Order of Crown of Italy, 1946; Pro Pontifice et Ecclesia (Papal medal), 1946; Knight of Malta, 1952; Knight of the Holy Sepulchre, 1952; Knight of Grand Cross of St. Rita, 1953; Order of St. George (Britain); Legion of Honor (France); honorary LL.D., St. Mary's College of California.

WRITINGS: *The Origins of Charity,* 1927; *The Resurrection,* 1933; *I Believe!,* Paulist Press, 1935; *The Unified Gospel of Jesus,* Paulist Press, 1939; *The Creed of a Catholic,* Daughters of St. Paul, 1965; *Catholic Devotional Life,* Daughters of St. Paul, 1965. Also author of *The Catholic Way of Life,* Paulist Press, *The Ten Commandments,* Paulist Press, and other religious books.

WORK IN PROGRESS: *Facts Which Fortify the Faith;* and *Sanctity.*†

(Died September 1, 1973)

* * *

HURWITZ, Samuel J(ustin)   1912-1972

PERSONAL: Born August 23, 1912, in New York, N.Y.; son of Jacob and Celia (Feldman) Hurwitz; married Edith Farber (a teacher); children: Arthur, Shelah. *Education:* Brooklyn College (now Brooklyn College of the City University of New York), A.B., 1934; St. Lawrence University, LL.B., 1936; Columbia University, A.M., 1940, Ph.D., 1946.

CAREER: Brooklyn College of the City University of New York, Brooklyn, N.Y., beginning 1940, former professor of history. Lecturer in history, Columbia University, 1945-46; visiting professor at State Teachers College (now State University of New York College at Fredonia), 1946, New York University, 1956-57, Syracuse University, 1957-58, University of Puerto Rico, 1960-61, and University of Hawaii, 1967-69. Director of research, American Association for Social Security, New York, N.Y., 1934-35. Consultant to Prentice-Hall, Simon & Schuster, Random House, and other publishers. *Member:* American Historical Association, American Association of University Professors, Phi Beta Kappa. *Awards, honors:* Faculty fellow, Fund for the Advancement of Education, 1953-54; Fulbright fellowship to Jamaica, West Indies, 1963-64.

WRITINGS: *State Intervention in Great Britain: A Study of Economic Control and Social Response, 1914-1919,* Columbia University Press, 1949; (contributor) *Making of Modern Europe,* Dryden Press, 1951; (contributor) *Some Modern Historians of Britain,* Dryden Press, 1951; (contributor) *Making of English History,* Dryden Press, 1952; (contributor) *Comparative Education,* Dryden Press, 1952; (editor) *A History of Bolshevism,* Anchor Books, 1967; (editor and translator) G. Ferrero, *The Two French Revolutions,* Basic Books, 1968; (editor) Solomon Frank Bloom, *A Liberal in Two Worlds,* Public Affairs Press, 1968; (with wife, Edith F. Hurwitz) *Jamaica: A Historical Portrait,* Praeger, 1971. Contributor of articles to scholarly journals.

WORK IN PROGRESS: Writing on twentieth-century Britain and the Abolitionist movement in Great Britain.†

(Died, 1972)

* * *

HUSTON, Luther A.   1888-

PERSONAL: Born November 18, 1888, in Paullina, Iowa;

son of Luther Allen and Alice (Noble) Huston; married Dora Lee Carey (an interior decorator), February 15, 1929; children: Ann Noble. *Education:* University of Southern California, Los Angeles, student, three years. *Politics:* Republican. *Religion:* Episcopalian. *Home:* 111 Golf View Dr., Franklin, N.C. 28734.

CAREER: Bellingham Herald, Bellingham, Wash., reporter, 1912-14; *Seattle Times,* Seattle, Wash., reporter, later sports editor, 1914-17; International News Service, 1914-34, successively bureau manager in Chicago, Ill., assistant news manager in New York, N.Y., assistant bureau manager in London, England, Far East manager in Tokyo, Japan, and sales manager in New York, N.Y.; *Washington Post,* Washington, D.C., city editor, 1934-35; *New York Times,* New York, N.Y., Washington correspondent, 1935-57; U.S. Department of Justice, Washington, D.C., information director, 1957-61; Washington correspondent for *Editor and Publisher,* 1966-74. *Member:* National Press Club (member of board of governors, 1953-57; chairman, 1957), Sigma Delta Chi (fellow; national president, 1947-48). *Awards, honors:* George Polk Memorial Award of Long Island University, 1954, for coverage of school segregation cases before the Supreme Court; Wells Key of Sigma Delta Chi.

WRITINGS: Pathway to Judgment: A Study of Earl Warren, Chilton, 1966; *The Department of Justice,* Praeger, 1967; (with others) *Roles of the Attorney General of the United States,* American Enterprise Institute for Public Policy Research, 1968. Contributor to *American Bar Journal, Quill, New York Times Magazine,* and other journals and newspapers.

* * *

HUSZAR, George B(ernard) de 1919-19(?)

PERSONAL: Born March 15, 1919, in Bern, Switzerland; son of William and Jolanda (Kepf) de Huszar; married Barbara Esser. *Education:* Studied at University of Budapest, 1936, University of Geneva, 1937, and University of Chicago, 1938-40; Northwestern University, M.A., 1954, additional graduate study, 1955. *Politics:* Republican. *Religion:* Lutheran.

CAREER: European and Asiatic Area Study (conducted by University of Chicago and U.S. Army), staff member, 1943-44; Encyclopaedia Britannica, Inc., Chicago, Ill., in charge of development of *Encyclopaedia of International Affairs,* 1945-46; Spencer Press of Sears, Roebuck & Co., Chicago, Ill., history editor of *American Peoples Encyclopedia,* 1947-48; Northwestern University, University College, Chicago, Ill., lecturer, 1950-52; U.S. Government, research analyst and consultant, 1953-54, and 1963; Chicago City College, Loop Campus, assistant professor of political science, beginning, 1966; writer, editor, and researcher under foundation grants, 1955-62, 1964-65. *Member:* Council for Basic Education, American Association of University Professors, Chicago Press Club (charter member).

WRITINGS: (Editor and co-author) *New Perspectives on Peace,* University of Chicago Press, 1944; *Practical Applications of Democracy,* Harper, 1945; (compiler) *Anatomy of Racial Intolerance,* Wilson, 1946; (editor and co-author) *Persistent International Issues,* Harper, 1947; (compiler) *Equality in America,* Wilson, 1949; (editor) Joseph Roucek, *Introduction to Political Science,* Crowell, 1950; (with Alfred de Grazia) *An Outline of International Relations,* Barnes & Noble, 1951, 2nd edition with title *International Relations,* 1953; (with Thomas Stevenson) *Political Science,*

Littlefield, 1951, 4th edition, 1965; (editor with others) *Basic American Documents,* Littlefield, 1953; (co-author and co-editor) *Soviet Power and Policy,* Crowell, 1955; (editor) *National Strategy in an Age of Revolutions,* Praeger, 1957; (editor and co-author) *The Intellectuals,* Free Press, 1960; (editor) *Fundamentals of Voluntary Health Care,* Caxton, 1962; (editor) Frederic Bastiat, *Selected Essays on Political Economy,* Van Nostrand, 1964. Contributor to professional journals.

WORK IN PROGRESS: Philosophical and literary essays.†

(Deceased)

* * *

HUTCHISON, Chester Smith 1902-

PERSONAL: Born May 18, 1902, in Ashville, Ohio; son of Ransford Lewis (a blacksmith) and Lillie (Smith) Hutchison; married Virginia Black, June 24, 1928; children: Virginia (Mrs. Frank Bazler), Nancy (Mrs. Harold Richard). *Education:* Ohio State University, B.S., 1924, M.A., 1930. *Politics:* Republican. *Religion:* Presbyterian. *Home:* 510 Evening St., Worthington, Ohio 43085.

CAREER: West Liberty (Ohio) public schools, teacher of vocational agriculture, 1924-26, teacher and superintendent of schools, 1926-30; State Department of Education, Columbus, Ohio, district supervisor of vocational agriculture, 1930-36; Ohio State University, College of Agriculture, Columbus, assistant professor and teacher trainer, 1936-40, junior dean, 1941-47, associate dean, 1947-51, assistant dean, 1951-64. Mayor of Worthington, Ohio, 1956-57; owner and operator of farm in Ohio. Former member of Ohio Governor's Committee on Highway Safety, and of Southern Ohio Selective Service Appeal Board. Consultant to International Cooperation Administration Food and Agriculture Evaluation Panel, 1960. *Member:* Association of Land-Grant Colleges and Universities (chairman of agricultural careers committee), Ohio Vocational Association (president, 1939-40), Central Ohio School Boards Association (former president), American Rose Society (national convention chairman, 1953, 1963), Gamma Sigma Delta (former national president), Alpha Zeta, Delta Theta, Masons.

WRITINGS: Training for Service, Ohio State University Press, 1945; *Vegetable Science,* Lippincott, 1949; *Your Future in Agriculture,* Rosen, 1965. Also author of *Where Our Graduates Go,* 1964, and career pamphlets for prospective students in agriculture. Editor, *Ohio Vocational News,* 1937-38.

AVOCATIONAL INTERESTS: Young people, roses (and other gardening), photography, and conservation of soil and water.

* * *

IMMROTH, John Phillip 1936-1976

PERSONAL: Born September 30, 1936, in La Junta, Colo.; son of Phillip Andreas (a railroad official) and Margaret (Boyd) Immroth; married Barbara Froling (an indexer and librarian), November 26, 1964; children: Christopher James, Andrew Stephen. *Education:* Pueblo Junior College, A.A., 1956; University of Colorado, B.A., 1959, M.A. (English literature), 1962; University of Denver, M.A. (librarianship), 1965; University of Pittsburgh, advanced certificate in library and information science, 1969, Ph.D., 1970. *Politics:* Democrat. *Religion:* Anglican. *Home:* 513 Roslyn Pl., Pittsburgh, Pa. 15232. *Office:* Graduate School of Library and

Information Sciences, University of Pittsburgh, Pittsburgh, Pa. 15213.

CAREER: Pueblo Municipal Band, Pueblo, Colo., music librarian, summers, 1960-64; McClelland Public Library, Pueblo, library clerk, 1961-62, senior library clerk, summers, 1961-62; Tarleton State College (now University), Stephenville, Tex., instructor in speech and drama, 1962-64; University of Denver, Denver, Colo., cataloger in libraries, 1965, instructor, Graduate School of Librarianship, 1965-66; State University of New York College at Geneseo, assistant professor of library science, 1966-68; University of Pittsburgh, Graduate School of Library and Information Sciences, Pittsburgh, Pa., instructor, 1968-70, assistant professor, 1970-71, associate professor of library and information sciences, beginning 1971, assistant dean, 1971-73, coordinator of library research projects, Office of Communications Programs, 1970-71. Lecturer at institutes on librarianship and related subjects, Kent State University, 1968, University of Pittsburgh, 1969, University of Kansas, 1970, University of Maryland, 1970; speaker at state, regional and national library conferences.

MEMBER: American Library Association (chairman, Scholarship Committee, 1970-72; chairman, Library Education Division/Teachers Media Research Committee, beginning 1971), Association of College and Research Libraries, Association of American Library Schools, American Association of University Professors, Bliss Classification Society, Printing Historical Society, Pittsburgh Bibliophiles, various regional library associations. *Awards, honors:* Esther J. Piercy Award, American Library Association, 1971.

WRITINGS: A Guide to Library of Congress Classification, Libraries Unlimited 1968, 2nd edition, 1971, 3rd edition, in press; (with Jay E. Daily) *Library Cataloging: A Guide to the Basic Course,* Libraries Unlimited, 1968, 2nd edition, 1971; *An Analysis of Vocabulary Control in Library of Congress Classification and Subject Headings,* Libraries Unlimited, 1971; (compiler) *Ronald Brunlees McKerrow: Collected Essays,* Scarecrow, 1974. Also author of an unpublished dramatization of "Alice in Wonderland," 1959, and of a drama, *Kremhilde,* privately printed, 1960. Author of several syllabi for library science courses, and of four unpublished studies on literary and library topics. Contributor of articles to professional periodicals and the *Encyclopedia of Library and Information Science;* contributor of reviews to *American Reference Books Annual,* and *Reprint Bulletin.*

WORK IN PROGRESS: Editing *The Collected Essays of Ronald B. McKerrow;* two books, *A Student's Laboratory Manual for Cataloging,* and *A Reader in Descriptive Bibliography.*

SIDELIGHTS: John Phillip Immroth was interested in music and the theatre and was actively involved in college and community theatre from 1955-64. He had been a member of musical organizations since 1944, and was an accomplished flautist.†

(Died April 2, 1976)

* * *

IVAN, Martha Miller Pfaff   1909-
(Martha Miller; Gus Tavo, sometimes a joint pseudonym)

PERSONAL: Born June 11, 1909, in St. Louis, Mo.; daughter of A. G. Pfaff; married Gustave E. Ivan (a writer), March 6, 1937 (deceased). *Education:* Texas Technological College (now Texas Tech University), B.A., 1930, M.A., 1931; University of Texas, graduate study. *Religion:* Methodist. *Agent:* McIntosh & Otis, Inc., 18 East 41st St., New York, N.Y. 10017. *Office:* Kilgore College, Kilgore, Tex.

CAREER: Kilgore College, Kilgore, Tex., director of guidance, beginning 1953. *Member:* Texas Personnel and Guidance Association, Texas Junior College Teachers Association, Texas State Teachers Association. *Awards, honors:* Named best Texas author by Theta Sigma Phi, Austin Chapter, with husband, 1960, for *Hunt the Mountain Lion,* and 1963, for *The Buffalo Are Running.*

WRITINGS—With husband, Gustave E. Ivan, under joint pseudonym Gus Tavo: *Hunt the Mountain Lion,* Knopf, 1959; *The Buffalo Are Running,* Knopf, 1960; *Track the Grizzly Down,* Knopf, 1963; *Trail to Lone Canyon,* Knopf, 1964.

Sole author: (Under Martha Miller) *Timberline Hound,* Knopf, 1963; (under pseudonym Gus Tavo) *Ride the Pale Stallion,* Knopf, 1968.

WORK IN PROGRESS: Danger Stalks the Texas Hills, for publication under the Gus Tavo pseudonym.

AVOCATIONAL INTERESTS: Hunting, fishing, swimming.†

* * *

JACOBSEN, O(le) Irving   1896-

PERSONAL: Born April 2, 1896, in Dannebrog, Neb.; son of Lauritz S. (a contractor) and Marie Inger (Andersen) Jacobsen; married Marie W. Wentworth, June 10, 1928; children: Joan Marie (Mrs. Gilbert F. Bourcier). *Education:* University School of Music, Lincoln, Neb., B.Mus., 1924; University of Nebraska, B.S., 1925; University of Chicago, M.A., 1926; University of Iowa, Ph.D., 1933. *Politics:* Republican. *Religion:* Presbyterian. *Home:* 2736 North Shepard Ave., Milwaukee, Wis. 53211. *Office:* Veterans Administration Center, Wood, Wis. 53193.

CAREER: High school director of music in Elmhurst, Ill., 1933-38; Shurtleff College, Alton, Ill., head of departments of education and psychology, 1938-42; U.S. Government, Vocational Counseling Service, beginning 1946, psychologist at Veterans Administration Hospital in Wood, Wis., beginning 1957. *Military service:* U.S. Army, 1917-18, 1942-46; became major. *Member:* American Psychological Association (fellow), Sigma Xi, Phi Beta Kappa, Tau Kappa Epsilon, Phi Delta Kappa, Phi Mu Alpha, Masons, Shriners.

WRITINGS: Honor Above All (epic poems), Humphries, 1946; *The Power of Your Mind,* Parker Publishing, 1968. Contributor of about 125 articles to professional journals; has written more than one thousand reviews for *Psychological Abstracts,* including translations from Danish, Swedish, Norwegian, Finnish, German, French, Spanish, and Dutch.

WORK IN PROGRESS: A book on personality.

AVOCATIONAL INTERESTS: Gardening, music, travel, nature.

* * *

JAEGER, Edmund C(arroll)   1887-

PERSONAL: Born January 28, 1887, in Loup City, Neb.; son of John Phillip (a banker) and Catherine (Gunther) Jaeger. *Education:* Occidental College, B.Sc., 1918; graduate study at Pomona College and University of California, 1922-23, and University of Colorado, 1924. *Home:* 4464 Sixth St., Riverside, Calif. 92501.

CAREER: Riverside City College, Riverside, Calif., teacher of biology and zoology and head of department of zoology, 1921-53; Riverside Municipal Museum, Riverside, curator of plants, beginning 1953. *Member:* American Society of Mammalogists, American Ornithological Union, American Nature Study Society, Nature Conservancy, Desert Protective Council, Cooper Ornithological Society, California Botanical Society, Southern California Botanists, Phi Beta Kappa, Sigma Xi. *Awards, honors:* D.Sc., Occidental College, 1953; LL.D., University of California, 1967.

WRITINGS: Mountain Trees of Southern California, Star-News Publishing, 1919; *Denizens of the Desert,* Houghton, 1922; *Denizens of the Mountains,* C. C Thomas, 1929; *The California Deserts,* Stanford University Press, 1933, 4th edition, 1965; *Desert Wild Flowers,* Stanford University Press, 1940, revised edition, 1958; *A Sourcebook of Biological Names and Terms,* C. C Thomas, 1944, 3rd edition, 1959; *Our Desert Neighbors,* Stanford University Press, 1950; *Desert Wildlife,* Stanford University Press, 1950, 2nd edition, 1961; *Sourcebook of Medical Terms,* C. C Thomas, 1953; *A Naturalist's Death Valley,* Desert Magazine Press, 1957; *The North American Deserts,* Stanford University Press, 1957; *The Biologist's Handbook of Pronunciations,* C. C Thomas, 1960; (with Arthur C. Smith) *Introduction to the Natural History of Southern California,* University of California Press, 1966. Author of monthly articles for *Desert* magazine, 1956-65; contributor to other periodicals, including *Pacific Discovery, National Geographic,* and *Paisano.*

SIDELIGHTS: Jaeger has spent much time in North American deserts, with other extensive travels in Europe, Mexico, Australia, New Zealand, and Africa (southwest and south part of continent). He is the discoverer of the phenomenon of hibernation in birds.

*   *   *

JAGGARD, Geoffrey (William)   1902-1970

PERSONAL: Born March 31, 1902, in Liverpool, Lancashire, England; son of William (a Shakespeare bibliographer) and Emma Frances (Cook) Jaggard; married Dorothy Lilian Sleath, 1928; children: Rosalind Vallia (Mrs. David Maxwell Turner), Timothy Swithun. *Education:* Attended King Edward VI School, Stratford on Avon, 1910-20. *Home:* 8, The Parade, Court Rd., Brockworth, Gloucestershire, England.

CAREER: Leicester Mercury, Leicestershire, England, sub-editor, 1923-25; *Liverpool Daily Post & Echo,* Liverpool, England, leader-writer and drama critic, 1925-39; British Forces, Headquarters of Southern Command, public relations officer (as civilian), 1939-45, deputy assistant director of public relations, 1942-45; United Nations Relief and Rehabilitation Administration, chief information officer, British Zone of Germany, 1945-47; British Broadcasting Corp., London, England, news editor, 1947-50; London Airport, London, England, chief public relations officer, 1950-54; head of public relations at Associated Rediffusion Television, 1954-56. British Broadcasting Corp., occasional broadcaster and script writer, beginning 1945, regular member of "Round Britain Quiz" panel, beginning 1961. Co-director, Shakespeare Quatercentenary Exhibition, London, 1964.

WRITINGS: Companion to Stratford: Shakespeare's Town as He Knew It, Shakespeare Press, 1964; *Wooster's World: A Companion to the Wooster-Jeeves Saga of P. G. Wodehouse, LL.D.,* Macdonald & Co., 1967; *Blandings the*

Blest and the Blue Blood: A Companion to the Blandings Castle Saga of P. G. Wodehouse, LL.D., Macdonald & Co., 1968. "The Magnetic South," an ecological and sociological survey of southern England, for Southern Television Ltd.

SIDELIGHTS: Jaggard was a descendant of William Jaggard I, printer and publisher of Shakespeare's First Folio, 1623. Jaggard has catalogued, in *Wooster's World,* the characters, places, and animals of the Jeeves stories. Wilfred De'Ath believes that one of the best things about the book is "a complete peerage, baronetage, and knightage which assembles for the first time all of Wodehouse's titled characters, among them some of his finest creations." *The Books and Bookmen* reviewer called this volume a "delightful bedside book. One can dip into it anywhere and pull out a plum."

BIOGRAPHICAL/CRITICAL SOURCES: Books and Bookmen, November, 1967, December, 1968.†

(Died January, 1970)

*   *   *

JARMAN, Cosette C(otterell)   1909-

PERSONAL: Born February 18, 1909, in Dunedin, New Zealand; daughter of Samuel (a clergyman) and Gertrude Ann (Cotterell) Bailey; married Frederick Walter Jarman (a government draughtsman), December 23, 1943; children: Christopher John Bailey. *Education:* Educated at public and private schools in New Zealand, and at nurses' training school. *Religion:* Methodist. *Home:* The Muse, 254 The Parade, Wellington S.2, New Zealand. *Agent:* Curtis Brown Ltd., 1 Craven Hill, London W2 3EW, England.

CAREER: Former professional nurse in New Zealand, and sometime elocution and vocal tutor. Member of broadcasting staff, 1942-45. *Member:* New Zealand Women Writers.

WRITINGS: Tomorrow Comes the Song (nonfiction), A. H. & A. W. Reed, 1965. Also author of *Said the Robin to the Sparrow.*

SIDELIGHTS: Tomorrow Comes the Song, the story of her musical son, Christopher, who suffered from encephalitis, was serialized in Britain in the magazine *Annabel.* She has written the lyrics for a number of her son's compositions.†

*   *   *

JAYNES, Ruth   1899-

PERSONAL: Born October 17, 1899, in Santa Ana, Calif.; daughter of William Henry (a businessman) and Addie May (Boxley) Barry; married Joseph Jaynes, March 2, 1920; children: Alverta (Mrs. Paul G. Williamson). *Education:* Studied at University of Southern California, 1917, 1942, 1950; University of California, Los Angeles, California Teaching Credential, 1929; Los Angeles State College (now California State University, Los Angeles), B.A. and M.A. *Politics:* Republican. *Religion:* Protestant. *Home:* 2895 East Sierra Dr., Westlake Village, Calif. 91361. *Office:* 7120 Hayvenhurst St., Van Nuys, Calif.

CAREER: Board of Education, Los Angeles, Calif., elementary teacher, 1929-50, academic consultant, 1950-53, academic supervisor, 1953-65; California State University, Northridge, Office of Economic Opportunity training counselor, beginning 1965. *Member:* Delta Kappa Gamma.

WRITINGS—All for children; all published by Lawrence

Publishing: *Yo-Ho and Kim,* 1965; *Yo-Ho and Kim at Sea,* 1965. Also author of *Yo-Ho and Kim in Hidden Valley,* and *Yo-Ho and Kim on Vacation.*

General editor, "Bowmar Early Childhood" series, thirty books, Bowmar Publishing, 1965-68; author of teacher's manual and the following books in series: *Do You Know What . . .?,* 1967; *What Is a Birthday Child?,* 1967; *Friends! Friends! Friends!,* 1967; *Watch Me Outdoors,* 1967; *Watch Me Indoors,* 1967; *Benny's Four Hats,* 1967; *Where Is Whiffen?,* 1967; *Three Baby Chicks,* 1967; *The Biggest House,* 1968; *My Tricycle and I,* 1968; *Melinda's Christmas Stocking,* 1968; *A Box Tied with a Red Ribbon,* 1968; *Tell Me Please! What's That?,* 1968; *That's What It Is!,* 1968. Also author of study guide for "Fifty Stars and Thirteen Stripes," produced by Sigma Educational Films.†

* * *

JELLICOE, Sidney 1906-1973

PERSONAL: Born August 25, 1906, in Liverpool, England; son of William (a business manager) and Marianne (Turner) Jellicoe; married Winifred Charlesworth, August 26, 1939; children: Andrea, Ruth. *Education:* Educated at Liverpool Institute and St. Chad's College, Durham, England; University of Durham, B.A. (with honors), 1933, M.A., 1936, B.D., 1944. *Home and office:* Faculty of Theology, Bishop's University, Lennoxville, Quebec, Canada J0B 1Z0.

CAREER: Ordained a deacon, 1933, and Anglican priest, 1934; curate of Pocklington, Diocese of York, England, 1933-37; Sheffield Cathedral, Sheffield, England, percentor, 1937-39; Vicar of Sherburn-in-Elmet, Yorkshire, England, 1939-40; priest-in-charge of New Maltby and private chaplain to Earl of Scarbrough, K. G., Sandbeck, Yorkshire, England, 1940-44; Diocesan Inspector of Schools, Sheffield, England, 1941-44; Bishop Otter College, Chichester, England, chaplain and senior lecturer in divinity, 1944-52; examiner, University of Reading and Associated Training Colleges, Reading, England, 1945-52; Bishop's University, Lennoxville, Quebec, Harrold Professor of Divinity and dean of Faculty of Theology, 1952-71, dean emeritus, 1971-73, chairman, Division of Graduate Studies and Research, 1971-73. Member of General Synod of Anglican Church of Canada, 1955-61. Grinfield Lecturer on the Septuagint, University of Oxford, Oxford, England, 1969-73.

MEMBER: Society for Old Testament Study, Studiorum Novi Testamenti Societas (director, Permanent International Seminar on Greek New Testament and Septuagint, 1969-73), Society of Biblical Literature, American Textual Criticism Seminar, Humanities Association of Canada, Canadian Theological Society, Canadian Society of Biblical Studies, Society for the Scientific Study of Religion, International Organization for Septuagint and Cognate Studies (member of executive committee, 1968-73). *Awards, honors:* D.D., Montreal Diocesan Theological College, McGill University, 1955; Canada Council award for manuscript research in European libraries, 1967, and renewed for same and for study tour of Palestine, 1969; D.C.L., Bishop's University, Lennoxville, 1970.

WRITINGS: The Septuagint and Modern Study, Clarendon Press, 1968; (with Sebastian Brock and Charles T. Fritsch) *A Classified Bibliography of the Septuagint,* E. J. Brill, 1972; (contributor) *Wort, Lied und Gottesspruch,* Echter Verlag (Wuerzburg), 1972; (editor) *Studies in the Septuagint,* Ktav, 1973. Contributor of articles to *Journal of Theological Studies* (Oxford), *New Testament Studies* (Cambridge), *Expository Times* (Edinburgh), *Journal of Bib-*

lical Literature, Journal of the American Oriental Society, Catholic Biblical Quarterly, Jewish Quarterly Review, Textus, and other religious journals. Member of editorial board, *Arbeiten zur Literatur and Geschichte des hellenistischen Judentums* (Muenster), 1969-73; editor and contributor, *Bulletin* of the International Organization for Septuagint and Cognate Studies.

WORK IN PROGRESS: Research on the origins and transmission history of the Old Testament in Greek.

SIDELIGHTS: Sidney Jellicoe was interested in comparative semitic philology and cultural anthropology. He had a knowledge of modern German and French, ancient Greek, Latin, Hebrew, Arabic, and Syriac. *Avocational interests:* Music, and history of railways, travel.†

(Died November, 1973)

* * *

JENKINS, Frances Briggs 1905-

PERSONAL: Born October 15, 1905, in San Diego, Calif.; daughter of Edwin Cary and Theresa (Giehl) Briggs; married Hilerd Westley Jenkins (a physician), July 8, 1939 (deceased). *Education:* University of Illinois, B.S., 1926, Ph.D., 1937; Tulane University, M.S., 1928; University of California, Berkeley, B.L.S., 1947; Columbia University, graduate study, 1951. *Home:* 2410 Albatross St., Apt. 11, San Diego, Calif. 92101.

CAREER: University of Tennessee, Knoxville, assistant biochemist in Agricultural Experiment Station, 1928-29; University of Illinois, College of Medicine, Chicago, instructor in department of biological chemistry, 1929-41; U.S. Navy, Eleventh District Headquarters, San Diego, Calif., supervisor in communications office, 1941-43; University of California Library, Berkeley, head of science reference service, 1947-49, acting head of branch libraries, 1949-51; University of Illinois, Graduate School of Library Science, associate professor, 1951-57, professor of library science, 1957-71, professor emeritus, 1971—. *Military service:* U.S. Naval Reserve, 1944-46; became lieutenant.

MEMBER: American Library Association (council member, 1954-57, 1963-69; executive board member, 1965-69), American Chemical Society, Medical Library Association, Special Libraries Association, Catholic Daughters of America, National Audubon Society, Native Daughters of the Golden West, Zoological Society of San Diego, Sigma Xi, Beta Phi Mu, Sigma Delta Epsilon. *Awards, honors:* Isadore Gilbert Mudge Citation of the American Library Association, 1966.

WRITINGS: Science Reference Sources, Illini Union, 1956, 5th edition, M.I.T. Press, 1969; (editor with Robert Bingham Downs) *Bibliography: Current State and Future Trends,* University of Illinois Press, 1967. Member of editorial staff, "ACRL Monograph" series, 1952-60; member of publication board, *Library Trends,* 1955-71, and American Library Association, 1968-69.

* * *

JENSEN, Ad(olph) E. 1899-1965

PERSONAL: Born January 1, 1899, in Kiel, Germany; son of Peder and Margarete (Hansen) Jensen; married Elisabeth Pauli, July 24, 1952; children: Ellinor (Mrs. Kurt Hoffman). *Education:* University of Kiel and Bonn, Dr.Phil., 1922; University of Frankfort am Main, Dr.phil. habil., 1933. *Religion:* Evangelical Lutheran. *Home:* Schulstrasse 15, Mammolshain (Taunus), Germany. *Office:* Frobenius-Institut, Liebigstrasse, 41, Frankfort am Main, Germany.

CAREER: Forschungsinstitut fuer Kulturmorphologie, Frankfort am Main, Germany, research assistant; Staedtisches Museum fuer Voelkerkunde, Frankfort am Main, director, beginning 1945; Johann Wolfgang Goethe Universitaet, Frankfort am Main, Germany, professor and chairman of the department of anthropology, beginning 1946. *Military service:* German Unteroffizier, E.K. II. Klasse. *Honorary member:* Royal Anthropological Institute (London), Anthropologische Gesellschaft Wien. *Awards, honors:* Commandeur de l'Ordre National du Senegal.

WRITINGS: (Editor) *Im Lande des Gada,* Strecker & Schroeder, 1936; (editor) *Hainuwele,* Klostermann, 1939; *Die drei Stroeme,* Harrassowitz, 1948; *Das religioese Weltbild einer fruehen Kultur,* August Schroeder, 1948; *Mythos und Kult bei Naturvoelkern,* Franz Steiner, 1951 published as *Myth and Cult among Primitive Peoples,* University of Chicago Press, 1963; (editor) *Altvoelker Sued-Aethiopiens,* Kohlhammer, 1958; *Die getoetete Gottheit,* Kohlhammer, 1966.

SIDELIGHTS: Jensen made expeditions to South Africa, Tripoli, Ethiopia, Moluccas and Dutch New Guinea.†

(Died, 1965)

* * *

JENSEN, Pauline Marie (Long) 1900-
(Ann Marie Long)

PERSONAL: Born January 21, 1900, in Gretna, Neb.; daughter of Albert Newton (a grain dealer) and Mary LaVinia (Manley) Long; married Dewey Martin Jensen (semiretired and a credit consultant), August 12, 1924; children: Jeanne Marie (Mrs. Jack R. Cagle, Jr.), Marilynn Ann. *Education:* Attended public schools in Nebraska, and studied creative writing at University of Minnesota, 1955-56. *Politics:* Republican. *Religion:* Episcopalian. *Home:* 5220 Abbott Ave., South, Minneapolis, Minn. 55410.

CAREER: Free-lance writer. Young Women's Christian Association, Minneapolis, Minn., teacher of creative writing, 1962-64. Girl Scouts of America, former district chairman, Brentwood, Mo., and member of Minneapolis board of directors, 1949-53. *Member:* National League of American Pen Women (Minnesota branch president, 1964-66), Minnesota Authors' Guild. *Awards, honors:* Writer's Award, Minnesota Authors' Guild, 1961, 1962.

WRITINGS: Out of House and Home, Bobbs-Merrill, 1965; *Thicker than Water,* Bobbs-Merrill, 1966. Has sold about 150 stories and articles to magazines, with one of the stories anthologized in *Teen-Age Tales,* Heath, 1959, and an article, "Little Smidgeons," syndicated by *Guideposts* to U.S. newspapers and published in Thai and Chinese editions of the magazine; work has appeared in *Parents', Jack and Jill, National Humane Review, Wildlife, Wee Wisdom, Popular Gardening,* and other magazines.

WORK IN PROGRESS: Two juvenile books—a mystery for teen-agers, and a story about an American-Mexican boy and his pet burro.

SIDELIGHTS: Pauline Jensen chose a particular era, 1914-18, in which to set her books, because she feels that period has been somewhat neglected by writers. *Avocational interests:* Nature and animals; politics and religions.††

* * *

JOHNSON, Olga Weydemeyer 1901-
PERSONAL: Born August 19, 1901, in Tortine, Mont.; daughter of H. P. (a rancher) and Margaret (Campbell) Johnson; married Peter W. Johnson, April, 1941 (deceased). *Education:* Montana State University, B.S., 1925. *Religion:* No affiliation. *Home:* 3168 Williams Hwy., Grants Pass, Ore. 97526.

WRITINGS: (Editor) *The Story of the Tobacco Plains Country,* privately printed, 1950; *Early Libby and Troy, Montana,* privately printed, 1958; *Bears in the Rockies,* privately printed, 1960; *Flathead and Kootenay: The Rivers, the Tribes and the Region's Traders,* Arthur Clark, 1969. Contributor to newspapers in Spokane, Wash., and Great Falls, Mont.

AVOCATIONAL INTERESTS: Gardening, wilderness conservation.

* * *

JOHNSON, Virginia 1914-1975
(Jinna Johnson)

PERSONAL: Born April 17, 1914, in Moline, Ill.; daughter of Edward Herman (a patternmaker) and Alma (Arnold) Wellnitz; married Bert Johnson (president of an engineering company), May 2, 1936; children: Alan, Bruce. *Education:* Studied at Augustana College, Rock Island, Ill. *Politics:* Republican. *Religion:* Lutheran. *Home:* 706 Third St.A, Moline, Ill. 61265.

WRITINGS—Under pseudonym Jinna Johnson: *A Thousand Petals* (haiku), Tuttle, 1971.

WORK IN PROGRESS: Two books of Japanese-style poetry; a third book of poetry concerning Japanese customs; research on Gypsy culture for a fourth book of poetry; research on Eskimo culture for a self-illustrated children's book.†

(Died June 6, 1975)

* * *

JOHNSTON, Bernice Houle 1914-1971
PERSONAL: Born July 4, 1914, in Winona, Mich.; daughter of Thomas (a laborer) and Sarah (Meville) Houle; married Ray A. Johnston (associated with financial investment funds), October 30, 1939; children: Douglas R., Gordon P. *Education:* Attended public schools in Detroit, Mich. *Home:* 1212 East Hedrick Dr., Tucson, Ariz. 85719. *Office:* Arizona State Museum, University of Arizona, Tucson, Ariz. 85721.

CAREER: Worked as a typist and stenographer for a radio station and various firms in Detroit, Mich., 1933-42; Arizona State Museum, Tucson, museum assistant, 1963-71. *Member:* National Federation of Press Women; Arizona Press Women; Arizona Archaeological and Historical Society. *Awards, honors:* Awards from Arizona Press Women, annually, 1965-70; Arizona Newspaper Association Award, 1970, for best column entry; first place for public relations material, National Federation of Press Women, 1970; first place awards from Arizona Press Women and National Federation of Press Women, both 1971, for *The Seri Indians.*

WRITINGS: Speaking of Indians, University of Arizona Press, 1970; *The Seri Indians,* Arizona State Museum, 1970. Author of weekly column "Museum Piece," in *Arizona Daily Star,* 1963-71. Contributor to *Kiva, Arizona Highways, Desert Magazine,* and other magazines. Bulletin editor, Tucson Gem and Mineral Society.

SIDELIGHTS: Clara Lee Tanner of the University of Arizona said of Bernice Johnston's work: "Most significant among her writings was Mrs. Johnston's weekly column . . . titled 'Museum Piece'. . . . It dealt with a multitude of subjects and usually centered on an object in the Arizona State Museum collection. Each object was interpreted in a factual but delightfully appealing manner, with her writing often punctuated with sparkling humor. Much research went into each of these writings, for Mrs. Johnston had no formal training in either Anthropology or museum work."†

(Died December 23, 1971)

* * *

JOHNSTON, (William) Denis 1901-

PERSONAL: Born June 18, 1901, in Dublin, Ireland; son of William John (a judge of the Supreme Court) and Kathleen (King) Johnston; married Shelah Kathleen Richards, 1928 (divorced); married Betty Chancellor, 1945; children: (first marriage) one son, one daughter; (second marriage) two sons. *Education:* Educated at St. Andrew's College, Dublin, Ireland, and Merchiston Castle, Edinburgh, Scotland; attended Harvard University Law School, 1923-24; Christ's College, Cambridge, M.A., 1926, LL.M., 1926. *Home:* 8 Sorrento Ter., Dalkey County, Dublin, Ireland.

CAREER: Barrister-at-law, Inner Temple and King's Inns, 1925, and Northern Ireland, 1926; Dublin Gate Theatre, Dublin, Ireland, director, 1931-36; British Broadcasting Corp., London, England, staff member, 1936-47, as war correspondent in Middle East, Italy, France, and Germany, 1942-45, and program director of Television Service, 1946-47; Provincetown Playhouse, Provincetown, Mass., director, 1952; Mount Holyoke College, South Hadley, Mass., professor of English, 1950-60; Smith College, Northampton, Mass., head of theater department, 1961-66; visiting professor at Amherst College, Amherst, Mass., 1966-67, University of Iowa, Iowa City, 1967-68, University of California, Davis, 1970-71; New York University, New York City, Berg Professor, 1971-72; Whitman College, Walla Walla, Wash., Arnold Professor, 1972-73. *Member:* Royal Irish Yacht Club. *Awards, honors:* Mentioned in dispatches and recipient of Order of the British Empire for work as war correspondent; Guggenheim fellowship, 1955.

WRITINGS: Nine Rivers from Jordan (autobiography), Verschoyle, 1953, Little, Brown, 1955; *In Search of Swift* (biography), Hodges & Figgis (Dublin), 1959; *John Millington Synge* (biography), Columbia University Press, 1965; *The Brazen Horn* (autobiography), privately printed, 1968, Humanities, 1976.

Published plays: *The Moon in the Yellow River* [and] *The Old Lady Says "No!"*, J. Cape, 1932; *The Moon in the Yellow River* (acting version), Samuel French, 1933, included in *Three Irish Playwrights*, Penguin, 1959; *Storm Song* [and] *A Bride for the Unicorn*, J. Cape, 1935; *The Golden Cuckoo, and Other Plays*, J. Cape, 1954; *Collected Plays*, two volumes, J. Cape, 1960, published as *The Old Lady Says "No!", and Other Plays*, Little, Brown, 1961.

Plays in order of production: "The Old Lady Says 'No!'," 1929; "The Moon in the Yellow River," 1931; "A Bride for the Unicorn," 1933; "Storm Song," 1934; "Blind Man's Buff," 1936; "The Golden Cuckoo," 1938; "Weep for the Cyclops," 1938, revived in 1946 as "The Dreaming Dust"; "A Fourth for Bridge," 1948; "Strange Occurence on Ireland's Eye," 1956; "The Scythe and the Sunset," 1958; "Ulysses in Nighttown" (adaptation of parts of *Ulysses* by James Joyce), 1958; "Finnegan's Wake" (adaptation of the novel by James Joyce), 1959.

Radio plays: "Death at Newtownstewart," 1937; "Lillibulero," 1937; "Weep for Polyphemus," 1938; "Nansen of the 'Fram,'" 1940; "The Gorgeous Lady Blessington," 1941; "The Autobiography of Mark Twain," 1941; "Abraham Lincoln," 1941; "In the Train," 1946; "Verdict of the Court" series, 1960.

Television plays: "The Last Voyage of Captain Grant," 1938; "The Parnell Commission," 1939; "Weep for the Cyclops," 1946; "The Unthinking Lobster," 1948.

Screenplays: "Guest of the Nation," 1933; "River of Unrest," 1937; "Ourselves Alone," 1937. Librettist for operatic version of Pirandello's "Six Characters in Search of an Author," with score by Hugo Weisgall, published by T. Presser, 1957; librettist for "Nine Rivers from Jordan," score by Weisgall.

AVOCATIONAL INTERESTS: Sailing.

* * *

JOHNSTON, H(ugh) A(nthony) S(tephen) 1913-1967 (A Fighter Pilot, Hugh Sturton)

PERSONAL: Born December 7, 1913, in Belfast, Northern Ireland; son of James (in Indian Civil Service) and Edith Alma (Sturton) Johnston; married Berrice Jacqueline Lincoln, October 3, 1942; children: Carolyn, Robin (son). *Education:* Brasenose College, Oxford, B.A., 1935, M.A., 1943. *Home:* 40 Middleway, London N.W. 11, England.

CAREER: H.M. Overseas Civil Service, various posts in Nigeria, 1936-40, 1945-60, including deputy governor, 1960; Overseas Services Resettlement Bureau, London, England, director, 1961-65; City Parochial Foundation (charitable organization), London, England, chief executive, 1965-67. *Military service:* Royal Air Force, pilot, 1940-45; commanded a flight in the American Eagle Squadron, 1941-42; shot down over Malta in 1942 and wounded; became wing commander; received Distinguished Flying Cross and bar. *Member:* Royal Commonwealth Society, East India Sports Club (London). *Awards, honors:* Companion of St. Michael and St. George, 1959; Officer of Order of the British Empire, 1964.

WRITINGS: (Under pseudonym A Fighter Pilot) *Tattered Battlements*, P. Davies, 1943; (editor and translator) *A Selection of Hausa Stories*, Clarendon Press, 1966; (under pseudonym Hugh Sturton) *Zomo the Rabbit* (children's book), Atheneum, 1966; *The Fulani Empire of Sokoto*, Oxford University Press, 1967.††

(Died December 9, 1967)

* * *

JONES, Cyril Meredith 1904-

PERSONAL: Born April 17, 1904, in Newport, Monmouthshire, Wales; son of James Meredith (a Baptist minister) and Alice (Hughes) Jones; married Jane Humphrys, August 30, 1940; children: Ann Jones Klassen, Ronald Hugh Meredith, Alice Meredith. *Education:* University College of South Wales and Monmouthshire, B.A. (first class honors), 1924, M.A., 1927; Sorbonne, University of Paris, Docteur de l'Universite de Paris (mention tres honorable), 1936. *Politics:* Liberal. *Home:* 347 Niagara St., Winnipeg, Manitoba, Canada. *Office:* University of Manitoba, Winnipeg, Manitoba, Canada.

CAREER: Brecon High School, Brecon, Wales, senior French master, 1925-28; University of Manitoba, Winnipeg, lecturer, 1928-32, assistant professor, 1932-41, associate professor, 1941-43, professor of French and head of department, 1943-72, professor emeritus, 1972—, chairman of Division of Modern Languages, 1963-72, director of Evening Institute, 1934-54. Member of Council of Defence Associations of Canada, 1958-64. Chairman, Manitoba French Curriculum and Examination Committees, for twenty years. *Military service:* Canadian Army, Intelligence Corps Reserve; became lieutenant colonel.

MEMBER: Modern Language Association, Canadian Humanities Association, Canadian Association of University Teachers of French (president, 1964-66), Mediaeval Academy of America, Council for Western Canadian Studies (member of executive committee), Canadian Military Intelligence Association (president, 1962-64), Alliance Francaise. *Awards, honors:* American Council of Learned Societies fellow, 1933; Royal Society of Canada fellow, 1953-54; Canada Council fellow, 1960.

WRITINGS: La Chronique du pseudo-Turpin, Droz, 1937, reprinted, Slatkine (Geneva), 1973; (contributor) R. C. Lodge, editor, *Manitoba Essays,* Macmillan, 1937; (general editor) *En Avant,* Ryerson Press, 1950; (contributor) *Thought from the Learned Societies of Canada,* Gage, 1961; (reviser) K. L. O'Brien and M. S. La France, *Junior French,* Ginn, 1961; (with O'Brien and La France) *Senior French,* Gill, 1963; (with C.A.E. Jensen) *Les Lettres en France,* Macmillan, 1967. Contributor of articles and reviews to *Culture, Speculum, Canadian Bookman, Manitoba Arts Review, Modern Language Journal,* and other journals. Founder and chairman of editorial board, *Mosaic* (quarterly review), University of Manitoba Press, beginning 1966; member of advisory committee on publications, *Francais International* (Montreal).

* * *

JONES, Emlyn (David)   1912-1975

PERSONAL: Born November 27, 1912, in Seattle, Wash.; son of David and Anna (Gabriel) Jones; married Gertrude Ey, August 4, 1941; children: Gregory, Monica. *Education:* Western Washington State College, student, 1930-33; University of Washington, Seattle, B.A., 1936; Stanford University, M.A., 1942, Ph.D., 1953. *Politics:* Independent. *Religion:* Christian. *Home address:* P.O. Box 98, Auburn, Wash. 98002.

CAREER: Elementary teacher in Selleck and Woodinville, Wash., 1937-40; Seattle (Wash.) public schools, high school teacher and department head, 1945-49, director of social studies, 1950-60; University of Wisconsin—Madison, professor of history of education, 1960-65; Green River College, Auburn, Wash., professor and chairman of Division of History and Social Sciences, beginning 1965. Visiting summer instructor at Stanford University, 1953, University of Maine, 1955, 1957, Seattle University, 1960, University of Hawaii, 1966, Western Washington State College, 1965-68. Adviser to Hoover Commission, 1949-52, and Educational Policies Commission, 1956-59. *Military service:* U.S. Naval Reserve, active duty, 1942-45; became lieutenant commander; received four battle stars.

MEMBER: National Council for the Social Studies (president, 1961), National Education Association, American Historical Association, Washington State Social Studies Council, Puget Sound Council for the Social Studies (honorary life member), North Cascades Conservation Council.

WRITINGS: Our Washington, Cascade Pacific, 1950; *We Live in Washington,* Cascade Pacific, 1954; *Beyond Our Borders,* Rand McNally, 1956; *Beyond the Oceans,* Rand

McNally, 1959; *Within Our Borders,* Rand McNally, 1961; *Exploring the Northwest,* Follett, 1962, revised edition, 1967; *Within the Americas,* Rand McNally, 1962; *America de Todos,* Rand McNally, 1962. Contributor to professional journals. Editor, Scholastic and Civic Education Service Publications, 1959-64; consulting editor, United World Films, 1960-69, and McGraw-Hill Text Films, 1964-66; advisory editor, Universal Education and Visual Arts, 1966-70.

AVOCATIONAL INTERESTS: Photography, hunting, fishing, hiking.†

(Died March 26, 1975)

* * *

JONES, J(ohn) Ithel   1911-

PERSONAL: Middle name is pronounced with a short "I"; born January 1, 1911, in Merthyr Tydfil, Wales; son of David and Elizabeth Catherine (Jones) Jones; married Hannah Mary Rees, September 6, 1938. *Education:* University College of South Wales and Monmouthshire, B.A. (summa cum laude), 1933; South Wales Baptist College, B.D., 1936, M.A., 1946. *Home:* 54 Richmond Rd., Cardiff, Wales. *Office:* Office of the Principal, South Wales Baptist College, Cardiff, Wales.

CAREER: Baptist clergyman; minister in Porthcawl, Wales, 1936-40, Bristol, England, 1940-50, and London, England, 1950-58; South Wales Baptist College, Cardiff, principal and professor of theology and the philosophy of religion, beginning 1958. Dean of divinity, University of Wales, Cardiff, 1964-67; visiting professor, Baptist Seminary, Ruschlikon-Zurich, 1969. Gay Lecturer, Southern Baptist Seminary, Louisville, Ky., 1965; lecturer and preacher on several tours in United States, and in Australia and New Zealand, 1968. Moderator, Free Church Council of England and Wales; president, Baptist Union of Great Britain and Ireland, 1967-68. *Awards, honors:* D.D. from Eastern Baptist Theological Seminary, Philadelphia; LL.D. from Baylor University.

WRITINGS: (Contributor) *New Bible Commentary,* Inter-Varsity Fellowship, 1953; *Temple and Town,* Carey Kingsgate Press, 1961; *The Holy Spirit and Christian Preaching,* Epworth, 1967; *Facing the New World,* Word Books, 1968.††

* * *

JORDAN, Clarence L(eonard)   1912-1969

PERSONAL: Born July 29, 1912, in Talbotton, Ga.; son of James Weaver (a merchant) and Maude (Jossey) Jordan; married Florence Kroeger, July 21, 1936; children: Eleanor (Mrs. Mufit Kesim), James, Janet (Mrs. Farrel Zehr), Frank. *Education:* University of Georgia, B.S., 1933; Southern Baptist Theological Seminary, M.Th., 1936, Ph.D., 1939. *Home and office:* Koinonia Farm, Americus, Ga. 31709.

CAREER: Southern Baptist minister. Koinonia Farm (integrated colony of negroes and whites), Americus, Ga., director, 1942-69. Active in civil rights, peace, and church revitalization movements in the south.

WRITINGS: Lord and Master, Judson, 1950; *Sermon on the Mount,* Judson, 1952, revised edition, 1970; *The Cotton Patch Version of Paul's Epistles,* Association Press, 1968; *The Cotton Patch Version of Luke and Acts,* Association Press, 1969; *The Cotton Patch Version of Matthew and John,* Association Press, 1970; *The Cotton Patch Evidence,* edited by Dallas Lee, Harper, 1971; *The Substance of Faith and Other Cotton Patch Sermons,* edited by Lee, Association Press, 1972; *The Cotton Patch Version of Hebrews and the General Epistles,* Association Press, 1973. Has made five long-playing recordings, "The Rich Man and Lazarus," "The Great Banquet," "Jesus and the Rebel," "Metamorphosis," and "Judas."

BIOGRAPHICAL/CRITICAL SOURCES: Newsweek, February 25, 1957, February 26, 1968; *Christian Century,* March 6, 1957; *Time,* April 29, 1957, March 1, 1968; *Redbook,* October, 1957; *Action,* January, 1968.†

(Died October 29, 1969)

* * *

JORDAN, Mildred 1901-

PERSONAL: Born March 18, 1901, in Chicago, Ill.; daughter of Charles William (a poster printer) and Aurelia (Anderson) Jordan; married J. Lee Bausher (a hosiery manufacturer), November 17, 1923; children: Phyllis (Mrs. Ivor Petrak), Elaine, Jordan Lee, Noel (Mrs. Rudolf Szundy). *Education:* Attended Northwestern University, 1918-20; Wellesley College, B.A., 1922. *Politics:* Republican. *Religion:* Methodist. *Home:* 1802 Hill Rd., Reading, Pa. 19602.

CAREER: Civic and community worker in Reading, Pa.; former member of boards of Children's Aid Society, Family Service, Council of Social Agencies, Council of Historical Society of Berks County, Homemaker Service, and Reading Musical Foundation. *Member:* Authors Guild, Midland Authors (Chicago).

WRITINGS—Novels: *One Red Rose Forever,* Knopf, 1941; *Apple in the Attic,* Knopf, 1942; *Asylum for the Queen,* Knopf, 1948; *Miracle in Brittany,* Knopf, 1950; *Echo of the Flute,* Doubleday, 1958.

Children's books: *The Shoofly Pie,* Knopf, 1944; *"I Won't," Said the King,* Knopf, 1945; *Proud to be Amish,* Crown, 1968. Author of comedy drama, "Apple in the Attic," with Lucile Logan, 1960. Former member of editorial staff, *Berks County Historical Society Magazine.*

WORK IN PROGRESS: First draft of satirical fantasy; a nonfiction book on the Pennsylvania Dutch.

AVOCATIONAL INTERESTS: Painting, tennis, ice skating, community and church work especially with underprivileged mothers.

* * *

JORDAN, Weymouth T(yree) 1912-1968

PERSONAL: Born October 31, 1912, in Hamlet, N.C.; son of William Daniel and Mary (Utley) Jordan; married Louise Riggan (a newspaper reporter), August 11, 1935; children: Weymouth Tyree, Jr., Elizabeth (Mrs. David P. Edwards), William Royster. *Education:* North Carolina State University, B.S., 1933; Vanderbilt University, M.A., 1934, Ph.D., 1937. *Politics:* Democrat. *Religion:* Episcopalian. *Home:* 542 East Park Ave., Tallahassee, Fla. *Office:* Department of History, Florida State University, Tallahassee, Fla.

CAREER: Pembroke State College (now University), Pembroke, N.C., professor of history and head of department, 1937-38; Judson College, Marion, Ala., 1938-42, began as instructor, became associate professor of history and department head; Auburn University, Auburn, Ala., 1942-49, began as assistant professor, became research professor; Florida State University, Tallahassee, professor of history, 1949-68, head of department, 1954-64. Fulbright professor at University of Erlangen-Nurnberg, 1964-65. Visiting pro-

fessor at Transylvania College, 1936; visiting summer professor at University of Oklahoma, 1941, University of Missouri, 1958. Member of advisory board, Guggenheim Foundation, 1959-68, of advisory council, U.S. Civil War Centennial Commission, 1959-61. Regional associate American Council of Learned Societies, 1957-59. *Military service:* U.S. Navy, 1943-45; became lieutenant commander.

MEMBER: American Historical Association, Organization of American Historians, Agricultural History Society (vice-president, 1959-60; president, 1962-63; executive council member, 1948-49 and 1959-67), Southern Historical Association (executive council member, 1953-55), Mississippi Valley Historical Association, Florida Historical Association, Kappa Phi Kappa, Phi Alpha Theta, Sigma Pi Alpha. *Awards, honors:* C. M. McClung Award for best article in East Tennessee Historical Society's *Publications,* 1939-41; Social Science Research Council fellowships, 1940, 1941, 1947, 1950; General Education Board fellowships, 1947, 1948; Guggenheim fellowship, 1957-58.

WRITINGS: Hugh Davis and His Alabama Plantation (History Book Club selection), University of Alabama Press, 1948; *George Washington Campbell of Tennessee: Western Statesman,* Florida State University Press, 1955; *Ante-Bellum Alabama: Town and Country,* Florida State University Press, 1957; *Rebels in the Making: Planters' Conventions and Southern Propaganda,* University of Alabama Press, 1958; (contributor) Robert West Howard, editor, *This Is the South,* Rand McNally, 1959; *Herbs, Hoecakes and Husbandry: The Daybook of a Planter of the Old South,* Florida State University Press, 1960; (editorial adviser with Marvin Meyers and others) *Sources of the American Republic,* Scott, Volume I, 1960, Volume II, 1961; (editor) Herbert Bruce Fuller, *The Purchase of Florida,* University of Florida Press, 1964; *The United States: From Revolution to Civil War, 1783-1861,* Pageant, 1964.

Contributor to *Encyclopaedia Britannica.* Also contributor of some fifty articles and sixty reviews to historical and other learned journals. Co-editor of *Florida State University Studies,* 1951, editor, 1953-55. Member of board of editors, East Tennessee Historical Society's *Publications,* 1947-52, *Alabama Review,* 1948-50, *Agricultural History,* 1957-62, *Florida Historical Society's Quarterly,* 1959-63, *Journal of Southern History,* 1961-64, and *Southern Humanities Review,* 1966-68.

SIDELIGHTS: Jordan was competent in French and German. *Avocational interests:* Travel, sports.†

(Died November 22, 1968)

* * *

JOSEPHSON, Hannah 1900-1976

PERSONAL: Born June 6, 1900, in New York, N.Y.; daughter of Abraham David and Anna (Levinson) Geffen; married Matthew Josephson (a writer), May 6, 1920; children: Eric, Carl. *Education:* Studied at Hunter College (now Hunter College of the City University of New York), 1916-18, and Columbia University, 1918-19. *Home:* Church Rd., Sherman, Conn. 06784. *Agent:* Ivan von Auw, Jr., Harold Ober Associates, Inc., 40 East 49th St., New York, N.Y. 10017.

CAREER: Worked as newspaper reporter and magazine editor. American Academy of Arts and Letters, New York, N.Y., 1949-66, began as librarian, became editor of publications and director of manuscript exhibitions. *Awards, honors:* Van Wyck Brooks Award of University of Bridgeport, 1969, for *Al Smith, Hero of the Cities.*

WRITINGS: (With Malcolm Cowley) *Aragon: Poet of the Resistance*, Duell, Sloan, & Pearce, 1945; *The Golden Threads*, Duell, Sloan & Pearce, 1949, published as *The Golden Threads: New England's Mill Girls and Magnates*, Russell, 1967; (with husband, Matthew Josephson) *Al Smith, Hero of the Cities: A Political Portrait Drawing on the Papers of Frances Perkins*, Houghton, 1969; *Jeanette Rankin: First Lady in Congress* (biography), Bobbs-Merrill, 1974.

Translator: Louis Aragon, *The Century Was Young*, Duell, Sloan & Pearce, 1941; Philippe Soupault, *Age of Assassins*, Knopf, 1946; Gabrielle Roy, *The Tin Flute*, Reynal, 1948.

BIOGRAPHICAL/CRITICAL SOURCES: *Christian Science Monitor*, December 24, 1969; *Time*, January 19, 1970; *New York Times Book Review*, February 1, 1970; *New York Times*, October 31, 1976.†

(Died October 29, 1976)

*   *   *

JOY, Kenneth Ernest   1908-

PERSONAL: Born May 10, 1908, in South Berwick, Me.; son of Herbert E. (a merchant) and Mary (Burnham) Joy; married Edith Dennett, December 31, 1932; children: Beryl Louise (Mrs. Francis Oswell). *Education:* Attended schools in Kennebunk, Me. *Religion:* Baptist. *Home:* Alewive Rd., Kennebunk, Me. 04043.

CAREER: Writer and lecturer on local history, Kennebunk, Me.; Kennebunk town historian, beginning 1967; teacher of history in adult education classes, Kennebunkport, Me. Member of Kennebunk Planning Board. *Military service:* U.S. Army, Infantry, 1943-45; wounded in Luxembourg and in France; received Bronze Star, European Theater Medal with two stars, Purple Heart with oak-leaf cluster.

WRITINGS: *The Kennebunks—Out of the Past*, Wheelwright, 1967. Columnist, *York County Coast Star*, beginning 1961; contributor of historical items to other area newspapers.

WORK IN PROGRESS: Compiling notes and photographs for a history of the Kennebunk area, 1850-1950.

*   *   *

JOYCE, Ernest   1899-1975

PERSONAL: Born September 24, 1899, in Cheshire, England; son of Edward Ernest (a journalist) and Catherine Jane Joyce; married Kathleen Boyle, May 28, 1929; children: Timothy, Christopher. *Education:* Educated in Sidcup, Kent, England. *Religion:* Church of England. *Home:* 24 Chenies Close, Frant Rd., Tunbridge Wells, Kent, England.

CAREER: Furniture designer in Brenchley, Kent, England, 1948-64; Brighton Polytechnic, Moulsecoombe, Brighton, England, senior lecturer in furniture design, 1955-70. *Military service:* British Army, 1917-19. *Member:* Art Workers Guild, Society of Industrial Artists and Designers.

WORK IN PROGRESS: Several novels.

AVOCATIONAL INTERESTS: Hand craftsmanship; "standards of quality generally."†

(Died, 1975)

*   *   *

JUDD, Frances K.
  [Collective pseudonym]

WRITINGS—"Kay Tracey Mystery Stories" series; published by Cupples & Leon, except as indicated: *The Secret of the Red Scarf*, 1934; *The Strange Echo*, 1934; *The Mystery of the Swaying Curtains*, 1935; *The Shadow on the Door*, 1935; *The Six Fingered Glove Mystery*, 1936; *The Green Cameo Mystery*, 1936; *Beneath the Crimson Brier Bush*, 1937; *The Secret at the Windmill*, 1937; *The Murmuring Portrait*, 1938; *The Message in the Sand Dunes*, 1938; *In the Sunken Garden*, 1939; *When the Key Turned*, 1939; *The Sacred Feather*, 1940; *The Forbidden Tower*, 1940; *The Lone Footprint*, 1941; *The Double Disguise*, 1941; *The Mansion of Secrets*, 1942; *The Mysterious Neighbors*, Garden City Books, 1951.

SIDELIGHTS: See **ADAMS, Harriet S., STRATEMEYER, Edward L.,** and **SVENSON, Andrew E.**†

*   *   *

KALMIJN, Jo   1905-

PERSONAL: Born May 26, 1905, in The Netherlands; married Joseph Kalmijn (deceased); children: Joseph, Jr., Leonard, Ad, Frederica (Mrs. Henk van Faassen). *Education:* Took teacher training in The Netherlands. *Home:* van Bynkershoeklaan 155, Utrecht, The Netherlands.

CAREER: Writer for children.

WRITINGS: *Die Kinder von der Steinalp*, Boje-Verlag (Stuttgart), 1956; *Een Lorf vol Sprookjes* (fairy tales), Callenbach (The Netherlands), 1966, translation by Marian Powell published as *Sunbeams and Raindrops*, Oliver & Boyd, 1967. Author of plays, television scripts, poetry, booklets, fairy tales, and newspaper features, all for children.

SIDELIGHTS: Mrs. Kalmijn told *CA* that she is "fond of all living and growing things—animals, plants, and most of all, children!"

*   *   *

KALYANARAMAN, Aiyaswamy   1903-

PERSONAL: Born January 18, 1903, in Madras, India; son of Rajagopala Iyer (a government official) and Mangalambal (Ammal) Kalyanaraman; married Jnanambal Ammal, May 16, 1923; children: Gurumurthi (son), Baskaran (son), Rajagopalan (son), Nirmala Kalyanaraman Krishnamurthi (daughter). *Education:* St. Joseph's College, Tiruchirapalli, India, B.A. (honors), 1923; University of Madras, law student, 1924-25. *Politics:* "No remarks." *Religion:* Hindu. *Home:* 39 Thirumalai Pillai Rd., T Nagar, Madras 17, India.

CAREER: Assistant accountant general and deputy accountant general in various states of India, 1926-43; Bombay government, Bombay, India, 1943-55, began as deputy secretary, became secretary to government; Madras State, India, accountant general, 1955-58; deputy controller and auditor general of India, 1958-60; Khadi and Village Industries Commission, Bombay, financial adviser, 1960-61.

WRITINGS: *Aryatarangini: The Saga of the Indo-Aryans*, Asia Publishing House, Volume I, 1969, Volume II, 1970.

WORK IN PROGRESS: Further ideological research.††

*   *   *

KANE, John Joseph   1909-

PERSONAL: Born April 20, 1909, in Philadelphia, Pa.; son of John Joseph (a fire department lieutenant) and Marie C. (O'Hara) Kane; married Anne Marie Hilly, October 16, 1941; children: Marianne, Joan, Patricia Louise. *Education:* St. Joseph's College, Philadelphia, Pa., A.B., 1939; Temple

University, M.A., 1946; University of Pennsylvania, Ph.D., 1950. *Politics:* Democrat. *Religion:* Roman Catholic. *Home:* 230 Ardennes Ave., Mishawaka, Ind. *Agent:* McIntosh & Otis, Inc., 18 East 41st St., New York, N.Y. 10017.

CAREER: U.S. Navy, 1930-34; St. Joseph's College, Philadelphia, Pa., instructor in sociology, 1946-48; University of Notre Dame, Notre Dame, Ind., beginning 1948, became professor of sociology and head of department. National Conference of Christians and Jews, Indiana director, 1950-52. *Member:* American Sociological Association, American Catholic Sociology Society (president, 1952), Society for the Study of Social Problems, Alpha Sigma Nu.

WRITINGS: Marriage and the Family, Dryden Press, 1952; *Catholic-Protestant Conflicts in America,* Regnery, 1955; *Together in Marriage,* Fides, 1957; *Social Problems: A Situational-Value Approach,* Prentice-Hall, 1962; *A Story of Shame: The Negro in America,* Ave Maria Press, 1966. Writer of syndicated column on marital problems appearing in more than forty Catholic newspapers in United States, England, and Santo Domingo. Contributor to sociology journals and Catholic magazines.

WORK IN PROGRESS: A book, *Catholic-Jewish Relations in the U.S.;* a textbook, *Sociology of Marriage and Family.*

*   *   *

KANTOR, James   1927-1974

PERSONAL: Born February 26, 1927, in Johannesburg, South Africa; son of Abraham and Pauline (Braude) Kantor; married Barbara I. Bramley (a film executive), September 15, 1961; children: Brett, Earl, Tanya, Lara. *Education:* University of the Witwatersrand, qualified as attorney-at-law, 1948. *Politics:* Liberal. *Religion:* Jewish. *Home:* Broom Point, Broom Water West, Teddington, Middlesex, England. *Office:* James Kantor & Associates Ltd., 18 Soho Sq., London W.1, England.

CAREER: James Kantor & Partners (attorneys-at-law), Johannesburg, South Africa, senior partner, 1948-63; James Kantor & Associates Ltd. (publishers), London, England, managing director, beginning 1965. *Military service:* South African Air Force, air gunner, 1943-45; became warrant officer.

WRITINGS: A Healthy Grave (autobiographical), Hamish Hamilton, 1967.

SIDELIGHTS: Kantor's book is an account of his detention and lingering imprisonment in South Africa as a political prisoner, suspected of having aided the prison escape of his brother-in-law and legal partner, Harold Wolpe. Found not guilty and discharged during the course of the now-famous Rivonia Trial, Kantor looked back on South Africa (where his book is banned) as "one of the unhealthiest political climates in the world."†

(Died April 15, 1974)

*   *   *

KARLIN, Jules   1899-

PERSONAL: Born January 27, 1899, in Minsk, Russia; son of Samuel (a teacher) and Dora (Rubenstein) Karlin; married Dorothy Pikowsky (a teacher), February 16, 1938; children: Gloria (Mrs. Seymour Sacks), Joan (Mrs. Edward J. Dorman). *Education:* New School for Social Research, student, 1921-23; Illinois Institute of Technology, B.S., 1931; Columbia University, M.A., 1932.

CAREER: Social worker with delinquent and pre-delinquent boys, 1924-28; Illinois Institute of Technology, Chicago, assistant professor of sociology, 1932-38; Chicago Teachers College (now Chicago State University), Chicago, faculty member, 1938-43; Chicago City Junior College, Chicago, instructor, 1947-66, and head of department of social science at one period. *Member:* American Psychological Association.

WRITINGS: Chicago: Backgrounds of Education, Werkman Publishing, 1940; (editor) *Field Manual for Teachers,* Werkman Book House, 1941; (editor with Elgin Hunt) *Society Today and Tomorrow,* Macmillan, 1961; *Changing Framework of Human Nature: The Community,* Dean Publishing, 1962; *Man's Behavior,* Macmillan, 1967. Also author of guides for educational television courses on psychology and social science, 1961-62.

WORK IN PROGRESS: Man's Changing Image.††

*   *   *

KAY, (Albert) William   1930-1976

PERSONAL: Born February 17, 1930, in London, England; son of Albert Ernest (a company director) and Amy Rosina (Summers) Kay; married Pamela Constance Want, August 13, 1955; children: Graham Albert Lindsay, Bryony Rosina Valerie. *Education:* University of London, Teaching Certificate, Bachelor Degree (first class honors in theology and psychology), 1952; University of Nottingham, Diploma in Educational Studies, 1963, M.Ed. 1968. *Home:* 41 Fabis Dr., The Grove, Clifton, Nottingham NG118NY, England.

CAREER: Methodist clergyman; head of religious education department in a county secondary school in England, then headmaster of a primary school; Nottingham College of Education, Nottingham, England, senior lecturer in divinity, beginning 1961. Part-time lecturer, Institute of Education and in adult education department, University of Nottingham. Director on the boards of two London companies. *Member:* Royal Society of Arts (fellow), Social Morality Council, Society for Old Testament Study, Teilhard de Chardin Association, British Psychological Society, Psychiatrists' Association.

WRITINGS: Moral Development: A Psychological Study of Moral Growth from Childhood to Adolescence, Allen & Unwin, 1968, 2nd edition 1971, Schocken, 1969; *Moral Education,* Allen & Unwin, 1975. Contributor to *Teilhard Review, Lumen Vitae, Moral Education,* and *Learning For Living.*

WORK IN PROGRESS: Child Development and Early Education.†

(Died December 28, 1976)

*   *   *

KEHM, Freda (Irma) S(amuels)

PERSONAL: Born in Chicago, Ill.; daughter of M. E. and Hannah Samuels; married Milton M. Kramer, 1916 (divorced, 1935; deceased); married Harry Clayton Kehm, June 6, 1942 (died June, 1949); stepchildren: Mary (Mrs. David C. Echols), Ann (Mrs. Myron Bostwick, Jr.). *Education:* University of Illinois, B.A., 1916; University of South Dakota, M.A., 1935; Northwestern University, Ph.D., 1941. *Residence:* Chicago, Ill.

CAREER: South Dakota Child Welfare Commission, executive director, 1931-33; district supervisor of Federal Emergency Relief Administration, South Dakota, and acting director of South Dakota Public Health Association, 1933-34; University of South Dakota, Vermillion, instructor in social work, 1934-35; Carleton College, Northfield, Minn., 1935-42, started as instructor, became associate professor in department of sociology and anthropology; public relations consultant, Chicago, Ill., 1944-47; Association for Family Living, Chicago, director, 1948-65; child development consultant appearing on daily radio program, "Call Dr. Kehm," WBBM, Chicago, 1962-71. Lecturer on the individual, marriage, and the family, Northwestern University, beginning 1956. Member of advisory board of Child Study Association of America, of board of governors of National Forum Foundation, and of board of directors of Dyslexia Memorial Institute. Delegate to three White House Conferences on Children and Youth.

MEMBER: American Academy of Political and Social Science, American Sociological Association (fellow), National Council on Family Relations (former member of executive committee), American Association of Marriage and Family Counselors (life member), American Association of Marriage Counselors, American Association for the Advancement of Science, Child Care Association of Illinois, American Legion Auxiliary (former national vice-president; former national president of Eight and Forty), Phi Beta Kappa, Delta Delta Delta, Chicago Press Club. *Awards, honors:* South Dakota Distinguished Alumni Service Award, 1974.

WRITINGS: (With Joe L. Mini) *Let Children Be Children,* Association Press, 1968. Contributor of articles to other books, to *Childcraft* and *World Book,* and to periodicals. Columnist, *Chicago's Sunday American,* 1963.

* * *

KEIR, David Lindsay 1895-1973

PERSONAL: Born May 22, 1895, in Spennymoor, Durham, England; son of William (a clergyman, Church of Scotland) and Elizabeth Craig (Reid) Keir; married Anna Clunie Dale, April 3, 1930; children: Ann Elizabeth (Mrs. I. M. Lewis), Michael Ian Stenhouse. *Education:* Studied at University of Glasgow, 1913-14; New College, Oxford, B.A., 1921, M.A., 1925. *Politics:* None. *Religion:* Presbyterian. *Home:* Hillsborough, Boars Hill, Oxford, England.

CAREER: Oxford University, Oxford, England, fellow in history, University College, 1921-39, and dean of University College, 1925-33, university lecturer in English constitutional history, 1931-39; The Queen's University of Belfast, Belfast, Northern Ireland, president and vice-chancellor, 1939-49; Oxford University, master of Balliol College, 1949-65. Exchange tutor, Harvard University, 1923-24. Chairman, Advisory Committee for Overseas Colleges, 1953-65; trustee of Oxford Union Society and R. V. Stanley's Match. *Military service:* British Army, King's Own Scottish Borderers, 1915-19; became major.

MEMBER: Scottish History Society (president, 1958-62), Hansard Society, Ulster Society for Irish Historical Studies (life vice-president), Royal Institute of British Architects (honorary associate member). *Awards, honors:* Knighted, 1946. M.A. and D.C.L., Oxford University; D.Litt., University of Sussex; LL.D. from University of Glasgow, University of Dublin, Queen's University of Belfast, Queen's University at Kingston, and University of New Brunswick; honorary fellow of University College, Balliol College, and New College, Oxford University.

WRITINGS: (With F. H. Lawson) *Cases in Constitutional Law,* Clarendon Press, 1928, 5th edition, 1967; *Constitutional History of Modern Britain since 1485,* A. & C. Black, 1938, 9th edition, 1969. Contributor to history and law journals, and to magazines.

WORK IN PROGRESS: His memoirs.

SIDELIGHTS: David Keir traveled widely as a member of educational commissions, committees, and councils concerned with medical education in Malaya, and technical education in Southeast Asia, Malta, Sudan, West Indies, and East, Central, and West Africa.†

(Died October 2, 1973)

* * *

KELLAWAY, George P(ercival) 1909-

PERSONAL: Born October 21, 1909, in Dorsetshire, England; son of Walter John and Elizabeth Mary (Hewlett) Kellaway; married Ellen Elizabeth Young, March 31, 1934; children: Susan Diana (Mrs. Robert Macdonald Cumming). *Education:* University of Southampton, B.Sc. (general), 1931, Postgraduate Certificate of Education, 1932, B.Sc. (special honors), 1937. *Politics:* "Not a member of any party." *Religion:* Church of England. *Home:* Brown Fold, Blackrod, Bolton, Lancashire, England.

CAREER: Held teaching appointments in England, 1932-42; College of Education, York, England, lecturer, 1942-46; College of Education, Weymouth, England, principal, 1947-49; Fourah Bay College, Freetown, Sierra Leone, head of teacher training department, 1950-56; Nigerian College of Arts, Science, and Technology, head of department of education, 1956-63; Local Education Authority administration posts in England, beginning 1964. *Member:* Royal Geographical Society (fellow).

WRITINGS: A Background of Physical Geography, Macmillan, 1946, 2nd edition, 1968; *Map Projections,* Methuen 1947, 2nd edition, 1970; *Purposeful Education,* University of London Press, 1958; *Education for Living,* Cambridge University Press, 1967.

SIDELIGHTS: On his return from Africa, Kellaway bought a Queen Anne farmhouse on twenty-five acres of land in Lancashire, and has been modernizing the home "while preserving its character intact." *Avocational interests:* Travel, photography.†

* * *

KELLEY, Joanna (Elizabeth) 1910-

PERSONAL: Born May 23, 1910, in Murree, India (now Pakistan); daughter of William Musgrave (a lieutenant colonel) and Joanna Elizabeth (Ballard) Beadon; married Harper Kelley, November 6, 1934 (died, 1962). *Education:* Girton College, Cambridge, B.A. (honors in economics), 1931; Sorbonne, University of Paris, Diplome pour etrangers, 1932. *Politics:* None. *Religion:* Church of England. *Home:* 31 Westmoreland Ter., London S.W.1, England.

CAREER: Musee de l'Homme, Paris, France, assistant in department of prehistory, 1934-39; Young Women's Christian Association, mixed youth club leader, 1939-42; British Admiralty, welfare officer in Bath, England, 1942-47; H.M. Prison Holloway (women's prison), London, England, assistant governor, 1947-52; H.M. Prison Askham Grange (open prison for women), York, England, governor, 1952-59; H.M. Prison Holloway, governor, 1959-66; Home Office, London, England, assistant director of Prison Department, 1967-74. *Member:* Society of Antiquaries (fellow), Pierre Teilhard de Chardin Association of Great Britain (vice-chairman, 1965). *Awards, honors:* LL.D., University of Hull, 1960; honorary fellow, Girton College, Cambridge University, 1968; Order of the British Empire, 1972.

WRITINGS: When the Gates Shut, Longmans, Green, 1967. Contributor of articles on women in prison and on lesbianism to *Medical Women's Journal* and other periodicals.

SIDELIGHTS: Joanna Kelley is competent in French. *Avocational interests:* Archaeology, travel, and religion.

* * *

KELLOGG, Charles Flint 1909-

PERSONAL: Born October 28, 1909, in Pittsfield, Mass.; son of Charles Theodore (a merchant) and Bertie K. (Hawver) Kellogg; married Mary-Margaret Cashell (formerly a dean of women), November 28, 1946. *Education:* Columbia University, A.B. (honors), 1931; Harvard University, M.A., 1933; General Theological Seminary, New York, N.Y., diploma, 1936; Johns Hopkins University, Ph.D., 1963; other study at Cincinnati General Hospital, 1934, and Massachusetts State Hospital for Mental Diseases, 1935. *Home:* 100 Moreland Ave., Carlisle, Pa. 17013. *Office:* Department of History, Dickinson College, Carlisle, Pa. 17013.

CAREER: Episcopal clergyman. Rector or curate of churches in New York, N.Y., 1936-43, in Washington, D.C., 1943-45; St. Peter's Preparatory School, Peekskill, N.Y., assistant to headmaster and head of department of history, 1945-46; Dickinson College, Carlisle, Pa., instructor, 1946-47, assistant professor, 1947-52, associate professor, 1952-62, professor of history, beginning 1962, Boyd Lee Spahr Professor of American History, beginning 1968, acting chairman of department of history, 1960-61, chairman, beginning 1961. Bard College, Columbia University, member of president's council, beginning 1965, member of board of trustees, beginning 1975; trustee, Association of Episcopal College, beginning 1967.

MEMBER: American Historical Association, Organization of American Historians, American Studies Association, Association for Asian Studies, American Association of Teachers of Chinese Language and Culture (vice-president; member of executive committee of board of directors), American Association for Middle East Studies, Association of Asian Studies, American Association of University Professors, China Institute in America, U.S. Conference on Asian Intercollegiate Programs, American Institute of Pakistan Studies (member of board of directors; treasurer), Southern Historical Association, Association for the Study of Negro Life and History, Bard-St. Stephen's College Alumni Association (president, 1964-66; member of executive committee, beginning 1965), Pi Gamma Mu, Harvard Club (New York), University Club (Washington, D.C.). *Awards, honors:* Fund for the Republic grant, 1956-57; L.H.D., Bard College, 1960; Fulbright grant for summer institute in Chinese civilization at Tunghai University, Taiwan, Formosa, 1964; grant from Hebrew Union College (Jerusalem) for summer institute in Near Eastern civilizations, 1965; grant from American Philosophical Society for research in race relations, 1968.

WRITINGS: NAACP: A History of the National Association for the Advancement of Colored People, Johns Hopkins Press, Volume I, 1967.

WORK IN PROGRESS: Research on the life of John Bard, founder of the College of Physicians and Surgeons at Columbia University.

KEMBLE, James

PERSONAL: Born in Newcastle, New South Wales, Australia; married Dorothy Eleanor Wright, 1935; children: James Victor Harvey, Robert William Sydney. *Education:* University of Sydney, M.B., Ch.M. (honors), both 1921; Royal College of Surgeons of Edinburgh, F.R.C.S., 1928, Royal College of Surgeons of England, F.R.C.S., 1930. *Home:* 24 Keswick Rd., London S.W.15, England. *Office:* 152 Harley St., London W.1, England.

CAREER: Consultant surgeon and urologist, practicing in London, England; presently consultant surgeon and surgeon in charge of urological department of Battersea General Hospital and surgeon in department of genito-urinary surgery of West London Hospital. Lecturer in history of medicine, Faculty of History of Medicine of Worshipful Society of Apothecaries. *Wartime service:* Emergency Medical Service, surgeon, 1939-45. *Member:* Royal Society of Medicine (fellow), British Medical Association, British Association of Urological Surgeons, Society of Authors, West London Medico-Chirurgical Society (former vice-president), Osler Club (London).

WRITINGS: Idols and Invalids (on Byron, Columbus, and others), Methuen, 1933, Doubleday, Doran, 1936; *Hero-Dust,* Methuen, 1936; *Surgery for Nurses,* Williams & Wilkins, 1949; *Napoleon Immortal: The Medical History and Private Life of Napoleon Bonaparte,* J. Murray, 1960; (editor) Gideon Gorrequer, *St. Helena during Napoleon's Exile: Gorrequer's Diary,* Heinemann, 1969, Shoe String, 1970. Contributor to medical journals, beginning 1931. Editor, *West London Medical Journal.*

SIDELIGHTS: In preparing Major Gorrequer's diary for publication, James Kemble had to ferret out the identification of almost two hundred persons mentioned in the papers under cover names and, as the *Times Literary Supplement* points out, make sense of the "sometimes obscure text." Gorrequer, aide-de-camp to the governor of St. Helena during Napoleon's exile, kept a record whose history the *Times* critic says "is almost as remarkable as its contents." Kept secret for many years by Gorrequer's heirs, the manuscript was impounded in the vaults of the British Court of Chancery in 1881—sixty years after Napoleon's death. By an Act of Parliament the diary was finally transferred to the Public Record Office and opened to scrutiny.

AVOCATIONAL INTERESTS: Skiing, golf, painting.

BIOGRAPHICAL/CRITICAL SOURCES: Times Literary Supplement, August 29, 1969.

* * *

KEMPNER, Mary Jean 1913-1969

PERSONAL: Born in 1913, in Galveston, Tex.; daughter of Daniel W. Kempner (a businessman and philanthropist); married Oakleigh L. Thorne (a banker); married second husband Alan Pryce-Jones (a literary critic), October 26, 1968; children: (first marriage) Daniel Kempner Thorne. *Residence:* Sintra, Portugal.

CAREER: War correspondent accredited to the Navy during World War II, reporting for *Vogue* and Newspaper Enterprise Association from China, Japan, Okinawa, and the Pacific; following the war was on the staff of *Vogue* until 1952; free-lance writer, contributing chiefly to *Harper's, Harper's Bazaar,* and *House Beautiful,* 1952-69.

WRITINGS: Invitation to Portugal (young adult book), introduction by husband, Alan Pryce-Jones, Atheneum, 1969.††

(Died September 11, 1969)

KENNELL, Ruth Epperson   1893-1977

PERSONAL: Born September 21, 1893, in Oklahoma City, Okla.; daughter of Julius (a farmer) and Sara Ellen (Seeger) Epperson; married Frank Risley Kennell (a teacher), July 7, 1917 (deceased); children: James Epperson, David Epperson. *Education:* Attended University of California, Berkeley, 1913. *Politics:* Democratic Party. *Religion:* Unitarian Universalist. *Agent:* Ruth Cantor, 156 Fifth Ave., New York, N.Y. 10010.

CAREER: Richmond (Calif.) Public Library, children's librarian, 1914-17; American Colony Kuzbas, Kemerovo, Siberia, librarian and secretary, 1922-24; International Library, Moscow, Soviet Union, reference librarian, 1925-27; secretary and guide to Theodore Dreiser on his Russian tour, 1927-28; Newspaper Enterprise Association (N.E.A.; a syndicate), correspondent in Moscow, Soviet Union, 1930-32; writer of children's books and short stories, 1931-58, and of nonfiction. Correspondent for *Nation* in American Colony Kuzbas and later Moscow, 1922-31. Active in war relief work in China and Russia, 1941-45. *Member:* Women's International League for Peace and Freedom (literature chairman of Palo Alto branch, 1965-71), League of Women Voters, Civic League (Palo Alto).

WRITINGS—Juvenile fiction, except as noted: *Vanya of the Streets*, Harper, 1931; *Comrade One-Crutch*, Harper, 1932; *That Boy Nikolka and Other Tales of Soviet Children* (originally published in *Story Parade*), 1943, Russian War Relief, Inc., 1945; *Adventure in Russia: The Ghost of Kirghizia*, Messner, 1947; *The Secret Farmyard*, Abelard, 1956, published with teacher's guide, Houghton, 1968; *Dreiser and the Soviet Union 1927-1945: A Personal Chronicle* (adult nonfiction), International Publishers, 1969.

One of her short stories, "Lisa's Song," has been included in six collections and school readers, 1942-71; other stories originally published in *Story Parade* and *Child Life* have been reprinted in *Invitation to Reading*, Harcourt, 1945, *Youth Replies I Can*, Knopf, 1945, *Story Parade Yellow Book, Story Parade Star Book,* and in texts. Writer of short stories and serials for church school papers published by Methodist Book Concern, 1932-42, and stories for Junior Red Cross magazines, 1940-45, and other juvenile periodicals.

WORK IN PROGRESS: A book about the American Colony Kuzbas, Kemerovo, Siberia, for International Publishers.

BIOGRAPHICAL/CRITICAL SOURCES: American Mercury, April, 1932; *Youth Replies I Can,* Knopf, 1945.†

(Died March 5, 1977)

*   *   *

KENT, Margaret   1894-

PERSONAL: Born April 15, 1894, in Wells, Somersetshire, England; daughter of Fred and Margaret (Hall) Hatwell; married Charles Henry Kent (a schoolmaster), August 6, 1916 (deceased); children: Margaret (Mrs. A. L. Watson), Sylvia (Mrs. Courvoisier), Joan (Mrs. G. Stubbings), John. *Education:* University of Bristol, teacher training, 1911-13; studied music privately; became Licentiate of Royal Academy of Music, 1933. *Politics:* Conservative. *Religion:* Church of England. *Home:* Meon, 3 Alexandra Way, Botley, Southampton SO3 2ED, England.

CAREER: During her early career, assisted her husband at his school in Wales; headmistress of Shipley School, Sussex, England, 1945-54; writer, mainly for children. Voluntary village librarian in Somersetshire, and lecturer for women's groups and library associations.

WRITINGS: "Milly-Molly-Mandy" series; published by Harrap: *The Twins at Hillside Farm,* 1942; *The Twins at the Seaside,* 1943; *The Twins at Home,* 1947; *The Twins and Felicity,* 1959; *The Twins and the Move,* 1962.

"Children's Nature" series; published by Harrap: *Birds,* 1944; *Animals of Hedge, Pond and Moor,* 1944; *Trees,* 1945; *Flowers,* 1945; *Pond Life,* 1948; *Insects,* 1948; *The Seashore,* 1949; *Animals of the Farm,* 1949.

"Stories for Language Training" series; published by Macmillan: *Little Red Shoes,* 1949; *Timothy Tibbetts,* 1949; *The Tin Whistle,* 1949; *Megab the Sky Cleaner,* 1950; *The Fizzlewugs of Fettleby,* 1950; *Lucky the Cat,* 1950; *Teacher's Book,* 1953.

Other children's series; published by Harrap: *Spring at Cherry Tree Farm,* 1942; *Summer at Cherry Tree Farm,* 1942; *Autumn at Cherry Tree Farm,* 1942; *Winter at Cherry Tree Farm,* 1943.

Published by Wheaton & Co.: *The Six Sherlocks,* 1957; *The Six Sherlocks Again,* 1957; *The Six Sherlocks Carry On,* 1957; *The Six Sherlocks Win Through,* 1957.

Children's books: *Musical Reading Games,* Paxton & Co., 1942; *Playlets for the Classroom,* two books, Thomas Nelson, 1943; *Ten Minute Stories,* Harrap, 1943; *Stories for the Nursery School,* Harrap, 1947; *Nursery Rhyme Nature Stories,* Harrap, 1948; *Stories for Language Training,* Macmillan, 1949; *Melody Making in the Infant School,* Paxton & Co., 1949; *Melody Making in the Junior School,* Paxton & Co., 1949; *Melody Making in the Senior School,* Paxton & Co., 1949; *At Tweedles Farm,* Macmillan, 1949; *The Baby Moses* (scripture play with music), Paxton & Co., 1951; *The Jack-a-Nory Story Book,* Harrap, 1952; *Two Modern Plays for Schools* ("Spring Cleaning" and "A Song of Sixpence"), Macmillan, 1952; *When Queens Cook!; or, a Question of Pages* (with music), Paxton & Co., 1953; *Playlets for the Classroom,* Thomas Nelson, 1953; *Little Plays for Many Players,* Harrap, 1954; *Out-of-Doors Stories,* Pitman, 1954; *The Nativity* (scripture play with music), Paxton & Co., 1955; *The Tinker Tailor Story Book,* Harrap, 1955; *Seaside Stories,* Pitman, 1957; *The Lucky Thirteen: Stories from Around the World,* Pantheon, 1960 (published in England as *Kashi the Mongoose, and Other Stories,* Harrap, 1961); *Nuts to Crack* (puzzles and quizzes), Harrap, 1961; *The Jolly Clown's Picture Crosswords for Children,* two books, Wheaton & Co., 1965; *Scamp: A Dog's Story,* Robert Gibson, 1968; *Favourite Crosswords,* two books, Benn, 1968.

Author of *Two Way Songs for Infants, Toy Shop Songs, Zoo Nonsense Songs, Little All-Purpose Songs, The Loving Father* (play), and *Two Dramatised Singing Games—Simple Simon and Red Riding Hood,* published by Paxton & Co.; also author of *Little Nature Stories,* published by Charles. Writer of *Arrangements for Percussion Bands,* two books, Augener.

Contributor of articles, stories, verse, and plays to numerous adult and children's periodicals and to education journals; also contributor of weekly adult crossword puzzle to *Television Weekly,* 1965-68, and puzzles to children's periodicals and annuals.

KEPHART, Newell C.   1911-1973

PERSONAL: Born January 24, 1911, in Parker, Kan.; son of Harvey C. (a minister) and Ella (Duvall) Kephart; married Martha A. Menke, September 29, 1945. *Education:* University of Denver, A.B., 1932, M.A., 1933; University of Iowa, Ph.D., 1936. *Home:* 2940 State Rd. 26 West, West Lafayette, Ind. 47906. *Office:* Achievement Center for Children, Purdue University, Lafayette, Ind.

CAREER: Wayne County Training School, Plymouth, Mich., mental hygienist, 1936-41; Purdue University, Lafayette, Ind., 1945-73, started as assistant professor, professor of psychology and education, 1955-73, executive director of Achievement Center for Children, 1959-73. Achievement Camp for Children, Glenhaven, Colo., director, 1957-73. Member of national advisory board of National Society for Crippled Children and Adults and National Association for Children with Learning Disabilities. *Military service:* U.S. Navy, 1942-45. *Member:* American Psychological Association, American Association on Mental Deficiency, Council for Exceptional Children, Sigma Xi, Phi Delta Kappa.

WRITINGS: (With Alfred Strauss) *Psychopathology and Education of the Brain Injured Child*, Volume II, Grune, 1955; *The Slow Learner in the Classroom*, C. E. Merrill, 1960, 2nd edition, 1971; (with D. H. Radler) *Success Through Play*, Harper, 1960; (with E. G. Roach) *The Purdue Perceptual-Motor Survey*, C. E. Merrill, 1966; *Learning Disability: An Educational Adventure*, Kappa Delta Pi Press, 1968; (with Clara M. Chaney) *Motoric Aids to Perceptual Training*, C. E. Merrill, 1968; (with Marylou Ebersole) *Steps to Achievement for the slow Learner*, C. E. Merrill, 1968; (with Barbara B. Godfrey) *Movement Patterns and Motor Education*, Appleton, 1969.†

(Died April 12, 1973)

*   *   *

KEPPLE, Ella Huff   1902-

PERSONAL: Born July 10, 1902, in Waukomis, Okla.; daughter of William Tipton (a realtor) and Mary (Thain) Huff; married Paul Clarence Kepple (a missionary, now retired), August 24, 1930; children: Margaret, Phyllis (Mrs. Charles Worrell), Paul, Jr. *Education:* University of Oklahoma, B.A., 1925; Hartford Seminary Foundation, M.A., 1930. *Office:* United Christian Missionary Society, 222 South Downey, Indianapolis, Ind.

CAREER: Teacher in Oklahoma and Texas, alternating with university study, 1921-28; Christian Churches (Disciples of Christ), missionary in Mexico, 1930-61; United Christian Missionary Society, Indianapolis, Ind., writer and editor of children's missionary education materials, including "Friends Around the World" section of *Junior World*, beginning, 1961.

WRITINGS: Programas de Adoracion para los Niños, Casa Unida de Publicaciones, 1949; *Mateo of Mexico*, Friendship, 1958; *Balti*, Christian Board of Publication, 1959; *Three Children of Chile*, Friendship, 1961; *Fun and Festival from Latin America*, Friendship, 1961.††

*   *   *

KEREKES, Tibor   1893-1969
(Rotarius)

PERSONAL: Born February 5, 1893, in Budapest, Hungary; son of Geza and Ilona (Polonyi) de Kerekes; married Contessa Teresa Maria Ardizzone, 1923; children: Stephanie Elena Kerekes Kerns, Tibor, Jr., Richard Karl. *Edu-*

cation: University of Budapest, B.A., 1915, Ph.D., 1921; University of Vienna, LL.B., 1919. *Politics:* Republican. *Religion:* Roman Catholic.

CAREER: Tutor in Imperial House of Habsburg, 1916-22; Georgetown University, Washington, D.C., lecturer, 1927-29, assistant professor, 1929-30, associate professor, 1930-34, professor of history, 1934-60, professor emeritus, 1960-69, acting head of history department, 1934-36, head of history department, 1937-58, director of Institute of Ethnic Studies, 1958-61; Boston College, Chestnut Hill, Mass., professorial lecturer in Graduate School, 1961-69. Lecturer in American and European universities. Consultant to U.S. Senate Judiciary Committee. *Military service:* Austro-Hungarian Army, 1914-16; became first lieutenant. *Member:* American Historical Association, American Military Institute (trustee), Phi Alpha Theta, Cosmos Club (Washington, D.C.). *Awards, honors:* L.H.D. from Georgetown University, 1955; Danforth Foundation fellowship, 1960-61.

WRITINGS: Modern European History, H. W. Wise, 1937; (co-author) *Contemporary Europe*, Van Nostrand, 1947; (contributor) *Contemporary Political Ideologies*, Littlefield, 1961; (editor) *The Arab Middle East and Muslim Africa*, Praeger, 1961. Former editor of Institute of Ethnic Studies publications; former member of editorial board, Phi Alpha Theta.

AVOCATIONAL INTERESTS: Gardening.†

(Died October 5, 1969)

*   *   *

KERR, Jessica   1901-

PERSONAL: Born February 2, 1901, in Dublin, Ireland; daughter of Thomas E. (a surgeon) and Eleanor (Blake) Gordon; married Alexander C. Kerr, April 19, 1922 (died, 1967); children: Mary-Joy (Mrs. P. Andreas Bucher), David Clement Gordon, Jenny Nell (Mrs. R. R. Streiff). *Education:* Royal College of Music, London, A.R.C.M. (for solo violin), 1922. *Politics:* Independent. *Religion:* Episcopalian. *Home:* 880 Mandalay Ave., Clearwater Beach, Fla. 33515.

CAREER: Lived for many years in Germany, Netherlands, Belgium, and Switzerland; has lectured in Europe and America on Shakespeare's flowers and gardens. *Member:* National League of American Pen Women (Clearwater branch). *Awards, honors:* Gold Medal of Literary Guild (England) for the best nonfiction children's book of 1969, for *Shakespeare's Flowers.*

WRITINGS: Shakespeare's Flowers, illustrated by Anne Ophelia Dowden, Crowell, 1969. Contributor to *Music and Letters* and *Musical Times* (both London).

SIDELIGHTS: K. S. White of the *New Yorker* says of *Shakespeare's Flowers:* "This slender volume is the best of the many books on Shakespeare's flowers I have encountered. [It] is backed by well-concealed scholarly research by both author and illustrator. The prose is relaxed and entertaining." A Japanese edition of *Shakespeare's Flowers* has been published in Tokyo.

BIOGRAPHICAL/CRITICAL SOURCES: New York Times Book Review, November 9, 1969; *New Yorker*, March 28, 1970.

*   *   *

KERR, Rose Netzorg   1892-1974

PERSONAL: Born May 9, 1892, in Mecosta, Mich.; daughter of Isaac (a merchant) and Anna (Bendetson) Netzorg; married James W. Kerr (an artist), June 24, 1922; children: Paul F. *Education:* Western Michigan University, Life Certificate in Education, 1912; studied at Art Institute of Chicago, 1918, 1919, and Parsons School of Design, 1920. *Politics:* "Any humane party at the time." *Religion:* "Liberal—any religion, preferably Unitarian." *Home:* 7017 Bellrose Ave. N.E., Albuquerque, N.M.

CAREER: Western Michigan University, Kalamazoo, faculty member, 1912-22, director of department of art, 1916-22; free-lance artist, mainly in collaboration with husband, in New York, N.Y., and vicinity, 1923-60; free-lance artist and designer in Albuquerque, N.M., beginning 1960. *Member:* Albuquerque Museum Association. *Awards, honors:* 100 *Years of Costumes in America* was nominated for a Pulitzer Prize, 1951; numerous prizes for Christmas card designs and egg tempera paintings.

WRITINGS: (Author and illustrator) *100 Years of Costume Design,* Davis Press (Worcester, Mass.), 1951; (with Katharine M. Lester) *Historic Costume,* Charles A. Bennett, 1961, 6th edition, 1967. Also wrote and illustrated a looseleaf text on interpretive costume design published by Fairbairn, 1925, and has done other educational articles. Former associate editor, *School Arts* (magazine).†

(Died May 16, 1974)

*   *   *

KERTESZ, Stephen D(enis)   1904-

PERSONAL: Born April 8, 1904, in Putnok, Hungary; son of Lajos and Maria (Stolcz) Kertesz; married Margaret Cornelia de Fulop, October 7, 1931; children: Marianne (Mrs. Endre Sipos), Agnes (Mrs. Peter Serenyi). *Education:* University of Budapest, LL.D., 1926; University of Paris, diploma, 1928; graduate study at Yale University, Oxford University, and University of Geneva, 1935-37. *Home:* 1246 Woodlawn Blvd., South Bend, Ind. 46617. *Office:* Department of Political Science, University of Notre Dame, Notre Dame, Ind. 46556.

CAREER: Law practice in Budapest, Hungary, 1928-31; with Hungarian Foreign Ministry, 1931-47, as first secretary of Hungarian Legation in Bucharest, 1942, member of Political Section, 1943-44, secretary-general of Hungarian delegation to Peace Conference, 1946, and Hungarian minister to Italy, 1947; resigned from Hungarian Foreign Service, 1947; Yale University, New Haven, Conn., visiting associate professor, 1948-50; University of Notre Dame, Notre Dame, Ind., associate professor, 1950-51, professor of political science, 1951-75, professor emeritus, 1975—, acting head of department, 1962-64, Franklin Miles Professor, 1963, Cardinal O'Hara Professor of Government and International Studies, 1969, director, Institute on International Studies, beginning 1968. Consultant, Ford Foundation Foreign Area Training Fellowship Program, 1961-64; member of Catholic commission on intellectual and cultural affairs.

MEMBER: American Political Science Association, American Academy of Political and Social Science, American Historical Association, American Association for the Advancement of Slavic Studies, American Society of International Law, International Free Academy of Science and Letters. *Awards, honors:* Rockefeller fellowships, 1935-37; Guggenheim fellowship for study of parliamentary diplomacy in the United Nations, 1958-59; University of Notre Dame, lay faculty award, 1963, special presidential award, 1975; Rockefeller grant for research on modern diplomacy in Europe and North America, 1965-66.

WRITINGS—All published by University of Notre Dame Press, except as noted: *Az Allam Nemzetkozi Felelossege* (title means "The International Responsibility of the State"), [Budapest], 1938; *Diplomacy in a Whirlpool: Hungary between Nazi Germany and the Soviet Union,* 1953; (editor and contributor) *The Fate of East Central Europe: Hopes and Failures of American Foreign Policy,* 1956; (editor with M. A. Fitzsimons, and contributor) *Diplomacy in a Changing World,* 1959; (editor with Fitzsimons, and contributor) *What America Stands For,* 1959.

(Editor and contributor) *American Diplomacy in a New Era,* 1961; (editor and contributor) *East Central Europe and the World: Developments in the Post-Stalin Era,* 1962; (contributor) David M. Abshire and Richard V. Allen, editors, *National Security: Political, Military, and Economic Strategies in the Decade Ahead,* Praeger, 1963; *The Quest for Peace through Diplomacy,* Prentice-Hall, 1967; (editor and contributor) *Nuclear Non-Proliferation in a World of Nuclear Powers,* 1967; (contributor) Robert F. Byrnes, editor, *The United States and Eastern Europe,* Prentice-Hall, 1967; (editor) *The Task of Universities in a Changing World,* 1971.

Contributor of articles to *Grolier's Encyclopedia, New Catholic Encyclopedia, American Perspective, Current History,* and political science journals; contributor of about forty reviews to professional journals. Contributing editor, *Current History,* beginning 1958; advisory editor, *Review of Politics,* beginning 1960.

WORK IN PROGRESS: The Foundations and Practices of Diplomacy, and *The Development of International Systems.*†

*   *   *

KIEFER, Tillman W.   1898-
(Bill Kiefer)

PERSONAL: Born April 15, 1898, in Wooster, Ohio; son of W. W. and Sadie S. (Crater) Kiefer; married Naomi F. Tinkey, August 9, 1930; children: Richard, Carolyn. *Education:* Ashland College, Ashland, Ohio, B.A., 1926; further courses at Western Reserve University (now Case Western Reserve University), 1933, and at Ohio Northern University. *Religion:* Protestant. *Home:* 17314 Riverway Dr., Cleveland, Ohio 44107.

CAREER: Professional baseball player, pitched with three minor league teams, for sixteen years; chief accountant and secretary-treasurer with manufacturing corporations; Maerkle-White-Huxtable-Auble, Inc., head of investment property department, 1959.

WRITINGS: Apartments Can Make You Rich, Adams Press, 1969.††

*   *   *

KILANDER, H(olger) Frederick   1900-1969

PERSONAL: Born November 24, 1900, in St. Peter, Minn.; son of Karl August (a college professor) and Augusta Louise (Anderson) Kilander; married Juanita Claire Miller, January 1, 1930; children: Holger Frederick, Jr., Carole Lousie (Mrs. Cole Iver Iverson). *Education:* Gustavus Adolphus College, A.B., 1922; Columbia University, M.A., 1925, Ph.D., 1931. *Politics:* Republican. *Religion:* Lutheran. *Home:* 77 Grymes Hill Rd., Staten Island, N.Y. 10301. *Office:* Wagner College, Staten Island, N.Y. 10301.

CAREER: High School science instructor in Montevideo, Minn, 1922-23; Upsala College, East Orange, N.J., professor of biology, 1923-33; Panzer College, East Orange,

N.J., dean 1933-42; U.S. War Food Administration, regional chief, 1942-45; National Tuberculosis Association, New York, N.Y., associate in health education, 1945-47; U.S. Office of Education, Washington, D.C., specialist in health education, 1947-53; American National Red Cross, Washington, D.C., assistant national director of First Aid Service, 1951-52; New York University, New York, N.Y., professor of education, 1953-62; Wagner College, Staten Island, N.Y., dean of Graduate School, 1962-69. Consultant to Coronet Films; chairman, National Lutheran Committee on Scouting, 1952-54; National Young Men's Christian Association Camp Committee, 1954-59.

MEMBER: American School Health Association (president, 1954-56), American Academy of Physical Education, American Association for Health, Physical Education and Recreation, American Association of School Administrators, American Association of University Professors, American College Health Association, National Education Association, International Platform Association, International Union for Health and Health Education, Royal Society of Health, Council of Lutheran Church Men (president, 1957-62), American Scandinavian Foundation (fellow). *Awards, honors:* Howe Award of American School Health Association, 1960; Gustavus Adolphus College, distinguished alumnus citation, 1962.

WRITINGS: Science Education in Sweden, Bureau of Publications, Teachers College, Columbia University, 1931; (with Morey R. Fields and Jacob A. Goldberg) *Youth Grows into Adulthood,* Chartwell House, 1950; *Nutrition for Health,* McGraw, 1951; (with Reuel A. Benson and Goldberg) *The Camp Counselor,* McGraw, 1951; *Health Services in City Schools,* U.S. Office of Education, 1952; *Health for Modern Living,* Prentice-Hall, 1957, revised edition and *Teachers Manual,* 1965; (editor) *Alcohol and Narcotics Education: A Guide for Teachers,* Oklahoma State Department of Education, 1958; (editor) *Preparing the Health Teacher,* American Association for Health, Physical Education and Recreation, 1961; *School Health Education: Its Contents, Methods and Materials,* Macmillan, 1962, 2nd edition, 1968; *Sex Education in the Schools,* Macmillan, 1969.

Contributor: Charles C. Wilson, editor, *School Health Services,* National Education Association, 1953; Charles C. Wilson, editor, *Healthful School Living,* National Education Association, 1957; Fred V. Hein, editor, *Fit to Teach,* American Association for Health, Physical Education and Recreation, 1957; Milton A. Gabrielson and Caswell M. Miles, editors, *Sports and Recreation Facilities for School and Community,* Prentice-Hall, 1958.

Compiler of "Kilander Health Knowledge Tests," for college and high school students. Consultant on film scripts for "Fact or Fancy in Foods," Academy Film Productions, 1954, and "Let's Keep Food Safe to Eat," Coronet Films, 1965. Contributor to periodicals, including *Higher Education, Journal of Public Health, Lutheran Companion, School Life,* and other journals in fields of health, nutrition, education, and recreation.

WORK IN PROGRESS: A revision of *School Health Education,* for Macmillan, completion expected in 1967.

SIDELIGHTS: Kilander's research since 1936 focused on the health misconceptions of the American public. He tested more than a quarter million individuals in America; studied education and public health in Europe during three years residence abroad. He was competent in Swedish, Danish, and Norwegian. *Avocational interests:* Sailing, canoeing, superstitions.†

(Died December, 1969)

KING, Martin Luther, Jr. 1929-1968

PERSONAL: Given name, Michael, changed to Martin when he was six years old; born January 15, 1929, in Atlanta, Ga.; son of Martin Luther (a minister) and Alberta (Williams) King; married Coretta Scott (a concert singer), June 17, 1953; children: Yolanda Denise, Martin Luther III, Dexter Scott, Bernice Albertine. *Education:* Morehouse College, A.B., 1948; Crozer Theological Seminary, B.D., 1951; Boston University, Ph.D., 1955, D.D., 1959; Chicago Theological Seminary, D.D., 1957; special student at University of Pennsylvania and Harvard University.

CAREER: Ordained Baptist minister in his father's church in Atlanta, Ga., 1947; Dexter Avenue Baptist Church, Montgomery, Ala., pastor, 1954-60; Southern Christian Leadership Conference (SCLC), Atlanta, founder and director, 1957-68; Ebenezer Baptist Church, Atlanta, co-pastor with his father, 1960-68. Vice-president, National Sunday School and Baptist Teaching Union Congress of National Baptist Convention; president, Montgomery Improvement Association. *Member:* National Association for the Advancement of Colored People (NAACP), Alpha Phi Alpha, Sigma Pi Phi, Elks. *Awards, honors:* Selected one of ten outstanding personalities of 1956 by *Time,* 1957; L.H.D., Morehouse College, 1957, and Central State College, 1958; L.L.D., Howard University, 1957, and Morgan State College, 1958; *Time* Man of the Year, 1963; Nobel Prize for Peace, October, 1964; Judaism and World Peace Award, Synagogue Council of America, 1965; Nehru Award for International Understanding (posthumous), 1968; received numerous awards for leadership of Montgomery Movement; two literary prizes were named in his honor by National Book Committee and Harper & Row.

WRITINGS: Our Struggle: The Story of Montgomery (originally appeared in *Liberation,* April, 1956), Congress of Racial Equality (CORE), 1957; *Stride Toward Freedom: The Montgomery Story,* Harper, 1958; *The Measure of a Man,* Christian Education Press (Philadelphia), 1959, memorial edition, Pilgrim Press, 1968; *Letter from Birmingham City Jail,* American Friends Service Committee, 1963, published as *Letter from Birmingham Jail,* Overbrook Press, 1968; *Why We Can't Wait,* Harper, 1964; *Where Do We Go from Here: Chaos or Community?,* Harper, 1967, new edition with an introduction by wife, Coretta Scott King, Bantam, 1968 (published in England as *Chaos or Community?,* Hodder & Stoughton, 1968); *The Trumpet of Conscience,* foreword by Coretta Scott King, Harper, 1968; (author of introduction) William Bradford Huie, *Three Lives for Mississippi,* New American Library, 1968.

Omnibus volumes: *"Unwise and Untimely?"* (letters; originally appeared in *Liberation,* June, 1963), Fellowship of Reconciliation, 1963; *Strength to Love* (sermons), Harper, 1963; *A Martin Luther King Treasury,* Educational Heritage (New York), 1964; *The Wisdom of Martin Luther King in His Own Words,* edited by staff of Bill Alder Books, Lancer Books, 1968; *"I Have a Dream": The Quotations of Martin Luther King, Jr.,* edited and compiled by Lotte Hoskins, Grosset, 1968; *We Shall Live in Peace: The Teachings of Martin Luther King, Jr.,* edited by Deloris Harrison, Hawthorn, 1968; *Martin Luther King, Jr.: His Three-Pronged Attack on I: Christ and the Bible, II: The United States of America, III: Law and Order,* Church League of America (Wheaton, Ill.), 1968; *Speeches about Vietnam,* Clergy and

Laymen Concerned about Vietnam (New York), 1969; *A Martin Luther King Reader,* edited by Nissim Ezekiel, Popular Prakashan (Bombay), 1969; *Words and Wisdom of Martin Luther King,* Taurus Press, 1970; *Speeches of Martin Luther King, Jr.,* commemorative edition, Martin Luther King, Jr. Memorial Center (Atlanta), 1972.

Other writings; speeches, except as indicated: *The Montgomery Story,* [San Francisco, Calif.], 1956; *Pilgrimage to Nonviolence* (monograph; originally appeared in *Christian Century*), Fellowship of Reconciliation, 1960; *I Have a Dream,* John Henry and Mary Louise Dunn Bryant Foundation (Los Angeles), 1963; *Nobel Lecture,* Harper, 1965; *Address at Valedictory Service,* University of the West Indies (Mona, Jamaica), 1965; *The Ware Lecture,* Unitarian Universalist Association (Boston), 1966; *Conscience for Change,* Canadian Broadcasting Co., 1967; *Beyond Vietnam,* Altoan Press, 1967; *Declaration of Independence from the War in Vietnam,* [New York], 1967; *A Drum Major for Justice,* Taurus Press, 1969; *A Testament of Hope* (originally appeared in *Playboy,* January, 1969), Fellowship of Reconciliation, 1969.

Recorded speeches: "I Shall Die, but That Is All I Shall Do for Death," Center for the Study of Democratic Institutions (Santa Barbara, Calif.), 1969; "A Knock at Midnight," Creed Records, c. 1970; "Remaining Awake through a Great Revolution," Creed Records, c. 1970; "Martin Luther King, Jr. in Conversation with Arnold Michaelis," Xerox, 1972.

Work represented in numerous anthologies, including: *Crisis in Modern America,* edited by H. John Heinz, III, Yale University, 1959; *Civil Disobedience: Five Essays,* edited by Robert A. Goldwin, Public Affairs Conference Center, Kenyon College, 1968; *Shall Not Perish: Nine Speeches by Three Great Americans,* edited by William B. Thomas, Gyldendalske Boghandel, 1969.

SIDELIGHTS: "On December 5, 1955, to the amused annoyance of the white citizens of Montgomery, Alabama, an obscure young Baptist minister named Martin Luther King, Jr., called a city-wide Negro boycott of its segregated bus system. To their consternation, however, it was almost one hundred percent successful; it lasted for 381 days and nearly bankrupted the bus line," a *Playboy* interviewer wrote. From that time until his assassination on April 4, 1968, in Memphis, Tennessee, where he was organizing striking garbage workers, Martin Luther King stood on the front lines of a non-violent Black revolution against social injustice. King became the universally acknowledged leader of the American civil rights movement, and chief spokesman for the nation's 20,000,000 Negroes. He represented what the *New Yorker* called "a new kind of political leader in America."

Any progress was made the hard way. In the course of his civil rights work King was jailed at least fourteen times, stabbed once in the chest, and his home was bombed three times. He had to come to terms with the probability of his own violent death. He told Gerald Priestland in an interview: "I'm realistic enough to know that I can meet a violent end. I live every day under the threat of death, and I have no illusions about it. There are enough sick people in the world for me to come to a violent end just as other leaders have done." Mrs. King reported that the day her husband left for his fatal trip to Memphis, he sent her flowers. "They were beautiful red carnations," she wrote, "but when I touched them, I realized they were artificial. In all the years we had been together, Martin had never sent me artificial flowers. . . . Martin said, 'I wanted to give you something that

you could always keep.' . . . Somehow, in some strange way, he seemed to have known how long they would have to last."

Martin Luther King grew up in a middle income home in Atlanta and was fourteen before he himself experienced racial prejudice. He and a teacher were returning home from Dublin, Georgia, where he had participated in and won an oratorical contest sponsored by the Negro Elks. He told the *Playboy* interviewer: "Mrs. Bradley and I were on a bus returning to Atlanta, and at a small town along the way, some white passengers boarded the bus, and the white driver ordered us to get up and give the whites our seats. We didn't move quickly enough to suit him, so he began cursing us. . . . I intended to stay right in that seat, but Mrs. Bradley finally urged me up, saying we had to obey the law. And so we stood up in the aisle for the 90 miles to Atlanta. . . . It was the angriest I have ever been in my life."

"King was a believer in nonviolence," a *Life* editorial stated, "and perfected the technique, learned from Gandhi, of using it as a weapon in his war for social change. . . . King insisted on nonviolent means because he took the Sermon on the Mount seriously, and that can be a daring and unpopular thing to do." The *New Yorker* writer commented: "To the last, Dr. King assumed that when the legal and extra legal barriers to communication were hewn down, people would begin to see their brotherhood beneath the skin and begin to know 'the majestic heights of being obedient to the unenforceable.' . . . A refined civility ran through him to the core; he didn't need to dissemble, to conceal hatreds, for none smoldered within him—except the hatred of evil."

King's books expressed his beliefs and opinions not only on civil rights, but on other issues as well. *Stride Toward Freedom,* his account of the 1958 Negro boycott of the Montgomery bus lines, is, according to Abel Plenn, "a document of far-reaching importance for present and future chroniclings of the struggle for civil rights in this country." King told *Playboy* that he thought three important things came about as a result of *Letter from a Birmingham Jail,* which was written during one of the terms he served for civil disobedience, in reply to eight clergymen who had been critical of his work in Birmingham. "It helped to focus greater international attention upon what was happening in Birmingham," said King. "Without Birmingham, the march on Washington would not have been called. . . . It was also the image of Birmingham which . . . helped to bring the Civil Rights Bill into being in 1963." Stone said of *Why We Can't Wait,* "The book's logic and eloquence strike hard at the jugular veins of two American dogmas—racial discrimination, and that even more insidious doctrine which nourished it, gradualism."

Herbert Warren Richardson called King "the most important theologian of our time . . . because of his creative proposals for dealing with the structure of evil generated by modern relativism, *viz.,* ideological conflict. . . . King created not only a new theology, but also new types of piety, new styles of Christian living." Because the struggle against racism was a struggle against such an ideological conflict, King had to carry this struggle into other areas as well, and so was the first to join the civil rights struggle with the struggle against the Vietnam war. *Where Do We Go from Here: Chaos or Community* expressed his views on both subjects. He wrote: "The worth of an individual does not lie in the measure of his intellect, his racial origin or his social position. Human worth lies in relatedness to God. An individual has value because he has value to God." Andrew Salkley called the book "another of [his] continuing 'understated blasts' at the subterranean decency of pan-American life. He has always seen it as essentially a puritanical, hypocritical, powerful and, albeit, a forgiving society, capable of feeling and showing great shame and nobility and co-operative heroism.... Dr. King's concerns are overtly for the total American commonwealth of its citizens, eschewing sectional armed revolt and chaos, and advocating the full use of the traditional institutions of law and democracy by the society's underprivileged and dispossessed." David Steinberg found King to be in conflict in this book. King's "perception and definition of the problems" of race seem to fit with the advocates of black power. Yet King, being non-violent, could not possibly identify with this group. Steinberg commented that "we are left with the open question of whether his definition of the problem and his philosophy of action are compatible or contradictory."

A reviewer for *Virginia Quarterly Review*, commenting on *The Trumpet of Conscience* wrote: "King saw clearly, four months before he died, that the white man's hate and the rich man's dollar remain the West's most powerful forces, despite the preaching and example of his movement and the many moral outcries preceding him."

Time said of King: "The nation may take greater heart from the luminous words he flung into the face of white America: 'We will meet your capacity to inflict suffering with our capacity to endure suffering. We will meet your physical force with soul force. We will not hate you, but we cannot in all good conscience obey your unjust laws. We will soon wear you down by our capacity to suffer. And in winning our freedom, we will so appeal to your heart and your conscience that we will win you in the process.' In his death, if not in life, Martin Luther King may have gone far toward that goal."

King was originally buried in Southview Cemetery in Atlanta; he is presently buried in property adjacent to Ebenezer Baptist Church.

In April, 1970, a documentary entitled "King: A Filmed Record—Montgomery to Memphis" played one time simultaneously in over 1000 theatres in North America and Europe. The proceeds, which amounted to about $3,500,000, went to the Martin Luther King, Jr., Special Fund, the purpose of which is to finance organizations carrying on Dr. King's civil rights work.

Strength to Love has been translated into Italian; *Why We Can't Wait* has been translated into Polish, Yugoslavian, and French; *Where Do We Go from Here: Chaos or Community?* has been translated into Spanish, French, and German; King's writing has also been published in Brazil and Russia.

BIOGRAPHICAL/CRITICAL SOURCES—Periodicals: *New York Times*, October 12, 1958, April 12, 1968, April 13, 1968; *America*, August 17, 1963, July 22, 1967; *Critic*, August, 1964; *New Yorker*, June 22, 1967, July 22, 1967, April 13, 1968; *Christian Science Monitor*, July 6, 1967; *Saturday Review*, July 8, 1967; *Book World*, July 9, 1967, September 28, 1969; *Christian Century*, August 23, 1967, January 14, 1970, August 26, 1970; *New York Review of Books*, August 24, 1967; *New York Times Book Review*, September 3, 1967, February 16, 1969; *Commonweal*, November 17, 1967, May 3, 1968; *Choice*, February, 1968; *New Statesman*, March 22, 1968; *Punch*, April 3, 1968; *London Times*, April 6, 1968; *Economist*, April 6, 1968; *Listener*, April 11, 1968, April 25, 1968; *Time*, April 12, 1968, October 3, 1969; *Times Literary Supplement*, April 18, 1968; *Life*, April 19, 1968, September 12, 1969, September 19, 1969; *A B Bookman's Weekly*, April

22, 1968; *Negro Bulletin*, May, 1968; *Antioch Review*, spring, 1968; *Esquire*, August, 1968; *Virginia Quarterly Review*, autumn, 1968; *Washington Post*, January 14, 1970; *Books Abroad*, autumn, 1970.

Books: Lerone Bennett, Jr., *What Manner of Man*, Johnson Publishing Co. (Chicago, Ill.), 1964; *Playboy Interviews*, Playboy Press, 1967; Lionel Lokos, *House Divided: The Life and Legacy of Martin Luther King*, Arlington House, 1968; William Robert Miller, *Martin Luther King, Jr.: His Life, Martyrdom, and Meaning for the World*, Weybright, 1968; Edward T. Clayton, *Martin Luther King, Jr.: The Peaceful Warrior*, Prentice-Hall, 1968; Louis E. Lomax, *To Kill a Black Man*, Holloway, 1968; Deloris Harrison, editor, *We Shall Live in Peace: The Teachings of Martin Luther King, Jr.*, Hawthorn, 1968; *Martin Luther King, Jr., 1929-1968*, Johnson Publishing Co. (Chicago, Ill.), 1968; *Martin Luther King, Jr.: The Journey of a Martyr*, Universal Publishing & Distributing, 1968; Mary Luins Small, *Creative Encounters with "Dear Dr. King": A Handbook of Discussions, Activities, and Engagements on Racial Injustice, Poverty, and War*, edited by Sanders Redding, Buckingham Enterprises, 1969; Coretta Scott King, *My Life with Martin Luther King, Jr.*, Holt, 1969; Lenwood G. Davis, *I Have a Dream: The Life and Times of Martin Luther King, Jr.*, Adams Book Co., 1969; David L. Lewis, *King: A Critical Biography*, Praeger, 1970; Eric C. Lincoln, editor, *Martin Luther King, Jr.: A Profile*, Hill & Wang, 1970; John A. Williams, *The King God Didn't Save*, Coward, 1970; Jim Bishop, *The Days of Martin Luther King, Jr.*, Putnam, 1971; Robert M. Bleiweiss, editor, *Marching to Freedom: The Life of Martin Luther King, Jr.*, New American Library, 1971; Kenneth L. Smith and Ira G. Zepp, Jr., *Search for the Beloved Community: The Thinking of Martin Luther King, Jr.*, Judson, 1974; Alan Westin and Barry Mahoney, *The Trial of Martin Luther King*, Crowell, 1975; Gary Paulsen and Dan Theis, *The Man Who Climbed the Mountain: Martin Luther King*, Raintree, 1976; Flipp Schulke, editor, *Martin Luther King, Jr.: A Documentary.... Montgomery to Memphis*, Norton, 1976; *Martin Luther King, Jr.*, Norton, 1976.†

(Assassinated April 4, 1968 in Memphis, Tenn.)

*   *   *

KINNEAR, Elizabeth K. 1902-

PERSONAL: Born November 26, 1902, in Xenia, Ohio; daughter of Hugh Alexander (a minister) and Luella (Espy) Kelsey; married James Ernest Kinnear, September 24, 1932. *Education:* Muskingum College, B.A. (magna cum laude), 1924; School of Oriental Studies, Cairo, diploma in Arabic and Islamics, 1928. *Religion:* Protestant. *Office:* National Council of Churches, 475 Riverside Dr., New York, N.Y. 10027.

CAREER: United Presbyterian Church, educational missionary in Egypt, 1924-46; Columbia University, Teacher's College, New York City, secretary for student loans, 1947-51, executive assistant to chaplain, 1952-56; National Council of Churches, New York City, associate secretary for South Asia and the Near East, 1956-61; World Council of Churches, New York City, executive assistant to International Missionary Council and Division of World Mission, 1961-66; National Council of Churches, program assistant in world literacy and Christian literature, beginning 1966.

WRITINGS: She Sat Where They Sat: A Memoir of Anna Young Thompson of Egypt, Eerdmans, 1971. Assistant to literature and literacy committee, National Council of Churches *Quarterly Newsletter*.†

KINNEY, Lucien Blair   1895-1971

PERSONAL: Born January 15, 1895, in Hudson, Wis.; son of Andrew Jackson and Susan (Pierce) Kinney; married Ida Ormsrud, June 3, 1922 (died, 1967); married Joyce Valentine, December 14, 1968. *Education:* University of Minnesota, B.Sc., 1923, M.A., 1925, Ph.D., 1931; University of Chicago, graduate study, 1929-30. *Politics:* Democrat. *Home:* 400 Miramonte Ave., Palo Alto, Calif. 94306.

CAREER: University of Minnesota, Minneapolis, instructor in education, 1931-37; State University of New York College at Oswego, head of department of mathematics and acting registrar, 1937-40; Stanford University, Stanford, Calif., associate professor, 1940-45, professor of education, 1945-64, professor emeritus, 1964-71. Former member, California Committee on Accreditation. *Military service:* U.S. Aviation Service, World War I. *Awards, honors:* Outstanding Achievement Award, University of Minnesota, 1960.

WRITINGS: Business Mathematics, Holt, 1936, 2nd edition, 1937; *Senior Mathematics,* Holt, 1945; (editor with Katherine Dresden and Jean D. Grambs) *Better Learning Through Current Materials,* Stanford University Press, 1949, revised edition, 1954; (with H. R. Douglass) *The High School Curriculum,* Ronald, 1950, revised edition, 1964; (with C. Richard Purdy) *Teaching Mathematics in the Secondary School,* Rinehart, 1952; (with Douglass and James Lentz) *Everyday Arithmetic,* Books 1 and 2, Holt, 1953; *Everyday Mathematics,* Holt, 1955; (with Vincent Ruble and M. Russell Blythe) *Holt Arithmetic,* two books, grades seven and eight, Holt, 1961; (with Vincent Ruble) *General Mathematics,* Holt, 1961; (with Lawrence Thomas and Arthur Coladarci) *Perspective on Education,* Prentice-Hall, 1961; *Certification in Education,* Prentice-Hall, 1964; (with John L. Marks and Purdy) *Teaching Elementary School Mathematics for Understanding,* 2nd edition, McGraw, 1965; (with Ruble and Gerald W. Brown) *General Mathematics,* Books 1 and 2, Holt, 1968.

AVOCATIONAL INTERESTS: Golf, traveling in America.†

(Died December 24, 1971)

* * *

KIRK, T(homas) H(obson)   1899-
(K. H. Thomas)

PERSONAL: Born January 13, 1899, in West Hartlepool, County Durham, England; son of Henry (a coke-oven manager) and Harriet (Hobson) Kirk; married Ethel Winifred Daniels, June 15, 1925; children: June Margaret (Mrs. William Walker), Peter John Daniels. *Education:* University of Durham, M.B., B.S., 1921, M.D., 1930. *Religion:* Church of England. *Home:* Oakfield, Meadowfield Rd., Stocksfield, Northumberland, England. *Agent:* John Johnson, 51-54 Goschen Buildings, 12-13 Henrietta St., London WC2E 8LF, England.

CAREER: Medical practitioner in Barton-on-Humber, Lincolnshire, England, 1922-64; writer. *Military service:* Royal Naval Volunteer Reserve, 1917-18; became sub-lieutenant. *Member:* British Medical Association (chairman for Lincolnshire area, 1950). *Awards, honors:* Serving Brother, Order of St. John of Jerusalem.

WRITINGS—Fiction: Back to the Wall, Faber, 1967; *The River Gang,* Faber, 1968; *The Ardrey Ambush,* Faber, 1969. Author of a play, under pseudonym K. H. Thomas, entitled "Slack Water," produced by British Broadcasting Corp.,

1955; also author of a dozen other plays produced by amateur dramatic societies.†

* * *

KISSANE, Leedice McAnelly   1905-

PERSONAL: Born May 26, 1905, in Denison, Iowa; daughter of Jefferson Roy (an educator) and Minnie (Bigler) McAnelly; married Donald P. Kissane, June 16, 1926 (died June 15, 1968); children: Esther L. (Mrs. Robert D. Hodgkinson), John M., James D. *Education:* Cornell College, Mount Vernon, Iowa, B.A., 1926; University of Idaho, M.A., 1937; University of Minnesota, Ph.D., 1967. *Religion:* Presbyterian. *Home:* 249 South Seventh Ave., Pocatello, Idaho 83201.

CAREER: Pocatello (Idaho) public schools, substitute teacher, 1933-37; Idaho State University, Pocatello, instructor, 1941-47, assistant professor, 1947-62, associate professor, 1962-67, professor of English, 1967-70, director of American studies program, 1966-70; University of Iceland, Reykjavik, senior Fulbright lecturer, 1970-72. *Member:* National Council of Teachers of English, American Studies Association, American Association of University Professors, American Association of University Women, Idaho State Historical Society, Phi Beta Kappa, Phi Kappa Phi, Delta Kappa Gamma, P.E.O. Sisterhood.

WRITINGS: Ruth Suckow, Twayne, 1969. Contributor to *Idaho Yesterdays* (magazine of Idaho State Historical Society), and other journals.

WORK IN PROGRESS: Editing memoirs; book reviews.

AVOCATIONAL INTERESTS: American culture, especially music, fine arts, and theater; regional history, travel, and the study of foreign cultures.

* * *

KITAGAWA, Daisuke   1910-

PERSONAL: Born October 3, 1910, in Taihoku, Japan; became U.S. citizen in 1954; son of Chiyokichi (a priest of Nippon Seikokai) and Kumiko (Nazaki) Kitagawa; married Fujiko Sugimoto, July 1, 1944; children: Karen, John. *Education:* St. Paul's University, Tokyo, Japan, B.A., 1933; Central Theological College, Tokyo, Japan, B.D., 1933; General Theological Seminary, S.T.B., 1939; additional study at University of Chicago Divinity School, 1952, 1954-55, and Ecumenical Institute, Celingny, Switzerland, 1955-56.

CAREER: Ordained deacon, The Protestant Episcopal Church, 1939, priest, 1940. Priest-in-charge of missions to Japanese Americans in Washington State, 1939-42; clergyman at Tulelake War Relocation Center in California, 1942-43; field secretary, National Council of Churches' Committee on Japanese American Resettlement, 1943-44; director of United Christian Ministry to Japanese Americans in Minneapolis and St. Paul, Minn., 1944-49; pastor in Minneapolis, Minn., 1949-54; director, Department on Christian Social Relations, Episcopal Diocese of Minnesota, 1953-54; priest-in-charge of Japanese Episcopal Church, Chicago, Ill., 1954-56; World Council of Churches, Geneva, Switzerland, secretary in Division of Studies, 1956-60, secretary of Secretariat on Racial and Ethnic Relations, 1960-62; The Protestant Episcopal Church, Executive Council, New York, N.Y., executive secretary, Division of Domestic Mission, 1962-65, executive secretary of College and University Division, beginning 1965. *Awards, honors:* D.D., St. Paul's University, Tokyo, Japan, 1962.

WRITINGS: Race Relations and Christian Mission, Friendship, 1964; The Pastor and the Race Issue, Seabury, 1965; Issei and Nisei: The Internment Years, Seabury, 1967.

SIDELIGHTS: Issei and Nisei is the story of Kitagawa's experiences in the Japanese-American internment camps during the Second World War.†

* * *

KLEBE, Charles Eugene 1907-
(Gene Klebe)

PERSONAL: Born September 18, 1907, in Philadelphia, Pa.; son of Charles William (an engineer) and Clara (Wittemann) Klebe; married Mary Frothingham Klaer (an antique dealer), February 12, 1938; children: Margot Nowland (Mrs. Robert Clark Ernst). Education: Attended Philadelphia College of Art, four years, and University of Pennsylvania, one year. Politics: Republican. Home: Bristol Rd., Bristol, Me. 04539.

CAREER: Free-lance artist, specializing in marine and nature painting, and photographer. Did civilian art work for U.S. Navy and Surgeon General's Department during World War II; civilian combat artist for U.S. Navy, beginning 1960, including assignments to Antarctica, 1960-61, 1961-62, Middle East, 1964, Vietnam, 1965, and Gemini XI, 1966; executed two murals for Expo '67 and diarama for Bath Marine Museum. President, Pemaquid Group Artists, beginning 1955; member, Government Council on Art and Culture, 1965-69; chairman, Maine State Art Commission, 1966-71; member, Maine State Commission on the Arts and the Humanities. Member: American Watercolor Society, Allied Artists of America, Academic Artists Association, Maine Art Gallery, Philadelphia Watercolor Club, Baltimore Watercolor Club, Explorers Club and Salmagundi Club (both New York). Awards, honors: More than 100 art awards, including: Gold Medal of American Artists Professional League, 1961; Fox Purchase Prize of Farnsworth Museum, 1966; Navy Art Gold Medal, 1967; Salmagundi First Watercolor Prize, 1968; Franklin Mint Gold Medal, 1974. Also recipient of Academic Artists Awards, 1967-72.

WRITINGS: (Under name Gene Klebe; with daughter, Margot Klebe Ernst) Penguin Family (juvenile), Putnam, 1968. Photographs included in Grolier's Book of Knowledge, 1967 edition. Contributor to American Artists Magazine.

BIOGRAPHICAL/CRITICAL SOURCES: Down East Magazine, summer, 1968.

* * *

KLEES, Fredric (Spang) 1901-

PERSONAL: Born June 25, 1901, in Reading, Pa.; son of James A. (a wagon manufacturer) and Kate (Spang) Klees. Education: Bowdoin College, B.A., 1925; Exeter College, Oxford, graduate study, 1925-26. Politics: Democrat. Religion: Society of Friends (Quaker). Residence: Swarthmore, Pa.

CAREER: Swarthmore College, Swarthmore, Pa., instructor in English, 1926-27, Brown University, Providence, R.I., instructor in English, 1927-28; Swarthmore College, instructor, 1928-45, assistant professor of English literature, 1963-66, professor emeritus, 1966—.

WRITINGS: The Pennsylvania Dutch, Macmillan, 1950; The Round of the Year, Macmillan, 1963. Contributor to Holiday and Saturday Evening Post.

AVOCATIONAL INTERESTS: Gardening, painting, and travel.

* * *

KLEIN, Ernest 1899-

PERSONAL: Born July 26, 1899, in Szatmar, Hungary; son of Ignaz Isaac (a rabbi) and Rose (Friedrich) Klein; married Ella Schattin, 1935 (died, 1944); children: Joseph (died, 1944). Education: University of Vienna, Ph.D., 1925. Home: 119 Barse St., Toronto, Ontario, Canada.

CAREER: Rabbi of Nove Zamky, Czechoslovakia, 1931-44; deported by the Nazis to Auschwitz concentration camp, where his wife and son died, and later to Dachau; liberated by American troops in 1945; emigrated to Paris, France, where he was a rabbi of Congregation Rue de Montevideo, 1950-51; rabbi in Toronto, Ontario, beginning 1951, became rabbi of Beth Yitshak. Awards, honors: Canada Council grant, 1961.

WRITINGS: A Comprehensive Etymological Dictionary of the English Language: Dealing with the Origin of Words and Their Sense Development, Thus Illustrating the History of Civilization and Culture, Elsevier, Volume I, 1966, Volume II, 1967, published in one volume, 1971.

WORK IN PROGRESS: Etymological Dictionary of the Hebrew Language.

SIDELIGHTS: Ernest Klein spent twenty years of research on his dictionary; the manuscript was typed with the aid of a $4,000 grant from the Canada Council. Klein has read in Sumerian, Ethiopian, Syriac, Sanskrit, and Old Norse, among the lesser known languages, and in many others.

BIOGRAPHICAL/CRITICAL SOURCES: Toronto Telegram, March 12, 1966.†

* * *

KLUWE, Mary Jean 1905-1975

PERSONAL: Born August 12, 1905; daughter of John Joseph (a builder) and Beatrice (Wade) Upson; children: Nancy Smith, Richard Smith. Education: Wayne State University, B.S., 1941, M.E., 1945, Ed.D., 1957.

CAREER: Detroit (Mich.) Board of Education, beginning 1945, supervisor of language arts. Member: National Council of Teachers of English, National Education Association, Association for Supervision and Curriculum Development, Friends of the Detroit Public Library, Delta Kappa Gamma, Beta Sigma Phi.

WRITINGS: (With Byron H. Van Rockel) From Elephants to Eskimos, Harper, 1966; (with Van Rockel) From Fins to Feathers, Harper, 1966; (with Van Rockel) From Bicycles to Boomerangs, Harper, 1966.

WORK IN PROGRESS: Research in beginning reading.†

(Died January 22, 1975)

* * *

KNAPP, Robert Hampden 1915-1974

PERSONAL: Born April 16, 1915, in Portland, Ore.; son of Joseph B. (a lumberman) and Cornelia (Pinkham) Knapp; married Johnsia Rachel Nelson, March 19, 1945 (divorced, 1972); children: Robert H., Jr., Abigail Pinkham, Hiatt Jefferson, Sarah Elizabeth. Education: University of Oregon, B.A., 1938, M.A., 1939; Harvard University, M.A., 1940, Ph.D., 1948. Home: 31 Magnolia Hill, Cromwell, Conn. 06457. Office: Department of Psychology, Wesleyan University, Middleton, Conn. 06457.

CAREER: Massachusetts Commission on Public Safety, director of Propaganda Research Division, 1941-42; Wesleyan University, Middleton, Conn., lecturer, 1946-47, assistant professor, 1947-50, associate professor, 1950-55, professor of psychology 1955-74, chairman of department, 1956-74. Ford Foundation, deputy director of Behavioral Sciences Division, 1953-54; University of California at Berkeley, staff psychologist, Institute of Personality Assessment and Research, 1957-58. Director of science faculty fellowship panel, National Science Foundation and Association of American Colleges, 1956-74; member of Connecticut Board of Examiners of Psychologists, 1959-74. Consultant to Ford Foundation, U.S. Air Force, Educational Testing Service, and other agencies and institutions. Democratic candidate for Massachusetts Assembly, 1956; chairman of Planning and Zoning Commision, Haddam, Conn., 1956-58. Wartime service: U.S. Office of Strategic Services, 1943-46, area operations officer with Morale Branch in Middle East, agent in Greece, Indo-China, and China.

MEMBER: American Psychological Association (secretary-treasurer of esthetics division, 1964-67), American Ortho-Psychiatric Association, American Society for Aesthetics, American Association for Humanistic Psychology, Eastern Psychological Society, Connecticut State Psychological Society (council, 1954-58; president, 1956-57), Phi Beta Kappa (president of Wesleyan chapter, 1964-66), Sigma Xi, Sigma Nu, Harvard Club (New York). Awards, honors: M.A., Wesleyan University 1956; research contracts from U.S. Office of Naval Research, Carnegie Foundation, Ford Foundation, Fund for the Advancement of Education, National Institute of Mental Health, and Office of Education.

WRITINGS: (With H. B. Goodrich) The Origins of American Scientists, University of Chicago Press, 1953; (with J. Greenbaum) The Younger American Scholar, University of Chicago Press, 1954; (contributor) Identification of Creative Scientific Talent, edited by Calvin W. Taylor, University of Utah Press, 1955; (contributor) Motives in Fantasy, Action and Society, edited by J. W. Atkinson, Van Nostrand, 1958.

(Contributor) The American College, edited by R. Nevitt Sanford, Wiley, 1962 (condensed edition published as College and Character, 1964); (contributor) B. Barber and W. Hirsch, The Sociology of Science, Free Press of Glencoe, 1962; (contributor) Bernard Berelson, editor, Behavioral Science Today, Basic Books, 1963; (contributor) Taylor and Barron, editors, Scientific Creativity: Its Recognition and Development, Wiley, 1963; The Origins of the American Humanistic Scholars, Prentice-Hall, 1964.

Contributor to conference proceedings and about forty articles and reviews to Public Opinion Quarterly, Science, Scientific Monthly, and psychology and sociology journals.

WORK IN PROGRESS: Research on the psychology of aesthetics and personality.

SIDELIGHTS: Knapp was competent in German, "fair" in Italian.†

(Died September 8, 1974)

* * *

KNIGHT, H(erbert) Ralph   1895-

PERSONAL: Born January 13, 1895, in Glens Falls, N.Y.; son of Herbert William (an insurance company official) and Minnie (Carpenter) Knight; married Dorothy Weed, April 28, 1923; children: David, Joan (Mrs. William Abbott), William. Education: Attended Union College and University, Schenectady, N.Y., three years, and Columbia University,

1918. Politics: Registered Democrat, votes independently. Religion: Episcopalian. Home and office: 456 Rockland Rd., Merion Station, Pa. Agent: Collins-Knowlton-Wing, Inc., 60 East 56th St., New York, N.Y. 10022.

CAREER: Editor of a suburban magazine, 1920-23; editor, The Chesterfieldian, White Plains, N.Y.; sports editor, then editor-in-chief, of hometown morning newspaper, Glens Falls Post-Star, Glens Falls, N.Y., 1923-44; Saturday Evening Post, New York, N.Y., associate editor, 1945-61.

WRITINGS: The Burr-Hamilton Duel: A Tragedy that Stunned the American Nation, F. Watts, 1968; Learning to Talk to the World Beyond: An Introduction to the Joy of Immortality, Stackpole, 1969. Also author of A Pamphlet of Selected Poems, 1962. Contributor of short stories to Saturday Evening Post, 1940-44.

WORK IN PROGRESS: A group of short stories about his wife and himself, which he intends to eventually fit together as a novel.

SIDELIGHTS: Several of Knight's short stories were selected by the Saturday Evening Post for inclusion in pocket books sent to troops overseas during World War II.†

* * *

KNIGHT, Hattie M.   1908-1976

PERSONAL: Born May 23, 1908, in Malad, Idaho; daughter of John and Ann (Clark) Madson; married Eldred V. Knight, April 20, 1929 (deceased); children: Larry V. Education: Brigham Young University, B.S. (history and education), 1941; University of Denver, B.S. in L.S., 1943; George Peabody College for Teachers, M.S. in L.S., 1951; Rutgers University, graduate study, 1961-62. Religion: Church of Jesus Christ of Latter-day Saints. Home: 430 East Fifth N., Provo, Utah 84601.

CAREER: Public school teacher in Idaho, 1926-34, 1936-39; Brigham Young University, Provo, Utah, circulation librarian, 1941-49, reference librarian, 1949-58, assistant professor, 1958-69, associate professor of library science, 1969-73, acting director of library and information sciences, 1970-71. Instructor, George Peabody College for Teachers, summer, 1951, College of Idaho, summer, 1962, 1963. Advisor and consultant, Knapp School Libraries Project, 1965-67. Member: American Association of University Professors, American Library Association, Association of American Library Schools, Utah Library Association (past president), Utah Academy of Letters, Arts and Sciences, Mountain Plains Library Association, Brigham Young University Women, Delta Kappa Gamma, Phi Kappa Phi, Beta Phi Mu.

WRITINGS: The 1-2-3 Guide to Libraries, Brigham Young University Press, 1963, 4th edition, W. C. Brown, 1970; (with Jane Vance and Maude Jacobs) Better Libraries for Utah Schools: Standards and Goals, Utah Library Association, 1965. Contributor to Brigham Young University Extension publications and to journals. Editor, Utah Libraries, 1957-61.

WORK IN PROGRESS: A collection of readings in Utah history.†

(Died December 2, 1976)

* * *

KNIGHT, Norman L(ouis)   1895-

PERSONAL: Born September 21, 1895; son of Louis Ruthven (a pharmacist) and Mary Elizabeth (Stauber)

Knight; married Marie Sarah Yenn; children: Paula Marie (Mrs. John E. Hendrickson). *Education:* St. Joseph Junior College, St. Joseph, Mo., A.A., 1918; George Washington University, B.S. in Chem. Eng., 1925. *Politics:* Independent. *Religion:* Independent ("probably more akin to Unitarian than any other").

CAREER: U.S. Department of Agriculture, posts with Weather Bureau and Insecticide Division, 1919-64. Weather Bureau, assistant observer, Davenport, Iowa, 1919-20, observer and translator, Washington, D.C., 1920-25; Insecticide Division (now Pesticide Regulation Division), analytical chemist in Washington, D.C., 1925-29, Chicago, Ill., 1929, St. Louis, Mo., 1929-40, Chicago, Ill., 1940-50, and Beltsville, Md., 1950-64. *Military service:* U.S. Army, Field Artillery, 1918-19; served in France. *Member:* Science Fiction Writers of America. *Awards, honors:* Merit award from U.S. Department of Agriculture, 1962.

WRITINGS: (With James Blish) *A Torrent of Faces* (science fiction), Doubleday, 1967. Contributor of serials and novelettes to science fiction magazines.

AVOCATIONAL INTERESTS: Reading, microscopy, and oil painting.††

* * *

KNOLLENBERG, Bernhard 1892-1973

PERSONAL: Born November 26, 1892, in Richmond, Ind.; son of George H. (a businessman) and Agnes (Steen) Knollenberg; married Mary Lightfoot Tarleton (a sculptor), 1933; children: Bernhard Walter. *Education:* Earlham College, A.B., 1912; Harvard University, M.A., 1914, LL.B., 1916. *Politics:* "Mugwump." *Religion:* None. *Home:* Parkers Point Lane, Chester, Conn. 06412.

CAREER: Lawyer, 1916-1938; Lord, Day & Lord (law firm), New York, N.Y., lawyer, 1921-1938; Yale University, New Haven, Conn., library director, 1938-42; U.S. Lend-Lease Administration, Washington, D.C., deputy administrator, 1942-44, historian, 1945-73.

WRITINGS: Washington and the Revolution: A Re-Appraisal, Macmillan, 1940; *Whitewater Valley,* Indiana Historical Society, 1945; (editor) *The Correspondence of Governor Samuel Ward,* Rhode Island Historical Society, 1952; *Origins of the American Revolution,* Macmillan, 1960; *George Washington: The Virginia Period,* Duke University Press, 1964; *Growth of the American Revolution, 1766-1775,* Free Press, 1975.†

(Died July 6, 1973)

* * *

KNUTSON, Kent S(iguart) 1924-1973

PERSONAL: "K" in surname is pronounced; born August 7, 1924, in Goldfield, Iowa; son of Gunner and Gertrude (Thorsheim) Knutson; married Norma E. Arnesen, September 15, 1951; children: Kirsten, Kristofer, Kent, Kaia, Kimberly, Karl. *Education:* State University of Iowa, B.S., 1947; Luther Theological Seminary, B.Th., 1951; Columbia University and Union Theological Seminary, Ph.D., 1961, postdoctoral study, 1964-65; also attended University of Oslo, 1949, University of Minnesota, 1950, and University of Heidelberg, 1952-53. *Home:* 1566 Sumter Ave. N., Minneapolis, Minn. 55406. *Office:* 422 South Fifth St., Minneapolis, Minn. 55406.

CAREER: Standard Oil of Indiana, Whiting, Ind., chemical engineer, 1947; ordained a Lutheran minister, 1954; Our

Saviour Lutheran Church, Staten Island, N.Y., pastor, 1954-58; Luther Theological Seminary, St. Paul, Minn., faculty member, 1958-69; Wartburg Theological Seminary, Dubuque, Iowa, president, 1969-71; American Lutheran Church, Minneapolis, Minn., president, 1971-73. *Military service:* U.S. Navy, 1944-46; served in South Pacific Theater. *Member:* Minneapolis Athletic Club. *Awards, honors:* American Association of Theological Schools fellow, 1964-65; Doctor of Humane Letters, Luther College; Doctor of Divinity, St. Olaf College, Wartburg College.

WRITINGS—All published by Augsburg, except as indicated: (Contributor) Elwin W. Mueller and Giles C. Ekola, editors, *The Silent Struggle for Mid-America,* 1962; (contributor) James H. Burtness and John P. Kildahl, editors, *The New Community in Christ,* 1963; *His Only Son Our Lord,* 1966; *Eucharist and Sacrifice,* U.S.A. National Committee, Lutheran World Federation, 1968; (contributor) W. Kent Gilbert, editor, *Confirmation and Education,* Fortress, 1969; *God's Drama in Seven Acts,* 1970; *The Shape of the Question: The Mission of the Church in a Secular Age,* 1972; (contributor) William H. Weiblen, editor, *Gospel, Church, Mission,* 1976. Editor and contributor, *Dialog* (journal of theology), 1966-69.†

(Died March 12, 1973)

* * *

KOCH, Helen L(ois) 1895-

PERSONAL: Born August 26, 1895, in Blue Island, Ill.; daughter of Louis George (an estate manager) and Sophia (Uhlich) Koch. *Education:* University of Chicago, Ph.B., 1918, Ph.D., 1921. *Office:* Department of Psychology, University of Chicago, Chicago, Ill. 60637.

CAREER: University of Texas, Austin, instructor, 1922-23, adjunct professor, 1924-25, associate professor, 1926-27, professor of educational psychology, 1928-29; University of Chicago, Chicago, Ill., associate professor, 1929-42, professor of child psychology, 1942-60, professor emeritus, 1960—, director of Nursery School, 1933-48, coordinator, 1938-48. Exchange professor at University of Frankfurt, 1948-49, 1958; lecturer at University of Marburg, 1948-49, University of Wurzburg, 1948-49, and University of Southern California, summer, 1962. Member of Greater Metropolitan Area Child Care Committee, Office of Civilian Defense, 1942-47.

MEMBER: American Psychological Association (fellow; president of division of developmental psychology, 1960-61), American Association for the Advancement of Science (fellow), Society for Research in Child Development (fellow; charter member; secretary, 1934-35; president, 1937; board member, 1942-46), Illinois Society for Consulting Psychologists (president, 1940-41), Chicago Association of Child Study and Parent Education, Deutsche Gesellschaft fuer Psychologie, Phi Beta Kappa, Sigma Xi, Pi Lambda Theta, Delta Kappa Gamma (founder; member of national administrative board, 1965-69), Chicago Psychological Club, Quadrangle Club. *Awards, honors:* Citation for public service by University of Chicago, 1950, Chicago Psychological Club and Delta Kappa Gamma, 1960; G. Stanley Hall Medal of the American Psychological Association, 1967.

WRITINGS: (Contributor) T. G. Andrews, editor, *Methods of Psychology,* Wiley, 1947; *Twins and Twin Relations,* University of Chicago Press, 1966. Contributor to *Encyclopedia of Educational Research,* Macmillan, 1941, *Encyclopedia of Child Guidance,* Philosophical Library, 1943, *Junior Encyclopaedia Britannica,* 1943, *Dictionary of*

Education, McGraw, 1945, and *Encyclopaedia Britannica;* also contributor of about 50 monographs and articles to professional journals. Associate editor of *Journal of Experimental Child Psychology*, 1963, *Psychological Record, Journal Research in Child Development*, 1964, and *Child Development*, 1968.

WORK IN PROGRESS: Continued research on problems dealing with effects, biological and psychological, of twinning.

AVOCATIONAL INTERESTS: Travel; study of ancient history, natural history, geopolitics, and present social and economic trends.†

*   *   *

KOENIG, Samuel   1899-1972

PERSONAL: Born March 29, 1899, in Galicia, Austria; came to United States, 1921; son of Berl (a merchant) and Rebecca (Liebster) Koenig; married Miriam Nelson, October 13, 1932; children: Paul Maimon. *Education:* Attended University of Minnesota, 1924-27; Marquette University, Ph.B., 1929; Yale University, M.A., 1931, Ph.D., 1935. *Politics:* Independent. *Home:* 1890 East 21st St., Brooklyn, N.Y. 11229.

CAREER: Director of sociological studies, Federal Writers' Project, State of Connecticut, 1936-41, and research fellow Yale University, New Haven, Conn., 1937-40; Brooklyn College of the City University of New York, Brooklyn, N.Y., instructor in sociology and anthropology, 1941-48, assistant professor, 1949-51, associate professor, 1952-59, professor, 1960-70, deputy chairman of department, 1948-65. Fulbright professor, Bar-Ilan University, Israel, 1957-58, Karnatak University, India, 1964-65, Osmania University, India, 1968-69. Research associate, Study of Recent Immigration from Europe, 1944-46; member of executive committee, National Commission for the Study of Jewish Education in the United States, 1952-54; Yivo Institute for Jewish Research, member of commission on research, 1953-54, member of board of directors, 1953-72; member of board of directors, American Friends of the Hebrew University, Brooklyn chapter, 1953-58.

MEMBER: American Sociological Association (fellow), American Academy of Political and Social Science, American Association of University Professors, American Jewish Historical Society, Eastern Sociological Society, New York Academy of Sciences, American Society of Criminology, Sigma Xi, Alpha Kappa Delta. *Awards, honors:* Social Science Research Council grant for research in Israel, 1950-51.

WRITINGS: Immigrant Settlements in Connecticut, Connecticut State Department of Education, 1938, reprinted, R & E Research Associates, 1970; (co-editor) *Sociology: A Book of Readings,* Prentice-Hall, 1953; (co-editor) *Criminology: A Book of Readings,* Dryden, 1953; *Sociology: An Introduction to the Science of Society,* Barnes & Noble, 1957.

Contributor: *Studies in the Science of Society,* Yale University Press, 1937; *Jews in a Gentile World,* Macmillan, 1942; *The Refugees Are Now Americans,* Public Affairs Committee, 1945; *One American,* Prentice-Hall, 1945; *Contemporary Sociology,* Philosophical Library, 1958; *Readings in Contemporary American Sociology,* Littlefield, Adams, 1961; *Sociology of Crime,* Philosophical Library, 1961.

Contributor to professional journals in United States and abroad. Member of editorial board, *Slavonic Encyclopedia,* 1947-48; book review editor, *Social Problems,* 1953-56.

WORK IN PROGRESS: Minority problems in various parts of the world.

SIDELIGHTS: Koenig spoke German, Polish, Ukrainian, Yiddish, Hebrew. He had traveled in Latin America and Europe and Asia (particularly the Near East and India). His book, *Sociology: An Introduction to the Science of Society,* has been translated into Hebrew, Chinese, and Hindi.†

(Died December 28, 1972)

*   *   *

KOGOS, Frederick   1907-1974

PERSONAL: Born January 4, 1907, in Kiev, Russia; son of Joseph A. (a piano salesman) and Minnie (Piatigorsky) Kogos; married Sarah Ellen Pollock, August 5, 1934; children: Bonnie (Mrs. Richard Beckman). *Education:* Harvard University, B.A., 1929. *Politics:* Americanism. *Religion:* Hebrew. *Home and office:* 77 Maple Dr., Great Neck, N.Y. 11021.

CAREER: Kogos Publications Co., Great Neck, N.Y., president, 1943-74. Specialist and consultant on mergers and acquisitions in the textile-apparel industry.

WRITINGS: (Editor) *The Anatomy of Sports Outerwear,* Kogos Publications, 1963; *Instant Yiddish,* Citadel, 1966; *A Dictionary of Yiddish Slang and Idioms,* Citadel, 1968; *How to Get Along in Israel in English, in Yiddish, in Hebrew,* Kogos Publications, 1969; *1001 Yiddish Proverbs,* Citadel, 1970. Author of column, "Around the Apparel World with Fred Kogos." Editor, *Apparel Manufacturer Magazine* and *Apparel Securities Review.*†

(Died October 11, 1974)

*   *   *

KOLLEK, Theodore   1911-
   (Teddy Kollek)

PERSONAL: Born May 27, 1911, in Vienna, Austria; son of Alfred (a banker) and Margaret (Fleischer) Kollek; married Tamar Schwartz, May, 1936; children: Amos, Osnat (daughter). *Education:* Attended secondary schools in Austria. *Politics:* Israel Labour Party. *Religion:* Jewish. *Home:* 6 Rashba St., Jerusalem, Israel. *Office:* City Hall, Municipality of Jerusalem, Jerusalem, Israel.

CAREER: Settled in Palestine in 1934, and became a founder-member of Kibbutz Ein Gev in Galilee, 1937; returned to Europe on education mission to Zionist youth groups, 1938-40; member of staff of political department, Jewish Agency for Palestine, 1940-47; established office in Istanbul for contact with Jewish underground in Europe, 1942; member of mission to United States on behalf of Haganah, 1947-48; head of U.S. desk, Ministry for Foreign Affairs, Jerusalem, Israel, 1948-50; minister plenipotentiary, Israel Embassy, Washington, D.C., 1950-52; director-general of Prime Minister's office, Jerusalem, 1952-64; mayor of municipality of Jerusalem, beginning 1965. Chairman of Israel Government Tourist Corp., 1955-65, and Israel Water Desalination Joint Project with U.S. Government, beginning, 1964. Chairman of the board of Africa-Israel Investment Co. Ltd., 1964-65, and the board of Israel Museum, beginning 1965. *Military service:* Israeli Defense Army; became lieutenant colonel. *Awards, honors:* Solomon Bublick Hebrew University Award, 1971; Henrietta Szold Citation and Award, 1974; Roman Guardini Prize from the Catholic Academy of Bavaria, 1976.

*WRITINGS—*Under name Teddy Kollek: (With Moshe

Pearlman) *Jerusalem: A History of Forty Centuries,* Random House, 1968; (with Pearlman) *Pilgrims to the Holy Land: The Story of Pilgrimage Through the Ages,* Harper, 1970.

AVOCATIONAL INTERESTS: Archaeology, and ancient maps and books.

BIOGRAPHICAL/CRITICAL SOURCES: Terence Prittie, *Isreal: Miracle in the Desert,* Praeger, 1968; *New York Times,* December 14, 1968; *Saturday Review,* February 1, 1969; *Israel Magazine,* September, 1971.

* * *

KORGES, James 1930-1975
(Peter J. Longleigh, Jr.)

PERSONAL: Born September 13, 1930, in Seguin, Tex.; son of Ervin H. and Thelma (Hendrix) Korges; married Patricia Reeves, November 21, 1962 (divorced); children: Willard Allen Holmes, Philip Michael Laurence. *Education:* Rice Institute (now Rice University), B.A., 1953, M.A., 1955; also studied at University of Minnesota, 1956-57 and 1960-68, and at Control Data Educational Institute, 1969. *Home address:* Box 14063, University Station, Minneapolis, Minn. 55414.

CAREER: University of Alabama, University, instructor in English, 1956-59; University of Minnesota, Minneapolis, instructor in English, 1959-68; Control Data Corp., Hopkins, Minn., engineering writer, beginning 1968.

WRITINGS: Erskine Caldwell, University of Minnesota Press, 1969. Poetry editor, *Minnesota Review,* 1963; editor-in-chief, *Critique: Studies in Modern Fiction,* beginning 1964. Writer of articles under pseudonym Peter J. Longleigh, Jr.

WORK IN PROGRESS: Essays.†

(Died February 19, 1975)

* * *

KOSHI, George M. 1911-

PERSONAL: Born June 16, 1911; son of Philip T. and Matsu (Kuwahara) Koshi; married Ai Takizawa, December 20, 1946; children: Joyce A., Robert P., Sharon R. *Education:* University of Denver, B.A., 1938, LL.B., 1940 (converted to J.D., 1970). *Religion:* Protestant.

CAREER: U.S. Air Force, Tokyo, Japan, attorney adviser in international law, beginning 1952. *Military service:* U.S. Army, 1942-46. *Member:* American Bar Association, American Society of International Law, International Legal Society of Japan (member of board of directors, beginning 1952).

WRITINGS: The Japanese Legal Adviser: Crimes and Punishment, Tuttle, 1970.††

* * *

KOZELKA, Paul 1909-

PERSONAL: Surname is accented on second syllable, Ko-*zel*-ka; born September 11, 1909, son of Frank Joseph (a merchant) and Barbara (Cizek) Kozelka; married Faith E. Kuter, September 4, 1943; children: Stefan Paul. *Education:* Lawrence University, B.A., 1932; Northwestern University, M.A., 1937; Yale University, Ph.D., 1943. *Religion:* Congregational. *Home:* 100 LaSalle St., New York, N.Y. 10027.

CAREER: Hardware clerk in Chicago, Ill., 1932-36; Rosary College, River Forest, Ill., department assistant, 1937-40; American Red Cross, an assistant field director, 1943-45; Allegheny College, Meadville, Pa., assistant professor of speech, 1945-47; Columbia University, Teachers College, New York, N.Y., assistant professor, 1947-50, associate professor, 1950-57, professor of speech, 1957-63, professor of theatre, 1963-74, professor emeritus, 1974—, acting chairman of department of speech and theatre, 1963-68. Established Drama Workshop of Teachers College, 1947, designed workshop stage and auditorium, and has presented more than ninety-five plays.

MEMBER: American Theatre Association (president, 1965; national director of Children's Theatre Conference, 1955-57; chairman of Committee on Theatre for the Retiree, beginning 1974; fellow), American Society for Theatre Research (secretary-treasurer, 1956-60), American National Theatre and Academy (member of executive committee), National Council of Teachers of English, Speech Association of the Eastern States (past member of executive council), Sigma Phi Epsilon. *Awards, honors:* Eaves Junior Award of American Educational Theatre Association (now American Theatre Association), 1961; Secondary School Theatre Association founders award, 1971; Lawrence University distinguished service award, 1975.

WRITINGS: (Contributor) *History of Speech Education in America,* Appleton, 1954; *A Glossary to the Plays of Bernard Shaw,* Teachers College, Columbia University, 1959, reprinted, Norwood, 1974; (editor) *Fifteen American One-Act Plays,* Washington Square, 1961; (editor) *Four Plays by Bernard Shaw,* Washington Square, 1965; *The Theatre Student: Directing,* Richards Rosen, 1968. Editor of more than twenty drama guides for high school teachers and students, including Karl Bruder's *The Theatre Student: Properties and Dressing the Stage,* Richards Rosen, 1968, and Peter Kline's *The Theatre Student: Scenes to Perform,* Richards Rosen, 1969. Contributor to *Encyclopaedia Britannica* and to professional journals. Member of revision committee, *Guide to Play Selection,* National Council of Teachers of English.

AVOCATIONAL INTERESTS: Organizing and directing groups of senior citizens for theatre activities, collecting theatre memorabilia.

* * *

KRAMRISCH, Stella 1898-

PERSONAL: Born 1898, in Kikulov, Moravia; daughter of Jacques (a scientist) and Berta Kramrisch; married Lazlo Nemenyi, 1929 (died, 1950). *Education:* University of Vienna, Ph.D. *Home address:* R.R. 1, Box 111, Malvern, Pa. 19355. *Office:* Philadelphia Museum of Art, Box 7646, Philadelphia, Pa. 19101; and Institute of Fine Arts, New York University, 1 East 78th St., New York, N.Y. 10021.

CAREER: University of Calcutta, Calcutta, India, professor of Indian art, 1923-50; Courtauld Institute, London, England, lecturer on Indian art, 1937-40; University of Pennsylvania, Philadelphia, professor of South Asia art, 1950-69; Philadelphia Museum of Art, Philadelphia, Pa., curator of Indian art, beginning 1954; New York University, Institute of Fine Arts, New York, N.Y., professor of Indian art, beginning 1964. Consultant on the teaching of art and on art in industry to the Government of India. *Member:* American Oriental Society, College Art Association, Ecole Francaise d'Extreme Orient (honorary member), Oriental Club (Philadelphia). *Awards, honors:* D.Litt., Visva-Bharati University, 1974.

WRITINGS: (With others) *Indian Art and Art-crafts,* Theosophical Publishing, 1923; (editor and translator) *Puranas, The Vishnudharmottara, Part III: A Treatise on Indian Painting and Image-Making,* Calcutta University Press, 2nd edition, 1928; *Indian Sculpture,* Oxford University Press, 1933; *A Survey of Painting in the Deccan,* India Society, 1937; *The Hindu Temple,* University of Calcutta, 1946; *The Arts and Crafts of Travancore,* Royal India Society, 1948, revised edition published as *The Arts and Crafts of Kerala,* Paico Publishing House, 1970; *Dravida and Kerala in the Art of Travancore,* Artibus Asiae, 1953; *The Art of India: Traditions of Indian Sculpture, Painting and Architecture,* Phaidon, 1954, 3rd edition, 1965; *Indian Sculpture in the Philadelphia Museum of Art,* University of Pennsylvania Press, 1960; *The Art of Nepal,* Philadelphia Museum of Art, 1964; *Unknown India: Ritual Art in Tribe and Village,* [Philadelphia], 1968.

Also author or editor of *Principles of Indian Art,* 1924; *History of Indian Art,* 1929; *Asian Miniature Painting,* 1932; *Indian Terracottas,* 1939; *Kantha,* 1939; and *The Triple Structure of Creation,* 1962. Contributor of articles to art, history, and philosophy journals. Editor, *Journal of the Indian Society of Oriental Art,* 1932-50; editor of Indian section, *Artibus Asiae.*

WORK IN PROGRESS: Symbolism of the Rig Veda.

*   *   *

KRATZENSTEIN, Jossef J. 1904-

PERSONAL: Born April 2, 1904, in Germany; son of Selig and Dina (Strauss) Kratzenstein; married Rachel Mueller, October 28, 1929; children: J. Walter Kaye. *Education:* Attended teachers' seminary in Germany, 1918-24, University of Berlin, 1927-29, Lehranstalt fuer die Wissenschaft des Judentums, 1927-29; University of Zuerich, Ph.D., 1932. *Home:* 2151 Fifth St., Bay City, Mich. 48706. *Office:* Temple Israel, 2500 Center, Bay City, Mich. 48706.

CAREER: Israelitische Cultusgemeinde, Zuerich, Switzerland, 1929-46; chief rabbi of Luxembourg, 1947-48; Beth Jacob Congregation, Cumberland, Md., rabbi, 1948-51; Temple Israel, Bay City, Mich., rabbi, 1951-56; West End Synagogue, Nashville, Tenn., rabbi, 1957-58; Community Synagogue, Atlantic City, N.J., rabbi, 1958-62; Temple Israel, Bay City, Rabbi beginning 1962. University of Maryland, College Park, lecturer in philosophy and education, 1950-51; Central Michigan University, Mt. Pleasant, associate professor of philosophy, 1962-64; frequent lecturer at universities, clubs, church organizations, and other assemblies. President, Bay-Midland Counties Economic Opportunity Commission, 1965-66. *Member:* Rabbinical Assembly of America, Rotary Club, Torch Club.

WRITINGS: The Age of Idolism, David, 1965.

WORK IN PROGRESS: An enlarged edition of *The Age of Idolism.*

SIDELIGHTS: Kratzenstein writes: "Experiences in Europe between World War I and World War II, the failure of western civilization to humanize *homo sapiens,* man's inability to prevent his thoughts from deteriorating into idols or ill ideas, have essentially motivated my work." He speaks German, French, Hebrew, and Latin.††

*   *   *

KRAUS, Hans P(eter) 1907-

PERSONAL: Born October 12, 1907, in Vienna, Austria; came to United States in 1939, naturalized in 1945; son of Emil and Hilda (Rix) Kraus; married Hanni Zucker Hale, August 28, 1940; children: Mary Ann Mitchell, Barbara Gstalder, Evelyn Rauber, Susan, Hans Peter, Jr. *Education:* Attended Academy of Commerce, Vienna. *Residence:* Sugar Hill, Ridgefield, Conn. 06877. *Office:* H. P. Kraus, 16 East 46th St., New York, N.Y. 10017.

CAREER: H. P. Kraus (rare books and manuscripts dealer), New York, N.Y., partner, beginning 1940. President of Kraus Periodicals, Inc., 1948-68, and Kraus Reprint Corp., 1962-68, both New York; chairman of board, Kraus Thomson Organization Ltd., New York, beginning 1968. Member of board of trustees, Yale Library Associates, beginning 1969. *Member:* Bibliographical Society of America, Bibliographical Society of London, Gutenberg Society, Grolier Club (New York), Golden's Bridge Hounds (North Salem, N.Y.). *Awards, honors:* Chevalier, Legion of Honor (France), 1951; D.Litt., University of Bridgeport, 1969.

WRITINGS: Inter-American and World Book Trade (booklet), privately printed, 1944; *On Book Collecting: The Story of My Drake Library* (James Ford Bell lecture 6), Associates of James Ford Bell Library (Minneapolis), 1969; *Sir Francis Drake: A Pictorial Biography,* historical introduction by David W. Waters and Richard Boulind, Kraus Periodicals, 1970.

SIDELIGHTS: Hans Kraus, the well-known New York bookman, took most of the documentation for *Sir Francis Drake: A Pictorial Biography* from his personal Drake collection. Most of it dates from Drake's own lifetime; the rest comes from various accounts of his expeditions published soon after his death. Waters and Boulind state in their introduction to the book: "This history contains much unknown material.... That this task should have been achieved in a span of less than twelve years, when it might well be supposed that there is no original material to be found outside the great public collections, is indeed a notable feat of antiquarian percipience and industry.... The collection ... draws together much otherwise scattered material into a coherent record which enables the story of Drake's life to be seen as a whole ... from the points of view of his contemporaries. This presentation of so outstanding a collection is a fresh and original contribution to scholarship."

*   *   *

KREFETZ, Ruth 1931-1972
(Ruth Marossi)

PERSONAL: Born October 6, 1931, in Vienna, Austria; daughter of Maurice (a manufacturer and businessman) and Alice (Eichberg) Marossi; married Gerald Krefetz (a writer), June 19, 1959; children: Nadine Carol, Adriene Dora. *Education:* Cooper Union, Certificate in Fine Arts, 1952; Yale University, B.F.A., 1954; Columbia University, M.A., 1960. *Home:* 463 West St., New York, N.Y. 10014. *Office:* Page Proofs Literary and Art Agency, 25 East 10th St., New York, N.Y. 10003.

CAREER: Page Proofs Literary and Art Agency, New York, N.Y., partner, beginning 1962; free-lance writer and illustrator; formerly employed as international conference interpreter.

WRITINGS—Under name Ruth Marossi; with husband, Gerald Krefetz: *Investing Abroad: A Guide to Financial Europe,* Harper, 1965; *Money Makes Money and the Money Money Makes More Money: The Men Who Are Wall Street,* World Publishing, 1970. Contributor to *Esquire, Harper's, Parents' Magazine,* and other periodicals.

WORK IN PROGRESS: In the Name of Art, a book on the current art scene.†

(Died June 10, 1972)

* * *

KRENKEL, John H(enry) 1906-

PERSONAL: Born April 9, 1906, in Atlanta, Ill.; married Margaret E. Aistrope (a secretary), March 18, 1939. Education: University of Illinois, B.S., 1933, Ph.D., 1937; Claremont Graduate School, M.A., 1935. Home: 619 East Erie Dr., Tempe, Ariz. 85282. Office: Department of History, Arizona State University, Tempe, Ariz. 85281.

CAREER: Iowa Wesleyan University, Mount Pleasant, professor of history, 1937-38; Chicago Teachers College (now Chicago State University), Chicago, Ill., professor of history, 1938-43; Valparaiso University, Valparaiso, Ind., lecturer in history, 1943-44; New Mexico State Teachers College (now Western New Mexico University), University Park, professor of history, 1944-45; Fort Hays Kansas State College, Hays, assistant professor of history, 1945-46; University of Oklahoma, Norman, assistant professor of history, 1946-47; Arizona State University, Tempe, associate professor of social studies, 1947-52, professor of history, beginning 1952. Special lecturer, Arizona State College (now University), 1945; visiting summer professor at University of Florida, 1946, and University of Wyoming, 1960.

MEMBER: American Historical Association, Organization of American Historians, Western Historical Association, Southern Historical Association, Illinois State Historical Society, Phi Beta Kappa, Phi Kappa Phi, Phi Eta Sigma. Awards, honors: Distinguished Service Award, Phi Eta Sigma, 1972.

WRITINGS: Illinois Internal Improvements, 1818-1848, Torch Press, 1956; (editor) Richard Yates: Civil War Governor, Interstate, 1966; (editor) Serving the Republic: Richard Yates the Younger, Interstate, 1968; (editor) The Life and Times of Joseph Fish, Mormon Pioneer, Interstate, 1970. Contributor to historical journals; contributor of about four hundred abstracts to Historical Abstracts.

WORK IN PROGRESS: A biography of George Flower.

* * *

KROCK, Arthur 1887-1974

PERSONAL: Born November 16, 1887, in Glasgow, Ky.; son of Joseph (an accountant) and Caroline (Morris) Krock; married Marguerite Polleys, April 22, 1911 (died, 1938); married Martha McCullock Granger, 1939; children: (first marriage) Thomas Polleys. Education: Princeton University, student, 1904-05; Lewis Institute, A.A., 1907. Politics: "Democrat (Wilsonian-Liberal type)." Religion: None. Home: 2029 Connecticut Ave. N.W., Washington, D.C. 20008. Office: New York Times Bureau, 1920 L St. N.W., Washington, D.C. 20036.

CAREER: Reporter in Louisville, Ky., 1907-10; Washington correspondent for Louisville Times, Louisville, 1910-15, and for Louisville Courier-Journal, Louisville, 1911-15, editorial manager for both newspapers, 1915-19; Louisville Times, editor-in-chief, 1919-23; New York World, New York City, assistant to president, 1923-27; New York Times, New York City, member of board of editors, beginning 1927, Washington correspondent and bureau chief, 1932-53, author of column, "In the Nation," 1932-67, Washington commentator, 1953-67. Member of Pulitzer Prize Board, Columbia University School of Journalism, 1940-53. Assis-

tant to chairman of the Democratic National Committee, 1920.

MEMBER: Metropolitan Club, Gridiron Club, 1925 F St. Club (all Washington); Ivy Club, Nassau Club (both Princeton). Awards, honors: Pulitzer Prize, 1935, for general excellence of Washington coverage, 1938, for exclusive interview with President Franklin D. Roosevelt; Pulitzer award, 1950 (declined), for exclusive interview with President Harry S Truman, 1955, for distinguished correspondence from Washington, D.C. M.A., Princeton University, 1937; D.Litt., University of Louisville, 1939; D.H.L., University of Kentucky, 1956, Centre College of Kentucky, 1957, Northwestern University, 1967; D.L., Hamilton College, 1967. Legion d'Honneur (France), decorated officer, 1937, for coverage of Versailles Peace Conference, named commandant, 1967; Commander Polonia Restituta (Poland), 1950; Knight's Cross in Order of St. Olav (Norway), 1950; John Peter Zenger Award, University of Arizona, 1967; Freedoms Foundation Medal, 1970; Presidential Medal of Honor, 1971.

WRITINGS: (Compiler) The Editorials of Henry Watterson, G. H. Doran, 1923; In the Nation, 1932-1966 (collection of columns), McGraw, 1966; Memoirs: Sixty Years on the Firing Line, Funk, 1968; The Consent of the Governed and Other Deceits, Little, Brown, 1971; Reminiscences, Microfilming Corp., 1972; Myself When Young: Growing Up in the 1890's, Little, Brown, 1973. Contributor of articles to newspapers and magazines.

SIDELIGHTS: In a review of Memoirs: Sixty Years on the Firing Line, Ronald Steel said: "Krock is the ultimate insider, the man who knew eleven presidents, had lunch with the members of the cabinet, and played poker with generals and congressmen. He was privy to military secrets long before they could be revealed, solicited for his opinions on matters of state, and a confidant to the mighty. . . . In this book of reminiscences and opinions we are treated to a revealing portrait of the journalist as Establishment insider." However, Steel also believed that "for anyone who does not share the conservative values of Arthur Krock, [the memoirs] are marred by bad temper, narrowness of vision, and a crippling nostalgia for the past. . . . What makes Krock's book seem so dated is not that many of the stories he relates happened long ago, but that the personality which infuses these memoirs seems to have stopped its development somewhere in the early 1950's, if not before." Arthur Schlesinger, Jr. wrote: "Arthur Krock's career as a political reporter spans the long years from Theodore Roosevelt to Lyndon B. Johnson. By extension and reference, his acquaintance with American politics goes back a good deal further. . . . Much of the distinctive quality of the 'Memoirs' comes from the way the author sees himself as a continuator and defender of the American political tradition."

Philip Gyaelin, reviewing The Consent of the Governed and Other Deceits, explained that "nobody but Arthur Krock could write a collection of sketches about politics and newspapering and the nation's Capitol covering a period of more than 60 years and sprinkle it with personal recollections all along the way. When Krock talks about presidents he has known, he begins with Theodore Roosevelt; when he talks about the period during which he was an active journalist, he gives you first-hand reminiscences about the movers and the shakers—Supreme Court justices, senators, governors, presidential candidates, Secretaries of State, Speakers of the House, White House counselors, ambassadors, or whatever—back through the last dozen administrations in Washington. . . . Arthur Krock has been one of a tiny handful of genuinely towering figures of journalism in this century." In another review of *The Consent of the Governed*, John Chamberlain wrote: "His enemy FDR once picked him for an exclusive interview [the only exclusive interview given during Roosevelt's presidency] primarily because he represented the *Times*, which was the most desirable medium for presidential purposes. Well, it is true that Arthur got his share of beats simply because he was the *Times* man in Washington, and even presidents who disliked him had to deal with him. But it is also true that the *Times* was often favored because Krock was Krock."

BIOGRAPHICAL/CRITICAL SOURCES—Periodicals: *New York Times Book Review*, September 22, 1968; *New York Times*, September 24, 1968, December 27, 1968; *National Observer*, September 30, 1968; *Newsweek*, October 7, 1968; *Washington Post*, October 10, 1968, July 23, 1971; *National Review*, November 19, 1968, June 15, 1971; *Best Sellers*, December 1, 1968; *New York Review*, February 13, 1969; *Times Literary Supplement*, September 18, 1970.

Books; all written by Arthur Krock: *In the Nation*, McGraw, 1966; *Memoirs: Sixty Years on the Firing Line*, Funk, 1968; *The Consent of the Governed and Other Deceits*, Little, Brown, 1971; *Reminiscences*, Microfilming Corp., 1972; *Myself When Young: Growing Up in the 1890's*, Little, Brown, 1973.†

(Died April 11, 1974)

* * *

KROOSS, Herman E. 1912-1975

PERSONAL: Surname is pronounced like "cruise"; born July 12, 1912, in New York, N.Y.; son of Albert (a businessman) and Wilhelmina (Hinck) Krooss; married Helen A. Bausher, June 16, 1939. *Education:* Muhlenberg College, Ph.B., 1934; University of Pennsylvania, M.A., 1935; New York University, Ph.D., 1947. *Office:* New York University, 100 Trinity, New York, N.Y. 10006.

CAREER: Educational supervisor for Penn Mutual Life Insurance Co., New York, N.Y., 1935-40, Union Central Life Insurance Co., New York, N.Y., 1940-41; New York University, New York, N.Y., instructor, 1947-50, assistant professor, 1950-51, associate professor, 1951-53, professor of economics, 1953-75. Member of Council of Research in Economic History; member of board of trustees, MONY Mortgage Investors, Inc., 1971-75. *Member:* Economic History Association (treasurer, 1948-50; executive secretary-treasurer, 1970-72), American Economic Association, American Finance Association, Business History Conference (president-elect, 1973). *Awards, honors:* LL.D., Muhlenberg College, 1970.

WRITINGS: (With Paul Studenski) *Financial History of the United States*, McGraw, 1950, 2nd edition, 1960; (with E. A. Johnson) *Origins and Development of the American Economy*, Prentice-Hall, 1953; *American Economic Development*, Prentice-Hall, 1955, 2nd edition, 1966; (with Johnson) *The American Economy*, Prentice-Hall, 1961; (with Jules Bogen) *Security Credit*, Prentice-Hall, 1961; (with Bogen) *Savings and Other Time Deposits in Commercial Banks*, Graduate School of Business Administration, New York University, 1962; (editor) *Documentary History of Banking and Currency in the United States*, four volumes, Chelsa House, 1969; *Executive Opinion*, Doubleday, 1970; (with Martin R. Blyn) *A History of Financial Intermediaries* Random House, 1971; (with Charles Gilbert) *American Business History*, Prentice-Hall, 1972. Contributor to

Dictionary of American Biography, Collier's Encyclopedia, and to professional journals.†

(Died March 21, 1975)

* * *

KUIPER, Gerard Peter 1905-1973

PERSONAL: Surname is pronounced *Koi*-per; born December 7, 1905, in Harencarspel, Netherlands; came to United States in 1933, naturalized in 1937; son of Gerard and Ann (de Vries) Kuiper; married Sarah Parker Fuller, June 20, 1936; children: Paul, Lucy. *Education:* University of Leiden, B.Sc., 1927, Ph.D., 1933. *Home:* 721 North Sawtelle, Tuscon, Ariz. *Office:* Lunar and Planetary Laboratory, University of Arizona, Tucson, Ariz.

CAREER: Member of Dutch Solar Eclipse Expedition to Sumatra, 1929; University of California, research fellow at Lick Observatory, Mount Hamilton, 1933-35, research associate, 1935; Harvard University, Cambridge, Mass., lecturer in astronomy, 1935-36; University of Chicago, assistant professor of astronomy at Yerkes Observatory, Williams Bay, Wis., 1936-37, associate professor, 1937-43, professor, 1943-60, director of Yerkes Observatory and of McDonald Observatory, Fort Davis, Tex. (affiliated with University of Chicago), 1947-49, 1957-60; University of Arizona, Tucson, founder, and director of Lunar and Planetary Laboratory, 1960-73. Research associate, Harvard University Radio Research Laboratory, 1943-45; consultant to Eighth Air Force in England, 1944; member of Office of Scientific Research and Development mission to Europe, 1945. Dryden research lecturer, American Institute of Aeronautics and Astronautics, 1969. Principal investigator of Ranger Program, National Aeronautics and Space Administration.

MEMBER: National Academy of Sciences, American Academy of Arts and Sciences, International Astronomical Union, American Astronomical Society, Astronomical Society of the Pacific, Royal Astronomical Society (London; associate), Royal Netherlands Academy of Sciences (foreign member). *Awards, honors:* Commander, Order of Orange Nassau (Netherlands), Janssen Medal of French Astronomical Society for discovery of the satellites of Uranus and Neptune; Rittenhouse Medal, for his theory of the origin of the solar system.

WRITINGS: (Editor) *The Atmospheres of the Earth and Planets*, University of Chicago Press, 1949, revised edition, 1952; (editor) *The Solar System*, University of Chicago Press, Volume I, *The Sun*, 1953, Volume II, *The Earth as a Planet*, 1954, Volume III, *The Planets and Satellites*, 1961, Volume IV, (with Middlehurst) *The Moon, Meteorites and Comets*, 1963; (general editor with Barbara M. Middlehurst) *Telescopes*, University of Chicago Press, 1961.

(Editor) *Photographic Lunar Atlas*, University of Chicago Press, 1960; *Orthographic Atlas of the Moon*, (supplement to *Photographic Lunar Atlas*), University of Arizona Press, 1961; *Rectified Lunar Atlas* (supplement to *Photographic Lunar Atlas*), University of Arizona Press, 1963.

Also author of *Consolidated Lunar Atlas*. General editor with Barbara M. Middlehurst of *Stars and Stellar Systems*, University of Chicago Press, beginning 1960.

SIDELIGHTS: Dr. Kuiper was the first astronomer to accurately measure the diameter and mass of Pluto, the outer planet of our solar system. He also discovered new satellites to the planets Uranus and Neptune; and charted the equator and the position of the poles on Venus. He once described the surface of the moon as being like "crunchy snow." This observation was later confirmed by Neil A. Armstrong and other astronauts after their walks on the moon. A *New York Times* writer estimated that "[Kuiper] became one of the foremost authorities on the earth's moon."†

(Died December 24, 1973)

* * *

KUJOTH, Jean Spealman   1935-1975

PERSONAL: Born April 20, 1935, in Champaign, Ill.; daughter of Max Lang (a consulting chemical engineer) and Dorothy (Flickinger) Spealman; married Richard Kenneth Kujoth (a counselor), February 22, 1964 (divorced). *Education:* University of California, Berkeley, B.A., 1957; University of Michigan, M.S.W., 1959; University of Wisconsin—Milwaukee, M.A.L.S., 1966. *Home:* 920 North 37th St., Milwaukee, Wis. 53208.

CAREER: Milwaukee Boys' Club, Milwaukee, Wis., librarian, 1966-68; University of Wisconsin—Milwaukee, designer of documentation system for Office of Grants and Contracts, 1967-68. *Member:* Wisconsin Regional Writers Association, Phi Beta Kappa.

WRITINGS—All published by Scarecrow, except as indicated: (Editor) *Readings in Nonbook Librarianship*, 1968; *Subject Guide to Periodical Indexes and Review Indexes*, 1969; (editor) *Libraries, Readers, and Book Selection*, 1969; (editor) *The Teacher and School Discipline*, 1970; (editor) *Reading Interests of Children and Young Adults*, 1970; (editor) *Book Publishing: Inside Views*, 1971; (editor) *The Recreation Program Guide: Organizing Activities for School, Camp, Park, Playground or Children's Club*, 1972; *Best-Selling Children's Books*, 1973; *The Boys' and Girls' Book of Clubs and Organizations* (juvenile), Prentice-Hall, 1975; *Subject Guide to Humor: Anecdotes, Facetiae and Satire from 365 Periodicals, 1968-74*, 1976.

WORK IN PROGRESS: Editing *The Camp Program Encyclopedia*, for Scarecrow.†

(Died September 27, 1975)

* * *

KULSTEIN, David J.   1916-1974

PERSONAL: Born October 28, 1916, in St. Louis, Mo.; son of Morris (a merchant) and Lena (Rothman) Kulstein; married Edith Marx (a teacher); children: Deborah Monique. *Education:* University of Missouri, student, 1937-40; Washington University, St. Louis, Mo., B.A., 1948, M.A., 1950; Sorbonne, University of Paris, student, 1947-48; Harvard University, Ph.D., 1955. *Home:* 13648 Camino Rico, Saratoga, Calif. 95070.

CAREER: Amherst College, Amherst, Mass., instructor in history and humanities, 1955-58; San Jose State University, San Jose, Calif., associate professor, 1958-66, professor of history, beginning 1966. *Military service:* U.S. Army Air Forces, 1942-45. *Member:* American Historical Association, Society for French Historical Studies, Societe d'Histoire Moderne.

WRITINGS: Napoleon Third and the Working Class: A Study of Government Propaganda under the Second Empire, Ward Ritchie, 1969. Contributor of articles and reviews to historical journals.

WORK IN PROGRESS: A monograph on "le Moniteur universel" during the French Revolution.†

(Died February 23, 1974)

KVALE, Velma R(uth)   1898-

PERSONAL: Surname is pronounced Ka-*wah*-lee; born May 12, 1898, in Hastings, Neb.; daughter of Charles Cloke (a farmer) and Margaret (a music teacher; maiden name, Matlock) Mountjoy; married Ora F. Kvale (deceased); children: Kenneth Glenn, Noel Thomas (deceased), Verna Joy. *Education:* Attended University of Washington, Seattle, 1919, Spokane University, 1921-23, and University of Montana, 1924; Eastern Washington College of Education (now Eastern Washington State College), B.A. (with honors), 1954. *Politics:* Republican. *Religion:* Christian. *Home:* 1212 24th St., Ronan, Mont. 59864.

CAREER: Teacher in Montana and Washington, 1918-21, 1923-26, 1954-63, 1964. *Member:* Montana Press Women, Classroom Teachers of North-Western Montana (director, 1960-63), Northwestern Montana Retired Teachers Association (president, 1968-70), Alaska Crippled Children's Association (charter member), Delta Kappa Gamma, Pi Delta Epsilon, Order of the Eastern Star, Anchorage (Alaska) Garden Club (honorary life member), Ronan Garden Club, Ronan Woman's Club, Republican Women's Club of Ronan (president, 1967-69). *Awards, honors: Tobuk, Reindeer Herder* took first place in the juvenile book division of Montana Press Women's contest, 1969, and second place in National Federation of Press Women's contest, 1969.

WRITINGS: Tobuk, Reindeer Herder (juvenile), Denison, 1968.

WORK IN PROGRESS: Pioneer Women of Alaska; with Margaret Brooke, *History of Early Ronan.*

* * *

LACY, A(lexander) D(acre)   1894-1969

PERSONAL: Born May 6, 1894, in Weymouth, Dorset, England; son of Saumarez Dacre (a captain, Royal Navy) and Meta (Henry) Lacy; married Katharine Margaret Anne Goodenough, 1927; children: Diana (Mrs. Ronald Cookson), Elizabeth (Mrs. Cornelius de Witt Hastie), Monica. *Education:* Received preparatory education in Switzerland and England, and attended Royal Naval College, Dartmouth. *Home:* Croft, Farningham, Kent, England.

CAREER: Royal Navy, 1909-45, retiring as commander; training officer for an industrial firm in England, 1945-48; Ministry of Defence, London, England, secretary and interpreter in Military Agency for Standardisation of North Atlantic Treaty Organisation, 1948-52, intelligence officer, 1952-56; manager of tours to Greece and Turkey, 1962-69. During World War II was British naval liaison officer to Free French in London, 1940-42, and member of British Admiralty delegation in Washington, D.C., 1942-45. *Member:* Society for Promotion of Hellenic Studies, Anglo-Hellenic League, Society of Authors. *Awards, honors:* Admiralty Prize for naval history essay; Legion of Honor for services rendered to Free French Navy, 1948.

WRITINGS: The Canteen Worker's Manual, Croft Press, 1946; *Greek Pottery in the Bronze Age*, Barnes & Noble, 1967. Contributor to *Geographical Magazine, History Today,* and *Daily Mail.*

WORK IN PROGRESS: The Island of Rhodes.

SIDELIGHTS: Lacy held interpreter's rating in French and Spanish.††

(Died July 3, 1969)

LAFARGE, Rene 1902-

PERSONAL: Born January 26, 1902, in St. Vincent, Cantal, France; son of Antonin (engaged in agriculture) and Marie (Meynial) Lafarge. *Education:* Sorbonne, University of Paris, Licence en philosophie, 1930; Catholic Institute of Paris, Doctorat en philosophie, 1946. *Politics:* Liberal. *Home:* Institution St. Eugene, 15, Aurillac, Cantal, France.

CAREER: Ordained Roman Catholic priest; Institution St. Eugene, Aurillac, Cantal, France, professor of philosophy, 1930-70. *Military service:* French Army, 1939; prisoner of war, 1940-45; received medal for services to other prisoners of war.

WRITINGS: En pays Rheinay: Souvenirs de captivite, Bonis, 1947; *La Philosophie de Jean-Paul Sartre,* Editions Edouard Privat, 1967, translation by Marina Smyth-Kok published as *Jean-Paul Sartre: His Philosophy,* University of Notre Dame Press, 1970.

WORK IN PROGRESS: A study of Jacques Maritain and modern thought.††

*   *   *

LAHEE, Frederic Henry 1884-1968

PERSONAL: Born July 27, 1884, in Hingham, Mass.; son of Henry Charles (an author, and head of Boston Musical Bureau) and Selina Ida Mary (Long) Lahee; married Lucasta Karr Hodge, December 23, 1912 (deceased); children: Genevieve (Mrs. Charles W. Allen), Henry, Ruth Holden (Mrs. J. D. Marble), John Aspinwall. *Education:* Harvard University, A.B., 1907, M.A., 1908, Ph.D., 1911. *Politics:* "Mainly Democratic." *Religion:* Unitarian Universalist. *Home and office:* 7219 Kenny Lane, Dallas, Tex.

CAREER: Harvard University, Cambridge, Mass., instructor in geology, 1906-12; part-time instructor in geology at Radcliffe College, Cambridge, Mass., and Wellesley College, Wellesley, Mass., 1906-18; Massachusetts Institute of Technology, Cambridge, instructor, 1912-15, assistant professor of geology, 1915-18; Sun Oil Co., Philadelphia, Pa., field geologist, 1918-20, chief geologist, 1920-47, geological counselor, 1947-55. Geological consultant, expert witness in gas-rate cases, and writer. Chairman of committee on exploration for District III, U.S. Petroleum Administration for War, 1942-45.

MEMBER: Geological Society of America (fellow), American Institute of Professional Geologists, Society of Economic Geologists, American Institute of Mining, Metallurgical and Petroleum Geologists, American Petroleum Institute (chairman, committee on petroleum reserves, 1946-55), American Association of Petroleum Geologists (president, 1932-33; representative on National Research Council, 1936-40), Phi Beta Kappa. *Awards, honors:* Sidney Powers Memorial Award of American Association of Petroleum Geologists, 1953; citations from American Petroleum Institute.

WRITINGS: Field Geology, McGraw, 1916, 6th edition, 1961; *Statistics of Exploratory Drilling in the United States, 1945-1960,* American Association of Petroleum Geologists, 1962. Contributor of more than one hundred articles to professional journals. Editor, *Bulletin,* American Association of Petroleum Geologists, 1929-32.

WORK IN PROGRESS: A book on geology for high schools, Boy Scouts, and the traveling public.

SIDELIGHTS: Lahee's *Field Geology,* revised every ten years since its initial publication, served to introduce him to hundreds of geologists all over the world. He said that he lost any fluency he once had in foreign languages ("out of practice"). *Avocational interests:* Ice skating, dancing, golf.

BIOGRAPHICAL/CRITICAL SOURCES: Bulletin of American Association of Petroleum Geologists, Volume XXXVII, July, 1953.†

(Died December 3, 1968)

*   *   *

LAMBERT, Jacques Edward 1901-

PERSONAL: Born March 5, 1901, in Lyons, France; son of Edward (a professor) and Valerie (Decart) Lambert; married Valentine Neuville, May 1, 1924; children: Rene, Denis. *Education:* University of Lyon, D.J., 1925; Harvard University, research fellow, 1928. *Home:* Place Bellecour 30, Lyons 69, France.

CAREER: University of Lyons, Faculty of Law, Lyons, France, professor, 1925-39; National University of Brazil, Rio de Janeiro, professor of sociology, 1939-45; University of Lyons, professor of comparative law, beginning 1945. Expert, Center for Educational Inquiry, Rio de Janeiro, 1958. *Member:* International Population Association, International Political Science Association, Societe Francaise de Statistiques, Societe de Demographie Historique. *Awards, honors:* Doctor Honoris Causa, National University of Brazil and University of Guanabara.

WRITINGS: La Regle catonienne, Giard, 1925; *Histoire constitutionnelle des Etats-Unis,* four volumes, Sirey, 1930-37; *Les Nations contre la paix,* Alcan, 1933; *Les Origines du controle de constitutionnalite des lois d'etat par la judicature federale aux Etats-Unis,* Giard, 1933; *La Vengeance privee et les fondements du droit international public,* Sirey, 1936; *Problemes demographiques contemporains,* [Rio de Janeiro], 1944; *Quatre conferences faites en juillet 1944,* Secretario du Interior (Recife), 1945; *Le Bresil: Structure social et institutions politiques,* Fondation Nationale des Sciences Politiques, 1953; *Os Dois Brasis,* Ministerio de Educacao e Cultura (Rio de Janeiro), 1959, 2nd edition, Companhia Editora Nacional (Sao Paulo), 1967; *Amerique Latine: Structures sociales et institutions politiques,* Presses Universitaires de France, 1963, translation by Helen Katel published as *Latin America: Social Structure and Political Institutions,* University of California Press, 1967; (editor) Joseph Servos, *Le Statut juridique de l'energie atomique: Utilisations pacifiques,* Institut de Droit, for University of Lyons, 1966.

WORK IN PROGRESS: Political Life in Latin America; and *Demographic Problems.*

SIDELIGHTS: Jacques Lambert is competent in English, Portuguese, Spanish, and Italian. He has traveled in the United States, Near East, and Latin America.††

*   *   *

LAMSA, George M(amishisho) 1893-

PERSONAL: Born circa August 5, 1893, in Kurdistan, Turkey; came to United States in 1916, naturalized in 1923; son of Jando Peshah and Sarah Peshah (Yokhanan) Lamsa. *Education:* Archbishop of Canterbury's College, Urmiah, Iran, A.B. equivalent, 1907; Archbishop of Canterbury's College, Turkey, Ph.D. equivalent in theology, 1908; studied at Episcopal Theology Seminary in Virginia and University of Pennsylvania, 1918, and Dropsie College, 1942-44. *Home:* 1821 North Berkley, Turlock, Calif. 95380. *Office:* Aramaic Bible Society, Inc., P.O. Box 6406, St. Petersburg Beach, Fla. 33736.

CAREER: Left Turkey at beginning of World War I and migrated to South America; served in British Merchant Marine for a time, and worked on railroads, in mines, and later in printing shops in United States; field secretary of Archbishop of Canterbury's Assyrian Mission in United States, 1925-31; Aramaic Bible Society, Inc., St. Petersburg Beach, Fla., founder, 1943, chairman of the board; writer, translator, and lecturer. *Member:* Royal Society of Arts (London; fellow).

WRITINGS: The Secret of the Near East: Slavery of Women, Social, Religious and Economic Life in the Near East, Ideal Press, 1923; (with William C. Emhardt) *The Oldest Christian People,* Macmillan, 1926; *The Origin of the Gospel,* Winston, 1927.

Key to the Original Gospels, Winston, 1931; *My Neighbor Jesus: In the Light of His Own Language, People, and Time,* Harper, 1932, reprinted, Aramaic Bible Society, 1973; *Gospel Light: Comments on the Teachings of Jesus from Aramaic and Unchanged Eastern Customs,* A. J. Holman, 1936, reprinted, 1962; *Shepherd of All: The Twenty-Third Psalm,* A. J. Holman, 1939; *Modern Wisdom,* Association Press, 1939.

Second Reader in Aramaic, A. J. Holman, 1942; *New Testament Commentary from the Aramaic and the Ancient Eastern Customs,* A. J. Holman, 1945; *New Testament Origin,* Ziff-Davis, 1947; (editor) *The Short Koran: Designed for Easy Reading,* Ziff-Davis, 1949.

A Brief Course in the Aramaic Language, Aramaic Bible Society, 1961; *Old Testament Light: A Scriptural Commentary Based on the Aramaic of the Ancient Peshitta,* Prentice-Hall, 1964; *The Kingdom on Earth,* Unity, 1966; *Gems of Wisdom,* Unity, 1966; *And the Scroll Opened,* Doubleday, 1967; *The Hidden Years of Jesus,* revised edition, Unity, 1968; *More Light on the Gospel,* Doubleday, 1968.

The Man from Galilee: A Life of Jesus, Doubleday, 1970; *Idioms in the Bible Explained,* Aramaic Bible Society, 1971. Also author of *Roses of Gulistan* (poetry), Aramaic Bible Society.

Translator from the Aramaic: *The Four Gospels,* A. J. Holman, 1933; *Book of Psalms, According to the Eastern Version,* A. J. Holman, 1939; *New Testament According to the Eastern Text,* A. J. Holman, 1940; *The Old Testament,* A. J. Holman, 1955; *The Holy Bible from the Peshitta,* A. J. Holman, 1957, 5th edition, 1961.

SIDELIGHTS: George Lamsa spent more than thirty years laboring on his translation of the Bible from ancient Aramaic, a project conceived while he was also trying to learn the idioms of the English language. Besides Aramaic, he is competent in Hebrew, Turkish, Arabic, and Spanish.

*   *   *

LANDES, Ruth   1908-

PERSONAL: Born October 8, 1908, in New York, N.Y.; daughter of Joseph (a union founder and writer) and Anna (Grossman) Schlossberg; married 1929 (divorced). *Education:* New York University, B.S., 1928; New York School of Social Work, M.S.W., 1929; Columbia University, Ph.D., 1935. *Office:* Department of Anthropology, McMaster University, Hamilton, Ontario, Canada.

CAREER: Social worker in New York City, 1929-31; Columbia University, New York City, research fellow in anthropology, 1933-40; Coordinator of Inter-American Affairs, Washington, D.C., research director, 1941; President Roosevelt's Fair Employment Practices Committee, Washington, D.C., representative for Negro and Mexican-American affairs, 1941-45; director of private interim fair employment practices program, New York City, 1945; Los Angeles Metropolitan Welfare Council, Los Angeles, Calif., researcher on Mexican-American affairs, 1946-47; American Jewish Committee, New York City, study director in science research department, 1948-51; University of Edinburgh, Edinburgh, Scotland, Fulbright senior research scholar on colored colonial migration, 1951-52; lecturer at William Alanson White Psychiatric Institute, New York City, 1953-54, and New School for Social Research, New York City, 1953-55; University of Southern California, Los Angeles, visiting professor of anthropology, 1957-58; Los Angeles City Health Department, Los Angeles, director of geriatrics program, 1958-59; Claremont Graduate School, Claremont, Calif., visiting professor of anthropology, 1959-62; extension lecturer and consultant at University of California, Los Angeles, and University of California, Berkeley, 1962, and at Los Angeles State College (now California State University, Los Angeles), 1963; McMaster University, Hamilton, Ontario, professor of anthropology, beginning 1965. Instructor in anthropology at Brooklyn College (now Brooklyn College of the City University of New York), 1937, and Fisk University, 1937-38; visiting professor at Columbia University, summer, 1963, and Tulane University, 1964. Researcher on study of the American Negro, Carnegie Corp., 1939. Has done field work on Indian cultures in Ontario, Minnesota, and Kansas, 1932-36, on Negro communities in Brazil, 1938-39, on colored migrations and settlements in England, Scotland, Wales, and France, 1951-52, and on plurilingualism in South Africa, Canada, Spain, Switzerland, and Louisiana, 1968-74.

AWARDS, HONORS: McMaster University grant for research in Brazil, 1966; Canada Council grants for research in Switzerland, 1968, Spain, 1969, and South Africa, 1970, 1974.

WRITINGS: Ojibwa Sociology, Columbia University Press, 1937, reprinted as "Columbia University Contributions to Anthropology" series, Volume XXIX, 1969; *The Ojibwa Woman,* Columbia University Press, 1938, reprinted, AMS Press, 1969; *The City of Women,* Macmillan, 1947; *Culture in American Education,* Wiley, 1965; *The Latin-Americans of the Southwest,* Webster, 1965; *Ojibwa Religion and the Midewiwin,* University of Wisconsin Press, 1968; *The Mystic Lake Sioux: Sociology of the Mdewakantonwan Santee,* University of Wisconsin Press, 1968; *Prairie Potawatomi: Tradition and Ritual in the Twentieth Century,* University of Wisconsin Press, 1969.

Contributor: Margaret Mead, editor, *Cooperation and Competition Among Primitive Peoples,* McGraw, 1937, enlarged edition, Beacon Press, 1961; George F. Kneller, editor, *Foundations of Education,* Wiley, 1963, 2nd edition, 1967; J. H. Chilcott, Norman Greenberg, and Herbert Wilson, editors, *Readings in the Socio-Cultural Foundations of Education,* Wadsworth, 1965; Peggy Golde, editor, *Women in the Field,* Aldine, 1969. Contributor of reviews and articles to professional journals.

WORK IN PROGRESS: Studies in bilingualism and biculturalism in Switzerland, Spain, South Africa, and the American Far West and comparison with developments in Canada.

SIDELIGHTS: The City of Women has been translated into Portuguese and published in Brazil.

LANTIS, Margaret (Lydia) 1906-

PERSONAL: Born September 1, 1906, in Dayton, Ohio; daughter of Lee Ora (a teacher) and Betsy (Ames) Lantis. *Education:* University of Minnesota, B.A., 1930; University of California, Berkeley, Ph.D., 1939.

CAREER: University of California, Berkeley, research associate and instructor in anthropology, 1940-41; University of Minnesota, Minneapolis, instructor in anthropology, 1942; Reed College, Portland, Ore., assistant professor of sociology and anthropology, 1943-44; War Relocation Authority, Washington, D.C., community analyst, 1944-45; social science analyst in Georgia and Kentucky, U.S. Department of Agriculture, 1945-46; social-economic analyst for Bureau of the Census, 1946-47, and Bureau of Indian Affairs, 1948, both Washington, D.C.; Harvard University, Cambridge, Mass., social anthropologist, 1948-52; anthropologist in Washington, D.C., Seattle, Wash., and Anchorage, Alaska, for Public Health Service, U.S. Department of Health, Education, and Welfare, 1954-63; University of Kentucky, Lexington, professor of anthropology, 1965-74. Visiting professor, Boston University, 1950, University of California, Berkeley, 1950, 1964-65, University of Alaska, 1955, University of Minnesota, 1958, George Washington University, 1961, University of Washington, 1962, and McGill University, 1963-64. Consultant, Arctic Health Research Center, U.S. Public Health Service, 1966, Alaska Psychiatric Institute, 1967, and Encyclopaedia Britannica Educational Corp., 1973-75.

MEMBER: American Anthropological Association (fellow), Arctic Institute of North America (fellow; member of research committee, 1959-62; consultant, 1963-64), American Association for the Advancement of Science (fellow), American Ethnological Society (president, 1964-65), Society for Applied Anthropology (fellow; president, 1973-74), Arctic Circle (Canada), Anthropological Society of Washington (member of executive council, 1948, 1960-61), Phi Beta Kappa, Sigma Xi. *Awards, honors:* Fellow, Social Science Research Council, University of Chicago, 1942-43, Werner-Gren Foundation, Washington School of Psychiatry, 1947, Carnegie Foundation, McGill University Arctic Geography Program, 1952.

WRITINGS: Transactions, Volume XXXV: *Social Culture of the Nunivak Eskimo,* American Philosophical Society, 1946; *Alaskan Eskimo Ceremonialism* (monograph), J. J. Augustin, 1947; *Folk Medicine and Hygiene: Lower Kuskokwim and Nunivak-Nelson Island Areas,* University of Alaska, 1959; *Eskimo Childhood and Interpersonal Relationships: Nunivak Biographies and Genealogies* (monograph), University of Washington Press, 1960; (editor and contributor) *Ethnohistory in Southwestern Alaska and the Southern Yukon: Method and Content,* University Press of Kentucky, 1970.

Contributor: Edward H. Spicer, editor, *Human Problems in Technological Change,* Russell Sage, 1952; Diana Rowley, editor, *Arctic Research,* Arctic Institute of North America, 1955; H. P. Hansen, editor, *Arctic Biology,* Oregon State College, 1957; Ronald Macdonald, editor, *The Arctic Frontier,* University of Toronto Press, 1966. Contributor of articles and scientific papers to numerous journals, including *American Anthropologist, Africa, Psychiatry, Scientific Monthly, Journal of Home Economics, Archives of Environmental Health, Human Organization,* and *Smithsonian.*

LARSON, Andrew Karl 1899-

PERSONAL: Born December 11, 1899, in Washington, Utah; son of Andrew Hyrum (a farmer) and Mary Emily (Covington) Larson; married Katharine Miles, November 14, 1928; children: Arthur F. Crosby (foster son), Judith (Mrs. Gene Schneiter). *Education:* Attended Dixie Junior College, 1920-22; Brigham Young University, A.B., 1926, M.A., 1947; attended University of Utah, 1948, 1950, 1952. *Politics:* Democrat. *Religion:* Mormon. *Home:* 212 South 200 East, St. George, Utah 84770.

CAREER: Teacher in Washington County School District, Utah, 1922-25, 1926-46; Dixie Junior College, St. George, Utah, instructor in history, government, and literature, 1946-65. Member, Washington County (Utah) Centennial (arts chairman), 1946-47, Washington (Utah) Centennial Committee (historian), 1956-57, and St. George (Utah) Centennial Committee (history chairman), 1960-61. *Member:* Utah Historical Society (fellow, beginning 1965), Utah Academy of Sciences, Arts and Letters, American Heritage Society, National Sons of Utah Pioneers, Utah Heritage Society.

WRITINGS: The Red Hills of November, Deseret News Press, 1957; *I Was Called to Dixie, the Virgin River Basin: Unique Experiences in Mormon Pioneering,* Deseret News Press, 1961; (contributor) Thomas Cheney and Austin Fife, editors, *Lore of Faith and Folly,* University of Utah Press, 1971; *Erastus Snow: The Life of a Missionary and Pioneer for the Early Mormon Church,* University of Utah Press, 1971. Contributor of articles to *Utah Historical Quarterly* and *Western Folklore.*

WORK IN PROGRESS: Erastus Beman Snow: Son of the Dixie Cotton Mission; an autobiography, *Education of a Second Generation Swede.*

SIDELIGHTS: Andrew Larson told *CA* his major interest was United States history, especially that of the American West and the area of Utah which his ancestors helped to colonize. Larson's maternal great-grandfather, Robert D. Covington, founded the town where Larson was born in 1857. Prior to moving to Utah, Covington had been an overseer on a cotton plantation in Noxubee County, Miss., and "understood cotton culture. Raising cotton for the needs of the Mormon people led to his call to this area, which became known as Utah's Dixie because of the cotton grown here."††

* * *

LARSON, Henrietta M(elia) 1894-

PERSONAL: Born September 24, 1894, in Ostrander, Minn.; daughter of Hans Olaf (a businessman) and Karen Marie (Nordgaarden) Larson. *Education:* St. Olaf College, B.A., 1918; University of Minnesota, graduate study, 1922-24; Columbia University, Ph.D., 1926. *Politics:* Republican. *Religion:* Lutheran. *Home:* 1110 West First, Northfield, Minn. 55057.

CAREER: Instructor at Augustana College, Sioux Falls, S.D., 1921-22, Bethany College, Lindsborg, Kan., 1925-26, and Southern Illinois University, Carbondale, 1926-28; Harvard University, Graduate School of Business Administration, Boston, Mass., associate in research, 1928-39, assistant professor, 1939-42, associate professor, 1942-60, professor of business history, 1960-61, professor emeritus, 1961—. Ford Foundation consultant, Indian Institute of Management, Ahmedabad, 1966. Business History Foundation, trustee and officer, beginning 1947, editorial director,

1947-56. *Member:* American Historical Association, Economic History Association (vice-president, 1961-62), Economic History Society (England), Norwegian-American Historical Association, Phi Beta Kappa. *Awards, honors:* Litt.D., St. Olaf College, 1943; M.A., Harvard University, 1961.

WRITINGS: The Wheat Market and the Farmer in Minnesota, 1858-1900, Columbia University Press, 1926; *Jay Cooke, Private Banker,* Harvard University Press, 1936; (with N. S. B. Gras) *Casebook in American Business History,* Crofts, 1939; *Guide to Business History,* Harvard University Press, 1948; (with Kenneth Wiggins Porter) *History of Humble Oil and Refining Company,* Harper, 1959; (with Evelyn H. Knowlton and Charles S. Popple) *History of Standard Oil Company (New Jersey),* Volume III: *New Horizons, 1927-1950,* Harper, 1971. Editor, *Harvard Studies in Business History,* 1950-61.

SIDELIGHTS: Henrietta Larson is competent in Scandinavian languages and has a reading knowledge of French and German. She has traveled extensively in Europe. *Avocational interests:* Gardening.

BIOGRAPHICAL/CRITICAL SOURCES: Business History Review, spring, 1962.

*   *   *

LAST, Josephus Carel Franciscus   1898-1972
(Jef Last)

PERSONAL: Born in 1898, in The Hague, Netherlands; son of Carel and Helena Verstijnen; married Ida ter Haar, 1923; children: Femke, Annete, Hermien (all daughters). *Education:* Studied Chinese in Leiden, but interrupted his studies to travel for many years; University of Hamburg, Ph.D., 1957. *Politics:* Socialist (turned Communist at one point, then renounced the party). *Address:* Laren N.H., Rosa Spierhuis, Esseboom 2, Netherlands. *Agent:* Prins & Prins, de Lairessestrasse 6, Amsterdam, Netherlands.

CAREER: Poet, author, and translator. Worked as miner, sailor, assistant manager of a factory, teacher, and adviser on Dutch literature to Society of Writers in Moscow; captain in Spanish Republican Army, 1936-38; during German occupation of the Netherlands he edited *Vonk,* an underground newspaper; editor of Netherlands weekly, *Vlam,* 1945-46; counselor to President Sukarno of Indonesia on the culture and art of Bali, 1950-54. *Member:* Dutch Society of Journalists.

WRITINGS—All under pseudonym Jef Last; poetry: *Bakboordslichten,* Arbeiderspers, 1927; *Liedjes op de maat van de rottan,* Eigen Beheer, 1928; *De Wind speelt op het galentouw,* Eigen Beheer, 1929; *Kameraden,* W. L. Brusse, 1930; *Verleden tijd,* W. L. Brusse, 1932; *Twee werelden,* W. L. Brusse, 1933; *Onder de koperen ploert,* Pegasus, 1933; *De Bevrijde Eros,* W. L. Brusse, 1936; *Bloedkoraal,* De Ploeger, 1937; *Tau Kho Tau,* Kroonder, 1944; *Les Poetes maudits,* Kroonder, 1945; *Oog in oog,* Kroonder, 1945; *Vuur en Vlam,* Arbeiderspers, 1958; *Tegen de draad,* Arbeiderspers, 1960.

Fiction: *Branding,* Van Loghum Slaterus, 1930; *Marianne,* Servire, 1930; *Liefde in de portieken,* Servire, 1930; *Partij remise,* Contact, 1933; *Zuiderzee,* preface by Andre Gide, Querido, 1934; *Voor de mast,* Querido, 1935; *Een Huis zonder vensters,* Querido, 1935; *Een Flirt met den duivel,* Querido, 1936; *De Laatste waarheid,* Contact, 1939; *De Vliegende Hollander,* Kroonder, 1939; (with Harry Wilde) *Kruisgang der Jeugd,* W. L. Brusse, 1939; *Onvoldoende*

voor liefde, Kroonder, 1940; *Elfstedentocht,* Arbeiderspers, 1941; *Van een jongen die een man werd,* Nederlandse Uitgeverij, 1941; *Leeghwater maalt de meren leeg,* Arbeiderspers, 1942; *Het eerste schip op de Newa,* Arbeiderspers, 1945, translation by Fernand G. Renier and Anne Cliff published as *The First Ship Up the Neva,* Secker & Warburg, 1949; *Acht werken,* Kroonder, 1947; *Vingers van de linkerhand,* Kroonder, 1947; *In de zevende hemel,* Kroonder, 1949; *Schuim op de kust* (story collection), Driehoek, 1949; *De Rode en de witte lotus,* Kroonder, 1951; *Een Lotje uit de loterij,* Stols, 1957; *De Jeugd van Judas,* Enclave, 1962; *Doodvonnis voor een Provo,* Interland, 1967; *Drie over rood: Marianne, Elfstedentocht, Zuiderzee* (three novels; supra 1930, 1941, 1934), Kosmos, 1968.

Juvenile fiction: (With A. Kloots-Ehrenfest) *El Pintor's reizen* [and] *Matsa boemi op de Tafelberg* (latter story by Last), Corunda, 1946; (with Kloots-Ehrenfest) *El Pintor's reizen* [and] *Wat Hassan zag* (latter story by Last), Corunda, 1946; (with Pandji Tisma Udeyana) *I Bonto en I Koese,* Peet, 1958, translation by Marietta Moskin published as *The Bamboo School in Bali,* John Day, 1969.

Nonfiction: *Het Stalen fundament,* Vrieden van de Sowjet Unie, 1933; *De Spaanse Tragedie* (letters to his wife from Spain), Contact, 1937, translation by David Hallett published as *The Spanish Tragedy,* Routledge & Sons, 1939, revised edition, Contact, 1962; *Kinderen van de middernachtzon,* Wereld Bibliotheek, 1940; *Gedachten onder water* (essay), Distelvink, 1945; *Aan de bronnen van het herzet* (essay), Breughel, 1945; *De socialistische renaissance* (essay), Breughel, 1945; *Inleiding tot het denken van Confucius* (booklet on Confucius and Confucianism), Born, 1953; *Bali in de kentering* (Bali history), Bezige Bij, 1955; *Zo zag ik Indonesiee* (Indonesia history), van Hoeve, 1956; *La Hsun: Dichter und Odol* (Last's thesis at University of Hamburg, 1957, under title "Der Wandel in der Beurteilung Lu Hsun's und seine Ursachen"), Metzner, 1959; *Lieh tze en Yang Tsjoe,* Kluwer, 1959; *Japan in kimono en overall,* Kosmos, 1960; *Confucius,* Kruseman, 1961; *Inleiding bij het werk van Pearl Buck,* Heideland, 1961; *Lau-tse en de Tauisten,* Kruseman, 1962; *De Tweede dageraad van Japan: Een poging tot het rechtzetten van misverstanden,* Moussalut, 1966; *Mijn vriend Andre Gide,* van Ditmar, 1966; *China: Land van de eeuwige omwenteling,* Boom, 1966; (with Harry Wilde) *Rinus van der Lubbe: Doodstraf voor een provo,* Interland, 1967; *Strijd, handel en zeeroverij: De Hollandse tijd op Formosa,* Van Gorcum, 1968; *Vuurwerk achter de Chinese muur,* Wolters & Noordhoff, 1970; *Tjoebek in het Tijgerbos,* Strengholt, 1972. Also author of several pamphlets on Asian topics, 1967.

Plays: *De Draak ontwaakt,* Chinese Victory Committee, 1945; (with A. den Doolaard [pseudonym of C. Spoelstra] and C. A. B. Bantzinger) *Dit is Walcheren* (radio play), Willink & Zoon, 1945; *Djajaprana,* van Hoeve, 1954; *Een Aziatt wint de nobelprijs* (radio play), Vara-Hilversum, 1962.

Translations from French: Andre Gide, *Nieuwe spijzen,* Driehoek, 1939; Gide, *De Verloren zoon,* Driehoek, 1939; Gide, *Vrouwenschool,* Driehoek, 1945; Gide, *Oedipus en Theseus,* Driehoek, 1948; Pierre de Ronsard, *Les Amours,* Sythoff, 1948; Gide, *De Hadsji,* Driehoek, 1949; Gide, *Stories and Essays,* Heideland, 1963; Gide, *Corydon,* N.V.S.H., 1968; Victor Hugo, *Essays,* Heideland, 1972.

Translations from Russian: D. Masjlanenko, *De Vrolijke Brigade,* Moskwa, 1934; Tolstoi, *Linnenmeter,* Driehoek, 1941.

Translations from English: Joseph Conrad, *Aan het eind van de last,* Arbeiderspers, 1941; Lin Yu Tang, *Peking onder bliksemlicht,* Arbeiderspers, 1941; Edward Seidensticker, *Japan,* Parool, 1962; J. D. Brown, *India,* Parool, 1962; Brown, *China,* Parool, 1962.

Translations from German: Martin Buber, *Geschiedenis van Rabbi Nachmann,* Driehoek, 1946; Theodoor Plivier, *Honden waren mijn troost,* Bezige Bij, 1955.

Translations from Norwegian: *Liederen van het verzet* (Resistance poems), van Ditmar, 1947; *Opstand en revolutie,* van Gorkum, 1965.

Translations from Spanish: Ramon del Valle-Inclan, *Lentesonate, Zomer-sonate, Herfst-sonate,* and *Winter-sonate,* all four books published by Kroonder, 1950.

Translations from Chinese: Lieh Tze, *Het boek der grote Leegte,* Kluwer, 1959; *Golven der Gele Rivier* (collection of poetry), Boucher, 1962; Loe Sjuun, *Te Wapen* (stories), Bruna, 1970.

Translations from Japanese: *Meesters der Japanse vertelkunst* (collection of stories), Meulenhof, 1960; *Vloog een bloesem terug naar haar tak* (collection of haiku), Boucher, 1960; Yukio Mishima, *Na het banket,* Meulenhof, 1965; Mishima, *Vijf moderne Noh-spelen,* Bezige Bij, 1965; Mishima, *Bekentenissen van een gemaskerde,* Bezige Bij, 1967.

Co-author of "Andre Gide: Etudes gidiennes," published in *Revue des Lettres Modernes,* 1970. Contributor to other periodicals.

WORK IN PROGRESS: Reiziger in cultuur; translation of Mencius.

SIDELIGHTS: Josephus Last renounced the Communist Party after his trip with Andre Gide through the Soviet Union, and later served as a member of the International Bureau of the Socialist Movement for a United Europe. In his later years his writings and translations were aimed at bringing about a better understanding between East and West.†

(Died, 1972)

*   *   *

LATOURETTE, Kenneth Scott   1884-1967

PERSONAL: Born August 9, 1884, in Oregon City, Ore.; son of DeWitt Clinton (a lawyer and banker) and Rhoda Ellen (a teacher before marriage; maiden name, Scott) Latourette. *Education:* Linfield College, B.S., 1904; Yale University, B.A., 1906, M.A., 1907, Ph.D., 1909. *Politics:* Republican. *Home and office:* 409 Prospect St., New Haven, Conn. 06511; and Oregon City, Ore.

CAREER: Student Volunteer Movement for Foreign Missions, traveling secretary in United States and Canada, 1909-10; Yale in China, Changsha, Hunan, staff member, 1910-12; after partial recovery from illness contracted in China was part-time lecturer at Reed College, Portland, Ore., 1914-15, and assistant professor of history, 1915-16; Denison University, Granville, Ohio, associate professor, 1916-17; professor of history and chairman of department of history and political science, 1917-21, chaplain, 1918-21; ordained Baptist minister, 1918; Yale University, New Haven, Conn., D. Willis James Professor of Missions in Divinity School, 1921-27, professor of missions and Oriental history, 1927-49, Sterling Professor of Missions and Oriental History, 1949-53, professor emeritus, 1953-67, chairman of department of religion, Graduate School, 1938-46, director of graduate studies, 1946-53, fellow of Berkeley College, 1944-67. Professorial lecturer, Union Theological Seminary,

1955-64; distinguished lectureships include Cadbury Lecturer at University of Birmingham, 1947, Condon Lecturer at University of Oregon, 1949, Tipple Lecturer at Drew University, 1950, Carnahan Lecturer at Instituto Theologico Buenos Aires, 1956, and many others. President of American Baptist Convention, 1951-52. Trustee of Yale in China beginning 1921; Japanese International Christian University Foundation, trustee, beginning 1948, president, beginning 1953; trustee of Oberlin in China Association, 1949-56, and United Board of Christian Colleges in China.

MEMBER: American Historical Association (president, 1948-49), American Society of Church History (president, 1945), Association for Asian Studies (president, 1955), American Academy of Arts and Sciences, American Oriental Society, Connecticut Academy of Arts and Sciences (vice-president, 1938-45). *Awards, honors:* Order of the Jade (Republic of China), 1938. D.D. from Linfield College, 1922, McMaster University, Colgate University, Oxford University, 1947, Yale University, 1957, and University of Wales, 1962; LL.D. from Denison University, 1942; Litt.D. from Baylor University, 1945, Princeton University, 1947, and Boston University, 1953; S.T.D. from University of Glasgow, 1947; D.Science in Religion from University of Marburg, 1952; and others.

WRITINGS: The History of Early Relations between the United States and China, 1784-1844, Yale University Press, 1917; *The Development of China,* Houghton, 1917, 6th edition, 1946; *The Development of Japan,* Macmillan, 1918, reprinted as *The History of Japan,* 1947, revised edition, 1957; *The Christian Basis of World Democracy,* Association Press, 1919; *Japan: Suggested Outlines for a Discussion of Japan, Her History, Culture, Problems, and Relations with the United States,* Japan Society, 1921, 7th edition, 1934; *A History of Christian Missions in China,* Macmillan, 1929.

The Chinese: Their History and Culture, two volumes, Macmillan, 1934, 4th edition, 1964; *Missions Tomorrow,* Harper, 1936; *A History of the Expansion of Christianity,* seven volumes, Harper, 1937-45; *Toward a Christian Fellowship,* Association Press, 1938; *Anno Domini: Jesus, History and God,* Harper, 1940; *The Unquenchable Light* (William Belden Noble lectures), Harper, 1941; (editor) John Foster, *Then and Now,* Harper, 1942; (editor) *The Gospel, the Church, and the World,* Harper, 1946; *A Short History of the Far East,* Macmillan, 1946, 4th edition, 1964; *The U.S. Moves across the Pacific,* Harper, 1946; *The Christian Outlook,* Harper, 1948 (published in England as *Prospect for Christianity,* Eyre & Spottiswoode, 1949); (with William Richy Hogg) *Tomorrow Is Here,* Friendship, 1948; *Missions and the American Mind,* National Foundation Press, 1949; *The Emergence of a World Christian Community* (Rockwell lectures), Yale University Press, for Rice Institute, 1949; *The China That Is to Be,* Oregon State System of Higher Education, 1949.

These Sought a Country, Harper, 1950; *The American Record in the Far East, 1945-51,* Macmillan, 1952; *A History of Christianity,* Harper, 1953; *The Christian World Mission in Our Day,* Harper, 1954; *A History of Modern China,* Penguin, 1954; *Challenge and Conformity,* Harper, 1955; *Introducing Buddhism,* Friendship, 1956; *Desaffo a los Protestantes,* La Aurora (Buenos Aires), 1957; *World Service: A History of the Foreign Work and World Service of the Young Men's Christian Associations of the United States and Canada,* Association Press, 1957; *Christianity in a Revolutionary Age: A History of Christianity in the Nineteenth and Twentieth Centuries,* five volumes, Harper:

Volume I: *The Nineteenth Century in Europe: A Background and the Roman Catholic Phase,* 1958, Volume II: *The Nineteenth Century in Europe: The Protestant and Eastern Churches,* 1959, Volume III: *The Nineteenth Century outside Europe: The Americas, the Pacific, Asia, and Africa,* 1961, Volume IV: *The Twentieth Century in Europe: The Roman Catholic, Protestant, and Eastern Churches,* 1961, Volume V: *The Twentieth Century outside Europe: The Americas, the Pacific, Asia, and Africa,* 1962; *China,* Prentice-Hall, 1964; *Christianity through the Ages,* Harper, 1965; *Beyond the Ranges,* Eerdmans, 1967; *On the History of Missions: A Bibliography,* Eerdmans, 1968.

Author of a number of shorter works appearing in *League of Nations, American Historical Review,* and other journals, and then issued as separate reprints. Advisory editor, *International Review of Missions,* beginning 1928; member of editorial board, *Religion in Life.*

SIDELIGHTS: Dr. Latourette's books have been translated into German, Spanish, Norwegian, Chinese, Japanese, and Hindi. One of the nation's foremost church historians, he died in Oregon when struck by a car in front of the house where he had been reared.

BIOGRAPHICAL/CRITICAL SOURCES: Time, November 16, 1962; *New York Times,* January 1, 1968.†

(Died December, 1967)

* * *

LAUGESEN, Mary E(akin) 1906-

PERSONAL: Born May 4, 1906, in Bangkok, Thailand; daughter of John Anderson (a teacher and missionary) and Altha (Rhamey) Eakin; married Gudmund Laugesen (a shipping manager), October 22, 1932. *Education:* Wooster College, B.A., 1927; additional study at Columbia University, 1928, 1943-44, University of California, Berkeley, 1947-48, College of San Mateo, 1966-67, and Chabot College, Hayward, Calif., 1969-70.

CAREER: Poet and author. Assistant to treasurer of Presbyterian Pension Board in Philadelphia, Pa.; founded and taught private school for American children in Bangkok, Thailand, 1928-32; treasurer of Nielsen Hays Library, head of concert and performing arts section of Women's Club, Bangkok, 1928-41; part-time organist in Bangkok, 1923-41, and Livermore, Calif., 1964-66; Chulalongkorn University, Bangkok, lecturer in English literature, 1934-41; lived in Denmark, organized fund-raising bazaars in Copenhagen, 1949-62; moved to California, where "active in writing petitions and canvassing for causes." *Member:* American Association of University Women, National Retired Teachers Association, California Writers, Springtown Women's Club. *Awards, honors:* California Poetry Association award, 1966, for poem, "Fog on the Bay Bridge"; first prize, California Writers, 1967, for *The Chrisamat Tree.*

WRITINGS: The Chrisamat Tree, Bobbs-Merrill, 1970. Contributor of poems to *Kansas City Poetry Magazine, Tidens Kvinder* (Copenhagen), *Foreign Guide Posts,* religious periodicals and Bangkok newspapers and magazines. Translator of King Vajiravudth's *High Born Waifs;* author of an unpublished epic poem on Thai history.

WORK IN PROGRESS: A biography of John Anderson Eakin (father); novel about a Thai dancer, Tevada; children's books on Thai mythology; story of an American girl born in Thailand, *The Golden Bracelet;* a novel about the life and times of Christian IV of Denmark, *Igdrasil;* a biography of Anna's Prince of Siam, King Chulalongkorn.

SIDELIGHTS: Mary Laugesen told *CA* that her father, John Eakin, went to Siam to help start and teach in a school for princes; he later started the Bangkok Christian College, a school for commoners, and joined the Presbyterian Mission. Mary Laugesen has lived on three continents and visited twenty-five nations. *Avocational interests:* Painting, singing, drama.

BIOGRAPHICAL/CRITICAL SOURCES: The Eakin Family in Thailand, Prachandra Press (Bangkok), 1955.††

* * *

LAWSHE, C(harles) H(ubert) 1908-

PERSONAL: Born May 26, 1908, in Swayzee, Ind.; son of Charles Hubert (a pharmacist) and Rachel Lewis (Spears) Lawshe; married Muriel Grace Knight, January 30, 1930; children: Jane Ann Lawshe Kelbaugh. *Education:* Purdue University, B.S., 1929, Ph.D., 1940; University of Michigan, M.A., 1936. *Home:* 1005 Vine St., West Lafayette, Ind. 47906.

CAREER: Administrator and teacher in Indiana secondary schools, 1930-37, 1939-41; Purdue University, Lafayette, Ind., guest professor, 1941-44, associate professor, 1944-47, professor of industrial psychology, 1947-74, research associate in statistical laboratory, 1948-55, assistant to dean of Graduate School, 1954-57, dean of University Extension, 1958-66, dean of School of Technology, 1964-66, dean of continuing education, 1966-68, vice-president of university, 1966-74. Diplomate, American Board of Examiners in Professional Psychology. Member of board of directors of Clergy Economic Education Foundation, 1959-70, East Chicago Housing Corp., 1960-74, Housing Progress, Inc., 1964-74, National University Extension Association, 1965-68, Duncan Electric Manufacturing Co., beginning 1966, Indianapolis Center for Advanced Research, 1970-74, Duncan Foundation, and Purdue Aeronautics Corp. Chairman of board of directors, Indiana Higher Education Telecommunication System, 1972-74. Chairman of Indiana State Board of Vocational and Technical Education, 1965-69. President of Purdue-Calumet Development Foundation, 1965-73. Civilian Advisory Board, Air Training Command of U.S. Air Force, member, 1956-67, chairman, 1967-69. Member, National Advisory Council for Extension and Continuing Education, beginning, 1973.

MEMBER: American Psychological Association (fellow; president of industrial psychology division, 1957), Sigma Xi, Sigma Delta Chi, Phi Delta Kappa. *Awards, honors:* Award of merit, Air Training Command of U.S. Air Force, 1965; L.L.D., Kent State University, 1974; D.Sc., Purdue University, 1975.

WRITINGS: (With Harold Spears) *High School Journalism,* with teacher's manual, Macmillan, 1939, 3rd edition, 1966; *A Review of the Literature Related to the Various Psychological Aspects of Highway Safety,* Purdue University, 1939; (with Easton J. Asher and Joseph Tiffin) *Workbook for the Psychology of Normal People,* Heath, 1946; *Principles of Personnel Testing,* McGraw, 1947, 2nd edition, 1966; (contributor) *Planning Wage and Extra Compensation Policies,* American Management Association, 1948; (with Frank J. Harris) *Contributions of Military Psychology to Personnel Training,* American Management Association, 1948.

(With W.H.E. Holmes, Jr. and George M. Turmoil) *An Analysis of Employee Handbooks,* American Management Association, 1951; (with E. J. McCormick and others) *The Psychology of Industrial Relations,* McGraw, 1953; (with

Harold W. Porter and Orville D. Lascoe) *Machine Shop Operations and Setups,* American Technical Society, 1954, 2nd edition, 1960; (with Leon Thomas) *Applied Psychology for Employees,* American Technical Society, 1954. Author or co-author of eleven personnel and psychological tests published by Science Research Associates and Purdue Research Foundation. Contributor of some sixty articles to personnel, education, and psychology journals.

* * *

LAWTON, Sherman P(axton) 1908-
(Jack Paxton, Dr. John Paxton)

PERSONAL: Born July 13, 1908, in Muskegon Heights, Mich.; son of Henry James and Emma (Bruce) Lawton; married Kathleen E. Ewbank (an interviewer for U.S. Department of Commerce), November 15, 1930; children: Stephan Bruce and Sherman Ewbank (twins). *Education:* Albion College, A.B., 1929; University of Michigan, M.A., 1930; University of Wisconsin, Ph.D., 1939. *Politics:* Democrat. *Religion:* Episcopalian. *Home:* 530 Chautauqua, Norman, Okla. 73069. *Office:* Kaufman Hall, University of Oklahoma, Norman, Okla. 73069.

CAREER: Bradley Polytechnic Institute (now Bradley University), Peoria, Ill., instructor, 1930-32; Stephens College, Columbia, Mo., instructor, 1934-38, coordinator of radio and visual education, 1939-45; University of Oklahoma, Norman, professor of radio, beginning 1946, coordinator of broadcasting instruction, beginning 1950, research associate archaeologist, Stovall Museum, beginning 1955. Visiting summer professor at University of Vermont, 1947, Stephen F. Austin College, 1958; visiting lecturer at University of Wisconsin, 1948, 1949, and a number of other universities and colleges. Conductor of various broadcast series, beginning 1933, including "This Is Oklahoma" (radio), 1949-50, "The Open Window" (educational television), 1950-62, "Director's Debut" (educational television), 1962-65, and "Museum," 1963-64; regional representative, Peabody Awards, 1949-60. Member of board of directors, Oklahoma League for the Blind, 1952-54. Chairman of Board of Public Safety, Norman, beginning 1962.

MEMBER: Association for Professional Broadcasting Education (member of board), National Association of Educational Broadcasters, Instituto Interamericano (fellow), Oklahoma Anthropological Society (president, 1956), Texas Archaeological Society, Arkansas Archaeological Society, Delta Sigma Rho, Theta Alpha Phi, Pi Kappa Delta, Alpha Epsilon Rho (founder; past executive secretary), Classical Club. *Awards, honors:* Citation of Merit, U.S. Department of the Treasury, for radio series, "This is Oklahoma"; Golden Trowel Award as outstanding amateur in archaeology, Oklahoma Anthropological Society, 1966.

WRITINGS: Radio Speech (textbook), Expression, 1932; *Radio Drama* (textbook), Expression, 1938; *Radio Continuity Types,* Expression, 1938; (with others) *Projects for Radio Speech,* Harper, 1940; (with Henry Lee Ewbank) *Broadcasting: Radio and Television* (textbook), Harper, 1952; (with others) *Broadcasting Projects, Radio and Television,* Harper, 1953; *The Modern Broadcaster,* Harper, 1961; *Introduction to Modern Broadcasting,* Harper, 1963.

Editor of *Proceedings,* Annual Radio Conference, 1942-51. Contributor of articles and occasional reviews to speech, education, broadcasting, film, and archaeology journals. Former radio editor, *Speaker* (Pi Kappa Delta journal); member of editorial board, American Council for Better Broadcasts, 1953-57, of editorial committee on radio and television, *Central States Speech Journal,* 1956-57, and of editorial advisory committee, *Journal of Broadcasting,* 1957-60.

SIDELIGHTS: Lawton's work in archaeology has led to his name being given to a prehistoric culture, now known as Lawton Aspect of the Southern Plains Archaic. *Avocational interests:* Fishing, camping, and bridge.††

* * *

LAYTON, Felix 1910-

PERSONAL: Born September 10, 1910, in Devonshire, England; son of Wilfred and Ethel (Lancaster) Layton; married Eunice Shipp (a teacher), October 21, 1950. *Education:* University of Michigan, B.S., 1933; Stanford University, M.A., 1950. *Residence:* Wheaton, Ill.

CAREER: Spent seventeen years in India, seven of them as teacher and principal of Besant Memorial School, dedicated to revival of Indian Culture, and three years as principal of Olcott Memorial School for poor and outcastes; vice-president of Theosophical Society in America, Wheaton, Ill., 1966-72. *Military service:* British Army (in India), 1940-47. *Member:* Humane Society of the United States.

WRITINGS: Einstein's Theories in the Light of Theosophy, Theosophical Press, 1954; (with wife, Eunice Layton) *Some Basic Concepts of Theosophy,* Theosophical Publishing House (India), 1960; (with Eunice Layton) *Theosophy: Key to Understanding,* Theosophical Publishing House, 1967.

WORK IN PROGRESS: Another book on theosophy.

* * *

LEE, Ruth (Wile) 1892-

PERSONAL: Born November 8, 1892, in Chicago, Ill.; married Sylvanus George Lee (a lawyer), November 14, 1917 (deceased); children: Joan Lee Winter, Ruth Lee Optner, Mary Lee Winik. *Education:* Vassar College, A.B., 1914. *Home:* 766 Whiteoaks Lane, Highland Park, Ill. 60035.

CAREER: J. Walter Thompson Co. (advertising agency), Chicago, Ill., consultant and writer for public relations department, 1941-65; Haeger Potteries, Inc., Dundee, Ill., publicity director, beginning 1952; Joanna Western Mills Co., Chicago, Ill., publicity director, beginning 1960. Director of home furnishings sales seminar at Northwestern University, 1941-48, Chicago Retail Furniture Association, 1948-60, and American Furniture Mart, 1960-68; editorial scout, *Better Homes and Gardens,* 1941-68. *Member:* Illinois Home Fashions League (founder; past president), Chicago Vassar Club (past president). *Awards, honors:* Bolender Award for services to home fashions industries.

WRITINGS: (With Louise T. Bolender) *Fashions in Furnishings,* McGraw, 1948; (with Bolender) *Ten Keys to Home Decorating,* privately printed, 1949; *Exploring the World of Pottery,* Childrens Press, 1967. Author of home decorating booklets; contributor to *Better Homes and Gardens Annual,* 1941-68; regular contributor to *Better Homes and Gardens,* 1941-68, and *Design for Living,* 1958-68.

AVOCATIONAL INTERESTS: Travel: Ruth Lee made twenty-five trips to Europe, four to the Far East, three to the Middle East, one around the world, and one to South America in 1975.

LEE, S(idney) G(illmore) M(cKenzie)   1920-1973

PERSONAL: Born December 26, 1920, in Durban, South Africa; son of Sidney George (a farmer) and Grace (Goodland) Lee; married Margaret Thorp (an artist), May 22, 1948; children: Susan, Francis Jeremy. *Education:* University of Natal, B.A., 1946, M.A., 1948; University of London, Ph.D., 1954. *Politics:* Liberal. *Home:* Knighton Church Rd., Leicester, England. *Office:* Department of Psychology, University of Leicester, Leicester, England.

CAREER: University of London, London, England, lecturer in psychology, 1951-54, 1956-60; University College of Fort Hare, Alice, South Africa, senior lecturer in psychology, 1955-56; University of Leicester, Leicester, England, professor of psychology, beginning 1960. *Military service:* British Army, 1940-42; South African Air Force, 1942-46; became lieutenant. *Member:* International African Institute, British Psychological Society, American Psychological Society.

WRITINGS: Manual of a Thematic Apperception Test for African Subjects, University of Natal Press, 1953; (with Derek William Forrest) *Mechanism of Defense and Readiness in Perception and Recall* (monograph), American Psychological Association, 1962; *Stress and Adaption,* Humanities, 1962; (editor with M. Herbert) *Freud and Psychology,* Penguin, 1970; (with others) *Introducing Psychology,* Penguin, 1970; (compiler with Andrew R. Mayes) *Dreams and Dreaming: Selected Readings,* Penguin, 1973.

WORK IN PROGRESS: Research in African psychopathology, attachment behavior in young children, cross-cultural studies, and psychosomatic medicine.

SIDELIGHTS: Sidney Lee traveled widely in Africa and was competent in Zulu and Afrikans. *Avocational interests:* Shooting and collecting Africana and antiques.†

(Died March, 1973)

*   *   *

LEE, Samuel J(ames)   1906-

PERSONAL: Born February 26, 1906, in Toronto, Ontario, Canada; son of Isaac and Minnie (Rittenberg) Lee; married Leonie Lawrence, July 27, 1929; children: Jeffrey, Martin. *Education:* Attended special classes at McGill University and Cooper Union.

CAREER: President of Sam Lee Associates, beginning 1948, and Sentry Leasing, Inc., beginning 1964, both firms lease industrial equipment and motor vehicles, both in Los Angeles, Calif. *Member:* National Association of Fleet Administrators (honorary life member), Society of Automotive Engineers, American Automotive Leasing Association, American Jewish Historical Society, Southern California Jewish Historical Society.

WRITINGS: Automotive Transportation in Industry, L. Wolf, 1950; *Introduction to Leasing,* Coda Publications, 1965, revised edition, 1965; *Fleet and Lease Manager's Handbook,* Coda Publications, 1968; *Moses of the New World: The Work of Baron de Hirsch,* Yoseloff, 1970.

WORK IN PROGRESS: A book on highway safety, *The Other Side of the Story;* research in ecology.††

*   *   *

LeGALLEY, Donald P(aul)   1901-

PERSONAL: Born June 30, 1901, in Norwalk, Ohio; son of Marian E. and Mabel A. (Nunamaker) LeGalley; married Evangeline Cook, September 1, 1927; children: David M.,

Paul R. *Education:* Heidelberg College, Tiffin, Ohio, B.S., 1925; Pennsylvania State University, M.S., 1930, Ph.D., 1935. *Home:* 10402 Curaco Drive, Sun City, Ariz. 85351.

CAREER: Capital University, Columbus, Ohio, head of physics department, 1926-28; Pennsylvania State University, University Park, instructor in physics, 1935-37; Philadelphia College of Pharmacy and Science, Philadelphia, Pa., professor of physics, 1937-46; U.S. Navy, physicist in Research Division, Bureau of Ordance, 1946-50; scientist in Office of Chief of Naval Operations, 1950-56; General Motors Corp., A.C. Spark Plug Electronic Division, scientific staff consultant, 1956-59; Space Technology Laboratories, Redondo Beach, Calif., member of technical staff, 1959-64. Associate professor of physics, Haverford College, 1943-44; research physicist, U.S. Office of Scientific Research and Development, 1943-44. *Member:* American Rocket Society (senior member; chairman of guidance and control committee, 1960-62), American Society for Engineering Education, American Institute of Aeronautics and Astronautics, Sigma Xi, Sigma Pi Sigma.

WRITINGS: (Editor) *Ballistic Missiles and Space Technology,* four volumes, Academic Press, 1960; (editor and contributor) *Space Science,* Wiley, 1962; (co-editor and contributor) *Space Physics,* Wiley, 1964; (co-editor and contributor) *Space Exploration,* McGraw, 1964. Contributor of articles on guided missiles, nuclear physics, and allied subjects to journals.

*   *   *

LEGARET, Jean   1913-1976

PERSONAL: Born August 29, 1913, in Ambert, France; son of Gustave (a professor and inspector-general of national education) and Rose (Hardy) Legaret; married Jacqueline Hurel (an administrator, City of Paris), August 21, 1948; children: Sylvie, Jean-Francois, Jean-Philippe. *Education:* University of Paris, Licencie es lettres, 1933, Docteur en droit, 1936; School of Political Science, Paris, diplome, 1934; French War College, diplome, 1952. *Politics:* Independent. *Religion:* Roman Catholic. *Home:* 1 rue des Prouvaires, 75001 Paris, France.

CAREER: French Government, Paris, auditor, 1946, technical adviser to various ministeries, 1949-52, maitre des requetes (law post) for Council of State, 1956; Deputy of Paris, 1956-62, municipal councillor, Paris, 1964-65, president of Municipal Council of Paris, 1964-65; senator representing Paris, 1968-76. Professor at School of Higher Commercial Studies and at Academy of International Commerce. President of Commission of Cultural Affairs, and vice-president of Office of Tourism for Paris, beginning 1972. *Military service:* French Army, Engineers, 1939-45; commandant of Air Branch of Army, beginning 1957; received Croix de guerre and Croix du Combattant Volontaire de la Resistance for World War II service. *Awards, honors:* Chevalier of the Legion of Honor.

WRITINGS: Paul-Louis Target (1821-1908): Essau sur l'un fondateurs de la republique conservatrice, Les Presses Modernes, 1936; *La Communaute Europeene de Defense,* Librairie J. Vrin, 1953; *Le Statut de Paris,* Librairie Generale de Droit et de Jurisprudence, 1959; *Rapport sur les Halles de Paris et le probleme de leur transfert,* Imprimerie Municipale, 1960; *Le District de Paris,* Imprimerie Municipale, c. 1960; *Paris an 2000* (booklet), Imprimerie Moderne de la Presse, 1965; *Le Conde,* Laffont, 1967, translation by Helen Eustis published as *The Tightrope: A Novel of Intrigue in the Paris Underworld,* Little, Brown, 1970. Contributor to periodicals.

WORK IN PROGRESS: L'Innocent, a novel.†

(Died February 16, 1976)

* * *

LEHMANN, Arno 1901-

PERSONAL: Born May 23, 1901, in Dresden, Germany; son of Otto Theodore (a bank officer) and Hulda (Morgner) Lehmann; married Gertrude Harstall (an author), June 4, 1928 (died, 1965); married Wendula Nolte, August 25, 1967; children: (first marriage) Johannes, Theodor, Joachim. *Education:* Theological Seminary and University at Leipzig, student, 1919-25; University of Leipzig, Dr.theol., 1947. *Home:* Kirschbergweg 18, 402 Halle an der Salle, East Germany.

CAREER: Turned from a "worldly" profession to theology and became a missionary in southern India, 1926-34; *Blaetter fuer Mission,* Dresden, Germany, editor, 1935-40; full-time writer and editor, 1940-50; University of Halle-Wittenberg, Halle an der Salle, East Germany, professor of religions, missions, and Dravidology, 1950-71. *Member:* Deutsche Gesellschaft fuer Missionswissenschaft, International Association of Tamil Research. *Awards, honors:* Honorary doctorate, University of Jena, 1957; D.D., St. Louis University, 1966.

WRITINGS: (Translator) *Die Hymnen des Tayumanavar,* Bertelsmann-Guetersloh, 1935; (editor) *Die Mission der Kirche,* twelve volumes, Ungelenk, 1936-39; (editor) *Gott will es,* Ungelenk, 1939; *Das Wunder des Unscheinbaren,* Heimatdienstverlag, 1940; (editor) *Dem Befehl gehorsam,* eight volumes, Heimatdienstverlag, 1940-41; *Die Sivaitische Froemmigkeit der tamulischen Erbauungsliteratur,* Heimatdienstverlag, 1948; *Der Start ueber die Altergrenze,* [Leipzig], 1952.

(Editor) *Lutheran World Missions Handbook,* Mission, Breklum, 1952; *Ihla Formosa,* Missionsverlag, 1952; *Es begann in Tranquebar,* Evangelische Verlagsanstalt, 1955, 2nd edition, 1956, translation by M. J. Lutz published as *It Began at Tranquebar: The Story of the Tranquebar Mission and the Beginnings of Protestant Christianity in India,* Christian Literature Society (Madras), 1956; *Die Kunst der Jungen Kirchen* (title means "The Art of the Younger Churches"), Evangelische Verlagsanstalt, 1955, 2nd edition with supplement, 1957; (editor) *Gottes Volk in vielen Laendern,* Evangelische Verlagsanstalt, 1955; *Lebendige Kirche in der weiten Welt,* Lutherisches Verlagshaus, 1956; *Wie die Lutherisch Kirche nach Indien kam,* Mission, Erlangen, 1956; (editor) *Alte Briefe aus Indien,* Evangelische Verlagsanstalt, 1957; (translator) *Religion und christlicher Glaube,* Vandenhoek & Ruprecht, 1959; (editor) *Gottes ist der Orient,* Evangelische Verlagsanstalt, 1959; *Die Welt des Hinduismus,* MBK-Verlag, 1961; *Afroasiatische Christliche Kunst* (continuation of *Die Kunst der Jungen Kirchen*), Evangelische Verlagsanstalt, 1966, translation by Eric Hopka and others published as *Christian Art in Africa and Asia,* Concordia, 1969.

Contributor to *Religion in Geschiche und Gegenwart, Neue Deutsche Bibliographie,* and *The Concise Dictionary of the Christian World Missions.* Contributor of almost eight hundred articles and reviews to journals and newspapers.

WORK IN PROGRESS: Further research on the history of missions.

SIDELIGHTS: Christian Art in Africa and Asia "makes its predecessors seem like the work of hobbyists," Robert Steele writes in the *Christian Century.* Arno Lehmann, con-sidered a specialist in religious art since publication of *Die Kunst der Jungen Kirchen,* also is a jazz devotee, likes to smoke Brazilian cigars, and play tennis. He speaks English and Tamil fluently; his other languages are Latin, Greek, and Hebrew.

BIOGRAPHICAL/CRITICAL SOURCES: Theologische Literaturzeitung (Leipzig), 1961, 1966, 1971; *Christian Century,* October 8, 1969; *Deutsches Pfarrerblatt* (Essen), May 2, 1971.

* * *

LEIBERT, Julius A(mos) 1888-

PERSONAL: Surname is pronounced Lee-bert; name originally was Zalko Lebyotko; born March 20, 1888, in Lithuania; came to United States in 1904; son of Chayim and Leah Lebyotko; married Leona Goodman, 1919; children: Sharon Leah Leibert Israel, Carol Marti (Mrs. Donald G. Day). *Education:* University of Cincinnati, B.A., 1915; Hebrew Union College, Cincinnati, Ohio, Rabbi, 1916; also studied at University of Notre Dame. *Residence:* Pensacola, Fla.

CAREER: Rabbi, beginning 1916, serving congregations in South Bend, Ind., Spokane, Wash., Long Beach, Calif., Los Angeles, Calif., Pensacola, Fla., San Rafael, Calif. and Santa Cruz., Calif. Admitted to California Bar, 1919, and practiced law at intervals between synagogue posts; also sometime chaplain with the Civilian Conservation Corps and at San Quentin, Folsom, and Alcatraz prisons in California; former teacher of elementary philosophy at Pensacola Junior College, Pensacola, Fla. *Military service:* U.S. Army, chaplain, World War I, and 1941-45; became lieutenant colonel. *Member:* Veterans of Foreign Wars (state chaplain, Florida).

WRITINGS: Facing the Sun, De Vorss, 1933; *The Lawgiver* (novel), Exposition, 1953; *The Wives of King David,* Philosophical Library, 1962; (with Emily Kingsbery) *Behind Bars: What a Chaplain Saw in Alcatraz, Folsom, and San Quentin,* Doubleday, 1965.††

* * *

LEMAITRE, Georges E(douard) 1898-1973

PERSONAL: Born November 26, 1898, in Algiers, Algeria; became U.S. citizen, 1944; son of George Emile (a businessman) and Clemence (Vadam) Lemaitre; married Wynifred Eaves, June, 1937 (divorced September, 1947). *Education:* University of Algiers, Bachelier es-Lettres, 1916; University of Paris, Agrege de l'Universite, 1921, Docteur es-Lettres, 1931. *Politics:* Republican. *Religion:* Episcopalian. *Home:* 576 Tennyson Ave., Palo Alto, Calif. 94301. *Office address:* P.O. Box 2524, Stanford University, Stanford, Calif. 94305.

CAREER: French Institute, London, England, lecturer in French history, 1925-27; Dalhousie University, Halifax, Nova Scotia, lecturer in French, 1927-28; University of Wisconsin—Madison, lecturer in French, 1928-29; McGill University, Montreal, assistant professor, 1929-31, associate professor of French, 1931-38; Stanford University, Stanford, Calif., professor of Romance languages, 1938-64, professor emeritus, 1964-72. *Military service:* French Army, 1921-23; became lieutenant. *Member:* American Academy of Political and Social Science, Authors Club (London).

WRITINGS: Four French Novelists, Oxford University Press, 1938, Kennikat, 1969; *From Cubism to Surrealism in French Literature,* Harvard University Press, 1941; *Beaumarchais,* Knopf, 1949; *Maurois: The Writer and His Work,*

Ungar, 1968; *Giraudoux: The Writer and His Work,* Ungar, 1972.

SIDELIGHTS: Lemaitre believed that his best book was *Beaumarchais,* "owing mainly to its connection with American history." He traveled in Russia, Japan, India, the South Pacific, and Brazil.†

(Died August, 1973)

* * *

LEONARD, Eugenie Andruss 1888-

PERSONAL: Born February 22, 1888, in Dallas, Tex.; daughter of Eugene D. (a dentist) and Elizabeth (Medley) Andruss; married Robert J. Leonard, August 14, 1912 (deceased); children: Eugenie Leonard Mitchell, Robert J., Jr. *Education:* University of California, Berkeley, B.A., 1920; Columbia University, Ph.D., 1930.

CAREER: Syracuse University, Syracuse, N.Y., professor of education and dean of women, 1930-35; San Francisco Junior College, San Francisco, Calif., vice-president and dean of women, 1935-38; Catholic University of America, Washington, D.C., professor in Graduate School and dean of women, 1939-58.

WRITINGS: Concerning Our Girls and What They Tell Us, Teachers College, Columbia University, 1930, reprinted AMS Press, 1972; *Problems of College Freshman Girls,* Teachers College, Columbia University, 1932; *Vocational Citizenship,* Kenedy, 1947; *Origins of Personnel Services in American Higher Education,* University of Minnesota Press, 1956; (co-author) *The American Woman in Colonial and Revolutionary Times,* University of Pennsylvania Press, 1962; *Dear Bought Heritage,* University of Pennsylvania Press, 1965.†

* * *

LEONARD, Ruth S(haw) 1906-

PERSONAL: Born August 24, 1906, in Boston, Mass.; daughter of Fred Bickford (an accountant) and Mary (Shaw) Leonard. *Education:* Simmons College, S.B., 1928; Columbia University, M.S.L.S., 1944. *Politics:* Independent. *Religion:* Episcopalian. *Home:* 370 Longwood Ave., Boston, Mass. 02215.

CAREER: Bentley School of Accounting and Finance (now Bentley College), Boston, Mass., research director, 1930-37; Simmons College, School of Library Science, Boston, instructor, 1937-41, assistant professor, 1941-48, associate professor of library science, 1948-71. Organizer of library and consultant to Massachusetts Taxpayers Foundation, 1945-46. *Member:* American Library Association, Association of College and Research Libraries, Association of American Library Schools (chairman of recruiting committee, 1945-47; chairman of committee on instruction, 1951-52), Special Libraries Association (second vice-president, 1946-47; chairman of professional standards committee, 1966-69), American Association of University Professors, New England Library Association, Massachusetts Library Association. *Awards, honors:* Special Libraries Association Professional Award, 1965.

WRITINGS: (With H. C. Bentley) *Bibliography of Works on Accounting by American Authors,* two volumes, privately printed, 1934-35, reprinted, Augustus Kelley, 1970; (with M. P. Hazen) *Library Work,* Bellman Publishing, 1945, revised edition published as *The Library Profession,* 1954; (compiler) *Profiles of Special Libraries,* New York Special Libraries Association, 1965. Contributor to professional journals.

LESESNE, J(oab) Mauldin 1899-

PERSONAL: Surname is pronounced Le-*sane;* born September 25, 1899, in Kingstree, S.C.; son of Nabor DeKalb and Hortense (Mauldin) Lesesne; married Henrietta Fennell, November 13, 1935; children: Joab Mauldin, Jr., William W. *Education:* Wofford College, A.B., 1919; University of South Carolina, M.A., 1932, Ph.D., 1948. *Religion:* A.R. Presbyterian. *Home address:* Box 246, Due West, S.C. 29639.

CAREER: History teacher in public high schools in Rock Hill and Greenville, S.C., 1921-40; Erskine College, Due West, S.C., head of history department, 1940-54, president, 1954-66, president emeritus, 1966—. Town of Due West, S.C., served as mayor and as chairman of School Board. *Military service:* U.S. Army, 1918; served in World War I. *Member:* Southern Intercollegiate Athletic Association (former president), South Carolina Historical Association (former president). *Awards, honors:* LL.D., Wofford College, 1956; Litt.D., Lander College, 1956.

WRITINGS: Bank of the State of South Carolina: A General and Political History, University of South Carolina Press, for South Carolina Tricentennial Commission, 1970. Contributor of historical articles to periodicals, and to *Proceedings* of South Carolina Historical Association.

WORK IN PROGRESS: The Antebellum Churches of Upcountry South Carolina.

AVOCATIONAL INTERESTS: Travel.†

* * *

LESSEL, William M. 1906-

PERSONAL: Born May 15, 1906, in Strassburg, France; son of Michael (a railroad employee) and Louise (Brechenmacher) Lessel; married Vivian Gertrude Craig, September 3, 1932 (deceased); married G. G. Rathy, December 6, 1975. *Education:* Chicago School of Printing, graduate; also attended Northwestern University. *Politics:* Republican. *Religion:* Protestant. *Home:* 10 North Maguire Ave., Apt. 411, Tucson, Ariz. 85710.

CAREER: Moody Bible Institute, Chicago, Ill., foreman of printing plant, 1928-48, director of service department, 1948-71.

WRITINGS: Christmas Program Helps, three books, Moody, 1959; *Church Publicity,* Nelson, 1971; *Hi, Sugar,* B & B Publishing, 1971.

* * *

LESSERE, Samuel E. 1892-

PERSONAL: Born February 22, 1892, in London, England; son of Maurice and Dora (Lenowitz) Lessere; married Frances A. Auerbach, April 19, 1920; children: Eugene V. *Education:* Attended high schools in Bronx, N.Y. *Politics:* "Leftist Democrat." *Religion:* None. *Home and office:* Metacomet Rd., Farmington, Conn. 06032.

CAREER: Journeyman printer in earlier days, working around the country; later director of typography for Ketterlinus Litho Co., Philadelphia, Pa.; Typographical Designers, Inc., New York, N.Y., founder, 1930, and president, 1930-47; traveler and travel writer since retirement. *Member:* Advertising Typographers Association of America, Society of American Travel Writers.

WRITINGS: What You Must Know to Travel with a Camera, Harian, 1952, 7th edition, 1969; *Foreign Language Speak-Easy,* Harian, 1958; *We Retired to Travel,* Doubleday, 1962. Contributor to magazines.

SIDELIGHTS: For fifteen years Lessere and his wife lived and traveled abroad four to five months each year, collecting travel posters and notes on keeping down the cost of extended vacations. Their travels spanned most of Europe, various points in the Mediterranean, Near East, North Africa, Mexico, and Puerto Rico.

*   *   *

LETHBRIDGE, T(homas) C(harles)   1901-1971

PERSONAL: Born March 23, 1901, in Timberscombe, Devonshire, England; son of Ambrose Yarburgh (an officer in the Grenadier Guards) and Violet (Murdoch) Lethbridge; married Sylvia Frances Robertson, 1923 (divorced, 1944); married Mina Elizabeth Leadbitter, July 18, 1944; children: (first marriage) two sons (one son deceased), one daughter. *Education:* Trinity College, Cambridge, M.A., 1922. *Home:* Hole House, Branscombe, Seaton, Devonshire, England. *Agent:* Curtis Brown Ltd., 1 Craven Hill, London W2 3EW, England.

CAREER: Cambridge Antiquarian Society, Cambridge, England, excavator, 1925-56; Cambridge University Museum of Archaeology and Ethnology, Cambridge, excavator and honorary keeper of Anglo-Saxon collections, 1925-56. Member of Cambridge expeditions to Jan Mayen Island in the Arctic Ocean, 1921, East Greenland and Iceland, 1923, Baffin Island, 1937, and Iceland, 1939; made voyages to the Baltic in square-rigged sailing ships to obtain information on the handling of such vessels, summers, 1933-34, and field trips to the Outer Hebrides most other summers. *Military service:* Royal Naval Volunteer Supplementary Reserve; Naval Intelligence Division, 1939-45; became major. *Member:* Society of Antiquaries of London (fellow), Cambridge Antiquarian Society (honorary member).

WRITINGS: (Contributor) Charles Lucas, *Memories of a Fenland Physician*, Jarrolds, 1930; (compiler and illustrator) *Recent Excavations in Anglo-Saxon Cemeteries in Cambridgeshire and Suffolk*, Bowes, for Cambridge Antiquarian Society, 1931; (compiler and illustrator) *A Cemetery at Shudy Camps, Cambridgeshire* (booklet), Bowes, for Cambridge Antiquarian Society, 1936; *Merlin's Island: Essays on Britain in the Dark Ages*, Methuen, 1948; *Herdsmen and Hermits: Celtic Seafarers in the Northern Seas*, Bowes, 1950; (compiler and illustrator) *A Cemetery at Lackford, Suffolk*, Bowes, for Cambridge Antiquarian Society, 1951; *Coastwise Craft* (booklet), Methuen, 1952; (self-illustrated) *Boats and Boatsmen*, Thames & Hudson, 1952; *The Painted Men*, Philosophical Library, 1954; *Gogmagog: The Buried Gods*, Routledge & Kegan Paul, 1957, revised edition, 1975; *Ghost and Ghoul*, Routledge & Kegan Paul, 1961, Doubleday, 1962; *Witches: Investigating an Ancient Religion*, Routledge & Kegan Paul, 1962, published as *Witches*, Citadel, 1968; *Ghost and Divining-Rod*, Routledge & Kegan Paul, 1963, Hobbs, Dorman, 1967; *ESP: Beyond Time and Distance*, Routledge & Kegan Paul, 1965; *A Step in the Dark*, Routledge & Kegan Paul, 1967; *The Monkey's Tail: A Study in Evolution and Para-psychology*, Routledge & Kegan Paul, 1969; *The Legend of the Sons of God: A Fantasy?*, Routledge & Kegan Paul, 1972. Author of monographs and articles on Anglo-Saxon, Scottish, and Eskimo archaeology.

WORK IN PROGRESS: Research on dreams.

AVOCATIONAL INTERESTS: Water color sketches of localities and of sailing vessels.

BIOGRAPHICAL/CRITICAL SOURCES: Times Literary Supplement, August 31, 1967; *Antiquaries Journal*, Volume LII, 1972.†

(Died September 30, 1971)

LEVENSON, William B.   1907-

PERSONAL: Born May 5, 1907, in Cleveland, Ohio; son of Sam and Frieda (Seskin) Levenson; married Ruth Haas, July 4, 1938; children: Linda Seidman, Alice. *Education:* Ohio State University, B.Sc., 1927; Western Reserve University (now Case Western Reserve University), M.A., 1933, Ph.D., 1937. *Office:* Department of Education, Case Western Reserve University, Cleveland, Ohio 44106.

CAREER: Cleveland (Ohio) public schools, high school teacher of history, 1928-37; Station WBOE, Cleveland, director, 1938-47; Cleveland public schools, assistant superintendent, 1947-54, deputy superintendent, 1954-61, superintendent, 1961-64; Case Western Reserve University, Cleveland, lecturer in graduate school, 1940-60, professor of education and coordinator of urban education studies, 1964-75, professor emeritus, 1975—. Former member of U.S. National Commission for UNESCO, of Canada-U.S. Committee on Education, and of Radio Manufacturers Association-U.S. Office of Education Joint Committee; member of advisory committee on guidance and counseling, U.S. Office of Education; consultant on social studies texts, Ginn & Co. Trustee of City Club Forum Foundation, Cleveland Mental Health Association, Cleveland Welfare Federation, Council on Human Relations, and Cleveland Zoological Society; member of advisory council, Cleveland Girl Scouts. *Member:* American Association of School Administrators, Ohio Education Association (life member).

WRITINGS: Teaching Through Radio, Farrar & Rinehart, 1945, revised edition (with Edward Stasheff) published as *Teaching Through Radio and Television*, Rinehart, 1952; *Steve Sears, Ace Announcer*, King Co., 1948; (with Florence French and Vera Rockwell) *Radio English*, McGraw, 1952; *The Spiral Pendulum: The Urban School in Transition*, Rand McNally, 1968. Contributor of about thirty articles to professional journals, largely on school use of mass media.

*   *   *

LEVER, J(ulius) W(alter)   1913-1975
(Walter Lever)

PERSONAL: Born July 24, 1913, in Salford, England; son of Jack (a pharmacist) and Gertrude (Finestone) Lever; married Anita Caplan, July 17, 1940; children: Constance (Mrs. Noel Tracy), Rachel (Mrs. Sean Matgamna). *Education:* Lincoln College, Oxford, B.A., 1934, M.A., 1954; University of Manchester, M.A., 1945; University of Birmingham, Ph.D., 1955.

CAREER: Hebrew University, Jerusalem, Israel, lecturer, 1947-53; University of Khartoum, Khartoum, Sudan, professor of English, 1955-58; University of East Africa, Makerere, Uganda, senior lecturer in English, 1958-60; University of Durham, Durham, England, lecturer in English, 1960-65; Simon Fraser University, Burnaby, British Columbia, professor of English, 1972-75.

WRITINGS: (Under name Walter Lever) *Jerusalem Is Called Liberty*, Massada Press, 1951; *The Elizabethan Love Sonnet*, Methuen, 1956, 2nd edition, 1966; (editor) William Shakespeare, *A Midsummer Night's Dream*, Longmans, Green, 1961; (editor) Shakespeare, *Measure for Measure*, Harvard University Press, 1965; (translator) S. Y. Agnon, *Two Tales*, Schocken, 1966; (editor) Shakespeare, *As You*

Like It, Longmans, Green, 1967; *The Tragedy of State*, Methuen, 1971; (editor) Ben Johnson, *Every Man in his Humor: A Parallel-text Edition of the 1601 Quarto and the 1616 Folio*, University of Nebraska Press, 1971; (editor) Shakespeare, *The Rape of Lucrece*, Penguin, 1971; *Sonnets of the English Renaissance*, Athlone Press, 1974.

Under name Walter Lever, author of plays, "The Guy," performed at Ealing, England, and at Mercury Theatre, and "The Rary," performed at Manchester University Theatre, London. Contributor to *Shakespeare Survey*, *Shakespeare Quarterly*, and other journals.

WORK IN PROGRESS: Edition of Ben Jonson's *Every Man out of His Humor*, for University of Nebraska Press.†

(Died November 11, 1975)

* * *

LEVY, D(arryl) A(llen)   1942-1968

PERSONAL: Name written in lower-case letters: d. a. levy; born October 29, 1942, in Cleveland, Ohio; son of Joseph and Caroline Levy. *Education:* High school graduate, 1960, and "long talks with angels." *Politics:* "passive anarchist." *Religion:* "Yes."

CAREER: Poet, painter, and printer. Publisher with r. j. sigmund of underground newspaper *The Buddhist Third Class Junk Mail Oracle*. *Military service:* U.S. Navy, seven months, 1960-61.

WRITINGS: More Withdrawed or Less, Renegade Press, 1963; *5 Cleveland Prints*, Renegade Press, 1964; (with Alden Kirby Congdon and Carl Larsen) *3 One Act Plays*, Hors Commerce Press, 1964; *The North American Book of the Dead: Part 1 and 2*, Free Lance Press, 1965; *Chalchihuitlicue*, Renegade Press, 1965; (with Kent Taylor) *Fortuitous Mother F——er*, Renegade Press, 1965; *Cleveland Undercovers*, 7 Flower Press, 1966; *Visualized Prayers and Hymn for the American God*, Renegade Press Death Book, 1966; *Black Hat at the End of the Bar*, [Cleveland], 1966; *The Cement F——*, [Cleveland], 1966.

Cleveland: The Rectal Eye Visions, Press Today, 1966; (with D. R. Wagner) *The Egyptian Stroboscope*, Asphodel Book Shop, 1966; (editor) *465: An Anthology of Cleveland Poets*, 7 Flowers Press, 1966; *The Great Tibetan Train Robbery Mystery Play in Color: A Mandala Hernia Ruptured Word Game*, Ganglia Press, 1966; *The North American Book of the Dead*, 7 Flowers Press, 1966; *Plastic Saxophone in an Egyptian Tomb is a Collection of Egyptian, Tibetan and American Concrete/Mandala's, Shrieks, Poems, Prayers, Sound and Light Rays Re-Translated and Hallucinated by d. a. levy*, Accident, 1966; *White Light*, [Cleveland], 1966; (author of introduction) George Montgomery, *The Mary-Jane Papers: Poems and a Play*, 7 Flowers Press, 1966; *The Box Lunch: Travel-og of Fremont Gulch*, [Cleveland], 1967; *Kibbutz in the Sky*, Free Love Press, 1967; *Poems for Julie*, Grass Coin Publishing, 1967.

(Editor and contributor) *Poetry Survival Pamphlet*, Grass Coin Publishing, 1967; *Tantric Strobe (Horizons): Part 1 and 2*, Ghost Press, 1967; (compiler) *Three-oh-six: An Anthology of Cleveland Poets*, 7 Flowers Press, 1967; *Tomb Stone as a Lonely Charm: A Poem*, Runcible Spoon (Sacramento), 1967; (with Carl Woideck and Taylor) *Three Poems by Cleveland Poets*, 7 Flowers Press, 1967; *d. a. levy, a Tribute to the Man: An Anthology of his Poetry*, edited by rjs (Robert J. Sigmund), Ghost Press, 1967; *The Beginning of Sunny Dawn, a Short Story*, Ghostflower Press, 1968; *Poems for Beverly*, Cold Mountain Publishing, 1968;

Poems, Quixote Press, 1968; *Prose: On Poetry in the Wholesale Education and Culture System*, Gunrunner Press, 1968.

7 Concrete Poems, Quixote Press, 1968; *Suburban Monastery Death Poem*, Zero Edition, 1968; *The Tibetan Stroboscope*, Ayizan Press, 1968; *Zen Concrete: Translations and a New Interpretation of Buddhist Doctrines*, Blewointmentpress, 1968; *For John R. Scott Who Painted Flowers: A Written Testimonial*, Ghost Press, 1968; *The Beginning of Sunny Dawn* [and] *Red Lady*, Open Skull Press, 1969; *The Madison Poems of d. a. levy*, edited by Morris and Betsy Edelson and others, Quixote Press, 1969; *Postcard*, Ganglia Press, 1969; *Red Lady*, Para-Shakti Press, 1969; *Songs for Dead Children* (a poem), Black Rabbit Press, 1969; *Notes: Variations on a Short Poem*, Runcible Spoon (Sacramento), 1970; *Private No Parking* (poems), RPM Print, 1972.

Also author of *Stone Sarcophagus*, Radical America, and *Tune in Today for Tomorrow's Episode*, Radical America. Also illustrator of *Head Second* (poems), by Judson C. Crews, Staatsburg, N.Y. Editor, *Marrahwannah Quarterly*.

SIDELIGHTS: Levy was interested in the legalization of psychedelics for medicinal and religious purposes, legalizing love, concluding the illusion. While out on bond for the possession and distribution of his poems, he was arrested March 27, 1967, for publishing "obscene" literature. The Cleveland police at the same time confiscated the poetry of Robert Duncan who had received a $10,000 federal grant.

New York Times reported that "after he tidied up his world, mailed letters off to friends across the country saying he was leaving Cleveland, drove away his common-law wife in anger and shipped his belongings to friends, he placed a .22-caliber rifle between his eyes and pulled the trigger. He died at age 26."

BIOGRAPHICAL/CRITICAL SOURCES: Andrew Curry, *Raging Against the Dying of the Light*, L. Fulton, 1969; *New York Times*, March 3, 1969.†

(Died, 1968)

* * *

LEWIS, June E(thelyn)   1905-

PERSONAL: Born June 5, 1905, in Boyne City, Mich.; daughter of William Nelson (a lumber mill superintendent) and Ethelyn (Hooper) Lewis. *Education:* Attended Alma College, 1923-25; Western Michigan University, A.B., 1932; Columbia University, M.A., 1935; Harvard University, Ed.D., 1953. *Politics:* Republican. *Religion:* Presbyterian. *Home:* 7150 Northeast Seventh Ave., Boca Raton, Fla. 33431.

CAREER: Elementary teacher in Three Rivers, Mich., 1925-27; elementary science specialist in Kalamazoo, Mich., 1927-33; State University of New York College at Plattsburgh, instructor, 1935-38, assistant professor, 1938, associate professor, 1938-53, professor of physical science, 1954-63. Visiting professor, Wheelock College, 1950-51. Director of elementary science workshops, Ministry of Education of Indonesia. Adviser to New York State Research Foundation and to Ford Foundation. *Member:* Association for Education of Teachers in Science (president, 1955-56), Council for Elementary Science International (president, 1957-58), National Association for Research in Science Teaching, National Science Teachers Association, American Association of University Professors, Pi Lambda Theta, Kappa Delta Pi.

WRITINGS: (With Gerald S. Craig) *The Earth Then and*

Now, Ginn, 1940; (with Craig) *Going Forward in Science,* Ginn, 1947; (with Irene C. Potter) *The Teaching of Science in the Elementary School,* Prentice-Hall, 1961, 2nd edition, 1970. Author of script and teacher's guide for film, "What Makes a Rocket Go?," National Aeronautics and Space Administration, 1963.

WORK IN PROGRESS: Revision of second edition of *The Teaching of Science in the Elementary School.*

* * *

LEWIS, Marvin 1923-1971

PERSONAL: Born January 28, 1923, in Camden, N.J.; son of Isaac (a merchant) and Lillian (Barsh) Lewis; married Ruta Arija Ievina, November 23, 1959; children: Marvin Victor, Andrew Eric. *Education:* Montana State College (now University), B.A., 1945; University of Pennsylvania, M.A., 1948; University of Southern California, M.L.S., 1961. *Home:* 2337 Hickory St., San Diego, Calif. 92103.

CAREER: Denver (Colo.) public schools, teacher in secondary schools, 1952-62; San Diego Junior Colleges, San Diego, Calif., librarian and history instructor, 1963-71. *Member:* Organization of American Historians, American Federation of Teachers, California Junior College Association.

WRITINGS: (Editor) *The Mining Frontier: Contemporary Accounts from the American West in the Nineteenth Century,* University of Oklahoma Press, 1967. Contributor to *Western Folklore, Arizona Quarterly,* and *Western Humanities Review.*

WORK IN PROGRESS: A study of family life and pioneer society in Nevada between 1864-1874, tentatively titled *A Pioneer Family;* readings in California history, politics, and government.†

(Died July 29, 1971)

* * *

LEWIS, Walker 1904-

PERSONAL: Born February 10, 1904, in Hoboken, N.J.; son of Edwin A. S. (a lawyer) and Alice S. (Walker) Lewis; married Eleanor R. Nelson, October 7, 1938; children: Edwin A. S., John N., Fielding, Henry McI. *Education:* Princeton University, A.B., 1925; Harvard University, LL.B., 1928. *Religion:* Episcopalian. *Home:* 103 St. Johns Rd., Baltimore, Md. 21210. *Agent:* A. Watkins, Inc., 77 Park Ave., New York, N.Y. 10016.

CAREER: Attorney, beginning 1928, practicing in Baltimore, Md., and Washington, D.C.; Chesapeake & Potomac Telephone Co., Washington, D.C., general solicitor, 1955-68. *Military service:* U.S. Army, 1941-45; became lieutenant colonel. *Member:* Maryland Historical Society, 14 West Hamilton St. Club (Baltimore), Army and Navy Club (Washington, D.C.).

WRITINGS: Without Fear or Favor: A biography of Chief Justice Roger Brooke Taney, Houghton, 1965; (editor) *Speak for Yourself, Daniel: A Life of Webster in His Own Words,* Houghton, 1969.

* * *

LEWISTON, Robert R(ueben) 1909-

PERSONAL: Born January 18, 1909, in Detroit, Mich.; son of Jacob Abram (a union officer) and Rose (Bloom) Levin; married Patricia Kolodin (a teacher), December 25, 1930; children: Michael B., Richard M., David H. *Education:*

University of Michigan, A.B., 1928; Detroit College of Law, LL.B., 1930. *Politics:* Democrat. *Religion:* Jewish. *Home:* 19320 Lancaster Dr., Southfield, Mich. *Office:* 3200 Guardian Building, Detroit, Mich. 48226.

CAREER: Admitted to Michigan State Bar, 1930; private practice as attorney in Detroit, Mich., and suburbs, beginning 1930. Trustee of Cerebral Palsy Society. *Member:* American Bar Association, Detroit Bar Association, Town and Country Club (director, 1965-68).

WRITINGS: Hit from Both Sides: An Expose of Our Insurance System, Abelard, 1967.

WORK IN PROGRESS: The Paper Curtain: Suburbia's Jericho Wall, as related to American housing, future, and racism.

SIDELIGHTS: Lewiston listed among his interests, "relationships between man and rats in their respective proclivities toward self-destruction, the probability of mankind enduring to the twentieth-first century, the subservience of man to ignorant and superior authority, and the accidental evolutionary development of man."

* * *

LEWITON, Mina 1904-1970
(Mina Lewiton Simon)

PERSONAL: Born March 22, 1904, in New York, N.Y.; daughter of Leonard and Sara (Cass) Lewiton; married Howard Simon (an artist), January 20, 1936; children: Bettina (Mrs. James Niederer). *Education:* Attended New School for Social Research. *Politics:* Independent. *Religion:* None. *Residence:* Stanfordville, N.Y. 12581.

CAREER: Author. New School for Social Research, New York City, instructor, 1960-67; New York University, Division of Adult Education, New York City, instructor, 1961-65. *Awards, honors:* Literary award, National Council on the Arts, 1968.

WRITINGS—Juveniles, except as noted: *John Philip Sousa, the March King,* illustrated by husband, Howard Simon, Didier, 1944; *Elizabeth and the Young Stranger* (a novel for young adults), McKay, 1961; *Lighthouses of America,* illustrated by H. Simon, Criterion, 1964; *Especially Humphrey,* illustrated by H. Simon, Delacorte, 1967; *A Young Girl Going Out of the Door,* Delacorte, 1969.

Under name Mina Lewiton Simon: *The Divided Heart,* McKay, 1947; *A Cup of Courage,* McKay, 1948; *The Tough and the Tender* (novel), F. Watts, 1950; *First Love,* illustrated by H. Simon, McKay, 1952; *Beasts of Burden,* illustrated by H. Simon, Lothrop, 1954; *Rachel,* illustrated by H. Simon, F. Watts, 1954; *Penny's Acres* (novel), McKay, 1955; *Rachel and Herman* (a sequel to *Rachel*), illustrated by H. Simon, F. Watts, 1957; *Candita's Choice,* illustrated by H. Simon, Harper, 1959; *Faces Looking Up,* illustrated by H. Simon, Harper, 1960; *Animals of the Field and Forest,* illustrated by H. Simon, Whitman, 1961; (with H. Simon) *If You Were an Eel, How Would You Feel?,* Follett, 1963; *That Bad Carlos,* illustrated by H. Simon, Harper, 1964; (with H. Simon) *Who Knows When Winter Goes?,* Follett, 1966; *Is Anyone Here?,* illustrated by H. Simon, Atheneum, 1967; *Humphrey on the Town* (a sequel to *Especially Humphrey*), illustrated by H. Simon, Delacorte, 1971.

Also, editor of *Song of Hiawatha, The Ancient Mariner,* and *Evangeline,* during 1967. Story anthologized in *Fiction of the Forties.* Contributor of short stories to *New Yorker* and articles to *Library Journal.*

WORK IN PROGRESS: Two novels, The Sweet and Poisoned Air and another, as yet untitled; a fictionalized biography of Felix Mendelssohn.

SIDELIGHTS: Miss Lewiton told CA: "I believe the best books for children are still to be written with themes that take for granted certain basic human achievements to come: that warfare will be considered barbaric and of the childhood of the race; that ethical behavior has been learned in the beginning grades together with writing and reading; that the knowledge and enjoyment of art and music are equally needed for growth and achievement of human maturity as are food and clothing." She added that all her New Yorker stories and portions of the novel The Tough and the Tender are "clearly autobiographical."†

(Died February 11, 1970)

*   *   *

LEYBURN, Ellen Douglass   1907-1966

PERSONAL: Born September 21, 1907, in Durham, N.C.; daughter of Edward R. (a minister) and Nancy (Harlan) Leyburn. Education: Agnes Scott College, B.A., 1927; Radcliffe College, M.A., 1928; Yale University, Ph.D., 1934. Home: 380 South Candler St., Decatur, Ga. Office: Agnes Scott College, Decatur, Ga. 30030.

CAREER: Beaver Country Day School, Brookline, Mass., teacher, 1928-29; Buffalo Seminary, Buffalo, N.Y., teacher of English, 1929-32; Agnes Scott College, Decatur, Ga., instructor, 1934-39, assistant professor, 1939-43, associate professor, 1943-57, professor of English, 1957-66. Member: Modern Language Association of America, South Atlantic Modern Language Association, American Association of University Women, Phi Beta Kappa. Awards, honors: Huntington Library fellow, 1953-54.

WRITINGS: Satiric Allegory: Mirror of Man, Yale University Press, 1956; Strange Alloy: The Relation of Comedy to Tragedy in the Fiction of Henry James, University of North Carolina Press, 1968. Contributor to learned journals.††

(Died, 1966)

*   *   *

LEYPOLDT, Martha M.   1918-1975

PERSONAL: Born October 2, 1918, in Hanover, Ontario, Canada; daughter of John (a minister) and Huldah (Kusch) Leypoldt. Education: Linfield College, B.A., 1944; Northern Baptist Theological Seminary, M.R.E., 1949; University of Chicago, M.A., 1959; Indiana University, Ed.D., 1964. Politics: Republican. Office: Eastern Baptist Theological Seminary, City Line and Lancaster Ave., Philadelphia, Pa. 19151.

CAREER: High school teacher of algebra in Gresham, Ore., 1944-46; North American Baptist Headquarters, Forest Park, Ill., assistant in youth and Sunday school work, 1946-49, editorial staff assistant, 1949-53; director of education at Baptist church in Anaheim, Calif., 1953-55; North American Baptist Seminary, Sioux Falls, S.D., registrar and professor of Christian education, 1955-66; Eastern Baptist Theological Seminary, Philadelphia, Pa., professor of Christian education, beginning 1966. Member of Committee on Ministry with Adults, American Baptist Convention, 1966-69. Member: Religious Education Association, Adult Education Association of the United States, Association for Supervision and Curriculum Development, Pennsylvania Adult Education Association, Pi Lambda Theta, Zonta Club.

WRITINGS: Forty Ways to Teach in Groups, Judson, 1967; Learning is Change, Judson, 1971. Contributor to journals.†

(Died July 15, 1975)

*   *   *

LIEBERG, Owen S.   1896-1973

PERSONAL: Surname is pronounced Lee-berg; born July 21, 1896, in London, England; son of Frederick H. and Isobel (Wilson) Lieberg; married Madge N. Coggins, February 3, 1917. Education: The Polytechnic, London, England, Diploma in Electrical Engineering, 1923. Residence: La Tour de Peilz, Switzerland.

CAREER: Consulting mechanical engineer in London, England, 1931-39; partner in consultant mechanical engineering firms in Pasadena, Calif., 1946-52, and New York, N.Y., 1952-57. Lecturer in engineering, University of California, Los Angeles, 1950-51. Military service: British Army, assistant director of fortifications and works, War Office, 1939-45; became major. Member: American Society of Heating, Refrigerating and Air Conditioning Engineers, Institute of Electrical Engineers, Institute of Mechanical Engineers, Institute of Heating and Ventilating Engineers.

WRITINGS: High Temperature Water Systems, Industrial Press (New York), c.1958, revised edition, 1964; Wonders of Heat and Light (youth book), Dodd, 1965; Wonders of Magnets and Magnetism (youth book), Dodd, 1967; Wonders of Measurement, Dodd, 1972; The First Air Race: The International Competition at Reims, 1909, Doubleday, 1974. Contributor of technical articles to American journals, and of short stories and novelettes to magazines.†

(Died August 3, 1973)

*   *   *

LIEBERSON, Goddard   1911-

PERSONAL: Born April 5, 1911, in Hanley, Staffordshire, England; brought to America in 1915, naturalized in 1936; son of Davis (a manufacturer) and Rachel (Lewis) Lieberson; married Vera Zorina (an actress and stage director); children: Peter, Jonathan Sears. Education: Attended University of Washington, Seattle, Eastman School of Music, and University of Rochester.

CAREER: Taught music in private schools and was music critic for Rochester Journal-American, Rochester, N.Y.; Columbia Records, New York City, joined staff in 1939, became director of masterworks and education department, and vice-president, 1948-56, president, 1956-66, 1973-75; CBS/Columbia Group, New York City, president, 1966-1973; Columbia Broadcasting System, Inc., senior executive vice-president and member of board of directors, 1956-75; Goddard Productions, New York City, founder and president, beginning 1975. Composer of orchestral suites, including "Five Modern Painters," 1929, "Three Chinese Poems," 1936, and "Homage to Handel"; program annotator for New York Philharmonic broadcasts, 1943, and Philadelphia Orchestra broadcasts, 1954. Lecturer at universities in New York area. Member of board of directors and chairman of board of Music Theater, Lincoln Center for the Performing Arts. Director of Dartmouth College Arts Council, of advisory council for the performing arts, University of Pennsylvania, and of advisory board, New York City Theater. Honorary curator and chairman of special committee, Yale University Library; trustee, Professional Children's School.

MEMBER: Record Industry Association of America (former president and director), Civil War Roundtable. *Awards, honors:* Mus. D. from Temple University, 1957, and Cleveland Institute of Music, 1965; L.H.D. from Lincoln College, 1969; Gold Record Award of Record Industry Association of America and Grammy Award of National Academy of Recording Arts and Sciences, both seven times.

WRITINGS: (Editor) *Columbia Book of Musical Masterworks,* Allen, Towne & Heath, 1947; *Three for Bedroom C* (novel), Doubleday, 1947; (editor with J. Meyers) *John Fitzgerald Kennedy ... As We Remember Him,* Atheneum, 1965; *The Irish Uprising: 1916-1922,* Macmillan, 1966. A number of musical compositions have been published, and "String Quartet" and "Piano Pieces for Advanced Children or Retarded Adults" were recorded. Contributor to *Reporter, Theatre Arts, New York Times Magazine,* and other magazines and newspapers. Editor, *International Cyclopedia of Music and Musicians.*

SIDELIGHTS: Goddard Lieberson is competent in French, German, Italian, Spanish, and Japanese.

BIOGRAPHICAL/CRITICAL SOURCES: Esquire, July, 1956; *Time,* March 16, 1959; *Hi-Fi/Stereo Review,* January, 1965; *Columbia Journal of World Business,* fall, 1966; *Business Week,* October 7, 1967.†

*　　*　　*

LINCKE, Jack   1909-

PERSONAL: Born October 10, 1909, in Butte, Mont.; son of Clarence J. (a newspaper man) and Mabel (McMinn) Lincke; divorced; children: Mabel, Jack, Jr. *Education:* Attended Kemper Military Academy, Montana State University, 1922-24; University of Montana, student, 1925-27, B.A., 1971. *Religion:* Protestant. *Home:* 1766 North Allen Ave., Pasadena, Calif. 91104.

CAREER: Began flying at the age of fifteen and has been an aviator for forty years; commissioned first lieutenant of Infantry, U.S. Army, 1928, and took Army Air Corps flight training, 1928-29; commissioned ensign, U.S. Naval Reserve, on graduation from Navy Flight Training School, 1931, promoted to lieutenant junior grade, 1937; flier for Nationalist Chinese Air Force; owner and operator of a public relations business, Pasadena, Calif., beginning 1947; also operates an airplane for business and pleasure. *Member:* Combat Pilots Association, Kiwanis International, Quiet Birdmen, OX-5 Club, Silver Wings.

WRITINGS: Aircraft Manual for Inspection Maintenance and Repair, Aviation Press, 1935; *Jenny Was No Lady: The Story of the JN-4D,* Norton, 1970. Also author of "The Wings of the Dragon" (play), produced in serial form on NBC-TV. Contributor of articles and stories to *Liberty, Saturday Evening Post, American, Coronet,* and national news syndicates.

WORK IN PROGRESS: From Where the Sun Now Stands, an historical novel on the Nez Perce Indians; *Fathers of Flight,* a biography of the Wright brothers and an engineering treatise on their invention of the airplane; and *Publicity,* a book intended as a text, manual, or "self-help" work for those in publicity and public relations work.

SIDELIGHTS: Jack Lincke told *CA:* "[I was] selected from among graduates of Kemper Military School ... for inclusion in *History of Cooper County.* They overrated me greatly since the second one chosen was Will Rogers. ...."

LINCOLN, Murray D.   1892-1966

PERSONAL: Born April 18, 1892, in Raynham, Mass.; son of Minot Jackson (a storekeeper) and Helen (Andrews) Lincoln; married Anne Hurst, October 9, 1915; children: Betty. *Education:* University of Massachusetts, B.S., 1914. *Politics:* Democrat. *Religion:* Protestant. *Home:* 5099 Sunbury Rd., Gahanna, Ohio 43020.

CAREER: Insurance executive for many years, and longtime president of Nationwide Insurance, Columbus, Ohio. Former chairman of board, Cooperative for American Relief Everywhere (CARE), *Member:* Columbus Athletic Club, Masons.

WRITINGS: Vice President in Charge of Revolution, McGraw, 1960.

AVOCATIONAL INTERESTS: United Nations, agriculture, cooperatives.††

(Died November 7, 1966)

*　　*　　*

LINDERMAN, Winifred B.

PERSONAL: Born in Harmony, Minn.; daughter of James E. (a grain dealer) and Emma L. (Mark) Linderman. *Education:* Carleton College, B.A., 1919; Columbia University, B.S. in L.S., 1935, M.S. in L.S., 1940, Ph.D., 1959. *Home:* Hotel Ansonia, Broadway at 73rd St., New York, N.Y. 10023.

CAREER: Teacher of English at high schools in Minnesota, North Dakota, and South Dakota, 1919-24; high school librarian in Fresno, Calif., 1924-29; Brooklyn (N.Y.) Public Library, assistant, 1929-30; New York (N.Y.) Public Library, assistant reference librarian, 1931-36; high school librarian in Garden City, N.Y., 1936-44; Vassar College, Poughkeepsie, N.Y., reference librarian, 1944-45; U.S. Information Service, cultural officer and library director, Cape Town, South Africa, 1945-47; Columbia University, School of Library Service, New York, N.Y., associate, 1947-59, associate professor, 1959-65, professor, 1965-66, professor emeritus, 1966—. Visiting professor, Emory University, Division of Librarianship, Atlanta, Ga., 1967-68; visiting professor, University of Illinois, Graduate School of Library Science, Urbana, 1968-71, summer 1973.

MEMBER: American Library Association, American Historical Association, American Association of Library Schools, American Association of University Professors, American Association of University Women, New York Library Club, Phi Beta Kappa.

WRITINGS: (Editor) *The Present Status and Future Prospects of Reference/Information Service,* American Library Association, 1967. Contributor to library journals.

WORK IN PROGRESS: A biography of Melvil Dewey; *Childhood Recollections of Life on a Dakota Homestead.*

AVOCATIONAL INTERESTS: The theater, music, travel.

*　　*　　*

LINKLATER, Eric (Robert Russell)   1899-1974

PERSONAL: Born March 8, 1899, in Penarth, South Wales; son of Robert Baikie (a master mariner) and Elizabeth (Young) Linklater; married Marjorie MacIntyre, June 1, 1933; children: Alison, Kristin, Magnus, Andro. *Education:* Aberdeen University, studied medicine for a time, received M.A., 1925. *Politics:* Conservative. *Religion:* Church of

England. *Home:* The Mains of Hadd, Tarves, Aberdeenshire, Scotland. *Agent:* A. D. Peters, 10 Buckingham St., Adelphi, London WC2N 6DD, England.

CAREER: Times of India, Bombay, India, assistant editor, 1925-27; Aberdeen University, Aberdeen, Scotland, assistant to professor of English literature, 1927-28, rector, 1945-48; Commonwealth Fellow at Cornell University and University of California, 1928-30. *Military service:* The Black Watch, private, 1917-19; Royal Engineers, major, 1939-41; in War Office, 1941-45; temporary lieutenant colonel during Korean Conflict, 1951. *Member:* Royal Society of Edinburgh (fellow), Savile (London), New Club (Edinburgh). *Awards, honors:* LL.D., Aberdeen University, 1946; received Territorial Decoration; Commander, Order of the British Empire, 1954; Carnegie Medal, Library Association, 1945, for *The Wind on the Moon.*

WRITINGS: White-Maa's Saga, J. Cape, 1929; *A Dragon Laughed, and Other Poems,* J. Cape, 1930; *Poet's Pub,* J. Cape & H. Smith, 1930; *Ben Jonson and King James,* J. Cape & H. Smith, 1931, Kennikat, 1972; *Juan in America* (novel), J. Cape & H. Smith, 1931; *The Men of Ness: The Saga of Thorlief Coalbiter's Sons,* J. Cape, 1932, Farrar & Rinehart, 1933; *The Crusader's Key,* Knopf, 1933; *Mary, Queen of Scots,* Appleton, 1933; *Magnus Merriman,* Farrar & Rinehart, 1934; *The Revolution,* White Owl Press, 1934; *The Devil's in the News* (comedy), J. Cape, 1934; *Robert the Bruce,* Appleton, 1934; *Lion and the Unicorn, or, What England Has Meant to Scotland,* Routledge, 1935; *God Likes Them Plain* (stories), J. Cape, 1935; *Ripeness is All,* Farrar & Rinehart, 1935; *Juan in China,* Farrar & Rinehart, 1937; *The Sailor's Holiday,* J. Cape, 1937, Farrar & Rinehart, 1938; *The Impregnable Women,* Farrar & Rinehart, 1938; *Judas,* Farrar & Rinehart, 1939.

The Cornerstones: A Conversation in Elysium, Macmillan, 1941; *The Defence of Calais,* H.M.S.O., 1941; *The Man on My Back* (autobiography), Macmillan, 1941; *The Northern Garrisons,* Garden City Publishing, 1941; *The Highland Division,* H.M.S.O., 1942; *The Raft, and Socrates Asks Why: Two Conversations,* Macmillan, 1942; *Crisis in Heaven: An Elysian Comedy,* Macmillan, 1944; *The Great Ship, and Rabelais Replies: Two Conversations,* Macmillan, 1944; *The Wind on the Moon* (juvenile), Macmillan, 1944; *Private Angelo* (novel), Macmillan, 1946; *Art of Adventure,* Macmillan, 1947; *Sealskin Trousers, and Other Stories,* Hart-Davis, 1947; *A Spell for Old Bones,* J. Cape, 1949, Macmillan, 1950; *The Pirates in the Deep Green Sea* (juvenile), Macmillan, 1949.

Love in Albania (comedy), English Theatre Guild, 1950; *Mr. Byculla: A Story,* Hart-Davis, 1950; *The Thistle and the Pen: An Anthology of Modern Scottish Writers,* Nelson, 1950; *Two Comedies: Love in Albania,* and, *To Meet the MacGregors,* Macmillan, 1950; *The Campaign in Italy,* H.M.S.O., 1951; *Laxdale Hall* (novel), 1951; *Our Men in Korea,* H.M.S.O., 1952; *The Mortimer Touch* (comedy), S. French, 1952; *The House of Gair* (novel), J. Cape, 1953; *A Year of Space: A Chapter in Autobiography,* Harcourt, 1953; *The Sultan and the Lady,* Harcourt, 1954 (published in England as *The Faithful Ally,* J. Cape, 1954); *The Ultimate Viking,* Macmillan, 1955; *The Dark of Summer,* J. Cape, 1956; *A Sociable Plover, and Other Stories and Conceits,* Hart-Davis, 1957; *Karina With Love,* Macmillan, 1958; *Breakspear in Gascony* (play), Macmillan, 1958; *Position at Noon* (novel), J. Cape, 1958, published as *My Fathers and I,* Harcourt, 1959; *The Merry Muse,* J. Cape, 1959.

Edinburgh, Newnes, 1960; *Roll of Honour,* Hart-Davis,

1961; *A Man Over Forty* (novel), Macmillan, 1963; *Husband of Delilah* (novel), Harcourt, 1963; (author of text) *Gueller's Sweden,* Almqvist & Wiksell, 1964; *The Conquest of England,* Doubleday, 1966; *The Prince in the Heather,* Hodder & Stoughton, 1965, Harcourt, 1966; *A Terrible Freedom,* Macmillan, 1966; *Orkney and Shetland: An Historical, Geographical, Social, and Scenic Survey,* R. Hale, 1965, 2nd edition, 1971; *The Survival of Scotland: A New History of Scotland from Roman Times to the Present Day,* Doubleday, 1968 (published in England as *The Survival of Scotland: A Review of Scottish History from Roman Times to the Present Day,* Heinemann, 1968); *The Stories of Eric Linklater,* Macmillan (London), 1968, Horizon Press, 1969; (author of introduction) *Scotland,* Viking, 1968.

(Editor) *John Moore's England: A Selection from His Writings,* Collins, 1970; *Fanfare for a Tin Hat,* Macmillan, 1970; *The Royal House,* Doubleday, 1970 (published in England as *The Royal House of Scotland,* Macmillan, 1970); *The Corpse on Clapham Common: A Tale of Sixty Years Ago,* Macmillan, 1971; *The Voyage of the Challenger,* Doubleday, 1972.

SIDELIGHTS: Patrick Dennis wrote that Linklater "is incapable of writing an unentertaining book, a dull page, or even an unstylish line." P. G. Wodehouse describes Linklater's charm thus: "Mr. Linklater just goes on talking in a gentle voice, and it is impossible not to listen to his every word. He holds you, not with a glittering eye but by some subtle magic which is difficult to analyze." Of *Husband of Delilah,* the *Times Literary Supplement* wrote: "There is no convincing delineation of character, [but] of course every page is amusing."

BIOGRAPHICAL/CRITICAL SOURCES: Saturday Review, March 14, 1959; *New York Tribune Book Review,* February 14, 1960; *Spectator,* September 2, 1960; *Times Literary Supplement,* September 16, 1960, October 5, 1962; *New Yorker,* September 30, 1961.†

(Died November 7, 1974)

* * *

LIPPHARD, William B(enjamin) 1886-1971

PERSONAL: Born October 29, 1886, in Evansville, Ind.; son of William A. (a clergyman) and Martha (Liefield) Lipphard; married Helen Dickinson, October 15, 1914; children: Dickinson, Stella (Mrs. LeRoy D. Clarke). *Education:* Yale University, B.A., 1908, M.A., 1910; Colgate Rochester Divinity School, B.D., 1920. *Politics:* Republican. *Home:* 88 Franklin Ave., Yonkers, N.Y. 10505.

CAREER: American Baptist Foreign Mission Societies, assistant secretary, 1913-19, associate secretary, 1919-33, department editor of *Missions Magazine,* 1913-22, associate editor, 1922-32, editor-in-chief, 1932-52, editorial columnist, 1952-63, editor emeritus, 1963-71. Secretary of World Relief Committee, American Baptist Convention, 1940-52; Associated Church Press, president, 1947-49, executive secretary, beginning 1952; former member of various committees and commissions, National Council of Churches. *Member:* American Baptist Historical Society (vice-president, 1948-52), Foreign Policy Association. *Awards, honors:* D.D. from Franklin College, 1932; Litt.D. from Ottawa University, 1949; Associated Church Press Award, 1951, for first place in editorial writing.

WRITINGS: The Ministry of Healing, Judson Press, 1920; *The Second Century of Baptist Foreign Missions,* Judson Press, 1926; *Communing with Communism,* Judson Press,

1931; *Out of the Storm in China,* Judson Press, 1932; *Fifty Years an Editor* (autobiographical), Judson Press, 1963; *Disillusioned World,* Exposition, 1967. Also contributor to *The Religions of America,* 1954, *Why I Am a Baptist,* 1957, and *Why I Believe in Prayer,* 1958. Contributor to *Look, New York Sun,* and other secular and religious publications.

SIDELIGHTS: William Lipphard believed that he held the record for editorial association with a single publication—fifty years. He crossed the Atlantic more than seventy times and the Pacific three times, always by sea (he was never in a plane).†

(Died April 15, 1971)

*   *   *

LITTLE, Paul E.   1928-1975

PERSONAL: Born December 30, 1928, in Philadelphia, Pa.; son of Robert James (a minister) and Margaret (Eagleson) Little; married Marie Huttenlock, December, 1953; children: Deborah Ann, Paul Robert. *Education:* University of Pennsylvania, B.S., 1950; Wheaton College, Wheaton, Ill., M.A., 1958. *Office:* Department of Evangelism, Trinity Evangelical Divinity School, 2045 Half Day Rd., Deerfield, Ill. 60015.

CAREER: Inter-Varsity Christian Fellowship, staff member in Illinois, 1950-53, foreign student director in New York, 1955-57, South Central regional director in Dallas, 1957-60, director of evangelism in Chicago, beginning 1960. Trinity Evangelical Divinity School, Deerfield, Ill., assistant professor of evangelism, teaching one quarter each year, beginning 1964. Speaker at universities in Latin America, Africa, and Europe. *Member:* National Association for Foreign Student Affairs, Evangelical Theological Society, Association of College and University Religious Administrators.

WRITINGS: Lost Audience, Inter-Varsity, 1959; *Who's Got the Answer?,* Moody, 1964; *How to Give Away Your Faith,* Inter-Varsity, 1966; *Know What You Believe,* Victor Books, 1967; *Know Why You Believe,* Scripture Press, 1967, revised edition, Inter-Varsity, 1968. Weekly columnist, *Sunday School Times,* 1964-67; columnist for *Power,* beginning 1967; contributor to other religious periodicals.†

(Died July 11, 1975)

*   *   *

LIVERMORE, Shaw   1902-

PERSONAL: Born September 1, 1902, in Wellesley Hills, Mass.; son of Arnold and Lucy (Heilig) Livermore; married Evelyn Taylor, February 20, 1926 (divorced, 1956); married Rosalind Robb Salant, March 23, 1957; children: (first marriage) Shaw, Jr., Gloria Livermore Duclos. *Education:* Dartmouth College, A.B. (summa cum laude), 1922; Harvard University, M.B.A. (with highest distinction), 1924; Columbia University, Ph.D., 1939. *Politics:* Democrat. *Home:* 4545 Osage Drive, Tucson, Ariz. 85718.

CAREER: Analyst for a wholesale firm, 1925-26, an investment firm, 1926-28; University of Buffalo, Buffalo, N.Y., professor of economics and business organization, 1929-41; War Production Board, Washington, D.C., director of review and analysis staff, 1941-45, vice-chairman of requirements committee, 1944-45; Dun and Bradstreet, Inc., New York, N.Y., assistant director, then co-director of marketing and research division, 1945-49; Economic Cooperation Administration, deputy director, later director of Program Division in Paris, France, then director of Foreign

Supply and Requirements Committee, Washington, D.C., 1949-51; RAND Corp., research staff in Washington, D.C., and Santa Monica, Calif., 1951-52, consultant, beginning 1966; Office of Defense Mobilization, Washington, D.C., assistant to director, Office of Emergency Planning, member and chairman of program advisory committee, 1954-63; Rockefeller Brothers, New York, N.Y., economic staff, 1953-57; University of Arizona, Tucson, professor of business administration, 1957-64, professor of management, 1964-69, professor of public administration, 1969-71, dean of College of Business and Public Administration, 1957-63. Visiting professor at Cornell University, 1946, University of Buffalo, 1947-48, American University of Beirut, 1963-64, Alabama A&M University, 1973, 1974-75. Member of economic committee, U.S. Chamber of Commerce, 1953-55, of second Hoover Commission, 1954-55; Advisor to Government of Thailand, 1968. *Member:* Phi Beta Kappa, Beta Gamma Sigma, Alpha Delta Delta, Cosmos Club (Washington, D.C.).

WRITINGS: (With C. S. Tippetts) *Business Organization and Public Control,* Van Nostrand, 1933, revised edition, 1941; *Investment,* Irwin, 1938; *Early American Land Companies: Their Influence on Corporate Development,* Commonwealth Fund, 1939, reprinted, Harvard University Press, 1965; *Management of Science* (monograph), George Washington University Studies in Science and Technology, 1965. Contributor to economics and business journals.

*   *   *

LLOYD, Francis V(ernon), Jr.   1908-

PERSONAL: Born June 19, 1908, in York Harbor, Me.; son of Francis Vernon (a lawyer) and Mary Emlen (Lowell) Lloyd; married Elisabeth Boardman, December 28, 1933; children: Francis Vernon III, Malcolm, Boardman, Mary Lowell. *Education:* Stanford University, B.A., 1933; New College, Oxford, graduate study, 1934-35; Harvard University, M.Ed., 1949; Washington University, St. Louis, Mo., graduate study, 1957. *Politics:* Independent. *Religion:* Episcopalian. *Home:* 222 Pleasant St., South Yarmouth, Mass. 02664.

CAREER: St. Paul's School, Concord, N.H., successively teacher of English, head of Lower School, director of studies, and vice-rector, 1935-57; Clayton (Mo.) School District, superintendent, 1957-63; University of Chicago, Laboratory Schools, Chicago, Ill., director of pre-collegiate education, 1963-70; Educational Consultants, South Yarmouth, Mass., director, beginning 1970. Lecturer, Harvard University, 1950, University of Virginia, 1968, University of Michigan, 1968-70. Trustee of Webster College and Eaglebrook School, Deerfield, Mass. *Military service:* U.S. Coast Guard, 1942-45. *Member:* American Association of School Administrators, Modern Language Association of America, National Education Association (life member), American Studies Association, National Association of Principals of Schools for Girls (member of board), Independent Schools Association of Central States (member of board), Phi Delta Kappa, Sigma Delta Chi, Hyde Park Neighborhood Club, Checkerboard Club, Harvard Club (Boston, Mass. and New York, N.Y.). *Awards, honors:* Samuel Ells Award of Alpha Delta Phi, 1964.

WRITINGS: (Co-author) *Preparation of Teachers of Secondary Schools,* National Council of Independent Schools, 1958; *Forward to Teach,* Little, Brown, 1967. Author of column, "An Apple For—," for *Independent School Bulletin,* beginning 1967; contributor to other professional journals.

SIDELIGHTS: Lloyd traveled in Russia to attend the fourth Soviet-American Citizen's Conference in Leningrad, 1964, and in Australia as guest of honor at the Conference of Australian Independent School Headmasters, 1967. *Avocational Interests:* Photography, sailing, bird- and flower-watching.†

* * *

LOCKE, Clinton W.
[Collective pseudonym]

WRITINGS—"Perry Pierce Mystery" series; published by Henry Altemus Co., except as indicated: *Who Closed the Door?*, 1931; *Who Opened the Safe?*, 1931; *Who Hid the Key?*, 1932; *Who Took the Papers?*, M. A. Donohue, 1934.

SIDELIGHTS: See **ADAMS, Harriet S., STRATEMEYER, Edward L.,** and **SVENSON, Andrew E.**†

* * *

LOCKERT, (Charles) Lacy (Jr.)   1888-1974

PERSONAL: Born May 18, 1888, in Clarksville, Tenn.; son of Charles Lacy (a druggist) and Nannie (Smith) Lockert. *Education:* Southwestern Presbyterian University, A.B., 1907, A.M., 1909; Princeton University, Ph.D., 1916.

CAREER: Kenyon College, Gambier, Ohio, assistant professor of English, 1916-25; retired early in order to study and write. *Member:* Modern Language Association of America, Sierra Club.

WRITINGS—Translator and author of critical material, except as noted: (Author of commentary) Massinger and Field, *The Fatal Dowry*, New Era Press, 1918; (contributor) H. Craig, editor, *Essays in Dramatic Literature: The Parrott Presentation Volume*, Princeton University Press, 1935; Dante Alighieri, *The Inferno*, Princeton University Press, 1936; Jean Baptiste Racine, *Best Plays*, Princeton University Press, 1936; Pierre Corneille, *Chief Plays*, Princeton University Press, 1952, 2nd edition, 1957; (editor) Orville Ernest Watson, *Selected Sermons*, Kenyon College, 1955; *The Chief Rivals of Corneille and Racine*, Vanderbilt University Press, 1956; (author) *Studies in French-classical Tragedy*, Vanderbilt University Press, 1958; Racine, *Mid-career Tragedies*, Princeton University Press, 1958; Corneille, *Moot Plays*, Vanderbilt University Press, 1959; *More Plays by Rivals of Corneille and Racine*, Vanderbilt University Press, 1968. Contributor to *Sewanee Review, North American Review,* and other journals.

AVOCATIONAL INTERESTS: Great natural scenery, and photographing it; history of American intercollegiate football; Wagnerian opera.†

(Died April 21, 1974)

* * *

LOCKWOOD, William W(irt)   1906-

PERSONAL: Born February 24, 1906, in Shanghai, China; son of William Wirt and Mary Rebecca (Town) Lockwood; married Virginia Chapman, October 23, 1934; children: William W., Jr., Stephen C., Julia D. *Education:* De Pauw University, A.B., 1927; Harvard University, A.M., 1929, Ph.D., 1950. *Home:* 74 Jefferson Rd., Princeton, N.J. 08540.

CAREER: Bowdoin College, Brunswick, Me., instructor, 1929-32, assistant professor, 1932-34; American Council, Institute of Pacific Relations, New York, N.Y., research secretary, 1935-40, executive secretary, 1941-43; American

Committee for International Studies, Princeton, N.J., executive secretary, 1940-41; U.S. Office of Strategic Services, Washington, D.C., assistant chief of Far East Division, Research and Analysis Branch, 1943; U.S. Department of State, Washington, D.C., assistant chief of Division of Japanese and Korean Economic Affairs, 1946; Princeton University, Woodrow Wilson School of Public and International Affairs, Princeton, N.J., assistant director, 1946-57, associate professor, 1949-54, professor of politics and international affairs, 1955-71, professor emeritus, 1975—, lecturer, 1971-75. Consultant to U.S. Office of Export Control, 1940, Ford Foundation, 1953-54, and Foreign Area Fellowship Program, 1971-72; trustee of American Institute of Pacific Relations, 1946-53, 1955-61; Princeton-in-Asia trustee, beginning 1947, vice-president, 1954-70. McCosh faculty fellow, 1965-66. Member of East Asia panel, U.S. Department of State, 1968-69, National Committee on U.S.-China Relations, beginning 1969, senior specialist, East-West Center, Honolulu, Hawaii, 1969-70, and of executive committee on international affairs division of American Friends Service Committee, beginning 1970. Delegate to Fourth U.S.-Japan Conference on Education and Cultural Exchange, 1968. *Military service:* U.S. Army, 1943-45; became major.

MEMBER: Association for Asian Studies (director, 1948-49, 1957-59; president, 1963-64), American Economic Association, American Political Science Association, Council on Foreign Relations, Japan Society (director, beginning 1967), Joint Committee on Japanese Studies (member of Social Science Research Council, 1967-68), Phi Beta Kappa, Phi Kappa Psi. *Awards, honors:* Ford Foundation fellow, 1956-57; Fulbright research scholar in Japan, 1961-62.

WRITINGS: The Economic Development of Japan, Princeton University Press, 1954; (editor) *The State and Economic Enterprise in Japan,* Princeton University Press, 1965; (editor) *The United States and Communist China,* Princeton University Conference, 1965. Also author of numerous monographs, articles, and chapters on modernization in Asia. Member of editorial board, Princeton University Press, 1962-65.

WORK IN PROGRESS: Politics and Economic Development in Asia.

* * *

LOEWENFELD, Claire   1899-1974

PERSONAL: Born September 27, 1899, in Berlin, Germany; daughter of Arthur (a manufacturer) and Jeannette (Jacobi) Lewis; married G. E. Loewenfeld (a landscape designer), July 5, 1921; children: Verena C. (Mrs. Timothy Wilkinson). *Education:* Attended high school in Berlin, Germany; Dr. Bircher-Benner Institute, Zurich, Switzerland, special diploma, 1939. *Home:* Springwood, Buckland Common, near Tring, Hertfordshire, England. *Office:* Chiltern Herb Farms Ltd., near Tring, Hertfordshire, England. *Agent:* David Higham Associates Ltd., 5-8 Lower John St., London W1R 4HA, England.

CAREER: Worked in Germany at a Berlin institute providing slides and illustrations for a university, and later as a diet therapist for coeliac diseases at Hospital for Sick Children, London, England; founder and director of Chiltern Herb Farms Ltd., Hertfordshire, England. Founder of Garden Services Ltd., dietitian, designing and promoting convenience foods. *Member:* Soroptimist International.

WRITINGS: Britain's Wild Larder "Fungi," Faber, 1956; *Britain's Wild Larder "Nuts,"* Faber, 1957; (editor and translator) Ruth Bircher, *Eating Your Way to Health,* Faber, 1961; *Herb Gardening: Why and How to Grow Herbs,* Faber, 1964, Branford, 1965; (with Philippa Back) *Herbs for Health and Cookery,* Pan Books, 1965, published as *Herbs, Health and Cookery,* Hawthorn, 1967; (with Back) *The Complete Book of Herbs and Spices,* Putnam, 1974. Author of a series of leaflets on the nutritional value of wild herbs and berries, 1940-43.†

(Died August 20, 1974)

*   *   *

LOEWENSTEIN, Rudolph M(aurice)   1898-1976

PERSONAL: Born January 17, 1898, in Lodz, Poland; came to United States in 1942; naturalized, 1948; son of Maurice and Charlotte (Taube) Loewenstein; married Elisabeth Rozetta Geleerd (a psychoanalyst), July 13, 1946; children: Dominique-Therese Kolin, Elisabeth-Charlotte (Mrs. Jack Novick), Marie-Francoise (Mrs. Vincent Galizia), Richard Joseph. *Education:* Studied at University of Zurich, 1917-20, Berlin Psychoanalytic Institute, 1920-23; University of Berlin, M.D., 1923; University of Paris, M.D., 1935. *Religion:* Jewish.

CAREER: Berlin Psychoanalytic Institute, Berlin, Germany, assistant, 1923-25; Paris Psychoanalytic Institute, Paris, France, training analyst and lecturer, 1926-40; New York Psychoanalytic Institute, New York City, training analyst and instructor, beginning 1943, president, 1950-52; private practice in psychoanalysis, New York City, beginning 1943. Associate clinical professor of psychiatry, Yale University, Medical School, 1948-52. *Military service:* French Army, 1939-40; served as Medecin de Bataillon; received Croix de Guerre.

MEMBER: International Psycho-Analytical Association (vice-president, 1965-67), American Psychoanalytic Association (life member; president, 1957-58), American Psychiatric Association, American Medical Association, American Association for the Advancement of Science, Federation of American Scientists, Conference on Jewish Social Studies, New York State Medical Society, New York Psychoanalytic Society (life member; president, 1959-61), New York Society for Clinical Psychiatry, New York County Medical Society, Paris Psychoanalytic Society (corresponding member), Israel Psychoanalytic Society (corresponding member).

WRITINGS: Christians and Jews: A Psychoanalytic Study, International Universities Press, 1951; *Psychanalyse de l'Antisemitisme,* Presses Universitaires de France, 1952; (editor) *Drives, Affects, Behavior: Contributions to the Theory and Practice of Psychoanalysis and Its Applications,* International Universities Press, 1953; (with Heinz Hartmann and Ernst Kris) *Papers on Psychoanalytic Psychology,* International Universities Press, 1964; (editor with others) *Psychoanalysis—A General Psychology: Essays in Honor of Heinz Hartmann,* International Universities Press, 1966. Contributor since 1923 of articles in English, French, and German to psychoanalytic and psychiatric periodicals.

WORK IN PROGRESS: A book on psychoanalytic technique.

(Died April 14, 1976)

*   *   *

LOHMAN, Joseph D(ean)   1910-1968

PERSONAL: Born January 31, 1910, in New York, N.Y.; son of Isaac and Lena (Dean) Lohman; married Fern

Bernice Campbell, September 14, 1932; children: Barbara Susan. *Education:* University of Denver, B.A., 1930; University of Wisconsin, M.A., 1931; University of Chicago, graduate study, 1931-33. *Office:* School of Criminology, University of California, Berkeley, Calif. 94720.

CAREER: Behavior Research Fund, research criminologist, 1932-33; State of Illinois, Institute of Juvenile Research, senior research sociologist, 1934-39; University of Chicago, Chicago, Ill., instructor, 1939-42, assistant professor of sociology, 1942-45; American University, Washington, D.C., associate professor of sociology and chairman of department, 1945; University of Wisconsin—Madison, associate professor of sociology, 1946; associate director for human relations, Rosenwald Fund, and executive secretary of National Committee on Segregation in the Nation's Capital, both Chicago, Ill., 1946-48; State of Illinois, chairman of Division of Corrections, 1949-52, and of Parole and Pardon Board, 1952-53; sheriff of Cook County, Ill., 1954-58; State of Illinois, treasurer, 1958-61; University of California, Berkeley, professor of criminology and dean of School of Criminology, 1961-68. Professorial lecturer at University of Chicago, 1947-59; visiting professor at University of Michigan, University of Louisville, and University of Denver. Member of public panel of National War Labor Board, 1943-45; chairman of National Capital Planning Commission, 1952-53. Consultant to U.S. Department of Interior, 1950-53, Civil Government of Guam, 1951, Ford Foundation, 1954-60, U.S. Atomic Energy Commission, and Human Resources Research Office, Department of the Army; also consultant to foundations on crime and delinquency problems. Conductor of various television series on delinquency and penitentiaries.

MEMBER: American Social Health Association (member of board of directors), American Correctional Association, National Academy of Arbitrators, American Sociological Association, National Sheriffs' Association. *Awards, honors:* Medal of Freedom from U.S. Department of the Army for work as adviser to United Nations Repatriation Group in Korea, 1953; National Service Award of National Broadcasting Co. for television work, 1958.

WRITINGS: (With others) *The Police and Minority Groups,* Chicago Park District, 1947, revised edition published as *Principles of Police Work with Minority Groups,* Division of Police (Louisville, Ky.), 1950; (compiler) *Cultural Patterns in Urban Schools,* University of California Press, 1967. Also author of *Juvenile Delinquency: Its Dimensions, Its Conditions, Techniques of Control—Proposals for Action, A Metropolitan Police Force for Cook County,* both 1957, and *Cultural Patterns of Differentiated Youth,* 1966. Journal and encyclopedia contributions include articles on crime, human relations, and community relations. Member of editorial advisory board, *Trans-Action* and *Issues in Criminology.*††

(Died April 26, 1968)

*   *   *

LOLL, Leo M(arius), Jr.   1923-1968

PERSONAL: Born April 12, 1923, in Fergus Falls, Minn.; son of Leo Marius (a business executive) and Aldine (Paul) Loll; married Kay Betts, February 17, 1943; children: Scott Betts, Kristen, Jan. *Education:* Weber State College, student, 1940-42; University of Colorado, B.S. in B.A., 1947; Ohio State University, M.B.A., 1949; New York University, further graduate study, 1955-61. *Religion:* Church of Jesus Christ of Latter-day Saints.

CAREER: Ohio State University, Columbus, instructor in business organization and management, 1948-49; Utah State University, Logan, assistant professor of economics, 1949-55; New York University, Graduate School of Business Administration, New York City, variously director of admissions, assistant to dean, and instructor, 1955-61; Financial Training Associates of New York, New York City, president, 1962; University of Alaska, College, associate professor, 1963-66, professor of business administration and dean of College of Business, Economics and Government, 1966-68, vice-president for finance and comptroller of the university, 1968. Consultant, National Association of Securities Dealers, 1955-61. Member of Alaska Governor's Employment Advisory Commission, 1966-68 (Loll was traveling with the commission when he and five other members perished in the crash of a bush plane). *Military service:* U.S. Army, 10th Mountain Infantry Division (ski troops), 1943-46; became sergeant; received Bronze Star with two oak-leaf clusters.

WRITINGS: (With Julian G. Buckley) *The Over-the-Counter Securities Market,* Prentice-Hall, 1961, 2nd edition, 1967; *Industries of Alaska,* University of Alaska Press, 1966; *A Study of Technical and Economic Problems—State of Alaska,* University of Alaska Press, 1967; (with Buckley) *Questions and Answers about the Securities Markets,* Prentice-Hall, 1968. Contributor of articles about finance, investments, and current Alaskan economic development to journals. Editor, *Economic Review* (University of Alaska), 1966-68.

WORK IN PROGRESS: *Investing in Mutual Funds;* and *Handbook on Municipal Funds.*

SIDELIGHTS: Many of Loll's articles on the economy of Alaska have been translated into Japanese and Russian. *Avocational interests:* Hunting, fishing.††

(Killed in a plane crash at Point Barrow, Alaska, November 21, 1968)

* * *

LOLLIS, Lorraine 1911-

PERSONAL: Born April 28, 1911, in Topeka, Kan.; daughter of David (a minister) and Sara (Reynolds) Lyon; married James A. Lollis (a minister), June 23, 1936; children: David Lanier, Wayne Lyon, James Alan. *Education:* Arizona State University, student, 1928-31; Milligan College, A.B., 1932; University of Kentucky, M.A., 1954. *Politics:* Democrat. *Religion:* Christian Church (Disciples). *Home:* 880 Mandalay Ave. Apt. 825, Clearwater, Fla. 33515.

CAREER: Livingston Academy, Livingston, Tenn., teacher of Spanish and English, 1932-34; cashier for life insurance company and teacher in public schools in North Carolina, 1934-42; teacher of English and Spanish in public schools in Perryville, Danville, and Lexington, Ky., 1954-60; Transylvania College, Lexington, Ky., instructor in Spanish, 1960-61; Georgetown College, Georgetown, Ky., instructor in Spanish, 1966-67; director of Voluntary Service, Christian Church (Disciples of Christ), 1971-73. President, Church Women United, Bowling Green, Ky. *Member:* League of Women Voters (president of Bowling Green chapter, 1949-51), Lexington YWCA (president, 1968).

WRITINGS: *The Shape of Adam's Rib: A Lively History of Women's Work in the Christian Church,* Bethany Press, 1970.

SIDELIGHTS: Mrs. Lollis has co-directed ecumenical work camps in Jamaica and Scotland, and has been a member of various organizations, including interracial and peace groups, and those concerned about ecology, population, and pollution control. She has traveled in Europe, Mexico, Canada, and many parts of the United States.

* * *

LOMAX, Louis E(manuel) 1922-1970

PERSONAL: Born August 16, 1922, in Valdosta, Ga.; son of James (a teacher and clergyman) and Fannie (Hardon) Lomax; divorced from third wife, April, 1967; married fourth wife, Robinette G. Kirk, March 1, 1968; stepchildren: William Kirk, Robinette Kirk. *Education:* Paine College, A.B., 1942; graduate study at American University and Yale University. *Residence:* Baldwin Harbor, N.Y.

CAREER: Newspaperman, 1941-58; free-lance writer, 1958-70. News commentator on WNTA-TV, New York City, 1958-60, and for Metromedia Broadcasting, 1964-68. Former assistant professor of philosophy at Georgia State University, and former professor of humanities and social sciences at Hofstra University. *Awards, honors:* Annisfield-Wolf Award for best book concerned with racial problems, 1960, for *The Reluctant African;* awarded two honorary doctorates.

WRITINGS: *The Reluctant African,* Harper, 1960; *The Negro Revolt,* Harper 1962; *When the World Is Given,* World Publishing, 1964; *Thailand: The War That Is, The War That Will Be,* Random House, 1966; *To Kill a Black Man,* Holloway, 1968. Contributor to *Life, Look, Saturday Evening Post,* and newspapers.

WORK IN PROGRESS: A three-volume history of the Negro.

BIOGRAPHICAL/CRITICAL SOURCES: *Virginia Quarterly Review,* spring, 1968.†

(Died July 30, 1970)

* * *

LONDON, Joan 1901-1971

PERSONAL: Born January 15, 1901, in Oakland, Calif.; daughter of Jack (an author) and Elizabeth (Maddern) London; married Charles Lortz Miller, April, 1952; children: Bart Abbott. *Education:* University of California, Berkeley, A.B., 1921.

CAREER: California State Federation of Labor (became California Labor Federation, AFL-CIO, 1958), San Francisco, publications editor and research librarian, 1941-52. *Member:* Phi Beta Kappa.

WRITINGS: *Jack London and His Times: An Unconventional Biography,* Doubleday, Doran, 1939, reprinted, with a new introduction, University of Washington Press, 1969; (with Henry Anderson) *So Shall Ye Reap,* Crowell, 1970.

WORK IN PROGRESS: A book about Jack London as a father; continuing research on the history of organized labor, on biography, and on Latin America.†

(Died January, 1971)

* * *

LONG, Fern

PERSONAL: Born in Cleveland, Ohio; daughter of Francis J. (a tailor) and Louise (Sakryd) Long. *Education:* Radcliffe College, A.B. (magna cum laude), 1926; Charles University, Prague, Czechoslovakia, Ph.D., 1930; Western Reserve

University (now Case Western Reserve University), B.S. in L.S., 1940. *Home:* 2364 Queenston Rd., Cleveland Heights, Ohio 44118. *Office:* Cleveland Public Library, Cleveland, Ohio 44114.

CAREER: Ames Social Service League, Ames, Iowa, executive secretary, 1934-38; Cleveland Public Library, Cleveland, Ohio, library assistant, 1939-41, field worker in adult education department, 1941-44, supervisor of adult education department, 1944-70, deputy director, beginning 1970. Case Western Reserve University, School of Library Science, instructor, 1944-63, consultant, beginning 1963; member of advisory board of University of Wisconsin library materials research project, beginning 1967. Delegate to UNESCO Seminar, Malmo, Sweden, 1950, and to White House Conference on the Aging, 1961. Board member of Anti-Tuberculosis League of Cuyahoga County, and Cleveland Center on Alcoholism; director of Reading Centers Project for Functionally Illiterate Adults, 1965-66. *Member:* American Library Association (president of adult services division, 1963-64), Ohio Library Association, Phi Beta Kappa, Delta Kappa Gamma. *Awards, honors:* Radcliffe Alumnae Award, 1960; named Cleveland Woman of Achievement, 1961; Distinguished Daughter of Ohio award, 1975.

WRITINGS: (Translator) Hostovsky, *Seven Times the Leading Man,* L. B. Fischer, 1943; (translator) Hostovsky, *The Hideout,* Random House, 1943; (translator) Rezac, *If the Mirror Break,* Chilton, 1954; *All about Meetings: A Practical Guide,* Oceana, 1967; (with Bernice Bollenbacher) *The Proud Years, 1869-1969: A Pictorial History of the Cleveland Public Library,* Cleveland Public Library, 1969. Contributor to library journals.

WORK IN PROGRESS: Research on Rudolf II of Bohemia; translating Brezovsky's *The Eternal Lovers.*

*   *   *

LONG, Helen Beecher
[Collective pseudonym]

WRITINGS: The Girl He Left Behind, G. Sully, 1918.

"The Do Something" series; published by G. Sully: *Janice Day,* 1914; *How Janice Day Won,* 1916; *The Mission of Janice Day,* 1917; *The Testing of Janice Day,* 1918; *Janice Day, the Young Homemaker,* 1919.

SIDELIGHTS: See **ADAMS, Harriet S., STRATEMEYER, Edward L.,** and **SVENSON, Andrew E.**†

*   *   *

LOOKER, (Reginald) Earle   1895-1976

PERSONAL: Born February 11, 1895, in Washington, D.C.; son of Henry Brigham (a civil engineer) and Katharine (Earle) Looker; married Edith Applegate, December 5, 1917 (divorced, 1946); married Antonina Hansell, February 5, 1947; children: (first marriage) Edith Beaumont (Mrs. Arthur Mitchell), Katharine Earle (Mrs. Nelson Hyde). *Education:* Attended public schools in Washington, D.C. *Home:* Hillhouse, Lakemont, Ga. 30552. *Agent:* Marie Rodell, 141 East 55th St., New York, N.Y. 10022; and Laurence Pollinger Ltd., 18 Maddox St., London W1R 0EU, England.

CAREER: Cleveland News, Cleveland, Ohio, reporter, 1913; free-lance war correspondent, 1914-15; National Defense Committee, New York City, executive secretary, 1915; *Asia Magazine,* New York City, associate editor, 1919; Frank Presbrey Co., New York City, advertising ex-

ecutive, 1920-28; free-lance writer of biographies and articles for periodicals, 1928-37; *Fortune Magazine,* New York City, contributing editor, 1937; Carl Byoir & Associates, New York City, public relations counsel, 1937-39; full-time writer. Speech writer for Franklin Delano Roosevelt, 1932-40. *Military service:* Volunteer ambulance driver in France, 1914-15; Reserve Corps, 1916; U.S. Army, American Expeditionary Forces, 1917-19; became captain; Bureau of Public Relations, Chief of Intelligence Branch, 1940-41, Bureau of Economic Warfare, Chief of Intelligence Branch, 1941-42, Psychological Warfare Branch, Military Intelligence Service, 1942-43, joint Army-Navy Mission to United Kingdom, chief of mission, 1944-45, Morale Service of the Pacific Ocean Areas, director, 1944-45; became colonel. *Member:* Roosevelt Memorial Association (trustee), Rotary International (president of Northampton, Mass., chapter, 1933), Franklin-Hampshire Council of Boy Scouts of America (president, 1934-35).

WRITINGS: The White House Gang, Revell, 1929; *Colonel Roosevelt, Private Citizen,* Revell, 1932; *This Man Roosevelt,* Brewer, Warren, & Putnam, 1932; *The American Way: Franklin Roosevelt in Action,* John Day, 1933; (with wife, Antonina H. Looker) *Revolt* (novel), Hart-Davis, 1968.

WORK IN PROGRESS: A novel, *Stand Fast* (alternate title: *Slowly I Awoke*), with wife, Antonina Looker.

SIDELIGHTS: Earle Looker told *CA* that he was "disgusted by the defeatist attitude of writers who see no hope for the future, who deny the power and glory of man, who foul his dignity, who sneer at virtue. . . ."†

(Died May 22, 1976)

*   *   *

LOVELL, John, Jr.   1907-1974

PERSONAL: Born July 25, 1907, in Asheville, N.C.; son of John, Sr. and Zula (Pope) Lovell; married Nancy G. Merritt, September 6, 1940 (divorced, 1951); married Marian Giles Mouzon, July 31, 1954 (deceased, 1966); children: (first marriage) Taunya Marita (Mrs. Fred L. Banks, Jr.). *Education:* Northwestern University, B.A., 1926, A.M., 1927; University of Pennsylvania, graduate student, 1929-30; University of California, Berkeley, Ph.D., 1938. *Politics:* Democrat. *Office:* Department of English, Howard University, Washington, D.C. 20001.

CAREER: West Virginia State College, Institute, instructor in English, 1927-28; Howard University, Washington, D.C., assistant professor, 1930-46, associate professor, 1946-58, professor of English, 1958-74, acting head of department, 1968-69, 1972-74, director of adult education, 1952-56, cofounder, director and business representative of Washington Repertory Players, 1953-55, associate dean of College of Liberal Arts, 1965-68. Visiting professor, American Friends Service Committee, Iowa and Calif., 1948; Fulbright lecturer, Osaka University of Foreign Studies, Osaka, Japan, 1960-61. Visiting instructor, Prairie View State Normal and Industrial College (now Prairie View Agricultural and Mechanical College), 1930-31; lecturer, Pendle Hill School, 1934; visiting professor, College of the Pacific (now University of the Pacific), 1950, 1956; researcher and lecturer in Europe; lecturer and participant in various panel discussions, institutes, and radio broadcasts. *Military service:* U.S. Army, 1943-46; became first lieutenant; received Commendation Ribbon.

MEMBER: Modern Language Association of America,

Association for Asian Studies, American Studies Association, American National Theatre and Academy, International Theatre Institute, American Society for Theatre Research, American Society for African Culture (charter member), National Association for the Advancement of Colored People (secretary, District of Columbia branch, 1939-42; treasurer, 1942-43), Authors Guild, National Council of Teachers of English, Conference on College Composition and Communication, American Educational Theatre Association, National Collegiate Honors Council (member of founding group; executive committee member, 1966-68), Folklore Society of Greater Washington, District of Columbia Council of Teachers of English, Kappa Alpha Psi. *Awards, honors:* Rockefeller Foundation fellowship, 1935-36; Evening Star award, 1959, for study, "America in Drama."

WRITINGS: Digests of Great American Plays: Complete Summaries of More than 100 Plays from the Beginnings to the Present, Crowell, 1961, published as *Great American Plays in Digest Form: Complete Summaries of More than 100 Plays from the Beginnings to the Present,* Apollo, 1965; (contributor) Bernard Katz, editor, *Social Implications of Early American Negro Music,* Arno, 1969; *Black Song: The Forge and the Flame* (study of Afro-American spirituals), Macmillan, 1972. Editor, compiler, and publisher of *Who's Who at Howard University,* 1947; also author of *Dedicatory History of the College of Dentistry of Howard University,* 1955. Contributor of articles to *Theatre Annual, Theatre Survey, Unitas* (Manila), *Publication of the Modern Language Association, Theatre Arts, Mainichi Daily News* (Osaka), *Crisis, Negro-American Literature Forum, Journal of Negro Education, Modern Language Quarterly, Midwest Journal, Chicago Defender, Journal of Negro History,* and other journals and newspapers. Contributing annotator, *American Literary Realism, 1870-1910* (University of Texas publication).

WORK IN PROGRESS: A series of books describing the dramas of the world, excluding those of Europe and America, the first book to be entitled *African Drama: Past and Present.*

SIDELIGHTS: John Lovell, Jr. studied the national dramas of Hong Kong, Indonesia, Thailand, India, Iran, Egypt, Greece, England, Denmark, Sweden, Germany, and Austria, in those countries. As Fulbright lecturer at Osaka University of Foreign Studies, he attended more than one-hundred Japanese dramatic productions and interviewed thirty to forty outstanding personalities in the Japanese theatre, including actors, producers, playwrights, directors, translators, and drama critics. He traveled extensively in Africa, Europe, South America and the West Indies while writing *Black Song.*

BIOGRAPHICAL/CRITICAL SOURCES: Jordan Y. Miller, *Eugene O'Neill and the American Critic,* Shoe String-Archon, 1962.†

(Died June 6, 1974)

* * *

LOW, Elizabeth Hammond 1898-

PERSONAL: Born August 3, 1898, in Brooklyn, N.Y.; daughter of Howard Dexter (a lawyer) and Margaret (Roberts) Hammond; married Kenneth Brooks Low (a lawyer), June 16, 1923; children: Marilyn (Mrs. R. C. Geeslin), Elizabeth (Mrs. F. J. Mahaffey), Kenneth Brooks, Jr. *Education:* Vassar College, A.B., 1919. *Politics:* Democrat. *Religion:* Protestant. *Home:* 11 Elm Hill Dr., Port Chester, N.Y.

Agent: McIntosh & Otis, Inc., 18 East 41st St., New York, N.Y. 10017.

CAREER: Packer Collegiate Institute (now Packer College), Brooklyn, N.Y., teacher of English, 1920-23; writer of juvenile fiction.

WRITINGS: High Harvest, Harcourt, 1948; *Hold Fast the Dream,* Harcourt, 1955; *Mouse, Mouse, Go Out of My House,* Little, Brown, 1958; *Snug in the Snow* (Junior Literary Guild selection), Little, Brown, 1963. Contributor of articles to *American Home, Better Homes and Gardens,* and other periodicals.

WORK IN PROGRESS: Another story for children.

AVOCATIONAL INTERESTS: Sculpture (has done a number of portrait heads, mostly of children).††

* * *

LOWE, Gustav E. 1901-

PERSONAL: Born January 20, 1901, in Teschen, Poland; son of Emanuel (a professor) and Regina (Krasny) Lowe; married Elizabeth Lowenhaupt (a physician specializing in psychiatry), December 21, 1949; children: Robert A. *Education:* University of Vienna, Dr. of politics, 1926. *Religion:* Unitarian Universalist. *Home:* 863 Bates Ave., El Cerrito, Calif. 94530.

CAREER: Transportation assignments in Austria, Belgium, Germany, Yugoslavia, Bulgaria, and teacher of transportation law at Commercial Academy, Vienna, 1921-1940; Kaiser Aluminum & Chemical Corp., Oakland, Calif., manager of rates, 1942-66; Golden Gate College, San Francisco, Calif., member of transportation faculty, 1947-63; self-employed traffic consultant, specializing in organization of traffic departments and in European traffic problems, beginning 1966; International Institute of the East Bay, Oakland, president, 1969-72. *Member:* American Society of Traffic and Transportation (president of California chapter, 1960; regional vice-president, 1962), Association of Interstate Commerce Commission Practitioners (regional vice-president, 1960; chairman of San Francisco Bay chapter, 1961), Commonwealth Club of California. *Awards, honors:* Verein der Tarifeure (Vienna, Austria) Franz Krempler Medal for services in European transportation and education, 1972.

WRITINGS: Practice and Procedure before Rail Rate-Making Bodies, Traffic Service Co., 1959, revised edition published as *Practice and Procedure before Rate-Making Associations,* 1965, 3rd edition, 1967. American correspondent, *Verkehr* (weekly traffic magazine published in Vienna, Austria); contributor to *Traffic World.*

* * *

LOWELL, Mildred Hawksworth 1905-1974

PERSONAL: Born November 11, 1905, in Chicago, Ill.; daughter of Thomas William (a machinist) and Jessie (Mahoney) Hawksworth; married Wayne Russell Lowell (a geologist), December 24, 1934; children: Brent, Cym, Seth. *Education:* University of Puget Sound, A.B., 1927; University of Wisconsin, Library Science Certificate, 1928; University of Chicago, A.M., 1939, Ph.D., 1957. *Politics:* Independent. *Religion:* Episcopal. *Home:* 1248 East Wylie, Bloomington, Ind. 47401. *Office:* Library 023, Indiana University, Bloomington, Ind. 47401.

CAREER: Tacoma Public Library, Tacoma, Wash., part-time clerical assistant, 1924-27; Bradley University, Peoria, Ill., assistant librarian, 1928-30; Eastern Oregon College of

Education (now Eastern Oregon College), La Grande, Ore., librarian and assistant professor of library science, 1930-40; University of Chicago, Graduate Library School, Chicago, Ill., research assistant to dean, 1940-42; Indiana University, Bloomington, Ind., Graduate Library School, librarian, ICA-Thailand Project, 1954-60, associate professor, 1960-69, professor of library science, beginning 1969, Institute for Sex Research, library consultant, 1963. *Member:* American Library Association (treasurer, International Relations Round Table, 1964-66; member of board of directors, Association of College and Research Libraries, 1964-66; chairman, Nominating Committee for Teachers Section, Library Education Division, 1965-66; panel member on UNESCO, 1966-68), Association of American Library Schools, Indiana Library Association, Pi Kappa Delta, Beta Phi Mu.

WRITINGS: College and University Library Consolidations, Oregon State System of Higher Education, 1942; (with Louis Round Wilson and Sarah Rebecca Reed) *The Library in College Instruction: A Syllabus on the Improvement of College Instruction through Library Use,* H. W. Wilson, 1951; *Key Word-Analytic Subject Index to the Library of Education,* Center for Applied Research in Education, 1967; *The Management of Libraries and Information Centers,* Scarecrow, Volume I: *The Case Method in Teaching Library Management,* 1968, Volume II: *The Process of Managing: Syllabus and Cases,* 1968, Volume III: *Personnel Management: Syllabus and Cases,* 1968, Volume IV: *Role Playing and Other Management Cases,* 1971; *Library Management Cases,* Scarecrow, 1975.

Contributor: William S. Gray, compiler and editor, *Adjusting Reading Programs to Individuals,* University of Chicago Press, 1941; Hakam Singh, editor, *Academic Libraries,* Punjam Library Association, 1963. Contributor of articles and reviews to numerous journals, including *PNLA Quarterly* (publication of the Pacific Northwest Library Association), *Oregon Education Journal, Special Libraries, College and Research Libraries, Library Quarterly, American Library Association Bulletin, Library Occurrent, Focus on Indiana, Curriculum Journal,* and *Library Journal.*

WORK IN PROGRESS: Research on simulation in library education.

AVOCATIONAL INTERESTS: Travel.†

(Died October 31, 1974)

* * *

LUCAS, E(dna) Louise   1899-1970

PERSONAL: Born August 31, 1899, in Middletown, Ohio; daughter of William A. (a surgeon) and Edna Vail (Bonnell) Lucas. *Education:* Radcliffe College, A.B., 1921; Simmons College, graduate study in library science, 1924-25. *Home:* Straitsmouth Way, Rockport, Mass. 01966.

CAREER: Brookline Public Library, Brookline, Mass., staff member of circulation and catalog departments, 1921-27; Harvard University, Fogg Museum of Art (now Harvard Fine Arts Library), Cambridge, Mass., librarian, 1927-64. Associate member of Simmons College, 1944-65. Special project consultant to Toledo Museum of Art, Toledo Public Library, New York Graphic Society, and department of archaeology, Indiana University. *Member:* American Library Association, American Association of Museums (chairman of library group, 1930-36), Massachusetts Library Association, Phi Beta Kappa.

WRITINGS—Compiler: *Books on Art: A Foundation List,* Fogg Museum of Art, Harvard University, 1938; *Guides to*

Harvard Libraries: Fine Arts, Harvard University Press, 1949; *Harvard List of Books on Art,* Harvard University Press, 1952; *Art Books: A Basic Bibliography on the Fine Arts,* New York Graphic Society, 1968.†

(Died January 24, 1970)

* * *

LUCAS, Ruth (Baxendale)   1909-

PERSONAL: Born February 22, 1909, in Eastleigh, England, daughter of J. F. N. (an army officer and farmer) and Margaret M. H. (Heathcote) Baxendale; married John Lucas (an engineer), August 8, 1930; children: James G., Jennifer. *Education:* Educated privately at home, and at Pension pour Jeunes Filles, Paris, France, 1925-26. *Religion:* Church of England. *Residence:* Petersfield, Hampshire, England.

CAREER: Operator, with husband, of a farm, Petersfield, Hampshire, England. *Member:* National Farmers Union.

WRITINGS: Who Dare to Live, Houghton, 1965.

WORK IN PROGRESS: A novel.

SIDELIGHTS: Ruth Lucas is competent in French.††

* * *

LUCHSINGER, Elaine King   1902-

PERSONAL: First syllable of surname is pronounced Luck; born January 14, 1902, in Sweden; daughter of Gustaf Arvid (a blacksmith) and Anna Elizabeth (Skarin) Lind; married Lloyd Myrt King, 1920 (died, 1923); married Alfred Luchsinger, 1928 (died, 1953); children: (first marriage) Lloyd William King. *Education:* Attended Iowa State Teachers College (now State College of Iowa), 1920, Morningside College, 1924-25; Iowa State University, B.A., 1954, M.S., 1955; graduate study at University of Denver, 1957, Pennsylvania State University, 1961, and Iowa State University, 1962. *Religion:* Methodist. *Residence:* Whiting, Iowa 51063 (permanent home). *Office:* South Dakota State University, Brookings, S.D. 57006.

CAREER: Elementary and high school teacher during her early career; manager of her own farm property in Iowa, 1953-62; South Dakota State University, Brookings, associate professor of home economics and head of home management, equipment, and family housing, beginning 1955. Member of board of Woodbury (Iowa) Rural Electric Association. *Member:* American Home Economics Association, American Association of University Professors, American Association of Housing Educators, South Dakota Home Economics Association, Phi Upsilon Omicron, Omicron Nu, Phi Gamma Mu, Sigma Kappa.

WRITINGS: (With Iosbel McGibney) *Family Account Book,* South Dakota Extension Service, 1962; (with Tessie Agan) *The House: Principles/Resources/Dynamics,* Lippincott, 1965. Consultant for homemaking section, *Electrical Textbook for Farming and Home-Making,* South Dakota Rural Electric Association, 1960, 2nd edition, 1965.††

* * *

LYCAN, Gilbert L(ester)   1909-

PERSONAL: Born December 31, 1909, in Fort Gay, W.Va.; son of Henry Willard (a nurseryman) and Anna May (Loar) Lycan; married Sallie Belle Yale, August 4, 1937; children: David Edward, George Gilbert, Ella May (Mrs. Frederick C. Matthews), Barbara Janice (Mrs. Marlyn Miller). *Education:* Lincoln Memorial University, student,

1930-31; Berea College, A.B., 1934; Yale University, M.A., 1936, Ph.D., 1942. *Politics:* Democrat. *Religion:* Baptist. *Home:* 534 North Florida Ave., DeLand, Fla. 32720. *Office:* Department of History, Stetson University, 421 North Boulevard, DeLand, Fla. 32720.

CAREER: Valley City State College, Valley City, N.D., instructor in history and political science, 1937-40, 1941-42; U.S. Department of State, Washington, D.C., drafting officer, 1942-43; Queens College, Charlotte, N.C., associate professor, 1943-44, professor of history and chairman of department of social science, 1944-45; Northwest Missouri State College (now University), Maryville, chairman of department of history and social science, 1945-46; Stetson University, DeLand, Fla., professor of history, beginning 1946. Fulbright lecturer, Silliman University, Dumaguete City, Philippines, 1963-64. Chairman, Florida Committee for Alexander Hamilton Bicentennial, 1957; member Florida State Commission on Antiquities. Mayor of Lake Helen, Fla., 1951-53; president of Volusia County Tuberculosis and Health Association, 1956-57.

MEMBER: American Historical Association, American Society of International Law, Southern Historical Association, Florida Historical Association (president, 1960-62), Phi Alpha Theta, Omicron Delta Kappa, DeLand Chamber of Commerce, DeLand Rotary Club (president, 1957-58).

WRITINGS: (With Ernest Trice Thompson, Patrick H. Carmichael, Kenneth J. Foreman, J. M. Godard, and Lawrence I. Stell) *Bases of World Order,* John Knox, 1945; (with Walter C. Grady) *Inside Racing: Sports and Politics,* Pageant, 1961; *Twelve Major Turning Points in American History,* Everett Edwards, 1968; *Alexander Hamilton and American Foreign Policy: A Design for Greatness,* University of Oklahoma Press, 1970. Contributor to regional history journals.

WORK IN PROGRESS: A book on Florida in U.S. history.

AVOCATIONAL INTERESTS: Chess, propagating citrus trees.

*　　*　　*

LYNN, Conrad J.　1908-

PERSONAL: Born November 4, 1908, in Newport, R.I.; son of Joseph (a gardener) and Nellie (Irving) Lynn; married Mary Louise Garretson, March, 1948; married second wife, Yolanda Moreno, April 10, 1952; children: (first marriage) Suzanne; (second marriage) Alexander, Gabrielle. *Education:* Syracuse University, A.B., 1930, LL.B., 1932. *Politics:* Independent. *Religion:* None. *Home:* Skyview Acres, Pomona, N.Y. 10970.

CAREER: Attorney, practicing in New York, N.Y., beginning 1933. Guest lecturer at colleges; radio commentator, beginning 1966. *Military service:* U.S. Army, World War II; became sergeant. *Member:* American Civil Liberties Union.

WRITINGS: Black Justice Exposed, Elks Press, 1947; *Monroe: Turning Point,* Garrison Press, 1962; *Brief: David Mitchell Case,* Ackerman Press, 1965; *How to Stay Out of the Army: A Guide to Your Rights under the Draft Law,* Monthly Review Press, 1968. Contributor to *American Socialist, Dissent, Politics, Challenge,* and other magazines.

WORK IN PROGRESS: There Is a Fountain, memoirs.

SIDELIGHTS: Lynn told *CA* that his "major preoccupation is study of Revolutions." He added that he was "interrogated by the House Committee on Un-American Activities in 1963," and "exonerated."

How to Stay out of the Army not only provided useful tips for avoiding the draft, but, according to Edward F. Sherman, it was "also an examination by an experienced lawyer of some of the principal legal and constitutional issues raised by draft resistance."

Following his bent for traveling and studying in Socialist or Communist countries, Lynn visited Cuba in 1960 and 1962, and traveled in Europe and Asia in 1967, including Cambodia and North Vietnam.

BIOGRAPHICAL/CRITICAL SOURCES: New Republic, May 18, 1968.

*　　*　　*

LYNN, Jeannette Murphy　1905-

PERSONAL: Born September 27, 1905, in Boulder, Mont.; daughter of Joseph Harold (an attorney) and Louisa (Torrence) Murphy; married C. Lawrence Lynn (a professor and librarian), June 20, 1935. *Education:* Tabor College, Tabor, Iowa, B.A., 1926; University of Wisconsin, B.A. in L.S., 1928; University of Chicago, M.A., 1935. *Religion:* Roman Catholic. *Home:* 631 Austin, Park Ridge, Ill. 60068.

CAREER: Head cataloger, University of Notre Dame, Notre Dame, Ind., 1928-32, St. Mary's College, Notre Dame, 1932-33, and Cossitt Library, Memphis, Tenn., 1935-37; Siena College, Memphis, librarian, 1937-39; Catholic Library Association, executive secretary, 1952-54; Crerar Library, Chicago, Ill., head cataloger, 1954-59; catalog librarian in Park Ridge, Ill., beginning 1959.

WRITINGS: Alternative Classification for Catholic Books, American Library Association, 1937, 3rd edition, Catholic University of America Press, 1965; (with others) *Code for the Construction and Maintenance of the Classified Catalogue,* American Library Association, 1956. Editor, *Catholic Library World,* 1951-52.

*　　*　　*

LYNSKEY, Winifred　1904-

PERSONAL: Surname is of Irish origin (O'Loinscigh in Gaelic); born November 30, 1904, in Minneapolis, Minn.; daughter of N. Thomas (a railroad administrator) and Elizabeth (Grosse) Lynskey. *Education:* University of Minnesota, B.A. (summa cum laude), 1926, M.A., 1927; Radcliffe College, graduate study, 1930-31; University of Chicago, Ph.D., 1940. *Politics:* Independent. *Religion:* Roman Catholic. *Home:* 622 6th St. S.E., Minneapolis, Minn. 55414.

CAREER: Instructor in English at College of St. Benedict, St. Joseph, Minn., 1927-28, and University of Minnesota, Minneapolis, 1928-30, 1932-33, 1935-38; Purdue University, West Lafayette, Ind., instructor, 1938-41, assistant professor, 1941-52, associate professor, 1952-60, professor of English, beginning 1960. *Member:* Modern Language Association of America, National Council of Teachers of English, American Association of University Professors, Midwest Modern Language Association, Phi Beta Kappa, Theta Sigma Phi, Pi Epsilon Delta.

WRITINGS: (Editor) *Reading Modern Fiction: Thirty-One Stories with Critical Aids* (anthology), Scribner, 1952, 4th edition, 1968. Contributor to professional journals. Advisory editor, *Modern Fiction Studies,* 1956-63, and *College English,* 1960-62.

WORK IN PROGRESS: A mystery-detective novel.

AVOCATIONAL INTERESTS: Wild flowers, collecting Verdi operas recorded at La Scala, sports, politics.

MAAS, Audrey Gellen   1936-1975

PERSONAL: Born December 7, 1936, in New York, N.Y.; daughter of Michael David (a stockbroker) and Edith (Plotkin) Gellen; married Peter Maas (a journalist and novelist), April 4, 1962; children: John Michael. *Education:* Attended Cornell University; Barnard College, B.A., 1954; graduate study at Harvard University. *Politics:* "Registered Democrat leaning toward the left." *Agent:* Julian Bach Literary Agency, Inc., 3 East 48th St., New York, N.Y. 10017. *Home and office:* 444 East 57th St., New York, N.Y.

CAREER: "[Audrey Maas was] an ex-singer, ex-television producer, ex-television writer turned novelist, . . . no civic responsibilities except not to litter the streets." *Member:* Quoque Pool and Tennis Club. *Awards, honors:* Putnam Award for *Wait 'Til the Sun Shines Nellie.*

WRITINGS: Wait 'Til the Sun Shines Nellie (novel), New American Library, 1966. Writer of television adaptations of "Ethan Frome," "Billy Budd," "Dorian Grey," "Member of the Wedding," "Fallen Idol," "Philadelphia Story," "The Four Poster," "The Browning Version," and other fiction.

WORK IN PROGRESS: A novel-play, *Do You Have a Girl Friend Named Patsy?;* a novel, *The Unpublished Papers of a True Square,* by Thelma Thrilling; a screen treatment, with husband, Peter Maas.

SIDELIGHTS: David Susskind, television producer, said of Audrey Maas: "She blazed a trail for women in television as writers and producers. She was a liberated woman in the best sense—free, open and creative." Mrs. Maas developed the television series "East Side West Side" which starred George C. Scott and Cicely Tyson.†

(Died July 2, 1975)

*   *   *

MACBETH, Norman   1910-

PERSONAL: Born November 3, 1910, in Los Angeles, Calif.; son of Norman (an executive) and Lucia (Holliday) Macbeth; married Agnes Biedenkapp (a teacher), December 30, 1940; children: Angus, Christa C. *Education:* Stanford University, B.A., 1932; Harvard University, J.D., 1935. *Politics:* Independent. *Religion:* Christian. *Address:* Box 478, Rte. 1, Springfield, Vt. 05156.

CAREER: Admitted to Bar of State of California, 1936; O'Melveny & Myers (law firm), Los Angeles, Calif., associate, 1935-38; Douglas Aircraft Co., Santa Monica, Calif., attorney, 1941-46; private practice of law in own firm, Los Angeles, 1946-58; manager of private trusts, beginning 1958. *Member:* Society for the Study of Evolution, Conservation Society of Southern Vermont, Crown Point Country Club.

WRITINGS: Darwin Retried: An Appeal to Reason, Gambit, 1971. Contributor of articles to bar association journals.

WORK IN PROGRESS: Heredity versus environment; the tides; migration over the Bering Strait.

AVOCATIONAL INTERESTS: Tree farming; conservation.

*   *   *

MacGILLIVRAY, John H(enry)   1899-

PERSONAL: Born January 27, 1899, in Ithaca, N.Y.; son of Alexander Dyer (a professor) and Fanny (Edwards) MacGillivray; married Frances Gower, November 12, 1927 (died, 1974); children: Anne Ellis (Mrs. William Alexander), Harriet Jean (Mrs. Donald Stevens), Mary Margaret (Mrs. Thomas Cox), Donald Bruce. *Education:* University of Illinois, B.S., 1921, M.S., 1922; Cornell University, additional study, 1922-23; University of Wisconsin, Ph.D., 1925. *Politics:* Republican. *Religion:* Unitarian Universalist. *Home:* 7 Meadowbrook Dr., Davis, Calif. 95616. *Office:* Department of Vegetable Crops, University of California, Davis, Calif. 95616.

CAREER: Purdue University, Lafayette, Ind., associate professor and horticulturist, 1925-36; University of California, Davis, College of Agriculture, assistant professor, 1936-43, associate professor, 1943-49, professor of truck crops, 1949-66, olericulturist, 1943-66. Collaborator with U.S. Department of Agriculture, 1929-32, 1939-43; adviser to Taiwan National University, 1956-57; researcher. *Military service:* U.S. Naval Reserve, 1918. *Member:* American Association for the Advancement of Science (fellow), American Society of Horticultural Science (fellow), Institute of Food Technology, American Potato Association, Commonwealth Club (San Francisco).

WRITINGS: Vegetable Production, McGraw, 1953; *Agricultural Labor and Its Effective Use,* National Press Publications, 1964. Contributor of about 150 research papers on aspects of vegetable production to journals.

WORK IN PROGRESS: Research on the effective use of harvest labor in vegetable production.

*   *   *

MACKENZIE, Compton (Edward Montague)   1883-1972

PERSONAL: Born January 17, 1883, in West Hartlepool County, Durham, England; son of Edward Compton (an actor, using stage surname, Compton) and Virginia Frances (Bateman) Mackenzie; married Faith Stone, November 30, 1905 (died, 1960); married Christina MacSween, January 23, 1962 (died, 1963); married Lilian MacSween, March 4, 1965. *Education:* Magdalen College, Oxford, B.A. (honours in history), 1904. *Politics:* Independent. *Religion:* Catholic. *Home:* 31 Drummond Place, Edinburgh, Scotland.

CAREER: Settled on the island of Barra in the Outer Hebrides and helped to found Scottish Nationalist Party; Glasgow University, Glasgow, Scotland, rector, 1931-34; *Daily Mail,* London, England, literary critic, 1931-35; was reputedly BBC's first disc jockey; president of Dickens Fellowship, 1939-46, Wexford Festival, beginning 1951, Croquet Association, 1954-66, Songwriters Guild, beginning 1956, and Greek League of Democracy; Poetry Society, president, 1961-64, patron, beginning 1964; governor-general, Royal Stuart Society, beginning 1961. Founder of *Gramophone* Magazine (still published in Middlesex), 1923, and editor, 1923-62. *Wartime service:* Served with First Hertfordshire Regiment, 1900-01, with Royal Marines, 1915 (invalided, 1915); became captain, 1916; served as Military Control Officer, Athens, 1916, and director of Aegean Intelligence Service, Syra, 1917. Captain of Home Guard, 1940-44. *Member:* Royal Society of Literature (fellow), Royal Scottish Academician (honorary member), Savile Club, Pratt's Club, Authors' Club (president), New Club (Edinburgh), Scottish Arts (Edinburgh), Siamese Cat Club of Great Britain (president). *Awards, honors:* Named Officer of the Order of the British Empire, 1919; knighted, 1952; LL.D. from University of Glasgow, St. Francis Xavier University, Antigonish, Nova Scotia, Canada; Legion of Honor (France); Knight Commander of the Phoenix (Greece); designated Professor of Literature to the Royal Scottish Academy.

WRITINGS—Novels: *The Passionate Elopement* (adaptation of own play, "The Gentleman in Grey"), Lane, 1911, Putnam, 1916, with new foreword by the author, Macdonald & Co., 1953, new edition, Chivers, 1967; *Carnival*, Appleton, 1912, 3rd edition, Secker, 1912, reprinted, Macdonald & Co., 1951; *Youth's Encounter*, Appleton, 1913 (published in England as *Sinister Street*, Volume I, Secker, 1913, 3rd edition, Macdonald & Co., 1968); *Sinister Street*, Appleton, 1914 (published in England as *Sinister Street*, Volume II, Secker, 1914); *Plashers Mead*, Harper, 1915 (published in England as *Guy and Pauline*, Secker, 1915), published as *Guy and Pauline*, with new introduction by the author, Oxford University Press, 1938, reprinted, Scholarly Press, 1972; *The Early Life and Adventures of Sylvia Scarlett*, Harper, 1918 (published in England as *The Early Adventures of Sylvia Scarlett*, Hamish Hamilton, 1963; also Part I published as *Sylvia Scarlett*, New English Library, 1971, and Part II as *Sylvia and Arthur*, New English Library, 1971; also see below); *Sylvia and Michael: The Later adventures of Sylvia Scarlett* (a sequel to *The Early Life and Adventures of Sylvia Scarlett*), Harper, 1919 (published in England as *Sylvia and Michael*, New English Library, 1971) (also see below); *Poor Relations*, Harper, 1919.

The Vanity Girl, Harper, 1920, reprinted, Remploy, 1973; *Rich Relatives*, Harper, 1921, new edition, Macdonald & Co., 1966; *The Altar Steps*, Doran, 1922, new edition, Macdonald & Co., 1956; *The Parson's Progress* (a sequel to *The Altar Steps*), Cassell, 1923, Doran, 1924; *The Seven Ages of Woman*, Stokes, 1923, reprinted, Macdonald & Co., 1968; *The Old Men of the Sea: A Romance of Adventure in the South Pacific*, Stokes, 1924 (published in England as *Paradise for Sale*, Macdonald & Co., 1963); *The Heavenly Ladder*, Doran, 1924, reprinted, Remploy, 1973; *Coral: A Sequel to "Carnival,"* Doran, 1925, reprinted, Macdonald & Co., 1965; *Fairy Gold*, Doran, 1926, reprinted, Macdonald & Co., 1961; *Rogues and Vagabonds*, Doran, 1927, reprinted, New English Library, 1971; *Vestal Fire*, Doran, 1927; *Extremes Meet*, Doubleday, Doran, 1928, reprinted, Chatto & Windus, 1970; *Extraordinary Women: Theme and Variations*, Macy-Masius, 1928, reprinted, Icon Books, 1967; *The Three Couriers*, Doubleday, Doran, 1929, reprinted, New English Library, 1966.

April Fools: A Comedy of Bad Manners, Doubleday, Doran, 1930 (published in England as *April Fools: A Farce of Manners*, Cassell, 1930); *For Sale*, Doubleday, Doran, 1931 (published in England as *Buttercups and Daisies*, Cassell, 1931, reprinted, R. Hale, 1973); *Our Street*, Cassell, 1931, Doubleday, Doran, 1932, reprinted, New English Library, 1973; *Water on the Brain*, Doubleday, Doran, 1933, reprinted, Chatto & Windus, 1967; *The Darkening Green*, Doubleday, Doran, 1934; *Figure of Eight*, Cassell, 1936, reprinted, Mayflower, 1970.

The Four Winds of Love, Volume I: *The East Wind*, Dodd, 1937 (published in England as *The East Wind of Love: Being Book One of "The Four Winds of Love,"* Rich & Cowan, 1937), Volume II: *The South Wind of Love*, Dodd, 1937 (published in England as *The South Wind of Love: Being Book Two of "The Four Winds of Love,"* Rich & Cowan, 1937), Volume III: *The West Wind of Love*, Dodd, 1940 (published in England as *The West Wind of Love: Being Book Three of "The Four Winds of Love,"* Chatto & Windus, 1940, published in two volumes as *The West Wind of Love: Being Volume III of the "Four Winds of Love,"* Chatto & Windus, 1949-69), Volume IV: *West to North: Being Book Four of "The Four Winds of Love,"* Chatto & Windus, 1940, published as *West to North*, Dodd, 1941,

Volume V: *The North Wind of Love: Being Book(s) V [VI] of "The Four Winds of Love"* (containing two volumes, *The North Wind of Love* and *Again to the North*), Chatto & Windus, 1944-45, published as *The North Wind of Love: Being Volume IV of "The Four Winds of Love,"* two volumes, Chatto & Windus, 1944-45, 1949-68, published as *The North Wind of Love*, Dodd, 1945, Volume VI: *Again to the North*, Dodd, 1946 (published in England as Volume II of *The North Wind of Love*; see above).

The Red Tapeworm, Chatto & Windus, 1941; *The Monarch of the Glen*, Chatto & Windus, 1941, Houghton, 1951; *Keep the Home Guard Turning*, Chatto & Windus, 1943, reprinted, 1968; *Whiskey Galore*, Chatto & Windus, 1947, published as *Tight Little Island*, Houghton, 1950; *Hunting the Fairies*, Chatto & Windus, 1949.

Adventures of Sylvia Scarlett (containing *The Early Life and Adventures of Sylvia Scarlett* and *Sylvia and Michael: The Later Adventures of Sylvia Scarlett*), Macdonald & Co., 1950; *The Rival Monster*, Chatto & Windus, 1952; *Ben Nevis Goes East*, Chatto & Windus, 1954; *Thin Ice*, Chatto & Windus, 1956; Putnam, 1957; *Rockets Galore*, Chatto & Windus, 1957, reprinted, Tandem, 1972; *The Lunatic Republic*, Chatto & Windus, 1959.

Mezzotint, Chatto & Windus, 1961; *The Stolen Soprano*, Chatto & Windus, 1965; *Paper Lives*, Chatto & Windus, 1966.

Juveniles: *Santa Claus in Summer*, Constable, 1924, Stokes, 1925; *Mabel in Queer Street*, Blackwell, 1927; (with Mabel Marlowe) *Unpleasant Visitors* [and] *Posset's Toby Jug* (the former by Mackenzie; the later by Marlowe), Blackwell, 1928; *The Adventures of Two Chairs*, Blackwell, 1929.

The Enchanted Blanket, Blackwell, 1930; *Told* (children's tales and verses; verses originally published in *Kensington Rhymes*), Appleton, 1930; *The Conceited Doll*, Blackwell, 1931; *The Fairy in the Window Box*, Blackwell, 1932; *The Dining-Room Battle*, Blackwell, 1933; *The Enchanted Island*, Blackwell, 1934; *The Naughtymobile*, Blackwell, 1937; *The Stairs That Kept on Going Down*, Blackwell, 1937, reprinted, Doubleday, 1973.

Cat's Company, Elek Books, 1960, Taplinger, 1961; *Catmint*, Barrie & Rockliff, 1961, Taplinger, 1962; *Look at Cats*, Hamish Hamilton, 1963; *Little Cat Lost*, Macmillan, 1965; *The Secret Island*, Kaye & Ward, 1969.

Butterfly Hill, Kaye & Ward, 1970; *Achilles: Retold by Compton Mackenzie*, Aldus Books, 1972; *Jason: Retold by Compton Mackenzie*, Aldus Books, 1972; *Perseus: Retold by Compton Mackenzie*, Aldus Books, 1972; *Theseus: Retold by Compton Mackenzie*, Aldus Books, 1972.

History: *Gallipoli Memories* (first volume in series of memoirs of the European War, 1914-18), Cassell, 1929, Doubleday, Doran, 1930, reprinted, Panther Books, 1965.

First Athenian Memories (second volume in series of memoirs of the European War, 1914-18), Doubleday, Doran, 1931; *Prince Charlie, de jure Charles III, King of Scotland, England, France, and Ireland*, Peter Davies, 1932, Appleton, 1933; *Greek Memories* (third volume in series of memoirs of the European War, 1914-18), Cassell, 1932, withdrawn in 1932, published by Chatto & Windus, 1939; *Prince Charlie and His Ladies*, Cassell, 1934, Knopf, 1935; *Marathon and Salamis* (the Battle of Salamis, 480 B.C., and the Battle of Marathon, 490 B.C.), Peter Davies, 1934; *Catholicism and Scotland*, Routledge, 1936, reprinted, Kennikat, 1971; *Pericles*, Hodder & Stoughton, 1937; *The Windsor Tapestry: Being a Study of the Life, Heritage and Abdication of H.R.H. the Duke of Windsor, K.G.*, Stokes, 1938.

Aegean Memories (fourth and final volume in series of memoirs of the European War, 1914-18), Chatto & Windus, 1940; (with wife, Faith Compton Mackenzie) *Calvary*, Lane, 1942; *Wind of Freedom: The History of the Invasion of Greece by the Axis Powers, 1940-1941*, Chatto & Windus, 1943; *Mr. Roosevelt*, Harrap, 1943, Dutton, 1944; *Brockhouse*, J. Brockhouse, 1944; *Dr. Benes*, Harrap, 1946; *The Vital Flame*, F. Muller for the British Gas Council, 1947; *All Over the Place: Fifty Thousand Miles by Sea, Air, Road, and Rail*, Chatto & Windus, 1949.

Eastern Epic, Volume I: *Defense, September, 1939-March, 1943* (World War II), Chatto & Windus, 1951; *The House of Coalport, 1750-1950* (Coalport China Company), Collins (London), 1951, Collins (New York), 1952; *I Took a Journey: A Tour of National Trust Properties*, Naldrett Press for the National Trust, 1951; *The Queen's House: A History of Buckingham Palace*, Hutchinson, 1953; *The Savoy of London* [Savoy Hotel], Harrap, 1953; *Realms of Silver: One Hundred Years of Banking in the East*, Routledge & Kegan Paul, 1954.

Greece in My Life, Chatto & Windus, 1960; *Robert Louis Stevenson*, Morgan-Grampian Books, 1968, A. S. Barnes, 1969.

Essays: (With Archibald Marshall) *Gramophone Nights*, Heinemann, 1923; *Unconsidered Trifles*, Secker, 1932; *Literature in My Time*, Rich & Cowan, 1933, Mussey, 1934, reprinted, Books for Libraries, 1967; *Reaped and Bound*, Secker, 1933; *A Musical Chair* (pieces originally published in *The Gramophone*), compiled by Joyce Weiner, Chatto & Windus, 1939; *Birthday Book*, edited by Margery Weiner, Hutchinson, 1951; *Certain Aspects of Moral Courage*, Doubleday, 1962 (published in England as *On Moral Courage*, Collins, 1962).

Plays: "The Gentleman in Grey," first produced in Edinburgh, 1907; "Carnival," first produced in New York, 1912, produced as "Columbine," in Nottingham, 1922; *The Lost Cause: A Jacobite Play* (first broadcast, 1931), Oliver & Boyd, 1933.

Screenplays: (With Angus MacPhail) "Tight Little Island" (adapted from own novel), Universal, November 23, 1949 (released in England as "Whiskey Galore").

Poetry: *Poems*, Blackwell, 1907; *Kensington Rhymes*, Secker, 1912.

Autobiography: *My Life and Times*, Chatto & Windus, *Octave One: 1883-1891*, 1963, *Octave Two: 1891-1900*, 1963, *Octave Three: 1900-1907*, 1964, *Octave Four: 1907-1914*, 1965, *Octave Five: 1915-1923*, 1966, *Octave Six: 1923-1930*, 1967, *Octave Seven: 1930-1938*, 1968, *Octave Eight: 1939-1946*, 1969, *Octave Nine: 1946-1952*, 1970, *Octave Ten: 1953-1963*, 1971.

Other: (With J. L. Campbell) *The Book of Barra*, Routledge, 1936; *Echoes*, Chatto & Windus, 1954; *My Record of Music*, Hutchinson, 1955, Putnam, 1956; *Sublime Tobacco*, Chatto & Windus, 1957, Macmillan, 1958; *The Strongest Man on Earth: Based on the BBC Television "Jackanory" Programme*, Chatto & Windus, 1968.

Also author, with others, of *The New Decameron*, three volumes, published by Bretanos. Editor, *Oxford Point of View*, 1902-04.

SIDELIGHTS: Mackenzie came from a family of ample literary and dramatic talent. His father was a well-known actor and the author of several plays; his sister, Fay Compton, was a distinguished actress; his American aunt, Kate Bateman, was famous for her portrayal of Lady Macbeth; and his uncle, C. G. Compton, was a novelist. Mackenzie himself began reading nursery rhymes at the age of twenty-two months, and, allegedly, by the age of six he had already read Scott, Dickens, and Thackeray. These classics greatly influenced his later work. The *New Republic* writer, for instance, said that *Rogues and Vagabonds* "abounds in Dickensian characters, actors, garrulous land-ladies and one recognizable blood brother to Uriah Heap." As a youth in school he was most impressed with Oscar Wilde's *Intentions*. According to the *New Republic* writer, the various themes of Mackenzie's works encompassed everything from "human fancy-dresses to masquerade in the ranks of the serious novels," from high tragedy to farce; biographies and war records, to children's stories. The *New Republic* writer added that "[Mackenzie also] "proves himself . . . a writer . . . responsive to youth's emotions and . . . sensitive to external beauty."

Criticism of Mackenzie's work is as full of paradoxes as the subjects that he chose to write about. The *Boston Transcript* writer noted that Mackenzie wrote *Sinister Street* "with the zeal of the biographer who has known intimately his subject, and with the skill of the novelist who knows [his character] none the less intimately because he has created him out of his own mind and his own experience with life." But J. A. Smith commented that *West to North* "seems to have about as much life as a bundle of newspaper cuttings . . . [and the main character] remains a collection of opinions rather than a fully-imagined person."

Mackenzie also fluctuated from character studies of one or two people, "portrayed and analyzed with a delicacy and subtlety leaving little or nothing to be desired," to a medley of characters, according to a *New York World* reviewer, "caricatured as Charles Dickens never would have dared, and they bounce and grimace and mouth their quaintly mannered platitudes like well-trained puppets."

Critics have also debated about the virtues of Mackenzie's style of writing. The *New York Times Book Review* writer wrote of *Carnival:* "It is not too much to claim for Mr. Mackenzie that his delineation is as minute and as thorough as anything to be found. . . . *Carnival* should be carefully examined because of its artistic construction and its artistic wording." However, he complained that "one soon wearies" of *West to North* because it is "all too informative, too educative." The *Times Literary Supplement* writer added (in 1922) that Mackenzie's "prose is still sometimes deplorable and seldom other than commonplace; and his power of selection is still in its infancy." In contrast, Stanley Went said that "as his art approaches maturity, he adds to his native wit and cleverness a sure mastery of technique which puts him unmistakably in the forefront of the English novelists of the day." The *Athenaeum* reviewer voiced a recurrent criticism: "We will pay Mr. Mackenzie the compliment of believing he could have conveyed in half the number of pages all that is essential to the understanding of the two phases of his hero's life here treated," but, he continues, "we can also affirm that there are few pages which do not carry the reader on with fresh zest."

One of Mackenzie's greatest attributes was that he "[had] the requisite experience to distill farce—good, robust, mid-Victorian farce—from life," stated K. C. Tomlinson. And the *Springfield Republican* writer noted that" *Poor Relations* is engagingly light-hearted in all its phases, with a discernable grain of reality beneath the shell of comedy and satire," and his more serious novels, according to the *Independent* reviewer, were told "with a light sophistication and an ironic smile which make them amusing."

Critics do not know how to classify Mackenzie. His works involve a vast assortment of subjects as well as varying times and methods of treatment. E. C. Beckwith said that he wrote with "a gentle, sometimes broad humor." The *Boston Transcript* writer called him "racy, sometimes witty, always quite merciless." Some claimed him to be uproariously funny, others said he was dull and gloomy. In *Parson's Progress* he was accused of being overly religious; in *Extraordinary Women,* of being pornographic; in *Mr. Roosevelt,* of writing a campaign biography. But in all cases Mackenzie proved himself to be an artist capable of adapting his tone and treatment to his subject matter. Doris Webb noted: "Mr. Mackenzie may object to the expression: 'this well-known author writes in an entirely new vein,' but it seems to fit the occasion. He handles his hero ... with affectionate jocularity bordering on farce. Yet the complete picture of [the character] is fine, human and lovable—perhaps just because of its convincing defects."

Of *My Life and Times,* William Trevor felt that "his [Mackenzie's] scene has been wider by far than that of the professional literary man, and it is this, matched by the versatility of his talent, that makes his autobiography such good reading." David Williams was equally positive: "The advantages of [Mackenzie's] method—and in particular the amazing sense of immediacy and completeness it produces in the reader—far more than outweigh any blurrings or false emphasis which might with some writers result from too strict an adherence to chronological order."

On the publication of *Greek Memories* in 1932, according to Alden Whitman of the *New York Times,* "[Mackenzie] was prosecuted under the Official Secrets Act for divulging information about the war and was fined 100 pounds sterling; but he took his revenge in a novel, *Water on the Brain,* which satirized official spy-hunting." *Greek Memories* was reissued in 1939.

Film adaptations of Mackenzie's novels include "Sinister Street," R.C., October 26, 1919; "Carnival," United Artists, July 3, 1921; "Sylvia Scarlett" (adapted by Gladys Unger, John Collier, and Mortimer Offner), RKO, 1936; as well as "Tight Little Island."

Mackenzie's novel, *Tight Little Island,* was adapted for the stage by Sherman L. Sergel as *Tight Little Island: A Play in Three Acts,* Dramatic Publishing, 1966.

AVOCATIONAL INTERESTS: Mackenzie said he hated blood sports, golf, and imperialism. His favorite game was rugby football. He loved billiards, and preferred cats to dogs. His favorite composers were Beethoven, Mozart, and Sibelius.

BIOGRAPHICAL/CRITICAL SOURCES—Books: Leo Robertson, *Compton Mackenzie: An Appraisal of His Literary Work,* Richards, 1955; Compton Mackenzie, *My Life and Times,* Chatto & Windus, *Octave One: 1883-1891,* 1963, *Octave Two: 1891-1900,* 1963, *Octave Three: 1900-1907,* 1964, *Octave Four: 1907-1914,* 1965, *Octave Five: 1915-1923,* 1966, *Octave Six: 1923-1930,* 1967, *Octave Seven: 1930-1938,* 1968, *Octave Eight: 1939-1946,* 1969, *Octave Nine: 1946-1952,* 1970, *Octave Ten: 1953-1963,* 1971; Kenneth Young, *Compton Mackenzie,* Longmans, Green, 1968.

Periodicals: *New York Times Book Review,* April 28, 1912; *Boston Transcript,* November 19, 1913, December 16, 1914; *Athenaeum,* November 21, 1914, June 28, 1930; *New York Herald Tribune Books,* November 7, 1915, November 1, 1925, July 10, 1932; *New Republic,* December 4, 1915, July 20, 1927, November 7, 1928; *Publishers' Weekly,* March 20, 1920; *Springfield Republican,* May 2, 1920; *Times Literary Supplement,* May 6, 1920, June 8, 1922, September 6, 1928, November 19, 1931, September 7, 1940, February 23, 1967, January 25, 1968; *New York Evening Post,* September 25, 1920; *Literary Review,* March 3, 1923, August 7, 1926; *New York World,* November 9, 1924; *Independent,* September 8, 1928; *Nation,* June 28, 1930, January 16, 1937; *Spectator,* July 6, 1934, September 6, 1940, March 1, 1968, February 7, 1969; *New Statesman,* January 16, 1937; *Listener,* March 2, 1967; *Punch,* February 7, 1968, March 5, 1969; *Books and Bookmen,* March, 1968, June, 1969, March, 1970; *Observer Review,* January 31, 1971; *Bookseller,* February 6, 1971; *Evening Standard* (London), November 30, 1972.†

(Died November 30, 1972)

*   *   *

MacKENZIE, Fred   1905-

PERSONAL: Born January 27, 1905, in Franklin, Pa.; son of John Lewis (employed in metallurgy industry) and Minnie (Webber) MacKenzie; married Sarah Olson, June 2, 1928; children: Frederic P., Carol (Mrs. Harold J. Abramson). *Education:* Graduated from public high school in Tulsa, Okla. *Politics:* Democrat. *Religion:* Protestant.

CAREER: Began newspaper career at eighteen; Associated Press, Pittsburgh, Pa., day editor, 1925-32; *Pittsburgh Sun-Telegraph,* Pittsburgh, rewrite man, 1932-34; *Franklin News-Herald,* Franklin, Pa., city editor, 1934-42; *Buffalo Evening News,* Buffalo, N.Y., war correspondent, and later foreign correspondent, 1942-48; City of Buffalo, N.Y., deputy city comptroller, 1948-51; *Buffalo Courier-Express,* Buffalo, editorial writer, 1951-69. *Member:* 101st Airborne Division Association (honorary member).

WRITINGS: The Men of Bastogne, McKay, 1968.

WORK IN PROGRESS: A post-Civil War novel, *Chariot of Fire.*

SIDELIGHTS: Fred MacKenzie was the sole civilian correspondent in Bastogne during the period of its encirclement in December, 1944.

BIOGRAPHICAL/CRITICAL SOURCES: Barney Oldfield, *Never a Shot in Anger,* Duell, Sloan & Pearce, 1956; John Toland, *Battle: The Story of the Bulge,* Random House, 1959.††

*   *   *

MacLACHLAN, James Angell   1891-1967

PERSONAL: Surname legally changed, 1948; born August 15, 1891 in Ann Arbor, Mich.; son of Andrew Cunningham (a professor) and Lois Thompson (Angell) McLaughlin; married Mary Jane Carrier, February 9, 1928; children: Helen Campbell (Mrs. Paul Stelson), David Blair, Bruce Birge, James Angell, Jr., Rhoda Wilson. *Education:* University of Michigan, A.B., 1912; Harvard University, LL.B., 1916. *Politics:* Republican. *Home:* 2117 Devonshire Rd., Ann Arbor, Mich. *Office:* Hutchins Hall, Ann Arbor, Mich.

CAREER: Eastern High School, Bay City, Mich., coach and teacher of mathematics and astronomy, 1912-13; practicing lawyer in Chicago, Ill., 1916-17, 1919-24; Harvard Law School, Cambridge, Mass., assistant professor, 1924-27, professor of law, 1927-60, professor emeritus, 1960-67; Hastings College of Law, San Francisco, Calif., professor of law, 1960-67. Visiting professor, Rutgers University, 1964, University of Cincinnati, 1964-65, Washington University, St. Louis, Mo., 1966. *Military and wartime service:* U.S. Army, heavy field artillery, 1917-19 (on detached service with French Artillery Information, 1918); served as captain. Office of Price Administration, Washington, D.C., special counsel, 1942; United States Maritime Commission, Washington, D.C., chief business specialist on contract renegotiation, 1943-45. *Member:* International Movement for Atlantic Union, National Bankruptcy Conference (chairman, committee on preference, lien, and title, 1932-60), Federal Union, Michigan Bar Association, Phi Beta Kappa, Psi Upsilon.

WRITINGS: (Editor and annotator) *Cases on the Federal Anti-Trust Laws,* 1930, 2nd edition, 1933; (editor with John Hanna) *Cases and Materials on Creditors' Rights,* Foundation Press, 1939, 5th edition, 1957; (editor with Hanna) *Cases and Materials on Creditors' Rights and Corporate Reorganization,* 3rd edition (Maclachlan was not connected with earlier editions), Foundation Press, 1939, 5th consolidated edition, 1957; (editor) *The Bankruptcy Act,* Foundation Press, 1939, 8th edition, 1965; *Handbook of the Law of Bankruptcy,* West Publishing, 1956. Editor, *Harvard Law Review,* 1914-16; contributing editor, *Commercial Law Journal,* 1960-66. Author of substantial amendments to the Bankruptcy Act (as enacted July 2, 1898) which were embodied in the Chandler Act of 1938 and the amendment to the law of preferences in 1950. Contributor of articles to professional journals.†

(Died April 17, 1967)

*   *   *

MacPEEK, Walter G.   1902-1973
(Hugo Jumpp)

PERSONAL: Born March 14, 1902, in Stockton, Ill.; son of Perry Oliver and Louisa Anna (Brunner) MacPeek; married Virginia Ruth Stevens, October 24, 1941; children: Walter Lawrence. *Education:* University of Chicago, Ph.B., 1924; graduate study at University of Michigan, 1939-40, New York University, 1953, and Rutgers University, 1960. *Politics:* Republican. *Religion:* Presbyterian. *Home:* 3 Linwood Pl., North Brunswick, N.J. 08902; and Apt. 5, Twin Oaks Villas, 11200 102nd Ave. N., Seminole, Fla. 33540.

CAREER: Professional leader with Boy Scouts of America council staffs, 1924-53, serving in Chicago, Ill., Highland Park, Ill., Washington, D.C., Ann Arbor, Mich., and Grand Rapids, Mich.; Boy Scouts of America, National Council, New Brunswick, N.J., staff editor, 1953-60, associate editor of *Scouting* (magazine), 1953-67, assistant to director of editorial services, 1960-67; *New Brunswick Sunday Home News,* New Brunswick, editor of book column, 1967-73; *Boy's Life,* New Brunswick, stamp and coin editor, 1967-73. Consultant, American Humanities Foundation, 1967-73. *Member:* Sigma Delta Chi. *Awards, honors:* Gold Medal, Freedom Foundation, 1960.

WRITINGS—Youth books: *George Washington: Real Boy,* Franklin Press (Washington, D.C.), 1932; *Glimpses into Boyland: A Collection of Brief Incidents of Boy Life* (includes *George Washington: Real Boy*), Franklin Press, 1932; *Stories Stamps Tell,* Franklin Press, 1933; *Fetching Up Fred,* Peak Press, 1940; *Celebrating Boy Scout Week,* Boy Scouts of America, 1955; (compiler) *The Scout Law in Action,* Abingdon, 1966; (compiler) *The Scout Oath in Action,* Abingdon, 1967; *Scout Leaders in Action,* Abingdon, 1969; *Resourceful Scouts in Action,* Abingdon, 1972. Contributor of articles to magazines under pseudonym Hugo Jumpp. Contributing editor, *Quote,* 1967-73.

WORK IN PROGRESS: A book on human relations; other books, including one related to writing procedures.†

(Died January 31, 1973)

MADDOX, James G(ray)   1907-1973

PERSONAL: Born February 4, 1907, in Rison, Ark.; son of Ernest Ray and Eve (Gray) Maddox; married Alice Batten, June 15, 1934; children: Susanna, Jeannie (Mrs. Walter P. Sy), Melinda (Mrs. A. S. Boyers, Jr.), Swanee (Mrs. John H. Austin). *Education:* University of Arkansas, B.S.A., 1927; University of Wisconsin, M.S., 1930; Harvard University, M.P.A., 1948, Ph.D., 1950. *Politics:* Democrat. *Religion:* None. *Home address:* Route 6, Box 266, Raleigh, N.C.

CAREER: Economist with Farm Credit Administration, 1933-36, Agricultural Adjustment Administration, 1936-37, and Resettlement Administration, 1937-39; Farm Security Administration, Washington, D.C., division director, 1939-43; Bureau of Agricultural Economics, Washington, D.C., assistant to chief, 1943-47; American International Association, New York, N.Y., assistant director, 1949-52; American Universities Field Staff, New York, N.Y., member, 1953-58; North Carolina State University at Raleigh, 1958-73, began as professor of economics, became professor emeritus, director of Agricultural Policy Institute, 1966-70. *Member:* American Economic Association, American Farm Economics Association, Southern Economic Association.

WRITINGS: Technical Assistance by Religious Agencies in Latin America, University of Chicago Press, 1956; (with E. E. Liebhafsky, Vivian Henderson, and H. M. Hamlin) *The Advancing South: Manpower Prospects and Problems,* Twentieth Century Fund, 1967. Contributor to farm and economics journals.†

(Died December 15, 1973)

*   *   *

MADGE, Violet   1916-19(?)

PERSONAL: Born April 15, 1916, in Gloucester, England; daughter of Philip William (a Methodist minister) and Priscilla (Richards) Madge. *Education:* Westhill College, Preschool Teacher's Certificate, 1936; Teacher Training College, Exmouth, England, Ministry of Education Teacher's Certificate, 1949; Westhill College, Birmingham, National Froebel Foundation Teacher's Certificate, Certificate in Leadership in Christian Education, 1952; advanced course in education at University of Leeds, 1961-62. *Home and office:* Rolle College of Education, Exmouth, Devonshire, England.

CAREER: Social work as minister's assistant, 1936-40; Borough Polytechnic, London, England (evacuated to Exeter), secretary, 1940-42; Ministry of Education Regional Office, Exeter, Devonshire, England, secretary, 1942-47; Westhill College, Selly Oak, Birmingham, England, teacher in demonstration school and part-time lecturer in college, 1947-48, 1949-53, full-time lecturer in Froebel and Christian education departments, 1953-55; Rolle College of Education, Exmouth, Devonshire, senior lecturer in education and warden, 1955-64, senior woman tutor and principal lecturer in education and religious education, beginning 1965. Consultant to British Broadcasting Corp. on religious educational broadcasts.

WRITINGS: Children in Search of Meaning, S.C.M. Press, 1965, Morehouse, 1966; *Introducing Young Children to Jesus,* Morehouse, 1971. Contributor to *Child Education* and *Learning for Living.*

WORK IN PROGRESS: Research in religious conceptions and attitudes to religious education of teachers in training.†

(Deceased)

* * *

MADIGAN, Marian East 1898-

PERSONAL: Born June 2, 1898, in Weston, Neb.; daughter of Thomas and Maggie O. (East) Madigan. *Education:* University of Nebraska, A.B., 1924; Columbia University, M.A., 1927; University of Chicago, Ph.D., 1936. *Politics:* "Liberal conservative." *Religion:* "Student of the historical Jesus." *Residence:* Weston, Neb.

CAREER: Teacher in rural and city schools of Nebraska, 1916-20, 1924-26; Dana Hall, Wellesley, Mass., instructor in mathematics, 1927-30; Fermata School, Aiken, S.C., head of department of mathematics, 1930-32; Milwaukee Vocational Technical and Adult Schools, Milwaukee, Wis., mathematics teacher, 1936-38, doing testing, counseling, and special assignments in research programs, including achievement testing and multimedia techniques research beginning, 1938. Summer instructor, Stout State University, 1945, 1947; visiting professor, University of Arizona, 1948, 1949. *Member:* American Psychological Association (fellow), International Council of Psychologists (fellow), Milwaukee County Psychological Association (charter member), Milwaukee County Association for Mental Health, Phi Beta Kappa.

WRITINGS: Psychology: Principles and Applications (text for student nurses), Mosby, 1950, 5th edition, 1970. Author of three achievement test manuals published by Milwaukee Vocational and Adult Schools, *Industrial Courses,* 1949, revised edition, 1961, *Clothing and Allied Courses,* 1952, and *Foods and Nutrition Courses,* 1954.

SIDELIGHTS: Marian Madigan's achievement test manuals, each running about two hundred pages in length, are used in developing countries. She attended the International Congress of Psychology in Bonn, 1960, and Moscow, 1966. She still retains most of the Nebraska farm where she grew up, and manages the farm operation.

* * *

MAGGAL, Moshe M(orris) 1908-

PERSONAL: Surname rhymes with de Gaulle; born March 16, 1908, in Nagyecsed, Hungary; son of David (a merchant) and Esther (Fulop) Gelberman; married Rachel Diamond, July 8, 1951; children: Davida Elizabeth, Michelle Judith, Elana Ilene. *Education:* Studied at rabbinical colleges in Hungary, 1925-29; Jewish Theological Seminary, Budapest, Hungary, Rabbi, 1935; further study at German University, Zurich, Switzerland, 1936, and Hebrew University of Jerusalem, 1936-37.

CAREER: Iton Meyuhad (weekly), Tel Aviv, Palestine (now Israel), editor, 1939-42; rabbi of congregations in Claremont, N.H., 1950-52, Billings, Mont., 1952-54, Alhambra, Calif., 1955-56, and Canoga Park, Calif., 1959-61; Congregation Ahavath Israel, Hollywood, Calif., rabbi, beginning 1966. Editor, Heritage-Southwest Jewish Press, Los Angeles, 1958-60; founder and president, National Jewish Information Service (Jewish missionary organization), Los Angeles, beginning 1960. *Military service:* Israeli Defence Forces, 1948-50. *Member:* International Platform Association, Beverly Hills Zionist Organization (member of board, 1957), Greater Los Angeles Press Club. *Awards, honors:* Reward of Merit, Spiritual Mobilization, 1952; citation, Crusade for Freedom, 1952.

WRITINGS: Acres of Happiness, Hawthorn, 1967. Also author of *Prophecy and Fulfillment,* 1968. Contributor to *National Jewish Post & Opinion,* and other newspapers and magazines. Editor, *Voice of Judaism.*

SIDELIGHTS: Besides his native Hungarian, Maggal speaks Hebrew, Yiddish, and German, and knows some Arabic. *Avocational interests:* Travel, theatre.†

* * *

MAGOUN, F(rederick) Alexander 1896-

PERSONAL: Born March 4, 1896, in Oberlin, Ohio; son of Herbert William and Martha R. (Mann) Magoun; married Flora R. Lindsay, February 14, 1919; married Carolyn L. Warren, October 12, 1936; children: (first marriage) Priscilla, Richard M. (deceased), Theodore R. *Education:* Massachusetts Institute of Technology, S.B., 1918, M.S., 1923; Harvard University, B.S., 1918. *Politics:* Republican. *Religion:* Protestant. *Residence:* Jaffrey Center, N.H. *Office:* Social Science Department, Franklin Pierce College, Rindge, N.H.

CAREER: Apprentice engineer, 1918; Lowell Textile Institute, Lowell, Mass., instructor in applied mechanics, 1919-20; Massachusetts Institute of Technology, Cambridge, instructor in naval architecture, 1920-30, associate professor of human relations in industry, 1930-50; Hawthorne College, Antrim, N.H., professor of human relations, 1962-64; Franklin Pierce College, Rindge, N.H., head of social science department, beginning 1964. U.S. Department of State, consultant, 1942-44; Human Relations, Inc., Boston, Mass., president, 1946-50. Lecturer. *Member:* Society for the Advancement of Management (honorary life member), American Institute of Management (fellow).

WRITINGS: The Frigate "Constitution" and Other Historic Ships, Marine Research Society (Salem, Mass.), 1928; (with Eric Hodgins) *Sky High,* Little, Brown, 1929, revised edition, 1935; (with E. Hodgins) *A History of Aeronautics,* McGraw, 1931, published as *A History of Aircraft,* Arno, 1972; (with his students) *Problems in Human Engineering,* Macmillan, 1932; (with E. Hodgins) *Behemoth: The Story of Power,* Doubleday, 1932; *Balanced Personality,* Harper, 1943; (with Richard Magoun) *Love and Marriage,* Harper, 1948, revised edition, 1956; *The Teaching of Human Relations by the Case Demonstration Method,* Beacon, 1959; *Successfully Finding Yourself and Your Job,* Harper, 1959; *Living a Happy Life,* Harper, 1960; *Cooperation and Conflict in Industry,* Harper, 1960; *Christmas Poems, 1940-60,* privately printed, 1960; *Amos Fortune's Choice: The Story of a Negro Slave's Struggle for Self-Fulfillment* (photographs by the author), Wheelwright, 1964; *The Whispering Leaves* (poems), privately printed, 1964. Contributor to junior encyclopedias and to magazines. Editor, *Knollwood Pathway,* 1959-60.

WORK IN PROGRESS: A first novel; a book on human relations for the use of authors.

SIDELIGHTS: Parts of *Love and Marriage* have been translated into eleven languages, including Japanese. *Avocational interests:* Formerly, mountain-climbing; currently photography, collecting U.S. stamps and pennies.†

* * *

MALRAUX, (Georges-) Andre 1901-1976
   (Colonel Berger)

PERSONAL: Born November 3, 1901, in Paris, France; son of Fernand-Georges (a businessman, from a seafaring family) and Berthe (Lanny) Malraux; married Clara Goldschmidt (an author), October 26, 1921 (divorced, 1930's); married Josette Clotis (a writer; killed in a rail accident during World War II); married Marie-Madeleine Lioux (a concert pianist; widow of his half-brother, Roland), March, 1948; children: (first marriage) Florence; (second marriage) Gautier and Vincent (both killed in an automobile accident, 1961); Alain (stepson). *Education:* Attended Lycee Condorcet, and Ecole des Langues Orientales, where he developed his interest in archaeology and oriental art. *Address:* 2, rue d'Estienne d'Orves, Verrieres-le-Buisson, 91370, France.

CAREER: After leaving school worked for the bookseller, Rene-Louis Doyon, and in the art department of the publisher, Kra, in Paris, France; in 1923, left, with wife, Clara Goldschmidt Malraux, for Indochina on an archaeological expedition sponsored by the French Government; was imprisoned on a charge of taking ancient sculptures, which were regarded as official property by the colonial regime; his wife returned to France in 1924 to organize a petition of writers (including Andre Gide), which led to his release; returned to France, but set off again for Indochina two months later; collaborated in Saigon with the nationalist "Jeune-Annam" movement on the newspaper, *L'Indochine* (later became *L'Indochine enchainee*); joined the Kuomintang in Indochina and Canton; returned to France in 1927; in 1928, became art editor at the publishing firm, Gallimard, for whom he continued to work—in between numerous archaeological expeditions, and other activities—both as literary editor, and director of the series, "La Galerie de la Pleiade." Devoted the Prix Goncourt money to a trip in search of the lost city of the Queen of Sheba, in Southern Arabia; spoke at the 1934 Writers' Congress in Moscow (where he was listed as a "Marxist humanist"), and at the June, 1935 Congress of Writers in Defence of Culture, Paris; was involved in the activities of anti-Fascist organizations, including the "Comite mondial antifasciste," and "La Ligue internationale contre l'anti-semitisme." Became Minister of Information in de Gaulle's government, November, 1945-46; was Minister of Culture in the de Gaulle cabinet, 1958-59. *Wartime activity:* In 1936, organized the foreign division of the Republican air-force in the Spanish Civil War; at the outbreak of World War II he joined the French Army; was wounded, imprisoned, then escaped; after further wounds and imprisonment, organized the Resistance in S.W. France, heading the Alsace-Lorraine brigade in 1945, under the pseudonym, "Colonel Berger." *Awards, honors*—Military: Officier de la Legion d'honneur, Compagnon de la Liberation, Medaille de la Resistance, Croix de guerre (1939-45), Distinguished Service Order. Civilian: Prix Goncourt, 1933, for *La Condition humaine:* Prix Louis-Delluc, 1945, for the film *L'Espoir;* Prix Nehru, 1974, for promoting international understanding.

WRITINGS—Fiction: *Lunes en papier* (fantastic tale; also see below), Simon, 1921; *La Tentation de l'Occident* (philosophical tale; also see below), Grasset, 1926, reprinted, Les Bibliophiles Comtois, 1962, translation and introduction by Robert Hollander published as *The Temptation of the West,* Vintage Books, 1961; *Les Conquerants* (novel; also see below), Grasset, 1928, revised, "definitive" edition (contains a "postface" by Malraux consisting of his March 5, 1948 speech in defense of Gaullism), 1949, reprinted, Gallimard, 1967, translation by Winifred Stephen Whale published as *The Conquerors,* Harcourt, 1929, revised edition (with "postface" translated by Jacques Le Clerq), Beacon Press, 1956; *Royaume faufelu* (fantastic tale; also see below), Gallimard, 1928; *La Voie royale* (novel; also see below), Grasset,

1930, reprinted, 1968, translation by Stuart Gilbert published as *The Royal Way,* Smith & Haus, 1935; *La Condition humaine* (novel; also see below), Gallimard, 1933, revised edition, 1946, translation by Haakon M. Chevalier published as *Man's Fate,* Smith & Haus, 1934, reprinted, Random House, 1968, translation by Alistair Macdonald published as *Storm in Shanghai,* Methuen, 1934, published as *Man's Estate,* 1948, reprinted, Hamish Hamilton, 1968; *Le Temps du mepris* (novel), Gallimard, 1935, translation by Chevalier, with a foreword by Waldo Frank, published as *Days of Wrath,* Random House, 1936 (published in England as *Days of Contempt,* Gollancz, 1936); *L'Espoir* (novel; also see below); Gallimard, 1937, reprinted, 1974, translation by Gilbert and Macdonald published as *Man's Hope,* Random House, 1938, reprinted, 1968 (published in England as *Days of Hope,* Routledge & Kegan Paul, 1938); *La Lutte avec l'ange* (philosophical novel; part of a larger project, the rest of which was destroyed by the Gestapo), Editions du Haut Pays, 1943, published as *Les Noyers de l'Altenburg,* Gallimard, 1948, translation by A. W. Fielding published as *The Walnut Trees of Altenburg,* John Lehmann, 1952.

Art criticism: *Esquisse d'une psychologie du cinema,* Gallimard, 1946; *La Psychologie de l'art,* Skira, Volume I: *Le Musee imaginaire,* 1947, Volume II: *La Creation artisque,* 1948, Volume III: *La Monnaie de l'absolu,* 1949, translation by Stuart Gilbert published as *The Psychology of Art,* Pantheon, Volume I: *Museum without Walls,* 1949, Volume II: *The Creative Act,* 1950, Volume III: *The Twilight of the Absolute,* 1951, revised and enlarged French edition published as *Les Voix du silence* (contains an additional section, "Les Metamorphoses d'Apollon"), Galerie de la Pleiade, Gallimard, 1951, translation by Gilbert published as *The Voices of Silence,* Doubleday, 1953, Volume I: *Museum without Walls,* Volume II: *The Metamorphoses of Apollo,* Volume III: *The Creative Process,* Volume IV: *The Aftermath of the Absolute; Saturne,* Skira, 1949, translation by C. W. Chilton published as *Saturn: An Essay on Goya,* Phaidon, 1957; *Tout Vermaer de Delft,* Gallimard, c.1950; *Le Musee imaginaire de la sculpture mondiale,* Volume I, Gallimard, 1952, Volume II published as *Des bas-reliefs aux grottes sacree,* Gallimard, 1954, Volume III published as *Le Monde chretien,* 1954; *Le Metamorphose des dieux* (philosophy and religion in art), Gallimard, Volume I: *Le Surnaturel,* 1957, translation by Gilbert published as *The Metamorphosis of the Gods,* Doubleday, 1960, Volume II: *L'Ireel,* 1974, Volume III: *L'Intemporal,* 1976; *Le Triangle noir,* Gallimard, 1970; *La Tete d'obsidienne,* Gallimard, 1974, translation published as *Picasso's Mask,* Holt, 1976.

Political writings and official speeches: (In dialogue with James Burnham) *The Case for De Gaulle,* Random House, 1949; *Brasilia, la capitale de l'espoir* (French text followed by Spanish and English translations), Presidencia de Republicia, Servico de Documentacao, 1959; *Discours, 1958-1965,* Action Etudiante Gaullistes, 1966; *Oraisons funebres,* Gallimard, 1970; *Paroles et ecrits politiques, 1947-1972,* Plon, 1973.

Author of prefaces, including: D. H. Lawrence, *L'Amant de Lady Chatterley,* translation by Roger Cornaz, Gallimard, 1932, preface published as "Preface to *Lady Chatterley's Lover,*" in *Yale French Studies,* Number 11, 1953; William Faulkner, *Sanctuaire,* translation by R. M. Raimbault and Henri Delgove, Gallimard, 1933, preface published as "Preface to Faulkner's *Sanctuary,*" in *Yale French Studies,* Number 10, 1952; Andree Viollis, *Indochine S.O.S.,* Gallimard, 1935; *Goya: Dissins du Musee du Prado,* Skira, 1947; Manes Sperber, *Q'une larme dans l'ocean,* translation by author and Blanche Gidon, Calmann-Levy, 1952; *Tout Vermeer de Delft*, Gallimard, 1952; *Tout l'oeuvre peint de Leonard de Vinci*, Gallimard, 1952; General P. E. Jacquot, *Essai de strategie occidentale*, Gallimard, 1953; Albert Olivier, *Saint-Just et la force des choses* (also see below), Gallimard, 1954; Izis Bidermanas, *Israel*, Clairefontaine, 1955; Andre Parrot, *Sumer*, Gallimard, 1960; *Le Triangle noir* (contains prefaces on Laclos, Goya, and Saint-Just), Gallimard, 1970; Pierre Bockel, *L'Enfant du rire*, Grasset, 1973; Maria Van Ryssellberghe, *Les Cahiers de la petite dame, 1918-1929*, Gallimard, 1973; Georges Bernanos, *Journal d'un cure de campagne*, Plon, 1974; *Correspondance Romain Rolland-Jean Guehenno*, Albin Michel, 1975.

Other: *Les Chenes qu'on abat . . .*, Gallimard, 1970, translation by Irene Clephane published as *Fallen Oaks: Conversation with De Gaulle*, Hamish Hamilton, 1972, published as *Felled Oaks: Conversation with De Gaulle*, revised by Linda Asher, Holt, 1972; *Roi, je t'attends a Babylone*, Skira, 1973; *Lazare*, Gallimard, 1974.

Autobiography: *Le Miroir des limbes*, Gallimard, Volume I: *Antimemoires*, 1967, translation by Terrence Kilmartin published as *Anti-memoirs*, Holt, 1968, Volume II: *La Corde et le souris*, 1976.

Omnibus volumes: *Oeuvres completes*, Skira, 1945; *Scenes choisies*, Gallimard, 1946; *Romans* (contains *Les Conquerants, La Conditions humaine*, and *L'Espoir*), Gallimard, 1947, reprinted, 1969; *Lectures choisies*, edited by Anne Prioleau Jones, Macmillan, 1965; *Oeuvres* (contains *Lunes en papier, Tentation de l'Occident, Les Conquerants, Royaume farfelu, La Voie royale, La Condition humaine, L'Espoir*, and *Antimemoires*) four volumes, Gallimard, 1970.

General editor, *The Arts of Mankind*, beginning 1960. Contributor to *Action, L'Intransigeant, Commune, Les Conferences de l'Unesco, Liberte de l'esprit, Carrefour, Europe, Nouvelle Revue Francaise, L'Express*, and many other journals and publications.

WORK IN PROGRESS: Precarious Man and Literature.

SIDELIGHTS: W. M. Frohock wrote, "For Americans, Malraux has the special interest of being what America rarely produces, an artist who is also an intellectual."

All of Malraux's major novels were strongly biographical—though not personal. Gaetan Picon suggested that "the events which provided the material for the work are directly lived through, but remain external. The encounter between Malraux and History becomes the history of Malraux himself." His experience in Indochina, wrote the *Times Saturday Review*, "turned Malraux from a dilettante into a revolutionary." Donald Schier continued: "*L'Espoir* makes it plain that by 1938 Malraux was finding it impossible to identify himself with the Communist Party, although he continued to share, rather suspiciously, in its struggle against Fascism. . . . [In *Les Conquerants*, the] forcing of other people into paths they would not otherwise have taken (. . . not by party discipline but by individual leadership) is the real justification for the hero's existence. . . . Malraux sees himself as a hero." With respect to General de Gaulle, the *Times Saturday Review* commented how "Malraux has come to regard him not as a politician but as a 'mythe vivant'."

In an interview with Roger Stephane, Malraux noted: "I couldn't say that man is what he does, because, to the question, what is man? I would apply that we are the first civilization which says it doesn't know. . . . We are the only civilization in which man has no purpose. Not that he cannot have one, but that we are still trying to find out what it is. All other civilizations have rested in the end on religion." In an age without faith, he accorded a supreme role to the artist: "Art lives because its function is to let men escape from their human condition, not by means of evasion, but through a possession. All art is a way of possessing destiny."

Malraux was described in the *Times Saturday Review* as "a slight, intense hollow-eyed man, a chain-smoker who looks like a character from a Malraux novel." Janet Flanner wrote: "No other French writer is so rapid, compulsive, fascinating and rewarding a monologist. . . . As he walks, words and ideas rush from his brain and out of his mouth in extemporaneous creation, as though they were long quotations from books he had not yet written. . . ." Flanner continued: "He could work at his publishing job by day, and at his writing more than half the night at home. . . . It was in these circumstances that he wrote *La Condition humaine*."

It is well known that Malraux was not prepared to discuss his personal life with the public. Flanner reported that, "if a question of a biographical nature is inadvertently asked in an interview, Malraux will reply by saying 'Vie Privee' and nothing more. In his own view, which is aloof, his *vie publique* lies in his books." His autobiography revealed the same attitude towards what he called "confessions": "What interests me in a man is the human condition . . . and some features which express less an individual character, than a particular relationship with the world. . . . I call this book *Antimemoires* because it replies to questions that memoirs do not put, and does not answer those they do." David Caute noted: "These *Antimemoires* break away entirely from the traditional biography or memoir form. Not only is orthodox chronology rejected: there is in addition no attempt to provide a factually coherent outline of the author's life." Schier added: "The various sections of the *Antimemoires* bear the titles of his books but he does not discuss them. Rather the *Antimemoires* provide variations on the novelistic themes: individual action versus party discipline, terrorism as a political technique, art as a surrogate for religion, *fraternite verile*." Malraux told Stephane: "My problem is this: what answer can life give to the basic question posed by death? This question was always subordinate in great religious cultures which preceded our culture. My intention is to answer it in a fundamental way. This has been made easier for me because my memoirs don't follow a chronological sequence. . . . Up to a point, we can say that memoirs are essentially novels about the education of the author's personality. But I am concerned with something different, and I have taken another title because of that."

As de Gaulle's minister of culture, Malraux was probably best known for organizing the cleaning of Paris buildings, creating what was alluded to in the *Times Saturday Review* as "Paris blanchi." In the same article, it was reported that *Antimemoires* sold a quarter of a million copies in the first two months of publication.

There are a number of recordings of Malraux's work, including a reading by Malraux himself from *Les Voix du silence*, in the series "Auteurs du 20e Siecle," Philips. A film scenario of *L'Espoir* was made in Barcelona in 1938.

BIOGRAPHICAL/CRITICAL SOURCES—Books: W. M. Frohock, *Andre Malraux and the Tragic Imagination*, Stanford University Press, 1952, revised edition, with new preface, 1967; Gaetan Picon, *Malraux par lui-meme* (with annotations by Malraux), Editions du Seuil, 1953; Janet Flanner, *Men and Monuments*, Harper, 1957; Geoffrey Hartman, *Andre Malraux*, Hillary, 1960; *The Novelist as Philosopher*, edited by John Cruickshank, Oxford University Press, 1962; Charles D. Blend, *Andre Malraux: Tragic Humanist*, Ohio State University Press, 1963; Clara Malraux, *Le Bruit de nos pas*, Grasset, Volume I: *Apprendre a vivre*, 1963, Volume II: *Nos vingt ans*, 1966, translation by Patrick O'Brian published in a single volume as *Memoirs*, Bodley Head, 1967; R.W.B. Lewis, editor, *Malraux: A Collection of Critical Essays*, Prentice-Hall, 1964; Walter G. Langlois, *The Indochina Adventure*, Praeger, 1966; Andre Malraux, *Antimemoires*, Gallimard, 1967; Denis Boak, *Andre Malraux*, Oxford University Press, 1968; P.S.R. Payne, *A Portrait of Andre Malraux*, Prentice-Hall, 1970; Carolyn Riley, editor, *Contemporary Literary Criticism*, Gale, Volume I, 1973, Volume IV, 1975; T. J. Kline, *Andre Malraux and the Metamorphosis of Death*, Columbia University Press, 1973; Jean Lacouture, *Andre Malraux*, Editions du Seuil, 1973, translation by Alan Sheridan published under same title, Pantheon, 1975; Guy Suares, *Malraux, Past, Present, Future*, translated by Derek Coltman, Little, Brown, 1974; C. J. Greshoff, *An Introduction to the Novels of Andre Malraux*, Balkema, 1976; *Malraux*, Harcourt, 1976.

Articles: *Esprit* (nearly entire issue devoted to Malraux), October, 1948; *Modern Language Quarterly*, June, 1953; *Burlington Magazine*, December, 1954; *University of Kansas City Review*, Volume XXVIII, number 1, 1961; *Observer Weekend Review*, April 5, 1964; *Times Literary Supplement*, November 26, 1964; *Le Nouvel Observateur*, September 11, 1967; *Encounter* (interview), Volume XXX, number 1, 1967; *Times Saturday Review*, November 18, 1967; *Listener*, January 25, 1968, October 31, 1968; *Carleton Miscellany*, winter, 1969; *Melanges-Malraux-Miscellany*, 1969—; *New York Times*, November 25, 1976; *Newsweek*, December 6, 1976.†

(Died November 23, 1976)

* * *

MALTEN, William   1902-

PERSONAL: Born August 9, 1902, in Frankfurt, Germany; married Charlotte Gross (a ceramic sculptor), 1935. *Education:* University of Berlin, M.A., 1923; Sorbonne, University of Paris, Certificat de Licence, 1934; Columbia University, graduate student, 1947-48. *Residence:* West Nyack, N.Y. *Office:* Iona College, New Rochelle, N.Y. 10804.

CAREER: Actor and director in Germany, Austria, Czechoslovakia, and France before coming to United States in 1940; subsequently appeared in eight Broadway shows, including Theatre Guild productions, in radio and television series, and in motion picture, "T-Men"; instructor in French at Briarcliff College, Briarcliff Manor, N.Y., 1946-48, and in German at City College (now City College of the City University of New York), New York, N.Y., 1948-50; Iona College, New Rochelle, N.Y., instructor in German, 1954-59, assistant professor of modern languages, 1959-68, associate professor emeritus, 1968—. Writer, broadcaster in French and German, and occasional director of broadcasts for Office of War Information during World War II, and then for U.S. Information Agency's "Voice of America" until 1967; became reporter for Belgian state radio and television network, Brussels. Consultant to Linguaphone Institute, 1945-50; founding member of "Players from Abroad," presenting foreign plays at City College of the City University of New York and Barbizon Plaza Theatre. *Member:* Modern Language Association of America, Societe des Pro-

fesseurs Francais en Amerique, Foreign Press Association (New York). *Awards, honors:* Iona College faculty fellowship for research, 1966-67.

WRITINGS: (Compiler) *Literarische Kleinkunst*, with accompanying one-hour tape, commentary by the author, Harper, 1968. Contributor to *Aufbau* (New York German-language newspaper).

WORK IN PROGRESS: My Nine Lives, an autobiography covering his theatrical and academic career.†

* * *

MANGAN, James Thomas   1896-

PERSONAL: Born November 17, 1896, in Chicago, Ill.; son of John (a labor leader) and Amelia (Scanlan) Mangan; married Carol Marie Jackson, April 19, 1928; children: James Carroll, Ruth Marie (Mrs. Donald James Stump). *Education:* Loyola University, Chicago, Ill., A.B., 1917. *Politics:* Independent. *Religion:* Roman Catholic. *Home and office:* 10613 South Laramie Ave., Oak Lawn, Ill. 60453.

CAREER: Copywriter with Mitchell Faust Advertising Co., Chicago, Ill., 1918-22, and Mills Industries (manufacturers of coin operated devices), Chicago, 1922-25; Loftis Brothers Jewelry Co., Chicago, Ill., advertising manager, 1925-29; Mills Industries, advertising manager, 1929-44; Mangan & Eckland (advertising, public relations, and industrial design), Chicago, Ill., partner, 1944-55; Mangan & Mangan (sales promotion and public relations), Oak Lawn, Ill., president, beginning, 1956. Illinois chairman of special events and bond drives, U.S. Treasury, 1942-44; national promotion consultant, U.S. Department of Labor, 1942-45. *Military service:* U.S. Navy, 1918. U.S. Naval Reserve, 1918-22. *Member:* American Numismatic Society, Society of Typographic Arts, Veterans of World War I.

WRITINGS: Automatic Merchandising, Mills Novelty Press, 1931; *Unknown Sales Formula*, Mills Novelty Press, 1932; *You Can Do Anything*, Dartnell, 1932; *Thoughts on Salesmanship*, Dartnell, 1934; *The Knack of Selling Yourself*, Dartnell, 1936, revised edition, 1966; *Learn to Write*, Black Cat Press, 1936; *Push*, Black Cat Press, 1936; *Design: The New Grammar of Advertising*, Dartnell, 1939; *Sell by Giving*, Dartnell, 1948; *First Report to Universe*, Celestia Press, 1956; *The Golden Rule in Selling*, Dartnell, 1956; *How to Win Self-Confidence for Selling*, Prentice-Hall, 1957; *State of the Sky*, Celestia Press, 1958; *Secrets of Selling Yourself to People*, Prentice-Hall, 1961; *The Secret of Perfect Living*, Prentice-Hall, 1963. In teens wrote jokes for *Life* (humor magazine) and *Judge*, and filmscript condensations for *Feature Movie Magazine;* later contributor to *Coronet, Market Place*, and *American Legion Magazine*.

WORK IN PROGRESS: Five books, *How We Laugh, 60 Ways to Fall Asleep, How to Think Up Ideas That Click, Imagined*, and *The Uneasy Catholic*.

SIDELIGHTS: Mangan once described his special style of writing as "heroin prose" (he assumes that he has "swallowed" enough heroin to be completely out of this world). Some years ago he was featured in *Life* as the champion top-spinner of the world; he also claims to have written the most frequently stolen library book in America, declaring that *Design: The New Grammar of Advertising* has been filched from more than one hundred library reference rooms. His stunts have included a war stamp raffle in which Gertrude Lawrence participated, dropping seven thousand prizes from airplanes over a picnic ground and outer space mail stamps. In 1948 he and some colleagues founded a new nation, Celestia, staking claim to all the space in the sky. From time to time, new elaborations emerge on the scheme; Mangan has issued passports to the moon, and his stationery bears the return address, The Nation of Celestial Space, with the capitol listed as his home in suburban Chicago.

Author of song, "We're All American, All True Blue," 1939. Irving Berlin called it the worst song ever written. It sold 500,000 records.

BIOGRAPHICAL/CRITICAL SOURCES: Advertising Age, July 7, 1947; *Chicago Tribune,* November 3, 1966.

*   *   *

MANHEIM, Leonard (Falk)   1902-

PERSONAL: Born April 22, 1902, in New York, N.Y.; son of Mark (a businessman) and Sophie (a teacher and school principal; maiden name Cohen) Manheim; married Eleanor Blackman (a college professor), July 9, 1927; children: Michael. *Education:* Columbia University, A.B., 1921, M.A., 1923, J.D., 1924, Ph.D., 1950. *Politics:* "Norman Thomas Socialist." *Religion:* Unitarian Universalist. *Home:* 31 Applewood Rd., Bloomfield, Conn. 06002. *Office:* University of Hartford, West Hartford, Conn. 06117.

CAREER: High school teacher of English and other subjects, New York, N.Y., 1923-59; practice of law, New York, N.Y., 1924-32; City College (now City College of the City University of New York), New York, N.Y., lecturer in English and comparative literature, 1946-65; University of Massachusetts, Amherst, visiting professor of English and comparative literature, 1965-67; University of Hartford, West Hartford, Conn., professor of English and comparative literature, 1967-72, professor emeritus, 1972—. Visiting lecturer, George Peabody College for Teachers, 1959-60; visiting professor, Emory University, 1973. Former semi-professional singer; producer and director for little theater, and for educational radio and television. *Member:* Modern Language Association of America, New York City Association of Teachers of English (past president), Phi Beta Kappa.

WRITINGS: (Editor with wife, Eleanor B. Manheim) *Hidden Patterns: Studies in Psychoanalytic Literary Criticism,* Macmillan, 1966; (contributor) James D. Page, editor, *Approaches to Psychopathology,* Temple University Press, 1966. Wrote scripts for Columbia Broadcasting System in early days of television. Contributor to *American Imago, Shenandoah, Psychoanalytic Review,* and other journals. Editor, *Literature and Psychology,* 1951-68 and *Hartford Studies in Literature,* beginning 1968.

WORK IN PROGRESS: Editing and contributing to *A New Anatomy of Melancholy: Suicide and the Writer.*

SIDELIGHTS: Leonard Manheim is competent in German and French; he knows some Latin, Hebrew, and Italian.

*   *   *

MANRY, Robert   1918-1971

PERSONAL: Born June 2, 1918, in Landour, India; came to United States in 1936; son of James C. (a missionary-educator) and Margaret (King) Manry; married Virginia Place, January 7, 1950; children: Robin King, Douglas James. *Education:* Antioch College, A.B., 1948. *Home:* 31003 Royalview Dr., Willowick, Ohio 44094. *Agent:* Brandt & Brandt, 101 Park Ave., New York, N.Y. 10017.

CAREER: Worked at *Morning News,* Erie, Pa., *Pittsburgh*

Press, Pittsburgh, Pa., and as copy reader at *Cleveland Plain Dealer,* Cleveland, Ohio; writer, photographer, lecturer. *Military service:* U.S. Army, 1944-46. *Awards, honors:* Adventurers Club of New York gold medal, 1965.

WRITINGS: Tinkerbelle, Harper, 1966.

SIDELIGHTS: In 1965 Robert Manry undertook a seventy-eight-day solo voyage across the Atlantic Ocean aboard his thirteen-foot boat, "Tinkerbelle." He said he decided to make the crossing because "I was becoming a crashing bore; sitting at a desk is inclined to make a man desperate."

In a review of *Tinkerbelle,* Manry's account of his crossing, C. J. Maguire wrote that "the narrative as a whole is a delight. The style is perfectly tailored to material for a general audience. The story is told with all modesty and restraint, but unmistakably conveys a portrait of courage, sincerity, and, most of all, humanity. *Tinkerbelle,* the tale of a stout craft and its stout one-man crew, is commendable to all kinds of readers, not merely to those interested in things of the sea but to anyone concerned with the problems of what humans are and how they tick."

BIOGRAPHICAL/CRITICAL SOURCES: Best Sellers, July 15, 1966; *Book Week,* July 31, 1966; *Washington Post,* February 23, 1971.†

(Died February 21, 1971)

*   *   *

MARBERRY, M. M(arion)   1905-1968

PERSONAL: Born April 16, 1905, in Carbondale, Ill.; son of William Thomas and Myrtle (Brewer) Marberry; married Virginia Gardner, 1938; married second wife, Therese Pol (an editor and translator), April 24, 1965; children: (first marriage) John. *Education:* University of Illinois, B.A., 1930. *Politics:* Independent. *Religion:* None. *Home:* 170 Second Ave., New York, N.Y. 10003. *Agent:* Sterling Lord Agency, 660 Madison Ave., New York, N.Y. 10021.

CAREER: Full-time writer, 1930-68. Worked on newspapers in Chicago and was Sunday editor of *Chicago Times* in the early 1930's; in the late 1930's he worked for the *World Telegram, PM,* both New York City; worked on the national desk of Office of War Information during World War II. *Member:* Sigma Delta Chi.

WRITINGS: The Golden Voice: A Biography of Isaac Kalloch, Farrar, Straus, 1947; *Splendid Poseur: Joaquin Miller, American Poet,* Crowell, 1953; *Fool's Gold,* Day, 1960; *Vicky: A Biography of Victoria C. Woodhull,* Funk, 1967. Contributor to magazines, including *American Heritage, Horizon, Sports Illustrated, Script.*

AVOCATIONAL INTERESTS: Chess, reading.††

(Died August 16, 1968)

*   *   *

MAREK, Kurt W(illi)   1915-1972
(C. W. Ceram)

PERSONAL: Born January 20, 1915, in Berlin, Germany; came to United States in 1954; son of Max R. (a carpenter) and Anna (Mistol) Marek; married Hannelore Schipmann (a stage designer), December, 1952; children: Max Alexander. *Education:* Educated at Hohenzollern-Oberreal-Schule and Lessing-Hochschule in Berlin, Germany, and at University of Berlin. *Residence:* Reinbek, Germany. *Agent:* Sanford Jerome Greenburger, 757 Third Ave., New York, N.Y. 10017.

CAREER: Began writing career in Germany in 1932, with a brief period as a literary, theater, and film critic for Berlin newspapers, although his work was aborted because of Nazi curbs on free criticism; wrote for the Ullstein chain of newspapers and worked for several German publishing firms between 1933-38; after war service did writing, editing, and publishing in Hamburg, where he was a staff writer on *Die Welt* (British-licensed daily newspaper), 1946-50, editor-in-chief for Rowohlt Verlag, 1946-52, licensee and co-owner of *Benjamin* (British-sponsored magazine for young people), 1947-48, and regular contributor to the Nordwestdeutscher Rundfunk (radio), 1948-52; free-lance writer, 1952-72, living in Western Bavaria, 1952-54, in America, 1954-71, and in Germany, 1971-72. *Military service:* German Army, 1938-45; assigned to anti-aircraft unit, later combat correspondent in Norway and Soviet Union; became first lieutenant; wounded at Battle of Cassino in Italy and taken prisoner by Allies. *Member:* P.E.N. (United States and Germany), Archaeological Institute of America, American Anthropological Association. *Awards, honors:* Barcarella Book Award (Italy) for 1952, shared with Ernest Hemingway.

WRITINGS: Wir hielten Narvik, Stalling Verlag, 1941; (editor and author of introduction) David Low, *Low's Kleine Weltgeschichte,* Rowohlt Verlag, 1949; (editor and author of introduction) Mirko Szewczuk, *Stars und Sterne,* Rowohlt Verlag, 1955; *Provokatorische Notizen,* Rowohlt Verlag, 1960, published as *Yestermorrow,* Knopf, 1961; (author of introduction) Ernest Hemingway, *Das Ende von Etwas,* Reclam, 1962.

Under pseudonym C. W. Ceram: *Goetter, Graeber und Gelehrte,* Rowohlt Verlag, 1949, translation by E. B. Garside published as *Gods, Graves and Scholars,* Knopf, 1951, revised edition, 1967; (author of introduction) Richard Lewinsohn, *Eine Geschichte der Tiere,* Rowohlt Verlag, 1952, published as *Animals, Men and Myths,* Harper, 1954; (author of introduction) *A Woman in Berlin,* published anonymously, Harcourt, 1954; *Enge Schlucht und Schwarzer Berg,* Rowohlt Verlag, 1955, translation by Richard Winston and Clara Winston published as *The Secret of the Hittites,* Knopf, 1956 (published in England as *Narrow Pass, Black Mountain: The Discovery of the Hittite Empire,* Gollancz, 1956); *Goetter, Graeber und Gelehrte im Bild,* Rowohlt Verlag, 1957, translation by Richard Winston and Clara Winston published as *March of Archaeology,* Knopf, 1958 (published in England as *Picture History of Archaeology,* Thames & Hudson, 1958); *Archaeology,* Odyssey, 1964; *Eine Archaeologie des Kinos,* Rowohlt Verlag, 1965, translation published as *Archaeology of the Cinema,* Harcourt, 1965; (editor and author of introduction) *Goetter, Graeber und Gelehrte in Dokumenten,* Rowohlt Verlag, 1965, translation published as *Hands on the Past: Pioneer Archaeologists Tell Their Own Story,* Knopf, 1966 (published in England as *The World of Archaeology: The Pioneers Tell Their Own Story,* Thames & Hudson, 1966); *The First American: A Story of North American Archaeology,* translated from the German manuscript by Richard Winston and Clara Winston, Harcourt, 1972.

Also wrote introductions to German editions of works by Sinclair Lewis, Marjorie Kinnan Rawlings, and other American writers while he worked for Rowohlt Verlag. Under pseudonym C. W. Ceram, wrote and directed six television documentaries, "Auf den Spuren der Antike," produced by NDR-Fernsehen, Hamburg, 1962-63 (American version produced as "Footsteps in the Past," Channel 13, New York, 1964).

SIDELIGHTS: Gods, Graves and Scholars has been trans-lated into 25 languages, *The Secret of the Hittites* into twelve; all of his other books have been translated into at least five languages. *Avocational interests:* Traveling.†

(Died April 12, 1972)

*   *   *

MARILLA, E(smond) L(inworth)   1900-

PERSONAL: Born February 19, 1900, in Chatham, Va.; son of Henry (a farmer) and Bettie Lee Marilla; married Theopa Collins (a librarian), April 6, 1958. *Education:* University of Richmond, B.A., 1925; Harvard University, M.A., 1929; Ohio State University, Ph.D., 1941. *Home:* 626 Kimbro Dr., Baton Rouge, La. 70808. *Office:* Department of English, Louisiana State University, Baton Rouge, La. 70803.

CAREER: Ohio State University, Columbus, instructor, 1938-42; Louisiana State University, Baton Rouge, assistant professor, 1946-51, associate professor, 1951-57, professor of English, beginning 1957. *Member:* Modern Language Association of America, Milton Society of America, Renaissance Society of America.

WRITINGS: (Editor) *The Secular Poems of Henry Vaughan,* University of Uppsala Press, 1958; *Milton and Modern Man,* University of Alabama Press, 1968. Contributor to journals. Member of editorial board, *Milton Studies,* beginning 1969.

BIOGRAPHICAL/CRITICAL SOURCES: Thomas Austin Kirby and William John Olive, editors, *Essays in Honor of Esmond Linworth Marilla,* Louisiana State University Press, 1970.†

*   *   *

MARKHAM, James W(alter)   1910-1972

PERSONAL: Born August 12, 1910, in Holland, Tex.; son of William Walter and Mabel (Goodnight) Markham; married Myrtle Sturges, March 14, 1941; children: David, Sara. *Education:* University of Texas, B.J., 1932, M.A., 1940; University of Missouri, Ph.D., 1952. *Politics:* Democrat. *Residence:* Iowa City, Iowa. *Office:* 302 Communications Center, University of Iowa, Iowa City, Iowa 52240.

CAREER: Teacher in Texas public schools, 1934-36, 1937-40; *Fort Worth Press,* Fort Worth, Tex., newsman, 1936; *Dallas Journal,* Dallas, Tex., newsman, 1940-42; University of Texas, Austin, editorial director of student publications, 1942-43; State Board of Control, Texas, executive secretary, 1943-46; Baylor University, Waco, Tex., assistant professor, 1946-48; University of Missouri, Columbia, 1948-53, began as assistant professor, became associate professor; Pennsylvania State University, University Park, 1953-62, began as associate professor, became professor and head of journalism department; University of Iowa, School of Journalism, Iowa City, professor and head of international mass communication studies, 1962-72. Consultant, Chilton Publishing Co., Philadelphia, Pa., 1956-60, and U.S. Department of Agriculture, 1968-72; lecturer, International American Federation of Working Newspapermen, Panama City, 1962; member of workshop, Swedish Institute for Peace and Conflict Research, 1967; member of selection committee, Fulbright awards in journalism, 1967-70; member of advisory board, Center for International Studies.

MEMBER: American Association for Education in Journalism (chairman of advisory board; chairman of standing committee on professional freedom and responsibility; head of international communication division, 1967), International Press Institute, World Association for Public Opinion Research, International Association for Mass Communication Research, American Association for Public Opinion Research, American Association of University Professors, International Studies Association, Sigma Delta Chi, Kappa Tau Alpha (national secretary, 1956-67). *Awards, honors:* Research award of Kappa Tau Alpha, 1954, 1967; John Cotton Dana Award, 1959; first prize, Iowa Authors Contest, 1966, for manuscript of *Voices of the Red Giants.*

WRITINGS: Bovard of the Post-Dispatch, Louisiana State University Press, 1954; (with Guido Stempel III) *Pennsylvania Press Coverage of the Presidential Campaign: A Measurement of Performance,* Pennsylvania State University Press, 1956; *Foreign News in the U.S. and South American Press: A Comparative Analysis,* Pennsylvania State University Press, 1960; *Voices of the Red Giants: Communications in Russia and China,* Iowa State University Press, 1967, revised edition, 1970; *International Images and Mass Communication Behavior: A Five-Year Study of Foreign Students,* Mass Communication Research Bureau, University of Iowa School of Journalism, 1967; (editor) *International Communication as a Field of Study,* International Communications Division, Association for Education in Journalism, University of Iowa, 1970. Contributor to *Journalism Quarterly, St. Louis Post-Dispatch,* and other publications. Editor and founder, *International Communications Bulletin,* 1966-72.

WORK IN PROGRESS: With Adriano Bruttini, *The Communist Press of Italy.*†

(Died February 7, 1972)

* * *

MARKMAN, Sidney David 1911-

PERSONAL: Born October 10, 1911, in New York, N.Y.; son of Samuel (a builder) and Eva (Bodie) Markman; married Malvina Man, March 10, 1945; children: Sarah Dinah, Alexander Jacob, Charles William. *Education:* Union College, Schenectady, N.Y., A.B., 1934; Columbia University, M.A., 1936, Ph.D., 1943. *Politics:* None. *Religion:* Jewish. *Home:* 919 Urban Ave., Durham, N.C. 27701. *Office:* Art Department, Duke University, Durham, N.C. 27706.

CAREER: Universidad Nacional de Panama, Panama City, Panama, professor of art history, and archaeology, 1941-45; did research in Hispano-American art in Central America and Mexico, 1945-47; Duke University, Durham, N.C., assistant professor, 1947-52, associate professor, 1952-64, professor of art history and archaeology, beginning 1964. Chairman, Committee on Restoration and Preservation of Historic Monuments of Panama, 1942-45; lecturer, American Institute, Guatemala, 1949; archaeological architect, Khirbet Shema Excavations, Israel, 1970. *Member:* Archaeological Institute of America, Society of Architectural Historians, Society for American Archaeology, Conference on Latin American History, International Congress of Americanists, College Art Association of America, Sociedad de Geografia e Historia de Guatemala (corresponding member). *Awards, honors:* Institute of International Education grant to Sorbonne, University of Paris, 1939; Carnegie grants in fine arts, 1936-41; American Council of Learned Societies publication grant, 1943; American Philosophical Society grants, 1959, 1968; Fulbright scholar in Spain, 1961-62.

WRITINGS: The Horse in Greek Art, Johns Hopkins Press, 1943, reprinted, Biblo & Tanen, 1969; *San Cristobal de las Casas y su arquitectura,* Escuela de Estudios

Hispano-Americanos (Seville), 1963; *The Colonial Architecture of Antigua Guatemala,* American Philosophical Society, 1966. Contributor of articles on Latin American art and architecture to various periodicals, including *Journal of the Society of Architectural Historians* and *Boletin de Instituto de Investigaciones Historicas y Esteticas* (Caracas).

WORK IN PROGRESS: Research on the colonial architecture of Central America.

* * *

MARKOVA, Alicia 1910-

PERSONAL: Original name, Lilian Alicia Marks; name changed when she was taken into Russian Ballet at fourteen; born December 1, 1910, in London, England; daughter of Arthur Tristman (an engineer) and Eileen (Barry) Marks. *Education:* Educated privately in England; studied ballet under Seraphine Astafieva and Enrico Cecchetti. *Address:* c/o Barclays Bank Ltd., 451 Oxford St., London W. 1, England.

CAREER: Danced with Diaghilev's Russian Ballet Co., 1924-29; prima ballerina with Vic-Wells Ballet Co. (now Royal Ballet), in England, 1933-35; toured with Markova-Dolin Ballet Co., 1935-37, Ballet Russe de Monte Carlo, 1938-41, Ballet Theatre (American company), 1941-46, danced with Anton Dolin in guest and concert performances, 1948-50; founder with Dolin, and prima ballerina, Festival Ballet Co., 1950-52; made guest appearances, 1952-60, including performances at Metropolitan Opera House, New York, 1953-54, 1955, 1957, 1958, and in London, Milan, Rio de Janeiro, and Denmark. Vice-president of Royal Academy of Dancing, London, beginning 1958; director of Metropolitan Opera Ballet, New York, 1963-69; Cincinnati University, Cincinnati, Ohio, professor of ballet and performing arts, 1970-73; Royal Ballet, London, England, governor, beginning 1973. *Awards, honors:* Commander, Order of the British Empire, 1958; Dame Commander, Order of the British Empire, 1963; Doctor of Music, University of Leicester, 1966.

WRITINGS: Giselle and I, Barrie & Rockliff, 1960, Vanguard, 1961.

BIOGRAPHICAL/CRITICAL SOURCES: Gordon Anthony, *Alicia Markova,* British Book Center, 1951.

* * *

MARLOWE, Amy Bell
[Collective pseudonym]

WRITINGS—All published by Grosset: *The Girl from Sunset Ranch,* 1914; *A Little Miss Nobody,* 1914; *The Oldest of Four,* 1914; *Frances of the Ranges,* 1915; *The Girls of Rivercliff School,* 1916.

SIDELIGHTS: See **ADAMS, Harriet S., STRATEMEYER, Edward L.,** and **SVENSON, Andrew E.**†

* * *

MARSH, Willard 1922-1970

PERSONAL: Born March 5, 1922, in Oakland, Calif.; son of Louis and Goldie (Greene) Marsh; married George Rae Williams (a former actress at Pasadena Playhouse), September 4, 1948. *Education:* Chico State College (now California State University, Chico), student prior to World War II; University of Iowa, B.A., 1959, M.A., 1960. *Politics:* Liberal.

CAREER: Winthrop College, Rock Hill, S.C., assistant

professor of English, 1959-61; University of Southern California, Los Angeles, assistant professor of English, 1961-64; North Texas State University, Denton, assistant professor of English, 1968-70. Free-lance writer in Mexico before and between these years. *Military service:* U.S. Army Air Forces, 1942-45; served in South Pacific; became staff sergeant. *Member:* American Association of University Professors.

WRITINGS: Week with No Friday (novel), Harper, 1965; *Beachhead in Bohemia* (stories), Louisiana State University Press, 1970. Stories anthologized in: *Best American Short Stories 1953,* Houghton, 1953; *The Antioch Review Anthology,* World Publishing, 1953; *Best Saturday Evening Post Stories 1954,* Random House, 1954; *S-F: The Year's Greatest Science-Fiction and Fantasy,* Dell, 1956; *Prize Stories 1957: The O. Henry Awards,* Doubleday, 1957; *Midland,* Random House, 1961; *Best American Short Stories 1961,* Houghton, 1961; *Beachhead in Bohemia: Stories,* Louisiana State University Press, 1969. Contributor of short stories, poems, and articles to several dozen magazines, ranging from *Playboy* to *Yale Review.*

WORK IN PROGRESS: Fiction, both short and long.

SIDELIGHTS: Willard Marsh worked part way through Chico State College as a dance band musician. He took up writing as an antidote to boredom while serving as a radio operator at Pacific outposts during the war.

BIOGRAPHICAL/CRITICAL SOURCES: First Novelist, spring, 1965; *New York Times Book Review,* July 19, 1970.†

(Died, 1970)

*   *   *

MARSHALL, Howard D(rake)   1924-1972

PERSONAL: Born April 9, 1924, in Poughkeepsie, N.Y.; son of Smith J. (a real estate broker) and Florence (Drake) Marshall; married Natalie Junemann (a professor), August 6, 1954; children: Frederick S., Alison B. *Education:* Columbia University, A.B., 1947, M.A., 1949, Ph.D., 1954. *Home:* 87 Raymond Ave., Poughkeepsie, N.Y. 12601.

CAREER: Vassar College, Poughkeepsie, N.Y., instructor, 1949-54, assistant professor, 1954-59, associate professor, 1959-66, professor of economics, 1966-72. Visiting assistant professor, Wesleyan University, Middletown, Conn., 1955-56. *Military service:* U.S. Army, 1943-46. *Member:* American Economic Association, Industrial Relations Research Association, National Tax Association, American Association of University Professors.

WRITINGS: The Mobility of College Faculties, Pageant, 1964; *The Great Economists,* Pitman, 1967; (editor with wife, Natalie J. Marshall) *The History of Economic Thought: A Book of Readings,* Pitman, 1968; (editor) *Business and Government: The Problem of Power,* Heath, 1970; (with Natalie J. Marshall) *Collective Bargaining* (text), Random House, 1971. Contributor to economic and political science journals.†

(Died August 15, 1972)

*   *   *

MARSHALL, Lenore Guinzburg   1899-1971

PERSONAL: Born September 7, 1899, in New York, N.Y.; daughter of Henry Aaron (a businessman) and Leonie (Kleinert) Guinzburg; married James Marshall (a lawyer and political scientist), August 20, 1919; children: Ellen (Mrs. Roger Scholle), Jonathan. *Education:* Barnard College,

B.A., 1919. *Religion:* Jewish and Quaker. *Agent;* McIntosh & Otis, Inc., 18 East 41st St., New York, N.Y. 10017.

CAREER: Jonathan Cape & Harrison Smith (publishers), New York, N.Y., literary editor, 1929-34; author. Founder with Clarence Pickett and Norman Cousins, and member of executive committee, National Committee for a Sane Nuclear Policy, 1956. Founder and co-chairman with John W. Gofman and Charles E. Goodell, Committee for Nuclear Responsibility, 1971. *Member:* P.E.N. (member of board of directors), Poetry Society of America, Authors Guild of the Authors League of America, Pen and Brush Club.

WRITINGS: Only the Fear (novel), Macmillan, 1935; *Hall of Mirrors* (novel), Macmillan, 1937; *No Boundary* (poetry), Holt, 1943; *Other Knowledge* (poetry), Noonday Press, 1957; *The Hill Is Level* (novel), Random House, 1959; *Latest Will* (poetry), Norton, 1969. Contributor of short stories and articles to periodicals. A recording of her poems has been produced by Spoken Arts.

WORK IN PROGRESS: A novel; short stories.

BIOGRAPHICAL/CRITICAL SOURCES: Christian Science Monitor, August 7, 1969.†

(Died September 25, 1971)

*   *   *

MARSHALL, Ronald   1905-

PERSONAL: Born March 16, 1905; son of Barton and Lucy (Sunderland) Marshall. *Education:* Cambridge University, B.A., 1926, M.A., 1930. *Politics:* Northern Ireland Alliance Party. *Religion:* Church of Ireland.

CAREER: Stranmillis College of Education, Belfast, Northern Ireland, principal lecturer in history and head of social studies department, 1946-66. *Member:* Italian Institute (London), Society for Italian Studies, Belfast Literary Society (past president).

WRITINGS: Massimo d'Azeglio: An Artist in Politics, 1798-1866, Oxford University Press, 1966; *Methodist College, Belfast: A Centenary History,* Methodist College, 1968.

WORK IN PROGRESS: A History of Stranmillis College, Belfast, 1922-72; and *Rome, 1815-1846: The Political and Social Background.*††

*   *   *

MARSHALL, Thomas F(rederic)   1908-

PERSONAL: Born June 3, 1908, in Waterbury, Conn.; son of T. Frederic (a businessman) and May (Russell) Marshall; married Elizabeth Johnson (a landscape architect), August 14, 1937. *Education:* Temple University, B.A., 1931; University of Pennsylvania, M.A., 1932, Ph.D., 1941. *Politics:* Republican. *Religion:* Episcopalian. *Home:* Skyfield Emory Rd., Upperco, Md. 21155.

CAREER: Teacher in public schools of Pennsylvania and Delaware, 1932-36; Valley Forge Military Academy and Junior College, Wayne, Pa., head of English department, 1937-43; Western Maryland College, Westminster, associate professor, later professor of American literature, 1943-55; Kent State University, Kent, Ohio, professor of English, 1955-72, professor emeritus, 1972—, head of department, 1955-62. Faculty fellow, Duke University, 1953; Fulbright professor of American literature, University of Athens, 1953-54; Smith-Mundt Visiting Professor of American Studies, National University of Mexico, 1962-63. *Member:* Modern Language Association of America (chairman of literature and society section, 1960; chairman of English drama section, 1968), American Studies Association (member of executive committee, 1964-68), American Society for Theatre Research (archivist, 1956-70; chairman, 1970-73; member of international executive committee, beginning 1971), National Council of Teachers of English, Modern Humanities Research Association, American Association of University Professors, College English Association (director, 1949-54, 1959-61), Middle Atlantic College English Association (president, 1947-49), Ohio-Indiana American Studies Association (president, 1958-59), Northeast Ohio College English Group (president, 1959), Sigma Phi Epsilon.

WRITINGS: A History of the Philadelphia Theatre, 1878-79, [Westminster, Md.], 1943; *An Analytical Index to American Literature*, Duke University Press, 1954, revised and enlarged edition, 1963; *Three Voices of the American Tradition: Poe, Melville and Hemingway*, Ikaros Press (Athens), 1955; *Literature and Society, 1950-1955: A Selective Bibliography*, Miami University Press, 1956; *Literature and Society, 1955-60: A Selective Bibliography*, Miami University Press, 1962; *Compassion, Sacrificio y Perseverencia: La Obra de Faulkner*, Aguillar (Mexico), 1963.

WORK IN PROGRESS: Analytical Index to the "American Quarterly"; The Philadelphia Theatre from 1878 to 1890: A History and Day-Book.†

*   *   *

MARTIN, Eugene
[Collective pseudonym]

WRITINGS—"Sky Flyers" series; published by Henry Altemus Co.: *Randy Starr above Stormy Seas*, 1931; *. . . after an Air Prize*, 1931; *. . . Leading the Air Circus*, 1932.

SIDELIGHTS: See **ADAMS, Harriet S., STRATEMEYER, Edward L.,** and **SVENSON, Andrew E.**†

*   *   *

MASEFIELD, John (Edward)   1878-1967

PERSONAL: Born June 1, 1878 (although this is his official birthday, he notes in his autobiography that "there is some doubt of the day"), in Ledbury, Herefordshire, England; son of George Edward (a solicitor) and Carolyn (Parker) Masefield; raised by an uncle, William, after the death of his parents; married Constance de la Cherois-Crommelin, 1903 (died, 1960); children: Lewis (killed in action, 1942), Judith (illustrator of several of Masefield's books). *Education:* Briefly attended King's School, Warwick, England (ran away when he was about thirteen). *Home:* Burcote Brook, Abingdon, Berkshire, England.

CAREER: Indentured to a merchant ship, "Conway," about 1892; apprenticed aboard a windjammer about a year and a half later and sailed around Cape Horn to Chile where he became ill and returned to England by steamer; shipped aboard the White Star liner "Adriatic" as sixth officer but left the ship when she docked in New York; lived in Greenwich Village, New York City, 1895-97 (except for an interval in which he traveled as a hobo to California and back), and worked in a bakery, in a livery stable, on the waterfront, and in the saloon of Luke O'Connor's Columbian Hotel; moved to Yonkers, New York, where he worked as a "mistake finder" in a carpet factory; returned to England in 1897 and became friendly with John Millington Synge in London, then spent one summer in Devonshire with William Butler Yeats; about 1900 he became literary editor of the *Speaker* and was subsequently recommended to the *Manchester*

Guardian for which he wrote articles and organized a "Miscellany" feature (he served on the permanent staff of the *Guardian* for about six months); in 1930 King George appointed him Poet Laureate of England succeeding Robert Bridges. Appointed chairman of the committee acting on the awards of the King's medals for poetry, 1933; member of British Council's Books and Periodicals Committee; lectured in Turkey and other European countries for the British Council; frequent lecturer in the United States. *Military service:* During World War I served with the Red Cross in France and on the Gallipoli Peninsula. *Member:* Royal Society of Literature (member of academic committee, 1913; Companion, 1961), Incorporated Society of Authors, Playwrights and Composers (president, 1937-67). *Awards, honors:* Polignac Prize for Poetry, 1912; D. Litt., Oxford University, 1922; LL.D., University of Aberdeen, 1922; Order of Merit, 1935; Hanseatic Shakespeare Prize, Hamburg University, 1938; William Foyle Prize, 1961, for *The Bluebells and Other Verses*.

WRITINGS—Poetry: *Salt-Water Ballads*, Grant Richards, 1902, Macmillan, 1913; *Ballads and Poems*, Mathews, 1910; *The Everlasting Mercy*, Sidgwick & Jackson, 1911; *The Story of a Round-House*, Macmillan, 1912, revised edition, 1913; *The Widow in the Bye Street*, Sidgwick & Jackson, 1912; *The Daffodil Fields*, Macmillan, 1913; *Dauber: A Poem*, Heinemann, 1913; *Philip the King, and Other Poems*, Macmillan, 1914 (*Philip the King* published separately in England, Heinemann, 1927); *Good Friday: A Dramatic Poem*, Macmillan, 1915, published with additional poems as *Good Friday, and Other Poems*, 1916; *Sonnets* (from *Good Friday, and Other Poems*), Macmillan, 1916; *Sonnets and Poems* (from *Good Friday, and Other Poems*), privately printed, 1916; *Salt-Water Poems and Ballads*, Macmillan, 1916, published as *Salt-Water Ballads and Poems*, 1923; *Lollingdon Downs, and Other Poems*, Macmillan, 1917; *The Cold Cotswolds*, Express Printing Works, 1917; *Rosas*, Macmillan, 1918; *Reynard the Fox*, Macmillan, 1919, new edition, 1920; *Enslaved*, Macmillan, 1920, published with additional poems as *Enslaved, and Other Poems*, 1923; *Right Royal*, Macmillan, 1920; *King Cole*, Macmillan, 1921; *The Dream*, Macmillan, 1922, published with additional poems as *The Dream, and Other Poems*, 1923; *Sonnets of Good Cheer to the Lena Ashwell Players, From Their Well-Wisher, John Masefield*, Mendip Press, 1926; *Midsummer Night, and Other Tales in Verse*, Macmillan, 1928; *South and East*, Macmillan, 1929; *The Wanderer of Liverpool*, Macmillan, 1930; *Minnie Maylow's Story, and Other Tales and Scenes*, Macmillan, 1931; *A Tale of Troy*, Macmillan, 1932; *A Letter From Pontus, and Other Verse*, Macmillan, 1936; *The Country Scene in Poems*, Collins (London), 1937, Collins (New York), 1938; *Tribute to Ballet in Poems*, Macmillan, 1938; *Some Verses to Some Germans*, Macmillan, 1939; *Gautama the Enlightened, and Other Verse*, Macmillan, 1941; *Generation Risen*, Collins, 1942, Macmillan, 1943; *Land Workers*, Heinemann, 1942, Macmillan, 1943; *Wonderings*, Macmillan, 1943; *On the Hill*, Macmillan, 1949; *The Bluebells, and Other Verses*, Macmillan, 1961; *Old Raiger, and Other Verse*, Heinemann, 1964, Macmillan, 1965; *In Glad Thanksgiving*, Macmillan, 1967. Also author of *Animula*, 1920.

Novels: *Captain Margaret*, Grant Richards, 1908, Macmillan, 1916, reprinted, Scholarly Press, 1972; *Multitude and Solitude*, Grant Richards, 1909, Macmillan, 1916; *The Street of To-Day*, Dutton, 1911; *Sard Harker*, Macmillan, 1924, reprinted, Heinemann, 1956; *Odtaa*, Macmillan, 1926, reprinted, Penguin, 1966; *The Midnight Folk*, Macmillan,

1927; *The Hawbucks,* Macmillan, 1929; *The Bird of Dawning,* Macmillan, 1933, reprinted, 1967; *The Taking of the Gry,* Macmillan, 1934; *The Box of Delights,* Macmillan, 1935, reprinted, Heinemann, 1957; *Victorious Troy, or, The Hurrying Angel,* Macmillan, 1935; *Eggs and Baker,* Macmillan, 1936; *The Square Peg, or, The Gun Fella,* Macmillan, 1937; *Dead Ned,* Macmillan, 1938, reprinted, Heinemann, 1970; *Live and Kicking Ned,* Macmillan, 1939, reprinted, Heinemann, 1970.

Short stories: *The Mainsail Haul,* Mathews, 1905, revised edition, Macmillan, 1913; *A Tarpaulin Muster,* B. W. Dodge, 1908, reprinted, Books for Libraries, 1970.

Plays: *The Tragedy of Nan,* Kennerley, 1909; *The Tragedy of Pompey the Great,* Little, Brown, 1910, revised edition, Macmillan, 1914, reprinted Sidgwick & Jackson, 1964; *The Faithful* (three-act tragedy), Heinemann, 1915; *Good Friday: A Play in Verse,* Garden City Press, 1916, reprinted, Heinemann, 1955; *The Locked Chest* [and] *The Sweeps of Ninety-Eight* (prose plays), Macmillan, 1916; *Melloney Holtspur,* Macmillan, 1922; *A King's Daughter* (verse play), Macmillan, 1923; *The Trial of Jesus,* Macmillan, 1925; *Tristan and Isolt* (verse play), Heinemann, 1927; *The Coming of Christ,* Macmillan, 1928; *Easter: A Play for Singers,* Macmillan, 1929; *End and Beginning,* Macmillan, 1933; *A Play of Saint George,* Macmillan, 1948. Also author of "The Campden Wonder," 1907.

Juvenile: *A Book of Discoveries,* F. A. Stokes, 1910; *Lost Endeavor,* Nelson, 1910; *Martin Hyde: The Duke's Messenger,* Little, Brown, 1910; *Jim Davis,* F. A. Stokes, 1912, reprinted, Penguin, 1966, published as *The Captive of the Smugglers,* Page, 1918.

Essays and studies: *Sea Life in Nelson's Time,* Methuen, 1905, Macmillan, 1925, reprinted, Books for Libraries, 1969, 3rd edition, U.S. Naval Institute, 1971; *On the Spanish Main, or, Some English Forays on the Isthmus of Darien,* Macmillan, 1906, new edition, Naval Institute Press, 1972; *William Shakespeare,* Holt, 1911, reprinted, Fawcett, 1964, quartercentenary edition, Barnes & Noble, 1969; *John M. Synge,* Macmillan, 1915, reprinted, Folcroft Press, 1970; *Gallipoli,* Macmillan, 1916, 13th edition, 1925; *The Old Front Line, or, The Beginning of the Battle of the Somme,* Macmillan, 1917, published as *The Battle of the Somme,* Heinemann, 1919, reprinted, C. Chivers, [Bath], 1968; *The War and the Future,* Macmillan, 1918 (published in England as *St. George and the Dragon,* Heinemann, 1919); *John Ruskin,* Yellowsands Press, 1920; *Shakespeare and Spiritual Life,* Oxford University Press, 1924, reprinted, Folcroft Press, 1969; *With the Living Voice: An Address,* Macmillan, 1925; *Chaucer,* Macmillan, 1931; *Poetry,* Heinemann, 1931, Macmillan, 1932; *The Conway: From Her Foundation to the Present Day,* Macmillan, 1933; *The Nine Days Wonder* (story of the Dunkirk retreat), Macmillan, 1941; *Conquer: A Tale of the Nika Rebellion in Byzantium,* Macmillan, 1941; *Thanks Before Going: Notes on Some of the Original Poems of Dante Gabriel Rosetti,* Heinemann, 1946, Macmillan, 1947, reissued as *Thanks Before Going, With Other Gratitude for Old Delight,* Heinemann, 1947; *Baden Parchments,* Heinemann, 1947; *St. Katherine of Ledbury, and Other Ledbury Papers,* Heinemann, 1951; *An Elizabethan Theatre in London,* Oxford University, 1954; *The Western Hudson Shore,* [New York], 1962; *The Twenty-five Days,* Heinemann, 1972.

Other: *The Taking of Helen,* Macmillan, 1923, new edition with additional material published as *The Taking of Helen, and Other Prose Selections,* Macmillan, 1924; *Recent Prose,* Heinemann, 1924, revised edition, 1932, Macmillan, 1933; *Prologue to a Book of Pictures of Adventure by Sea,* [New York], 1925; *Any Dead to Any Living,* [New Haven], 1928; *A Masque of Liverpool,* Brown Brothers, 1930; *Lines on the Tercentenary of Harvard University,* Macmillan, 1936; *Basilissa: A Tale of the Empress Theodore* (fictional biography), Macmillan, 1930; *Some Memories of W. B. Yeats,* Macmillan, 1940, reprinted, Irish University Press, 1971; *In the Mill* (autobiography), Macmillan, 1941; *Shopping in Oxford,* Heinemann, 1941; *Natalie Maisie and Pavilastukay,* Macmillan, 1942; *I Want! I Want!,* National Book League, 1944, Macmillan, 1945; *Macbeth Production,* Heinemann, 1945, Macmillan, 1946; *New Chum,* Macmillan, 1945; *Book of Both Sorts,* Heinemann, 1947; *In Praise of Nurses,* Heinemann, 1950; *A Book of Prose Selections,* Heinemann, 1950; *The Ledbury Scene as I Have Used It in My Verse,* Hereford, 1951; *So Long to Learn: Chapters of an Autobiography,* Macmillan, 1952; *Grace Before Ploughing* (autobiographical sketches), Macmillan, 1966.

Collections: *The Everlasting Mercy* [and] *The Widow in the Bye Street,* Macmillan, 1912, new edition, 1919; *Poems of John Masefield,* Macmillan, 1917; *The Poems and Plays of John Masefield,* Macmillan, 1918; *A Poem and Two Plays,* Heinemann, 1919; *Dauber* [and] *The Daffodil Fields,* Macmillan, 1923; *Selected Poems,* Heinemann, 1922, Macmillan, 1923, 3rd edition, Heinemann, 1950, new edition, 1961; *King Cole, The Dream, and Other Poems,* Macmillan, 1923; *Philip the King, and Other Poems; Good Friday: A Play in Verse; Lollingdon Downs, and Other Poems, with Sonnets,* Macmillan, 1923; *The Collected Poems of John Masefield,* Heinemann, 1923, new edition, 1932, revised edition published as *Poems,* 1946; *Poems,* two volumes, Macmillan, 1925, published in one volume, 1930, 3rd edition with new poems, 1958; *Prose Plays,* Macmillan, 1925; *Verse Plays,* Macmillan, 1925; *Plays,* Heinemann, 1937; *Dead Ned* [and] *Live and Kicking Ned,* Macmillan, 1941; *Dauber* [and] *Reynard the Fox,* Heinemann, 1962, Macmillan, 1963.

Editor: (With wife, Constance Masefield) *Lyrists of the Restoration from Sir Edward Sherbourne to William Congreve,* Grant Richards, 1905; W. Dampier, *Voyages,* Dutton, 1906; *A Sailor's Garland,* Methuen, 1906, Macmillan, 1924, reprinted, Books for Libraries, 1969; (with Constance Masefield) *Essays, Moral and Polite, 1660-1714,* Grant Richards, 1906, reprinted, 1930, and Books for Libraries, 1971; *Defoe* (selections), Macmillan, 1909; (and translator) Jean Racine, *Esther* (play), Heinemann, 1922; (and translator) Racine, *Berenice* (play), Macmillan, 1922; *My Favourite English Poems,* Macmillan, 1950; (and author of introductions) Shakespeare, *Three Tragedies,* Dodd, 1965; (and author of introductions) Shakespeare, *Three Comedies,* Dodd, 1965; (and author of introductions) Shakespeare, *Three Histories,* Dodd, 1966; (and author of introductions) Shakespeare, *Tragedies II,* Dodd, 1966; (and author of introductions) Shakespeare, *Commedies II,* Dodd, 1967. Editor of several collections for Dent's "Everyman's Library" series.

Author of introduction: *Chronicles of the Pilgrim Fathers,* Dutton, 1910; George Anson, *Voyage Round the World in the Years 1740-1744,* Dutton, 1911; Richard Hakluyt, *Voyages,* Dutton, 1962. (See also Shakespeare collections, above.)

SIDELIGHTS: In 1913 an *American Review of Reviews* writer noted: "[*The Daffodil Fields*] is filled with Masefield's own peculiar literary beauties that mark his passionate gift of simple utterance; the art to tell a simple tale and yet reflect all of heaven and earth within it as a pool of water reflects the sky." For over seventy years Masefield told stories that excited his readers. His prosody was variously praised and deprecated, but his talent as a storyteller remains unquestioned. More than fifty years ago, a *New York Times* reviewer wrote: "[Masefield's work] bears the stamp of verity wherever the scene may be, and holds one's attention breathlessly in every part, in spite of its simplicity." And in 1961 Donald Davie recognized Masefield's venerability: "For the most part Masefield's poems still belong to the world of the 'Come all ye,' the street-ballad and modern folk-lyric. . . . It's delightful to be reminded that we have with us still a professional improviser of this ancient sort. He is probably the last of his kind."

In the autobiographical sketch included in Schreiber's *Portraits and Self-Portraits,* Masefield described his earliest poetic inclination: "While living in Yonkers in 1896, I first became acquainted with the works of the English poet Chaucer. The reading of his poems turned me to a systematic study of the English poets and also made me determined to attempt to write poetry." Masefield later spoke of the three distinct eras that composed his long career as a poet. In the preface to the 1958 edition of his collected poems he noted that his first period was characterized by an intense desire for escape and freedom. Later he devoted himself to the composition of long tales in verse and finally turned to "dramatic production and verse-speaking." (For many years Masefield maintained a small theater in his home for the production of verse plays.)

Although his early work won far more acclaim than his later verse, Masefield's poems were rarely greeted with unqualified praise. In 1913 the *Saturday Review of Literature* writer noted: "In Mr. Masefield it is the rush of his lines, their momentum and energy, that makes his poem. Our only doubt, which often runs to certainty, is that this momentum is less the momentum of genius than the momentum of an extremely clever writer exploiting an amazing facility of style and emotion." But the later poems frequently exhibited only what John Malcolm Brinin called "tired competence." Anthony Thwaite wrote of one narrative poem, "It has a kind of stately flatness, which sometimes takes one step down into bathos." And Dudley Fitts deplored Masefield's increasing ineptitude as early as 1950: "No man living has served poetry longer and with more devotion than has the present Laureate, but the publication of this book of new poems [*On the Hill*] is regrettable. Whatever ardor, whatever creative energy Mr. Masefield has displayed in the past . . . is shown here either in sad dilution or in an unconscious and cruel kind of self-parody. There are occasional passages of beauty, and of course the essential sweetness of the man is apparent everywhere; but these are not enough to outweigh the appalling mediocrity of the verse, both in content and execution."

A few critics of the later work were willing to examine the poems apart from the context of contemporary poetry. Thomas Lask wrote: ". . . Though he may have looked at the 20th-century world, it was with 19th-century eyes. The forms, the mold, the very rhythms carried with them old-fashioned comfort. 'Poets,' [Masefield] wrote, 'are great or little according to the nobleness of their endeavor to build a mansion for soul.' It is not only the didacticism of this sentiment but also the language in which it is couched that indicates his distance from the contemporary world." Margery Fisher added: "Over the years, Masefield has been defining imagination for us, by precept and example. I think he can never have been afraid of the tug between reality and fantasy that bedevils so many writers. He is a formidably straight and simple visionary."

Nevertheless, the modern critic is constantly aware that most of Masefield's verse is now "unfashionable." Paul Engle wrote: "There are many lines of great verbal attractiveness [in *The Bluebells and Other Verses*] in which the traditional subjects are treated in the traditional manner. Nothing is here to startle or amaze. Conventional beauty is conventionally reported. Many fine lyrical passages occur, but the dominant tone is one of subdued mediation on bluebells, ships, farms—the usual substance of John Masefield's books. All of that world has tremendous attractiveness, and yet it is very hard to accept the result as poetry which has truly confronted this actual world." Robert Hillyer, on the other hand, saw a purer sort of beauty in this collection. "Age has renewed Masefield's laurels more richly than ever," he wrote. "Here is the delight in fine stanza forms—the couplet, the rime royal, the Spenserian stanza and several of his own invention—and here the well-modulated rise from realistic effects to the high apostrophes of rapture."

It is, however, the earliest poems with which Masefield's name will most readily be associated. More than fifty years ago an *American Review of Reviews* writer said prophetically of *Salt-Water Ballads,* "These ballads of the sea, torn freshly from his . . . recent experiences, will quite likely remain to the end of his life the freshest and purest of all the Masefield posey." Indeed, Masefield's *Sea Fever* was published in this 1902 collection and there are few today who do not recognize its opening statement: "I must go down to the seas again, to the lonely sea and the sky. And all I ask is a tall ship and a star to steer her by." According to one *Time* reviewer, "Masefield led English poetry out of its Victorian sententiousness and thus earned his modest place in the poets' pantheon." When he was awarded the Laureateship in 1930 he was already "safe from obscurity," continued the *Time* reviewer, "[and] thus turned out only occasionally the dutiful doggerel that has so often been the lot of poets laureate." Masefield himself wrote in one of his last books, "It is time now to pipe down and coil up."

In his novels, as in his poems, Masefield's achievement was his ability to tell a fresh and energetic tale in unpretentious language. His most famous novel is probably *Sard Harker,* but in 1924 P. A. Hutchinson wrote of this book: "*Sard Harker* will not live; it will not go down as a great novel, or even as a great romance. Masefield has drunk a little too freely of the milk of Paradise. But the yarn—yes, that will have to be the final designation—must not be missed. Assuredly it must not be missed." The *Times Literary Supplement* reviewer cited the "matter-of-fact precision" with which *Sard Harker* was composed. "You must have greatness of mind, and greatness of art as well," he wrote, "to be capable of telling a simple adventure story about simple people in simple sentences, and making of the whole a great heroic tale."

Dead Ned and its sequel, *Live and Kicking Ned,* were also praised as excellent stories, imaginatively conceived. The *Boston Transcript* reviewer wrote: "In a day when a goodly portion is patently written in exposition of a thesis, it is refreshing to pick up a book that has no social, economic or emotional problem, past or present, in need of interpretation. Adventure, pure and simple, is the stuff of which John Masefield's latest romance, *Dead Ned,* is compounded." The *Times Literary Supplement* writer stated that "Mr. Masefield's is the art of reflecting life in a double glass so as to capture a twice-faithful image. It with the lessons of philosophy learned by experience, full of gentle skepticism also." William Soskin, impressed with the orignality shown in the

Ned sequence, even implied that Masefield's prose showed more skill than his poems. "Masefield contrives to incorporate nuances of satirical and reflective meaning," Soskin wrote, "which suggests he would be more wholesomely occupied as a Homer of adventure than an official poet for his native little island."

Masefield's autobiographical pieces were among his last writings, and those who read them were impressed with his ability to recall the excitement of the many "bright festivals" in his past. Chinua Achebe, in his review of *Grace Before Ploughing,* recalled the entire achievement of Masefield's career: "[He] took me along and I saw with wide-eyed wonder the sights of his childhood and felt something of the terror planted in his young mind by protective, well-meaning adults. . . . Masefield's art astonishes by the simplicity of its line. I think it comes from a rare gift of sight that reveals to those who possess it 'the unutterable worth of humble things.'"

A memorial service for Masefield was held at Westminster Abbey on June 20, 1967; Robert Graves gave the address and C. Day Lewis read from Masefield's works.

BIOGRAPHICAL/CRITICAL SOURCES: New York Times, April 16, 1913, March 12, 1950, May 13, 1967; *American Review of Reviews,* June, 1913, November, 1913; *Saturday Review (of Literature),* November 8, 1913, November 4, 1961; *Times Literary Supplement,* October 16, 1924, September 24, 1938, June 22, 1967; *International Book Review,* December, 1924; Georges Schreiber, editor, *Portraits and Self-Portraits,* Houghton, 1936; *Boston Transcript,* November 5, 1938; *New Yorker,* November 4, 1939; *New York Herald Tribune Books,* November 12, 1939; *Spectator,* June 9, 1961; *New Statesman,* June 16, 1961, June 17, 1966; *Chicago Sunday Tribune,* October 1, 1961; *New York Times Book Review,* October 15, 1961; *Kenyon Review,* March, 1967; *Publishers' Weekly,* April 10, 1967; *Time,* May 19, 1967; *Newsweek,* May 22, 1967.†

(Died May 12, 1967)

* * *

MASON, Edwin A. 1905-

PERSONAL: Born April 25, 1905, in Nottingham, England; son of Robert Augustus and Nora E. (Rayworth) Mason; married Mina L. Venot, December 23, 1933; children: Sylvia Margaret Mason Chisholm, Patsy Joyce. *Education:* Educated in England. *Politics:* Independent. *Religion:* Unitarian Universalist. *Office:* Massachusetts Audubon Society, Gordon Hall, South Lincoln, Mass. 01773.

CAREER: Professional wildlife manager, working since 1926 with the conservation movement; in charge of Wharton Bird Banding Station in Groton, Mass., 1926-43; creator and director of Audubon's Arcadia Wildlife Sanctuary in Northampton, Mass., 1944-62, arranging interpretive conservation programs, nature tours, a day camp, and other programs; director of department of wildlife management, Massachusetts Audubon Society, South Lincoln, beginning 1962. Lecturer and consultant on land management, natural resources conservation, forestry, and horticulture; assisted in formation of first South American conservation movement, headquartered in Buenos Aires. *Member:* Wildlife Society (charter member), American Ornithologists' Union, American Nature Study Society, Association of Interpretive Naturalists, Northeastern Bird-Banding Association (past president).

WRITINGS: Robins (juvenile), Follett, 1966; *Swans and*

Wild Geese (juvenile), Follett, 1970. Contributor to *Audubon Encyclopedia;* contributor of about seventy articles to scientific and popular publications, including *New York Times, Christian Science Monitor, Yankee,* and *Junior Natural History.* Columnist, *Hampshire Gazette,* 1947-48.††

* * *

MASSEY, Mary Elizabeth 1915-197(?)

PERSONAL: Born December 25, 1915, in Morrilton, Ark.; daughter of Charles Leonidas and Mary (McClung) Massey. *Education:* Hendrix College, B.A., 1937; University of North Carolina, M.A., 1940, Ph.D., 1947. *Home:* 505 College Ave., Rock Hill, S.C. 29730.

CAREER: High school teacher in Arkansas, 1937-39; Hendrix College, Conway, Ark., head of department of history in Training School, 1940-42; Flora Macdonald College, Red Springs, N.C., professor of history, 1942-44; University of North Carolina, Chapel Hill, teaching fellow, 1944-46; Washington College, Chestertown, Md., assistant professor of history, 1947-50; Winthrop College, Rock Hill, S.C., associate professor, 1950-54, professor of history, beginning 1954, chairman of department, 1960-64. Member of advisory council, National Civil War Centennial Commission, 1960-66; member, South Carolina Tricentennial Commission.

MEMBER: American Historical Association, Organization of American Historians, Southern Historical Association (executive council, 1959-61; chairman of program committee, 1962), South Carolina Historical Association, Phi Alpha Theta. *Awards, honors:* Henry E. Huntington research grant, 1963; Guggenheim fellowship, 1963-64; Distinguished Alumna Award, Hendrix College, 1967.

WRITINGS: Ersatz in the Confederacy, University of South Carolina Press, 1952; (contributor) Rinaldo Simenini, editor, *Education in the South,* Longwood College, 1959; *Refugee Life in the Confederacy,* Louisiana State University Press, 1964; *Bonnet Brigades: American Women and the Civil War,* Knopf, 1966. Contributor to *New Index* (London), and regional history journals.†

(Deceased)

* * *

MATHEW, David 1902-1975

PERSONAL: Born January 15, 1902, in Lyme Regis, Dorsetshire, England; son of Francis (a barrister-at-law) and Agnes (Woodroffe) Mathew. *Education:* Balliol College, Oxford, B.A., 1923, M.A., 1927; Trinity College, Dublin, Litt.D., 1933. *Home:* Stonor Park, near Henley on Thames, Oxfordshire, England.

CAREER: Ordained to Roman Catholic priesthood, 1929; assistant priest at St. David's Cathedral, Cardiff, Wales, 1930-34; chaplain to Catholics at University of London, London, England, 1934-44; titular bishop of Aeliae and auxiliary bishop of Westminster, 1938-46; apostolic visitor to Ethiopia, 1945; archbishop of Apamea and apostolic delegate to British East and West Africa, 1946-53; bishop to Her Majesty's Forces, 1954-63. Ford's Lecturer in Modern History, Oxford University, 1944-45; Ballard Mathews Lecturer, University College of North Wales, Bangor, 1952-53. Conventual chaplain of Knights of Malta, beginning 1936. *Military service:* Royal Navy, midshipman, 1918-19. *Member:* Royal Society of Literature (fellow), Society of Antiquaries (fellow), Athenaeum Club (London). *Awards, honors:* LL.D., University of Glasgow, 1958; Grand Officer of Order of Polonia Restituta.

WRITINGS: The Celtic Peoples and Renaissance Europe, Sheed, 1933, reprinted, Phaeton, 1974; (with Gervase Mathew) *The Reformation and the Contemplative Life,* Sheed, 1934; *Catholicism in England,* Longmans, Green, 1936, 3rd edition, Eyre & Spottiswoode, 1955; *Steam Packet* (novel), Longmans, Green, 1936; *The Jacobean Age,* Longmans, Green, 1938, reprinted, Kennikat, 1973; *British Seamen,* Collins, 1943; *The Naval Heritage,* Collins, 1944; *Acton: The Formative Years,* Eyre & Spottiswoode, 1945, reprinted, Greenwood Press, 1974; *Ethiopia: The Study of a Polity, 1540-1935,* Collins, 1947, reprinted, Greenwood Press, 1974; *The Social Structure in Caroline England* (Ford lectures), Clarendon Press, 1948; *Sir Tobie Mathew,* Clarke, Irwin, 1950; *The Mango on the Mango Tree* (fiction), Collins, 1951; *The Age of Charles I,* Eyre & Spottiswoode, 1951; *The Prince of Wales' Feathers* (fiction), Collins, 1953; *In Vallombrosa* (novel), Collins, 1952; *Scotland Under Charles I,* Eyre & Spottiswoode, 1955; (editor) *The Westminster Hymnal,* new and revised edition, Burns & Oates, 1965; *James I,* Eyre & Spottiswoode, 1967, University of Alabama Press, 1968; *Lord Acton and His Times,* University of Alabama Press, 1968; *The Courtiers of Henry VIII,* Eyre & Spottiswoode, 1970; *Lady Jane Grey: The Setting of the Reign,* Methuen, 1972.

BIOGRAPHICAL/CRITICAL SOURCES: New Statesman, December 6, 1968; *Spectator,* February 14, 1969; *Yale Review,* October, 1969; *Observer Review,* December 20, 1970; *Bookseller,* January 9, 1971.†

(Died December, 1975)

*   *   *

MATHEWS, Evelyn Craw   1906-
(Nancy Cleaver)

PERSONAL: Born September 27, 1906, in St. Helen's, Ontario, Canada; daughter of Robert Wilson (a minister of United Church of Canada) and Ethel (Plewes) Craw; married Arnold A. Mathews (a minister of United Church of Canada); children: David Craw, Rosemary (Mrs. David MacBrien Knight), Nancy. *Education:* University of Toronto, B.A. (honors in modern history), 1930. *Religion:* United Church of Canada.

CAREER: United Church of Canada, national girls work secretary, 1930-36; Winnipeg (Manitoba) Public Library, librarian in children's department, 1960-65; part-time teacher in Winnipeg, Manitoba, and Espanola, Ontario, 1965-66; free-lance writer. Onetime youth camp counselor. *Member:* Canadian Authors Association. *Awards, honors:* Prize for best radio series promoting appreciation of French language and culture from Province of Quebec, 1964; first prize for public speaking from Toronto Women's Liberal Club.

*WRITINGS—*Under pseudonym Nancy Cleaver: *The Treasury of Family Fun,* Revell, 1960; *Fell's Guide to Camping and Family Fun Outdoors,* Fell, 1965; (with Alvin Tresselt) *The Legend of the Willow Plate,* Parents' Magazine Press, 1968. Writer of weekly syndicated newspaper column, "For Parents Only." Contributor to magazines, including *Blackie's, Rod and Gun, American Home, Star Weekly, Chatelaine;* also contributor to juvenile periodicals and to church and Sunday school weeklies.

SIDELIGHTS: Evelyn Mathews has traveled in Germany as guest of West German government, and in Holland as guest of the bulb growers of Holland. *Avocational interests:* Conservation of natural resources (especially wild flowers).

BIOGRAPHICAL/CRITICAL SOURCES: Chatelaine, June, 1966.†

MATHEWS, John Joseph   1895-

PERSONAL: Born November 16, 1895, in Pawhuska, Okla.; son of William Shirley and Eugenia (Girard) Mathews; married Elizabeth Palmour, April 5, 1945; children: Virginia H., John H. *Education:* University of Oklahoma, B.A. 1920; Oxford University, B.A., 1923; summer study at University of Sewanee, 1915, University of Geneva, 1923. *Politics:* Democrat. *Home:* Blackjacks, Pawhuska, Okla. 74056. *Agent:* Robert T. Center, 240 East 76th St., New York, N.Y. 10021. *Office:* P.O. Box 1247, Pawhuska, Okla.

CAREER: Realtor in Los Angeles, Calif., and Pasadena, Calif., 1926-28; rancher, and writer since 1928. Member of Osage Tribal Council, 1934-42, and Oklahoma State Board of Education, 1935. *Military service:* U.S. Air Service, pilot, 1918; became second lieutenant. *Member:* Order of Daedalians, American Legion, Phi Beta Kappa. *Awards, honors:* Guggenheim fellowship, 1939-40; Distinguished Service Citation, University of Oklahoma, 1962; Award of Merit, American Association for State and Local History, 1962, for *The Osages.*

WRITINGS: Wah'Kon-Tah: The Osage and the White Man's Road (Book-of-the-Month Club selection), University of Oklahoma Press, 1932; *Sundown* (novel), Longmans, Green, 1934; *Talking to the Moon,* University of Chicago Press, 1945; *Life and Death of an Oilman,* University of Oklahoma Press, 1951; *The Osages: Children of the Middle Waters,* University of Oklahoma Press, 1961.

WORK IN PROGRESS: Boy, Horse and Dog, Volume I of a three-volume autobiography.

SIDELIGHTS: Mathews told *CA:* "My very first memory was of the Osage Indian prayer-chant to the morning star, which induced deep emotion, chiefly because this Neolithic petition was cut short before it was finished by sobbing and weeping. . . . The little boy memory of the prayer-chant that ended in a sob of frustration . . . has tinted all of my writing."††

*   *   *

MATTHEWS, Honor   1901-

PERSONAL: Born January 9, 1901. *Education:* University of London, B.A. *Home:* 65 Lansdowne Lane, Charlton, London S.E.7, England.

CAREER: University of London, Goldsmiths' College, London, England, principal lecturer in department of drama, 1953-63, examiner in English and drama, and extramural tutor in English. Examiner in English and Drama, Cambridge University; lecturer in department of drama, University of Hull.

WRITINGS: Character and Symbol in Shakespeare's Plays, Cambridge University Press, 1962; *The Primal Curse: The Myth of Cain and Abel in the Theatre,* Schocken, 1966; *The Hard Journey: The Myth of Man's Rebirth,* Barnes & Noble, 1968.†

*   *   *

MATTIS, George   1905-

PERSONAL: Born February 26, 1905; son of George (a dairy farmer) and Veronica (Wahl) Mattis. *Education:* University of Wisconsin, B.A., 1928. *Religion:* Catholic. *Home:* Route 1, Birchwood, Wis. 54817.

CAREER: Free-lance outdoor and nature writer and wildlife photographer. Has shown his own wildlife slides to conservation and other interested groups. *Military service:* U.S.

Army, 1941, 1942-45; received Purple Heart and four overseas bars. *Member:* Outdoor Writers Association of America, Association of Great Lakes Outdoor Writers.

WRITINGS: Whitetail: Fundamentals and Fine Points for the Hunter, World Publishing, 1969. Regular contributor to *Sport and Recreation* (magazine), beginning 1955.

WORK IN PROGRESS: A book, *Along the Trout Stream.*††

*   *   *

MAURIAC, Francois (Charles)   1885-1970
(Forez)

PERSONAL: Surname is pronounced Mo-*ryak;* born October 11, 1885, in Bordeaux, France; son of Jean-Paul (a businessman) and Marguerite (Coiffard) Mauriac; married Jeanne Lafon, June 2, 1913; children: Claude (a novelist and critic), Claire (widow of Prince Jean Wiazemsky), Luce (Mme. Alain Le Ray), Jean. *Education:* Attended church school at Cauderan; University of Bordeaux, Licence es Lettres; studied briefly at Ecole National des Chartes, Paris. (Originally intended to prepare for a career in paleography and medieval archaeology.) *Religion:* Roman Catholic. *Home:* Chateau de Malagar, par Saint-Maixant, Gironde, France; and 38 ave. Theophile Gautier, Paris 16e, France.

CAREER: Novelist, playwright, poet, essayist, scenarist, and journalist. Went to Paris, 1906; was a journalist for *Temps Present,* 1908, and *Lettres Francais,* 1940; regular contributor to *Figaro,* beginning 1944, and was a director until 1955; wrote "Bloc-Notes" column (political and literary commentary) for *L'Express,* 1954-61, then for *Figaro Litteraire,* 1961-70. *Wartime activity*—World War I: Served for two years as a hospital orderly in the Balkan campaigns; returned to France, March, 1917, after contracting illness at Salonika. World War II: Played an active part in the French resistance as a journalist, writing under the pseudonym Forez, and sending articles abroad. *Member:* Societe des Gens de Lettres (president, 1932-70), Academie Francaise, American Institute of Art and Letters, American Academy of Arts and Letters, L'Academie des Sciences, Lettres es Arts de Bordeaux, L'Academie du Vin de Bordeaux. *Awards, honors:* Grand Prix du Roman de l'Academie Francaise, 1926, for *Le Desert de l'amour;* Nobel Prize for Literature, 1952; D.Litt., Oxford University; Grand Croix de la Legion d'Honneur.

WRITINGS—Fiction: *L'Enfant charge de chaines,* Grasset, 1913, translation by Gerard Hopkins published as *Young Man in Chains,* Farrar, Straus, 1963; *La Robe pretexte,* Grasset, 1914, translation by Hopkins published as *The Stuff of Youth,* Eyre & Spottiswoode, 1960, original French edition published in *Les Chefs-d'oeuvre de Francois Mauriac,* 1967 (see Omnibus volumes, below).

La Chair et la sang, Emile-Paul, 1920, translation by Hopkins published as *Flesh and Blood,* Farrar, Straus, 1955, original French edition reprinted, with a preface by Henriette Geux-Rolle, Cercle du Bibliophile, 1967; *Preseances,* Emile-Paul, 1921, translation by Hopkins published as *Questions of Precedence,* Eyre & Spottiswoode, 1958, Farrar, Straus, 1959, original French edition reprinted, Flammarion, 1972; *Le Baiser au lepreux,* Grasset, 1922, translation by James Whitall published as *The Kiss to the Leper,* Heinemann, 1923, translation by Louis Galantiere published as "The Kiss to the Leper" in *The Family,* 1930 (see Omnibus volumes, below), translation by Hopkins published as *A Kiss for the Leper,* Eyre & Spottiswoode, 1950, original French edition reprinted, Grasset, 1966, original French edi-

tion published in *Les Chefs-d'oeuvres de Francois Mauriac,* 1967 (see Omnibus volumes, below), French language edition, edited by R. A. Escoffey, Oxford University Press, 1970; *Le Fleuve de feu,* Grasset, 1923, translation by Hopkins published as *The River of Fire,* Eyre & Spottiswoode, 1954, original French edition published in *Les Chefs-d'-oeuvres de Francois Mauriac,* 1967 (see Omnibus volumes, below), original French edition reprinted, Grasset, 1970; *Genitrix,* Grasset, 1923, translation by Galantiere published as "Genitrix" in *The Family,* 1930 (see Omnibus volumes, below), French language edition, edited by John Porter Houston and Mona Tobin Houston, Prentice-Hall, 1966, translation by Hopkins published as "Genetrix" (variant spelling is correct) in *A Mauriac Reader,* 1968 (see Omnibus volumes, below), excerpts from original French edition published as *Genitrix,* edited by Andre Lanly, Bordas, 1975.

Le Desert de l'amour, Grasset, 1925, translation by Samuel Putnam published as *The Desert of Love,* Covici, Friede, 1929, translation by Hopkins published as *The Desert of Love,* Pellegrini & Cudahy, 1951, French language edition, with an introduction by Kjell Stroemberg and a speech (originally delivered at the presentation of the Nobel Prize to Mauriac) by Anders Oesterling, Presses du Compagnonnage, 1964, original French edition reprinted, Grasset, 1971; *Therese Desqueyroux,* Grasset, 1927, translation by Eric Sutton published as *Therese,* Boni & Liveright, 1928, translation by Hopkins published as "Therese" in *Therese: A Portrait in Four Parts,* 1947 (see Omnibus volumes, below), French language edition, edited by Jean Collignon, Macmillan, 1963, another French language edition, edited by Cecil Jenkins, University of London Press, 1964, excerpts from original French edition published as *Therese Desqueyroux,* edited by Lanly, Bordas, 1973, another French language edition, edited by Bernard Delvaille, J. Tallandier, 1974, original French edition reprinted, Le Livre de Poche, 1974; *Destins,* Grasset, 1928, translation by Sutton published as *Destinies,* Covici, Friede, 1929, translation by Hopkins published as *Lines of Life,* Farrar, Straus, 1957, original French edition reprinted, Grasset, 1967; *La Nuit du borreau soi-meme,* Flammarion, 1929; *Trois recits,* Grasset, 1929.

Ce qui etait perdu, Grasset, 1930, translation by Harold F. Kynaston-Snell published as *Suspicion,* Nash & Grayson, 1931, translation by J.H.F. McEwen published as "That Which Was Lost" in *That Which Was Lost* [and] *The Dark Angels,* 1951 (see Omnibus volumes, below), translation by Hopkins published as *The Mask of Innocence,* Farrar, Straus, 1953; *Le Noeud de viperes,* Grasset, 1932, translation by Warre B. Wells published as *Viper's Tangle,* Sheed & Ward, 1933, translation by Hopkins published as *The Knot of Vipers,* Eyre & Spottiswoode, 1951, French language edition, edited by John T. Stoker and Robert Silhol, Harrap, 1959, Heath, 1961, another French language edition, edited by Gabriel Spille, Bordas, 1971, original French edition reprinted, Grasset, 1972; *Le Mystere Frontenac,* Grasset, 1933, translation by Hopkins published as *The Frontenac Mystery,* Eyre & Spottiswoode, 1952, same translation published as *The Frontenacs,* Farrar, Straus, 1961, French language edition, edited by Anthony M.C. Wilcox, Harrap, 1964, original English edition reprinted, Eyre & Spottiswoode, 1971; *Le Drole* (short story for children), Paul Hartmann, 1933, French language edition, edited by Isabelle H. Clarke, Heath, 1957, translation by Anne Carter published as *The Holy Terror,* J. Cape, 1964, Funk, 1967.

La Fin de la nuit, Grasset, 1935, translation by Hopkins published as "The End of the Night" in *Therese: Portrait in*

Four Parts, 1947 (see Omnibus volumes, below); *Le Mal,* Grasset, 1935, translation by Hopkins published as "The Enemy" in *The Weakling* [and] *The Enemy,* 1952 (see Omnibus volumes, below); *Les Anges noirs,* Grasset, 1936, translation by Hopkins published as "The Dark Angels" in *That Which Was Lost* [and] *The Dark Angels,* 1951 (see Omnibus volumes, below); *Therese a l'hotel,* originally published in *Plongees,* 1938 (see Omnibus volumes, below), translation by Hopkins published as "Therese at the Hotel" in *Therese: A Portrait in Four Parts,* 1947 (see Omnibus volumes, below), original French version published separately in France, 1961; *Les Chemins de la mer,* Grasset, 1939, translation by Hopkins published as *The Unknown Sea,* Holt, 1948, French language edition, edited by L. Clark Keating and James O. Swain, Heath, 1953.

La Pharisienne, Grasset, 1941, translation by Hopkins published as *A Woman of the Pharisees,* Holt, 1946, original French edition reprinted, Grasset, 1970, French language edition, edited by Wilcox, Harrap, 1971; *Le Sagouin,* Palatine-Plon, 1951, Cercle du Livre de France (New York), c.1951, translation by Hopkins published as *The Little Misery,* Eyre & Spottiswoode, 1952; *Galigai,* Flammarion, 1952, translation and postscript by Hopkins published as *The Loved and the Unloved,* Pellegrini & Cudahy, 1952, reprinted, Eyre & Spottiswoode, 1971, original French edition reprinted, Flammarion, 1972; *L'Agneau,* Flammarion, 1954, translation by Hopkins published as *The Lamb,* Farrar, Straus, 1955, original French edition reprinted, Flammarion, 1973; *Un Adolescent d'autrefois,* Flammarion, 1969, translation by Jean Stewart published as *Maltaverne,* Farrar, Straus, 1970, original French edition reprinted, University of London Press, 1972, French language edition published as *Maltaverne,* Flammarion, 1972.

Plays: *Asmodee* (first produced in Paris at Comedie Francaise, March 1, 1945), Grasset, 1938, translation by Basil Bartlett published as *Asmodee; or, The Intruder,* Secker & Warburg, 1939, translation by Beverly Thurman published as *Asmodee* (produced in New York at Theatre 74, March 25, 1958), Samuel French, 1957; *Les Mal aimes* (first produced in Paris at Comedie Francaise), Grasset, 1945, translation by Ursule Molinaro, entitled "The Egoists," distributed in typescript, [New York], 1959, original French edition reprinted, Grasset, 1965; *Passage du malin* (first produced in Paris at Theatre de la Madeleine, December 9, 1947), Editions de la Table Ronde, 1948; *Le Feu sur la terre* (first produced in Paris at Theatre Hebertot, November 7, 1950), Grasset, 1951, French language edition, edited by Robert J. North, published as *Le Feu sur la terre; ou, Le Pays sans chemin,* Harrap, 1962.

Films: *Le Pain vivant* (scenario and dialogue), Flammarion, 1955; (co-author of scenario) "Therese" (based on *Therese Desqueyrous*), 1963.

Poetry: *Les Mains jointes,* published at Mauriac's expense by Falque, 1909; *L'Adieu a l'adolescence,* Stock, 1911, revised edition, 1970; *Orages,* Champion, 1925; *Le Sang d'Atys,* Grasset, 1940.

Nonfiction: *De Quelques coeurs inquiets: Petits essais de psychologie,* Societe Litteraire de France, 1920; *Le Jeune homme,* Hachette, 1926; *Proust,* M. Lesage, 1926; *La Province,* Hachette, 1926; *Bordeaux,* Emile-Paul, 1926; *La Vie de Jean Racine,* Plon, 1928, reprinted as *La Vie de Racine,* Plon, 1962; *Le Roman,* L'Artisan du Livre, 1928; *Dieu et Mammon,* Editions du Capitole, 1929, translation by Barnard Wall and Barbara Wall published as *God and Mammon,* Sheed & Ward, 1936; *Mes plus lointains souvenirs,* E. Hazan, 1929.

Trois grands hommes devant Dieu, Editions du Capitole, 1930; *Blaise Pascal et sa soeur Jacqueline,* Hachette, 1931; *Le Jeudi-saint,* Flammarion, 1931, translation by Kynaston-Snell published as *Maundy Thursday,* Burns & Oates, 1932; *Souffrances et bonheur du chretien,* Grasset, 1931, translation by Harold Evans published as *Anguish and Joy of the Christian Life,* Dimension, 1964; *Rene Bazin,* F. Alcan, 1931; *Pelerins,* Editions de France, 1932; *Commencements d'une vie,* Grasset, 1932; *Petits essais de psychologie religieuse,* L'Artisan du Livre, 1933; *Le Romancier et ses personnages,* Correa, 1933, excerpts published as *L'Education des filles,* Correa, 1936, original edition reprinted, Buchet/Chastel, 1970; *Discours de reception a l'Academie Francaise et reponse de M. Andre Chaumeix,* Grasset, 1934; *Journal: Volume I,* Grasset, 1934, *Volume II,* Grasset, 1937, *Volume III,* Grasset, 1940, *Volume IV,* Flammarion, 1950, *Volume V,* Flammarion, 1953, excerpts published in *Malagar,* 1972 (see Omnibus volumes, below); *La Vie de Jesus,* Flammarion, 1936, translation by Julie Kernan published as *Life of Jesus,* Longmans, Green, 1937; *L'Homme et le peche,* Plon, 1938; (with others) *Communism and Christians,* translated by J. F. Scanlan, Sands, 1938; *Les Maisons fugitives,* Grasset, 1939.

Lacordaire et nous, Gallimard, 1940; (editor) *Les Pages immortelles de Pascal,* Correa, 1940, translation published as *Living Thoughts of Pascal,* Cassell, c.1940; (under pseudonym Forez) *Le Cahier noir,* published clandestinely by Editions de Minuit, 1943, published with parallel French and English texts as *Le Cahier noir: The Black Notebook,* Burrup, Mathieson, 1944; *La Nation francaise a une ame,* published clandestinely, c.1944; *Ne pas se renier,* Editions de la Revue Fontaine (Algeria), 1944; *Coups de couteau,* Editions Lumiere (Brussels), 1944; *The Eucharist: The Mystery of Holy Thursday,* translated by Marie-Louise Dufrenoy, Longmans, Green (New York), 1944; *Sainte Marguerite de Cortone,* Flammarion, 1945, translation by Bernard Fruchtman published as *Saint Margaret of Cortona,* Philosophical Library, 1948, translation by Barbara Wall published as *Margaret of Cortona,* Burns & Oates, 1948; *Pages de Journal,* Editions du Rocher (Monaco), 1945; *La Rencontre avec Barres,* Editions de la Table Ronde, 1945, published in *Ecrits intimes,* 1953 (see Omnibus volumes, below); *Le Baillon denoue, apres quatre ans de silence* (articles originally published in *Figaro,* August, 1944, to March, 1945), Grasset, 1945; *Reponse a Paul Claudel: Academie Francaise, seance du 13 mars 1947,* Editions de la Table Ronde, 1947; *Du cote de chez Proust,* Editions de la Table Ronde, 1947, translation by Elsie Pell published as *Proust's Way,* Philosophical Library, 1950; *Mes grands hommes,* Editions du Rocher, 1949, translation by Pell published as *Men I Hold Great,* Philosophical Library, 1951 (published in England as *Great Men,* Rockliff, 1952), reprinted, Kennikat, 1971.

Terres franciscaines, Plon, 1950; *La Pierre d'achoppement,* Editions du Rocher, 1951, translation by Hopkins published as *The Stumbling Block,* Philosophical Library, 1952; *La Mort d'Andre Gide,* Editions Estienne, 1952; (with others) *Bordeaux: Porte ouverte sur le monde,* R. Picquot (Bordeaux), 1952; *Lettres ouvertes,* Editions du Rocher, 1952, translation by Mario A. Pei published as *Letters on Art and Literature,* Philosophical Library, 1953, reprinted, Kennikat, 1970; *Mauriac par lui-meme* (with notes by Mauriac), edited by Pierre Henri Simon, Editions de Seuil, 1953; *Paroles catholiques,* Plon, 1954, translation by Edward H. Flannery published as *Words of Faith,* Philosophical Library, 1955; *Bloc-notes, 1952-1957* (articles originally published in *La Table Ronde* and *L'Express*), Flammarion, 1958; (contributor) *Trois ecrivains devant Lourdes,* Plon, 1958; *Le Fils de l'homme,* Grasset, 1958, translation by Bernard Murchland published as *The Son of Man,* World Publishing, 1960; *Memoires interieures,* Flammarion, 1959, translation by Hopkins published with original French title, Eyre & Spottiswoode, 1960, Farrar, Straus, 1961, excerpts from original French edition published in *Malagar,* 1972 (see Omnibus volumes, below).

Rapport sur les prix de vertu (paper read at a meeting of Institut de France, December 17, 1960), Firmin-Didiot, 1960; *Le Nouveau bloc-notes, 1958-1960,* Flammarion, 1961; *Second Thoughts: Reflections on Literature and on Life,* translated by Adrienne Foulke, World Publishing, 1961; *Ce que je crois,* Grasset, 1962, translation with an introduction by Wallace Fowlie published as *What I Believe,* Farrar, Straus, 1963; *Cain, Where Is Your Brother?,* Coward, 1962; *De Gaulle,* Grasset, 1964, translation by Richard Howard published as *De Gaulle,* Doubleday, 1966; *Les Plus belles pages de Maurice et Eugenie Guerin,* Mercure de France, 1965; *Nouveaux memoires interieures,* Flammarion, 1965, translation by Herma Briffault published as *The Inner Presence: Recollections of My Spiritual Life,* Bobbs-Merrill, 1968, excerpts from original French edition published in *Malagar,* 1972 (see Omnibus volumes, below), original French edition reprinted, Gallimard, 1974; *D'Autres et moi,* Grasset, 1966; *Memoires politiques,* Grasset, 1967; *Le Nouveau bloc-notes, 1961-1964* (articles originally published in *L'Express* and *Figaro*), Flammarion, 1968.

Le Nouveau bloc-notes, 1965-1967, Flammarion, 1970; *Le Dernier bloc-notes, 1968-1970,* Flammarion, 1971; *Correspondance Andre Gide-Francois Mauriac, 1912-1950,* edited by Jacqueline Morton, Gallimard, 1971; *Francois Mauriac en verve* (quotations), edited by Jean Touzot, P. Horay, 1974.

Prefaces and forewords: Pierre Mauriac, *Aux confins de la medicine,* Grasset, 1926; C. Planes-Burgade, *Bordeaux historique et descriptif,* R. Picquot, 1934; Pierre Mornand, *Le Visage du Christ,* Tisne, 1938, translation published as *Christ's Image,* French & European Publications, 1939; Pierre Henri Simon, *Prepare l'apres-guerre,* Bloud & Gay, 1940; Jacques Boell, *Oisans,* Susse, 1945; Claude Mauriac, *Aimer Balzac,* Editions de la Table Ronde, 1945; Abbe Remy Pasteau, *Vigile sous les armes,* Beauchesne, 1945; J. de la Ville de Mirmont, *L'Horizon chimerique,* R. Picquot, 1947; *Almanach des lettres, 1949,* Editions de Flore, 1948; P. J. Dominque, *Les Chaines qui tombent,* Editions Siloe, 1948; Graham Greene, *La Fond du probleme* (translation of *The Heart of the Matter*), Laffont, 1949; Graham Greene, *La Puissance et la gloire* (translation of *The Power and the Glory*), Laffont, 1949; Bela Just, *Un Proces fabrique,* Editions du Temoingnage Chretien, 1949; Louis Pauwels, *Les Voies de petite communication,* Editions du Seuil, 1949.

Maurice de Guerin, *Le Centaure,* Falaize, 1950; Lapoujade, *Cinquante dessins,* Editions du Seuil, c.1950; Boris Bouieff, *Pays de rigeur,* Editions du Seuil, 1950; Nelly Cormeau, *L'Art de Francois Mauriac,* Grasset, 1951; Marie-Anne Gonhier, *Charles DuBos,* Vrin, 1951; Bernard Grasset, *Amenagement de la solitude,* Grasset, 1951; Leon Poliakov, *Breviare de la haine,* Calmann-Levy, 1951; Francois Vallery-Rado, *Le Coeur de pretre,* Editions du Levain, 1951; Henri Dominique Laval, *Le Rosaire; ou, Les Trois mysteres de la rose,* Plon, 1952; Joris Karl Huysmans, *En Route,* Bibliotheca Alphonsiana (Louvain), 1953; Robert Barrat, *Justice pour le Maroc,* Editions du Seuil, 1953;

Victor de Pange, *Graham Greene,* Editions Universitaire, 1953; Louis Desgraves, *Bordeaux au cours des siecles,* Cledes (Bordeaux), 1954; Jacques Chevalier, *Bergson et le Pere Pouget,* Plon, 1954; Nathaniel Hawthorne, *La Lettre ecarlate* (translation of *The Scarlet Letter*), translated by Marie Canavaggia, Sauret (Monte Carlo), 1955; Jacques Dumaine, *Quai d'Orsay,* Sequana, 1955; *Chroniques de Port-Royal,* edited by Helen Laudenbach, Club des Libraires de France, 1955; Andre Lafon, *L'Eleve Gilles,* Club Francais du Livre, 1956; *Pages israeliennes,* Seghers, 1956; Jacques Rabemananjara, *Antsa: Poeme,* Presence Africaine, 1956; *Israel,* Ides et Calendes, 1957; Micheline Maurel, *Un Camp tres ordinaire,* Editions de Minuit, 1957; Jean Guerin and Bernard Guerin, *Des Hommes et des activites autour d'un demi-siecle,* Societe Bordelaise d'Editions Biographiques (Lormont), 1957; Elie Wiesel, *La Nuit,* Editions de Minuit, 1958; Francis Jammes, *Clara d'Ellebeuse,* Sauret (Monte Carlo), 1958; Fritiof Billquist, *Greta Garbo: Vedette solitaire,* Fayard, 1959; Daniel Fleg, *Journal,* Correa, 1959.

Ville de Bordeaux, *Francis Jammes et Bordeaux,* Bibliotheque Municipal (Bordeaux), 1960; Denise Marie-Louise Bourdet, *Visages d'aujourd'hui,* Plon, 1960; Abbe Henry de Julliot, *D'un coeur qui t'aime,* Casterman, 1960; Alfred Dreyfus, *Cinq annees de ma vie (1894-1899),* Fasquelle, 1962; Henri Moreau, *Le Pecheur d'or* (poems), R. Picquot, c.1962; Henri Guillemin, *Flaubert devant la vie et devant Dieu,* Nizet, 1962; Jacques Nantet, *Histoire de Liban,* Editions de Minuit, 1963; Jean-Jacques Rousseau, *Les Confessions,* Livre de Poche, 1963; Jean-Rene Huguenin, *Journal,* Editions du Seuil, 1964; Paul Claudel, *Premieres oeuvres: 1886-1901* (catalogue), University of Paris Library, 1965; Michel Suffran, *Sur une generation perdue,* Samie (Bordeaux), 1966; Leon Ernest Halkin, *A l'Ombre de la mort,* Duculot, 1966; Georges Lacour-Gayet, *Talleyrand,* Editions Rencontre (Lausanne), 1968; Michel Suffran, editor, *Jean de la Ville de Mirmont,* Seghers, 1968.

Omnibus volumes: *The Family* (contains "The Kiss to the Leper" and "Genitrix"), translations by Louis Galantiere, Covici, Friede, 1930; *Plongees* (stories; contains "Therese chez le docteur," "Therese a l'hotel," "Insomnie," "Le Rang," and "Conte de Noel"), Grasset, 1938, published in *Les Chef-d'oeuvres de Francois Mauriac,* 1967 (see below); *Therese: A Portrait in Four Parts* (contains *The End of the Night,* "Therese and the Doctor," and "Therese at the Hotel"), translations by Hopkins, Holt, 1947, reprinted, Penguin, 1975; *Oeuvres completes* (complete works), Fayard, 1950-59; *That Which Was Lost* [and] *The Dark Angels,* the former translated by J.H.F. McEwen, the latter by Hopkins, Eyre & Spottiswoode, 1951; *The Weakling* [and] *The Enemy,* translations by Hopkins, Pellegrini & Cudahy, 1952; *Ecrits intimes* (contains *Commencements d'une vie, La Rencontre avec Barres,* "Journal d'un homme de trente ans," and *Du cote de chez Proust*), Palatine, 1953; *Therese Desqueyroux* [suivi de] *Therese chez le docteur, Therese a l'hotel* [et] *La Fin de la nuit,* Grasset, 1956.

Marc Alyn, editor, *Francois Mauriac* (selections and a study of Mauriac by the editor), Seghers, 1960; *Asmodee: Piece en cinq actes de Francois Mauriac* [et] *Sur un banc: Comedie en un acte de Charles Mahieu,* [Paris], 1961; *Therese Desqueyroux* [et] *La Fin de la nuit,* introduction by Pierre Henri Simon, Club des Amis du Livre, 1963; *Oeuvres romanesques,* Flammarion, 1965; *Les Chefs d'oeuvre de Francois Mauriac* (contains *La Robe pretexte, Le Baiser au lepreux, Le Fleuve de feu,* and *Plongees*), Cercle du Bibliophile, 1967; *A Mauriac Reader* (contains *A Kiss for the Leper,* "Genetrix," *The Desert of Love, The Knot of Vi-*

pers, and *A Woman of the Pharisees*), translations by Hopkins, introduction by Wallace Fowlie, Farrar, Straus, 1968; *Five Novels,* translations by Hopkins, Eyre & Spottiswoode, 1969.

La Vie de Jesus, Le Jeudi-saint, Sainte Marguerite de Cortone, [et] *La Pierre d'achoppement,* Cercle du Bibliophile, 1970; *Malagar: Ma maison de champs* (contains selections from *Memoires interieurs, Nouveaux memoires interieurs,* and his *Journal*), Arcaehon, 1972.

Contributor to many books; contributor to more than forty newspapers and periodicals, including *Le Figaro, La Table Ronde, L'Express, Lettres Francaises, Le Temps Present,* and *L'Echo de Paris.*

SIDELIGHTS: Rayner Hoppenstall wrote: "The deep seam of regionalism in the French novel runs right through Mauriac. Even when they are to be found upon the pavements of Paris, his characters invariably come from the Landes in the neighborhood of Bordeaux and most of his characters stay there." It was this environment which provided the special atmosphere of his novels; the *Books Abroad* reviewer commented that "the monotonous *landes . . .* with their extremes of rain and drought are the perfect reflection of solitary brooding temperaments struggling against barely repressed passions, and this creates an atmosphere of intensity, a kind of poetry that is very difficult to translate." According to Cecil Jenkins, writing in 1965, Mauriac has constantly expressed through his writing his own relationship with his native region: "Sixty books have scarcely exhausted the love-hate relationship with this region which Mauriac abandoned almost as many years ago at the age of twenty-one. If Paris has been the privileged platform for the man of letters, the human reality behind the writings has never ceased to be Bordeaux."

Consequently, his writing involved a continuing exercise of memory; Jenkins reported that, in an interview with Malcolm Cowley, Mauriac stated: "I don't observe and I don't describe: I rediscover. I rediscover the narrow Jansenist world of my devout, unhappy and introverted childhood." His method of working was instinctive, rather than based on conscious organization; Jenkins continued: "He describes himself today as an 'instinctive writer'. . . . He says that, if he was never horrified by what he wrote, he was often surprised. He wrote extremely fast—in some cases completing the draft of a novel in three weeks—and, as indeed some of his hasty endings suggest, he was never very concerned with the deliberate ordering of the structure of his work. . . . Control, in the Mauriac novel, is purely organic, and quality a function of the intensity of concentrating upon a theme."

As the *Books Abroad* writer noted, Mauriac was "closely indentified with Roman Catholicism and mention of his name invariably provokes lengthy arguments about the role of the Catholic novelist." (Mauriac himself, however, disputed the notion that he is a "Catholic novelist." Mauriac told Alden Whitman: "I am a novelist who is a Catholic. . . . With the aid of a certain gift for creating atmosphere, I have tried to make the Catholic universe of evil palpable, tangible, odorous.") Many critics consider that the main interest of his work is psychological, but Paul-Andre Lesort made this interesting observation on the part played by the religious emphasis in his writing: "The novels of Mauriac offer us not a psychology of the passions, but a theology of the passions—or, more exactly, the opposite of a theology: a demonology."

John Weightman, explaining some French critics' condemnation that Mauriac was only a writer of "superior novelettes," wrote: "He provides neatly packaged anguish, couched in limpid, graceful French, which flatters the usual French desire to be at once anti-bourgeois and bourgeois. He satirises the traditional family as being materialistic and purely formal in its Catholicism and yet, in the end, he seems to want to believe that it is a permanent social necessity and can occasionally be touched with grace, even in its awfulness. It is almost as if, subconsciously and because of early conditioning, he believed more in the family than in God. He never sees the kind of ingrown, festering family he is dealing with as a temporary, local French phenomenon that might be radically questioned in the name of a more cheerful worldview. . . ." Weightman continued by saying that if "the Mauriacian family becomes an historical curiosity, the chances are that some readers will still turn to the novels because of the macabre fascination of the patterns made by Mauriac out of the various elements of his local colour: the smell of the pine trees, claustrophobic interiors, migrating doves and lustful sin."

Mauriac's career as a journalist has also been the subject of controversy. Robert North reported: "Mauriac's point of view often led him into opposition to the majority. At the time of the Spanish Civil War when most eminent Catholics supported General Franco, Mauriac denounced him, and supported the Republican Government in Spain. . . . On many occasions of public controversy, he has taken the unpopular view, never afraid to be in a minority, and always urging what seemed to him the Christian and charitable policy." In the early 1950's, he became more deeply involved as a commentator on public affairs and, from this time, wrote Jenkins, "his journalism acquires its distinctive cutting edge and its real bitterness." Mauriac himself described how this involvement came about at the time when he won the Nobel Prize, as he sought "to turn it into a beginning rather than accept it as an ending." He said: "I received the Nobel Prize on the day, almost at the very hour, that an unhappy crowd in Casablanca was walking straight into the ambush laid for it. I returned to find that an irrefutable dossier had been brought to me, as if in answer to my secret prayer amid the pomp of Stockholm. . . . Henceforth, I was committed."

Mauriac has been described by Hoppenstall as "tall, thin, dark, nervous, a brilliant conversationalist, afflicted with melancholy." The French commentator, Jean-Francois Revel, who often disapproved of Mauriac's journalistic style (though not the causes he espoused), affirmed that Mauriac was "honest, almost always sincere, and highly intelligent."

Time reported that "Mauriac provided his own eulogy in a recording he made 20 years ago to be released after his death. It reflected a lifelong preoccupation with the possibilities of grace that he had explored in his essays, if not in his other work. 'I believe,' he said, 'as I did as a child, that life has meaning, a direction, a value; that no suffering is lost, that every tear counts, each drop of blood, that the secret of the world is to be found in St. John's "*Deus caritas est*"—"God is Love."'"

BIOGRAPHICAL/CRITICAL SOURCES—Books: Francois Mauriac, *Journal,* five volumes, Grasset, 1934, 1937, 1940, Flammarion, 1950, 1953; Rayner Hoppenstall, in *The Double Image,* Secker & Warburg, 1947; Elsie Pell, *Francois Mauriac: In Search of the Infinite,* Philosophical Library, 1947; Graham Greene, *The Lost Childhood, and Other Essays,* Eyre & Spottiswoode, 1951; Pierre-Henri Simon, *Mauriac par lui-meme,* Editions du Seuil, 1953; Martin Jarret-Kerr, *Francois Mauriac,* Bowes & Bowes, 1954; Martin Turnell, *The Art of French Fiction,* Hamish

Hamilton, 1959; Francois Mauriac, *Memoires interieures,* Flammarion, 1959, translation by Gerard Hopkins published under the French title, Farrar, Straus, 1961; Xavier Grall, *Francois Mauriac, Journaliste,* Editions du Cerf, 1960; Francois Mauriac, *Second Thoughts: Reflections on Literature and on Life,* translated by Adrienne Foulke, World Publishing, 1961; *Le Feu sur la terre* (critical edition), edited with an introduction by Robert J. North, Harrap, 1962; Cecil Jenkins, *Mauriac,* Oliver & Boyd, 1965; A. M. Caspary, compiler, *Francois Mauriac,* Herder, 1968; J. E. Flower, *Intention and Achievement: An Essay on the Novels of Francois Mauriac,* Oxford University Press, 1969; Maxwell A. Smith, *Francois Mauriac,* Twayne, 1970; Roger Bichelberger, *Rencontre avec Mauriac,* Editions de l'Ecole, 1973; *Contemporary Literary Criticism,* Volume IV, Gale, 1975.

Articles: *Illustrated London News,* November 15, 1952; *La Table Ronde* (special number devoted to Mauriac), January, 1953; *La Parisienne* (special number on Mauriac), May, 1956; *Time,* August 12, 1957, September 14, 1970; *New Yorker,* June 21, 1958; *Kenyon Review,* fall, 1959; *Commonweal,* March 17, 1961, December 25, 1970, November 16, 1973; *Modern Language Review,* October, 1963; *Yale French Studies,* April, 1964-March, 1965; *Nation,* March 28, 1966; *L'Express,* June 19, 1967; *Books Abroad,* winter, 1967; *New York Times Book Review,* June 28, 1970; *New York Times,* September 1, 1970; *Washington Post,* September 3, 1970, September 2, 1970; *Observer Review,* September 6, 1970; *Esquire,* December, 1970; *Christianity Today,* August 8, 1975.†

(Died September 1, 1970)

*   *   *

MAUROIS, Andre   1885-1967

PERSONAL: Original name, Emile Salomon Wilhelm Herzog; name legally changed in 1947; born July 26, 1885, in Elbeuf (Seine-Inferieure), France; son of Ernest (a textile manufacturer) and Alice-Helene (Levy) Herzog; married Jeanne-Marie Wande de Szymkievicz, October 30, 1912 (died 1924); married Simone de Caillavet, September 6, 1926; children: (first marriage) Michelle, Gerald, Oliver; (second marriage) Francoise (child of a previous marriage of his second wife; died, 1930). *Education:* Lycee Corneille, Rouen (Prix d'honneur de philosophie), 1897-1902, diplome; l'Universite de Caen, licence in philosophy, 1902. *Home:* 86 Boulevard Maurice Barres, Neuilly sur seine, France (winter); and Essendieras, Excideuil, Dordogne, France (summer).

CAREER: Industrial manager in family textile factory, 1904-14, 1919-26; made a lecture tour in the United States (his first visit to America), 1927; lectured in New York, Schenectady, Worcester, Ottawa, Montreal, and at Dartmouth College, Smith College, and Cornell University, 1927-32; Clark Lecturer, Trinity College, Cambridge University, 1928; held Meridith Howland Pyne chair of French literature, Princeton University, October, 1929 to February, 1931; elected to the French Academy, June 23, 1938; Lowell Lecturer, Harvard University, 1940; professor of French literature, Mills College, Oakland, California, summer, 1941; pleaded the cause of France and Marshal Henri Petain to the Americans in his writings and lectures, 1940-43; professor of French literature, University of Kansas City, 1945-46; after World War II, Maurois devoted full time to writing and lecturing. *Military service:* French Army, volunteered and served with the Seventh Division, Rouen, 1903-04; inter-

preter for the Ninth Scottish Division, then liaison officer to the British Army Headquarters, 1914-18, received Distinguished Conduct Medal; Bureau of Information, attached to British Headquarters, 1939-40; volunteered for service in North Africa, Corsica, Italy, captain, 1943-44; went to the United States under the orders of General Giraud to relate to the Americans the effects of the lend-lease program and the extent of the French military effort in Italy. *Member:* Association France-Etats-Unis (president), Societe des Gens de Lettres, Comite de Lecture de la Comedie-Francaise, Portuguese Academy, Brazilian Academy. *Awards, honors:* Honorary degrees from Edinburgh University, 1928, Princeton University, 1933, Oxford University, 1934, University of Saint Andrews, 1934, University of Louisiana, and other institutions; Grand Officer of the Legion of Honor awarded by the French Ministry of Commerce and Industry, 1937; Knight of the Order of the British Empire, 1938; Commandeur des Arts et des Lettres; Commandeur du Merite Sportif; Prix des Ambassadeurs.

WRITINGS—Novels: *Les Silences du Colonel Bramble,* Grasset, 1918, new edition edited by E. A. Phillips and E. G. Le Grand, Cambridge University Press, 1920, revised edition, Brentano's, 1943, translation by Thurfrida Wake and Wilfrid Jackson published as *The Silence of Colonel Bramble,* Lane, 1920, revised edition of translation, 1927; *Ni ange, ni bete,* Grasset, 1919; *Le General Bramble,* Grasset, 1920, translation by Jules Castier and Ronald Boswell published as *General Bramble,* Lane, 1921, enlarged edition published as *Les Discours du Docteur O'Grady,* Grasset, 1922, translation by Castier and Boswell published as *The Discourses of Doctor O'Grady* in one volume with the above translation of *The Silence of Colonel Bramble,* Bodley Head, 1965; *Le Hausse et la baisse,* Les Oeuvres Libres, 1922, revised edition published as *Bernard Quesnay,* Gallimard, 1926, translation by Brian W. Downs published as *Bernard Quesnay,* Appleton, 1927; *Climats,* Grasset, 1928, translation by Joseph Collins published as *Atmosphere of Love,* Appleton, 1929, translation by J. Collins published in England as *Whatever Gods May Be,* Cassell, 1929, translation by Violet Schiff and Esme Cook published in England as *The Climates of Love,* Barrie, 1957; *Le Cercle de famille,* Grasset, 1932, translation by Hamish Miles published as *The Family Circle,* Appleton, 1932; *L'Instinct du bonheur,* Grasset, 1934, translation by Edith Johannsen published as *A Time for Silence,* Appleton, 1942; *Terre promise,* Maison Francaise (New York), 1945, translation by Joan Charles published as *Woman without Love,* Harper, 1945; *Nouveaux discours du Docteur O'Grady,* Grasset, 1950, translation by Gerard Hopkins published as *The Return of Doctor O'Grady,* Bodley Head, 1951; *Les Roses de septembre,* Flammarion, 1956, translation by Hopkins published as *September Roses,* Harper, 1958.

Short stories: *Par la faute de Monsieur Balzac,* Paillart (Amiens), 1923; *Meipe; ou, La Delivrance,* Grasset, 1926, new edition, augmented with *Les Derniers jours de Pompei* and published as *Les Mondes Imaginaires,* Grasset, 1929, translation of first edition, by Eric Sutton, published as *Mape: The World of Illusion,* Appleton, 1926; *Les Souffrances du jeunne Werther,* Schiffrin, 1926; *Les Chapitre Suivant,* Kra, 1927, translation by K. Paul published as *The Next Chapter: The War Against the Moon,* Dutton, 1927; *Voyage au pays des Articoles,* J. Schiffrin, 1927, translation by David Garnett published as *A Voyage to the Island of the Articoles,* Appleton, 1929; *Deux fragments d'une histoire universelle 1922,* Portiques, 1928; *Les Derniers jours de Pompei,* Lapina, 1928; *Le Peseur d'ames,* Gallimard, 1931, translation by Hamish Miles published as *The Weigher of Souls* (includes *The Earth Dwellers* and an autobiographical introduction by the author), Macmillan, 1963; *L'Anglaise et d'autres femmes*, Nouvelles Societes, 1932, translation by Miles published as *Ricochets: Miniature Tales of Human Life*, Harper, 1935; *Premiers Contes*, Defontaine (Rouen), 1935; *La Machine a lire les pensees*, Gallimard, 1937, translation by James Whitall published as *The Thought-Reading Machine*, Harper, 1938; *Toujours l'inattendu arrive* (stories and novellas), Maison Francaise (New York), 1943; *La Campagne, Transfert, Love in Exile* (three novellas), Maison Francaise (New York), 1945; *Tu ne commettras point d'adultere*, A. Michel, 1946, translation included in *The Ten Commandments* (ten short stories by various authors), Simon & Schuster, 1944, also published as *Les Dix commandments*, Maison Francaise, 1944; *Les Mondes impossibles: Recits et nouvelles fantastiques* (five short stories previously published), Gallimard, 1947; *La Malediction de l'or*, France Illustration, 1948; *L'Amour en exile*, Les Oeuvres Libres, 1950; *Le Diner sous les marronniers*, Deux-Rives, 1951; *Les Erophages*, Passerelle, 1966; *The Collected Stories of Andre Maurois*, Washington Square Press, 1967.

Biography: *Ariel; ou, La Vie de Shelley*, Grasset, 1923, translation by Ella d'Arcy published as *Ariel: The Life of Shelley*, Appleton, 1924, translation by E. d'Arcy published in England as *Ariel: A Shelley Romance*, Lane, 1924; *Portrait d'une actrice*, Tremois, 1925; *Lord Byron et le Demon de la tendresse*, Porte Etroite, 1925; *Un Essai sur Dickens*, Grasset, 1927, published as *Dickens*, Ferenczi (Paris), 1935, translation by Miles published as *Dickens*, Lane, 1934, Harper, 1935; *La Vie de Disraeli*, Gallimard, 1927, translation by Miles published as *Disraeli: A Picture of the Victorian Age*, Appleton, 1928; *La Vie de Joseph Smith*, Champion, 1927; *Byron*, two volumes, Grasset, 1930, translation by Miles published under same title, Appleton, 1930, new edition with preface by the author, Bodley Head, 1963, published as *Don Juan; ou, La Vie de Byron*, Grasset, 1952; *Lyautey*, Plon, 1931, abridged edition, 1935, translation by Miles published as *Lyautey*, Appleton, 1931, same translation published in England as *Marshall Lyautey*, Lane, 1931; *Tourgueniev*, Grasset, 1931; *Voltaire*, translation by Miles, P. Davies, 1932, published in French by Gallimard, 1935; *Edouard VII et son temps*, Editions de France, 1933, new edition, Grasset, 1937, translation by Miles published as *The Edwardian Era*, Appleton, 1933, same translation published in England as *King Edward and His Times*, Cassell, 1933; *Byron et les femmes*, Flammarion, 1934; *Chateaubriand*, Grasset, 1938, translation by Vera Fraser published as *Chateaubriand: Poet, Statesman, Lover*, Harper, 1938, published as *Rene; ou, La Vie de Chateaubriand*, Grasset, 1956.

A la recherche de Marcel Proust, Hachette, 1949, translation by Hopkins published as *Proust: Portrait of a Genius*, Harper, 1950, same translation published in England as *The Quest for Proust*, Cape, 1950, published as *Proust: A Biography*, Meridian, 1960; *Destins exemplaires*, Plon, 1952, translation by Helen Temple Patterson published in England as *Profiles of Great Men*, Tower Bridge, 1954; *Lelia; ou, La Vie de George Sand*, Hachette, 1952, translation by Hopkins published as *Lelia: The Life of George Sand*, Harper, 1953; *La Vie de Cecil Rhodes*, Les Oeuvres Libres, 1953, translation by Rohan Wadham published as *Cecil Rhodes*, Macmillan, 1953; *Alexandre Dumas: Great Life in Brief*, translation by Jack Palmer White, Knopf, 1954; *Olympio; ou, La Vie de Victor Hugo*, Hachette, 1954, translation by Hopkins published in England as *Victor Hugo*, J. Cape,

1956, same translation published as *Olympio: The Life of Victor Hugo*, Harper, 1956, translation by Oliver Bernard published as *Victor Hugo and His World*, Viking, 1966; *Louis XIV a Versailles*, Hachette, 1955; *Robert et Elizabeth Browning: Portraits suivis de quelques autres*, Grasset, 1955; *Les Troi Dumas*, Hachette, 1957, translation by Hopkins published as *The Titans: A Three-Generation Biography of the Dumas*, Harper, 1957, same translation published in England as *Three Musketeers: A Study of the Dumas Family*, J. Cape, 1957; *La Vie de Sir Alexander Fleming*, Hachette, 1959, translation by Hopkins published as *The Life of Sir Alexander Fleming, Discoverer of Penicillin*, Dutton, 1959, same translation published in England as *Fleming, the Man Who Cured Millions*, Methuen, 1961; *Adrienne; ou, La Vie de Madame de La Fayette*, Hachette, 1961, translation by Hopkins published as *Adrienne: The Life of the Marquise de La Fayette*, McGraw, 1961; (with others) *Beethoven*, Hachette, 1961; *Promethee; ou, La Vie de Balzac*, Hachette, 1965, translation by Norman Denny published as *Prometheus: The Life of Balzac*, Harper, 1966.

Literary history and criticism: *Essais sur la litterature anglaise*, Le Livre, 1924; *Etudes anglaises*, Grasset, 1927; *Quatre etudes anglaises*, Artisan du Livre, 1927 (this work subsumes *Etudes anglaises*); *Aspects de la biographie* (lectures given at Cambridge University, 1928), Au Sans Pariel, 1928, translation by Sidney Castle Roberts published as *Aspects of Biography*, Appleton, 1929; *Le Roman et le romancier* (lecture), Imprimerie de Monaco, 1929; *Supplement a melanges et pastiches de Marcel Proust*, Trianon, 1929, published as *Le Cote de Chelsea*, Gallimard, 1932, translation by Miles published in England as *Chelsea Way*, Matthews & Marrot, 1930; (with Luc Durtain, Victor Llona, and Bernard Fay) *Romanciers americains*, Denoel et Steele, 1931; *Introduction a la methode de Paul Valery*, Editions Libres, 1933; *Magiciens et logiciens*, Grasset, 1935, translation by Miles published as *Prophets and Poets*, Harper, 1935, same translation published in England as *Poets and Prophets*, Cassell, 1936; *Etudes litterairs*, Maison Francaise (New York), Volume I, 1941, Volume II, 1944, published as *Grands ecrivains du demi-siecle*, Club du Livre du Mois, 1957; *Cinq visages de l'amour* (lectures given at Princeton, 1930-31), Didier (New York), 1942, new edition published as *Sept visages de l'amour*, 1942, translation by Haakon M. Chevalier published as *Seven Faces of Love*, Didier, 1944; *Etudes americaines*, Maison Francaise, 1945; *Alain*, Domat, 1949; *Biographie*, Editions Estienne, 1957; *Lecture, mon doux plaisir*, Fayard, 1957, translation by Hopkins of most of the essays published as *The Art of Writing*, Dutton, 1960, published in French as *De La Bruyere a Proust*, Fayard, 1964; *Le Monde de Marcel Proust*, Hachette, 1960; *Choses vues*, Gallimard, 1963; *De Proust a Camus*, Perrin, 1963, translation by Carl Morse and Renaud Bruce published as *From Proust to Camus*, Doubleday, 1966; *De Gide a Sartre*, Perrin, 1965.

History: *Histoire d'Angleterre*, Fayard, 1937, translation by Miles published as *The Miracle of England: An Account of Her Rise to Preeminence and Present Position*, Harper, 1937, revised edition of this translation, Garden City, 1940, translation by Miles published as *A History of England*, J. Cape, 1937, revised edition of this translation, Farrar, Straus, 1958, published in a condensed version as *An Illustrated History of England*, Bodley Head, 1963; *L'Empire francais*, Hachette, 1939; *Les Origines de la guerre de 1939*, Gallimard, 1939; *The Battle of France*, translated by F. R. Ludman, Lane, 1940; *Tragedie en France*, Maison Francaise, 1940, translation by Denver Lindley published as

Tragedy in France, Harper, 1940, same translation published in England as *Why France Fell,* Lane, 1941; *Defense de la France,* [Buenos Aires], 1941; (with Christian Megret) *Petit traite sur les politiques d'hier et les libertes de demain,* Maison Francaise, 1942; *Histoire des Etats-Unis,* two volumes, Maison Francaise, 1943-44, translation by Denver Lindley and Jane Lindley published as *The Miracle of America,* Harper, 1944, same translation published in England as *A New History of the United States,* Lane, 1948, revised edition published as *Histoire des Etats-Unis, 1492-1954,* Michel, 1954, published as *Histoire de peuple americain: Etats-Unis,* two volumes, Editions Litteraires, 1955-56; *Histoire de la France,* Wapler, 1947, translation by Henry Binsse published as *The Miracle of France,* Harper, 1948, same translation published in England as *A History of France,* J. Cape, 1950, revised edition, two volumes, Club du Livre Selectionne, 1957, translation by Binsse and Hopkins published as *A History of France,* Farrar, Straus, 1957, published in a condensed form as *An Illustrated History of France,* Viking, 1960; *Rouen devaste,* [Rouen], 1947; (with Louis Aragon) *L'Histoire parallele des Etats-Unis et de l'U.R.S.S., 1917-1960,* four volumes, Presses de la Cite, 1962, published as *Les Deux Geants,* three volumes, Pont Royal, 1962, Volume I published as *Histoire des Etats-Unis de 1917 a 1961,* 1963, translation by Patrick O'Brien published as *From the New Freedom to the New Frontier,* McKay, 1963, same translation published in England as *A History of the USA: From Wilson to Kennedy,* Weidenfeld & Nicolson, 1964; (with Aragon) *Conversations avec quelques Americains eminents et apercus donnes par quelques Sovietiques eminents,* Presses de la Cite, 1963; *Histoire de l'Allemagne,* Hachette, 1965, translation by Stephen Hardman published as *An Illustrated History of Germany,* Viking, 1966.

Other works: *Les Bourgeois de Witzheim,* Grasset, 1920; *Dialogues sur le commandement,* Paillart (Abbeville), 1923, translation by John Lewis May published as *Captains and Kings,* Appleton, 1925; *Arabesques,* Marcelle Lesage, 1925; *Anarchie,* Editions de la Lampe d'Argile, 1926; *Une Carriere,* La Cite des Livres, 1926; *Les Anglais* (includes "Opinion sur les Francais," by L. Washburn, translation by Andre Maurois), Cahiers Libres, 1927; *Ce qu'on appelle charme: Pensees,* Claude Aveline, 1927; *Conseils a un jeune francais partant pour l'Angleterre,* Paillart, 1927; *La Conversation,* Hachette, 1927, translation by Yvonne Dufour published as *Conversation,* Dutton, 1930; *Decors,* Emile-Paul, 1927; *Petite histoire de l'espece humaine,* Cahiers de Paris, 1927; *Rouen,* Emile-Paul, 1927; *Contact,* Stols, 1928; *L'Amerique inattendue,* Mornay, 1931; "*Sur le vif"*: *L'Eposition coloniale de Paris, 1931,* Librairie Eos, 1931; *Chantiers americains,* Gallimard, 1933; *En Amerique* (contains of *Contact* and *L'Amerique inattendue*), Flammarion, 1933, published in French by American Book Co. (Cincinnati), 1936; *Mes Songes que voici,* Grasset, 1933; *Sentiments et Coutumes* (five lectures), Grasset, 1934; *Malte,* Editions Alpina, 1935; *La Jeunesse devant notre temps,* Flammarion, 1937; *Three Letters on the English,* Chatto & Windus, 1938, Transatlantic, 1943; *Un Art de vivre,* Plon, 1939, translation by James Whitall published as *The Art of Living,* Harper, 1940; *Chef-d'oeuvre des aquarellistes anglais: Turner et ses contemporains,* Plon, 1939; *Espoirs et souvenirs* (lecture), Maison Francaise, 1943; *The Role of Art in Life and Law* (address), translation by Arthur Cowan, Brandeis Lawyers Society (Philadelphia), 1945; *Conseils a un jeune Francais partant pour les Etats-Unis,* Jeune Parque, 1947; *Quand la France s'enrichissait,* Les Oeuvres

Libres, 1947; *Retour en France,* Maison Francaise, 1947; *J.-L. David,* Le Divan, 1948; *Can Our Civilization Be Saved?,* Brandeis Lawyers Society, 1949; *Centenaire de la mort de Frederic Chopin,* Firmin Didot, 1949; *Ce que je crois,* Grasset, 1951, new edition augmented with objections made by some readers and replies to these objections, 1952; *Cours de bonheur conjugal* (radio play), Hachette, 1951, translation by Crystal Herbert published as *The Art of Being Happily Married,* Harper, 1953; *La Divine Comtesse,* Georges Blaizot, 1951; *Metamorphoses,* Goossens (Brussels), 1951; *Paris,* Nathan (Paris), 1951; *Lettres a l'inconnue,* Jeune Parque, 1953, translation by John Buchanan-Brown published as *To an Unknown Lady,* Dutton, 1957, same translation published in England as *To the Fair Unknown,* Bodley Head, 1957; *Rio de Janeiro,* Nathan, 1953; *Centenaire de la mort de Lamennais,* Firmin Didot, 1954; *Femmes de Paris,* Plon, 1954, translation by Norman Denny published as *The Women of Paris,* Bodley Head, 1954; *Le Poeme de Versailles* (text for the performances of the Sound and Light Festival given at Versailles), Grasset, 1954, published as *Versailles aux lumieres,* Editions Tel, 1954, translation by A. S. Alexander published in France as *A Vision of Versailles,* Amelot (Brionne), 1955; *Aux innocents les mains pleines* (play), La Table Ronde, 1955; *Hollande,* Hachette, 1955; *Paris Capitale,* Foret, 1955; *Perigord,* Hachette, 1955; *Portrait de la France et des francais,* Hachette, 1955; *La France change de visage,* Gallimard, 1956; *Wit and Humor* (lecture), 1958; *Dialogues des vivants,* Fayard, 1959; *France,* Foret, 1959; *Cent cinquantenaire de Barbey d'Aurevilly a Saint-Sauveur-Le-Vicomte,* Firmin Didot, 1959; *La Bibliotheque publique et sa mission,* UNESCO, 1961, translation published in Paris as *Public Libraries and Their Mission,* UNESCO, 1961; (with J. M. Gavin) *A Civil War Album of Paintings by the Prince de Joinville,* Atheneum, 1964, published as *Princely Service: Excerpts from the Civil War Album of Paintings by the Prince de Joinville,* American Heritage, 1964; *Lettre ouverte a un jeune homme, sur la conduite de la vie,* Albin Michel, 1966; *Illusions* (lectures prepared just before his death, and never presented), Columbia University Press, 1966; *Memoirs, 1885-1967* (autobiography), translation by Denver Lindley, Harper, 1970.

Juvenile books: *Le Pays de trente-six mille volontes,* Portiques, 1928, translation by Pauline Fairbanks published as *The Country of Thirty-six Thousand Wishes,* Appleton, 1930; *Patapoufs et filifers,* Hartmann, 1930, translation by Rosemary Benet published as *Fatapoufs and Thinifers,* Holt, 1940, translation by Norman Denny published in England as *Fattypuffs and Thinifers,* Lane, 1941; *Frederic Chopin,* Brentano's, 1941, translation by Ruth Green Harris published as *Frederic Chopin,* Harper, 1942; *Eisenhower,* Didier (New York), 1945, translation by Eileen Lane Kinney published as *Eisenhower, the Liberator,* Didier, 1945; *Franklin: La Vie d'un optimiste,* Didier, 1945, translation by Haakon M. Chevalier published as *Franklin: The Life of an Optimist,* Didier, 1945; *Washington: The Life of a Patriot,* translation by Henry C. Pitz, Didier, 1946; *Nico, le petit garcon change en chien,* Calmann-Levy, 1955, translation published as *The French Boy,* Sterling, 1957; *Nico a New York,* Calmann-Levy, 1958; *Napoleon,* Hachette, 1964, translation by D.J.S. Thomson published as *Napoleon: A Pictorial Biography,* Viking, 1964.

Autobiography: *Fragments d'un journal de vacances,* Emile Hazan, 1929; *Relativisme,* Kra, 1931; *Etats-Unis 39: Journal d'un voyage en Amerique,* Editions de France, 1939, new edition, 1940; *Memoires,* two volumes, Maison Francaise, 1942, revised edition, Flammarion, 1948, translation by Denver and Jane Lindley published as *I Remember, I Remember*, Harper, 1942, same translation published in England as *Call No Man Happy*, J. Cape, 1943; *Journal: Etats-Unis 1946*, Bateau Ivre, 1946, translation, with additional material, by Joan Charles published as *From My Journal*, Harper, 1948, same translation published in England as *My American Journal*, Falcon, 1950; *Retour en France*, Maison Francaise, 1947, translation by J. Charles included in *From My Journal*, Harper, 1948; *Souvenirs d'enfance et de jeunesse*, Les Oeuvres Libres, 1947; *Journal d'un tour en Amerique Latine*, Bateau Ivre, 1948, translation by Frank Jackson published in England as *My Latin-American Diary*, Falcon, 1953; *Journal d'un tour en Suisse*, Portes de France, 1948; *Portrait d'un ami qui s'appelait moi*, Wesmael-Charlier, 1959.

Omnibus volumes: J. H. Brown, editor, *Selections from Andre Maurois*, [London], 1928; Gerard Le Grand, editor, *Morceaux choisis*, Cambridge University Press, 1931; H. Miles, translator, *A Private Universe* (essays), Appleton, 1932; Edouard Maynial, editor, *Textes choisis*, Grasset, 1936; Louis Chaigne, editor, *Poesie et action: Choix de textes*, Le Roux, 1949; *The Maurois Reader*, introduction by Anne Fremantle, Didier, 1949; *Oeuvres completes*, sixteen volumes, Fayard, 1950-56; *L'Angleterre romantique* (biographies), Gallimard, 1953; *Pour piano seul* (nouvelles), Flammarion, 1960; *Romans* (novels), Gallimard, 1961; *The Collected Stories of Andre Maurois*, Washington Square Press, 1967.

Contributor: *L'Art cinematographique* (Volume III, *Pesie du cinema*, by Maurois), Alcan, 1927; *Hommage a Andre Gide*, Editions du Capitole, 1928; *La Jeunesse litteraire devant la politique*, Cahiers Libres, 1928; *Contes et nouvelles du pays normand*, P. Duval (Elbeuf), 1930; *D'Ariane a Zoe: Alphabet galant et sentimental*, Libraire de France, 1930; *Divorce as I See It*, Douglas (London), 1930; *L'Ambassadeur*, Bossard, 1931; *Le Coeur selon . . .*, Baudiniere, 1931; *Enquete sur la France en danger*, Attinger, 1934; *L'Esprit, l'ethique et la guerre*, Stock, 1934; *Tableau de la litterature francaise*, Gallimard, 1939; *Hommage a Eugene Dabit*, Gallimard, 1939; *Europe unie, 1949-1950: Etude pour la formation d'une conscience europeenne*, Alsatia, 1949; *Marcel Proust de 1906 a 1922*, France Illustration, 1949; *Savoir vivre international*, Ode, 1950; *La Cuisine consideree comme un des beaux-arts*, Tambourinaire, 1951; *Figure dans l'oeuvre de Leger*, Carre, 1952; *Problemes d'aujourd'hui*, Larousse, 1952; *Le Tour du monde du rire*, Hachette, 1953; *Hommage a George Sand*, Faculte des Lettres, 1954; *Paris . . . Toujours*, Alpina, 1954; *Discours de reception de M. Jean Cocteau a l'Academie francaise et reponse de M. Andre Maurois*, Gallimard, 1955; *Le Dernier quart d'heure de . . .*, La Table Ronde, 1955; *Cinquantenaire du 6 octobre*, Flammarion, 1956; *Maurice Utrillo*, Foret, 1957; *S. Mendjisky*, Grou-Radenez, 1961; M. B. Shaw, editor, *Types et Personnages*, Longmans, Green, 1963; *My Most Inspiring Moment* (collection of articles from *Family* Magazine), Doubleday, 1965; *Discours de reception de M. Jacques Rueff a l'Academie francaise, et reponse de M. Andre Maurois*, Gallimard, 1965. Contributor to various numbers of *Les Oeuvres libres: Nouvelle serie*.

Editor, with prefaces, forewords, and introductions: Maurice Barine, *Daphne Adeane*, [Paris], 1928; Paul Louis Courier, *Conversation chez le Comtess d'Albany*, Plon, 1928; *Zinovi Pechkoff*, La Legion etrangere au Maroc, [Paris], 1928; Jean-Francois-Paul de Gondi, cardinal de Retz, *Memoires*, four volumes, Charpentier (Paris), 1928-

29; Joseph Durey de Saurpy du Terrail, *The Masked Lady*, translation by Eric Sutton, Chapman & Hall (London), 1929; Arnold Bennett, *L'Escalier de Riceyman*, translation by Maurice Remon, [Paris], 1929; Virginia Woolf, *Mrs. Dalloway*, translation by S. David, [Paris], 1929; Alain (Emile Chartier), *Mars, or the Truth about War*, translation by Doris Mudies and Elizabeth Hill, J. Cape & H. Smith, 1930; Jacques-Emile Blanche, *Aymeris*, [Paris], 1930; Benjamin Disraeli (Lord Beaconsfield), *Lettres intimes*, translation by Mme. William Laparra, [Paris], 1930; Jacques Lefebvre, *Neptune and Co.*, Berger-Levrault (Paris), 1930; (with Sir Daniel Stevenson) Robert de Traz, *The Spirit of Geneva*, translation by Fried-Ann Kindler, Oxford University Press, 1935; *Londres*, Arthaud, 1936; *Voltaire: Pages immortelles choisies et expliques par Andre Maurois*, Correa, 1938, translation by Barrows Mussey and Richard Aldington published as *Voltaire: Living Thoughts, Presented by Andre Maurois*, Longmans, Green (New York), 1939; Gustave Flaubert, *Madame Bovary*, translation by Eleanor Marx Aveling, Limited Editions Club (New York), 1938; Victor Hugo, *Les Miserables*, translation by Lascelles Wraxall, Limited Editions Club, 1938; Balzac, *Ten Droll Tales*, translation by J. Lewis May, [New York], 1940; Marcel Proust, *Jean Santeuil*, three volumes, Gallimard, 1952; Tolstoi, *Le Bonheur conjugal* [suivi de] *La Sonate a Kreutzer*, Vial, 1953; (with others) *French Thought in the Eighteenth Century*, McKay, 1953; Alexandre Dumas, fils, *La Dame aux Camelias*, translation by Edmund Gosse, Limited Editions Club, 1955; Edmond Pognon, *Chateaux de l'ancienne France*, Credit Lyonnais, 1957; Oscar Wilde, *The Picture of Dorian Gray*, Limited Editions Club, 1957; (with Georges Duhamel and Jean Huguet) *Rives et Courants*, Alsatia, 1960; Rosamond Lehmann, *Poussiere*, Club des Amis du Livre, c.1961; Andre Brissaud, *L'Amerique de Kennedy*, Club des Amis du Livre, 1962; Jack Kolbert, *Edmond Jaloux et sa critique litteraire*, Minard (Paris), 1962; Norman Mailer, *Les Nues et les morts*, translation by Jean Malaquais, Le Livre de Poche, 1962; Alphonse Seche, *Ces jours lointains*, Michel, 1962; Soulange-Bodin, *Chateaux anciens de France connus et inconnus*, Editions de Jura, 1962; Marcel Thiebaut, *Entre les lignes*, Hachette, 1962; Pierre Boisdeffre, *Metamorphose de la litterature*, Editions Alsatia, 1963; Lewis Carroll, *Alice au pays des merveilles*, translation by Andre Bay, Verviers (Belgium), 1963; Robert Choquette, *Metropolitan Museum* (poems), Grasset, 1963; Georges Gontier, *Alain a la guerre*, Mercure de France, 1963; Marcel Proust, *A la recherche du temps perdu*, three volumes, Gallimard, 1963; Jean Damas-Hinard, *Dictionnarie ou recueil alphabetique des opinions et jugements de Napoleon Ier*, Au Club de l'Honnete Homme, c.1964; Anne Heurgon-Desjardins, *Paul Desjardins et les decades de Pontigny*, Presses Universitaires de France, 1964; Paul B. Metadier, *Balzac au petit matin*, La Palatine (Geneva), 1964; Ivan Tourgueniev, *Premier amour* [suivi de] *Nouvelles et poemes en prose*, translation by R. Hofmann, Le Livre de Poche, 1964; Honore de Balzac, *Le Lys dans la vallee*, Le Livre de Poche, 1965; Paul Helot, *Un Humaniste: Le Docteur Paul Helot*, Colombes, Morin, 1965; Jacques Sallebert and Phillippe Berard, *U.S.A.*, Gerard, 1965.

Translator: (With G. Richet under the name E. Herzog) Ian Hay, *Les premiers mille . . .*, [Paris], 1917; (with Jeanne-Simone Bussy) David Garnett, *La Femme changee en renard*, Grasset, 1924; (with Virginia Vernon) Laurence Housman, *Victoria Regina* (play), Plon, 1937; Elizabeth Barrett Browning, *Sonnets a la Portugaise*, Brentano's, 1946.

Contributor of articles to *Adam International Review, A La*

Page, American Heritage, Les Annales, Annales du Centre Universitaire Mediterraneen, Atlantic, Atlas Magazine, Biblio, Cahiers Charles Du Bos, Family, Le Figaro Litteraire, Forum, La Grive, Harper's, Holiday, House and Garden, L'Illustration, Irish Writing, Ladies' Home Journal, Lettres Francaises, Listener, Living Age, McCall's, New York Times Book Review, New York Times Magazine, Nouvelles Litteraires, Opera News, Reader's Digest, La Revue Hebdomadaire, La Revue de Holland, La Revue de Paris, Revue Politique et Parlementaire, Revue des Visages, Rotarian, Saturday Review, Spectator, La Table Ronde, Theatre Arts, U.N. World, Vital Speeches, Woman's Home Companion, Yale Review, and other publications.

SIDELIGHTS: The scope and volume of Andre Maurois's writings are certainly two of the most striking features of his literary output. His versatility as a biographer, novelist, popular historian, literary critic, practical philosopher, and writer of fantastic tales, is all the more remarkable considering that he was thirty-three years of age when his first book was published and that he did not devote the major part of his time to writing until almost ten years later. Despite his superior achievements as a student, his childhood desire to be a writer, and his ambition to become a professor, Maurois, out of a deep sense of family loyalty, devoted the first ten years of his professional life to assisting his father and uncles with the management of their cloth factory. It was the first World War which catapulted him out of the humdrum routine of the small provincial town of Elbeuf, exposed him to the British character and customs, and inspired him to write *The Silence of Colonel Bramble.* This witty and penetrating commentary on warfare and the British character and prejudices was received with unexpected enthusiasm on both sides of the Channel and immediately ushered Maurois into literary circles. It was at this time that Emile Herzog adopted the pseudonym Andre Maurois, because he was an officer in the French Army when this book, which could have offended the English, was originally published. (Maurois is the name of a French village, and Herzog reportedly liked its somber sound.) It was the first of a series of works on the English and American cultures that brought Maurois the reputation of being the foremost intellectual link between France and the English-speaking world.

In an article written for the *Revue de Paris* (May, 1959), Maurois attributed the wide scope of his writings to his innate and universal curiosity, his desire to understand, and his need to explain. In a sense, writing had been for him a means of self-education, the fruits of which he offered to the public. Robert Kemp described him as being "above all, a great professor." The most profound influence on Maurois was Emile Chartier, one of the finest teachers of modern times, who wrote under the pseudonym Alain. Maurois studied under Alain at Rouen and it was to him, Maurois stated, that he owed "everything" and to him that Maurois consistently made references in his writings and interviews. Maurois related in his *Memories* that Alain encouraged him to pursue a non-academic vocation, following the examples of Balzac and Dickens, so that he could see men at work, experience life, and avoid writing before he was mature enough to write. Maurois was further influenced by the personality and writings of Charles Du Bos who, like himself, interpreted foreign thought and literature to the French nation. As a result of the success of his early writings, his travels, and the captivating charm of his person, Maurois also came into close contact with such writers as Andre Gide, Rudyard Kipling, Virginia Woolf, H. G. Wells, Maurice

Baring, Anatole France, Paul Valery, and Francois Mauriac.

It was as a biographer that Maurois made his most significant contribution to literature, and in America his nonscholarly biographies have been more widely read than either his novels or essays. With his first two biographies, *Ariel: The Life of Shelley* and *Disraeli: A Picture of the Victorian Age,* Maurois was instrumental in revolutionizing the basic concept and content of biography as a literary media, lending to it the qualities of a good novel. Professor Le Sage commented that Maurois had a talent for "imparting to biography the illusion of living reality characteristic of fiction. . . . Facts in his hands change from statistics into vital indications of some real human being." Because of his superior gift of intuition and projection, "a vivid idea of the person behind the personage" emerges in his prose. The *Times Literary Supplement,* however, noted that his work on Napoleon contains "many misstatements of facts . . . [and] instances of sheer carelessness." In his *Aspects of Biography* Maurois clearly specified the essentials of this form of "novelized" or interpretive biography. Primarily, the form requires strict adherence to facts even though these may be objectionable to descendants of the subject or threatening to the subject's legendary image. No attempt should be made to present a morally exemplary life. Whereas older biographers insisted on the homogeneity of character, Maurois stressed the multiplicity of the personality, its contradictory extremes, and its interior struggles. However, transcending these diversities of character, every life, according to Maurois, possesses a fundamental harmony or unifying thread that the biographer must discover and reveal. By choosing subjects with whom he could personally identify, Maurois further transformed biography, as Georges Lemaitre has indicated, into a medium that could "serve the writer as a vehicle for the outpouring of his suppressed emotions and desires." The quality of his biographies, in Lemaitre's opinion, varies directly with the degree of his personal affinity with the subjects. Notwithstanding these standards, Maurois maintained that there exists no possible scientific truth in biography, but only a psychological or poetic truth, and he believed that it is impossible to achieve the kind of synthesis of a person's inner life that one often finds in novels.

Maurois's histories were largely based on secondary sources which were not necessarily the most recent ones. In his histories of England, America, France, and Germany, he made effective use of his ability to empathize with other times, individuals, and cultures. Michel Droit pointed out that Maurois saw the essence of man's history as the struggle of individuals. In portraying the changing characteristics of men and nations, it was Maurois's goal to reveal the permanent features of a people. Utilizing his discriminate and artful choice of the clever anecdote and quick quotation, he injected color and drama into his texts. There is in his histories, a cool detachment and an absence of distortion.

Maurois's novels are most often set within the framework of French provincial life. Maurois was a novelist of the bourgeoisie, of marriage, and of the family. Many of his characters and circumstances are autobiographical, but, as Lemaitre stated, it is not possible to draw an unbroken parallel between his own life and any of the lives he created. *Bernard Quesnay,* the story of a young man who aspires to a literary career but is tied to a family textile industry is the most obviously autobiographical. The theme of reconciliation of opposing interests runs throughout his novels. Maurois once said: "I have felt an acute need to describe certain conflicts and sentiments which have divided and troubled me." In *Bernard Quesnay* he described the conflict between the propertied and working classes, in *The Family Circle,* that of two generations, in *The Atmosphere of Love,* that of two lovers, in *The Silence of Colonel Bramble,* that of two cultures, and, in *The Return of Doctor O'Grady,* that of the deterministic materialist and the spiritualist. Although his protagonists often exhibit attitudes of acceptance and resignation in the face of the unchangeable, Maurois, as Droit commented, did not resolve the problems he posed or postulate any moral or political doctrines. Rather, he tacitly urged the reader to find his own resolution. He reserved the explication of theories for his essays.

The most subtle of Maurois's talents as a biographer are given free play in his novels. Commenting on *The Atmosphere of Love,* Elmer Davis said: "You must go back to Stendhal to find so painstaking an analysis of the causes and workings of love and jealousy." This statement would have pleased the author, for Maurois, like his preceptor, Alain, venerated Stendhal and Balzac above all other writers. Alain instructed Maurois to copy out, word for word, passages from *La Chartreuse de Parme or Le Rouge et le Noir* "in order to learn the technique of writing, as young painters copy the pictures of their masters." Maurois's admiration of Balzac prompted him to write a biography of the author of *The Human Comedy.* At one time Maurois stated, "I would have liked to write a *Human Comedy.*" Maurois's novels display a balance, a restrained dynamism, and a technical skill that is usually concentrated on the development of character and psychological analyses rather than on action. His biographies, however, are generally considered to be superior to his novels which, as Margaret Wallace judged to be the case with *The Family Circle,* do not always impart a vivid or lasting sensation of life. Henri Peyre stated that Maurois wrote family novels with only moderate success and that, in his opinion, the novels of Maurois will not survive as outstanding literary achievements.

Practically all of Maurois's writings are lauded for their clarity and precision; he is a thoroughly readable author no matter what his subject may be. His style of exposition is compressed, graceful, urbane—"exquisitely civilized." His irony and wit, charm and delight. His structure is neatly ordered and balanced; nothing is superfluous. Louis Chaigne said that Maurois "knows how to put silences between his sentences and in his sentences." One critic commented that he has "the gift of skimming lightly over the most difficult ground and so making everything seem extraordinarily easy and pleasant." One seldom gets the feeling that he is deeply emersed in the pathos of the human condition. Because of his detached restraint, his polished elegance, and his disinclination to offend, Maurois's works are often devoid of intensity and are reproached for their superficiality, pseudosophistication, and artificiality.

Despite the fact that Maurois's novels are more popular in France than in the United States, the French regard him primarily as an analyst and moralist, not as an exceptionally creative writer. In the late twenties the originality of his work was challenged in a series of articles in the *Mercure de France.* Lemaitre stated that "frequently it is possible to trace the essentials of his plots and characters to certain well-known and definite sources . . . [but Maurois] has in no case consciously adapted to his own use fragments of some other author's work." The full force of Maurois's imagination is seen best in his science fiction tales like *The Weigher of Souls* and *The Earth Dwellers* which hold the reader in a sustained state of suspense and almost force him to surrender his rational faculties. Maurois excelled as a storyteller and his *contes fantastiques* represent, according to Droit, an absolutely original genre in modern French literature.

In Maurois's own life one can discern a dichotomy between his artistic nature and his conservative bourgeois background and sympathies. As a spokesman of his social class, he wrote that "a horror of disorder has always been one of my strongest emotions." Describing his own youth, he commented that he had been "Frivolous? Yes. Perhaps. But above all, a conformist, exactly the opposite of a rebel." Similarly, he saw man as a brutish animal that has been civilized only gradually by philosophers, priests, rituals, and by society in general. He therefore defended conventions in an age when they were being challenged, and believed that the rejection of traditional customs is tantamount to a return to savagery. This is not to say that Maurois opposed reform; but change, he contended, should come about slowly, in accordance with traditional roots, and under the aegis of a firm and just power. It follows that his criticism of present society and the bourgeoisie was muted. One sympathetic critic, Louis Chaigne, wrote that, in Maurois's works, "one would like a sharper, more vigorous reprobation of [middle class] conformism and prejudices."

Maurois neither subscribed to nor formulated any formal philosophic system. He was most frequently labeled an agnostic and, according to Michel Droit, he accepted only one absolute—that all truth is relative. Maurois nonetheless stated that he believed in "the existence in man of something which transcends man. . . ." "I am ready," he added "to call this common conscience God, but my god is imminent, not transcendent." The universe, he believed, is neither hostile nor moral. It does not determine man's destiny. The individual, rather, has the power to create his fate to the degree that he refuses to create his unhappiness. That is, if one accepts what cannot be altered and does not ask, in an Epicurean sense, too much of life, he will then be capable of reaching some level of happiness which Maurois thought was man's duty to do. He attributed his optimism and confidence to Alain, who taught him that "the human condition is such that if one does not adopt an attitude of invincible optimism, the blackest pessimism would at once be justified, because despair . . . engenders despair and failure."

Many of the particulars of Maurois's practical philosophy are contained in the essays which compose *The Art of Living.* These have been described by some critics as tolerant, urbane, and sensible, and by others as unreasonably reasonable, complacent, and opportunistic. Some critics also discounted him as a "literary factory," an allegation not altogether groundless. He told the *New York Times* a few months before his death at the age of eighty-two: "I get up at seven and am at my desk at eight and work all day long. I write every day except for Sunday. . . . The job of a writer is to write."

BIOGRAPHICAL/CRITICAL SOURCES—Books: David G. Larg, *Andre Maurois,* Harold Shaylor (London), 1931; John Bakeless, *Andre Maurois,* Appleton, 1932; J. Sauvenier, *Andre Maurois,* Editions de Belgique, 1932; Louis Chaigne, *Vie et oeuvres d'ecrivains,* 1933; Maurice Roya, *Andre Maurois,* Editions de la Caravelle, 1934; Amelie Fillon, *Andre Maurois, romancier,* [Paris], 1937; Georges Lemaitre, *Andre Maurois,* Stanford University Press, 1939; Victor Dupuis, *Un Ecrivain tonique: Andre Maurois,* Editions de l'Efficience (Lausanne), 1945; Suzanne Guery, *La Pensee d'Andre Maurois,* Deux Rives, 1951; Michel Droit, *Andre Maurois,* Editions Universitaires, 1953, revised edition, 1958; Henri Peyre, *The Contemporary French Novel,* Oxford University Press, 1955; Jacques Suffel, *Andre Maurois avec des remarques par Andre Maurois,* Flammarion, 1963; Andre Maurois, *Memoirs, 1885-1967,* translation by Denver Lindley, Harper, 1970.

Periodicals: *Saturday Review of Literature,* September 6, 1919, July 21, 1928, September 7, 1929, April 24, 1937, September 5, 1953, May 5, 1956; *Living Age,* July 3, 1926, July 12, 1926, April 15, 1928, July 5, 1928; *Independent Review,* December 17, 1927; *Mercure de France,* March 1, 1928, April 1 and 15, 1928, May 1, 1928, June 1 and 15, 1928; *Annales,* May 15, 1928; *Le Correspondant,* June 10, 1928; *Sewanee Review,* October, 1928; *Everyman,* September 11, 1930, July 22, 1965; *Times Literary Supplement,* April 21, 1932, December 2, 1960, August 13, 1964; *New York Times Book Review,* August 7, 1932, May 22, 1966; *Etudes,* June 20, 1935, January 20, 1938; *Nouvelle Revue Francaise,* September 1, 1937; *Paris-Soir,* June 23, 1939; *Time,* March 25, 1940; *Life,* January 19, 1948, October 4, 1954; *New York Herald Tribune Weekly Book Review,* February 8, 1948; *Newsweek,* April 10, 1950; *Hommes et Mondes,* January, 1955; *Revue de Paris,* February, 1958, May, 1959; *La Nouvelle Critique,* November, 1960; *New Yorker,* January 26, 1963; *Le Figaro Litteraire,* June 3-9, 1965; *Biblio,* June-July, 1965; *Manchester Guardian,* July 26, 1965; *New York Times,* October 10, 1967; *Time,* November 17, 1967.†

(Died October 9, 1967)

*   *   *

MAY, Elizabeth   1907-

PERSONAL: Born August 23, 1907, in Denver, Colo.; daughter of Henry (a lawyer) and May (Rickard) May. *Education:* Attended Ecole Normale de Musique, Paris, France, 1927-28; Mills College, A.B., 1935; University of California, Berkeley, M.A., 1940; University of California, Los Angeles, Ph.D., 1958. *Office:* Santa Monica Unified School District, 1723 Fourth St., Santa Monica, Calif.

CAREER: Teacher of music in Oakland (Calif.) public schools, 1935-39, 1940-42; assistant director, United Service Organizations (USO), in various California cities, 1942-45; teacher of music in Oakland (Calif.) public schools, 1945-47, at San Jose State College (now University) San Jose, Calif., 1947-48, Sacramento State College (now California State University, Sacramento), 1948-50, San Jose State College (now University) 1950-53, and University of California, Los Angeles, 1954-55; Santa Monica (Calif.) Unified School District, teacher of music, beginning 1958. Summer professor at Stanford University, 1956, and University of Washington, Seattle, 1961; Fulbright lecturer at University of Western Australia, 1965. *Member:* Society for Ethnomusicology, International Folk Music Council, International Society for Music Education, Music Educators National Conference, Southern California Recorder Society (music director, 1956-58). *Awards, honors:* Grant from Australian Institute of Aboriginal Studies, 1965, to record aboriginal music.

WRITINGS: The Influence of the Meiji Period on Japanese Children's Music, University of California Press, 1963. Contributor to *Western Folklore, Ethnomusicology, American Journal of Physical Medicine, Volta Review, Music Educators Journal, Journal of Research in Music Education,* and other journals.

WORK IN PROGRESS: Writing on Australian music and music education.††

MAYER, Clara Woollie   1895-

PERSONAL: Born June 1, 1895, in New York, N.Y.; daughter of Bernhard and Sophia (Buttenwieser) Mayer. *Education:* Columbia University, B.A., 1915, graduate study, 1915-19. *Politics:* Democrat. *Religion:* Jewish. *Home:* 41 East 72nd St., New York, N.Y. 10021.

CAREER: New School for Social Research, New York, N.Y., trustee, 1924-30, assistant director, 1931-36, associate director, 1937-43, dean, 1943-61, vice-president, 1950-61; writer. *Awards, honors:* D.H.L. from New School for Social Research, 1948.

WRITINGS: The Manmade Wilderness, Atheneum, 1964. Assistant editor, *Encyclopedia of Social Sciences,* 1928-29.

WORK IN PROGRESS: A book on adult education.

SIDELIGHTS: Clara Mayer has competency in German, French, Spanish, Italian, and Latin.††

*   *   *

MAYFIELD, L(afayette) H(enry) II   1910-

PERSONAL: Born December 19, 1910, in Green, S.C.; son of Lafayette Henry (a judge) and Pearl (Wilson) Mayfield; married Glady G. Manney; children: D. Jean (Mrs. William G. Donohoo), Lafayette Henry III, Geoffrey Lynn. *Education:* Attended Clemson College (now University), 1928-32, Marian College, 1935-38, and Garrett Theological Seminary, 1943-47. *Home:* 5500 Kirby Rd., Cincinnati, Ohio 45239. *Office:* Christ Hospital, Auburn Ave., Cincinnati, Ohio 45219.

CAREER: The Methodist Church, Ohio Conference, Columbus, minister, beginning 1947. Chaplain, Christ Hospital, Cincinnati, Ohio; chief of chaplains, Villa Hope Methodist Convalescent Hospital; conductor of annual workshops on pastoral care and counseling. *Member:* American Protestant Hospital Association, Methodist Hospital and Homes Association (past chairman, chaplains division). Lecturer on and demonstrator of candle-making.

WRITINGS: Behind the Clouds, Light, Abingdon, 1965.

AVOCATIONAL INTERESTS: Candle-making, photography, growing roses, carpentry.††

*   *   *

MAZZULLA, Fred   1903-

PERSONAL: Born December 14, 1903, in Trinidad, Colo.; son of Enrico and Angela (Perri) Mazzulla; married Leona Williams, February 21, 1929; married second wife, Josephine D'Andrea (a writer under the name Jo Mazzulla), November 19, 1939; children: Arlene (Mrs. Robert Christen), Julia Noland. *Education:* University of Denver, LL.B., 1937. *Politics:* Republican. *Home:* 1930 East Eighth Ave., Denver, Colo. 80206. *Office:* 1430 Western Federal Savings Building, Denver, Colo. 80202.

CAREER: Admitted to the Colorado State Bar, 1938; attorney in Denver, Colo., beginning 1938. Free-lance photographer; writer. Member of draft board and government appeal board, Denver, beginning 1944; member of Denver Landmark Commission, beginning 1967. Trustee, American Museum of Photography. *Member:* American Bar Association, National Press Photographers Association, Colorado Bar Association, Westerners (former president of Denver Posse), Denver Press Club, Elks.

WRITINGS: (Editor with William Kostka) *Mountain Charley or the Adventures of Mrs. E. J. Guerin, Who Was*

Thirteen Years in Male Attire, University of Oklahoma Press, 1968.

Western books and booklets with wife, Jo Mazzulla: *The First 100 Years: A Photographic Account of the Rip-Roaring, Gold-Plated Days in the World's Greatest Gold Camp,* Hirschfeld Press, 1956; *Colorado's Century of Cities,* Smith-Brooks Publishing, 1958; *Centennial Album of Colorado,* Kistler Publishing, 1959; *Outlaw Album,* Hirschfeld Press, 1966; *Brass Checks and Red Lights,* Hirschfeld Press, 1966; *Al Packer: A Colorado Cannibal,* Hirschfeld Press, 1968.

SIDELIGHTS: Fred Mazzulla and his wife spent over thirty years collecting more than 250,000 photographs and negatives of the western scene and taping more than 850 hours of interviews with pioneer residents and widely known personalities. Both the photographs, which have been used to illustrate numerous books and magazine articles, and the tapes have been acquired by the Amon Carter Museum of Western Art in Fort Worth, Texas.

BIOGRAPHICAL/CRITICAL SOURCES: Max Miller, *Holladay Street,* New American Library, 1962; *Seattle Times,* August 8, 1968; *Book World,* September 8, 1968; *Rocky Mountain News,* October 12, 1973.

* * *

McALEAVY, Henry   1912-1968

PERSONAL: Born January 11, 1912, in Manchester, England; son of Denis and Catherine (Sheridan) McAleavy; married Ayako Ikeda (a teacher of Japanese), May 16, 1942. *Education:* University of Manchester, B.A., 1933; National University of Peking, graduate study, 1936-37; Trinity College, Cambridge, M.A., 1938. *Politics:* Labour. *Religion:* Catholic.

CAREER: British Embassy, Press Attache's Office, Chinese specialist in Shanghai and Chungking, China, 1940-45; Chinese National Bureau of Compilation and Translation, translator in Peip'ei, Szechwan, 1945-46; British Embassy, Shanghai, Chinese secretary (information), 1947-50; British Museum, assistant keeper, department of Oriental printed books and manuscripts, 1951-54; barrister-at-law, Gray's Inn, beginning 1954; University of London, London, England, reader in Oriental laws, beginning 1954.

WRITINGS: A Dream of Tartary, Allen & Unwin, 1963; *The Modern History of China,* Praeger, 1967.

Translator: *That Chinese Woman,* Crowell, 1960; *The Chinese Bigamy of Mr. David Winterlea,* Allen & Unwin, 1961; *Black Flags in Vietnam,* Macmillan, 1968. Contributor of articles on Chinese history to *History Today,* and papers on Chinese law and history to academic publications.

WORK IN PROGRESS: The Warlords of China.

SIDELIGHTS: McAleavy was competent in French, Chinese, Latin, and Greek.

BIOGRAPHICAL/CRITICAL SOURCES: London Times, October 28, 1968.†

(Died October 25, 1968)

* * *

McAULIFFE, Clarence   1903-

PERSONAL: Born March 16, 1903, in Omaha, Neb.; son of Robert (a postman) and Anna (Helin) McAuliffe. *Education:* St. Louis University, A.B., 1925, A.M., 1928, S.T.D., 1939.

CAREER: Roman Catholic priest of Society of Jesus (Jesuits); St. Louis University, St. Mary's College, St. Marys, Kan., professor of sacramental theology, 1940-67.

WRITINGS: Sacramental Theology, B. Herder, 1958, revised edition, 1961; *De Sacramentis in Genere,* B. Herder, 1960. Contributor of learned and popular articles to Catholic and other periodicals. Editorial consultant, *Theology Digest.*

WORK IN PROGRESS: Research articles on Catholic doctrine.

SIDELIGHTS: McAuliffe lived for three years on the Island of Jersey in the English Channel. He reads French, German, Spanish, Italian, and Latin, and "can make way through" Greek.†

* * *

McBROOM, R. Curtis   1910-
(Nathaniel Dring)

PERSONAL: Born September 8, 1910, in Lowpoint, Ill.; son of Elam Rowland (a country doctor) and Clara (Curtis) McBroom; married Esther Adams, August 25, 1931; children: Robert, Paul, William. *Education:* University of Chicago, student, 1928-29; University of Illinois, A.B., 1932, law studies, 1932-33. *Religion:* Disciples of Christ. *Agent:* Berkley Associates, 132 West Broadway, San Diego, Calif. 92101. *Office:* 2409 Medford Court West, Fort Worth, Tex. 76109.

CAREER: Admitted to Texas Bar, 1934, and Bar of U.S. Supreme Court, 1944; attorney in private practice, Fort Worth, Tex., beginning 1934; also officer in oil companies, Fort Worth, beginning 1950. Assistant to U.S. Solicitor of Labor, Texas office, 1939-40; Texas Royalty Co., director, beginning 1950; Producers, Inc. (subsidiary of Signal Oil & Gas Co.), president, 1951-53; Ambassador Oil Corp., vice-president, 1953-57; WFA Oil Co., president, 1957-64. *Military service:* U.S. Army, 1944-45. *Member:* American Bar Association, American Arbitration Association (panel member, arbitrator), American Institute of Mining Engineers, American Petroleum Landmans Association (charter member), Fort Worth Chamber of Commerce.

WRITINGS—Under pseudonym Nathaniel Dring: *The Earth Is Your Spaceship,* Space Age Press, 1967. Contributor of technical articles to legal and education journals.

WORK IN PROGRESS: Space Age Philosophy, nonfiction; *Migration to Venus,* a sequel, also in science fiction form, to *The Earth Is Your Spaceship.*

SIDELIGHTS: McBroom told *CA:* "My interest in geology stirred my interest in the space age. . . . I have taken this 'story' [science fiction] method to present several new geological theories as well as a provocative idea that some of our ancestors actually came from outer space only some 12,000 years ago."

* * *

McCAW, Mabel Niedermeyer   1899-

PERSONAL: Born March 13, 1899, in Bloomington, Ill.; daughter of Charles (a bookkeeper) and Anna L. (Ammann) Niedermeyer; married Clayton Claire McCaw (a minister), February 3, 1948; stepchildren: John E., Rossie Elizabeth (Mrs. John W. Johannabar), Franklin C., Herbert P. *Education:* Illinois Wesleyan University, B.S., 1924; Yale University, M.A., 1926. *Religion:* Disciples of Christ.

CAREER: First Christian Church, Bloomington, Ill.,

director of education, 1927-35; United Christian Missionary Society, Indianapolis, Ind., national director of children's work, 1935-48; free-lance writer in religious education field.

WRITINGS: Then I Think of God, Bethany, 1942; *This Is God's World*, Bethany, 1944, revised edition, 1960; *Sometime Every Day*, Bethany, 1948; *Our Happy Family*, Bethany, 1958; *God's Way*, Whitman Publishing, 1961; *God's Loving Care*, Gibson, 1961; *Orange Juice for Terry*, Broadman, 1962; *My Friend at Church* (picture-story book), Bethany, 1968; *My Friend Next Door* (picture-story book), Bethany, 1968; *I Know What Love Is*, Broadman, 1968. Contributor of stories, poems, songs, and devotionals to church school papers.†

*   *   *

McCLAIN, Russell H(arding)   1910-

PERSONAL: Born September 1, 1910, in Benton, Ark.; son of William (a railroad track foreman) and Cora V. (Burrow) McClain; married Lillian Alyene Yarbrough, October 8, 1933; children: Marilyn Russell. *Education:* Centenary College of Louisiana, B.A., 1944; Columbia University, M.A., 1945, Ph.D., 1955. *Politics:* Republican. *Religion:* Methodist. *Home:* 1220 Indian Hill Rd., Toms River, N.J. 08753. *Office:* Ocean County College, Toms River, N.J. 08753.

CAREER: Worked in various capacities for the *New York Times*, New York City, 1946-61; Typo-Publishers' Welfare and Pension Fund, administrator, 1961-66; New York University, New York City, teacher of economics in school of education, 1961-66; Ocean County College, Toms River, N.J., professor of psychology and sociology, beginning 1966, chairman of department of public administration and department of social sciences, beginning 1966. *Member:* Academy of Political Science, American Historical Association, American Orthopsychiatric Association.

WRITINGS: (With George G. Dawson) *Colliers' Quick and Easy Guide to Economics*, Collier, 1964, published as *Economics for Businessmen and Investors*, 1966.

WORK IN PROGRESS: J. and E. Brooks: A Study in Mid-Nineteenth-Century Journalism.

*   *   *

McCLINTOCK, Robert (Mills)   1909-

PERSONAL: Born August 30, 1909, in Seattle, Wash.; son of John Mills and Christine (Chamberlain) McClintock; married Elena Barrios, April 29, 1936; children: John Martin, Robert David. *Education:* Stanford University, B.A., 1931. *Home:* 2429 California St. N.W., Washington, D.C. 20007. *Agent:* Julian Bach Literary Agency, 3 East 48th St., New York, N.Y. 10017. *Office:* U.S. Department of State, Washington, D.C.

CAREER: U.S. Department of State, foreign service officer, beginning 1931, had various diplomatic assignments in Panama, 1932, Japan, 1933-35, Chile, 1935-37, Dominican Republic, 1937-39, Finland, 1939-44, and Sweden, 1944; assigned to United Nations as member of international secretariat at Conference on International Organization, San Francisco, Calif., 1945, as political advisor to U.S. delegation, London, England, 1945-46, and New York, N.Y., 1946-48; secretary of American Embassy, Brussels, Belgium, 1949-57; assigned to National War College, 1951-52; deputy chief of mission and counselor at U.S. Embassy, Cairo, Egypt, 1952; deputy chief of mission, Saigon, Vietnam, 1953; ambassador to Cambodia, 1954-56, Lebanon, 1958-61, and Argentina, 1962-64; advisor to Naval War Col-

lege, 1964-66; senior foreign service inspector, 1966-67; co-director of Special State Defense Study of U.S. Overseas Bases, 1968-69; chairman of interdepartmental group of Symington Subcommittee on Overseas Commitments, 1969-70; ambassador to Venezuela, beginning 1970.

MEMBER: American Foreign Service Association (life member), U.S. Naval Institute (life member), Phi Beta Kappa, Sigma Chi, Metropolitan Club (Washington, D.C.), Chevy Chase Club (Chevy Chase, Md.), Annapolis Yacht Club. *Awards, honors:* Gold Medal of U.S. Naval Institute, 1942; Superior Service Award, U.S. Department of State, 1959.

WRITINGS: The Meaning of Limited War, Houghton, 1967.

SIDELIGHTS: Robert McClintock speaks French, Spanish, Italian, Portuguese, and Swedish. He has traveled in seventy-six countries. *Avocational interests:* Sailing, skiing, submarine archaeology, swimming, shooting.†

*   *   *

McCLOY, Shelby Thomas   1898-19(?)

PERSONAL: Born January 27, 1898, in Monticello, Ark.; son of Joseph Dixon and Sarah Tommie (Tool) McCloy; married Minnie Lee Fagan, March 25, 1933. *Education:* Davidson College, A.B., 1918, A.M., 1919; Union Theological Seminary, Richmond, Va., further study, 1919-20, 1922-23; Oxford University, B.Litt., 1922, B.A., 1924; Columbia University, Ph.D., 1933. *Religion:* Presbyterian. *Home:* 201 West Fourth St., Fordyce, Ark. 71742.

CAREER: Robert College, Constantinople (now Istanbul), Turkey, Young Men's Christian Association secretary and instructor in Bible, 1924-25; Duke University, Durham, N.C., instructor, 1927-41, assistant professor of history, 1941-45; University of Kentucky, Lexington, visiting professor, 1944-45, professor of history, 1945-66, professor emeritus, beginning 1966, Hallam Professor of History, 1959-61. *Member:* Phi Beta Kappa. *Awards, honors:* Social Science Research Council grants-in-aid, 1937, 1939, 1946; Fulbright research award for work in Paris, 1956-57; Kentucky Research Foundation award, 1963-64, for work in France.

WRITINGS: Gibbon's Antagonism to Christianity, Williams & Norgate, 1933; *Government Assistance in Eighteenth-Century France*, Duke University Press, 1946; *French Inventions of the Eighteenth Century*, University of Kentucky Press, 1952; *The Humanitarian Movement in Eighteenth-Century France*, University of Kentucky Press, 1957; *The Negro in France*, University of Kentucky Press, 1961; *The Negro in the French West Indies*, University of Kentucky Press, 1966. Contributor to historical journals.†

(Deceased)

*   *   *

McCULLOCH, Warren S(turgis)   1898-1969

PERSONAL: Born November 16, 1898, in Orange, N.J.; son of James W. and Mary Hughes (Bradley) McCulloch; married Rook Metzger, May 29, 1924. *Education:* Yale University, B.A., 1921; Columbia University, M.A., 1923, M.D., 1927; New York University, graduate work in mathematical physics, 1931-32; Rockland State Hospital, psychiatric training, 1932-34. *Home:* Whippoorwill Rd., Old Lyme, Conn. 06371. *Office:* Massachusetts Institute of Technology, Room 26-027, Cambridge, Mass. 02139.

CAREER: Licensed to practice medicine in state of New

York. Bellevue Hospital, New York City, intern and resident, Neurological Service, 1927-28; experimental work in epilepsy and head injuries in laboratories of Columbia University, New York City, and Bellevue Hospital, 1928-30; Seth Low Junior College, instructor in physiological psychology, 1930-31; Yale University, New Haven, Conn., honorary research fellow, Laboratory of Neurophysiology, 1934-35, Sterling Fellow, 1935-36, instructor, 1936-40, research assistant with title of assistant professor, 1941-45, professor of psychiatry and clinical professor of physiology, 1945-52; Massachusetts Institute of Technology, Cambridge, staff member of Division of Sponsored Research, Research Laboratory of Electronics, continuing research on central nervous system, beginning 1952. Diplomate, National Board of Medicine. *Military service:* U.S. Naval Reserve, active duty, World War I.

MEMBER: American Academy of Neurology, American Neurological Association, American Physiological Society, American Orthopsychiatric Association (honorary member), Association for Research in Nervous and Mental Disease, Electroencephalographic Society (England), Society for Biological Psychiatry, American Association of Anatomists, Aerospace Medical Association, Civil Aerospace Medical Association, American Association for the Advancement of Science (fellow), American Academy of Arts and Sciences, American Mathematical Society, Institute of Electrical and Electronics Engineers (fellow), New York Academy of Sciences, Sigma Xi, Chicago Literary Club.

WRITINGS: (With P. Bailey and G. von Bonin) *The Isocortex of the Chimpanzee,* University of Illinois Press, 1950; (with Wayne Dennis and others) *Current Trends in Psychological Theory,* University of Pittsburgh Press, 1951; *Finality and Form,* C. C Thomas, 1952; (with Brockway McMillan and others) *Current Trends in Information Theory,* University of Pittsburgh Press, 1954; (author of preface) Gordon Pask, *An Approach to Cybernetics,* Harper, 1961; *Embodiments of Mind,* M.I.T. Press, 1965.

Contributor: *The Precentral Motor Cortex,* edited by Paul C. Bucy, University of Illinois Press, 1944; *Cerebral Mechanisms in Behavior: The Hixon Symposium,* edited by Lloyd A. Jeffress, Wiley, 1951; *The Biology of Mental Health and Disease,* Hoeber Medical Division, 1952; *The Validation of Scientific Theories,* edited by Phillip G. Frank, Beacon Press, 1956; *Information Theory,* edited by Colin Cherry, Academic Press, 1956; *Mechanisation of Thought Processes,* H.M.S.O., 1959.

Self-Organizing Systems, edited by Marshall C. Yovits and Scott Cameron, Pergamon, 1960; *Lectures on Experimental Psychiatry,* University of Pittsburgh Press, 1961; *Mental Patients in Transition,* edited by Greenblatt and others, C. C Thomas, 1961; *Sensory Communication,* edited by W. A. Rosenblith, Wiley and M.I.T. Press, 1961; *Self-Organizing Systems 1962,* edited by M. C. Yovits, George J. Jacobi, and Gordon D. Goldstein, Spartan Books, 1962; *Aspects of the Theory of Artificial Intelligence,* edited by C. A. Muses, Plenum, for Barth Foundation, 1963; *Information Storage and Neural Control,* edited by William S. Fields and Walter Abbott, C. C Thomas, 1963; *Cross-cultural Understanding: Epistemology in Anthropology,* edited by F.S.C. Northrop and Helen H. Livingston, Harper, 1964; *Disorders of Communication,* edited by David McKenzie Rioch and Edwin A. Weinstein, Williams & Wilkins, 1964. Contributor of more than 200 articles to scientific journals; papers and poetry published by Chicago Literary Club.†

(Died September 26, 1969)

McDONALD, John D(ennis) 1906-

PERSONAL: Born December 5, 1906, in Detroit, Mich.; son of John E. (a builder) and Kate (Brown) McDonald; married Lorraine Oven, November 1, 1928 (divorced, 1936); married Dorothy Eisner (a painter), November 6, 1936; children: (first marriage) Joan McDonald Miller; (second marriage) Christie McDonald Vance. *Education:* University of Michigan, A.B., 1928, M.A., 1931. *Residence:* New York, N.Y.

CAREER: J. E. McDonald Drug Co., Detroit, Mich., assistant manager, 1928-29, 1931-32; free-lance journalist, New York, N.Y., 1932-38; *Film News,* editor, 1939-45; American Film Center, associate director, 1943-45; *Fortune* (magazine), New York, N.Y., associate editor, 1945-48, member of board of editors, 1948-66. Member of advisory council to department of economics, Princeton University, 1960-62.

WRITINGS: (Editor) *The Complete Fly Fisherman,* Scribner, 1947; *Strategy in Poker, Business and War,* Norton, 1950; *The Origins of Angling,* Doubleday, 1963; (editor) A. P. Sloan, *My Years with General Motors,* Doubleday, 1964.††

*   *   *

McDOWELL, Edward Allison, Jr. 1898-

PERSONAL: Born August 20, 1898, in Mitford, S.C.; son of Edward Allison (a minister) and Eva Holmes (Scott) McDowell; married Doris Price, June 18, 1925; children: Edward Allison III, Elizabeth (Mrs. A. Robert Smith). *Education:* Furman University, A.B., 1919; Southern Baptist Theological Seminary, Th.M., 1928, Ph.D., 1931; Union Theological Seminary, New York, N.Y., postdoctoral study, 1946-47. *Politics:* Democrat. *Home:* 270 Peachtree Hills Ave. N.E., Apt. D., Atlanta, Ga. 30305. *Office:* First Baptist Church, 754 Peachtree N.E., Atlanta, Ga. 30308.

CAREER: Baptist minister. Reporter on newspapers in Greenville, S.C., 1919-22; private secretary to Governor McLeod of South Carolina, Columbia, 1923-25; pastor of Baptist churches in Vinton, Va., 1931-34, and Union, S.C., 1934-35; Southern Baptist Theological Seminary, Louisville, Ky., instructor, 1935-37, assistant professor, 1937-41, associate professor, 1941-46, professor of New Testament, 1946-52, head of department, 1951-52; Southeastern Baptist Theological Seminary, Wake Forest, N.C., professor of New Testament, 1952-64, professor emeritus, 1964—; First Baptist Church, Atlanta, Ga., minister of teaching, beginning 1964. Visiting lecturer, Union Theological Seminary, New York, N.Y., 1946-47; member of faculty, Atlanta Baptist College, 1968-72; distinguished professor of religion, Mercer University, 1972-73. Member, Interracial Commission of the South, 1935-43; chairman, Kentucky Council on Interracial Cooperation, 1941-43. *Military service:* U.S. Army, 1918; became second lieutenant. *Member:* Society of Biblical Literature, Southern Regional Council (life fellow). *Awards, honors:* D.D., Furman University, 1946.

WRITINGS: Son of Man and Suffering Servant, Broadman, 1944, published as *Jesus and His Cross,* 1958; (with W. H. Davis) *A Source Book of Interbiblical History,* Broadman, 1948; *The Meaning and Message of The Book of Revelation,* Broadman, 1951. Author of study guide and writer of lessons for Sunday School Board of Southern Baptist Convention. Contributor to *Broadman Comments,* Broadman, 1957, 1968; also contributor to theological journals.

WORK IN PROGRESS: A book on cosmic Christianity,

with special emphasis on Pierre Teilhard de Chardin's synthesis of science and religion.†

* * *

McEVOY, James III   1940-1976

PERSONAL: Born April 16, 1940, in Detroit, Mich.; son of James, Jr. (an attorney) and Helen (Huff) McEvoy. *Education:* University of Michigan, A.B., 1963, A.M., 1964, Ph.D., 1968. *Home:* 645 Oak Ave., Davis, Calif. 95616. *Office:* Department of Environmental Studies, University of California, Davis, Calif. 95616.

CAREER: University of Michigan, Ann Arbor, adult education instructor, 1962-67, university extension service instructor at Federal Prison, Milan, 1966, 1967; University of California, Davis, assistant professor, 1967-72, associate professor of environmental studies, 1972-76, associate dean of research, beginning 1972. Assistant professor of political science, University of California, Berkeley, 1968-70. Partner, Ecological Research Associates, Davis, Calif., beginning 1970. Project director, National Commission on the Causes and Prevention of Violence, beginning 1968. *Member:* American Sociological Association, American Association for the Advancement of Science, Sierra Club, Friends of the Earth.

WRITINGS: (Editor with Abraham Miller) *Black Power and Student Rebellion: Conflict on the American Campus,* Wadsworth, 1969; *Radicals or Conservatives: The Contemporary American Right,* Rand McNally, 1971; (editor with Peter J. Richerson, and author of introduction) *Human Ecology: An Environmental Approach,* Duxbury, 1973; (editor with C. R. Goldman and Richerson) *Environmental Quality and Water Development,* W. H. Freeman, 1973; (editor) *Handbook for Environmental Planning,* Wiley, 1976.

Contributor: W. J. Crotty, editor, *Assassinations and the Political Order,* Harper, 1969; *Report of the Task Force on Political Assassination of the National Commission on the Causes and Prevention of Violence,* U.S. Government Printing Office, 1969; Robert A. Schoenberger, editor, *The American Right Wing: Readings in Political Behavior,* Holt, 1969; James Conyers and Morris L. Medley, editors, *Dynamic Sociology in Modern America,* Wiley, 1970; Howard S. Becker, editor, *Campus Power Struggle,* Aldine, 1970; W. R. Burch and others, editors, *Social Behavior, Natural Resources, and the Environment,* Harper, 1971; James F. Short and Marion Wolfgang, editors, *Collective Violence: A Sociological Perspective,* Aldine, 1971. Contributor to social and political science journals.†

(Died March, 1976)

* * *

McFARLAND, Ross A(rmstrong)   1901-

PERSONAL: Born July 18, 1901, in Denver, Colo.; son of James and Helen (Russell) McFarland; married Emily Frelinghuysen, October 14, 1950. *Education:* Park College, student, 1919-21; University of Michigan, A.B., 1923; Trinity College, Cambridge, research fellow, 1927-28; Harvard University, Ph.D., 1928. *Residence:* Dublin, N.H. 03444. *Office:* Harvard School of Public Health, 665 Huntington Ave., Boston, Mass. 02115.

CAREER: Columbia University, New York, N.Y., instructor in psychology, 1928-37; Harvard University, Boston, Mass., assistant professor of industrial research, 1937-46, School of Public Health, assistant professor of industrial

hygiene, 1947-49, associate professor, 1949-58, professor of environmental health and safety, 1958-62, Daniel and Florence Guggenheim Professor of Aerospace Health and Safety, 1962-72, professor emeritus, 1972—, director of Guggenheim Center for Aerospace Health and Safety, 1957-72. Summer lecturer, School of International Studies, Geneva, Switzerland, 1930-34; distinguished lecturer at Walter Reed Army Medical Center and Colby College, and for American College of Preventive Medicine and Ergonomics Research Society of Great Britain. Member of International High Altitude Expedition to Chile, 1935; conducted fatigue tests for Pan American Airways on global routes, 1937-42; director of Commission on Accidental Trauma, Armed Forces Epidemiological Board, 1950-70; member of medical advisory council, Office of the Civil Air Surgeon, Federal Aviation Agency, beginning 1960; member of research and advisory committee on biotechnology and human research, National Aeronautics and Space Administration, beginning 1963. Consultant to U.S. and British airlines, 1936-51, Surgeon General, U.S. Army, 1950-1970, and to U.S. Air Force, Department of State, Public Health Service, and other government agencies. Member of board of governors, Flight Safety Foundation, beginning 1946; member of board of directors, Health Research Foundation, beginning 1957, and National Safety Council, 1959-74. *Military service:* U.S. Naval Reserve, 1930-41, active duty, 1940; became lieutenant commander.

MEMBER: Aerospace Medical Association (fellow; executive council, 1956-59), American Physiological Society, American Psychological Association (fellow; chairman of division on aging, 1957-58), Airlines Medical Directors Association (honorary fellow), American Academy of Arts and Sciences (fellow), American Association for the Advancement of Science, American Association of Physical Anthropologists, American Geographical Society (fellow), American Psychosomatic Society, American Public Health Association (fellow), American Institute of Aeronautics and Astronautics (senior member), Ergonomics Research Society (Great Britain), Gerontological Society (fellow), Human Factors Society (founder member; executive council member, beginning 1958; president, 1969-71), Institute of the Aerospace Sciences (associate fellow), International Academy of Aviation Medicine, Optical Society of America, Royal Aeronautical Society (fellow), Society of Automotive Engineers, New York Academy of Sciences (fellow; vice-president, 1935-56), New York Academy of Medicine, Massachusetts Medical Society (honorary fellow), American Association for Automotive Medicine (honorary member), Sigma Xi, Delta Omega.

AWARDS, HONORS: Longacre Award of Aero Medical Association, 1947; Flight Safety Foundation Award, 1953; John Jeffries Award of Institute of Aeronautical Sciences, 1956; Walter M. Boothby Award of Aerospace Medical Association, 1962; special aerospace honor citation from American Medical Association, 1962; Arthur Williams Memorial Gold Medal of American Museum of Safety, 1965; Franklin V. Taylor Award, Society of Engineering Psychologists, 1968; Exceptional Service Award, U.S. Air Force, 1969; Distinguished Civilian Service Award, U.S. Army, 1971. Sc.D. from Park College, 1942, Rutgers University, 1964, Trinity College, 1965, and University of Denver, 1971.

WRITINGS: Human Factors in Air Transport Design, McGraw, 1946; *Human Factors in Air Transportation: Occupational Health and Safety,* McGraw, 1953; (with others) *Human Body Size and Capabilities in the Design and Operation of Vehicular Equipment,* Harvard School of Public Health, 1953; (with Alfred L. Moseley) *Human Factors in Highway Transport Safety,* Harvard School of Public Health, 1954; (with Roland C. Moore and A. Bertrand Warren) *Human Variables in Motor Vehicle Accidents: A Review of the Literature,* Harvard School of Public Health, 1955, revised edition, 1966; (with others) *Human Factors in the Design of Trucks,* Harvard School of Public Health, 1957; (with Albert Damon and Howard W. Stoudt) *The Human Body in Equipment Design,* Harvard University Press, 1966.

Contributor: J. S. Simmons, editor, *Public Health in the World Today,* Harvard University Press, 1949; *Industry and Tropical Health,* Harvard School of Public Health, Volume I, 1950, Volume II, 1954; *The Biology of Mental Health and Disease,* Paul B. Hoeber, 1952; F. A. Patty, editor, *Industrial Hygiene and Toxicology,* 2nd edition, Interscience, 1958; James E. Birren, editor, *Handbook of Aging and the Individual: Psychological and Biological Aspects,* University of Chicago Press, 1959; R.S.F. Schilling, editor, *Modern Trends in Occupational Health,* Butterworth & Co., 1960; E. Ginzberg, editor, *Values and Ideals of American Youth,* Columbia University Press, 1960; M. H. Halsey, editor, *Accident Prevention: The Role of Physicians and Public Health Workers,* McGraw, 1961; C. T. Morgan and others, editors, *Human Engineering Guide to Equipment Design,* McGraw, 1963; E. M. Bennett, J. Degan, and J. Spiegal, editors, *Human Factors in Technology,* McGraw, 1963; J. Pemberton, editor, *Epidemiology: Reports on Research and Teaching,* Oxford University Press, 1963; L. G. Norman, editor, *Medicine in Transport: Rail, Road, and Sea,* Butterworth & Co., 1965; H. R. Leavell and E. G. Clark, editors, *Preventive Medicine for the Doctor in His Community,* revised edition, McGraw, 1965. Contributor of more than 130 articles to journals, mainly in the field of highway and air safety and health hazards in industry.

SIDELIGHTS: McFarland made an investigation tour of scientific institutes in Moscow and Leningrad in 1934; he has spanned the world several times, and traveled in North and South America, Europe, Africa, and the Middle and Far East.

* * *

McGAFFIN, William 1910-1975

PERSONAL: Born October 2, 1910, in David City, Neb.; son of Hugh Martin (a newspaperman) and Nelle Mae (Derby) McGaffin; married Jean Fuller, July 22, 1949; children: Christopher M., Nicholas P. *Education:* University of Nebraska, A.B., 1932; Columbia University, B.Sc., 1935. *Religion:* Episcopalian. *Home:* 6208 Beachway Dr., Falls Church, Va. 22041. *Office: Chicago Daily News,* 1229 National Press Building, Washington, D.C. 20004.

CAREER: Reporter for *Nebraska State Journal,* Lincoln, 1931-32, *Lincoln Star,* Lincoln, 1932-33, and *Omaha World Herald,* Omaha, Neb., 1933-34; *Columbus Telegram,* Columbus, Neb., telegraph editor, 1934; Associated Press, editor and writer in New York, N.Y., 1935-37, correspondent in London, Paris, French North Africa, Egypt, Libya, India, China, and Russia, 1937-44; *Chicago Daily News,* Chicago, Ill., correspondent with U.S. forces in the Pacific, Japan, China, Manchuria, Czechoslovakia, Russia, and Britain, 1944-53, London Bureau chief, 1947-53, United Nations correspondent, 1953-56, Washington correspondent, 1956-75. Chairman of Standing Committee of Correspondents, U.S. Congress, 1969-70. *Member:* National Press

Club, Overseas Writers Club, Sigma Delta Chi, Sigma Nu. *Awards, honors:* Fiftieth Anniversary Award, Columbia Graduate School of Journalism, 1963.

WRITINGS: (With Erwin Knoll) *"Anything But The Truth": The Credibility Gap,* Putnam, 1968; (with Knoll) *Scandal in the Pentagon,* Fawcett, 1969.

BIOGRAPHICAL/CRITICAL SOURCES: Washington Post, July 13, 1968; *New York Times Book Review,* November 3, 1968; *New Republic,* April 25, 1970.†

(Died April 10, 1975)

* * *

McGEOWN, Patrick 1897-

PERSONAL: Surname is pronounced McGowan; born September 9, 1897, in Craigneuk, Scotland; son of Peter (a steelman) and Mary Ann (Donnelly) McGeown; married Aileen Hopton, January 1, 1929; children: Josephine, Bernadette (Mrs. John Pennington). *Education:* Attended Catholic schools in Scotland, 1902-12. *Politics:* Supporter of British Labour Party. *Religion:* Roman Catholic. *Home:* 57 Rothiemay Rd., Flixton, Manchester, England. *Agent:* A. P. Watt & Son, 26-28 Bedford Row, London WC1R 4HL, England.

CAREER: Steel worker, tending open hearth furnaces, 1915-63. Writer.

WRITINGS: Heat the Furnace Seven Times More (autobiography), Hutchinson, 1967. Contributor to *New Statesman, Man and Metal, Safety,* and to B.B.C. Radio.

SIDELIGHTS: McGeown told *CA:* "I have had only one trade in my working lifetime, and that was steelmaking. Found it exciting, dramatic, and creative.... As a steelmaker turned writer I love every minute. Love the cheques, too."

* * *

McGINN, Donald Joseph 1905-

PERSONAL: Born April 1, 1905, in Indian Lake, N.Y.; son of James and Mary Elizabeth (McCarthy) McGinn; married Margaret Howley, June 27, 1940; children: Mary Kathleen (Mrs. Donald P. Spring), Donald Joseph, Jr. *Education:* Cornell University, A.B., 1926, M.A., 1929, Ph.D., 1930. *Politics:* Democrat. *Religion:* Roman Catholic. *Home:* 2 President Ave., Lavallette, N.J. 08732. *Office:* Department of English, Georgian Court College, Lakewood, N.J.

CAREER: New York Telephone Co., New York, N.Y., business office employee, 1926-28; Rutgers Preparatory School, New Brunswick, N.J., head of English department, 1930-36; Rutgers University, New Brunswick, instructor, 1936-40, assistant professor, 1940-46, associate professor, 1946-51, professor of English, 1951-73, professor emeritus, 1973—. Georgian Court College, Lakewood, N.J., lecturer, 1945-52, professor of English, beginning 1952. *Member:* Modern Language Association of America, Renaissance Society of America, Shakespeare Association of America, Catholic Commission on Intellectual and Cultural Affairs (secretary, 1961-62), College Conference on English in the Central Atlantic States (secretary-treasurer, 1942-55; president, 1955-58), Phi Beta Kappa.

WRITINGS: Shakespeare's Influence on the Drama of His Age, Rutgers University Press, 1938; *The Admonition Controversy,* Rutgers University Press, 1949; (with G. Howerton) *Literature as a Fine Art,* Row, Peterson & Co., 1959; *John Penry and the Marprelate Controversy,* Rutgers University Press, 1966. Contributor to journals.

WORK IN PROGRESS: Thomas Nashe: A Critical Study.

AVOCATIONAL INTERESTS: Walking on the beach, bird watching.

*   *   *

McGLINCHEE, Claire

PERSONAL: Born in Boston, Mass.; daughter of Andrew J. and Eleanor H. (McBride) McGlinchee. *Education:* Radcliffe College, A.B., 1921; Longy School of Music, Diploma, 1922; Columbia University, M.A., 1924, Ph.D., 1940. *Religion:* Roman Catholic. *Home:* 30 East 68th St., New York, N.Y. 10021. *Office:* English Department, Hunter College of the City University of New York, 695 Park Ave., New York, N.Y. 10021.

CAREER: Achard School for Girls, Brookline, Mass., teacher of English, 1921-22; Academy of the Holy Child, New York City, teacher of English and choral music, 1922-23; Hunter College of the City University of New York, New York City, beginning 1924, began as instructor, professor of English, 1961-69, professor emeritus, 1969—. Speaker at international conferences in France, Holland, Scotland, and Sweden. *Member:* Modern Language Association of America, Shakespeare Association of America, Renaissance Society of America, American Society for Aesthetics, American Society for Theatre Research, Society for Theatre Research (London), American Association of University Professors; Metropolitan Museum, Renaissance Club, Radcliffe Club, and Harvard Club (all New York). *Awards, honors:* George N. Shuster Fund grant, 1963.

WRITINGS: The First Decade of the Boston Museum, Humphries, 1940; *James Russell Lowell,* Twayne, 1967. Contributor to journals of music and literature.

AVOCATIONAL INTERESTS: Music and travel.

*   *   *

McGLOTHLIN, William J(oseph) 1908-

PERSONAL: Born August 18, 1908, in Louisville, Ky.; son of William Joseph and Maybelle (Williams) McGlothlin; married Nell Winn, 1948. *Education:* Furman University, B.A. (summa cum laude), 1927; Columbia University, M.A., 1928; Duke University, graduate study, 1933-34; University of Chicago, graduate study, 1934-35. *Religion:* Unitarian Universalist. *Home:* 521 Belgravia Ct., Louisville, Ky. 40208. *Office:* 201 White Hall, University of Louisville, Louisville, Ky. 40208.

CAREER: University of Tennessee, Knoxville, instructor in English, 1928-31; Furman University, Greenville, S.C., instructor in English, summers, 1930-31; Tennessee Valley Authority, Knoxville, research aide, administrative assistant, training officer, 1935-42, assistant chief of training division, 1942-43, chief of training and educational relations branch, 1943-48; Southern Regional Education Board, Atlanta, Ga., associate director of mental health program, 1948-57, on leave, 1957, deputy director, 1957-58; Columbia University, New York, N.Y., instructor in educational administration, 1957; Study on Education for Professions, New York, N.Y., director, 1957; University of Louisville, Louisville, Ky., vice-president, 1958-68, professor of higher education, 1968-76, professor emeritus, 1976—. Red Cross campaign, division chairman, 1959, member of board of directors, 1961. Member of board of directors, Louisville School of Art. *Member:* National Institute of Mental Health (member of sub-committee on in-service training), National League for Nursing (second vice-president), Kentucky Mental Health Manpower Commission (vice-chairman), Kentucky Commission on Higher Education, Phi Kappa Phi, Kappa Delta Pi.

WRITINGS: (With Maurice F. Seay) *Elementary Education in Two Communities of the Tennessee Valley,* Bureau of School Service, University of Kentucky, 1942; *Large Was Our Bounty: Natural Resources and Our Schools,* Association for Supervision and Curriculum Development, 1948; *Patterns of Professional Education,* Putnam, 1960; *The Professional Schools,* Center for Applied Research in Education, 1964. Corresponding and contributing editor, *Journal of Higher Education,* beginning 1962; member of editorial board, *Journal of Social Work Education,* 1965-68. Contributor to professional journals.

AVOCATIONAL INTERESTS: Choral singing, bicycling.

*   *   *

McGUFFIE, Tom H(enderson) 1902-

PERSONAL: Born May 30, 1902, in Carlisle, Cumberland, England; son of James (a civil servant) and Martha Anne (Henderson) McGuffie; children: Duncan. *Education:* University of London, B.A., 1925, M.A., 1940.

CAREER: Schoolmaster in Middlesex, England, and Hertfordshire, England, 1922-48; during period 1948-55, did teaching at Trent Park College, Middlesex, England, and University of Birmingham Institute of Education, Birmingham, England, and was Simon research fellow at University of Manchester, Manchester, England; schoolmaster in Birmingham, England, beginning 1955. *Member:* Royal Historical Society (fellow), Royal Commonwealth Society, Royal United Service Institution, United Service Club, and Naval and Military Club (all London). *Awards, honors:* Leverhulme research grant.

WRITINGS: Peninsular Cavalry General, Harrap, 1951; *History for Today* (texts), six books, Macmillan, 1963-64, 2nd edition of book five published as *Our World Since 1939,* 1966; (editor) *Rank and File: The Common Soldier at Peace and War, 1642-1914,* Hutchinson, 1964, St. Martin's, 1966; *The Siege of Gibraltar, 1779-1783,* Batsford, 1965; *Stories of Famous Mutinies,* Barker, 1966. Contributor of articles and reviews to history journals. Honorary editor, Society for Army Historical Research, beginning 1952.†

*   *   *

McINNES, Graham (Campbell) 1912-1970

PERSONAL: Born February 18, 1912, in London, England; son of James Campbell (a concert singer) and Angela (Mackail) McInnes; married Joan Burke; children: two sons, one daughter. *Education:* University of Melbourne, B.A. (first class honors), 1933, M.A., 1940. *Office:* 1 rue Chanez, Paris 16, France.

CAREER: A would-be jazz composer in his youth, McInnes went on to specialize in the fine arts and then in diplomacy; he emigrated from Melbourne (his mother's second husband was an Australian) to Canada in 1934; spent almost a year studying fine arts in Europe and became art editor of *Saturday Night,* Toronto, Ontario, 1935-40; University of Toronto Extension, Toronto, lecturer in fine arts, 1938-41; National Film Board of Canada, senior producer of industrial and art films and coordinator of graphic projects, 1942-48; Canadian Department of External Affairs, 1948-70, first secretary in New Delhi, India, 1952-54, first secretary and later counsellor in Wellington, New Zealand, 1954-55, head of Commonwealth Division, Ottawa, Ontario, 1955-58, assigned to Imperial Defence College, London, England, 1958-59, counselor in London, 1959-62, and minister, 1962, first Canadian high commissioner to Jamaica, 1962-65, minister plenipotentiary and permanent delegate of Canada to UNESCO, Paris, France, 1965-70.

WRITINGS: A Short History of Canadian Art, Macmillan (Toronto), 1939, revised and expanded edition published as *Canadian Art,* 1950; *Lost Island: An Adventure,* World Publishing, 1954; *Sushila* (novel), Putnam, 1957; *The Road to Gundagai* (autobiographical), Hamish Hamilton, 1965, London House (New York), 1966; *Humping My Bluey* (autobiographical), Hamish Hamilton, 1966; *Finding A Father* (autobiographical), Hamish Hamilton, 1967; *Goodbye, Melbourne Town,* Hamish Hamilton, 1968. Contributor of articles and stories to Canadian periodicals.

SIDELIGHTS: McInnes traveled to Canada on a small legacy to seek his father, whom he had not seen for eighteen years, and discovered a homeland. His affection for his adopted country is so evident in *Finding a Father,* the third volume of his autobiography, that a *Times Literary Supplement* reviewer suggested that a more accurate title would be "Finding a Fatherland." The reviewer continued: "He found himself as a journalist, art critic and broadcaster, discovering Canada first through the work of Canadian painters and then at first hand in a series of transcontinental journeys." The reviewer also mentioned an instance of McInnes' penchant for starting at the top as a young man, even if he had to work his way down. He went to New York with his jazz compositions and presented them to George Gershwin, Rudy Vallee, and Ethel Waters, introducing himself as the one and only overseas correspondent of the *Australian Music Maker and Dance Band News.*

BIOGRAPHICAL/CRITICAL SOURCES: Times Literary Supplement, April 27, 1967; *Observer Review,* May 21, 1967; *New Statesman,* June 7, 1968.†

(Died February 28, 1970)

* * *

McINTOSH, John   1930-1970

PERSONAL: Born September 4, 1930, in Gatooma, Southern Rhodesia; citizen of South Africa; son of Dan (a bank manager) and Gladys (McGrath) McIntosh. *Education:* Attended University of Cape Town, 1948, and University of the Witwatersrand, 1952, 1961. *Politics:* Progressive Party ("but not a member"). *Religion:* Roman Catholic. *Home:* c/o Boy's Town, P.O. Box 57, Magaliesburg, Transvaal, Republic of South Africa. *Agent:* Ann Elmo Agency, Inc., 52 Vanderbilt Ave., New York, N.Y. 10017.

CAREER: Journalist on *Star,* Johannesburg, South Africa, 1953-61, working in London, England, 1957; teacher at Boy's Town, Magaliesburg, Transvaal, South Africa, 1962-70. Novelist. *Awards, honors:* C.N.A. Literary Award, 1970, for *The Stonefish.*

WRITINGS—Novels: *Blood Brothers,* Anthony Blond, 1965; *The Thorn Trees,* Harcourt, 1967; *Come to My House,* Harcourt, 1968; *The Stonefish,* Harcourt, 1970. Short stories represented in many anthologies, including: *Winter's Tales 14,* edited by Kevin Crossley-Holland, Macmillan, 1968; *Winter's Tales 16,* edited by A. D. MacLean, Macmillan, 1970; *Short Stories from Seven Countries,* edited by A. Lennox-Short, Juta & Co., 1972.

WORK IN PROGRESS: A novel set in south-west Africa.

SIDELIGHTS: John McIntosh lived on "sort of" a farm of twenty acres, near the school for underprivileged children

where he taught part-time. He visited most of the game parks in Africa, preferred country life to city, and spoke Afrikaans. A two-year film option was taken out on *The Thorn Trees. Avocational interests:* Tennis, swimming, walking, reading.†

(Died September 5, 1970)

* * *

McKINLEY, David Hopwood   1906-

PERSONAL: Born September 24, 1906, in Uniontown, Pa.; son of John Milton (a manufacturer) and Margaret Wiley (Hopwood) McKinley; married Margaret Elizabeth Moore, June 24, 1931; children: Joan Elliott (Mrs. John B. Nesbitt), Madge Virginia. *Education:* Pennsylvania State University, B.A., 1927, M.A., 1932; Western Reserve University (now Case Western Reserve University), LL.B. (since converted to J.D.), 1932. *Politics:* Republican. *Religion:* Methodist. *Home:* 642 Fairway Rd., State College, Pa. 16801. *Office:* College of Business Administration, Pennsylvania State University, University Park, Pa. 16802.

CAREER: Admitted to Ohio Bar, 1932; practicing attorney in Cleveland, Ohio, 1932-42; Cleveland Trust Co., Cleveland, economist and statistician, 1938-42; Pennsylvania State University, University Park, 1946—, began as assistant professor of economics, professor of banking, 1955-72, associate dean of College of Business Administration, 1957-72, associate emeritus professor and emeritus dean, 1972—. Pennsylvania Conference of Economists, secretary, 1959-67, president, 1967-69. Lecturer at banking schools; consultant to National Association of Manufacturers and bankers associations. *Military service:* U.S. Army Air Forces, 1942-46; became lieutenant colonel. U.S. Air Force Reserve, 1946-56. *Member:* American Economic Association, American Finance Association, Appalachian Finance Association.

WRITINGS: (Editor) *Administration of German Air Force* (classified publication), U.S. Army Air Forces, 1946; (with George Leffler) *Your Bank,* Pennsylvania Bankers Association, 1960; (contributor) H. V. Procknow, editor, *The Federal Reserve System,* Harper, 1960; (with Murray Lee and Helene Duffy) *Forecasting Business Conditions,* American Bankers Association, 1964.

* * *

McLAREN, Homer D.   1887-

PERSONAL: Born December 2, 1887, in Summon, Ill.; son of C. C. (a manufacturer) and Louise (Clary) McLaren; married Matilda Rose (a teacher), July 1, 1916; children: Arthur Douglas, Nina Kaiser, Robert Bruce, Homer F., David R. *Education:* Illinois State University, student, 1915-17; Lincoln College of Law, LL.B., 1921, LL.M., 1922. *Home:* 1709 Fayette, Springfield, Ill. 62704.

CAREER: Lawyer in private practice, Springfield, Ill., beginning 1922. Assistant attorney general, State of Illinois, 1934-39. *Member:* Illinois Bar Association, Lions Club.

WRITINGS: (With son, Robert B. McLaren) *All to the Good: A Guide to Christian Ethics,* World Publishing, 1969.

WORK IN PROGRESS: Stories of the past.

AVOCATIONAL INTERESTS: Painting, wood carving, travel in United States.††

* * *

McLEAN, Beth Bailey   1892-

PERSONAL: Born April 15, 1892, in Superior, Wis.;

daughter of Stewart J. (a contractor) and Amanda (Catt) Bailey; married John Alexander McLean, October 27, 1923 (deceased); children: John Cameron, Janet (Mrs. James Christensen). *Education:* Stout Institute (now Stout State University), Menomonie, Wis., B.S., 1917; University of Pittsburgh, graduate study, summer, 1918; Iowa State College (now University), M.S., 1934. *Politics:* Republican. *Home:* 2545 Southwest Terwilliger Blvd., Portland, Ore. 97201.

CAREER: School for Dependent Children, Owatonna, Minn., dietitian, 1912-13; Janeville (Wis.) public schools, supervisor of home economics, 1913-16; School of Forestry, Battineau, N.D., economist, 1916-17; University of Pittsburgh, Pittsburgh, Pa., assistant professor of home economics, 1917-18; Iowa State College (now University), Ames, associate professor of home economics, 1918-23; Southern Rice Industry, New Orleans, La., director of home economics, 1933-36; Swift & Co., Chicago, Ill., director of home economics, 1936-57; Oregon State University, Corvallis, assistant professor of home economics, 1957-62. *Member:* Home Economists in Business. *Awards, honors:* Sc.D., Iowa State University, 1958.

WRITINGS: Meal Planning and Table Service, Bennett, 1923, latest revision, 1963; *Good Manners*, Bennett, 1929; *Modern Homemaker's Cookbook*, Barrows, 1950; *Martha Logan's Meat Cookbook*, Pocket Books, 1952; (with Thora Campbell) *The Complete Meat Cookbook*, Bennett, 1953; *The Young Woman in Business*, Iowa State University Press, 1954, revised edition (with Jeanne Paris), 1962; (with Thora Campbell) *Meat and Poultry Cookbook*, Pocket Books, 1960, revised edition, 1962. Author of booklets; contributor of articles to periodicals.

AVOCATIONAL INTERESTS: Traveling, world affairs.††

*   *   *

McLEAN, Kathryn (Anderson)   1909-1966
(Kathryn Forbes)

PERSONAL: Born March 10, 1909, in San Francisco, Calif.; daughter of Leon Ellis and Della (Jesser) Anderson; married Robert McLean (a contractor), 1926 (divorced May, 1946); children: Robert, Jr., Richard. *Education:* Graduated from Mount View High School, San Francisco, 1925. *Residence:* Burlingame, Calif.

CAREER: Full-time professional writer.

WRITINGS—Under pseudonym Kathryn Forbes: *Mama's Bank Account* (short stories), Harcourt, 1943; *Transfer Point*, Harcourt, 1947. Also wrote articles for magazines and scripts for radio.

SIDELIGHTS: Miss Forbes' semi-autobiographical *Mama's Bank Account* concerns a Norwegian-American family in the early years of the twentieth century and a mother's financial stratagem for giving her children a sense of security when times were hard and it seemed almost impossible to stretch the father's earnings to cover expenses. A *Book Week* reviewer noted that although the book was frankly sentimental it was not offensively so. "It's amusing, gently ironic and well written, making real people of Mama, Papa, the girls and Nels, and all the aunts. If there are any who may excusably be called 100 per cent American, they are people like this Norwegian family, who brought with them from the old country traits of courage, honesty and straight thinking which we like to think make up the American character." *Mama's Bank Account* was dramatized by

John Van Druten, produced by Richard Rodgers and Oscar Hammerstien II, and reached the Music Box Theater on Broadway as "I Remember Mama" in 1944. It was filmed by RKO as "I Remember Mama" in 1948 and became a popular television show for the Columbia Broadcasting Company which ran from July 1, 1949, to June 1, 1957.

BIOGRAPHICAL/CRITICAL SOURCES: Book Week, March 21, 1943.††

(Died May 15, 1966)

*   *   *

McNEIL, Elton B(urbank)   1924-1974

PERSONAL: Born January 1, 1924, in Royal Oak, Mich.; son of Elton Burwell and Grace I. (Hueston) McNeil; married Marjorie E. Snider, September 14, 1946; children: Douglas, Timothy, Laurie. *Education:* Harvard University, A.B. (cum laude), 1948; University of Michigan, Ph.D., 1952. *Home:* 2269 Westaire Ct., Ann Arbor, Mich. 48103. *Office:* Psychology Department, University of Michigan, Ann Arbor, Mich. 48104.

CAREER: University of Michigan, Ann Arbor, instructor, 1952-53, assistant professor, 1954-58, associate professor, 1958-62, professor of psychology, 1962-74. Field selection officer, Peace Corps. *Military service:* U.S. Army Air Forces, 1943-45; received Croix de Guerre. *Member:* American Psychological Association.

WRITINGS: The Nature of Human Conflict, Prentice-Hall, 1965; *The Concept of Human Development*, Wadsworth, 1966; *The Quiet Furies: Man and Disorder*, Prentice-Hall, 1967; (with D. N. Fader) *Hooked on Books: Program and Proof*, Putnam, 1968; *Human Socialization*, Brooks-Cole, 1969; *The Psychoses*, Prentice-Hall, 1970; *Neurosis and Personality Disorder*, Prentice-Hall, 1970; *Readings in Human Socialization*, Brooks-Cole, 1971; *Being Human: The Psychological Experience*, Canfield Press, 1972; *The Psychology of Being Human*, Rand McNally, 1974.

WORK IN PROGRESS: Hostility in Society.

BIOGRAPHICAL/CRITICAL SOURCES: Best Sellers, January 1, 1968.†

(Died March, 1974)

*   *   *

MEACHAM, Harry M(onroe)   1901-1975

PERSONAL: Born July 19, 1901, in Petersburg, Va.; son of Bejamin Thomas (a sales executive) and Julia (Webb) Meacham; married Lucy Allen Davies, March 8, 1924; children: Frances Christian (Mrs. John C. McWhorter). *Education:* Took special courses in Greek and Greek literature at St. John's College, Annapolis, Md., 1942, and in philosophy at Richmond Professional Institute, 1950 ("like Yeats, self-educated!").

CAREER: Dun & Bradstreet, Inc., financial reporter, Washington, D.C., 1933-38, salesman in Baltimore, Md., 1938-44, sales manager of Baltimore branch, 1944-48, district manager in Richmond, Va., 1948-66. Lecturer on sales management in evening school, University of Richmond, 1950-51. U.S. Small Business Administration, member of board of field advisers, 1955-63, chairman of Richmond chapter of Service Corps of Retired Executives (SCORE), 1965-66. Lecturer at more than two hundred small business clinics in the South; also lecturer on contemporary poetry. Consultant to small businesses. Member of board of Poe Foundation, beginning 1950, and Richmond Professional Institute, 1950-

63; chairman of Port of Richmond Advisory Commission, 1956-60.

MEMBER: Academy of American Poets (organizer and chairman of affiliated societies group), Poetry Society of America, National Federation of Poetry Societies (chancellor), Poetry Society of Virginia (president, 1955-58, beginning 1969), Virginia Writers Club (president, 1965-67), Virginia Historical Society, New Hampshire Poetry Society (honorary life member), Distributive Education Clubs of America (honorary life member), Cabell Society. *Awards, honors:* Chosen by Virginia's governor as SCORE volunteer of the year, 1965.

WRITINGS: (Executive editor) *Lyric Virginia Today,* two volumes, Dietz, 1956; *Ezra Pound, un memoire,* L'Herne (Paris), 1965; (co-editor) *One-Hundred Years of Alaska Poetry,* A. Swallow, for Poetry Society of Alaska, 1967; *The Caged Panther: Ezra Pound at St. Elizabeths,* Twayne, 1968. Poetry included in several anthologies, including *The Golden Year,* Poetry Society of America, 1960. Poetry reviewer, *Richmond News Leader;* contributor of poetry and literary criticism to *Lyric, American Weave, Commonwealth, New York Times,* and other publications. Editor, *Dentonator* (publication of Academy of American Poets); member of editorial advisory board, *Lyric,* beginning 1945.

WORK IN PROGRESS: Research on Samuel Davies, father of Presbyterianism in Virginia, for a possible biography.

SIDELIGHTS: Harry Meacham kicked off a small business broadcast in Hagerstown, Md., filmed by U.S. Small Business Administration for use throughout the county. His lecture, "Why Businesses Fail," has been reprinted in whole or in part in a number of manuals issued by the U.S. Government.†

(Died, 1975)

* * *

MEADE, Robert Douthat 1903-197(?)

PERSONAL: Born August 16, 1903, in Danville, Va.; son of Edmund Baylies (in real estate) and Helen (Douthat) Meade; married Lucy Boyd, December 29, 1934; children: Lucy Boyd (Mrs. Rogers Vaden, Jr.). *Education:* Virginia Military Institute, A.B., 1924; University of Virginia, M.A., 1926; University of Chicago, Ph.D., 1935. *Politics:* Democrat. *Religion:* Episcopalian. *Home:* 408 Trents Ferry Rd., Lynchburg, Va. 24504. *Office:* Randolph-Macon Woman's College, Lynchburg, Va. 24504.

CAREER: Instructor in French at Episcopal School, Lynchburg, Va., 1926-27, and in history at University of Illinois, Urbana, 1927-28, Vanderbilt University, Nashville, Tenn., 1928-29, and University of North Carolina, Chapel Hill, 1929-31; U.S. Department of Interior, Washington, D.C., historical assistant with National Park Service, 1932-34; University of North Carolina, instructor in history, 1935-36; Randolph-Macon Woman's College, Lynchburg, associate professor, 1936-39, professor of history and chairman of department, beginning 1939. Member of advisory council, National Civil Service League, 1935-63.

MEMBER: American Historical Association, Southern Historical Association, Virginia Historical Society, Virginia Social Science Association (president, 1952-53). *Awards, honors:* Southern Authors Award, 1943, for *Judah P. Benjamin, Confederate Statesman;* Guggenheim fellowships, 1953-54, 1960-61; Distinguished Service Award of Virginia

Social Science Association, 1969; grants from Library of Congress, Rosenwald Foundation, Patrick Henry Memorial Foundation, Carnegie Foundation, American Philosophical Society, and American Council of Learned Societies.

WRITINGS: Judah P. Benjamin, Confederate Statesman, Oxford University Press, 1943, reprinted Arno, 1975; *Patrick Henry,* Lippincott, Volume I: *Patriot in the Making,* 1957, Volume II: *Practical Revolutionary,* 1969; (contributor) Ralph Newman, editor, *Lincoln for the Ages,* Doubleday, 1960. Author of twenty-four biographical articles for *Dictionary of American Biography,* two historical articles for Broadcast Music, Inc., and syndicated newspaper articles; contributor to journals, including *Atlantic.*

WORK IN PROGRESS: A book on the European backgrounds of American Revolutionary soldiers; several newspaper and magazine articles.†

(Deceased)

* * *

MEEKER, Alice (MacCutcheon) 1904-

PERSONAL: Born August 23, 1904, in Brooklyn, N.Y.; daughter of Henry Newton and Fannie (MacCutcheon) Meeker. *Education:* Columbia University, B.S., 1929; New York University, M.A., 1939; additional study at City College of the City University of New York, Mills College of Education, and New York University. *Office:* William Paterson College of New Jersey, Wayne, N.J. 07473.

CAREER: Drew University, Madison, N.J., evening division, instructor in elementary education, beginning 1944; New York University, New York, N.Y., evening division instructor in elementary education, 1952-55; William Paterson College of New Jersey, Wayne, professor of education, 1954-75, professor emeritus, 1975—. Trustee, Mills College of Education, eight years; member, Paterson Model Cities Program. *Member:* National Education Association (life member), Association for Childhood Education International, Association of New Jersey Colleges, New Jersey Education Association. *Awards, honors:* Outstanding Alumna Award, Mills College of Education, 1955; award from New Jersey Council of Teachers of English, 1963, for *How Hospitals Help Us;* honorary doctorate, William Paterson College, 1970.

WRITINGS: I Like Children, Row, Peterson & Co., 1953; *Teachers at Work in the Elementary School,* Holt, 1958; *How Hospitals Help Us* (juvenile), Benefic, 1962; *How Doctors Help Us* (juvenile), Benefic, 1964; *Enjoying Literature with Children,* Odyssey, 1969. Contributor to *Family Circle* and other publications in United States, England, and Canada.

* * *

MEEKER, Richard Kilburn 1925-19(?)

PERSONAL: Born February 21, 1925, in Lackawanna, N.Y.; son of David Magee (a purchasing agent) and Helen (Kilburn) Meeker; married Barbara Ann Southern, June 11, 1955; children: Stephen, Philip. *Education:* Lafayette College, A.B., 1948; University of Pennsylvania, M.A., 1949, Ph.D., 1955; additional study at University of Vermont, Georgetown University, and Middlebury College. *Home:* 60 Elm St., Oneonta, N.Y. 13820.

CAREER: Springfield College, Springfield, Mass., instructor in English, 1950-51; Bay Path Junior College, Longmeadow, Mass., head of department of English, 1951-52; Longwood College, Farmville, Va., assistant professor,

1953-56, associate professor of English, 1956-62; State University of New York College at Potsdam, professor of English, 1962-66; Hartwick College, Oneonta, N.Y., associate professor, beginning, 1966. *Military service:* U.S. Army, Infantry, 1943-45. *Member:* Modern Language Association of America, College English Association, National Council of Teachers of English, American Association of University Professors, Pi Delta Epsilon, Kappa Phi Kappa. *Awards, honors:* Research grants from University Center, Virginia, 1957, 1958, State University of New York Research Foundation, 1963, 1964.

WRITINGS: (Contributor) *The South in Perspective,* Institute of Southern Culture, Longwood College, 1958; (editor, author of introduction, and contributor) *The Dilemma of the Southern Writer,* Institute of Southern Culture, Longwood College, 1961; (editor and author of introduction) *The Collected Stories of Ellen Glasgow,* Louisiana State University Press, 1963.

WORK IN PROGRESS: Several editions of eighteenth-century novels; a study of point of view in eighteenth-century fiction.†

(Deceased)

*   *   *

MEISSNER, Kurt   1885-1976

PERSONAL: Born March 9, 1885, in Hamburg, Germany; son of Otto (a publisher) and Agnes Meissner; married June 28, 1923; wife's name, Johanna; children: Hans Ingeborg (Mrs. Frank R. Freehauf), Wolfgang. *Education:* Attended Realgymnasium of Johanneum, Hamburg. *Politics:* None. *Religion:* Lutheran. *Residence:* Orselina, Switzerland.

AWARDS, HONORS: Dr. honoris causa, University of Hamburg, 1955.

WRITINGS: Lehrbuch der Grammatik der japanischen Schriftsprache (Japanese language text in German), Deutsche Gesellschaft fuer Natur- & Voelkerkunde Ostasiens, 1927; *Grundlagen der nationalen erziehung in Japan* (booklet on Japanese nationality and education), Deutsch-Japanischen Gesellschaft (Berlin), 1934; *Nationale erziehung in Japan* (on education in Japan), Weidmann, 1934; (translator) *Die "heilige" Sutra und andere japanische Geschichten,* Kyo Bun Kwan, 1937; *Deutsche in Japan, 1639-1939,* Deutsche Verlagsanstalt, 1940, updated edition published as *Deutsche in Japan, 1639-1960,* Harrassowitz, 1961; *Unterricht in der japanischen umgangssprache* (Japanese grammar and phrase book), Harrassowitz, 1941; *Einfuehrung in die japanische Umgangssprache* (on spoken Japanese), Harrassowitz, 1954; (author of section on Yokohama; section on Kobe by Otto Refardt) *Die Deutschen in Yokohama* [and] *Die Deutschen in Kobe* (booklet), Harrassowitz, 1956; *Erwachsenenbildung in einer dynamischen Gesellschaft* (on education of adults), Ernst Klett, 1964; *Japanese Woodblock Prints in Miniature: The Genre of Surimono,* Tuttle, 1969. Also author of *Kokutani,* 1976.†

(Died August 13, 1976)

*   *   *

MELIN, Grace Hathaway   1892-1973

PERSONAL: Surname pronounced Meh-leen; born February 19, 1892, in Columbus, Ohio; daughter of William (a painter) and Elizabeth (Martin) Hathaway; married Carl G. Melin (a retired chemist), August 23, 1939. *Education:* Attended Columbus Normal School, 1910-12, and Oregon State College (now Oregon State University), 1918-19;

George Washington University, B.A., 1941. *Politics:* Independent. *Religion:* Protestant. *Home:* R.F.D., Clarksville, Md.

CAREER: Public school teacher in Columbus, Ohio, 1912-18; reporter for *Benton County Courier,* Corvallis, Ore., 1919-23; public school teacher in Washington, D.C., 1941-43, Edmonston, Md., 1943-46, and Laurel, Md., 1946-62. *Member:* National Education Association, Maryland Teachers Association, Delta Kappa Gamma. *Awards, honors:* Third prize for a travel article in *Instructor,* 1949.

WRITINGS—All published by Bobbs-Merrill: *Maria Mitchell, Girl Astronomer,* 1954; *Dorothea Dix, Girl Reformer,* 1963; *Henry Wadsworth Longfellow, Gifted Young Poet,* 1968; *Carl Sandburg, Young Singing Poet,* 1973. Author of four plays published in *Instructor.*

AVOCATIONAL INTERESTS: Reading, nature study, travel.†

(Died December 1, 1973)

*   *   *

MENZEL, Donald H(oward)   1901-1976

PERSONAL: Born April 11, 1901, in Florence, Colo.; son of Charles Theodore (an accountant) and Ina Grace (Zint) Menzel; married Florence Elizabeth Kreager, June 17, 1926; children: Suzanne Kay (Mrs. James E. Lindeman), Elizabeth Ina (Mrs. Bernard Davis). *Education:* University of Denver, A.B., 1920, A.M., 1921; Princeton University, A.M., 1923, Ph.D., 1924. *Home:* 1010 Memorial Dr., Cambridge, Mass.

CAREER: University of Iowa, Iowa City, instructor in astronomy, 1924-25; Ohio State University, Columbus, assistant professor of astronomy, 1925-26; Lick Observatory, Mount Hamilton, Calif., assistant astronomer, 1926-32; Harvard University, Cambridge, Mass., assistant professor of astronomy, 1932-35, associate professor of astrophysics, 1935-38, professor of astrophysics, 1938-71, Paine Professor of Practical Astronomy, 1956-71, director of Harvard Observatory, 1954-66, research scientist, Smithsonian Astrophysical Observatory, 1966-71. Chief scientist, Geophysics Corporation of America, 1959-69; vice-president and member of board of directors, Colorado Instruments, Inc. and Silver Bell Mines. Member or director of solar eclipse (total) expeditions in France, Italy, Peru, Canada, Mexico, Greece, West Africa, and Russia. State Department specialist for Latin America, lecturing there in 1964. Boy Scout field executive in Colorado, 1920, and long active in work of Boy Scouts of America and American Red Cross. *Military service:* U.S. Naval Reserve, 1942-55; with active duty, 1942-45; became commander; received unit and individual citations.

MEMBER: International Astronomical Union (president of commission on solar eclipses, 1948-55; president of commission 17-the moon, 1964-67), American Astronomical Society (president, 1954-56; director-at-large, beginning 1959), American Philosophical Society (vice-president, 1965-68), National Academy of Sciences (vice-president, 1935-38), American Mathematical Society, American Physical Society, American Geophysical Union, American Association of Variable Star Observers, Royal Astronomical Society (England), American Academy of Arts and Sciences, Phi Beta Kappa, Sigma Xi. *Awards, honors:* A. Cressy Morrison Prize of New York Academy of Sciences, 1926, 1928, 1947; A.M., Harvard University, 1942; D.Sc., University of Denver, 1954; James H. Rand scholarship in astrophysical computation, 1955; Thomas Alva Edison Foundation Award, 1957; John Evans Award, University of Denver, 1965; Minor Planet Center of International Astronomical Union named an asteroid for him in honor of his contribution to astrophysics.

WRITINGS: A Study of Line Intensities in Stellar Spectra, [Cambridge], 1924; *A Study of Solar Chromosphere,* University of California Press, 1931; *Stars and Planets: Exploring the Universe,* University Society, 1931, 3rd edition, 1938; *Mathematical Physics,* Prentice-Hall, 1947; *Elementary Manual of Radio Propagation,* Prentice-Hall, 1948; *Our Sun,* Blakiston, 1949, 2nd edition, Harvard University Press, 1959; *Flying Saucers,* Harvard University Press, 1953; (with F. Shirley Jones) *Classification of Solar Prominences,* Solar Department of Harvard College Observatory, 1956; *The Edge of the Sun,* [Washington], 1957; *The Universe in Action,* Rushton Lectures Foundation, 1957; *Final Report Under ARDC Contract AF19(604) for the Operation of a Solar Observatory at Sacramento Peak, New Mexico,* [Cambridge], 1958; *Cosmic Noise Survey,* Harvard College Observatory, 1958; (with Howard Mumford Jones and Lyle G. Boyd) *Writing a Technical Paper,* McGraw, 1961; *Selected Papers on the Transfer of Radiation,* Dover, 1962; (with Prabhu Lal Bhatnagar and Hari K. Sen) *Stellar Interiors,* Chapman, 1963, Wiley, 1964; (with Boyd) *The World of Flying Saucers: A Scientific Examination of a Major Myth of the Space Age,* Doubleday, 1963; *A Field Guide to the Stars and Planets, Including the Moon, Satellites, Comets, and Other Features of the Universe,* Houghton, 1964; (author of revision) Martha E. Martin, *The Friendly Stars,* 2nd edition (not associated with first edition), Dover, 1964; (author of revision) Antony E. Fanning, *Planets, Stars, and Galaxies: Descriptive Astronomy for Beginners,* 2nd edition (not associated with first edition), Dover, 1967; (with Ali R. Arnir-Maez) *Fun with Numbers, Lines and Angles,* Highlights, 1969; *Astronomy,* Random House, 1970; *Survey of the Universe,* Prentice-Hall, 1971.

Editor: David Peck Todd, *The Story of the Starry Universe,* 2nd edition, P. F. Collier, 1948; *Osnovnye formuly Fiziki,* [Moscow], 1957; *Fundamental Formulas of Physics,* Dover, 1960; *The Radio Noise Spectrum,* Harvard University Press, 1960; (with Gerald de Vaucouleurs) *Final Report on the Occulation of Regulus by Venus, July 7, 1959,* U.S. Department of Commerce, Office of Technical Services, 1961; *Selected Papers on Physical Processes in Ionized Plasmas,* Dover, 1962; (with Ernest K. Smith, Jr.) *Conference on Non-Linear Processes in the Ionosphere, December 16-17, 1963,* U.S. Government Printing Office, 1964; Rose Wyler and Gerald Ames, *The New Golden Book of Astronomy: An Introduction to the Wonders of Space,* Golden Press, 1965. Editor, "Prentice-Hall Physics Series," 1947-54. Editor, *Telescope,* 1937-41; member of editorial board, *Sky and Telescope,* 1941-59; member of editorial advisory board, *Journal of Atmospheric and Terrestrial Physics,* 1951-65, *Galaxy Magazine* (science-fiction journal).

WORK IN PROGRESS: Research in astrophysics, with specialization on problems of the sun and interpretation of stellar and nebular spectra; planetary atmospheres; wave mechanics and atomic spectra; radio propagation; magneto-hydrodynamics of sunspots and solar corona; theory of reactions and equilibria at high temperatures; ionosphere, spectroscopy, geophysics; and theory of relativity.

AVOCATIONAL INTERESTS: Painting, playing guitar, and dancing; amateur radio operator.

BIOGRAPHICAL/CRITICAL SOURCES: New York Times, March 7, 1970.

(Died December 14, 1976)

* * *

MERRITT, LeRoy Charles 1912-1970

PERSONAL: Born September 10, 1912, in Milwaukee, Wis.; son of Arthur F. and Amanda (Polze) Schimmelpfennig; married Mary Averill Liebenberg, September 14, 1935; children: James LeRoy, Lauren Vail, Jeannette Averill (Mrs. William Eugene Heinkel). *Education:* University of Wisconsin, B.A. and Library Diploma, 1935; University of Chicago, Ph.D., 1942. *Home:* 3935 Mill St., Eugene, Ore. 97405. *Office:* School of Librarianship, University of Oregon, Eugene, Ore. 97403.

CAREER: University of Colorado, Boulder, assistant librarian, 1937-38; Longwood College, Farmville, Va., librarian and associate professor of librarianship, 1942-46; University of California, School of Librarianship, Berkeley, associate professor, 1946-51, professor of librarianship, 1951-66, associate dean of school, 1964-66; University of Oregon, School of Librarianship, Eugene, professor of librarianship and dean of school, 1966-70. *Military service:* U.S. Army, 1944-45; served in European theater.

MEMBER: American Library Association, Association of American Library Schools (president, 1966), American Association of University Professors, Association of College and Reference Libraries, Society of American Archivists, American Documentation Institute, Pacific Northwest Library Association, Oregon Library Association, Oregon Association of School Libraries. *Awards, honors:* Robert Downs Award of University of Illinois, 1969, for outstanding contribution to the cause of intellectual freedom in libraries.

WRITINGS: (Contributor) *Public Documents,* American Library Association, 1938; (contributor) Robert B. Downs, editor, *Union Catalogs in the United States,* American Library Association, 1942; *The United States Government as Publisher,* University of Chicago Press, 1943; (contributor) Herman H. Fussler, editor, *Library Buildings for Library Service,* American Library Association, 1947; (with Martha Boaz and Kenneth S. Tisdel) *Reviews in Library Book Selection,* Wayne State University Press, 1958; *Book Selection and Intellectual Freedom,* H. W. Wilson, 1970. Contributor to professional journals. Editor of American Library Association's *Newsletter on Intellectual Freedom,* 1962-70.

BIOGRAPHICAL/CRITICAL SOURCES: Drexel Library Quarterly, January, 1970.††

(Died May 22, 1970)

* * *

METALIOUS, Grace (de Repentigny) 1924-1964

PERSONAL: Born September 8, 1924, in Manchester, N.H.; daughter of Alfred Albert and Laurette (Royer) de Repentigny; married George Metalious, 1942; children: Marsha Metalious Dupuis, Christopher, Cynthia. *Education:* Attended public schools in New Hampshire. *Home address:* R.F.D. 1, Gilmanton, N.H.

CAREER: Writer.

WRITINGS: Peyton Place, Messner, 1956; *Return to Peyton Place,* Messner, 1959; *The Tight White Collar,* Messner, 1960; *No Adam in Eden,* Trident, 1963. Also author of two autobiographical articles for the *American Weekly* and a short story for *Glamour.*

SIDELIGHTS: "More Americans, we find, have purchased *Peyton Place* than the works of . . . Fitzgerald, Hemingway, Melville, Dreiser or James Joyce," said Paul D. Zimmerman. Carlos Baker wrote, "If Mrs. Metalious can turn her emancipated talents to less lurid purposes, her future as novelist is a good bet." The *Times Literary Supplement* commented that Grace Metalious' "writing is for the most part flat, the construction casual and confusing, and the characterization, where it exists, conventional to a degree." Elizabeth Bayard concluded that "Mrs. Metalious' prose flows along easily, but it lacks freshness and is often ungainly. Her characters are apt to run instead of walk, yell instead of exclaim; they invariably express the obvious emotion in the most appropriate cliche."

Mrs. Metalious told *CA* in 1962: "I've been married and raising children forever," and she also noted that she had "lost count of the number of radio and TV things I've been on."

Peyton Place was filmed in 1957, and *Return to Peyton Place* was filmed in 1961, both by Twentieth Century-Fox. "Peyton Place" was also a television series.

BIOGRAPHICAL/CRITICAL SOURCES: New York Times Book Review, September 23, 1956, November 29, 1959, September 25, 1960; *San Francisco Chronicle,* September 28, 1956, December 6, 1959; *Saturday Review,* December 12, 1959; *Times Literary Supplement,* January 15, 1960; *Chicago Sunday Tribune,* September 25, 1960; *New Yorker,* October 5, 1963; *Newsweek,* February 19, 1968.††

(Died February 25, 1964)

* * *

MEWS, Hazel 1909-1975

PERSONAL: Born December 25, 1909, in London, England; daughter of John Wharton and Charlotte (Freeman) Mews. *Education:* University of London, B.A. (honors), 1931, M.A., 1934. *Religion:* Church of England. *Office:* 12 Morden College, Blackheath, London SE3 0PW, England.

CAREER: South African Council for Scientific and Industrial Research, Pretoria, South Africa, head of library information division, 1945-58; University of the Witwatersrand, Johannesburg, South Africa, senior lecturer in English and librarianship, 1958-64; Cambridge University, Girton College, Cambridge, England, fellow and librarian, 1965-66; Reading University Library, Reading, England, bibliographical consultant, 1966-72; Morden College, Blackheath, London, England, honorary archivist, 1973-75. *Member:* Library Association (fellow). *Awards, honors:* D.Litt., University of Pretoria, 1964.

WRITINGS: (Editor with P. E. Krige) *Directory of Scientific, Technical and Medical Libraries in the Union of South Africa,* South African Council for Scientific and Industrial Research, 1949; *Books Are Tools: The Organization of Small Technical Libraries for South African Industry,* South African Council for Scientific and Industrial Research, 1951; *Frail Vessels: Woman's Role in Women's Novels from Fanny Burney to George Eliot,* Athlone Press, 1969; *Reader Instruction in Colleges and Universities,* Clive Bingley, 1972. Former editor, *South African Libraries.*

WORK IN PROGRESS: A biography of Priscilla Wakefield.

SIDELIGHTS: Hazel Mews was competent in German, French, Italian, Russian, Latin, and Afrikaans.†

(Died December 16, 1975)

MEYER, Harold D(iedrich) 1892-1974(?)

PERSONAL: Born November 20, 1892, in Augusta, Ga.; son of John Henry (a broker) and Mena (Sancken) Meyer; married Helen Wright, September 27, 1917; children: Harold Diedrich (deceased), George Wright. *Education:* University of Georgia, A.B., 1912, A.M., 1915; Columbia University, graduate study, 1925-26. *Religion:* Episcopalian. *Home:* 513 Dogwood Dr., Chapel Hill, N.C. *Office address:* Box 1139, Chapel Hill, N.C.

CAREER: Statesville (Ga.) public schools, principal, 1912-13, superintendent, 1913-15; State Normal School, Athens, Ga., professor of history, 1916-18, professor of sociology, 1919-21; University of North Carolina, Chapel Hill, associate professor, 1921-26, professor of sociology, 1926-65, first Taylor Grandy Professor of the Art and Philosophy of Living, 1962, professor emeritus, 1965-74, also identified with recreation curriculum at the university for more than three decades, heading all-university Division of Recreation, 1947-65. Summer professor at Emory University, University of Colorado, New York University, and other universities and colleges. Director of recreation for southern region, Works Progress Administration, 1935-38, for North Carolina Office of Civil Defense, 1943-45; chairman of National Conference on State Recreation, Federal Security Agency, 1945, and of International Recreation Conference, Geneva, Switzerland, 1949; delegate to other international and national conferences, including White House Conference on Aging. Member of National Council, Boy Scouts of America, 1925-55, and National Board, Camp Fire Girls, 1948-51; member of board of directors, North Carolina Conference for Social Service, North Carolina Congress of Parents and Teachers, 1924-52, and Penick Home for the Aging, 1963-67. Consultant to National Congress of Parents and Teachers, 1941-49, and Veterans Administration, 1962-74. Speaker and lecturer throughout United States.

MEMBER: International Recreation Association, American Recreation Society (past president), American Sociological Society, American Association for Health, Physical Education and Recreation, National Industrial Recreation Association, Southern Sociological Society, Southern Association for Health, Physical Education and Recreation, Delta Tau Delta, Alpha Kappa Delta, Alpha Phi Omega, Phi Delta Kappa, Omicron Delta Kappa. *Awards, honors:* Silver Beaver Award, Boy Scouts of America, 1940; National Distinguished Service Award from National Recreation and Park Association, 1973; honorary degrees from Florida Southern College, Salem College, and Catawba College; various awards from American Recreation Society.

WRITINGS: A Handbook of Extra-Curricular Activities in the High School, A. S. Barnes, 1926; *School Club Programs,* A. S. Barnes, 1931; *Financing Extra-Curricular Activities,* A. S. Barnes, 1933; *Regional Recreation: Leisure Time in the Southeast,* [Washington, D.C.], 1937; (with H. W. Odum and others) *American Democracy Anew,* Henry Holt & Co., 1940; (with Charles K. Brightbill) *Community Recreation: A Guide to its Organization and Administration,* Heath, 1949, 3rd edition, 1974; (with Charles K. Brightbill) *State Recreation,* A. S. Barnes, 1950; (with Charles K. Brightbill) *Recreation—Text and Readings,* Prentice-Hall, 1953; (with C. K. Brightbill) *Recreation Administration,* Prentice-Hall, 1956, 2nd revised edition, 1969. Editor, "Extra Curricular Library," twenty volumes, A. S. Barnes, 1926-35. Writer of brochures and pamphlets; contributor to sociology, recreation, health, and youth journals. Editor, *North Carolina Recreation and Park Review,* 1954-74.

(Died, 1974[?])

MEYER, Herbert W(alter)   1892-

PERSONAL: Born June 10, 1892, in Minneapolis, Minn.; son of August Ferdinand (a shop foreman) and Martha Augusta (Beutel) Meyer; married Elfriede Struss, November 16, 1918; children: Marilyn Annette (Mrs. W. E. Klosterman), Carol Louise. *Education:* University of Minnesota, B.Sc., 1914. *Politics:* Republican. *Religion:* Lutheran. *Home:* 4905 Garfield Ave. S., Minneapolis, Minn. 55409.

CAREER: Stone & Webster, Boston, Mass., power station and substation electrician, 1911; Draftsman Electric Machinery Co., generator and switchboard layout engineer, 1912-13; Byllesby Engineering and Management Corp., Chicago, Ill., power station and substation construction engineer, 1914-16; Northern States Power Co., Minneapolis, Minn., statistical engineer, 1917-57. Instructor in night school classes in electricity at Dunwoody Institute, 1916-22, Northern States Power Co., 1922-26. *Member:* Institute of Electrical and Electronics Engineers (life member; chairman of Minnesota section, 1923), National Electric Light Association (chairman of education committee, North Central Division, 1925), Minnesota Federation of Engineering Societies, Minneapolis Engineer's Club (director, 1923, 1969). *Awards, honors:* Engineer of the Year, Minneapolis Engineer's Club, 1976.

WRITINGS: Builders of Northern States Power Company, Northern States Power Co., 1957; *A History of Electricity and Magnetism,* M.I.T. Press, 1971. Also author of *Early History of the Electric Machinery Co.,* 1960. Contributor of articles on various subjects for technical press, newspapers, and magazines.

AVOCATIONAL INTERESTS: Music, geology, astronomy, and wild flowers.

* * *

MEYER, Ruth F(ritz)   1910-

PERSONAL: Born December 22, 1910, in Brooklyn, N.Y.; daughter of John Henry Charles (a clergyman and seminary professor) and Emilie (Koerber) Fritz; married Adolph Ralph Meyer (a clergyman), November 14, 1937; children: Adolph Ralph, Jr., Carol Ann (Mrs. John F. Beilharz). *Education:* Attended Lutheran parochial schools and public schools in St. Louis and Clayton, Mo. *Religion:* The Lutheran Church-Missouri Synod. *Home:* 9263 Cottonwood Dr., St. Louis, Mo. 63136.

CAREER: Stenographer in St. Louis, Mo., 1928-30; teacher at Lutheran school in Chester, Ill., 1931-32; Walther League (national headquarters), Chicago, Ill., secretary, 1932-33; Concordia Seminary, St. Louis, Mo., secretary to dean, 1934-37; kindergarten teacher at Lutheran schools in Augusta, Ga., 1944-45, and Honolulu, Hawaii, 1949-50. *Member:* Lutheran Women's Missionary League, Concordia Historical Society (St. Louis).

WRITINGS: Women on a Mission, Concordia, 1967. Contributor to Lutheran publications and to *Hawaiian Digest.*

WORK IN PROGRESS: A biography of her father, John H. C. Fritz, first dean of Concordia Seminary, St. Louis.

* * *

MEYERHOFF, Howard A(ugustus)   1899-

PERSONAL: Born May 27, 1899, in New York, N.Y.; son of Augustus Henry and Grace Edith (Berry) Meyerhoff; married Sophie Theilen, October 6, 1923; children: Arthur A. *Education:* University of Illinois, B.A., 1920; Columbia University, M.A., 1923, Ph.D., 1935. *Politics:* Republican. *Religion:* Protestant. *Home:* 3625 South Florence Pl., Tulsa, Okla. 74105.

CAREER: Columbia University, New York, N.Y., curator in paleontology, 1921-24; Smith College, Northampton, Mass., professor of geology, 1924-49; American Association for the Advancement of Science, Washington, D.C., administrative secretary, 1949-53; Scientific Manpower Commission, Washington, D.C., executive director, 1953-62; University of Pennsylvania, Philadelphia, professor of geology and chairman of department, 1963-67, professor emeritus, 1967—. Propper-McCallum Hosiery Co., chairman of board, 1938-46; GeoSurveys (mineral consultants), president, beginning 1955. National War Labor Board, mediator, 1942-45; Committee to Investigate Copyright Problems, president, beginning 1960; Office of Emergency Planning, member of Executive Reserve, 1960-69; Joint Board on Scientific Education, chairman, 1961-62. Consulting geologist, Scientific Survey of Puerto Rico and Virgin Islands, 1924-43, Dominican Government, 1937-38, 1942-51.

MEMBER: American Association for the Advancement of Science, American Association of Petroleum Geologists, American Institute of Mining, Metallurgical and Petroleum Engineers, Geological Society of America (chairman of Northeast section, 1965-67), American Institute of Professional Geologists, Society of Economic Geologists, Paleontological Society, Geochemical Society, American Geophysical Union; New York, Pennsylvania, and Washington Academies of Sciences. *Awards, honors:* LL.D., Drexel Institute of Technology, 1955.

WRITINGS: Geology of Puerto Rico, University of Puerto Rico Press, 1932; (with G. W. Bain) *Flow of Time in the Connecticut Valley,* Hampshire Bookshop (Springfield, Mass.), 1941, 2nd edition, 1964; (contributor) Ralph Linton, editor, *Most of the World,* Columbia University Press, 1949; (translator) *Geology of Cuba,* Joint Publication Research Service, U.S. Department of Commerce, 1968. Contributor of some 175 articles to journals. Editor, *Science* and *Scientific Monthly,* 1950-53; consulting editor, American Association of Petroleum Geologists, 1968-75.

WORK IN PROGRESS: Continuing research on Caribbean and Appalachian geology; new research on geomorphology and tectonics.

SIDELIGHTS: As a geologist, Meyerhoff has covered a great deal of ground from Alaska to Patagonia; his work in the Eastern Hemisphere has been limited to Morocco, Cyprus, and Italy.

* * *

MEYERS, Roy (Lethbridge)   1910-1974
(Rex Lethbridge)

PERSONAL: Born November 17, 1910, in Hounslow, Middlesex, England; son of Percy F. Cambridge (an engineer) and Maude (Lethbridge) Meyers; married Mary Isobel Leasor (a physician and surgeon), February 14, 1942; children: Christopher J.L. *Education:* Attended University College, London, and St. Bartholomew's Hospital Medical College; received L.R.C.P., 1940; M.R.C.S., 1940. *Home:* The Manor Linneys, Stogumber, Taunton, Somerset, England.

CAREER: Physician and surgeon in general practice in Stogumber, Taunton, Somerset, England, 1944-74. Chairman of Medical Board, Ministry for Social Security, 1945-74; regional medical officer, Ministry of Health, 1971-74. Former director, Periwinkle Press. *Member:* British Medical Association.

WRITINGS: The Man They Couldn't Kill, Blackfriars Press, 1942; *Dolphin Boy,* Ballantine, 1967; *Dolphin Rider,* Rapp & Whiting, 1968; *Daughter of the Dolphin,* Ballantine, 1968; *Destiny of the Dolphins,* Ballantine, 1969. Author of short stories syndicated by *Daily Express;* has also written under the pseudonym Rex Lethbridge.

WORK IN PROGRESS: Alien Pleasures, a science fiction novel; *Footsteps in the Sands of Time,* a novel.

SIDELIGHTS: Meyers told *CA* that his "Dolphin" trilogy was written as a "wonderful escape from reality."†

(Died February 13, 1974)

* * *

MEYNELL, Francis Meredith Wilfrid 1891-1975

PERSONAL: Born May 12, 1891, in London, England; son of Wilfrid (an editor) and Alice (a poet and essayist; maiden name Thompson) Meynell; married Hilda Saxe, 1914; married Vera Mendel, 1925; married Alix Hester Marie Kilroy (a barrister and civil servant), 1946; children: (first marriage) Cynthia (Mrs. David Lloyd); (second marriage) Benedict. *Education:* Attended Trinity College, Dublin, 1908-10. *Politics:* Socialist. *Religion:* Humanist agnostic. *Home:* The Grey House, Lavenham, Suffolk, England.

CAREER: Burns & Oates Ltd., London, England, typographer, 1911-13; Pelican Press, London, founder and designer, 1914; *Daily Herald,* London, director and assistant editor, 1918-20; Nonesuch Press, London, founder, designer, director, 1923-75; *News Chronicle* (now *Daily Mail and News Chronicle*), London, columnist, 1934; Mather & Crowther Ltd. (advertising agency), London, a director, 1939-60; Bodley Head Ltd., London, a director, 1960-75. British Broadcasting Corp. Brains Trust, London, chairman, 1942-43; H.M. Stationery Office, London, honorary typography advisor, 1945-66; Cement and Concrete Association, director-general, 1946-58; Royal Mint, London, member of advisory council, 1954-70. Royal College of Art, London, member of council, 1959-61. *Wartime service:* Board of Trade, advisor on consumer needs, 1940-46. *Member:* Art Workers Guild (honorary member), Society of Typographer Designers (president, 1958-62), Poetry Society (vice-president), Savile Club. *Awards, honors:* Appointed Royal Designer for Industry, 1945; knighted, 1946; D.Litt., University of Reading, 1964.

WRITINGS: (Editor) *The Week-End Book,* Nonesuch, 1923; (editor) George Herbert, *The Temple,* Nonesuch, 1927; (editor) Beedome, *Poems,* Nonesuch, 1928; *The Nonesuch Century,* Nonesuch, 1936; *Seventeen Poems,* Dent, 1945; *English Printed Books,* Collins, 1946; (editor) *The New Week-End Book,* Nonesuch, 1955; *Poems and Pieces,* Nonesuch, 1961; *My Lives,* Random House, 1971. Designer of all Nonesuch Press editions. Contributor of articles on typographical subjects to *Encyclopaedia Britannica* and *Manchester Guardian;* contributor of poems to various publications.

SIDELIGHTS: Sir Francis presented many radio broadcasts, speaking on literary and design topics and on family background. *Avocational interests:* Cricket, bridge, table tennis.

(Died July 10, 1975)

MICHALOPOULOS, Andre 1897-

PERSONAL: Born March 1, 1897, in London, England; married, 1924; children: one son, two daughters. *Education:* Oriel College, Oxford, B.A. (first class honors), 1920, M.A., 1927. *Home:* Grasshopper Hill, Irvington-on-Hudson, N.Y. 10533.

CAREER: Private secretary to Eleutherios Venizelos, Prime Minister of Greece, 1917, 1921-24; governor of Greek provinces, 1918-19, 1924-25; managing director of Athens-Piraeus Water Co., and director of several banking and business corporations in Athens, Greece, 1925-41; joined Greek forces in Crete, 1941, and later that year became general secretary of National Committee of Greeks in Egypt; member of Greek cabinet as minister of information in London, Washington, D.C., and Cairo, 1941-43; Greek minister plenipotentiary in charge of information in America, 1945-46; special adviser on American affairs, Royal Greek Embassy, Washington, D.C., 1950-67; professor of classical literatures and civilizations at Fairleigh Dickinson University, Teaneck, N.J., 1957-64, professor emeritus, 1965—. Visiting professor at University of Kansas City (now University of Missouri—Kansas City), 1949; lecturer at Harvard, Princeton, Columbia, and Georgetown Universities and other universities throughout America; also public lecturer in United States, Britain, Canada, and South Africa. Broadcast nightly English news commentary from Athens during Greco-Italian War, 1940-41; broadcast regularly in English, French, and Greek for British Broadcasting Corp., London, 1941-43; broadcast to Greece for Voice of America, 1950-55; former moderator of Columbia Broadcasting System program, "Invitation to Learning."

MEMBER: Royal Society of Arts (London; fellow), Poetry Society of America, American Academy of Poets (founding member), Ancient Monuments Society (London; fellow). *Awards, honors:* Officer, Order of the British Empire, 1919, Commander, 1937; Chevalier of Legion Honor (France), 1934; Commander of Order of the Phoenix (Greece), 1936; Commander of Order of Orange-Nassau (Netherlands), 1939; Commander of Order of George I, with swords (Greece), 1941.

WRITINGS: Poems in English by a Greek, Librarie des Bibliophiles (Lausanne), 1923; *Verses in English by a Greek,* Kaufman (Athens), 1928; *Greece's Role as a Balkan and Mediterranean Power,* Manchester University Press and John Rylands Library, 1942; *Greek Fire* (collection of broadcast articles; foreword by Compton Mackenzie), M. Joseph, 1943; *Homer,* Twayne, 1966. Contributor to other books, to *Encyclopedia Americana,* and to magazines and newspapers in eight countries; weekly book reviewer for King Features Syndicate, 1959.

* * *

MICHAUD, Charles Regis 1910-

PERSONAL: Surname is pronounced Me-*show;* born August 8, 1910, in Greenwich, Conn.; son of Regis (an author and professor) and Jennie Wells (Chase) Michaud. *Education:* Studied at Lycee Louis le Grand, Paris, France, 1924-30; University of Illinois, B.A., 1932; Northwestern University, M.A., 1933; Columbia University, graduate study, 1938-40. *Religion:* Protestant.

CAREER: Instructor in French at Northwestern University, Evanston, Ill., 1932-34, Union College, Schenectady, N.Y., 1935-36, and Lafayette College, Easton, Pa., 1936-38; U.S. Naval Academy, Annapolis, Md., began as instructor, 1941, became associate professor, beginning, 1948. Trident

Associates, Annapolis, Md., consultant and translator; Carleton Grant Associates, Annapolis, Md., director of Translation Division. *Military service:* U.S. Naval Reserve, active duty, 1942-45; became lieutenant commander. *Member:* Modern Language Association of America, American Association of Teachers of French, American Association of University Professors, U.S. Naval Institute, Phi Beta Kappa; Colonial Players, Mayo Players, and Annapolitan Club (all Annapolis).

WRITINGS: (With Marie Louise Michaud Hall) *Lectures Classiques et Modernes,* Odyssey, 1956; (with William H. Buffum) *Practical Conversational French,* Odyssey, 1962. Associate editor and writer of "Exits and Entrances" column, *Chespeake Log.*

WORK IN PROGRESS: Choix de Contes Francais, an anthology of French short stories; review of French grammar and reader for second- or third-year students.

AVOCATIONAL INTERESTS: The theatre—acting, directing, and reviewing plays.††

* * *

MICHELSON, Florence B.

PERSONAL: Born in Chicago, Ill.; daughter of Barnett and Rose E. (Brodsky) Slesnick; married William Michelson, November 7, 1926 (died October, 1974); children: Aaron I. *Education:* Audited courses at Western Reserve University (now Case Western Reserve University) for many years. *Home:* 16207 Van Aken Blvd., Apt. 102, Shaker Heights, Ohio 44120. *Agent:* Ruth Cantor, 156 Fifth Ave., New York, N.Y. 10010.

CAREER: Writer for young people. *Member:* National League of American Pen Women, Women in Communications, Cleveland College Writers Club. *Awards, honors:* National League of American Pen Women award for picture book, *The More the Merrier,* 1966; Cleveland Public Library poetry award; a number of first prizes for short stories (juvenile and adult), verse, and essays in Cleveland College Writers Club annual contests.

WRITINGS—All published by Whitman Publishing: *The Defiant Heart* (teenage novel), 1964; *The More the Merrier* (picture book), 1964; *Andy's Hospital Adventure* (juvenile), 1966; *Lassie and the Cub Scout* (juvenile), 1966. Also author of juvenile novel, *Lassie and the Firefighters.* Publications include light verse, short stories, and feature articles.

WORK IN PROGRESS: Completed manuscripts include a teenage novel, *Dody's Difficult Summer,* and a children's fantasy, *Winklesnap;* research on the American Indian of today for a children's biography of Chief Cornplanter, a Seneca friend of George Washington and Thomas Jefferson.

* * *

MIDGETT, Elwin W. 1911-
(Wink Midgett)

PERSONAL: Born December 31, 1911, in Watertown, Tenn.; son of Edell Wilburn and Martha (Ellis) Midgett; married Nell Grandstaff, October 28, 1933; children: Don Carter, Dan Earl. *Education:* Tennessee Technological University, B.S., 1934; University of Kentucky, M.A., 1938. *Religion:* United Methodist. *Home:* 510 Woodmore, Murfreesboro, Tenn. 37130. *Office:* Department of Business Education, Middle Tennessee State University, Murfreesboro, Tenn. 37130.

CAREER: Teacher of business subjects and coach at Le-

banon High School, Lebanon, Tenn., 1934-36, and Castle Heights Military Academy, Lebanon, 1936-38; Middle Tennessee State University, Murfreesboro, beginning 1939, began as faculty member of department of business, became professor, chairman of department of business education, beginning 1946. Chairman, Evaluating Committee for Business Schools for the State of Tennessee. *Military service:* U.S. Naval Reserve, 1944-46; became lieutenant. *Member:* Administrative Management Society, Alpha Kappa Psi, Pi Omega Pi, Lions Club. *Awards, honors:* Inducted into Sports Hall of Fame, Tennessee Technological University, 1976.

WRITINGS: An Accounting Primer, New American Library, 1968, hardcover edition, World Publishing, 1969; (under pseudonym Wink Midgett) *Corkus (Punt, Pitch, Pass and Putt),* Dehoff, 1970.

* * *

MIKESELL, Rufus Merrill 1893-1972

PERSONAL: Born April 17, 1893, near Union City, Ind.; son of Curtis Otwell (a farmer) and Martha Ann (McConnell) Mikesell; married Minnie M. Shigley, September 8, 1940; children: John Lee. *Education:* Indiana University, A.B., 1920, M.S., 1926; graduate study at New York University, 1923-24, 1925, and Northwestern University, 1937-38. *Politics:* Republican. *Religion:* Presbyterian. *Home address:* R.R. 12, Bloomington, Ind. 47401.

CAREER: Public school teacher in Indiana, 1912-24; Link-Belt Co., Indianapolis, Ind., assistant traffic manager, 1920-22, 1923; United Electric Light and Power Co., New York, N.Y., statistical clerk, 1924; Indiana University, Bloomington, 1924-63, began as instructor, professor of accounting, 1951-63. *Military service:* U.S. Army, 1918-19, 1942-46; became major. *Member:* Municipal Finance Officers Association of United States and Canada, American Accounting Association, American Institute of Certified Public Accountants, Beta Gamma Sigma.

WRITINGS: (With A. L. Prickett) *Principles of Accounting,* Macmillan, 1929, 2nd edition, 1937; *Accounting Manual for Farm Bureau Credit Unions,* Indiana Farm Bureau, 1948; (with L. E. Hay) *Governmental Accounting,* Irwin, 1951, 5th edition, 1974; (with C. H. Spencer and Glen Babcock) *Financial Management,* Indiana State Highway Commission, 1965.

AVOCATIONAL INTERESTS: Agriculture and agricultural cooperatives.†

(Died May 8, 1972)

* * *

MIKESELL, William H(enry) 1887-1969

PERSONAL: Born October 29, 1887, in Westminster, Maryland; son of William Augustus (a carpenter) and Lucinda Magdalene (Harner) Mikesell; married Nellie Rand Patterson, June 16, 1923; children: Ritchie P., William Henry, Jr. *Education:* Western Maryland College, B.A. (cum laude), 1909; Westminster Theological Seminary, Philadelphia, Pa., B.D. (cum laude), 1912; Harvard University, M.A., 1914; University of Illinois, Ph.D., 1926. *Politics:* Independent. *Residence:* Roswell, N.M.

CAREER: Ordained to Congregational ministry, 1912. Instructor in public speaking at University of Texas, Austin, 1916-18, University of Illinois, Urbana, 1923-26; instructor in public speaking and dramatics at University of Kentucky, Lexington, 1920-22, University of Missouri, Columbia,

1922-23; Municipal University of Wichita (now Wichita State University), Wichita, Kan., professor of psychology and head of department, 1926-47, dean of College of Liberal Arts, 1926-29; Washburn University of Topeka, Topeka, Kan., head of department of psychology, 1947-53; Mississippi State College for Women, Columbus, director of guidance, 1953-58; Anderson College, Anderson, Ind., director of guidance, beginning, 1958; Roswell Community College, Roswell, N.M., director of guidance, beginning, 1964. Chief psychologist in Mental Hygiene Clinic, U.S. Veterans Administration, Denver, Colo., 1946-47. Public lecturer on applied psychology. *Military service:* U.S. Army, psychologist, 1942-46; became captain. *Member:* Masons.

WRITINGS: Compulsory Arbitration of Labor Disputes for Public Utilities [Lexington, Ky.], 1921; (editor) *Psychology and Life,* ten volumes, Department of Psychology, Municipal University of Wichita, 1933; *Mental Hygiene* (college textbook), Prentice-Hall, 1939; *How to Study,* McGuin Publishing Co., 1940; (editor) *Modern Abnormal Psychology,* Philosophical Library, 1950; (with Gordon Hanson) *Psychology of Adjustment,* Van Nostrand, 1952; *Techniques of Living,* Stackpole, 1953; *The Power of High Purpose,* Warner Press, 1961; *Counseling for Ministers,* Christopher, 1961.

SIDELIGHTS: Mikesell had a working knowledge of French and German. *Avocational interests:* Fishing, walking, singing.†

(Died March, 1969)

*   *   *

MILLER, Charles Henderson   1905-

PERSONAL: Born October 26, 1905, in Salisbury, N.C.; son of Charles Henderson and Laura (Klutz) Miller; married Maude McCracken, April 14, 1949; children: Charles Henderson III, John Merriman. *Education:* Duke University, A.B., 1928, LL.B., 1934. *Politics:* Independent. *Religion:* Methodist. *Home:* 4622 Wye Way Lane, Knoxville, Tenn. 37920.

CAREER: Admitted to bar, North Carolina, 1933, Tennessee, 1949. Duke University, Durham, N.C., associate professor of law and assistant in legal aid clinic, 1933-45; director of North Carolina state department institutions, 1945-46; University of Tennessee, Knoxville, professor of law and director of legal aid clinic, beginning 1947. Private law practice, beginning 1934. Consultant to National Probation Association, New York, N.Y., 1945-47; president of Knoxville Council of Community Agencies, 1949-51; member of board of directors of Knoxville Community Chest, Salvation Army of Knoxville, and Family Service Association; trustee of Medical Research Foundation. *Member:* American Bar Association, North Carolina Bar Association, Knoxville Bar Association, National Council of Legal Clinics, Order of Coif, Phi Kappa Phi, Phi Delta Theta.

WRITINGS: (With William E. Cole) *Social Problems: A Sociological Interpretation,* McKay, 1965. Also author of a book, "Anatomy of a Criminal Case," as yet not published. Contributor to legal periodicals.

*   *   *

MILLER, Edward   1905-1974
(Eddie Miller)

PERSONAL: Born September 5, 1905, in De Soto, Mo.; son of Edward (a barber) and Louise Ann (Craig) Miller;

married Lucille A. Kaufman, September 24, 1934. *Education:* Attended Central Methodist College, Fayette, Mo., 1926; studied art in night classes at Art Institute of Chicago and St. Louis School of Fine Arts. *Politics:* Liberal. *Religion:* Protestant. *Home address:* Route 2, Peter Moore Lane, De Soto, Mo. 63020.

CAREER: Architectural Decorating Co. (general displays and exhibits), Chicago, Ill., designer and art director, 1931-40; Sears, Roebuck & Co., Chicago, art director of headquarters display department, 1940-42; free-lance artist in De Soto, Mo., 1942-74, doing advertising agency commissions, painting in water colors, and illustrating books. Has done whimsical paper sculpture and more conventional advertising designs for Ford Motor Co., United Airlines, U.S. Steel, Purina Mills, and other corporations; also drew a comic strip for six years for Falls City Brewing Co.; designer of television slides and film strips for TV Arts, Inc., St. Louis, Mo., 1958-59; when illness forced him to give up advertising art in 1960, he formed Storybook Associates to create ideas for children's picture books. De Soto Public Library Board, member, 1952-61, former secretary. *Member:* State Historical Society of Missouri. *Awards, honors:* Awards for water colors at various art exhibitions.

WRITINGS—"Halls of Greatness" series for young people; author and illustrator with Betty Jean Mueller; all published by Meredith Press: *The Franklin Delano Roosevelt Home and Library,* 1967; *The Harry S Truman Library,* 1967; *The Dwight D. Eisenhower Library,* 1967; *The Halls of Lincoln's Greatness,* 1968; *Mount Vernon,* 1968.

Illustrator of more than thirty books and texts, including a twelve-book animal adventure series for Benefic Press, three books, *Jerry Goes Riding, Apron Strings and Rowdy,* and *Carlos of Mexico* for Beckley-Cardy, and science, language, spelling, and history books for Webster Division of McGraw-Hill; also illustrator of magazine articles for *This Day,* Concordia Publishing House. Under the byline Eddie Miller, writer and illustrator of a weekly historical feature, "As You Were," for *De Soto Press-Dispatch,* 1967-74.

WORK IN PROGRESS: Gettysburg Today and *Kennedy Memorial at Arlington,* for "Halls of Greatness" series; a light-hearted book about the art game, tentatively entitled *Is It True About Artists?*.

BIOGRAPHICAL/CRITICAL SOURCES: Illustrator, spring, 1959, summer, 1969; *American Artist,* May, 1962; *Chicago Tribune,* May 7, 1967.†

(Died February 14, 1974)

*   *   *

MILLER, Haskell M(orris)   1910-

PERSONAL: Born July 10, 1910, in Hubbard, Tex.; son of John Thomas (a farmer) and Roxie Prudence (Wright) Miller; married Ada Wilson Anderson, June 2, 1930; children: James Morris (deceased), Mary Jo (Mrs. Edward H. Kicklighter), Helen Ann (Mrs. Robert L. Quave), Lucian Thomas. *Education:* Attended Bethel College, McKenzie, Tenn.; Southern Methodist University, B.A., 1932, M.A., 1933; New York University, Ph.D., 1941. *Politics:* Democrat. *Home:* 32 Grant Circle N.W., Washington, D.C. 20011. *Office:* Department of Sociology, Wesley Theological Seminary, 4400 Massachusetts Ave. N.W., Washington, D.C. 20016.

CAREER: Methodist clergyman, serving pastorates in Texas, Tennessee, New Jersey, Virginia, and Maryland, and currently member of Baltimore Conference of The

Methodist Church; Emory and Henry College, Emory, Va., professor of sociology, vice-president, and chaplain, 1945-49; University of Chattanooga, Chattanooga, Tenn., professor of sociology and head of department and chaplain, 1949-56, chairman of Social Science Division, 1955; Wesley Theological Seminary, Washington, D.C., professor of sociology and social ethics, beginning 1956; Wesley Institute of Urban Ministry, Washington, D.C., director, beginning 1966. Research consultant, Methodist Board of Christian Social Concerns, beginning 1962; Chairman of Board of Christian Social Concerns, Baltimore Conference of The Methodist Church. *Member:* American Sociological Association, American Academy of Political and Social Science, National Council on Family Relations, American Society of Christian Ethics, Southern Sociological Society.

WRITINGS: The Texas Gang Boy, Department of Sociology, Southern Methodist University, 1935; *The Test of Love,* Cumberland Presbyterian Publishing House, 1942; *Understanding and Preventing Juvenile Delinquency,* Abingdon, 1958; *Compassion and Community,* Association Press, 1961; *Barriers and Bridges to Brotherhood,* Abingdon, 1962; *A Christian Critique of Culture,* Abingdon, 1965; *Social Welfare Ministries in a Time of Radical Social Change,* Committee on Social Welfare, National Council of the Churches of Christ in the U.S.A., 1969. Contributor to *Christendom, Religion in Life, Journal of Educational Sociology,* and a number of Methodist publications. Editor of a research monograph series for Methodist Board of Social Concerns.

WORK IN PROGRESS: Man in Community.†

* * *

MILLER, J. Innes 1892-1976

PERSONAL: Born November 4, 1892, in Glasgow, Scotland; son of David (a business manager) and Margaret Macmillan (Dunlop) Miller; married Betty Stuart Milne, June 25, 1918; children: Hilary Stuart (Mrs. John Peter Davies). *Education:* University of Edinburgh, M.A. (first class honors in classics and history), 1915; Oxford University, M.A. (by decree), 1955. *Religion:* Church of England. *Home:* Little Lane Cottage, Brightwell-cum-Sotwell, Wallingford, Berkshire, England.

CAREER: Malayan Civil Service, 1919-48 (interned by Japanese, 1942-45); British Foreign Office, commissioner of trade and supplies in Tripolitania, 1951; Oxford University, Oxford, England, researcher in ancient history and teacher of Malay language and literature, 1954-69. *Military service:* Royal Field Artillery, serving in Gallipoli and Mesopotamia, 1915-18. *Member:* Royal Asiatic Society (life member, Malayan Branch), Royal Commonwealth Society (life member). *Awards, honors:* D.Phil., Oxford University, 1964.

WRITINGS: (Contributor) S. Durai Raja Singam, *A Hundred Years of Ceylonese in Malaysia and Singapore (1867-1967),* [Kuala Lumpur], 1967; *The Spice Trade of the Roman Empire, 29 B.C.-A.D. 641,* Clarendon Press, 1969.

WORK IN PROGRESS: Editing *The Periplus of the Erythraean Sea,* a first century Greek treatise on Roman Imperial trade in the Indian Ocean, for the Hakluyt Society, London.

BIOGRAPHICAL/CRITICAL SOURCES: Times Literary Supplement, March 13, 1969; *Journal of the Royal Geographical Society,* September, 1969; *Choice,* January, 1970; *Classical World,* January, 1970; *American Historical Review,* March, 1970; *Journal of Asian Studies,* December, 1970; *English Historical Review,* April, 1971.†

(Died October 9, 1976)

MILLER, Minnie M. 1899-

PERSONAL: Born August 26, 1899, in Olpe, Kan.; daughter of William Elonzo (a merchant) and Sarah Virginia (White) Miller. *Education:* Kansas State Normal College (now Kansas State Teachers College), B.S. in Ed., 1919; University of Chicago, M.A., 1923, Ph.D., 1928. *Home:* 824 Mechanic St., Apt. 5, Emporia, Kan. 66801.

CAREER: High school teacher in Kansas, 1919-22; member of Romance language faculty at Upper Iowa College (now University), Fayette, 1922-26, and Southwestern College, Winfield, Kan., 1927-29; Kansas State Teachers College, Emporia, 1929-68, professor of foreign languages and head of department, 1931-67. *Member:* American Association of Teachers of French, Modern Language Association of America (former national chairman of Franco-American literature section), International Federation of University Women (former chairman, International Relations Committee), American Association of University Women (former national secretary). *Awards, honors:* Palmes Academiques (silver and gold), French Government.

WRITINGS: (Editor) Gustave Flaubert, *Trois Contes* (text edition), Appleton, 1930; (with J. R. Nielson) *Outlines and Tests on French Civilization,* Appleton, 1940, 2nd edition, 1948; (editor) *First Readings in French Literature,* Appleton, 1940; (editor with Geraldine Farr) *First Readings in Spanish Literature,* Heath, 1941; (with Nielson and Jean M. Leblon) *Precis de civilisation francaise,* Appleton, 1966. Contributor of some thirty articles and numerous reviews to learned journals.

* * *

MILLER, Nyle H. 1907-

PERSONAL: Born November 16, 1907, in Anthony, Kan.; son of Alfred and Lulu Pearl (Blankinship) Miller; married Esther Isbell Pennock, June 11, 1932; children: Virginia (Mrs. Hector Correa), Nyle David, Janis Esther. *Education:* Friends University, Wichita, Kan., student, 1925-27; College of William and Mary, A.B., 1929. *Religion:* Methodist. *Home:* 635 Horne, Topeka, Kan. 66604. *Office:* Kansas State Historical Society, 120 West Tenth, Topeka, Kan. 66612.

CAREER: Kansas State Historical Society, Topeka, staff member, beginning 1931, managing editor of publications, beginning 1939, executive secretary, beginning 1951.

WRITINGS: (With Edgar Langsdorf and Robert W. Richmond) *Kansas: A Pictorial History,* Kansas Centennial Commission, 1961; (with Langsdorf and Richmond) *Kansas in Newspapers,* Kansas State Historical Society, 1963; (with Joseph W. Snell) *Why the West Was Wild,* Kansas State Historical Society, 1963; *Kansas: A Student's Guide to Localized History,* Teachers College, Columbia University, 1965; (with Snell) *Great Gunfighters of the Kansas Cowtowns, 1867-1886,* University of Nebraska Press, 1967; *Kansas: The Thirty-Fourth Star,* Kansas State Historical Society, 1976. Editor, *Kansas Historical Quarterly;* regional editor, *Montana Magazine of Western History;* member of editorial board, *The American West.*

WORK IN PROGRESS: Further study of Kansas history.

* * *

MILLER, Shane 1907-

PERSONAL: Born January 25, 1907, in Reading, Pa.; son

of Benjamin Franklin and Edith (Shane) Miller; married Janet Sinclair (an editorial assistant), May 22, 1937. *Education:* Studied art at Pennsylvania School of Industrial Art, Art Student's League, New York, N.Y., and New School for Social Research. *Religion:* Presbyterian. *Residence:* New York, N.Y.

CAREER: Advertiser's Art Service, Philadelphia, Pa., partner, 1927-32; free-lance illustrator, and writer of short stories for magazines, New York City, 1932-37; Paramount Pictures, scenic artist and scriptwriter for animation unit in New York City and Florida, 1937-45; free-lance book illustrator and writer, beginning 1945, currently in New York City.

WRITINGS—All self-illustrated: *Peter Stuyvesant's Drummer,* Coward, 1959; *The Romans,* Coward, 1963; (with Edward Ochsenschlager) *The Egyptians,* Coward, 1963; *The Hammer of Gaul,* Hawthorn, 1964, published as *Charles the Hammer: The Story of Charles Martel,* Guild Press, 1964; *Desert Fighter: The Story of General Yigael Yadin and the Dead Sea Scrolls,* Hawthorn, 1967; *Tristan Dan'l and the King of the Mill,* Rand McNally, 1969.

Co-author of animated motion picture script for Paramount Pictures, "Enchanted Square." Author of short stories, religious articles, and studies on the Bible.

Illustrator: Robert Green, *Hawk of the Nile,* St. Martin's, 1962; Harry E. Neal, *The Pennsylvania Colony,* Hawthorn, 1967. Also illustrator of *The Blue Goufalon,* Doubleday, and several other books.

WORK IN PROGRESS: Author-illustrator of a book series for children eight-to-twelve.

SIDELIGHTS: Shane Miller's film work for Paramount included set designs for two feature pictures, "Gulliver's Travels" and "Mr. Bug Goes to Town." He made a trip to Israel to research material on the archaeologist, Yigael Yadin, 1966, and also did archaeological research on a sect known as Essenes.†

*　　　*　　　*

MILLIKEN, William Mathewson 1889-

PERSONAL: Born September 28, 1889, in Stamford, Conn.; son of Thomas Kennedy (a linen merchant) and Mary Spedding (Mathewson) Milliken. *Education:* Princeton University, A.B., 1911. *Politics:* Democrat. *Religion:* Presbyterian. *Home:* 1890 East 107th St., Number 1140, Cleveland, Ohio 44106.

CAREER: Metropolitan Museum of Art, New York, N.Y., assistant curator of decorative arts, 1913-17; Cleveland Museum of Art, Cleveland, Ohio, curator of decorative arts, 1919-58, director of museum, 1930-58, director emeritus, 1958—. Member, U.S. National Committee for UNESCO, 1954-59; first vice-president, International Council of Museums, 1956-59 (honorary member, 1959); organizer, Masterpieces of Art Exhibition, Seattle World's Fair, 1962; Regents Professor, University of California, Berkeley, 1963. *Military service:* U.S. Army, 1917-18; commanded 282nd Air Squadron in England.

MEMBER: American Association of Museums (president, 1953-57; now honorary member), Association of Art Museum Directors (president, 1946-49; now honorary member), American Academy of Arts and Sciences, Royal Society of Arts (London), Renaissance Society of America, American Federation of Arts (honorary member), German National Museum (honorary member), Karamu House (honorary trustee for life). *Awards, honors:* Commander's Cross,

Hungarian Order of Merit, 1937; Order of Cavalierato of the Crown of Italy, 1938; New Sweden Tercentenary Medal, 1939; Chevalier of French Legion of Honor, 1950, and Officer, 1955; Commander, Civil Order of Alphonse X (Spain), 1954. Honorary M.A., Princeton University, 1942; L.H.D., Western Reserve University (now Case Western University), 1942; Ohio State University, 1959, and Bowling Green State University, 1963; D.F.A., Yale University, 1946, Oberlin College, 1955, and Kenyon College, 1958.

WRITINGS: The Cleveland Museum of Art, Abrams, 1958; *Unfamiliar Venice,* Press of Case Western Reserve University, 1967. Also author of *A Time Remembered: A Cleveland Memoir,* Western Reserve Historical Society. Former member of editorial advisory committee, *American Art Annual,* and editor of *Bulletin* of Cleveland Museum of Art.

WORK IN PROGRESS: A book on Greece, tentatively entitled *Greece Many-Blossomed Spring.*

SIDELIGHTS: Milliken has made more than fifty trips abroad. He is proficient in French, German, Italian, and knows some modern Greek.

*　　　*　　　*

MIRSKY, Jeannette 1903-

PERSONAL: Born September 3, 1903, in Bradley Beach, N.J.; daughter of Michael David (a businessman) and Frieda (Ittleson) Mirsky; married Edward Bellamy Ginsburg, February 14, 1942 (died, 1959). *Education:* Columbia University, B.A., 1924, graduate study in anthropology, 1935-38. *Home and office:* 230 Nassau St., Princeton, N.J. 08540.

CAREER: Author. Princeton University, Princeton, N.J., visiting fellow, department of Oriental studies, 1964-67, department of east Asian studies, 1970-71, 1972-73. Lecturer for U.S. Department of State and on radio and television; consultant to *Encyclopaedia Britannica. Member:* Society of Woman Geographers, Society for the History of Discoveries, Royal Central Asian Society, P.E.N., Phi Beta Kappa. *Awards, honors:* Guggenheim fellowships, 1947-48 and 1949-50; Rockefeller Foundation grant, 1964-67; National Endowment for the Humanities grant, 1970-72.

WRITINGS: To the North!, Viking, 1934, revised edition published as *To the Arctic!,* Knopf, 1946; *The Westward Crossings: Balboa, Mackenzie, Lewis and Clark,* Knopf, 1944; (with Allan Nevins) *The World of Eli Whitney,* Macmillan, 1952; *Elisha Kent Kane and the Seafaring Frontier,* Little, Brown, 1954; *Balboa, Discoverer of the Pacific,* Harper, 1964; (editor and compiler) *The Great Chinese Travelers* (anthology), Pantheon, 1964; (author of introduction) M. Aurel Stein, *On Ancient Central Asian Tracks,* Pantheon, 1964; *Houses of God,* Viking, 1965; *The Gentle Conquistadors: The Ten Year Odyssey Across the American Southwest of Three Spanish Captains and Esteban, a Black Slave,* Pantheon, 1969.

WORK IN PROGRESS: Research for a critical biography of Sir M. Aurel Stein.

SIDELIGHTS: Jeannette Mirsky has pursued her interest in historical geography and cultural anthropology in the Middle East, Central America, Europe, and India. *To the North!* was published in England, and in German and Spanish editions, and *The Westward Crossings,* in England. Arabic and French editions of *The World of Eli Whitney* were distributed overseas by U.S. Information Agency.†

MOBERLY, Walter (Hamilton) 1881-1974

PERSONAL: Born October 20, 1881, in Great Budworth, Cheshire, England; son of Robert Campbell (canon of Christ Church, Oxford) and Alice Sidney (Hamilton) Moberly; married Gwendolen Gardner, December 29, 1921; children: Edward, John, Richard, Robert. *Education:* New College, Oxford, B.A. (first class honors), 1903, M.A., 1907. *Religion:* Church of England. *Home:* 7 Fyfield Rd., Oxford, England.

CAREER: University of Aberdeen, Aberdeen, Scotland, lecturer in political science, 1905-06; Oxford University, Oxford, England, fellow of Lincoln College, 1906-21; University of Birmingham, Birmingham, England, professor of philosophy, 1921-24; University College of the South-West of England, Exeter, principal, 1925-26; University of Manchester, Manchester, England, vice-chancellor, 1926-34, chairman, University Grants Committee, 1935-49; St. Catherine's, Cumberland Lodge, Windsor, England, principal, 1949-55. Fellow, Merton College, Oxford University, 1904-07, and Winchester College, 1942-66. *Military service:* British Army, Oxford and Bucks Light Infantry, World War I; served in France and Belgium; received Distinguished Service Order, 1917, and was mentioned in dispatches twice.

AWARDS, HONORS: Knighted, 1934; Knight Commander of the Bath, 1944; Knight Grand Cross, Order of the British Empire, 1949. Oxford University, honorary fellow of Lincoln College, 1930, Merton College, 1937, and New College, 1942; LL.D., Queen's University of Belfast; D.Litt. from University of Manchester, University of Nottingham, and University of Keele.

WRITINGS: (With others) Burnett H. Streeter, editor, *Foundations: A Statement of Christian Belief in Terms of Modern Thought by Seven Oxford Men,* Macmillan, 1912; (with William Bragg and Lord Kennet) *Moral Rearmament,* S.C.M. Press, 1938; *Plato's Conception of Education and Its Meaning for To-day* (presidential address to Classical Association), Oxford University Press, 1944; *The Crisis in the University,* S.C.M. Press, 1949; *Universities Ancient and Modern* (Ludwig Mond lecture), Manchester University Press, 1950; *The Universities and Cultural Leadership* (Walker Trust lectures), Oxford University Press, 1951; *Responsibility* (Riddell Memorial lectures), Oxford University Press, 1951, Seabury, 1956, published as *Legal Responsibility and Moral Responsibility,* Fortress, 1965; (editor with Oliver de Selincourt) James Black Baillie, *Reflections on Life and Religion,* Verry, 1952; *The Ethics of Punishment,* Archon Books, 1968.

BIOGRAPHICAL/CRITICAL SOURCES: New Statesman, February 14, 1969.†

(Died, 1974)

* * *

MOGER, Allen W(esley) 1905-

PERSONAL: Born May 12, 1905, in Nansemond County, Va.; son of Lorenzo D. and Martha (Johnson) Moger; married Marguerite Neale (a library assistant), June 19, 1936; children: Alice Neale (Mrs. Arthur F. Marotti), Esther (Mrs. James S. Stokes IV). *Education:* Randolph-Macon College, A.B., 1927; Johns Hopkins University, graduate student, 1927-28; Columbia University, M.A., 1935, Ph.D., 1940. *Religion:* Presbyterian. *Home:* 506 Jackson Ave., Lexington, Va. 24450.

CAREER: Virginia Episcopal School, Lynchburg, instructor in Latin, 1928-29; Washington and Lee University, Lexington, Va., instructor, 1929-35, assistant professor, 1935-46, associate professor, 1946-51, professor of history, beginning 1951, head of department, 1969-70. Civilian head of testing department, School for Personnel Services, Army Service Forces, Lexington, Va., 1944-46; visiting professor at University of Virginia, summer, 1956, 1957-58, and summer, 1966, and Columbia University, summer, 1958. *Member:* American Historical Association, Southern Historical Association, Virginia Social Science Association (president, 1948-49), Virginia Historical Society, Rockbridge Historical Society (president, 1973-76).

WRITINGS: The Rebuilding of the Old Dominion, 1880 to 1902, Edwards Brothers, 1940; *Virginia: Bourbonism to Byrd, 1870 to 1925,* University Press of Virginia, 1968. Educational collaborator on seven instructional films and six film strips for Coronet Films, Chicago. Contributor to professional journals.

* * *

MOKGATLE, Nyadioe Naboth 1911-

PERSONAL: Born April 1, 1911, in Phokeng, South Africa; married; two children. *Politics:* Socialist. *Home:* 23B, Aquinas St., London S.E.1, England.

CAREER: Trade unionist and writer. *Awards, honors:* Anisfield-Wolf Award, *Saturday Review.*

WRITINGS: Autobiography of an Unknown South African, University of California Press, 1970.

WORK IN PROGRESS: Several manuscripts.

SIDELIGHTS: Nyadioe Mokgatle told *CA:* "I have been motivated by love for people, hatred for injustices, lack of comfort, sufferings of my people in South Africa.... Circumstances which cause me at all times to write are to provoke discussions; about the past, present, about things I think are neglected or never taken notice of by the Governors and the Governed. Particularly, and specifically laws resting on the rock of the doctrine of Apartheid in South Africa."

AVOCATIONAL INTERESTS: Reading history and biographies, the social sciences.

* * *

MOLLOY, Robert (William) 1906-1977

PERSONAL: Born January 9, 1906, in Charleston, S.C.; son of Robert William (a businessman) and Edith Estelle (Johnson) Molloy; married Marion Knapp Jones (a librarian), June 29, 1929; children: Brian Frederick, Thomas Lawrence. *Education:* Student at private and public schools in Charleston, Philadelphia, and New York. *Politics:* Independent Democrat. *Religion:* None. *Residence:* Paramus, N.J. *Agent:* Paul R. Reynolds, Inc., 599 Fifth Ave., New York, N.Y. 10017.

CAREER: New York Sun, New York, N.Y., assistant literary editor, 1936-43, literary editor, 1943-45; and free-lance copy editor for newspapers including *World Telegram* and *Daily News;* translator and novelist.

WRITINGS—Novels, except as noted: *Pride's Way,* Macmillan, 1945; *Uneasy Spring,* Macmillan, 1946; *Charleston: A Gracious Heritage* (nonfiction), Appleton, 1947; *The Best of Intentions,* Lippincott, 1949; *Pound Foolish,* Lippincott, 1950; *A Multitude of Sins,* Doubleday, 1953; *An Afternoon in March,* Doubleday, 1958; *The Reunion,* Doubleday, 1959; *The Other Side of the Hill,* Doubleday, 1962.

Translator: (And adapter with Madeleine Boyd) Lucien Pemjean, *Captain d'Artagnan,* Doubleday, 1933; Romulo Gallegos, *Dona Barbara,* Peter Smith, 1948; Denis F. Bernard, *Suspended Man,* Putnam, 1960. Contributor to *Columbia Encyclopedia, Encyclopedia Americana,* and *British Authors of the Nineteenth Century.*

AVOCATIONAL INTERESTS: Music.†

(Died January 27, 1977)

* * *

MONRO, Isabel S(tevenson)   1884-

PERSONAL: Born October 6, 1884, in Wallace, Nova Scotia, Canada; daughter of James David and Kate (Stevenson) Monro. *Education:* Simmons College, S.B., 1907. *Politics:* Republican. *Religion:* Presbyterian. *Home:* Winter Park Towers, 1111 South Lakemont Ave., Winter Park, Fla.

CAREER: Cataloger at University of Maine Library, Orono, 1907-09, and University of Minnesota Library, Minneapolis, 1911-13; New York (N.Y.) Public Library, classifier, 1914-34; H. W. Wilson Co. (publishers), New York, N.Y., editorial assistant, 1935-45. Member of board, Winter Park Public Library. *Member:* American Association of University Women, Woman's Club of Winter Park, Garden Club of Winter Park.

*WRITINGS—*All with sister, Kate M. Monro: *Index to Reproductions of American Paintings,* H. W. Wilson, 1948; *Index to Reproductions of European Painting,* H. W. Wilson, 1956; *The Clubwoman's Manual,* Macmillan, 1957; *Costume Index,* supplement, H. W. Wilson, 1957; *Supplement to Reproductions of American Paintings,* H. W. Wilson, 1964.

* * *

MONRO, Kate M.   1883-19(?)

PERSONAL: Born February 26, 1883, in Wallace, Nova Scotia, Canada; daughter of James David and Kate (Stevenson) Monro. *Education:* Mount Holyoke College, B.A., 1906. *Politics:* Republican.

CAREER: Onetime teacher of English in high schools, with last position as administrative assistant, Haaren High School, New York, N.Y., 1933-45. Also taught secretarial correspondence in Extension Division, Columbia University. *Member:* National League of American Pen Women, American Association of University Women.

WRITINGS: (With Sarah Augusta Taintor) *The Secretary's Handbook,* Macmillan, 1929, 9th edition, 1969; (with Taintor) *The Handbook of Social Correspondence,* Macmillan, 1936; *English for Secretaries,* McGraw, 1944; (sole author of first and second editions; subsequent editions with Mary A. Wittenberg) *A Workbook Course in Modern English,* McGraw, 1947, 3rd edition published as *Modern Business English: A Text-Workbook in English Usage,* 1962, 4th edition published as *Modern Business English: A Text-Workbook for Colleges,* 1967, 5th edition, 1972; (with sister, Isabel S. Monro) *Index to Reproductions of American Paintings,* supplement, H. W. Wilson, 1948; (with I. S. Monro) *Index to Reproductions of European Paintings,* H. W. Wilson, 1956; (with I. S. Monro) *The Clubwoman's Manual,* Macmillan, 1957; (with I. S. Monro) *Costume Index,* supplement, H. W. Wilson, 1957; (with I. S. Monro) *Supplement to Reproductions of American Printings,* H. W. Wilson, 1964.†

(Deceased)

MONTEUX, Doris (Hodgkins)   1894-

PERSONAL: Surname is pronounced Moan-ter; born November 8, 1894, in Eden, Me.; daughter of Eugene-Hamilton (a decorator) and Bethia Marie (Emery) Hodgkins; married Pierre Monteux (conductor of San Francisco Symphony Orchestra, 1934-52, and other orchestras in American and Europe), September, 1926 (died July, 1964). *Education:* Studied at Boston Latin School for Girls, New England Conservatory of Music, and in Europe. *Politics:* Democrat. *Religion:* Roman Catholic. *Home:* Winterhaven, Hancock, Me.

CAREER: Writer in recent years. President of Pierre Monteux Memorial Foundation, and director of Domaine School for Conductor and Orchestra Musicians.

WRITINGS: Everyone is Someone, Farrar, Straus, 1962; *It's All in the Music: The Life and Work of Pierre Monteux,* Farrar, Straus, 1965.

WORK IN PROGRESS: Two books *A Jocular Outpouring,* and *Small Town Scamp.*

SIDELIGHTS: Doris Monteux speaks French, Italian, Dutch, German, and understands Russian. *Avocational interests:* Helping young conductors.

* * *

MOONEY, Chase C(urran)   1913-1972

PERSONAL: Born December 30, 1913, in Davidson County, Tenn.; son of Aurelius A. (a schoolteacher) and Alma (Ainsworth) Mooney; married Loraine Binkley, September 9, 1939; children: Barbara Ellen (Mrs. Jon C. Underwood), L. Wayne. *Education:* Vanderbilt University, B.A. (magna cum laude), 1935, M.A., 1936, Ph.D., 1939. *Home:* 910 South Highland, Bloomington, Ind. 47401.

CAREER: Brenau College, Gainesville, Ga., professor of history and political science, 1939-42; U.S. Army Air Forces, senior historian, 1942-46; Southern Methodist University, Dallas, Tex., assistant professor of history, 1946; Indiana University, Bloomington, assistant professor, 1946-51, associate professor, 1951-61, professor of history, 1961-72. Summer visiting professor at University of Mississippi, 1939, 1940, Vanderbilt University, 1942, Alaska Methodist University, 1950, and Johns Hopkins University, 1955. *Member:* American Historical Association, Organization of American Historians (chairman of prize studies awards committee, 1956-63), Southern Historical Association, Phi Beta Kappa. *Awards, honors:* Social Science Research Council grant, 1941; Guggenheim fellowship, 1959-60.

WRITINGS: Slavery in Tennessee, Indiana University Press, 1957; *Civil Rights and Liberties,* Holt, 1963, 2nd edition, 1965; *William H. Crawford, 1772-1834,* University Press of Kentucky, 1973. Contributor to historical journals. Book review editor, *Historian,* 1955-58; associate editor and book review editor, *Mississippi Valley Historical Review* (now *Journal of American History*), 1963-66.

AVOCATIONAL INTERESTS: Carpentry, cabinet work, and golf. †

(Died, 1972)

* * *

MOORE, Cora R.   1902-

PERSONAL: Born April 7, 1902, in Dexter, Mo.; daughter of Walter Andrew (a farmer) and Rebecca (Hendrick) Stewart; married Roscoe Moore, June 12, 1921; children: Lila M. (Mrs. Wendell P. Decker), Lucille R. (Mrs. Edwin

F. Christian). *Education:* Attended high school in Bakersfield, Calif. *Religion:* Protestant. *Home:* 515 South Ross, Santa Ana, Calif. 92701.

WRITINGS: Inspiring Devotional Programs for Women's Groups, Zondervan, Book I, 1966, Book II, 1967, Book III, 1968.

* * *

MOORE, Fenworth
[Collective pseudonym]

WRITINGS—"Jerry Ford Wonder Stories" series; published by Cupples & Leon: *Cast Away in the Land of Snow,* 1931; *Lost in the Caves of Gold,* 1931; *Wrecked on a Cannibal Island,* 1931; *Prisoners on the Pirate Ship,* 1932.

SIDELIGHTS: See **ADAMS, Harriet S., STRATEMEYER, Edward L.,** and **SVENSON, Andrew E.**†

* * *

MOORE, Ward 1903-

PERSONAL: Born August 10, 1903, in Madison, N.J.; son of Samuel Ward and Stella Adelaide (Lemlein) Moore; married Lorna Lenzi (a librarian), September, 1942 (divorced); married Raylyn Crabbe (a writer), June 14, 1967; children: Fredrica, Rebekah (deceased), David (deceased), Samuel Benjamin, Hannah, Sara. *Education:* "None." *Politics:* "Registered Democrat, whatever that means." *Religion:* Jewish. *Home:* 302 Park St., Pacific Grove, Calif. 93950. *Agent:* Virginia Kidd, P.O. Box 278, Milford, Pa. 18337.

CAREER: Writer.

WRITINGS: Breathe the Air Again, Harper, 1942; *Greener Than You Think,* Sloane, 1947; *Bring the Jubilee,* Farrar, Straus, 1953; *Cloud by Day,* Heinemann, 1956; (with Avram Davidson) *Joyleg,* Pyramid Publications, 1962. His short stories have been included in numerous anthologies. Contributor of fiction to *Saturday Evening Post, Harper's Bazaar,* and other magazines, and nonfiction to magazines and newspapers, including *Reporter* and *Nation.*

SIDELIGHTS: Ward Moore says that he has had no difficulty publishing satire "so long as it can be labeled science fiction. When it cannot, editors agree that it is superb, but not for their public." *Greener Than You Think* also was published in England and Argentina, and *Bring the Jubilee* in England and Italy.

* * *

MORENO, Jacob L. 1892-1974

PERSONAL: Born May 20, 1892, in Bucharest, Rumania; came to United States, 1927, naturalized, 1935; son of Nissim (a merchant) and Pauline (Wolf) Moreno; married Zerka Toeman (a psychodramatist), December 8, 1949; children: Regina (Mrs. Mathew Zachariah), Jonathan David. *Education:* University of Vienna, M.D., 1917. *Home and office:* 259 Wolcott Ave., Beacon, N.Y., 12508.

CAREER: Mitterndorf State Hospital, Vienna, Austria, superintendent, 1918; officer of health, Voeslau, Austria, 1918-25; practicing psychiatrist, Voeslau and Vienna, 1918-25; founder of Das Stegreiftheater (The Spontaneity Theater), 1921-25; originator of first "living newspaper", and the idea of psychodrama, 1923; licensed as physician by New York State, 1927, practicing as a psychiatrist and working in psychodramatics, 1927-74; Moreno Sanitarium, Beacon, N.Y., physician in charge, 1936-68; Moreno Institute, Beacon, N.Y., and New York, N.Y., chairman, 1942-

74; New York University, Graduate School of Arts and Sciences, adjunct professor of sociology, 1952-66; founder of Impromptu Theatre (Carnegie Hall), 1929-31, and Therapeutic Theatre, 1936. Publisher of *Daimon* (monthly magazine of philosophy and literature) 1918, and *Impromptu* magazine, 1931; made Sociometric studies at Sing Sing Prison, 1931-32; advisor, Subsistence Homestead Division, U.S. Department of Interior, 1934; president, International Council on Group Psychotherapy; honorary president, First International Congress of Psychodrama, Paris, 1964. Special lecturer at New School for Social Research, 1937-38, Columbia University, 1939-40; lecturer at other universities in America; lecturer in Europe, including Soviet Russia (at invitation of Academy of Sciences) and Czechoslovakia, 1959, Czechoslovakia and Hungary, 1963.

MEMBER: American Psychiatric Association (life fellow; secretary, psychotherapy section, 1954-60), American Medical Association (life member), American Society of Group Psychotherapy and Psychodrama (founder; former president), American Sociometric Association (president, 1945), American Sociological Association, New York Medical Society (life member).

WRITINGS: Das Stegreiftheater, Gustav Kiepenheur, 1923 (English translation by the author, *The Theatre of Spontaneity,* Beacon House, 1947); *Group Method and Group Psychotherapy,* Beacon House, 1932, subsequent editions published as *The First Book on Group Psychotherapy,* with 4th edition, 1959; *Who Shall Survive?: Foundations of Sociometry, Group Psychotherapy and Sociodrama,* Nervous and Mental Disease Publishing, 1934, revised edition, Beacon House, 1953; *The Words of the Father,* Beacon House, 1941; (with Zerka Toeman, later Zerka Toeman Moreno) *The Group Approach to Psychodrama,* Beacon House, 1942; (with Zerka Toeman) *Psychodrama,* Volume I, Beacon House, 1945, 4th edition, 1972, Volume II, 1959, Volume III, 1969; (editor) *Group Psychotherapy, a Symposium,* Beacon House, 1945, 2nd edition, 1960; *Life-situation Test,* Beacon House, 1947.

(With James Enneis) *Hypnodrama and Psychodrama,* Beacon House, 1950; *Sociometry, Experimental Method and the Science of Society,* Beacon House, 1951; *Grundlagen der Soziometrie,* Westdeutscher Verlag, 1953; (co-editor) *Progress in Psychotherapy,* Volumes I-V, Grune, 1955-60; *Preludes to My Autobiography,* Beacon House, 1955; (editor) *Sociometry and the Science of Man,* Beacon House, 1956; *Sociometry of Subhuman Groups,* Beacon House, 1958; *Discovery of the Spontaneous Man,* Beacon House, 1958; *Gruppenpsychotherapie und Psychodrama,* Thieme Verlag, 1959; (contributor) *American Handbook of Psychiatry,* edited by S. Arieti, Basic Books, 1959; (co-editor) *The Sociometry Reader,* Free Press of Glencoe, 1960; *New Introduction to Psychodrama,* Beacon House, 1963; (with others) *The First Psychodramatic Family,* Beacon House, 1964; (editor with A. Friedemann) *The International Handbook of Group Psychotherapy,* Philosophical Library, 1966.

Author of a number of short monographs. Editor, "Classics of Sociometry," eighteen volumes, Beacon House, 1937-56. Founding editor, *Sociometry,* 1937-55; editor, *Group Psychotherapy,* beginning 1947, and *International Journal of Sociometry and Sociatry,* beginning 1956.

WORK IN PROGRESS: The American Revolution as approached by group and action methods.

SIDELIGHTS: Jacob Moreno's books have been translated into more than fifteen languages, with *Sociometry, Experimental Method and the Science of Society* appearing in Russian, Turkish, Serbo-Croatian, and Japanese, among other languages; Moreno received 12,000 rubles for the Russian publication, although the book contains a criticism of Marxism. He spoke German, Italian, French, and Rumanian.

BIOGRAPHICAL/CRITICAL SOURCES: Horoscope, November, 1951; Jacob L. Moreno, *Preludes to My Autobiography,* Beacon House, 1955; P. Renouvier, *The Group Psychotherapy Movement, J. L. Moreno, Its Pioneer and Founder,* Beacon House, 1958; Jacob L. Moreno and others, *The First Psychodramatic Family,* Beacon House, 1964. †

(Died May 14, 1974)

* * *

MORGAN, Lenore H. 1908-1976

PERSONAL: Born October 3, 1908, in Princeton, N.J.; daughter of David (a law professor and college president) and Laura (Mooney) Hutchison; married David H. Morgan (a director, Dow Chemical Co.), December 30, 1933; children: Ann (Mrs. Charles D. Dever), Dale (Mrs. Sandford T. Waddell). *Education:* State University of New York, B.A., 1929; Vanderbilt University, M.A., 1930; University of Paris, Dr. en Droit, 1932; Academy of International Law, The Hague, Netherlands, Certificat, 1932; Colorado State University, M.S., 1949; additional graduate study at Columbia University, London School of Economics and Political Science, and University of California. *Politics:* Republican. *Religion:* Presbyterian. *Home:* 714 West St. Andrews, Midland, Mich. 48640.

CAREER: Employed as program director for Station KRE, Berkeley, Calif., programmer for Radio Station WOKO, Albany, N.Y., and staff member of U.S. Office of War Information, San Francisco, Calif.; worked in special children's health radio programming in New York; teacher of writing for children, Writer's Conference, Judson, N.Y., 1966-69. Actress with little theaters and stock companies in New York, Tennessee, London, England, and Paris, France; holder of U.S. patents for toy designs. *Member:* Authors League of America, Midland Women's Club, Kings Daughters, Phi Beta Kappa.

WRITINGS—Juveniles: *The Mouse Who Was Stirring,* Baker Book, 1961; *The Shepherds Brought a Song,* Baker Book, 1962; *Peter's Pockets,* Oddo, 1965; *Dragons and Stuff,* Oddo, 1970. Contributor of short stories to "SRA Reading Series." Contributor of more than 125 stories and articles to national magazines. Writer-producer of Midland Centennial Pageant, 1968.

WORK IN PROGRESS: A juvenile novel on the Revolution; a humorous personal-essay type novel on the life of a college president and his wife.

AVOCATIONAL INTERESTS: Designing toys; theatre; golf.†

(Died February 21, 1976)

* * *

MORRAH, Dermot (Michael Macgregor) 1896-1974 (Yorkist)

PERSONAL: Born April 26, 1896; son of Herbert Arthur and Alice Elsie (Macgregor) Morrah; married Ruth Houselander (a justice of the peace), January 18, 1923; children: Deirdre, Brigid (Mrs. Thomas Edwin Utley). *Education:* New College, Oxford, M.A. (first class honors), 1921. *Poli-*

tics: Reactionary. *Religion:* Roman Catholic. *Home:* 131A Ashley Gardens, Westminster, London S.W.1, England. *Agent:* Curtis Brown Ltd., 1 Craven Hill, London W2 3EW, England.

CAREER: Oxford University, All Souls College, Oxford, England, fellow, 1921-28; assistant principal, Home Civil Service, 1922-28; *Daily Mail,* London, England, leader-writer, 1928-31; *Times,* London, leader-writer concerned largely with imperial affairs, constitutional law, and penal theory, 1932-61; *Daily Telegraph,* London, leader-writer, 1961-67. Arundel Herald Extraordinary (herald to the Queen on all state occasions), 1953-74. Freeman of City of London, 1960. *Military service:* Royal Engineers, 1915-19; served with Mediterranean and Egyptian Expeditionary Forces; became lieutenant. *Member:* Society of Antiquaries (fellow), Commonwealth Press Union (member of council, beginning 1945; chairman of press freedom committee, beginning 1956), Wine Society (director, 1943-63; chairman, 1959-63), Monarchist League (councillor of honor, beginning 1965).

WRITINGS: If It Had Happened Yesterday: Extracts from the Apocrypha of "The Daily Mail," George Newnes, 1931; *The Mummy Case,* Harper, 1933, reprinted, Garland Publishing, 1972; (with Campbell Dixon) *Caesar's Friend* (play), Samuel French, 1933; *Chorus Angelorum* (a nativity play for young performers), Samuel French, 1936; *The British Red Cross,* Collins, 1944; *The Royal Family in Wartime,* Odhams, 1945; *Princess Elizabeth,* Odhams, 1947, enlarged edition published as *Princess Elizabeth, Duchess of Edinburgh,* 1950; *The Royal Family in Africa,* Hutchinson, 1947; *The Royal Family,* Odhams, 1950; *Most Excellent Majesty: The Crown, from First Beginnings to Its Place in the Modern World* (booklet), H.M.S.O., 1953, revised edition published as *Crown and People,* 1959; *A History of Industrial Life Assurance,* Allen & Unwin, 1955; *The Work of the Queen,* Kimber & Co., 1958; (with others) *The Queen's Visit: Elizabeth II in India and Pakistan,* Asia Publishing House, 1961; (editor of English translation) Jiri Louda, *European Civic Coats of Arms,* Hamlyn, 1966; (editor of English translation) Vaclav Mericka, *Orders and Decorations,* Hamlyn, 1967; *To Be a King,* Hutchinson, 1968, updated edition, Arrow Books, 1969.

Contributor to *The History of "The Times,"* five volumes, Times Newspapers Ltd., 1935-52, and former editor of *Times Style Book* (also has written letters to the *Times* under the pseudonym Yorkist). Writer of films, "Royal Heritage" and "The Coronation Ceremony," both 1953. Regular contributor to technical wine journals. Leader-writer, *Round Table,* 1942-44, editor, 1944-65.

SIDELIGHTS: Morrah represented the *Times* and King George's Jubilee Trust on the royal tour of southern Africa in 1947. From time to time he visited most of the principal winefields of France, Spain, Portugal, and Hungary.

BIOGRAPHICAL/CRITICAL SOURCES: Books and Bookmen, June, 1969.†

(Died September 30, 1974)

* * *

MORTON, C(lement) Manly 1884-1976

PERSONAL: Born February 25, 1884, in Newport, N.C.; son of Leonard and Joannah (Garner) Morton; married Selah Louise Beam, August 21, 1916 (deceased). *Education:* Atlantic Christian College, B.A., 1909; College of Missions, M.A., 1916; Hartford Seminary Foundation, M.R.E., 1927;

also studied at University of Paraguay, 1919-20, and University of Chicago, 1932-33. *Politics:* Independent. *Home and office:* 712 Southeast Seventh St., Fort Lauderdale, Fla. 33301.

CAREER: Evangelist and pastor of Christian churches (Disciples of Christ) in the United States and South America, 1909-18; International College, Asuncion, Paraguay, founder, 1920; Evangelical Seminary of Puerto Rico, Rio Piedras, head of department of practical theology, 1923-44. Executive secretary, Interdenominational Committee on Christian Education for the Island of Puerto Rico, 1934-39. *Awards, honors:* D.D., Atlantic Christian College, 1951; Order of Merit, Government of Paraguay, 1960, for outstanding service.

WRITINGS: Paraguay: Inland Republic, Powell & White, 1926; *Kingdom Building in Puerto Rico,* United Christian Missionary Society, 1949; *Adventures in Prayer,* Revell, 1967; *Isle of Enchantment: Stories and People of Puerto Rico,* Bethany Press, 1970.

WORK IN PROGRESS: His autobiography, tentatively entitled *Life: Adventure and Challenge.*

SIDELIGHTS: C. Manly Morton said that he had little time for writing most of his life, but at eighty "resolved to write and publish three books . . . to prove that man is not dead at eighty."†

(Died February, 1976)

* * *

MORTON, William C(uthbert) 1875-1971

PERSONAL: Born March 1, 1875, in San Fernando, Trinidad; son of John (a Presbyterian missionary) and Sarah Etter (Silver) Morton; married Mary Jarvie Brodie, September 28, 1904; children: Norah Cuthbert, Mary Silver Cuthbert. *Education:* Attended Queen's Royal College, Port-of-Spain, Trinidad; University of Edinburgh, M.A. (first class honors in classics), 1896, M.D., 1910; further study at University of Berlin and University of Freiburg.

CAREER: General practice of medicine in Leeds, England, 1907-57. *Military service:* British Army, 1914-19; stationed at 2nd Northern General Hospital; became captain; made Commander, Order of the British Empire, 1919.

WRITINGS: The Harmony of Verse, University of Toronto Press, 1968. Also author of *The Language of Anatomy,* 1922. Contributor to medical journals.

WORK IN PROGRESS: Upon the Face of the Waters, a book on the influence of animism and anthropomorphism on the language of the Bible; a book of verse for old and young.†

(Died, 1971)

* * *

MOSER, Shia 1906-

PERSONAL: Born October 17, 1906, in Jagielnica, Austria-Hungary; son of Chaim and Sheva Moser. *Education:* John Casimir University, M.A. in Philosophy, 1933, M.A. in Germanic Studies, 1936; McGill University, M.A., 1952; University of Buffalo (now State University of New York at Buffalo), Ph.D., 1958. *Religion:* Jewish. *Home:* Lafayette Hotel, Buffalo, N.Y. 14205. *Office:* Department of Philosophy, State University of New York, Buffalo, N.Y. 14222.

CAREER: State University of New York at Buffalo, lecturer, 1957-58, assistant professor, 1958-63, associate professor, 1963-67, professor of philosophy, beginning 1967.

Member: American Association of University Professors, American Philosophical Association (Eastern division).

WRITINGS: Absolutism and Relativism in Ethics, C. C Thomas, 1958. Contributor to philosophy journals.

SIDELIGHTS: Shia Moser speaks German, Polish, and Yiddish, and has some knowledge of French, Russian, Hebrew, and Ukrainian.

* * *

MOSLEY, Oswald (Ernald) 1896-
(European)

PERSONAL: Born November 16, 1896, in London, England; son of Sir Oswald and Maud (Heathcote) Mosley; succeeded to title held by his father, 1928, becoming the sixth baron; married Lady Cynthia Curzon, May 11, 1920 (died, 1933); married the Honorable Diana Mitford, October 6, 1936; children: (first marriage) Nicholas (Lord Ravensdale), Vivien (Mrs. Forbes-Adams), Michael; (second marriage) Alexander, Max. *Education:* Educated at Winchester College and Royal Military Academy at Sandhurst. *Politics:* "Union of Europe." *Home:* 1 rue des Lacs, Orsay 91, Essonne, France.

CAREER: Entered the House of Commons at the age of twenty-one as a supporter of Lord George's Coalition Government and served as Conservative member from Harrow Division of Middlesex, 1918-22; estranged by what he considered outrages committed by Crown agents in Ireland, he left the Conservative Party and was returned to Parliament as an independent member from Harrow, 1922-24, and then as Labour member from Smethwick Division, 1924, 1926-31; as chancellor of the Duchy of Lancaster, 1929-30, he was one of the ministers charged with dealing with Britain's unemployment problem; when his ideas for reform, based on a planned economy along Keynesian lines, were rejected, he resigned from Parliament to form the New Party; the New Party failing to gain support, he organized and led the British Union of Fascists (Blackshirts) and was interned by his own government during World War II; after the war, he founded the Union Movement to promote the Union of Europe and campaigned continuously for advanced policy of "Europe A Nation," a phrase that he coined in 1948. *Military service:* British Army, 16th Lancers and Royal Flying Corps, World War I; served in France.

WRITINGS: The Greater Britain, B.U.F. (British Union of Fascists) Publications, 1932; *Blackshirt Policy,* B.U.F. Publications, 1932; *Fascism: 100 Questions Asked and Answered,* B.U.F. Publications, 1936; *Tomorrow We Live,* Greater Britain Publications, 1936; *My Answer,* Mosley Publications, 1946; *Mosley: What They Say, What They Said, What He Is,* Raven Books, 1947; *The Alternative,* Mosley Publications, 1947, reprinted, AMS Press, 1972; *Policy and Debate* (essays), Euphorion, 1954; *Mosley: The Facts,* Euphorion, 1957; *Europe: Faith and Plan,* Euphorion, 1958; *Mosley: Right or Wrong?,* Lion Books, 1961; *My Life,* Thomas Nelson, 1968.

Pamphlets and other short publications: *Revolution by Reason,* Borough Labour Party (Birmingham, England), 1925; *Menace of Russian Communism,* Mosley Publications, 1947; *A Policy for Britain: The Way Out from England on the Dole,* Mosley Publications, 1947; *Union of Europe,* Mosley Publications, 1947; *The European Situation: The Third Force,* Mosley Publications, 1950; *European Socialism,* Sanctuary Press, 1951; *What Chance of Peace?,* Sanctuary Press, 1951; *Wagner and Shaw: A Synthesis,* Sanctuary Press, c. 1956; *European Socialism: A Summary of the*

Policy, and a Reply to Comment and Criticism for Britain, Germany, Italy and America, Sanctuary Press, 1956. Occasionally used the pseudonym European for articles.

SIDELIGHTS: Lord Boothby writes of Oswald Mosley: "I discerned in him . . . this kind of quality of leadership that I discerned in only two other men during all my period of political life. One is Lloyd George and the other is Churchill." Michael Foot equally admires Mosley: "[*My Life*] could cast a dazzling gleam across the whole century. . . . Within a few years of joining the Labour Party, he came near to diverting the whole course of British history. More surely than any other comparable figure of the time, Mosley had grasped the reality of Britain's economic plight. Vigour, intelligence, dramatic gesture and coruscating wit combined to give to this would-be Caesar a touch of Cicero as well. . . . What Mosley so valiantly stood for could have saved his country from the Hungry Thirties and the Second World War . . . the deep-laid middle-class love of mediocrity and safety-first which consigned political genius to the wilderness and the nation to the valley of the shadow of death."

BIOGRAPHICAL/CRITICAL SOURCES: Allan Young, *A National Policy: An Account of the Emergency Programme Advanced by Sir Oswald Mosley,* Macmillan, 1931; James Drennan (pseudonym of William E.D. Allen), *B.U.F.: Oswald Mosley and British Fascism,* J. Murray, 1934; Arthur K. Chesterton, *Oswald Mosley: Portrait of a Leader,* Action Press, 1937; Dennis N. Pritt, *The Mosley Case,* Labour Monthly, 1947; Thomas E.N. Driberg, *Mosley? No!,* W. H. Allen, 1948; *Observer Review,* October 20, 1968; *Panorama,* October 21, 1968; *Evening Standard,* October 22, 1968; *Times Literary Supplement,* October 24, 1968; *New Statesman,* October 25, 1968; *Listener,* October 31, 1968; *New Republic,* December 7, 1968; Robert Skidelsky, *Oswald Mosley,* Macmillan, 1975.

* * *

MOYER, Claire B. (Inch)   1905-

PERSONAL: Born June 29, 1905, in Boston, Mass.; daughter of James W. (a mine boss and steel worker) and Elizabeth (Jones) Inch; married Roy D. Moyer (an Air Force civilian employee), May 8, 1926; children: Marcia (Mrs. John Winterhouse, Jr.), Lois (Mrs. William Kirk Crane), Gail (Mrs. Phillip C. Christner). *Education:* Studied at Wayne University (now Wayne State University), 1923-25, and University of Utah, 1947-49; University of Denver, B.A., 1954; University of Washington, Seattle, graduate study, 1957-63.

CAREER: Teacher in public and private schools in Detroit, Mich., 1925-26, Salt Lake City, Utah, 1945-49, Englewood, Colo., 1952-55, Port Angeles, Wash., 1956-60, Sequim, Wash., 1962-63, Point Arena, Calif., 1964-65; U.S. Department of Defense Overseas School System, elementary teacher, Ulm, Germany, beginning 1965. Active in astronomical societies in various states of residence, and director of junior astronomers for Denver Astronomical Society, 1953-54. *Member:* National Education Association, American Guild of Organists.

WRITINGS: Silver Domes: A Directory of Observatories of the World, Big Mountain Press, 1955; *Ke-Wee-Naw* (nonfiction; the story of copper mining and undersea cables), A. Swallow, 1966.

SIDELIGHTS: As a winner in the *Denver Post's* "Heart's Desire Contest," held in connection with *Life* (magazine), Claire Moyer was guest conductor of the Denver Symphony Orchestra in March, 1953. She has taught music at times in the schools, been a church organist and choir director, and lists music appreciation as her prime hobby.††

* * *

MOYNE, Ernest J(ohn)   1916-1976

PERSONAL: Born May 3, 1916, in Hanko, Finland; son of Ernest A. and Ida (Korpi) Moyne; married Kathleen M. McCormick (a teacher), January 30, 1943; children: Elizabeth. *Education:* Yale University, B.A., 1938, M.A., 1940; Harvard University, Ph.D., 1948. *Home:* 3 Tanglewood Lane, Newark, Del. 19711 *Office:* Department of English, University of Delaware, Newark, Del. 19711.

CAREER: Williams College, Williamstown, Mass., instructor in English, 1942-43; University of Delaware, Newark, instructor, 1948-51, assistant professor, 1951-56, associate professor, 1956-64, professor of English, 1964-72, H. F. DuPont Winterthur Professor of American Literature, beginning 1972. *Military service:* U.S. Army, 1943-46; became master sergeant; received Army Commendation Ribbon. *Member:* Modern Language Association of America, American Studies Association, Modern Language Society of Helsinki, Kalevala Society, Thoreau Society, Society for the Advancement of Scandinavian Studies, Historical Society of Delaware, Delaware Swedish Colonial Society.

WRITINGS: (Translator and editor) Alexandra Gripenberg, *A Half Year in the New World,* University of Delaware Press, 1954; *Hiawatha and Kalevala: A Study of the Relationship between Longfellow's "Indian Edda" and the Finnish Epic,* Academia Scientiarum Fennica, 1963; (editor and annotator) *The Journal of Margaret Hazlitt: Recollections of England, Ireland, and America,* University of Kansas Press, 1967. Contributor to professional journals.

WORK IN PROGRESS: An edition of *The Correspondence of Richard Somers Smith and August Fredrik Soldan, 1851-1877; Studies in Cultural Relations between Finland and America;* a translation of Peter Kalm's *Travels in North America.*

AVOCATIONAL INTERESTS: Book collecting and travel.†

(Died June 28, 1976)

* * *

MUIR, Jean   1906-1973

PERSONAL: Born March 4, 1906, in Portland, Ore.; daughter of William Torbert (a lawyer) and Jane (Whalley) Muir. *Education:* Attended Reed College, 1923-24, and Sorbonne, University of Paris, 1930-31. *Politics:* Independent. *Religion:* Episcopalian. *Home:* 1120 Taylor St., San Francisco, Calif. 94108. *Agent:* Lurton Blassingame, 60 East 42nd St., New York, N.Y. 10017.

CAREER: Oregon Journal, Portland, Ore., feature writer, 1941-45; free-lance writer, beginning 1945. *Member:* Mystery Writers of America (member of board of directors, 1969-71), Women's National Book Association.

WRITINGS: (With Helen King Hastings) *A Little Widow Is a Dangerous Thing,* Putnam, 1959; (with Irma Lee Emmerson) *The Woods Were Full of Men,* McKay, 1963; *The Smiling Medusa,* Dodd, 1969; *The Adventures of Grizzly Adams,* Putnam, 1970; *Stranger, Tread Light,* Dodd, 1971. Contributor to *Ladies' Home Journal, Reader's Digest, True, Saturday Evening Post, Gourmet,* and other magazines.

WORK IN PROGRESS: A romantic suspense novel.

SIDELIGHTS: Jean Muir lived in various countries of Europe for a total of about five years. In the years preceding her death, she was wholly involved in romantic suspense fiction, possibly because of "a reaction from having written so much in the magazine article line, often slanted toward a male audience." *Avocational interests:* Bridge, cooking and eating.

BIOGRAPHICAL/CRITICAL SOURCES: Time, March 6, 1944.†

(Died March 24, 1973)

* * *

MURPHY, Robert Cushman 1887-1973

PERSONAL: Born April 29, 1887, in Brooklyn, N.Y.; son of Thomas Daniel (an educator) and Augusta (Cushman) Murphy; married Grace Emeline Barstow (a writer), February 17, 1912; children: Alison Barstow (Mrs. Steven L. Connor), Robert Cushman, Jr., Amos Chafee Barstow. *Education:* Brown University, Ph.B., 1911; Columbia University, A.M., 1917. *Politics:* Independent Democrat. *Religion:* Unitarian Universalist. *Home:* 16 Sound St., Stony Brook, Long Island, N.Y.

CAREER: American Museum of Natural History, New York City, assistant, 1906-07; Brooklyn Museum, Brooklyn, N.Y., curator of mammals and birds, 1911-17, curator of the department of natural science, 1917-20; American Museum of Natural History, New York City, associate curator of birds, 1921-26, assistant director, 1924-26, curator of oceanic birds, 1926-42, chairman of the department of birds, 1942-54, Lamont Curator of Birds, 1942-55, Lamont Curator of Birds Emeritus and research associate, 1955-73. Leader of an expedition to the tropical and sub-antarctic Atlantic, for the American Museum of Natural History and the Brooklyn Museum, 1912-13; member of many other expedition teams including Operation Deep Freeze in Antarctica, when he was biologist for the U.S. Navy, 1960. President, Cold Spring Harbor Laboratory, 1940-52; advisor to Fire Island National Seashore Commission, U.S. Department of the Interior; member of the Pacific Science Board, National Resources Council; member of the executive council, Long Island University at Brookhaven, N.Y.; consultant on conservation problems to the governments of New Zealand, Peru, Chile, Venezuela, and Bharatpur. Delegate to various international conferences, 1924-62.

MEMBER: American Ornithologists Union (fellow; president, 1948-50), National Audubon Society (honorary president), American Association for the Advancement of Science, Association of American Geographers, American Geographic Society (fellow), American Geophysical Union, American Philosophical Society, Zoology Society of London, British Ornithology Union (honorary member), Ornithology Society of France, Deutsche Ornithologische Gesellschaft, Royal Society of New Zealand, Royal Australasian Ornithologists Union, Sociadad Ornitologica del Plato (Argentina), Royal Hungarian Institute (honorary member), Venezuelan Society of Natural Science, California Academy of Sciences, New York Academy of Science (vice-president, 1924), New York Zoology Society, Linnaean Society of New York, Long Island Biology Association, Phi Beta Kappa, Sigma Xi, Boone and Crockett Club, Century Association. *Awards, honors:* Brewster Medal, American Ornithologists Union, 1937; bronze medal, Burroughs Association, 1938; Cullum Medal, American Geographic Society, 1940; Hutchinson Conservation Medal, Garden Club of America, 1941; Elliot Medal, Na-

tional Academy of Science, 1943; Raimondi Medal, Geographic Society of Peru, 1953; Explorer's Medal, Explorer's Club, N.Y., 1966; D.Sc. from University of San Marco, 1925, Brown University, 1941, and Long Island University, 1964.

WRITINGS: (Editor) *A Report on the South Georgia Expedition,* Museum of the Brooklyn Institute of Arts and Sciences, 1915; *Bird Islands of Peru: The Record of a Sojourn on the West Coast,* Putnam, 1925; *Oceanic Birds of South America,* American Museum of Natural History, 1936; *Logbook for Grace: Whaling Brig Daisy, 1912-1913,* Macmillan, 1947, reprinted with a new introduction by George Gaylord Simpson, Time, Inc., 1965; (with Dean Amadon) *Land Birds of America,* McGraw, 1953; *Fish-shape Paumanok: Nature and Man on Long Island,* American Philosophical Society, 1964; *Rare and Exotic Birds,* Odyssey Press, 1964; *A Dead Whale or a Stove Boat: Cruise of Daisy in the Atlantic Ocean, June 1912-May 1913,* Houghton, 1967; (author of foreword) *The Larousse Encyclopedia of Animal Life,* McGraw, 1967. Also author of pamphlets and papers on nature and wildlife published by the Museum of Natural History. Contributor to journals in his field. Former contributing editor, *Geography Review.*†

(Died March 20, 1973)

* * *

MURRAY, John F(rancis) 1923-1977
(Daisy Backgammon, Nick Carryaway)

PERSONAL: Born June 25, 1923, in Brooklyn, N.Y.; son of John Francis (an electrical engineer and commissioner of the Port of New York) and Jeanne (Durand) Murray; married Alison E. Gray (an art instructor), April 3, 1948; married second wife, Marie A. Harriman (a painter), March 8, 1969 (died September 20, 1970); married Frederica Bishop Mason (separated); children: (first marriage) Melinda G., John Francis III, Matthew D. *Education:* Yale University, B.A., 1948. *Politics:* "Usually Democrat." *Religion:* "Unorganized." *Agent:* Raines & Raines, 475 Fifth Ave., New York, N.Y. 10017.

CAREER: Free-lance copywriter and staff copywriter at various agencies in New York City, 1950-68, including Benton & Bowles and Cunningham & Walsh; Ogilvy & Mather, Inc., New York City, copywriter, 1969-74; Bishop-Hayden, Inc., Smithtown, Long Island, N.Y., chief copyeditor, 1974-77. Founder, East Egg Publishing Co., Wainscott, N.Y., 1971. *Military service:* U.S. Army, World War II; served in Belgium and Germany.

WRITINGS: The Devil Walks on Water (fiction), Little, Brown, 1969; (under pseudonyms Daisy Backgammon and Nick Carryaway) *Sh!: An Intimate Service Book to the Hamptons That Tells It Like It Is,* East Egg, 1974. Editor, twenty-fifth reunion book of class of 1945, Yale University. Also author of a weekly column, *East Hampton Star;* Suffolk county correspondent, *Newsday.* Contributor of short stories to *Gentleman, Dude, New Yorker,* and other magazines.

WORK IN PROGRESS: Gallagher's Grain (fiction).

AVOCATIONAL INTERESTS: Good movies, the theater; books and stories by John O'Hara, F. Scott Fitzgerald, Donleavy, and James M. Cain; skiing, tennis, golf, snorkeling.

BIOGRAPHICAL/CRITICAL SOURCES: New York Times, April 30, 1977.†

(Died, 1977)

MURRAY, Keith A.   1910-

PERSONAL: Born October 31, 1910, in Nez Perce, Idaho; son of James (a clergyman) and Olive (Kidd) Murray; married Olive M. Clarke, June 18, 1937 (died March 6, 1969); married Shirley Anderson, March 14, 1970; children: (first marriage) Anne Murray Brubacher, Carolyn O. *Education:* Whitworth College, B.A., 1935; University of Washington, Seattle, M.A., 1940, Ph.D., 1946. *Politics:* Independent. *Religion:* Presbyterian. *Home:* 1240 Undine St., Bellingham, Wash. 98225. *Office:* Department of History, Western Washington State College, Bellingham, Wash. 98225.

CAREER: Whitworth College, Spokane, Wash., director of admissions, 1936-39; teacher in public schools in state of Washington, 1940-45; Western Washington State College, Bellingham, assistant professor, 1946-50, associate professor, 1950-53, professor of history, beginning 1953, chairman of department, 1960-69. Chairman, Historic Sites Advisory Board, Washington State Parks and Recreation Commission, 1950-54; ranger and historian, National Park Service, summers, 1954-58. Member of board of trustees, Whitworth College, beginning 1958. Moderator, Presbytery of North Puget Sound, United Presbyterian Church, U.S.A., 1971. *Member:* American Historical Association, Washington State Historical Society (member of board of curators, beginning 1969), Whatcom County Historical Society (president, 1966-68), Phi Alpha Theta, Bellingham Rotary Club (president, 1963). *Awards, honors:* Award of merit from Pacific Northwest History Conference, 1965; Alumni Distinguished award, 1967, from Whitworth College.

WRITINGS: The Story of Banking in Whatcom County, Cox Brothers, 1954; *The Modocs and Their War,* University of Oklahoma Press, 1959; *The Pig War,* Washington State Historical Society, 1968. Contributor to *Encyclopaedia Britannica* and *Reader's Encyclopedia of the American West;* contributor to history journals.

WORK IN PROGRESS: A history of Alaska, tentatively entitled *Reindeer and Gold; Diplomatic History of Pacific Northwest.*††

*   *   *

MYER, Dillon S(eymour)   1891-

PERSONAL: Born September 4, 1891, in Hebron, Ohio; son of John Hyson (a farmer) and Harriet Estella (Seymour) Myer; married Mary Jenness Wirt, September 4, 1924; children: Mary Jenness (Mrs. Melvin Sandmeyer), Elizabeth Ann (Mrs. W. Luther Hall), Margaret Wirt (Mrs. David McFaddin). *Education:* Ohio State University, B.Sc., 1914; Columbia University, M.A., 1926. *Politics:* Democrat. *Religion:* Protestant. *Home:* 3025 Daniel Lane N.W., Washington, D.C. 20015.

CAREER: Kentucky Agriculture College, instructor in agronomy, 1914-16; county agricultural agent, Vanderburgh County, Ind., 1916-17; Purdue University, Lafayette, Ind., assistant county agent leader, Agricultural Extension Service, 1917-20; county agricultural agent, Franklin County, Ohio, 1920-22; Ohio State University, Columbus, district supervisor, Extension Service, 1922-34; U.S. Department of Agriculture, Washington, D.C., chief of compliance section and then assistant chief of Planning Division, Agricultural Adjustment Administration, 1934-36, division chief and assistant chief, Soil Conservation Service, 1936-41; War Relocation Authority, Washington, D.C., director, 1942-46; Public Housing Administration, Washington, D.C., commissioner, 1946-47; Institute of Interamerican Affairs,

Washington, D.C., president, 1947-50; U.S. Department of the Interior, Washington, D.C., commissioner, Bureau of Indian Affairs, 1950-53. Consultant to U.S. Information Agency and Agency for International Development. *Awards, honors:* Medal of Merit from U.S. Government, 1946, for work as director of War Relocation Authority.

WRITINGS: Uprooted Americans: The Japanese Americans and the War Relocation Authority, University of Arizona Press, 1970.

*   *   *

MYERS, Garry Cleveland   1884-1971

PERSONAL: Born July 15, 1884, in Sylvan, Pa.; son of John A. (a farmer) and Sarah A. (Besore) Myers; married Caroline Elizabeth Clark (managing editor of *Highlights for Children*), June 26, 1912; children: John Edgar, Elizabeth (Mrs. Kent L. Brown), Garry C. (deceased). *Education:* Cumberland Valley State Normal School (now Shippensburg State College), graduate, 1905; Ursinus College, A.B., 1909; University of Pennsylvania, graduate study, 1909-10; Columbia University, Ph.D., 1913. *Home:* Boyds Mills, Pa., 18406. *Office: Highlights for Children,* 803 Church St., Honesdale, Pa. 18431.

CAREER: Juniata College, Huntington, Pa., professor of psychology and social sciences, 1912-14; Brooklyn Training School for Teachers, Brooklyn, N.Y., professor of psychology and education, 1914-18; Western Reserve University (now Case Western Reserve University), Cleveland, Ohio, chairman of Division of Psychology at Senior College and at Cleveland School of Education, 1920-27, head of Division of Parent Education at Cleveland College, 1927-40; *Highlights for Children,* Honesdale, Pa., co-founder and editor-in-chief, beginning 1946. Certified consulting psychologist and lecturer on child psychology. Leader of public forums for U.S. Office of Education, 1937-39. *Military service:* U.S. Army, Sanitary Corps, 1918; became captain.

MEMBER: American Association for the Advancement of Science (fellow), American Educational Research Association, American Psychological Association, Society for Research in Child Development, National Society for the Study of Education, National Association for Better Broadcasting (member of executive committee; second vice-president), Rotary International. *Awards, honors:* Citation of Merit from National Association for Gifted Children, 1966.

WRITINGS: A Study in Incidental Memory, Science Press, 1913; (with wife, Caroline Elizabeth Myers) *Measuring Minds* (examiner's manual), Newson, 1921; (with C. E. Myers) *The Language of America* (lessons in elementary English and citizenship for adults), Newson, 1921; *The Prevention and Correction of Errors in Arithmetic,* Plymouth Press, 1925; *The Learner and His Attitude,* B. H. Sanborn, 1925; (with C. E. Myers) *My Work Book in Arithmetic,* Harter Publishing, 1929; *The Modern Parent,* Greenberg, 1930; *Developing Personality in the Child at School,* Greenberg, 1931; *Building Personality in Children,* Greenberg, 1931; *Marriage and Parenthood,* World Publishing, 1934; *The Modern Family,* Greenberg, 1934; *I Am Growing Up,* School & College Service, 1934; *Learning to Be Likable,* School & College Service, 1935; (with Clarence W. Sumner) *Books and Babies,* McClurg, 1938.

Marriage and Parenthood, World Publishing, 1941; (with C. E. Myers) *Homes Build Persons,* Dorrance, 1950; *For Beginning the School Day,* Highlights for Children, 1966; *Headwork for Elementary School Children,* Highlights for Children, 1968; *Headwork for Preschoolers,* Highlights for

Children, 1968; (with C. E. Myers) *Your Child and You,* Hewitt House, 1969; *Wishes,* Hewitt House, 1969.

Author of pamphlets on child care published by Child Development Foundation, U.S. Bureau of Education, and National Committee for Mental Hygiene. Writer of syndicated daily newspaper column, "The Parent Problem," for King Features, beginning 1932. Contributor to psychology and educational journals and popular magazines.†

(Died July 19, 1971)

* * *

NEFF, Walter S(cott) 1910-

PERSONAL: Born June 8, 1910, in Philadelphia, Pa.; son of Joseph (a physician) and Hetty (Krasne) Neff; married Mary Himoff, April 26, 1946; children: Richard, Alan. *Education:* University of Pennsylvania, B.A., 1930, M.A., 1931; Cornell University, Ph.D., 1936; University of Chicago, post-doctoral study, 1947-48. *Residence:* East Hampton, N.Y. 11937.

CAREER: Instructor in psychology at University of Maine, Orono, 1936-37, and City College (now City College of the City University of New York), New York City, 1937-40; Jewish Vocational Service, Chicago, Ill., clinical psychologist, later chief psychologist, 1948-57, director of research, 1957-60; New York University, New York City, 1960—, began as professor of psychology, now professor emeritus. Lecturer in clinical psychology, Illinois Institute of Technology, 1953-56; lecturer in the behavioral sciences, University of Chicago, 1959-60. Institute for the Crippled and Disabled of New York City, director of research, 1960-64, research consultant, 1964-68; principal research scientist, New York State Department of Mental Hygiene, beginning 1968. *Military service:* U.S. Army, psychologist, 1944-47.

MEMBER: American Psychological Association (fellow), American Orthopsychiatric Association (fellow), American Association for the Advancement of Science, American Academy of Political and Social Science, New York Academy of Sciences, Sigma Xi.

WRITINGS: (With others) *Adjusting People to Work,* Jewish Vocational Service (Chicago), 1957; (contributor) B. Wolman, editor, *Handbook of Clinical Psychology,* Mc-Graw, 1965; *Work and Human Behavior,* Atherton, 1968; (editor) *Rehabilitation Psychology,* American Psychological Association, 1970. Contributor of about thirty articles to psychology, rehabilitation, and other journals.

WORK IN PROGRESS: Culture, Society and Mental Disorder.

* * *

NELIGAN, David 1899-

PERSONAL: Born October 14, 1899, in Limerick, Ireland; son of David and Elizabeth (Mullane) Neligan; married Sheila Rogan, June 5, 1935; children: Maeve (Mrs. L. Brown), Carol (Mrs. B. Byrne), Joan, David. *Education:* "My parents were school-teachers, so I could not escape a certain amount of education, though I tried." *Politics:* None. *Religion:* Roman Catholic. *Home:* 15 St. Helen's Rd., Booterstown, County Dublin, Ireland.

CAREER: Joined the Metropolitan Police of Dublin, Ireland, in 1919, and applied for the British Secret Service in 1920; was a double agent for the British and Irish during the fight for Irish independence, 1920-21, much of the time as a spy in Dublin Castle, the seat of British rule; chief of Irish

Criminal Investigation Branch, 1923-32. *Military service:* Irish Army; became colonel.

WRITINGS: The Spy in the Castle (autobiography), MacGibbon & Kee, 1968.

WORK IN PROGRESS: A sequel to *The Spy in the Castle.*

SIDELIGHTS: David Neligan's book is a best seller in Ireland. After a lifetime of studying secret service and allied subjects, he says that he knows enough "to advise people to have nothing to do with them."

BIOGRAPHICAL/CRITICAL SOURCES: Spectator, December 20, 1968.

* * *

NELSON, Alvin F(redolph) 1917-1973

PERSONAL: Born June 27, 1917, in Oakland, Neb.; son of John N. (a farmer) and Bena (Anderson) Nelson. *Education:* University of Nebraska, A.B. (with distinction), 1938, M.A., 1939; Ohio State University, Ph.D., 1942. *Residence:* Fort Worth, Tex.

CAREER: Wesleyan College, Macon, Ga., assistant professor of philosophy, 1949-51; Newberry College, Newberry, S.C., professor of education and psychology, 1951-53; Berry College, Mount Berry, Ga., acting chairman of division of education, 1953-54; Yankton College, Yankton, S.D., Fiske Professor of Philosophy and Psychology, 1954-60; Texas Christian University, Fort Worth, Tex., associate professor, 1960-65, professor of philosophy, 1965-73. *Member:* American Philosophical Association, Metaphysical Society of America, History of Science Society, American Association of University Professors, Southern Society for Philosophy and Psychology, Southwestern Philosophical Society, North Texas Philosophical Association (president, 1969-70).

WRITINGS: The Structure of Normative Ethics, Edwards Brothers, 1943; (with D. L. Evans and W. S. Gamertsfelder) *Elements of Logic,* W. C. Brown, 1957; (with G. A. Ferre) *Basic Philosophical Issues,* Educational Publishers, 1962; *The Development of Lester Ward's World View,* Branch-Smith, 1968, revised edition, 1970; (editor) Albert Edwin Avey, *Primary Questions, Historical Answers,* Christopher, 1968; *Inquiry and Reality: A Discourse in Pragmatic Synthesis,* Texas Christian University Press, 1976.†

(Died April 19, 1973)

* * *

NELSON, Herbert B(enjamin) 1903-

PERSONAL: Born March 27, 1903, in Boulder, Colo.; son of Ben S. and Barbara (Haas) Nelson; married Roberta Orr, August 26, 1928; children: Robert B., Molly E. (Mrs. Dale Hannon). *Education:* University of Colorado, A.B., 1926, M.A., 1927; University of Washington, Seattle, Ph.D., 1944. *Politics:* Republican. *Religion:* Presbyterian. *Home:* 130 North 31st St., Corvallis, Ore. *Office:* Oregon State University, Corvallis, Ore.

CAREER: Oregon State University, Corvallis, beginning 1927, as instructor, professor of English, beginning 1947, head of department of English, beginning 1951. *Member:* National Council of Teachers of English (Oregon chapter president, 1952), Oregon State Employees Association, Alpha Phi Omega, Theta Xi.

WRITINGS: (With R. R. Reichart) *Teach Yourself Grammar,* Oregon State University Cooperative, 1937; (with R. R. Reichart) *Foundations of Good English,* Ginn, 1938;

The Literary Impulse in Pioneer Oregon, Oregon State University Press, 1948; *English Essentials,* Littlefield, 1955; (with Preston E. Onstad) *A Webfoot Volunteer,* Oregon State University Press, 1965. Contributor to *Pacific Northwest Quarterly, Idaho Yesterdays, Portland Oregonian* and other publications. Consulting editor, Albany Metallurgy Research Center, 1965.

WORK IN PROGRESS: Articles for magazines and newspapers.

* * *

NEMIR, Alma 1902-1971

PERSONAL: Born April 21, 1902, in Omaha, Neb.; daughter of Ferris (a merchant) and Bertha (Shabook) Nemir; married Leslie H. Bryer, January 21, 1939. *Education:* Rice University, B.A. (with distinction), 1922; University of California, M.D., 1931. *Home:* 1420 South Thirteenth East St., Salt Lake City, Utah 84105.

CAREER: San Francisco General Hospital, San Francisco, Calif., intern, 1930-31; Mount Zion Hospital, San Francisco, resident in pathology, 1931-34; University of Utah, Salt Lake City, health educator and medical consultant, 1934-70, supervisor of Division of Health Education, 1948-56, acting director of Student Health Service, 1956-59, professor emeritus, 1970-71. Private medical practice, Salt Lake City, 1935-56. Medical consultant to Family Service Society and Children's Service Society, Salt Lake City, 1935-56; member of advisory committee and director, Utah Social Hygiene Association, 1947-52.

MEMBER: American Medical Association, American School Health Association, American College Health Association, American Association for Health, Physical Education and Recreation (vice-president, Southwest district, 1948-49, 1952-53), Pacific Coast College Health Association (president, 1958-59), Utah State Medical Association, Utah Public Health Association, Utah Council on Family Relations, Alpha Omega Alpha, Phi Kappa Phi. *Awards, honors:* Honor Award, Southwest district, American Association for Health, Physical Education and Recreation, 1959.

WRITINGS: The School Health Program, Saunders, 1959, 4th edition (with Warren E. Schaller), 1975. Contributor to medical and health education journals.†

(Died October, 1971)

* * *

NERUDA, Pablo 1904-1973

PERSONAL: Real name, Ricardo Eliezer Neftali Reyes y Basoalto; born July 12, 1904, in Parral, Chile; son of Jose del Carmen Reyes (a railroad worker) and Rosa de Basoalto; married (second marriage) Matilde Urrutia. *Education:* Attended local schools at Temuco, Chile; attended Instituto Pedagogica (Santiago, Chile) in the early 1920's. *Politics:* Communist (member of central committee of Chilean party). *Home:* Marquez de la Plata 0192, Santiago, Chile; and at Isle Negra, near Valparaiso, Chile.

CAREER: Went to Rangoon, Burma, as Chilean consul, 1927; consul in Colombo, Ceylon, 1929, Batavia, Java, 1930 (visiting China, Japan, and Indo-China); during the early 1930's he was consul in Buenos Aires, Siam, Cambodia, Anam, and Madrid; helped Spanish refugees in Paris, 1939; sent to Chilean Embassy, Mexico City, Mexico, 1939-41, consul, 1941-44; when he returned to Chile he was elected to the Senate as a Communist; he wrote letters (1947-49) charging President Gonzalez Videla with selling out to the United States, and carried his case to the Chilean Supreme Court which upheld Videla's position; escaped to Mexico; also traveled in Italy, France, U.S.S.R., Red China; returned to Chile in 1953, after the victory of the anti-Videla forces; Chilean ambassador to France, 1971-72. Came to New York for the P.E.N. Congress, 1966. Member of World Peace Council, 1950-73. *Member:* Union de Escritores Chilenos (president, 1959-73), Modern Language Association of America (honorary fellow), International P.E.N. *Awards, honors:* First prize for poetry in the Students' Federation spring festival, Instituto Pedagogica, 1921, for *La Cancion de la fiesta;* International Peace Prize, 1950; Lenin and Stalin Peace Prize, 1953; Premio Municipal de Literatura (Chile), 1944; Premio Nacional de Literatura (Chile), 1945; Litt.D., Oxford University, 1965; awarded Czechoslovakia's highest decoration, 1966; Nobel Prize in Literature, 1971.

WRITINGS: La cancion de la fiesta (poetry), Federacion de Estudiantes de Chile (Santiago), 1921; *Crepuscular io* (poetry), Nascimento (Santiago), 1923, 4th edition, Losada (Buenos Aires), 1971; *Viente poemas de amor y una cancion desesperada,* Nascimento, 1924, definitive edition, 1932, 16th edition, Losada, 1972, translation by W. S. Merwin published as *Twenty Love Poems and a Song of Despair,* J. Cape, 1969; *Tentativa del hombre infinito* (poem), Nascimento, 1925, new edition, Editorial Orbe (Santiago), 1964; *El habitante y su esperanza* (prose), Nascimento, 1925, 2nd edition, Ercilla (Santiago), 1939; (with Tomas Lago) *Anillos* (prose), Nascimento, 1926; *Prosas de Pablo Neruda* (prose), Nascimento, 1926.

El hondero entusiasta, 1923-24 (poetry), Ercilla, 1933, 3rd edition, 1938; *Residencia en la tierra* (poetry and prose), Ediciones del Arbol (Madrid), Volume I (1925-31), 1933, Volume II (1931-35), 1935, published in one volume, Losada, 1944, 3rd edition, 1969; *Poesias de Villamediana presentadas por Pablo Neruda,* Cruz y Raya (Madrid), 1935; *Homenaje a Pablo Neruda de los poetas espanoles: Tres cantos materiales* (poetry), Plutarco (Madrid), 1935, translation by Angel Flores published as *Tres cantos materiales: Three Material Songs,* East River Editions, 1948; *Sonetos de la Muerte de Quevedo, presentados por Pablo Neruda,* Cruz y Raya, 1935; *Espana en el corazon: Himno a las glorias del pueblo en 'a guerra* (poetry), first printed by Spanish Republican soldiers on the battlefront, Ercilla, 1937, 2nd edition, 1938; *Las furias y las penas* (poetry), Nascimento, 1939; (with Emilio Oribe and Juan Marinello) *Neruda entre nosotros* (prose), A.I.A.P.E. (Montevideo), 1939; *Homenaje a Garcia Lorca* (prose), A.I.A.P.E., 1939; *Chile os acoge* (prose), [Paris], 1939.

Un canto para Bolivar (poetry), Universidad Nacional Autonoma de Mexico, 1941; (contributor of poetry) *Presencia de Garcia Lorca,* Darro (Mexico), 1943; *Nuevo canto de amor a Stalingrado* (poem), Comite de ayuda a Rusia en guerra (Mexico), 1943; *Canto general de Chile* (poem), privately printed, 1943; *Cantos de Pablo Neruda* (poetry), Hora del Hombre (Lima), 1943; *Cantico,* La Gran Colombia (Bogota), 1943; *Pablo Neruda: Sus mejores versos,* La Grand Colombia, 1943; *Saludo al Norte y Stalingrado,* privately printed, 1945; (with Pedro Pomar and Jorge Amado) *O Partido Comunista e a liberdade de criacao* (prose), Horizonte (Rio de Janeiro), 1946; *Carta a Mexico,* Fondo de Cultura Popular (Mexico), 1947; *Tercera residencia, 1935-1945* (poetry), Losada, 1947, 5th edition, 1971; *Viajes al corazon de Quevedo y por las costas del mundo* (prose), Sociedad de Escritores de Chile (Santiago), 1947; *28 de Enero,* Partido Comunista de Chile, 1947; *Los heroes de carcon encarnan los ideales de democracia e independencia nacional* (prose), El Tranviario (Santiago), 1947; *La verdad sobre las rupuras* (prose), Principios (Santiago), 1947; *La crisis democratica de Chile,* Hora del Hombre, 1947, translation published as *The Democratic Crisis of Chile,* Committee for Friendship in the Americas (New York), 1948; *Dura elegia,* Cruz del Sur (Santiago), 1948; *Himno y regreso,* Cruz del Sur, 1948; *Que despierte el lenador!* (poetry), Coleccion Yagruma (Havanna), 1948, translation published as *Peace for Twilights to Come!,* Jayant Bhatt for People's Publishing House (Bombay, India), 1950; *Alturas de Macchu-Picchu* (poetry), Libreria Neira (Santiago), 1948, definitive edition, Nascimento, 1954, translation by Nathaniel Tarn published as *The Heights of Macchu Picchu,* J. Cape, 1966, Farrar, Straus, 1967; *Coral de Ano Nuevo para mi Patria en tinieblas,* privately printed, 1948; *Pablo Neruda acusa,* Pueblos Unidos (Montevideo), 1948; *Y ha llegado el monento en que debemos elegir,* privately printed, 1949; *Gonzalez Videla, el Laval de America Latina: Breve biografia de un traidor,* Fondo de Cultura Popular, 1949; *Dulce patria,* Editorial del Pacifico (Santiago), 1949.

Neruda en Guatemala (prose), Saker-Ti (Guatemala), 1950; *Patria prisionera,* Hora del Hombre, 1951; *A la memoria de Ricardo Fonseca,* Amistad (Santiago), 1951; *Cuando de Chile,* Austral (Santiago), 1952; *Poemas,* Fundamentos (Buenos Aires), 1952; *Los versos del Capitan: Poemas de amor* (anonymously published until 3rd edition, 1963), privately printed in Naples, 1952, 7th edition, Losada, 1972, translation by Donald D. Walsh published as *The Captain's Verses,* New Directions, 1972; *Todo el amor* (poetry), Nascimento, 1953; *En su muerte,* Partido Comunista Argentino (Buenos Aires), 1953; *Poesia politica: Discursos politicos,* two volumes, Austral, 1953; *Las uvas y el viento* (poetry), Nascimento, 1954; *Odas elementales* (poetry), Losada, 1954, 3rd edition, 1970; *Discurso inauguracion Fundacion Pablo Neruda,* Universidad de Chile (Santiago), 1954; *Alli murio la muerte,* Ediciones del Centro de Amigos de Polonia (Santiago), 1954; *Regreso la sirena* (poetry), Ediciones del Centro de Amigos de Polonia, 1954; *Viajes* (prose), Nascimento, 1955; *Nuevas odas elementales,* Losada, 1956, 3rd edition, 1971; *Oda a la tipografia* (poetry), Nascimento, 1956; *Dos odas elementales,* Losada, 1957; *Estravagario* (poetry), Losada, 1958, 3rd edition, 1971, translation by Alastair Reid published as *Extravagaria,* J. Cape, 1972, Farrar, Straus, 1974; *Tercer libro de las Odas* (poetry), Losada, 1959; *Algunas Odas* (poetry), Edicion del 55 (Santiago), 1959; *Cien sonetos de amor* (poetry), Losada, 1959, 6th edition, 1971; *Odas: Al libro, a las Americas, a la luz* (poetry), Homenaje de la Asociacion de Escritores Venezolanos (Caracas, Venezuela), 1959; *Todo lleva tu nombre* (poetry), Ministerio de Educacion (Caracas), 1959; *Navegaciones y regresos* (poetry; 4th volume of *Odas Elementales*), Losada, 1959; (with Federico Garcia Lorca) *Discurso al Alimon sobre Ruben Dario,* Semana Dariana (Nicaragua), 1959.

(With Pablo Picasso) *Toros: 15 lavis inedits,* Au Vent d'Arles (Paris), 1960; *Cancion de gesta* (poetry), Imprenta Nacional de Cuba (Havana), 1960, 3rd edition, Siglo (Montevideo), 1968; *Oceana* (poem), La Tertulia (Havana), 1960, 2nd edition, 1962; *Los primeros versos de amor* (poetry), Austral, 1961; *Las piedras de Chile* (poetry), Losada, 1961; *Primer dia de La Sebastiana,* privately printed, 1961; *Cantos ceremoniales* (poetry), Losada, 1961, 2nd edition, 1972; *Plenos poderes* (poetry), Losada, 1962, 2nd edition, 1971, translation by Alastair Reid published as *Fully Empowered,* Farrar, Straus, 1975; (with Toral) *Poema con grabado* (poetry), Ediciones Isla Negra (Santiago), 1962; *La*

insepulta de Paita (poetry), Losada, 1962; *Con los catolicos hacia la paz,* [Santiago], 1962, published as *Cuba: Los obispos,* Paz y Soberania (Lima), 1962; (with Nicanor Parre) *Discursos: Pablo Neruda y Nicanor Parra* (prose), Nascimento, 1962; *Mensaje de Paz y unidad, internacionalismo proletario, el poeta de la revolucion* (addresses), Esclarecimiento (Lima), 1963; (with Gustavo Hernan and Guillermo Atias) *Presencia de Ramon Lopez Velarde en Chile,* Universitaria (Santiago), 1963; *Memorial de Isla Negra* (poetry), Volume I: *Donde nace la lluvia,* Volume II: *La luna en el laberinto,* Volume III: *El fuego cruel,* Volume IV: *El cazador de raices,* Volume V: *Sonata critica,* Losada, 1964; *Arte de pajaros,* Sociedad de Amigos del Arte Contemporaneo (Santiago), 1966; *Una casa en la arena,* Lumen (Barcelona), 1966, 2nd edition, 1969; *La Barcarola* (poem), Losada, 1967; *Fulgor y muerte de Joaquin Murieta: Bandido chileno injusticiado en California el 23 de julio de 1853,* (play), Zig-Zag (Santiago), 1967, translation by Ben Belitt published as *Splendor and Death of Joaquin Murieta,* Farrar, Straus, 1972; *Las manos del dia* (poetry), Losada, 1968, 2nd edition, 1970; *Aun: Poema* (poem), Nascimento, 1969; *Fin de Mundo* (poem), Losada, 1969; *La copa de sangre* (poetry and prose), privately printed, 1969.

La espada encendida, Losada, 1970, 2nd edition, 1972; *Las piedras del cielo,* Losada, 1970; *Discurso pronunciado con ocasion de la entrega del premio Nobel de literature, 1971,* Centre de recherches hispaniques (Paris), 1972, translation published as *Toward the Splendid City: Nobel Lecture,* Farrar, Straus, 1974; *Geografia infructuosa* (poetry), Losada, 1972; *Libro de las odas,* Losada, 1972; *El mar y las campanas: Poemas,* Losada, 1973; *La rosa separada* (poetry), Losada, 1973; *El corazon amarillo* (poetry), Losada, 1974; *Elegia* (poetry), Losada, 1974; *Incitacion al Nixonicidio y alabanza de la revolucion chilena,* Grijalbo (Barcelona), 1974; *Oda a la lagartija* (poem), P. R. Martorell (Camp Rico de Canovanas), 1974; *Jardin de invierno,* Losada, 1974; *Libro de las preguntas,* Losada, 1974; *Cartas de amor de Pablo Neruda* (love correspondence), compiled by Sergio Lorrain, Rodas (Madrid), 1974; *Confieso que he vivido: Memorias,* Seix Barral (Barcelona), 1974, translation published as *Memoirs,* Farrar, Straus, in press.

Omnibus volumes: *Seleccion* (poetry), compiled by Arturo Aldunate, Nascimento, 1943; *Coleccion Residencia en la tierra: Obra poetica,* ten volumes, Cruz del Sur, 1947-48; *Canto general* (poetry), Comite Auspiciador (Mexico), 1950, 5th edition in two volumes, Losada, 1971; *Poesias Completas,* Losada, 1951; *Los versos mas populares* (poetry), Austral, 1954; *Los mejores versos de Pablo Neruda* (poetry), [Buenos Aires], 1956; *Obras completas* (complete works), Losada, 1957, 3rd updated edition in two volumes, 1968; *El habitante y su esperanza, El hondero entusiasta, Tentativa del hombre infinito,* [and] *Anillos,* Losada, 1957, 4th edition, 1971; *Antologia* (poetry), Nascimento, 1957, 4th enlarged edition, 1970; *Antologia poetica* (poetry), selected by Pablo Luis Avila, Gheroni (Torino, Italy), 1962; *Poesias* (poetry), selected by Roberto Retamar, Casa de las Americas (Havana), 1965; *Antologia esencial* (poetry), selected by Hernan Loyola, Losada, 1971; *Poemas immortales* (poetry), selected by Jaime Concha, Quimantu (Santiago), 1971; *Obras escogidas* (poetry), selected by Francisco Coloane, A. Bello (Santiago), 1972; *Pablo Neruda* (includes poems, Nobel prize acceptance speech, interview, and chronologies), Noroeste (Buenos Aires), 1973; *Poesia* (poetry), two volumes, Noguer (Barcelona), 1974.

Other translations into English: *Selected Poems* (from *Residencia en la tierra*), translated by Angel Flores, privately printed, 1944; *Residence on Earth and Other Poems* (includes "Residence on Earth I and II," "Spain in the Heart," "General Song of Chile," and "Recent Poems"), translated by Angel Flores, New Directions, 1946; *Let the Splitter Awake & Other Poems* (selected from *Que despierte el lenador!* and *Canto general*), Masses & Mainstream, 1950; *Let the Rail-Splitter Awake*, World Student News, 1951; *Selected Poems*, edited and translated by Ben Belitt, Grove, 1961; *Elementary Odes* (selections), translated by Carlos Lozano, G. Massa, 1961; *Residence on Earth* (selections), translated by Clayton Eshleman, Amber House Press, 1962; *Bestiary/Bestiario: A Poem*, translated by Elsa Neuberger, Harcourt, 1965; *Nocturnal Collection: A Poem*, translated by Angel Flores, [Madison, Wis.], 1966; *We Are Many* (poem), translated by Alastair Reid, Cape Goliard Press, 1967, Grossman, 1968; *Twenty Poems* (selected from *Residencia en la tierra, Canto general*, and *Odas elementales*) translated by James Wright and Robert Bly, Sixties Press, 1967; *A New Decade: Poems, 1958-67*, edited by Belitt, translation by Belitt and Reid, Grove, 1969; *The Early Poems*, translated by David Ossman and Carlos B. Hagen, New Rivers Press, 1969; *Selected Poems*, edited by Nathaniel Tarn, translated by Anthony Kerrigan and others, J. Cape, 1970, Delacorte Press, 1972; *Nerda & Vallejo: Selected Poems*, compiled by Bly, translated by Bly and others, Beacon Press, 1971; *New Poems, 1968-70*, edited and translated by Belitt, Grove, 1972; *Residence on Earth* (includes *Residencia en la tierra*, Volumes I and II, and *Tercera residencia*), translated by Donald D. Walsh, New Directions, 1973; *Five Decades, a Selection: Poems, 1925-70*, edited and translated by Belitt, Grove, 1974; *For Neruda, For Chile: An International Anthology*, edited by Walter Lowenfels, Beacon Press, 1975; *Fully Empowered: Plenos Poderes*, Farrar, Straus, 1975.

Translator into Spanish: William Blake, *Visiones de las hijas de Albion y el viajero mental*, Cruz y Raya, 1935; William Shakespeare, *Romeo y Julieta*, Losada, 1964; *Cuarenta y cuatro* (Rumanian poetry), Losada, 1967.

Contributor of poems and articles to numerous periodicals, worldwide, including *Poetry, Nation, Commonweal, Canadian Forum*, and *California Quarterly*, Work represented in many anthologies including *Anthology of Contemporary Latin American Poetry*, edited by Dudley Fitts, New Directions, 1942; *Three Spanish American Poets: Pellicer, Neruda, and Andrade*, Sage Books, 1942; *Modern European Poetry*, edited by Willis Barnstone, Bantam, 1966. Founder and editor with Manuel Altolaguirre of *El Caballo Verde* (poetry periodical), six issues, 1935-36.

SIDELIGHTS: "No writer of world renown is perhaps so little known to North Americans as the Chilean poet Pablo Neruda," observed Selden Rodman. "Yet on a recent visit to New York he held a capacity audience enthralled at the Y.M.H.A.'s Poetry Center as he read—in Spanish—from his works. Only Dylan Thomas and Robert Frost (reading in English, of course) had evoked a similar state of euphoria or aroused the standing ovation that was accorded Neruda on that memorable night." Neruda was generally considered to be the greatest living poet writing in the Spanish language, even though readers in the United States found it difficult to dissociate his poetry from his political views. His poems are also difficult to translate, so the volume of his work available in English is small compared to his output (his 1962 edition of collected poems contains 1,832 pages in small print and does not include his *Cancion de gesta* or *Isla Negra*). His work has been praised by Garcia Lorca, Paul Eluard, Stephen Spender, Archibald MacLeish, and Louis Aragon. Alastair

Reid said that Neruda "has never bothered his head about the state of poetry. He has just gone on exuding it, as naturally as he draws breath." He was, wrote Geoffrey Barraclough, "a one-man Renaissance—the MacDiarmid of half a hemisphere—who has modified the outlook of three generations of Latin Americans. His roots are firmly planted in Chile ['What could I ever say without my roots?' he asked]; his appeal is to the whole continent."

As a child he would say, "I'm going out hunting poems." And he found them everywhere. "All his books are testimonials," suggested Luis Monguio, "all his chants are material, all his songs, love songs: love of atoms, barbed wire, lemons, moons, cats, pianos, printing presses, man, life, and poetry....Between *The Heights of Macchu Picchu* and 'I Am,' Neruda has packed the whole history and life of America, all the politics and myths dearest to him. In *Canto general* he interprets history according to Karl Marx, writes a new *Legende des siecles* like Victor Hugo, and prophesies like William Blake: it is one and the same. The truths he encountered were known to him instinctively as a child: 'Nature there [in Temuco] went to my head like strong whisky. I was barely ten at the time, but already a poet.' " Sandra Hochman called him "a child grown wise."

Tempered by reason, intelligence, wit, and humor, his poetry is nevertheless "committed to the satisfaction of man's emotional needs, and not his discursive intelligence," asserts Monguio. "Its medium is a literature that structures itself on emotive association, like the subconscious, and works in the flux of sensation and thought—simultaneously or by discontinuous bursts; by accumulation or short circuit; by repetitive and chaotic enumeration; or by spontaneous synthesis—a process, to all appearance arbitrary and wayward, but moved, nevertheless, by real states of being that find their justification simply by coming to be." Ben Belitt believes Neruda's vision was like Whitman's "'hankering, gross, mystical, nude,' but his art shows the stresses of a more protean identity, the anguish of a more unappeasable commitment....Though he is master of the Goya-esque cartoon ('The Dictators') in which compassion bites like an etcher's corrosive, he has also Whitman's capacity for moving from dimension-in-length to dimension-in-breadth-and-depth, opening the stanza to enormous increments of detail and floating the burden of the phenomenal world on the unanswerable pathos of a mystery.... He transcends both the programmatic materialism of his political stance and the histrionics of his attitude."

Neruda wrote in 1954 that "we come upon poetry a step at a time, among the beings and things of this world: nothing is taken away without adding to the sum of all that exists in a blind extension of love." He never shunned what was "impure" or in "bad taste." In his essay on "impure poetry" he wrote: "Let [this] be the poetry we search for: worn with the hand's obligations, as by acids, steeped in sweat and in smoke, smelling of lilies and urine, spattered diversely by the trades that we love by, inside the law or beyond it. A poetry impure as the clothing we wear, or our bodies, soup-stained, soiled with our shameful behavior, our wrinkles and vigils and dreams, observations and prophecies, declarations of loathing and love, idyls and beasts, the shocks of encounter, political loyalties, denials and doubts, affirmations and taxes." Beneath politics, people of flesh and bone, vanity—anything provisional—was what he called the "interminable artichoke" which is the heart of poets.

Neruda was not fond of English and American poets who have worked predominantly in the symbolist tradition, and called them "too purely intellectual for [the Latin American]

sensibility. It seemed to us a limitation that they could never deal directly with the world they lived in. . . . Somewhere after the turn of the century, our modernism and yours parted company. You might say that we were retarded in not pursuing French symbolism to its logical conclusions. But then again someone might say that your most influential poets dropped the burden of being human and socially alert, dropped it too easily. As a young man in the early twenties my gods were Walt Whitman and Ruben Dario." Being human, for Neruda, meant using the senses, looking closely, at certain hours of the day, at "objects at rest," because "from them flow the contacts of man with the earth, like a text for all harassed lyricists. . . . Blossom and water and wheat kernel share one precious consistency, the sumptuous appeal of the tactile." And rain, he believed, "is very important for poetry."

The contemporary world "has changed, and so has my poetry," he said. He was first published at the age of fifteen, and until 1925 his poetry was in many ways an imitation of French poetry—symbolistic, quiet. But even then, noted Fernando Alegria, "a mysterious, dedicated madness . . . set him apart from French decadentism. His mind was moving in an extravagant, shapeless orbit." *Veinte Poemas de amor y una cancion desesperada* showed the influence of Tagore, and in the opinion of Alegria, marked the transition between Neruda's symbolist and surrealist periods. These poems "are records of emotional pressures seeming to originate in material objects which the poet knew intimately in his youth. Neruda was approaching the mastery of a system of materialistic images which was to attain ideal organization in *Residencia en la tierra*. In 1962 he published . . . *El Habitante y su esperanza*, which represents a further step in this process of organizing chaos." Amado Alonso believes Neruda's chaos was definite, but Alegria observed that, "in the light of what Neruda has produced after *Residencia en la tierra*, we know that his surrealistic chaos was an 'organized chaos,' a calculated process of destruction which, in itself, carried the impulse for the creation of a new world. . . . For Neruda, in conceiving this monumental chaos, has expressed, as no one had done before, the metaphysical anguish of the Spanish American man. . . . The *Elementary Odes* represent still another phase in the evolution of Neruda's poetic art. He has left behind the episodic tendencies of *Canto general*, but not its social connotations. His lyrical register shows a sharp change in volume; the high pitched tone of *Macchu Picchu* has now become subdued." Because, as Reid noted there are so many Nerudas, "his work has provoked the whole gamut of criticism, from hatred to idolatry, to all of which he is indifferent. He has to be taken whole, or not at all. But there is such a lot to take! What Neruda has done is to keep bursting at the seams, breaking the sound barrier, swallowing the world whole and regurgitating it in an endless stream of poems that he seems to leave behind him like footprints—one might as well mix the metaphor, for Neruda certainly would not hesitate to do so." Even as late 1960 a Cuban poet told Jose Yglesias that he must read *Estravagario* because it is "an intensely personal book. Think of it!—in his 50s Neruda breaks new ground, when we'd thought he had hardened into a political poet, a writer of public poetry."

The social element was present in his poetry as early as 1925. His poems have influenced the climate of opinion in his country and indeed throughout Latin America. Belitt believes that *Canto general* "is a work inseparable from the national scene." In *Canto general* he renounced the poetry he had written prior to 1937 and declared that he was a poet

of the people. His tone became more affirmative. Monguio said, "No one will deny that on many occasions the verse of Neruda is closer to political reportage and homily than to poetry. . . . Nevertheless, it would be hard to deny that in most of these poems, the circumstantial detail, the politics, the propaganda, the truth, the bias, the anger, the hate (call it what you please) have in no way impaired his poetic intensity." Neruda believed that almost all Latin American writers are "radicals if not social revolutionaries. Poverty and tyranny impinge upon us much more closely than they do with you. We can't afford the luxury of being uncommitted. . . . [But] for me it's very difficult to associate a writer's work with a movement. *Indigenismo*, social realism, are only words. . . . I don't believe in social realism. Why? Because this label, this way of looking at things, is prefabricated. I want to taste the wine before it is bottled. The great writer—a Whitman, a Blake, a Quevedo, a Gongora—is not very conscious of what he is saying. He just has to say it—and that way. For myself, I can be realist and subjectivist, political and non-political, sometimes all in the same poem."

Neruda said he tried not to be sectarian or dogmatic, "but it is very difficult." He distrusted abstractions; his roots were in a physical world. His *Elementary Odes*, wrote Alegria, "are a song to matter, to its dynamism and to the life and death cycles which perpetuate it. His concept of universality does not always refer to a philosophical order." He sometimes said he was a realistic poet, but by realistic he did not mean objective, but rather concrete, basic. Alegria observed that "everything in the *Elementary Odes* is a seed, or functions as a seed." Whereas his earlier poetry sometimes sacrificed intelligibility in order to present an immediate experience, he later wanted to be simple and understood by all "He does not describe, he glorifies." wrote Alegria. Rodman added: "Neruda . . . has his naivetes and inconsistencies. But above all else are his affirmation, an internationalism brought down to earth, and the extension of love of Man's body to Man's world."

Neruda's books have been translated into Italian, Russian, German, French, Swedish, Esperanto, and at least eighteen other languages. Some of his works have been recorded, including "Pablo Neruda Reads His Poems in Spanish," Spoken Arts, 1972, Rafael de Penagos reading "Poesias escogidas," Discos Aguilar, 1972, and "Loretta Pauker Reads Extended Excerpts of 'Let the Rail Splitter Awake' [and] 'The Dead in the Square,'" Khalan Records, 1973. Neruda has also been recorded by the Library of Congress.

Christopher Logue's twenty poems, *The Man Who Told His Love* [Middle Scorpion Press, 1958] is based on Neruda's *Los cantos d' amores*, and Rudolph Holzmann's *Tres madrigales para canto y piano* [Editorial Argentina de Musica, 1946] is Neruda's *Residencia en la tierra* set to music.

AVOCATIONAL INTERESTS: Sailing.

BIOGRAPHICAL/CRITICAL SOURCES: Poetry, June, 1947, February, 1963, October, 1967, June, 1968; Stanley Burnshaw, editor, *The Poem Itself*, Holt, 1960; *New Statesman*, June 4, 1965; *Encounter*, September, 1965; *Books*, June, 1966; *New York Times*, June 18, 1966, August 1, 1966; *Saturday Review*, July 9, 1966; *New York Times Book Review*, July 10, 1966, May 21, 1967; *Nation*, July 11, 1966; *Evergreen Review*, December, 1966; *Book Week*, May 28, 1967; *New Leader*, July 3, 1967; Rachel Benson, translator, *Nine Latin American Poets*, Las Americas, 1968; Nancy Willard, *Testimony of the Invisible man*, University of Missouri Press, 1970; Frank Reiss, *The Word and the Stone:*

Language and Imagery in Neruda's "Canto General," Oxford University Press, 1972; David P. Gallagher, *Modern Latin American Literature*, Oxford University Press, 1973; *Ramparts*, September, 1974; Carolyn Riley, editor, *Contemporary Literary Criticism*, Gale, Volume I, 1973, Volume II, 1974, Volume V, 1976, Volume VII, 1977; Pablo Neruda, *Confieso que he vivado: memorias*, Seix Barral (Barcelona), 1974, translation published as *Memoirs*, Farras, Straus, in press.†

(Died September 23, 1973)

* * *

NETTELL, Richard (Geoffrey)   1907-
(Richard Kenneggy)

PERSONAL: Surname is pronounced Ne-*tell;* born November 1, 1907, in Shirebrook, Notts, England; son of John Patten (a physician) and Grace (Austen) Nettell; married Martha Ferguson, September 27, 1932; children: Stephanie (Mrs. Alex Hamilton). *Education:* "Neglected." *Politics:* Left of center. *Religion:* "Unorthodox." *Home:* Adgestone, Sandown, Isle of Wight, England. *Agent:* Jonathan Clowes Ltd., 19 Jeffrey's Pl., London NW1 9PP, England.

CAREER: Breeder of pedigreed Rhode Island Reds in Isle of Wight, England, 1923-40; British Ministry of Aircraft Production, assistant examiner in Bristol, England, and Dumbarton, Scotland, 1941-42, examiner-in-charge in Newarthill, Lanarkshire, Scotland, 1942-45; novelist.

WRITINGS: Wait for the Wagon, R. Hale, 1938; *Drive the Dead Leaves*, Low, 1939; *Midsummer Spring*, Low, 1943; *Your Career in Poultry Breeding*, Jordan, 1946; *Garfin's God*, Low, 1948; *The Hearthstone Heart*, Benn, 1952; *Naked to Mine Enemy*, Hodder & Stoughton, 1968.

"Forbye" series: *Rum and Green Ginger*, Low, 1946; *Brose and Butter*, Low, 1947; *Girl in Blue Pants*, Hodder & Stoughton, 1967.

Author of *Pictorial Guide to Isle of Wight* and *Come for a Walk (Isle of Wight)*. Short stories included in *My Blood Ran Cold*, Corgi Books, 1966, *Splinters*, Hutchinson, 1968, Walker, 1969, and *Triangles*, Hutchinson, 1973. Contributor of short stories to *Courier, Woman's Mirror, Woman's Illustrated, Flair,* and British Broadcasting Corp.'s "Late Night Story." Regular reviewer for *Books and Bookmen;* author of criticism under pseudonym Richard Kenneggy.

SIDELIGHTS: Nettell told *CA:* "Circumstances governed by disability of right arm and leg through polio (1910); four years of treatment in Switzerland restored leg and partial use of two fingers. Motivation coloured by arbitrary scrubbing of seventeen years work in 1940 . . . and by social attitudes towards those disabled, other than by industry or road accident. Wartime removal from a rural setting in southern England to industrial Scotland changed social and political outlook. Convinced that 'Love thy neighbour as thyself' is the most important and exacting rule of life."

"The early years of life are the worst," Nettell writes in *Books and Bookmen.* "Grown-ups talk over a child's head, and his friends tell him the truth. I can remember, at the beginning of my scratchy education, . . . an adored little girl said, 'Of course, no one will marry you!' As it turned out, one I wanted, did. I cheated, naturally, by asking her at a moment when she was terrified by a violent thunderstorm; but the marriage lines were handed to her before she could change her mind."

BIOGRAPHICAL/CRITICAL SOURCES: Books and Bookmen, June, 1968, July, 1968.

NETTL, J(ohn) P(eter)   1926-1968
(Paul Norwood)

PERSONAL: Born February 10, 1926, in Dresden, Germany; son of Kurt (a businessman) and Gertrude (Kafka) Nettl; married Marietta Lux, January, 1950; children: Andrea, Stephen, Francis. *Education:* St. John's College, Oxford, B.A. (first class honors), 1950, M.A., 1955. *Home:* Windyridge, Ladder Hill, Wheatley, near Oxford, England. *Office:* Department of Sociology, University of Pennsylvania, Philadelphia, Pa. 19104.

CAREER: Nettl, Dyson & Co. Ltd., Bradford, England, managing director prior to 1963; University of Leeds, Leeds, England, reader in politics, 1963-67; University of Pennsylvania, Philadelphia, professor of sociology and political science, 1967-68. *Military service:* British Army, 1943-47; became major; mentioned in dispatches.

WRITINGS: The Eastern Zone and Soviet Policy in Germany, Oxford University Press, 1950; *Rosa Luxemburg* (biography), two volumes, Oxford University Press, 1966, abridged edition, 1969; *Political Mobilization*, Basic Books, 1967; *The Soviet Achievement*, Harcourt, 1968; (with Roland Robertson) *International Systems and the Modernization of Societies*, Basic Books, 1968.

Novels under pseudonym Paul Norwood: *Tenner's Kingdom*, Heinemann, 1958; *The Prize-Giving*, Heinemann, 1960; *God the Father, cha cha cha,* Anthony Blond, 1963.

WORK IN PROGRESS: A book on current politics; a major study on power.

BIOGRAPHICAL/CRITICAL SOURCES: Commentary, October, 1968; *Times* (London), November 4, 1968; *New York Times*, August 13, 1969.††

(Died in plane crash in Hanover, N.H., October 25, 1968)

* * *

NEUMEYER, M(artin) Henry   1892-

PERSONAL: Born October 8, 1892, in Jackson, Mo.; son of Henry (a farmer) and Martha (Bohnsack) Neumeyer; married Esther Sternberg, July 15, 1919. *Education:* DePauw University, A.B., 1919; Garrett Theological Seminary, B.D., 1921; Northwestern University, A.M., 1922; University of Chicago, Ph.D., 1929. *Politics:* Usually Republican. *Home:* 6263 La Tijera Blvd., Los Angeles, Calif. 90056. *Office: Sociology and Social Research*, Los Angeles, Calif. 90007; and University of Southern California, University Park, Calif.

CAREER: Ordained Methodist minister, 1917; held student pastor appointments, 1917-23; Chicago Training School, Chicago, Ill., instructor in sociology and social work, 1923-27; University of Southern California, Los Angeles, assistant professor, 1927-32, associate professor, 1932-37, professor of sociology, 1937-62, professor emeritus, beginning 1962; *Sociology and Social Research* (international journal), Los Angeles, Calif., managing editor, 1934-60, associate editor, 1960-61, editor, beginning 1961. National Child Guidance Foundation, member of advisory board, beginning 1955; Los Angeles County Federation of Community Coordinating Councils, former officer, life member; member of National Council on Family Relations, National Council on Crime and Delinquency, and Los Angeles Council of Churches.

MEMBER: American Sociological Association, Society for the Study of Social Problems (chairman, crime and delinquency committee), Pacific Sociological Association (president, 1941), Alpha Kappa Delta (national vice-president, 1948-54; president, 1954-58; member of executive committee, beginning 1958), Theta Phi, Pi Gamma Mu. *Awards, honors:* Alumni awards from Northwestern University, 1939, and DePauw University.

WRITINGS: (With Loran D. Osborn) *Community and Society,* American Book Co., 1933; (with wife, Esther S. Neumeyer) *Leisure and Recreation,* A. S. Barnes, 1936, 3rd edition, Ronald, 1958; *Juvenile Delinquency in Modern Society,* Van Nostrand, 1949, 3rd edition, 1961; *Social Problems in a Changing Society,* Van Nostrand, 1953. Contributing editor, *Dictionary of Sociology,* 1944, 1955; contributor of sections on crime and delinquency prevention to *Americana Annual,* 1962-66; contributor to other encyclopedias and to journals.

* * *

NEWBERRY, Clare Turlay   1903-1970

PERSONAL: Born April 10, 1903, in Enterprise, Ore.; daughter of Chester Clare (a business executive) and Daisy (Wasson) Turlay; divorced; children: (first marriage) Richard Stephen Newberry; (second marriage) Felicia Noelle Trujillo. *Education:* Studied at University of Oregon, 1921-22, School of the Portland Art Museum, 1922-23, California School of Fine Arts, 1923-24, and at La Grand Chaumiere, Paris, France, 1930-31. *Home:* 2961 Barnard St., San Diego, Calif. 92110. *Agent:* McIntosh & Otis, Inc., 18 East 41st St., New York, N.Y. 10017.

CAREER: Began drawing at the age of two, particularly cats, which she has always loved; at sixteen sold her first drawings, a series of paper dolls for *John Martin's Book;* studied art and worked on her first book in Paris, France, 1930-31; after returning to the United States concentrated on portrait painting until 1934; writer and illustrator of juvenile books, mostly about cats, beginning 1934.

WRITINGS—All self-illustrated; all published by Harper, except as noted: *Herbert the Lion,* Brewer, Warren & Putnam, 1931; *Mittens,* 1936; *Babette,* 1937; *Barkis,* 1938; *Cousin Toby,* 1939; *April's Kittens,* 1940; *Drawing a Cat,* Studio, 1940; *Lambert's Bargain,* 1941; *Marshmallow,* 1942; *Pandora,* 1944; *The Kittens,* ABC, 1946, revised edition, 1965; *Smudge,* 1948; *T-Bone the Babysitter,* 1950; *Percy, Polly, and Pete,* 1952; *Ice Cream for Two,* 1953; *Widget,* 1958; *Frosty,* 1961.

Portfolios of drawings: *Cats,* Harper, 1943; *Cats & Kittens,* Harper, 1956.

WORK IN PROGRESS: The Blue Cat, a fantasy for children from eight to twelve.

SIDELIGHTS: Mrs. Newberry once told *CA:* "Most of my stories are based on personal experience, and all my illustrations, except those in *Herbert the Lion* and *Lambert's Bargain,* are done from life, many of them being drawings of my own children and pets. The effect of fur in *Mittens, April's Kittens,* and other books, is achieved by painting rapidly with watercolor on wet paper."

BIOGRAPHICAL/CRITICAL SOURCES: Scribner's, June, 1940; *Christian Science Monitor,* December 23, 1944.†

(Died, 1970)

* * *

NEWCOMB, Covelle   1908-

PERSONAL: Born September 7, 1908, in San Antonio, Tex.; married Addison Burbank. *Education:* Hunter College (now Hunter College of the City University of New York), B.A. and M.A. ("never troubled to collect the two diplomas and am uncertain of the correct years in which I received the degrees—but I believe they were approximately, 1939 and 1941"). *Residence:* New York, N.Y.

CAREER: Taught creative writing at Aquinas College, Grand Rapids, Mich., and at Fordham University, New York. Full-time writer, beginning 1940. *Member:* Authors League of America. *Awards, honors:* D. Litt., Incarnate Word College, San Antonio, Tex., 1957.

WRITINGS: Black Fire: A Story of Henri Christophe, Longmans, Green, 1940, reprinted, 1966; *The Red Hat: A Story of John Henry Cardinal Newman,* Longmans, Green, 1941, McKay, 1962; *Vagabond in Velvet: The Story of Miguel de Cervantes,* Longmans, Green, 1942; *Silver Saddles,* Longmans, Green, 1943; *Larger Than the Sky: A Story of James Cardinal Gibbons,* Longmans, Green, 1945; (with Addison Burbank) *Narizona's Holiday* (fiction), Longmans, Green, 1946; *The Secret Door,* Dodd, 1946; *Cortez the Conqueror,* Random House, 1947; *Running Waters,* Dodd, 1947; *The Broken Sword,* Dodd, 1955; *Brother Zero,* Dodd, 1959; *Christopher Columbus, the Sea Lord,* Dodd, 1963; *Leonardo da Vinci, Prince of Painters,* Dodd, 1965; *Explorer with a Heart: The Story of Giovanni da Verrazzano,* McKay, 1969.

WORK IN PROGRESS: A book about four contemporary artists entitled *A Gallery of Four.*

* * *

NEWMAN, Stewart A(lbert)   1907-

PERSONAL: Born January 26, 1907, in Jermyn, Tex.; son of Virgil Albert (a farmer) and Willie (Bayless) Newman; married Sara Knupp (a public school teacher), August 15, 1930; children: Charles Virgil, Stewart A., Jr., Harvey Knupp. *Education:* Hardin-Simmons University, A.B., 1930; Southwestern Baptist Theological Seminary, Th.M., 1935, Th.D., 1939; also studied at Northwestern University, Duke University, and University of Rochester. *Home and office:* Box 535, Buies Creek, N.C. 27506.

CAREER: Baptist minister. Southwestern Baptist Theological Seminary, Fort Worth, Tex., 1935-52, became professor of religion and history; Southeastern Baptist Theological Seminary, Wake Forest, N.C., professor of philosophy of religion, 1952-66; Campbell College, Buies Creek, N.C., professor of philosophy, 1966-74; Meredith College, Raleigh, N.C., lecturer in philosophy, beginning 1974. *Awards, honors:* D.D. from Hardin-Simmons University, 1947.

WRITINGS: Walter Thomas Conner, Theologian of the Southwest, Broadman, 1964.

WORK IN PROGRESS: Faith and a Freer Church; and *Religion and the Problem of Meaning in Western Culture.*

* * *

NEWSOM, Carroll V(incent)   1904-

PERSONAL: Born February 23, 1904, in Buckley, Ill.; son of Curtis Bishop (an educator) and Mattie Fitzallen (Fisher) Newsom; married Francis Higley, August 15, 1928; children: Jeanne Carolyn (Mrs. William A. Challener III), Walter Burton, Gerald Higley. *Education:* College of Emporia, B.A., 1924; University of Michigan, M.A., 1927, Ph.D., 1931. *Politics:* Independent. *Religion:* Congregationalist. *Home:* Candlewood Isle, New Fairfield, Conn.

CAREER: Instructor in mathematics at College of Emporia, Emporia, Kan., 1924, and University of Michigan, 1927-28; University of New Mexico, Alburquerque, instructor, 1928-29, assistant professor, 1929-30, associate professor, 1931-32, professor of mathematics and head of department, 1932-44; Oberlin College, Oberlin, Ohio, professor of mathematics, 1944-48; New York State Department of Education, Albany, assistant commissioner for higher education, 1948-50, associate commissioner for higher and professional education, 1950-55; New York University, New York, N.Y., executive vice-president, 1955-56, president, 1956-62; Prentice-Hall, Inc., Englewood Cliffs, N.J., senior vice-president, 1962-64, president, 1964-65; Radio Corporation of America, director, 1961-71; educational consultant, 1965-66, vice-president in education, 1966-71. Director of National Broadcasting Co., 1961-71, M. Lowenstein & Sons, 1962-73, New York World's Fair (1964-65) Corp., and African-American Chamber of Commerce. Vice-president and trustee of Thomas Alva Edison Foundation; trustee of Guggenheim Foundation, National Association of Educational Broadcasters, and Dropsie University; chairman of American Friends of Ethiopia.

MEMBER: National Council of Teachers of Mathematics, American Mathematical Society, Mathematical Association of America, American Association for the Advancement of Science (fellow), Royal Society for the Encouragement of the Arts (Benjamin Franklin fellow), American Academy of Arts and Sciences (fellow), New York University Club; University Club and Century Association (both New York). *Awards, honors:* Pasteur Medal of Pasteur Institute (Paris), 1952; Chevalier of the Legion of Honor (France); honorary degrees from some twenty-four universities and colleges.

WRITINGS: An Introduction to Mathematics: A Study of the Nature of Mathematics, University of New Mexico Press, 1936; *An Introduction to Mathematics for College Students,* University of New Mexico Press, 1939; (with J. C. Knode and others) *An American Philosophy of Education,* Van Nostrand, 1942; (with H. D. Larsen) *A Manual of Mathematics for Prospective Air Corps Cadets,* Prentice-Hall, 1942; (with H. D. Larsen) *Basic Mathematics for Pilots and Flight Crews,* Prentice-Hall, 1943; *An Introduction to College Mathematics,* Prentice-Hall, 1946, revised edition, 1954; (contributor) *Our Great Heritage,* Harper, 1948; (reviser) *Slobin-Wilbur Freshman Mathematics,* Rinehart, 1948.

(Editor) *A Television Policy for Education,* American Council on Education, 1952; (with Howard Eves) *Foundations and Fundamental Concepts of Mathematics,* Rinehart, 1958, revised edition, 1965; *A University President Speaks Out,* Harper, 1961; *Mathematical Discourses: The Heart of Mathematical Science,* Prentice-Hall, 1964.

Contributor to *Yearbook of National Society for the Study of Education,* 1952. Editor of *Pentagon,* 1938-40; associate editor, *American Mathematics Monthly,* 1942-47, editor-in-chief, 1947-52; member of editoral committee, "Slaught Mathematics Papers," sponsored by Mathematical Association of America, 1942-52.

WORK IN PROGRESS: The Evolution of Christian Tradition.

AVOCATIONAL INTERESTS: Gardening and all country life activities; music, the theater.

NICHOLS, Dale (William) 1904-
   (Willem de Polman)

PERSONAL: Born July 13, 1904, in David City, Neb.; son of John Dale and Edith (Pohlman) Nichols; married fifth wife, Maria Gandara Herrera; children: (first marriage) Joan Lucille (Mrs. Keith Smith); (third marriage) Carla Dale. *Education:* Studied at Art Institute of Chicago and Chicago Academy of Fine Arts, 1924, and under Joseph Binder, Vienna, Austria, 1936. *Religion:* "Type of Zoroastrian." *Home:* Antigua Guatemala, Sacatepequez Department, Guatemala, Central America.

CAREER: Painter, designer, and illustrator, who started earning his living as a popular pianist. Advertising artist in Chicago, Ill., for *Chicago Tribune,* 1927, Crafton Studios, 1927-28, and Stevens, Sundblom Stultz, 1932-33; Carnegie visiting professor and artist in residence, University of Illinois, Urbana, 1939-40; art editor, Encyclopaedia Britannica, Inc., Chicago, Ill., 1942-48; artist in residence, Northern Michigan University, Marquette, 1954. Art director, Tucson (Ariz.) Regional Planning Board, 1940-44. Works owned by Metropolitan Museum of Art, Art Institute of Chicago, and other museums; exhibitor at Carnegie Institute, Denver Art Museum, and Dallas Museum of Fine Arts, among others. Consultant to American School, Guatemala, and designer and illustrator of school magazine, *Caminos;* also illustrator of books by other authors. *Member:* American Artists Professional League, Society of Typographic Arts. *Awards, honors:* Various awards for painting and for design in printing.

WRITINGS: A Philosophy of Esthetics, Black Cat Press, 1938; *Figure Drawing,* Watson, 1957. Writer of several pamphlets on art including "The Pyramid Text of the Ancient Maya"; contributor to *Coronet, Better Homes and Gardens, Printers' Ink, True, American Printer,* and other journals.

Books illustrated include *Two Years Before the Mast, The Shining Trail, Blood Brother,* and textbooks for Ginn.

WORK IN PROGRESS: The Psychoscope; The Animystics, a book on art as instinct; *Meditations on Eros,* poetry; and *Ophelia Bumps,* adventures in a Model A Ford.

SIDELIGHTS: Nichols told *CA* that he was a student of motivational psychology, anthropology, and comparative religions "as a means of bringing more effectual communication to art, prose, and poetry...." Also believes that "obedience to Natural Law must supersede transitory ideas in religion, politics and social patterns. He practices this dictum in painting and design, poetry, prose and music." Nichols is a member of the Nation of Celestial Space, and was the group's ambassador pro tem in Guatemala.

*   *   *

NICHOLSON, Arnold 1902-

PERSONAL: Born October 11, 1902, in Philadelphia, Pa.; son of Edgar W. and Ruth (Arnold) Nicholson; married Elisabeth White, December 30, 1927; children: Frederic A., John Berryhill. *Education:* Princeton University, B.S., 1924. *Agent:* Ann Elmo Agency, Inc., 545 Fifth Ave., New York, N.Y. 10017.

CAREER: Evening Public Ledger, Philadelphia, Pa., reporter and rewrite man, 1924-26; U.S. National Park Service, Yellowstone National Park, public relations writer, 1926; *Kansas City Star,* Kansas City Mo., feature writer, 1927; Curtis Publications, Philadelphia, Pa., associate editor of *Country Gentleman,* 1929-42, managing editor, 1942-55, associate editor of *Saturday Evening Post*, 1955-62. Restorer (for use) of four eighteenth-century dwellings in the 1950's. Chairman of Philadelphia Air Pollution Control Board, 1958-63; director and vice-president of Citizens Council on City Planning, Philadelphia, 1958-64; consultant to Old Philadelphia Development Corp., beginning 1963. Editorial consultant, Action, Inc., 1963, and Purdue University, 1964-65. *Member:* Society of Architectural Historians, National Trust for Historic Perservation. *Awards, honors:* American Institute of Architects award for article in *Saturday Evening Post*, 1957.

WRITINGS: Adventures with a Prophet, Curtis Publishing Co., 1939; *American Houses in History,* Viking, 1965; *Acme Markets, Inc., 1891-1967: From Corner Grocery to Supermarket Chain,* Acme Markets, 1967. Contributor to national magazines.†

* * *

NIEDECKER, Lorine 1903-1970

PERSONAL: Born May 12, 1903, in Fort Atkinson, Wis.; daughter of Henry E. (a commercial fisherman) and Theresa (Kunz) Niedecker; married Albert Millen (painter in an industrial shop), May 26, 1963. *Education:* Beloit College, student for two and one-half years. *Residence:* Fort Atkinson, Wis.

CAREER: Formerly employed in a library and hospital, and at Radio Station WHA, Madison, Wis.

WRITINGS—Poetry: New Goose, Decker Press, 1946; *My Friend Tree,* Wild Hawthorn, 1962; *North Central,* Fulcrum Press, 1968; *Tenderness and Gristle: The Collected Poems,* Jargon Society, 1970; *Collected Poems 1968,* Fulcrum Press, 1970; *Blue Chicory,* Elizabeth Press, 1976. Featured poet in *Origin,* July, 1966.

BIOGRAPHICAL/CRITICAL SOURCES: Nation, April 13, 1970.†

(Died December 31, 1970)

* * *

NIELSEN, Oswald 1904-

PERSONAL: Born November 28, 1904 in Sioux City, Iowa; son of Anders Peter (a minister) and Mariane (Jensen) Nielsen; married Irene Allen (a teacher), July 8, 1933; children: Helen (Mrs. Alan M. McNeil), John A. *Education:* University of Chicago, Ph.B., 1929; University of Minnesota, Ph.D., 1936. *Religion:* Baptist. *Office:* Graduate School of Business, Stanford University, Stanford, Calif. 93405.

CAREER: Member of faculty, Stanford University, Graduate School of Business, Stanford, Calif. Trustee of American Baptist Homes and Hospitals of Northern California and of Berkeley Baptist Divinity School. *Member:* American Institute of Certified Public Accountants, American Accounting Association, Financial Executives Institute, Budget Executives Institute, California Society of Certified Public Accountants.

WRITINGS: (Editor) *University Administration in Practice,* Graduate School of Business, Stanford University, 1959; *Cases in Auditing,* Irwin, 1965; (editor) *Research in Accounting Measurement,* American Accounting Association, 1966. Writer of monographs, articles, and book reviews.†

NIESS, Robert Judson 1911-

PERSONAL: Born August 25, 1911, in Mason City, Iowa; son of George (a businessman) and Mary Ann (Thibodeau) Niess; married Martha I. Laing (a secretary); children: Martha Caroline (Mrs. Harold Gene Moss), Barbara Steele Niess Buys. *Education:* University of Minnesota, A.B. (magna cum laude), 1933, A.M., 1934, Ph.D., 1937. *Politics:* Democrat. *Home:* 2709 Spencer St., Durham, N.C. 27705. *Office:* Department of Romance Languages, Duke University, Durham, N.C. 27706.

CAREER: Washington University, St. Louis, Mo., instructor in French, 1936-39; Mundelein College, Chicago, Ill., assistant professor of French, 1939-42; U.S. Military Academy, West Point, N.Y., instructor in French, with rank of captain, 1942-46; University of Kentucky, Lexington, associate professor of French, 1946-47; Harvard University, Cambridge, Mass., visiting lecturer, 1947-49; University of Michigan, Ann Arbor, associate professor, 1949-55, professor of French, 1955-72; Duke University, Durham, N.C., professor of French, beginning 1972. *Member:* American Association of Teachers of French, Modern Language Association of America, American Association of University Professors, South Atlantic Modern Language Association, Phi Beta Kappa. *Awards, honors:* Palmes Academiques of French Government; University of Michigan Press Prize, 1970.

WRITINGS: Zola's Letters to J. Van Santen Kolff, Washington University Press, 1940; *Julien Benda,* University of Michigan Press, 1956; (editor with F.W.J. Hemmings) Emile Zola, *Salons,* Droz, 1959; (editor) *France: L'individu et le destin, 1918-1960,* Houghton, 1962; *Zola, Cezanne and Manet: A Study of l'Oeuvre,* University of Michigan Press, 1968. Contributor to scholarly journals.

WORK IN PROGRESS: Research on the relationship between Emile Zola and Edmond de Goncourt.

BIOGRAPHICAL/CRITICAL SOURCES: Georgia Review, summer, 1969.

* * *

NIGGLI, Josefina

PERSONAL: Born in Monterrey, Neuvo Leon, Mexico; daughter of Frederick Ferdinand (a cement manufacturer) and Goldie (Morgan) Niggli. *Education:* Incarnate Word College, San Antonio, Tex., B.A., 1931; University of North Carolina, M.A., 1937; special work in drama abroad at University of Bristol and Old Vic Theatre School. *Politics:* Democrat. *Religion:* Roman Catholic. *Address:* Box 35, Cullowhee, N.C. 28723. *Agent:* Ashley Famous Agency, Inc., 1301 Avenue of the Americas, New York, N.Y. 10019. *Office:* Department of Speech and Theatre Arts, Western Carolina University, Cullowhee, N.C. 28723.

CAREER: University of North Carolina, Chapel Hill, instructor in radio, 1942-44; Metro-Goldwyn-Mayer Studios, Culver City, Calif., writer, 1951-52; University of North Carolina, Woman's College, Greensboro, assistant professor of drama, 1955-56; Western Carolina University, Cullowhee, N.C., associate professor and chairman of department of drama, beginning 1957. Guest teacher in playwriting, Bristol University, 1955-56. Did Latin America broadcasts for U.S. Department of State, 1942. *Member:* American Educational Theatre Association, Authors Guild, Photographic Society of America, Carolina Dramatic Association (past president). *Awards, honors:* Rockefeller fellowship in Europe, 1950-51; Mayflower Cup for best work of nonfiction by a North Carolinian, 1946, for *Mexican Village;* Alumni Award, University of North Carolina, for work in drama.

WRITINGS: Mexican Silhouettes, Silhouette Press (San Antonio), 1931; (editor) *Mexican Folk Plays,* University of North Carolina Press, 1938, reprinted, Arno, 1976; *Red Velvet Goat* (one-act Mexican folk play), S. French, c.1938; *Sunday Costs Five Pesos* (one-act Mexican folk comedy), S. French, 1939; *Miracle at Blaise* (morality play), S. French, c.1940; *Mexican Village,* University of North Carolina Press, 1945; *Pointers on Playwriting,* The Writer (Boston), 1945, revised and enlarged edition published as *New Pointers on Playwriting,* 1967; *Pointers on Radio Writing,* The Writer, 1946; *Step Down, Elder Brother* (novel), Rinehart, 1947; *Miracle for Mexico,* New York Graphic Society, 1964. Author of film and television scripts. Contributor of short stories and articles to *Vogue* and other periodicals.

WORK IN PROGRESS: A drama text on period and style.

SIDELIGHTS: Josefina Niggli is bi-lingual in English and Spanish; she travels to England almost every year. *Avocational interests:* Color photography.†

*   *   *

NIXON, Ivor Gray   1905-

PERSONAL: Born August 5, 1905, in London, England; son of John and Marian (Barber) Nixon; married Margaret Joan Smith, October 30, 1935; children: John Kevin, Irving Philip, Christina Helen (Mrs. Anthony Keith Wilson). *Education:* University of London, B.Sc. (first class honors), 1926; Clare College, Cambridge, B.A., 1928. *Home:* ler, Stock Ost, "Matterhorngruss," Zermatt 3920, Valais, Switzerland.

CAREER: Royal Dutch Shell Petroleum Co., The Hague, Netherlands, chemical engineer, 1928-63, working at various times in California, Mexico, West Indies, England, and the Netherlands, and head of Manufacturing Operations Division, The Hague, 1963. British Iron and Steel Research Association, consultant, 1968-70. *Wartime service:* British Home Guard, Heavy Anti-Aircraft Battery, 1940-45. *Member:* Institute of Petroleum and Institution of Mechanical Engineers (both United Kingdom). *Awards, honors:* Senior research fellowship from University of Sussex; associate senior research fellow, Brunel University, 1976.

WRITINGS: The Rise of the Dorians, Praeger, 1968. Also author of research papers in the field of chemistry and iron and steel making.

WORK IN PROGRESS: Study of the Mycenaean/Minoan period preceding the Dark Ages, with particular reference to the date of the fall of Knossos; research at the University of Sussex and Brunel University on the reduction of iron ore and the manufacture of steel.

AVOCATIONAL INTERESTS: Archaeology, ancient history, color photography.

*   *   *

NOBLE, G(eorge) Bernard   1892-1972

PERSONAL: Born July 11, 1892, in Leesburg, Fla.; son of Charles Samuel (a civil engineer) and Eva Susanna (Hall) Noble; married Matilda Thomas, December 24, 1917. *Education:* Attended University of Washington, Seattle, 1910-13; Oxford University, B.A., 1915, M.A., 1923; University of Wisconsin, graduate study, 1916-17; Columbia University, Ph.D., 1935. *Politics:* Generally Democratic ("not

hard liner"). *Religion:* Unitarian Universalist. *Home:* 3101 Worthington Circle, Falls Church, Va. 22044.

CAREER: Served in Paris with U.S. Commission to Negotiate Peace, 1918-19, reporting to the delegation daily on trends of French opinion: University of Nebraska, Lincoln, assistant professor of international law and comparative government, 1920-22; Reed College, Portland, Ore., assistant professor, 1922-28, professor of international law, diplomacy, and comparative government, 1928-43; chairman, Twelfth Regional War Labor Board, 1943-45; U.S. Department of State, Washington, D.C., chief of Division of Historical Policy Research, 1946-58, director of Historical Office, 1958-62, consultant to Public Affairs Bureau, 1962-65. Visiting lecturer, Barnard College, 1926-27. Oregon State senator, 1941-42. *Military service:* U.S. Army, Infantry, World War I; became first lieutenant; received Distinguished Service Cross.

MEMBER: American Society of International Law, American Political Science Association (member of executive board, 1936-40), American Historical Association, Phi Beta Kappa, Alpha Delta Phi, Cosmos Club (Washington, D.C.). *Awards, honors:* Rhodes scholar at Oxford University, 1913-16; LL.D., Reed College, 1962.

WRITINGS: Policies and Opinions at Paris, 1919, Macmillan, 1935, reprinted, Fertig, 1968; *Christian A. Herter,* Cooper Square, 1970. Contributor of articles and reviews to periodicals.

WORK IN PROGRESS: Post-World War II diplomatic developments, especially trends of U.S. policy, and relations between Congress and the Executive.†

(Died November 28, 1972)

*   *   *

NOLDE, O(tto) Frederick   1899-1972

PERSONAL: Born June 30, 1899, in Philadelphia, Pa.; son of Antone Harry and Ida (Fuchs) Nolde; married Ellen Jarden, June 21, 1927 (deceased); married Nancy Lawrence, January 12, 1966; children: (first marriage) Anthony Derf, Susanne von Loehr, Fredericka Jane (Mrs. Bruce Berger), Walter Hahn Jarden (deceased). *Education:* Muhlenberg College, A.B., 1920; Lutheran Theological Seminary, Philadelphia, B.D., 1923; University of Pennsylvania, Ph.D., 1928. *Home:* 7602 East Lane, Philadelphia, Pa. 19118.

CAREER: Ordained minister of Lutheran Church, 1923; University of Pennsylvania, Philadelphia, instructor, 1925-28, assistant professor, 1929-35, lecturer in religious education, 1936-43; Lutheran Theological Seminary, Philadelphia, Pa., instructor, 1925-28, assistant professor, 1928-31, professor of religious education, 1931-68, professor emeritus, 1968-72, dean of Graduate School, 1943-62. Pastor, Grace Evangelical Lutheran Church, Wyndmoor, Pa. World Council of Churches, director of Commission of Churches on International Affairs, 1946-68, associate secretary-general for international affairs, 1948-68. Associate consultant to U.S. delegation at United Nations Conference, San Francisco, 1945. Carnegie Endowment for International Peace, member of executive committee of board of trustees, 1951-69, vice-chairman, 1959-69, honorary trustee, beginning 1969.

MEMBER: International Institute of Arts and Letters (fellow), Academy of Political and Social Sciences, Phi Delta Kappa, Century Association (New York), Philadelphia Cricket Club, Mantoloking Yacht Club. *Awards, honors:* Muhlenberg College, D.D., 1932, LL.D., 1946; L.H.D.,

Wittenberg University, 1951; Litt.D., Temple University, 1957.

WRITINGS: A Guide Book in Catechetical Instruction, Board of Publication, United Lutheran Church in America, 1932, enlarged edition, 1939; *Yesterday, Today, Tomorrow* (course of study), Board of Publication, United Lutheran Church in America, 1933; *Truth and Life: The Meaning of the Catechism,* United Lutheran Publication House, 1937; *Christian World Action: The Christian Citizen Builds for Tomorrow,* Muhlenberg Press, 1942, 3rd edition, 1944; *Power for Peace: The Way of the United Nations and the Will of Christian People,* Muhlenberg Press, 1946; (editor) *Toward World-Wide Christianity,* Harper, 1946, reprinted, 1969; *Freedom's Charter: The Universal Declaration of Human Rights,* introduction by Eleanor Roosevelt, Foreign Policy Association (New York), 1949; *Free and Equal: Human Rights in Ecumenical Perspective,* introduction by Charles Habib Malik, World Council of Churches, 1968; *The Churches and the Nations,* introduction by W. A. Visser 't Hooft, Fortress, 1970.

With Paul J. Hoh; all published by United Lutheran Publication House, except as noted: *My Pupils,* 1934; *My Life,* 1934; *My Work,* 1935; *My Preparation,* 1935; *My Bible,* 1935; *My Material,* 1936; *My Group Sessions,* 1936; *My Progress,* 1937; *God's Master Builders: Methods of Leading Group Sessions* (based on *My Group Sessions,* 1936), Muhlenberg Press, 1950.

BIOGRAPHICAL/CRITICAL SOURCES: Lutheran, November 22, 1961.†

(Died June 17, 1972)

* * *

NOLING, A(lfred) W(ells)   1899-

PERSONAL: Born September 11, 1899, in East Orange, N.J.; son of Isaac Oliver (a dentist) and Alice (Mandeville) Noling; married Jean Louise Luther, December 22, 1926; children: Lawrence J., Katharine Noling Smith. *Education:* Took evening courses at Columbia University. *Office:* Hurty-Peck & Co., 16950 Armstrong Ave., Irvine, Calif. 92713.

CAREER: Hurty-Peck & Co., Indianapolis, Ind., beginning 1926, presently chairman of board of directors.

WRITINGS: Beverage Literature: A Bibliography, Scarecrow, 1971.

SIDELIGHTS: A. W. Noling has assembled "the largest library in the world" of beverage literature in English, about six thousand titles collected in Canada, Great Britain, Australia, New Zealand, South Africa, and the United States.

* * *

NORRIS, Dorothy E. Koch   1907-

PERSONAL: Born January 12, 1907, in Mineral Ridge, Ohio; daughter of Bruno Richard and Ida M. (Maggs) Koch; married Paul G. Norris, 1956 (died, 1958). *Education:* Oberlin College, A.B., 1930; Columbia University, M.A., 1936, Professional Diploma, 1961. *Home:* 2691 Elmwood Ave., Apt. 3, Kenmore, N.Y. 14217.

CAREER: High school teacher in Berea, Ohio, 1930-35; University of Tennessee, Knoxville, instructor, 1936-39; assistant professor of health and physical education, 1939-41; Boston University, Sargent College, Cambridge, Mass., assistant professor, 1941-45, associate professor, 1945-49, professor of physical education, 1949-59, director of Modern Dance Club, 1941-57; Young Women's Christian Association, Wilmington, Del., director of physical education, 1958-59; State University of New York College at Buffalo, associate professor, 1959-69, professor of health, physical education, and recreation, beginning 1969. Choreographer and director of dance concerts. *Member:* American Association for Health, Physical Education and Recreation, National and Eastern Association for Physical Education of College Women, National Education Association, New York State Teachers Association, New York State Association for Health, Physical Education and Recreation, Association for Women in Physical Education of New York State, Pi Lambda Theta, Kappa Delta Pi.

WRITINGS: (With Reva P. Shiner) *Keynotes to Modern Dance,* Burgess, 1965, 3rd edition, 1969, recordings to accompany text, with music by Cola Heiden, Educational Activities, 1966. Contributor of articles on dance to education journals.

WORK IN PROGRESS: A book on tap dance.

AVOCATIONAL INTERESTS: Collecting dance books, photography, reading, traveling, attending dance and other theatrical productions.

* * *

NORTHMORE, Elizabeth Florence   1906-1974
(Elizabeth Stucley)

PERSONAL: Born February 9, 1906, in England; daughter of Hugh (a baronet and naval officer) and Gladys (Bankes) Stucley; married J. G. L. Northmore (a portrait painter), February 16, 1955. *Education:* Attended London School of Economics and Political Science, 1933-35. *Politics:* Conservative. *Religion:* Church of England. *Home:* St. Cuthbert's, Bathampton, Bath, Somersetshire, England. *Agent:* A. M. Heath & Co. Ltd., 40-42 William IV St., London WC2N 4DD, England.

CAREER: British author; headmistress of St. Cuthbert's Finishing School, Bathampton, England, 1960-64. Much of her adult life has revolved around work with and for children—Guides' creche service, social welfare in London's poor areas, and occupational therapy in a children's hospital. During World War II, was a driver with the Mechanical Transport Corps in France, and assisted in a French maternity hospital. *Awards, honors:* Mentioned in dispatches (British) for services during the retreat from France, June, 1940, as a mechanised transport driver.

*WRITINGS—*All under name Elizabeth Stucley: *The Village Organizer* (handbook for social workers), Methuen, 1935; *The House Will Come Down* (novel), Duckworth, 1938; *Louisa* (novel), Duckworth, 1939; *Trip No Further* (novel), Low, 1946; *Hebridean Journey with Johnson and Boswell* (travel), Christopher Johnson, 1956; *To End the Storm* (novel), Hutchinson, 1957; *Teddy Boy's Picnic* (autobiography), Anthony Blond, 1958; *Life is for Living: The Erratic Life of Elizabeth Stucley,* Anthony Blond, 1959.

Books for young people: *Pollycon: A Book for the Young Economist,* Basil Blackwell, 1933; *Star in the Hand,* Collins, 1946; *Penfeather Family,* Nicholson & Watson, 1947; *Secret Pony,* Faber, 1950; *Magnolia Buildings,* Bodley Head, 1960, published as *Family Walk-Up: A Story of the Berners Family,* F. Watts, 1961; *Springfield Home,* Bodley Head, 1961, published as *The Contrary Orphans,* F. Watts, 1962; *Miss Georgie's Gang,* Abelard, 1970.

SIDELIGHTS: Elizabeth Northmore traveled extensively in Europe, Asia, United States, and Canada.

BIOGRAPHICAL/CRITICAL SOURCES: Elizabeth Stucley, *The Village Organizer,* Methuen, 1935, *Teddy Boy's Picnic,* Anthony Blond, 1958, and *Life Is for Living,* Anthony Blond, 1959.†

(Died July 26, 1974)

* * *

NOTH, Martin D.   1902-1968

PERSONAL: Born August 3, 1902, in Dresden, Germany; son of Gerhard Friedrich and Coelestine (Hochmuth) Noth; married Helga Binterim, 1934; children: Eva, Albrecht, Christian, Mechthild. *Education:* Studied at University of Erlangen, 1921-22, University of Rostock, 1922, and University of Leipzig, 1922-25; University of Greifswald, D.Theol., 1930; University of Lund (Sweden), Dr.Teol., 1959; University of Frankfurt, Dr. iur., 1964.

CAREER: University of Greifswald, Greifswald, Germany, privatdozent, 1927-28; University of Leipzig, Leipzig, Germany, privatdozent, 1928-30; taught in Koenigsberg, East Prussia (now Kaliningrad, U.S.S.R.), 1930-45; University of Bonn, Bonn, Federal Republic of Germany, professor of Old Testament, beginning 1945.

WRITINGS: Die Israelitischen Personennamen, Kohlhammer, 1928, reprinted, Georg Olms, 1966; *Das System der Welt des zwoelf Staemme Israel,* Vandenhoeck & Ruprecht, 1950, reprinted, Wissenschaftliche Buchgesellschaft, 1966; *Gesammelte Studien zum Alten Testament,* Kaiser, 1957, 4th edition, 1969, translation by D. R. Ap-Thomas, published as *The Laws in the Pentateuch, and Other Studies,* Oliver & Boyd, 1967; *Die Welt des Alten Testament,* Topelmann, 1962; *Das dritte Buch Mose: Leviticus, Ubers und erklart,* Vandenhoeck & Ruprecht, 1966; *Das vierte Buch Mose: Numeri, Ubers und erklart,* Vandenhoeck & Ruprecht, 1966, translation by James D. Martin, published as *Numbers: A Commentary,* Westminster, 1968; *Geschichte Israels,* Vandenhoeck & Ruprecht, 1966; *Ueberlieferungsgeschichte des Pentateuch,* Hebrew Union College, 1966, translation by Bernhard W. Anderson, published as *A History of Pentateuchal Traditions,* Prentice-Hall, 1972; *Aufsatze zur biblischen Landes- und Altertumskunde,* Neukirchener Verlag, 1971.†

(Died, 1968)

* * *

NOVOTNY, Louise Miller   1889-

PERSONAL: Born April 26, 1889, in Bondurant, Iowa; daughter of James A. (a farmer) and Isabel (Brown) Miller; married Joseph A. Novotny, 1925. *Education:* Highland Park College (now Des Moines University), degree in Education and Dramatic Art, 1914; Cincinnati Bible College, B.S.L. *Home:* 1603 23rd St., Des Moines, Iowa.

CAREER: Formerly a teacher in public schools, church schools, and summer camps.

WRITINGS—All published by Standard Publishing, except where noted: *Primary Playlets and Dramatizations,* 1936; *Women and the Church,* 1940; *Special Days in Church Schools,* 1943; *Fifty-two Practical Programs for Young People,* Zondervan, 1957; *Meditations and Programs for Women's Groups,* 1959; *Worship in Art and Music,* Zondervan, 1959; *Guide to Prayer,* 1959; *Programs for Women,* 1962. Writer of more than sixty pageants and playlets for *Lookout,* and many articles.††

NUTTING, Willis D(wight)   1900-1975

PERSONAL: Born March 10, 1900, in Iowa City, Iowa; son of Charles (a professor) and Eloise (Willis) Nutting; married Eileen Barry (a librarian), August 1, 1934; children: Theresa M. (Mrs. Michel Marcy), Charles J., Theodore M. *Education:* University of Iowa, B.A., 1921, Ph.D., 1933; Oxford University, B.A., 1923, B.Litt., 1924. *Politics:* Independent. *Religion:* Roman Catholic. *Home:* 53240 Juniper Rd., South Bend, Ind. 46637. *Office:* University of Notre Dame, Notre Dame, Ind. 46556.

CAREER: Episcopal clergyman in West Indies and Colorado, 1924-30; College of St. Teresa, Winona, Minn., instructor, 1933-36; University of Notre Dame, Notre Dame, Ind., faculty member, beginning 1936. *Military service:* U.S. Army, 1918. *Awards, honors:* Rhodes scholar, 1921-24.

WRITINGS: How Firm a Foundation? Sheed, 1939; *Reclamation of Independence,* Berliner & Lanigan, 1947; *Schools and the Means of Education,* Fides, 1959; *The Free City,* Templegate, 1967.

WORK IN PROGRESS: My Neighbor and Myself, an investigation of Christian action; study on belief in God.

AVOCATIONAL INTERESTS: Farming.†

(Died December 6, 1975)

* * *

NYE, Hermes   1908-

PERSONAL: Born February 11, 1908; son of Howard H. (a freight-rate official) and Nora (Cheney) Nye; married Mary Elizabeth Beasley (owner of an art gallery), December 30, 1937; children: Eric Beasley. *Education:* Attended Washburn College, 1925-29; University of Kansas, B.A., 1930, LL.B., 1933. *Politics:* Democrat. *Religion:* Unitarian Universalist. *Home:* 5906 Norway Rd., Dallas, Tex. 75230. *Agent:* Barthold Fles Literary Agency, 507 Fifth Ave., New York, N.Y. 10017. *Office:* Room 201, Cookston Smith Building, 3603 Lemmon Ave., Dallas, Tex. 75219.

CAREER: Attorney, in private practice of law, Dallas, Tex., beginning 1933. Folksinger for more than twenty years, making personal appearances in North Texas area, and broadcasting on Dallas radio and television stations; recording artist for five long-playing albums issued by Folkways Records. Teacher of private class in creative writing, Dallas. *Military service:* U.S. Navy, 1943-44. *Member:* Texas Bar Association, Texas Folklore Society (past president).

WRITINGS: Fortune Is a Woman (novel), Signet Books, 1958; *How to Be a Folksinger,* Oak, 1965; *TS: A Faith for the Desperate,* privately printed, 1965. Book reviewer for *Dallas Times Herald* and *Dallas Morning News,* 1945-65; contributor of articles on folklore, and occasional travel pieces, to Texas periodicals.

WORK IN PROGRESS: Expanding *TS: A Faith for the Desperate.*††

* * *

OBERMEYER, Henry   1899-

PERSONAL: Born March 5, 1899, in New York, N.Y.; son of George (a merchant) and Mina (Emmerich) Obermeyer; married Marion Dickens, March 25, 1926; children: Judith Ann (Mrs. Alex Drust), Louise Henrietta (Mrs. Robert Smith). *Education:* Columbia University, B.Litt., 1921. *Politics:* Republican. *Religion:* Episcopalian. *Home:* 49 Longview Dr., Simsbury, Conn. 06070.

CAREER: Consolidated Edison Co., New York City, director of advertising, 1926-49; Bozell & Jacobs Advertising Agency, New York City, senior vice-president, 1949-68. Member of board, Child and Family Services, Inc. Director of Communications, Hartford Graduate Center. Member: Public Relations Society of America, Public Utilities Advertising Association, Alpha Delta Sigma, Alpha Chi Rho, Advertising Club of Greater Hartford.

WRITINGS: Successful Advertising Management, McGraw, 1969.

* * *

OBOURN, Ellsworth Scott 1897-

PERSONAL: Born September 5, 1897, in Mansfield, Pa.; son of George E. and Etta (Thurston) Obourn; married M. Cora Price, 1918 (died, 1940); married Honora W. Camden, 1942; children: (first marriage) Robert L., Malcolm R., Norma Obourn Harrington, Marlyn Obourn Oliver. Education: Attended Pennsylvania State College (now University), 1916-20; Columbia University, B.S., 1923; New York University, M.A., 1947, Ph.D., 1950. Home: 2100 South Ocean Dr., Apt. 2 CD, Sky Harbor East, Fort Lauderdale, Fla.

CAREER: Head of science department at high schools in New York and Pennsylvania, 1919-22; John Burroughs School, Clayton, Mo., head of science department, 1923-54; UNESCO, program specialist in science teaching, Paris, France, 1954-55; U.S. Office of Education, Washington, D.C., science specialist, 1955-65. Science adviser (under UNESCO) to Minister of Education, Thailand, 1951-52.

MEMBER: National Science Teachers Association (charter and life member; member of board of directors, 1948), American Association for Advancement of Science (fellow), National Association for Research in Science Teaching (charter member; vice-president, 1946-47, 1961-62; president, 1962-63), National Education Association, Association for Education of Teachers in Science, American Chemical Society, Council for Elementary Science International, Science Society of Thailand (honorary life member), British Science Masters Association (honorary life member), Central Association of Science and Mathematics Teachers, Washington Academy of Science, Philosophical Society of Washington, D.C., Phi Delta Kappa, Cosmos Club. Awards, honors: Science Education Recognition Award, National Association for Research in Science Teaching, 1963.

WRITINGS: (Co-author) Science Problems of Modern Life, Volumes I and II, Webster Publishing, 1923; Civic Science in the Home, privately printed, 1923; (co-author) Instructional Tests in High Schools Physics, World Book Co., 1931; Modern Science Problems, Webster Publishing, 1933; (co-author) Our World of Living Things, Webster Publishing, 1936; (co-author) Modern Science Teaching, Macmillan, 1940, revised edition, 1950; (co-author) Introduction to Machines, Webster Publishing, 1942; (co-author) Introduction to Electricity, Webster Publishing, 1942.

(Co-author) Science in Everyday Life, and Workbook, Van Nostrand, 1953; (co-author) Everyday Problems in Science, and Teacher's Manual, Von Nostrand, 1953, revised edition, 1958; UNESCO Source Book for Science Teaching, UNESCO, 1956, revised and enlarged edition, 1962; (co-author) Exploring the World of Science, Van Nostrand, 1963; (co-author) Discovering the World of Science, Van Nostrand, 1963; (with John H. Woodburn) Teaching the Pursuit of Science, Macmillan, 1965; (co-author) Investi-

gating the World of Science, Van Nostrand, 1966; My World of Science, McCormick-Mather, 1968.

Author or co-author of science education bulletins issued by U.S. Office of Education, 1948-66. Contributor to yearbooks in education, and to science education journals.†

* * *

O'BRIEN, Frances (Kelly) 1906-

PERSONAL: Born October 7, 1906; daughter of James Joseph and Alice (Downing) Kelly; married William O'Brien, January 13, 1934; children: Dorothy Ann (Mrs. Louis Logue Doyle). Education: Teachers College of the City of Boston (now Boston State College), B.S. in Ed., 1928, Ed.M., 1929; summer study at Sorbonne, University of Paris, 1930, Middlebury College, 1956, 1960. Politics: Republican. Religion: Roman Catholic. Home: 120 Hillside Ave., Needham Heights, Mass. 02194.

CAREER: Teacher of French in Boston and Newton, Mass., in earlier years; Wellesley High School, Wellesley, Mass., teacher of French, beginning 1954. Member: American Association of Teachers of French, National Education Association, Massachusetts Teachers Association, Amicale of Middlebury.

WRITINGS: (With James Etmekjion and Raymond Caefer) Speaking French, Allyn & Bacon, 1963; (with J. Etmekjion and R. Caefer) Le Francais Courant I, Allyn & Bacon, 1964.

AVOCATIONAL INTERESTS: Attending the theater.††

* * *

O'CONNOR, Sister Mary Catharine (Catharine Farrell)

PERSONAL: Born in Newark, N.J.; daughter of William Farrell (a business executive) and Mary Catherine (Brady) O'Connor. Education: College of St. Elizabeth, A.B., 1917; Fordham University, A.M., 1924; Columbia University, Ph.D., 1940. Politics: Republican. Home: College of St. Elizabeth, Convent Station, N.J.

CAREER: Roman Catholic nun; Academy of St. Elizabeth, Convent Station, N.J., teacher, 1920-24; College of St. Elizabeth, Convent Station, instructor, 1924-30, assistant professor, 1930-35, professor of English, 1935-69, professor emeritus, 1969—, chairman of department, 1952-69, member of board of trustees, 1940-46, 1962-67. Member: Modern Language Association of America, National Council of Teachers of English, English Graduate Union of Columbia University. Awards, honors: D.H.L. from College of St. Elizabeth, 1974.

WRITINGS: The Art of Dying Well: The Development of the Ars Moriendi, Columbia University Press, 1942; The Kinderbeast Prize, Sheed, 1962. Contributor of short stories and articles to Catholic World, Ave Maria, Critic, and under name Catharine Farrell to New Yorker.

SIDELIGHTS: Sister O'Connor reads French, German, Spanish, and Latin.

* * *

O'DEA, Thomas F(rancis) 1915-1974

PERSONAL: Born December 1, 1915, in Amesbury, Mass.; son of Patrick Joseph (a merchant) and Mary (Quinn) O'Dea; married Georgia Stillman, June 5, 1936; married second wife, Janet Koffler (a researcher and teacher), August 5, 1967. Education: Harvard University, A.B. (summa cum laude), 1949, M.A., 1951, Ph.D., 1953. *Religion:* Roman Catholic. *Home:* 420 Rosario Dr., Santa Barbara, Calif. 93105. *Office:* University of California, Santa Barbara, Calif. 93106.

CAREER: Massachusetts Institute of Technology, Cambridge, Carnegie fellow in sociology, 1951-53, assistant professor of sociology, 1953-56; Fordham University, New York City, associate professor of sociology, 1956-59; University of Utah, Salt Lake City, professor of sociology, 1959-64; Columbia University, New York City, professor of sociology and religion, 1964-66, chairman of department of religion, 1965-66; University of California, Santa Barbara, professor of sociology and religious studies, beginning 1967, director of Institute of Religious Studies. Fellow, Center for Advanced Study in the Behavioral Sciences, Stanford University, 1955-56. Consultant and researcher on social change in Saudi Arabia, Arabian American Oil Co., 1963. *Military service:* U.S. Army Air Forces, 1943-45; served in North Africa, India, China, Australia, and the Marianas; received Silver Star and Distinguished Unit Badge. *Member:* Phi Beta Kappa.

WRITINGS: The Sociology of Mormonism, M.I.T. Press, 1955; *The Mormons,* University of Chicago Press, 1957; *American Catholic Dilemma,* Sheed, 1958; *The Sociology of Religion,* Prentice-Hall, 1966; *The Catholic Crisis,* Beacon, 1968; *Alienation, Atheism, and the Religious Crisis,* Sheed, 1969; *Sociology and the Study of Religion: Theory, Research, Interpretation,* Basic Books, 1970; (with others) *Religion and Man: Judaism, Christianity, and Islam,* Harper, 1972; (editor with wife, Janet K. O'Dea) *Readings on the Sociology of Religion,* Prentice-Hall, 1973. Contributor to *Encyclopedia Americana, New Catholic Encyclopedia,* and *International Encyclopedia of the Social Sciences;* also contributor to anthologies, professional journals, and magazines.

SIDELIGHTS: O'Dea lived in Mexico, Ireland, and Saudi Arabia, and traveled also in Canada and Europe.

BIOGRAPHICAL/CRITICAL SOURCES: Christian Century, August 28, 1968; *Commonweal,* October 11, 1968.†

(Died November 12, 1974)

*　　*　　*

OLDFIELD, R(ichard) C(harles)   1909-1972

PERSONAL: Born September 26, 1909, in London, England; son of Sir Francis (a lawyer) and Frances (Cayley) Oldfield; married Lady Kathleen Balfour, August 23, 1933; children: Frances Elizabeth (Mrs. Roderick Whitfield), Margaret Cayley (Mrs. Agbo Folarin). *Education:* Peterhouse College, Cambridge, B.A., 1931, M.A., 1935; Oxford University, M.A., 1946. *Politics:* None. *Religion:* None. *Home:* Woodhall Cottage, Pencaitland, East Lothian, Scotland.

CAREER: Leverhulme research student in industrial psychology, 1936; Rockefeller research fellow in psychology, 1938; Oxford University, Oxford, England, lecturer in psychology, 1946-50, director of Institute of Experimental Psychology and professor of psychology, 1956-66, fellow of Magdalen College; University of Reading, Reading, England, professor of psychology, 1950-56; Medical Research Council, Edinburgh, Scotland, director of speech and communication research unit, beginning 1966. Honorary professor, University of Edinburgh, 1967. *Military service:* Royal Air Force Volunteer Reserve, Radar Branch, 1941-46; be-

came flight lieutenant; mentioned in dispatches. *Member:* Experimental Psychology Society, Royal Society of Medicine, Royal Automobile Club.

WRITINGS: Psychology of the Interview, Methuen, 1941; (editor with J. C. Marshall) *Language,* Penguin, 1968. Contributor to scientific journals. *Quarterly Journal of Experimental Psychology,* editor, 1947-49, associate editor, 1949-56.

WORK IN PROGRESS: The Pathology of Language.

AVOCATIONAL INTERESTS: Gardening.†

(Died April 27, 1972)

*　　*　　*

OLIVER, G(uillaume) Raymond   1909-

PERSONAL: Born March 27, 1909, in Langon, Gironde, France; son of Louis (a hotel owner) and Cecile (Cavernes) Oliver; married Mari Tsunoda, July, 1972; children: (previous marriage) Michel, Dominique, Chantal, Sophie. *Education:* Attended College de Jesuites and Ecole superieure de Talence. *Home:* 156 Rue de Rivoli, Paris, France. *Office:* 17 Rue de Beaujolais, Paris 1, France.

CAREER: Owner of Hotel Oliver and Hotel Lion d'Or, in Langon, France, and of Grand Vefour, in Paris, France, since 1948. *Military service:* Armee de l'Air, pilot. *Member:* Institute of Directors, Comite du Palais Royal (president), Club Paul Tissandier, Number Ten Club. *Awards, honors:* Chevalier de la Legion d'Honneur; Chevalier des Palmes academiques; Commandeur du Merite agricole et du Merite touristique; Commandeur de Saint-Georges; Gold Medal of the city of Bordeaux; Silver Medal of the city of Paris; Medaille de vermeil Arts-Sciences-Lettres.

WRITINGS: Art et magie de la cuisine, translation by Ambrose Heath published as *The Art and Magic of Cookery,* Muller, 1959; *La Cuisine pour les hommes,* translation by Carol Chevalier published as *A Man's Cookbook,* Muller, 1959; *La Gastronomie a travers le monde,* Hachette, 1963, translation by Claude Durrell published as *Gastronomy of France,* World Publishing, 1967; *La Cuisine a quatre vents,* Flammarion, 1963; (with Edouard Longue) *La Cuisine du bonheur,* Casterman, 1964; *La Cuisine,* Bordas, 1965, abridged version published as *Mes Recettes preferees,* 1967, translated and edited by Nika Standen Hazelton and Jack van Bibber, Tudor, 1969; *Agenda de la cuisine francais,* Bordas, 1965; *The French at Table,* M. Joseph, 1967; *Classic Sauces,* M. Joseph, 1968. Also author of *Celebration de la nouille.* Collaborator for O.R.T.F., the French television network, notably with "La Cuisine a quatre mains," a television show, since 1953.

WORK IN PROGRESS: The most important and most complete collection of books on cuisine, approximately seven thousand books.

AVOCATIONAL INTERESTS: Painting and drawing, collecting ceramics, aviation, fishing, riding.

BIOGRAPHICAL/CRITICAL SOURCES: Best Sellers, October 1, 1967; *Listener,* December 28, 1967.

*　　*　　*

O'LOUGHLIN, Carleen

PERSONAL: Born in Liverpool, England. *Education:* Cambridge University, B.A., M.A., and M.Sc.; Australian National University, Ph.D. *Permanent address:* c/o Clare Hall, Herschel Rd., Cambridge, England.

CAREER: Formerly teacher of economics at Massey University of Manawatu, Palmerston North, New Zealand; Food and Agriculture Organization, Rome, Italy, section chief, 1966-68; University of Ghana, Institute of Statistical, Social and Economic Research, Legon, director, 1969-71; World Bank, Washington, D.C., economic consultant, beginning 1971.

WRITINGS: Economics of Sea Transport, Pergamon, 1967; *Economic and Political Change in the Leeward and Windward Islands*, Yale University Press, 1968; *National Economic Accounting*, Pergamon, 1970.†

(Deceased)

* * *

OLSEN, R(obert) Arthur 1910-

PERSONAL: Born December 1, 1910, in Brooklyn, N.Y.; son of Martinius (a seaman) and Clara (Hansen) Olsen; married Helen Fehleisen, June 25, 1938; children: Karen Marie. *Education:* New York University, B.S., 1939, M.A., 1940, Ed.D., 1942. *Religion:* Lutheran. *Home:* 1333 Parkview Dr., Macomb, Ill. 61455. *Office address:* P.O. Box 202, Macomb, Ill. 61455.

CAREER: Teaching principal in Elwood, N.Y., 1935-37; instructor in social science in North Merrick, N.Y., 1937-43; Pratt Institute, Brooklyn, N.Y., instructor in geography, 1943-44; Rayonier, Inc. (wood cellulose), New York, N.Y., production worker, 1944-47; Western Illinois University, Macomb, beginning 1947, began as assistant professor, became professor of economics, professor emeritus, 1970—. Illinois State Education Office, consultant in economic education. *Member:* American Economic Association, American Academy of Political and Social Science, National Education Association, Association for Higher Education (director, Illinois conference, 1968), Missouri Economic Association, Illinois Council for Social Studies (executive board member, 1968; president, 1970), Mason.

WRITINGS: Introduction to Sociology, edited by James Bossard, Stackpole, 1952; *Knowing Your Community*, Western Illinois University Press, 1959; (with J. H. Dodd and John W. Kennedy) *Applied Economics*, 6th edition (not associated with earlier editions), South-Western Publishing, 1962, 8th edition, 1972; *Understanding NATO at the Secondary School Level*, Western Illinois University Press, 1963; *Development in Economic Education*, Superintendent of Public Instruction (Illinois), 1966. Contributor to educational journals.

AVOCATIONAL INTERESTS: Photography, world travel, gardening.

* * *

O'NEAL, Charles E. 1904-

PERSONAL: Born January 6, 1904, in Raeford, N.C.; son of Charles Samuel (a salesman) and Elizabeth M. (Duffy) O'Neal; married Patricia R. O'Callaghan (an actress), April 20, 1941; children: Ryan, Kevin. *Education:* Attended University of Iowa, 1923-28. *Politics:* "Reformed Democrat (now Republican)." *Religion:* Roman Catholic. *Agent:* Reece Halsey Agency, 8733 Sunset Blvd., Los Angeles, Calif. 90069.

CAREER: Free-lance writer, mostly for films and television. *Member:* Dramatists Guild, Authors Guild, Writers Guild of America, West. *Awards, honors:* Christopher Book Award, 1949, for *The Three Wishes of Jamie McRuin*.

WRITINGS: The Three Wishes of Jamie McRuin, Mess-

ner, 1949; (with Victor Trivas) *The Thirty-second Day*, Doubleday, 1964.

Plays: (With Abe Burrows) "Three Wishes for Jamie" (musical; adaptation of *The Three Wishes of Jamie McRuin*), produced, 1951; "Praise Hoyes," produced, 1953, but closed before reaching Broadway.

Films: "The Missing Juror," Columbia Pictures, 1944; "I Have a Mystery," Columbia Pictures, 1945; "Return of the Badmen," R.K.O., 1948; "Montana," Warner Bros., 1950; "Golden Girl," Twentieth Century-Fox, 1951.

Has written several scripts for "The Untouchables," "Lassie," and other programs.

WORK IN PROGRESS: Research for an Irish historical novel; a family novel "which could be longer than *War and Peace*."††

* * *

O NUALLAIN, Brian 1911-1966
(Brian Nolan, Brian O'Nolan; pseudonyms: Myles na Gopaleen [sometimes written na gCopaleen], Flann O'Brien)

PERSONAL: Born October 5, 1911, in Strabane, County Tyrone, Northern Ireland; moved to Dublin with his family while still a child; son of Michael Victor and Agnes (Gormley) O Nuallain; married Evelyn McDonnell, 1949. *Education:* University College, Dublin, M.A. (Celtic studies), 1929. *Home:* 21 Watersland Rd., Stillorgan, County Dublin, Ireland.

CAREER: While at University College, edited a magazine called *Blather;* Government of the Republic of Ireland, senior civil servant, serving four successive Ministers for Local Government, 1937-53; *Irish Times*, Dublin, columnist, writing "Cruiskeen Lawn" (sometimes in Latin or German; often in Irish) under the pseudonym Myles na Gopaleen, 1940-66.

WRITINGS—Novels; all under pseudonym Flann O'Brien, except where otherwise noted: *At Swim-Two-Birds*, Longmans, Green, 1939, Pantheon, 1951; (under pseudonym Myles na gCopaleen) *An Beal Bocht; no, An Milleanach*, National Press (Dublin), 1941, 3rd edition, Dolmen (Dublin), 1964, translation by Patrick C. Power published as *The Poor Mouth: A Bad Story about the Hard Life*, Viking, 1974; *The Hard Life: An Exegesis of Squalor*, MacGibbon & Kee, 1961, Pantheon, 1962; *The Dalkey Archive*, MacGibbon & Kee, 1964, Macmillan, 1965; *The Third Policeman* (written in 1940), MacGibbon & Kee, 1967, Walker & Co., 1969.

Others: "Thirst" (sketch), originally written for Edwards-MacLiammoir Show at Gate Theatre, 1942, rewritten for radio and television; "The Insect Play" (adapted from Capek), produced in Dublin, 1943; *Faustus Kelly* (play; first produced in Dublin at Abbey Theatre, 1943), Cahill & Co., 1943; *The Best of Myles* (selections from his *Irish Times* columns; includes one section in Irish), edited by his brother, Kevin O'Nolan, Walker & Co., 1968; *Stories and Plays* (contains selected chapters from an unfinished novel, "The Great Sago Saga," as well as work previously published elsewhere), MacGibbon & Kee, 1973; *Myles: Portraits of Brian O'Nolan*, edited by T. O'Keeffe, Martin Brian & O'Keeffe, 1973.

SIDELIGHTS: O'Nolan, according to Saul Maloff, "is like no one else." He was compared to Joyce, Nabokov, even John Barth. One character in *At Swim-Two-Birds* (the title itself was a blitz on Irish place names) discussed the form which the novel should take: "A satisfactory novel should be a self-evident sham to which the reader could regulate at will the degree of his credulity. It was undemocratic to compel characters to be uniformly good or bad or poor or rich. Each should be allowed a private life, self-determination and a decent standard of living.... Characters should be interchangeable as between one book and another. The entire corpus of existing literature should be regarded as a limbo from which discerning authors could draw their characters as required, creating only when they failed to find a suitable existing puppet." As Vivian Mercier pointed out, "whether he believed in these principles or not, Mr. O'Nolan certainly acted upon them.... By doing so, [he] contrived a method of demonstrating that the realistic novel, the moralizing novel spiced with sin, the Western cowboy yarn, the hero-tale, the myth, the folk or fairy tale, each has its own equally valid or invalid convention, its own formula. Each formula in turn is illustrated and then parodied. It is hardly possible to conceive a more purely *literary* use of oral and traditional material than that made by the author of *At Swim-Two-Birds.*"

In other words, as Benedict Kiely said, O'Nolan "plays whack with the novel"; resultantly, he produced some of the most fantastic fiction of our time. Timothy Hilton called *At Swim-Two-Birds* "the most purely comic book of the century." Anthony Burgess also believed that the novel was "one of the 10 great comic books of the century," and, he added, "it is one of the five outrageous fictional experiments of all time to come completely and triumphantly off." In *At Swim-Two-Birds* O'Nolan was writing a novel about an undergraduate at University College (identified only as "I") who was writing a novel about one Dermot Trellis, an Irish novelist who perfected the technique of "aestho-autogamy" and was therefore able to create his characters so literally that they actually came to life. Trellis then used this technique to write a novel about, among others, Pooka Fergus MacPhellimey who, in the course of his "life" within Trellis' novel, begins a novel about Trellis. This last work was thus a novel within a novel, within a novel, within a novel! That the book satirized the realistic, conventional novel can hardly be disputed. Hilton wrote: "*At Swim-Two-Birds* has been one of those books doomed to an underground existence, with treasured copies lent only to trusted friends.... It remains the property of isolated bunches of cognoscenti. They hold readings from it round kitchen tables. They huddle giggling, in the corners of bars. They—quite literally—know extensive passages by heart, and use it for hours of jesting." Maloff, who called the novel a "frenetic, dazzling, unconscionably funny ... underground classic," wrote: "[O'Nolan's] crown jewel was the sort of book one stumbled across, glanced at, fell in love with, borrowed with the solemn promise to return, and then chose exile rather than do so."

The Third Policeman, written contemporaneously with *At Swim-Two-Birds* but published posthumously, was according to John Raymond, "a dark riotous fantasy, a grim feast of allegorical clowning or a bogsong with shamanic variations—anything you please but a novel." Burgess noted that the speech of the characters in this novel was "Irish solecistic sesquipedalian to the ultimate power." O'Nolan's attack on both the form and the language of the traditional novel consisted in his creation of "a whole bogus scholarship," Burgess wrote, "centred on the writings of an impossible savant called de Selby." The narrator, again called only "I" (because, said Maloff, "he has forgotten his name

and lost his identity"), was obsessed with the teachings of de Selby and filled his story with dense footnotes which sometimes ran to several pages. O'Nolan's "sense of humour is a sharp instrument; it penetrates the myth, its explicable and implacable violence and desolation, leaves it intact and makes it comic" according to Hilton. He added: "One feels that [O'Nolan] could not bring himself to believe in the real world at all. His prose is the equal of his doubts, at its best in the succession of hauntingly wild fantasies that deny the existence of matter, that existence matters." Kay Dick concluded that O'Nolan has simply "[introduced] an almost new perspective to the art of definition."

In 1940 O'Nolan became involved in a literary dispute chronicled in the *Irish Times* correspondence section. As a result, the editor of the *Times* engaged him to write a daily column. These columns delighted Irish readers for 26 years and served as a vehicle for some of O'Nolan's most brilliant writing. Mercier told of one wonderful series which recorded the adventures of the rather decadent companion poets Keats and Chapman. "The story which inaugurated this series," Mercier wrote, "tells how Keats and ... Chapman were medical students together; Chapman's pet homing pigeon fell ill of a throat ailment, and Keats was asked for a medical opinion; after carefully examining the bird, he wrote that immortal sonnet, 'On First Looking into Chapman's Homer.'" Mercier recalled another memorable column in which O'Nolan remarked that "two famous Dublin scholars had proved that there were two Saint Patricks and no God." The columnist O'Nolan was also deeply concerned with the invention of useful machinery. On one occasion, Hilton noted, Myles was working on a device for "collecting, measuring and storing the *neiges d'antan.*" O'Nolan continued to sign his column Myles na Gopaleen long after his identity was well known to the Irish (who revered him as "The Sage of Santry"). The name Myles na Gopaleen, according to O'Nolan's English publishers, Mssrs MacGibbon & Kee, was originally used in Gerald Griffin's novel, *The Collegians.* It was also used in *The Colleen Bawn,* by Dion Boucicault, and in Sir Julius Benedict's opera, "Lily of Killarney." The name was usually translated as Myles of the Little Horses, but Kiely related this story: "Once I referred to [O'Nolan] in print under one of his personalities, as Myles of the Little Horses. He refuted me in a considerable article pointing out that the name meant Myles of the Ponies, and [called] forth authors, ancient and modern, to defend the autonomy of the pony against the imperialism of the horse. That was his way."

When O'Nolan died in 1966, there were few outside Ireland who recognized his name(s). Burgess wrote: "What a fuss the French anti-novelists make about their tedious exercises in *chosisme;* how little fuss has been made about Flann O'Brien's humour, humanity, metaphysics, theology, bawdry, mythopoeia, word-play and six-part counterpoint." In *The Dalkey Archive* (which Brigid Brophy called "one of Irish literature's grand triumphs"), O'Nolan stated that James Joyce is not dead at all; he lives in a small Irish town, works as a bartender, attends Mass daily, and is embarrassed by his Parisian past. Miss Brophy duly noted that O'Nolan died on All Fools' Day, 1966. But, she added, "no preposterousness would more delight me than that he should have done no such thing but be working in a restaurant in Dublin (*specialite de la maison:* Flann O'Brien)."

Hugh Leonard's play, "When the Saints Go Cycling In," is a dramatization of *The Dalkey Archive;* it was first produced for the Dublin Theatre Festival in 1965.

As noted above, O'Nolan was competent in English, Gaelic

(and dialectal Irish), Greek, Latin, and German. It is said that he once wrote his *Times* column in Irish transliterated into Greek script. That was his way.

BIOGRAPHICAL/CRITICAL SOURCES: Vivian Mercier, *The Irish Comic Tradition*, Clarendon, 1962; *New York Times*, April 2, 1966; *New York Herald Tribune*, April 3, 1966; *Observer*, September 3, 1967; *Punch*, September 6, 1967; *Spectator*, September 15, 1967; *Listener*, September 28, 1967; *Books and Bookmen*, November, 1967; *New York Times Book Review*, November 12, 1967; *New Statesman*, December 8, 1967; *Newsweek*, January 1, 1968; Carolyn Riley, editor, *Contemporary Literary Criticism*, Gale, Volume I, 1973, Volume IV, 1975, Volume V, 1976, Volume VII, 1977.†

(Died April 1, 1966)

* * *

ORTMAN, E(lmore) Jan 1884-
(Elmer John Ortman)

PERSONAL: Born August 29, 1884, in Crescent City, Ill.; son of William Frederick (a farmer) and Ernstina (Bachus) Ortman; married Esther Anna Wabel (a former teacher), June 25, 1908; children: Garwood Elmore, Roberta Ernstina (Mrs. Charles Newell Dauton). *Education:* Callow Business College, graduated as commercial accountant, 1900; Illinois State Normal University (now Illinois State University), Life Teaching Certificate, 1912; University of Oregon, B.A., 1917; Columbia University, M.A., 1918, Ph.D., 1921. *Politics:* Independent. *Religion:* Presbyterian.

CAREER: Teacher, principal, and then superintendent in various school systems, 1900-17; college dean, 1920-23; college founder and president, 1923-28; University of Oklahoma, Norman, professor of philosophical principles of education, beginning 1928; University of California, Los Angeles, professor of philosophical principles of education, until 1950. Law worker in Presbyterian churches for more than fifty years. *Member:* Phi Delta Kappa, Kappa Delta Pi.

WRITINGS—Under name Elmer John Ortman: *To Rear the Tender Thought: The Autobiography of a Modern Educator*, Exposition Press, 1962; *Philosophy of Teaching*, Philosophical Library, 1962; *Challenges of Democracy*, Philosophical Library, 1968. Contributor to magazines and newspapers.

WORK IN PROGRESS: Jesus, My Advocate; an expanded edition of *Challenges of Democracy.*

SIDELIGHTS: Elmore Ortman is a longtime amateur actor. He told *CA* that he is also "deeply interested in landscaping, home decorating, poetry (hold 1000 bits of poetry in mind now). . . . Have taken thousands of colored movies and still pictures. Have written a dozen lectures on democracy and its historicity, helped along with my own pictures. Am very fond of athletics, and fishing for muskies, northern pike, and walleyes in the lakes of northern Minnesota and southern Canada."†

* * *

OSBORN, James M(arshall) 1906-1976

PERSONAL: Born April 22, 1906, in Cleveland, Ohio; son of Clare Marshall (a civil engineer) and Mildred (Sleeper) Osborn; married Marie-Louise Montgomery, November 20, 1929 (died, 1968); children: J. Marshall, Jr., Thomas M. *Education:* Wesleyan University, Middletown, Conn., B.A., 1928; Columbia University, M.A., 1934; Oxford University, B.Litt., 1937. *Home:* 123 York St., Apt. 12A, New Haven, Conn. 06511. *Office:* 1914 Yale Station, New Haven, Conn.

CAREER: Guaranty Trust Co., New York, N.Y., investment adviser, 1928-32; Yale University, New Haven, Conn., research associate in English literature, 1938-72, fellow of Silliman College, 1957-76, curator of Osborn Collection, now housed in Beinecke Library, 1962-72, curator emeritus, 1972-76. Visiting lecturer in English literature, Wesleyan University, Middletown, Conn., 1939-40; director of training programs, Connecticut State War Council, 1941-44; fellow, St. Catherine's College, Oxford University, 1968-76. Owner of Whirlwind Hill Farm, Wallingford, Conn., and breeder of registered Holsteins, 1940-59. Member of executive committee, National Municipal League, beginning 1954; New Haven Symphony, member of board of directors, beginning 1957, vice-president, beginning 1963; vice-president, New Haven Free Public Library, beginning 1959.

MEMBER: Modern Language Association of America, Modern Humanities Research Association, English Institute (trustee), Bibliographical Society (London), Society of Antiquaries (London; fellow), Royal Society of Arts (London; fellow), Oxford Bibliographical Society, Connecticut Academy of Arts and Sciences, Johnson Club of London, Johnsonians (New York), Athenaeum Club (London), Metropolitan Club and Grolier Club (both New York), Graduates Club, Lawn Club, Elizabethan Club, and Mory's (all New Haven). *Awards, honors:* National Municipal League distinguished citation award, 1962; D.H.L., Kenyon College, 1963; D.Litt. from Oxford University, 1968, and McGill University, 1972.

WRITINGS: Dryden Facts and Problems, University of Colorado Press, 1940, revised edition, University of Florida Press, 1965; *The Beginnings of Autobiography in England*, University of California Press, 1959; (editor) *The Autobiography of Thomas Whythorne, 1528-1596*, Oxford University Press, 1961, modern spelling edition, 1962; (editor) Joseph Spence, *Observations, Anecdotes, and Characters of Books and Men*, two volumes, Oxford University Press, 1966; *Young Philip Sidney*, Yale University Press, 1972. Also author of *Holstein Handbook*, 1947. Contributor of articles on literary and agricultural topics to journals. Editor of *Work in Progress in the Modern Humanities*, 1932-42, *Seventeenth Century News-Letter*, 1942-46, and *New England Holstein Bulletin*, 1943-46.

WORK IN PROGRESS: Two books, *The Boswell-Malone Correspondence*, and *A Life of Edmond Malone, 1741-1812.*

SIDELIGHTS: James Osborn began building up the Osborn Collection of literary and historical manuscripts in 1934. Four years later he acquired the Joseph Spence papers, sold by the Duke of Newcastle at Sothebys; the papers are considered to be the richest collection of literary memorabilia of their time. According to Werner Bamberger, Osborn's other literary accomplishments included the discoveries of "the earliest known autobiography in English" and of a "hitherto unknown manuscript" by Thomas Traherne.

BIOGRAPHICAL/CRITICAL SOURCES: Book Collector, winter, 1959; *Times Literary Supplement*, February 2, 1967; *Yale Review*, summer, 1967; *New York Times*, October 19, 1976.

(Died October 17, 1976)

* * *

OSBORNE, George E(dward) 1893-

PERSONAL: Born June 11, 1893, near Akron, Colo.; son of

George E. (an educator) and Mary Catherine (Morrison) Osborne. *Education:* University of California, Berkeley, A.B., 1916; Harvard University, LL.B., 1919, S.J.D., 1920. *Home:* Bohemian Club, 624 Taylor, San Francisco, Calif. 94102.

CAREER: Admitted to Massachusetts Bar, 1919; West Virginia University, Morgantown, assistant professor of law, 1920-21; University of Minnesota, Minneapolis, associate professor of law, 1921-23; Stanford University, Stanford, Calif., professor of law, 1923-58, William Nelson Cromwell Professor, 1953-58, professor emeritus, 1958—; University of California, Hastings College of Law, San Francisco, professor of law, beginning 1959. Visiting professor, Duke University, 1931-32; Charles Inglis Thompson Professor of Law, University of Colorado, 1953; summer visiting professor at Columbia University, 1923, University of Chicago, 1927, University of Washington, Seattle, 1933, University of California, 1953. Chairman of commissions to set national minimum wages for railway carriers, motor carriers, and lumber and clay products industries, 1939-43; mediator for National War Labor Board, 1943-45; arbitrator in various labor and commercial disputes, 1946, member of President's railroad emergency boards, 1949, 1952.

MEMBER: American Bar Association, Phi Beta Kappa, Phi Delta Phi, Bohemian Club, Menlo Country Club, Palo Alto Club (president, 1956), Stanford Faculty Club (president, 1947), University of California Faculty Club, Harvard Club (San Francisco). *Awards, honors:* LL.D. from University of California, Berkeley, 1966.

WRITINGS—All published by West Publishing, except as indicated: *Cases on Property Security,* 1940, 2nd edition, 1954; *Text on Mortgages,* 1951; *American Law of Property,* Volume IV, Little, Brown, 1952; (with Henry M. Ballantine) *Law Problems,* 1956; *Cases on Suretyship,* 1966; *Cases on Secured Transactions,* 1967. Contributor of notes, articles, and reviews to law periodicals, Editor-in-chief, *Harvard Law Review,* 1918-19.

WORK IN PROGRESS: Revising *Text on Mortgages.*

*   *   *

O SIOCHAIN, P(adraig) A(ugustine)   1905-
(Patrick Augustine Sheehan)

PERSONAL: Born May 26, 1905, in Cork, Ireland; son of Daniel Desmond (a member of Parliament, barrister-at-law, and editor), and Mary (O'Connor) Sheehan; married Marjorie Griffin, June 30, 1931; children: Niall, Donal, Orla, Parra, Ruairi. *Education:* Attended Capuchin College and Farranferris College, Cork, Ireland, five years, and University of London, three years; University College of Dublin, Barrister-at-Law, 1936. *Politics:* Labour-Socialist-Nationalist. *Religion:* Roman Catholic. *Home:* 44 Paire Rathfearnan, Dublin, Ireland.

CAREER: Part-time reporter for *Daily Sketch,* London, England, and *Enniscorthy Echo,* Wexford, Ireland, 1923-24; reporter in Dublin, Ireland, for *Irish Times,* 1925-31, and *Irish Press,* 1931-32; *Garda Review* (official journal of Irish National Police Force), Dublin, editor, beginning 1932; The Law Courts, Dublin, barrister-at-law and senior counsel, beginning 1936. Chairman of board of directors, Galway Bay Products Ltd. (exporters of handcrafts and knitwear). *Military service:* Irish Army Local Defence Force, 1940-46. *Member:* Honorable Society of the King's Inns, P.E.N., Grange Golf Club, Dublin Gliding Club.

WRITINGS: (Under name Patrick Augustine Sheehan) *Dli*

Coiriuil na hEireann (title means "Criminal Law of Ireland"), Ofig an tSolathair, 1940 (subsequent editions under name P. A. O Siochain), 5th edition, 1966; *Dli na Fianaise in Eireann* (title means "Law of Evidence Practice and Procedure in Ireland"), Ofig an tSolathair, 1953; *Aran Islands of Legend,* Foilsiuchain Eireann, 1962, Devin, 1963. Contributor to *Irish Aviation, New Irish Magazine, International Criminal Police Review,* and other periodicals.

WORK IN PROGRESS: A book on aviation pioneers, and the first attempts and successes in transatlantic aviation, which he covered as air correspondent; personal viewpoints on the Irish political scene since 1925; a popular history of Irish Celts.

SIDELIGHTS: Both of P. A. O Siochain's law books have been officially translated into Gaelic. He is "dedicated to the restoration of Gaelic in Ireland." He is the founder of National Language Revival Movement.††

*   *   *

OSTRINSKY, Meir Simha   1906-

PERSONAL: Born July 7, 1906, in Poland; son of Joel (a businessman) and Sarah Jessica (Novor) Ostrinsky; married Martha Krawitz, December 7, 1941; children: Renah, Avi, Sarah Jessica. *Education:* New York University, B.S., 1934; Yeshiva University, rabbinical degree, 1941. *Politics:* "Religious Zionist." *Religion:* Jewish Orthodox. *Home:* 2639 East 24th St., Brooklyn, N.Y. 11235.

CAREER: Ordained as rabbi, 1941; Congregation B'nai Israel, Sheepshead Bay, Brooklyn, N.Y., rabbi, beginning 1947. *Member:* Rabbinical Conference of America (president), Flatbush Board of Rabbis, Religious Zionist Chapter of Sheepshead Bay (president).

WRITINGS: Sambatyon-2: A Documentary Novel, Bloch Publishing, 1970.††

*   *   *

OTTEMILLER, John H(enry)   1916-1968

PERSONAL: Born September 17, 1916, in York, Pa.; son of Walter Franklin and Maude (Robey) Ottemiller; married Frances Tompson (director of Shoe String Press, Inc.), March 24, 1943; children: Joan, John T. *Education:* Middlebury College, A.B., 1938; Columbia University, B.S. in L.S., 1940. *Politics:* Republican. *Religion:* Protestant. *Office:* Yale University Library, 120 High St., New Haven, Conn. 06520.

CAREER: New York (N.Y.) Public Library, assistant in Preparations Division, 1939-40; Columbia University Library, New York, N.Y., circulation and reference assistant, 1940-42; Brown University, Providence, R.I., assistant to librarian, 1942-44; U.S. Office of Strategic Services, Washington, D.C., assistant to chief, later section chief of interdepartmental Committee for Acquisition of Foreign Publications, 1944-45; U.S. Department of State, Washington, D.C., acting chief of Reference Division, 1946, chief, 1947, acting chief of Division of Library and Reference Services, 1948-51; Yale University, New Haven, Conn., associate librarian, 1951-57, associate university librarian, 1957-68. Shoe String Press, Inc., Hamden, Conn., president, 1958-68. Instructor in library science at Simmons College, 1953-55, and Southern Connecticut State College, 1961, 1963, 1965. Member of U.S. Civil Service Commission of Expert Examiners, 1948-51. Founder and secretary-treasurer, Tompsons Malone, Inc., 1957-68.

MEMBER: Bibliographical Society of America, American

Library Association, New England Library Association (chairman of regional planning committee), Connecticut Library Association, Yale Library Associates, Alpha Sigma Phi, Mory's Association, Yale Club and Grolier Club (both New York).

WRITINGS: Index to Plays in Collections, 1900-1942, H. W. Wilson, 1943, 4th edition published as *Index to Plays in Collections, 1900-1962,* Scarecrow, 1964; *Yale's Selective Book Retirement Program,* Shoe String, 1963; (managing editor) *Who's Who in Library Service,* 4th edition, Shoe String, 1966. Contributor to library journals.†

(Died July 22, 1968)

* * *

OTTO, Henry J. 1901-

PERSONAL: Born March 20, 1901, in Brownton, Minn.; son of Christoph H. and Anna (Uecker) Otto; married Mildred Alice Wagner, August 18, 1932 (died, 1958); married Cecelia R. Henderson, April 6, 1963; children: (first marriage) Gordon, Byron. *Education:* Carleton College, B.A., 1923; University of Minnesota, M.A., 1927, Ph.D., 1931. *Home:* 3404 Windsor Rd., Austin, Tex. 78702. *Office:* University of Texas, Austin, Tex. 78712.

CAREER: High school teacher of science and mathematics in Long Prairie, Minn., 1923-25; superintendent of schools in Buffalo Lake, Minn., 1925-28; Northwestern University, Evanston, Ill., assistant professor of education, 1930-34; W. K. Kellogg Foundation, Battle Creek, Mich., consultant on education, 1934-42; University of Texas, Austin, professor of elementary curriculum and administration, 1942-69, professor emeritus, 1969—, chairman of department of educational administration, 1959-66. *Member:* American Association of School Administrators, American Educational Research Association, National Education Association (life member), Texas State Teachers Association. *Awards, honors:* Outstanding Achievement Award, University of Minnesota, 1951.

WRITINGS: Elementary School Organization and Administration, Appleton, 1934, 4th edition (with David C. Saunders), 1964; *Promotion Policies and Practices in Elementary Schools,* Educational Test Bureau, 1935; (with S. A. Hamrin) *Co-Curricular Activities in Elementary Schools,* Appleton, 1937.

(With others) *Community Workshops for Teachers,* University of Michigan Press, 1942; *Principles of Elementary Education,* Rinehart, 1949, revised edition (with Hazel Floyd and Margaret Rouse), 1955.

(With Thomas D. Horn and others) *Spelling Instruction: A Curriculum Wide Approach,* University of Texas Press, 1954; (with others) *Class Size Factors in Elementary Schools,* University of Texas Press, 1954; (editor) *Curriculum Enrichment for Gifted Elementary School Children in Regular Classes,* University of Texas Press, 1955; *Social Education in Elementary Schools,* Rinehart, 1956; (contributor) Clarence W. Hunnicutt, editor, *Education 2000 A.D.,* Syracuse University Press, 1956; (with others) *Four Methods of Reporting to Parents,* University of Texas Press, 1957; (with others) *Underage First Grade Enrollees: Their Achievement and Personal and Social Adjustment,* University of Texas Press, 1957; (with Bruce C. Browning) *Organization for Instructional Supervision in Elementary Schools,* College of Education, University of Texas, 1957; *Methods of Reporting Elementary School Children's Progress to Parents,* Texas Congress of Parents and Teachers,

1957; *You and Your Child's Report Card,* Compton, 1958; (with Frances Flournoy and others) *Meeting Individual Differences in Arithmetic,* University of Texas Press, 1959.

(With James M. Ward and John E. Suttle) *The Curriculum Integration Concept Applied in the Elementary School,* University of Texas Press, 1960; *The Education of the Exceptional Child in Casis School,* University of Texas Press, 1964.

Scripts for Coronet Instructional Films: "Sounds All About Us," 1954; "Light All About Us," 1954; "Air All About Us," 1955; "Understanding Our Universe," 1956; "What Do We See in the Sky," 1957; "The Moon and How It Affects Us," 1958; "The Sun and How It Affects Us," 1958. Contributor to *Dictionary of Education* and *Encyclopedia of Educational Research.* Contributor of more than 120 articles to education journals.

WORK IN PROGRESS: A monograph on value orientations in four elementary schools.†

* * *

OVERACKER, Louise 1891-

PERSONAL: Born November 18, 1891, in Centerville, Calif.; daughter of Howard (a farmer) and Louise (Matthews) Overacker. *Education:* Stanford University, A.B., 1915, A.M., 1917; University of Chicago, Ph.D., 1924. *Politics:* Democratic. *Home:* Building M 3, 110 Wood Rd., Los Gatos, Calif. 95030.

CAREER: Vassar College, Poughkeepsie, N.Y., instructor, 1920-22; Wilson College, Chambersburg, Pa., professor of political science, 1924-25; Wellesley College, Wellesley, Mass., assistant professor, 1925-31, associate professor, 1931-40, professor of political science, 1940-57, professor emeritus, 1957—. Bacon Lecturer, Boston University, 1945; visiting professor at Bethany College, Bethany, W.Va., 1957-58, University of California, Los Angeles, 1960-61, and Inter American University of Puerto Rico, 1963; visiting fellow at Australian National University, 1965. *Member:* American Political Science Association (second vice-president, 1939), Australasian Political Studies Association, American Academy of Arts and Sciences, Phi Beta Kappa. *Awards, honors:* Guggenheim fellowship, 1950.

WRITINGS: The Presidential Primary, Macmillan, 1926; (with C. E. Merriam) *Primary Elections,* University of Chicago Press, 1928; *Money in Elections,* Macmillan, 1932; *Presidential Campaign Funds* (Gaspar G. Bacon lecture), Boston University Press, 1946; *The Australian Party System,* Yale University Press, 1952; *Australian Parties in a Changing Society: 1945-67,* Verry, 1968.

WORK IN PROGRESS: Further research in Australian parties and politics.

SIDELIGHTS: Dr. Overacker has made three visits to Australia, two to New Zealand, and spent a year in England studying British political parties.

* * *

OWEN, William Vern 1894-

PERSONAL: Born September 3, 1894, in Tipton, Iowa; son of John Taylor (a businessman) and Myrtle Minerva (Neiman) Owen; married Bernice Winifred Johnson, June 5, 1919; children: Louise Carolyn. *Education:* Attended University of Iowa, 1914-15; University of Chicago, Ph.B., 1920; University of Wisconsin, Ph.M., 1924. *Home:* 9916 Columbus Circle N.W., Albuquerque, N.M. 87114.

CAREER: Purdue University, Lafayette, Ind., instructor, 1921-25, assistant professor, 1925-30, associate professor, 1930-39, professor of economics, 1939-63, Loeb Professor of Industrial Management, 1959-63, professor emeritus, 1963—; Reynolds Electrical and Engineering Co., Inc., Santa Fe, N.M., industrial relations specialist, 1963-71. Visiting professor, University of New Mexico, 1963-64. Arbitrator in labor disputes, 1948-63. *Military service:* U.S. Army, Medical Corps, 1917-19; became sergeant. *Member:* Industrial Relations Research Association.

WRITINGS: *Labor Problems,* Ronald, 1946; (with others) *Labor Management Economics,* Ronald, 1956; *Modern Management,* Ronald, 1958; (with Howard V. Finston) *Industrial Relations: Management, Labor, and Society,* Appleton, 1964. Contributor of numerous articles on industrial relations and industrial management to journals.†

* * *

PADDOCK, Paul (Ezekiel, Jr.)   1907-1975

PERSONAL: Born October 31, 1907, in Des Moines, Iowa; son of Paul Ezekiel and Sarah (Lee) Paddock. *Education:* Attended University of Minnesota, 1926-27; Princeton University, B.A., 1932; also studied at Canadian National Defence College, 1950-51. *Religion:* Presbyterian. *Home:* 9 Ober Rd., Princeton, N.J.

CAREER: Worked for business firms, 1934-37; U.S. Department of State, Foreign Service officer, 1937-58. Held posts in Mexico, 1937-38, Netherlands, East Indies, 1939-41, Australia, 1942, New Zealand, 1942-43, Morocco, 1943-44, Soviet Union, 1944-45, Afghanistan, 1946-47, Communist China, 1948-49, Korea, 1951-52, Malta, 1953-54, Laos, 1954-55, and the Philippines, 1955; also assigned to two General Assemblies of United Nations, 1956-58. Member of board of directors, Time Insurance Co., Milwaukee, Wis. *Member:* Overseas Press Club and Princeton Club (both New York), University Club (Washington, D.C.), Nassau Club (Princeton).

WRITINGS—With brother, William Paddock: *Hungry Nations,* Little, Brown, 1964; *Famine, 1975—America's Decision: Who Will Survive?,* Little, Brown, 1967.

WORK IN PROGRESS: *Time of Famine: America and the Continuing Food Crisis.*

SIDELIGHTS: In her review of *Famine, 1975,* Henrietta Buckmaster wrote: "It is very hard for the average person, or even the specialist, to grasp the fact that the world is faced with a catastrophe even more terrible than nuclear holocaust—worldwide famine. The warning signals have been going up for a long time, but even those who know the intensity of the situation have tried to stave off alarm by the somewhat desperate optimism—'some answer will turn up.' Only the date is speculative. . . . The Paddocks set 1975 as the year when 'the worst famine in history will be nearing its peak.' . . . The Paddocks end on a demoralizing note. They claim some countries cannot be saved, and they put India at the top of the list." A. John Giunta noted that the Paddocks suggest that we classify all needy countries into three categories, similar to the "triage" system used by doctors treating battlefield casualties. "Those countries which cannot improve their condition, even with our help, . . . should be dropped from our list of food recipients; those that can improve their condition with our help will have first priority to our food surplus; the third group, which may not have reached famine level as yet, would have to manage for themselves." Miss Buckmaster suggested that the Paddocks have, at times, neglected their responsibility to accurate sta-

tistical analysis. However, she added, "the book is . . . a fireball in the night to which we should give instant heed. Its warning message should be read as far as possible and *demand* the imagination and inspiration which are deeply needed as the source of practical answers. This is a rare instance in which the ideal and the practical must move as one, and must move over the face of the earth."

Paddock's more unconventional travels included a trip by small boat down the west coast of Africa from Tangier to Portuguese Guinea, and an overland journey from Moscow to Kabul, through central Asia. He was competent in Spanish and French and studied several other languages.

BIOGRAPHICAL/CRITICAL SOURCES: *Best Sellers,* June 1, 1967; *Christian Science Monitor,* November 9, 1967.†

(Died August 29, 1975)

* * *

PAGE, Robert Morris   1903-

PERSONAL: Born June 2, 1903, in St. Paul, Minn.; son of Clarence Quincy (a farmer and minister) and Lillian (Wintermute) Page; married Signe Astrid Benson, 1928 (divorced, 1962); married Esther Cornelia Strand Britt, March 21, 1963; children: (first marriage) John Robert; (stepchildren) Donald Victor Britt. *Education:* Hamline University, B.S., 1927; George Washington University, M.A., 1932. *Politics:* Independent. *Religion:* Christian. *Home:* 10222 Berkshire Rd., Bloomington, Minn. 55437.

CAREER: U.S. Naval Research Laboratory, Washington, D.C., physicist, 1927-38, physicist and head of Radar Research Section, 1938-45, superintendent of Radio Division III, 1945-52, associate director of research in electronics, 1952-57, director of research, 1957-66. U.S. Office of Scientific Research and Development, civilian scientist, 1943-46. Played a major role in development of radar in United States and holds seventy-five patents in precision electronics.

MEMBER: Institute of Electrical and Electronics Engineers (fellow; chairman of Washington section, 1958-59), American Association for the Advancement of Science (fellow), American Scientific Affiliation (fellow), Scientific Research Society of America, Franklin Institute (life fellow), Washington Academy of Sciences. *Awards, honors:* D.Sc., Hamline University, 1943; Distinguished Civilian Service Award, U.S. Navy, 1945; Presidential Certificate of Merit, 1946; Harry Diamond Memorial Award of Institute of Radio Engineers, 1953; Stuart Ballantine Medal of Franklin Institute, 1957; Captain Robert Dexter Conrad Award, U.S. Navy, 1959; Distinguished Federal Civilian Service Award (presidential), 1960; Centennial Award, Wheaton College, Wheaton, Ill., 1960; W. Randolf Lovelace II Award, 1967; George Washington University alumni achievement award, 1967.

WRITINGS: (Contributor) John C. Monsma, editor, *Evidence of God in an Expanding Universe,* Putnam, 1958; (contributor) *Airborne Radar,* Van Nostrand, 1961; *The Origin of Radar,* Doubleday, 1962. Contributor to *Harper Encyclopedia of Science, Crowell-Collier Young People's Encyclopedia, Zondervan Pictorial Encyclopedia of the Bible,* to society proceedings and to professional journals. Institute of Radio Engineers, member of editorial board, 1946-53, editorial reviewer, 1954-67.

BIOGRAPHICAL/CRITICAL SOURCES: *New York Times,* January 18, 1960.

PALFFY-ALPAR, Julius 1908-

PERSONAL: Born May 19, 1908, in Kristyor, Hungary; son of Joseph Alpar and Marie Gagyi Palffy; married Eva Ilona Talos (a secretary), May 10, 1943. *Education:* Royal Hungarian Sport Institute, M.A. equivalent, 1935. *Religion:* Roman Catholic. *Home:* 105 Kenyon Ave., Kensington, Calif. 94708. *Office:* University of California, Berkeley, Calif. 94720.

CAREER: Royal Hungarian Military Academy, professor (with rank of captain), 1935-45; Recreational Center for American Army in Europe, Eibsee, Germany, director of sports, 1945-48; University of Toronto, Toronto, Ontario, instructor in fencing, 1949-60; San Francisco Sport Academy, San Francisco, Calif., head coach, 1960-62; University of California, Berkeley, lecturer in dramatic art and supervisor of physical education, beginning 1962. Fencing instructor for American Conservatory Theater, San Francisco, Calif., 1967-68. *Member:* California Association for Health, Physical Education and Recreation, Association Mondiale des Academy d'Armes Nationales, National Fencing Coaches Association of America.

WRITINGS: Sword and Masque, F. A. Davis, 1967.

WORK IN PROGRESS: A book on stage movements.

*   *   *

PALMER, Everett W(alter) 1906-1970

PERSONAL: Born January 25, 1906, in Menomonie, Wis.; son of John S. (a Methodist minister) and May (Sanders) Palmer; married Florence Ruth Wales, June 30, 1927; children: Joanne (Mrs. Clifford C. Cate), Elizabeth (Mrs. A. Ross Cash), Ruth (Mrs. John P. McKean). *Education:* Dakota Wesleyan University, B.A., 1932; Drew Theological Seminary, B.D. (cum laude), 1935, part-time graduate study, 1935-39; also studied at Union Theological Seminary, New York, N.Y., 1942, and Oxford University, 1950. *Office:* The Methodist Church, 800 Olympic National Building, 920 Second Ave., Seattle, Wash. 98104.

CAREER: Began herding steers at twelve and was top ranch hand at seventeen; later worked as a hard rock miner and contractor at Homestake Gold Mine in the Black Hills of South Dakota until 1928; pastor in Artesian, S.D., 1929-32, and of Silverton Circuit, N.J., 1933-34; ordained deacon of The Methodist Church, 1934, and elder, 1935; held pastorates in Highland Park, N.J., 1934-42, Camden, N.J., 1942-46, Asbury Park, N.J., 1946-51, and Glendale, Calif., 1951-60; resident bishop, Seattle area, The Methodist Church, Seattle, Wash., 1960-70. Member of various commissions and boards of The Methodist Church, 1960-70, including chairman of department of ministerial education, Board of Education, and vice-chairman of Commission on Ecumenical Affairs; chairman of 1966 Urban Life Convocation; a Methodist representative, Consultation on Church Union; member of World Methodist Council. Member of summer faculty, Iliff School of Theology, 1964, and Garrett Theological Seminary, 1965. Exchange preacher to England, 1950; member of preaching mission to U.S. Air Force in Far East, 1954; made episcopal visitation to South Asia, 1963.

MEMBER: Rainier Club and Harbor Club (both Seattle). *Awards, honors:* D.D., Dakota Wesleyan University, 1952; D.S.T., University of Puget Sound, 1961; LL.D., Morningside College, 1963; Alumnus of the Year, Dakota Wesleyan University, 1964.

WRITINGS: Spiritual Life Through Witnessing, Tidings, 1955; *You Can Have a New Life,* Abingdon, 1959; *There Is*

an Answer, Abingdon, 1962; *The Glorious Imperative,* Abingdon, 1967. About 250 articles have been published since 1937, in *Christian Century Pulpit, Pulpit Digest, Religion in Life, Music Ministry,* and other periodicals.

WORK IN PROGRESS: Several lecture series.†

(Died January 5, 1970)

*   *   *

PANNELL, Anne Gary 1910-

PERSONAL: Born September 15, 1910, in Durham, N.C.; daughter of Alexander Henry and Anne Roche (Thomas) Gary; married Henry Clifton Pannell, 1936 (died, 1946); children: Henry Gary, Clifton Wyndham. *Education:* Barnard College, A.B., 1931; Institute of Historical Research, University of London, Oxford scholar, 1932-33; St. Hugh's College, Oxford, D.Phil., 1935. *Religion:* Episcopalian. *Home:* 4800 Sillmore Ave., Alexandria, Va. 22311.

CAREER: Alabama College (now University of Montevallo), Montevallo, instructor in history, 1934-36; University of Alabama, University, instructor, 1939-45, assistant professor, 1946-47, associate professor of history, 1947-49; Goucher College, Towson, Md., professor of history and academic dean, 1949-50; Sweet Briar College, Sweet Briar, Va., president, 1950-71. Trustee of Barnard College, Virginia Foundation for Independent Colleges, and Maryland Foundation for Independent Colleges; member of Maryland Governor's Committee for Financing Private Colleges. Consultant to Title IV advisory commission, U.S. Department of Health, Education, and Welfare.

MEMBER: American Association of University Women (president, 1967-71). *Award, honors:* LL.D. from University of Alabama, 1952, University of North Carolina, 1960, Cedar Crest College, 1968, Washington College, 1971, and Bridgewater College, 1972; Litt.D. from Western Reserve University (now Case Western Reserve University), 1963; L.H.D. from University of Chattanooga, 1963, and Women's Medical College of Pennsylvania, 1968.

WRITINGS: The Political and Economic Relations of English and American Quakers, Clarendon Press, 1935; *Canada: America's Northern Neighbor,* Oxford University Press, 1951; (with D. E. Wyatt) *Julia Tutwiler and Social Progress,* University of Alabama Press, 1961.

WORK IN PROGRESS: The Need to Support Independent Education.

AVOCATIONAL INTERESTS: Travel (Europe and Asia), gardening (roses, camellias, tulips).

*   *   *

PARKER, Dorothy (Rothschild) 1893-1967

PERSONAL: Born August 22, 1893, in West End, N.J.; daughter of J. Henry and Eliza A. (Marston) Rothschild; married Edwin Pond Parker II, 1917 (divorced, 1928); married Alan Campbell (a motion picture actor and scenarist), October, 1933 (divorced, 1947); remarried Campbell, August, 1950 (died, 1963). *Education:* Attended Miss Dana's School, Morristown, N.J., and Blessed Sacrament Convent, New York, N.Y. *Politics:* Generally far left. *Home:* Volney Hotel, 23 East 74th St., New York, N.Y.

CAREER: Vogue, New York, N.Y., member of editorial staff, 1916-17; *Vanity Fair,* New York, N.Y., member of editorial staff and drama critic, 1917-20 (she was fired for writing unfavorable reviews of three important plays); *New Yorker,* New York, N.Y., book reviewer, writing "Constant Reader" column, about 1925-27; free-lance writer, 1927-67. Lived in Hollywood, Calif., for many years, beginning in the early 1930's, while writing for motion pictures and magazines; taught English at Los Angeles State College (now California State University, Los Angeles), about 1960. (She said that she didn't lecture; instead, "the students read things and then they fight. It's called discussion.") Founder, with Robert Benchley and Robert E. Sherwood, of the Algonquin Round Table in the Algonquin Hotel, New York, N.Y. (resigned during the 1930's). *Awards, honors:* O. Henry Memorial Award, 1929, for short story "Big Blond."

WRITINGS: (Author of text with George Chappell and Frank Crowninshield) *High Society* (illustrations by Anne Harriet Fish), Putnam, 1920; *Men I'm Not Married To; Women I'm Not Married To,* Doubleday, Page, 1922; *Enough Rope* (poems), Boni & Liveright, 1926, new edition, 1934; *Sunset Gun* (poems), Boni & Liveright, 1928, new edition, 1934; (with Elmer Rice) *Close Harmony, or The Lady Next Door* (play; originally copyrighted as "Soft Music," 1924, but never published or produced with that title; first produced as "Close Harmony" in New York at Gaiety Theater, December 1, 1924), Samuel French, 1929; *Laments for the Living* (stories), Viking, 1930; *Death and Taxes* (poems), Viking, 1931; *After Such Pleasures* (stories), Viking, 1932; *Collected Poems: Not So Deep as a Well,* Viking, 1936; *Here Lies* (stories), Viking, 1939; (with Arnaud d'Usseau) *Ladies of the Corridor* (play; first produced in New York at Longacre Theater, October 21, 1953), Viking, 1954.

Omnibus volumes: *Collected Stories,* Modern Library, 1942; *Collected Poetry,* Random House, 1944; *Dorothy Parker* (selected poetry and prose), introduction by W. Somerset Maugham, Viking, 1944, revised and enlarged edition published as *The Portable Dorothy Parker,* 1973; *The Best of Dorothy Parker,* Methuen, 1952; *Constant Reader* (selected stories from the *New Yorker*), Viking, 1970; *A Month of Saturdays,* Macmillan (London), 1971.

Editor: *The Portable F. Scott Fitzgerald,* Viking, 1945; Cazenove Gardner Lee, *Lee Chronicle: Studies of the Early Generations of the Lees of Virginia,* New York University Press, 1957; (with F. B. Shroyer) *Short Story: A Thematic Anthology,* Scribner, 1965.

Unpublished plays: (Lyricist) "Round the Town" (revue), first produced in New York at Century Roof Theater, May 21, 1924; (contributor of sketches) "Shoot the Works" (revue), first produced in New York at George M. Cohan Theater, July 21, 1931; (contributor of sketches) "After Such Pleasures" (revue based on Mrs. Parker's short stories; adaptation by Edward F. Gardner, first produced in New York at Bijou Theater, February 7, 1934; (with Ross Evans) "The Coast of Illyria" (play based on the life of Charles Lamb), first produced in Dallas, 1949; (lyricist with John La Touche and Richard Wilbur) "Candide," first produced in New York at Martin Beck Theater, December 1, 1956.

Screenplays; all with husband, Alan Campbell: "Here is My Heart," Paramount, 1934; "One Hour Late," Paramount, 1935; "Big Broadcast of 1936," Paramount, 1935; "Mary Burns, Fugitive," Paramount, 1935; "Hands Across the Table," Paramount, 1935; "Paris in Spring," Paramount, 1935; "Three Married Men," Paramount, 1936; "Lady Be Careful," Paramount, 1936; "The Moon's Our Home," Paramount, 1936; "Suzy," Metro-Goldwyn-Mayer, 1936; "A Star is Born," United Artists, 1937; "Sweethearts," Metro-Goldwyn-Mayer, 1938; "Crime Takes a Holiday," Columbia, 1938; "Trade Winds," United Artists, 1938;

"Flight into Nowhere," Columbia, 1938; "Five Little Peppers and How They Grew," Columbia, 1939; "Weekend for Three," RKO, 1941; "Saboteur," Universal, 1942; "A Gentle Gangster," Republic, 1943; "Mr. Skeffington," Warner Bros., 1944; "Smash-Up: The Story of a Woman," Universal, 1947; "The Fan," Twentieth Century-Fox, 1949.

Television plays: Mrs. Parker adapted her stories "The Lonely Leave," "A Telephone Call," and "Dusk Before Fireworks" for the Festival of Performing Arts, WNEW-TV, May 8, 1962.

Mrs. Parker was a regular contributor to the *New Yorker* from its second issue, February 28, 1925, until December 14, 1957. She regularly contributed book reviews to *Esquire* for several years, beginning in 1958.

SIDELIGHTS: "Dorothy Parker was small, dark, and fragile, with a sharp, pretty face and an air of being almost too sensitive to what went on about her," wrote Anita Loos. It was this sensitivity that produced one of the sharpest, most biting wits in modern letters. Miss Loos concluded that "Dorothy's presence anywhere tended to produce an atmosphere of tension." The *Time* reporter noted that "hers was the tongue heard round the world. . . . During the long Victorian era, wit had hardly been considered a feminine attribute. Dorothy Parker proved again that bitchiness could be the soul of wit."

Mrs. Parker came to deplore the reputation accorded her wit. She once said that "it got so bad that they began to laugh before I opened my mouth." She held in similar contempt her reputation as a serious writer. She told her *Paris Review* interviewer that her play, *Ladies of the Corridor,* was "the only thing I have ever done in which I had great pride." (The play's Broadway run was only modestly successful.) She added that she "fell into writing, . . . being one of those awful children who wrote verses." She always referred to her rhyming as "verse"; "I cannot say poems," she told the *Paris Review.* "Like everybody was then, I was following in the exquisite footsteps of Miss Millay, unhappily in my own horrible sneakers. My verses are no damn good. Let's face it, honey, my verse is terribly dated—as anything once fashionable is dreadful now. I gave it up [her last published poem was written in 1944], knowing it wasn't getting any better, but nobody seemed to notice my magnificent gesture."

But her harsh self-derogation was enthusiastically contradicted by critics and acquaintances. ("Acquaintances" because Anita Loos doubts that she had any real *friends;* "she had no belief at all in friendship and knew herself to be a lone wolverine.") Ogden Nash once wrote: "To say that Mrs. Parker writes well is as fatuous, I'm afraid, as proclaiming that Cellini was clever with his hands. . . . The trick about her writing is the trick about Ring Lardner's writing or Ernest Hemingway's writing. It isn't a trick." And Edmund Wilson found beauty in her work: "She is not Emily Bronte or Jane Austen, but she had been at some pains to write well, and she has put into what she has written a voice, a state of mind, an era, a few moments of human experience that nobody else has conveyed." Somerset Maugham wrote: "Perhaps what gives her writing its peculiar tang is her gift for seeing something to laugh at in the bitterest tragedies of the human animal." If Mrs. Parker's laughter seemed merciless, it was because she truly believed that humor and compassion are inharmonious sentiments. Alden Whitman recalled Mrs. Parker's own definition of her particular talent: "Humor to me, Heaven help me, takes in many things. There must be courage, there must be no awe. There must be criticism, for humor, to my mind, is encapsulated in criticism. There must be a disciplined eye and a wild mind. There must be a magnificent disregard of your reader, for if he cannot follow you, there is nothing you can do about it." Whitman summarized: "Her lifelong reputation as a glittering, annihilating humorist in poetry, essays, short stories and in conversation was compiled and sustained brickbat by brickbat." (Although, Whitman added, she was not altogether without sentimentality; "she truly loved flowers, dogs and a good cry.")

Although many have called Mrs. Parker's wit ageless, some critics attribute her immense success to the peculiarities of the 'thirties and 'forties, her most expressive and influential years. The *Time* writer noted: "If one wonders what so captivated her contemporaries, the answer is probably that she viewed the period as it liked to picture itself: a time of grace and intelligence, when irony could conquer sentimentality and laughter would always overwhelm tears." Wilson, analyzing Mrs. Parker's work in retrospect, concluded that her writing "has a value derived from rarity—a rarity like that of steel penknives, good erasers and real canned sardines, articles of which the supply has almost given out and of which one is only now beginning to be aware of how excellent the quality was." But Mrs. Parker could never complain of a dearth of admirers (if she entered any complaint, it was that she was overrated). In 1931 Henry Seidel Canby wrote: "In verse of a Horatian lightness, with an exquisite certainty of technique, which, like the lustre on a Persian bowl, is proof that civilization is itself a philosophy, Dorothy Parker is writing poetry deserving high praise.... I suspect that one should quote Latin rather than English to parallel the edged fineness of Dorothy Parker's verse. This belle dame sans merci has the ruthlessness of the great tragic lyricist whose work was allegorized in the fable of the nightingale singing with her breast against a thorn. It is a disillusion recollected in tranquility where the imagination has at last controlled the emotions. It comes out clear, and with the authentic sparkle of a great vintage." Louis Kronenberger expressed similar admiration for her work in 1936, concluding that "there is no one else in Mrs. Parker's special field who can do half as much." And Alexander Woollcott, a fellow Algonquin Round Table luminary, wrote in the early 1940's: "Mrs. Parker's published work does not bulk large. But most of it has been pure gold and the five winnowed volumes of her shelf ... are so potent a distillation of nectar and wormwood, of ambrosia and deadly nightshade, as might suggest to the rest of us that we all write far too much. Even though I am one who does not profess to be privy to the intentions of posterity, I do suspect that another generation will not share the confusion into which Mrs. Parker's poetry throws so many of her contemporaries, who, seeing that much of it is witty, dismiss it patronizingly as 'light' verse, and do not see that some of it is thrilling poetry of a piercing and rueful beauty."

Although Mrs. Parker's formidable wit had found a large audience as early as 1927, her enthusiasm for politically liberal causes did not amuse certain United States authorities. Whitman reported that "from the late nineteen-twenties, when Mrs. Parker was fined $5 for 'sauntering' in a Boston demonstration against the execution of Nicola Sacco and Bartolomea Vanzetti, she was active in liberal causes. In the Spanish Civil War and afterward, she was national chairman of the Joint Anti-Fascist Refugee Committee and active in its behalf. This had repercussions in 1951 when she was cited, by the House Un-American Activities Committee, with 300 other writers, professors, actors and artists, for affiliation with what the committee designated as 'Communist-

front' organizations." In 1944 Edmund Wilson offered an explanation, if not an apology, for her activites: "A decade or more ago she went out to Hollywood and more or less steadily stayed there, and, once away from her natural habitat, New York, she succumbed to the expiatory mania that has become epidemic with film-writers and was presently making earnest appeals on behalf of those organizations which talked about being 'progressive' and succeeded in convincing their followers that they were working for the social revolution, though they had really no other purpose than to promote the foreign policy of the Soviet Union." Much later Mrs. Parker spoke bitterly of her years in California: "I can't talk about Hollywood," she told the *Paris Review*. "It was a horror to me when I was there and it's a horror to look back on. I can't imagine how I did it. When I got away from it I couldn't even refer to the place by name. 'Out there,' I called it."

Mrs. Parker frequently expressed a desire to be rich. When asked to name "the source of most of [her] work," she replied: "Need of money, dear." She explained: "I'd like to have money. And I'd like to be a good writer. These two can come together, and I hope they will, but if that's too adorable, I'd rather have money. I hate almost all rich people, but I think I'd be darling at it."

For the most part, Mrs. Parker had as little respect for contemporary writers as for any other group. She admitted that she usually turned to older writers "for comfort" and cited *Vanity Fair* as her favorite novel. She added: "I was a woman of eleven when I first read it," and speculated that she has since read Thackeray's book "about a dozen times a year." But she would not discount younger writers without qualification. She told the *Paris Review* interviewer: "I will say of the writers of today that some of them, thank God, have the sense to adapt to their times. Mailer's *The Naked and the Dead* is a great book. And I thought William Styron's *Lie Down in Darkness* an extraordinary thing. The start of it took your heart and flung it over there. He writes like a god ... I love Sherlock Holmes. My life is so untidy and he's so neat. But as for the living novelists, I suppose E. M. Forster is the best, not knowing what that is, but at least he's a semi-finalist, wouldn't you think?"

Edmund Wilson once noticed that all of Mrs. Parker's books had "funereal titles," but that "the eye was always wide open and the tongue always quick to retort. Even those titles were sardonic exclamations on the part of an individual at the idea of her own demise." Indeed, Mrs. Parker's suggestions for her own epitaph have become famous; perhaps "Excuse my dust" and "If you can read this, you've come too close" are most often quoted. When she died, more that 150 literary and theatrical acquaintances attended the brief funeral; it was Zero Mostel who remarked: "If she had had her way, I suspect she would not be here at all."

Mrs. Parker, left the bulk of her estate to Martin Luther King, Jr.; upon his death, whatever remained went to the National Association for the Advancement of Colored People.

Mrs. Parker read from her work for "The World of Dorothy Parker," Verve, 1962, and for "Poems and a Story," Spoken Arts, 1962. "As Dorothy Parker Said," a musical revue based on her works, was first produced in London at Fortune Theatre, July 21, 1969.

BIOGRAPHICAL/CRITICAL SOURCES: Saturday Review, June 13, 1931, November 4, 1933; *New York Times,* December 13, 1936, June 8, 10, 27, 1967; Malcolm Cowley, editor, *Writers at Work: The "Paris Review" Interviews,*

Viking, 1957; Anita Loos, *A Girl Like I* (autobiography), Viking, 1966; *Time,* June 16, 1967; *Esquire,* July, 1968; John Keats, *You Might as Well Live,* Simon & Schuster, 1970; *McCall's,* October, 1970.†

(Died June 7, 1967)

*   *   *

PARKER, Thomas Maynard   1906-

PERSONAL: Born March 7, 1906, in London, England; son of Thomas Maynard and Emily Mary Parker. *Education:* Exeter College, Oxford, B.A., 1927, M.A., 1931, D.D., 1956. *Office:* University College, Oxford OX1 4BH, England.

CAREER: Ordained deacon, Church of England, 1930, and priest, 1931; Chichester Theological College, Chichester, England, librarian and tutor, 1930-32; curate in London, England, 1932-35; Pusey House, Oxford, England, librarian, 1935-52, and custodian of Pusey Memorial Library, 1946-52; Oxford University, Oxford, England, assistant chaplain, Exeter College, 1946-52, acting chaplain and lecturer in medieval history and political science, Pembroke College, 1951-52, lecturer in theology, Pembroke College, 1952-61, university lecturer in theology, beginning 1950, chaplain, 1952-70, fellow and praelector in theology and modern history, University College, 1952-73, professor emeritus of theology and modern history, 1973—, examiner for bachelors of philosophy in European history, beginning 1972. Bampton lecturer, Oxford University, 1950; Birkbeck lecturer, Trinity College, Cambridge University, 1956-57; select preacher, Cambridge University, 1955, and Oxford University, 1960-61; external examiner at Queen's University, Belfast, 1964-66, and at St. David's College, Lampeter, 1968-70. Member of Central Advisory Council for Training of Ministry, 1948-55. Liveryman of Worshipful Company of Butchers, beginning 1927, member of court of assistants, 1955-65, master, 1962-63, past master, beginning 1963. *Member:* Royal Historical Society (fellow; member of council, 1964-68), Society of Antiquaries of London (fellow), Athenaeum Club (London).

WRITINGS: The Re-Creation of Man, Dacre Press, 1941; *The English Reformation to 1558,* Oxford University Press, 1950, 2nd edition, 1966; *Christianity and the State in the Light of History* (Bampton lectures for 1950), Harper, 1955.

Contributor: *Union of Christendom,* S.P.C.K., 1938; *The Apostolic Ministry,* Hodder & Stoughton, 1946; *Ideas and Beliefs of the Victorians,* Sylvan Press, 1949, Dutton, 1966; *Augustinus Magister,* Volume II, Etudes Augustiniennes (Paris), 1955; *Miscellanea Historiae Ecclesiastiae,* Revue d'Histoire Ecclesiastique (Louvain), 1960; *Studies in Church History,* Volume I, Nelson, 1964; Schafer Williams, editor, *The Gregorian Epoch: Reformation, Revolution, Reaction,* Heath, 1964; Beryl Smalley, editor, *Trends in Medieval Political Thought,* Basil Blackwell, 1965; G. B. Bennett and J. D. Walsh, editors, *Essays in Modern English Church History in Memory of Norman Sykes,* Oxford University Press, 1966; J. Coulson and A. M. Allchin, editors, *The Rediscovery of Newman,* S.P.C.K., 1967; John Roach, editor, *The New Cambridge Modern History,* Volume III, Macmillan, 1968. Also contributor to *Oxford Dictionary of the Christian Church, Chambers's Encyclopaedia, Encyclopaedia Britannica,* and to journals.

WORK IN PROGRESS: Two books, *God, Man and the State in Later Medieval Thought* and *The Late Middle Ages: The English Reformation, 1558-1688.*

AVOCATIONAL INTERESTS: Railways.†

PARKER, William Riley   1906-1968

PERSONAL: Born August 17, 1906, in Roanoke, Va.; son of Frank Benjamin (a physician) and Bertha (Riley) Parker; married Mary Ann Blakesley, September 20, 1932; children: Pamela Lucile, Robin Blakesley. *Education:* Roanoke College, B.A., 1927; Princeton University, M.A., 1928; Oxford University, B.Litt., 1934. *Office:* Department of English, Indiana University, Bloomington, Ind. 47401.

CAREER: Northwestern University, Evanston, Ill., instructor, 1928-32, researcher in English, 1934-35; Ohio State University, Columbus, instructor, 1935-36, assistant professor, 1936-41, associate professor, 1941-43, professor of English, 1943-46; New York University, New York, N.Y., professor of English, 1946-56; Indiana University, Bloomington, professor of English, 1956-58, Distinguished Service Professor, 1958-68, chairman of department, 1966-68. Visiting professor at Johns Hopkins University, 1937; visiting summer professor at Duke University, 1938, 1941, University of Southern California, 1946. U.S. Office of Education, chief of Language Development Program, 1958-59, member of National Advisory Committee on Language Development, 1959-64. American Council of Learned Societies, member of board of directors, 1950-56; U.S. National Commission for UNESCO, member of executive committee, 1954-58, vice-chairman, 1957-58.

MEMBER: Modern Language Association of America (executive secretary, 1947-56; president, 1959), National Council of Teachers of English, American Association of Teachers of French (honorary), Bibliographical Society (London), Phi Beta Kappa (member of senate, 1961-67), Andiron Club and Century Association (both New York). *Awards, honors:* D.Litt., Middlebury College, 1953; LL.D., University of Michigan, 1956; L.H.D., Roanoke College and Miami University, Oxford, Ohio, both 1962; Guggenheim fellowship and Fulbright research award, 1962-63; Goethe Gold Medal, 1966; Distinguished National Service award, New York State Federation of Foreign Language Teachers, 1967.

WRITINGS: Milton's Debt to Greek Tragedy in Samson Agonistes, Johns Hopkins Press, 1937; *Milton's Contemporary Reputation,* Ohio University Press, 1940, reprinted, Folcroft Press, 1969; (editor) G. S., *The Dignity of Kingship Asserted,* Columbia University Press, 1942 (also published as *Monarchy Triumphing Over Traiterous Republicans*); *The National Interests and Foreign Language,* Government Printing Office, 1954, 3rd edition, 1962; (author of introduction) William Winstanley, *The Lives of the Most Famous English Poets,* Scholars, 1963; *The Language Curtain and Other Essays,* Modern Language Association of America, 1966; *Milton: A Biography,* two volumes, Clarendon Press, 1968. Editor, *PMLA,* 1947-56; compiler of *The MLA Style Sheet,* 1951, revised edition, 1954.

WORK IN PROGRESS: Samson Agonistes: Variorum Notes and Commentary and *A History of English Studies.*

BIOGRAPHICAL/CRITICAL SOURCES: London Times, November 1, 1968; *AB Bookman's Weekly,* December 9, 1968.†

(Died October 28, 1968)

*   *   *

PARMELEE, Alice   1903-

PERSONAL: Born January 11, 1903, in New York, N.Y.; daughter of Henry Douglas (a manufacturer) and Gussie (Thom) Parmelee. *Education:* Bryn Mawr College, A.B., 1926. *Home:* 26 East 81st St., New York, N.Y. 10028.

CAREER: Miss Hewitt's Classes, New York City, English teacher, 1928-30; Calvary Episcopal Church, New York City, director of religious education, 1930-35; *Episcopal Church Annual*, New York City, managing editor, 1941-55. Advisory editor to Harper & Row Publishers, Inc., 1952-65.

WRITINGS: *Building the Kingdom*, Morehouse-Gorham, 1940; *Fellowship of the Church*, Morehouse-Gorham, 1941; *Patriarchs, Kings and Prophets*, Morehouse-Gorham, 1943; *A Guidebook to the Bible*, Harper, 1948, 2nd edition, Hodder & Stoughton, 1963; *All the Birds of the Bible*, Harper, 1959; *They Beheld His Glory*, Harper, 1967. Assistant editor, *Harper's Bible Dictionary*, 1949-52.

AVOCATIONAL INTERESTS: Bird watching and visiting museums.

* * *

PARRIS, Addison W(ilson) 1923-1975

PERSONAL: Born November 30, 1923, in Baltimore, Md.; son of Paul Southerland (an insurance executive) and Angela Everett (Wilson) Parris; married Ellen Ann Moynihan, September 7, 1950; married second wife, Judith Ann Heimlich (a political scientist), October 12, 1968; children: (first marriage) Susan Phipps, Addison Wilson, Jr. Education: Mississippi State College (now Mississippi State University), student, 1943-44; Tufts College, (now Tufts University), A.B., 1947, M.A., 1949; Columbia University, graduate study, 1947-48. Politics: Democrat. Religion: Methodist. Home: 3105 Northampton St. N.W., Washington, D.C. 20015. Office: U.S. Small Business Administration, 1441 L St. N.W., Washington, D.C. 20416.

CAREER: National Association of Manufacturers, New York City, research associate in international relations, 1949-53, assistant director, 1953-55; American Management Association, New York City, assistant manager, finance division, 1955-57; Committee for Economic Development, Washington, D.C., international economist, 1957-61; U.S. Department of Commerce, Washington, D.C., 1961-63, began as consultant, became director of Office of Commercial and Financial Policy; Office of the Special Representative for Trade Negotiations, Washington, D.C., executive secretary of Trade Expansion Act Advisory Committee, 1963; U.S. Small Business Administration, Washington, D.C., economist, beginning 1963. Senior economic consultant in Somali Republic for program sponsored by United Nations, 1967. Military service: U.S. Army, 1942-46. Member: American Economic Association.

WRITINGS: *Topics of Current Interest in International Economic Relations*, National Association of Manufacturers, 1953; *The European Common Market and Its Meaning to the United States*, McGraw, 1959; *National Objective and the Balance of Payments Problem*, Committee for Economic Development, 1960; *Cooperation for Progress in Latin America*, Committee for Economic Development, 1961; *The Small Business Administration*, Praeger, 1968.

WORK IN PROGRESS: Studies on the position of the United States in the world economy, especially in relation to other developed countries; strategies of economic development of less-developed nations.†

(Died, 1975)

* * *

PARRISH, Wayland Maxfield 1887-?

PERSONAL: Born March 7, 1887, in Coshocton County, Ohio; son of John J. (a farmer and manufacturer) and Rebecca (Moore) Parrish; married Greeta Leigh, August 8, 1913; children: Katharine (Mrs. A. H. Schulz), Stephen Maxfield, Joan Leigh (Mrs. William H. Hay; deceased). Education: Ohio Wesleyan University, B.L., 1908; Cornell University, Ph.D., 1929. Politics: Liberal. Religion: None. Home: 1831 Northwest 12th Rd., Gainesville, Fla. 32601.

CAREER: Dartmouth College, Hanover, Mass., assistant professor of speech, 1922-23; University of Pittsburgh, Pittsburgh, Pa., 1923-36, began as assistant professor, became professor of speech; University of Illinois, Urbana, 1936-55, began as associate professor, became professor of speech, professor emeritus, beginning 1955. Visiting professor, University of Florida, Gainesville, 1955-58. Member: Speech Association of America, Southern Speech Association.

WRITINGS: *Reading Aloud*, Ronald, 1932, 4th edition, 1966; *The Teacher's Speech*, Harper, 1939; *Speaking in Public*, Scribner, 1947; (with Marie Hochmuth) *American Speeches*, Longmans, Green, 1954. Contributor to speech journals.†

(Deceased)

* * *

PATTERSON, Emma L. 1904-

PERSONAL: Born March 27, 1904, in Windham, N.Y.; daughter of George Thompson (a carpenter) and Emma (Munson) Patterson. Education: Mount Holyoke College, B.A., 1925; Columbia University, graduate study, 1932. Politics: Independent. Religion: Christian. Residence: Windham, N.Y. 12496.

CAREER: High school teacher of English, Montgomery, N.Y., 1926-28; high school librarian, Peekskill, N.Y., 1929-59. Peekskill Public Library, member of board of trustees, 1940-47, secretary of board for two years. Member: American Association of University Women (charter member of Peekskill branch), Authors Guild of the Authors League of America, Phi Beta Kappa. Awards, honors: First place in national short story contest, American Association of University Women, 1940.

WRITINGS—Youth books, except as noted: *Peekskill: In the American Revolution* (adult), Friendly Town Association, 1944; *Midnight Patriot*, McKay, 1949; *The World Turned Upside Down*, McKay, 1953; *Sun Queen: Nefertiti*, McKay, 1967. Author of several one-act plays, including "The Printer's a Devil," short stories, and professional articles.

WORK IN PROGRESS: Continuing research into the background of the Sun Queen.††

* * *

PATTERSON, Samuel White 1883-1975

PERSONAL: Born December 25, 1883, in New York, N.Y.; son of Matthew (a dry goods merchant) and Mary (Maxwell) Patterson; married May Blauvelt, 1919 (died, 1940). Education: City College (now City College of the City University of New York), A.B., 1903; New York University, M.A., 1906, Ph.D., 1913; Columbia University, A.M., 1910; special student at Union Theological Seminary, New York, N.Y., 1961-63, Metropolitan Museum of Art, 1961-65. Politics: Republican. Religion: Episcopalian. Residence: Paramus, N.J.

CAREER: Teacher in New York, N.Y., for more than forty years, retiring in 1952 as professor of education at Hunter College of the City University of New York. New York

Board of Education, high school teacher, 1909-20, lecturer in American history and institutions, 1909-26, head of English department of Evening High School for Men, 1910-12; Columbia University, instructor in English, 1914-18; New York Teachers College, professor of English and head of department, 1920-30; Hunter College of the City University of New York, New York, N.Y., member of faculty, 1930-52, professor of education, 1948-52, professor emeritus, 1952-75. Vice-president of New York Episcopal Church board of religious education, 1919-26. Member of board of directors, Greater New York Federation of Churches, 1920-30, and International Daily Vacation Bible Schools; member of auxiliary council, American Christian Palestine Committee, 1925-30. Commissioner-at-large, Interstate Rochambeau Memorial Bridge Commission, Alexandria, Va., 1955-58, and speaker at dedication of the bridge, 1958.

MEMBER: American Historical Association, Poetry Society of America (associate member), Pilgrims of the United States, St. Andrew's Society, Near East Foundation (honorary member), Institute of Arts and Letters (Zurich; life fellow), Metropolitan Museum of Art, American Friends of Bodley's (Oxford University), Phi Beta Kappa. *Awards, honors:* U.S. Treasury Department citation and medal for work in directing the raising of nearly five million dollars in war bonds, 1946; Freedoms Foundation medal for "An Open Letter to American Youth," 1964.

WRITINGS: The Spirit of the American Revolution as Revealed in the Poetry of the Period, Badger, 1915; *Over There to Over Here,* U.S. Surgeon General's Office, 1918; (editor) *Adam Bede,* Macmillan, 1922; *Famous Men and Places in the History of New York City,* Noble, 1923; *Teaching the Child to Read,* Doubleday, Doran, 1928; *Geography of New York and Far-Away Lands,* Noble, 1929.

(Editor) *Autobiography of Olin S. Roche,* Friebele, 1930; *Old Chelsea and St. Peter's Church,* Friebele, 1935; *Etchings in Verse,* Friebele, 1939; *Horatio Gates: Defender of American Liberties,* Columbia University Press, 1941, reprinted, AMS Press, 1966.

Hunter College: Eighty-five Years of Service, Lantern, 1955; *The Poet of Christmas Eve: A Life of Clement Clarke Moore,* Morehouse, 1956; *Knight Errant of Liberty: The Truimph and Tragedy of General Charles Lee,* Lantern, 1958; *When Saint Nicholas Got Back,* Comet, 1958; *Occasions Glimpsed from the Mount,* St. Onge, 1961. Editor of "Junior High School Literature Series," Bobbs-Merrill, 1928. Contributor of articles and reviews to history and education journals.

WORK IN PROGRESS: Three books, *The Good Samaritan and His Friends, My Beloved Valley,* and *Jesus Christ Across the Centuries.*†

(Died November 20, 1975)

* * *

PATTIE, Alice 1906-

PERSONAL: Born October 9, 1906, in St. Louis, Mo.; daughter of Heusted T. (a railroad executive) and Jessie M. (Condell) Young; married John R. Pattie, May 26, 1931 (deceased); children: John Heusted, Mary Alice (Mrs. Henry S. McDonald), Jane Seed (Mrs. Victor A. Vyssotsky). *Education:* Miami University, Oxford, Ohio, A.B., 1928; Columbia University, M.A., 1965. *Religion:* Protestant.

CAREER: Episcopal City Mission Society, New York City, member of staff, 1962-63; St. Luke's Home, New

York City, acting superintendent, summer, 1963; Riverside Church, New York City, director of Town League (program for the elderly), 1963-65; St. Mark's Church, Augusta, Me., superintendent of St. Mark's Home and director of Open Door program, 1966; Town of Huntington, Long Island, N.Y., supervisor of program for the elderly, 1967-68. Director, Friday Friends (program for aging), Millburn, N.J., beginning 1970. *Member:* National Council on the Aging, Essex County Committee on Aging (chairman of education committee), American Association of Retired Persons, Alpha Delta Sigma.

WRITINGS: (Editor) *Sermons of John R. Pattie,* privately printed, 1962; (with Bernadine Kreis) *Up from Grief: Patterns of Recovery,* Seabury, 1969. Contributor of articles and reviews to National Council on the Aging newsletters.

AVOCATIONAL INTERESTS: Painting, travel.†

* * *

PATTY, Ernest N(ewton) 1894-1976

PERSONAL: Born March 27, 1894, in La Brande, Ore.; son of Thomas Franklin and Zora E. (Beach) Patty; married Kathryn Stanton, December 28, 1918 (died July, 1961); married Virginia Wiley Price, January 20, 1968; children: (first marriage) Ernest N. (deceased), Stanton, Dale. *Education:* University of Washington, Seattle, B.S., 1919, E.M., 1925. *Politics:* Republican. *Religion:* Presbyterian. *Home:* 1600 Windemere Dr. E., Seattle, Wash. 98102. *Agent:* Lurton Blassingame, 60 East 42nd St., New York, N.Y. 10017.

CAREER: Mining engineer with Washington State Geological Survey, 1919-20, and engineer in charge of Black Rock Mine, Northport, Wash., 1921; Alaska Agricultural College and School of Mines (now University of Alaska), Fairbanks, professor of geology and mineralogy, 1922-25, dean of School of Mines, 1925-35; president and general manager of Gold Placers, Inc., and Alluvial Gold, Inc., both Fairbanks, beginning 1935, Clear Creek Placers Ltd., 1940-53, and Yukon Placers Ltd., Dawson, Yukon Territory, 1946-54; University of Alaska, president, 1953-60, president emeritus, 1960-76. Consultant to mining companies. Member of board of directors, First National Bank of Fairbanks.

MEMBER: Arctic Institute of North America (fellow), American Association for the Advancement of Science, American Institute of Mining and Metallurgical Engineers, American Mining Congress, Alaska Miners Association (past president; past member of board of directors), Pioneers of Alaska, Explorers Club (New York), Rainier Club (Seattle). *Awards, honors:* D.Sc., University of Alaska, 1953.

WRITINGS: North Country Challenge, McKay, 1969. Contributor of articles to magazines and to mining and geology journals.

BIOGRAPHICAL/CRITICAL SOURCES: New York Times, January 14, 1976.†

(Died January 12, 1976)

* * *

PAULSEN, Lois (Thompson) 1905-

PERSONAL: Born August 11, 1905, in Concordia, Kan.; daughter of Edward W. (a county judge) and Mary (Van Fleet) Thompson; married Clarence Paulsen (a lawyer), June 4, 1930; children: Richard E. *Education:* University of Kansas, A.B., 1927. *Home:* 312 West Ninth St., Concordia, Kan. 66901.

WRITINGS: Sonnets to My Son, Big Mountain Press, 1963. Occasional contributor to magazines.

SIDELIGHTS: Lois Paulsen has some proficiency in Spanish and French.

* * *

PEARL, Leonard 1911-

PERSONAL: Born December 5, 1911, in Chicago, Ill.; son of Morris Alvin and Ida (Robbins) Pearl; married Florence Brisker, August 26, 1946; children: Linda Dina (Mrs. James Thomas). *Education:* Attended Northwestern University, 1930-31, and Chicago Technical College, 1933-35. *Residence:* San Diego, Calif.

CAREER: South Shore Outlook, Chicago, Ill., editor, 1938-41; Outlook News Service, San Diego, Calif., manager, 1941-43; Ace Auto Supply, El Cajon, Calif., president, 1950-65; free-lance writer, beginning 1965. *Member:* Benevolent and Protective Order of Elks.

WRITINGS: The Big Secret of Good Golf, privately printed, 1962; (with Archie Moore) *Any Boy Can: The Archie Moore Story,* Prentice-Hall, 1971. Co-author of newspaper column, "In the Ring with Archie Moore."

WORK IN PROGRESS: Sugar and Spite; The Ghost Wore Red; The Flammers.

AVOCATIONAL INTERESTS: Football, baseball, hockey, basketball, and other spectator sports, playing golf, bowling, sailing, flying (former pilot).††

* * *

PECK, Kathryn Blackburn 1904-1975

PERSONAL: Born July 9, 1904, in Jacksonville, Ill.; daughter of Charles E. (a teacher) and Mary (Cary) Blackburn; married Harlan C. Peck, August 23, 1919; children: Marlin E., Lillian M. (Mrs. Calvin Mathews), Dolores (Mrs. M. Alsobrook). *Education:* Attended public schools in Illinois and Missouri. *Politics:* Republican. *Home:* 1634 Ewing Ave., Kansas City, Mo.

CAREER: Writer of church school material for teachers and pupils at the primary level for more than twenty years; Church of the Nazarene, Department of Church Schools, Kansas City, Mo., member of curriculum committee, 1946-74.

WRITINGS: Golden Windows, Nazarene Publishing, 1941; *Along the Winding Pathway,* Beacon Hill, 1947; *In Favor with God and Man,* Beacon Hill, 1952; *Better Primary Teaching,* Beacon Hill, 1957; *Every Day and Sunday,* Warner Press, 1959; *God Made This Lovely, Lovely World,* Warner Press, 1960; *Up in the Jumby Tree,* Beacon Hill, 1960; *Mother Memories,* Beacon Hill, 1960; *Candles in the Dark,* Beacon Hill, 1962; *I, Too, Can Sing!,* Beacon Hill, 1964; *You Can Be a Happy Shut-in,* Beacon Hill, 1967; *Joy in the Morning,* Beacon Hill, 1969. Author of vacation Bible school manuals, lyrics for about forty published children's songs, and lyrics for about twenty adult songs. Poetry has been published in religious periodicals for several decades.

WORK IN PROGRESS: Bible story leaflets and other primary teaching aids.

AVOCATIONAL INTERESTS: Painting, color photography.†

(Died September 21, 1975)

* * *

PEERY, Paul D(enver) 1906-

PERSONAL: Born August 9, 1906, in Denver, Colo.; son of Rufus Benton (a minister, college president, and author) and Letitia (Rich) Peery; married Jessie Kneedler Cummins (an artist), June 22, 1929 (deceased); children: Barbara Lee (Mrs. Walter D. Bowne). *Education:* Attended Lenoir Rhyne College, 1922-24; United States Military Academy, B.S., 1928. *Politics:* Republican. *Religion:* Lutheran. *Home and office:* 1414 Tenth St., Coronado, Calif. 92118.

CAREER: U.S. Army, commissioned second lieutenant in Air Corps, 1928, later transferred to Coast Artillery, and was retired because of physical disability, 1935; head of his own creative writing school, Coronado, Calif., beginning 1935; organ teacher and recitalist, Coronado, beginning 1945; official carillonneur, San Diego, Calif., beginning 1946; consulting carillonneur, Maas-Rowe Carillons, Los Angeles, Calif., beginning 1946, and maker of most of the disks and rolls for operating their mechanical players. Visiting lecturer and carillon recitalist during Organ Week at Claremont College, 1957, 1960, 1962-67; has made about fifty chimes recordings for commercial records, and played at most carillon dedications in southern California since 1946. Member of Coronado Library Board for twelve years. *Member:* American Guild of Organists.

WRITINGS: Chimes and Electronic Carillons, John Day, 1948; *Billy Casper: Winner* (biography), Prentice-Hall, 1969. Author of more than two hundred columns, articles, and short stories published in this country and abroad.

WORK IN PROGRESS: A novel, *Kinsmen Stand Afar.*

SIDELIGHTS: Paul Peery has five brothers who are musicians, some avocationally and some professionally, and his daughter is a pianist. At West Point he was a pianist in the plebe orchestra, member of the cadet chapel choir, and also played the chapel chimes. For more than a decade he has been tenor soloist at the Episcopal Church in Coronado, and he was director of the church choir for three years.

AVOCATIONAL INTERESTS: Growing roses and camellias; breeding Siamese cats.

* * *

PELGER, Lucy J. 1913-1971

PERSONAL: Born September 22, 1913, in Cleveland, Ohio; daughter of John Herman and Mathilda (Huge) Kleinmyer; married William Matthew Pelger, September 8, 1934; children: (adopted) John William, Barbara Lynne (Mrs. David Scott). *Religion:* Lutheran. *Office:* Trinity Lutheran Church, 32nd and University, Des Moines, Iowa 50311.

CAREER: Paul P. Sogg, Attorney, Cleveland, Ohio, secretary, 1933-34; U.S. Army Air Forces Training Command, Fort Worth, Tex., secretary, 1943-44; Trinity Lutheran Church, Des Moines, Iowa, church secretary, beginning 1958.

WRITINGS: Living for a Living Lord, Concordia, 1967. Contributor to religious journals.

WORK IN PROGRESS: The Encounter (tentative title).†

(Died May 25, 1971)

* * *

PELISSIER, Roger 1924-1972

PERSONAL: Born December 30, 1924, in France; son of Michel and Andree (Massaloux) Pelissier; married Jytte Toennesen (in public relations), December 29, 1952; children: Yan, Brigette, Marc. *Education:* Ecole Nationale des Langues Orientales, Diplome de Chinois, 1953; Sorbonne, Universite de Paris, Lincence-es-Lettres, 1955; Ecole Nationale de Bibliothecaires, Diplome superieur de Bibliothecaire, 1957. *Office:* Ecole Nationale des Langues Orientales, 2, rue de Lille, Paris 7, France.

CAREER: Ecole Superieure de Guerre, Paris, France, librarian, 1959-65; Ecole Nationale des Langues Orientales, Paris, France, librarian for Chinese section, 1965-72; Ecole des Hautes Etudes, Sorbonne, Universite de Paris, assistant director of Centre de Documentation sur la Chine, 1958-72. *Member:* Centre d'Etudes de Politiques Etranger.

WRITINGS: La Chine Entre en Scene, Julliard, 1963, translation by Martin Kieffer published as *The Awakening of China,* Putnam, 1967; *2000 Revues d'Asie,* Bibliotheque Nationale, 1964; *Le Troiseme Geant: La Chine,* Presses de France, 1966; *De la Revolution Chinoise,* Julliard, 1967; *Les bibliotheques en Chine pendant la premiere moitie du XX siecle,* Mouton, 1971. Co-editor, *Newsletter for Chinese Studies in Europe.* Contributor of articles on modern China to French periodicals.

WORK IN PROGRESS: A history of the Chinese People's Republic.

SIDELIGHTS: Besides Chinese, Pelissier was proficient in English, German, and the Scandinavian languages.†

(Died August 29, 1972)

* * *

PENDLEBURY, B(evis) J(ohn) 1898-

PERSONAL: Born June 6, 1898, in Handsworth, Staffordshire, England; son of James (a clerk) and Clara (Topping) Pendlebury; married Enid Mary Smith, December 27, 1923; children: Ronald John, Isabel Mary Scoffham, Elizabeth Jane (Mrs. Gerald Watkins). *Education:* University of Birmingham, B.A. (first class honors), 1920, M.A., 1921. *Home:* 8 King's Rydon Close, Stoke Gabriel, Totnes, England.

CAREER: College de Thonon, Thonon-les-Bains, France, English assistant, 1921; Harrogate Grammar School, Harrogate, Yorkshire, England, English master, 1921-31; Douglas High School for Boys, Isle of Man, England, senior English master, 1931-59. *Military service:* British Army, Gordon Highlanders, 1916-19; became lieutenant. Home Guard, 1940-45; became captain. Also commandant of Isle of Man Army Cadet Force, 1942-47.

WRITINGS: To Enid (poems), Erskine Macdonald, 1922; *Dryden's Heroic Plays: A Study of the Origins,* Selwyn & Blount, 1923, reprinted, Russell & Russell, 1967; (editor and author of introduction) *English Lyrical Types,* Blackie & Son, 1934; *A Junior Course of Analysis,* Macmillan (London), 1935; *A Revision Course of French Grammar,* Blackie & Son, 1940; *Simple Ditties,* Heath Cranton, 1944; *English Test Papers,* Thomas Nelson, 1949; *English Test Papers for the Middle Forms,* Thomas Nelson, 1953; *A Grammar School English Course,* Thomas Nelson, Books I-II, 1956, Book III, 1957, Book IV, 1958; *G.C.E. English Practice for Technical Candidates,* University of London Press, 1963; *C.S.E. English Practice,* University of London Press, 1964; *English Language Revision,* Thomas Nelson, 1965; *Fourth-Year English Practice,* University of London Press, 1966; *Understanding and Appreciation,* three books, Thomas Nelson, 1967; *Comprehension and Comment,* Thomas Nelson, 1968; *Advanced Comprehension and Comment,* Thomas Nelson, 1969; *English Practice for Middle Forms,* University of London Press, 1970; *The Art of the Rhyme,* Scribner, 1971.

Writer of short stories, produced by British Broadcasting Corp., 1955, 1956. Occasional contributor to *Punch* and *Times Educational Supplement.*

WORK IN PROGRESS: A study of syntax in English poetry.

AVOCATIONAL INTERESTS: Travel, particularly in France and Italy.

* * *

PENROSE, Margaret
[Collective pseudonym]

WRITINGS—All published by Cupples & Leon, except as noted: *Burglar's Daughter; or, A True Heart Wins Friends,* Caldwell, 1899.

"Dorothy Dale" series: *Dorothy Dale, a Girl of Today,* 1908; *... at Glenwood School,* 1908; *... and Her Chums,* 1909; *Dorothy Dale's Great Secret,* 1909; *... Queer Holidays,* 1910; *... Camping Days,* 1911; *... School Rivals,* 1912; *Dorothy Dale in the City,* 1913; *Dorothy Dale's Promise,* 1914; *Dorothy Dale in the West,* 1915; *Dorothy Dale's Strange Discovery,* 1915; *... Engagement,* 1917; *Dorothy Dale to the Rescue,* 1924.

"Motor Girls" series: *The Motor Girls; or, a Mystery of the Road,* 1910; *... on a Tour,* 1910; *... at Lookout Beach; or, In Quest of the Runaways,* 1911; *... through New England; or, Held by the Gypsies,* 1911; *... on Cedar Lake; or, The Hermit of Fern Island,* 1912; *... on the Coast,* 1912; *... on Crystal Bay,* 1912; *... on Waters Blue,* 1912; *... on Camp Surprise,* 1912; *... in the Mountains,* 1912.

"Radio Girls" series: *The Radio Girls at Forest Lodge; or, The Strange Hut in the Swamp,* 1924; *... of Roselawn,* 1924; *... on Station Island,* 1924; *... on the Program,* 1924.

"Campfire Girls" series, four volumes, Goldsmith, 1930.

SIDELIGHTS: See **ADAMS, Harriet S., STRATEMEYER, Edward L.,** and **SVENSON, Andrew E.**†

* * *

PEPPARD, Murray B(isbee) 1917-1974

PERSONAL: Born May 23, 1917, in Concord, Mass.; son of Victor Edwin (a farmer) and Edna (Bisbee) Peppard; married Josette Smith (a teacher), October 25, 1942; children: Victor Edwin, Josette Marie, George Neville. *Education:* Amherst College, A.B., 1939; Yale University, M.A., 1942, Ph.D., 1948. *Home:* Harkness Rd., Pelham, Mass. 01002. *Office:* Amherst College, Amherst, Mass. 01002.

CAREER: Amherst College, Amherst, Mass., instructor in German, 1942; Yale University, New Haven, Conn., instructor in German, 1945-46; Amherst College, instructor, 1946-49, assistant professor, 1949-55, associate professor, 1955-62, professor of German, 1962-74. Member of Pelham Planning Board, 1962-64. *Military service:* U.S. Naval Reserve, active duty, 1942-45; became lieutenant; received Commendation Ribbon. *Member:* Modern Language Association of America, American Association of Teachers of German.

WRITINGS: N. A. Nekrasov, Poet and Publisher, Twayne, 1967; *Friedrich Durrenmatt,* Twayne, 1969; *Paths Through the Forest: A Biography of the Brothers Grimm,* Holt, 1971; (translator with Laszlo Tikos) Andrei Sinyavsky, *For Freedom of Imagination,* Holt, 1971. Contributor of articles and reviews to *Monatshefte.*

SIDELIGHTS: Peppard lived in Germany on three occasions. In addition to his fluency in German, he read Russian well, and some Turkish, Sanskrit, and Hindu.†

(Died September 3, 1974)

PERKINS, Virginia Chase 1902-
(Virginia Lowell Chase)

PERSONAL: Born July 31, 1902, in Blue Hill, Me.; daughter of Edward Everett (a lawyer) and Edith (Lord) Chase; married Wallace W. Perkins (an engineer), January 22, 1927; children: Mary Ellen (Mrs. Robert E. Sutton). *Education:* University of Minnesota, B.A. (magna cum laude), 1924; University of Michigan, graduate study, 1933-35, 1938-40; Wayne University (now Wayne State University), M.A., 1935. *Politics:* Independent. *Religion:* Unitarian Universalist. *Home:* 46 Hickory Lane, West Hartford, Conn. 06107. *Agent:* McIntosh & Otis, Inc., 475 Fifth Ave., New York, N.Y. 10017.

CAREER: High school principal in Steuben, Me., 1920-21; head of English department in public high school in Livermore Falls, Me., 1924-25; English teacher in public schools in Detroit, Mich., 1925-38; Colleges of the City of Detroit (now Wayne State University), Detroit, Mich., instructor in English, 1926-29; University of Michigan, Ann Arbor, teaching assistant in English, 1946-47; Hartford College for Women, Hartford, Conn., part-time lecturer in English, 1950-70. Visiting lecturer, Smith College, 1949-50. *Member:* Authors' League of America, English Speaking Union, Bronte Society, Mark Twain Memorial Society, Urban League. *Awards, honors:* Avery Hopwood Award for Fiction, University of Michigan, 1940.

WRITINGS: The Writing of Modern Prose, Henry Holt, 1935; *The American House,* Duell, Sloan & Pearce, 1944; *Discovery,* Macmillan, 1948; *The End of the Week,* Macmillan, 1953; *The Knight of the Golden Fleece,* Little, Brown, 1959; *One Crow, Two Crow,* Vanguard, 1971. Contributor of stories to anthologies, and articles and stories to national periodicals, including *Atlantic Monthly, Literary Review, Commonweal, New England Quarterly, Good Housekeeping, Seventeen,* and *Woman's Day.*

AVOCATIONAL INTERESTS: Archaeology, especially Roman remains in Great Britain.††

* * *

PERLMAN, Samuel 1905-1975

PERSONAL: Born October 18, 1905, in New York, N.Y.; son of Jacob (a tailor) and Rachel L. (Golub) Perlman; married Katherine Barbour (a social worker), May 27, 1941; children: Rachel Lee (Mrs. Lawrence White), Stephen M., Lois Beth. *Education:* College of the City of New York (now City College of the City University of New York), B.S.S., 1926; Hebrew Union College-Jewish Institute of Religion, New York, Rabbi and M.H.L., 1930; Columbia University, Ph.D., 1950. *Politics:* Independent.

CAREER: Rabbi of congregations in New York, New Jersey, and Pennsylvania, 1930-44; B'nai B'rith Hillel Foundations, director of foundation at University of Alabama, University, 1944-48, of foundations at University of North Carolina, Chapel Hill, Duke University, Durham, and other North Carolina colleges, 1948-52, and of foundation at Boston University and counselorships at Emerson College and State College of Boston (now Boston State College), all Boston, Mass., 1952-70. Boston University, lecturer in School of Theology and lecturer in Jewish history at Metropolitan College. *Member:* National Association of Hillel Directors (past president), Central Conference of American

Rabbis. *Awards, honors:* D.D., Hebrew Union College-Jewish Institute of Religion, 1956.

WRITINGS: Students versus Parents: Problems and Conflicts, Howard Doyle, 1969.

WORK IN PROGRESS: Contemporary Judaism.†

(Died February 4, 1975)

* * *

PERRY, Ben Edwin 1892-1968

PERSONAL: Born February 21, 1892, in Fayette, Ohio; son of Edwin Stewart (in hardware business) and Delle (Wickizer) Perry; married Lillian Pierce, July 19, 1922. *Education:* University of Michigan, A.B., 1915, A.M., 1916; Princeton University, Ph.D., 1919. *Politics:* Conservative Republican. *Religion:* Christian. *Home:* 504 West Vermont St., Urbana, Ill. 61801.

CAREER: Instructor in Latin at Urbana University School, Urbana, Ohio, 1919-20, Dartmouth College, Hanover, N.H., 1920-22, and Western Reserve University (now Case Western Reserve University), Cleveland, Ohio, 1922-24; University of Illinois, Urbana, assistant professor, 1924-28, associate professor, 1928-41, professor of classics, 1941-60, professor emeritus, 1960-68. Sather Visiting Professor, University of California, Berkeley, 1951; visiting professor, University of Michigan, 1967. Member of managing committee of American School of Classical Studies at Athens; member of advisory council of School of Classical Studies of American Academy in Rome. *Military service:* U.S. Army, 1918-19.

MEMBER: American Philological Association (member of board of directors, 1943-47; second vice-president, 1951-53), American Oriental Society, International Society for Folk-Narrative Research, Classical Association of the Middle West and South, Phi Beta Kappa. *Awards, honors:* Guggenheim fellow, 1930-32, 1954-55; Award of Merit of American Philological Association, 1955; presented festschrift in his honor by former students and colleagues at University of Illinois, 1968.

WRITINGS: The Metamorphoses Ascribed to Lucius of Patrae, Its Content, Nature, and Authorship, [Lancaster Pa.], 1920; (with W. A. Oldfather and H. V. Canter) *Index Apuleianus,* American Philological Association, 1934; *Studies in the Text History of the Life and Fables of Aesop,* American Philological Association, 1936; (editor) *Aesopica: A Series of Texts Relating to Aesop or Ascribed to Him or Closely Connected with the Literary Tradition That Bears His Name; Collected and Critically Edited with a Commentary and Historical Essay,* University of Illinois Press, Volume I, 1952; *The Origin of the Book of Sinbad,* W. de Gruyter, 1960; (editor and translator) *Secundus, the Silent Philosopher. The Greek Life of Secundus Critically Edited and Restored so far as Possible,* American Philological Association, 1964; (author of foreword; translation by A. K. Shalian) *David of Sassoun: The Armenian Folk Epic,* Ohio University Press, 1964; (editor) *Babrius and Phaedrus, Newly Edited and Translated into English, Together with an Historical Introduction and a Comprehensive Survey of Greek and Latin Fables in the Aesopic Tradition,* Harvard University Press, 1965; *The Ancient Romances: A Literary-Historical Account of Their Origins* (Sather Lectures), University of California Press, 1967.

Contributor: *Classical Studies in Honor of William Abbott Oldfather,* University of Illinois Press, 1943; *Essays in Literature, Folklore, Bibliography, Honoring Archer Taylor,* J.

J. Augustin, 1960; *Festschrift fuer Franz Dolger*, Carl Winter (Heidelberg), 1966. Contributor to *Dictionary of World Literature* and *Encyclopaedia Britannica;* contributor of about sixty articles and reviews to professional journals in America and abroad. Associate editor, *Classical Philology*, 1948-50.

WORK IN PROGRESS: A critical edition of Johannes Georgides' prose anthology; a critical edition and translation of the oldest version of *Sinbad and the Seven Wise Masters; Aesopica*, Volume II, and Volume III.

SIDELIGHTS: Perry had varying competence in Greek, Latin, German, French, Italian, Spanish, Russian ("very weak"), Hebrew, Syrica, Arabic, Armenian, and Persian ("very little"). *Avocational interests:* Outdoor life and exercise in Vermont and Florida.

BIOGRAPHICAL/CRITICAL SOURCES: Comparative Literature, summer, 1968; John L. Heller, editor, *Classical Studies Presented to Ben Edwin Perry by His Students and Colleagues at the University of Illinois, 1924-1960*, University of Illinois Press, 1969.†

(Died November 1, 1968)

*   *   *

PERRY, Henry Ten Eyck   1890-1973

PERSONAL: Born December 18, 1890, in Albany, N.Y.; son of John Treadwell (a banker) and Gertrude (Ten Eyck) Perry; married Elizabeth McAfee Bigelow, December 23, 1922. *Education:* Yale University, B.A., 1912; Harvard University, M.A., 1914, Ph.D., 1916. *Home:* 21 Autumn St., New Haven, Conn. 06511.

CAREER: Yale University, New Haven, Conn., instructor, 1916-21, assistant professor of English, 1921-24; University of Wisconsin, Madison, associate professor of English, 1924-26; University of Buffalo (now State University of New York at Buffalo), professor of English literature, 1926-59, head of department of English, 1926-56, professor emeritus, 1959-73. *Military service:* U.S. Army, 1918-19.

WRITINGS: The First Duchess of Newcastle and Her Husband, Ginn, 1918; (editor) Shakespeare, *The Taming of the Shrew*, Yale University Press, 1921; *The Comic Spirit in Restoration Drama*, Yale University Press, 1925; *Masters of Dramatic Comedy*, Harvard University Press, 1939; (editor) *The Way of the World*, Crofts, 1951.†

(Died June 21, 1973)

*   *   *

PERRY, Kenneth F(rederick)   1902-1974

PERSONAL: Born November 1, 1902, in Pueblo, Colo.; son of John A. (an architect) and Bessie (Polkinghorn) Perry; married Lorena K. Mason, September 26, 1924; children: Joyce Elaine, John Kenneth, Kathryn Ann (Mrs. John S. Girault). *Education:* Colorado State College (now University of Northern Colorado), A.B., 1924, A.M., 1927; Columbia University, Ph.D., 1941. *Home:* 2118 Glen Fair Dr., Greeley, Colo. 80631. *Office:* University of Northern Colorado, Greeley, Colo. 80631.

CAREER: Teacher of industrial arts at high school in Fort Worth, Tex., 1925-26, and at junior high school in Denver, Colo., 1926-27; University of Northern Colorado, Greeley, began 1927, as instructor, became professor of industrial arts, 1933, chairman of Division of the Arts, beginning 1941. *Member:* American Industrial Arts Association (president, 1959), American Council on Industrial Arts Teacher Educa-

tion, American Vocational Association, National Association of Industrial Teacher Educators, Greeley Chamber of Commerce (past president), Lions Club (past district governor).

WRITINGS: (With Clarence T. Baab) *The Binding of Books*, Manual Arts Press, 1940, revised edition, McKnight & McKnight, 1967; *A Diversified Art Program*, Teachers College, Columbia University, 1943.†

(Died May 16, 1974)

*   *   *

PERSON, Amy L.   1896-

PERSONAL: Born August 23, 1896, in Hector, Minn.; daughter of Ola and Hannah (Lundstrom) Person. *Education:* Asbury College, A.B., 1923; University of Kentucky, M.A., 1927; George Peabody College for Teachers, graduate study, 1935-36. *Politics:* Prohibition. *Religion:* Church of the Nazarene. *Home:* 4515 Bryant Ave. N., Minneapolis, Minn. 55412.

CAREER: Asbury College, Wilmore, Ky., registrar, 1927-29; Trevecca Nazarene College, Nashville, Tenn., registrar, 1931-62, instructor in English, 1933-66. *Member:* Phi Beta Lambda.

WRITINGS: Illustrations from Literature, Baker Book, 1966.††

*   *   *

PETTITT, George A(lbert)   1901-1976

PERSONAL: Born June 7, 1901; son of George J. (a ship carpenter) and Catherine (McGuire) Pettitt; married Eleanor K. Graves, April 12, 1935; children: Nancy Kyle, Jennifer Graves. *Education:* University of California, Berkeley, B.A., 1926, Ph.D., 1940. *Home:* 1429 Euclid Ave., Berkeley, Calif. 94708. *Agent:* Gerard McCauley Agency, Inc., 159 West 53rd St., New York, N.Y. 10019.

CAREER: U.S. Navy, 1943-46, served active duty in Air Corps, became lieutenant commander; entered U.S. Naval Reserve, 1943, retired from service, 1946; serving on Selective Service Draft Board, number forty-seven; served on city council of Berkeley, Calif., 1949-58; director of Berkeley Chamber of Commerce, Berkeley, 1949-51; San Francisco Bay Area Educational Television Association, 1956-60, began as member of board of trustees, became first vice-president; University of California, Berkeley, assistant to president, lecturer in anthropology, 1940-66. President of board of directors, Cazadero Music Camp Fund, Inc., 1970-71. Former vice-president of Public Relations Society of America; former treasurer of American College Public Relations Association. *Member:* American Anthropological Association, American Ethnological Society, San Francisco Press Club, Phi Beta Kappa, Sigma Xi, Berkeley Breakfast Club (president, 1966), Berkeley Rotary Club (secretary, 1964-66), Faculty Club (University of California, Berkeley), Mira Vista Golf and Country Club.

WRITINGS: So Boulder Dam Was Built, Press of Lederer, Street & Zeus, 1935; *Primitive Education in North America*, University of California Press, 1946; *The Quileute of La Push, 1775-1945*, University of California Press, 1950; *Twenty-Eight Years in the Life of a University President* (biography of Robert Gordon Sproul), University of California Press, 1966; *Clayton, Not Quite Shangri-La: The Story of a California Town*, Contra Costa County Historical Society, 1969; *Prisoners of Culture*, Scribner, 1970; *Berkeley: The Town and Gown of It*, North-Howell, 1973;

History of Berkeley, Alameda County Historical Society, 1976. Contributor to *Encyclopaedia Britannica,* 15th edition, 1974.

SIDELIGHTS: Pettitt told *CA* he was one of the co-originators of the "University Explorer," the "longest lived radio network program in the U.S., 1933 to date."†

(Died May 6, 1976)

* * *

PEYTON, Patrick J(oseph) 1909-

PERSONAL: Born January 9, 1909, in Carracastle, County Mayo, Ireland; son of John and Mary (Gillard) Peyton. *Education:* Holy Cross Seminary, Notre Dame, Ind., graduate, 1932; University of Notre Dame, A.B., 1937; Holy Cross College, Washington, D.C., graduate theological study, 1937-42. *Home and office:* Family Rosary Crusade, 773 Madison Ave., Albany, N.Y. 12208.

CAREER: Left Ireland at nineteen, expecting to "make a million dollars in real estate" in America, but ended up mining coal in Scranton, Pa., and later working as a church janitor and door-to-door salesman of American flags; entered Seminary of Holy Cross Fathers at Notre Dame, Ind., and was ordained to Roman Catholic priesthood, 1941; after recovering from tuberculosis contracted shortly before ordination, he began his far-flung crusade for family unity through prayer (originated the slogan, "The family that prays together . . . stays together"); founder and director of Family Rosary Crusades, Albany, N.Y., beginning 1942, conducting rallies in United States, Canada, Africa, India, Australia, New Zealand, Philippines, and other countries of Asia, Europe, and South America; founder and producer of "Father Peyton's Family Theater," weekly radio program, beginning 1947; producer of television shows originating in his Hollywood-based Family Theater Productions, including a series of fifteen films on the rosary for television and radio in Spain, 1956, and the series, "Prayer of the Ages," 1964.

MEMBER: Knights of Columbus. *Awards, honors:* George Washington Honor Medal of Freedoms Foundation, 1954; Thomas Alva Edison Foundation National Mass Media Award, 1955; LL.D., Stonehill College, 1963; Bronze Medal at Venice International Film Festival, 1964, for television film, "The Soldier."

WRITINGS: The Ear of God, Doubleday, 1951; *Father Peyton's Rosary Prayer Book,* Family Rosary, Inc., 1954; *Family Prayer Book,* Benziger, 1964; *All for Her,* Doubleday, 1967.

SIDELIGHTS: Father Peyton drew an attendance of two million people at a prayer rally in Sao Paulo, and an estimated one and a half million in Rio de Janeiro; the largest gathering to hear him in the United States was five hundred thousand at Golden Gate Park in San Francisco in 1961.

* * *

PFEILSCHIFTER, Boniface 1900-

PERSONAL: Born April 22, 1900, in Cleveland, Ohio; son of Alois (an organist) and Elizabeth (Kramer) Pfeilschifter. *Education:* Our Lady of Angels Seminary, Cleveland, Ohio, B.A., 1923; attended St. Anthony Seminary, St. Louis, Mo., 1923-27. *Home:* 3140 Meramec St., St. Louis, Mo. 63118.

CAREER: Roman Catholic priest; missionary in Shantung, China, 1928-47; home missionary in Chicago, Ill., 1947-55, and in St. Louis, Mo., beginning 1955.

WRITINGS: (With Norbert Schmals) *Shen-Fu's Story* (memoirs of two missionaries in China), Franciscan Herald, 1966.

* * *

PHELPS, D(udley) Maynard 1897-

PERSONAL: Born May 8, 1897, in Manton, Mich.; son of Charles Dellen (a businessman) and Cora Lee (Ladd) Phelps; married Mildred Irene Hendrick, February 6, 1934; children: Marcia Lee Phelps Schmidt, Richard Ladd. *Education:* University of Michigan, A.B., 1925, M.B.A., 1926, Ph.D., 1931; University of Minnesota, additional study, 1926. *Home:* 1475 Roxbury Rd., Ann Arbor, Mich. 48104. *Office:* Graduate School of Business Administration, University of Michigan, Ann Arbor, Mich. 48104.

CAREER: Manager of grain, lumber, and fuel business, 1918-22; University of Michigan, Ann Arbor, instructor, 1926-28, assistant professor, 1929-35, associate professor, 1935-40, professor of marketing, 1940-67, professor emeritus, 1967—. U.S. Department of State, senior economic analyst at U.S. Embassy, Caracas, Venezuela, 1942-43, associate chief of Division of Financial and Monetary Affairs, Washington, D.C., 1944-45, chief of Division of Foreign Economic Development, Washington, D.C., and deputy U.S. representative to Allied Commission, 1945-46. Visiting professor and adviser, Foundation for Business Administration, Rotterdam, Netherlands, 1966-67, 1968-69; visiting professor or lecturer at several universities, including University of Colorado, and Columbia University. Trustee of Marketing Science Institute, Philadelphia, 1962-65.

MEMBER: American Marketing Association (president, 1957-58), Delta Sigma Pi, Pi Kappa Alpha, Beta Gamma Sigma, Rotary Club (Ann Arbor). *Awards, honors:* Social Science Research Council research fellow in South America, 1932-33; Marketing Educator of the Year Award of National Sales Executives, 1960; Distinguished Faculty Service Award, University of Michigan, 1961; Parlin Award of Philadelphia chapter, American Marketing Association, 1964; named to Hall of Fame in Distribution.

WRITINGS: Marketing Research (Purpose, Scope, and Method), Bureau of Business Research, University of Michigan, 1937; *Planning the Product,* Irwin, 1948; *Sales Management: Policies and Procedures,* Irwin, 1951, 2nd edition (with J. Howard Westing) published as *Marketing Management,* Irwin, 1960, 3rd edition, 1968; *Rubber Developments in Latin America,* Bureau of Business Research, University of Michigan, 1956; (editor) *Product Management: Selected Readings,* American Marketing Association, 1970. Contributor to journals in his field. Contributing editor, *Handbook of Latin American Studies,* 1936-40.

WORK IN PROGRESS: Product Planning and Development.

* * *

PHILIP, J(ames) A(llenby) 1901-

PERSONAL: Born December 18, 1901, in Galt, Ontario, Canada; son of William (a banker) and Ruth (Allenby) Philip; married Erika ter Hell, July 17, 1952; children: William, James. *Education:* University of Toronto, B.A., 1923; University of Florence, D.Litt., 1935. *Religion:* Anglican. *Home:* Stonehurst Farm, R.R. 1, Victoria Harbour, Ontario, Canada L0K 2A0.

CAREER: Canadian Pacific Railway, managing director, Rome, Italy, 1925-40; University of Toronto, Trinity College, Toronto, Ontario, lecturer, 1949-59, associate professor of classics, 1959-70; Bishop's University, Lennoxville, Quebec, professor of ancient philology, 1970-72, dean, 1971-72. *Military service:* Canadian Army, 1941-47; became major. *Member:* Classical Association (Canada), American Philological Association. *Awards, honors:* Canada Council fellowship, 1968.

WRITINGS: Pythagoras and Early Pythagoreanism, University of Toronto Press, 1966. Contributor to scholarly journals.

WORK IN PROGRESS: An edition of *Plato—Sophistes,* with commentary.†

* * *

PHILLIPS, Jewell Cass   1900-

PERSONAL: Born October 8, 1900, in Eldorado, Okla.; son of Jewell William (a merchant) and Ritchie Mary (Goar) Phillips; married Winifred Sudderth, December 27, 1922 (deceased); married Grace Noble Verbryck, February 29, 1968 (divorced). *Education:* University of Oklahoma, B.A., 1921, M.A., 1929; University of Pennsylvania, Ph.D., 1935. *Politics:* Democrat. *Religion:* Christian. *Home:* 2276-P, Via Mariposa E., Laguna Hills, Calif. 92563.

CAREER: Principal and superintendent of schools in Wyoming and Oklahoma, 1921-28; University of Oklahoma, Norman, instructor in government, 1928-30; University of Pennsylvania, Philadelphia, instructor, 1930-37, assistant professor, 1937-45, associate professor, 1945-53, professor of political science, 1953-66, professor emeritus, 1966—. Visiting professor of American studies, University of Bombay, 1964-65. Public service supervisor, Public Works Reserve for State of Pennsylvania, 1941-42; chairman, Citizenship Clearing House Committee for Eastern Pennsylvania, 1955-57. Member of Citizens Charter Committee of Philadelphia, 1951-55, and Philadelphia Committee of Seventy, beginning 1952.

MEMBER: American Political Science Association, American Academy of Political and Social Science, American Society for Public Administration, American Association of University Professors, National Municipal League, Alpha Kappa Psi, Pi Sigma Alpha, Pi Gamma Mu.

WRITINGS: State and Local Government in America, American Book Co., 1954; *Municipal Government and Administration in America,* Macmillan, 1960; (with Cortez A. M. Ewing and Henry J. Abraham) *Essentials of American Government,* American Book Co., 1962, 3rd edition, Van Nostrand, 1971. Contributor of articles to law, tax, and economic journals.

* * *

PHILLIPS, Velma   1894-

PERSONAL: Born October 28, 1894, in Knox County, Ill.; daughter of William T. and Serah Dell (Maxey) Phillips. *Education:* Knox College, Ph.B., 1914; University of Chicago, A.M., 1915; Columbia University, Ph.D., 1927. *Politics:* Republican. *Religion:* Methodist.

CAREER: Instructor in home economics, Lenox College, Hopkinton, Iowa, 1915-16, Baker University, Baldwin, Kan., 1916-17, Horace Mann High School, New York, N.Y., 1917-18; Montana State College (now University), Bozeman, director of home economics and dean of women, 1918-24; Abraham and Straus, Inc., Brooklyn, N.Y., educational advertising, 1924-28; Ohio University, Athens, director of home economics, 1929-39; Washington State

University, Pullman, director of College of Home Economics, 1939-61; California State University, Northridge, professor of home economics, beginning 1961. Visiting professor, Long Beach State College (now California State University, Long Beach), 1965. Delegate to International Home Economics Congress, Copenhagen, 1939, Stockholm, 1949, University of Maryland, 1959. *Member:* American Home Economics Association, American Association of University Women, Consumer Council, California Home Economics Association (research chairman).

WRITINGS: Evidence of the Need of Education for Efficient Purchasing, Teachers College, Columbia University, 1931, reprinted, AMS Press, 1972; (With Mildred Graves Ryan) *Clothes for You,* Appleton, 1947, sole author of revised edition, 1954; *Consumer Buying,* Washington State University Press, 1951, revised edition (with Walter J. Wills), 1958; *Home Economics Careers for You,* Harper, 1957, revised edition, 1962. Contributor to *Journal of Home Economics.*†

* * *

PHILLIPS, Wendell   1921-1975

PERSONAL: Born September 25, 1921, in Oakland, Calif.; son of Merley H. and Sunshine (Chrisman) Phillips; married Shirley Au, September 14, 1968 (divorced December, 1968). *Education:* University of California, Berkeley, A.B. (with honors), 1943; University of Brussels, Ph.D., 1972. *Religion:* Presbyterian. *Home:* 2969 Kalakaua Ave., Honolulu, Hawaii 96815. *Agent:* Collins-Knowlton-Wing, Inc., 60 East 56th St., New York, N.Y. 10022. *Office:* American Foundation for the Study of Man, International Market Place, Suite 207, Halau Building, Honolulu, Hawaii 96815.

CAREER: Explorer and archaeologist; holder of oil and other concessions in Oman, Libya, and Venezuela; founder and president of American Institute for the Study of Man, 1949-75, with headquarters in Honolulu, Hawaii. Served in U.S. Merchant Marine, 1943-45, and collected marine zoological specimens in the South Pacific; organized and led an archaeological expedition that spanned Africa from Cairo to the Cape, 1947-49; leader of other expeditions in Sinai, 1950 (microfilmed the ancient library at the Monastery of St. Catherine's for the Library of Congress), Yemen, 1951-52, and Oman, 1952-53, 1958, 1961; president of Philpryor Corp., 1951-58, and Middle East American Oil Co., 1955-56; chairman of the board, P.T.P. Corp., Reno, Nev., and Phillips Pacific, Sacramento, Calif. Director of antiquities for the sultantate in Oman, 1953-70, and economic adviser to Sultan of Oman, 1956-70. Lecturer at New York University, 1958; visiting professor of archaeology at University of Wyoming, 1968. Trustee, Hawaii Loa College, Honolulu, 1968, and San Francisco Theological Seminary, 1970.

MEMBER: American Geographical Society (fellow), American Association for the Advancement of Science, American Anthropological Association, Society for American Archaeology, Royal Geographical Society (fellow), Royal Anthropological Institute (fellow), Royal Asiatic Society (fellow), Royal Central Asian Society (fellow), Oriental Society, Society of Vertebrate Paleontology, Middle East Institute, Royal Archaeological Institute, Hakluyt Society, New York Academy of Sciences, Honolulu Academy of Arts; Explorers Club, Dutch Treat Club, and Circumnavigators Club (all New York), Adventurers Club (Honolulu), Alpha Gamma Nu (honorary member).

AWARDS, HONORS: Sheik of Bal-Harith Tribe; Knight of the Order of St. Catherine (Greece); University of Brussels

Commemorative Medal, 1969; American Academy of Achievement Gold Plate Award, 1972. American Library Association named *Qataban and Sheba* one of the best books of the year, 1955. Honorary degrees from twenty-six universities and colleges, including Sc.D., Marietta, College, 1952, Ed.D., Kyungpook National University, Korea, 1966, and D.Sc., University of Utah, 1972.

WRITINGS: Qataban and Sheba: Exploring the Ancient Kingdoms on the Biblical Spice Routes of Arabia, Harcourt, 1955; *Unknown Oman,* McKay, 1966; *Oman: A History,* Reynal, 1968; *An Explorer's Life of Jesus,* Two Continents Publishing, 1975. Contributor to scientific journals.

SIDELIGHTS: Featured in a *Time* article under the heading "Entrepeneurs," Phillips was quoted as saying, "I am the largest private oil concessionaire in the world." Phillips was also the only American to be named an Arab sheik. In 1968, University of the Pacific established the Wendell Phillips Center for Intercultural Studies and the Wendell Phillips Lectureship in Intercultural Studies; the Wendell Phillips Centre for Advanced Theological Studies in Berkeley was also established in 1968.

Of his book, *Unknown Oman,* E. P. Stickney noted, "Though rambling in its slight organization, it will be a readable and absorbing account for the informed layman as well as the specialist."

BIOGRAPHICAL/CRITICAL SOURCES: Economist, September 3, 1966; *Times Literary Supplement,* September 15, 1966; *Time,* September 30, 1966; *Business Week,* September 25, 1971, October 16, 1971; *Newsweek,* February 14, 1972.†

(Died December 4, 1975)

* * *

PICK, John 1911-

PERSONAL: Born September 18, 1911, in West Bend, Wis.; son of Edwin and Tessa (Hickish) Pick; married the Marchesa Cecilia Barbara, April 18, 1956. *Education:* University of Notre Dame, B.A., 1933; University of Wisconsin, M.A., 1934, Ph.D., 1938; graduate study at Harvard University and Oxford University. *Home:* Le Redan, Madliena, Malta.

CAREER: Boston College, Boston, Mass., professor of English, 1939-41; Groton School, Groton, Mass., master, 1941-45; Marquette University, Milwaukee, Wis., associate professor, 1945-52, professor of English, 1952-75, professor emeritus, 1975—, chairman of university committee on fine arts, 1951-75. Cultural attache, Embassy of Malta, Washington, D.C., beginning 1968. Fulbright lecturer, Royal University of Malta, 1955-56; visiting professor at Harvard University, University of St. Edmunds (England), Cambridge University, 1976, and Oxford University, 1977. Trustee, Milwaukee Art Center. *Member:* Modern Language Association of America, English-Speaking Union, American Association of University Professors, Royal Society (London; fellow).

WRITINGS: Gerard Manley Hopkins: Priest and Poet, Oxford University Press, 1942, 2nd edition, 1966; (editor) Gerard Manley Hopkins, *A Hopkins Reader,* Oxford University Press, 1953, revised edition, Image Books, 1966; *Marquette University Art Collection,* Marquette University Press, 1964; (editor) *Hopkins: The Windhover,* C. E. Merrill, 1968. Editor, *Renascence: A Critical Journal of Letters,* 1948-69.

PIKE, Norman 1901-

PERSONAL: Born August 9, 1901, in Malden, Mass.; son of Eleazer Stuart (in insurance) and Emma (Veazie) Pike; married Merle Bronson, September 4, 1926 (deceased); children: Norman Bronson. *Education:* Attended Amherst College, four years. *Politics:* Republican. *Religion:* Episcopalian. *Home:* Main St., Ashfield, Mass. 01330.

CAREER: Wico Electric Co., West Springfield, Mass., engineer, 1924-35; Equitable Life Assurance Society, Springfield, Mass., salesman, 1935-36; Westinghouse Electric Co., East Springfield, Mass., buyer, 1936-37; Bunting Brass & Bronze Co., Toledo, Ohio, salesman, 1937-39; Worthington Pump & Machinery Corp., Holyoke, Mass., time study supervisor, 1939-48; Ford Motor Co., proprietor of dealership in Ashfield, Mass., 1949-63. *Member:* Ashfield Grange (master, 1949-50), Ashfield Historical Society (president, 1962-63), Ashfield Golf Club (treasurer, 1947-52).

WRITINGS: The Joy of Woodworking, Pantheon, 1969.

WORK IN PROGRESS: Research on the birth of religious freedom in Massachusetts; an alphabetical illustrated description of common insects.

AVOCATIONAL INTERESTS: Creation of articles from choice native wood.

* * *

PILKINGTON, E(dward) C(ecil) A(rnold) 1907-

PERSONAL: Born November 1, 1907, in Lancashire, England; son of Alfred Cecil (a glass manufacturer) and Olive Mary Christine (Medley) Pilkington; married Mabel Joyce Newman, February, 1945; children: Arnold Philip, Brian. *Education:* Oxford University, B.A., 1929, graduate study, 1929-30. *Home:* Dordtwyck, Elm Park Rd., Pinner, Middlesex, England.

CAREER: Schoolmaster in England, teaching German, economics, politics, and government, beginning 1932; Merchant Taylors' School, Northwood, Middlesex, head of modern studies department, 1962-68, part time faculty member, beginning 1968. *Military service:* Royal Air Force, 1941-45; became flight lieutenant; received Africa Star.

WRITINGS: The Economic Problem in Outline, Pergamon, 1966.

WORK IN PROGRESS: A translation of stories by E.T.A. Hoffmann.

SIDELIGHTS: Edward Pilkington was a middle distance runner for Oxford University, 1930, and was captain of his college rugby team. He has been partially paralyzed since 1950 as the result of polio.††

* * *

PILKINGTON, Francis Meredyth 1907-

PERSONAL: Born June 16, 1907, in Kingstown County, Dublin, Ireland; daughter of Guy Brabazon (a solicitor) and Charlotte Edith (Cotton-Walker) Pilkington. *Education:* Attended French School, Bray, Ireland. *Religion:* Church of England. *Home:* Brookleaze, Nettlebridge, Oakhill, near Bath, Somersetshire, England. *Agent:* Anthony Sheil, 52 Floral St., Covent Garden, London WC2E 9DA, England.

WRITINGS: Three Sorrowful Tales of Erin (youth book), Bodley Head, 1965, Walck, 1966; *Shamrock and Spear: Tales and Legends from Ireland* (youth book), Bodley Head, 1966, Holt, 1968.

AVOCATIONAL INTERESTS: Music, reading, gardening.

PILPEL, Harriet F(leischl)

PERSONAL: Born in New York, N.Y.; daughter of Julius (a businessman) and Ethel (Loewy) Fleischl; married Robert Pilpel (a social service executive), June 15, 1933; children: Judith Ethel (Mrs. Alan Appelbaum), Robert Harry. *Education:* Vassar College, A.B., 1932; Columbia University, A.M., 1933, LL.B., 1936. *Politics:* Democrat. *Religion:* Ethical Culture. *Home:* 70 East 96th St., New York, N.Y. 10028. *Office:* Greenbaum, Wolff & Ernst, 437 Madison Ave., New York, N.Y. 10022.

CAREER: Admitted to New York Bar, 1936; Greenbaum, Wolff & Ernst, New York, N.Y., associate, 1936-43, senior partner, beginning 1943. Counsel to Planned Parenthood Federation of America, Sex Information and Education Council of the United States, Association for the Study of Abortion, and Association for Voluntary Sterilization; member of International Advisory Committee of Law and Population Programme of Fletcher School of Law and Diplomacy; vice-chairman, Alan Guttmacher Institute. Lecturer on marriage and family law, civil liberties, birth control, and related subjects. Member of national board and chairman of radio and television committee, American Civil Liberties Union; member of board of visitors, Columbia University School of Law; member of advisory board, Arthur and Elizabeth Schlesinger Library on History of Women in America.

MEMBER: American Bar Association, Federal Bar Council, New York County Lawyers Association, American Association of Marriage Counselors (affiliate), Authors League of America, P.E.N., Society of Magazine Writers, Phi Beta Kappa.

WRITINGS: (With Theodore Zavin) *Your Marriage and the Law,* Rinehart, 1952; *Rights and Writers,* Dutton, 1960; (with Morton David Goldberg) *A Copyright Guide,* Bowker, 1960, 4th edition, 1969; (with Minna Post Peyser) *Know Your Rights,* Women's Bureau, U.S. Department of Labor, 1965. Also author of pamphlet, *When Should Abortion Be Legal?,* for Public Affairs Committee, 1969. Monthly columnist writing "You Can Do That" for *Publishers' Weekly;* contributor to other magazines and to legal journals. Formerly an editor of *Columbia Law Review;* member of board of editors, *Performing Arts Review,* and of advisory board, *Journal of Marriage and Family Counseling.*

* * *

PIMSLEUR, Paul 1927-1976

PERSONAL: Born October 17, 1927, in New York, N.Y.; son of Solomon (a composer) and Meira (Goldwater) Pimsleur; married Beverly Fleishman (a teacher of ancient history), December 27, 1962; children: Marc-Andrew, Julia. *Education:* City College (now City College of the City University of New York), BS., 1949; Columbia University, M.A., 1952, Ph.D., 1956, M.A., 1957. *Residence:* Loudonville, N.Y. *Office:* School of Education, State University of New York at Albany, Albany, N.Y. 12222.

CAREER: University of California, Los Angeles, instructor, 1957-59, assistant professor of French, 1959-61; Ohio State University, Columbus, associate professor, 1961-67, professor of Romance languages and education, 1967-70; State University of New York at Albany, professor of education and Romance languages, 1970-76. Fulbright professor, University of Heidelberg, 1965-67; visiting professor, Sorbonne, 1976. Company manager, Salzburg Marionette Theatre, 1952-56. Director, The Language Lab, Ohio Bell Telephone Co., 1960-70. *Military service:* U.S. Army, 1946-

47; became sergeant. *Member:* Modern Language Association, American Educational Research Association, American Association of Teachers of French, American Council on Teaching of Foreign Languages.

WRITINGS: Pimsleur Language Aptitude Battery, Harcourt, 1966; *Pimsleur Language Proficiency Tests,* Harcourt, 1967; *C'est la Vie,* Harcourt, 1970, second edition, 1976; (editor with Terence Quinn) *Psychology of Second Language Learning,* Cambridge University Press, 1971; *Sol y Sombra: Lecturas de hoy,* Harcourt, 1972; (with Giose Rimanelli) *Poems Make Pictures: Pictures Make Poems,* Pantheon, 1972; *Pimsleur Language Programs,* Center for Curriculum Development, 1972; *Le Pont Sonore,* Harcourt, 1972; (with Donald Berger) *Encounters: A Basic Reader,* Harcourt, 1974. Contributor of articles on foreign language learning to professional journals.

WORK IN PROGRESS: Sense Modality Endowment.†

(Died June 22, 1976)

* * *

PINSENT, Arthur 1888-

PERSONAL: Born September 16, 1888, in Leicester, England; children: two sons. *Education:* University College of Wales, Aberystwyth, B.Sc., 1911; University of London, M.A., 1921. *Residence:* Aberystwyth, Wales.

CAREER: Taught school at primary, secondary, and adult levels; vice-principal, Emergency Training College for Ex-Service Men, 1921-23; University College of Wales, Aberystwyth, began as lecturer, became senior lecturer in education, 1926-49; National Foundation for Educational Research in England and Wales, Slough, England, research officer, 1949-50; University College of Wales, secretary of Faculty of Education, 1950-53. Former member, Cardiganshire Education Committee. *Military service:* British Army, Royal Engineers, 1915-19; became captain. *Member:* American Psychological Association (foreign affiliate).

WRITINGS: Principles of Teaching-Method, Harrap, 1941, 3rd revised and enlarged edition published as *Principles of Teaching Method: With Special Reference to Secondary Education,* Verry, 1969; (editor and contributor) *A Survey of Rewards and Punishments in Schools,* National Foundation for Educational Research in England and Wales, 1952. Contributor to *British Journal of Educational Psychology* and *Journal of the Institute of Sociology.*

WORK IN PROGRESS: Application of scientific concepts to the general theory of education.†

* * *

PIPPIN, Frank Johnson 1906-1968

PERSONAL: Born July 22, 1906, in Round Oak, Ga.; son of George Thomas (a civil servant and merchant) and Dora (Jackson) Pippin; married Anne Ozelle Weems, July 22, 1933 (died September, 1962); married Ann Hedgecock Foster, October 25, 1966; children: Elizabeth (Mrs. Bill Gentry), Julia Lilla (Mrs. Carel Sellenraad, Jr.). *Education:* Emory University, A.B., 1927; Southern Methodist University, B.D., 1929; graduate study at Phillips University, 1938, and Harvard University, 1943. *Home:* 307 King Ave., Belton, Mo. 64012. *Office:* Community Christian Church, 4601 Main St., Kansas City, Mo. 64112.

CAREER: Ordained as minister of Christian Churches (Disciples of Christ), 1933; minister in Tulsa, Okla., 1933-39, and in Bristow, Okla., 1939-41; Community Christian Church,

Kansas City, Mo., minister, 1946-68. Trustee, Culver-Stockton College. *Military service:* U.S. Army Reserve, chaplain, 1932-56; on active service, 1941-45; became lieutenant colonel; received three combat stars and special citation for meritorious service. *Member:* Military Order of the World Wars (chaplain, Kansas City chapter, 1965), Disciples Chaplains Association of United States (president, 1959-60), Masons, Sertoma Club. *Awards, honors:* D.D., Culver-Stockton College, 1955.

WRITINGS: Only This Throne, Burton, 1949; *Thoughts in the Night,* Christopher, 1953; *In the Night His Song,* Christopher, 1955; *The Christmas Light and the Easter Hope,* Crowell, 1959; *The Roads We Travel,* Bethany, 1966. Regular columnist, *Christian;* feature writer, *Tulsa World,* 1935-38.

WORK IN PROGRESS: Please Don't Move the Candlesticks, for younger ministers only; *The Best of Thoughts in the Night.*†

(Died June 28, 1968)

* * *

PIQUET, Howard S. 1903-

PERSONAL: Born July 4, 1903, in New York, N.Y.; son of Samuel D. (a physician) and Laura E. (Mann) Piquet; married Dorothy Burke, December 23, 1930; children: Dorothy Vanna (Mrs. Norman S. Damon), Howard S., Jr., Barbara. *Education:* New York University, B.S. (summa cum laude), 1924; University of California (now University of California, Berkeley), M.A., 1926; Princeton University, Ph.D., 1930. *Politics:* Independent. *Religion:* Protestant. *Home:* 2045 Yorktown Rd., N.W., Washington, D.C. 20012.

CAREER: Princeton University, Princeton, N.J., instructor, 1928-32; New York University, New York, N.Y., assistant professor of economics, 1932-34; U.S. Tariff Commission, Washington, D.C., senior economist, 1934-37, chief of Economics Division, 1937-43; United Nations Food and Agriculture Organization, Interim Commission, Washington, D.C., executive secretary, 1943-45; U.S. Office of War Mobilization and Reconversion, Washington, D.C., consultant, 1945-46; Library of Congress, Washington, D.C., senior specialist in international economics, Legislative Reference Service, 1946-1969. American University, Graduate School, Washington, D.C., adjunct professor of economic theory, 1934-56. Deputy staff director, House of Representatives Select Committee on Foreign Aid; member of professional staff, House Committee on Foreign Affairs. *Member:* Council on Foreign Relations (New York), National Press Club, Phi Beta Kappa.

WRITINGS: Building and Loan Associations in New Jersey, Princeton University Press, 1930, 2nd edition, 1931; *Outline of New Deal Legislation,* McGraw, 1934, 2nd edition, 1935; *Aid, Trade and the Tariff,* Crowell, 1953; *The Trade Agreements Act and the National Interest,* Brookings, 1958; *The European Free Trade Association: Implications for U.S. Exports,* American Management Association, 1960; *Foreign Trade and Foreign Policy,* National Planning Association, 1962; *The U.S. Trade Expansion Act of 1962: How Will It Affect Canadian-American Trade?,* National Planning Association, 1963; *The U.S. Balance of Payments and International Monetary Reserves,* American Enterprise Institute, 1966.

Contributor: *The European Common Market,* American Management Association, 1958; *Economic Development and International Trade,* Southern Methodist University Press, 1959; *Foreign Trade: Special Analysis,* American Enterprise Association, 1962; *Current Business Studies,* Society of Business Advisory Professions, 1963; *The Common Market: Friend or Competitor?,* New York University Press, 1964. Writer of government reports and staff papers. Contributor to government publications and to periodicals, including *Challenge, Reporter, World Affairs, Nation's Business, Saturday Review,* and *Harvard Business Review.*

WORK IN PROGRESS: Axioms of Economic Science.

* * *

PITMAN, (Isaac) James 1901-

PERSONAL: Born August 14, 1901, in London, England; son of Ernest (a publisher) and Frances Isabel (Butler) Pitman; married Margaret Beaufort Lawson-Johnston, April 28, 1927; children: Peter John, Michael Ian, David Christian, Margaret (Mrs. Timothy Duncan Miller). *Education:* Christ Church, Oxford, B.A. (honors), 1922. *Politics:* Conservative. *Religion:* Church of England. *Home:* 58 Chelsea Park Gardens, London SW3 6A3, England.

CAREER: Sir Isaac Pitman & Sons Ltd. (publishers), London, England, chairman and managing director, 1934-66; Initial Teaching Alphabet Foundation, London, chairman, beginning 1963, and member of University of London Institute of Education-National Foundation for Educational Research committee conducting research into early reading failure. Conservative member of Parliament from Bath, 1945-64. Bursar for Duke of York's and King's Camp, 1933-39; director, Bank of England, 1941-45; director of organization and methods, His Majesty's Treasury, 1943-45. Pro-chancellor, University of Bath; member of committee of management, and committee of building and finance, University of London Institute of Education; chairman, Royal Society of Teachers, 1948. Director, Equity & Law Life Assurance Society; former director of Methuen & Co. Ltd., Bath Gas Co., Bovril Ltd., and Boots Pure Drug Co.; former chairman, British and Foreign School Society. *Military service:* Royal Air Force, 1940-43; became acting squadron leader.

MEMBER: British Association for Commercial and Industrial Education (vice-president), National Union of Teachers, Institute of Administrative Management (president, 1965-69), Association of Technical Institutions (former president), Carlton Club, Harlequins Club, Achilles Club, Ski Club of Great Britain. *Awards, honors:* Knight Commander, Order of the British Empire, 1961; D.Hum.Litt., Hofstra University, 1969; Litt.D., University of Strathclyde and University of Bath, both 1970.

WRITINGS: (With Emily D. Law) *Modern Course in Pitman's Shorthand,* Pitman, 1939; (contributor) *The Character of England,* Oxford University Press, 1947; (with John St. John) *Alphabets and Reading: The Initial Teaching Alphabet,* Pitman, 1969. Also author of *Learning to Read,* 1962, which originally appeared in *Journal of the Royal Society of Arts.* Contributor to educational journals.

SIDELIGHTS: Isaac James Pitman won the middle-weight public schools boxing championship in England, 1919, and was a member of the Oxford University rugby, running, and skiing teams, 1922. He served on the advisory committee to the trust set up under the will of George Bernard Shaw for design and publication of a proposed British alphabet.

AVOCATIONAL INTERESTS: Breeding Gordon setters and Conemora ponies.

PLANK, Emma N(uschi) 1905-

PERSONAL: Born November 11, 1905, in Vienna, Austria; came to United States in 1938, naturalized citizen in 1944; daughter of Emil (a telephone office director) and Doris (Langbein) Spira; married Robert Plank (a university professor), September 17, 1932. *Education:* International Montessori Course, diploma, 1929; Psychoanalytic Seminar for Educators, diploma, 1938; Mills College, Oakland, Calif., M.A., 1947. *Home:* 2387 Overlook Rd., Cleveland, Ohio 44106.

CAREER: Montessori School, Vienna, Austria, teacher, 1925-31, director, 1931-38; Presidio Hill School, San Francisco, Calif., director, 1939-47; Mills College, Oakland, Calif., instructor in child development, 1947-48; American Friends Service Committee, Vienna, director of special projects, 1948-50; Case Western Reserve University, Cleveland, Ohio, assistant professor, 1950-63, associate professor of child development, 1963-72, professor emeritus, 1972—. Director of child life and education, Cleveland Metropolitan General Hospital, 1956-72. Visiting professor, University of California, Davis, winter, 1976; lecturer at colleges and universities. *Member:* American Association for Child Care in Hospitals (president, 1969-70), American Academy of Child Psychoanalysis, American Orthopsychiatric Association (fellow), Northern Ohio Pediatrics Society. *Awards, honors:* Grace Owen Award, Mills College, 1947.

WRITINGS: Working with Children in Hospitals, Press of Case Western Reserve University, 1962, 2nd edition, Year Book Medical Publishers, 1971. Author of numerous professional papers.

SIDELIGHTS: Working with Children in Hospitals has been published in Britain, and translated into Spanish and German.

*   *   *

PLATH, Sylvia   1932-1963
(Victoria Lucas)

PERSONAL: Born October 27, 1932, in Boston, Mass.; daughter of Otto Emil (a professor of biology and scientific German at Boston University) and Aurelia (a teacher of medical secretarial courses at Boston University; maiden name, Schober) Plath; married Ted Hughes (a poet), June 16, 1956 (separated, 1962); children: Frieda Rebecca, Nicholas Farrar. *Education:* Smith College, B.A. (summa cum laude), 1955; attended Harvard University, summer, 1954; Newnham College, Cambridge, Fulbright scholar, 1955-57, M.A., 1957. *Religion:* Unitarian Universalist. *Home:* Court Green, North Tawton, Devonshire, England.

CAREER: Worked as a volunteer art teacher at the People's Institute, Northampton, Mass., while in college; served as guest editor with *Mademoiselle,* summer, 1953; taught English at Smith College, 1957-58; lived in Boston, 1958-59; spent some time at Yaddo, 1959; settled in London, England, 1959, then in Devon. *Member:* Phi Beta Kappa. *Awards, honors: Mademoiselle* College Board contest winner in fiction, 1953; Irene Glascock Poetry Prize, Mount Holyoke College, 1955; Bess Hokin Award, *Poetry* magazine, 1957; first prize in Cheltenham Festival, 1961; Eugene F. Saxon fellowship, 1961.

WRITINGS—All poetry, unless otherwise noted: *The Colossus,* Heinemann, 1960, published in a somewhat different form under title *The Colossus and Other Poems,* Knopf, 1962; (editor) *American Poetry Now,* supplement number 2 to *Critical Quarterly,* Oxford University Press, 1961; (under pseudonym Victoria Lucas) *The Bell Jar* (novel), Heinemann, 1963, republished under real name, Faber, 1966, Harper, 1971; *Ariel,* Faber, 1965, Harper, 1966; *Uncollected Poems* (booklet), Turret Books (London), 1965; *Three Women: A Monologue for Three Voices* (radio play first broadcast by British Broadcasting Corporation in 1962; limited edition), Turret Books, 1968; *Wreath for a Bridal* (limited edition), Sceptre Press, 1970; *Crossing the Water: Transitional Poems,* Harper, 1971; *Crystal Gazer and Other Poems* (limited edition), Rainbow Press (London), 1971; *Lyonnesse* (limited edition), Rainbow Press, 1971; *Million Dollar Month* (limited edition), Sceptre Press, 1971; *Winter Trees,* Faber, 1971, Harper, 1972; *Letters Home: Correspondence, 1950-1963,* selected and edited, with a commentary, by Aurelia Schober Plath, Harper, 1975.

Poetry is represented in anthologies, including *The New Yorker Book of Poems,* Viking, 1969. *Early Poems,* a collection of Plath's work, was published as the May, 1967 issue of *Harvard Advocate;* fifty of her early unpublished poems appeared in *Times Literary Supplement,* July 31, 1969. Contributor to *Seventeen, Christian Science Monitor, Mademoiselle, Harper's, Nation, Atlantic, Poetry, London Magazine,* and other publications.

SIDELIGHTS: When Sylvia Plath ended her life in 1963, she was already becoming a legend. Robert Lowell, who knew her when she audited a class he was teaching, recalls her as a "distinguished, delicate, complicated person" who gave no indication of what would come later. Her final achievement, he admits, startled him. Yet she was precocious as a child (her first published poem appeared in the *Boston Traveller* when she was eight-and-a-half), and A. Alvarez notes that while at Smith she "remorselessly" won all the prizes, and that beneath "a nervous social manner . . . she was ruthless about her perceptions, wary and very individual."

Alvarez believes that with the poems in *Ariel* she made "poetry and death inseparable. The one could not exist without the other. And this is right. In a curious way, the poems read as though they were written posthumously." Robert Penn Warren calls *Ariel* "a unique book, it scarcely seems a book at all, rather a keen, cold gust of reality as though somebody had knocked out a window pane on a brilliant night." George Steiner writes: "It is fair to say that no group of poems since Dylan Thomas's *Deaths and Entrances* has had as vivid and disturbing an impact on English critics and readers as has *Ariel....* Reference to Sylvia Plath is constant where poetry and the conditions of its present existence are discussed." Already younger poets are trying to write as she did. But, as Steiner maintains, her "desperate integrity" cannot be imitated. "No artifice alone could have conjured up such effects," writes Peter Davison.

Like other major poets she consistently courted death. She once said: "When I was learning to creep, my mother set me down on the beach to see what I thought of it. I crawled straight for the coming wave and was just through the wall of green when she caught my heels." At nineteen she first attempted suicide. In her final poems, writes Charles Newman, "death is preeminent but strangely unoppressive. Perhaps it is because there is no longer dialogue, no sense of 'Otherness'—she is speaking from a viewpoint which is total, complete. Love and Death, all rivals, are resolved as one within the irreversibility of experience. To reverse Blake, the Heart knows as much as the Eye sees." Alvarez believes that "the very source of her creative energy was, it turned out, her self-destructiveness. But it was, precisely, a source of *living* energy, of her imaginative, creative power. So, though death itself may have been a side issue, it was also an unavoidable risk in writing her kind of poem. My own impression of the circumstances surrounding her eventual death is that she gambled, not much caring whether she won or lost; and she lost," he adds, only because the possibility of future poems has been lost. Steiner, however, believes that from these final poems she could never return.

As a very young poet she experimented with the villanelle and other forms. She had been "stimulated" by such writers as Lawrence, Joyce, Dostoevski, Virginia Woolf, Henry James, Theodore Roethke, Emily Dickinson, and later by Robert Lowell and Anne Sexton. She has been linked with Lowell and Mrs. Sexton as a member of the so-called "confessional" school of poetry. Ted Hughes notes that she shared with them a similar geographical home land as well as "the central experience of a shattering of the self, and the labour of fitting it together again or finding a new one." And nothing more.

Although her first volume of poems is extremely accomplished, erudite, imaginative, it was not yet entirely the product of an individual voice. Afterwards, she developed her technique until the tone of her poems was transformed. She later said: "I can't read any of the poems [in *The Colossus*] aloud now. I didn't write them to be read aloud. In fact, they quite privately bore me. Now these very recent ones—I've got to say them. . . . Whatever lucidity they may have comes from the fact that I say them aloud." Alvarez also notes that, in her later poems, the relevance of the experience recounted becomes terribly direct, and cites the poem "Ariel" as an example: "The rider is one with the horse, the horse is one with the furrowed earth, and the dew on the furrow is one with the rider. The movement of the imagery, like that of the perceptions, is circular. There is also another peculiarity: although the poem is nominally about riding a horse, it is curiously 'substanceless' to use her own word. You are made to feel the horse's physical presence, but not to see it. . . . It is as though the horse itself were an emotional state. So the poem is not about 'Ariel'; it is about what happens when the 'stasis in darkness' ceases to be static. . . ." At such times she was able to overcome the "tension between the perceiver and the thing-in-itself by literally becoming the thing-in-itself," writes Newman. "In many instances, it is nature who personifies her." She uses history in the same way, "to explain herself." She writes about the Nazi concentration camps as though she had been therein incarcerated. She said: "I think that personal experience shouldn't be a kind of shut box and mirror-looking narcissistic experience. I believe it should be generally relevant, to such things as Hiroshima and Dachau, and so on." Newman explains that "in absorbing, personalizing the socio-political catastrophes of the century, she reminds us that they are ultimately metaphors of the terrifying human mind." Alvarez notes that the "anonymity of pain, which makes all dignity impossible, was Sylvia Plath's subject." Her reactions to the smallest desecrations, even in plants, were "extremely violent," writes Hughes. "Auschwitz and the rest were merely the open wounds." In sum, Newman believes, she evolved in poetic voice from the precocious girl, to the disturbed modern woman, to the vengeful magician, to—*Ariel*—God's Lioness."

Her earlier poems, Ted Hughes reports, were written "very slowly, Thesaurus open on her knee, in her large, strange handwriting, like a mosaic, where every letter stands separate within the work, a hieroglyph to itself. If she didn't like a poem, she scrapped it entire. . . . Every poem grew complete from its own root, in that laborious inching way, as if she were working out a mathematical problem, chewing her lips, putting a thick dark ring of ink around each word that stirred for her on the page of the Thesaurus." After she had written "The Stones," the last poem she completed in America before becoming a complete exile, she repudiated everything prior to this poem as juvenilia. With the birth of her first child in 1960, "she received herself," writes Hughes, "and was able to turn to her advantage all the forces of a highly-disciplined, highly intellectual style of education which had, up to this point, worked mainly against her. . . . The birth of her second child, in January of 1962, completed the preparation." In 1961 she wrote "Tulips" without consulting the Thesaurus, "and at top speed, as one might write an urgent letter. From then on, all her poems were written in this way."

Newman considers her novel, *The Bell Jar,* a "testing ground" for her poems. It is, according to Newman, "one of the few American novels to treat adolescence from a mature point of view. . . . It chronicles a nervous breakdown and consequent professional therapy in non-clinical language. And finally, it gives us one of the few sympathetic portraits of what happens to one who has genuinely feminist aspirations in our society, of a girl who refuses to be an *event* in anyone's life. . . . [Ms. Plath] remains among the few woman writers in recent memory to link the grand theme of womanhood with the destiny of modern civilization." She told Alvarez that she published the book under a pseudonym partly because "she didn't consider it a serious work . . . and partly because she thought too many people would be hurt by it. . . ."

The novel was published one month before her death. After its publication she began to write poems with intense, almost demonic speed, as many as three per day. "One is reminded," Newman suggests, "of Beethoven's atonal explosions in the last quartets, of Turner's last seascapes as they became abstractionist holocausts. In the last poems, there is not the slightest gap between theory and realization, between myth and the concrete particular—they utterly escape the self-consciousness of craft." During the final week of her life she wrote five poems, all included in *Ariel*. Davison notes that these last poems are "a triumph for poetry . . . at the moment that they are a defeat for their author. . . . No matter to whom these may be addressed, they are written for nobody's ears except the writer's. They have a ritual ring, the inevitable preface to doom." A. E. Dyson's phrase, "a terrible beauty," is practically apt when speaking of these poems. Lowell calls her final manner of feeling "controlled hallucination, the autobiography of a fever." "These last poems stun me," writes Anne Sexton. "They eat time,"

Alvarez reports that Ms. Plath seemed convinced that the basis for her suffering was the death of her father when she was eight. The most powerful of her last poems, "Daddy," is explained by her as an "awful little allegory" that she had to act out before she was free of it. Steiner calls the poem an achievement in "the classic act of generalization, translating a private, obviously intolerable hurt into a code of plain statement, of instantaneously public images which concern us all. It is the 'Guernica' of modern poetry."

Ted Hughes summarizes her unique personality and talent thus: "Her poetry escapes ordinary analysis in the way clairvoyance and mediumship do: her psychic gifts, at almost any time, were strong enough to make her frequently wish to be rid of them. In her poetry, in other words, she had free and controlled access to depths formerly reserved to the primitive ecstatic priests, shamans and Holy men. . . .

"Surveyed as a whole, . . . I think the unity of her opus is clear. Once the unity shows itself, the logic and inevitability of the language, which controls and contains such conflagrations and collisions within itself, becomes more obviously what it is—direct, and even plain, speech. This language, this unique and radiant substance, is the product of an alchemy on the noblest scale. Her elements were extreme: a violent, almost demonic spirit in her, opposed a tenderness and capacity to suffer and love things infinitely, which was just as great and far more in evidence. Her stormy, luminous senses assaulted a downright, practical intelligence that could probably have dealt with anything. . . . She saw her world in the flame of the ultimate substance and the ultimate depth. And this is the distinction of her language, that every word is *Baraka:* the flame and the rose folded together. Poets have often spoken about this ideal possibility but, where else, outside these poems, has it actually occurred? If we have the discrimination to answer this question, we can set her in her rightful company.''

BIOGRAPHICAL/CRITICAL SOURCES: Poetry, March, 1963, January, 1967; *Writers on Themselves,* British Broadcasting Corporation, 1964; *Critical Quarterly,* Volume VII, number 1, 1965; *Reporter,* October 7, 1965; *Time,* June 10, 1966; *New Republic,* June 18, 1966; *Newsweek,* June 20, 1966; *Atlantic,* August, 1966; *Tri-Quarterly,* fall, 1966; *Partisan Review,* winter, 1967; Charles Newman, editor, *The Art of Sylvia Plath: A Symposium,* Indiana University Press, 1970; A. Alvarez, *The Savage God: A Study of Suicide,* Weidenfeld & Nicolson, 1971, Random House, 1972; *Ms.,* September, 1972; E. M. Aird, *Sylvia Plath,* Harper, 1973; N. H. Steiner, *A Closer Look at Ariel: A Memory of Sylvia Plath,* Harper's Magazine Press, 1973; *Contemporary Literary Criticism,* Gale, Volume I, 1973, Volume II, 1974, Volume III, 1975, Volume V, 1976.†

(Died February 11, 1963, in London, England)
[Original sketch approved by Mrs. Aurelia S. Plath]

*   *   *

PLOMER, William Charles Franklin   1903-1973

PERSONAL: Surname is pronounced to rhyme with rumour; born December 10, 1903, in Northern Transvaal, Africa; son of Charles (magistrate specializing in native affairs) and Edythe (Waite-Browne) Plomer. *Education:* Attended Rugby. *Address:* c/o Jonathan Cape, 30 Bedford Square, London W.C.1, England.

CAREER: Writer. After schooling returned to Africa, became farmer in Stormberg mountains, and joined a Settler's Association; lived in Johannesburg, and was a trader in Zululand; published a literary review with Roy Campbell; spent two years traveling and teaching in Japan; returned to England through Manchuria, Siberia, Russia, and Poland; was offered Chair of English Literature at Imperial University, Tokyo (formerly held by Lafcadio Hearn), but refused it and, after visiting France, Germany, and Italy, went to live in Greece; later returned to England. Served at the Admiralty, 1941-45. *Member:* Royal Society of Literature (fellow), Kilvert Society (president), Society of Authors, International P.E.N., Poetry Society (president, 1968-71). *Awards, honors:* D.Litt., University of Durham; Queen's Gold Medal for Poetry, 1963; Commander of the Order of the British Empire, 1968.

WRITINGS: Turbott Wolfe, introduction by Laurens van der Post, Hogarth, 1925, Harcourt, 1926, reprinted, Morrow, 1965; *I Speak of Africa,* Hogarth, 1927; *The Family Tree* (poetry), Hogarth, 1929; *Paper Houses* (stories), Cow-

ard, 1932; *The Case Is Altered,* Farrar & Rinehart, 1932, revised edition, Chatto & Windus, 1970; *The Fivefold Screen* (poetry), Hogarth, 1932; *The Child of Queen Victoria and Other Stories,* J. Cape, 1933; *Cecil Rhodes,* Appleton, 1933; *The Invaders,* J. Cape, 1934; *Ali the Lion: Ali of Tebeleni, Pasha of Jannina, 1741-1822,* J. Cape, 1936, published as *The Diamond of Jannina: Ali Pasha, 1741-1822,* Taplinger, 1970; *Visiting the Caves* (poetry), J. Cape, 1936; *Selected Poems,* Hogarth, 1940; *Double Lives: An Autobiography,* J. Cape, 1943, Noonday Press, 1956, reprinted, Books for Libraries, 1971; *Dorking Thigh and Other Satires* (poetry), J. Cape, 1945; *Four Countries,* J. Cape, 1949.

Museum Pieces, J. Cape, 1952, Noonday Press, 1954; *A Shot in the Park* (poetry), J. Cape, 1955; *Borderline Ballads* (poetry), Noonday Press, 1955; *Coming to London* (stories), edited by John Lehmann, Phoenix House, 1957; *At Home: Memoirs,* Noonday Press, 1958, reprinted, Books for Libraries, 1971; *Collected Poems,* J. Cape, 1960; *Taste and Remember* (poetry), J. Cape, 1966; (translator) Ingrid Jonker, *Selected Poems,* J. Cape, 1968; *Celebrations,* J. Cape, 1972; (with Richart Fitter) *The Butterfly Ball and the Grasshopper Feast,* J. Cape, 1973; *Collected Poems,* J. Cape, 1973.

Editor: (And author of introduction) H. Ichikawa, *Japanese Lady in Europe,* Dutton, 1937; (and author of introduction) R. F. Kilvert, *Diary,* J. Cape, 1938, revised edition, 1961; Herman Melville, *Selected Poems,* Hogarth, 1943; W. D'Arfey, *Curious Relations,* J. Cape, 1945, Sloane, 1947, reprinted, Sphere Books, 1968; *New Poems, 1960-1961* (a P.E.N. anthology), Transatlantic, 1961; (and author of introduction) Richard Rumbold, *A Message in Code,* Weidenfeld & Nicolson, 1964.

Librettos; all with Benjamin Britten: *Gloriana* (opera in three acts), Boosey & Hawkes, 1953; *Curlew River,* Faber Music, 1964; *The Burning Fiery Furnace,* Faber Music, 1966; *The Prodigal Son,* Faber Music, 1968.

SIDELIGHTS: Reviewing Plomer's first book, *Turbott Wolfe,* Walter Yust commented: "The 'story' is the least important portion of the book. The impressions of Turbott Wolfe, a good and thoughtful man torn by disillusion and with only a half faith in humankind, are rich and warm. Some are harsh but many are beautiful. His are the moods and honesty of a Dostoievsky and the delight in firm color of a Henri Rousseau." *Double Lives,* his autobiography, described an exciting epoch in South African history just before the turn of the century. "Here both his wit and his sympathy are fully engaged; his ability at characterization is in full play," wrote Elizabeth Barthelme. The *San Francisco Chronicle* reviewer pointed out that "the scenes shift from Victorian salons to the African bush. [The book] juxtaposes the amenities of a liberal England with the life on a frontier in which the racial conflicts present in Africa today were already foreshadowed." *The New York Times* commented on *Paper Houses:* "One cannot read very far in Mr. Plomer's book without observing that his stories are 'different,' that they attempt through the guise of fiction to adumbrate certain peculiar spiritual and mental attitudes of the Japanese, and that an unsensational honesty is behind every paragraph." Vincent Sheean stated that Plomer "writes whole pages of English prose, which for hard, solid beauty have not been surpassed since the early James Joyce. . . ."

Ernestine Evans wrote of *The Case is Altered:* "By the clear consciousness of its telling and the courage of its perceptions, no one can fail to be moved, in pain for the matter, and in pleasure for the manner, of its telling.'' According to H. C. Webster, *At Home: Memoirs,* a sequel to *Double Lives,* ''deserves to rank with the best literary autobiographies that have come out of England.''

Gloriana was performed during the coronation celebration for Queen Elizabeth II in 1953. *Conversation with My Younger Self* was broadcast on the BBC Third Programme on December 12, 1962.

BIOGRAPHICAL/CRITICAL SOURCES: Literary Review, April 24, 1926; *Times Literary Supplement,* March 21, 1929; *Books,* June 2, 1929, September 1, 1936; *New York Times,* July 28, 1929, January 1, 1956, November 16, 1958; *Commonweal,* December 28, 1956; *San Francisco Chronicle,* March 10, 1957; Carolyn Riley, editor, *Contemporary Literary Criticism,* Volume IV, 1975.†

(Died September 21, 1973)

* * *

PLUMMER, L. Gordon 1904-

PERSONAL: Born August 8, 1904, in San Diego, Calif.; son of Fred Gordon (a civil engineer and geographer in U.S. Forest Service) and Emily R. (Sherman) Plummer; married Esther V. Kean, December 22, 1950. *Education:* Theosophical University, San Diego, B.A., 1929, M.A., 1935, Ph.D., 1944. *Religion:* Theosophy. *Home:* 1254 Robinson Ave., Apt. 7, San Diego, Calif. 92103.

CAREER: Former teacher at Theosophical University, San Diego, Calif., and at private schools in California; San Diego (Calif.) Camp Commission, teacher, 1951-61, and also active in summer camp program for many years. Education representative, San Diego Hall of Science. Lecturer.

WRITINGS: From Atom to Cosmos, Theosophical University Press, 1940; *Star Habits and Orbits,* Theosophical University Press, 1944; *The Mathematics of the Cosmic Mind,* privately printed, 1968, revised edition, Theosophical Publishing, 1970. Contributor to theosophical journals.

* * *

PLUMMER, Margaret 1911-

PERSONAL: Born January 12, 1911, in Leicester, England; daughter of Herbert Edward (a postmaster) and Alice Maud Mary (Sands-Basford) Cave; married Cyril Charles Plummer, November 26, 1938; children: Lesly Margaret (Mrs. Edgar Biro), Christopher Charles Kennedy, Matthew Stewart Ottaway. *Education:* Attended secondary school in Newark, England. *Politics:* Conservative. *Religion:* Church of England. *Home:* 66A Curzon Ave., Birstall, Leicester, England.

CAREER: Went to India to be married in 1938, and lived there until 1963. *Awards, honors:* Norman King Literary Award, 1966, for manuscript of *One Rupee and a Bundle of Rice,* and 1968, for *Rama and the White Bullock.*

WRITINGS: One Rupee and a Bundle of Rice (juvenile), Odhams, 1967; *Rama and the White Bullock* (juvenile), Odhams, 1968. Contributor to *Lady.*

WORK IN PROGRESS: There's a Killer in the Jungle; other books with Indian background.††

* * *

POCHMANN, Ruth Fouts 1903-

PERSONAL: Surname is pronounced Pock-man; born March 20, 1903, in Nacogdoches, Tex.; daughter of Wilbur Courtland (a merchant) and Lela (Roquemore) Fouts; married Henry August Pochmann (a professor of American literature), September 11, 1928; children: Virginia Ruth (Mrs. Theodore Patrick Weis). *Education:* Southern Methodist University, student, 1920-23; Stephen F. Austin State College (now University), B.A., 1925; Columbia University, M.A., 1927; University of Wisconsin, further study. *Religion:* Protestant. *Home:* 524 Inwood Lane, Nacogdoches, Tex. 75961.

CAREER: High school teacher in Nacogdoches, Tex., 1923-24; Stephen F. Austin State College (now University), Nacogdoches, teacher of Spanish, 1924-25, of English, 1925-26, 1927-28; during depression years taught in substitute capacity at University of Mississippi, University, and Mississippi State College (now University), Starkville; during World War II was correspondence teacher for U.S. Armed Forces Institute; free-lance writer, beginning 1930. Lecturer on conservation and nature subjects, writing, quilting, gardening, and dollmaking.

MEMBER: International Doll Club, Audubon Society, East Texas Writers Association, Stephen F. Austin State University Women's Faculty Club (honorary member), President's Club (Stephen F. Austin State University chapter), Pines Garden Club (Nacogdoches, Tex.), Nacogdoches Art League, Nacogdoches Bicentennial Committee (chairman of arts and crafts), Alpha Chi, Alpha Delta Pi. *Awards, honors:* Best acting award in 1927 Texas Little Theatre Tournament; named woman of the year in conservation by Wisconsin Federation of Women's Clubs, 1966; Wisconsin Council for Writers Award ($500), 1968, for best published book of nonfiction; *Triple Ridge Farm* was selected for the 1968 Ambassadors' List; first place in Wisconsin Press Women's State Contest, 1969; Hull Award from National Council of Garden Clubs 1970, for *Triple Ridge Farm;* award of appreciation from Stephen F. Austin State University Alumni Association; state award for best bird habitat among Texas gardeners.

WRITINGS: Some Early Texas Families, privately printed, 1942; *Triple Ridge Farm* (autobiographical), Morrow, 1968. Contributor of verse, articles, and reviews to magazines and newspapers, with some of the verse and articles anthologized.

WORK IN PROGRESS: Birds of Triple Ridge, for Morrow; a book on edible and medicinal plants; a book for doll collectors; a novel.

SIDELIGHTS: Ruth Pochmann kept a daily journal for twelve years before writing *Triple Ridge Farm,* the story of the Pochmanns' experiment in converting 100 acres of eroded land into a productive farm, forest, and wildlife refuge.

Mrs. Pochmann has established a $10,000 scholarship at Stephen F. Austin State University. She also gives an annual award to the Nacogdoches High School student with the greatest creative writing potential.

BIOGRAPHICAL/CRITICAL SOURCES: Capital Times (Madison, Wis.), December 8, 1967; *Daily Sentinel* (Nacogdoches, Tex.), February 6, 1968, January 14 and 23, 1969; *Jackson Daily News* (Jackson, Miss.), March 17, 1968; *Waushara Argus* (Wautoma, Wis.), April 25, 1968 (all newspaper sources are feature stories).

* * *

POE, Charlsie 1909-

PERSONAL: Born May 28, 1909, in Jones County, Tex.; daughter of Charles Luther (a grocer) and Eula Mae (Cooke)

Graham; married George W. Poe (a farmer; mayor of Winters, Tex., 1954-59), August 21, 1927 (died January 22, 1973); children: Jeannine, Dennis. *Education:* Attended Hardin-Simmons University for one year; has since taken a number of correspondence courses and several extension courses in creative writing. *Politics:* Democrat. *Religion:* Baptist. *Home:* 207 West Truett, Winters, Tex. 79567.

CAREER: High school teacher of mathematics and government, 1941-48; correspondent for *Abilene Reporter-News,* Abilene, Tex., 1955-70. Member of Texas Historical Foundation; secretary of Runnels County Historical Survey Committee, beginning 1962. Superintendent of intermediate department in local Baptist Sunday school, 1945-71; president of Woman's Missionary Union of Runnels (county) Baptist Association, 1956-62; member of board of West Texas Rehabilitation Center. *Member:* West Texas Historical Association, Writers Guild, Edwards Plateau Historical Association (first vice-president). *Awards, honors: Angel to the Papagos* received third place for adult nonfiction in Texas Press Women awards, 1965; Texas state award for best regional history of the year, 1970, for *Runnels Is My County.*

WRITINGS: Angel to the Papagos (biography of Goldie Richmond), Naylor, 1964; *Runnels Is My County,* Naylor, 1970. Articles have appeared in magazines, and features in *Abilene Reporter-News;* writer of all historical articles in the special issue of *Winters Enterprise* commemorating the 75th anniversary of the founding of the town.

WORK IN PROGRESS: A biography of Orrel A. Parker, inventor of wheels and tires for cars.

*   *   *

POLITELLA, Joseph   1910-

PERSONAL: Born September 20, 1910, in Roccamonfina, Italy; came to United States, 1919; son of Anthony (a sales manager) and Catherine (Ionta) Politella; married Ellen Sue Duke (a college history teacher), September 2, 1950. *Education:* Massachusetts State College (now University of Massachusetts), B.S., 1933; Amherst College, M.A., 1935; University of Pennsylvania, Ph.D., 1938. *Politics:* Republican. *Religion:* Episcopalian. *Home:* 544 Rellim Dr., Kent, Ohio 44240. *Office:* Department of Philosophy, Kent State University, Kent, Ohio 44240.

CAREER: Northland College, Ashland, Wis., instructor in English, 1941-42; Kent State University, Kent, Ohio, professor of philosophy and religion, 1946-73, professor emeritus, 1973—, chairman of graduate studies in philosophy, 1970-73. *Military service:* U.S. Army Air Forces, 1942-46; became captain. *Member:* Royal Asiatic Society, American Academy of Religion (president of Midwest section), Ohio Philosophical Association.

WRITINGS: Platonism, Aristotelianism and Kabbalism in the Philosophy of Leibniz, University of Pennsylvania Press, 1938; *Seven World Religions,* Kent State University Press, Volume I, 1960, Volume II, 1963; *Mysticism and the Mystical Consciousness Illustrated from World Religions,* Kent State University Press, 1964; *Hinduism: Its Scriptures, Philosophy and Mysticism,* Sernoll, 1966; *Buddhism: A Philosophy of the Spirit and a Way to the Eternal,* Sernoll, 1966; *Taoism and Confucianism: The Way of Heaven and the Way of Man,* Sernoll, 1967; *Mystical Foundation of World Religions,* Sernoll, 1968. Contributor to *Muslim World, Darshana International, Encounter, Philosophy East and West,* and other religious and philosophical publications.

WORK IN PROGRESS: A book, *What Zen Buddhism Is Bringing into Western Intellectual and Religious Thinking.*†

*   *   *

POLLOCK, James K(err)   1898-1968

PERSONAL: Born May 25, 1898, in New Castle, Pa.; married Agnes Marie Hahn (deceased); children: Robert Newton, Ann Appleyard (deceased). *Education:* University of Michigan, A.B., 1920, A.M., 1921; Harvard University, Ph.D., 1925. *Office:* Department of Political Science, University of Michigan, Ann Arbor, Mich. 48104.

CAREER: Ohio State University, Columbus, instructor, 1923-25; University of Michigan, Ann Arbor, instructor, 1925-27, assistant professor, 1927-29, associate professor, 1929-34, professor, 1934-48, James Orin Murfin Professor of Political Science, beginning 1948, chairman of department, 1948-61. Visiting summer professor at Stanford University, 1938, 1947. Election official, Saar Plebiscite, 1935; special adviser to U.S. Military Governor for Germany, 1945-46, 1947, 1948, and to U.S. High Commissioner for Germany, 1950. Member of first Hoover Commission, 1947-49; vice-chairman of Advisory Commission on Intergovernmental Relations (appointed by President Eisenhower), 1959-61; consultant to Secretary of the Army, Secretary of State, and other officials and government agencies. Chairman of Michigan Civil Service Study Commission, 1935-37; delegate to Michigan Constitutional Convention, 1961. Lecturer at U.S. Army, Air, and National War Colleges. Director of Governmental Affairs Institute, 1950-68.

MEMBER: International Political Science Association (president, 1955-58), American Political Science Association (member of executive council, 1935-38; second vice-president, 1945; president, 1950), Phi Beta Kappa, Pi Sigma Alpha. *Awards, honors:* Social Science Research Council fellow in Europe, 1927-28; U.S. Medal of Merit, in recognition of work in Germany during Occupation, 1946; Grand Cross of Order of Merit, 1956, and Knight Commander's Cross of Order of Merit (West Germany), 1959; award for distinguished faculty achievement, University of Michigan, 1959; LL.D., University of Pittsburgh, 1957, University of Massachusetts, 1963, Adrian College, 1965, Olivet College, 1966, Iowa Wesleyan College, 1967; Litt.D., Ohio Northern University, 1960.

WRITINGS: Party Campaign Funds, Knopf, 1926; (editor) *Readings in American Government,* Holt, 1927; *Money and Politics Abroad,* Knopf, 1932, reprinted, Books for Libraries, 1972; *German Election Administration,* Columbia University Press, 1934; (with W. E. Rappard and others) *Source Book on European Governments,* Van Nostrand, 1937; *The Government of Greater Germany,* D. Van Nostrand, 1938; (with James Meisel) *Germany Under Occupation: Illustrative Materials and Documents,* Wahr, 1947; (editor) *Change and Crisis In European Government,* Rinehart, 1948; (with Homer L. Thomas and others) *Germany in Power and Eclipse,* D. Van Nostrand, 1952; (editor) *German Democracy at Work,* University of Michigan Press, 1956; *Making Michigan's New Constitution, 1961-1962,* Wahr, 1962; (compiler with John C. Lane) *Source Materials on the Government and Politics of Germany,* Wahr, 1964. Contributor to professional journals. Member of board of editors, American Political Science Association, 1943-45.†

(Died October 4, 1968)

POLLOCK, Norman H(all), Jr. 1909-

PERSONAL: Born February 14, 1909, in Philadelphia, Pa.; son of Norman H., Sr. and Jane G. (Roberts) Pollock; married Jean King (a teacher and organist), July 10, 1945; children: Robert K. *Education:* Denison University, A.B., 1931; Harvard University, A.M., 1934; University of Pennsylvania, Ph.D., 1948. *Politics:* Republican. *Religion:* Baptist. *Home:* 435 West College St., Granville, Ohio 43023.

CAREER: Admiral Farragut Academy, Pine Beach, N.J., history teacher, 1934-38; Gudebrod Brothers Silk Co., Philadelphia, Pa., sales promotion, 1938-40; Rutgers University, branch in Atlantic City, N.J., lecturer in history, 1947-48; Denison University, Granville, Ohio, assistant professor, 1948-55, associate professor, 1955-66, professor of history, 1966-74. *Military service:* U.S. Navy, 1942-46; became lieutenant commander. *Member:* American Historical Association, American Association of University Professors, African Studies Association, Ohio Academy of History.

WRITINGS: The Struggle Against Sleeping Sickness in Nyasaland and Northern Rhodesia, Ohio University Press, 1969; *Nyasaland and Northern Rhodesia: Corridor to the North,* Duquesne University Press, 1971.

SIDELIGHTS: Norman Pollock has traveled extensively through Africa, Latin America, the Caribbean, and western Europe. *Avocational interests:* Camping, hiking, canoeing, bird-watching.

* * *

POLLOCK, Thomas Clark 1902-

PERSONAL: Born March 31, 1902, in Monmouth, Ill.; son of Thomas Cithcart (a clergyman) and Mary (Heade) Pollock; married Katherine Gantz (an author), October 23, 1930. *Education:* Muskingum College, A.B., 1922; Ohio State University, M.A., 1927; University of Pennsylvania, Ph.D., 1930. *Religion:* Episcopalian. *Home:* Estate Carlton, Frederiksted, St. Croix, Virgin Islands 00840.

CAREER: Punjab University, Gordon College, Punjab, India, professor of philosophy, 1922-24; Muskingum College, New Concord, Ohio, instructor in public speaking, 1924-25; Ohio State University, Columbus, instructor in English, 1926-28; University of Pennsylvania, Philadelphia, assistant professor of English, 1928-31, university fellow for research, 1931-32; University of Omaha (now University of Nebraska at Omaha), associate professor of English and chairman of humanities division, 1932-33; Ohio State University, assistant professor, 1933-36, associate professor of English, 1936-38; Montclair State College, Montclair, N.J., professor of English, 1938-43, head of department, 1938-41; New York University, New York, N.Y., professor of English education, 1941-43, professor of English, 1944-70, professor emeritus, 1970—, chairman of department of English education, 1941-43, 1944-47, dean of Washington Square College, 1947-62, University vice-president and secretary, 1962-67, archivist, 1947-70. Council on Religion and International Affairs, trustee, beginning 1949, chairman of executive committee, beginning 1966; trustee of College Retirement Equities Fund, 1962-70.

MEMBER: National Council of Teachers of English (president, 1948), Modern Language Association of America (vice-president, 1952), Phi Beta Kappa; Century Association, Metropolitan Club, Church Club, University Club, and The Players (all New York); Upper Montclair Country Club. *Awards, honors:* American Council of Learned Societies grant for *The Philadelphia Theatre in the Eighteenth*

Century; honorary degrees from Muskingum College, 1948, and University of Bahia and University of Brazil, 1959; commander, Order of Cruzeiro do Sul (Brazil).

WRITINGS: The Philadelphia Theatre in the Eighteenth Century, University of Pennsylvania Press, 1933, reprinted, Greenwood Press, 1968; *The Nature of Literature,* Princeton University Press, 1942, reprinted, Gordian, 1965; (with Oscar Cargill) *Thomas Wolfe at Washington Square,* New York University Press, 1954; (editor with Cargill) *Correspondence of Thomas Wolfe and Homer Andrew Watt,* New York University Press, 1954; (senior author) "Macmillan English Series" (elementary and high school texts), eleven books, Macmillan, 1954, 3rd revised edition, 1967. Editor of Prentice-Hall series, "Introduction to Literature and Composition." Contributor of articles on English education to magazines.†

* * *

POPOVIC, Nenad D(ushan) 1909-
(Spectator)

PERSONAL: Surname is pronounced Pop-o-vich; born June 17, 1909, in Srem Mitrovica, Serbia, Yugoslavia; son of Dushan L. (a government official) and Angelina S. (Yovanovic) Popovic; married March 23, 1948; wife's name, Tatyana V. (a librarian); children: Deyan N. (son), Gina Popovic-Thonis, Sanya Lillian. *Education:* University of Belgrade, LL.B. (summa cum laude), 1932. *Religion:* Eastern Orthodox (Serbian). *Home:* 319 Wedgewood Ter., Syracuse-DeWitt, N.Y. 13214. *Office:* Maxwell Hall, Syracuse University, Syracuse, N.Y. 13210.

CAREER: Research assistant in National Bank of Yugoslavia, Belgrade, 1930-37, and Agrarian Bank of Yugoslavia, Belgrade, 1938-41; prisoner of war in Germany, 1941-45; Yugoslav War Reparation Board, Belgrade, director, 1945-46; State Planning Commission of Serbia, Belgrade, vice-president, 1946-50; State Economic Council of Serbia, Belgrade, vice-president, 1950; International Monetary Fund, Washington, D.C., executive director, 1950-52; National Bank of Yugoslavia, Belgrade, vice-governor, 1953-55; Yugoslav Ministry of Foreign Affairs, Belgrade, plenipotentiary minister, 1955-56; Yugoslav Ministry of Foreign Trade, Belgrade, assistant state secretary, 1956-60; Yugoslav Ministry of Foreign Affairs, Belgrade, plenipotentiary minister, 1960-61; Syracuse University, Maxwell Graduate School of Citizenship and Public Affairs, Syracuse, N.Y., visiting professor, 1961-69, adjunct professor of socialist and western economics and economic development of undeveloped countries, 1969-75, professor emeritus, 1975—. Representative of Turkey, Thailand, Ceylon, and Yugoslavia in International Monetary Fund, and of West Germany and Yugoslavia in International Bank for Reconstruction and Development (World Bank), 1950-53; governor or alternate for Yugoslavia in both organizations, 1950-61; appointed member of Committee on Special United Nations Fund for Economic Development, 1955. Teacher of economics at University of Belgrade, 1946-50, and at labor union schools and other institutions in Yugoslavia. Member of editorial board, Book of Science Publishing House, 1954-58.

WRITINGS: (Under pseudonym Spectator) *Istina o Abisiniji* (title means "Truth About Ethiopia"), Popularna Binlioteka, 1935; (with Vladeta Vuksanovic) *Kontrola Zagranicnog Platnog Prometa* (title means "Control of Payments Abroad"), Izdavacko Pr. Radenkovic, 1936; (translator from the English into Serbo-Croatian) Louis Bromfield, *The Rains Came,* Edicija, 1940; (translator from the English into

Serbo-Croatian) Somerset Maugham, *The Trembling of a Leaf*, Edicija, 1940; *Uloga statistike i evidencije u nar, privredi* (title means "The Role of Statistics and Accounting in the National Economy"), People's University, 1948; *International Financial Organizations*, Maxwell Graduate School of Citizenship and Public Affairs, Syracuse University, 1964, 2nd edition, 1966; *Yugoslavia: The New Class in Crisis*, Syracuse University Press, 1968.

Weekly columnist in *Politika*.(Belgrade), 1951-53. Contributor to economic, political, and other journals in Yugoslavia, Rome, and Paris. Financial editor of *Vreme* ("Times"; Belgrade), 1936-37.

WORK IN PROGRESS: His autobiography; research on workers' self-management and other forms of decision-making decentralization in socialist and state-planned economies; a study of theoretical and practical implications of Marxist-type capital expropriations; a study of recent economic reforms in eastern Europe, especially in Yugoslavia.

SIDELIGHTS: Nenad Popovic, one of Yugoslavia's leading economic experts, helped negotiate U.S. loans and credits for the Tito regime in 1960. The following year he defected to the West. "With hardly another alternative," he says, he gravitated in his youth toward Marxism and the Soviet-type planned economy "which promised his country a way out of poverty and a short cut to freedom and affluency." His two greatest hopes failed "when the Tito-Stalin conflict brought about a new class instead of freedom, and when Djilas' request for a multi-party system was answered by prison."

In addition to Serbo-Croatian and English, he speaks German, Russian, and Italian. He is fond of classical Chinese humor, music, and Roman history.

*   *   *

PORTER, C(edric) L(ambert) 1905-

PERSONAL: Born January 15, 1905, in Gujranwala, West Pakistan; son of Edwin Lytle and Winifred (Lambert) Porter; married Marjorie Woollett, June 10, 1929; children: Richard B., Kenneth R., Carol L. (Mrs. Jerry Murray). *Education:* College of Wooster, student, 1924-26; University of Michigan, B.S., 1928, M.S., 1929; University of Washington, Seattle, Ph.D., 1937.

CAREER: University of Wyoming, Laramie, instructor, 1929-32, assistant professor, 1932-38, associate professor, 1939-42, professor of botany and curator of Rocky Mountain Herbarium, 1943-68. *Member:* American Association for the Advancement of Science (fellow), American Society of Plant Taxonomists, International Association for Plant Taxonomy, California Botanical Society, Torrey Botanical Club.

WRITINGS: Taxonomy of Flowering Plants, W. H. Freeman, 1959, 2nd edition, 1967; *Spring Flora of Southeastern Wyoming*, University of Wyoming Press, 1968. Contributor of research papers to journals and bulletins.

WORK IN PROGRESS: Further volumes on the flora of Wyoming, for University of Wyoming Press.

AVOCATIONAL INTERESTS: Photography, travel (has been around the world and covered most of America; partial to sailing on Great Lakes).††

*   *   *

PORTER, Ethel K. 1901-

PERSONAL: Born February 22, 1901, in Wilmette, Ill.; daughter of Henry Lincoln (a realtor) and Annie E. (Gerken) Flentye; married Hugh Porter, August 20, 1932 (deceased); children: David Hugh. *Education:* Northwestern University, A.B., 1923; American Conservatory of Music, B.M., 1927; attended Juilliard Graduate School (now Juilliard School), 1927-31. *Religion:* Protestant. *Home:* 549 West 123rd St., New York, N.Y. 10027.

CAREER: Dalton School, New York City, teacher of music, 1931-45; Union Theological Seminary, New York City, lecturer at School of Sacred Music, beginning 1953. Music teacher of church school, Riverside Church, New York City.

WRITINGS: (Editor of music, with Hugh Porter) *Pilgrim Hymnal*, United Church Press, 1958; (with Albert C. Ronander) *Guide to the Pilgrim Hymnal*, United Church Press, 1966.

*   *   *

POST, Homer A(very) 1888-

PERSONAL: Born July 6, 1888, in Dayton, Mich.; son of Elijah Jay (a physician) and Grace (Eaton) Post; married Laura Drum; children: Rachel Ellen (Mrs. Samuel McChestney Rust), Patricia Grace (Mrs. Donald Harding Heselwood). *Education:* Attended University of Michigan, 1910-12, and University of Washington, Seattle, summer, 1913; Whitman College, B.A., 1915. *Home:* 4825 Bell St., Tacoma, Wash. 98408.

CAREER: Teacher in secondary schools of Oregon, California, and Washington, 1915-53. Reporter, copy desk man, and correspondent for daily newspapers in Tacoma, San Francisco, Olympia, and other western cities, while teaching, and later, during summers, and weekends; judge of college and high school newspaper contests. *Military service:* World War I, 1918. *Member:* Quill and Scroll Society (president, 1936-37), Journalism Education Association, Washington Association of Journalism Directors, Columbia Scholastic Press Association Advisers, Sigma Delta Chi. *Awards, honors:* Gold Key of Columbia Scholastic Press Association, 1934, and of National Scholastic Press Association, 1936, both in recognition of work as adviser of high school publications; other awards for service to journalism from School of Communications, University of Washington, Seattle, and from Journalism Education Association, Future Journalists of America, and Western Washington Chapter of Sigma Delta Chi; National Scholastic Press Association, named to scroll of honor and, in 1970, honored as one of fifty pioneers in scholastic journalism.

WRITINGS: (With Harold R. Snodgrass) *News in Print*, Allyn & Bacon, 1961, revised edition, 1967. Contributor to journalism periodicals. Advisory editor, *Scholastic Editor; JEA Digest*, editor, 1954-68, honorary editor, beginning 1968.

*   *   *

POTTER, M(aurice) David 1900-

PERSONAL: Born January 1, 1900, in New York, N.Y.; son of Jules and Ada (Brownstone) Potter; married Rosanne Yules, June 29, 1936 (deceased); married Ingrid Klumpp, September, 1968; children: (first marriage) Carol Ann; (second marriage) David John, Stephanie Luise, Marcus Rene. *Education:* Harvard University, B.S., 1921; Columbia University, M.A., 1934; New York University, Ed.D., 1940. *Home:* 446 Fensalir Ave., Pleasant Hill, Calif. 94523. *Office:* San Francisco State University, San Francisco, Calif. 94132.

CAREER: Chico State College (now California State University, Chico), associate professor, 1940-51; San Francisco State University, San Francisco, Calif., professor of business, 1951-71, professor emeritus, 1971—. Faculty member of Diable Valley College, Pleasant Hill, Calif. and Los Medanos College, Pittsburg, Calif. Executive director, National Home Furnishings Education Association. *Military service:* U.S. Army, Infantry, 1918-19.

WRITINGS: *Merchandising Guide,* Ronald, 1941; *Textiles,* Gregg, 1945, 4th edition (with Bernard P. Corbman) published as *Textiles: Fiber to Fabric,* McGraw, 1967; (with others) *Retailing,* Pitman, 1961; (with others) *Advertising,* Pitman, 1962.

WORK IN PROGRESS: Procedural aspects in retail merchandising.

* * *

POULTON, Helen Jean 1920-1971

PERSONAL: Born April 22, 1920, in Warren, Ohio; daughter of Fred (a fireman) and Elma (Wilson) Poulton. *Education:* San Jose State College (now University), A.B., 1942; University of Oregon, M.A., 1946, Ph.D., 1949; University of Michigan, M.A.L.S., 1951.

CAREER: Westminster College, Salt Lake City, Utah, assistant professor of history, 1948-51; Oklahoma A. & M. (now Oklahoma State University), Stillwater, senior reference librarian, 1951-52, social sciences librarian, 1953, reference librarian, 1954-58; Washington University, St. Louis, Mo., reference chief, 1953-54; University of Nevada, Reno, agricultural librarian, 1958-62, social sciences librarian, 1962-63, reference librarian, 1963-69, university archivist, 1969-71. *Member:* Pi Gamma Mu, Pi Lambda Theta, Phi Kappa Phi, Phi Alpha Theta.

WRITINGS: (With Russell R. Elliott) *Writings on Nevada: A Selected Bibliography,* University of Nevada Press, 1963; *Nevada State Agencies: From Territory Through Statehood,* University of Nevada Press, 1964; *James Edward Church: Bibliography of a Snow Scientist,* University of Nevada Press, 1964; *The Historian's Handbook: A Descriptive Guide to Reference Works,* University of Oklahoma Press, 1972. Contributor of book reviews to *Choice.*†

(Died April 25, 1971)

* * *

POUND, Merritt B(loodworth) 1898-1970

PERSONAL: Born December 17, 1898, in Barnesville, Ga.; son of Jere Madison (an educator) and Ada (Murphey) Pound: married Marjorie Carroll, April 12, 1922; children: Marjo, Merritt Bloodworth, Jr. *Education:* University of Georgia, A.B., and M.A., 1924; University of North Carolina, Ph.D., 1939. *Politics:* Democrat. *Religion:* Protestant. *Home:* 652 Milledge Circle, Athens, Ga. 30601.

CAREER: University of Georgia, Athens, assistant professor, 1926-30, associate professor, 1930-39, professor of history, 1939-40, professor of political science and head of department, 1941-64; professor emeritus, 1964-70. Visiting instructor at University of North Carolina, 1931-32, 1938. Member of Athens City Council for six years, and Athens Tax Appeal Board, 1960-70. *Military service:* U.S. Army, Infantry, 1918. U.S. Army Air Corps, active duty, 1942-45; became colonel, U.S. Air Force. *Member:* Southern Political Science Association (president, 1950).

WRITINGS: (With M. E. Thompson) *Georgia Citizenship,* Johnson Publishing, 1939; (with A. B. Saye) *Handbook on Constitutions of United States and Georgia,* University of Georgia Press, 1946, 9th edition, 1967; *Benjamin Hawkins: Indian Agent,* University of Georgia Press, 1950; (with Saye and J. F. Allums) *Principles of American Government,* Prentice-Hall, 1950, 7th edition, 1974; (with J. T. Askew) *The Government of Georgia,* Harlow Publishing, 1959.†

(Died, 1970)

* * *

POWELL, Norman J(ohn) 1908-1974

PERSONAL: Born September 28, 1908, in New York, N.Y.; married, 1932; children: David. *Education:* New York University, B.S., 1928; Columbia University, M.A., 1929, Ph.D., 1936.

CAREER: Sing Sing Prison, Ossining, N.Y., psychologist, 1931-36; New York Civil Service Commission, examiner, 1936-39, director of research, 1939-41, director of classification and research, 1941-42; City College of the City University of New York, New York City, instructor, 1942-46, assistant professor, 1947-51, associate professor, 1952-57, professor of political science, 1957-68; Bernard M. Baruch College of the City University of New York, New York City, professor of political science, beginning 1968. Summer visiting professor at University of New Mexico, 1950, Portland State College (now University), 1957, University of Puerto Rico, 1959. Consultant to New Hampshire State Government, 1942-43, New York State Legislative Commission, 1942-45, Welfare Council of Community Chests and Councils of America, 1947-48, New York City Board of Higher Education, 1952-55, and Institute of International Education, 1954-55. Consultant and occasional lecturer, New York City Department of Personnel, 1956-68. *Member:* American Political Science Association, American Psychological Association, American Sociological Association.

WRITINGS: *Anatomy of Public Opinion,* Prentice-Hall, 1951; *Personnel Administration in Government,* Prentice-Hall, 1956; (senior editor) *Major Aspects of American Government,* McGraw, 1963; *Responsible Public Bureaucracy in the United States,* Allyn & Bacon, 1967; (with Robert A. Holmes) *Black Politics and Public Policy: Between Catastrophe and Civilization,* Emerson Hall, 1973.†

(Died May 23, 1974)

* * *

POWERS, David Guy 1911-1967

PERSONAL: Born January 13, 1911, in New York, N.Y.; son of Patrick Guy (a restaurateur) and Ellen (Cowmey) Powers; married second wife, Julia Joyce Barata, August 9, 1963; children: (first marriage) Guy David. *Education:* University of Notre Dame, A.B., 1933; Columbia University, A.M., 1934, Ed.D., 1938; postdoctoral study, 1939-40; New York University, Ph.D., 1950; also studied at Sorbonne, University of Paris, 1952, and University of Strasbourg, 1953. *Politics:* Democrat. *Religion:* Roman Catholic.

CAREER: Fordham University, Bronx, N.Y., assistant professor of English, 1935-39; Manhattan College, Bronx, N.Y., adjunct professor of English, 1937-48; Brooklyn Polytechnic Institute, Brooklyn, N.Y., professor of logic, 1939-41; Queens College of the City University of New York, Flushing, N.Y., 1939-67, started as assistant professor, became professor of American rhetoric. Member of National Defense Research Committee, 1943-46, and Office of Scientific Research and Development, 1943-67. Educational director, SICO (oil company) Scholarship Fund, Mount Joy, Pa. *Member:* American Association of University Professors. *Awards, honors:* Member, Advanced School of Education, Columbia University, 1939-40; L.H.D., Ohio College of Podiatry.

WRITINGS: Situational Speech, Pitman, 1937, 5th edition, 1944; *Signal Speech,* Pitman, 1943; *Live a New Life,* Doubleday, 1949; *Fundamentals of Speech,* McGraw, 1951; *How to Say a Few Words,* Doubleday, 1953; (with Donald A. Laird and Herbert N. Casson) *Persoonlijke Efficiency,* Maanblad Success (The Hague), 1955; *The First Book of How to Make a Speech,* F. Watts, 1963; *The First Book of How to Run a Meeting,* F. Watts, 1967. Author with Suzanne E. Martin of six texts for upper elementary grades in "Your Speech" series, Pitman, 1940; co-author of three technical manuals for U.S. Navy; author or co-author of four booklets published by Queens College Library.

WORK IN PROGRESS: The More Abundant Life (an expansion of lectures given at National Safety Congress, 1956, and published by National Safety Council, 1957), for Doubleday.

SIDELIGHTS: Live a New Life was serialized and syndicated to Scripts-Howard newspapers throughout the country, published in condensed form in *Your Life,* and excerpted in *Coronet.* Extracts from the book also appeared in more than one thousand trade journals and newspapers. Powers was competent in French, Italian, German, and Spanish. For over a period of four years he visited twenty-five universities in England, Italy, France, Germany, Colombia, and Peru, to study university administration.†

(Died December 14, 1967)

*   *   *

POWERS, William Edwards 1902-

PERSONAL: Born March 25, 1902, in Florence, Ala.; son of William Edwards (a teacher) and Annie (Smith) Powers; married Marian Louise Drisko, September 5, 1932; children: William Edwards, Jr. *Education:* Northwestern University, B.S., 1925, M.A., 1928; Harvard University, Ph.D., 1931. *Religion:* Presbyterian.

CAREER: Northwestern University, Evanston, Ill., instructor, 1926-29, assistant professor, 1931-40, associate professor, 1940-45, professor of geography, 1945-72. Field researcher in middlewestern United States, New England, Colorado Rockies, Hawaii, New Zealand, and north Greenland; worked summers for U.S. Geological Survey. *Member:* Geological Society of America, Association of American Geographers. *Awards, honors:* Library of Congress fellow, 1940-41; Fulbright grant for research in New Zealand, 1961.

WRITINGS: (With C. F. Kohn) *Aerial Photointerpretation of Landforms and Rural Cultural Features,* Northwestern University Press, 1959; *Physical Geography,* Appleton, 1966.†

*   *   *

PRESSER, (Gerrit) Jacob 1899-1970
(J. Drukker, J. van Dam, J. van Wageningen)

PERSONAL: Born February 24, 1899, in Amsterdam, Netherlands; son of Gerrit and Aaltje (Stempel) Presser; married Debora Susanna Appel, July 30, 1936 (killed by the Nazis in Poland in World War II); married Bertha Hartog, January 22, 1954. *Education:* Studied at University of Amsterdam. *Home:* Frankenstate, Lindenlaan 40 B, Bergen (N.H.), Netherlands. *Agent:* Robert Harben, 3 Church Vale, London N2 9PD, England.

CAREER: Vossiusgymnasium, Amsterdam, Netherlands, teacher, 1926-47; University of Amsterdam, Amsterdam, professor of modern history, 1947-69. *Member:* Historisch Genootschap (historical association), Maatschappij der Nederlandse Letterkunde (literary society), Royal Dutch Academy of Science. *Awards, honors:* Wynaends Francken Award for *Napoleon: Historie en legende;* Van der Hoogt Award for *De Nacht der Girondijnen;* Jan Campert Award and $2,500 Remembrance Award of World Federation of Bergan-Belsen Associations for *Ondergang: De Vervolging en Verdelging van het Nederlandse jodendom.*

WRITINGS: Das Buch "De Tribus Impostoribus (Von den drei Detruegern) (doctoral dissertation), H. J. Paris, 1926; *De Tachtigjarige Oorlog* (Netherlands wars of independence, 1556-1648), Elsevier, 1941; (under pseudonym J. van Wageningen) *Orpheus en Ashasverus* (poems), Querido, 1945; *Napoleon: Historie en legende,* Elsevier, 1946; *Amerika: Van Kolonie tot Wereldmacht* (American history), Elsevier, 1949; *Historia hodierna* (inaugural speech), E. J. Brill, 1950; *Gewiekte wielen: Richard Arkwright* (biography), Van Loghum Slaterus, 1951; (author of introduction) Heinrich Heine, *Ich weiss Nicht was Soll es Bedeuten* (text in German; introduction in Dutch), Daamen, 1956; *De Nacht der Girondijnen* (novel), 1957, English translation by Barrows Mussey published as *The Breaking Point,* World Publishing, 1958; (editor) *Antwoord aan het Kwaad: Getuigenissen 1939-1945* (World War II prisoners and poetry), J. M. Meulenhoff, 1961; *Schrijfsels en schrifturen* (essays), Moussault, 1961; (author of introduction) *Portret van een Tijdperk,* De Bezige Bij, 1963; *Ondergang: De Vervolging en Verdelging van het Nederlandse jodendom, 1940-45,* two volumes, Nijhoff, 1965, translation by Arnold Pomerans published as *Ashes in the Wind,* Souvenir Press, 1968, same translation published as *The Destruction of the Dutch Jews,* Dutton, 1969; *Meit hek werk van Dr. Jacques Presser* (essays, addresses, and lectures), Atheneum, 1969. Also author of *Europa in een Boek,* 1963. Co-editor-in-chief, Winkler Prins encyclopedias.

WORK IN PROGRESS: The Golden Age of the Netherlands.

SIDELIGHTS: As a Jew, Presser was in hiding for twenty-three months in World War II. His chronicle of the destruction of his countrymen (about 100,000 of Holland's 140,000 Jews were killed) took fifteen years to compile. The work was commissioned by the Netherlands State Institute of War Documentation.

BIOGRAPHICAL/CRITICAL SOURCES: Jacques Presser, J. M. Meulenhoff, 1959; *Punch,* November 13, 1968; *Observer Review,* February 23, 1969; *New York Times,* February 25, 1969; *Book World,* March 23, 1969; *Commentary,* January, 1970; Philo Bregshein, *Gesprekken meh Jacques Presser* (interviews), Atheneum, 1972.†

(Died April 30, 1970)

*   *   *

PROCTOR, Lillian Cummins 1900-

PERSONAL: Born December 20, 1900, in Seymour, Tex.; daughter of James McDonald and Anne Elizabeth (Bagby) Cummins; married Fred J. Proctor, June 6, 1918. *Education:* Attended University of Texas. *Religion:* Presbyterian. *Home:* 5510 Merrimac Ave., Dallas, Tex. 75206.

CAREER: Taught school for four years; has taught adult Bible classes and reviewed books.

WRITINGS: No Uncertain Sound (novel), Augsburg, 1966.††

* * *

PRYOR, Helen Brenton 1897-1972

PERSONAL: Born July 31, 1897, near Green Mountain Falls, Colo.; daughter of William Henry and Mary C. (Foster) Brenton; married Roy Jay Pryor, December 1, 1922; children: Dorothy Elizabeth (Mrs. George L. Bartlett), Richard Brenton. Education: University of Oregon, B.A., 1919; University of Minnesota, M.D., 1924. Politics: Republican. Religion: Protestant. Office: Department of Pediatrics, Medical School, Stanford University, Stanford, Calif. 94305.

CAREER: University of Minnesota Hospital, Minneapolis, intern, 1923-24; Rockefeller Foundation Hospital, Peiping, China, resident, 1924-25; Nanking University Hospital, Nanking, China, visiting physician in pediatrics and obstetrics, 1925-29; University of California Medical School, San Francisco, assistant in pediatrics, 1929-35, research associate, Institute of Child Welfare, 1931-39; Children's Hospital, San Francisco, Calif., visiting pediatrician, 1930-35; Stanford University, Stanford, Calif., professor of hygiene and director of Women's Health Service, 1935-45; Medical Clinic, Redwood City, Calif., pediatrician and partner in clinic, 1945-65; Stanford University Medical School, Stanford, clinical professor of pediatrics, beginning 1966. Chief of staff for pediatrics, Sequoia Hospital, 1952-64. Diplomate, American Board of Pediatrics. President of board of directors, San Mateo County Heart Association, 1957-59, Volunteer Bureau, 1958-60, Mid-Peninsula YWCA, 1960-62, and Palo Alto Neighbors Abroad, 1966; chairman of Senior Division, Community Welfare Council, 1963-65.

MEMBER: American Academy of Pediatrics (fellow), American Student Health Association (national secretary-treasurer, 1942-44), Society for Research in Child Development, American Medical Association, National League of American Pen Women, California Congress of Parent-Teacher Association (honorary life member), Sigma Xi, Palo Alto Quota Club (president, 1956-58). Awards, honors: Medallions for distinguished achievement and distinguished service, American Heart Association, 1964; Creative Living Award, American Association of University Women, 1968, for contributions toward better health for the world's children; Matrix Award, Theta Sigma Phi, 1970, for Lou Henry Hoover: Gallant First Lady and other writings; California Commission on Aging Award for work in behalf of senior citizens.

WRITINGS—All published by Bobbs-Merrill, except as indicated: (With Wilson and Almack) Health at Home and School, 1942; (with Wilson and Almack) Health at Work and Play, 1942; (with Wilson and Almack) Growing Healthfully, 1943; (with Wilson and Almack) Health Progress, 1943; (with Wilson and Almack) Modern Ways to Health; As the Child Grows, Silver Burdett, 1943; Lou Henry Hoover: Gallant First Lady (teen book), Dodd, 1969. Contributor to Encyclopedia of Sport Sciences and Medicine, World Book Encyclopedia, medical journals, and magazines.

BIOGRAPHICAL/CRITICAL SOURCES: Pen Woman, November, 1969.†

(Died July 7, 1972)

PUCKEY, Walter (Charles) 1899-

PERSONAL: Born December 28, 1899, in Fowey, Cornwall, England; son of Thomas Edward (a master mariner) and Anne (Keast) Puckey; married Alice Rebecca Richards, May 24, 1926. Education: Attended technical colleges in England. Religion: Church of England. Home: Silverdale, Beech Dr., Kingswood, Surrey, England. Office: 17 Stratton St., London W.1, England.

CAREER: Director and general manager, Hoover Ltd., England, 1938-51; Management Selection Group Ltd., London, England, founder and chairman, beginning 1954; Hay-MLS, London, founder and chairman, beginning 1954. Director of International Computers, 1954-68, and Black & Decker, 1955-65. Chartered engineer. Member: Institute of Production Engineers (fellow), Institute of Directors (fellow), Savile Club. Awards, honors: Knighted, 1954.

WRITINGS: What Is This Management?, Chapman & Hall, 1944; So You Are Going to a Meeting, Institute of Production Engineers, 1946; Management Principles: A Primer for Directors and Potential Directors, Hillary, 1962, revised edition, Hutchinson, 1970; Organization in Business Management: A Guide for Managers and Potential Managers, Hillary, 1963, revised edition, Hutchinson, 1970; The Board-Room: A Guide to the Role and Function of Directors, Hutchinson, 1969. Contributor to technical journals.

WORK IN PROGRESS: A biography.

AVOCATIONAL INTERESTS: Golf, gardening.

BIOGRAPHICAL/CRITICAL SOURCES: Times Literary Supplement, June 5, 1969.†

* * *

PURKEY, Roy (Delbert) 1905-

PERSONAL: Born December 1, 1905; son of William L. and Minnie J. (Strickler) Purkey; married Gretchen Louise Frentzel (a teacher). Education: Illinois Wesleyan University, B.A., 1928; University of Iowa, M.A., 1939. Politics: Republican. Religion: Methodist. Home: 1506 North Gilbert St., Danville, Ill. 61832.

CAREER: Former instructor in English and speech at Danville (Ill.) High School, and in speech at Danville Junior College; former summer representative, Interstate Printers & Publishers, Inc., Danville, Ill. Member: National Education Association, Illinois Education Association, Phi Delta Kappa, Toastmasters Club, Elks, Masons, Grotto, Red Mask Players, Vermilion Hills Country Club (Danville).

WRITINGS: (With Dudley) Workbook on Speech, Interstate, 1935; Winning Future Farmer Speeches, Interstate, 1951; Handbook on Speech for Future Farmers of America, Interstate, 1959, revised edition, 1966. Contributor to professional journals.

AVOCATIONAL INTERESTS: Sound recording, golf, tennis, swimming.††

* * *

PUTNAM, Donald F(ulton) 1903-

PERSONAL: Born August 15, 1903, in Lower Onslow, Nova Scotia, Canada; son of Albert (a farmer) and Ella (Fulton) Putnam; married Jean Wiles, December 29, 1931; children: Robert Garth, Ardith Jean (Mrs. Lynn A. Ralph). Education: Nova Scotia Agricultural College, Diploma, 1924; Ontario Agricultural College, B.S.A., 1927; McGill University, graduate study, 1929-30; University of Toronto, Ph.D., 1935. Address: P.O. Box 896, Oakville, Ontario,

Canada L5L 1C6. *Office:* Department of Geography, Erindale College, University of Toronto, 3359 Mississauga Rd., Mississauga, Ontario, Canada L5L 1C6.

CAREER: University of Toronto, Toronto, Ontario, instructor, 1938-39, lecturer, 1939-42, assistant professor, 1942-47, associate professor, 1947-53, professor of geography and head of department, 1953-66, Erindale College, Mississauga, Ontario, professor of geography, 1966-72, professor emeritus, 1972—. Summer professor at Royal Military College of Canada, 1952, University of Alberta, 1954, 1957, Dalhousie University, 1955, and University of Waterloo, 1961.

MEMBER: Royal Canadian Geographical Society, (fellow), Canadian Association of Geographers, American Association of Geographers, American Association for the Advancement of Science, Canadian Institute of Agriculture, Ontario Institute of Agrology, Conservation Council of Ontario. *Awards, honors:* National Research Council of Canada grants, 1930, 1931; Ontario Research Council grant, 1933-49; Canada Department of Mines and Resources grant, 1950; Coronation Medal in Geography, 1953; Massey Medal, Royal Canadian Geographical Society, 1969; LL.D., York University, 1974.

WRITINGS: (With Lyman J. Chapman) *The Physiography of Southern Ontario,* University of Toronto Press, 1951, 3rd edition, 1966; (editor and contributor) *Canadian Regions: A Geography of Canada,* Dent, 1952, 4th edition, 1960; (with Donald P. Kerr) *A Regional Geography of Canada,* Dent, 1956, 3rd edition, 1964; (with Robert G. Putnam) *Canada: A Regional Analysis,* Dent, 1970.

WORK IN PROGRESS: Continued research in agricultural geography, geography of natural resources, and regional geography of Canada.

*   *   *

PYLE, (William) Fitzroy 1907-

PERSONAL: Born May 7, 1907, in Aylesbury, Buckinghamshire, England; son of Ernest Edgar (a dealer in musical instruments) and Kathleen (Mitchell) Pyle; married Amy Patricia Conerney, July 7, 1931; children: Patrick David Fitzroy, Fergus Patrick D'Esterre, Hilary Ann (Mrs. Maurice Carey). *Education:* Trinity College, Dublin, B.A., 1929, M.A. and Ph.D., 1933. *Religion:* Christian (Church of Ireland). *Residence:* Blackrock, County Dublin, Ireland. *Office:* Trinity College, University of Dublin, Dublin 2, Ireland.

CAREER: University of Dublin, Trinity College, Dublin, Ireland, lecturer, 1930-51, reader, 1951-71, associate professor of English, beginning 1971, fellow, beginning 1951. *Member:* Royal Irish Academy.

WRITINGS: "The Winter's Tale": A Commentary on the Structure, Barnes & Noble, 1969. Contributor of articles on metrics, Milton, Shakespeare, and other topics to journals.

WORK IN PROGRESS: A commentary on the growth and structure of *Paradise Lost;* other studies on the metrics of the Chaucerian tradition, on Milton's versification, and on Shakespearean comedy.

*   *   *

QUEST, Rodney

HOME: 96 Gregories Rd., Beaconsfield, Buckinghamshire, England. *Agent:* John Cushman Associates, Inc., 24 West 43rd St., New York, N.Y. 10036; and Curtis Brown Ltd., 1 Craven Hill, London W2 3EW, England.

CAREER: Writer. *Military service:* British Army, 1914-19; received military cross; Royal Air Force, 1939-45.

WRITINGS—Novels: *Men Are Different,* John Long, 1933; *Secret Establishment,* Hutchinson, 1961; *The Venus of Samos,* Hutchinson, 1962; *Just Off Bond Street,* Hutchinson, 1963; *Countdown to Doomsday,* Harrap, 1966; *The Fenton Affair,* Harrap, 1967; *The Cerberus Murders,* Harrap, 1969, McCall Publishing, 1970; *Murder with a Vengeance,* Harrap, 1971; *Death of a Sinner,* Harrap, 1971.

*   *   *

QUIMBY, Myrtle 1891-

PERSONAL: Born January 21, 1891, in Howard, Kan.; daughter of Joseph Henry (a farmer) and Mary Louisa (Perkins) Chambers; married Frank Eugene Quimby, October 9, 1910 (deceased); children: Clayton, Don, Mary (Mrs. E. B. Martin), Eugene, Dale. *Education:* Attended Oklahoma Agriculture and Mechanical College (now Oklahoma State University), 1908. *Home:* 2505 East Hartford, Meadows Apartments, Ponca City, Okla. 74601.

WRITINGS: The Cougar (juvenile), Criterion, 1968; *The White Crow,* Criterion, 1970.

*   *   *

RABE, Olive H(anson) ?-1968

PERSONAL: Surname is pronounced Robbie; born in Chicago, Ill.; daughter of Henry Byer (a teaming contractor) and Sarah Louise (Haen) Hanson; divorced. *Education:* Northwestern University, LL.B., 1916; University of Chicago, Ph.B., 1937. *Politics:* Democrat (usually). *Religion:* New Thought. *Home and office:* Sunshine Canyon Rd., Boulder, Colo. 80302.

CAREER: Labor Bureau of the Middle West, Chicago, Ill., partner, 1921-26; Zimring and Rabe (law firm), Chicago, Ill., partner, 1926-32. Free-lance writer. *Member:* Phi Beta Kappa.

WRITINGS—All with Aileen Fisher: *United Nations Plays and Programs,* Plays, 1954; *Patriotic Plays and Programs,* Plays, 1956; *We Dickinsons,* Atheneum, 1965; *United Nations Day,* Crowell, 1965; *Human Rights Day,* Crowell, 1966; *We Alcotts,* Atheneum, 1968. Contributor of popular legal articles to national magazines, including *Reader's Digest.*

AVOCATIONAL INTERESTS: Extrasensory perception, hiking (especially on mountain trails), world affairs, country living.†

(Died December, 1968)

*   *   *

RABINOVICH, Isaiah 1904-1972

PERSONAL: Born November 22, 1904, in Khodorkof, Ukraine; became Canadian citizen; son of Eisig (a merchant) and Sheindel (Rabinovich) Rabinovich; married Sara Unick, November 14, 1924; children: Solomon. *Education:* Teachers Seminary, Kiev, Ukraine, graduate, 1923; University of Manitoba, B.A., 1930; University of Toronto, M.A., 1946; Jewish Theological Seminary of America, D.R.E., 1950. *Home:* 6328 North Kedzie Ave., Chicago, Ill. 60645; and 4190 Bathurst St., Apt. 608, Downsview, Ontario, Canada. *Office:* College of Jewish Studies, 72 East 11th St., Chicago, Ill. 60605.

CAREER: Began teaching in Hebrew schools in Canada, 1925; principal of Hebrew schools in Winnipeg, Manitoba, and then Toronto, Ontario, 1934-60; Canadian Jewish Congress, Central Division, Toronto, director of department of education and culture, 1940-47; Hebrew Teachers Seminary, Toronto, lecturer in Hebrew literature, 1953-60; College of Jewish Studies, Chicago, Ill., Solomon Professor of Hebrew Literature, 1960-69, professor emeritus, 1969-72. *Member:* World Union of Jewish Studies, American Jewish Historical Society, Histadrut for Israel, Association of Hebrew Writers, Hebrew P.E.N. Club of America (member of executive committee), Labor Zionist Organization of America. *Awards, honors:* Louis Lamed Award for Literature, 1947.

WRITINGS: Ha-Sifrut be-Mashber ha-Dor (title means "Literature in the Crisis of Our Generation"), Ohel, 1948; *Yetzer Vitzirah* (title means "Creativity and Impulse"), Bialik Institute (Jerusalem), 1951; *Ner Dolek* (collection of tales; title means "A Burning Candle"), Am Oved (Tel-Aviv), 1954, translation into Yiddish by Rabinovich published under same title, Peretz (Tel-Aviv), 1975; *Be-Hevle Doram* (studies in Hebrew poetry; title means "In the Pangs of Their Generation"), Am Oved, 1959; *Shorashium u-Megamot* (title means "Roots and Aims"), Bialik Institute, 1967; *Ha-Sipporet Ha-Ivrit Me-Happet Gibbor,* Association of Hebrew Writers and Massadah, 1967, translation by M. Roston published as *Major Trends in Modern Hebrew Fiction,* University of Chicago Press, 1968; *Adam mul nufo* (title means "Man and His Environment"), Makibbutz Hameuchad (Tel-Aviv), 1976. Also author of *Aley Adamoth,* 1963. Contributor to Hebrew journals.

WORK IN PROGRESS: Major Trends in Modern Hebrew Poetry; and *Detachment and Attachment in the Creation of Poetic Metaphor.*

BIOGRAPHICAL/CRITICAL SOURCES: Books Abroad, autumn, 1968.†

(Died, 1972)

* * *

RADFORD, John 1901-1967

PERSONAL: Born March 6, 1901, in Burton on Trent, Staffordshire, England; son of Leonard (a business executive) and Mary Jane (Howlett) Radford; married Kathleen May Kirby, September 18, 1939; children: John Kirby, Mark, Rosemary Alison, Christine Margaret. *Education:* Attended Burton on Trent schools until fifteen; qualified for both Masters and Extra Masters Foreign-going Certificates, 1926. *Politics:* "Independent. Liberal and Progressive." *Religion:* None. *Home and office:* Leaholme, Appley Rd., Ryde, Isle of Wight, England.

CAREER: Went to sea as cadet on a cargo ship on the South American run, 1916; sailed on all kinds of ships in every ocean for almost twenty years, resigning his appointment with the Cunard Line to enter the pilotage service in 1935; pilot with Corporation of Trinity House, England, 1935-39, 1946-67, finally as senior Trinity House inward sea pilot for the Isle of Wight District, and the first selected inward pilot for Cunard and several other lines. *Military service:* Royal Naval Reserve, 1925-46; active duty at sea, 1939-45; retired as commander. *Member:* Society for Nautical Research, British Sailors' Society, Ryde Lawn Tennis and Croquet Club (president, 1963-67).

WRITINGS: Pilot Stations of the British Isles, Brown, Son & Ferguson, 1939; *Pilot Aboard* (autobiographical), W. Blackwood, 1965. Stories about the sea, and articles have appeared in *Trident, Nautical Magazine, Wide World, Navy, Blackwood's Magazine,* and other periodicals.

WORK IN PROGRESS: Project S.T.F., a book of fiction dealing with use of lasers at sea.

SIDELIGHTS: Pilot Stations of the British Isles still is in print, incorporated in *The Nautical Almanac,* published by Brown, Son & Ferguson. With fifty years of sea-going and two wars behind him, Radford deplored "violence in drama and art, the apparent disregard all over the world of the value of human lives, and the acceptance of war as a way of settling disagreements amongst nations." He spoke some French and Spanish.††

(Died November, 1967)

* * *

RADWANSKI, Pierre A(rthur) 1903-
(Dr. Pierre A. Radwanski-Szinagel; pseudonyms: Al-Van-Gar, Chochlik, O'Key)

PERSONAL: Born January 4, 1903, in Latoszyn, Poland; immigrated to Canada, 1951, naturalized, 1956; son of Henry (a gentleman farmer) and Maria Victoria (Kawecka) Radwanski; married Isabella Latoszynska, August 2, 1937; children: George. *Education:* Jagellonian University, Cracow, Poland, L.Ph., 1926, D.Sc., 1931. *Religion:* Roman Catholic. *Home:* 4855 Grosvenor Ave., Montreal, Quebec, Canada. *Office:* Department of Social Sciences, Dawson College, Westmont, Quebec, Canada D0670.

CAREER: Jagellonian University, Cracow, Poland, assistant in physical anthropology, 1922-31, professor of cultural and physical anthropology, College of Sciences, 1931-39; Royal Institute of Natural Sciences, Brussels, Belgium, research fellow, 1947-51; University of Ottawa, Faculty of Arts, Ottawa, Ontario, professor of cultural and physical anthropology, 1952-54; University of Montreal, Faculty of Arts and Letters, Montreal, Quebec, professor of anthropology and Slavic ethnology, 1952-69, head of Slavic section, 1962-68; Dawson College, Montreal, Quebec, professor of anthropology, beginning 1969. Former secretary-general, Polish Institute of Arts and Sciences in America, 1960-62.

MEMBER: Royal Anthropological Society of Belgium, International Platform Association, Polish Association of Intellectuals Veritas (president), Canadian Center of Anthropological Research, Canadian Association of Slavists, New York Academy of Sciences, Association of Polish University Professors (London, England), French Canadian Association for the Advancement of Sciences (counselor). *Awards, honors:* Francqui Foundation fellowship (Belgium), 1950; Queen Elizabeth of Belgium Award, 1951; grants from Canadian Department of Resources and Development, 1953, Canada Council, 1966, and Research Council for Humanities, 1968.

WRITINGS: Man, the Known, Universum Press, 1966. Contributor of more than one hundred articles and papers to publications, including the proceedings of international congresses in Moscow, Paris, Vienna, Tokyo, and journals in Belgium, United States, Canada, England. Contributor of short stories to publications under pseudonyms Al-Van-Gar, Chochlik, and O'Key, and scientific books under name Dr. Pierre A. Radwanski-Szinagel.

WORK IN PROGRESS: Cultural Process and Systematics of Culture; and practical commentary to some theoretical points of his book, *Man, the Known.*†

RAFFELOCK, David 1897-
(R. E. Locke)

PERSONAL: Born July 7, 1897, in Topeka, Kan.; son of Jacob (a merchant) and Molly (Claimont) Raffelock; married Esse R. Dorfman, November 16, 1924; children: Maxine (Mrs. Fred T. Davine). *Education:* Graduated from a junior college in St. Joseph, Mo., 1917; attended Columbia University, 1919-20, and University of Wyoming, 1922. *Home:* 1090 Lafayette St., Denver, Colo. 80218. *Office:* National Writers Club, 1365 Logan St., Denver, Colo. 80203.

CAREER: Author & Journalist (periodical), Denver, Colo., associate editor, 1921-49, editor, 1950-51; *Echo* (periodical), Denver, editor and publisher, 1925-28; Writers Colony, Indian Hills, Colo., founder and director, 1926-29; National Writers Club (writers' service), Denver, founder and president, beginning 1937. *Military service:* U.S. Army, Infantry, World War I; became sergeant. *Member:* Outdoor Writers Association of America, Authors Guild of the Authors League of America, Colorado Authors' League (president, 1966-67).

WRITINGS: (Editor) *The Echo Anthology of Verse,* Echo, 1926; *Conscious Short Story Technique,* Author & Journalist, 1928; *Practical Magazine Writing,* Author & Journalist, 1928; *The Creative Ability Developer,* Simplified Training Course, 1935; *Writing for the Markets,* Funk, 1969. Contributor of stories and serials, some under pseudonym R. E. Locke, as well as articles, to *Ace High, Look, Youth's Comrade, Mailbag, Midwest Review, Canadian Bookman,* and other periodicals.

WORK IN PROGRESS: Encyclopedia of Creative Writing.

AVOCATIONAL INTERESTS: Photography, pre-Columbian and Indian arts and artifacts, theater, coins.

BIOGRAPHICAL/CRITICAL SOURCES: Denver Post, April 9, 1967; *Rocky Mountain News,* April 9, 1967.

* * *

RAGEN, Joseph E(dward) 1897-1971

PERSONAL: Born November 22, 1897, in Trenton, Ill.; son of William (in livestock business) and Mollie (Rinesmith) Ragen; married Loretta Heyer, November 25, 1926; children: Jane (Mrs. Gerald Fahrner), William. *Education:* Educated in public and parochial schools, Carlyle, Ill. *Politics:* Independent. *Religion:* Roman Catholic. *Home and office:* 1317 Mayfield Ave., Joliet, Ill.

CAREER: Clinton County, Ill., deputy sheriff, 1922-26, sheriff, 1926-30, county treasurer, 1930-33; Illinois State Penitentiary, Menard, warden, 1933-35; Illinois State Penitentiary, Joliet, warden, 1935-61; with exception of eighteen months with U.S. Department of Justice, 1941-42; Illinois Department of Public Safety, director, 1961-65; Louis Joliet Bank, Joliet, Ill., vice-president of marketing, 1965-71. Private counselor for penal institutions, beginning 1965. *Military service:* U.S. Navy, 1918-19. *Member:* Warden's Association of America (past president), American Congress of Corrections (past president), American Legion. *Awards, honors:* Various awards from U.S. Government, state of Illinois, and other states where he made prison surveys.

WRITINGS: (With Charles Finston) *Inside the World's Toughest Prison,* C. C Thomas, 1962.

BIOGRAPHICAL/CRITICAL SOURCES: G. A. Erickson, *Warden Ragen of Joliet,* Dutton, 1957.†

(Died September 22, 1971)

RAGHAVAN, Manayath D. 1892-

PERSONAL: Born January 23, 1892, in Tellicherry, Malabar (now Kerala), India; son of Kanary D. (a merchant) and Chemmarathy (Bappu) Raghavan; married Kausalya Raman, May 11, 1919; children: Jayachandran, Vijara, Padma (Mrs. M. P. Sadanandan). *Education:* Studied at Government Brennen College, Tellicherry, India, 1909-10, St. Aloysius College, Mangalore, India, 1911-13, and Oxford University, 1930-31. *Religion:* Hinduism. *Home:* "Padma Sudan," 12 F. Halls Rd., Kilpauk, Madras 600010, Tamil Nadu, India.

CAREER: Government Museum, Madras, India, administrative and anthropology posts, 1918-45; University of Madras, Madras, India, head of department of anthropology, 1945-46; Department of National Museums, Ceylon, ethnologist and assistant director of national museums at Colombo, Kandy, Ratnapura, and Jaffna, 1946-55, working mainly on official Ethnological Survey of Ceylon, and doing the technical and administrative work on Ceylon's four national museums; University of Ceylon, Peradeniya, Hilda Obeyasekhara research fellow, 1956-57; retired from official assignments, 1958, to devote time to writing. Member of North Malabar section of German State Expedition in India, 1928; traveled in jungles of Wynad, Malabar, and in the jungle areas of ancestral Vedda settlements on later expeditions. President of ethnology and folklore section of All India Oriental Conference XI; member of folk dances and songs panel, Ceylon Arts Council, 1952-58. Adviser, Backward Communities Welfare Board, Ceylon, 1951-56. Co-founder of Kerala Association, 1918, to aid in the higher education of students from Kerala.

MEMBER: Royal Asiatic Society (council member of Ceylon branch, 1950-53), Archaeological Society of South India (council member, 1964-66), Social Sciences Association (Madras; council member, 1964-66). *Awards, honors:* Granted distinguished citizenship by Government of Ceylon for services to the country, 1953.

WRITINGS: Folk Plays and Dances of Kerala, Rama Varma Research Institute (Trichur), 1947; *Handsome Beggars: The Rodiyas of Ceylon,* K.V.G. De Silva & Sons (Colombo), 1955; *The Karava of Ceylon: Society and Culture,* K.V.G. De Silva & Sons, 1958; *Ceylon: A Pictorial Survey of the Peoples and Arts,* M. D. Gunasena & Co. (Colombo), 1960; *India in Ceylonese History, Society and Culture,* India Council for Cultural Relations, 1964, 2nd revised edition, Asia Publishing House, 1969; *Sinhala Natum: Dances of the Sinhalese,* M. D. Gunasena & Co., 1967. Also author of *Jaffna: Its History, Peoples, and Arts* and *Ceylon and the Mukkuver,* both published by Ila Nadu (Jaffna).

Monographs in "Ethnological Survey of Ceylon" series; published by Department of National Museums, Ceylon: *The Sigiriya Frescoes,* 1947; *Cultural Anthropology of the Rodiyas,* 1948; *Kinnarayas: The Tribe of Mat Weavers,* 1949; *The Paltini Cult as a Socio-Religious Institution,* 1950; *An Antique Kandyan Vase: A Study in Kandyan Art Designs,* 1950; *The Ahikuntakaya: Ceylon Gypsy Tribe,* 1951; *Folk Sports,* 1951; *Traditions and Legends of Nagercoil, Northern Province,* 1952; *A Kalvettu (Folk Chronicle) of the Seerpadam of the Eastern Province,* 1952; *The Sinhalese Social System: A Sociological Review,* 1953; *Traditions and Chronicles of the Dance in Ceylon,* 1956.

Contributor to *Man* (London), *Indian Antiquary, Current Science, Ceylon Today,* and other journals; also contributor to the press in India and Ceylon.

WORK IN PROGRESS: Tamil Culture in Ceylon, for publication by Kala Nilagam.

SIDELIGHTS: In addition to Malayalam, Raghavan is competent in Tamil and Sinhalese and he has a working knowledge of French.

BIOGRAPHICAL/CRITICAL SOURCES: Christoph Von Furer Haimendorff, *Bibliography of South East Asian Anthropology,* Mouton & Co., 1956, enlarged edition, 1964.

* * *

RAGO, Henry Anthony 1915-1969

PERSONAL: Born October 5, 1915, in Chicago, Ill.; son of Louis and Theresa (Argenzio) Rago; married Juliet Maggio, October 7, 1950; children: Maria Christina, Maria Carmela, Anthony Pascal, Maria Martha. *Education:* DePaul University, LL.B., 1937, Litt.D., 1965; University of Notre Dame, M.A. (magna cum laude), 1939, Ph.D. (magna cum laude), 1941. *Home:* 1707 North Park Ave., Chicago, Ill. 60614. *Office:* 1018 North State St., Chicago, Ill. 60610.

CAREER: University of Notre Dame, South Bend, Ind., teaching fellow, 1939-41; DePaul University, Chicago, Ill., instructor in English, 1941-42; Barat College of the Sacred Heart (now Barat College), Lake Forest, Ill., lecturer in philosophy, 1941-42; University of Chicago, Chicago, assistant professor of humanities, 1947-54, Divinity School, professor of theology and literature, 1956-59; St. Xavier College, Chicago, professor of humanities, 1954-56; *Poetry* magazine, Chicago, associate editor, 1954-55, editor, 1955-69. Staff member, Breadloaf Writers Conference, Middlebury, Vt., 1965-69; fellow, School of Letters, Indiana University, 1965-69; Isabelle Kellogg Thomas Lecturer, Goucher College, 1965. Member of national poetry council of Rockefeller Foundation, 1960-69; member of Chicago Motion Picture Appeal Board. *Military service:* U.S. Army, 1942-46; became first lieutenant; received Bronze Star. *Awards, honors:* Rockefeller Foundation travel grant, 1960-61; Clarence B. Randall Award for poetry, Society for Midland Authors, 1965.

WRITINGS: The Philosophy of Esthetic Individualism, University of Notre Dame Library, 1941; *The Travelers* (poems), Golden Goose Press,1949; *Conoscenza della luce* (poems in English and Italian), Libreria Antiquaria Palmaverdi (Bologna), 1959; *A Sky of Late Summer* (poems), Macmillan, 1963; (editor) *Poetry: The Golden Anniversary Issue* (originally October-November, 1962, issues of *Poetry*), University of Chicago Press, 1967. Editor, with Stanley Kunitz and Richard Wilbur, of *Poems in Folio,* 1956-57. Contributing editor, *New City,* 1960-69.

WORK IN PROGRESS: The Vocation of Poetry.

SIDELIGHTS: "Henry Rago was a man of many devotions: To his art, to the magazine he edited with skill and imagination, to teaching, and, more intimately, to his friends and family," Ralph J. Mills said. "One could sense this devotedness, I think, even at first encounter, for it was so evident in his manner of speech, the way in which he talked. . . . In him, the voice was the man—authentic, impassioned, articulate, precise." Hayden Carruth commented, "I remember too how Henry talked, how when he was excited he blocked out his words in the air with his stonemason's hands."

"The ultimate implications of poetry were, to Henry Rago's mind, symbolic, metaphysical, religious," Mills wrote. Denise Levertov said much the same thing in her review of *A Sky of Late Summer:* "[His] poems are essentially, though

in no obvious way, religious. They celebrate the light of Nature as a reflection of inner light; they celebrate the word as the expression of a living Silence." Although she found the lack of "evil, anguish, *Angst*" to be a fault, she concluded that "the recurring vision—the common source of his many images of light, of transparency, of ecstatic dazzle—does convince, in and of itself." Mills pointed out Rago's "desire to work in a line of descent from those great pioneer modernists he admired so much—Eliot, Pound, Stevens, the late Williams." Mills said that one notices at once two "qualities that are inseparable and that enrich each other" in Rago's own poems—"the contemplative and the visual"; in "The Green Afternoon," "we begin with a reflected image on a wall, one of those happy, fortuitous combinations of sunlight, wind, and leaves that seduces the vision, calms the body, draws the mind into itself, toward contemplation." Dudley Fitts found *A Sky of Late Summer* to be "a quiet and graceful collection, especially effective in its disposition of melodic nuances. . . . One perceives that the poet knew what he wanted to do and did it, which happens less often that you would think."

Carruth concluded that Rago "was of course more than the rescuer of *Poetry,* more than a loved teacher, a valiant and failing poet, a scholar of the great humane, Catholic and catholic tradition, and a literary arbiter whose authority was widely acknowledged. Fidelity was what meant most to him, I think, fidelity to men, to poetry, and to his knowledge of spiritual reality."

BIOGRAPHICAL/CRITICAL SOURCES: Nation, February 3, 1964; *Saturday Review,* May 2, 1964; *New York Times,* May 28, 1969; *Poetry,* August, 1969, December, 1969.††

(Died May 26, 1969)

* * *

RAKNES, Ola 1887-1975
(Carl Arnold)

PERSONAL: Born January 17, 1887, in Bergen, Norway; son of Erik Askildsen and Magdali Raknes; married Vaa Aslaug, December 20, 1911; married second wife, Gjertrud Bonde, October 30, 1941; children: (first marriage) Magli (Mrs. Torolf Elster), Anne, Tora, Erik, Tor; (second marriage) Ada. *Education:* University of Oslo, M.A., 1915, Ph.D., 1928; also attended University of Paris, University College, London, Psychoanalytic Institute, Berlin, and Orgone Institute, New York. *Home and office:* Nilserudkleiva 22, Oslo 8, Norway.

CAREER: High school teacher, 1916-17, 1922-27; lecturer at University of Paris, Paris, France, 1917-21, and University of London, London, England, 1921-22; Norsk Psykologforening (psychotherapy), Oslo, Norway, member, beginning 1935; American College of Orgonomy, New York, N.Y., fellow, 1968-75. *Military service:* Served as private soldier in Norway, summers, 1910-16. *Member:* Norsk Maldyrkingslag, Det Norske Samlaget (honorary member), Studentmallaget (honorary member).

WRITINGS: Norsk-Fransk Ordliste, Det Norske Samlaget, 1914; (with Illit C. Grondahl) *Chapters in Norwegian Literature,* Gyldendal (London), 1923; *Engelsk-Norsk Ordbok,* H. Aschehoug & Co., 1927; *Motet med det heilage,* Norsk Gyldendal, 1927; *Fransk-Norsk Ordbok,* Det Norske Samlaget, 1939-42; *Fri Vokster* (essays), J. G. Tanum, 1949; *Wilhelm Reich and Orgonomy,* St. Martin's, 1970.

Contributor, under pseudonym Carl Arnold, to *Interna-*

tional Journal of Sex Economy and Orgone Research, Orgone Energy Bulletin, Syn og Segn, published in Oslo in 1919, and *Orgonomic Medicine,* Volume 1.

SIDELIGHTS: Ola Raknes told *CA:* "Three books have had a decisive influence on my life and work: 1) Ivar Flem: *Determinismen* (which I read at 17, and which helped me trust my own thinking and feeling; 2) William James: *The Varieties of Religious Experience* (which I read at 30, and which made me look upon religions as a natural human phenomenon; 3) Wilhelm Reich: *The Discovery of the Orgone, Vol. I-II* (the contents of which I partially knew before publication, and which made me view in a new light man's place in the universe, and the role of religion in human life)."†

(Died January 28, 1975)

*   *   *

RAMSEYER, Lloyd L. 1899-

PERSONAL: Surname is pronounced *Ram*-sire; born November 5, 1899, in Normal, Ill.; son of M. L. (a farmer) and Anna (Stahly) Ramseyer; married Ferne Yoder, June 4, 1927; children: Robert L., Mary Jean, William. *Education:* Bluffton College, A.B., 1924; Ohio State University, M.A., 1932, Ph.D., 1938. *Religion:* Mennonite. *Home:* 488 West Elm St., Bluffton, Ohio 45817. *Office:* Bluffton College, Bluffton, Ohio 45817.

CAREER: High school teacher and coach in Heyworth, Ill., 1924-27, and high school principal, Heyworth, 1927-36; Bluffton College, Bluffton, Ohio, president, 1938-65, professor of psychology and president emeritus, beginning 1965. Summer faculty, Bowling Green State University, 1938-39, Ohio State University, 1940-41. Did relief work in Korea, February-July, 1966. Interim pastor at Bethel College Mennonite Church, North Newton, Kan., 1929-71, and Grace Mennonite Church, Pandora, Ohio, 1972-73; acting president, Mennonite Biblical Seminary, Elkhart, Ind., 1971-72. *Member:* Phi Delta Kappa, Torch Club, Lions Club. *Awards, honors:* D.D., Bethel College, North Newton, Kan., 1952; L.H.D., Findlay College, 1964.

WRITINGS: The More Excellent Way, Faith & Life, 1965. Contributor to educational and religious magazines.

*   *   *

RAPPAPORT, David 1907-

PERSONAL: Born June 13, 1907, in Kiev, Russia; son of Aaron and Esther Rappaport; married Ayala Pekarsky; children: Dahlia (Mrs. Albert Derin), Mildred (Mrs. Sheldon Goldstein). *Education:* University of Chicago, B.S., 1928; Northwestern University, M.A., 1954, Ed.D., 1957. *Politics:* Democrat. *Religion:* Jewish. *Home:* 2747 Coyle, Chicago, Ill. 60645. *Office:* 5500 North St. Louis Ave., Chicago, Ill. 60625.

CAREER: Chicago (Ill.) public schools, elementary teacher, 1937-40, high school teacher, 1940-56; Illinois Teachers College, Chicago-North (now Northeastern Illinois University), Chicago, professor of mathematics education, 1957-73, professor emeritus, 1973—. Coronet Instructional Films, collaborator on mathematics films, 1964-73. *Member:* National Council of Teachers of Mathematics, Central Association of Science and Mathematics Teachers, Men's Mathematics Club of Chicago (president, 1949-50).

WRITINGS: (Contributor) M. Vere De Vault, editor, *Improving Mathematics Programs,* C. E. Merrill, 1961; (contributor) Robert E. Chasnoff, editor, *Elementary Curriculum,* Pitman, 1964; *Understanding and Teaching Ele-*

mentary School Mathematics, Wiley, 1966. Compiler of diagnostic test in arithmetic published by Science Research Associates, 1959; contributor of some fifteen articles to educational journals.

WORK IN PROGRESS: A popular book on the new mathematics, for parents and teachers.

SIDELIGHTS: Rappaport speaks and reads Hebrew.

*   *   *

RATCLIFFE, T(om) A(rundel) 1910-

PERSONAL: Born August 6, 1910, in England; son of Thomas S. and Mary Joanna (Arundel) Ratcliffe; married Norah V. Greenall, October 3, 1935; children: Judith Ann Ratcliffe Jolley. *Education:* St. John's College, Cambridge, B.A. (first class honors), 1931, M.B. and B.Ch., 1934, M.A., 1947; St. Thomas Hospital Medical School, London, M.R.C.S. and L.R.C.P., 1934, D.P.M., 1936, D.Ch., 1938. *Home and office:* The Croft, Croft Rd., Edwalton, Nottingham NG12 4BW, England.

CAREER: Physician specializing in child psychiatry. Consultant child psychiatrist to Nottingham Paediatric Hospital and Nottinghamshire Clinical Area; part-time lecturer at University of Nottingham, University of Leicester, and elsewhere. Consultant to World Federation for Mental Health. *Military service:* British Army, specialist psychiatrist, World War II; became lieutenant colonel. *Member:* Royal Medico-Psychological Society, Association of Child Psychology and Allied Disciplines (founder member).

WRITINGS: Discipline and the Child, National Association for Mental Health (London), 1960; *The Development of Personality,* Humanities, 1967; *Parents under Stress,* National Marriage Guidance Council (London), 1968; *Child and Reality: Lectures by a Child Psychiatrist,* Humanities, 1970. Contributor to professional and other journals.

*   *   *

RAUCH, Basil 1908-

PERSONAL: Born September 6, 1908, in Dubuque, Iowa; son of William H. (a businessman) and Elizabeth (Wordehof) Rauch; married Elisabeth Hird (a sculptor and architect), October 2, 1964. *Education:* University of Notre Dame, B.A., 1929, Yale University, graduate study, 1929-33; Columbia University, Ph.D., 1946. *Home:* Outer Island, Stony Creek, Conn. 06405. *Office:* 420 Lehman, Barnard College, Columbia University, New York, N.Y. 10027.

CAREER: Columbia Grammar School, New York, N.Y., instructor, 1933-40; Columbia University, New York, N.Y., instructor in history, School of General Studies, 1941, member of history faculty, Barnard College, beginning 1941, became professor of history, 1952, chairman of department, 1949-52, chairman of American studies program, beginning 1952. Salzburg Seminar in American Studies, faculty member, 1955. *Military service:* U.S. Army, Field Artillery and Cavalry, 1925-26. U.S. Naval Reserve, instructor at U.S. Naval Academy, 1943-45; became lieutenant. *Member:* American Studies Association, American Civil Liberties Union, Century Association, Lawn Club (New Haven), Phi Beta Kappa (honorary member). *Awards, honors:* Edmund Campion Award, 1972.

WRITINGS: History of the New Deal, 1933-1938, Farrar, Straus, 1944, edition with new introduction, Putnam, 1963; *American Interest in Cuba, 1848-1855,* Columbia University Press, 1948; *Roosevelt: From Munich to Pearl Harbor,* Farrar, Straus, 1950, revised edition, Barnes & Noble, 1967;

(editor) *Franklin Roosevelt: Selected Speeches, Messages, Press Conferences, and Letters,* Rinehart, 1957; (editor) *The Roosevelt Reader,* Holt, 1957; (with Dumas Malone) *Empire for Liberty,* two volumes, Appleton, 1960, revised edition in six volumes, Prentice-Hall, 1965.

AVOCATIONAL INTERESTS: Horseback riding, mosaics, beekeeping, woodworking, canoeing, traveling, collecting U.S. and British gold coins.

* * *

RAWLINS, Jennie Brown 1910-

PERSONAL: Born January 24, 1910, in Ogden, Utah; daughter of John A. (a farmer) and Jeanette (Gatchell) Brown; married Alma Narvel Rawlins (a farmer), December 29, 1934; children: Lane, Barbara (Mrs. Jerry Matson). *Education:* Attended Weber College, 1928-30, and took various courses at Ricks College. *Religion:* Church of Jesus Christ of Latter-day Saints. *Home address:* Route 2, Rigby, Idaho 83442.

CAREER: Elementary teacher at schools in Ogden, Utah, 1930-31, Ririe, Idaho, 1931-32, Rigby, Idaho, 1932-36, and Bonneville County, Idaho, 1947-48, 1957-61. *Member:* Idaho Writers League (president, 1967-68). *Awards, honors:* Named writer of year by Idaho Writers League, 1967.

WRITINGS: Talk Topics, Deseret, 1959; *High Button Shoes,* Deseret, 1962; *Exploring Idaho's Past,* Deseret, 1963; *The Secret in the Cave,* Deseret, 1967; *Tame the Wild Wind,* Bouregy, 1969. Writer of column for *Deseret News,* 1959-61; also author of plays, stories, and articles.

WORK IN PROGRESS: Three books, *Flame on the Mountain, A Mother for Jeru,* and *The Never-Say-Die O'Roulians.*††

* * *

RAY, Kenneth Clark 1901-

PERSONAL: Born November 17, 1901, in McConnelsville, Ohio; son of Thomas Vincent (a farmer) and Mary (Harmon) Ray; married Hope Walker, June 24, 1931; children: John Walker, Beverly Ann (Mrs. Daniel Paul Klineko). *Education:* Muskingum College, B.S. in Ed., 1925; Ohio University, M.A., 1931; Ohio State University, Ph.D., 1943. *Politics:* Republican. *Religion:* Methodist. *Home:* 263 East Main St., McConnelsville, Ohio 43756.

CAREER: Principal and teacher at high schools in Morgan County, Ohio, McKeesport, Pa., and Coolville, Ohio, 1921-32; superintendent of schools, Athens County, Ohio, 1932-38, and Zanesville, Ohio, 1938-41; superintendent of public instruction, state of Ohio, 1941-45; Grolier Society, Inc., New York, N.Y., director of education, 1945-54; U.S. Department of State, Washington, D.C., director of Educational Services, International Cooperation Administration, 1954-59; Ohio University, Athens, visiting lecturer in education, 1959-69. Member of Ohio House of Representatives, 1928-32. *Member:* National Education Association, National Organization on Legal Problems in Education, Association for Higher Education, Ohio Education Association, Kappa Delta Pi, Phi Delta Kappa. *Awards, honors,* L.H.D., Central State University, 1973.

WRITINGS: (With Drury) *Principles of School Law,* Appleton, 1965. Co-editor of workbooks in English, State Publishing, 1962, and consultant for "Stories of Young Americans," State Publishing, 1964.

RAY, Philip A(lexander) 1911-1970

PERSONAL: Born May 27, 1911, in Salt Lake City, Utah; son of William Wallace (a lawyer) and Leda (Rawlins) Ray; married Denece Sanford, September 12, 1935. *Education:* Attended University of Utah, 1928-31; Stanford University, A.B. (cum laude), 1932, LL.B., 1935. *Politics:* Republican. *Home:* 520 Roekampton Rd., Hillsborough, Calif. *Office:* Kelso, Cotton, Seligman & Ray, Alcoa Building, 1 Maritime Plaza, San Francisco, Calif. 94111.

CAREER: Admitted to California Bar, 1935; McCutchen, Olney, Mannon & Green, and successor law firms, San Francisco, Calif., associate, 1935-42, partner, 1946-54, 1957; U.S. Department of Commerce, Washington, D.C., general counsel, 1954-56; J. H. Pomeroy & Co. (contractors and engineers), San Francisco, vice-president, 1957-58; U.S. Department of Commerce, Washington, D.C., Undersecretary of Commerce, 1958-61; private practice of law, San Francisco, 1961-67; Kelso, Cotton, Seligman & Ray (law firm), San Francisco, partner, 1967-70. Chairman of International Bond & Share, 1961-64; member of board of directors, Commonwealth Mutual Funds, beginning 1961, and General Brewing Corp., 1966-70. Trustee of World Affairs Council of Northern California, 1957-70, American Enterprise Institute, 1961-70, and San Francisco Symphony Foundation, 1966-70. *Military service:* U.S. Navy, World War II; served as combat intelligence officer; became lieutenant commander; received Bronze Star.

MEMBER: Inter-American Bar Association, American Law Institute, American Society of International Law, American Bar Association, State Bar of California. *Awards, honors:* Research fellowship at Hoover Institution on War, Revolution and Peace, 1963-65.

WRITINGS: South Wind Red, Regnery, 1962.

WORK IN PROGRESS: A book on strategic aspects of Mexico, for Hoover Institution.†

(Died July 16, 1970)

* * *

RAY, Wilbert S(cott) 1901-

PERSONAL: Born July 21, 1901, in Rochester, Pa.; son of James Francis (a clergyman) and E. Jane (Sturgeon) Ray; married Dorothy Philips Clark, May 19, 1928 (died June 13, 1975); children: Susan (Mrs. Robert L. Marquardt), David Scott. *Education:* Washington and Jefferson College, A.B., 1923; University of Wisconsin, M.A., 1929, Ph.D., 1930. *Religion:* United Presbyterian Church in the U.S.A. *Office:* Psychology Department, Bethany College, Bethany, W.Va. 26032.

CAREER: High school teacher in Pennsylvania, 1924-28; Yale University, New Haven, Conn., assistant in clinic of child development, 1930-31; New Jersey State Hospital, Trenton, clinical psychologist, 1931-37; Hillsdale College, Hillsdale, Mich., professor of psychology, 1937-44; Adelphi University, Garden City, N.Y., associate professor of psychology, 1944-45; Trinity College, Hartford, Conn., assistant professor of psychology, 1946-51; U.S. Air Force Personnel and Training Research Center, Lackland Air Force Base, Tex., research psychologist, 1951-56; Bethany College, Bethany, W.Va., professor of psychology and head of department, beginning 1956. *Member:* American Psychological Association (fellow; secretary-treasurer, Division of the Teaching of Psychology, 1966-72), British Psychological Society (fellow), American Association for the Advancement of Science (fellow), American Association of University Professors.

WRITINGS: A Laboratory Manual for Social Psychology, American Book Co., 1951; (contributor) W. J. McKeachie and others, *Undergraduate Curricula in Psychology,* Scott, Foresman, 1961; *The Experimental Psychology of Original Thinking,* Macmillan, 1967. Contributor to journals. Associate editor, *Psychological Record.*†

* * *

RAYMOND, William O. 1880-1970

PERSONAL: Born November 23, 1880, in Stanley, New Brunswick, Canada; son of William O. (a clergyman) and Julia (Nelson) Raymond; married Florence J. Gillespie, September, 1907; children: Eleanor (Mrs. E.C.G. Barrett), Nelson. *Education:* University of New Brunswick, B.A., 1902; Montreal Diocesan College, L.Th., 1905; University of Michigan, M.A., 1914, Ph.D., 1916.

CAREER: Anglican clergyman in McAdam, New Brunswick, 1905-07, in Ann Arbor, Mich., 1907-14; University of Michigan, Ann Arbor, instructor, then assistant professor of English, 1914-28; Bishop's University, Lennoxville, Quebec, professor and head of department of English, 1928-50, professor emeritus, 1950-1970. Visiting summer professor at University of Texas and Queen's University, Kingston, Ontario. *Member:* Royal Society of Canada (fellow). *Awards, honors:* D.C.L., Bishop's University, 1950.

WRITINGS: (Editor, and author of introduction and notes) *Selections from Swinburne,* Harcourt, 1925; *The Infinite Moment and Other Essays in Robert Browning,* University of Toronto Press, 1950, enlarged edition, 1965. Contributor of articles and reviews to university journals.

WORK IN PROGRESS: Further research on the life and poetry of Robert Browning.†

(Died, 1970)

* * *

REDFORD, Polly 1925-1972

PERSONAL: Born November 26, 1925, in Evanston, Ill.; daughter of Laurens and Mildred (Smith) Hammond; married James F. Redford (a real estate broker), May 6, 1954; children: Adam, Matthew. *Education:* Illinois Institute of Technology, M.S., 1950. *Home:* 3975 Little Ave., Miami, Fla. 33133. *Agent:* McIntosh & Otis, Inc., 475 Fifth Ave., New York, N.Y. 10017.

CAREER: University of Miami, Division of Applied Ecology, Coral Gables, Fla., editor and consultant, 1971-72. *Member:* Tropical Audubon Society (conservation chairman), Izaak Walton League. *Awards, honors:* Rembert W. Patrick Memorial Award of Florida Historical Society, 1971, for *Billion Dollar Sandbar.*

WRITINGS—All published by Dutton: *Raccoons and Eagles,* 1965; *Christmas Bower,* 1967; *Billion Dollar Sandbar,* 1970. Contributor to national magazines, including *Harper's, Atlantic,* and *Gourmet.*

WORK IN PROGRESS: Research on the environmental crisis in Florida.†

(Died August 19, 1972)

* * *

REDISH, Bessie Braid 1905-1974

PERSONAL: Born September 21, 1905, in Summerville, S.C.; daughter of Jefferson Davis (a furniture designer) and Ida Priscilla (Meyer) Braid; married Harry Carl Redish,

April 15, 1934 (deceased); stepchildren: Barbara (Mrs. Harry Lyman Kirkland II). *Education:* Davis Secretarial School, Charleston, S.C., graduate; also attended Augusta College and College of Charleston. *Politics:* Republican. *Religion:* Presbyterian. *Home:* 1907 McDowell St., Augusta, Ga. 30904. *Office address:* Continental Can Co., P.O. Box 1425, Augusta, Ga. 30903.

CAREER: News and Courier and *Charlotte Evening Post,* Charlotte, S.C., secretary to publisher, 1924-34; Atlantic Coast Line (railroad), Augusta, Ga., secretary, 1942-45; Continental Can Co., Inc., Augusta, secretary, 1959-74. Did secretarial and editorial work for William E. Woodward and other authors at various times. *Member:* National Secretaries Association, Georgia Writers Association, Georgia Poetry Society.

WRITINGS: Along the Way (collection of poems), Doubleday, 1969. Contributor of poetry to magazines, newspapers, and trade journals.

WORK IN PROGRESS: A second collection of poems, *Lyrics from Life.*

BIOGRAPHICAL/CRITICAL SOURCES: Augusta Chronicle-Herald, February 23, 1969; *News and Courier,* March 2, 1969.†

(Died, 1974)

* * *

REEVES, Joan Wynn 1910-1972

PERSONAL: Born April 26, 1910, in England; daughter of Herbert Wynn (a musician) and Charlotte P. (Child) Reeves. *Education:* Bedford College, London, B.A. (first class honors), Ph.D., 1935. *Office:* Bedford College, Regents Park, London N.W. 1, England.

CAREER: Teacher at various schools in England, 1935-36; National Institute of Industrial Psychology, London, England, librarian and assistant editor, 1936-41, psychologist, 1946-50; University of London, Bedford College, London, England, beginning 1948, became reader in psychology. *Military service:* Auxiliary Territorial Service (British women's service), specialist officer (psychologist) in War Office, 1941-46; became senior commander. *Member:* British Psychological Society, Aristotelian Society.

WRITINGS: Body and Mind in Western Thought, Pelican, 1958; *Thinking about Thinking,* Secker & Warburg, 1965, Braziller, 1966. Assistant editor, *Occupational Psychology,* 1936-41, and *British Journal of Psychology,* 1950-54.

WORK IN PROGRESS: Theories of Pleasure, Pain and Emotion; and *Attitudes to Music and the Visual Arts.*†

(Died January, 1972)

* * *

REEVES, John K(night) 1907-

PERSONAL: Born April 7, 1907, in Beaver Falls, Pa.; son of John T. (a banker) and Lula (Knight) Reeves; married Alice Phelps, August 31, 1932 (died October 12, 1960); married Janet Ahlefeld, June 17, 1967; children: (first marriage) John P., Virginia (Mrs. Stephen Vishanoff), Susan (Mrs. John Williams). *Education:* Williams College, A.B., 1929; Oxford University, B.Litt., 1932; Harvard University, Ph.D., 1938. *Politics:* Independent. *Religion:* Presbyterian. *Home:* 5 Oakland Dr., Saratoga Springs, N.Y. 12866.

CAREER: University of Pittsburgh, Pittsburgh, Pa., assistant in English, 1932-33; Skidmore College, Saratoga Springs, N.Y., assistant professor, 1938-47, associate professor, 1947-61, professor of English, 1961-63. Fulbright lecturer, University of Ankara, 1962-63. Reeves Bank, Beaver Falls, Pa., president, 1933-69, became chairman of board, 1969, currently chairman emeritus. *Member:* Modern Language Association of America, College English Association, Williams Club of New York.

WRITINGS: (Editor and author of introduction) William Dean Howells, *Their Wedding Journey*, Indiana University Press, 1968. Contributor to literary journals.

* * *

REID, James W. 1912-197(?)

PERSONAL: Born August 12, 1912, in Camden, N.J.; son of James W. and Viola W. (McConahy) Reid; married Geraldine Denison, December 27, 1943; children: James W. III, Ellen E., Thomas D., Susan L. *Education:* Drexel Institute of Technology (now Drexel University), B.S. in Mechanical Engineering, 1953. *Religion:* Protestant. *Home:* 2912 Sheffield Dr., Norristown, Pa. 19403.

CAREER: New York Shipbuilding Corp., Camden, N.J., shop engineering manger, 1935-43; National Aeronautics and Space Administration (NASA), Langley Field, Va., mechanical engineer, 1944-48; consultant in mechanical engineering, 1948-55; Design Engineering Co., Trenton, N.J., general manager, 1951-55; General Electric Co., Missile & Space Division, King of Prussia, Pa., manager of research equipment development in Space Sciences Laboratory, 1956-69, member of speakers bureau; writer and lecturer, beginning 1969. *Military service:* U.S. Army Air Forces, 1944. *Member:* American Institute of Aeronautics and Astronautics (associate fellow), American Association for the Advancement of Science, American Society of Mechanical Engineers, Franklin Institute, Pi Tau Sigma.

WRITINGS—All published by Zondervan: *God, the Atom, and the Universe*, 1968; *The Quiet Revolution*, 1970; *Does Science Confront the Bible*, 1971. Author of technical papers. Also author of monthly column on science and Bible in *Eternity*. Contributor of articles on the relation between the Bible and science to periodicals.†

(Deceased)

* * *

REILLY, William J(ohn) 1899-

PERSONAL: Born March 6, 1899, in Pittsburgh, Pa.; son of William John (a gas company executive) and Anna Jean (Kelly) Reilly; married Gladys Margaret Bogue, May 1, 1926; children: Ann Bogue (Mrs. Richard F. Pratt), Myrtle Jean (Mrs. William Durant Radebaugh), Norman Bogue. *Education:* Carnegie Institute of Technology (now Carnegie-Mellon University), B.S., 1921, M.S., 1923; University of Chicago, Ph.D., 1927. *Politics:* Independent. *Religion:* Presbyterian.

CAREER: Procter & Gamble Co., Cincinnati, Ohio, research associate, 1925-27; University of Texas, Austin, associate professor of marketing, 1927-29; Erickson Co., New York, N.Y., director of research, 1929-32; *American Weekly*, New York, N.Y., St. Louis manager, 1933-36; Townsend & Townsend, Inc., New York, N.Y., vice-president and general manager, and chairman of board of Townsend Advertising Research Institute, 1937-39; Lennen & Mitchell, New York, N.Y., account executive, 1939-41; personnel consultant to Bristol-Myers Co., 1939-62, Vick Chemical Co., 1942, Sales Affiliates, 1942-54, Super Market Institute, beginning 1955, and Armour & Co., beginning

1964. National Institute for Straight Thinking, New York, N.Y., founder and director, beginning 1932. Consultant on career planning at high school, college, and adult levels. *Military service:* U.S. Naval Reserve, 1918-1921; active duty, 1918. *Member:* American Management Association, Institute of Management, Phi Eta, Masonic Lodge, Columbia University Club (New York). *Awards, honors:* Junior Achievement Awards, 1948, for *How to Find and Follow Your Career*, and, 1953, for *Career Planning for High School Students;* Paul D. Converse Award, University of Illinois chapter of American Marketing Association, 1959.

WRITINGS: Marketing Investigations, Ronald, 1929; *Methods for the Study of Retail Relationships*, University of Texas, 1929; *What Place Has the Advertising Agency in Market Research?*, University of Texas, 1929; *The Law of Retail Gravitation*, privately printed, 1931, 2nd edition, Pilsbury Publishers, 1953; *The Effects of the Advertising Agency Commission System*, privately printed, 1931; *What's Stopping You?*, privately printed, 1931; *Straight Thinking*, Harper, 1935; *How to Find and Follow Your Career*, Harper, 1936; *How to Use Your Head to Get What You Want*, Harper, 1938; *How to Improve Your Human Relations by Straight Thinking*, Harper, 1942; *The Law of Intelligent Action Applied in Business Relations*, Harper, 1945; *The Twelve Rules for Straight Thinking*, Harper, 1947; *How to Avoid Work*, Harper, 1949.

Successful Human Relations, Harper, 1952; *Career Planning for High School Students*, Harper, 1953; *Life Planning for College Students*, Harper, 1954; *How to Make Your Living in Four Hours a Day Without Feeling Guilty About It*, Harper, 1955; *How to Get What You Want Out of Life*, Prentice-Hall, 1957; *In Search of a Working Philosophy of Life*, Harper, 1959; *Opening Closed Minds and Persuading Others to Act Favorably*, Harper, 1964.

WORK IN PROGRESS: Definition and propagation of the fundamental laws of human environment.

SIDELIGHTS: Many of Reilly's books have been published in Japan, India, Denmark, and South America.

BIOGRAPHICAL/CRITICAL SOURCES: Time, August 1, 1938; *Parade*, May 15, 1949; *Fortune*, May, 1953; *New Yorker*, January 7, 1956.††

* * *

REISCHAUER, August Karl 1879-1971

PERSONAL: Born September 4, 1879, in Jonesboro, Ill., son of Rupert and Maria (Gattermeier) Reischauer; married Helen Oldfather, August 17, 1905; children: Robert Karl, Edwin O., Felicia Miriam. *Education:* Hanover College, B.A., 1902, M.A., 1905; McCormick Theological Seminary, B.D., 1905; University of Chicago, graduate study, 1912-13. *Religion:* Presbyterian. *Home:* 130 Oakley Rd., Belmont, Mass.

CAREER: Professor of philosophy in Japan at Meiji Gakuin College, 1907-13, and professor of comparative religions at Meiji Gakuin Theological Seminary, 1913-35, and Nihon Shingakko (Japan Theological Seminary), 1928-41; United Presbyterian Church in the U.S.A., secretary of Commission on Ecumenical Missions and Relations, 1941-51; Union Theological Seminary, New York, N.Y., professor of comparative religions, 1943-52. Co-founder of Tokyo Woman's Christian College, 1918, and executive secretary of board of trustees, 1918-41; chairman of Federated Missions in Japan. *Member:* Asiatic Society of Japan (vice-president). *Awards, honors:* Imperial decoration, Order of the Sacred Treasure

(Japan); honorary citizen and Certificate of Merit, city of Tokyo; D.D. from New York University and Nihon Shingakko; LL.D. from Hanover College.

WRITINGS: Studies in Japanese Buddhism, Macmillan, 1917, reprinted, AMS Press, 1970; *The Task in Japan,* Revell, 1925; (contributor) *The Great Religions of the Modern World,* Princeton University Press, 1946; *The Nature and Truth of the Great Religions,* Tuttle, 1966. Also author of "A Catechism of the Shin Sect" (in Japanese), and *Genshin's Ojo Yoshu.* Contributor of entry on religion in Japan to *Encyclopedia Americana,* 1951.†

(Died July 10, 1971)

* * *

RESNICK, Nathan 1910-

PERSONAL: Born June 13, 1910, in New York, N.Y.; son of Abraham and Fanny (Weinberg) Resnick; married Ernestine R. Cederholm (a teacher), May 4, 1943. *Education:* Long Island University, B.S., 1933; Columbia University, B.S., 1937; New York University, M.A., 1945. *Home:* 72 Barrow St., New York, N.Y. 10014. *Office:* Long Island University, Brooklyn, N.Y. 11201.

CAREER: Long Island University, Brooklyn, N.Y., beginning 1933, assistant librarian, instructor, 1938-48, associate professor of English, 1948-52, associate professor of art, 1950-56, professor of art, beginning, 1956, department chairman, beginning, 1958, director of libraries and university press, beginning 1948, university director of planning, beginning 1965, became dean, Development of Learning Center, 1974. President, Walt Whitman Birthplace Association. *Member:* American Library Association, National Education Association, American Association for the Advancement of Science, American Studies Association, New York Folklore Society.

WRITINGS: Walt Whitman and the Authorship of the Good Gray Poet, Long Island University Press, 1948; (with E.S.M. Gatner and F. Cordasco) *Study Guide to English Literature,* Lamb, 1948; (editor) Allen and Kellogg, *Songbirds of America, in Color, Sound, and Story,* Cornell University Press, 1953; (with M. Komroff and K. Cramer) *The Third Eye: A New World of Exploratory Photography,* Walker & Co., 1962; (editor) Kosok, *Life, Land and Water in Ancient Peru,* Long Island University Press, 1966. Contributor to professional and other periodicals.

WORK IN PROGRESS: Three books, *The Philosophy of Photography, The Living Habits of Birds,* and *The Ideas of Walt Whitman.*

* * *

REYNOLDS, Bertha Capen 1885-

PERSONAL: Born December 11, 1885, in Brockton, Mass.; daughter of Franklin Stewart (an organ and piano tuner) and Mary L. B. (Capen) Reynolds. *Education:* Smith College, A.B., 1908, Certificate in Social Work, 1919; Simmons College, B.S., 1914. *Home:* 760 Pleasant St., Stoughton, Mass. 02072.

CAREER: Children's Aid Society, Boston, Mass., social worker, 1913-18; Massachusetts Department of Mental Diseases, Boston, social worker, 1918-25; Smith College, Northampton, Mass., associate director of School for Social Work, 1925-38; visiting lecturer and institute leader in twenty-eight states, 1938-43; United Seamen's Service, casework supervisor, 1943-48. Secretary, Stoughton Fair Housing and Human Rights Association. *Member:* Academy of Certified Social Workers, National Association of Social Workers, American Orthopsychiatric Association, Stoughton Historical Society, Phi Beta Kappa.

WRITINGS: Learning and Teaching in the Practice of Social Work, Farrar & Rinehart, 1942, new edition, Russell & Russell, 1965; *Social Work and Social Living,* Citadel, 1951; *An Uncharted Journey* (autobiography), Citadel, 1963. Contributor of about fifty articles to periodicals. Contributor to "Smith College Studies in Social Work," 1932, 1934.

* * *

REZNIKOFF, Charles 1894-1976

PERSONAL: Born August 31, 1894, in Brooklyn, N.Y.; son of Nathan (a businessman) and Sarah Yetta (Wolvosky) Reznikoff; married Marie Syrkin (a professor emeritus at Brandeis University), May 27, 1930. *Education:* Attended University of Missouri, 1910-11; New York University, LL.B., 1915. *Politics:* Democrat. *Religion:* Jewish.

CAREER: Admitted to Bar of the State of New York, 1916, but did not practice law; American Law Book Co., Brooklyn, N.Y., member of editorial staff in early 1930's; *Jewish Frontier,* New York, N.Y., member of editorial staff, beginning 1955. *Awards, honors:* Morton Dauwen Zabel Award for Poetry, National Institute of Arts and Letters, 1971.

WRITINGS—Verse: Rhythms, privately printed, 1918; *Poems,* Samuel Roth, 1920; *Uriel Acosta: A Play and a Fourth Group of Verse,* Cooper Press, 1921; *Chatterton, the Black Death, and Meriwether Lewis: Three Plays,* Sunwise Turn, 1922; *Coral, and Captive Israel: Two Plays,* Sunwise Turn, 1923; *Five Groups of Verse,* privately printed, 1927; *Nine Plays,* privately printed, 1927; *Jerusalem the Golden,* Objectivist, 1934; *In Memoriam: 1933,* Objectivist, 1936; *Going To and Fro and Walking Up and Down,* privately printed, 1941; *Inscriptions: 1944-1956,* privately printed, 1959; *By the Waters of Manhattan: Selected Verse,* New Directions, 1962; *Testimony: The United States (1885-1890),* New Directions, 1965; *Testimony: The United States (1891-1900),* privately printed, 1968; *By the Wall of Living and Seeing: New and Selected Poems 1918-1973,* edited by Seamus Cooney, Black Sparrow Press, 1974; *Holocaust,* Black Sparrow Press, 1975; *Poems 1918-1936: Volume I of the Complete Poems,* edited by Cooney, Black Sparrow Press, 1976; *Poems 1937-1975: Volume II of the Complete Poems,* Black Sparrow Press, 1977.

Other books: *By the Waters of Manhattan* (prose; partly fiction), Charles Boni, 1930; *Testimony* (prose), Objectivist, 1934; (with parents, Nathan and Sarah Reznikoff) *Family Chronicle,* privately printed, 1936, reprinted, Universe Books, 1971; *The Lionhearted* (historical novel), Jewish Publications Society, 1944; (with Uriah Engelman) *The Jews of Charleston* (history), Jewish Publication Society, 1950.

Translator, Emil Cohn, *Stories and Fantasies from the Jewish Past,* Jewish Publication Society of America, 1961.

SIDELIGHTS: Charles Reznikoff explained that he didn't practice law "because I wanted to use whatever mental energy I had for my writing." "I did not continue with journalism," he said, "because—to change the old adage—I was more interested in dog bites man than in man bites dog."†

(Died January 22, 1976)

* * *

REZNY, Arthur A(dolph) 1910-

PERSONAL: Born September 16, 1910, in Chicago, Ill.;

son of Martin Bernard (a plumbing contractor) and Helen (Pikas) Rezny; married Sally Matthews (a substitute teacher), June 22, 1935; children: Marilyn (Mrs. Gerald Hahn), Carolyn (Mrs. Lonnie Benson). *Education:* J. S. Morton Junior College, diploma, 1930; University of Illinois, B.S., 1932, M.S., 1939; University of Michigan, Ph.D., 1958. *Politics:* Liberal. *Religion:* Protestant. *Office:* Arkansas State University, State University, Ark.

CAREER: Elmwood Park (Ill.) public schools, teacher of social studies, 1934-37; Ann Arbor (Mich.) public schools, teacher, later administrative assistant, 1937-49; Royal Oak (Mich.) public schools, director of instruction, 1949-53; University of Wisconsin-Milwaukee, assistant professor, 1953-59, associate professor of education administration and supervision, beginning 1959; Arkansas State University, State University, professor of education administration, beginning 1974. Visiting professor at University of Alberta, 1949, and University of Wisconsin, Madison, 1959; visiting dean of student affairs at Northland College, 1963-64. *Military service:* U.S. Navy, 1942-45; became lieutenant commander. *Member:* American Association of School Administrators, National Education Association, Phi Kappa Phi, Phi Delta Kappa, Problems in Education (chairman, research committee, 1962; co-chairman, national convention, 1965), Association of Professors of School Administration, Wisconsin Education Association, Phi Kappa Phi, Phi Delta Kappa, Schoolmasters Club of Wisconsin (president, 1962-63).

WRITINGS: (With Madaline Kinter Remmlein) *A Schoolman in the Law Library,* Interstate, 1962; (contributor) *The Law of Counseling and Guidance,* W. H. Anderson, 1964; (editor-in-chief) *Legal Problems of School Boards,* W. H. Anderson, 1966. Contributor to educational journals.

* * *

RHOADS, Dorothy M(ary) 1895-

PERSONAL: Born March 19, 1895, in Pekin, Ill.; daughter of Franklin Koons (an estate management realtor) and Frances May (Cook) Rhoads. *Education:* Wellesley College, B.A., 1917. *Home:* 451 Arroyo Tenorio, Santa Fe, N.M. 87501.

CAREER: U.S. Government, translator of French and Spanish in New York, N.Y., 1917-19; *Rock Island Argus,* Rock Island, Ill., reporter and society editor, 1920-21; owner-manager of gift shop in Rock Island, Ill., 1922-27; free-lance writer. U.S. Government, census enumerator, 1950, 1960. *Member:* Authors Guild of the Authors League of America, American Association of University Women, Business and Professional Womens Association (Rock Island, Ill.). *Awards, honors: The Corn Grows Ripe* was runner-up for Newbery Award of American Library Association, 1957.

WRITINGS: The Bright Feather and Other Maya Tales, Doubleday, Doran, 1932; *The Story of Chan Yuc,* Doubleday, Doran, 1941; *The Corn Grows Ripe,* Viking, 1956. Contributor of stories and articles to *Catholic Digest, Children's Activities, Country Life, Junior Catholic Messenger,* and *Tomorrow.*

WORK IN PROGRESS: A juvenile book about Yucatan archaeology; a novel; editing correspondence of Sylvanus G. and Frances Rhoads Morley, describing their early exploration and jungle trips in Mexico and Central America.

SIDELIGHTS: An inveterate traveler, Miss Rhoads re-

members riding a donkey into the Grand Canyon at age five, and touring national parks on horseback with her parents and sister. She was in Rome when Mussolini took over the government in 1922; lived and traveled in Central America with her sister and sister's archaeologist-husband during the 1930's and 1940's. *Avocational interests:* Animals, wild and tame (especially cats).††

* * *

RICE, Elmer 1892-1967

PERSONAL: Born Elmer Leopold Reizenstein, September 28, 1892, in New York, N.Y.; son of Jacob and Fanny (Lion) Reizenstein; married Hazel Levy, June 16, 1915 (divorced January 10, 1942); married Betty Field (actress), January 12, 1942 (divorced, 1955); married Barbara A. Marshall; children: (first marriage) Robert, Margaret; (second marriage) John, Judith, Paul. *Education:* New York Law School, LL.B. (cum laude), 1912; attended Columbia University. *Politics:* Liberal. *Religion:* "I could never bring myself to an acceptance of ritual, dogma, and denominationalism; nor was I ever willing to submit to the authority of self-appointed spiritual guides." *Home:* 815 Long Ridge Rd., Stamford, Conn.

CAREER: Samstag and Hilder Bros., New York City, claims clerk, 1907; law clerk, 1908-12, admitted to New York Bar, 1913; was dramatic director, University Settlement, and chairman, Inter-Settlement Dramatic Society, New York City; Samuel Goldwyn Pictures Corp., Hollywood, Calif., scenarist, 1918-20; Famous Players-Lasky Corp. and Real Art Films, Hollywood, Calif., free-lance writer, 1920; organized the Morningside Players with Hatcher Hughes, New York City; purchased and operated David Belasco Theatre, New York City, 1934-37(?); Works Progress Administration, Federal Theatre Project, regional director, New York City, 1935-36; Playwright's Producing Co., director and co-founder with Robert E. Sherwood, Maxwell Anderson, S. N. Behrman and Sidney Howard, 1937-59. Lecturer in English, University of Michigan, Ann Arbor, 1954; adjunct professor, New York University, New York City, 1957-58. Directed numerous plays, including: Robert E. Sherwood's "Abe Lincoln in Illinois" (produced on Broadway at Plymouth Theatre, October 15, 1938, starring Raymond Massey); Maxwell Anderson's "Journey to Jerusalem" (produced on Broadway at National Theatre [now Billy Rose Theatre], October 5, 1940); S. N. Behrman's "The Talley Method" (produced on Broadway at Henry Miller's Theatre, February 24, 1941); "Second Fiddle" for Theatre Guild (closed out of town, 1953).

MEMBER: Dramatists Guild (founding member; contract committee, president, 1939-43), Authors League of America (Dramatists Guild representative on council; president, 1945-46), P.E.N. (international vice-president, New York), American National Theatre and Academy (executive committee member), League of British Dramatists, National Council on Freedom from Censorship (chairman), National Institute of Arts and Letters, American Civil Liberties Union (board member), American Arbitration Association, Writer's War Board (advisory council member). *Awards, honors:* Pulitzer Prize, 1929, for *Street Scene;* Canada Lee Foundation Award, 1954, for *The Winner;* Litt.D., University of Michigan, 1961.

WRITINGS—Plays: On Trial (first produced in New York at Candler Theatre, August 19, 1914; produced in London's West End at Lyric Theatre, April 29, 1915), Samuel French, 1919.

The Adding Machine (first produced Off-Broadway at Garrick Theatre, March 19, 1923), Doubleday, Page & Co., 1923; (with Hatcher Hughes) *Wake Up, Jonathan* (three-act comedy; first produced on Broadway at Henry Miller's Theatre, January 17, 1920), Samuel French, 1928; (with Dorothy Parker) *Close Harmony,* or *The Lady Next Door* (first produced in New York at Gaiety Theatre, December 1, 1924), Samuel French, 1929; (with Philip Barry) *Cock Robin* (three-act; first produced on Broadway at Forty-Eighth Street Theatre, January 12, 1928), Samuel French, 1929; *Street Scene* (three-act; directed by Rice; first produced on Broadway at Plymouth Theatre, January 10, 1929), Samuel French, 1929 (adapted as musical with music by Kurt Weill, libretto by Rice, and lyrics by Langston Hughes; first produced in London's West End at Adelphi Theatre, January 9, 1947), Chappell, 1948; *The Subway* (first produced Off-Broadway at Cherry Lane Theatre, January 25, 1929; later produced on Broadway), Samuel French, 1929.

See Naples and Die (three-act comedy; first produced in New York at Vanderbilt Theatre, September 24, 1929), Samuel French, 1930; *The Left Bank* (first produced by Rice on Broadway at Little Theatre, October 5, 1931), Samuel French, 1931; *Counsellor-at-Law* (three-act; first produced on Broadway at Plymouth Theatre, November 6, 1931 and at Royale Theatre, November 24, 1942), Samuel French, 1931; *House in Blind Alley* (three-act comedy), Samuel French, 1932; *We, the People* (first produced in New York at Empire Theatre, January 21, 1933), Coward, 1933; *The Home of the Free* (first produced in repertory by the Washington Square Players in New York at Comedy Theatre, 1917-18), Samuel French, 1934; *Judgment Day* (three-act melodrama; first produced on Broadway at Belasco Theatre, September 12, 1934; produced in London's West End at Strand Theatre, 1935), Coward, 1934; *The Passing of Chow-Chow* (one-act comedy written in 1913 for Columbia University one-act play contest), Samuel French, 1935; *Between Two Worlds* (first produced on Broadway at Belasco Theatre, October 25, 1934), published with "Not for Children," as *Not for Children* [and] *Between Two Worlds,* Coward, 1935; "Life is Real" (first produced in San Francisco, 1937; produced under title "Not for Children," directed by Rice, on Broadway at Coronet Theatre [now Eugene O'Neill Theatre], February 13, 1951), published with "Between Two Worlds" as *Not for Children* [and] *Between Two Worlds,* Coward, 1935, published as *Not for Children,* Samuel French, 1951; *Black Sheep* (three-act comedy; first produced on Broadway at Morosco Theatre, October 13, 1932), Dramatists Play Service, 1938; *American Landscape* (three-act; directed by Rice; first produced on Broadway at Cort Theatre, December 3, 1938), Coward, 1939.

Two on an Island (directed by Rice; first produced on Broadway at Broadhurst Theatre, January 22, 1940), Coward, 1940; *Flight to the West* (directed by Rice; first produced on Broadway at Guild Theatre [now American National Theatre & Academy, ANTA], December 30, 1940), Coward, 1941; *A New Life* (directed by Rice; first produced on Broadway at Royale Theatre, September 9, 1943), Coward, 1944; *Dream Girl* (comedy; directed by Rice; first produced on Broadway at Coronet Theatre [now Eugene O'Neill Theatre], December 14, 1945), Coward, 1946, final script, Feuer & Martin Productions, 1965.

The Grand Tour (two-act; directed by Rice; first produced on Broadway at Martin Beck Theatre, December 10, 1951), Dramatists Play Service, 1952; *The Winner* (directed by Rice; first produced on Broadway at Plymouth Theatre, February 17, 1954), Dramatists Play Service, 1954; *Cue for*

Passion (directed by Rice; first produced on Broadway at Henry Miller's Theatre, November 25, 1958), Dramatists Play Service, 1959.

Love Among the Ruins (two-act; first produced at University of Rochester, 1963), Dramatists Play Service, 1963; *The Iron Cross* (first produced in New York at Comedy Theatre, February 13, 1917), Proscenium Press, 1965.

Plays produced only: "For the Defense," first produced on Broadway at Playhouse Theatre, December 19, 1919; "It Is the Law" (dramatization of Hayden Talbot's unpublished novel), first produced in New York at Ritz Theatre, November 19, 1922; "The Mongrel" (adaptation of play by German dramatist, Hermann Bahr), first produced on Broadway at Longacre Theatre, December 15, 1924; "Is He Guilty?" (adaptation of play "The Blue Hawaii," by German dramatist, Rudolph Lothar), closed in Boston, Mass., September, 1927.

Also author of plays "Find the Woman," neither published nor produced, written c. 1918, and "A Diadem of Show" (one-act), published in *The Liberator,* 1918.

Other writings: "Papa Looks for Something" (novel), unpublished, c. 1926; (editor) *One Act Plays for Stage and Study* (fifth series), Samuel French, 1929; *A Voyage to Purilia* (novel; serialized in *New Yorker*), Cosmopolitan Book, 1930; *Imperial City* (novel), Coward, 1937; *The Show Must Go On* (novel), Viking, 1949; *Supreme Freedom,* Graphics Group, 1949; *The Living Theatre,* Harper, 1959; *Minority Report* (autobiography), Simon & Schuster, 1963. Contributor of articles and stories to *Collier's, New Yorker,* and other periodicals.

Omnibus volumes: *Plays* (contains *The Adding Machine, Street Scene, See Naples and Die,* and *Counsellor-at-Law*), Gollancz, 1933; *Three Plays Without Words* (contains "Landscape with Figures," "Rus in Urbe," and "Exterior"), Samuel French, 1934; *Two Plays: Not for Children* [and] *Between Two Worlds,* Coward, 1935; *Other Plays, and Not for Children: Being Four Plays* (contains *Between Two Worlds, Judgment Day, We, the People,* and *Not for Children*), Gollancz, 1935; *Seven Plays,* Viking, 1950; *Three Plays* (contains *The Adding Machine, Street Scene,* and *Dream Girl*), Hill & Wang, 1965.

Screenplays: Collaborated on "Help Yourself," adapted from Wallace Irwin's "Trimmed with Red," Goldwyn Pictures Corp., 1920; "Doubling for Romeo" starring Will Rogers, produced by Goldwyn Pictures Corp., 1921; "Street Scene," United Artists, 1931, directed by King Vidor; "Counsellor-at-Law," Universal Pictures, 1933, directed by William Wyler and starring John Barrymore.

SIDELIGHTS: "There have always been at least three Rice's to keep track of," wrote *Newsweek.* "One is the professional Rice—prolific, erratic, a restless innovator, a superb craftsman, winner of the Pulitzer Prize.... The second is the public Rice—unselfish, bold, a socialist who has held fast to principles.... Finally, there is the private Rice—cool, casual, emotionally uncommitted. His life was often dictated by happenstance, and he sometimes seems, in his autobiography, hardly to exist at all."

The public Rice regarded the Broadway theatre as a platform to express his views. "Justice was the subject to which he was most passionately devoted," commented Brooks Atkinson, "and he wrote for a theatre that believed in taking sides and making partisan statements." He began championing causes early in his career. "I had been one of a small male contingent that had marched up Fifth Avenue in a woman-suffrage parade headed by the beautiful Inez Milholland astride a white horse," wrote Rice in his autobiography, *Minority Report*. He fought child labor with his play, "The House in Blind Alley."

Along with the American Civil Liberties Union he was instrumental in instituting a screening process by which many Japanese internees were released from West Coast concentration camps during World War II. His longest battle, perhaps, was against blacklisting and the "new wave of anti-liberalism" that swept the country in the 1940's and 50's. Because of his left wing views (established in youth through the writings of George Bernard Shaw and H. G. Wells), Rice was constantly on everyone's "red" or "front" list. He insisted, however, that his penchant for socialism did not include Marxism or Leninism, or "any historical or economic dogma, but the development of a society in which the implements of production are employed primarily for the satisfaction of human needs, rather than for the enrichment and aggrandizement of a few individuals. There is no greater fallacy than the identification of the imperialism and totalitarianism of the Soviet Union with true socialism." He was never a member of the Socialist or any other party and claimed his socialism was of the "utopian variety." The many right-wing booklets and exposes released in that period placed Rice in excellent company, however, for among others named as possible dupes of the Kremlin were Clifford Odets, Lillian Hellman, Garson Kanin, Arthur Miller, Oscar Hammerstein II, and Gypsy Rose Lee. Rice was incredulous that "Freud and Gandhi were not included."

Rice has been praised for his role in opposing censorship throughout his lifetime. When Albert Deutsch, a New York columnist, called the film version of *Oliver Twist* flagrantly anti-Semitic and caused delay in the American opening, Rice became active in the campaign to release the picture. He convinced the Jewish organizations "That it was one thing to criticize and condemn the picture, to urge people not to see it, even to picket the theatres in which it might be shown, but quite another to prevent it from being shown at all. . . . In a democratic society there should be no sacred cows; no one should claim immunity from criticism or even from ridicule." Rice also encountered censorship with his own works. While filming 'Street Scene" he was notified that Miss Simpson would not be characterized as a social worker "unless she is shown as a kindly and tolerant person." With his views on censorship it is ironic that Rice felt that the highest honor ever paid him was the Nazis' inclusion of his published works in a book-burning.

Although his political plays, *We, the People, Judgment Day, Between Two Worlds,* and *Flight to the West,* were powerful advocates for social change, he is more apt to be remembered for his expressionism and theatrical innovations. His play, *On Trial,* presented the first attempt at the flashback technique on the stage. Louis Sherwin of the *New York Globe* wrote: "Can you imagine the wickedness of a play that has the sheer audacity to be original? A play that breaks well-nigh every rule of construction that has been dinned into our ears by the professors? A play that has the impertinence to be a good play instead of a well-made play? . . . 'On Trial' contains the most radical innovation in play construction, the most striking novelty that has been seen for years. Undoubtedly, it will bring about important changes in the technique of the theatre."

Rice, however, was not entirely impressed with his success, noting that "a good theatrical craftsman is not necessarily a worthy dramatist, a distinction that the reviewers failed to make." After a few failures, Rice began to take his writing

seriously with *The Adding Machine,* which, he recalled, "flashed into my mind—characters, plot, incidents, title, and some of the dialogue." The play, which concerns a man who is replaced by a machine and subsequently kills his boss, was written in the stylized, intensified form of expressionism. An allegation has persisted that he borrowed liberally from the German expressionists, but Rice insisted that, although he had heard of expressionism, he had not read any of the German plays until after the play was written. Since its inception, *The Adding Machine* has had innumerable productions.

His most notable success (601 consecutive performances on Broadway), however, was *Street Scene,* a panoramic impression of New York. The set, designed by Jo Mielzner (as were many other sets for Rice's plays), contained a typical Manhattan brownstone walk-up apartment house that was an integral part of the play. "I was excited by the concept of a large number of diverse individuals whose behavior and relationships were largely conditioned by their accidental common occupancy of a looming architectural pile," wrote Rice. "To some extent, the play adhered to the classical unities. The single setting was analogous to the traditional temple or palace; the elapsed time was less than a day. There even the superficial resemblance ended, for instead of unity of action there was a multitude of varied and seemingly irrelevant incidents. Blending and arranging these unrelated elements into a patterned mosaic and introducing the many characters in a seemingly natural way posed technical problems of the greatest difficulty. The play is, by all odds, the most experimental I have ever attempted, a fact not readily apparent to the reader or spectator, for its construction depends not upon novel or striking technological devices, but upon concealed architectonics." *Street Scene* was originally rejected by the Theatre Guild for lack of content, and, after numerous other rejections, William A. Brady, a one-time leading producer who had not had a success for twelve years, agreed to take on the play. The critics, although praising the play themselves, expressed doubts concerning its popular appeal. For example, *Variety* wrote: "Whether this play which starts so interestingly will catch high public favor is questionable," but the line in front of the box office did not break for six months.

Because of his caustic remarks and one unfortunate speech at Columbia University, Rice was often regarded as a chronic critic-baiter. At Columbia, Rice had remarked that "the critics were fostering the theatre of sterile entertainment" and were "discouraging innovators and rebels. With a few honorable exceptions, they were stupid and illiterate." The private Rice, however, was a modest man who wrote in his autobiography: "Since I became aware early of my artistic limitations, I have not essayed to scale unattainable heights or attempted Icarian flights. If it is true that a man's reach should exceed his grasp, I deserve commendation, for my aspirations have always exceeded my achievements."

On Trial was made into a motion picture by Essanay Film Manufacturing Co. in 1917, by Warner Bros., 1928, and remade by Warner Bros., 1939; "For the Defense" was filmed by Famous Players-Lasky Corp., 1922, by Paramount, 1930; *It is the Law* was filmed by Fox Film Corp., 1924; *See Naples and Die* was made into a movie by Warner Bros. under the title "Oh! Sailor, Behave," starring Olsen and Johnson, 1930; *Dream Girl* was filmed by Paramount Pictures in 1948 and was the basis for the musical "Skyscraper," 1966; *The Adding Machine* was filmed by Universal Pictures, 1969. *The Grand Tour* was adapted for television on the "U.S. Steel Hour," August 17, 1954. The

Theatre Guild presented many of Rice's best known plays on radio, 1949-54.

BIOGRAPHICAL/CRITICAL SOURCES: Newsweek, August 26, 1963; *Time,* August 30, 1963, May 19, 1967; *New York Times,* May 9, 1967; *Village Voice,* May 11, 1967; Frederick Lumley, *New Trends in 20th Century Drama,* Oxford University Press, 1967; *Contemporary Literary Criticism,* Volume VII, Gale, 1977.†

(Died May 8, 1967)

* * *

RICHARDS, H(arold) M(arshall) S(ylvester) 1894-

PERSONAL: Born August 28, 1894, in Davis City, Iowa; son of Halbert Marshall Jenkin (a minister) and Bertie C. (Sylvester) Richards; married Mabel Eastman; children: Virginia (Mrs. Walter Cason), Harold, Jr., Kenneth, Justus. *Education:* Columbia Union College, B.A., 1920. *Office:* Voice of Prophecy, 1500 East Chevy Chase, Glendale, Calif. 91206.

CAREER: Ordained to Seventh-day Adventist ministry, 1918; did pastoral and evangelistic work in United States and Canada; Voice of Prophecy, Glendale, Calif., founder and director and broadcaster, beginning 1942. Inaugurated the Richards Lectureship at Columbia Union College, 1956, and gave the tenth-year series, 1966. *Awards, honors:* D.D., Andrews University.

WRITINGS: Revival Sermons, Review & Herald, 1947; *30,000 Miles of Miracles,* Voice of Prophecy, 1950; *Radio Sermons,* Review & Herald, 1952; *Have Faith in God* (poems), Review & Herald, 1952; *30 Sermons,* Voice of Prophecy, 1953; *The Promises of God: The Morning Watch Texts with a Devotional Reading for Each Day,* Review & Herald, 1956; *Day after Tomorrow and Other Sermons,* Review & Herald, 1956; *What Jesus Said,* Southern Publishing Association, 1957; *Feed My Sheep,* Review & Herald, 1958; *Look to the Stars,* Review & Herald, 1964; *Why I Am a Seventh-day Adventist,* Review & Herald, 1965. Also author of *The Indispensable Man,* and recordings on religious subjects.

SIDELIGHTS: Richards has traveled in Europe, Africa, India, the Far East, Australia, New Zealand, the Middle East, and South America.

* * *

RIDLEY, Nat, Jr.
[Collective pseudonym]

WRITINGS—"Nat Ridley Detective Stories" series; published by Garden City Publishing: *The Crime on the Limited,* 1926; *A Daring Abduction,* 1926; *The Double Dagger,* 1926; *The Great Circus Mystery,* 1926; *Guilty or Not Guilty?,* 1926; *In the Nick of Time,* 1926; *A Scream in the Dark,* 1926; *Tracked to the West,* 1926; *The Western Express Robbery,* 1927; *The Mountain Inn Mystery,* 1927.

SIDELIGHTS: See ADAMS, Harriet S., STRATEMEYER, Edward L., and SVENSON, Andrew E.†

* * *

RIDOUT, Albert K(ilburn) 1905-

PERSONAL: Born August 8, 1905, in Mays Landing, N.J.; son of George Whitefield (a clergyman) and Laura (Smith) Ridout; married Ruth Una Moss (an editor and free-lance writer), August 29, 1928. *Education:* Asbury College, B.A., 1927; Ohio State University, LL.B., 1929, M.A., 1935; Co-

lumbia University, graduate courses. *Religion:* Protestant. *Office:* Pelham Memorial High School, Pelham, N.Y. 10803.

CAREER: Pelham Memorial High School, Pelham, N.Y., teacher of English, beginning 1935, chairman of department, beginning 1953. Director of amateur theaters in Westchester County and summer theaters in New York State and Vermont; teacher of speech in adult classes, Scarsdale, N.Y., for ten years. Field director, American Red Cross Services to Armed Forces, 1943-45; local director of Disaster Service, American Red Cross. *Member:* National Education Association, National Council of Teachers of English, New York State Teachers Association.

WRITINGS—Editor: F. Scott Fitzgerald, *The Great Gatsby* (school edition), Scribner, 1961; Jesse Stuart, *The Thread That Runs So True* (school edition), Scribner, 1963; (with Jesse Stuart) *Short Stories for Discussion,* Scribner, 1965; *Introducing Biography,* Scribner, 1968. Contributor to *Junior Libraries* and education journals.†

* * *

RIEDEL, Richard Langham 1908-

PERSONAL: Surname is pronounced Ruh-*del;* born December 3, 1908, in Chicago, Ill.; son of Richard Reinhold (a Baptist minister) and Carrie Edna (Langham) Riedel; married Angela Cody Bachman (a teacher), June 12, 1953; children: Angela Lynn, Kathleen Cody. *Education:* Self-educated. *Politics:* Nonpartisan. *Religion:* Baptist. *Home:* 14027 Braddock Rd., Centreville, Va. 22020.

CAREER: Worked in U.S. Senate, 1918-65; began as the youngest Senate page at the age of nine and retired as press liaison officer, 1965. Lecturer about the Senate to college, club, and church groups.

WRITINGS: Halls of the Mighty: My Forty-Seven Years at the Senate, foreword by Senator Everett Dirksen, Robert B. Luce, 1969.

WORK IN PROGRESS: A documentary sixteen-millimeter color film of pictures he made at the Capitol since 1940.

SIDELIGHTS: Don Keown commented: "Riedel offers us some very valuable insights into the men and women who have inhabited the Senate chambers.... One must admit that the title of U.S. Senator has been applied to a most colorful cast, kooks and statesmen, hacks and geniuses, demagogues and patriots. It is this rich diversity that makes *Halls of the Mighty* such enjoyable reading." A *Publishers' Weekly* reviewer wrote that Riedel's book is "fair, perceptive, always interesting, sometimes shrewd, [and that] Riedel writes of patronage, ceremonies, filibusters, Senators who've gone all the way to the White House (or made the try), and Senatorial 'mavericks.' His book is a uniquely detailed portrait of our most august legislative body."

Raymond P. Brandt stated: "Richard Riedel, the Washington reporter's friend, has written a real 'Inside story' about the Senate that no other person could have produced.... Because of its acute observation, occasional humor and its wealth of human interest, the book will be a valuable aid to historians and political scientists. It is enjoyable reading for those who remember the 'giants of yesteryear.' Riedel believes the present and future senates will produce equally heroic and mighty men."

AVOCATIONAL INTERESTS: Travel, photography, camping, swimming, gardening, jogging.

BIOGRAPHICAL/CRITICAL SOURCES: Publishers Weekly, April 7, 1969; St. Louis Post-Dispatch, July 27, 1969; Independent Journal (San Rafael, Calif.), August 2, 1969.

* * *

RIEDL, John O(rth)   1905-

PERSONAL: Born June 10, 1905, in Milwaukee, Wis.; son of Lucas Henry and Olive (Orth) Riedl; married Clare Carmelita Quirk, August 17, 1932; children: Annelore, John Orth, Joseph, Paul, Rose, William. Education: Marquette University, A.B., 1927, A.M., 1928, Ph.D., 1930; additional study at University of Wisconsin, 1930-32, University of Toronto, 1930, 1937, Columbia University, 1934, 1936, and University of Breslau, 1938-39. Home: 42-19 219th St., Bayside, N.Y. 11361. Office: Department of Philosophy, Queensborough Community College of the City University of New York, Bayside, N.Y. 11364.

CAREER: Marquette University, Milwaukee, Wis., instructor, 1930-33, assistant professor, 1933-44, associate professor, 1944-46 (on leave, 1942-45); Office of Military Government for Germany, chief of Catholic affairs, 1946-48, chief of Education Branch, 1948-49; Office of U.S. High Commissioner for Germany, chief of Education Branch, 1949-52; Public Affairs Field Center, Freiburg, Germany, public affairs officer and director, 1952-53; researcher and writer, New York, N.Y., 1953-54; Marquette University, professor of philosophy, 1954-66, dean of Graduate School, 1954-60; Queensborough Community College of the City University of New York, Bayside, professor of philosophy and dean of faculty, beginning 1966, dean-in-charge, 1966-67. Tower Press, Milwaukee, Wis., editor and co-owner, beginning 1941. Member of Citizen Consultation Committee, U.S. National Commission for UNESCO, 1957-61, and board of foreign scholarships, U.S. Department of State, 1958-63. Member of Catholic Commission on Intellectual and Cultural Affairs, beginning 1947. Military service: U.S. Navy, 1942-45; became lieutenant commander.

MEMBER: American Catholic Philosophical Association (president, 1935), American Philosophical Association, Metaphysical Society of America, Societe Thomiste (Belgium), Society for Phenomenology and Existential Philosophy, Charles S. Peirce Society, American Association of University Professors, National Conference of Christians and Jews, American Association for the United Nations. Awards, honors: Brotherhood Award, Wisconsin region of National Conference of Christians and Jews, 1965; with wife, received B'nai B'rith Interfaith Award, Milwaukee B'nai B'rith Councils of Men and Women, 1966.

WRITINGS—All published by Marquette University Press, except as noted: Exercises in Logic, first series, 1935, second series, 1947; A Catalogue of Renaissance Philosophers, 1940; (translator) Josef Koch, Giles of Rome, Errores Philosophorum, 1944; The University in Process, 1965.

Contributor: The Press in the Service of Faith and Reason, 1939; Gerard Smith, editor, Jesuit Thinkers of the Renaissance, 1939; Robert E. Brennan, editor, Essays in Thomism, Sheed, 1942; We Hold Those Truths, National Conference of Christians and Jews, 1954; Donald A. Gallagher, editor, Some Philosophers on Education, 1956; (author of foreword) From Disorder to World Order, 1956; James Collins, editor, Readings in Ancient and Mediaeval Philosophy, Newman, 1960; The Environment Change, Time-Life Books, 1964. Contributor of articles and reviews to professional journals.

RIEMER, George   1920-1973
(Seth Poole, Clint Schirmerhorn)

PERSONAL: Surname rhymes with "schemer"; born October 29, 1920, in Milwaukee, Wis.; son of George (a salesman) and Mary (Wasinger) Riemer; married Margaret M. Flanagan, 1971. Education: St. Louis University, Ph.L. Politics: "Free-lance." Religion: Roman Catholic. Home: 149 Clinton St., Brooklyn Heights, N.Y. 11201.

CAREER: Member of the Society of Jesus (Jesuits), 1940-47; Haydn Society, Inc., New York, N.Y., manager, 1950-52; free-lance writer. Member: Society of Magazine Writers, Education Writers Association, Mystery Writers of America.

WRITINGS: How They Murdered the Second R, Norton, 1968; (illustrated with photographs by the author) Dialog: Dating and Marriage, Holt, 1969; The Case for the Private High, Association Press, 1970; Dialog and Decision-Making, Holt, 1970; Beginning Communication, Pitman, 1971; The New Jesuits, Little, Brown, 1971. Contributor of articles on food and cooking and on other topics to Good Housekeeping, Ladies' Home Journal, men's magazines, and pulps.

WORK IN PROGRESS: The Interrogator, for Little, Brown.

BIOGRAPHICAL/CRITICAL SOURCES: New York Times Book Review, March 14, 1971; Best Sellers, March 15, 1971.†

(Died March 31, 1973)

* * *

RIGGS, Dionis Coffin   1898-

PERSONAL: Born August 6, 1898, in Edgartown, Mass.; daughter of Thomas Martin and Mary Wilder (Cleaveland) Coffin; married Sidney Noyes Riggs (an educator, artist, and print-maker), June 25, 1922 (died June, 1975); children: Alvida Cleaveland (Mrs. Ralph J. Jones), Ann Lewis (Mrs. William A. Fielder), Cynthia (Mrs. George E. Stoertz). Education: New Jersey Teachers' College (now Newark State College), graduate, 1920; additional study at New York University and Columbia University. Politics: "Independent voter, registered Republican." Religion: Congregational. Residence: West Tisbury, Mass. 02575.

CAREER: Elementary teacher in West Portal, N.J., 1920, in Lyndhurst, N.J., 1921-22. Former chairman, West Tisbury Conservation Commission. Member: Poetry Society of America, Academy of American Poets, New England Poetry Club, Poetry Society of Virginia, Dukes County Historical Society. Awards, honors: Poet Lore, Stephen Vincent Benet Narrative Poem Award, 1968, for "Herring Run," and honorary mention, 1973, for "Flower Seller."

WRITINGS: (With husband, Sidney N. Riggs) From Off Island: The Story of My Grandmother, Whittlesey House, 1940 (published in England as Martha's Vineyard, John Lane, 1941); (with Marion Lineaweaver, Barbara Bradley, and Robert Hyde; prints by S. N. Riggs) Martha's Vineyard: Poems by Four, Noone House, 1965; (prints by Riggs) Sea Born Island (poems), Noone House, 1969. Regular contributor to Vineyard Gazette; poems also have appeared in McCall's, Good Housekeeping, Saturday Evening Post, Nation, Kenyon Review, New York Times, and other periodicals and newspapers.

WORK IN PROGRESS: Translations of poetry from Turkish.

SIDELIGHTS: Mrs. Riggs' poems reflect her attachment to Martha's Vineyard, where she spent her childhood and most of her summers as an adult. When her husband retired, they returned to the island to live in the old Cleaveland family homestead in West Tisbury. Mrs. Riggs has crossed the Atlantic a number of times (once by freighter), has traveled about England for six months tracing the King Arthur Legends, and has spent a winter in Ankara, Turkey where she presented a program, "Poems in Two Languages," with the Turkish poet Ozcan Yalum at the Turkish-American Association.

* * *

RINKOFF, Barbara Jean (Rich)   1923-1975

PERSONAL: Born January 25, 1923, in New York, N.Y.; daughter of John J. and Sophia B. (Frank) Rich; married Herbert Rinkoff (a dentist); children: Robert, Richard, June. *Education:* New York University, B.A., 1943. *Home:* 25 Langland Dr., Mount Kisco, N.Y. 10549.

CAREER: Beeckman-Downtown Hospital, New York, N.Y., medical social worker, 1943-47; professional writer. Teacher of after-school course in creative writing for fifth and sixth graders in Mount Kisco, 1965-66. *Member:* American Association of University Women, Alpha Kappa Delta.

WRITINGS: A Map Is a Picture, Crowell, 1965; *The Remarkable Ramsey,* Morrow, 1965; *The Dragon's Handbook,* Nelson, 1966; *Birthday Parties Around the World,* Barrows, 1967; *The Troublesome Tuba,* Lothrop, 1967; *Elbert, The Mind-Reader,* Lothrop, 1967; *Member of the Gang,* Crown, 1968; *The Family Christmas Book,* Doubleday, 1969; *Name: Johnny Pierce,* Seabury, 1969; *Harry's Homemade Robot,* Crown, 1969; *Sandra's View,* McGraw, 1969.

Headed for Trouble, Knopf, 1970; *The Pretzel Hero,* Parents' Press, 1970; *A Guy Can Be Wrong,* Crown, 1970; *I Need Some Time,* Seabury, 1970; *Tricksters and Trappers,* Abelard, 1970; *Rutherford T. Finds 21 B,* Putnam, 1970; *The Case of the Stolen Code Book,* Crown, 1971; *Guess What Grasses Do,* Lothrop, 1972; *The Watchers,* Knopf, 1972; *Let's Go to a Jetport,* Putnam, 1973; *Guess What Trees Do,* Lothrop, 1974; *Red Light Says Stop,* Lothrop, 1974; *No Pushing—No Ducking,* Lothrop, 1974; *Guess What Rocks Do,* Lothrop, 1975. Contributor of stories and travel articles to a number of national magazines.

BIOGRAPHICAL/CRITICAL SOURCES: New York Times, February 22, 1975; *AB Bookman's Weekly,* March 17, 1975; *Publishers Weekly,* April 28, 1975.

(Died February 18, 1975)

* * *

RISTIC, Dragisha N.   1909-

PERSONAL: Born January 9, 1909, in Serbia, Yugoslavia; son of Nikola K. (a civil servant in Yugoslav Treasury Department) and Leposava (a teacher; maiden name, Churchic) Ristic. *Education:* Belgrad Military Academy, B.S., 1928; began U.S. studies at Wayne (now Wayne State) University, 1942-43; University of California, Los Angeles, B.A., 1950, M.A., 1953; University of Paris, graduate study, 1955-56; Western Colorado University, Ph.D., 1973. *Home address:* P.O. Box 1342, Monterey, Calif. 93940.

CAREER: Served in Royal Yugoslav Air Force, 1928-45, in Zagreb, 1928-33, in Novi Sad, 1933-35, as aide-de-camp to RYAF Commander in Zemun, 1935-38 and 1940-41, as aide-de-camp to Chief of the General Staff, 1938-40, as aide-de-

camp and executive secretary to D. T. Simovic, Prime Minister of Yugoslavia, 1941-42, as a member of the Yugoslav Military Mission to the U.S. and Canada, 1942-43, working in headquarters in Cairo, Egypt, 1943-45; Defense Language Institute, Monterey, Calif., professor of language and culture, beginning 1951. *Member:* American Association of International Law, American Association of University Professors, Navy League of the United States, Commonwealth Club of California, Caterpillar Club, Northern Golf Association.

WRITINGS: Yugoslavia's Revolution of 1941, Pennsylvania State University Press, for Hoover Institution, 1966.

WORK IN PROGRESS: Nicholas, Lenin, Kerensky: The Duma, and the Revolution.

* * *

RITCHIE, James T. R.   1908-

PERSONAL: Born January 13, 1908, in Edinburgh, Scotland; son of James and Alice (Henderson) Ritchie. *Education:* Edinburgh University, B.Sc., 1929, Ph.D., 1931. *Home:* 16 Cairnmuir Rd., Edinburgh, Scotland.

CAREER: North Park Secondary School, Edinburgh, Scotland, science teacher, beginning 1935.

WRITINGS: The Singing Street, Oliver & Boyd, 1964; *Golden City,* Oliver & Boyd, 1965. Contributor to *Scots Magazine, Saltire Review,* and other Scottish reviews.

Documentary film scripts: "Happy Week End," "The Singing Street," "The Grey Metropolis," "The Flower and the Straw."

WORK IN PROGRESS: Playground, a book dealing with games, rhymes, songs, and language of Edinburgh school children; *A Cinema of Days,* a collection of poems in Scots-English.

SIDELIGHTS: An *Antiquarian Bookman* reviewer wrote of *The Singing Street:* "For all those . . . who have fallen in love with Edinburgh and who sneak back every time they can squeeze a day in, this is a book for you, about the language, today, and how difficult it is for Scots to live two languages, their street names, riddles, sayings, games which live on with a vitality on the streets that does not apply elsewhere." Norman MacCaig noted: "In Mr. Ritchie's . . . book *The Singing Street,* he gives us, through songs, chants, games, customs and cheeky and cryptic sayings and rhymes, a vivid and lively close-up of the life vigorously flourishing among the tenements and closes and grim back greens of Edinburgh." *Avocational interests:* Film-making and collecting Scottish folk lore.

BIOGRAPHICAL/CRITICAL SOURCES: Times Literary Supplement, January 14, 1965, November 18, 1965; *Antiquarian Bookman,* July 5, 1965; *New Statesman,* November 12, 1965.††

* * *

RITCHIE, M(iller) A(lfred) F(ranklin)   1909-

PERSONAL: Born July 24, 1909, in Churchville, Va.; son of Wiley W. J. (a minister) and Anna Marie (Henkel) Ritchie; married Josephine Marie Barnett, June 6, 1938; children: John, Jo Ann, Elizabeth Jane (Mrs. Jerry Hanson). *Education:* Roanoke College, A.B. (with honors), 1932; College of William and Mary, M.A., 1942; graduate study at Columbia University, Florida State University, and New York University, 1947-53. *Religion:* Protestant. *Home:* 216 Northeast 17th Ave., Hillsboro, Ore. 97123. *Office:* 319 Yeon Bldg., Portland, Ore. 97204.

CAREER: Teacher of English and chairman of department at high school in Waynesboro, Va., 1932-35; *News Virginian,* Waynesboro, managing editor, 1935-36; Roanoke College, Salem, Va., alumni secretary and director of public relations, 1936-39; College of William and Mary, Matthew Whaley School, Williamsburg, Va., supervising teacher of language arts, 1939-40; Roanoke College, director of admissions and alumni director, 1940-42; University of Miami, Coral Gables, Fla., assistant professor, 1946-47, associate professor, 1947-50, professor of human relations and head of department, 1950-53; Hartwick College, Oneonta, N.Y., president, 1953-59; Pacific University, Forest Grove, Ore., president, 1959-70, president emeritus, 1970—; University of Miami, professor of education, 1970-75; Oregon Community Foundation, Portland, executive secretary, beginning 1975. Member of Commission on the Arts, Association of American Colleges, 1961-63. *Military service:* U.S. Naval Reserve, active duty, 1942; became lieutenant commander.

MEMBER: National Education Association (life member), Association for Higher Education, National Retired Teachers Association. *Awards, honors:* L.H.D. from Florida Memorial College, 1953; LL.D. from Roanoke College, 1957; Litt.D. from Wagner College, 1958; Sc.D. from Parsons College, 1960. Meritorious Service Award of Hartwick College Alumni Association, 1956; Ernest O. Melby Award in Human Relations, New York University, 1960; Distinguished Alumni Award of Tau Kappa Alpha, 1962; special award for work in field of human relations, Oregon Education Association and Anti-Defamation League of B'nai B'rith, 1969.

WRITINGS: (Editor with Paul Leonard and others) *Readings in English* (reference book for grades 8-11), Virginia State Board of Education, 1935; (editor) *Toward Better Inter-Group Education,* University of Miami Press, 1952; (contributor) *Regional Problems and Issues in Human Relations Education,* Anti-Defamation League of B'nai B'rith, 1957; *Six Exciting Years: 1953-1959,* Hartwick College, 1959; *The College Presidency: Initiation into the Order of the Turtle,* Philosophical Library, 1970; *Decade of Development,* Pacific University, 1970. Contributor of about fifty articles to education and other journals.

WORK IN PROGRESS: Book outlines on higher education and on human relations.

SIDELIGHTS: M.A.F. Ritchie told *CA:* "I have always believed that educators have a special obligation to put their ideas and commitments before their peers and the public. One way to do this is to write books and articles on education and related subjects. . . . Writing by educators emeriti is a useful outlet and hopefully a helpful way for them to share their wealth of experience with others."

BIOGRAPHICAL/CRITICAL SOURCES: *Oregon Journal,* June 15, 1970.

*   *   *

RIVETT-CARNAC, Charles Edward   1901-

PERSONAL: Born August 13, 1901, in Eastbourne, Sussex, England; son of John Thurlow and Edith Emily (Brownlow) Rivett-Carnac; married Mary Dillon Ware, November 16, 1932; children: Beverly Ann Rivett-Carnac Griffin, Mary Frances Rivett-Carnac Beeney. *Education:* Educated in England at St. Cyprian's Preparatory School and Eastbourne College. *Religion:* Anglican. *Home:* Apt. 206, 1035 Belmont Ave., Victoria, British Columbia, Canada. *Agent:* General Artists Corp., 600 Madison Ave., New York, N.Y. 10022; and Robert P. Mills, 20 East 53rd St., New York, N.Y. 10022.

CAREER: Joined Royal Canadian Mounted Police as constable in 1923, and rose through the ranks to become commissioner, terminated association, 1960. Canadian Corps of Commissionaires, Victoria, member of board, 1963-65; Canadian Red Cross, vice-president of Victoria branch, 1963-65. *Wartime service:* Red Cross ambulance driver attached to French Army, World War I.

WRITINGS: *Pursuit in the Wilderness,* Little, Brown, 1965.

*   *   *

ROBB, Mary K(unkle)   1908-

PERSONAL: Born September 8, 1908, in New Kensington, Pa.; married Theodore Robb, August 21, 1951 (deceased), married George W. Graham, 1969. *Education:* Slippery Rock State College, B.S.; additional study at Pennsylvania State University, University of Pittsburgh, and Edinboro State College. *Politics:* Republican. *Religion:* Lutheran. *Home:* 3104 Rudolph St., Erie, Pa. 16508.

CAREER: Erie (Pa.) School District, physical education teacher, 1930-69. Conductor of party service for church, club, community, and school groups, Erie, Pa. Has had summer employment as playground supervisor, camp counselor, juvenile court worker, director of camp for handicapped children, and social hostess for hotels and resorts.

WRITINGS: *Put Your Party in Orbit,* privately printed, 1964; *Making Teen Parties Click,* Stackpole, 1965.

*   *   *

ROBBINS, Mildred Brown
(Millie Robbins)

PERSONAL: Born in San Francisco, Calif.; daughter of Alexander Mortlock and Frida (Herrmann) Brown; married Theodore A. Robbins, April 9, 1929 (deceased); children: Alexandra (Mrs. Irving Hunter). *Education:* University of California, A.B., 1926. *Religion:* Protestant. *Home:* 2154 32nd Ave., San Francisco, Calif. 94116. *Office:* San Francisco Chronicle, Fifth and Mission, San Francisco, Calif. 94119.

CAREER: *San Francisco Chronicle,* San Francisco, Calif., society editor, 1938-56, columnist, beginning 1956. *Awards, honors:* California Historical Society Award of Merit, 1964, for newspaper columns; Laura Bride Powers Memorial Award, 1966; member, Exalted Order of the Grizzly, California Heritage Council, 1969.

WRITINGS: *Tales of Love and Hate in Old San Francisco,* San Francisco Chronicle, 1971.

*   *   *

ROBERTS, Cecil (Edric Mornington)   1892-1976

PERSONAL: Born May 18, 1892, in Nottingham, England; son of John Godber and Elizabeth Roberts. *Education:* Attended Mundella Grammar School and University College, Nottingham. *Home:* The Athenaeum, Pall Mall, London S.W.1, England. *Agent:* Curtis Brown Ltd., 1 Craven Hill, London W2 3EW, England.

CAREER: Literary editor, *Liverpool Post,* Liverpool, England, 1915-18; official war correspondent with British Army, Royal Air Force, and Royal Navy, 1916-18; examining officer to Civil Liabilities Commission, 1919; editor, *Nottingham Journal,* Nottingham, England, 1920-25; member of British Mission to United States, 1939-45; author. Parliamentary candidate for Nottingham, East Division, 1922. Lecturer on tours in United States and Canada, 1920, 1924, 1928, 1934, 1936, 1938. *Member:* Society of Authors (member of council). *Awards, honors:* LL.D. from Washington and Jefferson College, 1927; Gold Medal and Diploma of City of Rome; honorary citizen of Alassio, Italy; honorary Freeman of Nottingham.

WRITINGS: The Trent, Needham, 1912; *Phyllistrata and Other Poems,* James Clarke, 1913; *Through Eyes of Youth* (poems), James Clarke, 1914; *The Youth of Beauty* (poems), James Clarke, 1915; *Collected War Poems,* James Clarke, 1916; *A Week with the Fleet* (nonfiction), James Clarke, 1917; *Twenty-six Poems,* Grant Richards, 1917; *The Chelsea Cherub* (novel), Grant Richards, 1917; *Charing Cross and Other Poems of the Period,* Grant Richards, 1918; *Training the Airmen* (nonfiction), J. Murray, 1919.

Collected Poems (preface by John Masefield), Stokes, 1920; *A Tale of Young Lovers* (four-act tragedy in verse; produced by Compton Company, 1921), Heinemann, 1922; *Scissors* (novel), Stokes, 1923, reprinted, Hodder & Stoughton, 1968; *Sails of Sunset* (novel), Stokes, 1924; *The Love Rack* (novel), Stokes, 1925; "The Right to Kiss" (comedy), produced by Dean Company, 1926; *Little Mrs. Manington* (novel), Doran, 1926; (editor) *The Diary of Russell Beresford,* Doran, 1927, revised edition, Hodder & Stoughton, 1928; *Sagusto* (novel), Doubleday, 1928; *David and Diana* (novel), Hodder & Stoughton, 1928, published as *Goose Fair,* Stokes, 1929; *Indiana Jane* (novel), Heinemann, 1929, Appleton, 1930; *Pamela's Spring Song* (novel), Hodder & Stoughton, 1929, Appleton, 1930.

Havana Bound (novel), Appleton, 1930; *Half Way* (autobiography; foreword by Philip Gibbs), Appleton, 1931; *Bargain Basement* (novel), Hodder & Stoughton, 1931, Appleton, 1932; *Alfred Fripp* (biography), Hutchinson, 1932; *Spears Against Us* (play; produced by Liverpool Repertory Company, 1939), Appleton, 1932, reprinted, Hutchinson, 1973; *Pilgrim Cottage* (novel; also see below), Appleton, 1933; *Gone Rustic* (nonfiction), Appleton, 1934; *The Guests Arrive* (novel; also see below), Hodder & Stoughton, 1934, Appleton, 1935; *Volcano* (novel; also see below), Hodder & Stoughton, 1935, Appleton, 1936; *Gone Rambling* (travel), Appleton, 1935; *Gone Afield* (travel), Appleton, 1936; *Gone Sunwards* (travel in Florida), Macmillan, 1936; *Victoria, Four-Thirty* (novel), Macmillan, 1937; *The Pilgrim Cottage Omnibus* (contains *Pilgrim Cottage, The Guests Arrive,* and *Volcano*), Hodder & Stoughton, 1938; *They Wanted to Live* (novel), Macmillan, 1939.

And So to Bath (travel), Macmillan, 1940; *A Man Arose* (poem on Winston Churchill), Macmillan, 1941; *One Small Candle* (novel), Macmillan, 1942; *The Labyrinth* (novel), Doubleday, Doran, 1944 (published in England as *So Immortal a Flower,* Hodder & Stoughton, 1944); *And So to America* (travel), Hodder & Stoughton, 1947; *Eight for Eternity* (novel), Doubleday, 1948.

And So to Rome (travel), Macmillan, 1950; *A Terrace in the Sun* (novel), Macmillan, 1951; *One Year of Life: Some Autobiographical Pages,* Macmillan, 1952; *The Remarkable Young Man* (novel), Macmillan, 1954; *Portal to Paradise: An Italian Excursion,* Hodder & Stoughton, 1955; *Love Is Like That* (novel), Hodder & Stoughton, 1957, Coward, 1958.

Selected Poems, 1910-1960 (preface by Lord Birkett), Hutchinson, 1960; *Wide Is the Horizon* (novel), Coward, 1962; *The Grand Cruise* (travel), Hodder & Stoughton, 1963; *A Flight of Birds* (novel), Hodder & Stoughton, 1965, Coward, 1966; *The Growing Boy: Being the First Book of*

an Autobiography, 1892-1908, Hodder & Stoughton, 1967; *The Years of Promise: Being the Second Book of an Autobiography, 1908-1919,* Hodder & Stoughton, 1968; *The Bright Twenties: Being the Third Book of an Autobiography, 1920-1929,* Hodder & Stoughton, 1970; *Sunshine and Shadow: Being the Fourth Book of an Autobiography, 1930-1946,* Hodder & Stoughton, 1972; *The Pleasant Years: Being the Final Book of an Autobiography, 1947-1972,* Hodder & Stoughton, 1974. Also author of memoir in *Finale: Self Portrait of N. Malacrida,* published in 1935.

SIDELIGHTS: Cecil Roberts' novels have been translated into French, German, Italian, Spanish, Dutch, Hungarian, Swedish, Danish, Norwegian, Finnish, Czech, Portuguese, Rumanian, and Russian.

BIOGRAPHICAL/CRITICAL SOURCES: Times Literary Supplement, November 2, 1967, October 16, 1970; *Spectator,* October 18, 1968.

(Died December, 1976)

* * *

ROBERTS, Edward Barry   1900-1972

PERSONAL: Born December 19, 1900, in Ardmore, Okla; son of Edward William and Daisy Fredericka (Barry) Roberts. *Education:* Attended University of Texas, 1922-24; Yale University, drama studies, 1927-29. *Residence:* New York, N.Y.

CAREER: Writer for stage in 1930's; television playwright, 1948-54; "Armstrong's Circle Theatre," television editor, 1950-54; Columbia Broadcasting System, New York, N.Y., Eastern story editor and manager of story department, 1956-58; manager of CBS writing grants competition, 1959; special new material editor, "U.S. Steel-Theatre Guild Television Show," 1959-62; Batten, Barton, Durstine & Osborn, New York, N.Y., writer and researcher in public relations department; free-lance writer. Founder of course in television playwriting at Yale Drama School, 1954, now subsidized by American Broadcasting Co. *Member:* Dramatists Guild of the Authors League of America, Writers Guild of America, East, Academy of Television Arts and Sciences, The Players (New York).

WRITINGS: Television Writing and Selling (textbook), Writer, 1954; (with Elspeth Woodward) *The Pink Rose* (novel of manners), Lothrop, 1955.

Plays produced on Broadway: (With Frank Cavett) "Forsaking All Others," 1933; (translator from the Hungarian of Bush-Fekete) "The Lady Has a Heart," 1937. Also author of other plays for television.

Short stories have been published in *Ladies' Home Journal, Cosmopolitan, Holland's Magazine,* and British periodicals.

WORK IN PROGRESS: A musical comedy adaptation of *The Pink Rose;* several other plays.

SIDELIGHTS: Both "Forsaking All Others" and "The Lady Has a Heart" were made into motion pictures, the first by M-G-M, 1934.†

(Died August 6, 1972)

* * *

ROBERTS, Harold S(elig)   1911-1970

PERSONAL: Born March 14, 1911, in Zdunska-Wola, Poland; came to United States in 1921, naturalized in 1926; son of S. Wolf and Adela (Erlich) Roberts; married Margery Prescott, April 4, 1939; children: Joyce Rider (Mrs. Jack

McLarty), Penny Elizabeth (Mrs. Donald Kennedy), Pamela Jean. *Education:* City College (now City College of the City University of New York), B.S.S., 1934; Columbia University, M.A., 1938, Ph.D., 1944. *Home:* 2646 Oahu Ave., Honolulu, Hawaii 96822. *Office:* Industrial Relations Center, University of Hawaii, 2404 Maile Way, Honolulu, Hawaii 96822.

CAREER: U.S. Government, Washington, D.C., analyst for Subcommittee on Railroad Finance, U.S. Senate Commission on Interstate Commerce, 1936-38, economist in Division of Economic Research, National Labor Relations Board, 1938-41, administrative officer and consultant with National War Labor Board, 1942-45, chief of Collective Bargaining Division, Bureau of Labor Statistics, Department of Labor, 1945-47; University of Hawaii, Honolulu, professor, 1948-64, senior professor of business economics and industrial relations, 1964-70, director of Industrial Relations Center, 1948-70, dean of College of Business Administration, 1950-59, chairman of department of personnel and industrial relations, 1960-64. Economist and consultant (during sabbatical), U.S. Department of Labor, 1962-63; arbitrator for National Mediation Board, Federal Mediation and Conciliation Service, and for American Arbitration Association. Chairman, Tripartite Territorial Employment Security Advisory Council, 1948-60; elected delegate, Hawaii State Constitutional Convention, 1949-50; chairman, Organization of Government Health and Welfare Services, 1954-59; vice-president, Oahu Health Council, 1956-60; member, Hawaii State Judicial Council, beginning 1961; consultant, City and County Personnel Management Evaluation Program, beginning 1965.

MEMBER: American Economic Association, Academy of Political and Social Science, Industrial Relations Research Association, Hawaii Economic Association (president, 1964-65), Industrial Relations Association of Hawaii, Phi Kappa Phi, Rotary Club. *Awards, honors:* Wills Memorial Award in Industrial Relations, University of Hawaii, 1959; Outstanding Citizen of the Year Award of Hawaiian Government Employees Association, 1967; American Society of Public Administration Award of 1968, for Hawaii.

WRITINGS: The Rubber Workers: Labor Organization and Collective Bargaining in the Rubber Industry, Harper, 1944; *Manual for Mediation and Emergency Boards,* Hawaii Department of Labor, 1948; *The First Year under the Taft-Hartley Act,* Extension Division, University of Hawaii, 1948; *Compulsory Arbitration of Labor Disputes,* Legislative Reference Bureau, University of Hawaii, 1949; *Dictionary of Labor-Management Relations,* Parts III-IX, Industrial Relations Center, University of Hawaii, 1957-63, reissued in one volume as *Roberts' Dictionary of Industrial Relations,* Bureau of National Affairs, 1966; *The Doctrine of Preemption,* University of Hawaii Press, 1957; *Compulsory Arbitration: Panacea or Millstone?,* Industrial Relations Center, University of Hawaii, 1965; *Reapportionment and the Revision and Amending Procedures of the Hawaii State Constitution,* 2nd edition, University of Hawaii, 1966; *Who's Who in Industrial Relations,* Industrial Relations Center, University of Hawaii, Volume I, 1966, Volume II, 1967; *Hawaii Constitutional Convention Studies. Article XII: Organization, Collective Bargaining,* Legislative Reference Bureau, University of Hawaii, 1968.

Editor: *Arbitration of Grievances under Existing Contracts: Source Book,* Extension Division, University of Hawaii, 1950, 3rd edition, 1962; *Government Intervention in Industrial Relations: Source Book,* Industrial Relations Center, University of Hawaii, 1950, 3rd edition, 1962; *Plant Grievances: Source Book,* Extension Division, University of Hawaii, 1952; *Labor-Management Relations in Hawaii,* Industrial Relations Center, University of Hawaii, Part II, 1955, Part III, 1956; *Proceedings on the Institute of the Older Worker,* Industrial Relations Center, University of Hawaii, 1960; *Selected Readings on Problems of the Aged and Aging,* University of Hawaii, 1960; *Labor in a Changing Society,* Industrial Relations Center, University of Hawaii, 1960; *Labor and Anti-Trust Legislation: Selected Readings,* Industrial Relations Center, University of Hawaii, 1961; (and compiler) *A Manual for Employee-Management Cooperation in the Federal Service,* Industrial Relations Center, University of Hawaii, 1964, 3rd edition, 1967, enlarged edition published as *Labor-Management Relations in the Public Service,* 1968; *Automation: Some of Its Effects on the Economy and Labor,* Industrial Relations Center, University of Hawaii, 1964; (with Paul F. Brissenden) *The Challenge of Industrial Relations in Pacific-Asian Countries,* East-West Center Press, 1965; *Proceedings of Conference on the Challenge of Industrial Relations in Pacific-Asian Countries,* four volumes, Industrial Relations Center, University of Hawaii, 1962-65; *Manpower Utilization in Government Agencies,* Industrial Relations Center, University of Hawaii, 1967; *New Perspectives in Industrial Relations,* Industrial Relations Center, University of Hawaii, 1968; *The Collective Bargaining Relationship in the Hawaiian Electrical Industry,* Industrial Relations Center, University of Hawaii, 1968; *Proceedings of Conference on Collective Bargaining and Dispute Settlement in the Public and Private Sectors: A Review and Evaluation,* University of Hawaii, 1970.

Author or editor of manuals, reports, and surveys. Contributor to labor and government journals. Co-editor, *American Labor Year Book,* 1941-42; consulting editor, *American Arbitration Journal.*†

(Died February 5, 1970)

* * *

ROBERTSON, James Louis 1907-

PERSONAL: Born October 31, 1907, in Broken Bow, Neb.; son of Andrew J. (a rancher, banker, and public official) and Dora May (Reese) Robertson; married Julia Jenson, July 24, 1928; children: James Young, Frederick Young, Alan Young. *Education:* Grinnell College, student, 1925-27; George Washington University, A.B. and LL.B., 1931; Harvard Law School, LL.M., 1932. *Politics:* Independent. *Religion:* Presbyterian. *Home:* 5114 Brookview Dr., Washington, D.C. 20016.

CAREER: Admitted to the Bar of the U.S. Court of Appeals, 1931, and the Bar of the U.S. Supreme Court, 1935; Federal Bureau of Investigation, Washington, D.C., special agent, 1932-33; U.S. Department of Treasury, Comptroller of the Currency, assistant counsel, 1933-42, assistant chief counsel, 1942-43, deputy comptroller, 1944-52; Federal Reserve System, Washington, D.C., member of board of governors, 1952-66, vice-chairman, 1966-73; economic and legal consultant, beginning 1973. *Military service:* U.S. Naval Reserves, 1943-44; became lieutenant junior grade. *Member:* American Bar Association, Federal Bar Association, Kappa Sigma, Cosmos Club (Washington, D.C.). *Awards, honors:* LL.D., Grinnell College, 1964; Distinguished Service Award, U.S. Department of Treasury, 1969; Freedoms Foundation Award, 1971, for article "A Concerned Citizen Speaks about America's Turmoil."

WRITINGS: Monetary and Fiscal Operations of the Fed-

eral Reserve System, [Washington, D.C.], 1958; *What Generation Gap?: A Dialogue on America,* Acropolis Books, 1970. Contributor of articles to national magazines and law reviews.

SIDELIGHTS: James Louis Robertson told *CA:* "While my vocation is in the field of banking and finance, I have become deeply concerned in recent years with strong signs of diminishing respect for the rule of law and for the values that underlie our civilization. I have spoken out strongly on these questions. One of these speeches was reprinted in full in the *U.S. News and World Report,* and it produced such a response that I ended up publishing the speech and the ensuing correspondence as a book. Much of the correspondence was with young people and dealt with the pressing problems troubling youth today; hence, the title of the book [*What Generation Gap?: A Dialogue on America*]. . . . The title bespeaks my conviction that it is possible for people of my generation to communicate with today's youth, but I think we have been doing a poor job of it. I am not one of those who would write the younger generation off. On the contrary, I think we must redouble our efforts to communicate to them an understanding of the great principles and value systems that have made the flowering of civilization possible."

*   *   *

ROBERTSON, Priscilla (Smith)   1910-

PERSONAL: Born May 16, 1910, in Paris, France; daughter of Preserved (a historian) and Helen (Kendall) Smith; married Cary Robertson (a newspaper editor), May 26, 1934; children: Charlotte, Henry Preserved Smith, Cary, Jr. *Education:* Vassar College, A.B., 1930; graduate study at Columbia University, 1933-34, Radcliffe College, 1945-46, and Radcliffe Institute for Independent Study, 1965-67. *Home:* 12627 Osage Rd. N., Anchorage, Ky. 40223.

CAREER: Jefferson County (Ky.) public schools, junior high school teacher, 1931-34; *Louisville Courier-Journal,* Louisville, Ky., assistant literary editor, 1934-41; *Humanist,* editor, 1956-59; Indiana University, Bloomington, lecturer in history, 1962-68; Kentucky Southern College (now closed), Anchorage, faculty member, 1968-69. Chairman, Anchorage (Ky.) Children's Theatre, 1948-53. *Member:* American Historical Association, American Friends Service Committee, Kentucky Civil Liberties Union (chairman, 1960-63). *Awards, honors:* Award for creative writing in history, National Institute of Arts and Letters, 1956; honorable mention, Herbert Baxter Adams Prize of American Historical Association, 1956.

WRITINGS: The Revolutions of 1848: A Social History, Princeton University Press, 1952; *Lewis Farm: A New England Saga,* privately printed, 1952; *The Kendall Book,* privately printed 1959. Contributor of articles to *Harper's* and *American Scholar.*

WORK IN PROGRESS: A social history of nineteenth-century Europe, stressing cross-cultural relationships, a book researched during her two years at Radcliffe Institute for Independent Study.

*   *   *

ROBERTS-WRAY, Kenneth (Owen)   1899-

PERSONAL: Born June 6, 1899, in Bexley, Kent, England; son of Thomas Henry (an electrical engineer and a captain in Royal Naval Volunteer Reserve) and Florence Grace (Vincent) Roberts-Wray; married Joan Tremayne Waring, July 16, 1927 (died, 1961); married Mary Howard Williams (widow of Sir Ernest Williams), December 3, 1965; children: (first marriage) Christopher Waring, Peter Kenneth, Brian Philip; stepchildren: Hilary Mary Williams (Mrs. Edward Julian Walter). *Education:* Merton College, Oxford, qualified for B.A., 1922, B.A. conferred (first class honors in jurisprudence), 1925, M.A., 1931, B.C.L. and D.C.L. (both degrees by "accumulation"; conferred simultaneously), 1967. *Religion:* Church of England. *Home:* The Old Golf House, Forest Row, Sussex, England. *Office:* 5 King's Bench Walk, Temple, London E.C.4, England.

CAREER: Called to the Bar (certificate of honor), 1924; private practice of law, 1924-26; Ministry of Health, London, England, member of Legal Branch, 1926-31; Dominion Office (later Commonwealth Relations Office) and Colonial Office, London, second assistant legal adviser, 1931-43, assistant legal adviser, 1943-45, legal adviser, 1945-60; practice of law, London, beginning 1961. Appointed Queen's counsel, 1959. Chairman of Law Officers Conference in Trinidad, 1944, and of Judicial Advisers Conference in Uganda, 1953, and Nigeria, 1956. *Military service:* British Army, 1918-20; first lieutenant when retired on account of wounds, 1920. Home Guard, captain in antiaircraft unit, 1940-44.

MEMBER: British Institute of International and Comparative Law (member of advisory board of comparative law section). *Awards, honors:* Companion of Order of St. Michael and St. George, 1946; Knight Commander of Order of St. Michael and St. George, 1949; Knight Grand Cross of Order of St. Michael and St. George, 1960; L·L.D., University of Birmingham, 1968.

WRITINGS: (With R. O. Roberts and A. D. Gibb) *The Law of Collisions on Land,* Sweet & Maxwell, 1925; (contributor) J.N.D. Anderson, editor, *Changing Law in Developing Countries,* Humanities, 1963; *Commonwealth and Colonial Law,* Praeger, 1966. Contributor to *Journal of African Law* and other legal journals.

SIDELIGHTS: Kenneth Roberts-Wray traveled extensively for the Colonial Office, 1944-59—in Bermuda, the West Indies, East and West Africa, East Asia, the Pacific and the Mediterranean; he made official visits to the United States in 1944 and 1946.

*   *   *

ROBICHAUD, Gerard   1908-

PERSONAL: Surname is pronounced Row-bee-show; born September 12, 1908, in Quebec, Canada; son of Michel and Celestine (Mathieu) Robichaud; married Elizabeth Eckard (a social worker), June 13, 1953. *Education:* Attended Seminary of St. Hyacinth, Quebec, Canada, 1923-28; Columbia University, special courses, 1951-54. *Home:* 7 Peter Cooper Rd., New York, N.Y. 10010. *Agent:* Curtis Brown Ltd., 60 East 56th St., New York, N.Y. 10022.

CAREER: Bank employee, 1945-68. Novelist. *Military service:* U.S. Army, 1942-45; served in Hawaii and on Iwo Jima; received Bronze Star Medal.

WRITINGS: Papa Martel, Doubleday, 1961; *The Apple of His Eye,* Doubleday, 1965.

SIDELIGHTS: Robichaud told *CA:* "My bent is decidedly offbeat. There is no rape, sexual deviation, sadism, or incitement to juvenile or adult delinquency in my work, nor is there the tiresome despair, the confessional boredom. . . . A writer should parade before his readers real people, involved in real situations, in a development that is going somewhere, preferably upward."

ROBIE, Edward H(odges) 1886-

PERSONAL: Born November 30, 1886, in Whitney Point, N.Y.; son of Harry Adams (an engineer and farmer) and Alma (Hodges) Robie; married Agnes Purcell Parks, October 10, 1914; children: Robert Hodges, Theodore Parks (deceased), Edward Adams, John Adams (deceased). *Education:* Cornell University, student, 1907-08; University of Michigan, B.Ch.E., 1911. *Politics:* Liberal. *Religion:* Protestant. *Home and office:* Birdsall Loop, Rural Route 1, Box 43, Yorktown Heights, N.Y. 10598.

CAREER: Harrison Safety Boiler Works, Philadelphia, Pa., chemical engineer, 1911-13; Canadian Copper Co. (International Nickel Co.), Copper Cliff, Ontario, assistant metallurgist, 1913-19; *Engineering and Mining Journal,* New York, N.Y., staff, 1919-31, successively assistant, associate and acting editor, 1927-31; American Institute of Mining and Metallurgical Engineers, New York, N.Y., assistant secretary, and editor of *Mining and Metallurgy,* 1932-48, secretary, 1948-55, secretary emeritus, 1956—, secretary of Mining Branch, 1955, secretary of gifts committee, United Engineering Center, 1956-62, secretary and assistant to chairman, Corrosion Research Council, 1958-63. *Member:* American Institute of Mining, Metallurgical, and Petroleum Engineers, Canadian Institute of Mining and Metallurgy (life member). *Awards, honors:* First Mineral Economics Award, American Institute of Mining, Metallurgical, and Petroleum Engineers, 1966; Certificate of Service, Society of Petroleum Engineers, 1966.

*WRITINGS—*All published by American Institute of Mining, Metallurgical, and Petroleum Engineers: (Editor) *The Porphyry Coppers in 1956,* 1957; (editor) *Economics of the Mineral Industries,* 1959, 2nd edition, 1964; *History of the Institute, 1947-1961,* 1961.

AVOCATIONAL INTERESTS: Gardening, and caring for thirteen acre country home.

* * *

ROBINSON, Donald H(oy) 1910-

PERSONAL: Born March 4, 1910, in Hunters, Wash.; son of Luke Hoy (a farmer) and Ama (Linton) Robinson; married Martha Jantz (a nurse), November 7, 1940; children: Marjorie (Mrs. Joseph Haines), Myra (Mrs. Joseph Boone), Paul. *Education:* Gonzaga University, student, 1929-30; University of Washington, Seattle, B.S., 1938. *Religion:* Baptist. *Home:* 6516 129th St. S.E., Bellevue, Wash. 98006.

CAREER: Glacier National Park, Mont., park ranger, 1939-50, park naturalist, 1950-57; Blue Ridge Parkway, Va., park naturalist, 1957-66; National Park Service, Southeast Region, Richmond, Va., interpretive specialist, 1966-72. *Member:* Association of Interpretive Naturalists, National Audubon Society, Toastmasters International (past president), Lions Club (past secretary).

WRITINGS: Trees of Glacier National Park, Glacier Natural History Association, 1935; *History of Glacier National Park,* Glacier Natural History Association, 1940; (editor and contributor) *Wildflowers in Color,* Harper, 1965; *Campers' and Hikers' Guide to Blue Ridge Parkway,* Chatham Press, 1971.

AVOCATIONAL INTERESTS: Cultural and folk history, travel, photography, nature study, gardening, woodworking, oil painting.

* * *

ROBINSON, Elwyn B(urns) 1905-

PERSONAL: Born October 13, 1905, in Russell, Ohio; son of Walter Perry (a photographer) and Mabel L. (Robinson) Robinson; married Eva S. Foster, September 2, 1935; children: Stephen W., Gordon F. *Education:* Oberlin College, B.A., 1928; Western Reserve University (now Case Western Reserve University), M.A., 1932, Ph.D., 1936. *Politics:* Democratic party. *Religion:* Episcopal. *Home:* 425 Princeton St., Grand Forks, N.D. 58201. *Office:* University of North Dakota, Grand Forks, N.D. 58201.

CAREER: University of North Dakota, Grand Forks, instructor, 1935-36, assistant professor, 1936-48, associate professor, 1948-51, professor of history, 1951-67, University Professor, 1967-70, chairman of department, 1962-64. Episcopal lay reader. Secretary of North Dakota State Historical Board, 1965-70. *Member:* Organization of American Historians (chairman of membership committee, 1964-65). *Awards, honors:* University of North Dakota Alumni Award for distinguished teaching, 1958.

WRITINGS: History of North Dakota, University of Nebraska Press, 1966. Contributor to *Britannica Yearbook,* 1958-63; also contributor to historical and educational journals.

SIDELIGHTS: Robinson worked off and on for almost twenty years on *History of North Dakota.*

* * *

ROBINSON, Joseph William 1908-

PERSONAL: Born June 16, 1908, in St. Paul, Minn.; son of Joseph William (a mining engineer) and Emma (Weston) Robinson; married Jeanne E. Keever, March 21, 1936 (died February, 1963); children: William W., Alven Leonard. *Education:* Stanford University, A.B., 1930, M.A., 1931, Ph.D., 1936; Harvard University, graduate student, 1931-32; summer study at University of Wisconsin, University of California, Los Angeles, and University of Chicago. *Home:* 10115 Santa Gertrudes Ave., Whittier, Calif. 90603. *Office:* Department of Political Science, Whittier College, Whittier, Calif. 90608.

CAREER: Stanford University, Stanford, Calif., acting instructor in government, 1932-35; University of Idaho, Moscow, instructor, 1935; Purdue University, Lafayette, Ind., instructor, 1937-39, assistant professor, 1939-42, associate professor, 1942-46, professor of governemnt, 1946-47; Whittier College, Whittier, Calif., professor of political science and chairman of department of political science and international relations, beginning 1947, director of Whittier European Program, Copenhagen, 1970. University of Southern California, member of executive committee, Institute of World Affairs, beginning 1950, visiting summer professor, 1964, 1968. Instructor, University of California Extension, beginning 1961; professor, Rio Hondo College, beginning 1975. Trustee, Coro Foundation.

MEMBER: American Political Science Association, American Society of International Law, Council on Foreign Relations, American Association for the United Nations, International Political Science Association, International Studies Association, Society for the Advancement of Education, American Association of University Professors, Commission to Study the Organization of Peace (New York), Western College Association, Western Political Science Association, Midwest Political Science Conference, Southern California Political Science Association (president, 1959-60; member of executive committee, beginning 1960), Pi Sigma Alpha, Sigma Delta Chi, Kappa Alpha Delta, Alpha Tau Omega.

WRITINGS: (With Hugh McD. Clokie) *Royal Commissions of Inquiry,* Stanford University Press, 1937; (with James T. Watkins IV) *General International Organization: A Source Book,* Van Nostrand, 1956; *The Roots of International Organization,* Public Affairs Press, 1968. Also author of pamphlets. Contributor of articles and reviews to journals.

WORK IN PROGRESS: With James T. Watkins IV, a revised edition of *General International Organization: A Source Book.*

BIOGRAPHICAL/CRITICAL SOURCES: New York Times Book Review, June 2, 1968.

*   *   *

ROCHE, T(homas) W(illiam) E(dgar)   1919-197(?)

PERSONAL: Born December 9, 1919, in Exeter, Devonshire, England; son of Thomas and Dorothy (Hatton) Roche; married Henriette Bopp (a teacher of French), October 1, 1941; children: Margaret (Mrs. Barry Desmond Brook), Delphine (Mrs. Norman Wynne Griffith), Elizabeth. *Education:* Exeter College, Oxford, M.A., 1948. *Religion:* Church of England. *Home:* 41 Grantchester St., Cambridge CB3 9H2, England.

CAREER: In British Immigration Service, beginning 1941, became H.M. assistant chief inspector. Immigration officer, 1941-50; chief immigration officer at London Airport, Northolt Airport, Dover, and in East Africa, 1950-57; inspector in charge of London Airport Number 1 District, 1959-67; assistant chief inspector in charge of London Airport, and Birmingham and Luton Airports, beginning 1967. Director, Great Western Preservations Ltd. Vice-chairman, Dorney School Managers, beginning 1964. *Member:* Great Western Society (chairman of Reading, Berkshire group, 1966-67), Exeter College Association, Oxford Society, Old Exonian Club, Civil Service Club, Southampton Master Mariners' Club.

WRITINGS: Ships of Dover, Adlard Coles, 1959; *Plymouth & Launceston,* Branch Line Handbooks, 1962; *Go Great Western,* West Country Handbooks, 1965; *The King of Almayne,* J. Murray, 1966; *The Precious Blood* (history of Burnham Abbey), Luff & Co., 1966; *The Withered Arm,* West Country Handbooks, 1967; *The Key in the Lock: A History of Immigration Control in England,* J. Murray, 1969, published as *The Key in the Lock: Immigration Control in England from 1066 to the Present Day,* Transatlantic, 1970; *More Great Westernry,* Town & Country, 1969; (with A. S. Caswell) *Through Western Windows: Verses of the G.W.K.,* Town & Country, 1969; *Cornish Riviera Limited: A Review of the Life of a Famous Train,* Town & Country, 1969.

Samuel Cunard and the North Atlantic, Macdonald & Co., 1971; *Philippa: Dona Filipa of Portugal,* Phillimore, 1971; *A Pineapple for the King,* Phillimore, 1971; *A Shipman's Tale: Reminiscences of Ships of Devon from the 1920's to the Present Day,* Town & Country, 1971; *The Golden Hind,* Praeger, 1973. Contributor to *Railway Magazine, Amateur Historian,* and *Great Western Echo.*

SIDELIGHTS: Roche spoke French, German, Dutch, Swedish, Norwegian, and some Danish and Spanish. As an immigration official he traveled extensively in Europe and East Africa, and to America. *Avocational interests:* West of England, archaeology (especially medieval), ships, railways (in connection with interest in railways, Roche worked as a guard on the privately-owned Bluebell Railway in Sussex).†

(Deceased)

ROCKWELL, Wilson (Miller)   1909-

PERSONAL: Born June 26, 1909, in Bradford, Pa.; son of Robert Fay (a rancher) and Aileen (Miller) Rockwell; married Enid Wolverton, April 26, 1948; children: Daniel. *Education:* Attended Whittier College, 1930-32; Stanford University, B.A., 1933; University of Denver, M.A., 1938. *Politics:* Republican. *Religion:* Protestant. *Address:* P.O. Box 869, Creston, British Columbia, Canada.

CAREER: Cattle rancher near Maher, Colo., beginning 1938. Member of Colorado State Senate, beginning 1962. Member of board of directors, Delta County Memorial Hospital. *Military service:* U.S. Army Air Forces, 1942-46; became first lieutenant. *Member:* Colorado Authors' League, Phi Delta Phi, American Legion, Elks, Rotary Club (local president, 1960-61).

WRITINGS: New Frontier, World Press, 1940; *No Way Back,* Bradford-Robinson, 1950; *Sunset Slope,* Sage Books, 1956; *Memoirs of a Lawman,* Sage Books, 1962; *The Utes—A Forgotten People,* Sage Books, 1965; *Uncompahgre Country,* Sage Books, 1965. Writer of radio and television series on western history. Also contributor to *The 1967 Denver Westerner's Brand Book.*

WORK IN PROGRESS: A book entitled *We Hold These Truths . . . ,* about an American family who moves to Canada in search of a simple, quiet life.

*   *   *

ROCKWOOD, Roy
[Collective pseudonym]

WRITINGS: The Wizard of the Sea, Mershon, 1900; *A Schoolboy's Pluck,* Mershon, 1900; *Rival Ocean Divers,* Stitt, 1905; *Through the Air to the North Pole,* Cupples & Leon, 1906; *Under the Ocean to the South Pole,* Cupples & Leon, 1907; *Jack North's Treasure Hunt,* Chatterton-Peck, 1907; *Adrift on the Pacific,* Grosset, 1908; *Five Thousand Miles Underground,* Cupples & Leon, 1908; *Lost on the Moon,* Cupples & Leon, 1911.

"Dave Fearless" series; published by Garden City Publishing Co., except as indicated: *The Cruise of the Treasure Ship,* Mershon, 1906; *Dave Fearless after Sunken Treasure,* 1926; *. . . among the Icebergs,* 1926; *. . . and the Cave of Mystery,* 1926; *. . . and the Mutineers,* 1926; *. . . on a Floating Island,* 1926; *. . . Wrecked among Savages,* 1926.

"Great Marvel" series; published by Cupples & Leon: *Through Space to Mars,* 1910; *The City beyond the Clouds,* 1925; *By Air Express to Venus,* 1929; *By Space Ship to Saturn,* 1935.

"The Bomba Books" series; published by Cupples & Leon: *Bomba the Jungle Boy on Terror Trail,* 1928; *. . . among the Slaves,* 1929; *. . . in the Swamp of Death,* 1929; *. . . and the Lost Explorers,* 1930; *. . . on the Underground River,* 1930; *. . . in a Strange Land,* 1931; *. . . among the Pygmies,* 1931; *. . . and the Cannibals,* 1932; *. . . and the Painted Hunters,* 1932; *. . . and the River Demons,* 1933; *. . . and the Hostile Chieftain,* 1934; *. . . Trapped by the Cyclone,* 1935; *. . . in the Land of Burning Lava,* 1936; *. . . in the Perilous Kingdom,* 1937; *. . . in the Steaming Grotto,* 1938.

"Speedwell Boys" series also written under this pseudonym.

SIDELIGHTS: See **ADAMS, Harriet S., STRATEMEYER, Edward L.,** and **SVENSON, Andrew E.**†

RODIMER, Eva 1895-

PERSONAL: Born May 25, 1895, in Andover Township, N.J.; daughter of Albert Puder (a farmer) and Mida (Vail) Walker; married Jacob V. Rodimer, November 22, 1917 (deceased). *Education:* Paterson State College (now William Paterson College of New Jersey), B.S., 1957, M.S., 1958. *Politics:* Republican. *Religion:* Protestant. *Home:* 184 Main St., Newton, N.J. 07860.

CAREER: Teacher in a New Jersey country school, 1913-21; Newton (N.J.) Elementary School, teacher of science and history, 1921-61, supervisor of instruction, 1961-63. Republican committeewoman, Newton, N.J., 1940-54. *Member:* New Jersey Retired Teachers Association, New Jersey Audubon Society, Sussex County Garden Club, Sussex County Bird Club (vice-president, 1966-67). *Awards, honors:* Freedoms Foundation Teacher's Award, 1961.

WRITINGS: The Year Outdoors, Rutgers University Press, 1966. Author of a monthly column, "Nature's Notebook," in *New Jersey Herald,* beginning 1964.

WORK IN PROGRESS: A nature novel, *Tiger of the Air,* the story of a year in the life of the great horned owl.

SIDELIGHTS: Eva Rodimer has traveled throughout the United States studying natural science. *Avocational interests:* Amateur theatricals, horticulture, and flower arranging.††

* * *

RODMAN, Bella (Kashin) 1903-

PERSONAL: Born December 25, 1903, in Warsaw, Poland; daughter of Morris and Rose (Eisenband) Kashin; married Samuel Rodman, November, 1926; children: Karl. *Home:* 7 West 81st St., New York, N.Y. 10024.

AWARDS, HONORS: Charles W. Follett award, 1967, Nancy Bloch award, 1967, and Boys' Clubs of America Junior Book Award, 1967, for *Lions in the Way.*

WRITINGS: (With Philip Sterling) *Fiorello LaGuardia,* Hill & Wang, 1962; *Lions in the Way,* Follett, 1966.

* * *

ROE, Harry Mason
[Collective pseudonym]

WRITINGS—"Lanky Lawson" series; published by Barse & Co.: *Lanky Lawson, the Boy from Nowhere,* 1929; . . . *with the One-Ring Circus,* 1929; . . . *and His Trained Zebra,* 1930.

SIDELIGHTS: See **ADAMS, Harriet S., STRATEMEYER, Edward L.,** and **SVENSON, Andrew E.**†

* * *

ROEMER, Norma H. 1905-1973

PERSONAL: Born June 1, 1905, in Detroit, Mich.; daughter of Alfred P. (a restauranteur) and Bertha Roemer. *Education:* Attended Wayne State University, 1923-25; University of Michigan, A.B. in Ed., 1929, M.A., 1931. *Politics:* Democratic. *Religion:* Protestant. *Home:* 999 Hampton Rd., Grosse Pointe, Mich. 48236.

CAREER: High school teacher of geography and social studies in Detroit, 1937-68. *Member:* Pi Lambda Theta.

WRITINGS: (With Saul Israel and Loyal Durand, Jr.) *World Geography Today,* Holt, 1960, 4th edition, 1971.

AVOCATIONAL INTERESTS: Globe trotting and photography (travels cover the United States and Canada, Mexico, West Indies, South America, Asia, and Europe; visited Australia, New Zealand, and the Pacific Islands in the spring of 1967).†

(Died May 11, 1973)

* * *

ROESELER, Robert O. 1882-

PERSONAL: Born July 30, 1882, in Germany; son of Albert and Mathilde (Gundlach) Roeseler; married Anna-Marie Methschl, 1917; children: Herbert, Gerhart, Nancy Roeseler Beutler. *Education:* Teachers College, Bromberg, Germany, graduate, 1902; University of Posen, graduate (passed state examination), 1908; Ohio State University, Ph.D., 1929.

CAREER: Teacher of European history at schools in Czarnikau, Germany, 1908-09, Riga, Russia, 1909-10, Odessa, Russia, 1910-11, Krotoschin, Germany, 1911-13, and at Milwaukee Teachers Seminary, Milwaukee, Wis., 1913-20; Ober-Realschule, Mexico City, Mexico, rektor (headmaster), 1920-25; National Military Officer Training School, Chapultepec, Mexico, instructor, 1923-25; Ohio State University, Columbus, associate professor of German language and literature, 1925-34; University of Wisconsin, Madison, professor of German language and literature, 1934-52, professor emeritus, 1952—. *Member:* Modern Language Association of America (chairman of Middle West section, 1933), American Association of Teachers of German, Modern Language Teachers Association of Wisconsin (chairman, 1935), Phi Kappa Phi, Phi Delta Kappa.

WRITINGS: (With M. B. Evans) *College German,* Crofts, 1931, revised edition, 1939; (with Evans) *Das Rheinland,* Crofts, 1934; (edited with Adelaide Ber) *Altes und Neues,* Holt, 1934; (with A. A. Duckert) *Moderne Deutsche Erzaehler,* Norton, 1935; *Deutsche Novellen des 19. Jahrhunderts,* Holt, 1941; *Altes Deutsches Kulturgut,* Norton, 1948; (editor) Gertrud von le Fort, *Das Gericht des Meeres,* Appleton, 1959; *German Grammar,* Holt, 1961; (with G. A. Scherer) *Germany: The Country and Its People,* Ronald, 1962; *German in Review,* 4th edition, Holt, 1967. Contributor to *Jahrbuch fur physische Geographie* and other publications in Germany during earlier teaching days, later to *Monatschefte,* a journal he edited (at University of Wisconsin), 1934-52.

WORK IN PROGRESS: Gottfried Herder, 1744-1803, als Kulturphilosoph der slawischen Volker; a guide to composition and essay writing, in German, for American students.

SIDELIGHTS: Roeseler, in addition to German, reads, speaks, and understands Polish, Russian, and Spanish.†

* * *

ROGERS, Berto 1903-1974

PERSONAL: Born April 3, 1903, in Walton County, Ga.; son of Thomas Perry and Bert (Cocroft) Rogers; married Margaret Stuart Clark, June 2, 1934; children: Stuart Clark. *Education:* Mercer University, LL.B., 1926, J.D., 1970. *Politics:* Democrat (usually). *Religion:* Baptist. *Home and office:* 11 Rutledge Ave., Northport, N.Y. 11768.

CAREER: Admitted to Georgia Bar, 1926, and New York Bar, 1940; editor of law books, 1926-38; Milbank, Tweed, Hadley & McCloy, New York City, associate, 1938-56; Chase Manhattan Bank, New York City, member of legal department, 1956-68, retiring from his post as second vice-president, 1968. Trustee, Village of Northport, N.Y., 1946-

48; treasurer and trustee, National Committee on Employment of Youth (formerly National Child Labor Committee), 1961-66. *Member:* American Bar Association.

WRITINGS: Forms of Registration for Corporate Stock, Chase Manhattan Bank, 1957, 3rd edition, 1967; *Forms for Use in Claiming Exemption from Federal and New York Stock Transfer Taxes,* Chase Manhattan Bank, 1959; *Proxy Guide for Meetings of Stockholders,* Prentice-Hall, 1969; *Opinions and Stories of and from the Georgia Courts and Bar,* Equity Publishing (New Hampshire), 1973. Contributor to *Law Notes,* 1927-38, and to other legal periodicals.

WORK IN PROGRESS: Cyclopedia of Small Business; an untitled novel; short stories.†

(Died June 24, 1974)

* * *

ROGERS, Matilda 1894-1976

PERSONAL: Born March 3, 1894, in Budapest, Hungary; daughter of Leopold and Sali Rosenfeld. *Education:* Attended evening classes at Columbia University and New York University, and summer classes at University of Michigan; attended writers conferences at Bread Loaf, 1950, Boulder, 1951, and Mexico City College (now University of the Americas), 1954. *Home:* Hotel Sovereign, 205 Washington Ave., Santa Monica, Calif. 90403.

CAREER: Began as a medical secretary in New York City, then was executive secretary for community councils, and fund-raiser for United Hospital Fund, Knickerbocker Hospital, Amherst College, and Mount Vernon (N.Y.) Hospital; conducted the programs, "Careers for Women," "Hobbies of Prominent Men," and "Book Chats for Children" on Radio Station KFRC, San Francisco, Calif., 1926-30; wrote column, "Careers for Women," in *San Francisco Bulletin;* representative of Equitable Life Assurance Society in California before returning in 1940 to New York City, where she taught flower arrangement, worked for a federal contract renegotiation office during World War II, and was a volunteer job resume counselor for the Job Forum of the New York Advertising Club; in 1945 became a job resume specialist on a full-time professional basis; after a trip around the world in 1960, settled permanently in Santa Monica, Calif.

WRITINGS: Flower Arrangement Manual, International Press, 1942; *Flower Arrangement: A Hobby for All* (based on 1942 book), Women's Press, 1948; *A First Book of Tree Identification* (juvenile), Random House, 1951; *The First Book of Cotton* (juvenile), F. Watts, 1954; *Flower Arrangements Anyone Can Do Anywhere,* Dodd, 1954; *Trees of the West, Identified at a Glance,* Ward Ritchie, 1966. Contributor of articles on life insurance, flower arrangement, job finding, and other topics to *Think, Christian Science Monitor, New York Herald Tribune, Family Circle, Printers' Ink,* and other periodicals and newspapers.

WORK IN PROGRESS: A book on flower arrangement; a book on job-finding.†

(Died, 1976)

* * *

ROLLISON, William D(ewey) 1897-1971

PERSONAL: Born July 1, 1897, in Bloomfield, Ind.; son of Jesse and Charlotte (Benham) Rollison; married Edwin Latimer. *Education:* Indiana University, LL.B., 1921, A.B., 1924; Harvard University, LL.M., 1930. *Religion:* Baptist.

Home and office: Samford University, Birmingham, Ala. 35209.

CAREER: Admitted to Indiana Bar, 1919, and Alabama Bar, 1925. University of Alabama, University, assistant professor, 1922-26, associate professor of law, 1926-30; University of Notre Dame, Notre Dame, Ind., professor of law, 1930-63; Samford University, Birmingham, Ala., distinguished professor of law, beginning 1963. Member of probate study committee, state of Alabama. *Member:* Phi Alpha Delta. *Awards, honors:* Lay faculty award, 1949, for distinguished service to University of Notre Dame; LL.D., University of Notre Dame, 1969.

WRITINGS: Law of Wills, Callaghan & Co., 1939; *Clauses in Wills and Forms of Wills, Annotated,* Bender, 1946, *Cumulative Supplement,* 1949; *Illinois Estate Planning and Drafting of Wills and Trusts,* Banks & Co., 1952; *Cases and Materials on Estate Planning,* Volume I, University of Notre Dame Press, 1959, Volume II, 1960; (with William D. Rollinson and Elizabeth Eshelman) *Forms for Wills and Estate Planning,* Harrison, 1967.†

(Died January 21, 1971)

* * *

ROLPH, Earl R(obert) 1910-

PERSONAL: Born May 23, 1910, in Milwaukee, Wis.; son of John Robert (a machinist) and Rosa (Leid) Rolph; married Margaret Brainerd (an editor), August 29, 1936; children: John Eric, James Alan. *Education:* College of Wooster, B.S. (with honors), 1931; Princeton University, M.A., 1932; Cornell University, Ph.D., 1936. *Home:* 4 Arlington Ct., Berkeley, Calif. *Office:* Department of Economics, University of California, Berkeley, Calif. 94720.

CAREER: Instructor in economics at Cornell University, Ithaca, N.Y., 1934-36, and Colgate University, Hamilton, N.Y., 1935-36; University of California, Berkeley, instructor, 1937-40, assistant professor, 1940-47, associate professor, 1947-55, professor of economics, beginning 1955, chairperson of department, beginning 1975. Economist, U.S. Office of Price Administration, 1942-45. Consultant to U.S. Treasury Department, 1950-52, 1966-67, and to Brookings Institution. *Member:* International Institute of Public Finance, American Economic Association, National Tax Association, American Finance Association, American Association for the Advancement of Science, Western Economic Association (president, 1971-72), Canadian Political Science and Economic Association. *Awards, honors:* Guggenheim fellowship, 1957-58; Ford Foundation research professor, 1962-63.

WRITINGS: (Contributor) *Readings in the Theory of Income Distribution,* Blakiston Co., 1946; (contributor) *The Limits of Taxable Capacity,* Princeton University Press, 1954; *The Theory of Fiscal Economics,* Bureau of Business and Economic Research, University of California, Berkeley, 1954; (with George Break) *Public Finance,* Ronald, 1961; (contributor) Joseph Scherer and James A. Papke, editors, *Public Finance and Fiscal Policy,* Houghton, 1966. Contributor to professional journals. Member of editorial board, *National Tax Journal,* beginning 1957; referee, *Journal of Political Economy.*

WORK IN PROGRESS: Studies in local government; the concept of a government budget constraint and other fallacies; the relevance of distinctions between fiscal and monetary policies.

RONGEN, Bjoern 1906-

PERSONAL: Born July 24, 1906, in Voss, Norway; married Charlotte Schanche Olsen, March 9, 1940; children: Thana (Mrs. Ola Brdeveien), Ole. *Education:* Attended University of Oslo. *Religion:* None. *Home:* Skogvaegen 22, Droebak, Norway 1440.

CAREER: Author and free-lance journalist. *Member:* Den norske Forfatterforening, Ungdomslitteraturens forfatterlag, P.E.N.

WRITINGS—Novels; all published by Gyldendal, except as indicated: *To semester,* O. Norli, 1934, reprinted, Samleget, 1966; *Embetsfolk,* 1935; *Stille smil,* 1936; *Det drar ifra Vest,* 1939; *Nettenes natt,* 1940; *Tolv liv,* 1946; *Hun moeter deg alltid,* 1946; *Fager er lien,* 1948; *Kunnskapens tre,* 1949; *Driftekarens hoest,* 1951; *Kvinnen og pisken,* 1953; *Ragnhilds rike,* 1955; *Toget over vidda,* 1956; *I joekulens skygge,* 1957; *Klart for tog,* 1958; *Store Ma,* Tiden, 1960; *Nei men Johanne,* 1962.

Juvenile books: *Bergtatt I Risehola,* Damm, 1953, translation by Evelyn Ramsden published as *Olaf and the Echoing Cave,* McGraw, 1968; *Utvandrergutten: Knute Nelsons Saga,* Gyldendal, 1959; *Fem doegn paa isfjell: Tegninger av Arne Johnson,* Aschehoug, 1959; *De hemmelige flyktningene,* Gyldendal, 1962; *Anne Villdyrjente,* Damm, 1962, Gyldendal, 1966, translation by Ramsden published as *Anna of the Bears,* Methuen, 1965, Farrar, Straus, 1967; *Den store brannen,* Norsk Barneblad, 1967; *Ola den heldige,* Norsk Barneblad, 1970. Also author of *Slalaam for livet.* Author of radio plays and of several hundred short stories.

BIOGRAPHICAL/CRITICAL SOURCES: Young Readers Review, February, 1969.

* * *

ROSE, Camille Davied 1893-
(Camille Davied)

PERSONAL: Born March 8, 1893, in Chattanooga, Tenn.; daughter of John Felix and Elizabeth (Williams) Davied; married Egmont Arens, October 25, 1930 (deceased); married Marc A. Rose (an editor), May 22, 1953 (deceased); children: (first marriage) Patricia (Mrs. Edward C. Cumming). *Education:* Attended University of Kentucky, 1918-19, and Barnard College, 1921-22. *Home:* 115 East 82nd St., New York, N.Y. 10028.

CAREER: Began as editorial assistant on *Survey Graphic;* managing editor of *World Review,* 1925-26, *American Girl,* 1926-29 (also editor at one period), and *Vogue,* 1929-30; *Charm,* Newark, N.J., editor, 1930-32; *Arts & Decoration,* New York City, editor, 1932-33; *McCall's,* New York City, executive editor, 1933-58, consultant, 1958-62; free-lance writer, and free-lance editor of *Amerika,* Washington, D.C., 1962-64; New York University, New York City, lecturer on writing for today's magazines, 1963-66; Hunter College of the City University of New York, New York City, lecturer on writing for publication, beginning 1966. Former editor, Family Book Club. *Member:* Overseas Press Club of America, Women's National Press Club (Washington, D.C.), National Arts Club (New York).

WRITINGS: How to Write Successful Magazine Articles, Writer Inc., 1967. Contributor of articles, often under name Camille Davied, to magazines.

WORK IN PROGRESS: A book on Kentucky history since 1900.

ROSEBURY, Theodor 1904-1976

PERSONAL: Born August 10, 1904, in London, England; naturalized U.S. citizen; son of Aaron (an editor and translator) and Emily (Dimesets) Rosebury; married Lily Aaronson, December 26, 1926; married second wife, Amy Loeb (a psychotherapist), November 21, 1949; children: Joan (Mrs. Myron Lebow), Celia (Mrs. Stephen Lighthill). *Education:* Attended City College of New York (now City College of the City University of New York), 1921-23, and New York University, 1924; University of Pennsylvania, D.D.S., 1928; Columbia University, postdoctoral study, 1928-30. *Politics:* Independent. *Residence:* Conway, Mass. *Office:* School of Dentistry, Washington University, St. Louis, Mo. 63130.

CAREER: Columbia University, College of Physicians and Surgeons, New York, N.Y., instructor, 1930-35, assistant professor, 1935-44, associate professor of bacteriology, 1944-50; Washington University, School of Dentistry, St. Louis, Mo., professor of bacteriology, 1950-67, professor emeritus, 1967-76, chairman of department, 1951-67. Bacteriologist, U.S. Department of Interior, 1936; U.S. War Department, civilian bacteriologist, 1943-45, consultant, 1945-46. Diplomate in medical microbiology of American Academy of Microbiology. *Member:* American Association for the Advancement of Science (fellow), American Public Health Association, American Society for Microbiology, Society for Experimental Biology and Medicine, International Association for Dental Research, Society for Social Responsibility in Science, Physicians for Social Responsibility, Harvey Society, American Recorder Society, Sigma Xi. *Awards, honors:* Decoration from U.S. War Department for exceptional civilian service in World War II; special commendation from National Book Awards Committee, 1971, for *Life on Man.*

WRITINGS: (Contributor) F. P. Gay and others, *Agents of Disease and Host Resistance,* C. C Thomas, 1935; (contributor) S. Gordon, editor, *Dental Science and Dental Art,* Lea & Febiger, 1938; *Experimental Air-Borne Infection,* Williams & Wilkins, 1947; (contributor) R. Dubos and J. G. Hirsch, editors, *Bacterial and Mycotic Infections of Man,* Lippincott, 1948, 4th edition, 1965; *Peace or Pestilence,* McGraw, 1949; *Microorganisms Indigenous to Man,* McGraw, 1962; *Life on Man,* Viking, 1969; *Microbes and Morals: The Strange Story of Venereal Disease,* Viking, 1971. Contributor of about one hundred fifty articles to professional journals.

WORK IN PROGRESS: Science and Prejudice; an autobiographical account of his medical practice.

SIDELIGHTS: Life on Man, according to John Leonard, is "sane, elegant and informative: a joy to read, making intellectual ripples that go on widening long after the words have dropped into the mind." Robert Stock wrote: "Theodor Rosebury is a veteran bacteriologist who is disgusted with 'civilized' man's fetishes about cleanliness. He would root them out—with irony, sarcasm, and a heavy dose of purgative fact. . . . [This book's] mission is not so much to entertain as to protest." "It is Rosebury's contention," Lee Ash said, "that we have carried our fetish of hygiene too far in modern society and that the toll on our money and our psychological well-being is too great." Ash continued: "In relating the story of the symbiotic values (or harmlessness) of the body's microbes, and of the joy of scatological habits (or thoughts!), as quoted or described from the works of the great scatologists, he proposes a code for greater freedom of action and speech." "The questions he raises are not easily dismissed," Stock acknowledged. "Must we continue to loathe and hide from our bodies and their functions as if they were unnatural? Does obscenity lie in microbes and the normal acts and products of the body—or is it not simply the emanation of our twisted minds?"

Of *Microbes and Morals,* a *New York Times* reviewer wrote: "Why has Dr. Rosebury taken the trouble to tell such a story in this age of medical miracles when all that it takes to destroy the 'fastidious' bacteria that cause syphillis and gonorrhea is an adequate dose of penicillin? Quite simply because V.D., after having been nearly eradicated in the 1950's, seems to be on the rise again throughout most of the world . . . moral prudery, which Dr. Rosebury regards as the major impediment to a successful war on V.D., should find itself overwhelmed by the detective work, the scholarship, the clarity of explanation, and the pure wit that Rosebury has combined in this logical successor to his prize-winning *Life on Man.*" The reviewer concluded that "if *Microbes and Morals* serves any single purpose other than to throw light where darkness prevails, it is to make clear how intimately venereal disease is connected with the profoundest problems that now afflict us—problems such as war, poverty, race discrimination, male chauvinism, and ecology—and that its ultimate eradication may require equally profound responses."

BIOGRAPHICAL/CRITICAL SOURCES: New York Times, June 26, 1969, July 13, 1969, December 4, 1969, September 13, 1971, November 28, 1976; *Life,* July 11, 1969; *New York Times Book Review,* July 16, 1969; *Best Sellers,* August 1, 1969; *New Republic,* August 9, 1969.†

(Died November 25, 1976)

*   *   *

ROSENBAUM, Nathan 1897-

PERSONAL: Born August 15, 1897, in Russia; brought to United States, 1903, naturalized, 1907; son of Morris (a manufacturer) and Anna (Schatz) Rosenbaum; married Elizabeth Scher, May 27, 1923; children: Arthur S. and J. Paul (twins). *Education:* Temple University, student, 1916-18.

CAREER: Member of staff of *Philadelphia Inquirer* and later of *Evening Ledger,* Philadelphia, Pa., 1917-24; mortgage broker, 1924-29; Colonial Trust Co., Wilmington, Del., president, 1930-31; Rosenbaum & Co. (finance), Philadelphia, Pa., head, beginning 1932. *Member:* Poetry Society of America, B'nai B'rith, Temple University Down Town Club.

WRITINGS: Songs and Symphonies, Ferris & Leach, 1919; *Each in His Time,* Ariel Books, 1925; *My Hand and Seal,* Beechurst Press, 1947; *A Man from Parnassus,* Bookman Associates, 1951; *Create the World,* Whittier Books, 1956; *Collected Poems 1947-67,* A. S. Barnes, 1968.

WORK IN PROGRESS: Short stories and poetry.

AVOCATIONAL INTERESTS: Collecting first editions.†

*   *   *

ROSENHOUSE, Archie 1878-

PERSONAL: Born May 27, 1878, in Russia; son of Jacob (a teacher) and Libby (Strongin) Rosenhouse; married Molly Cohen, February 3, 1913; children: Miriam (Mrs. Edwin Lasker), Estelle (Mrs. Sidney Gelfan). *Education:* Northwestern University, D.D.S., 1915. *Politics:* Democrat. *Home:* 172 North Normandie Ave., Los Angeles, Calif. 90004.

CAREER: Doctor of dental surgery. *Member:* Centro Studi e Sambit Interrazionali (Rome), American Poetry League, Poets Haven, California Federation of Chaperral Poets (fourth vice-president). *Awards, honors:* Received second prize for best poems of the year in *Stepladder* (Knox College magazine), 1957.

WRITINGS: Aubade For Eve, Olivant, 1966; *. . . and Nothing Human Is Alien to Me,* Olivant, 1969; *Portrait of a Kiss,* Swordsman, 1972.

WORK IN PROGRESS: With Eddie Lou Cole, *200 X 2;* and *Love Poems—Cycle M.*†

*   *   *

ROSENQUIST, Carl M(artin) 1895-1973

PERSONAL: Born June 2, 1895, in Ethan, S.D.; son of Nils Maason (a wheelwright) and Anna Christina (Johnson) Rosenquist; married Helen Elisabeth Barrett, January 29, 1930; children: Martha Christina (Mrs. Charles Clifford Oldenburg), Carl John. *Education:* University of Illinois, A.B., 1921; University of Texas, M.A., 1925; University of Chicago, Ph.D., 1930. *Politics:* Democrat. *Home:* 248 Los Angeles Blvd., San Anselmo, Calif. 94960.

CAREER: University of Texas at Austin, tutor, then assistant professor, 1925-34, associate professor, 1935-36, professor of sociology, 1937-65, professor emeritus, 1965-73. U.S. Department of Agriculture, assistant chief of rice and sugar section, Agricultural Adjustment Administration, 1934, chief agricultural economist, 1934-35; price officer, U.S. Office of Price Administration, 1942-43. *Awards, honors:* Smith-Mundt and Fulbright grants.

WRITINGS: Social Problems, Prentice-Hall, 1940; (with Walter G. Browder) *Family Mobility in Houston, Texas, 1922-1938,* Bureau of Research in the Social Sciences, University of Texas, 1942; (with others) *Fundamentals of Sociology,* Crowell, 1950; (with Edwin I. Megaree) *Delinquency in Three Cultures,* University of Texas Press, for Hogg Foundation for Mental Health, 1969. Editor-in-chief with Megaree, *Southwestern Social Science Quarterly,* 1939-42.†

(Died September 16, 1973)

*   *   *

ROSS, Eva J(eany) 1903-1969

PERSONAL: Born June 2, 1903, in Belfast, Northern Ireland; came to United States in 1930, naturalized in 1950; daughter of Charles Alexander (an artist) and Eva Elizabeth (Woodland) Ross. *Education:* Bedford College, London, B.Com., 1930; Chartered Institute of Secretaries, A.C.I.S., 1930; St. Louis University, M.A., 1934; Yale University, Ph.D., 1937. *Politics:* Democrat. *Religion:* Roman Catholic. *Office:* Sociology Department, Trinity College, Washington, D.C. 20017.

CAREER: Moody's Investor's Service, London, England, secretary and staff manager, 1925-27; Dillon Read Corp., Paris, France, head of information department, 1928-30; Nazareth College, Nazareth, Mich., instructor in economics and sociology, 1930-32; instructor in economics and sociology of St. Louis University, Maryville College, and Fontbonne College, St. Louis, Mo., 1932-33; Albertus Magnus College, New Haven, Conn., faculty member, 1935-36; College of St. Elizabeth, Convent Station, N.J., professor of economics, 1936-39; Trinity College, Washington, D.C., professor of sociology and head of department, 1940-69. Summer professor, St. Michael's College, 1944-46, 1948; Fulbright professor, University of Colombia, 1961.

Member: American Sociological Association (fellow), American Association of University Women, American Catholic Sociological Society (president, 1943). *Awards, honors:* D.Litt., St. Bonaventure University, 1956; National Science Foundation travel grant, 1959; Pro Ecclesia Et Pontifice Medal (a papal honor).

*WRITINGS—*All published by Bruce, except as indicated: *A Survey of Sociology,* 1932; *Rudiments of Sociology,* 1934, revised edition, 1939; *Social Origins,* Sheed, 1936; *Fundamental Sociology,* 1939; *What is Economics? A Brief Survey of our Economic Life,* 1939; *Belgian Rural Cooperation: A Study in Social Adjustment,* 1940; *Sound Social Living,* 1941, published with teacher's manual, 1942, revised and enlarged edition, 1951, new revised edition, 1963; *American Democracy: Its Problems and Its Achievements,* 1944, revised edition, 1952; *Sociology and Social Problems,* 1948, revised and enlarged edition, 1960; *Basic Sociology,* 1953, revised and enlarged edition, 1958; (with Ernest Kilzer) *Western Social Thought,* 1954; *Living in Society,* 1966; *Introducing Sociology,* 1967. Book review editor, *American Catholic Sociological Review,* 1943-50.

Translator: Robert Kothen, *Marriage, The Great Mystery,* Newman, 1947; Marie Michel Philipon, *The Message of Ste. Therese,* Newman, 1947; Francois Jamart, *The Life and Spirit of Carmel,* Newman, 1951.

WORK IN PROGRESS: Belgian Rural Cooperatives: Agricultural Cooperation in Colombia, to be published in Spanish; and a third book, *Sociology in Great Britain.*

SIDELIGHTS: Eva Ross traveled in Latin America, Europe, the Middle East and the Orient. She had a thorough knowledge of French, Spanish, Latin, German, and Italian. She was buried at Taormina, Sicily, according to her wish. *Avocational interests:* Walking and reading.†

(Died June, 1969)

* * *

ROSS, Harold Raymond 1904-

PERSONAL: Born June 19, 1904, in Fort Recovery, Ohio; son of James and Winnie (Sortor) Ross. *Education:* Attended Ohio State University, 1922-27; New York University, A.B. and A.M., 1946; Columbia University, graduate study, 1951-53. *Office:* New York University, Washington Sq., New York, N.Y. 10003.

CAREER: Barnes & Noble, Inc. (publishers), New York, N.Y., staff, 1927-42; New York University, New York, N.Y., instructor, 1946-47, assistant professor of speech, beginning 1948. Private teacher of voice and speech, beginning 1935. *Member:* Speech Association of America, Linguistic Society of America, National Society for the Study of Communication, American Dialect Society, American Association of University Professors, Speech Association of Eastern States, New York State Speech Association, Linguistic Circle of New York, Delta Sigma Rho-Tau Kappa Alpha, Alpha Psi Omega.

WRITINGS: (With Watt and Holzknecht) *Outlines of Shakespeare's Plays,* Barnes & Noble, 1935; (with Williamson and Fritz) *Speaking in Public,* Prentice-Hall, 1949; (with Warren Bower and others) *How to Write,* Lippincott, 1951; (with Fritz) *Practice Manual for Speech Improvement,* New York University Bookstore, 1952; (with George Fluharty) *Public Speaking,* Barnes & Noble, 1966.

WORK IN PROGRESS: Research in five areas—spoken English as a second language, stressed vowels in most frequent words, word as a combining form in English, native plant names, and specificity of vowels in English.

SIDELIGHTS: Ross is competent in French, Spanish, German, Italian, and Latin. *Avocational interests:* Singing, playing piano, and acting.††

* * *

ROSS, Marvin C(hauncey) 1904-1977

PERSONAL: Born November 21, 1904, in Moriches, N.Y.; son of William Edwin (a farmer) and Mary K. Ross; married Lotus Robb, September 11, 1937. *Education:* Harvard University, A.B., 1928, A.M., 1930; also studied at University of Berlin, 1927, Centro de Estudios Historicos, Madrid, Spain, 1930, and New York University Institute of Fine Arts, 1933-34. *Politics:* Republican. *Religion:* Protestant. *Home:* 2230 California St., Washington, D.C. 20008.

CAREER: Curator at Brooklyn Museum, Brooklyn, N.Y., 1934, and Walters Art Gallery, Baltimore, Md., 1934-52; Los Angeles County Museum, Los Angeles, Calif., chief curator of art, 1952-55; free-lance researcher and writer, 1955-60; Hillwood, Washington, D.C., curator, 1960-73; Smithsonian Institution, Washington, D.C., consultant, 1973-77. University of Vienna, Fulbright professor, 1959-60. Dumbarton Oaks Collection, Washington, D.C., member of advisory committee, 1941-64. *Military service:* U.S. Marine Corps Reserve, active duty, 1942-46; became major. *Member:* College Art Association, American Association of Museums, Archaeological Institute of America.

WRITINGS: Catalogue of Exhibition of Early Christian and Byzantine Art, Walters Art Gallery, 1947; (with Anna W. Rutledge) *The Sculpture of W. H. Rinehart,* Walters Art Gallery, 1951; (editor) *The West of Alfred Jacob Miller,* University of Oklahoma Press, 1951, revised edition, 1967; (with Joan F. Erdberg) *A Catalogue of Italian Majolica in the Walters Art Gallery,* Walters Art Gallery, 1952; (with E. S. King) *A Catalogue of American Art in the Walter's Gallery,* Walters Art Gallery, 1956; *The Life of Christ in Masterpieces of Art,* Harper, 1957; (editor) George Catlin, *Last Rambles with the Indians,* University of Oklahoma Press, 1959; *Catalogue of Folkwandering Antiquities,* Walters Art Gallery, 1961; *Catalogue of the Byzantine Antiquities in the Dumbarton Oaks Collections,* Volume I, [Washington, D.C.], 1962, Volume II, 1965; *The Art of Karl Faberge and His Contemporaries,* University of Oklahoma Press, 1965; *Russian Porcelains,* University of Oklahoma Press, 1967. Contributor to art periodicals. Member of editorial board, *Art Quarterly.*

WORK IN PROGRESS: Compiling a work on Byzantine art.

(Died April 24, 1977)

* * *

ROSS, Phyllis (Freedman) 1926-1970

PERSONAL: Born August 28, 1926, in New York, N.Y.; daughter of Harry and Josephine (Sachs) Freedman; married Herbert S. Ross (an exporter), August 31, 1949; children: Harry, Josephine, Mary. *Education:* Wellesley College, B.A., 1946; Columbia University, M.A., 1959. *Politics:* Democrat. *Religion:* Jewish. *Home:* 110 Riverside Dr., New York, N.Y. 10024. *Agent:* Roberta Pryor, Ashley Famous Agency, Inc., 1301 Avenue of the Americas, New York, N.Y. 10019.

CAREER: Writer.

WRITINGS: Sybil Larson, Hospital Nurse, Pocket Books, 1963; *Priscilla White, TV Secretary,* Pocket Books, 1964; *Channing,* New American Library, 1964; *Headline Nurse,* Pocket Books, 1965; *Miranda Clair,* Pocket Books, 1965.†

(Died February, 1970)

ROTH, Ernst   1896-1971

PERSONAL: Born June 1, 1896, in Prague, Czechoslovakia; son of Karl (a merchant) and Pauline (Kohn) Roth; married Kate Henrietta Low (a teacher). *Education:* University of Prague, Dr.Iuris, 1921. *Religion:* Jewish. *Home:* 26 Meadowside, Twickenham, England.

CAREER: Universal-Edition (publishers), Vienna, Austria, 1922-38, became production manager and chief editor of Wiener Philharmonischer Verlag (a subsidiary of Universal-Edition); Boosey & Hawkes Ltd. (music publishers), London, England, chairman, 1964-71.

WRITINGS: Magalhaes, Colligen, 1919; *Die Grenzer der Kuenste,* Engelhorn, 1925; *Vom Vergaenglichen in der Musik,* Atlantis Verlag, 1949; *Richard Strauss Stage Works,* Boosey & Hawkes, 1954; (with William Shuh) *Richard Strauss: Complete Catalogue,* Boosey & Hawkes, 1964; *Musik als Kunst und Ware,* Atlantis Verlag, 1966; (translator) *Composers' Autographs,* Fairleigh Dickinson University Press, Volume I, edited and annotated by Walter Gerstenberg, 1968, Volume II, edited by Martin Hurlimann, 1968; *The Business of Music: Reflections of a Music Publisher,* Cassell, 1969; *Tale of Three Cities,* Cassell, 1971; *Von Prag bis London Erfahrungen Autobiographische Fragmente* (posthumous collection of selected writings), Atlantis Verlag, 1974.

SIDELIGHTS: Ernst Roth spoke German, French, and Italian.†

(Died July 17, 1971)

*   *   *

ROTHMAN, Theodore   1907-

PERSONAL: Born April 28, 1907, in Paterson, N.J.; son of Abram (a stationer) and Rebecca (Geber) Rothman; married Jean Gershfield (a real estate manager), December 25, 1934; children: Stephanie (Mrs. Charles Swartz). *Education:* Clark University, B.A., 1928; New York Medical College, M.D., 1932. *Politics:* Registered Democrat. *Religion:* Jewish. *Residence:* Los Angeles, Calif. *Office:* 9201 Sunset Blvd., Los Angeles, Calif. 90069.

CAREER: Licensed to practice medicine in New York and California. Metropolitan Hospital, New York, N.Y., intern, 1932-33, resident, 1933-36; private practice in psychiatry, Los Angeles, Calif., beginning 1936. Emeritus clinical professor of psychiatry, University of California, School of Medicine. Attending psychiatrist, Los Angeles County and University of Southern California Medical Center. Psychiatric consultant to various hospitals. Post-graduate preceptorships at New York Medical College, New York Neurological Institute, Mount Sinai Hospital, University of California, Los Angeles, and University of Southern California. Executive director, Rush Research Foundation. *Member:* American Medical Association, American College of Neuropsychopharmacology (vice-president and secretary, beginning 1961), American Association of the History of Medicine, Society of Biological Psychiatry, Dante Alighieri Society (former president and member of board of directors), California Medical Association, Southern California Psychiatric Association, Los Angeles Society of Neurology and Psychiatry. *Awards, honors:* Order of Merit, first class, Republic of Italy, 1963; Physicians Recognition Award, American Medical Association, 1969; Paul Hoch Distin-

guished Service Award, American College of Neuropsychopharmacology, 1973; Selective Service Medal, U.S. Congress.

WRITINGS: (Contributor) Abraham Stone and Roberta Graves, editors, *Sex in Our Culture,* Emerson, 1955; (contributor) Paul H. Hoch and Joseph Zubin, editors, *Psychopathology of Communication,* Grune, 1957; (contributor) P. B. Bradley and others, *Neuro-Psychopharmacology,* Van Nostrand, 1960; (contributor) Hoch and Zubin, editors, *The Future of Psychiatry,* Grune, 1962; (contributor) Nathan K. Rickles, editor, *The Management of Anxiety for the General Practitioner,* C. C Thomas, 1963; (contributor) John Nodine and John Moyes, editors, *Psychosomatic Medicine,* Lea & Febiger, 1965; (editor) *Changing Patterns in Psychiatric Care: An Anthology of Evolving Scientific Psychiatry in Medicine,* Crown, 1970. Contributor to *Endocrinology, Modern Hospital, Journal of the American Medical Association, American Journal of Neurology and Psychiatry, American Journal of Physiology, Psychosomatics, Journal of Neuropsychiatry,* and other professional journals.

SIDELIGHTS: Theodore Rothman has traveled and lectured in most countries of Europe as well as in Japan. *Avocational interests:* Playing piano, chamber music, history of ideas, the philosophy of science, bibliophile, and collecting graphics.

*   *   *

ROTHSCHILD, J(acquard) H(irshorn)   1907-

PERSONAL: Born December 22, 1907, in Cincinnati, Ohio; son of Julius Joseph (a clothing designer) and Gertrude (Hirshorn) Rothschild; married Phyllis Mills, September 18, 1938; children: Ronald Mills. *Education:* University of Illinois, student, 1925-26; U.S. Military Academy, B.S., 1930; Massachusetts Institute of Technology, S.M. in Chemical Engineering, 1942. *Politics:* Democrat. *Religion:* Unitarian Universalist. *Home and office:* 2323 North Central Ave., Phoenix, Ariz. 85004.

CAREER: U.S. Army, Chemical Corps, career service, 1930-57, retiring as brigadier general; University of Colorado, Boulder, lecturer in chemical engineering and business management, 1958-60; management and industrial consultant, based in Phoenix, Ariz., and lecturer on chemical and biological warfare, arms control, and disarmament, beginning 1959; now a tennis pro. Assignments during Chemical Corps service included commanding officer of Development Laboratory, Massachusetts Institute of Technology, 1941-44; chief of Technical Division, Washington, D.C., 1945-46; assistant professor of chemistry, U.S. Military Academy, West Point, N.Y., 1947-50; commanding officer, Chemical and Radiological Laboratories, 1950-51; chemical officer, Far East Command, 1951-54; commanding general, U.S. Army Chemical Corps Research and Development Command, Washington, D.C., beginning 1954.

MEMBER: American Chemical Society, American Institute of Chemical Engineers, United World Federalists (national advisory board member, beginning 1960), Arizona Civil Liberties Union (board member, beginning 1962), Sigma Xi, Phoenix Urban League (board member, beginning 1961). *Awards, honors—*Military: Legion of Merit with two oak leaf clusters, Bronze Star.

WRITINGS: Tomorrow's Weapons, Chemical and Biological, McGraw, 1964. Contributor to *Harper's, Survival, Marine Corps Gazette,* and *Bulletin of the Atomic Scientists.* Consulting editor, *Journal of Arms Control.*

ROUX, Willan Charles 1902-

PERSONAL: Surname is pronounced Rue; born August 18, 1902, in Newark, N.J.; son of Louis Alexander (a professor) and Gertrude (Willan) Roux; married Gertrude Smith, June 28, 1929; children: John W., Suzanne Roux Spurlock. Education: Brown University, Ph.B., 1923. Politics: Republican. Religion: Protestant. Home: 2 Wilshire Rd., Madison, Conn.

CAREER: L. Bamberger & Co. (department store), Newark, N.J., advertising staff, 1923-26; self-employed in own advertising agency, Newark, N.J., 1926-32; National Broadcasting Co., New York, N.Y., advertising, promotion, and sales staff, 1932-47; Colyer-Roux Printing Co., Newark, N.J., president, 1947-62. Member: Sigma Nu.

WRITINGS: What's Cooking Down in Maine?, Wheelwright, 1964; Fried Coffee and Jellied Bourbon, Barre, 1967; (editor) Barbara Flood, Game in the Kitchen, Barre, 1968. Contributor to Yankee, Down East, Vista, U.S.A., Rural Vermonter, and New York Times.

* * *

ROYSTER, Salibelle 1895-1975

PERSONAL: Born August 7, 1895, in Smith Mills, Ky.; daughter of L. C. (a physician) and Sallie (Martin) Royster. Education: Evansville College (now University of Evansville), A.B., 1924, M.A., 1926; graduate study at University of Chicago, 1930, and Cambridge University, 1936; Columbia University, M.A. and Teachers College Diploma, 1938. Religion: Protestant. Home: 620 Southeast First Street, Apt. B, Evansville, Ind. 47713.

CAREER: Reitz High School, Evansville, Ind., teacher of English, 1924-62, head of department, 1940-62; University of Evansville, Evansville, Ind., part-time instructor in English, 1962-69. Member: American Association of University Women, National League of American Pen Women (vice-president of Southern Indiana branch, 1972-74), Tyro Press Club (president, 1972), Pi Lambda Theta. Awards, honors: Second award in published book division (poetry), National League of American Pen Women's biennial contest, 1968, for Skyway to Poetry.

WRITINGS: In Kodachrome (poems), Lantern Press, 1954; Skyway to Poetry (collection of her own poems and her translations of French poetry), South & West, 1966. Author of "Cliff's Notes" for eight books by Shakespeare, Sir Walter Scott, Mark Twain, and others, 1962-65. Articles and poems have been published in Poet Lore, Chicago Tribune, English Journal, and other periodicals and newspapers.

WORK IN PROGRESS: A new collection of poetry.

AVOCATIONAL INTERESTS: Travel and photography.

BIOGRAPHICAL/CRITICAL SOURCES: Evansville Press, February 14, 1967.†

(Died May 3, 1975)

* * *

RUARK, Robert (Chester) 1915-1965

PERSONAL: Born December 29, 1915, in Wilmington, N.C.; son of Robert C. and Charlotte (Adkins) Ruark; married Virginia Webb, August 12, 1938 (divorced). Education: University of North Carolina, A.B., 1935. Religion: Episcopalian. Residence: Palamos, Spain. Agent: Harold Matson Co., Inc., 22 East 40th St., New York, N.Y. 10016.

CAREER: Spent early years as an accountant for Works Progress Administration; served with the Merchant Marine; Washington Daily News, Washington, D.C., sports writer, columnist, 1937-42; Newspaper Enterprise Association Service, Washington correspondent, 1942; Scripps-Howard Newspaper Alliance, Washington correspondent, 1945; Scripps-Howard Newspapers and United Features Service, New York, N.Y., columnist, 1946-65. Military service: U.S. Navy, 1942-45. Member: Phi Kappa Sigma.

WRITINGS: Grenadine Etching: Her Life and Loves, Doubleday, 1947; I Didn't Know It Was Loaded, Doubleday, 1948; One for the Road, Doubleday, 1949; Grenadine's Spawn, Doubleday, 1952; Horn of the Hunter, Doubleday, 1953; Something of Value (Book-of-the-Month Club selection), Doubleday, 1955; The Old Man and the Boy (autobiographical), Holt, 1957; Poor No More, Holt, 1959; The Old Man's Boy Grows Older (autobiographical), Holt, 1961; Uhuru: A Novel of Africa (Book-of-the-Month Club selection), McGraw, 1962; The Honey Badger (Book-of-the-Month Club selection), McGraw, 1965; Use Enough Gun: On Hunting Game, New American Library, 1966; Women, New American Library, 1967. Contributor to national magazines.

SIDELIGHTS: Self-described as "a pretty ordinary hack," Ruark wrote 4,000 columns for the United Feature Syndicate. He boasted that, on the average, he could type a daily column in eleven minutes and once wrote 16 columns in a single day in Rome. "There was a time," Ruark recalled, "when I would go anywhere, eat airline food, use gin as a substitute for sleep, fight against the Mau Mau, chase elephants on horseback, slug athletes, enjoy being jailed, and wrestle with leopards, all for love of the newspaper business."

Hemingway was his hero and Ruark relentlessly imitated his writing style and mode of life. "If Ernest Hemingway [had not existed]," wrote Time, "it is difficult to see how Robert Ruark . . . could ever have been invented." Something of Value, a novel of the Mau Mau uprising in Kenya, resembled Hemingway's style, although Ruark's novel, unlike Hemingway's books, emphasized blood and torture. Orville Prescott, who felt it was the most loathsome novel he had read in nearly 25 years of reviewing, remarked that Ruark had "drenched his book in blood and crammed it with scenes of killing, butchering, . . . obscene rituals and every kind of torture." Similarly, T. E. Cassidy wrote: "This is not a journey into Kenya via the novel; it is a trip through an abattoir. The stench overwhelms the mind. Worse, it remains." Charging that the text was "literally horrible," Bruce Bliven commented: "It's hard to say exactly how much bad taste is excusable as accurate reporting; but not nearly this much, in my opinion. . . . Apart from horror, Something of Value has little to offer."

Some critics were more favorably impressed. John Barkham, a critic and lecturer on Africa, declared that he would not hesitate to nominate it the "most sensational novel of the year. Those familiar with the author's wisecracking columns or his lighthearted earlier novels will find a brand new Ruark here. Gone is the happy gun-toter whose African safaris were racily recorded in Horn of the Hunter. . . . In the interim the Mau Mau descended on Kenya and turned it into a land of terror. The story of that human blight and what it did to Kenyans, white and black alike, is recounted in this huge and frightening novel." And, noted Percy Wood, although "it shocks and revolts, . . . it also has beauty and love and a warm appreciation of friendship, bravery and courage." Apparently anticipating critical reaction to the book, Ruark wrote in the foreword: "There is much blood in the book.

There is much killing. But the life of Africa was washed earlier by blood, and its ground was, and still is, fertilized by the blood of its people and its animals. This is not a pretty book, nor was it written for the pre-bedtime amusement of small children.''

His autobiographical novels dealing with his philosophical grandfather have found more critical favor. "One has the impression that although *The Old Man and the Boy* may not have outsold Mr. Ruark's best-selling novels, it became the most widely liked book he had written,'' noted Dan Wickenden. A Kirkus reviewer said of the same book: ''Dismiss from your mind any preconception of Ruark as the author of *Something of Value.* Enjoy to the hilt this enchanting and nostalgic recreation of his own boyhood . . . under the supervision of a remarkable grandfather.''

Something of Value was sold to Metro-Goldwyn-Mayer for $300,000 and made into a motion picture in 1957.

BIOGRAPHICAL/CRITICAL SOURCES: Saturday Review, April 23, 1955; *Chicago Sunday Tribune,* April 24, 1955; *Commonweal,* May 13, 1955; Kirkus Service, September 1, 1957; *Time,* November 11, 1957, May 5, 1961; *New York Herald Tribune Lively Arts,* April 23, 1961; *New York Times,* July 1, 1965.††

(Died July 1, 1965)

*   *   *

RUBICAM, Harry Cogswell, Jr. 1902-

PERSONAL: Born February 27, 1902, in Denver, Colo.; son of Harry Cogswell (an insurance man) and Kittie Emma (Whallon) Rubicam; married Elizabeth Louise Bell, June 24, 1930; children: Harry Cogswell III. *Education:* Attended high school in Denver, Colo. *Politics:* Republican. *Religion:* Episcopalian. *Residence:* Grafton, Vt. 05146. *Agent:* McIntosh & Otis, Inc., 475 Fifth Ave., New York, N.Y. 10017.

CAREER: Denver Post, Denver, Colo., reporter, then assistant state editor, 1926-28; Western Air Express, Denver, Colo., publicity director, Rocky Mountain region, 1929-31; Young & Rubicam, Inc. (advertising agency), New York, N.Y., 1932-59, began as copywriter, became manager of copy department; retired, 1959, to live on 400-acre farm in Vermont. *Member:* Sons of the American Revolution.

WRITINGS: Pueblo Jones, Knopf, 1939; *Two Spot, Wolf Dog of the Circle Y,* Knopf, 1941; *Find a Career in Advertising,* Putnam, 1960; *Men at Work in Hawaii,* Putnam, 1960; *Men at Work in the Mountain States,* Putnam, 1960; *Men at Work in the Great Plains States,* Putnam, 1961. Two novels on Westernlore in *West Magazine,* 1948, 1950; about forty short stories published in *National Sportsman* and *Hunting and Fishing;* poems published in *Hartford Courant,* Hartford, Conn.

WORK IN PROGRESS: Further research on the West and the plains Indians.

AVOCATIONAL INTERESTS: Carpentry, photography, philately, gardening.

*   *   *

RUBINSTEIN, Stanley (Jack) 1890-1975

PERSONAL: Born January 17, 1890, in London, England; son of Joseph Samuel (a solicitor of the Supreme Court of England) and Isabelle Alexandra (Marks) Rubinstein; married Vera Rachel Solomon, June 24, 1915 (died April 5, 1953); children: Joan Stanley, Anthony Benno, John Stanley. *Education:* Studied in Hanover, Germany, 1906-07,

and in Tours, France, 1907-08. *Politics:* Conservative. *Religion:* Jewish. *Home:* 31 Rodney Gardens, Eastcote-Pinner, Middlesex, England. *Agent:* Christine Campbell-Thompson, D. C. Benson & Campbell Thomson Ltd., Clifford's Inn, Fleet St., London E.C.4, England. *Office:* Rubinstein, Nash & Co., 5/6 Raymond Buildings, Gray's Inn, London W.C.1, England.

CAREER: Solicitor, 1913-68, and former senior partner in firm of Rubinstein, Nash & Co. (solicitors), London, England, copyright consultant, 1968-75. Chairman, Burke Publishing Co. Ltd., London. Composer of dance music, marches, light musicals, and songs. Past master, Worshipful Company of Musicians; trustee, Royal Opera House Covent Garden Benevolent Fund; founder member, Council for Music in Hospitals; honorary solicitor and vice-president, British Council for Rehabilitation, 1946-75; committee member, Lord Soper's West London Mission Creche, 1944-75.

MEMBER: Performing Right Society (composer member), Society of Authors, International P.E.N., Romantic Novelists' Association (founder member; honorary solicitor), Confederation Internationale des Societes d'Auteurs et Compositeurs, Gesellschaft fuer Musikalische Auffuehrungs und Mechanische Vervielfaeltigungsrechte, Association Litterraire et Artistique Internationale, Savage Club (honorary solicitor), London Sketch Club (honorary solicitor), Shoreditch Rotary Club (past president), Law Society.

WRITINGS: Bubbson: An Extravaganza, Jarrolds, 1927; *Love-in-Law,* Jarrolds, 1932; *Merry Murder,* Jarrolds, 1947; *The Street Traders' Lot: London, 1851,* Sylvan Press, 1947; *A Letter to the Editor,* Allan Wingate, 1952; *Historians of London,* Volume I, Shoe String, 1968. Contributor to *Listener, Times, London Opinion, Strand,* and other magazines and newspapers, and to law journals.

WORK IN PROGRESS: Volume II of *Historians of London;* an autobiography.†

(Died, 1975)

*   *   *

RUKEYSER, Merryle Stanley 1897-1974

PERSONAL: Surname pronounced *Roo*-ky-ser; born January 3, 1897, in Chicago, Ill.; son of Isaac and Pauline (Solomon) Rukeyser; married Berenice Simon, June 25, 1930 (died, 1964); married Marjorie B. Leffler, August 1, 1965; children: (first marriage) Merryle Stanley Jr., Louis, William Simon, Robert James; stepchildren: William Leffler II, Walter Leffler. *Education:* Columbia University, B.Litt., 1917, M.A., 1925.

CAREER: New York Morning Telegraph, New York City, assistant sports editor and correspondent, 1915-17; *New York Tribune,* New York City, reporter, 1917-20, financial editor, 1920-23; *New York Evening Journal,* New York City, financial editor, 1923-26; financial columnist for Hearst Newspapers and International News Service, 1927-58, and editorial writer for the Hearst chain, 1931-52; writer of syndicated newspaper column, ''Everybody's Money,'' beginning 1958. Professional lecturer, broadcaster, and consultant. Staff member, Columbia University, School of Journalism, 1918-35. President, National Outlook Corp., beginning 1963; member of board of directors, Deuterium Corp. and Consolidated Halliwell Corp. President, New Rochelle Board of Education, 1960-62. *Member:* Academy of Political Science, Sigma Delta Chi, Columbia University Club, Beachpoint Club.

WRITINGS: *The Common Sense of Money and Investments*, Simon & Schuster, 1924; *Financial Advice to a Young Man*, Simon & Schuster, 1927; *The Doctor and His Investments*, Blakiston Co., 1929; *Investment and Speculation*, Alexander Hamilton Institute, 1930; *The Diary of a Prudent Investor*, Hellman Curl, 1937; *Financial Security in a Changing World*, Greenberg, 1940; *Life Insurance Property: The Hallmark of Personal Success*, Home Life Insurance Co., 1958; *The Kennedy Recession*, Monarch Books, 1962; *The Attack on Our Free Choice*, Monarch Books, 1963; *Collective Bargaining: The Power to Destroy*, Delacorte, 1968.†

(Died April, 1974)

* * *

RUNYAN, Harry (John) 1913-(?)

PERSONAL: Born March 8, 1913, in Spring Green, Wis.; son of Harry Arthur (a stock buyer) and Lillian (Hood) Runyan. *Education:* University of Wisconsin, B.A., 1940, Ph.D., 1949; University of Michigan, M.A., 1941. *Home:* 1350 North Lake Shore Dr., Chicago, Ill. 60610. *Agent:* Eleanor Langdon Associates, 8 West Oak St., Chicago, Ill. 60611. *Office address:* University of Illinois, Box 4348, Chicago, Ill. 60680.

CAREER: University of Wisconsin—Madison, instructor in English, 1947-48; University of Utah, Salt Lake City, assistant professor of English, 1948-52; University of Illinois at Chicago Circle, assistant professor, 1955-61, associate professor, 1961-66, professor of English, beginning 1966. Visiting lecturer, University of Wisconsin, 1953. *Military service:* U.S. Army Air Forces, 1943-45; became sergeant; received Bronze Star Medal. *Member:* Modern Language Association of America, American Association of University Professors, Art Institute of Chicago.

WRITINGS: *A Faulkner Glossary*, Citadel, 1964; (author of critical commentary) William Faulkner, *Absalom, Absalom!*, American R.D.M., 1966; (author of critical commentary) William Faulkner, *Intruder in the Dust*, American R.D.M., 1967. Staff reviewer, *Choice*.†

(Deceased)

* * *

RUPERT, Raphael Rudolph 1910-
(Istvan Tatray)

PERSONAL: Born July 1, 1910, in Szekesfehervar, Hungary; son of Rudolph (a lawyer and liberal politician) and Edith (de Kompolthy) Rupert; married Anne Clancy, June 10, 1961; children: Rudolph, Paul, Anne. *Education:* Cardinal Pazmany University, Budapest, Hungary, Doctor of Law and Political Science, 1933. *Politics:* Liberal. *Religion:* Roman Catholic. *Home:* 7 Caherdavin Park, Caherdavin, Limerick, Ireland.

CAREER: Became member of Chamber of Lawyers, Budapest, Hungary, 1939, and practiced law in Budapest; Shannon Industrial Estate, Shannon Free Airport, Limerick, Ireland, company manager of Lana-knit (Ireland) Ltd., beginning 1960, and director of board of Clare Chemicals Ltd. Former legal adviser to Pester Hungarian Commercial Bank, Budapest. *Military service:* Royal Hungarian Hussar Regiment, became senior lieutenant; awards include citation from Field Marshal Alexander, on behalf of British Commonwealth, for rescue of several British and Allied soldiers from the Germans. *Member:* Hungarian Association of Sovereign Order of Knights of Malta.

WRITINGS: *A Hidden World*, edited by Anthony Rhodes, World Publishing, 1962. Author, under pseudonym Istvan Tatray, of series of articles on matters behind the Iron Curtain, in *The Observer* (London) and several U.S. newspapers.

WORK IN PROGRESS: European history in general and its political motivations.††

* * *

RUSKAY, Joseph A. 1910-

PERSONAL: Born June 7, 1910, in New York, N.Y.; son of Cecil B. (a lawyer) and Sophie (Liebovitz) Ruskay; married Margot Stern (a social worker), August 15, 1947; children: Deborah, David. *Education:* Attended Dartmouth College, 1927-29, University of Munich and University of Bonn, Germany, 1929-30; Columbia University, B.S., 1931, LL.B., 1934. *Politics:* Democrat. *Religion:* Jewish. *Home and office:* 115 Oak St., Woodmere, N.Y. 11598.

CAREER: Admitted to the New York Bar; lawyer, beginning 1934. *Military service:* U.S. Army, 1942-46; became first lieutenant. *Member:* Americans for Democratic Action (member of national board, beginning 1963), Bar Association of the City of New York, National Ski Patrol.

WRITINGS: (With Richard A. Osserman) *Half-Way to Tax Reform*, Indiana University Press, 1970. Contributor of articles to *New Republic, Nation, New Leader,* and *Minority of One*.

WORK IN PROGRESS: Research for a book on minority stockholders and the courts.

* * *

RUSSELL, (Sydney) Gordon 1892-

PERSONAL: Born May 20, 1892, in London, England; son of Sydney Bolton (a company director) and Elizabeth (Shefford) Russell; married Constance Elizabeth Jane Vere Denning, August 8, 1921; children: Michael, Robert Henry, Oliver (deceased), Katherine (Mrs. Kenneth Baynes). *Education:* Attended schools in Gloucestershire, England. *Religion:* Church of England. *Home and office:* Kingcombe, Chipping Campden, Gloucestershire, England.

CAREER: The background for his craftsmanship was laid at sixteen when he was put in charge of the workshop at his father's inn, the Lygon Arms in Broadway, Worcestershire, England; on demobilization from the Army in 1919, he started designing furniture in a contemporary manner, expanding the production as designer and managing director of Gordon Russell Ltd. in Broadway, England, 1926-40, became chairman; partner in Russell & Sons (inn ownership), 1919-46; Lygon Arms Ltd., director and became chairman; industrial design consultant, beginning 1960. British Board of Trade, member of utility furniture advisory committee and furniture production committee, 1942-47, chairman of design panel, 1943-47 (as chairman played a major part in the national production of wartime utility furniture by six hundred firms); Council of Industrial Design (government body), member, beginning 1944, director, 1947-59. Crafts Council of Great Britain, chairman, 1964-68, member of crafts advisory committee, 1971-74; original member of executive committee for 1951 Festival of Britain, 1948-51; member of art panel, Arts Council of Great Britain, 1948-53, of fine arts committee, British Council, 1948-58, of design panel, British Railways Board, 1956-66, of arts advisory committee, United Kingdom National Commission for UNESCO, 1960-66, of bank note design committee, Bank of

England, 1960-70. Member of council, Royal College of Art, 1948-51, 1952-63, and Royal School of Needlework, 1951-68; member of National Council for Diplomas in Art and Design, 1961-68. Served on jury of International Low-Cost Furniture Competition at Museum of Modern Art, New York, 1948. *Military service:* British Army, Worcestershire Regiment, 1914-19; became lieutenant; received Military Cross.

MEMBER: Society of Industrial Artists and Designers (fellow), Design and Industries Association (president, 1960-62), Royal Society of Arts (fellow; member of council, 1947-49, 1951-55), Art Workers Guild (master, 1962), Royal Institute of British Architects (honorary associate, 1953; honorary fellow, 1965), Institute of Landscape Architects (honorary associate, 1955), Society of Designer Craftsmen (honorary member), Svenska Slojdforeningen (corresponding member), Landsforeningen Dansk Kunsthaandvaerk (corresponding member), Arts Club.

AWARDS, HONORS: Royal Designer for Industry, 1940, master of faculty, 1947-49; Order of the British Empire, Commander, 1947, Knight Bachelor, 1955; Royal College of Art, honorary fellow, 1952, senior fellow, 1960; Chevalier of Swedish Royal Order of Vasa, 1954; Bronze Medal, Parsons School of Design (New York), 1956; Commander of Norwegian Royal Order of St. Olav, 1957; Society of Industrial Artists Medal, 1959; LL.D., University of Birmingham, 1960; Gold Albert Medal of Royal Society of Arts, 1962, for services to industrial design; honorary doctorate, University of York, 1969.

WRITINGS: The Things We See: Furniture, Penguin, 1947, 3rd revised edition published as *Looking at Furniture,* Lund, Humphries, 1964; *How to Buy Furniture* (booklet), H.M.S.O., for Council of Industrial Design, 1947, revised edition, 1951; (with Jacques Groag) *The Story of Furniture* (picture book), Puffin, 1947; (with Alan Jarvis) *How to Furnish Your Home,* Newman Neame, 1953; *Designer's Trade* (autobiography), Fernhill, 1968.

SIDELIGHTS: "In recent years mainly concerned with industrial design, but still deeply interested in the crafts," Sir Gordon Russell told *CA.* "Garden design and gardening a particular personal interest—including execution personally of stone carving, stone wall building and paving. Also architecture." As the *Times Literary Supplement* points out, "Sir Gordon's professional work (which he modestly designates 'trade') and his public life belong already, in a sense, to history.... His life's work has been much more than furniture or industrial design.... It is the quality of life in this country, whether urban or rural, industrial or individual, that has been his lifelong concern and it is quality in the fullest, roundest sense that is the real thread running through *Designer's Trade.*" Christopher Wordsworth notes that Russell's autobiography, "at once fresh and mellow like the scent of wood shavings" concludes with a look ahead and "a rallying call against planned obsolescence and other impending horrors of subtopia."

BIOGRAPHICAL/CRITICAL SOURCES: Observer Review, July 7, 1968; *Times Literary Supplement,* July 25, 1968; Gordon Russell, *Designer's Trade,* Fernhill, 1968.

*   *   *

RUTENBER, Culbert G(erow) 1909-

PERSONAL: Surname is pronounced *Rut*-en-bur; born May 6, 1909, in Grove City, Pa.; son of Ralph Dudley (a clergyman) and Margaret (Gerow) Rutenber; married Duron Sparks, June 28, 1970. *Education:* Kenyon College, Ph.B.,

1930; Eastern Baptist Theological Seminary, B.D., 1933; University of Pennsylvania, M.A., 1938, Ph.D., 1945. *Home:* Eastern Baptist Theological Seminary, Lancaster Ave. at City Line, Philadelphia, Pa. 19151.

CAREER: Ordained Baptist minister, 1933; pastor in Camden, N.J., 1931-39; Eastern Baptist Theological Seminary, Philadelphia, Pa., 1939-58, became professor of philosophy of religion and social ethics; Andover Newton Theological School, Newton Centre, Mass., professor of philosophy of religion, 1959-69; American Baptist Seminary of the West, Covina, Calif., professor of philosophy of religion, 1969-74; Eastern Baptist Theological Seminary, professor of philosophy of religion, beginning 1974. H. I. Hester Lecturer of Association of Schools and Colleges of the Southern Baptist Convention, 1974; Edwin S. Griffiths Memorial Lecturer of South Wales Baptist College, Cardiff, Wales, 1975. President of American Baptist Convention, 1968-69. *Member:* American Philosophical Association, Society for the Scientific Study of Religion, American Society of Christian Ethics, Common Cause, Phi Beta Kappa, Sigma Pi.

WRITINGS: The Doctrine of the Imitation of God in Plato, King's Crown Press, 1946; *The Dagger and the Cross,* Fellowship Press, 1950; *The Price and the Prize,* Judson, 1953; *The Reconciling Gospel,* Judson, 1960; *Peace Keeping or Peace Making,* Friendship, 1968. Contributor to *Christian Century, Current Religious Thought, Journal of Chemical Education,* and other journals in his field.

*   *   *

RYWELL, Martin 1905-1971
(Taylor Hemingway, Deane Sears)

PERSONAL: Born December 3, 1905, in New York, N.Y.; son of H. P. and Augusta Lord (Nass) Rywell; married Ethel Stone; children: Sanford Spencer. *Education:* Studied at New York University, 1923, Columbia University, 1924-25, City College (now City College of the City University of New York), New York, N.Y., 1928-31, University of Grenoble and University of Paris, 1923; Cumberland University, LL.B., 1924. *Home and office:* Harriman, Tenn.

CAREER: Editor of *New York Municipal Review,* 1933-35, Political Digest Syndicate, 1936-40, *Current Humor,* 1954-58, and *Listen,* beginning 1959; editor, Pioneer Press, Harriman, Tenn., beginning 1948. Author, and specialist on American firearms. *Awards, honors:* Ph.D., University of Bari (Italy), 1958.

WRITINGS—Published by Pioneer Press, except as noted: (Compiler) *Anthology of Short Stories,* 1935; *Investigators Law Manual,* 1938.

Decimal Indexes, 1947; *Judah Benjamin, Unsung Rebel Prince,* Stephens Press, 1948; *Mortar in American Foundations,* 1949; *American Antique Gems,* 1949.

(With Harry L. Golden) *Jews in American History,* privately printed, 1950; *United States Military Muskets, Rifles, Carbines,* 1950; *American Antique Rifles,* 1951; *Firearms in American History,* 1951; (compiler) *Tennessee Cook Book,* 1951; *Samuel Colt: A Man and an Epoch,* 1952; (compiler) *Mexican Cook Book,* 1952; *Confederate Guns and Their Current Prices,* 1952, 10th updated edition, 1962; (compiler) *Wild Game Cook Book,* 1952, 23rd edition published as *Wild Game, Wild Fowl Cookbook,* 1970; (editor) *Samuel Colt, Colt Guns,* 1953, 2nd edition, 1957; *Smith & Wesson: The Story of the Revolver,* 1953, 2nd edition, 1957; *Trial: Complete Report of the Trial of Samuel Colt vs. Massachusetts Arms Co.,* 1953; (under pseudonym Taylor Hemingway) *Sex*

Control: Curious Customs of Medieval Times, 1953; *Gun Collectors' Guide*, 1954, 5th edition, 1961; (editor) *Laughing With Tears* (anthology of Jewish writing), 1955; *Sabotage in the American Revolution*, 1955; *Muzzle Loader Gun Guide*, 1955; (editor) Henry Lee Scott, *Civil War Military Dictionary*, 1956; (editor) Henry Lee Scott, *Civil War Military Dictionary*, 1956; (with H. J. Blanch) *English Guns and Gun Makers*, 1956; *The Gun That Shaped American Destiny*, 1957; *American Antique Guns and Their Current Prices*, 1957, 17th updated edition, 1969; (compiler, under pseudonym Deane Sears) *Where to Find Bargains in the United States*, 1957; (published as joint work of Deane Sears [pseudonym for Martin Rywell] and Martin Rywell) *Coin Collector's Guide, 1958-59*, 1958, updated edition, 1960; *The Kentucky Rifle*, 1958; *Powder Flask: The Complete Guide for the Collector of the Principal Accessory to the Firearm*, 1959.

Guns in American History, 1960; *The Truth About John Brown*, 1962; *Joy and Profit of Collecting American Antique Guns*, 1962; *Winchester Guns*, 1962; *Confederate Weapons*, 1962; *Fell's Collector's Guide to American Antique Firearms*, 1963; (with Maude D. Key) *Grandmother's Amazing Household Secrets*, 1963; *Indian Artifact Collectors Handbook*, 1964; (compiler) *First Texas Cook Book*, 1965; (compiler) *First American Cook Book*, 1966; *Tell It Like It Is*, 1967; *Directory of Every American Automobile Ever Manufactured*, 1969, revised edition, 1970.

Contributor of stories, articles, and essays to periodicals.†

(Died, 1971)

* * *

SACHS, Nelly 1891-1970

PERSONAL: Born December 10, 1891, in Berlin, Germany; became a Swedish subject; daughter of William (an industrialist and inventor) and Margarethe (Karger) Sachs. *Education:* Attended Hoch Toechterschule; educated privately. *Religion:* Jewish.

CAREER: Through the aid of Selma Lagerloef and Prince Eugene of Sweden, Miss Sachs escaped with her mother from Germany to Sweden in 1940, when she was about to be placed in a concentration camp. She and her mother were the only survivors in her family. Visited Germany in 1961 to attend a ceremony in her honor. Writer. *Member:* Bayrische Adademie fuer schoene Kuenste (Munich), Freie Akademie der Stadt Hamburg, Darmstaedter Akademie fuer Sprache und Dichtung. *Awards, honors:* Prize of the Poets' Association (Sweden); Jahrespring Literature Prize, 1959; Kulturpreis der deutschen Industrie, 1959; Annette Droste Prize for Poetry, 1960; won the first Nelly Sachs Prize for Literature (created in her honor by the town of Dortmund, Germany), 1961; Peace Prize of the West German Booksellers, 1965; Nobel Prize for Literature, 1966.

WRITINGS—All poetry unless otherwise noted: *Legenden und Erzaehlungen* (legends and stories dedicated to Selma Lagerloef), Meier Verlag (Berlin), 1921; *In den Wohnungen des Todes* (title means "In the Dwellings of Death"; also see below), Aufbau-Verlag (Berlin), 1946; *Sternverdunkelung* (title means "Eclipse of the Stars"; also see below), Bermann-Fischer, 1949; *Eli: Ein Mysterienspiel vom Leiden Israels* (play; title means "Eli: A Mystery Play of the Sufferings of Israel"; broadcast over German radio, 1951, first produced in Dortmund, West Germany, 1962; also see below), privately printed, 1951; *Und niemand weiss weiter* (title means "And No One Knows How To Go On"), Ellerman (Hamburg), 1957, 2nd edition, 1966; *Flucht und Ver-*

wandlung (title means "Flight and Metamorphosis"), Deutsche Verlags-Anstalt (Stuttgart), 1959.

Fahrt ins Staublose: Die Gedichte der Nelly Sachs (collected poems; title means "Journey to Staublose"), Suhrkamp (Frankfurt am Main), 1961; *Die Gedichte der Nelly Sachs*, Suhrkamp, two volumes, 1961-71; *Zeichen im Sand: Die szenischen Dichtungen der Nelly Sachs* (collected plays; title means "Sketches in Sand"), Suhrkamp, 1962; *Das Leiden Israels* (includes *Eli, In den Wohnungen des Todes,* and *Sternverdunkelung*), Suhrkamp, 1962; *Ausgewaehlte Gedichte* (title means "Selected Poems"), Suhrkamp, 1963, U.S. edition, edited by Guy Stern and Gustave Mathieu, published under same title, Harcourt, 1968; *Gluehende Raetsel* (title means "Glowing Riddle"), Insel-Buecherei, 1964; *Spaete Gedichte* (title means "Later Poems"), Suhrkamp, 1965; *Die Suchende* (title means "The Seeker"; also see below), Suhrkamp, 1966; *Wie leicht wird Erde sein: Ausgewaehlte Gedichte*, Bertelsmann (Guetersloh), 1966; *Simson faellt durch Jahrtausende und andere szenische Dichtungen*, Deutscher Taschenbuch (Munich), 1967; *O the Chimneys: Selected Poems, Including the Verse Play, Eli,* translated by Michael Hamburger and others, Farrar, Straus, 1967 (published in England as *Selected Poems: Including the Verse Play 'Eli,'* J. Cape, 1968).

The Seeker and Other Poems (selections), translated by Ruth Mead, Matthew Mead, and Michael Hamburger, Farrar, Straus, 1970; *Verzauberung: Spaete szenische Dichtungen*, Suhrkamp, 1970; *Teile dich Nacht: Die letzten Gedichte*, edited by Margaretha Holmqvist and Bengt Holmqvist, Suhrkamp, 1971; *Suche nach Lebenden: Die Gedichte der Nelly Sachs*, edited by Margaretha Holmqvist and Bengt Holmqvist, Suhrkamp, 1971.

Work represented in anthologies, including *Contemporary German Poetry*, edited and translated by Gertrude C. Schwebell, New Directions, 1964.

Translator into German: *Von Wolle und Granit: Querschnitt durch die schwedische Lyric des 20. Jahrhunderts* (title means "From Wool and Granite: A Cross Section of Swedish Poetry of the 20th Century"), Aufbau-Verlag, 1947; (and editor) *Aber auch diese Sonne ist heimatlos: Schwedische Lyric der Gegenwart* (title means "Once Again the Sun is Homeless: Swedish Poetry of Today"), Buechner (Darmstadt), 1957; (with others) Johannes Edfelt, *Der Schattenfischer* (poetry; title means "The Shadowy Fisherman"), Bonniers (Stockholm), 1959; Gunnar Ekelof, *Poesie* (bilingual edition in German and Swedish), Suhrkamp, 1962; Erik Lindegren, *Gedichte* (poetry), Bonniers, 1962; Karl Vennberg, *Poesie,* Suhrkamp, 1965; (and editor) *Schwedische Gedichte* (title means "Swedish Poetry"), 1965.

SIDELIGHTS: Although Miss Sachs had written poetry and puppet plays since she was seventeen, though she was first discovered by Stefan Zweig and inspired by Selma Lagerloef with whom she carried on a correspondence, and while she contributed to such papers as *Berliner Tageblatt,* she remained largely unknown in Europe until after World War II and, in America, until she won the Nobel Prize. J. P. Bauke reported that she "did not seek fame and did not receive it and apparently lived in such seclusion that no memorialist remembers meeting her." Yet Harry Zohn wrote, "There is little doubt that Nelly Sachs ranks with Else Lasker-Schueler and Gertrud Kolmar, the foremost German-Jewish poetess of our century." Hans Magnus Enzenberger called her "the greatest author writing today in the German language." What began as a bitter lament for the sufferings of the Jewish people "has gradually given way to expressions of sympathy for the suffering of all," the *New York Times* wrote. "There have been tones of reconciliation and forgiveness."

Kurt Pinthus called her "the presumably final expression in the German language of the ancestral sequence of 6000 years which began with the psalmists and the prophets." Zohn believed Miss Sachs was regarded "as a sort of soul sister of Franz Kafka, and surely her statement 'Writing was my mute outcry—I only wrote because I had to free myself' is eminently Kafkaesque. [She] regards herself as the vessel of a higher idea: she did not seek to become the poetess of the Holocaust; the subject sought her out. From the outset her poetry has not been easy of access. Highly personal, mystical, and visionary in quality, her poems sought to embody her conception of 'the invisible universe.' She strove for universal dimensions and incorporated an intricate symbolism born of a desire to go to the roots of our age and of the human condition." Her later work became quieter and more cryptic and condensed than her earlier poetry, according to Michael Hamburger.

"In her verse," wrote Bauke, "Miss Sachs has raised a monument to the Jews that is at once modern and timeless. Combining impulses from the German world of Hoelderlin, Novalis and Rilke, from surrealism, Chassidism, and the Old Testament, she has found a language uniquely her own. Totally free of irony, understatement and anger, her verse reaches the hymnic pathos of prophecy. In visions of cosmic sweep her lines associate the hunting scenes on the walls of prehistoric caves with the horrors of Auschwitz and Belsen. Her sibylline incantations invoke in ever new variations 'the sound at the heart of the world' and approach the mysteries of evil and suffering with the resignation of Job." Her work was not derivative but rather what she called "a sheaf of lightning on this acre of paper." She "creates on a large canvas," wrote Zohn, "and raises the tragedy of her time, of her people, from chaos and formlessness, from subjective emotion to a higher plane where it can be contemplated for its universal significance."

Of *Spaete Gedichte*, Zohn wrote: "This is curiously compressed, elliptic and enigmatic poetry which seeks to penetrate to the mystic border region where language touches silence. These poems reduce everything earthly to its barest substance, and the horror of the concentration camps is made the more vivid and searing by this searching beyond material fact and realistic description." *Die Welt* (a Hamburg newspaper) wrote of her work in general: "Her volumes of lyrics are dominated by a single theme: Israel. Not today's state bearing that name, but the people of the Old Testament—a God-chosen, tried and afflicted people; not a militant people, but one that has known suffering and sacrifice, mockery, persecution, destruction.... To the millions of the nameless and voiceless who are generally recalled only in the form of merciless, six-digit figures, Nelly Sachs has given mouth and voice. It is her one theme. For 20 years her allegorical and metaphorical variations on it have been unusually daring and extremely beautiful."

Nelly Sachs recorded some of her poetry for a recording entitled "Nelly Sachs liest Gedichte." Her scenario, "Eli," was made into an opera by the Swedish composer Moses Pergament.

BIOGRAPHICAL/CRITICAL SOURCES: Nelly Sachs zu Ehren (festschrift for her seventieth birthday), Suhrkamp, 1961; *Nelly Sachs zu Ehren II*, Suhrkamp, 1966; *New York Times*, October 21, 1966, December 11, 1966; *New York Times Book Review*, November 6, 1966; *Congress Bi-*

Weekly, November 7, 1966; *Books Abroad*, winter, 1967; *Chicago Review*, December, 1969; *Washington Post*, March 6, 1972.†

(Died May 12, 1970)

*   *   *

SACKS, Benjamin   1903-

PERSONAL: Born October 6, 1903, in Philadelphia, Pa.; son of Morris and Dora (Clayman) Sacks; married Jeanette Nelson, September 7, 1955; children: Allan, Betsy. *Education:* University of New Mexico, B.A., 1926; McGill University, M.A., 1927; Stanford University, Ph.D., 1934. *Office:* Department of History, Arizona State University, Tempe, Ariz. 85281.

CAREER: High school teacher of history, Albuquerque, N.M., 1929-32; University of New Mexico, Albuquerque, 1932-63, began as instructor, associate professor, 1937-47, professor of history, 1947-63; Arizona State University, Tempe, professor of history, beginning 1963. *Military service:* U.S. Army Air Forces, 1943-45; became lieutenant. *Member:* American Historical Association, Southwest Social Science Association, Phi Alpha Theta, Phi Kappa Phi.

WRITINGS: J. Ramsay MacDonald, University of New Mexico Press, 1952; *Religious Issue in the State Schools of England and Wales, 1902-1914*, University of New Mexico Press, 1961; *Peace Plans of the 17th and 18th Centuries*, Coronado Press, 1962; *South Africa, an Imperial Dilemma: Non-Europeans and the British Nation, 1902-1914*, University of New Mexico Press, 1967.†

*   *   *

SAINT-DENIS, Michel Jacques   1897-1971
(Jacques Duchesne)

PERSONAL: Born September 13, 1897, in Beauvais, France; son of Charles and Margaret (Copeau) Saint-Denis; married Marie Ostroga, 1923; married Suria Magito (a theatre director); children: Jerome, Christine de la Potterie, Blaise Gautier (son). *Education:* Educated in France at College Rollin, Paris, and Lycee Hoche, Versailles. *Agent:* A. P. Watt & Son, 26-28 Bedford Row, London WC1R 4HL, England. *Office:* Royal Shakespeare Theatre, Stratford on Avon, Warwickshire, England.

CAREER: Theatrical producer and director identified with the founding of national companies in three countries. Career began in 1920 with Theatre du Vieux-Colombier in France, where he became assistant director (also appeared as actor, making debut in 1922); founder, 1930, and director, producer, and actor with La Compagnie des Quinze, France; founder and managing director of London Theatre Studio, Islington, England, 1935-39; head of French section, broadcasting under pseudonym Jacques Duchesne, British Broadcasting Corp., London, England, 1940-45, and head of BBC English section in Paris, France, 1945-46; helped to rebuild Old Vic after World War II; founder of Old Vic Theatre Centre and School, London, England, and director-general, 1946-52; founder of school of Centre Nationale Dramatique de l'Est, Strasbourg, France, and director-general, 1952-57; inspector-general of theater, under French Ministry for Cultural Affairs, Paris, 1959-65; Royal Shakespeare Theatre, Stratford on Avon and London, England, co-director, beginning, 1962, consultant director, beginning, 1966. Helped establish National Theatre and Theatre School, Montreal, Canada, 1960, and was president of the school, beginning, 1960. President of International Commission on Training, attached to UNESCO, Paris; special consultant in establishment of Lincoln Center Repertory Theatre and Drama School, New York, 1960: Juilliard School, New York, N.Y., adviser, 1959-68, co-director of drama division, beginning, 1968. His British productions have included "Macbeth," with Laurence Olivier, "Twelfth Night," with Michael Redgrave, "Electra" and "The Cherry Orchard," with Peggy Ashcroft, "The Three Sisters," with John Gielgud and Michael Redgrave.

MILITARY SERVICE: French Army, 1914-18; also served in Infanterie Coloniale as liaison officer at British Headquarters, 1939-40; decorations include Croix de Guerre (World War I), Officier de la Legion d'honneur, Medaille Resistance, Rosette de la Resistance, Chevalier de l'Ordre de Leopold (Belgium), and Commander of Order of the British Empire. *Member:* Royal College of Arts (London; fellow). *Awards, honors:* D. Litt., University of Birmingham, 1962; L.H.D., Dartmouth College, 1962; World Theatre Award, International Theatre Institute and American Theatre Association, 1969.

WRITINGS: Theatre: Rediscovery of Style, Theatre Arts, 1960; (under pseudonym Jacques Duchesne) *Le Quadrille* (play), Cercle du Livre de France, 1968. Author of introductions to other books on the theater; author and adaptor of plays; contributor to periodicals.

WORK IN PROGRESS: A comprehensive book on the training of actors, directors, designers, and stage technicians.†

(Died July 31, 1971)

*   *   *

SALSBURY, Edith Colgate   1907-1971

PERSONAL: Born August 14, 1907, in Bedford, N.Y.; daughter of Lathrop and Edith C. (Leonard) Colgate; married Charles Baker Salsbury (an architect), May 26, 1934 (died, 1967); children: Colgate, Sherrod (daughter), Baker. *Education:* Smith College, B.A., 1929; studied painting at American School, Fontainebleau, France, 1929-33, at Art Students League, New York, N.Y., and privately with Jonas Lie. *Politics:* Independent. *Religion:* Episcopalian.

CAREER: Paintings exhibited at National Arts Club and with National Women Painters and Sculptors; Mark Twain Memorial, Hartford, Conn., vice-president and researcher for restoration of Twain's home in Hartford, 1958-71.

WRITINGS: (Editor) *Susy and Mark Twain: Family Dialogues,* Harper, 1965. Occasional reviewer for *Hartford Courant.*

SIDELIGHTS: Edith Salsbury was competent in French and Italian. *Avocational interests:* Genealogy.†

(Died September 26, 1971)

*   *   *

SAMFORD, Clarence D(ouglas)   1905-

PERSONAL: Born March 31, 1905, in Fairfield, Ill.; son of John F. (a teacher) and Eva Myrtle (Talbert) Samford; married Inez Moss (a teacher); children: Lynn, Lester, Lloyd, John. *Education:* Southern Illinois University, B.Ed., 1926; University of Michigan, M.A., 1930; New York University, Ph.D., 1940. *Politics:* Republican. *Religion:* Christian. *Home:* 1220 West Church St., Champaign, Ill. 61820. *Office:* Department of Secondary Education, Southern Illinois University, Carbondale, Ill. 62901.

CAREER: Teacher and superintendent in public schools of Springerton, Ill., 1923-25, Carbondale, Ill., 1926-29, Mounds, Ill., 1929-31; Ohio University, Athens, supervising critic teacher, 1931-45; University of Wyoming, Laramie, senior teacher of social studies, 1945-47, principal of University High School and professor of education, 1947-51; Southern Illinois University, Carbondale, professor of education, beginning 1951, chairman of department of secondary education, 1957-69. Visiting summer professor, Wilmington College, 1945, University of Wisconsin, 1961. *Member:* National Association of Secondary School Principals, National Council for Social Studies, National Education Association, Association for Supervision and Curriculum Development, Illinois Council of Social Studies, Illinois Education Association, Phi Delta Kappa, Kappa Delta Pi, Masons.

WRITINGS: (With Eugene Cottle) *Social Studies in the Secondary Schools,* McGraw, 1952; (with V. Randolph) *Teaching Elementary School Social Studies,* W. C. Brown, 1957; *Social Studies in the Elementary Schools,* W. C. Brown, 1958; *Teaching of Social Studies* (bibliography), Southern Illinois University Press, 1959.

(With others) *Secondary Education,* W. C. Brown, 1963; (with Edith McCall and Ruth Gue) *You and the Community,* Benefic, 1963; (with McCall and Gue) *You and the Neighborhood,* Benefic, 1963; (with McCall and Gue) *You Are Here,* 1963; (with McCall and Floyd Cunningham) *You and Regions Near and Far,* Benefic, 1964; (with McCall and Cunningham) *You and the United States,* Benefic, 1964; (with McCall and Cunningham) *You and the Americas,* Benefic, 1965; (with McCall and Cunningham) *You and the World,* Benefic, 1966. Author of curriculum guides and tests. Contributor to education journals.†

*   *   *

SAMUEL, Yeshue   1907-
(Athanasius Y. Samuel)

PERSONAL: Born December 25, 1907, in Hilwah, Syria; son of Soumay (a farmer) and Khatoun (Malky) Samuel. *Education:* Studied at St. Mark's Syrian Orthodox Seminary, Jerusalem, 1923-29, 1932-36, and Coptic College, Cairo, 1927-29. *Home and office:* 293 Hamilton Pl., Hackensack, N.J. 07601.

CAREER: Archbishop of Syrian Orthodox Church in the United States and Canada, with ecclesiastical title of Mar Athanasius (Mar Athanasius Yeshue Samuel, Archbishop). Fled Syria with mother at close of World War I, and lived in an orphanage in Adana, 1918-20; admitted to St. Mark's Syrian Orthodox Monastery in Jerusalem, 1923, ordained a novice of the Syrian Orthodox Church of Antioch, 1926, and elevated to the priesthood, 1932; remained at St. Mark's Seminary in Jerusalem, 1932-45, doing administrative and educational work; Archbishop and Metropolitan of Palestine and Transjordan, 1946-48; Archbishop (apostolic delegate) in the United States and Canada, beginning 1949, with headquarters at St. Mary's Church, West New York, N.J., 1949-54, and in Hackensack, N.J., beginning 1954. Toured Syrian Orthodox churches of India with Patriarch Elias III, 1931-32, and churches in South America with Patriarch Ignatius Jacob III, 1958; delegate to World Council of Churches, New Delhi, 1961, Uppsala, 1968.

WRITINGS: (Under name Athanasius Y. Samuel) *Treasure of Qumran: My Story of the Dead Sea Scrolls,* Westminster, 1966. Author of a series of Syriac-Aramaic textbooks published by St. Mark's Printing Press (Jerusalem), 1939-45. Also translator of the Liturgy of St. James,

1967 and rituals of the Syrian Orthodox Church of Antioch, 1974.

SIDELIGHTS: In 1947, while Archbishop of Palestine and Transjordan, Yeshue Samuel succeeded in purchasing four Dead Sea Scrolls, which were discovered in a cave northwest of the Dead Sea—an event, he says, "that changed my entire life." He carried the Dead Sea Scrolls with him on his voyage to America in 1949.

* * *

SANDERS, Jennings B(ryan)   1901-

PERSONAL: Born March 18, 1901, in Martin County, Ind.; son of Jefferson D. (a merchant) and Emma (Horsey) Sanders; married Mary Purviance, June 6, 1923. *Education:* Franklin College of Indiana, A.B., 1923; University of Chicago, A.M., 1925, Ph.D., 1928. *Politics:* Democrat. *Religion:* Baptist. *Home:* 10408 Hebard, Kensington, Md. 20795.

CAREER: Denison University, Granville, Ohio, assistant professor of history, 1926-27; University of Chicago, Chicago, Ill., instructor in history, 1928-30; University of Alabama, Tuscaloosa, 1930-35, began as assistant professor, became associate professor of history; University of Tennessee, Knoxville, professor of history and chairman of department, 1935-43; Memphis State College (now University), Memphis, Tenn., president, 1943-46; University of Washington, Seattle, acting professor of history, 1947; U.S. Office of Education, Washington, D.C., specialist in college history and social sciences, 1948-59; independent research historian, beginning 1959. *Military service:* U.S. Army, 1942-43. *Member:* American Historical Association, Southern Historical Association. *Awards, honors:* LL.D., Franklin College of Indiana, 1953.

WRITINGS: The Presidency of the Continental Congress, privately printed, 1930; *Evolution of Executive Departments of the Continental Congress, 1774-1789,* University of North Carolina Press, 1935; *Early American History, 1492-1789,* Prentice-Hall, 1938, reprinted, Scholarly Press, 1971; *A College History of the United States,* two volumes, Row, Peterson & Co., 1962; *Historical Interpretations and American Historianship,* Antioch Press, 1966. Contributor to professional journals.

WORK IN PROGRESS: A short history of the United States; essays on history and historiography.

* * *

SANDFORD, William P(hillips)   1896-1975

PERSONAL: Born October 27, 1896, in Champaign, Ill.; son of William Emanuel and Eva Regine (Phillips) Sandford; married Kathryn Selden Johnson, September 15, 1920; children: John William, Kathryn Frances, Priscilla (deceased), Susanna. *Education:* University of Michigan, A.B., 1920, A.M., 1923; Ohio State University, Ph.D., 1929. *Home:* 6124 Pershing Ave., St. Louis, Mo. 63112.

CAREER: University of Minnesota, Minneapolis, instructor in speech, 1920-21; Ohio State University, Columbus, instructor, 1921-25, assistant professor of speech, 1925-26; University of Illinois, Champaign, assistant professor, 1926-29, associate professor of speech, 1929-34; in business, 1934-41; Illinois Agricultural Association, director of sales service, 1941-46; St. Louis University, St. Louis, Mo., professor of speech, 1946-65, professor emeritus, 1965-75. *Military service:* U.S. Army, American Expeditionary Forces, 1917-19.

WRITINGS: (With W. H. Yeager) *Effective Business Speech,* McGraw, 1928, 4th edition, 1960; (with W. H. Yeager) *Principles of Effective Speaking,* Ronald, 1928, 6th edition, 1963; *English Theories of Public Address, 1530-1828,* H. L. Hedrick, 1931, 3rd edition, 1965; *Speak Well and Win,* McGraw, 1944; *Real Estate Salesman's Complete Ideas Handbook,* Prentice-Hall, 1958. Writer of sales manuals, guides, and training films.

WORK IN PROGRESS: Research on Jesuit rhetorics.†

(Died February, 1975)

* * *

SARETT, Alma (Johnson)   1908-

PERSONAL: Surname is pronounced Sa-*rett;* born July 21, 1908, in Durant, Fla.; daughter of Joseph Edward (a farmer) and Elizabeth (Barnes) Johnson; married Lew Sarett (poet, professor of speech, and professional lecturer), April 19, 1946 (died, 1954); married Clarence W. Anderson, July 3, 1969; stepchildren: Lewis H., Helen (Mrs. John Stockdale), Carter W., Beryl (Mrs. Robert Jackson), Jacqueline (Mrs. Louis Melchio). *Education:* Florida Southern College, B.S., 1934; Northwestern University, M.A., 1938, Ph.D., 1942. *Politics:* Democrat. *Religion:* Protestant. *Home:* 1810 Mapleleaf Blvd., Oldsmar, Fla. 33557.

CAREER: Florida Southern College, Lakeland, assistant professor of speech, 1936-40; Northwestern University, Evanston, Ill., instructor in speech, 1942-43; assistant professor of speech at State College of Iowa (now University of Northern Iowa), Cedar Falls, 1945-46, University of Florida, Gainesville, 1955-60; University of South Florida, Tampa, associate professor, 1960-64, professor of speech, 1964-70, professor emeritus, 1970—. Florida State Department of Education, member of Committee on Secondary School Curriculum in Speech and Dramatics, 1964-67. Florida Poetry Festival (annual), founder and director, 1964-70.

MEMBER: Speech Communication Association (member of legislative assembly, 1960-63), American Association of University Professors, Southern Speech Communication Association (member of executive council, 1939-40), Florida Speech Communication Association (executive secretary, 1938-39; president, 1939-40), Tau Kappa Alpha, Zeta Phi Eta, Alpha Psi Omega. *Awards, honors:* Recipient of first national Zeta of the Year Award, 1960; University of South Florida professor emeritus award, 1972.

WRITINGS: Jo's Boys (three-act play), Row, Peterson & Co., 1939; (editor) *Covenant with Earth: A Selection from the Poems of Lew Sarett,* University of Florida Press, 1956; (reviser) Lew Sarett and William Trufant, *Basic Principles of Speech* (college text), 3rd edition (Alma Sarett was not associated with earlier editions), Houghton, 1958, 4th edition, 1966. Two poems included in anthologies; contributor of short stories and numerous poems to magazines and newspapers, and monographs and articles to professional journals.

WORK IN PROGRESS: A fictionalized history of the Johnson-Johnston family from the first settlement in North Carolina in 1670 to the present; a test of reflective thinking ability.

AVOCATIONAL INTERESTS: Ceramic sculpture, painting, writing personal verse.

BIOGRAPHICAL/CRITICAL SOURCES: Cameo (published by Zeta Phi Eta), spring, 1958, fall, 1960; *Tampa Times,* July 20, 1963; *Florida Lives,* Historical Record Association, 1966.

SAUNDERS, John Turk 1929-1974

PERSONAL: Born October 26, 1929, in Cleveland, Ohio; son of Leroy R. (a salesman) and Adele (Turk) Saunders; married Marilynn Goldstein, September 12, 1952; married second wife, Valerie Neill, April 3, 1965; children: (second marriage) Sean Turk. *Education:* University of California, Los Angeles, B.A., 1956, Ph.D., 1961. *Religion:* Atheist. *Residence:* Los Angeles, Calif. *Office:* Department of Philosophy, California State University, Northridge, Calif. 91326.

CAREER: California State University, Northridge, instructor, 1960-61, assistant professor, 1961-64, associate professor, 1964-67, professor of philosophy, beginning 1967. Instructor in Extension Division, University of California, Los Angeles, beginning 1959. *Member:* American Philosophical Association. *Awards, honors:* American Council of Learned Societies fellow, 1967-68.

WRITINGS: (With Donald F. Henze) *The Private-Language Problem: A Philosophical Dialogue,* Random House, 1967. Contributor to philosophical journals.

WORK IN PROGRESS: A study of rationality for a book, *Standards of Rationality.*†

(Died March, 1974)

*   *   *

SAVAGE, Henry, Jr. 1903-

PERSONAL: Born August 1, 1903, in Camden, S.C.; son of Henry and Helen (Alexander) Savage; married Elizabeth C. Anderson, August 21, 1929 (died April 16, 1932); married Elizabeth Clarke Jones, October 7, 1933; children: (first marriage) William Henry; (second marriage) Carroll J. Elizabeth Hope, Virginia B., Samuel P., Henry III, Helen A. *Educaiton:* University of Virginia, B.S. and LL.B., 1926. *Home:* 1707 Lyttleton St., Camden, S.C. 29020. *Office:* Savage, Royall & Kinard, 1111 Church St. (P.O. Box 590), Camden, S.C. 29020.

CAREER: Admitted to South Carolina Bar, 1926; general practice of law in Camden, S.C., beginning 1926, as senior partner of Savage, Royall & Kinard, beginning 1953. Mayor of Camden, 1948-58. Pioneer in tree farming and still extensively engaged in it. Director of First Federal Savings & Loan Association, Camden, of Citizens & Southern National Bank of South Carolina, Camden, and of Hospital Service Plan, Columbia, S.C.; trustee of Ashley Hall School for Girls, Charleston, S.C., and Medical University of South Carolina, Charleston; University of South Carolina, member of advisory council; South Carolina Municipal Association, president, 1958. *Member:* South Carolina Bar Association, South Carolina Forestry Association (president, beginning 1969), Kershaw County Bar Association, Kershaw County Forest Protection Association (former chairman).

WRITINGS: America Goes Socialistic, Dorrance, 1933; *River of the Carolinas: The Santee,* Rinehart, 1956; *Seeds of Time: The Background of Southern Thinking,* Holt, 1959; *Lost Heritage,* Morrow, 1970.

AVOCATIONAL INTERESTS: Fishing, nature studies.

*   *   *

SAVAGE, Leonard J(immie) 1917-1971

PERSONAL: Born November 20, 1917, in Detroit, Mich.; son of Louis and Mae (Rugawitz) Savage; married second wife, Jean Strickland, July 10, 1964; children: (first marriage)

Sam L., Frank Albert. *Education:* University of Michigan, B.S., 1938, Ph.D., 1941. *Home:* 305 Lawrence St., New Haven, Conn.

CAREER: Cornell University, Ithaca, N.Y., instructor in mathematics, 1942-43; resident mathematician at Brown University, Providence, R.I., 1943-44, Columbia University, New York, N.Y., 1944-45, and New York University, New York, N.Y., 1945-46; Rockefeller fellow at Marine Biological Laboratory, Woods Hole, Mass., and University of Chicago, Chicago, Ill., 1946-47; University of Chicago, research associate, 1947-49, assistant professor, 1949-53, associate professor, 1953-54, professor of statistics, 1954-60, chairman of department, 1956-59; University of Michigan, Ann Arbor, professor of statistics, 1960-64; Yale University, New Haven, Conn., Eugene Higgins Professor of Statistics, 1964-71.

MEMBER: American Academy of Arts and Sciences, Institute of Mathematical Statistics (fellow; president, 1957-58), American Mathematical Society, American Statistical Association, International Statistical Institute. *Awards, honors:* Guggenheim fellow, Paris and Cambridge, 1951-52; Fulbright award to France, 1951-52.

WRITINGS: (With Milton Friedman) *Planning Experiments Seeking Maxima,* McGraw, 1947; (with others) *Sampling Inspection,* McGraw, 1948; *Foundations of Statistics,* Wiley, 1954, 2nd revised edition, Dover, 1972; (with Lester E. Dubins) *How to Gamble If You Must,* McGraw, 1965.

Contributor: *Abandoning an Experiment Prior to Completion,* McGraw, 1947; *La probabilita soggettiva nei problemi practici della statistica,* Instituto Matematico dell' Universita (Rome), 1959; Earl J. Hamilton and others, editors, *Landmarks in Political Economy,* University of Chicago Press, 1962; *The Foundations of Statistical Inference: A Discussion,* Wiley, 1962; R. Machol and P. Gray, editors, *Decision and Information Processes,* Macmillan, 1962; *La matematica negli instituti tecnici commerciali,* Ministry of Public Education (Rome), 1962; Henry E. Kyburg and Howard E. Smokler, editors, *Studies in Subjective Probability,* Wiley, 1964. Contributor to *Proceedings* of International Congress of Mathematicians, 1958, and to other symposia and journals.†

(Died November 3, 1971)

*   *   *

SAWYER, Charles 1887-

PERSONAL: Born February 10, 1887, in Cincinnati, Ohio; son of Edward Milton (a schoolteacher) and Caroline (Butler) Sawyer; married Margaret Johnston, July 15, 1918 (died July 6, 1937); married Elizabeth L. de Veyrac, June 10, 1942; children: (first marriage) Anne Sawyer (Mrs. John Bradley Greene), Charles, Jr. (deceased), Jean Johnston (Mrs. John Weaver), John, Edward. *Education:* Oberlin College, B.A., 1908; University of Cincinnati, LL.B., 1911. *Politics:* Democrat. *Religion:* Episcopalian. *Home:* 95 East Fountain Ave., Glendale, Ohio 45246. *Office:* Dixie Terminal Bldg., Cincinnati, Ohio 45202.

CAREER: Admitted to Ohio Bar, 1911, and to Bar of U.S. Supreme Court; practice of law in Cincinnati, Ohio, beginning 1911, currently partner in law firm of Taft, Stettinius & Hollister. Member of City Council, Cincinnati, 1911-15; Lieutenant Governor of Ohio, 1933-34; member of Democratic National Committee, 1936-44; Democratic candidate for governor of Ohio, 1938 (defeated by John Bricker); U.S. Ambassador to Belgium and Minister to Luxembourg, 1944-

45; member of President's Loyalty Review Board, 1947-48; U.S. Secretary of Commerce, 1948-53. Former owner of eighteen newspapers in Ohio; currently owner of radio stations in Dayton, Springfield, and Columbus, Ohio, in Louisville, Ky., and in Milwaukee, Wis.; chairman of the board, Coney Island, Inc.; director of numerous corporations. Former member of Hoover Commission Task Force, National Housing Council, National Munitions Control Board, Commission on Money and Credit, and a number of other government boards and commissions; former chairman of the board of United Appeal of Greater Cincinnati and leader in other civic enterprises. *Military service:* U.S. Army, 1917-19; served in France and Germany; became major.

MEMBER: American Bar Association, Ohio State Bar Association, Cincinnati Bar Association, Masons, American Legion, Veterans of Foreign Wars, Queen City Club (past president; member of board of governors), Cincinnati Country Club, Commercial Club and Commonwealth Club (both Cincinnati), National Press Club and Alfalfa Club (both Washington, D.C.), Everglades Club and Bath and Tennis Club (both Palm Beach). *Awards, honors:* LL.D., University of Cincinnati, 1950.

WRITINGS: Concerns of a Conservative Democrat (foreword by John L. Snyder and Dean Acheson), Southern Illinois University Press, 1968.

BIOGRAPHICAL/CRITICAL SOURCES: National Review, December 31, 1968; Alan F. Westin, *The Anatomy of a Constitutional Law Case: Youngstown Sheet and Tube Co. v. Sawyer, the Steel Seizure Decision,* Macmillan, 1968.†

*   *   *

SAYLES, E(dwin) B(ooth)   1892-
(Ted Sayles)

PERSONAL: Born May 14, 1892, in Abilene, Tex.; son of Henry (a lawyer) and Hattie (MacAlpine) Sayles; married Gladys Cheatham, January 19, 1918 (deceased). *Education:* Attended University of Texas, 1913-14; further study through extension courses at University of Texas and Columbia University. *Home:* 106 West Washington St., Tucson, Ariz. 85701.

CAREER: Sayles Co. (real estate), Abilene, Tex., secretary and office sales manager, 1919-31; Gila Pueblo (archaeological research), Globe, Ariz., archaeologist, 1931-42; Miami Cooper Co., Miami, Ariz., wartime development work, 1942-43; University of Arizona, Tucson, curator of Arizona State Museum, 1943-61, acting director of museum, 1949-50, assistant director of Field School of Archaeology, 1946-49. *Military service:* U.S. Army, Infantry, 1917-19; became captain; received Croix de Guerre. *Member:* Society for American Archaeology (fellow), American Anthropological Association (fellow), Arizona Archaeological and Historical Society, Sigma Xi, Tucson Camera Club (co-founder and president). *Awards, honors:* Cokesbury Juvenile Award, 1960, for *Throwstone, the First American Boy 25,000 Years Ago.*

WRITINGS: (With Mary Ellen Stevens) *Throwstone, the First American Boy 25,000 Years Ago* (juvenile), Reilly & Lee, 1960; (with Stevens) *Little Cloud and the Great Plains Hunters, 15,000 Years Ago* (juvenile), Reilly & Lee, 1962; (with Muriel Thayer Painter) *Faith, Flowers and Fiestas: The Yaque Indian Year, a Narrative of Ceremonial Events,* University of Arizona Press, 1962; (with Joan Ashby Henly) *Fantasies of Gold, Legends of Treasure and How They Grew,* University of Arizona Press, 1968. Also author with

others, *The Cochise Culture,* University of Arizona Press. Writer of a number of archaeological reports and articles published 1929-59; his photographs have been published in *American Anthropologist* and *Arizona Highways.*

WORK IN PROGRESS: Continuation of the "Ago Books," fictional stories based on archaeology and related sciences to tell the story of the settlement of America before Columbus for juvenile readers; research in the origins of legends and in the Spanish-Mexican relationship with the Anglo settlement west of the Mississippi River following the Mexican War of 1848.

BIOGRAPHICAL/CRITICAL SOURCES: Reader's Digest, August, 1949.††

*   *   *

SCHEINFELD, Aaron   1899-1970

PERSONAL: Born August 12, 1899, in Louisville, Ky.; son of Solomon I. and Sanna (Sachs) Scheinfeld; married Sylvia Rosenberg, September 5, 1924; children: James D., Ruth S. (Mrs. Stephen J. Pollak), Daniel R. *Education:* University of Wisconsin, LL.B. (later changed to Dr.Jur.), 1923.

CAREER: Attorney for a number of insurance companies, 1923-33; Scheinfeld & Winter (law firm), Chicago, Ill., and Milwaukee, Wis., senior partner, 1933-56; Manpower, Inc., Milwaukee, co-founder and chairman of the board, 1948-70. Co-founder, Sylvia and Aaron Scheinfeld Foundation; founding member, Center for the Study of Democratic Institutions; fellow, Aspen Institute; creator of Urban Opportunities Plan. *Member:* American Bar Association, Foreign Policy Association, Authors Guild, Wisconsin Bar Association, Illinois Bar Association, Arts Club and Cliff Dwellers (both Chicago), M & M Club.

WRITINGS: Get Ahead in Business!, Hawthorn, 1969.†

(Died September 23, 1970)

*   *   *

SCHINHAN, Jan Philip   1887-1975

PERSONAL: Surname is pronounced Shin-ann; born October 17, 1887, in Vienna, Austria; naturalized U.S. citizen; son of Adolph (director of a steamship company) and Hermine (Ublein-Stein) Schinhan; married Camilla von Egloffstein, July 12, 1915 (deceased); married second wife, Elizabeth Logan (a teacher), December 22, 1949; children: (first marriage) Philip Camill. *Education:* Studied music privately for two years, then at Church Music School, Regensburg, Bavaria, for one year, and at Munich Academy of Music, 1908-10; University of California, A.B., 1931, M.A., 1933; Columbia University graduate study, 1935-36; University of Vienna, Ph.D., 1937.

CAREER: Conductor for opera companies in Wurtemberg, Germany, 1911-13, and in Cincinnati, Ohio, 1913-15; private teacher of music, San Francisco, Calif., 1913-25; San Francisco Conservatory of Music, San Francisco, Calif., head of organ department, 1925-33; University of North Carolina, Chapel Hill, assistant professor, 1935-42, associate professor, 1942-46, professor of music, 1946-58, professor emeritus, 1958-75, director of Institute of Folk Music, 1958, member of advisory board of institute, beginning 1958. Visiting professor of music at Davidson College, Davidson, N.C., 1958-59, and Mars Hill College, Mars Hill, N.C., 1959-60. Guest organist, Palace of Legion of Honor, San Francisco, 1924-33; organ soloist, San Francisco Symphony Orchestra, 1930-33. Composer of more than eighty songs, including anthems.

MEMBER: International Society for Ethnology and Folklore, American Musicological Society, American Folklore Society, National Federation of Music Clubs (life member; archivist and chairman of folk music research, 1963-67), International Platform Association. *Awards, honors:* Benjamin Award in composition, 1959, for "Fantasy for Orchestra"; Award of Merit, National Federation of Music Clubs, 1966.

WRITINGS: (Editor) *Frank C. Brown Collection of North Carolina Folklore,* Duke University Press, Volume IV: *Music of the Ballads,* 1957, Volume V: *Music of the Folksongs,* 1962.

WORK IN PROGRESS: A work on the music of the Papago and Yurok.

AVOCATIONAL INTERESTS: Anthropology and archaeology.

BIOGRAPHICAL/CRITICAL SOURCES: Washington Post, March 29, 1975.†

(Died March 26, 1975)

*   *   *

SCHOLES, Walter V(inton)   1916-1975

PERSONAL: Born July 26, 1916, in Bradford, Ill.; son of John H. (a druggist) and Sadie (Sutherland) Scholes; married Marie Vielmetti (a writer), June 21, 1941. *Education:* Western Illinois University, student, 1934-36; University of Michigan, B.A., 1938, M.A., 1940, Ph.D., 1943. *Home:* 1515 Ross, Columbia, Mo. 65201. *Office:* Department of History, University of Missouri, Columbia, Mo. 65201.

CAREER: Stephens College, Columbia, Mo., assistant professor of history, 1943-45; University of Missouri, Columbia, assistant professor, 1945-50, associate professor, 1950-54, professor of history, beginning 1954. *Member:* American Historical Association.

WRITINGS: The Diego Ramirez Visita, University of Missouri, 1946; (editor) Jose F. Ramirez, *Mexico during the War with the U.S.,* University of Missouri, 1951; *Mexican Politics during the Juarez Regime, 1855-1872,* University of Missouri, 1957; (contributor) Norman A. Graebner, editor, *An Uncertain Tradition: American Secretaries of State in the Twentieth Century,* McGraw, 1961; (with wife, Marie V. Scholes) *Foreign Policies of the Taft Administration,* University of Missouri Press, 1970; *United States Diplomatic History: Readings for the Twentieth Century,* Volume II, Houghton, 1973.

WORK IN PROGRESS: Foreign Policies of Secretary of State, Charles Evans Hughes.†

(Died January 24, 1975)

*   *   *

SCHOLZ, Albert A(ugust)   1899-19(?)

PERSONAL: Born October 20, 1899, in Gottesberg, Germany; son of August and Anna (Hanel) Scholz; married Agnes Scholz, August 26, 1903; children: Conrad K. *Education:* Teachers College, Habelschwerdt, Germany, B.A., 1921; Columbia University, further study, 1929-30; Yale University, A.M., 1935, Ph.D., 1942. *Politics:* Republican. *Religion:* Roman Catholic. *Office:* Le Moyne College, Syracuse, N.Y. 13214.

CAREER: Bookkeeper and bank teller in Europe, 1921-25; laborer and streetcar motorman in Brooklyn, N.Y., 1926-27; Cherry Lawn School, Darien, Conn., teacher of French, German, and music, 1927-39; St. Louis University, St.

Louis, Mo., instructor in modern languages, 1939-45; Syracuse University, Syracuse, N.Y., assistant professor, 1945-47, associate professor of German, 1947-65, associate professor emeritus, beginning 1965; East Carolina University, Greenville, associate professor of German, 1965-67; Le Moyne College, Syracuse, N.Y., guest professor of German, beginning 1967. *Member:* Modern Language Association of America, American Association of Teachers of German (president of Central New York State branch, 1958-60), American Association of University Professors, New York State Federation of Foreign Language Teachers (treasurer, 1952-54), Syracuse Liederkranz (honorary member).

WRITINGS: Silesia Yesterday and Today, Nijhoff, 1964; *Luise Rinsers Leben und Werk: Eine Einfuehrung,* Peerless Press (Syracuse), 1968. Contributor of articles and reviews to *Music & Letters* and to language journals.†

(Deceased)

*   *   *

SCHRECK, Everett M.   1897-
(Richard Morrill)

PERSONAL: Born September 3, 1897, in Washington, Kan.; son of Benjamin Jacob (a farmer) and Lilian (Watkins) Schreck; married Dorothy Cashen (died August 30, 1976); children: Richard A., Phoebe A., Schreck-Pierce. *Education:* Kansas Wesleyan University, B.S., 1923; Kansas State University, M.S., 1925; Yale University, M.F.A., 1932; Cornell University, Ph.D., 1942. *Religion:* Episcopalian. *Home:* 1840 North Garfield Pl., Hollywood, Calif. 90028.

CAREER: Ohio State University, Columbus, associate professor, 1946-67. *Military service:* U.S. Army, 1918. *Member:* Actors' Equity Association, Screen Actors Guild, American Federation of Television and Radio Artists.

WRITINGS: Principles and Styles of Acting, Addison-Wesley, 1970.

*   *   *

SCHROEDER, Henry A(lfred)   1906-1975

PERSONAL: Born June 18, 1906, in Short Hills, N.J.; son of Henry Alfred (a merchant) and Natalie M(unde) Schroeder; married Jessie F. Keena, June 27, 1931 (divorced); married Janet Gregg Wallace (a sculptor), May 20, 1949; children: (first marriage) Henry Alfred, Jr., David A.; adopted children: Eugenie Wallace (Mrs. Marius S. Darrow). *Education:* Yale University, A.B., 1929; Columbia University, M.D., 1933. *Politics:* Independent liberal. *Religion:* Episcopalian. *Residence:* Ginseng Hill, West Brattleboro, Vt. 05301. *Office:* 9 Belmont Ave., Brattleboro, Vt. 05301.

CAREER: Presbyterian Hospital, New York City, intern, 1934-36; University of Pennsylvania Medical School, Philadelphia, research fellow in pharmacology, 1936-37; Hospital of Rockefeller Institute, New York City, assistant resident, 1937-39, assistant in medicine, 1939-42, associate in medicine, 1942-46; Washington University, St. Louis, Mo., associate professor of medicine, Medical School, and assistant physician, Barnes Hospital, 1946-58; Dartmouth College Medical School, Hanover, N.H., associate professor, 1958-66, professor of physiology, 1966-71, professor emeritus, 1971-75; Brattleboro Memorial Hospital, Brattleboro, Vt., director of research, 1965-75. Diplomate in cardiovascular disease, American Board of Internal Medicine,; diplomate in aviation medicine, American Board of Preventive Medicine. Consultant to U.S. Department of Defense, 1948-53, and U.S. Navy, 1949-51. Trustee of Marlboro College, 1960-61. Lay reader in Episcopal church, 1965-75. *Military service:* U.S. Naval Reserve, Medical Corps, active duty as flight surgeon, 1942-46; became commander.

MEMBER: American Medical Association, American Heart Association (fellow; member of board of directors, 1950-51), American College of Physicians (fellow), American Association for the Advancement of Science (fellow), Aero Medical Association (fellow), Gerontological Society, American Physiological Society, American Institute of Nutrition, Society for Experimental Biology and Medicine, American Society for Preventive Medicine, New York Academy of Sciences, New York Academy of Medicine, Harvey Society, Sigma Xi. *Awards, honors:* St. Louis College of Pharmacy and Chemistry Award, 1958; M.A., Dartmouth College, 1967.

WRITINGS: (With Laurance A. Peters) *Shirt-tail and Pigtail,* Minton, 1930; (with others) *Personality in Arterial Hypertension,* Josiah Macy, Jr. Foundation, 1945; *Hypertensive Diseases: Causes and Control,* Lea & Febiger, 1953; *Mechanisms of Hypertension,* C. C Thomas, 1957; *A Matter of Choice,* Stephen Greene, 1968; *Pollution, Profits, and Progress,* Stephen Greene, 1971; *Trace Elements and Man,* Devin-Adair, 1973; *The Poisons around Us: Toxic Metals in Food, Air, and Water,* Indiana University Press, 1974; *Elements in Living Systems,* Plenum, 1976.

Contributor to thirteen medical books, 1951-70. Contributor of more than two hundred articles to scientific and medical journals.

WORK IN PROGRESS: The A.B.C. of G., for Stephen Greene.

SIDELIGHTS: Henry Schroeder made a medical survey in the Orient, 1956-57; he traveled around the world in 1928 and 1933-34, and visited Europe many times.†

(Died April 20, 1975)

*   *   *

SCHULER, Edgar A(lbert)   1905-

PERSONAL: Born April 9, 1905, in Garner, Iowa; son of John Adam and Lydia (Schaeffer) Schuler; married Kathryn Etta Reinhart, August 31, 1932; children: John Hampton, Virginia Ruth, Kathryn Lydia. *Education:* Morningside College, A.B., 1928; University of Minnesota, A.M., 1929; Harvard University, Ph.D., 1933; Thammasat University, Bangkok, Thailand, postdoctoral study, 1957-58. *Politics:* Democrat. *Religion:* Methodist. *Home:* 629½ East University, Wooster, Ohio 44691.

CAREER: Louisiana State University, Baton Rouge, instructor, 1933-36, assistant professor of sociology, 1937-43; U.S. Department of Agriculture, Bureau of Agricultural Economics, senior social scientist, 1943-46; Michigan State University, East Lansing, associate professor of sociology and associate director of social research service, 1946-49; Wayne State University, Detroit, Mich., professor of sociology and anthropology and chairman of department, 1949-59; Michigan State University, professor of education, sociology, and anthropology, 1959-72, professor emeritus, 1972—. Ford Foundation Pakistan Project, adviser to Pakistan Academy for Village Development, 1959-62. *Member:* American Sociological Association, Rural Sociological Society, American Civil Liberties Union, American Association of University Professors. *Awards, honors:* Fulbright scholar, 1957-58.

WRITINGS: Social Status and Farm Tenure: Attitudes and Social Conditions of Corn Belt and Cotton Belt Farmers, [Washington], 1938; *Survey of Radio Listeners in Louisiana,* Louisiana State University, 1943; (with Robert J. Mowitz and Albert J. Mayer) *Medical Public Relations of the Public Relations Program of the Academy of Medicine of Toledo and Lucas County, Ohio,* [Detroit], 1952; (editor with Duane L. Gibson, Thomas F. Hoult, and Wilbur B. Brookover) *Outside Readings in Sociology,* Crowell, 1952, 2nd edition published as *Readings in Sociology,* 1960, 5th edition, 1974; (with Vibul Thamavit) *Public Opinion Among Thai Students: A Study of Opinions, Attitudes and Values Held by a Random Sample of Students in Colleges and Universities, Thailand, 1958,* Thammasat University, 1958; (with Raghu Singh) *The Pakistan Academies for Rural Development, Comilla and Peshawar,* Michigan State University, 1965; (with wife, Kathryn R. Schuler) *Public Opinion and Constitution Making in Pakistan, 1958-1962,* Michigan State University Press, 1967.

*   *   *

SCHULTZ, George F(ranklin)   1908-

PERSONAL: Born March 14, 1908, in Columbia City, Ind. *Education:* U.S. Naval Academy, B.S., 1931; Indiana University, A.B., 1950, A.M., 1955; University of Michigan, A.M., 1956. *Religion:* Lutheran.

CAREER: Career officer in U.S. Navy, 1927-40, retired for physical disability with rank of lieutenant; Vietnamese-American Association (sponsored by U.S. Information Agency), Saigon, Vietnam, director, 1956-58; Purdue University, Lafayette, Ind., associate professor of Russian and chairman of department, 1959-62. *Member:* American Association of Teachers of Slavic and East European Languages (president, Indiana chapter, 1961).

WRITINGS: Vietnamese Legends, Tuttle, 1965. Contributor of legends and articles to *Viet-My* (journal of Vietnamese-American Association).

WORK IN PROGRESS: Vietnamese Fairy Tales and *Vietnamese Folktales.*††

*   *   *

SCHULZ, Florence   1908-

PERSONAL: Born November 3, 1908, in Chicago, Ill.; daughter of Frederick Ernst and Flora Aurora (Reinhardt) Stolley; married Burton A. Schulz (an assistant building manager), February 8, 1930; children: Kenneth Burton, Constance Mary (Mrs. Glenn R. Wiesner), James Alan, Roger Carl. *Education:* Took special courses at Northwestern University, University of Chicago, and National College of Education, between 1926-67, accumulating about two years of college credits. *Politics:* Democrat. *Religion:* United Church of Christ. *Home:* 842 Oak St., Winnetka, Ill. 60093.

CAREER: Did catalog and advertising work, Chicago, Ill., 1926-30; church secretary, Glenview, Ill., 1945-50; nursery school teacher in Winnetka (Ill.) Public Schools, 1957-67. Teacher in laboratory schools for church school teachers in Illinois, Minnesota, and Michigan, 1955-65. *Member:* National Association for the Education of Young Children.

WRITINGS—Juveniles: Tim, United Church Press, 1961; *And Jesus Was Born,* United Church Press, 1961; *Twinkle Loon,* United Church Press, 1961; *No and Yes,* United Church Press, 1962; *Mr. Right-Hand Man,* United Church Press, 1962; *They Came to See Jesus,* United Church Press,

1962; *Sunday Morning,* Covenant Life Curriculum Press, 1965; *I Am Andrew,* Covenant Life Curriculum Press, 1965; *Who Is Jesus?,* Covenant Life Curriculum Press, 1965; *Families and Friends,* Covenant Life Curriculum Press, 1965; *Nobody Else Is Just Like Me,* Covenant Life Curriculum Press, 1966.

Guides and other teacher's books: *Summer with Nursery Children,* Pilgrim Press, 1958; *Growing in the Fellowship,* United Church Press, 1961; *Living in the Christian Community,* United Church Press, 1962; *Friends and Neighbors,* Pilgrim Press, 1962; *Claiming the Inheritance,* Covenant Life Curriculum Press, 1965; *Preschool Children in School,* Covenant Life Curriculum Press, 1965. Author of other instructional material, and contributor to religious education journals.

WORK IN PROGRESS: Studies in learning and development before the age of five.††

*   *   *

SCHWARTZ, Delmore   1913-1966

PERSONAL: Born December 8, 1913, in Brooklyn, N.Y.; son of Harry and Rose (Nathanson) Schwartz; married Gertrude Buckman; married second wife, Elizabeth Pollet, 1949. *Education:* Attended University of Wisconsin, 1931; New York University, B.A. in philosophy, 1935; attended Harvard University, 1935-37.

CAREER: Editor of *Mosaic* (a little magazine) while still a student; Harvard University, Cambridge, Mass., Briggs-Copeland Instructor in English Composition, 1940, assistant professor of English composition, 1946-47; *Partisan Review,* New Brunswick, N.J., editor, 1943-47, associate editor, 1947-55; associated with *Perspectives,* a Ford Foundation publication, 1952-53; poetry editor of *New Republic,* 1955-57. Visiting lecturer at New York University, Kenyon School of English, Indiana School of Letters, Princeton University, and University of Chicago; visiting professor, Syracuse University. Literary consultant to New Directions (publishers). *Awards, honors:* Guggenheim fellow, 1940 and 1941; National Institute of Arts and Letters grant in literature, 1953; *Kenyon Review* fellow, 1957; Levinson Prize (*Poetry*), 1959; Bollingen Prize in poetry, 1959, and Shelley Memorial Award, 1960, both for *Summer Knowledge.*

WRITINGS: In Dreams Begin Responsibilities (story, poem, lyrics, and a play), New Directions, 1938; (translator) Jean Rimbaud, *A Season in Hell,* New Directions, 1939, 2nd edition, 1940; *Shenandoah* (one-act verse play; produced Off-Off Broadway at American Theatre Club, April, 1969), New Directions, 1941; *Genesis, Book I* (prose and poetry), J. Laughlin (New York), 1943; *The World is a Wedding* (stories), New Directions, 1948.

Vaudeville for a Princess, and Other Poems, New Directions, 1950; (with John Crowe Ransom and John Hall Wheelock) *American Poetry at Mid-Century,* Gertrude Whittall Poetry and Literature Fund, 1958; *Summer Knowledge: New and Selected Poems, 1938-1958,* Doubleday, 1959, published as *Selected Poems: Summer Knowledge, 1938-1958,* New Directions, 1967; *Successful Love, and Other Stories,* Corinth, 1961; (compiler and author of foreword) *Syracuse Poems, 1964,* Department of English, Syracuse University, 1965; *Selected Essays of Delmore Schwartz,* edited by Donald A. Dike and David H. Zucker, University of Chicago Press, 1970. Author of an unpublished manuscript, "The Imitation of Life, and Other Problems of Literary Criticism." Contributor to *New York Times Book Review, Commentary, New Yorker, Poetry, Southern Review,* and other publications.

SIDELIGHTS: Delmore Schwartz had, writes Alfred Kazin, "a feeling for literary honor, for the highest standards, that one can only call *noble*—he loved the nobility of example presented by the greatest writers of our century, and he wanted in this sense to be noble himself, a light unto the less talented.... So he suffered, unceasingly, because he had often to disappoint himself—because the world turned steadily more irrational and incomprehensible—because the effort of his intellectual will, of his superb intellectual culture, was not always enough to sustain him.... He was the prisoner of his superb intellectual training, a victim of the logic he respected beyond anything else. He was of the generation that does not come easily to concepts of the absurd...."

Mental illness had haunted him for approximately twenty years. Marlene Nadle reported that it sent him "in and out of sanatoriums and into and out of the isolation of hotel rooms. It was an illness he accepted almost fatalistically." "Lost he was," said Kazin, "but he was not enough 'lost' in the demonic poet's tradition of losing himself to this world and finding himself in a richer world of private vision.... He was not a seer, not a visionary of 'the lost traveller's dream under the hill,' of the 'holy madness' that Yeats claimed to find in Ireland itself—the madness that Christopher Smart knew, and Hoelderlin, and Blake."

He possessed a dazzling intellect that was equally fascinated by the ideas of Marx and Freud and by popular culture. He spoke quickly and emotionally, his words often running together, and was once clocked talking for eight hours straight. After the death of Dylan Thomas he inherited the role of house poet at the White Horse Tavern in New York. He was known to amuse his friends with a dialogue in which he played both himself and T. S. Eliot. He could turn his humor on himself; Miss Nadle recalls how "he couldn't quite see Delmore as a name for a nice Jewish boy. To explain this exotic happening he embroidered elaborate tales about his being named after a Tammany politician. Other times the story would be that he was named after a pullman car, or a building on Riverside Drive."

Kazin remembers him as one who "believed in nothing so much as the virtue and reason of poetry.... In Delmore's world of writer-heroes, none was greater than Joyce. [Schwartz was known to carry with him a heavily-annotated copy of *Finnegans Wake.*] Joyce, after all, had proved that naturalist art could attain to the condition of poetry. But beyond this intense loyalty to the great modern tradition—this was Delmore's religion and his faith—it was his need to be intellectually *serious,* in his favorite form of irony, that explains the extraordinary style of *The World is a Wedding.*"

His view of life was a tragic one. Morton Seiff called him a "desperate counterpart of Rimbaud.... Both are aware that the supports of their respective cultures are tottering and new beliefs must be found to nourish the religious impulse of man." He wrote of the city, about which he had no illusions. He was "concerned with fundamentals, with the problem of identity, of knowledge and belief, haunted by the noise time makes, able to write wittily and movingly," according to Babette Deutsch. He chose as his theme "the wound of consciousness," he once said, and he wanted to show the miraculous character of daily existence. M. L. Rosenthal has said that Schwartz "has many moments of pure music to offer, and some moments in which he speaks in the accents of greatness, and he holds us even in his failures with the honesty and contemporaneity of his voice."

He died, ostensibly of a heart attack, outside a stranger's door with no one to come to his aid. For three days no one came to claim his body. His friends, who reported that he had dropped out of sight for a year prior to his death, learned of his death by reading the obituaries. He died at the Columbia Hotel in New York, in the city whose artifacts were contributing to "our anguished diminution until we die."

In 1975, when Saul Bellow's novel, *Humboldt's Gift*, was published by Viking, Karyl Roosevelt stated that Humboldt is "a thinly disguised portrait of the late poet Delmore Schwartz, with whom Bellow had a complex friendship in real life." Walter Clemmons and Jack Kroll wrote of that same character as "a loving portrait of Delmore Schwartz, whose precocious early poems prefigured the flowering of the powerful generation of poets who came to the fore in the '40s—Robert Lowell, Randall Jarrell, John Berryman. A woman who remembers Schwartz's electrifying youth says that Humboldt's talk in this novel brings him back with heartbreaking clarity."

BIOGRAPHICAL/CRITICAL SOURCES: New York Herald Tribune Books, March 5, 1939; *Saturday Review*, April 29, 1939; *Poetry*, May, 1939, February, 1960, December, 1966; *New York Times Book Review*, November 5, 1950; *Commentary*, December, 1950; *Jewish Social Studies*, October, 1951; *New Republic*, November 9, 1959; *Nation*, June 11, 1960; *Village Voice*, July 21, 1966; *Publisher's Weekly*, July 25, 1966; *Book Week*, October 9, 1966; *Books Abroad*, spring, 1967; *Contemporary Literary Criticism*, Gale, Volume II, 1974, Volume IV, 1975.†

(Died July 11, 1966)

*   *   *

SCOTT, Clinton Lee 1890-

PERSONAL: Born September 28, 1890, in Newport, Vt.; son of Robert Dent (a farmer) and Florence (Rexford) Scott; married second wife, Mary Slaughter (a curator of Innes paintings), October 2, 1930; children: (first marriage) Florence (Mrs. Wilfred Tapper), Martha (Mrs. Tom Coble); (second marriage) Peter Lee. *Education:* Goddard Seminary (now Goddard College), student, 1908-09; Tufts University, A.B., 1913, S.T.B., 1915; graduate study at Harvard University and University of Chicago, 1915-17, and University of Southern California, 1925-26. *Politics:* Democrat. *Residence:* Mattapoisett, Mass. 02739.

CAREER: Universalist clergyman; minister in Buffalo, N.Y., 1916-20, Philadelphia, Pa., 1920-23, Los Angeles, Calif., 1923-28, Atlanta, Ga., 1928-31, Peoria, Ill., 1931-40; superintendent of Universalist churches in Massachusetts and Connecticut, 1942-57. Trustee of Universalist conventions, 1929-37, and of Unitarian Universalist Association, 1961-65. Director of Peoria (Ill.) Sunday Evening Forum, 1930-40; co-founder of National Research Forum, 1935. *Member:* Theta Delta Chi, Masons (32nd degree). *Awards, honors:* D.D. from St. Lawrence University, 1930; Founders Award of American Humanist Association, 1963.

WRITINGS: Parish Parables, Murray Press, 1946; *Religion Can Make Sense*, Universalist Publishing House, 1949; *The Universalist Church of America: A Short History*, Universalist Historical Society, 1957; *These Live Tomorrow*, Beacon, 1964. Editor, *Messenger*, 1931-37, *Cape Ann Universalist*, 1942-46, and *Universalist Trumpet*, 1946-57.

AVOCATIONAL INTERESTS: Civil rights, birth control, human relations, United Nations.††

SCOTT, Dan
[Collective pseudonym]

WRITINGS—"Bret King" series; published by Grosset: *The Mystery of Ghost Canyon*, 1960; *The Mystery of Rawhide Gap*, 1960; *The Range Rodeo Mystery*, 1960; *The Secret of Hermit's Peak*, 1960; *The Secret of Fort Pioneer*, 1961; *The Mystery at Blizzard Mesa*, 1961; *The Mystery of Comanche Caves*, 1962; *The Phantom of Wolf Creek*, 1963; *The Mystery of Bandit Gulch*, 1964.

SIDELIGHTS: See **ADAMS, Harriet S., STRATEMEYER, Edward L.,** and **SVENSON, Andrew E.†**

*   *   *

SCOTT, Lalla (McIntosh) 1893-

PERSONAL: Born January 25, 1893, in Collins, Miss.; daughter of Dan (a lawyer) and Venia (Tarver) McIntosh; married Andrew Humbert Scott (an assayer for the U.S. Government), December 29, 1920 (deceased). *Education:* Belhaven College, Certificate in Expression, 1908; studied at Curry College, 1909, 1911, and Posse School of Gymnastics, Boston, Mass., 1919. *Politics:* Democrat. *Religion:* Methodist. *Home:* 475 13th St., Lovelock, Nev. 89419.

CAREER: Roswell (N.M.) public schools, supervisor of physical education, 1919-21; during Depression taught classes in physical education and literature under the Works Progress Administration; director of local talent plays in a number of communities where she has lived. *Member:* National League of American Pen Women, Lovelock Study Club (charter member).

WRITINGS: Karnee—A Paiute Narrative, University of Nevada Press, 1966.

WORK IN PROGRESS: Research for a biography of her husband, *My Scotty: A Man of Mystery*, and for her autobiography.††

*   *   *

SCOTT, Natalie Anderson 1906-
(Natalie B. Sokoloff)

PERSONAL: Born September 7, 1906, in Ekaterinoslav, Ukraine, Russia; came to United States in 1915, naturalized in 1942; daughter of Boris Kamyshansky (an inventor) and Nadjeshda (Mochugovskai) Sokoloff. *Education:* Educated at schools in England up to 1915, and then in New Jersey. *Politics:* "Vote for personalities." *Religion:* Greek Orthodox. *Residence:* Larchmont, N.Y.

CAREER: Worked at various jobs, including salesgirl and hostess until publication of first short story in 1929; wrote stories for *Adventure*, 1929-35; novelist, beginning 1935. Contributor of articles and reviews to periodicals. *Member:* Authors Guild. *Awards, honors:* First prize for short story (her first published) in a small magazine contest, 1929; Bread Loaf fellowship, 1935, for first novel, *So Brief the Years*.

WRITINGS: (Under name Natalie B. Sokoloff) *So Brief the Years*, Dodd, 1935; *The Sisters Livingston*, Dutton, 1945; *The Story of Mrs. Murphy* (Book-of-the-Month Club selection), Dutton, 1947, reprinted, Popular Library, 1971; *The Husband*, Dutton, 1949; *Romance*, Dutton, 1951; *The Little Stockade*, Dutton, 1954; *Salvation Johnny*, Doubleday, 1958; *Golden Trollop* (historical), Doubleday, 1961; *Firebrand: Push your Hair Out of your Eyes*, Ure Smith, 1968, Carolrhoda Books, 1969.

WORK IN PROGRESS: A new novel (theme is "The individual against the status quo").

SIDELIGHTS: "Wish I had time for travel or gardening," Miss Scott told CA, "but I write all the time, and since all my novels (except the historical *Golden Trollop*) are on controversial contemporary subjects, have to do a lot of research. Can't imagine greater joy than just writing."†

* * *

SEALOCK, Richard Burl 1907-

PERSONAL: Born June 15, 1907, in Lexington, Ill.; son of Burl H. (a clergyman) and Irene (Ridgley) Sealock; married Mary Margaret Morrow, September, 1932; children: Mary Margaret (Mrs. David Powell), David, Sarah (Mrs. Richard Amos). Education: Eureka College, A.B., 1929; University of Illinois, B.S. in L.S., 1930; Columbia University, M.S. in L.S., 1935. Religion: Presbyterian. Office: Forest Press, Albany, N.Y.

CAREER: Queens Borough Public Library, New York, N.Y., order assistant, 1930-32, general assistant, 1932-34, curator of Long Island Collection, 1934-39; Enoch Pratt Free Library, Baltimore, Md., head of department of history, travel, and biography, 1939-43; Gary Public Library, Gary, Ind., assistant librarian, 1943-45, librarian, 1945-49; Kansas City Public Library, Kansas City, Mo., librarian, 1950-68; Forest Press, Albany, N.Y., executive director, beginning 1968. Member: American Library Association (treasurer, 1956-60; second vice-president, 1963-64), Missouri Library Association (president, 1955; chairman of development committee, 1965-68), Rotary Club. Awards, honors: L.H.D., Eureka College, 1967.

WRITINGS: (With Grace Osgood Kelley and Harry Devereaux) *Woodside Does Read*, Queens Borough Public Library, 1933; (with P. A. Seely) *Long Island Bibliography*, privately printed, 1940; (with Seely) *Bibliography of Place Name Literature in United States and Canada*, American Library Association, 1948, 2nd edition, 1967. Contributor to professional journals.

WORK IN PROGRESS: Western American explorations; a history of printing in Missouri to 1876; development of music printed in Missouri; supplement to United States and Canada place name bibliography.

* * *

SEAMAN, Sylvia S(ybil)
(Francis Sylvin, a joint pseudonym)

PERSONAL: Born in New York, N.Y.; daughter of Nathaniel (in textiles) and Felicia (Bleet) Bernstein; married William Seaman (a research chemist); children: Gideon, Jonathan. Education: Cornell University, B.A.; Columbia University, M.A. Home: 244 West 74th St., New York, N.Y. 10023. Agent: Muriel Fuller, Box 193, Grand Central Station, New York, N.Y.

CAREER: Writer; former high school teacher of English in New York, N.Y., and book reviewer in Bound Brook, N.J. Recording for talking books, Congressional Library, division for the blind.

WRITINGS: (With Frances Schwartz, under joint pseudonym Francis Sylvin) *Rusty Carrousel*, Dutton, 1943; (with Frances Schwartz, under joint pseudonym Francis Sylvin) *Miracle Father*, McBride, 1952, published as *Test-Tube Father*, New American Library, 1968; *Always a Woman: What Every Woman Should Know About Breast Surgery*, Argonaut, 1965. Contributor of articles to newspapers and magazines.

WORK IN PROGRESS: A humorous book, *How to be a Jewish Grandmother*.

AVOCATIONAL INTERESTS: Travel (has visited more than 100 countries with husband).

* * *

SEIBEL, C(lifford) W(inslow) 1890-

PERSONAL: Born November 10, 1890, in Kansas City, Mo.; son of Richard M. and Lida (Kittle) Seibel; married Ruth Bowdle, December 22, 1915 (died, 1951); married Thelma Porter Pallette, November 29, 1952; children: (first marriage) Richard M. II, Margaret D. (Mrs. Frank P. Wilson, Jr.). Education: University of Kansas, B.S., 1913, M.S., 1915. Politics: Republican. Religion: Presbyterian. Home and office: 1520 Lamar, Amarillo, Tex. 79102.

CAREER: University of Kansas, Lawrence, instructor in chemistry, 1913-17; U.S. Bureau of Mines, 1917-59, began as junior gas chemist, established first helium analysis laboratory in Fort Worth, Tex., directed design and construction of four new helium plants during World War II, regional director in charge of six-state area, 1948-54, assistant director of Bureau of Mines, in charge of helium program, Washington, D.C., 1954-59. Member: American Chemical Society, Sigma Xi, Rotary Club, Cosmos Club (Washington, D.C.). Awards, honors: D.Sc., Texas Technological College (now Texas Tech University), 1937; Distinguished Service Award of U.S. Department of the Interior, 1954; National Civil Service Award, 1956; citation for distinguished service from University of Kansas Alumni Association.

WRITINGS: *Helium: Child of the Sun*, University Press of Kansas, 1968.

* * *

SELBY, Hazel Barrington 1889-1972

PERSONAL: Born March 8, 1889, in Grand Forks, N.D.; daughter of Frederick William and Alice Elizabeth (Ransier) Barrington; married Albert E. Selby, March 25, 1910; children: Jean (Mrs. John Mancieri), Anne (Mrs. Finch). Education: University of North Dakota, Teacher's Certificate. Politics: Democrat. Agent: McIntosh & Otis, Inc., 475 Fifth Ave., New York, N.Y. 10017.

CAREER: During her early career was a teacher, and advertising manager of *Broadcaster* (magazine); free-lance writer. Member: National League of American Pen Women. Awards, honors: First prize for poetry in national contest of National League of American Pen Women.

WRITINGS: *Stalks of Wind* (poetry), Humphries, 1941; *Home to My Mountains*, Van Nostrand, 1962. Contributor of short stories and features to anthologies and to national magazines, including *Town and Country*.

WORK IN PROGRESS: A book.†

(Died, 1972)

* * *

SELLERY, C. Morley 1894-

PERSONAL: Born August 6, 1894, in Guelph, Ontario, Canada; son of Samuel (a clergyman) and Margaret (Swann) Sellery; married Gladys I. Taylor, June 11, 1921; children: Bruce, Austin, Joan (Mrs. W. Allen Austill). Education: Queen's University, Kingston, Ontario, B.A., 1913, M.D., 1916. Home: 1467 Oakhurst Dr., Los Angeles, Calif. 90035.

CAREER: Physician; superintendent of Indian Reserve Hospital, Norway House, Manitoba, 1920-21, and Jenshow Hospital, Jenshow, Sze, China, 1921-27; Los Angeles

(Calif.) city schools, assistant director of health services, 1929-40, director of health education and health services, 1940-60. Former assistant clinical professor of preventive medicine and public health at College of Medical Evangelists, Loma Linda, Calif., and summer lecturer in school health administration at University of California, Los Angeles. *Military service:* Canadian Army, Medical Corps, 1916-19; became captain.

MEMBER: American Public Health Association (fellow), American School Health Association (fellow, past president), California School Health Association (past president), Southern California Public Health Association (past president), Los Angeles County Tuberculosis and Health Association (past president). *Awards, honors:* William A. Howe Award from American School Health Association, 1951.

WRITINGS: (With C. E. Turner and Sara Louise Smith) *School Health and Health Education,* Mosby, 1966. Contributor to *Journal of School Health.*††

* * *

SELVER, (Percy) Paul 1888-1970

PERSONAL: Born March 22, 1888; son of Wolfe and Catherine (Minden) Selver; married Maria Dunin-Vonsovitch. *Education:* University of London, B.A. (honors in English and German). *Religion:* Jewish. *Home:* 31 Ormsby Lodge, The Avenue, Bedford Park, London W.4, England. *Agent:* A. M. Heath & Co. Ltd., 40-42 William IV St., London, WC2N 4DD, England.

CAREER: Teacher in secondary schools in England, 1910-17; writer and translator. *Military service:* British Army, World War I; served in Infantry and Royal Engineers as interpreter of French and German languages, and finally in the War Office as an expert on the Czech language; demobilized with a disability pension.

WRITINGS: (Compiler) *An Anthology of Modern Bohemian Poetry,* H. J. Drane, 1912; (compiler, translator, and author of introduction) *Modern Russian Poetry* (Russian text and translation), Dutton, 1917; *Personalities* (in verse), Allen & Unwin, 1918; (compiler, translator, and author of introduction and notes) *Anthology of Modern Slavonic Literature in Prose and Verse,* Dutton, 1919; (compiler, translator, and author of introduction) *Modern Czech Poetry,* Dutton, 1920; *Otakar Brezina: A Study in Czech Literature,* Basil Blackwell, 1921; *Schooling* (novel), Jarrolds, 1924, Boni, 1925; *One, Two, Three* (novel), Jarrolds, 1926, Doran, 1927; *Czech Self Taught, by the Natural Method,* Marlborough & Co., 1927; *Private Life* (novel), Jarrolds, 1929, Harper, 1930; (compiler, translator, and author of introduction) *An Anthology of Czechoslovak Literature,* Paul, Trench, Trubner, 1929.

A Baker's Dozen of Tin Trumpets, and Two Others of Different Metal (sonnets and other poems), Stanley Nott, 1936; *Masaryk* (biography of Tomas Masaryk) introduction by Jan Masaryk, M. Joseph, 1940, reprinted, Greenwood Press, 1975; *Slovnicek Anglickeho Slangu* (glossary of English slang with Czech equivalents), Allen & Unwin, 1942; *Czechoslovak Literature: An Outline,* Allen & Unwin, 1942; (translator and author of introduction) *A Century of Czech and Slovak Poetry,* New Europe Publishing, 1946; *English Phraseology* (dictionary), Brodie, 1957, supplement published as *More English Phraseology,* 1965; *Orage and the New Age Circle: Reminiscences and Reflections,* Allen & Unwin, 1959; *The Art of Translating Poetry,* John Baker, 1966, Writer, Inc., 1967.

Translator: (And author of introduction, notes, and vocabulary) Anton P. Chekhov, *The Chameleon and Four Other Tales,* Paul, Trench, Trubner, 1916; Josip Kosor, *People of the Universe* (plays), 1917.

Sigrjohn Obstfelder, *Poems* (in Norwegian and English), Oxford University Press, 1920; Jens P. Jacobsen, *Poems* (in Danish and English), Oxford University Press, 1920; Joseph S. Machar, *The Jail,* Basil Blackwell, 1922; Karel Capek, *R.U.R.* (play), Oxford University Press, 1923, reprinted, 1961; Karel and Josef Capek, *'And so ad Infinitum': The Life of the Insects* (three-act play adapted for the English stage by Nigel Playfair and Clifford Bax), Oxford University Press, 1923, translation included in *International Modern Plays,* Dent, 1950; Karel Capek, *Letters from England,* Bles, 1925, reprinted, Allen & Unwin, 1957; Josef Capek, *The Land of Many Names,* Allen & Unwin, 1926; Karel Capek, *The Macropoulous Secret* (comedy), Holden & Co., 1927; Edvard Benes, *My War Memoirs,* Houghton, 1928; Emanuel Lesehradu, *Music of the Heart* (selected poems), [Prague], 1929; (and compiler and author of introduction) *An Anthology of Czechoslovak Literature,* Routledge, 1929.

Jaroslav Hasek, *The Good Soldier, Schweik,* Doubleday, 1930; Karel Capek, *Letters from Spain,* Bles, 1931, Putnam, 1932; Karel Capek, *Tales from Two Pockets,* Faber, 1932; Jan Welzl, *Thirty Years in the Golden North,* Macmillan, 1932; Karel Capek, *Letters from Holland,* Putnam, 1933; Edmond Konrad, *The Wizard of Menlo,* Bhat, 1935; Francis de Croisset, *The Wounded Dragon,* Bles, 1937; Genevieve R. Tabouis, *Blackmail or War,* 4th edition, Penguin, 1938; (translator and adapter with Ralph Neale) Karel Capek, *Power and Glory* (version of Capek's play, "The White Scourge"), Allen & Unwin, 1938, Macmillan, 1939; Jacqueline Vincent (pseudonym of R.M.J. Desmazieres), *And This, Our Life,* Bles, 1939.

Karel Capek, *The Mother* (play), Allen & Unwin, 1940, Macmillan, 1941; Vicki Baum, *Central Stores,* Bles, 1940; Johannes Urzidil Hollar, *A Czech Emigre in England,* Czechoslovak Independent Weekly, 1942; Vlado Clementis, *"Panslavism," Past and Present,* Czechoslovak Committee for Slav Reciprocity (London), 1943; Frantisek Kubka, *A Complicated Affair,* [Czechoslovakia and London], 1944; Theophile Gautier, the Elder, *Mademoiselle de Maupin,* Hamish Hamilton, 1948.

Aime Michel, *The Truth About Flying Saucers,* Criterion, 1956; (with Wade Baskin) Victor Alexandrov, *Khrushchev of the Ukraine,* Philosophical Library, 1957; Hans Kades (pseudonym of Hans Werlberger), *House of Crystal,* Angus & Robertson, 1957; Jean de La Fontaine, *The Fables of La Fontaine,* Brodie, 1961. Also translator of several educational books.

Former London correspondent, *Das Literarische Echo* (Berlin). Contributor to *Times Literary Supplement.*

SIDELIGHTS: Paul Selver attributed "such literary success as I have achieved" to his knowledge of the Czech language, which he greatly admired, both as a literary medium, and also in its colloquial aspect.

BIOGRAPHICAL/CRITICAL SOURCES: Times Literary Supplement, June 29, 1967; *Antiquarian Bookman,* May 25, 1970.†

(Died April 9, 1970)

* * *

SEOANE, Rhoda 1905-

PERSONAL: Born November 2, 1905, in Brooklyn, N.Y.;

daughter of William Gilman (a banker) and Rhoda (Howe) Low; married Consuelo Andrew Seoane (an army colonel), February 12, 1952 (died July 5, 1964). *Education:* Educated in New York, N.Y. *Religion:* Episcopalian. *Residence:* Topton, N.C. 28781.

CAREER: Artist; works exhibited at Argent Gallery, New York City, beginning 1946, Lynn Kottler Gallery, New York City, 1967, and Arts Club Washington, beginning 1969. *Member:* American Watercolor Society, Colonial Dames of America, Army and Navy Club, York Club, Ibizan Hound Club of America (president).

WRITINGS: The Whole Armor, Speller, 1965; *Uttermost East and the Longest War,* Vantage, 1968.

* * *

SEWALL, Mary Franklin   1884-19(?)

PERSONAL: Born July 14, 1884, in Seaford, Del.; daughter of George Ward (a civil engineer) and Mary Franklin (Cottingham) Sewall. *Education:* Kensington Hospital, Philadelphia, Pa., Diploma in Nursing, 1907; Columbia University, B.S., 1935. *Religion:* Religious Science.

CAREER: Registered nurse and teacher of nursing education, 1907-50; Methodist Hospital, Los Angeles, Calif., director of nursing education, 1944-50. *Military service:* U.S. Army, Nurse Corps, 1917-19; served at Base Hospital, Beaune, France. *Member:* American Nurses Association, National League for Nursing, Daughters of the American Revolution, American Legion.

WRITINGS: (With Elizabeth Jamieson) *Trends in Nursing History,* Saunders, 1940, 6th edition (with Suhrie), 1966.

WORK IN PROGRESS: A book on both ethical and historical aspects of nursing.†

(Deceased)

* * *

SHACKLEFORD, Bernard L.   1889-1975

PERSONAL: Born March 3, 1889, in Carroll County, Ga.; son of Richard Jones (a farmer) and Sallie (Jones) Shackleford; married Winnifred Madden; children: Winnifred P. (Mrs. Waverly S. Brown). *Education:* Fourth District A&M College (now West Georgia College), diploma, 1916; Mercer University, Premedical Certificate, 1917; Medical College of Georgia, M.D., 1921. *Politics:* Independent. *Religion:* Baptist. *Home:* 216 Broadland Ct. N.W., Atlanta, Ga. 30342.

CAREER: Taught school before beginning practice as a physician and surgeon in Georgia. *Member:* American Medical Association, International College of Surgeons, American College of Surgeons, Southern Medical Association, Georgia Medical Association, Fulton County Medical Association (former president).

WRITINGS: To My Patients and Friends: Poems, Scott-Roberts, 1968.†

(Died May 1, 1975)

* * *

SHAFFER, K(atherine) Stevenson   1902-

PERSONAL: Born November 20, 1902, in Clifton Heights, Pa.; daughter of Wilfred S. and Kate A. (Donnell) Stevenson; married William R. Shaffer, July 29, 1926 (died, 1964); children: Betty Shaffer Reichert, William Richard, Katherine Anne Reynal. *Education:* Studied piano and organ at Philadelphia Academy of Music, 1910-16; Ursinus College, B.S., 1925; also special study at University of Pennsylvania. *Home:* Snyder Rd., Green Lane, Pa. 18054.

CAREER: Teacher in Lansdowne, Pa., 1926, as substitute in Conover, N.C., and with La Cour Team in Japan, 1959. Lecturer and book reviewer. *Member:* National League of American Pen Women (vice-president of Philadelphia branch).

WRITINGS: Lift the Latch, Christian Education Press, 1963. Contributor of plays, poetry, and stories for children to religious magazines and other periodicals.

WORK IN PROGRESS: Children's stories.

SIDELIGHTS: Katherine Shaffer has traveled extensively in Europe, Holy Land, Latin America, United States, and the Far East, using materials gathered on trips as basis for illustrated lectures.††

* * *

SHAKABPA, Tsepon W(angchuk) D(edan)   1907-

PERSONAL: Given names, Wangchuk Dedan (Tsepon is a title); born January 11, 1907, in Lhasa, Tibet; son of Tashi Phuntsok Shakabpa. *Education:* Studied at Government Official Academy (lay school) in Tibet for nine years, and then privately for three years with scholars at two monasteries and with Co-ne Dge-bshes Rinpoche, Tibet's most famous scholar. *Home:* Shakabpa House, Kalimpong, West Bengal, India.

CAREER: Former Tibet government official, who went into exile in 1951 rather than collaborate with the Chinese. Government posts included: finance secretary of Tibet; leader of Tibetan trade delegation on world trip; leader of peace delegation in talks with Prime Minister Jawaharlal Nehru and the Chinese ambassador in Delhi; spokesman of Tibet National Assembly; assistant representative of the Dalai Lama at the United Nations debate on the Tibet question; representative of the Dalai Lama to the Government of India, New Delhi.

WRITINGS: Lord Buddha's Relics in Tibet, Baptist Mission Press (Calcutta), 1951; *Tibet, A Political History,* edited by Turrell V. Wylie, Yale University Press, 1967.

WORK IN PROGRESS: Further research on Tibetan history.

SIDELIGHTS: Tibet: A Political History was written in Tibetan, and then translated into English; the book carried the official approval of the fourteenth Dalai Lama. Shakabpa's research after retirement from active service to his government included histories of those countries—such as China, Sikkim, Ladakh, Bhutan, and Nepal—having relevance to the history of Tibet. He traveled over much of Asia, and in the United States, United Kingdom, France, West Germany, Switzerland, and Italy.

BIOGRAPHICAL/CRITICAL SOURCES: Times Literary Supplement (London), August 31, 1967.††

* * *

SHANK, Joseph E(lmer)   1892-

PERSONAL: Born April 18, 1892, in Dayton, Va.; son of Adam and Mary (Brunk) Shank; married Eloise Hill, September 13, 1921. *Education:* Attended public schools in Virginia. *Politics:* Independent. *Religion:* Presbyterian. *Home:* 1522 DeGrasse Ave., Norfolk, Va. 23509.

CAREER: Newspaperman in Virginia for almost fifty years, starting as reporter for *Harrisonburg Daily Times,* 1912; news editor of *Harrisonburg News-Record,* 1914-17, 1919-

20, and *News and Advance,* Lynchburg, 1920-22; variously city editor, news editor, and assistant managing editor of *Ledger-Dispatch* and *Ledger-Star,* Norfolk, 1922-58. *Military service:* U.S. Air Service, with duty in France, 1918; became sergeant major. *Member:* Norfolk Historical Society, Norfolk Round Table (president, 1967), Sigma Delta Chi, American Legion, Virginia Club.

WRITINGS: (With Lenoir Chambers) *Salt Water and Printer's Ink: Norfolk and Its Newspapers, 1865-1965,* University of North Carolina Press, 1967.

* * *

SHANK, Margarethe Erdahl 1910-

PERSONAL: Born July 21, 1910, in Turtle Lake, N.D.; daughter of Bertinus N. and Gyda (Jaastad) Erdahl; married Oliver Renolds Shank; children: Stephen Henry. *Education:* University of Arizona, B.A., 1931; University of California, Berkeley, extension study, 1940; Arizona State University, M.A., 1959. *Religion:* Lutheran. *Home:* 6011 West Pierson Circle, Phoenix, Ariz. 85033. *Office:* Glendale Community College, Glendale, Ariz.

CAREER: High school teacher of English in Chandler, Ariz., 1932-35, Chula Vista, Calif., 1942-45, and Phoenix, Ariz., 1958-59; instructor in English at Phoenix College, Phoenix, Ariz., 1959-65, and Glendale Community College, Glendale, Ariz., beginning 1965. *Member:* Authors Guild, Alpha Delta Kappa.

WRITINGS: The Coffee Train, Doubleday, 1953; *Call Back the Years,* Augsburg, 1966. Work anthologized in college texts, *Writing from Experience, Experience and Expression,* and *The Process of Creative Writing.*

WORK IN PROGRESS: A novel.

SIDELIGHTS: Margarethe Shank speaks Norwegian, and knows some German. *Avocational interests:* Norse mythology, the Viking Age, Anglo-Saxon history.

* * *

SHANKEL, George Edgar 1894-

PERSONAL: Born June 17, 1894, in Halifax, Nova Scotia, Canada; son of Stewart Wilson and Eva (Hubley) Shankel; married Win Osborn (a music teacher), June 17, 1919; children: Virginia (Mrs. Harvey L. Rittenhouse). *Education:* Walla Walla College, B.A., 1920; University of Washington, Seattle, M.A., 1933, Ph.D., 1945. *Home:* Kendall Hill Rd., Sterling, Mass. 01565.

CAREER: Canadian Union College, Lacombe, Alberta, instructor in English, 1921-25; Helderberg College, Somerset West, Cape Province, South Africa, instructor in English, 1925-33, president of college, 1934-42; Atlantic Union College, South Lancaster, Mass., dean, 1946-54; West Indies College, Mandeville, Jamaica, dean, 1954-56; Southern Missionary College, Collegedale, Tenn., dean, 1956-60; Columbia Union College, Takoma Park, Md., professor of history, 1960-62; Atlantic Union College, professor of history, 1963-72.

WRITINGS: God and Man in History, Southern Publishing, 1967.

* * *

SHAPPIRO, Herbert (Arthur) 1899(?)-1975
(Burt Arthur, Herbert Arthur, Arthur Herbert)

PERSONAL: Born circa 1899, in Texas; wife's name, Hortene; children: Budd (a writer under name Budd Arthur).

CAREER: Novelist. Also worked as a newspaperman, advertising agency executive, editor, screen writer, and playwright.

WRITINGS: The Black Rider, Arcadia, 1941; *The Valley of Death,* Arcadia, 1941; *Chenango Pass,* Arcadia, 1942; *Mustang Marshall,* Phoenix, 1943; *Trouble at Moon Pass,* Phoenix, 1943; *Silver City Agents,* Phoenix, 1944; *Gunsmoke Over Utah,* Phoenix, 1945 (published under pseudonym Burt Arthur, Macfadden, 1969); *Woman in the White House,* Tech Books, 1945; *High Pockets,* McBride, 1946 (published under pseudonym Burt Arthur, Macfadden, 1968); *The Texan,* McBride, 1946; *The Buckaroo,* Arcadia, 1947; *Boss of the Far West,* Phoenix, 1948 (published under pseudonym Burt Arthur, Macfadden, 1969); *Sheriff of Lonesome,* Phoenix, 1948; *The Long West Trail,* Phoenix, 1948.

Under name Burt Arthur: *Lead-Hungry Lobos,* Phoenix, 1945; *Nevada,* Doubleday, 1949, published as *Trigger Man,* New American Library, 1957; *Stirrups in the Dust,* Doubleday, 1950; *Trouble Town,* Doubleday, 1950; *Thunder Valley,* Doubleday, 1951; *The Drifter,* Ace, 1955; *Texas Sheriff,* Avalon, 1956; *Return of the Texan,* New American Library, 1956; *Gunsmoke in Nevada,* New American Library, 1957; (with son, Budd Arthur) *The Stranger,* Doubleday, 1959; *Swiftly to Evil,* Consul, 1961; *Quemado,* Wright & Brown, 1961; (with Budd Arthur) *Three Guns North,* R. Hale, 1962; (with Budd Arthur) *Big Red,* Signet, 1962; *Shadow Valley,* Wright & Brown, 1962; *Flaming Guns,* Paperback Library, 1964; (with Budd Arthur) *Ride a Crooked Trail,* Avon, 1964; (with Budd Arthur) *Requiem for a Gun,* Avon, 1964; *Sing a Song of Six-Guns,* Macfadden, 1964; *Empty Saddles,* Macfadden, 1964; *Two-Gun Outlaw,* Paperback Library, 1964; *Gun-Law on the Range,* Paperback Library, 1964; (with Budd Arthur) *Walk Tall, Ride Tall,* New American Library, 1965; *Gunsmoke in Paradise,* Macfadden, 1965; (with Budd Arthur) *Ride a Crooked Mile,* Avon, 1966; (with Budd Arthur) *Action at Truxton,* Avon, 1966; *The Free Lands,* New American Library, 1966; *Action at Ambush Flat,* Paperback Library, 1967; *Outlaw Fury,* Paperback Library, 1967; *Duel on the Range,* Paperback Library, 1967; *Silver City Rangers,* Macfadden, 1968; *Killer's Crossing,* Macfadden, 1969.

Under name Herbert Arthur: *The Killer,* Doubleday, 1952; *No Other Love,* Pleiades Books, 1952; *Action at Spanish Flat,* Allen, 1953.

Under name Arthur Herbert: *Bugles in the Night,* Rinehart, 1950; *The Gunslinger,* Rinehart, 1951; *Freedom Run,* Rinehart, 1951.

Also author of more than fifty additional westerns, and of numerous plays and screenplays, some in collaboration with his son, Budd Arthur.

SIDELIGHTS: Shappiro's books have been issued in many countries and in many languages, and he estimated that about thirty-two million copies of his books have been sold. Many of his books have been adapted for motion pictures and television.†

(Died March 15, 1975)

* * *

SHARMA, Shripad Rama 1879-

PERSONAL: Born August 8, 1879, in Mangalore, Mysore State, India; son of R. S. (a priest); children: R. S., V. S., Meera S. (Mrs. S. S. Kalbag). *Education:* Attended Bombay University. *Home:* 39/19 Ashraya, Kacharwadi, Poona 4, Maharashtra, India.

CAREER: University of Poona, Fergusson College, Poona, Maharashtra, India, professor of history, 1934-58. *Member:* Deccan Education Society (former secretary).

WRITINGS: Swami Rama Tirtha: The Poet Apostle of Practical Vedanta, Dharma Prakash Press, 1921, 2nd edition, Bharatiya Vidya Bhavan, 1965; *The Founding of Maratha Freedom,* 1934, revised edition, Orient Longmans, 1964; *A Bibliography of Mughal India,* Karnatak Publishing House, 1934, revised edition published as *Mughal Empire in India,* three volumes, 1940-41, 2nd revised edition, Lakshmi Narain Agarwal, 1966; *The Crescent In India: A Study in Medieval History* (partly abridged from *Mughal Empire in India*), Karnatak Publishing House, 1937, revised 3rd edition, Hind Kitabs, 1966; *A Brief Survey of Human History,* Karnatak Publishing House, 1938, 4th edition, 1963.

Janism and Karnataka Culture, N. S. Kamalapur, 1940; *Maratha History Re-examined, 1295-1707,* Karnatak Publishing House, 1944; *Our Educational Effort: Fergusson College through Sixty Years,* Karnatak Publishing House, 1945; *Ancient Indian History and Culture,* Hind Kitabs, c. 1945, 3rd revised edition, 1956; *Shivaji,* National Information and Publications (Bombay), 1947; *Our Heritage and Its Significance,* Hind Kitabs, 1947, revised edition, 1963.

The Making of Modern India, Orient Longmans, 1951, 2nd edition, 1965; *India as I See Her,* Lakshmi Narain Agarwal, 1956, published as *The Soul of Indian History,* Bharatiya Vidya Bhavan, 1967; *Wisdom beyond Reason,* Lakshmi Narain Agarwal, 1957.

Focus on Tukaram from a Fresh Angle, Popular Book Depot, 1962; *Our Human Heritage: A Synoptic Study,* Bharatiya Vidya Bhavan, 1964; *Tukaram's Teachings,* Bharatiya Vidya Bhavan, 1964; *Mughal Government and Administration,* Hind Kitabs, 1965. Also author of *Abkar the Great, Ranade: A Modern Mystic, Makers of Maratha History,* and *All about Akbar We Need to Know.*

* * *

SHARWOOD SMITH, Bryan Evers   1899-

PERSONAL: Born January 5, 1899, in Hull, England; son of Edward (a schoolmaster) and Lucy (Evers) Sharwood Smith; married Sylvia Powys-Smith, July 20, 1926; married second wife, Winifred Joan Mitchell, August 26, 1939; children: (first marriage) Sarah Elizabeth (Mrs. Victor Hibbs); (second marriage) Michael Anthony, Geoffrey Hugh, Angela Eve (Mrs. Colin D. J. Rennie). *Education:* Educated in Elstree, Hertsfordshire, England. *Religion:* Church of England. *Home:* 47 Cooden Dr., Bexhill on Sea, Sussex, England.

CAREER: St. Cuthbert's Preparatory School, Malvern, England, assistant master, 1920; entered British Colonial Service, 1920, and was administrative officer in the British Cameroons, 1920-27, and in Northern Nigeria, 1927-57; president of Northern Nigerian House of Assembly, 1950-52; lieutenant governor of Northern Nigeria and president of House of Chiefs, 1952-54, governor, 1954-57. *Military service:* Royal Flying Corps (now Royal Air Force), flying officer, 1917-20; served in France, on the Rhine, and in India. Nigerian Regiment, captain serving on intelligence duties, 1939-42. *Awards, honors:* Awarded Open Classical Scholarship to Emmanuel College, Cambridge University, 1917; not accepted. Companion of St. Michael and St. George, 1950; Knight Commander, Order of the British Empire, 1953; Knight Commander of St. Michael and St. George, 1954; Knight Commander of the Royal Victorian Order, 1956.

WRITINGS: Recollections of British Administration in the Cameroons and Northern Nigeria, 1921-1957: But Always as Friends, Duke University Press, 1969 (published in England as *But Always as Friends: Northern Nigeria and the Cameroons, 1921-1957,* Allen & Unwin, 1969).

* * *

SHELDON, Ann
[Collective pseudonym]

WRITINGS—"Linda Craig" series; published by Doubleday: *Linda Craig and the Clue on the Desert Trail,* 1962; *. . . and the Palomino Mystery,* 1962; *. . . and the Mystery of Horseshoe Canyon,* 1963; *. . . and the Secret of Rancho del Sol,* 1963; *. . . and the Ghost Town Treasure,* 1964; *. . . and the Mystery in Mexico,* 1964.

SIDELIGHTS: See **ADAMS, Harriet S., STRATEMEYER, Edward L.,** and **SVENSON, Andrew E.**†

* * *

SHEPHARD, Esther   1891-1975

PERSONAL: Born July 29, 1891, in Minneapolis, Minn.; daughter of John August (engaged in farming) and Justina (Lindberg) Lofstrand; married R. T. Shepherd, October 19, 1914 (died, 1915); married C. Ellis Shephard, December 16, 1921 (died February, 1938); children: (second marriage) Richard J. *Education:* University of Washington, Seattle, B.A., 1920, M.A., 1921, Ph.D., 1938. *Politics:* Democratic. *Religion:* None. *Home:* 55 South Sixth St., San Jose, Calif. 95112; Shepherd's Bush, Suquamish, Wash. 98392 (summer).

CAREER: Teacher in public schools of Minnesota and Montana; Reed College, Portland, Ore., instructor in English, 1921-22; University of Washington, Seattle, associate in verse and drama, 1928-30, summer, 1931; Lower Columbia College, Longview, Wash., professor of English, 1934-35; San Jose State University, San Jose, Calif., 1939-59, began as instructor, became professor of English, professor emeritus, 1959-75. *Member:* American Oriental Society, Modern Language Association of America, Renaissance Society of America, Shakespeare Association of America, California Folklore Society, Phi Beta Kappa.

WRITINGS: Paul Bunyan, McNeil Press, 1924, reprinted with illustrations by Rockwell Kent, Harcourt, 1926; *Pierrette's Heart* (play), Samuel French, 1924; (contributor) *Golden Tales of Our America,* Dodd, 1929, reprinted, 1963; *Walt Whitman's Pose,* Harcourt, 1938; *The Cowherd and the Sky Maiden,* Pacific Rim, 1950; *An Oriental Tale and a Romantic Poet,* Pacific Rim, 1967; *Selected Poems,* Pacific Rim, 1968. Short story included in *Golden Tales of Our America,* Dodd, 1929, reprinted, 1963. Also author of librettos for operas produced at University of Washington, Seattle, 1952 and 1958. Contributor to professional journals.

SIDELIGHTS: Esther Shephard learned Swedish from her parents, studied Latin and German in school, and Greek, French, Icelandic, and Chinese in graduate courses.

BIOGRAPHICAL/CRITICAL SOURCES: Golden Tales of Our America, Dodd, 1929, reprinted, 1963; *Christian Science Monitor Magazine,* June 10, 1945.†

(Died February 10, 1975)

* * *

SHER, Eva
PERSONAL: Born in New York, N.Y.; daughter of Jacob

(a farmer) and Anna (Abrahamson) Goldblatt; married Henry Sher (with Schenley Industries, Inc.), June 25, 1932; children: Lawrence, Joanne (Mrs. Stanley Scott Grumet). *Education:* Studied at Rutgers University, 1929-30, Newspaper Institute of America, 1946-47, New School for Social Research, 1953-54, 1955. *Politics:* Democrat. *Religion:* Jewish. *Home:* 713 Nantucket Circle, Lake Worth, Fla. 33460. *Agent:* Seligmann & Collier, 280 Madison Ave., New York, N.Y. 10016.

CAREER: Henry Sher Associates (interior decorators), New York, N.Y., vice-president and secretary, 1963-67. Lecturer and panelist on television and radio. *Member:* Hadassah (life member), Women's American ORT.

WRITINGS: Poetry—American Vanguard 1953, Dial, 1953; *Life with Farmer Goldstein,* Funk, 1967. Also editor of *Covered Bridge Reflections.*

WORK IN PROGRESS: A novel, *In Separate Compartments;* a book of poetry.

*   *   *

SHERMAN, T. P. 1917-1976

PERSONAL: Born November 20, 1917, in London, England; son of William (a printer) and Bridget (Donovan) Sherman; married Jessica Taylor, June 12, 1948; children: Catherine Mary, Michael James. *Education:* University of London, student, 1934. *Home:* 12 Lower Park Rd., Chester CH4 7BB, England. *Office:* Management Advisory Unit, Cheshire County Council, 54 Nicholas St., Chester, England.

CAREER: London County Council, London, England, personnel, training, organization, and methods officer, 1934-59; Cheshire County Council, Chester, England, director of organization and methods, and then of management advisory unit incorporating work study and operational research, beginning 1959. Lecturer on management topics. *Military service:* British Army, Intelligence Corps, 1943-46; became captain. Territorial Army, 1947-52. *Member:* Organization and Methods Society, Local Government Work Study Group (national chairman, 1970).

WRITINGS: O and M in Local Government, Pergamon, 1969. Contributor to periodicals.

WORK IN PROGRESS: General and continual research into ways of improving management and administration.

SIDELIGHTS: T. P. Sherman told *CA* that he was a "fervent believer in [the] importance of high productivity/efficiency in helping to improve [the] standard of living nationally and globally." His travels included the Far East, U.S., Canada, and Middle East.†

(Died August 2, 1976)

*   *   *

SHERWOOD, Michael 1938-1976

PERSONAL: Born August 23, 1938, in Milwaukee, Wis.; son of Samuel Schefrin and Lillian (Friedland) Franklin. *Education:* Princeton University, A.B. (summa cum laude), 1960; Oxford University, B.Litt., 1965; Harvard University, M.D. (magna cum laude), 1967. *Religion:* None. *Home:* 9 Knox St., Boston, Mass. 02116.

CAREER: Massachusetts Mental Health Center, Boston, resident physician, beginning 1968; Harvard Medical School, Boston, teaching fellow in psychiatry, beginning 1968. Co-owner of Nine Knox Restaurant, Boston, and Casa Mexico Restaurant, Cambridge. *Member:* Phi Beta

Kappa. *Awards, honors:* Rhodes scholarship, 1962-65; Borden Research prize, 1967.

WRITINGS: The Logic of Explanation in Psychoanalysis, Academic Press, 1969. Contributor to *Human Relations* and *Cortex.*

WORK IN PROGRESS: A psychoanalytic interpretation of creation myths; and a behavioral approach to treatment of impulsivity.†

(Died March, 1976)

*   *   *

SHIPTON, Clifford K(enyon) 1902-1973

PERSONAL: Born August 5, 1902, in Pittsfield, Mass.; son of George and Edith May (Kenyon) Shipton; married Dorothy George Boyd MacKillop, June 11, 1927; children: Ann Boyd (Mrs. Nord Davis), Nathaniel Niles, George MacKaye. *Education:* Harvard University, S.B., 1926, A.M., 1927, Ph.D., 1933. *Politics:* Republican. *Religion:* Unitarian Universalist. *Home:* The Common, Shirley Center, Mass. 01465. *Office:* American Antiquarian Society, 185 Salisbury, Worcester, Mass.

CAREER: Brown University, Providence, R.I., instructor in history, 1927-30; Massachusetts Historical Society, Boston, Mass., editor, beginning 1930; Harvard University, Cambridge, Mass., archivist, 1938-69; American Antiquarian Society, Worcester, Mass., librarian and director, 1940-67; Clark University, Worcester, Mass., professor of history, 1961-65. Shirley Town Finance Committee, member, 1941-49, chairman, 1944-49; clerk, First Parish of Shirley, 1949-60; trustee, Fruitlands Museum; member of council, Williamsburg Institute; director, Shirley Tax-payers Association, Historic Sights Committee, and Committee to Provide Employment for World War II Veterans. *Member:* American Antiquarian Society (council), Society of American Archivists (fellow; council), American Academy of Arts and Sciences, Grolier Club, Club of Odd Volumes, Massachusetts Historical Society (member of council), Colonial Society of Massachusetts (former president), Phi Beta Kappa, Worcester Torch Club. *Awards, honors:* D.Litt. from Harvard University, 1964, and Clark University, 1969.

WRITINGS: (Editor) *Sibley's Harvard Graduates: Biographical Sketches of Those Who Attended Harvard College, 1690-1771,* Volumes IV-XVII, Harvard University Press, 1933-75; *Andrew Oliver,* American Antiquarian Society, 1943; *Roger Conant,* Harvard University Press, 1945; *Isaiah Thomas,* Printing House of Leo Hart, 1948; (author of bibliography and notes) *The American Bibliography of Charles Evans,* P. Smith, 1962; *New England Life in the Eighteenth Century,* Harvard University Press, 1963; *Harvard Loyalists in New Brunswick,* University of New Brunswick, 1964; *National Index of American Imprints Through 1800: The Short-Title Evans,* American Antiquarian Society, 1969. Member of editorial board, *William and Mary Quarterly,* 1946-54, *New England Quarterly,* 1958-69.

WORK IN PROGRESS: Continuing Harvard biographies; editing the "Early American Imprints" series, microprint reproductions of All American printing, 1640-1805; *Index to the Proceedings* of the American Antiquarian Society.†

(Died December 4, 1973)

*   *   *

SHIRKEY, Albert P(atterson) 1904-

PERSONAL: Born January 8, 1904, in Staunton, Va.; son

of John Joseph and Jessie Hewitson (Close) Shirkey; married Leona Lauck, June 21, 1929; children: Albert Lauck, John Adams, Charles Patterson. *Education:* Randolph-Macon College, student, 1925-28; Union Theological Seminary, Richmond, Va., graduate, 1931. *Home:* 10401 Grosvenor Pl., Apt. 609, Rockville, Md. 20852. *Office:* Mount Vernon Place Methodist Church, 900 Massachusetts Ave., N.W., Washington, D.C. 20001.

CAREER: Ordained elder of the Methodist Church, 1932; pastor in Richmond, Va., 1927-35, Washington, D.C., 1935-38, San Antonio, Tex., 1938-49, Houston, Tex., 1949-50; Mount Vernon Place Methodist Church, Washington, D.C., pastor, 1950-69, minister emeritus, 1969—. Richards lecturer, Washington Missionary College, 1959; Freitas lecturer, Asbury Theological Seminary, 1959. Director of Religious Commission for World Brotherhood, 1950 and 1951; delegate to World Methodist Conferences, 1961 and 1966, and to sessions of General Conference of The Methodist Church; president, Washington Ministerial Union, 1952-54; Washington Council of Churches, executive committee member, beginning 1950, president, 1955-57; president, Baltimore Conference Board of Social Concerns, 1956-57, Baltimore Conference Board of Evangelism, 1957-65; member of executive council of Methodist Commission on Chaplains, 1956-64, Commission of Chaplains and Armed Forces Personnel, 1961-68, also member of Commission on Chaplains and Committee on Spiritual Life, National Council of Churches, and of President's Committee on Juvenile Delinquency. Trustee of The American University, 1952-73; vice-president of Sibley Memorial Hospital, 1952-70; member of board of governors, Wesley Theological Seminary, 1956-72; trustee of Asbury College, 1956-73; member of board of directors, Washington Institute for Scientific Studies, 1960-65; president of board of trustees, Asbury Methodist Home, 1962-68; vice-president of District of Columbia's Council on Alcohol Studies, 1964-69; sponsor of Atlantic Council U.S. Inc., beginning 1964. *Member:* International Inventors, Association for a United Church of America (director), Sigma Phi Epsilon, Theta Phi, Inter-Church Club, Statesman's Club, Masons. *Awards, honors:* D.D., Trinity University, San Antonio, Tex., 1943, The American University, 1954; LL.D., Asbury College, 1966.

WRITINGS: The Lord Is My Shepherd, Upper Room, 1963; *Meditations on the Lord's Prayer,* Upper Room, 1964. Also author of *Wings of the Soul,* 1966, and *Love Never Fails,* 1967. Contributor to religious journals.†

*   *   *

SHOOLBRED, C(laude) F(rederick) 1901-

PERSONAL: Born April 27, 1901; married Alice Justina Russell, April 10, 1943; children: Patience Justina, Charles Frederick. *Education:* Attended Harrow School, 1915-19; Pembroke College, Cambridge, B.A. and LL.B., 1923. *Religion:* Church of England. *Home:* 1 Oakdene, Burgh Heath, Tadworth, Surrey, England.

CAREER: Practicing barrister-at-law, 1923-35; Court of Middlesex Quarter Sessions, assistant clerk of the peace, 1935-58, deputy clerk of the peace, 1958-65; Middlesex Area Quarter Sessions of Greater London, clerk of the peace, 1965-68. *Awards, honors:* Commander, Order of the British Empire.

WRITINGS: Lotteries and the Law, Solicitors' Law Stationery Society, 1932; *The Law of Gaming and Betting,* Pitman, 1935; *Criminal Justice in England and Wales,* Pergamon, 1966; (with R. W. Vick) *Civil Justice in England and*

Wales, Pergamon, 1968; *A Guide to Recent Criminal Legislation,* Pergamon, 1968.

*   *   *

SHRYOCK, Richard Harrison   1893-1972

PERSONAL: Born March 29, 1893, in Philadelphia, Pa.; son of George Augustus (a merchant) and Mary (Chipman) Shryock; married Rheva Ott, September 10, 1921; children: Barbara Ott Shryock Koelle, Richard Wallace. *Education:* Attended Philadelphia School of Pedagogy, 1911-13; University of Pennsylvania, B.S. in Ed., 1917, Ph.D., 1924. *Home:* 2401 Pennsylvania Ave., 15 B33, Philadelphia, Pa. 19130. *Office:* American Philosophical Society, 105 South Fifth St., Philadelphia, Pa.

CAREER: Instructor in history at Ohio State University, Columbus, 1921-24, and University of Pennsylvania, Philadelphia, 1924-25; Duke University, Durham, N.C., associate professor of history, 1925-32, professor, 1932-38; University of Pennsylvania, professor of American history, 1938-49, lecturer on medical history, 1941-49; Johns Hopkins University, Baltimore, Md., Welch Professor of Medical History and director of Institute of History of Medicine, 1949-58, professor emeritus, 1958-72; American Philosophical Society, Philadelphia, Pa., librarian, 1958-65, consultant librarian, 1966-72. Lecturer on medical history, Woman's Medical College of Pennsylvania, 1944-49; Anson G. Phelps lecturer, New York University, 1959. Member of board, Russell Sage Foundation, 1956-65. *Military service:* U.S. Army, Field Ambulance Corps, 1917-18. U.S. Coast Guard Reserve, 1942-45; became lieutenant commander.

MEMBER: International Association of University Professors (president, 1958), International Union of the History and Philosophy of Science (vice-president, 1958), History of Science Society (president, 1941-42), American Association for the History of Medicine (president, 1946-47), American Historical Association (chairman, executive committee, 1956), American Association of University Professors (president, 1950), Phi Beta Kappa, Cosmos Club (Washington, D.C.), 14 West Hamilton Street Club (Baltimore), Rittenhouse Club (Philadelphia). *Awards, honors:* William H. Welch Medal, American Association for the History of Medicine, 1960; Sarton Medal, History of Science Society, 1961; LL.D., Duke University, 1962.

WRITINGS: Georgia and the Union in 1850, Duke University Press, 1925; (editor) *The Letters of Richard D. Arnold, M.D.,* Duke University Press, 1929; *The Development of Modern Medicine,* University of Pennsylvania Press, 1936, 2nd edition, 1947; *American Medical Research: Past and Present,* Commonwealth Fund, 1947; *Unique Influence of the Johns Hopkins University on American Medicine,* Munksgaard (Copenhagen), 1953; (with O. T. Beale) *Cotton Mather: First Significant Figure in American Medicine,* Johns Hopkins Press, 1954; *The National Tuberculosis Association, 1904-1954,* National Tuberculosis Association, 1957; *The University of Pennsylvania Faculty: A Study in Higher Education,* University of Pennsylvania Press, 1959.

The History of Nursing: An Interpretation of the Social and Medical Factors Involved, Saunders, 1959; *Medicine and Society in America, 1660-1860,* New York University Press, 1960; (editor) *The Status of University Teachers,* Ghent, 1961; *Medicine in America: Historical Essays,* Johns Hopkins Press, 1966; *Medical Licensing in America, 1650-1965,* Johns Hopkins Press, 1967; (editor) Richard Dennis Arnold, *Letters,* AMS Press, 1970. Contributor to professional journals. Editor, *Pennsylvania Magazine of History and Biography,* 1940, 1943-45.†

(Died January 30, 1972)

SICILIANO, Vincent Paul   1911-

PERSONAL: Born July 25, 1911, in Astoria, N.Y.; son of Paul Vincent (a restaurateur) and Theresa (Rosati) Siciliano; married Fay Fortunato, February, 1929. *Politics:* Democrat. *Religion:* Catholic. *Home:* 30-91 Crescent St., Astoria, N.Y. 11102. *Office:* Nassau Offset Corp., 18-18 Astoria Blvd., Long Island City, N.Y. 11102.

CAREER: Broker Plate Making Corp., New York, N.Y., sales representative, beginning 1968; Nassau Offset Corp., Long Island City, N.Y., sales representative, beginning 1968.

WRITINGS: Unless They Kill Me First, Hawthorn, 1970.

SIDELIGHTS: According to a review of *Unless They Kill Me First* in *Best Sellers:* "Vincent Siciliano, runt of the brood sired by Paul Siciliano, once the King of Ravenswood (New Jersey), began his life of crime at an early age as a sort of natural development of his environment. . . . From sneak thief and truant, to robber, hold-up man, organizer of brothels, heister of crap games, he also graduated from jail, running the gamut from Welfare Island to Riker's Island to Dannemora, and to Sing Sing. He knows the field he writes about as thoroughly as anyone can, and he writes of it with a frank and, towards the end, angry gusto that rings true to the echo. . . . Siciliano scores the cops-on-the-take, the district attorneys who suppress evidence for pay, the jealousy between the agents of the Narcotics Bureau and the FBI or other Federal agents. . . . This is a shocking indictment of our hedonistic society. It should be read by every citizen, and a good many of the citizenry who read it will recognize themselves somewhere in the book."

BIOGRAPHICAL/CRITICAL SOURCES: Best Sellers, July 15, 1970.†

*   *   *

SIKORA, Joseph (John)   1932-1967

PERSONAL: Born December 6, 1932, in Chicago, Ill.; son of Joseph John (a factory guard) and Rose (Beck) Sikora. *Education:* St. Mary of the Lake Seminary, B.A., 1953; University of Chicago, graduate study, 1953-54; University of Notre Dame, M.A., 1956, Ph.D., 1958; postdoctoral study at West Baden College, 1962-64, and at Bellarmine School of Theology, 1964-66.

CAREER: Entered Society of Jesus (Jesuits), 1959, ordained priest, 1965. Loyola University, Chicago, Ill., began as instructor, became assistant professor of philosophy, 1957-59; philosophical and theological study, research and writing, 1959-67. Instructor in philosophy, Xavier University, 1961.

WRITINGS: Inquiry into Being, Loyola University Press (Chicago), 1965; *The Scientific Knowledge of Physical Nature,* Desclee, 1966; *The Christian Intellect and the Mystery of Being,* Martinus Nijhoff, 1966; *Calling: A Reappraisal of Religious Life,* Herder & Herder, 1968; *Theological Reflections of a Christian Philosopher,* Martinus Nijhoff, 1968. Contributor to *Thomist, Thought, New Scholasticism,* and other journals in America and Canada.

SIDELIGHTS: Joseph Sikora was competent in Latin, Greek, French, German, Hebrew, and Italian. *Avocational interests:* Amateur astronomy, mathematics, and physical sciences.†

(Died August 16, 1967)

SILONE, Ignazio   1900-

PERSONAL: Name originally Secundo Tranquilli; pseudonym pronounced See-*low*-nay; born May 1, 1900, in Pescina, Italy; son of Paolo (a small landowner) and Annamaria (a weaver; maiden name, Delli Quadri) Tranquilli; orphaned at age 14; married Darina Laracy (an Irish writer), 1944. *Education:* Attended Jesuit and other Catholic schools in the Abruzzi and in Rome. *Politics:* Independent Socialist. *Home:* Via di Villa Ricotti, 36, Rome, Italy. *Office:* c/o Harper & Brothers, 49 East 33rd St., New York, N.Y. 20016.

CAREER: Secretary of the Federation of Land Workers of the Abruzzi, 1917; member of the Italian Socialist Youth Movement, 1917-21; editor of *Avanguardia,* a leftist weekly paper published in Rome, and *Il Lavoratore,* a Trieste daily leftist paper, 1921-22; during this period he became a communist and helped establish the Italian Communist Party which in 1921 sent him to Russia and in 1923 to Spain; in Spain he was twice imprisoned for political reasons, first in Madrid and then in Barcelona; in 1925 he returned to Rome and engaged in work against the Facist Regime as a militant communist; from 1921-29 he contributed to various newspapers and magazines in Italy and abroad, many of them printed clandestinely; in 1930 he broke away from the Communist Party, then was smuggled across the border to Switzerland in 1941; he was Political Secretary in Zurich of the Foreign Center of the Italian Socialists which was in touch with the Resistance movements in Germany, Austria, France, and the Balkans; he broadcasted an appeal for civil resistance in Italy in 1942 and was consequently briefly imprisoned by the Swiss; after the Liberation he returned to Rome and joined the Socialist Party in 1945, becoming editor of *Avanti,* the Socialist daily newspaper. Founder of Teatro del Popolo, 1945, and president. Member of the Italian Constituent Assembly, 1946-48, and active participant in the political life of the country; secretary of the Unitary Socialist Party in 1950, in 1950, however, he gave up politics and devoted himself to literature; until 1970 he was co-editor of the magazine *Tempo Presente. Member:* National Institute of Arts and Letters, P.E.N., Italian Pen Club (president, 1945-59), Association for the Freedom of Italian Culture (chairman). *Awards, honors:* Marzotto Prize, 1965; honorary doctorates from Yale University, 1965, and University of Toulouse, 1969; Campiello award, 1968.

WRITINGS—Novels, except as indicated: *Fontamara,* first published in German, translation by Nettie Sutro, Oprecht & Helbling, 1930, first Italian edition published abroad by Nuove Edizione Italiani (Zurich and Paris), 1933, English translation by Eric Mosbacher and Gwenda David, Methuen, 1934, translation by Michael Wharf, Smith & Haas, 1934, revised Italian edition, Mondadori (Milan), 1958, revision translated by Harvey Fergusson II, with a preface by Malcolm Cowley, Atheneum, 1960; *Mr. Aristotle* (short stories), translation by Samuel Putnam, with a biographical note on Silone by Sutro, R. M. McBride (New York), 1935 (never published in Italian); *Pane e vino,* first published in translation by Mosbacher and David as *Bread and Wine,* Methuen, 1936, Harper, 1937, first Italian edition, by Nuove Edizioni di Capolago (Lugano), 1937, revised Italian edition published as *Vino e pane,* Mondadori, 1955, revision translated by Fergusson, with a new preface by Silone, Atheneum, 1962; *Il Seme sotto la neve,* first published in German translation as *Der Samen unterm Schnee,* [Zurich], 1941, translation by Frances Frenaye published as *The Seed Beneath the Snow,* Harper, 1942, first Italian edition, Faro (Rome), 1945, new translation by Fergusson published as *The Seed Beneath the Snow*, Atheneum, 1965; *Una Manciata di more*, Mondadori, 1952, translation by Silone's wife, Darina Silone, published as *A Handful of Blackberries*, Harper, 1953; *Il Segreto di Luca*, Mondadori, 1956, translation by D. Silone published as *The Secret of Luca*, Harper, 1958; *La Volpe e le camelie*, Mondadori, 1960, translation by Mosbacher published as *The Fox and the Camelias*, Harper, 1961.

Others: *Der Fascismus: Seine Entstehung und seine Entwicklung*, Europa-Verlag (Zurich), 1934; *Un Viaggio a Parigi*, [Zurich], 1934; *La Scuola dei dittatori*, [Zurich], 1938, translation by Mosbacher and David published as *The School for Dictators*, Harper, 1938, translation by William Weaver, published under same title, with a preface by Silone, Atheneum, 1963; (editor) *Mazzini*, 1939, translation published as *The Living Thoughts of Mazzini*, with an introductory essay by Arthur Livingstone, Longmans, Green, 1939; *Ed Egli si nascose* (4-act play), first published in German translation, Buechergilde Gutenberg (Zurich), 1944, first Italian edition, [Rome], 1945, English translation by D. Silone published as *And He Hid Himself*, Harper, 1946, (published in England as *And He Did Hide Himself*, J. Cape, 1946), Italian version published in *Teatro*, Nos. 12 and 13, 1950, revised Italian version, Edizioni Mondiali, 1966; *Uscita di sicurezza* (essay), first published in translation in *The God That Failed: Six Studies in Communism*, by Silone, Arthur Koestler, Andre Gide ("presented by Enid Starkie"), Richard Wright, Louis Fischer, and Stephen Spender, edited by Richard Crossman, Harper, 1949, Italian edition, [Florence], 1951, Associazione Italiana per la Liberta della Cultura (Rome), 1955, new edition, Vallecchi (Florence), 1965, translation published as *Emergency Exit: Autobiographical Fragments that Combine The Chronicle of a Life with a Spiritual Self-portrait*, Harper, 1968; (with Anissimov) *Un Dialogo difficile: Sono liberi gli scrittori russi?* (dialogue concerning Communism and Russian literature), [Rome], 1950, published as *An Impossible Dialogue Between Ivan Anissimov and Ignazio Silone*, Institute of Political and Social Studies, 1957; *La Scelta dei compagni*, Associazione Italiana per la Liberta della Cultura, 1954; (editor) *A trent'anni dal Concordata*, Parenti (Florence), 1959; *Mi Paso por el comunismo*, Asociacion Argentina por la Libertad de la Cultura (Buenos Aires), 1959; (with others) *Per una legge sull'obiezione di coscienza*, Associazione Italiana per la Liberta della Cultura, 1962; *L'Avventura d'un povero cristiano* (play), Mondadori, 1968, translation by Weaver published as *The Story of a Humble Christian*, Harper, 1971; *Paese dell'anima*, edited by Maria Letizia Cassata, U. Mursia (Milan), 1968.

Contributor to anthologies: *Modern Italian Short Stories*, edited by Marc Slonim, Simon & Schuster, 1954; *New World Writing*, New American Library, 1955; *Italian Short Stories*, edited by Raleigh Trevelyan, Penguin, 1965. Contributor to numerous Italian journals, magazines, and newspapers. Editor, with Nicola Chiaromonte, *Tempo Presente* (magazine), until 1970.

SIDELIGHTS: Silone wrote his first novel *Fontamara* in 1930 when he was a political exile in Davos, Switzerland. "Since I was alone there," he wrote in the preface to the revised edition which appeared several years later, "—a stranger with an alias to evade the efforts of the Fascist police to find me—writing became my only means of defense against despair." At that time Silone believed he had not long to live and he wrote hurriedly, "with unspeakable affliction and anxiety, to set up as best I could that village into which I put the quintessence of myself and my native heath

so that I could at least die among my own people." The village which he created, Fontamara (the name means "bitter fountain"), is not unlike Pescina, the village of his own youth, with the same endless cycle of life, work, poverty, and death. "A village, in short, like many others," Silone has said, "but for those who are born and die there, the world." The story concerns the life of the peasants and their hopeless struggles against the tyrannies of the landowners and petty officials. But, underlying this theme is an affirmation of the dignity of man even among the indignities of life and, above all, a profound compassion for suffering humanity. Sergio Pacifici has called *Fontamara* "a kind of classic, a book that illuminates its own time and man's condition." Silone's vision in *Fontamara* was of a world where ultimately the peasants would unite with their fellow sufferers and would triumph over officialdom and fascism. In his review of the book, Anthony West wrote: "It is one of those rare novels that really deserves to be called important." Another reviewer commented: "It is written with passion and also with wonderful realism of language and economy of means. Its vitality transcends the circumstances of its creation."

A storm of controversy attended the publication of *Fontamara*. "Nobody not rabidly anti-fascist can be conceived either as believing it or as liking it," said Mark Van Doren. Nevertheless, *Fontamara* was translated into sixteen languages and became a best seller in fourteen European countries. Few today would deny the propagandist character of the book, even in the revised edition which omitted many of the unrelieved political passages, but would now agree with H. E. Bates who wrote: "It is lifted right out of the ordinary propagandist class by Silone's art. His simple, bitterly humorous, savagely satirical style is without a flaw." Silone himself made no secret of the fact that his fiction has a message, social, political, and human. Brotherhood and freedom were the ideals he strove for and the themes he wove into his writing and, as Pacifici has observed, his stories dramatize the need for action.

During his years as a communist, Silone entirely identified with the Party which became his "family, school, church, and barracks." The day he broke away was, he admits, "a very sad day for me, a day of deep mourning, of mourning for my youth." He has described his involvement and eventual disillusionment with communism in a lengthy essay which was published along with testimonies from other former communists under the title *The God That Failed*. Iris Origo feels that Silone was possibly never meant, by temperament, to be a Party man. "Nevertheless," she continues, "it is not possible to separate his positions as a political rebel and as a writer: both spring from the same patient, persistent preoccupation with the condition and destiny of man."

Later novels by Silone repeat in essence the themes implicit in *Fontamara*, although some were less successful. Reviewing *The Fox and the Camelias*, Marc Slonim observed that Silone "appears again as a moralist deeply concerned with ethical problems and the political reality of our times," but, comparing this with the earlier novel, Slonim considered this effort "more limited in scope and less comprehensive in its vision of life." *Bread and Wine*, however, which first appeared in English, and *School for Dictators*, a political discussion rather after the style of Plato's *Republic*, both met with praise from reviewers.

Of Silones' latest work, a six-act play entitled *The Story of a Humble Christian*, Emile Capouya wrote: "In his earlier books the polity that might incarnate our values had come more and more to appear incompatible with government. In this play, his conclusion is more explicitly anarchist: men cannot find God or the good while their institutions separate them from their fellows. It is our privilege that so sound a moralist is also a great artist."

Silone is best known as the author of *Bread and Wine,* a document against Italian Fascism. "To readers of any political faith *Bread and Wine* must needs be a compelling novel" wrote Fanny Butcher. "The peasants live in these pages as naturally as a trillium grows on the banks of the Des Plaines river. They are neither sentimentalized nor looked at through a miscroscope." H. S. Canby believed that, "in spite of the tragedy depicted, it is also a humorous book, and often tender and very touching." The *Forum* reviewer called it "a grand, resounding parable. . . . Here is the voice of Italy's Sinclair Lewis, repeating more subtely, more poetically—'It *has* happened here.'" Silone wrote "this compassionate, sunny, wonderfully sensitive book," said Alfred Kazin, "in a spirit that is as rare in modern letters as it is in modern consciousness. It is not easy to name that spirit, with its supple, tragic sense of good feeling that pervades everything he writes. Part of it is the serenity and the gaiety of the folk writer, the joyous tenderness of a man who is fond of his own people, his hosts in time of danger. It is the tenderness of a man who has an immense faith in the masses, who is democratic by instinct." With this novel Philip Rahv believes that Silone became recognized "as one of the most truly contemporary and significant writers of our time."

To a great extent the extraordinary power of Silone's writing lies in the incredible simplicity of his style. The language is often rich in imagery and vividly colloquial but it is always immediate and direct. At times, it reveals a sad and melancholy poetry. Silone avoids complex grammatical structure and self-conscious symbolism allowing the natural, vigorous dialect of the peasants to lend strength and vibrancy to the narration. The stark and somber background against which their lives are led is depicted with bitter irony, occasionally illuminated by flashes of humor or heightened by descriptive passages of rare and haunting beauty.

The mistrust with which Silone was once regarded in Italy has now been replaced by a very genuine admiration. Iris Origo noted wryly: "To admire Silone has now become not only the fashion, but almost a certificate of integrity," but for too long, she said, he was "undervalued both as a thinker and a writer." Silone continues to survey the political and social scene and to write "in order to understand."

Le Grain sous la neige, a play by Daniel Guerin (Del Duca, 1961), was based on *Il Seme sotto la neve.*

AVOCATIONAL INTERESTS: Football.

BIOGRAPHICAL/CRITICAL SOURCES: Nation, October 3, 1934, April 10, 1937; *New Stateman and Nation,* November 10, 1934; *Saturday Review,* April 3, 1937, November 9, 1968, April 24, 1971; *Chicago Daily Tribune,* April 3, 1937; *Books,* April 11, 1937, October, 1969; *Forum,* June, 1937; *Partisan Review,* fall, 1939; Nathan A. Scott, *Rehearsals of Discomposure: Alienation and Reconciliation in Modern Literature: Franz Kafka, Ignazio Silone, D. H. Lawrence, and T. S. Eliot,* John Lehmann (London), 1952; *Personalist,* XXXVI, 1953; *New York Times Book Review,* May 28, 1961, December 29, 1968; Sergio Pacifici, *A Guide to Contemporary Italian Literature,* Meridian, 1962; *Times Literary Supplement,* January 7, 1965; *Atlantic,* March, 1967; *Book World,* December 5, 1968; *New York Times,* December 26, 1968, March 22, 1972; *Variety,* April 2, 1969; *London Magazine,* June, 1969; *Books and Bookmen,* July,

1969, February, 1971; *Observer Review,* August 3, 1969; *Best Sellers,* May 5, 1971; *Contemporary Literary Criticism,* Volume IV, Gale, 1975.†

*   *   *

SILVERMAN, David 1907-

PERSONAL: Born March 13, 1907, in Brooklyn, N.Y.; son of Benjamin and Hannah (Kahan) Silverman; married Pauline Manos, July 3, 1940; children: Jonathan, Ben. *Education:* Western Reserve University (now Case Western Reserve University), A.B., 1928, LL.B., 1930. *Religion:* Jewish. *Home:* 17307 Lomond Blvd., Shaker Heights, Ohio.

CAREER: West Publishing Co. (law books), St. Paul, Minn., legal editor, 1931-44; U.S. Department of the Navy, civilian employee in Office of General Counsel, 1946; president of a chain of retail stores, 1946-64. *Military service:* U.S. Army, Infantry, 1944-45. *Member:* Order of the Coif, Sigma Delta Chi, Delta Sigma Rho.

WRITINGS: Pitcairn Island, World Publishing, 1967.

WORK IN PROGRESS: Continuing study in the history of the Pacific Islands.†

*   *   *

SIMPSON, (Robert) Smith 1906-

PERSONAL: Born November 9, 1906, in Arlington, Va.; son of Hendree Paine (an engineer) and Edith (Smith) Simpson; married Henriette Lanniee, November 7, 1934; children: Margaret Lanniee (Mrs. Mario Maurin), Zelia Tinsley (Mrs. Hugh R. Elsea, Jr.). *Education:* University of Virginia, B.S., 1927, M.S., 1928; Cornell University, LL.B., 1931; Columbia University, graduate study, 1931-32. *Mailing address:* Annandale, Va.

CAREER: National Recovery Administration, Washington, D.C., special labor adviser and junior administrator, 1933-34; Asphalt Roofing and Shingle Industry, New York, N.Y., adviser to Code Authority, 1934-35; University of Pennsylvania, Wharton School of Finance and Commerce, Philadelphia, instructor, 1935-38, assistant professor, 1938-42; War Shipping Administration, Washington, D.C., assistant director of Foreign Division, 1942-43; U.S. Department of State, Washington, D.C., principal divisional assistant, International Security and Organization Branch, 1943-44, chief of International Labor Organization Branch, 1944-45; U.S. Foreign Service officer with embassy posts in Brussels, Belgium, 1945-47, Athens, Greece, 1947-49, Mexico City, Mexico, 1949, deputy principal officer, U.S. Consulate General, Bombay, India, 1952-54, and U.S. Consul General, Lourenco Marques, Mozambique, 1954-57; U.S. Department of Labor, Washington, D.C., adviser on African affairs, 1958-60, director of Office of Country Programs, 1960-62; U.S. Department of State, Washington, D.C., deputy examiner, Board of Foreign Service Examiners, 1961-62. Participated in drafting of United Nations Charter; co-drafter of Pennsylvania Unemployment Compensation Law, 1936. U.S. Government delegate and advisor to various international conferences. Active in civic and community projects, Fairfax County, Va., beginning 1962. *Member:* Phi Beta Kappa, Raven Society (University of Virginia). *Awards, honors:* Commendable Service Award, U.S. Department of Labor, 1961.

WRITINGS: (With Arthur J. Altmeyer, William Haber, Robert Watt, and John J. Corson) *War and Post-War Social Security,* American Council on Public Affairs, 1942; *El Movimiento Obrero en los Estados Unidos de Norteamer-*

ica, American Embassy, Mexico City, 1951; *Anatomy of the State Department*, Houghton, 1967; *Resources and Needs of American Diplomacy*, American Academy of Political and Social Science, 1968. Contributor to *American Journal of International Law, American Political Science Review, American Federationist, Nation, Foreign Service Journal,* and *Social Service Review.* Co-founder and editor, *Spectator* (University of Virginia) and *Cornell Contemporary* (Cornell University).

SIDELIGHTS: Simpson was one of the architects of the plan that rid the Greek labor movement of communist control by the democratic technique of free trade union elections. He is fluent in French and Spanish.

* * *

SINGLETON, Betty 1910-
(Mary Reens, Dodge Rutland)

PERSONAL: Born August 8, 1910; daughter of Lionel Loraine (in cable and wireless telegraphy business) and Helen (Russell) Weaver; married George Kirkby Singleton (a retired engineer), September 25, 1942; children: Richard Kirkby Lionel. *Education:* Attended Woodford House, School, Croydon, Surrey, England. *Politics:* Right-wing Conservative. *Religion:* Church of England. *Home:* South View, The Green, Tockington, Avon, England. *Agent:* John Johnson, 51-54 Goschen Buildings, 12-13 Henrietta St., London WC2E 8LF, England.

CAREER: Did secretarial work for London newspaper and insurance and banking firms prior to marriage; novelist. *Awards, honors:* Mid-Somerset Eisteddfodd Literary Award, 1957.

WRITINGS: Cross of Fire, R. Hale, 1957, published as *A Note of Grace*, World Publishing, 1958; *The Salt of the Hide*, R. Hale, 1958, Ace Books, 1959; *Mutiny in the Attic*, P. Davies, 1960; (under pseudonym Mary Reens) *Kill for the Cub*, Pall Mall, 1961; *Gift Horses*, Bles, 1965; *The Hat*, Bles, 1967.

WORK IN PROGRESS: The Monthly Nurse.

SIDELIGHTS: Cross of Fire was adapted for television in Britain. *Gift Horses* was read for the BBC's "Woman's Hour" and is presently under film option. After seven years in Malta, Betty Singleton has returned to England to live in a Victorian cottage in Avon.

AVOCATIONAL INTERESTS: Local history, silent cinema, archeology, and the occult.

BIOGRAPHICAL/CRITICAL SOURCES: Books and Bookmen, January, 1968.

* * *

SITWELL, (Francis) Osbert (Sacheverell) 1892-1969

PERSONAL: Born December 6, 1892, in London, England; son of Sir George Reresby (fourth baronet of the peerage established in 1808) and Lady Ida Sitwell (formerly Lady Ida Emily Augusta Denison); brother of Dame Edith and Sacheverell Sitwell. *Education:* Studied at Eton. *Address:* Castello di Montegufoni, 50020 Montagnana, Val di Pesa, near Florence, Italy.

CAREER: Fifth baronet of Renishaw Hall, Derbyshire, England, succeeded to title in 1943. Served as justice of the peace in Derbyshire, 1939, and as trustee of the Tate Gallery, 1951-58; was chairman of the management committee, Society of Authors, 1944-45, 1946-48, 1951-53. In 1919, Sitwell, his brother Sacheverell, and others, organized the Ex-

hibition of Modern French Art at the Mansard Gallery at Heal's. *Military service:* Entered the yeomanry regiment, the Sherwood Rangers, 1911; served as captain in the Grenadier Guards, 1912-18; fought in France. *Member:* Society of Authors, Royal Society of Literature (fellow), Royal Institute of British Architects (fellow), American Institute of Arts and Letters (honorary associate member, 1950-69), St. James's Club. *Awards, honors:* Received the first *Sunday Times* annual award and gold medal for English literature, 1947; Commander of the Order of the British Empire, 1956; Companion of Honour, 1958; Companion of Literature, 1967; LL.D., University of St. Andrews, 1946; D.Litt., University of Sheffield, 1951.

*WRITINGS—*Poems: (With Edith Sitwell) *Twentieth Century Harlequinade, and Other Poems*, Blackwell, 1916; *The Winstonburg Line* (satire), Hendersons (London), 1919; *Argonaut and Juggernaut*, Chatto & Windus, 1919, Knopf, 1920; *At the House of Mrs. Kinfoot* (satire), privately printed at the Favil Press, Kensington (London), 1921; *Out of the Flame*, Grant Richards (London), 1923; *Who Killed Cock Robin? Remarks on Poetry*, C. W. Richards (London), 1923, Doran, 1925; (with Edith and Sacheverell Sitwell) *Poor Young People*, Fleuron, 1925; *Winter the Huntsman*, The Poetry Bookshop (London), 1927; *England Reclaimed* (first volume in trilogy; also see below), Duckworth, 1927, Doubleday, Doran, 1928, published as *England Reclaimed, and Other Poems*, Little, Brown, 1949, reprinted, Greenwood Press, 1972; *Miss Mew*, published by Stanford Dingley at the Mill House Press, 1929.

Collected Satires and Poems, Duckworth, 1931; *Dickens*, Chatto & Windus, 1932, reprinted, Folcroft, 1969; *Mrs. Kimber*, Macmillan, 1937, reprinted, Folcroft, 1971; *Selected Poems, Old and New*, Duckworth, 1943; *A Letter to My Son*, Home & Van Thal, 1944; *Four Songs of the Italian Earth*, Banyon Press, 1948; *Demos the Emperor: A Secular Oratorio*, Macmillan, 1949; *Wrack at Tidesend* (second volume in trilogy; also see below), Macmillan (London), 1952, Caedmon Publishers, 1953; *On the Continent* (final volume in trilogy; also see below), Macmillan, 1958; *Poems about People; or, England Reclaimed* (trilogy; includes *England Reclaimed, Wrack at Tidesend*, and *On the Continent*), Hutchinson, 1965.

Short stories: *Triple Fugue*, Grant Richards, 1924, Doran, 1925, reprinted, Books for Libraries Press, 1970; *Dumb-animal, and Other Stories*, Duckworth, 1930 (the publishers withdrew all the unsold copies of this collection in March, 1931, after the author had been sued for libel on account of the satirical story, "Happy Endings"; the latter has not since been reprinted in England, but appeared in the American edition, *Dumb-animal, and Other Stories*), Lippincott, 1931; *Penny Foolish* (sketches), Macmillan, 1935, reprinted, Books for Libraries Press, 1967; *Open the Door!*, Macmillan, 1941, reprinted, Books for Libraries Press, 1970; *A Place of One's Own*, Macmillan, 1941, published as *A Place of One's Own, and Other Stories*, Icon Books, 1961; *Alive-Alive Oh!* (stories previously printed in *Triple Fugue* and *Dumb-animal*), Pan Books, 1947; *Death of a God, and Other Stories*, Macmillan, 1949; *Collected Stories*, Harper, 1953; *Fee Fi Fo Fum! A Book of Fairy Stories*, Macmillan, 1959; *Tales My Father Taught Me*, Little, Brown, 1962; *Queen Mary and Others*, M. Joseph, 1974.

Novels: *Before the Bombardment*, Doran, 1926; *The Man Who Lost Himself*, Duckworth, 1929, Coward, 1930; *Miracle on Sinai* (satire), Duckworth, 1933, Holt, 1934, new edition, Duckworth, 1948; *Those Were the Days*, Macmillan, 1938.

Plays: (With Sacheverell Sitwell) *All at Sea: A Social Tragedy in Three Acts for First-Class Passengers Only* (containing preface by Osbert Sitwell, "A Few Days in an Author's Life"), Duckworth, 1927, Doubleday, Doran, 1928; (with Rubeigh J. Minney) *Gentle Caesar,* Macmillan, 1942; *The Cinderella Complex,* Dramatic Publishing, 1960.

Travel: *Discursions on Travel, Art and Life,* Doran, 1925, reprinted, Greenwood Press, 1970; *Winters of Content,* Lippincott, 1932, published with additional material as *Winters of Content, and Other Discursions,* Duckworth, 1950; *Escape with Me! An Oriental Sketchbook,* Macmillan, 1939, Harrison-Hilton, 1940, new edition, Pan Books, 1948; *The Four Continents,* Harper, 1954, reprinted, Kennikat, 1972.

Autobiographies; all published by Little, Brown: *Left Hand! Right Hand!,* 1944; *The Scarlet Tree,* 1946; *Great Morning!,* 1947, reprinted, Greenwood Press, 1972; *Laughter in the Next Room,* 1948, reprinted, Greenwood Press, 1972; *Noble Essences,* 1950, reprinted, Greenwood Press, 1972.

History: (With Margaret Barton) *Brighton,* Faber, 1925, general edition, Houghton, 1935; *C.R.W. Nevinson,* Benn, 1925; *The People's Album of London Statues,* illustrated by Nina Hamnett, Duckworth, 1928; *Three-Quarter Length Portrait of Michael Arlen,* Doubleday, Doran, 1931; *Three-Quarter Length Portrait of the Vicountess Wimborne,* privately printed at the University Press, Cambridge, 1931; *The True Story of Dick Whittington* (Christmas story), Home & Van Thal, 1945.

Essays: (With Edith and Sacheverell Sitwell) *Trio: Dissertations on Some Aspects of National Genius* (Northcliffe Lectures at the University of London, 1937), Macmillan, 1938, reprinted, Books for Libraries Press, 1970; *Sing High! Sing Low!,* Macmillan, 1944; *The Novels of George Meredith* (presidential address to the English Association, 1947), Oxford University Press, 1947, reprinted, Folcroft, 1969; *Pound Wise,* Little, Brown, 1963.

Contributor: O. Simon and H. H. Child, editors, *The Bibliophile's Almanack for 1927,* Fleuron, 1926; (author of biographical memoir) *The Works of Ronald Firbank,* Volume I, Brentano, 1929; (author of introduction) *Thomas Rowlandson,* The Studio (London), 1929; (editor with Barton, and author of preface) *Sober Truth: A Collection of Nineteenth-Century Episodes,* Duckworth, 1930; (text editor) *Belshazzar's Feast,* musical score by William Walton, Oxford University Press, 1931; (author of introduction) Ria Sysonby, *Lady Sysonby's Cook Book,* Putnam, 1935; (author of foreword) Ralph Dutton, *The English Country House,* Batsford, 1935, Scribner, 1936; (editor and author of preface) *Two Generations* (containing the reminiscences of Mrs. Georgiana Swinton [Sitwell] and the journal of Miss Florence Sitwell), Macmillan, 1940; (author of foreword) James Agate, *Here's Richness!* (an anthology of Agate's work), Harrap, 1942; (author of introduction) William Henry Davies, *Collected Poems of W. H. Davies,* J. Cape, 1943; (author of preface) John Piper, *The Sitwell Country* (catalogue published for exhibition of Piper's works at the Leicester Galleries), Ernest Brown & Phillips, 1945; (editor and author of character portrait) Walter Richard Seckert, *A Free House!; or, The Artist as Craftsman,* Macmillan, 1947; (author of introduction) Sir George Reresby Sitwell, *On the Making of Gardens,* Scribner, 1951.

Also author of introduction of *Catalogue of the Frick Collection,* 1949. Contributor to other books and to the *Times* and *Sunday Times* (London), *Spectator, Harper's, New Yorker, Atlantic Monthly,* and many other journals in England and America. Joint literary editor with Herbert Read of the quarterly, *Arts and Letters,* beginning 1919.

SIDELIGHTS: Sir Osbert was deeply attached both to English and European tradition. He recalled the first morning he awakened at the Castle of Montegufoni (a Tuscan fortress bought by his father before World War I): "I realized that Italy was my second country, the complement and perfect contrast to my own." Yet, as Roger Fulford notes: "No one [had his] mind more firmly based in England and the English countryside."

His autobiographies have been praised for the portrait of England that they give. Fulford maintains: "Certain it is that future generations wishing to recapture the true spirit of English life in the great days before 1914 and the tarnished rather breathless years afterwards will turn to Sir Osbert's graceful volumes." V. S. Pritchett, who comments upon the "elaborate and ornate style" of the books, notes other characteristics: "[Sir Osbert] is the most Dickensian of contemporary writers and Renishaw is a kind of gilded Bleak House seen from the inside. . . . To the English comic tradition, Sir Osbert has added the tremendous."

He had criticized the denigration of men of the past (such as in the mode of biography made fashionable by Lytton-Strachey) which takes the form of "a kind of *tutoyer*-ing through the centuries, the style of the gossip-writer applied to history."

Yet he was a rebel against many facets of English life, notably the public school system. R. L. Megroz writes of "Happy Endings": "Reading that emotional and witty story as thinly-disguised autobiography, the author's dislike of the Eton-followed-by-military-college sort of education is revealed as a consequence of having it thrust upon him." He was also bitterly opposed to war; World War I roused him, Fulford writes, "to a sense of frustrated fury with the older generation who were in some way responsible."

Sir Osbert started on his single-minded literary career against parental opposition. Writing of the period around 1918, he revealed that, "though . . . my father was determined to prevent it, as far as lay within his power, I was resolved to devote my future, my whole life, to writing." He remained true to his resolution, despite standing, unsuccessfully, as Liberal candidate for parliament (having failed to gain Labour support) in the election of 1919.

As a writer, solitude was an essential condition for his work. Fulford reports that Sir Osbert wrote "*Before the Bombardment* in a monastic cell in S. Italy and *Escape With Me!* in a disused kitchen in Guatemala, under the curious and rather hungry eye of a friendly vulture which hovered outside the window." One of his pet aversions was the telephone, and he maintained, says Sir Charles Petrie, "that to ring a man up without notice is just as much an invasion of his privacy as it would be to shout at him through his window as he sits and reads."

Travel always held a peculiar fascination for Sir Osbert; it is, he wrote, "like a drug that permeates the mind with an indefinite but unusual tinge, stimulating and releasing, imparting a greater significance than they possess to the things that interest and amuse it."

Selections from his works have been recorded, including a reading by Sitwell from *England Reclaimed, and Other Poems,* Caedmon, 1953; a musical arrangement of *Winter the Huntsman* was made by Elisabeth Lutyens in 1934.

BIOGRAPHICAL/CRITICAL SOURCES—Books: R. L. Megroz, *The Three Sitwells,* Richards Press (London),

1927; Megroz, *Five Novelist Poets of Today*, Joiner & Steele (London), 1933; Osbert Sitwell, *Left Hand! Right Hand!*, Little, Brown, 1944; Osbert Sitwell, *The Scarlet Tree*, Little, Brown, 1946; Osbert Sitwell, *Great Morning!*, Little, Brown, 1947, reprinted, Greenwood Press, 1972; Osbert Sitwell, *Laughter in the Next Room*, Little, Brown, 1948, reprinted, Greenwood Press, 1972; Osbert Sitwell, *Noble Essences*, Little, Brown, 1950, reprinted, Greenwood Press, 1972; Roger Fulford, *Osbert Sitwell*, Longmans, Green, for the British Council and the National Book League, 1951; Max Wykes-Joyce, *Triad of Genius*, P. Owen, 1953; John Lehmann, *A Nest of Tigers: The Sitwells in Their Times*, Atlantic-Little, Brown, 1968.

Periodicals: *Illustrated London News*, April 7, 1945, February 9, 1963; *New Statesman*, July 2, 1949; *New Republic*, December 14, 1953; *Sunday Times* (London), June 2, 1968; *New York Times Book Review*, September 22, 1968; *London Times*, May 6, 1969; *New York Times*, May 6, 1969; *Washington Post*, May 6, 1969.†

(Died May 4, 1969, in Montagnana, Italy)

* * *

SIZEMORE, Margaret D(avidson)

PERSONAL: Born in Birmingham, Ala.; daughter of Julius Weston (an attorney) and Ruth (Lee) Davidson; married James Middleton Sizemore, June 19, 1937 (deceased, 1968); children: James M., Ruth Lee (Mrs. Kenneth House). *Education:* Howard College (now Samford University), A.B., 1928, M.A., 1930; Sorbonne, University of Paris, D.N.; further study at Western Reserve (now Case Western Reserve) University. *Politics:* Independent. *Religion:* Presbyterian. *Home:* 3084 Sterling Rd., Birmingham, Ala. 35213. *Office:* Samford University, Birmingham, Ala. 35209.

CAREER: Teacher at public and private schools in Florida and Alabama, 1930-42; Samford University, Birmingham, Alabama, beginning 1947, began as instructor, became associate professor of French, dean of women, 1950-70, assistant to president for community affairs, beginning 1970. Member of U.S. Defense Advisory Committee on Women in the Services, 1965-68; chairman, Alabama Commission on Women, 1971-74. Member of Birmingham Museum of Art, Alabama Constitution Commission, Bicentennial Commission, and advisory board of Alabama Historical Commission. *Member:* National Association of Women Deans, American Association of University Women, National League of American Pen Women (state president, 1974-76), Alabama Association of Women Deans, Alabama Guidance Association (president, 1953), Alabama Writers' Conclave (president, 1961-62), Hypatia, Phi Kappa Phi, Phi Delta Phi, Kappa Delta Epsilon, Beta Pi Theta. *Awards, honors:* Cited Ami de France, City of Paris, 1951; scroll, Archbishop of Canterbury, 1951; George Washington Medal of Honor, Freedoms Foundation of Valley Forge, 1962; State Daughters of the American Revolution Distinguished Award, 1965; Distinguished Service Award, Forney Historical Society, 1971; Service to Mankind Award, Sertoma Clubs, 1971; and many other awards from civic and social organizations for contributions of outstanding service and patriotism.

WRITINGS: Victor Hugo and His Dramas, Howard College, 1928; *The New Education in France*, Howard College, 1930; (with Nell S. Graydon) *The Amazing Marriage of Marie Eustis and Josef Hofmann*, University of South Carolina Press, 1965. Author of articles, historical sketches, and genealogical studies.

WORK IN PROGRESS: A book, *Collecting Antiques: Outline Studies*.

* * *

SKORNIA, Harry J(ay) 1910-

PERSONAL: Born April 2, 1910, in Boyne City, Mich.; son of Charles (a farmer) and Josephine (Schluttenhofer) Skornia; married second wife, Lorene Krafft (in university administration), June 18, 1961; children: (previous marriage) Mary, Lee. *Education:* Michigan State University, A.B., 1932; University of Michigan, M.A., 1933, Ph.D., 1937. *Religion:* Presbyterian. *Home:* 224 South Pebble Beach Blvd., Sun City Center, Fla. 33570. *Office:* Department of Communication, University of South Florida, Tampa, Fla. 33620.

CAREER: Faculty member at University of Michigan, Ann Arbor, 1932-34, 1936-37, Arkansas City Junior College, Arkansas City, Kan., 1934-36, and DePauw University, Greencastle, Ind., 1938-40; radio station WIRE, Indianapolis, Ind., program director, 1940-41; Indiana University, Bloomington, associate professor of radio and television, chairman of department, and director of broadcasting, 1941-51; radio adviser and visiting expert, U.S. Military Government in Germany and Austria, 1948-49; radio attache, U.S. Embassy, Vienna, Austria, 1951-53; University of Illinois, Urbana, lecturer in radio and television, and director of Kellogg Project in Educational Radio, 1953-60, professor of radio and television, 1960-69, professor of radio and television at Chicago, 1969-75, professor emeritus, 1975—. Executive director and president, National Association of Educational Broadcasters, 1953-60; chairman of Mass Communications Committee, U.S. National Commission for UNESCO, 1961-63; member of Advisory Committee on New Educational Media, U.S. Office of Education, 1961-64; senior specialist, East-West Center, 1967.

MEMBER: National Association of Educational Broadcasters (director, 1946-50; executive director, 1951-59; president, 1959-60; chairman of international relations, 1960-63), International Radio and Television Society, National Association for Better Radio and Television (board member, beginning 1964), Association for Education in Journalism, National Education Association, Illinois News Broadcasters Association, Alpha Tau Omega, Kappa Tau Alpha, Delta Phi Alpha. *Awards, honors:* Rockefeller Foundation, Fund for Adult Education, and two Ford Foundation grants.

WRITINGS: Manual for German Radio (in German), U.S. Office of Military Government, 1949; (with Robert H. Lee and Fred A. Brewer) *Creative Broadcasting*, Prentice-Hall, 1950; *Television and Society*, McGraw, 1965; *Television and the News*, Pacific Books, 1968; (editor with Jack W. Kitson) *Problems and Controversies in Television and Radio*, Pacific Books, 1968. Contributor of about 150 articles and reviews to education and broadcasting journals.

WORK IN PROGRESS: Readings in U.S. Television and Radio; developing new courses in media analysis; research in basic uses of television and radio.

* * *

SLADE, Richard 1910-1971

PERSONAL: Born July 19, 1910, in England; son of Richard Simon (a chef) and Ellen (Reardon) Slade. *Education:* Weymouth Teacher Training College, Ministry of Education Certificate, 1947. *Residence:* Barking, Essex, England.

CAREER: Waiter in Belgium and Austria, 1928-31; Gascoigne Junior School, Barking, Essex, England, teacher, 1948-69. Elementary exchange teacher in Los Angeles, Calif., 1965-66. *Military service:* British Army, Royal Corps of Signals, 1941-46; took part in Normandy invasion.

WRITINGS—All published by Faber, except as noted: *You Can Make a String Puppet,* 1957; *Clever Hands,* 1959; *Your Book of Heraldry,* 1960; *Masks and How to Make Them,* 1964; *Take an Egg Box,* 1965; *Your Book of Modelling;* 1967, published as *Modeling in Clay, Plaster, and Papiermache,* Lothrop, 1968; *Toys from Balsa,* 1968; *Tissue Paper Craft,* 1968; *Patterns in Space,* 1969; *Geometrical Patterns,* 1970; *Paper Aeroplanes: How to Make Aeroplanes from Paper,* 1970, St. Martin's, 1971; *Carton Craft,* 1972, S. G. Phillips, 1973; *Take a Tin Can,* 1973. Contributor to *Art Craft and Education;* also contributor of travel articles to *Lady,* and articles on photography and motorcycling to British national magazines.

WORK IN PROGRESS: Other books on handicraft.

SIDELIGHTS: Richard Slade covered most of Europe by motorcycle during school holidays, and traveled in Russia, Palestine, Egypt, Japan, India, Hawaii, Central America, and most of North America. He told *CA:* "I look upon art and crafts for children as means rather than ends, as method rather than subject. I see the use of the hand as promoting the development of thought. . . ."†

(Died October, 1971)

* * *

SMALLEY, Ruth E(lizabeth)   1903-

PERSONAL: Born November 14, 1903, in Chicago, Ill.; daughter of Joseph Henry (a business manager) and Grace (Hollister) Smalley. *Education:* University of Minnesota, B.A., 1924; Smith College, M.S.S., 1929; University of Pittsburgh, D.S.W., 1949. *Home:* 630 Glenmary Rd., Radnor, Pa.

CAREER: Newark (N.J.) Board of Education, Bureau of Child Guidance, school social worker, 1929-32; University of Chicago, Chicago, Ill., social worker and field instructor, 1932-35; Rochester (N.Y.) Board of Education, director of visiting teacher department, 1935-37; Smith College, School of Social Work, Northampton, Mass., faculty member, 1937-38; University of Pittsburgh, School of Social Work, Pittsburgh, Pa., 1939-50, began as associate professor, became professor of social work; University of Pennsylvania, Philadelphia, professor of social work, 1950-67, professor emeritus, 1967—, acting dean, 1957-58, dean, 1958-67; Council on Social Work Education, New York, N.Y., acting director of Division of Education Services, 1967-68. Fulbright lecturer on social work education in Rome, Italy, 1966-67. Consultant to Children's Bureau of U.S. Department of Health, Education, and Welfare, and to National Institute of Mental Health.

MEMBER: American Orthopsychiatric Association (fellow), National Association of Social Workers (vice-president, 1955-57), National Conference on Social Welfare (vice-president, 1965-66), Council on Social Work Education (president, 1961-64), American Association of University Professors, Phi Beta Kappa, Gamma Phi Beta, Mortar Board. *Awards, honors:* Distinguished Alumni Award of University of Minnesota, 1962; Distinguished Service Award of Council on Social Work Education, 1964; Fulbright fellowship, 1966-67.

WRITINGS: (Contributor) *Papers in Honor of Everett*

Kimball, Smith College Press, 1943; *Theory for Social Work Practice,* Columbia University Press, 1967. Writer of pamphlets for Council on Social Work Education. Contributor to professional journals.

* * *

SMITH, Arthur M(umford)   1903-

PERSONAL: Born September 19, 1903, in Scott, Ind.; son of Ora Lynn (a lawyer) and Genevieve (Mumford) Smith; married Elizabeth Barbara Allan, June 14, 1926; children: Carrol Jean (Mrs. Dwight A. Lewis), Arthur Allan. *Education:* University of Michigan, A.B., 1924, LL.B., 1926. *Politics:* Republican. *Religion:* Methodist. *Office:* U.S. Court of Customs and Patent Appeals, Washington, D.C. 20439.

CAREER: Admitted to bars of Michigan and Illinois, 1926; admitted to practice, U.S. Supreme Court, 1942, U.S. Court of Customs and Patent Appeals, 1958. Practice of patent law, Chicago, Ill., 1926-29, of general and patent law, Detroit, Mich., 1929-33; Gray & Smith, Detroit, Mich., junior partner, 1933-46; Smith, Wilson, Lewis & McRae (and predecessor firms), Dearborn, Mich., senior partner, 1946-59; U.S. Court of Customs and Patent Appeals, Washington, D.C., associate judge, beginning 1959. Lecturer in patent law, University of Michigan Law School, 1952-59. *Member:* American Bar Association, Federal Bar Association, American Patent Law Association, Inter-American Bar Association, American Judicature Society, Michigan Patent Law Association (president, 1929; life member), Lincoln Group of Washington, D.C. (vice-president, 1963-64), Gamma Eta Gamma. *Awards, honors:* Jefferson Medal, New Jersey Patent Law Association, 1961.

WRITINGS: Patent Law, Cases, Comments & Materials, Overbeck, 1954, revised edition, 1964; *The Art of Writing Readable Patents,* Practising Law Institute, 1958; (co-editor) *Patent Licensing,* Practising Law Institute, 1958. Contributing editor, *Encyclopedia of Patent Practice.* Author of series of articles on patent law published in *Tool Tec* (magazine), 1958, and other articles in legal journals.

WORK IN PROGRESS: A history of U.S. patent law and the philosophic basis of its development; articles on Abraham Lincoln and the U.S. patent system, and on George Washington and the patent system.††

* * *

SMITH, Florence Margaret   1902-1971
(Stevie Smith)

PERSONAL: Born in 1902, in Hull, Yorkshire, England; daughter of Charles Ward (a shipping agent) and Ethel Rahel (Spear) Smith. *Education:* Attended high school in Palmers Green, London, and North London Collegiate School. *Home:* 1 Avondale Rd., Palmers Green, London N.13, England.

CAREER: Prior to 1953 worked in a publisher's office in London, England; writer and broadcaster. Gave poetry readings for British Broadcasting Corp. radio and television; read and sang poems set to music (based on plainsong and folk music) at festivals in London, Edinburgh, Stratford on Avon, and elsewhere in England. Member of literature panel of Arts Council. *Awards, honors:* Cholmondeley Poetry Award, 1966; Queen's Gold Medal for Poetry, 1969.

WRITINGS—All under name Stevie Smith: *Novel on Yellow Paper,* J. Cape, 1936, Morrow, 1937, reprinted, J. Cape, 1969; *Over the Frontier* (novel), J. Cape, 1938; *The Holiday* (novel), Chapman & Hall, 1949; *Some Are More*

Human than Others (drawings and captions), Gaberbocchus, 1958; (editor) *T. S. Eliot: A Symposium for His 70th Birthday,* Hart-Davis, 1958; (author of introduction) *Cats in Color* (photographs), Batsford, 1959, Studio, 1960; (editor) *The Poet's Garden,* Viking, 1970 (published in England as *The Batsford Book of Children's Verse,* Batsford, 1970).

Poetry; all self-illustrated: *A Good Time Was Had by All,* J. Cape, 1937; *Tender Only to One,* J. Cape, 1938; *Mother, What is Man?,* J. Cape, 1942; *Harold's Leap,* Chapman & Hall, 1950; *Not Waving But Drowning,* Deutsch, 1957; *Selected Poems* (also see below), Longmans, Green, 1962, New Directions, 1964; *The Frog Prince and Other Poems* (also see below), Longmans, Green, 1966; (with Edwin Brock and Geoffrey Hill) *Penguin Modern Poets 8,* Penguin, 1966; *The Best Beast,* Knopf, 1969; *Two in One* (includes *Selected Poems* and *The Frog Prince and Other Poems*), Longman, 1971; *Scorpion and Other Poems,* Longman, 1972.

Poetry represented in many anthologies, including: *Distaff Muse,* compiled by Clifford Bax and Meum Stewart, Hollis & Carter, 1949; *Faber Book of Twentieth-Century Verse,* compiled by John F. A. Heath-Stubbs and David Wright, 2nd edition, Faber, 1965; *Poetry 1900 to 1965,* compiled by George MacBeth, Longmans, Green, 1967; *Poems from Hospital,* compiled by Jean Sergeant and Howard Sergeant, Allen & Unwin, 1968; *Blue Guitar,* compiled by Donald G. Rutledge and John M. Bassett, McClelland & Stewart, 1968. Contributor of poems and reviews to *Observer, Times Literary Supplement, Listener, New Yorker, Nation,* and other periodicals.

SIDELIGHTS: David Wright called *Not Waving But Drowning* "the best collection of new poems to appear in 1957." He wrote: ". . . As one of the most original women poets now writing [Stevie Smith] seems to have missed most of the public accolades bestowed by critics and anthologists. One reason may be that not only does she belong to no 'school'—whether real or invented as they usually are—but her work is so completely different from anyone else's that it is all but impossible to discuss her poems in relation to those of her contemporaries. . . . Perhaps her nearest equivalent among contemporary poets is John Betjeman, who surfaces with deceptive gaiety an inherent gloom, except that in the case of Stevie Smith the gaiety is fundamental and does not deceive the gloom but defines it. . . . The uninhibited wit and gaiety which she brings to her best poems plus the optimism they often express provides an appearance of frivolity which is in reality a mask worn to further the impact of truth which, were it declaimed from a lugubrious tripod, would be vitiated or diluted. The apparent geniality of many of her poems is in fact more frightening than the solemn keening and sentimental despair of other poets, for it is based on a clearsighted acceptance, by a mind neither obtuse nor unimaginative, but sharp and serious, innocent but far from naive, and because feminine having a bias towards life and survival, of the facts as they are and the world as it is. . . . Stevie Smith is the possessor of a subtle ear and easily produces lines of astonishing auditory beauty. . . ."

Florence Smith recorded, with three other poets, a reading of her own poems, "The Poet Speaks," Arco, 1965; a recorded poetry reading was released by Marwell Press, 1966, and she recorded her poems for Listener Records, 1967.

BIOGRAPHICAL/CRITICAL SOURCES: Poetry, August, 1958, March, 1965; *Contemporary Literary Criticism,* Volume III, Gale, 1975.†

(Died March 7, 1971)

SMITH, Gerald B. 1909-

PERSONAL: Born May 7, 1909, in Northville, S.D.; son of Clifford E. and Aura (Halpenny) Smith; married Karine Snipstad, July 21, 1928; married second wife, Mildred Harrod (employed on a college staff), April 23, 1965; children: six. *Education:* Attended St. Paul Bible College, St. Paul, Minn., 1930-33, and Bethel College, St. Paul, 1945-48.

CAREER: Ordained to ministry of Christian and Missionary Alliance, 1934; pastor of churches in Owen, Green Bay, and Oconto, Wis., 1933-44; *St. Paul Pioneer Press and Dispatch* (daily newspaper), St. Paul, Minn., religion editor and feature writer, 1944-61; Christian and Missionary Alliance (headquarters), New York, N.Y., assistant for public relations to the president, beginning 1961. Member of board, Christian Publications, Inc., Harrisburg, Pa., beginning 1962.

WRITINGS: (Compiler and editor) *The Tozer Pulpit,* Christian Publications, Volume I, 1966, Volume II, 1969; (with Mabel Francis) *One Shall Chase a Thousand,* Christian Publications, 1968. Writer of films and filmstrips produced by Christian and Missionary Alliance. Member of editorial board, *Alliance Witness,* beginning 1962.††

*   *   *

SMITH, Guy-Harold 1895-

PERSONAL: Born January 1, 1895, in La Farge, Wis.; son of John William (a farmer) and Harriet (Waddell) Smith; married Elizabeth Baker, August 5, 1926 (died July 26, 1965); children: John Waddell. *Education:* University of Wisconsin, Ph.B., 1921, Ph.D., 1927; University of Pennsylvania, graduate student, 1922-23. *Politics:* Republican. *Religion:* Protestant. *Home:* 2340 Canterbury Rd., Columbus, Ohio 43221. *Office:* Ohio State University, 1775 College Rd., Columbus, Ohio 43210.

CAREER: Instructor in geography at University of Pennsylvania, Philadelphia, 1922-23, and University of Wisconsin, Madison, 1923-27; Ohio State University, Columbus, assistant professor of geography, 1927-28; University of Illinois, Urbana, associate in geography, 1928-29; Ohio State University, assistant professor, 1929-34, associate professor, 1934-37, professor of geography, 1937-65, professor emeritus, 1965—, chairman of department, 1934-63. Summer professor or lecturer at Columbia University, University of Washington, Seattle, and other universities. Consultant to Military Intelligence Service, U.S. Army, 1943-45, 1948-49. *Military service:* U.S. Army, 1917-18; became second lieutenant.

MEMBER: American Association for the Advancement of Science (fellow; vice-president, 1963), American Geographical Society (fellow), Association of American Geographers (vice-president, 1937), National Council for Geographic Education, American Polar Society, Ohio Academy of Science (fellow; president, 1961-62), Phi Beta Kappa, Sigma Xi, Beta Gamma Sigma, Faculty Club (Ohio State University). *Awards, honors:* Centennial Achievement Award, Ohio State University, 1970.

WRITINGS: (With Dorothy Good) *Japan: A Geographic View,* American Geographical Society, 1943; (editor and principal contributor) *Conservation of Natural Resources,* Wiley, 1950, 4th edition, 1971; *The First Fifty Years of the College of Commerce and Administration,* Ohio State University, 1966. Contributor of several population and physiographic maps to other publications; about eighty articles have been published in *Ohio Journal of Science* and in geographic and other journals.

SMITH, Hugh L(etcher)   1921-1968

PERSONAL: Born June 20, 1921, in Dallas, Tex.; son of Hugh L. (an airlines executive) and Goldie (Capers) Smith; married Margaret Young, June 11, 1941; married second wife, Deborah Keniston (a college art instructor), December 21, 1962; children: Hugh Letcher III. *Education:* University of Missouri, student, 1939-42; University of Tulsa, B.A., 1951, M.A., 1952; University of New Mexico, Ph.D., 1955. *Office:* Department of English, California State University, Long Beach, Calif. 90804.

CAREER: American Airlines, New York, N.Y., ground instructor, 1942-46, outside sales representative, 1946-48; Wichita State University, Wichita, Kan., instructor in English, 1955-56; California State University, Long Beach, assistant professor, 1956-60, associate professor, 1960-65, professor of English, 1965-68. *Member:* National Council of Teachers of English. *Awards, honors:* $500 Distinguished Teaching Award, California State College, Long Beach (now California State University, Long Beach), 1967.

WRITINGS: "Jazz and Popular Music" in *The College and Adult Reading List in Literature and the Fine Arts,* Edward Lueders, editor, Washington Square, 1962; (compiler with Steven Dunning and Edward Lueders) *Reflections on a Gift of Watermelon Pickle . . . and Other Modern Verse* (collection for ages eleven and up), Lothrop, 1966. Essay included in *His Firm Estate,* University of Tulsa Monograph, 1967; (compiler with Dunning and Lueders) *Some Haystacks Don't Even Have a Needle,* Lothrop, 1969. Contributor to professional journals.

WORK IN PROGRESS: A textbook on jazz history and development, with Stanford Helm.†

(Died, 1968)

*   *   *

SMITH, Lillian (Eugenia)   1897-1966

PERSONAL: Born December 12, 1897, in Jasper, Fla.; daughter of Calvin Warren (a businessman) and Anne (Simpson) Smith. *Education:* Attended Piedmont College, Peabody Conservatory, Columbia University. *Politics:* Liberal Democrat. *Address:* P.O. Box 766, Clayton, Ga. *Agent:* McIntosh & Otis, Inc., 475 Fifth Ave., New York, N.Y. 10017.

CAREER: Director and owner, Laurel Falls Camp for Girls, Clayton, Ga., twenty-five years; Virginia School, Huchow, Chekiang, China, music teacher, 1922-25; founder, editor, and publisher of "little" magazine titled successively, *Pseudopodia, North Georgia Review,* and *South Today,* 1936-46. Taught creative writing at University of Indiana and University of Colorado; lectured at Vassar College, 1955. Frequent radio and television appearances; frequent public speaker on human relations. Rabun County (Ga.) Hospital, board member, founder of hospital auxiliary. *Member:* American Civil Liberties Union (former vice-president; member of the national board), Congress of Racial Equality (member of advisory board; resigned, 1966), Author's Guild, P.E.N. *Awards, honors:* Honorary degrees from Oberlin College, Howard University, Atlanta University; Page One Award, 1944, Constance Skinner Lindsay Award for "best book by a woman," 1945, both for *Strange Fruit;* Southern Award, 1949, for *Killers of the Dream;* Sidney Hillman Award for magazine writing, 1962; citation from National Book Award Committee for "distinguished contribution to American letters"; Rosenwald Foundation fellowship, two years.

WRITINGS: Strange Fruit, Reynal, 1944; *Killers of the Dream,* Norton, 1949, revised edition, Doubleday, 1963; *The Journey,* World Publishing, 1954; *Now Is the Time,* Viking, 1955; *One Hour,* Harcourt, 1959; *Memory of a Large Christmas,* Norton, 1962; *Our Faces, Our Words,* Norton, 1964; *The Journey,* Norton, 1965. Contributor to *Saturday Review, Redbook, Life, New Republic, The Nation, New York Times.*

SIDELIGHTS: "I was born on the rim of that mysterious terrain which spills over from Georgia's Okefenokee Swamp into Florida," Miss Smith wrote in the essay, "The Mob and the Ghost." "As a child, I walked on earth that trembled. . . . There were other fabulous things: a river that, now and then, disappeared into the earth and came up thirty miles away. Suddenly it happened: the fish were feeling secure and comfortable, then *whsst!* there they were, left wriggling on white hot sand with no water within miles. I learned early not to stake much on security; if fish didn't have it, why should I? And there were the sinks: a piece of land, ordinary land, was there today, with perhaps a house on it; tomorrow, sunk into the earth forty feet down. Today, solid fact; tomorrow, emptiness. I learned my lessons early, those the existentialists have been reminding us of in recent decades. . . . I think what impressed me most was this: On that trembling earth of the Great Swamp, although a child could scarcely walk on it, heavy trees and jungled growth were supported by it. Is it not a superb image of civilization: all that men have dreamed and created, springing out of and supported by massive uncertainties? In this mythic and surreal place I lived as a child. In a world full of not only spiritual but physical ambiguities, each casting a shadow on the other. Eyes and muscles and heart knew them long before I heard that word. . . .

"I do not remember when I first heard the word segregation, but I knew its meaning from babyhood. I learned it the hard way, for I was separated from people I loved by death. These were my first lessons in segregation. Other lessons came quickly. I learned of the segregation that cuts one off from knowledge. There were things I wanted to know which no one would tell me; questions no one would answer. . . . Then came another question, more and more often, that concerned me every day: the question about race and its ritual of segregation. My first concern with it was because it affected *me,* not because it affected Negroes. I just did not like to be segregated. . . . I did not like being restricted to members of the white race. . . . I wanted the people I loved to come through the front door. . . . My earth was trembling—not only out near Big Swamp but in the bigger swamp of my interior life. . . . [There] were not only the unchangeable uncertainties on which the human condition is based, but another uncertainty that *need not be.* It was this that hurt me, this knowledge that racial separation does not belong in the category of the archetypal and unchangeable separations: birth, death, a universe which we can never know save in small fragments, a God whose existence we can never prove, a *why was I born?* which even a man's vocation does not answer in full. This separation was different; it could be *changed.*"

The outcome of this antipathy toward segregation was *Strange Fruit,* a book destined for the best-seller lists because of attempts to suppress it. It was "unofficially" banned in Boston and Detroit; used as a test-case by Bernard De Voto in Cambridge, Massachusetts; banned from the mails by an ambitious U.S. postal clerk; and caused a fellow townsman of Miss Smith's to remark: "I'll give you the real facts. Miss Lil is a deeply religious woman. She would never have written that vulgar sexy stuff. Her publishers wrote it. They stuck it in to make the books sell.'' The novel told of the love of an educated Negro girl for a white man, with murder and lynching a result of that love. The loud protestations in the North centered around Miss Smith's use of a four-letter word that was regarded unprintable in 1944. Said Joseph McSorley in the *Catholic World:* ''Presumably for the purpose of appealing to a vulgar multitude, she sins against good taste so grossly as to make her story quite unfit for general circulation. It seems curious enough that 'the daughter of one of the South's oldest families' should . . . employ phrases which decent people regard as unprintable.'' Edward Weeks differed strongly: ''I find nothing in the novel that is pornographic. . . . Without the shock, I doubt if the moral would have gone home. At the speed things are moving today, I suspect we shall be needing a new *Uncle Tom's Cabin* for each decade. This one comes from the South, and this time New England seems afraid of it.'' Protest in the South was not concerned so much with sex as with story. Miss Smith noted that ''the lunatic fringe of the fascist groups and the White supremacy crowd . . . were writing editorials and reviews that *Strange Fruit* advocates the mongrelizing of the white race. . . . The *Southern Watchman* screamed in headlines that Alabama must not vote for Roosevelt because the author of *Strange Fruit* once wrote a piece in praise of our President. . . . I thought of my book as a fable about a son in search of a mother, about a race in search of surcease from pain and guilt—both finding what they sought in death and destruction. So when people ask 'Is *Strange Fruit* a race book; is it about the Negro problem?' I say, 'I don't think so.' For it seems to me a book about human beings journeying also back to childhood, always back to the room where they were born, seeking to find, wherever they travel, that which they left there, so long ago.''

Elaborating on this theme, Miss Smith once told *CA:* ''My deep concern in writing is not simply race relations but the curious and dramatic and subtle ways men have of dehumanizing themselves and others. This is my real theme; and I am fascinated by the deep meanings attached to the word, *segregation.* My writings tend toward depth analysis, the philosophic and ethical implications of segregation, the curious ideas about the body image, etc. I am not a 'reformer' and hate organizations and groups, although sometimes my conscience makes me do chores for them.''

This same conscience could also cause her to break relations with an organization. She had worked with Congress on Racial Equality (CORE) for twenty years but resigned in 1966 when she could no longer sanction its militancy. In a letter to Floyd B. McKissick, CORE's national director, she wrote: ''I strongly protest the dangerous and unwise position CORE has taken on the use of violence in effecting racial change. . . . CORE has been infiltrated by adventurers and by nihilists, black nationalists and plain old-fashioned haters, who have finally taken over.'' She described the new leaders of CORE as ''new killers of the dream. . . . We are working for something bigger than civil rights. We are working for better human beings, we are working for excellence in our cultural life.''

Miss Smith's personal life evolved around operations, cobalt treatments, and hormone treatments. ''I have been struggling with cancer since 1953,'' she wrote *CA* in 1963, ''but during this time have written four books, partially written several others, lectured a number of times, been on television and radio, made tapes, and even went to India for five months. I still have cancer but find it rather a friendly enemy to live with. I have often said more people die of fear of cancer than of the cancer itself; I cannot 'prove' that, but I believe it.'' She had weaker moments in her prolonged fight as is evidenced in a letter to a friend: ''One wants to yowl, sometimes, at this never-ending struggle. It has to be; God, I wish I were as courageous as my friends think I am. But when I can work I am happy and content.''

She was also ''happy and content'' with her surroundings. ''My home is on a lovely old mountain in north Georgia, where, in spite of my 'controversial' books, the people are friendly and also take me seriously enough to read me. Large quantities of my books are sold in my home town. I love the quietness of the mountain. It affords me a needed seclusion for writing, thinking, studying, painting, listening to music; but I get out into the world often, get into all sorts of activities, know people from the top crust to the bottom ooze; it is my job to, as a writer; but it is also my pleasure to find ways of relating myself to all kinds of people, mean, nasty, bigoted, brave, warm, human, ignorant, brilliant, 'normal' and 'abnormal'—two words I do not believe in.''

While discussing her stature as a person and a writer, she wrote: ''I am small, in height and weight; am called 'vivid, warm, unpretentious.' And this is true, I think; but I have a devil of a temper if people really get too mean; I hate the idea of being a martyr myself and do not like to stress my 'difficult times.' After all, who doesn't have them? After *Strange Fruit,* tons of stuff was written about me. Some fantastic things have been written, too. I have in recent years been 'smothered' somewhat; the critics don't know how to categorize me—and in this age not to be able to file somebody away in a category or pinch them into a stereotype is the signal to bury them! I feel I have been influenced greatly by Dostoevsky, Kafka, and to a certain extent by Freud, Jung, Fromm, Erik Erikson, Maritain, and Charles Williams. Camus I admire; I have not been influenced by him. Faulkner I do not admire; too superficial and anti-woman.''

Miss Smith's manuscripts are in the library of the University of Florida, which also has a complete file of the little magazine edited by her and materials related to it. Some nine thousand of her letters pertaining to the period when she was most deeply involved in race relations, which had been gathered at the request of the Library of Congress, were destroyed along with other materials when her house was burned by two white boys in 1955.

At her request, passages of *The Journey* were read at a memorial service for her on September 30, 1966. The following excerpt denoted her thought on the existence of man. ''To believe in something not yet proved and to underwrite it with our lives; is the only way we can leave the future open. Man, surrounded by facts, permitting himself no surmise, no intuitive flash, no great hypothesis, no risk is in a locked cell. Ignorance cannot seal the mind and imagination more surely. To find the point where hypothesis and fact meet; the delicate equilibrium between dream and reality; the place where fantasy and earthy things are metamorphosed into a work of art; the hour when faith in the future becomes knowledge of the past; to lay down one's powers for others in need; to shake off the old ordeal and get ready for the new; to question, knowing that never can the full answer be found; to accept uncertainties quietly, even our incomplete knowledge of God: this is what man's journey is about, I think.''

Strange Fruit was dramatized on Broadway, 1945-46.

BIOGRAPHICAL/CRITICAL SOURCES: Time, March 20, 1944; *Publisher's Weekly,* March 25, 1944, May 27, 1944,

December 2, 1944; *Atlantic Monthly*, May, 1944; *Catholic World*, May, 1944; *Newsweek*, May 29, 1944; *Saturday Review*, February 17, 1945, October 22, 1966; *New York Herald Tribune Book Review*, October 30, 1949; *Collier's*, January 28, 1950; *Christian Century*, October 2, 1957; *Life*, December 15, 1961; Bradford Daniel, editor, *Black, White and Gray*, Sheed & Ward, 1964; Robert B. Downs, editor, *The First Freedom*, American Library Association, 1966; *New York Times*, July 6, 1966.†

(Died September 28, 1966)

* * *

SMITH, Mary Benton   1903-

PERSONAL: Born August 19, 1903, in Madill, Okla.; daughter of John Wiley and Mary Jane (Scobee) Benton; married Thor Merritt Smith (retired vice-president and director of development, Mills College), April 17, 1930; children: Deanne (Mrs. Jay McMurren), Suzanne (Mrs. Richard P. Mueller), Marianne (Mrs. Henry Hudson Hubbard III). *Education:* University of California, Los Angeles, student, 1924-25; University of Oregon, B.S., 1928. *Politics:* Democrat. *Religion:* Episcopalian. *Home:* 74 La Cumbre Circle, Santa Barbara, Calif. 93105.

CAREER: University of Nevada, Reno, instructor in journalism and English, 1942-43; Associated Press, acting correspondent and chief of bureau, Reno, Nev., 1943-45, accredited correspondent at signing of Japanese Peace Treaty, 1951; *Sunset* (magazine), Menlo Park, Calif., travel scout, 1945-51; Macy's, San Francisco, Calif., senior publicity executive, 1951-52; Western Business Publications, San Francisco, Calif., assistant editor of *Pacific Travel News*, 1963-73, editor of *All Ashore!* (Pacific & Orient Lines publication), 1964-66; assistant editor, *Pacific Commerce*, 1966-68. American Red Cross, publicity co-chairman for Nevada, 1942-45; San Francisco Protestant Orphanage, publicity director, 1950; Peninsula Young Men's Christian Association, Burlingame, director, 1952. *Member:* Audubon Society, Museum of Natural History, Museum of Art, Botanic Garden (all Santa Barbara), Channel City Women's Forum, Theta Sigma Phi.

WRITINGS—"Sunset Travel Books"; all published by Lane: (With Mary Ellen Fox) *New Zealand*, 1964, revised edition, 1965; (with Fox) *Australia*, 1964; (with Mimi Bell) *Japan*, 1964; *Hong Kong*, 1965; *Islands of the South Pacific*, 1965; *Southeast Asia*, 1968; *Taiwan*, 1968.

(Research associate), Richard Travis Atkins and Jane McGlennon Atkins, *The World Traveler's Medical Guide*, Simon & Schuster, 1958.

SIDELIGHTS: Mary Smith has done research for travel writing in Europe, Indonesia, Japan, Hong Kong, Macao, Philippines, Taiwan, and the major islands of the Pacific.

* * *

SMITH, Ruth Leslie   1902-

PERSONAL: Born March 1, 1902, in Brooklyn, N.Y.; married David Gellar (a lawyer), August, 1920 (deceased); married Joseph L. Smith (a retired pharmacist), July, 1967; children: (first marriage) Doris L. Gellar Pertz, Elsie Gellar Wilner, Ralph. *Education:* Studied classical art at Cooper Union Women's Art School.

CAREER: Legal stenographer for a number of years, assisting her lawyer-husband; often entertained her children and their friends with original stories and puppet plays, told stories in settlement houses, and performed her puppet plays in schools.

*WRITINGS—*For children: *Hurry! Dinner Is at Six* (fantasy), Bobbs-Merrill, 1969.

WORK IN PROGRESS: Two more children's books, *Mollie, Pretzel and the Diving Saucer*, and a mystery for boys.

BIOGRAPHICAL/CRITICAL SOURCES: Commonweal, May 23, 1969.†

* * *

SMITH, Warren L(ounsbury)   1914-1972

PERSONAL: Born March 23, 1914, in Watertown, N.Y.; son of Burt W. and Fannie (Allen) Smith; married Ann Elizabeth Schwartz, August 27, 1943; children: Andrew L., Samuel W., Catherine A. *Education:* University of Michigan, B.A., 1947, M.A., 1949, Ph.D., 1952. *Politics:* Democrat. *Religion:* Unitarian Universalist. *Home:* 1584 Marian, Ann Arbor, Mich. 48103. *Office:* Department of Economics, University of Michigan, Ann Arbor, Mich. 48104.

CAREER: University of Michigan, Ann Arbor, instructor in economics, 1952-53; University of Virginia, Charlottesville, assistant professor of economics, 1953-56; Ohio State University, Columbus, associate professor of economics, 1956-57; University of Michigan, associate professor, 1957-59, professor of economics, 1959-72, chairman of department, 1963-68, 1970-71. Visiting lecturer, Harvard University, 1958-59. Council of Economic Advisors, senior staff member, 1962-63, member, 1968-69. Consultant to U.S. governmental agencies, beginning 1958. *Military service:* U.S. Army Air Forces, 1942-45; became sergeant. *Member:* American Economic Association, Econometric Society, American Finance Association, American Association of University Professors, Phi Beta Kappa.

WRITINGS: Debt Management in the United States, Joint Economic Committee, Congress of the United States, 1960; *Reserve Requirements in the American Monetary System*, Prentice-Hall, 1963; (editor with Richard L. Teigen) *Readings in Money, National Income, and Stabilized Policy*, Irwin, 1965, 3rd edition, 1974; *Macroeconomics*, Irwin, 1970. Contributor to professional journals.

WORK IN PROGRESS: Further research on U.S. monetary and fiscal policy.

BIOGRAPHICAL/CRITICAL SOURCES: New York Times, April 24, 1972; *Washington Post*, April 25, 1972.†

(Died April 23, 1972)

* * *

SMITH, William Stevenson   1907-1969

PERSONAL: Born February 7, 1907, in Indianapolis, Ind.; son of Louis Ferdinand and Edna (Stevenson) Smith. *Education:* Attended University of Chicago, 1924-26; Harvard University, A.B., 1928, Ph.D., 1940. *Home:* 6 Avon Pl., Cambridge, Mass. 02140. *Office:* Museum of Fine Arts, 479 Huntington Ave., Boston, Mass. 02115.

CAREER: Museum of Fine Arts, Boston, Mass., staff of Egyptian department, 1941-69, as assistant curator, 1941-54, associate curator, 1954-56, curator of Egyptian art, 1956-69. Lecturer in fine arts at Harvard University, 1948-69. Member of Egyptian expedition to Giza Pyramids, 1930-39, 1946-47. President of American Research Center in Egypt, Inc., 1963-66. *Military service:* U.S. Naval Reserve, active duty, 1942-46; became lieutenant commander. *Member:* Archaeological Institute of America, American Academy of Arts and Sciences (fellow), American Oriental Society, German Archaeological Institute.

WRITINGS: *Ancient Egypt as Represented in the Museum of Fine Arts, Boston*, Museum of Fine Arts, 1942, 4th revised edition, 1968; *A History of Egyptian Sculpture and Painting in the Old Kingdom*, Oxford University Press, 1946, 2nd edition, 1949, Chapter XIV included in Volume I of *Cambridge Ancient History*, 2nd edition, Cambridge University Press, 1962; (with George A. Reisner) *A History of the Giza Necropolis*, Volume II, Harvard University Press, 1955; *The Art and Architecture of Ancient Egypt*, Penguin, 1958; *Interconnections in the Ancient Near East*, Yale University Press, 1965.†

(Died January 13, 1969)

* * *

SMURTHWAITE, Ronald 1918-1975

PERSONAL: Born December 13, 1918, in Twickenham, England; son of Thomas and Ann (Smith) Smurthwaite; married Molly Hayward, October 22, 1939; children: Favel Paul, Nicholas. *Education:* Chartered Insurance Institute, A.C.I.I. *Religion:* Church of England. *Home:* 114 High St., Hampton, Middlesex, England. *Office:* Corporation of Insurance Brokers, 15 St. Helens Pl., London E.C. 3, England.

CAREER: Chartered Insurance Institute, London, England, careers advisory officer, 1958-64; Corporation of Insurance Brokers, London, 1965-75, began as national secretary, became director. *Military service:* British Army, Intelligence Corps, 1939-46; became captain. *Member:* Chartered Insurance Institute.

WRITINGS: *Insurance*, Sunday Times Book Co., 1960; *Target for Careers—Insurance*, R. Hale, 1961; *Nicholas in Insurance* (novel), Chatto & Windus, 1963; *Commerce as a Career*, Batsford, 1965; (with Rita Udall) *Starting Work*, Batsford, 1966; *The Services of an Insurance Broker*, Hodder & Stoughton, 1966. Author of sixty radio and television scripts for British Broadcasting Corp.

AVOCATIONAL INTERESTS: Visiting prisons and oil painting.†

(Died October, 1975)

* * *

SNAVELY, Ellen Bartow 1910-

PERSONAL: Born June 23, 1910, in Milan, Ohio; daughter of Winfield Bronson and Gertrude (Strong) Bartow; married Robert Hamilton Snavely (a teacher), May 27, 1934; children: Pamela Jane (Mrs. Phillip C. Ashley), Gretchen Elizabeth (Mrs. Russell E. Coney). *Education:* Bowling Green State University, Elementary Education Certificate. *Politics:* Republican. *Religion:* Protestant. *Home:* 34 West Broadway, Westerville, Ohio 40381. *Agent:* Scott Meredith Literary Agency, Inc., 845 Third Ave., New York, N.Y. 10022.

CAREER: Teacher in Ohio public schools at intervals, beginning 1932; private home tutor at intervals, beginning 1952; Otterbein College, Westerville, Ohio, part-time preschool teacher, beginning 1959. *Member:* National League of American Pen Women, Council of Religious Education (secretary). *Awards, honors:* Two awards for short-short stories from *Writer's Digest;* three first awards from Midwest Regional Conference of Pen Women.

WRITINGS: *Shoes for Angela*, Follett, 1962. Author of several dozen skits for youth fellowship groups, local clubs, and civic groups. Contributor to *Humpty Dumpty's, Jack and Jill, Children's Friend, Sunday Digest, Lookout,* and other periodicals.

WORK IN PROGRESS: *Come On, Let's Teach*, a handbook for beginning elementary teachers; *With a Walk, Trot, and Canter*, a book of family experiences in the horse world, as done on a limited budget.†

* * *

SNOW, Sinclair 1909-1972

PERSONAL: Born August 28, 1909, in Pulaski, Va.; son of William Henry and Rosa (Harkrader) Snow; married Kimberley Hartzog (a graduate student), June 2, 1966; children: Kimberley, Simms. *Education:* Virginia Polytechnic Institute, student, 1948-49; Roanoke College, B.A., 1951; Escuela Interamerican Saltillo, Mexico, graduate student, 1952; University of North Dakota, M.A. 1955; University of Virginia, Ph.D., 1960. *Office:* Social Sciences Department, Eastern Kentucky University, Richmond, Ky. 40476.

CAREER: In earlier years worked as merchant seaman, forester, telephone lineman, electrician, broadcast technician, and in other fields; Virginia Intermont College, Bristol, professor of Spanish, 1956-57; University of Virginia, Roanoke, instructor in history and Spanish, 1959-61; University of Virginia, Charlottesville, assistant professor of history, summer, 1961; Martha Washington College, Fredericksburg, Va., assistant professor of history, 1962; Memphis State University, Memphis, Tenn., assistant professor of history, 1962-63; Lander College, Greenwood, S.C., associate professor of history, 1963-66; University of North Dakota, Grand Forks, associate professor of history, 1966-69; Eastern Kentucky University, Richmond, professor of history, 1969-72. *Military service:* U.S. Army, Signal Corps, World War II. *Member:* American Historical Association, American Association of University Professors.

WRITINGS: *The Pan-American Federation of Labor*, Duke University Press, 1964; (editor) John Kenneth Turner, *Barbarous Mexico*, University of Texas Press, 1969. Contributor to professional journals.†

(Died February, 1972)

* * *

SOBOL, Louis 1896-

PERSONAL: Born August 10, 1896, in New Haven, Conn.; son of Jacob (a clock-maker) and Sonya (Secol) Sobol; married Helen Lee Cantor, April 26, 1919 (died, 1948); married Peggy Marlowe Antman, July 28, 1950; children: (first marriage) Natalie Muriel Sobol Spritzler (deceased). *Education:* Attended school in Waterbury, Conn. *Politics:* Independent. *Home:* 333 West 56th St., New York, N.Y. 10019.

CAREER: Member of editorial staff of newspapers in Waterbury, Conn., 1919-23, and New London, Conn., 1923-25; newspaperman and columnist in New York City, for more than forty years, first as city editor of *Automotive Daily News*, 1925-26, then writer for Famous Features Syndicate, 1926-27; began with *New York Evening Graphic* as a rewrite man, 1929, but shortly succeeded Walter Winchell as that paper's Broadway columnist and drama critic, 1929-31; Broadway columnist for *New York Journal*, 1931-35, *New York Journal American*, 1935-66, and *New York World Journal Tribune*, 1966-67; editor, Simon & Flynn, Inc. (publishers), New York City, 1968-70; director of features, Robert S. Taplinger Associates, Inc., New York City, beginning 1970. *Military service:* U.S. Army, 1917-18. *Member:* American Legion, Skeeters. *Awards, honors:* Knight Commander, Order of St. Andrew of Caffa.

WRITINGS: Six Lost Women, C. Kendall, 1936; *Some Days Were Happy* (autobiographical), Random House, 1947; *Along the Broadway Beat,* Avon, 1951; *The Longest Street* (memoirs; foreword by Jim Bishop), Crown, 1968. Author of play, "The High Hatters," produced, 1927. Contributor of fiction and feature articles to *Cosmopolitan, Photoplay, Redbook, Collier's, Town and Country, Signature, American Legion Magazine,* and other national magazines.

SIDELIGHTS: Louis Sobol has given his collection of Broadway memorabilia to New York University. He drew on the collection and his recollections for *The Longest Street,* a book that Maurice Zolotow described as "probably the longest Broadway column ever written . . . an authentic warehouse of souvenirs" about a bygone era.

BIOGRAPHICAL/CRITICAL SOURCES: Louis Sobol, *Some Days Were Happy,* Random House, 1947; Sobol, *The Longest Street,* Crown, 1968; *New York Times Book Review,* December 29, 1968.

* * *

SONNEBORN, Ruth (Cantor)   1899-1974

PERSONAL: Born October 14, 1899, in New York, N.Y.; daughter of Jacob A. and Lydia (Greenebaum) Cantor; married Lawrence H. Sonneborn, March 1, 1929; children: John Andrew, Eve Sonneborn Wenett. *Education:* Ethical Culture Normal School, Teacher's Certificate, 1920. *Politics:* Democrat. *Home:* 45 Barrow St., New York, N.Y. 10014. *Office:* Bank Street College of Education, 216 West 14th St., New York, N.Y. 10014.

CAREER: Bank Street College of Education, New York, N.Y., member of publications staff and director of bookstore, beginning 1944, became special consultant.

WRITINGS: (Contributor) L. S. Mitchell, editor, *Know Your Children in School,* Macmillan, 1954; (contributor)I. S. Black and Mitchell, editors, *Believe and Make Believe,* Dutton, 1956; *Question and Answer Book of Everyday Science,* Random House, 1961; *Question and Answer Book of Space,* Random House, 1965; *The Lollipop Party* (illustrated by Brinton Turkle), Viking, 1967; *Seven in a Bed,* Viking, 1968; *Friday Night is Papa Night* (Junior Literary Guild selection), Viking, 1970; *I Love Gram,* Viking, 1971. Editor of book page, *Journal of Nursery Education.*

BIOGRAPHICAL/CRITICAL SOURCES: Lee Bennett Hopkins, *Books Are by People,* Citation Press, 1969.†

(Died February 24, 1974)

* * *

SOULE, George (Henry, Jr.)   1887-1970

PERSONAL: Born June 11, 1887, in Stamford, Conn.; son of George Henry (a manufacturer) and Ellen (Smyth) Soule; married M. Flanders Dunbar (a physician), July, 1940 (deceased); children: Marcia Winslow Dunbar-Soule. *Education:* Yale University, A.B., 1908. *Residence:* (Summer) South Kent, Conn.

CAREER: Frederick A. Stokes Co. (publishers), New York City, 1908-14, became advertising manager; *New Republic,* New York City, assistant editor, 1914-18, an editor, 1924-46; Bennington College, Bennington, Vt., professor of economics, 1949-57; visiting professor at Colgate University, Hamilton, N.Y., 1958, Washington College, Chestertown, Md., 1958-59, and University of Tennessee, Knoxville, 1961-62. Author of books, mainly on economics, 1920-70. Summer teacher at Columbia University, 1948-52. Co-founder,

Labor Bureau, Inc., 1920; director-at-large, National Bureau of Economic Research, 1922-70; consultant to Twentieth Century Fund, 1948-57. *Military service:* U.S. Coast Artillery Corps, 1918; became second lieutenant. *Member:* American Economic Association, American Association for the Advancement of Science (fellow). *Awards, honors:* Fund for Advancement of Education grant, 1958-59.

WRITINGS: (Co-author) *The New Unionism in the Clothing Industry,* Harcourt, 1920, reprinted, Russell, 1968; *The Intellectual and the Labor Movement,* League for Industrial Democracy (New York), 1923; *The Accumulation of Capital,* League for Industrial Democracy, 1924; *Wage Arbitration,* Macmillan, 1928; *The Useful Art of Economics,* Macmillan, 1929; *A Planned Society,* Macmillan, 1932, reprinted, Peter Smith, 1965; *The Coming American Revolution,* Macmillan, 1934; *The Future of Liberty,* Macmillan, 1936; *An Economic Constitution for Democracy,* Yale University Press, 1939; *Sidney Hillman, Labor Statesman,* Macmillan, 1939; *The Strength of Nations: A Study in Social Theory,* Macmillan, 1942; *America's Stake in Britain's Future,* Viking, 1945; (with David Efron and Norman T. Ness) *Latin America in the Future World,* Farrar & Rinehart, for National Planning Association, 1945; *Prosperity Decade; From War to Depression: 1917-1929,* Rinehart, 1947; *Introduction to Economic Science,* Viking, 1948, revised edition published as *The New Science of Economics: An Introduction,* Viking, 1964, revised edition, Fawcett, 1965; *The Costs of Health Insurance,* [New York], 1949; (with Max W. Thornburg) *Turkey: An Economic Appraisal,* Allen & Unwin, 1949, reprinted, Greenwood Press, 1968.

Compilation Showing Progress and Status of the Defense Minerals Production Program, U.S. Government Printing Office, 1952; *Ideas of the Great Economists,* Viking, 1952; *Gypsum: Information Concerning Gypsum and a New All-Purpose Building Material,* U.S. Government Printing Office, 1952; *Economic Forces in American History,* Sloane, 1952, revised edition, with Vincent P. Carosso, published as *American Economic History,* Dryden, 1957; *Men, Wages, and Employment in the Modern U.S. Economy,* New American Library, 1954; *Economics for Living,* Abelard, 1954, 2nd edition, 1961; *Time for Living,* Viking, 1955; *What Automation Does to Human Beings,* Sidgwick & Jackson, 1956; *U.S.A. in New Dimension: The Measure and Promise of America's Resources,* Macmillan, 1957; *The Shape of Tomorrow,* New American Library, 1958; *Longer Life,* Viking, 1958; *Economics: Measurement, Theories, Case Studies,* Holt, 1961; *Planning: U.S.A.,* Viking, 1967.†

(Died April 14, 1970)

* * *

SOUTHGATE, W(yndham) M(ason)   1910-

PERSONAL: Born May 26, 1910, in Birmingham, Ala.; son of James Taylor (a businessman) and Lizzie Morris (Mason) Southgate; married Joan Prosper Rudisill, May 11, 1941. *Education:* Attended Birmingham-Southern College, 1927-28; Harvard University, A.B. (cum laude), 1931, A.M., 1932, Ph.D., 1948. *Politics:* Democrat. *Religion:* Episcopalian. *Home:* 5 Sheppard Pl., Granville, Ohio 43023.

CAREER: Instructor in history at Birmingham-Southern College, Birmingham, Ala., 1932-33, Scripps College, Claremont, Calif., 1938-41, and California Institute of Technology, Pasadena, 1941-42; Denison University, Granville, Ohio, beginning 1946, began as assistant professor, professor of history, 1954-75, professor emeritus, 1975—, head of department, 1960-63. Educational consultant to Owens-

Corning Fiberglas, 1953-55; visiting lecturer in history, Kenyon College, 1966. *Military service:* U.S. Naval Reserve, active duty, 1942-46; became commander. *Member:* American Historical Association, American Association of University Professors. *Awards, honors:* American Philosophical Society grant, 1950.

WRITINGS: (Contributor) R. L. Schuyler and H. Ausubel, editors, *The Making of English History,* Dryden, 1952; *John Jewel and the Problem of Doctrinal Authority,* Harvard University Press, 1962. Contributor of articles and reviews to historical journals.

WORK IN PROGRESS: Research in Elizabethan puritanism.

*   *   *

SOUTHWORTH, James G(ranville)   1896-

PERSONAL: Born October 18, 1896, in Monroe, Mich.; son of Clinton Byron and Phily (Osgood) Southworth; married Bernice Weis, April 12, 1924 (died May 16, 1925); married Janet Miller Dixon (divorced March 12, 1946). *Education:* University of Michigan, A.B., 1918; Oxford University, B.A. (honors), 1927, M.A., 1933; Harvard University, Ph.D., 1931. *Home:* 625 Virginia, Toledo, Ohio 43620.

CAREER: Employed in business firms, 1918-25; College of Puget Sound (now University of Puget Sound), Tacoma, Wash., professor of English, 1928-29; Heidelberg College, Tiffin, Ohio, professor of English, 1931-33; University of Toledo, Toledo, Ohio, professor of English, 1934-66, chairman of the department, 1961-63. Fulbright visiting lecturer, Kyushu University, 1958-59, Tokyo University of Foreign Studies, 1964-65. *Military service:* U.S. Aviation Service, flying cadet, World War I. *Member:* Modern Language Association of America, American Association of University Professors, College English Association, Pi Mu Epsilon.

WRITINGS: Sowing the Spring: Studies in British Poets from Hopkins to MacNeice, Basil Blackwell, 1940, Books for Libraries, 1968; *Vauxhall Gardens: A Chapter in the Social History of England,* Columbia University Press, 1941, reprinted, Octagon, 1971; *The Poetry of Thomas Hardy,* Columbia University Press, 1947; *Some Modern American Poets,* Basil Blackwell, 1950, Books for Libraries, 1968; *More Modern American Poets,* Basil Blackwell, 1954, Books for Libraries, 1968; *Verses of Cadence: An Introduction to the Prosody of Chaucer and His Followers,* Basil Blackwell, 1954, reprinted, Folcroft, 1973; *The Prosody of Chaucer and His Followers,* Basil Blackwell, 1962.

WORK IN PROGRESS: Aristotle and Mr. Shakespeare.

SIDELIGHTS: Southworth traveled in Europe, Japan, and the Far East. He once gave his motivation as "general intellectual curiosity," and his viewpoint as "to live as full and well-rounded [a] life as possible." *Avocational interests:* Ceramics.

*   *   *

SOWERBY, E(mily) Millicent   1883-

PERSONAL: Born September 7, 1883, in Beverley, East Yorkshire, England; daughter of Henry and Emily (Mills) Sowerby. *Education:* Girton College, Cambridge, M.A., 1912; University of Grenoble, summer study. *Home:* 211 Merrywood Lane, Muncie, Ind. 47304.

CAREER: W. M. Voynich, London, England, rare book cataloger, 1912-14; Sotheby & Co., London, book cataloger,

1916-23; American Art Galleries, New York City, book cataloger, 1923-24; New York (N.Y.) Public Library, worked in reserve room and in rare books, 1924; Rosenbach Co., Philadelphia, Pa., and New York City, bibliographer, 1925-42; U.S. Library of Congress, Washington, D.C., Jefferson bibliographer, 1942-55. *Member:* Bibliographical Society (England), Bibliographical Society of America.

WRITINGS: (Compiler and annotator) *Catalogue of the Library of Thomas Jefferson,* five volumes, Library of Congress, 1952-59; *Rare Books and Rare People* (memoirs), Constable, 1967. Also wrote three books published under the name of Abraham Simon Wolf Rosenbach (Dr. Rosenbach of the Rosenbach Co.), *An American Jewish Bibliography,* American Jewish Historical Society, 1926, *The Earliest Christmas Books,* privately printed, 1927, and *Early American Children's Books,* Southworth Press, 1933.

SIDELIGHTS: Miss Sowerby was 84 when her memoirs were published, a book that the *Times Literary Supplement* found distinguished by breeding and good manners and certain to find a "permanent niche in the annals of the rare-book trade during three of the most exciting decades of its history." The *Times* critic mentions that her friendship with Dr. Rosenbach endured despite his bland assumption that it was entirely reasonable that she should write his books and articles ("a large number of articles," Miss Sowerby recalls). She adds that she didn't sell her memoirs to Constable but that "someone else did." "A knowledge of most foreign languages was essential in my Rare Book life," she writes, "however French is the only one I really remember now."

BIOGRAPHICAL/CRITICAL SOURCES: Times Literary Supplement, January 18, 1968.

*   *   *

SPARKE, (George) Archibald   1871-1970

PERSONAL: Born July 19, 1871, in Cardiff, Wales; son of Edward (a shipping clerk) and Victoria (Cochrane) Sparke; married Beatrice Kate Andrews, July, 1896 (died, 1948); children: Beatrice Muriel (Mrs. Franz Minoprio; died, 1963), Dorothy (Mrs. Kenneth Marshall). *Education:* Attended Tredegarville School, Cardiff; studied with private tutors. *Home:* 11 Conyers Ave., Birkdale, Southport, Lancashire, England.

CAREER: Trained in Cardiff Public Library; former librarian of Kidderminster, Carlisle, Bury, and Bolton. Lecturer, Victoria University, Manchester. Freeman of City of Exeter, 1907. Former member, Council of the Library Association. *Member:* Lancashire Parish Register Society (honorary secretary, 1931-57), Royal Society of Literature (fellow), Library Association (fellow). *Awards, honors:* M.A., Manchester University.

WRITINGS: (Compiler) *The Index to the First 16 Volumes of Transactions of the Cumberland and Westmorland Antiquarian and Archaeological Society (1866-1900),* T. Wilson, 1901; *A Bibliography of the Dialect Literature of Cumberland, Westmorland, and Lancashire North of the Sands,* T. Wilson, 1907; (transcriber and editor) *The Township Booke of Halliwell (1640-1762),* Chetham Society, 1911; *Bibliographia Boltoniensis,* University Press (Manchester), 1913; (transcriber) *The New Church in Rosendale Parish Registers (1653-1723),* Lancashire Parish Register Society, 1913; (editor and indexer) *The Bolton Parish Registers (1573-1660),* Lancashire Parish Register Society, 1913; (with Albert Reginald Corns) *A Bibliography of Unfinished Books,* Quaritch, Ltd., 1915, reprinted, Gale, 1968; (editor) *The Deane Parish Registers (1604-1750),* Lancashire Parish Register Society, two volumes, 1917, Volume III: ... *(1751-1812)*, 1940; *The Bowyer Bible*, Libraries Committee (Bolton, England), 1920; (with H. Hamer) *The Book of Bolton*, Tillotson, 1929; *Index to Garstang Parish Registers (1660-1734)*, Lancashire Parish Register Society, 1932; (editor) *Warrington Parish Registers (1591-1653)*, Lancashire Parish Register Society, 1933, ... *(1653-1680)*, Preston, 1955, ... *(1681-1700)*, 1962; (editor and indexer) *North Meols Parish Registers (1732-1812)*, Lancashire Parish Register Society, 1935; (editor) *Great Harwood Parish Registers (1547-1812)*, Lancashire Parish Register Society, 1937; (transcriber, editor, and indexer) *Leigh Parish Registers (1626-1700)*, Preston, 1948.

Also author of *The Uses of Public Libraries*, 1895; *Handbook to Turner's "Liber Studiorum,"* 1902; *John Kay, Inventor: An Appreciation*, 1904; *The Bury Art Gallery and the Wrigley Collection of Pictures*, 1904; (editor and transcriber) *The Bury Parish Registers (1647-1698)*, 1905; *Town Bibliographies*, 1913; *How the Public Library Can Help the Business Man*, 1917, 3rd edition, 1919; *Broken Arcs*, 1918; *Bibliography of Walt Whitman*, 1931; *Guide to Iwerne Minster*, 1934; (transcriber, editor and indexer) *Turton Parish Registers (1720-1812)*, 1943; *Notes from My Memory Box*, 1963. Author of many pamphlets and articles on librarianship and bibliography. Contributor to *Notes and Queries* and other professional journals.

BIOGRAPHICAL/CRITICAL SOURCES: Library World, April, 1963.†

(Died November 28, 1970)

* * *

SPEARMAN, Arthur Dunning   1899-

PERSONAL: Born August 26, 1899, in Wheaton, Ill.; son of Frank Hamilton and Eugenie Amelia (Lonergan) Spearman. *Education:* Attended Loyola Academy, Chicago, Ill., Loyola University of Los Angeles, and University of Santa Clara; Gonzaga University, B.A., 1926, M.A., 1927; St. Louis University, B.S.Th., 1931, Licentiate in Theology, 1932. *Home:* 820 Alviso St., Santa Clara, Calif. 95053. *Office:* University of Santa Clara, Santa Clara, Calif. 95053.

CAREER: Entered Society of Jesus (Jesuits), 1918, ordained priest in St. Louis, Mo., 1931. Seattle Preparatory School, Seattle, Wash., teacher of English, 1927-29; Loyola University of Los Angeles, Los Angeles, Calif., director of library, 1935-47; archdiocesan director of sodality youth organizations, Los Angeles, 1941-47; parish work with Spanish-speaking groups, San Diego, Calif., 1949-54; research in geneology and California Jesuit history, beginning 1954; University of Santa Clara, Santa Clara, Calif., archivist, beginning 1957. Chairman of Santa Clara Historical Landmarks Commission, 1960-64. *Member:* Society of Colonial Wars (California; life member), American Aviation Historical Society.

WRITINGS: The Spanish-English Confessor's Guide, Saint Anthony Guild Press, 1942, revised edition, 1960; *The Five Franciscan Churches of Mission Santa Clara*, National Press Publications, 1963; *John Joseph Montgomery, Father of Basic Flying*, University of Santa Clara Press, 1967. Author of pamphlets on Jesuits and Jesuit history including, *Our Lady Patroness of the Californias, Padre Magin Catala*, and *Bernard R. Hubbard*.

WORK IN PROGRESS: A family history, *Rails to the West*.

AVOCATIONAL INTERESTS: Archaeology, Bible sources, trees (forest and garden).

SPEARMAN, Walter (Smith)   1908-

PERSONAL: Born January 9, 1908, in Newberry, S.C.; son of Walter Smith (a farmer) and Minnie Agnes (Cuthbertson) Spearman; married Mary Elizabeth Dale, August 7, 1937 (deceased); married Jean Johnson, August 29, 1969; children: (first marriage) Robert Worthington, Mary Lindsay. *Education:* University of North Carolina, A.B., 1929, M.A., 1937; University of Lyon, Certificate, 1930; Harvard University, further study, 1957-58. *Politics:* Democrat. *Religion:* Presbyterian. *Home:* 418 Whitehead Cir., Chapel Hill, N.C. 27514. *Office:* School of Journalism, 102 Howell Hall, University of North Carolina, Chapel Hill, N.C. 27514.

CAREER: Charlotte News, Charlotte, N.C., reporter, drama critic, and book editor, 1930-35; University of North Carolina, Chapel Hill, instructor, 1935-37, assistant professor, 1937-40, associate professor, 1940-48, professor of journalism, beginning 1948. Editorial writer, *New Orleans Item*, summer, 1955, and *Greensboro Daily News*, summer, 1965; director of Writers' Workshop, Chautauqua, N.Y., 1956-61. Director, North Carolina Scholastic Press Institute, beginning 1940; secretary, North Carolina Editorial Writers Conference; chairman, North Carolina Writers Conference; moderator, Annual Town Meeting on Books, Greensboro, beginning 1948. *Military service:* U.S. Army, Quartermaster Corps, 1942-45; became second lieutenant.

MEMBER: Association for Education in Journalism, American Association of University Professors, Sigma Delta Chi, Kappa Tau Alpha, Chi Psi, Chapel Hill Country Club (president, 1947). *Awards, honors:* Fund for Adult Education fellowship at Harvard University, 1957-58; Tanner Award for excellence in teaching, 1967.

WRITINGS: Racial Crisis and the Press, Southern Regional Council, 1960; (with Samuel Selden) *The Carolina Playmakers: The First Fifty Years*, University of North Carolina Press, 1970.

Plays: *Death of a Swan*, Herald Press, 1932; *Transient*, Herald Press, 1933; *Dead Man's Bluff*, Herald Press, 1934; *Country Sunday*, Association of Southern Women for the Prevention of Lynching, 1936. Author of University of North Carolina Library Extension booklets, including *The Film Yesterday, Today and Tomorrow*, 1941, *Understanding the News*, 1942, and *North Carolina Writers*, 1949. Author of weekly book review column for four North Carolina newspapers and drama reviewer for *Chapel Hill Weekly*.

WORK IN PROGRESS: A book, *Reviewing Books, Plays and Movies*, also the title of a course he has taught for a number of years.

AVOCATIONAL INTERESTS: Acting (appears from time to time with Carolina Playmakers and had a character role in the American International film, "Killers Three").

* * *

SPEARS, Edward (Louis)   1886-1974

PERSONAL: Born August 7, 1886; son of Charles McCarthy and Marguerite Milicent (Hack) Spears; married Mary Borden (an American-born novelist), 1918 (died, 1968); married Nancy Maurice, 1969; children: (first marriage) Michael Justin Aylmer (deceased). *Education:* Educated privately in England and in the south of France, where he had to spend winters as a boy because of respiratory trouble following diphtheria. *Religion:* Church of England. *Home:* 12 Strathearn Pl., Hyde Park Square, London W.2, England. *Office:* 164 St. Stephen's House, Westminster, London S.W.1, England.

CAREER: Joined Kildare militia before his seventeenth birthday, and served in the regular British Army, initially with 8th Hussars, and then with 11th Hussars, 1906-20; retired from Army following three years as head of British Military Mission to Paris, 1917-20; member of Parliament, representing Loughborough division of Leicester, 1922-24, and Carlisle, 1931-45; named major general and British Prime Minister's personal representative with French Prime Minister and Minister of Defence, 1940; head of British Mission to General de Gaulle, 1940, and Spears Mission to Syria and Lebanon, 1941; first British minister to Republics of Syria and Lebanon, 1942-45; created baronet, 1953, with title Major General Sir Edward Spears; former president of British Bata Shoe Co. Ltd. and chairman of Ashanti Goldfields Corp. Ltd., both London. Institute of Directors, president, 1953-54, chancellor, 1966; life president of Commercial Union Assurance Co. Ltd., West End Board, 1972.

MEMBER: Royal Institute of International Affairs (founding member), Royal United Service Institution, United Service Corps (president), Cavalry Club, Carlton Club. *Awards, honors*—Military: Commander, Order of the British Empire, 1919; Companion of the Bath, 1921; Knight Commander, Order of the British Empire, 1942; mentioned in British dispatches five times (four times wounded), in French Army orders three times, and in Polish dispatches; Croix de Guerre with three palms (France); Etoile Noir; Grand Cross of White Eagle of Serbia; Czecho-Slovak Croix de Guerre.

WRITINGS: Lessons of the Russo-Japanese War, Hugh Rees Ltd., 1906; *Cavalry Tactical Schemes,* Hugh Rees Ltd., 1914; *Liaison 1914,* Heinemann, 1931, 2nd edition, Stein & Day, 1968; *Prelude to Victory,* J. Cape, 1939; *Assignment to Catastrophe,* Heinemann, 1954; *Two Men Who Saved France,* Eyre & Spottiswoode, 1966; *The Picnic Basket* (autobiographical), Secker & Warburg, 1967; W. W. Norton, 1968. Writer of scripts for British Broadcasting Corp. radio and television, and broadcasting companies abroad. Contributor to the British press, including *Times, Daily Telegraph, Daily Express,* and *Evening Standard.*†

(Died July, 1974)

* * *

SPECK, Gordon 1898-

PERSONAL: Born December 26, 1898, in Norfolk, Neb.; son of Loren J. (an engineer) and Mary Katherine (Show) Speck; married Lillian Lehman, August 17, 1925; children: Jane (Mrs. Leo L. McIntee), Jon. *Education:* Eastern Washington College, student, 1920-23; University of Idaho, B.S., 1927, M.S., 1931; University of Washington, Seattle, graduate student, 1928. *Home:* 9901 224th St., S.W., Edmonds, Wash. 98020.

CAREER: Junior and senior high school teacher of American history in Bend, Ore., 1924-26, in Everett, Wash., 1927-29, in Seattle, Wash., 1929-51. Has also worked in building and dry cleaning trades, landscape gardening, retail selling, and in a paper mill. Lecturer for Americanization classes. *Military service:* U.S. Navy, 1918-19. *Member:* American Archivists Society, Authors Guild, English Westerner's Society (London), Pacific Northwest Writers Conference, Washington State Historical Society.

WRITINGS: Northwest Explorations, Binfords, 1954, revised edition, 1970; *Samuel Hearne and the Northwest Passage,* Caxton, 1963; *Breeds and Halfbreeds,* Clarkston N. Potter, 1969. Contributor to *Journal of Natural Science in the Pacific Northwest.*

WORK IN PROGRESS: A history of the myths which resulted in New World explorations.

* * *

SPECTORSKY, A(uguste) C(omte) 1910-1972

PERSONAL: Born August 13, 1910, in Paris, France; son of American citizens, Isaac (an educator) and Frances (an opera singer in Paris, later an educator; maiden name, Herbert) Spectorsky; married Lucille Hill, August 6, 1937 (divorced); married Elizabeth Bullock, October 8, 1944 (divorced); married Theo Feigenspan (a personnel director), January, 1956; children: (first marriage) Susan Ann; (second marriage) Kathrine Michelle; (third marriage) Brooke Edwin, Lance Douglas. *Education:* New York University, B.S., 1934. *Politics:* Independent. *Religion:* None.

CAREER: New Yorker, New York, N.Y., editorial associate, 1938-41; *Chicago Sun* (now *Sun-Times*), Chicago, Ill., literary editor, 1941-46; Twentieth Century-Fox Film Corp., New York, N.Y., associate Eastern story editor, 1946-48; Street & Smith Publications, New York, N.Y., managing editor of *Living for Young Homemakers* and promotion director of *Charm,* 1948-51; *Park East* (magazine; now defunct), New York, N.Y., editor, 1951-54; National Broadcasting Co., New York, N.Y., staff member, 1952-54, senior editor, 1954-56; Playboy Enterprises, Inc., Chicago, Ill., senior vice-president, 1956-72, associate publisher and editorial director of *Playboy,* 1956-72. Author and editor. Member of board of directors, Urban Gateways.

MEMBER: American Institute of Management (executive member), International Society for General Semantics, Authors Guild, International P.E.N., Society of Midland Authors (director), Shaw Society of Chicago (vice-president), Phi Beta Kappa; Arts Club, Cliff Dwellers, Chicago Press Club, Columbia Yacht Club, Great Lakes Cruising Club (all Chicago).

WRITINGS: (Contributor) *North, East, South, West,* Howell, Soskin, 1945; (with Fred Iselin) *Invitation to Skiing,* Simon & Schuster, 1947; (editor) *Man into Beast,* Doubleday, 1948; (editor) *The Book of the Sea,* Appleton, 1954; *The Exurbanites,* Lippincott, 1955; (editor) *The Book of the Mountains,* Appleton, 1955; (editor) *The Book of the Sky,* Appleton, 1956; (editor) *The Book of the Earth,* Appleton, 1957; (editor) *The College Years* (anthology), Hawthorn, 1958; (with Iselin) *The New Invitation to Skiing,* Simon & Schuster, 1958, revised edition published as *Invitation to Modern Skiing,* 1965.

Author of radio and television scripts. Contributor to many national magazines, including *Cosmopolitan, Harper's Bazaar, Reader's Digest, Good Housekeeping, Collier's,* and to *New York Times Book Review, This Week,* and the daily press.

WORK IN PROGRESS: Three books of popular sociology, in the same vein as *The Exurbanites,* but on different subjects.†

(Died January 17, 1972)

* * *

SPERRY, Raymond, Jr.
[Collective pseudonym]

WRITINGS—"Larry Dexter" series; published by Garden City Publishing: *Larry Dexter and the Land Swindlers,* 1926; *. . . at the Big Flood,* 1926.

"White Ribbon Boys" series also written under this pseudonym.

SIDELIGHTS: See **ADAMS, Harriet S., STRATEMEYER, Edward L.,** and **SVENSON, Andrew E.**†

* * *

SPINKS, G(eorge) Stephens 1903-

PERSONAL: Born December 30, 1903, in Cambridge, England; son of George (a marine engineer) and Edith (Stephens) Spinks; married Mrs. Annie Nightingale, 1968. *Education:* Educated at Manchester College and St. Catherine's College, Oxford, and at University College and King's College, London; University of London, M.A., 1939, Ph.D., 1946; Oxford University, Hibbert research student, 1944-45. *Politics:* None. *Home:* 35 Greenmount Dr., Greenmount, Bury, Lancashire BL8 4HA, England.

CAREER: Unitarian minister, 1932-51; Anglican clergyman, beginning 1951. Minister in London, England, 1937-47; Oxford University, Oxford, England, Upton lecturer at Manchester College, 1947-48, 1949-50; rector of Great Lever, Bolton, England, 1952-55, and of Clovelly, 1955-59; priest-in-charge, Littleham, England, 1962-64; Vicar of Scouthead, near Oldham, 1966-69. Extension lecturer, University of Exeter, 1956-66; examining chaplain to Bishop of Manchester, 1967-70. Broadcaster for British Broadcasting Corp. European Service.

WRITINGS: (With E. L. Allen and James Parkes) *Religion in Britain since 1900,* Dakers, 1952; *The Fundamentals of Religious Belief,* Hodder & Stoughton, 1961; *Psychology and Religion,* Methuen, 1963, Beacon Press, 1965, 2nd edition, 1967. Contributor to various periodicals in England. Editor, *Hibbert Journal,* 1948-51.

WORK IN PROGRESS: The Thread of Ariadne, a study of philosophy in the Western world; *Religion and Analytical Psychology.*†

* * *

SPITZER, E(rwin) E(dwin) 1910-

PERSONAL: Born July 29, 1910, in New York, N.Y.; son of Ignatz Rudolph (a baron) and Cecelia (Lowy) Spitzer; married Eve Merriam, 1940; married second wife, Lee Brown (a musician), June 30, 1946; children: (second marriage) Elinor Claire. *Education:* Columbia University, B.A., 1933. *Home:* 411 East 57th St., New York, N.Y. 10022. *Agent:* Lucy Kroll Agency, 390 West End Ave., New York, N.Y. 10024.

CAREER: Kudner (advertising) Agency, New York City, vice-president, 1952-59; Papert, Koenig, Lois, Inc. (advertising agency), New York City, vice-president, beginning 1960. *Military service:* U.S. Army, 1943-45.

WRITINGS: Once You Shave a Cactus (novel), Crown, 1966; "The Interview" (one-act play), first produced in New York at Gene Frankel Theater Workshop, November 8, 1968. Contributor to *Saturday Evening Post, Harper's,* and *Contemporary Reader.*

WORK IN PROGRESS: A second novel; a one-act play.†

* * *

SPOTTS, Charles D(ewey) 1899-1974(?)

PERSONAL: Born April 26, 1899, in Cambridge, Pa.; son of Joseph Edgar (a blacksmith) and Mary E. (Gault) Spotts; married Lucy Musselman, June 17, 1925; children: Mary Jane Spotts Merrill, Nancy Lou Spotts Bare. *Education:* Franklin and Marshall College, A.B., 1922; Lancaster Theological Seminary, B.D., 1925; University of Pennsylvania,

A.M., 1933. *Politics:* Democrat. *Residence:* Smoketown, Pa. *Office:* Department of Philosophy, Millersville State College, Millersville, Pa.

CAREER: Clergyman of United Church of Christ. St. Peter's Reformed Church, Lancaster, Pa., pastor, 1925-31; Franklin and Marshall College, Lancaster, Pa., professor of religion, 1931-64; Millersville State College, Millersville, Pa., professor of philosophy, beginning 1964. Lancaster Board of Education, member, 1933-39. *Member:* American Academy of Religion, American Association of University Professors, Phi Beta Kappa, Phi Delta Kappa. *Awards, honors:* D.D., Catawba College, 1948.

WRITINGS: You Can Read the Bible, Christian Education Press, 1949; *God's Wonder World,* Christian Education Press, 1952; *Science in God's World,* Christian Education Press, 1952; *The Earth Is the Lord's,* Christian Education Press, 1952; *Called to Teach,* United Church Press, 1963. Also editor of *Denominations Originating in Lancaster County,* 1963.

AVOCATIONAL INTERESTS: Farming and natural history.†

(Deceased)

* * *

STANIFORTH, (John Hamilton) Maxwell 1893-

PERSONAL: Born June 23, 1893, in Hinderwell, Yorkshire, England; son of John William (a surgeon) and Mary Jane (Maxwell) Staniforth; married Ruby Stephens, July 1, 1922; children: Rosamund Ann (Mrs. Charles Edward Byron Du Cane). *Education:* Christ Church, Oxford, M.A., 1919; Chichester Theological College, Holy Orders, 1938. *Politics:* Conservative. *Home:* Five Chimneys, Pilley, Lymington, Hampshire, England.

CAREER: Entre Rios Railway, Concordia, Argentina, assistant traffic manager, 1926-31; International Broadcasting Co., Fecamp, France, studio chief, 1932-34; Sylvan Publications Ltd., London, England, director, 1934-36; Church of England, vicar in Flimwell, Sussex, 1941-45, chaplain and tutor at St. Michael's School, Petworth, Sussex, 1945-47, and Beehive School, Bexhill, Sussex, 1947-52, vicar of Handley, Dorsetshire, 1952-63, rural dean of Blandford, Dorsetshire, 1954-63. Member, Salisbury Diocesan Dilapidations Board, 1954-63; secretary, Salisbury Diocesan Bishops and Rural Deans Conference, 1955-63. *Military service:* British Army, Infantry, Connaught Rangers, 1914-15, Prince of Wales Leinster Regiment, 1915-18; became major; mentioned in dispatches.

WRITINGS—Translator: Marcus Aurelius, *Meditations,* Penguin, 1964; *Early Christian Writings: The Apostolic Fathers,* Penguin, 1968. Contributor to *Theology, Times* (London), and *Guardian.* Editor, *Concordia Chronicle* (Argentina), 1929-31.

SIDELIGHTS: Staniforth lived in Argentina for a total of seven years, with occasional professional visits to Brazil, Chile, Uruguay, and Paraguay; he has also traveled extensively in Europe and North Africa. He is competent in Latin, Greek, French, Spanish, and Italian, and reads German.

* * *

STEEFEL, Lawrence D. 1894-

PERSONAL: Born June 25, 1894, in Rochester, N.Y.; son of Simon L. (a merchant) and Estelle (Dinkelspiel) Steefel;

married Genevieve Fallon, June 17, 1925; children: Lawrence D., Jr., Nina Moore. *Education:* Harvard University, B.A., 1916, M.A., 1917, Ph.D., 1923. *Politics:* Independent. *Religion:* Unitarian Universalist. *Home:* 3420 Heritage Dr., Edina, Minn. 55435.

CAREER: University of Minnesota, Minneapolis, instructor, 1923-25, assistant professor, 1925-32, associate professor, 1932-44, professor of history, 1944-59, professor emeritus, 1959—. *Military service:* U.S. Army, 1918-19. *Member:* American Historical Association, Society of American Historians, Royal Historical Society (fellow), American Association of University Professors, Minnesota Historical Society, Phi Beta Kappa. *Awards, honors:* Guggenheim fellow, 1929-30; Fulbright research grant, for Germany, 1954-55.

WRITINGS: The Schleswig-Holstein Question, Harvard University Press, 1932; (contributor) E. P. Schmidt, editor, *Man and Society,* Prentice-Hall, 1937; (contributor) Arshas O. Sarkissian, editor, *Studies in Diplomatic History and Historiography in Honor of G. P. Gooch,* Longmans, Green, 1961; *Bismark, The Hohenzollern Candidacy and the Origins of the Franco-German War of 1870,* Harvard University Press, 1962. Contributor to journals.

SIDELIGHTS: Steefel is competent in German, and has knowledge of French and Danish.

* * *

STEELE, A(rchibald) T(rojan) 1903-
PERSONAL: Born 1903, in Toronto, Ontario, Canada; son of James A. and Clara (Trojan) Steele; married Esther Johnston, January 16, 1933. *Education:* Stanford University, B.A., 1924. *Residence:* Portal, Ariz.

CAREER: Correspondent in China for Associated Press, 1932-34, and *New York Times,* 1935-37; roving correspondent for *Chicago Daily News,* Chicago, Ill., 1938-45, and *New York Herald Tribune,* New York, N.Y., 1945-59. *Awards, honors:* George Polk Memorial Award of Long Island University for achievements in journalism; Maria Moors Cabot Prize of Columbia University for journalistic contribution to international relations in the Americas.

WRITINGS: The American People and China, McGraw, 1966.††

* * *

STEGALL, Carrie Coffey 1908-
PERSONAL: Born March 13, 1908, in Dallas, Tex.; daughter of Edwin L. and Lucetta (Hollar) Coffey; married Willie Everett Stegall (a druggist); children; Nancy Ann. *Education:* Attended Hardin-Simmons University, 1926-27; North Texas State Teacher's College (now North Texas State University), B.S., 1940; Midwestern University, M.A., 1953. *Politics:* Democrat. *Religion:* Baptist. *Residence:* Pecan, Holliday, Tex. 76366.

CAREER: Elementary teacher in various Texas public school systems, 1927-73, teaching at all levels in Holliday, 1940-73. Member of Texas Commission on English rewriting the state course of study, 1957-58, and of Texas State Board of Examiners for Teacher Education, 1966-69. *Member:* National Council of Teachers of English (past national director), Texas Council of Teachers of English (secretary, 1964-65).

WRITINGS: (Co-author) *Sequential Tests of Educational Progress,* Educational Testing Service, 1957; *The Adven-*

tures of Brown Sugar: Adventures in Creative Writing, National Council of Teachers of English, 1967. Contributor to English and educational journals. Member of national advisory board of Scholastic Magazines, 1956-57, 1959-60.

* * *

STEINBICKER, Paul G(eorge) 1906-
PERSONAL: Born October 24, 1906, in Cincinnati, Ohio; son of Bernard J. (a builder) and Flora (Dassell) Steinbicker; married Marcella Helmers, August 15, 1934; children: Paul G., Jr., Ruth D. (Mrs.John R. Scharf). *Education:* Xavier University, A.B., 1929; University of Cincinnati, A.M., 1931, Ph.D., 1934. *Religion:* Roman Catholic. *Home:* 4141 Renwood Dr., Kettering, Ohio 45429.

CAREER: University of Detroit, Detroit, Mich., instructor in history, 1931-32; St. Louis University, St. Louis, Mo., instructor, 1934-36, assistant professor, 1936-39, associate professor, 1939-42, professor of political science, 1946-68. Visiting professor at University of California, Los Angeles, 1958, University of Dayton, 1968-73. State of Missouri, Merit System supervisor, 1942-45, member of Personnel Board, beginning 1946, chairman of Personnel Board, beginning 1958; St. Louis County Charter Revision Committee, chairman, 1962-64. *Member:* American Political Science Association (member of council, 1959-61), Public Personnel Association.

WRITINGS: (With others) *Federation,* University of Oklahoma Press, 1946; (with H. J. Schmandt) *Fundamentals of Government,* Bruce, 1955; (with Schmandt and G. D. Wendel) *Metropolitan Reform,* Holt, 1962; (editor) *Readings in Political Science,* Newman, 1964. Contributor to professional journals.

* * *

STEINHARDT, Herschel S. 1910-
PERSONAL: Born May 21, 1910, in Zambrow, Poland; emigrated to the United States in 1920; son of Abraham (a rabbi and teacher) and Zelda (Shafran) Steinhardt; wife deceased; children: Joyce Steinhardt Garber, Judie Steinhardt Goldstein. *Education:* Attended Wayne State University, 1930-31, New School for Social Research, 1938-40, Hunter College (now Hunter College of the City University of New York), 1946-47. *Religion:* Jewish. *Home:* 1131 Junction, Detroit, Mich. 48210. *Office:* 5610 W. Fort St., Detroit, Mich. 48209.

CAREER: Newsboy and theater usher in Detroit, Mich., and cook on a dredging boat in Florida before moving to New York City to write plays; worked with Federal Theater Project as a writer in playwriting department, New York City, 1938-40; press representative for Displaced Persons Program, New York City, 1944-52; Little Book Shop, Detroit, Mich., owner. *Member:* Dramatists Guild.

WRITINGS—Plays: No One Walks Alone (originally produced on radio), American Jewish Committee, 1946; *Sons of Men* (three-act; originally produced with title "Precinct" on National Broadcasting Co. network television program, "Robert Montgomery Presents"), Bookmen Associates, 1959; *A Star in Heaven* (three-act; originally produced at Concept East, Detroit, 1963), New Voices, 1967.

Unpublished plays: "Six Men Seated on a Subway" (one-act), first produced at Henry Street Settlement Playhouse, New York; "The Wind and the Rain," first produced by student theater at Wayne State University, 1955; "God's in His Heaven," first produced by student theater at Wayne

State University, 1962. "The Voice of the Bell" was recorded and distributed by Citizens Committee for Displaced Persons, 1946; six one-act plays were published in *Young Israel Viewpoint,* 1948-49, and a one-act play in *Impresario* (magazine), 1961. Also author of "Man on Earth," "Song of the Street," "The Power of the Dog," and "Before the Morning."

WORK IN PROGRESS: "The Third Hour of the Night."

SIDELIGHTS: No One Walks Alone has been broadcast on radio in Switzerland, West Germany, Netherlands, and Jerusalem. Steinhardt has written several other unproduced full-length plays and a number of one-act plays.

*   *   *

STEINITZ, Kate T(rauman)   1889-1975

PERSONAL: Born August 2, 1889, in Beuthen, Germany (now Poland); daughter of Arnold (a judge) and Magdalene (Mannheimer) Trauman; married Ernest Steinitz (a physician), February, 1942; children: Ilse (Mrs. Fred Berg), Lotte Maria (Mrs. Ernest Sears), Ernest. *Education:* Studied art privately in Germany, and art history in Berlin, Hanover, and Paris. *Politics:* Democrat. *Home:* 11842 Goshen Ave., Los Angeles, Calif. 90049. *Office:* Elmer Belt Library of Vinciana, Art Library, University of California, Los Angeles, Calif. 90024.

CAREER: Elmer Belt Library of Vinciana, Los Angeles, Calif., librarian, beginning 1945, also honorary curator since the library was donated to University of California, Los Angeles, 1961. Teacher of art history at Pomona College; free-lance lecturer on art. Member of advisory board, Junior Arts Council, Los Angeles. *Member:* American Federation of Arts, American Society for Aesthetics, Special Libraries Association, Kestner Gesellscheft (Hanover), Museum of Modern Art (New York), Los Angeles County Museum. *Awards, honors:* Award for libretto in opera texts competition, Vienna, 1928; Ninth Lettura Vinciana in Vinci, Italy (Italian Air Force fly-by salute), 1969; Medal of Merit (Germany), 1970.

WRITINGS: (With Kurt Schwitters) *Der Hahnepeter* (juvenile), Apos & Merz Verlag (Hanover), 1924; (with Schwitters) *Die Maerchen vom Paradies* (juvenile), Apos & Merz Verlag, 1925; (with Schwitters and Theodore van Doesburg) *Die Scheuche* (juvenile), Apos & Merz Verlag, 1928; *Kurt Schwitters, Erinnerungen und Gespraeche,* Arche Verlag (Zurich), 1963, translation by Robert Haas published as *Kurt Schwitters: A Portrait from Life* [and] *Collision: A Science Fiction Opera-Libretto in Banalities, and Other Writings,* University of California Press, 1968; (compiler of catalogue) Elmer Belt, *Manuscripts of Leonardo da Vinci,* Andersen & Ritchie, 1948; *Leonardo da Vinci's Trattate della Pittura: A Bibliography,* University of Copenhagen Library, 1958. Collaborator with Kurt Schwitters on opera libretto, "Der Zusammenstoss," 1928. Compiled catalogues for exhibits at University of California and in Netherlands. Contributor to *Technology and Culture, Renaissance News,* and art journals in America and abroad.

WORK IN PROGRESS: A book in German on Leonardo da Vinci as stage designer and technician, for Arche Verlag in Zurich.

BIOGRAPHICAL/CRITICAL SOURCES: Wilson Library Journal, January, 1970; *Los Angeles Times,* April 27, 1975.†

(Died April 7, 1975)

STENE, Edwin O(tto)   1900-

PERSONAL: Surname is pronounced Steen; born December 21, 1900, in Ashby, Minn.; son of C. J. (a farmer) and Oliana (Rohn) Stene; married Jessie Anderson, June 11, 1927 (died June 2, 1961); married Elin Jorgensen (a professor emeritus of music education), December 21, 1963; children: (first marriage) Edwin A. *Education:* University of Minnesota, B.A., 1923, Ph.D., 1931. *Politics:* Independent. *Religion:* Protestant. *Home:* 1644 University Dr., Lawrence, Kan. 66044.

CAREER: High school teacher in South Dakota, 1923-28; University of Cincinnati, Cincinnati, Ohio, instructor in political science, 1931-34; University of Kansas, Lawrence, acting assistant professor, 1934-37, assistant professor, 1937-43, associate professor, 1943-49, professor of political science, 1949-69, university professor, 1969-71, professor emeritus, 1971—. Faculty fellow at Harvard University, 1947; visiting professor at University of the Philippines, 1954-55, 1957-58, University of Indiana, 1960, University of Hawaii, 1964, and Purdue University, 1975. Public administration consultant in the Philippines, 1954, 1958, in Indonesia, 1962. *Member:* American Political Science Association, American Society for Public Administration, International City Managers Association (honorary member), American Association of University Professors (council member, 1949-53), Pi Sigma Alpha, Sigma Iota Epsilon, Kiwanis Club.

WRITINGS: Kansas State Board of Agriculture, Government Research Center, University of Kansas, 1948; *Railroad Commission and Corporation Commission,* Government Research Center, University of Kansas, 1954; (editor and contributor) *Public Administration in the Philippines,* Institute of Public Administration, University of the Philippines, 1955; *Case Problems of City Management,* International City Managers Association, 1964; *The City Manager: Professional Training and Tenure,* Government Research Center, University of Kansas, 1966; *Selecting a Professional Municipal Administrator* (pamphlet), International City Managers Association, 1972. Contributor to political science journals.

*   *   *

STERN, Boris   1892-

PERSONAL: Born October 1, 1892, in Russia; married Malcka Razovsky; children: Naomi E. (Mrs. Edmund F. Rovner), Elizabeth (Mrs. Leonard Uhr). *Education:* Harvard University, A.B. (cum laude), 1918; Columbia University, Ph.D., 1924. *Home:* 6308 Owen Pl., Bethesda, Md. 20034.

CAREER: U.S. Department of Labor, Washington, D.C., economist and statistician, 1924-54. United Nations Technical Assistance Administration, staff member in Israel, 1952-53. *Military service:* U.S. Army, 1918-19; wounded in Argonne Forest. *Awards, honors:* Distinguished Service Award, U.S. Department of Labor, 1951, for *Mobilizing Labor for Defense;* Scroll of Honor from Israel Government, 1952-53, for United Nations work.

WRITINGS—All published by U.S. Department of Labor, except as noted: *Works Council Movement in Germany,* 1925, *Productivity of Labor in Glass Industry,* 1927, *Cargo Handling and Longshore Labor Conditions,* 1932, *Problems of Labor in Automotive Tire Industry,* 1934, *Mobilizing Labor for Defense,* 1951, *The Kibbutz That Was,* Public Affairs, 1965. Editor, *Labor Information Bulletin,* 1934-47.

SIDELIGHTS: Stern writes and speaks German, French, Russian, Yiddish, and Hebrew.††

*   *   *

STERN, George G(ordon) 1923-1974

PERSONAL: Surname originally Sternberg; born October 3, 1923, in New York, N.Y.; son of Frederick (a signmaker) and Dorothy (Gordon) Sternberg; married Shirley Rosenthal (a teacher), November 13, 1942; children: Sally (Mrs. Gordon La Bedz), Frederick, Patricia. *Education:* University of Chicago, Ph.D., 1949. *Politics:* Independent. *Religion:* None. *Home:* 421 Buffington Rd., DeWitt, N.Y. 13224. *Office:* Department of Psychology, 209 Sims IV, Syracuse University, Syracuse, N.Y. 13210.

CAREER: University of Chicago, Ill., statistician, International Harvester Research Center, 1947-48, supervisor of research (assistant professor), examiner's office, 1949-53, lecturer in department of psychology, 1951-53; Syracuse University, Syracuse, N.Y., associate professor, 1953-59, professor of psychology, 1959-74, head of psychological evaluation and assessment laboratory, Psychological Research Center, 1953-74, director of social psychology training program, 1968-70. Visiting professor, Michigan State University, summer, 1953, and State University of New York at Buffalo, 1970. Danforth visiting lecturer, 1964-65. Certified psychologist, State of New York, 1959. Member of education panel, President's Science Advisory Council, 1966-68; member of research development panel, Educational Policy Research Center, 1968-74. Research consultant, Menninger Foundation, 1952-54, College of Medicine, State University of New York at Syracuse, 1953-68, and Veterans Administration Training Program, Syracuse, 1964-66. *Military service:* U.S. Army Air Forces, 1943-46.

MEMBER: American Association for the Advancement of Science (fellow), American Psychological Association (fellow), Society for the Psychological Study of Social Issues (fellow), American Sociological Association (fellow), American Association for Higher Education, American Educational Research Association, National Council for Measurement in Education, American Association of University Professors, Sigma Xi, Psi Chi. *Awards, honors:* Borden Medal, American Council on Education, 1970, for *People in Context: Measuring Person-Environment Congruence in Education and Industry;* research grants from U.S. Air Force, U.S. Office of Education, Carnegie Foundation, Social Science Research Council, and other agencies and foundations.

WRITINGS: (With Morris I. Stein and Benjamin S. Bloom) *Methods in Personality Assessment,* Free Press of Glencoe, 1956; (with N. G. Haring and William M. Cruickshank) *Attitudes of Educators toward Exceptional Children,* Syracuse University Press, 1958; (with Joseph M. Masling) *Unconscious Factors in Career Motivation for Teaching,* Psychological Research Center, Syracuse University, 1958; *Scoring Instructions and College Norms: Activities Index, College Characteristics Index,* Psychological Research Center, Syracuse University, 1963; (with others) *Sociological and Educational Factors in the Etiology of Juvenile Delinquency,* Psychological Research Center, Syracuse University, 1966; (with Masling) *The Pedagogical Significance of Unconscious Factors in Career Motivation for Teachers,* Psychological Research Center, Syracuse University, 1966; *People in Context: The Measurement of Environmental Interaction in School and Society,* two volumes, Psychological Research Center, Syracuse University, 1967, revised edition published in one volume as *People in Context: Measuring Person-Environment Congruence in Education and Industry,* Wiley, 1970; (with S. D. Cook, T. F. Green, and A. J. Wiener) *Dilemmas of American Policy: Crucial Issues in Contemporary Society,* Syracuse University Press, 1969; (with others) *Shared Authority on Campus,* American Association for Higher Education, 1971.

Contributor: H. T. Sprague, editor, *Research on College Students,* Western Interstate Commission for Higher Education, 1960; N. C. Brown, editor, *Orientation to College Learning: A Reappraisal,* American Council on Education, 1961; Samuel J. Messick and John Ross, editors, *Measurement in Personality and Cognition,* Wiley, 1962; R. Nevitt Sanford, editor, *The American College: A Psychological and Social Interpretation of the Higher Learning,* Wiley, 1962; N. L. Gage, editor, *Handbook of Research in Teaching,* Rand McNally, 1963; G. K. Smith, editor, *Agony and Promise: Current Issues in Higher Education, 1969,* Jossey-Bass, 1969; W. A. Hunt, editor, *Human Behavior and Its Control,* Schenkman, 1972.

Author or co-author of a number of other studies published by Psychological Research Center, Syracuse University. Contributor of more than thirty articles to professional journals, some of them reprinted in books. Associate editor, *Sociology of Education,* 1963-68; member of editorial advisory board, *Change,* 1968-74.

WORK IN PROGRESS: To Be a Man: A Curriculum for Humankind.†

(Died July 20, 1974)

*   *   *

STERN, Michael 1910-

PERSONAL: Born August 3, 1910, in New York, N.Y.; son of Barnet and Annie (Agulansky) Stern; married Estelle Goldstein, November 11, 1934; children: Michael David, Margaret Leslie (Mrs. David Dorsen). *Education:* Syracuse University, B.S., 1932. *Home:* Via Zandonai, 95, Rome, Italy.

CAREER: Sportswriter for newspapers in Syracuse, N.Y., New York City, and Middletown, N.Y., 1929-32; MacFadden Publications, New York City, reporter and staff writer, 1934-41; war correspondent in Africa, Italy, France, Germany, and Austria, 1941-45; chief European correspondent for Fawcett Publications, 1945-54; chief European correspondent for *Argosy* (magazine), with headquarters in Rome, Italy, 1954-55; Fawcett Publications, European correspondent, beginning 1955. Radio and television commentator on European affairs, 1945-54. *Member:* Overseas Press Club of America, Acqua Santa Country Club and Olgiata Golf Club (both Rome). *Awards, honors:* Academy of Motion Picture Arts and Sciences Award (Oscar), 1943, for writer of original story, "The Memphis Belle."

WRITINGS: White Ticket: Commercialized Vice in the Machine Age, National Library Press, 1936; (with Otto Strasser) *Flight from Terror,* McBride, 1943; *Into the Jaws of Death,* McBride, 1944; *No Innocence Abroad,* Random House, 1953; *An American in Rome* (autobiography; foreward by Robert Ruark), Geis, 1964; *Farouk,* Bantam, 1965; *Via Veneto,* Bantam, 1969.

*   *   *

STEVENSON, David Lloyd 1910-1975

PERSONAL: Born June 10, 1910, in Escondido, Calif.; son

of Lloyd Adair (a banker) and Nellie-Louise (Baldridge) Stevenson; married Joan Thorsen, September 4, 1937; children: John Fergus-Lloyd. *Education:* University of California, Berkeley, A.B., 1933, M.A., 1935; Columbia University, Ph.D., 1941. *Politics:* Democrat. *Religion:* Protestant. *Home:* 40 East 68th St., New York, N.Y. 10021; Pudders' Lane, Falls Village, Conn. 06031. *Office:* English Department, Hunter College of the City University of New York, 695 Park Ave., New York, N.Y. 10021.

CAREER: Instructor in English at California Institute of Technology, Pasadena, 1937-39, University of Wisconsin, Madison, 1939-40, Wayne State University, Detroit, Mich., 1940-41, and University of California, Berkeley, 1941-43; U.S. War Production Board, Compliance Division, chief regional analyst, San Francisco, Calif., 1943-47; Western (now Case Western) Reserve University, Cleveland, Ohio, associate professor, 1947-57, professor of English, 1957-63, coordinator of graduate studies in English, 1956-63; Hunter College of the City University of New York, New York, N.Y., professor of English, 1963-75, chairman of the department, beginning 1967. *Member:* Modern Language Association of America, Renaissance Society of America, Shakespeare Society of America, English Institute, Malone Society, Phi Beta Kappa.

WRITINGS: The Love Game Comedy, Columbia University Press, 1946; (editor with Herbert Gold, and author of introduction and commentary) *Stories of Modern America,* St. Martin's, 1961; (editor and author of introduction) Shakespeare, *Much Ado about Nothing,* Signet Books, 1964; (editor and author of introduction) *The Elizabethan Age,* Fawcett, 1966; *The Achievement of Shakespeare's "Measure for Measure,"* Cornell University Press, 1967. Contributor of articles on current American fiction to periodicals, including *Lettres Modernes, New York Times Book Review,* and *Nation;* contributor of scholarly articles to journals, including *Journal of Aesthetics,* and *Shakespeare Quarterly.* Literary editor, *San Francisco Argonaut,* 1942-43.†

(Died April 28, 1975)

*   *   *

STILES, Joseph 1903-

PERSONAL: Born November 10, 1903, in Little Rock, Ark.; son of John Newton and Edith Rosa (Carson) Stiles; married Emma Jeane Batte, January 15, 1926; children: JoAnn (Mrs. Clifford L. Payne), Patricia Jean (Mrs. Edward Owens). *Education:* Ouachita Baptist College, B.A., 1935; Southern Baptist Theological Seminary, Th.M., 1938, Th.D., 1942; University of Louisville, postgraduate study, 1939-41. *Office:* Southern Baptist Theological Seminary, 2825 Lexington Rd., Louisville, Ky.

CAREER: Baptist minister, beginning, 1942. Park Place Baptist Church, Houston, Tex., pastor, 1942-56; Southern Baptist Theological Seminary, Louisville, Ky., professor of Church Administration, beginning 1956. *Member:* Association of Seminary Professors in Practical Fields.

WRITINGS: Acquiring and Developing Church Real Estate, Prentice-Hall, 1965.††

*   *   *

STIRLING, (Thomas) Brents 1904-

PERSONAL: Born March 30, 1904, in Walla Walla, Wash.; son of William Lee and Myrtle (Brents) Stirling; married Alice Watson, July 13, 1929. *Education:* University of

Washington, Seattle, LL.B., 1926, Ph.D., 1934. *Address:* Box 65, Arch Cape, Ore. 97102. *Office:* Department of English, University of Washington, Seattle, Wash. 98105.

CAREER: University of Washington, Seattle, instructor, 1934-37, assistant professor, 1937-43, associate professor, 1943-49, professor of English literature, 1949-70, professor emeritus, 1970—. *Member:* Modern Language Association of America (chairman of Shakespeare group, 1955-56), Shakespeare Association of America.

WRITINGS: The Populace in Shakespeare, Columbia University Press, 1949; *Unity in Shakespearian Tragedy,* Columbia University Press, 1956; *The Shakespeare Sonnet Order: Poems and Groups,* University of California Press, 1968. Contributor to professional journals.

*   *   *

STOLZ, Lois Meek 1891-
(Lois Hayden Meek)

PERSONAL: Born October 19, 1891, in Washington, D.C.; daughter of Alexander Kennedy (a lawyer) and Fannie (Price) Meek; married Herbert R. Stolz (a physician), March 7, 1938. *Education:* George Washington University, A.B., 1921; Columbia University, M.A., 1922, Ph.D., 1925. *Office:* Department of Psychology, Stanford University, Stanford, Calif. 94305.

CAREER: Educational secretary, American Association of University Women, 1924-29; Columbia University, Teachers College, New York, N.Y., professor of education and director of Child Development Institute, 1929-39; University of California, Berkeley, research associate, Institute of Child Welfare, 1941-46; Stanford University, Stanford, Calif., professor of psychology, 1945-57, professor emeritus, 1957—. *Member:* American Psychological Association (fellow), Society for Research in Child Development, American Association for the Advancement of Science (fellow). *Awards, honors:* American Psychological Association, Award of Merit and G. Stanley Hall Award.†

WRITINGS: (Under name Lois Hayden Meek) *How Children Build Habits,* [Washington, D.C.], 1925; (under name Lois Hayden Meek) *A Study of Learning and Retention in Young Children,* Teachers College, Columbia University, 1925, reprinted, AMS Press, 1972; (contributor under name Lois Hayden Meek) Paul S. Achilles, editor, *Psychology at Work,* Whittlesey House, 1932, reprinted, Books for Libraries, 1971; *Your Child's Development and Guidance,* Lippincott, 1941; *Interpersonal Relations of Boys and Girls,* Progressive Education Association, 1943; (with husband, Herbert R. Stolz) *Somatic Development of Adolescent Boys,* Macmillan, 1951; *Father-relations of War Born Children,* Stanford University Press, 1954; (contributor) J. F. Rosenblith and W. Allinsmith, editors, *The Causes of Behavior,* Allyn & Bacon, 1962; (contributor) F. Ivan Nye and Lois Wladis Hoffman, editor, *The Employed Mother in America,* Rand McNally, 1963; *Influences on Parent Behavior,* Stanford University Press, 1967; (contributor) Mary Cover Jones and others, editors, *The Course of Human Development,* Xerox College Publishing, 1971. Editor, *Preschool and Parent Education,* yearbook of National Society for the Study of Education, 1929.

*   *   *

STONE, Alan
[Collective pseudonym]

WRITINGS—"Tolliver" series; published by World: *The*

Tollivers and the Mystery of Pirate Island, 1967; . . . *and the Mystery of the Lost Pony,* 1967; . . . *and the Mystery of the Old Jalopy,* 1967.

SIDELIGHTS: See **ADAMS, Harriet S., STRATEMEYER, Edward L.,** and **SVENSON, Andrew E.**†

* * *

STONE, Grace Zaring 1891-
(Ethel Vance)

PERSONAL: Born January 9, 1891, in New York, N.Y.; daughter of Charles Wesley (a lawyer) and Grace (Owen) Zaring; married Ellis Spenger Stone (a captain, U.S. Navy), April 1, 1917 (deceased); children: Eleanor (Baroness Perenyi). *Education:* Educated at Sacred Heart Convent, New York, N.Y., and Sacre Coeur, Paris. *Home:* 53 Main St., Stonington, Conn. 06378. *Agent:* Curtis Brown Ltd., 60 East 56th St., New York, N.Y. 10022.

CAREER: Writer. *Member:* Royal Society of Literature (fellow).

WRITINGS—Novels: The Heaven and Earth of Dona Elena, Bobbs-Merrill, 1929; *The Bitter Tea of General Yen,* Bobbs-Merrill, 1930; *The Almond Tree,* Bobbs-Merrill, 1931; *The Cold Journey,* Morrow, 1934; (under pseudonym Ethel Vance) *Escape,* Little, Brown, 1939; (under pseudonym Ethel Vance) *Reprisal,* Little, Brown, 1943; *Winter Meeting,* Little, Brown, 1946; *The Secret Thread,* Harper, 1948; *The Grotto,* Harper, 1951; *Althea,* Harper, 1962; *Dear Deadly Cara,* Random House, 1968. Contributor to. magazines.

SIDELIGHTS: Grace Stone, partly from inclination and partly because of her late husband's career, has lived and traveled in China, Japan, Indonesia, Australia, New Zealand, the Carribean and Mexico, nearly all of Europe, the Near East, and Egypt. She also once studied to be a concert pianist, but says she now is "only a fairly competent amateur." Three of her books were filmed: *The Bitter Tea of General Yen,* by Columbia, 1933, *Escape,* by M-G-M, 1940, and *Winter Meeting,* by Warner Bros., 1948.

* * *

STONE, Raymond
[Collective pseudonym]

WRITINGS—"Tommy Tiptop" series; published by Graham & Matlack: *Tommy Tiptop and His Baseball Nine,* 1912; . . . *and His Football Eleven,* 1912; . . . *and His Winter Sports,* 1912.

SIDELIGHTS: See **ADAMS, Harriet S., STRATEMEYER, Edward L.,** and **SVENSON, Andrew E.**†

* * *

STOUGHTON, Gertrude K. 1901-

PERSONAL: Born June 3, 1901, in Brooklyn, N.Y.; daughter of Milton and Paula (von Kapff) Knapp; married Philip N. Rawson (an artist and builder), May 21, 1926; married second husband, Perry O. Stoughton (an inventor, now manufacturing gunite equipment), September 15, 1939; children: (first marriage) Stanley (deceased), Sylvia (Mrs.

Richard L. Rudolph). *Education:* Swarthmore College, B.A. (summa cum laude), 1924; Somerville College, Oxford, graduate research, 1924-26, 1928-29; University of Chicago, graduate study, 1936-37; University of California, M.A., 1939; University of Southern California, M.S. in L.S., 1960. *Home:* 279 Floramar Ter. S., New Port Richey, Fla. 33552.

CAREER: Advertising copywriter for various department stores in Los Angeles, Calif.; Pasadena (Calif.) Public Library, librarian, 1958-68. *Member:* California Library Association, Southern California Library Council for Californiana and Local History (founder; past secretary), Phi Beta Kappa, Beta Phi Mu.

WRITINGS: The Books of California, Ward, 1968.

SIDELIGHTS: Mrs. Stoughton was involved for three years in Southern California Library Council project to check for old and rare material, such as that listed in Robert Cowan's *Bibliography of California, 1510-1930,* in some seventy libraries of southern California. *Avocational interests:* Outdoor life, music, books.††

* * *

STRAIN, Frances Bruce ?-1975

PERSONAL: Born in Milwaukee, Wis.; daughter of Charles Chapin (an importer) and Marcia (Rolfe) Bruce; married Horace L. Strain (a minister; deceased); children: Bruce, Margery (Mrs. Donald K. Ross). *Education:* University of Iowa, B.A., 1919; graduate study at Colorado College and University of Colorado, 1920-23. *Religion:* Congregational.

CAREER: Writer and lecturer. Colorado University Psychopathic Hospital, Denver, acting psychologist, 1924. Lecturer for Cleveland Community Chest, Social Hygiene Society of Cincinnati Community Chest, University of Vermont, Mills College, Los Angeles Public Schools, University of Southern California. Conducted seminars and institutes at University of Denver, University of California, Berkeley, Santa Barbara Public Schools, Glendale Public Schools. *Member:* National Council of Women of the United States, National Association of Marriage Counselors (fellow), Delta Kappa Gamma, Kappa Kappa Gamma. *Awards, honors:* Iowa Press and Author's Club Award, 1919; *Parents' Magazine* Award, 1934, for *New Patterns in Sex Teaching;* American Association of Marriage and Family Counselors Award, 1967.

WRITINGS: New Patterns in Sex Teaching, Appleton, 1934, revised edition published as *New Patterns in Sex Teaching: A Guide to Answering Children's Questions on Human Reproduction,* 1951; *Being Born,* Appleton, 1936, 3rd edition, Hawthorn, 1970; *Sex Education in the Home,* Grolier Society, 1938; *Love at the Threshold: A Book on Social Dating, Romance, and Marriage,* Appleton, 1939, revised and enlarged edition, 1952; *Sex Guidance in Family Life Education: A Handbook for Schools,* Macmillan, 1942; *Your Child: His Family and Friends,* Appleton, 1943; *Teen Days: A Book for Boys and Girls,* Appleton, 1946; *Normal Sex Interests of Children from Infancy to Childhood,* Appleton, 1949; "*But You Don't Understand": A Dramatic Series of Teenage Predicaments,* Appleton, 1950; *Marriage Is for Two: A Forward Look at Marriage in Transition,* Longmans, Green, 1955; (with Charles Lee Eggert) *Framework for Family Life Education: A Survey of Present-day Activi-*

ties in Sex Education, National Association of Secondary School Principals, 1956. Contributor to *Good Housekeeping, Parents' Magazine,* and *Better Homes and Gardens.*†

(Died May 6, 1975)

*   *   *

STRANG, Gerald   1908-

PERSONAL: Born February 13, 1908, in Claresholm, Alberta, Canada; U.S. citizen; son of Mark A. and Gertrude (Stevens) Strang; married Clara Weatherwax, September, 1930; married second wife, Eileen Kelly (a cellist), December, 1958; children: (first marriage) Mark Lorenzo (deceased). *Education:* Principia Junior College, St. Louis, Mo., A.A., 1926; Stanford University, A.B., 1928; University of California (now University of California, Berkeley), graduate study, 1928-29; University of Southern California, Ph.D., 1948. *Home:* 6500 Mantova St., Long Beach, Calif. 90815.

CAREER: University of California, Los Angeles, teaching assistant to Arnold Schoenberg, 1936-38; Long Beach City College, Long Beach, Calif., teacher of music, 1938-58, chairman of department, 1954-58; San Fernando Valley State College (now California State University, Northridge), professor of music, 1958-65, chairman of department, 1958-62; California State College, Long Beach (now California State University, Long Beach), professor of music, 1965-69, chairman of department, 1965-68. Lecturer on electronic music, University of California, Los Angeles. Composer. Managing editor, New Music Edition (music publisher), 1935-40; engineer, Douglas Aircraft Co., 1942-45; acoustical consultant to Bell Telephone Laboratories, summer, 1963, and to universities and colleges. *Member:* International Society for Contemporary Music, American Composers Alliance, American Musicological Society, Alpha Mu, Pi Epsilon Theta, Phi Mu Alpha.

WRITINGS: (Editor) Ernst Toch, *Shaping Forces in Music,* Criterion, 1948; (editor) Peter Yates, *Amateur at the Keyboard,* Pantheon, 1964; (editor) Arnold Schoenberg, *Fundamentals of Musical Composition,* St. Martin's, 1967; (contributor) H. M. Von Foerster and J. W. Beauchamp, editors, *Music by Computers,* Wiley, 1969; (contributor) H. B. Lincoln, editor, *The Computer and Music,* Cornell University Press, 1970.

Composer: "Mirrorrorrim," New Music Edition, 1931; "Two Piano Pieces," New Music Edition, 1931; "Sonatina for Clarinet Alone," New Music Edition, 1932; "Percussion Music for Three Players," New Music Edition, 1935; "Three Pieces for Flute and Piano," New Music Edition, 1937; "Overland Trail," AMI Edition, 1943; "Three Excerpts from Walt Whitman," AMI Edition, 1950; "Sonata for Flute Alone," AMI Edition, 1953; "Intermezzo," New Music Edition, 1953. Also composer of other performed works and computer music on tape. "Concerto for Cello" and "Percussion Music for Three Players" have been recorded. Contributor to professional publications.

WORK IN PROGRESS: Research in computer sound synthesis, computer composition of music, and acoustics of music.

STRATEMEYER, Edward L.   1862-1930

(Manager Henry Abbott, Captain Ralph Bonehill, Jim Bowie, Franklin Calkins, Allen Chapman, Louis Charles, James A. Cooper, Jim Daly, Spencer Davenport, Julie Edwards, Albert Lee Ford, Robert W. Hamilton, Hal Harkaway, Harvey Hicks, Dr. Willard Mackenzie, Ned St. Myer, Chester K. Steele, E. Ward Strayer, Arthur M. Winfield, Edna Winfield, Nat Woods; Oliver Optic, joint pseudonym. Stratemeyer Syndicate pseudonyms: Victor Appleton, Victor Appleton II, Richard Barnum, Philip A. Bartlett, May Hollis Barton, Charles Amory Beach, Captain James Carson, Lester Chadwick, Allen Chapman, John R. Cooper, Elmer A. Dawson, Franklin W. Dixon, Julia K. Duncan, Alice B. Emerson, James Cody Ferris, Graham B. Forbes, Frederick Gordon, Alice Dale Hardy, Mabel C. Hawley, Brooks Henderley, Grace Brooks Hill, Laura Lee Hope, Francis Hunt, Frances K. Judd, Carolyn Keene, Clinton W. Locke, Helen Beecher Long, Amy Bell Marlowe, Eugene Martin, Fenworth Moore, Gert W. Morrison, Margaret Penrose, Nat Ridley, Jr., Roy Rockwood, Harry Mason Roe, Dan Scott, Ann Sheldon, Raymond Sperry, Jr., Alan Stone, Raymond Stone, Richard A. Stone, Helen Louise Thorndyke, Frank A. Warner, Frank V. Webster, Jerry West, Janet D. Wheeler, Ramy Allison White, Clarence Young)

PERSONAL: Born October 4, 1862, in Elizabeth, N.J.; married Magdalene Baker Van Camp; children: Harriet Stratemeyer Adams, Edna C. Stratemeyer Squier.

CAREER: Began writing short stories for magazines about 1884, articles for boys for Street & Smith in 1893; wrote also for Lee & Shepard and Beadle & Adams before founding Stratemeyer Syndicate in 1906.

WRITINGS: Reuben Stone's Discovery; or, The Young Miller of Torrent Bend, Merriam, 1895; (with William Taylor Adams, under pseudonym Oliver Optic) *An Undivided Union,* Lee & Shepard, 1899; *The Minute Boys of Bunker Hill,* D. Estes & Co., 1899; *The Last Cruise of the Spitfire; or, Luke Forster's Strange Voyage,* Lee & Shepard, 1900; *On to Peking; or, Old Glory in China,* Lee & Shepard, 1900; *True to Himself; or, Roger Strong's Struggle for Place,* Lee & Shepard, 1900; *Between Boer and Briton; or, Two Boys' Adventures in South Africa,* Lee & Shepard, 1900; *American Boys' Life of William McKinley,* Lee & Shepard, 1901; *Under Scott in Mexico,* D. Estes & Co., 1902; *Bound to be an Electrician; or, Franklin Bell's Success,* Lee & Shepard, 1903; *Fighting for His Own; or, The Fortunes of a Young Artist,* Lee & Shepard, 1903; *The Young Auctioneer; or, The Polishing of a Rolling Stone,* Lee & Shepard, 1903; *Joe the Surveyor; or, The Value of a Lost Claim,* Lee & Shepard, 1903; *American Boy's Life of Theodore Roosevelt,* Lee & Shepard, 1904, revised, 1906; *Under the Mikado's Flag,* Lee & Shepard, 1904; *Larry the Wanderer; or, The Rise of a Nobody,* Lee & Shepard, 1904; *Under Togo for Japan; or, Three Young Americans on Land and Sea,* Lee & Shepard, 1906; *Defending His Flag; or, A Boy in Blue and a Boy in Gray,* Lothrop, Lee & Shepard, 1907; *First at the North Pole; or, Two Boys in the Arctic Circle,* Lothrop, Lee & Shepard, 1909; *For the Liberty of Texas,* Lothrop, Lee & Shepard, 1909.

"Bound to Win" series: *Richard Dare's Venture; or, Striking Out for Himself*, Merriam, 1894; *Schooldays of Fred Harley; or, Rivals for All Honors*, W. L. Allison, 1897; *Shorthand Tom; or, The Exploits of a Bright Boy*, W. L. Allison, 1897; *Gun and Sled; or, The Young Hunters of Snow-Top Island*, W. L. Allison, 1897; *Leo the Circus Boy; or, Life Under the Great White Canvas*, Lee & Shepard, 1897; *Oliver Bright's Search; or, the Mystery of a Mine*, Lee & Shepard, 1899; *To Alaska for Gold; or, The Fortune Hunters of the Yukon*, Lee & Shepard, 1899.

"Colonial" series; published by Lee & Shepard: *With Washington in the West; or, A Soldier Boy's Battles in the Wilderness*, 1901; *Marching on Niagara; or, The Soldier Boys of the Old Frontier*, 1902; *At the Fall of Montreal; or, A Soldier Boy's Final Victory*, 1903; *On the Trail of Pontiac; or, The Pioneer Boys of the Ohio*, 1904; *At the Fall of Port Arthur; or, A Young American in the Japanese Navy*, 1905; *The Fort in the Wilderness; or, The Soldier Boys of the Indian Trails*, 1905; *Trail and Trading Post; or, The Young Hunters of the Ohio*, 1906.

"Dave Porter" series; published by Lothrop, Lee & Shepard, formerly Lee & Shepard: *Dave Porter at Oak Hall; or, The Schooldays of an American Boy*, 1905; *. . . in the South Seas; or, The Strange Cruise of the Stormy Petrel*, 1906; *Dave Porter's Return to School; or, Winning the Medal of Honor*, 1907; *Dave Porter in the Far North; or, The Pluck of an American Schoolboy*, 1908; *. . . and His Classmates; or, For the Honor of Oak Hall*, 1909; *. . . at Star Ranch; or, the Cowboy's Secret*, 1910; *. . . and His Rivals; or, The Chums and Foes of Oak Hall*, 1911; *. . . on Cave Island; or, a Schoolboy's Mysterious Mission*, 1912; *. . . and the Runaways; or, Last Days at Oak Hall*, 1913; *. . . in the Gold Fields; or, The Search for the Landslide Mine*, 1914; *. . . at Bear Camp; or, The Wild Man of Mirror Lake*, 1915; *. . . and His Double; or, The Disappearance of the Basswood Fortune*, 1916; *Dave Porter's Great Search; or, The Perils of a Young Civil Engineer*, 1917; *Dave Porter under Fire; or, A Young Army Engineer in France*, 1918; *Dave Porter's War Honors; or, At the Front with the Fighting Engineers*, 1919.

"Lakeport" series; published by Lothrop, Lee & Shepard, except as noted: *The Baseball Boys of Lakeport; or, The Winning Run*, A. S. Barnes, 1905; *The Boat Club Boys of Lakeport; or, The Water Champions*, 1908; *The Gun Club Boys of Lakeport; or, The Island Camp*, 1908; *The Football Boys of Lakeport; or, More Goals Than One*, 1909; *The Automobile Boys of Lakeport; or, A Run for Fun and Fame*, 1910; *The Aircraft Boys of Lakeport; or Rivals of the Clouds*, 1912.

"Old Glory" series; published by Lee & Shepard: *A Young Volunteer in Cuba; or, Fighting for the Single Star*, 1898; *Under Dewey at Manila; or, The War Fortunes of a Castaway*, 1898; *Under Otis in the Philippines; or, A Young Officer in the Tropics*, 1899; *Fighting in Cuban Waters; or, Under Schley on the Brooklyn*, 1899; *The Campaign of the Jungle; or, Under Lawton through Luzon*, 1900; *Under MacArthur in Luzon; or, Last Battles in the Philippines*, 1901.

"Pan-American" series; published by Lothrop, Lee & Shepard: *Lost on the Orinoco; or, American Boys in Venezuela*, 1902; *The Young Volcano Explorers; or, American Boys in the West Indies*, 1902; *Young Explorers of the Isthmus; or, American Boys in Central America*, 1903; *Young Explorers of the Amazon; or, American Boys in Brazil*, 1904; *Treasure Seekers of the Andes; or, American Boys in Peru*, 1907; *Chased across the Pampas; or, American Boys in Argentina and Homeward Bound*, 1911.

Under pseudonym Captain Ralph Bonehill: *Young Hunters in Puerto Rico; or, The Search for a Lost Treasure*, Donohue Brothers, 1900; *For the Liberty of Texas*, D. Estes & Co., 1900; *With Taylor on the Rio Grande*, D. Estes & Co., 1901; *Three Young Ranchmen; or, Daring Adventures in the Great West*, Saalfield, 1901; *Tour of The Zero Club; or, Adventures amid Ice and Snow*, McKay, 1902; *The Boy Land Boomer; or, Dick Arbuckle's Adventures in Oklahoma*, Saalfield, 1902; *Lost in the Land of Ice; or, Daring Adventures around the South Pole*, A. Wessels, 1902; *Neka, the Boy Conjurer; or, a Mystery of the Stage*, McKay, 1902; *With Boone on the Frontier; or, The Pioneer Boys of Old Kentucky*, Mershon, 1903; *Pioneer Boys of the Great Northwest; or, With Lewis and Clark across the Rockies*, Mershon, 1904; *Pioneer Boys of the Gold Fields; or, The Nugget Hunters of '49*, Chatterton-Peck, 1906.

"Boy Hunters" series, under pseudonym Captain Ralph Bonehill: *The Island Camp; or, The Young Hunters of Lakeport*, A. S. Barnes, 1904; *Four Boy Hunters; or, The Outing of the Gun Club*, Cupples & Leon, 1906; *Guns and Snowshoes; or, The Winter Outing of the Young Hunters*, Cupples & Leon, 1907; *Young Hunters of the Lake; or, Out with Rod and Gun*, 1908; *Out with Gun and Camera; or, The Boy Hunters in the Mountains*, 1910.

"Flag of Freedom" series, under pseudonym Captain Ralph Bonehill: *A Sailor Boy with Dewey; or, Afloat in the Philippines*, Mershon, 1899; *When Santiago Fell; or, The War Adventures of Two Chums*, Mershon, 1899; *The Young Bandmaster; or, Concert Stage and Battlefield*, Mershon, 1900; *Boys of the Fort; or, a Young Captain's Pluck*, Mershon, 1901; *With Custer in the Black Hills; or, A Young Scout among the Indians*, Grosset, 1902; *Off for Hawaii; or, The Mystery of a Great Volcano*, Mershon, 1905.

Under pseudonym Allen Chapman: *Bound to Rise; or, The Young Florists of Spring Hill and Walter Loring's Career*, Mershon, 1900.

Under pseudonym Louis Charles: *Fortune Hunters of the Philippines; or, The Treasure of the Burning Mountain*, Mershon, 1900; *The Land of Fire*, Mershon, 1900.

Under pseudonym James A. Cooper; published by G. Sully & Co.: *Cap'n Abe, Storekeeper*, 1917; *Cap'n Jonah's Fortune*, 1919; *Tobias o' the Light*, 1920; *Sheila of Big Wreck Cove*, 1922.

Under pseudonym Robert W. Hamilton: *Belinda of the Red Cross*, Sully & Kleinteich, 1917.

Under pseudonym Chester K. Steele: *The Mansion of Mystery*, Cupples & Leon, 1911; *The Diamond Cross Mystery*, G. Sully & Co., 1918; *The Golf Course Mystery*, G. Sully & Co., 1919; *The Crime at Red Towers*, E. J. Clode, 1927. Also author of *House of Disappearances*, 1927.

Under pseudonym E. Ward Strayer: *Making Good with Margaret*, G. Sully & Co., 1918.

Under pseudonym Arthur M. Winfield: *The Missing Tin Box; or, The Stolen Railroad Bonds*, W. L. Allison, 1897; *By Pluck, Not Luck; or, Dan Granbury's Struggle to Rise*, W. L. Allison, 1897; *A Young Inventor's Pluck; or, The Mystery of the Willington Legacy*, Saalfield, 1901; *Bob, The Photographer; or, A Hero in Spite of Himself*, A. Wessels, 1902; *Larry Barlow's Ambition; or, The Adventures of a Young Fireman*, Saalfield, 1902; *Mark Dale's Stage Venture; or, Bound to Be an Actor*, Street & Smith, 1902; *The Young Bank Clerk; or, Mark Vincent's Strange Discovery*,

Street & Smith, 1902; *The Young Bridge-Tender; or, Ralph Nelson's Upward Struggle*, Street & Smith, 1902.

"Putnam Hall" series, under pseudonym Arthur M. Winfield: *The Putnam Hall Cadets; or, Good Times in School and Out*, Stitt Publishing Co., 1905; *The Putnam Hall Rivals; or, Fun and Sport Afloat and Ashore*, Mershon, 1906; *The Putnam Hall Champions; or, Bound to Win Out*, Grosset, 1908; *The Putnam Hall Rebellion; or, The Rival Runaways*, Grosset, 1909; *The Putnam Hall Encampment; or, The Secret of the Old Mill*, Grosset, 1910; *The Putnam Hall Mystery; or, The School Chums' Strange Discovery*, Grosset, 1911.

"Rover Boys" series, under pseudonym Arthur M. Winfield: *The Rover Boys on the Ocean; or, A Chase for a Fortune*, Mershon, 1899; *. . . in the Jungle; or, Stirring Adventures in Africa*, Mershon, 1899; *. . . at School; or, The Cadets of Putnam Hall*, Mershon, 1899; *. . . out West; or, The Search for a Lost Mine*, Mershon, 1900; *. . . on the Great Lakes; or, The Secret of the Island Cave*, Mershon, 1901; *. . . in the Mountains; or, A Hunt for Fun and Fortune*, Mershon, 1902; *. . . on Land and Sea; or, The Crusoes of Seven Islands*, Mershon, 1903; *. . . in Camp; or, The Rivals of Pine Island*, Mershon, 1904; *. . . on the River; or, The Search for the Missing Houseboat*, Grosset, 1905; *. . . on the Plains; or, The Mystery of Red Rock Ranch*, Mershon, 1906; *. . . in Southern Waters; or, The Deserted Steam Yacht*, Grosset, 1907; *. . . on the Farm; or, Last Days at Putnam Hall*, Grosset, 1908; *. . . on Treasure Isle; or, The Strange Cruise of the Steam Yacht*, Grosset, 1909; *. . . at College; or, The Right Road and the Wrong*, Grosset, 1910; *. . . Down East; or, The Struggle for the Stanhope Fortune*, Grosset, 1911; *. . . in the Air; or, From College Campus to the Clouds*, Grosset, 1912; *. . . in New York; or, Saving Their Father's Honor*, Grosset, 1913; *. . . in Alaska; or, Lost in the Fields of Ice*, Grosset, 1914; *. . . in Business; or, The Search for the Missing Bonds*, Grosset, 1915; *. . . at Colby Hall; or, The Struggles of the Young Cadets*, Grosset, 1917; *. . . under Canvas; or, The Mystery of the Wrecked Submarine*, Grosset, 1919; *. . . on Sunset Trail; or, The Old Miner's Mysterious Message*, Grosset, 1925.

Under pseudonym Edna Winfield: *The Little Cuban Rebel; or, A War Correspondent's Sweetheart*, Street & Smith, 1898.

"Holly Library" series under pseudonym Edna Winfield; published by Mershon: *Temptations of a Great City; or, The Love that Lived Through All*, 1899; *A Struggle for Honor; or, The World against Her*, 1900; *An Actress' Crime; or, All for Name and Gold*, 1900; *Lured from Home; or, Alone in a Great City*, 1900; *The Girl from the Ranch; or, The Western Girl's Rival Lovers*, 1900; *Because of Her Love; or, The Mystery of a Spell*, 1900.

Author of numerous other books, some pertaining to the above mentioned series. Also author, before 1912, of books with James Otis Kaler, including "Minute Boys" series.

SIDELIGHTS: Stratemeyer was a follower and admirer of Horatio Alger and of the works which William Taylor Adams wrote as Oliver Optic. He finished and had published an Optic novel, *An Undivided Union*, left uncompleted at the time of Adams' death, edited 18 Alger stories after that author's death, and completed his last story. At that time Stratemeyer was writing dime novels as Jim Bowie, Nat Woods and Jim Daly, and also serials aimed at women for the *Weekly* under the name Julie Edwards. His full length books included the "Rover Boys" and "Dave Porter" books, and many historical series totaling about 400 books.

His daughter, Harriet S. Adams supplied *CA* with information regarding the Stratemeyer Syndicate. Because of the success of the serials in the early twentieth century, Stratemeyer founded the syndicate to supply long and short stories for boys and girls. He outlined and edited all of the works by himself. Some were partially ghostwritten from his outlines. Stratemeyer continued to supply ideas for plots and outlines until his death. By 1930, he and his syndicate had published over 700 books, with "Tom Swift" and "Bobbsey Twins" series the most popular. Sales on each of these had reached over 6,000,000 copies.

After his death the syndicate was carried on by Stratemeyer's two daughters under the same set-up their father had established. But because of the depression of the thirties and World War II, with its paper and metal shortages, the number of series was cut down. Carried on were "Tom Swift," "The Bobbsey Twins," "Ted Scott," "The Hardy Boys" (nine volumes by Stratemeyer), and "Nancy Drew" (three volumes by Stratemeyer). During this period the "Dana Girls" and the "Kay Tracey" series were started.

In 1942, Mrs. Squier became an inactive partner and Mrs. Adams ran the syndicate alone, writing the "Nancy Drew" and "Dana Girls" series, and many of the "Bobbsey Twins" and other stories, as well as preparing outlines for ghostwriters. In 1948, Andrew E. Svenson joined the syndicate and acted as a partner from 1961 until his death in 1975. As Jerry West he was the author of the syndicate's "Happy Hollister" series. Beginning in 1954, Mrs. Adams and Mr. Svenson created six other new series: "Tom Swift, Jr.," "Bret King," "Linda Craig," "The Tollivers," "Christopher Cool," and "Honey Bunch and Norman." Other work of the syndicate includes rewriting and updating the early books in the older series. In all, the syndicate has produced over twelve hundred books. The "Nancy Drew" series has sold 60,000,000 copies, and the "Hardy Boys" and "Bobbsey Twins" series have each sold around 50,000,000 copies to date.

See **ADAMS, Harriet S.** and **SVENSON, Andrew E.**

BIOGRAPHICAL/CRITICAL SOURCES—Books: Albert Johannsen, *The House of Beadle and Adams*, Volume II, University of Oklahoma Press, 1950, Volume III, 1962; Quentin Reynolds, *The Fiction Factory*, Street & Smith, 1955; Raymond L. Kilgour, *Lee and Shepard*, Shoe String Press, 1965; Arthur Prager, *Rascals at Large*, Doubleday, 1971.

Periodicals: *New York Times*, May 13, 1930; *Saturday Review*, July 10, 1971; *New York Times Book Review*, May 4, 1975; *Detroit Free Press*, October 10, 1975.†

(Died May 10, 1930)

*   *   *

STRATMAN, Carl J(oseph) 1917-1972

PERSONAL: Born December 19, 1917, in Detroit, Mich.; son of Carl William (an accountant) and Helen (Taylor) Stratman. *Education:* De Paul University, A.B., 1940; University of Illinois, M.A., 1943, Ph.D., 1947; Catholic University of America, M.A., 1945. *Home:* 6219 Sheridan Rd., Chicago, Ill. 60626. *Office:* Loyola University, 6525 North Sheridan Rd., Chicago, Ill. 60626.

CAREER: Roman Catholic priest, member of Clerics of St. Viateur (C.S.V.); Fournier Institute, professor of English, 1947-49; Loyola University, Chicago, Ill., associate professor, 1949-61, professor of English, beginning 1961. *Member:* Modern Language Association of America, Mediaeval

Academy of America, Society for Theatre Research (England), American Society for Theatre Research, National Council of Teachers of English, Renaissance Society, Malone Society, Oxford Bibliographical Society, Harvard Club of Chicago. *Awards, honors:* Folger Library fellow, 1959.

WRITINGS: Bibliography of Medieval Drama, two volumes, University of California Press, 1954, 2nd edition, revised and enlarged, Unger, 1972; *A Bibliography of British Dramatic Periodicals,* New York Public Library, 1962; (editor with David E. Spencer) *Research in Restoration and 18th Century Drama and Theatre,* Loyola University Press, 1963; *Bibliography of the American Theatre,* Loyola University Press, 1965; *Dramatic Play Lists: 1591-1963,* New York Public Library, 1966; *Bibliography of English Printed Tragedy, 1565-1900,* two volumes, Southern Illinois University Press, 1966; (editor) Edmund A. Napieralski and Jean E. Westbrook, compilers, *Restoration and 18th Century Theatre Research Bibliography, 1961-1968,* Whitston Publishing, 1969; *American Theatrical Periodicals, 1789-1967: A Bibliographical Guide,* Duke University Press, 1970; (editor with Spencer and Mary Elizabeth Devine) *Restoration and Eighteenth Century Theatre Research: A Bibliographical Guide, 1900-1968,* Southern Illinois University Press, 1971. Contributor to learned journals. Editor, *Restoration and Eighteenth-Century Theatre Research.*†

(Died, 1972)

* * *

STRATTON, Roy (Olin)

PERSONAL: Born in Richmond, Ind.; son of Roy Olin (a cigar store owner) and Grace (Fleming) Stratton; married second wife, Monica Dickens (an author-journalist), December 7, 1951; children: (first marriage) Roy Olin III; (second marriage) Pamela Dickens, Prudence Dickens. *Education:* Attended public schools in Richmond, Ind. *Politics:* Republican. *Home:* 237 Main Rd., North Falmouth, Mass. 02556. *Agent:* Scott Meredith Literary Agency, Inc., 845 Third Ave., New York, N.Y. 10022.

CAREER: Ran away from home at fifteen and enlisted in U.S. Navy, serving for thirty years and retiring with rank of commander; during World War II was assigned to Navy supply facilities in Northern Ireland, Scotland, and England; in 1944 was sent to Chungking, China, to become paymaster for guerillas and pirates operating in the Admiral Milton Miles-General Tai Li underground network against the Japanese; during the period 1950-53, conducted comparative studies of German staff planning and logistics during World War II, and the Royal Navy's various supply systems; president of Brookdeal of America, Inc. (branch of British firm manufacturing phase sensitive detectors), North Falmouth, Mass., beginning 1966; treasurer of Dickstra, Inc. (family corporation); writer and lecturer. Secretary-treasurer of Harvey School, Hawthorne, N.Y. Director of Falmouth Taxpayers Association, 1954-56; former president and holder of other offices in North Falmouth Library Association, 1956-65; trustee of Falmouth Hospital Association, 1959-61; president of Falmouth Historical Society, 1965-68.

MEMBER: Royal Thames Yacht Club and Steering Wheel Club (both London). *Awards, honors—Military:* Commendation Medal (three times) from secretary of the Navy; Distinguished Service Medal from Republic of China; twelve campaign ribbons.

WRITINGS: The Rice Paddy Navy, C. S. Palmer Publishing, 1951; *The Decorated Corpse,* M. S. Mill, 1962; *One Among None,* M. S. Mill, 1965. Author of U.S. Navy special reports on operations and organization of the German Naval Supply System in World War II, 1953, and similar reports on the British Navy, 1954. Contributor to *Sports Illustrated, Woman's Own, Yankee, LaPrensa,* and other periodicals.

WORK IN PROGRESS: The Cold Green Eye, a novel about naval under-the-snow camps in Antarctica; research for possible motion picture script about the Navy; *The What the Hell Pennant,* a biography of Admiral Milton E. Miles, U.S. Navy.

SIDELIGHTS: Stratton and his wife have a flat in London and visit England and the Continent two or three times every year. They covered Australia, New Zealand, Singapore, Calcutta, and Beirut on a tour in 1964. He lived in China seven years in the course of his naval career. Stratton told *CA:* "Gene Stratton Porter, a member of my father's family, inspired my initial writing efforts, all of which were bad."

* * *

STRAUSS, Frances 1904-
(Bell Wiley)

PERSONAL: Born August 31, 1904, in Chicago, Ill.; daughter of Albert Lee and Bell (Miracle) Goetzmann; married Bertram Wiley Strauss, July 14, 1931; children: Helen (Mrs. Michael Seitz), Emily. *Education:* Wells College, student, 1922-23; Vassar College, B.A., 1926; Drake University, M.A., 1929. *Politics:* Democrat. *Religion:* None. *Home:* 3129 Sleepy Hollow Rd., Falls Church, Va. 22042.

CAREER: American National Junior Red Cross, Washington, D.C., public relations work, 1944-47; American Association of University Women, Washington, D.C., part-time public relations work, 1951-55; U.S. Information Agency, Washington, D.C., feature writer, 1956-61; teacher of Latin and English at a high school for Africans in Rhodesia, 1961, and at University of the Punjab, Lahore, West Pakistan, 1963. Staff member for magazine section at Summer Course in Publishing Procedures, Cambridge, Mass., 1947-53; instructor in English literature at University of Virginia Extension, Arlington, 1951-59.

WRITINGS: (Under pseudonym Bell Wiley) *So You're Going to Get Married,* Lippincott, 1938; (under pseudonym Bell Wiley; with Clare Newman) *Cookbook of Leftovers,* Little, Brown, 1941; (with husband, Bert Strauss) *New Ways to Better Meetings,* Viking, 1951, revised edition, 1965; *My Rhodesia,* Gambit, 1969; *Where Did the Justice Go?: The Story of the Giles-Johnson Case,* Gambit, 1970. Contributor to periodicals.

WORK IN PROGRESS: Two Corners of Spain, a travel and guide book on Galicia in northwest Spain and Catalonia and Aragon in northeast Spain, with illustrations by her husband, Bert Strauss; a biography of Diego Gelmirez (1075-113?), the first archbishop of Galicia.

BIOGRAPHICAL/CRITICAL SOURCES: Washington Post, January 23, 1970; *Gambit,* January-June, 1970.††

* * *

STRAUSS, Maurice B(enjamin) 1904-1974

PERSONAL: Born March 5, 1904, in Brooklyn, N.Y.; son of Henry M. (a merchant) and Ida (Igelheimer) Strauss; married Ruth Franc, September 8, 1927; children: Peter Franc, Barbara Franc. *Education:* Amherst College, A.B., 1924; Johns Hopkins University, M.D., 1928. *Home:* 151 Tremont St., Boston, Mass. 02111. *Office:* School of Medicine, Tufts University, 136 Harrison Ave., Boston, Mass. 02111.

CAREER: Boston City Hospital, Boston, Mass., intern, 1928-30, resident, 1930-36, visiting physician, 1936-37; Harvard University, Medical School, Boston, instructor, 1936-39, associate, 1939-52, lecturer, 1952-74; chief of medical service, Cushing Veterans Administration Hospital, Framingham, Mass., 1946-52, Boston Veterans Administration Hospital, Boston, 1952-66; Boston University, School of Medicine, Boston, professor of medicine, 1952-66, lecturer, 1967-70; Tufts University, School of Medicine, Boston, lecturer, 1953-67, professor of medicine and associate dean, 1967-74. Peters Lecturer, Yale University, 1959; Myers Lecturer, Washington Hospital Center, 1971; Ratner Lecturer, Mt. Sinai Hospital, Cleveland, Ohio, 1972. Consulting physician, Faulkner Hospital, 1939-74, New England Center Hospital, 1967-74, Boston City Hospital, 1968-74. *Military service:* U.S. Army, Medical Corps, 1943-46; became lieutenant colonel. *Member:* American College of Physicians, Association of American Physicians, American Society for Clinical Investigation, American Federation for Clinical Research, American Medical Association, Massachusetts Medical Society. *Awards, honors:* Boston City Hospital citation, 1964.

WRITINGS: (With L. G. Raisz) *Clinical Management of Renal Failure,* C. C Thomas, 1956; *Body Water in Man,* Little, Brown, 1957; (editor with L. G. Welt) *Diseases of the Kidney,* Little, Brown, 1963, 2nd edition, 1971; (editor) *Familiar Medical Quotations,* Little, Brown, 1968. Contributor of more than 150 articles to medical journals. Member of editorial board, *New England Journal of Medicine,* 1966-69.†

(Died April 19, 1974)

*   *   *

STURT, Mary 1896-

PERSONAL: Born September 8, 1896, in Bushey, Hertfordshire, England; daughter of Henry (a university teacher) and Florence (May) Sturt. *Education:* Somerville College, Oxford, M.A., 1924; University of Birmingham, Ph.D., 1932. *Home:* Glebe House, Exbourne, near Okehampton, Devonshire, England.

CAREER: University of Birmingham, Birmingham, England, lecturer in education, 1930-50; St. Mary's College, Bangor, Wales, vice-principal, 1950-63.

WRITINGS: The Psychology of Time, Routledge & Kegan Paul, 1925; (with E. C. Oakden) *Modern Psychology and Education,* Routledge & Kegan Paul, 1926, revised edition, 1962; *Francis Bacon,* Routledge & Kegan Paul, 1932; (with Margaret Hobling) *Practical Ethics,* Routledge & Kegan Paul, 1949; *The Education of the People,* Humanities, 1966.

WORK IN PROGRESS: An educational psychology book from the standpoint of ethology; a history of Oxford University.

SIDELIGHTS: "[I] am interested in people," Dr. Sturt told *CA*; "thus my work has been in education where men's characters are formed, or in history where they are displayed."

*   *   *

STUTLER, Boyd B. 1889-1970

PERSONAL: Born July 10, 1889, in Coxs Mills, W.Va.; son of Daniel Elias (a lawyer) and Emily Bird (Heckert) Stutler; married Catheolene Huffman, November 26, 1911; children: William Morris, Warren Harding (deceased). *Education:* Attended public schools. *Politics:* Republican. *Home and office:* 517 Main St., Charleston, W.Va. 25302.

CAREER: Newspaper and magazine editor; *American Legion Magazine,* New York, N.Y., managing editor, 1936-54; Education Foundation, Inc., Charleston, W.Va., managing editor of publications and director, beginning 1954. War correspondent with General MacArthur's Pacific Command, 1944-45. Mayor of Grantsville, W.Va., 1911-12; president of Grantsville Board of Education, 1915-16. Chairman of West Virginia War History Commission, 1944-50, and John Brown Centennial Commission, 1958-59. *Military service:* U.S. Army, 1917-19; fought in St. Mihiel offensive and Meuse-Argonne battle. U.S. Army Reserve and West Virginia National Guard, 1921-35. *Member:* West Virginia Historical Society (president, 1958-59), and a number of other state historical societies. *Awards, honors:* U.S. Navy Certificate of Commendation, 1945; Litt.D., Alderson-Broaddus College, 1961.

WRITINGS: Captain John Brown and Harper's Ferry, Storer College Press, 1930; (with P. M. Conley and M. Y. Sandrus) *West Virginia Yesterday and Today* (text), West Virginia Review Press, 1931, 4th edition, Education Foundation of West Virginia, 1966; *Glory! Glory! Hallelujah!: The Story of the John Brown Song,* C. J. Krebhill, 1960; *West Virginia in the Civil War,* Education Foundation of West Virginia, 1963, 2nd edition, 1966; *Kinman Massacre,* McClain Printing, 1969. Writer of radio scripts; editor of "The American Story" radio series, 1954-57.

WORK IN PROGRESS: A biography of John Brown, 1800-1859.†

(Died February 19, 1970)

*   *   *

SULLIVAN, A(loysius) M(ichael) 1896-

PERSONAL: Born August 9, 1896, in Harrison, N.J.; son of William Henry (a businessman) and Mary Elizabeth (Flynn) Sullivan; married Catherine Veronica McNamee, October 8, 1919 (deceased); children: Catherine Rose, Mary Rose (Mrs. Patrick J. Tuohy). *Education:* Graduated from St. Benedict's Preparatory School, Newark, N.J., 1913. *Politics:* Independent. *Religion:* Catholic. *Home:* 65 North Fullerton Ave., Montclair, N.J. 07042; also maintains a summer residence in the Musconetcong Valley, N.J.

CAREER: Held odd jobs in New Jersey, including selling newspaper space in Newark, reading gas meters in Jersey City, and selling pianos in Hoboken; became a free-lance writer, 1917; Submarine Boat Corp., Port Newark, N.J., founder and editor of a house organ, *Speed-Up,* 1918-24; J. P. Muller Advertising Agency, New York City, copywriter, 1924-34; founder and director, "New Poetry" radio program on WOR and the Mutual Network, 1933-42; Dun & Bradstreet, Inc., New York City, 1934-61, began as advertising and public relations director, *Dun's Review,* associate editor, 1938-54, editor, 1954-61, editorial consultant, 1961-71. Member of board of directors, Schalkenbach Foundation, New York City, beginning 1961, and Flight Insulation Corp., Marietta, Ga., 1965-76.

MEMBER: P.E.N., Poetry Society of America (member of executive board, beginning 1935; president, 1939-41, 1950-51), Catholic Poetry Society of America (president, 1961-68), Brendan Society (Irish Cultural Organization; former president, fifteen years), American Irish Historical Society (member of board of directors, beginning 1941; historian, beginning 1943), Irish-American Cultural Institute, New Jersey Historical Society (fellow, 1976), American Revolutionary Roundtable, Warren County (N.J.) Historical Society (vice-president, beginning 1963), Advertising Club of

New York, Craftsmen (former president), Browning Society (honorary), James Joyce Society. *Awards, honors:* Poetry Society of America, Silver Medal, 1941, Alexander Droutskoy Memorial Gold Medal, 1951, for distinguished service to poetry, Gold Medal of Achievement, 1976; Annual Poetry Citation, Catholic Press Association, 1950; *Spirit* Magazine Award of Merit, Catholic Poetry Society, 1958; L.L.D., St. Edward's University, 1964; New Jersey State Senate Citation, 1968, for *Songs of the Musconetcong, and Other Poems of New Jersey;* Litt.D., Montclair State College, 1970.

WRITINGS—Poetry: *Sonnets of a Simpleton,* D. S. Colyer, 1924; *Progression, and Other Poems,* Chisholm Press, 1929; *Elbows of the Wind,* Kingsley Press, 1932; *New Jersey Hills,* J. A. Decker, 1940; *The Ballad of a Man Named Smith,* J. A. Decker, 1940; *A Day in Manhattan,* Dutton, 1941; *This Day and Age: A Collection of Poems of Science and Industry,* privately printed for *Dun's Review,* 1943; *The Ballad of John Castner: An Unrecorded Incident of the American Revolution,* Fine Editions, 1943; *Stars and Atoms Have No Size: Poems of Science and Industry,* Dutton, 1946; *Tim Murphy, Morgan Rifleman, and Other Ballads,* Declan X. McMullen, 1947; *Incident in Silver: A Book of Lyrics,* Declan X. McMullen, 1950; *Three Choral Poems,* McMullen Books, 1951; *Psalms of the Prodigal, and Other Poems,* Kenedy, 1954; *The Ballad of Dick Dowling,* American Irish Historical Society, 1955; *The Bottom of the Sea,* Dun & Bradstreet, 1966; *Songs of the Musconetcong, and Other Poems,* photographs by Sullivan, Guinea Hollow Press, 1968, sight and sound edition (book and tapes), 1973; *Selected Lyrics and Sonnets of A. M. Sullivan,* Crowell, 1970.

Prose: (With Robert L. Tebeau) *Opportunities in Retail Trade for Service Men,* Dun & Bradstreet, 1945; *The Three-Dimensional Man* (essays), Kenedy, 1956; *Human Values in Management: The Business Philosophy of A. M. Sullivan* (essays), edited by Harold Lazarus, foreword by Peter F. Drucker, Dun & Bradstreet, 1968.

Screenplays; all produced by Wilding for Dun & Bradstreet: "Man's Confidence in Man," 1951; "Of Time and Salesmen," 1954; "Small Business, U.S.A.," 1957. Also author of a choral poem for radio, "Transcontinental," broadcast on Norman Corwin's "Words Without Music" in the late 1930's, published in *A Day in Manhattan.*

WORK IN PROGRESS: Research in American history as the basis for historical balladry; a revision of a novelized group of short stories about his father's country store at the turn of the century.

SIDELIGHTS: As originator and director of the "New Poetry" radio series, A. M. Sullivan presented over 300 American and foreign poets reading their own works, including Robert Frost, Edgar Lee Masters, William Carlos Williams, Robert P. Tristam Coffin, John Hall Wheelock, Mark Van Doren, Edwin Markham, Percy MacKaye, Alfred Noyes, Countee Cullen, Robert Hillyer, Harriet Monroe, Padraic and Mary Colum, Richard Aldington, the Benets, and Louis MacNeice. Many of these poets are represented, several by books personally inscribed to Sullivan, in the 800 volumes of twentieth-century poetry which he donated to Montclair State College in 1966. The collection also includes many rare, out-of-print books by important but lesser-known poets.

Sullivan's poems are known for their wide range of subject matter and form. His verse spans half a century of American thought and varies from sonnets and epigrammatic quatrains

to historical ballads and long chorales. One of his most popular works is *The Bottom of the Sea,* an epic poem dealing with the scientific and historical as well as legendary aspects of the sea. Still another of Sullivan's interests is explored in his most recent collection, *Selected Lyrics and Sonnets,* which concerns metaphysical concepts of space, time, identity, eternity, and man's spiritual identity in a material world.

Most of the poems from *Songs of the Musconetcong, and Other Poems of New Jersey* were written at Sullivan's family home, an 1830's farmhouse in the Musconetcong Valley where the poet has summered for fifty years. A personal tribute to the beauty of northern New Jersey, the volume also contains several of Sullivan's ballads about American pioneers and Revolutionary War heroes. The book was recently honored in an unusual gesture by the New Jersey State Senate for its "valuable contribution to American literature" and "the distinction which [Sullivan's] verse lends to his home State."

"Transcontinental," originally written as a radio chorale and broadcast on Norman Corwin's "Words Without Music," was also produced as a recording and adapted for use as a film short. Filmed by Fox-Movietone in 1959, it was shown at the Locarno Film Festival, where it won an award. Two other choral poems from *A Day in Manhattan* were also aired on radio programs around 1940, "Midnight Caravan" by Norman Corwin, and the title poem, "A Day in Manhattan," by the Columbia Workshop. A film about Sullivan, "Song of the Musconetcong," is being made by New Jersey Public Television.

BIOGRAPHICAL/CRITICAL SOURCES: Daily News, April 23, 1976; *New York Times,* April 25, 1976.

* * *

SULLIVAN, Dulcie Turner   1895-1969

PERSONAL: Born June 11, 1895, in Tascosa, Tex.; daughter of A. L. (a rancher) and Annie B. (Cole) Turner; married Ross A. Sullivan, June 15, 1928 (deceased). *Education:* St. Anthony School of Nursing, Amarillo, Tex., R.N. *Politics:* "Variable." *Religion:* Catholic. *Home:* 1509 Travis, Amarillo, Tex. 79102.

CAREER: Registered nurse and supervisor in Texas, 1928-69. *Member:* Professional Nurse Association of Texas. *Awards, honors:* Commendation of the American Association for State and Local History, 1970, for *The LS Brand: Story of Panhandle Ranch.*

WRITINGS: The LS Brand: Story of Panhandle Ranch, University of Texas Press, 1968. Contributor of stories on local history to *Amarillo Daily News* and *Cattleman.*

SIDELIGHTS: Partially blind, Dulcie Sullivan worked with a reading glass to write stories based on memory and interviews with old-timers from the Texas Panhandle.††

(Died October 30, 1969)

* * *

SULLIVAN, Francis John   1892-1976
(Frank Sullivan)

PERSONAL: Born September 22, 1892, in Saratoga Springs, N.Y.; son of Dennis and Catherine (Shea) Sullivan. *Education:* Cornell University, A.B., 1914. *Politics:* Democrat. *Religion:* Roman Catholic. *Home and office:* 135 Lincoln Ave., Saratoga Springs, N.Y. 12866.

CAREER: Reporter for *Saratogian,* Saratoga Springs,

N.Y., 1910-17; following World War I wrote for metropolitan New York dailies, as reporter for *New York Herald*, 1919, feature writer for *New York Evening Sun*, 1920-22, and feature writer and columnist for *New York World*, 1922-31; contributor to *New Yorker*, 1926-74, writing among other features the annual "Christmas Greeting" page (in verse) for thirty-seven years; author and humorist. Member of Corporation of Yaddo, Saratoga Springs. *Military service:* U.S. Army, Infantry, 1917-19; became second lieutenant. *Member:* Authors League of America; The Players, Dutch Treat Club, and Silurians (all New York). *Awards, honors:* D.H.L., Skidmore College, 1967.

WRITINGS—Under name Frank Sullivan: *The Life and Times of Martha Hepplethwaite*, Liveright, 1926; (with Herb Roth) *Adventures of an Oaf*, Macy-Masius, 1927; *Innocent Bystanding*, Liveright, 1928; *Broccoli and Old Lace*, Liveright, 1931; *In One Ear*, Viking, 1933; *A Pearl in Every Oyster*, Little, Brown, 1938; *Sullivan at Bay*, Dent, 1939; *A Rock in Every Snowball*, Little, Brown, 1946; *The Night the Old Nostalgia Burned Down*, Little, Brown, 1953; (with Sam Berman) *Sullivan Bites the News*, Little, Brown, 1954; *A Moose in the Hoose*, Random House, 1959; *Frank Sullivan Through the Looking Glass* (poems, pieces, and letters), edited by George Oppenheimer, introduction by Marc Connelly, Doubleday, 1970, published as *Well, There's No Harm in Laughing*, Doubleday, 1972. Contributor to *Saturday Evening Post, Good Housekeeping, Town & Country*, and other periodicals.

SIDELIGHTS: Frank Sullivan is best remembered by many readers for his Christmas greetings, which appeared annually in *New Yorker* magazine from 1932 through 1974. These carols strung together the names of celebrities in a somewhat incongruous, but always amusing fashion. The tone was light, half-mocking, with an air of friendliness extended to the world. The concluding couplet of his first greetings read, "I greet you all, mes *petits choux*, I greet the whole goddam *Who's Who*."

Also well loved was his fictional character, Mr. Arbuthnot, the expert on the commonplace and particularly on well-worn cliches, who allowed himself to be interviewed on such issues as crime, war, love, the atom, and Roosevelt haters. Charles Poore wrote of Frank Sullivan (and Mr. Arbuthnot), "It is his notion that every proverb has what he calls an antidote proverb that cancels it out. . . . Tell him that Satan finds work for idle hands and he'll say all work and no play makes Jack a dull boy. . . . Mr. Sullivan is a master of undersimplification. He can take the clearest and most obvious commonplace and—in slightly more than no time at all—reduce it to its ultimate complexity."

Although he began his career as a news reporter, Frank Sullivan turned to wit after an obituary which he wrote of a prominent woman for the *New York World* made page one of the paper. "It was an excellent obituary," Sullivan remembered. "The only thing wrong with it was that she wasn't dead." Upset over the folding of the *World* in 1931, he never again worked regularly for a newspaper. "When I die," he once remarked, "I want to go where the *World* has gone and work on it again."

The playwright, Marc Connelly, called Sullivan, "a generous personality, the least bitter man I ever knew," and this aspect of his character is accentuated in his personal letters, many of which are included in *Frank Sullivan Through the Looking Glass*. J. Bryan III wrote: "The lucky people who get letters from Sullivan never throw them away; they keep them forever, to warm their hands and hearts by. No bitterness comes in Sullivan's envelopes, no sneers or snarls, no gossip or spite, . . . nothing but sunniness and gentle merriment."

Speaking from his semi-retirement, Frank Sullivan once said, "The autumn coloring is at its height and I am simply beautiful, all red and gold. People come from miles just to see me." P. G. Wodehouse once stated: "There is only one Frank Sullivan. To my mind—and it is not a mind to be sneezed at—he is America's finest humorist."

BIOGRAPHICAL/CRITICAL SOURCES: Corey Ford, *The Time of Laughter*, Little, Brown, 1967; *New York Times Book Review*, October 22, 1972; *New York Times*, February 20, 1976; *Washington Post*, February 22, 1976; *Time*, March 1, 1976; *Newsweek*, March 1, 1976; *New Yorker*, March 8, 1976.†

(Died February 19, 1976)

*   *   *

SULLIVAN, Vincent F. 1899-

PERSONAL: Born December 23, 1899, in New York, N.Y.; son of Timothy F. (a banker) and Margaret (Kilbride) Sullivan; married Corina Bazin, August 15, 1927; children: Robert A., James J. *Education:* Columbia University, student, 1922-23. *Politics:* Independent.

CAREER: New York Daily News, New York, N.Y., manager of business office, 1922-27, assistant to advertising director, 1927-50, manager of advertising and promotion, 1950-60, consultant to management, 1960-69. *Military service:* U.S. Army, 1917-19. *Member:* American Legion, Larchmont Shore Club.

WRITINGS: With the Yanks in France, Square Publishing, 1919; *How to Sell Your Way into the Big Money* (Book-of-the-Month Club selection), Citadel, 1954; *Big Money*, Prentice-Hall, 1960; *How to Stop Problem Drinking*, Fell, 1969.

WORK IN PROGRESS: Valley of Retirement.††

*   *   *

SULLY, (Lionel Henry) Francois 1927-1971

PERSONAL: Born August 7, 1927, in Paris, France; son of Fernand and Germaine (Garchey) Sully. *Education:* Attended a business school in Paris, France, 1941-45, and Harvard University, 1962-63. *Home:* 106 Nguyen-Hue, Saigon, Vietnam; and Porto Cervo, Sardegna, Italy.

CAREER: Tea planter in Indo-China, 1947-49; officer of French Information Service, 1949-51; Time, Inc., New York City, correspondent in Vietnam, 1952-57; correspondent in Southeast Asia for United Press International, New York City, 1959-61, and *Newsweek*, New York City, 1961-71. *Military service:* French Army, World War II; wounded during Liberation of Paris; served with French Expeditionary Forces in the Far East, 1944-47. *Member:* Association of Foreign Correspondents in Vietnam (secretary general, 1958-62; vice president, 1970-71).

WRITINGS: Age of the Guerrilla: The New Warfare (young adult book), Parents' Magazine Press, 1968; (editor with Marjorie Weiner Normand) *We the Vietnamese: Voices from Vietnam* (young adult book), Praeger, 1971. Contributor to *Living History of the World, Business Week*, and other publications.

WORK IN PROGRESS: A book on Vietnam, for young adults.

SIDELIGHTS: As a teenager Francois Sully fought in the

French underground. He joined the French Army in 1944 and was part of a French Expeditionary Force that landed in Saigon in 1946. After giving up his tea-farm he began coverage of the war in Southeast Asia which continued until his death. In 1962 Francois Sully became the first foreign newsman to be expelled from South Vietnam.

BIOGRAPHICAL/CRITICAL SOURCES: John Mecklin, *Mission in Torment,* Doubleday, 1965.†

(Died February 23, 1971)

* * *

SURMELIAN, Leon (Zaven) 1907-
(Cyril Vandour)

PERSONAL: Sometimes uses both given names, and sometimes Leon Z. Surmelian; born 1907 (day and month unknown), in Trebizond, Turkey; son of Karapet (a pharmacist) and Zevart (Diradourian) Surmelian. *Education:* Received elementary and secondary education in Trebizond and Constantinople; Kansas State University of Agriculture and Applied Science, B.S., 1941. *Religion:* Armenian Apostolic Orthodox Church. *Office:* English Department, California State University, Los Angeles, Calif. 90032.

CAREER: Orphaned in the Turkish massacre, Surmelian was sheltered for a time by a Greek peasant family, and at the age of sixteen became an assistant secretary in the Commissariat of the Interior, Soviet Armenian Republic; editor of an Armenian-American weekly newspaper, 1931-32; deputy probation officer, Los Angeles County, Calif., 1944-45; junior screen writer for Metro-Goldwyn-Mayer, Culver City, Calif., 1945-46; University of California Extension, Los Angeles, teacher of creative writing and fiction, 1958-64; California State University, Los Angeles, professor of English and director of Pacific Coast Writers Conference, beginning 1960. *Member:* American Association of University Professors, American Federation of Teachers, Association of California State College Professors.

WRITINGS: I Ask You, Ladies and Gentlemen (autobiographical), introduction by William Saroyan, Dutton, 1945; *98.6°* (novel), Dutton, 1950; (translator) Davit' Sasowntsi, *Daredevils of Sassoun: The Armenian National Epic,* A Swallow, 1964; *Techniques of Fiction Writing: Measure and Madness,* introduction by Mark Schorer, Doubleday, 1968; *Apples of Immortality: Folktales of Armenia,* University of California Press, 1968. Short stories, some of them anthologized in *Best American Short Stories* and other collections, have appeared in *Prairie Schooner, New Mexico Quarterly Review, Hairenik, Tanager,* and other literary magazines; contributor of articles to *Holiday* and the Armenian press. Some magazine writing was done under the pseudonym Cyril Vandour, 1934-45.

WORK IN PROGRESS: A novel.

SIDELIGHTS: "I preach holy poverty for the writer. Profit motive pulls down all values in the arts. Holy poverty does not mean that the writer must not be paid or poorly paid . . . but he should not fear poverty and even welcome it, to keep his integrity as a writer." UNESCO editions of *Daredevils of Sassoun* and *Apples of Immortality* were published in London by Allen & Unwin as part of the series of national classics.

BIOGRAPHICAL/CRITICAL SOURCES: Times Literary Supplement, September 1, 1966; *New York Times Book Review,* October 6, 1968.††

SWAIN, James E(dgar) 1897-1975

PERSONAL: Born August 20, 1897, in Judson, Ind.; son of Daniel M. (a farmer) and Lucinda (Payton) Swain; married D. Esther Wimmer (a school administrator), September 9, 1919; children: James E. *Education:* Indiana University, A.B., 1921, A.M., 1922; University of Pennsylvania, Ph.D., 1926; Sorbonne, University of Paris, postdoctoral study, 1928. *Politics:* Republican. *Religion:* Presbyterian. *Home:* 1100 South 24th St., Allentown, Pa. 18103.

CAREER: University of Pennsylvania, Philadelphia, instructor in history, 1922-24; Muhlenberg College, Allentown, Pa., 1925-67, began as instructor, became professor of history, chairman of department, 1933-66, professor emeritus, 1967-75; Swain Country Day School, Allentown, director of curriculum, 1967-75. *Member:* American Historical Association, American Association of University Professors. *Awards, honors:* Benjamin Rush Award, 1951; LL.D., Muhlenberg College, 1967.

WRITINGS: The Struggle for Control of the Mediterranean, Stratford Press, 1933; *A History of World Civilization,* McGraw, 1938, revised edition, 1947; (co-author) *Essays in Modern History,* Indiana University Press, 1946; *Little Man, Where Art Thou?,* Muhlenberg College Press, 1964; *A History of Muhlenberg College,* Appleton, 1967.

WORK IN PROGRESS: A biography of Talleyrand; *Memoirs of an Indiana Farm Boy in the Early Twentieth Century.*

SIDELIGHTS: A History of World Civilization has been translated into Hebrew and Hindi. James E. Swain had done research in the government archives of the United States, England, France, Spain, Austria, and the Vatican; he also studied the private papers of Talleyrand in Valencay, France.

BIOGRAPHICAL/CRITICAL SOURCES: Muhlenberg College News, May, 1962; *Indiana University Magazine,* January, 1963.†

(Died March, 1975)

* * *

SWAIN, Joseph Ward 1891-1971

PERSONAL: Born December 16, 1891, in Yankton, S.D.; son of Henry Huntington and Mira (Olmsted) Swain; married Margaret Hatfield, August 15, 1921; children: Henry Huntington, Richard Hatfield (deceased), Martha Swain Carlson, Theodore Merryman. *Education:* Attended Beloit College, 1908-10; Columbia University, A.B., 1912, Ph.D., 1916; Harvard University, A.M., 1913; Ecole Pratique des Hautes Etudes, graduate study, 1913-14. *Religion:* Episcopalian. *Home:* 308 West Delaware Ave., Urbana, Ill.

CAREER: Wabash College, Crawfordsville, Ind., instructor in modern languages, 1916-17; University of Montana, Missoula, instructor in history, 1917-18; University of Illinois, Urbana, instructor, 1919-25, assistant professor, 1925-29, associate professor, 1929-37, professor of history, 1937-60, chairman of department, 1956-60, professor emeritus, 1960-71. Visiting summer professor, Columbia University, 1945; research scholar, Huntington Library, 1962-63. *Military service:* U.S. Army, 1918-19; became sergeant. *Member:* American Historical Association, Phi Beta Kappa.

WRITINGS: (Translator into English) Emile Durkheim, *The Elementary Forms of Religious Life,* Allen & Unwin, 1915, reprinted, Collier Books, 1961; *Beginning the Twen-*

tieth Century, Norton, 1933; *The Ancient World,* two volumes, Harper, 1950; *Harper History of Civilization,* two volumes, Harper, 1958; (with William H. Armstrong) *The Peoples of the Ancient World,* Harper, 1959; *Edward Gibbon, the Historian,* St. Martin's, 1967.†

(Died September 4, 1971)

* * *

SWEENEY, Henry Whitcomb 1898-1967

PERSONAL: Born September 12, 1898, in Springfield, Mass.; son of Anthony Joseph (a salesman) and Edna Inez (Stacy) Sweeney; married Mae Edith Fichter, June 12, 1934; children: Diana Mae. *Education:* Amherst College, student, 1915-17; Columbia University, A.B., 1919, B.S., 1920, M.S., 1921, A.M., 1924, Ph.D., 1936, LL.M., 1960; Georgetown University, LL.B., 1940. *Home:* 1112 Park Ave., New York, N.Y. 10028.

CAREER: Certified public accountant, and attorney admitted to practice before U.S. Supreme Court, U.S. Court of Claims, and U.S. Tax Court. Assistant professor at University of Wisconsin, Madison, 1921-23, and University of Pittsburgh, Pittsburgh, Pa., 1924-25; supervisor for firms of certified public accountants, New York, N.Y., 1925-34, and assistant comptroller of C.I.T. Corp., New York, 1934-35; U.S. government, Washington, D.C., bank examiner for Farm Credit Administration, 1935-39, chief accountant for Compensation Board, Department of the Navy, 1939-43; Leve, Hecht & Hadfield (attorneys), Washington, D.C., partner, 1943-44; Henry W. Sweeney & Co. (certified public accountants), New York, N.Y., head partner, beginning 1943; Stassen, Kephart, Sarkis & Kostos (attorneys), Philadelphia, Pa., counsel, beginning 1965. U.S. Department of Defense, Washington, D.C., deputy assistant Secretary of Defense, 1964-65. Professor of accounting, Georgetown University, 1936-44, and of law, 1941-58; adjunct professor of accounting, Columbia University, 1956. *Military service:* U.S. Army, 1918.

MEMBER: American Institute of Certified Public Accountants, American Accounting Association, National Association of Business Economists, Financial Executives Institute, Federal Bar Association, Association of the Bar of the City of New York, Federal Government Accountants Association, Armed Forces Management Association, American Association of University Professors, New York State Society of Certified Public Accountants, Society of Mayflower Descendants, Sons of the Revolution, and a number of other lineage and patriotic societies, Beta Gamma Sigma, Pi Gamma Mu; Cosmos Club and Army-Navy Country Club (both Washington, D.C.), Union League Club and Grolier Club (both New York), Sleepy Hollow Country Club.

WRITINGS: Bookkeeping and Introductory Accounting, McGraw, 1924; *Stabilized Accounting,* Harper, 1936, reissued with a new foreword, Holt, 1964; (with H. Shockey) *Tax Effects of Operating as a Corporation or Partnership,* Prentice-Hall, 1957; (with Shockey and G. P. Brady) *Taxation and Business Planning,* Prentice-Hall, 1963. Contributor of several dozen articles to business and accounting journals. Federal legislation editor, *Georgetown Law Journal,* 1937-39; assistant editor, *Accounting Review,* 1937-40.

WORK IN PROGRESS: The Defense Contract: A Critique.†

(Died September 1, 1967)

SWEET, Frederick A(rnold) 1903-

PERSONAL: Born June 20, 1903, in Sargentville, Me.; son of Frederick A. and Julia (Harkness) Sweet; married Esther Stephenson, September 6, 1928; children: Ann Macdonald (Mrs. Eugene J. Reilly), Jessica Harkness Goss. *Education:* Harvard University, B.A., 1925, M.A., 1930; studied at Sorbonne, University of Paris, 1926, and Institute of Fine Arts, New York University, 1934-36. *Home:* Sargentville, Me. 04673.

CAREER: Brooklyn Museum, Brooklyn, N.Y., curator of Renaissance art, 1932-36; Portland Art Museum, Portland, Ore., director, 1936-39; Art Institute of Chicago, Chicago, Ill., associate curator of paintings, 1939-52, curator of American paintings, 1952-68; sculptor. *Member:* Harvard Club (Boston).

WRITINGS: The Hudson River School, Art Institute of Chicago, 1945; (with Carl O. Schniewind) *George Bellows,* Art Institute of Chicago, 1946; (with Hans Huth) *From Colony to Nation,* Art Institute of Chicago, 1949; *Sargent, Whistler and Mary Cassatt,* Art Institute of Chicago, 1954; *Ivan Albright,* Art Institute of Chicago, 1964; *Miss Mary Cassatt: Impressionist from Pennsylvania,* University of Oklahoma Press, 1966; *James McNeill Whistler,* Art Institute of Chicago, 1968. Contributor to *Vogue, Art Quarterly,* and *Antiques.*

* * *

SWINSON, Arthur 1915-1970

PERSONAL: Born May 11, 1915, in England; son of Hugh (a printer) and Lilla (Fisher) Swinson; married Joy Budgen, September 16, 1950; children: Sabra, Antonia, Sheridan. *Education:* Attended St. Albans School, St. Albans, Hertfordshire, England. *Politics:* "Not affiliated to any party." *Religion:* Church of England. *Home:* 23 Camlet Way, St. Albans, Hertfordshire, England. *Agent:* John Johnson, 51-54 Goschen Buildings, 12-13 Henrietta St., London WC2E 8LF, England.

CAREER: Professional writer; playwright, 1946-49; British Broadcasting Corp., London, England, writer and producer, 1949-61; free-lance writer, 1961-70. Member of executive committee, St. Albans Arts Council, 1966-70. *Military service:* British Army, 1939-44, Indian Army, 1944-46; served principally in Far East; became captain. *Member:* Writers Guild of Great Britain, Society of Authors, Screen Writer's Guild, Radiowriters Association, Royal Central Asian Society, International P.E.N. (member of executive committee), Old Albanian Rugby Football Club (president, 1961-64), Company of Ten Theatre Club (St. Albans; co-founder and honorary life member), Savage Club, BBC Club.

WRITINGS: Writing for Television, A. & C. Black, 1955.

Writing for Television Today, A. & C. Black, 1963; *Scotch on the Rocks: The True Story of the "Whisky Galore" Ship,* P. Davies, 1963; *Six Minutes to Sunset: The Story of General Dyer and the Amritsar Affair,* P. Davies, 1964; *Television* (juvenile), Wheaton & Co., 1964; *A Casebook of Medical Detection,* P. Davies, 1965; *Sergeant Cork's Casebook* (fiction), Arrow Books, 1965; *History of Public Health* (juvenile), Wheaton & Co., 1965; *Sergeant Cork's Second Casebook* (fiction), Arrow Books, 1966; *Kohima* (military history), Cassell, 1966, published as *The Battle of Kohima,* Stein & Day, 1967; *North-West Frontier: People and Events, 1839-1947,* Praeger, 1967; *Four Samurai: A Quartet of Japanese Army Commanders in the Second World War,* Hutchinson, 1968; *The Great Air Race: England-Australia,*

1934, Cassell, 1968; *The Raiders: Desert Strike Force*, Ballantine, 1968; (editor) Robert Waterfield, *The Memoirs of Private Waterfield*, Cassell, 1968.

Defeat in Malaya: The Fall of Singapore, Ballantine, 1970; Frederick Sander, *The Orchid King: The Record of a Passion*, Hodder & Stoughton, 1970; *The Temple*, M. Joseph, 1970; *Beyond the Frontiers: The Biography of Colonel F. M. Bailey, Explorer and Special Agent*, Hutchinson, 1971; *Mountbatten*, Ballantine, 1971; (editor) *A Register of the Regiments and Corps of the British Army: The Ancestry of the Regiments and Corps of the Regular Establishment*, Archive Press, 1972; (editor) Derek Tulloch, *Wingate in Peace and War*, Macdonald & Co., 1972.

Plays: *The Sword Is Double-Edged*, Samuel French, 1939; *The Senora*, Evans Brothers, 1948; *The Bridge of Estaban*, H. W. F. Deane, 1951. Other plays professionally produced: (With Roy Plomley) "Lock, Stock and Barrel"; "Conflict at Kalanadi." Author of about 140 television plays, documentaries, and films, and 150 radio plays and features.

WORK IN PROGRESS: Sections on Far Eastern campaigns for *History of the Second World War*, for Purnell & Sons.

SIDELIGHTS: Swinson once told *CA:* "Always known I had to write as I can't do anything else. The trouble has always been that I didn't know which was my right field. I still don't. . . . Was an athlete and games player (still a fanatical follower of rugby football), and soldier, and it is the world of action which interests me."†

(Died August 12, 1970)

* * *

SWISHER, (Frank) Earl 1902-

PERSONAL: Born July 22, 1902, in Lyons, Kan.; son of Frank Eldon (a farmer) and Myrtia (Ball) Swisher; married Leis Chapin, August 13, 1929; children: Leland Anthony, Robin Ann. *Education:* University of Colorado, B.A., 1924, A.M., 1929; Washington University, St. Louis, Mo., graduate study, 1929-30; Harvard University, Ph.D., 1940. *Politics:* Democrat. *Religion:* Episcopalian. *Office:* Hellems 242, University of Colorado, Boulder, Colo. 80302.

CAREER: Instructor, Lingnam University, China, 1924-28; American Council of Learned Societies, research assistant at Library of Congress, Washington, D.C., 1934-35; University of Colorado, Boulder, assistant professor, 1935-45, associate professor, 1945-51, professor of history, beginning 1951. Asia Foundation representative, Taipei, Taiwan, 1956-58. *Military service:* U.S. Marine Corps, 1942-46; became lieutenant colonel; received four battle stars and Bronze Star Medal. *Member:* Association for Asian Studies, American Historical Association, Phi Beta Kappa. *Awards, honors:* Harvard-Yenching Institute fellow, 1931-34; Rockefeller Foundation research grant for work in Palace Archives, Peking, 1937-38, 1947-48; Social Science Research Council research grant for work at Academia Sinica, Taipei, 1965-66.

WRITINGS: (Translator and editor) *China's Management of the American Barbarians: A Study of Sino-American Relations, 1841-1861*, Yale University Press, 1951, reprinted, Octagon, 1972; *Communist and Nationalist China*, Ginn, 1963; *China: World in Focus*, Ginn, 1964. Editor, *Notes on Far Eastern Studies in America*, American Council of Learned Societies, 1940-42; associate editor, *Journal* of Pacific Coast branch of American Historical Association, beginning 1950.

WORK IN PROGRESS: American Policy in Asia.†

SYMINGTON, David 1904-
(James Halliday)

PERSONAL: Born July 4, 1904, in Bombay, India; son of James Halliday (an insurance manager and merchant) and Maud McGrigor (Aitken) Symington; married Anne Ellen Harker, August 18, 1929; children: David Arthur, Bridget (Mrs. Grant Edward Newbury). *Education:* Attended Oriel College, Oxford, 1923-26. *Religion:* Church of England. *Home:* 5 Paragon Ter., Cheltenham, England.

CAREER: Held various posts with Indian Civil Service, 1926-47, including backward classes officer for Bombay Province, 1934-37, municipal commissioner for city of Bombay, 1938, secretary to Home Department, government of Bombay, 1942, secretary to governor of Bombay, 1943-47; John Lewis Partnership, London, England, member, 1948-52; Northern Rhodesia Chamber of Mines, Kitwe, director, 1953-60. Chairman, Copperbelt Technical Foundation, 1955-60; member of council, Cheltenham College, 1961-1977. *Awards, honors:* Companion of the Order of the Indian Empire, 1943; Companion of the Order of the Star of India, 1947.

WRITINGS: Report on Aboriginal Tribes of the Bombay Province, Government of Bombay, 1938; (under pseudonym James Halliday) *I Speak of Africa*, W. Blackwood, 1965; (under pseudonym James Halliday) *A Special India* (memoirs), Chatto & Windus, 1968; "The Brahmin Widow" (play), produced on Anglia Television, 1968. Contributor of short stories and articles to *Blackwood's Magazine*.

SIDELIGHTS: A Special India is being published in Marathi (an Indic language).

* * *

TABB, Jay Yanai 1907-

PERSONAL: Born January 1, 1907, in Holoskov, Ukraine; son of Ezriel (a rabbi) and Kressel (Zabarsky) Tabb; married Jean Goldberg, July 15, 1934. *Education:* Long Island University, B.S., 1932; University of Chicago, M.A., 1947, Ph.D., 1952. *Religion:* Jewish. *Office:* Technion-Israel Institute of Technology, Haifa, Israel.

CAREER: University of Chicago, Chicago, Ill., assistant professor of industrial relations, 1950-54; settled in Israel, 1954; Technion-Israel Institute of Technology, Haifa, faculty member and director of extension division, 1954-56, associate professor, 1956-64, professor of industrial relations, beginning 1964, Tulin Professor, beginning 1969, chairman of department of general studies, 1957-61. Adviser on manpower development, government of Ceylon, 1961-62. Member of council, Israel Management Center; member of board of directors, Israel Electric Corp. *Member:* International Industrial Relations Association (member of executive board), Israel Industrial Relations Research Association (president).

WRITINGS: (With Yosef Ami and Gil Shall) *Yahase ha-'avodah be-Yisrael* (title means "Labor Relations in Israel"), Dvir Publishing, 1961; *Personnel Relations in a Growing Enterprise: A Case Study of an Israel Undertaking*, International Labour Office (Geneva), 1962; (compiler) *Handbook of Personnel Management*, Ceylon Institute of Scientific and Industrial Research (Colombo), 1964; (with Betty Mannheim) *Ha-Gorem ha-enoshi ba-avodah* (title means "The Human Factor in Production"), Dvir Publishing, 1965; (with Amira Goldfarb) *Workers' Participation in Management: Expectations and Experience*, Technion Research and Development Foundation (Haifa), 1968, Pergamon, 1970. Also author of *Techniques of Conference Leadership*, 1966, and *Israel's Socio-Economic Planning*. Contributor to professional journals.

WORK IN PROGRESS: Studies on collective bargaining models and their empirical application and on stewards committees as focus of tension.†

* * *

TALLAND, George A(lexander) 1917-19(?)

PERSONAL: Born November 22, 1917, in Budapest, Hungary; married Non D. Chamberlain (a family caseworker), November 21, 1953; children: Claudia, Valentine. *Education:* Queens' College, Cambridge, B.A. (economics), 1939, M.A., 1943; University of London, B.A. (psychology), University College, 1951, Ph.D., Institute of Psychiatry and Maudsley Hospital, 1953.

CAREER: Harvard University Medical School, Boston, Mass., assistant professor of psychology, beginning 1962; Massachusetts General Hospital, Boston, psychologist, beginning 1962. *Awards, honors:* National Institutes of Health career development award, 1963; American Academy of Arts and Sciences monograph award for manuscript of *Deranged Memory*.

WRITINGS: Deranged Memory, Academic Press, 1965; (editor) *Human Aging and Behavior*, Academic Press, 1968; *Disorders of Memory and Learning*, Penguin, 1968; (editor with Nancy C. Waugh) *The Pathology of Memory*, Academic Press, 1969.†

(Deceased)

* * *

TARTRE, Raymond S. 1901-1975

PERSONAL: Born March 2, 1901, in Biddeford, Me.; son of J. B. Edmund and Maria S. (Lalanne) Tartre. *Education:* Studied at Eymard Seminary, Suffern, N.Y., for six years, and Immaculate Conception College, Montreal, Quebec, four years; International University Angelico, Rome, Italy, S.Th.B., 1926, S.Th.L., 1926. *Home:* 184 East 76th St., New York, N.Y. 10021. *Office:* 194 East 76th St., New York, N.Y. 10021.

CAREER: Roman Catholic priest, member of Fathers of the Blessed Sacrament. *Emmanuel*, New York, N.Y., editor, beginning 1954. Retreat master and lecturer in Catholic seminaries; director of pilgrimages to International Eucharistic Congresses in Munich, 1960, Bombay, 1964, and Bogota, 1968. *Military service:* U.S. Army, chaplain, 1941-46; served in Pacific Theater; became major. *Member:* Priests' Eucharistic League (national director, beginning 1953), Knights of Columbus (council chaplain, beginning 1960). *Awards, honors:* Catholic Press Association award for best editorial, 1965.

WRITINGS: Priestly Prayers, Sentinel, 1958; *Secret of Divine Love*, Sentinel, 1962; *The Postconciliar Priest*, Kenedy, 1966; *The Eucharist Today*, Kenedy, 1967. Contributor to Catholic periodicals. Editor, *Monstrance*, Melbourne, Australia, 1935-39.†

(Died January 6, 1975)

* * *

TAYLOR, Alice J. 1909-1969

PERSONAL: Born April 8, 1909, in Albany, N.Y.; daughter of Sydney Tucker (in wholesale paper business) and Guennola (Smith) Jones; married George Alfred Taylor

(Episcopal bishop of Easton, Md.), June 28, 1933; children: Frank Webb, Sydney Tucker. *Education:* Sweet Briar College, A.B.; State Normal School (now State University of New York College at Oneonta), teaching license. *Religion:* Episcopalian. *Home:* 514 Trippe Ave., Easton, Md. 21601. *Agent:* American Authors, Inc., 342 Madison Ave., New York, N.Y. 10017.

WRITINGS: How to be a Minister's Wife and Love It, Zondervan, 1968. Also author of a pamphlet, *Starting the Prayer Group*, 1959.††

(Died June 18, 1969)

* * *

TAYLOR, Henry J(unior) 1902-

PERSONAL: Born September 2, 1902, in Chicago, Ill.; son of Henry Noble (in coal industry) and Eileen (O'Hare) Taylor; married Olivia Fay Kimbro, March 2, 1928; married Marion J. E. Richardson, July 3, 1970; children: (first marriage) Henry Noble (died, 1961). *Education:* Attended University of Virginia. *Politics:* Republican. *Home:* 150 East 69th St., New York, N.Y. 10021. *Office:* 45 Rockefeller Plaza, New York, N.Y. 10020.

CAREER: Industrialist, long associated with pulp and paper business; correspondent for Scripps-Howard Newspaper Syndicate on assignment in various war theaters, 1945; U.S. Ambassador to Switzerland, 1957-61; delegate to Disarmament and Nuclear Control Conference, Geneva, 1958-60, and other international conferences in Geneva, Quebec, Cairo, San Francisco, Paris, Berlin, and London; syndicated columnist, United Features Syndicate, beginning 1961. Chairman of board, Silicone Paper Co. of America; member of board of directors, Clinchfield Coal Co., Pittston Corp., and Waldorf-Astoria Hotel; member of advisory board, Chemical New York Trust Co.; trustee of Manhattan Savings Bank, and Carnegie Lifesavings Foundation; lifetime trustee, University of Virginia Endowment Fund; trustee emeritus, Thomas Jefferson Memorial Association. Member of alumni council, Lawrenceville School.

MEMBER: Foreign Policy Association, National Institute of Social Sciences, Academy of Political Science, Military Order of Foreign Wars, Delta Kappa Epsilon (member of national council), Piping Rock Club (Long Island); Overseas Press Club, Economic Club, Dutch Treat Club, Racquet and Tennis Club, and The Pilgrims (all New York); Farmington Country Club (Charlottesville).

AWARDS, HONORS: Alfred I. Dupont radio award; war department citation for conspicuous service in a theatre of combat; Freedom Foundation gold medal, 1972; American Society of Mechanical Engineers gold medal for public service; Sons of the American Revolution, Paul Revere Bowl for good citizenship; Military Order of Foreign Wars General Douglas MacArthur medal; Wallace award, American-Scottish Foundation; Order of LaFayette (France); Order of the Rose (Finland); Pope Pius XII Papal Medal; United Nations Association for Oppressed Nations Hungarian Freedom Medal.

WRITINGS: It Must Be a Long War, Christopher, 1939; *Why Hitler's Economy Fooled the World*, Christopher, 1941; *Time Runs Out*, Doubleday, 1942; *Men in Motion*, Doubleday, 1943; *Men and Power*, Dodd, 1946; *An American Speaks His Mind*, Doubleday, 1960; *The Big Man* (novel), Random House, 1965; *Men and Moments*, Random House, 1966. Contributor to *Life*, *Saturday Review of Literature*, *Saturday Evening Post*, *This Week*, *Reader's Digest*,

Cosmopolitan, and other magazines; also contributor to economic journals in America, Switzerland, Sweden, and England.†

* * *

TAYLOR, James R(owe) 1907-

PERSONAL: Born August 1, 1907, in Hartford, Mich.; son of Samuel H. (a minister) and Alma A. (Rowe) Taylor; married Hedwig J. Geisinger (a high school teacher), January 25, 1941; children: Ann Louise, Kathleen Julia. *Education:* St. Joseph Junior College, St. Joseph, Mo., A.A., 1929; University of Kansas, A.B., 1931; University of Michigan, A.M., 1933, Ph.D., 1951. *Politics:* Republican. *Religion:* Presbyterian. *Home:* 10414 Kingston, Huntington Woods, Mich. 48070.

CAREER: High school teacher in Kansas, 1929-31, in Port Huron, Mich., 1931-33, and in Detroit, Mich., 1933-42; Wayne State University, Detroit, 1947-63, began as assistant professor, chairman of department of general business, 1951-63, professor of business administration, 1958-63; Accrediting Commission for Business Schools, Detroit, executive commissioner, 1963-67; National Cosmetology Accrediting Commission, executive director, beginning 1967. Management consultant to Republic of Chile, sponsored by U.S. Department of State, 1957. Chairman of trustees, Detroit College of Applied Science. *Military service:* U.S. Army Air Forces, 1942-47; served in western Pacific; became lieutenant colonel; received Bronze Star. *Member:* American Society of Association Executives, Administrative Management Society, National Office Management Association (international president, 1961-62), National Education Association, Michigan Education Association, Michigan Business Education Association, Alpha Kappa Lambda, Phi Delta Kappa, Delta Pi Epsilon (chapter president, 1948), Delta Sigma Pi, Phi Theta Pi.

WRITINGS: The Training of Clerical Workers, Prentice-Hall, 1961.

WORK IN PROGRESS: Orientation to Office Practice, for Prentice-Hall.

* * *

TAYLOR, Katharine Whiteside 1897-

PERSONAL: Born December 24, 1897, in Louisville, Ky.; daughter of Harry Robert (a merchant) and Adelaide (a teacher; maiden name, Schroeder) Whiteside; married Paul Schuster Taylor (a professor), May 15, 1920 (divorced September, 1935); children: Katharine Page (Mrs. John George Loerch), Ross Whiteside (deceased), Margot Agnes (Mrs. Donald Fanger). *Education:* University of Wisconsin, B.A., 1919; University of California, graduate study, 1933; Columbia University, M.A., 1936, Ed.D., 1937. *Politics:* Democrat. *Religion:* Society of Friends. *Home and office:* 1591 Shrader St., San Francisco, Calif. 94117.

CAREER: Seattle (Wash.) public schools, consultant in family life education, 1940-45; Long Beach City College, Long Beach, Calif., coordinator of family life education, 1946-51; Baltimore (Md.) public schools, supervisor in parent education, 1951-63; Fulbright lecturer in New Zealand universities, 1964; University of California Extension, San Francisco, lecturer, beginning 1966. Psychotherapist in private practice, San Francisco. Lecturer at University of Maryland, University of Wisconsin, Columbia University, and elsewhere; consultant to U.S. Office of Education and U.S. Attorney General; founder and former chairman of international relations, Parent Cooperative Preschools International. *Member:* National Council on Family Relations (vice-president 1945-46), American Psychological Association, National Education Association, American Association of Marriage Counselors, Phi Beta Kappa, Theta Sigma Phi, Kappa Delta Pi.

WRITINGS: Do Adolescents Need Parents?, Appleton, 1938; (contributor) Howard Becker and R. L. Hill, editors, *Family, Marriage and Parenthood,* Heath, 1948; *Parent Cooperative Nursery Schools,* Teachers College, Columbia University, 1954, revised and enlarged edition published as *Parents and Children Learn Together,* 1967; (contributor) Ernest W. Burgess and Morris Fishbein, editors, *Successful Marriage,* 2nd revised and enlarged edition, Oxford University Press, 1957. Editor, *Parent Cooperative Newsletter,* 1958-63.

* * *

TAYLOR, Norman 1883-1967

PERSONAL: Born May 18, 1883, in Hereford, England; brought to United States in 1889, naturalized in 1896; son of James Durham (a merchant) and Mary Ann (Preece) Taylor; married Bertha Fanning, 1908; married second wife, Margaretta Stevenson, July 31, 1943; children: (first marriage) Norman, Jr., Alice, Marian (Mrs. Nicola Abbagnano). *Education:* Cornell University, student, 1901-02. *Politics:* Republican. *Religion:* Episcopalian. *Home:* Elmwood, Princess Anne, Md. 21853. *Office:* 20 West Tenth St., New York, N.Y. 10011.

CAREER: New York Botanical Garden, New York City, assistant curator, 1905-11; Brooklyn Botanic Garden, Brooklyn, N.Y., curator of plants, 1911-29; botany, horticulture, and forestry editor for second edition of *Webster's New International Dictionary,* 1933-36; Cinchona Products Institute, Inc., New York City, director, 1937-50; Cinchona Instituut, Amsterdam, Netherlands, adviser, 1951-53; writer on botanical subjects. Conducted botanical expeditions to Bolivia, Peru, Ecuador, Brazil, the Bahamas, Haiti, Cuba, and the countries of Central America.

MEMBER: American Association for the Advancement of Science (fellow), New York Academy of Sciences (fellow), New York Academy of Medicine (associate fellow), Massachusetts Horticultural Society, Torrey Botanical Club; Century Association, Players Club, and Explorers Club (all New York); Cosmos Club (Washington, D.C.). *Awards, honors:* Massachusetts Horticultural Society Gold Medal, 1936; D.Sc., Washington College, Chestertown, Md., 1958; Distinguished Service Award, New York Botanical Garden, 1961; Liberty Hyde Bailey Gold Medal, American Horticultural Society, 1963.

WRITINGS: Flora of the Vicinity of New York: A Contribution to Plant Geography, [New York], 1915; *Botany: The Science of Plant Life,* P. F. Collier, 1922, published as *The Story of Our Plants: The Science of Botany, the Forms, Functions and Economic Importance of Vegetable Life,* 1930; *A Guide to the Wild Flowers East of the Mississippi and North of Virginia,* Greenberg, 1928; *The Vegetation of the Allegany State Park,* University of the State of New York, 1928; (editor) *The Garden Dictionary,* Houghton, 1936, 2nd edition published as *Taylor's Encyclopedia of Gardening, Horticulture and Landscape Design,* 1948, 4th edition, 1961; *Cinchona in Java: The Story of Quinine,* Greenberg, 1945; *Flight from Reality,* Duell, Sloan & Pearce, 1949, revised edition published as *Narcotics: Nature's Dangerous Gifts,* Dell, 1963.

Color in the Garden, Van Nostrand, 1953; *Fragrance in the Garden,* Van Nostrand, 1953; *The Permanent Garden,* Van Nostrand, 1953; *Herbs in the Garden,* Van Nostrand, 1953; *Fruit in the Garden,* Van Nostrand, 1954; *The Ever-blooming Garden,* Van Nostrand, 1954; *Wild Flower Gardening,* Van Nostrand, 1955; (editor) Ferdinand Schuyler Mathews, *Field Book of American Wild Flowers,* revised and enlarged edition, Putnam, 1955; *Garden Guide,* Van Nostrand, 1957, revised edition, Dell, 1962; *The Guide to Garden Flowers: Their Identity and Culture,* Houghton, 1958; *The Ageless Relicts: The Story of Sequoia,* St. Martin's, 1963; *1001 Questions Answered about Flowers,* Dodd, 1963; *The Guide to Garden Shrubs and Trees,* Houghton, 1965; *Plant Drugs that Changed the World,* Dodd, 1965. Contributor to *Encyclopaedia Britannica* and *Book of Knowledge;* also contributor of scientific papers to journals, and articles to popular magazines.

AVOCATIONAL INTERESTS: Sailing, sixteenth- to eighteenth-century music, running a three-hundred acre farm and forest.

BIOGRAPHICAL/CRITICAL SOURCES: Washington Post, November 7, 1967; *New York Times,* November 9, 1967.†

(Died November 5, 1967)

* * *

TAYLOR, Ray Ward   1908-

PERSONAL: Born September 12, 1908, in Kalamazoo, Mich.; son of Freeman Ward and Anna Louise (Powell) Taylor; married Florence Murer, March 17, 1947; children: Keith Powell and Lane Chatten (daughters). *Education:* Attended Indiana University, 1926-28, and University of Wisconsin, 1928. *Home:* 3856 North Glebe Rd., Arlington, Va. 22207. *Agent:* Raines & Raines, 475 Fifth Ave., New York, N.Y. 10017.

CAREER: Monthly (magazine), Memphis, Tenn., sales manager, 1930-40; U.S. Army Air Forces and U.S. Air Force, pilot and intelligence officer, 1940-61, serving in the Pacific as a B-29 combat pilot during World War II, and retiring as lieutenant colonel; Radio Station WAMU-FM, Washington, D.C., book editor, beginning, 1966; independent producer of weekly radio book review program. *Awards, honors*—Military: Air Medal.

WRITINGS: Roll Back the Sky (novel), Holt, 1956; *Doomsday Square* (novel), Dutton, 1966. Contributor of short stories and articles on aviation to magazines.

WORK IN PROGRESS: A novel, *Willie Willie Willie.*

SIDELIGHTS: Taylor speaks German and Spanish. *Avocational interests:* Sailing, gun collecting, sports cars, and flying.

* * *

TAYLOR, Robert Martin   1909-

PERSONAL: Born August 8, 1909, in Los Angeles, Calif.; son of Martin Julian (a realtor) and Charlotte Marie (Newman) Taylor; married Lebbie Lowry (former teacher of foreign languages), April 12, 1941; children: Leslie (daughter), Edward Martin, Lowry (daughter). *Education:* University of Washington, Seattle, B.A., 1930, M.A., 1931, Ph.D., 1956. *Religion:* Protestant Episcopal. *Home:* 12001 Maplerock Ct., San Antonio, Tex. 78230.

CAREER: U.S. Department of State, career foreign service officer with posts in Mexico, France, China, Africa, West

Germany, India, and Washington, D.C., 1931-53; University of Toronto, Toronto, Ontario, assistant professor of geography, 1956-57; University of Texas, Austin, associate professor of marketing administration, 1957-66; Texas Christian University, Fort Worth, professor of geography and chairman of department, 1966-74. Visiting lecturer, University of Delaware, summer, 1956; visiting associate professor, Portland State College (now University), summer, 1962. *Member:* American Foreign Service Association, Association of American Geographers, American Association of University Professors, Southwestern Social Science Association, Southwestern Council of Latin American Studies (secretary, 1967-68), Delta Sigma Pi, Gamma Theta Upsilon.

WRITINGS: (Editor and compiler with Norton E. Marks) *Physical Distribution and Marketing Logistics: An Annotated Bibliography,* American Marketing Association, 1966; (editor with Marks) *Marketing Logistics: Perspectives and Viewpoints,* Wiley, 1967.

WORK IN PROGRESS: Research on the geography of Texas.

* * *

TEDDER, Arthur William   1890-1967
(Lord Tedder)

PERSONAL: Born July 11, 1890, in Scotland; son of Sir Arthur John (a member of Commission of Customs and Excise) and Emily (Bryson) Tedder; married Rosalind Wilamina MacLardy, June 4, 1915 (died, 1942); married Marie de Seton Black, January, 1943 (died, 1963); children: (first marriage) Arthur (killed in action, 1940), Mina Una Margaret, John Michael; (second marriage) Richard Seton. *Education:* Cambridge University, B.A., 1912. *Religion:* Church of England.

CAREER: Entered Britain's Colonial Service, 1913, serving in Fiji, 1913-14; commissioned first lieutenant in Dorsetshire Regiment, 1914; transferred to Royal Flying Corps, 1916, and Royal Air Force, 1919, rising in RAF to deputy supreme commander of Allied Forces in Europe under General Eisenhower, 1943-45, and chief of British Air Staff, 1946-50; retired from active duty with Royal Air Force, 1950, but was designated marshal, 1960 (giving him the dual title of Lord Tedder and Marshal of the Royal Air Force); chairman of British Joint Services Mission in Washington, D.C., and United Kingdom representative on the standing group of the Military Committee, North Atlantic Treaty Organization, 1950-51; chancellor of Cambridge University, Cambridge, England, 1953-67. During World War I served in France and Egypt; squadron commander in Constantinople, 1922-23, followed by posts in England at service colleges and with Air Ministry, 1923-36; commander, Royal Air Force in Far East, 1936-38; director-general of research and development, Air Ministry, 1938-40; air commander-in-chief, Royal Air Force in Middle East, 1941-43; air commander-in-chief of Mediterranean Air Command just prior to appointment to Supreme Headquarters, Allied Expeditionary Force in Europe, 1943. Member of board of governors, British Broadcasting Corp., 1945-51; member of board of directors, Distillers Co., 1953-60; president of Standard Triumph Motor Co., 1954-61.

AWARDS, HONORS: During World War I was twice mentioned in dispatches and received Italian Medaille Militaire, 1916; created Commander of the Bath, 1937, Knight Commander of the Bath, 1942, and first Baron of Glenguin, 1946; military honors in World War II also included Distinguished

Service Medal and Legion of Merit (United States), Legion of Honor (France), Crown with Palm and Croix de Guerre (Belgium), Order of Orange Nassau (Netherlands), and Order of Kutusov (Soviet Union); LL.D. from Cambridge University, Oxford University, University of Glasgow, University of Leeds, and University of Sheffield, all 1946.

WRITINGS: Navy of the Restoration, Cambridge University Press, 1915; *Air Power in War,* Hodder & Stoughton, 1949; *With Prejudice* (autobiographical military history, 1932-45), Cassell, 1966, Little, Brown, 1967.

BIOGRAPHICAL/CRITICAL SOURCES: Roderic Owen, *Tedder,* Collins, 1952.††

(Died June 3, 1967)

* * *

TEDLOCK, E(rnest) W(arnock), Jr. 1910-

PERSONAL: Born December 20, 1910, in St. Joseph, Mo.; son of Ernest Warnock (a businessman) and Ethel Clare (Byrne) Tedlock; married Agnes Peterson, January 8, 1938; children: Dennis Ernest, Susan Ann, David Peter. *Education:* University of Missouri, B.A., 1932, M.A., 1933; University of Chicago, graduate study, 1935-37; University of Southern California, Ph.D., 1950. *Politics:* Independent. *Address:* P.O. Box 53, Cerrillos, N.M. 87010.

CAREER: University of New Mexico, Albuquerque, instructor, 1943-47, assistant professor, 1947-52, associate professor, 1952-59, professor of English, 1959-72, professor emeritus, 1972—. Publisher, San Marcos Press, Cerrillos, N.M. Visiting associate professor, New York University, summer, 1956. *Member:* American Studies Association, Modern Language Association of America (chairman, English II, 1967-68), American Association of University Professors, Rocky Mountain Modern Language Association. *Awards, honors:* Rockefeller Foundation fellowship, 1944-45.

WRITINGS: The Frieda Lawrence Collection of D. H. Lawrence Manuscripts, University of New Mexico Press, 1948; (editor with C. V. Wicker) *Steinbeck and His Critics: A Record of Twenty-Five Years,* University of New Mexico Press, 1956; (editor) *Dylan Thomas, the Legend and the Poet: A Collection of Criticism,* Heinemann, 1962; *D. H. Lawrence: Artist and Rebel,* University of New Mexico Press, 1963; *Frieda Lawrence: The Memoirs and Correspondence,* Heinemann, 1963, Knopf, 1964; *D. H. Lawrence's "Sons and Lovers": Sources and Criticism,* New York University Press, 1965.

SIDELIGHTS: Tedlock told *CA:* "My motivation has always been the excitement and pleasure, perhaps even insight, gained from the felt values created in poetry and fiction.... [I] suppose this is a kind of unorganized, secular religious feeling, something found and in a sense relied on in the midst of modern realism, relativism, and skepticism. Anyhow, it seems to lie at the center of my existence. [Have] an interest in what might be called the literature of fantasy, as Graham's *The Wind in the Willows,* and its perennial appeal."

* * *

TEETERS, Negley K(ing) 1896-1971

PERSONAL: Born November 16, 1896, in Steubenville, Ohio; son of Harry Negley (a dentist) and Margaret (Wyeth) Teeters; married Ruth Schendel, September 1, 1927; children: Robert Duane, Ralph Negley. *Education:* Oberlin College, A.B., 1920; Ohio State University, M.A., 1925,

Ph.D., 1931. *Home:* 15 Maple St., Oneonta, N.Y. *Office:* Hartwick College, Oneonta, N.Y. 13820.

CAREER: Playground Association of America, New York, N.Y., field work, 1920-23; Chamber of Commerce, Steubenville, Ohio, secretary, 1923-24; Moorhead State College, Moorhead, Minn., instructor, 1926-27; Temple University, Philadelphia, Pa., beginning 1927, began as instructor, professor of sociology, 1946-64, professor emeritus, 1964-71, chairman of department of sociology, 1948-56; Hartwick College, Oneonta, N.Y., visiting professor of sociology, 1964-71, H. Claude Hardy Professor of Sociology, 1971. Member of Pennsylvania Governor's Committee on Correctional Matters, 1955-58. *Member:* American Sociological Association, American Association of University Professors, Pennsylvania Prison Society (past president). *Awards, honors:* U.S. Department of State grant to study prisons and penal codes in South America, 1942; August Vollmer Award of American Society of Criminology, 1962; Eastern Sociological Society Merit award, 1969.

WRITINGS: They Were in Prison, Winston & Co., 1937; (with Harry W. Barnes) *New Horizons in Criminology,* Prentice-Hall, 1943, 3rd edition, 1959; *World Penal Systems,* Pennsylvania Prison Society, 1944; *Penology from Panama to Cape Horn,* University of Pennsylvania Press, 1946; (with John O. Reinemann) *The Challenge of Delinquency,* Prentice-Hall, 1950; *The Cradle of the Penitentiary,* Pennsylvania Prison Society, 1955; (with John D. Shearer) *The Prison at Philadelphia: Cherry Hill,* Columbia University Press, 1957; *Scaffold and Chair,* sponsored by Pennsylvania Prison Society and privately printed, 1963; (with J. H. Hedblom) *Hang by the Neck,* C. C Thomas, 1967. Editor, *Deliberations of the International Penal and Penitentiary Congresses,* sponsored by American Prison Association and privately printed, 1949. Contributor to prison and criminal law journals.

(Died October 30, 1971)

* * *

TEISSIER du CROS, Janet 1906-

PERSONAL: Born January 26, 1906, in Aberdeen, Scotland; daughter of Sir Herbert John Clifford (a professor of literature) and Mary Letitia (Ogston) Grierson; married Francois Teissier du Cros (a physicist), December 9, 1930; children: Henri, Andre, Nicolas, Marie-Elisabeth. *Education:* Studied piano privately in Vienna, Austria, and with Sir Donald Francis Tovey in Edinburgh, Scotland; studied theory of music at University of Edinburgh. *Religion:* Catholic. *Home:* 40, rue Vaneau, Paris, France; Mandiargnee, par St. Hippolyte-du-Fort 30170, France. *Agent:* Richmond Tower & Benson Ltd., 14 Essex St., London W.C. 2, England.

CAREER: Former broadcaster of "Paris Letter," for British Broadcasting Corp., for three years; author of column, "Paris Letter," for *Glasgow Herald;* concert pianist.

WRITINGS: Divided Loyalties (nonfiction), Hamish Hamilton, 1960, Knopf, 1963.

WORK IN PROGRESS: A semi-autobiographical novel dealing with family history.

SIDELIGHTS: Janet Teissier du Cros told *CA:* "My passion is my country house and the part of the world where it stands, which is the Cevennes. I speak French as fluently as English. My German was fluent but has grown rusty." *Avocational interests:* History, religion, and music.

TELFER, Dariel   1905-
(Caleb Forrest)

PERSONAL: Born September 5, 1905, in Pueblo, Colo.; daughter of Albert L. (a steelworker) and Minnie (Birdsall) Pugh; married Forrest C. Telfer (deceased); children: Forrest C., Jr., Penelope Ann Telfer Brunette. *Home:* 217 Dupps Ave., Pueblo, Colo. 81005.

CAREER: Author. *Member:* Authors Guild.

WRITINGS: The Caretakers, Simon & Schuster, 1959; *The Guilty Ones,* Simon & Schuster, 1961; *Love Is for Hating,* Muller, 1962; *The Corruptors,* Simon & Schuster, 1964; *The Night of the Comet,* Doubleday, 1969. Also author of filmscript, "The Caretakers" based on her book by the same title, for United Artists.

WORK IN PROGRESS: Two books of detective fiction; and research for sequel to *The Night of the Comet.*

SIDELIGHTS: The Caretakers has been published in other languages, and all of Telfer's books except *The Night of the Comet* are in paperback printings.

BIOGRAPHICAL/CRITICAL SOURCES: New York Times Book Review, March 9, 1969; *Best Sellers,* March 15, 1969.†

* * *

TERBORGH, George (Willard)   1897-

PERSONAL: Born May 6, 1897, in Portland, Mich.; son of Isaac (a farmer) and Lillie (Thompson) Terborgh; married Dorothy Poor, 1930. *Education:* Oberlin College, B.A., 1922; University of Chicago, M.A., 1925; Brookings Institution, Ph.D., 1928; *Politics:* Independent. *Home:* 4582 26th St. N., Arlington, Va. 22207. *Office:* Machinery and Allied Products Institute, 1200 18th St. N.W., Washington, D.C.

CAREER: Federal Reserve Board, Washington, D.C., research economist, 1930-33; Brookings Institution, Washington, D.C., staff member, 1933-36; Federal Reserve Board, research economist, 1936-41; Machinery and Allied Products Institute, Washington, D.C., secretary, 1941-43, research director, 1943-70, consultant, beginning 1970. Teacher of economics at University of Illinois, 1923-24, University of Chicago, 1924-25, Ohio State University, 1925-26, University of New Mexico, 1928-29, and Antioch College, 1929-30. *Military service:* U.S. Army, 1918-19. *Member:* National Association of Business Economists (fellow), Conference of Business Economists, National Economists Club, Mont Pelerin Society.

WRITINGS—All published by Machinery and Allied Products Institute, except as noted: (With John Henry Gray) *First Mortgages in Urban Real Estate Finance* (pamphlet), Brookings, 1929; *Price Control Devices in NRA Codes* (pamphlet), Brookings, 1934; (co-author) *The National Recovery Administration,* Brookings, 1935; *Fluctuation in Housing Construction,* 1938; *The Bogey of Economic Maturity,* 1945, 2nd edition, 1950; (with William F. Yelverton) *Technological Stagnation in Great Britain,* 1948; *Dynamic Equipment Policy: A MAPI Study,* McGraw, 1949; *MAPI Replacement Manual,* 1950; *Amortization of Defense Facilities,* 1952; *Realistic Depreciation Policy: A MAPI Study,* 1954; *Business Investment Policy,* 1958; *The Automation Hysteria,* Norton, 1966; *Business Investment Management,* 1967; *The New Economics,* 1968; *Capitalism Revisited,* 1968; *Essays on Inflation,* 1970. Author of about twenty pamphlets, 1947-65. Contributor to *Fortune* and to economic and financial journals.

AVOCATIONAL INTERESTS: Travel, mountain climbing, hiking, swimming.

* * *

TERBOVICH, John B.   1933-1969

PERSONAL: Born June 16, 1933, in Lyndora, Pa.; son of Walter B. and Mary B. (Agich) Terbovich. *Education:* St. Fidelis Seminary and College, A.B., 1955; Capuchin College, Washington, D.C., S.T.B., 1960, M.A. (religious education), 1960; graduate study at Catholic University of America, summers, 1957-60, Duquesne University, 1960-61; Fort Hays Kansas State College, M.A. (English), 1962; further summer study at University of Michigan, 1962, and University of Dijon, 1965. *Home:* St. Joseph's Military Academy, Hays, Kan. 67601.

CAREER: Roman Catholic priest; member of Capuchin Franciscan Order. St. Joseph's Military Academy, Hays, Kan., professor of English and journalism, 1961-69. Fort Hays Kansas State College, director of Newman Club, 1961-69, campus chaplain, 1964-69. Lecturer and youth counselor. Director of academic board of advisers, American Institute for Foreign Studies, 1963-69. *Member:* National Council of Teachers of English, National Newman Chaplains Association, Kansas Association of Teachers of English, Kansas Association of Journalism, Knights of Columbus. *Awards, honors:* Ronald E. Knox Award of National Newman Federation, 1966, for *The Faces of Love.*

WRITINGS: The Faces of Love (Catholic Literary Guild selection), Doubleday, 1966. Contributor of more than seventy articles to magazines and journals, including *Ave Maria, Western Folklore, Our Sunday Visitor, Catholic Educator, Eastern Churches Quarterly.*

WORK IN PROGRESS: A novel, tentatively entitled, *Angry Blood.*

SIDELIGHTS: John Terbovich traveled throughout Germany, France, Scotland, Wales, and England during the summer of 1966, as inspector of campuses for American Institute for Foreign Studies. He spoke six foreign languages and had studied fourteen. *Avocational interests:* Playing harmonica and guitar for hootenanies at local Newman functions.†

(Died April 5, 1969)

* * *

TERRY, Luther L(eonidas)   1911-

PERSONAL: Born September 15, 1911, in Red Level, Ala.; son of James Edward (a physician) and Lula M. (Durham) Terry; married Beryl Janet Reynolds, June 29, 1940; children: Janet Terry Kollock, Luther Leonidas, Jr., Michael D. *Education:* Birmingham-Southern College, B.S., 1931; Tulane University, M.D., 1935. *Office:* University Associates, Inc., 475 L'Enfant Plaza N., Suite 2100, Washington, D.C. 20024.

CAREER: Hillman Hospital, Birmingham, Ala., intern, 1935-36; University Hospital, Cleveland, Ohio, assistant resident, 1936-37; City Hospital, Cleveland, resident in medicine, 1937-38, intern in pathology and assistant admitting officer, 1938-39; Washington University, St. Louis, Mo., instructor in medicine and research fellow in pneumonia, 1939-40; University of Texas Medical Branch at Galveston, instructor, 1940-41, assistant professor, 1941-42, associate professor of medicine and preventive medicine, 1942-46 (on military leave, 1943-46); U.S. Public Health Service Hospital, Baltimore, Md., member of medical service staff, 1942-

43, chief of medical services, 1943-53; Johns Hopkins University, School of Medicine, Baltimore, part-time instructor, 1944-53, assistant professor of medicine, 1953-61; National Heart Institute, Bethesda, Md., chief of general medicine and experimental therapeutics, 1950-58, assistant director of Institute, 1958-61; U.S. Public Health Service, Washington, D.C., surgeon general, 1961-65; University of Pennsylvania, Philadelphia, vice-president for medical affairs, 1965-71, and professor of medicine and of community medicine in School of Medicine, 1965-75, adjunct professor, beginning 1975; president, University Associates, Inc. (consulting firm), Washington, D.C. Member of Medical Division, U.S. Strategic Bombing Survey to Japan, 1945-46; U.S. Public Health Service, member of committee on civilian health requirements, 1955-58, and of advisory committee on nutrition, Division of Indian Health, 1957-61; World Health Organization, chief of U.S. delegation, 1961-65, member of expert committee, 1974; member, National Board of Medical Examiners; chairman, National Interagency Council on Smoking and Health, 1967. Member of board of directors of Medic Alert Foundation and United Health Services, among others; public trustee, Nutrition Foundation. Member at large of national council, Boy Scouts of America; honorary vice-president, National Tuberculosis Association. Diplomate, American Board of Internal Medicine, 1943.

MEMBER: American College of Cardiology (fellow), American College of Physicians (former governor; honorary master), American Heart Association, American Public Health Association, American Social Health Association (member of board of directors), Association of American Physicians, National Society for Medical Research (member of board of directors), Pan American Medical Association, U.S. Public Health Service Clinical Society (past president), National Resuscitation Society, Royal Society of Health (England; honorary fellow), American College of Chest Physicians, and other medical associations; Alpha Kappa Kappa, Pi Kappa Alpha, Omicron Delta Kappa.

AWARDS, HONORS: Fourteen honorary degrees, 1961-70, including D.Sc. from Birmingham-Southern College, 1961, Tulane University, 1964, University of Rhode Island, 1964, McGill University, 1966, University of Alabama, 1966, and LL.D. from University of Alaska, 1964, and Marquette University, 1968; Distinguished Achievement Award, Pi Kappa Alpha, 1962; Robert D. Bruce Award, American College of Physicians, 1965; Distinguished Service Medal, U.S. Public Health Service, 1965.

WRITINGS: (Contributor) Lewis Herker, editor, *Crisis in Our Cities,* Prentice-Hall, 1965; (contributor) Seymour Tilson, editor, *Toward Environments Fit for Men,* Johns Hopkins Press, 1968; (with Daniel Horn) *To Smoke or Not to Smoke* (youth book), Lothrop, 1969; (contributor) Gerald Leinwand, editor, *Air and Water Pollution,* Washington Square Press, 1969. Contributor to *Encyclopedia of Careers and Vocational Guidance* and *New Book of Knowledge;* contributor of more than one hundred articles to medical journals.

* * *

THAYER, George (Chapman, Jr.) 1933-1973

PERSONAL: Born September 18, 1933, in Philadelphia, Pa.; son of George Chapman (a banker) and Mary Hazelhurst (Steel) Thayer; married Carol Edgerton (an editor and writer), September 9, 1972. *Education:* University of Pennsylvania, B.A., 1955; Center of Industrial Studies, Geneva,

Switzerland, Certificate of International Business, 1958; London School of Economics and Political Science, graduate study, 1963. *Religion:* Episcopalian. *Residence:* Washington, D.C. *Agent:* International Famous Agency, Inc., 1301 Sixth Ave., New York, N.Y. 10020.

CAREER: Research assistant to Randolph S. Churchill on biography of his father, Sir Winston Churchill, 1964-65; writer. Speechwriter for Governor Nelson A. Rockefeller, 1968, Senator Claiborne Pell of Rhode Island, 1969, and Representative Lawrence R. Coughlin of Pennsylvania, 1969-72. *Military service:* U.S. Army, 1955-57. *Member:* Sierra Club.

WRITINGS: The British Political Fringe, Anthony Blond, 1965; *The Farther Shores of Politics: The American Political Fringe Today,* Simon & Schuster, 1967; *The War Business,* Simon & Schuster, 1969; *Who Shakes the Money Tree?,* Simon & Schuster, 1974.

BIOGRAPHICAL/CRITICAL SOURCES: Nation, March 11, 1968; *Spectator,* May 10, 1968; *Books and Bookmen,* July, 1968; *New York Times,* June 6, 1969; *Life,* June 13, 1969; *Saturday Review,* September 6, 1969; *Commonweal,* September 26, 1969.†

(Died August 13, 1973)

* * *

THAYER, V(ivian) T(row) 1886-

PERSONAL: Born October 13, 1886, in Tomora, Neb.; son of Oscar (a minister) and Rose Standish (Munson) Thayer; married Florence Adams, April 18, 1914; children: Robert Adams, Horace Standish, Lois Lilian (Mrs. Joseph Papaleo, Jr.). *Education:* University of Wisconsin, A.B., 1916, M.A., 1917, Ph.D., 1922. *Politics:* Democrat. *Religion:* Ethical Culture Movement. *Address:* P.O. Box 3427, Nalcrest, Fla. 33856.

CAREER: Ashland (Wis.) public schools, superintendent, 1912-14, 1918-19; University of Wisconsin, Madison, instructor in philosophy, 1919-22; Ethical Culture Schools, New York, N.Y., principal of high school, 1922-24; Ohio State University, Columbus, faculty of department of education, 1924-28; Ethical Culture Schools, New York, N.Y., director, 1928-48. Visiting professor or lecturer at University of Hawaii, 1948-49, University of Virginia, 1951-56, Fiske University, 1956-57, and Johns Hopkins University, University of Maryland, and other universities. Progressive Education Association, chairman of Commission on Secondary School Curriculum, 1932-40. *Member:* National Education Association, Philosophy of Education Society, John Dewey Society, American Civil Liberties Union, Beta Phi Kappa. *Awards, honors:* Designated Humanist of the Year by American Humanist Society, 1964; distinguished lifetime service award from John Dewey Society, 1969.

WRITINGS: Passing of the Recitation, Heath, 1928; (with H. B. Albertz) *Supervision in the Secondary School,* Heath, 1931; (with Caroline B. Zackry and Ruth Kolinsky) *Reorganizing Secondary Education,* Appleton, 1939; *American Education under Fire,* Harper, 1944; *Religion in Public Education,* Viking, 1947; *The Attack upon the American Secular School,* Beacon, 1951; *Public Education and Its Critics,* Macmillan, 1954; *The Role of the School in American Society,* Dodd, 1960, revised edition, with Martin Levit, Dodd, 1966; *Formative Ideas in American Education,* Dodd, 1965. Contributor to *Harper's, Humanist, School and Society,* and other education journals.

THEDE, Marion Draughon   1903-
(Marion Unger)

PERSONAL: Surname rhymes with "speedy"; born November 11, 1903, in Davis, Indian Territory (now Oklahoma); daughter of James and Lena (Erdwurm) Draughon; married former husband, Johnston Murrray, 1923; remarried, former husband's name, Buchanan, 1933; married former husband, George H. Unger, 1947; married John Frederick Thede (a musician), March 12, 1960; children: (first marriage) Johnston Murray, Jr.; (second marriage) James H. G. Buchanan. *Education:* University of Oklahoma, M.B., 1922; further study at Chicago Musical College, 1929, and Oklahoma City University, 1938. *Politics:* Democrat. *Religion:* "Religious Science." *Home:* 1824 Northwest 23rd St., Oklahoma City, Okla. 73106.

CAREER: Violinist and violist with Oklahoma City Symphony, Oklahoma City, Okla., 1937-67, and Tulsa Philharmonic Symphony, Tulsa, Okla., 1967-70. Teacher of stringed instruments for Board of Education, Oklahoma City, and privately in a studio operated with her husband in Oklahoma City; also played in summer Lyric Theatre Orchestra, Oklahoma City, 1961-66. State folk archivist, Oklahoma, beginning 1965; lecturer on musical subjects and traditional arts and crafts of the Southwest; recording artist; producer of folk festivals. *Member:* International Folk Music Council, International Musicological Council, National Folk Festival Association (member of board of advisers), National Federation of Music Clubs (national folk archivist and chairman of folk music, 1968-71; national committee member, beginning 1971), American Federation of Musicians of the United States and Canada, American Folklore Society, Music Educators National Conference, Society for Ethnomusicology, American String Teachers Association, Oklahoma Federation of Music Clubs (chairman of state folk music, beginning, 1964), Oklahoma Writers Association, Oklahoma Folk Council (organizer and chairman), Oklahoma Fiddlers' Association (organizer, 1971), Oklahoma Historical Society, Mu Phi Epsilon, Alpha Gamma Delta. *Awards, honors:* Award for folk research from National Federation of Music Clubs and its Oklahoma branch, 1966, 1967, 1968, 1969.

WRITINGS: The Fiddle Book, Oak, 1967. Contributor to *Ethnomusicology,* under name Marion Unger until 1960; also contributor of articles to music and Western periodicals.

WORK IN PROGRESS: Volume II of *The Fiddle Book;* writing on an aspect of American Indian music, in collaboration with husband, John Frederick Thede; directing National Federation of Music Clubs project on the compilation of fifty sets of folk material, one representing each state; a history of fine arts in the Southwest, beginning in pre-Columbian times.

BIOGRAPHICAL/CRITICAL SOURCES: Viltis, October-November, 1959.†

* * *

THESIGER, Wilfred (Patrick)   1910-

PERSONAL: Born June 3, 1910, in Addis Ababa, Ethiopia; son of Wilfred Gilbert (a British diplomat) and Kathleen Mary (Vigors) Thesiger. *Education:* Magdalen College, Oxford, M.A., 1933. *Politics:* Conservative. *Religion:* Church of England. *Home:* 15 Shelley Court, Tite St., London S.W. 3, England. *Agent:* Curtis Brown Ltd., 1 Craven Hill, London W2 3EW, England.

CAREER: Explored Danakil Desert and Aussa Sultanate in eastern Africa, 1933-34; Sudan Political Service, 1935-40, serving in Darfur and Upper Nile Provinces; explored in southern Arabia and Hejaz, 1945-50; lived with Marsh Arabs in Iraq, 1950-58; traveler in other remote areas of Middle East, Africa, and Asia. *Military service:* British Army, 1940-43; served in Ethiopian, Syrian, and Western Desert campaigns; became major; received Distinguished Service Order. *Member:* Royal Society of Literature (fellow), Royal Geographical Society (fellow), Royal Central Asian Society, Brooks' Club, Travellers' Club, Pratt's Club. *Awards, honors:* Back grant, Royal Geographical Society, 1935; Founder's Gold Medal of Royal Geographical Society (for explorations in southern Arabia and dual crossing of the Empty Quarter), 1948; Lawrence of Arabia Medal of Royal Central Asian Society, 1955; Livingstone Gold Medal of Royal Scottish Geographical Society, 1960; Royal Society of Literature award, 1965, for *The Marsh Arabs;* Burton Memorial Medal of Royal Asiatic Society, 1966; D.Litt. from University of Leicester, 1968.

WRITINGS: Arabian Sands, Dutton, 1959; *The Marsh Arabs,* Dutton, 1964. Papers on explorations published in *Geographical Journal* and *Journal of the Royal Central Asian Society.*

* * *

THOMAS, Dorothy Swaine   1899-1977

PERSONAL: Born October 24, 1899, in Baltimore, Md.; daughter of John Knight (a salesman) and Sarah (Swaine) Thomas; married William Isaac Thomas, February, 1938 (deceased). *Education:* Columbia University, A.B., 1922; University of London, Ph.D., 1924. *Residence:* Bethesda, Md.

CAREER: Federal Reserve Bank, New York, N.Y., research assistant, 1924-25; Social Science Research Council, fellow, 1925-26; Columbia University, Teachers College, New York, N.Y., assistant professor and research associate, 1927-30; Yale University, New Haven, Conn., research associate, 1931-35, director of research in social statistics, 1935-39; Carnegie Corp., staff member, Study of Negro in America, 1939-40; University of California, Berkeley, lecturer in sociology, 1940-41, professor of rural sociology, 1941-48; University of Pennsylvania, Philadelphia, research professor of sociology, 1948-71, professor emeritus, 1971-77, co-director of Study of Population Redistribution and Economic Growth, 1952-59, research director, Population Studies Center, 1959-71; Georgetown University, Center for Population Research, Washington, D.C., professorial lecturer, 1972-77. Visiting professor at Social Science Institute, University of Stockholm, 1933, 1935, 1936, and at University of Gothenburg, 1964. Demographer, United Nations Technical Assistance Administration, Bombay, India, 1957, and consultant in demography for United Nations in Bombay and Cairo, Egypt, 1963-64; consultant to U.S. Bureau of the Budget, National Resources Committee, Bureau of the Census, beginning 1965, Department of Agriculture, beginning 1966, and other national and state agencies.

MEMBER: American Philosophical Society (councillor, 1966-67), American Statistical Association (fellow; vice-president, 1946), American Sociological Society (president, 1952), Population Association of America (president, 1958-59), Social Science Research Council (former director).

WRITINGS: Social Aspects of the Business Cycle, Routledge & Kegan Paul, 1925, Knopf, 1928, reprinted, Gordon & Breach, 1968; (with husband, W. I. Thomas) *The Child in America,* Knopf, 1928, reprinted, Johnson Reprint Co.,

1970; *Some New Techniques for Studying Social Behavior*, Teachers College, Columbia University, 1929; (with A. M. Loomis and R. E. Arrington) *Observational Studies of Social Behavior*, Institute of Human Relations, Yale University, 1933; *Research Memorandum on Migration Differentials*, Social Science Research Council, 1938; *Social and Economic Aspects of Swedish Population Movements, 1750-1933*, Macmillan, 1941; (with Richard S. Nishimoto) *Japanese American Evacuation and Resettlement: The Spoilage*, University of California Press, 1946; (with Charles Kikuchi and James Sakoda) *Japanese American Evacuation and Resettlement: The Salvage*, University of California Press, 1952; (editor with others) *Population Redistribution and Economic Growth, United States, 1870-1950*, American Philosophical Society, Volume I: *Methodological Considerations and Reference Tables*, 1957, Volume II: *Analysis of Economic Change*, 1960, Volume III: *Demographic Analyses and Interrelations*, 1964.

Contributor: *Economic Essays in Honor of Wesley Clair Mitchell*, Columbia University Press, 1935; (author of introduction) B. Malzberg and E. S. Lee, *Migration and Mental Disease*, Social Science Research Council, 1956; J. B. Gittler, editor, *Understanding Minority Groups*, Wiley, 1956; Philip Hauser, editor, *Population and World Politics*, Free Press of Glencoe, 1958. Contributor to U.S. government reports on population and census studies; also contributor of about forty papers to proceedings, yearbooks, and professional journals.

WORK IN PROGRESS: Studies of migration and urbanization.†

(Died May 1, 1977)

*   *   *

THOMPSON, James D(avid)   1920-1973

PERSONAL: Born January 11, 1920, in Indianapolis, Ind.; son of Earl Carroll and Alta (Wilson) Thompson; married Mary L. Mettenbrink, April 18, 1946; children: Gregg R., Janet C. *Education:* Indiana University, B.S., 1941, M.A., 1947; University of North Carolina, Ph.D., 1953. *Office:* Department of Sociology, Vanderbilt University, Nashville, Tenn. 37235.

CAREER: University of Wisconsin, Madison, assistant professor of journalism, 1947-49; University of North Carolina, Chapel Hill, research associate in behavioral sciences, 1951-54; Cornell University, Ithaca, assistant professor, 1954-56, associate professor of administration, 1956-57; University of Pittsburgh, Pittsburgh, Pa., associate professor, 1957-60, professor of sociology, 1960-62, director of Administrative Science Center, 1957-62, acting chairman of department of sociology, 1961-62; Indiana University, Bloomington, professor of business administration, 1962-68; Vanderbilt University, Nashville, Tenn., professor of sociology, 1968-73. *Military service:* U.S. Army, 1941-45; became first lieutenant. *Member:* American Sociological Association (fellow).

WRITINGS: (Co-editor) *Comparative Studies in Administration*, University of Pittsburgh Press, 1959; (editor) *Approaches to Organizational Design*, University of Pittsburgh Press, 1966; *Organizations in Action*, McGraw, 1967; (with D. R. Van Houten) *The Behavioral Sciences*, Addison-Wesley, 1970. Contributor to professional journals. Editor, *Administrative Science Quarterly*, 1955-57.†

(Died September, 1973)

THOMPSON, Roy Anton   1897-

PERSONAL: Born July 1, 1897, in Minneapolis, Minn.; son of Peter (a tailor) and Anna (Nelson) Thompson; married Ruby Elizabeth Carlson, June 30, 1927; children: Anna Josephine (Mrs. Donald O. Johnson), Nancy Elizabeth (Mrs. Vernon L. Larson). *Education:* Bible Institute of Evangelical Free Church, graduate, 1922; Moody Bible Institute, graduate, 1923; University of Chicago, B.Ph., 1933. *Politics:* Republican. *Religion:* Protestant. *Home:* 5202 Elliot Ave., Minneapolis, Minn. 55417.

CAREER: Evangelical Free Church of America, Minneapolis, Minn., editor of *Evangelical Beacon*, 1931-58, director of publications, 1958-64; Trinity Evangelical Divinity School, Deerfield, Ill., archivist and member of faculty, 1964-69. *Member:* American Society of Archivists. *Awards, honors:* Litt.D. from Trinity College (Deerfield) and Trinity Evangelical Divinity School.

WRITINGS: The Diamond Jubilee Story, Free Church Publications, 1959; *Toward New Horizons*, Free Church Publications, 1969. Also author of devotional messages for Every Sunday Bulletin Service.

*   *   *

THORNDYKE, Helen Louise
[Collective pseudonym]

WRITINGS—"Honey Bunch" series; all published by Grosset: *Honey Bunch: Her First Days in Camp*, 1925; ... *Her First Trip West*, 1928; ... *Her First Summer on an Island*, 1929; ... *Her First Trip on the Great Lakes*, 1930; ... *Her First Trip on an Airplane*, 1931; ... *Her First Visit to the Zoo*, 1932; ... *Her First Big Adventure*, 1933; ... *Her First Big Parade*, 1934; ... *Her First Little Mystery*, 1935; ... *Her First Little Circus*, 1936; ... *Her First Little Treasure Hunt*, 1937; ... *Her First Little Club*, 1938; ... *Her First Trip in a Trailer*, 1939; ... *Her First Trip to a Big Fair*, 1940; ... *Her First Twin Playmate*, 1941; ... *Her First Costume Party*, 1943; ... *Her First Trip on a Houseboat*, 1945; ... *Her First Winter at Snowtop*, 1946; ... *Her First Trip to the Big Woods*, 1947; ... *Her First Little Pet Show*, 1948; ... *Her First Trip to a Lighthouse*, 1949, published as *Honey Bunch and Norman on Lighthouse Island*, 1957; ... *Her First Visit to a Pony Ranch*, 1950; ... *Her First Tour of Toy Town*, 1951, published as *Honey Bunch and Norman Tour Toy Town*, 1951; ... *Her First Visit to Puppyland*, 1952; ... *Her First Trip to Reindeer Farm*, 1953, published as *Honey Bunch and Norman Visit Reindeer Farm*, 1958; ... *and Norman Ride with the Sky Mailman*, 1954; ... *and Norman Visit Beaver Lodge*, 1955; ... *and Norman Play Detective at Niagara Falls*, 1957; ... *and Norman*, 1957; ... *and Norman in the Castle of Magic*, 1959; ... *and Norman Solve the Pine Cone Mystery*, 1960; ... *and Norman and the Paper Lantern Mystery*, 1961; ... *and Norman and the Painted Pony*, 1962; ... *and Norman and the Walnut Tree Mystery*, 1963.

SIDELIGHTS: See ADAMS, Harriet S., STRATEMEYER, Edward L., and SVENSON, Andrew E.†

*   *   *

TIERNEY, John Lawrence   1892-1972
(Brian James)

PERSONAL: Born June 17, 1892, near Mudgee, New South Wales, Australia; son of John and Elizabeth (Rheinberger) Tierney; married Effie I. Brodie, September 6, 1932; children: Margaret J. H., Brian J. H., Alan J. H. *Education:*

Sydney Teachers College, student; University of Sydney, B.A., 1914, M.A., 1922; Oxford University, diploma in education, 1923. *Home:* 17 Kirkham St., Beecroft, Sydney, New South Wales 2119, Australia.

CAREER: Writer, 1942-72. Former teacher in New South Wales. *Wartime activity:* Served in Voluntary Aid Detachment during World War II. *Member:* Bread and Cheese Club. *Awards, honors:* Prior Memorial Prize, 1946, for *Cookabundy Bridge, and Other Stories.*

WRITINGS—All under pseudonym Brian James: *First Furrow,* Clarendon, 1944; *Cookabundy Bridge, and Other Stories,* Angus & Robertson, 1946; *The Advancement of Spencer Button* (novel), Angus & Robertson, 1950; *The Bunyip of Barney's Elbow* (stories), Angus & Robertson, 1956; (editor) *Selected Australian Stories,* Oxford University Press, 1959; *Australian Orchards,* Oxford University Press, 1962; *Hopeton High* (novel), Angus & Robertson, 1963; (editor) *Australian Short Stories,* Oxford University Press, 1963; *The Big Burn* (stories), Angus & Robertson, 1965. Also author of "Cookabundy Chronicles" (fiction), serialized in *Sydney Bulletin.* Contributor of articles to newspapers.

AVOCATIONAL INTERESTS: Bush tramping.

BIOGRAPHICAL/CRITICAL SOURCES: Douglas Stewart, *Flesh and the Spirit: An Outlook on Literature,* Angus & Robertson, 1948; Clement Semmler, *The Art of Brian James and Other Essays on Australian Literature,* University of Queensland Press, 1972.†

(Died February 11, 1972)

* * *

TILLEY, (William) Roger (Montgomerie) 1905-1971

PERSONAL: Born April 21, 1905, in London, England; son of Sir John Anthony Cecil (a diplomat) and Edith (Montgomery-Cuninghame) Tilley; married Rozella Josephine Blount, March 9, 1929 (died, 1953); married Jean Frances Elise Knowles, October 15, 1953; children: (first marriage) John Roger, Joseph Christopher. *Education:* Cadet at Royal Naval College, Osborne, and Royal Naval College, Dartmouth, 1919-23. *Politics:* Conservative. *Religion:* Church of England. *Home:* Thames Cottage, High St., Thames Ditton, Surrey, England.

CAREER: British Diplomatic Service, honorary attache at British Embassy, Tokyo, Japan, 1926-27; De La Rue Co., London, England, deputy archivist, 1950-66. *Military service:* Royal Navy, 1923-25, invalided out as sub-lieutenant. Royal Air Force, 1940-45; served as liaison officer with French fleet, Dakar; became squadron leader. *Member:* Printing History Society, Chicago Playing Card Collectors.

WRITINGS: Playing Cards, Putnam, 1967.

WORK IN PROGRESS: Manuscript on an entirely new approach to the Tarot; articles for an encyclopedia, *Man, Myth, Magic.*

SIDELIGHTS: Tilley told *CA:* "Always interested in customs of the past. . . . Come of a writing family. My father [Sir John Tilley] published two books and his half-brother, my uncle Arthur Augustus Tilley, a couple of dozen or so on French literature. . . . My grandfather, another Sir John Tilley, married the sister of Anthony Trollope."†

(Died August, 1971)

* * *

TOBEY, Kathrene McLandress 1908-

PERSONAL: Born August 18, 1908, in Oconto, Wis.; daughter of Robert John (a clergyman) and Katharine (Smith) McLandress; married Hamlin George Tobey, June 24, 1933; children: Robert George. *Education:* University of Illinois, student, 1925-27; Boston University, B.R.E., 1929; McCormick Theological Seminary, M.A., 1932; additional graduate study at University of Pennsylvania, 1959, Union Theological Seminary, New York, 1960, and Columbia University, 1964. *Religion:* Presbyterian. *Home:* Valley Rd., R.D. 1, Lakeville, Conn. 06039.

CAREER: Director of Christian education at Presbyterian church in Hammond, Ind., 1929-31; San Francisco Theological Seminary, San Anselmo, Calif., teacher, 1946; teacher in nursery schools in Llanerch, Pa., and New York City, 1959-61, 1963-64; teacher in Thailand, 1961-62, 1970-71; Madison Avenue Presbyterian Church, New York City, director of children's work, 1965-70.

WRITINGS: When They Are Four and Five, Westminster, 1950; *When We Teach Kindergarten Children,* Westminster, 1957; *The Church Plans for Kindergarten Children,* Westminster, 1959; *The Church and Children under Two,* Covenant Life Curriculum Press, 1964; *Learning and Teaching through the Senses,* Westminster, 1970. Also author of kindergarten textbooks for vacation schools, Westminster, 1951-53. Contributor to *Westminster Dictionary of Christian Education,* and to magazines.

* * *

TOBIN, James Edward 1905-1968
(Alan Rayne)

PERSONAL: Born January 17, 1905, in Fall River, Mass.; son of William J. J. and Mary L. (Kelleher) Tobin; married C. Lorraine Walsh, September 9, 1929; children: Jean (Mrs. Eugene A. Galletta), Robert E., Richard J., David W., Philip D. *Education:* Boston College, B.A., 1925; Fordham University, M.A., 1928, Ph.D., 1933. *Residence:* Tuckahoe, N.Y. *Office:* Queens College of the City University of New York, Flushing, N.Y. 11367.

CAREER: Associated Press, staff writer, 1925-27; Fordham University, Bronx, N.Y., English faculty member, 1928-46, chairman of department of English, Graduate School, 1936-46; McMullen Books, Inc., New York, N.Y., editor and vice-president, 1946-48; Queens College of the City University of New York, Flushing, N.Y., assistant professor, 1948-53, associate professor, 1954-58, professor of English literature, 1959-68, director of School of General Studies, 1962-66, dean, 1966-68. Notre Dame College of Staten Island, visiting lecturer, 1929-31, 1942-43; Molloy College, member of advisory board, 1955-67, visiting professor, 1957-60, trustee, 1967-68. Woodrow Wilson Fellowship Foundation, member of selection committee, 1961-68. Tuckahoe (N.Y.) Library Board, trustee, 1949-68, president, 1963-68. *Member:* Modern Language Association (member of bibliography committee, 1943-49; chairman, 1948-49), Modern Humanities Research Association, Bibliography Society, Catholic Poetry Society of America (chairman of board, 1951), Catholic Renascence Society (member of board of directors, 1958-65), Lotos Club (New York). *Awards, honors:* Thomas More Association Medal for most distinguished contribution to Catholic publishing for *Dictionary of Catholic Biography;* William F. O'Brien/Newman Foundation Award, 1966.

WRITINGS: Ardent Marigolds (poetry), White Fawn Press, 1933; *Eighteenth Century English Literature and Its Cultural Backgrounds,* Fordham University Press, 1939; (with F. X. Connolly) *To an Unknown Country,* Cosmopolitan, 1942; *Alexander Pope: A List of Critical Studies,* Cosmopolitan, 1945; (with Louis A. Landa) *Jonathan Swift: A List of Critical Studies,* Cosmopolitan, 1946; (with J. J. Delaney) *Dictionary of Catholic Biography,* Doubleday, 1961.

Editor: (With Charles B. Hale) *Contrast and Comparison,* Prentice-Hall, 1931; Thomas F. Woodlock, *Thinking It Over,* McMullen Books, 1947; (with William H. Hines and Victor M. Mann) *College Book of English Literature,* American Book Co., 1949; *The Happy Crusaders,* McMullen Books, 1952; *Joyce Kilmer's Anthology of Catholic Poets,* Doubleday, 1955; (with John G. Brunini) *Sealed unto the Day,* Catholic Poetry Society, 1955; *Second America Book of Verse,* America Press, 1956; (with John G. Brunini) *Invitation to the City,* Catholic Poetry Society, 1960.

Translations included in *Thought and Culture of the English Renaissance, Anthology of German Poetry from Holderlin to Rilke, Anthology of Spanish Poetry from Garcilaso to Garcia Lorca, Anthology of Medieval Lyrics,* and other anthologies. Contributor to *Collier's Encyclopedia* and *Catholic Encyclopedia for School and Home;* articles and poems published in *America, Catholic World, Polish Review, Thought, Baltimore Sun, New York Herald Tribune, Classical Bulletin,* and other journals and newspapers.

Associate editor, Fordham University Press, 1928-50; member of editorial board, *Thought,* 1939-46, and acting editor, 1945-46; managing editor, *Comparative Literature News Letter,* 1943-46; member of editorial board, *Fathers of the Church* (patristic translations series), 1945-62, and Catholic Book Club, 1947-52; associate editor, *Spirit,* 1951-68.

BIOGRAPHICAL/CRITICAL SOURCES: New York Times, October 31, 1968.†

(Died October 30, 1968)

*   *   *

TOLKIEN, J(ohn) R(onald) R(euel)   1892-1973

PERSONAL: Surname pronounced *Tohl*-keen; born January 3, 1892, in Bloemfontein, South Africa; brought to England in 1896; son of Arthur Reuel (a bank manager) and Mabel (a part-time missionary; maiden name, Suffield) Tolkien; married Edith Mary Bratt, March 22, 1916; children: three sons, one daughter. *Education:* Exeter College, Oxford, B.A., 1915, M.A., 1919. *Religion:* Roman Catholic. *Home:* 76 Sandfield Rd., Headington, Oxford, England.

CAREER: Assistant on *Oxford English Dictionary,* 1918-20; University of Leeds, Leeds, England, reader in English, 1920, professor of English, 1924-25; Oxford University, Oxford, England, Rawlinson and Bosworth Professor of Anglo-Saxon, 1925-45, Merton Professor of English Language and Literature, 1945-59, fellow of Pembroke College, 1926-45. Leverhulme research fellow, 1934-36; Andrew Lang Lecturer, St. Andrews University, 1939; W. P. Ker Lecturer, University of Glasgow, 1953. *Military service:* Lancashire Fusiliers, 1915-18. *Member:* Royal Society of Literature (fellow), Philological Society (vice-president), Hid Islenzka Bokmenntafelag (honorary). *Awards, honors:* *New York Herald Tribune* Children's Spring Book Festival award, 1938; for *The Hobbit;* Dr. en Phil. et Lettres, Liege, 1954; D.Litt., University College, Dublin, 1954; International Fantasy Award, 1957, for *The Lord of the Rings;* honorary fellow, Exeter College, Oxford.

WRITINGS: A Middle English Vocabulary, Milford, 1922; (editor with Eric V. Gordon) *Sir Gawain and the Green Knight,* Oxford University Press, 1925, 2nd edition, revised by Norman Davis, 1967; *Chaucer as a Philologist,* Philolog-

ical Society, 1934; *Beowulf: The Monsters and the Critics,* Oxford University Press, 1937; (self-illustrated) *The Hobbit; or, There and Back Again,* Allen & Unwin, 1937, Houghton, 1938, 4th edition, Allen & Unwin, 1972, collectors edition, Houghton, 1972; (contributor) *Essays Presented to Charles Williams* (essay entitled "On Fairy-Stories"), Oxford University Press, 1947; *Farmer Giles of Ham,* Allen & Unwin, 1949, Houghton, 1950.

The Lord of the Rings, Houghton, Volume I: *The Fellowship of the Ring,* 1954, Volume II: *The Two Towers,* 1954, Volume III: *The Return of the King,* 1955, with new foreword by author, Ballantine, 1966, 2nd edition, in three parts, Allen & Unwin, 1966, Houghton, 1967; (editor) *Ancrene Wisse,* Oxford University Press, 1962; *The Adventures of Tom Bombadil, and Other Verses from the Red Book,* Allen & Unwin, 1962, Houghton, 1963; *Tree and Leaf* (reprint of "On Fairy-Stories" and "Leaf By Niggle," the latter originally published in *The Dublin Review,* 1945), Allen & Unwin, 1964, Houghton, 1965; *The Tolkien Reader,* introduction by Peter S. Beagle, Ballantine, 1966; *Smith of Wooten Major,* Houghton, 1967; *Smith of Wooten Major and Farmer Giles of Ham,* Ballantine, 1970; *The Father Christmas Letters,* edited by Baillie Tolkien, Houghton, 1976. Also author of "The Homecoming of Beorhtnoth" in *Essays and Studies,* English Association, 1953. Contributor to *Shenandoah.*

WORK IN PROGRESS: The Silmarillion, a further work about Middle-Earth; *Akallabeth,* the story of the downfall of Numenor.

SIDELIGHTS: Some thirty years ago a Middle English scholar began writing tales about hobbits, elves, dragons and other creatures. For many years most of his colleagues knew nothing of these activities. The stories were at first a philological game: "The invention of languages is the foundation," wrote Tolkien. "The 'stories' were made rather to provide a world for the languages than the reverse. I should have preferred to write in 'Elvish'."

Tolkien not only invented languages, with their own alphabets and rules, but a world that existed prior to our own, Middle-Earth, a region that has its basis in rural England and in Norse and Germanic mythologies; and he peopled this world with special species, explaining at length their genealogies. Along with C. S. Lewis and Charles Williams, he revived the romance. His trilogy, *The Lord of the Rings,* recounts the adventures of an ordinary and even unwilling hobbit named Frodo, who, with his party, embarks on a journey to destroy the Ring of Power and becomes involved "in cosmic struggles on whose outcome depends the welfare of the created universe." Edmund Fuller reported that "the sheer creative feat of bringing a new creature into the realm of fairy story is almost too much for some to accept." Sir Stanley Unwin, Tolkien's publisher, told him that "the first negotiations for German publication of *The Hobbit* were broken off abruptly when the publishers wrote that they had searched through all the encyclopedias and found that there was no such thing as a hobbit."

When asked what his story was about, he replied: "It is not 'about' anything but itself. Certainly it has *no* allegorical intentions, general, particular or topical, moral, religious or political." Douglass Parker considered the trilogy "probably the most original and varied creation ever seen in the genre, and certainly the most self-consistent; yet it is tied up with and bridged to reality as is no other fantasy. . . . Tolkien has made his world a prodigious and, so far as I can judge, unshakable construct of the imagination." Richard Hughes believed nothing of this kind had been attempted since *The Faerie Queen.* C. S. Lewis found it "good beyond hope," and added, "If Ariosto rivalled it in invention (in fact, he does not), he would still lack its heroic seriousness." Discussing Tolkien's artistry, Guy Davenport wrote: "The reader soon learns that the spirit he meets in Tolkien is fine and particular, capable of every modulation in the spellbinder's repertory: a country scene from Brueghel or Deloney, a forest out of Mahler, an imaginary tree worthy of Odilon Redon, pages that out-boiardo Boiardo, that are as dread as Old English elegies, pages where Dante would have envied the economy of detail, Berlioz the tone."

Critics who were less favorably disposed to the trilogy reminded the reader of the "bad verse," "flat characterizations," the scarcity of women, and the lack of any real conflict within the characters. (Tolkien said that "a lot of the criticism of the verses shows a complete failure to understand the fact that they are all dramatic verses: they were conceived as the kind of things people would say under the circumstances.") But R. J. Reilly maintained that the trilogy remains "an anomaly heartily liked or disliked not so much on literary grounds as on fundamental religious or ideological ones. It demanded extra-literary value judgments, and it got them." But there was one among the critics, called Edmund Wilson, who cried fie upon it and said, "juvenile trash." And so greatly displeased were Tolkien's admirers that Wilson was likened to an orc.

Tolkien fans in America now amount to something of a cult: some have banded together to form the Tolkien Society (a group which includes among its members W. H. Auden, a former student of Tolkien's), and even persuaded Tolkien to join; the hard-core admirers memorize the six appendices to the trilogy and contribute such studies as "The Heredity Pattern of Immortality in Elf-Human Crosses"; and there are many who appear behind buttons that proclaim "Frodo Lives." The American interest in Tolkien has never really been explained except by suggesting that he offers an escape from the real and provides enough material for months of study and conversation.

Tolkien believed the faerian drama offered the reader Recovery, Escape, and Consolation. Recovery he called the "regaining of a clear view" after one's vision has become blurred by familiarity. The appeal of this form of escape is that it "opens a door on Other Time, and if we pass through, though only for a moment, we stand outside our own time, outside Time itself, maybe." And we are rewarded with the Consolation of the Happy Ending, which no other literary form offers to the same degree. The fairy-story, he said, must offer a happy ending. "Since we do not appear to possess a word that expresses this opposite [of tragic drama]—I will call it *Eucatastrophe.* The *eucatastrophic* tale is the true form of fairy-tale, and its highest function." What is important is its "inherent morality, not any allegorical *significatio.*" For "in the 'eucatastrophe' we see in brief vision that the answer . . . may be a far-off gleam or echo of *evangelium* in the real world."

His fondness for the form developed early in life. He wrote that while still quite young, he "desired dragons with a profound desire. Of course, I in my timid body did not wish to have them in the neighborhood, intruding into my relatively safe world. . . . But the world that contained even the imagination of Fafnir was richer and more beautiful, at whatever cost or peril."

Fantasy, according to Tolkien, is "the making or glimpsing of Other-worlds"; this process is "not a lower but a higher form of Art, indeed the most nearly pure form, and so (when achieved) the most potent." It is, however, not easily achieved. Tolkien wrote in "On Fairy-Stories": "Anyone inheriting the fantastic device of human language can say *the green sun.* [But] to make a Secondary World inside which the green sun will be credible, commanding Secondary Belief will . . . certainly demand a special skill, a kind of elvish craft. Few attempt such difficult tasks. But when they are attempted and in any degree accomplished then we have a rare achievement of Art: indeed narrative art, story-making in its primary and most potent mode."

Tolkien said he spent his days "working like hell." *The Lord of the Rings,* which Tolkien typed with two fingers, took 14 years to complete. Neither the trilogy nor *The Hobbit* was written for children, as some have reported. "That's all sob stuff," said Tolkien. "If you're a youngish man and you don't want to be made fun of, you say you're writing for children. . . . *The Hobbit* was written in what I should now regard as bad style, as if one were talking to children. There's nothing my children loathed more. They taught me a lesson."

Tolkien modestly said he was not a storyteller. J.I.M. Stewart, however, praised Tolkien as an Oxford orator. "He could turn a lecture room into a mead hall in which he was the bard and we were the feasting, listening guests."

The trilogy has been translated into nine languages. Tolkien recorded a number of his works for Caedmon Records, including "The Hobbit," "The Fellowship of the Ring," "Lord of the Rings," and "Poems and Songs of Middle Earth." Donald Swann has put six of the verses to music, one to be sung in Elvish. And *The Hobbitt: or, There and Back Again* has been broadcast on radio as a play.

BIOGRAPHICAL/CRITICAL SOURCES—Books: Edmund Fuller, *Books with Men behind Them,* Random House, 1962; Charles Moorman, *The Precincts of Felicity: The Augustinian City of the Oxford Christians,* University of Florida Press, 1966; Neil D. Isaacs and Rose A. Zimbardo, editors, *Tolkien and the Critics,* University of Notre Dame Press, 1968; William B. Ready, *The Tolkien Relation: A Personal Inquiry,* Regnery, 1968; Catherine R. Stimpson, *J.R.R. Tolkien,* Columbia University Press, 1969; Lin Carter, *A Look behind "The Lord of the Rings,"* Ballantine, 1969; Richard C. West, compiler, *Tolkien Criticism: An Annotated Checklist,* Kent State University Press, 1970; Gracia F. Ellwood, *Good News from Tolkien's Middle Earth: 2 Essays on the Applicability of "The Lord of the Rings,"* Eerdmans, 1970; Robert Foster, *A Guide to Middle Earth,* Mirage Press, 1971; Gunnar Urang, *Shadows of Heaven: Religion and Fantasy in the Writing of C. S. Lewis, Charles Williams, and J.R.R. Tolkien,* Pilgrim Press (Boston), 1971; Paul H. Kocher, *Master of Middle-Earth: The Fiction of J.R.R. Tolkien,* Houghton, 1972; Roger Sale, *Modern Heroism: Essays on D. H. Lawrence, William Empson, and J.R.R. Tolkien,* University of California Press, 1973; Paul H. Kocher, *Master of Middle-Earth: The Achievement of J.R.R. Tolkien,* Thames & Hudson, 1973; *Contemporary Literary Criticism,* Gale, Volume I, 1973, Volume II, 1974, Volume III, 1975; Richard L. Purtill, *Lord of the Elves and Eldils: Fantasy and Philosophy in C. S. Lewis and J.R.R. Tolkien,* Zondervan, 1974; Edmund Fuller and others, *Myth, Allegory and Gospel: An Interpretation of J.R.R. Tolkien, C. S. Lewis, G. K. Chesterton [and] Charles Williams,* Bethany Fellowship, 1974.

Periodicals: *Time and Tide,* October 22, 1955; *New Republic,* January 16, 1956; *Nation,* April 14, 1956; *Hudson Re-*

view, IX (1956-57); *South Atlantic Quarterly*, summer, 1959; *Critique*, spring-fall, 1959; *Sewanee Review*, fall, 1961; *Thought*, spring, 1963; *Atlantic*, March, 1965; *New York Times Book Review*, March 14, 1965, October 31, 1965; *National Review*, April 20, 1965; *Kenyon Review*, summer, 1965; *Commonweal*, December 3, 1965; *Saturday Evening Post*, July 2, 1966; *Esquire*, September, 1966; *New York Times Magazine*, January 15, 1967; *Commentary*, February, 1967; *Book Week*, February 26, 1967; *South Atlantic Quarterly*, spring, 1970.†

(Died September 2, 1973)

* * *

TOMKIEWICZ, Mina 1917-1975
(Meta, Dona Quichot)

PERSONAL: Born September 18, 1917, in Warsaw, Poland; daughter of Bernard (a merchant) and Felicja (Kornberg) Tomkiewicz; married Moshe Mieczyslaw Tomkiewicz, February 28, 1937 (died, 1943); married Stanislaw Krysztal, January 1, 1966; children (first marriage) Marceli-Robert. *Education:* Alliance Francaise, Paris, Diploma, 1933; University of Warsaw, magister juris, 1937; Cambridge Proficiency Diploma (London), 1965; also took courses at London School of Economics and Political Science and City Literary Institute, London, 1965. *Religion:* Jewish. *Home:* 136 Richmond Hill, Richmond, Surrey, England.

CAREER: During the war was interned in Bergen-Belsen concentration camp, then settled in Israel after a period in a displaced person camp; turned to free-lance journalism in 1950, and wrote a weekly column for *Nowiny-Kurier* (Polish-language daily), Israel, 1950-65, and articles and essays for Hebrew magazines and newspapers; correspondent in England for *Nowiny-Kurier*, beginning 1965, and writer for Polish emigre newspapers and magazines in London. Translator from French and English into Polish. Secretary and chief clerk of Teus (Histadruth-sponsored company), Israel, 1950-65. *Member:* Association of Jewish Journalists and Authors in England, Polish Union of Journalists (London).

WRITINGS: Gam sham hayu hayim (title means "There Was Life There, Too"; autobiographical book on Bergen-Belsen concentration camp), Tversky, 1946; *Petsatsot ve-akhbarim*, Tversky, 1955, translation by Stefan F. Gazel from Polish edition published as *Of Bombs and Mice: A Story of the Warsaw Ghetto*, edited by Tomkiewicz and Patrick Wyndham, Yoseloff, 1970. Contributor of articles, short stories, essays, and features to *Davar Hashavua* (Hebrew magazine), *Maariv* (Hebrew daily), *Przeglad*, and other periodicals in Israel and England, writing sometimes under the pseudonyms Dona Quichot, Meta, and others; articles also have been reprinted in Polish emigre newspapers in the United States.

WORK IN PROGRESS: Studies on the absorption of refugees and displaced persons in different countries, with emphasis on their mental and social adjustment.

SIDELIGHTS: Gam sham hayu hayim also was published in Polish in the weekly *Nasza Trybuna* in the United States in 1947, in a Polish emigre magazine *Orzel Bialy* in 1969, and in Yiddish in Germany. Mina Tomkiewicz lost most of her family to the Nazis, but she and her small son managed to survive the concentration camp. Her first book was written in a British military camp in Beit Nabala, and the second book at night in the kitchen of a hostel for immigrant women. She visited the United States and Canada, and wrote travelogues and essays about the places she saw.

BIOGRAPHICAL/CRITICAL SOURCES: Observer Review, July 12, 1970.†

(Died October 6, 1975)

* * *

TOMLINSON, Jill 1931-1976

PERSONAL: Born December 27, 1931, in Twickenham, Middlesex, England; daughter of Idris (a bank accountant) and Myfanwy (Jones) Griffiths; married Rolfe C. Tomlinson (a research executive), July 26, 1952; children: Kate, Philip, Andy. *Education:* Attended Lady Eleanor Holles School in Hampton, Middlesex, and studied voice for three years at Royal College of Music, London. *Politics:* Liberal. *Religion:* Church of England. *Home:* Kirbygate, Ducks Hill Rd., Northwood, Middlesex HA6 2NW, England.

CAREER: Trained as an opera singer; fitted professional singing engagements "between babies" until multiple sclerosis prevented her from accepting any but amateur engagements; writer of children's books. *Member:* Society of Authors, British Federation of University Women, Disablement Income Group, Multiple Sclerosis Society, Zoological Society of London, Oxford and Cambridge Music Club.

WRITINGS—Juvenile books: The Bus That Went to Church, Faber, 1965; *Pyjams*, Faber, 1966; *Patti Finds an Orchestra*, Faber, 1966; *The Dog Who Couldn't Swim*, Faber, 1966; *Hilda the Hen*, Methuen, 1967, published as *The Hen Who Wouldn't Give Up*, 1977; *Fanny*, Faber, 1967; (with Gillian Shanks) *Suli and the Kitchen Cats*, Faber, 1968; *The Owl Who Was Afraid of the Dark*, Methuen, 1968, Bobbs-Merrill, 1970; *Lady Bee's Bonnets*, Faber, 1971; *The Cat Who Wanted to Go Home*, Methuen, 1972; *The Aardvark Who Wasn't Sure*, Methuen, 1973; *Penguin's Progress*, Methuen, 1975; *The Gorilla Who Wanted to Grow Old*, Methuen, 1977.

SIDELIGHTS: Jill Tomlinson's husband wrote *CA:* "Jill Tomlinson started writing children's stories when it was diagnosed that she had multiple sclerosis and would no longer have the strength to sing professionally. She took a correspondence course and had the good fortune to be given a tutor who recognised talent. One of her first exercises was *The Bus That Went to Church* which was accepted for publication—though not by the first publisher she tried—and is still in print ten years after publication. That first book was written in manuscript but as she moved to longer stories she taught herself to type, producing what her publishers described as 'immaculate' manuscripts.

"Multiple sclerosis is a deteriorating disease, however, and the time came when she could no longer control her hands enough to type. Then she dictated her stories and was just able to correct the drafts by hand. A while after this, she could no longer read typescript so she listened to her own tapes and corrected them by dictating into another machine. Finally she relied on her husband reading the stories. She claimed to be the only successful author who could neither read nor write.

"It may seem paradoxical that, in the circumstances, her stories were so funny. But they were—as she herself was. Despite her terrible disease, which kept her paralyzed on her bed—she remained the focus of her family and the person to whom doctors and nurses and social workers came to be cheered up. She fought every inch of the way.

"It was no accident that most of her books were about young animals. She was fascinated by animal behaviour—and researched all her books thoroughly. But more than this, she found that this approach enabled to transcend barriers of class, colour and nationality. She was able to treat problems that children face—even such things as one-parent families, or night fears—without being sentimental or over-earnest. Certainly the stories appear to be endless and have been translated into such disparate languages as Spanish and Japanese.

"In one sense her animal characters are like their author—so funny and loveable on first acquaintance, that it is only on second thoughts that you realise the underlying seriousness of what they are doing and the courage and determination needed to do it."

All of Jill Tomlinson's books have been published in German, and some in Norwegian, Swedish, Danish, Spanish, and Japanese. *The Owl Who Was Afraid of the Dark* has been published in Danish and German, and five stories from the book have been used twice on the British Broadcasting Corp. television program, "Playschool." *Patti Finds an Orchestra* and *Hilda the Hen* also were used on "Playschool."

BIOGRAPHICAL/CRITICAL SOURCES: Books and Bookmen, July, 1968.†

(Died, 1976)

* * *

TRACEY, Hugh (Travers) 1903-

PERSONAL: Born January 29, 1903, in Willand, Devonshire, England; son of Henry Eugene (a doctor in general practice) and Emily Alice (Martin) Tracey; married Ursula Campbell, April 14, 1935; children: Andrew Travers Norman, Paul Hugh Lawrence. *Education:* Educated in Bath, England. *Office address:* International Library of African Music, Box 138, Roodepoort, 1725 Transvaal, South Africa.

CAREER: South African Broadcasting Corp., Natal, South Africa, regional director of broadcasting, 1935-47; International Library of African Music, Roodepoort, Transvaal, South Africa, director, beginning 1947. Lecturer on African music at more than fifty universities, including thirty-six in the United States on four visits here between 1960-71 (among the American universities are Harvard, Yale, Columbia, Northwestern, and University of California, Los Angeles); also has done radio and television broadcasts in America, South Africa, and England. *Military service:* South African Army, 1939-45; became captain. *Member:* African Music Society (founder and honorary secretary, beginning 1947), Durban Club. *Awards, honors:* D.Mus., University of Cape Town.

WRITINGS: (Translator) *Antonio Fernandes: Descobridor do Monomotapa, 1514-1515,* Imprensa Nacional (Lisbon), 1940; (with K. E. Masinga) *Chief Above and Chief Below* (musical play), Shuter & Shooter, 1944; *Chopi Musicians: Their Music, Poetry, and Instruments,* Oxford University Press, 1948, reprinted, International African Institute, 1970; (compiler and translator) *Lalela Zulu: 100 Zulu Lyrics,* African Music Society, 1948; *Ngoma: An Introduction to Music for Southern Africans,* Longmans, Green, 1948; *Zulu Paradox,* Silver Leaf Books (Johannesburg), 1948; *African Dances of the Witwatersrand Gold Mines,* African Music Society, 1952; *The Evolution of African Music and Its Function in the Present Day* (booklet), Institute for the Study of Man in Africa, 1961; *Father's First Car,* Routledge & Kegan Paul, 1966; *The Lion on the Path, and Other African Stories,* Routledge & Kegan Paul, 1967, Praeger, 1968; (with Gerhard Kubik and Andrew T. N. Tracey) *Codification of*

African Music and Textbook Project, International Library of African Music, 1969. Has made and directed the recording of more than two hundred long-playing records in "Music of Africa" and "Sound of Africa" series, issued by International Library of African Music. Contributor of articles to *African Music* and other periodicals. Editor, *African Music.*

WORK IN PROGRESS: Further research and recordings in African music.

BIOGRAPHICAL/CRITICAL SOURCES: Best Sellers, March 1, 1969.†

* * *

TRACY, Thomas Henry 1900-

PERSONAL: Born September 23, 1900, in Boston, Mass.; son of Frank (a lawyer) and Nellie (Rattigan) Tracy; married Margaret Ray (the late Steve Hannagan's "Girl Friday" for twenty-five years), June 9, 1945. *Education:* Hebron Academy, graduate, 1922; Georgetown University, LL.B., 1926. *Politics:* Republican. *Religion:* Roman Catholic. *Home:* 118 East 60th St., New York, N.Y. 10022.

CAREER: Federal Bureau of Investigation, agent, 1926-35, as agent in charge, Seattle, Wash., 1929-32; private law practice in New York, N.Y., beginning 1935. *Awards, honors:* Honorary Doctor of Laws, Georgetown University, 1967.

WRITINGS: How to Be a G-Man, McBride, 1940; *The Book of the Poodle,* Viking, 1951; *The Seventh Commandment,* Abelard, 1963.

WORK IN PROGRESS: Oyez, Oyez, a book on the U.S. Courts.

* * *

TRALBAUT, Mark-Edo 1902-1976

PERSONAL: Born January 3, 1902, in Auvers-sur-Oise, France; son of Louis (a naturalized American) and Isabella (Odufre) Tralbaut; married Paula Van Dijck, August 23, 1947; children: Ivo (writes under the pseudonym Ivo Berg). *Education:* Studied at several universities; University of Ghent, doctorate in archeology and history of art, 1943. *Home:* Mas du Lezard Aile, Route du Destat, Mausanne-Les-Alpilles, France; and 1 Schuttershofstraat, Antwerp, Belgium. *Office:* International Van Gogh Archives, The Hague, Netherlands.

CAREER: Founder, 1934, and managing editor until 1937 of Flemish newspaper *De Dag;* curator of the Dutch State Institute for Fine Arts at The Hague, The Hague, Netherlands; International Van Gogh Archives, The Hague, founder and director, 1937-76. *Awards, honors:* Award of National Academy for Fine Arts of Belgium, 1944; first prize in Society for Authors Rights play competition, 1958, for *In Raven's Shadow* (translation by son, Ivo Berg).

WRITINGS: Onbekende archivalia betreffende Michiel van der Voort den Oude, F. de Backer, 1946; *Verdi's Othello,* F. de Backer, 1946; *Michiel van der Voort de Oude als dierenbeeldouwer,* De Sikkel, 1946; *De amors & putti, serafijnen & cherubijnen, van Michael van der Voort den Oude,* De Sikkel, 1946; *In kortgeding: Zo was "de Fee,"* Herinnengen aan Felix Timmermans, 1947; *Vincent van Gogh in zijn Antwerpsche periode,* Strengtholt, 1948; *De Antwerpse "meester constbeldthouwer" Michiel van der Voort de Oude (1667-1737): Zijn leven en werken,* Standaard-Boekhandel, 1950; *Vincent van Gogh en de Vlamingen,* Colibrant, 1955; *Van Gogh: Reflekties op Van*

Ostaijen, Drukkerijen Govaerts, 1956; *Van Gogh te Antwerpen,* Ontwikkeling, 1958; *Vincent van Gogh und die Gesellschaft* (booklet), Kulturamt der Stadt Dortmund, 1958; *Van Gogh: Eine Bildbiographie,* Kindler, 1958, translation by Margaret Shenfield published as *Van Gogh: A Pictorial Biography,* Viking, 1959; *Vincent van Gogh in Drenthe,* De Torenlaan, 1959; *Huit fois Vincent van Gogh* (five lectures in French and three in Flemish), Enterprises de Peinture B. & P. Pere, 1962; *Un Peintre devant les cathedrales de France, ou Le Pelerinage de Marie Howet,* Colas, 1962; *Richard Wagner im Blickwinkel fuenf grosser Maler* (booklet), [Dortmund], 1965; *Comment identifier Van Gogh?,* International Van Gogh Archives, 1967; *Van Gogh, le mal aime,* Edita, 1969, translation published as *Vincent van Gogh,* Viking, 1969.

Plays and librettos of musical works: *Servaz Brikoda* (play), Snoeck-Ducaju, 1941; *De stier van Minos* (play), Snoeck-Ducaju, 1941; *Ikaros* (oratorio), Snoeck-Ducaju, 1942; (with Jef Schampaert) *Mateo Falcone* (opera), Snoeck-Ducaju, 1942; (with Van Looy) *Nophriet's tweede dood* (opera), Snoeck-Ducaju, 1942.

Other: (Translator) Jean Capart, *Horti, jongetje uit het oude Egypte,* Snoeck-Ducaju, 1942; (compiler) *Vincent van Gogh* (catalogue), Stedelijk Museum (Amsterdam), 1958. Contributor to journals. Tralbaut's complete bibliography runs to more than one thousand items.

BIOGRAPHICAL/CRITICAL SOURCES: Newsweek, December 15, 1969.†

(Died May 5, 1976)

* * *

TRAVELL, Janet (Graeme) 1901-

PERSONAL: Born December 17, 1901, in New York, N.Y.; daughter of Willard (a physician) and Janet (Davidson) Travell; married John William Gordon Powell, June 6, 1929 (deceased); children: Janet (Mrs. Vinicio Pinci; stage name, Gianna Pinci), Virginia Gordon (Mrs. Edward Hunt Street; professional name, Gina Street). *Education:* Wellesley College, B.A., 1922; Cornell University, M.D., 1926. *Politics:* Democrat. *Religion:* Episcopalian. *Residence:* Washington, D.C. *Office:* 4525 Cathedral Ave. N.W., Washington, D.C. 20016.

CAREER: New York Hospital, New York City, intern and house physician, 1927-29; Bellevue Hospital, New York City, fellow working on digitalis-pneumonia study, 1929-30; physician in private practice, beginning 1933, in New York City, and more recently in Washington, D.C.; physician to President John F. Kennedy at the White House, 1961-63, and to President Lyndon B. Johnson, 1963-65. Cornell University Medical College, New York City, instructor in pharmacology, 1930-47, assistant professor, 1947-51, associate professor of clinical pharmacology, 1951-63 (on leave, 1961-63); Beth Israel Hospital, New York City, Josiah Macy, Jr. Foundation fellow working on arterial disease study, 1939-41, associate physician in cardiovascular medicine, beginning 1941 (on leave, beginning 1961); George Washington University Medical Center, Washington, D.C., associate professor of clinical medicine at the university, 1961-70, professor emeritus, 1970—, and at University Hospital, beginning 1964. Assistant, became associate visiting physician, Sea View Hospital, Staten Island, 1936-45; physician to outpatients, New York Hospital, 1941-66. Member of scientific advisory board, Joseph P. Kennedy, Jr. Foundation, 1959-61; special consultant to the U.S. Air Force, Office of the Surgeon General, 1962-64; chairman of medical care and

public health committee, Inaugural Committee for President Johnson, 1965. Member of national board, Medical College of Pennsylvania.

MEMBER: American Medical Association, American Medical Women's Association, American Rheumatism Association, American Society for Pharmacology and Experimental Therapeutics, American Society for Clinical Pharmacology and Therapeutics, American Association for the Advancement of Science, Pan American Medical Association, American Association for the Study of Headache, North American Academy of Manipulative Medicine (founder; president, 1968-69), International Association for the Study of Pain, New York Academy of Medicine, Medical Society of the County of New York (associate member), Medical Society of the District of Columbia, Rheumatism Society of the District of Columbia, Phi Beta Kappa, Alpha Omega Alpha.

AWARDS, HONORS: U.S. Public Health Service grant for research at Heart Institute, 1951-57; Spirit of Achievement Award from Albert Einstein College of Medicine, Yeshiva University, 1961; D.M.S. from Woman's Medical College of Pennsylvania, 1961; D.Sc. from Wilson College, 1962.

WRITINGS: Office Hours: Day and Night (autobiography), World Publishing, 1969. Contributor of medical, pharmacological, and popular articles to periodicals.

BIOGRAPHICAL/CRITICAL SOURCES: Best Sellers, January 1, 1969.

* * *

TRAVEN, B.   ?-1969
(Ret Marut, Berick Traven Torsvan; also see SIDELIGHTS)

PERSONAL—A compilation of conjectural statements, not intended to be definitive: Born March 5, 1890, in Chicago, Ill.; son of Burton and Dorothy Torsvan; or born May 3, 1882, in Germany; perhaps the son of Burton and Dorothy (Ottarent) Marut; married Rosa Elena Lujan, May 16, 1957. *Education:* Little formal education. *Politics:* Left wing. *Residence:* Near Reforma Blvd., Mexico City, Mexico.

CAREER: Went to sea as cabinboy, around 1900 or 1912; later became a seaman; spent some time in London and Berlin, before settling in Mexico, about 1920-22. Author.

WRITINGS—All under name B. Traven: *Das Totenschiff: Die Geschichte eines amerikanischen Seemans,* Buechergilde Gutenberg (Berlin), 1926, 2nd edition, W. Krueger (Hamburg), 1951, U.S. edition, prepared by author, published as *The Death Ship: The Story of an American Sailor,* Knopf, 1934, translation from the German by Eric Sutton published under same title, Chatto & Windus, 1934; *Der Wobbly,* Buchmeister Verlag (Berlin), 1926, published as *Die Baumwollpfluecker,* 1929, translation by Eleanor Brockett published as *The Cotton-Pickers,* R. Hale, 1956, U.S. edition, prepared by author, published under same title, Hill & Wang, 1969; *Der Schatz der Sierra Madre,* Buechergilde Gutenberg, 1927, translation by Basil Creighton published as *The Treasure of Sierra Madre,* Chatto & Windus, 1935, U.S. edition, prepared by author, published under same title, Knopf, 1935; *Land des Fruehlings,* Buechergilde Gutenberg, 1928; *Die Bruecke im Dschungel,* Buechergilde Gutenberg, 1929, English language edition, prepared by author, published as *The Bridge in the Jungle,* Knopf, 1938; *Die weisse Rose,* Buechergilde Gutenberg, 1929, H. Fel Kraus, 1946, English language edition, prepared by author, published as *The White Rose,* R. Hale, 1965.

Der Busch (short stories), Buechergilde Gutenberg, 1930; *Der Karren,* Buechergilde Gutenberg, 1931, translation by Basil Creighton published as *The Carreta,* Chatto & Windus, 1935, U.S. edition, prepared by author, published under same title, Hill & Wang, 1970; *Regierung,* Buechergilde Gutenberg, 1931, translation by Basil Creighton published as *Government,* Chatto & Windus, 1935, Hill & Wang, 1971; *Der Marsch ins Reich der Caoba: Ein Kriegsmarsch,* Buechergilde Gutenberg, 1933, translation published as *March to Caobaland,* R. Hale, 1960; *O Cloveku Ktery Stvoril Slunce* (South American Indian legends), translated from the English manuscript by Vincenc Svoboda, F. J. Mueller (Prague), 1934, English language edition published as *The Creation of the Sun and the Moon,* Hill & Wang, 1968; *Die Troza,* Buechergilde Gutenberg, 1936; *Die Rebellion der Gehenkten,* Buechergilde Gutenberg, 1936, translation from the German by Charles Duff published as *The Rebellion of the Hanged,* R. Hale, 1952, translation from the Spanish edition published under same title, Knopf, 1952; *Djungelgeneralen,* translated from the German manuscript by Arne Holmstrom, Axel Holmstrom (Stockholm), 1939, translation by Desmond Vesey published as *General from the Jungle,* R. Hale, 1954, Hill & Wang, 1972.

Macario, Buechergilde Gutenberg, 1950, translation by author's wife, Rosa Elena Lujan, published under same title, Houghton, 1971; *Der Banditendoktor: Mexikanische Erzaehlungen,* Limmat-Verlag (Zurich), 1957.

Aslan Norval, Desch (Munich), 1960; *Stories by the Man Nobody Knows: Nine Tales,* Regency Books, 1961; *Khundar: Das erste Buch Begegnungen,* Clou Verlag (Egnach, Switzerland), 1963; *March to the Monteria,* Dell, 1963; (editor) Fritz Thurn, *Die Weisheiten der Aspasia,* Inter-Verlag (Luxembourg), 1966; *The Night Visitor and Other Stories,* Hill & Wang, 1966; *Erzaehlungen,* Limmat-Verlag, 1968; *The Kidnapped Saint and Other Stories,* Lawrence Hill, 1975.

Work included in *Vagabunden: Three Modern German Stories,* edited by Wolfgang Paulsen, Holt, 1950.

SIDELIGHTS: B. Traven's work has been published in 36 languages and over 500 editions since April, 1926. He is "probably the most mysterious and baffling of all modern writers," E. R. Hagemann once commented, "a man who has seemingly courted obscurity as another might court fame and notoriety, courted oblivion with an almost pathological intensity. Occasionally, this mysteriousness has been lessened by a letter or communication from him (irritating in its vagueness), or by an article either by one who puts forth claims of personal acquaintanceship or second-hand familiarity, or by one who seems deliberately to confuse the picture even more with wild and totally imaginative writing. The result, for one interested in Traven as a man and as a writer, is more than another 'quest for Corvo.' At best, one can only patch together a chaotic *melange* of what appear to be facts, guesses, legends, myths, and downright unadorned lies; and after completing his patchwork, can but suggest that his *may* be Traven's biography, but nothing more." Traven has been thought to be: Jack London, who, some believe, only pretended to die; ex-President Lopez Mateos of Mexico, who reasonably pointed out in a press conference in 1960 that he was only five years old when Traven's first book was published, although he did admit that his sister, Esperanza Lopez Mateos, had assisted the writer in translations; Ret Marut, a Bavarian socialist; a Negro fleeing from American injustice; an expatriate of the old Industrial Workers of the World (a Wobbly); a leper; a fugitive Austrian archduke; an American capitalist who wrote prole-

tarian novels to salve his conscience; and the illegitimate son of Kaiser Wilhelm II of Germany. At one time the *Times Literary Supplement* added facetiously that "two highly promising lines of speculation that have so far not been explored are that Traven is T. E. Lawrence and that Traven is the Empress Anastasia."

When *The Death Ship* went to press, his German publishers wrote the author in Mexico asking him for photographs and biographical material. Traven replied: "My personal history would not be disappointing to readers, but it is my own affair which I want to keep to myself. . . . I am in fact in no way more important than is the typesetter for my books, the man who works the mill; . . . no more important than the man who binds my books and the woman who wraps them and the scrubwoman who cleans up the office." Another reason for his reluctance to identify himself might have been attributed to his opinion of American publicity methods which, he claimed, reduced "authors to the status of tight rope walkers, sword swallowers, and trained animals." "Such resolute shunning of the limelight," the *Times Literary Supplement* continued, "has, of course, made the limelight search for him all the more avidly. And in the forty years since the publication of *The Death Ship,* Traven has had a steady following of detective readers. *Life* magazine even offered a large prize to anyone who could identify him."

Although Traven was thought to be a German, he always claimed to be a native-born American. He insisted that he always wrote in English and that he tried to interest an American publisher in *The Death Ship* before a German-Swiss translator encouraged a German firm to publish it. "This being the case," wrote William Weber Johnson, "it is strange that British editions of his books appeared as translations from German by different translators—Eric Sutton, Basil Creighton, Charles Duff, Eleanor Brockett. Why it was necessary to translate from the German when the originals, according to Traven, were written in English, has never been explained—though it led to one of the more fanciful theories about Traven: that he is really Jack London, . . . the linguistic migration from English to German and back to English again occurring in order to disguise his readily identifiable style. Traven's writing did not appear in the United States until the early 1930's, when Alfred A. Knopf, hearing in Europe of Traven's popularity, began publishing some of the mysterious author's novels. The Knopf texts differed from the British translations and may have been taken from Traven's original manuscripts. In *The Night Visitor and Other Stories* . . . it is curious to find that one of the stories appears to be taken from the British translation of a German translation. . . . There are enough Traven textual mysteries to occupy a generation of Ph.D. candidates." Harlan Ellison once said, while speaking of *Stories by the Man Nobody Knows:* "I let Scott Meredith, Traven's agent in New York, know that I wanted to publish some new material in the collection as well as those they had recently gotten published in magazines. These three stories came then, and they simply amazed me. They were so crudely written. I had heard that Traven took editing, but nothing that Knopf got from him could have looked like these. I had to do everything to them, short of rewriting them myself." Ellison suspected someone else was writing from Traven's notes.

Warner Bros. purchased the rights to *The Treasure of Sierra Madre* for $5,000 and, in 1947, John Huston, scenarist and director, began filming. By correspondence, Traven expressed admiration for Huston's script and thus was invited to serve as consultant on the film. In Mexico City, Huston was confronted by a man who claimed to be Traven's representative and whose card read "Hal Croves, Translator, Acapulco." It was suspected that Croves was Traven and upon completion of the film, Huston wrote an article to this effect. Following this lead and knowing that Croves traveled on an American passport, a Mexican novelist, Luis Spota, checked Mexican immigration records and found that Mexican "Form-14" passport gave his full name as Traven Torsvan, born in Chicago on March 5, 1890. His parents were listed as Burton and Dorothy Torsvan described as Norwegian-Swedish immigrants. Spota found that he also used the name Berick Traven Torsvan at times. Traven had denied that his name was B. Traven (or Ben or Benno or Bruno).

Years ago, William Weber Johnson received an unsigned letter that he assumed was written by Traven or Esperanza Lopez Mateos. "On reading Traven," it read, "one will find it some times not very easy. His style, his way to express himself, is now and then clumsy, cumbersome, twisted, mangled, and his English will frequently shock men and women of culture, although the ideas he wished to drive home are always clear.... Yet one must not forget that he has been a sailor for many years, that he has had to earn his own living and stand on his own two feet since he was seven.... Until he was thirty-five [he] had no more than twenty-six days of education in grammar school.... He came to Mexico for the first time when he was twelve, then being cabin boy on a Dutch freighter. He jumped ship on the West Coast of Mexico, stayed for a good time in Mexico, working as an electrician's assistant before returning to his home country. Since then, with occasional interruptions to sail ships again, he has lived in Latin America the greater half of his life, most of the time in Mexico."

The Traven myths evolve around the untraceable years, 1910-1920. The German theory was that Traven's true identity was to be found under the name Ret Marut. As reported in *Stern* by Gerd Heidemann, Richard Maurhut, Robert Marut, or Ret Marut was an actor and writer of obscure origins. Before World War I he was improperly registered with the German police as English, born in San Francisco in 1882. With the outbreak of the war, Marut changed his passport to read "American" and thus was a neutral. He then started his own paper, *Der Ziegelbrenner (The Brickmaker)* which attacked Hindenberg, the war, and the Pope. Because of his post-war Bavarian revolutionary career he was forced to flee the country and escaped to Mexico in 1923. Here, according to the Heidemann theory, he took the name of Traven Torsvan. Heidemann claimed that there was a good reason for Traven to hide his identity. Traven's wife, Rosa Elena Lujan, told Heidemann that in "a weak hour in Berlin" Traven had told her that his father's name was William—Kaiser Wilhelm II. Heidemann also claimed that the birthdate on Spota's discovered passport was false and that Traven was born May 3, 1882. A two-part *Ramparts* article claimed that Judy Stone "was given an unprecedented series of interviews with the mysterious novelist." The man she interviewed, however, was Hal Croves who still insisted that he was only a close friend of Traven's. His wife's name was Rosa Elena Lujan.

Reporting Traven's death in 1969, many newspapers and magazines identified him as Traven Torsvan (one account reported Rosa Elena had given out the information). Even that did not end the mystery. Donald D. Chankin, author of *Anonymity and Death: The Fiction of B. Traven,* told *CA:* "Senora Lujan also admitted that he was in fact Ret Marut; thus he was most likely born in 1882. She does not seem to

have noticed the contradiction—in 1907 Ret Marut was already appearing as actor and director in Essen. Throughout his life Traven always maintained that he was born in Chicago, but there is no birth certificate or other documentary proof (for the probable reasons for lack of documents, see *The Death Ship*). I think he should be accepted as American, not because he was born here, but because his main protagonists are American—Gales, Dobbs, Howard.''

In Russia, Traven is regarded as an important American proletarian writer. His books have sold well and have been enthusiastically received in Germany and elsewhere, though not in the United States. Many critics believe a possible explanation for this is that Americans are used to hard-sell campaigns and are unaccustomed to discovering an author's excellence without some knowledge of his personal life.

Traven's books have recurrent themes: sickness, death, cruelty, hard work for low wages, loneliness, fear, and superstition. He passionately defended the underdog. "It is an anarchist message," noted the *Times Literary Supplement,* "the anarchism of the Wobblies, of Thoreau and of Tolstoy (though without Tolstoy's Christianity). It is totally committed to the proletariat, the oppressed, committed to life and to enjoyment of physical reality: it is equally committed to opposing capitalism, authority, bureaucracy, the state, the oppressor. *The Treasure of Sierra Madre,* for example, is a polemic against the concept of gold as a commercial substance. Gold is a pretty metal, useful for making ornaments but not much more; the ignorant Mestizo murderers of Dobbs are right in their valuation when they mistake gold dust for sand and scatter it to the winds. Similarly Traven's references to capitalism are frequent, and never complimentary: 'Sing Sing . . . is the residence of all New Yorkers who get caught. The rest have offices in Wall Street'."

As the unsigned letter to Johnson maintained, his style is often clumsy. The opening chapter of *The Treasure of Sierra Madre* reads: "The manager . . . was a very young man, hardly more than twenty-five. He was short and very lean, and he had a long thin nose.... He looked as if he might die any minute. Your mistake, mister, for he could wallop any tough sailor who opened his swear-hold farther than was considered decent by the clerk." This same style might encourage literary buffs to include the opening sentence of *Sierra Madre* in their collection of favorite first lines: "The bench on which Dobbs was sitting was not so good." Bruce Cook wrote: "His 'untranslated' English versions read as though they had been worked out laboriously by someone who was fairly fluent in English yet not entirely at home with it. There is a good deal of self-conscious use of dated slang, . . . This sort of thing, intended to make the text idiomatically up-to-date and very American, actually stamps it indelibly as foreign and quite old-fashioned. On the other hand, B. Traven writes a good standard literary German, free from slang and replete with those long dependent clauses with which Mark Twain had so much fun in his essay, 'The Awful German Language'." But "the gift for spinning a yarn," wrote Johnson, "outweighs the occasional awkwardness of language." Desmond MacNamara was also impressed. "Of all the proletarian writers he alone shares honors with Jack London. Indeed, for me he is far better. As a storyteller he is superb and his feeling for Latin American politics on a backyard or jungle-clearing level is the best available. He can make the sun-sodden realities of the cactus lands as logical as an eviction in Kentish Town."

Anthony West, however, voiced scathing dissension against the popular view: "The Traven mystery, insofar as there is one, resides in the question of how Mr. Traven has been able to make himself a reputation with writing of this order, even if only in the wide and windy open spaces of Texas and the Southwest, where he has become the subject of a cult in university English departments. A possible answer is suggested by the history of Mr. Traven's success. In the twenties, when [Traven] . . . was settling himself into his newly adopted Mexican habitat, his work, unpublished in the United States, was being lapped up in Germany. An immense vogue for adventure stories in general, and for Westerns in particular, swept over Germany in the postwar decade. Dreamstuff about a free zone beyond the advancing frontiers of civilization, a place outside the urbanized world of rules and restraints where there was elbowroom and where action was all-important, had an enormous appeal for disillusioned and frustrated people in Europe. Mr. Traven's stories are about men who leave their law- and custom-bound selves behind and prove their virility with guns and knives while regaining contact, through the Indians, with an ancient wisdom of the instincts whose secrets Europeans have forgotten in the process of becoming civilized. [At that time,] this particular brand of baloney could not be sold in a Southwest whose distances were only just beginning to surrender to the Model T Ford. . . . Mr. Traven's West is a region of the mind, wholly unrelated to the West of reality—an un-place that might best be described as its creator's anti-Chicago. . . .''

The Treasure of Sierra Madre was made into a motion picture by Warner Bros., 1948, directed by John Huston and starring Humphrey Bogart. It received the New York Film Critics' Award and the National Board of Review Award for the best picture of 1948. *Rebellion of the Hanged* was filmed in 1954. *Das Totenschiff* was filmed by a German company in 1959 and starred Horst Buchholz. *Macario* was made into an award-winning Mexican film. *The White Rose*, filmed in Mexico under the title ''Rosa Blanca'' in 1962, was purchased by the Mexican government and not released until 1972, allegedly for political reasons. The movie versions of two other Traven novels also shared government censorship problems. The script for *Bridge in the Jungle*, written by director Pancho Kohner and rejected by the Mexican Motion Picture Bureau, was filmed only after a battle over modifications almost cancelled production. The film was released by United Artists in 1970. The same Mexican bureau confiscated ten rolls of a German production of *The Cotton-Pickers* in 1969 for presenting a false impression of modern Mexico.

BIOGRAPHICAL/CRITICAL SOURCES: Bibliographical Society of America, January, 1959; *New York Times Book Review*, April 17, 1966, June 11, 1967; *New York Times*, May 7, 1967; *Times Literary Supplement*, June 22, 1967; *New Statesman*, June 23, 1967; *New Yorker*, July 22, 1967; *Ramparts*, September, October, 1967; *The National Observer*, November 27, 1967; *New York Post*, April 3, 1969; *Los Angeles Times*, July 19, 1970; Donald D. Chankin, *Anonymity and Death: The Fiction of B. Traven*, Pennsylvania State University Press, 1975; Michael L. Baumann, *B. Traven: An Introduction*, University of New Mexico Press, 1976; Judy Stone, *The Mystery of B. Traven*, William Kaufmann, 1977; *Time*, April 11, 1977.†

(Died March 27, 1969)

*   *   *

TRAXLER, Arthur E(dwin)   1900-

PERSONAL: Born February 19, 1900, in Irving, Kan.; son of Edwin Clifford (a school superintendent) and Ora (Wells)

Traxler; married Bobbi Yearout, June 1, 1924; children: Karen (Mrs. David F. Ellett). *Education:* Kansas State Normal School (now Kansas State Teachers College of Emporia), B.S. in Ed., 1920; University of Chicago, M.A., 1924, Ph.D., 1932. *Politics:* Republican. *Religion:* Methodist. *Home:* 6825 Southwest 59th St., Miami, Fla. 33143.

CAREER: Superintendent of school systems in Kansas, 1918-28; University of Chicago High School, Chicago, Ill., psychologist, 1932-36; Educational Records Bureau, Inc., New York, N.Y., research associate, 1936-38, assistant director, 1938-41, associate director, 1941-50, executive director, 1950-64, president, 1964-65, president emeritus, beginning 1965; University of Miami, Coral Gables, Fla., part-time lecturer, 1965-72. Visiting instructor at University of Chicago, University of Arkansas, summer, 1935, University of Alabama, summer, 1936, Temple University, 1941-42, University of California, Berkeley, summer, 1942, Columbia University, and Syracuse University, 1948-49. Regional director, Army and Navy Qualifying Tests, 1943-45; assistant director of college and professional testing programs, American Institute of Accounting, 1946-65. Member of Board of Education, Hartsdale, N.Y., 1958-60.

MEMBER: American Educational Research Association (president, 1950-51), American Association for the Advancement of Science (vice-president, 1956-57), American Psychological Association, American Personnel and Guidance Association, International Reading Association, National Council on Measurement in Education (president, 1959-60), Phi Delta Kappa, Kappa Delta Pi. *Awards, honors:* Award for outstanding service to secondary education from Williston Academy, 1965; certificate as honorary admissions officer, U.S. Military Academy at West Point, 1968.

WRITINGS: The Measurement and Improvement of Silent Reading at the Junior-High-School Level, [Chicago], 1932; *The Use of Test Results in Diagnosis and Instruction in the Tool Subjects*, Educational Records Bureau, 1936, 3rd edition, 1949; *The Use of Test Results in Secondary Schools*, Educational Records Bureau, 1938; *The Use of Tests and Rating Devices in the Appraisal of Personality*, Educational Records Bureau, 1938; *The Nature and Use of Anecdotal Records*, Educational Records Bureau, 1939; *The Nature and Use of Reading Tests*, Science Research Associates, 1941; *Ten Years of Research in Reading: Summary and Bibliography*, Educational Records Bureau, 1941; *Techniques of Guidance: Tests, Records, and Counseling in a Guidance Program*, Harper, 1945, 3rd edition, 1966.

Co-author: (With P. E. Knight) *Read and Comprehend*, Little, Brown, 1937, 2nd edition, 1949; (with P. E. Knight) *Develop Your Reading*, Little, Brown, 1941; (with Agatha Townsend) *Another Five Years of Research in Reading: Summary and Bibliography*, Educational Records Bureau, 1946; (with others) *Introduction to Testing and the Use of Test Results in Public Schools* (revision of the work by M. Selover and others, Educational Records Bureau, 1950), Harper, 1953; (with J. Anthony Humphreys and R. D. North) *Guidance Services*, Science Research Association, 1954, 3rd edition, 1967; (with Agatha Townsend) *Eight More Years of Research in Reading: Summary and Bibliography*, Educational Records Bureau, 1955; (with Ann Jungeblut) *Research in Reading During Another Four Years: Summary and Bibliography*, Educational Records Bureau, 1960; (with Ruth Strang and Constance McCullough) *The Improvement of Reading*, McGraw, 1946, 4th edition, 1967.

Editor: *The Public School Demonstration Project in Educa-*

tional Guidance: A Progress Report, Educational Records Bureau, 1937; *Guidance in Public Secondary Schools: A Report of the Public School Demonstration Project in Educational Guidance,* Educational Records Bureau, 1939; *Goals of American Education,* American Council on Education, 1950; *Measurement and Evaluation in the Improvement of Education,* American Council on Education, 1951; *Education in a Period of National Preparedness,* American Council of Education, 1952; *Modern Educational Problems,* American Council on Education, 1953; (with Agatha Townsend) *Improving Transition From School to College: How Can School and College Best Cooperate?,* Harper, 1953; *Strengthening Education at All Levels,* American Council on Education, 1955; *Education in a Free World,* American Council on Education, 1955; *Selection and Guidance of Gifted Students for National Survival,* American Council on Education, 1956; *Vital Issues in Education: A Report of the Twenty-First Educational Conference,* American Council on Education, 1957; *Long-Range Planning for Education: A Report of the 22nd Educational Conference, 1957,* American Council on Education, 1957; *The Positive Values in the American Educational System,* American Council on Education, 1959; *Curriculum Planning to Meet Tomorrow's Needs,* American Council on Education, 1960; (with Geraldine Spaulding) *Measurement and Research in Today's Schools,* American Council on Education, 1961; *Improving the Efficiency and Quality of Learning,* American Council on Education, 1962; *Frontiers on Education,* American Council on Education, 1963; *Keeping Abreast of the Revolution in Education,* American Council on Education, 1964; *Innovation and Experiment in Modern Education,* American Council on Education, 1965.

Author of publications issued by Educational Records Bureau; contributor of more than three hundred articles and reviews to educational and psychological journals.

WORK IN PROGRESS: A book on educational measurement.†

* * *

TREFFLICH, Henry (Herbert Frederick) 1908-

PERSONAL: Born January 9, 1908, in Hamburg, Germany; became U.S. citizen, 1934; son of Heinrich (an animal dealer) and Caroline (Jahn) Trefflich; married Alberta Stetin, June 27, 1942; children: Richard, Carol, Arno, Marlene. *Education:* Attended elementary school in Hamburg, Germany. *Home address:* R.D. 1, P.O. Box 2605, Whitehouse Station, N.J. 08889.

CAREER: Trefflich's Bird & Animal Co., Inc. (import-export), New York City, president, beginning 1931. Left school at fourteen to sign on as mess boy on German tramp steamer; came to United States in 1923 and worked at restaurants in New York City; went to India with father, an animal dealer in Hamburg, Germany, to hunt animals, 1928, 1929, and made several more trips alone to obtain animals on consignment; established Henry Trefflich's Bird & Animal Co., Inc., New York City, 1931; set up animal collecting agencies, first in Far East, then West Africa, and later world-wide; pioneered importation of animals by air transport, and of rhesus monkeys in large quantities for research; during World War II supplied U.S. Government and National Foundation for Infantile Paralysis with research animals; established monkey reconditioning center near Accomac, Va., for 1,000 monkeys, 1950; in addition to research, supplies animals for zoos, circuses, carnivals, and for pets. *Member:* Players Club (New York).

WRITINGS: (With Baynard Kendrick) *They Never Talk Back,* Appleton, 1952; (with Edward Anthony) *Jungle for Sale,* Hawthorn, 1967.

AVOCATIONAL INTERESTS: Collecting hand organs.

* * *

TRUAX, Charles B. 1933-197(?)

PERSONAL: Born June 28, 1933, in Springfield, Ill.; son of Charles B. and Dortha (Parrish) Truax; married Jane Lynn Vuchetich, August 29, 1959; children: Theresa Lynn, Tamara Lynn. *Education:* Arizona State University, B.S. (with high distinction), 1955; University of Wisconsin, M.S., 1956, Ph.D., 1960. *Office:* Department of Educational Psychology, University of Calgary, 2920 24th Ave. N.W., Calgary, Alberta, Canada T2N 1N4.

CAREER: University of Iowa, Iowa City, research assistant professor, 1959-60; University of Wisconsin, Madison, co-director of schizophrenic research project, 1961-63, director of joint University of Wisconsin-University of Kentucky group psychotherapy research program, 1962-65; University of Kentucky, Lexington, associate professor and director of psychotherapy research group, 1963-65; University of Arkansas, Fayetteville, 1965-69, began as associate professor, became professor of psychology; University of Calgary, Alberta, professor of educational psychology, beginning 1970. Visiting professor, University of Florida, 1969-70. Executive director, Kentucky Mental Health Institute, 1964-65; director of research, Arkansas Rehabilitation Research and Training Center, 1965-69. *Member:* American Psychological Association, Canadian Psychological Association, Midwestern Psychological Association, Kentucky Psychological Association, Sigma Xi. *Awards, honors:* American Rehabilitation and Counseling Association research award for report, "Counseling and Psychotherapy: Process and Outcome," 1966-67; National Research Award, American Rehabilitation Association.

WRITINGS: (With R. R. Carkhuff) *Toward Effective Counseling and Psychotherapy: Training and Practice,* Aldine, 1967; (with C. R. Rogers, E. T. Gendlin, and D. J. Kiesler) *The Therapeutic Relationship and Its Impact: A Study of Psychotherapy with Schizophrenics,* University of Wisconsin Press, 1967; (contributor) Allen E. Bergen and others, editors, *Psychotherapy, 1971: An Aldine Annual,* Aldine-Atherton, 1972.†

(Deceased)

* * *

TRUETT, Fred M(oore) 1899-

PERSONAL: Born July 31, 1899, in Whitewright, Tex.; son of John Harvey (a lawyer) and Purcie (McMurry) Truett; married Mayme Twichell, December 3, 1925; children: Diane (Mrs. A. D. Roberts, Jr.). *Education:* Baylor University, B.A., 1920; Columbia University, graduate study in School of Business, 1921-22. *Politics:* Independent. *Religion:* Methodist. *Home:* 6046 DeLoache Ave., Dallas, Tex. 75225. *Office:* Southwestern Drug Corp., 8000 Carpenter Freeway, Dallas, Tex. 75247.

CAREER: Waco Drug Co., Waco, Tex., 1916-45, began as laborer, became assistant to the president; Southwestern Drug Corp., Dallas, Tex., president, 1945-63, chairman of board, beginning 1963. Director, Texas Industrial Corp. and Druggists Service Council. President of Children's Bureau, Dallas, and chairman of Public Health Advisory Board; secretary of Dallas unit, American Cancer Society; trustee of

Wadley Research Institute. *Military service:* U.S. Army, Infantry, second lieutenant, 1918. *Member:* National Wholesale Druggists' Association (president, 1953-54), Beta Gamma Sigma, Dallas Petroleum Club, Dallas Country Club, Executive Club.

WRITINGS: The Arithmetic of Sales Management, American Management Association, 1967.

WORK IN PROGRESS: Writing a section for *Creative Pricing,* for the American Management Association; *Mexico: A Travel Wise Guide.*

AVOCATIONAL INTERESTS: Travel, archaeology, architecture.

*   *   *

TUNYOGI, Andrew C(sapo)   1907-

PERSONAL: Born March 4, 1907, in Hungary; naturalized American citizen; son of Janos Csapo and Louisa (Sandor) Tunyogi; married Adele Orosz, November 2, 1932; children: Ildiko (Mrs. Frank Foldvary). *Education:* Theological Seminary of the Hungarian Reformed Church in Rumania, B.D., 1929, M.Th., 1936, M.Ed., 1937; Westminster College, Cambridge, England, further study, 1929-30; University of Debrecen, Th.D., 1942. *Home:* 624 Pennsylvania Ave., Norfolk, Va. 23508. *Office:* Department of Philosophy, Old Dominion University, Norfolk, Va. 23508.

CAREER: Minister of Hungarian Reformed Church in Rumania, 1932-36; professor of theology, Seminary of the Hungarian Reformed Church in Czechoslovakia, 1936-38; Deak Ter College, Budapest, Hungary, professor of religion, 1938-44; minister to refugees in Germany, 1945-50; Presbyterian minister in Cincinnati, Ohio, 1950-56; Pikeville College, Pikeville, Ky., professor of Bible, philosophy, and psychology, 1956-58; Old Dominion University, Norfolk, Va., professor of philosophy, 1958-73, professor emeritus, 1973—, chairman of department, 1966-73. *Military service:* Hungarian Army, chaplain. *Member:* Society for Biblical Literature, American Academy of Religion, Virginia Philosophical Association, Torch Club, Theophylus Club of Norfolk.

WRITINGS: Az Oszovetsegi Aldozat (title means "Sacrifice in the Old Testament"), Bethlen Press (Budapest), 1941; *Israel Bolcsessege* (title means "The Wisdom of Israel"), Bethlen Press, 1942; *The Rebellions of Israel,* John Knox, 1969. Contributor to *Journal of Biblical Literature.*

WORK IN PROGRESS: The Divine Struggle for Human Salvation; and a text on the history of western religious thought.

SIDELIGHTS: Andrew Tunyogi speaks German and Rumanian and reads biblical Hebrew, Greek, and Latin.

*   *   *

TURING, John (Ferrier)   1908-

PERSONAL: Born September 1, 1908, in Coonoor, South India; son of Julius Mathieson (in Indian civil service) and Ethel Sara (Stoney) Turing; married Joan Humphreys, August 25, 1934; married second wife, Beryl Mary Ada Hann (a teacher), July, 1960; children: (first marriage) Inagh Jean (Mrs. Warren Gray), Shuna, Janet Ferrier; (second marriage) John Dermot. *Education:* Attended Marlborough College, 1922-26. *Politics:* "Variable." *Religion:* Church of England. *Home:* 267 Stradbroke Grove, Clayhall, Ilford, Essex, England. *Office:* Fladgate & Co., 8 Waterloo Pl., London S.W.1, England.

CAREER: Solicitors' articled clerk, London, England, 1926-31, and solicitors' managing clerk, London, 1931-39, 1945-47; solicitor in private practice, London, and elsewhere in England, beginning 1947. *Military service:* British Army, 1939-45; became colonel. *Member:* Law Society.

WRITINGS: Moving House, Hodder & Stoughton, 1965; *Nothing Certain But Tax,* Hodder & Stoughton, 1966; *101 Points on Buying a House,* Dickens Press, 1967, hardcover edition, Arthur Barker, 1968; *My Nephew Hamlet,* Dent, 1967, A. S. Barnes, 1968.

SIDELIGHTS: In his review of *My Nephew Hamlet,* Norman Marshall writes: "This ingenious and entertaining book purports to be the diary of King Claudius. According to Mr. Turing, Shakespeare's reconstruction of what happened at Elsinore was often erratic and inaccurate." The diary, then, gives us "the events as they really happened, chronicled by a contemporary observer." Marshall notes that the book "is more than just witty entertainment because it provides perfectly feasible explanations to problems which have worried Shakespearean commentators—such as why Hamlet was passed over for the succession and why he turned against Ophelia. By the end of the diary one has a very vivid impression of what life was like in that gloomy chilly castle." Turing himself told *CA:* "I deplore the depraved taste of the reading public for sex, sadism, and 'James Bond Escapism,' the subordination of authorship to commercial considerations, and the obscenity of much current literature. I consider that, generally speaking, style is more imporant than subject."

BIOGRAPHICAL/CRITICAL SOURCES: Quarterly Theatre Review, winter, 1967.

*   *   *

TURNER, Katharine Charlotte   1910-

PERSONAL: Born March 11, 1910, in Normal, Ill.; daughter of Edwin Arthur and Charlotte (Griggs) Turner. *Education:* Illinois State Normal University (now Illinois State University), B.Ed., 1930; University of Michigan, M.A., 1931, Ph.D., 1939. *Home:* 1216 Maple, Tempe, Ariz. 85281. *Office:* Department of English, Arizona State University, Tempe, Ariz. 85281.

CAREER: High school English teacher in Farmer City, Ill., 1931-32, and Lincoln, Ill., 1932-35; Central Michigan University, Mount Pleasant, assistant professor of English, 1939-43; U.S. War Department, Arlington, Va., cryptographer, 1943-46; Arizona State University, Tempe, assistant professor, 1946-49, associate professor, 1950-55, professor of English, beginning 1955. Smith-Mundt Lecturer in American Literature, Tamkang College and National Taiwan University, 1955-56. *Member:* American Association of University Professors, American Association of University Women, Phi Kappa Phi, Delta Kappa Gamma, P.E.O. Sisterhood.

WRITINGS: Red Men Calling on the Great White Father, University of Oklahoma Press, 1951; *Writing: The Shapes of Experience,* Pruett, 1967. Contributor to *Colorado Quarterly, Best Articles and Stories, Southern Humanities Review,* and other journals.

WORK IN PROGRESS: Practicum to Poetry.

AVOCATIONAL INTERESTS: Handwork, including hooked-rug making and quilting; writing poems, and fossil hunting.

TUTTLE, W(ilbur) C(oleman) 1883-19(?)

PERSONAL: Born November 11, 1883, in Glendive, Montana Territory; son of Henry Clay (a lawman) and Anna (Dineen) Tuttle; married Bertha M. Stutes, June 23, 1927; children: Gene. *Education:* "My education was all garnered in a Montana cow-town school, where you stayed until the seats got so short that you grew calluses on your knees. No graduation—you quit." *Politics:* None. *Religion:* None. *Home:* 5428½ Hermitage Ave., North Hollywood, Calif.

CAREER: Worked as sheepherder, cowpuncher, salesman, railroader, forest ranger, baseball player and manager, and at other jobs; free-lance writer of fiction, mainly westerns, beginning 1915. President of Pacific Coast Baseball League, 1935-43.

WRITINGS—Variously under Wilbur C. Tuttle and W. C. Tuttle; all published by Houghton, except as indicated: *Reddy Brant, His Adventures,* Century, 1920; *Straight Shooting,* Garden City Publishing, 1926; *Sad Sontag Plays His Hunch,* Garden City Publishing, 1926; *Thicker Than Water: A Story of Hashknife Hartley,* 1926; *The Morgan Trail: A Story of Hashknife Hartley,* 1928.

The Red Head from the Sun Dog, 1930; *The Valley of Twisted Trails,* 1931; *Mystery at the JHC Ranch,* 1932; *The Silver Bar Mystery,* 1933; *The Santa Dolores Stage: A Story of Hashknife Hartley,* 1934; *Rifled Gold,* 1934; *Tumbling River Range,* 1935; *Hashknife of Stormy River,* 1935; *Henry the Sheriff,* 1936; *Hashknife of the Double Bar 8,* 1936; *The Keeper of Red Horse Pass,* 1937; *Bluffer's Luck,* 1937; *The Wild Horse Valley: A Henry Story,* 1938; *Wandering Dogies,* 1938; *The Medicine Man: A Hashknife Story,* 1939; *Singing River,* 1939.

Shotgun Gold, 1940; *Ghost Trails,* 1940; *The Tin God of Twisted River,* 1941; *The Mystery of the Red Triangle,* 1942; *Straws in the Wind,* 1948; *The Trail of Deceit,* 1951; *Salt for the Tiger,* Bouregy, 1952; *Renegade Sheriff,* Bouregy, 1953; *Thunderbird Range,* Avalon Books, 1954; *Mission River Justice,* Avalon Books, 1955. Author of many other books, and contributor of more than one thousand stories to magazines.†

(Deceased)

* * *

UNDERHILL, Harold 1926-1972
(Hal Underhill)

PERSONAL: Born January 25, 1926; son of Harold N. (in gift business) and Katherine (Luddy) Underhill; married Agnes Maurin (a fashion designer), February 18, 1967; children: Pamela. *Education:* New York University, B.S., 1948, graduate courses, 1951-55. *Politics:* Democrat. *Agent:* Bertha Klausner International Literary Agency, Inc., 71 Park Ave., New York, N.Y. 10016. *Office:* Puerto Rico Information Service, 18 East 48th St., New York, N.Y. 10014.

CAREER: Various employment, 1951-59, including public relations work for American Can Co. and New York State Thruway Authority; Puerto Rico Information Service (Puerto Rican government agency), New York, N.Y., account executive, 1959-63; director of public relations, Government of Jamaica, 1963-64; public relations work for Netherlands Antilles, 1965-67; Puerto Rico Information Service, account executive, 1967-72. Former Caribbean correspondent for American Broadcasting Co., U.S. Information Agency, Voice of America, Reuters, and *Diplomat* (magazine published in Washington, D.C.). *Military service:* U.S.

Army, 1944-46; received battle star for Po Valley campaign in Italy. *Member:* Society of American Travel Writers.

WRITINGS—Under name Hal Underhill: *Jamaica White* (novel), Macmillan, 1968. Author of short stories appearing in *Nugget* and *The San Juan Review.*

WORK IN PROGRESS: A novel; a book in collaboration with a psychiatrist.

AVOCATIONAL INTERESTS: Existential psychoanalysis, chess, swimming, dancing.†

(Died September 23, 1972)

* * *

UNGARETTI, Giuseppe 1888-1970

PERSONAL: Born February 10, 1888, in Alexandria, Egypt; son of Antonio (an immigrant from Tuscany; laborer and worker on the Suez Canal project) and Maria (Lunardini) Ungaretti; married Anne Jeanne Dupois, June 3, 1920 (died, 1958); children: Ninon (a daughter), Antonietto (died, 1939). *Education:* Attended the Ecole Suisse Jacob in Alexandria; studied at the College de France and the Sorbonne, 1912-14. *Home:* Via della Sierra Nevada 1, Rome, Italy.

CAREER: Paris correspondent for the *Popolo d'Italia,* 1919-20; attached to the Ministry of Foreign Affairs in Rome, 1922-30; at the invitation of the *Gazzetto del Popolo* in Turin he visited a number of foreign countries and wrote a series of travel articles, 1931-35; joint managing editor of the international literary review, *Mesures* (published in Paris), 1935-36; professor of Italian literature and language at the University of Sao Paulo, Brazil, 1936-42; professor of contemporary Italian literature at the University of Rome, 1942-59; paid a four month visit to New York as guest lecturer of Columbia University, 1964. *Military service:* Italian Army, infantryman, 1915-18. *Member:* Italian Academy, Bayerische Akademie des Schoenen Kuenste, European Community of Writers (president, 1962-63), P.E.N. Club. *Awards, honors:* Premio del Gondoliere, 1932; Grand Prix International de Poesie, 1956; Tor Margana Prize; Etna-Taormina International Prize, 1967, for *Visioni di William Blake;* nominated for Nobel Prize in Literature, 1969; Chevalier de la Legion d'Honneur; Books Abroad International Prize for Literature, 1970.

WRITINGS—Poetry: *Il Porto Sepolto,* Stabilimento Tipografico Friulano (Udine), 1916; *Allegria di Naufragi,* Vallecchi (Florence), 1919, expanded edition published as *L'Allegria,* Preda (Milan), 1931; *La Guerre* (poems in French), Etablissements LUX (Paris), 1919; *Sentimento del Tempo,* Vallecchi, 1933; *Frammenti per la Terra Promessa,* Concilium Lithographicum (Rome), 1945; *Derniers Jours 1919* (poems in French), Garzanti (Milan), 1947; *Gridasti Soffoco,* Fiumara (Milan), 1951; *Un Grido e Paesaggi,* Schwarz (Milan), 1952; *Les Cinq Livres* (French translations of Ungaretti's poems by the author in collaboration with Jean Lescure), Editions de Minuit (Paris), 1954; *Life of a Man* (a selection from *Vita d'un Uomo,* translated into English by Allen Mandelbaum), New Directions, 1958; *Il Taccuino del Vecchio* (contains tributes to Ungaretti from foreign poets including T. S. Eliot, Ezra Pound, and Rene Char), Mondadori, 1960; *Quattro Poesie,* All'insegna del Pesce d'Oro (Milan), 1960; *Ungaretti,* edited by Elio Filippo Accrocca, Nuova Accademia (Milan), 1964; *Inni di Ungaretti,* F. Riva (Verona), 1965; *Il carso non e piu un inferno,* All'insegna del Pesce d'Oro, 1966; *Croazia segreta,* M'arte Edizione, 1970; *Per conoscere Ungaretti,* edited by Leone Piccioni, Mondadori, 1971.

Other: *Piccola Roma,* Urbinati (Rome), 1944; (editor with Davide Lajolo) *I poeti scelti,* Mondadori, 1949; *Pittori italiani contemporanei,* Cappelli (Bologna), 1950; *Il povero nella citta* (collection of essays), Edizione della Meridiana (Milan), 1951; (editor) *Le voci tragiche di Guido Gonzato,* Il Milione (Milan), 1952; (author of introduction) *Anna Salvatore,* De Luco (Rome), 1965; (editor) Dante Alighieri, *La Divina commedia,* six volumes, Fabbri (Milan), 1963-65; (author of introduction) *Fontane d'Italia,* Editalia (Rome), 1967; (author of text) *Carlo Guarienti,* Fondazione Querini Stampalia (Venice), 1968; (author of introduction) *Zeichnungen, 1930-1970,* Propylaen Verlag (Berlin), 1970; *Lettere a un fenomenologo: Con un saggio de Enzo Paci,* All'insegna del Pesce d'Oro (Milan), 1972.

Translator into Italian: *Traduzioni* (poems from other literatures), Novissima (Rome), 1936; *XXII Sonetti di Shakespeare,* Documento (Rome), 1944; *L'Apres-Midi et le Monologue d'un Faune di Mallarme,* Il Balcone (Milan), 1947; (with T. S. Eliot) Alexis Saint-Leger, *Anabase,* Le rame (Verona), 1967.

Omnibus volumes, all published by Mondadori, except as indicated: "Vita d'un Uomo," twelve volumes, (poetry) Volume I: *L'Allegria,* 1942, Volume II: *Il sentimento del tempo,* 1943, Volume III: *Poesie disperse,* 1945, Volume IV: *Il dolore,* 1947, Volume V: *La terra promessa,* 1950, Volume VI: *Un grido e paesaggi,* 1954, Volume VII: *Il taccuino del vecchio,* 1960, (prose) Volume I: *Il deserto e dopo,* 1961, 2nd edition published as *Prose di viaggi e saggi: Il deserto e dopo, 1931-46,* 1969, (translations) Volume I: *40 Sonetti di Shakespeare,* 1946, Volume II: *Da Gongora e dal Mallarme,* 1948, Volume III: *Fedra di Jean Racine,* 1950, Volume IV: *Visioni de William Blake* (with a critical study), 1965; *Poesie,* edited by Elio Filippo Accrocca, Nuova Accademia (Milan), 1964; *Vita D'un uomo: 106 poesie,* 1966, 4th edition, 1970; *Morte deile Stagioni* (includes *La terra promessa, Il taccuino del vecchio,* and "Apocalissi"), Fogola (Torino), 1967; *Vita d'un uomo: Tutte le poesie,* edited by Leone Piccione, 1970.

Contributor: *Dopo il Diluvio,* Garzanti, 1947; *Il Simbolo,* Vol. IV, Edizioni pro Civitate Christiana (Assisi), 1947; *Il problema di Dio,* Editrice Universale (Rome), 1949; *Panorama dell'arte italiana,* Editori Lattes (Turin), 1951; *L'Artiste dans la societe contemporaine,* UNESCO (Paris), H. Vaillant Carmanne (Lieges), 1954; *Omaggio a Rimbaud,* Scheiwiller (Milan), 1954; *Preghiera e Poesia,* Tipografia L'Impronta (Florence), 1954; *Lettere dantesche (Inferno),* Sansoni (Florence), 1955.

Contributor (anthologies): *Antologia popolare di poeti del Novecento,* edited by V. Masselli and G. A. Cibotto, Vallechi, 1955; *Antologia poetica della Resistenza Italiana,* edited by E. F. Accrocca and V. Volpini, Landi (Arezzo), 1955; *La giovane poesia (Saggio e Repertorio),* edited by Enrico Falqui, Colombo (Rome), 1956; *The Promised Land and Other Poems: An Anthology of Four Contemporary Poets* (bilingual edition), edited by Sergio Pacifici, Vanni, 1957; *Poesia italiana del dopoguerra,* edited by Salvatore Quasimodo, Schwarz, 1958; *Dal Carducci ai Contemporanei: Antologia della lirica moderna,* edited by G. Getto and F. Portinari, Zanichelli (Bologna), 1958; *The Penguin Book of Italian Verse* (bilingual edition), edited by George Kay, Penguin, 1958; *Poesia italiana contemporanea,* edited by Giacinto Spagnoletti, Guanda (Parma), 1959; *La Lirica del Novecento,* edited by Luciano Anceschi and Sergio Antonielli, Vallecchi, 1961; *Modern European Poetry,* edited by Willis Barnstone, Bantam, 1966; *L'ermetismo: La poesia del Novocento,* edited by Tommaso Santilli, Trebi (Pescara), 1966.

Contributor of over 250 articles, essays, poems, and translations to more than forty journals, literary magazines, and newspapers such as *Comprende* (Venice), *L'Italia Letteraria* (Rome), *Litterature* (Paris), *La Nouvelle Revue Francaise* (Paris), *Gazzetta del Popolo* (Turin), *Il Popolo d'Italia* (Milan), and *Il Tevere* (Rome).

SIDELIGHTS: "Ungaretti's poetry," wrote Glauco Cambon, "born in the ordeal of World War I and its trenches, . . . marked a turning point in modern Italian literature." Breaking away from the traditional Italian form of the hendecasyllable, Ungaretti experimented with syntax and meter, seeking a new purity and meaning in word and phrase. "To capture the pure note," continues Cambon, "he lowered the tone of his poetry to a bare whisper, slowed down its pace to potentially infinite duration; filled each pause with meaning." He seemed to be taking meter apart to examine the single word in isolation. John Frederick Nims has commented that the full effect of these early and extremely brief poems, some of them consisting of only one line, was intended to be conveyed "as much by the silences and the blankness surrounding them as by the words."

Ungaretti himself described poetry as the ability to express oneself "with absolute candor, as if it were the first day of creation." In this quest for purity and attempt to restore to words their original virginity, Ungaretti was following the paths traced out by the French symbolists, Rimbaud, Mallarme, and Apollinaire. Like them, he believed that a poem should suggest rather than describe, and that words have an evocative content beyond their everyday significance. However, when Ungaretti had done his essential work of purification, a change occurred in his diction. "The lean syntax grew complex, the tenuous surface opaque, and the heart of the matter crowded, contorted with sorrows and perplexity."

His *Sentimento del Tempo,* published in 1933, "created a furore in the world of Italian letters," noted Nims. "Magazines were founded with the express purpose of attacking Ungaretti, who was accused of being a 'hermetic' poet and the leader of the 'hermetic school'." His style became "abstruse, constricted, and elliptical" and he withdrew "into the inner sanctum of the contemplative soul," said Cambon, "refusing the public myths, to look at the world as a realm of mysterious essences." Although Ungaretti insisted that he was never obscure on purpose, his conception of poetry was intensely personal. His preoccupation with the mysteries of life, the condensation of his ideas, and his desire to suppress the superfluous, sealed him off from his contemporaries.

Economy, even severity of line, was always a characteristic of Ungaretti's style and he contended that "the ideal writer should use the minimum number of words." His advice to writers was that they be more concise; he considered prolixity one of the greatest defects in a writer and was critical of those who digress from their subject. Allen Mandelbaum, Ungaretti's English translator, commented: "Ungaretti purged the language of all that was but ornament, of all that was too approximate for the precise tension of his line. Through force of tone and sentiment, and a syntax stripped to its essential sinews, he compelled words to their primal power."

One of the central themes in Ungaretti's poetry is the longing for lost innocence and his mood is often nostalgic and wistful. Yet underlying this sadness is a lyricism which at times rivals Mallarme's in its magical and musical intensity. *Il Dolore* ("Sorrow"), a collection of poems deriving its title from the tragedy of his little son's death in Brazil at the age of nine, contains some of his most beautiful verse; in *Tu ti spezzasti* ("You were broken") he suggests with one phrase or word an infinity of passion, melancholy or aspiration, extracting a poetic magic even from the hideous realities of life and death.

Ungaretti once remarked that he had four countries: Egypt, the land of his birth; Italy, the country of his parents and his permanent home; France, the place of his education and formative years, and where, through such friends as Apollinaire, he was in intimate contact with the whole artistic movement in France; and Brazil, his home for six years while teaching at the University of Sao Paulo. He recorded his impressions, in prose and poetry, of all these countries, and many others as well. He also wrote enthusiastically about his visit to New York in 1964, in an article for *Epoca*. His reputation traveled equally far. In a tribute to Ungaretti on his seventieth birthday, T. S. Eliot called him "one of the most authentic poets of Western Europe," and reviewers hailed his *Visioni di William Blake*, a critical study of Blake with Italian translations of his poems, as a work of international significance.

BIOGRAPHICAL/CRITICAL SOURCES: Gigi Cavalli, *Ungaretti*, Fabbri (Milan), 1958; Ioan Gutia, *Linguaggio di Ungaretti*, Le Monnier (Florence), 1959; Stanley Burnshaw, editor, *The Poem Itself*, Holt, 1960; A. F. Acrocca, editor, *Ritratti su misura di scrittori italiani*, Soldalizio del Libro (Venice), 1960; Renzo Frattarolo, *Dal volgare ai moderni*, Edizioni dell'Ateneo (Rome), 1962; Luciano Rebay, *Le origini della poesia di Giuseppe Ungaretti*, Edizione di Storia e Letteratura (Rome), 1962; Sergio Pacifici, *A Guide to Contemporary Italian Literature*, Meridian, 1962; Willis Barnstone, editor, *Modern European Poetry*, Bantam, 1966; *Times Literary Supplement*, May 19, 1966; Glauco Cambon, *Giuseppe Ungaretti*, Columbia University Press, 1967; *Books Abroad*, spring, 1970, autumn, 1970, winter, 1970, spring, 1971; *Washington Post*, June 4, 1970; *Contemporary Literary Criticism*, Volume VII, 1977.†

(Died June 1, 1970)

* * *

UPTON, Albert 1897-

PERSONAL: Born November 13, 1897, in Denver, Colo.; son of Albert Ezra (a banker) and Anabel (Fitzgerald) Upton; married Alleene Tweedy, 1933; married second wife, Anne Fiedler (a teacher), January 28, 1955; children: (first marriage) James Tweedy, Thomas Walker. *Education:* University of Denver, B.A., 1921; University of California, Berkeley, Ph.D., 1928. *Politics:* Republican. *Religion:* Congregational. *Home:* 2404-2E Via Mariposa West, Laguna Hills, Calif. 92653.

CAREER: Whittier College, Whittier, Calif., professor of English, 1929-70, head of department, 1933-60, director of general studies, 1960-68. *Military service:* U.S. Navy Reserve Force, 1918-22. U.S. Navy, 1922-23. *Member:* National Council of Teachers of English, Conference on College Composition and Communication, National Society for the Study of Communication, American Association of University Professors, Beta Theta Pi.

WRITINGS: Design for Thinking, Stanford University Press, 1961, revised edition, Pacific Books, 1973; (with Richard Samson) *Creative Analysis*, Dutton, 1962. Contributor to professional journals.

WORK IN PROGRESS: Books on concept analysis, on paragraph construction, and on organization and content of compulsory general studies program in the college of liberal arts.

* * *

UPTON, Monroe 1898-

PERSONAL: Born August 15, 1898, in Bandon, Ore.; son of James Monroe (a lawyer) and Eleanor Augusta (Reed) Upton; married Emerita Correa; children: Jonika. *Education:* Attended high schools in Marshfield and Roseburg, Ore. *Politics:* Democrat. *Religion:* Episcopalian.

CAREER: U.S. Merchant Marine, radio officer, at sea and in Shanghai, China, 1918-26; radio writer and comedian, 1926-41; U.S. Office of War Information, San Francisco, Calif., broadcaster to Philippines, 1941-45; free-lance writer and manager of rental properties in San Francisco, Calif., and Tucson, Ariz., beginning 1945.

WRITINGS: Electronics for Everyone, Devin, 1954, 3rd revised edition, 1963; *Inside Electronics*, Devin, 1963. Writer of scripts for radio, mostly comedy.

SIDELIGHTS: Upton reads and speaks Spanish, and has some competence in Italian. *Electronics for Everyone* has been published in England and in German, Arabic, Hebrew, and Portuguese.†

* * *

VALENTINE, Sister Mary Hester 1909-
(Helen Valentine)

PERSONAL: Born September 5, 1909, in Pueblo, Colo.; daughter of Frank Edgar and Hester (Yockey) Valentine. *Education:* Mount Mary College, B.A., 1937; Loyola University, Chicago, Ill., M.A., 1942; additional graduate study at University of Detroit, Wayne State University, De Paul University, University of Notre Dame, Fordham University, and Columbia University. *Politics:* "Not committed; a liberal a little left of center, but more center than left." *Office:* Department of English, Mount Mary College, 2900 Menomonee River Pkwy., Milwaukee, Wis. 53222.

CAREER: Roman Catholic religious member of School Sisters of Notre Dame. Mount Mary College, Milwaukee, Wis., instructor, 1951-53, assistant professor, 1954-58, associate professor, 1959-70, professor of English and chairman of department, beginning 1971. Visiting professor of writing, St. Mary College (Kansas), 1958; lecturer, Savage Consolini University, 1960-64; composition consultant of curriculum committee, Wisconsin Language-Arts, 1963; lecturer, U.S. Information Service, 1970-71; visiting professor of English, Sogang University and Song Sim College (Korea), 1970-71. Reader, Educational Testing Service, Princeton, N.J., for College Entrance Examination Board and Advanced Placement, Educational Testing Service, Princeton, N.J. *Member:* National Council of Teachers of English (member of executive council of Wisconsin branch, 1960-66; co-chairman of national convention, 1968; member of curriculum committee, 1970-73), Modern Language Association of America, Conference on College Composition and Communication, English Association of Greater Milwaukee.

WRITINGS: Mother Stanislaus Kostka (biography), University of Notre Dame Press, 1945; *Canticle for the Harvest*, Kenedy, 1951; (editor) *Program for Progress*, Fordham University Press, 1966; *The Post-Conciliar Nun*, Hawthorn, 1968; (editor) *Local Superior, Capstone of Formation*, Fordham University Press, 1968. Short stories, verse, critical and historical essays, and reviews have been published in professional journals and general interest magazines. Editor, *Sister Formation Conferences,* 1965-70.†

*   *   *

VANDER, Harry J(oseph) III   1913-19(?)

PERSONAL: Born September 6, 1913, in Slidell, La.; son of Harry J. II and Augusta (Phillips) Vander. *Education:* Southern University and Agricultural and Mechanical College, B.A., 1939; Wayne State University, M.Ed., 1947; graduate study at University of Michigan, 1947-48, Michigan State University, 1951-52, and Syracuse University, 1952-54; Interamerican University, Saltillo, Mexico, Ph.D., 1967. *Politics:* Democrat. *Religion:* Roman Catholic. *Office:* Department of Geography, Jackson State College, Jackson, Miss. 39217.

CAREER: Detroit (Mich.) Board of Education, substitute teacher of social studies, 1946-48; Texas State University, Houston, associate professor of geography, 1948-51; New York State Mental Health Commission, Syracuse, research assistant, 1953-54; Tennessee Agricultural and Industrial State University (now Tennessee State University), Nashville, associate professor of geography, 1954-55; Talladega College, Talladega, Ala., associate professor of education, 1955-56; Jackson State College, Jackson, Miss., associate professor of geography, beginning 1956. *Military service:* U.S. Army, 1941-45; became sergeant major. *Member:* Association of American Geographers, Association of Social and Behavioral Scientists (president), American Association of University Professors, International Platform Association, Phi Delta Kappa, Gamma Theta Upsilon, Pi Gamma Mu, Sigma Rho Sigma, Omega Psi Phi. *Awards, honors:* Gamma Theta Upsilon annual award for excellence in geography; honorary doctorate from Instituto de Estudios Iberoamericanos, Mexico.

WRITINGS: Ethnology of the Pacific Basin, Burgess, 1956; *Writing Scholarly Papers,* Burgess, 1958; (with V. Horatio Henry) *Human Geography Workbook,* Burgess, 1967; *Political and Economic Progress of the American Negro, 1940-1963,* W. C. Brown, 1968. Contributor to *Journal of Social Science Teachers.*

WORK IN PROGRESS: A geography of Mississippi.

SIDELIGHTS: Harry J. Vander traveled extensively in Hawaii, Australia, and many of the Pacific islands.†

(Deceased)

*   *   *

VAN PRAAGH, Margaret   1910-
(Peggy Van Praagh)

PERSONAL: Born September 1, 1910, in London, England; daughter of Harold John (a physician) and Ethel (Shanks) Van Praagh. *Education:* Attended King Alfred School, London, England, 1919-27. *Politics:* Liberal. *Religion:* Church of England. *Home:* 48 Neville Ct., Abbey Rd., London, England, and 24/248 The Avenue, Parkville, Victoria 3052, Australia. *Agent:* David Higham Associates Ltd., 5-8 Lower John St., London W1R 4HA, England.

CAREER: Solo dancer in England with Ballet Rambert, 1933-38, London Ballet, 1938-40, and Sadler's Wells Ballet, 1940-46; ballet mistress and assistant director, Sadler's Wells Theatre Ballet (later Royal Ballet School and Company), London, England, 1946-56; artistic director of Borovansky Company, 1960-61; artistic director, Australian Ballet, Melbourne, 1962-74. Teacher and lecturer on ballet in

London, 1945-60, and at Jacob's Pillow, Mass., 1959. *Member:* Imperial Society of Teachers of Dancing (fellow). *Awards, honors:* Royal Academy of Dancing-Queen Elizabeth Coronation Award for services to ballet, 1965; Officer, Order of the British Empire (Queen's Birthday Honors, 1966), for services to ballet in Australia; Dame of the British Empire, 1970; D.Litt., University of New England, Australia, 1974; Distinguished Artist award of Australia Council, 1975, for services to dance in Australia.

WRITINGS: How I Became a Dancer, Thomas Nelson, 1954; (with Peter Brinson) *The Choreographic Art,* Knopf, 1963; *Ballet in Australia,* Longmans, Green, 1965. Contributor to ballet magazines in England, United States, and Australia.

SIDELIGHTS: As artistic director of the Australian Ballet, Dame Van Praagh has toured throughout Australia, and on world tour, 1965, visiting Baalbeck, London, Paris, Copenhagen, Los Angeles, and Honolulu. *Avocational interests:* Leisure motoring and sunbathing.

BIOGRAPHICAL/CRITICAL SOURCES: Agnes de Mille, *Dance to the Piper,* Little, Brown, 1952.

*   *   *

VAUDRIN, William   1943-1976
(Bill Vaudrin)

PERSONAL: Surname rhymes with "squadron"; born May 31, 1943, in Akron, Ohio; son of William Douglas (a realtor) and Margery (Johnston) Vaudrin; married Kathleen Ann Chesnut (a student), June 9, 1969; children: Bristol Dawn. *Education:* Alaska Methodist University, B.A., 1966; University of Oregon, M.F.A., 1968. *Address:* Pedro Bay, Alaska 99647.

CAREER: Commercial fisherman in Bristol Bay, Alaska for more than ten seasons, and sled-dog racer; University of Oregon, Eugene, part-time instructor in English, 1967-68; Anchorage Community College, Anchorage, Alaska, instructor in English, 1968-70. Director of community liason, Alaska's State Operated School System, 1971; educational chairman, Cook Inlet Native Association (Anchorage), 1972-73; chairman of the board, Alaskan Federation of Native Education, 1972-73. *Member:* Modern Language Association of America, American Association of University Professors, Phi Alpha Theta.

WRITINGS—Under name Bill Vaudrin: *Tanaina Tales from Alaska,* University of Oklahoma Press, 1969; (editor) *Racing Alaskan Sled Dogs,* Alaska Northwest Publishing, 1976. Poetry, short stories, folklore, and reviews have been published in *Alaska Review, Alaska Sportsman, Gauntlet, Viltis, Contemproary Alaskan Literature,* and other periodicals.

WORK IN PROGRESS: A novel, *Somewhere I Have Never Travelled.*

SIDELIGHTS: William Vaudrin was of Indian descent—Chippewa and Cree. He hunted, trapped, and worked as a longshoreman in Alaska.†

(Died January 26, 1976)

*   *   *

VAZAKAS, Byron   1905-

PERSONAL: Born September 24, 1905, in New York, N.Y.; son of Alfred (a professor of languages at Columbia University and at his own school in New York, N.Y.) and Margaret (Keffer) Vazakas. *Address:* c/o Alexander K. Vazakas, 1623 Mineral Spring Rd., Reading, Pa. 19602.

CAREER: Poet. Has given poetry readings at Harvard University, Brown University, and (with Tennessee Williams) at Young Men's Hebrew Association Poetry Center, New York. *Awards, honors:* Amy Lowell traveling scholarship to Europe, 1962-64, among other awards.

WRITINGS—Poetry: *Transfigured Night,* introduction by William Carlos Williams, Macmillan, 1946; *The Equal Tribunals,* Clarke & Way, 1961; *The Marble Manifesto,* October House, 1966; *Nostalgias for a House of Cards,* October House, 1969. Several of his more than two hundred published poems have been anthologized in *100 Modern Poems,* edited by Seldon Rodman, *Modern American Poetry,* edited by Oscar Williams, *Modern Poetry,* edited by John Malcolm Brinnin and Kimon Friar, *American Writing, Accent Anthology, Contemporary Poetry,* and other collections. Poems have appeared in forty-five periodicals, including *Poetry* (Chicago), *Kenyon Review, Harper's Bazaar, Nation, Virginia Quarterly Review,* and *Partisan Review.*

WORK IN PROGRESS: A fifth volume of poetry, all poems previously published in periodicals.

SIDELIGHTS: "My poetry is my biography," Vazakas told *CA.* "There really is very little 'official' to tell . . . since I am . . . in the romantic tradition of poets who do nothing but write poetry. . . . I have avoided . . . occupations. . . . This is largely because I don't want to work at these things, especially anything on the periphery of the arts, and also because a poet requires leisure. I know that most of my colleagues would be delighted not to have to teach. At a college reading recently, I replied to a question as to why I write poetry that, 'I am totally unfitted for any other occupation!' . . . My existence consists of the '3 R's': Writing, Reading, and Roaming. . . . Unhappily, the connection between my life and my work will probably not be recognized except posthumously. I am an advocate of what I call 'Organic Poetry,' . . . the association between the artist's life and his work, and poetry as an extension of the personality."

Vazakas commented on his economic situation: "While we lived well in my father's time near the Cloisters in upper New York City, when he died we were bankrupt, and though my grandmother . . . 'had money,' this prevented an academic career, for better or worse; but that's the way it is. I sometimes think it is worse to have lost than never to have had (in an economic sense)."

William Carlos Williams, in his introduction to *Transfigured Night,* described Vazakas as "that important phenomenon among writers, an inventor." Vazakas has "picked up the thread where Whitman dropped it," and he has discovered "a measure based not upon convention, but upon music." H. C. Webster found the book "an exciting fulfillment as well as a promise." He also quoted Williams as naming Vazakas creator of a "line loose as Whitman's but measured as his was not." Babette Deutsch felt that "what distinguishes his work is his ability to convey the more delicate nuances of a mood, to suggest the sensitively apprehended atmosphere of a doctor's waiting-room, a photographer's studio, a railway terminal. . . . Perhaps the lack of a unifying belief that characterizes our time, the sense of our diversion, together with a lively awareness of the need for some common basis of communication and action while retaining our integrity, make distinctions between the public and the private matter of peculiar significance for us. Mr. Vazakas' emphasis upon this double aspect of everyday life, and his hints, never obvious or insistent, at the absurd and tragic quality of that life, are what gives his poems value for us. As a result they sometimes read like excerpts from a psychological novel or like notations on the insights of Kafka and Kierkegaard." F. C. Golffing wrote: "Vazakas' cadenced prose—if we may call it that in default of a better term—is for the most part extremely perceptive. . . . Both his imagination and his craftsmanship are remarkable. He is a master of definition. . . . He knows how to sustain a mood and stick to his frame—usually one of scenery, either actual or allegorical."

Vazakas told *CA* that he has plenty of material for a "rip-roaring autobiography in depth." He said that "the more time passes the more [a writer's] idiosyncrasies are written about." He explained that this demonstrates his theory of "Organic Poetry."

BIOGRAPHICAL/CRITICAL SOURCES: Book Week, October 27, 1946; *New York Times,* November 24, 1946; *Poetry,* December, 1946.

* * *

VELIE, Lester 1908-

PERSONAL: Born January 1, 1908, in Kiev, Ukraine; came to United States, 1913, naturalized U.S. citizen, 1922; son of Samuel and Sarah (Spector) Velie; married Frances Rockmore, October 29, 1932; children: Alan R., Franklin Bell. *Education:* University of Wisconsin, B.A., 1929. *Home:* 42 Pond Rd., Kings Point, N.Y. *Agent:* William Morris Agency, 1350 Ave. of the Americas, New York, N.Y. 10019. *Office: Reader's Digest,* Pleasantville, N.Y.

CAREER: Reporter in Albany and New York, N.Y., 1930-32; *Brooklyn Eagle,* Brooklyn, N.Y., suburban editor, 1932-35; *Literary Digest,* New York, N.Y., business and financial editor, 1936-37; *Journal of Commerce,* New York, N.Y., associate editor, 1937-46; *Collier's,* Philadelphia, Pa., associate editor, 1946-52; *Reader's Digest,* Pleasantville, N.Y., roving editor, beginning 1953. Radio lecturer, and analyst on program, "Ahead of Time," WQXR, New York, N.Y., 1941-45; economic analyst for British Broadcasting Corp., 1943. *Member:* Overseas Press Club, Sigma Delta Chi. *Awards, honors:* Sigma Delta Chi Public Service Through Journalism Award and Best Magazine Article Award, both 1949; Bell award from Newspaper Enterprise Association, 1966, for magazine journalism; American Bar Association Gavel award, 1972, Silver Gavel award, 1973.

WRITINGS: Labor U.S.A., Harper, 1959, revised edition published as *Labor U.S.A. Today,* 1964; *Countdown in the Holy Land,* Funk, 1969.†

* * *

VENABLE, Vernon 1906-

PERSONAL: Born September 15, 1906, in Cincinnati, Ohio; son of Bryant (in advertising) and Gertrude (Spellmire) Venable; married Ruth Dillard (a college professor), June 15, 1933; children: Ann Dillard, Jean Hardy. *Education:* University of Cincinnati, Extraordinary B.A. (honors), 1928; Columbia University, Ph.D., 1945. *Office:* Department of Philosophy, Vassar College, Poughkeepsie, N.Y. 12601.

CAREER: Free-lance writer, 1928-29; copywriter, 1929-30; teacher, writer, and student in France and Switzerland, 1930-32; Vassar College, Poughkeepsie, N.Y., faculty member, beginning 1932, chairman of department of philosophy, 1946-47, 1949-66, 1967-69, James Munroe Taylor Professor of Philosophy, 1949-72, professor emeritus, 1972—. Research fellow in France, 1939-40, 1948-49. *Member:*

American Philosophical Association, American Association of University Professors, Phi Beta Kappa.

WRITINGS: Human Nature: The Marxian View, Knopf, 1945, new edition, World Publishing, 1966. Contributor to journals.

WORK IN PROGRESS: Human nature in modern thought.

AVOCATIONAL INTERESTS: Ornamental tree growing, landscape designing.†

* * *

VENNARD, Edwin   1902-

PERSONAL: Born September 4, 1902, in New Orleans, La.; son of George H. and Rhoda (Wickliffe) Vennard; married Alyce Richard, December 19, 1929; children: Katherine Beatrice (Mrs. Joseph R. LeBlanc), Barbara Alyce (Mrs. Warren Brown). *Education:* Tulane University, B.E., 1924. *Politics:* Republican. *Religion:* Episcopalian. *Home:* Khakum Wood, Greenwich, Conn. 06830. *Office:* 283 Greenwich Ave., Greenwich, Conn. 06830.

CAREER: General Electric Co., Schenectady, N.Y., member of testing department, 1924-25; Gulf States Utilities Co., Lake Charles, La., power sales engineer, 1925-26; Southwestern Gas & Electric Co., Shreveport, La., power sales engineer, 1926-28, general commercial manager, 1928-33; Middle West Utilities Co., Chicago, Ill., head of rate department, 1933-37; Middle West Service Co., Chicago, vice-president, 1937-53, president, 1953-56; Edison Electric Institute (trade association), New York City, vice-president and managing director, 1956-69; Commonwealth Management Consultants, New York City, president, 1969-71; Commonwealth Services, Inc., New York City, vice-president and board member, 1969-71; industrial consultant, beginning 1971. Consultant, Charles T. Main, Inc., New York City, beginning 1972. Vice-president, Electric Light and Power, 1961-65. Trustee, Insurance Trust Fund, 1953-56. Honorary member, U.S. National Committee, World Energy Conference; member, International Platform Association. Member of board of trustees and executive committee, Thomas Alva Edison Foundation. Former member of board of visitors and former member of advisory committee of school of engineering, Tulane University.

MEMBER: Institute of Electrical and Electronics Engineers, American Management Association, American Institute of Electrical Engineers, Tau Beta Pi, Kappa Alpha, Tulane Alumni Club of Greater New York (president), Union League, Greenwich Country Club. *Awards, honors:* Seven awards from Freedoms Foundation.

WRITINGS: (Contributor) *The American Economic System,* Row, Peterson, 1957; *The Electric Power Business,* McGraw, 1962, revised and enlarged edition, 1970; *Government in the Power Business,* McGraw, 1968.

* * *

VENTON, W. B.   1898-1976

PERSONAL: Born December 28, 1898, in London, England; daughter of William Cawthorne Unwin; married; husband deceased; children: Josephine Maria (Mrs. Geoffrey Bogh). *Education:* Attended Slade School of Art and University College, London. *Religion:* Church of England. *Home:* 53 Woodberry Ave., Winchmore Hill, London N.21, England. *Office:* Sardinia House, Kingsway, London W.C.2, England.

CAREER: Artist and writer in London, England.

WRITINGS: The Analyses of Shakespeare's Sonnets Using the Cipher Code, Mitre Press, 1968.

WORK IN PROGRESS: An extension of *The Analyses of Shakespeare's Sonnets Using the Cipher Code* from the original eight sonnets to all 154.†

(Died April 24, 1976)

* * *

VESSELO, I(saac) Reginald   1903-

PERSONAL: Born December 20, 1903, in London, England; son of Lazarus and Ada Vesselo; married Constance Mason Minetta Hughes, April 4, 1936. *Education:* University of London, B.Sc. (honors in mathematics), 1923; University of Manchester, M.Ed., 1952. *Home:* 36 Damer Gardens, Henley-on-Thames, Oxfordshire, England.

CAREER: Teacher at Pitman's College, London, England, 1924-28, Ongar School, Essex, England, 1928-34, and Stationers' Company's School, Hornsey, Middlesex, England, 1935-48; Cheshire College of Education, Stoke-on-Trent, Staffordshire, England, principal lecturer and head of mathematics department, 1948-65; Penguin Books Ltd., West Drayton, Middlesex, England, senior science editor, 1965-69. Part-time lecturer in statistics, University of Surrey. Visiting lecturer at University of Victoria, British Columbia, Canada, 1961-62. *Member:* Royal Statistical Society (fellow), Institute of Mathematics and Its Application (fellow).

WRITINGS: Air Training Mathematics, Pitman, 1941; *Air Cadets Handbook on Radio,* Allen & Unwin, 1942; *A.T.C. General Science,* Hutchinson, 1943; *A.T.C. Air Navigation,* Hutchinson, 1943; (editor) *Chess in Schools,* Allen & Unwin, 1945; (editor) *New Builders Handbook,* Allen & Unwin, 1945-47; (with S. H. Glenister) *Examples in Engineering Mathematics,* Book 2, Harrap, 1947; *Secondary School Mathematics,* Books 1-4, Allen & Unwin, 1955; *How to Read Statistics,* Harrap, 1962, Van Nostrand, 1965; (editor) *Studies in Applied Statistics,* Penguin, 1968; (editor) *The Further Training of Mathematics Teachers at Secondary Level,* UNESCO, 1969.

WORK IN PROGRESS: Dictionary of Modern Mathematics.

* * *

VESTAL, Edith Ballard   1884-1970

PERSONAL: Born April 19, 1884, in Snohomish, Wash.; daughter of Samuel and Harriet (Martin) Vestal. *Education:* Whitman College, B.L., 1907. *Politics:* Republican. *Religion:* Presbyterian. *Home:* 2315 Northeast 65th St., Seattle, Wash. 98115.

CAREER: Elementary teacher in Snohomish, Wash., 1907-14, and Seattle, Wash., 1914-49. *Member:* National Retired Teachers Association.

WRITINGS: Rattley, Rattlety, Rattlety Bang!, and Other Stories, Highlights for Children, 1968.†

(Died December 19, 1970)

* * *

VILLERS, Raymond   1911-

PERSONAL: Born February 12, 1911, in Rheims, France; came to United States in 1943, naturalized in 1944; son of Alphonse G. and Anne (Giesmar) Villers-Allerand; married second wife, Garda Graaff Schmidt, November 14, 1950; children: (first marriage) Ann; (second marriage) Philippe. *Education:* University of Paris, B.S., 1928, D.E.S., 1936;

University of Leipzig, D.Jur., 1931; Columbia University, M.B.A., 1948. *Address:* Box 167, R.F.D. 1, Bellows Falls, Vt. 05101. *Office:* Rautenstrauch & Villers, 185 East 85th St., New York, N.Y. 10028.

CAREER: Huilcombus, Paris, France, operating executive, 1938-39; Rautenstrauch & Villers (industrial management consultants), New York City, partner, 1947-51, owner, beginning 1951; Columbia University, New York City, assistant professor, 1947-52, lecturer in industrial engineering, 1952-65; Stevens Institute of Technology, Hoboken, N.J., assistant professor of industrial engineering, 1952-57; Syracuse University, Syracuse, N.Y., professor of industrial engineering, 1965-66; Pace College (now Pace University), New York City, professor in Graduate School of Business Administration, 1966-72. Lecturer to armed forces, civil service agencies, and management associations. Consultant, U.S. Army, 1965-66. Trustee, Marlboro College, 1952-67. *Military service:* French Army and Free French naval staff, 1939-43; liaison officer with U.S. Navy Amphibious Force, 1943. U.S. Navy, 1944-45.

MEMBER: American Institute of Industrial Engineers (vice-president, 1952), American Society of Mechanical Engineers, American Management Association, American Society for Engineering Education, Institute of Management Sciences, Newcomen Society in North America, American Association of University Professors, Alpha Pi Mu (honorary member). *Awards, honors:* DuPont de Nemours-General Motors joint research fellowship, 1946; American Management Association seminar award, 1958.

WRITINGS: (With Walter Rautenstrauch) *The Economics of Industrial Management,* Funk, 1949, revised edition, 1957; (with Rautenstrauch) *Budgetary Control,* Funk, 1950, revised edition, 1968; (contributor) *Big Business Methods for the Small Business,* Harper, 1952; *The Dynamics of Industrial Management,* Funk, 1954; (contributor) *Handbook of Industrial Engineering and Management,* Prentice-Hall, 1955; (contributor) *The Factory of the Future,* American Management Association, 1957; *Dynamic Management in Industry,* Prentice-Hall, 1960; *Research and Development: Planning and Control,* Financial Executives Research Foundation, 1964; (contributor) *Executive Skills Handbook,* Management Engineering Training Agency, U.S. Army, 1967; (contributor) *Handbook of Business Administration,* McGraw, 1967. Also contributor to *American Management Association Handbook,* 1970. Contributor to *Dun's Review & Modern Industry, Harvard Business Review,* and other journals.

SIDELIGHTS: Four of Raymond Villers's books have been translated into other languages, with *Dynamic Management in Industry* appearing in Japanese and Spanish editions.

* * *

VILLIARD, Paul 1910-1974
(J. H. deGros)

PERSONAL: Surname pronounced Vee-yarh; born January 16, 1910, in Spokane, Wash.; married Gertrude vanden Bergen, October 27, 1941; children: Paul, Jr., William John, Frederick. *Address:* P.O. Box 164, Saugerties, N.Y. 12477.

CAREER: Writer and photographer; in addition to illustrating his own work, supplied technical and scientific photographs to publishers and agents for use in books and magazines.

*WRITINGS—*All self-illustrated: (Under pseudonym J. H.

deGros) *Today's Woman Candy Cook Book,* Fawcett, 1953; (under pseudonym J. H. deGros) *Holiday Candy and Cookie Cook Book,* Fawcett, 1954; *Handy Man's Plumbing and Heating Guide,* Fawcett, 1967; *A Manual of Veneering,* Van Nostrand, 1968; *A First Book of Ceramics,* Funk, 1969; *A First Book of Jewelrymaking,* Funk, 1969; *Reptiles as Pets* (juvenile), Doubleday, 1969; *Moths, and How to Rear Them,* Funk, 1969; *Through the Seasons with a Camera,* Doubleday, 1970; *Growing Pains,* Funk, 1970; *Exotic Fishes as Pets,* Natural History Press, 1971; *Shells: Homes in the Sea,* Addison-Wesley, 1972; *Wild Mammals as Pets,* Doubleday, 1972; *Raising Small Animals for Fun and Profit,* Winchester Press, 1973; *Collecting Stamps,* Doubleday, 1974; *The Hidden World,* Van Nostrand, 1975. Contributor to *Reader's Digest, Natural History, Audubon Magazine, Popular Homecraft,* and other magazines.

WORK IN PROGRESS: A First Book of Leatherwork, A First Book of Fly-Tying, A First Book of Enamelling, Candy Cook Book, all for Abelard; *Shells Built by Mollusks, Shells: Homes on Land, Shells: The Poisonous Ones,* all elementary grade texts with teachers' manuals, for Addison-Wesley; *Contemporary Furniture Design,* for Funk; *Flowers by the Way; A Manual of Marquetry; After the Camera; Nature Photography: A Manual.†

(Died August 18, 1974)

* * *

VINCENT, Elizabeth Lee 1897-
(E. Lee Vincent, Leona Vincent)

PERSONAL: Born August 6, 1897, in Victor, Colo.; daughter of John Michel (a chemist) and Elizabeth (Stevens) Vincent. *Education:* University of Colorado, A.B., 1919, A.M., 1921; Columbia University, Ph.D., 1924. *Politics:* Non-partisan. *Religion:* Protestant.

CAREER: Merrill-Palmer Institute, Detroit, Mich., head of psychology department, 1924-46; New York State College of Home Economics, Cornell University, Ithaca, dean, 1946-53. *Member:* Society for Research in Child Development (member of council, 1944-51), New York Academy of Sciences, Phi Beta Kappa, Sigma Xi.

WRITINGS: (Under name Leona Vincent) *A Study of Intelligence Test Elements,* Teachers College, Columbia University, 1924, reprinted, AMS Press, 1972; (under name E. Lee Vincent, with Winifred Rand and Mary E. Sweeny) *Growth and Development of the Young Child,* Saunders, 1930, 4th edition, 1946, 5th edition, revised by Marian E. Breckenridge and Margaret Nesbitt Murphy, 1953, 6th edition, by Breckenridge and Murphy, published as *Rand, Sweeny and Vincent's Growth and Development of the Young Child,* 1958; *Mental Hygiene for Nurses,* Saunders, 1938; (under name E. Lee Vincent, with Breckenridge) *Child Development: Physical and Psychological Growth Through the School Years,* Saunders, 1943, 4th edition published as *Child Development: Physical and Psychological Growth Through Adolescence,* 1960, 5th edition, 1965; (with Phyllis C. Martin) *Human Development,* Ronald, 1960; (with Martin) *Human Psychological Development,* Ronald, 1961.†

* * *

VISSER, W(illem) F(rederik) H(endrik) 1900-1968

PERSONAL: Born January 15, 1900, in Zwaqgwesteinde, Netherlands; son of Anne and Aaltje (Lemstra) Visser; married Bieuwkje Kerkhof, September 18, 1928; children: Wim,

Peter. *Education:* Educated at a teacher training college in Leeuwarden, Netherlands, 1914-18. *Home:* Park Boswijk 484, Boorn, Netherlands.

CAREER: Among the papers left by the Dutch teacher his widow found the following biographical memo (intended for his young readers), which she copied for *CA:* "I was born in Zwaqgwesteinde, a little Frisian village, in the year 1900 (Friesland is one of the eleven provinces of Holland). So you can easily calculate how 'young' I am. Probably I was in my youth as good and as naughty as you are now. I was already a form master being eighteen years old. After that I had the function of head-teacher at Oranjewoud (also in Friesland) and at The Hague. At first I had my trouble at school, of course, but one thing came very easy to me: telling a story! Doing that the most troublesome pupils were singing small. From telling stories till writing them is not a long step. I began with short stories. For writing larger books I hardly had time before my retirement. That's all of it! Read pleasantly?" *Awards, honors:* Dutch Association for the Promotion of Books award for the best book of the year for young people, 1964 for *Niku, de koerier.*

WRITINGS: Onder de laars van Napolean (title means "Under the Boot of Napoleon"), Van Goor Zonen, 1960; *De tijdbaan* (readers; title means "The Course of Time"), two books, Van Goor Zonen, 1960; *William van Oranje* (title means "William of Orange"), Van Goor Zonen, 1960; *Sikke en ik* (title means "Sikke and I"), Arbeiderspers, 1961; *Het gezin Algera* (novel; title means "The Family Algera"), Strengholt, 1961; *Het spook van de burcht* (title means "The Ghost of the Castle"), Van Goor Zonen, 1961; *Schippersjongens* (title means "Bargeman's Boys"), Kruseman, 1961; *Op de vleugels van de tijd* (history of Holland in stories; title means "On the Wings of Time"), Van Goor Zonen, 1962; *Robie en de tovenaar* (title means "Robin and the Sorcerer"), Van Goor Zonen, 1963; *Niku, de zigeunerjongen* (title means "Niku, the Gypsy Boy"), Van Goor Zonen, 1964; *Niku, de koerier,* Van Goor Zonen, 1964, translation by Marian Powell published as *Niku, the Messenger,* Oliver & Boyd, 1966, same translation published as *Gypsy Courier,* Follett, 1969; *Niku, de zwerver* (title means "Niku, the Wanderer"), Van Goor Zonen, 1964; *Hans van de Polle,* De Fontein, 1970; *Storm Over de Polle,* De Fontein, 1970.

Author with M. Bijpost of a language series, "Taal voor allemaal," twelve books, all but two of the volumes published by Van Goor Zonen. Contributor to *Kinders van die werelt* (title means "Children of the World"), published by Albertijn (Capetown, South Africa).†

(Died December 13, 1968)

*   *   *

VOILS, Jessie Wiley

PERSONAL: Born in Caldwell, Kan.; daughter of Daniel Wesley and Lillie (Hawks) Wiley; married Willard H. Voils, March 3, 1920 (died July, 1973); children: Patricia June (Mrs. John S. Tillman). *Education:* Attended Emporia Teacher's College, 1919-20, Columbia University, 1936, and New York University, 1940-57. *Home:* 609 Morningside Dr., Wellington, Kan. 67152.

CAREER: Delineator, New York City, midwestern editor and columnist, 1935-37; *Pictorial Review,* New York City, contributing editor, 1937-39; National Broadcasting Co., New York City, 1940-49, associate editor and broadcaster of "Streamline Journal of the Air," 1940-43, writer and co-producer of children's program, "Yankee Doodle Quiz," 1944-45, and associate editor and broadcaster of "Highways to

Famous Homes"; Young Women's Christian Association, New York City, radio director for national board, 1949-54. *Member:* Author's League of America, English-Speaking Union, Kansas State Historical Society, Kansas Author's Club.

WRITINGS: Summer on the Salt Fork (juvenile novel), illustrations by Leonard Vosburgh, Meredith Press, 1969. Contributor of more than one hundred articles to *McCall's, Christian Science Monitor, Coronet,* and other publications.

WORK IN PROGRESS: An adult historical novel and sequel to *Summer on the Salt Fork,* tentatively entitled *Border Queen;* a children's book.

AVOCATIONAL INTERESTS: Collecting fine china, especially Wedgwood, and plates showing the homes of U.S. presidents; Americana, of which she has a large research library; travel.

BIOGRAPHICAL/CRITICAL SOURCES: Christian Science Monitor, December 29, 1937; *Sunday Oklahoman,* January 25, 1970.†

*   *   *

von BERTALANFFY, Ludwig   1901-1972

PERSONAL: Born September 19, 1901, in Atzgersdorf, Austria; became Canadian citizen; son of Gustav and Charlotte (Vogl) von Bertalanffy; married Maria M. Bauer, 1925; children: Felix D. *Education:* Educated at Universities of Innsbruck and Vienna; University of Vienna, Ph.D., 1926. *Religion:* Roman Catholic. *Home:* 65 Chestnut Hill Lane S., Williamsville, N.Y. 14221. *Office:* Center for Theoretical Biology, State University of New York at Buffalo, 4248 Ridge Lea Rd., Buffalo, N.Y. 14226.

CAREER: University of Vienna, Vienna, Austria, docent, later professor of biology, 1934-48; University of London, London, England, guest professor, 1948-49; University of Ottawa, Ottawa, Ontario, professor of biology and director of research department, 1949-54; University of Southern California, Los Angeles, professor of physiology, 1955-58; Mount Sinai Hospital, Los Angeles, director of biological research, 1955-58; Menninger Foundation, Topeka, Kan., Sloan Professor and research associate, 1958-60; University of Alberta, Edmonton, professor of theoretical biology, then university professor, 1961-69, member of Center for Advanced Study in Theoretical Psychology, 1967-69; State University of New York at Buffalo, professor, 1969-72.

MEMBER: Society for General Systems Research (founder; vice-president, 1956-60), International Academy of Cytology (fellow), American Association for the Advancement of Science (fellow), New York Academy of Sciences, Deutsche Akademie der Naturforscher, American Psychiatric Association (honorary fellow), and other scientific organizations. *Awards, honors:* Fellow of Notgemeinschaft der Deutschen Wissenschaft, 1930-33, Rockefeller Foundation, 1937-38, Lady Davis Foundation, 1949, and Center for Advanced Study in the Behavioral Sciences, 1954-55; Gold Medal of Postal History Society of the Americas, 1963.

WRITINGS: Kritische Theorie der Formbildung, Gebrueder Borntraeger (Berlin), 1928, translation published as *Modern Theories of Development,* Oxford University Press, 1933, Torchbooks, 1962; *Nikolaus von Kues,* George Mueller (Munich), 1928; *Lebenswissenschaft und Bildung,* Kurt Stenger (Erfurt), 1930; *Theoretische Biologie,* Gebrueder Boentraeger, Volume I: *Allgemeine Theorie, Physiko-Chemie, Aufbau und Entwicklung des Organismus,*

1932, Volume II: *Stoffwechsel, Wachstum,* 1942, 2nd enlarged edition, A. Francke (Bern), 1951; *Das Gefuege des Lebens,* Teubner (Leipzig), 1937; *Vom Molekuel zur Organismenwelt: Grundfragen der modernen Biologie,* 1942, 2nd edition, Akademische Verlagsgesellschaft Athenaion (Potsdam), 1949; *Biologie und Medizin,* Springer Verlag (Vienna), 1946; *Das biologische Weltbild,* A. Francke, 1949, translation published as *Problems of Life: An Evaluation of Modern Biological Thought,* Wiley, 1952; *Auf den Pfaden des Lebens: Ein biologisches Skizzenbuch,* Universum Verlag (Vienna), 1951; *Biophysik des Fliessgleichgewichts,* Vieweg (Braunschweig), 1953; *Robots, Men and Minds: Psychology in the Modern World,* Braziller, 1967; *Organismic Psychology and System Theory,* Clark University Press, 1968; *General System Theory: Foundations, Development, Applications,* Braziller, 1968, revised edition, 1969; (editor with J. R. Royce) *Toward the Unification of Psychology,* University of Toronto Press, 1969; *. . . Aber vom Menschen wissen wir nichts,* Econ-Verlag (Duesseldorf), 1970; *Perspectives on General System Theory,* edited by wife, Maria von Bertalanffy, and Edgar Taschdjian, Braziller, 1976.

Contributor: *Kuchentkal's Handbuch der Zoologie,* de Gruyter (Berlin), 1957; *Fundamental Aspects of Normal and Malignant Growth,* edited by W. W. Nowinski, Elsevier (Amsterdam), 1960; *Discussions on Child Development IV,* edited by J. M. Tanner and B. Inhelder, Tavistock Publications, 1960; *Chronic Schizophrenia,* edited by L. Appleby and others, Free Press of Glencoe, 1960; *Psychology and the Symbol,* edited by Royce, Random House, 1965; *American Handbook of Psychiatry,* Volume III, edited by S. Arieti, Basic Books, 1966; *Beyond Reductionism,* edited by Arthur Koestler and J. R. Smythies, Hutchinson, 1969, Macmillan, 1970. Also contributor of more than 200 papers on biophysics, growth, cancer, general system theory, behavioral theory, and history and philosophy of science to scientific journals. Founder and editor, *Handbuch der Biologie,* Akademische Verlagsgesellschaft Athenaion, twelve volumes, beginning 1942; editor, *General Systems,* yearbook of Society for General Systems Research, beginning 1956; co-editor, *Fortschritte der experimentellen und theoretischen Biophysik,* Thieme (Leipzig), beginning 1969.

SIDELIGHTS: Alan A. Stone wrote that "von Bertalanffy's importance results from his creative use of his position to look to both sides of his own scientific area and to refine the framework in which scientific observations and . . . theories have been made and shaped. He can appropriately be called the father of the 'general systems' approach. . . ." Ludwig von Bertalanffy's writings have been translated into French, Italian, Spanish, Dutch, Czech, Japanese, German, Swedish, and Portuguese.

BIOGRAPHICAL/CRITICAL SOURCES: C. Fries, *Metaphysik als Naturwissenschaft: Gedanken zu L. von Bertalanffys Theoretischer Biologie,* [Berlin], 1936; S.E.M. Gorleri de Tribino, *Una Nueva Orientation de la Filosofia Biologica: El Organicismo de L. Bertalanffy,* [Buenos Aires], 1946; A. Pi Suner, *Classics of Biology,* Philosophical Library, 1955; A. Bendmann, *L. von Bertalanffys organismische Auffassung des Lebens in ihren philosophischen Konsequenzen,* Fischer (Jena), 1967; *Book World,* October 6, 1968; *Die Wissenschaft vom Leben,* Volume III, [Freiburg-Munich], 1969; W. Gray, F. J. Duhl, and N. Rizzo, editors, *General Systems Theory and Psychiatry,* [Boston], 1970; Gray and Rizzo, editors, *Unity Through Diversity: A Festschrift in Honor of L. von Bertalanffy,* Gordon & Breach, 1973.†

(Died June 12, 1972)

* * *

von HORN, Carl 1903-

PERSONAL: Born July 15, 1903, in Vittskovle, Sweden; son of Carl Henning (an army captain) and Martha (Stjernsward) von Horn; married Gun Elisabeth Liljeroth, April 21, 1964; previously twice married; children: (first marriage) Agneta Madeleine (Mrs. G. Beskow), Katarina (Mrs. Gert Heiberg); (second marriage) Carl Johan Carlsson; (third marriage) Clara Catharina Elisabeth. *Education:* Royal Swedish Military Academy, graduate, 1923; Royal Swedish Staff College, graduate, 1930; also attended Royal Swedish Defence College, 1956. *Religion:* Protestant. *Home:* Jordberga, Klagstorp, Sweden.

CAREER: Swedish Army, commissioned lieutenant in Royal Swedish Horse Guards, 1923, retired as major general, 1963. Rose to lieutenant colonel during World War II; military director of State Railway Board and executive assistant to Count Bernadotte on various repatriations, 1943-46; director of movements, Defence Staff, 1945-47; Army Attache at Swedish Embassy in Oslo, Norway, 1947-49, and Copenhagen, Denmark, 1948-49; commanding colonel of Kronobergs Regiment, 1950-57, and Malmo Defence District, 1957-58; chief of staff, United Nations Truce Supervisory Organization in Palestine, 1958-60, 1960-63; also supreme commander, United Nations Forces in Congo, 1960; and commander of United Nations Mission to Yemen, 1963; resigned from United Nations, 1963.

WRITINGS: Fredens Soldater, Norstedts (Stockholm), 1966, translation published as *Soldiering for Peace,* Cassell, 1966, McKay, 1967. Contributor to military journals.

WORK IN PROGRESS: Historical research.

SIDELIGHTS: Carl von Horn speaks Danish, Norwegian, English, German, and French; he also knows smatterings of Finnish, Russian, Italian, Spanish, and Malay. His interests include military history, transportation, comparative linguistics, geography, poetry, and military slang.

* * *

von STORCH, Anne B. 1910-
(Anne Malcolmson)

PERSONAL: Born December 16, 1910; daughter of Charles and Edna (Lagenberg) Burnett; married Charles Malcolmson (a newspaperman), June 20, 1936 (died May 31, 1946); married Earl von Storch, June 11, 1954. *Education:* Bryn Mawr College, A.B., 1933.

CAREER: Girls Latin School, Chicago, Ill., fifth grade teacher, 1935-37; The Potomac School, Washington, D.C., junior high school English teacher, 1940-46; The Potomac School, McLean, Va., junior high school English teacher, 1955-63. *Wartime service:* Volunteer work including rations board and Red Cross, 1942-45. *Member:* Children's Book Guild of Washington, D.C. (president, 1968-69).

WRITINGS—All under name Anne Malcolmson: *Yankee Doodle's Cousins,* Houghton, 1941; *Son of Robin Hood,* Houghton, 1947; (with Dell McCormick) *Mr. Stormalong,* Houghton, 1952; *Miracle Plays,* Houghton, 1959; (editor) *A Taste of Chaucer,* Houghton, 1964; (editor) *William Blake: An Introduction,* Harcourt, 1967; *Captain Ichabod Paddock,* Walker & Co., 1970.

WORK IN PROGRESS: Research into the folk tales and tall stories connected with travel in and around North America.

SIDELIGHTS: Anne von Storch told *CA:* "After majoring in English literature at college, I had the good fortune to spend a summer at a girls' camp in New Hampshire, whose handyman claimed to have worked as a lumberjack for Paul Bunyan. He had many stories to tell. Shortly thereafter I began my chief career as a schoolteacher. Being unable to find any collection of American stories for my kids to read, I plunged and wrote my first book to fill the gap. Since then most of my writing has come about in the same way—to supply a book I thought I needed in teaching. My two chief fields of interest, so far as writing is concerned, are American folklore and English literature."

AVOCATIONAL INTERESTS: Florida winter vacations and French cooking.††

* * *

WADSWORTH, James J.   1905-

PERSONAL: Born June 12, 1905, in Groveland, N.Y.; son of James W. (a public servant) and Alice (Hay) Wadsworth; married Harty Tilton, June 16, 1927 (deceased); married Mary A. Donaldson, May 27, 1967; children: Alice Tilton (Mrs. Trowbridge Strong). *Education:* Yale University, B.A., 1927. *Politics:* Republican. *Religion:* Episcopalian. *Home:* 3909 Avon Road, Geneseo, N.Y. 14454.

CAREER: Member of New York State Legislature, 1931-41; Curtiss Wright Corp., Buffalo, N.Y., manager of industrial relations, 1941-45; U.S. War Assets Administration, Public Service Division, Washington, D.C., director, 1945-46; Air Transport Association of America, New York, N.Y., director of department of government affairs, 1946-48; U.S. Government, Washington, D.C., special assistant to administrator, Economic Cooperation Administration, 1948-50, acting director, Office of Civil Defense, 1950, deputy administrator, Federal Civil Defense Agency, 1951; deputy U.S. representative to United Nations, 1953-60, permanent representative, 1960-61; Federal Communications Commission, Washington, D.C., commissioner, 1965-70. Chairman of board of trustees, Freedom House, 1961; president of Peace Research Institute, 1961-62; trustee of People to People and U.S. Committee for Dag Hammarskjold Foundation. Chairman of board of directors, Genesee Valley National Bank, beginning 1973. Lecturer on international affairs.

MEMBER: International Club of Washington (president, 1963-71), United Nations Association of the U.S.A. (vice-president, 1964-65), Yale Club (New York), Chevy Chase Club. *Awards, honors:* LL.D. from Alfred University, 1937, Bowdoin College, 1962, Wilmington College, 1964; Eleanor Roosevelt Peace Award, 1963; United World Federalists Award for promotion of peace and disarmament, 1964.

WRITINGS: The Price of Peace, Praeger, 1961; (contributor) Arthur Larsen, editor, *A Warless World,* McGraw, 1963; (contributor) Alan Westin, editor, *Power and Order,* Praeger, 1964; *The Glass House,* Praeger, 1966. Contributor to *Saturday Review* and other magazines.

WORK IN PROGRESS: Research for a historical novel of post-Revolutionary era (1785-1810).

SIDELIGHTS: Arising from public service families on both sides, Wadsworth's main thrust has been to government activity, regardless of politics—he has worked under presidents from both parties. He told *CA* that he is impelled to write because of his conviction that the public gets little chance to understand international policy of the United States, even less the why's of the United Nations. *Avocational interests:* Sports, painting, ceramics, sculpture.

* * *

WAIFE-GOLDBERG, Marie   1892-

PERSONAL: Born October 29, 1892, in Kiev, Russia; daughter of Solomon (the Yiddish writer, Sholom Aleichem) and Olga (Loyeff) Rabinowitz; married Benjamin Waife-Goldberg (an author and columnist), December 23, 1917; children: S. O. Waife, Mitchell M. Waife. *Education:* University of Lausanne, B.es L., 1914. *Religion:* Jewish. *Home:* 375 Riverside Dr., New York, N.Y. 10025.

AWARDS, HONORS: Hyim Greenberg Literary Award of Pioneer Women of America.

WRITINGS: My Father, Sholom Aleichem, Simon & Schuster, 1968.

SIDELIGHTS: Marie Waife-Goldberg speaks, reads, and writes French in addition to Russian and Yiddish; she has traveled in all countries of Europe, and in Latin America and Israel.††

* * *

WALINSKY, Louis J(oseph)   1908-

PERSONAL: Born April 19, 1908, in London, England; came to United States, 1912, became citizen, 1921; son of Ossip J. (a labor leader) and Rosa (Newman) Walinsky; married Michelle Benson, 1936 (divorced); married Dorothy Monie, September 22, 1947; children: (first marriage) Adam; (second marriage) Marian, Louisa. *Education:* Cornell University, B.A. (honors), 1929; New School for Social Research, graduate study, 1940-41. *Home:* 100 Elm St., Cohasset, Mass. 02025.

CAREER: New York (N.Y.) public schools, teacher of economics, 1930-43; U.S. War Production Board, Washington, D.C., economic consultant, 1943-47; World Organization for Rehabilitation through Training Union, New York, N.Y., and Paris, France, financial director, 1947-49; Robert R. Nathan Associates, Washington, D.C., chief economist, 1949-63, economic consultant, beginning 1963. Chief economic adviser to government of Burma, 1953-58; has made economic survey, advisory, and planning missions to Korea, Afghanistan, Iran, El Salvador, Bolivia, Venezuela, Brazil, India, and eastern Africa. Consultant to World Bank. *Member:* American Economic Association, Society for International Development, Americans for Democratic Action (chapter president, 1951).

WRITINGS: Economic Development in Burma, Twentieth Century, 1962; *Planning and Execution of Economic Development,* McGraw, 1963; (contributor) E. E. Hagen, editor, *Planning Economic Development,* Irwin, 1963. Author of plays, "Heil Hitler," 1936, "Brave New World," 1938. Contributor to *Saturday Review, New Republic, Business and Society,* and other journals.

WORK IN PROGRESS: Getting From Here to There.

* * *

WALKER, Charles R(umford)   1893-1974

PERSONAL: Born July 31, 1893, in Concord, N.H.; son of Charles Rumford (a physician) and Frances (Sheafe) Walker; married Adelaide Haley George, October 28, 1928; children: Charles Rumford III, Daniel Sheafe. *Education:*

Yale University, B.A., 1916; graduate study at Harvard University and Columbia University. *Politics:* Independent. *Religion:* Episcopalian. *Office:* Yale University, 333 Cedar St., New Haven, Conn.

CAREER: Worked in steel mills after college; editorial posts with magazines, as assistant editor of *Atlantic Monthly,* 1922-23, associate editor of *Independent,* 1924-25, and *Bookman,* 1928-29; Yale University, New Haven, Conn., assistant secretary of university, 1942-45, director of Yale Technology Project and senior research fellow in industrial relations, 1945-62, curator of Technology Society Collection, 1962-74, fellow emeritus of Berkeley College; author and editor. Consultant in automation, United Nations World Health Organization, 1957. *Military service:* U.S. Army, 1917-19; became first lieutenant. *Member:* Society for Applied Anthropology (president, 1955), American Sociological Association, Industrial Relations Research Association, Phi Beta Kappa, Elizabethan Club (New Haven), Yale Club (New York), Tavern Club (Boston). *Awards, honors:* Guggenheim fellowship, 1938-39; Bollingen grant, 1960.

WRITINGS: Steel, the Diary of a Furnace Worker, Atlantic Monthly Press, 1922; *Bread and Fire* (novel), Houghton, 1927; *Our Gods Are Not Born* (short stories), Harrison Smith, 1930; *American City,* Farrar & Rinehart, 1936; (with F. L. W. Richardson) *Human Relations in an Expanding Company,* Yale Labor and Management Center, 1948; *Steeltown: An Industrial Case History,* Harper, 1950; (with Robert H. Guest) *The Man on the Assembly Line,* Harvard University Press, 1952; (with R. H. Guest and A. N. Turner) *The Foreman on the Assembly Line,* Harvard University Press, 1956; *Towards the Automatic Factory,* Yale University Press, 1957; *Modern Technology and Civilization,* McGraw, 1962, revised edition, with wife, Adelaide G. Walker, published as *Technology, Industry, and Man: The Age of Acceleration,* 1968.

(Contributor) David Grene and Richmond Lattimore, editors, *The Complete Greek Tragedies,* University of Chicago Press, 1958; (translator and editor) Sophocles, *Oedipus the King* [*and*] *Oedipus at Colonus: A New Translation for Modern Audiences and Readers,* Anchor Books, 1966; (editor) H. Phelps Putnam, *The Collected Poems of H. Phelps Putnam,* Farrar, Strauss, 1971.

AVOCATIONAL INTERESTS: Greece and Greek tragedy, the American theater, sketching, and travel.†

(Died November 26, 1974)

*   *   *

WALKER, Eric Anderson   1886-1976

PERSONAL: Born September 6, 1886, in London, England; son of William (secretary of Union-Castle Steamship Co.) and Jessie (Goodman) Walker; married Lucy Stapleton, April 10, 1913; children: Jean Jessie (Mrs. John England), Hilary (Mrs. Andre Bruler). *Education:* Attended Merton College, Oxford, 1905-08. *Politics:* Liberal. *Religion:* Church of England. *Home:* 76 Manning Rd., Durban, South Africa.

CAREER: University of Bristol, Bristol, England, lecturer in modern history, 1908-11; University of Cape Town, Cape Town (now at Rondebosch), South Africa, King George V Professor of History, 1911-36; Cambridge University, Cambridge, England, Vere Harmsworth Professor of Imperial and Naval History, 1936-51, professor emeritus, 1951—, fellow of St. John's College, beginning 1936. *Military service:* British Army, 1914-18, 1939-45; became captain.

Member: Royal Commonwealth Society, Leander Club. *Awards, honors:* Gold Medal of Royal Empire Society, 1937.

WRITINGS: Historical Atlas of South Africa, Oxford University Press, 1922; *Lord de Villiers and His Times,* Constable, 1925; *A Modern History for South Africans,* Blackwell, 1927; *A History of South Africa,* Longmans, Green, 1928, 3rd edition published as *A History of Southern Africa,* Longmans, Green, 1957, new impression with corrections, 1962; *The Frontier Tradition in South Africa,* Oxford University Press, 1930; *The Great Trek,* A. & C. Black, 1934, 5th edition, 1965; *W. P. Schreiner: A South African,* Oxford University Press, 1937, condensed edition, 1960, reprinted, 1969; *South Africa,* Oxford University Press, 1940; *Britain and South Africa,* Longmans, Green, 1941; *The British Empire: Its Structure and Spirit,* Bowes, 1943, 2nd edition, Cambridge University Press, 1953, Harvard University Press, 1956; *Colonies,* Macmillan, 1944; (editor) *South Africa, Rhodesia and the High Commission Territories,* 2nd edition, Cambridge University Press, 1963.

South African adviser to the editors of Volume VIII of *Cambridge History of the British Empire,* 1936, joint editor and contributor, Volume III, 2nd edition, 1959, and editor and contributor, Volume VIII, 2nd edition, 1963.

AVOCATIONAL INTERESTS: Painting and rowing.

(Died March, 1976)

*   *   *

WALL, Martha   1910-

PERSONAL: Born March 22, 1910, in Alsen, N.D.; daughter of Gerhardt G. (a farmer) and Stella (Lóewen) Wall. *Education:* Salem Hospital Nurses Training School, Hillsboro, Kan., R.N., 1931; Tabor College, student, 1937-38. *Politics:* Republican. *Religion:* Protestant. *Home:* 3710 Gross Rd., Santa Cruz, Calif. 95062.

CAREER: Medical missionary for Sudan Interior Mission, West Africa, in Katsina Leper Settlement, Kano Eye Hospital, and a bush dispensary on the lower fringe of the Sahara, 1939-54; worked briefly as an assistant editor for Scripture Press, Wheaton, Ill., 1955, and then as writer on assignment, 1955-57; full-time writer, beginning 1957. Working as a volunteer tutoring foreign students in English.

WRITINGS: Splinters from an African Log, Moody, 1960; *As a Roaring Lion,* Moody, 1967; *In a Cross Fire of Hate,* Moody, 1970; *Strong Tower,* Herald Press, 1970. Author of Sunday school materials and articles for religious magazines.

WORK IN PROGRESS: Fragrant Forever, a devotional book; ghostwriting a biography for young people, *George Washington,* to be published by Mott.

SIDELIGHTS: Martha Wall speaks German, French, Spanish, Hausa (West African dialect), and a dialect of Dutch learned in a German Mennonite community as a child. She lived in Paris, France for ten months in 1950 to learn French, in San Jose, Costa Rica, for eight months in 1963 to learn Spanish, and then spent nine months collecting interviews as the basis for *As a Roaring Lion* and *In a Cross Fire of Hate.*

AVOCATIONAL INTERESTS: Travel, photography, pastel drawing.

*   *   *

WALLACE, Helen Kingsbury   1897-

PERSONAL: Born April 25, 1897, in Peabody, Mass.;

daughter of Orvin Henry and Carrie Estelle (Hatch) Wallace. *Education:* Pembroke College, Ph.B., 1920; New York University, A.M., 1938; attended Brown University; also studied summers at Columbia University, 1922, 1931, 1935, and at Courtauld Institute of Art, University of London, 1936. *Home:* The Navesink House, 40 Riverside Ave., Red Bank, N.J. 07701.

CAREER: Franklin College, Franklin, Ind., associate professor of fine arts and dean of women, 1922-24; Hofstra College (now University), Hempstead, N.Y., assistant professor of fine arts and dean of women, 1939-41; Maryland College for Women, Lutherville, dean, 1945; American Baptist Convention, various positions with Board of Education and Publication in New York, N.Y., Philadelphia, Pa., and Valley Forge, Pa., at intervals, 1921-62. Instructor at St. David's Christian Writer's Conference, 1968-69, and at Christian Authors' Guild. *Member:* Religious Public Relations Council (past president of Philadelphia branch), American Association of University Women, National League of American Pen Women (president of Philadelphia branch, 1966-68), St. David's Christian Writers' Association (member of board of directors), Women's University Club (Philadelphia). *Awards, honors:* Carnegie scholarship for study at University of London, 1936; first place in fiction and third place in nonfiction in National League of American Pen Women (Philadelphia branch) contest, 1970.

WRITINGS—All published by Revell, except as indicated: (With R. Donald Williamson) *Stewardship in the Life of Youth,* 1926; *Stewardship in the Life of Women,* 1928; *Junior Stewards of the Bible,* 1930; *If I Were Eighteen,* 1943; *Stewardship for Today's Woman,* 1960; *Meditations on New Testament Symbols,* 1962; *Prayers for Women's Meetings,* 1964; *Keys in Our Hands,* Judson, 1967. Contributor of articles and stories to *John Martin's Book, Child Welfare, Christian Herald,* and a number of American Baptist periodicals. Former profile editor, *Pen Woman.*

* * *

WALLACE, Lewis Grant   1910-

PERSONAL: Born March 29, 1910, in London, England; son of Vincent and Florence Blanche (Cartwright) Grant Wallace. *Education:* Attended University College, Oxford. *Politics:* Conservative. *Religion:* Church of England. *Agent:* Margaret Ramsey Ltd., 14 Goodwin Ct., London W.C.2, England; and Margery Vosper Ltd., 53A Shaftesbury Ave., London W.1, England.

CAREER: Dover College, Kent, England, assistant master, 1930-31; private tutor, 1931-33; full-time playwright and scriptwriter, beginning 1933. Co-founder in 1939 of two documentary film companies, Public Relationship Films Ltd. and Everyman Films Ltd., and producer and script editor for both. *Military service:* Royal Navy, 1942-43. *Member:* Society of Authors, Old Dovorian Society, Bury Horticultural Society.

WRITINGS—All plays: "Interlude," produced at Duke of York's Theatre, 1938; *Young Chippie: A Play in One Act,* Samuel French, 1949 (produced on television and radio, 1948); *First Person Singular: A Comedy in Three Acts,* Samuel French, 1952 (produced same year at Duke of York's Theatre); "The Long View," produced at Alexandra Theatre, 1960. Author of film scripts, chiefly documentary, including "Fear and Peter Brown," "Sailors Without Uniform," and "Cambridge"; also author of eleven television plays produced by British Broadcasting Corp.

SIDELIGHTS: "Having left London to live in country

(1962)," Wallace wrote, "[my] interests have widened to embrace village life and activities. My Sussex home built in 1934. Dearest companion: a miniature dachshund. Having lived in France and Germany, speak French and German, but traveling days are over until British quarantine laws concerning dogs are changed. As years increase find writing more and more difficult. Have become my own severest critic, with depressing results on amount of creative writings I allow to be seen, even by my literary agents. Not quite dried-up, but the possibility comes to mind constantly."††

* * *

WALLIS, Robert   1900-

PERSONAL: Born January 9, 1900, in Paris, France; son of Victor Jacques (a physician) and Marguerite (Pereire) Wallis; married Celestina Wainwright, June 4, 1956: children: Eric, Emmanuel, Victor, Spencer. *Education:* Paris Lycee, B.A., 1916; University of Paris, M.Sc., 1918, M.D., 1930. *Home and office:* 11 East 67th St., New York, N.Y. 10021. *Agent:* Mrs. William Aspenwall Bradley, 18 Quai de Bethune, Paris IV, France.

CAREER: Physician in private practice, specializing in internal medicine, New York, N.Y. *Military service:* French Air Force, physician, World War II; named officer of French Legion of Honor. *Member:* American College of Chest Physicians (fellow), New York Academy of Medicine (fellow), New York Academy of Sciences (fellow), Lotos Club.

WRITINGS: Time: Fourth Dimension of the Mind, Harcourt, 1968. Contributor to medical journals in France, 1926-39, and in United States, 1945-59.

* * *

WALMSLEY, Robert   1905-1976

PERSONAL: Born July 31, 1905, in Westhoughton, Lancashire, England; son of Henry (an insurance agent) and Elizabeth (Barcroft) Walmsley; married Mary Seddon, July 29, 1931 (died, 1940); married Melissa Frances Gregory, February 24, 1945; children: (first marriage) Robert Seddon, William Seddon; (second marriage) James. *Education:* Attended the parochial school in Westhoughton, England, until thirteen. *Religion:* Church of England. *Home:* 231 Newbrook Rd., Atherton, Lancashire, England. *Office:* Shaw's Bookshop Ltd., 95 Bridge St., Manchester M3 2GX, England.

CAREER: Printing and publishing trade, 1918-1942; Shaw's Bookshop Ltd., Manchester, England, managing director, 1947-70, chairman of board of directors. Trustee, Deane School, Lancashire; manager, Hart Common School, Westhoughton. *Military service:* British Army, 1942-46. *Member:* Antiquarian Booksellers' Association (member of executive committee), Manchester Society of Book Collectors (founder and chairman). *Awards, honors:* M.A. from University of Manchester for service to scholarship.

WRITINGS: Memorials of the Ditchfield Family, privately printed, 1941; *Peterloo: The Case Reopened,* Augustus M. Kelley, 1969. Contributor to historical journals and the local press.

WORK IN PROGRESS: A bibliography of the British Temperance Movement; histories of the parishes of Deane and Westhoughton.

BIOGRAPHICAL/CRITICAL SOURCES: Observer Review, July 20, 1969; *Spectator,* July 26, 1969.†

(Died April 19, 1976)

WALSH, Warren Bartlett   1909-

PERSONAL: Born December 21, 1909, in Brookfield, Mass.; son of William L. (a minister) and Lucy (Bartlett) Walsh; married Elizabeth Cantril, June 6, 1936; children: Lucy E. (Mrs. Stephen E. Phinney), Elizabeth C. (Mrs. James R. Colquhoun), Sara B. (Mrs. Lewis B. Hayes). Education: Tufts University, A.B., 1930; Harvard University, A.M., 1931, Ph.D., 1935. Home: 11 Pebble Hill Rd. S., DeWitt, N.Y. 13214. Office: 304 Maxwell, Syracuse University, Syracuse, N.Y. 13210.

CAREER: Tufts University, Medford, Mass., assistant in history, 1933-35; Syracuse University, Syracuse, N.Y., beginning 1935, professor of Russian history, beginning 1946, chairman of board of Russian studies, 1944-63, chairman of department of history, 1963-67, director of projects at Research Institute, 1955-65. National War College, member of civilian faculty, 1952-55, director of Political Affairs Division, 1953-55, member of board of consultants, 1963-65. Occasional lecturer to the War College of Air University, the Army War College, the Naval War College, the Foreign Service Institute, the Inter-American Defense College, the NATO Defense College, the National War College. Member of panel of visiting scholars, State University of New York, 1963-65. Member of national council of Unitarian Laymen's League, 1943-46; American Unitarian Association, member of board of directors, 1947-53, member of publications council, 1950-54; president of Unitarian Congregational Society in Syracuse, 1942-44, 1962-64; consultant, American Council on Education, beginning 1967; chairman, Secretary of the Army's Advisory Committee for U.S. Army Military History Research Collection, 1971-73. Member: American Historical Association, American Association for the Advancement of Slavic Studies, Phi Beta Kappa, Phi Alpha Theta. Awards, honors: U.S. Department of the Army, commendation for meritorious civilian service, 1954; award for outstanding service from National War College, 1964; United States Air Force, honorary member of 960th A.E.W.&C. Squadron, 1965; Outstanding Civilian Service Medal, Department of the Army, 1973.

WRITINGS: (With C. G. Haines) The Development of Western Civilization, Holt, 1940; Readers' Guide to Russia (bibliography), Syracuse University Press, 1945; Russia Under Tsars and Commissars (bibliography), Syracuse University Press, 1946; (editor) Readings in Russian History, Syracuse University Press, 1948, 4th revised edition, 1963; Russia and the Soviet Union: A Modern History, University of Michigan Press, 1958, new edition, 1968; Perspectives and Patterns: Discourses on History, Syracuse University Press, 1962; (editor with K. Heberle) International Conflict and Cooperation, Maxwell Graduate School, Syracuse University, 1963; Science and International Public Affairs, Maxwell Graduate School, Syracuse University, 1967.

Contributor: Russia: A Handbook, Syracuse University Press, 1948, and later editions; Michael Shapovalov, Let's Read about Russia, Fideler, 1953; Great Issues, Harper, 1953; Communism in the USSR, U.S. Department of Defense, 1955; In the Iron Grip of the Kremlin, U.S. Department of Defense, 1955; Psychological Aspects of Global Conflict, Industrial College of the Armed Forces, 1955; R. J. Shafer, editor, A Guide to Historical Method, Dorsey, 1969.

Scriptwriter and narrator of U.S. Department of Defense film, "The Communist Weapon of Allure," 1956. Author of series of articles on Soviet Russia, syndicated nationally by North American Newspaper Alliance, 1947; contributor to encyclopedias and to periodicals, including Russian Review, Pacific Historical Review, Antioch Review, New York Times Sunday Magazine, and Journal of Modern History. Associate editor, Russian Review, beginning 1946; member of editorial board of Christian Register, 1947-48.

WORK IN PROGRESS: Psychohistorical and Biohistorical Essays on Persons and Groups during the Reign of the Last Romanovs; Essays on the State Duma.

AVOCATIONAL INTERESTS: Humanistic psychology, color photography, and small boat sailing.

*   *   *

WARBURG, James Paul   1896-1969
(Paul James)

PERSONAL: Born August 18, 1896, in Hamburg, Germany; brought to United States in infancy; son of Paul M. (a banker) and Nina (Loeb) Warburg; married Katherine Faulkner Smith, June, 1918 (divorced, 1934); married Phyllis Baldwin Browne; married Joan Melber, August 28, 1948; children: (first marriage) April (Mrs. B. Gagliano), Andrea (Mrs. Sydney Kaufman), Kay (Mrs. Robert A. Levin); (third marriage) James Paul, Jr., Jennifer Joan, Philip Neff, Sarah Neff. Education: Harvard University, A.B. (magna cum laude), 1916. Politics: Democrat. Residence: John St., Greenwich, Conn.; and Deerfield Beach, Fla. (winter). Also maintained an apartment at 34 East 70th St., New York, N.Y. Office: 60 East 42nd St., New York, N.Y. 10017.

CAREER: With Baltimore & Ohio Railroad Co., 1916, National Metropolitan Bank, Washington, D.C., 1919, and First National Bank of Boston, Boston, Mass., 1919-21; International Acceptance Bank, New York City, vice-president, 1921-29, president, 1931-32; International Manhattan Co., New York City, president, 1929-31; Bank of the Manhattan Co., New York City, vice-chairman of board, 1932-35; became member of President Roosevelt's first "Brain Trust," 1933, serving as financial adviser to U.S. Delegation at World Economic Conference in London; U.S. Office of War Information, Washington, D.C., special assistant to coordinator of information, 1941-42, deputy director of Overseas Branch, 1942-44. Writer on world affairs and domestic politics and economics, 1935-69. Trustee, Institute for Policy Studies, Washington, D.C. Director of Bydale Co., Fontenay Corp., and Polaroid Corp. Former chairman of board, Julliard School. Military service: U.S. Naval Flying Corps, 1917-18; became lieutenant junior grade.

MEMBER: American Academy of Political Science (director), Phi Beta Kappa, Authors' Club (London); Economic Club, Harvard Club, and Wings Club (all New York); Cosmos Club (Washington, D.C.), Faculty Club (Cambridge, Mass.), Stanwich Club (Greenwich, Conn.).

WRITINGS: Wool and Wool Manufacture, First National Bank of Boston, 1920; Cotton and Cotton Manufacture, First National Bank of Boston, 1921; Hides and Skins and the Manufacture of Leather, First National Bank of Boston, 1921.

(Under pseudonym Paul James) And Then What? (verse), Knopf, 1931; (under pseudonym Paul James) Shoes and Ships and Sealing Wax (verse), Knopf, 1932; The Money Muddle, Knopf, 1934; It's Up to Us, Knopf, 1934; Hell Bent for Election, Doubleday, 1935; Still Hell Bent, Doubleday, 1936; Peace in Our Time?, Harper, 1939.

Our War and Our Peace, Farrar & Rinehart, 1941; The Isolationist Illusion and World Peace, Farrar & Rinehart, 1941;

Man's Enemy and Man (verse), Farrar & Rinehart, 1942; *Foreign Policy Begins at Home*, Harcourt, 1944; *Unwritten Treaty*, Harcourt, 1946; *Germany: Nation or No-Man's-Land?*, Foreign Policy Association, 1946; *Germany: Bridge or Battleground*, Harcourt, 1947; *Put Yourself in Marshall's Place*, Simon & Schuster, 1948; *How to Achieve One World*, privately printed, circa 1948; *Listen to the People*, privately printed, circa 1948; *Our Role in World Affairs*, privately printed, circa 1948; *The United States and the World Crisis*, privately printed, circa 1948; *Deadlock over Germany*, Canadian Association for Adult Education, 1948; *"Point Four": Our Chance to Achieve Freedom from Fear and What You Can Do About It*, privately printed, 1949; *Last Call for Common Sense*, Harcourt, 1949.

Faith, Purpose and Power, Farrar, Straus, 1950; *Victory Without War*, Franklin and Marshall College, and Current Affairs Press, 1951; *How to Co-Exist Without Playing the Kremlin's Game*, Beacon Press, 1952; *Germany: Key to Peace*, Harvard University Press, 1953; *The United States in a Changing World*, Putnam, 1954; *Turning Point Toward Peace*, Current Affairs Press, 1955; *The Middle East Crisis*, Current Affairs Press, 1956; *Danger and Opportunity*, Current Affairs Press, 1956; *Agenda for Action*, Academy Books, 1957; *Proposal for a United Nations Development Authority*, Current Affairs Press, circa 1957; *A New Age of Opportunity*, Roosevelt University, 1957; *Our Last Chance in Europe: What Are We Waiting For?*, Current Affairs Press, 1957; *Prognosis for the United Nations*, Current Affairs Press, 1958; *Toward a Revised Foreign Aid Program*, Current Affairs Press, 1958; *United States Postwar Policy in Asia*, Current Affairs Press, 1958; *The Bare Essentials of a New Approach to Peace*, Current Affairs Press, 1958; *The Lesson We Must Learn, or Perish*, Current Affairs Press, 1958; *The German Crisis in Perspective*, Current Affairs Press, 1959; *The West in Crisis*, Doubleday, 1959; *A Call to Leadership Action*, Current Affairs Press, 1959.

Reveille for Rebels, Doubleday, 1960; *How Useful Is NATO?*, Current Affairs Press, 1960; *Disarmament: Challenge of the Nineteen Sixties*, Doubleday, 1961; *Pending the Establishment of World Law: How Lawless Can We Be?*, Current Affairs Press, 1961; *The First Three Months of the Kennedy Administration*, Current Affairs Press, circa 1961; *What Progress toward Disarmament?*, Current Affairs Press, circa 1961; *Cuba: Time for Restraint and Fortitude*, Current Affairs Press, 1962; *Farewell to the Postwar Period*, Current Affairs Press, 1963; *Toward a Strategy of Peace*, Current Affairs Press, 1964; *The Long Road Home: The Autobiography of a Maverick*, Doubleday, 1964; *Time for Statesmanship*, Current Affairs Press, 1965; *The United States in the Postwar World*, Atheneum, 1966; *Western Intruders: America's Role in the Far East*, Atheneum, 1967; *Crosscurrents in the Middle East*, Atheneum, 1968. Also author of *Acceptance Financing*, 1922, *Three Textile Materials*, 1923, and *A Memorandum to the 85th Congress*, 1957. Contributor to magazines.

BIOGRAPHICAL/CRITICAL SOURCES: Arthur Schlesinger, *The Age of Roosevelt*, Volume II, Houghton, 1959; Herbert Feis, editor, *1933: Characters in Crises*, Little, Brown, 1966.†

(Died June 3, 1969)

*   *   *

WARD, Theodora   1890-1974

PERSONAL: Born November 13, 1890, in South Orange, N.J.; daughter of Bleecker (a publisher) and Kate (Holland)

Van Wagenen; married Jasper D. Ward (an engineer), February 7, 1931 (deceased); stepchildren: Allen, Jasper D., Jr. *Education:* Studied in private schools. *Agent:* McIntosh & Otis, Inc., 475 Fifth Ave., New York, N.Y. 10017.

CAREER: Artist and writer; woodcuts are in collections of Boston and Baltimore art museums.

WRITINGS: (Editor) Emily Dickinson, *Letters to Dr. and Mrs. Josiah Gilbert Holland*, Harvard University Press, 1951; (assistant editor) Emily Dickinson, *Poems: Including Variant Readings Critically Compared with All Known Manuscripts*, edited by Thomas H. Johnson, three volumes, Belknap Press, 1955; (associate editor) *Letters of Emily Dickinson*, edited by Johnson, three volumes, Belknap Press, 1958; *The Capsule of the Mind: Chapters in the Life of Emily Dickinson*, Harvard University Press, 1961; *Men and Angels*, Viking, 1969.

BIOGRAPHICAL/CRITICAL SOURCES: Time, December 26, 1969; *New York Times Book Review*, February 8, 1970.†

(Died August 16, 1974)

*   *   *

WARE, Runa Erwin

PERSONAL: Born in Bainbridge, Ga.; daughter of Howell Cobb (a manufacturer) and Runa (Patterson) Erwin; married Frederick A. Ware (an auto dealer and banker), March 14, 1931 (deceased); children: Frederick A., Jr., Howell Cobb. *Education:* Attended Washington Seminary, Atlanta, Ga., and Hollins College. *Religion:* Presbyterian. *Home:* 812 Aumond Pl. E., Augusta, Ga. 30904. *Agent:* George Scheer Associates, Box 750, Chapel Hill, N.C. 27514.

CAREER: Teacher of parliamentary law to women's groups, beginning 1957; lecturer on flower arranging and gardening; gives humorous talks on women's clubs; book reviewer. Volunteer nurses aide for American Red Cross, 1941-65. *Member:* National Council of State Garden Clubs, Dixie Council of Authors and Journalists, Garden Club of Georgia (honorary life member), Georgia Writers Association, Augusta Authors Club, Kappa Delta. *Awards, honors:* Annual award of Dixie Council of Authors and Journalists for best nonfiction book by a Georgia writer, 1969, for *All Those in Favor Say Something*.

WRITINGS: All Those in Favor Say Something, Geron-X, 1968. Contributor to *Atlanta Constitution*, gardening magazines, and other periodicals. Former book review editor, *Augusta Chronicle*; assistant editor, *Georgia Magazine*, 1971.

SIDELIGHTS: Mrs. Ware lived in Australia for a number of years.†

*   *   *

WARK, Ian W(illiam)   1899-

PERSONAL: Born May 8, 1899, in Melbourne, Victoria, Australia; son of William John (an agent) and Florence Emily (Palmer) Wark; married Elsie Evelyn Booth, May 27, 1927; children: Elizabeth Helen (Mrs. Keith W. Stedwell). *Education:* Attended Scotch College, Melbourne; University of Melbourne, M.Sc., 1921, D.Sc., 1924; University of London, Ph.D., 1923; University of California, postdoctoral study, 1924. *Home:* 31 Linum St., Blackburn, Victoria 3130, Australia.

CAREER: University of Sydney, Sydney, Australia, lecturer in chemistry, 1925; researcher for Australian mining industry, 1925-40; Commonwealth Scientific and Industrial Research Organization, Melbourne, Australia, chief of Division of Industrial Chemistry, 1939-58, first director of Chemical Research Laboratory, 1958-60, member of executive board, 1961-65; Commonwealth Advisory Committee on Advanced Education, Canberra, Australia, chairman, 1965-71; Commonwealth Scientific and Industrial Research Organization, honorary consultant, beginning 1971. Fellow, University College, University of London, 1965. Governor, Ian Potter Foundation. *Member:* Australian Academy of Science (fellow; treasurer, 1958-63), Royal Australian Chemical Institute (fellow; general president, 1958), Australasian Institute of Mining and Metallurgy (honorary member). *Awards, honors:* H. G. Smith Medal, Syme Medal, and Grimwade Prize, all 1933, for research in physical chemistry and metallurgy; Commander, Order of the British Empire, 1963; Companion of St. Michael and St. George, 1967; Knight Bachelor, 1969; Anzaas Medal, 1973.

WRITINGS: Principles of Flotation, Australasian Institute of Mining and Metallurgy, 1938, revised edition (with K. L. Sutherland), 1955; *Why Research?,* Educational Explorers, 1968. Contributor of more than fifty papers to scientific journals.

AVOCATIONAL INTERESTS: Trout fishing, golf.

* * *

WARNER, Frank A.
[Collective pseudonym]

WRITINGS: "Bobby Blake" series; published by Barse & Hopkins: *Bobby Blake on a Plantation; or, Lost in the Great Swamp,* 1922; *. . . in the Frozen North; or, The Old Eskimo's Last Message,* 1923.

"Bob Chase" series; published by Barse & Co.: *Bob Chase after Grizzly Bears,* 1929; *. . . in the Tiger's Lair,* 1929; *. . . with the Big Moose Hunters,* 1929; *. . . with the Lion Hunters,* 1930.

SIDELIGHTS: See ADAMS, Harriet S., STRATEMEYER, Edward L., and SVENSON, Andrew E.†

* * *

WARREN, William Stephen   1882-1968
(Billy Warren)

PERSONAL: Born September 6, 1882, in Carrollton, Ark.; son of James Henry (a cattleman) and Mary Lou (Eddelman) Warren; married Agnes Kirkland, May 14, 1913 (deceased); married Anne Kirkland, March 5, 1952. *Education:* Academy of Fine Arts, Chicago, Ill., student, 1918-20. *Politics:* Democrat. *Religion:* Episcopalian. *Home:* 483 University Circle, Claremont, Calif. 91711.

CAREER: Cowboy on Colorado range, 1895-1910; Colorado State Penitentiary, Canon City, superintendent of road construction by convict labor, 1910-18; political cartoonist for *Chicago Tribune,* Chicago, Ill., part-time, 1920-22, *Cleveland News,* Cleveland, Ohio, 1922-28, *Philadelphia Morning Public Ledger,* Philadelphia, Pa., 1928-32, and *Buffalo Evening News,* Buffalo, N.Y., 1932-40; owner of a peach orchard at Palisade, Colo., and a cattle ranch at Collbran, Colo., 1941-48; writer and illustrator of books for young people, 1942-68. *Member:* Authors Guild, University Club (Claremont). *Awards, honors:* Boys' Clubs of America Junior Book Award, 1950, for *Tony Gay on the Longhorn Trail.*

WRITINGS—All under name Billy Warren and all self-illustrated, except as indicated: *Ride, Cowboy, Ride!,*

Reynal, 1946; *Saddles Up! Ride 'em High,* McKay, 1948; *Tony Gay on the Longhorn Trail,* McKay, 1949; *Silver Spurs,* McKay, 1950; *The Golden Palomino,* McKay, 1951; *Ride West into Danger* (Junior Literary Guild selection), McKay, 1953; *Headquarters Ranch,* McKay, 1954; *Black Lobo* illustrations by Bernard Garbutt, Golden Gate, 1967.

Contributor: *All Around Me,* Macmillan, 1951; *Time to Read: Finding Favorites,* edited by Bernice E. Leary, Edwin C. Reichert, and Mary K. Reely, Lippincott, 1953; *Aboard the Story Rocket,* L. W. Singer, 1960; *Stories of Fun and Adventure,* Copp Clark, 1964; *Around the World Readers,* Book I, A. H. & A. W. Reed, 1967.

WORK IN PROGRESS: Rosita, a sequel to *Black Lobo,* the life story of an old Indian woman with a sixth sense.

SIDELIGHTS: Ride, Cowboy, Ride! was made into a movie and was published in Braille. Warren was competent in Spanish. *Avocational interests:* Golf and bridge.††

(Died October 18, 1968)

* * *

WASSERMAN, Earl R(eeves)   1913-1973

PERSONAL: Born November 11, 1913, in Washington, D.C.; son of Samuel (a businessman) and Jennie (Applestein) Wasserman; married Eleanor B. Franklin, October 15, 1937. *Education:* Johns Hopkins University, Ph.D., 1938. *Home:* 602 Providence Rd., Towson, Md. 21204. *Office:* Johns Hopkins University, Baltimore, Md. 21218.

CAREER: University of Illinois, Urbana, 1938-48, began as instructor, became associate professor of English; Johns Hopkins University, Baltimore, Md., associate professor, 1948-53, professor of English, 1953-69, Caroline Donovan Professor of English, 1969-73, chairman of department, 1959-64. Visiting summer professor at Columbia University, 1959, 1961, University of Washington, Seattle, 1962, University of Colorado, 1963, Harvard University, 1966, and other universities. *Military service:* U.S. Navy, 1944-46; became lieutenant junior grade. *Member:* International Association of University Professors of English, Modern Language Association of America, Phi Beta Kappa, Tudor and Stuart Club. *Awards, honors:* Guggenheim fellow, 1967-68.

WRITINGS: Elizabethan Poetry in the 18th Century, University of Illinois Press, 1947; *The Finer Tone: Keats's Major Poems,* Johns Hopkins Press, 1953; *The Subtler Language,* Johns Hopkins Press, 1959; *Pope's Epistle to Bathurst,* Johns Hopkins Press, 1960; *Shelley's Prometheus Unbound: A Critical Reading,* Johns Hopkins Press, 1965; (editor) *Aspects of the Eighteenth Century,* Johns Hopkins Press, 1965; *Shelley: A Critical Reading,* Johns Hopkins Press, 1971. Member of editorial board, *Modern Language Notes, College English, Studies in English Literature,* and *ELH, A Journal of English Literary History.*†

(Died March 3, 1973)

* * *

WATLAND, Charles D(unton)   1913-1972

PERSONAL: Born April 26, 1913, in Albert Lea, Minn.; son of Albert O. (a businessman) and Myrtie (Jorgensen) Watland. *Education:* Swarthmore College, B.A., 1934; University of Minnesota, M.A., 1937, Ph.D., 1953; Johns Hopkins University, graduate study, 1937-41. *Politics:* Democrat. *Religion:* Roman Catholic. *Home:* 2330 Terrace Way, Columbia, S.C. 29205. *Office:* University of South Carolina, Columbia, S.C. 29208.

CAREER: U.S. Embassy, Santiago, Chile, cryptographer, 1942-45; Goucher College, Baltimore, Md., instructor in modern languages, 1945-46; Union College, Schenectady, N.Y., assistant professor, 1946-56, associate professor of foreign languages, 1956-62; Marquette University, Milwaukee, Wis., associate professor of foreign languages, 1962-66; University of South Carolina, Columbia, professor of foreign languages, 1966-72. *Member:* American Association of Teachers of Spanish and Portuguese, Modern Language Association of America, American Association of University Professors, South Atlantic Modern Language Association, South Carolina Association of Spanish Teachers. *Awards, honors:* Order of Ruben Dario (Nicaragua), Certificate of Honor, 1957, and Knight Commander, 1967.

WRITINGS: Poet-Errant: A Biography of Ruben Dario, Philosophical Library, 1965; *Formacion literaria de Ruben Dario,* Imprenta Nacional (Managua), 1966. Contributor of articles and reviews to language journals. Editor, *Bulletin* of Wisconsin Association of Modern Foreign Language Teachers, 1963-65.

WORK IN PROGRESS: A novel; research on several Spanish-American poets.†

(Died December 26, 1972)

*   *   *

WATTERSON, Joseph   1900-1972

PERSONAL: Born August 7, 1900, in Cleveland, Ohio; son of William Ruggles (an architect) and Mary (Batchelor) Watterson; married Kathleen T. Howes, June 6, 1923 (deceased); married Gertrude Harris, December 30, 1948; children: (first marriage) David S., Stephen W., Joseph. *Education:* University of Pennsylvania, architecture student, 1924. *Office:* National Park Service, 801 19th St. N.W., Washington, D.C. 20006.

CAREER: Draftsman with Abram Garfield, Cleveland, Ohio, 1922-24, and Frederick L. Ackerman, New York City, 1924-27; designer with Schultze & Warren, New York City, 1927-30, and Reinhard & Hoffmeister, New York City, 1931; City College (now City College of the City University of New York), New York City, instructor in history and art appreciation, 1931-36; independent practice of architecture in Mineola, N.Y., 1936-56; American Institute of Architects, Washington, D.C., editor of *AIA Journal,* 1956-65; U.S. Department of the Interior, Washington, D.C., special assistant to Secretary of the Interior, 1965-68, chief of Division of Historic Architecture, National Park Service, 1968-71. Chief engineer, Dade Brothers, Inc., Mineola, 1941-45; U.S. member of Commission on Parks and Recreation, Union Internationale des Architectes, 1965-71; director, Society of Architectural Historians, 1967-70. Adjunct professor, Graduate School of Environmental Studies, University of Notre Dame, 1969-70; lecturer at University of Florida, Syracuse University, Iowa State University, and University of Texas.

MEMBER: American Institute of Architects (fellow), Association of Collegiate Schools of Architecture, National Trust for Historic Preservation, Society of Architectural Historians, Association for State and Local History, New York State Historical Association, Architectural League of New York, Delta Kappa Epsilon, Cosmos Club (Washington, D.C.). *Awards, honors:* Kemper Award, American Institute of Architects, 1965, for distinguished service to the Institute; National Endowment for the Arts fellow, 1969.

WRITINGS: Architecture–5000 Years of Building, Norton,

1950, revised edition published as *Architecture: A Short History,* 1968; (co-editor) *With Heritage So Rich,* Random House, 1967; (editor and contributor) *The Potomac* (report of Potomac Planning Task Force), U.S. Government Printing Office, 1967. Contributor to architectural journals and other periodicals.†

(Died May 30, 1972)

*   *   *

WATTS, Franklin (Mowry)   1904-

PERSONAL: Born June 11, 1904, in Sioux City, Iowa; son of John Franklin (a minister) and Amanda (Mowry) Watts; married Helen Hoke (an editor), May 25, 1945. *Education:* Boston University, B.B.A., 1925. *Office:* 200 Park Ave. S., Room 1705, New York, N.Y. 10003.

CAREER: Book buyer for George Innes Co. and L. S. Ayers & Co., 1925-32; sales manager for the New York City publishing firms, Vanguard Press, Inc., 1932-34, Julian Messner, Inc., 1934-50, and Heritage Press, 1936-50; Franklin Watts, Inc. (publishers specializing in children's books), New York City, founder and president, beginning 1942. A director, Grolier Enterprises, Inc.; former member; of advisory committee, U.S. Department of State international book projects. *Member:* Publishers Lunch Club.

WRITINGS: (Editor) *Voices of History,* F. Watts, 1941, 3rd edition, 1943; (editor) *The Complete Christmas Book,* F. Watts, 1958; *Let's Find Out About Christmas,* F. Watts, 1967; *Let's Find Out About Easter,* F. Watts, 1969. Editor, *Pocket Book Magazine,* 1954-56.

*   *   *

WATTS, Harold H(olliday)   1906-

PERSONAL: Born May 18, 1906, in Urbana, Ill.; son of Charles Holliday (a county superintendent of schools) and Blanche (Irwin) Watts; married Helen I. Sempill (member of staff of Krannert School, Purdue University); children: Felicia Margaret Watts Smith, Stephen Sempill. *Education:* University of Illinois, B.A., 1927, M.A., 1928, Ph.D., 1932. *Religion:* Episcopalian. *Home:* 2020 North River Rd., West Lafayette, Ind.

CAREER: Purdue University, Lafayette, Ind., beginning 1929, began as instructor, professor of English, 1946-72, professor emeritus, 1972—. Visiting lecturer at University of Wisconsin, summer, 1963. *Member:* Phi Beta Kappa.

WRITINGS: The Modern Reader's Guide to the Bible, Harper, 1949, revised edition, 1959; *Ezra Pound and the Cantos,* Regnery, 1951; *Hound and Quarry,* Routledge & Kegan Paul, 1952; *The Modern Reader's Guide to Religions,* Barnes & Noble, 1969; *Aldous Huxley,* Twayne, 1969. Also author of "Witches Go Silently," a three-act play produced by Pasadena Playhouse, 1941. Co-editor, *First Stage, a Quarterly of New Plays.*

SIDELIGHTS: Watts resided in Europe during the year 1955, and spent 1965 in Italy. He has reading competence in French, Spanish, Italian.

*   *   *

WEBB, Holmes   1904-

PERSONAL: Born October 23, 1904, in Winfield, Tex.; son of Joseph Edgar (a farmer) and Mary Susan (Holmes) Webb; married Doris Johnson (an elementary school counselor), June 26, 1933; children: Susan (Mrs. Leonard Smith), Holmes, Jr., Sarah (Mrs. Larry Jones). *Education:* Texas

Technological College (now Texas Tech University), B.A., 1930, M.A., 1935; University of Southern California, Ed.D., 1953. *Religion:* United Methodist. *Home:* 3412 55th St., Lubbock, Tex. 79413. *Office:* Department of Secondary Education, Texas Tech University, Lubbock, Tex. 79409.

CAREER: Principal of rural schools in Texas, 1928-32, of elementary schools in Hamlin and Abilene, Tex., 1932-41, of junior high school in Abilene, Tex., 1941-45, of senior high schools in Gladewater and Tyler, Tex., 1945-60; Texas Tech University, Lubbock, professor of secondary education and chairman of department, 1960-70, professor emeritus, 1970—. Member of Accreditation Commission, Texas Education Agency, 1955-60. *Member:* National Education Association, National Association of Secondary School Principals (advisory council member, 1958-59, 1960), Texas Association of Secondary School Principals (president, 1960-61; executive committee member, 1961-62), Texas State Teachers Association (district president, 1949), Phi Delta Kappa.

WRITINGS: (With wife, Doris Johnson Webb) *School Administration: A Casebook,* International Textbook, 1967; (with Doris Johnson Webb) *The Secondary Teacher: A Casebook,* Intext, 1970. Contributor to education journals.

AVOCATIONAL INTERESTS: Local history.

* * *

WEBSTER, Cyril Charles 1909-

PERSONAL: Born December 28, 1909, in England; son of Ernest (an accountant) and Ethel (Cox) Webster; married Mary Wimhurst, March 8, 1947; children: Deborah Mary, Colin Phillip. *Education:* Wye College, London, B.Sc. (honors), 1931, Ph.D., 1949; Selwyn College, Cambridge, graduate study, 1931-32; Imperial College of Tropical Agriculture, Trinidad, A.I.C.T.A., 1933. *Religion:* Church of England. *Home:* 5 Shenden Way, Sevenoaks, Kent, England.

CAREER: Agricultural officer, Ibadan, Nigeria, 1936-38; senior agricultural officer, Limbe, Nyasaland, 1938-50; chief agricultural research officer, Nairobi, Kenya, 1950-55; deputy director of agriculture for Malaya, Kuala Lumpur, 1956; University of West Indies, St. Augustine, Trinidad, professor of agriculture, 1957-60; Rubber Research Institute, Kuala Lumpur, Malaya, director, 1961-65; Agricultural Research Council, London, England, scientific adviser, 1965-71, chief scientific officer, 1971-75. *Member:* Association of Applied Biologists, British Society of Soil Science, British Grassland Society. *Awards, honors:* Companion of St. Michael and St. George.

WRITINGS: Agriculture in the Tropics, Longmans, Green, 1965; *The Effects of Air Pollution on Plants and Soil,* Agricultural Research Council (London), 1967. Author of various papers on tropical agriculture.

* * *

WEBSTER, Frank V.
[Collective pseudonym]

WRITINGS—"Books for Boys" series; published by Cupples & Leon: *Jack the Runaway,* 1909; *The Newsboy Partners,* 1909; *Only a Farm Boy,* 1909; *Tom the Telephone Boy,* 1909; *Two Boy Gold Miners,* 1909; *The Young Firemen of Lakeville,* 1909; *The Young Treasure Hunter,* 1909; *Bob the Castaway,* 1909; *The Boy from the Ranch,* 1909; *The Boy Pilot of the Lakes,* 1909; *Boys of Bellwood School,* 1910; *Comrades of the Saddle,* 1910; *Airship Cindy,*

1911; *Ben Hardy's Flying Machine,* 1911; *Bob Chester's Grit,* 1911; *Darry, the Life Saver,* 1911; *Dick, the Bank Boy,* 1911; *High School Rivals,* 1911; *The Boys of the Wireless,* 1912; *Harry Watson's High School Days,* 1912.

SIDELIGHTS: See ADAMS, Harriet S., STRATEMEYER, Edward L., and SVENSON, Andrew E.†

* * *

WEIGERT, Edith 1894-

PERSONAL: Born February 6, 1894, in Duesseldorf, Germany; daughter of Eduard (a bank director) and Auguste (Pieper) Vowinckel; married Oscar Weigert (a labor expert), November 24, 1931 (died, 1968); children: Wolfgang. *Education:* University of Berlin, M.D., 1922; University of Maryland, M.D., 1938; psychiatric residency and psychoanalytic training in Berlin, Germany. *Religion:* Protestant. *Home and office:* 12 Oxford St., Chevy Chase, Md. 20015.

CAREER: Psychiatrist and psychoanalyst in private practice in Maryland, beginning 1938; Washington School of Psychiatry, Washington, D.C., chairman of faculty, beginning 1960. Training analyst, Washington Psychoanalytic Training Institute. *Member:* American Psychiatric Association (life member), American Psychoanalytic Association (life member).

WRITINGS: The Courage to Love: Selected Papers, Yale University Press, 1970.††

* * *

WEINBERG, Ian 1938-1969

PERSONAL: Born January 8, 1938, in London, England; married Mary Louise Meyer, January 26, 1964; children: Paul Henry Field, Laurie Lovell. *Education:* Exeter College, Oxford, B.A. (honors), 1961; Princeton University, M.A., 1963, Ph.D., 1964. *Office:* Department of Sociology, University of Toronto, Toronto, Ontario, Canada.

CAREER: University of Michigan, Ann Arbor, assistant professor of sociology, 1964-66; Russell Sage Foundation, New York, N.Y., research associate, 1966; University of Toronto, Toronto, Ontario, assistant professor, 1966-68, associate professor of sociology, 1968-69. *Military service:* Royal Air Force, National Service. *Member:* American Sociological Association. *Awards, honors:* Fulbright travel scholarship; Ogden Porter Jacobus fellowship at Princeton.

WRITINGS: The English Public Schools: The Sociology of Elite Education, Atherton, 1967; *Perspectives on Modernization,* University of Toronto Press, 1972. Associate editor, *American Sociologist.*

WORK IN PROGRESS: Medieval Philanthropy, supported by Russell Sage Foundation; *Sociology of Education,* for Atherton; *British Girls' Public Schools.*†

(Died, 1969)

* * *

WEISS, Miriam (Strauss) 1905-

PERSONAL: Born May 9, 1905, in Tupelo, Miss.; daughter of Henry (a salesman) and Nannie (Strauss) Weiss. *Education:* University of Wisconsin, B.A., 1926; Memphis State University, M.A., 1964. *Politics:* "Recalcitrant Democrat, Liberal." *Religion:* Jewish. *Home:* 2153 Washington, Apt. 15, Memphis, Tenn. 38104.

CAREER: Hebrew Watchman (Anglo-Jewish newspaper), Memphis, Tenn., editor, 1927-33; Sears, Roebuck & Co., Memphis, buyer in catalog order plant, 1933-65; Joint University Center, Memphis, instructor in English, 1965-73; teacher in religious school. Member, Brandeis University Women's National Committee. *Member:* B'nai B'rith Women (district past president), Friends of the Pink Palace Museum (educational chairman, 1970-71), Salon Circle (corresponding secretary, 1973-77).

WRITINGS: A Lively Corpse: Religion in Utopia, A. S. Barnes, 1969. Contributor to *Mississippi Quarterly* and *Journal of Mississippi History.*

SIDELIGHTS: Miriam Weiss worked as a camp store clerk at Two Medicine in Glacier National Park in 1967, "a thing I was not able to do as a young woman but enjoyed thoroughly as a not-so-young one." She has traveled to Japan, Hong Kong, and the Philippines by freighter, and made extensive trips to Greece, Israel, Turkey, and the Galapagos Islands.

AVOCATIONAL INTERESTS: Collecting books on literary subjects, Judaica, archaeology, and history. Miriam Weiss has a special interest in cats, having one of her own, as well as a collection of more than 300 replicas in ceramic, glass, rope, fur, and brass.

*   *   *

WEITZ, Martin Mishli   1909-

PERSONAL: Surname is pronounced Waits; born August 7, 1909, in Denver, Colo.; son of Joseph (a bag dealer) and Rachel (Kauffman) Weitz; married Margaret Kalach, August 5, 1934; children: Mimi Weitz Levinson, Jonathan David. *Education:* Attended Colorado State College (now University of Northern Colorado), 1925-27; University of Cincinnati, A.B., 1932; Hebrew Union College-Jewish Institute of Religion, Cincinnati, Ohio, M.A. and Rabbi, 1934. *Politics:* Independent.

CAREER: Hillel Foundation at Northwestern University, Evanston, Ill., director, 1934-37; rabbi at Kenosha, Wis., 1937-43, Des Moines, Iowa, 1946-48, Hot Springs, Ark., 1948-51, Atlantic City, N.J., 1951-63, Syosset, N.Y., 1963-65; Lincoln University, Lincoln University, Pa., director of religious studies, 1967-74; Temple of Israel, Wilmington, N.C., rabbi, beginning 1974; University of North Carolina, Wilmington, resident lecturer, beginning 1974. Lecturer at Drake University, 1947-48, Rutgers University Extension, 1953-61, New York Institute of Technology, beginning 1965; historian, Hebrew Union College Alumni Association, 1953-65. Founder, and president of Atlantic County Board of Rabbis, 1953-57; organizer, and chairman of Atlantic City chapter of Brotherhood Council, National Conference of Christians and Jews, 1953-64; president of board, Atlantic Community College, 1954-63. *Military service:* U.S. Army Chaplains Corps, 1943-46; became captain; received commendation for interfaith work in Solomon Islands.

MEMBER: Central Conference of American Rabbis (executive board, 1953-55), World Union for Progressive Judaism (American board), Jewish War Veterans (national deputy chaplain), Alumni Association of Hebrew Union College (trustee, beginning 1964), International Platform Association, Rotary. *Awards, honors:* Citation, National Conference of Christians and Jews, 1948; D.D., Hebrew Union College (now Hebrew Union College-Jewish Institute of Religion), 1959; D.H.L., Colorado State College (now University of Northern Colorado), 1964; D.D., Lincoln University, 1967.

WRITINGS: Timberline: A Chapbook, Ralston Press, 1932; (editor and compiler) Abraham Cronbach, *Religion and Its Social Setting,* Social Press, 1933; *Jewish Commu-*

nity Studies (pupil's workbook and teacher's manual), Hebrew Union College Press, 1935; *Wind Whispers* (radio broadcasts), Connelly Press, 1951; (with Albert G. Minda) *Ten Commandments for Today,* Bloch Publishing, 1952; *Year Without Fear,* Bloch Publishing, 1955; *Life Without Strife,* Bloch Publishing, 1957; *Decalogues for Our Day,* Bloch Publishing, 1961; *Campus-on-a-Compass,* Lincoln University, 1968.

Author of booklets and pamphlets; contributor of about two hundred articles to religious journals and popular magazines. Editor of *Youth Leader,* 1932-37, *Mosaic,* 1936-38, *Annals of College of Jewish Studies,* 1938-42, *Hebrew Union College Alumni Notes,* beginning 1952; also editor of manuals for World Union for Progressive Judaism.

WORK IN PROGRESS: Itinerary or Pilgrimage, a three-volume work, with volume titles of *Journeys to Promised Lands, Journeys to Lost Horizons,* and *Journeys to Living Legends;* and *A Century of the Lincoln Legend.*

*   *   *

WELLBORN, Grace Pleasant   1906-19(?)

PERSONAL: Born May 10, 1906, in Chico, Tex.; daughter of Acie Melvin and Annie Lee (Cox) Pleasant; married Don A. Wellborn, September 17, 1933; children: William Don. *Education:* Hardin-Simmons University, B.A. (magna cum laude), 1928, M.A., 1933; Texas Technological College (now Texas Tech University), graduate study, 1952-53. *Politics:* Democrat. *Religion:* Baptist. *Home:* 2323 10th St., Lubbock, Tex. *Office:* Texas Tech University, Lubbock, Tex.

CAREER: Hardin-Simmons University, Abilene, Tex., manager of book store, 1929-32; Howard Payne College, Brownwood, Tex., registrar, 1934-36, instructor in English and speech, 1937-44, head of speech department, 1945-46; Texas Tech University, Lubbock, instructor, 1947-58, became assistant professor of English, 1959. *Member:* Modern Language Association of America, American Folklore Society, Western Literature Association, South Central Modern Language Association, Rocky Mountain Modern Language Association, American Association of University Women, American Association of University Professors, Texas Folklore Association, Alpha Chi, Lubbock Women's Club, Twentieth Century Study Club. *Awards, honors:* Four research grants to study Hawthorne and Willa Cather.

WRITINGS: (With L. B. Green and Kline Nall) *A Manual for Technical Writing,* Rogers Co., 1957; (with Ruth Russell) *Essential Tools for the Technical Writer,* Tinsley Publishing, 1959; (with L. B. Green and K. Nall) *Technical Writing,* Houghton, 1961; *Trees of the Bible,* Baker, 1966. Contributor to *Texas Folklore, Southern Folklore Quarterly, Delphian, Forum,* and other journals. Abstractor, *Abstracts of English Studies;* reviewer, *Western Folklore.*

WORK IN PROGRESS: Plant Lore; other writing on folklore, Hawthorne, and Cather.

AVOCATIONAL INTERESTS: Playing piano and pipe organ, oil painting, writing poetry.†

(Deceased)

*   *   *

WELLINGTON, John H.   1892-

PERSONAL: Born in 1892, in Truro, Cornwall; married Jessica Whincup, 1918. *Education:* Christ's College, Cambridge, B.A., 1921. *Home:* 7 Cotswold Dr., Saxonwold, Johannesburg, South Africa.

CAREER: University of the Witwatersrand, Johannesburg, South Africa, professor of geography, 1925-57, professor emeritus, 1957—. *Military service:* British Army, King's Own Yorkshire Light Infantry, 1915-19; served in France during World War I; received Military Cross and bar. *Member:* Royal Geographical Society (honorary fellow). *Awards, honors:* Sc.D., Cambridge University, 1958.

WRITINGS: Southern Africa: A Geographical Study, two volumes, Cambridge University Press, 1955; *South West Africa and Its Human Issues,* Oxford University Press, 1967. Editor, *South African Geographical Journal,* 1922-48.

WORK IN PROGRESS: A revised edition of *Southern Africa: A Geographical Study.*

*　*　*

WELTY, Susan F. 1905-
(S. F. Welty)

PERSONAL: Born January 20, 1905, in Fairfield, Iowa; daughter of Charles Jacobs and Hermine (Stichter) Fulton; married Joel Carl Welty (a professor), September 2, 1930. *Education:* Parsons College, B.S., 1926; University of Utah, M.A., 1927; summer graduate study at University of Southern California, 1929, and University of Iowa, 1930. *Politics:* Independent. *Religion:* Congregational (United Church of Christ). *Home:* R.R. 1, Beloit, Wis. 53511. *Agent:* McIntosh & Otis, Inc., 475 Fifth Ave., New York, N.Y. 10017.

CAREER: High school speech teacher and drama coach in Oklahoma City, Okla., 1928; Parsons College, Fairfield, Iowa, speech instructor and drama coach, 1928-34; Washington State College (now University), Pullman, instructor in English, 1946-47; instructor in parliamentary procedure at Community College, Beloit, Wis., 1955-56, and Beloit Vocational School, 1961; free-lance writer. *Member:* Wisconsin Academy of Sciences, Arts, and Letters, Beloit Federation of Women (past president), Beloit College Faculty Women's Club, Ned Hollister Bird Club, Spring Brook Watershed Association.

WRITINGS: (Under name S. F. Welty) *Knight's Ransom,* Wilcox & Follett, 1951; *Look Up and Hope: The Life of Maud Ballington Booth,* Thomas Nelson, 1961; *Birds with Bracelets: The Story of Bird-Banding,* Prentice-Hall, 1965; *A Fair Field, in Jefferson County, State of Iowa,* Harlo Press, 1968, Bicentennial edition, 1975.

Plays: *The Light Shines,* David C. Cook, 1938; *St. Francis Spreads Christmas Joy,* Row, Peterson & Co., 1944; *A Candle for the Christmas Guest,* Row, Peterson & Co., 1945.

Contributor to *Reader's Digest, Magazine Digest, Nature, Christian Science Monitor, American Forests, Car Life, Woman's Press, American Swedish Monthly, This Month, Wisconsin Academy Review,* and to religious journals.

*　*　*

WEST, Edward Nason 1909-

PERSONAL: Born November 5, 1909, in Boston, Mass.; son of Edward Nason and Dora da Vincento Bellizia (Willey) West. *Education:* Boston University, B.S., 1931; General Theological Seminary, S.T.B., 1934. *Office:* Cathedral Church of St. John the Divine, Cathedral Heights, New York, N.Y. 10025.

CAREER: Ordained deacon of Protestant Episcopal Church, 1934, priest, 1935; Trinity Church, Ossining, N.Y.,

curate, 1934-37, rector, 1937-41; Cathedral Church of St. John the Divine, New York, N.Y., sacrist, 1941-43, canon residentiary, beginning 1943, sub-dean, beginning 1967, deputy to general convention, beginning 1969. Episcopal Diocese of New York, head of Division of Adult Education, 1954-56; General Theological Seminary, lecturer in liturgics, 1957-60; New York University, lecturer in education, 1961-62; Union Theological Seminary, New York, N.Y., lecturer in Anglican doctrine and worship, beginning 1965; Purser Shortt Lecturer, University of Dublin, 1971. Designer of chapels for Royal Navy, American Merchant Marine, and U.S. Military Academy at West Point; chairman of Joint Commission on Church Architecture and Allied Arts (Episcopal). Select preacher, University of Dublin, 1952, 1971. Trustee of St. Vladimir's Orthodox Theological Seminary and Academy. *Military service:* U.S. Army Reserve (National Guard), chaplain, beginning 1947; became major.

MEMBER: Royal Society of Arts (fellow), Society of the Cincinnati, Protestant Episcopal Society for Promoting Religion and Learning in the State of New York (member of board), St. Andrews Society, St. George Society; Century Association, University Club, and Columbia University Faculty Club (all New York); Athenaeum (London). *Awards, honors:* D.D., Ripon College, 1946; fellow, Trinity College, London, 1948; Litt.D., Boston University, 1950; Th.D., Institut de Theologie Orthodoxe, Paris, 1953; S.T.D., General Theological Seminary, 1963. Decorations include: Officer of the Order of Orange-Nassau (Netherlands); Officer, Order of the British Empire; Chevalier, Legion of Honor (France); Silver Medal of the Red Cross of Japan; Medal of Merit of the Order of St. Gregory the Illuminator.

WRITINGS: Meditations on the Gospel of St. John, Harper, 1955; *Things I Always Thought I Knew,* Morehouse, 1957; *Byzantine Religious Art* (monograph), Cathedral of St. John the Divine, 1958; *A Glossary of Architectural and Liturgical Terms,* Seabury, 1958; (author of text) *The History of the Cross* (illustrations by Norman la Liberte), Macmillan, 1960; *God's Image in Us,* World Publishing, 1960; *The Far-Spent Night,* Seabury, 1960; (contributor) H. R. Landon, editor, *Living Thankfully,* Seabury, 1961; (contributor) K. B. Cally, editor, *Confirmation: History, Doctrine, and Practice,* Seabury, 1962. Contributor to *Encyclopedia Americana* and *Funk & Wagnall's Universal Standard Encyclopedia.*†

*　*　*

WEST, Herbert Faulkner 1898-1974

PERSONAL: Born January 6, 1898, in Jamaica Plain, Mass.; son of Arthur Richard (a merchant) and Annie Leila (Faulkner) West; married Carin af Robson (curator, Dartmouth Art Gallery), May 23, 1925; children: Herbert Faulkner, Jr. *Education:* Attended Pennsylvania State College (now University), 1917-19; Dartmouth College, A.B., 1922, M.A., 1924; studied in London and Berlin, 1924-25; Harvard University, M.A., 1933. *Politics:* Independent. *Religion:* Episcopalian. *Home:* 15 Buell St., Hanover, N.H. 03755.

CAREER: Dartmouth College, Hanover, N.H., instructor, 1925-28, assistant professor, 1928-37, professor of comparative literature, 1937-64, professor emeritus, 1964-74, chairman of department, 1953-57. Westholm Publications, Hanover, N.H., founder, 1955, and president. Artist, writer, and rare book dealer. *Military service:* U.S. Army, American Expeditionary Forces, 1918-19. *Member:* Friends of the Dartmouth Library (founder; director, 1938-64), Thoreau Society (past president), Book Club of California, Boston Society of Independent Artists, Delta Upsilon, Century Association (New York), American Club (London).

WRITINGS: The Dreamer of Devon: An Essay on Henry Williamson, Ulysses Press, 1932; *A Modern Conquistador: Robert Bontine Cunninghame Graham, His Life and Works,* Cranely & Day, 1932; *An Apology for Book Collecting, Being Random Reflections Together with an Account of London Bookmen in Their Native Haunts,* Arts Press, 1933; *Modern Book Collecting for the Impecunious Amateur,* Little, Brown, 1936; *Don Roberto,* Dartmouth Press, 1936; *The Nature Writers: A Guide to Richer Reading,* Stephen Daye Press, 1939; *The George Matthew Adams Vachel Lindsay Collection,* Dartmouth College Library, 1945; *The Mind on the Wing,* Coward, 1947; *W. H. Hudson's Reading,* privately printed, 1947; *A Stephen Crane Collection,* privately printed, 1948; *John Sloan's Last Summer,* Prairie Press, 1952; *Rebel Thought,* Beacon Press, 1953; *The Coronary Club,* Westholm, 1956; *What Price Teaching?,* Westholm, 1957; *Learning My ABC's,* Westholm, 1958; *For a Hudson Biographer,* Westholm, 1958; *Here's to Togetherness: A Modern Fable,* Westholm, 1961; *The Impecunious Amateur Looks Back,* Westholm, 1966; *Notes from a Bookman,* Westholm, 1967; *HMS Cephalonia,* Westholm, 1969; *Sunny Interval,* Westholm, 1972.

Editor: W. H. Hudson and R. B. Cunninghame Graham, *Two Letters on an Albatross,* Westholm, 1955; *Emerson at Dartmouth,* Westholm, 1956; Robert Watchorn, *Autobiography,* Robert Watchorn Charities, 1959; Graham, *Three Fugitive Pieces,* Westholm, 1960. Reviewer for *New York Times Sunday Book Magazine.*†

(Died November 9, 1974)

*   *   *

WESTERN, J(ohn) R(andle)   1928-1971

PERSONAL: Born October 28, 1928, in London, England. *Education:* St. John's College, Oxford, B.A. (first class honors in history), 1949; University of Edinburgh, Ph.D., 1953. *Politics:* Socialist. *Religion:* Sceptic. *Home:* Townscliffe Farm, Townscliffe Lane, Stockport, Cheshire, England. *Office:* History Department, University of Manchester, Manchester, England.

CAREER: University of Edinburgh, Edinburgh, Scotland, assistant in history, 1949-53; University of Manchester, Manchester, England, lecturer in history, 1954-71. *Member:* Society for Army Historical Research.

WRITINGS: The English Militia in the Eighteenth Century: The Story of a Political Issue, 1660-1802, Routledge & Kegan Paul, 1965; *The End of European Primacy, 1871-1945,* Humanities, 1965; (editor) *The New Cambridge Modern History,* Volume VIII, Cambridge University Press, 1965; *Monarchy and Revolution: The English State in the 1680's,* Rowman & Littlefield, 1972. Contributor of notes, reviews, and articles to historical journals.

WORK IN PROGRESS: A chapter on the military for *The Eighteenth Century,* edited by A. Cabbau, for Thames & Hudson; editing a diary of the Siege of Ladysmith, for Routledge & Kegan Paul; editing *Memoirs of General A. C. Jackson (1772-1827),* for Manchester University Press.

BIOGRAPHICAL/CRITICAL SOURCES: Michael R. D. Foot, editor, *War and Society: Historical Essays in Honour and Memory of J. R. Western, 1928-1971,* Elek, 1973.†

(Died, 1971)

WESTFALL, Don C.   1928-1973

PERSONAL: Born June 17, 1928, in Beaver Dam, Wis.; son of Harold Irvin (a barber) and Irma (Gallasch) Westfall; married Lois Smith (a writer and secretary), December 13, 1949; children: Marta K., Kirk M., Lanson J., John D., Julie Ann. *Education:* Carroll College, Waukesha, Wis., B.A., 1949; McCormick Theological Seminary, B.D., 1952. *Office:* 131 Adams N.E., Albuquerque, N.M.

CAREER: Minister of United Presbyterian Church in the U.S.A., 1952-73; field director of Board of Christian Education, Presbyterian Church, Albuquerque, N.M., 1962-65; director of education, U.S. Office of Economic Opportunity grant to H.E.L.P., Albuquerque, N.M., 1965-73. Member of Washington Conference on Civil Rights and Albuquerque Board on Crime Prevention. *Member:* Exchange Club (Albuquerque).

WRITINGS: (With Vic Jameson) *Bull at a New Gate,* Fortress, 1965; (editor) *Help Through Learning English,* Socorro, 1966; *Help Through Learning Woodworking,* Socorro, 1966. Contributor to religious journals.

WORK IN PROGRESS: With Vic Jameson, *Like a Herd of Turtles.*†

(Died August, 1973)

*   *   *

WESTPHAL, Clarence   1904-

PERSONAL: Born June 16, 1904, in Manson, Iowa; son of Otto Max (a farmer) and Susie (DeWall) Westphal; married Marion Hammond (a nurse), October 25, 1958; children: Kimberly and Sunia (orphaned Koreans adopted by the Westphals). *Education:* Westmar College, B.A., 1927; Boston University, M.A., 1928. *Politics:* Independent Republican. *Religion:* First Evangelical Free Church. *Home and office:* R.F.D. 1, Manson, Iowa 50563.

CAREER: During his early career traveled as a horseman with Ringling Bros. and Barnum and Bailey Circus; high school teacher in Manchester, N.H., 1929-36; American Red Cross field director in United States and European Theater, 1943-46; farmer in Manson, Iowa, beginning 1962. Lecturer, beginning 1960. *Military service:* U.S. Army, 1942; became sergeant. *Member:* American Legion, Farm Bureau, Gideons. *Awards, honors:* Ford Foundation grant, 1957, to do a series of radio programs in Africa on Africa's contribution to modern life.

WRITINGS: African Heritage, Denison, 1960; *Come Along to the Congo,* Denison, 1963; *Mooney the Pet Lion,* Denison, 1963; *Norman Vincent Peale, Christian Crusader,* Denison, 1964. Contributor of some twenty articles to magazines, and more than three hundred to newspapers.

WORK IN PROGRESS: Come Along to Korea.

SIDELIGHTS: Clarence Westphal has made four trips to Africa, two to South America, four to Europe, and one to Korea.

BIOGRAPHICAL/CRITICAL SOURCES: Marcus Bach, *Adventures in Faith,* Denison, 1959.

*   *   *

WHEELER, Charles (Thomas)   1892-1974

PERSONAL: Born March 14, 1892, in Codsall, Staffordshire, England; son of Sam Phipps (a journalist) and Anne Florence (Crowther) Wheeler; married Muriel Bourne (an artist), August 22, 1918; children: Neil Bourne, Carol Rosemary. *Education:* Educated in primary and secondary schools in Wolverhampton, England; graduated from Wolverhampton School of Art; Royal College of Art, London, diploma in art education, 1917. *Home:* Woodreed Farmhouse, Mayfield, Sussex, England. *Studio:* 22 Cathcart Rd., London S.W.10, England.

CAREER: Sculptor and painter. Exhibited at Royal Academy, 1914-74; executed sculptures on Winchester College War Memorial Cloisters, 1924, R.A.F. Memorial on Malta, Jellicoe Fountain in Trafalgar Square, Bishop Jacob Memorial Church at Ilford, Indian Memorial at Neuve Chapelle, India House, South Africa House, Rhodes House, Oxford, Haileybury College Chapel, Royal Empire Society, Merchant Navy Memorial, Tower Hill, sculpture in Queen's Park, Invercargill, New Zealand, and others; bust, "Infant Christ," purchased for nation under Chantrey Bequest, 1924, also bronze statue, "Spring," 1930, stone sculpture, "Aphrodite II," 1944, and "Earth and Water," 1952. Trustee, Tate Gallery, Milbank, England, 1942-49; member of Royal Fine Art Commission, 1946-52.

MEMBER: Royal Academy (associate, 1934; academician, 1940; president, 1956-66), Royal Society of British Sculptors (fellow; president, 1944-49), Royal Institute of British Architects (honorary fellow), Royal Engineers (honorary member), Royal Society of Painters in Water Colors (honorary member), Royal Institute of Painters in Water Colors (honorary member), Royal Scottish Academy (honorary member), Royal Academy of San Fernando, Madrid (honorary corresponding academician), Athenaeum, Arts, Chelsea Arts, and Savage Clubs. *Awards, honors:* Commander, Order of the British Empire, 1948; Gold Medal, Royal Society of British Sculptors, 1949, for distinguished services to sculpture; Knight Commander of the Royal Victorian Order, 1958; D.C.L., Oxford University, 1960; L.L.D., Trinity College, Dublin, 1961; D.Litt., Keele University, 1961; Gold Medal, U.S.A. National Academy of Design, 1963; Officier de la Legion d'Honneur; Knight Commander of the Crown of Siam; Commendatore Al Merito della Repubblica Italiana.

WRITINGS: High Relief: The Autobiography of Sir Charles Wheeler, Sculptor, Country Life (Southampton), 1968.

WORK IN PROGRESS: A book of poems.

SIDELIGHTS: In a review of *High Relief,* Christopher Wordsworth observed that Wheeler "writes evocatively about his Wolverhampton boyhood, the pleasures and minor privations of the artist's Chelsea 50 years back, Whistler's boatman, the Italian colony of Academy models: the storm over the Leonardo Cartoon provides the drama. If he has his private views about 'intellectual codswallop' he is less ready to howl it down than some of his generation."

BIOGRAPHICAL/CRITICAL SOURCES: Observer Review, July 7, 1968.†

(Died August 22, 1974)

* * *

WHEELER, Janet D.
[Collective pseudonym]

WRITINGS—"Billie Bradley" series; published by Cupples & Leon, except as noted: *Billie Bradley on Lighthouse Island; or, The Mystery of the Wreck,* G. Sully, 1920; . . . *and Her Classmates; or, The Secret of the Locked Tower,* G. Sully, 1921; . . . *at Twin Lakes; or, Jolly Schoolgirls Afloat and Ashore,* G. Sully, 1922; . . . *at Treasure Cove; or,*

The Old Sailor's Secret, 1928; . . . *at Sun Dial Lodge; or, School Chums Solving a Mystery,* 1929; . . . *and the School Mystery; or, The Girl from Oklahoma,* 1930; . . . *Winning the Trophy; or, Scoring against Big Odds,* 1932.

SIDELIGHTS: See ADAMS, Harriet S., STRATEMEYER, Edward L., and SVENSON, Andrew E.†

* * *

WHEELER, Margaret 1916-

PERSONAL: Born September 23, 1916, in England; daughter of William Edmund and Mary (Heydon) Collingridge; married Robert Galliano Norfolk (an officer in the Royal Navy), August 20, 1940 (deceased); married Sir Mortimer Wheeler (secretary of British Academy), October 6, 1945 (deceased); children: (first marriage) Elizabeth (deceased). *Education:* Attended St. Mary's Convent, Princethorpe, England, and University College, University of London. *Religion:* Roman Catholic. *Home:* Rose Hill Coach House, Erbistock, Wrexham, North Wales.

CAREER: Archaeologist. Worked on excavations in France, Cyprus, India, and Rome; member of Jericho and Jerusalem excavations under director of British School of Archaeology, Jerusalem; conductor of excavations in Rome for Academia Britannica of Rome. Lecturer under auspices of Foyles and Frosts agencies, London.

WRITINGS: Walls of Jericho, Chatto & Windus, 1955; *A Book of Archaeology,* Cassell, 1956; *A Second Book of Archaeology,* Cassell, 1957; (compiler) *History Was Buried: A Source Book of Archaeology,* Hart, 1967.

WORK IN PROGRESS: A book on a journey alone with eight Sherpas to the base camp of Everest, for Constable.

* * *

WHEELWRIGHT, Philip (Ellis) 1901-1970

PERSONAL: Born July 6, 1901, in Elizabeth, N.J.; son of Charles Edward (a stockbroker) and Jessamine (Meeker) Wheelwright; married Maude McDuffee, June 8, 1940; children: Linda Jean. *Education:* Princeton University, A.B., 1921, Ph.D., 1924. *Politics:* Liberal Democrat. *Religion:* "Hard to define." *Home:* 2663 Tallant Rd., Santa Barbara, Calif. 93105.

CAREER: Princeton University, Princeton, N.J., instructor in philosophy, 1924-25; New York University, New York, N.Y., instructor, 1925-27, assistant professor, 1927-28, associate professor, 1928-31, professor of philosophy, 1931-35, chairman of department, 1927-32; Dartmouth College, Hanover, N.H., professor of philosophy and humanities, 1937-53, chairman of humanities division, 1944-47; University of California, Riverside, professor of philosophy and humanities, 1953-66, professor emeritus, 1966-70. Lecturer in philosophy, Bread Loaf School, summers, 1930 and 1942; visiting professor, Pomona College, 1953-54; W. A. Neilson Research Professor, Smith College, 1958; Carleton College, Cowling Visiting Professor, 1959, and Winston Churchill Birthday Foundation visiting lecturer in English, 1960. Teacher of pre-navigational mathematics to Navy and Marine units.

MEMBER: American Philosophical Association, American Society for Aesthetics (president of Pacific division, 1966), English Institute, Metaphysical Society of America, Foundation for the Arts, Religion and Culture, Phi Beta Kappa. *Awards, honors:* LL.D., University of California, 1968.

WRITINGS: (With James Burnham) *Introduction to Philo-*

sophical Analysis, Holt, 1932; (editor) George Berkeley, *Treatise Concerning the Principles of Human Knowledge,* Doubleday, 1935; *A Critical Introduction to Ethics,* Odyssey, 1935, 3rd edition, revised, 1959; (editor) *Jeremy Bentham: An Introduction to the Principles of Morals and Legislation; James Mill: Essays on Government Jurisprudence, Liberty of the Press and Law of Nations; John Stuart Mill: On Liberty and Utilitarianism,* Doubleday, 1935; (translator and editor) Aristotle, *From Natural Science, Psychology,* [and] *The Nicomachean Ethics,* Doubleday, 1935; (contributor) Allen Tate, editor, *The Language of Poetry,* Princeton University Press, 1942; (editor and translator) *Aristotle: Selections,* Odyssey, 1951; *The Burning Fountain: A Study in the Language of Symbolism,* Indiana University Press, 1954, revised edition, 1968; *The Way of Philosophy,* Odyssey, 1954, revised edition, 1960; *Philosophy as the Art of Living* (Tully Cleon Knoles lectures), College of the Pacific, 1956; *Heraclitus,* Princeton University Press, 1959; *Metaphor and Reality,* Indiana University Press, 1962; *Valid Thinking,* Odyssey, 1962; (editor with Peter Fuss) *Five Philosophers,* Odyssey, 1963; (editor and translator) *Heraclitus,* Atheneum, 1964; (editor) *The Presocratics,* Odyssey, 1966. Co-editor, *Symposium* (Quarterly), 1930-33.

WORK IN PROGRESS: Revisions of certain published volumes.

BIOGRAPHICAL/CRITICAL SOURCES: The Hidden Harmony (volume of essays presented on his retirement from teaching), Odyssey, 1966.†

(Died January 6, 1970)

*   *   *

WHITCOMB, Hale C(hristy)   1907-

PERSONAL: Born August 16, 1907, in Pittsburgh, Pa.; son of Eugene Pitt (president of Union Natural Gas Corp.) and Mary Evelyn (Wise) Whitcomb; married Margaret Elizabeth Murphey (an artist and graphic designer), 1934; children: Roger Pitt, Julia Hale (Mrs. George A. Evans, Jr.). *Education:* Yale University, B.A. (with honors), 1929; Northwestern University, M.B.A. (with honors), 1949; Georgia State University, D.B.A., 1965. *Politics:* Republican. *Religion:* Protestant.

CAREER: Fillmore Foundry, Inc., Buffalo, N.Y., assistant secretary-treasurer, 1929-34; Roger W. Somers & Co., Chicago, Ill., partner and manager of tax department, 1934-42; Owens-Corning Fiberglas Corp., Toledo, Ohio, member of controller's staff, 1942-44; management consultant, 1944-51, and certified public accountant, 1949-51; Murray Corporation of America, Home Appliance Division, Scranton, Pa., controller, 1951-52; management consultant and certified public accountant, 1952-58; Northwestern University, Evanston, Ill., research associate in accounting, 1958-59; University of Evansville, Evansville, Ind., associate professor of economics, 1959-62; Purdue University, Lafayette, Ind., associate professor of accounting, 1964-66; Mississippi State University, Starkville, professor of finance, 1966-69; Duquesne University, Pittsburgh, Pa., professor of accounting, analytic methods, and finance, 1969-72; University of Wisconsin—Whitewater, visiting professor of finance, 1972-75.

MEMBER: American Institute of Certified Public Accountants, American Accounting Association, American Economic Association, American Finance Association, Financial Executives Institute, Delta Mu Delta, Alpha Kappa Psi.

WRITINGS: (Contributor) *Quantitative Controls for Business,* Irwin, 1965; (with Perry P. Greiner) *The Dow Theory*

and the Seventy Year Forecast Record, Investors Intelligence, 1969.

WORK IN PROGRESS: The Dow Theory Revisited, an extension of *The Dow Theory and the Seventy Year Forecast Record.*†

*   *   *

WHITE, John Albert   1910-

PERSONAL: Born August 14, 1910, in Providence, R.I.; son of Benjamin L. and Mary (Worsley) White; married Dorothea Niehaus, July, 1934; married second wife, Dorothy Lewis, December 28, 1949; children: (first marriage) Geoffrey Allan; (second marriage) Kenneth Warren. *Education:* University of California, Los Angeles, B.A., 1933; Columbia University, M.A., 1940; Stanford University, Ph.D., 1947. *Politics:* Republican. *Religion:* Protestant. *Office:* History Department, 2550 Campus Rd., University of Hawaii, Honolulu, Hawaii 96822.

CAREER: University of Hawaii, Honolulu, associate professor, 1947-56, professor of history, beginning 1956. *Military service:* U.S. Naval Reserve, 1942-66; active duty, 1942-46. *Member:* American Historical Association, American Association for the Advancement of Slavic Studies, Association for Asian Studies, Retired Officers Association, Phi Kappa Phi. *Awards, honors:* Rockefeller Foundation research grants, Japan, 1946-47, 1954-55, England, 1963-64; Hoover Institution research grants, 1948, 1949.

WRITINGS: The Siberian Intervention, Princeton University Press, 1950, reprinted, Greenwood Press, 1976; (with Shunzo Sakamaki) *Asia,* Webster Publishing, 1953; *The Diplomacy of the Russo-Japanese War,* Princeton University Press, 1964. Contributor of articles and reviews to Slavic and historical journals.

WORK IN PROGRESS: The Anglo-Russo-Japanese Agreements of 1907.

*   *   *

WHITE, K(enneth) Owen   1902-

PERSONAL: Born August 29, 1902, in London, England; son of Malcolm (a physician) and Ethel (Budd) White; married Pearl Woodworth, July 14, 1926; children: Stanley Owen, Ruth (Mrs. Jack J. Marslender). *Education:* Bible Institute of Los Angeles, student, 1921-24; University of Louisville, B.A., 1933; Southern Baptist Theological Seminary, Th.M., 1932, Ph.D., 1934. *Politics:* Republican.

CAREER: Ordained Baptist minister, 1925; pastor in Atlanta, Ga., 1936-44, Washington, D.C., 1944-50, Little Rock, Ark., 1950-53, and Houston, Tex., 1953-65; Metropolitan Missions, Los Angeles, Calif., coordinator, beginning 1965. Conducted evangelistic and mission crusades in Hawaii, 1955, Japan, 1958, and British Isles, 1959. President, Baptist General Convention of Texas, 1962-64; Southern Baptist Convention, 1963-64; chairman of New Life Movement.

WRITINGS: Studies in Hosea, Convention Press, 1957; *The Book of Jeremiah,* Baker Book, 1961; *Messages on Stewardship,* Baker Book, 1963; *Nehemiah Speaks Again,* Broadman, 1964.†

*   *   *

WHITE, Ramy Allison
[Collective pseudonym]

WRITINGS—"Sunny Boy" series; published by Barse &

Hopkins: *Sunny Boy and His Games*, 1923; . . . *in the Far West*, 1924; . . . *on the Ocean*, 1925; . . . *with the Circus*, 1926; . . . *in the Snow*, 1928; . . . *at Willow Farm*, 1929; . . . *and His Cave*, 1930.

SIDELIGHTS: See ADAMS, Harriet S., STRATEMEYER, Edward L., and SVENSON, Andrew E.†

* * *

WHITEHALL, Harold 1905-
(Fritz)

PERSONAL: Born May 14, 1905, in Ramsbottom, Lancashire, England; son of Charles H. (a Civil Service administrator) and Beatrice E. (Fallows) Whitehall; married Nancy Moore (a teacher and poet), September 6, 1925. *Education:* Attended Nottingham University, 1923; University of London, B.A. (honors), 1927; Cambridge University, Diploma in Higher Education, 1928; University of Iowa, Ph.D., 1931. *Politics:* None. *Religion:* None. *Office:* % British Embassy, Monrovia, Liberia.

CAREER: University of Iowa, Iowa City, instructor in English, 1928-31; University of Michigan, Ann Arbor, assistant editor of *Middle English Dictionary*, 1931-39; Queens College (now of the City University of New York), Flushing, N.Y., assistant professor of English, 1940-41; University of Indiana, Bloomington, associate professor, 1941-49, professor of English, 1949-59, professor of English and linguistics, 1959-66, fellow of School of Letters, 1952-66; University of Ibadan, Ibadan, Nigeria, professor of English language, 1966-70, head of department, 1967-68. Visiting lecturer and research associate, University of Wisconsin, 1939-40; Kenyon College, special lecturer in analytical linguistics, 1944; summer professor at University of Texas, University of Notre Dame, and Ohio University. Editor-in-chief, Lexicographical Division, World Publishing Co., 1945-49. Broadcaster of educational and other programs on radio and television.

MEMBER: Modern Language Association of America (secretary and chairman, Middle English and aesthetic sections, 1941-50), American Dialect Society (life member). *Awards, honors:* Guggenheim fellow, 1939-40; Rockefeller fellow in criticism on staff of *Kenyon Review*, 1944.

WRITINGS: Middle English " u " and Related Sounds: Their Development in Early Modern British and American English, Linguistic Society of America, 1939; (author of preface) Bertha M. Watts, *Modern Grammar at Work*, Houghton, 1944; (contributor) *Gerard Manley Hopkins, by the Kenyon Critics*, New Directions, 1945; *Structural Essentials of English*, Harcourt, 1956; (contributor) Northrop Frye, editor, *The Sound of Poetry*, Columbia University Press, 1957; (contributor) Harold B. Allen, editor, *Applied Linguistics*, Appleton, 1958, 2nd edition, 1962.

Lexicographical works: (Contributor) *Webster's Imperial Dictionary of the English Language*, World Publishing, 1945, and subsequent editions, 1946, 1947, Standard Reference Works, 1961, 1962; (linguistic and etymological editor, and author of section on the English Language) *Webster's New World Dictionary of the American Language*, two-volume encyclopedia edition, World Publishing, 1951, collegiate editions, 1953-61.

Plays; first produced by community and university theaters, unless otherwise noted: "Life and Peter Waller" (one-act), 1935; (translator from the Middle English) "Towneley Second Shepherds' Play" (eight scenes), produced by Federal Theater in major U.S. cities, 1935; "Where the Tree Falleth" (folk-tragedy in three acts), 1936; "Master Peter Pathelin" (three-act), 1938; (translator from the French) Rostand, "Cyrano de Bergerac," published in *World's Great Plays*, edited by George Jean Nathan, World Publishing, 1944; "Times and Seasons" (dance drama in five scenes), 1950. Translator of other plays from Middle French, Old Irish, German, and Anglo-Saxon, for publication in *Folio Magazine*.

Radio and television scripts: "Cyrano de Bergerac" (radio version), included in *Creative Broadcasting*, Prentice-Hall, 1950; "Introduction to the Study of Language" (lecture series for credit), 1953; "Elementary Composition on Linguistic Principles" (lecture series for credit), 1954; "Language for Writing" (lecture series), 1954; "The Poet Speaks" (lectures, readings and commentary), 1957-59; "Poetry to Jazz" (readings accompanied by a chamber jazz quartet), 1960.

Other writings include three mimeographed textbooks; "The Language of the Shuttleworth Accounts," Parts 1-5, in *Philological Quarterly*, 1932, 1933; "The Orthography of John Bate of Sharon, Connecticut, 1700-1784," issued as a supplement to *American Speech*, Volume XXII, 1947. Contributor of articles, essays, and poems to other journals.

WORK IN PROGRESS: Etymological Dictionary of the English Language; Marriage Revisited, a novelle in verse; *Three Medieval Plays for Modern Actors;* enlargement and revision of *Structural Essentials of English;* translations from Chinese, Arabic, and French.†

* * *

WHITTEN, Jamie L(loyd) 1910-

PERSONAL: Born April 18, 1910, in Cascilla, Miss.; son of Alymer Guy (a merchant-farmer) and Nettie (Early) Whitten; married Rebecca Thompson, June 20, 1940; children: James Lloyd, Beverly Rebecca (Mrs. Walter McDonald Merritt III). *Education:* University of Mississippi, student in literary and law schools, 1927-32. *Politics:* "Mississippi Democrat." *Religion:* Presbyterian. *Home:* Charleston, Miss. 38921. *Office:* 2413 Rayburn Building, Washington, D.C. 20515.

CAREER: High school principal, 1931; elected to Mississippi State Legislature, 1931; admitted to Mississippi State Bar, 1933; practicing attorney, beginning 1933; district attorney (elected) for 17th District of Mississippi, 1933-41; member of U.S. Congress from 2nd Mississippi District, Washington, D.C., beginning 1941. *Member:* Phi Alpha Delta, Beta Theta Phi, Omicron Delta Kappa, Masons, Lions, Rotary International.

WRITINGS: That We May Live, Van Nostrand, 1966. Writer of House of Representatives annual report on U.S. agriculture, beginning 1949, and report on Russia, 1957.

* * *

WHITTON, John Boardman 1892-

PERSONAL: Born February 25, 1892, in Oakland, Calif.; son of Charles Francis and Helen (Blakeslee) Whitton; married Dangla de Laplane Laguerre, 1926 (deceased); married Lila Galitzine, 1959; children: (first marriage) Helene Andree (Mrs. John S. Baker). *Education:* University of California, A.B., 1916, J.D., 1920; University of Paris, Diplome en Droit Internationale, 1926. *Home:* 14 South Stanworth Dr., Princeton, N.J. 08540.

CAREER: Admitted to California Bar, 1919; private practice of law, San Francisco, Calif., 1920-23; Princeton University, Princeton, N.J., instructor, 1927-28, assistant professor, 1928-30, associate professor of international law, 1930-60, associate professor emeritus, 1960—. Director, Geneva Research Center, 1936-38; head of political science department, U.S. Army University, Biarritz, 1945-46. Lecturer at Institut des Hautes Etudes Internationales, Paris, 1927, 1932, 1934, Academy of International Law, The Hague, 1927, 1934, 1948, Graduate Institute of International Studies, Geneva, 1936-38, and U.S. Army Constabulary School, Germany, 1946. Member of Neutral Commission, France-Indian Plebiscite, 1950-54. Trustee, Princeton Foundation, beginning 1962, president, 1963-70. *Wartime service:* American Ambulance Field Service, American Red Cross, and French Army, 1917-19.

MEMBER: American Society of International Law, Alpha Delta Phi, Phi Delta Phi, Nassau Club. *Awards, honors:* Docteur honoris causa, University of Bordeaux, 1946; Knight, Legion of Honor (France).

WRITINGS: Doctrine de Monroe, Pedone (Paris), 1933; (editor with H. L. Childs) *Propaganda by Short Wave,* Princeton University Press, 1942, reprinted, Arno, 1972; (editor) *The Second Chance: America and the Peace,* Princeton University Press, 1944, reprinted, Books for Libraries, 1970; (editor) *Propaganda and the Cold War: A Princeton University Symposium,* Public Affairs, 1963; (with Arthur Larson) *Propaganda Towards Disarmament in the War of Words,* Oceana, 1964; (translator) Paul Mantoux, *Proceedings of the Council of Four (March 24—April 18, 1919),* Librairie E. Droz, 1964. Member of editorial board, *American Journal of International Law.*†

*   *   *

WIGHT, (Robert James) Martin 1913-1972

PERSONAL: Born November 26, 1913, in Brighton, England; son of Edward (a physician) and Margaretta (Scott) Wight; married Gabriele Ritzen, December 23, 1952; children: Susannah, Katharine, Jeremy, Daniel, Barbara, Felicity. *Education:* Hertford College, Oxford, B.A. (first class honors in history), 1935. *Politics:* Grotian. *Religion:* Church of England. *Home:* Harwarton, Speldhurst, near Tunbridge Wells, Kent, England. *Office:* Department of History, University of Sussex, Falmer, Brighton, Sussex BN1 9QN, England.

CAREER: Royal Institute of International Affairs, London, England, research staff, 1936-38; Haileybury College, Hertfordshire, England, assistant master, 1938-41; Oxford University, Nuffield College, Oxford, England, research staff, 1941-46; *Observer,* London, England, diplomatic and United Nations correspondent, 1946-47; Royal Institute of International Affairs, research staff, 1946-49; University of London, London School of Economics and Political Science, London, reader in international relations, 1949-61; University of Sussex, Brighton, England, professor of history, beginning 1961, dean of School of European Studies, 1961-69. Visiting professor, University of Chicago, 1956-57. Member of academic planning board, University of Kent.

MEMBER: Royal Institute of International Affairs (councilor, beginning, 1952), Institute for Strategic Studies, David Davies Memorial Institute, Historical Association, Hellenic Society, Roman Society, Classical Association, Society for Nautical Research, Virgil Society.

WRITINGS: Power Politics, Royal Institute of International Affairs, 1946; *The Development of the Legislative Council, 1606-1945,* Faber, 1946; *The Gold Coast Legislative Council,* Faber, 1947; (with W. A. Lewis, M. Scott, and

C. Legum) *Attitude to Africa,* Penguin, 1951; (editor) H. J. Laski, *An Introduction to Politics,* revised edition, Allen & Unwin, 1951; *British Colonial Constitutions 1947,* Clarendon Press, 1952; (contributor) Arnold Joseph Toynbee, editor, *The World in March 1939,* Oxford University Press, for Royal Institute of International Affairs, 1952; (editor with H. Butterfield) *Diplomatic Investigations,* Harvard University Press, 1966.

AVOCATIONAL INTERESTS: Gardening, travel.

WORK IN PROGRESS: The Balance of Power.†

(Died, 1972)

*   *   *

WIGNER, Eugene Paul 1902-

PERSONAL: Born November 17, 1902, in Budapest, Hungary; came to United States in 1930, naturalized in 1937; son of Anthony and Elizabeth (Einhorn) Wigner; married Amelia Z. Frank, 1936 (died, 1937); married Mary Wheeler, June 4, 1941; children: (second marriage) David Wheeler, Martha Faith. *Education:* Technische Hochscule, Berlin, Germany, Dr.Ing., 1925. *Home:* 8 Ober Rd., Princeton, N.J. 08540.

CAREER: Princeton University, Princeton, N.J., lecturer, 1930, part-time professor of mathematical physics, 1931-37; University of Wisconsin—Madison, professor of physics, 1937-38; Princeton University, Thomas D. Jones Professor of Mathematical Physics, 1938-71, professor emeritus, 1971—; visiting lecturer at numerous universities, beginning 1971. During World War II was on staff of Metallurgical Laboratory, University of Chicago, and director of research and development at Clinton Laboratories; member of general advisory committee, U.S. Atomic Energy Commission, 1952-57, 1959-64; director of Civil Defense Research Project, Oak Ridge, 1964-65. Member of visiting committee, National Bureau of Standards, 1948-52, of mathematical section, National Research Council, 1952-54, and of physics panel, National Science Foundation, 1953-64.

MEMBER: American Physical Society (president, 1956), American Nuclear Society, American Mathematical Society, American Philosophical Society, National Academy of Sciences, American Association for the Advancement of Science, American Academy of Arts and Sciences, Royal Netherlands Academy of Science and Letters, Austrian Academy of Sciences, Royal Society (London), Akademie der Wissenschaften in Goettengen, Franklin Society, Sigma Xi, and other scientific groups.

AWARDS, HONORS: U.S. Government medal for merit, 1946; Franklin Medal, Franklin Institute, 1950; Enrico Fermi Award, U.S. Atomic Energy Commission, 1958; Atoms for Peace Award, Ford Motor Co. Fund, 1960; Max Planck Medal, German Physical Society, 1961; Nobel Prize for Physics, 1963; George Washington Award, American Hungarian Studies Foundation, 1964; Semmel Weiss Medal, American Hungarian Medical Association, 1965; National Medal of Science, 1969. D.Sc. from University of Wisconsin, 1949, Washington University (St. Louis), 1950, Case Institute of Technology (now Case Western Reserve University), 1955, University of Chicago, 1957, Colby College, 1959, University of Pennsylvania, 1961, Thiel College, 1964, University of Notre Dame, 1965, Technical University of Berlin and Swarthmore College, both 1966, University of Louvain and University of Liege, both 1967, University of Illinois, 1968, Seton Hall University and Catholic University, both 1969, Rockefeller University, 1970, and Technion

(Haifa), 1973; Dr.Laws, University of Alberta, 1957; D.H.L., Yeshiva University, 1963.

WRITINGS: Gruppentheorie und ihre Anwendung auf die Quantenmechanik der Atomspektren, Friedrich Vieweg (Brunswick), 1931, translation by J. J. Griffin published as *Group Theory,* Academic Press, 1959; (with L. Eisenbud) *Nuclear Structure,* Princeton University Press, 1958; (with Alvin M. Weinberg) *The Physical Theory of Neutron Chain Reactors,* University of Chicago Press, 1958; (contributor) Charles E. Porter, editor, *Statistical Theories of Spectra: Fluctuations,* Academic Press, 1965; (contributor) L. C. Biedenharn and H. Van Dam, editors, *Quantum Theory of Angular Momentum,* Academic Press, 1965; *Symmetries and Reflections,* Indiana University Press, 1967; *Who Speaks for Civil Defense?,* Scribner, 1968; (contributor) Ernest M. Loebl, editor, *Group Theory and Its Applications,* Academic Press, 1968; (editor and contributor) *Survival and the Bomb: Methods of Civil Defense,* Indiana University Press, 1969. Contributor to symposia and scientific journals.

* * *

WILDER, Robert (Ingersoll) 1901-1974

PERSONAL: Born January 25, 1901, in Richmond, Va.; son of William Wallace and Estrella (Mendoza) Wilder; married Sally Peters, August 22, 1927; children: Robert Wallace. *Education:* Attended John B. Stetson University, 1918, and Columbia University, 1920-22. *Home:* 2031 Paseo Dorado, La Jolla, Calif. *Office:* G. P. Putnam's Sons, 200 Madison Ave., New York, N.Y. 10016. *Agent:* Ashley-Steiner-Famous Artists Inc., 9255 Sunset Blvd., Los Angeles, Calif.

CAREER: International Press Service, reporter, 1922-26; Radio Station WOR, New York, N.Y., publicity director, 1927-35; *New York Sun,* New York, N.Y., columnist "On the Sun Deck," and foreign correspondent, 1935-45; associated with Metro-Goldwyn-Mayer, Paramount, and Warner Brothers Studios, 1944-48; *Miami Herald,* Miami, Fla., correspondent in Mexico, 1950-55; author. *Military service:* U.S. Army, 1917-18. *Member:* Theta Xi.

*WRITINGS—*All published by Putnam, except as indicated: *God Has a Long Face,* 1940; *Out of the Blue,* 1942; *Flamingo Road,* 1943; *Written on the Wind,* 1945; *Mr. G. Strings Along,* 1946; *Bright Feather,* 1948; *Wait for Tomorrow,* 1950, new edition, Bantam, 1968; *And Ride a Tiger,* 1951; *Autumn Thunder,* 1953; *The Wine of Youth,* 1954; *Walk with Evil,* 1956; *The Sun Is My Shadow,* 1958; *A Handful of Men,* 1959; *Plough the Sea,* 1961; *Wind From the Carolinas,* 1964; *Fruit of the Poppy,* 1965; *The Sea and the Stars,* 1967; *An Affair of Honor,* 1969; *The Sound of Drums and Cymbals,* 1974.

Also author of *Thread for Ariadne,* 1953; *Redemption Cay,* 1955; *Shadow in Copper,* 1956; *A Handful of Men,* 1960.

Plays; produced in New York: "Sweet Chariot," 1930; "Stardust," 1943; "Flamingo Road," 1950. Screenplays: "Flamingo Road," starring Joan Crawford; "The Big Country," starring Gregory Peck and Jean Simmons. Contributor of short stories to *Smart Set, New Yorker,* and other magazines.

SIDELIGHTS: Written on the Wind was made into a motion picture with the same title, Universal, 1956, and the motion picture "Sol Madrid," Metro-Goldwyn-Mayer, 1968, was based on Wilder's novel *Fruit of the Poppy.*†

(Died August 22, 1974)

WILKINS, Mesannie 1891-

PERSONAL: Born December 13, 1891, in Minot, Me.; daughter of George Wallace Stuart (a laborer) and Sarah Libby (Stuart) Wilkins. *Education:* Attended a district ungraded school in Grafton, N.H. *Politics:* "Best man for the job." *Religion:* "Any sincere." *Home:* 33 First St., Bangor, Me. 04401.

CAREER: Spent most of her life on a Maine farm; in earlier years peddled fish, cut lumber, drove oxen, and was an auto mechanic ("had a permit to wear pants before all women did"); later worked in a shoe shop and raised cucumbers for a pickle factory; left the farm shortly before her sixty-third birthday to ride horseback to California, traveling almost seven thousand miles on the seventeen-month journey.

WRITINGS: (With Mina Titus Sawyer) *Last of the Saddle Tramps* (autobiography), Prentice-Hall, 1967.

WORK IN PROGRESS: Another book of memoirs, with Mina Titus Sawyer.

SIDELIGHTS: About the collaboration that produced *Last of the Saddle Tramps,* Mesannie Wilkins explains: "I write the facts; Mrs. Sawyer brings or rather shortens it down to reasonable size. . . . [I] have the notes for five books, but at my age who can tell."††

* * *

WILL, Lawrence Elmer 1893-

PERSONAL: Born January 31, 1893; son of Thomas Elmer (an educator and Everglades developer) and Marie (Rogers) Will; married Anne F. Williams, December 23, 1928; children: Barbara Anne (Mrs. Albert C. Stevens), Charles R. *Education:* Attended high school in Washington, D.C. *Office:* 200 South Main St., Belle Glade, Fla. 33430.

CAREER: Went to Florida Everglades when reclamation was starting, helped found Okeelanta (the first settlement in the sawgrass), farmed, ran freight, passenger, and dredge boats, and hunted and trapped; founder, 1928, and still president of Pioneer Motor Sales Co. (auto parts), the oldest business firm in Belle Glade, Fla. One-time member of Belle Glade City Council; Belle Glade fire chief, 1931-61. *Military service:* U.S. Army, Infantry, 1918; became second lieutenant.

*WRITINGS—*All published by Great Outdoors Publishing: *Okeechobee Hurricane and the Hoover Dike,* 1961; *Cracker History of Okeechobee,* 1964; *Okeechobee Boats and Skippers,* 1965; *Okeechobee Catfishing,* 1965; *A Dredgeman of Cape Sable,* 1967; *Swamp to Sugar Bowl: Pioneer Days in Belle Glade,* 1968. Author of some forty articles in historical series, "Custard Apple Days," *Belle Glade Herald,* 1957-58.†

* * *

WILLEY, R(oy) DeVerl 1910-197(?)

PERSONAL: Born in 1910, in Byron, Wyo.; son of Roy and Clarissa (Robison) Willey; married Helen Ann Young, June 4, 1944; children: Robert, Kim, Sara Jennis, Quentin, Dorothy, Blair. *Education:* University of Wyoming, B.A., 1929; Brigham Young University, M.A., 1936; Stanford University, Ph.D., 1942. *Religion:* Church of Jesus Christ of Latter-day Saints (Mormon).

CAREER: San Jose State College (now University), San Jose, Calif., instructor in elementary curriculum, 1938-42; University of Utah, Salt Lake City, member of faculty in psychology, 1947-53, chairman of department of educational psychology, 1953-54; University of Nevada, Reno, professor of elementary education, beginning, 1955, chairman of department of elementary education, 1955-65, acting dean, College of Education, 1965-67. *Military service:* U.S. Naval Reserve; was retired with the rank of lieutenant commander. *Member:* International Committee for Early Childhood Education (member of board of governors), Association for Childhood Education International, International Reading Association, National Education Association, American Association of University Professors, Phi Kappa Phi, Phi Delta Kappa, Alpha Phi Alpha.

WRITINGS: (With Young) *Radio in Elementary Education,* Heath, 1948; *Teaching Arithmetic with the Tachistoscope,* Keystone View Co., 1949; *Guidance in Elementary Education,* Harper, 1952, revised edition, 1963; (with Andrew) *Modern Methods and Techniques in Guidance,* Harper, 1955; *Organization and Administration of the Guidance Program,* Harper, 1958; *Group Guidance,* Harper, 1958; (with Melvin Dunn) *The Role of the Teacher in the Guidance Program,* McKnight & McKnight, 1964; (with Kathleen Barnette Waite) *The Mentally Retarded Child: Identification, Acceptance, and Curriculum,* C. C Thomas, 1964; *Understanding Children: A Guide to their Rearing,* Deseret, 1965; *Child-Centered Reading,* Pitman, 1970. Contributor to yearbooks, to the proceedings of learned associations, and to educational journals.

WORK IN PROGRESS: The Elementary School Curriculum; and *Curriculum for the Mentally Retarded.*†

(Deceased)

*   *   *

WILLIAMS, Clyde C.   1881-1974
(Slim Williams)

PERSONAL: Born January 14, 1881, in Fresno, Calif.; son of Charles (a rancher) and Alverta (Bigelow) Williams; married Gladys Pennington (manager of a lecture agency). *Education:* Attended public grade schools in California. *Residence:* Chicago, Ill.

CAREER: Spent a quarter century in Alaska, working as trader, trapper, prospector, farmer, and mail carrier; lecturer on Alaskan experiences, 1934-59. *Member:* Adventurers Club of Chicago.

WRITINGS—Under name Slim Williams: (With Elizabeth C. Foster) *The Friend of the Singing One* (juvenile), Atheneum, 1967; (with E. C. Foster) *The Long Hungry Night* (juvenile), Atheneum, 1973.

BIOGRAPHICAL/CRITICAL SOURCES: Richard Morenus, *Alaska Sourdough: The Story of Slim Williams,* Rand McNally, 1956; *Chicago Sun-Times,* May 2, 1973.†

(Died October 9, 1974)

*   *   *

WILLIAMS, Griffith Wynne   1897-1972

PERSONAL: Born February 12, 1897, in Clynderwen, Wales; came to United States in 1923; son of David and Anne (Morris) Williams; married Hanna Stiglitz, April 29, 1944; children: Gresham Verne, Mona Rae (Mrs. Donald O. Brown). *Education:* Attended Regents Park College, London, 1920-23; Hartford Seminary Foundation, B.Pd., 1924, M.Pd., 1925; University of Wisconsin (now University of Wisconsin—Madison), Ph.D., 1929. *Politics:* Independent. *Religion:* Unitarian Universalist. *Home:* 1428 South Ave., Apt. 3F, Plainfield, N.J. 07062.

CAREER: Atlanta University, Atlanta, Ga., instructor in psychology, 1925-27; Yale University, New Haven, Conn., research associate, 1929-30; assistant professor of psychology at University of Illinois, Urbana, 1930-31, and University of Rochester, Rochester, N.Y., 1931-37; Rutgers University, New Brunswick, N.J., assistant professor, 1937-41, associate professor, 1941-59, professor of psychology, 1959-60, professor emeritus, 1960-72. Diplomate, American Board of Examiners in Professional Psychology. *Military service:* British Army, Medical Corps, 1916-20. *Member:* American Psychological Association, Society for Clinical and Experimental Hypnosis, Eastern Psychological Association. *Awards, honors:* Society for Clinical and Experimental Hypnosis, award for outstanding contribution to scientific hypnosis, 1958, Bernard G. Raginsky Award, 1963, for pioneering in the field of hypnosis.

WRITINGS: Suggestibility in the Normal and Hypnotic States (monograph), Archives of Psychology, 1930; *Psychology: A First Course,* edited by Claude E. Buxton, Harcourt, 1960; "Hypnosis in Perspective" (recorded lecture), Sound Seminars, 1968. Contributor to professional journals. Advisory editor, *International Journal of Clinical and Experimental Hypnosis,* beginning 1954.

AVOCATIONAL INTERESTS: Chinese and Japanese art.†

(Died April 22, 1972)

*   *   *

WILLIAMS, Hugh (Anthony Glanmor)   1904-1969

PERSONAL: Born March 6, 1904, in Sussex, England; son of Hugh D. A. and Hilda (Lewis) Williams; married Gwynne Whitby, 1925 (divorced, 1940); married Margaret Vyner (a playwright and actress), June 21, 1940; children: (first marriage) two daughters; (second marriage) Hugo, Simon, Pollyanna. *Education:* Educated in England and Switzerland; studied for stage at Royal Academy of Dramatic Art. *Politics:* "Through disgust, none (English)." *Religion:* Church of England. *Home:* Albufeira, Algarve, Portugal. *Agent:* Margery Vosper Ltd., 26 Charing Cross Rd., Suite 8, London WC2H 0DG, England.

CAREER: Stage and screen actor; playwright, in collaboration with his wife, beginning 1956. Made stage debut in England in "The Charm School," 1921, and film debut in Hollywood in "Charlie's Aunt," 1930; member of Liverpool Repertory Theatre company, 1923-26; toured in Australia, 1927-29, then played Captain Stanhope in "Journey's End" in United States and Canada, 1929-30; since then has appeared on London stage in more than fifty productions, including "The Matriarch," 1929, "Hawk Island," 1931, "Grand Hotel," 1932, "While Parents Sleep," 1932, "Pride and Prejudice," 1937, "Dear Octopus," 1939, "The Cocktail Party," 1951, "The Seagull," 1956, "Plaintiff in a Pretty Hat," 1957, "The Happy Men," 1957, "The Grass Is Greener," 1958, "The Irregular Verb to Love," 1961, "Past Imperfect," 1964, "The Cherry Orchard," 1966, "Getting Married," 1967, "Let's All Go Down to the Strand," 1967, and "His, Hers, and Theirs," 1969; had role of "Julian" in "The Green Bay Tree" at Martin Beck Theatre, New York, 1935, subsequently appearing on Broadway in "Old Music," 1938, and a revival of "The Green Bay Tree," 1950; also appeared in a number of films, 1930-54, including "Wuthering Heights," "One of Our Aircraft Is Missing," "Charley's Aunt," "The Holly and the Ivy," "Outcast Lady," "An Ideal Husband," and "Take My Life." *Military service:* British Army, 1939-45; served in North Africa, Italy,

Normandy, and northwest Europe; became captain. *Member:* Bath Club (London).

WRITINGS—Plays; all written with wife, Margaret Williams; all first produced in England: *Plaintiff in a Pretty Hat* (two-act comedy; produced in 1956), Evans Brothers, 1957; *The Happy Man* (two-act comedy; first produced in 1957 as "Father's Match"), Evans Brothers, 1958; *The Grass Is Greener* (two-act comedy; produced in 1958), Evans Brothers, 1960, Samuel French, 1966; *Double Yolk* (contains two plays, "By Accident" and "With Intent," both produced in 1959), Evans Brothers, 1960; *The Irregular Verb to Love* (first produced in 1959; produced on Broadway, 1963), Evans Brothers, 1962, Samuel French, 1966; *Past Imperfect* (two-act comedy), Samuel French, 1965; *Let's All Go Down to the Strand* (produced in 1967), Evans Brothers, 1969; *The Flip Side* (two-act comedy; produced on Broadway at Booth Theatre, October 10, 1968), Evans Brothers, 1969; *His, Hers, and Theirs* (comedy; produced on the West End at Apollo Theatre, 1969), Evans Brothers, 1972; (author of libretto with M. Williams and Ray Cooney) *Charlie Girl,* music and lyrics by David Heneker, Chappell, 1972. Also author with M. Williams of a screenplay of "The Flip Side" for Twentieth Century-Fox.

SIDELIGHTS: Hugh Williams told *CA:* "Have a large family and like to live well and travel extensively. Have therefore always been a commercially minded actor and commercial playwright—which mostly I do not regret. Have a working knowledge of American; also Casino French." Williams appeared in British productions of all of his own plays. *The Grass Is Greener* was filmed by Universal Pictures, 1960.

BIOGRAPHICAL/CRITICAL SOURCES: New York Times, October 11, 1968, December 8, 1969; *Variety,* December 10, 1969; *Punch,* December 10, 1969; *New Statesman,* December 12, 1969; *Christian Science Monitor,* December 27, 1969.†

(Died December 7, 1969)

* * *

WILLIAMS, John G(ordon) 1906-

PERSONAL: Born April 20, 1906, in London, England; son of Charles Frederick (an artist) and Margaret (Reynolds) Williams; married Alice May Irene Walker (a nurse), May 6, 1943 (died, 1968); married Loretta Janice Paul, 1972; children: (first marriage) Christopher, Margaret (deceased), Bernard and Martin (twins). *Education:* University of London, B.A. (first class honors), University College, 1927, and Diploma in Education, Institute of Education, 1928. *Home:* 28 Borrage Lane, Ripon, Yorkshire, England.

CAREER: Priest of Church of England. Assistant priest in London, England, 1932-40; British Broadcasting Corp., London, assistant to director of religious broadcasting, 1940-50; field secretary of National Society in London, 1950-53; vicar in Liverpool, 1953-57; Society for Promoting Christian Knowledge, London, chaplain and education officer, 1957-72. Honorary minor canon of Ripon Cathedral, beginning 1972.

WRITINGS: God and His World, S.P.C.K., 1937; *The Life of Our Lord,* S.P.C.K., 1939; *Children's Hour Prayers,* S.C.M. Press, 1946; *What Next?,* S.P.C.K., 1949; *Listen on Wednesday,* S.C.M. Press, 1949; *Switch on for the News,* S.C.M. Press, 1950; *Worship and the Modern Child,* S.P.C.K., 1957; *God and the Human Family,* S.P.C.K., 1958; *Hungry World,* S.P.C.K., 1961; *Thinking Aloud,*

S.C.M. Press, 1963; *The Faith and the Space Age,* S.P.C.K., 1964, published as *Christian Faith and the Space Age,* World Publishing, 1967.

* * *

WILLIAMS, Loring G. 1924-1974

PERSONAL: Born December 10, 1924, in Hyannis, Mass.; son of Ralph W. and Lillian (Lincoln) Williams; married Elsie Roberts (a clerk), March 5, 1944; children: Sherman R., Jackson L. *Education:* Attended Davis Vocational School, Dover, N.H., 1947-49, and took summer and extension courses at Keene State College, Keene, N.H., 1957-66. *Home:* 35 Main St., Hinsdale, N.H. 03451. *Agent:* Jay Garon-Brooke Associates, Inc., 415 Central Park W., New York, N.Y. 10025.

CAREER: High school teacher of industrial arts in Portsmouth and Hinsdale, N.H., and Bellows Falls and Fair Haven, Vt., 1955-69; consulting hypnotist, 1964-74. *Military service:* U.S. Army, 1945-46; served in Italy; became sergeant. *Member:* New Hampshire Industrial Education Association (vice-president, 1961), American Legion.

WRITINGS: (With Brad Steiger) *Other Lives,* Hawthorn, 1969. Also author with Steiger of *Minds Through Space,* Award Books.

WORK IN PROGRESS: A book on hypnotherapy and self-hypnosis; continued psychic research.

BIOGRAPHICAL/CRITICAL SOURCES: Brad Steiger, *We Have Lived Before,* Ace Books, 1967.†

(Died January 5, 1974)

* * *

WILSON, Charles McMoran 1882-1977
(Charles McMoran Wilson Moran)

PERSONAL: Born November 10, 1882, in Skipton-in-Craven, Yorkshire, England; son of John Forsythe (a physician) and Mary (Hanna) Wilson; married Dorothy Dufton, July 15, 1919; children: Richard John McMoran, Geoffrey Hazlitt. *Education:* University of London, M.D. (Gold Medal), 1913, L.R.C.P. and F.R.C.P. *Home:* Newton Valence Manor, near Alton, Hampshire, England.

CAREER: University of London, St. Mary's Hospital Medical School, London, England, dean, 1920-45, consulting physician, beginning, 1945. Personal physician to Sir Winston Churchill, 1940-65. President, Royal College of Physicians, London, England, 1942-51. Sometime examiner in medicine for Cambridge University and University of Birmingham. Consultant to British Ministry of Health. *Military service:* Royal Army Medical Corps, attached to Royal Fusiliers, 1914-17, medical officer at military hospital, Boulogne, France, 1917-18; became major; received Military Cross, Italian Silver Medal for military valor, and was mentioned in dispatches (twice). *Member:* Royal Society of Medicine (fellow), Royal College of Surgeons, Association of Physicians, Medical Society of London, Harveian Society; honorary fellow of American College of Physicians, Royal Australasian College of Physicians, Royal College of Physicians (Edinburgh), and Royal College of Physicians (Glasgow). *Awards, honors:* Knighted, 1938, created first baron of Manton (Lord Moran of Manton), 1943.

WRITINGS—Under name Charles McMoran Wilson Moran: *Anatomy of Courage,* Constable, 1945, Houghton, 1967, 2nd edition, Constable, 1966; *Churchill: The Struggle for Survival, 1940-1965,* Houghton, 1966 (published in England as *Winston Churchill: The Struggle for Survival, 1940-1965,* Constable, 1966). Contributor of articles to professional journals.

(Died April 12, 1977)

*   *   *

WILSON, Wilfrid George   1910-

PERSONAL: Born September 6, 1910, in Holborn, London, England; son of Herbert Henry (a police sergeant) and Minnie (Ellis) Wilson; married Emily Florence Gallivan, March 26, 1932; married Daisy Irene Howell, September 3, 1949. *Education:* Attended county grammar school, Ealing, London, England, 1922-28. *Religion:* Church of England. *Home:* 42 Willow Grove, Ruislip, Middlesex, England. *Office:* Greater London Council, County Hall, London S.E.1, England.

CAREER: London County Council, London, England, various posts, 1928-65; Greater London Council, London, Highways and Traffic Committee, clerk, 1965-68, Planning and Transportation Committee, clerk, 1968-70, principal clerk, beginning 1970. *Military service:* British Army, 1940-46; became Quartermaster sergeant; received Africa Star and Italy Star. *Member:* Central Council of Church Bell Ringers (life member), Oxford Diocesan Guild of Church Bell Ringers (vice-president), London County Association of Church Bell Ringers (past master; treasurer).

WRITINGS: On Conducting, Central Council of Church Bell Ringers, 1954; *Hints to Beginners,* Central Council of Church Bell Ringers, circa 1955; *Change Ringing: The Art and Science of Change Ringing on Church and Hand Bells,* October House, 1965. Contributor to *Ringing World* (weekly publication of Central Council of Church Bell Ringers).

WORK IN PROGRESS: With Frederick Sharpe, *Bells.*

AVOCATIONAL INTERESTS: Motoring.

*   *   *

WINSTON, Alexander   1909-

PERSONAL: Born February 15, 1909, in Seattle, Wash.; son of Joseph Byrd (a newspaperman) and Hal (Porter) Winston; married Cornell Wiese (a teacher), June 26, 1939; children: Annaleigh (Mrs. Lawrence Erdmann), Joseph Byrd, Patrick Henry. *Education:* University of Washington, Seattle, B.A., 1930, M.A., 1932, Ph.D., 1949; Meadville Theological School (now Meadville/Lombard Theological School), B.D., 1935. *Residence:* New Haven, Conn.

CAREER: Clergyman of American Unitarian Association, 1936-53, and of United Church of Christ, 1953-61. Lecturer in philosophy, Tufts University, 1942-46. Free-lance writer. *Member:* Alpha Delta Phi, Graduate Club (New Haven).

WRITINGS: You Are the Key, Falmouth Publishing House, 1949; *I Leave You My Heart,* Juniper Press (Portland), 1951; *No Man Knows My Grave: Sir Henry Morgan, Captain William Kidd, Captain Woodes Rogers in The Great Age of Privateers and Pirates, 1665-1715,* Houghton, 1969 (published in England as *No Purchase, No Pay: Sir Henry Morgan, Captain William Kidd, Captain Woodes Rogers in The Great Age of Privateers and Pirates, 1665-1715,* Eyre & Spottiswoode, 1970). Contributor to *American Heritage, Harper's, Christian Century,* and other publications.

WORK IN PROGRESS: The Life and Times of Admiral Hiram Paulding.

AVOCATIONAL INTERESTS: Squash, badminton, travel ("get to Europe every year or so, knapsack on back").†

*   *   *

WINSTON, R(obert) A(lexander)   1907-1974
(Col. Victor J. Fox)

PERSONAL: Born October 25, 1907, in Washington, Ind.; son of John Leonidas and Laura Grant (Scudder) Winston; married Annrika Boberg, October 20, 1940; children: Roderick Duncan, Cecilia Anne (Mrs. B. Magnus Floren), Frederick Blix, Carolina Jeanne (Mrs. George Van B. Cochran). *Education:* Indiana University, A.B., 1935. *Home:* Back Acres, R.F.D. 2, Bedford, N.Y. 10506. *Office:* Fargo Press, Inc., Box 425, Pleasantville, N.Y. 10570.

CAREER: New York Daily News, New York City, feature writer, assistant manager of merchandising department, manager of Information Bureau, 1930-35; U.S. Navy, 1935-50, squadron commander and air group commander, U.S.S. Cabot, 1943-44, assistant naval air attache in U.S. Embassy, Stockholm, Sweden, 1945-48, special assistant to director of public relations, Washington, D.C., 1949-50, retiring as captain; Central Intelligence Agency, Washington, D.C., classified assignment, 1951-52; free-lance writer, 1953-54; General Foods Corp., White Plains, N.Y., manager of corporate press relations, 1955-58; Freedom Press, Inc., New York City, president and publisher, 1958-67; Fargo Press, Inc., Pleasantville, N.Y., president and publisher, 1968-74. President, Nerico Co. *Member:* U.S. Fighter Aces Association (charter member). *Awards, honors*—Military: Distinguished Flying Cross, Air Medal with two Gold Stars, Bronze Star, Presidential Unit Citation, Royal Order of the Sword (Sweden), Mannerheim Medal and Winter War Medal (Finland).

WRITINGS—Nonfiction: *Dive Bomber,* Holiday House, 1939; *Aces Wild,* Holiday House, 1941; *Aircraft Carrier,* Harper, 1942; *Fighting Squadron,* Holiday House, 1946; *Fun in the Water,* June & Osborn, 1952.

Under pseudonym Col. Victor J. Fox: *The Pentagon Case* (fiction), Freedom Press, 1958; *The Welfare Staters,* Freedom Press, 1962; *The White House Case* (fiction), Fargo Press, 1968. Contributor under his own name to fifteen magazines, among them *Saturday Evening Post, Ken, Reader's Digest,* and *This Week.*

SIDELIGHTS: R. A. Winston was the author of the articles recommending seat belts for automobiles (*This Week,* 1950; *Ken,* 1957), and the designer of several features of a new two-place amphibian seaplane marketed in 1969.†

(Died June 3, 1974.)

*   *   *

WITMER, Helen L(eland)   1898-

PERSONAL: Born July 17, 1898, in Lansford, Pa.; daughter of I. K. and Nellie (Seager) Witmer. *Education:* Dickinson College, A.B., 1919; University of Wisconsin (now University of Wisconsin—Madison), M.A., 1923, Ph.D., 1925; Bryn Mawr College, Certificate in Social Work, 1924; London School of Economics and Political Science, postdoctoral study, 1927-29. *Office:* 433 South Lee St., Alexandria, Va. 22306.

CAREER: Statistician, Division of Corrections, Commonwealth of Massachusetts, 1925; University of Minnesota, Minneapolis, assistant research professor of sociology, 1926-27; Smith College, School for Social Work, Northampton, Mass., director of research and editor, "Smith College Studies in Social Work," 1929-49; University of California,

Los Angeles, School of Social Welfare, professor of social welfare, 1949-51; U.S. Children's Bureau, Washington, D.C., director of Division of Research, 1951-67, director of research utilization, beginning 1967. Researcher and writer for National Council of Parent Education, National Committee for Mental Hygiene, Commonwealth Fund, and other agencies, 1929-49; director of fact-finding, White House Conference on Children and Youth, 1949-51. *Awards, honors:* Social Science Research Council fellowship in England, 1927-29.

WRITINGS: The Field of Parent Education, University of Minnesota Press, 1936; *Psychiatric Clinics for Children,* Commonwealth Fund, 1940; *Social Work: An Analysis of a Social Institution,* Farrar & Rinehart, 1942; *Psychiatric Interviews with Children,* Commonwealth Fund, 1946; (editor) *Pediatrics and the Emotional Needs of the Child,* Commonwealth Fund, 1948; (editor) *Teaching Psychotherapeutic Medicine,* Commonwealth Fund, 1949; (with Edwin Powers) *An Experiment in the Prevention of Delinquency: The Cambridge-Somerville Youth Study,* Columbia University Press, 1951; (with Ruth Kotinsky) *Personality in the Making: The Fact-Finding Report of the Midcentury White House Conference on Children and Youth,* Harper, 1952; (with Kotinsky) *Community Programs for Mental Health: Theory, Practice, Evaluation,* Commonwealth Fund, 1955; *Independent Adoptions,* Russell Sage, 1963; (editor with Charles P. Gershenson) *On Rearing Infants and Young Children in Institutions,* U.S. Children's Bureau, 1967. Author or editor of series of Children's Bureau publications on delinquency, 1954-66; editor, "Children's Bureau Research Reports," beginning 1967. Contributor to *Journal of Criminal Law and Criminology, Quarterly Journal of Economics, Mental Hygiene,* and other journals.†

* * *

WITTENBERG, Philip 1895-

PERSONAL: Born April 4, 1895, in Brooklyn, N.Y.; son of William and Elizabeth (Plesetzkaya) Wittenberg; married Ruth Budinoff, November 22, 1919; children: Susana (Mrs. Jason C. Berger), Jonathan B. *Education:* New York University, LL.B., 1916. *Home:* 35 West Tenth St., New York, N.Y. 10011. *Office:* 36 West 44th St., New York, N.Y. 10036.

CAREER: Admitted to New York Bar, 1916; New Playwrights Theatre, New York, N.Y., organizer and director, 1927-34; Wittenberg, Carrington & Farnsworth (law firm), New York, N.Y., partner, beginning 1935. Lecturer at New School for Social Research, Columbia University, and Cooper Union, beginning 1939; counsel to Bill of Rights Fund and Mystery Writers of America. Trustee of American Academy of Dramatic Arts and Copyright Society of the United States. *Member:* Washington Square Association (director). *Awards, honors:* Edgar Allen Poe Award of Mystery Writers of America, for *The Lamont Case.*

WRITINGS: Literary Property, Messner, 1938; *Guilty Men,* Stokes, 1940; *Dangerous Words,* Columbia University Press, 1947; *The Lamont Case,* Horizon, 1957; *The Law of Literary Property,* World Publishing, 1957; *The Protection of Literary Property,* Writer, Inc., 1968. Contributor to *Encyclopedia of Social Sciences,* magazines, and law reviews.†

* * *

WITTY, Robert G(ee) 1906-

PERSONAL: Born October 6, 1906, in Glasgow, Ky.; son of Robert Lee and Maude (Lawrence) Witty; married Katherine Henderson, December 24, 1943; children: Mary, Edith, Robert, Daniel, Ann; stepchildren: Robert Hoover. *Education:* Willamette University, A.B., 1928; studied at Kimball School of Theology, 1928, Princeton Theological Seminary, 1929, and Garrett Biblical Institute, 1930; Asbury Theological Seminary, B.D., 1932; Burton College and Seminary, Th.D., 1952; University of Florida, Ph.D., 1959. *Home:* 357 Tidewater Dr., Jacksonville, Fla. 32211. *Office:* Luther Rice Seminary, 1050 Hendricks Ave., Jacksonville, Fla. 32207.

CAREER: Clergyman of Southern Baptist Convention. Central Baptist Church, Jacksonville, Fla., pastor, 1943-70; Luther Rice Seminary, Jacksonville, Fla., dean of graduate studies, 1962-68, chairman of trustees, 1962-68, president, beginning 1968. President of Witty Evangelistic Enterprises, Jacksonville, Fla., beginning 1966. Former radio evangelist in about forty states; also made missionary tours in Cuba and Jamaica. Florida Baptist Convention, chairman of committee on democracy, 1959-63, and committee on fellowship, 1965. *Member:* Jacksonville Ministerial Alliance, American Association of Independent College and University Presidents.

WRITINGS: Power for the Church, Broadman, 1967; *Church Visitation: Theory and Practice,* Broadman, 1968; (with John Havlik) *Revival Preparation Plan Book* (pastor's guide), Convention Press, 1968; *Help Yourself to Happiness,* Broadman, 1968; *Signs of the Second Coming,* Broadman, 1969. Contributor to denominational magazines.

WORK IN PROGRESS: Purposive Preaching, a textbook on homiletics; a collection of sermons.

SIDELIGHTS: Witty is competent in Spanish and in Classic and New Testament Greek.

* * *

WOLFE, (George) Edgar 1906-

PERSONAL: Born August 27, 1906, in Ottawa, Kan.; son of George Mitchel and Elizabeth Sue (Ashby) Wolfe; married Nina Ruth Winters, June 2, 1929. *Education:* University of Kansas, A.B., 1928, M.A., 1950. *Religion:* Unitarian Universalist. *Home:* 1712 Tennessee, Lawrence, Kan. 66044. *Office:* Department of English, University of Kansas, Lawrence, Kan. 66044.

CAREER: High school teacher in Stoneville, S.D., 1928-30, and Axtell, Kan., 1930-31; superintendent of schools, Weta, S.D., 1931-32; dealer in Watkins Products, Topeka, Kan., 1933-35; Wyandotte County Welfare Board, Kansas City, Kan., social worker, 1935-42; U.S. Disciplinary Barracks, Fort Leavenworth, Kan., instructor in English, 1942-47; University of Kansas, Lawrence, assistant instructor, 1947-49, instructor, 1949-58, assistant professor, 1958-63, associate professor, 1963-69, professor of English, beginning 1969. Chairman of Douglas County branch, National Multiple Sclerosis Society, 1957-62. *Member:* American Association of University Professors.

WRITINGS: Widow Man (novel), Little, Brown, 1953; (contributor) A. C. Edwards, Edgar Wolfe, and Natalie Calderwood, editors, *Write Now,* Holt, 1954. Novelette anthologized in *Kansas Renaissance,* Coronado Press, 1961. Poems have appeared in more than a dozen periodicals, including *American Weave, Sports Illustrated, Christian Century, Descant,* and *Arts and Crafts,* and short stories and occasional articles in other publications. With Ayseli Usluata, has done translations from the Turkish of short stories and poems by Sait Faik for *Prairie Schooner* and *Smoky Hill Review.*

WORK IN PROGRESS: Poetry and a novel.

* * *

WOLFERT, Helen 1904-

PERSONAL: Born January 31, 1904, in New York, N.Y.; daughter of Alexander and Rosa (Ganzfried) Herschdorfer; married Ira Wolfert (a writer), February 18, 1928; children: Ruth, Michael. *Education:* Hunter College (now of the City University of New York), B.A., 1923; attended Columbia University, University of Maine, New School for Social Research, and Cornell University.

CAREER: Taught English in one high school and several elementary schools, all in New York, N.Y., during a period covering about thirteen years. *Member:* Authors League, Poetry Society of America, Hadassah, Alumni Association of Hunter College of the City University of New York.

WRITINGS: Nothing is a Wonderful Thing (narrative poem), Simon & Schuster, 1946; *The Music* (poems), Norton, 1965. Work represented in anthologies, including *Cross Section,* edited by Edwin Seaver, L. B. Fisher, 1944 and 1945; *Rising Tides,* edited by L. Chester and S. Barba, Washington Square Press, 1973. Poetry reviewer, *P.M.;* contributor of reviews, articles, short stories, and poems to *New York Times, New York Herald Tribune, New York Post, Poetry, Harper's Bazaar, New Republic, Nation, Flame, Trace, Voices, Poet Lore,* and *Quarterly Review of Literature.*

WORK IN PROGRESS: Translation of "The Song of Songs."

SIDELIGHTS: Helen Wolfert has given poetry readings before academic, literary, artistic, and religious audiences, as well as on the air. She has traveled extensively in the United States, Canada, Europe, the Middle East, Asia, Polynesia, Australia, and New Zealand.

* * *

WOLFSON, Harry Austryn 1887-1974

PERSONAL: Born November 2, 1887, in Austryn, Russia; came to United States in 1903; son of Menahem Mendal and Sarah Deborah (Savitsky) Wolfson. *Education:* Harvard University, A.B. and A.M., 1912, Ph.D., 1915; University of Berlin, graduate study, 1912-13. *Religion:* Jewish. *Office:* Widener K, Harvard University, Cambridge, Mass. 02138.

CAREER: Harvard University, Cambridge, Mass., instructor, 1915-22, assistant professor, 1922-25, Nathan Littauer Professor of Hebrew Literature and Philosophy, 1925-58, Littauer Professor emeritus, 1958-74. Professor, Jewish Institute of Religion, New York, N.Y., 1923-25. *Military service:* U.S. Army, 1918-19.

MEMBER: American Philosophical Society (fellow), American Philosophical Association, Society of Biblical Literature, American Academy of Arts and Sciences (fellow), Polish Institute of Arts and Sciences, American Academy for Jewish Research (fellow; president, 1935-37), Mediaeval Academy of America (fellow), American Oriental Society (president, 1957-58). *Awards, honors:* D.H. Litt., Jewish Institute of Religion, 1935, Jewish Theological Seminary of America, 1945; D.H.L., Hebrew Union College, 1945, Brandeis University, 1958, Columbia University, 1970; L.H.D., Yeshiva University, 1950, University of Chicago, 1950; D.Litt., Dropsie College, 1952; Litt.D., Har-

vard University, 1956; Faculty Prize, Harvard University Press, 1956, for *The Philosophy of the Church Fathers;* American Council of Learned Societies Prize, 1958.

WRITINGS: Crescas' Critique of Aristotle, Harvard University Press, 1929; *The Philosophy of Spinoza,* two volumes, Harvard University Press, 1934; *Philo,* two volumes, Harvard University Press, 1947, revised edition, 1968; *The Philosophy of the Church Fathers,* Volume I, Harvard University Press, 1956, 3rd edition, 1970; *Religious Philosophy,* Harvard University Press, 1961; *Judah Halevi on Causality and Miracles,* College of Jewish Studies Press, 1966; *Studies in the History and Philosophy of Religion,* edited by Isadore Twersky and G. H. Williams, Harvard University Press, 1973; *The Philosophy of the Kalam,* Harvard University Press, 1975. Editor-in-chief, *Corpus Commentariorum Averrois in Aristotelem,* published by Mediaeval Academy of America.

WORK IN PROGRESS: The Philosophy of the Church Fathers, Volume II.†

(Died September 19, 1974)

* * *

WOOD, Frederic C(onger), Jr. 1932-1970

PERSONAL: Born December 26, 1932, in New Rochelle, N.Y.; son of Frederic C. (a consulting engineer) and Evan (Trend) Wood; married Jane Barber (a schoolteacher), June 19, 1954; children: Jennifer Elizabeth, Barbara. *Education:* Cornell University, B.A., 1954; Protestant Episcopal Seminary in Virginia, B.D., 1960; Union Theological Seminary, New York, N.Y., S.T.M., 1961, Th.D., 1964. *Politics:* Democratic (liberal). *Home:* Lindgren Blvd., Sanibel, Fla. 33957.

CAREER: Ordained deacon in Protestant Episcopal Church, 1960, and priest, 1961; served churches in Richmond, Va., 1959-60, and New York, N.Y., 1960-63; Cornell University, Ithaca, N.Y., acting Episcopal chaplain, 1963-64; Goucher College, Towson, Md., chaplain and assistant professor of religion, 1964-67; Vassar College, Poughkeepsie, N.Y., chaplain and associate professor of religion, 1967-70; full-time writer, 1970. Reader and interviewer, Danforth Foundation, 1965-67. Member of Bishop's committee on college work, Episcopal Diocese of New York, 1967-70. *Military service:* U.S. Navy, 1954-57; served at sea and as Russian cryptolinguist with National Security Agency; became lieutenant. *Member:* National Association of College and University Chaplains, Evangelical Education Society, National Campus Ministry Association, American Association of University Professors, Fellowship of Reconciliation, American Civil Liberties Union.

WRITINGS: (Contributor) William Greenspun and Cynthia Wedel, editors, *Second Living Room Dialogues,* Paulist/Newman, 1967; *Sex and the New Morality,* Association Press, 1968; (contributor) G. Kerry Smith, editor, *Agony and Promise,* American Association of Higher Education, 1969; *Living in the Now,* Association Press, 1970. Contributor to magazines and religious publications.

WORK IN PROGRESS: Research in the life of Soren Kierkegaard.

SIDELIGHTS: Frederic C. Wood Jr. was competent in Russian, Indonesian, German, Biblical Greek, and Hebrew.

During his illness, Frederic Wood kept a chronological journal of his thoughts and experiences. His father is presently arranging this journal topically for publication.†

(Died October 10, 1970)

WOODROOF, Horace M(alcolm) 1906-

PERSONAL: Born November 17, 1906, in White Creek, Tenn.; son of Ethel W. and Kate (Blunkall) Woodroof; married Mabel Nichols (divorced). *Education:* Left school to help support family after completing fourth grade in Nashville, Tenn. *Politics:* Independent. *Religion:* Church of Christ.

CAREER: Worked at odd jobs on a farm and as a commercial sign painter's helper; convicted on a charge of murder and spent thirty-two years in prison in Tennessee, and taught electronics during last years of confinement; released from prison, 1962; worked as shipping clerk in a food factory and as a file clerk at Ford dealership in Nashville, Tenn., until 1968. *Military service:* U.S. Marine Corps, fifteen months.

WRITINGS: Stonewall College, Aurora Publishing, 1970. Contributor of articles and letters to local newspapers and national magazines. Editor of a prison magazine, *"Inside News,"* in Nashville, Tenn.

SIDELIGHTS: Horace M. Woodroof told *CA* that he is especially interested in the "seemingly insolvable race issue in America. This issue can be resolved only by a complete separation of the races—but with full assistance, of course. [This] is only an opinion—but it represents serious thinking and continued research. The present status of the colored race—not only in America but in other countries like England, for example—is precarious indeed, and much of it can be attributed to the historical dependence of the Negro upon the white race. . . . But aside from this interest, I have another interest in American prison systems. I have an *open* mind here, too—even though I spent over thirty years in a Tennessee prison!"††

* * *

WORKMAN, Samuel K(linger) 1907-

PERSONAL: Born August 28, 1907, in Gambier, Ohio; son of Irvin Samuel and Ruth (Klinger) Workman; married Julia Lord, June 13, 1931; married second wife, Lillian Garrett (an artist, designer, and teacher), March 12, 1953; children: (first marriage) Allen Klinger, Charles Lord. *Education:* Kenyon College, B.A., 1926; Ohio State University, M.A., 1927; Princeton University, Ph.D., 1935. *Politics:* Democrat. *Home:* R.D. 1, Riegelsville, Pa. 18077.

CAREER: University of Kentucky, Lexington, instructor in English, 1927-28; Northwestern University, Evanston, Ill., instructor, 1935-40, assistant professor of English, 1940-48; Illinois Institute of Technology, Chicago, associate professor of English, 1948-61; Newark College of Engineering, Newark, N.J., professor of English, 1961-67, distinguished professor, 1967-72, distinguished professor emeritus, 1973—, chairman of department, 1961-72. Editorial consultant, McGraw-Hill Book Co., 1963-70. *Member:* Modern Language Association of America, College English Association, American Society for Engineering Education. *Awards, honors:* Ford Foundation faculty fellowship, 1952-53.

WRITINGS: Fifteenth Century Translation, Princeton University Press, 1940, reprinted, Octagon, 1971; (with Henry Knepler) *A Range of Writing,* Prentice-Hall, 1959; (author of introduction) *Moll Flanders,* Collier, 1962. Contributor of articles and reviews to *Modern Language Notes, Chicago Sun,* and *Chicago Jewish Forum.*

* * *

WORRALL, Ambrose A(lexander) 1899-1972

PERSONAL: Born January 18, 1899, in Barrow-in-Furness, Lancashire, England; son of Alexander (a proprietor of a retail store) and Rebecca Brown (Mattocks) Worrall; married Olga Nathalie Ripich (a writer), June 7, 1928; children: Ambrose K., Alexander M. (twins, both deceased). *Education:* Attended Barrow-in-Furness Technical School, England, 1916-18, St. Ignatius College, 1923-24, and Cleveland College (now Cleveland College of Case Western Reserve University), 1927-29; National Radio Institute, Washington, D.C., diploma in electronics, 1964. *Religion:* Methodist. *Home:* 1208 Havenwood Rd., Baltimore, Md. 21218.

CAREER: Vickers Ltd., Aeronautical Engineering Department, Barrow-in-Furness, England, engineer, 1918-20; Martin Co., Baltimore, Md., department manager, 1924-64; K. & W. Enterprises, Inc., Baltimore, Md., vice-president, beginning 1964; Makari Research Laboratories, Inc., Englewood, N.J., vice-president, beginning 1966; Life Energies Research, Inc., New York, N.Y., director, beginning 1968. Consultant for Martin Marietta Corp., 1964-68, and Westinghouse Electric Co., Aerospace Division, 1968-69, both in Baltimore, Md.; associate director of New Life Clinic, Mt. Washington United Methodist Church, Baltimore, Md. Member of corporate board of Springfield College, Springfield, Mass., beginning 1962; member of Wainwright House for Development of Human Resources, Rye, N.Y. *Military service:* British Army, 1918-19. *Member:* Spiritual Frontiers Fellowship, Free and Accepted Masons of Ohio.

WRITINGS: (With wife, Olga Worrall) *The Gift of Healing: A Personal Story of Spiritual Therapy,* Harper, 1965; (with O. Worrall) *Miracle Healers,* New American Library, 1968; (with O. Worrall and Will Oursler) *Explore Your Psychic World,* Harper, 1970. Also author of *Essay on Prayer,* 1952, *Meditation and Contemplation,* 1956, *The Philosophy and Methodology of Spiritual Healing,* 1961, *Silentium Altum* (title means "Deep Silence"), 1961, and *Basic Principles of Spiritual Healing,* 1963, all privately printed.

SIDELIGHTS: Ambrose A. Worrall told *CA:* "I lecture frequently throughout the U.S.A. and occasionally abroad on E.S.P. and spiritual healing, to colleges, churches, and other associations. I am doing research on the relationship of mind, soul, body, and the creative energies that influence them, particularly those that maintain a healthy mind in a healthy body. I am also interested in life after death conditions, and the immortality of the soul and its personal characteristics. Personal experience is the motivating factor behind this research which I started in 1916."

BIOGRAPHICAL/CRITICAL SOURCES: Will Oursler, *The Healing Power of Faith,* Hawthorn, 1957.†

(Died, 1972)

* * *

WRIGHT, Bruce S(tanley) 1912-1975

PERSONAL: Born September 17, 1912, in Quebec, Province of Quebec, Canada; son of Arthur Stanley (an army officer), and Dorothy (Ahern) Wright; married Marjorie Hatheway McMurray, October 19, 1937; children: Victor Bruce Stanley, Barbara Hatheway. *Education:* University of New Brunswick, B.Sc., 1936; University of Wisconsin, M.Sc., 1947. *Home:* 6 Elmcroft Pl., Fredericton, New Brunswick, Canada. *Office:* Northeastern Wildlife Station, University of New Brunswick, Fredericton, New Brunswick, Canada.

CAREER: University of New Brunswick, Fredericton, director of Northeastern Wildlife Station, 1947-74, honorary research fellow in biology. Field work includes trips to British Columbia to study cougar-hunting techniques, 1955, and six months in Kenya and Tanganyika studying lions, 1957. *Military service:* Royal Canadian Naval Reserve, active duty, 1940-45; commanded British frogman unit in California, the Bahamas, and Far East for three years; became lieutenant commander; received Atlantic Star and Burma Star. *Member:* Canadian Society of Wildlife and Fishery Biologists (founding member; first senior director, Atlantic region), Wildlife Society, American Ornithologists' Union (life member), American Society of Mammalogists, Canadian Institute of Forestry (chairman, wildlife committee, 1961-65), Outdoor Writers of Canada.

WRITINGS: High Tide and an East Wind—The Story of the Black Duck, Stackpole and Wildlife Management Institute, 1954; *The Ghost of North America—The Story of the Eastern Panther,* Vantage, 1959; *Wildlife Sketches Near and Far,* Brunswick Press, 1962; *The Monarch of Mularchy Mountain,* Brunswick Press, 1963; *Black Duck Spring,* Dutton, 1966; *The Frogmen of Burma,* Clark, Irwin, 1968; *The Eastern Panther,* Clark, Irwin, 1972. Author of research reports on waterfowl breeding conditions and other investigations, published by U.S. Fish and Wildlife Service, Canadian Wildlife Service, and National Research Council, Ottawa. Contributor of forty-odd articles, most self-illustrated with photographs, to *Atlantic Advocate, Sports Afield, Audubon Magazine, Field and Stream,* and other magazines in Canada and United States.

WORK IN PROGRESS: Studies on various aspects of raccoon, ruffed grouse, white-tailed deer, harbor porpoise in the Bay of Fundy, woodcock, and waterfowl biology.

SIDELIGHTS: Along with his Canadian research projects, Wright was interested in the possible survival of the West Indian monk seal—the result of several trips to the West Indies. Once an avid grouse and woodcock hunter, he raised and trained his own bird dogs. *Avocational interests:* Underwater photography, bird, beast, and fish watching.†

(Died April 19, 1975)

*   *   *

WRIGHT, David McCord   1909-1968

PERSONAL: Born August 1, 1909, in Savannah, Ga.; son of Anton Pope (a lawyer and banker) and Hannah McCord (Smythe) Wright; married Caroline Noble Jones, June 27, 1940; children: Antony Pope, Peter Meldrim, Anna Habersham. *Education:* Attended University of Pennsylvania, 1927-30; University of Virginia, LL.B., 1935; Harvard University, M.A., 1940, Ph.D., 1941. *Politics:* Republican. *Religion:* Episcopalian. *Home:* 420 Fortson Dr., Athens, Ga.; (summer residence) Cotuit, Mass. *Office:* University of Georgia, Athens, Ga.

CAREER: Admitted to Georgia bar, 1935; Reconstruction Finance Corp., attorney, 1936-37; University of Virginia, Charlottesville, assistant professor of business administration, 1939-42, associate professor of economics, 1942-46, professor of economics, 1946-55, lecturer in Law School, 1940, 1947-55; McGill University, Montreal, Quebec, William Dow Professor of Economics and Political Science, 1955-62; University of Georgia, Athens, professor of economics, 1962-68. Fulbright lecturer at Oxford University, 1953-54; visiting summer lecturer at Columbia University, Harvard University, University of California, and for U.S. Department of State in France and Germany, 1956. Economic consultant, National Resources Planning Board,

1943; economic adviser, Federal Reserve Bank of Atlanta, 1963-65.

MEMBER: American Economic Association (member of executive committee, 1952-55), Royal Economic Society, Southern Economic Association (president, 1950), Huguenot Society of South Carolina (life member), Society of Colonial Wars, Phi Delta Phi, Alpha Kappa Psi, Delta Psi, Beta Gamma Sigma, Oglethorpe Club, Savannah Yacht Club. *Awards, honors:* Rockefeller Foundation fellow, 1954-55; Earhart fellow, 1954-55.

WRITINGS: The Creation of Purchasing Power, Harvard University Press, 1942; *The Economics of Disturbance,* Macmillan, 1947; *Democracy and Progress,* Macmillan, 1948; *Capitalism,* McGraw, 1951; (editor) *The Impact of the Union,* Harcourt, 1951; *The Key to Modern Economics,* Macmillan, 1954; *The Keynesian System,* Fordham University Press, 1962; *Growth and the Economy: Principles of Economics,* Scribner, 1964; *The Trouble with Marx,* Arlington House, 1967. Contributor to economic, legal, and other journals. Member of editorial committee, *UNESCO Dictionary of the Social Sciences,* 1959-63.

SIDELIGHTS: Wright once told *CA* that he aimed in his work to carry analysis beyond the economic quantities to the social forces that change and shape them, and to "explain aggregative (Keynesian) analysis *in depth* and proportion. . . . *Second hand* Keynes is as shabby a product as most second hand clothes. . . ."

BIOGRAPHICAL/CRITICAL SOURCES: New York Times, January 8, 1968; *Virginia Quarterly Review,* spring, 1968.†

(Died January 7, 1968)

*   *   *

WRIGHT, Enid Meadowcroft (LaMonte)   1898-1966
(Enid LaMonte Meadowcroft)

PERSONAL: Born March 31, 1898, in New York, N.Y.; daughter of Horace G. (a realtor) and Enid (Smith) LaMonte; married Kirk Meadowcroft (deceased); married Donald Wright, June 16, 1941 (deceased). *Education:* Lesley College, Cambridge, Mass., student, 1916-18. *Politics:* Republican. *Religion:* Episcopalian. *Home:* Lakeville, Conn. *Agent:* McIntosh & Otis, Inc., 475 Fifth Ave., New York, N.Y. 10017.

CAREER: Primary teacher at Bergen School, Jersey City, N.J., 1922-26, Catlin School, Portland, Ore., 1926-28, and Browning School for Boys, New York, N.Y., 1928-41; writer for young people, and editor.

WRITINGS—Under name Enid LaMonte Meadowcroft; all published by Crowell: *The Adventures of Peter Whiffen,* 1936; *The Gift of the River—A History of Ancient Egypt,* 1937; *The First Year,* 1937; *By Wagon and Flatboat,* 1938; *Aren't We Lucky,* 1939; *Along the Erie Towpath,* 1940; *Benjamin Franklin,* 1941; *Abraham Lincoln,* 1942; *Shipboy with Columbus,* 1942; *Silver for General Washington,* 1944; *China's Story,* 1946; *On Indian Trails with Daniel Boone,* 1947; *By Secret Railway,* 1948.

Texas Star, Crowell, 1950; *The Story of George Washington,* Grosset, 1952; *The Story of Benjamin Franklin,* Grosset, 1952; *The Story of Thomas Alva Edison,* Grosset, 1952; *The Story of Davy Crockett,* Grosset, 1952; *The Story of Andrew Jackson,* Grosset, 1953; *The Story of Crazy Horse,* Grosset, 1954; *We Were There at the Opening of the Erie Canal,* Grosset, 1958; *Holding the Fort with Daniel Boone,* Crowell, 1958; *Land of the Free,* Crowell, 1961; *Scarab for*

Luck, Crowell, 1964; *Crazy Horse—Sioux Warrior,* Garrard, 1965; *When Nantucket Men Went Whaling,* Garrard, 1966.

Supervising editor of Grosset's "Signature Books" series, with fifty biographies published, 1952-66, and Garrard's "How They Lived" series. Author of radio scripts for "This Is America," program sponsored by U.S. Rubber Co. Contributor of articles about children to *Household* and *Parents'.*

AVOCATIONAL INTERESTS: Music and travel.†

(Died November 23, 1966)

* * *

WYATT, Dorothea E(dith) 1909-

PERSONAL: Born July 25, 1909, in San Francisco, Calif.; daughter of Thomas Grant (a builder) and Mary Elizabeth (Healey) Wyatt. *Education:* Stanford University, A.B., 1930, M.A., 1931, Ph.D., 1936. *Religion:* Episcopalian. *Home:* 1901 Woodslea Dr., Flint, Mich. 48507.

CAREER: Stanford University, Stanford, Calif., acting instructor in history, 1936-37; Radcliffe College, Cambridge, Mass., tutor, 1937-39; Milwaukee-Downer College (now Lawrence University), Milwaukee, Wis., instructor in history and political science, 1939-40; Goucher College, Baltimore, Md., 1940-52, began as instructor, became professor; College of William and Mary, Williamsburg, Va., professor of history and dean of women, 1952-56; University of Michigan, Flint, professor of history, 1956-75. Member of Genessee County (Mich.) Library Board, beginning 1959; vice-president of Flint Friends of the Library, 1967-68. *Military service:* U.S. Coast Guard, Women's Reserve, 1942-45; became lieutenant. *Member:* American Historical Association, Organization of American Historians, American Association of University Women, Zonta International.

WRITINGS: (With Anne Gary Pannell) *Julia S. Tutwiler and Social Progress in Alabama,* University of Alabama Press, 1961.

WORK IN PROGRESS: American cultural history since 1865.

AVOCATIONAL INTERESTS: Oil painting, photography, and golf.

* * *

WYCKOFF, Charlotte Chandler 1893-1966

PERSONAL: Born April 30, 1893, in Kodaikanal, India; daughter of John Henry (a missionary) and Gertrude (Chandler) Wyckoff. *Education:* Wellesley College, A.B., 1915. *Home:* Presbyterian Home, 49 East 73rd St., New York, N.Y.

CAREER: Missionary in India, working under Board of World Missions, Reformed Church in America, 1915-60. *Member:* American Association of Retired Persons.

WRITINGS: Jothy, Longmans, Green, 1932; *History of Ascot Mission,* Diocesan Press (Madras), 1953; *History of Kodaikanal,* London Mission Press, 1965; *Kumar,* Norton, 1965. Writer of textbooks, and pamphlets and articles on education subjects published in India.††

(Died July 22, 1966)

* * *

WYLIE, Philip (Gordon) 1902-1971

PERSONAL: Born May 12, 1902, in Beverly, Mass.; son of Edmund Melville (a Presbyterian minister) and Edna (a writer; maiden name Edwards) Wylie; married Johanna Ondeck (a model), April 17, 1928 (divorced, 1937); married Frederica Ballard, April 7, 1938; children: (first marriage) Karen (Mrs. Taylor A. Pryor). *Education:* Attended Princeton University, 1920-23. *Residence:* South Miami, Fla. *Agent:* Harold Ober Associates, 40 East 49th St., New York, N.Y. 10017.

CAREER: New Yorker, staff member, 1925-27; Cosmopolitan Book Corp., advertising manager, 1927-28; Paramount Pictures Corp., writer, 1931-33; Metro-Goldwyn-Mayer Corp., writer, 1936-37. Member, Defense Council of Dade County; chairman, Dade County chapter of Commission to Defend America, 1940; president, Dade County Conservation Council, 1942; member of board, Office of Facts and Figures, 1942; expert consultant, Federal Civil Defense Administration, 1949-71; consultant to Oceanic Institute of Hawaii; member of steering committee, Lerner Marine Laboratory; editor, Farrar & Rinehart, 1944. *Member:* International Game Fish Association (governor), United Nations Association, Authors Guild (member of council, 1945), Tropical Audubon Society (director), Academy of Political Science of the City of New York, Sigma Tau Delta, Sigma Delta Chi, Outdoor Writer's Club, Angler's (director). *Awards, honors:* Litt.D., University of Miami, and Florida State University; Gold Medal of the Freedom Foundation, 1953; Henry H. Hyman Memorial Trophy, 1959; Lotos Club medal, 1966.

WRITINGS: Heavy Laden, Knopf, 1928; *Babes and Sucklings,* Knopf, 1929, reprinted as *The Party,* Popular Library, 1967; *Gladiator,* Knopf, 1930, reprinted with a new introduction, Hyperion Press, 1974; *Footprint of Cinderella,* Farrar & Rinehart, 1931, reprinted as *Nine Rittenhouse Square,* Popular Library, 1967; *Murderer Invisible,* Farrar & Rinehart, 1931; *The Savage Gentleman,* Farrar & Rinehart, 1932; (with Edwin Balmer) *Five Fatal Words,* R. R. Smith, 1932; (with Balmer) *When Worlds Collide,* Stokes Publishing, 1933; (with Balmer) *Golden Hoard,* Stokes Publishing, 1934; (with Balmer) *After Worlds Collide,* Stokes Publishing, 1934; *Finnley Wren; His Notions and Opinions Together with a Haphazard History of His Career and Amours in These Moody Years, as Well as Sundry Rhymes, Fables, Diatribes and Literary Misdemeanors: A Novel in a New Manner,* Farrar & Rinehart, 1934; *As They Reveled,* Farrar & Rinehart, 1936; *Too Much of Everything,* Farrar & Rinehart, 1936; (with Balmer) *Shield of Silence,* Stokes Publishing, 1936; *An April Afternoon,* Farrar & Rinehart, 1938; *Big Ones Get Away!,* Farrar & Rinehart, 1939.

(With W. W. Muir) *Army Way: A Thousand Pointers for New Soldiers,* Farrar & Rinehart, 1940; *Danger Mansion* (abridged edition), Bantam, 1940; *The Other Horseman,* Farrar & Rinehart, 1941; *Salt Water Daffy,* Farrar & Rinehart, 1941; *Generation of Vipers,* Farrar & Rinehart, 1942, new annotation by author, Pocket Books, 1959; *Corpses at Indian Stones,* Farrar & Rinehart, 1943; (contributor) *Fifth Mystery Book: Four Short Stories by Philip Wylie and Others,* Farrar & Rinehart, 1944; *Night Unto Night,* Farrar & Rinehart, 1944; *Fish and Tin Fish: Crunch and Des Strike Back,* Farrar & Rinehart, 1944; (author of introduction) *American Thought,* Gresham, 1947; *An Essay on Morals,* Holt, 1947; *Crunch and Des: Stories of Florida Fishing,* Holt, 1948; *Opus 21: Descriptive Music for the Lower Kinsey Epoch of the Atomic Age; A Concerto for a One Man Band; Six Arias for Soap Operas, Fugues, Anthems, and Barrelhouse,* Holt, 1949.

(With Balmer) *When Worlds Collide* [and] *After Worlds Col-*

lide (omnibus volume), Lippincott, 1951; *Three to Be Read* (contains the *The Smuggled Atom Bomb, Sporting Blood* and *Experiment in Crime,* all separately published in paperback editions), Holt, 1951; *The Disappearance,* Holt, 1951; *Denizens of the Deep,* Holt, 1953; *Best of Crunch and Des,* Holt, 1954; *Tomorrow!,* Holt, 1954; *The Answer,* Holt, 1956; *Treasure Cruise, and Other Crunch and Des Stories,* Holt, 1956; *Innocent Ambassadors,* Rinehart, 1957; *The Lerner Marine Laboratory at Bimini, Bahamas: A Field Station of the American Museum of Natural History,* American Museum of Natural History, c. 1960; *Triumph,* Doubleday, 1963; *They Both Were Naked,* Doubleday, 1965; *Autumn Romance,* Lancer Books, 1967; *The Magic Animal: Man Revisited,* Doubleday, 1968; *The Spy Who Spoke Porpoise,* Doubleday, 1969; *Sons and Daughters of Mom,* Doubleday, 1971; *The End of a Dream,* Doubleday, 1972. Contributor of stories and articles to *Redbook, Saturday Evening Post, Reader's Digest, Look,* and other magazines.

Screenplays: (With Waldemar Young) "Island of Lost Souls," Paramount, 1932; "Murders in the Zoo," Paramount, 1933; (with Fred Niblo, Jr.) "King of the Jungle," Paramount, 1933. Also author of "L.A. 2017," for National Broadcasting Co. series "Name of the Game."

SIDELIGHTS: Wylie created a sensation with his observations in *Generation of Vipers.* The book became compulsory reading in many college English classes. During the first year after its publication Wylie answered more than 10,000 letters concerning the book.

After a period of working for government war information agencies, Wylie returned to Miami "ill, discouraged and frustrated" and dashed off the book between May 12th and July 4, 1942. "This book represented private catharsis," wrote Wylie, "a catalogue of what I felt to be wrong morally, spiritually and intellectually with my fellow citizens. Since it did not enter my head that millions shared my vexations and anxieties, that they would read the list and remark over it to this day, I did not make . . . that careful literary effort such an audience has the right to expect," maintaining that, "without criticism, progress is impossible," Wylie pointed out "what's wrong," and during that pursuit, was not interested in "what's right." "That *deliberate* fixation of my mind appalled many readers. They could see no 'hope' in a book written to indicate *which way real hope lay.* . . . Three or four times, in the past thirteen years I have had to rush to the telephone . . . to get in touch with correspondents whose despondency, after reading this book, was so great that I honestly feared they meant to carry out plans for suicide. . . . I talked to one young lady for an hour while she sat on the window sill of a high floor of a Manhattan skyscraper with a copy *Vipers* on her lap!"

The chapter entitled "Common Women" added the word "Momism" to the English language. In this section, he noted that "mom was an American creation. Megaloid momworship has got completely out of hand. Men live for her and die for her, dote upon her and whisper her name as they pass away, and I believe she has now achieved . . . a spot next to the Bible and the Flag. . . . [Congressmen] take cracks at their native land and make jokes about Holy Writ, but nobody among them . . . from the first day of the first congressional meeting to the present ever stood in our halls of state and pronounced that one indubitably most-needed American verity: 'Gentlemen, mom is a jerk.'"

Thomas Sugrue wrote of *Vipers:* "Mr. Wylie . . . is a good showman, and he cracks his prose over his opinions like a bull whip. . . . Each reader will find a place where he will

wince, but that will be made up for by the places where he can laugh at his neighbor. . . . Mr. Wylie wrote the whole thing at the top of his voice." A *Time* reviewer, on the other hand wrote: "His religious perceptions, useful as far as they go, are rudimentary. His prose ranges between brilliant neo-Menckenism and embarrassing vulgarity. Too often, when he intends to insult the reader's stupidity, he insults his intelligence instead."

Sometimes referred to as a "pot-boiler," Wylie was a prolific author who worked 250 days a year and once wrote a 25,000-word novelette in one day. His output included hundreds of short stories, serials, articles, syndicated newspaper columns, radio programs and advertising copy. The National Broadcasting Co. television serial, "Crunch and Des," 1955-56, was based on his stories. Film adaptations of Wylie's work include: "Come on Marines," Paramount, 1933; "Fair Warning," Twentieth Century-Fox, 1937; "Springtime in the Rockies," Twentieth Century Fox, 1942; "Cinderella Jones," Warner Bros., 1946; "Night unto Night," Warner Bros., 1949; "When Worlds Collide," Paramount, 1951. His manuscripts have been collected in the Firestone Memorial Library, Princeton University.

BIOGRAPHICAL/CRITICAL SOURCES: Books, January 10, 1943; *Time,* January 18, 1943, November 5, 1965; *New York Times Book Review,* August 11, 1968; *New York Times,* February 4, 1971.†

(Died October 25, 1971)

*   *   *

WYLY, Rachel Lumpkin 1892-

PERSONAL: Born November 7, 1892, in La Fayette, Ga.; daughter of Hugh P. (a lawyer) and Emma (Black) Lumpkin; married Robert M. Wyly, February 12, 1918 (died, 1938); children: Emmalee (Mrs. Thomas G. Whatley). *Education:* Attended Wesleyan College, Macon, Ga., 1909-10, and Shorter College, Rome, Ga., 1910-11; Tift College, B.S. (cum laude), 1954; summer graduate study at University of Georgia and Mercer University. *Religion:* Methodist. *Home:* 184 West Main St., Forsyth, Ga. 31029.

CAREER: Public school teacher in La Fayette, Ga., and Forsyth, Ga., 1930-46; visiting teacher for Monroe County, Ga., 1946-60. Georgia co-chairman, National Poetry Day Committee. *Member:* National League of American Pen Women, Dixie Council of Authors and Journalists, Georgia Writers Association, Atlanta Writers Club, Daughters of the American Revolution, Daughters of the Confederacy. *Awards, honors:* Awards for poetry and articles from Atlanta Writers Club and Atlanta branch of National League of American Pen Women.

WRITINGS: Garlands of Christmas Verses, Banner Press, 1935; *Worlds of Song,* Monroe Advertiser, 1945; *Fifty Little Lyrics,* Daniel Business Services, 1962; *Sifted Memories* (poem), Branden Press, 1968. Writer of Christmas and Easter church programs. Contributor of articles and poems to magazines and newspapers.

WORK IN PROGRESS: Articles on early Methodism in the United States, with the view of eventually publishing a collection of articles.

SIDELIGHTS: Two of her poems, "Listen to the Angels Sing" and "Sing Your Sleepy Song," have been set to music. *Avocational interests:* Genealogical research, music, flowers.

BIOGRAPHICAL/CRITICAL SOURCES: Monroe Advertiser, Forsyth, Ga., May 8, 1969.

YALE, Wesley W(oodworth) 1900-

PERSONAL: Born October 6, 1900, in Syracuse, N.Y.; son of Wesley A. (a corporation executive) and Jane (Wagner) Yale; married Lillian Lackey, February 9, 1927; children: John W., Thomas H. *Education:* U.S. Military Academy, West Point, B.A., 1922; attended Command and General Staff College, 1937-38, Naval War College, 1941-42. *Religion:* Roman Catholic. *Home:* 1083 Trapper's Trail, Pebble Beach, Calif. 93953.

CAREER: U.S. Army, 1922-54, served in Cavalry-Armor, retiring as colonel; Stanford Research Institute, Menlo Park, Calif., senior operations analyst, 1956-66; self-employed military operations research consultant, beginning 1966. Member of Citizens' Committee, Carmel, Calif., 1956-58. *Member:* Operations Research Society of America. *Awards, honors*—Military: Two Silver Stars, Legion of Merit, Bronze Star, Purple Heart, several foreign decorations.

WRITINGS: (With others) *Alternative to Armageddon*, Rutgers University Press, 1970. Contributor of articles to numerous professional publications. Editor, *Armor*, 1948-49; guest editor of *Washington Report*, American Security Council, February, 1971.

WORK IN PROGRESS: Farewell to Boots and Saddles, a story of the cavalry days on the Mexican border during the 1920's and 1930's; *Clambake*, a book about the evolution of the Crosby Golf Tournament and colorful personalities.

SIDELIGHTS: Wesley Yale told *CA* he is interested in "writing on geopolitics and national defense matters (nuclear weapons control, implications of all-volunteer Army, public relations and national defense, etc.)," his experiences as an executive for the disposal of surplus property in Europe after World War II, research on strategic communications and nuclear strike control for Stanford Research in NATO and the Pacific, and service with Germany Army research in 1966.

BIOGRAPHICAL/CRITICAL SOURCES: America, October 24, 1970; *Army*, November, 1970; *San Francisco Examiner*, December 1, 1970; *New York Review of Books*, February 11, 1971.

* * *

YANAGA, Chitoshi 1903-

PERSONAL: Born May 9, 1903, in Waiohinu, Hawaii; son of Torakichi (a farmer) and Yoshi (Inouye) Yanaga; married Clara Yoshie Sato, June 13, 1931; children: Mary Toshiko (Mrs. Lawrence C. George), Keiko Elizabeth. *Education:* University of Hawaii, B.A., 1928, M.A., 1930; University of California, Berkeley, Ph.D., 1934; Tokyo University, postdoctoral study, 1935-37. *Home:* 70 Mt. Vernon St., Boston, Mass. 02108.

CAREER: Teacher of social studies in junior high schools, Honolulu, Hawaii, 1928-32; University of California, Berkeley, instructor in Japanese history and government, 1937-42; U.S. Office of War Information, director of Japanese translation and research in San Francisco, Calif., and Denver, Colo., 1942-44; Federal Communications Commission, Foreign Broadcast Intelligence Service, Washington, D.C., Far Eastern advisor, 1944; U.S. Office of Strategic Services and Department of State, Washington, D.C., chief of special Japan research section, Far East Division of Research and Analysis Branch, 1944-45; Yale University, New Haven, Conn., lecturer, 1945-49, associate professor, 1949-62, professor of political science, 1962-71, professor emeritus, 1971—.

MEMBER: Association for Asian Studies (member of board of directors), American Association of University Professors. *Awards, honors:* Carnegie traveling fellow in Japan, 1936-37; Fulbright research scholar in Japan, 1955-56; Yale senior faculty research fellow in Tokyo, 1962-63.

WRITINGS: Japan since Perry, McGraw, 1949; *Japanese People and Politics*, Wiley, 1956; *Big Business in Japanese Politics*, Yale University Press, 1968. Contributor to encyclopedias and to political science and Asian affairs journals.

BIOGRAPHICAL/CRITICAL SOURCES: National Review, April 7, 1970.

* * *

YAREMKO, Michael 1914-1970

PERSONAL: Born April 24, 1914, in West Ukraine; son of Michael (a farmer) and Anne (Pacholok) Yaremko; married Lois Muriel Hokanson (a psychiatrist), July 12, 1954; children: John, Lisa, Susie. *Education:* University of Basel, student, 1934-37; University of Vienna, M.Th., 1939, Ph.D., 1945; University of Toronto, B.L.Sc., 1953. *Home:* 1513 North Prairie St., Galesburg, Ill. 61401.

CAREER: Former librarian in college and public libraries; minister of United Church of Canada, 1948-54; United College, Winnipeg, Manitoba, teacher of Greek and Hebrew, 1957-59; University of Manitoba, Winnipeg, teacher of history and Russian, 1959-60; University of South Dakota, Vermillion, associate professor of Russian and German, 1960-64; Western Illinois University, Macomb, associate professor of Russian and German, 1965-69. *Member:* American Historical Association, American Association for the Advancement of Slavic Studies, Modern Language Association of America.

WRITINGS: From Moscow to Evanston, Winnipeg Christian Press, 1957; *Galicia-Halychyna: From Separation to Unity*, Shevchenko Scientific Society, 1967 (published in Canada as *From Separation to Unity: Galicia Halychyna*, Christian Press, 1967).

WORK IN PROGRESS: Studies on the Ukrainian philosopher, Skovovoda, and on the literary heritage of W. Narizhny.†

(Died December, 1970)

* * *

YEAGER, W(illard) Hayes 1897-

PERSONAL: Born July 6, 1897, in Lewistown, Ohio; son of Lovinus Reed (a minister) and Addie Caroline (Baker) Yeager; married Clara Elizabeth Pritchard, February 3, 1923; children: Hayes Pritchard, James Lee. *Education:* Ohio State University, A.B., 1919, M.A., 1926; studied at Columbia University, 1919-20, and University of Illinois, 1927-28. *Home:* 3905 Mountview Rd., Columbus, Ohio 43221.

CAREER: High school teacher in Ohio, 1922, and West Virginia, 1922-23; Ohio State University, Columbus, instructor in English, 1923-27; University of Illinois, Urbana, associate in English, 1927-29; George Washington University, Washington, D.C., Chauncey M. Depew Professor of Public Speaking and executive officer of department of public speaking, 1929-45; Ohio State University, professor of speech and chairman of department, beginning 1945. U.S. Air Force lecturer, 1948-50, consultant 1952-56. *Member:* Speech Association of America (president, 1941; executive vice-president, 1945-48), Delta Theta Phi, Phi Delta

Gamma, Pi Gamma Mu, Omicron Delta Kappa, Acacia. *Awards, honors:* LL.D., Morris Harvey College, 1956.

WRITINGS: (With William Phillips Sandford) *Successful Speaking* (high school text), Nelson, 1927; (with Sandford) *Principles of Effective Speaking* (college text), Nelson, 1928, 6th revised edition, Ronald, 1963; (with Sandford) *Business and Professional Speaking,* McGraw, 1929, 2nd edition published as *Practical Business Speaking,* 1937, 4th edition published as *Effective Business Speech,* 1960; (compiler with Sandford) *Business Speeches by Business Men,* McGraw, 1930; (with Sandford) *Problems in Business and Professional Speaking,* McGraw, 1931; (with Sandford) *Problems for Debate Practice,* Nelson, 1933; (editor) *Chauncey Mitchell Depew, the Orator,* George Washington University Press, 1934.

Effective Speaking for Every Occasion, Prentice-Hall, 1940, 2nd edition, 1951; (editor with others) *Papers and Addresses of the Eastern Public Speaking Conference,* Wilson, 1940; (contributor and member of editorial board) *History and Criticism of American Public Address,* McGraw, 1943; (with Kendall B. Taft, John F. McDermott, and Dana O. Jensen) *English Communication: A Handbook of Writing and Speaking,* Farrar & Rinehart, 1943; (editor with William E. Utterback) *Communication and Social Action,* American Academy of Political and Social Science, 1947; (consulting editor) William E. Utterback, *Committees and Conferences: How to Lead Them,* Rinehart, 1950, also published as *Committees and Conferences: Group Thinking and Conference Leadership: Techniques of Discussion.* Contributor to *World Book Encyclopedia, American Railroads,* and other publications.††

*   *   *

YOUMANS, E(lmer) Grant   1907-

PERSONAL: Born October 2, 1907, in Elling, N.D.; son of George E. (in insurance business) and Jennie (Perchie) Youmans; married Elsie Markesi (a secretary), August 5, 1945; children: Douglas, Beverly. *Education:* University of Chicago, A.B., 1937, A.M., 1938; Michigan State University, Ph.D., 1953. *Religion:* Unitarian Universalist. *Home:* 1226 Scoville Rd., Lexington, Ky. 40502. *Office:* Department of Sociology, University of Kentucky, Lexington, Ky. 40506.

CAREER: Englewood Junior College, Chicago, Ill., instructor in social science, 1939-40; U.S. Government, Washington, D.C., organization analyst, 1940-46, 1951-53; Michigan State University, East Lansing, instructor in social science, 1946-51; National Institute of Mental Health, Bethesda, Md., research sociologist, 1953-57; University of Kentucky, Lexington, lecturer, 1957-61, associate professor, 1961-68, adjunct professor of sociology, beginning 1968. *Member:* American Sociological Association, Gerontological Society, Rural Sociological Society, Southern Sociological Society.

WRITINGS: (Editor) *Older Rural Americans,* University of Kentucky Press, 1967. Contributor to professional journals.

WORK IN PROGRESS: Research into generation, race, and social change, the morale of widows, and the achievements of youth.

*   *   *

YOUNG, Clarence
[Collective pseudonym]

WRITINGS—All published by Cupples & Leon: "Jack

Ranger" series: *Jack Ranger's Schooldays,* 1907; . . . *Western Trip,* 1908; . . . *School Victories,* 1908; . . . *Ocean Cruise,* 1909; . . . *Gun Club,* 1910; . . . *Treasure Box,* 1911.

"Motor Boys" series: *The Motor Boys; or, Chums through Thick and Thin,* 1906; . . . *Overland,* 1906; . . . *in Mexico,* 1906; . . . *across the Plain,* 1907; . . . *Afloat,* 1908; . . . *on the Atlantic,* 1908; . . . *in Strange Waters,* 1909; . . . *on the Pacific,* 1909; . . . *in the Clouds,* 1910; . . . *over the Rockies,* 1911; . . . *over the Ocean,* 1911; . . . *on the Wing,* 1912; . . . *after a Fortune,* 1912; . . . *on the Border,* 1913; . . . *on Road and River,* 1915; . . . *on Thunder Mountain,* 1924.

"Racer Boys" series: *The Racer Boys at Boarding School,* 1912; . . . *or, The Mystery of the Wreck,* 1912; . . . *to the Rescue,* 1912; . . . *on the Prairie,* 1913.

SIDELIGHTS: See **ADAMS, Harriet S., STRATEMEYER, Edward L.,** and **SVENSON, Andrew E.**†

*   *   *

YOUNG, Harold H(erbert)   1903-

PERSONAL: Born May 30, 1903, in Laconia, N.H.; son of Herbert Rufus (a machinist) and Fannie (Cawley) Young; married Esther Maurer, September 23, 1933; children: Leanna (Mrs. W. Stanley Brown), Lucinda (Mrs. Thorpe M. Kelly). *Education:* Brown University, Ph.B., 1923, M.B.A., 1925. *Politics:* Republican. *Religion:* Baptist. *Home:* Wastena, Ednam Forest, Charlottesville, Va. 22903.

CAREER: Bodell & Co. (investment bankers), Providence, R.I., security analyst, 1925-43; Bear, Stearns & Co. (investment bankers), New York, N.Y., security analyst, 1943-45; Eastman Dillon & Co. (now Eastman Dillon, Union Securities & Co.), New York, N.Y., security analyst and general partner, 1945-60, later became a limited partner. Director of Commonwealth Telephone Co., Dallas, Pa., 1951-61, and North Penn Gas Co., Port Allegany, Pa., 1953-63. Chairman of United Givers Fund, Charlottesville, Va., 1964. *Member:* Phi Beta Kappa, Rotary Club; Farmington Country Club and Boar's Head Club (both Charlottesville).

WRITINGS: Forty Years of Public Utility Finance, University Press of Virginia, 1965. Bi-weekly contributor for thirteen years to *Investment Dealers' Digest.*

AVOCATIONAL INTERESTS: Travel (in eighty countries).††

*   *   *

YOUNG, Seymour Dilworth   1897-

PERSONAL: Born September 7, 1897, in Salt Lake City, Utah; son of Seymour Bicknell (in real estate business) and Carlie L. Y. (Clawson) Young; married Gladys Pratt, May 31, 1923 (deceased); married Hulda Parker, January 4, 1965; children: (first marriage) Dilworth Randolph (deceased), Leonore (Mrs. Blaine P. Parkinson). *Education:* Weber College (now Weber State College), Ogden, Utah, student for one year. *Home:* 575 J St., Salt Lake City, Utah 84103.

CAREER: Missionary Church of Jesus Christ of Latter-day Saints, 1920-22; Boy Scouts of America, executive in Ogden, Utah, 1923-45; Church of Jesus Christ of Latter-day Saints, Salt Lake City, Utah, member of First Council of Seventy, beginning 1945. *Military service:* U.S. Army, Field Artillery, World War I, 1917-19.

WRITINGS—All published by Bookcraft (Salt Lake City), except as indicated: *An Adventure in Faith,* 1956; *Family Night Reader,* 1958; *More Precious than Rubies: A Mormon Boy and His Priesthood,* 1959; (self-illustrated)

Young Brigham Young (juvenile fiction), 1962; *Here Stand I, Looking* (poetry), Deseret, 1963; *Here Is Brigham: Brigham Young, the Years to 1844,* 1964; *The Long Road: From Vermont to Nauvoo* (poetry), 1967. Also author and illustrator of booklet, *The Beehive House,* in series on Salt Lake City's historic homes.

* * *

YOUNGDAHL, Benjamin E(manuel) 1897-1970

PERSONAL: Born July 12, 1897, in Minneapolis, Minn.; son of John C. (a retail merchant) and Elizabeth (Johnson) Youngdahl; married Livia Bjorquist, August 25, 1925; children: James Edward, Kent Benjamin, Mark Alexander. *Education:* Gustavus Adolphus College, A.B., 1920; Columbia University, A.M., 1923; additional graduate study at University of Minnesota, University of Iowa, and University of Wisconsin. *Office:* George Warren Brown School of Social Work, Washington University, St. Louis, Mo. 63130.

CAREER: Marietta (Minn.) public schools, high school principal, 1921, superintendent of schools, 1922; Gustavus Adolphus College, St. Peter, Minn., professor of sociology and economics, 1923-33; Minnesota State Emergency Relief Administration, St. Paul, director of social service, 1933-37; Minnesota State Board of Control, St. Paul, director of public assistance, 1937-39; Washington University, St. Louis, Mo., associate professor, 1939-43, professor of social work, 1943-65, dean of School of Social Work, 1945-62, professor emeritus, 1965-70. Visiting summer professor, Universities of Minnesota and Southern California, 1938, 1939, 1941, and University of California, 1950. Attached to Supreme Headquarters, American Expeditionary Forces, Europe (SHAEF) as liaison officer with United Nations Relief and Rehabilitation Administration, 1944-45; consultant to Neuropsychiatric Division, Surgeon General's Office, U.S. Department of the Army, 1949-50. Member of national committee, Midcentury White House Conference on Children and Youth, 1949-50; member of board, St. Louis Social Planning Council, 1946-49, 1950-53, 1954-57; member of St. Louis Race Relations Commission, 1947-49. *Military service:* U.S. Army, Field Artillery, 1918; became second lieutenant.

MEMBER: National Conference of Social Work (member of executive committee, 1950-52; president, 1955-56), American Associations of Schools of Social Work (president, 1947-48), Child Welfare League of America (member of board, 1949-51), Council on Education for Social Work (first vice-president, 1952-54; member of board, 1954-56), American Association of Social Workers (president, 1951-53), American Civil Liberties Union (member of national committee, 1953-70), St. Louis Urban League (member of board, 1948-54), Phi Beta Kappa. *Awards, honors:* Certificate of Merit from General Eisenhower, 1945; Gustavus Adolphus College, L.L.D., 1954, and distinguished alumni citation, 1960; Washington University, Alumni Federation distinguished faculty award, 1961, L.L.D., 1968; Florina Lasker Award in Social Work, 1963; George Warren Brown Alumni Award, presented at time of the first Benjamin E. Youngdahl lecture (by Vice-President Hubert Humphrey), at Washington University, 1965.

WRITINGS: (Contributor) *Social Work as Human Relations,* Columbia University Press, 1949; (contributor) J. E. Russell, editor, *National Policies for Education, Health and Social Services,* Doubleday, 1955; *Social Action and Social Work,* Association Press, 1966. Contributor to *Social Work Year Book,* 1949, 1951, and to professional journals.†

(Died September 18, 1970)

ZARA, Louis 1910-

PERSONAL: Born August 2, 1910, in New York, N.Y.; son of Benjamin Jacob and Celia (Glick) Rosenfeld; married Bertha Robbins, September 23, 1930; married Marlene Brett, March 22, 1958; children: Paul, Philip Edward, Daniel, Jon. *Education:* Attended Crane Junior College, 1927-30, University of Chicago, 1930-31. *Home:* 1521 Brightwater Ave., Brooklyn, N.Y.

CAREER: Ziff-Davis Publishing Co., Chicago, Ill., and New York, N.Y., vice-president, 1946-53, general manager of book division, 1959-61; Publisher's Consultants, Inc., New York, N.Y., president, 1955-56; Follet Publishing Co., New York, N.Y., editor-in-chief, General Trade Division, 1962-65. *Member:* Authors Guild of Authors League of America, Society of Midland Authors, Overseas Press Club, National Commission of Anti-Defamation League (life member), American Numismatic Society (fellow), Royal Numismatic Society (fellow). *Awards, honors:* Chicago Foundation of Literature Award, 1940, for *This Land is Ours;* Daroff Memorial Fiction Award of Jewish Book Council of America, 1955, for *Blessed Is the Land.*

WRITINGS—Novels: *Blessed Is the Man,* Bobbs-Merrill, 1935; *Give Us This Day,* Bobbs-Merrill, 1935; *Some for the Glory,* Bobbs-Merrill, 1937; *This Land Is Ours,* Houghton, 1940; *Against This Rock,* Creative Age Press, 1943; *Ruth Middleton,* Creative Age Press, 1946; *Rebel Run,* Crown, 1951; *In the House of the King,* Crown, 1952; *Blessed Is the Land,* Crown, 1954; *Dark Rider,* World Publishing, 1961; (with Carroll Land Fenton) *Rocks, Minerals, and Gems,* Doubleday, 1965; *Jade,* Walker, 1969; *Locks and Keys,* Walker, 1969. Editor-in-chief of *Masterpieces, Home Collection of Great Art,* 1950. Author of other radio scripts, dramas, scenarios, and short stories.

WORK IN PROGRESS: A novel.

SIDELIGHTS: Zara has appeared on the radio-television show, "Stump the Authors."†

* * *

ZAWADZKI, Edward S. 1914-1967

PERSONAL: Born April 14, 1914, in Detroit, Mich.; son of Stanley and Zofia (Filipowicz) Zawadzki; married Clara E. Halapi; children: Anthony, Mary. *Education:* Wayne State University, B.A., 1936, M.S., 1940, M.D., 1942. *Home:* 14961 Piedmont, Detroit, Mich. 48223. *Office:* 400 East Lafayette, Detroit, Mich. 48226.

CAREER: Florence Crittenton Hospital, Detroit, Mich., pathologist, 1948-57; chief medical examiner, Wayne County, Mich., 1948-67; Wayne State University, Detroit, Mich., assistant professor of pathology, 1955-67. Federal Aviation Agency, Washington, D.C., consulting pathologist, 1961. *Military service:* U.S. Army, Medical Corps, 1942-46; became captain. *Member:* International Academy of Pathology, College of American Pathologists (fellow), American Society of Clinical Pathologists (fellow), American Academy of Forensic Sciences (fellow), American Medical Society, Michigan Society of Pathologists, Michigan Medical Society, Wayne County Medical Society, Sigma Xi.

WRITINGS: (With Jerome E. Bates) *Criminal Abortion: A Study in Medical Sociology,* C. C Thomas, 1964.†

(Died February 5, 1967)

ZEIDMAN, Irving 1908-

PERSONAL: Born September 30, 1908, in New York, N.Y.; son of Morris (a manufacturer) and Pauline (Goodman) Zeidman; married Henrietta Hertz, October 2, 1938; children: Heywood, Cynthia. *Education:* City College (now City College of the City University of New York), A.B., 1928; Brooklyn Law School, LL.B., 1931. *Politics:* Democrat. *Religion:* Jewish. *Agent:* Scott Meredith Literary Agency, Inc., 845 Third Ave., New York, N.Y. 10022.

CAREER: Attorney in private practice, Brooklyn, N.Y., beginning 1932; W. S. Cory Equipment Corp., Brooklyn, president, beginning 1960.

WRITINGS: The American Burlesque Show, Hawthorn, 1967.†

*   *   *

ZELIGS, Meyer A(aron) 1909-

PERSONAL: Born March 20, 1909, in Cincinnati, Ohio; son of Joseph (a merchant and scholar) and Betty (Mirkin) Zeligs; married Elizabeth Winifred Anderson, June 21, 1946; children: Betsy, Michael, Joseph, David. *Education:* University of Cincinnati, B.A., 1928, B.M., 1931, M.D., 1932; further study at National Hospital, London, England, 1936-37, and San Francisco Psychoanalytic Institute, 1947-55. *Home:* 3941 Washington St., San Francisco, Calif. 94108; and Country Club Dr., Carmel Valley, Calif. 93920. *Agent:* James Brown Associates, Inc., 22 East 60th St., New York, N.Y. 10022.

CAREER: Psychiatrist and neurologist in private practice, Cincinnati, Ohio, 1938-42, and San Francisco, Calif., 1946-52; private practice of psychoanalysis, San Francisco, Calif., beginning 1952. *Military service:* U.S. Naval Reserve, Medical Corps, active duty, 1942-46; became commander. *Member:* International Psycho-analytic Association, American Medical Association, American Psychiatric Association, American Psychoanalytic Association, American Psychosomatic Society, San Francisco Psychoanalytic Society and Institute, Phi Delta Epsilon, Concordia Argonaut Club.

WRITINGS: (Contributor) *History of World War II,* U.S. Naval Medical Department, 1944; *Friendship and Fratricide: An Analysis of Whittaker Chambers and Alger Hiss,* Viking, 1967. Contributor to *Psychoanalytic Forum* and other scientific journals.

WORK IN PROGRESS: Psychobiography of historical characters; *Nixon, Hiss, and Chambers,* a sequel to *Friendship and Fratricide.*

SIDELIGHTS: Zeligs told *CA* that he is most interested in "the role of psychoanalytic investigation in the research of contemporary as well as historical figures; the application of psychoanalytic skills and technique to biography and ongoing history." In *Friendship and Fratricide* he has written an "analytic biography" of the protagonists in the controversial 1950 trial of Alger Hiss, whose conviction was due to the accusations of Whittaker Chambers. David Cort says that "it would be easy to find fault with [the book] as literary psychoanalysis; but it is as a compilation of significant data about Chambers and Hiss that the book is important.... Dr. Zeligs' facts are so shocking, so consistent, convincing and well documented, as to make psychiatry a mere distraction." Although Zeligs says that "it was not my intent to confirm the guilt or establish the innocence of Hiss," his biography is, according to Mark Harris, "a persuasive expo-

sition of the author's thesis that [Hiss] was a victim of Chambers' pathological need to destroy." Sidney Hook points out that "despite the fact that Zeligs never laid eyes on Chambers, most of the analysis is devoted to him. The analysis of Hiss, for all the hours and letters [involved] is comparatively meagre." Zeligs tries to refute any charge of "selective reporting" when he remarks on the "irony" of Chambers' continued refusals to speak privately to him, after his personal life had already been so widely publicized. The pertinence of this study to contemporary events is emphasized by Harris, who says that "hidden or unconscious passions are as real as assassins' bullets.... The main service of Dr. Zeligs' book is its directing our attention along the right lines.... Dr. Zeligs' care and labor must win the respect of open minds."

BIOGRAPHICAL/CRITICAL SOURCES: Newsweek, January 30, 1967; *Harper's* February, 1967; *New York Times Book Review,* February 5, 1967; *Time,* February 10, 1967; *Saturday Review,* February 11, 1967; *Christian Science Monitor,* February 16, 1967; *New York Review of Books,* February 23, 1967; *America,* February 25, 1967; *Nation,* March 26, 1967.

*   *   *

ZUCKER, Paul 1888-1971

PERSONAL: Born August 14, 1888, in Berlin, Germany; came to United States, 1937, became U.S. citizen, 1944; son of Julius and Anna (Samter) Zucker; married Rose Walter (a concert and oratorio singer), September 16, 1916 (died, 1962). *Education:* Studied at universities and institutes of technology in Berlin and Munich; University of Berlin, Ph.D., 1913. *Residence:* New York, N.Y.

CAREER: Lecturer in history of art and architecture at Leasing Hochschule, Berlin, Germany, 1917-1935, and State Academy of Arts, Berlin, 1928-33; architect in private practice, Berlin, Germany, 1920-37; New School for Social Research, New York City, lecturer in history of art, architecture, and theater, beginning 1937; Cooper Union Art School, New York City, lecturer, 1938-48, adjunct professor, 1948-63, visiting professor of architecture and history of art, 1963-69. *Member:* College Art Association of America, Society of Architectural Historians, American Society for Aesthetics. *Awards, honors:* Numerous first and second prizes in architectural competitions in Germany, 1913-33; Brunner scholarship award of American Institute of Architects, 1953; Rossi Prize, 1969.

WRITINGS: Die Bruecke: Typologie und Geschichte ihrer kuenstlerischen Gestaltung, E. Wasmuth, 1921; *Die Theaterdekoration des Barock,* R. Kaemmerer, 1925; *Die Theaterdekoration des Klassizismus,* R. Kaemmerer, 1925; *Entwicklung des Stadtbildes: Die Stadt als Form,* Drei Masken Verlag, 1929; *Lichtspielhaeuser, Tonfilmtheater,* E. Wasmuth, 1931; *American Bridges and Dams,* Greystone, 1941; (editor with William H. Hendelson) *The Music Lovers Almanac,* Doubleday, Doran, 1943; (editor) *New Architecture and City Planning: A Symposium,* Philosophical Library, 1944; *Styles in Painting: Comparative Study,* Viking, 1950, 2nd edition, 1962; *Town and Square from the Agora to the Village Green,* Columbia University Press, 1959; *Fascination of Decay: Ruins—Relic, Symbol, Ornament,* Gregg, 1968.†

(Died February 14, 1971)

ZYLBERBERG, Michael 1907-1971

PERSONAL: Born April 29, 1907, in Plock, Poland; son of Abraham and Hinda (Kilbert) Zylberberg; married Henrietta Erlich, October 21, 1940. *Education:* Attended Rabbinical College, Warsaw, 1923-28, Institute of Jewish Studies, Warsaw, 1928-30, and Institute of Education, London, 1951-52. *Home:* 14 Clorane Gardens, London N.W.3, England.

CAREER: Teacher in secondary schools, Warsaw, Poland, 1931-39, and headmaster of a Hebrew day school in the Warsaw Ghetto, 1940-42; active in Polish underground, 1944; Council of Religious Communities, Warsaw, general secretary, 1945-48; Yiva Institute, London, England, secretary, 1954-71. Lecturer in South America, 1948-49, South Africa and Southern Rhodesia, 1952, and for London County Council, 1951-60. Correspondent for Jewish daily newspapers in New York and Buenos Aires. *Member:* Association of Jewish Journalists (London).

WRITINGS: A Warsaw Diary, 1939-1945 (originally published in Yiddish in serial form by the daily New York newspaper, *Forward*), Valentine, Mitchell, 1969. Also author of "The Melody of the Warsaw Ghetto" (radio script), 1954, broadcast by Radio Free Europe and Kol Israel. Contributor of articles and essays to publications in United States, England, South Africa, and Australia.

WORK IN PROGRESS: Christian Missions to Jews in England; and his memoirs, 1945-50.

BIOGRAPHICAL/CRITICAL SOURCES: Spectator, June 7, 1969; *Jewish Chronicle,* June 13, 1969; *Times Literary Supplement,* August 7, 1969.†

(Died October 22, 1971)

* * *